BUSINESS LAW

PRINCIPLES
CASES
LEGAL ENVIRONMENT

ELEVENTH EDITION

RONALD A. ANDERSON
Professor of Law and Government,
Drexel University
Member of the Pennsylvania and Philadelphia Bars

IVAN FOX
Professor of Law and Chairman,
Business Law Department, Pace University
Member of the New York Bar

DAVID P. TWOMEY
Professor of Law, Carroll School of Management,
Boston College
Member of the Massachusetts and Florida Bars

COLLEGE DIVISION South-Western Publishing Co.

Cincinnati Ohio

Sponsoring Editor: Jeanne R. Busemeyer
Developmental Editor: Dr. Carol A. Cromer
Production Editor: Thomas E. Shaffer
Production House: Graphic Typesetting Service, Inc.
Cover and Interior Designer: Craig LaGesse Ramsdell
Marketing Manager: Scott D. Person

LA70KA
Copyright © 1992
by South-Western Publishing Co.
Cincinnati, Ohio

Library of Congress Cataloging-in-Publication Data

Anderson, Ronald Aberdeen
    Business law : principles, cases, legal environment / Ronald A.
    Anderson, Ivan Fox, David P. Twomey.—11th ed.
        p.   cm.
    Includes index.
    ISBN 0-538-81270-2
    1. Commercial law—United States—Cases.   I. Fox, Ivan.
II. Twomey, David P.   III. Title.
KF888.A44   1992
346.73'07—dc20   91–31285
[347.3067]   CIP

1 2 3 4 5 6 7 8 9 Ki 9 8 7 6 5 4 3 2 1

Printed in the Unites States of America

This book is printed on acid-free paper that meets Environmental Protection Agency standards for recycled paper.

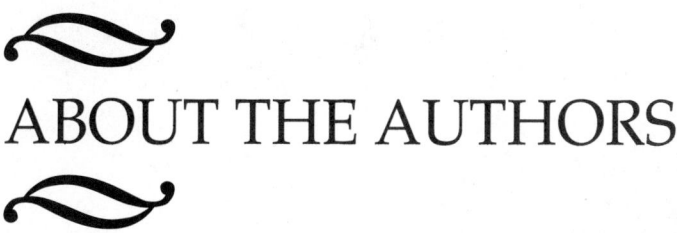

ABOUT THE AUTHORS

Ronald A. Anderson, Professor of Law and Government, Drexel University, taught the subjects covered by this book for 40 years. He is the internationally renowned author of the definitive, 11-volume treatise on the Uniform Commercial Code and other well-respected professional works.

Professor Anderson was graduated from the University of Pennsylvania in 1933 and earned his *Juris Doctor* from that school in 1936. He is a member of the American Bar Association and is an active member of the legal community.

Ivan Fox, with Pace University since 1958, and currently Professor of Law and Chairman of the Business Law Department, is widely known for his work with the Fox-Gearty CPA Review Course and has lectured extensively to professional and banking groups on various business law topics.

Professor Fox was graduated from Pace University in 1954, earned his *Juris Doctor* from New York Law School in 1957, and received his LL.M. from New York University in 1963. He is a member of the New York Bar and the New York State Bar Association.

David P. Twomey is Professor of Law at Boston College and is a nationally known labor arbitrator. He has written a great number of books and articles on labor law and business law topics, and he was elected to membership in the National Academy of Arbitrators in 1979.

Professor Twomey was graduated from Boston College in 1962 and earned his MBA at the University of Massachusetts at Amherst in 1963. After two years of business experience, he entered Boston College Law School and earned his *Juris Doctor* in 1968. He is a member of the Massachusetts, Florida, and Federal Bars. Professor Twomey joined the faculty of the Boston College School of Management in 1968 and was promoted to professor in 1978. He has a special interest in curriculum development, having recently served three terms as chairman of his school's Educational Policy Committee. He is chairman of the Business Law Department.

PREFACE

Our focus in preparing this Eleventh Edition of BUSINESS LAW: PRINCIPLES, CASES, LEGAL ENVIRONMENT continues to be to create a flexible teaching tool with universally desirable qualities that can be adapted to each instructor's personal teaching philosophy. We have sought, in presenting a broad range of materials, to make this book (1) accurate, (2) understandable, (3) balanced, (4) life-oriented, and (5) thought provoking.

By *accurate*, we mean that we have done everything possible to insure that the content of the book is as up-to-date as modern publishing technology will permit. Accurate also means that new doctrines and minority trends have been identified. Accordingly, we have endeavored to make this book anticipatory as well as retrospective. In the process of so doing, we hope to emphasize the dynamic character of the law.

Understandable means that legalistic jargon and words of art must be translated into ordinary English. We have replaced linguistic provincialisms and obscure words with ordinary language that can be understood by the modern student.

Balanced means that from the myriad discrete legal topics that might have some significance for undergraduate students of business law, those with the greatest relevance have been selected. If all the volumes of professional treatises relating to business were added together, the number would exceed 1,000. The business law student is given one book. Obviously, careful choice is necessary to bring the great mass of the law down into a one-volume text for beginners. In addition, great care must be exercised to treat all portions of the student's book with the appropriate degree of intensity.

Life-oriented requires the book to be devoted to those areas that the undergraduate student of today will most likely meet in future years. Consequently, it means avoiding the unusual, the bizarre, the headline cases that have no real value for the business person. Above all, life-oriented brings out the interrelationship between the law and life: the law is shaped by the environment, and the law gives direction to the environment. For the purpose of curriculum compartmentalization, "law" is a separate subject but as far as life is concerned it is an inseparable part of living. The more the student can appreciate this interrelationship, the better will be the student's understanding both of law and of life.

Thought provoking means there are end-of-chapter materials that call for the student's developing skill in the analysis of data to identify basic questions, to apply existing principles to the solution of such basic questions, and to make intelligent decisions when there are no preexisting principles to govern the exact basic questions that are involved. This system not only brings the student back to the orientation of law to life but also assures the teaching of law a permanent place in the pattern of higher education.

The objectives set forth above have guided the writing of this book for more than a third

iv

of a century. Though our focus on these objectives has never wavered, the specific content of the book has evolved to keep pace with changing times. The early 1960s witnessed the integration of the Uniform Commercial Code in the Seventh Edition as a result of the growth in the number of states adopting the UCC. In subsequent years that coverage has been continually updated to keep pace with amendments to the UCC and other uniform and model acts. Curriculum trends have us placing increasing emphasis upon environmental and regulatory topics.

The Legal and Regulatory Environment of Business

Part I of the book brings together various chapters relating to societal or public law that form the general background for individual business transactions. To borrow terms familiar to the economist, Part I deals with macro law while much of the balance of the book relates to micro law. It is important that the student see the background of macro law. It is also important that the student recognize that the legal environment of business is the sum total of the macro and micro areas.

More specifically, Part I deals with the regulatory environment in which business operates. The social forces behind the creation and evolution of the specific principles and substantive rules that govern disputes and transactions between individuals are explored. A comprehensive discussion of the federal and state court structure and the procedures involved in a lawsuit, from commencement to execution of the judgment, is included. The Constitution, as the foundation of the legal environment of business, is presented. The increasing role played by the administrative agencies in the government regulation of business is fully discussed.

This allocation of the indicated material to Part I is in harmony with the increased concern for an environmental approach to the teaching of business law. At the same time, this focusing on societal or public law is not made at the expense of the treatment of the areas of private law. There has been no lessening of attention to accuracy of content, clarity of expression, and thoroughness of subject matter coverage.

In addition to the topics discussed in Part I, other chapters throughout the book are appropriate for a course that focuses on public law. Although every chapter in the text possesses the potential for an environmental approach, some chapters lend themselves to this mode of teaching more readily than others. A list of chapters emphasizing public law follows:

Suggested Legal Environment Outlines

Chapters:

1. Law and Determination of Legal Rights
2. Ethics, Social Forces, and the Law
3. The Constitution as the Foundation of the Legal Environment
4. Government Regulation
5. Administrative Agencies
6. The Legal Environment of International Trade
7. Crimes
8. Torts
20. Personal Property (Protection of Trademarks, Copyrights, Patents)
21. Computers and the Law (Protection of Computer Software and Chips)
29. Consumer Protection
37. Bankruptcy
42. Employment (Government Regulation of Employment)
48. Securities Regulation
51. Environmental Law and Community Planning

An introductory course that emphasizes societal or public law may include the chapters above and other appropriate chapters selected for the course. An introductory course emphasizing private law may cover selected chapters from Part I, "The Legal and Social Environment of Business," and chapters on contracts, personal property, or agency. The instructor may choose to cover additional topics in this introductory course, depending upon the ability level of the students and the time allotted to the course at the institution. The remainder of the book may be covered in advanced courses.

Preparation for CPA Exam

As was true in previous editions, this Eleventh Edition continues to provide strong preparation for the business law section of the CPA exam. This text is used as an authoritative source for the business law section of the exam. Topics generally tested on this exam are:

The CPA and the Law
Business Organizations
Contracts
Debtor-Creditor Relationships
Government Regulation of Business
Uniform Commercial Code
Property

As this list suggests, the breadth and depth of CPA testing in the business law section necessitate inclusion of a great deal of material in any text purporting to prepare students for the exam. Adequate coverage of all these topics requires at least six semester hours. Consequently, this text is designed to accommodate a two-semester program in business law.

New Topics

New in this Eleventh Edition are a chapter on Securities Regulation and coverage of the following topics: new articles of the UCC; international trade topics such as the Single European Act, the U.S.-Canada Free Trade Agreement, and export regulations; insurance relating to transportation of goods; anti-takeover statues; S corporations; priorities; secured loans; electronic fund transfers; recreational use statutes; self-proved and living wills; and 1990 statutes, such as the Americans with Disabilities Act.

Up-To-Date with the Code

Within the last few years, a wave to reform the UCC began. Thus far, five new articles or revisions have been adopted as official parts of the Code. The first footnote in Appendix 3 of this text lists the states that have adopted these new articles. This book is up-to-date with these changes in the Code. Selected sections of the statute are presented in Appendix 3. In addition, Article 2A, "Leases," is covered by Appendix 4; Article 4A is covered by the text of Chapter 34; and Article 6 is handled briefly in Chapter 24. Appendices 5 and 6 provide tables listing the sections of the 1990 Articles 3 and 4 that make significant changes or additions to the prior Code versions covered by this text. Appendices 7 and 8 provide explanations of these changes in Articles 3 and 4.

Instructors in states adopting the new code Articles will of course be interested in these up-to-date materials. But, in addition, the comparison of the new Articles with the former versions furnishes an excellent opportunity for the student to see how business practices and the new technologies give rise to new situations that call for new law.

Cases

As in previous editions, this Eleventh Edition contains ample cases—including case questions—integrated with the text of each chapter. Popular, precedent-setting cases have been retained while at the same time adding many new decisions (a substantial number of which have been decided since 1988).

Features

An outline presented at the beginning of each chapter gives an overview of the topics covered. Points in the text have been enhanced by the use of illustrations. End-of-chapter summaries designed to assist students in assimilating the material are presented in each chapter.

A section on "Analysis of Court Opinions" is presented on pages ix–xi. This section includes a chart designed to assist students in identifying and analyzing ethical issues in the cases.

A glossary, a case index, and a subject index are included, as well as appendices

"How to Find the Law," the "U.S. Constitution," and selected model or uniform business statues.

Students' Supplements

Accompanying this Eleventh Edition is a new student study guide authored by Ronald L. Taylor of Metropolitan State College of Denver. The study guide contains an outline of each chapter in the text, expanded by general rules, limitations on these rules, and study hints. Review and application questions are given for each chapter. Answers are in a separate key.

The Legal Tutor™ on Contracts and *The Legal Tutor™ on Sales*, also authored by Ronald Taylor, provide the opportunity to develop analytical ability, improve academic performance, and expand knowledge through the use of interactive IBM-compatible software.

Instructor's Materials

An instructor's manual was prepared by Kim Tyler of Shasta College in conjunction with the text authors. This manual contains chapter outlines, lecture notes and teaching suggestions, case briefs, and answers to end-of-chapter questions and case questions.

A printed test bank of over 2,800 questions, prepared by Wayne L. Anderson of Southwest Missouri State University, is available. The test questions may also be obtained in an easy-to-use software package, MicroSWAT III.

A set of color transparencies has been developed to enhance classroom presentation of text concepts.

Videos, custom-designed for use with this text, are available to adopters. Video topics include an introduction to business law, employment law, and the business law portion of the CPA exam.

Acknowledgments

We thank the faculty and students who have provided valuable suggestions that have influenced this text. In particular we wish to thank the following reviewers:

Wayne L. Anderson
Southwest Missouri State University

Thomas M. Branton
Alvin Community College

Thomas Brucker
The University of Washington

George F. Conlin
Savannah State College

Nancy P. Cooper
Edison State Community College

John C. Folkenroth
Loyola University

Jerry L. Furniss
University of Montana

Gamewell Gantt
Idaho State University

James M. Highsmith
California State University, Fresno

Susan S. Jarvis
The University of Texas
Pan American

Burton M. Leiser
Pace University

Keith A. Maxwell
University of Puget Sound

Beverly McCormick
Morehead State University

Sharlene A. McEvoy
Fairfield University

Gregory C. Mosier
Oklahoma State University

Gregory J. Naples
Marquette University

Sheelwant B. Pawar
Idaho State University

Charles H. Sturgeon
Frostburg State University,
Hagerstown Center
Hagerstown Junior College

Nancy A. Wainwright
Eastern Washington University

William H. Walker
Indiana University-Purdue University at Fort Wayne

ANALYSIS OF COURT OPINIONS

Beginning with page 5, you will find opinions that were handed down by judges in actual cases. Some of these opinions show how the courts apply a rule of law that has been stated in the text. Other opinions extend or expand the rule stated in the text.

Components of a Court Opinion

The information for each case is presented in three parts: (a) the heading, (b) the facts of the case, and (c) the opinion. In this explanation the case *Manrique v Fabbri*, beginning on page 9, will be used as an example.

(a) HEADING. The heading of the case consists of the title and the source.

(1) Title. The title of the case usually consists of the names of the parties to the action. In the illustrative case Manrique, as plaintiff, sued Fabbri as defendant.

The title of an appealed case may not reveal who the plaintiff was in the original or lower court or who the defendant was. When the action is begun in the lower court, the first party named is the plaintiff and the second is the defendant. When the case is appealed, the name of the party who takes the appeal may appear first on the records of the higher court, so that if the defendant takes the appeal, the original order of the names of the parties is then reversed.

(2) Source. The second part of the heading gives the source of the opinion. *Manrique v Fabbri* was decided by the Florida Supreme Court and is found in "493 So 2d 437." This means that the opinion is found in the 493rd volume of the second series of the Southern (So) reporter[1] beginning at page 437.

(b) FACTS. The paragraph following the heading is a summary of the facts of the case, which provides a background for an understanding and analysis of the opinion. Read the statement of facts. Keep in mind the principles of law that you studied in the chapter. Then read the opinion carefully to see how the court made its decision, what it decided, and whether it agrees with what you thought would be decided.

(c) OPINION. The opinion of the court includes the name of the judge, excerpts from the reasoning of the court, and the judgment.

(1) Judge. At the beginning of the opinion is the surname of the judge who wrote it. The opinion in the *Manrique* case was written by Judge Barkett.

The letter or letters following the name of the judge indicate the judge's rank or title. *J.* stands for Judge or Justice. (*JJ.* is the plural form.) Other abbreviations include *C.J.* for Chief Justice or Circuit Judge, *D.J.* for District Judge, *P.J.* for Presiding Judge or President Judge, *A.J.* for Associate Judge or less often Auditing Judge, and *C.* for Chancellor or Commissioner.

When a case is perfectly clear and obvious, the opinion will frequently be filed without naming the writing judge and will then have

---

[1] See Appendix, "How to Find the Law," footnote 1, for sectional reporters.

a heading of "memorandum" or "per curiam."

(2) Body of the Opinion. The material following the judge's name is quoted from the opinion of the court. Words enclosed in brackets [ ] did not appear in the original opinion but have been added to explain a legal term, to identify a party, or to clarify a statement. Ellipses (three or four periods) are used to indicate that, for use in the textbook, something has been omitted that is not pertinent to the point of law with which we are concerned at this time.

Decisions vary in length from less than a page to more than a hundred pages, and opinions frequently involve several points of law. Each case in this book has been carefully edited so that the excerpts reprinted here will be convenient for student use.

Opinions do not follow a standard pattern of organization; but usually the well-written opinion will carefully examine the arguments presented by all parties and then explain why the court accepts or rejects those arguments in whole or in part. In this process the opinion may discuss the opinion of the lower court, the decisions in similar cases in other courts, and material from other sources.[2]

(3) Judgment. The case is concluded with a statement of the court's decision. If the case has been appealed and if the court agrees with the lower court, the decision may simply be "Judgment affirmed" or a similar expression. If the appellate court disagrees, the decision may be expressed as "Judgment reversed." "Case remanded" means that the case is returned to the lower court to proceed further in harmony with the appellate court's decision. In lower court cases when the judgment is on a narrow issue, the judgment of the court may be limited to "Objection sustained" or "Objection dismissed."

[2]   See Appendix, "How to Find the Law."

A judge of the court who disagrees with the majority may file a dissenting opinion.

Checklist for Case Study

The questions in the following checklist will serve as a guide for the analysis of each case. It should be understood, however, that not every case will provide answers to all these questions.

(a) COURT. In what court was the action brought originally, and which court filed the opinion being studied?

(b) PARTIES. Who were the parties to the action? Were they the parties to the original transaction, or were they strangers such as creditors?

(c) PURPOSE OF THE ACTION. What was the relief or remedy sought in the action?

(d) ACTION APPEALED FROM. What was done in the lower court that the appellant deemed wrong and from which the appeal was taken?

(e) ARGUMENTS OF THE PARTIES. What were the arguments made by the respective parties?

(f) DECISION OF THE COURT. What did the court decide?

(g) BASIS FOR DECISION. On what authority or ground did the court base its decision? Was it common law, decision, statute, Restatement of the Law, text, logic, or the personal belief of the court?

(h) APPRAISAL OF THE DECISION. What social objectives are advanced by the decision? What social objectives are hindered or defeated by the decision? What ethical principles are involved in the case? Is the decision socially desirable? Is it practical in application? Does it give rise to any dangers?

FIGURE 1   GUIDELINES TO BUSINESS ETHICS

Business Ethics	
Selected Ethical Principles or Issues to Discuss in Relation to Cases	Elementary Guidelines for an Ethical Analysis of Contemplated Action
1. Integrity and truthfulness.	1. Identify the ethical principle(s) involved in the case.
2. Promise-keeping.	2. Define the problem from the decision maker's point of view.
3. Loyalty.	3. Identify who could be injured by the contemplated action.
4. Fairness.	4. Define the problem from the opposing point of view.
5. Doing no harm.	
6. Maintaining confidentiality.	5. Would you (as the decision maker) be willing to tell your family, your supervisor, your CEO, and the board of directors about the planned action?
7. Avoiding conflict of interest.	
8. Whistleblowing.	6. Would you be willing to go before a community meeting, a congressional hearing, or a public forum to describe the action?
9. Efficiency and effectiveness (create new jobs and the products necessary for a humane life).	
10. Innovation.	7. With moral common sense and full consideration of the facts and alternatives, reach a decision about whether the contemplated action should be taken.

BRIEF CONTENTS

APPENDICES

CONTENTS

PART ONE

THE LEGAL AND SOCIAL ENVIRONMENT OF BUSINESS

1

LAW AND DETERMINATION OF LEGAL RIGHTS

Why have law?

If you have ever been stuck in a traffic jam or jostled in a crowd leaving a stadium, then you have been in a position to observe the need for order to keep things running smoothly and efficiently. What is true on a small scale for traffic jams and crowds is true on a large scale for society in general. The order, or pattern of rules, that society establishes to govern the conduct of individuals and the relation-ships among them we call law. Law is society's way of keeping things running smoothly and efficiently.

Stated another way, law is merely management at the societal level. You personally have objectives and make decisions to manage your life. Business people have objectives and make decisions to manage their businesses. Likewise, when society governs itself, it determines its objectives and makes management decisions, albeit through a much more complex process. That which we call law is merely a particular aspect of the broad problem of management: the management of society.

In this text we will look generally at the process of managing society through the system of laws and enforcement agencies. We will examine specifically those aspects of the system that deal with business. Perhaps the best place to start is with an explanation of the nature of law and legal rights.

A.   NATURE OF LAW AND LEGAL RIGHTS

Law consists of the body of principles that govern conduct and that can be enforced in courts or by administrative agencies. Much of the difficulty in seeking to understand the law is the result of regarding it as an absolute and exact science. The ideal of a definite body of law is attractive not only to the student but to everyone. Long-revered is the maxim that "in the known certainty of the law lies the safety of all." The purpose of establishing our Constitution was to enable us to have a government of laws and not of people.

Actually, the certainty, the precision, and the logic of the law are very relative matters. In truth the law is an arbitrary set of rules that we have agreed upon to govern ourselves. Our reason for so doing is the quest for justice and the advancement of our social objectives.

1.   Legal Rights

What are legal rights? Who has them? In answering these questions, we tend to make the mistake of thinking of the present as being characteristic of what was and what will be. But consider the evolution of the concept of the "rights of the human being" and the right of privacy.

(a) THE "RIGHTS OF THE HUMAN BEING" CONCEPT. Our belief in the American way of life and in the concepts on which our society or government is based should not obscure the fact that at one time there was no American way of life. In the past many reli-

gious leaders, philosophers, and poets spoke of the rights and dignity of people, but rulers disregarded such pretensions and held people tightly in a society based on status. A noble had the rights of a noble. A warrior had the rights of a warrior. A slave had very few rights at all. In each case, the law saw only status; rights attached not to the human beings but to their status.

In the course of time, serfdom displaced slavery in much of the Western world. Eventually feudalism disappeared and, with the end of the Thirty Years War, the modern nation-state began to emerge. Surely one might say that in such a "new order," a human being had legal rights. But the person had rights not as a human being—only as a subject. Even when the English colonists settled in America, they brought with them not the rights of human beings but the rights of British subjects. Even when the colonies were within one year of war, the Second Continental Congress presented to King George III the Olive Branch Petition, which asked the king to recognize the colonists' rights as English subjects. For almost a year the destiny of the colonies hung in the balance, with the colonists unable to decide between remaining loyal to the Crown, seeking to obtain recognition of their rights as English subjects (a "status" recognition), or doing something else.

Finally, the ill-advised policies of George III and the eloquence of Thomas Paine's *Common Sense* tipped the scales. The colonists spoke on July 4, 1776, not in terms of the rights of English subjects but in terms of the rights of people existing independently of any government. Had the American Revolution been lost, the Declaration of Independence would have gone rattling down the corridors of time with many other failures. But the American Revolution was won, and the new government that was established was based upon *human beings* rather than upon *subjects* as the building blocks. The concept of rights of human beings replaced the concept of rights of subjects. With this transition, the obligations of a monarch to faithful subjects were replaced by the rights of human beings existing without regard to the will or authority of any king. Since then,

America has been going through additional stages of determining what is embraced by the concept of "rights of human beings."

(b) THE RIGHT OF PRIVACY. One legal right recognized by all Americans today is the right of privacy. Before 1890, however, this right did not exist in American law. Certainly those who wrote the Declaration of Independence and the Bill of Rights were conscious of rights. How can we explain that the law did not recognize a right of privacy until a full century later?

The answer is that at a particular time people worry about the problems that face them. Note the extent of the fears and concern of the framers of the Bill of Rights. The Fourth Amendment states, "The right of the people to be secure in their persons, houses, papers, and effects, against unreasonable searches and seizures, shall not be violated, and no warrants shall issue, but upon probable cause, supported by oath or affirmation, and particularly describing the place to be searched and the persons or things to be seized." The people of 1790 were afraid of a recurrence of the days of George III.

The framers of the Fourth Amendment declared what we today would regard as a segment of privacy—protection from police invasion of privacy. The people of 1790 were simply not concerned with invasion of privacy by a private person. While a snooping person could be prosecuted to some extent under a Peeping Tom statute, this was a criminal liability. The victim could not sue for damages for invasion of privacy.

If we are honest in reviewing history, all we can say is that modern people think highly of privacy and want it to be protected. Knowing that the law is responsive to the wishes of society, we can also say that the right is protected by government. But note that we should go no further than to say that it is a right that society wishes to protect at the present time. If circumstances arise in our national life of such a nature that the general welfare is opposed to the right of privacy, we can expect that the "right" of privacy will be limited or modified. For example, although the right of privacy prevents a bank from giving out information about a customer's bank account, the federal government, acting under a 1969 statute, can require such information to see if income taxes are due or if money has been paid or received in criminal transactions.[1]

(c) ABOLITION OF RIGHTS. When not protected by a constitutional provision, rights may be abolished by statute. The *Strock* case turned on whether a legislature could destroy a right to sue.

---

[1]   United States v Bisceglia, 420 US 141 (1975). But see Chapter 34, Section 4(a) of this book.

STROCK v PRESSNELL
38 Ohio 3d 207, 527 NE2d 1235 (1988)

Strock and his wife were unhappily married. Strock sued Pressnell for alienation of affections, claiming that it was Pressnell's fault that Strock's wife no longer loved him. Pressnell raised the defense that the action for alienation of affections had been abolished by state statute. Strock claimed that the statute was unconstitutional. The court held the statute was constitutional. Strock appealed.

WRIGHT, J. . . . The challenges to the constitutionality of [the statute] are that abolition of these common-law actions without providing an alternative remedy is violative of both state and federal Constitutions. The challengers contend that the statute denies due process and/or equal protection under the Fourteenth Amendment to the United

States Constitution and due course of law and equal protection under Sections 2 and 16, Article I of the Ohio Constitution. . . .

The United States Supreme Court has emphatically declared that no person has a vested right in any of the rules of the common law:

> A person has no property, no vested interest, in any rule of the common law. . . . Rights of property which have been created by the common law cannot be taken away without due process; but the law itself, as a rule of conduct, may be changed at the will, or even at the whim, of the legislature, unless prevented by constitutional limitations. Indeed, the great office of statutes is to remedy defects in the common law as they are developed, and to adapt it to the changes of time and circumstances. *Munn v. Illinois* (1876), 94 U.S. 113, 134, 24 L.Ed. 77; . . .

The federal Constitution does not forbid the abolition of common-law rights so long as it is to attain a permissible legislative objective. . . .

Similarly, we have consistently held that the legislative branch of state government, unless prohibited by constitutional limitations, may modify or entirely abolish common-law actions. . . . As we stated in . . . *Leis v. Cleveland Ry. Co.* (1920), 101 Ohio St. 162, 128 N.E. 73: "Rights of property cannot be taken away or interfered with without due process of law. But there is no property or vested right in any of the rules of the common law, as guides of conduct, and they may be added to or repealed by legislative authority."

Thus, we hold that actions for alienation of affections and criminal conversation are not "property interests" and the General Assembly enacted [the statute] with a permissible legislative objective. This holding is consistent with virtually every other court decision that has addressed the constitutionality of these statutes. . . .

Therefore, we hold that . . . the statute that abolished amatory actions, is constitutional; it does not violate either . . . the Ohio Constitution, or the Equal Protection or Due Process Clauses of the Fourteenth Amendment to the United States Constitution.

[Judgment affirmed as to constitutionality of statute]

QUESTIONS

1. Did Strock claim that the legislature could not change the law? Explain.
2. How would the case have been decided if the court had held that the rule of law involved was a property right?

2.   What Is the Law?

The expression "a law" is ordinarily used to indicate a statute enacted by a state legislature or the Congress of the United States, such as an act of the federal Congress to provide old-age benefits. However, the statutes enacted by legislative bodies are not the only source of law.

Constitutional law includes the constitutions in force in a particular area or territory. In each state, two constitutions are in force—the state constitution and the national constitution.

Statutory law includes legislative acts declaring, commanding, or prohibiting something. Each state has its own legislature, and the United States has the Congress; both of these bodies enact laws. In addition, every city, county, or other subdivision has some power to adopt ordinances that, within their sphere of operation, have the same binding effect as legislative acts.

Of great importance are **administrative**

regulations, such as rules of the Securities and Exchange Commission and the National Labor Relations Board. The regulations promulgated by national and state administrative agencies generally have the force of statute and are therefore part of "the law."

Law also includes principles that are expressed for the first time in court decisions. This is **case law.** For example, when a court decides a new question or problem, its decision becomes a **precedent,** which stands as the law for that particular problem in the future. This rule that a court decision becomes a precedent to be followed in similar cases is the doctrine of *stare decisis.*

Court decisions do not always deal with new problems or make new rules. In many cases courts apply rules as they have been for many years—even centuries. These time-honored rules of the community are called the **common law.** Statutes will sometimes repeat or redeclare the common law rules. Many statutes depend upon the common law for definition of the terms in the statute.

Law also includes treaties made by the United States and proclamations and orders of the President of the United States or of other public officials.

3.   Uniform State Laws

To secure uniformity as far as possible, the National Conference of Commissioners on Uniform State Laws, composed of representatives from every state, has drafted statutes on various subjects for adoption by the states. The best example of such laws is the Uniform Commercial Code (UCC).[2] The UCC regulates the fields of sales and leasing of goods; commercial paper, such as checks; funds transfers; secured transactions in personal property; bulk transfers; and particular aspects of banking, letters of credit, warehouse receipts, bills of lading, and investment securities.

National uniformity has also been brought about in some areas of consumer protection by the adoption of the federal Consumer Credit Protection Act (CCPA), Title I of which is popularly known as the Truth in Lending Act.[3] A Uniform Consumer Credit Code (UCCC) has been proposed and is now before the states for adoption. To the extent that it is adopted, it will complement the Uniform Commercial Code.[4]

4.   Classifications of Law

Law is classified in many ways. For example, **substantive law,** which creates, defines, and regulates rights and liabilities, is contrasted with **procedural law,** which specifies the steps that must be followed in enforcing those rights and liabilities. Law may also be classified in terms of its origin, as coming from the Roman (or civil) law, the English common law of principles based on customs and usages of the community, or the law merchant. Law may be classified as to subject matter, such as the law of contracts, the law of real estate, and the law of wills.

Law is at times classified in terms of principles of law and principles of equity. At one

---

2   The Code has been adopted in every state except Louisiana. It has also been adopted for Guam, the Virgin Islands, and the District of Columbia. Louisiana has adopted Articles 1 and 3 to 9, inclusive, of the Code. The National Conference of Commissioners on Uniform State Laws has adopted amendments to Article 8, Investment Securities (1977) and Article 9, Secured Transactions (1972). It has also adopted new articles: 2A, Leases; 4A, Funds Transfers; and 6, Bulk Sales. Revisions of Articles 3, Commercial Paper (now called Negotiable Instruments), and 4, Bank Collections, have been adapted in 1990. The states that have adopted these later articles are listed on the first page of Appendix 3 of this book.

Uniformity has also reached international scope. The United Nations Convention on Contracts for the International Sale of Goods (CISG) applies to contracts between parties in the United States and those in the other nations that have approved the Convention. The provisions of this Convention, or international agreement, have been strongly influenced by Article 2 of the Uniform Commercial Code.

3   15 United States Code Section 1601 et seq. and 18 USC Section 891 et seq.

4   As of January, 1990, the 1968 version of the Uniform Consumer Credit Code has been adopted in Colorado, Indiana, Oklahoma, South Carolina, Utah, Wisconsin, and Wyoming. It has also been adopted for Guam. The 1968 version of the UCCC has been replaced by a 1974 version that has been adopted in Idaho, Iowa, Kansas, and Maine. In 1985 Idaho replaced the UCCC with the Idaho Credit Code.

time there were separate law courts and separate equity courts. Except in a few states, these courts have been combined so that one court applies principles of both law and equity. Even though administered by the same court, the two systems of principles remain distinct. That is, if the plaintiff seeks what historically would be equitable relief, the case is governed by equitable principles. If the plaintiff brings what historically would have been an action at law, the action is governed by law principles rather than equity.[5] To illustrate the difference, consider the case of a homeowner making a contract to sell the home to a buyer. If the owner refuses to go through with the contract, the rules of law will permit the buyer to sue the owner for damages. Rules of equity will go further and will compel the owner to actually transfer the ownership of the house to the buyer. This equitable remedy is called "specific performance."

B.   DETERMINATION OF LEGAL RIGHTS

Legal rights are meaningless unless they can be enforced. Government, therefore, provides a system by which the rights of the parties under the law can be determined and enforced. Generally the instrumentality of government by which this is accomplished is a court; the process involved is an action or a lawsuit. Administrative agencies have also been created to enforce law and to determine rights within certain areas. In addition, various alternative means have developed as out-of-court methods of dispute resolution.

5.   Contract Selection of Law or Forum

The parties to a contract may to some extent control the determination of their legal rights by specifying (a) the law that should apply to

the contract and (b) the **forum,** or the court in which any lawsuit should be brought.

(a) CHOICE OF LAW. In order to reduce the uncertainty of transactions or to further the convenience of the parties, it is customary for the modern contract to state that the contract should be governed by the law of a particular state or nation. This becomes important for an enterprise that does business in many states. Such an enterprise will typically specify that all contracts are governed by the law of the state in which the home office is located. For example, a life insurance company may issue policies to people all across the country. These policies will ordinarily state that they are governed by the law of the home office state. This means the legal staff of the insurance company need only concern itself with the law of one state rather than the law of 50 different states. As long as the state whose law is selected bears a reasonable relationship to the transaction, the designation by the contract will be followed.[6] Without regard to whether there is a reasonable relationship to the transaction, courts will ignore the law of the state selected by the parties when the selected law is contrary to a strong public policy of the forum.[7]

(b) CHOICE OF FORUM. The parties to a contract may specify that any lawsuit must be brought in the court of a particular state or country. This will generally be done for the convenience of the stronger party who will specify a local jurisdiction. If the choice is made in order to block lawsuits by the weaker party, the court selection provision will be held invalid. Thus, a provision that if a consumer in State A would bring a lawsuit against the manufacturer located in State B the suit must be brought in a distant State C, is invalid because it sets up an unconscionable

---

[5]   Gibbons v Stillwell, 149 Ill App 3d 411, 102 Ill Dec 864, 500 NE2d 965 (1986).

[6]   This concept is restated in the Uniform Commercial Code, Section 1–105. In contrast, however, Article 4A approves the selection made by the parties to a funds transfer without regard to whether there is a reasonable relationship to the transaction.

[7]   Mencor Enterprises, Inc. v Hets Equities Corp. 190 Cal App 3d 432, 235 Cal Rptr 464 (1987).

FIGURE 1-1   DISPUTE RESOLUTION PROCEDURES

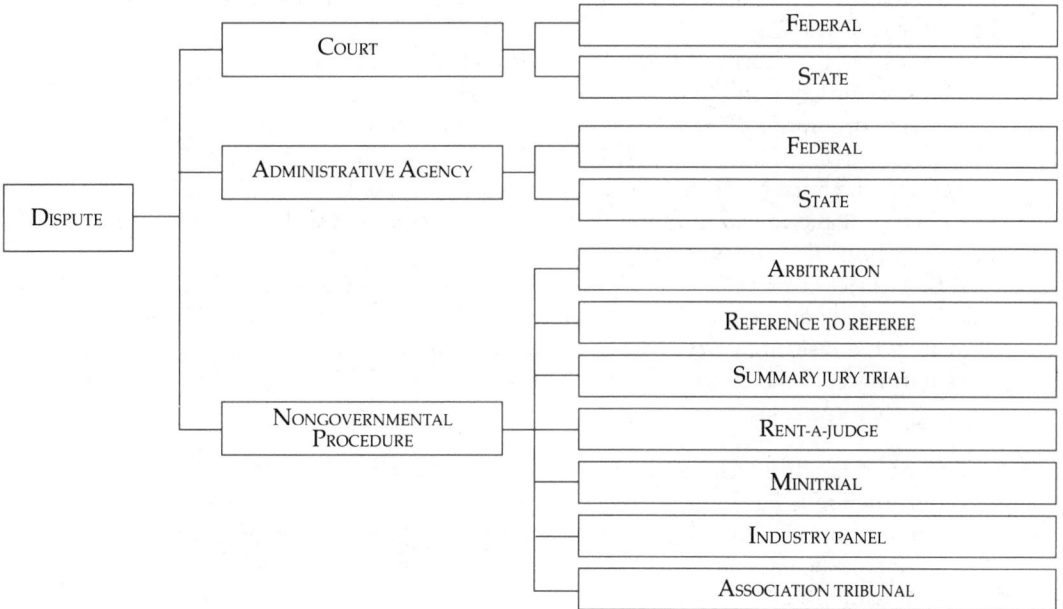

hurdle to the bringing of the lawsuit. If, however, there is a reasonable relationship between the parties or the transaction and the jurisdiction of the court selected, the forum selection clause is valid and will be enforced. In the *Manrique* case the plaintiff claimed that he was not bound by the forum selection clause of the contract.

MANRIQUE v FABBRI
(Fla) 493 So 2d 437 (1986)

Fabbri made a contract to sell Florida land to Manrique. The contract specified that any lawsuit should be brought in the courts of the Netherlands Antilles. A dispute arose, and Manrique sued Fabbri in a Florida court. Fabbri raised the defense that suit could not be brought in Florida. An appeal was taken to the state supreme court.

BARKETT, J. . . . The Third District Court of Appeal has consistently held that contractual provisions requiring that future disputes be resolved in specified foreign jurisdictions are void as impermissible attempts to oust Florida of subject matter jurisdiction. On the other hand, the Fourth District in *Maritime [Limited Partnership v Greenman Advertising Associates, Inc.* (Fla App) 455 So 2d 1121] has held that parties to a contract may agree to submit to the jurisdiction of a chosen forum provided that (1) the forum was not chosen because of one party's overwhelming bargaining power; (2) enforcement would not contravene public policy; (3) the purpose of such an agreement is not to transfer a local dispute to a remote and alien forum in order to inconvenience one or both of the parties.

In *Maritime,* the Fourth District relied upon and adopted the reasoning of the United States Supreme Court in *The Bremen v Zapata Off-Shore Co.,* 407 U.S. 1 (1972). In *Zapata,* a German corporation (Unterweser) contracted with Zapata, an American Corporation, to tow an oil rig across the Atlantic Ocean to Italy. The contract provided: "Any dispute arising must be treated before the London Court of Justice." The rig was damaged in transit and towed to Tampa. Zapata, notwithstanding such provision, instituted proceedings for damages against Unterweser in the United States District Court, Middle District of Florida. . . . The United States Supreme Court . . . held that forum selection clauses are prima facie valid and should be enforced unless enforcement is shown by the resisting party to be unreasonable under the circumstances. In *Zapata,* the Court rejected the same policy position adopted by the Third District in the case presently before us, saying:

> The argument that such clauses are improper because they tend to "oust" a court of jurisdiction is hardly more than a vestigial legal fiction. It appears to rest at core on historical judicial resistance to any attempt to reduce the power and business of a particular court and has little place in an era when all courts are overloaded and when businesses once essentially local now operate in world markets. It reflects something of a provincial attitude regarding the fairness of other tribunals. . . .

The Supreme Court gave compelling reasons why a freely negotiated private agreement unaffected by fraud, undue influence, or overweening bargaining power should be given full effect. It noted that at the very least such clauses represent efforts to eliminate uncertainty as to the nature, location, and outlook of the forum in which parties of differing nationalities might find themselves. Moreover, such clauses might be vital parts of agreements fixing monetary terms, with the consequences of the forum clause figuring prominently in the parties' calculations. The Court concluded:

> The correct approach would have been to enforce the forum clause specifically unless [the party] could clearly show that enforcement would be unreasonable and unjust, or that the clause was invalid for such reasons as fraud or overreaching.

The view articulated by the Court in *Zapata* enables freely contracting parties to conduct their interstate and international business affairs more efficiently. . . . Because the *Zapata* rule is based on a realistic assessment of modern commercial culture, and because the rule enhances contractual predictability within the culture, it is not surprising that it is rapidly becoming a majority view. . . .

We reject the position espoused by the Third District and adopt the view enunciated in *Zapata* and *Maritime.* Florida courts should recognize the legitimate expectations of contracting parties. The trial courts of this state can effectively protect a party by refusing to enforce those forum selection provisions which are unreasonable or result from unequal bargaining power. We hold that forum selection clauses should be enforced in the absence of a showing that enforcement would be unreasonable or unjust. . . .

We remand with directions that the matter be returned to the trial court for proceedings consistent herewith.

[Action remanded]

6. Courts

A **court** is a tribunal established by government to hear and decide matters properly brought before it, to give redress to the injured or enforce punishment against wrongdoers, and to prevent wrongs. A **court of record** is one in which the proceedings are preserved in an official record. In a **court not of record** the proceedings are not officially recorded.

Each court is empowered to decide certain types or classes of cases. This power is called **jurisdiction.** A court may have original or appellate jurisdiction, or both. A court with **original jurisdiction** has the authority to hear a controversy when it is first brought into court. A court having **appellate jurisdiction,** on the other hand, has authority to review the judgment of a lower court.

The jurisdiction of a court may be general, as distinguished from limited or special. A court having **general jurisdiction** has power to hear and decide all controversies involving legal rights and duties. A court of **limited** or **special jurisdiction** has authority to hear and decide only those cases that fall within a particular class, such as cases in which the amounts are below a specified sum.

Courts are frequently classified in terms of the nature of their jurisdiction. A **criminal court** is one that is established for the trial of crimes, which are regarded as offenses against the public. A **civil court,** on the other hand, is authorized to hear and decide issues involving private rights and duties and also noncriminal public matters. In like manner, courts are classified as equity courts, juvenile courts, probate courts, and courts of domestic relations, on the basis of their limited jurisdiction.

Each court has inherent power to establish rules necessary to preserve order in the court or to transact the business of the court. An infraction of these rules or the disobedience to any other lawful order, as well as a willful act contrary to the dignity of the court or tending to pervert or obstruct justice, may be punished as **contempt of court.**

7. Administrative Agencies

It is difficult for courts to administer laws regulating all phases of the economy. This difficulty led Congress and the state legislatures to establish commissions or agencies of experts to make the rules and to pass judgment upon violations of the rules. Thus, the Interstate Commerce Commission (ICC) now regulates interstate commerce and passes upon whether conduct of a carrier is a violation of ICC regulations. The ICC acts as a lawmaker, an executive that enforces the law, and a court that interprets and applies the law. This is also true of the Federal Trade Commission, the Securities and Exchange Commission, the National Labor Relations Board, and many other federal and state administrative agencies.

8. Alternate Means of Dispute Resolution

Because of the rising costs, delays, and complexities of litigation, business people often seek to resolve disputes out of court.

(a) ARBITRATION. By the use of **arbitration,** a dispute is brought before one or more arbitrators (disinterested persons selected by the parties to the dispute). The parties have agreed in advance to accept the decision of the arbitrators as final. Arbitration first reached extensive use in the field of commercial contracts. This procedure is encouraged as a means of avoiding expensive litigation and easing the workload of courts. Arbitration enables the parties to present the facts before trained experts familiar with the practices that form the background of the dispute.

A Uniform Arbitration Act has been adopted in a number of states.[8] Under this Act and similar statutes, the parties to a contract may agree in advance that all disputes arising thereunder will be submitted to arbitration. In some instances the contract will name the arbitrators for the duration of the contract.

The Federal Arbitration Act[9] declares that an arbitration clause in a contract relating to an interstate transaction is "valid, irrevocable, and enforceable." When the contract of the parties subject to the Federal Arbitration Act provides for the arbitration of disputes, the parties are bound to arbitrate in accordance with the federal statute, as against the claim that the arbitration was not binding under state law.[10]

(1) Mandatory Arbitration. In contrast with statutes that merely regulate arbitration when selected voluntarily by the parties, some statutes require that certain kinds of disputes be submitted to arbitration. In some states, by rule or statute, the arbitration of small claims is required.

(2) Scope of Arbitration. When arbitration is required by the statute, the terms of the statute will define the scope of the arbitration. When the parties have voluntarily agreed to arbitrate, their agreement will control the scope. In such case, questions may arise as to what disputes are covered thereby. This was the issue involved in the *Gross* case.

---

[8]   The 1955 version of the Uniform Arbitration Act has been adopted in Alaska, Arizona, Arkansas, Colorado, Delaware, Idaho, Illinois, Indiana, Iowa, Kansas, Maine, Maryland, Massachusetts, Michigan, Minnesota, Missouri, Montana, Nebraska, Nevada, New Mexico, North Carolina, North Dakota, Oklahoma, Pennsylvania, South Carolina, South Dakota, Tennessee, Texas, Utah, Vermont, Virginia, Wyoming, and the District of Columbia. The earlier 1925 version of the Act is in force in Wisconsin.

[9]   9 USC Sections 1–14.

[10]   Heily v Superior Court, 202 Cal App 3d 225, 248 Cal Rptr 673 (1988).

GROSS v RECABAREN

206 Cal App 3d 771, 253 Cal Rptr 820 (1988)

In 1984, Gross went to Doctors Fister and Recabaren to have certain growths removed from his face. At that time, Gross signed a written agreement to submit to arbitration "any dispute as to medical malpractice." Two growths were removed and further treatment was not required. In 1986 Gross returned to these two doctors for the removal of other growths on his head and face. Gross was not satisfied with the result of the surgery used to remove the growths. He sued the doctors for malpractice. The doctors raised the defense that Gross was bound by the 1984 agreement to arbitrate the claim. From a judgment for the defendants, Gross appealed.

GATES, J. . . . This state has a strong public policy favoring arbitration over litigation as a speedy and relatively inexpensive means of dispute resolution which eases court congestion. . . .

Code of Civil Procedure section 1295 . . . "encourages and facilitates the *arbitration* of medical malpractice disputes by specifying uniform language to be used in binding arbitration contracts to assure that the patient knows what he is signing and what its ramifications are."* . . .

---

*   Section 1295 provides: "(a) Any contract for medical services which contains a provision for arbitration of any dispute as to professional negligence of a health care provider shall have such provision as the first article

(continued at the bottom of page 13)

Because the scope of arbitration is a matter of agreement between the parties, the court should attempt to give effect to [their] intentions, in light of the usual and ordinary meaning of the contractual language and the circumstances under which the agreement was made. . . .Any doubts concerning the scope of arbitrable issues must be resolved in favor of arbitration. . . .

It is manifest that the contract signed by Steven Gross cannot, on its face, reasonably be said to be limited only to those services provided contemporaneous to its signing. . . .We are satisfied that . . . it was intended to encompass those situations where Gross, in the course of an ongoing doctor-patient relationship, sought treatment for a condition of the type which initially brought him to Dr. Fister's office. As we stressed in *Hilleary v. Garvin* ". . . To impose upon a physician, during a continuous doctor-patient relationship, the extra burden of having to renew the arbitration agreement each time there is a variation in treatment or ailment would be impractical, and would frustrate the purpose of the statute, which is to facilitate, not emasculate, the arbitration process."

Although the course of treatment Gross received in 1984 and 1986 differed, in each instance he sought medical services for the treatment of similar problems, i.e., potentially malignant skin lesions on his face and head. . . .

There was simply no objective evidence from which a reasonable person could conclude either of the parties viewed their relationship as having terminated in 1984. The mere fact that they did not anticipate Gross would return in the absence of further dermatological problems requiring the attention of an oncologist does not demonstrate otherwise. Obviously, Gross *hoped* additional treatment would not be necessary. When it was, however, he once again sought Dr. Fister's services. This was persuasive evidence of an ongoing relationship. Likewise, the manner in which Steven Gross' medical and billing records were maintained by Dr. Fister was indicative of a continuing association. . . .

[Judgment affirmed]

QUESTIONS

1. What are the reasons for the California policy with regard to arbitration?
2. Was the decision in the *Gross* case inevitable?
3. When the patient signed the paper in 1984, do you think he read it with sufficient care to realize what it said about arbitration and that he remembered what it said when he came back for treatment in 1986?

of the contract and shall be expressed in the following language: 'It is understood that any dispute as to medical malpractice, that is as to whether any medical services rendered under this contract were unnecessary or unauthorized or were improperly, negligently or incompetently rendered, will be determined by submission to arbitration as provided by California law, and not by a lawsuit or resort to court process except as California law provides for judicial review of arbitration proceedings. Both parties to this contract, by entering into it, are giving up their constitutional right to have any such dispute decided in a court of law before a jury, and instead are accepting the use of arbitration.'

"(b) Immediately before the signature line provided for the individual contracting for the medical services must appear the following in at least 10-point bold red type:

" 'NOTICE: BY SIGNING THIS CONTRACT YOU ARE AGREEING TO HAVE ANY ISSUE OF MEDICAL MALPRACTICE DECIDED BY NEUTRAL ARBITRATION AND YOU ARE GIVING UP YOUR RIGHT TO A JURY OR COURT TRIAL. SEE ARTICLE I OF THIS CONTRACT.'

"(c) Once signed, such a contract governs all subsequent open-book account transactions for medical services for which the contract was signed until or unless rescinded by written notice within 30 days of signature. Written notice of such rescission may be given by a guardian or conservator of the patient if the patient is incapacitated or a minor. . . ."

(3) Finality of Arbitration. When arbitration is based upon the agreement of the parties, it is generally held or provided that the decision of the arbitrator is final. This is so even though it was wrong, unless there is clear proof of fraud, arbitrary conduct, or a significant procedural error.

In contrast, when arbitration is mandatory under statute or rule, it is generally provided that the losing party may appeal from such compulsory arbitration to a court, and the appeal will proceed just as though there never had been any prior arbitration. This is called a **trial** *de novo* and is required to preserve the constitutional right to a jury trial.[11] As a practical matter, however, relatively few appeals are taken from the arbitration decision.

(b) REFERENCE TO THIRD PERSON. An out-of-court determination of disputes under construction contracts is often made under a term of the contract that any dispute shall be referred to the architect in charge of the construction and that the architect's decision shall be final.

Increasingly, other types of transactions provide for a third person or a committee to decide rights of persons. Thus, employees and an employer may have agreed as a term of the employment contract that claims of employees under retirement and pension plans shall be decided by a designated board or committee. The seller and buyer may have selected a third person to determine the price to be paid for goods. Ordinarily the parties agree that the decision of such a third person or board shall be final and that no appeal or review may be had in any court. In most cases, referral to a third person is used in situations that involve the determination of a particular fact, in contrast to arbitration, which seeks to end a dispute.

(c) ASSOCIATION TRIBUNALS. Many disputes never reach the law courts because both parties to the dispute belong to a group or association, and the tribunal created by the group or association disposes of the matter.

Thus, a dispute between members of a labor union, a stockbrokers' exchange, or a church may be heard by some board or committee within the association or group. Courts will review the action of such tribunals to determine that a fair and proper procedure was followed, but generally the courts will not go any further and will not examine the facts of the case to see if the association tribunal reached the same conclusion that the court would have reached.

Trade associations commonly require their members to employ out-of-court methods of dispute settlement. Thus, the National Association of Home Builders requires its member builders to employ arbitration. The National Automobile Dealers Association provides for panels to determine warranty claims of customers. The decision of such panels is final as to the dealer, but the consumer is allowed to bring a regular lawsuit upon losing before the panel.

(d) SUMMARY JURY TRIAL. A summary jury trial is in effect a dry run or mock trial in which the lawyers present their claims before a jury of six persons. The object is to get the reaction of a sample jury. No evidence is presented before this jury, and it bases its opinion solely on what the lawyers state. The determination of the jury has no binding effect, but it has value in that it gives the lawyers some idea of what a jury might think if there were an actual trial. This has special value when the heart of a case is whether something is reasonable under all the circumstances. When the lawyers see how the sample jury reacts, the lawyers may moderate their positions and reach a settlement.

(e) RENT-A-JUDGE. Under the rent-a-judge plan, the parties hire a judge to hear the case. In many states this is done by the parties' voluntarily choosing the judge as a "referee," with the judge acting under a statute authorizing the appointment of referees.[12] Under such a statute the referee hears all the evidence just as though there were a regular trial,

---

[11]   Firelock, Inc. v District Court (Colo) 778 P2d 1090 (1989) (mandatory arbitration of claims under $50,000).

[12]   See Section 8(b) of this chapter.

and the judge's determination is binding on the parties unless reversed on appeal. In some jurisdictions, special provision is made for the parties to agree that the decision of the judge selected as referee shall be final.

(f) MINITRIAL. When only part of a case is disputed, the parties may stay within the framework of a lawsuit but agree that only the disputed issues be submitted to a jury. For example, when there is no real dispute over the liability of the defendant but the parties disagree as to the damages, the issue of damages alone may be submitted to the jury.

In some states, instead of submitting the matter to a regular jury, the attorneys will agree to hold a minitrial. Under this system, the parties agree that a particular person, frequently a retired judge, should listen to the evidence on the disputed issues and decide the case. The agreement of the parties for the minitrial may specify whether this decision is binding on the parties. As a practical matter, the evaluation of the case by a neutral person will often bring the opposing parties together to reach a settlement.

(g) CONTRACT PROVISIONS. The parties' contract may pave the way for the settlement of future disputes by containing clauses requiring the parties to submit disputes to arbitration or to make use of one of the procedures described above. In addition, contracts may provide that no action may be taken until after the expiration of a specified cooling-off period, or that the parties shall continue in the performance of their contract even though there is a dispute between them.

9.   Disposition of Complaints and Ombudsmen

In contrast with the traditional and alternative procedures for resolving disputes are the procedures aimed at removing the ground for complaint before it develops into a dispute that requires resolution. For example, the complaint department in a department store will often be able to iron out the difficulty before the customer and the store are locked in an adversary position that could end in a law-suit. Grievance committee procedures will often be effective to bring about an adjustment or removal of grounds for complaint. A statute may create a government official for the purpose of examining complaints. Such an official is often called an *ombudsman*.[13] The few federal statutes that have created such an officer have not given the ombudsman any judicial power. Typically the ombudsman is limited to receiving complaints, supervising the administration of the system, and making recommendations for improvements. Two of the federal statutes expressly declare that the creation of the office of ombudsman does not impair any right existing by law.[14] In addition, when the complaint involves a right that would require a jury trial at common law, the Seventh Amendment to the United States Constitution guarantees that right, and an ombudsman could not be given the power to decide such a matter. Moreover, the trend in America is to create special tribunals or administrative agencies rather than to give the ombudsman greater power.

C.   COURT ORGANIZATION

Courts in the United States are organized in two distinct systems: the federal courts and the state courts. Although created under separate governments, the methods of operation and organization of these two systems are similar.

10.   Personnel of Courts

Both the federal and state court systems require the assistance of many people. These include not only those individuals in the direct employ of the court, but also those described as officers of the court and, in many cases, a jury as well.

---

[13]   This name is Swedish for "commissioner."

[14]   For example, see the Solid Waste Disposal Act of November 8, 1984, PL 98–616, Section 703(a), 98 Stat 3225, 42 USC Section 6917; and the Panama Canal Commission Act of September 17, 1979, PL 96–70, Section 1113, 93 Stat 460, 22 USC Section 3623.

(a) OFFICERS OF THE COURT. The **judge** is the primary officer of the court. A judge is either elected or appointed. **Attorneys** or counselors at law are also officers of the court. They are usually selected by the parties to the controversy—but in some cases by the judge—to present the issues of a case to the court.

The **clerk** of the court is appointed in some of the higher courts but is usually elected to office in the lower courts. The principal duties of the clerks are to enter cases upon the court calendar, to keep an accurate record of the proceedings, to attest the same, and, in some instances, to approve bail bonds and to compute the amount of costs involved.

The **sheriff** is the chief executive of a county. In addition to the duty of maintaining peace and order within the territorial limits of a county, the sheriff has many other duties in connection with the administration of justice in county courts of record: summoning witnesses, taking charge of the jury, preserving order in court, serving writs, carrying out judicial sales, and executing judgments. The **marshals** of the United States perform these duties in the federal courts. In county courts not of record, such as the courts of justices of the peace, these duties, when appropriate, are performed by a **constable.** Some of the duties of the sheriff are now performed by persons known as **court criers,** or by deputy sheriffs, known as **bailiffs.**

(b) THE JURY. The **jury** is a body of citizens sworn by a court to try to determine by verdict the issues of fact submitted to them. A trial jury consists of not more than twelve persons. The first step in forming a jury is to make a **jury list.** This involves the preparation by the proper officers or board of a list of qualified persons from which a jury may be drawn.

A certain number of persons drawn from the jury list constitute the **jury panel.** A trial jury is selected from members of the panel.

11.   Federal Courts

The Supreme Court of the United States is the highest court in the federal system. The courts of appeals are intermediate courts. The district courts and special courts are the lower courts.

(a) SUPREME COURT OF THE UNITED STATES. The Supreme Court is the only court expressly established by the Constitution. Congress is authorized by the Constitution to create other federal courts.

The Supreme Court has original jurisdiction in all cases affecting ambassadors, other public ministers, and consuls, and in those cases in which a state is a party. Except as regulated by Congress, the Supreme Court has appellate jurisdiction in all cases that may be brought into the federal courts in accordance with the terms of the Constitution. The Supreme Court also has appellate jurisdiction in certain cases that have been decided by the supreme courts of the states. Thousands of cases are filed with the Court each year.

(b) COURTS OF APPEALS. The United States, including the District of Columbia, is divided into 13 judicial circuits. Each of the circuits has a court of appeals. These courts are courts of record. There is also a court of appeals for all federal circuits. It has nationwide jurisdiction for certain subject areas such as patents and copyrights.

A court of appeals has appellate jurisdiction only and is empowered to review the final decisions of the district courts, except in cases that may be taken directly to the Supreme Court. The decisions of the courts of appeals are final in most cases. An appeal may be taken as a matter of right on certain constitutional questions. Otherwise, review depends on the discretion of the Supreme Court and, in some cases, of the court of appeals.

(c) DISTRICT COURTS. The United States, including the District of Columbia, is further divided into a number of judicial districts. Some states form a single district, whereas others are divided into two or more districts. District courts are also located in the territories.

The district courts have original jurisdiction in practically all cases that may be maintained in the federal courts. They are the trial courts for civil and criminal cases.

Civil cases that may be brought in these district courts are (a) civil suits in which the United States is a party; (b) actions brought by citizens of the same state claiming land under grants by different states; (c) proceedings under the bankruptcy, postal, copyright, and patent laws; (d) civil cases of admiralty and maritime jurisdiction; (e) actions against national banking associations; (f) cases between citizens of different states or between citizens of one state and a foreign state involving $50,000 or more; and (g) cases that arise under the federal Constitution or laws and treaties made thereunder.

(d) OTHER FEDERAL COURTS. In addition to the Supreme Court, the courts of appeals, and the district courts, the following tribunals have been created by Congress to determine other matters as indicated by their titles: Court of International Trade, Claims Court, Tax Court, Court of Military Appeals, and the territorial courts.

12.   State Courts

The system of courts in the various states is organized along lines similar to the federal court system, although differing in details such as the number of courts, their names, and jurisdiction.

(a) STATE SUPREME COURT. The highest court in most states is known as the supreme court. In a few states it may have a different name, such as "Court of Appeals" in New York. The jurisdiction of a supreme court is ordinarily appellate, although in a few instances it is original. In some states the supreme court is required to render an opinion on certain questions that may be referred to it by the legislature or by the chief executive of the state. The decision of a state supreme court is final in all cases not involving the federal Constitution, laws, and treaties.

(b) INTERMEDIATE COURTS. In some states intermediate courts have original jurisdiction in a few cases, but in the main they have appellate jurisdiction of cases removed for review from the county or district courts.

The intermediate courts are known as superior, circuit, or district appellate courts. As a general rule, their decisions may be reviewed by the highest state court.

(c) COUNTY AND DISTRICT COURTS. County and district courts of record have appellate jurisdiction of cases tried in the justice of the peace and police courts, as well as general original jurisdiction of criminal and civil cases. They also have jurisdiction of wills and guardianship matters except when, as in some states, the jurisdiction of such cases has been given to special orphans', surrogate, or probate courts.

(d) OTHER STATE COURTS. In addition to the foregoing, the following, which are ordinarily not courts of record, have jurisdiction as indicated by their titles: city or municipal courts, police courts, traffic courts, small claims courts, and justice of the peace courts.

D.   COURT PROCEDURE

Detailed laws specify how, when, and where a legal dispute can be brought to court. These rules of procedure are necessary in order to achieve an orderly, fair determination of litigation and in order to obtain, as far as humanly possible, the same decisions on the same facts. It is important to remember, however, that there is no uniform judicial procedure. While there are definite similarities, the law of each state may differ from that of the others. For the most part the uniform laws that have been adopted do not regulate matters of procedure.

13.   Steps in a Lawsuit

The following are the steps in a lawsuit. Not every step is taken in every suit. The facts of a case may be such that the case ends before every possible step is taken. The parties may not want to fight it out to the very end or to raise every possible point.

(a) COMMENCEMENT OF ACTION. An action is begun by filing a complaint with the clerk of the appropriate court. The complaint generally consists of a description of the acts complained of by the plaintiff and a request for some sort of reparation or relief.

(b) SERVICE OF PROCESS. The defendant must be served with **process** (a writ, notice, or summons, or the complaint itself) to give notice that the action is pending and to subject the defendant to the power of the court.

(c) PLEADINGS. After the plaintiff has filed a complaint and process has been served on the defendant, the defendant must make some reply, generally within 15 or 20 days. If the defendant fails to do so, the plaintiff ordinarily wins the case by default.

Before answering the plaintiff's complaint, the defendant may make certain preliminary objections, such as that the action was brought in the wrong court or that service was not properly made. If the objection is sustained, the case may be ended, depending upon the nature of the objection, or the plaintiff may be allowed to correct the mistake if that is possible. The defendant may also raise the objection, sometimes called a **motion to dismiss** or **demurrer,** that even if the plaintiff's complaint is accepted as true, the plaintiff is still not entitled to any relief.

If the defendant makes an objection that is overruled or dismissed, or if the defendant makes no objection, the defendant must file an **answer.** An answer either admits or denies the facts asserted by the plaintiff. For example, if the plaintiff declared that the defendant made a contract on a certain date, the defendant may either admit making the contract or deny having done so. An admission of having made the contract does not end the case, for the defendant may then be able to plead defenses— for example, that at a later date the plaintiff and defendant had agreed to set the contract aside.

Without regard to whether the defendant pleads a defense, the defendant may generally assert a **counterclaim** or **cross complaint** against the plaintiff. Thus, the defendant may contend that the plaintiff owes money or is liable for damages and that this liability should be offset against any claim the plaintiff may have.

After the defendant files an answer, the plaintiff may generally file preliminary objections to the answer. Just as the defendant could raise objections, the plaintiff may, in certain instances, argue that a counterclaim raised by the defendant could not be asserted in that action, that the answer is fatally defective in form, or that it is not legally sufficient. Again the court must pass upon the preliminary objections. When these are disposed of, the pleading stage is ordinarily over.

Generally, all of the pleadings in an action may raise only a few or perhaps one question of law, or a question of fact, or both. Thus, the entire case may depend on whether a letter admittedly written by the defendant amounted to an acceptance of the plaintiff's offer, thereby constituting a contract. If this question of law is answered in favor of the plaintiff, a judgment will be entered for the plaintiff; otherwise, for the defendant. By way of contrast, it may be that a certain letter would be an acceptance if it had been written by the defendant, but the defendant may deny having written it. Here the question is one of fact, and the judgment is entered for the plaintiff if it is determined that the facts happened as claimed by the plaintiff. Otherwise the judgment is entered for the defendant.

If the only questions involved are questions of law, the court will decide the case on the pleadings alone, since there is no need for a trial to determine the facts. If questions of fact are involved, then there must be a trial to determine what the facts really were.

(d) PRETRIAL PROCEDURE. Many states and the federal courts have adopted other procedural steps that may be employed before the trial, with the purpose of eliminating the need for a trial, simplifying the issues to be tried, or giving the parties information needed for preparation for trial.

(1) Motion for Judgment on the Pleadings. After the pleadings are closed, many courts permit either party to move for a **judgment on the pleadings.** When such a motion is made,

the court examines the record and may then enter a judgment according to the merits of the case as shown by the record.

(2) Motion for Summary Judgment. In most courts a party may shorten a lawsuit by showing that there is no substantial dispute as to the material facts relating to the claim or defense asserted by that party. This is ordinarily done by filing in court sworn statements and affidavits that show that the claim or defense of the adverse party is false or a sham. If the court concludes that there is no substantial dispute as to the material facts involved, it will enter such judgment as is proper on the actual facts of the case. If the court decides that there is a substantial dispute as to a material fact, it will dismiss the motion, and the case will then continue as though the motion had not been filed.

(3) Pretrial Conference. In many courts either party may request the court to call a **pretrial conference,** or the court may take the initiative in doing so. This conference is a discussion by a judge of the court and the attorneys in the case. The object of the conference is to eliminate matters that are not in dispute and to determine what issues remain for litigation. Some cases are settled at this stage.

(4) Discovery. The Federal Rules of Civil Procedure and similar rules in a large number of states permit one party to inquire of the adverse party and of all witnesses about anything relating to the action. This includes asking the adverse party the names of witnesses; asking the adverse party and the witnesses what they know about the case; examining, inspecting, and photographing books, records, buildings, and machines; and making an examination of the physical or mental condition of a party when it has a bearing on the action. These procedures are classed as **discovery.**

(5) Depositions. Ordinarily a witness testifies in court at the time of the trial. In some instances it may be necessary or desirable to take such testimony out of court before the time of the trial. It may be that the witness is aged or infirm or is about to leave the state or country and will not be present when the trial is held. In such a case the interested party is permitted to have the testimony, called a **deposition,** of the witness taken outside of the court.

(e) DETERMINATION OF FACTS. A legal system must provide for someone to determine the facts of a case when the parties do not agree on the facts.

(1) The Trier of Facts. If the legal controversy is one that under the common law would have been tried by a jury, either party to the action has the constitutional right today to demand that the action be tried before a jury. If all parties agree, however, the case may be tried by the court or judge alone without a jury, and in some instances may be referred to a master or a referee appointed by the court to hear the matter.

In equity there is no constitutional right to a jury trial, but a chancellor or equity judge may submit questions to a jury. There is the basic difference that in such cases the verdict or decision of the jury is only advisory to the chancellor; that is, the chancellor is not bound by the verdict. In contrast, the verdict of a jury in an action at law is binding on the court unless a basic error is present.

When new causes of action are created by statute, such as the right of an employee to obtain workers' compensation for an injury arising in the course of employment without regard to whether the employer was negligent, there is no constitutional right to a trial by jury. The trier of facts may accordingly be a judge without a jury, or a special administrative board or agency, such as a Workers' Compensation Board.

(2) Basis for Decision. The trier of fact, whether a jury, a judge, a referee, or a board, can only decide questions of fact on the basis of evidence presented before it. Each party offers evidence. The evidence usually consists of the answers of persons to questions in court. Their answers are called **testimony.** The evidence may also include **real evidence,** that is, tangible things, such as papers, books, and records. It is immaterial whether the records are kept in ordinary ledger books or stored in a computer, because a computer printout made

for trial is admissible as evidence of the information contained in the computer.[15] In some cases, such as a damage action for improper construction of a building, the trier of fact may be taken to view the building so that a better understanding of the evidence can be obtained.

The witness who testifies in court is usually a person who had some direct contact with the facts in the case, such as a person who saw the events occur or who heard one of the parties say something. In some instances, it is also proper to offer the testimony of persons who have no connection with the case, when they have expert knowledge and their opinions as experts are desired.

A witness who refuses to appear in court may be ordered to do so by a **subpoena,** and may also be compelled to bring relevant papers to the court by a **subpoena** *duces tecum.* If the witness does not obey the subpoena, the witness may be arrested for contempt of court. In some states the names of the order upon the witness and the procedure for contempt have been changed, but the substance remains the same.

(f) CONDUCT OF THE TRIAL. The conduct of a trial will be discussed in terms of a jury trial. Generally a case is one of several assigned for trial on a certain day or during a certain trial period. When the case is called, the opposing counsel seat themselves at tables in front of the judge, and the jury is selected. After the jury is sworn, the attorneys usually make **opening addresses** to the jury. Details vary in different jurisdictions, but the general pattern is that each attorney tells the jury what will be proven. When this step has been completed, the presentation of the evidence by both sides begins.

The attorney for the plaintiff starts with the first witness and asks any questions pertinent to the case. This is called the **direct examination** of the witness, since it is made by the attorney calling the witness. After the direct examination has been finished, the opposing counsel asks the same witness other questions

in an effort to disprove the prior answers. This is called **cross-examination.**

After the cross-examination has been completed, the attorney for the plaintiff may ask the same witness other questions to overcome the effect of the cross-examination. This is called **redirect examination.** This step in turn may be followed by further examination by the defendant's attorney, called **recross-examination.**

After the examination of the plaintiff's witness has been concluded, the plaintiff's second witness takes the witness stand and is subjected to an examination in the same way as the first. This continues until all of the plaintiff's witnesses have been called. Then the plaintiff "rests," and the defendant calls the first defense witness. The pattern of examination of witnesses is repeated except that now the defendant is calling the witnesses, and the defendant's attorney conducts the direct and redirect examination while the questioning by the plaintiff's attorney is cross- or recross-examination.

After the witnesses of both parties have been examined and all the evidence has been presented, each attorney makes another address to the jury. This is called a **summation,** which sums up the case and suggests that a particular verdict be returned by the jury.

(g) CHARGE TO THE JURY AND VERDICT. The summation by the attorneys is followed by a charge of the judge to the jury. This **charge** is a résumé of what has happened at the trial and an explanation of the applicable law. At its conclusion, the judge instructs the jury to retire and study the case in the light of the charge and then return a **verdict,** or a finding. By such instructions, the judge leaves to the jury the problem of determining the facts but states the law that they must apply to such facts as they may find. The jury then retires to secret deliberation in the jury room.

(h) TAKING THE CASE FROM THE JURY AND ATTACKING THE VERDICT. At several points during the trial, or immediately after it, a party may take a step to end the case or to set aside the verdict the jury has returned.

(1) Voluntary Nonsuit. A plaintiff who is

---

[15]   See Chapter 21, Section 4.

dissatisfied with the progress of the trial may wish to stop the trial and begin again at a later date. In most jurisdictions this can be done by taking a **voluntary nonsuit.**

(2) Compulsory Nonsuit. After the plaintiff has presented the testimony of all witnesses, the defendant may request the court to enter a nonsuit on the ground that the case presented by the plaintiff does not entitle the plaintiff to recover. This is called a **compulsory nonsuit.**

(3) Mistrial. When necessary to avoid great injustice, the trial court may declare that there has been a **mistrial** and thereby terminate the trial and postpone it to a later date. While either party may move the court to enter a mistrial, it is discretionary with the court whether it does so. A mistrial is commonly entered when the evidence has been of a highly prejudicial character and the trial judge does not believe that the jury can ignore it even when instructed to do so, or when a juror has been guilty of misconduct.

(4) Directed Verdict. After the presentation of all the evidence at the trial, either party may request the court to direct the jury to return a verdict in favor of the requesting party. When the plaintiff would not be entitled to recover even if all the testimony in the plaintiff's favor were believed, the defendant is entitled to have the court direct the jury to return a verdict for the defendant. The plaintiff is entitled to a directed verdict when, even if all the evidence on behalf of the defendant were believed, the jury would still be required to find for the plaintiff. In some states, the defendant may make a motion for a directed verdict at the close of the plaintiff's proof.

(5) New Trial. After the verdict has been returned by the jury, a party may move for a new trial if not satisfied with the verdict or with the amount of damages awarded. If it is clear that the jury made a mistake or if material evidence that could not have been discovered before the trial becomes available later, the court will award a new trial, and the case will be tried again before another jury.

(6) Judgment n.o.v. If the verdict returned by the jury is clearly wrong as a matter of law, the court may set aside the verdict and enter a judgment contrary to the verdict. In some states this is called a **judgment** *non obstante veredicto* (notwithstanding the verdict), or as it is abbreviated, a judgment n.o.v.

(i) JUDGMENT AND COSTS. The court enters a judgment conforming to the verdict unless a new trial has been granted, a mistrial declared after the return of the verdict, or a judgment n.o.v. entered. Generally the winning party will also be awarded costs in the action. In equity actions or those that had their origin in equity, and in certain statutory proceedings, the court has discretion to award costs to the winner or to divide them between the parties.

Costs ordinarily include the costs of filing papers with the court, the cost of having the sheriff or other officers of the court take official action, the statutory fees paid to the witnesses, the cost of a jury fee, if any, and the cost of printing the record when this is required on appeal. Costs do not include compensation for the time spent by the party in preparing the case or in being present at the trial, the time lost from work because of the case, or the fee paid to an attorney. Sometimes when a special statutory action is brought, the statute authorizes recovery of a small fee for the attorney. Thus, a mechanics' lien statute may authorize the recovery of an attorney's fee of 10 percent of the amount recovered, or a "reasonable attorney's fee." As a general rule, the costs that a party recovers represent only a small part of the total expenses actually incurred in the litigation.

(j) APPEAL. After a judgment has been entered, any party who is aggrieved thereby may appeal. This means that a party who wins the judgment but is not awarded as much as had been hoped, as well as a party who loses the case, may take an appeal.

The appellate court does not hear witnesses. It examines the record of the proceedings before the lower court (that is, the file of the case containing all the pleadings, the testimony of witnesses, and the judge's charge) to see if there was an error of law. To assist the court, the attorneys for the parties file arguments or briefs and generally make arguments orally before the court.

If the appellate court does not agree with the application of the law made by the lower court, it generally sets aside or modifies the action of the lower court and enters such judgment as it concludes the lower court should have entered. It may set aside the action of the lower court and send the case back to the lower court with directions to hold a new trial or with directions to enter a new judgment in accordance with the opinion that is filed by the appellate court.

(k) EXECUTION. After a judgment has been entered or after an appeal has been decided, the losing party generally complies with the judgment of the court. If not, the winning party may then take steps to execute or carry out the judgment.

(1) Money Judgment. If the judgment is for the payment of a sum of money, the plaintiff may direct the sheriff or other judicial officer to sell as much of the property of the defendant as is necessary to pay the plaintiff's judgment and the costs of the proceedings and of the execution. Acting under this authorization, the sheriff may make a public sale of the defendant's property and apply the proceeds to the payment of the plaintiff's judgment. In most states the defendant is allowed a limited monetary exemption and an exemption for certain articles, such as personal clothing and tools of trade.

(2) Garnishment of Debt. When a money judgment is entered in favor of *A* against *B*, it may happen that *B* is owed money by *C*. *A* can garnish or attach this debt of *C* to *B*. To the extent that money paid by *C* then goes to *A* instead of *B*, both the debt of *C* to *B* and the judgment liability of *B* to *A* are reduced or discharged.

(3) Non-Money Judgment. If the judgment is for the recovery of specific property, the judgment will direct the sheriff to deliver the property to the plaintiff.

If the judgment directs the defendant to carry out or to refrain from an act, it is commonly provided that failure to obey the order is a contempt of court punishable by fine or imprisonment.

14.   Declaratory Judgment

In this century, a court procedure for settling disputes, authorized by statute, has made its appearance. This is the **declaratory judgment** procedure. Under it a person, when confronted with the early stages of an actual controversy, may petition the court to decide the question or declare the rights of the parties before loss is actually sustained. A copy of the petition is served on all parties. They may file answers. After all the pleadings have been filed, the court then decides the questions involved just as though a lawsuit had been brought.

15.   Judicial Control of Procedure

Just as a police patrol watches over traffic, the judge of the court watches over the proceedings to be sure that everyone is following proper rules. In order to prevent abusive use of court actions or obstruction of their conduct, courts may impose a variety of penalties. These include imposing court costs on the wrongdoer, fining and imprisoning for contempt, barring a claim or a defense, or refusing to listen to evidence that had been improperly withheld earlier in the action.[16]

16.   Mootness as a Bar to Court Reflief

Courts have the power to determine controversies. Under declaratory judgment statutes, courts have the power to determine budding controversies that have not yet become full-blown disputes. Courts do not have the power to decide matters after the dispute has disappeared. When this occurs, the case is described as being **moot.**

17.   Immunity for Wrong Decision

The fact that a judge, jury, or arbitrator makes a wrong decision does not impose any liability upon the decision maker. If the decision maker is involved in a crime, such as bribery,

---

[16]   Dwyer v Crocker National Bank, 194 Cal App 3d 1418, 240 Cal Rptr 297 (1987).

the wrongdoer may be prosecuted for that offense. However, there is no liability for merely making a wrong decision. For example, the fact that a judge does not know the law and makes a mistake does not entitle the loser to sue the judge. Even if the decision is later reversed on appeal, the winning party cannot go back and sue the judge. That is, the judge has immunity from liability while acting within the scope of judicial authority.[17]

[17]   Grane v Grane, 143 Ill App 3d 979, 98 Ill Dec 91, 493 NE2d 1112 (1986).

SUMMARY

Law consists of the pattern of rules established by society to govern conduct and relationships. These rules can be expressed as constitutional provisions, statutes, case decisions, and administrative regulations. Law can be classified as substantive or procedural, and it can be described in terms of its historical origins, by the subject to which it relates, or in terms of law or equity.

Courts have been created to hear and resolve legal disputes. A specific court's power is defined by its jurisdiction, which may be original or appellate, general or special, and criminal or civil. The judge is the primary officer of a court. A jury may serve to determine issues of fact.

Courts in the United States are organized in two distinct systems, federal and state. The Supreme Court of the United States is the highest federal court. The United States courts of appeals are the intermediate courts and the United States district courts are the trial-level courts. Most state court systems are similarly organized.

A lawsuit is begun by filing a complaint. The defendant named in the complaint must be served with process; that is, the defendant must be notified that an action has been commenced. The issues to be tried are developed through pleadings and pretrial procedures. Testimony and real evidence are presented at trial, where attorneys for the parties introduce evidence and examine the witnesses.

Because a formal trial can be time-consuming and costly, the parties sometimes agree to an alternative method of resolving the dispute. Among common alternatives are arbitration, reference to a third person or association tribunal, the summary jury trial, the private judge/referee, and the minitrial.

QUESTIONS AND CASE PROBLEMS

1. How can parties to a dispute avoid the expense of litigation?
2. What is the difference between original and appellate jurisdiction of a court?
3. What is the most significant uniform law?
4. On learning of the many steps of a lawsuit, Elaine exclaimed that all lawsuits must take a very long time. Is she correct?
5. Tenton owes Orlando $1,000. Orlando has a friend, Helen, who is a judge in the Court of International Trade. Orlando wants to sue Tenton in that court. May he do so?
6. Carolyn, Elwood, and Isabella are involved in a real estate development. The development is a failure, and Carolyn, Elwood, and Isabella want to have their rights determined. They could bring a lawsuit but they are afraid that the case is so complicated that a judge and jury not familiar with the problems of real estate development would not reach a proper result. What can they do?
7. Attorneys are, and at the same time are not, officers of the court. Explain this contradictory statement.
8. Ames brought an action against Jarvis Co. to recover damages resulting from a breach of contract. No process was served on the defendants, but Ames published notice of the action in the newspaper. Ames secured a judgment against the defendants. Later it was contended that the

judgment was not valid. Do you agree? Why?

9. The entry of a judgment on a motion for summary judgment is a violation of the right to trial by jury. Appraise this statement.

10. A witness who is willing to testify concerning certain facts in a case lives in another state. How can the testimony be secured for use as evidence in the trial?

11. James Waters repaired the roof of the home of Rosalyn Albanese. She owed him $1,000 for the work, but she did not pay him. James owed $1,000 to the Ajax Supply House, from which he had purchased roofing materials for several jobs. Can Ajax require Rosalyn to pay it the money she owes James?

12. The right of privacy is a fundamental right that has always been recognized by American law. Appraise this statement.

13. The right to trial by jury is a fundamental procedure that must always be used whenever any issue of fact is to be determined. Appraise this statement.

14. Mostek Corporation, a Texas corporation, made a contract to sell computer-related products to the North American Foreign Trading Corporation, a New York corporation. North American used its own purchase order form, on which appeared the statement that "any dispute arising out of this order shall be submitted to arbitration as provided in the terms set forth on the back of this order." Acting on the purchase order, Mostek delivered almost all of the goods but failed to deliver the final installment. North American then demanded that the matter be arbitrated. Mostek refused to do so. Was it required to arbitrate? [Re Mostek Corporation, 120 App Div 2d 383, 502 NYS2d 181]

15. What ethical value or values are involved in providing parties with the many procedural steps described in this chapter?

2

ETHICS, SOCIAL FORCES, AND THE LAW

In Chapter 1 we defined *law* as a body of *enforceable* principles of conduct. In a democratic society these principles of conduct are determined by the people. Laws represent an expression of the collective desires of the people to encourage conduct that is right, good, and just and to discourage conduct that is wrong, evil, or unjust. In this sense, the law has its underpinnings in ethics—the ethics of a society constitutes a force that molds that society's law. Ethics in turn reflects social forces.

A. ETHICS AND LAW

To what extent do ethical values affect the law?

1. What Is Ethics?

Ethics consists of moral principles. More fully stated, ethics constitutes the branch of philosophy dealing with values relating to human conduct, with respect to the goodness and the rightness of motives and actions. Thus far the matter is easy. The difficulty arises in defining *goodness*. The definition changes over time and with different societies. For example, the ancient Spartans believed that it was good that sickly infants be allowed to die. The England of two centuries ago believed it was good to punish some 250 offenses by death. Our society used to believe it was good for the marketplace to be governed by the rule of "Let the buyer beware." Gradually, public opinion came to regard this as not good, and much of modern law, with its protection of the consumer, is based on "Let the *seller* beware."

Consider the Founding Fathers who obtained our national independence and established our Constitution. We certainly respect, admire, and praise them. But they thought of "inalienable rights" as being the "rights of man"—white, free men over 21; women and slaves excluded. To them, labor unions were illegal conspiracies and employees could not strike or picket against their employers. It was to take almost a century after they lived, a civil war, and a constitutional amendment to delegalize the institution of slavery and abolish the concept that a slave was a thing or chattel owned by a master. It was to take the 20th century to give employees the right to unionize, strike, and picket, and to recognize the legal rights of women.[1]

Further study of history and of different societies will emphasize that goodness, and therefore ethics, does not have the same meaning at all times to all peoples.

2.   Why Ethical Concepts Change

What makes the content of ethics change? This is important to a study of law because as ethical concepts change, so does the law.

If we look closely at why one society or one generation believes something is bad although another society or generation thought it was good, we come to the conclusion that there are certain underlying currents that run through the pages of history. These currents are described in this chapter as social forces. Depending upon the importance attached to the different forces at different times, the content of the community's code of ethics changes. Thus, the underlying reason for changed ethics is the change in the value placed upon the different social forces. To understand why society's evaluation of social forces changes requires a thorough study of practically every field of knowledge and therefore lies beyond the scope of this book. It is sufficient for our purpose to recognize that there are social forces, that these forces give rise to the ethical patterns of the day, that the evaluation of the social forces changes, and that with such changes there are corresponding changes in the field of ethics.

3.   Ethics and Modern Law

The social forces considered in this chapter give rise to our ethical concepts. These concepts in turn influence and give rise to the rules of law. The law existing at any one time is part of the social environment in which people live and work. The goals and objectives inspired by the environment will seek to advance certain social forces. Thus, there is an endless circle of interaction between social environment, social forces, ethics, and the law.

FIGURE 2-1   THE ENDLESS CIRCLE OF SOCIETAL INTERACTION

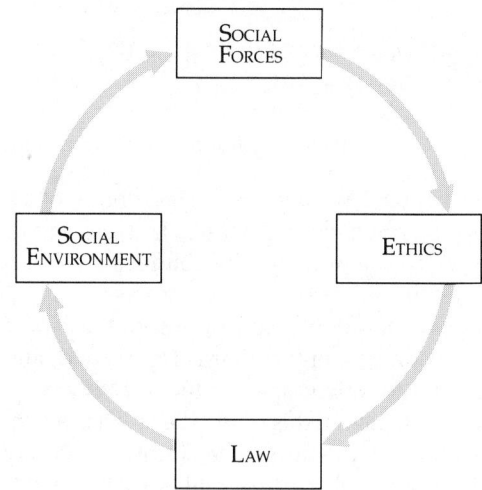

By their very nature, ethical concepts are vague and general. The law, as opposed to broad ethical standards, must be more definite and stable in order to be capable of consistent enforcement. Notwithstanding this dis-

---

[1]   One quotation will be sufficient to show that our views of what is right or good today are much different from views in former years. In 1869, a woman lawyer was refused admission to the bar of the state of Illinois because she was a woman. On appeal the United States Supreme Court held that this was proper. Justice Bradley stated that: "The paramount destiny and mission of woman are to fulfill the noble and benign office of wife and mother. This is the law of the Creator." (Bradwell v Illinois, 16 Wall 130 (1873), affirming 55 Ill 535).

tinction between law and ethics, it is clear that there is a strong relation between them. Laws are made and remade as notions of justice change. A society's sense of justice is in turn influenced by its laws. The interactions are unquestionably complex, but a few observations can nonetheless be made.

(a) LAW AS THE CRYSTALLIZATION OF ETHICS. Not all ethical values are capable of expression as laws, but certainly the more elemental ethical principles find their way into a society's legal framework. An ethical regard for the value of human life is crystallized in criminal codes detailing precisely defined degrees of offense—murder, manslaughter, negligent homicide. Similarly, an ethical obligation to look after the well-being of others takes the form of the legally enforceable duty of parents to care for their children. In these areas the law approaches the attainment of ethical values of society and locks the ethical concepts into binding rules of conduct.

But the law cannot equal the reach of ethical values, at least partly because some things are better left to individual choice and initiative. Criminal penalties for behavior that actively or negligently endangers human life stop short of imposing a general duty to intervene to save a life already in danger. Legal obligations to further the well-being of others are not extended to members of society generally, but only to those with a dependent relationship. In fact, it might be said that if a society's ethical codes constitute its concept of ideal behavior, then that society's law is its minimum standard of conduct.

(b) SOCIETAL ETHICS AS THE BLUEPRINT FOR FUTURE LAW. As was noted earlier, a society's ethical values change over time. The law similarly evolves to keep pace with changing technologies and values, though at a much more deliberate pace. Because of the close relationship between law and ethics, the ethical values of today's society can be regarded as a blueprint for the law of tomorrow.

(c) PARTICULAR APPLICATIONS. As you study business law, you will find many

instances of established legal principles that became inadequate to serve society's changing notions of what was right or just. As public sentiment against a particular law or legal principle grew, a legal system that was otherwise resistant to change found various ways to relieve the pressure. The change sometimes took the form of a judicial decision that found a new exception to an established rule or simply overturned an earlier decision. Or the change may have been manifested as a new statute or a constitutional amendment. Consider the following illustrations.

As was discussed in Chapter 1, there has not always been a legally recognized right of privacy. The very rapid dissemination of information to great numbers of people made possible by the development of the modern newspaper, and much later by radio and television, created a need for enforceable protection against unwarranted intrusion upon private lives. Privacy is now a constitutionally protected right.[2]

Another example of changes in societal ethics resulting in changes in the law involves consumerism. As of 1776, the concept of what was "right" in the marketplace meant that everyone was equal. That was the year in which the Declaration of Independence proclaimed the political equality of everyone; and Adam Smith, in *The Wealth of Nations*, declared that every person was the economic equal of every other person and should be allowed to move about in the marketplace freely and without restraint. But all this was before the rise of mass production, modern distribution, and giant sellers. Beginning in the middle of this century, society began to feel that it was just not "right" to treat the consumer as the equal of the giant seller. The result, consumer protection laws, gave the consumer special protection because of such inequality. The Uniform Commercial Code placed special duties on merchants. Our American ideal of equality was modified in recognition of the fact that equality does not exist in the marketplace.

---

[2]   Griswold v Connecticut, 381 US 479 (1965).

(d) IMPLICATIONS FOR BUSINESS. As the size, resources, and business patterns of society change, what seems right today may seem wrong in the future. While society's changing notions of what is right and just do not create binding obligations on businesses and business people, they do constitute a force that will help to mold future law. Businesses that act irresponsibly and with disregard for society's view of what is right will speed the transition from ethical concept to enforceable law. Business can only avoid society's tendency toward more stringent regulation by acting responsibly and in harmony with societal ethics. Today many companies have established codes of ethics as guides for their employees, requiring that company business be conducted not only in compliance with the law, but also in accordance with the highest standards of business integrity and honest dealings.

In the remainder of this chapter, we will examine some of the basic principles that our society regards as important in making its ethical decisions and its laws.

B.   SOCIAL FORCES AND THE LAW

Every rule of law seeks some goal or objective. General objectives are the creation and maintenance of order, stability, and justice.

4.   Social Forces

The desires or forces that motivate society in making its laws can be called **social forces.** These social forces influence the ethical concepts of society, which in turn produce society's laws.

The social forces and objectives of the law are, in effect, the opposite sides of the same coin. Because certain forces are pushing society, society seeks certain objectives. Asking what is the objective of a law is thus another way of asking what social force in society seeks that result. The sum of these societal drives gives us the ethical pattern or environment of society.

(a) PROTECTION OF THE STATE. A number of laws are designed to protect the existing governments, both state and national. Laws condemning treason, sedition, and subversive practices are examples of society's taking measures to preserve governmental systems. Less dramatic are the laws that impose taxes to provide for the support of those governments.

Under the national social security system, a number is assigned to each person. The same number is used by other government programs and agencies, such as the Internal Revenue Service and various relief programs. The numbering system solves the problem of distinguishing between two persons with the same name. As the assigned numbers are shorter than the names of most people, the numbering system speeds up the process of storing and retrieving information. The use of the same identifying numbers by the various government programs makes it easier for the government to spot fraudulent claims. However, various attacks have been made on this numbering system on the ground that it is dehumanizing or violates religious principles. The *Bowen* case deals with a conflict between the plaintiff's religious beliefs and the governmental requirement of using a social security number in order to obtain financial assistance.

BOWEN v ROY
476 US 693 (1986)

Federal law provides financial assistance to poor families through the food stamp program and Aid to Families with Dependent Children. In order to obtain benefits under these programs, the federal law requires a recipient to give a social security number to any state welfare agency involved. Roy, an American Indian, was refused federal benefits for his two-year-old daughter because he would not furnish a social security number. He claimed that the use of a number was contrary to his religious belief, and that freedom of religion gave him the right to refuse to furnish a social security number. From a decision against him, he appealed.

BURGER, C. J. . . . Roy is a Native American descended from the Abenaki Tribe, and he asserts a religious belief that control over one's life is essential to spiritual purity and indispensable to "becoming a holy person." Based on recent conversations with an Abenaki chief, Roy believes that technology is "robbing the spirit of man." In order to prepare his daughter for greater spiritual power, therefore, Roy testified to his belief that he must keep her person and spirit unique and that the uniqueness of the social security number as an identifier, coupled with the other uses of the number over which she has no control, will serve to "rob the spirit" of his daughter and prevent her from attaining greater spiritual power. . . .

Never to our knowledge has the Court interpreted the First Amendment to require the Government *itself* to behave in ways that the individual believes will further his or her spiritual development or that of his or her family. The Free Exercise Clause simply cannot be understood to require the Government to conduct its own internal affairs in ways that comport with the religious beliefs of particular citizens. Just as the Government may not insist that appellees engage in any set form of religious observance, so appellees may not demand that the Government join in their chosen religious practices by refraining from using a number to identify their daughter. "The Free Exercise Clause is written in terms of what the government cannot do to the individual, not in terms of what the individual can extract from the government." Sherbert v Verner, 374 US 398, 412 (1963) (Douglas, J., concurring). . . .

The statutory requirement that applicants provide a social security number is wholly neutral in religious terms and uniformly applicable. There is no claim that there is any attempt by Congress to discriminate invidiously or any covert suppression of particular religious beliefs. . . .It may indeed confront some applicants for benefits with choices, but in no sense does it affirmatively compel appellees, by threat of sanctions, to refrain from religiously motivated conduct or to engage in conduct that they find objectionable for religious reasons. Rather, it is [Roy and his daughter] who seek benefits from the Government and who assert that, because of certain religious beliefs, they should be excused from compliance with a condition that is binding on all other persons who seek the same benefits from the Government.

This is far removed from the historical instances of religious persecution and intolerance that gave concern to those who drafted the Free Exercise Clause of the First Amendment. . . .

Governments today grant a broad range of benefits; inescapably at the same time the administration of complex programs requires certain conditions and restrictions. Although in some situations a mechanism for individual consideration will be created, a policy decision by a government that it wishes to treat all applicants alike and that it does not wish to become involved in case-by-case inquiries into the genuineness of each religious objection to such condition or restrictions is entitled to substantial deference. Moreover, legitimate interests are implicated in the need to avoid any appearance of favoring religious over nonreligious applicants. . . .

The social security number requirement clearly promotes a legitimate and important public interest. No one can doubt that preventing fraud in these benefits programs is an important goal. . . .
[Judgment affirmed]

QUESTIONS

1. Does the court agree or disagree with the religious beliefs of Roy?
2. How does the decision affect Roy's religious freedom?
3. Who would be harmed if Roy were allowed to receive governmental benefits and still follow his beliefs?

(b) PROTECTION OF THE PERSON. At an early date, laws were developed to protect the individual from being injured or killed. The field of criminal law is devoted to a large extent to the protection of the person. In addition, under civil law a suit can be brought to recover damages for the harm done by criminal acts. For example, a person who steals an automobile is subject to a penalty imposed by the state in the form of imprisonment or a fine, or both. In addition, the thief is liable to the owner for the money value of the automobile. Over the course of time, the protection of personal rights has broadened to include protection of reputation and privacy, and protection of contracts and business relations from malicious interference by outsiders. The right to privacy is protected against news media seeking to learn and communicate what is happening.[3]

In the *Rasmussen* case the privacy interest of blood donors and the public welfare interest were in conflict with the interest of an AIDS victim seeking to learn the identity of the donors.

---

[3]   Miller v National Broadcasting Co. 187 Cal App 3d 1463, 232 Cal Rptr 668 (1986).

RASMUSSEN v SOUTH FLORIDA BLOOD SERVICE, INC.
(Fla) 500 So 2d 533 (1987)

Donald Rasmussen was hit by an automobile. In the hospital he was given a number of blood transfusions. Some time thereafter it was determined that he had AIDS. He filed a petition for a court order against the blood bank that had furnished the blood to the hospital. He wanted to learn the names and addresses of all blood donors so that he could determine if any had AIDS. He hoped by this to prove that he had contracted AIDS as the result of one of the transfusions in the hospital. He died from the AIDS, and his estate continued the proceeding. The court of appeals certified the question to the state supreme court.

BARKETT, J. . . . The court must balance the competing interests that would be served by granting discovery or by denying it. . . .

The Supreme Court first recognized a right of privacy based on the United States Constitution in *Griswold v Connecticut*, 381 U.S. 479 (1965). This right of privacy has been described as "the most comprehensive of rights and the right most valued by civilized man." *Stanley v. Georgia*, 394 U.S. 557, 564 (1969). . . . In recent cases, the Court has discussed the privacy right as one of those fundamental rights that are "'implicit in the concept of ordered liberty' such that 'neither liberty nor justice would exist if [they] were sacrificed.'" *Bowers v. Hardwick*, [478] U.S. [186], 106 S.Ct. 2841, 2844 (1986). . . .

In 1980, the voters of Florida amended our state constitution to include an express right of privacy. Art. V, Section 23, Fla.Const. In approving the amendment, Florida became the fourth state to adopt a strong, freestanding right of privacy as a separate section of its state constitution, thus providing an explicit textual foundation for those privacy interests inherent in the concept of liberty which may not otherwise be protected by specific constitutional provisions.

Although the general concept of privacy encompasses an enormously broad and diverse field of personal action and belief, there can be no doubt that the Florida amendment was intended to protect the right to determine whether or not sensitive information about oneself will be disclosed to others. . . .

It is now known that AIDS is a major health problem with calamitous potential. At present, there is no known cure and the mortality rate is high. As noted by the court below, medical researchers have identified a number of groups which have a high incidence of the disease and are labeled "high risk" groups. . . .

The [court order requested] gives petitioner access to the names and addresses of the blood donors with no restrictions on their use. There is nothing to prohibit petitioner from conducting an investigation without the knowledge of the persons in question. We cannot ignore, therefore, the consequences of disclosure to nonparties, including the possibility that a donor's co-workers, friends, employers, and others may be queried as to the donor's sexual preferences, drug use, or general life-style.

The threat posed by the disclosure of the donors' identities goes far beyond the immediate discomfort occasioned by third party probing into sensitive areas of the donors' lives. Disclosure of donor identities in any context involving AIDS could be extremely disruptive and even devastating to the individual donor. If the requested information is released, and petitioner queries the donors' friends and fellow employees, it will be functionally impossible to prevent occasional references to AIDS. As the district court recognized:

> AIDS is the modern day equivalent of leprosy. AIDS, or a suspicion of AIDS, can lead to discrimination in employment, education, housing and even medical treatment. . . .

We conclude, therefore, that the disclosure sought here implicates constitutionally protected privacy interests.

Our analysis of the interests to be served by denying discovery does not end with the effects of disclosure on the private lives of the fifty-one donors implicated in this case. Society has a vital interest in maintaining a strong volunteer blood supply, a task that has become more difficult with the emergence of AIDS. . . . It is clearly "in the public interest to discourage any serious disincentive to volunteer blood donation." *Rasmussen*, 467 So.2d at 804. Because there is little doubt that the prospect of inquiry into one's private life and potential association with AIDS will deter blood donation, we conclude that society's interest in a strong and healthy blood supply will be furthered by the denial of discovery in this case.

In balancing the competing interests involved, we do not ignore Rasmussen's interest in obtaining the requested information. . . . However, we find that the discovery order requested here would do little to advance that interest. The probative value of the discovery sought by Rasmussen is dubious at best. The potential of significant harm to most, if not all, of the fifty-one unsuspecting donors in permitting such a fishing expedition is great and far outweighs the plaintiff's need under these circumstances. . . .

[Discovery refused]

QUESTIONS

1. What social forces were involved in the *Rasmussen* case?
2. Assume that Rasmussen had obtained the names and addresses of the donors. If one of them had AIDS, would that prove that Rasmussen had contracted AIDS from the blood transfusions?

In cases similar to *Rasmussen*, if the court has greater sympathy with the plaintiff than with the donors, discovery may be obtained subject to restrictions to prevent the information from going beyond the parties to the action and their attorneys.[4]

It is a federal offense to knowingly injure, intimidate, or interfere with anyone who is exercising a basic civil right (such as voting), taking part in any federal governmental program, or receiving federal assistance. Interference with attendance in a public school or college, participation in any state or local governmental program, service as a juror in a state court, or the use of any public facility (common carrier, hotel, or restaurant) is prohibited when based on race, color, religion, or national origin discrimination.[5]

Protection of the person is expanding to protect economic interests. Laws prohibiting discrimination in employment, in furnishing hotel accommodations and transportation, and in commercial transactions in the sale of property are an extension of the concept of protecting the person. Because membership in a professional association, a labor union, or a trade or business group has economic importance to its members, an applicant can no longer be excluded arbitrarily from the membership or be expelled without notice of the charges made and an opportunity to be heard.[6]

(c) PROTECTION OF PUBLIC HEALTH, SAFETY, AND MORALS. The law seeks to protect the public health, safety, and morals in many ways. Laws relating to quarantine, food inspection, and compulsory inoculation protect the public health. Laws regulating highway speeds and laws requiring fire escapes or guard devices around moving parts of factory machinery are for the safety of the public. Laws prohibiting the sale of liquor to minors and those prohibiting obscenity protect the morals of the public.

(d) PROTECTION OF PROPERTY. Just as laws have been developed to protect the individual's physical well-being, laws have been developed to protect one's property from damage, destruction, and other harmful acts. As already noted, a thief who steals an automobile is civilly liable to the owner of the automobile for its value and is criminally responsible to the state.

(e) PROTECTION OF TITLE. Because of the importance of ownership of property, one of the objectives of the law has been to protect

---

[4]   Gulf Coast Regional Blood Center v Houston (Tex App) 745 SW2d 557 (1988). In some states, statutes prohibit such discovery. Belle Bonfils Memorial Blood Center v District Court (Colo) 763 P2d 1003 (1988).

[5]   Civil Obedience Act of 1968, PL 90–284, 18 USC Section 245.

[6]   Silver v New York Stock Exchange, 373 US 341 (1963); Cunningham v Burbank Board of Realtors, 262 Cal App 2d 211, 68 Cal Rptr 653 (1968).

the title of the owner of property. Thus, if property is stolen, the true owner may recover it from the thief, and even from a person who purchased it in good faith from the thief.

(f) FREEDOM OF PERSONAL ACTION. In the Anglo-American stream of history, the desire for freedom from political domination gave rise to the American Revolution, and the desire for freedom from economic domination gave rise to the free enterprise philosophy. Today freedom is the dominant element in the constitutional provisions for the protection of freedom of religion, press, and speech, and also in such laws as those against trusts or business combinations in restraint of trade by others.

Freedom of action is also given to a patient who is competent to choose to die, in which case that person may refuse to take medical treatment that might prolong life.[7]

This right of freedom of personal action, however, cannot be exercised by one person in such a way that it interferes to an unreasonable extent with the rights of others. Freedom of speech, for example, does not mean freedom to speak or write a malicious, false statement about another person's character or reputation. In effect, this means that one person's freedom of speech must be balanced with another person's right to be free from defamation of character or reputation.

(g) FREEDOM OF USE OF PROPERTY. Freedom of action is often stated in terms of freedom of use of property. For example, the owner of an automobile is free to drive the car or not, to say who shall ride in it, to sell or give it away, and so on.

It must be remembered, however, that there are often restrictions on the use of property, such as speed laws governing the automobile, zoning laws regulating buildings, and antipollution laws restricting factories.

(h) ENFORCEMENT OF INTENT. When persons voluntarily enter into a transaction, the law usually seeks to enforce their intent. This objective is closely related to the concept that the law seeks to protect the individual's freedom of action. For example, if a person provides by will for the distribution of property upon death, the law will generally allow the property to pass to the persons intended by the deceased owner. The law will likewise seek to carry out the intention of the parties to a business transaction.

In looking for the intent of the lawmaker in adopting a law, the court will go behind first appearances. For example, although "intoxicating liquor" does not ordinarily suggest cough medicine, a motorist will be held to have been driving under the influence of intoxicating liquor when the blood test shows twice the allowable maximum of alcohol in the blood in consequence of the motorist's taking cough syrup having a high alcohol content.[8]

The extent to which the intent of one person or of several persons will be carried out has certain limitations. Sometimes the intent is not effective unless it is manifested by a particular written formality. For example, a deceased person may have intended to leave property to a friend, but in most states that intent must be shown by a written will signed by the deceased owner. Likewise, in some cases the intent of the parties may not be carried out because the law regards the intent as illegal.

(i) PROTECTION FROM EXPLOITATION, FRAUD, AND OPPRESSION. Many rules of law have developed in the courts, and many statutes have been enacted, to protect certain groups or individuals from exploitation or oppression by others. Thus, in order to protect **minors** (persons under legal age), the law developed that minors could set aside their contracts, subject to certain exceptions.

Persons buying food that is packed in cans are given certain rights against the seller and the manufacturer. Since the contents of the cans are not visible, buyers of such products need special protection from unscrupulous canners. The consumer is also protected by

---

[7]   Re Milton, 29 Ohio 3d 20, 505 NE2d 255 (1987).

[8]   Thornton v North Dakota State Highway Commissioners (ND) 399 NW2d 861 (1987).

laws against adulteration and poisons in food, drugs, and household products. Laws prohibiting unfair competition and discrimination, both economic and social, are also designed to protect from oppression.

(j) FURTHERANCE OF TRADE. Society seeks to further trade in a variety of ways, such as establishing a currency as a medium of payment; recognizing and giving legal effect to installment sales; adopting special rules for checks, notes, and similar instruments so that they can be widely used as credit devices and substitutes for money; and by enacting laws to mitigate the harmful effects of alternating periods of depression and inflation.

Laws that have been considered in connection with other objectives may also serve to further trade. For example, laws protecting against unfair competition have the objective of furthering trade, as well as the objective of protecting certain classes from oppression by others.

(k) PROTECTION OF CREDITORS. Society seeks to protect the rights of creditors and to protect them from dishonest or fraudulent acts of debtors. Initially, creditors are protected by the law that makes contracts binding and that provides machinery for the enforcement of contracts, and by the provision of the federal Constitution that prohibits states from impairing the obligation of contracts. Further, creditors may compel a debtor to go into bankruptcy. If the debtor has concealed property or transfers it to a friend in order to hide it from creditors, the law permits the creditors to claim the property for the payment of the debts due them.

(l) REHABILITATION OF DEBTORS. Society has come to regard it as unacceptable that debtors should be ruined forever by the burden of their debts. Imprisonment for debt has been abolished. Bankruptcy laws have been adopted to provide the debtor with a means of starting a new economic life. In times of widespread depression, the same objective has been served by special laws prohibiting the foreclosure of mortgages.

(m) STABILITY. Stability is particularly important in all business transactions. When you buy a house, for example, you not only want to know the exact meaning of the transaction under today's law, but you also want the transaction to have the same meaning in the future.

Because of the desire for stability, courts will ordinarily follow former decisions unless there is a strong reason to depart from them. Likewise, when no former case directly bears on the point involved, a court will strive to reach a decision that is a logical extension of some former decision or that follows a former decision by analogy, rather than to strike off on a fresh path to reach a decision unrelated to the past.

(n) FLEXIBILITY. If stability were always required, the cause of justice would often be defeated. The reason that originally gave rise to a rule of law may have ceased to exist.[9] Also, a rule may later appear unjust because it reflects a concept of justice that is outmoded or obsolete. For example, capital punishment, which one age believed just, has been seriously questioned by another age. We must not lose sight of the fact that the rule of law under question was created to further the sense of social justice existing at that time, and that our concepts of justice change.

(1) Means of Attaining Flexibility. Changes by legislative action are relatively easy to make. Furthermore, some statutes recognize the impossibility of laying down in advance a hard-and-fast rule that will do justice in all cases. The typical modern statute, particularly in the field of regulation of business, often contains an "escape clause" by which a person can escape from the operation of the statute under certain circumstances. Thus, a rent control law may impose a rent ceiling—that is, a maximum above which landlords cannot charge. The same law may also authorize a greater charge when special circumstances

---

[9]   "It is revolting to have no better reason for a rule of law than that it was laid down in the time of Henry IV. It is still more revolting if the grounds upon which it was laid down have vanished long since, and the rule simply persists from blind imitation of the past." Holmes, Collected Papers 187 (1920).

"The law must be stable, but it must not stand still." Roscoe Pound, *Introduction to the Philosophy of Law* (Connecticut: Yale University Press, 1922).

make it just to allow such exception, as when the landlord has made expensive repairs to the property or when taxes have increased substantially.

The rule of law may be stated in terms of what a reasonable or prudent person would do. Thus, whether you are negligent in driving your automobile is determined in court by whether you exercised the degree of care that a prudent person would have exercised in the same situation. This is a vague and variable standard as to how you must drive your car, but it is the only standard that is practical. The alternative would be a detailed motor code specifying how you should drive your car under every situation that might arise. A code obviously could not foresee every possibility, and it certainly would be too long for any driver to remember.

Even constitutions are flexible to the extent that they can be changed by amendment or judicial construction. Constitutions state the procedures for their amendment. Making changes in constitutions is purposely made difficult, so as to serve the objective of stability, but change can be made when the need for change is generally recognized by the people of the state or nation.

(2) Conflicting Social Forces. The social force of protecting the person is frequently the controlling factor in determining whether a court should adhere to the common law, thereby furthering stability; or whether it should change the law, thereby furthering flexibility. Thus, it will be seen that many times the courts retain the common law when that will further the protection of the person.

In other instances, the courts change the common law because a change will give the person greater protection. One court retained the common law definition of *person* with the result that a reckless driver injuring a mother and killing her unborn child was not guilty of manslaughter with respect to the death of the unborn child, because such a child was not a *person* under the common law of crimes.[10] By this decision, the person of the defendant was protected because the common law definition of *person* required him to be acquitted of the crime of manslaughter. However, in so doing, the court turned its back on protecting the person of the unborn child. Which person should the law protect? The social force of stability tipped the scales in favor of protecting the defendant.

(3) Evolution of Servant to Employee. At common law the parties to an employment contract were called master and servant. The servant was in fact regarded as a chattel or thing owned by the master rather than as a human being or a person. With the growth in this century of the rights of the person, the common law servant has been replaced by the modern employee who is a person and has all the rights of a person. In the *Cravens/Pocock* case the court was faced with the question of whether an employer could sue a third person who had negligently injured an employee. The employer sought to recover damages for the loss of the services of the injured employee.

[10]   Meadows v Arkansas, 291 Ark 105, 722 SW2d 584 (1987).

CRAVENS/POCOCK INS. AGENCY, INC. v JOHN F. BEASLEY CONSTRUCTION CO., INC.

(Tex App) 766 SW2d 309 (1989)

George Pocock was the president of Cravens/Pocock Insurance Agency. He was a passenger in an automobile that was struck by a negligently driven truck of the Beasley Construction Company. The Cravens agency sued Beasley for damages representing the value of Pocock's services that were lost because he was injured.

Beasley claimed that Cravens, as an employer, could not recover damages for such loss. Judgment was entered against Cravens, and it appealed.

LAGARDE, J. . . . Cravens based its proposed theory of recovery on the ancient common law principle of *per quod servitium amisit*. . . .

The common law does contain the doctrine of *per quod servitium amisit*, and Texas adopted the English common law as precedent in 1840.* The theory that a master may recover damages for the loss of services of a servant injured by a negligent third party harks back to a common law principle known as *per quod servitium amisit*. . . . This remedy originated in early Roman law when children, servants, and slaves were so closely identified with the domestic head of the house that an injury to them gave rise to an action by the *paterfamilias*, the male head of the house, who alone was entitled to recover for these damages. . . . Subsequently, this idea was taken wholly into the English common law so that a master had a cause of action for loss of services.

Over time, as English common law progressed, the rule of *per quod servitium amisit* came to be stated as follows:

A master also may bring an action against any man for beating or maiming his servant: but in such a case he must assign, as a special reason for so doing, his own damage by the loss of his service; and the loss must be proved upon the trial.

. . . Eventually, however, the social and economic relationship between master and servant which formed the basis of the negligent tort of *per quod servitium amisit* evolved into a contractual relationship between employer and employee with a significant juridical difference.

. . . The action of *per quod servitium amisit* fell into disuse in the United States. . . . Several policy considerations also strongly suggest that we should refrain from applying the rule. First, adoption of such a rule could cause the judicial floodgates to open and release a torrent of actions to swamp already crowded dockets. . . .

We should consider public policy factors such as the remoteness of foreseeability of injury, the disproportion of injury to culpability, the extraordinary nature of the result, the unreasonable burden on the negligent tortfeasor, the likelihood of fraudulent claims, and the fact that this theory of recovery has no sensible or just stopping point. . . . We have considered all those factors.

Thus, in conclusion, we decline to apply the common law rule of *per quod servitium amisit*. The rule may have made sense in a society where servants, children, and wives were considered mere chattels, but, fortunately, people think differently today. Nothing now resembles what was once thought of as the status of the servant. Consequently, we decline to apply this obsolete, archaic, and outmoded theory.

[Judgment affirmed] . . .

QUESTIONS

1. The court in the *Cravens* case was required to follow the common law. Appraise this statement.
2. What is the basis of the court's decision in the *Cravens* case?

---

*   An Act to Adopt the Common Law of England, to Repeal Certain Mexican Laws, and Regulate the Marital Rights of Parties. 1840 Tex.Gen.Laws 1, 2 H. Gammel, Laws of Texas 177 (1898).

(o) PRACTICAL EXPEDIENCY. Frequently the law is influenced by what is practical or expedient in the situation. Often the law will strive to make its rules fit the business practices of society. For example, a signature is frequently regarded by the law as including a stamping, printing, or typewriting of a name, in recognition of the business practice of "signing" letters and other instruments by mechanical means. A requirement of a handwritten signature would impose a burden on business that would not be practically expedient.

With the advent of the computer, the law of evidence has changed to allow a computer printout to be admitted in evidence. The old law was that records could not be produced in court unless the person who prepared them was present as a witness.[11]

5.   Conflicting Objectives

The specific objectives of the law sometimes conflict with each other. When this is true, the problem is one of social policy, which in turn means weighing social, economic, and moral forces to determine which objective should be furthered.

At times a conflict develops between the objective of the state in seeking protection from the conduct of individuals or groups and the objective of freedom of action by those individuals and groups. For example, although protection of the freedom of the individual seeks the utmost freedom of religious belief, society will impose limitations on religious freedom where it believes such freedom will cause harm to the public welfare. Hence, state laws requiring vaccination against smallpox were enforced despite the contention that this violated religious principles. Similarly, parents failing to provide medical care for a sick child will be held guilty of manslaughter if the child dies, even though the parents sincerely believed as a matter of religious principle that medical care was improper. In contrast, when the harm contemplated is not direct or acute, religious freedom will prevail. For example, a compulsory child education law will not be enforced against Amish parents who as a matter of religion are opposed to state education.[12] A statute may constitutionally authorize owners of mobile parks to adopt a rule limiting residents within the park to adults, even though this limits the freedom of action of nonadults.[13]

As another example of conflicting objectives, that of protecting title may conflict with the objective of furthering trade. Consider again the example of the stolen property that was sold by the thief to a person who purchased it for value and in good faith, without reason to know that the goods had been stolen. If we are to further the objective of protecting the title to the property, we will conclude that the owner can recover the property from the innocent purchaser. This rule, however, will discourage trade, for people will be less willing to buy goods if they run the risk that the goods were stolen and may have to be surrendered. If we instead think only of taking steps to encourage buying and selling, we will hold that the buyer takes a good title because the buyer acted in good faith and paid value. If we do this, we then destroy the title of the original owner and obviously abandon our objective of protecting title to property. As a general rule, American society has followed the objective of protecting title. In some instances, however, the objective of furthering trade is adopted by statute and the buyer is given good title, as in certain cases of commercial paper (notes, drafts, and checks) or of the purchaser from a regular dealer in other people's goods.

6.   Law as an Evolutionary Process

Law changes as society changes. Let us consider an example of this type of change. When the economy was patterned on a local community unit in which everyone knew each other and each other's product, the concept of "let the buyer beware" expressed a proper basis on which to conduct business. Much of the early law of the sale of goods was based

---

[11]   See Chapter 21, Section 4.

[12]   Wisconsin v Yoder, 406 US 205 (1972) (high school student).
[13]   Schmidt v Superior Court, 48 Cal 3d 438, 256 Cal Rptr 766, 769 P2d 948 (1989).

on this view. In today's economy, however, with its interstate, national, and even international character, the buyer has little or no direct contact with the manufacturer or seller, and the packaging of articles makes their presale examination impossible. Under these circumstances, the consumer must rely on the integrity of others. Gradually, practices that were tolerated and even approved in an earlier era have been condemned, and the law has changed to protect the buyer.

Moreover, new principles of law are being developed to meet the new situations that arise. Every new invention and every new business practice introduces a number of situations for which there may be no existing rule of law. For example, how could there have been a law relating to stocks and bonds before those instruments came into existence? How could there have been a law with respect to the liability of radio and television broadcasters before such methods of communication were developed?

New inventions and new techniques for investigation have changed or produced new rules of law because it has become possible to prove facts that could not have been proven before. Thus, fingerprint identification, ballistics, and advanced chemical analysis techniques have made identification a certainty. The use of radar to determine speed is now commonplace. Within the last decade the DNA or "genetic fingerprint" test for identity of blood cells has become recognized as a highly reliable means of proving identity.[14]

7.　The Courts and the Making of the Law

In the early days of our country, courts were thought to merely declare the law. That is, they were to apply existing law to existing facts. They had no power to make new law.

Since the 1930s, it has been recognized and accepted that courts do make the law. Changing technology and cultural patterns produce new situations for which there is no law. A

---

[14]　Andrews v Florida (Fla App) 533 So 2d 841 (1988) (Expert testified that the chance that two persons would show the same on the DNA test was 1 out of 839,914,540).

---

strict court will wait until the lawmaker passes a law. The liberal court will create a new rule to fill the gap. Similarly, the rule of law followed by a former court may appear outmoded in the light of the new technology and cultural pattern. Here the strict court will follow the former decision until the lawmaker makes a change. The liberal court will take charge and make the change by revising the earlier decision. During the last three decades, more and more courts adopted the liberal approach, and their opinions openly recognized that they were making law to advance one or more of the social forces discussed in Section 4 of this chapter.

The extent to which courts can make the law is, of course, limited by existing statutes and constitutions. These cannot be ignored by the courts. In many instances, however, the courts may reinterpret the statute or constitution so that the net result is the same as if they were amended.

8.　Law as a Synthesis

Many rules of law do not further one objective alone. Some rules are a combination of two or more objectives, with each objective working toward the same result. In other instances, the objectives oppose each other, and the rule of law that emerges is a combination or synthesis of the different objectives.

Law as a synthesis may be illustrated by the law as it relates to a contract for the sale of a house. Originally such a contract could be oral; that is, merely spoken words with nothing in writing to prove that there was such a contract. Of course, there was the practical question of proof—that is, whether the jury would believe that there was such a contract—but no rule of law said that the contract had to be evidenced by a writing. This situation made it possible for a witness in court to swear falsely that Jones had agreed to sell Jones' house for a specified sum. Even though Jones had not made such an agreement, the jury might believe the false witness, and Jones would be required to give up the house on terms to which Jones had never agreed. To prevent such a miscarriage of justice, a statute was passed declaring that contracts for the sale of houses had to be evidenced by a writing.

This law ended the evil of persons lying that there was an oral agreement for the sale of a house, but was justice achieved? Not always, for cases arose in which Jones did in fact make an oral agreement to sell land to Smith. Smith would take possession of the land and would make valuable improvements at great expense and effort, and then Jones would have Smith thrown off the land. Smith would defend on the ground that Jones had orally agreed to sell the land. Jones would then say, "Where is the writing that the statute requires?" To this, Smith could only reply there was no writing. No writing meant no binding legal agreement; and therefore Smith lost the land, leaving Jones with the land and all the improvements that Smith had made. That certainly was not just.

Gradually, the courts developed the rule that even though the statute required a writing, the courts would enforce an oral contract for the sale of land when the buyer had gone into possession and made valuable improvements of such a nature that it would be difficult to determine what amount of money would be required to make up the loss to the buyer if the buyer were to be put off the land.

Thus, the law passed through three stages. The original concept held that all land contracts could be oral and did not require any written evidence. Because the perjury evil arose under that rule, the law swung to the opposite rule that no such contract could be oral without any written evidence. This rule gave rise to the hardship case of the honest buyer under an oral contract who made extensive improvements. The law then swung back, not to the original rule, but to a middle position, combining the writing requirement as to the ordinary transaction, but allowing oral contracts in special cases to prevent hardship.

This example is also interesting because it shows the way that the courts amend the law by decision. The flat requirement of the statute was eroded by an exception created by the courts in the interest of furthering justice.

SUMMARY

A society's ethical code constitutes the foundation on which its laws are built. In contrast to ethics, however, the law must be more definite and stable in order to be enforceable. Nevertheless, a society's evolving ethical code can serve as a blueprint for the future form of its laws.

Some of the underlying principles that society regards as important in making its ethical decisions and formulating its laws include: protection of the state; protection of the person; protection of public health, safety, and morals; protection of property and title; freedom of personal action; freedom of use of property; enforcement of intent; protection from exploitation, fraud, and oppression; furtherance of trade; creditor protection; debtor rehabilitation; stability; flexibility; and practical expediency. These individual concerns sometimes conflict with one another and so, as laws are created and evolve, society is continually seeking a proper balance or synthesis of its ultimate objectives.

QUESTIONS AND CASE PROBLEMS

1. What is the general purpose of law?
2. What social force is involved in the rule that a professional association cannot arbitrarily exclude a person from membership?
3. Give an illustration of the social force of protection of title.
4. The social force in favor of freedom of personal action permits you to say anything you wish. Appraise the statement.
5. Does the law remain constant?
6. Of the specific objectives of the law, which do you consider to be the most important? Why?

7. (a) How can law be dynamic if stability is one of its specific objectives? (b) How do some statutes provide for built-in flexibility?

8. McCarthy owned a motor scooter. He obtained an insurance policy from the Foundation Reserve Insurance Company. This policy covered medical expenses when the insured was "struck by an automobile." McCarthy rode his scooter into an automobile. The insurance company refused to pay his medical expenses on the ground that he had struck the automobile and had not been struck by an automobile. What social forces are involved in deciding the case?

9. The Reader's Digest Association published an article on truck hijacking. In the article it stated that John Doe, giving his actual name, had taken part in a truck hijacking 11 years before and had thereafter reformed. John Doe sued the Reader's Digest Association for damages. Reader's Digest Association raised the defense that it was not liable because the information was true. What was the theory on which John Doe sued? What social forces are involved? Is John Doe's claim valid?

10. Lopez wrote bad checks on the United Bank of Pueblo and on the Colorado National Bank. He was prosecuted for the crime of issuing bad checks. The prosecution offered in evidence bank statements obtained from the two banks showing the condition of the accounts of Lopez. He objected to this evidence which would show that his checks were bad on the ground that his right of privacy was violated when the banks furnished the statements. Decide. [Colorado v Lopez (Colo) 776 P2d 390]

11. The Federal Bureau of Investigation (FBI) has criminal records on over 24 million persons. A CBS television news correspondent and the Reporters Committee for Freedom of the Press requested to see the information held by the FBI on certain named persons. The request was made under the Freedom of Information Act. That Act provides generally for the disclosing of governmental agency records subject to certain exceptions, one of which is that disclosure could be refused where it could reasonably be expected to constitute an unwarranted invasion of privacy. The FBI refused to disclose the records. In the lawsuit brought against the FBI it was claimed that each case should be examined separately on its facts to see if there would be a danger of an unreasonable invasion of privacy. The FBI claimed that there should be a flat rule that none of its criminal records had to be disclosed. Decide. What social forces are involved? [United States Department of Justice v Reporters Committee for Freedom of the Press, 489 US 749, 103 L Ed 2d 774]

12. The New York Social Services Law authorized the Social Services officials to replace necessary furniture and clothing of welfare recipients who lost such items by fire, flood, or other like catastrophe. Howard was on state welfare. Her clothing was stolen from her apartment by a burglar. She claimed that this was a catastrophe and that the Social Service official was required to replace the stolen clothing. Was she correct? [In re Howard, 28 NY2d 434, 271 NE2d 528]

13. The United States Congress has passed several laws aimed at preventing the sale of narcotics and harmful drugs. One of these laws makes it illegal for an unauthorized person to sell or supply marijuana or LSD. Judith Kuch was prosecuted for violating this Act. She admitted that she had transferred the substances covered by the Act and that she did not have a license as required by the Act. She claimed, however, that she was protected by religious freedom. She was, in fact, an ordained minister of the Neo-American Church and the substances were used by her only as part of the religious services in her church. Decide. [United States v Kuch (DC Dist Col) 288 F Supp 439]

14. As you read the explanation of how modern scientific tests work, you will become impressed with the fact that only people working in science can understand the way the tests work. (See, for example, the explanation of the DNA (genetic fingerprint) test in Andrews v Florida (Fla App) 533 So 2d 841 (1988).) The result is that the typical jury will accept the conclusion of the expert. In a case that turns on the identity of a wrongdoer, the net result is that it is the expert and not the jury that determines that the defendant is the person who is guilty or who is at fault. Discuss the ethical implications.

15. Norma Wons was admitted to the Jackson Memorial Hospital because of extreme internal bleeding. The doctors believed that without blood transfusions she would die. Norma's mind was not affected by her illness. She was 38 years of age. She refused to take the transfusion because of her religious belief. Her husband shared her religious belief. They had two boys, ages 12 and 14. The hospital sought a court order to authorize giving Norma the necessary transfusions without her consent. Should the court issue such authorization? [Wons v Public Health Trust of Dade County (Fla App) 500 So 2d 679]

3

THE CONSTITUTION AS THE FOUNDATION OF THE LEGAL ENVIRONMENT

A basic principle of the American Revolution was that there should be limits to governmental power. Americans saw the need for a central government but did not want that government to have unlimited power. Consequently, the document creating that central government, the Constitution of the United States, sets forth not only the structure and powers of government but also limitations on those powers. This Constitution, together with the constitutions of each of the states, forms the foundation of our legal environment.

A. THE FEDERAL SYSTEM

By creating a central government to coexist with the governments of the individual states, the U.S. Constitution created a federal system. In a **federal system** a central government is given power to administer to national concerns while the individual states retain the power to administer to local concerns.

1.   What a Constitution Is

The term **constitution** refers to either the structure of the government and its relation to the people within its sphere of power or the written document setting forth that structure. When capitalized, the word refers to the written document that specifies the structure and powers of the United States national government and its relation to the people within the territory of the United States.

In speaking of the Constitution it is often necessary to distinguish between the written Constitution and the living Constitution. This is required because the Constitution has grown and changed as described in Section 7 of this chapter.

2.   The Branches of Government

The written Constitution establishes a **tripartite** (three-part) division of government. That is, there is a **legislative branch** (Congress) to make the laws, an **executive branch** (the President) to execute the laws, and a **judicial branch** (courts) to interpret the laws. The national legislature or Congress is a **bicameral** (two-house) body consisting of a Senate and a House of Representatives. Members of the Senate are popularly elected for a term of six years. Members of the House of Representatives are popularly elected for a term of two years. The President is elected by an Electoral College whose membership is popularly elected. The President serves for a term of four years and is eligible for re-election for a second term. Judges of the United States are appointed by the President with the approval of the Senate and serve for life, subject to removal only by impeachment because of misconduct.

B.   THE STATES AND THE CONSTITUTION

The effect of the adoption of the Constitution was to take certain powers away from the states and to give them to the national government.

3.   Delegated and Shared Powers

The national government possesses only the powers given by the states. These powers are set forth in the United States Constitution.

(a) DELEGATED POWERS. The powers given by the states to the national government are described as **delegated powers.** Some of these delegated powers are given exclusively to the national government. Thus, the national government alone may declare war or establish a currency.

(b) SHARED POWERS. Some of the powers delegated to the national government may still be exercised by the states. For example, the grant of power to the national government to impose taxes did not destroy the state power to tax. Some of the shared powers may only be exercised by the states as long as there is no federal exercise. Thus, a state appliance-safety law may apply until a federal law on the subject is adopted by Congress. In other cases, a state may provide regulation along with, but subject to the supremacy of, federal law. Regulation of navigation on navigable waterways within a state is an example.[1]

(c) PROHIBITED POWERS. The Constitution prohibits states from doing certain acts, even though the federal government is also similarly prohibited. Thus, neither states nor the national government may adopt *ex post facto* laws. *Ex post facto* laws make criminal an act already committed that was not criminal when committed or increase the penalty for an act already committed above the penalty in force at the time it was committed.

4.   Federal Supremacy

Federal law will bar conflicting state action when there is a federal law regulating the particular subject. Federal law will also bar state action when the silence of Congress is seen as showing the congressional intent that there should be no regulation by anyone.

---

[1]   Re Income Tax Cases, 157 Mich App 525, 403 NW2d 182 (1987).

FIGURE 3-1   GOVERNMENTS OF THE UNITED STATES

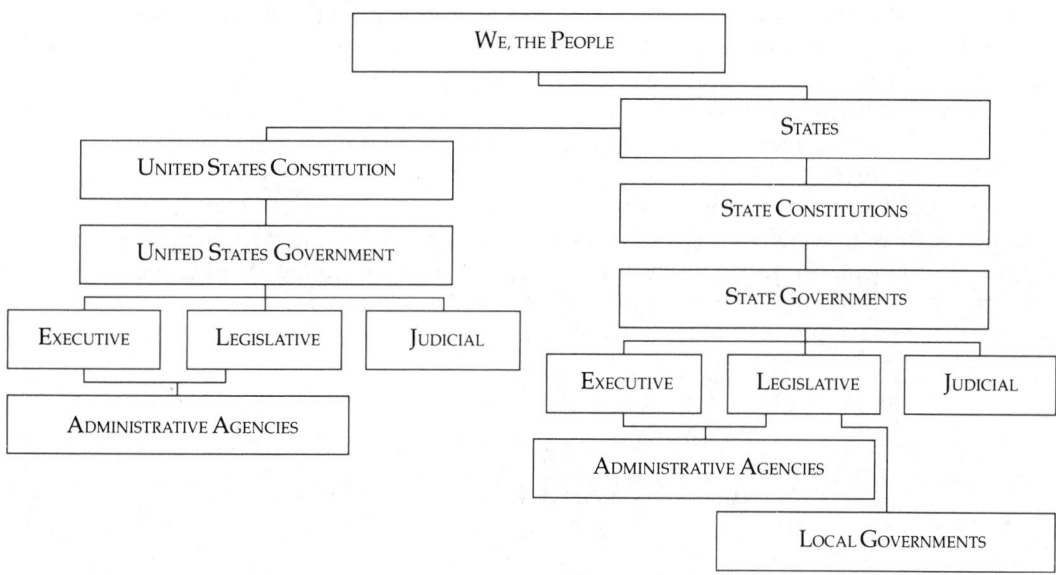

(a) EXPRESS FEDERAL REGULATION. The Constitution and statutes properly adopted by Congress are the supreme law of the land. They cancel out any conflicting state law.

This **federal supremacy** is expressly declared by the Constitution.[2] When there is a direct conflict between federal and state statutes, the decision as to which prevails is thus easy to make.[3]

If there is no obvious conflict because the federal statute covers only part of the subject matter, the question arises whether a state law can regulate the areas not regulated by Congress or whether the partial regulation made by Congress **preempts** the field so as to prohibit state legislation.

(b) SILENCE OF CONGRESS. In some situations, the silence of Congress in failing to cover a particular phase of the subject, or in failing to have any law on the subject at all, is held to indicate that Congress does not want any law on the matter. Therefore, no state law will be allowed to regulate the matter. When national uniformity is essential, it is generally held that the silence of Congress means that the subject has been preempted by Congress and that no state law on the subject may be adopted.

C.   INTERPRETING AND AMENDING THE CONSTITUTION

The Constitution as it is interpreted today has changed greatly from the Constitution as originally written. This change has been brought about by interpretation, amendment, and practice.

5.   Conflicting Theories

Shortly after the Constitution was adopted, conflict arose as to whether the Constitution was to be interpreted strictly, so as to give the federal government the least power possible, or broadly, so as to give the federal government the greatest power that the words would permit. These two views may be given the names of (a) the bedrock view and (b) the living document view.

By the bedrock view, the purpose of a constitution is to state certain fundamental principles for all time. By the living document view, a constitution is merely a statement of

---

[2]   US Const, Art VI, Cl 2. Michigan Canners and Freezers Ass'n., Inc. v Agricultural Marketing and Bargaining Board, 467 US 461 (1984).
[3]   Perry v Thomas, 482 US 483 (1987)

goals and objectives and is intended to grow and change with time.

Whether the Constitution is to be liberally interpreted, under the living document view, or narrowly interpreted, under the bedrock view, has a direct effect upon the Constitution. For the last century, the Supreme Court has followed the living document view. This has resulted in strengthening the power of the federal government, permitting the rise of administrative agencies, and expanding the protection of human rights. If the Constitution had been strictly interpreted according to the bedrock theory, the central or federal government would have relatively little power today, administrative agencies would not be allowed, and many human rights would not be protected from governmental invasion. The living document view has given us the living Constitution described in Section 7 of this chapter. The living document view was first stated by the United States Supreme Court in the *McCulloch* case.

McCULLOCH v MARYLAND
4 Wheat 316 (1819)

The first bank of the United States was chartered in 1791 and again in 1816. Hostile state legislation attempted to drive it out of existence. In 1818, Maryland adopted a law imposing a tax on bank notes issued by any bank not chartered by the state legislature. McCulloch, the cashier of the Baltimore branch of the National Bank, issued bank notes on which this tax had not been paid. Suit was brought by the state of Maryland against him to recover the statutory penalties imposed for violation of the statute.

MARSHALL, C. J. . . . The first question . . . is, has Congress power to incorporate a bank? . . .

This government of the Union . . . is acknowledged by all to be one of enumerated powers. . . .

Among the enumerated powers, we do not find that of establishing a bank or creating a corporation. . . . A constitution, to contain an accurate detail of all the subdivisions of which its great powers will admit, and of all the means by which they may be carried into execution, would partake of the prolixity of a legal code, and could scarcely be embraced by the human mind. It would probably never be understood by the public. Its nature, therefore, requires, that only its great outlines should be marked, its important objects designated, and the minor ingredients which compose those objects be deduced from the nature of the objects themselves. . . .

Although, among the enumerated powers of government, we do not find the word "bank" or "incorporation," we find the great powers to lay and collect taxes; to borrow money; to regulate commerce; to declare and conduct a war; and to raise and support armies and navies. The sword and the purse, all the external relations, and no inconsiderable portion of the industry of the nation, are intrusted to its government . . . A government, intrusted with such ample powers, on the due execution of which the happiness and prosperity of the nation so vitally depends, must also be intrusted with ample means for their execution. The power being given, it is the interest of the nation to facilitate its execution. . . . Can we adopt that construction [of the Constitution] (unless the words imperiously require it) which would impute to the framers of that instrument, when granting these powers for the public good, the intention of impeding their exercise by withholding a choice of means? If, indeed, such be the mandate of the Constitution, we have only to obey; but that instrument does not profess to enumerate the means by which the powers it confers may be executed; nor does it prohibit the creation of a corporation, if the existence of such a being be essential to the beneficial exercise of those powers. It is, then, the subject of fair inquiry, how far such means may be employed. . . .

The government which has a right to do an act, and has imposed on it the duty of performing that act, must, according to the dictates of reason, be allowed to select the means; and those who contend that it may not select any appropriate means, that one particular mode of effecting the object is excepted, take upon themselves the burden of establishing that exception. . . .

But the Constitution of the United States has not left the right of Congress to employ the necessary means, for the execution of the powers conferred on the government, to general reasoning. To its enumeration of powers is added that of making "all laws which shall be necessary and proper, for carrying into execution the foregoing powers, and all other powers vested by this Constitution, in the government of the United States, or in any department thereof."

. . . This provision is made in a constitution intended to endure for ages to come, and, consequently, to be adapted to the various crises of human affairs. To have prescribed the means by which government should, in all future time, execute its powers, would have been to change, entirely, the character of the instrument, and give it the properties of a legal code. It would have been an unwise attempt to provide, by immutable rules, for exigencies which, if foreseen at all, must have been seen dimly, and which can be best provided for as they occur. [The Court rejected the contention that "necessary" means "absolutely necessary."] . . . Sound construction of the Constitution must allow to the national legislature that discretion, with respect to the means by which the powers it confers are to be carried into execution, which will enable that body to perform the high duties assigned to it, in the manner most beneficial to the people. Let the end be legitimate, let it be within the scope of the Constitution, and all means which are appropriate, which are plainly adapted to that end, which are not prohibited, but consist with the letter and spirit of the Constitution, are constitutional.

. . . It can scarcely be necessary to say, that the existence of state banks can have no possible influence on the question. No trace is to be found in the Constitution of an intention to create a dependence of the government of the Union on those of the states, for the execution of the great powers assigned to it. . . . The choice of means implies a right to choose a national bank in preference to state banks, and Congress alone can make the election.

[Judgment against Maryland on the basis that, as Congress had authority to create a bank, a state law designed to harm that bank was unconstitutional, and therefore Maryland could not recover the penalty authorized by that state statute]

QUESTIONS

1. What section of the Constitution authorizes Congress to create a national bank?
2. Does the Court say that the creation of a national bank system is the best way to do the job?

Can we decide that we should adopt the bedrock view or the living document view? We cannot select one view to the exclusion of the other for the simple reason that we want both. Contradictory as this sounds, it is obvious that we want our Constitution to be durable. We do not want a set of New Year's resolutions that will be forgotten shortly. At the same time, we know that the world changes, and therefore we do not want a constitution that will hold us tied in a straightjacket of the past.

In terms of social forces that make the law, we are torn between our desire for stability and our desire for flexibility. We want a constitution that is stable. At the same time we want one that is flexible. There is probably no one living today who believes that the Constitution should be either 100 percent stable or 100 percent flexible. Everyone wants both qualities, and the problem is how to reach a compromise. Some people will favor more change than others. That is why we have conflict.

It is essential that we recognize that our Constitution is in a sense torn between the conflicting desires of change and no change. To look only at the Constitution as it was written in 1787 and to ignore the stresses and strains of the change-no change conflict is misleading. If we do not see the conflict, we do not see the Constitution as it really is today. Even more important, we lack the understanding needed to meet the problems of tomorrow.

6.   Amending the Constitution

The United States Constitution has been amended in three ways: (a) expressly, (b) by interpretation, and (c) by practice.

(a) CONSTITUTIONAL METHOD OF AMENDING. Article V of the Constitution sets forth the procedure to be followed for making amendments to the Constitution. Relatively few changes have been made to the Constitution by this formal amending process, although thousands of proposals have been made.

(b) AMENDMENT BY JUDICIAL INTERPRETATION. The greatest change to the written Constitution has been made by the Supreme Court in "interpreting" the Constitution. Generally, interpretation is used to apply the Constitution to a new situation that could not have been foreseen when the written Constitution was adopted.

(c) AMENDMENT BY PRACTICE. In practice, the letter of the Constitution is not always followed. Departure from the written Constitution began as early as 1793, when Washington refused to make treaties, as required by the Constitution, "by and with the consent of the Senate." Washington began the practice that has been followed since that time of the President's negotiating the treaty with the foreign country and then submitting it to the Senate for approval. Similarly, the Electoral College that was intended to exercise independent judgment in selecting the President now automatically elects the official candidate of the party that elected the members of the Electoral College.

Other aspects of practice have added to the Constitution things that are not there. As written, the Constitution contemplates that Congress will originate and adopt laws. With the rise of the party system, which was not anticipated by the framers of the Constitution, the President has become the leader of the legislative program. This position of leadership has been strengthened greatly by modern media, beginning with Roosevelt's radio "fireside chats" of the 1930s and broadening into television in later years.

7.   The Living Constitution

The Constitution that has developed in the manner described in the preceding section is radically different from that which was written on paper. The living Constitution has the following characteristics:

(a) STRONG GOVERNMENT. One of the characteristics of the new Constitution is strong government. Adam Smith's concept of **laissez faire**—of a "hands off" policy of government—has been largely forgotten. Freedom of the individual as a human being has expanded, but business enterprises can now be regulated and the economy controlled.

(b) STRONG PRESIDENT. Instead of being merely an officer who carries out the laws, the President has become the political leader of a party, exerting a strong influence on the lawmaking process. If the President's political party is in control of both Houses of the Congress, the President acts as the leader of the lawmaking process.

(c) ECLIPSE OF THE STATES. Under the new Constitution, all governments have powers that they never possessed before, but the center of gravity has shifted from the states to the nation. When the Constitution was adopted in 1789, the federal government was to have only the very limited powers specified in Article I, Section 8 of the Constitution. What regulation of business was permissible was to be imposed by the states. Today, the great bulk of the regulation of business is adopted by the federal government through Congress or its administrative agencies. As the American economy moved from the local community stage to the nationwide stage, the individual states were unable to provide effective regulation of business. It was inevitable that regulation would be drawn to the central government. Consequently, when we speak of government regulation of business, we ordinarily mean the national government, not the state or local governments.

(d) ADMINISTRATIVE AGENCIES. These were virtually unheard of in 1789, and no mention is made of them in the Constitution of 1789. The vast powers of the new Constitution are exercised to a very large degree by administrative agencies. They are in effect a fourth branch of the government, not provided for in the written Constitution. More importantly, it is the administrative agencies that come in contact with the majority of business persons and citizens. The agencies are the "government" for most people.

In other words, the vast power of government to regulate business is not exercised di-

rectly by the legislatures, the courts, or the executive officers. Rather, this power is exercised by agencies. The members of the agencies—or the boards, commissions, or persons heading the agencies—are not elected by the voters, and their decisions are to a large degree not subject to effective review or reversal by the courts.

(e) HUMAN RIGHTS. The scope of human rights protected from governments has dramatically broadened. These rights are protected from invasion by not merely the federal government, but by any government. Most significant of all, unwritten rights are protected, although they are not guaranteed by any express constitutional provision.

Statutes regulating conduct must be carefully drawn to avoid invading these rights. For example, a city ordinance making it unlawful to interrupt police officers in the performance of their duties is unconstitutional because it is so broad that it prohibits speech.[4]

The study of the evolution of the Constitution will serve as a guide to understanding the present; to foreseeing, even if dimly, the future; and to appreciating the problems that are involved. As people working in a business world, it is essential that we have this understanding. As citizens living and voting in an organized democratic society, it is our duty to ourselves and our nation to understand these problems so that we can intelligently take part in their solution.

D.   FEDERAL POWERS

The federal government possesses powers necessary to administer matters of national concern. Some of those powers are of particular interest to businesses.

8.   Power to Regulate Commerce

The desire to protect commerce from restrictions and barriers set up by the individual states was a prime factor leading to the adop-

---

[4]   City of Houston v Hill, 482 US 451 (1987).

tion of the Constitution of 1789. To protect commerce, Congress was given, by Article I, Section 8, Clause 3, the power "to regulate commerce with foreign nations, and among the several states, and with the Indian tribes."

Until 1937, the Supreme Court held that this provision gave Congress the power to control or regulate only that which crossed a state line, such as an interstate railway train or an interstate telegraph message.

(a) THE COMMERCE POWER BECOMES A GENERAL WELFARE POWER. In 1937 the Supreme Court began expanding the concept of interstate commerce. By 1946 the power to regulate interstate commerce had become very broad. By that year the power had expanded to the point that it gave authority to Congress to adopt regulatory laws that were "as broad as the economic needs of the nation."[5] By virtue of this broad interpretation, Congress can regulate manufacturing, agriculture, mining, stock exchanges, insurance, loan sharking,[6] monopolies, and conspiracies in restraint of trade. If desired, Congress can set standards, quotas, and priorities for industries.

The case that was the starting point in this transition of the commerce clause was the *Jones & Laughlin Steel Corp.* case.

[5] American Power & Light Co. v Securities and Exchange Commission, 329 US 90 (1946). The wide scope of this view is seen in such statutes as The Food, Agriculture, Conservation, and Trade Act of 1990. Act of November 28, 1990, PL 101–624, 104 Stat 3359, ___ USC §§ ___.
[6] Perez v United States, 402 US 146 (1971).

NLRB v JONES & LAUGHLIN STEEL CORP.
301 US 1 (1937)

The National Labor Relations Board found that Jones & Laughlin Steel Corporation had discharged ten employees to discourage membership in a union. The Board ordered these employees reinstated with full back pay and ordered that the employer cease and desist from such conduct. When the employer failed to comply with the order, the Board petitioned the court of appeals to enforce the order. The court of appeals denied the petition, holding that the Board's order exceeded federal power. The Supreme Court granted certiorari.

HUGHES, C. J. . . . The scheme of the National Labor Relations Act . . . may be briefly stated. The first section sets forth findings with respect to the injury to commerce resulting from the denial by employers of the right of employees to organize and from the refusal of employers to accept the procedure of collective bargaining. There follows a declaration that it is the policy of the United States to eliminate these causes of obstruction to the free flow of commerce. The Act then defines the terms it uses, including the terms "commerce" and "affecting commerce." Section 2. It creates the National Labor Relations Board and prescribes its organization. Sections 3–6. It sets forth the right of employees to self-organization and to bargain collectively through representatives of their own choosing. Section 7. It defines "unfair labor practices." Section 8. It lays down rules as to the representation of employees for the purpose of collective bargaining. Section 9. The Board is empowered to prevent the described unfair labor practices affecting commerce and the Act prescribes the procedure to that end. . . .

. . . The respondent [Jones & Laughlin Steel Corp.] argues (1) that the Act is in reality a regulation of labor relations and not of interstate commerce; . . .

The facts as to the nature and scope of the business of the Jones & Laughlin Steel Corporation have been found by the Labor Board.

[The Court discussed in detail the interstate organization of the employer with various plants in different states.]

Summarizing these operations, the Labor Board concluded that the works in Pittsburgh and Aliquippa "might be likened to the heart of a self-contained, highly integrated body. They draw in the raw materials from Michigan, Minnesota, West Virginia, Pennsylvania in part through arteries and by means controlled by the respondent; they transform the materials and then pump them out to all parts of the nation through the vast mechanism which the respondent has elaborated."

. . . The Scope of the Act.—The Act is challenged in its entirety as an attempt to regulate all industry, thus invading the reserved powers of the States over their local concerns. . . .

. . . The grant of authority to the Board does not purport to extend to the relationship between all industrial employees and employers. Its terms do not impose collective bargaining upon all industry regardless of effects upon interstate or foreign commerce. It purports to reach only what may be deemed to burden or obstruct that commerce and, thus qualified, it must be construed as contemplating the exercise of control within constitutional bounds. It is a familiar principle that acts which directly burden or obstruct interstate or foreign commerce, or its free flow, are within the reach of the congressional power. Acts having that effect are not rendered immune because they grow out of labor disputes. . . . It is the effect upon commerce, not the source of the injury, which is the criterion. Whether or not particular action does affect commerce in such a close and intimate fashion as to be subject to federal control, and hence to lie within the authority conferred upon the Board, is left by the statute to be determined as individual cases arise. . . .

. . . Although activities may be intrastate in character when separately considered, if they have such a close and substantial relation to interstate commerce that their control is essential or appropriate to protect that commerce from burdens and obstructions, Congress cannot be denied the power to exercise that control.

. . . The stoppage of [respondent's] operations by industrial strife would have a most serious effect upon interstate commerce. In view of respondent's far-flung activities, it is idle to say that the effect would be indirect or remote. It is obvious that it would be immediate and might be catastrophic. We are asked to shut our eyes to the plainest facts of our national life and to deal with the question of direct and indirect effects in an intellectual vacuum. Because there may be but indirect and remote effects upon interstate commerce in connection with a host of local enterprises throughout the country, it does not follow that other industrial activities do not have such a close and intimate relation to interstate commerce as to make the presence of industrial strife a matter of the most urgent national concern. When industries organize themselves on a national scale, making their relation to interstate commerce the dominant factor in their activities, how can it be maintained that their industrial labor relations constitute a forbidden field into which Congress may not enter when it is necessary to protect interstate commerce from the paralyzing consequences of industrial war? We have often said that interstate commerce itself is a practical conception. It is equally true that interferences with that commerce must be appraised by a judgment that does not ignore actual experience.

Experience has abundantly demonstrated that the recognition of the right of employees to self-organization and to have representatives of their own choosing for the purpose of collective bargaining is often an essential condition of industrial peace. Refusal to confer and negotiate has been one of the most prolific causes of strife. . . . And of what avail is it to protect the facility of transportation, if interstate commerce is throttled with respect to the commodities to be transported!

. . . It is not necessary again to detail the facts as to respondent's enterprise. . . . [I]t presents in a most striking way the close and intimate relation which [an] industry may have to interstate commerce, and we have no doubt that Congress had constitutional authority. . . .

[The National Labor Relations Act was constitutional as applied to the respondent steel company and was within the scope of the power of Congress over interstate commerce]

QUESTIONS

1. What statute was involved in the *Jones & Laughlin Steel Corp.* case?
2. Was the decision of the Court inevitable?
3. Why was it important to hold that the labor relations were interstate commerce?

(b) THE COMMERCE POWER AS A LIMITATION ON STATES. The federal power to regulate commerce not only gives Congress the power to act but also prevents states from acting in any way that interferes with federal regulation or burdens interstate commerce. For example, if the federal government establishes safety device regulations for interstate carriers, a state cannot require different devices.

Because modern commerce is typically interstate in character, the fact that Congress does not impose any regulation is generally interpreted as excluding state action with respect to interstate commerce.

States may not use their tax power for the purpose of discriminating against interstate commerce, as such commerce is within the protection of the national government.[7] For example, a state cannot impose a higher tax on goods imported from another state than it imposes on the same kind of goods produced in its own territory.

The fact that a local law may have some effect upon out-of-state markets does not mean that the local law is unconstitutional as a burden on interstate commerce.

State regulations designed to advance local interests may come into conflict with the interstate commerce clause. This occurred in the *Healy* case.

[7]   Tyler Pipe Industries, Inc. v Washington Dept. of Revenue, 483 US 232 (1987).

HEALY v THE BEER INSTITUTE, INC.
491 US 324 (1989)

The legislature of Connecticut determined that the retail price of beer in the three bordering states was consistently lower than in-state retail prices. By statute, Connecticut then required out-of-state importers to post in Connecticut the prices they were charging and to affirm that at the time of such posting, the prices charged in the neighboring states were not lower than the posted prices. The Beer

Institute and others brought an action to have the Connecticut posting requirement declared unconstitutional as an unreasonable burden on interstate commerce. The state law was invalidated by the court of appeals. A further appeal
was taken to the United States Supreme Court.

BLACKMUN, J. . . . A state law that has the "practical effect" of regulating commerce occurring wholly outside that State's borders is invalid under the Commerce
Clause. . . . Taken together, our cases concerning the extraterritorial effects of state economic regulation stand at a minimum for the following propositions: First, the "Commerce Clause . . . precludes the application of a state statute to commerce that takes
place wholly outside of the State's borders, whether or not the commerce has effects
within the State," . . . and, specifically, a State may not adopt legislation that has the
practical effect of establishing "a scale of prices for use in other states." . . . Second, a
statute that directly controls commerce occurring wholly outside the boundaries of a
State exceeds the inherent limits of the enacting State's authority and is invalid regardless of whether the statute's extraterritorial reach was intended by the legislature. The
critical inquiry is whether the practical effect of the regulation is to control conduct
beyond the boundaries of the State. Third, the practical effect of the statute must be
evaluated not only by considering the consequences of the statute itself, but also by
considering how the challenged statute may interact with the legitimate regulatory
regimes of other States and what effect would arise if not one, but many or every State
adopted similar legislation. Generally speaking, the Commerce Clause protects against
inconsistent legislation arising from the projection of one state's regulatory regime into
the jurisdiction of another State. . . . And, specifically, the Commerce Clause dictates
that no State may force an out-of-state merchant to seek regulatory approval in one
State before undertaking a transaction in another. . . .

[The Court examined the tax laws in the border states to show that it was likely that
importers would establish their prices in the border states with the Connecticut statute
in mind.]

The Commerce Clause problem with the Connecticut statute appears in even stark-
er relief when it is recalled that if Connecticut may enact a contemporaneous affirmation statute, so may each of the border States and, indeed, so may every other State in
the Nation. Suppose, for example, that the border States each enacted statutes essentially identical to Connecticut's. Under those circumstances, in January, when a brewer
posts his February prices in Connecticut and the border States, he must determine
those prices knowing that the lowest bottle, can, or case price in any State would become the maximum bottle, can, or case price the brewer would be permitted to charge
throughout the region for the month of March. This is true because in February, when
the brewer posts his March prices in each State, he will have to affirm that no bottle,
can, or case price is higher than the lowest bottle, can, or case price in the region—and
these "current" prices would have been determined by the January posting. Put differently, unless a beer supplier declined to sell in one of the States for an entire month, the
maximum price in each State would be capped by previous prices in the other State.
This maximum price would almost surely be the minimum price as well, since any
reduction in either State would permanently lower the ceiling in both. Nor would such
"price gridlock" be limited to individual regions. The short-circuiting of normal pricing decisions based on local conditions would be carried to a national scale if and when
a significant group of States enacted contemporaneous affirmation statutes that linked
in state prices to the lowest price in any State in the country. This kind of potential

regional and even national regulation of the pricing mechanism for goods is reserved by the Commerce Clause to the Federal Government and may not be accomplished piecemeal through the extraterritorial reach of individual state statutes.

The Connecticut statute, moreover, violates the Commerce Clause in a second respect: On its face, the statute discriminates against brewers and shippers of beer engaged in interstate commerce. . . . By its plain terms, the Connecticut affirmation statute applies solely to interstate brewers or shippers of beer, that is, either Connecticut brewers who sell both in Connecticut and in at least one border State. Under the statute, a manufacturer or shipper of beer is free to charge wholesalers within Connecticut whatever price it might choose so long as that manufacturer or shipper does not sell its beer in a border State. . . . We perceive no neutral justification for this patent discrimination. Connecticut has claimed throughout this litigation that its price-affirmation laws are designed to ensure the lowest possible prices for Connecticut consumers. While this may be a legitimate justification for the statute, it is not advanced by, in effect, exempting brewers and shippers engaging in solely domestic sales from the price regulations imposed on brewers and shippers who engage in sales throughout the region. . . .

[Judgment affirmed]

QUESTIONS

1. What provision of the United States Constitution regulating state taxation was involved in the *Healy* case?
2. In the *Healy* case, the Connecticut statute affected the actions of the beer sellers in the border states. Appraise this statement.
3. A state law regulating commerce within the state is valid as far as the federal commerce power is concerned when the statute is adopted solely for the purpose of regulating commerce within that state. Appraise this statement.

9.   The Financial Powers

The financial powers of the federal government include the powers to tax, borrow, spend, and coin money.

(a) THE TAXING POWER. The federal Constitution provides that "Congress shall have power to lay and collect taxes, duties, imposts and excises, to pay the debts and provide for the common defense and general welfare of the United States. . . ."[8] Subject to the express and implied limitations arising from the Constitution, the states may impose such taxes as they desire and as their own individual constitutions and statutes permit. In addition to express constitutional limitations, both national and local taxes are subject to the un-written limitation that they be imposed for a public purpose.

The federal government is subject to certain limitations on the form of the taxes it imposes. Capitation or poll taxes and all direct taxes must be apportioned among the states according to the census-determined population.[9] Today, direct taxes include taxes on real estate or personal property and taxes imposed on persons because of their ownership of property. Income taxes, to the extent that they tax the income from property, are direct, although by virtue of the Sixteenth Amendment their apportionment is no longer required.

All other taxes imposed by the federal government are regarded as indirect taxes. These include customs duties, taxes on consumption

---

[8]   US Const, Art 1, Section 8, Cl 1.

[9]   US Const, Art 1, Section 9, Cl 4.

(such as gasoline and cigarette taxes), taxes on the exercise of a privilege (such as an amusement tax), taxes on the transmission of property upon death (such as estate taxes), taxes upon the privilege of making a gift, or taxes upon the privilege of employing workers (such as the federal employer's social security tax). In the case of a federal tax upon the exercise of a privilege, it is immaterial whether the privilege arises by virtue of a state or a federal law.

The only restriction upon the form of indirect federal taxes is that they be uniform throughout the continental United States and the incorporated territories. This requirement of uniformity does not prohibit a progressively graduated tax, wherein the greater the monetary value of the tax base, the greater the rate of tax. The requirement of uniformity also is not violated by a provision allowing credits against the federal tax for taxes paid to a state, even though the amount of the federal tax paid will vary from state to state, depending upon the existence of a state tax for which credit is allowable.

The federal taxing power is subject to the implied limitation that state and municipal governments may not be directly taxed. In former years this concept was interpreted to exempt from federal income tax any money received from state or local governments by private persons. This immunity of private persons has been destroyed by decisions of the Supreme Court, so that the federal income tax reaches income received by private persons working for or dealing with state and municipal governments. If Congress wishes, it may subject income from state and municipal bonds to the general federal income tax.[10]

(b) THE BORROWING POWER. Congress is authorized "to borrow money on the credit of the United States."[11] No limitation is prescribed to the purposes for which the United States can borrow.

Obligations of the United States issued to those lending money to the United States are binding. Congress cannot attempt to repudiate these obligations or to make them repayable in a less valuable currency than called for by the obligations without violating the legal rights of the holders.

The states have an inherent power to borrow money. State constitutions and statutes may impose a limit on the amount that can be borrowed. Frequently, these limitations are evaded by the creation of independent authorities or districts that borrow money by issuing bonds. The bonded indebtedness of such independent authorities and districts is not regarded as a debt of the state and therefore is not subject to the limitations applicable to state borrowing.

(c) THE SPENDING POWER. The federal government may use tax money and borrowed money " . . . to pay the debts and provide for the common defense and general welfare of the United States."[12] From the earliest days of the Constitution there was disagreement over whether there was any limitation on the power of the United States to spend the money that it raised by taxation or borrowing. Madison claimed that the money of the United States could only be spent on a subject that could be directly regulated or legislated upon by Congress. Hamilton claimed that as long as the money was spent for a public purpose rather than a private purpose, it was immaterial whether Congress could legislate directly upon the object for which the money was spent.

This matter has become academic with the present interpretation of the commerce power as permitting federal regulation of anything. The situation can no longer arise in which Congress would be spending money for something that it could not regulate if it so chose.

Congress may reduce federal funds that would otherwise be distributed to a state if that state has a drinking age lower than 21. The object of Congress in so doing is to eliminate the hazard of persons under 21 driving to the lower-age states, becoming drunk, and

[10] South Carolina v Baker, 485 US 505 (1988).
[11] US Const, Art 1, Section 8, Cl 2.
[12] US Const, Art 1, Section 8, Cl 1.

then becoming involved in highway accidents.[13]

(d) THE CURRENCY POWER. The Constitution authorizes Congress "to coin money, regulate the value thereof" and "provide for the punishment of counterfeiting the securities and . . . coin of the United States."[14] This federal power is made exclusive by prohibiting the states from coining money, emitting bills of credit, or making anything but gold and silver coins legal tender in payment of debts.[15]

The national government can determine what shall be legal tender and is not restricted to the use of metallic money but may issue paper money.[16] Congress can establish such base as it desires for paper currency and may change the base of existing currency.

10.   The Power to Own Businesses

In a sense, government ownership of what would ordinarily be deemed private business represents the ultimate in the regulation of private business.

(a) CONSTITUTIONALITY OF GOVERNMENT OWNERSHIP. Speaking generally, there is no constitutional barrier against state or federal government ownership and operation of businesses. It had formerly been assumed that there were certain purposes that were not public or for the general welfare. These purposes were distinguished from those that were public or for the general welfare. It is impossible today to draw such a line between public and private and to prohibit a government from entering into any particular business on the ground that to do so is not in furtherance of a public purpose or does not advance the general welfare.

(b) CREATION OF NEW BUSINESS. The statement that the United States may constitutionally engage in business leads to the conclusion that it may constitutionally spend its

money in order to create a new business or build new plants. There is no requirement that limits the national government to acquiring existing businesses and plants.

(c) ACQUISITION OF EXISTING BUSINESSES AND PLANTS. The power to engage in and own businesses embraces the right to acquire existing businesses and plants by purchase or gift. The national government may also acquire the property by eminent domain if the owner will not voluntarily sell to the government at a price that is satisfactory to the government.

The United States, as a sovereign state, may acquire land or any other property by any means. It may do so by war, purchase, or treaty.

(d) SALE AND DISTRIBUTION OF GOVERNMENT PRODUCTION. A government may sell or otherwise dispose of the products that the government-owned business manufactures. Congress is authorized to "dispose of and make all needful rules and regulations respecting the territory or other property belonging to the United States."[17] The power of a government to dispose of its property permits the government to compete with a private enterprise and to dispose of its products at any price it chooses, without regard to whether the price is below cost. No constitutional privilege of the private business is violated by being underpriced by the national, a state, or local government.[18]

E.   CONSTITUTIONAL LIMITATIONS ON GOVERNMENT

The most significant limitations in the Constitution are found in the first ten amendments adopted in 1791 and in the post-Civil War amendments. Most state constitutions contain limitations similar to those of the national Constitution. The limitations discussed in the

[13]   South Dakota v Dole, 483 US 203 (1987).
[14]   US Const, Art 1, Section 8, Cls 5,6.
[15]   US Const, Art 1, Section 10.
[16]   Julliard v Greenman, 110 US 421 (1884).

[17]   US Const, Art 4, Section 3(2).
[18]   Puget Sound Power & Light Co. v Seattle, 291 US 619 (1934).

following sections are the limitations that are most important to the person and to business.

11.   Due Process

The most important limitation on the power of government is that found in the Fifth and Fourteenth Amendments to the Constitution. Those amendments prohibit the national government and the state governments, respectively, from depriving any person of life, liberty, or property without due process of law.

(a) EXPANSION OF DUE PROCESS. By virtue of liberal interpretation of the Constitution, the **due process clause** is now held to be a guarantee of protection from unreasonable procedures[19] and unreasonable laws, and a guarantee of equal protection of the law, and a guarantee of protection of significant interests. The Supreme Court has extended the due process clause to protect the record or standing of a student.

Through judicial construction, due process of law affords the individual a wide protection. However, the guarantee, affords no protection when the matter is reasonably debatable. Therefore, due process of law does not bar the regulation of business, for any regulation that would have sufficient support to pass a legislature or the Congress would have sufficient claim to validity as to be debatable. The fact that many persons would deem the law unsound, unwise, hazardous, or un-American does not in itself make the law invalid under the due process clause.

As the due process concept is a limitation upon governmental action, it does not apply to transactions between private persons or to private employment or other nonpublic situations. In some cases, however, statutes, such as the federal Civil Rights Act and consumer protection laws, apply due process concepts to private transactions.

(b) SHORTCUT PROCEDURES. Complaint has often been made of the delays of the law. Shortcut procedures are inspired by the legitimate desire to speed up litigation and to give everyone easy access to a day in court. However, procedures must not be so streamlined as to deprive defendants of reasonable notice and opportunity to be heard. In an era in which a defendant may be a resident or a business of a foreign state, statutes have generally been adopted to allow the plaintiff to sue a foreign defendant in the state where the plaintiff lives. Such state statutes are subject to the limitation that they can be applied only when the defendant has such a relationship, as by carrying on of business, within the state of the plaintiff that it is reasonable to require the defendant to appear in the plaintiff's state and defend an action in the courts of that state. Conversely, if the defendant does not have such a reasonable relation to the plaintiff's state, it is a denial of due process to require the defendant to go to the plaintiff's state.

12.   Equal Protection of the Law

The Constitution prohibits both the state and national governments from denying any person the equal protection of the law.[20] This guarantee prohibits a government from treating one person differently from another when there is no reasonable ground for classifying them differently.

In harmony with this concept of equality, it has been held that a wife may be held responsible for necessaries furnished her husband, matching the common law liability of the husband for necessaries furnished the wife.[21]

(a) REASONABLE CLASSIFICATION. The equal protection clause does not require that all persons be protected or treated equally, and a law is valid even though it does not apply to everyone or everything. Whether a classification is reasonable depends on whether the nature of the classification bears a rea-

---

[19]   Mennonite Board of Missions v Adams, 462 US 792 (1983).

[20]   US Const, Fourteenth Amendment as to the states; modern interpretation of due process clause of Fifth Amendment as to national government. Congress has adopted the Civil Rights Act to implement the concept of equal protection. Newport News Shipbuilding and Dry Dock Co. v EEOC, 462 US 669 (1983).

[21]   Webb v Hillsborough County Hospital Authority (Fla App) 521 So 2d 199 (1988).

sonable relation to the evil to be remedied or to the object to be attained by the law. In determining this, the courts have been guided generally by considerations of historical treatment and by the logic of the situation. The trend is to permit the classification to stand unless it is clear that the lawmaking body has been arbitrary or capricious.

(b) IMPROPER CLASSIFICATION. Laws that make distinctions in the regulation of business, the right to work, and the right to use or enjoy property on the basis of race, alienage, or religion are invalid. Also invalid are laws that impose restrictions on some but not all persons without any justification for the distinction.[22] A law prohibiting the ownership of land by aliens has been traditionally regarded as an exception to this rule. Large alien holdings of land is considered such a social evil as to justify legislation directly prohibit-

ing such holding, although it appears that in the course of time this discrimination may be declared invalid.[23] A state statute taxing out-of-state insurance companies at a higher rate than in-state insurance companies violates the equal protection clause.[24]

The lawmaker may not discriminate on the basis of moral standards and cultural patterns. People cannot be deprived of the same treatment given to other persons because they do not have the same moral standards or cultural patterns as the lawmaker. Lawmakers cannot penalize people because they do not live, think, and dress the same as the lawmakers. In the *Moreno* case, the validity of an entitlement plan was challenged by those who did not receive the benefits.

---

[22]   Carey v Brown, 447 US 445 (1980).

[23]   The alien land laws have been declared unconstitutional by the supreme courts of California, Montana, and Oregon, as being in violation of the Fourteenth Amendment of the United States Constitution.
[24]   Metropolitan Life Ins. Co. v Ward, 470 US 869 (1985).

UNITED STATES DEPARTMENT OF AGRICULTURE v MORENO
413 US 528 (1973)

The Federal Food Stamp Act provided for the distribution of food stamps to needy "households." In 1971, Section 3(e) of the statute was amended to define *households* as groups whose members were all related to each other. This was done because of congressional dislike for the life-styles of unrelated "hippies" who were living together in "hippie communes." Moreno and others applied for food stamps but were refused them because the relationship requirement was not satisfied. An action was brought to have the relationship requirement declared unconstitutional. The lower court held the statute unconstitutional and the Department of Agriculture appealed.

BRENNAN, J. . . . Appellees [the applicants for the food stamps] . . . consist of several groups of individuals who allege that, although they satisfy the income eligibility requirements for federal food assistance, they have nevertheless been excluded from the program solely because the persons in each group are not "all related to each other." Appellee Jacinta Moreno, for example, is a 56-year-old diabetic who lives with Ermina Sanchez and the latter's three children. They share common living expenses, and Mrs. Sanchez helps to care for appellee. Appellee's monthly income, derived from public assistance, is $75; Mrs. Sanchez receives $133 per month from public assistance. The household pay $135 per month for rent, gas, and electricity, of which appellee pays $50. Appellee spends $10 per month for transportation to a hospital for regular visits, and $5 per month for laundry. That leaves her $10 per month for food and other necessities. Despite her poverty, appellee has been denied federal food assistance solely because she is unrelated to the other members of her household. Moreover, although Mrs. Sanchez and her three children were permitted to purchase $108 worth of food stamps per month for $18, their participation in the program will be terminated if appellee Moreno continues to live with them.

Appellee Sheilah Hejny is married and has three children. Although the Hejnys are indigent, they took in a 20-year-old girl, who is unrelated to them, because "we felt she had emotional problems." The Hejnys receive $144 worth of food stamps each month for $14. If they allow the 20-year-old girl to continue to live with them, they will be denied food stamps by reason of Section 3(e).

Appellee Victoria Keppler has a daughter with an acute hearing deficiency. The daughter requires special instruction in a school for the deaf. The school is located in an area in which the appellee could not ordinarily afford to live. Thus, in order to make the most of her limited resources, appellee agreed to share an apartment near the school with a woman who, like appellee, is on public assistance. Since appellee is not related to the woman, appellee's food stamps will be cut off if they continue to live together. . . .

In essence, appellees contend, and the District Court held, that the "unrelated person" provision of Section 3(e) creates an irrational classification in violation of the equal protection component of the Due Process Clause of the Fifth Amendment. We agree.

Under traditional equal protection analysis, a legislative classification must be sustained if the classification itself is rationally related to a legitimate governmental interest. . . . The purposes of the Food Stamp Act were expressly set forth in the congressional "declaration of policy":

> It is hereby declared to be the policy of Congress . . . to safeguard the health and well-being of the Nation's population and raise levels of nutrition among low-income households. The Congress hereby finds that the limited food purchasing power of low-income households contributes to hunger and malnutrition among members of such households. The Congress further finds that increased utilization of food in establishing and maintaining adequate national levels of nutrition will promote the distribution in a beneficial manner of our agricultural abundances and will strengthen our agricultural economy, as well as result in more orderly marketing and distribution of food. To alleviate such hunger and malnutrition, a food stamp program is herein authorized which will permit low-income households to purchase a nutritionally adequate diet through normal channels of trade.

The challenged statutory classification (households of related persons versus households containing one or more unrelated persons) is clearly irrelevant to the stated purposes of the Act. As the District Court recognized, "the relationships among persons constituting one economic unit and sharing cooking facilities have nothing to do with their ability to stimulate the agricultural economy by purchasing farm surpluses, or with their personal nutritional requirements." . . .

If it is to be sustained, the challenged classification must rationally further some legitimate governmental interest other than those specifically stated in the congressional "declaration of policy." . . . The legislative history indicates . . . that that amendment was intended to prevent so-called "hippies" and "hippie communes" from participating in the food stamp program. . . . The challenged classification clearly cannot be sustained by reference to this congressional purpose. For if the constitutional conception of "equal protection of the laws" means anything, it must at the very least mean that a bare congressional desire to harm a politically unpopular group cannot constitute a *legitimate* governmental interest. As a result, "a purpose to discriminate against hippies cannot, in and of itself and without reference to [some independent] considerations in the public interest, justify the 1971 amendment." . . .

Traditional equal protection analysis does not require that every classification be drawn with precise "mathematical nicety." Dandridge v Williams, 397 US 471 (1970). But the classification here in issue is not only "imprecise," it is wholly without any rational basis. The judgment of the District Court holding the "unrelated person" provision invalid under the Due Process Clause of the Fifth Amendment is therefore affirmed.

[Judgment affirmed]

QUESTIONS

1. Is there a constitutional right to receive food stamps?
2. Is it lawful for you to give presents to three of your four nephews and not give the fourth anything because you do not like the way he lives?
3. How would the *Moreno* case have been decided if there had been reason to believe that the excluded claimants were agitating to overthrow the U.S. government?

13. Privileges and Immunities

The federal Constitution declares that "The citizens of each state shall be entitled to all privileges and immunities of citizens in the several states."[25] This means that a person going into another state is entitled to make contracts, own property, and engage in business, to the same extent as the citizens of that state. Thus, a state cannot bar a traveler from another state from engaging in local business or from obtaining a hunting or fishing license merely because the traveler is not a resident. Likewise, a law that requires an attorney to be a resident of the state in order to practice is unconstitutional as a violation of this provision.[26]

14. Protection of the Person

The Constitution does not contain any express provision protecting "persons" from governmental action. Persons are expressly protected by the Constitution with respect to particular matters, such as freedom of speech, ownership of property, right to a jury trial, and so on. There is, however, no general provision declaring that the government shall not impair "rights of persons." There is not a word in the Constitution as to the inalienable rights that were so important on July 4, 1776.[27]

[27]   The term *inalienable right* is employed in preference to *natural right, fundamental right,* or *basic right.* Apart from the question of scope or coverage, the adjective *inalienable* emphasizes the fact that the right is still possessed by the people, as opposed to the contention that people have surrendered or subordinated such rights to the will of society. The word *alien* is the term of the old common law for transferring title or ownership. Today we would say transfer and, instead of saying "inalienable" rights, would say "nontransferable" rights. Inalienable rights of the people were therefore those that not only were possessed by the people, but ones they could not give up, even if they wanted to. Therefore they are still owned by everyone.

[25]   US Const, Art IV, Section 2, Cl 1.
[26]   Supreme Court of New Hampshire v Piper, 470 US 274 (1985).

(a) RISE OF CONSTITUTIONAL PRO-
TECTION OF THE PERSON. During the last
four decades, the Supreme Court has been
finding constitutional protection for a wide
array of rights of the person that are not expressly protected by the Constitution. Examples are the right of privacy, the right to marry
the person one chooses,[28] protection from unreasonable zoning, protection of parental control, protection from durational residency requirements, protection from discrimination
because of poverty, and protection from sex
discrimination.[29]

(b) DEMOCRACY AND THE PROTEC-
TION OF THE PERSON. As the goal of a democracy is to promote the well-being and development of each individual, the concept of
protecting a person and the goal of democracy
would appear to be moving toward the same
objective. This is ordinarily true, but there
may be a conflict between the democratic system of government and the protection of the
person. We think of a democratic society as

one in which the majority of the people govern. But is being governed by the majority sufficient for those who cherish the American
ideal?

If we look closely at our individual and national desires, we see that the American way
of life is not a society run by the will of the
majority. Instead we find that the American
way divides life into two zones. In one zone
the democratic concept is that the majority
rules. In the other zone, that of the "person,"
not even the majority can interfere. To illustrate, the majority can declare by statute that
before you marry you must have a health certificate. This is perfectly reasonable for the
protection of the general health and welfare.
But no one, not the majority, nor even the
unanimous action of everyone in the United
States, can command you to marry or not
marry or choose your mate for you.

Most amazing is the fact that a relatively
short time ago the second zone was unheard
of and everything was thought to be in the
zone that was controlled by the majority unless there was an express prohibition of such
action by the Constitution. Even more star-
tling, the emergence of the second zone has
taken place for the most part within the lifetime of your parents and your lifetime. The expansion of the second zone will have a pro-
found effect on the rest of your life.

[28]   Akron v Akron Center for Reproductive Health, Inc.
462 US 416 (1983).
[29]   In some cases the courts have given the due process
and equal protection clauses a liberal interpretation in
order to find a protection of the person, thereby making up
for the fact that there is no express constitutional guarantee
of protection of the person. Davis v Passman, 442 US 228
(1979) (due process); Orr v Orr 440 US 268 (1979) (equal
protection).

SUMMARY

The U.S. Constitution created the structure of
our national government and gave it certain
powers. It also placed limitations on those
powers. It created a federal system, with a tripartite division of government and a bicameral national legislature.

Some governmental powers are possessed
exclusively by the national government, while
other powers are shared by both the states and
the federal government. In areas of conflict,
federal law is supreme.

The U.S. Constitution is not a detailed document. It takes much of its meaning from the
way in which it is interpreted. In recent years,

liberal interpretation has expanded the powers of the federal government.

Among the powers of the federal government that directly affect business are the
power to regulate commerce; the power to tax,
borrow, spend, and coin money; and the
power to own and operate businesses. Among
the limitations on government that are most
important to business are the requirement of
due process and the requirement of equal protection of the law.

The due process requirement stipulates
that no person shall be deprived of life, liberty,
or property without due process of law. The

due process requirement applies to both the state and federal governments but does not apply to private transactions.

The equal protection concept of the U.S. Constitution prohibits both the state and fed-

eral governments from treating one person differently from another unless there is a legitimate reason for doing so and unless the basis of classification is reasonable.

QUESTIONS AND CASE PROBLEMS

1. What are the characteristics of the Constitution as it is today?
2. Would a constitutional amendment that deleted the present Article V and in its place provided that an amendment could be adopted by a majority of those voting at a presidential election be valid?
3. Does equal protection prevent classification? If not, when is classification proper?
4. A federal law is adopted providing that no one may operate a television station without a federal license. Is that statute constitutional?
5. Does the due process clause protect a business from being destroyed by taxation?
6. Perez was sued for damages arising from an automobile collision. A judgment was entered against Perez. He then filed a petition in bankruptcy. In due course, he was given a discharge in bankruptcy that discharged him from all debts, including the judgment. The state of Arizona then suspended Perez's automobile registration and operator's license pursuant to a state statute providing for such suspension whenever a judgment remained unpaid for 60 days, even though the judgment had been discharged in bankruptcy. Perez claimed that the state statute was unconstitutional and that the suspension of his licenses was therefore improper. Was he correct? [Perez v Campbell, 402 US 637]
7. The home of the Crafts was supplied with gas by the city gas company. Because of some misunderstanding, the gas company believed that the Crafts were delinquent in paying their gas bill. The gas company had an informal complaint procedure for discussing such matters, but the Crafts had never been informed that such procedure was available. The gas company notified the Crafts that they were delinquent and that the company was shutting off the gas. The Crafts brought an action to enjoin the gas company from so doing on the theory that a termination without any hearing was a denial of due process. The lower courts held that the interest of the Crafts in receiving gas was not a

property interest protected by the due process clause and that the procedures that the gas company followed satisfied the requirements of due process. The Crafts appealed. Were they correct in contending that they had been denied due process of law? [Memphis Light, Gas and Water Division v Craft, 436 US 1]
8. Gladys Boddie lived on welfare in Connecticut. She wanted to obtain a divorce but did not have the $60 required to commence a divorce action. She claimed that the state requirement of the prepayment of such fees deprived her of her constitutional rights and that the statute was therefore invalid. Was she correct? [Boddie v Connecticut, 401 US 371]
9. The New York Civil Service law provided that only United States citizens could hold permanent civil service positions. Dougall was an alien who had lawfully entered and was lawfully residing in the United States. He held a job with the City of New York but was fired because of the state statute. He claimed that the statute was unconstitutional. Was he correct? [Sugarman v Dougall, 413 US 634]
10. Montana imposed a severance tax on every ton of coal mined within the state. The tax varied depending on the value of the coal and the cost of production. It could be as high as 30 percent of the price at which the coal was sold. Montana mine operators and some of the out-of-state customers claimed that this tax was unconstitutional as an improper burden on interstate commerce. Decide. [Commonwealth Edison Co. v Montana, 452 US 609]
11. What social force guided the court in deciding the *Commonwealth Edison* case?
12. Heald was the executor of the estate of a deceased person who had lived in Washington, D.C. Heald refused to pay federal tax owed by the estate on the ground that the tax had been imposed by an Act of Congress, but that, since residents of the District of Columbia had no vote in Congress, the tax law was necessarily adopted without their representation. In addition to having no voice in the adoption of the tax

laws, the proceeds from taxes collected in the District were paid into the general treasury of the United States and were not maintained as a separate District of Columbia fund. Heald objected that the tax law was void as contrary to the Constitution because it amounted to taxation without representation. Decide. [Heald v District of Columbia, 259 US 114]

13. California owns the Belt Railroad that serves San Francisco Harbor and, through connections with other lines, handles interstate traffic. It is a common carrier, and it files tariffs with the Interstate Commerce Commission. A collective bargaining agreement was entered into between the state and the employees of the Belt Railroad. A number of employees later presented to the National Railroad Adjustment Board claims arising under the agreement. The board refused to exercise jurisdiction over the matter, on the theory that the Railway Labor Act did not apply to a state-owned railroad. The employees then brought an action against the board to compel it to exercise jurisdiction. They claimed that the board had jurisdiction because (1) the Labor Act stated expressly that it applied to "any carrier by railroad" that was subject to the Interstate Commerce Act and (2) the Belt Railroad was in fact subject to the Interstate Commerce Act. Decide. [California v Taylor, 353 US 553]

14. Because of misconduct, Lopez and other public high school students were suspended for periods of up to ten days. A state statute authorized the principal of a public school to suspend a student for periods up to ten days without any hearing. A suit was brought by Lopez and others claiming that the statute was unconstitutional because it deprived them of due process by not giving them notice and a hearing to determine whether a suspension was justified. Was the state statute constitutional? [Gross v Lopez; 419 US 565]

15. An Illinois statute provides for the automatic revocation of a driver's license upon the driver's being convicted of a sexual offense. Lindner was convicted of such an offense. His driver's license was revoked although no automobile had been involved in the crime. He claimed that the revocation of his license violated the Constitution. Was he correct? [Illinois v Lindner, 127 Ill 2d 174, 535 NE2d 829].

4

GOVERNMENT REGULATION

In Chapter 3 you saw that government can regulate business and much of our lives. Whether government should exercise this power comes down to a question of policy—whether we, the people, want government to do so. This in turn involves questions of economics, political science, the humanities, and related subjects. If society decides that there should be regulation by government, then questions arise as to what should be regulated and how. These questions involve important decisions for the welfare of society, because in every decision some social interest loses and some interest gains. Society must make the difficult decision of how it should manage itself. For the last century the American people have called upon government to regulate more and more of their way of life. Although there is some movement toward deregulation, the overwhelming pattern continues to be regulation of business by government.

A. POWER TO REGULATE BUSINESS

The states possess the power to adopt laws to protect the general welfare, health, safety, and morals of the people. This is called the **police power**. By virtue of their police power, states may regulate all aspects of business, so long as they do not impose an unreasonable burden on interstate commerce or any activity of the federal government. Local governments may also exercise this power to the extent each state permits. The federal government may impose upon any phase of business any regulation that is required by "the economic needs of the nation."[1]

1.   Regulation, Free Enterprise, and Deregulation

The regulation of business is flatly opposed to the concept of free enterprise. Under a true free enterprise system there would not be any regulation of prices, safety of airplanes, safety for human consumption of foods and drugs, and so on. The 100 percent believer in free enterprise assumes that when a product or a service kills enough people, the public will stop buying and the bad provider will just go out of business. Although we all believe in free enterprise, it is obvious that no one believes in it 100 percent. Where to draw the line between 100 percent and 0 percent? That is a question of policy. Different people will place the boundary line at different points.

In recent years there has been some movement toward deregulation of industry. For many years the banking and savings industry was heavily regulated. Beginning in 1978, various acts were adopted to deregulate this industry. This did not produce the desired results, and Congress adopted several bank-regulating laws toward the end of the 80s. The broadest regulation was made by the Financial Institutions Reform, Recovery, and Enforcement Act of 1989 (FIRREA).[2] This Act regulates savings and loan associations and similar organizations to ensure their financial stability.

The regulation of rates of plane and truck transport has been removed. It seems unlikely that the move to deregulate will go much beyond removing restrictions on rates.[3]

2.   Regulation of Production, Distribution, and Financing

In order to protect the public from harm, government may prohibit false advertising and labeling, and goverment may establish health and purity standards for cosmetics, foods, and drugs. Without regard to the nature of the product, government may regulate business with respect to what materials may be used, the quantity of a product that may be produced or grown, and the price at which the finished product may be sold. Government may also engage in competition with private enterprises or own and operate an industry.

Regulation of production may take the form of providing encouragement or assistance for enterprises that would not prove attractive to private investors.[4]

FIGURE 4-1   GOVERNMENT REGULATION OF AMERICAN LIFE

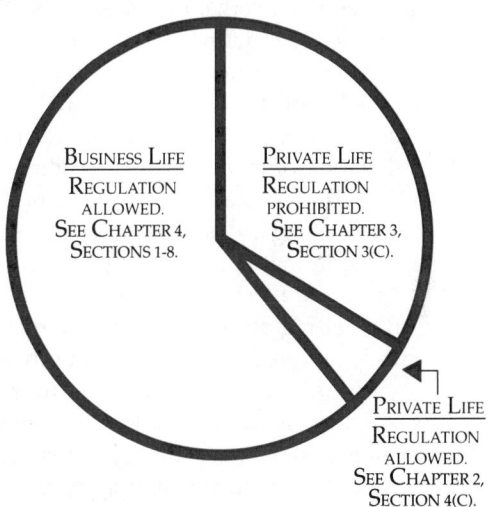

BUSINESS LIFE
REGULATION ALLOWED.
SEE CHAPTER 4, SECTIONS 1-8.

PRIVATE LIFE
REGULATION PROHIBITED.
SEE CHAPTER 3, SECTION 3(C).

PRIVATE LIFE
REGULATION ALLOWED.
SEE CHAPTER 2, SECTION 4(C).

Under its commerce power, the federal government may regulate all methods of interstate transportation and communication. A similar power is exercised by each state over its intrastate traffic. The financing of business

---

[1]   American Power & Light Co. v SEC, 329 US 90 (1946).
[2]   Act of October 9, 1989, PL 101–73, 103 Stat 183, Codified to various sections of titles 12 and 15 of USC.
[3]   Airline Deregulation Act of Oct. 24, 1978, PL 95–504, 92 Stat 1705, 49 USC §§ 1301 et seq.; Bus Regulatory Reform Act of Sept. 20, 1982, PL 97–261, 96 Stat 1102, 49 USC §§ 10101 et seq.

[4]   Orphan Drug Act of January 4, 1983, PL 97–44, 96 Stat 2049, 21 USC §§ 301, 306 (encouraging development of drugs to fight diseases that are so rare that there is no commercial interest in developing drugs to prevent or treat them).

is directly affected by the national government, which creates a national currency and maintains a federal reserve bank system. State and other national laws may also affect financing by regulating financing contracts and documents, such as bills of lading and commercial paper.

The federal government may also establish standards for weights and measures. The Metric Conversion Act of 1975 declares that it is the policy of the United States to convert to the metric system. Various agencies have adopted regulations to carry out this policy.

3.   Regulation of Competition

The federal government, and the states in varying degrees, prohibit unfair methods of competition. Frequently, a commission is established to determine whether a given practice comes within the general class of unfair methods of competition. In other instances, the statutes specifically define the practices condemned.

Congress has declared "unlawful" all "unfair methods of competition" and has created a Federal Trade Commission (FTC) to administer the law. The FTC has condemned harassing tactics, coercing by refusing to sell, boycotting, discriminating, disparaging of a competitor's products, enforcing payment wrongfully, cutting off or restricting the market, securing and using confidential information, spying on competitors, and inducing breach of customer contracts. The law also prohibits misrepresentation by appropriating business or corporate names, simulating trade or corporate names, appropriating trademarks, simulating the appearance of a competitor's goods, simulating a competitor's advertising, using deceptive brands or labels, and using false and misleading advertising.

A shift of emphasis is taking place in appraising methods of doing business. Instead of harm to competitors being the sole consideration, the effect on the consumer is being given increasing recognition. Many practices that were condemned earlier only because they would harm a competitor by diverting customers are now condemned because such practices prevent the customer from getting full value for the money spent.

4.   Regulation of Prices

Governments, both national and state, may regulate prices. This may be done directly by the lawmaker—that is, the Congress or the state legislature—or the power to do so may be delegated to an administrative officer or agency. This power extends to prices in any form. It includes not only what a buyer pays for goods purchased from a store, but also what a borrower pays as interest on a loan and what a tenant pays for rent.

(a) PROHIBITED PRICE DISCRIMINATION. The Clayton Act of 1914, applicable to interstate and foreign commerce, prohibits price discrimination between different buyers of commodities "where the effect of such discrimination may be substantially to lessen competition or tend to create a monopoly in any line of commerce."

The federal law prohibits the furnishing of advertising or other services that, when rendered to one purchaser but not another, will have the effect of granting the former a price discrimination or lower rate. It is made illegal for a seller to accept any fee or commission in connection with a sale except for services actually rendered and unless the services are equally available to all on the same terms. The Clayton Act makes both the giving and the receiving of any illegal price discrimination a crime.

A state's statute prohibiting selling below cost for the purpose of harming competitors is constitutional.[5]

(b) PERMITTED PRICE DISCRIMINATION. Price discrimination is expressly permitted when it can be justified on the basis of: (1) difference in grade, quality, or quantity involved; (2) the cost of the transportation involved in performing the contract; (3) a good-faith effort to meet competition; (4) differences

---

[5]   Alabama ex rel. Galanos v Mapco Petroleum, Inc. (Ala) 519 So 2d 1275 (1987).

in methods or quantities; (5) deterioration of goods; or (6) a close-out sale of a particular line of goods. The Robinson-Patman Act of 1936 reaffirms the right of a seller to select customers and to refuse to deal with anyone as long as the refusal is in good faith and not for the purpose of restraining trade.

The "meeting competition" defense is available where the seller lowers the price for a general competitive area, as distinguished from doing so on an individual customer basis.

When a supplier offers to sell to anyone at a reduced price if certain conditions are met, the fact that every buyer cannot meet the conditions does not condemn the supplier's pricing plan as discriminatory.

5.   Prevention of Monopolies and Combinations

To protect competitors and the public from monopolies and combinations in restraint of trade, the federal government and almost all of the states have enacted antitrust statutes.

(a) THE FEDERAL ANTITRUST ACT. The federal antitrust act, known as the Sherman Antitrust Act, is applicable to both sellers and buyers.[6] It provides that "[§1] Every contract,

combination in the form of trust or otherwise, or conspiracy, in restraint of trade or commerce among the several states, or with foreign nations, is declared to be illegal. [§ 2] Every person who shall monopolize or attempt to monopolize, or combine or conspire with any other person or persons to monopolize any part of the trade or commerce among the several states, or with foreign nations, shall be deemed guilty of a felony."[7]

(b) PROHIBITED CONDUCT. Section 1 of the Sherman Act applies only when two or more persons agree or conspire to restrain trade. Thus, there is no violation when there is only an agreement between a corporation and its own employees or officers.

Under Section 2, one person or corporation may violate the law by monopolizing or attempting to monopolize interstate commerce. As discussed in the *Mandeville* case, the Sherman Act applies not only to buying and selling activities generally associated with trade and commerce, but also to manufacturing and production activities, without regard to whether consumers, brokers, or manufacturers are involved.

---

[6]   This act has been amended by the Clayton Act, the Federal Trade Commission Act, the Shipping Act, and other legislation.

[7]   15 USC, Ch. 1, §§ 1,2. Free competition has been advanced by the Omnibus Trade and Competitiveness Act of August 23, 1988, as amended, PL 106–418, 102 Stat 1107, 19 USC §§ 2901 et seq. Gray v Marshall County Board of Education (W Va App) 367 SE2d 751 (1988).

MANDEVILLE ISLAND FARMS v AMERICAN CRYSTAL SUGAR CO.
334 US 219 (1948)

The raising of sugar beets is an important industry in California. Sugar refineries buy the beet crop of the farmers and make sugar from the beets. This sugar is then shipped out of California and sold in many states. In order to hold down the prices paid to the sugar beet farmers, the American Crystal Sugar Company and two other refiners agreed among themselves on the price that they would pay the farmers for sugar beets. Sugar beets were grown on Mandeville Island Farms. Mandeville claimed that the price-fixing agreement between the sugar refiners violated the Sherman Antitrust Act. Mandeville sued American Crystal for treble (triple) damages as authorized by the federal statute. Judgment was entered for Mandeville, and American Crystal appealed.

RUTLEDGE, J. . . . The refiners controlled the seed supply and the only practical market for beets grown in northern California. When the new contracts were offered to the farmers, they had the choice of either signing or abandoning sugar-beet farming. . . .

[American Crystal] claimed that the growing, purchasing, and refining of sugar beets were local activities and not within the reach of the Sherman Act, which applied only to transactions in interstate commerce, and that no illegal practice occurred in the subsequent interstate distribution of the refined sugar.

. . . The broad form of [American Crystal]'s argument cannot be accepted. It is a reversion to conceptions formerly held but no longer effective to restrict either Congress' power . . . or the scope of the Sherman Act's coverage. The artificial and mechanical separation of "production" and "manufacturing" from "commerce," without regard to their economic continuity, the effects of the former two upon the latter, and the varying methods by which the several processes are organized, related, and carried on in different industries, or indeed within a single industry, no longer suffices to put either production or manufacturing and refining processes beyond reach of Congress' authority or of the statute. . . .

. . . The inquiry whether the restraint occurs in one phase or another, interstate or intrastate, of the total economic process is now merely a preliminary step. . . . The vital question becomes whether the effect is sufficiently substantial and adverse to Congress' paramount policy . . . to constitute a forbidden consequence. If so, the restraint must fall; and the injuries it inflicts upon others become remediable under the act's prescribed methods, including the treble damage provision.

. . . It is clear that the [sugar refiners'] agreement is the sort of combination condemned by the act, even though the price fixing was by purchasers and the persons specially injured under the treble damage claim are sellers, not customers or consumers. . . .

. . . The statute does not confine its protection to consumers, or to purchasers, or to competitors, or to sellers. Nor does it immunize the outlawed acts because they are done by any of these. . . . The act is comprehensive in its terms and coverage, protecting all who are made victims of the forbidden practices by whomever they may be perpetrated. . . .

Nor is the amount of the nation's sugar industry which the California refiners control relevant, so long as control is exercised effectively in the area concerned. . . .

. . . Under the facts characterizing this industry's operation and the tightening of controls in this producing area by the new agreements and understandings, there can be no question that their restrictive consequences were projected substantially into the interstate distribution of the sugar. . . .

[Judgment affirmed]

QUESTIONS

1. Is the Sherman Antitrust Act limited to agreements between sellers that restrain trade?
2. Did American Crystal and other refiners intend to affect the price at which sugar was sold in the markets in other states?

> 3. Does the Sherman Antitrust Act apply to a combination of five manufacturers that agree to the price at which they will sell their furniture throughout the United States?

The Act also prohibits professional persons, such as doctors, from using a peer review proceeding to put pressure on another professional who competes with them in private practice and refuses to become a member of a clinic formed by them.[8]

The Sherman Act does not deprive a city of the power to impose rent ceilings, since such a regulation does not involve concerted action.

The fact that a manufacturer sells only through a particular distributor and refuses to sell through anyone else does not in itself constitute an illegal restraint of trade, even though other merchants are deprived of the benefit of selling the particular product.[9]

(c) BIGNESS. The Sherman Antitrust Act does not prohibit bigness. However, § 7 of the Clayton Act, as amended in 1950, provides that "no corporation . . . shall acquire the whole or any part of the assets of another corporation . . . , where in any line of commerce in any section of the country, the effect of such acquisition may be substantially to lessen competition, or to tend to create a monopoly."

If the Act is violated by acquiring the ownership or control of competing enterprises, the court may order the defendant to dispose of such interests.[10] Such a decree is called a **divestiture order**.

(1) Premerger Notification. When large-size enterprises plan to merge, they must give written notice to the Federal Trade Commission and to the attorney in charge of the Antitrust Division of the Department of Justice. This gives the Department the opportunity to block the merger and thus avoid the loss when enterprises merge and are then required to separate."[11]

(2) Takeover Laws. Antitrust laws are usually concerned with whether the combination or agreement is fair to society or to a particular class, such as consumers. Some legislation is aimed at protecting the various parties directly involved in the combining of different enterprises. There is concern that one enterprise may in effect be raiding another enterprise. Laws seeking to protect from unfairness in such situations have been adopted by Congress and four-fifths of the states. State laws are limited in effect because they can only operate within the area over which a state has control. In the *Edgar* case it was claimed that a state takeover law was unconstitutional because it went too far.

---

8   Patrick v Burget, 486 US 83 (1988).
9   Oakridge Investment, Inc. v Southern Energy Homes, Inc. (Okla App) 719 P2d 848 (1986).

10   California v American Stores Co. 495 US ____, 109 L Ed 2d 240 (1990).
11   Antitrust Improvement Act of 1976, PL 94–435, § 201, PL 94–435, 90 Stat 1383, 15 USC §§ 1311 et seq.

EDGAR v MITE CORP.
457 US 624 (1982)

An Illinois statute required a corporation seeking to buy out another corporation to file papers disclosing certain information. MITE Corporation, a Delaware corporation, offered to buy all the stock of the Chicago Rivet Company, an Illinois corporation. Edgar, the Illinois Secretary of State, sought an injunction to block MITE because it had not complied with the requirements of the Illinois statute. MITE claimed that the Illinois statute was unconstitutional because (1) it was in conflict with the federal Williams Act that amended the Securities and Exchange Act of 1934, and (2) it placed an unreasonable burden on interstate commerce. From a decision in favor of MITE, Edgar appealed.

WHITE, J. . . . The Williams Act, passed in 1968, was the congressional response to the increased use of cash tender offers in corporate acquisitions. . . . The Act imposes several requirements. First, it requires that upon the commencement of the tender offer, the offeror file with the SEC, publish or send to the shareholders of the target company, and furnish to the target company detailed information about the offer. The offeror must disclose information about its background and identity; the source of the funds to be used in making the purchase; the purpose of the purchase, including any plans to liquidate the company or make major changes in its corporate structure; and the extent of the offeror's holdings in the target company. . . .

There is no question that in imposing these requirements, Congress intended to protect investors. . . . But it is also crystal clear that a major aspect of the effort to protect the investor was to avoid favoring either management or the takeover bidder. . . . Congress disclaimed any "intention to provide a weapon for management to discourage takeover bids. . . ." and expressly embraced a policy of neutrality. . . .

The Illinois Act requires a tender offeror to notify the Secretary of State and the target company of its intent to make a tender offer and the material terms of the offer 20 business days before the offer becomes effective.

. . . By providing the target company with additional time within which to take steps to combat the offer, the precommencement notification provisions furnish incumbent management with a powerful tool to combat tender offers, perhaps to the detriment of the stockholders who will not have an offer before them during this period. These consequences are precisely what Congress determined should be avoided, and for this reason, the precommencement notification provision frustrates the objectives of the Williams Act.

. . . The Commerce Clause permits only *incidental* regulation of interstate commerce by the states; direct regulation is prohibited. . . . The Illinois Act violates these principles for two reasons. First, it directly regulates and prevents, unless its terms are satisfied, interstate tender offers which in turn would generate interstate transactions. Second, the burden the Act imposes on interstate commerce is excessive in light of the local interests the Act purports to further.

. . . The Illinois Act . . . directly regulates transactions which take place across state lines, even if wholly outside the State of Illinois. A tender offer for securities of a publicly-held corporation is ordinarily communicated by the use of the mails or other means of interstate commerce to shareholders across the country and abroad. Securities are tendered and transactions closed by similar means. Thus, in this case, MITE Corporation, the tender offeror, is a Delaware corporation with principal offices in Connecticut. Chicago Rivet is a publicly-held Illinois corporation with shareholders scattered around the country, 27 percent of whom live in Illinois. MITE's offer to Chicago Rivet's shareholders, including those in Illinois, necessarily employed interstate facilities in communicating its offer, which, if accepted, would result in transactions occurring across state lines. These transactions would themselves be interstate commerce. Yet the Illinois law, unless complied with, sought to prevent MITE from making its offer and concluding interstate transactions not only with Chicago Rivet's stockholders living in Illinois, but also with those living in other states and having no connection with Illinois. Indeed, the Illinois law on its face would apply even if not a single one of Chicago Rivet's shareholders were a resident of Illinois, since the Act applies to every tender offer for a corporation meeting two of the following conditions: the corporation has its principal executive office in Illinois, is organized under Illinois laws, or has at least 10% of its stated capital and paid-in surplus represented in Illinois. . . . Thus the Act could be applied to regulate a tender offer which would not affect a single Illinois shareholder.

It is therefore apparent that the Illinois statute is a direct restraint on interstate commerce and that it has a sweeping extraterritorial effect. Furthermore, if Illinois may impose such regulations, so may other states; and interstate commerce in securities transactions generated by tender offers would be thoroughly stifled. . . .

Because the Illinois Act purports to regulate directly and to interdict interstate commerce, including commerce wholly outside the state, it must be held invalid.

. . . When a state statute regulates interstate commerce indirectly, the burden imposed on that commerce must not be excessive in relation to the local interests served by the statute. The most obvious burden the Illinois Act imposes on interstate commerce arises from the statute's previously-described nationwide reach which purports to give Illinois the power to determine whether a tender offer may proceed anywhere.

The effects of allowing the Illinois Secretary of State to block a nationwide tender offer are substantial. Shareholders are deprived of the opportunity to sell their shares at a premium. The reallocation of economic resources to their highest-valued use, a process which can improve efficiency and competition, is hindered. The incentive the tender offer mechanism provides incumbent management to perform well so that stock prices remain high is reduced. . . .

Appellant [Edgar] . . . contends that Illinois has an interest in regulating the internal affairs of a corporation incorporated under its laws. The internal affairs doctrine is a conflict of laws principle which recognizes that only one state should have the authority to regulate a corporation's internal affairs—matters peculiar to the relationships among or between the corporation and its current officers, directors, and shareholders—because otherwise a corporation could be faced with conflicting demands. See Restatement (Second) of Conflict of Laws, § 302, Comment b at 307–308 (1971). That doctrine is of little use to the state in this context. Tender offers contemplate transfers of stock by stockholders to a third party and do not themselves implicate the internal affairs of the target company. . . . Furthermore, the proposed justification is somewhat incredible since the Illinois Act applies to tender offers for any corporation for which 10% of the outstanding shares are held by Illinois residents, . . . The Act thus applies to corporations that are not incorporated in Illinois and have their principal place of business in other states. Illinois has no interest in regulating the internal affairs of foreign corporations.

We conclude with the Court of Appeals that the Illinois Act imposes a substantial burden on interstate commerce which outweighs its putative local benefits. It is accordingly invalid under the Commerce Clause.

[Judgment affirmed]

QUESTIONS

1. Was the Illinois Act intended to regulate commerce?
2. What is the attitude of the court to corporate takeovers?
3. The Illinois Act was valid as a regulation of internal affairs of Illinois corporations. Appraise this statement.

(d) PRICE FIXING. Agreements fixing prices, whether horizontally or vertically, violate the federal antitrust law. Thus, manufacturers cannot agree among themselves on the price at which they will sell (horizontal price fixing); likewise, a wholesaler cannot require a dealer to agree not to resell below a stated price (vertical price fixing).[12]

(e) EXCEPTIONS TO THE ANTITRUST LAW. By statute or decision, associations of exporters, marine insurance associations, farmers' cooperatives, and labor unions are exempt from the Sherman Antitrust Act with respect to agreements between their members. Certain pooling and revenue-dividing agreements between carriers are exempt from the antitrust law when approved by the appropriate federal agency. The Newspaper Preservation Act of 1970 grants an antitrust exemption to operating agreements entered into by newspapers to prevent financial collapse. The Soft Drink Interbrand Competition Act[13] grants the soft drink industry a limited exemption when it is shown that, in fact, there is substantial competition in spite of the agreements.

The general approach of the Supreme Court of the United States to the trust problem has been that an agreement should not be automatically or per se condemned as a restraint of interstate commerce merely because it creates a power or a potential to monopolize interstate commerce. It is only when the restraint imposed is unreasonable that the practice is unlawful.

(f) PUNISHMENT AND CIVIL REMEDY. A violation of either of the Sherman Act provisions stated in Chapter 4, Section 5(a) of this text is punishable by fine or imprisonment or both, at the discretion of the court. The maximum fine for a corporation is $1 million. A person can be fined a maximum of $100,000 or imprisoned for a maximum term of three years or both. In addition to this criminal penalty, the law provides for an injunction to stop the unlawful practices and permits suing the wrongdoers for damages.

(1) Individual Damage Suit. Any person or enterprise harmed may bring a separate action for treble damages (three times the damages actually sustained).

(2) Class Action Damage Suit by State Attorney General. When the effect of an antitrust violation is to raise prices, the attorney general of a state may bring a class action to recover damages on behalf of those who have paid the higher prices. This action is called a *parens patriae* action, on the theory that the state is suing as the "parent" of its people.

6.   Regulation of Employment

Basically, parties are free to make an employment contract on any terms they wish. By statute, certain limitations are imposed on this freedom of contract. Persons under a certain age cannot be employed at certain kinds of labor. Statutes commonly specify minimum wages and maximum hours that the employer must observe. A state may require employers to pay employees' wages for the time that they are away from work for the purpose of voting.

(a) FAIR LABOR STANDARDS ACT. By this statute, which is popularly known as the Wage and Hour Act, Congress provides that, subject to certain exceptions, persons working in interstate commerce or in an industry producing goods for interstate commerce cannot be paid less than a specified minimum wage. Furthermore, they cannot be employed for more than 40 hours a week unless they are paid time and a half for overtime.[14] The Act prohibits the employment of children under the age of 14 years. It permits the employment of children between the ages of 14 and 16 years in all industries, except mining and

---

[12]   Vertical price-maintenance agreements were authorized by statutes in varying degrees from 1931 to 1975, but the Consumer Goods Pricing Act of 1975, PL 94–145, 89 Stat 801, abolished the immunity from the federal antitrust law that had been given to such agreements. Although the states may permit such agreements as long as interstate commerce is not involved, the area of intrastate commerce is so slight that for all practical purposes such agreements are now illegal.

[13]   Act of July 9, 1980, PL 96–308, 94 Stat 939, 15 USC §§ 3501 et seq.

[14]   Fair Labor Standards Amendment of 1977, PL 95–151, 91 Stat 1245, 29 USC §§ 201 et seq.

manufacturing, under certain prescribed conditions. This Act has been copied by a number of states in regulating those phases of industry not covered by the federal statute.

(b) FAIR EMPLOYMENT PRACTICES ACTS. With some exceptions, employers of 15 or more persons are forbidden to discriminate against any person because of race, religious creed, color, sex, national origin, or age with regard to compensation and other privileges or conditions of employment.[15] Special protection for migrant farm workers is provided by the Federal Migrant and Seasonal Agricultural Workers Protection Act.[16] The federal law does not cover all cases of improper employer conduct. For example, the liability of an employer for improper discharge is governed by state law when the decision of the claim does not require an interpretation of the collective bargaining agreement that had been made in accordance with the National Labor Relations Act.

(1) Sex Discrimination. An employer cannot discriminate on the basis of sex. An employer may not hire on the basis of a stereotypical pattern of what is "woman's work" and what is "man's work." Women, therefore, cannot be excluded from working as bartenders, and men cannot be excluded from working as airline flight attendants. Indirect sex discrimination is also prohibited, as when the employer establishes height and weight specifications that have no bearing on the performance of the work but have the effect of excluding women from the job.

The equality of the sexes is literally applied so that a law is unconstitutional when it gives to women a protection or an advantage that it does not give to men performing the same work. Likewise, it is a discriminatory labor practice to allow women seniority rights that are not available to men on the same terms, or

to prohibit women from working at jobs that involve the lifting of heavy weights. A standardized "compulsory pregnancy leave" regulation for public school teachers is unconstitutional. This is so because no consideration is given the fitness of the individual teacher to continue teaching; and there is no proof that pregnant teachers, as a class, are necessarily and universally unfit to teach.[17] The protection against sex discrimination is not limited to situations that are customarily regarded as employment. Thus, it is held that a law partnership violates the Act if it refuses to invite an associate to become a partner because the associate is a woman.[18]

(2) Disability Discrimination. Anyone employing 15 or more employees may not discriminate against any qualified person with respect to hiring, firing, or conditions of employment because of a disability of such person.[19]

(3) Allowable Distinctions. The federal law does not require that every employee be treated the same as every other. It does not prohibit the testing or screening of applicants or employees for the purpose of determining whether a person is qualified to be hired, promoted, given a wage increase, or given special training. The Civil Rights Act has no effect upon the employer's right to establish compensation scales, to provide bonus pay and incentive pay, or to pay different rates in different geographic areas. The employer may also recognize seniority status, voluntarily or as a result of collective bargaining.

(4) Proof of Discrimination. A person claiming discrimination in employment must first establish that any qualifications for the employment in question were satisfied. The claim that there has been improper discrimination against an applicant or employee is made in a court or before an administrative agency. The procedure is regulated by statute—the claimant does not have a choice as to whether to go to court or to an agency.

---

[15]   Federal Civil Rights Act of 1964, Title VII, as amended by the Equal Employment Opportunities Act of 1972 and 1986. TWA v Thurston, 469 US 111 (1985). With minor exceptions, the federal law prohibits age discrimination. In some states and cities, state statutes and local ordinances also prohibit age discrimination.
[16]   Act of January 14, 1983, PL 97–470, 96 Stat 2583, 29 USC § 1801.

[17]   Cleveland Board of Education v La Fleur, 414 US 632 (1974).
[18]   Hishon v King & Spalding, 467 US 69 (1984).
[19]   Americans with Disabilities Act of 1990, Act of July 26, 1990, PL 101–336, 104 Stat 329, ____USC § ____.

Who has the burden of proof when the claimant brings a lawsuit or files a complaint with an administrative agency? This is a vital question because, as a practical matter, there will be many cases in which it is impossible to prove exactly what happened. In such cases whoever has the burden of proving what did happen will lose, because it will not be possible to carry the burden of proof.

The *Price Waterhouse* case involved defending against an employee's claim of improper discrimination.

PRICE WATERHOUSE v HOPKINS
490 US 228, 104 L Ed 2d 268 (1989)

Ann Hopkins was employed as senior manager of a branch office of the national accounting firm of Price Waterhouse. She was proposed as a partner for the firm, but no action was taken on her application. This was apparently because some of the partners felt that she was too masculine and abrasive. It was suggested that her application would be acted on favorably in the following year if she would dress and act like a woman. The following year, however, no one would propose her for partner. She therefore quit the firm and brought suit against it under the Federal Civil Rights Act. Both the district court and the court of appeals decided in her favor and rejected the claim of the defendant that sex had nothing to do with its decision because the defendant had not proven that by clear and convincing evidence. Price Waterhouse petitioned the Supreme Court for review of the decision.

BRENNAN, J. . . . Congress' intent to forbid employers to take gender into account in making employment decisions appears on the face of the statute. In now-familiar language, the statute forbids an employer to "fail or refuse to hire or to discharge any individual, or otherwise to discriminate with respect to his compensation, terms, conditions, or privileges of employment," or to "limit, segregate, or classify his employees or applicants for employment in any way which would deprive or tend to deprive any individual of employment opportunities or otherwise adversely affect his status as an employee, because of such individual's . . . sex." . . . We take these words to mean that gender must be irrelevant to employment decisions. . . .

Our interpretation . . . is supported by the fact that Title VII does identify one circumstance in which an employer may take gender into account in making an employment decision, namely, when gender is a "bona fide occupational qualification [(BFOQ)] reasonably necessary to the normal operation of the particular business or enterprise." 42 USC § 2000e-2(e) [42 USCS § 2000e-2(e)]. The only plausible inference to draw from this provision is that, in all other circumstances, a person's gender may not be considered in making decisions that affect her. . . . The central point is this: while an employer may not take gender into account in making an employment decision (except in those very narrow circumstances in which gender is a BFOQ), it is free to decide against a woman for other reasons. We think these principles require that, once a plaintiff in a Title VII case shows that gender played a motivating part in an employment decision, the defendant may avoid a finding of liability only by proving that it would have made the same decision even if it had not allowed gender to play such a role. . . .

In deciding as we do today, we do not traverse new ground. We have in the past confronted Title VII cases in which an employer has used an illegitimate criterion to distinguish among employees, and have held that it is the employer's burden to justify decisions resulting from that practice. When an employer has asserted that gender is a bona fide occupational qualification . . . our assumption always has been that if an employer allows gender to affect its decisionmaking process, then it must carry the burden of justifying its ultimate decision. We have not in the past required women whose gender has proved relevant to an employment decision to establish the negative proposition that they would not have been subject to that decision had they been men, and we do not do so today.

We have reached a similar conclusion in other contexts where the law announces that a certain characteristic is irrelevant to the allocation of burdens and benefits. . . .

In saying that gender played a motivating part in an employment decision, we mean that, if we asked the employer at the moment of the decision what its reasons were and if we received a truthful response, one of those reasons would be that the applicant or employee was a woman. In the specific context of sex stereotyping, an employer who acts on the basis of a belief that a woman cannot be aggressive, or that she must not be, has acted on the basis of gender. . . .

As to the employer's proof, in most cases, the employer should be able to present some objective evidence as to its probable decision in the absence of an impermissible motive. Moreover, proving "that the same decision would have been justified . . . is not the same as proving that the same decision would have been made." . . . The employer instead must show that its legitimate reason, standing alone, would have induced it to make the same decision.

The courts below held that an employer who has allowed a discriminatory impulse to play a motivating part in an employment decision must prove by clear and convincing evidence that it would have made the same decision in the absence of discrimination. We are persuaded that the better rule is that the employer must make this showing by a preponderance of the evidence.

Although Price Waterhouse does not concretely tell us how its proof was preponderant even if it was not clear and convincing, this general claim is implicit in its request for the less stringent standard. Since the lower courts required Price Waterhouse to make its proof by clear and convincing evidence, they did not determine whether Price Waterhouse had proved by a *preponderance of the evidence* that it would have placed Hopkins' candidacy on hold even if it had not permitted sex-linked evaluations to play a part in the decision-making process. Thus, we shall remand this case so that that determination can be made. . . .

[Judgment reversed and action remanded]

QUESTIONS

1. When a rejected employee claims that there has been improper discrimination in violation of the federal law, the employee must prove that the rejection was caused only by a purpose to discriminate. Appraise this statement.
2. What error had been made by both lower courts?
3. What burden of proof is applied when it is claimed that there is discrimination because of race?

7.   Regulation of Labor Relations

Statutes declare the right of employees to form a union and require the employer to deal with the union as the bargaining representative of the employees. An employer cannot refuse in advance to bargain with the proper representative of the employees on the ground that the employer is afraid that improper demands will be made by the representative.

The federal labor law only preempts with respect to the contract of employment. A claim by an employee that her employer intentionally subjected her to emotional distress does not relate to the contract of employment but is a tort claim.[20] Therefore, the employee may sue the employer under state law in a state court for causing such distress.[21]

(a) MACHINERY TO ENFORCE COLLECTIVE BARGAINING. To protect the rights of workers to unionize and bargain collectively, the federal government created the National Labor Relations Board (NLRB). The NLRB determines the proper collective bargaining unit and eliminates unfair practices by which the employer and the union might interfere with employees' rights.

(b) SELECTION OF BARGAINING REPRESENTATIVE. Generally there is an election by secret ballot to select the bargaining representative of the employees within a particular collective bargaining unit.

(c) EXCLUSIVE AND EQUAL REPRESENTATION OF ALL EMPLOYEES. Any union selected by the majority of the workers within the unit is the exclusive representative of all the employees in the unit for the purpose of bargaining with respect to wages and hours or other conditions of employment. Whether or not all the workers are members of the representative union is immaterial because, in any case, this union is the exclusive representative of every employee. It is unlawful for any employee, whether a member or non-member of the union, to attempt to make a contract directly with the employer. Except as to grievances, every worker must act through the representative union with respect to the contract of employment. At the same time, the union is required to represent all workers fairly, nonmembers as well as members. It is unlawful for the union, in bargaining with the employer, to discriminate in any way against any employee. It makes no difference whether a particular worker is a member of the representative union. The union cannot use its position as representative of all workers to further its interest as a union.

The fact that the representative of the bargaining unit must represent all employees fairly does not bar it from exercising independent judgment and from failing to prosecute an employee's grievance if the union honestly believes the grievance has no merit.

(d) UNFAIR LABOR PRACTICES. The National Labor Relations Act prohibits certain practices as unfair and authorizes the NLRB to conduct proceedings to stop such practices.

(1) Unfair Employer Practices. The federal law declares that it is an unfair labor practice for an employer to interfere with unionization, to discriminate against any employee because of union activities, or to refuse to bargain collectively as to wages, hours, and other terms and conditions of employment.

(2) Unfair Union Practices. The federal law declares it to be an unfair labor practice for a union to interfere with employees in forming a union or in refraining from joining a union; to cause an employer to discriminate against an employee for belonging to another union or no union; to refuse to bargain collectively; and under certain circumstances to stop work or refuse to work on materials or to persuade others to stop work.

(3) Procedure for Enforcement. Under the National Labor Relations Act, the NLRB issues a complaint whenever it appears that an unfair labor practice has been committed. The complaint informs the respondent of the charges made and gives notice to appear at a hearing before an administrative law judge (ALJ). The ALJ conducts a hearing and sends

---

[20]   See Chapter 7 as to tort law generally.
[21]   Alpha Beta, Inc. v Superior Court, 198 Cal App 3d 1390, 244 Cal Rptr 414 (1988).

a report to the parties and the five-member Board in Washington, D.C. *recommending* either an order to cease and desist from an unfair labor practice or a dismissal of the complaint. Unless either party files timely exceptions to the ALJ's findings, the ALJ's recommended order becomes an order of the Board. When exceptions are filed, the five-member Board reviews the case and either finds the respondent guilty or not guilty. When the respondent is found guilty, the Board issues a cease and desist order, which can be enforced by the U.S. Court of Appeals.

Proceeding before the NLRB is the only way of enforcing rights under the federal statute. A lawsuit cannot be brought in a state court.

(4) Constitutional Protection. Any employment practice that violates a constitutional right of a worker can be stopped by court action if not within the control of an administrative agency.

(e) Union Organization and Management. In order to ensure the honest and democratic administration of unions, Congress adopted the Labor–Management Reporting and Disclosure Act of 1959. It regulates unions operating in or affecting interstate commerce. The Act protects the rights of union members within their unions by guaranteeing equality, the right to vote on specified matters, and the right to information on union matters and contracts. It also protects members from interference with the enjoyment of these rights.

In the *United Steelworkers* case, the court was faced with the question of whether the election procedure of the union violated the federal statute.

UNITED STEELWORKERS OF AMERICA v USERY
429 US 305 (1977)

The steelworkers union was run by officers elected from the members of the union. A rule of the union stated that a member was not eligible to be an officer unless the member had attended at least one-half of the regular meetings of the union in the preceding three years. When this rule was applied to a local branch of the union, Local 3489, the result was to disqualify 96.5 percent of the membership of the local union from holding office. This meant that only 23 members were eligible. Nine of these were already officers of the local. An election was held in the local to vote for new officers. The meeting-attendance rule was applied to determine those who were eligible. W. J. Usery, the Secretary of Labor of the United States, claimed that the election was invalid because of the meeting-attendance eligibility requirement. He claimed that it violated the Labor–Management Reporting and Disclosure Act, § 401(e), 29 USC § 481(e), which declared that "Every member in good standing shall be eligible to be a candidate and hold office . . . subject to . . . reasonable qualifications uniformly imposed." The district court sustained the meeting-attendance rule as a reasonable qualification uniformly imposed. On appeal, the court of appeals held the rule invalid. The local then appealed to the Supreme Court.

BRENNAN, J. . . . [The] LMRDA [Labor–Management Reporting and Disclosure Act] does not render unions powerless to restrict candidacies for union office. The injunction in § 401(e) that "every member in good standing shall be eligible to be a candidate and to hold office" is made expressly "subject to . . . reasonable qualifications uniformly imposed." . . . But "Congress plainly did not intend that the authorization . . . of 'reasonable qualifications . . .' should be given a broad reach. The contrary is implicit in the legislative history of the section and its wording. . . ." The basic objective of Title IV of LMRDA is to guarantee "free and democratic" union elections modeled on "political elections in the country" where "the assumption is that voters will exercise common sense and judgment in casting their ballots."

. . . Thus, Title IV is not designed merely to protect the right of a union member to run for a particular office in a particular election." . . . Congress emphatically asserted a vital public interest in assuring free and democratic union elections that transcends the narrower interest of the complaining union member." . . . The goal was to "protect the rights of rank-and-file members to participate fully in the operation of their union through processes of democratic self-government, and, through the election process, to keep the union leadership responsive to the membership." *Wirtz v Hotel Employees*, [291] US 492 at 497 [(1968)] . . .

Whether a particular qualification is "reasonable" within the meaning of § 402(e) must therefore "be measured in terms of its consistency with the Act's command to unions to conduct 'free and democratic' union elections." . . .

. . . The antidemocratic effects of the meeting attendance rule outweigh the interests urged in its support. . . . An attendance requirement that results in the exclusion of 96.5% of the members from candidacy for union office hardly seems to be a "reasonable qualification" consistent with the goal of free and democratic elections. A requirement having that result obviously severely restricts the free choice of the membership in selecting their leaders. . . .

Petitioners next argue that the rule is reasonable within § 401(e) because it encourages attendance at union meetings, and assures more qualified officers by limiting election to those who have demonstrated an interest in union affairs, and are familiar with union problems. But the rule has plainly not served these goals. It has obviously done little to encourage attendance at meetings, which continue to attract only a handful of members. Even as to the more limited goal of encouraging the attendance of potential dissident candidates, very few members, as we have said, are likely to see themselves as such sufficiently far in advance of the election to be spurred to attendance by the rule.

As for assuring the election of knowledgeable and dedicated leaders, the election provisions of LMRDA express a congressional determination that the best means to this end is to leave the choice of leaders to the membership in open democratic elections, unfettered by arbitrary exclusions. Pursuing this goal by excluding the bulk of the membership from eligibility for office, and thus limiting the possibility of dissident candidacies, runs directly counter to the basic premise of the statute. We therefore conclude that Congress, in guaranteeing every union member the opportunity to hold office, subject only to "reasonable qualifications," disabled unions from establishing eligibility qualifications as sharply restrictive of the openness of the union political process as is petitioners' attendance rule.

[Judgment affirmed]

QUESTIONS

1. What was the basis for the claim of the Secretary of Labor?
2. What was the object of Congress in adopting the statute involved in the *Steelworkers* case?

8.   Social Security and Unemployment Compensation

Employees and employers are required to pay social security taxes. These taxes provide employees with four types of insurance protection—retirement benefits, disability benefits, life insurance benefits, and health insurance (Medicare).

The federal Social Security Act established a federal program of aid for the needy aged, the blind, and the disabled. This is called the Supplemental Security Income program (SSI). Payments are administered directly by the Department of Health and Human Services.

The states also have plans of assistance for the unemployed, aged, and disabled. The federal law encourages the making of payments under state programs in addition to those received under the federal program. Such additional programs are called State Supplemental Payments (SSP). State plans typically establish an administrative board or agency with which claims for assistance are filed. If the board approves a claim, assistance is given to the applicant in the amount specified by the statute for the number of weeks or other period of time designated by the statute.

Unemployment compensation laws generally deny the payment of benefits when the employee was discharged for good cause, or abandoned work without cause, failed or refused to seek or accept an offer of suitable employment, or when the unemployment was the result of a labor dispute. A state may refuse to pay unemployment compensation to workers who financed the strike that caused their unemployment.[22]

B.   LIMITATIONS ON STATE POWER TO REGULATE

By virtue of their police power, the states may regulate business to prevent the sale of harmful products, to protect from fraud, and so on.

The power of the states is subject to important limitations.

9.   Constitutional Limitations

A state law, although made under the police power, cannot (a) impose an unreasonable burden on or discriminate against interstate commerce, or (b) invade a right that is protected by the federal Constitution.

A state statute cannot prohibit lawyers from making a direct-mail solicitation to the public to seek as clients persons with a specified kind of problem, such as foreclosure.[23]

10.   Federal Supremacy

A state law cannot conflict with a federal law or regulation on the same subject matter. Moreover, when the federal government regulates a particular activity, state regulation is generally excluded even as to matters not covered by the federal regulation. That is, the federal government occupies or preempts the entire field even though every detail is not regulated.

The federal authority that overrides state action may be a federal administrative agency regulation, as contrasted with an act of Congress. Thus the Federal Communications Commission (FCC) may prohibit states and cities from imposing stricter standards on cable television companies than those imposed by the FCC.[24]

11.   State and Local Governments as Market Participants

When a state or local government, such as a city or county, enters the marketplace to buy or sell goods, whether produced by itself or others, it is not acting as a government. It is a market participant, as contrasted with a government regulating the conduct of others. When a state or local government is a market participant, it is not subject to the limitations

---

[22]   Baker v General Motors Corp. 478 US 621 (1986) (workers contributed to union strike fund).

[23]   Shapero v Kentucky Bar Ass'n, 486 US 466 (1988).
[24]   City of New York v FCC, 486 US 57 (1988).

imposed upon state governments by the U.S. Constitution.

The *White* case raised the question of

whether a city was subject to limitations of the commerce clause when it was having a building constructed.

WHITE v MASSACHUSETTS COUNCIL OF CONSTRUCTION EMPLOYERS, INC.

460 US 204 (1983)

The mayor of Boston issued an executive order that on all construction work done by the city of Boston, at least one-half of the work force had to be bona fide residents of Boston. An employer organization claimed that this requirement was a violation of the commerce clause of the United States Constitution. From a decision holding the executive order invalid, the mayor appealed.

REHNQUIST, J. . . . We were first asked in Hughes v Alexandria Scrap Corp., 426 US 794 (1976), to decide whether state and local governments are restrained by the Commerce Clause when they seek to effect commercial transactions not as "regulators" but as "market participants." . . . In upholding the Maryland statute in the face of a Commerce Clause challenge, we said that "nothing in the purpose animating the Commerce Clause prohibits a State, in the absence of congressional action, from participating in the market and exercising the right to favor its own citizens over others." . . .

We faced the question again in Reeves, Inc. v Stake, 447 US 429 (1980), when confronted with a South Dakota policy to confine the sale of cement by a state operated cement plant to residents of South Dakota. We underscored the holding of Hughes v Alexandria Scrap Corp., saying:

> The basic distinction drawn in Alexandria Scrap between States as market participants and States as market regulators makes good sense and sound law. As that case explains, the Commerce Clause responds principally to state taxes and regulatory measures impeding free private trade in the national marketplace. There is no indication of a constitutional plan to limit the ability of the States themselves to operate freely in the free market.

We concluded that South Dakota, "as a seller of cement, unquestionably fits the 'market participant' label" and applied the "general rule of Alexandria Scrap." . . .

Alexandria Scrap and Reeves, therefore, stand for the proposition that when a state or local government enters the market as a participant it is not subject to the restraints of the Commerce Clause. As we said in Reeves, in this kind of case there is "a single inquiry: whether the challenged 'program constituted direct state participation in the market.'" We reaffirm that principle now.

. . . The Supreme Judicial Court of Massachusetts expressed reservations as to the application of the "market participation" principle to the city here, reasoning that "the implementation of the mayor's order will have a significant impact on those firms which engage in specialized areas of construction and employ permanent work crews composed of out-of-state residents." 384 Mass, at [479], 425 NE2d, at 354. Even if this conclusion is factually correct, it is not relevant to the inquiry of whether the city is participating in the marketplace when it provides city funds for building construction. If the city is a market participant, then the Commerce Clause establishes no barrier to conditions such as these which the city demands for its participation. Impact on out-of-state residents figures in the equation only after it is decided that the city is regulating the market rather than participating in it, for only in the former case need it be determined whether any burden on interstate commerce is permitted by the Commerce Clause.

. . . We hold that on the record before us the application of the mayor's executive order to the contracts in question did not violate the Commerce Clause of the United States Constitution. Insofar as the city expended only its own funds in entering into construction contracts for public projects, it was a market participant and entitled to be treated as such under the rule of Hughes v Alexandria Scrap Corp., supra. . . .

[Judgment reversed and action remanded]

QUESTIONS

1. Did the Court determine whether the mayor's order placed an unreasonable burden on interstate commerce?
2. Would it have made any difference if the mayor's order had required that all construction work performed in the city should be performed only by city residents?
3. In the situation in the *White* case, does it make any difference whose money is being used to pay for the work?

When a state or local government is a market participant, it is subject to all laws applicable to ordinary persons. For example, when a city owns and operates a mass transit system, it is in the position of a private employer and therefore is subject to the federal minimum wage law.[25]

[25]   Garcia v San Antonio Metropolitan Transit Authority, 469 US 528 (1985).

SUMMARY

Regulation by government has occurred primarily to protect one group from the improper conduct of another group. Until the middle third of this century, regulation of business was primarily directed at protecting competitors from misconduct of other competitors. Beginning with the middle third of this century, regulation has expanded in the interest of protecting consumers.

In the last 100 years, the federal government has regulated advertising and food, drugs, and cosmetics. This protects consumers from false claims and from untested and possibly unsafe drugs. Unfair methods of competition are prohibited.

Prices have been regulated both by the setting of the exact price or a maximum price and by prohibiting discrimination as to prices. Price discrimination between buyers is prohibited when the effect of such discrimination could tend to create a monopoly or lessen competition. Certain exceptions are made where the circumstances are such that the price discrimination does not have the purpose or result of harming someone else.

The Sherman Antitrust Act prohibits conspiracies in restraint of trade and the monopolization of trade. A partial attempt to solve the problem of bigness is made by the Clayton Act in prohibiting mergers or the acquisition of the assets of another corporation when such conduct would tend to lessen competition or give rise to a monopoly. Violation of these statutes subjects the wrongdoer to criminal prosecution and suit, by persons harmed, for treble damages. The application of these laws is modified to some extent by express exceptions and by the approach of the Supreme Court to antitrust cases.

Employment has been regulated in a variety of ways. The federal Fair Labor Standards Act, also known as the Wage and Hour Act, requires that employees be paid not less than a specified minimum wage. Fair employment practice acts prohibit discrimination in employment because of race, religion, color, sex, or national origin. Discrimination because of age is partially prohibited. Special protection is afforded by statute to migrant farm workers. The right of employees to bargain collectively with their employer and the right to choose their representative for such purpose is guaranteed by the National Labor Relations Act. The representative selected by the employees to bargain on their behalf is required to represent all employees fairly and equally without regard to whether particular employees are members of the representative union. The National Labor Relations Act prohibits both employers and unions from committing specified acts that would violate the rights of employees.

In order to protect union members from misconduct within their own unions, the federal Labor–Management Reporting and Disclosure Act imposes certain limitations on unions to ensure that they are run in an honest and democratic manner. As an aspect of regulating the rewards of labor, the social security system under federal law provides for payment to workers who retire because of age or disability. The federal Supplemental Security Income payment (SSI) is in some cases supplemented by payments made under state programs (SSP).

Many of the regulations imposed by the federal government are paralleled or duplicated by state laws making a similar regulation as to local matters. The action of the states is restricted by the limitations arising from the Constitution and by the doctrine of the supremacy of federal law.

QUESTIONS AND CASE PROBLEMS

1. Describe the objective of each of the following rules of law. (a) Horizontal price-fixing is illegal under the federal law without regard to whether the price fixed is fair and reasonable. (b) Farmers' and dairy farmers' cooperatives are exempt by statute from the operation of the Sherman Antitrust Act.

2. What government can regulate business?

3. The Danabo Corporation paid the workers in its Pennsylvania factory $.50 an hour more than workers doing the same work in its Mississippi factory. Was the Danabo Corporation guilty of unfair employment practices?

4. Hart is employed by the Bulldog Concrete Forms Company. Her employer refused to promote her because she belonged to a labor union. She claimed that the employer violated a fair employment practices act. Was she correct?

5. Cressler owns a factory. She refuses to obey the state safety laws on the ground that there is no constitutional provision that grants the state the power to make such laws. Does this justify Cressler's refusal to obey the state law?

6. Johnson was a school teacher. He applied to the Bozeman School District for a teaching position. His application was rejected. He claimed that this was done because his wife was employed by the school district, and the school district had followed a rule against nepotism (the hiring of a close relative of an employee). Johnson claimed that this violated the Montana Human Rights Statute, which prohibited refusing to hire an applicant "because of his . . . marital status." The school district had applicants take qualifying tests that were graded from 1 (superior) to 5 (poor). Johnson had scored 4. It was the policy of the school district to employ only persons scoring 1 or 2. Did the school district violate the state law? [Johnson v Bozeman School District No 7, 226 Mont 134, 734 P2d 209]

7. What limitations are imposed upon the purchasing of the assets of an existing enterprise?

8. Jim Mandell applied to the Conestoga Airlines for a job as a flight attendant. His application was rejected on the ground that the airline was employing only female attendants because the passengers preferred them. Jim claimed that the airline was guilty of an unlawful discrimination in its employment practices. Was he correct?

9. The Hines Cosmetic Company sold beauty preparations nationally to beauty shops at a standard or fixed price schedule. Some of the shops were also supplied with a free demonstrator and with free advertising materials. The shops that were not so supplied claimed that the giving of the free services and materials constituted unlawful price discrimination. Hines replied that there was no price discrimination because it charged everyone the same. What it was giving free was merely a promotional campaign that was not intended to discriminate against those who were not given anything free. Was Hines guilty of unlawful price discrimination?

10. Eleanor was an employee of the Basic Computer Company. The Computer Workers Union was elected as the bargaining representative of the employees of Basic Computer Company. Eleanor and a few other workers did not belong to the union. The union entered into a contract with Basic Computer Company under which it was agreed that in case of any reduction in workforce, the employer would discharge the nonunion workers first. Eleanor claimed that this was a violation of federal law because it discriminated against nonunion workers. The union claimed that it was justified in providing this seniority for union members because they were paying dues to the union and Eleanor was not. The union claimed that if Eleanor were given the same protection as the dues-paying union members, she would be given a "free ride." Decide.

11. Moore ran a bakery in Santa Rosa, New Mexico. His business was wholly intrastate. Mead's Fine Bread Company, his competitor, engaged in an interstate business. Mead cut the price of bread in half in Santa Rosa but made no price cut in any other place in New Mexico or in any other state. As a result of this price cutting, Moore was driven out of business. Moore then sued Mead for damages for violation of the Clayton and Robinson-Patman Acts. Mead claimed that the price cutting was purely intrastate and therefore did not constitute a violation of federal statutes. Was Mead correct? [Moore v Mead's Fine Bread Co. 348 US 115]

12. The El Paso Natural Gas Company acquired the stock and assets of the Pacific Northwest Pipe Line Company. El Paso, although not a California enterprise, supplied over half of the natural gas used in California; all the other natural gas was supplied by California sources. No gas was sold in California by Pacific Northwest, although it was a strong, experienced company within the Northwest area and had attempted several times to enter the California market. The United States claimed that the acquisition of Pacific by El Paso constituted a violation of § 7 of the Clayton Act, as amended, because the effect would be to remove competition between the two companies within California. The defense was raised that (a) California was not a "section" of the country within the Clayton Act, (b) the sale of natural gas was not a line of commerce, and (c) the acquisition did not lessen competition when there had not been any prior sales by Pacific within the area. Decide. [United States v El Paso Natural Gas Co. 376 US 651]

13. Copperweld Corp. purchased Regal Tube Co. Some time later the Independence Tube Corp. sued Copperweld and Regal for damages for conspiring in violation of the Sherman Antitrust Act. They denied liability for "conspiring" because Regal was the wholly owned subsidiary of Copperweld. Were they liable? [Copperweld Corp. v Independence Tube Corp. 467 US 752]

14. Lingle was employed in Illinois by the Norge Division of Magic Chef, Inc., under a collective bargaining agreement that prohibited the wrongful discharge of an employee. She was injured at work and filed a claim for Illinois worker's compensation. Norge fired her. She claimed that this was a wrongful discharge under the law of Illinois and sued for damages under that law. Norge claimed that the state law could not be applied because the employment was governed by the collective bargaining agreement made under the Labor Management Relations Act. Was Norge correct? [Lingle v Norge Division of Magic Chef, Inc. 486 US 399]

15. The Duke Power Company established standards for promotion from one department to another. In order to be promoted from one department to another, an employee had to have a high school education and had to pass two aptitude tests. These tests were prepared by professional test preparers. Willie S. Griggs and other blacks were employed in the labor department of Duke. They applied for promotion out of the labor department. They could not get the

necessary scores on the aptitude tests. They claimed that by requiring them to pass the tests, the employer was guilty of prohibited racial discrimination. Griggs and other employees brought a class action under Title VII of the federal Civil Rights Act of 1964. It was shown that the aptitude tests did not specifically test for any of the qualities needed in the department to which promotion was sought. It was also shown that white workers obtained better scores on the tests, apparently because of their having a better public school education. Griggs claimed that Duke was guilty of unlawful discrimination. Was he correct? [Griggs v Duke Power Co. 401 US 424]

5

ADMINISTRATIVE AGENCIES

In Chapter 4 we discussed the ability of governments--federal, state, and local—to regulate many aspects of business. Early in this country's history all of this regulation was accomplished through direct application of the powers of the legislative, executive, and judicial branches of government. However, the pace of advancing technology began to outstrip this cumbersome tripartite government's ability to keep up with it. A new type of governmental structure, designed to be able to specialize in a particular field, began to emerge—the administrative agency.

A. NATURE OF THE ADMINISTRATIVE AGENCY

An **administrative agency** is a governmental body charged with administering and implementing legislation. An agency may be a department, independent establishment, commission, administration, authority, board, or bureau. Agencies exist on the federal and state levels.

1. Importance of the Administrative Agency

In this new age of complex regulation, most people and businesses do not come into direct contact with the constitutional branches of government. Typically they deal with an administrative agency. To them, an agency is the government.

Large areas of the American economy are governed by federal administrative agencies created to carry out the general policies specified by Congress. A contract must be in harmony with the law declared by Congress and the courts and also with the regulations and decisions of the appropriate administrative agency. For example, a contract to market particular goods might not be prohibited by any statute or court decision, but it may still be condemned by the Federal Trade Commission as an unfair method of competition. A contract not in harmony with the guidelines of a specific commission, such as a contract of a carrier charging a higher or a lower rate than that approved by the Interstate Commerce Commission, is illegal. Other federal administrative agencies include the Federal Communications Commission, the Federal Maritime Commission, the Federal Power Commission, the National Labor Relations Board, and the Securities and Exchange Commission. The law governing these agencies is known as **administrative law**.

State administrative agencies may also affect business and the citizen. State agencies may have jurisdiction over fair employment practices, workers' compensation claims, and the renting of homes and apartments.

2. Uniqueness of Administrative Agencies

Federal and state governments alike are divided into three branches—executive, legislative, and judicial. Many of the offices in these branches are filled by persons who are elected. The judicial branch acts as a superguardian to prevent the executive and the legislative branches from exceeding the proper spheres of their power. In contrast to the situation in the tripartite structure, members of administrative agencies are ordinarily appointed (in the case of federal agencies, by the President of the United States with the consent of the Senate). The major agencies combine legislative, executive, and judicial powers; they may make the rules, police the community to see that the rules are obeyed, and sit in judgment to determine whether there have been violations of their rules.

In the *Withrow* case the challenge was made that it was unfair to have the same body both investigate and then decide the case.

WITHROW v LARKIN
421 US 35 (1975)

Doctors must obtain a license from the state in which they practice. These licenses are ordinarily issued by a licensing board that reviews the qualifications of each applicant. In addition, the statutes creating these licensing boards ordinarily give them the power to revoke a license when there is good reason to do so. The Wisconsin statute authorized the medical licensing board to investigate any case to see if there was cause for revoking a license. If it thought that the circumstances appeared sufficiently bad, the same board could then hold a hearing to see what should be done.

Duane Larkin was a doctor licensed under the laws of Wisconsin. The state medical licensing board conducted an investigation of Larkin. The board concluded that it should hold a hearing to determine whether Larkin's license should be suspended. Larkin claimed that his constitutional rights would be violated if the same body that had investigated the case against him were also to act as judge to determine whether his license should be suspended. He brought a lawsuit against Harold Withrow and the other members of the licensing board to enjoin them from holding the hearing. An injunction was granted, and Withrow and the other members of the board appealed.

WHITE, J. . . . Concededly, a "fair trial in a fair tribunal is a basic requirement of due process." . . .

The contention that the combination of investigative and adjudicative functions necessarily creates an unconstitutional risk of bias in administrative adjudication has a . . . difficult burden of persuasion to carry. It must overcome a presumption of honesty and integrity in those serving as adjudicators: and it must convince that, under a realistic appraisal of psychological tendencies and human weakness, conferring investigative and adjudicative powers on the same individuals poses such a risk of actual bias or prejudgment that the practice must be forbidden if the guarantee of due process is to be adequately implemented.

Very similar claims have been squarely rejected in prior decisions of this Court. . . .

More recently we have sustained against due process objection a system in which a social security examiner has responsibility for developing the facts and making a decision as to disability claims, and observed that the challenge to this combination of functions "assumes too much and would bring down too many procedures designed, and working well, for a government structure of great and growing complexity." . . .

That is not to say that there is nothing to the argument that those who have investigated should not then adjudicate. The issue is substantial, it is not new, and legislators and others concerned with the operations of administrative agencies have given much attention to whether and to what extent distinctive administrative functions should be performed by the same persons. No single answer has been reached. Indeed, the growth, variety, and complexity of the administrative processes have made any one solution highly unlikely. Within the Federal Government itself, Congress has addressed the issue in several different ways, providing for varying degrees of separation from complete separation of functions to virtually none at all. For the generality of agencies, Congress has been content with § 5 of the Administrative Procedure Act, 5 USC § 554(d), which provides that no employee engaged in investigating or prosecuting may also participate or advise in the adjudicating function, but which also expressly exempts from this prohibition "the agency or a member or members of the body comprising the agency."

. . . The case law, both federal and state, generally rejects the idea that the combination [of] judging [and] investigating functions is a denial of due process. . . ." Similarly, our cases . . . offer no support for the bald proposition applied in this case by the District Court that agency members who participate in an investigation are disqualified from adjudicating. . . .

When the Board instituted its investigative procedures, it stated only that it would investigate whether proscribed conduct had occurred. Later in noticing the adversary hearing, it asserted only that it would determine if violations had been committed which would warrant suspension of appellee's license. Without doubt, the Board then anticipated that the proceeding would eventuate in an adjudication of the issue; but there was no more evidence of bias or the risk of bias or prejudgment than inhered in the very fact that the Board had investigated and would now adjudicate. Of course, we should be alert to the possibilities of bias that may lurk in the way particular procedures actually work in practice. The processes utilized by the Board, however, do not in themselves contain an unacceptable risk of bias. The investigative proceeding had been closed to the public, but appellee and his counsel were permitted to be present throughout; counsel actually attended the hearings and knew the facts presented to the Board. No specific foundation has been presented for suspecting that the Board had been prejudiced by its investigation or would be disabled from hearing and deciding on the basis of the evidence to be presented at the contested hearing. The mere exposure to evidence presented in nonadversary investigative procedures is insufficient in itself to impugn the fairness of the board members at a later adversary hearing. Without a showing to the contrary, state administrators, "are assumed to be men of conscience and intellectual discipline, capable of judging a particular controversy fairly on the basis of its own circumstances."

We are of the view, therefore, that the District Court was in error when it entered the restraining order against the Board's contested hearing and when it granted the preliminary injunction based on the untenable view that it would be unconstitutional for the Board to suspend appellee's license "at its own contested hearing on charges evolving from its own investigation. . . ."

[Judgment reversed]

QUESTIONS

1. Who objected to the combining of the functions of investigating and adjudicating?
2. What is the practical basis for this objection?
3. How does the decision in the *Withrow* case compare with the theory of American government?

3.   Agency Powers

An agency has only such powers as have been granted by the statute creating the agency.[1] However, as technology and the economy have become more complicated, the powers given to agencies have broadened. The modern agency usually possesses legislative, executive, and judicial powers.

In order to meet the objection that the exercise of executive, legislative, and judicial powers by the same body is a potential threat to impartiality, some steps have been taken toward decentralizing the administrative func-

tions. Thus, the prosecution power of the National Labor Relations Board was withdrawn from the Board and entrusted to an independent General Counsel by the Labor-Management Relations Act of 1947. In a number of agencies, such as the Federal Trade Commission, the judicial function is assigned to administrative law judges.

4.   Right to Know

In order to avoid the evils of secret government, provision is made for public knowledge of the activity of administrative agencies. This is done through (a) open records, (b) open meetings, and (c) public announcement of agency guidelines. The more recently adopted statutes creating new agencies usually contain

[1]   Association for Retarded Citizens v Department of Developmental Services, 38 Cal 3d 384, 211 Cal Rptr 758, 696 P2d 150 (1985).

FIGURE 5–1   THE ADMINISTRATIVE CHAIN OF COMMAND

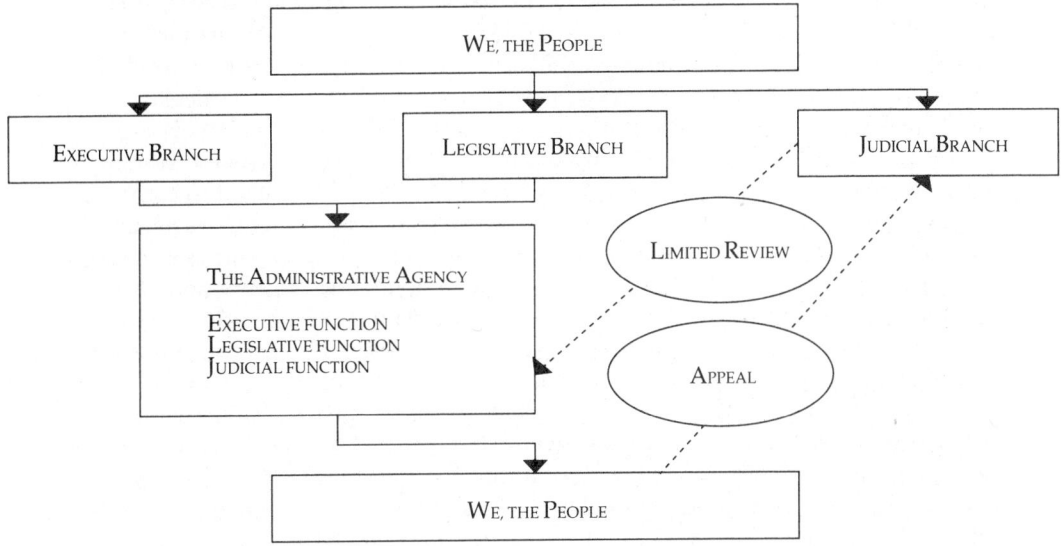

provisions regulating these matters. For most federal agencies not otherwise regulated, these matters are controlled by the Administrative Procedure Act (APA). Many states have adopted statutes that copy the provisions of the APA. By definition, these statutes relate only to government records. They do not allow a business to examine the records of a competitor.[2]

(a) OPEN RECORDS. The Freedom of Information Act[3] provides that information contained in records of federal administrative agencies shall be made available upon proper request. Numerous exceptions to this right are made in order to prevent persons from obtaining information that is not necessary to their legitimate interests. The state statutes typically exempt from disclosure information that would constitute an invasion of the privacy of others. However, freedom of information acts are broadly construed, and unless an exemption of particular papers is clearly given, the papers in question are subject to public inspection.[4] Moreover, the person claiming that there is an exemption that prohibits disclosure has the burden of proving that there is an exemption and that the facts of the case come within the scope of the exemption.[5]

In the *Baudin* case the court had to fix the procedure for considering a claim of exemption under a freedom of information statute.

[2]   KMEG Television, Inc. v Iowa State Board of Regents (Iowa) 440 NW2d 382 (1989)
[3]   Added to the APA by Act of December 31, 1974, PL 93-579, 88 Stat 1897, as amended, 5 USC §§ 552 et seq.

[4]   Legislative Joint Auditing Committee v Woosley, 291 Ark 89, 722 SW2d 581 (1987).
[5]   DeMaria Building Co. v Department of Management and Budget, 159 Mich App 129, 407 NW2d 72 (1987).

BAUDIN v CITY OF CRYSTAL LAKE

192 Ill App 3d 530, 139 Ill Dec 554, 548 NE2d 1110 (1989)

Baudin asked the City of Crystal Lake to tell him the policies and procedures followed by its police force in the handling of information and the follow-up as to hit-and-run cases. The city refused to disclose this information. Baudin requested the court to examine the relevant documents in the judge's chambers (*in camera*). This was refused. Baudin appealed.

DUNN, J. . . . Plaintiff originally sought information concerning the policies and procedures of the police department with respect to: (a) handling and receiving information from telephone callers regarding automobile accidents (hit-and-run); (b) receiving information in person concerning an accident; (c) follow-up on information received concerning automobile accidents; and (d) investigation guidelines with respect to automobile accidents, including hit-and-run accidents. Plaintiff also sought excerpts of radio tapes of the City's police department for June 17, 1988, for the period between 8 P.M. and 8:30 P.M., and for June 18, 1988, from 9:15 A.M. to 9:45 A.M.

In response to plaintiff's request, defendant . . . sent a letter to plaintiff on June 23, 1988, denying plaintiff's request and claiming that items (a) through (d) were exempt from disclosure under section 7(w) of the Information Act, which exempts information "related solely to the internal personnel rules and practices of the public body." [The] letter also stated that the radio tapes were exempt from disclosure under section 7(e) of the Act, which exempts records of "State and local law enforcement agencies and correctional agencies that are related to the detection and investigation of crime." . . .

The central issue to be determined is whether the procedures . . . were sufficient to provide plaintiff an adequate . . . determination of whether the requested information was discloseable under the Act; as a corollary, it must be determined whether the City met its burden of showing that the materials requested were exempted under the Act.

The purpose of the Information Act is to open governmental records to the light of public scrutiny. . . . In order to foster governmental accountability and an informed citizenry, the public policy of this State encourages a free flow and disclosure of information between the government and the people; the Information Act is to be liberally construed to achieve this goal, and there is a presumption that public records are open and accessible, subject only to exemptions that are to be read narrowly. . . .

The restraints on access to information are to be regarded as limited exceptions to the general rule that the people have a right to know the decisions, policies, procedures, rules, standards, and other aspects of governmental activity that affect the conduct of government and the lives of people. . . . If any public record is exempt from disclosure under section 7 of the Act . . . and it contains material which is not exempt, the public body shall delete the exempted material and make the remaining information available for inspection and copying. . . .

Under the Information Act, the burden of proof is on the City to establish that the material in question is exempt from disclosure; however, governmental agencies cannot clothe material regarding the affairs of government with an exemption from public disclosure by . . . statements that the material is exempt. . . . Reliance upon self-determination by public officials and employees as to what should or should not be disclosed to the public would frustrate the purposes of the Information Act. . . .

Section 11(f) of the Act requires the . . . court to consider the matter *de novo* and requires the court to conduct whatever *in camera* inspection of the requested records it finds appropriate to determine whether the records or any part of them may be withheld under the Act. . . . Whether the material is exempt under the Act is necessarily a factual determination to be made by the court based on its examination of the affidavits and, if required, based on an examination of the documents themselves *in camera*. . . .

In determining whether matter is exempt under the Act, a case-by-case approach is clearly warranted. . . . An agency such as a police department cannot simply take the position that, since it is involved in investigatory work and some of its records are exempt from disclosure under the Act, every document in its possession somehow comes to share in that exemption. . . . The classification of information as "law enforcement" or "investigatory" does not necessarily foreclose access unless it can be shown, in a particular case, that disclosure would interfere with law enforcement and would, therefore, not be in the public interest. . . .

We find from our examination of the City's affidavits that they were entirely conclusory and merely recite or paraphrase the language of the statute without giving any clue as to the discloseability of the requested documents. As such, they provided an insufficient factual basis to permit the trial court to grant . . . judgment to the City, particularly in the absence of an *in camera* inspection of the disputed material. The burden is on the governmental agency to prove that specific documents fit within one of the statutory exemptions. To meet this burden and to assist the court in making its determination, the agency must provide a *detailed* justification for its claim of exemption, addressing the requested documents specifically. . . .

It is obvious that the party with the greatest interest in obtaining disclosure is at a loss to argue with desirable legal precision for the revelation of the concealed information. . . . Therefore, aside from legal argument, where the sole support regarding the contents of documents and their exemption is contained in a conclusory affidavit, courts must no longer accept such conclusory or generalized allegations of exemption and must require a relatively detailed analysis of the documents in manageable segments. . . .

When an agency meets its burden by means of affidavits, *in camera* review is not necessary. . . . However, the affidavits will not suffice if the agency's claims are conclusory, merely reciting statutory standards, or if they are too vague or sweeping. . . .

If the disclosure significantly risks circumvention of the agency's regulations or of statutes, the material is exempt from mandatory disclosure.

Upon remand, the trial court must make a *de novo* review of the agency's classification decision, and the burden is on the agency to justify nondisclosure. The trial court shall require the agency to create as full a public record as possible concerning the nature of the documents and the justification for nondisclosure without compromising the secret nature of the information. If the affidavits show with reasonable specificity why the documents fall within the claimed exemption under the test announced here, then . . . judgment [against disclosure] is appropriate without *in camera* review. . . . If the agency fails to make a sufficient showing by affidavit to permit a responsible *de novo* review, the trial court may order *in camera* review of the documents. . . .

[Judgment reversed and action remanded]

McLAREN, J., concurring: I concur in the majority opinion. However, I believe one aspect of the opinion needs greater emphasis. The placement of detailed information in an affidavit is necessary if the trial court is to be sufficiently apprised of the nature and extent of the information contained in the contested documentation. Disclosure of such information in an affidavit may foreseeably result in disclosure of the information sought by the plaintiff. The defendant, in attempting to keep such information from the plaintiff, will find it extremely difficult to prepare affidavits that give the court sufficient information to determine that a privilege exists while simultaneously constricting the information to safeguard nondisclosure via the affidavit.

The trial court should be hesitant in determining a privilege exists based solely on the affidavits submitted by the defendant, for without an *in camera* review there is no external means to verify the truthfulness of the affidavits submitted by the defendant. I therefore believe that trial courts, except in rare instances, should not determine that a privilege exists without an *in camera* review of the contested documentation. . . .

QUESTIONS

1. When a citizen seeks the disclosure of public records, how important is it that the government officials in charge of the records say that the records are exempt?
2. How are exemptions in a freedom of information statute interpreted?
3. Compare the decision of the majority of the court with the concurring opinion of Justice McLaren.

(b) OPEN MEETINGS. The government, via the Government in the Sunshine Act of 1976, requires most of the meetings of the major administrative agencies to be open to the public. The object of this statute is to enable the public to know what is being done and to prevent administrative misconduct by making an agency aware that the public is watching. The term *meeting*, as used in these statutes, is liberally construed so that it does not matter whether a particular governmental unit is meeting alone or is discussing matters with an outsider, such as a consultant or a real estate developer.

(c) PUBLIC ANNOUNCEMENT OF AGENCY GUIDELINES. In order to inform the public of the way in which administrative agencies operate, the APA, with certain exceptions, requires that each federal agency publish in the *Federal Register* a statement of the rules, principles, and procedures followed by the agency.[6]

B. LEGISLATIVE POWER OF AN AGENCY

An administrative agency has power to make laws that regulate a particular segment of life or industry.

5. An Agency's Regulations as Law

An agency may adopt regulations within the scope of its authority. If the regulation is not authorized by the law creating the agency, the regulation is invalid.[7]

There once was a great reluctance to accept the fact that agencies made law because of our constitutional doctrine that only the lawmaker, namely the Congress or the state legislature, can make laws. It therefore seemed an improper transfer, or delegation, of power for the lawmaker to set up a separate body or agency and give it the power to make the laws.

The same forces that initially led society to create the administrative agencies caused society to clothe them with the power to make laws. Practical expediency gradually prevailed in favor of the conclusion that if an agency was to do a job, the agency must have sufficient power to do it.

In the early days of administrative regulation, the legislative character of the administrative rules was not clearly perceived. An agency's sphere of power was so narrow that the agency was, in effect, merely a thermostat. That is, the lawmaker told the agency when to do what, and all that the agency did was to act in the manner specified by such direction. For example, the cattle inspector was told to take

---

[6]   APA codified to 5 USC § 552, Act of September 13, 1976, PL 94-409, 90 Stat 1247. See Chapter 5, Section 7 for a description of the *Federal Register*.

[7]   Bowen v American Hospital Ass'n. 476 US 610 (1986).

certain steps when it was determined that cattle had hoof-and-mouth disease. Here it was clear that the lawmaker had set the standard, and the agency authority merely swung into action when the specified situation existed.

The next step in the growth of the administrative power was to authorize the cattle inspector to act upon the discovery of a contagious cattle disease. Thus, the inspector had to formulate a rule or guide as to which diseases were contagious. Here again, the discretionary and the legislative aspects of the agency's conduct were obscured by the belief that the field of science would define *contagious*, leaving no area of discretionary decision to the agency.

Today's health commission, an agency, is authorized to make such rules and regulations for the protection or improvement of the common health as it deems desirable. Its rules thus make up the health law. In regulating various economic aspects of national life, the agency is truly the lawmaker.

Gradually, the courts have come to recognize the authority of an agency, even though the lawmaker creating the agency did nothing more than state the goal or objective to be attained by the agency. Some courts still speak in terms of requiring a standard but then state that the fact that the standard is not precise has no significance when the standard is as precise as possible.[8]

It has been sufficient for a legislature to authorize an agency to grant licenses "as public interest, convenience, or necessity requires"; "to prohibit unfair methods of competition"; to regulate prices so that they, "in [the agency's] judgment, will be generally fair and equitable"; to prevent "profiteering"; "to prevent the existence of intercorporate holdings, which unduly or unnecessarily complicate the structure [or] unfairly or inequitably distribute voting power among security holders"; and to renegotiate government contracts to prevent "excessive profits."

In the state courts, however, greater emphasis is placed upon establishing "standards" to prevent the administrative agency from being arbitrary or capricious. In any case, an administrative regulation that goes beyond the power granted the agency is invalid. Thus, the fact that an insurance commissioner is authorized to regulate the forms of insurance policies and to prevent discrimination does not give the commissioner authority to adopt a regulation prohibiting insurers from considering whether an applicant for health insurance has human immunodeficiency virus (HIV). Such a condition clearly affects the health of an applicant and is properly considered by an insurer in deciding whether to accept an application.[9]

The authority of an agency is not limited to the technology existing when the agency was created. To the contrary, the sphere in which an agency may act expands with new scientific developments. So it has been held that although community cable television (CATV) was developed after the Federal Communications Commission was created by the Federal Communications Act of 1934, the Commission can regulate CATV. This power to regulate includes both the mechanical aspects of broadcasting and reception and also the content of the broadcast. Thus, the Commission may require such systems to originate local programs (cablecasting) in order to serve the local communities, in addition to their activity of transmitting programs from a distance.[10]

When the matter is a question of policy not specifically addressed by statute, the agency given the discretion to administer the statute may establish new policies covering such issues. This power is granted whether the lawmaker had intentionally left such matters to the discretion of the agency or had merely never foreseen the problem. In either case, the matter is one to be determined within the dis-

---

[8]   Fort Gratiot Charter Township v Kettlewell, 150 Mich App 648, 389 NW2d 468 (1986).

[9]   Health Insurance Ass'n. v Corcoran, 154 App Div 2d 61, 551 NYS2d 615 (1990).

[10]   United States v Midwest Video Corp. 406 US 649 (1972) (sustaining a Commission regulation that provided that "no CATV system having 3,500 or more subscribers shall carry the signal of any television broadcast station unless the system also operates to a significant extent as a local outlet by cablecasting and has available facilities for local production and presentation of programs other than automated services.").

cretion of the agency, and a court will not review an agency's policy decision.[11]

6.   Public Participation in Adoption of Regulations

In some instances, nongovernmental bodies or persons play a part in furnishing information or opinions that may ultimately affect the adoption of a rule by an agency. This pattern of public participation may be illustrated by the Federal Trade Commission practice, begun in 1919, of calling together members of each significant industry so that the members can discuss which trade practices are fair and which are not. The conclusions of these conferences are not automatically binding on the Federal Trade Commission. They do, however, serve as a valuable means of bringing to the Commission detailed information regarding the conduct of the particular industry or business in question. Under the Federal Trade Commission practice, the rules of fair practice agreed to at a trade conference may be approved or disapproved by the Commission. When the rules are approved, a further distinction is made between those rules that are "affirmatively approved" by the Commission and those that are merely "accepted as expressions of the trade." In the case of the former, the Commission will enforce compliance by the members of the industry. In the case of the latter, the Commission will accept the practices as fair trade practices but will not enforce compliance by persons not willing to comply. This technique of industry participation has recently been followed by several other major federal administrative agencies. In addition, the APA, with certain exceptions, requires that a federal agency planning to adopt a new regulation must give public notice of such intent. The agency must then hold a public hearing.[12]

---

[11]   Chevron, U.S.A., Inc. v National Resources Defense Council, Inc. 467 US 837 (1984).
[12]   APA codified to 5 USC §§ 553, 556, by Act of September 6, 1966, PL 89-554, 80 Stat 383, as amended. The Negotiated Rulemaking Act of 1990, Act of November 15, 1990, PL 101-552, 104 Stat 2736, _____ USC § _____, encourages federal agencies to formulate their regulations with the cooperation of those affected thereby.

7.   Public Knowledge of Regulations

When an agency adopts a regulation, a practical problem arises as to how to inform the public of its existence. Some regulations will have already attracted such public attention that the news media will give the desired publicity. The great mass of regulations, however, do not attract such attention. In order to provide publicity for all regulations, the Federal Register Act provides that an administrative regulation is not binding until it is printed in the *Federal Register*. This is a government publication, published five days a week, that lists all administrative regulations, all presidential proclamations and executive orders, and such other documents and classes of documents as the President or Congress may direct.

The Federal Register Act provides that the printing of an administrative regulation in the *Federal Register* is sufficient to give notice of the contents of the regulation to any person subject thereto or affected thereby. This means that no one can claim as an excuse ignorance of the published regulation. This is so even though the person in fact did not know that the regulation had been published in the *Register*.

C.   EXECUTIVE POWER OF THE AGENCY

The modern administrative agency has the power to execute the law and to bring proceedings against violators.

8.   Execution of the Law

The power of an agency to execute the law is, of course, confined to matters within an agency's jurisdiction. Within that sphere, an agency typically has the power to investigate, to require persons to appear as witnesses, to require witnesses to produce relevant papers and records, and to bring proceedings against violators of the law. In this connection, the phrase *the law* embraces regulations adopted by an agency as well as statutes and court decisions. Increasingly, agencies are required to file opinions and reports or to give explanations for their actions.

An agency may investigate in order to see if there is any violation of the law or of its rules generally, to determine whether there is need for the adoption of additional rules, to ascertain the facts with respect to a particular suspected or alleged violation, and to determine whether its decisions are being obeyed.

The federal Antitrust Civil Process Act is an example of the extent to which administrative investigation is authorized. The Act authorizes the attorney general or the assistant attorney general in charge of the Antitrust Division of the Department of Justice to make a civil investigative demand (CID) on any person believed to have knowledge relevant to any civil antitrust investigation. This might be in connection with an investigation before bringing a suit to enjoin a monopolistic practice or an investigation made upon receiving a premerger notification. The person so notified can be compelled to produce relevant documents, furnish written answers to written questions, or appear in person and give oral testimony.[13] Similar power to require the production of papers is possessed by the Federal Trade Commission, the Federal Maritime Commission, the National Science Foundation, the Treasury Department, the Department of Agriculture, the Department of the Army, the Department of Labor, and the Veterans Administration.

9. Constitutional Limitations on Administrative Investigation

The Constitution does not impose any significant limitations on the power of an agency to conduct an investigation.

(a) INSPECTION OF PREMISES. In general, a person has the same protection against unreasonable search and seizure by an administrative officer as that person has against unreasonable search and seizure by a police officer.

In contrast, when the danger of concealment is great, a warrantless search can be validly made of the premises of a highly regulated business, such as one selling liquor or firearms. Likewise, when violation of the law is dangerous to health and safety, the law may authorize inspection of the workplace without advance notice or a search warrant when such a requirement could defeat the purpose of the inspection.

(b) AERIAL INSPECTION. A search warrant is never required when the subject matter can be seen from a public place. For example, when a police officer walking on the public pavement can look through an open window and see illegal weapons, a search warrant is not required to enter the premises and seize the weapons. Utilizing the airplane and helicopter, the eyes of the law can see from the air. May an agency gather information in this manner? It has been held that a police officer may do so,[14] and there is no reason to believe the same power is not possessed by an agency.

(c) PRODUCTION OF PAPERS. For the most part, the constitutional guarantee against unreasonable search and seizure does not afford much protection with regard to papers and records being investigated by an agency. That guarantee does not apply if there is not an actual seizure. For example, a subpoena to testify or to produce records cannot be opposed on the ground that it is a search and seizure, as the constitutional protection is limited to cases of actual physical search and seizure rather than the obtaining of information by compulsion.

The protection afforded by the guarantee against self-incrimination is likewise narrow. It cannot be invoked when a corporate employee or officer in control of corporate records is compelled to produce the records, even though that person would be incriminated by them. It cannot be invoked if records that by law must be kept by the person subject to the administrative investigation are involved.

---

[13]   Antitrust Civil Process Act of 1962, as amended by the Antitrust Improvement Act of 1976, §§ 101, 102, PL 94-435, 90 Stat 1383, 15 USC § 1311 et seq.

[14]   California v Ciraolo, 476 US 207 (1986).

D.   JUDICIAL POWER OF THE AGENCY

The modern administrative agency possesses judicial powers.

10.   The Agency as a Specialized Court

An agency may be given power to sit as a court and to determine whether there have been any violations of the law or of the agency regulations. Thus, the National Labor Relations Board determines whether a prohibited labor practice has been committed, the Federal Trade Commission acts as a court to determine whether unfair competition exists, and so on.

The fact that an administrative agency exercises judicial power should not be interpreted to mean that every agency has all the powers of a court. For example, in many states an administrative agency cannot declare a statute unconstitutional.[15]

At first glance, the conferring of any judicial power on an administrative agency seems contrary to American tradition. When an administrative agency sits as judge to determine whether one of its regulations has been violated, there is some question that the agency is not impartial, since it is trying the accused for violating agency law rather than "the law." There is also the objection that an agency is determining important rights but does so without a jury, which seems inconsistent with the long-established emphasis of our history on the sanctity of trial by jury. In spite of these objections to an agency's exercise of judicial power, such exercise is now firmly established.

11.   Pattern of Administrative Procedure

At the beginning of the era of modern regulation of business, the power of agencies to ad-

judicate rested, to a large extent, on minor executives or police officers charged with the responsibility of enforcing laws applicable to limited fact situations. The example of the health officer empowered to condemn and destroy diseased cattle was typical. In view of the need for prompt action and because of the relative simplicity of the fact determination to be made, it was customary for such a person to exercise summary powers. Upon finding cattle believed to be diseased, the officer would destroy animals immediately, without delaying to find their true owner and without holding a formal hearing to determine whether the animals were in fact diseased.

Today, the exercise of summary powers is the exceptional case. Concepts of due process generally require that some notice be given those who will be adversely affected and that some form of hearing be held at which they may present their case.

(a) PRELIMINARY STEPS. It is commonly provided that either a private individual aggrieved by the conduct of another, or an agency, may file a written complaint. This complaint is then served on the alleged wrongdoer, who is given the opportunity to file an answer. There may be other phases of pleading between the parties and the agency, but eventually the matter comes before the agency to be heard. After a hearing, the agency makes a decision and enters an order either dismissing the complaint or directing the adverse party to carry out or refrain from certain acts.

The complaint filing and prehearing stage of the procedure may be more detailed. In many of the modern administrative statutes, provision is made for an examination of the informal complaint by some branch of the agency to determine whether the case comes within the scope of the agency's authority. It is also commonly provided that an investigation be made by the agency to determine whether the facts are such as to warrant a hearing of the complaint. If it is decided that the complaint is within the jurisdiction of the agency and that the facts appear to justify it, a formal

---

[15]   HOH Corp. v Motor Vehicle Industry Licensing Board (Hawaii) 736 P2d 1271 (1987).

complaint is issued and served on the adverse party. An answer is then filed as stated above.

With the increasing complexity of the subjects regulated by administrative agencies, the trend is to require greater preliminary examination on the basis of an informal complaint.

(b) THE ADMINISTRATIVE HEARING.

In order to satisfy the requirements of due process, it is generally necessary for an agency to give notice and to hold a hearing at which all persons affected may be present. A person indirectly affected by administrative action cannot take part in the administrative hearing. An existing enterprise has no standing to chal-

lenge the granting of a license to a new business that will be a competitor.[16]

A significant difference between an agency's hearing and a court hearing is that there is no right of trial by jury before an agency. For example, a workers' compensation board may decide a claim without any jury. The absence of a jury does not constitute a denial of due process. Similarly, there is no right to a jury trial in an action for violation of the Age Discrimination in Employment Act. A jury trial was demanded in the *Atlas Roofing* case.

[16]   Pie Mut. Ins. Co. v Kentucky Medical Ins. Co. (Ky App) 782 SW2d 51 (1990).

ATLAS ROOFING COMPANY, INC. v OCCUPATIONAL SAFETY AND HEALTH REVIEW COMMISSION
430 US 442 (1977)

In order to protect factory and industrial workers from unnecessary hazards and unsafe working conditions, Congress adopted the Occupational Safety and Health Act of 1970 (OSHA). The Act is administered by the Occupational Safety and Health Administration (also known as OSHA). If one of the OSHA examiners finds a dangerous condition in a place of employment, the employer is ordered to eliminate the bad condition. If the employer does not do so, OSHA can impose a fine or civil penalty on the employer. In the *Atlas Roofing* case, the OSHA examiner decided that a condition in the Atlas Roofing Company was hazardous and ordered its correction. Atlas Roofing refused to do so. OSHA imposed a fine on Atlas. Atlas claimed that it was entitled to a jury trial on the question of whether there was a hazardous working condition and whether the company had violated the law. Atlas claimed that this right to trial by jury was guaranteed by the Seventh Amendment of the federal Constitution. That amendment declares: "In suits at common law, where the value in controversy shall exceed twenty dollars, the right of trial by jury shall be preserved. . . ." The lower court decided against Atlas and it appealed.

WHITE, J. . . . The issue in this case is whether, consistent with the Seventh Amendment, Congress may create a new cause of action in the Government for civil penalties enforceable in an administrative agency where there is no jury trial. After extensive investigation, Congress concluded, in 1970, that work-related deaths and injuries had become a "drastic" national problem.

. . . Congress enacted the Occupational Safety and Health Act of 1970. . . . The Act created a new statutory duty to avoid maintaining unsafe or unhealthy working conditions, and empowers the Secretary of Labor to promulgate health and safety standards. Two new remedies were provided—permitting the Federal Government, proceeding before an administrative agency, (1) to obtain abatement orders requiring employers to correct unsafe working conditions and (2) to impose civil penalties on any employer maintaining any unsafe working condition. Each remedy exists whether or not an employee is actually injured or killed as a result of the condition, and existing state statutory and common law remedies for actual injury and death remain unaffected.

Under the Act, inspectors, representing the Secretary of Labor, are authorized to conduct reasonable safety and health inspections. . . . If a violation is discovered, the inspector, on behalf of the Secretary, issues a citation to the employer fixing a reasonable time for its abatement and, in his discretion, proposing a civil penalty. . . . Such proposed penalties may range from nothing for de minimis and nonserious violations, to not more than $1,000 for serious violations, to a maximum of $10,000 for willful or repeated violations. . . .

If the employer wishes to contest the penalty or the abatement order, he may do so by notifying the Secretary of Labor within 15 days, in which event the abatement order is automatically stayed. . . . An evidentiary hearing is then held before an administrative law judge of the Occupational Safety and Health Review Commission. The Commission consists of three members, appointed for six-year terms, each of whom is qualified to adjudicate contested citations and assess penalties "by reason of training, education or experience." . . . At this hearing the burden is on the Secretary to establish the elements of the alleged violation and the propriety of his proposed abatement order and proposed penalty; and the judge is empowered to affirm, modify, or vacate any or all of these items, giving due consideration in his penalty assessment to "the size of the business of the employer . . . , the gravity of the violation, the good faith of the employer, and the history of previous violations." . . . The judge's decision becomes the Commission's final and appealable order unless within 30 days a Commissioner directs that it be reviewed by the full Commission. . . .

If review is granted, the Commission's subsequent order directing abatement and the payment of any assessed penalty becomes final unless the employer timely petitions for judicial review in the appropriate court of appeals. . . . The Secretary similarly may seek review of Commission orders, . . . but, in either case, "the findings of the Commission with respect to questions of fact, if supported by substantial evidence on the record considered as a whole, shall be conclusive." . . . If the employer fails to pay the assessed penalty, the Secretary may commence a collection action in a federal district court in which neither the fact of the violation nor the propriety of the penalty assessed may be retried. . . . Thus, the penalty may be collected without the employer ever being entitled to a jury determination of the facts constituting the violation.

Congress has often created new statutory obligations, provided for civil penalties for their violation, and committed exclusively to an administrative agency the function of deciding whether a violation has in fact occurred. These statutory schemes have been sustained by this Court. . . .

. . . It is apparent from the history of jury trial in civil matters that factfinding, which is the essential function of the jury in civil cases . . . was never the exclusive province of the jury under either the English or American legal systems at the time of the adoption of the Seventh Amendment; and the question whether a fact would be found by a jury turned to a considerable degree on the nature of the forum in which a litigant found himself. Critical factfinding was performed without juries in suits in equity, and there were no juries in admiralty. . . . neither was there in the military justice system.

The jury was the factfinding mode in most suits in the common law courts, but it was not exclusively so: condemnation was a suit at common law but constitutionally could be tried without a jury. . . .

The Seventh Amendment was declaratory of the existing law, for it required only that jury trial in suits at common law was to be "preserved." It thus did not purport to require a jury trial where none was required before. . . .

The point is that the Seventh Amendment was never intended to establish the jury as the exclusive mechanism for factfinding in civil cases. It took the existing legal order as it found it, and there is little or no basis for concluding that the Amendment should now be interpreted to provide an impenetrable barrier to administrative factfinding under otherwise valid federal regulatory statutes. We cannot conclude that the Amendment rendered Congress powerless—when it concluded that remedies available in courts of law were inadequate to cope with a problem within Congress' power to regulate—to create new public rights and remedies by statute and commit their enforcement, if it chose, to a tribunal other than a court of law—such as an administrative agency—in which facts are not found by juries. . . .

Congress found the common law and other existing remedies for work injuries resulting from unsafe working conditions to be inadequate to protect the Nation's working men and women. It created a new cause of action, and remedies therefore, unknown to the common law, and placed their enforcement in a tribunal supplying speedy and expert resolutions of the issues involved. The Seventh Amendment is no bar to the creation of new rights or to their enforcement outside the regular courts of law.

[Judgment affirmed]

QUESTIONS

1. Who was the plaintiff in this case?
2. Who was the defendant in this case?
3. The right to trial by jury exists in all important cases. Appraise this statement.

An agency is ordinarily not subject to the rules of evidence.[17] Another significant difference between an administrative hearing and a judicial determination is that an agency may be authorized to make an initial determination without holding a hearing. If an agency's conclusion is challenged, the agency will then hold a hearing. A court, on the other hand, must have a trial before it makes a judgment. This has important practical consequences in that when a hearing is sought after an agency has acted, the objecting party has the burden of proof and the cost of going forward. The result is that fewer persons go to the trouble of

seeking such a hearing. This, in turn, reduces the number of hearings and the amount of litigation in which an agency becomes involved. Thus, from the government's standpoint, money and time are economized.

It is held that when the administrative action concerns only the individuals directly affected, rather than a class of persons or the community in general, it is necessary to have some form of hearing before an agency may make a judicial decision. Thus, it has been held that, since a civil service employee may only be removed for cause, it is a denial of due process for a statute to authorize an agency to remove the employee without a hearing. It is not sufficient that the employee is given the right to appeal such action. Because the em-

---

[17]   New South Communications, Inc. v Answer Iowa, Inc. (Miss) 490 So 2d 1225 (1986).

ployee has a significant interest in continued employment, there must be some preremoval hearing to determine that there is no basic error in the administrative action.[18]

(c) STREAMLINED PROCEDURE. Informal settlement and consent decrees are practical devices to cut across the procedures outlined above. In many instances, the alleged wrongdoer is willing to change on being informally notified that a complaint has been made. It is, therefore, sound public relations, as well as expeditious handling of the matter, for an agency to inform the alleged wrongdoer of the charge made prior to the filing of any formal complaint. A matter that has already gone into the formal hearing stage may also be terminated by agreement, and a stipulation or consent decree may be filed setting forth the terms of the agreement.

Streamlining of procedure is encouraged by The Administrative Dispute Resolution Act of 1990 authorizing federal agencies to use alternative means of dispute resolution.

(d) REHEARING AND CORRECTION OF ADMINISTRATIVE ACTION. Under some statutes, an agency is given power to rehear or correct a decision within a certain time.

12. Punishment and Enforcement Powers of Agencies

Originally, agencies could not impose punishment or to enforce decisions. If the person regulated did not voluntarily comply with an agency's decision, the agency could only petition a court to order that person to obey.

Within the last few decades, agencies have been increasingly given the power to impose a penalty and to issue orders that are binding on the regulated person unless an appeal is taken to a court and the administrative decision reversed. As an illustration of the power to impose penalties, the Occupational Safety and Health Act of 1970 provides for the assessment of civil penalties against employers

failing to put an end to dangerous working conditions when ordered to do so by the administrative agency created by that statute. Likewise, environmental protection statutes adopted by states commonly give the state agency the power to assess a penalty for a violation of the environmental protection regulations. As an illustration of the issuance of binding orders, the Federal Trade Commission can issue a **cease and desist order** to stop a practice that it decides is improper. This order to stop is binding unless reversed on an appeal.

(a) COMPLIANCE VERIFICATION. In order to assure itself that a particular person is obeying the law, including the agency's regulations and orders, an administrative agency may require proof of compliance. At times, the question of compliance may be directly determined by an agency investigation, either of a building or plant or by an examination of witnesses and documents. An agency may require the regulated person or enterprise to file reports in a specified form.[19] An agency may also hold a hearing or audit on the question of compliance and may require the filing of a detailed statement or plan of operation showing that the regulated person or enterprise is acting properly.

(b) COMPLAINANT INDEMNIFICATION. When the administrative decision is that the defendant has caused a loss to or harmed a particular person, can the administrative agency compensate or indemnify the harmed person for the loss sustained? Until the 1930s the answer to this question was that the administrative agency could stop further wrong but could not undo or compensate for past wrong. Beginning with the New Deal legislation of the 1930s, administrative agencies have been given the power in some cases to provide indemnity to the party harmed by the defendant's wrong. Such power is not unlimited, and its boundaries are defined by the statute creating the agency.

---

[18]   Cleveland Board of Education v Loudermill, 470 US 532 (1985).

[19]   United States v Morton Salt Co., 338 US 632 (1950).

13.   Exhaustion of Administrative Remedy

When the law creates an agency, all parties must follow the procedure specified by the law. An appeal may be taken to a court, but it cannot be taken until the agency has acted. The principle is that, as a matter of policy, parties are required to exhaust the administrative remedy before they may go into court or take an appeal.[20]

As long as an agency is acting within the scope of its authority or jurisdiction, a party cannot appeal before the agency has made a final decision. The fact that the complaining party does not want the agency to decide the matter, or is afraid that the agency will reach a wrong decision, is not grounds for bypassing the agency by going to court before the agency has acted. Neither can an appeal be made before the agency has made a final decision.

14.   Appeal from Administrative Action

The statute creating the modern administrative agency generally provides for the taking of an appeal from the administrative decision to a particular court. The statute may state that a party in interest or any person aggrieved by the administrative action may appeal. This requires the appellant to have a legally recognized right or interest that is harmed by the administrative action. The fact that a person or persons do not like the action of the agency does not entitle them to appeal.

15.   Finality of Administrative Determination

Basic to the Anglo-American legal theory is the belief that no one, not even a branch of the government, is above the law. Thus, the growth of powers of the administrative agency was frequently accepted or tolerated on the theory that if the administrative agency went too far, the courts would review the administrative action. The typical modern statute pro-

vides that an appeal may be taken from the administrative action.

When the question that an agency decides is a question of law, the court on appeal will reverse the agency if the court disagrees with the decision.[21] This concept is being eroded to some extent by modern technology. Thus, it is held that the court will accept the agency's interpretation of the statute when the statute relates to a technical matter. Here the court will tend to accept the agency's interpretation as long as it is reasonable, even though it is not the only interpretation that could have been made.[22]

In contrast with an agency's decision on matters of law, the controversy may turn on a question of fact or a mixed question of law and fact. In such cases, a court will accept the conclusion of an agency if it is supported by substantial evidence. This means that the court must examine the entire record of the proceedings before the administrative agency, including the evidence opposing the administrative findings as well as the supporting evidence, to see if the general conclusion to be drawn is that there was substantial evidence to support the administrative findings.[23] A court will not reverse an agency's decision merely because the court would have made a different decision on the same facts.[24] As most disputes before an agency are based on questions of fact, the net result is that the decision of the agency will be final in most cases.

The greatest limitation on court review of the administrative action is the rule that a decision involving discretion will not be reversed in the absence of an error of law or a clear abuse of, or the arbitrary or capricious

---

[20]   Vaught v Waites (SC App) 387 SE2d 91 (1989).

[21]   Re Minnesota Joint Underwriting Ass'n. (Minn App) 408 NW2d 599 (1987).

[22]   Chemical Mfrs. Ass'n. v Natural Resources Defense Council, Inc. 470 US 116 (1985).

[23]   Department of Health and Welfare v Sandoval (Idaho App) 742 P2d 992 (1987).

[24]   Service Employees International v State Educational Labor Relations Board, 153 Ill App 3d 744, 106 Ill Dec 112, 505 NE2d 418 (1987). The appellate court cannot review the evidence to determine the credibility of the witnesses who testified before the administrative agency. Hammann v City of Omaha, 227 Neb 285, 417 NW2d 323 (1987).

exercise of, discretion. The courts reason that since the members of the agencies were appointed because of expert ability, it would be absurd for the court, which is manifestly unqualified technically to make a decision in the matter, to step in and determine whether the agency made the proper choice. Courts will not do so unless the agency has clearly acted wrongly, arbitrarily, or capriciously. As a practical matter, the action of an agency is rarely found to be arbitrary or capricious. As long as an agency has followed the proper procedure, the fact that the court disagrees with the conclusion reached by the agency does not make that conclusion arbitrary or capricious. In areas in which economic or technical matters are involved, it is generally sufficient that the agency had a reasonable basis for the decision made. A court will not attempt to second-guess the agency as to complex criteria with which an administrative agency is intimately familiar. The judicial attitude is that, for protection from laws and regulations that are unwise, improvident, or out of harmony with a particular school of thought, the people must resort to the ballot box, not to the court.

Because of limited funding and staff, an agency must exercise discretion as to which cases should be handled. Ordinarily, the decision of an agency to do nothing about a particular complaint will not be reversed by a court.[25] That is, the courts will not override an agency's decision to do nothing. Exceptions are made, however, when it is obvious that the agency is refusing to act for an improper reason. If it is obvious that the agency wrongly believed that there was no authority to act, that the agency had taken a bribe to keep out, or that, on the basis of the facts, there was no logical explanation for the agency's refusal to act, then the court may override the decision.

16.   Liability of the Agency

The decision of an agency may cause substantial loss to a business by increasing its operating costs or by making a decision that later is shown to be harmful to the economy. An agency is not liable for such loss when it has acted in good faith in the exercise of discretionary powers. An administrator who wrongly denies a person the benefit of a government program is not personally liable to that person even though that person's constitutional rights have been violated.[26]

[25]   Heckler v Chaney, 470 US 821 (1985).
[26]   Schweiker v Chilicky, 487 US 412 (1988).

SUMMARY

The administrative agency is unique because it combines the three functions that are kept separate under the traditional system: legislative, executive, and judicial. By virtue of legislative power, an agency adopts regulations that have the force of law, although the members of the agency were not elected by those who are subject to the regulations. By virtue of the executive power, an agency carries out and enforces the regulations, makes investigations, and requires the production of documents. By virtue of the judicial power, an agency acts as a court to determine whether there has been a violation of any regulation. To some extent, an agency is restricted by constitutional limitations in making inspection of premises and in requiring the production of papers. These limitations, however, have a very narrow application. The protection against unreasonable search and seizure and the protection against self-incrimination are so narrowed by judicial construction as to have little protective value. When an agency acts as a judge, it is not required that there be a jury trial or that the ordinary courtroom procedures be followed. Typically, an agency will give notice to the person claimed to be acting improperly, and a hearing will then be held before the agency. When the agency has determined that there has been a violation, the stopping of the violation may be ordered. Under some statutes, the agency may go further and impose a penalty upon the violator.

An appeal may be taken from any decision of the agency by a person harmed thereby. Only a person with a legally recognized interest can appeal from the agency ruling. No appeal can be taken until every step available before the agency has been taken; that is, the administrative remedy must first be exhausted.

As a practical matter, an appeal from the administrative action will ordinarily have little value. When the controversy turns on a determination of facts, a court will not reverse the decision of an agency because it disagrees with the conclusion that the agency drew from those facts. When an agency is given discretion to act, a court will never reverse the agency just because it disagrees with the choice that the agency made. In contrast, if an agency made a wrong decision as to a question of law, a court will generally reverse the agency when the court disagrees with the decision. In the absence of an error of law, an agency's decision will be reversed only if the court decides that the administrative action was arbitrary and capricious.

Protection from secret government is provided by the right to know what is contained in most administrative agency records, by the requirement that most agency meetings be open to the public, by the invitation to the public to take part in rule making, and by publicity given, through publication in the *Federal Register*, to the guidelines followed by the agency and to regulations that have been adopted.

QUESTIONS AND CASE PROBLEMS

1. What social forces are affected by the principle that the same administrative agency may conduct an investigation to determine if there is reason to believe that there has been a violation, and then hold a hearing to determine whether in fact there was a violation?

2. Can an administrative agency make law?

3. Pennington is a licensed physician. She is appointed state health administrator in 1984 under a statute adopted in 1960. The statute authorizes the administrator to adopt regulations protecting from health hazards and disease. In 1985, certain candy manufacturers began using a new artificial sweetener, Doucetran. Tests conducted by Pennington convince her that Doucetran may cause cancer. She adopts a regulation prohibiting the use of Doucetran. The candy manufacturers claim that she cannot do this on the theory that she could only regulate those health hazards that were known in 1960 when the legislature adopted the statute. Are they correct?

4. The federal Department of Housing and Urban Development (HUD) decides to hold a conference of leading building contractors for the purpose of deciding patterns of urban development that should be encouraged by HUD. Culpepper wants to attend the meeting. She is denied admission because she is neither a government official nor a building contractor. Is she entitled to attend the meeting?

5. Adams is appointed the state price control administrator. By virtue of this position, he requires all sellers of goods and suppliers of services to keep records of the prices they charge. He suspects that the Ace Overhead Garage Door Corporation is charging more than the prices permitted by law. To determine this, he notifies the company to produce the records that it was required to keep. It refuses to do so on the ground that Adams does not have the authority to require the production of papers. Is this a valid defense?

6. Bell was employed by the Sinclair Radio Corporation. She was fired from her job and made a complaint to the National Labor Relations Board that she was fired because she belonged to a union. The examiner of the Board held a hearing at which Bell produced evidence of an anti-union attitude of the employer. The employer produced evidence that Bell was fired because she was chronically late and did poor work. The examiner and the Labor Relations Board concluded that Bell was fired because of her union membership. Sinclair appealed. The court reached the conclusion that, had the court been the Board, it would have held that the discharge of Bell was justified because it would not have believed the testimony of Bell's witnesses. Will the court reverse the decision of the National Labor Relations Board?

7. An agency created by an act of Congress: (a) can

be given only the power to carry out the terms of an act of Congress; (b) can be given only executive power; (c) can be given executive, legislative, and judicial powers. Is any of these three alternatives correct? Explain.

8. Santa Monica adopted a rent control ordinance authorizing the Rent Control Board to set the amount of rents that could be charged. At a hearing before the Board, the Board determined that McHugh was charging his tenant a rent greater than the maximum rent allowed. McHugh claimed that the action of the Board was improper because there was no jury trial. Decide. [McHugh v Santa Monica Rent Control Board, 49 Cal 3d 348, 261 Cal Rptr 318, 777 P2d 91]

9. The New York City charter authorizes the New York City Board of Health to adopt a health code and declares that it "shall have the force and effect of law." The board adopted a code in 1964 that provided for the fluoridation of the public water supply. A suit was brought to enjoin the carrying out of this program on the ground that it was unconstitutional and that money could not be spent to carry out such a program in the absence of a statute authorizing such expenditure. It was also claimed that the fluoridation program was unconstitutional because there were other means of reducing tooth decay; fluoridation was discriminatory in that it benefited only children; it unlawfully imposed medication on the children without their consent; and fluoridation "is or may be" dangerous to health. Was the code provision valid? [Paduano v City of New York, 257 NYS2d 531]

10. The Federal Trade Commission directs the Essex Manufacturing Company to install safety devices in its factory. Essex claims that the Commission's order can be ignored because the members of the Commission were not elected by the voters, and therefore the Commission cannot make an order that has the force of law. Is this defense valid?

11. By training and work experience Templeton was a plumbing and heating maintenance worker. Templeton sustained an injury, which made him unable to use his right arm. Because of this he left his regular employment and took a half-time job with Black Hills State College to run a program of preventive maintenance of equipment. The job required a knowledge of computer programming and data processing. Templeton resigned after a while because he could not live on the half-time pay. He filed a claim for disability benefits under the State Retirement System. The retirement statute defined "disability" as "any medically determinable physical or mental impairment which prevents a member from performing his usual duties for his employer, or the duties of a position of comparable level for which he is qualified by education, training, and experience. . . ." The Retirement Board denied his application because he could work for the State College. Templeton took an appeal. Decide. [Re Templeton (SD) 403 NW2d 398]

12. The Occupational Safety and Health Act of 1970 authorizes the secretary of labor to adopt job safety standards to protect workers from harmful substances. The secretary is directed by the statute to adopt that standard "which most adequately assures, to the extent feasible, on the basis of the best available evidence" that no employee will suffer material impairment of health. Acting under this authorization, the secretary adopted a Cotton Dust Standard to protect workers exposed to cotton dust. This dust causes serious lung disease that disables about one out of twelve cotton factory workers. The cotton industry attacked the validity of the Cotton Dust Standard on the ground that the secretary, in adopting the standard, had not considered the cost to the cotton industry of complying with the standard (a cost of $656.5 million). Was the Cotton Dust Standard valid? [American Textile Manufacturers Institute, Inc. v Donovan, 452 US 490]

13. The Macon County Landfill Corporation (MCL) applied for permission to expand the boundaries of its landfill. This was opposed by Tate and others. After a number of hearings, the appropriate agency granted the requested permission to expand. Tate appealed and claimed that the agency had made a wrong decision on the basis of the evidence presented. Will the court determine if the correct decision was made? [Tate v Illinois Pollution Control Board, 188 Ill App 3d 994, 136 Ill Dec 401, 544 NE2d 1176]

14. The planning commissioner and a real estate developer planned to meet to discuss the rezoning of certain land in order to permit the real estate developer to construct certain buildings that were not allowed under the then existing zoning law. A homeowners association claimed that it had the right to be present at the meeting. This claim was objected to on the theory that the state's Open Meetings Act applied only to meetings of the specified governmental units and

did not extend to a meeting between one of them and an outsider. Was this objection valid?

15. The Interstate Commerce Commission had to determine the valuation of the stock of a railroad and whether the stock should be split. The Commission informed the parties that instead of having an oral hearing, it would dispose of the matter on the basis of the sworn written statements of the parties. Laird owned some of the stock of the railroad. He claimed that he had a right to an oral hearing. Was he correct? [Laird v ICC (CA3 ICC) 691 F2d 147]

6

THE LEGAL ENVIRONMENT OF INTERNATIONAL TRADE

American business firms have become increasingly international in their orientation and operations. In world trade American businesses must compete with the business firms of other nations, including host-country firms. The success or failure of the American firms doing business in foreign countries may well depend on accurate information about the laws and customs of the host countries. In their domestic operations, American business firms compete against imports from other nations of the world. Such imported goods include Japanese automobiles, German steel, French wine, Taiwanese textiles, and Chilean copper. American business firms should be well aware of the business practices of foreign business firms in order to compete effectively, and also to ascertain if foreign firms are using

unfair methods of competition in violation of American antitrust laws, antidumping laws, or international trade agreements.

Individuals from all over the world participate in the U.S. securities markets. Special problems exist in the regulation and enforcement of American securities laws involving financial institutions of countries with secrecy laws.

A.   GENERAL PRINCIPLES

Nations enter into treaties and conferences to further international trade. The business world has developed certain forms of organizations for conducting that trade.

1.   The Legal Background

Because of the complexity and ever-changing character of the legal environment of international trade, this section will give consideration to certain underlying elements. Subsequent sections of this chapter will give particular attention to certain problems that are currently of international importance.

(a) WHAT LAW APPLIES. When there is a sale of goods within the United States, there is typically one law that applies to the transaction. Some variation may be introduced when the transaction is between parties in different states, but for the most part the law governing the transaction is the American law of contracts and the Uniform Commercial Code.[1] In contrast, when an international sale is made, it is necessary to determine whether it is the law of the exporter's state or the law of the importer's state that will govern. The parties to an international contract often resolve that question themselves as part of their contract, setting forth which state's law will govern should a dispute arise. Such agreement language is called a **choice of law clause**. As another alternative, the parties to the contract may agree to arbitrate any contractual dispute that may arise, according to dispute resolution procedures set forth in their contract.

In order to eliminate uncertainty, a number of treaties have been entered into by the major trading countries of the world. When their citizens deal with each other, their rights and liabilities are determined by looking at the treaty. These treaties are discussed in Section 2 of this chapter.

(b) CONFLICTING IDEOLOGIES. Law, for all people and at all times, is the result of the desire of the lawmaker to achieve certain goals. These are the social forces that make the law. In the eyes of the lawmaker, the attainment of these goals is proper and therefore ethical. This does not mean that we all can agree on what the international law should be, because different people have different ideas as to what is right. This affects our views as to

ownership, trade, and dealings with foreign merchants. For example, a very large part of the world does not share the American dislike for trusts. Other countries do not have our antitrust laws; therefore, their merchants can form a trust to create greater bargaining power in dealing with American and other foreign merchants.

(c) FINANCING INTERNATIONAL TRADE. There is no international currency. This creates problems as to what currency to use and how to make payment in international transactions. Centuries ago, buyers used precious metals, jewels, or furs in payment. Today the parties to an international transaction agree in their sales contract on the currency to be used to pay for the goods. They commonly require that the buyer furnish a **letter of credit**. By this, an issuer, typically a bank, agrees to pay the amounts of the drafts drawn against the buyer for the purchase price.[2] In trading with merchants in some countries, the foreign country itself will promise that the seller will be paid.

2.   International Trade Organizations, Conferences, and Treaties

A large number of organizations exist that affect the multinational markets for goods, services, and investments. A world view of multinational trade includes the *industrialized world*, which generally favors free trade; the currently changing centrally planned world, with its trade often focusing on providing for unplanned shortages or disposing of unplanned surpluses; and the developing countries of the world, sometimes called the *third world*, which are not in favor of free trade and seek to use trade to structurally improve their own economies. A survey of major international organizations, conferences, and treaties follows.

(a) GATT. **The General Agreement on Tariffs and Trade (GATT)** is a multilateral treaty, subscribed to by 96 governments, including the United States. Together, these countries account for more than four-fifths of world trade. The basic aim of the GATT is to

---

[1]   The law of sales under the UCC is analyzed in Chapter 24 et seq. Contract law is set forth in Chapters 9 et seq.

liberalize world trade and place it on a secure basis, thereby contributing to economic growth and development of the world's peoples. Negotiations are conducted in rounds, like the "Uruguay Round," which started in 1986 with the expectation of completion of the work in four years.

The GATT is based on the fundamental principles of trade without discrimination and protection through tariffs. The principle of trade without discrimination is embodied in its **most favored nation** clause. In the application and administration of import and export duties and charges, all contracting parties are bound to grant to each other treatment as favorable as they give to any country. Thus, no country is to give special trading advantages to another; all are to be on an equal basis and share the benefits of any moves toward lower trade barriers. Exceptions to this basic rule are allowed in certain special circumstances involving regional trading arrangements, such as the European Economic Community (the Common Market), and special preferences granted to developing countries. The second basic principle is that where protection is given for domestic industry, it should be extended essentially through a tariff, not through other commercial measures. The aim of this rule is to make the extent of protection clear and to make competition possible.

In the Uruguay Round, the GATT members agreed to substantial progressive reductions of agricultural protection and subsidies that distort trade. These changes were to take effect in 1991. A top priority of the United States in the Uruguay Round was the protection of intellectual property rights in world trade by the GATT.

(b) CISG. The **United Nations Convention on Contracts for the International Sale of Goods (CISG)**[3] sets forth uniform rules to govern the formation of international sales

contracts and the rights and obligations of the buyer and seller. The CISG became effective on January 1, 1988, between the United States and the other nations that had approved it.[4] The provisions of the CISG have been strongly influenced by Article 2 of the Uniform Commercial Code.

(c) UNCTAD. The **United Nations Conference on Trade and Development (UNCTAD)** represents the interests of the less-developed countries of the world. Its prime objective is the achievement of an international redistribution of income through trade. Through UNCTAD pressure, the developed countries of the world agreed to a system of preferences, with quota limits, for manufactured imports from the developing countries.

(d) EEC. The **European Economic Community (EEC)** was established in 1958 to remove trade and economic barriers between member countries and to unify their economic policies. The EEC's Treaty of Rome, as amended by the Single European Act of 1986, contains the governing principles of this regional trading group. The treaty was signed by the original six nations of Belgium, France, West Germany, Italy, Luxembourg, and the Netherlands. Membership in the EEC expanded by the entry of Denmark, Ireland, Great Britain, Greece, Spain, and Portugal.

There are four main institutions making up the formal structure of the EEC. The *European Council* consists of the heads of state of the member countries. The Council's decisions set broad policy guidelines for the EEC. The *European Commission* implements decisions of the Council and initiates actions against individuals, companies, or member states that violate community law. The *European Parliament* has an advisory legislative role. The *European Court of Justice* (ECJ) is the judicial arm of the EEC. *The Court of First In-*

---

[2]   Orders to pay or drafts are commercial paper and are discussed in Chapter 30 et seq. The agreement of a bank to pay drafts is a letter of credit and is discussed in Chapter 36.

[3]   52 Fed. Reg. 6262 (1987).

[4]   The contracting nations are currently Argentina, Australia, Austria, China, Egypt, Finland, France, Hungary, Italy, Lesotho, Mexico, Norway, Sweden, Syria, the United States, Yugoslavia, and Zambia. Ratification proceedings are presently under way in other countries.

stance (CFI) was created by the 1986 Act to relieve the excessive work load of the ECJ. The CFI has primary responsibility for competition cases.

Under the Single European Act the vast internal market of the EEC will be without internal barriers to the free movement of goods, persons, services, and capital by the end of 1992. Measures have been taken to eliminate physical barriers such as border controls on people and goods, as well as fiscal barriers such as excise duties.

(e) U.S.-CANADA FTA. Canada and the United States share the world's largest trading relationship between two countries. Under the United States-Canada Free Trade Agreement (FTA)[5] which took effect on January 1, 1989, it is hoped that two-way trade between these countries will be significantly increased. The key feature of the FTA is the progressive elimination of all duties and most nontariff barriers on virtually all trade in goods between the two countries over a ten-year period.[6] Also, the FTA ensures nondiscriminatory and open markets for a wide range of services, including advertising, public relations, computer and telecommunication services, and management services.[7] A very important provision of the FTA is the lowering of Canadian barriers to U.S. investments. In order to accommodate the movement of people as well as the exchange of goods and services, the FTA provides for workable immigration provisions for "business persons."[8]

(f) REGIONAL TRADING GROUPS OF DEVELOPING COUNTRIES. In recent years numerous trading arrangements between groups of developing countries have been established.

(g) IMF-WORLD BANK. The **International Monetary Fund (IMF)** was created after World War II by a group of nations meeting in Bretton Woods, New Hampshire. The Articles of Agreement of the IMF state that the purpose is to "facilitate the expansion and balanced growth of international trade" and to "shorten the duration and lessen the disequilibrium in the international balance of payments of members." The IMF helps to achieve such purposes by administering a complex lending system. A country can borrow money from other IMF members or from the IMF by means of **Special Drawing Rights (SDR)** sufficient to permit that country to maintain the stability of its currency's relationship to other world currencies. The Bretton Woods conference after World War II also set up the **International Bank for Reconstruction and Development (World Bank)** to facilitate the lending of money by capital surplus countries—such as the United States—to countries needing economic help and wanting foreign investments after the war.

(h) OPEC. The **Organization of Petroleum Exporting Countries (OPEC)** is a producer cartel or combination. Its two main goals have been to raise the taxes and royalties earned from crude oil production and to assume control from the major oil companies over production and exploration. Its early success in attaining these goals led other nations who export raw materials to form similar cartels. For example, copper- and bauxite-producing nations have formed cartels.

3.   Forms of Business Organizations

The decision to participate in international business transactions and the extent of that participation depend on the financial position of the individual firm, production and marketing factors, and tax and legal considerations. There are a number of forms of business organizations for doing business abroad.

(a) EXPORT SALES. A direct sale to customers abroad by an American firm, with terms of payment commonly based on an irrevocable letter of credit, is an **export sale**. No foreign presence exists for the American firm

---

[5]   Act of September 19, 1988, PL 100-449; 102 Stat 1815, 19 USC § 2112, 27 ILM 281.
[6]   FTA Art. 401.
[7]   FTA Art. 1402.
[8]   FTA Art 1502.

in such an arrangement. The export is subject to a tariff by the foreign country, but the exporting firm is not subject to local taxation by the importing country.

(b) AGENCY ARRANGEMENTS. A U.S. manufacturer may decide to make a limited entry into international business by appointing an **agent,** a person or firm with authority to make contracts, to represent it in a foreign market. The agent will receive commission income for sales made on behalf of the U.S. principal. The appointment of a foreign agent commonly constitutes "doing business" in that country and subjects the U.S. firm to local taxation.

(c) FOREIGN DISTRIBUTORSHIPS. A **distributor** takes title to goods and bears the financial and commercial risks for the subsequent sale of the goods. A U.S. firm may decide to appoint a foreign distributor in order to avoid making a major financial investment. A U.S. firm may also appoint a foreign distributor in order to avoid managing a foreign operation, with its complicated local business, legal, and labor conditions. Care is required in designing an exclusive distributorship for an EEC country, lest it be in violation of EEC antitrust laws.

(d) LICENSING. American firms may select licensing as a means of doing business in other countries. **Licensing** involves the transfer of technology rights in a product so that it may be produced by a different business organization in a foreign country in exchange for royalties and other payments as agreed. The technology being licensed may fall within the internationally recognized categories of patents, trademarks, and "know-how" (trade secrets and unpatented manufacturing processes outside the public domain). These intellectual property rights, which are legally enforceable, may be licensed separately or incorporated into a single, comprehensive licensing contract. **Franchising,** which involves granting permission to use a trademark, trade name, or copyright under specified conditions, is a form of licensing that is now very common in international business.

(e) WHOLLY OWNED SUBSIDIARIES. A firm seeking to maintain control and authority over its own operations, including the protection of its own technological expertise, may choose to do business abroad through a wholly owned subsidiary. In Europe the most common choice of foreign business organization, similar to the U.S. corporate form of business organization, is called the **société anonyme (S.A.).** In German-speaking countries this form is called **Aktiengesellschaft (A.G.).**

Corporations doing business in more than one country pose many taxation problems for the governments in the countries in which the firm does business. The United States has established tax treaties with many countries. These treaties grant corporations relief from double taxation. Credit is normally given to U.S. corporations for taxes paid to foreign governments.

There is a potential for tax evasion by U.S. corporations, by their selling goods to their overseas subsidiaries. Corporations could sell goods at less than the fair market value to avoid a U.S. tax on the full profit for such sales. By allowing the foreign subsidiaries located in countries with lower tax rates to make higher profits, the company as a whole would minimize its taxes. Section 482 of the Internal Revenue Code, however, allows the IRS to reallocate the income between the parent and its foreign subsidiary corporation. The parent corporation is insulated from such a reallocation if it can show, based on independent transactions with unrelated parties, that its charges were at arm's length."[9] In the *Du Pont* case, the IRS reallocation of income between the related corporations resulted in a $9 million tax deficiency for the parent corporation. In reading the decision, note the significance of tax considerations in the creation of the subsidiary corporation.

---

[9]   United States Steel Corp. v Commissioner (CA2 NY) 617 F2d 942 (1980).

E. I. DU PONT DE NEMOURS & CO. v UNITED STATES

(US Ct of Cl) 608 F2d 445 (1979)

Early in 1959 Du Pont de Nemours (taxpayer or plaintiff), an American chemical company, created a wholly owned Swiss marketing and sales subsidiary for foreign sales—Du Pont International S.A. (DISA). Most of the Du Pont chemical products marketed abroad were first sold by taxpayer to DISA, which then arranged for resale to the ultimate consumer through independent distributors. The profits of these Du Pont sales were divided for income tax purposes between plaintiff and DISA via the mechanism of the prices plaintiff charged DISA. For 1959 and 1960 the Commissioner of Internal Revenue, acting under § 482 of the Internal Revenue Code that gives authority to reallocate profits among commonly controlled enterprises, found these divisions of profits economically unrealistic. DISA was found to have been given too great a share. Accordingly, the Commissioner reallocated a substantial part of DISA's income to the taxpayer. This increased the latter's taxes for 1959 and 1960 by considerable sums. Du Pont contended that the prices it charged DISA were valid under the Treasury regulations implementing § 482. From a judgment in the Commissioner's favor, Du Pont appealed.

DAVIS, J. . . . Du Pont first considered formation of an international sales subsidiary in 1957.

A decreasing volume of domestic sales, increasing profits on exports, and the recent formation of the Common Market in Europe convinced taxpayer's president of the need for such a subsidiary. . . .

Neither in the planning stage nor in actual operation was DISA a sham entity; nor can it be denied that it was intended to, and did, perform substantial commercial functions which taxpayer legitimately saw as needed in its foreign (primarily European) market. Nevertheless, we think it also undeniable that the tax advantages of such a foreign entity were also an important, though not the primary, consideration in DISA's creation and operation. During the planning stages, plaintiff's internal memoranda were replete with references to tax advantages, particularly in planning prices on Du Pont goods to be sold to the new entity. The tax strategy was simple. If Du Pont sold its goods to the new international subsidiary at price below fair market value, that company, upon resale of the goods, would recognize the greater part of the total profit (i.e., manufacturing and selling profits). Since this foreign subsidiary could be located in a country where its profits would be taxed at a much lower level than the parent Du Pont would be taxed here, the enterprise as a whole would minimize its taxes. . . .

Consistently with that aim, plaintiff's prices on its intercorporate sales to DISA were deliberately calculated to give the subsidiary the lion's share of the profits. Instead of allowing each individual producing department to value its goods economically and to set a realistic price, Du Pont left pricing on the sales to DISA with the Treasury and Legal Departments. Neither department was competent to set an economic value on goods sold to DISA, and no economic correlation of costs to price was attempted. Rather, an official of the Treasury Department established a pricing system designed to leave DISA with 75 percent of the total profits. If the goods' cost was greater than DISA's selling price, the department would price the item at its cost less DISA's selling expense. This latter provision was designed to insulate DISA from any loss. On the whole, the pricing system was based solely on Treasury and Legal Department estimates of the greatest amount of profits that would be shifted to DISA without evoking IRS intervention. . . . It is not that there was anything "illegal" or immoral in Du Pont's plan; it is simply that that plan made it very difficult, perhaps impossible, to satisfy the controlling Treasury regulations under Section 482.

Section 482 gives the Secretary of the Treasury (or his delegate) discretion to allocate income between related corporations when necessary to "prevent evasion of taxes or clearly to reflect the income" of any of such corporations. . . .

The court concludes as a matter of law that plaintiff is not entitled to recover. . . . [Judgment affirmed]

QUESTIONS

1. Was DISA a sham corporation created for tax evasion purposes?
2. Explain the tax strategy behind the creation of DISA.
3. What is the source of the IRS's authority to reallocate the income of DISA to Du Pont?

(f) JOINT VENTURES. A U.S. manufacturer and a foreign entity may form a joint venture whereby the two firms agree to perform different functions for a common result. The responsibilities and liabilities of such operations are governed by contract. For example, Hughes Aircraft Co. formed a joint venture with two Japanese firms, C. Itoh & Co. and Mitsui, and successfully bid on a telecommunications space satellite system for the Japanese government.

B. GOVERNMENTAL REGULATION

Nations regulate trade to protect the economic interests of their citizens or to protect themselves in international relations and transactions.

4. Export Regulations

The Export Administration Act[10] (EAA) is the principal statute imposing export controls on

goods and technical data from the United States. The Bureau of Export Administration issues the *Export Administration Regulations*[11] to enforce export controls. Violations of the Export Administration Regulations carry both civil and criminal penalties.

Export licensing is an integral part of exporting. For reasons of national security, foreign policy, or short supply of certain domestic products, the United States controls the export of all goods and technology. There are two types of export licenses: general and validated.

A *general license* is a broad grant of authority to all exporters for certain categories of products to all or most destinations. Most U.S. exports are shipped abroad under general licenses, and no application is required for their use.

A *validated license* is a specific grant of authority from the government to a particular exporter to export a particular product to a certain destination. Licenses are granted on a case-by-case basis for a single transaction and generally have a two-year validity period. An

---

[10] Export Administration Act of 1979, PL 96–72, 93 Stat 503, 50 USC §§ 2401–20; The Export Administration Amendments Act of 1985, Act of July 12, 1985, PL 99–64, 99 Stat 120, 50 USC § 2401.

[11] The Export Administration regulations are available from the Superintendent of Documents, U.S. Government Printing Office, Washington, D.C. 20230.

exporter must apply to the U.S. Commerce Department's Office of Export Licensing for a validated export license.

(a) DETERMINING THE TYPE OF LICENSE NEEDED. In order to determine whether a product requires a general or validated license, a three-step procedure is followed.

(1) Destination of the Product. The exporter must check the schedule of "Country Groups" contained in the *Export Administration Regulations* to see under which category the export destination falls. The countries making up Country Group 2 (North Korea, Vietnam, Kampuchea, and Cuba) are subject to a virtual trade embargo, and no goods may be licensed for export there.

(2) The Product Being Exported. The exporter must check the "Commodity Control List" contained in the *Export Administration Regulations* to see whether the product requires a validated license for shipment to the "Country Groups" identified in the preceding step.

(3) Special Restrictions. The exporter must determine whether any "special restrictions" apply to the export transaction. An exporter probably will have to apply for a validated export license if exporting the following: a) a "strategic" commodity to any destination—or in a few cases, only to a destination where exports are restricted for national security purposes, such as certain communist countries; b) a "short supply" commodity to any destination; c) any other commodity to a destination where there are foreign policy concerns; or d) "unpublished" technical data to certain destinations. This refers to technical information, generally related to the design, production, or use of a product, that is not available to the public.

If after following the above procedures it is determined that a validated license is not required, the exporter may ship its product under a general license.

(b) SHIPPER EXPORT DECLARATION. If the shipment is valued at $500 or more or requires a validated export license, the exporter must complete a Shipper's Export Declaration (SED). The SED is used by the U.S. Customs Service to indicate the type of export license being used and to keep track of what products are exported. SEDs are also used by the Bureau of Census to compile statistics on U.S. trade patterns.

(c) CRIMINAL SANCTIONS. Validated export licenses are required for the export of certain high-technology and military products. A company intending to ship "maraging 350 steel" to a user in Pakistan would find by checking the Commodity Control List that such steel is used in making high-technology products and also has nuclear applications. Thus, a validated export license would be required. Since Pakistan is a non-signatory nation of the Nuclear Non-Proliferation Treaty, the Department of Commerce would be expected to deny an application for a validated license for the use of this steel in a nuclear plant. However, a license to export this steel for use in the manufacture of high-speed turbines or compressors might be approved. The prospective purchaser must complete a "Statement of Ultimate Consignee and Purchaser" form with the application for a validated license. The prospective purchaser must identify the "end use" for the steel and indicate where the purchaser is located and the location in Pakistan where a U.S. Embassy official can make an on-site inspection of the product's use. Falsification of the information in the license application process is a criminal offense. Were the exporter of maraging 350 steel to assert it was to be used in manufacturing high-speed turbines when in fact the exporter knew it was being purchased for use in a nuclear facility, the exporter would be guilty of a criminal offense.[12] In the *Mechanic* case, the defendants claimed that a mere attempt to violate U.S. export controls could not subject them to criminal sanctions.

---

[12]   See U.S. v Pervez (CA3 Pa) 871 F2d 310 (1989), on the criminal application of the Export Administration Regulations to an individual who made up a false end use for "maraging 350 steel" on his export application to ship this steel to Pakistan.

UNITED STATES v MECHANIC
(CA5 Tex) 809 F2d 1111 (1987)

> Barry and Mary Mechanic attempted to export a "sweep generator." This device
> is used in laboratories to develop radar and military communication systems,
> such as guided missile tracking systems. The Mechanics were caught trying to
> ship the device to Europe without a validated federal license, and they were
> charged with criminal violation of the Export Administration Regulations. They
> claimed that a mere *attempt* to violate export controls could not subject them to
> criminal sanctions. They were convicted, and they appealed.

GEE, C.J. . . . The facts relevant to this appeal are undisputed. Bahram (Barry) Mechanic
and his ex-sister-in-law, Mary Akers Mechanic, constituted the entire personnel roster
for Faratel, Inc., an operation located in a small office in Houston, Texas. In December
1984, Mary called Hughes Aircraft to obtain a quote for a plug-in sweep generator,
stating Faratel had a West German client who wanted one shipped to Switzerland.
Hughes gave a foreign price quotation, adding that the item was subject to United
States export control regulations and that delivery was contingent upon receipt of a
validated export license. In February 1985, Mary called Hughes again, but requested a
domestic price quotation, stating that Faratel had a foreign client who intended to use
the device in a Houston-based beeper-pager operation. This use is not compatible with
the requested equipment, which is primarily used in laboratories to develop radar and
military communication systems, such as guided missile tracking.

Hughes shipped the equipment in late March 1985. Executing a search warrant, the
U.S. Customs Service intercepted the crate at a Houston airport and installed a tracking
device. While maintaining surveillance, Customs Service personnel observed Barry
and Mary repack the generator in a footlocker. They later observed one Eugene Krug
check the footlocker as baggage on his flight to Zurich. Krug was detained at the airport and Barry and Mary were later arrested. The first trial resulted in a hung jury; the
jury at the second trial acquitted Krug, but convicted Barry and Mary.

When the Mechanics were busying themselves with the sweep generator in April
1985, the Export Administration Act of 1979 was not in effect of its own force. On the
expiration date of Congress's last extension of the Act, March 30, 1984, the President
issued Executive order No. 12470, pursuant to special powers granted him under the
International Economic Emergency Powers Act (IEEPA). . . . The Order declared a national economic emergency and continued the operation of the provisions of the EAA
of 1979 and all rules and regulations under it. The President revoked the Order after
signing into law the Export Administration Amendments Act of 1985 (EAAA). Pub.L.
No. 99–64, 99 Stat. 120 (July 12, 1985). Thus, at the time the offenses were committed in
April 1985, the EAA of 1979 rested solely upon the President's exercise of his powers
under the IEEPA.

Furthermore, a regulation, and not the EAA itself, denounced an *attempt* to violate
export controls as a criminal offense, as follows:

> Solicitation and attempt. No person may do any act that solicits the commission
> of, or that constitutes an attempt to bring about, a violation of the Export Admin-
> istration Act or any regulation, order, or license issued under the Act.

15 C.F.R. § 387.3(a) (1985).

The EAA of 1979 imposed criminal sanctions on those who knowingly violate any provision of the Act or any regulation issued under it. . . . The EAA goes on to establish that, in order to further these policies, the President may "prohibit or curtail" the exportation of any goods, technology, or other information subject to the jurisdiction of the United States. . . .

[Judgment affirmed]

QUESTIONS

1. Did Mary Mechanic know that a validated export license was required for the sweep generator?
2. How was the U.S. Customs Service alerted to the possible violation of export controls?
3. Was the Export Administration Act in effect of its own force in April 1985 when the Mechanics tried to ship the sweep generator?
4. Were the Mechanics' actions contrary to any of the "Selected Ethical Principles" set forth in the "Analysis of Court Opinions" in the introductory pages of this textbook?

(d) EXPERT ASSISTANCE. The Department of Commerce's Export Assistance Staff provides assistance to exporters needing help in determining the proper export license.[13] Licensed *foreign freight forwarders* are in the business of handling the exporting of goods to foreign destinations. They are experts on U.S. Department of Commerce export license requirements. Licensed foreign freight forwarders can attend to all of the essential arrangements required to transport a shipment of goods from the exporter's warehouse to the overseas buyer's specified port and inland destination. They are well versed in all aspects of ocean, air, and inland transportation as well as banking, marine insurance, and other services relating to exporting.

5.   Antitrust

As explained in Chapter 4, antitrust laws exist in the United States to protect the American consumer by assuring the benefits of competitive products from foreign competitors as well as domestic competitors. Competitors' private agreements designed to raise the price of imports or to exclude imports from our domestic markets in exchange for not competing in other countries are restraints of trade in violation of our antitrust laws. The antitrust laws also exist to protect American export and investment opportunities against privately imposed restrictions, whereby a group of competitors seeks to exclude another competitor from a particular foreign market. Antitrust laws also exist in other countries where American firms compete. These laws are usually not directed at breaking up cartels, but rather at regulating them in the national interest.

(a) JURISDICTION. In U.S. courts the U.S. antitrust laws have a broad extraterritorial reach. Our antitrust laws must be reconciled with the rights of other interested countries as embodied in international law.

(1) The Effects Doctrine. Judge Learned Hand's decision in *United States v Alcoa*[14] established the **effects doctrine**. Under this doctrine, U.S. courts will assume jurisdiction and will apply U.S. antitrust laws to conduct outside of the United States where the activity of the business firms outside the United States has a direct and substantial effect on U.S. commerce. This basic rule has been modified to require that the effect on U.S. commerce also be foreseeable.

---

[13]   Exporter Assistance Staff, U.S. Department of Commerce, Washington D.C. 20230.

[14]   (CA2 NY) 148 F2d 416 (1945).

(2) The "Jurisdictional Rule of Reason." The "jurisdictional rule of reason" addresses the problems arising when conduct taking place outside of the United States has the requisite effect on U. S. commerce, but a foreign state also has a significant interest in regulating the conduct in question. The **"jurisdictional rule of reason"** balances the vital interests, including laws and policies, of the United States with the vital interests of the foreign country involved. This rule of reason is based on the principle of comity. **Comity** is a principle of international law that the laws of all nations deserve the respect legitimately demanded by equal participants in international affairs.

(b) DEFENSES. Three defenses are commonly raised to the extraterritorial application of the U.S. antitrust laws. These defenses are also commonly raised to attack jurisdiction in other legal actions involving international law.

(1) Act of State Doctrine. The classic enunciation of the **act of state doctrine** is that:

Every sovereign state is bound to respect the independence of every other sovereign state, and the courts of one country will not sit in judgment of another government's acts done within its own territory.[15]

The act of state doctrine is based on the judiciary's concern over its possible interference with the conduct of foreign relations, considering such matters to be political, not judicial, questions.[16]

(2) The Sovereign Compliance Doctrine. This doctrine allows a defendant to raise as an affirmative defense to an antitrust action the fact that the defendant's actions were compelled by a foreign state.[17] In order to establish this defense, compulsion by the foreign government is required. The Japanese government uses informal and formal contacts within an industry to establish a consensus on a desired course of action. Such governmental action is not a defense for a U.S. firm, however, because the activity in question is not compulsory.

(3) The Sovereign Immunity Doctrine. This doctrine states that a foreign sovereign generally cannot be sued unless an exception to the Foreign Sovereign Immunities Act of 1976 applies.[18] The most important exception covers the commercial conduct of a foreign state.

The *Timberlane* decision discusses the factors considered by a U.S. court in deciding whether or not to take jurisdiction of a case concerning transactions that occurred outside U.S. borders. This case is an example of the "jurisdictional rule of reason" test. The *Timberlane* court also considers a number of defenses to its assuming extraterritorial jurisdiction.

---

[15]   Underhill v Hernandez, 108 US 250, 252 (1897).

[16]   First City Bank v Banco National de Cuba, 406 US 759 (1972).
[17]   Mannington Mills, Inc. v Congoleum Corp. (CA3 Pa) 595 F2d 1287 (1979).
[18]   See Verlinden B.V. v Central Bank of Nigeria, 461 US 574 (1983).

TIMBERLANE LUMBER CO. v BANK OF AMERICA
(CA9 Cal) 549 F2d 597 (1976)

The Timberlane Lumber Company, an Oregon partnership, brought an antitrust suit against the Bank of America, several employees of the Bank who worked for the Bank in Honduras, and others. The suit alleged violations of Sections 1 and 2 of the Sherman Act. Timberlane alleged that the defendants conspired to prevent Timberlane, through Honduras subsidiaries, from milling lumber in Honduras and exporting it to the United States. Timberlane alleged that the defendants were trying to keep control of the Honduran lumber business in the hands of individuals financed and controlled by the bank. The defendants contended that the action must be dismissed because of the act of state doctrine since a Honduran court approved certain of the challenged activities. Defendants also contended that the court lacked jurisdiction because these activities occurred in Honduras, and the court lacked subject matter jurisdiction under the effects doctrine. From a judgment in favor of Bank of America, Timberlane appealed.

CHOY, C.J. . . . The defendants argue—as the district court apparently held—that the injuries allegedly suffered by Timberlane resulted from acts of the Honduran government, principally in connection with the enforcement of the security interests in the Maya plant, which American courts cannot review. Such an application of the act of state doctrine seems to us to be erroneous. Even if the *coup de grace* to Timberlane's enterprise in Honduras was applied by official authorities, we do not agree that the doctrine necessarily shelters these defendants or requires dismissal of the Timberlane action.

The leading modern statement of the act of state doctrine appears in *Banco Nacional de Cuba v Sabbatino*, 376 U.S. 398 (1964). The Court concluded that the doctrine was not compelled by the nature of sovereignty, by international law, or by the text of the Constitution. Rather, it derives from the judiciary's concern for its possible interference with the conduct of foreign affairs by the political branches of the government:

> The doctrine as formulated in past decisions expresses the strong sense of the Judicial Branch that its engagement in the task of passing on the validity of foreign acts of state may hinder rather than further this country's pursuit of goals both for itself and for the community of nations as a whole in the international sphere.

The Court recognized that not every case is identical in its potential impact on our relations with other nations....

A corollary to the act of state doctrine in the foreign trade antitrust field is the often-recognized principle that corporate conduct which is compelled by a foreign sovereign is also protected from antitrust liability, as if it were an act of the state itself. Thus, in *Interamerican Refining Corp. v Texaco Maracaibo, Inc.*, 307 F. Supp. 1291 (D.Del. 1970), a refusal by defendants to sell Venezuelan crude oil to plaintiff was held not to be an illegal restraint of trade because it was a complete defense that the Venezuelan government had imposed a boycott forbidding such sales. The court there observed that "when a nation compels a trade practice firms there have no choice but to obey. Acts of business become effectively acts of the sovereign." . . .

On the basis of the foregoing analysis, we conclude that the court below erred in dismissing the instant suit. . . . Timberlane does not seek to name Honduras or any Honduran officer as a defendant or co-conspirator, nor does it challenge Honduran policy or sovereignty in any fashion that appears on its face to hold any threat to relations between Honduras and the United States. . . .

Under these circumstances, it is clear that the "act of state" doctrine does not require dismissal of the Timberlane action.

Extraterritorial Reach of the United States Antitrust Laws

There is no doubt that American antitrust laws extend over some conduct in other nations....

That American law covers some conduct beyond this nation's borders does not mean that it embraces all, however. Extraterritorial application is understandably a matter of concern for the other countries involved. Those nations have sometimes resented and protested, as excessive intrusions into their own spheres, broad assertions of authority by American courts. . . .

It is the effect on American foreign commerce which is usually cited to support extraterritorial jurisdiction. *Alcoa* [*United States v Alcoa*, 148 F2d 416 (1945)] set the course, when Judge Hand declared,

> It is settled law . . . that any state may impose liabilities, even upon persons not within its allegiance, for conduct outside its borders that has consequences within its borders which the state reprehends; and these liabilities other states will ordinarily recognize.

Despite its description as "settled law," *Alcoa*'s assertion has been roundly disputed by many foreign commentators as being in conflict with international law, comity, and good judgment. Nonetheless, American courts have firmly concluded that there is some extraterritorial jurisdiction under the Sherman Act.

Even among American courts and commentators, however, there is no consensus on how far the jurisdiction should extend. The district court here concluded that a "direct and substantial effect" on United States foreign commerce was a prerequisite, without stating whether other factors were relevant or considered. . . .

[But] an effect on United States commerce, although necessary to the exercise of jurisdiction under the antitrust laws, is alone not a sufficient basis on which to determine whether American authority *should* be asserted in a given case as a matter of international comity and fairness.

What we prefer is an evaluation and balancing of the relevant considerations in each case—in the words of Kingman Brewster, a "jurisdictional rule of reason." . . .

The elements to be weighed include the degree of conflict with foreign law or policy, the nationality or allegiance of the parties and the locations or principal places of business or corporations, the extent to which enforcement by either state can be expected to achieve compliance, the relative significance of effects on the United States as compared with those elsewhere, the extent to which there is explicit purpose to harm or affect American commerce, the foreseeability of such effect, and the relative importance to the violations charged of conduct within the United States as compared with conduct abroad. . . .

We conclude, then, that the problem should be approached in three parts: Does the alleged restraint affect, or was it intended to affect, the foreign commerce of the United States? Is it of such a type and magnitude so as to be cognizable as a violation of the Sherman Act? As a matter of international comity and fairness, should the extraterritorial jurisdiction of the United States be asserted to cover it? The district court's judgment found only that the restraint involved in the instant suit did not produce a direct and substantial effect on American foreign commerce. That holding does not satisfy any of these inquiries. . . .

[Dismissal vacated and action remanded]

QUESTIONS

1. Are the U.S. antitrust laws limited to transactions that take place within its territorial boundaries?
2. Did the act of state doctrine require the dismissal of the plaintiff's claim?

> 3. What are the relevant considerations to be used to determine whether or not to exercise juris-
>   diction in extraterritorial application of antitrust laws?

(c) LEGISLATION. In response to business uncertainty as to the applicability of the antitrust laws to international transactions, Congress passed the Foreign Trade Antitrust Improvements Act of 1982. This Act, in essence, codified the effects doctrine. The Act requires a direct, substantial, and reasonably foreseeable effect on U.S. domestic commerce or exports by U.S. residents before business conduct abroad may come within the purview of the U.S. antitrust laws.[19]

(d) FOREIGN ANTITRUST LAWS. Attitudes in different countries of the world vary toward cartels and business combinations. Because of this, antitrust laws vary in content and application. Japan, for example, has stressed consumer protection against such practices as price fixing and false advertising. However, with regard to mergers, stock ownership, and agreements among companies to control production, Japanese law is much less restrictive than American law.

Europe is a major market for American products, services, and investments. American firms doing business in Europe are subject to the competition laws of the EEC. The Treaty of Rome uses the term *competition* rather than *antitrust*. Articles 85 and 86 of the Treaty of Rome set forth the basic regulation on business behavior in the EEC.[20]

Article 85 (1) expressly prohibits agreements and concerted practices that:

1. Even indirectly fix prices of purchases or sales, or fix any other trading conditions.
2. Limit or control production, markets, technical development, or investment.
3. Share markets or sources of supply.

4. Apply unequal terms to parties furnishing equivalent considerations, thereby placing one at a competitive disadvantage.
5. Make a contract's formation turn upon acceptance of certain additional obligations that, according to commercial usage, have no connection with the subject of such contracts.

Article 85(3) allows for an individual exemption if the agreement meets certain conditions, such as improving the production or distribution of goods or promoting technical or economic progress, and reserving to consumers a fair share of the resulting economic benefits.

Article 86 provides that it is unlawful for one or more enterprises, having a dominant market position within at least a substantial part of the Common Market, to take improper advantage of such a position if trade between the member states may be affected.

6. Securities Regulation in an International Environment

Illegal conduct in the U.S. securities markets, whether this conduct is initiated in the United States or abroad, threatens the vital economic interests of the United States. Investigation and litigation concerning possible violations of the U.S. securities laws often have extraterritorial effects. Conflicts with the laws of foreign countries may occur.

(a) JURISDICTION. U.S. district courts have jurisdiction over violations of the antifraud provisions of the Securities Exchange Act where losses occur from sales to Americans living in the United States. This is true whether or not the actions occurred in this country. U.S. district courts also have jurisdiction where losses occur to Americans living abroad if the acts occurred in the United

---

[19]   PL 97-290, 96 Stat. 1233, 15 USC § 6(a).
[20]   See Osakeyhtio v EEC Commission, 1988 CCH Com Mkt Rptr 14, 491 for discussion of the extraterritorial reach of the EEC Commission.

States. The antifraud provisions do not apply, however, to losses from sales of securities to foreigners outside the United States unless acts within the United States caused the losses.

(b) IMPACT OF FOREIGN SECRECY LAWS IN SEC ENFORCEMENT. **Secrecy laws** are confidentiality laws applied to home-country banks. These laws prohibit the disclosure of business records or the identity of bank customers. **Blocking laws** prohibit the disclosure, copying, inspection, or removal of documents located in the enacting country in compliance with orders from foreign authorities. These laws impede, and indeed sometimes foreclose, the SEC's ability to police its securities markets properly.

The *Banca Della Suizzera* case demonstrates how the SEC, in certain circumstances, can obtain discovery from foreign financial institutions despite the existence of secrecy laws.

The SEC is not limited to litigation when a securities law enforcement investigation runs into secrecy or blocking laws. For example, the SEC may rely on the 1977 Treaty of Mutual Assistance in Criminal Matters between the United States and Switzerland.[21] Although this treaty has served to deter the use of Swiss secrecy laws to conceal fraud in the U.S., its benefits for securities enforcement have been limited. It applies only where there is a dual criminality—that is, the conduct involved constitutes a criminal offense under the laws of both the United States and Switzerland.

[21]   27 UST 2021.

SEC v BANCA DELLA SUIZZERA ITALIANA
92 FRD 111 (DC NY 1981)

Banca Della Suizzera Italiana (BSI) is a Swiss bank with an office in the United States. BSI purchased certain call options and common stock of St. Joe Minerals Corporation (St. Joe), a New York corporation. This purchase was made immediately prior to the announcement on March 11, 1981 of a cash tender offer by Joseph Seagram & Sons Inc. for all St. Joe common stock at $45 per share. On March 10, 1981, when BSI acted, the stock traded at approximately $30 per share. On March 11, 1981 the stock moved sharply higher in price. BSI instructed its broker to close out the purchases of the options and sell most of the shares of stock, resulting in an overnight profit of $2 million. The SEC noticed the undue activity in the options market, initiated suit against BSI, and obtained a temporary restraining order. The restraining order froze the proceeds in BSI's bank account at a New York bank. The SEC, through the Departments of State and Justice, and the Swiss government sought without success to learn the identity of BSI's customers involved in the transactions. The SEC believed that the customers had used inside information in violation of the Securities Exchange Act of 1934. The SEC filed a motion to compel disclosure. BSI, a Swiss bank, contended that it might be subject to criminal liability under Swiss penal and banking laws if it disclosed the requested information.

POLLACK, D.J. . . . BSI claims that it may be subject to criminal liability under Swiss penal and banking law if it discloses the requested information. However, this Court finds the factors in § 40 of the Restatement of Foreign Relations* to tip decisively in favor of the SEC. Moreover, it holds BSI to be "in the position of one who deliberately courted legal impediments . . . and who thus cannot now be heard to assert its good faith after this expectation was realized." BSI acted in bad faith. It made deliberate use of Swiss nondisclosure law to evade in a commercial transaction for profit to it, the strictures of American securities law against insider trading. . . .

The first of the § 40 factors is the vital national interest of each of the States. The strength of the United States interest in enforcing its securities laws to ensure the integrity of its financial markets cannot seriously be doubted. That interest is being continually thwarted by the use of foreign bank accounts. Congress, in enacting legislation on bank record-keeping, expressed its concern over the problem over a decade ago. . . .

The Swiss government, on the other hand, though made expressly aware of the litigation, has expressed no opposition. In response to BSI's lawyers' inquiries, the incumbent Swiss Federal Attorney General, Rudolf Gerber, said only that a foreign court could not change the rule that disclosure required the consent of the one who imparted the secret and that BSI might thus be subject to prosecution. The Swiss government did not "confiscate" the Bank records to prevent violations of its law. . . . NEITHER THE UNITED STATES NOR THE SWISS GOVERNMENT has suggested that discovery be halted. . . . The Court of Appeals in *United States v National City Bank*, 396 F2d 897 (2d cir. 1968), found the fact that the governments concerned had not intervened of great importance. It observed that "when foreign governments, including Germany, have considered their vital national interests threatened, they have not hesitated to make known their objections. . . to the issuing court." It is true that BSI may be subject to fines and its officers to imprisonment under Swiss law. However, this Court notes that there is some flexibility in the application of that law. Not only may the particular bank involved obtain waivers from its customers to avoid prosecution, but Article 34 of the Swiss Penal Code contains "State of Necessity" exception that relieves a person of criminal liability for acts committed to protect one's own good, including one's fortune, from an immediate danger if one is not responsible for the danger and one cannot be expected to give up one's good.

Of course, given BSI's active part in the insider trading transactions alleged here, the Swiss government might well conclude—as this Court has—that BSI is responsible for the conflict it is in and that therefore the "State of Necessity" exception should not apply. However, that is certainly no cause for this Court to withhold its sanctions since the dilemma would be a result of BSI's bad faith. A party's good or bad faith is an important factor to consider, and this court finds that BSI, which deposited the proceeds of these transactions in an American bank account in its name and which cer-

---

*   § 40 reads as follows:
§ 40. Limitations on Exercise of Enforcement Jurisdiction. Where two states have jurisdiction to prescribe and enforce rules of law and the rules they may prescribe require inconsistent conduct upon the part of a person, each state is required by international law to consider, in good faith, moderating the exercise of its enforcement jurisdiction, in the light of such factors as
(a) vital national interests of each of the states,
(b) the extent and the nature of the hardship that inconsistent enforcement actions would impose upon the person,
(c) the extent to which the required conduct is to take place in the territory of the other state,
(d) the nationality of the person, and
(e) the extent to which enforcement by action of either state can reasonably be expected to achieve compliance with the rule prescribed by that state.

tainly profited in some measure from the challenged activity, undertook such transactions fully expecting to use foreign law to shield it from the reach of our laws. Such "deliberate courting" of foreign legal impediments will not be countenanced.

The last three of the § 40 Restatement of Foreign Relations Law factors—the place of performance, the nationality of the resisting party, and the extent to which enforcement can be expected to achieve compliance with the rule prescribed by that state—appear to be less important in this Circuit. . . .

It would be a travesty of justice to permit a foreign company to invade American markets, violate American laws if they were indeed violated, withdraw profits and resist accountability for itself and its principals for the illegality by claiming their anonymity under foreign law. . . .

This decision shall constitute an order that BSI is directed to complete its answers to all of the demands in the SEC's First Interrogatories, pertaining to St. Joe.

[So ordered]

[*Note:* Confronted with the judge's opinion and the possibility of substantial fines, BSI obtained a waiver of the secrecy laws from its customer and produced the requested information.]

QUESTIONS

1. What are the dominant factors considered by a court when deciding on whether or not to issue a subpoena or discovery order to a foreign bank in a secrecy jurisdiction?
2. Did the court find that the Swiss interest in bank secrecy outweighed the U.S. interest?
3. Did BSI act in good faith?
4. Did the court give significant weight to BSI's potential liability under Swiss law?

7.   Barriers to Trade

The most common barrier to the free movement of goods across borders is the tariff. A wide range of nontariff barriers also restrict the free movement of goods, services, and investments.

Governmental export controls used as elements of foreign policy have proven to be a major barrier to trade with certain countries.

(a) TARIFF BARRIERS. A **tariff** is an import or export duty or tax placed on goods as they move into or out of a country. It is probably the most common method used by countries to restrict foreign imports. The tariff raises the total cost and thus the price of the imported product in the domestic market. Thus, the price of a domestically produced product, not subject to the tariff, is more advantageous. One goal of the General Agreement on Tariff and Trade (GATT) was the reduction of tariffs by its member nations.

(b) NONTARIFF BARRIERS. Nontariff barriers consist of a wide range of restrictions that inhibit the free movement of goods between countries. An import quota, such as the limitation of the number of automobiles that can be imported from one country to another, is such a barrier. More subtle nontariff barriers exist in all countries. For example, Japan's complex customs procedures resulted in the restriction of the sale of U.S.-made aluminum baseball bats in Japan. The customs procedures required the individual uncrating and "destruction testing" of bats at the ports of entry. Government subsidies are also nontariff barriers to trade. A major objective of the Tokyo Round of the GATT was to produce agreements on limiting the use of nontariff measures.

(c) EXPORT CONTROLS AS INSTRUMENTS OF FOREIGN POLICY. U.S. export controls have been used as instruments of foreign policy in recent years. For example, the United States has sought to deny goods and technology of strategic or military importance to unfriendly nations. The United States has also denied goods such as grain, technology, or machine parts to certain countries to protest or to punish activities it considered violative of human rights or world peace.

8. Relief Mechanisms for Economic Injury Caused by Foreign Trade

In the dynamic and profitable markets that the United States provides for foreign-produced goods, certain U.S. industries may suffer severe economic injury as a result of foreign competition. American law provides protection against unfair competition from foreigners' goods and provides economic relief for U.S. industries, communities, firms, and workers adversely affected by import competition. American law also provides certain indirect relief for American exporters and producers who encounter unfair foreign import restrictions.

(a) ANTIDUMPING LAWS AND EXPORT SUBSIDIES. Selling goods in another country at less than their fair value is called **dumping.** The dumping of foreign goods in the United States is prohibited under the Trade Agreement Act of 1979.[22] Proceedings in antidumping cases are conducted by two federal agencies, which separately examine two distinct components. The International Trade Administration (ITA) of the Department of Commerce investigates the matter of whether specified foreign goods are being sold in the United States at less than fair value (LTFV). The International Trade Commission (ITC) conducts proceedings to determine if there is an injury to a domestic industry as a result of such sales. Findings of both LTFV sales and injury must be present before remedial action is taken. Remedial action might include the addition of duties to reflect the difference between the fair value of the goods and the price being charged in the United States. Judicial review of both ITA and ITC decisions is before the Court of International Trade. Figure 6-1 provides an example of antidumping proceedings.

A settlement of the matter may be reached through a suspension agreement, whereby prices are revised to completely eliminate any LTFV sales and other corrective measures are taken.

The 1979 Act also applies to subsidy practices by foreign countries. If a foreign country sells subsidized goods in the United States at less than their fair value, the goods may be subject to a countervailing duty.

(b) RELIEF FROM IMPORT INJURIES. Title II of the Trade Act of 1974[23] provides relief for U.S. industries, communities, firms, and workers when any one or more of them are substantially adversely affected by import competition. The Department of Commerce, the Secretary of Labor, and the President have roles in determining eligibility. The relief provided may be temporary import relief through the imposition of a duty or quota on the foreign goods. Workers found to be eligible may seek assistance in the form of readjustment allowances, job training, job search allowances, or unemployment compensation.

(c) RETALIATION AND RELIEF AGAINST FOREIGN UNFAIR TRADE RESTRICTIONS. American exporters of agricultural or manufactured goods or of services may encounter unreasonable, unjustifiable, or discriminatory foreign import restrictions. At the same time, producers from the foreign country involved may be benefiting from trade agreement concessions that allow producers from that country access to U.S. markets. Prior trade acts and the Omnibus Trade and Competitiveness Act of 1988[24] contain broad authority to retaliate against "unreasonable," "unjustifiable," or "discriminatory" acts by a foreign country. The authority to retaliate is commonly referred to as "§ 301 authority." The fear or actuality of the economic sting of § 301 retaliation often leads offending foreign countries to open their markets to im-

---

[22]   PL 96–39, § 106, 93 Stat 193, 19 USC § 160.

[23]   PL 93–618, 88 Stat 1978, 19 USC § 2251–2298.
[24]   PL 100–418.

FIGURE 6-1   ANTIDUMPING PROCEEDINGS

PHASE I: INTERNATIONAL TRADE ADMINISTRATION

DATE	EVENT
DECEMBER 28, 1988	COMPLAINT BY U.S. MANUFACTURERS TO THE INTERNATIONAL TRADE ADMINISTRATION (ITA) ALLEGING DUMPING OF SMALL BUSINESS TELEPHONES ON THE U.S. MARKET BY NAMED ASIAN MANUFACTURERS.
JANUARY - JULY, 1989	ITA INVESTIGATES WHETHER THESE FOREIGN-MADE GOODS ARE BEING SOLD IN THE U.S. AT LESS THAN FAIR VALUE (LTFV). INVESTIGATION INCLUDES QUESTIONNAIRES ON COSTS AND PRICING FROM ALL PARTIES.
JULY 27, 1989	PRELIMINARY FINDING BY THE ITA THAT JAPANESE AND TAIWANESE FIRMS ARE DUMPING BUSINESS PHONES ON THE U.S. MARKET.
OCTOBER 11, 1989	FINAL DETERMINATION BY ITA THAT THE NAMED FIRMS ARE DUMPING PHONES ON THE U.S. MARKET.
OCTOBER 11, 1989	U.S. CUSTOMS SERVICE COMMENCES REQUIREMENT OF CASH DEPOSIT OR BOND ON IMPORTS EQUAL TO THE DIFFERENCE BETWEEN THE FAIR VALUE OF THE GOODS AS DETERMINED BY THE ITA AND THE PRICES BEING CHARGED FOR THE GOODS IN THE U.S.

PHASE 2: INTERNATIONAL TRADE COMMISSION

DATE	EVENT
OCTOBER 31, 1989	HEARING BEFORE THE ITC TO DETERMINE WHETHER THERE IS AN INJURY TO THE DOMESTIC PHONE MANUFACTURING INDUSTRY AS A RESULT OF THE LTFV SALES BY THE NAMED ASIAN FIRMS.
NOVEMBER 20, 1989	DECISION OF ITC THAT U.S. MANUFACTURERS OF SMALL BUSINESS TELEPHONE SYSTEMS ARE SUFFERING INJURY BECAUSE OF THE DUMPED EXPORTS.
NOVEMBER 20, 1989	U.S. CUSTOMS SERVICE COMMENCES THE ACTUAL COLLECTION OF ANTI-DUMPING DUTIES.

ports. Thus, indirect relief is provided to domestic producers and exporters adversely affected by foreign unfair trade practices.

The 1988 Act transferred the authority to make determinations and take retaliatory action under § 301 from the President to the United States trade representative (USTR). The USTR is appointed by the President. Under the 1988 Act mandatory retaliatory action is required if the USTR determines that: (1) United States rights under a trade agreement are being denied; or (2) actions or policies of a foreign country are unjustifiable and burden or restrict U.S. commerce.

The overall thrust of the trade provisions of the 1988 Act is to open markets and liberalize trade.

9.   Expropriation

A major concern of U.S. businesses that do business abroad is the risk of expropriation of financial assets by a host government. Firms involved in the extraction of natural resources, banking, communications, or defense-related industries are particularly susceptible to nationalization. Multinational corporations commonly have a staff of full-time political scientists and former Foreign Service officers studying the countries relevant to their operations to monitor and calculate risks of expropriation. Takeovers of American-owned businesses by foreign countries may be motivated by a short-term domestic political advantage or by the desire to demonstrate political clout in world politics. Takeovers may also be motivated by long-term considerations associated with planned development of the country's economy.

Treaty commitments, or provisions in other international agreements between the United States and the host country, may serve to narrow expropriation uncertainties. Treaties commonly contain provisions whereby property will not be expropriated except for public benefit and with the prompt payment of just compensation.

One practical way to mitigate the risk of investment loss due to foreign expropriation is to purchase insurance through private companies such as Lloyd's of London. Commercial insurance is also available against such risks as host governments' arbitrary recall of letters of credit and commercial losses due to embargoes.

The Overseas Private Investment Corporation (OPIC) is a U.S. agency under the policy control of the Secretary of State. OPIC supports private investments in less-developed, friendly countries. OPIC offers asset protection insurance against risk of loss to plant and equipment as well as losses of deposits in overseas bank accounts to companies that qualify on the basis of a "substantial U.S. interest" being involved.

10.   Government-Assisted Export Programs

The United States has massive trade deficits. U.S. exporters encounter strong competition from foreign, government-assisted enterprises that are aggressively structured to promote the export trade of the foreign country. Those factors have led the U.S. government to take legislative action to bolster the export performance of U.S. firms.

(a) EXPORT TRADING COMPANY ACT. The Export Trading Company Act of 1982 (ETCA)[25] is designed to stimulate and promote additional U.S. exports. The ETCA promotes the formation of U.S.-based export trading companies and allows banks to invest in these export trading companies. The ETCA also clarifies applicable antitrust restrictions and provides a limited exception from antitrust liability through a certificate of review process.

Trading companies exist in many European and East Asian countries. They are primary competitors of U.S. exporters. Japan's export trading companies, or *sogo shosha*, provide comprehensive export services and may serve as models for U.S. trading companies created under the 1982 Act. For example, a *sogo shosha* may participate in the purchase transaction of goods for export. It may then handle the paperwork and documents related to the export transaction. It may obtain insurance coverage and provide warehousing and transportation services. Through access to or ownership of banks, the *sogo shosha* may extend credit or make loans or loan guarantees to buyers, sellers, and suppliers. It has expertise in marketing research relative to target export markets and expertise in foreign exchange and tariff requirements. By encouraging exporters to form trading companies with banking institutions (banks have been prohibited by law from engaging in commercial as opposed to banking activities), and specifically allowing and encouraging the bank-related firms to perform comprehensive export services, Congress believes that increased export activity will be generated.

(b) FOREIGN SALES CORPORATIONS. The **Foreign Sales Corporation** created by the Foreign Sales Corporation Act of 1984[26] replaces the Domestic International Sales Corporation (DISC) created by the Revenue Act of 1971, in response to complaints from several of the United States' major trading partners. These trading partners viewed certain DISC indefinite tax deferment rules as creating an illegal export subsidy in violation of the GATT.

The 1984 Act provides export incentives for U.S. firms that form Foreign Sales Corpo-

---

[25]   PL 97–290, 96 Stat 1233 (1982).

[26]   Title VIII of the Tax Reform Act of 1984, PL 98–369, 98 Stat 678. See IRC §§ 921 through 927.

rations (FSC), so as to continue export incentives to U.S. firms without violating the GATT. In order to qualify for the tax incentives provided under the 1984 Act, an FSC subsidiary of an American firm must be organized under the laws of a U.S. possession (such as the Virgin Islands or Guam, but not Puerto Rico), or under the laws of an acceptable foreign country—that is, a country with an income tax treaty with the United States containing an exchange-of-information program. The FSC must satisfy certain other organizational requirements in order to be eligible for the tax incentives provided by the law.

(c) UNITED STATES EXPORT-IMPORT BANK (EXIMBANK). **Eximbank** is wholly owned by the U.S. government. Its primary purpose is to facilitate U.S. exports by making direct loans in the form of dollar credits to foreign importers for the purchase of U.S. goods and services. Payments are then made directly to the U.S. exporter of goods and services. Such loans are made where private financial sources are unwilling to assume the political and economic risks that exist in the country in question. Loans are also made by Eximbank to enable U.S. suppliers of goods and services to compete for major foreign contracts with foreign firms that have government-subsidized export financing.

(d) OTHER PROGRAMS. As stated previously, OPIC provides expropriation insurance for U.S. private investments in friendly, less-developed countries. The Commodity Credit Corporation (CCC) provides financing for agricultural exports. Also, the Small Business Administration has an export loan program.

11.   The Foreign Corrupt Practices Act

There are legal restrictions on U.S. firms doing business abroad, in connection with payments made to foreign government officials in the procurement of business from foreign governments. Passage of the Foreign Corrupt Practices Act of 1977[27] resulted from the bribery scandals connected to the Lockheed Aircraft Company's procurement of foreign government contracts. The Act requires strict accounting standards and internal control procedures to prevent the hiding of improper payments to foreign officials. The Act prohibits any offers, payments, or gifts to foreign officials, or third parties who might have influence with foreign officials, to influence a decision on behalf of the firm making the payment. It provides for sanctions of up to $1 million against the company, and for fines and imprisonment for the employees involved. The Act does not apply, however, to payments to low-level officials to expedite performance of routine government services.

[27]   PL 95–213, 94 Stat 1494.

SUMMARY

The General Agreement on Tariffs and Trade, a multilateral treaty subscribed to by the United States and most of the industrialized countries of the world, is based on the principle of trade without discrimination. The United Nations Convention on Contracts for the International Sale of Goods, influenced by UCC Article 2, provides uniform rules for international sales contracts between parties in contracting nations. The European Economic Community is a regional trading group that includes most of Western Europe. The U.S.-Canada FTA eliminates (over a ten-year period) duties on goods traded between the countries, opens markets for a wide range of services, lowers barriers to U.S. investments, and contains immigration provisions for business persons.

American firms may choose to do business abroad by making export sales or contracting with a foreign distributor to take title to their goods and sell them abroad. Such methods generally do not result in foreign presence for the U.S. firms. American firms may also license their technology or trademarks for foreign use. An agency arrangement, or the organization of a foreign subsidiary, may be required to participate effectively in foreign markets. This results in foreign presence for the U.S. firm, subjecting the firm to taxation in the host country. However, tax treaties commonly resolve the matter of double taxation.

The Export Administration Act is the principal statute imposing export controls on goods and technical data. The need for a validated license from the U.S. Department of Commerce (as opposed to a general license) is determined by a three-step process. This process involves determinations about the destination of the product, the product being exported, and whether special restrictions apply to the product. Falsification of information on a license application is a criminal offense.

In choosing the form for doing business abroad, U.S. firms must be careful not to violate the antitrust laws of host countries. Anticompetitive foreign transactions may have an adverse impact on competition in U.S. domestic markets. U.S. antitrust laws have a broad extraterritorial reach. The U.S. courts apply a "jurisdictional rule of reason" weighing the interests of the United States with the interests of the foreign country involved in making a decision on whether or not to hear the case. Illegal conduct may occur in the U.S. securities markets, which are used by citizens of most nations of the world. U.S. enforcement efforts sometimes run into foreign countries' secrecy and blocking laws that hinder effective enforcement.

Antidumping laws offer relief for domestic firms threatened by unfair foreign competition. In addition, economic programs exist to assist industries, communities, and workers injured by import competition. Programs also exist to bolster the export performance of U.S. firms.

QUESTIONS AND CASE PROBLEMS

1. What social forces are affected by the extraterritorial application of U.S. antitrust laws?
2. How does the most favored nation clause of the GATT work to foster the principle of trade without discrimination?
3. How does the selling of subsidized foreign goods in the United States adversely affect free trade?
4. Ronald Sadler, a California resident, owned a helicopter distribution company in West Germany, called Delta Avia. This company distributed American-made Hughes civilian helicopters in Western Europe. Sadler's West Germany firm purchased 85 helicopters from Hughes Aircraft Co. After validated export licenses were obtained in reliance on the purchaser's written assurance that the goods would not be disposed of contrary to the export license, the helicopters were exported to West Germany for resale in Western Europe. Thereafter Delta Avia exported them to North Korea (a country subject to a trade embargo by the United States). The helicopters were converted to military use. Sadler was charged with violating Export Administration regulations. In Sadler's defense, it was contended that the U.S. regulations have no effect as to what occurs in the resale of civilian helicopters in another sovereign country. Decide.

5. Mirage Investments Corporation (MIC) planned a tender offer for the shares of Gulf States International Corp. (GSIC). Archer, an officer of MIC, placed purchase orders for GSIC stock through the New York office of the Bahamian Bank (BB) prior to the announcement of the tender offer, making a $300,000 profit when the tender offer was made public. The Bahamas is a secrecy jurisdiction. The bank informed the SEC that under its law it cannot disclose the name of the person for whom it purchased the stock. What, if anything, may the SEC do to discover whether or not the federal securities laws have been violated?

6. National Dynamics Corp. (ND), a large defense contractor, has been selected by the oil-rich African nation of Nirombia to build and deliver 20 ND-21 jet fighter planes at an average price of $16 million per plane. ND's back orders are small, and it needs the contract to avoid layoffs of many hundreds of workers. At a meeting held in Nirombia to finalize the contract, the Prime Minister made it very clear to ND's senior representative that a "finder's fee" of .025 percent of the contract price would have to be deposited in his brother-in-law's account in Switzerland in order to finalize the contract. He pointed out that the contract was being made in

Nirombia where American law did not apply. He stated that such a payment was an ordinary business custom in his country and on the African continent and that such payment was offered by ND's European competitor if the contract were awarded to it. The Prime Minister laughed, saying "The percentage is so small you can consider it an entertainment expense if you want to." Advise National Dynamics.

7. Six major oil companies, four based in the United States and two in Western Europe, operate oil concessions in an African country. Five of these producers, concerned about the stability of their operations in this African country and seeking leverage in their dealings with its government, form a joint venture called Petro Supply Corp., incorporated in the Bahamas. The purpose of the joint venture is to arrange backup commitments from other African sources of scarce low-sulfur oil, which is required by environmental standards in the United States and Europe. They agree to pool such oil on a prorata basis among the participants. The three American firms (A, B, and C), the two European firms (D), in which the British government owns 50 percent of the stock, and E, in which the French government owns 50 percent of the stock, agree that the fourth American firm, Mesquite Petroleum of San Angelo, Texas, will not be included in the joint venture because of its cutthroat pricing tactics in both the United States and Europe and the reckless takeover ventures of the corporate chairman. The U.S. Justice Department contends in a court action that the joint venture is a violation of the Sherman Act. The joint venture contends that the U.S. court has no jurisdiction over a Bahamian corporation seeking oil supplies outside of the United States; it contends that the ownership by the British and French governments entitles the venture to sovereign immunity; and it contends that a joint venture to share the large and unusual risks involved in producing low-sulphur oil in the African nation is a justifiable business reason for the joint venture. Decide.

8. Assume that prior to the formation of the European Economic Community the lowest-cost source of supply for a certain product consumed in France was the United States. Explain the basis by which, after the EEC was formed, higher-cost German producers could have replaced the United States as the source of supply.

9. A complaint was filed with the U.S. Commerce Department's International Trade Administration (ITA) by U.S. telephone manufacturers AT&T, Comidial Corp., and Eagle Telephones, Inc. alleging that 12 Asian manufacturers of small business telephones, including the Japanese firms Hitachi, NEC, and Toshiba and the Taiwanese firm Sun Moon Star Corp, were dumping their small-business phones in the U.S. market at prices that were from 6 to 283 percent less than in their home markets. The U.S. manufacturers showed that the domestic industry's market share had dropped from 54 percent in 1985 to 33 percent in 1989. They asserted that it was doubtful if the domestic industry could survive the dumping. Later in a hearing before the International Trade Commission (ITC), the Japanese and Taiwanese respondents contended that the domestic industry was basically sound, and that the U.S. firms simply had to become more efficient to meet worldwide competition. They contended that the U.S. was using the procedures before the ITA and ITC as a nontariff barrier to imports. How should the ITC decide the case? [American Telephone and Telegraph Co. v Hitachi, 6 ITC 1511]

10. Timken Roller Bearing Co. of Ohio (American Timken) owns 30 percent of the outstanding shares of British Timken, a foreign competitor. In 1928 American Timken and British Timken organized French Timken, and since that time they have together owned all the stock of the French company. Since 1928 American Timken, British Timken, and French Timken have continuously kept operative "business agreements" regulating the manufacture and sale of antifriction bearings by the three companies and providing for the use by the British and French corporations of the trademark "Timken." Under these agreements the contracting parties have (1) allocated trade territories among themselves, (2) fixed prices on products of one of the parties sold in the territory of the others, and (3) cooperated to protect each other's markets and to eliminate outside competition. The United States Department of Justice contends that American Timken has violated Sections 1 and 3 of the Sherman Act. American Timken contends that its actions were legal, since it was entitled to enter a joint venture with British Timken to form French Timken, and was legally entitled to license the trademark "Timken" to the British and French companies. Decide. [Timken Roller Bearing Co. v United States, 341 US 593]

11. Roland Staemphfli was employed as the chief financial officer of Honeywell Bull S.A. (HB), a Swiss computer company operating exclusively

in Switzerland. Staemphfli purportedly arranged financing for HB in Switzerland through the issuance of promissory notes for DM 7,500,000. He had the assistance of Fidenas, a Bahamian company dealing in commercial paper. Unknown to Fidenas, the HB notes were fraudulent, having been prepared and forged by Staemphfli, who lost all of the proceeds in a speculative investment. Staemphfli was convicted of criminal fraud. HB denied responsibility for the fraudulently issued notes when they came due. Fidenas' business deteriorated because of its involvement with the HB notes. It sued HB and others in the United States for violations of the U.S. securities laws. HB defended that the U.S. court did not have jurisdiction over the transactions in question. Decide. [Fidenas v Honeywell Bull, S.A. (CA2 NY) 606 F2d 5]

12. Marc Rich & Co., A.G., a Swiss commodities trading corporation, refused to comply with a grand jury subpoena requesting certain business records maintained in Switzerland relating to crude oil transactions and possible violations of U.S. income tax laws. Marc Rich contends that a U.S. court has no authority to require a foreign corporation to deliver to a U.S. court documents located abroad. The court disagreed and imposed fines, froze assets, and threatened to close a Marc Rich wholly owned subsidiary that did business in the state of New York. The fines amounted to $50,000 for each day the company failed to comply with the court's order. Marc Rich appeals the judge's decision. Decide. [Marc Rich v United States (CA2 NY) 707 F2d 633]

13. The United States Steel Corporation formed Orinoco Mining Company, a wholly owned corporation, to mine large deposits of iron ore that U.S. Steel had discovered in Venezuela. Orinoco, which was incorporated in Delaware, was subject to Venezuela's maximum tax of 50 percent on net income. Orinoco was also subject to U.S. income tax, but the U.S. foreign tax credit offset this amount. U.S. Steel Corp. purchased the ore from Orinoco in Venezuela. U.S. Steel formed Navios, Inc., a wholly owned subsidiary, to transport the ore for it. Navios, a Liberian corporation, was subject to a 2.5 percent Venezuelan excise tax and was exempt from U.S. income taxes. Although U.S. Steel was Navios' primary customer, it charged other customers

the same price it charged U.S. Steel. U.S. Steel's investment in Navios was $50,000. In seven years Navios accumulated nearly $ 80 million in cash, but had not paid any dividends to U.S. Steel. The IRS used Internal Revenue Code Section 482 to allocate $52 million of Navios' income to U.S. Steel. U.S. Steel challenged this action, contending its charges to U.S. Steel were at arm's length and the same it charged other customers. Decide. [United States Steel Corp. v Commissioner (CA2 NY) 617 F2d 942]

14. On May 9, 1986 the Florida Citrus Mutual, which represents the U.S. concentrated orange juice industry, filed a petition with the ITA. The petition contended that Brazilian shipments of concentrated orange juice were selling at less than fair value (LTFV) and that increasing production and stock levels of the product in Brazil were undercutting the U.S. industry. The ITA ruled that the juice was being sold at LTFV. On April 13, 1987 the ITC concluded that the imported products were injuring or threatening to injure the U.S. industry. The importers contended that they had paid the significant shipping costs and all import duties and, in our free trade economy, they must be allowed to sell their products at any price they deem appropriate even if it should turn out to be less than the fair value of the product. Decide. [Florida Citrus Mutual v. Citrosuco Paulista S.A., 4 ITR 519]

15. Sensor, a Netherlands business organization wholly owned by Geosource, Inc. of Houston, Texas, made a contract with C.E.P. to deliver 2,400 strings of geophones to Rotterdam by September 20, 1982. The ultimate destination was identified as the U.S.S.R. Thereafter, in June of 1982, the President of the United States prohibited the shipment to the U.S.S.R. of equipment manufactured in foreign countries under license from U.S. firms. The President had a foreign policy objective of retaliating for the imposition of martial law in Poland. He was acting under regulations issued under the Export Administration Act of 1979. Sensor, in July and August of 1982, notified C.E.P. that as a subsidiary of an American corporation it had to respect the President's embargo. C.E.P. filed suit in district court of the Netherlands, asking that Sensor be ordered to deliver the geophones. Decide. [Compagnie Europeenne des Petroles v Sensor Nederland, 22 ILM 66]

7

CRIMES

Law sets the standards of conduct for all to follow. What happens when someone does not follow the law? There are two aspects to

* Computer crimes are discussed in Chapter 21.

the problem. On one hand, society wants to punish the wrongdoer and prevent others from repeating what was done. On the other hand, society, through the law, authorizes the victim to sue the wrongdoer for damages sus-

128

tained by the victim. The first phase of punishment and prevention is governed by principles of criminal law, discussed in this chapter. The second phase is governed by the principles of tort law, discussed in the next chapter.

It is important to bear in mind that society has made a choice of having both criminal law and tort law, as contrasted with having only one and not the other. By having both, society rejects any argument that it is unfair to punish a wrongdoer twice for one wrong.

A. GENERAL PRINCIPLES

A **crime** is an offense against the sovereign, a breach of public duty. Most crimes have certain common characteristics. These are discussed in the following sections.

1. Classification of Crimes

A crime may be classified according to the source of the criminal law, the seriousness of the offense, or the nature of the crime.

(a) SOURCE OF CRIMINAL LAW. Crimes are classified, in terms of their origin, as common law and statutory crimes. Some offenses that are defined by statute are merely declaratory of the common law. Each state has its own criminal law, although a common pattern among the states may be observed.

(b) SERIOUSNESS OF OFFENSE. Crimes are classified in terms of their seriousness as treason, felonies, and misdemeanors. Treason is defined by the Constitution of the United States, which states that "**Treason** against the United States, shall consist only in levying war against them, or in adhering to their enemies, giving them aid and comfort."[1] **Felonies** include the other more serious crimes, such as arson, murder, and robbery, which are punishable by confinement in prison or by death. Crimes not classified as treason or felonies are **misdemeanors**. Reckless driving, weighing and measuring goods with uninspected scales and measuring devices, and disturbing the

peace by illegal picketing are generally classified as misdemeanors. An act may be a felony in one state and a misdemeanor in another.

(c) NATURE OF CRIMES. Crimes are also classified in terms of the nature of the misconduct. **Crimes *mala in se*** are crimes that are inherently vicious or, in other words, that are naturally evil as measured by the standards of a civilized community. **Crimes *mala prohibita*** are acts that are only wrong because they are declared wrong by some statute.

2. Basis of Criminal Liability

A crime generally consists of two elements: (a) an act or omission, and (b) a mental state. Harm may occur as a result of a crime, but harm is not an essential element of a crime.

(a) MENTAL STATE. Mental state does not require an awareness or knowledge of guilt. In most crimes, it is sufficient that the defendant voluntarily did the act that is criminal, regardless of motive or intent. The lawmaker may make an act a crime even though the actor has no knowledge that a law is being broken. In some instances, a particular mental state is required, such as the necessity that a homicide be with **malice aforethought** in order to constitute murder. In some cases, it is the existence of a specific intent that differentiates one crime from other offenses. An assault with intent to kill is distinguished by that intent from an ordinary assault or from an assault with intent to rob.

Actions that are in themselves crimes are not made innocent by the claim that the defendant was exercising a constitutional right. Thus, freedom of speech does not give the right to send threatening letters.[2]

(b) HARM. Causing harm is typical of some crimes, such as murder or arson. Other crimes, however, are committed without harm to others. For example, a person may be guilty of speeding or reckless driving on the highway, although no one is hurt. In such case, it is the social judgment that the act condemned as a crime has such a potential for harm that the

---

[1] US Const, Art 3, § 3, Cl 1.

[2] Smith v Florida (Fla App) 532 So 2d 50 (1988).

FIGURE 7-1   THE LAW OF CRIMES

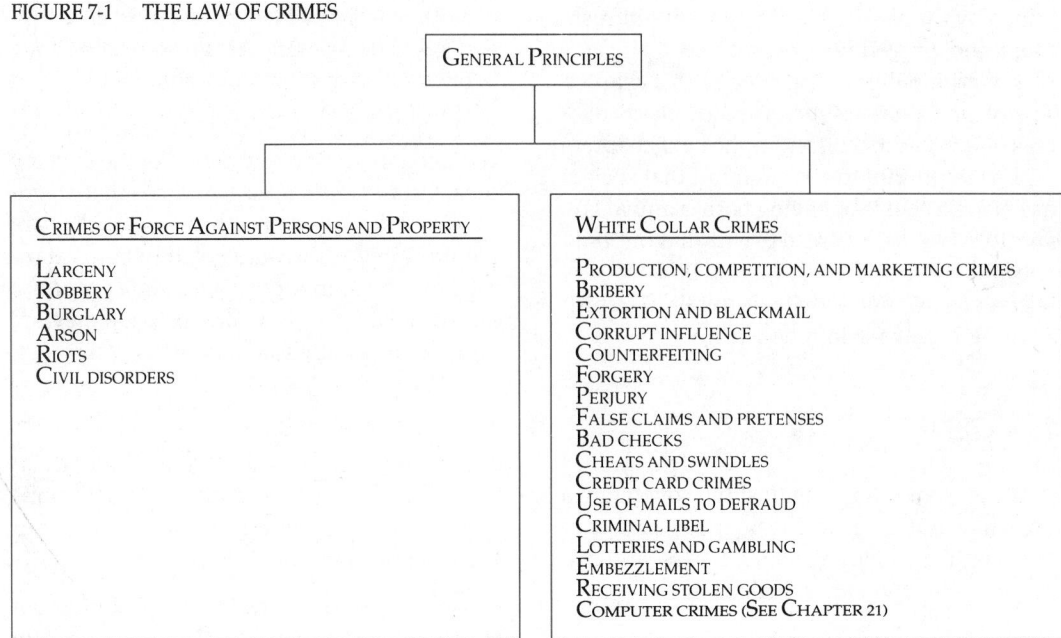

act should be prohibited before it does cause harm to others.

3.   Parties to a Crime

Two or more parties may directly or indirectly commit or contribute to the commission of a crime. At common law, participants in the commission of a felony may be principals or accessories. The statutory trend is to simplify or abolish these distinctions and to treat everyone taking part in a crime as being guilty of the crime. At times, the statutory change is basically a change of name, as when the crime of harboring a known fugitive is created in place of that of accessory after the fact. Sometimes a distinction is made in terms of first degree, second degree, and so on, to distinguish between different grades of conduct.

4.   Responsibility for Criminal Acts

In some cases particular persons are not held responsible for their criminal acts. In other cases, persons are held criminally responsible for acts committed by others.

(a) EMPLOYERS. An employer is liable for the crime committed by the employee when the employer directs or requires the commis-

sion of the crime. The fact that the employee is also guilty of a crime does not shield the employer; both the employer and the employee carrying out the wrongful plan are guilty of crimes. Thus, an employer is guilty of a crime when the employer gives the employee money to bribe a building inspector to overlook violations of the fire code. The employee is also guilty of the crime of bribery when the employee pays the money to the inspector.

When the employer has not directed the commission of the crime, the employer is not liable for an employee's crime that is committed outside of the scope of the employment of the employee.

(b) CORPORATIONS. The modern tendency is to hold corporations criminally responsible for their acts. A corporation may also be held liable for crimes based upon the failure to act. Thus, a corporation may be held criminally responsible when an employee is killed because of the corporation's failure to install the safety devices required by law.

In some instances the crime may be defined by statute in such a way that it requires, or is interpreted as requiring, a "living person" to commit the crime, in which case a corporation cannot be held criminally liable. Certain crimes, such as perjury, cannot be committed by corporations.

It is also usually held that crimes punishable only by imprisonment or corporal punishment cannot be committed by corporations. If the statute imposes a fine in addition to or in lieu of imprisonment or corporal punishment, a corporation may be convicted for the crime. Thus, a corporation may be fined for violating the federal antitrust law by conspiring to restrain interstate commerce.

(c) PERSONS UNDER INCAPACITY. Minors below a certain age, insane persons, and, to a limited extent, intoxicated persons are not responsible for their crimes. Intoxication generally does not relieve a person from criminal responsibility unless a crime requires specific intent that cannot be formed because of intoxication. Generally the law applicable to persons under incapacity comes from the common law, although there is an increasing trend toward statutory regulation.[3]

5.   Attempts and Conspiracies

Prior to the commission of an intended crime, there may be conduct that is itself a crime, such as an attempt or a conspiracy.

(a) ATTEMPTS. When the criminal fails to commit the crime intended, it may be that what has been done constitutes an **attempt**. Attempts are punished as distinct crimes. However, it is difficult to determine just what constitutes an attempt. Obviously, it is something less than committing the intended crime, but it must be more than merely preparing to commit that crime. Thus, the purchasing of a gun with which to kill the victim is not regarded as an attempt but as preparation and ordinarily is not itself a crime. However, when the criminal points the gun at the door through which the victim is expected to leave the building, an attempt has been committed. The modern trend is to condemn as an attempt any conduct that has reached such a point that the potential for harm to others is unreasonably great. Thus, a person attempt-

ing to fire a gun at the victim is guilty of an attempt even though the gun may malfunction. Likewise, a robber pointing a gun at the victim and demanding money is guilty of an attempt even though the robber changes his mind and does not take any money.

(b) CONSPIRACIES. A **conspiracy** is an agreement between two or more persons to commit an unlawful act or to use unlawful means to achieve an otherwise lawful result. The crime is the agreement, and generally it is immaterial that nothing is done to carry out the agreement. Some statutes, however, require that there be some act done to carry out the conspiracy before the crime is committed.

(c) NUMBER OF OFFENSES. If the criminal actually commits the intended crime, there is no criminal attempt. There can only be an attempt when the intended crime is not committed.

In contrast with the concept of an attempt, a conspiracy is a separate crime. Consequently, the fact that the intended crime is actually committed does not erase the conspiracy. Defendants may thus be prosecuted both for having conspired to commit the crime and for having committed the crime intended. They may be prosecuted for the conspiracy, although the contemplated crime, in fact, is not committed.

6.   Criminal Fines and Administrative Penalties Compared

The differences between a monetary penalty imposed by an administrative agency and a fine imposed by a court are very slight and largely theoretical. In both the administrative proceeding and the criminal court prosecution, the monetary penalty represents dollars paid by the defending party to the government. Both the fine and the penalty are imposed because the defending party failed to follow a standard of conduct required by the government.

In many instances, the administrative penalty will be significantly larger than fines im-

---

[3]   See, for example, Insanity Reform Act of 1984, § 401, PL 98–473, 98 Stat 2057, 18 USC § 402.

posed by a court. The reason is partly historical. The statute defining a particular crime and specifying the maximum fine ordinarily follows the pattern of an earlier statute that may be from the last century. What was then a large fine is today insignificant. Thus, a maximum fine inherited from the past may specify that the fine that can be imposed for armed robbery may not exceed $1,000. In contrast, the agency with power to impose a penalty is a creation of our time; therefore, any penalties are stated in terms of the modern purchasing power of the dollar. Thus, it is not unusual to authorize an agency to impose a penalty not to exceed $10,000. This difference in the maximum penalty may also be justified theoretically. For example, in the case of armed robbery there is one victim of the crime, whereas in the case of the administrative agency there may be many victims of the crime (e.g., factory's pollution of the environment).

7.   Indemnification of Crime Victims

Typically the victim of a crime does not benefit from the criminal prosecution and conviction of the wrongdoer. Any fine that is imposed upon the defendant is paid to the government and is not received in any way by the victim.

(a) STATUTORY ASSISTANCE. Several states have adopted statutes to provide a limited degree of indemnification to victims of crime in order to compensate them for the harm or loss sustained.[4] Under some criminal victim indemnification statutes, dependents of a deceased victim are entitled to recover the amount of the support that they were deprived of by the victim's death. The Victims of Crime Act of 1984 creates a federal Crime Victims Fund. This fund receives the fines paid into the federal courts and other moneys. From this fund, grants are made to the states to assist them in financing programs to provide indemnity to and assistance for victims of crime.[5] The Victim and Witness Protection Act of 1982 authorizes the sentencing judge in a federal district court to order, in certain cases, that the defendant make **restitution** (restoration) to the victim or pay the victim the amount of medical expenses or loss of income caused by the crime.[6]

Mob violence statutes frequently impose liability for property damage on the local government. The term *property* in such a statute generally applies to tangible property and does not authorize recovery for loss of profits or goodwill resulting from business interruption. The fact that the government was unable to prevent the harm or damage is not a defense to liability under such statutes.

(b) ACTION FOR DAMAGES. Although the criminal prosecution of a wrongdoer does not financially benefit the victim of the crime, the victim is typically entitled to bring a civil action for damages against the wrongdoer for the harm sustained. The modern pattern of statutes creating business crimes is to give the victim the right to sue for damages. Thus, the wrongdoer violating the federal antitrust act or the Racketeer Influenced and Corrupt Organizations Act (RICO) is liable to the victim for three times the damages actually sustained. A number of states have adopted statutes following the pattern of RICO. State statutes define racketeering broadly and cover both white collar and violent crimes.[7]

A damage suit may be brought under the federal act without proof of a "racketeering injury" or the prior conviction of the defendant.[8]

In the *Banderas* case the question was whether the Florida RICO authorized a civil

---

[4]   A Uniform Crime Victims Reparations Act has been adopted in Kansas, Louisiana, Montana, North Dakota, Ohio, and Texas.

[5]   Act of October 12, 1984, PL 98–473, 98 Stat 2170, 18 USC §§ 1401 et seq.

[6]   Act of October 12, 1982, PL 97–291, 96 Stat 1253, 18 USC § 3579, amended by Act of November 15, 1990, PL 101–581, 104 Stat 2865, 18 USC § ___. A defendant does not have a right to a jury trial to determine the restitution, as the right to a jury trial does not extend to the sentencing after conviction, and restitution is an element of sentencing. Iowa v Mayberry (Iowa) 415 NW2d 644 (1987).

[7]   Georgia v Shearson Lehman Brothers, Inc. 188 Ga App 120, 372 SE2d 276 (1988).

[8]   Sedima, S.P.R.L. v Imrex Co., Inc. 473 US 479 (1985).

action for damages when (1) the misconduct was making a false claim for payment and (2) there was no proof that the defendant was related to organized crime.

BANDERAS v BANCO CENTRAL DEL ECUADOR
(Fla App) 461 So 2d 265 (1985)

The Banco Central administered a humanitarian plan for the government of Ecuador. Fernando Banderas and his wife presented false claims that were paid by the bank. After the fraud was discovered, the bank sued Banderas and his wife for damages for fraud and treble damages under the Florida version of RICO. Defendants asserted that they were not liable for RICO damages because there was no proof that they were related to organized crime and because the wrong committed by them was merely ordinary fraud. They had not used any racketeering methods. From a judgment in favor of the bank, the defendants appealed.

HENDRY, J. . . . Appellants raise . . . on appeal: 1) whether the civil damages provisions of RICO were improperly applied to these defendants because there was no showing that they were connected to organized crime; 2) whether the civil damages provisions were improperly applied to a mere "garden variety" fraud case.

The Florida RICO Act, promulgated in 1977, is nearly identical to the federal RICO statute, 18 U.S.C. §§ 1961–1968 (1970), passed as Title IX of the Organized Crime Control Act of 1970. Thus, we can also look to a wealth of material on the federal RICO statute for guidance on this issue. The legislative history shows that Congress was clearly concerned, during the drafting of this bill, with the constitutional problems associated with trying to limit the statute's target to "organized crime" only; that is, that the statute would not survive attacks on the grounds that it was unconstitutionally overbroad or that it created status crimes. Status crimes, related as they are to the old English bills of attainder, are especially disfavored. *Cf. Robinson v California*, 370 U.S. 660 (1962) (state cannot make drug addiction a crime); *Lanzetta v New Jersey*, 306 U.S. 451 (1939) (state cannot make being a "gangster" a crime). Secondly, Congress deliberately made the scope of the statute as broad as possible "to avoid opening loopholes through which the minions of organized crime might crawl to freedom." Congress chose the only course available to it which would effectuate the broad purpose of the statute without creating serious constitutional issues. It imposed enhanced sanctions for the types of activities which were characteristic of "organized crime." Thus, all persons who engage, over a period of time, in activities which Congress has defined as being "racketeering activities" are subject to criminal prosecution or civil litigation under RICO.

Against this background, it is now well established in the federal courts that it is not necessary to prove a nexus to organized crime in order to obtain damages in a private civil RICO suit.

Appellants' second argument, that the trial court permitted Central Bank to turn a "garden variety" fraud case into a treble damage civil RICO action is, paraphrasing Mr. Justice Cardozo, to spread the study of horticulture to unaccustomed fields. *United States v Constantine*, 296 U.S. 287, 299 (1935) (Cardozo, J., dissenting). We cannot accept appellants' argument. The statute makes no distinction between levels or degrees of fraudulent activity. *See* § 895.02(1)(a)16. Thus, courts are not in a position to decide whether certain frauds are "garden variety" subject only to simple compensatory and possible punitive damages, and whether other frauds are "exotic arrangements" meriting the full range of enhanced penalties available under RICO. Fraud is not so easily parsed.

Section 895.02(4) defines "pattern of racketeering activity" as:

> Engaging in at least two incidents of racketeering conduct that have the same or similar intents, results, accomplices, victims, or methods of commission or that otherwise are interrelated by distinguishing characteristics and are not isolated incidents, provided at least one of such incidents occurred within 5 years after a prior incident of racketeering conduct.

This case fits precisely within the parameters of the statute. This was not a technical securities or business fraud. This was a well-organized, ongoing, systematic, criminal scheme devised by appellants to defraud the government of Ecuador—their own government.

At some time prior to June, 1981, appellants and Florida Aviation Corp. [FAVCO] and Banla formed a conspiracy for the express purpose of carrying out this scheme. In furtherance of this scheme, these appellants created four fictitious "hospitals" in three different states [Florida, Texas and Missouri]. Appellants sent "statements," in medical terminology, on invoices which they caused to be printed in the names of these non-existent hospitals. They sent seventy of these statements over the course of thirteen months, which the Central Bank paid in good faith. The bank didn't realize there was a problem with the medical assistance program until the spring of 1982 when an employee at Southeast Bank noticed that the address listed for St. John's Hospital corresponded to a vacant lot. Appellants earned over $851,000.00 on a few dollars invested in printing and a medical dictionary. Innocent banks were drawn into the scheme. As a result, there were also violations of the federal mail and wire fraud statutes. . . . This case presents one version of precisely the sort of activity that should, without controversy, fall within the statute's application.

[Judgment affirmed]

QUESTIONS

1. What is the importance of not requiring a RICO plaintiff to prove that the defendant was connected to organized crime?
2. Did the case present a simple common law fraud?
3. Is passing a bad check conduct that brings the wrongdoer under a RICO-type statute?

(c) INDEMNIFICATION OF UNJUSTLY CONVICTED. From time to time an innocent person is convicted of a crime. When the truth is learned, the person is, of course, released from prison. The state legislature typically pays the person indemnity to compensate for the wrong that has been done. In some states this right to indemnity is expressly established by statute, as in the case of the New York Unjust Conviction and Imprisonment Act.[9]

---

[9]   Carter v New York (Court of Claims) 528 NYS2d 292 (1988).

8. Sentencing

The problem of sentencing the convicted criminal is one of the most difficult problems in the administration of justice. The difficulty is that society is caught between conflicting social purposes. Uniformity and stability are desired. At the same time, flexibility is desired in order to make the punishment fit both the crime and the criminal. Earlier this century, the emphasis has been on flexibility in sentencing. This, however, has produced a very inconsistent pattern of sentencing. Various reform movements are underway to secure more uniform sentencing of criminals.[10]

(a) THE INDIGENT DEFENDANT. When a court imposes sentence, it cannot impose an alternative (1) fine or (2) imprisonment if the defendant does not have the money to pay the fine. For example, it is unconstitutional to sentence a defendant to "$30 or 30 days."[11] This conclusion is reached on the ground that such a sentence in the alternative discriminates on the basis of poverty by making the poor person, who cannot pay the fine, go to jail, while the rich person pays the fine and walks out of the court.

(b) WHITE COLLAR CRIMES. There is much criticism about the sentencing of white collar criminals on the ground that the penalties are not sufficiently large to serve the purpose of punishing the defendant or of deterring others from committing similar crimes. It can be recognized that there is a reluctance on the part of judges to send an otherwise respectable person to jail. But one of the fundamentals of our American system is equality before the law; therefore, no exception should be made because the defendant had a good standing or a good education. In some in-stances the lawmaker is at fault in failing to provide punishments that fit the crime.

(c) FORFEITURE OF CRIME-RELATED PROPERTY. When a defendant is convicted of a crime, the court may also declare that the defendant's rights in any instrument of that crime are forfeited. When the forfeited property can be used only for a criminal purpose, as in the case of engraved plates used for making counterfeit money, there is no question of the right of the government to confiscate the property. This confiscation is allowable even though this, in effect, increases the penalty imposed on the defendant.

Forfeiture is not limited to property that can be used only for crime. Thus, an automobile that is used to carry illegal merchandise may itself be seized by the government, even though it is obvious that the automobile could also be put to a lawful use.

As we move into the area of white collar crime, this problem of defining crime-related property becomes increasingly difficult because the property involved is not by itself criminal, or even potentially criminal, in character. Legislation in this area has been directed at depriving the wrongdoer of the gains obtained by the crime or of taking away the power to benefit from the crime. An example of the first type of legislation is the Sherman Antitrust Act, under which a defendant guilty of unlawfully acquiring the stock of competing corporations may be ordered by the court to sell or otherwise dispose of such shares. This is called a **divestiture order**. Illustrative of both the first and the second type of legislation is the federal RICO Act. Under RICO the court is required to enter an order against the defendant to forfeit any property acquired or used in exercising unlawful racketeering influence. Under RICO the fruits of the racketeering activity and related property may be forfeited regardless of their nature.[12]

In the *Kravitz* case the defendant attacked the validity and application of the RICO forfeiture provisions.

---

[10] The Sentencing Reform Act of October 12, 1984, Chapter 227, PL 98–473, 98 Stat 1987, 18 USC §§ 3551 et seq. contains provisions designed to produce greater uniformity in sentencing. Mistretta v United States, 488 US 361 (1989). The Commissioners on Uniform Laws have proposed a Model Sentencing and Corrections Act.

[11] Tate v Short, 401 US 395 (1971).

[12] 4447 Corporation v Goldsmith (Ind) 504 NE2d 559 (1987).

UNITED STATES v KRAVITZ

(CA3 Pa) 738 F2d 102 (1984)

Kravitz owned 100 percent of the stock of American Health Programs, Inc. (AHP). In order to obtain the Philadelphia Fraternal Order of Police as a customer for AHP, Kravitz paid money bribes to persons whom he thought were officers of that organization, but who, in fact, were federal undercover agents. He was prosecuted for violating RICO. He was convicted, and the court ordered the forfeiture of all of the shares of stock of AHP owned by Kravitz. He claimed that the court was not required to order the forfeiture and that the statute was unconstitutional as interpreted. From a decision against Kravitz, he appealed.

GIBBONS, C.J. . . . Charles Kravitz appeals from a judgment of sentence imposed following his conviction for violations of the Racketeer Influenced and Corrupt Organizations Act, 18 U.S.C. § 1961 *et seq.* (1982) ("RICO"). He contends that his conviction should be set aside, and that in any event the court erred in ordering forfeiture of his interest as a stockholder in American Health Programs, Inc. (AHP). We hold that his objections to the RICO convictions are without merit, and that the forfeiture order was proper.

A primary question presented by this appeal is whether forfeiture under section 1963 is mandatory upon a finding that the appellant's property was used to promote racketeering. We conclude, as have all other courts to decide the question, that forfeiture is mandatory.

Several factors compel that conclusion. The first is the plain meaning of the language employed in section 1963(a), stating that "whoever violates any provision of section 1962 . . . shall forfeit to the United States" the illegally used interest. As the Fifth Circuit pointed out in *United States v L'Noste,* 609 F2d 796 (CA5, 1980), although there are occasions where "shall" has been interpreted to vest discretionary, rather than mandatory, authority to act, the wording of the statute is the most persuasive evidence of Congressional intent. Nor does the legislative history ever discuss forfeiture in discretionary terms. The wording of the remaining penalties established under section 1963(a) also supports a mandatory interpretation of forfeiture: section 1963(a) states that a defendant "shall be fined not more than $25,000 or imprisoned not more than twenty years, *or both*" (emphasis added). Thus, where Congress intended for the penalty to be optional, as in the choice between fine or imprisonment, they specified that there was such a choice. The section's wording provides no choice regarding the imposition of forfeiture.

Moreover, a literal reading of section 1963(a) is consistent with RICO purposes. The criminal forfeiture provision was viewed as an innovative means of addressing the spread of organized crime that has infiltrated so many aspects of American society. Of foremost concern during Congressional hearings on RICO was the weakness of current efforts at curtailing the spread of organized crime to legitimate business endeavors. For instance, the Senate Judiciary Committee's report quoted the Attorney General's testimony that:

> While the prosecutions of organized crime leaders can seriously curtail the operations of the Cosa Nostra, as long as the flow of money continues, such prosecutions will only result in a compulsory retirement and promotion system as new people step forward to take the place of those convicted.

S.Rep. No. 91–617 91st Cong. 1st Sess. 78 (1969). The report stated that forfeiture as a penalty for the criminal offense—although disfavored throughout American history—was an innovative approach which could provide the linchpin in the renewed effort against organized crime:

> Title IX recognizes that present efforts to dislodge the forces of organized crime from legitimate fields of endeavor have proven unsuccessful. To remedy this failure, the proposed statute adopts the most direct route open to accomplish the desired objective. Where an organization is acquired or run by defined racketeering methods, then the persons involved can be legally separated from the organization, either by the criminal law approach of fine, imprisonment and forfeiture, or through a civil law approach of equitable relief broad enough to do all that is necessary to free the channels of commerce from all illicit activity.

In light of RICO's central goal of inhibiting organized crime's infiltration of legitimate business, it is certainly not likely that forfeiture was viewed by its drafters as an optional penalty. At the least, a mandatory interpretation of section 1963(a)'s forfeiture would promote, rather than discourage, RICO's intended purpose. Indeed, it is consistent with RICO's own construction clause, Pub.L. No. 91–452, § 904(a), 84 Stat. 922, 947 (1970), which states that the statute "shall be liberally construed to effectuate its remedial purposes."

When Congress has opted to provide for discretionary forfeiture, it has done so expressly. Thus, under the Internal Revenue Laws there is district court discretion to remit or mitigate the forfeiture. 18 U.S.C. § 3617 (1982). The Organized Crime Control Act itself elsewhere contains a permissive, rather than mandatory, forfeiture provision. In establishing penalties for illegal gambling, Congress provided that "any property . . . used in violation of the provisions of this section may be seized and forfeited to the United States." 18 U.S.C. § 1955(d) (1982).

Finally, we note that where Congress did provide for the remission or mitigation of the forfeiture order, it vested that decisionmaking authority with the Attorney General, not the federal courts. . . .

Kravitz also challenges the forfeiture on eighth amendment grounds. He argues that forfeiture constitutes a disproportionate penalty because AHP's contract with the FOP expired prior to indictment. Since AHP was no longer providing services pursuant to the illegally secured contract, Kravitz would have us accept that the taint upon the property had dissipated, and thus that the order of forfeiture was cruel and unusual punishment, in violation of the eighth amendment.

Kravitz's eighth amendment argument completely ignores the nature of RICO's forfeiture provision. Forfeiture under RICO is . . . designed as part of the punishment for the criminal offense committed. It is simply incorrect that the termination of the criminal conduct bars the imposition of punishment. Although . . . forfeiture is not commonly used in our system of jurisprudence, it is nonetheless a legitimate weapon in the enforcement of our criminal laws and, as with any punishment for criminal conduct, may be imposed despite the cessation of the criminal conduct charged in the indictment.

[Judgment affirmed]

QUESTIONS

1. What kind of property was ordered forfeited?

2.   Would you classify the property forfeited as an instrument of crime?
3.   Is it material whether the forfeited property is acquired by means of crime?

B.   WHITE COLLAR CRIMES

Those crimes that do not use, or threaten to use, force or violence or do not cause injury to persons or physical damage to property are called **white collar crimes**. Computer crimes, a type of white collar crime, are discussed in Chapter 21 of this text. A particular defendant may be guilty of both a white collar crime and a traditional crime of the kind described in Part C of this chapter.

9.   Crimes Related to Production, Competition, and Marketing

A person or enterprise in business may be guilty of various crimes relating to labor and employment practices, conspiracies and combinations in restraint of trade, price discrimination, and environmental pollution. These crimes are discussed in Chapters 4 and 51.

(a) IMPROPER USE OF INTERSTATE COMMERCE. The shipment of improper goods or the transmission of improper information in interstate commerce constitutes a crime under various federal statutes. Thus, it is a federal crime to send in interstate commerce a statement as part of a scheme to defraud; to send a blackmail or extortion threat; to ship adulterated or misbranded foods, drugs, or cosmetics; or to ship into a state child-labor-made or convict-labor-made goods or intoxicating liquor when the sale of such goods is prohibited by the destination state.

(b) SECURITIES CRIMES. In order to protect the investing public, both state and federal laws have regulated the issuance and public sale of stocks and bonds.[13] Between 1933 and 1940 seven such regulatory statutes were adopted by Congress. As a practical matter, these federal statutes have largely displaced state statutes by virtue of the principle of federal preemption. Violation of these statutes is typically made a crime.

10.   Bribery

Bribery is the act of giving money, property, or any benefit to a particular person to influence that person's judgment in favor of the giver of the bribe. At common law the crime was limited to doing such acts to influence a public official. In this century, the common law concept has expanded to include commercial bribery. Thus, it is now a crime to pay a competitor's employee money in order to obtain secret information about the competitor.

The giving and the receiving of a bribe each constitute a crime. In addition, the act of seeking to obtain a bribe may be a crime of solicitation of bribery. In some states bribery is broadly defined to include solicitation of bribes.[14]

The crime of bribery is complete when the bribe has been paid or received. Whether the person paying the bribe obtains what was bargained for does not affect the guilt of either the giver or the receiver of the bribe.

11.   Extortion and Blackmail

Extortion and blackmail are crimes by which the wrongdoer seeks to force the victim to do some act—typically paying money—that the victim would not otherwise desire to do.

(a) EXTORTION. When a public officer, acting under the apparent authority of the office, makes an illegal demand, the officer has committed the crime of **extortion**. For example, if a health inspector threatens to close down a restaurant on a false charge of violation of the sanitation laws unless the restaurant pays the inspector a sum of money, the inspector has committed extortion. If the res-

---

[13]   See Chapter 48, Section 10.

[14]   Martinez v Texas (Tex App) 696 SW2d 930 (1985).

taurant voluntarily offers the inspector the money to prevent the restaurant from being shut down because of actual violations of the sanitation laws, the crime committed would be bribery.

Modern statutes tend to ignore the "public officer" aspect of the common law and expand extortion to include obtaining anything of value by threat. This might be in connection with loansharking or labor racketeering. In a number of states, statutes extend the extortion concept to include the making of "terroristic threats."[15]

(b) BLACKMAIL. In jurisdictions where extortion is limited to conduct of public officials, a nonofficial commits **blackmail** by making demands that would be extortion if made by a public official. Ordinarily, the concept of blackmail is used in the context of a threat to give publicity to some matter that would damage the victim's personal or business reputation.

12.   Corrupt Influence

In harmony with changing concepts of right and wrong, society has increasingly outlawed practices on the ground that they exerted a corrupting influence on business transactions. To some extent this objective of the law was attained by applying the criminal law of extortion, blackmail, and bribery to business situations. In time the definitions of these crimes were expanded to include practices similar to the old crimes but not within the technical definition of such crimes. Thus, the crime of bribery was extended to include commercial bribery.

(a) IMPROPER POLITICAL INFLUENCE. In order to protect from the improper influencing of political or governmental action, various acts have been classified as crimes. For instance, it is a crime for the holder of a government office to be financially interested in or to receive money from an enterprise that is seeking to do business with the govern-

ment. Such conflict of interests is likely to produce a result that is harmful to the public. Thus, lobbyists and foreign agents must register in Washington, D.C.,[16] and must adhere to statutes regulating the giving and receiving of contributions for political campaigns. Violation of these regulatory statutes is a crime.

(b) IMPROPER COMMERCIAL INFLUENCE. The protection from improper influence is extended to the commercial world by statutes making it a crime to engage in commercial bribery, to engage in loansharking, to use gangster methods to influence legitimate business, or to run a legitimate business for the purpose of laundering gangster money.

Under federal statutes, it is a crime to obtain a benefit by means of a threat of economic or physical loss or harm, to use racketeering methods or money obtained from racketeering to acquire an interest in a legitimate business, or to travel in interstate commerce for the purpose of engaging in racketeering activities. A person convicted of such crimes is subject to punishment by fine, imprisonment, and the forfeiture of money obtained by the criminal conduct. The convicted defendant is also subject to civil liability to the victims of the crime.[17]

13.   Counterfeiting

It is a federal crime to make, to possess with intent to pass, or to pass counterfeit coins, bank notes, or obligations or other securities of the United States. Legislation has also been adopted against the passing of counterfeit foreign securities or notes of foreign banks.

The various states also have statutes prohibiting the making and passing of counterfeit coins and bank notes. These statutes often provide, as does the federal statute, a punishment for the mutilation of bank notes or the lightening or mutilation of coins.

[15]   Pennsylvania v Bunting, 284 Pa Super 444, 426 A2d 130 (1981).

[16]   Foreign Agents Registration Act, Act of June 8, 1938, 52 Stat 631, 22 USC §§ 611 et seq., as amended.
[17]   Act of June 25, 1948, 62 Stat 793, 18 USC § 1951; Travel Act of September 13, 1961, PL 87–228, 75 Stat 498, 18 USC § 1952; Racketeer Influenced and Corrupt Organizations Act of October 15, 1970, PL 91–452, 84 Stat 941, 18 USC §§ 1961 et seq., Criminal Control Act of 1990, Act of November 29, 1990, PL 101–647, 104 Stat 4789, 18 USC § ___.

14.   Forgery

Forgery consists of the fraudulent making or material altering of an instrument, such as a check, that apparently creates or changes a legal liability of another person. The instrument must have some apparent legal efficacy in order to constitute forgery.

Ordinarily, forgery consists of signing another's name with intent to defraud. It may also consist of making an entire instrument or altering an existing one. It may result from signing a fictitious name or the offender's own name with the intent to defraud.

When the nonowner of a credit card signs the owner's name on a credit card invoice without the owner's permission, such act is a forgery.

The issuing or delivery of a forged instrument to another person constitutes the crime of "uttering" a forged instrument. Any sending of a forged check through the channels of commerce or of bank collection constitutes an "uttering" of a forged instrument. Thus, the act of depositing a forged check into the forger's bank account by depositing it in an automatic teller machine constitutes "uttering" within the meaning of a forgery statute.[18]

15.   Perjury

Perjury consists of knowingly giving false testimony in a judicial proceeding after having been sworn or having affirmed to tell the truth. By statute, knowingly making false answers on any form filed with a government is typically made perjury or is subjected to the same punishment as perjury. In some jurisdictions, the out-of-court offense is called false swearing.

16.   False Claims and Pretenses

Many statutes declare it a crime to make false claims or to obtain goods by false pretenses.

(a) FALSE CLAIMS. A statute may expressly declare that the making of a false claim is a crime. The federal False Statement statute makes it a crime to knowingly and willfully

make a false, material statement as to any matter within the jurisdiction of any department or agency of the United States.[19] Thus, it is a crime for a contractor to make a false claim against the United States for payment for work that was never performed by the contractor. Other statutes indirectly regulate the matter by declaring that the signing of a false written claim constitutes perjury or is subject to the same punishment as perjury.

(b) OBTAINING GOODS BY FALSE PRETENSES. In almost all of the states, statutes are directed against obtaining money or goods by means of false pretenses. These statutes vary in detail and scope. Sometimes the statutes are directed against a particular form of deception, such as using a bad check. In some states the false pretense crime has been expanded to include obtaining anything of value or services by false pretenses. In any case an intent to defraud is an essential element of obtaining property by false pretenses.[20]

The Trademark Counterfeiting Act of 1984[21] makes it a federal crime to deal in goods and services under a counterfeit mark.

False representations as to future profits or the identity of the defendant are other common forms of false pretenses.

17.   Bad Checks

The use of a bad check is commonly made a crime by a statute directly aimed at the use of bad checks. In the absence of a bad check statute, the use of a bad check could generally be prosecuted under a false pretenses statute.

Under a bad check statute it is a crime to use or pass a check with knowledge that there will not be sufficient funds in the bank to pay the check when it is presented for payment. Knowledge that the bad check will not be paid when presented to the bank is an essential element of the crime.

A statute making the issuing of a bad check a crime punishable by imprisonment

---

18   Wisconsin v Tolliver (Wis App) 440 NW2d 571 (1989).

19   United States v Petullo (CA7 Ill) 709 F2d 1178 (1983).
20   North Carolina v Compton, 90 NC App 101, 367 SE2d 353 (1988).
21   Act of October 12, 1984, § 1502, PL 98–473, 98 Stat 2178, 18 USC § 113.

does not violate a constitutional prohibition against imprisonment for debt.[22]

The bad check statutes typically provide that if the check is not made good within a specified number of days after payment by the bank is refused, it is presumed that the defendant had acted with the intent to defraud.

18.   Cheats and Swindles

Various statutes are designed to protect the public from being deceived.

(a) FALSE WEIGHTS, MEASURES, AND LABELS. Cheating, defrauding, or misleading the public by use of false, improper, or inadequate weights, measures, and labels is a crime. Both the federal and state governments have adopted many statutes on this subject.

(b) SWINDLES AND CONFIDENCE GAMES. The act of a person who, intending to cheat and defraud, obtains money or property by trick, deception, fraud, or other device, is an act known as a **swindle** or **confidence game**. Bad stock and spurious works of art are frequently employed in swindling operations.

The essential elements of the crime of confidence game are (1) an intent to defraud, (2) the creation of confidence of the victim in the defendant, (3) intentional false statements as to past or existing facts, and (4) in some states, the sustaining by the victim of a loss of more than a stated amount, such as $50.[23]

19.   Credit Card Crimes

It is a crime to steal a credit card and, in some states, to possess the credit card of another person without the consent of that person. The use of a credit card without the permission of the rightful cardholder constitutes the crime of obtaining goods or services by false pretenses or with the intent to defraud. Likewise, a person continuing to use a credit card with knowledge that it has been canceled is guilty of the crime of obtaining goods by false pretenses.

When, without permission, the wrongdoer signs the name of the rightful cardholder on the slip for the credit card transaction, the wrongdoer commits the crime of forgery. The district attorney has the discretion to choose the particular crime for which to prosecute the wrongdoer.

The Credit Card Fraud Act of 1984[24] makes it a federal crime to obtain anything of value in excess of $1,000 in a year by means of a counterfeit credit card, to make or traffic in such cards, or to possess more than 15 counterfeit cards at one time.

20.   Use of Mails to Defraud

Congress has made it a crime to use the mails to further any scheme or artifice to defraud. To constitute this offense, there must be (a) a contemplated or organized scheme to defraud or to obtain money or property by false pretenses, and (b) the mailing or the causing of another to mail a letter, writing, or pamphlet for the purpose of executing or attempting to execute such scheme or artifice. Illustrations of schemes that come within the statute are false statements to secure credit, circulars announcing false cures, false statements to induce the sale of stock of a corporation, and false statements as to the origin of a fire and the value of destroyed goods for the purpose of securing indemnity from an insurance company. Federal law also makes it a crime to use a telegram or a telephone to defraud.

21.   Criminal Libel

A person who falsely defames another without legal excuse or justification may be subject to criminal liability as well as civil liability. Criminal libel is made a crime because of its tendency to cause a breach of the peace. Under some statutes, however, the offense appears to be based on the tendency to injure another.

No publication or communication to third persons is required in the case of criminal libel. The offense is committed when the de-

---

22   Steeley v Alabama (Ala Crim App) 533 So 2d 665 (1988).

23   Lane v Oklahoma (Okla Crim App) 742 P2d 577 (1987).

24   Act of October 12, 1984, § 1029, PL 98–473, 98 Stat 2183, 18 USC § 1029.

fendant communicates the libel directly to the person libeled as well as when it is made known to third persons.

The truth of the statement is a defense in civil libel. In order to constitute a defense to criminal libel, the prevailing view requires that a proper motive on the part of the accused be shown as well as proof that the statement was true.

In a number of states **slander** (oral defamation) or particular kinds of slander have also been made criminal offenses by statutes.

22.   Lotteries and Gambling

Running lotteries and gambling are common statutory crimes.

(a) LOTTERIES. There are three elements to a **lottery**: (a) a payment of money or something of value for an opportunity to win, (b) a prize, (c) by lot or chance. If these elements are present, it is immaterial that the transaction appears to be a legitimate form of business or advertising, or that the transaction is called by some name other than a lottery, such as a raffle. The sending of a chain letter through the mail is generally a federal offense, both as mail fraud and as an illegal lottery, when the letter solicits contributions or payments.

In many states, government lotteries are legal.

The question has frequently been raised, as in the *St. Augustine* case, whether bingo is a lottery.

SECRETARY OF STATE v ST. AUGUSTINE CHURCH
(Tenn) 766 SW2d 499 (1989)

The Tennessee constitution declares that "the legislatures shall have no power to authorize lotteries for any purpose." The Tennessee legislature adopted several statutes legalizing bingo when conducted for a charitable purpose. St. Augustine Church conducted bingo games for charitable purposes. The Secretary of State brought an action against the church for conducting a "lottery." The church raised the defense that it was protected by the charitable bingo statutes. The court held that the statutes were unconstitutional and that bingo was an illegal lottery. St. Augustine Church appealed. Several organizations intervened in the appeal to assert that bingo was not a lottery.

HARBISON, J. . . . [The constitution's] terms are sweeping and absolute. It simply removes from the General Assembly the authority to authorize lotteries for any purpose—charitable, public, private, or any other. . . .

We recognize, of course, that the constitutional provision did not prohibit all types of gambling. Except for lotteries, there is nothing in the constitution of the State prohibiting gambling, and the regulation of all other types of gambling, except lotteries, is a matter for determination by the General Assembly. The latter may prohibit all types of gambling, or it may legalize some and regulate others. Any form of gambling which consists of a lottery, however, may not be authorized or sanctioned by the General Assembly.

The statutes . . . in this case . . . purported to exempt the game of bingo from the general statutes against gambling and to regulate its conduct by a licensing system. Implicitly, of course, the General Assembly must have concluded that bingo was not a "lottery" but simply a form of gambling which it could authorize and regulate. In our opinion this conclusion was erroneous. . . . The more recent statutes proceeded on the theory that when cards for bingo play were sold by charitable, religious and similar organizations, the payment made by the customer constituted a charitable contribution rather than a wager, so long as the other terms and provisions of the regulatory statutes were observed.

It is the insistence of the appellants, . . . that the provisions of the state constitution . . . were designed to abolish and outlaw only the older forms of "ticket lotteries" which were prevalent in the early nineteenth century and which have again become enormously popular in some states. . . .

The state constitution does not define the term "lottery," but the word is one of general usage. . . .

> 1: a scheme for the distribution of prizes by lot or chance; *esp:* a scheme by which prizes are distributed to the winners among those persons who have paid for a chance to win them usu. as determined by the numbers on tickets as drawn at random (as from a lottery wheel) . . . 2: the occasion of selection of prizes by lot 3: an event or affair whose outcome is or seems to be determined by chance . . . (*Webster's Third New International Dictionary* 1338 (1981)).

. . . The first definition contained in *Black's Law Dictionary* 853 (5th ed. 1979) is as follows:

> A chance for a prize for a price. Essential elements of a lottery are consideration, prize and chance and any scheme or device by which a person for a consideration is permitted to receive a prize or nothing as may be determined predominantly by chance.

. . . In the statutes . . . under consideration . . ., the General Assembly undertook to remove the game of bingo from the definition of a lottery by terming the consideration paid by a customer as a charitable contribution rather than a wager. This, in our opinion, is an ineffective means to circumvent the constitutional prohibition, so long as the other elements of prize and chance are present.

Of course, the game "bingo" was not known in 1835 when the original Tennessee constitutional provision became effective. According to the briefs of the parties, the game was first introduced into the United States about 1928. It, of course, like many other games, may be played as a simple parlor game purely for the amusement of the participants. In this respect it is no different from dominoes, parcheesi, or any number of other perfectly innocent parlor games, although it demands less skill on the part of the player and turns almost wholly on the random drawing of numbers.

When conducted on a commercial scale,* however, for profit, and when chances, or tickets, are sold for a consideration, it is agreed by all parties that bingo becomes a form of gambling. In our opinion, "bingo" clearly constitutes a lottery within the meaning of the Tennessee Constitution. . . .

In several states, earlier constitutional prohibitions against lotteries have been amended or modified so that the playing of bingo, either through charitable organizations or under other regulatory schemes, could be legalized by the state legislature. *See e.g.,* Cal. Const. art IV, § 19(c) (1966, amended 1976).

The intervening appellants have relied primarily upon two decisions which held that constitutional prohibitions against lotteries were confined to the earlier form of ticket lotteries and did not include bingo. . . . We decline to follow these decisions.

---

* The record in this action shows that receipts from "bingo" operations in Tennessee totalled thirty-one million dollars in 1987.

This Court expresses no opinion, of course, as to the desirability of the legalization of bingo or any other form of gambling. . . . Under the present constitutional provisions, however, the General Assembly may not authorize any form of lottery. . . . The game of bingo . . . simply falls within the generally accepted definition of the term "lottery."

. . . In our opinion no legislative definition of "bingo" could remove the game as traditionally played from that form of gambling known as a lottery.

[Judgment affirmed]

QUESTIONS

1. What did the court hold and why?
2. The decision of the court was in harmony with the will of the people of Tennessee. Appraise this statement.
3. Could the state legislature reverse the decision of the *St. Augustine* case by adopting a statute declaring that bingo was not a lottery?

(b) GAMBLING. **Gambling** is a crime under modern statutes. It is similar to a lottery in that there are the three elements of payment, chance, and prize. Equipment used in gambling is generally declared by law to be contraband and may be confiscated by the government. If the winner of an electronic video card game receives something of value as a prize, the game is an illegal gambling device. Statutes commonly make it a crime to use a "device" as a means of aiding a gambler.

(c) CHARITABLE PURPOSE. Gambling conducted by a charity is unlawful gambling even though the purpose is to raise funds for a charitable purpose.[25]

23. Embezzlement

Embezzlement is the fraudulent conversion of another's property or money by a person to whom it has been entrusted. An example would be an employee's taking of the employer's money for the employee's own use. Embezzlement is a statutory crime designed to cover the case of unlawful takings that are not larceny because the wrongdoer did not take the property from the possession of another,

and not robbery because there is neither a taking nor the use of force or fear.

It is immaterial whether the defendant received the money or property from the victim or from a third person to deliver to the victim. Thus, an agent commits embezzlement when the agent receives and keeps payments from third persons—payments the agent should have remitted to the principal. Likewise, when an insured gives money to an insurance agent to pay the insurance company but the insurance agent uses the money to pay premiums on the policies of other persons, the agent is guilty of embezzlement. Generally, the fact that the defendant intends to return the property or money embezzled, or does in fact do so, is no defense.

Today, every jurisdiction has not only a general embezzlement statute but also various statutes applicable to particular situations, such as embezzlement by trustees, employees, and government officials.

24. Receiving Stolen Goods

The crime of **receiving stolen goods** is the receiving of goods that have been taken with the intent to deprive the owner of them. To be guilty of the crime of receiving stolen goods, a person must know or have reasonable cause to believe that the property was stolen. It is

---

[25]   Charnes v Central City Opera House Ass'n (Colo) 773 P2d 546 (1989).

immaterial that the receiver does not know the identity of the owner or of the thief.

C.   CRIMES OF FORCE AND CRIMES AGAINST PROPERTY

In contrast with the white collar crimes are those that involve the use of force, threat of force, or that cause injury to persons or damage to property. Such crimes that affect businesses are discussed in the following sections.

25.   Larceny

Larceny is the wrongful or fraudulent taking and carrying away of the personal property of another by any person with a fraudulent intent to deprive the owner of such property. The place from which the property is taken is generally immaterial, although by statute the offense is sometimes subjected to a greater penalty when property is taken from a particular kind of building, such as a warehouse. Shoplifting is a common form of larceny. In many states, shoplifting is made a separate crime.

Although the term is broadly used in everyday speech, not every unlawful taking is a larceny. At common law, a defendant who took property of another with the intent to return it was not guilty of larceny. This has been changed in some states so that a person who "borrows" a car for a joyride is guilty of larceny, theft, or some other statutory offense.

Statutes in many states penalize as **larceny by trick** the use of any device or fraud by which the wrongdoer obtains the possession of, or title to, personal property from the true owner. In some states all forms of larceny and robbery are consolidated into a statutory crime of theft.[26] At common law there was no crime known as "theft."

26.   Robbery

Robbery is the taking of personal property from the presence of the victim by use of force

or fear. In most states, there are aggravated forms of robbery, such as robbery with a deadly weapon. Snatching a necklace from the neck of the victim involves sufficient force to constitute robbery.[27] When the unlawful taking is not by force or fear, as when the victim does not know that the property is being taken, the offense is larceny, but it cannot be robbery. In contrast, when the property is taken from the victim by use of force or fear, there is both robbery and larceny. In such case the prosecuting attorney will determine for which crime the defendant is to be prosecuted.

27.   Burglary

At common law, **burglary** was the breaking and entering in the nighttime of the dwelling house of another, with the intent to commit a felony therein. When the wrongdoer inserts an automatic teller card in an automatic teller machine set in the wall of the bank, that insertion of the card constitutes an "entry" into the bank for the purpose of constituting burglary.[28] While one often thinks of burglary as stealing property, any felony would satisfy the definition. The criminalization of such an act was aimed primarily at protecting the habitation. Thus, it illustrates the social objective of protection of the person—in this case, the persons living or dwelling in the building.

Modern statutes have eliminated many of the elements of the common law definition,so that under some statutes it is immaterial when or whether there is an entry to commit a felony. The elements of breaking and entering are frequently omitted. Under some statutes, the offense is aggravated and the penalty is increased in terms of the place where the offense is committed, such as a bank building, freight car, or warehouse. Related statutory offenses have been created, such as the crime of possessing burglar's tools.

28.   Arson

At common law, **arson** was the willful and

---

[26]   Washington v Southard, 49 Wash App 59, 741 P2d 78 (1987).

[27]   Illinois v Taylor, 129 Ill 2d 80, 133 Ill Dec 466, 541 NE2d 677 (1989).

[28]   California v Ravenscroft, 198 Cal App 3d 642, 243 Cal Rptr 827 (1988).

malicious burning of the dwelling house of another. Thus, it was designed to protect human life, although the defendant was guilty if there was a burning of the building even though no one was actually hurt. In most states arson is a felony, so that if someone is killed in the resulting fire, the offense is murder by application of the felony-murder rule. Under the felony-murder rule, homicide, however unintended, occurring in the commission of a felony is automatically classified as murder. Statutes may expand the kind of property involved in arson. Thus, a statute may make it arson to burn a "structure" of such a nature that persons are commonly present.

In virtually every state, a special offense of **burning to defraud** an insurer has been created by statute. Such burning is not arson when the defendant burns the defendant's own house in order to collect the insurance money.

29. Riots and Civil Disorders

Damage to property in the course of a riot or civil disorder is ordinarily the same type of crime as though only one wrongdoer were involved. That is, there is a crime of larceny or arson and so on, depending on the nature of the circumstances, without regard to whether one person or many are involved. In addition, the act of assembling as a riotous mob and engaging in civil disorders is generally some form of crime in itself, without regard to the destruction or theft of property, whether under common law concepts of disturbing the peace or under modern antiriot statutes.

A statute may make it a crime to riot or to incite to riot. However, a statute relating to inciting must be carefully drawn, to avoid infringing upon constitutionally protected free speech.

SUMMARY

When a person does not live up to the standards set by the law, society may regard the conduct of the defendant as so dangerous to the government, to people, or to property that society will prosecute the defendant for such misconduct. This punishable conduct, called *crime*, may be common law or statutory in origin. Crimes are classified as treason, felony, and misdemeanor. A felony is a crime that is punishable by imprisonment or death.

In terms of the parties taking part in a crime, there are principals and accessories. The statutory trend is to abolish distinctions and to treat everyone taking part in a crime as being guilty of the crime.

Employers and corporations may be criminally responsible for their acts and the acts of their employees. Minors, the insane, and the intoxicated are held criminally responsible to a limited extent. This means that in some cases they will not be held responsible for a crime when a normal, adult person would be held responsible.

Crimes are often classified in terms of whether force or violence is involved. The phrase *white collar crime* is frequently used in reference to crimes that do not involve force or violence. Among white collar crimes are those relating to illegal methods of production, competition, and marketing, such as the illegal use of interstate transportation and communication. Other white collar crimes include crimes relating to securities, such as stocks and bonds; computer crimes; bribery; extortion; blackmail; and crimes relating to the exercise of improper influence in politics and in business. Also included as white collar crimes are counterfeiting, forgery, perjury, the making of false claims against the government, and the obtaining of goods or money by false pretenses. The use of bad checks; the use of false weights, measures, and labels; swindles and confidence games; dealing in counterfeit credit cards and possessing more than 15 such cards at one time; using the mails to defraud; making defamatory statements about another; engaging in lotteries and gambling; embezzlement; and receiving stolen goods are other white collar crimes.

In contrast with the foregoing crimes are the crimes of force and violence. Most common of these crimes, relating to property, are larceny, robbery, burglary, arson, and burning to defraud an insurer. Taking part in a riot or civil disorder may be a crime in itself, in addition to the traditional forms of crime that

may be committed in the course of the riot or disorder.

There is no uniform law of crimes. Each state and the federal government defines and punishes crimes as it chooses. Although there is a tendency to follow a common pattern, there are many variations as to details between the law of different states and the federal law.

QUESTIONS AND CASE PROBLEMS

1. What is the objective of the rule of law that a person buying a gun with the intent to kill a neighbor is not guilty of attempted murder?

2. What is a crime that is *malum in se*?

3. Hunter was employed by the Watson Corporation. He was killed at work by an explosion caused by the gross negligence of the corporation. The corporation was prosecuted for manslaughter. It raised the defense that only people could commit manslaughter and that it was therefore not guilty. Was this defense valid?

4. Johnny took a radio from the Englehart Music Store without the knowledge of any clerk that he was removing it. He was then prosecuted for larceny. He claimed that he could only be prosecuted for shoplifting because larceny was a serious felony, and all that he had done was to take merchandise from a store. Was this defense valid?

5. Garrison purchased goods that she knew had been stolen. When the police traced some stolen articles and discovered Garrison's activities, Garrison was prosecuted for embezzlement. Was she guilty?

6. Compare larceny, robbery, and embezzlement.

7. Gail drove her automobile after having had dinner and several drinks. She fell asleep at the wheel and ran over and killed a pedestrian. She was prosecuted for manslaughter and raised the defense that she did not intend to hurt anyone and because of the drinks did not know what she was doing. Was this a valid defense?

8. A state law made it a crime to use a "device to assist . . in analyzing the probability of the occurrence of an event relating to the game." The defendant took part in a card game played for money. Unknown to the other players, he had a microcomputer that he used to show the probabilities of cards appearing in the game. This was discovered, and he was prosecuted under the law quoted above. He raised the defense that a microcomputer was not a "device." Was he guilty of violating the statute? Why did the statute state "device" rather than listing the specific devices that were to be outlawed? [Sheriff, Clark County, Nevada v Anderson, 103 Nev Adv 119, 746 P2d 643]

9. Buckley took a credit card from the coat of its owner with the intent never to return it. He then purchased some goods at a department store and paid for them by presenting the credit card to the sales clerk and then signing the credit card slip with the name of the owner of the credit card. What crimes, if any, did Buckley commit? [Buckley v Indiana, 163 Ind App 113, 322 NE2d 113]

10. Berman organized Greatway Travel, Ltd. Greatway sold travel consultant franchises and promised that the franchisees would receive various discounts and assistance. None of these promises were ever kept because Greatway lost all its money through mismanagement. Berman was prosecuted for obtaining money by false pretenses. Was he guilty? [Berman v Maryland, 35 Md App 193, 370 A2d 580]

11. Lang and his wife lived in a trailer in a trailer park. Winhoven broke into the trailer in order to steal. He was prosecuted and convicted of breaking and entering "an occupied dwelling" with the intent to commit larceny. He raised the defense that he had not broken into an occupied dwelling but into a trailer. Was he correct? [Michigan v Winhoven, 65 Mich App 522, 237 NW2d 540]

12. Mary Jacobs was a tenant in New Martinsville Towers, a government-financed housing pro-

ject. The rent of tenants was determined by their ability to pay. Barnes was in charge of the management of the Towers. He borrowed $7,800 from Jacobs on the basis that he was going to buy Easter clothes and other items for his family, and he would see to it that the rent of Jacobs was not raised and that she would be given a particular job. He did not have any authority to prevent an increase in the rent nor to obtain the job, and he knew he had no such authority. The rent of Jacobs was thereafter increased, and she did not get the job. Barnes was prosecuted for obtaining property by false pretenses. He raised the defense that he had spent the money for the purpose that he had stated and therefore was not guilty of a crime. Was he correct? [West Virginia v Barnes (W Va) 354 SE2d 606]

13. Skelton attempted to rob a general store. He used a small wooden toy pistol. The attempt failed, and he was arrested. He was prosecuted for attempted armed robbery. Was he guilty? [Illinois v Skelton, 83 Ill 2d 58, 46 Ill Dec 571, 414 NE2d 455]

14. Jennings operated a courier service to collect and deliver money. The contract with his customers gave Jennings a day or so to deliver the money that had been collected. Instead of holding collections until delivered, Jennings made short-term investments with the money. He always made deliveries to the customers on time but kept the profit from the investments for himself. He was prosecuted for larceny. Was he guilty? [New York v Jennings, 69 NY2d 103, 512 NYS2d 652, 504 NE2d 1079]

15. A person is guilty of the crime of passing a bad check whenever there is not sufficient money in the bank to cover the amount of the check. Appraise this statement.

8

TORTS

When a wrong has been done that has caused harm to someone, the law generally allows the injured person to recover monetary damages from the wrongdoer. When the wrong that has been done is the breaking of a contract, the right of the aggrieved person is governed by contract law. When there is no contract, the right of the aggrieved person is typically governed by tort law.

A. GENERAL PRINCIPLES

In this chapter you will see many points at

which there is a gradual expansion of the law of torts. This expansion is being made in response to what society thinks is right as it strives to promote the social forces described in Chapter 2.

1.   Tort and Crime Distinguished

A crime is a wrong arising from a violation of a public duty, whereas a **tort** is a wrong arising from a violation of a private duty. More practically stated, a crime is a wrong of such a serious nature that the state steps in to take some action to punish the wrongdoer and to deter others from committing the same wrong. Whenever the act that is punished as a crime causes harm to an identifiable person, that person may sue the wrongdoer for monetary damages to compensate for the harm. As to the person harmed, the wrongful act is called a tort; as to the government, that same wrongful act is a crime. If, however, a crime does not hurt an identifiable person, it is not a tort. For example, bribing a public official is a crime, but no individual person is harmed, so no tort is committed. Conversely, there may be a tort even though there is no crime. For example, if

I walk away with your coat wrongly but honestly thinking that it is mine, I have committed the tort of conversion. That is, I have committed an act wrongful to you. However, I have not committed any crime because I did not have the mental state necessary to constitute a crime such as larceny or theft.

2.   Tort and Breach of Contract Distinguished

The wrongs or injuries caused by a breach of contract arise from the violation of an obligation or duty created by the agreement of the parties. In contrast, a tort arises from the violation of an obligation or duty created by law. The same act may be both a breach of contract and a tort. For example, when an agent exchanges property instead of selling it as directed by the principal, the agent is liable for breach of contract and for the tort of conversion.

3.   Basis of Tort Liability

The mere fact that a person is hurt or harmed in some way does not mean that such person

FIGURE 8-1   TORT LAW

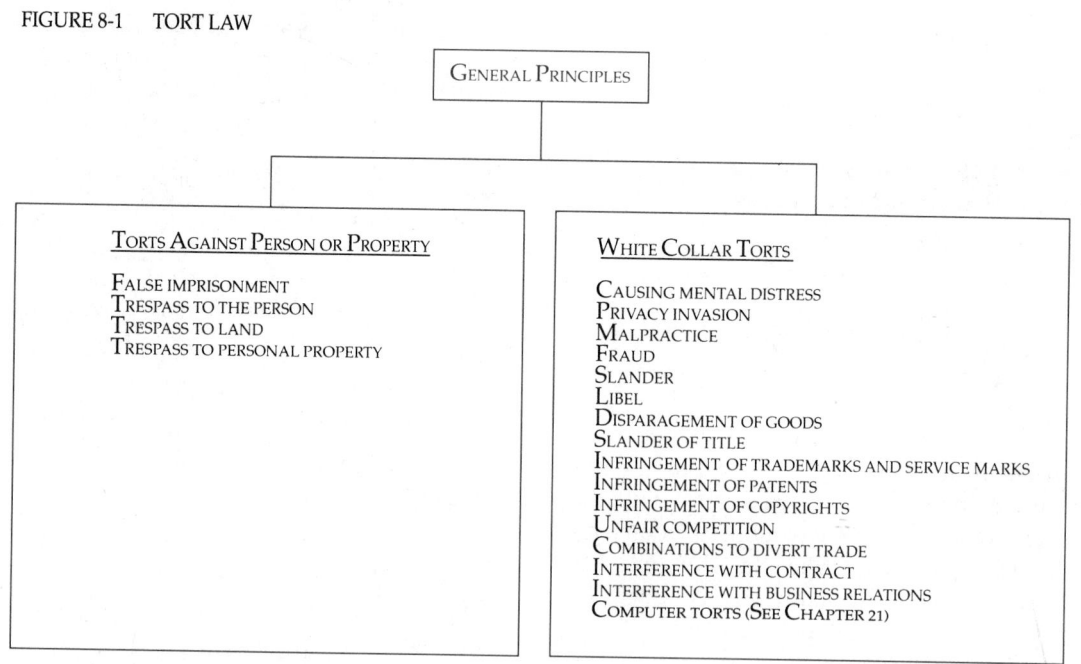

can sue and recover damages from the person causing the harm. There must exist a recognized basis for liability.

(a) DUTY. The mere fact that someone is hurt does not mean that someone else must pay for the harm. Society does not want to go that far. In trying to state how far society will go, many courts speak in terms of a duty having been broken. That is, the plaintiff will not be allowed to recover from the defendant if the defendant did not break a duty that was owed to the plaintiff. There is a strong modern trend to ignore whether there is a duty. By this view, the court looks directly at the facts and considers whether there are interests involved that should be protected from harm. If the defendant has harmed such an interest, the defendant is required to pay for the damages.

(b) VOLUNTARY ACT. The defendant must be guilty of a voluntary act or omission. Acts committed or omitted by one who is confronted with a sudden peril caused by another are considered involuntary acts.

(c) INTENT. Whether intent to do an unlawful act or intent to cause harm is required as a basis for tort liability depends on the nature of the tort involved. Liability is imposed for some torts even though the person committing the tort acted without any intent to do wrong. Thus, a person going on neighboring land without consent of the landowner is liable for the tort of trespass, even though such action was caused by an honest mistake as to the location of the boundary line.

In other torts, the intent of the actor is an essential element. Thus, in the case of slander and interference with contracts, it is necessary for the plaintiff to show that the defendant intended to cause harm or at least had the intent to do an act that a reasonable person would anticipate was likely to cause harm.

(d) MOTIVE. As a general rule, motive is immaterial except as evidence to show the existence of intent. In most instances, a legal right may be exercised even with bad motives, and an act that is unlawful is not made lawful by good motives.

(e) CAUSAL RELATIONSHIP. As a matter of elementary justice, liability for harm should not be imposed unless the defendant's conduct was in some way the cause of the harm. But should a defendant be held liable for every consequence that flows from the defendant's act? Assume that the defendant has negligently run over and killed the key employee of a large industrial enterprise. Assume further that because of that death, the enterprise goes out of business. This harms its other employees, stockholders, creditors, and the families of all of these, and also the stores where all of these people would buy goods. Should the defendant be held liable for every penny of harm suffered by all of these people because of the negligently caused death of the key employee?

The social force of protecting from hardship causes the law to draw the line at some point and say that no money can be recovered for harm sustained beyond that line. Courts are agreed as to this general objective, but there is conflict as to how and where to draw the dividing line between liability and nonliability.

(1) Proximate Cause. Some courts hold that the defendant's misconduct must be the **proximate cause** of the harm, using *proximate* to mean the cause that was immediately next to the harm. Some courts define *proximate* as conduct of such a nature that "but for" that conduct the harm would not have been sustained. The modern trend is to regard a cause as sufficient to impose liability when it was a substantial factor in producing the harm, as contrasted with being the sole cause of the harm.[1]

(2) Foreseeability. In many instances the courts define a causal relationship in terms of foreseeability. That is, if it was reasonably foreseeable that the conduct of the defendant could cause harm to the plaintiff, there is a sufficient causal relationship between the defendant's conduct and the plaintiff's harm to impose liability.

(3) Act of Third Person. A wrongful act of a third person may take effect between the

---

[1]   Domingue v Louisiana Department of Public Safety (La App) 490 So 2d 772 (1986).

time that the defendant acted or failed to act and the time the plaintiff is injured. This occurrence does not establish that the causative chain between the defendant's conduct and the plaintiff's harm has been broken. The action of a third person, therefore, does not insulate the defendant from liability for the plaintiff's harm. If the conduct of the third person was foreseeable, it does not relieve the defendant from liability to the plaintiff. To the contrary, both the defendant and the third person are liable to the plaintiff. The question of division of liability, discussed in Chapter 8, Section 7 of this book, then arises.

The fact that the plaintiff is harmed by a criminal act of a third person does not break the chain of liability when the defendant was under a duty to protect the plaintiff from the class of harm that was sustained. Thus, a multistory garage, operated on a park-it-yourself-and-lock basis, was liable to the plaintiff parking her car in the garage when she was robbed at gunpoint. The garage was negligent in failing to provide adequate security for the protection of its customers or to warn them that no security was provided.[2]

(f) LIABILITY FOR TORT OF EMPLOYEE OR CHILD. A person may be innocent of wrong yet be held liable for the tort committed by another person. As will be discussed later in the chapters on agency, the tort of an employee or agent may, in some cases, impose liability on the employer or principal.

A parent is ordinarily not liable for the tort committed by a child. That is, the mere fact that the person sued is the parent of the child committing the wrong does not in itself impose liability on the parent.[3]

There are several instances, however, in which a parent will be held liable. If the parent knows that the child has a dangerous characteristic, such as a disposition to set houses on fire, and does not take reasonable steps to prevent this, the parent will be held liable for the harm caused by the child. If the child is a reckless driver and the parent allows the child to use the parent's car, the parent is liable on the theory that the parent was negligent in entrusting the car to the child. In about half of the states, a parent supplying a family car is liable for any harm negligently caused by any member of the family while driving the car. In some states, any person lending an automobile is liable for the harm caused by the negligence of the person borrowing or renting the car. In some states, statutes make a parent liable for willful or malicious property damage caused by minor children. Such statutes generally specify a maximum limitation on such liability and are constitutional.[4]

4.   Liability-Imposing Conduct

Generally, American law imposes tort liability only when there is some fault on the part of the defendant. Thus, it is required either that the defendant intended to cause the harm of the plaintiff or that the defendant was negligent. In a number of instances the law of this century has made exceptions to the concept that liability can only be based on fault and has imposed liability solely because the plaintiff has been harmed by the act of the defendant. Although there is a duty to act in good faith, there is no tort of bad faith. Thus, a defendant who acts within legal or contract rights is not liable to the plaintiff on the theory that the defendant exercised those rights in bad faith.

5.   Absolute Liability

In some areas of the law, liability for harm is imposed without regard to whether there was any fault on the part of the defendant—that is, without regard to whether there was any negligence or intention to cause harm. For example, in most states when a contractor blasts with dynamite and debris is hurled onto the land of another, the landowner may recover damages from the contractor even though the contractor was not negligent and did not intentionally cause the harm.

---

[2]   Allright, Inc. v Pearson (Tex App) 711 SW2d 686 (1986).
[3]   Jackson v Moore, 190 Ga App 329, 378 SE2d 726 (1989).

[4]   Distinctive Printing and Packaging Co. v Cox, 232 Neb 846, 443 NW2d 566.

By this concept of absolute liability, society is saying that the activity is so dangerous to the public that liability must be imposed even though no fault is present. Yet society will not go so far as to outlaw the activity. Instead, a compromise is made. The activity is allowed to continue, but the one who stands to benefit from the activity must pay its injured victims regardless of the circumstances under which the injuries are inflicted.

(a) INDUSTRIAL ACTIVITY. Generally, there is absolute liability for harm caused by the storage of inflammable gas and explosives in the middle of a populated city; crop dusting when the chemical used is dangerous to life and the dusting is likely to be spread by the wind; and for factories emitting dangerous fumes, smoke, and soot in populated areas. However, the mere fact that activity is industrial in nature does not mean that absolute liability is to be applied. Thus, drilling and operating a natural gas well is not an activity that results in absolute liability.[5]

(b) CONSUMER PROTECTION. Pure food statutes may impose absolute liability on the seller of foods in favor of the ultimate consumer who is harmed by them. Decisions and statutes governing product liability impose liability although the defendant is not negligent and intends no harm.

(c) WILD ANIMALS. A person keeping a wild animal is absolutely liable for any harm caused by it. This liability is not affected by the fact that the animal was tamed and the owner had no reason to foresee that harm would occur.

(d) NO-FAULT LIABILITY. **No-fault liability** is another name for absolute liability. However called, the defendant is liable for harm caused the plaintiff by virtue of the fact that such harm was caused the plaintiff. Liability is imposed without regard to whether there is fault or intention to harm on the part of the defendant.

No-fault liability is based on statutes. Usually, recovery on no-fault liability is less than the liability that would exist if fault of the defendant could be established. Generally, the plaintiff is allowed to prove such fault and recover a greater amount when serious injury or death has been caused.

Today no-fault liability is associated with automobiles. A half century before the no-fault concept was applied to automobile liability, it became the basis for workers' compensation. Under such statutes, the worker is compensated when employment-related harm is sustained, without any question being raised as to the presence or absence of fault on the part of the employer. The amount recovered by a worker is smaller than could be recovered if a common law action could be prosecuted. The injured worker who is covered by workers' compensation is restricted to the recovery permitted by such law and does not have the choice of bringing a lawsuit to seek a larger recovery.

6.   Negligence

The widest range of tort liability today arises in the field of **negligence**, which exists whenever the defendant has acted with less care than would be exercised by a reasonable person under the circumstances. Such negligence must be causally related to the harm sustained by the plaintiff.

(a) THE "REASONABLE PERSON." The reasonable person whose behavior is made the standard is an imaginary person. In a given case that is tried before a jury, "reasonable" is what appears to the composite, or combined, minds of the jurors to be sensible or suitable under the circumstances.

This reasonable person does not represent any one of the jurors or an average of the jurors. The law is not concerned with what the jurors would do in a like situation, for it is possible that they may be more careful or less careful than the abstract reasonable person.

(b) VARIABLE CHARACTER OF THE STANDARD. By definition the standard is a variable standard, for it does not tell you in

5   Williams v Amoco Production Co. 241 Kan 102, 734 P2d 1113 (1987).

advance what should be done. This is confusing to everyone, in the sense that the exact answer in any borderline case is unknown until the lawsuit is over. From the standpoint of society, however, this flexibility is desirable because it is obviously impossible to foresee every possible variation in the facts that might arise and even more impossible to keep such a code of conduct up-to-date. Imagine how differently the reasonable person must act while driving today's automobile on today's superhighways than when driving a Model T on dirt roads three-quarters of a century ago.[6]

(c) DEGREE OF CARE. The degree of care required of a person is that which an ordinarily prudent person would exercise under similar circumstances. It does not mean such a degree of care as would have prevented the harm from occurring, nor is it enough that it is just as much care as everyone else exercises. It is not sufficient that one has exercised the degree of care that is customary for persons in the same kind of work or business, or that one has employed the methods customarily used. If one is engaged in services requiring skill, the care, of course, must measure up to a higher standard. In any case, the degree of care exercised must be commensurate with the danger that would probably result if such care were lacking. In all cases, it is the diligence, care, and skill that can be reasonably expected under the circumstances. Whether one has exercised the degree of care that is required under the circumstances is a question that is determined by the jury.

(d) CONTRIBUTORY NEGLIGENCE. At common law a plaintiff could not recover for injuries caused by another's negligence if the plaintiff's own negligence had contributed to the injury. The plaintiff guilty of contributory negligence was denied recovery without regard to whether the defendant was more negligent. The common law did not recognize comparative degrees of negligence, nor did it try to apportion the injury to the two parties in terms of the degree of their respective fault.

In order to avoid the harshness of the common law rule as to contributory negligence, there developed a doctrine variously called the doctrine of last clear chance, the humanitarian doctrine, and the doctrine of discovered peril. Under this concept, although the plaintiff was negligent, the defendant was liable if the defendant had the last clear chance to avoid the injury. When the defendant had such opportunity but did not make use of it, the theory was that the plaintiff's negligence was not the cause of the harm sustained.

(e) COMPARATIVE NEGLIGENCE. In most states the common law rule as to contributory negligence has been rejected. States rejecting the common law rule regard it as unjust that the plaintiff who has been contributorily negligent should forfeit all rights even when the plaintiff's negligence was slight in comparison to the defendant's negligence. These states provide that there should be a comparing of the negligence of the plaintiff and the defendant. The negligence of the plaintiff does not bar recovery but only reduces the plaintiff's recovery to the extent that the harm was caused by the plaintiff's fault. For example, if the jury decides that the plaintiff had sustained damages of $100,000 but that the plaintiff's own negligence was one-fourth the cause of the damage, the plaintiff would be allowed to recover $75,000. At common law the plaintiff in such case would have recovered nothing.

In some states the comparative negligence concept is modified by ignoring the negligence of the plaintiff if it is slight and the negligence of the defendant is great or gross. At the other extreme, some states refuse to allow the plaintiff to recover anything if the negligence of the plaintiff was more than 50 percent of the cause of the harm.

---

[6]   As the law is stated, in terms of "reasonableness" it is necessary to make a value judgment in which the extent of harm is measured against the cost and burden of taking precaution to prevent the harm. That is, "when the product of the possibility of escape multiplied times the gravity of the harm, if it happens, exceeds the burden of precautions, the failure to take those precautions is negligence." Levi v Southwest Louisiana Electric Membership Cooperative (La) 542 So 2d 1081 (1989).

The trend of the law is to apply the concept of comparative fault to all actions, even though the defendant's alleged liability is based on warranty, strict tort, or absolute liability.

In the *Langley* case, the argument was made that the court should abolish the defense of contributory negligence and substitute the concept of comparative negligence.

LANGLEY v BOYTER
(App) 284 SC 162, 325 SE2d 550 (1984)

Robin Langley and James Boyter were driving automobiles in opposite directions on a two-lane highway. At a curve in the road the two cars collided. Each driver claimed that the other had crossed into the wrong lane. Langley sued Boyter for the damages sustained. Langley requested the judge to instruct the jury that any negligence on her part would merely reduce the amount that she could recover. The judge refused to do so and instructed the jury that any negligence on Langley's part barred her from recovering anything. The jury returned a verdict against Langley. A judgment was entered in favor of Boyter, and Langley appealed.

SANDERS, C. J. . . . To paraphrase John Locke, there is nothing less powerful than an idea whose time is gone. In our opinion, the doctrine of contributory negligence is an idea whose time is gone in South Carolina. It is extinct almost everywhere it once existed. It no longer exists in England, the country of its birth. It survives only in parts of this country, where it is threatened and endangered. Indeed, the doctrine of contributory negligence exists today as the Ivory-Billed Woodpecker of the common law.

The continued existence of the doctrine of contributory negligence as presently applied in South Carolina cannot be justified on any logical basis. It is contrary to the basic premise of our fault system to allow a defendant, who is at fault in causing an accident, to escape bearing any of its cost, while requiring a plaintiff, who is no more than equally at fault or even less at fault, to bear all of its cost. . . .

While we agree that juries may often ignore the law because of its harshness, we view this proclivity as a compelling reason to abrogate the doctrine rather than retain it. There is something fundamentally wrong with a rule of law which is so contrary to the convictions of ordinary citizens that, when serving as jurors, they often refuse to enforce it in violation of their oaths. The disrespect for the law engendered by perpetuating such a rule is obvious. . . .

We are of the opinion that the common law doctrine of contributory negligence should no longer be applied in South Carolina, and the doctrine of comparative negligence should be adopted in its place. There remains the question of which form of the doctrine of comparative negligence should be adopted.

The four leading versions of the doctrine are the slight-gross version, two modified versions, and the pure version.

Under the slight-gross version, if the defendant's negligence is gross and the plaintiff's negligence is slight, then the plaintiff may recover, with his damages reduced in proportion to his own negligence. This version has been adopted by statute in only two states and has not been looked on with favor by the commentators and courts. There appears to be very little difference in this version from the exception to the doctrine of contributory negligence already recognized in South Carolina which provides that a plaintiff guilty of simple contributory negligence is not barred from recovery against a defendant whose conduct is reckless.

The two modified versions of the doctrine of comparative negligence are similar to each other. One allows recovery by the plaintiff if his negligence was *not as great as* the negligence of the defendant. The other modified version allows the plaintiff to recover if his negligence is *not greater than* the defendant's negligence. In both versions, recovery is reduced by the amount of the plaintiff's negligence. The majority of the states have adopted one of these two versions. The recent trend in the states has been toward the latter version.

Under the pure version of comparative negligence, the plaintiff may recover even if his negligence is greater than that of the defendant, with his recovery diminished by the amount of his negligence. This version is recognized in a minority of the states. . . .

We choose the not-greater-than version of the doctrine for essentially two reasons. Unlike the pure version, it does not allow a plaintiff to recover when he has been the most at fault in causing an accident. But, unlike the not-as-great-as version, it does not allow a defendant to escape all responsibility for an accident which he was equally at fault in causing. Instead, the not-greater-than version of the doctrine strikes the reasonable balance of providing that parties equally at fault in causing an accident share equally in its cost.

In choosing this modified version of the doctrine over the pure version, we are also influenced by the conservative approach taken by our Supreme Court in abrogating doctrines of common law. . . .

[Reversed and remanded]

QUESTIONS

1. Assume that two cars collide at an intersection. The driver of car No. 1 sues the driver of car No. 2. The jury decides that driver No. 1 was 60 percent at fault and that driver No. 2 was 40 percent at fault. The total damages to car No. 1 amounted to $10,000. How much does car owner No. 1 recover in the action?
2. What social forces underlie the concept of comparative negligence?
3. What kind of comparative negligence doctrine is preferable?

(f) PROOF OF NEGLIGENCE. The plaintiff ordinarily has the burden of proving that the defendant did not exercise reasonable care. In some instances, however, it is sufficient for the plaintiff to prove that the injury was caused by something that was within the control of the defendant. If injury ordinarily results from a particular object only when there is negligence, the proof of the fact that injury resulted is held sufficient proof that the defendant was negligent. This is expressed by the maxim *res ipsa loquitur* (the occurrence or the thing speaks for itself).

This concept does not establish that the defendant was negligent but merely allows the jury to conclude or infer that the defendant was negligent. The defendant is not barred from proving lack of negligence or from explaining that the harm was caused by some act for which the defendant was not responsible. The jury, if it believes the defendant's evidence, can refuse to infer negligence from the mere happening of the event and can conclude that the defendant was not negligent.

The burden of proving that the plaintiff was contributorily negligent is on the defendant, both under common law and under the comparative negligence concept.[7]

(g) VIOLATION OF STATUTE. By the general rule, if harm is sustained while the defendant is violating a statute, the defendant is deemed negligent and is liable for the harm. Many courts narrow this concept so that the defendant is liable only if the statute is intended to protect against the kind of harm that was sustained because of the violation of the statute and if the plaintiff was a member of the class that the statute was designed to protect. For example, in a suit over a collision of the automobiles of the plaintiff and defendant, the fact that the defendant was driving without proper tags in violation of an automobile registration law will be ignored. This is because the purpose of the registration statute was not to proscribe negligent driving or to protect other drivers from being negligently harmed.

(h) ASSUMPTION OF RISK. The plaintiff may have taken chances with a known danger. For example, the plaintiff may drive an automobile although its brakes are known to be bad. In such case, there is an assumption of risk by the plaintiff that harm may be sustained because of the defective brakes. Likewise, a farm employee attempting to hammer a metal bolt into shape without wearing any protective goggles assumes the risk that the bolt may splinter and that a flying splinter may cause an eye injury. Consequently, an employee injured in that manner is barred from suing the employer for negligence in failing to supply protective goggles to workers.[8]

At common law the plaintiff who had assumed risk was barred from recovering from the defendant for the harm sustained. Early in this century workers' compensation legislation abolished the defense of assumption of risk with respect to workers' compensation claims.

In many situations there is little or no difference between contributory negligence and assumption of risk. In situations in which that is true, a comparative negligence or comparative fault statute has the effect of abolishing the common law effect of assumption of risk and requires a comparison of the fault of the respective parties, with a reduction of the plaintiff's recovery to the extent directed by the statute.

7.   Division of Liability

In some instances, when two or more defendants have caused harm to the plaintiff, it is difficult or impossible to determine what damage was done by each of such wrongdoers or tortfeasors. For example, suppose automobile *A* strikes automobile *B*, which is then struck by automobile *C*. Ordinarily, it is impossible to determine how much damage to automobile *B* was caused by each of the cars. Similarly, a tract of farmland downriver may be harmed because two or more factories have dumped industrial wastes into the river. It is not possible to determine how much damage each of the factories has caused the farmland.

By the older view, a plaintiff was denied the right to recover from any of the wrongdoers in these situations. The courts followed the theory that a plaintiff is not entitled to recover from a defendant unless the plaintiff can prove what harm was caused by that defendant. The modern trend of the cases is to hold all the defendants jointly and severally (collectively and individually) liable for the total harm sustained by the plaintiff.

8.   Who May Sue

Ordinarily, the person who brings suit for a tort is the person whose property has been damaged or who has sustained personal injury.

In some torts, not only the immediate victim has the right to sue but also persons standing in certain relationships to the victim. Thus, under certain circumstances, one spouse can sue for an injury to the other spouse, or a parent can sue for an injury to the child. In a wrongful death action, members of the surviving group (typically the spouse, child, and

[7]   ITT Rayonier, Inc v Puget Sound Freight Lines, 44 Wash App 368, 722 P2d 1310 (1986).
[8]   Benjamin v Benjamin (ND) 439 NW2d 527 (1989).

parents of the person who has been killed) have a right to sue the wrongdoer for such death.

9.   Immunity from Liability

Basically, every person committing a tort is liable for damages for the harm caused thereby. However, certain persons and entities are not subject to tort liability. This is called **immunity** from liability.

Governments are generally immune from tort liability. This rule has been eroded by decision and in some instances by statutes, such as the Federal Tort Claims Act. Subject to certain exceptions, this Act permits the recovery of damages from the United States for property damage, personal injury, or death action claims arising from the negligent act or omission of any employee of the United States under such circumstances that the United States, "if a private person, would be liable to the claimant in accordance with the law of the place where the act or omission occurred." A fast-growing number of states have abolished governmental immunity, although many still recognize it.

At the beginning of this century charities were immune, and child and parent and spouses could not sue each other. These immunities are fast disappearing.[9] However, very young children are immune from tort liability to anyone.

B.   WHITE COLLAR TORTS

A classification of torts may be made, similar to that made in the law of crimes, between white collar torts and torts of force. Computer torts are discussed in Chapter 21.

10.   Causing of Mental Distress

When the defendant commits an act that by itself is a tort, there is ordinarily recovery for

the mental distress that is caused thereby. At common law, if no tort was committed, the plaintiff could not recover for mental distress.

(a) INTENTIONALLY CAUSED MENTAL DISTRESS. Since the turn of the century, and particularly in the last four decades, recovery has been allowed in a number of cases in which no ordinary or traditional form of tort was committed. The common element in these cases was that the defendant had willfully subjected the plaintiff to unnecessary emotional disturbance. This result was reached when an outrageous practical joke was played on the plaintiff; the corpse of a close relative was concealed or mistreated, or interference was made with the burial; or statements were made to humiliate the plaintiff because of race, creed, or national origin.

The concept of liability for intentionally caused distress is applicable in a commercial setting, as when a collection agency uses harassing techniques to collect the debt owed by a consumer. Another example is when a manufacturer engages in a continuing campaign, including illegal electronic eavesdropping, to intimidate a critic of the defendant's product. In either case the tort may be called the tort of outrageous conduct, or the tort of outrage. No distinction is made between causing mental distress or fear for the purpose of causing such distress or fear and coercing the victim into acting, or refraining from acting, in a particular way.

When there is liability for intentionally caused distress, there is also liability for any physical harm that is caused by the distress.

The fact that the plaintiff's rights have been violated and that the plaintiff was upset or made angry does not entitle the plaintiff to recover for emotional distress. For example, the fact that the plaintiff was wrongly denied the right to vote by the voting registrars does not in itself entitle the plaintiff to recover damages for outrageous conduct.

The *Miller* case turned on how bad conduct had to be in order to impose liability for emotional stress caused thereby.

---

[9]   Heino v Harper and Heino, 306 Or 347, 759 P2d 253 (1988).

MILLER v EQUITABLE LIFE ASSURANCE SOCIETY
181 Ill App 3d 954, 130 Ill Dec 558, 537 NE2d 887 (1989)

Sharon Graziani was employed by the Equitable Life Assurance Society. Because of the way she was treated by supervisors and fellow workers she suffered great emotional distress, to such an extent that a trustee, Miller, had to be appointed to manager her affairs. Miller sued Equitable and a number of its employees to recover damages on behalf of Sharon for the emotional distress that she had suffered. Judgment was entered against Miller and he appealed.

JIGANTI, J. . . . In order to state a cause of action for intentional infliction of emotional distress, the plaintiff must allege facts which establish: (1) the defendant's conduct was extreme and outrageous; (2) the emotional distress suffered by the plaintiff was severe; and (3) the defendant knew that severe emotional distress was certain or substantially certain to result from such conduct. . . .

With respect to the first requirement, the defendant's conduct must be " 'so outrageous in character, and so extreme in degree, as to go beyond all possible bounds of decency. . . .' " (*Public Finance Corp.*, 66 Ill.2d at 90, 4 Ill. Dec. at 654, 360 N.E.2d at 767, quoting Restatement (Second) of Torts § 46, comment *d* (1965).) Recovery under this theory does not extend to conduct which merely involves insults, indignities, threats, annoyances, petty oppressions, or other trivialities. . . . With respect to the severity of the plaintiff's distress, " 'the law intervenes only where the distress inflicted is so severe that no reasonable man could be expected to endure it.' " . . .

Determining whether a complaint states a cause of action essentially involves drawing a line "between the slight hurts which are the price of a complex society and the severe mental disturbances inflicted by intentional actions wholly lacking in social utility." . . . We recognize that our decision as to where that line should be drawn is based in large part on common sense and intuition more "subtle than any articulate major premise." . . .

The complaint essentially alleges that for approximately three and one-half years Graziani was surrounded by supervisors and co-workers who were inconsiderate, rude, vulgar, uncooperative, unprofessional and unfair. While we do not condone such behavior, we do not believe that the conduct alleged is so outrageous in character and so extreme in degree as to go beyond all bounds of human decency. Nor do we believe that the distress is so severe that no reasonable person could be expected to endure it. The fact that Graziani alleges that she was a victim of sexual harassment, battery, and retaliatory discharge does not necessarily mean that she has a cause of action for intentional infliction of emotional distress.

In employment situations, personality conflicts, job performance evaluations, or job transfers are unavoidable and often result in stress. However, if such stress formed the basis for the tort of intentional infliction of emotional distress, virtually every employee would have a cause of action. . . .

Because the complaint fails to allege extreme and outrageous conduct . . . we hold that Graziani has failed to allege a cause of action for intentional infliction of emotional distress. . . .

[Judgment affirmed]

QUESTIONS

1. In the *Miller* case was the emotional distress intentionally or negligently caused?
2. How does your answer to Question 1 affect the decision that you would make in the case?
3. Did the court have a precise definition for "extreme and outrageous" conduct?

(b) NEGLIGENTLY CAUSED MENTAL DISTRESS. In many jurisdictions the concept of liability for distress has been expanded to impose liability for negligently caused mental distress.

There is some indication that courts will impose wider liability for emotional distress when the circumstances are such as to exclude false claims, even though the defendant did not intentionally cause the distress. Thus, it has been held that when a mining company removed coal by burrowing under a graveyard, the company was liable for the subsi- dence and cracking of the graveyard caused by the failure to leave sufficient supporting pillars of coal and earth underneath the graveyard.[10]

In the *Schultz* case the plaintiff suffered a great emotional shock because of the negligence of the defendant. He claimed that he was entitled to damages for such emotional stress.

---

[10]   Bennett v 3 C Coal Co. (W Va App) 379 SE2d 388 (1989).

SCHULTZ v BARBERTON GLASS CO.
4 Ohio 3d 131, 447 NE2d 109 (1983)

A truck of the Barberton Glass Co. was transporting large sheets of glass down the highway. Elliot Schultz was driving his automobile some distance behind the truck. Because of the negligent way that the sheets of glass were fastened in the truck, a large sheet fell off the truck, shattered upon hitting the highway, and then bounced up and broke the windshield of Schultz's car. He was not injured but suffered great emotional shock. He sued Barberton to recover damages for such shock. Barberton denied liability on the ground that Schultz had not sustained any physical injury at the time or as the result of the shock. From a decision in favor of Barberton, Schultz appealed.

CELEBREZZE, C. J. . . . The issue raised in this appeal is whether a contemporaneous physical injury is a necessary condition precedent to liability for the negligent infliction of serious emotional distress. For the reasons which follow, we conclude that a contemporaneous physical injury is unnecessary.

In 1908, Ohio adopted the [impact] rule which requires the finding of contemporaneous physical injury before any recovery can be obtained for fright, shock, emotional distress, or mental suffering. *Miller v. Baltimore & Ohio S.W. R.R. Co.*, 78 Ohio St. 309, 85 N.E. 499 (1908). The court reasoned that ". . . 'if the right of recovery in this class of cases should be once established, it would naturally result in a flood of litigation in cases where the injury complained of may be easily feigned without detection, and where the damages must rest upon mere conjecture or speculation. The difficulty which often exists in cases of alleged physical injury, in determining whether they exist, and if so, whether they were caused by the negligent act of the defendant, would not only be greatly increased, but a wide field would be opened for fictitious or speculative claims. To establish such a doctrine would be contrary to principles of public policy.' "

We find that the reasons set forth in *Miller* are no longer valid. The first concern that a flood of litigation would result if recovery were permitted has not materialized. Commentators and courts in other jurisdictions have concluded that this argument lacks merit. As stated in *Falzone v. Busch* (1965), 45 N.J. 559, 567, 214 A.2d 12, "there is no indication of an excessive number of actions of this type in other states which do not require an impact as a basis for recovery." . . .

Even if there may be a possibility of increased litigation, it is not a valid reason for denying a judicial forum. The Supreme Court of Pennsylvania, quoting Prosser, Intentional Infliction of Mental Suffering: A New Tort (1939), 37 Mich.L.Rev. 874, stated: " 'It is the business of the law to remedy wrongs that deserve it, even at the expense of a "flood of litigation"; and it is a pitiful confession of incompetence on the part of any court of justice to deny relief upon the ground that it will give the courts too much work to do.' " *Niederman v. Brodsky* (1970), 436 Pa. 401, 412, 261 A.2d 84. Even if the caseload increases, the "proper remedy" is an expansion of the judicial machinery, not a decrease in the availability of justice.

Therefore, we are not convinced that the problem of increased litigation is real or inevitable. Moreover, even if the caseload increases, we believe it is an unacceptable reason for denying justice.

A second reason for the physical injury requirement is the fear of fictitious injuries and fraudulent claims. . . .

The danger of illusory claims for mental distress is no greater than in cases of physical injury, especially when the injury is slight. The opportunity for fraud is as likely in such a case as one absent any physical injury. "The problem is one of adequate proof, and it is not necessary to deny a remedy in all cases because some claims may be false." Prosser, Law of Torts (4 Ed.1971) 327–328, Section 54.

. . . The last argument urged by appellee for retaining the physical injury rule is that problems regarding the proof of emotional distress are insurmountable because damages must be based upon conjecture or speculation. . . .

Judges and juries will consider the credibility of witnesses and the genuineness of the proof as they do in other cases. In most instances, expert medical testimony will help establish the validity of the claim of serious emotional distress. Three medical doctors and a doctor of psychology testified, in the case *sub judice*, to the effect that appellant suffers from traumatic neurosis which was directly caused by the collision. Appellee did not offer expert testimony to the contrary.

Having carefully examined the arguments in support of the contemporaneous physical injury rule, it is clear that continued adherence to the rule makes little sense. Legal scholars who have considered the rule denying recovery in the absence of contemporaneous physical injury or impact are unanimous in condemning it as unjust and contrary to experience. The justifications for the doctrine are no longer valid and the reasons for abrogating it are strong. Consequently, the earlier cases upholding the doctrine are overruled. . .

For these reasons, we hold that a cause of action may be stated for the negligent infliction of serious emotional distress without a contemporaneous physical injury.

. . . We conclude that appellant has such a cause of action. . . .

[Judgment reversed and action remanded]

(c) BYSTANDER RECOVERY. When a bystander is a spectator to the negligent conduct of the defendant, and the witnessing of such conduct causes serious and reasonably foreseeable emotional distress, some courts hold that the bystander may recover damages for such harm from the wrongdoer. Most of these courts limit this liability to spectators who are closely related to the person directly endangered by the defendant's conduct.

A few courts have eliminated the requirement that the bystander actually see the event that causes shock. Thus, the relative arriving shortly after the actual occurrence may recover damages for the emotional distress caused by the negligence of the defendant.[11]

11.   Invasion of Privacy

As an aspect of protecting the person from unreasonable interference, the law has come to recognize a right of privacy. This right is most commonly invaded in one of the following ways: (a) invasion of physical privacy, as by planting a microphone in a person's home; (b) giving unnecessary publicity to personal matters of the plaintiff's life, such as financial status or past careers; (c) false public association of the plaintiff with some product or principle, such as indicating that the plaintiff endorses a product or is in favor of a particular law, when such is not the case; or (d) commercially exploiting the plaintiff's name or picture, as in using them in advertising without permission.

When a party has a legitimate business interest in making information known, such conduct is generally not regarded as an invasion of privacy. The conduct is protected by a privilege as long as good faith is exercised by the disclosing party.

12.   Malpractice

Malpractice liability is a tort liability imposed for a poor or bad performance of a legal duty when the performance results in harm. Usually, it will be a poor performance because of negligence, as distinguished from harm that is intentionally caused. Usually, the duty of performance is one that arises from a contract, and therefore the wrongdoer is guilty of both a breach of contract and a tort. The subject of malpractice will be considered in detail in Chapter 19.

13.   Fraud

A person is entitled to be protected from fraud and may recover damages for harm caused by fraud. This protects the plaintiff from false statements made with knowledge of their falsity or with reckless indifference as to whether or not they were true.[12]

In some instances, antifraud provisions have been adopted by consumer protection statutes. To illustrate, when the seller of a used car turns the odometer back with the intent to defraud, the seller is liable under the federal Motor Vehicle Information and Cost Savings Act to whomever purchases the automobile, without regard to whether the purchaser bought directly from that dealer or from an intermediate dealer.

Fraud is to be distinguished from racketeering. The fact that deceptive practices are used does not constitute racketeering activity within a RICO-type statute. Thus, a seller of a laundromat did not engage in racketeering activity when the seller created the false appearance of the profitable nature of the laundromat by stuffing the coinboxes with coins.

---

[11]   Thing v La Chusa, 48 Cal 3d 664, 257 Cal Rptr 865, 771 P2d 814 (1989).

[12]   The concept of fraud is more fully analyzed in Chapter 11, Section 5 of this book.

14.   Defamation by Slander

A person is liable for defamation of another. Reputation is injured by **defamation**, which is a publication tending to cause one to lose the esteem of the community.[13] **Slander** is a form of defamation consisting of the publication or communication to another of false, spoken words. Thus, a false statement by the manager of a business that the former manager had been fired for stealing is slander. The fact that language is offensive or derogatory does not in itself constitute slander.

(a) PRIVILEGE. Under certain circumstances no liability arises when false statements are made, even though they cause damage. This absolute privilege exists in the case of publication by a public officer when the publication is within the officer's line of duty. The rule is deemed necessary to encourage public officers in the performance of their public duties.

Other circumstances may afford a qualified or conditional privilege. A communication made in good faith, on a subject in which the party communicating has an interest or right, is privileged if made to a person with a corresponding interest or right.[14] Thus, the owner of a watch may in good faith charge another person with the theft of the watch. A mercantile agency's credit report is conditionally privileged when made to an interested subscriber in good faith in the regular course of the agency's business.

A Better Business Bureau that has carefully maintained its records has a qualified privilege to state to a consumer that a particular enterprise had a history of failing to remedy complaints.[15] Also, when a client tells an attorney that a customer of the client owes money, such statement does not impose liability for defamation, even though it is wrong. The former employer of a job applicant has a qualified privilege to tell the prospective employer of the applicant why the former employer discharged the applicant.

Statements made in pleadings filed in court are protected by a privilege. In the *Defend* case, the controversy turned on whether this protection was an absolute or a conditional privilege.

---

[13]   Shannon v Taylor AMC/Jeep, Inc. 168 Mich App 415, 425 NW2d 165 (1988). A person harmed by false advertising statements of a competitor may recover damages for commercial defamation under the Trademark Law Revision Act of 1988, Act of November 16, 1988, PL 100-667, 102 Stat 3935, 15 USC §§ 1051–1127.

[14]   Parry v George H. Brown & Associates, Inc. 46 Wash App 193, 730 P2d 95 (1986).
[15]   Patio World v Better Business Bureau, Inc. 43 Ohio App 3d 6, 583 NE2d 1098 (1989).

DEFEND v LASCELLES
149 Ill App 3d 630, 102 Ill Dec 819, 500 NE2d 712 (1986)

Lascelles and his wife were real estate developers. Defend and Johnson purchased homes constructed by them and later sued the Lascelles. Defend and Johnson claimed that in promoting the development, the defendants had committed mail and wire fraud and were guilty of violating the Racketeer Influenced and Corrupt Organizations Act (RICO). The defendants counterclaimed that the plaintiff's claim was made maliciously and that the defendants were entitled to damages for defamation. The plaintiffs replied that the statements in their complaint, although defamatory, were absolutely privileged. The court refused to dismiss the counterclaim, and the plaintiffs appealed.

MORTHLAND, J. . . . We begin our analysis by recognizing the oft-stated principle in Illinois that anything said or written in a legal proceeding, including pleadings, is protected by an absolute privilege against defamation actions, subject only to the qualification that the words be relevant or pertinent to the matters in controversy. . . .

The privilege itself is steeped in public policy: it is uniformly recognized that the judicial system would best be served if persons with knowledge of relevant facts could report those facts to the court without fear of civil liability.

Plaintiff calls our attention to another view in this area which substitutes a different yardstick for the "relevant and pertinent" inquiry relied upon by many courts. That analysis provides for an absolute privilege when otherwise defamatory material is published in a judicial proceeding if the statements have "some relation" to the litigation. Specifically, section 587 of the Restatement (Second) of Torts states the following:

> A party to a private litigation or a private prosecutor or defendant in a criminal prosecution is *absolutely privileged* to publish defamatory matter concerning another in communications preliminary to a proposed judicial proceeding, or in the institution of or during the course and as a part of, a judicial proceeding in which he participates, if the matter has *some relation* to the proceeding. (Emphasis added.) Restatement (Second) of Torts § 587, at 248 (1977).

The Restatement standard has gained wide acceptance, becoming the majority rule today. At least two appellate courts in Illinois have heretofore embraced versions of the Restatement rule.

Clearly, then, depending upon the analysis employed, the threshold inquiry concerns whether the complained-of allegations are "relevant and pertinent" or bear "some relation" to the litigation. If so, pleadings in a judicial proceeding are absolutely privileged and cannot ordinarily form the basis of a defamation action. Defendants steadfastly maintain, though, that any pleading filed maliciously should not be granted an absolute privilege.

As a general principle, certain types of statements are deemed so privileged that the person making the statement should not be deterred from speaking by the threat of civil liability. In such a case an absolute privilege is granted, and no cause of action for defamation will lie against the person making the statement even if it is made with malice. This immunity afforded *absolutely* privileged matter is complete. It is not conditioned upon an honest or reasonable belief that the defamatory matter is true, or upon the absence of ill will on the part of the speaker. On the other hand, where only a *qualified* privilege is granted based upon a lesser concern for the freedom of the speaker, the person making the statement is immune from liability unless the privilege is abused or some element such as malice is present. When a qualified privilege is shown, the plaintiff has the burden of alleging and proving actual malice.

The law thus clearly allows for an absolute privilege where there exists a significant interest in protecting the type of speech involved. In such cases, malice alone on the part of the speaker will not defeat the privilege. Accordingly, the prevailing rule in the United States today is that libelous material contained in a pleading is absolutely privileged so long as it is pertinent, relevant, or bears some reasonable relation to the judicial proceeding, irrespective of whether it is false and malicious. . . .

The weight of authority in Illinois clearly favors recognition of an absolute privilege for statements made in a judicial proceeding based upon public policy. The defense of privilege or immunity in defamation cases rests upon the idea that "conduct which otherwise would be actionable is to escape liability because the defendant is acting in furtherance of some interest of social importance," an interest to be protected "even at the expense of uncompensated harm to the plaintiff's reputation." (Prosser, Torts § 114, at 776 (4th ed. 1971).) Further, comment *a* to section 587 of the Restatement explains:

> The privilege stated in this Section is based upon the public interest in according to all men the utmost freedom of access to the courts of justice for the settlement of their private disputes. . . . It protects a party to a private litigation . . . from liability for defamation *irrespective of his purpose in publishing the defamatory matter, of his belief in its truth or even his knowledge of its falsity.*" (Emphasis added.) Restatement (Second) of Torts § 587, comment *a*, at 249 (1977); see also *Bond v. Pecaut* (N.D.Ill.1983), 561 F.Supp. 1037.

. . . We hold that otherwise defamatory statements made in a pleading filed in a judicial proceeding enjoy an absolute privilege if they are relevant, pertinent, or bear some relation to the subject in controversy. Whether or not the occasion gives rise to the privilege is solely a question of law for the court. If the complained-of statements are found not to reasonably relate to the issues, then the absolute privilege is no longer available, and a charge of malice will enter into consideration as if a qualified privilege were involved instead.

Under the precise question certified, then, we find that pleading a civil cause of action for violation of the applicable RICO provision is absolutely privileged from any counterclaim based on defamation so long as it has some relation to the matter in controversy. If such is the case, malicious intent in filing the pleading is irrelevant.

. . . Persons defamed in pleadings or trial testimony may be left without legal redress, even if their reputations are damaged, because of the public policy favoring free and open administration of justice.

[Judgment reversed and action remanded]

QUESTIONS

1. What tests did the court consider using to determine whether statements in a pleading in court are privileged?
2. What is the difference between the tests given in your answer to Question 1?
3. Is it ever important whether statements in a pleading in court were made maliciously?

If a consumer makes false statements about a seller, such as that a particular automobile dealer sold the consumer a "lemon," the consumer is liable for defamation. The fact that a person is a consumer does not give rise to any privilege to make false statements.

15.   Defamation by Libel

The reputation of a person or a business may be defamed by written statements. This is known as **libel**. Although the defaming statement is described as a writing, it may also be in print, picture, or in any other permanent, visual form. For example, to construct a gallows in front of another's residence is a libel. A written report falsely stating that an employee has falsified time work records is libelous.

16.   Disparagement of Goods and Slander of Title

In the transaction of business, one is entitled to be free from the interference of malicious, false statements made by others as to the title or the quality of goods sold by the business. Actual damage must be proved by the plaintiff to have resulted from the false communications by the defendant to a third person. The plaintiff must show that as a consequence of the statement, the third person refrained from dealing with the plaintiff.

17.   Infringement of Trademarks and Service Marks

A **trademark** or **service mark** is a word, name, device, symbol, or any combination of these, used by a manufacturer or seller of goods or a provider of services to distinguish those goods and services from those of other persons. When the mark of a particular person is used or substantially copied by another, it is said that the mark is **infringed**. The owner of the mark may sue for damages and enjoin its wrongful use.[16]

18.   Infringement of Patents

A grant of a **patent** entitles the patentee to prevent others from making, using, or selling a particular invention for a period of 17 years. Anyone so doing without the patentee's permission is guilty of a patent infringement. If the inventor does not have a patent or if the patent is invalid, anyone may copy the invention without liability.

An infringement occurs even though all parts or features of an invention are not copied if there is a substantial identity of names, operations, and result between the original and the new device. In the case of a process, however, all successive steps or their equivalent must be copied. In the case of a combination of an ingredient, the use of the same ingredient with others constitutes an infringement, except when the result is a compound essentially different in nature.

19.   Infringement of Copyrights

A wrong similar to the infringement of a patent is the infringement of a copyright. A copyright is the right given by statute to prevent others for a limited time from printing, copying, or publishing a production resulting from intellectual labor. The right exists for the life of the author and for 50 years thereafter.[17]

Infringement of a copyright in general consists of copying the form of expression of ideas or conceptions. There is no copyright in the idea or conception itself, but only in the particular way in which it is expressed. In order to constitute an infringement, the production need not be reproduced entirely or be exactly the same as the original. Reproduction of a substantial part of the original, although paraphrased or otherwise altered, constitutes an infringement, but appropriation of only a word or single line does not.

One guilty of infringement of copyright is liable to the owner for damages, which are to be determined by the court. The owner is also entitled to an injunction to restrain further infringement.

20.   Unfair Competition

Unfair competition is unlawful. The person injured thereby may sue for damages and an injunction to stop the practice, or may report the matter to the Federal Trade Commission or to an appropriate state agency.

It is unfair competition to imitate signs, storefronts, advertisements, and the packaging of goods of a competitor. Thus, when one adopts a box of distinctive size, shape, and color in which to market a product, and the package is imitated by a competitor, the latter is liable for unfair competition.

Not every similarity to a competitor, however, is necessarily unfair competition. For example, the term *downtown* is merely descriptive, so the Downtown Motel cannot obtain an injunction against the use of the name Downtown Motor Inn, because a name that is merely descriptive cannot be exclusively appropriated or adopted. As an exception, if the descriptive word has been used by a given business for such a long time as to be identified with the business in the public mind, a competitor cannot use that name.

The goodwill that is related to a trade name is an important business asset. There is

---

[16]   See Chapter 20, Section 8 of this book.

[17]   Copyright Act of 1976, Act of October 19, 1976, § 302, PL 94–553, 90 Stat 2541, 2572, 17 USC § 302.

a judicial trend in favor of protecting a trade name from a competitor's use of a similar name.

Historically, the law as to unfair competition was concerned only with protecting competitors from unfair competition by their rivals. Under consumer protection statutes, most states now give protection to the consumer who is harmed by unfair competitive practices.

21.   Combinations to Divert Trade

Business relations may be harmed by a combination to keep third persons from dealing with another. Such a combination, resulting in injury, constitutes an actionable wrong known as conspiracy if the object is unlawful or if a lawful object is sought by unlawful means.

If the object of a combination is to further a lawful interest of the combination, no actionable wrong exists so long as lawful means are employed. For example, when employees are united in a strike, they may peacefully persuade others to withhold their patronage from the employer. On the other hand, all combinations to drive or keep away customers or prospective employees by violence, force, threats, or intimidation are actionable wrongs.

Labor laws prohibit some combinations as unfair labor practices, and other combinations to divert trade are condemned as illegal trusts.

22.   Malicious Interference with Contract

The extent of tort law relating to interference with contracts and other economic relationships has increased greatly in recent years, as a result of society's seeking to impose on the marketplace higher ethical standards to prevent the oppression of victims of improper practices. In general terms, when the defendant interferes with and brings about the breach of the contract between a third person and the plaintiff, the circumstances may be such that the plaintiff has an action in tort against the defendant for interfering with contractual relations.

As the tort in question is the malicious interfering with contract, it follows that there is

no tort when the interference is not malicious but is done to safeguard or protect one's own financial or economic interest. However, the fact that the defendant is a competitor of the plaintiff does not constitute justification for the defendant's causing third persons to break their contracts with the plaintiff.

The fact that a contract is terminable at will does not deprive it of protection from interference.[18] Likewise, it is immaterial that the contract could be ignored because it is not evidenced by a writing that satisfies the statute of frauds.

In addition to protecting existing contracts from deliberate interference, tort liability is imposed for acts intentionally committed to prevent the making of a contract.

23.   Wrongful Interference with Business Relations

One of the fundamental rights of an individual is to earn a living by working or by engaging in trade or business. Any wrongful interference with this liberty is a tort.[19]

The right to conduct one's business is, nevertheless, subject to the rights of others. Hence, the injuries suffered by one in business through legitimate competition give no right to redress.

C.   TORTS AGAINST PERSON OR PROPERTY

In contrast with the white collar torts, some torts involve the use of force against persons or property.

24.   Trespass to the Person

Trespass to the person consists of any contact with the victim's person for which consent was not given. It thus includes what is technically described as a **battery**. It includes an **assault** in which the victim apprehends the commission of a battery but is in fact not touched.

---

[18]   Sterner v Marathon Oil Co. (Tex) 767 SW2d 686 (1989).
[19]   Tamiami Trail Tours, Inc. v Cotton (Fla App) 463 So 2d 1126 (1985).

It also includes false imprisonment. In some instances, as in cases of self-defense, a person has a right to use force that would otherwise constitute an unlawful battery.

25.　False Imprisonment

False imprisonment is the intentional, unprivileged detaining of a person without that person's consent.[20] It may take the extreme form of kidnapping. At the other extreme a shopper who is detained in a store manager's office and questioned about shoplifting is the victim of false imprisonment where there is no reasonable ground for believing that the shopper is a thief. Likewise, a merchant is liable for false imprisonment when a person detained under suspicion of shoplifting is detained after it is determined that the person was innocent and the original suspicion was a mistake.[21] False imprisonment also includes detention under an official arrest when there is no legal justification for the arrest.

(a) DETENTION. Any detention at any place by any means for any duration of time is sufficient to satisfy the detention element of false imprisonment. If a robber holds a bank teller at gunpoint for the purpose of preventing the teller from attacking the other robbers or from escaping, there is a sufficient detention.

(b) CONSENT AND PRIVILEGE. By definition no false imprisonment occurs when the person detained consents to it. For example, when a merchant without any justification detains a person on the suspicion of shoplifting, such detention is not a false imprisonment if the victim consents to it without any protest. If the merchant had reasonable grounds for believing that the victim was guilty of shoplifting, the action of the merchant was not false

imprisonment, even though the victim was detained under protest and did not consent to it. Statutes frequently give merchants a privilege to detain persons reasonably suspected of shoplifting. Likewise there is a privilege and it is not false imprisonment to confine a hospital patient in an emergency room in order to prevent harm to the patient and to others.[22]

26.　Trespass to Land

A **trespass to land** consists of any unpermitted entry below, on, across, or above land. This rule is modified to permit the proper flight of aircraft above the land so long as it does not interfere with a proper use of the land.

27.　Trespass to Personal Property

An illegal invasion of property rights with respect to property other than land constitutes a **trespass to personal property,** whether done intentionally or negligently. When done in good faith and without negligence, there is no liability. This is in contrast with the case of trespass to land, where good faith and absence of negligence is not a defense.

Negligent damage to personal property imposes liability for harm done. Intentional damage to personal property will impose liability for the damage done and also may justify exemplary or punitive damages.

A **conversion** occurs when personal property is taken by the wrongdoer and kept from its true owner or prior possessor.[23] For example, a bank clerk commits conversion by unlawfully taking money from the bank. Conversion is the civil side of the crimes relating to stealing. The good faith of the converter, however, is not a defense to civil liability. Thus, an innocent buyer of stolen goods is liable for damages for converting them.

---

[20]　Walker v Portland, 71 Or App 693, 693 P2d 1349 (1985).
[21]　Latek v K Mart Corp. 224 Neb 807, 401 NW2d 503 (1987).

[22]　Blackman v Rifkin (Colo App) 759 P2d 54 (1988).
[23]　Kendal/Hunt Publishing Co. v Rowe (Iowa) 424 NW2d 235 (1988).

SUMMARY

Conduct that harms other people or their property is generally called a tort. The injured

person may sue the wrongdoer to recover damages to compensate for the harm or loss caused. The conduct that is a tort may also be a crime and may sometimes be a breach of contract. Tort liability is generally imposed because of the fault of the wrongdoer; in some cases it is imposed when there is no fault. In any case, the harm-causing conduct of the defendant must be voluntary and must have a causal relationship to the harm sustained. Liability is imposed without fault in connection with industrial activity, consumer protection, wild animals, and certain areas of liability to workers or to victims of automobile collisions.

Negligence is the failure to follow the degree of care that would be followed by a reasonably prudent person in order to avoid foreseeable harm. If the negligence of the plaintiff contributes to the plaintiff's harm, the recovery obtained by the plaintiff may be reduced proportionately or barred, depending on the type of comparative negligence rule that is in force. In a minority of states, the common law contributory negligence rule is still followed. Under this law, any negligence of the plaintiff bars all recovery. Negligence must be proven as a fact, although the plaintiff may be aided by the doctrine of *res ipsa loquitur*. In most

states the violation of a statute is proof that the defendant was negligent, provided the statute is designed to protect from the kind of harm that has been sustained and the plaintiff is a member of the class that the statute sought to protect.

In general, any person aggrieved or harmed by a tort can sue the defendant. In some instances a relative of the injured person will have a right to sue the defendant because of the harm caused. When there are two or more persons causing harm in such a way that it is not possible to determine how much harm was caused by each person, all the persons causing the harm are jointly and severally liable to the plaintiff by the modern trend.

Ordinarily, any wrongdoer may be sued, but some wrongdoers have a limited immunity, while others may be liable for the tortious acts of third persons. Governments may be immune from suit. To some extent minors, parents of the aggrieved person, and the spouse of that person may be immune from suit. The trend of the law is to treat charities the same as other defendants and impose tort liability on them.

QUESTIONS AND CASE PROBLEMS

1. What is the objective of each of the following rules of law?
   (a) In some areas of law, liability for harm exists without regard to whether there was any negligence or intention to cause harm.
   (b) Geographical and descriptive names cannot ordinarily be adopted as trademarks.
2. Is proof of a bad motive essential to imposing tort liability?
3. The Coleman Construction Company was constructing a highway. It was necessary to blast rock with dynamite. The corporation's employees did this with the greatest of care. In spite of their precautions some flying fragments of rock damaged a neighboring house. The owner of the house sued the corporation for the damages. The corporation raised the defense that the owner was suing for tort damages and that such damages could not be imposed because the corporation had been free from fault. Was this defense valid?
4. Burnstein drove a car on a country road at 35

miles an hour. The maximum speed limit was 45 miles an hour. He struck and killed a cow that was crossing the road. The owner of the cow sued Burnstein for the value of the cow. Burnstein raised the defense that as he was not driving above the speed limit, there could be no liability for negligence. Was this defense valid?
5. The Brunswick Corporation manufactured and sold raincoats that it advertised to consumers as "waterproof" when in fact they were merely "water resistant." The Brunswick Corporation was sued for engaging in unfair competition. It raised the defense that it was not guilty because it was understood in the trade that "waterproof" meant only "water resistant," so no unfair advantage was taken of any competitor. Was this defense valid?
6. Jessica Sorensen was a minor. She was riding in an automobile driven by her father, Paul. The car collided with another car. Jessica was injured. She sued her father for her injuries. He raised the defense that a father could not be

sued by his child for negligence. Was he correct? [Sorensen v Sorensen, 369 Mass 350, 339 NE2d 907]

7. Henry Neiderman was walking with his small son. An automobile driven by Brodsky went out of control, ran up on the sidewalk, and struck a fire hydrant, a litter pole and basket, a newsstand, and Niederman's son. The car did not touch Niederman, but the shock and fright caused damage to his heart. He sued Brodsky for the harm that he sustained as the result of Brodsky's negligence. Brodsky defended on the ground that he was not liable because he had not touched Neiderman. Was this a valid defense? [Niederman v Brodsky, 436 Pa 401, 261 A2d 84]

8. Carrigan, a district manager of Simples Time Recorder Company, was investigating complaints of mismanagement of the Jackson office of the company. He called at the home of Hooks, the secretary of that office. She expressed the opinion that part of the trouble was caused by stealing of parts and equipment by McCall, another employee. McCall was later discharged and sued Hooks for slander. Was she liable? [Hooks v McCall (Miss) 272 So 2d 925]

9. Defendant #1 parked his truck in the street near the bottom of a ditch on a dark, foggy night. Iron pipes carried in the truck projected beyond the truck nine feet in back. Neither the truck nor the pipes carried any warning light or flag, thus violating both city ordinance and state statute. Defendant #2 was a taxicab owner whose taxicab was negligently driven at an excessive speed. Defendant #2 ran into the pipes, thereby killing the passenger in the taxicab. The plaintiff brought an action for the passenger's death against both defendants. Defendant #1 claimed he was not liable because it was the negligent act of defendant #2 that had caused the harm. Was this defense valid? [Bumbardner v Allison, 238 NC 621, 78 SE2d 752]

10. A statute required that air vent shafts on hotel roofs have parapets at least 30 inches high. Edgar Hotel had parapets only 27 inches high. Nunneley was visiting a registered guest at the Edgar Hotel. She placed a mattress on top of a parapet. When she sat on the mattress, the parapet collapsed and she fell into the air shaft and was injured. She sued the hotel, claiming that its breach of the statute as to the height of the parapets constituted negligence. Decide. [Nunneley v Edgar Hotel, 36 Cal 2d 493, 225 P2d 497]

11. A, B, and C owned land. Some construction work they did on their land prevented the free flow of surface water and caused a flooding of land owned by D. D sued A for the damage caused his land by the flooding. A claimed that D could not hold him liable for any damage, since D could not prove how much of the total damage had been caused by A and how much by B and C, and that in any event A could not be liable for more than one-third of the total damage sustained by D. Decide. [Thorson v Minot (ND) 153 NW2d 764]

12. Tom Lawrence took his automobile to Wayne Strand Pontiac-GMC, Inc., for repairs. Strand left the car on its lot with the key in the ignition. Two weeks later Lawrence's car was stolen. Ronald Williamson was driving his car and came into the vicinity of the stolen car just as the thieves abandoned it and ran away on foot. In order to avoid hitting the thieves, Williamson swerved. In so doing, he struck the abandoned car and was injured. He then sued Wayne Strand for damages. Was Strand liable for damages? [Williamson v Wayne Strand Pontiac-GMC, Inc. (Tex App) 658 SW2d 263]

13. Collete Bass worked in a building owned by Nooney Company. As part of her job she was going from one floor to another when the elevator stopped moving. She was alone in the elevator for about an hour before she was rescued. The emergency phone in the elevator was dead. She sued the Nooney Company for the mental distress to which she was subjected. The Nooney Company claimed that it was not liable because there was no proof that it had been negligent. Bass claimed Nooney had the burden of proving that it was not negligent. Was she correct? [Bass v Nooney Co. (Mo) 646 SW2d 765]

14. The Belmont County Fair was held in the week of September 5. Three helium-filled tanks were delivered to the fairground to be used to fill balloons to promote the political candidacy of Bob Olexo. The tanks remained on the fairgrounds after the close of the fair. Two weeks later, Jeffers, aged 14, entered the fairgrounds to watch a football game. He came across the tanks. He ignored the plain warning on the tanks that inhaling the gas could cause suffocation. He inhaled the gas, collapsed, and died. His father then brought suit against Olexo and all persons involved in supplying the helium. Decide. What ethical values are involved? [Jeffers v Olexo, 43 Ohio 3d 140, 539 NE2d 614]

15. A farmer sued five factories that were located several miles from his farm. He proved that industrial fumes from the factories had seriously damaged his crops. The defendants did not

deny that damage had been done, but each defendant claimed that the farmer could not recover from that defendant without proving how much of the total damage had been caused by that defendant. As this was not possible, the defendants claimed that judgment should be entered against the farmer. Were they correct? What are the ethics of the problem?

PART TWO

CONTRACTS

9

NATURE AND CLASSES OF CONTRACTS

Practically every personal business activity involves a contract: enrolling in college, purchasing a color television, renting an apartment. In each transaction relating to the acquisition of raw materials, their manufacture, and the distribution of the finished product by businesses, there are contracts that define the relationship and the rights and obligations of the parties.

A. NATURE OF CONTRACTS

As pervasive as contracts are in our lives, the legal language of contracts is not very familiar to most of us. For that reason, this introductory chapter is devoted primarily to the termi-

nology or vocabulary that is needed to work with contract law.

In addition, this chapter deals with something called **quasi contracts**. These, as you might guess, are not true contracts. They lack some essential element that the law requires of a true contract. Nevertheless, society, through its laws, has created this special class of obligations that are enforced in a limited way.

1. Definition of a Contract

A **contract** is a binding agreement.[1] By one

---

[1] The Uniform Commercial Code defines *contract* to mean "the total legal obligation which results from the parties' agreement as affected by [the Code] and any other applicable rules of law," UCC § 1–201(11).

definition "a contract is a promise or a set of promises for the breach of which the law gives a remedy, or the performance of which the law in some way recognizes as a duty."[2] Contracts arise out of agreements, so a contract may be defined as an agreement creating an obligation.

The substance of the definition of a contract is that by mutual agreement or assent the parties create enforceable duties or obligations. That is, each party is legally bound to do or to refrain from doing certain acts.

2.   Elements of a Contract

The elements of a contract are: (a) an agreement, (b) between competent parties, (c) based upon the genuine assent of the parties, (d) supported by consideration, (e) made for a lawful objective, and (f) in the form required by law, if any. These elements will be considered in the chapters that follow.

3.   Subject Matter of Contracts

The subject matter of a contract may relate to the performance of personal services, such as contracts of employment to work on an assembly line, to work as a secretary, to sing on television, or to build a house. The contract may provide for the transfer of ownership of property, such as a house (real property) or an automobile (personal property), from one person to another. A contract may also call for a combination of these things. For example, a builder may contract to supply materials and do the work involved in installing the materials, or a person may contract to build a house and then transfer the house and the land to the buyer.

4.   Parties to a Contract

A person who makes a promise is the **promisor**, and the person to whom the promise is made is called the **promisee**. If the promise is binding, it imposes upon the promisor a duty or obligation, and the promisor may be called the **obligor**. The promisee who can claim the

benefit of the obligation is also called the **obligee**. The parties to a contract are said to stand in privity with each other, and the relationship between them is termed **privity of contract**.

In written contracts parties may be referred to by name. More often, however, they are given special names that serve better to identify each party. For example, consider a contract by which one person agrees that another may occupy a house upon the payment of money. The parties are called landlord and tenant, or lessor and lessee, and the contract between them is known as a lease. Parties to other types of contracts also have distinctive names, such as vendor and vendee, the parties to a sales contract; shipper and carrier, the parties to a transportation contract; and insurer and insured, the parties to an insurance policy.

A party to a contract may be an individual, a partnership, a corporation, or a government. A party to a contract may be an agent acting on behalf of another person.

There may be one or more persons on each side of the contract. In some cases there are three-sided contracts, as in the case of a credit card transaction. A credit card transaction involves the company issuing the card, the holder of the card, and the business furnishing goods and services in reliance on the credit card. When a contract is written, the persons who are the parties and who are bound by it will ordinarily be determined by reading what the paper says and seeing how it is signed.

In addition to the original parties to the contract, other persons may have rights or duties with respect to it. For example, one party may to some extent assign rights under the contract to a third person. Also, the contract may have been made for the benefit of a third person, as in a life insurance contract, in which case the third person (the beneficiary) is permitted to enforce the contract.

5.   How a Contract Arises

A contract is based upon an agreement. An agreement arises when one person, the **offeror**, makes an offer and the person to whom the

---

[2]   Restatement, Contracts, 2d 1.

FIGURE 9-1   CONTRACTUAL LIABILITY

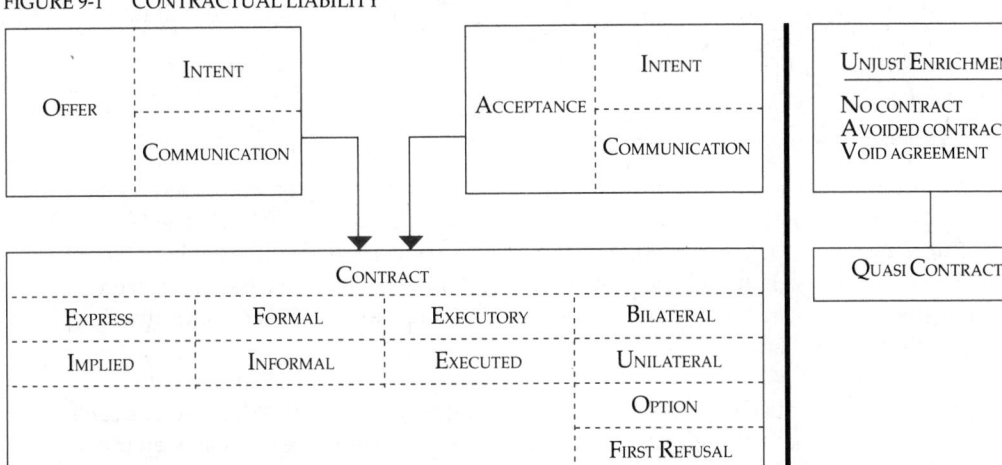

offer is made, the **offeree**, accepts. There must be both an offer and an acceptance. If either is lacking, there is no contract.

An offeror may make an offer to a particular person or it may be made to the public at large. The latter case arises, for example, when a reward is offered to the public for the return of lost property.

It is frequently said that a meeting of minds is essential to an agreement or a contract. Modern courts do not stress the meeting of the minds, however, because in some situations the law finds an agreement even though the minds of the parties have not in fact met. The real test is not whether a meeting of the minds occurred but whether, under the circumstances, one party was reasonably entitled to believe that there was an offer and the other to believe that there was an acceptance.

6.   Intent to Make a Binding Agreement

Because a contract is based on the consent of the parties and is a legally binding agreement, it follows that the parties must have an intent to enter into an agreement that is binding. Sometimes the parties are in agreement, but their agreement does not produce a contract. Sometimes there is merely a preliminary agreement, but the parties never actually make a contract. It may be merely an agreement as to future plans or intentions without any contractual obligation to carry out those plans or intentions. In the *Bowman* case there was a dispute as to whether an agreement was a contract.

BOWMAN v HILL
45 NC App 116, 262 SE2d 376 (1980)

William Hill and the Terrells owned two tracts of land in the town of Dayton. They sold one tract to Dr. Terry O. Bowman and made an agreement with him as to the second lot, which they kept. The agreement stated in part:

. . . whereas the parties of the second part [William Hill and the Terrells] desire to construct a building adjacent to the building of the party of the first part [Dr. Bowman] at some future time; and WHEREAS, all of the parties are *desirous* of having one large inter-connecting parking lot located in front of the buildings and sidewalks connecting to said parking lots;

WITNESSETH:

That for the mutual considerations *expressed hereinabove*, the parties do contract as follows: . . . [emphasis added]

The agreement went on to provide that when the Hill-Terrell lot was paved for a parking lot, Bowman would pave a similar parking area on his tract. The Hill-Terrell lot was thereafter sold, and the buyer constructed a building where the parking lot would have been. Bowman sued Hill and Terrell for having broken their contract. The lower court held the defendants liable for breach of contract, and they appealed.

HILL, J. . . . One of the elements of a valid contract is a promise, which has been defined as an assurance that a thing will or will not be done. "The mere expression of an intention or desire is not a promise. . . ."

An apparent promise which, according to its terms, makes performance optional with the promisor no matter what may happen, or no matter what course of conduct in other respects he may pursue, is in fact no promise. Such an expression is often called an illusory promise. Williston, Contracts § 1A (3d ed 1957).

When we give the ordinary and usual meaning to the words of the contract—desire and desirous—it is apparent that they express a wish or request. Certainly, they do not carry the thrust of a promise to do or refrain from doing anything with regard to the remaining property. There is no expressed obligation to develop the property at anytime.

In the case of *Jones v Realty Co.*, 226 NC 303, 37 SE2d 906 (1946), the plaintiff sued to recover a sales commission for procuring a purchaser who was ready, willing, and able to buy land on terms set out in an agreement. The trial court interpreted the agreement between the parties to mean that the commission was to be paid "when"—and only when—"the deal is closed up." The deal never closed, and the Court said . . . that,

It can make no difference whether the event be called a contingency or the time of performance. Certainly, under either construction, the result would be the same; since, if the event does not befall, or a time coincident with the happening of the event does not arrive, in neither case may performance be exacted. Nor will it do to say that a promise to pay "when the deal is closed up" is a promise to pay when it ought to be closed up according to the terms of the contract. Such is not the meaning of the words used. It is the event itself, and not the date of its expected or contemplated happening, that makes the promise to pay performable.

By the conveyance of the property . . . , the defendants served notice to the plaintiff, and to all the world, that they would never develop the property, and such conveyance and notice terminated the agreement, if any there was. . . .

[Judgment reversed]

QUESTIONS

1. Who were the defendants in this case?

2. Why didn't the plaintiff sue the purchaser of the second Hill-Terrell tract?

3. Did the purchaser of the second tract know of the agreement as to the parking lot?

7.   Additional Printed Matter

Frequently a contract is mailed or delivered by one party to the other in an envelope that contains additional printed matter. Similarly, when goods are purchased, the buyer often receives with the goods a manufacturer's manual and various pamphlets. What effect do all these papers have upon the contract? The same question arises when a worker gets a new job, and the employer hands the new employee a handbook or a set of rules. Is this material a part of the contract?

(a) INCORPORATION OF OTHER STATEMENT. The contract itself may furnish the answer. Sometimes the contract will expressly refer to and incorporate into the contract the terms of the other writing or printed statement. For example, a warehouse contract may expressly state that it covers the "goods of the customer," but instead of listing the goods, the contract will describe the goods "as set forth in Schedule A, which is delivered to the customer with this contract." Frequently such a schedule will be stapled or otherwise attached to the contract itself. The contract may say that the customer will be charged at the rates set forth in the approved tariff schedule posted on the premises of the warehouse, and may continue with the words, "a copy of which is attached hereto and made part of this contract."

(b) EXCLUSION OF OTHER STATEMENT. As the opposite of incorporation, the contract may declare that there is no agreement outside of the contract. This means that either there never was anything else or that any prior agreement was merely a preliminary step that is finally canceled out or erased. The contract in its final form is stated in the writing. For example, the seller of goods may state in the contract that no statements as to the goods have been made to the buyer and that the written contract contains all of the terms of the sale.

(c) REDUCTION OF CONTRACT TERMS. The effect of accompanying or subsequently delivered printed matter may be to reduce the terms of the written contract. That is, one party may have had a better bargain under the original contract. In this case, the accompanying matter will generally be ignored if it is not shown that the party who would be harmed had agreed that it be part of the contract.

This is so because a contract, once made, cannot be changed by unilateral action—that is, by the action of one party or one side of the contract without the agreement of the other.

(d) EMPLOYEE'S HANDBOOK. It is a common practice for large employers to hand a new employee a manual or handbook that sets forth various matters relating to the employment. The question can then arise whether the statements in the handbook are binding terms of the employment contract or whether they are merely statements of the employer's existing policies or practices. If the handbook constitutes part of the contract, it cannot be changed by the action of the employer alone. If they are merely a statement of policies or practices, the terms of the handbook can be changed at will. Litigation frequently arises when an employee who is fired or denied pension rights claims that this is a violation of the terms of the handbook.

Whether the handbook is part of the employment contract depends on the intent of the parties. If the handbook has been carefully written, it will specify whether it represents terms of the contract or merely policies. If this is not done by the handbook or other terms of the contract, it then becomes a question of fact as to what intent the parties had. This means that ordinarily the question is decided by the jury as a question of fact.

FIGURE 9-2   CONTRACT
Note that this contract includes the following important items of information: (1) the name and address of
each party, (2) the promise or consideration of the seller, (3) the promise or consideration of the buyer, (4) the
signature of the two parties, and (5) the date.

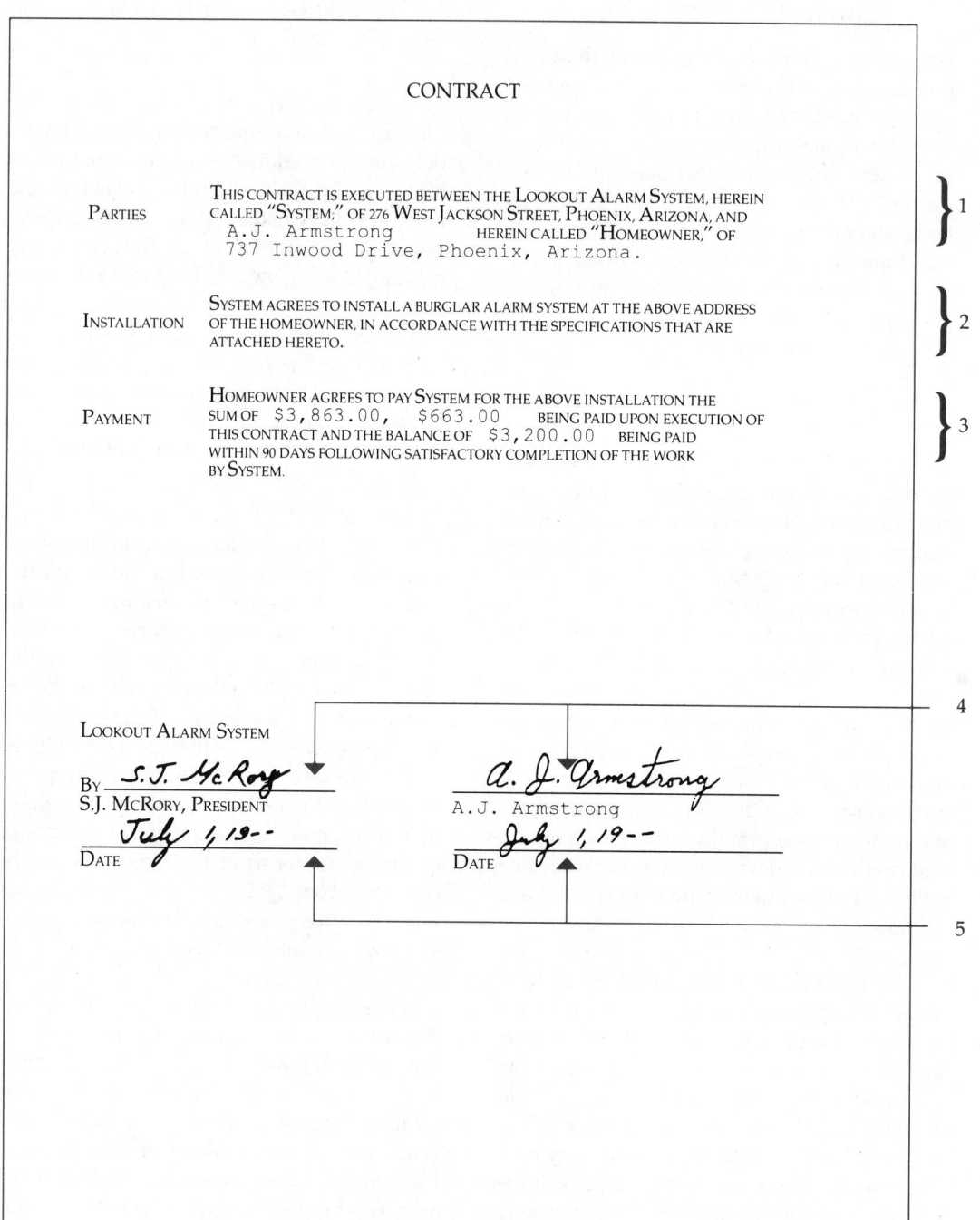

CONTRACT

PARTIES

THIS CONTRACT IS EXECUTED BETWEEN THE LOOKOUT ALARM SYSTEM, HEREIN
CALLED "SYSTEM," OF 276 WEST JACKSON STREET, PHOENIX, ARIZONA, AND
   A.J. Armstrong   HEREIN CALLED "HOMEOWNER," OF
   737 Inwood Drive, Phoenix, Arizona.   } 1

INSTALLATION

SYSTEM AGREES TO INSTALL A BURGLAR ALARM SYSTEM AT THE ABOVE ADDRESS
OF THE HOMEOWNER, IN ACCORDANCE WITH THE SPECIFICATIONS THAT ARE
ATTACHED HERETO.   } 2

PAYMENT

HOMEOWNER AGREES TO PAY SYSTEM FOR THE ABOVE INSTALLATION THE
SUM OF $3,863.00, $663.00   BEING PAID UPON EXECUTION OF
THIS CONTRACT AND THE BALANCE OF $3,200.00   BEING PAID
WITHIN 90 DAYS FOLLOWING SATISFACTORY COMPLETION OF THE WORK
BY SYSTEM.   } 3

LOOKOUT ALARM SYSTEM   4

BY _S.J. McRory_   _a. J. Armstrong_
S.J. McRORY, PRESIDENT   A.J. Armstrong
   July 1, 19--   _July 1, 19--_
DATE   DATE   5

Thus, an employee's handbook may become part of the contract of employment when the circumstances surrounding the hiring of the employee manifests the intent that the handbook be so regarded. The same conclusion may be reached when a handbook is distributed to existing employees, and they continue to work thereafter without any objection.[3]

B.   CLASSES OF CONTRACTS

Contracts are classified with respect to their form, their binding character, and the extent to which they have been performed.

8.   Formal and Informal Contracts

Contracts can be classified as formal or informal contracts.

(a) FORMAL CONTRACTS. **Formal contracts** are enforced because the formality with which they are executed is considered sufficient to signify that the parties intend to be bound by their terms. Formal contracts include (1) contracts under seal, (2) contracts of record, and (3) negotiable instruments.

(1) Contracts under Seal. A **contract under seal** is executed by affixing a seal or making an impression on the paper or on some adhering substance, such as wax, attached to the document. Although at common law an impression was necessary, the courts now treat various signs or marks to be the equivalent of a seal. Most states hold that there is a seal if a person's signature or a corporation's name is followed by a scroll or scrawl, the word *seal*, or the letters *L.S.* In some jurisdictions the body of the contract must recite that the parties are sealing the contract, in addition to their making a seal following their signatures.[4]

A contract under seal was binding at common law solely because of its formality. In many states this has been changed by statute. The Uniform Commercial Code abolishes the law of seals for the sale of goods. In some states the law of seals has been abolished generally, without regard to the nature of the transaction involved. Unless expressly required by statute or administrative regulation, a seal is not needed in order to make a binding contract. The parties have the freedom of choice to use or do without a seal.

(2) Contracts of Record. A **contract of record** is an agreement or obligation that has been recorded by a court. One form of contract of record arises when one acknowledges before a proper court the obligation to pay a certain sum unless a specified condition is met. For example, a party who has been arrested may be released on a promise to appear in court and may agree to pay a certain sum on failing to do so. An obligation of this kind is known as a **recognizance**.

Similarly, an agreement made with an administrative agency is binding because it has been so made. For example, when a business agrees with the Federal Trade Commission that the enterprise will stop a particular practice that the Commission regards as unlawful, the business is bound by its agreement and cannot thereafter reject it.

(3) Negotiable Instruments. **Negotiable instruments** are contracts governed by the law of commercial paper. These special-purpose contracts must meet certain formal requirements in order to be enforceable.

(b) INFORMAL CONTRACTS. All other contracts are called **informal** (or **simple**) **contracts**, without regard to whether they are oral or written. These contracts are enforceable, not because of the form of the transaction, but because they represent the agreement of the parties.

9.   Express and Implied Contracts

Simple contracts may be classified in terms of the way in which they are created, as express contracts or implied contracts.

(a) EXPRESS CONTRACTS. An **express contract** is one in which the agreement of the

---

[3]   Duldulao v Saint Mary of Nazareth Hospital Center, 115 I11 2d 482, 106 I11 Dec 8, 505 NE2d 314 (1987).
[4]   Lumbermen's Mutual Cas. Co. v Pattillo Constr. Co. 172 Ga App 452, 323 SE2d 649 (1984).

parties is manifested by their words, whether spoken or written.

(b) IMPLIED CONTRACTS. An **implied contract** (or, as sometimes stated, a contract implied in fact) is one in which the agreement is not shown by words, written or spoken, but by the acts and conduct of the parties. Such a contract arises, for example, when one person renders services under circumstances indicating that payment for them is expected, and the other person, knowing such circumstances, accepts the benefit of those services.[5] Similarly, when an owner requests a professional roofer to make repairs to the roof of a building, an obligation arises to pay the reasonable value of such services, although no agreement has been made as to compensation.

In terms of effect, there is no difference between an implied contract and an express contract. The difference relates solely to the manner of proving the existence of the contract.

An implied contract cannot arise when there is an existing express contract on the same subject.

No contract is implied when the relationship of the parties is such that by a reasonable interpretation, the performance of services or the supplying of goods was intended as a gift.[6]

In *Novak's Estate*, the mother died, and her daughter claimed compensation for services she had rendered to her mother.

[5]   Knight v Post (Utah App) 748 P2d 1097 (1988).
[6]   Hildebrand v Ballard (Mo App) 767 SW2d 62 (1989).

NOVAK'S ESTATE
(Minn App) 398 NW2d 653 (1987)

Clara Novak was sick. Her daughter Janie helped her in many ways. Clara died, and Janie then claimed that she was entitled to be paid for the services that she had rendered her mother. The court dismissed her claim, and she appealed.

SEDGWICK, J. . . . Clara Novak suffered kidney failure in 1971. Dialysis treatment was required since November 1977. She died on June 23, 1984, just before her 71st birthday.

Clara Novak's will provided $2,000 to her church and the residue of her estate to be divided equally among her children. One daughter, Janie Novak, claims she is entitled to a greater share because she was the primary caretaker for her mother for at least six years. Janie's claim against the estate for $26,105.50 for her services was denied. Her siblings claim Janie was simply doing her part and that three other children also helped their mother.

Janie Novak claims she averaged two hours a day helping her mother. Janie became a licensed practical nurse at her mother's suggestion. She worked nights in order to help her mother during the day. She drove her mother to the Little Falls hospital 96 times for dialysis and made seven trips to the Hennepin County Medical Center. Janie also reports the loss of 16 days, 5 hours of vacation time on her mother's behalf. She incurred phone expense because of her mother's condition. She lived a quarter mile distance from her mother and was a frequent visitor. Appellant argued:

> Janie . . . provided nursing services on a daily basis in Clara's home. Janie would also check her mother's blood pressure and other vital signs, bathe her, do her hair, clip her toe and fingernails, massage her scalp, and attended to other hygiene needs. Janie would do her mother's shopping for her, pay her bills, provide her with transport to and from various business establishments, and otherwise

attend to her mother's needs. After one of her mother's many hospitalizations, Janie kept her mother in her own home for a period of some three months, and personally attended to her mother's various medical ailments at the time. In short, Janie provided nursing services for her mother's well-being for a period in excess of thirteen years.

The family responded that Janie merely did her share; three other siblings also helped out. The trips for dialysis were thrice weekly and since other family members gave Clara rides, 96 trips over 6 years was not an unreasonable figure. The siblings state that Janie's son Jeffrey often made the dialysis trips rather than Janie. In 1978, Clara purchased a new car for the trips and paid for travel expenses. The family offered as evidence a number of checks, mostly for small amounts, payable to Janie Novak. From September 1983 to March 1984, another daughter took Clara in and cared for her. The family also points out that Clara's medical needs were satisfied by the Little Falls hospital, and that the medical services, such as blood pressure checks, temperature, etc., supplied by Janie were solely for her own peace of mind. She did not maintain records as a nurse would when providing professional services. . . .

The courts proceed on the premise that services provided between family/household member are gratuitous.

> The presumption of gratuity is dependent on the existence of a family relation and only arises when it is shown that the services rendered were of the type which members of a family usually and ordinarily render to each other by reason of family relation. The authorities stress the fact that the presence of those reciprocal duties within the family is essential to the creation of this presumption.

In re Estate of Tilghman, 240 Minn. 494, 495, 61 N.W.2d 743, 745 (1953). The presumption operates if the family relation exists. . . .

Appellant argues that "family" does not include a blood relation who lives independently from the person to whom the services were rendered, *i.e.,* a non-household member should not be saddled with the presumption. We believe the presumption properly applies to immediate family regardless of their residence. "Household" is simply a more inclusive term since it may include individuals residing with a family and participating in the exchange of services, but absent a blood tie. Whether or not family members reside in the same household, the question is the extent to which care furnished exceeds "reciprocal duties and mutual benefits." *Id.* at 499, 61 N.W.2d at 747. . . .

The evidentiary presumption arises where there is a family relationship, as evidenced by a close blood relation and/or a membership in a family's household. Once the "close" relationship is established where individuals are presumed to commonly share duties and provide services to other family members, the analysis shifts to an examination of whether the exchange of services was actually mutual and reciprocal. If one party rendered or received an obviously disproportionate share of services, the absence of mutuality may obviate the presumption.

The more distant the kinship or relationship, the easier it is to overcome the presumption since reciprocal benefits are more limited. A daughter-in-law . . . or a daughter with no parental contact for fifty years (*Tilghman*) will be able to avoid the presumption, while a child who has always been close to her parents will have a difficult task overcoming the presumption absent significant inequities. It must be remembered the presumption is an evidentiary device, and it is not an absolute bar to recovery.

In the present case, Janie Novak lived nearby and provided a number of services to her elderly, sick mother. Her care and assistance does not rise to the level in *Tilghman* . . . and does not appear to be disproportionate to the aid provided by her siblings. She also received one-sixth of the estate. Even if she provided more services, while others did less (and perhaps other siblings did nothing), the balancing of the equities does not justify an interference with the testamentary plan of the deceased.

[Judgment affirmed]

QUESTIONS

1. What is the basis for the presumption applied by the court?
2. What is the distinction between family and household?
3. Did the facts of the case confirm or rebut the presumption of gratuity?

10. Valid and Voidable Contracts and Void Agreements

Contracts may be classified in terms of enforceability or validity.

(a) VALID CONTRACTS. A **valid contract** is an agreement that is binding and enforceable.

(b) VOIDABLE CONTRACTS. A **voidable contract** is an agreement that is otherwise binding and enforceable, but because of the circumstances surrounding its execution or the lack of capacity of one of the parties, it may be rejected at the option of one of the parties. For example, a person who has been forced to sign an agreement which that person would not have voluntarily signed may in some instances avoid the contract.

(c) VOID AGREEMENTS. A **void agreement** is without legal effect. An agreement that contemplates the performance of an act prohibited by law is usually incapable of enforcement; hence it is void. Likewise, it cannot be made binding by later approval or ratification.[7]

11. Executed and Executory Contracts

Contracts may be classified, in terms of the extent to which they have been performed, as executed contracts and executory contracts.

(a) EXECUTED CONTRACTS. An **executed contract** is one that has been completely performed. In other words, an executed contract is one under which nothing remains to be done by either party. A contract may be executed at once, as in the case of a cash sale; or it may be executed or performed in the future.

(b) EXECUTORY CONTRACTS. In an **executory contract**, something remains to be done by one or both parties. For example, if a utility company agrees to furnish electricity to a customer for a specified period of time at a stipulated price, the contract is executory. If the entire price is paid in advance, the contract is still deemed executory; although, strictly speaking, it is executed on one side and executory on the other.

12. Bilateral and Unilateral Contracts

In making an offer, the offeror is in effect extending a promise to do something, such as to pay a sum of money, if the offeree will do what the offeror requests. Contracts are classified as bilateral or unilateral. Some bilateral contracts

---

[7]   See Section 1 of Chapter 13. Although the distinction between a void agreement and a voidable contract is clear in theory, there is frequently confusion. Some courts describe a given transaction as void, while others regard it as merely voidable.

look ahead to the making of a later contract. Depending on their terms, these are called option contracts or first-refusal contracts.

(a) BILATERAL CONTRACT. If the offeror extends a promise and asks for a promise in return and if the offeree accepts the offer by making the promise, the contract is called a **bilateral contract.** One promise is given in exchange for another, and each party is bound by the obligation. For example, when the house painter offers to paint the owner's house for $1,000, and the owner promises to pay $1,000 for the job, there is an exchange of promises, and the agreement gives rise to a bilateral contract.

(b) UNILATERAL CONTRACT. In contrast, the offeror may offer to do something only when something is done by the offeree. Because only one party is obligated to perform after the contract has been made, this kind of contract is called a **unilateral contract.** This is illustrated by the case of the reward for the return of lost property. The offeror does not wish to have promises by members of the public that they will try to return the property. The offeror wants the property and promises to pay anyone who returns the property. The offer of a unilateral contract calls for an act; a promise to do the act does not give rise to a contract.

(c) OPTION AND FIRST-REFUSAL CONTRACTS. The parties may make a contract that gives a right to one of the parties to enter into a second contract at a later date. If one party has an absolute right to enter into the later contract, the initial contract is called an **option contract.** Thus, a bilateral contract may be made today giving one of the parties the right to buy the other party's house for a specified amount. This is an option contract, as the party with the privilege has the freedom of choice, or option, to buy or not buy. If the option is exercised, the other party to the contract must follow the terms of the option and enter into the second contract. If the option is never exercised, no second contract ever aris-

es, and the offer protected by the option contract merely expires.[8]

In contrast with an option contract, a contract may merely give a **right of first refusal.** This only imposes the duty to make the first offer to the party having the right of first refusal. For example, the homeowner could make a contract providing that, should the owner desire to sell at some future time, the other party to the contract could buy either at a fixed price or at a price matching a good-faith bid by a third person. Here the homeowner cannot be required to sell, but if the owner attempts to sell, an option immediately comes into existence by which the other party can buy or not buy.[9]

The situation can arise in which there is a question as to whether there is a contract to sell, an option to buy, or a right of first refusal. In all cases the answer is determined by the intent of the parties.

13.   Quasi Contracts

In some cases the courts will pretend that there is a contract when in fact there is no contract. Such a make-believe contract is called a **quasi contract.**

(a) PREVENTION OF UNJUST ENRICHMENT. Such quasi contracts are recognized in a limited number of situations in order to attain an equitable or just result. These instances may be classified in terms of situations in which there is no contract between the parties; those in which there was a contract between the parties, but it has been avoided; and those in which there was an attempted contract, but for some reason the agreement is held illegal and therefore void. The power to prevent unjust enrichment, however, does not authorize a court to refuse to enforce the unambiguous terms of a lawful contract.[10]

(1) No Contract. In some cases the hoped-for contract is never formed. The parties ex-

---

[8]   Perkins v Daughtery (Ky App) 722 SW2d 907 (1987).
[9]   Lin Broadcasting Corp. v Metromedia, Inc. 74 NY2d 54, 544 NYS2d 316, 542 NE2d 629 (1989).
[10]   Rongotes v Pridemore, 88 NC App 363, 363 SE2d 221 (1988).

pect that there will be a contract, but something happens that prevents their reaching a final agreement. Meanwhile, one or more of the parties may have acted prematurely and begun performing as though there were a contract. When it is finally clear that there is no contract, a party who had rendered some performance will seek to be paid for what was done. The claim will be made that if payment is not made, the other party will be unjustly enriched.

The no-contract case may arise in a situation where there is a mistake as to the subject matter of the contract. For example, a painter may begin painting the house of *A* because of a mistake as to the address of the building. *A* sees the work going on and realizes the painter is making a mistake. Nevertheless, *A* does not stop the painter. When the painter finishes the work and presents a bill for painting, *A* then refuses to pay because there never was a contract. This is true because *A* never expressly agreed for the painting. Likewise, the conduct of *A* never caused the painter as a reasonable person to believe that *A* was entering into a contract. The painter just assumed that everything was all right.

In such a case the law deems it inequitable that *A* should have remained silent and then reaped the benefits of the painter's mistake. *A* will therefore be required to pay the painter the reasonable value of the painting. This liability is described as quasi-contractual.

The mistake that benefits the defendant may be the mistake of a third person.

(2) The Avoided Contract. In some situations one party to the contract may be able to avoid it or set it aside. As will be seen in Chapter 11, the contract of a minor can be avoided. If the contract was for something necessary received by the minor, the minor must pay the reasonable value of what was received. The minor is not required to pay the contract price, but only the reasonable value of the benefit received. As the liability enforced against the minor is not based on the contract, it is called quasi-contractual.

Likewise, when the parties rescind or set aside their contract, a party who has already conferred a benefit on the other party before the contract was rescinded may recover in quasi contract for the value of such benefit. Thus, a contractor may recover for the value of an irrigation system installed on the defendant's land before the construction contract was set aside.[11]

(3) The Void Agreement. In some instances, the parties make a contract, one party receives the benefit of the contract, and then the benefited party seeks to avoid paying on the ground that the contract was void because of illegality. For example, governmental units, such as cities, must generally advertise for the lowest responsible bidder when a contract is to be made to obtain supplies or to construct buildings. In some instances, the city officials may improperly skip the advertising. This might be done either because of a corrupt purpose or because the officials honestly, but wrongly, believed that the particular contract came within an exception to the requirement of advertising. Whatever the reason, the city officials enter into a contract with a contractor without following the statutory procedures. The contractor fully performs the contract. When the contractor requests to be paid, the city officials refuse to live up to the contract on the ground that the contract violated the statutory requirements and therefore was illegal and void. In such cases it will be held that although the contract is void, the city must pay the reasonable value of what has been done. In this way, the contractor gets paid for what the contractor really did. The city is not required to pay for any more than it has actually received. The danger of the city's paying inflated prices, which was the evil that the advertising statute sought to avoid, does not arise, because the court does not require the city to pay the contract price but only the reasonable value of the benefit conferred upon the city.

(b) WHEN QUASI-CONTRACTUAL LIABILITY DOES NOT EXIST. While the objective

---

[11]   Murdock-Bryant Construction Inc. v Pearson, 146 Ariz 48, 703 P2d 1197 (1985).

of the quasi contract is to do justice, one must not jump to the conclusion that a quasi contract arises every time there is an injustice. The mere fact that someone has benefited someone else and has not been paid will not necessarily give rise to a quasi contract.[12] For example, no quasi-contractual obligation arises when the plaintiff merely confers on the defendant a benefit to which the defendant was already entitled.

(1) Unexpected Cost. The fact that performance of a contract proves more difficult or more expensive than had been expected does not entitle a party to extra compensation when there was no misrepresentation as to the conditions that would be encountered or the events that would occur. Courts are particularly unwilling to allow extra compensation when the complaining party is experienced with the particular type of contract and the problems that are likely to be encountered. That is, the contractor is not entitled to quasi-contractual recovery for extra expense on the theory that the extra work had conferred a greater benefit than had been contemplated.

(2) Existing Contract. A plaintiff cannot sue in *quantum meruit*, or for reasonable value, when there is an express contract fixing the amount due. In other words, a person cannot recover for the reasonable value of goods or services when there is an existing contract that obligates the obligor of that contract to pay a set price for the goods or services rendered.

A subcontractor doing work that benefits the homeowner can only sue the contractor on the contract between the subcontractor and the contractor. The subcontractor cannot sue the owner merely because the owner was benefited by the work done by the subcontractor. Likewise, when a distributor of tires is not paid by a dealer, the distributor cannot sue the customer who bought the tires from the dealer for the bill that the dealer should have paid the distributor.[13]

In the *Niggel Associates* case it was claimed that a stranger to the transaction had been unjustly enriched by the performance of a contract between two other persons.

---

[12]   Kapral's Tire Service, Inc. v Aztek Tread Corp. 124 App Div 2d 1011, 508 NYS2d 777 (1986).

[13]   City of Damascus v Bivens, 291 Ark 600, 726 SW2d 677 (1987).

NIGGEL ASSOCIATES, INC. v POLO'S OF NORTH MYRTLE BEACH, INC.

(App) 296 SC 530, 374 SE2d 507 (1988)

Windy Hill held a long-term lease of a large tract of land from the local airport commission. Beach Investments leased part of this land from Windy Hill. Beach contracted with Niggel Associates and Mechanical Industrial to do tiling, heating, and cooling work in two buildings located on the part of the land rented by Beach. They were not paid and sued everyone related to the property. The lower court held that Windy Hill was unjustly enriched and required it to make restitution to the contractors. Windy Hill appealed.

BELL, J. . . . The plaintiff must show: (1) that he conferred a nongratuitous benefit on the defendant; (2) that the defendant realized some value from the benefit; and (3) that it would be inequitable for the defendant to retain the benefit without paying the plaintiff its value. . . .

The plaintiff must confer the benefit nongratuitously: that is, it must either be (1) at the defendant's request or (2) in circumstances where the plaintiff reasonably relies on the defendant to pay for the benefit and the defendant understands or ought to understand that the plaintiff expects compensation and looks to him for payment....

In this case, the Contractors did the work under contracts with Beach. They expected to be paid by Beach. They had no dealings whatever with Windy Hill. Indeed, they did not know Windy Hill had an interest in the property when they agreed to perform the work. Windy Hill did not request the work. It did nothing to cause the Contractors to rely on it for payment. It had no reason to suppose the Contractors looked to it for payment. The Contractors were not induced to furnish their labor and materials by any expectation that Windy Hill would pay for them. In these circumstances, Windy Hill had no duty to make restitution to the Contractors. Any benefit it received was an incidental result of dealings between others in which it did not participate and over which it assumed no control.

Additionally, the Contractors failed to prove the value of any benefit Windy Hill may have received from their work. In a case involving improvements to realty, the measure of recovery in restitution is the difference in the fair market value of the property before and after the improvements.... The Contractors introduced no evidence to show their work increased the value of Windy Hill's leasehold interest. They neglected to prove the value of the leasehold before and after the work. Accordingly, there was no proof that the defendant realized value from the benefit conferred.

Because Niggel and Mechanical Industrial failed to prove essential elements of their case, the [lower] court erred in granting restitution.

[Judgment reversed]

QUESTIONS

1. What was the basis for the court's decision in the *Niggel Associates* case?
2. Could the contractors have recovered from Beach for unjust enrichment if the facts otherwise remained the same?

---

(3) No Unjust Enrichment. In order to recover in quasi contract, the plaintiff must prove that the defendant was enriched, the extent or dollar value of such enrichment, and that such enrichment was unjust. If the plaintiff cannot prove all these elements, there can be no recovery in quasi contract. A creditor receiving the money that is owed is not unjustly enriched thereby.[14]

(4) Gift Benefit. There can be no recovery for unjust enrichment when the circumstances are such that it is reasonable to conclude that goods or services were furnished to the benefited party with the intent to make a gift and not in the expectation of being compensated.[15]

(c) Extent of Recovery. When recovery is allowed in quasi contract, the plaintiff recovers the reasonable value of the benefit conferred upon the defendant. The fact that the plaintiff may have sustained greater damages, or have been put to greater expense, is ignored.[16] Thus, the plaintiff cannot recover lost profits or other kinds of damages that would be recovered in a suit for breach of a contract.

---

[14] Lynch v Deaconess Medical Center, 113 Wash 2d 162, 776 P2d 681 (1989).

[15] Lewis' Estate v Mordy, 168 Mich App 70, 423 NW2d 600 (1988). As noted in Section 9(b) of this Chapter, no implied contract arises in this situation.

[16] Morphy, Makofsky & Masson, Inc. v Canal Place 2000 (La App) 522 So 2d 1223 (1988).

SUMMARY

A contract is a binding agreement between two or more parties. A contract arises when an offer is accepted with contractual intent (the intent to make a binding agreement). When a written contract is sent with additional printed matter, questions arise whether the additional matter is part of the contract. The contract itself may furnish the answer.

Contracts may be classified in a number of ways: as to form, manifestation, validity, and obligations. With respect to form, a contract may be formal, such as those under seal or those appearing on the records of courts or administrative agencies. The manifestation of the agreement distinguishes between agreements that are expressed by words—written or oral—and those that are implied or deduced from conduct. The question of validity requires distinguishing between contracts that are valid; those that are voidable; and those that are not contracts at all, but are merely void agreements. Contracts can be distinguished on the basis of the obligations created, as executed contracts, in which everything has been performed, and executory contracts,

in which something remains to be done. The bilateral contract is formed by exchanging a promise for a promise, so each party has the obligation of thereafter rendering the promised performance. In the unilateral contract, which is the doing of an act in exchange for a promise, no further performance is required of the offeree who performed the act. The only obligation is that of the promisor.

In certain situations the law regards it as unjust that a person should receive a benefit and not pay for it. In such case the law of quasi contracts allows the performing person to recover the reasonable value of the benefit conferred upon the benefited person, even though there is no contract between them requiring any payment. The unjust enrichment, which quasi contract is designed to prevent, sometimes arises when there never was any contract between the persons involved or when there was a contract, but for some reason it was avoided or held to be merely a void agreement. Quasi-contractual recovery is not allowed merely because someone loses money.

QUESTIONS AND CASE PROBLEMS

1. State the specific objective(s) of the law (from the list in Chapter 2, Section 4) illustrated by the following quotation: "A person shall not be allowed to enrich himself unjustly at the expense of another."

   Note: As you study the various rules of law in this chapter and the chapters that follow, consider each rule in relationship to its social, economic, and ethical background. Try to determine the particular objective(s) of each important rule. To the extent that you are able to analyze law as the product of society's striving for justice, you will have a greater insight into the law itself, the world in which you live, the field of business, and the human mind.

2. What is a contract?

3. Ackerman went to the phone book and sent letters to randomly selected names. The letter to each stated, "It is agreed that we will paint your house for a price based on the cost of our labor

and paint plus an additional 10 percent for profit." He sent such a letter to Maria. Is there a contract between Ackerman and Maria?

4. Henry made a written contract to paint Betty's house for $500. The reasonable value of such work was $1,000. Henry made the price low in the hope that Betty's neighbors would have him paint their houses. He painted Betty's house. He got no work from the neighbors. He then sent Betty a bill for $1,000 on the ground that an implied contract existed to pay him the reasonable value of his services. Was he entitled to recover $1,000?

5. Stephen said to Hilda, "I want to buy your old automobile." She replied, "It's yours for $400." Stephen replied, "I'll take it." Later Stephen changed his mind and refused to take or pay for the car. When Hilda sued him for damages, he raised the defense that he had never made a contract with her because they had never

pressly stated, "We hereby make a contract for the sale of the automobile." Stephen claimed that in the absence of such an express declaration showing that they intended to make a contract, there could be no binding agreement to purchase the automobile. Was he correct?

6. Legal stationery stores sell blank forms of contracts. In many states, at the end of such forms, following the lines on which the parties sign, will appear the letters "L.S." or the word "seal." When the parties to a contract sign such a form, it is held that they have signed a sealed contract. What social force is involved in this rule of law?

7. Compare an implied contract and a quasi contract.

8. *A* made a contract to construct a house for *B*. Subsequently, *B* sued *A* for breach of contract. *A* raised the defense that the contract was not binding because it was not sealed. Is this a valid defense? [Cooper v G. E. Construction Co. 116 Ga App 690, 158 SE2d 305]

9. Carlos Estaban was nine years old when his parents were killed in an auto crash. Maria Pedrillo, a friend of the family, took Carlos into her home and raised him. Carlos was never adopted by Maria, but all the neighbors thought he was related to Maria. About 20 years later Maria became very sick and, after a long period, died. During this time she was dependent on Carlos, who ran the house, prepared her meals, and did whatever had to be done. Carlos kept an itemized list of what he had done. He gave a copy of this list to the executor of Maria's estate and demanded that he be paid the reasonable value of his services. Was he entitled to compensation for such services?

10. Dozier and his wife, daughter, and grandson lived in the house Dozier owned. At the request of the daughter and grandson, Paschall made some improvements to the house. Dozier did not authorize these, but he knew that the improvements were being made and did not object to them. Paschall sued Dozier for the reasonable value of the improvements. Dozier defended on the ground that he had not made any contract for such improvements. Was he obligated to pay for such improvements?

11. Harriet went away for the summer. In her absence Landry, a housepainter, painted her house. Landry had a contract to paint a neighbor's house, but painted Harriet's house by mistake. The painting of Harriet's house was worth $1,200. When she returned from her vacation, Landry billed her for $1,200. She refused to pay.

He claimed that she had a quasi-contractual liability for that amount. Was he correct?

12. By his will Andrew Czapp left one-half of his land to his son Wesley and one-half to his daughter Anna. His will also gave Wesley "an option" to lease the land given to Anna and "a first option" to purchase that land at its fair market value. After Andrew's death, Wesley offered Anna the fair market value for her land. She refused to sell, and Wesley brought an action to compel her to recognize his option. Decide. [Czapp v Cox, 179 Mich App 216, 445 NW2d 218]

13. Margrethe and Charles Pyeatte were married. They agreed that she would work so that he could go to law school and that when he finished law school, she would go back to school for her master's degree. After Charles was admitted to the Bar and before Margrethe went back to school, the two were divorced. She sued Charles for breaking their contract. The court held that there was no contract because the agreement between them was too vague to be enforced. Margrethe then claimed that she was entitled to quasi-contractual recovery of the money that she had paid for Charles' support and law school tuition. He denied liability. Was she entitled to recover for the money she spent for Charles' maintenance and law school tuition? [Pyeatte v Pyeatte (App) 135 Ariz 346, 661 P2d 196]

14. Carriage Way was a real estate development of approximately 80 houses and 132 apartments. The property owners were members of the Carriage Way Property Owners Association. Each year, the association would take care of certain open neighboring areas that were used by the property owners, including a nearby lake. The board of directors of the association would make an assessment or charge against the property owners to cover the cost of this work. The property owners paid these assessments for a number of years and then refused to pay any more. In spite of this refusal, the association continued to take care of the areas in question. The association then sued the property owners and claimed that they were liable for the benefit that had been conferred on them. Were the owners liable? [Board of Directors of Carriage Way Property Owners Ass'n v Western National Bank, 139 Ill App 3d 542, 94 Ill Dec 97, 487 NE2d 974]

15. Janet went for a job interview with the Hebrides Manufacturing Company. She was hired, and

both she and the proper officer of the company signed a one-page contract of employment. In the course of the job interview it was explained to Janet that matters relating to sick leave, leave of absence, promotions, insurance, and so on, were all covered by an employee's handbook. When she signed the employment contract she was given a copy of the handbook to keep for herself. After she had been working for a year, a dispute arose as to her right to a leave of absence. She claimed that she was not bound by a restriction in the employee's handbook because that restriction was not in the contract she had signed and the signed contract did not refer in any way to the employee's handbook. Is Janet bound by the provisions of the employee's handbook?

10

THE AGREEMENT

As described in Chapter 9, a contract consists of enforceable obligations that have been voluntarily assumed. Thus, one of the essential elements of a contract is an agreement. The importance of requiring an agreement is that it shows that the parties have voluntarily surrendered a part of their freedom of action—they have bound themselves to act in the manner specified in the contract. Because freedom of action is so essential to the American way of life, society is very careful to be sure that there is a proper agreement whenever any part of that freedom is surrendered. Therefore, it is necessary to show that there was an offer and that while the offer was still existing, it was accepted without any qualification. Only then can it be said that both parties have assented to the terms of the contract, and only then is each party bound by the obligations stated in the contract.

A. REQUIREMENTS OF AN OFFER

An **offer** expresses the willingness of the offeror to enter into a contractual agreement regarding a particular subject. It is a promise that is conditional upon an act, a forbearance, or a return promise that is given in exchange for the promise or its performance.

1.   Contractual Intention

To make an offer, the offeror must intend to or must appear to intend to create a legal obligation. This intent may be shown by conduct. For example, when one party signs a written contract and sends it to the other party, such action is an offer to enter into a contract on the terms of the writing.[1]

There is no contract when a social invitation is made or when an offer is made in jest or excitement. A reasonable person would not regard such an offer as indicating a willingness to enter into a binding agreement.

(a) INVITATION TO NEGOTIATE. The first statement made by one of two persons is not necessarily an offer. In many instances, there may be a preliminary discussion or an *invitation* by one party to the other to *negotiate* or to make an offer. Thus, an inquiry by a school as to whether a teacher wished to continue the following year was merely a survey or invitation to negotiate and was not an offer that could be accepted. Therefore, the teacher's affirmative response did not create a contract.[2]

Ordinarily, a seller sending out circulars or catalogs listing prices is not regarded as making an offer to sell at those prices. The seller is merely indicating a willingness to consider an offer made by a buyer on those terms. The reason for this rule is, in part, the practical consideration that since a seller does not have an unlimited supply of any commodity, the seller cannot possibly intend to make a contract with everyone who sees the circular. The same principle is applied to merchandise that is displayed with price tags in stores or store windows and to most advertisements. A "For Sale" advertisement in a newspaper is merely an invitation to negotiate and is not an offer

that can be accepted by a reader of the paper, even if the seller in fact has only one of the particular item advertised.

The circumstances may be such, however, that even a newspaper advertisement constitutes an offer. Thus, the seller may make an offer when the advertisement states that specific items will be sold at a clearance sale at the prices listed and adds the words *first-come, first-served*.

Quotations of prices, even when sent on request, are likewise not offers in the absence of previous dealings between the parties or the existence of a trade custom that would give the recipient of the quotation reason to believe that an offer was being made. Whether a price quotation is to be treated as an offer or merely an invitation to negotiate is a question of the intent of the party making such quotation. Although sellers are not bound by quotations and price tags, they will, as a matter of goodwill, ordinarily make every effort to deliver the merchandise at those prices.[3]

In some instances it is apparent that an invitation to negotiate rather than an offer has been made. When construction work is done for the national government, for a state government, or for a political subdivision, statutes require that a printed statement of the work to be done be published and circulated. Contractors are invited to submit bids on the work, and the statute generally requires that the bid of the lowest responsible bidder be accepted. Such an invitation for bids is clearly an invitation to negotiate, both from its nature and from the fact that it does not specify the price to be paid for the work. The bid of each contractor is an offer, and there is no contract until the government accepts one of these bids.[4] This procedure of advertising for bids is also commonly employed by private persons when a large construction project is involved.

In some cases the fact that important terms are missing serves to indicate that the parties are merely negotiating and that an oral con-

[1]   Arga Co. v Limbach, 36 Ohio 3d 220, 522 NE2d 1074 (1988).
[2]   Knipmeyer v Diocese of Alexandria (La App) 492 So 2d 550 (1986).

[3]   Statutes prohibiting false or misleading advertising may also require adherence to advertised prices.
[4]   Dick Fischer Development Co. No. 2, Inc. v Department of Administration (Alaska) 778 P2d 1153 (1989).

FIGURE 10-1   OFFER AND ACCEPTANCE

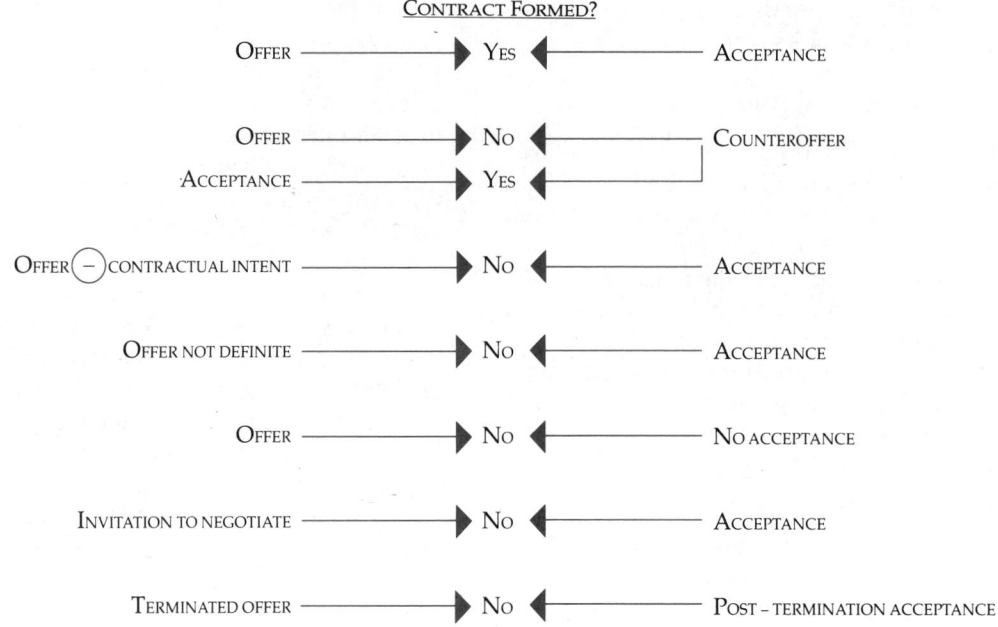

tract has not been made. When a letter or printed promotional matter of a party leaves many significant details to be worked out later, the letter or printed matter is merely an invitation to negotiate. It is not an offer that may be accepted and a contract thereby formed.

(b) STATEMENT OF INTENTION. In some instances a person may make a statement of intention but not intend to be bound by a contract. For example, a certain lease does not expressly allow the tenant to terminate the lease in the case of a job transfer. The landlord states that should the tenant be required to leave for that reason, the landlord would try to find a new tenant to take over the lease. This declaration of intention does not give rise to a binding contract. The landlord cannot be held liable for breach of contract should the landlord fail to obtain a new tenant or not even attempt to obtain a new tenant.

(c) AGREEMENT TO MAKE A CONTRACT AT A FUTURE DATE. No contract arises when the parties merely agree that at a future date they will consider making a contract or will make a contract on terms to be agreed on at that time. In such a case neither party is under any obligation until the future contract is made. Similarly, there is no contract between the parties if essential terms are left open for future negotiation.[5] Thus, a promise to pay a bonus or compensation to be decided on after three months of business operation is not binding. Likewise, no binding contract to renew a contract upon its expiration was created by a provision in the original contract that upon its expiration the parties intend to "negotiate in good faith to renew this agreement for an additional year upon terms and conditions to be negotiated."[6]

The *Beck* case raised the question of whether the parties had entered into a binding agreement.

[5]   Satellite Development Co. v Bernt, 229 Neb 778, 429 NW2d 334 (1988).
[6]   Yan's Video, Inc. v Hong Kong TV Video Programs, Inc. 133 App Div 2d 575, 520 NYS2d 143 (1987).

BECK v AMERICAN HEALTH GROUP INTERNATIONAL
211 Cal App 3d 1555, 260 Cal Rptr 237 (1989)

Beck sued the American Health Group for breach of an alleged contract to employ him as psychiatrist for the Palmdale Hospital Medical Center. He placed in evidence a letter written to him by the executive director of the defendant. The letter stated the terms that were being considered and concluded: "If this is a general understanding of the agreement, I ask that you sign a copy of this letter, so that I might forward to Corporate Counsel for the drafting of a contract. When we have a draft, we will discuss it, and hopefully shall have a completed contract and operating unit in the very near future." Beck claimed that there was a binding contract when he signed and mailed this letter as requested. The defendant denied that there was a contract. Judgment was entered for the defendant, and Beck appealed.

LILLIE, J. . . . "Whether a writing constitutes a final agreement or merely an agreement to make an agreement depends primarily upon the intention of the parties. In the absence of ambiguity this must be determined by a construction of the instrument taken as a whole." . . . "Preliminary negotiations or an agreement for future negotiations are not the functional equivalent of a valid, subsisting agreement. 'A manifestation of willingness to enter into a bargain is not an offer if the person to whom it is addressed knows or has reason to know that the person making it does not intend to conclude a bargain until he has made a further manifestation of assent.' " . . . The words of a written instrument are generally to be understood in their ordinary and popular sense. . . . The objective intent as evidenced by the words of the instrument, not the parties' subjective intent, governs our interpretation. "The outward manifestation or expression of assent is controlling . . . and . . . what the language of an [instrument] means is a 'matter of interpretation for the courts and not controlled in any sense by what either of the parties intended or thought its meaning to be. . . .' "

The letter under consideration begins: "It is a pleasure to draft the *outline of our future agreement.* . . ." (Emphasis added.) After outlining the terms of the proposed agreement the writer of the letter asks plaintiff to sign it "if this is a general understanding of the agreement," in order that the Hospital may "forward it to Corporate Counsel *for the drafting of a contract.*" (Emphasis added.) The letter concludes: "When we have a draft, we will discuss it, and *hopefully shall have a completed contract* and operating unit in the very near future." (Emphasis added.) Taken in their ordinary sense, the words of the letter manifest an intention of the parties that no binding contract would come into being until the terms of the letter were embodied in a formal contract to be drafted by corporate counsel. Assignment of the drafting to an attorney evidences an expectation that the terms set forth in the letter were subject to his approval. Even after counsel drafted a contract the letter contemplated further negotiations by its statement that "when we have a draft, we will discuss it." By signing the letter plaintiff assented to its terms, i.e., no binding agreement would result until a formal contract was drafted by counsel. That plaintiff may have intended or believed a binding contract came into existence upon his signing the letter is immaterial in the face of its language which plainly indicated otherwise.

We conclude that the letter did not constitute a binding contract, but was merely "an agreement to agree." . . .
[Judgment affirmed]

QUESTIONS

1. How did the court regard the letter relied on by the plaintiff?
2. What was the controlling factor in the decision of the *Beck* case?

2.   Definiteness

An offer, and the resulting contract, must be definite and certain. If an offer is indefinite or vague or if an essential provision is lacking,[7] no contract arises from an attempt to accept it. The reason is that the courts cannot tell what the parties are to do. Thus, an offer to conduct a business for such time as should be profitable is too vague to be a valid offer. The acceptance of such an offer does not result in a contract that can be enforced. Likewise, a promise to give an injured employee "suitable" employment that the employee is "able to do" is too vague to be a binding contract. A statement by a landlord to the tenant that "some day it [the rented land] will be your own" is too indefinite to be an offer, and no contract for the sale of the land arises when the tenant agrees to the statement.

The law does not favor the destruction of contracts, because that would go against the social force of carrying out the intent of the parties. Consequently, when it is claimed that a contract is too indefinite to be enforced, a court will do its best to find the intent of the parties and thereby reach the conclusion that the contract is not too indefinite.[8]

The question of how definite is *definite* was raised in the *Midland Hotel* case.

[7]   University National Bank v Ernst & Whinney (Tex App) 773 SW2d 707 (1989). The fact that certain terms are missing from a contract is immaterial when a statute or administrative regulation specifies what the missing terms must be. Inland Title Co. v Comstock (Idaho) 779 P2d 15 (1989).

[8]   Welsh v Northern Telecom, Inc. 85 NC App 310, 354 SE2d 746 (1987).

MIDLAND HOTEL v REUBEN H. DONNELLEY CORP.

149 Ill App 3d 53, 103 Ill Dec 742, 501 NE2d 1280 (1986)

Reuben Donnelley published a tourist guide to Chicago. The Midland Hotel made a contract with Donnelley to be listed in the guide. When the guide was published, Midland found that it was listed only under "Banquet Rooms," not under "Hotels." Midland sued Donnelley for the profit that it claimed to have lost because it was not properly listed. The defendant raised the defense that the agreement between them was too vague to be enforced because it did not specify any particular listing of Midland, but merely stated that there would be "appropriate" listing. Judgment was entered for Midland, and Donnelley appealed.

SCARIANO, J. . . . Defendant, citing *Panko v. Advanced Appliance Service* (1977), 55 Ill. App.3d 301, 13 Ill.Dec. 308, 371 N.E.2d 3, argues that a contract in which it agreed simply to provide plaintiff with "appropriate" listings is too vague and ambiguous to be enforced. We disagree. Whether a contract is ambiguous is a question of law for the court. The primary object in construing a contract is to give effect to the intention of the parties, and a contract is sufficiently definite and certain if the court is able, from its terms and provisions and allowable extrinsic evidence to ascertain what the parties agreed to. Plaintiff is known as the "Midland *Hotel*," and defendant's offer was made in the hotel itself; [an executive officer of the plaintiff] testified that a few days after the *Guide* was issued, the representative of defendant with whom he had originally negotiated acknowledged that failure to list the Midland under "Hotels" "was a mistake and he was sorry it happened;" and when asked whether a hotel should be listed under "Hotels," Donnelley's district sales manager testified, "You would think they should be there." Defendant argues that there are numerous other listings for the Midland that would also be appropriate, such as "Ballrooms," "Cocktail Lounges," "Coffee Shops," etc. However, plaintiff does not claim that it should have been listed under these headings as well, or that the listing under "Banquet Rooms" that it did receive was inappropriate. It is not necessary that a contract provide for every collateral matter and every future contingency to be sufficiently definite to be enforceable. We conclude that an offer to list the Midland Hotel in the "appropriate" places is not so ambiguous as to render the contract unenforceable.

[Judgment affirmed on vagueness issue]

QUESTIONS

1. Is the term *appropriate listing* sufficiently definite to be enforced?
2. What social force is involved in cases raising the question of the definiteness of the agreement?
3. How could the controversy in the *Midland Hotel* case have been avoided?

(a) DEFINITE BY INCORPORATION. An offer and the resulting contract that by themselves may appear "too indefinite" may be made definite by reference to another writing. For example, a lease agreement that was too vague by itself was made definite because the parties agreed that the lease should follow the standard form with which both were familiar. An agreement may also be made definite by reference to the prior dealings of the parties and to trade practices.

(b) IMPLIED TERMS. Although an offer must be definite and certain, not all of its terms need be expressed. Some of the omitted terms may be implied by law. For example, an offer "to pay $50 for a watch" does not state the terms of payment. A court, however, would not condemn this provision as too vague, but would hold that it required that cash be paid and that the payment be made

upon delivery of the watch. Likewise, terms may be implied from conduct. As an illustration, where the borrowed money was given to the borrower by a check on which there was written the word *loan*, the act of the borrower in indorsing the check constituted an agreement to repay the amount of the check.

(c) DIVISIBLE CONTRACTS. When the agreement consists of two or more parts and calls for corresponding performances of each part by the parties, the agreement is a **divisible contract**. Thus, in a promise to buy several separate articles at different prices at the same time, the agreement may be regarded as separate or divisible promises for the articles. When a contract contains a number of provisions or performances to be rendered, the question arises as to whether the parties intended merely a group of separate, divisible contracts or whether it was to be a package deal so that complete performance by each party is essential.

(d) UNIMPORTANT VAGUE DETAILS IGNORED. If a term that is too vague is not important, it may sometimes be ignored. If the balance of the agreement is definite, there can then be a binding contract. For example, where the parties agreed that one of them would manage a motel that was being constructed for the other, and where it was agreed that the contract would begin to run before the completion of the construction, the management contract did not fail because it did not specify any date on which it was to commence. It was apparent that the exact date was not essential and could not be determined at the time when the contract was made.

(e) EXCEPTIONS TO DEFINITENESS. The law has come to recognize certain situations where the practical necessity of doing business makes it desirable to have a contract, yet the situation is such that it is either impossible or undesirable to adopt definite terms in advance. In these cases, the indefinite term is often tied to the concept of good-faith performance or to some independent factor that will be definitely ascertainable at some time in the future. For example, the indefinite term might be tied to market price, cost to complete, or production requirements. Thus, the law recognizes binding contracts in the case of a **requirements contract**, a contract to buy all requirements of the buyer from the seller. The law also recognizes as binding an **output contract**, the contract of a producer to sell the entire production or output to a given buyer. These are binding contracts, although they do not state the exact quantity of goods that are to be bought or sold. Contracts are also binding although they run for an indefinite period of time, require a buyer to pay the costs plus a percentage of costs as profit, or require one person to supply professional services as needed.

An agreement is not made too indefinite to be binding because it does not specify exact prices or quantities. When these relate to the future or future events, it is obvious that the agreement cannot be precise. In such case, an agreement is deemed sufficiently definite if it specifies a standard or formula by which the variable factors are to be determined.

3.   Communication of Offer to Offeree

The offer must be communicated to the offeree. Otherwise, the offeree cannot accept, even though knowledge of the offer has been indirectly acquired. Internal management communications of an enterprise that are not intended for outsiders or employees do not constitute offers and cannot be accepted by them. Sometimes, particularly in the case of unilateral contracts, the offeree performs the act called for by the offeror without knowing of the offer's existence. Such performance does not constitute an acceptance.[9] Thus, without knowing that a reward is offered for the arrest of a particular criminal, a person may arrest the criminal. In most states, if that person learns thereafter that a reward has been offered for the arrest, the reward cannot be recovered.[10]

Not only must the offer be communicated, but it must be communicated by the offeror or at the offeror's direction.

B.   TERMINATION OF OFFER

An offer gives the offeree power to bind the offeror by contract. This power does not last forever, and the law specifies that under certain circumstances the power ends or is terminated.

Once the offer is terminated, the offeree cannot revive it. If an attempt is made to accept the offer after it has been terminated, this attempt is meaningless, unless the original offeror is willing to regard the late acceptance as a new offer, which the original offeror then accepts.

---

[9]   Richard D. Price, Jr. & Associates v East Peoria, 154 Ill App 3d 725, 107 Ill Dec 564, 507 NE2d 228 (1987).

[10]   With respect to the offeror, it should not make any difference as a practical matter whether the services were rendered with or without knowledge of the existence of the offer. Only a small number of states have adopted this view, however.

Offers may be terminated in any one of the following ways: (1) revocation of the offer by the offeror, (2) counteroffer by offeree, (3) rejection of offer by offeree, (4) lapse of time, (5) death or disability of either party, and (6) subsequent illegality.

4.   Revocation of Offer by Offeror

Ordinarily, the offeror can revoke the offer before it is accepted. If this is done, the offeree cannot create a contract by accepting the revoked offer. Thus, the bidder at an auction sale may withdraw (revoke) a bid (offer) before it is accepted. The auctioneer cannot thereafter accept that bid.

An ordinary offer may be revoked at any time before it is accepted, even though the offeror has expressly promised that the offer will be good for a stated period and that period has not yet expired. It may also be revoked even though the offeror has expressly promised to the offeree that the offer will not be revoked before a specified later date.

(a) WHAT CONSTITUTES A REVOCATION. No particular form or words are required to constitute a revocation. Any words indicating the offeror's termination of the offer are sufficient. A notice sent to the offeree that the property that is the subject of the offer has been sold to a third person is a revocation of the offer. A customer's order for goods, which is an offer to purchase at certain prices, is revoked by a notice to the seller of the cancellation of the order, provided such notice is communicated before the order is accepted.

(b) COMMUNICATION OF REVOCATION. A revocation of an offer is ordinarily effective only when it is made known to the offeree. Until it is communicated to the offeree, directly or indirectly, the offeree has reason to believe that there is still an offer that may be accepted, and the offeree may rely on this belief.

Except in a few states a letter or telegram revoking an offer made to a particular offeree is not effective until received by the offeree. It is not a revocation at the time it is written by the offeror or even when it is mailed or dispatched. A written revocation is effective, however, when it is delivered to the offeree's agent, or to the offeree's residence or place of business under such circumstances that the offeree may be reasonably expected to be aware of its receipt.

It is ordinarily held that there is a sufficient communication of the revocation when the offeree learns indirectly of the offeror's revocation. This is particularly true in a land sale, when the seller-offeror, after making an offer to sell the land to the offeree, sells the land to a third person, and the offeree indirectly learns of such sale. The offeree necessarily realizes that the seller cannot perform the original offer and therefore must be deemed to have revoked it.

If the offeree accepts an offer before it is effectively revoked, a valid contract is created. Thus, there may be a contract when the offeree mails or telegraphs an acceptance without knowing that a letter of revocation has already been mailed.

When an offer is made to the public, it may usually be revoked in the same manner in which it was made. For example, an offer of a reward that is made to the general public by an advertisement in a newspaper may be revoked in the same manner. A member of the public cannot recover the amount of the reward by thereafter performing the act for which the reward was originally offered. This exception is made to the rule requiring communication of revocation because it would be impossible for the offeror to communicate the fact that the offer was revoked to every member of the general public who knows of the offer. The public revocation of the public offer is effective even though it is not seen by the person attempting to accept the original offer.

(c) OPTION CONTRACTS. An **option contract** is a binding promise to keep an offer open for a stated period of time or until a specified date. An option contract requires that the promisor receive consideration—that is, something, such as a sum of money, as the price for the promise to keep the offer open. In other words, the option is a contract to refrain from revoking an offer.

When an option contract recites the giving of a specified consideration, but such consideration in fact was never paid, the option contract is merely an offer. It may be revoked at any time prior to acceptance.[11]

(d) FIRM OFFERS. As another exception to the rule that an offer can be revoked at any time before acceptance, statutes in some states provide that an offeror cannot revoke an offer prior to its expiration when the offeror makes a firm offer. A **firm offer** is an offer that states that it is to be irrevocable, or irrevocable for a stated period of time. Under the Uniform Commercial Code this doctrine of firm offers applies to a merchant's signed, written offer to buy or sell goods, but with a maximum of three months on its period of irrevocability.[12]

(e) DETRIMENTAL RELIANCE. There is growing authority that when the offeror foresees that the offeree will rely on the offer's remaining open, the offeror is obligated to keep the offer open for a reasonable time.

The concept of detrimental reliance can thus prevent the revocation of an offer. This was the issue in the *Arango Construction* case.

---

[11]   Hamilton Bancshares, Inc. v Leroy, 131 Ill App 3d 907, 87 Ill Dec 86, 476 NE2d 788 (1985).

[12]   UCC § 2–205.

ARANGO CONSTRUCTION CO. v SUCCESS ROOFING, INC.

46 Wash App 314, 730 P2d 720 (1986)

Arango Construction Company wanted to do certain construction work for the United States government. In preparing its bid, Arango phoned Success Roofing to see what it would charge for doing the roofing work involved. Success offered to do the work for a specified price. Arango then made a bid to the government. Its bid was accepted. Thereafter Success notified Arango that it was withdrawing its bid to do the roofing work because it had made a significant mistake in its calculation. Arango claimed it could not do this because Arango had used the bid in making its own bid to the United States. Arango sued Success for damages caused by the revocation of its bid. From a judgment for Success, Arango appealed.

COLEMAN, J. . . . In contract law, construction bidding is treated as a unique category. Since construction bidding deadlines make the drafting of written agreements impossible, contractors must rely on oral bids. Therefore, the courts consider the subcontractor's oral bid an irrevocable offer until the general contractor has been awarded the prime contract; then the courts apply promissory estoppel to ensure that the subcontractor does not raise the bid. This concept was explained in J. Feinman, *Promissory Estoppel and Judicial Methods*, 97 Harv.L.Rev. 678, (1984).

A recurrent example of the flexible approach to promise is found in the courts' treatment of construction bidding cases, which have repeatedly generated important promissory estoppel decisions. In the typical case, a general contractor preparing to bid on a construction project receives bids on parts of the job from subcontractors and suppliers. The general then prepares its own bid on the basis of the lowest reliable subcontract bids. Subcontractors occasionally miscalculate, in part because they often compute their bids and telephone them to the general only hours before the general's bid is due. A subcontractor may also intentionally submit a low bid in the hope of receiving the contract and renegotiating the price. Conflict typically arises when, after the general has calculated and submitted its own bid and won the contract, a subcontractor notifies the general that the subcontractor has made an error or an intentionally low bid and refuses to perform.

Under traditional contract analysis, the subcontractor could withdraw with impunity, because its bid was regarded as an offer, revocable until accepted, to enter into a bilateral contract. In the leading case of *Drennan v. Star Paving Co.*, [51 Cal.2d 409, 333 P.2d 757 (1958)], however, Justice Traynor held that the business context of the bid required that promissory estoppel apply to make the subcontractor's offer irrevocable until the general contractor had an opportunity to accept after being awarded the prime contract. The general's acceptance of the subcontractor's bid then created a traditional bilateral contract, for breach of which the subcontractor was required to pay as damages the difference between its bid and the higher price the general had to pay another subcontractor to perform the work. Cases since *Drennan* have held that promissory estoppel normally binds a subcontractor to the terms of its bid. Although the subcontractor does not make an explicit promise to keep its bid open, the court infers such a promise. . . .

This court has accepted the *Drennan* rationale in *Ferrer v. Taft Structural, Inc.*, 21 Wash.App. 832, 587 P.2d 177 (1978).

This concept [promissory estoppel] applies readily to the unique situation of a subcontractor and a general contractor, as exists here. A subcontractor submits a bid to the general contractor, knowing the general cannot accept the bid as an offer immediately, but must first incorporate it into the general's offer to the prospective employer. The general contractor incorporates the bid in reliance upon the subcontractor to perform as promised, should the prospective employer accept the general's offer. Thus, the elements of predictable and justifiable reliance and change of position are satisfied. Numerous courts and authorities have opined that a subcontractor's bid upon which a general contractor relies should be deemed irrevocable for a reasonable time pursuant to the doctrine of promissory estoppel. . . .

Thus, as a matter of law, a subcontractor's bid is considered an irrevocable offer until the award of the prime contract; then, the general contractor's acceptance of the bid results in a bilateral contract. . . . Thus, if the subcontractor refuses to perform following the award of the contract, the general contractor may recover damages under the doctrine of promissory estoppel. . . .

The *Ferrer* court listed the five elements of promissory estoppel:

. . . (1) A promise which (2) the promisor should reasonably expect to cause the promisee to change his position and (3) which does cause the promisee to change his position (4) justifiably relying upon the promise, in such a manner that (5) injustice can be avoided only by enforcement of the promise.

. . . Success's bid was a promise. Success could reasonably expect that promise to cause Arango to change position by including the Success bid in Arango's prime bid. Success confirmed its bid 2 days after it was given, and Arango informed Success that it would be including that bid in its prime bid to be submitted 13 days later. Arango did include Success's bid in its prime bid, thereby changing its position.

The only element of promissory estoppel in dispute is whether Arango justifiably relied on Success's bid. Success contends that as a prudent and experienced general contractor, Arango should have known that Success's bid was too low for the job involved. . . . Success had to present evidence supporting this assertion. Success, however, has submitted no evidence that Arango should have known. The only other bid found in the record was from Tin Benders. Its bid was for $38,500 . . . as compared to the $34,659 bid by Success. There is nothing in the record to support an inference that Arango knew or should have known that Success had made a mistake. . . .

The judgment of the trial court is reversed and the cause remanded with instruction to enter judgment in favor of Arango on its complaint for damages.

[Judgment reversed and action remanded]

QUESTIONS

1. Was the decision in the *Arango Construction* case in harmony with general contract law? Explain.
2. What social forces are advanced by the decision? Explain.
3. How could the problem in the *Arango Construction* case have been avoided?

5.   Counteroffer by Offeree

Ordinarily, if *A* makes an offer, such as to sell a used automobile to *B* for $1,000, and *B* in reply makes an offer to buy at $750, the original offer is terminated. *B* is in effect indicating refusal of the original offer and in its place making a different offer. Such an offer by the offeree is known as a **counteroffer**.

The making of a counteroffer terminates the offeree's power to accept the offer unless the intent is manifested that the counteroffer should not have the effect of a rejection.

Counteroffers are not limited to offers that directly contradict the original offers. Any departure from, or addition to, the original offer is a counteroffer, even though the original offer was silent as to the point added by the counteroffer. For example, when the offeree stated that the offer was accepted and added that time was of the essence, the acceptance was a counteroffer because the original offer had been silent on that point. A conditional acceptance is a counteroffer.[13]

6.   Rejection of Offer by Offeree

If the offeree rejects the offer and communicates this rejection to the offeror, the offer is terminated, even though the period for which the offeror agreed to keep the offer open has not yet expired. It may be that the offeror is willing to renew the offer, but unless this is done, there is no longer any offer, for the offeree to accept.

7.   Lapse of Time

When the offer states that it is open until a particular date, the offer terminates on that date if it has not yet been accepted. This is particularly so where the offeror declares that the offer shall be void after the expiration of the specified time. Such limitations are strictly construed. When a specified time limitation is imposed on an option, the option cannot be exercised after the expiration of that time, without regard to whether the late exercise was made within what would have been held a reasonable time if no time period had been specified.[14] It has been held that the buyer's attempt to exercise an option one day late had no effect.

When the offeree attempts to accept after the deadline for acceptance has passed, the act of the offeree has no effect as an acceptance but instead is the making of a counteroffer. If the original offeror accepts this counteroffer, there is a contract. If the counteroffer is not accepted, there is no contract.

---

13   Anand v Marple, 167 Ill App 3d 918, 118 Ill Dec 826, 522 NE2d 281 (1988).

14   Watson v Hatch (Utah) 728 P2d 989 (1986).

If the offer does not specify a time, it will terminate after the lapse of a reasonable time. What constitutes a reasonable time depends on the circumstances of each case—that is, on the nature of the subject matter, the nature of the market in which it is sold, the time of year, and other factors of supply and demand. If a commodity is perishable or fluctuates greatly in value, the reasonable time will be much shorter than if the subject matter is a staple article. An offer to sell a harvested crop of tomatoes would expire within a very short time. When a seller purports to accept an offer after it has lapsed by the expiration of time, the seller's acceptance is merely a counteroffer and does not create a contract unless that offer is accepted by the buyer.

8.   Death or Disability of Either Party

If either the offeror or the offeree dies or becomes insane before the offer is accepted, the offer is automatically terminated.

9.   Subsequent Illegality

If the performance of the contract becomes illegal after the offer is made, the offer is terminated. Thus, if an offer is made to sell alcoholic liquors but a law prohibiting such sales is enacted before the offer is accepted, the offer is terminated.

C.   ACCEPTANCE OF OFFER

Once the offeror expresses or appears to express a willingness to enter into a contractual agreement with the offeree, the latter may accept the offer. An **acceptance** is the assent of the offeree to the terms of the offer. No particular form of words or mode of expression is required, but there must be a clear expression that the offeree agrees to be bound by the terms of the offer.

10.   Privilege of Offeree

Ordinarily, the offeree may refuse to accept an offer. If there is no acceptance, by definition there is no contract. The fact that there had been a series of contracts between the parties and that one party's offer had always been accepted by the other does not create any legal obligation to continue to accept subsequent offers.

Certain partial exceptions exist to the privilege of the offeree to refuse to accept an offer.

(a) PLACES OF PUBLIC ACCOMMODATION AND PUBLIC UTILITIES. Places of public accommodation and public utilities are under a duty to serve any fit person. They cannot refuse to serve a person because of a disability.[15] When a fit person offers to register at a hotel (that is, offers to hire a room), the hotel has the obligation to accept the offer and to enter into a contract for the renting of the room. However, there is no duty on the part of the hotel to accept unless the person is fit and the hotel has space available.

(b) ANTIDISCRIMINATION. When offers are solicited from members of the general public, an offer generally may not be rejected because of the race, nationality, religion, or color of the offeror. If the solicitor of the offer is willing to enter into a contract to rent, sell, or employ, antidiscrimination laws compel the solicitor to accept an offer from any otherwise fit person.

(c) CONSUMER PROTECTION. Statutes and regulations designed to protect consumers from false advertising may require a seller to accept an offer from a customer to purchase advertised goods and may impose a penalty for an unjustified refusal.

11.   Effect of Acceptance

When an offer has been accepted, a binding agreement or contract is created, assuming that all of the other elements of a contract are present. Thereafter, neither party can withdraw from or cancel the contract without the consent of the other party (or the existence of such facts as under the law justify such unilateral action). For example, when an enterprise conducts a prize contest, its offer to conduct

---

[15]   Americans with Disabilities Act of 1990, Act of July 26, 1990, PL 101–336, 104 Stat 327, _____USC § _____.

the contest according to stated rules is accepted when an entrant sends in the entry form. The enterprise must then conduct the contest according to the announced contest rules because it is bound by a contract.[16]

12.   Nature of the Acceptance

An acceptance is the offeree's manifestation of intent to enter into a binding agreement on the terms stated in the offer. Whether there is an acceptance depends on whether the offeree has manifested an intent to accept. It is the objective or outward appearance that is controlling, rather than the subjective or unexpressed intent of the offeree.[17]

In the absence of a contrary requirement in the offer, an acceptance may be indicated by an informal "OK," by a mere affirmative nod of the head, or, in the case of an offer of a unilateral contract, by performing the act called

for. However, while the acceptance of an offer may be shown by conduct, it must be very clear that the offeree intended to accept the offer.

The acceptance must be absolute and unconditional. It must accept just what is offered. If the offeree changes any terms of the offer or adds any new term, there is no acceptance, because the offeree does not agree to what was offered.

Where the offeree does not accept the offer exactly as made, the addition of any qualification converts the "acceptance" into a counteroffer, and no contract arises unless such a counteroffer is accepted by the original offeror. The addition of new terms in the acceptance, however, does not always mean that the attempted acceptance fails. The acceptance is still unqualified if the new terms are merely those that (a) would be implied by law as part of the offer, (b) constitute a mere request, or (c) relate to a mere clerical detail.

What constituted an acceptance was the question involved in the *Holman Erection Company* case.

---

[16]   First Texas Savings Ass'n v Jergins (Tex App) 705 SW2d 390 (1986).
[17]   Schwandt Sanitation of Paynesville v City of Paynesville (Minn App) 423 NW2d 59 (1988).

HOLMAN ERECTION CO. v ORVILLE E. MADSEN & SONS, INC.
(Minn) 330 NW2d 693 (1983)

The city of Moorhead advertised for bids for the construction of a wastewater treatment facility. Orville E. Madsen submitted a bid. In the bid it listed Holman Erection Co. as the subcontractor for the steel work. The city awarded the contract to Madsen. Madsen then switched from Holman to another subcontractor in order to satisfy the contract provision that contractors should make an effort to comply with the federal Minority Business Enterprise (MBE) regulation. Holman then sued Madsen for breach of contract, claiming that its bid had been accepted by Madsen when it was included in Madsen's bid submitted to the city. From a judgment for Madsen, Holman appealed.

YETKA, J. . . . Appellant Holman argues that a binding contractual relationship was created between it and Madsen when Madsen utilized Holman's sub-bid in its general bid for the waste treatment plant project and listed Holman as a proposed subcontractor for steel erection work. Does the act of listing Holman in the general bid constitute an acceptance of Holman's offer to do the work when no other communication occurred after the offer and prior to the substitution of a different subcontractor? We think not.

To constitute an acceptance, Madsen's acts must be deemed a manifestation of assent when evaluated under an objective standard. . . .

Holman argues that listing Holman as a subcontractor, as required by the awarding authority, constitutes an acceptance. . . .

Appellant's argument flies in the face of a large body of precedent holding that no contract is formed by the listing of a subcontractor in a general contractor's bid. . . . This court has held, however, that the subcontractor may be bound to his bid as submitted to the general contractor by operation of promissory estoppel. . . .

In Minnesota, as well as most other jurisdictions, the subcontractor may be obligated to perform by application of promissory estoppel. The general, however, remains free to avoid the listed subcontractor and negotiate with other subcontractors. This one-sided arrangement seems, on its face, unfair. Why should one party be bound and other not? A close examination of the construction business and the nature of the bidding process, however, reveals several justifications for the unequal treatment of generals and subcontractors.

First, the reason a subcontractor is bound by its bid is the existence of justifiable reliance by the general on the subcontractor's price for specified work. The general makes his bid after gathering and evaluating a number of subcontract bids. Once the general wins the prime contract from the awarding authority, he is bound to his own bid. For the subcontractor to be able to refuse to perform would subject the general to a financial detriment.

In contrast, the subcontractor does not rely on the general and suffers no detriment. A subcontractor submits bids to all or most of the general contractors that it knows are bidding on a project. The subcontractor receives invitations to bid from some generals and submits bids to others without invitation. The time and expense involved in preparing the bid is not segregated to any particular general. The total cost is part of the overhead of doing business. The same bid is submitted to each general. Thus, whether or not any particular general wins the contract is of little or no concern to the subcontractor. The subcontractor engages in the same work and expense in preparing its bid regardless of who wins the general contract and whether the subcontractor wins the contract on which it bid. No further expense is incurred until a formal agreement is reached with the general and actual work commences. Clearly, the promissory estoppel concept is not applicable in this situation. . . . With no detrimental reliance, there can be no estoppel claim. Ample justification exists for binding the subcontractor and not binding the general. The two situations are very different.

Second, the nature of the bidding process compels allowing the general sufficient leeway to maintain its flexibility in executing subcontracts and selecting the subcontractors it will hire for a project. Typically, subcontractors submit their bids only a few hours before the general bid must be submitted to the awarding authority. The general's representatives take the bids over the telephone and hurriedly compile their own bid. This period of time is hectic and complex. The bids received consist of the contract price and a listing of work included. Specifics are left for future negotiation and clarification. . . .

The bidding process puts the subcontractor and the general in very different positions as to the content of the subcontract. The subcontractors have the luxury of preparing their bids on their own timetable, subject only to the deadline for submitting their bids to the general contractors. The same bid goes to all the general contractors and covers the same work. The generals, on the other hand, are dealing with all the various construction aspects of the project and with numerous potential subcontractors. They compile their bids, as the various subcontractor bids are received, within a few hours of the deadline for submission of the prime bid. Specifics are necessarily given less than thorough consideration and are left for future negotiations. Finally, the lowest dollar amount bidder is not always the one chosen to do the work or the one listed as the potential subcontractor. Reliability, quality of work, and capability to handle the job are all considerations weighed by the general in choosing subcontractors. MBE regulations requiring an effort to use a percentage of minority contractors are another potential consideration. . . .

If Madsen was bound to the bids listed in its prime bid, there is a possibility that the contract would have been lost due to failure to comply with MBE regulations. The next highest qualifying bidder would then have been selected, to the awarding authority's greater expense and to Madsen's detriment. Such a result imposes a greater cost on the project and a loss to the general contractor. The result under the prevailing law in most jurisdictions, and which we adopt here, would not impose any additional expenses on the rejected subcontractor.

A decision in favor of the subcontractor on this issue would place Minnesota in a minority position as perhaps the sole state to hold that a contract is formed by the mere listing of a subcontractor in a general contractor's bid to the awarding authority. Although supplying some certainty and symmetry to the construction industry, such a decision would also impose a rigidity on the process and result in greater cost to awarding authorities and potential detriment to general contractors. If such a change is to take place, it is one properly brought before the legislature.

[Judgment affirmed]

QUESTIONS

1. Why does the court hold that there was no acceptance when the subcontractor's bid was listed in the general contractor's bid?
2. Does promissory estoppel bar the general contractor from rejecting a subcontractor's bid after being awarded the general contract?
3. How would the *Holman* case have been decided if there were no requirement of employing minority workers?

13. Who May Accept

An offer may be accepted only by the person to whom it is directed. If anyone else attempts to accept it, no agreement or contract with that person arises.

If the offer is directed to a particular class, rather than a specified individual, it may be accepted by anyone within that class. If the offer is made to the public at large, it may be accepted by any member of the public at large having knowledge of the existence of the offer.

When a person to whom an offer was not made attempts to accept it, the attempted acceptance has the effect of an offer. If the original offeror is willing to accept this offer, a binding contract arises. If the original offeror does not accept the new offer, there is no contract.

14. Manner of Acceptance

The offeror may specify the manner for accepting the offer. Consequently, when the offeror required that certain documents be delivered to an agent in order to accept the offer, there is no acceptance if the offeree fails to satisfy that requirement.[18] When the offeror specifies that there must be a written acceptance,

---

[18] Crane v Timberbrook Village, Ltd. (Utah App) 774 P2d 3 (1989).

no contract arises when the offeree makes an oral acceptance. If the offeror calls for acceptance by a specified date, a late acceptance has no effect.[19] When an acceptance is required by return mail, it is usually held that the letter of acceptance must be mailed the same day that the offer was received by the offeree. If the offer specifies that the acceptance be made by the performance of an act by the offeree, the latter cannot accept by making a promise to do the act but must actually perform it.

When the offer calls for the performance of an act or of certain conduct, the performance thereof is an acceptance of the offer and creates a unilateral contract.[20]

When a person accepts services offered by another and it reasonably appears that compensation was expected, the acceptance of the services without any protest constitutes an acceptance of the offer, and a contract exists for the payment for such services.

When the offeror has specified a particular manner of acceptance, the offeree cannot accept in any other way. However, acceptance in some other way is effective (1) if the manner of acceptance specified was merely a suggested alternative and was not clearly the exclusive method of acceptance, or (2) if the offeror has proceeded on the basis that there had been an effective acceptance.

While it is ordinarily the offeror who is the person specifying the manner of acceptance, the person making an invitation to negotiate will sometimes state the way in which any acceptance of an offer will be made.

(a) SILENCE AS ACCEPTANCE. In most cases the offeree's silence and failure to act cannot be regarded as an acceptance. Ordinarily, the offeror is not permitted to frame an offer in such a way as to make the silence and inaction of the offeree operate as an acceptance.

In the case of prior dealings between the parties, as in a record or book club, the offeree may have a duty to reject an offer expressly,

and the offeree's silence may be regarded as an acceptance.

(b) UNORDERED GOODS AND TICKETS. Sometimes a seller writes to a person with whom the seller has not had any prior dealings stating that, unless notified to the contrary, the seller will send specified merchandise and the recipient is obligated to pay for it at stated prices. There is no acceptance if the recipient of the letter ignores the offer and does nothing. The silence of the person receiving the letter is not an acceptance, and the sender, as a reasonable person, should recognize that none was intended.

This rule applies to all kinds of goods, books, magazines, and tickets sent through the mail when they have not been ordered. The fact that the items are not returned does not mean that they have been accepted; that is, the offeree is neither required to pay for nor return the items. If desired, the recipient of the unordered goods may write "Return to Sender" on the unopened package and put the package back into the mail without any additional postage. The Postal Reorganization Act of 1970 provides that the person who receives unordered mailed merchandise from a commercial (noncharitable) sender has the right "to retain, use, discard, or dispose of it in any manner the recipient sees fit without any obligation whatsoever to the sender."[21] It provides further that any unordered merchandise that is mailed must have attached to it a clear and conspicuous statement of the recipient's right to treat the goods in this manner.

15.   Communication of Acceptance

If the offeree accepts the offer, must the offeror be notified? The answer depends on the nature of the offer.

If the offeror makes an offer of a unilateral contract, communication of acceptance is ordinarily not necessary. In such a case, the offeror calls for a completed or accomplished act. If that act is performed by the offeree with knowledge of the offer, the offer is accepted without any further action by way of notifying

---

[19]   Martin v Factory Mutual Research Corp. 401 Mass 621, 518 NE2d 846 (1988).

[20]   Peters v Mutual Benefit Life Ins. Co. (Minn App) 420 NW2d 908 (1988).

[21]   Federal Postal Reorganization Act § 3009.

the offeror. As a practical matter, there will eventually be some notice to the offeror, because the offeree who has performed the act will ask the offeror to pay for the performance that has been rendered.

If the offer pertains to a bilateral contract, an acceptance is not effective unless communicated. The acceptance must be communicated directly to the offeror or the offeror's agent.

The *Rothenbuecher* case raised the question of whether there was an acceptance when the offeree signed a written offer.

ROTHENBUECHER v TOCKSTEIN
88 Ill App 3d 968, 44 Ill Dec 186, 411 NE2d 92 (1980)

Tockstein offered to purchase a duplex from Rothenbuecher. The written offer stated that it was "subject to the approval of the owner [Rothenbuecher] within one day." The offer was given by Tockstein to Rothenbuecher's real estate agent on July 9. On July 10, Rothenbuecher signed the written offer and gave it back to the agent. On July 11, Tockstein was notified by telephone that the offer had been signed. On July 15, Tockstein informed the real estate agent that the offer was withdrawn. Two days later Rothenbuecher sued Tockstein for breach of contract. Physical delivery of the written acceptance signed by Rothenbuecher was not made to Tockstein until July 23. The lower court held that there was a binding contract. Tockstein appealed.

HARRISON, J. . . . The judgment . . . is challenged upon the grounds that no valid contract of sale existed between the parties under the facts presented. . . .

The mutual assent necessary to the formation of a bilateral contract, such as the one here contemplated, requires the communicated expression of a promise to purchase and an acceptance in the form of a promise to sell. . . . The appellant argues that no valid contract was formed under the present circumstances. We agree with that conclusion because of certain facts regarding the terms of the offer, its retraction and Rothenbuecher's failure to timely communicate acceptance.

Tockstein signed an instrument prepared by the seller's agent, thus creating the offer with which we are concerned. That offer was conditioned on "approval" by the seller within a 24-hour period. We can find no other logical meaning in the term "approval" than acceptance of the tendered offer. If it were to stand for less than acceptance, it would merely amount to a promise to consider the terms advanced as a legitimate offer. Therefore, acceptance is required in the very terms of the offer by means of a promise to perform communicated within a day. It is the essence of a valid acceptance that it be objectively manifested by or on behalf of the offeree. Otherwise an offeree's assent could remain undisclosed and while he might find the terms of an offer agreeable, he could, for example, hold assent in reserve while other offers were entertained. . . .

It is without dispute that no communication of acceptance occurred on July 10 as the offer required and that no physical delivery of acceptance occurred until July 23, six days after this suit was instituted. At best, the signed agreement constituting a purported acceptance was given to the seller's agent on the evening of July 10. However, this was inadequate to communicate acceptance since it cannot be said that as a matter of legal effect this put the manifestation of assent out of the offeree's [Rothenbuecher's] possession. While still in the hands of his agent, and without notice to the offeror, the seller could have at any time during the period of the condition given instructions that his acceptance be revoked. . . . The appellant withdrew her offer on July 15 and it is elementary that an offeree's power to accept is terminated by revocation of the offer. . . . And hence, under these facts no contract resulted between the parties. . . . There being no agreement to enforce, we find it necessary to reverse the judgment.

[Judgment reversed]

QUESTIONS

1. Did the owner intend to accept the offer?
2. On what ground did the court then hold that there was no contract?
3. How would the case have been decided if the offer had not contained any time limitation?

16. Acceptance by Mail or Telegraph

When the offeree sends an acceptance by mail or telegraph, questions may arise as to the right to use such means of communication and the time the acceptance is effective.

(a) RIGHT TO USE MAIL OR TELE-GRAPH. Express directions of the offeror, prior dealings between the parties, or custom of the trade may make it clear that only one method of acceptance is proper. For example, in negotiations with respect to property of rapidly fluctuating value, such as wheat or corporation stocks, an acceptance sent by mail may be too slow. When there is no indication that mail or telegraph is not a proper method, an acceptance may be made by either of those means without regard to the manner in which the offer was made. The trend of the modern decisions supports the following provision of the Uniform Commercial Code relating to sales of personal property: "Unless otherwise unambiguously indicated by the language or circumstances, an offer to make a sales contract shall be construed as inviting acceptance in any manner and by any medium reasonable in the circumstances."

(b) WHEN ACCEPTANCE BY MAIL OR TELEGRAPH IS EFFECTIVE. If the offeror does not specify otherwise, a mailed accep-

tance takes effect when the acceptance is properly mailed (the "mailbox rule"). Likewise, a telegraph acceptance takes effect when and where the telegram is dispatched or sent, unless the offeror specifies otherwise or unless custom or prior dealings indicate that acceptance by telegraph is improper. If the offeror specifies that an acceptance shall not be effective until received, there is no acceptance until the acceptance is received. Likewise, the "mailbox rule" does not apply when the offeror requires receipt of a payment to accompany an acceptance.[22]

The letter must be properly addressed to the offeror, and any other precaution that is ordinarily observed to ensure safe transmission must be taken. If it is not mailed in this manner, the acceptance does not take effect when mailed, but only when received by the offeror.

The rule that a properly mailed acceptance takes effect at the time it is mailed is applied strictly. The rule applies even if the acceptance letter never reaches the offeror.

(c) PROOF OF ACCEPTANCE BY MAIL OR TELEGRAPH. How can the time of mailing be established, or even the fact of mailing in the case of a destroyed or lost letter? A similar problem arises in the case of a telegraphic

---

[22] American Heritage Life Ins. Co. v Koch (Tex App) 721 SW2d 611 (1986).

acceptance. In either case the problem is not one of law but one of fact: a question of proving the case to the jury. The offeror may testify in court that an acceptance was never received or that an acceptance was sent after the offer had been revoked. The offeree may then testify that the acceptance letter was mailed at a particular time and place. The offeree's case will be strengthened if postal receipts for the mailing and delivery of a letter sent to the offeror can be produced, although these, of course, do not establish the contents of the letter. Ultimately, the case goes to the jury (or to the judge, if a jury trial has been waived) to determine whether the acceptance was made at a certain time and place as claimed by the offeree.

17. Acceptance by Telephone

Ordinarily, acceptance of an offer may be made by telephone unless the circumstances are such that, by the intent of the parties or the law of the state, no acceptance can be made or contract arise in the absence of a writing.

A telephoned acceptance is effective when and where the acceptance is spoken into the phone. Consequently, when a person who lived in Kansas applied for a job to work in Missouri and the employer telephoned from Missouri to Kansas accepting the application, the employment contract was a Missouri contract. Thus, the Kansas Workers' Compensation statute did not apply when the employee was subsequently injured.

18. Auction Sales

At an auction sale the statements made by the auctioneer to draw forth bids are merely invitations to negotiate. Each bid is an offer, which is not accepted until the auctioneer indicates that a particular offer or bid is accepted. Usually this is done by the fall of the auctioneer's hammer, indicating that the highest bid made has been accepted. As a bid is merely an offer, the bidder may withdraw the bid at any time before it is accepted by the auctioneer.

Ordinarily, the auctioneer may withdraw any article or all of the property from the sale if not satisfied with the amounts of the bids that are being made. Once a bid is accepted, however, the auctioneer cannot cancel the sale. In addition, if it had been announced that the sale was to be made "without reserve," the goods must be sold to the person making the highest bid, regardless of how low that may be.

SUMMARY

As a contract arises when an offer is accepted, it is necessary to find that there was an offer and that it was accepted. If either element is missing, there is no contract.

An offer does not exist unless the offeror has contractual intent. This intent is lacking if the statement of the person is merely an invitation to negotiate, a statement of intention, or an agreement to agree at a later date. Newspaper ads, price quotations, and catalog prices are ordinarily merely invitations to negotiate and cannot be accepted.

An offer must be definite. If an offer is indefinite, its acceptance will not create a contract, because it will be held that the resulting agreement is too vague to enforce. In some cases an offer that is by itself too indefinite is made definite because some writing or standard is incorporated by reference and made

part of the offer. In some cases the offer is made definite by implying terms that were not stated. In other cases the indefinite part of the offer is ignored when that part can be divided or separated from the balance of the offer. In other cases the requirement of definiteness is ignored, either because the matter that is not definite is unimportant or because there is an exception to the rule requiring definiteness.

Assuming that there is in fact an offer that is made with contractual intent and that it is sufficiently definite, it still does not have the legal effect of an offer unless it is communicated to the offeree by or at the direction of the offeror.

In some cases no contract arises because there is no offer that satisfies the requirements just stated. In other cases there was an offer, but it was terminated before it was accepted. By definition an attempted acceptance made after the offer has been terminated has no effect. The ordinary offer may be revoked at any time by the offeror. All that is required is the showing of intent to revoke and the communication of that intent to the offeree. The offeror's power to revoke is barred by the existence of an option contract under common law, a firm offer under the Uniform Commercial Code or local non-Code statute, and by the application of the doctrine of detrimental reliance by the offeree. An offer is also terminated by the express rejection of the offer or by the making of a counteroffer; by the lapse of the time stated in the offer, or of a reasonable time when none is stated; by the death or disability of either party; or by a change of law that makes illegal a contract based on the particular offer.

When the offer is accepted, a contract arises. Only the offeree can accept an offer, and the acceptance must be of the offer exactly as made without any qualification or change. Ordinarily, the offeree may accept or reject as the offeree chooses. Limitations on this freedom of action have been imposed by antidiscrimination and consumer protection laws.

The acceptance is any manifestation of intent to agree to the terms of the offer. Ordinarily, silence or failure to act does not constitute acceptance, and the recipient of unordered goods and tickets may make any disposition thereof without such action constituting an acceptance. An acceptance does not exist until the words or conduct manifesting assent to the offer are communicated to the offeror. Acceptance by mail or telegraph takes effect at the time and place when and where the letter is mailed or the telegram dispatched. A telephoned acceptance is effective when and where spoken into the phone.

In an auction sale, the auctioneer asking for bids makes an invitation to negotiate. A person making a bid is making an offer, and the acceptance of the highest bid by the auctioneer is an acceptance of that offer and gives rise to a contract. When the auction sale is without reserve, the auctioneer must accept the highest bid. If the auction is not expressly without reserve, the auctioneer may refuse to accept any of the bids.

QUESTIONS AND CASE PROBLEMS

1. What objective of the law (from the list in Chapter 2, Section 4) is illustrated by each of the following statements?
   (a) Economic life would be most uncertain if we did not have the assurance that contracts, once made, would be binding.
   (b) An offer is terminated by the lapse of a reasonable time, when no time has been stated.

2. The Hamilton store ran a newspaper ad stating that a certain television set was on sale for $400. Nora phoned the store to say that she wanted one of the sets. The store stated that it was sold out and could not fill her order. She sued Hamilton for breach of contract. Was it liable?

3. The Croft Cement Works agreed to supply Grover with as much cement as Grover would buy at a specified price per unit. Was this a requirements contract?

4. Katherine mailed Paul an offer that stated that it was good for ten days. Two days later she mailed Paul another letter stating that the original offer was revoked. That evening Paul phoned Katherine to say that he accepted the offer. She said that he could not do so because she had mailed him a letter of revocation and that he would undoubtedly receive the letter of revocation in the next morning's mail. Was the offer revoked by Katherine?

5. When an offer is rejected by the offeree, can the offeree thereafter accept the offer if the offeror refuses to make a better offer?

6. Nelson wanted to sell his home. Baker sent him a written offer to purchase the home. Nelson made some changes to Baker's offer and wrote him that he, Nelson, was accepting the offer as amended. Baker notified Nelson that he was dropping out of the transaction. Nelson sued Baker for breach of contract. Decide. What social forces and ethical values are involved? [Nelson v Baker (Mo App) 776 SW2d 52]

7. The Lessack Auctioneers advertised an auction sale that was open to the public and was to be conducted with reserve. Gordon attended the auction and bid $100 for a work of art that was worth much more. No higher bid, however, was made. Lessack refused to sell the item for $100

and withdrew the item from the sale. Gordon claimed that, as he was the highest bidder, Lessack was required to sell the item to him. Was he correct?

8. The Willis Music Co. advertised a television set at $22.50 in the Sunday newspaper. Ehrlich ordered a set, but the company refused to deliver it on the ground that the price in the newspaper ad was a mistake. Ehrlich sued the company. Was it liable? Reason? [Ehrlich v Willis Music Co. 93 Ohio App 246, 113 NE2d 252]

9. Hall, the owner of a tract of land, wanted to have an office building constructed on it. He advertised for bids for the construction of the building. Davis, a contractor, sent in a bid accompanied by a letter stating that he accepted Hall's offer and thanked him for the contract. Did Davis have a contract with Hall?

10. A movement was organized to build a Charles City College. Hauser and others signed pledges to contribute to the college. At the time of signing Hauser inquired what would happen if he should die or be unable to pay. The representative of the college stated that the pledge would not then be binding and that it was merely a statement of intent. The college failed financially, and Pappas was appointed receiver to collect and liquidate the assets of the college corporation. He sued Hauser for the amount due on his pledge. Hauser raised the defense that the pledge was not a binding contract. Decide. What ethical values are involved? [Pappas v Hauser, 293 Iowa 102, 197 NW2d 607]

11. *A* owned land. He signed a contract agreeing to sell the land but reserving the right to take the hay from the land until the following October. He gave the contract form to *B*, a broker. *C*, a prospective buyer, agreed to buy the land and signed the contract but crossed out the provision as to the hay crop. Was there a binding contract between *A* and *C*?

12. The Cobble Hill Nursing Home was run in a building rented from the Henry Warren Corporation. The lease gave Cobble "the option" to purchase the building at any time during the life of the lease "at a price determined by the [New York State] Department [of Health] in accordance with the Public Health Law and all applicable rules and regulations of the Department." Nothing in New York statutes nor in the regulations of the Department made any provision for determining the price of real estate. However, the department did make a determination as to a fair price, basing its decision in part on other regulations applicable to nursing homes. Cobble sued Warren to enforce the option. Decide. What social force is advanced by your decision? [Cobble Hill Nursing Home, Inc. v Henry Warren Corp. 74 NY2d 475, 548 NE2d 203]

13. A.H. Zehmer discussed selling a farm to Lucy. After a 40-minute discussion of a first draft of a contract, Zehmer and his wife, Ida, signed a second draft stating: "We hereby agree to sell to W. O. Lucy the Ferguson Farm complete for $50,000 title satisfactory to buyer." Lucy agreed to purchase the farm on these terms. Thereafter the Zehmers refused to transfer title to Lucy and claimed that they had made the contract for sale as a joke. Lucy brought an action to compel performance of the contract. The Zehmers claimed that there was no contract. Were they correct? [Lucy v Zehmer, 198 Va App 493, 84 SE2d 516]

14. Wheeler operated an automobile service station, which he leased from W.C. Cornitius, Inc. The lease ran for three years. Although the lease did not contain any provision for renewal, the lease was in fact renewed six times for successive three-year terms. The landlord refused to renew the lease for a seventh time. Wheeler brought suit to compel the landlord to accept his offer to renew the lease. Decide. [William C. Cornitius, Inc. v Wheeler, 276 Or 747, 556 P2d 666]

15. Cogdill made an offer to the Bank of Benton. The proper officer stated that he would "start the paperwork." Did Cogdill have a contract with the Bank of Benton? [Bank of Benton v Cogdill, 118 Ill App 3d 280, 73 Ill Dec 871, 454 NE2d 1120]

11

CAPACITY AND GENUINE ASSENT

In some cases a person may avoid or cancel an apparently binding agreement on the ground that contractual capacity was lacking. Avoidance might also be sought on the ground that there had been a mistake or misconduct of such a nature that the consent or agreement to the transaction was not genuine.

A. CONTRACTUAL CAPACITY

Some persons lack contractual capacity. This embraces both those who have a status incapacity, such as minors, and those who have a factual incapacity, such as insane persons.

1. Contractual Capacity Defined

Contractual capacity is the ability to understand that a contract is being made and to understand its general meaning. The fact that a person does not understand the full legal meaning of a contract does not mean that contractual capacity is lacking. Everyone is presumed to have capacity unless it is proven that capacity is lacking, or unless there is status incapacity.

(a) STATUS INCAPACITY. Over the centuries, the law has declared some classes of persons to lack contractual capacity in order to give them protection by giving them the power to get out of unwise contracts. Of these types, the most important today is the class identified as minors.

Until recent times, some other classes were held to lack contractual capacity in order to discriminate against them. Examples of such classes are married women and aliens. Still other classes, such as persons convicted and sentenced for a felony, were held to lack contractual capacity in order to punish them. Today these discriminatory and punitive incapacities have largely disappeared. Married women generally have the same contractual capacity as unmarried persons.[1]

By virtue of treaties between nations of the world, the discrimination against aliens has been removed. The destruction of contractual capacity as a punishment for crime still exists in some states, but recent cases regard it as unconstitutional, so it is likely that it will soon disappear.

(b) FACTUAL INCAPACITY. In contrast with incapacity imposed because of the class or group to which a person belongs is a factual incapacity. This may exist when because of mental or physical condition caused by shock, medication, drugs, alcohol, illness, or age, a person does not understand that a contract is being made or understand its general nature. If the factual incapacity later disappears, the party affected thereby can ordinarily avoid the contract. In some extreme cases, the contract made while the incapacity existed is void.

2.   Minors

For the protection of minors the law has always treated minors as a class as lacking contractual capacity.

(a) WHO IS A MINOR? At common law any person, male or female, under twenty-one years of age was a **minor** (or an infant). At common law minority ended the day before the twenty-first birthday. The "day before the birthday" rule is still followed, but the age of majority has been reduced from twenty-one years to eighteen years in most states and to nineteen in a few.

(b) MINOR'S POWER TO AVOID CONTRACTS. With exceptions that will be noted later, a contract made by a minor is voidable at the election of the minor. The minor may affirm or ratify the contract on attaining majority by performing the contract, by giving an express statement of approval, or by allowing a reasonable time to lapse without avoiding the contract. Once the contract is affirmed, it can no longer be avoided.

In some states a statute declares that certain kinds of contracts made by minors are void and not merely voidable. When such a statute is applicable, there is no need for a minor to declare that the contract is not binding, as there is nothing for the minor to avoid.[2]

(1) What Constitutes Avoidance. A minor may avoid or disaffirm a contract by any expression of an intention to repudiate the contract. Any act inconsistent with the continuing validity of the contract is also an avoidance. Thus, when a minor sold property to A and later, on reaching majority, made a sale of the same property to B, the second sale was an avoidance of the first.

(2) Time for Avoidance. The minor can avoid a contract only during minority and for a reasonable time after attaining majority. After the lapse of such reasonable time, the contract is deemed ratified and cannot be avoided by the minor. A few states permit the former minor to avoid a wholly executory contract thereafter in the absence of an express affirmance.

(3) Minor's Misrepresentation of Age. Generally, the fact that the minor has misrepresented age does not affect the minor's power to avoid the contract. A few states hold that such fraud of the minor prevents the

---

[1]   In a few states there is a limitation that a married woman cannot make a binding contract to pay the debt of her husband if he fails to do so.

[2]   Moran v Williston Cooperative Credit Union (ND) 420 NW2d 353 (1988).

minor from avoiding the contract. A few states permit the minor to avoid the contract in such a case but require the minor to pay for any damage to the property received under the contract.

In any case the other party to the contract may avoid it because of the minor's fraud.

(c) RESTITUTION BY MINOR AFTER AVOIDANCE. When a minor avoids a contract, the question arises as to what must be returned by the minor to the other contracting party.

(1) Original Consideration Intact. When a minor still has what was received from the other party, the minor, on avoiding the contract, must return it to the other party or offer to do so. That is, the minor must put things back to the original position, or as it is called, restore the **status quo ante.** If the minor who is able to return the consideration does not do so, the minor cannot avoid the contract. By virtue of this rule, when a contract is avoided, the minor must avoid all of it.

(2) Original Consideration Damaged or Destroyed. What happens if the minor cannot return what has been received because it has been spent, used, damaged, or destroyed? The minor's right to avoid the contract is not affected thereby. The minor can still avoid the contract and is only required to return what remains. The fact that nothing remains or that what remains is damaged does not bar the right to avoid the contract. In those states that follow the common law rule the minor can thus refuse to pay for what has been received under the contract or can get back what had been paid or given, even though the minor does not have anything to return or returns any property in a damaged condition. There is, however, a trend that would limit this rule.

In the *Star Chevrolet* case the dealer claimed a credit for the salvage value of the automobile purchased by the minor.

STAR CHEVROLET CO. v GREEN
(Miss) 473 So 2d 157 (1985)

Kevin Green purchased an automobile from Star Chevrolet Company. He later notified Star that he was a minor and was avoiding the contract. Star refused to take back the car and to refund the purchase price. Kevin continued to use the car. He was involved in a collision. His insurance paid his claim, and he transferred the car to the insurance company. The company later sold the car for salvage for $1,500. Kevin sued Star for the price that he had paid for the car. Star claimed that it was entitled to a setoff of $1,500 for the salvage value of the car. The lower court refused to allow this setoff, and Star appealed.

SULLIVAN, J. . . . Before reaching the precise question at hand, some general principles warrant restatement. First, the right of a minor to disaffirm his contract is based upon sound public policy to protect the minor from his own improvidence and the overreaching of adults. It is the policy of the law to discourage adults from contracting with minors and the adult cannot complain if, as a consequence of his violation of this rule of conduct, he is injured by the minor's exercise of the right of disaffirmance, since this injury might have been avoided if the adult had declined to enter into the contract.

Second, if upon disaffirmance the minor has in his possession the specific property or any part of it which he received he must return it. Thus, where a minor repudiates an automobile sales contract while the vehicle is still in his hands, he must tender the vehicle in order for his purchase price to be refunded. . . . The seller may not deduct from the refunded purchase price allowances for use and depreciation.

Third, the general rule is that upon disaffirmance of a minor's contract, he is required to return the consideration only if it is still in his possession. The minor who disaffirms a contract is not obliged to return the consideration received by him or its equivalent where during his minority he has wasted, squandered, destroyed, used, or otherwise disposed of the consideration.

Finally, depreciation in the value of the vehicle due to the minor's misuse or neglect, short of [an] intentional or grossly negligent act amounting to an independent tort, is not allowable by way of recoupment. In other words, the minor is not liable for damages due to the very improvidence and indiscretion of infancy against which the law seeks to protect him. On the other hand, a minor may not use infancy, which is a shield for protection, as a sword for attack; such conduct by the minor amounts to fraud.

Turning to the facts of this case, the minor clearly had the consideration, i.e. the vehicle, in his possession when he first notified appellant of the disaffirmance of the contract. Had appellant offered the minor, as the law required, a full refund of his purchase price, the minor clearly would have been required to return the vehicle. Instead, the appellant did not, and while suit was pending the minor repaired the vehicle and began to use it. There is no hint in the record that the accident which destroyed the vehicle was the result of any deliberate design on the minor's part to fraudulently deprive appellant of that which would have placed him in status quo. For aught that appears in the record, the accident was caused by the carelessness and improvidence with which the law expects a minor to deal with his property. Disaffirmance at this point would have required the appellant to refund the full purchase price and the appellee, in turn, to return the damaged Camaro, since the law does not condition a minor's right to disaffirm a contract upon placing the other party in status quo, but only requires the return of whatever consideration remains in the minor's hands.

This case goes one step further. Prior to trial, the minor transferred title to the vehicle to the insurance company and used the proceeds to purchase another vehicle. The insuror obtained $1500 salvage value for the damaged Camaro. We are urged to offset the minor's recovery by the $1500 salvage value of the car on the ground that the minor had the duty to tender this consideration to appellant in order to receive a refund of the full purchase price.

. . . We hold that the minor is liable, and the appellant is entitled to a setoff, for the salvage value of the consideration which he intentionally conveyed away. . . .

[Judgment reversed as to setoff claim]

QUESTIONS

1. What is the justification for the common law rule on avoidance of contracts by minors?
2. What is the common law rule as to the liability of a minor avoiding a contract for property that had been damaged?
3. Does the *Star Chevrolet* case follow the common law rule stated in your answer to Question 2?

(d) RECOVERY OF PROPERTY BY MINOR ON AVOIDANCE. When a minor avoids a contract, the other contracting party must return the money received from the minor. Any property received from the minor must also be returned. If the property has been sold to a third person who did not know of the minority of the original seller, the minor cannot get the property back, but in such cases the minor is entitled to recover the monetary value of the property or the money received by the other contracting party from the third person.

(e) CONTRACTS FOR NECESSARIES. A minor can avoid a contract for necessaries but must pay the reasonable value for furnished necessaries. This duty of the minor is a quasi-contractual liability.[3] It is a duty that the law imposes on the minor, rather than one created by contract.

(1) What Constitutes Necessaries. Originally, **necessaries** were limited to those things absolutely necessary for the sustenance and shelter of the minor. Thus limited, the term would extend only to the most simple foods, clothing, and lodging. In the course of time, the rule was relaxed to extend generally to things relating to the health, education, and comfort of the minor. Thus, the rental of a house used by a married minor is a necessary. Services reasonably necessary to obtaining employment by a minor have been held to be necessaries.

The rule has also been relaxed to hold that whether an item is a necessary in a particular case depends on the financial and social status, or station in life, of the minor.

Property other than food or clothing acquired by a minor is generally not regarded as a necessary. Although this rule is obviously sound in the case of jewelry and property used for pleasure, the same view has been held even though the minor is self-supporting and uses the property in connection with work. Examples are tools of trade or an automobile used to go to and from work. The more recent decisions hold that property used by a minor to earn a living is a necessary. Thus, it has been held that a tractor and farm equipment were necessaries for a married minor who supported a family by farming.

These changes have come about because, in this century, minors have taken a greater part in the business and working world, in many cases leaving the parental home to lead independent lives.

(2) Contract with Parent or Guardian. When a third person supplies the parents or guardian of a minor with goods or services that are needed by the minor, the minor is not liable for such necessaries. This is so because the contract of the third person is with the parent or guardian, not with a minor.[4]

(f) RATIFICATION OF FORMER MINOR'S VOIDABLE CONTRACT. A former minor cannot avoid a contract that has been ratified after reaching majority.

(1) What Constitutes Ratification. Ratification consists of any words or conduct of the former minor manifesting an intent to be bound by the terms of a contract made while a minor.

The making of payments after attaining majority may constitute a ratification. Many courts, however, refuse to recognize payment as ratification in the absence of further evidence of an intent to ratify, an express statement of ratification, or an appreciation that such payment might constitute a ratification.

An acknowledgment that a contract had been made during minority, without an intent to be bound thereby, is not a ratification.

(2) Form of Ratification. Generally, no special form is required for ratification of a minor's voidable contract, although in some states a written ratification or declaration of intention is required.

(3) Time for Ratification. A minor can avoid a contract any time during minority and for a reasonable time thereafter but, of necessity, can only ratify a contract after attaining majority. The minor must have attained majority, or the "ratification" would itself be regarded as voidable.

(g) CONTRACTS THAT MINORS CANNOT AVOID. Statutes in many states deprive a minor of the right to avoid an educational loan,[5] a contract for medical care, a contract

---

[3]   See Chapter 9, Section 13 as to quasi-contractual liability generally.

[4]   Hammond's Estate v Aetna Cas Co. 141 Ill App 3d 963, 96 Ill Dec 270, 491 NE2d 84 (1986).

[5]   A Model Student Capacity to Borrow Act makes educational loans binding on minors in Arizona, Mississippi, North Dakota, Oklahoma, and Washington. This uniform act was reclassified as a model act by the Commissioners on Uniform Laws, indicating that it was recognized that uniformity was not important and that the matter was primarily local in character.

made while running a business, a contract approved by a court, a contract made in performance of a legal duty, or a contract relating to bank accounts, insurance policies, or corporate stock. In most states the contract of a veteran, although a minor, is binding, particularly a contract for the purchase of a home. In some states, by court decision, a minor who is nearly an adult, or who appears to be an adult, cannot avoid a contract, particularly when it is made in connection with a business or employment.

Some courts take an intermediate position with respect to employment contracts. These courts allow the minor to avoid the contract, but prohibit the minor from using any secret information obtained in the course of the employment or from competing with the former employer when the avoided contract contained a noncompetition clause. It has also been held that when a minor has settled a claim and received the amount specified in a release, the release is binding on the minor and cannot be set aside when the minor attains majority.

As an exception to the right to disaffirm a contract during minority, a minor cannot fully avoid a conveyance for the transfer of land until majority is attained.

(h) LIABILITY OF THIRD PERSON FOR MINOR'S CONTRACT. The question arises whether parents are bound by the contract of their minor child. The question also arises whether a person cosigning a minor's contract is bound if the contract is avoided.

(1) Liability of Parent. Ordinarily, a parent is not liable on a contract made by a minor child. The parent may be liable, however, if the child is acting as the agent of the parent in making the contract. Also, the parent is liable to a seller for the reasonable value of necessaries supplied by the seller to the child if the parent had deserted the child.

(2) Liability of Cosigner. When the minor makes a contract, another person, such as a parent or a friend, may sign along with the minor to make the contract more attractive to the third person.

With respect to the other contracting party, the cosigner is bound independently of the minor. Consequently, if the minor avoids the contract, the cosigner remains bound by the contract. If the debt to the creditor is actually paid, the obligation of the cosigner is discharged.

If the minor avoids a sales contract but does not return the goods, the cosigner remains liable for the purchase price.

3.   Incompetents

A person who is mentally deranged is generally called an **incompetent** and lacks capacity to make a contract. The cause of the incapacity is immaterial. It may be the result of insanity, senile dementia, imbecility, excessive use of drugs or alcohol, or a stroke. If the person is so mentally deranged as to be unable to understand that a contract is being made or the general nature of the contract, the person lacks contractual capacity.

An incompetent may have lucid intervals. If a contract is made during such an interval and is not affected by any delusion, the contract is valid and binding.

(a) EFFECT OF INCOMPETENCY. An incompetent person may ordinarily avoid a contract in the same manner as a minor.[6] Upon the removal of the disability (that is, upon becoming normal), the formerly incompetent person can either ratify or disaffirm the contract.

There is a trend in the law to treat the incompetent's contract as fully binding when its terms and the surrounding circumstances are reasonable and the incompetent is unable to restore the other contracting party to the status quo ante.

As in the case of minors, the other party to the contract has no right to disaffirm the contract merely because the incompetent has the right to do so.

(b) APPOINTMENT OF GUARDIAN. If a court appoints a guardian for the incompetent person, a contract made by the incompetent before that appointment may be ratified or, in some cases, disaffirmed by the guardian. If the incompetent person makes a contract after a

---

[6]   Palmer v Palmer (Fla App) 479 So 2d 221 (1985).

guardian has been appointed, the contract is void and not merely voidable.

4.   Intoxicated Persons

The capacity of a party to contract and the validity of the contract are not affected by the party's being drunk at the time of making the contract, as long as the party knew that a contract was being made.

If the degree of intoxication is such that a person does not know that a contract is being made, the contract is voidable by that person. The situation is the same as though the person were insane at the time and did not know what was being done. Upon becoming sober, the person may avoid or rescind the contract. However, an unreasonable delay in taking steps to set aside a known contract entered into while intoxicated may bar the intoxicated person from asserting this right.[7]

---

[7]   Diedrich v Diedrich (Minn App) 424 NW2d 580 (1988).

FIGURE 11-1   AVOIDANCE OF CONTRACT

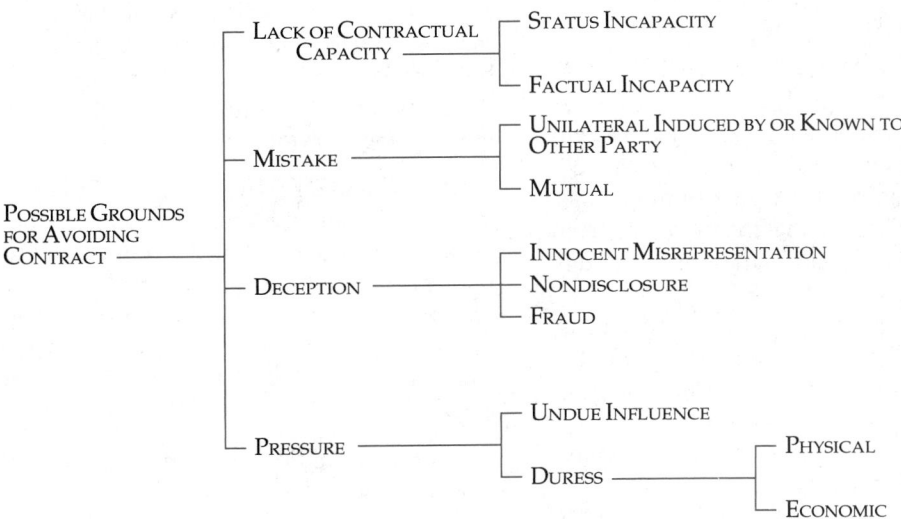

B.   MISTAKE

The validity of a contract may be affected by the fact that one or both of the parties made a mistake. In some cases the mistake may be caused by the misconduct of one of the parties.

5.   Unilateral Mistake

A unilateral mistake as to a fact does not affect the contract. For example, a customer orders a water-resistant coat, mistakenly thinking that this means it is waterproof. The customer cannot get out of the contract on the basis of this one-sided or unilateral mistake of fact as to the quality of the coat.

As exceptions to the statement that a unilateral mistake of fact does not affect the contract, the agreement has no effect if it states that it shall be void if the fact is not as believed. The party making the mistake may also avoid the contract if the mistake is known, or should be known or recognized, by the other contracting party.

A unilateral mistake as to expectations or the law does not have any effect on the contract. Thus, the fact that a signer of a contract would not have signed if the signer had understood the legal effect of the contract is not a defense.

A minority of states recognize unilateral mistake as a defense unless (1) the mistake is the result of inexcusable lack of due care, or (2) the other party has so changed position in reliance on the contract that rescission would be unconscionable.[8]

(a) MISTAKE AS TO NATURE OF PAPER. When a party makes a negligent mistake as to the nature of a paper, the party is bound according to its terms. For example, when the printed form for a corporation's loan application contained a guaranty by the president of the corporation of the corporate debt, the president signing the application without reading it was bound by this guaranty. This is true even though the president did not know that it was in the application and the application was headed merely "application for credit."

(b) MISTAKE AS TO TERMS OF PAPER. A person who has the ability and the opportunity to read a paper before signing is bound by its terms even though such person signed without reading. Such a signer cannot avoid liability on the ground that there had not been any explanation given of the terms of the writing.

A person unable to read or to understand the terms of a paper is bound by signing the paper without obtaining an explanation of it, unless the other contracting party knows, or has reason to know, of the signer's disability or educational limitation.

(c) MISTAKE AS TO RELEASE. An insurance claimant is bound by a release given to the insurance company when there is a unilateral mistake as to its meaning resulting from carelessness in reading the release. When a release is given and accepted in good faith, it is immaterial that the releasor or both of the parties were mistaken as to the seriousness or possible future consequences of a known injury or condition. If the release covers all claims "known or unknown," the courts following the common law view hold the releasor bound even though there were other injuries of which the releasor was unaware because the effects of the unknown injuries had not yet appeared. Some courts depart

from this and hold the release effective only with respect to the conditions or consequences that were known at the time the release was given.

6.   Mutual Mistake

When both parties make the same mistake of fact, the agreement is void. Thus, the contract is void if both parties mistakenly believe that the contract can be performed when, in fact, it is impossible to perform it. Assume that *A* meets *B* downtown and makes a contract to sell to *B* an automobile, which both believe is in *A*'s garage. Actually, the automobile was destroyed by fire an hour before the agreement was made. Since this fact is unknown to both parties, there is a mutual mistake as to the possibility of performing the contract, and the agreement is void.

(a) MISTAKE AS TO EXPECTATIONS. A mutual mistake with respect to expectations ordinarily has no effect on the contract unless the realization of those expectations is made an express condition of the contract. This means that the mistake has no effect unless the contract says that it shall be void if the matter is not as believed.

(b) MISTAKE OF LAW. When the mutual or bilateral mistake is one of law, the contract generally is binding. Thus, even if both parties to a lease mistakenly believe that the leased premises can be used for boarding animals because they are unaware of a zoning regulation that prohibits such a use of the property, the tenant does not have a right to rescind the lease for mutual mistake of law. In the eyes of the law, the parties should have known what the zoning regulations allowed. A few courts have refused to follow this rule. In several states statutes provide that a mutual mistake of law shall have the same effect as a mutual mistake of fact.

(c) COLLATERAL MATTERS. When a mutual mistake occurs as to a collateral matter, it has no effect on the contract. For example, where the plaintiff asks the fire insurer to issue a policy and both the insured and the insurance company wrongly believed that there

---

[8]   BMW of North America, Inc. v Krathen (Fla App) 471 So 2d 585 (1985).

was no other policy, the policy that was then issued was not void because of the mutual mistake that there was no other policy. That mistake related to a collateral matter.

C.   DECEPTION

One of the parties to a contract may have been misled by an innocent misrepresentation, a failure to disclose information, or a fraudulent statement.

7.   Innocent Misrepresentation

Suppose one party to a contract makes a statement of fact that is false but that is innocently made without intending to deceive the other party. Can the other party set aside the contract on the ground of being misled by the statement?

Equity will permit the rescission of the contract when the innocent misstatement of a material fact induces another to make the contract. If the deceived person is a defendant in an action *at law* for breach of contract, it is generally held that such innocent deception by the plaintiff cannot be asserted as a defense. There is a tendency, however, for the law courts to adopt the rule of equity. For example, it may be possible for an insurance company to avoid its policy because of an innocent misstatement of a material fact by the applicant. Contracts between persons standing in confidential relationships, such as guardian and ward, or parent and child, can be set aside for the same reason. Some courts go beyond this and permit the recovery of damages sustained because of the misrepresentation.

Modern law is increasingly concerned with the plight of the plaintiff and less concerned with whether the defendant was at fault. Courts that take this approach see no difference between an intentional fraudulent statement and innocent misrepresentation: The plaintiff is misled and harmed in either case.

In some states statutes have defined fraud so as to include innocent misrepresentation. Under such a statute a wrong statement of the model year of an automobile imposes liability on the seller, even though the misrepresentation was a mistake and no common law fraud or bad faith was present.[9]

8.   Nondisclosure

Under certain circumstances nondisclosure will serve to make a contract voidable, especially when the nondisclosure consists of active concealment.

(a) GENERAL RULE OF NONLIABILITY. Ordinarily, there is no duty on a party to a contract to volunteer information to the other. If *A* does not ask *B* any questions, *B* is not under any duty to make a full statement of material facts. Consequently, the nondisclosure of information that is not asked for does not impose fraud liability or impair the validity of a contract.

(b) EXCEPTIONS. In some instances the failure to disclose information that was not requested is regarded as fraudulent. In those cases the party to whom the information was not disclosed has the same remedies as if a known false statement were intentionally made.

(1) Unknown Defect or Condition. There is developing in the law a duty for one party who knows of a defect or condition to disclose that information to the other party where the defect or condition is obviously unknown to the other person and is of such a nature that it is unlikely that the other person would discover the truth or inquire about it.

Manufacturers and distributors of asbestos were guilty of fraud when they sold asbestos products without disclosing the information they possessed showing a relationship between cancer and asbestos products.[10]

In the *Reed* case the buyer of a house claimed that she should have been told by the seller that five people had been murdered in the house.

---

[9]   Myers v Liberty Lincoln-Mercury, Inc. 89 NC App 335, 365 SE2d 663 (1988).
[10]   Board of Education of City of Chicago v A, C, and S, Inc. 171 Ill App 3d 737, 121 Ill Dec 643, 525 NE2d 950 (1988).

REED v KING

145 Cal App 3d 261, 193 Cal Rptr 130 (1983)

> Robert King sold his house to Doris Reed. She was not told that, ten years earlier, a woman and her four small children had been murdered in the house. Some time after the sale Reed learned of the murders and sued to rescind the sale. She claimed that because of its bad reputation, the house was not worth what she had paid for it. From a judgment in favor of King, Reed appealed.

BLEASE, J. . . . The critical question is: does the seller have a duty to disclose here? Resolution of this question depends on the materiality of the fact of the murders.

In general, a seller of real property has a duty to disclose: "where the seller knows of facts *materially* affecting the value or desirability of the property which are known or accessible only to him and also knows that such facts are not known to, or within the reach of the diligent attention and observation of the buyer, the seller is under a duty to disclose them to the buyer." . . .

Whether information "is of sufficient materiality to affect the value or desirability of the property . . . depends on the facts of the particular case." Materiality "is a question of law, and is part of the concept of right to rely or justifiable reliance." Accordingly, the term is essentially a label affixed to a normative conclusion. Three considerations bear on this legal conclusion: the gravity of the harm inflicted by nondisclosure; the fairness of imposing a duty of discovery on the buyer as an alternative to compelling disclosure; and its impact on the stability of contracts if rescission is permitted.

Numerous cases have found non-disclosure of physical defects and legal impediments to use of real property are material.* However, to our knowledge, no prior real estate sale case has faced an issue of non-disclosure of the kind presented here. Should this variety of ill-repute be required to be disclosed? Is this a circumstance where "nondisclosure of the facts amounts to a failure to act in good faith and in accordance with reasonable standards of fair dealing[?]" (Rest.2d Contracts, § 161, subd. (b).) . . .

The murder of innocents is highly unusual in its potential for so disturbing buyers they may be unable to reside in a home where it has occurred. This fact may foreseeably deprive a buyer of the intended use of the purchase. Murder is not such a common occurrence that *buyers* should be charged with anticipating and discovering this disquieting possibility. Accordingly, the fact is not one for which a duty of inquiry and discovery can sensibly be imposed upon the buyer.

Reed alleges the fact of the murders has a quantifiable effect on the market value of the premises. We cannot say this allegation is inherently wrong and, in the pleading posture of the case, we assume it to be true. If information known or accessible only to the seller has a significant and measurable effect on market value and, as is alleged here, the seller is aware of this effect, we see no principled basis for making the duty to

---

*For example, the following have been held of sufficient materiality to require disclosure: the home sold was constructed on filled land . . . ; improvements were added without a building permit and in violation of zoning regulations . . . or in violation of building codes . . . ; the structure was condemned . . . ; the structure was termite-infested . . . ; there was water infiltration in the soil . . . ; the correct amount of net income a piece of property would yield. . . .

disclose turn upon the character of the information. Physical usefulness is not and never has been the sole criterion of valuation. . . .

Reputation and history can have a significant effect on the value of realty. "George Washington slept here" is worth something, however physically inconsequential that consideration may be. Ill-repute or "bad will" conversely may depress the value of property.

Whether Reed will be able to prove her allegation the decade-old multiple murder has a significant effect on market value we cannot determine. If she is able to do so by competent evidence she is entitled to a favorable ruling on the issues of materiality and duty to disclose.

[Judgment reversed]

QUESTIONS

1. How was the plaintiff harmed in the *Reed* case?
2. How does the *Reed* case compare with other nondisclosure cases?
3. Does this case stand for the proposition that a buyer can rescind a sales contract whenever the buyer learns of some fact that the seller had failed to volunteer to the buyer?

(2) Confidential Relationship. If *A* and *C* stand in a confidential relationship, such as that of attorney and client, *A* has a duty to reveal anything that is material to *C*'s interest when dealing with *C*. *A*'s silence has the same legal consequence as a knowingly made false statement that there was no material fact to be told to *C*.

The relationship between the buyer of a house and a financial institution lending the money to finance the purchase is not a confidential relationship. Therefore, the lender is not under any duty to disclose information possessed by it.

(3) Fine Print. An intent to conceal may be present when a printed contract or document contains certain clauses in such fine print that it is reasonable to believe that the other contracting party will neither take the time nor even be able to read such provisions.

In some instances legislatures have outlawed certain fine print contracts. Statutes commonly declare that insurance policies may not be printed in type of smaller size than designated by statute. Consumer protection statutes frequently require that particular clauses be set in large type. When a merchant selling goods under a written contract disclaims the obligation that goods be fit for their normal use, the Uniform Commercial Code requires the waiver to be set forth in "conspicuous" writing.[11] "Conspicuous" is defined as requiring "a term or clause . . . so written that a reasonable person against whom it is to operate ought to have noticed it. A printed heading in capitals . . . is conspicuous. Language in the body of a form is 'conspicuous' if it is in larger or other contrasting type or color . . ."[12]

There is a growing trend to treat a fine print clause as not binding on the party who would be harmed thereby, without considering whether fraud was involved. A provision freeing the other contracting party from liability is not binding when it is printed in type that is so small that a person with normal vision would have difficulty in reading it.

(4) Active Concealment. Nondisclosure may be more than the passive failure to volunteer information. It may consist of a positive act of hiding information from the other party by physical concealment, or it may consist of furnishing the wrong information. Such conduct constitutes fraud.

---

[11]   UCC § 2-316(2).
[12]   UCC § 1-201(10).

9.   Fraud

Fraud is (1) the making of a false statement of fact, (2) with knowledge of its falsity or with reckless indifference as to its truth, (3) with the intent that the listener rely thereon, (4) with the result that the listener does so rely, and (5) with the consequence that the listener is harmed.[13]

A seller committed fraud when selling a car as a "new" demonstrator when in fact the car had been damaged and repaired three times.[14]

(a) RELIANCE ON STATEMENT. The fact that a fraudulent statement has been made has no importance unless the other party relies on the statement's truth. Consequently, fraud is not present when the victim has the same knowledge of the true facts as the alleged wrongdoer or when the victim should have known such facts. When the false statements have been made after a contract has been signed, it is obvious that the making of the contract was not induced by the statements and that the other party to the contract had not relied thereon.

If the victim of the false statement could have easily determined that it was false, it will be held that there is no fraud liability. However, the fraud victim is not barred from relief because every possible step was not taken to determine whether statements were true. The modern American economy depends on a fast turnover of goods, and this is possible only when there is reliance by buyers upon statements of sellers. Thus, the buyer of a used car is entitled to rely on the statement of the seller that the car had never been in a wreck and that it had nothing wrong with it. This is true, even though if the buyer had had the car raised on a lift, the buyer could have seen the wreck-caused damage to the car and thus

learned that the statements of the seller were false.

(b) STATEMENT OF INTENTION OR PROMISE. A statement of intention or promise can constitute fraud when made by a person who does not intend to keep it. To illustrate, a customer purchases goods from a merchant on credit and agrees to pay for them in 60 days. If the customer does not intend to pay for the goods and does not do so, the customer is guilty of fraud by misrepresenting intention.[15]

The mere fact that the defendant has not performed a promise does not in itself establish that the defendant was guilty of fraud. It must be shown that the person made the promise with the intention of not keeping it.

(c) STATEMENT OF OPINION OR VALUE. Ordinarily, a misstatement of opinion or value is not regarded as fraudulent. The theory is that the person hearing the statement recognizes or should recognize that it is merely the speaker's personal view and not a statement of fact. A statement that is mere sales talk cannot be the basis of fraud liability.[16]

However, if the defendant, in making a statement as to future expectations, had knowledge not available to the plaintiff that showed that such expectations could not be realized, the statement can be held fraudulent. Thus, a statement that a business would make a stated profit in the future is actionable when the speaker knew that, on the basis of past events, such prediction was false. Likewise, a statement of opinion may be fraudulent when the speaker knows of past or present facts that make the opinion false.

In the *Master Abrasives* case a franchisee claimed that the sales pitch made by the franchisor was fraudulent. This was denied by the franchisor.

---

[13]   Rocky Mountain Helicopters, Inc. v Air Freight, Inc. (Wyo) 773 P2d 911 (1989).

[14]   Martin Chevrolet Sales, Inc. v Dover (Ind App) 501 NE2d 1122 (1986).

[15]   Goldome Credit Corp. v Hardy (Ala Civ App) 503 So 2d 1227 (1987).

[16]   Hill v Jay Pontiac, Inc. 191 Ga App 417, 381 SE2d 417 (1989).

MASTER ABRASIVES CORP. v WILLIAMS
(Ind App) 469 NE2d 1196 (1984)

Master Abrasives Corp. sold a dealership to Williams giving him the exclusive right to sell its products in 22 counties. Williams purchased the dealership because Robert F. Oldham, the vice president and national sales manager of Master, told him that there was the potential for earning $30,000 to $40,000 a year, and that the company had distributors who were currently earning that amount. Williams gave Master a down payment. Williams did not pay the balance. When Master sued him, he raised the defense of fraud. From a decision in favor of Williams, Master appealed.

CONOVER, J. . . . On September 18, 1982, Master and Williams entered into a sale and distribution agreement whereby Williams paid Master $1,000 and executed a 90-day note in favor of Master for $2,000. Master was to grant Williams exclusive selling rights to its trademarked product for two territories containing a total of 22 counties, provide product education, and sales assistance. At the time of the agreement, Master Abrasive's product line included grinding wheels and grinding points, in various grits, used in metal fabrication applications.

Prior to signing the agreement, Robert F. Oldham (Oldham), controller, vice president, and national sales manager of Master, represented to Williams there was a potential for earning $30,000 to $40,000 annually from a distributorship, and Master had distributors who were currently earning that amount. . . .

Williams argues Oldham's statements concerning profit potential and ease of earning back the investment are sufficient to support a finding of fraud. We disagree. These statements are mere opinion. Williams had no right to rely thereon. The essential elements of actual fraud are a material representation of past or existing *facts*, which representations are false, made with a knowledge or reckless ignorance of this falsity, which causes a reliance upon these representations, to the detriment of the person so relying.

While Oldham's statements as to the profit potential of the franchise are not sufficient for a finding of fraud, his statements about existing distributorships and their profitability will support such a finding. Testimony by Williams showed he relied on Oldham's representation Master had distributors earning $30,000 per year from the distributorships. Testimony by Johnson, however, shows there were only two distributors at the time, one of them being Oldham, and the *total sales* by these distributors during 1982 was only $10,000 to $15,000. Using Oldham's estimated cost of sales percentage of 40%, this shows earnings of only $6,000 to $9,000 for all the distributorships combined. Such a discrepancy is a clear misrepresentation by Oldham of an existing material fact.

A purchaser may rely on statements of fact made by the seller which are not obviously false and where the buyer lacks facilities for ascertaining the truth, as where facts are peculiarly within the knowledge of the seller. Here, the profitability of existing distributorships could have been known only by the principals of Master or the distributors themselves. Thus Williams reasonably could have relied upon such representations. That they were false statements renders them fraudulent. . . .

[Judgment affirmed]

QUESTIONS

1. What distinction did the court make between statements as to the potential earnings of Williams and the actual earnings of other dealers?
2. How would the case have been decided if nothing had been said as to the earnings of the other dealers?
3. Was Williams entitled to rely on the statements made to him as to the earnings of other dealers? Explain.

(d) STATEMENT OF LAW. A misstatement of law is treated in the same manner as a misstatement of opinion or value. Ordinarily, the listener is regarded as having an opportunity equal to that of the speaker of knowing what the law is, so that the listener is not entitled to rely on what the speaker says. Thus, a claim of fraud cannot be based on the assurance by a landlord that the tenant "should have no trouble" in obtaining a license desired by the tenant.[17] When the speaker has expert knowledge of the law or claims to have such knowledge, however, the misstatement of law can be the basis for fraud liability.

(e) UNCONSCIONABILITY AND CONSUMER PROTECTION. In many states greater protection than is allowed under the common law doctrine of fraud is given by applying the concept of unconscionability or the specific provisions of a consumer protection statute. That is, relief is at times given the victim in deception and hardship cases, even though some of the elements required to impose fraud liability are not present.

D.   PRESSURE

What appears to be an agreement may not in fact be voluntary because one of the parties entered into it because of undue influence or physical or economic duress.

10.   Undue Influence

An aged parent may entrust all business affairs to a trusted child; an invalid may rely on a nurse; a client may follow implicitly whatever an attorney recommends. The relationship may be such that for practical purposes, the one person is helpless in the hands of the other. When such a confidential relationship exists, it is apparent that the parent, the invalid, or the client is not exercising a free will in making a contract suggested by the child, nurse, or attorney, but is merely following the will of the other person. Because of the great possibility of unfair advantage, the law presumes that the dominating person exerts **undue influence** on the other person whenever the dominating person obtains any benefit from a contract made with the dominated person. The contract is then voidable. It may be set aside by the dominated person unless the dominating person can prove that, at the time the contract was made, no unfair advantage had been taken.

The class of confidential relationships is not well-defined. It ordinarily includes the relationships of parent and child, guardian and ward, physician and patient, attorney and client, and any other relationship of trust and confidence in which one party exercises a control or influence over another.[18]

Whether undue influence exists is a difficult question for the court (ordinarily the jury) to determine. The law does not regard every influence as undue. Thus, nagging may drive

---

[17]   Watkins v Gross (Mo App) 772 SW2d 22 (1989).

[18]   Misskelly v Rogers (Mo App) 721 SW2d 170 (1986).

a person to make a contract, but that is not ordinarily regarded as undue influence. Persuasion and argument are not in themselves undue influence.

An essential element of undue influence is that the person making the contract does not exercise free will. In the absence of a recognized type of confidential relationship, such as that between parent and child, the courts are likely to take the attitude that the person who claims to have been dominated was merely persuaded and there was therefore no undue influence.

11. Duress

A party may enter into a contract to avoid a threatened danger. The danger threatened may be a physical harm to person or property, called **physical duress;** or it may be a threat of financial loss, called **economic duress.**

(a) PHYSICAL DURESS. A person makes a contract under **duress** when there is such violence or threat of violence that the person is deprived of free will and makes the contract to avoid harm. The threatened harm may be directed at a near relative of the contracting party as well as against the contracting party. A contract is executed under duress when it is executed by parents under threat that their child will be prosecuted for a crime if they do not make the contract. If a contract is made

under duress, the resulting agreement is voidable at the victim's election.

Agreements made to bring an end to mass disorder or violence are ordinarily not binding contracts because they were obtained by duress.

(b) ECONOMIC DURESS. The economic pressure on a contracting party may be so great that it will be held to constitute duress. Economic duress occurs when the victim is threatened with irreparable loss for which adequate recovery could not be obtained by suing the wrongdoer.

Generally, a threat of economic loss or pressure caused by economic conditions does not constitute duress that makes a contract voidable. The fact that the plaintiff drove a hard bargain does not give rise to the defense of economic duress. When money is in fact owed a creditor, a threat by the creditor to sue the debtor to collect the amount owed does not constitute unlawful duress. It is merely a statement of what the law entitles the creditor to do.[19]

In the *Rich & Whillock* case, the creditor reduced the amount of the bill that was owed when the debtor refused to pay anything if the full bill was demanded.

---

[19] Avco Financial Services v Foreman-Donovan, 237 Mont 260, 772 P2d 862 (1989).

RICH & WHILLOCK, INC. v ASHTON DEVELOPMENT, INC.

157 Cal App 3d 1154, 204 Cal Rptr 86 (1984)

Ashton Development, Inc. and Bob Britton, Inc. were developing a tract of land. They made a contract with Rich & Whillock to perform grading and excavating work. Installment payments were made for this work as it progressed. When the project was completed, there was a balance due Rich & Whillock of approximately $72,000. Ashton and Britton offered to pay $50,000 and declared that it would be necessary to bring a lawsuit to get any more. Rich & Whillock informed Ashton and Britton that they would be forced into bankruptcy if they were not paid because they owed subcontractors, laborers, and suppliers of equipment in connection with the job. In order to avoid bankruptcy, Rich & Whillock accepted

$50,000 and signed a release of any additional amount. Some time later Rich & Whillock sued Ashton and Britton for $22,000. The defendants raised the defense that this claim was barred by the release.

WEINER, J. . . . At the outset it is helpful to acknowledge the various policy considerations which are involved in cases involving economic duress. Typically, those claiming such coercion are attempting to avoid the consequences of a modification of an original contract or of a settlement and release agreement. On the one hand, courts are reluctant to set aside agreements because of the notion of freedom of contract and because of the desirability of having private dispute resolutions be final. On the other hand, there is an increasing recognition of the law's role in correcting inequitable or unequal exchanges between parties of disproportionate bargaining power and a greater willingness to not enforce agreements which were entered into under coercive circumstances.

California courts have recognized the economic duress doctrine in private sector cases for at least 50 years. The doctrine is equitably based and represents "but an expansion by courts of equity of the old common law doctrine of duress.". . .

The underlying concern of the economic duress doctrine is the enforcement in the marketplace of certain minimal standards of business ethics. Hard bargaining, "efficient" breaches and reasonable settlements of good faith disputes are all acceptable, even desirable, in our economic system. That system can be viewed as a game in which everybody wins, to one degree or another, so long as everyone plays by the common rules. Those rules are not limited to precepts of rationality and self-interest. They include equitable notions of fairness and propriety which preclude the wrongful exploitation of business exigencies to obtain disproportionate exchanges of value. Such exchanges make a mockery of freedom of contract and undermine the proper functioning of our economic system. The economic duress doctrine serves as a last resort to correct these aberrations when conventional alternatives and remedies are unavailing. . . .

Nowadays, a wait of even a few weeks in collecting on a contract claim is sometimes serious or fatal for an enterprise at a crisis in its history. The business of a creditor in financial straits is at the mercy of an unscrupulous debtor, who need only suggest that if the creditor does not care to settle on the debtor's own hard terms, he can sue. This situation, in which promptness in payment is vastly more important than even approximate justice in the settlement terms, is too common in modern business relations to be ignored by society and the courts.

Here, Britton and Ashton acted in bad faith when they refused to pay Rich & Whillock, Inc.'s final billing and offered instead to pay a compromise amount of $50,000. At the time of their bad faith breach and settlement offer, Britton, and through him, Ashton, knew Rich & Whillock, Inc. was a new company overextended to creditors and subcontractors and faced with imminent bankruptcy if not paid its final billing. Whillock and Rich strenuously protested Britton's and Ashton's coercive tactics, and succumbed to them only to avoid economic disaster to themselves and the adverse ripple effects of their bankruptcy on those to whom they were indebted. Under these circumstances, the trial court found the July 10 agreement and August 20 release were the products of economic duress. That finding is consistent with the legal principles discussed above and is supported by substantial evidence. Accordingly, the court correctly concluded Ashton Development, Inc. and Bob Britton, Inc. were liable for the $22,286.45 balance due under the contract.

[Judgment affirmed]

QUESTIONS

1. What did the court decide?
2. What is the basis for the court's decision?
3. What is the basis for the doctrine that the court applied?

12.   Adhesion Contracts

Pressure on a contracting party may not be as extreme as physical duress or economic duress. It may still be sufficient to justify the conclusion that there was no genuine assent freely given, and that, accordingly, the basic element of a voluntary agreement was lacking, and that what appears to be a contract is merely a voidable transaction. Such a situation may involve a contract of adhesion. A **contract of adhesion** is one that is offered by a dominant party to a party with inferior bargaining power on a take-it-or-leave-it basis. The weaker person cannot go elsewhere to obtain the goods or services desired and therefore must deal on the terms dictated by the superior party or do without.

With the rise of the concept of unconscionability and the adoption of consumer protection laws, the need to apply the concept of the adhesion contract has diminished greatly. In most cases it is held that the concept is not applicable either because there is not a gross inequality of bargaining power or because the goods or services could be obtained elsewhere.

The modern view of the concept of the contract of adhesion is seen in the *Hartland Computer* case.

HARTLAND COMPUTER LEASING CORP., INC. v INSURANCE MAN, INC.

(Mo App) 770 SW2d 525 (1989)

In accordance with their prior agreement, Insurance Man selected a computer from Multitask, Inc., and Hartland Computer Leasing then purchased and leased the computer to Insurance Man. The lease between Hartland Computer and Insurance Man stated that Hartland Computer made no warranties, that if the computer did not work, Insurance Man had to continue to pay rent and could not sue anyone except Multitask. The leased computer failed to work properly, and Insurance Man stopped making rental payments. Hartland Computer then sued Insurance Man for breach of the lease. Insurance Man raised the defense that the computer did not work properly. Hartland computer claimed that Insurance Man could not raise that defense because of the provisions of the lease. Insurance Man replied that those terms were not binding because the lease was a contract of adhesion. Judgment was entered for Insurance Man, and Hartland Computer appealed.

GAERTNER, J. . . . An adhesion contract, as opposed to a negotiated contract, has been described as a form contract created and imposed by a stronger party upon a weaker party on a "take this or nothing basis," the terms of which unexpectedly or unconscionably limit the obligations of the drafting party. . . . Some writers view any pre-printed standardized form with filled-in blank spaces to be a contract of adhesion insofar as the pre-printed provisions are concerned. Thus, in *Corbin On Contracts*, § 559A at 660 (Supp. 1989), it is said "the bulk of contracts signed in this country, if not every major Western nation, are adhesion contracts. . . ." . . . Such form contracts are a natural concomitant of our mass production-mass consumer society. . . . Therefore, a rule automatically invalidating adhesion contracts would be completely unworkable. . . . Accordingly, courts do not view adhesion contracts as inherently sinister and automatically unenforceable. Rather, as with all contracts, the courts seek to enforce the reasonable expectations of the parties garnered not only from the words of a standardized form imposed by its proponent, but from the totality of the circumstances surrounding the transaction. . . . Only such provisions of the standardized form which fail to comport with such reasonable expectations and which are unexpected and unconscionably unfair are held to be unenforceable. . . . Because standardized contracts address the mass of users, the test for "reasonable expectations" is objective, addressed to the average member of the public who accepts such a contract, not the subjective expectations of an individual adherent. . . .

We look then to all the evidence surrounding this transaction to determine the objectively reasonable expectations of the parties and to the question of unconscionable unfairness imposed upon respondents under the terms of the form contract. [The court reviewed the facts and decided that the lease could not be condemned as unconscionable.]

[Judgment reversed and action remanded]

QUESTIONS

1. Was the provision excluding liability of Hartland Computer unreasonably unfair?
2. What insight does the *Hartland Computer* case give into the legal environment of business?
3. What is the significance of "contract of adhesion"?

E.   REMEDIES

When there is not a genuine agreement of the parties, the remedy may be a rescission of the contract, an action for damages, or an action for reformation of the contract.

Mistake, fraud, undue influence, and duress may make the agreement voidable or, in some instances, void. The following remedies are available.

13.   Rescission

If the contract is voidable, it can be **rescinded** or set aside by the party who has been injured or of whom advantage has been taken. The object of rescission is to restore the status quo ante.

If not avoided, however, the contract is valid and binding. In no case can the other party, the wrongdoer, set aside the contract. If the agreement is void, neither party can enforce it and no act of avoidance is required by either party to set the contract aside. The power to avoid a contract because of mistake or misrepresentation is lost if with knowledge or reason to know thereof, the aggrieved party delays an unreasonable time, affirms the transaction, or does any act inconsistent with an avoidance of the transaction.[20]

14.   Damages

Some states allow the person harmed by an innocent misrepresentation to recover compensatory damages. Since such a misrepresentation is, by definition, neither intentional nor

[20]   Thorstenson v Arco Alaska, Inc. (Alaska) 780 P2d 371 (1989).

reckless, punitive damages cannot be recovered.[21]

If the other party was guilty of a wrong, such as fraud, the injured party may sue for damages caused by such a wrong. In the case of the sale of goods, the aggrieved party may both rescind the contract and recover damages; but in other contracts, the victim must choose one of these two remedies.[22] Thus, a buyer rescinding a contract for the sale of a house because of fraud cannot also recover damages for the fraud.

15.   Reformation of Contract by Court

At times a written contract does not correctly state the agreement already made by the par-

---

[21]   Christopher v Heimlich (Ala Civ App) 523 So 2d 466 (1988).
[22]   UCC § 2-721; Potomac Leasing Co. v Thrasher, 181 Ga App 883, 354 SE2d 210 (1987).

---

ties. When this occurs either party can have the court correct or reform the writing to state the agreement actually made. A court action for reformation may be necessary because a change of circumstances or the occurrence of certain events may cause the other party to refuse to change the written contract voluntarily. For example, suppose *A* obtains a collision insurance policy on an automobile, but through mistake the policy describes the wrong car. *A* can obtain a decree of court declaring that the policy covers the car that *A* and the insurance company intended to insure rather than the car wrongly identified in the policy. The insurance company would gladly have made the correction prior to any loss' being sustained, but if the car *A* intended to insure has been damaged, court reformation would be necessary.

In the *Phil Bramsen* case the parties contracted in terms of a cost of living index that did not exist.

PHIL BRAMSEN DISTRIBUTOR, INC. v MASTRONI AND KUHSE

(App) 151 Ariz 194, 726 P2d 610 (1986)

Mastroni and Kuhse leased land to Phil Bramsen Distributor. The lease specified the amount of the rent and provided that such amount would be reset every five years according to the cost of living index prepared by the United States Department of Labor for the city of Phoenix. A dispute arose, and the lessee brought a suit to rescind the lease on the ground that there was no such cost of living index. The lessor counterclaimed, seeking a reformation of the lease. The lower court reformed the lease to refer to the Phoenix cost of living index prepared by the Bureau of Business and Economic Research at Arizona State University. The lessee appealed.

HATHAWAY, J. . . . Neither the Bureau of Labor Statistics (BLS) nor any other subdivision of the United States Government prepares a consumer price index (CPI) for Phoenix. . . .

After a trial to the court, judgment was entered . . . reforming the rent escalation clause by replacing the "consumer price index prepared by the United States Bureau of Labor Statistics" with the "consumer price index for Phoenix, Arizona." The court went on to hold that the metropolitan Phoenix consumer price index prepared by the Bureau of Business and Economic Research, Arizona State University, would be used in the reformed escalation clause. . . .

Before reformation can be granted, a court must be presented with clear and convincing evidence that (1) a mutual mistake was made by the parties in drafting the instrument, and (2) that the minds of the parties had met on a definite intention before the instrument was drafted. . . .

In the present case, the parties agreed to an escalation clause based on the rate of inflation. It was a mistake of fact that caused the clause to fail. The draftsman, Mastroni's attorney, inserted the term "cost of living index for the City of Phoenix prepared by the Bureau of Labor Statistics." There is no evidence that either appellees or appellants Bramsen had any independent knowledge of such an index or relied on anyone's word but the attorney's. Therefore, by mutual mistake the parties believed they had a workable formula. Appellants argue that because the attorney was Mastroni's agent, the mistake is still unilateral. Even if we were to agree that the drafter was Mastroni's agent, this argument fails. If a mutual mistake of the parties results from the mistake of the draftsman, it is immaterial, so far as reformation is concerned, which party employed him.

The parties clearly intended to have an escalation clause based on inflation. It was only the error of the scrivener that caused this escalation clause to be unenforceable and the trial court could have found that there was a mutual mistake.

Appellants also argue that there was no agreement by the parties to the lease concerning the escalation clause prior to the drafting of the lease. The parties did, however, agree that there would be an escalation clause based upon inflation. . . . No equitable reason appears for refusing to reform the lease agreement. On the contrary, equity favors the reformation, otherwise appellant would receive an unconscionable windfall if allowed to enforce his lease at the current rental price. . . .

We see no equitable, legal or factual reasons for precluding the trial court from reforming this contract.

[Judgment as to reformation affirmed]

QUESTIONS

1. Why was reformation granted in the *Bramsen* case?
2. What was the significance of the fact that the improper description of the cost of living index was added to the written lease by the attorney for one of the lessors? Explain.
3. Did the court regard the lease provision relating to the cost of living index as ambiguous?

A party seeking reformation of a contract must clearly prove both the grounds for reformation and what the agreement actually was.[23]

[23]   Omaha Door Co. v Mexican Food Manufacturers of Omaha, Inc. 232 Neb 153, 439 NW2d 776 (1989).

SUMMARY

An agreement that otherwise appears to be a contract may not be binding because a party thereto lacks contractual capacity. In such case the contract is ordinarily voidable at the election of that party who lacks contractual capacity. In some cases the contract is void. Ordinarily, contractual incapacity is the inability, for mental or physical reasons, to understand that a contract is being made and to understand its general terms and nature. This is typically the case when it is claimed that incapacity exists because of insanity or intoxication. The incapacity of minors arises because society is discriminating in favor of that class in order to protect them from unwise contracts.

In most states today the age of majority is eighteen years. Minors can avoid most contracts. If the minor received anything from the other party, the minor, upon avoiding the contract, must return what had been received from the other party, if the minor still has it.

When a minor avoids a contract for a necessary, the minor must pay the reasonable value of any benefit received. The concept of a necessary has expanded so that it now embraces needs reasonably necessary for the minor's existence and employment, taking into consideration the social position and background of the minor.

Only a minor is liable for the minor's contract. Parents of the minor are not liable on the contracts of the minor merely because they are the parents. Frequently, an adult will enter into the contract as a coparty of the minor. Such an adult, whether a parent or a nonrelative, is liable on the contract made by such person and the minor without regard to whether the minor has avoided the contract. However, the cosigner is released if everything in its original condition is returned by the minor to the other contracting party.

The contract of an insane person is voidable to much the same extent as the contract of a minor. An important distinction is that if a guardian has been appointed for the insane person, a contract made by the insane person is void and not merely voidable.

An intoxicated person lacks contractual capacity to make a contract if the intoxication is such that the person does not understand that a contract is being made.

The consent of a party to an agreement is not genuine or voluntary in certain cases of mistake, deception, or pressure. When this is so, the agreement of the parties does not give rise to a contract, and what appears to be a contract can be avoided by the victim of such circumstances or conduct.

As to mistake, it is necessary to distinguish between unilateral mistakes that are unknown to the other contracting party and those that are known. Mistakes that are unknown to the other party usually do not affect the binding character of the agreement. A unilateral mistake of which the other contracting party has knowledge or has reason to know makes the contract avoidable by the victim of the mistake.

The deception situation may be one of innocent misrepresentation, nondisclosure, or fraud. The innocent misrepresentation generally has no effect on the binding quality of an agreement, although there is a trend to recognize it as a ground for avoiding the contract. A few courts allow the recovery of damages. When one party to the contract knows of a fact that has a bearing on the transaction, the failure to volunteer information as to that fact to the other contracting party is called nondisclosure. The law ordinarily does not attach any significance to nondisclosure. Contrary to this rule, there is a duty to volunteer information when a confidential relationship exists between the possessor of the knowledge and the other contracting party. A strong modern trend in the law imposes a duty to disclose or volunteer information relating to matters that are not likely to be inquired about by the other contracting party.

When concealment goes beyond mere silence and consists of actively taking steps to hide the truth, the conduct may be classified as fraud rather than nondisclosure. There is a growing trend to hold fine print clauses not to be binding, on the theory that they are designed to hide the truth from the other contracting party. Consumer protection statutes often outlaw fine print clauses by requiring particular contracts or particular clauses in contracts to be printed in type of a specified size. A statement of opinion, value, or law cannot ordinarily be the basis for fraud liability, although it can be when the maker of the false statement claims to be an expert as to the particular subject matter and is making the statement as an expert.

The free will of a person, essential to the voluntary character of a contract, may be lacking because the agreement had been obtained by pressure. This may range from undue influence, through the array of threats of extreme economic loss (called economic duress), to the threat of physical force that would cause serious personal injury or damage to property (called physical duress). The mere fact that one party to the contract has great bargaining power and offers the other party a printed contract on a take-it-or-leave-it basis (an adhesion contract) does not prove that the agreement was not voluntary. However, some courts have held that in such cases the agreement is not voluntary if the weaker party cannot obtain the desired goods or services elsewhere.

When the voluntary character of an agreement has been destroyed by mistake, deception, or pressure, the victim may avoid or rescind the contract or may ratify the contract and obtain money damages from the wrongdoer. When the mistake consists of an error in putting an oral contract in writing, either party may ask the court to reform the writing so that it states the actual agreement of the parties.

QUESTIONS AND CASE PROBLEMS

1. Explain the objective of each of the following rules of law:
   (a) One party generally cannot set aside a contract because the other party failed to volunteer information that the complaining party would desire to know.
   (b) In certain close relationships that are regarded as confidential, it is presumed that a contract that benefits the dominating person was obtained by undue influence, and the dominating person has the burden of proving the contrary.

2. How is a contract affected by a unilateral mistake?

3. Lester purchased a used automobile from MacKintosh Motors. He asked the seller if the car had ever been in a wreck. The MacKintosh salesperson had never seen the car before that morning and knew nothing of its history, but quickly answered Lester's question by stating: "No. It has never been in a wreck." In fact, the auto had been seriously damaged in a wreck and, although repaired, was worth much less than the value it would have had if there had not been any wreck. When Lester learned the truth, he sued MacKintosh Motors and the salesperson for damages for fraud. They raised the defense that the salesperson did not know that the statement was false and had not intended to deceive Lester. Did the conduct of the salesperson constitute fraud?

4. Helen, age seventeen, wanted to buy a motorcycle. She did not have the money to pay cash but persuaded the dealer to sell a cycle to her on credit. The dealer did so partly because Helen said that she was twenty-two and showed the dealer an identification card that falsely stated her age as twenty-two. Helen drove the motorcycle away. A few days later she damaged it and then returned it to the dealer and stated that she avoided the contract because she was a minor. The dealer said that she could not do so because (a) she had misrepresented her age and (b) the motorcycle was damaged. Can she avoid the contract?

5. Yang and Richard make a contract for the sale of an automobile. They orally agree that the price Richard is to pay is $2,000, but when the written contract is typed, the amount is wrongly stated as $3,000. This contract is signed before anyone notices the mistake. Yang then claims that the written contract is binding and that Richard is required to pay $3,000. Richard claims that he is only required to pay the originally agreed-upon amount of $2,000. Is he correct?

6. Thompson bought an automobile on credit from Central Motor Co. The contract required him to pay 35 monthly installments of $125 and a final installment of $5,265. Thompson claimed that he agreed to buy because the sales manager falsely assured him that when the last payment was due it could be refinanced by signing another note for that amount at 8 percent interest. Thereafter, Central Motor refused to finance the final payment unless Thompson promised to pay 12 percent interest. He refused to do so and returned the car. Central sold the car and then sued Thompson for the balance remaining due. Is Thompson liable? What are the ethical values involved? [Central Motor Co. v Thompson (Tex Civ App) 465 SW2d 405]

7. Mary purchased a home from the Mitchell Developers. She was told that the house was free from termites. Actually, the house was infested with termites, and there was extensive termite damage in the house. This was known to Mitch-

ell and Mitchell had intentionally concealed the damage by paint and paper. When Mary learned of the actual termite condition, she sued Mitchell for damages for fraud and to set aside the contract. How will her claims be decided by the court?

8. Thomas Bell, a minor, went to work in the beauty parlor of Sam Pankas and agreed that when he left the employment, he would not work in or run a beauty parlor business within a ten-mile radius of downtown Pittsburgh, Pennsylvania, for a period of two years. Contrary to this provision, Bell and another employee of Pankas opened up a beauty shop three blocks from Panka's shop and advertised themselves as former employees of Pankas. Pankas sued Bell to stop the breach of the noncompetition or restrictive covenant. Bell claimed that he was not bound because he was a minor when he had agreed to the covenant. Was he bound by the covenant? [Pankas v Bell, 413 Pa 494, 198 A2d 312]

9. Aldrich and Company sold goods to Donovan on credit. The amount owed grew steadily, and finally Aldrich refused to sell any more to Donovan unless Donovan signed a promissory note for the amount due. Donovan did not want to do so but signed the note because he had no money and needed more goods. When Aldrich brought an action to enforce the note, Donovan claimed that the note was not binding because it had been obtained by means of economic duress. Was he correct? [Aldrich & Co. v Donovan, 238 Mont 431, 778 P2d 397]

10. *A* claimed that *B* owed him money. *A* was under the impression that *B* did not have much money. On the basis of this impression, *A* made a settlement agreement with *B* for a nominal amount. When *A* later learned that *B* was in fact reasonably wealthy, *A* sought to set the agreement aside. Was *A* entitled to do so?

11. An agent of Thor Food Service Corp. was seeking to sell Makofske a combination refrigerator-freezer and food purchase plan. Makofske was married and had three children. After being informed of the eating habits of Makofske and his family, the agent stated that the cost of the freezer and food would be about $95 to $100 a month. Makofske carefully examined the agent's itemized estimate and made some changes to it. Makofske then signed the contract and purchased the refrigerator-freezer. The cost proved to be greater than the estimated $95 to $100 a month, and Makofske claimed that the contract had been obtained by fraud. Decide. [Thor Food Service Corp. v Makofske, 28 Misc

2d 872, 218 NYS2d 93]

12. Kadish Pharmacy and other pharmacies made a contract with Blue Cross Blue Shield to provide prescription drugs to subscribers of Blue Cross Blue Shield, which in turn would reimburse the pharmacies. Kadish and the other pharmacies claimed that the contract with Blue Cross Blue Shield should have specified that the reimbursement to them would be at the customery rate charged by them. There was no proof that the parties had ever agreed to this as a term of their contract. Kadish sued to reform the contract. Decide. [Kadish Pharmacy, Inc. v Blue Cross Blue Shield, 114 App Div 2d 439, 494 NYS2d 354]

13. In 1622, a fleet of Spanish treasure ships sank, 40 nautical miles off the Florida coast. In 1971, Treasure Salvors, Inc. located one of the wrecked ships, the Atocha. Treasure Salvors and the Department of State of Florida believed that the wreck was located on the Florida coastal strip. On this basis, the State of Florida and Treasure Salvors made successive annual contracts giving Treasure Salvors the right to search for sunken treasure of the wreck in return for its giving Florida 25 percent of everything that was found. In a subsequent lawsuit, it was determined that the wreck was not on Florida land. Treasure Salvors claimed that it was not bound by its contract with Florida. Was it correct? [Florida v Treasure Salvors, Inc. (CA5 Fla) 621 F2d 1340]

14. Sippy was thinking of buying the house of Christich. He noticed water marks on the ceiling, but the agent showing the house stated that the roof had been repaired and was in good condition. Sippy was not told that the roof still leaked and that the repairs had not been able to stop the leaking. Sippy bought the house. Some time later, heavy rains caused water to leak into the house. Sippy claimed that Christich was guilty of fraud. Was he correct? [Sippy v Christich, 4 Kan App 2d 511, 609 P2d 204]

15. Pileggi owed money to Young. Young threatened to bring suit against Pileggi for the amount due. Pileggi feared the embarrassment of being sued and the possibility that he might be thrown into bankruptcy because of the suit. In order to avoid being sued, Pileggi executed a promissory note promising to pay to Young the amount due. He later asserted that the note was not binding because he had executed it under duress. Is this defense valid? [Young v Pileggi, 309 Pa Super 565, 455 A2d 1228]

12

CONSIDERATION

In Chapter 10, you saw that an agreement between the parties is one of the essential ingredients of a binding contract. The existence of an agreement ensures that the obligations created by the contract have been voluntarily assumed. Society will not, however, muster its resources to enforce every promise. As a condition for enforceability, society requires that a promise be supported by a consideration—that is, the promise must have been obtained in return for something else. Does it matter what is offered in return? Historically, it did not. In the days of Adam Smith the law left it to the contracting parties to determine what

each party wanted as consideration. Whether that was too much or too little was no concern of the law. In the last few decades this social desire for unrestricted bargaining freedom lost much of its appeal when it was seen that those with inferior economic power or education could not take care of themselves. In order to prevent consumer exploitation, consumer protection statutes and the concept of unconscionability have made the law examine the sufficiency or adequacy of the consideration. Going in the opposite direction, society has chosen to enforce promises made in certain situations even though no consideration at all was present. Thus, in some instances, no consideration is required to make a promise binding.

A.   GENERAL PRINCIPLES

As a general rule, one of the elements needed to make an agreement binding is consideration. This chapter discusses what this means.

1.   Definition

Consideration is what a promisor demands and receives as the price for the promise.[1] Consideration is something to which the promisor is not otherwise entitled, which the promisor specifies as the price for the promise. It is not necessary that the promisor expressly use the word *consideration*.

Since consideration is the price paid for the promise, it is unimportant who pays that price, as long as it has been agreed that it should be paid in that way. For example, consideration may be the extending of credit to a third person, as extending credit to the corporation of which the promisor is a stockholder. Likewise, when a bank lends money to a third person, such lending is consideration for the promise of its customer to repay the loan to the bank if it will loan the money to the third person.[2]

(a) NATURE OF CONTRACT. In a unilateral contract the consideration for the promise is the doing of the act called for. The doing of the act in such case is also the acceptance of the offer of the promisor.

In a bilateral contract, which is an exchange of promises, each promise is the consideration for the other promise. When a lawsuit is brought for breaking a promise, it is the consideration for the broken promise to which attention is directed.

(b) AGREED EXCHANGE. Consideration is what is agreed to in return for the promise.

In most cases this will directly benefit the promisor and will be some burden or detriment to the promisee. For example, an employer who promises to pay wages sustains detriment by promising to pay the wages in exchange for the benefit of receiving the employee's promise to work. The important thing, however, is that what is received is what was asked for as the price of the promise.

As long as someone gives what was asked for by the promisor, the promisor's obligation is supported by consideration, even though the economic benefit of the promise is not received by the person giving the consideration. Thus, when a third person comes to the financial aid of a debtor by making some promise *to* the creditor in exchange for some promise *from* the creditor, consideration exists. The contract is binding, even though the creditor's promise benefits the debtor rather than the third person. A promise guaranteeing repayment of a loan to a corporation is binding although the money loaned was all received by the corporation and nothing was received by the promisor, even though the promisor is not a shareholder of the corporation.[3]

2.   Effect of Absence of Consideration

The absence of consideration makes a promise not binding.[4] Thus, a person sued for breaking a promise will not be held liable when no consideration was received for the promise. For example, when the promise of an employee to refrain from competing with the employer is not supported by consideration, the promise is not binding, and the employee may compete with the employer. When a creditor promises the debtor that the debtor can have more time in which to pay the debt, the creditor is not bound by that promise because no consideration was given for it. Likewise, an offer that is to be held open for a specified number of days may be revoked at any time

---

[1]   The Advertiser Company v Electronic Engineers, Inc. (Ala Civ App) 527 So 2d 1317 (1988).
[2]   Peterson Bank v Langendorf, 136 Ill App 3d 537, 90 Ill Dec 961, 483 NE2d 279 (1985).

[3]   Dunkin Donuts of America, Inc. v Liberatore, 138 App Div 2d 559, 526 NYS2d 141 (1988).
[4]   Campbell v Matlock (Tenn App) 749 SW2d 748 (1987).

FIGURE 12-1   CONSIDERATION AND PROMISES

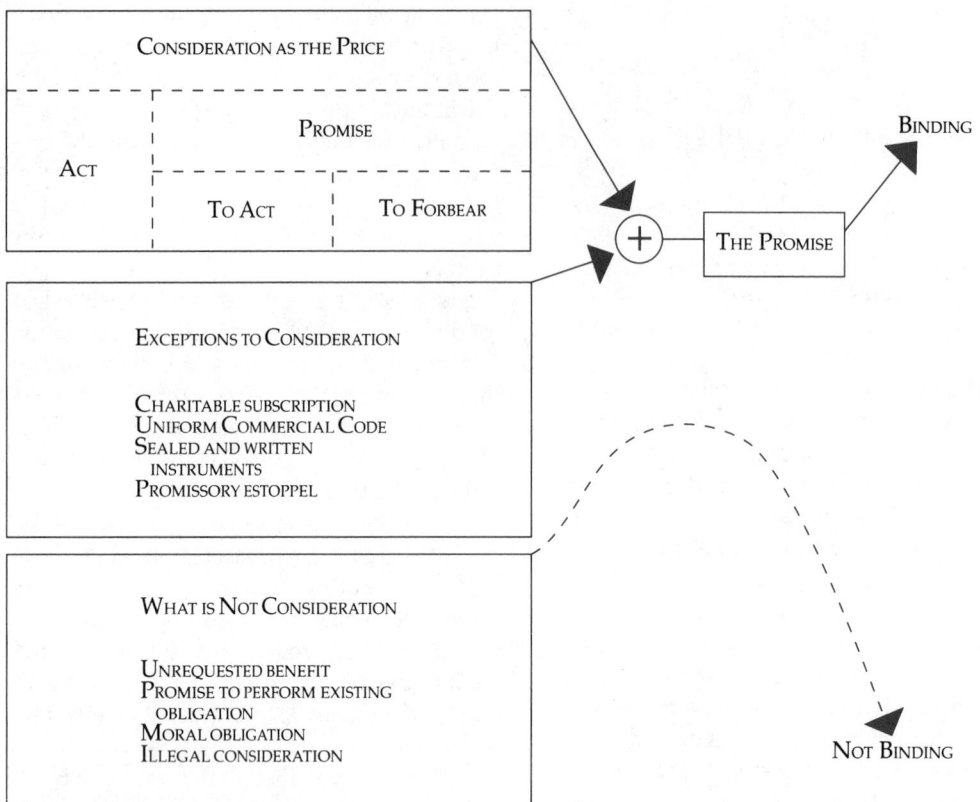

when no consideration is given for the promise to keep the offer open.

(a) MORAL OBLIGATION. The fact that the promisor feels morally obligated to make the promise does not make the promise binding when there is no consideration for it. Thus, a promise to pay money to an investor because the promisor feels responsible for the investor's loss is not binding. There is no consideration for the promise, and the moral obligation of the promisor does not constitute or take the place of consideration.

(b) LEGALITY DISTINGUISHED. While the absence of consideration ordinarily prevents enforcing a promise, the absence of consideration has no greater effect. That is, the agreement is not illegal because there was no consideration. Consequently, when a person keeps the promise, the performance rendered cannot be thereafter revoked on the ground that there was no consideration. To illustrate,

a promise to make a gift cannot be enforced because there is no consideration for the promise, but once the gift is made, the donor cannot take the gift back because there was no consideration.

3.   Legality of Consideration

The law will not permit persons to make contracts that violate the law. Accordingly, a promise to do something that the law prohibits or a promise to refrain from doing something that the law requires is not valid consideration, and the contract is illegal. This subject is further discussed in Chapter 13.

4.   Failure of Consideration

When a promise is given as consideration, the question arises as to whether the promisor will perform the promise.

(a) NONPERFORMANCE OF PROMISE. If the promise is not performed, the law describes the default as a "failure of consideration."

(b) BAD BARGAIN DISTINGUISHED. When the promisor performs the promise, there is never a failure of consideration. The fact that it turns out that the consideration is disappointing does not mean that there has been a failure of consideration. That is, the fact that the contract proves to be a bad bargain for the promisor does not constitute a failure of consideration, nor does it affect the binding character of the contract. Thus, the fact that a business purchased by the buyers does not prove profitable does not constitute a failure of consideration that releases them from their obligation to the seller.[5]

B.   WHAT CONSTITUTES CONSIDERATION

The sections that follow analyze certain common situations in which a lawsuit turned on whether the promisor received consideration for the promise sued upon.

5.   A Promise as Consideration

In a bilateral contract each party makes a promise to the other. The promise that one party makes is consideration for the promise made by the other.[6]

The fact that parties appear to be in agreement does not mean that there is a promise. Thus, a statement that a proposed step would be "no problem" does not constitute a promise.

(a) BINDING CHARACTER OF PROMISE. To constitute consideration, a promise must be binding; that is, it must impose a liability or create a duty. An unenforceable promise cannot be consideration. Suppose that a coal company promises to sell to a factory at a specific price all the coal that it orders, and that the factory agrees to pay that price for any coal that it orders from the coal company. The promise of the factory is not consideration because it does not obligate the factory to buy any coal from the coal company. However, if the factory promises to purchase all the coal it requires for a specific period, and the coal dealer agrees to supply it at a specific price per ton, there is a valid contract.

A promise that in fact does not impose any obligation on the promisor is often called an **illusory promise** because although it looks like a binding promise, it is not. The *Rosenberg* case turned on whether promises were binding or illusory.

---

[5]   Commerce Bank of Joplin v Shallenburger (Mo App) 766 SW2d 764 (1989).

[6]   Atlanta Six Flags Partnership v Hughes, 191 Ga App 404, 381 SE2d 605 (1989).

ROSENBERG v LAWRENCE
(Fla App) 541 So 2d 1204 (1988)

Charles Rosenberg and Cynthia Lawrence had married and then divorced. They made a 1978 agreement to share equally in the education, maintenance, support, and health care of their four sons. The agreement stated that the parents "shall consult one another before incurring a material expense." Disputes arose with respect to the consulting, and a 1982 amendment was made stating that the consulting provision meant that neither of them "will be obligated to pay for any material, unusual, or extraordinary expense to which he or she does not consent." At the time of this agreement, one of the sons, Howard, was a student at college. He left to go to work but later enrolled in another college. Cynthia paid all his expenses from September 1984 to November 1985, totaling $43,616.38. She demanded that Charles pay her half of this amount. He refused to pay her, on the ground that he had not been consulted and had not consented to the expense. Cynthia sued Charles for one-half of the expenses. Judgment was entered in favor of Cynthia. Charles appealed.

NESBITT, J. . . . Where one party retains to itself the option of fulfilling or declining to fulfill its obligations under the contract, there is no valid contract and neither side may be bound. . . ."One who in words promises to render a future performance, if he so wills and desires when the future time arrives, has made no real promise at all." 1 *Corbin on Contracts* § 149 (1963). *See also Port Largo Club, Inc. v. Warren*, 476 So.2d 1330 (Fla. 3d DCA 1985) (vendor's contract obligation wholly illusory where he could breach contract with impunity); *Young v. Johnston*, 475 So.2d 1309 (Fla. 1st DCA 1985) and cases cited therein (where one party retains to itself the option of fulfilling or declining to fulfill its obligations under the contract, there is no valid contract and neither side may be bound); *Spooner v. Reserve Life Ins. Co.*, 47 Wash.2d 454, 287 P.2d 735 (1955) (statement by insurance company that sales bonus was voluntary and could be withheld with or without notice rendered promise illusory and unenforceable). "An illusory promise is no promise at all as that term has been . . . defined. If the expression appears to have the form of a promise, this appearance is 'an illusion.' " 1 *Corbin on Contracts* § 16 (1963). "As a matter of course, no action will lie against the party making the illusory promise. Having made no promise, it is not possible for him to be guilty of a breach." 1 *Corbin on Contracts* § 145 (1963).

Under the 1982 modification, the parties were not "obligated for any material, unusual or extraordinary expense to which he or she does not consent." Because payment was contingent upon each parent's consent to undertake an obligation, Charles and Cynthia's "promise" represented no more than an illusion which did not obligate either party to act. The illusory nature of each parent's promise made that promise void and the mother has no right to seek reimbursement based on that illusory commitment, either by way of direct action for breach or under an estoppel theory. *See* 1A *Corbin on Contracts* § 201 (1963) (action in reliance on a supposed promise creates no obligation on a man whose only promise is wholly illusory). Their "obligation" meant nothing more than, "I will if I want to.". . . .

[Judgment reversed and action remanded]

QUESTIONS

1. What was the basis of the court's decision?
2. Could the court have decided the case on any other grounds?
3. Why does the law hold that an illusory promise is not binding?

(b) CONDITIONAL PROMISE. Can a conditional promise be consideration? Assume that an agreement states "buyer promises to buy, provided buyer can obtain financing." Is such a promise consideration for the seller's promise to sell, or is the buyer's promise not consideration because it does not impose any obligation on the buyer at the time that the promise is made?

The fact that a promise is conditional does not prevent it from being consideration, even though, as a practical matter, it is unlikely that the condition would ever be satisfied.[7] Thus, the promise of a fire insurance company to pay the homeowner in case of fire is consideration for the payment of premiums by the homeowner, even though it is probable that there will never be a fire.

(c) CANCELLATION PROVISION. Although a promise must impose a binding obligation, it may authorize one or either party to terminate or cancel the agreement under certain circumstances or upon giving notice to the other party. The fact that the contract may be terminated in this manner does not make the contract any less binding prior to such termination.

6.   Promise to Perform Existing Obligation

Ordinarily, doing or promising to do what one is already under a legal obligation to do is not consideration.[8] Similarly, a promise to refrain from doing what one has no legal right to do is not consideration. This preexisting duty or legal obligation can be based on statute, on general principles of law, on responsibilities of an office held by the promisor, or on a preexisting contract.

In the *Crookham & Vessels* case a promise was made to pay a subcontractor extra money because of difficulties encountered by the subcontractor.

[7]   Charles Hester Enterprises, Inc. v Illinois Founders Ins. Co. 114 Ill 2d 278, 102 Ill Dec 306, 499 NE2d 1319 (1986).

[8]   Waide v Tractor and Equipment Co. (Ala) 545 So 2d 1327 (1989).

CROOKHAM & VESSELS, INC. v LARRY MOYER TRUCKING, INC.

16 Ark App 214, 699 SW3d 414 (1985)

Crookham & Vessels had a contract to build an extension of railroad for the Little Rock Port Authority. They made a contract with Larry Moyer Trucking Co. to dig drainage ditches. The ditch walls collapsed because water would not drain off. This required that the ditches be dug over again. Larry Moyer refused to do this unless extra money was paid. Crookham & Vessels agreed to pay the additional compensation, but after the work was done they refused to pay it. Larry Moyer sued for the extra compensation promised. Judgment was entered in favor of Larry Moyer, and Crookham & Vessels appealed.

COOPER, J. . . . The appellant was the general contractor on a project to build an extension of a railroad for the Little Rock Port Authority. The appellee entered into a subcontract agreement with the appellant in January 1982 to do the excavation and dirt work on the project, which provided that the appellee would perform the work according to the plans and specifications provided by Garver & Garver, Inc. The problem in this case arose when the water would not drain out of the ditches the appellee constructed because the culverts through which they were to drain were clogged off of the jobsite. This caused the ditches to collapse, requiring the appellee to repeatedly have to redig the ditches. Larry Moyer, owner of the appellee, testified that, because of this problem, which began shortly after he started working, he told the appellant's representative, Alan McElhaney, that he would not continue to work without extra pay for redigging the ditches. He stated that McElhaney agreed to this.

The Port Authority's Invitation to Bid required each bidder to make an inspection of the jobsite, stating,

Each Bidder should visit the site of the proposed work and fully acquaint himself with the existing conditions there relating to construction and labor, and should fully inform himself as to the facilities involved, and the difficulties and restrictions attending the performance of the Contract. . . . The Contractor by the execution of the Contract shall not be relieved of any obligation under it due to his failure to receive or examine any form or legal instrument or to visit the site and acquaint himself with the conditions there existing and the Owner will be justified in rejecting any claim based on facts regarding which he should have been on notice as a result thereof.

Moyer testified that the contract required him to make this inspection, that he did do so, and that there was nothing stopping him from inspecting the culverts. He also admitted that he was required under the contract's plans and specification to build the drainage ditches to meet the specifications and be up to grade at the time the project closed. Moyer acknowledged that that was precisely what he accomplished.

Under Arkansas law, there must be additional consideration when the parties to a contract enter into an additional contract. . . . *Feldman v. Fox*, 112 Ark. 223, 164 S.W. 766 (1914). In *Feldman*, the court, in holding no consideration existed for a contract raising the price of crops that the seller was already obligated to sell to the buyer, stated:

If no benefit is received by the obligee except what he was entitled to under the original contract, and the other party to the contract parts with nothing except what he was already bound for, there is no consideration for the additional contract concerning the subject matter of the original one. *Thompson v. Robinson*, 34 Ark. 44; 1 Brandt on Suretyship and Guaranty, § 387; I Page on Contracts, § 312. "Mere performance of an existing contract or a part thereof," says Mr. Page in the section cited above, "is of itself no consideration for a new promise to the party performing. . . . If, without legal justification, one party to a contract breaks it, or threatens to break it, and to induce performance on his part the adversary party promises to pay more than was provided for by the original contract, there is in principle no consideration for such promise, as the party who threatens to break the contract does, when he finally performs it, no more than he was bound in law to do." 112 Ark. at 226, 164 S.W. 766.

Here, the contract admittedly required the appellee to dig the ditches so that he met the specifications at the time the project was approved, and it is undisputed that that is what the appellee did. Where the work performed is covered under the terms of the contract, as here, there can be no recovery for it as extra work. . . . The appellee had the duty to acquaint himself before bidding with the conditions, nature, and extent of the work to be performed, and the condition of the culverts in question could have been taken into account. In Arkansas, it is settled that "inconvenience or the cost of compliance with the contract or other like thing cannot excuse a party from the performance of an absolute and unqualified undertaking to do that which is possible and lawful." . . . Here, the appellee did no more than was required by its contract; the unforeseen clogged culverts merely made it more difficult. The appellant has received no additional consideration for its alleged promise to pay extra, having gotten no more than it bargained for in the first place. Therefore, the jury verdict . . . for the "extra ditching" must be overturned.

[Judgment reversed as to extra compensation claim]

QUESTIONS

1. Whose fault required the additional work?
2. Could the subcontractor have protected himself by examining the culverts before entering into the contract?
3. Was the amount of the extra compensation demanded by the subcontractor reasonable for the extra work done?

(a) COMPLETION OF CONTRACT. When a contractor refuses to complete a building unless the owner promises a payment or bonus in addition to the sum specified in the original contract, and the owner promises to make that payment, the question arises as to whether the owner's promise is binding. Most courts hold that the second promise of the owner is without consideration.

If the promise of the contractor is to do something that is neither expressly nor implicitly a part of the first contract, then the promise of the other party is binding.[9] For example, if a bonus of $1,000 is promised in return for the promise of a contractor to complete the building at a date earlier than that specified in the original agreement, the promise to pay the bonus is binding.

(1) Good Faith Adjustment. There is a trend to enforce a second promise to pay a

contractor a greater amount for the performance of the original contract when there are extraordinary circumstances caused by unforeseeable difficulties and when the additional amount promised the contractor is reasonable under the circumstances.

When parties to a contract, in a good faith effort to meet the business realities of a situation, agree to a reduction of contract terms, there is some authority that the promise of the one party to accept the lesser performance of the other is binding. These cases have held that the promise is binding, even though technically the promise to render the lesser performance is not consideration because the obligor was already obligated to render the greater performance. Thus, a landlord's promise to reduce the rent was binding when the tenant could not pay the original rent and the landlord preferred to have the building occupied even though receiving a smaller rental. A similar good faith adjustment to economic realities was made in the *Angel* case.

---

[9]   Penn Compression Moulding, Inc. v Mar-Bal, Inc. 73 NC App 291, 326 SE2d 280 (1985).

ANGEL v MURRAY
113 RI 482, 322 A2d 630 (1974)

John Murray was director of finance of the city of Newport. A contract was made with Alfred Maher to remove trash. Later, Maher requested that the city council increase his compensation. Maher's costs were greater than had been anticipated because four hundred new dwelling units had been put into operation. The city council voted to pay Maher an additional $10,000 a year. After two such annual payments had been made, Angel and other citizens of the city sued Murray and Maher for a return of the $20,000. They said that Maher was already obligated by his contract to perform the work for the contract sum, and there was, accordingly, no consideration for the payment of the increased compensation. From a decision in favor of the plaintiffs, the city and Maher appealed.

ROBERTS, C.J. . . . It is generally held that a modification of a contract is itself a contract, which is unenforceable unless supported by consideration. . . .

The preexisting duty rule is followed by most jurisdictions. . . .

The primary purpose of the preexisting duty rule is to prevent what has been referred to as the "hold-up game.". . . . A classic example of the "hold-up game" is found in *Alaska Packers' Ass'n v Domenico,* 117 F 99 (9th Cir 1902). There 21 seamen entered into a written contract with Domenico to sail from San Francisco to Pyramid Harbor, Alaska. They were to work as sailors and fishermen out of Pyramid Harbor during the fishing season of 1900. The contract specified that each man would be paid $50 plus two cents for each red salmon he caught. Subsequent to their arrival at Pyramid Harbor, the men stopped work and demanded an additional $50. They threatened to return to San Francisco if Domenico did not agree to their demand. Since it was impossible for Domenico to find other men, he agreed to pay the men an additional $50. After they returned to San Francisco, Domenico refused to pay the men an additional $50. The court found that the subsequent agreement to pay the men an additional $50 was not supported by consideration because the men had a preexisting duty to work on the ship under the original contract, and thus the subsequent agreement was unenforceable.

Another example of the "hold-up game" is found in the area of construction contracts. Frequently, a contractor will refuse to complete work under an unprofitable contract unless he is awarded additional compensation. The courts have generally held that a subsequent agreement to award additional compensation is unenforceable if the contractor is only performing work which would have been required of him under the original contract. . . .

These examples clearly illustrate that the courts will not enforce an agreement that has been procured by coercion or duress and will hold the parties to their original contract regardless of whether it is profitable or unprofitable. However, the courts have been reluctant to apply the preexisting duty rule when a party to a contract encounters unanticipated difficulties and the other party, not influenced by coercion or duress, voluntarily agrees to pay additional compensation for work already required to be performed under the contract. For example, the courts have found that the original contract was rescinded, . . . abandoned, . . . or waived.

Although the preexisting duty rule has served a useful purpose insofar as it deters parties from using coercion and duress to obtain additional compensation, it has been widely criticized as a general rule of law. . . . The modern trend appears to recognize the necessity that courts should enforce agreements modifying contracts when unexpected or unanticipated difficulties arise during the course of the performance of a contract, even though there is no consideration for the modification, as long as the parties agree voluntarily.

Under the Uniform Commercial Code, § 2–209(1), . . . "an agreement modifying a contract [for the sale of goods] needs no consideration to be binding.". . . Although at first blush this section appears to validate modifications obtained by coercion and duress, the comments to this section indicate that a modification under this section must meet the test of good faith imposed by the Code, and a modification obtained by extortion without a legitimate commercial reason is unenforceable.

The modern trend away from a rigid application of the preexisting duty rule is reflected by § 89D(a) of the American Law Institute's Restatement Second of the Law of Contracts, which provides: "A promise modifying a duty under a contract not fully performed on either side is binding (a) if the modification is fair and equitable in view of circumstances not anticipated by the parties when the contract was made. . . ."

We believe that § 89D(a) is the proper rule of law and find it applicable to the facts of this case. It not only prohibits modifications obtained by coercion, duress, or extortion but also fulfills society's expectation that agreements entered into voluntarily will be enforced by the courts. . . .

Section 89D(a), of course, does not compel a modification of an unprofitable or unfair contract; it only enforces a modification if the parties voluntarily agree and if (1) the promise modifying the original contract was made before the contract was fully performed on either side, (2) the underlying circumstances which prompted the modification were unanticipated by the parties, and (3) the modification is fair and equitable.

The evidence, which is uncontradicted, reveals that in June of 1968 Maher requested the city council to pay him an additional $10,000 for the year beginning on July 1, 1968, and ending on June 30, 1969. This request was made at a public meeting of the city council, where Maher explained in detail his reasons for making the request. Thereafter, the city council voted to authorize the Mayor to sign an amendment to the 1964 contract which provided that Maher would receive an additional $10,000 per year for the duration of the contract. Under such circumstances we have no doubt that the city voluntarily agreed to modify the 1964 contract.

Having determined the voluntariness of this agreement, we turn our attention to the three criteria delineated above. First, the modification was made in June of 1968 at a time when the five-year contract which was made in 1964 had not been fully performed by either party. Second, although the 1964 contract provided that Maher collect all refuse generated within the city, it appears this contract was premised on Maher's past experience that the number of refuse-generating units would increase at a rate of 20 to 25 per year. Furthermore, the evidence is uncontradicted that the 1967–1968 increase of 400 units "went beyond any previous expectation." Clearly, the circumstances which prompted the city council to modify the 1964 contract were unanticipated. Third, although the evidence does not indicate what proportion of the total this increase comprised, the evidence does indicate that it was a "substantial" increase. In light of this, we cannot say that the council's agreement to pay Maher the $10,000 increase was not fair and equitable in the circumstances.

[Judgment reversed and action remanded]

QUESTIONS

1. What was the basis for the plaintiff's suit?
2. How would the *Angel* case have been decided under the common law rule as to consideration?
3. Could the contract have been written in a way that would have avoided the problem involved in the *Angel* case?

(2) Contract for Sale of Goods. When the contract is for the sale of goods, any modification made by the parties to the contract is binding, without regard to the existence of consideration for the modification.

(b) COMPROMISE AND RELEASE OF CLAIMS. The rule that doing or promising to do what one is bound to do is not consideration applies to a part payment made in satisfaction of an admitted debt. For example, if one person owes another $100, the promise of the latter to accept $50 in full payment is not binding. It will not prevent the creditor from demanding the remainder later. The part payment made by the debtor was not consideration for the promise to release the balance of the claim.

If the debtor pays before the debt is due, there is consideration, since on the day when the payment was made, the creditor was not entitled to demand any payment. Likewise, if the creditor accepts some article (even of slight value) in addition to the part payment, consideration exists, and the agreement is held to be binding.

A debtor and creditor may have a bona fide dispute as to the amount owed or as to whether any amount is owed. In such a case payment by the debtor of less than the amount claimed by the creditor is consideration for the latter's agreement to release or settle the claim. It is generally regarded as sufficient if the claimant believes in the merit of the claim. Conversely, if the claimant knows that the claim does not have any merit and is merely pressing the claim in order to force the other party to make some payment to buy peace from the annoyance of a lawsuit, the settlement agreement based on the part payment is not binding.

(c) PART-PAYMENT CHECKS. The acceptance and cashing of a check for part of a debt releases the entire debt when the check bears a notation that it is intended as final or full payment and the total amount due is disputed or unliquidated. It probably has this same effect even though the debt is not disputed or liquidated.[10] In some jurisdictions this principle is applied without regard to the form of payment or whether the claim is disputed. The California Civil Code, § 1541, provides: "An obligation is extinguished by a release therefrom given to the debtor by the creditor upon a new consideration, or in writing, with or without new consideration."

(d) COMPOSITION OF CREDITORS. In a **composition of creditors** the various creditors of one debtor mutually agree to accept a fractional part of their claims in full satisfaction thereof. Such agreements are binding and are supported by consideration. When creditors agree to extend the due date of their debts, the promise of each creditor to forbear is likewise consideration for the promise of other creditors to forbear.

7.   Present Consideration versus Past Benefits

Consideration is what the promisor states must be received in return for the promise. Therefore, consideration must be given when or after the promisor states what is demanded.

(a) PAST CONSIDERATION. Past benefits already received by the promisor cannot be consideration for a later promise.

(b) COMPLEX TRANSACTIONS. In applying the rule that past benefits cannot be consideration, care must be taken to distinguish between the situation in which the consideration is in fact past and the situation in which the earlier consideration and subsequent promises were all part of one complex transaction. In such cases, the earlier consideration is not regarded as past and supports the later promises.[11]

In the *Medley* case a father guaranteed payment of his son's debts but later claimed that the guaranty was not binding because no consideration had been received by him.

---

[10]   Hearst Corp. v Lauerer, Martin & Gibbs, Inc. 37 Ohio App 3d 87, 524 NE2d 193 (1987).

[11]   Such a complex transaction is called "contemporaneous" in some states. Soukop v Snyder (Hawaii App) 709 P2d 109 (1985).

MEDLEY v SOUTHTRUST BANK OF QUAD CITIES
(Ala) 500 So 2d 1075 (1986)

Roy Medley borrowed money from the bank. His father, Oscar, gave the bank a guaranty that he would pay his son's existing and future bank loans if his son did not repay them. Roy Medley did not repay the loans, and the bank sued Oscar Medley on the guaranty. Oscar Medley raised the defense that the guaranty was not binding because he had not received any consideration for it. This defense was overruled and judgment was entered against Oscar Medley. He appealed.

JONES, J. . . . Medley contends that there is no consideration because the guaranty sued upon 1) included pre-existing debts, 2) was not made contemporaneously with any loan, and 3) contained no expression of new valuable consideration. SouthTrust, on the other hand, argues that its promise of future advances constitutes sufficient consideration.

That portion of the guaranty agreement here contested contains the following language:

> WHEREAS, the undersigned (if more than one, the undersigned jointly and severally) have requested . . . the Bank to extend credit from time to time to
>
> Roy D. Medley . . . (hereinafter referred to as the debtor), and have agreed to guarantee the payment when due of all such credits, and also of all other indebtedness of every kind and character now or at any time hereafter (before revocation hereof) owing by the debtor to the Bank; and
>
> WHEREAS, the Bank is willing to extend such credit to the debtor from time to time as, in the Bank's discretion, is prudent and wise, provided this instrument of guaranty is executed to the Bank.
>
> NOW, THEREFORE, in consideration of the premises, and in order to induce the Bank to extend to the debtor from time to time in the future as requested by the debtor, such loans, extensions of loans and forbearances as to the Bank may seem prudent and wise, the undersigned (if more than one, the undersigned jointly and severally) guarantee(s) the prompt payment on demand of the principal of and interest on any indebtedness of the debtor now, or at any time hereafter, outstanding, and any and all renewals thereof, together with all costs of collection, including a reasonable attorney's fee, as may be provided for in the face of any and all notes heretofore taken, or hereafter executed by the debtor, evidencing any such indebtedness, or any part thereof.

It is true that when someone not a party to the original transaction signs an instrument as guarantor after the original contract has been duly executed and delivered, without agreement at the time of the execution of the original contract that additional security would be furnished, he is entering a new and independent contract; and, to be binding, this agreement must be supported by consideration, independent of the original contract.

When dealing with a guarantee of a pre-existing debt, consideration is essential to sustain the obligation. In the instant case, however, the guaranty agreement is not limited solely to pre-existing debts. Rather, it covers the "indebtedness of debtor now, or at any time hereafter, . . . and any and all renewals thereof. . . ." In other words, Medley agreed to guarantee all of his son's past and future indebtedness to SouthTrust.

This Court has repeatedly held that the promise of extension of credit in the future to the principal debtor is good consideration in a guaranty contract. . . .

[Judgment affirmed]

8.   Forbearance as Consideration

In most cases consideration consists of the performance of an act or the making of a promise to act. Consideration may also consist of forbearance, which is refraining from doing an act, or a promise of forbearance. In other words, the promisor may desire to buy the inaction or a promise of inaction of the other party.

The waiving or giving up of any right can be consideration for the promise of another. Thus, the relinquishment of a right in property or of a right to sue for damages will support a promise given in return for it.

The promise of a creditor to forbear collecting the debt is consideration for a promise by the debtor to modify the terms of the transaction.[12]

When the creditor agrees to extend the time for paying the debt in return for the debtor's promise of a higher return of interest, the agreement to extend is consideration for the promise to pay the higher rate of interest.

When a supplier has the right to terminate the contract with the dealer selling its products, the promise of the supplier to refrain from revoking the contract with the dealer is consideration for the dealer's agreement to reduce the commissions deducted on the resale of the supplier's product.

The right that is surrendered in return for a promise may be a right against a third person, as well as against the promisor.

As under the rule governing compromises, forbearance to assert a claim is consideration when the claim has been asserted in good faith, even though it is without merit.[13] In the absence of a good faith belief, forbearance with respect to a worthless claim is not consideration.

(a) WHAT CONSTITUTES CONSIDERATION. The consideration for forbearance is anything that constitutes consideration under the general rules discussed in this chapter. Usually it is a payment of money to the promisor or a third person to guarantee the debt of another.

(b) CONSIDERATION IN EMPLOYMENT CONTRACTS. In employment contracts an employee may promise not to compete with the employer upon leaving the employment. What is the consideration for this promise? When the promise is made at the time of the making of the contract of employment, the promise of the employer to employ and to pay compensation is consideration for the employee's promise to refrain from competing upon leaving the employment. If the employee's promise is made after the contract of employment has been made, it is necessary to see whether the contract (a) is for an indefinite duration with no job security provision, or (b) is for a definite period of time, such as five years, or contains job security provisions that prevent the employer from discharging the employee at will. If the employment contract is for a definite period or is covered by job security provisions, the employee's promise not to compete when made after the contract of employment has been made is not binding on the employee unless the employer gives some consideration for the promise not to compete. In the case of the indefinite duration contract that has no job security provision, the employer can ordinarily terminate the contract at will. Therefore, according to some courts, the employer's continuing to employ the employee after the employee's making of the promise not to compete is consideration for that prom-

---

[12]   Bank of Crockett v Cullipher (Tenn App) 752 SW2d 84 (1988).
[13]   Matey v Pruitt (Fla App) 510 So 2d 351 (1987).

ise, even though the parties did not express these thoughts in words.[14] Other courts, however, do not make a distinction based on the type of employment contract. These courts follow the common law rule that a restrictive covenant agreed to by an employee already under contract of employment is not binding because it is not supported by consideration.

9.   Adequacy of Consideration

Ordinarily, courts do not consider the adequacy of the consideration given for a promise. The fact that the consideration supplied by one party is slight when compared with the burden undertaken by the other party is immaterial. It is a matter for the parties to decide when they make their contract whether each is getting a fair return. In the absence of fraud or other misconduct, the court usually will not interfere to make sure that each side is getting a fair return.

C.   EXCEPTIONS TO THE LAW OF CONSIDERATION

The ever-changing character of law clearly appears in the area of consideration, as the rules stated earlier in this chapter are seen slowly eroding.

10.   Exceptions to Adequacy of Consideration Rule

The insufficiency or inadequacy of the consideration may lead a court to the conclusion that a contract is not binding because it is unconscionable. Inadequate consideration may also indicate that fraud was practiced on the promisor.

The inadequacy of the consideration may be evidence of the exercise of undue influence or the taking advantage of the condition of the other contracting party. Several factors may combine to challenge the validity of the contract.

11.   Exceptions to Requirement of Consideration

By statute or decision, consideration is no longer required in a number of situations.

(a)   CHARITABLE   SUBSCRIPTIONS. When charitable enterprises are financed by voluntary subscriptions of a number of persons, the promise of each is generally enforceable. For example, when a number of people make pledges or subscriptions for the construction of a church, for a charitable institution, or for a college, the subscriptions are binding.

The theories for sustaining such promises vary. Consideration is lacking according to the technical standards applied in ordinary contract cases. Nevertheless, the courts enforce such promises as a matter of public policy.

(b) UNIFORM COMMERCIAL CODE. In a number of situations the Uniform Commercial Code abolishes the requirement of consideration. For example, under the Code, consideration is not required for (1) a merchant's written, firm offer as to goods, stated to be irrevocable; (2) a written discharge of a claim for an alleged breach of a commercial contract; or (3) an agreement to modify a contract for the sale of goods.[15]

(c)   SEALED AND WRITTEN INSTRUMENTS. At common law consideration was not necessary to support a promise under seal. In a state that gives the seal its original common law effect, the gratuitous promise or a promise to make a gift is enforceable when it is set forth in a sealed instrument.

In some states a promise under seal must be supported by consideration, just as though it did not have a seal. Other states take a middle position and hold that the presence of a seal is prima facie proof that there is consideration to support the promise. This means that if nothing more than the existence of the sealed promise is shown, it is deemed supported by consideration. The party making the promise, however, may prove that there

---

[14]   Computer Sales International, Inc. v Collins (Mo App) 723 SW2d 450 (1986).

[15]   UCC § 2–209(1).

was no consideration. In that case the promise is not binding.

In some states a rebuttable presumption arises, whenever a contract is in writing, that the promises of the parties are supported by consideration.[16]

12.   Promissory Estoppel

Most courts enforce some promises that are not supported by consideration by applying the doctrine of **promissory estoppel**. A person may make a promise to another under such circumstances that the promisor should reasonably foresee that the promisee will be induced to rely thereon and that the promisee will then sustain substantial loss if the promise is not kept. Under the doctrine of promissory estoppel, such a promise is binding, even though there is no consideration for it.[17] In applying the doctrine of promissory estoppel, courts are ignoring the requirement of consideration in order to attain a just result.

Legal difficulties often arise because parties take certain things for granted. Frequently they will be sure that they have agreed to everything and that they have a valid contract. However, sometimes they do not. The courts are then faced with the problem of leaving them with their broken dreams or coming to their rescue, as in the *Hoffman* case.

---

[16]   Nordwick v Berg, 223 Mont 337, 725 P2d 1195 (1986).

[17]   Kaluzny Bros, Inc. v Mahoney Grease Service, Inc. 165 Ill App 3d 390, 116 Ill Dec 289, 518 NE2d 1269 (1988).

HOFFMAN v RED OWL STORES, INC.
26 Wis 2d 683, 133 NW2d 267 (1965)

Joseph H. Hoffman wanted to acquire a franchise for a Red Owl Grocery Store. (Red Owl was a corporation that maintained a system of chain stores.) The agent of Red Owl informed Hoffman and his wife that if they would sell their bakery in Wautoma, acquire a certain tract of land in Chilton, another city, and put up a specified amount of money, they would be given a franchise as desired. Hoffman sold his business and acquired the land in Chilton, but was never granted a franchise. He and his wife sued Red Owl, which raised the defense that there had only been an assurance that Hoffman would receive a franchise, but no promise supported by consideration. Thus, there was no binding contract to give him a franchise. From a judgment in the Hoffmans' favor Red Owl appealed.

CURRIE, C.J. . . . The development of the law of promissory estoppel "is an attempt by the court to keep remedies abreast of increased moral consciousness of honesty and fair representations in all business dealings." *Peoples National Bank of Little Rock v Lineberger Constr. Co.*, 219 Ark. 11, 240 SW2d 12, (1951). . . .

The Restatement avoids use of the term "promissory estoppel," and there has been criticism of it as an inaccurate term. . . . Use of the word "estoppel" to describe a doctrine upon which a party to a lawsuit may obtain affirmative relief offends the traditional concept that estoppel merely serves as a shield and cannot serve as a sword to create a cause of action. . . .

Because we deem the doctrine of promissory estoppel, as stated in Sec 90 of Restatement, 1 Contracts, as one which supplies a needed weapon which courts may employ in a proper cause to prevent injustice, we endorse and adopt it.

The record here discloses a number of promises and assurances given to Hoffman by Lukowitz in behalf of Red Owl upon which plaintiffs relied and acted upon to their detriment. . . .

Originally the doctrine of promissory estoppel was invoked as a substitute for consideration rendering a gratuitous promise enforceable as a contract. . . . In other words, the acts of reliance by the promisee to his detriment provided a substitute for consideration. . . . [Under] Sec 90 of Restatement, 1 Contracts, . . . the conditions imposed are:

(1) Was the promise one which the promisor should reasonably expect to induce action or forbearance of a definite and substantial character on the part of the promisee?
(2) Did the promise induce such action or forbearance?
(3) Can injustice be avoided only by enforcement of the promise? . . .

We conclude that injustice would result here if plaintiffs were not granted some relief because of the failure of defendants to keep their promises which induced plaintiffs to act to their detriment. . . .

[Judgment affirmed on this phase of the case]

QUESTIONS

1. Could the court in the *Hoffman* case have reached the same conclusion by applying the common law rule as to consideration?
2. Compare the concept of firm offer with promissory estoppel.
3. How could Hoffman have avoided the problem that arose in his case?

(a) PROMISSORY ESTOPPEL DISTINGUISHED FROM CONSIDERATION. Promissory estoppel differs from consideration in that, with promissory estoppel, the reliance of the promisee is not the bargained-for price or response sought by the promisor. Under promissory estoppel it is sufficient that the promisor foresees that there will be such reliance. The doctrine of promissory estoppel applies only when (1) the promisor has reason to foresee the detrimental reliance by the promisee, and (2) the promisee in fact would sustain a substantial loss because of such reliance if the promise were not performed.

(b) DETRIMENTAL RELIANCE ESSENTIAL. Promissory estoppel cannot be applied merely because the promisor has not performed the promise. In the absence of the promisee's detrimental reliance on the promise, the doctrine of promissory estoppel is not applicable. Thus, a promise made to the debtor by the creditor that the creditor would collect only $20 a month on the debt of approximately $12,000 was not binding because there was no proof that the debtor relied in any manner on such promise.[18]

What constitutes detrimental reliance sufficient to satisfy the promissory estoppel rule has been diluted in recent years. In the early promissory estoppel cases it was necessary to show that if the defendant did not perform the promise, the plaintiff would suffer a substantial loss—of a nature that could not be compensated for by the payment of money. Many courts are now willing to accept any financial loss as sufficient to show detrimental reliance.

---

[18]   Lawrence v Board of Education, 152 Ill App 3d 187, 105 Ill Dec 195, 503 NE2d 1201 (1987). Some courts hold the promisor liable for tort damages when the promisee has sustained harm because the promisee relied on the promise, but the promise was never kept. ITT Terryphone Corp. v Tri-State Steel Drum, Inc. 178 Ga App 694, 344 SE2d 686 (1986). The explanation for these differing views is that those courts do not believe it is just for the promisor to break a promise on which the promisee had detrimentally relied, but at the same time they do not feel that they can flatly state that consideration is not required to make the broken promise binding on the defendant.

Thus, it has been held that when the plaintiff quit a job in reliance on the defendant's promise to employ the plaintiff, there was sufficient detrimental reliance to make the defendant's promise binding.[19]

[19]   Roberts v Geosource Drilling Services, Inc. (Tex App) 757 SW2d 48 (1988).

SUMMARY

A promise is not binding if there is no consideration for the promise. Consideration is the price required by the promisor as the price for the promise. That price may be the doing of an act, refraining from the doing of an act, or merely a promise to do or to refrain. In a bilateral contract it is necessary to find that the promise of each party is supported by consideration. If either promise is not so supported, it is not binding, and the agreement of the parties is not a contract. Consequently, the agreement cannot be enforced. When a promise is the consideration, it must be a binding promise. The binding character of a promise is not affected by the circumstance that there is a condition precedent to the performance promised. Likewise, the binding character of the promise and of the contract is not affected by a provision in the contract for its cancellation by either one or both of the parties. A promise to do what one is already obligated to do is not consideration, although some exceptions are made—when the rendering of a partial performance or a modified performance is accepted as a good faith adjustment to a changed situation, a compromise and release of claims, a part-payment check, or a compromise of creditors. As consideration is the price that is given to obtain the promise, past benefits conferred upon the promisor cannot be consideration. In the case of a complex transaction, however, the past benefit and the subsequent transaction relating to the promise may in fact have been intended by the parties as one transaction. In such a case the earlier benefit is not past consideration but is the consideration contemplated by the promisor as the price for the promise subsequently made.

A promise to refrain from doing an act can be consideration. A promise to refrain from suing or asserting a particular claim can be consideration. Generally the promise to forbear must be for a specified time, as distinguished from agreeing to forbear at will. When consideration is forbearance to assert a claim, it is immaterial whether the claim is valid, as long as the claim has been asserted in good faith in the belief that it was valid.

When the promisor obtains the consideration specified for the promise, the law is not ordinarily concerned with the value or adequacy of that consideration. Exceptions are sometimes made in the case of fraud or unconscionability and under consumer protection statutes.

There is a trend to abandon the requirement of consideration. Promissory estoppel is the most extensive repudiation of the requirement of consideration.

All transactions must be lawful; therefore, consideration for a promise must be legal. If it is not, there is no consideration, and the promise is not binding.

When the promisor does not actually receive the price promised for the promise, it is said that there is a failure of consideration. This is merely a default in performance, and the binding character of the agreement is not affected by the subsequent failure of consideration. Such failure constitutes a breach of the contract.

Although consideration is required to make a promise binding, the promise that is not supported by consideration is not unlawful or illegal. If the promisor voluntarily performs the promise, the promisor cannot undo the performance and restore matters to their original position prior to the making of the agreement. The parties are free to perform their agreement, but the courts will not help either of them, because there is no contract.

QUESTIONS AND CASE PROBLEMS

1. What is the objective of each of the following rules of law?
   (a) An executed gift or a performance that has been rendered without consideration cannot be rescinded for lack of consideration.
   (b) In the absence of fraud, the adequacy of consideration is usually immaterial.
2. What is consideration?
3. Sarah's house caught on fire. Through the prompt assistance of her neighbor, Odessa, the fire was quickly extinguished. In gratitude, Sarah promised to pay Odessa $1,000. Can Odessa enforce this promise if Sarah does not pay the money?
4. Clifton agreed to work for Acrylics Incorporated for $400 a month. Clifton later claimed that there was no contract because the consideration for the services to be rendered was inadequate. Is there a binding contract?
5. Ravitts was employed by Richards of Rockford under a contract prohibiting him from competing with Richards for one year after termination of his employment. Thereafter, the parties terminated the employment by mutual agreement and signed a release of all obligations under the contract. The business and all the contract rights of Richards were later sold to Aqua-Aerobic Systems. Meanwhile, Ravitts had begun to compete with the business of Richards and was now competing with Aqua-Aerobic. Aqua-Aerobic sued Ravitts to stop him from such competing. Ravitts raised the defense that he had been released from the contract that imposed the restriction against competing. Aqua-Aerobic claimed that the release was not binding because there had not been any consideration for the release. Was the release binding? What social force is involved? [Aqua-Aerobic Systems, Inc. v Ravitts, 166 Ill App 3d 168, 117 Ill Dec 77, 520 NE2d 67]
6. Compare (a) adequate consideration, (b) moral obligation, and (c) past consideration.
7. Galloway induced Marian to sell Marian's house to Galloway by false statements that a factory was going to be built on the vacant lot adjoining Marian's house. No factory was ever built, and Marian then sued Galloway for damages for fraud. Marian offered to prove that Galloway had paid Marian only a fraction of the true value of Marian's house. Galloway claimed that this evidence as to value could not be admitted because it was immaterial whether the

consideration paid Marian was adequate. Is Galloway correct?
8. Koedding hired West Roofers to put a roof on her house. She later claimed that the roofing job was defective and threatened to sue West. Both parties discussed the matter in good faith. Finally West guaranteed that the roof would be free from leaks for 20 years in return for the guarantee by Koedding not to sue West for damages. The roof leaked the next year. Koedding sued West on the guarantee. West claimed that the guarantee was not binding because there was no consideration for it. According to West, Koedding's promise not to sue had no value because Koedding in fact did not have any valid claim against West; therefore, she was not entitled to sue. Was this defense valid?
9. Fedun rented a building to Gomer, who did business under the name of Mike's Cafe. Later, Gomer was about to sell out the business to Brown and requested Fedun to release him from his liability under the lease. Fedun agreed to do so. Brown sold out shortly thereafter. The balance of the rent due by Gomer under the original lease agreement was not paid, and Fedun sued Gomer on the rent claim. Could he collect after having released Gomer? [Fedun v Mike's Cafe, 204 Pa Super 356, 204 A2d 776]
10. Alexander Proudfoot Company was in the business of devising efficiency systems for industry. It told the Sanitary Linen Service Company that it could provide an improved system for Sanitary Linen that would save it money. It made a contract with Sanitary Linen to provide a money-saving system. The system was put into operation, and Proudfoot was paid the amount due under the contract. The system failed to work and did not save money. Sanitary Linen sued to get the money back. Was it entitled to do so? [Sanitary Linen Service Co. v Alexander Proudfoot Co. (CA5 Fla) 435 F2d 292]
11. Allen owned land that was being developed. Allen's brother, Norburn, wrote to the vice president of Investment Properties of Asheville, Inc., stating that "this is to certify that I will stand personally liable" for the land preparation expenses. When Investment Properties sued Norburn on this guaranty, he raised the defense that he did not receive any consideration for his promise, so it was not binding. Was this a valid defense? [Investment Properties of Asheville, Inc. v Norburn, 281 NC 300, 188 SE2d 342]

12. Sears, Roebuck & Co. promised to give Forrer "permanent employment." Forrer sold his farm at a loss in order to take the job. Shortly after commencing work, he was discharged by Sears, which claimed that the contract could be terminated at will. Forrer claimed that promissory estoppel prevented Sears from terminating the contract. Was he correct? [Forrer v Sears, Roebuck & Co. 36 Wis 2d 388, 153 NW2d 587]

13. Kemp leased a gas filling station from Baehr. Kemp, who was heavily indebted to the Penn-O-Tex Oil Corporation, transferred to it his right to receive payments on all claims. When Baehr complained that the rent was not paid, he was assured by the corporation that the rent would be paid to him. Baehr did not sue Kemp for the overdue rent but later sued the corporation. The defense was raised that there was no consideration for the promise of the corporation. Decide. [Baehr v Penn-O-Tex Corporation, 258 Minn 533, 104 NW2d 661]

14. Bogart owed several debts to the Security Bank & Trust Company. He applied to the bank for a loan to pay the various debts. The bank's employee stated that he would take the application for the loan "to the loan committee and within two or three days, we ought to have something here, ready for you to go with." The loan was not made. The bank sued Bogart for his debts. He filed a counterclaim on the theory that the bank had broken its contract to make a loan to him, and that promissory estoppel prevented the bank from going back on what the employee had said. Was this counterclaim valid? [Security Bank & Trust Co. v Bogart (Ind App) 494 NE2d 965]

15. Through a mistake, Midwest Recovery Bureau wrongfully took Cobb's truck. In so doing the truck was damaged. Later Cobb gave Midwest a release, by which he released Midwest from liability for wrongfully taking his truck. The release was given in consideration of the repairing and the returning of the truck. After the truck was repaired and returned, Cobb sued Midwest for damages. It raised the defense that Cobb had released it from liability. Was Midwest correct? [Cobb v Midwest Recovery Bureau Co. (Minn) 295 NW2d 232]

13

LEGALITY AND PUBLIC POLICY

If society were totally committed to free enterprise and freedom of contract, anyone could make a contract on any subject. But as you might suspect, society does not wish to go that far. In Chapters 7 and 8 you saw that certain conduct is prohibited as crimes and torts. Logically, it follows that society will not allow the making of a contract that calls for conduct that would be a crime or a tort.

In its most obvious form, the rule has developed that a contract calling for the commission of a crime is void. However, the criminal law generally lags behind the societal judgment of what is right and what is wrong. What happens when a court is faced with a contract that it believes is wrong, but there is no statute making the transaction illegal? In such a case the court will declare that the contract is void as contrary to public policy. In recent years the judges have ventured even further in order to declare a contract or a contract provision invalid because it was unconscionable. All three limitations—illegality, contravention of public policy, and unconscionability—represent society speaking through the lawmaker or the judge for the purpose of striking a balance between freedom of contract and protection of the public.

A.   GENERAL PRINCIPLES

An agreement is illegal when either its formation or performance is a crime or a tort, or it is contrary to public policy or unconscionable.

1.   Effect of Illegality

Ordinarily, an illegal agreement is void.

When an agreement is illegal, the parties are usually not entitled to the aid of the courts. If the illegal agreement has not been performed, neither party can sue the other to obtain performance or damages.[1] If the agreement has been performed, neither party can sue the other for damages or to set it aside.

In the *Jackson Purchase* case, the validity of a contract provision was challenged on the ground that it called for a practice that was unlawful.

---

[1]   P.C.B. Partnership v City of Largo (Fla App) 549 So 2d 738 (1989).

JACKSON PURCHASE ELECTRIC COOPERATIVE v LOCAL UNION 816
(CA6 Ky) 646 F2d 264 (1981)

When employees belong to a union, it is common for the union and the employer to agree that the employer shall deduct the union dues of the employees from their wages and pay such amounts directly to the union. This is called a checkoff of union dues. Under federal law, this is unlawful if done without written authorization from the employees affected. Moreover, if a checkoff of union dues is willfully made without such written authorization, the employer is guilty of a crime. The employees of Jackson Purchase Rural Electric Cooperative Association belonged to Local Union 816 of the electrical workers union. For sixteen years the employer made a checkoff of union dues without any written authorization. The practice was unilaterally terminated by the employer in 1978. The union protested, and the matter was referred to an arbitrator. The arbitrator ordered the employer to reinstate dues checkoff, but also provided that such checkoff should only be made upon the submission of a written authorization of the employees affected. The union appealed to the district court on other grounds. The district court held that the checkoff practice that had been followed in the prior years was illegal and therefore could not be reinstated. A further appeal was taken by the union.

KENNEDY, J. . . . Section 302(a)(1) of the Labor Management Relations Act, 29 U.S.C. § 186(a)(1), states that

it shall be unlawful for any employer . . . to pay, lend, or deliver, or agree to pay, lend, or deliver, any money or any other thing of value to any representative of any of his employees who are employed in an industry affecting commerce.

Subsection (c)(4) creates an exception

with respect to money deducted from the wages of employees in payment of membership dues in a labor organization: *Provided*, That the employer has received from each employee, on whose account such deductions are made, a written assignment which shall not be irrevocable for a period of more than one year, or beyond the termination date of the applicable collective bargaining agreement, whichever occurs sooner. . . .

Subsection (d) makes it a misdemeanor willfully to violate the above provisions.

Local 816 first argues that because subsection (d) makes it a crime willfully to violate § 302, a willful violation is the only violation that Congress contemplated. Because the District Court found that Jackson Purchase and Local 816 did not *intend* to violate § 302, Local 816 claims that [the District Court] erred in finding that the Local *did* violate that section. This argument is devoid of merit. The fact that willful violations of § 302 are to be met with a criminal sanction does not render an unwitting violation lawful. Congress need not prescribe a criminal penalty, or any penalty for that matter, to make an action illegal. As noted above, subsection (a) expresses Congress' intent that an agreement to check off union dues without written employee authorization "shall be unlawful." . . .

Local 816 next observes that the long-continued practice of checking off union dues necessarily implies an underlying agreement to check off union dues. It argues that although the implementation of the agreement in this case was unlawful, the agreement itself is not, because the agreement does not specify that unlawful means shall be used to accomplish its ends. Thus, Local 816 contends that we should sever the agreement to check off from the manner in which the checking off was accomplished, and enforce only the agreement to check off through the past practice doctrine. The distinction that the union is making may have merit in the appropriate case, where there is evidence of a lawful agreement which is independent of the illegal act. However, that is not the case here. The only implied agreement that could be said to have become, by long-continued practice, a part of the contract is the agreement to check off without written authorizations from the employees. Such agreement to check off without written authorizations, although not willful and therefore not criminal, is clearly unlawful under the terms of the applicable statute. . . .

However, it is not the case that all unlawful agreements are *ipso facto* void. If the denial of relief is disproportionately inequitable the right to recover will not be denied. 14 *Williston on Contracts* § 1630A (3d ed. 1972). Factors a court should consider in performing this balancing include: the justified expectations of the parties; the forfeiture that would result from nonenforcement of the agreement; any special public interest in enforcement; the strength of the public policy that the agreement violates, as shown by legislation or court decision; the likelihood that refusal to enforce will further that policy; and the seriousness of the misconduct. *Restatement (Second) of Contracts* § 320(1) (Tent. Draft No. 12, 1977).

. . . There is a strong presumption that agreements in violation of a statute will not be sanctioned by the courts. That presumption is stronger than usual in this case, as Congress not only made the act of unauthorized checking off of union dues illegal, it also made the agreement to do that act illegal. This is not a case where a party is trying to have an entire contract declared illegal on the basis that a minor provision violates the law. . . . Local 816 is trying to enforce the illegal agreement itself. There is no specific public interest in enforcing this agreement. Rather, the public's interest is promoted by non-enforcement. The public policy advanced by § 302 is to protect employees in deal-ings between the union and employer. The relief ordered by the arbitrator is prospec-tive and there is no contention that any employee was actually injured by this past practice. However, enforcement of an illegal agreement on the ground that the evil concerned did not follow would destroy the safeguards of law and lessen the preven-tion of abuses. Local 816 had no justified expectation that its agreement with Jackson Purchase was lawful, nor was it misled in any way by Jackson Purchase. No forfeiture or unjust enrichment will result to any party if this past practice or agreement is not made a part of future collective bargaining agreements. ... In short, Local 816 has given us no reason to disregard the presumption that courts will not give legal effect to illegal acts.

[Judgment affirmed]

QUESTIONS

1. What is the difference in stating that checking off union dues without written authorization is unlawful and saying that when done willfully it is criminal?
2. Did the arbitrator authorize a continuation of the past practice of checking off union dues?

2.   Exceptions to Effect of Illegality

In some situations, the rules stated in Section 1 of this chapter produce a result that society deems too harsh and unjust. Thus, the follow-ing exceptions are made.

(a) PROTECTION OF ONE PARTY. When the law that the agreement violates is intend-ed for the protection of one of the parties, that party may seek relief. For example, when, in order to protect the public, the law forbids the issuance of securities or notes by certain clas-ses of corporations, a person who has pur-chased them may recover the money paid.

(b) UNEQUAL GUILT. When the parties are not *in pari delicto*—not equally guilty—the least guilty party is granted relief when public interest is advanced by so doing. For example, when a statute is adopted to protect one of the parties to a transaction, such as a usury law adopted to protect borrowers, the person to be protected will not be deemed to be *in pari delicto* with the wrongdoer when en-tering into a transaction that is prohibited by the statute.

(c) KNOWLEDGE OF ILLEGAL PUR-POSE OF OTHER CONTRACTING PARTY. A contract that is in itself lawful is not made un-lawful by the fact that one of the parties in-tends to make unlawful use of the subject mat-ter of the contract, and this intention is known to the other contracting party.

3.   Partial Illegality

An agreement may involve the performance of several promises, some of which are illegal and some legal. The legal parts of the agree-ment may be enforced, provided that they can be separated from the parts that are illegal. The same rule applies when the consideration is illegal in part. The rule is not applied, how-ever, to situations in which the illegal act or consideration is said to taint and strike down the entire agreement. Thus, an employee could not recover for services when the em-ployee had performed some lawful work but had also taken part in a fraudulent scheme of the employer.[2]

If a contract is susceptible to two interpre-tations, one legal and the other illegal, the court will assume that the legal meaning was intended unless the contrary is clearly indicated.

---

[2]   Sacks v Dallas Gold & Silver Exchange, Inc. (Tex App) 720 SW2d 177 (1986).

4. Crimes and Civil Wrongs

An agreement is illegal, and therefore void, when it calls for the commission of any act that constitutes a crime. To illustrate, one cannot enforce an agreement by which the other party is to commit an assault, steal property, burn a house, or kill a person.

An agreement that calls for the commission of a civil wrong is also illegal and void. Examples are agreements to slander a third person; defraud another; infringe another's patent, trademark, or copyright; or fix prices.

5. Good Faith and Fairness

The law is evolving toward requiring that contracts be fair and made in good faith. The law is becoming increasingly concerned with whether *A* has utilized a superior bargaining power or superior knowledge to obtain better terms from *B* than *A* would otherwise have obtained.

In the case of goods, the seller must act in good faith, which is defined as to merchant sellers as "honesty in fact and the observance of reasonable commercial standards of fair dealing in the trade."[3]

6. Unconscionable and Oppressive Contracts

Ordinarily, a court will not consider whether a contract is fair or unfair, wise or foolish, or operates unequally between the parties. However, in a number of instances the law holds that contracts or contract clauses will not be enforced because they are too harsh or oppressive to one of the parties. This principle is most commonly applied to invalidate a clause providing for the payment by one party of a large penalty upon breaking the contract or a provision declaring that a party shall not be liable for the consequences of negligence. This principle is extended in connection with the sale of goods to provide that "if the court . . . finds the contract or any clause of the contract to have been unconscionable at the time it was made, the court may refuse to enforce the contract, or it may enforce the remainder of the contract without the unconscionable clause, or it may so limit the application of any unconscionable clause as to avoid any unconscionable result."[4]

A provision that gives what the court believes is too much of an advantage over a buyer is likely to be held void as **unconscionable.** In order to bring the unconscionability provision into operation, it is not necessary to prove that fraud was practiced. When there is a grossly disproportionate bargaining power between the parties, so that the weaker or inexperienced party cannot afford to risk confrontation with the stronger party but just signs on the dotted line, courts will hold that grossly unfair terms obtained by the stronger party are void as unconscionable.

Under the UCCC a particular clause or an entire agreement relating to a consumer credit sale, a consumer lease, or a consumer loan is void when such provision or agreement is unconscionable.[5]

However, the fact that a contract is a bad bargain does not make it unconscionable. Moreover, unconscionability is to be determined in the light of the circumstances existing at the time when the contract was made. The fact that later events make the contract unwise or undesirable does not make the contract unconscionable. Hence, the fact that there is a sharp rise in the market price of goods after the contract has been made does not make the contract unconscionable. The decision that a provision or a contract is unconscionable can only be made by a court after holding a hearing in order to determine the real effect of the contract when viewed in its commercial setting. In a particular state the

---

[3] UCC § 2–103(1)(b). Higher standards are also imposed on merchant sellers by other provisions of the UCC. See § 2–314, as to warranties; § 2–603, as to duties with respect to rightfully rejected goods; and § 2–509(3), as to the transfer of risk of loss. The provisions of the Code noted above do not apply to contracts generally. However, there is a growing trend of courts to extend Article 2 of the Code, which relates only to the sale of goods, to contract situations generally. This extension is based on the theory that the Code represents the latest restatement of the law of contracts made by expert scholars and the legislators of the land.

[4] UCC § 2–302(1).
[5] UCCC § 5.108.

concept of unconscionability may be based on the Uniform Commercial Code, the Uniform Consumer Credit Code, local nonuniform code statutes, or general principles of equity absorbed by the common law. The concept of unconscionability is given the same interpretation by the courts regardless of the source of the concept. This is seen in the *Williams* case.

WILLIAMS v WALKER-THOMAS FURNITURE CO.
(CA Dist Col) 350 F2d 445 (1965)

The Walker-Thomas Furniture Co. sold furniture on credit under contracts that contained a provision that a customer did not own the purchase as long as any balance on any purchase remained due. It sold goods to Ora Lee Williams. At the time when the balance of her account was $164, Walker-Thomas Furniture Co. sold her a $514 stereo set with knowledge that she was supporting herself and seven children on a government relief check of $218 a month. From 1957 to 1962, Williams had purchased $1,800 worth of goods and made payments of $1,400. When she stopped making payments in 1962, Walker-Thomas sought to take back everything she had purchased since 1957. From a judgment in favor of Walker-Thomas, Williams appealed.

WRIGHT, J. . . . The notion that an unconscionable bargain should not be given full enforcement is by no means novel. In *Scott v United States*, 79 U.S. (12 Wall) 443, 445 (1870), the Supreme Court stated: "If a contract be unreasonable and unconscionable, but not void for fraud, a court of law will give to the party who sues for its breach damages, not according to its letter, but only such as he is equitably entitled to." . . .

Congress has recently enacted the Uniform Commercial Code, which specifically provides that the court may refuse to enforce a contract which it finds to be unconscionable at the time it was made. . . . The enactment of this section, which occurred subsequent to the contracts here in suit, does not mean that the common law of the District of Columbia was otherwise at the time of enactment, nor does it preclude the court from adopting a similar rule in the exercise of its powers to develop the common law for the District of Columbia. In fact, in view of the absence of prior authority on the point, we consider the congressional adoption of § 2–302 persuasive authority for following the rationale of the cases from which the section is explicitly derived. Accordingly, we hold that where the element of unconscionability is present at the time a contract is made, the contract should not be enforced.

Unconscionability has generally been recognized to include an absence of meaningful choice on the part of one of the parties together with contract terms which are unreasonably favorable to the other party. Whether a meaningful choice is present in a particular case can only be determined by consideration of all the circumstances surrounding the transaction. In many cases the meaningfulness of the choice is negated by a gross inequality of bargaining power. *Henningsen v Bloomfield Motors, Inc.* [32 NJ 358 (1960)]. The manner in which the contract was entered is also relevant to this consideration. Did each party to the contract, considering his obvious education or lack of it, have a reasonable opportunity to understand the terms of the contract, or were the important terms hidden in a maze of fine print and minimized by deceptive sales practices? Ordinarily, one who signs an agreement without full knowledge of its terms might be held to assume the risk that he has entered a one-sided bargain. But when a party of little bargaining power, and hence little real choice, signs a commercially unreasonable contract with little or no knowledge of its terms, it is hardly likely that his consent, or even an objective manifestation of his consent, was ever given to all the terms. In such a case the usual rule that the terms of the agreement are not to be questioned should be abandoned and the court should consider whether the terms of the contract are so unfair that enforcement should be withheld. . . .

Because the trial court and the appellate court did not feel that enforcement could be refused, no findings were made on the possible unconscionability of the contracts in [this case]. Since the record is not sufficient for our deciding the issue as a matter of law, the [case is] remanded to the trial court for further proceedings.

So ordered.

QUESTIONS

1. Did the court hold that the contract in the *Williams* case was illegal?
2. What is the difference between holding that a contract is unconscionable and holding that the contract is illegal?
3. Why did the court not say that the contract was or was not unconscionable?

7.   Social Consequences of Contracts

The social consequences of a contract are an important element today in determining the contract's validity and the power of government to regulate it. The social consequences of a contract are related to the concept of unconscionability. This is true even although unconscionability would seem to be concerned with the effect of the contract as between the parties, whereas social consequences have a broader concern for the effect of the particular contract and other similar contracts on society in general.

(a) THE PRIVATE CONTRACT IN SOCIETY. The law of contracts was originally oriented to private relations between private individuals. Now it is moving from the field of bilateral private law to multiparty societal considerations. The Supreme Court has held that private contracts lose their private, do-not-touch character when they become such a common part of our way of life that society deems it necessary to regulate them.

The significance of the socioeconomic setting of the contract is seen in the minimum wage law decisions. The Supreme Court at first held such laws unconstitutional as an improper interference with the rights of two adult contracting parties. Thereafter it changed its point of view to sustain such laws because of the consequences of substandard wages on the welfare of the individual, society, and the nation.

This reevaluation of old standards is part of the general move to make modern law more "just."

(b) THE *n* FACTOR. There has been expansion of the concepts of "against public policy" and unconscionability on the one hand and government regulation of business on the other. With this change, the number of times (n) that the given contract is used in the modern business world becomes increasingly significant in determining the validity of the contract as between the parties. Less and less are courts considering a contract as only a legal relationship between A and B. More and more, the modern court is influenced in its decision by the recognition of the fact that the contract before the court is not one in a million but is one of a million.

For example, J Company makes an insurance contract with K that is of the same nature as one that J makes with M. Also, these contracts are the same as the one that Company R makes with S, and so on. A like industry-wide pattern is seen in the case of the bank loan made by bank *O* to borrower *P*, by bank *Q* to borrower *T*, and so on.

The appreciation that a particular contract is merely one of many has not only influenced the courts in the interpretation of such contracts but has also been held to justify regulation of the contract by government. The view has been adopted that "when a widely diffused public interest has become enmeshed in a network of multitudinous private arrangements, the authority of the state 'to safeguard the vital interests of its people' . . . is not to be gainsaid by abstracting one such agreement from its public context and treating it as though it were an isolated private contract constitutionally immune from impairment."[6]

FIGURE 13-1   ILLEGAL AGREEMENTS AFFECTING PUBLIC WELFARE

AGREEMENTS CONTRARY TO PUBLIC POLICY
AGREEMENTS EVADING STATUTES
AGREEMENTS INJURING PUBLIC SERVICE
AGREEMENTS INVOLVING CONFLICTS OF INTEREST
AGREEMENTS OBSTRUCTING LEGAL PROCESS
AGREEMENTS INVOLVING ILLEGAL DISCRIMINATION
WAGERS AND PRIVATE LOTTERIES

B.   AGREEMENTS AFFECTING PUBLIC WELFARE

Agreements that may harm the public welfare are condemned as contrary to public policy and are not binding. Agreements that interfere with public service or the duties of public officials, obstruct legal process, or discrimi-

nate against members of minority groups are considered detrimental to public welfare and, as such, are not enforceable.

8.   Agreements Contrary to Public Policy

A given agreement may not violate any statute but may still be so offensive to society that the courts feel that enforcing the contract would be contrary to public policy.

(a) THE CONCEPT OF PUBLIC POLICY. **Public policy** cannot be defined precisely but is loosely described as protecting from that which tends to be injurious to the public or contrary to the public good, or which violates any established interest of society.[7] Contracts condemned as contrary to public policy frequently relate to the protection of the public welfare, health, or safety; to the protection of the person; and to the protection of recognized social institutions. For example, a contract that prohibits marriage under all circumstances or that encourages divorce is generally held invalid as contrary to public policy. Courts are slow and cautious in invalidating a contract on the ground that it is contrary to public policy. This is so because the courts recognize that on the one hand, they are applying a very vague standard, and on the other hand, they are restricting the freedom of the contracting parties to contract freely as they choose.[8]

When a statute makes conduct illegal, how far will that statute reach to affect contracts? That was the question underlying the *Bovard* case.

---

[6]   East New York Savings Bank v Hahn, 326 US 230, 232 (1945).

[7]   O'Hara v Ahlgren, Blumenfeld and Kempster, 127 Ill 2d 333, 130 Ill Dec 401, 537 NE2d 730 (1989).

[8]   United Steelworkers of America v Quadna Mountain Corp. (Minn App) 435 NW2d 120 (1989).

BOVARD v AMERICAN HORSE ENTERPRISES, INC.

201 Cal App 3d 832, 247 Cal Rptr 340 (1988)

American Horse Enterprises was predominantly engaged in manufacturing devices for smoking marijuana and to a minor degree in making jewelry. A state law made it illegal to possess, use, or transfer marijuana. There was no statute prohibiting manufacturing equipment for smoking marijuana. Bovard owned the stock of American Horse Enterprises and contracted to sell the corporation to Ralph. Ralph did not make the payments required by the contract. Bovard then brought suit to enforce the contract. The trial judge raised the question whether the contract sued upon was void for illegality. The trial judge held the contract void as contrary to public policy. Bovard appealed.

BUGLIA, J. . . . The trial court concluded the consideration for the contract was contrary to the policy of the law as expressed in the statute prohibiting the possession, use and transfer of marijuana. Whether a contract is contrary to public policy is a question of law to be determined from the circumstances of the particular case. . . . Whenever a court becomes aware that a contract is illegal, it has a duty to refrain from entertaining an action to enforce the contract. . . .

The question whether a contract violates public policy necessarily involves a degree of subjectivity. Therefore, ". . . courts have been cautious in blithely applying public policy reasons to nullify otherwise enforceable contracts. This concern has been graphically articulated by the California Supreme Court as follows: 'It has been well said that public policy is an unruly horse, astride of which you are carried into unknown and uncertain paths.' . . ." While contracts opposed to morality or law should not be allowed to show themselves in courts of justice, yet public policy requires and encourages the making of contracts by competent parties upon all valid and lawful considerations, and courts so recognizing have allowed parties the widest latitude in this regard; and, unless it is entirely plain that a contract is violative of sound public policy, a court will never so declare. "The power of the courts to declare a contract void for being in contravention of sound public policy is a very delicate and undefined power, and . . . should be exercised only in cases free from doubt." . . .

> Before labeling a contract as being contrary to public policy, courts must carefully inquire into the nature of the conduct, the extent of public harm which may be involved, and the moral quality of the conduct of the parties in light of the prevailing standards of the community. . . .

These factors are more comprehensively set out in the Restatement Second of Contracts section 178:

(1) A promise or other term of an agreement is unenforceable on grounds of public policy if legislation provides that it is unenforceable or the interest in its enforcement is clearly outweighed in the circumstances by a public policy against the enforcement of such terms.

(2) In weighing the interest in the enforcement of a term, account is taken of
   (a) the parties' justified expectations,
   (b) any forfeiture that would result if enforcement were denied, and
   (c) any special public interest in the enforcement of the particular term.

(3) In weighing a public policy against enforcement of a term, account is taken of
   (a) the strength of that policy as manifested by legislation or judicial decisions,
   (b) the likelihood that a refusal to enforce the term will further that policy,
   (c) the seriousness of any misconduct involved and the extent to which it was deliberate, and
   (d) the directness of the connection between that misconduct and the term.

Applying the Restatement test to the present circumstances, we conclude the interest in enforcing this contract is very tenuous. Neither party was reasonably justified in expecting the government would not eventually act to geld American Horse Enterprises, a business harnessed to the production of paraphernalia used to facilitate the use of an illegal drug. Moreover, although voidance of the contract imposed a forfeiture on Bovard, he did recover the corporate machinery, the only assets of the business which could be used for lawful purposes, i.e., to manufacture jewelry. Thus, the forfeiture was significantly mitigated if not negligible. Finally, there is no special public interest in the enforcement of this contract, only the general interest in preventing a party to a contract from avoiding a debt.

On the other hand, the Restatement factors favoring a public policy against enforcement of this contract are very strong. . . .The public policy against manufacturing paraphernalia to facilitate the use of marijuana is strongly implied in the statutory prohibition against the possession, use, etc., of marijuana, a prohibition which dates back at least to 1929. . . . Obviously, refusal to enforce the instant contract will further that public policy not only in the present circumstances but by serving notice on manufacturers of drug paraphernalia that they may not resort to the judicial system to protect or advance their business interests. Moreover, it is immaterial that the business conducted by American Horse Enterprises was not expressly prohibited by law when Bovard and Ralph made their agreement since both parties knew that the corporation's products would be used primarily for purposes which were expressly illegal. We conclude the trial court correctly declared the contract contrary to the policy of express law and therefore illegal and void. . . .

[Judgment affirmed]

QUESTIONS

1. Who raised the winning argument in the *Bovard* case? What was it?
2. What provision of the contract in the *Bovard* case was illegal?
3. Did the court in *Bovard* overstep its bounds and infringe on the role of the legislature?

(b) AGREEMENTS EVADING STATUTORY PROTECTION. Statutes frequently confer benefits or provide protection. If an agreement is made that deprives a person of such a statutory benefit, it is generally held that the agreement is invalid because it is contrary to the public policy declared by the statute. For example, a state law provides that automobile insurance policies should cover certain persons. A policy provision that would exclude certain persons who would be covered by the statutory provision is not valid, because it is contrary to the public policy declared in the statute.

The waiver of statutory provisions designed to protect debtors, creditors, consumers may be held void as contrary to public policy.[9]

9.   Agreements Injuring Public Service

An agreement that tends to interfere with the proper performance of the duties of a public officer—whether legislative, administrative, or judicial—is contrary to public policy and void. Thus, an agreement to procure the award of a public contract by corrupt means is not enforceable. Other examples are agree-

[9]   Coastal Caisson Drill Co., Inc. v American Cas. Co. of Reading (Fla App) 523 So 2d 791 (1988).

ments to sell public offices, to procure pardons by corrupt means, or to pay a public officer more or less than legal fees or salary.

One of the most common agreements within the class is the **illegal lobbying agreement.** This term is used to describe an agreement to use unlawful means to procure or prevent the adoption of legislation by a lawmaking body, such as Congress or a state legislature. Such agreements are clearly contrary to the public interest, since they interfere with the workings of the democratic process. They are accordingly illegal and void.

Some courts hold illegal all agreements to influence legislation, regardless of the means contemplated or employed. Other courts adopt the rule that such agreements are valid in the absence of the use of improper influence or the contemplation of using such influence.

10.   Agreements Involving Conflicts of Interest

Various statutes prohibit government officials from being personally interested, directly or indirectly, in any transaction entered into by such officials on behalf of the government. When there is a prohibited conflict of interest, a contract is invalid, without regard to whether its terms are fair or advantageous to the public.

11.   Agreements Obstructing Legal Processes

Any agreement intended to obstruct or pervert legal processes is contrary to public interest and therefore void. Agreements that promise to pay money in return for the abandonment of the prosecution of a criminal case, for the suppression of evidence in any legal proceeding, for initiating litigation, or for the perpetration of any fraud on the court are therefore void.

An agreement to pay an ordinary witness more than the regular witness fee allowed by law, or a promise to pay a greater amount if the promisor wins the lawsuit, is void. The danger here is that the witness will lie in order to help win the case.

12.   Illegal Discrimination Contracts

A contract specifying that a property owner will not sell to a member of a particular race cannot be enforced, because it violates the Fourteenth Amendment of the Constitution.[10] Hotels and restaurants may not deal with their customers on terms that discriminate because of race, religion, color, or national origin.[11]

13.   Wagers and Lotteries

Largely as a result of the adoption of antigambling statutes, wagers or bets are generally illegal. Private lotteries involving the three elements of prize, chance, and consideration (or similar affairs of chance) are also generally held illegal. In many states public lotteries (lotteries run by a state government) have been legalized by statute. Raffles are usually regarded as lotteries. Sales promotion schemes calling for the distribution of property according to chance among the purchasers of goods are held illegal as lotteries, without regard to whether the scheme is called a guessing contest, a raffle, or a gift.

Giveaway plans and games are lawful as long as it is not necessary to buy anything or to give anything of value in order to participate. If participation is free, the element of consideration is lacking, and there is no lottery.

An activity is not gambling when the result is solely a matter of skill. In contrast, it is gambling when the result is solely a matter of luck. Rarely is any activity 100 percent skill or 100 percent luck. In the *Seattle Times* case the court was faced with the problem of how to classify a contest that involved both skill and chance.

---

10   Shelley v Kraemer, 334 US 1 (1948).
11   Federal Civil Rights Act of 1964, 42 USC §§ 2000a et seq.

SEATTLE TIMES COMPANY v TIELSCH
80 Wash App 2d 502, 495 P2d 1366 (1972)

The *Seattle Times* ran a football game forecasting contest, called "Guest-Guesser." George Tielsch, the Seattle Chief of Police, claimed that this was illegal as a lottery. The *Times* brought a declaratory judgment action to determine the legality of the contest. The court held that the contest was a lottery, and the *Seattle Times* appealed.

ROSELLINI, J. . . . The result of a football game may depend upon weather, the physical condition of the players and the psychological attitude of the players. It may also be affected by sociological problems between and among the members of a football team. The element of chance is an integral part of the game of football as well as the skill of the players.

The lure of the "Guest-Guesser" contest is partially the participant's love of football, partially the challenge of competition and partially the hope enticingly held out, which is often false or disappointing, that the participant will get something for nothing or a great deal for a very little outlay. . . .

The elements of a lottery are prize, consideration and chance.

. . . Where a contest is multiple or serial, and requires the solution of a number of problems to win the prize, the fact that skill alone will bring contestants to a correct solution of a greater part of the problems does not make the contest any the less a lottery if chance enters into the solution of another lesser part of the problems and thereby proximately influences the final result. . . .

Our research has revealed only one case involving a football forecasting game and the game there was a "pool," that is, a gambling game wherein wagers were placed. The Superior Court of Pennsylvania held that it was a lottery. What is most relevant in the case for our consideration here is the court's discussion of the element of chance in forecasting the result of football games. That court said: It is true that for an avid student of the sport of football the chance taken is not so great as for those who have little interest in the game. However, it is common knowledge that the predictions even among these so-called "experts" are far from infallible. Any attempt to forecast the result of a single athletic contest, be it football, baseball, or whatever, is fraught with chance. This hazard is multiplied directly by the number of predictions made. The operators of the scheme involved in this case were all cognizant of this fact for the odds against a correct number of selections were increased from 5 to 1 for three teams picked up to 900 to 1 for fifteen teams. *Commonwealth v Laniewski*, 173 Pa Super 245, 98 A2d 215 (1953).

The trial court in the instant case recognized the same basic realities attendant upon the enterprise of football game-result forecasting. We are convinced that it correctly held that chance, rather than skill, is the dominant factor in the Times' "Guest-Guesser" contest. The very name of the contest conveys quite accurately the promoter's as well as the participants' true concept of the nature of the contest.

We conclude that the contest, however harmless it may be in the opinion of the participants and the promoters, is a lottery. . . .

[Judgment against *Seattle Times*]

FIGURE 13-2   ILLEGAL AGREEMENTS AFFECTING BUSINESS

CONTRACTS WITH UNLICENSED PERSONS IN LICENSED CALLINGS OR DEALINGS

FRAUDULENT SALES

AGREEMENTS RESTRAINING TRADE

AGREEMENTS NOT TO COMPETE

USURIOUS AGREEMENTS

C.   REGULATION OF BUSINESS

Local, state, and national laws regulate a wide variety of business activities and practices. A person violating such regulations may under some statutes be subject to a fine or criminal prosecution, or under others to an administrative agency's or commission's order to cease and desist.

Whether an agreement made in connection with business conducted in violation of the law is binding or void depends on how strongly opposed the public policy is to the prohibited act. Some courts take the view that the agreement is not void unless the statute expressly so specifies. In some instances the statute expressly preserves the validity of the contract. For example, if someone fails to register a fictitious name under which the business is done, the violator, after registering the name as required by the statute, is permitted to sue on a contract made while illegally conducting business.

14.   Statutory Regulation of Contracts

In order to establish uniformity or to protect one of the parties to a contract, statutes frequently provide that contracts of a given class must follow a statutory model or must contain specified provisions. For example, statutes commonly specify that particular clauses must be included in insurance policies in order to protect the persons insured and their beneficiaries. Other statutes require that contracts executed in connection with credit buying and loans contain particular provisions designed to protect the debtor.

Consumer protection legislation gives the consumer the right to rescind the contract in certain situations. Laws relating to truth in lending, installment sales, and home improvement contracts commonly require that an installment-sale contract specify the cash price, the down payment, the trade-in value (if any), the cash balance, the insurance costs, and the interest and finance charges.

When the statute imposes a fine or imprisonment for violation, the court should not hold that the contract is void, since that would increase the penalty that the legislature had imposed. If a statute prohibits the making of certain kinds of contracts or imposes limitations on contracts that can be made, the attorney general or other government official may generally be able to obtain an **injunction**, or court order, to stop the parties from entering into a prohibited contract.

15.   Licensed Callings or Dealings

Statutes frequently require that a person obtain a license, certificate, or diploma before practicing certain professions, such as law or medicine, or before carrying on a particular business or trade, such as that of a real estate broker, peddler, stockbroker, hotelkeeper, or pawnbroker. If a license is required to protect the public from unqualified persons, a contract made by an unlicensed person is void. For example, it has been held that when a statute required that contractors be licensed, and an unlicensed contractor made a contract to make repairs, the contractor could not recover from the owner either the price agreed to in their contract or the reasonable value of the services actually performed. A corporation that does not hold a required real estate broker's license cannot sue to recover fees for services as a broker.[12]

Likewise, an agreement with an unlicensed physician for services cannot be enforced by the physician. The patient of the unlicensed physician, however, may sue for damages if the contract is not properly performed.

The illegality of contracts often comes into the picture when parties seek to set up some arrangement to evade government regulations or prohibitions of the criminal law, or to avoid paying taxes.

In contrast with the protective license, a license may be required solely as a revenue measure by requiring the payment of a fee for the license. In that event an agreement made in violation of the statute by one not licensed is generally held valid. The contract may also sometimes be held valid when it is shown that no harm has resulted from the failure to obtain a permit to do the work contemplated by the particular contract.

16. Fraudulent Sales

Statutes commonly regulate the sale of certain commodities. Scales and measures of grocers and other vendors must be checked periodically, and they must be approved and sealed by the proper official. Certain articles must be inspected before they are sold. Other articles must be labeled in a particular way to show their contents and to warn the public of the presence of any dangerous or poisonous substance. Since these laws regulaating sales are generally designed for the protection of the public, transactions in violation of such laws are void.

17. Administrative Agency Regulation

Large segments of the American economy are governed by federal administrative agencies created to carry out the general policies specified by Congress. A contract must be in harmony with public policy, not only as declared by Congress and the courts, but also as applied by the appropriate administrative agency. For example, a particular contract to market goods might not be prohibited by any statute or court decision but may still be condemned by the Federal Trade Commission as an unfair method of competition. When the proper commission has made its determination, a contract not in harmony therewith, such as a contract of a railroad charging a higher or a lower rate than that approved by the Interstate Commerce Commission, is illegal.

18. Contracts in Restraint of Trade

An agreement that unreasonably restrains trade is illegal and void on the ground that it is contrary to public policy. Such agreements take many forms, such as a combination to create a monopoly or to obtain a corner on the market, or an association of merchants to increase prices. In addition to the illegality of the agreement based on general principles of law, statutes frequently declare monopolies illegal and subject the parties to various civil and criminal penalties.[13]

19. Agreements Not to Compete

In the absence of a valid restrictive covenant, the seller of a business may compete with the

---

12   Unifund General, Inc. v Orr, 191 Ga App 836, 383 SE2d 199 (1989).

13   Sherman Antitrust Act, 15 USC §§ 1–7; Clayton Act, 15 USC §§ 12–27; Federal Trade Commission Act, 15 USC §§ 41–58.

buyer, or an ex-employee may solicit customers of the former employer.[14]

When a going business is sold, it is commonly stated in the contract that the seller shall not go into the same or a similar business again within a certain geographical area, or for a certain period of time, or both. In early times, such agreements were held void because they deprived the public of the service of the person who agreed not to compete, impaired the latter's means of earning a livelihood, reduced competition, and exposed the public to monopoly. To the modern courts the question is whether, under the circumstances, the restriction imposed on one party is reasonably necessary to protect the other party. If the restriction is reasonable, it is valid.

Restrictions to prevent competition by an employee are held valid when reasonable and necessary to protect the interest of the employer. For example, a provision that a doctor employed by a medical clinic would not practice medicine for one year within a 50-mile radius of the city in which the clinic was located is reasonable and will be enforced. Likewise, a provision is valid that prohibited an employee for two years from calling on any customer of the employer called on by the employee during the last six months of employment. Thus, an agreement is valid by which an accountant employed by an accounting firm promised that for three years after termination of employment, the accountant would not perform any accounting services for any client of the firm or, in the alternative, would pay the firm 50 percent of the fees received from such clients.[15]

The more unusual the business, the greater the geographic area that will be allowed. This is so because the more unusual the business is, the more likely it is to draw customers from a greater distance than an ordinary business.

If there is no sale of a business or making of an employment contract, an agreement not to compete is illegal as a restraint of trade and a violation of the antitrust law. The agreement is therefore void. A restrictive covenant is not binding when it places a restriction on the employee that is broader than reasonably necessary to protect the employer. The employer cannot prohibit competition by a former employee for all time or for the entire world merely because some customer might follow the former employee.[16]

When a restriction of competition agreed to by the parties is invalid because its scope as to time or geographical area is too great, how does this affect the contract? Some courts trim the restrictive covenant down to a scope that the court deems reasonable and require the parties to abide by that revision. This rule is nicknamed the *blue pencil rule*. Other courts refuse to apply the blue pencil rule and hold that the restrictive covenant is void or that the entire contract is void. There is also authority that a court should refuse to apply the blue pencil rule when the restrictive covenant was manifestly unfair and would virtually keep the employee from earning a living.[17]

20.   Usurious Agreements

Usury is committed when money is loaned at a greater rate of interest than is allowed by law. Most states prohibit by statute the taking of more than a stated amount of interest. These statutes provide a maximum contract rate of interest that is the highest annual rate that can be exacted or demanded under the law of a given state. This maximum is often stated as a flat percentage rate, although there is a trend to tie the usury ceilings to current market rates. Intentionally charging greater interest on a loan than allowed by law constitutes usury. It is not necessary to prove that the defendant knew that there was a violation of the usury law.

When a lender incurs expenses in the making of a loan, such as the cost of appraising property or making a credit investigation of the borrower, the lender will require the borrower to pay the amount of such expenses. Lenders may attempt to obtain more than the

[14]   Hart v McCormack (Tex App) 746 SW2d 330 (1988).
[15]   Perry v Moran, 109 Wash 2d 691, 748 P2d 224 (1987).
[16]   Hill v Mobile Auto Trim, Inc. (Tex) 725 SW2d 168 (1987).
[17]   North American Paper Co. v Unterberger, 172 Ill App 3d 410, 122 Ill Dec 362, 526 NE2d 621 (1988).

expenses from the borrowers. Any fee charged by a lender that goes beyond the reasonable expense of making the loan constitutes "interest" for the purpose of determining whether the transaction is usurious.[18]

21.   Credit Sale Contracts

Sales of goods and services on credit are not technically within the scope of the usury laws, as the seller does not make an express "loan" to the buyer. When the sale is made on credit, the price that the seller charges is ordinarily not controlled by the usury law.

(a) CREDIT SALE PRICE. A seller may charge one price for cash sales and a higher price for credit or installment sales. The difference between these two prices is called the **time-price differential.** Since the usury law is not applicable, the time-price differential may be greater than the maximum amount of inter-

est that could be charged on a loan equal to the cash price.

A few states, however, hold that the time-price differential is subject to the usury law, or have amended their usury laws or have adopted statutes to regulate the differential between cash and time prices charged by the seller. Such statutes are sometimes limited to sales by retailers to consumers or apply only to sales under a stated dollar maximum.

Many states have adopted installment-sale laws that apply whenever the sale price is to be paid in installments and the seller retains a security interest in the goods. These laws frequently fix a maximum for the time-price differential, thereby remedying the situation created by the fact that the differential is not subject to the usury laws.

In the *Midland Guardian Company* case the buyer defended an action brought by the finance company on the ground that any liability to the plaintiff could not be enforced because it was usurious. The buyer asserted that she was entitled to statutory damages.

---

[18]   First American Bank & Trust v Windjammer Time Sharing Resort, Inc. (Fla App) 483 So 2d 732 (1986).

MIDLAND GUARDIAN CO. v THACKER
280 SC App 584, 314 SE2d 26 (1984)

Sarah Thacker purchased a mobile home from a dealer, Colonial. Thacker paid for it with the money borrowed from a finance company, Midland Guardian Co. When she stopped making payments on the loan, Midland sued to get the home. Thacker asserted that the transaction was usurious and counterclaimed against Midland to recover the statutory damages authorized in cases of usury. From a decision in favor of Midland, Thacker appealed.

GOOLSBY, J. . . . [The counterclaim for usury damages raises the question] whether a transaction involving the sale of a mobile home on deferred payments constitutes a sale at a time price or a loan and cloak for usury. . . .

We recognize . . . that a bona fide sale of property on credit at a price which exceeds the cash price by more than the legal rate of interest does not constitute usury. But the sale will be considered usurious when the sale is in fact at an agreed cash price and the form of a sale on credit is employed for the purpose of evading the usury statute. . . .

A close relationship between the seller of personal property and the financing institution can trigger an application of the usury statute despite language in the contract appearing to invoke the time price exception. Indeed, the time price exception has no application to a lending company that purchases the loan instrument from the merchant for the actual cash price when it is privy to the terms of the original transaction.

Here, the evidence shows that Colonial, the seller, and Midland Guardian, the finance company, were so closely allied that the original transaction was, in substance, a direct loan from Midland Guardian to the Thackers. As the record discloses, the finance company furnished the seller with security agreement forms and rate charts. And while the seller undertook to obtain credit information from the buyer, the seller did nothing with the data except transmit it to the finance company. Further, the finance company conducted the credit check and indicated approval of the credit application before any contract was made. Also, the security agreement was assigned to the finance company on the same day of its execution. . . .

Moreover, there are other indicia that the purported time price sale involved a usurious loan. The time price, here referred to as the "deferred payment price," was determined by adding amounts for insurance and a "finance charge" to the "cash price." Additionally, Colonial received from Midland Guardian in exchange for the security agreement its cash price and nothing else. Finally, and in many ways the most revealing, Colonial never contemplated that it would extend credit to the Thackers. This fact is made clear by the following exchange between the buyers' attorney and the mobile home salesman:

Q. . . . You stated that if the finance company turned you down on a customer's application for credit, you would go to another finance company?
A. Yes, M'am.
Q. . . . If all the finance companies that you normally dealt with turned you down, would you indeed make a credit sale to that customer?
A. No, m'am.

Thus, the correct conclusion to be drawn from the undisputed facts is "that the real transaction was a sale at a cash price accompanied by a loan or extension of credit to which the [finance company] was privy throughout." When so viewed, the finance charge of Six Thousand One Hundred Sixty-six Dollars ($6,166) on a mobile home costing, exclusive of insurance, Six Thousand Four Hundred Forty-two and 80/100 Dollars ($6,442.80) clearly emerges as usurious interest on a loan and not as an additional price paid for credit. The trial judge, therefore, erred as a matter of law in not holding that the time price rule was inapplicable. . . .

Because we have concluded that the transaction involved here did not constitute, under the particular facts shown, a valid time price sale, the judgment appealed from is reversed and the case is remanded to the Court of Common Pleas for a determination of the amount to which the appellant is entitled on her counterclaim as statutory damages.

[Judgment reversed and action remanded]

QUESTIONS

1. What was the basis for Thacker's claim that the transaction was usurious?
2. Would it affect the decision of the court if Colonial had sold the mobile home to Thacker on credit?
3. The parties agreed to a transaction in the form of a sale. Why doesn't the court accept the agreement and treat the transaction as a sale?

(b) REVOLVING CHARGE ACCOUNTS. When a merchant sells on credit, puts the bill on a charge account, and then adds a charge to the unpaid balance due by the customer, most courts hold that the amount of such charge is not controlled by the usury law.

SUMMARY

When an agreement is illegal, it is ordinarily void, and no contract arises therefrom. Courts will not allow one party to an illegal agreement to bring suit against the other party. There are some exceptions to this, as when the parties are not equally guilty or when the law's purpose in making the agreement illegal is to protect the person who is bringing suit. When possible, an agreement will be interpreted as being lawful. Even when a particular provision is held unlawful, the balance of the agreement will generally be saved, so that the net result is that there is a contract minus the clause that was held illegal.

The term *illegality* embraces situations in which a statute declares that certain conduct is unlawful or a crime; contracts requiring the commission of a tort; contracts that are contrary to public policy; contracts that are unconscionable; and, to some extent, contracts that are oppressive, unfair, or made in bad faith. The question of the legality of an agreement is not considered in the abstract, but the effect of the decision on the rest of society is considered. Increasingly, a given contract is not considered to be in a class by itself but is the same as thousands and even millions of other contracts.

Whether a contract is contrary to public policy may be difficult to determine, because *public policy* is not precisely defined. That which is harmful to the public welfare or general good is contrary to public policy. Contracts condemned as contrary to public policy include those designed to deprive the weaker party of a benefit that the lawmaker desired to provide; agreements injuring public service, such as an agreement to buy a government job for an applicant; agreements involving conflicts of interests, as when the purchasing officer of a government buys from a company that the officer privately owns; agreements obstructing legal process, such as an agreement with a witness to disappear; illegal discrimination contracts; and wagers and private lotteries. Statutes commonly make the wager illegal, as a form of gambling. The lottery is any plan under which, for a consideration, a person has a chance to win a prize.

Illegality may consist of the violation of a statute or administrative regulation adopted to regulate business. Statutes may make it illegal to do business unless a particular form of contract is used or unless the party promoting the transaction is licensed. The protection of buyers from fraud of sellers may make it unlawful to sell under certain circumstances or without making certain disclosures. Contracts in restraint of trade are generally illegal as violating federal or state antitrust laws. An agreement not to compete is illegal as a restraint of trade, except when reasonable in its terms and when it is incidental to the sale of a business or to a contract of employment.

The charging by a lender of a higher rate of interest than allowed by law is usury. Courts must examine transactions carefully to see if there is a usurious loan disguised as a legitimate transaction.

When sellers of goods offer their buyers one price for a cash sale and another, higher price for a credit sale, the higher price is lawful. The credit price is not usurious, even though the difference between the cash price and the credit price is greater than the amount that could be charged as interest on a loan equal to the cash price. This concept is called the time-price differential. A minority of states reject or abolish it or limit the increase of the credit price over the cash price to a specified percentage or to the maximum amount that could be charged on a loan equal to the cash price. Most states do not apply the usury law to a revolving charge account. A minority do so, with the result that the charges imposed on the account must not exceed the amount that could be charged as interest on a loan of the amount due on the account.

QUESTIONS AND CASE PROBLEMS

1. What social forces are affected by the rule that a credit sale price is not usurious, although the difference between the credit price and the cash price is greater than the interest that could be charged on a loan in the amount of the cash price?

2. When are the parties to an illegal agreement *in pari delicto*?

3. Alman made a contract to purchase an automobile from Crockett Motors on credit. Alman failed to make payments on time. When Crockett sued to enforce the contract, Alman raised the defense that the price of the car had been increased because she was buying on credit and that this increase was unconscionable. Crockett proved that the automobile was exactly what it was represented to be and that no fraud had been committed in selling the car to Alman. Does Crockett's evidence constitute a defense to Alman's claim of unconscionability?

4. The Civic Association of Plaineville raffled an automobile in order to raise funds to build a hospital. Lyons won the automobile, but the Association refused to deliver it to her. She sued the Association for the automobile. Can Lyons enforce the contract?

5. Ewing was employed by Presto-X-Company, a pest exterminator. His contract of employment specified that he would not solicit or attempt to solicit customers of Presto-X for two years after the termination of his employment. After working several years, his employment was terminated. Ewing then sent a letter to customers of Presto-X stating that he no longer worked for Presto-X and that he was still certified by the state. Ewing then set forth his home address and phone number, which the customers did not previously have. The letter then ended with the statement "I thank you for your business throughout the past years." Presto-X brought an action to enjoin Ewing from sending such letters. He raised the defense that he was only prohibited from soliciting and that there was nothing in the letters that constituted a seeking of customers. Decide. What ethical values are involved? [Presto-X-Company v Ewing (Iowa) 442 NW2d 85]

6. The Creswell Department Store sold merchandise for cash and for credit. A customer purchasing on credit paid in 12 monthly installments and paid a purchase price that was 20 percent higher than a person buying for cash. Rose purchased a refrigerator from Creswell on the credit plan. After paying for it in full, she sued Creswell for the penalties prescribed by the state usury law. She claimed that the price increase of 20 percent for the credit sale violated the state usury law that allowed a maximum of only 6 percent interest on loans. Was she entitled to recover the penalties?

7. Compare the legality of prize drawings with winners selected by a random drawing from (a) names in the telephone book, (b) names of persons attending a television show, and (c) names of persons written on entry blanks obtained when purchasing goods from the sponsoring store.

8. The Minnesota Adoption Statute requires that any agency placing a child for adoption must make a thorough investigation and cannot give a child to an applicant unless such placement is in the best interests of the child. Tibbetts applied to Crossroads, Inc., a private adoption agency, for a child to adopt. He later sued the agency for breach of contract, claiming that the agency was obligated by contract to supply a child for adoption. The agency claimed that it was only required to use best efforts to locate a child and was not required to supply a child to Tibbetts unless it found him to be a suitable parent. Decide. [Tibbetts v Crossroads, Inc. (Minn App) 411 NW2d 535]

9. Florida law prohibits discrimination in a wide range of business transactions. The Florida Human Rights Act prohibits discrimination because of religion. The Florida Fair Housing Act states that it is the "policy" of Florida to provide "fair housing throughout the state." Skolnick and his wife wanted to buy land in the residential section of Bal Harbour. They were told that they could not buy the land unless they were members of the Bal Harbour Club. They applied for membership in the club but were rejected because of their religion. They then sued the

club, claiming that it had improperly discriminated against them and that the requirement of membership in the club in order to buy the land was merely a device to evade the prohibition of discrimination in the sale of land. The club settled the suit by paying Skolnick $25,000. The club then demanded that the Ranger Insurance Company pay that amount to the club on the theory that the club's policy from that company covered all claims that could be made against the club by third persons. The insurance company refused to pay, on the ground that such payment would be compensating the club for its unlawful discrimination. Was the insurance company liable? [Ranger Ins. Co. v Bal Harbour Club, Inc. (Fla) 549 So 2d 1005]

10. *A* entered a retirement home operated by *B*. The contract between *A* and *B* required *A* to make a specified monthly payment that could be increased by *B* as the cost of operations of the home increased. The contract and the payment plan were thoroughly explained to *A*. As the cost of operations rose, the monthly payments were continually raised by *B* to cover these costs. *A* objected to the increases on the ground that the increases were far more than had been anticipated and that the contract was therefore unconscionable. Was his objection valid? [Onderdonk v Presbyterian Homes, 171 NJ Super 529, 410 A2d 252]

11. Smith was employed as a salesman for Borden, Inc., which sold food products in 63 counties in Arkansas, 2 counties in Missouri, 2 counties in Oklahoma, and 1 county in Texas. Smith's employment contract prohibited him from competing with Borden after leaving its employ. Smith left Borden and went to work for a competitor, Lady Baltimore Foods. Working for this second employer, Smith sold in three counties of Arkansas. He had sold in two of these counties while he worked for Borden. Borden brought an injunction action against Smith and Lady Baltimore to enforce the anticompetitive covenant in Smith's former contract. Was Borden entitled to the injunction? [Borden, Inc. v Smith, 252 Ark 295, 478 SW2d 744]

12. Doherty ran a lounge and bar, known as the Orchid Room, in California, where betting is illegal. Bradley, a patron in the Orchid Room, made bets with Doherty on the scores he could attain on the pinball machine. Bradley lost $70,000 on such bets. He later sued Doherty to recover the money. Doherty raised the defense that Bradley was *in pari delicto* and therefore could not recover. Bradley claimed that this defense did not apply because the pinball machines were fixed by electronic devices, and also because he, Bradley, was a compulsive gambler. Was Bradley correct? [Bradley v Doherty, 30 Cal App 3d 991, 106 Cal Rptr 725]

13. Credit Alliance Corporation loaned money to Westland Machine Company, Inc. Both companies had business experience, and the contract was signed on behalf of Westland by its president, who was also an attorney. He apparently did not read the contract and did not see that, buried in standard clauses, there was a provision waiving trial by jury. Credit Alliance later sued Westland on the debt. Westland demanded a jury trial and claimed that the waiver was invalid because it was unconscionable and contrary to public policy. Should a jury trial be granted? [Credit Alliance Corp. v Westland Machines Co. Inc. (Fla App) 439 So 2d 332]

14. Vodra was employed as a salesperson and contracting agent for American Security Services. As part of his contract of employment Vodra signed an agreement that for three years after leaving this employment, he would not solicit any customer of American. Vodra had no experience in the security field when he went to work for American. To the extent that he became known to American's customers, it was by virtue of being the representative of American rather than because of his own reputation in the security field. After some years Vodra left American and organized a competing company that solicited American's customers. American sued him to enforce the restrictive convenant. Vodra claimed that the restrictive convenant was illegal and not binding. Was he correct? [American Securities Services, Inc. v Vodra, 222 Neb 480, 385 NW2d 73]

15. The Potomac Leasing Company leased an automatic telephone system to Vitality Centers. Claudene Cato signed the lease as guarantor of payments. When the rental was not paid, Potomac Leasing brought suit against Vitality and Cato. They raised the defense that the rented equipment was to be used for an illegal purpose—namely, the random sales solicitation by means of an automatic telephone in violation of state statute; that this purpose was known to Potomac Leasing; and that Potomac Leasing could therefore not enforce the lease. Was this defense valid? [Potomac Leasing Co. v Vitality Centers, Inc. 290 Ark 265, 718 SW2d 928]

14

FORM OF CONTRACT

There was a time in the history of the common law when there was no requirement that a promise be in writing in order to be enforceable—a promise was a promise, irrespective of its form (oral or written). Experience proved that this degree of freedom created too great an opportunity for abuse. Perjury became commonplace. In order to prevent this type of fraud, the law was changed to require that certain kinds of contracts be evidenced by a writing. In practice this flat requirement was found also to open the door to fraud. At times there was an oral contract, but the existence of the contract was falsely denied. So the law shifted once again and now recognizes certain exceptions to the writing requirement. As an example, the requirement may be satisfied by a sufficient part performance. Some courts have gone further and ignore the writing requirement in certain cases of detrimental reliance on an oral contract.

Assuming that a contract had been evidenced by a writing, whether or not the writing was required by statute, society was next faced with the policy of what effect was to be given the writing. Specifically, was the writing the final word, or could it be modified or contradicted by the testimony of witnesses? Society has made a compromise between two extremes, holding by what is called the *parol*

FIGURE 14-1   HURDLES IN THE PATH OF A CONTRACT

WRITING REQUIRED:

STATUTE OF FRAUDS

MORE THAN ONE YEAR TO PERFORM
SALE OF LAND
ANSWER FOR ANOTHER'S DEBT OR DEFAULT
PERSONAL REPRESENTATIVE TO PAY DEBT
    OF DECEDENT
PROMISE IN CONSIDERATION OF MARRIAGE
SALE OF GOODS FOR $500 OR MORE
MISCELLANEOUS

EXCEPTIONS

PART PERFORMANCE
PROMISOR BENEFIT
DETRIMENTAL RELIANCE

PAROL EVIDENCE RULE

EVERY COMPLETE, FINAL WRITTEN
    CONTRACT

EXCEPTIONS

INCOMPLETE CONTRACT
AMBIGUOUS TERMS
FRAUD, ACCIDENT, OR MISTAKE
TO PROVE EXISTENCE OR NONBINDING
    CHARACTER OF CONTRACT
MODIFICATION OF CONTRACT
ILLEGALITY

evidence rule that the writing is ordinarily the final word, but that in certain circumstances it is not.

A.   STATUTE OF FRAUDS

In Chapter 9 it was stated that a contract is a binding agreement. Must the agreement be evidenced by a writing?

1.   Validity of Oral Contracts

Generally, a contract is valid whether it is written or oral. By statute, however, some contracts must be evidenced by a writing. The statutes do not apply when an oral agreement has been voluntarily performed by both parties.

The failure to sign and return a written contract does not establish that there is no contract, as there may have been an earlier oral contract. Whether such a prior oral contract exists is to be determined from all the circumstances. The test is what intent was manifested by the parties.[1] If one of the parties, with the knowledge or approval of the other contracting party, undertakes performance of the contract before it is reduced to writing, it is generally held that the parties intended to be bound from the moment the oral contract was made.

Although oral agreements are ordinarily binding and are therefore contracts, an exception will arise when it is the intent of the parties that there is no binding agreement until a written contract is prepared and signed. If, in fact, the parties intend not to be bound until a written contract is executed, their preliminary oral agreement does not constitute a contract. Such a preliminary agreement cannot be enforced when no writing is thereafter executed.[2]

---

[1]   Williams v Jones, 322 NC 42, 366 SE2d 433 (1988).
[2]   Lal v Naffah, 149 Ill App 3d 245, 102 Ill Dec 803, 500 NE2d 699 (1986).

2.   Contracts That Must Be Evidenced by a Writing

Ordinarily, a contract, whether oral or written, is binding if the existence and terms of the contract can be established to the satisfaction of the trier of fact—usually the jury. In some instances a statute, commonly called a **statute of frauds**,[3] requires that certain kinds of contracts be evidenced by a writing, or else they cannot be enforced. This means that either the contract itself must be in writing and signed by both parties, or there must be a sufficient written memorandum of the oral contract signed by the person being sued for breach of contract.

(a) AGREEMENT THAT CANNOT BE

[3]   The name is derived from the original English Statute of Frauds and Perjuries, which was adopted in 1677 and became the pattern for similar legislation in America. The seventeenth section of that statute governed the sale of goods, and its modern counterpart is § 2-201 of the UCC, discussed in Chapter 24. The fourth section of the English statute provided the pattern for American legislation with respect to contracts other than for the sale of good described in this section of the chapter. The English statute was repealed in 1954, except as to land sale and guaranty contracts. The American statutes remain in force, but the liberalization by UCC § 2-201 of the pre-Code requirements with respect to contracts for the sale of goods may be regarded as a step in the direction of the abandonment of the statute of frauds concept.

When the English Statute of Frauds and Perjuries was adopted, the parties to a lawsuit were not permitted to testify on their own behalf, with the result that a litigant had difficulty in disproving perjured testimony of third persons offered as evidence on behalf of the adverse party. The statute was repealed in England partly because it was felt that it permitted the assertion of a "technical" defense as a means of avoiding just obligations, and partly on the ground that since parties in interest now have the right to testify, there is no longer the need for a writing to protect the parties from perjured testimony of third persons. Azevedo v Minister, 86 Nev 576, 471 P2d 661 (1970).

PERFORMED WITHIN ONE YEAR AFTER THE CONTRACT IS MADE. A writing is required when the contract, by its terms or subject matter, cannot be performed within one year after the date of the agreement. Thus, a joint venture agreement to construct a condominium complex was subject to the one-year provision of the statute of frauds where the contract could not reasonably have been performed within one year. This was due to the complex nature of the project. The plans of the parties projected a development over the course of three years.

The year runs from the time the oral contract was made rather than from the date when performance is to begin. In computing the year, the day on which the contract was made is excluded. The year begins with the following day and ends at the close of the first anniversary of the day on which the agreement was made.

The statute of frauds does not apply if it is possible under the terms of the agreement to perform the contract within one year. Thus, a writing is not required when no time for performance is specified and the performance will not necessarily take more than a year. In this case the statute is inapplicable without regard to the time when performance is actually begun or completed.

When a contract may be terminated at will by either party, the statute of frauds is not applicable, because the contract may be terminated within a year. In the *Boening* case it was claimed that there was no binding contract. There was an oral agreement to continue the plaintiff's franchise for so long as performance thereunder was satisfactory.

D & N BOENING, INC. v KIRSCH BEVERAGES, INC.

63 NY2d 449, 483 NYS2d 164, 472 NE2d 992 (1984)

D & N Boening, Inc. was franchised by the American Beverage Corporation to sell the "Yoo-Hoo" beverage in a certain portion of New York state. The franchise was to continue as long as the franchisee rendered satisfactory performance. This agreement was oral, and several requests by Boening to put it in writing were refused. Thereafter Kirsch Beverages bought out American Beverage Corporation and notified Boening that its franchise was terminated. No cause for termination was given. Boening then sued Kirsch and American for breach of the franchise. From a judgment for the defendants, the plaintiff appealed.

JASEN, J. . . . The ancient Statute of Frauds . . . was intended to prevent fraud in the proving of certain legal transactions particularly susceptible to deception, mistake and perjury and, with regard specifically to the requirement for a signed writing for a contract not to be performed within one year, "the design of the statute was, not to trust to the memory of witnesses for a longer time than one year."

Unfortunately, the Statute does not in many cases provide an effective means of serving that purpose. There is no necessary relationship between the time of the making of a contract, the time within which its performance is required, and the time when it might come to court to be proven. Accordingly, the courts have generally been reluctant to give too broad an interpretation to this provision of the Statute and instead have limited it to those contracts only which by their very terms have absolutely no possibility in fact and law of full performance within one year.

> The parties may well have expected that the contract would continue in force for more than one year; it may well have been very improbable that it would not do so; and it did in fact continue in force for a much longer time. But they made no stipulation which in terms, or by reasonable inference, required that result. The question is not what the probable, or expected, or actual performance of the contract was; but whether the contract, according to the reasonable interpretation of its terms, required that it should not be performed within the year. . . .

. . . Moreover, consistent with that narrow interpretation, this court has continued to analyze oral agreements to determine if, according to the parties' terms, there might be any possible means of performance within one year. Wherever an agreement has been found to be susceptible of fulfillment within that time, in whatever manner and however impractical, this court has held the one-year provision of the Statute to be inapplicable, a writing unnecessary, and the agreement not barred. . . .

On the other hand, while the foregoing oral agreements and similar ones which are performable within one year are saved from the writing requirement of the Statute of Frauds, clearly there are others which simply are impossible of completion within that time by their own terms and are, therefore, void if unwritten. Prominent among these latter agreements falling within the Statute are those which are terminable within one year only upon a breach by one of the parties. A breach can in no way be equated with an option to discontinue or cancel, the exercise of which would constitute an alternative performance of the agreement. . . .

As this court early explained, "termination is not performance, but rather the destruction of the contract . . . where there is no provision authorizing either of the parties to terminate as a matter of right." And, more recently, in deciding that the contract then under review fell within the Statute because not truly performable within one year, this court held that "the contract was not, then, one which might be *performed* within a year, but rather one which could only be *terminated* within that period by a breach of one or the other party to it [emphasis in original]. *The possibility of such wrongful termination is not, of course, the same as the possibility of performance* within the statutory period."

Here, as the Appellate Division correctly held, the oral agreement between the parties called for performance of an indefinite duration and could only be terminated within one year by its breach during that period. . . .

According to its terms, the agreement required defendants to continue plaintiff's subdistributorship indefinitely. It provided for no expiration and there was no contemplation of any completion or final discharge. The sole limitation on the agreement's duration was its explicit requirement—especially crucial to an exclusive agency—that plaintiff conduct its subdistributorship satisfactorily, exerting its best efforts and acting in good faith. Only upon plaintiff's failure to do so within the first year could the agreement have been terminated during that period.

Such a failure would not have constituted a permitted manner of performance or exercise of an option, but rather, a breach of the agreement. And other than such a breach, there was no provision under the terms of the agreement for it to come to an end. Neither party had an option to cancel, and there was no specified time or event which automatically would cause the agreement to terminate. Instead, under a reasonable interpretation of its own terms, the agreement would extend beyond the first year and, indeed, would continue in perpetuity unless plaintiff failed to perform its part of the bargain.

Being terminable only by plaintiff's breach, the agreement alleged in the complaint was not one which by its terms could be *performed* within one year. As such, it came within the ambit of the Statute of Frauds and is void for being unwritten. . . .

[Judgment affirmed]

QUESTIONS

1. What was the evil against which the statute of frauds was intended to guard in connection with the provision involved in the *Boening* case?
2. What has been the attitude of the courts to the one-year provision of the statute of frauds?
3. Why didn't the court sustain the oral contract in view of the fact that it could have ended in less than a year if Boening's performance was not satisfactory to Kirsch?

The fact that a contract for a specified number of years would be terminated by the death of a party thereto does not affect the statute of frauds requirement. Thus, a contract of employment not to compete with the employer for five years would have to be evidenced by a writing even though the contract would be discharged by the death of the employee, which could occur within one year.[4]

(b) AGREEMENT TO SELL OR A SALE OF ANY INTEREST IN REAL PROPERTY. All contracts to sell, as well as sales of land, buildings, or interests in land, such as mortgages, must be evidenced by a writing.

The statute applies only to the agreement between the owner and purchaser or between their agents. It does not apply to agreements to pay for an examination or search of the title of the property or to agreements between the buyer and an attorney. Similarly, a partnership agreement to deal in real estate is generally not required by this provision of the statute of frauds to be in writing. The statute ordinarily does not apply to a contract between a real estate agent and one of the parties to the sales contract employing the agent.

An agreement to cancel or set aside a contract for the sale of land must satisfy the statute of frauds.

(c) PROMISE TO ANSWER FOR THE DEBT OR DEFAULT OF ANOTHER. When *A*

[4]   Frantz v Parke (Idaho App) 729 P2d 1068 (1986).

promises *C* to pay *B*'s debt to *C* if *B* does not do so, *A* is promising to answer for the debt of another. Such a promise must usually be evidenced by a writing to be enforceable.[5] Thus, the oral promise of the president of a corporation to pay the debts owed by the corporation to its creditors if they will not sue the corporation does not bind the president. A promise to pay an attorney the fee owed by a third person cannot be enforced when there was no writing to satisfy the statute of frauds.

If the promise is made directly to the debtor that the promisor will pay the creditor of the debtor what is owed, the statute of frauds is not applicable.[6] In contrast, if the promisor makes the promise to the creditor, it comes within the category of a promise made for the benefit of another. It must therefore be evidenced by a writing that satisfies the statute of frauds.

(d) PROMISE BY THE EXECUTOR OR ADMINISTRATOR OF A DECEDENT'S ESTATE TO PAY A CLAIM AGAINST THE ESTATE FROM PERSONAL FUNDS. The personal representative (executor or administrator) has the duty of handling the affairs of a deceased person, paying the debts from the proceeds of the estate, and distributing any balance remaining. The executor or administrator is not personally liable for the claims against the estate of the decedent. If the personal representative promises to pay the decedent's debts with the representative's own money, the promise cannot be enforced unless it is evidenced by a writing.

If the personal representative makes a contract on behalf of the estate in the course of administering the estate, a writing is not required. The representative is then contracting on behalf of the estate. Thus, if the personal representative employs an attorney to settle the estate or makes a burial contract with an undertaker, no writing is required.

(e) PROMISE MADE IN CONSIDERATION OF MARRIAGE. If a person makes a promise to pay a sum of money or to give property to another in consideration of marriage or a promise to marry, the agreement must be evidenced by a writing. This provision of the statute of frauds is not applicable to ordinary mutual promises to marry. It is not affected by the statutes in some states that prohibit the bringing of any action for breach of promise of marriage.

(f) SALE OF GOODS. When the contract price for goods is $500 or more, the contract must ordinarily be evidenced by a writing.

(g) MISCELLANEOUS STATUTES OF FRAUDS. In a number of states, special statutes require other agreements to be in writing or evidenced by a writing. Thus, a statute may provide that an agreement to name a person as beneficiary in an insurance policy must be evidenced by a writing.

The Uniform Commercial Code contains three statutes of frauds relating to sales of personal property. These deal with: (1) goods; (2) securities, such as stocks and bonds; and (3) personal property other than goods and securities. Under the UCC it has been held that an oral contract for the sale of a business could be enforced up to $5,000 by virtue of UCC § 1–206. This was true even though the oral contract could not be enforced under the general statute of frauds because it called for payment over three years and thus could not be fully performed within one year.[7]

In some states contracts with brokers relating to the sale of land are also subject to the statute of frauds.

3.   Note or Memorandum

The statute of frauds requires a writing to evidence those contracts that come within its scope. This writing may be a note or memorandum, as distinguished from a contract. It may be in any form, because its only purpose is to serve as evidence of the contract. The statutory requirement is, of course, satisfied if there is a complete written contract signed by both parties.

(a) SIGNING. The note or memorandum must be signed by the party sought to be

[5]   Lichtman v Grossbard, 129 App Div 2d 437, 514 NYS2d 9 (1987).
[6]   Allen v Rosen (Fla App) 526 So 2d 1050 (1988).
[7]   Beldengreen v Ashinsky, 528 NYS2d 744 (1987).

bound by the contract or that person's agent.[8] A letter from an employer setting forth the details of an oral contract of employment satisfies the statute of frauds in a suit brought by the employee against the employer. The writing was signed by the party "sought to be charged." If the employer had sued the employee in such case, the employer's letter would not satisfy the statute of frauds, since it would not be signed by the employee.

Some states require that the authorization of an agent to execute a contract coming within the statute of frauds must also be in writing. In the case of an auction, it is the usual practice for the auctioneer to be the agent of both parties for the purpose of signing the memorandum.[9]

Ordinarily, the signature may be made at any place on the writing. In some states it is expressly required that the signature appear at the end of the writing. The signature may be an ordinary one or any symbol that is adopted by the party as a signature. It may consist of initials, figures, or a mark. When a signature consists of a mark made by a person who is illiterate or physically incapacitated, it is commonly required that the name of the person be placed on the writing by someone else, who may be required to sign the instrument as a witness. A person signing a trade or assumed name is liable to the same extent as though the contract had been signed with the signer's name. In the absence of a local statute that provides otherwise, a signature may be made by pencil, pen, typewriter, print, or stamp.

(b) CONTENT. Except in the case of a sale of goods, the note or memorandum must contain all the material terms of the contract so that the court can determine just what was agreed. A writing that does not describe the land or identify the buyer does not satisfy the statute of frauds. Likewise, a writing is insufficient if the contract is partly oral and partly written. The subject matter must be identified either within the writing itself or in other writings to which it refers. A writing is not sufficient if it does not identify the subject of the contract. A deposit check given by the buyer to the seller does not take the oral land sales contract out of the statute of frauds. This is because the check does not set forth the terms of the sale.

The note or memorandum may consist of one writing or of separate papers, such as letters or telegrams, or of a combination of such papers.[10] The writing that satisfies the statute of frauds may be a letter written by a party's attorney.

Separate writings cannot be considered together unless they are linked. Linkage may be by express reference in each writing to the other or by the fact that each writing clearly deals with the same subject matter.

It is not necessary that the writing be addressed to the other contracting party or to any other person. It is not necessary that the writing be made with the intent to create a writing to satisfy the statute of frauds. For example, a corporation made an oral contract of employment with an employee. The minutes of the corporation reciting the adoption of the resolution to employ the employee (which minutes were signed by the president of the corporation), together with the salary check paid the employee, constituted a sufficient writing to satisfy the statute of frauds.

(c) TIME OF WRITING. The memorandum may be made at the time of the original transaction or at a later date. It must, however, ordinarily exist at the time a court action is brought upon the agreement.

4.   Effect of Noncompliance

The majority of states hold that a contract that does not comply with the statute of frauds is voidable.[11] A small minority of states hold that such an agreement is void. Under either view,

---

[8]   Sales Service, Inc. v Daewood Int'l (America) Corp. (Mo App) 770 SW2d 453 (1989).

[9]   Rohfling v Tomorrow Realty & Auction Co., Inc. (Fla App) 528 So 2d 463 (1988).

[10]   Machan Hampshire Properties, Inc. v Western Real Estate & Development Co. (Utah App) 779 P2d 230 (1989).

[11]   The UCC creates several statutes of frauds of limited applicability in which it uses the term *not enforceable*. § 1-206 (sale of intangible personal property); § 2-201 (sale of goods); and § 8-319 (sale of securities). The Official Code Comment, point 4, to § 2-201 describes *not enforceable* as meaning what would ordinarily be called *voidable*.

if an action is brought to enforce the contract, the defendant can raise the objection that it is not evidenced by a writing. However, when it is held that the oral contract is not void but merely voidable, it can be enforced if the defendant does not raise the statute of frauds. That is, the court will not refuse to enforce the contract when it notices that it is oral unless the opposing party objects thereto. No one other than the defendant, however, can make the objection.

(a) RECOVERY OF VALUE CONFERRED. In most instances a person who is prevented from enforcing a contract because of the statute of frauds is nevertheless entitled to recover from the other party the value of any services or property furnished or money given under the oral contract. Recovery is not based on the terms of the contract but on a quasi-contractual obligation. The other party is to restore to the plaintiff what was received in order to prevent unjust enrichment at the plaintiff's expense. For example, when an oral contract for services cannot be enforced because of the statute of frauds, the person performing the work may recover the reasonable value of the services rendered.

(b) PROOF OF FRAUD. The statute of frauds does not bar proof that the promisor had no intention to pay the debt of the third person but had made such promise fraudulently to induce the promisee to supply goods.

5. Judicial Relief from Statute of Frauds

The requirements of the statute of frauds are easily met. Often, however, because people are in a hurry or do not know the law, transactions consist only of spoken words. No writing is made that satisfies the statute of frauds. If one of the parties claims that the transaction is not binding because of the statute of frauds, a real injustice can be inflicted. To prevent this hardship, the courts have created certain exceptions to the statute of frauds.

(a) PART PERFORMANCE OF CONTRACT. In spite of the statute of frauds, an oral contract for the sale of an interest in land will be enforced if the buyer has taken possession of the land, has made substantial valuable improvements to the land, and the value of such improvements cannot be easily measured in dollars.

In some states, the concept of part performance has been expanded to bar the defense of the statute of frauds when the plaintiff has fully performed the obligations under the oral contract. To illustrate, the president of a corporation orally promised the insurer to pay the premiums on insurance to be furnished the corporation. The insurer, after having furnished the corporation with the specified insurance in reliance on the promise of the president, could enforce that promise. Enforcement could be obtained even though there was no writing to satisfy the statute of frauds.[12]

(b) PROMISOR BENEFITED BY PROMISE TO PAY DEBT OF ANOTHER. If a person orally promises a creditor to pay the debt owed to that creditor by a debtor, the promise is ordinarily not binding because of the statute of frauds. If the promise is made primarily to benefit the promisor, the courts refuse to apply the statute of frauds. In such case, the promise to pay the debt of the third person is binding even though it is oral and benefits the debtor by discharging the debt that was due.[13] For example, when the purpose of a majority stockholder's promise to pay the debt of the corporation is to benefit the stockholder, the statute of frauds is not applicable to that promise.

(c) DETRIMENTAL RELIANCE ON ORAL CONTRACT. The extent to which judicial relief from the statute of frauds will be granted in cases other than land sales and debt guaranties is not clear. The same forces that gave rise to the doctrine of promissory estoppel in connection with the law of consideration are to some extent causing courts to recognize detrimental reliance as excusing noncompliance with the statute of frauds. In

[12]   Jakubik v Rounis, 175 Ill App 3d 551, 125 Ill Dec 8, 529 NE2d 1084 (1988).
[13]   Heese Produce Co. v Lueders, 233 Neb 12, 443 NW2d 278 (1989).

the *Kiely* case, it was claimed that an oral contract could be enforced in spite of the statute of frauds because of the plaintiff's reliance on the contract.

KIELY v ST. GERMAIN
(Colo) 670 P2d 764 (1983)

Joel St. Germain was employed by the Public Service Company. William Boshouwers owned 100 percent of the stock of Boshouwers Color Laboratory, Inc. St. Germain and Boshouwers, in the office of St. Germain's attorney, reached an agreement that they would begin a new business venture, that St. Germain would come to work for Boshouwers Color Laboratory, and that William Boshouwers would sell 49 percent of the stock of the laboratory to St. Germain for $25,000. At the end of the meeting, Boshouwers stated to St. Germain "We have a deal and you can tell your employer that you are leaving." St. Germain then quit his job and obtained a second mortgage on his home to raise the money to purchase the stock of the laboratory. A document was prepared setting forth the terms of the oral agreement, but Boshouwers then refused to sign it and denied that there was ever such an agreement. St. Germain brought suit on the oral contract. With respect to the shares of the laboratory stock, he claimed the profit that he would have made if Boshouwers had sold the stock as orally agreed. Boshouwers raised the defense that the statute of frauds, UCC, § 8–319, required that the contract be evidenced by a writing, and that in the absence of a writing, there was no contract. St. Germain claimed that because of his reliance on the oral contract, the doctrine of promissory estoppel barred Boshouwers from raising the defense of the statute of frauds. The trial court held that the statute of frauds barred proof of the oral contract for the sale of stock but awarded other damages for lost wages and legal costs. By this time Boshouwers and the laboratory had become bankrupt, and Kiely, as the trustee in bankruptcy, then appealed.

KIRSHBAUM, J. . . . Although the doctrine of promissory estoppel is based in part upon the premise that statute of frauds provisions need not defeat meritorious claims for enforcement of oral promises, the results are far from uniform in cases wherein a claim based on promissory estoppel is challenged by a defense based squarely on the provisions of a particular statute of frauds. Some jurisdictions suggest that in such circumstances the absence of compliance with statute of frauds requirements invariably will result in the defeat of the promissory estoppel claim. . . . Other jurisdictions have permitted recovery on the promissory estoppel claim when the evidence establishes that the defendant relying on the statute of frauds defense orally agreed to reduce the operative promise to writing.

The majority of jurisdictions faced with resolving a confrontation between promissory estoppel claims and statute of frauds defenses have adopted a more flexible, albeit a more complex, approach. The courts in those jurisdictions are required to examine the policies furthered by the doctrine of promissory estoppel and by the particular statute of frauds in the total context of the case and to render a decision which is basically fair to all the parties. . . . The effort to compare the strengths of the doctrine and of the statute in particular cases gives maximum recognition to the central policy furthered by each—preventing unjust results when parties deal with each other by means of oral rather than written communication.

In response to judicial development of the doctrine of promissory estoppel, the American Law Institute in 1979 adopted a new section articulating principles directly applicable to the promissory estoppel claim/statute of frauds defense quagmire. . . . In essence, section 139 provides the equitable balancing test utilized by the majority of jurisdictions. This court has previously recognized that a plaintiff's full or partial performance of an oral agreement, when done in reasonably justifiable reliance thereon, is sufficient to overcome a statute of frauds defense. . . . Thus, the principle embodied in section 139 of the *Restatement (Second) of Contracts* that detrimental action performed in justifiable reliance upon oral promises may be sufficient to compel full or partial performance of the promise in spite of the applicability of a statute of frauds defense is but a slight extension of the principles well settled in Colorado. Thus, we conclude that the Court of Appeals correctly concluded that section 139 of the *Restatement (Second) of Contracts* is applicable to this case.

The statute of frauds relied on by defendants, [UCC § 8–319] states in pertinent part as follows:

> A contract for the sale of securities is not enforceable . . . unless: (a) There is some writing signed by the party against whom enforcement is sought or by his authorized agent or broker sufficient to indicate that a contract has been made for sale of a stated quantity of described securities at a defined or stated price. . . .

The statute, a part of the Uniform Commercial Code (the Code), is designed to ensure certainty in the sale and purchase of securities. It prohibits the sale of or purchase of this type of asset in the absence of a complete written agreement concerning the essential terms of such transaction. However, [UCC § 1–103] contains the following provision concerning construction of other provisions of the Code:

> Unless displaced by the particular provisions of this title, the principles of law and equity, including . . . the law relative to . . . estoppel . . . shall supplement its provisions.

This recognition that general principles of estoppel should be considered in applying the provisions of the Code indicates a strong legislative concern that the statute not be utilized to perpetrate a fraud or to achieve inequitable results in particular cases. Section 8–319 contains no indication that transactions involving the sale of securities are exempt from the general caveat of section 1–103. Thus, this particular statute of frauds may be "supplemented" by the doctrine of promissory estoppel—a virtual requirement that courts utilize a balancing test to prevent use of the statute to effect inequitable results.

The trial court has not had an opportunity to analyze the merits of St. Germain's claim for "lost profits" under the principles enunciated in section 139 of the *Restatement (Second) of Contracts*. It must be permitted to do so in light of the evidence adduced at trial or in light of any additional evidence it might in its discretion permit to be presented on the matter.

[Judgment reversed and action remanded]

QUESTIONS

1. List and explain the different views as to the relationship of promissory estoppel to the statute of frauds.

2. Compare promissory estoppel and part performance.
3. State whether (a) St. Germain's claim was based on promissory estoppel or whether (b) St. Germain relied on promissory estoppel as a defense against Boshouwers' claim that the statute of frauds barred enforcement of an oral contract.

There is a conflict of authority as to whether detrimental reliance excuses noncompliance with the statute of frauds. Some courts refuse to apply the doctrine of detrimental reliance to avoid the defense of the statute of frauds because that would defeat the purpose of the statute.[14]

The mere fact that the promisee relies on the oral promise is generally not sufficient to entitle the promisee to enforce the oral promise. The promisee must show that (1) because of the reliance on the promise, substantial or unconscionable injury would be sustained by the promisee, or (2) the promisor would be unjustly enriched if the oral promise were not enforced.

(d) PROMISE TO EXECUTE WRITING. Some courts enforce an oral contract in spite of the statute of frauds when the defendant promised to execute a writing that would satisfy the statute but failed to do so.[15]

B.   PAROL EVIDENCE RULE

When the contract is evidenced by a writing, may the contract terms be changed by the testimony of witnesses? The answer depends on the circumstances surrounding the execution of the writing and the nature of the writing.

6.   Exclusion of Parol Evidence

The general rule is that spoken words, that is, **parol evidence,** will not be allowed to modify or contradict the terms of a written contract that is complete on its face. This rule is not followed if there is clear proof that because of fraud, accident, or a mistake, the writing is not in fact the contract or the complete or true contract.[16] This is called the **parol evidence rule**. It excludes words spoken before or at the time the contract was made.

The parol evidence rule prevents a party from avoiding liability on a written contract by evidence that the writing does not mean what it says. Thus, the parol evidence rule bars proof that the obligee stated that a guaranty contract signed by the defendant was a "mere technicality" and that the defendant would not be required to make payment.

In the *Gerlund* case, evidence was offered that contradicted the express provision of an employment contract.

---

[14]   Meinhold v Huang (Mo App) 687 SW2d 596 (1985). Courts commonly refer to this doctrine as "promissory estoppel." The term *detrimental reliance* is used in the text, because the promissor estoppel applied in connection with the question of consideration requires greater detriment than is required by those courts recognizing reliance as avoiding the statute of frauds. See Section 12 of Chapter 12 as to consideration and promissory estoppel.

[15]   Magcobar North American v Grasso Oilfield Services, Inc. (Tex App) 736 SW2d 787 (1987).

[16]   McNeil & Associates, Inc. v ITT Life Ins. Corp. (Minn App) 446 NW2d 181 (1989).

GERLUND v ELECTRONIC DISPENSERS INTERNATIONAL
190 Cal App 3d 263, 235 Cal Rptr 279 (1987)

Leroy and Susan Gerlund were sales representatives of Electronic Dispensers International (EDI). They worked under a contract that specified that the employment could be terminated for any reason. The Gerlunds were the best sales representatives of EDI. After some years, EDI wanted to change the rate of commissions paid to sales representatives. When the Gerlunds did not agree to the changes, EDI discharged them. They sued EDI and offered evidence that EDI had stated they would be employed as long as they did a good job. From a judgment in the Gerlunds' favor, EDI appealed.

BRAUER, J. . . . We quote here the pertinent portions of the agreement:

11. EFFECTIVE PERIOD: TERMINATION

This agreement shall be effective until thirty (30) days after notice of termination given by either party. Notice of termination may be given at any time and for any reason, and the date of any such notice shall be the postmark date if mailed, or the transmission date if wired. . . .

13. THE AGREEMENT COMPLETE.

This agreement contains the entire agreement between the Company and the Representative. There are no oral or collateral agreements of any kind. . . .

. . . The parol evidence rule generally prohibits the introduction of any extrinsic evidence to vary or contradict the terms of an integrated written instrument. It is based upon the premise that the written instrument *is* the agreement of the parties. Its application involves a two part analysis: 1) was the writing intended to be an integration, i.e. a complete and final expression of the parties' agreement, precluding any evidence of collateral agreements, and 2) is the agreement susceptible of the meaning contended for by the party offering the evidence? . . .

In regard to the question of integration, the written agreement of the parties contained an expression of their intent that it supersede any and all other agreements between them and that it constitute their entire agreement. It specifically recited that "there are no oral or collateral agreements of any kind." Our Supreme Court held in *Masterson v Sine*, 68 Cal.2d 222, . . . that such a clause, while it certainly helps to resolve the issue, does not of itself establish an integration; the collateral agreement itself must be examined in order to determine whether the parties intended it to be a part of their bargain. *Masterson*, however, does not go so far as to permit proof of a collateral agreement which contradicts an express provision of the written agreement. The reason for this is clear: it cannot reasonably be presumed that the parties intended to integrate two directly contradictory terms in the same agreement. Under *Masterson* then, parol evidence can be admitted only "'to prove the existence of a separate oral agreement as to any matter on which the document is silent and which is not inconsistent with its terms. . .'"

The contract provides that either party can give written notice of termination *for any reason*. Thus there is no room for a separate collateral agreement regarding reasons for termination; the precise subject is already covered in the writing.

. . . We find that the alleged oral agreement is completely inconsistent with the language of the written contract. Thus the proffered parol understanding as to grounds for termination would be inadmissible to vary the contractual terms even if the contract were *not* an integration.

We now move on to the second part of our analysis: whether the offered evidence is nonetheless admissible to explain the meaning of the contractual language.

We do not find that the language of the contract lends itself to the proposed meaning. The term "any reason" is plainly all-inclusive, encompassing all reasons "*of what-*

ever kind," good, bad, or indifferent. (quoting Webster's Dictionary definition of "any"). Adding the modifier "good" has a delimiting effect which changes the meaning entirely. As written the contract is one which is terminable at will; the interpretation sought by the Gerlunds is that the contract is terminable only for good cause. The two are totally inconsistent. The trial court admitted the evidence on the ground that "both parties have testified as to what they interpreted the contract to mean." Testimony of intention which is contrary to a contract's express terms, however, does not give meaning to the contract: rather it seeks to substitute a different meaning. It follows . . . that such evidence must be excluded.

[Judgment reversed]

QUESTIONS

1. What does the court mean when it speaks of the contract as being an "integration"?
2. How would the *Gerlund* case have been decided if Paragraph 13, stating that it was the complete contract, had not been included?
3. Could the parol evidence in the *Gerlund* case have been admitted to explain the meaning of the terms used in the written contract?

(a) REASON FOR THE PAROL EVIDENCE RULE. The parol evidence rule is based on the theory that either there never was an oral agreement, or if there was, the parties purposely abandoned it when they executed their written contract. The social objective of the parol evidence rule is to give stability to contracts and to prevent the fraudulent assertion of oral terms that never actually existed. Some courts apply the parol evidence rule strictly.

To illustrate the parol evidence rule, assume that L, the landlord who is the owner of several new stores in the same vicinity, discusses leasing one of them to T (tenant). L agrees to give to T the exclusive right to sell soft drinks. L agrees to stipulate in the leases with the tenants of other stores that they cannot do so. L and T then execute a detailed written lease for the store. The lease with T makes no provision with respect to an exclusive right of T to sell soft drinks. Thereafter L leases the other stores to A, B, and C, without restricting them as to the sale of soft drinks. They begin to sell soft drinks, causing T to lose money. T sues L, claiming that the latter has broken the contract by which T was to have the exclusive right to sell soft drinks. L defends on the ground that there was no prior oral agreement

to that effect. Will the court permit T to prove that there was such an oral agreement?

On the facts as stated, if nothing more is shown, the court will not permit such parol evidence to be presented. The operation of this principle can be understood more easily if the actual courtroom procedure is followed. When T sues L, the first step will be to prove that there is a lease between them. Accordingly, T will offer in evidence the written lease between T and L. T will then take the witness stand and begin to testify about an oral agreement giving an exclusive right. At this point, L's attorney will object to the admission of the oral testimony by T because it would modify the terms of the written lease. The court will then examine the lease to see if it appears to be complete. If the court decides that it is, the court will refuse to allow T to offer evidence of an oral agreement. The only evidence before the court then will be the written lease. T will lose because nothing is in the written lease about an exclusive right to sell soft drinks.

If a written contract appears to be complete, the parol evidence rule prohibits its alteration not only by oral testimony but also by proof of other writings or memorandums made before or at the time the written contract was executed. An exception is made when the written contract refers to and identifies other writings or memorandums and states that they are to be regarded as part of the written contract. In such a case it is said that the other writings are integrated or incorporated by reference.

(b) CONFLICT BETWEEN ORAL AND WRITTEN CONTRACTS. Initially, when there is a conflict between the prior oral contract and the later written contract, the variation is to be regarded as (1) a mistake, which can be corrected by reformation, or (2) an additional term in the written contract, which is not binding because it was not part of the agreement.

Conflicts between written contracts and spoken words frequently arise when an agent or employee gives an explanation that is not what the written contract says.

7.   Liberalization of Parol Evidence Rule

The strictness of the parol evidence rule has been relaxed in a number of jurisdictions. A trend is beginning to appear that permits parol evidence as to the intention of the parties when the claimed intention is plausible from the face of the contract, even though there is no ambiguity.

There is likewise authority that parol evidence is admissible as to matters occurring before the execution of the contract, in order to give a better understanding of what the parties meant by their written contract.[17]

The liberalization approach is not followed by all courts, and some apply the **four corners rule.** Under this rule the court must look for the contract within the four corners of the

writing. The court may not look beyond the paper, in the absence of an exception to the parol evidence rule.

8.   When the Parol Evidence Rule Does Not Apply

The parol evidence rule may not apply in certain cases. The most common of these are discussed in the following paragraphs.

(a) INCOMPLETE CONTRACT. The parol evidence rule necessarily requires that the written contract sum up or integrate the entire contract. If the written contract is on its face or is admittedly not a complete summation, the parties naturally did not intend to abandon the points on which they agreed but that were not noted in the contract; and parol evidence is admissible to show the actual agreement of the parties.[18]

A contract may appear on its face to be complete and yet not include everything the parties agreed on. It must be remembered that there is no official standard by which to determine when a contract is complete. All that the court can do is to consider whether all essential terms of the contract are present. That is, the court can determine whether the contract is sufficiently definite to be enforceable and whether it contains all provisions that would ordinarily be included in a contract of that nature.

The fact that a contract is silent as to a particular matter does not mean that it is incomplete, for the law may attach a particular legal result (called *implying a term*) when the contract is silent. In such a case, parol evidence that is inconsistent with the term that would be implied cannot be shown. For example, when the contract is silent as to the time of payment, the obligation of making payment concurrently with performance by the other party is implied, and parol evidence is not admissible to show that there was an oral agreement to make a payment at a different time.

(b) AMBIGUITY. If a written contract may have two different meanings, parol evidence

---

[17]   This is also the view followed by UCC § 2-202 (a), which permits terms in a contract for the sale of goods to be "explained or supplemented by a course of dealing or usage of trade . . . or by course of performance." Such evidence is admissible not because there is an ambiguity, but "in order that the true understanding of the parties as to the agreement may be reached." Official Code Comment to § 2-202.

It has also been held that UCC § 1-205 permits proof of trade usage and course of performance with respect to non-Code contracts even though there is no ambiguity. Chase Manhattan Bank v First Marion Bank (CA5 Fla) 437 F2d 1040 (1971).

[18]   Marani v Jackson, 183 Cal App 3d 695, 228 Cal Rptr 518 (1986).

may generally be admitted to clarify the meaning. This is particularly true when the contract contains contradictory measurements or descriptions, or when the contract uses symbols or abbreviations that have no general meaning known to the court.

Parol evidence may also be admitted to show that a word used in a contract has a special trade meaning or a meaning in the particular locality that differs from the common meaning of that word.

The fact that the parties disagree as to the meaning of the contract does not mean that it is ambiguous.

(c) FRAUD, ACCIDENT, OR MISTAKE. A contract apparently complete on its face may have omitted a provision that should have been included. Parol evidence may be admit-

ted to show that a provision was omitted as the result of fraud, accident, or mistake, and to further show what that provision stated.

When one party claims to have been fraudulently induced by the other to enter into the contract, the parol evidence rule does not bar proof that there was fraud. For example, the parol evidence rule does not bar proof that the seller of land negligently misrepresented that the land was zoned to permit use as an industrial park.[19]

In the *Touche Ross* case the claim was made that both the terms of the contract and the parol evidence rule barred proof that the underlying transaction had been induced by fraud.

[19]   Formento v Encanto Business Park (App) 154 Ariz 495, 744 P2d 22 (1987).

TOUCHE ROSS LIMITED v FILIPEK
(Hawaii App) 778 P2d 721 (1989)

Holdings and Thriftway borrowed money from the Northland Bank. Filipek and others guaranteed that the loans would be paid back. The bank stopped doing business because of financial problems. Touche Ross was appointed to liquidate the assets of the bank. The loan to Holdings and Thriftway was not repaid when due. Touche Ross sued Filipek and the other guarantors on their obligation to repay the loan. They raised the defense that they were not bound by their guarantees because they and the borrowers had been induced to enter into the transactions because of the fraudulent statements and promises of the bank. Touche Ross claimed that the parol evidence rule barred any evidence that the parties had been induced by fraud. Judgment was entered in favor of Touche Ross. Filipek and the others appealed.

TANAKA, J. . . . The Loan Agreement included an integration clause which read as follows:

This Agreement constitutes the entire agreement between the parties hereto relating to the subject matter hereof and supersedes all prior and contemporaneous agreements, understandings, negotiations and discussions, whether oral or written, of the parties and there are no warranties, representations or other agreements among the parties in connection with the subject matter hereof except as specifically set forth herein.

. . . Appellants assert that since the Bank fraudulently induced Holdings and Thriftway to execute the First and Second Notes, those Notes are invalid and voidable and, consequently, their personal guarantees of those Notes are also invalid and unenforceable. . . .

Touche Ross argues, however, that since the loan documents are unambiguous in their terms and contain integration clauses, the parol evidence rule precludes all prior or contemporaneous representations and agreements from varying the terms therein. We disagree.

The general rule is that the parol evidence rule is inapplicable "where the issue is whether the contract was procured by fraud." 37 Am.Jur.2d *Fraud and Deceit* § 451 at 620 (1968) (footnote omitted). . . . Professor Sweet explains the inapplicability of the parol evidence rule where fraud is involved as follows:

> It is clear that a contract can be attacked if there are formation defects of a serious nature. If consent is not freely given, then no contract is formed, and consent is not freely given if it is induced by fraud. It follows that evidence establishing such a defect cannot be excluded by the parol evidence rule. The rule presupposes a contract, since it is grounded on the intention of the parties that the writing is to contain their complete agreement.

Sweet, *Promissory Fraud and the Parol Evidence Rule*, 49 Calif.L.Rev. 877, 887 (1961) . . .

The courts are divided, however, where promissory fraud is involved. Some courts preclude the introduction of parol or extrinsic evidence when the alleged fraud involves a promise which varies the terms of an integrated written instrument. . . . But the majority rule admits the parol or extrinsic evidence even though it conflicts with the terms of the integrated written instrument. . . .

We choose to follow the majority rule because as an Oregon appellate court stated:

> Oral promises made without the promisor's intention that they will be performed could be an effective means of deception if evidence of those fraudulent promises were never admissible merely because they were at variance with a subsequent written agreement.

[Judgment reversed and action remanded to permit proof of alleged fraud]

QUESTIONS

1. What is the purpose of an integration clause in a contract?
2. What effect does the decision have on the integration clause?
3. How can a party to a contract be protected from a fraudulent claim that the contract was induced by fraud?

(d) EXISTENCE OF CONTRACT. Parol evidence is admissible to identify the writing of the parties. When several documents are executed as part of one transaction, parol evidence is admissible to show the relationship of the documents as forming one transaction.

When it is claimed that there is in fact no contract because of a mutual mistake, parol evidence is admissible to show the existence of such a mistake.

The parol evidence rule does not bar proof that the written contract is in fact not a binding agreement. Thus, it can be shown that there was no consideration for the contract, that the contract was void because it was illegal, or that the contract was voidable because of the incapacity of a party or because of fraud. Likewise, parol evidence may be used to show in a lawsuit between the original parties that a promissory note signed by the defendant was never to be enforced, and that it was merely a dummy note intended to create a paper loss for tax purposes.[20]

(e) MODIFICATION OF CONTRACT. The parol evidence rule prohibits only the contradiction of a complete written contract. It does not prohibit proof that the contract was thereafter modified or terminated.

Written contracts commonly declare that they can be modified only by a writing. In the case of construction contracts, there is ordinar-ily a statement that no payment will be made for extra work unless there is a written order from the owner or architect calling for such extra work. If the parties proceed in disregard of such a clause requiring a writing, it may be shown by parol evidence that they have done so, and the contract will be modified accordingly.

(f) ILLEGALITY. The parol evidence rule does not bar proof of conduct that violates the law. In the *Honeywell* case evidence of precontract statements was offered to show that the defendant had violated the state Deceptive Trade Practices Act.

---

[20]   Bill Shannon, Inc. v San Clemente (Tex App) 724 SW2d 941 (1987).

HONEYWELL, INC. v IMPERIAL CONDOMINIUM ASS'N
(Tex App) 716 SW2d 75 (1986)

Honeywell made a contract with the Imperial Condominium Association to install and service a heating and cooling system. The system did not function properly, and Imperial Condominium sued Honeywell for treble damages under the Texas Deceptive Trade Practices Act (DTPA). Imperial offered in evidence the promotional literature of Honeywell to show that false statements had been made to induce the making of the contract and that this constituted deceptive trade practices. The trial court admitted this evidence, and the jury returned a verdict in favor of Imperial. From the judgment against it, Honeywell appealed.

HOWELL, J. . . . I. *Extrinsic Evidence of Misrepresentation*

Honeywell first complains that the trial court violated the parol evidence rule by admitting extrinsic evidence of Honeywell's pre-contractual representations. Over Honeywell's objection, the court allowed the consumer to introduce Honeywell's promotional literature for the limited purpose of proving that Honeywell's representations concerning the quality and benefits of its services did not accurately depict those actually received. We find no merit in Honeywell's complaint.

The [Texas] supreme court recently decided that the parol evidence rule does not prevent a consumer from introducing statements made before the formation of a contract to show that the provider of goods or services engaged in a deceptive trade practice. . . . This holding was based upon the differences between the nature of an action for a breach of contract and that of an action for a deceptive trade practice.

The Supreme Court reasoned that the justifications for the parol evidence rule do not apply in deceptive trade practices cases where the consumer sues on the basis of pre-contractual representations because the consumer's recovery is not dependent upon the alteration or contradiction of a contract but rather upon conduct which was itself actionable under the DTPA without regard to the obligations imposed on the parties by the contract.

In other words, the supreme court recognized that contractual liability and liability under the DTPA derive from two different sources. Contractual liability turns solely on the agreement of the parties whereas liability under the DTPA springs from the statute. As a general proposition, liability under the DTPA is neither increased nor diminished by the presence of a formal written contract covering the identical subject matter.

Unlike contractual liability, resulting from the voluntary agreement of the parties, liability for false, misleading and deceptive acts is provided by the legislature for the breach of a duty imposed by it. These duties cannot be altered by the agreement of the parties. To apply the parol evidence rule in DTPA cases would frustrate the legislature's purpose in passing the statute without furthering the objectives of the parol evidence rule. As the [Texas] supreme court succinctly announced . . . "traditional contractual notions do not apply" when the consumer seeks recovery for the breach of duty imposed by the DTPA. . . . We hold that trial court did not err when it allowed the consumer to introduce Honeywell's promotional literature for the purpose of proving that Honeywell violated the DTPA.

II. *Misrepresentation Under the DTPA*

Honeywell next contends that as a matter of law the consumer could not recover under the DTPA because a mere breach of contract, without more, is not a false, misleading or deceptive act. Honeywell argues that this case involves a mere breach of contract because all of the representations in its promotional literature were incorporated into the terms of the contract and, therefore, the consumer can show no failure to comply with a pre-contractual representation that was not also a breach of contract. This proposition is untenable in light of the supreme court's decision in *Smith v Baldwin*, 611 S.W.2d at 615–16.

The consumer there counterclaimed against his builder alleging that the builder failed to build a home which, as promised both in the contract and in discussions with the consumer, would qualify for financing by the Veteran's Administration. The consumer sought to recover on the grounds that the builder both breached the construction contract and misrepresented his services in violation of section 17.46 (b)(7) of the DTPA. . . . The supreme court reversed and . . . held that the consumer was entitled to his DTPA remedies. The court ruled that "representing that goods or services are of a particular standard, quality or grade . . . if they are of another" applies to goods and services to be provided in the future, and concluded that the builder committed a deceptive act by representing that the house when built would qualify for V.A. financing.

. . . Honeywell by its literature and by the formal contract represented that it would provide proper water treatment to extend equipment life. These representations later proved to be false. . . . We reject Honeywell's argument that intentional, reckless or negligent conduct must be proved in order to invoke the act. . . .

[Judgment affirmed]

QUESTIONS

1. Does the parol evidence rule bar proof of statements that constitute a violation of a consumer protection statute? Explain.
2. Were the precontract statements oral or written?
3. What significance is there to the fact that precontract statements are or are not included in the written contract?

SUMMARY

An oral agreement can be a contract unless it is the intention of the parties that they should not be bound by the agreement unless a writing is executed by them. If the parties intend to be bound by the oral agreement, it is a contract. As an exception to this statement, certain contracts must be evidenced by a writing, or else they cannot be enforced. The statutes that declare this exception are called statutes of frauds. Statutes of frauds commonly require that a contract be evidenced by writing in the case of (a) an agreement that cannot be performed within one year after the contract is made, (b) an agreement to sell or a sale of any interest in real property, (c) a promise to answer for the debt or default of another, (d) a promise by the executor or administrator of a decedent's estate to pay a claim against the estate from personal funds, (e) a promise made in consideration of marriage, and (f) a contract for the sale of goods for a purchase price of $500 or more. Local statutes may expand the above list to include other types of contracts, such as a contract between a landowner and a real estate agent employed to sell the land.

In order to evidence a contract so as to satisfy a statute of frauds, there must be a writing of all material terms. This must be signed by the defendant against whom suit is brought for enforcement of the contract or damages for its breach. The signing may be made by printing, stamping, typewriting, or any other means that is intended to identify the particular party. Two or more writings can be combined to form a writing sufficient to satisfy the statute of frauds, provided there is an express internal reference in the writings that ties them together.

If the applicable statute of frauds is not satisfied, the oral contract cannot be enforced. In order to avoid unjust enrichment, a plaintiff barred from enforcing an oral contract may recover from the other contracting party the reasonable value of the benefits conferred by the plaintiff upon the defendant. In order to prevent the statute of frauds from being used to defraud a party to an oral contract, the courts by decision have made certain exceptions to the statute of frauds.

When there is a written contract, the question arises as to whether that writing is the exclusive statement of the agreement of the parties. If the writing is the complete and final statement of the contract, parol evidence as to matters agreed to before or at the time the writing was signed is not admissible to contradict the writing. This is called the parol evidence rule. Some courts have liberalized the rule so that parol evidence is admitted when it will aid in interpreting the writing. In any case, the parol evidence rule does not bar parol evidence when (a) the writing is incomplete; (b) the writing is ambiguous; (c) the writing is not a true statement of the agreement of the parties because of fraud, accident, or mistake; or (d) the existence, modification, or illegality of a contract is in controversy. The fact that the parties disagree as to the meaning of a contract or that a court decision is required to settle the point does not make the writing ambiguous. The exception as to mistake permits proof that there is in fact no contract because there is a mutual mistake or that the writing that has been executed does not correctly set forth the terms of the contract.

QUESTIONS AND CASE PROBLEMS

1. What social forces are affected by the following rule of law? "Parol evidence is not admissible for the purpose of modifying a written contract when that evidence relates to an agreement made before or at the time that the written contract was executed."

2. What is the primary purpose exception to the statute of frauds?

3. In a telephone conversation Roderick agreed to buy Dexter's house. All the details of the transaction were agreed to in the conversation. The next day Dexter wrote Roderick a letter stating,

"This confirms the agreement we made last night that I should sell you my home." Later, Dexter refused to go through with the transaction. Roderick sued Dexter. Will Roderick recover?

4. Kelly made a written contract to sell certain land to Brown. Kelly gave Brown a deed to the land. Thereafter, Kelly sued Brown to get back a 20-foot strip of land. Kelly claimed that before making the written contract it was agreed that Kelly would sell all of his land to Brown in order to make it easier for Brown to get a building permit, but that after that was done, the 20-foot strip would be reconveyed to Kelly. Was Kelly entitled to the 20-foot strip? What ethical values are involved? [Brown v Kelly (Fla App) 545 So 2d 518]

5. Martin made an oral contract with Cresheim Garage to work as its manager for two years. Cresheim wrote Martin a letter stating that the oral contract had been made and setting forth all its terms. Cresheim later refused to recognize the contract. Martin sued Cresheim for breach of the contract and offered Cresheim's letter in evidence as proof of the contract. Cresheim claimed that the oral contract was not binding because the contract was not in writing and the letter referring to the contract was not a contract but only a letter. Was the contract binding?

6. Lawrence loaned money to Moore. Moore died without repaying the loan. Lawrence claimed that when he mentioned the matter to Moore's widow, she promised to pay the debt. She did not do so, and Lawrence sued her on her promise. Does she have any defense? [Moore v Lawrence, 252 Ark 759, 480 SW2d 941]

7. Investors Premium Corporation purchased computer equipment from Burroughs Corporation. It made the purchase because of various statements made by the Burroughs sales representative. A written contract was executed for the purchase of the system. The contract stated that there were no warranties that were not stated in the contract and that the written contract was the complete statement of the obligation of Burroughs. The system did not work properly, and Investors claimed that Burroughs was liable because the system did not perform as the salesman had warranted. Is Burroughs liable for breach of the agent's warranty? [Investors Premium Corp. v Burroughs Corp. (DC SC) 389 F Supp 39]

8. Boeing Airplane Co. contracted with Pittsburgh-Des Moines Steel Co. for the latter to con-

struct a supersonic wind tunnel. R.H. Freitag Mfg. Co. sold materials to York-Gillespie Co., which subcontracted to do part of the work. In order to persuade Freitag to keep supplying materials on credit, Boeing and the principal contractor both assured Freitag that he would be paid. When Freitag was not paid by the subcontractor, Freitag sued Boeing and the contractor. They defended on the ground that the assurances given Freitag were not written. Decide. What ethical values are involved? [R.H. Freitag Mfg. Co. v Boeing Airplane Co. 55 Wash 2d 334, 347 P2d 1074]

9. An accounting firm sold out its business to a new firm. The sales contract stated that it was the intention of the parties that the new firm should provide service for clients of the old firm. The new firm agreed to pay the old firm 15 percent of the gross billings for assignments performed by the new firm for a period of 84 months. Later a dispute arose as to whether the 15 percent of gross billings was limited to the billings of those who were originally clients of the old firm or whether it also included billings of new clients of the new firm. In a lawsuit over this point, parol evidence was offered to show what the contract covered. Was this evidence admissible? [Rullman v LaFrance, Walker, Jackley & Saville, 206 Neb 180, 292 NW2d 19]

10. When will improvements made by a buyer of land bar the seller from claiming that the purchase contract was not binding because it was oral?

11. Roth made a contract to sell her house to Eric. They signed a written contract but left the purchase price blank because they had agreed that the selling price was to be reduced by the cost of certain necessary repairs that the buyer would be required to make. They later agreed on this amount, but the amount was never filled in on the written contract. Is the contract binding?

12. With respect to the applicability of the statute of frauds, compare (a) a promise made by an aunt to her niece to pay the niece's bill owed to a department store; (b) a promise made by the aunt to the department store to pay the amount the aunt owes the store for a television set the aunt purchased as a present for her niece; and (c) a promise made by the aunt to the department store that she would pay her niece's bill if the niece did not do so.

13. Louise Pulsifer owned a farm. She desired to sell the farm and ran an ad in the local newspa-

per. Russell Gillespie agreed to purchase the farm. Louise then wrote him a letter stating that she would not sell the farm. He sued her in order to enforce the contract. Louise raised the defense of the statute of frauds. The letter signed by her did not contain any of the terms of the sale. Gillespie, however, claimed that the newspaper ad could be combined with her letter to satisfy the statute of frauds. Was he correct? [Gillespie v Pulsifer (Mo App) 655 SW2d 123]

14. McLarty claimed that he and Wright made an oral contract to start a business under the name of DeKalb Textile Mill, Inc., to incorporate the business, and to divide the stock equally. The alleged contract was not performed. McLarty sued Wright for breach of contract. Wright raised the defense of the statute of frauds, asserting that it was not specified that the contract should be performed within one year of making. Was this defense valid? [McLarty v Wright (Ala Civ App) 321 So 2d 687]

15. In February or March, Corning Glass Works orally agreed to retain Hanan as management consultant from May 1 of that year to April 30 of the next year for a total fee of $25,000. Was this agreement binding? Is this decision ethical? [Hanan v Corning Glass Works, 63 Misc 2d 863, 314 NYS2d 804]

15

INTERPRETATION OF CONTRACTS

When it has been decided that there is a contract between the parties, the next step is to determine the terms of that contract. Should a contract be interpreted to mean what one of the parties intended it to mean, or should it mean what a reasonable person would believe was intended? Should the contract be held to mean only what it expressly says, or can additional terms be implied or read into the contract? What if additional terms are needed to protect one of the parties to the contract from hardship or oppression?

If the parties disagree as to the terms, society has the task of determining just what the contract means. Society must also decide if the contract should be enforced according to its terms. The rules of law that have evolved in finding answers to these questions are the rules governing the interpretation of contracts.

A. RULES OF CONSTRUCTION AND INTERPRETATION

An understanding of the rules discussed in the following paragraphs will help contracting parties avoid many of the difficulties that may arise when a contract is not drafted carefully.

1.   Intention of the Parties

When persons enter into an agreement, it is to be presumed that they intend that their agreement should have some effect. A court will strive to determine what that intent was and give effect to it.[1] A contract is therefore to be enforced according to its terms. A court cannot remake or rewrite the contract of the parties under the pretense of interpreting it. If there is a dispute as to the meaning of a contract, the court examines the contract to determine what the parties intended. It will then give effect to what the parties intended, as long as it is lawful.

No particular form of words is required, and any words manifesting the intent of the parties are sufficient. In the absence of proof that a word has a peculiar meaning or that it was employed by the parties with a particular meaning, a common word is given its ordinary meaning.

A word will not be given its literal meaning when it is clear that the parties did not intend such a meaning. For example, *and* may be substituted for *or*, *may* for *shall*, and *void* for *voidable*, and vice versa, when it is clear that the parties so intended.

(a) OBJECTIVE INTENT. When it is stated that the law seeks to enforce the intent of the parties, this means the intent that is outwardly manifested. That is, what would a reasonable third person believe the parties intended? It is this **objective intent** that will be enforced. A party cannot claim that something else was secretly intended. Such secret or **subjective intent** cannot be proven.

The use of the objective intent standard means that an unambiguous contract must be interpreted as written.[2] It cannot be given a different meaning that one party thinks it has. In the *Sterling Merchandise* case the court was faced with the question of whether an insurance policy meant just what it said.

---

[1]   Hunt v Shamblin (W Va) 371 SE2d 591 (1988).

[2]   Edgewater Health Care, Inc. v Health Systems Management, Inc. (Mo App) 752 SW2d 860 (1988).

STERLING MERCHANDISE CO. v HARTFORD INS. CO.
30 Ohio App 3d 131, 506 NE2d 1192 (1986)

Sterling Merchandise Company obtained policies of insurance from the Hartford Insurance Company and from Underwriters at Lloyd's of London to protect the contents of the safe in its jewelry store from burglary. The policy stated that there was coverage of theft from the safe provided that there were visible marks on the safe of a forcible entry. The Sterling safe was robbed. The robber set off the electronic alarm system, but there were no visible marks of forcible entry. The insurer refused to pay for the loss. Sterling claimed that it reasonably expected that the contents of the safe would be covered whenever there was an opening of the safe by a robber. Sterling sued the insurers. From a decision in favor of Sterling, the insurers appealed.

GEORGE, P.J. . . . The insurance contracts issued to Sterling by Underwriters define a "safe burglary" as follows:

'SAFE BURGLARY' means the felonious abstraction of the insured property from within a safe or vault in the premises (or after removal therefrom by burglars) by any person or persons making felonious entry into such safe and also into the vault, if any, containing such safe, when all doors of such safe and vault are duly closed and locked by at least one combination, key or timelock thereof; provided that such entry shall be made by actual force or violence of which there shall be visible marks made by tools, explosives, electricity, gas or chemicals, upon the exterior of (1) all of said doors of such safe and vault, if any, containing such safe if entry is made through such doors, or (2) the top, bottom, or walls of such safe and of the vault through which entry is made, if not made through such doors.

. . . The trial court's decision is based entirely on the doctrine of reasonable expectations. . . .

The doctrine of reasonable expectations is a theory of recovery employed in contract actions. It has been articulated in the following passage contained in the Restatement of the Law 2d, Contracts (Tent. Drafts Nos. 1–7 Rev. 1973), Section 237 ("Standardized Agreements"), Comment *f*, at 540–541:

> *Terms excluded.* . . . Although customers typically adhere to standardized agreements and are bound by them without even appearing to know the standard terms in detail, they are not bound to unknown terms which are beyond the range of reasonable expectation. A debtor who delivers a check to his creditor with the amount blank does not authorize the insertion of an infinite figure. Similarly, a party who adheres to the other party's standard terms does not assent to a term if the other party has reason to believe that the adhering party would not have accepted the agreement if he had known that the agreement contained the particular term. Such a belief or assumption may be shown by the prior negotiations or inferred from the circumstances. Reason to believe may be inferred from the fact that the term is bizarre or oppressive, from the fact that it eviscerates the nonstandard terms explicitly agreed to, or from the fact that it eliminates the dominant purpose of the transaction. The inference is reinforced if the adhering party never had an opportunity to read the term, or if it is illegible or otherwise hidden from view. This rule is closely related to the policy against unconscionable terms and the rule of interpretation against the draftsman. . . .

This doctrine is grounded on several beliefs. First, that most people never read the insurance contracts they sign, but merely adhere to them. Second, that insurers write the terms of the contracts and usually offer the consumer only a standard preprinted form which the latter is ill-equipped to understand. Third, that the insured lacks any real bargaining power in such a situation because the insurer assumes a take-it-or-leave-it attitude. Fourth, that to enforce the terms of the contract in favor of the insurer is somehow unconscionable. . . .

Although Ohio has adopted rules of construction of insurance contracts which favor the insured, it has not implicitly adopted the theory of recovery known as the reasonable expectations doctrine. That doctrine is based on principles which go far beyond the liberal rules of construction employed by Ohio courts. . . .

The reasonable expectation doctrine requires a court to rewrite an insurance contract which does not meet popular expectations. Such rewriting is done regardless of the bargain entered into by the parties to the contract. Such judicial activism has not been adopted in Ohio by its courts and the courts' use of liberal rules of construction. Further, this court declines to do so. . . .

The facts of this case, as evidenced by the stipulations of the parties, do not indicate any misrepresentation, overreaching, or other conduct on behalf of the insurer which would justify abrogating the parties' agreement. Nor was there any evidence that Sterling was beguiled into believing it had more protection than it actually did.

Sterling tacitly refused to read its policies. The provision defining "safe burglary" was written in the same style and size type as the rest of the policy provisions. The definition was not hidden away in fine print in an obscure place, but was plainly set out. The definition was not so complex or esoteric that a competent businessman could not understand it. . . .

The record in the instant case also reveals that there was comprehensive crime coverage available to Sterling, but at an additional cost. This additional coverage was noted in part seven of Sterling's policy. . . .

The trial court did not find the "safe burglary" definition to be ambiguous. Neither does this court. Provisions requiring visible marks of entry by actual force or violence before coverage is allowed are not ambiguous. Because the definition is not ambiguous, it must be given its plain and ordinary meaning. . . .

[Judgment reversed]

QUESTIONS

1. Was the "safe burglary" paragraph of the policy ambiguous?
2. Why does the court mention the fact that Sterling could have obtained comprehensive crime coverage by paying an additional amount?
3. What effect would the adoption of the Restatement rule have on the business world?

Society balances the risks involved in enforcing a contract that does not accurately state the intent of the parties with the danger of giving effect to a subjective intent that is falsely asserted. The enforcing of the objectively determined intent appears to society to hold the smaller risk of harm and injury. Giving effect to a subjective intent would open the door to fraudulent claims that a contract was secretly intended to mean something else. Thus, the objectively shown intent controls, and the secret or subjective intent is ignored.[3]

(b) MEANING OF WORDS. Ordinary words are to be interpreted according to their ordinary meaning.

In the *Bartlett* case, property owners claimed to be covered by insurance when a breaking dam caused damage to the property. The insurance company claimed there was no liability for "flood damage."

---

[3] American States Ins. Co. v Breesnee, 49 Wash App 642, 745 P2d 518 (1987).

BARTLETT v CONTINENTAL DIVIDE INS. CO.
(Colo App) 697 P2d 412 (1984)

Perry Bartlett and his wife owned and operated a resort. They obtained a policy of insurance from the Continental Divide Insurance Company protecting the resort from damage. A nearby dam broke, and water from the dam and the debris carried by the water damaged the resort. The Bartletts claimed the insurance company was liable for the loss. It denied liability on the ground that the policy expressly excluded flood damage. The Bartletts claimed that what had happened was not a flood and brought suit against the insurance company. The court decided in favor of the insurance company, and the Bartletts appealed.

STERNBERG, J. . . . Continental denied coverage because the policy contained an exclusion for losses "caused by, resulting from, contributed to, or aggravated by . . . flood, surface water [or] . . . overflow of streams or other bodies of water. . . .

The plaintiffs filed this action for declaratory relief and damages. . . . The court found that the insurance policy expressly excluded damage due to flood, the term "flood" was not vague or ambiguous in this case, and the failure of Lawn Lake Dam did in fact cause a flood resulting in damage to plaintiff's property. . . .

The term "flood" is not defined within the policy, and it therefore retains its ordinary, customary meaning. . . . Ordinarily, "flood" means "a body of water (including moving water) . . . overflowing or inundating land not usually covered," . . . and no distinction is made between natural and artificial causes. . . .

Notwithstanding the ordinary meaning of "flood," plaintiffs urge us to distinguish between natural and artificial causes when reading the terms of the insurance policy. However, there is no such distinction in the contract, and the event in question falls well within the ordinary use of the term; therefore, to make such distinction would be to rewrite terms of the policy, and that is beyond our power. Although the use of the term may in some cases result in ambiguity, we agree with the trial court's conclusion that there was no ambiguity here.

. . . The only event alleged as the cause of the loss was the flood caused by the failure of the dam; and loss by flood was specifically excluded from coverage.

[Judgment affirmed]

QUESTIONS

1. Why wasn't the word *flood* defined in the insurance policy?
2. What effect does the decision have on the social force of protecting from hardship?
3. How would it have affected the decision of the court if the dam had failed because of sabotage by discontented workers?

If technical or trade terms are used in a contract, they are to be interpreted according to the area of technical knowledge or trade from which the terms are taken. If there is a common meaning to a term, that meaning will be followed, even though the dictionary may give a different meaning.

The prior relationships of the parties may give meaning to the words used by the parties.[4]

(c) INCORPORATION BY REFERENCE. The contract may not cover all the terms agreed upon. The missing terms may be found in another document. Frequently the parties executing the contract will state that it em-

braces or incorporates the other document. Thus, a contract for storage will simply state that a storage contract is entered into and that the contract applies to the goods that are listed in the schedule that is attached to and made part of the contract. Likewise, a contract for the construction of a building will simply state that the building is to be constructed according to the plans and specifications "which are incorporated herein and made part of this contract." When there is such an **incorporation by reference**, the contract consists of both the original or skeleton document and the detailed statement that is incorporated therein.

2. Whole Contract

The provisions of a contract must be con-

---

[4] See Section 6 of this chapter.

strued as a whole.[5] This rule is followed even when the contract is partly written and partly oral. Every word of a contract is to be given effect if reasonably possible.

(a) DIVISIBLE CONTRACT. A contract may contain a number of provisions or performances to be rendered. If so, the question arises as to whether the parties intended merely a group of separate contracts (a *divisible contract*). Possibly they intended a package deal so that complete performance of every provision of the contract was essential.

A significant indication that the parties intended a divisible contract is the fact that the consideration given by one party can be apportioned among the performances to be rendered by the other, or a separate consideration is stated for each performance.[6] For example, when an insurer provides coverage for a house and garage, and the premium charged is the sum of one amount specified for insuring the house and another amount charged for insuring the garage, it will be held that the insurance contract is divisible into two contracts. One contract covers the house, and the other covers the garage.

(b) WHAT CONSTITUTES THE WHOLE CONTRACT. The question may arise as to whether separate papers or particular parts of a paper constitute part of the whole contract.

Terms in a printed letterhead or billhead or on the reverse side of the printed contract form are not part of a contract written thereon unless a reasonable person would regard such terms as part of the contract. An employer's manual that is shown to the job applicant after the signing of an employment contract is not part of that contract. Similarly, provisions in a manufacturer's instruction manual, or in invoices, or on labels that are not seen or called to the attention of a buyer until after a contract of sale has been made are not part of the contract. They do not bind the buyer.

3. Conditions

When the occurrence or nonoccurrence of an event affects the existence of a contract or the obligation of a party to a contract, the event is called a **condition**.

Courts do not favor conditions, because they cause a loss of rights. Therefore, courts will interpret a contract provision as not creating a condition when that interpretation is reasonably possible.[7]

(a) CONDITION PRECEDENT. An obligation-triggering event may be described as a **condition precedent.** It precedes the existence of the obligation to perform or the existence of any contract.

In a fire insurance policy there is no obligation on the insurer to make any payment until there is a fire loss. The occurrence of such a loss is thus a condition precedent to the insurer's duty to pay under the policy. Likewise, when an employee is required to give notice to the employer in order to obtain a particular benefit, the giving of notice is a condition precedent to the employer's duty to provide the benefit.

(b) CONDITION SUBSEQUENT. The parties may specify that the contract shall terminate when a particular event occurs or does not occur. Such a provision is a **condition subsequent**. If government approval is required, the parties may specify that the contract shall not bind them if the government approval cannot be obtained.

A contract for the purchase of land may contain a condition subsequent that cancels the contract if the buyer is not able to obtain a zoning permit to use a building for a particular purpose.

In the *K & K Pharmacy* case the presence of a condition affected the existence of the contract.

---

[5]   Transamerica Insurance Corp. v Buckley, 169 Mich App 540, 426 NW2d 696 (1988).

[6]   Parker's Estate, 171 Ill App 3d 538, 121 Ill Dec 842, 525 NE2d 1149 (1988).

[7]   Vergote v K Mart Corp. 158 Mich App 96, 404 NW2d 711 (1987).

K & K PHARMACY, INC. v BARTA

222 Neb 215, 382 NW2d 363 (1986)

> K & K ran a pharmacy in space rented from the Millard Shopping Center. K & K made a contract with Barta to sell the pharmacy to him. Barta did not go through with the purchase. K & K sued him for breach of contract. He raised the defense that there was no contract because a condition in the agreement of the parties had not been satisfied. The lower court entered judgment for Barta, and K & K appealed.

BOSLAUGH, J. . . . On June 8, 1983, the plaintiff, K & K Pharmacy, Inc., entered into a written contract with the defendant, James R. Barta, for the sale of the pharmacy to the defendant. The contract contained the following provision regarding a new lease of the premises to be obtained by the defendant:

> 13. *New Lease.* This Agreement shall be contingent upon Buyer's ability to obtain a new lease from Larsen Enterprises, Inc., for the premises presently occupied by Seller. In the event Buyer is unable to obtain a new lease satisfactory to Buyer, this Agreement shall be null and void.

The defendant owned a number of full-line pharmacies and employed a specific marketing strategy which he intended to use in the operation of the pharmacy to be purchased from the plaintiff. The defendant carried high-traffic grocery items, such as bread, milk, and coffee, and sold those items at a low price in order to generate volume traffic into the drugstore.

Early in the negotiations for the sale of the pharmacy, the defendant advised the agent of the seller that the defendant would require the right or privilege to sell food-stuffs in the pharmacy. However, prior to signing the contract, the defendant did not know that Millard Food Mart, a grocery store located in the same shopping center as plaintiff's pharmacy, had a lease giving it the exclusive right to sell grocery items in the shopping center.

The record also shows that after signing the purchase agreement, the defendant entered into negotiations with the owner of the shopping center and other interested parties for the purpose of agreeing upon a satisfactory lease. At the first meeting of the parties, the grocer, who had the exclusive right to sell grocery items, indicated that he also used high-traffic items such as milk and bread as loss leaders to attract traffic into his store, that the exclusive right to sell groceries was important to him, and that he was not willing to give up any of his rights under his lease. Although lease negotiations continued, the grocer never agreed to allow Barta to carry any food items.

The original agreement provided for the closing of the sale on or about June 24, 1983. On the 24th of June the parties added an addendum to the agreement providing that the defendant would take possession of the pharmacy beginning June 25 and oper-ate the pharmacy until the anticipated closing on Monday, June 27. The defendant did go into possession on the 25th and operated the business until June 30, at which time he ceased operations in the drugstore because he had not been able to obtain a satisfac-tory lease.

This action was commenced on January 26, 1984, to recover damages resulting from the defendant's alleged breach of the contract. . . .

The case turns on the meaning and effect of the "New Lease" provision in the contract. Generally, in negotiating a contract the parties may impose any condition precedent, a performance of which is essential before the parties become bound by the agreement. . . .The provision entitled "13. *New Lease*" was clearly a condition precedent to the existence of binding contractual obligations between the parties. The contract was *contingent* upon the defendant obtaining a new lease *satisfactory* to him. This court has held that "where a contract is executed but its effectiveness is dependent upon the fulfillment of an agreed condition before it can become a binding contract, such contract cannot be enforced unless the condition is performed." . . .

The party seeking to enforce a contract containing a condition precedent bears the burden of proof as to the occurrence of the condition, and if there is no evidence of the occurrence of the condition, the contract is not binding and cannot be enforced. In the present case the plaintiff had the burden to prove that the condition precedent contained in the contract had been met before the contract was enforceable. . . .

[Judgment affirmed]

QUESTIONS

1. Did the defendant break his contract?
2. What effect was the condition in this case intended to have?
3. Do you agree with the court's classification of that condition?

(c) CONCURRENT CONDITIONS. In most bilateral contracts the performances by the parties are **concurrent conditions.** That is, the duty of each party to perform is dependent on the other party's performing. Thus, neither is required to perform until the other performs or tenders performance. Frequently the contract will specify or indicate that one person must perform first. In such case, that performance is a condition precedent and the conditions are not concurrent. For example, in a contract to pay a painter $1,000 for painting a house, the painter must perform the painting work before the owner is required to perform the promise of paying for the work. Performance by the painter is thus a condition precedent to the owner's obligation to pay.

4.   Contradictory and Ambiguous Terms

One term in a contract may conflict with another term, or one term may have two different meanings. It is then necessary for the court to determine whether there is a contract and, if so, what the contract really means. When the terms of a contract are contradictory or conflict as to a significant matter, the existence of such conflict prevents there being any contract.

In some instances the conflict between the terms of a contract is eliminated by the introduction of parol evidence or by applying an appropriate rule of construction.

(a) NATURE OF WRITING. When a contract is partly printed or typewritten and partly written, and the written part conflicts with the printed or typewritten part, the written part prevails. When there is a conflict between a printed part and a typewritten part, the latter prevails. Consequently, when a clause typewritten on a printed form conflicts with what is stated by the print, the conflicting print is ignored, and the typewritten clause controls. When there is a conflict between an amount or quantity expressed both in words and figures, as on a check, the amount or quantity expressed in words prevails.

(b) AMBIGUITY. A contract is **ambiguous** when the intent of the parties is uncertain and the contract is capable of more than one reasonable interpretation. Disagreement as to the legal effect of the terms used by the parties does not make the contract ambiguous.[8] This is so because the court, by applying the law to their terms, can reach a conclusion as to the intent manifested by the contract. In contrast, if the intent would still be uncertain even after rules of law were applied, the contract is ambiguous.

Whether a contract is ambiguous cannot always be determined merely by looking at it. In some cases the written contract will look perfectly clear, and the ambiguity does not become apparent until the contract is applied to the facts or the property concerned.

The fact that a particular situation is not provided for by the contract does not make it ambiguous. For example, a summer camp contract is not ambiguous because it does not contain any provision relating to refunds upon cancellation.

The background from which the contract and the dispute arose may assist in determining the intention of the parties. Thus, when suit was brought in Minnesota on a Canadian policy of insurance, the question arose as to whether the dollar limit of the policy referred to Canadian or American dollars. The court concluded that Canadian dollars were intended. Both the insurer and the insured were Canadian corporations; the original policy, indorsements to the policy, and policy renewals were written in Canada; over the years, premiums had been paid in Canadian dollars; and a prior claim on the policy had been settled by the payment of an amount computed on the basis of Canadian dollars.[9]

(c) STRICT CONSTRUCTION AGAINST DRAFTING PARTY. An ambiguous contract is interpreted strictly against the party who drafted it.[10] Thus, printed forms of a contract, such as insurance policies, which are supplied by the insurer, are interpreted against the insurer and in favor of the insured when two interpretations are reasonably possible. If the contract is clear and unambiguous, it will be enforced according to its terms, even though this benefits the party who drafted the contract.

In the *Grove* case the court was required to interpret a contract that could have either of two meanings.

---

8   Knox v Cook, 233 Neb 387, 446 NW2d 1 (1989).

9   Davis v Outboard Marine Corp. (Minn App) 415 NW2d 719 (1987).
10   Investors Associates Ltd. v B.F. Trappey's Sons, Inc. (La App) 500 So 2d 909 (1987).

GROVE v CHARBONNEAU BUICK-PONTIAC, INC.
(ND) 240 NW2d 853 (1976)

The Dickinson Elks Club conducted an annual Labor Day golf tournament. Charbonneau Buick-Pontiac offered to give a new car as a prize to any one making a hole in one on hole No. 8. The golf course of the club was only nine holes. In order to play eighteen holes, the players would go around the course twice, although they would play from different tees or locations for the second nine holes. On the second time around, what was originally the eighth hole became the seventeenth hole. Lloyd Grove was a contestant in the tournament. On the first day he scored three on the No. 8 hole, but on approaching it for the second time as the seventeenth hole, he made a hole in one. He claimed the prize car from Charbonneau. The latter claimed that Grove had not won the prize because he did not make the hole in one on the eighth hole. Grove sued Charbonneau for the value of the prize car. From a judgment in favor of Grove, Charbonneau appealed.

SAND, J. . . . The general rule of the law of contracts which provides that where an offer or promise for an act is made, the only acceptance of the offer that is necessary is the performance of the act, applies to prizewinning contests. When a word is used in an agreement between two parties, . . . such word is to be given its ordinary, popular meaning. The words are given the common prevailing meaning as generally understood among people.

Grove contends that the words of the offer, when used in their ordinary sense, mean that any time in the process of an official play in the tournament a ball is hit into the eighth hole in one stroke, from either tee No. 8 or tee No. 17, the conditions of the offer are satisfied. Charbonneau, however, contends that the language of the offer has a technical meaning under the rules of golf and that there cannot be a hole-in-one on hole No. 8 unless the ball, with a single stroke, is hit from tee area No. 8 and lands in hole No. 8.

. . . Where a contract contains ambiguous terms which are in dispute it is the duty of the court to construe them. . . . The ambiguous terms of a contract will be interpreted most strongly against the party who caused the ambiguity. . . .

The crucial or pivotal point in this case rests upon the meaning of the language "a hole-in-one on Hole No. 8," where the 9-hole golf course was converted to or used as an 18-hole course without adding any additional holes. Does this language, "on Hole No. 8," refer to the actual, physical designation of the hole, which is generally identified with the number on the flagstick, or does it refer to the hypothetical number given to the hole because of the sequence in which it is "played"? . . .

The offer does not contain any qualifications, restrictions, or limitations as to what is meant by the phrase "on hole No. 8." Neither does the award or offer make any statement restricting or qualifying that the hole-in-one on hole No. 8 may be accomplished only from tee No. 8. If Charbonneau had in mind to impose limitations, restrictions, or qualifications he could have made this in the offer so that a person with ordinary intelligence would have been fully apprised of the offer in every respect.

The distance from tee No. 17 to hole No. 8 was greater than the distance from tee No. 8 to hole No. 8. Thus an argument cannot be made that a player had an advantage playing from tee No. 17 to hole No. 8, as compared to playing from tee No. 8 to hole No. 8. Actually, it would be a disadvantage. . . .

We have no reason to suspect that anyone other than Charbonneau deliberately chose the ambiguous language. We are not suggesting that Charbonneau intended to trifle with the public, but if we do not apply the rule of law on ambiguous contracts, as set out earlier herein, to this situation we would permit promoters to trifle with the public, which we do not believe the law should permit, and in fact, does not permit.

If this rule of law were not applied it would permit the promoter who is so inclined, where there has been a performance, to keep adding requirements or conditions which were not stated in the offer. As an example, such as, "must use a certain club. . . ."

Both of the constructions and interpretations of the language in the offer as contended by the parties are reasonable and each has some strong convincing points. . . .

By interpreting and construing the ambiguous provisions of the offer most strongly against the party who caused them . . . we construe it to mean that an entrant in the golf tournament who had paid the fee and who during regular tournament play drives the ball in one stroke into hole No. 8 from either the 8th or 17th tee has made a hole-in-one on hole No. 8, and has met the conditions of the offer and is entitled to the award or the equivalent in money damages. . . .

[Judgment affirmed]

5. Implied Terms

In some cases the court will imply a term to cover a situation for which the parties failed to provide or when needed to give the contract a construction or meaning that is reasonable.

A term will not be implied in a contract when the court concludes that the silence of the contract on the particular point was intentional.

(a) DURATION OF CONTRACT. When a contract does not state any time for its duration, three alternatives are possible. It could be held that there is no contract at all because an essential term is missing, and without the term the agreement is too vague to enforce. It could also be held that as no termination is stated, the contract runs on forever. Neither of these views is adopted by the law.

Instead, when no duration is specified in the contract, courts will imply that the contract is to be performed or will continue for a reasonable time. But either party may terminate the contract by giving notice to the other party. Thus, an employment contract that specifies only the rate of pay but not the duration of employment may be terminated by the employer or the employee at any time.[11]

Note that in effect the court is trying to salvage the transaction and give some effect to the intent of the parties to have a contract. But one should not jump to the conclusion that whenever a term is missing from a contract the word *reasonable* is to be implied. For example, an agreement to sell your house is not a contract when no price is stated. The omission of the price will not be cured by implying that a reasonable price is to be paid.

(b) DETAILS OF PERFORMANCE. Details of performance of a contract not expressly stated in the contract will often be implied by the court. Thus, an obligation to pay a specified sum of money is implied to mean payment in legal tender. In a contract to perform work there is an implied promise to use such skill as is necessary for the proper performance of the work. In a "cost plus" contract an undertaking is implied that the costs will be reasonable and proper. When payment is made "as a deposit on account," there is an implied term that if the payment is not used for the purpose stated, the payment will be returned to the person who made the deposit. When a contract does not specify where money is to be paid, it will be implied that the payment is to be made to the creditor at the creditor's office or place of business.

A local custom or trade practice, such as that of allowing 30 days' credit to buyers, may form part of the contract. This occurs when it is clear that the parties intended to be governed by this custom or trade practice or when a reasonable person would believe that they had so intended.

When a written contract does not specify the time for performance, a reasonable time is implied.[12]

(c) GOOD FAITH. In every contract there is an implied obligation that neither party shall do anything that will have the effect of destroying or injuring the right of the other

---

[11]   Khalifa v Henry Ford Hospital, 156 Mich App 485, 401 NW2d 884 (1987). Note that there is a modern trend to prevent the employer from firing an employee without cause when the discharge violates public policy. See Section 3 of Chapter 42.

[12]   Donaldson v Farm Bureau Life Ins. Co. 232 Neb 140, 440 NW2d 187 (1989).

party to receive the fruits of the contract. This means that in every contract there exists an implied covenant of good faith and fair dealing.

When the satisfaction of a condition involves action by a party to the contract, the implied duty to act in good faith requires that such party make an honest, good faith effort to bring about the satisfaction of the condition. For example, when a contract is made subject to the condition that one of the parties obtain financing, that party must make reasonable, good faith efforts to obtain financing. The party is not permitted to do nothing and then claim that the contract is not binding because the condition has not been satisfied. When a contract may reasonably be interpreted in different ways, a court should make that interpretation which is in harmony with good faith and fair dealing. The court should avoid an interpretation that imputes bad faith to a party or produces an inequitable result.[13]

The obligation to act in good faith does not require a party to agree to a modification of the contract or to surrender any right. Likewise, a franchisor having a right to terminate the franchise without cause is not barred from so doing because of the duty of good faith. When a franchisee has been granted a nonexclusive franchise, good faith does not prevent the franchisor from granting another franchise that competes with the original franchise.

The breach of an oral promise to renew short-term credit until the debtor could obtain long term financing does not constitute a breach of the implied covenant of fair dealing.[14]

(d) GOVERNMENTAL APPROVAL. In some situations the ability to perform a contract will depend on obtaining a governmental permit or approval. When this is so, the failure to obtain such approval or permit may be made an express condition subsequent. The contract is then discharged by such failure. An implied term generally arises that one party to the contract will cooperate with the other in obtaining any necessary governmental permit or approval.

(e) STATUTORY TERMS Statutes commonly require that certain kinds of contracts contain particular clauses. For example, automobile insurance contracts are often required by statute to contain clauses with respect to no-fault liability and uninsured motorists. When a contract is written that does not contain the required statutory terms, the courts will ordinarily imply the statutory terms and interpret the contract as though it complied with the statute. Similarly, a provision in a contract that would be contrary to a required statutory provision will be ignored.[15]

6. Conduct and Custom

The conduct of the parties and the customs and usages of a particular trade may give meaning to the words of the parties and thus aid in the interpretation of their contract.

(a) CONDUCT OF THE PARTIES. The conduct of the parties in carrying out the terms of a contract may be considered in determining just what they meant by the contract.[16] When performance has been repeatedly tendered and accepted without protest, neither party will be permitted to claim that the contract was too indefinite to be binding. For example, a travel agent made a contract with a hotel to arrange for junkets to the hotel. Any claim that it was not certain just what was intended must be ignored when some 80 junkets had already been arranged and paid for by the hotel at the contract price, without any dispute as to whether the contract obligation was satisfied. Moreover, when the conduct of the parties is inconsistent with the original written contract, proof of such conduct may

---

[13] Srivastava v Russell's Barbecue, Inc. 168 Ill App 3d 726, 119 Ill Dec 562, 523 NE2d 30 (1988).
[14] Mitsui Manufacturers Bank v Superior Court, 212 Cal App 3d 726 260 Cal Rptr 793 (1989).

[15] Florida Beverage Corp. v Division of Alcoholic Beverages (Fla App) 503 So 2d 396 (1987). See UCC § 2-208(1) as to course of performance in the interpretation of contracts for the sale of goods and UCC § 1-205 as to both Code and non-Code transactions.
[16] Okun v Morton, 203 Cal App 3d 805, 250 Cal Rptr 220 (1988).

justify concluding that the parties had orally modified the original agreement.

(b) CUSTOM AND USAGE OF TRADE. The customs and usages of the trade or commercial activity to which the contract relates may be used to interpret the terms of a contract. For example, when a contract for the construction of a house calls for a "turn-key construction," industry usage is admissible to show what this means. It is a construction in which all the owner need do is "turn the key" in the lock to open the building for use, and that all risks are assumed by the contractor.[17]

Custom and usage, however, cannot override express provisions of a contract that are inconsistent with such customs and usage.

7.   Avoidance of Hardship

As a general rule a party is bound by a contract, even though it proves to be a bad bargain. If possible, a court will interpret a contract to avoid hardship, particularly when the hardship will hurt the weaker of the two parties to the contract. Courts will if possible interpret a vague contract in such a way as to avoid any forfeiture. Accordingly, a court will avoid holding that a statement or a promise is a condition precedent, which if unsatisfied would mean that no rights would arise under

the contract; or a condition subsequent, which if satisfied would mean that all rights under the contract would be terminated.[18]

When there is ambiguity as to the meaning of a contract, a court will avoid the interpretation that gives one contracting party an unreasonable advantage over the other or that causes a forfeiture of a party's interest. When there is an inequality of bargaining power between the contracting parties, courts will sometimes classify the contract as a contract of adhesion. This means that it was offered on a take-it-or-leave-it basis by the stronger party. The court will then interpret the contract as providing what appeared reasonable from the standpoint of the weaker bargaining party.

In some instances, if hardship cannot be avoided in this manner, the court may hold that the contract or a particular provision is not binding because it is unconscionable or contrary to public policy. The extent to which this protection is available is uncertain.

When the hardship arises because the contract makes no provision for the situation that has occurred, the court will sometimes imply a term in order to avoid the hardship.

In the *Perkins* case the weaker party claimed that the court should imply or read into the contract a protective term that was not there.

---

[17]   Blue v R.L. Glossen Contracting, Inc. 173 Ga App 622, 327 SE2d 582 (1985).

[18]   Security State Bank v Valley Wide Electric Supply Co., Inc. (Tex App) 752 SW2d 661 (1988).

PERKINS v STANDARD OIL CO.
235 Or 7, 383 P2d 107 (1963)

Standard Oil made a jobbing or wholesale dealership contract with Clyde Perkins. The contract limited Perkins to selling Standard's products and required him to maintain certain minimum prices. Standard Oil had the right to approve or disapprove of Perkins' customers. In order to be able to perform under this contract, Perkins had to make a substantial monetary investment, and his only income was from the commissions on the sales of Standard's products. Standard Oil made some sales directly to Perkins' customers. When Perkins protested, Standard Oil pointed out that the contract did not contain any provision making his rights exclusive. Perkins sued Standard Oil to compel it to stop dealing with his customers. From a decision in Standard's favor, Perkins appealed.

ROSSMAN, J. . . . The contract authorized the plaintiff [Perkins] to sell without Standard's written consent "on a nonexclusive basis" the products which Standard consigned to him but only to service stations or consuming accounts. Standard's written consent was required before the plaintiff could sell to any other account. The plaintiff promised in the contract to use his "best efforts to promote the sale of products consigned hereunder" and to sell a specified minimum amount during each year. . . . The plaintiff was required to deliver to Standard a complete list of the names and addresses of all his distributors and submit to it the names of any new potential distributors. . . .

The plaintiff claims that the contract by its very nature contains an implied condition that Standard would not solicit business directly from his (plaintiff's) customers. Standard protests that such an implied condition would be contrary to the express terms of the contract since the latter (1) provides that the plaintiff was authorized to sell Standard's products only "on a nonexclusive basis" and (2) reserved to Standard the "right to select its own customers." Plaintiff proposes a more restricted interpretation. . . . He concedes that the contract reserved to Standard the right to sell to any new accounts which it found, and to accept or reject any new accounts which he (the plaintiff) might obtain, but he insists that it does not permit Standard to solicit accounts which it had approved as his customers. . . .

In order to be successful in his business and to comply with the terms of his contract, the plaintiff was obliged to make substantial investments in storage facilities, delivery trucks, and other equipment. He was also obliged to hire employees. He was required to use his "best efforts" to promote the sale of Standard's products. Only if he sold Standard's products exclusively could it be said that he was using his best efforts to promote their sale. It is clear, then, that the contract limited his dealership to Standard products. Plaintiff was also required to sell a minimum quantity of other designated Standard petroleum products. If he at any time failed to sell the minimum quantity, Standard was at liberty to terminate its contract with him. Plaintiff's compensation was based exclusively on the sales he made to customers, which he secured through his own efforts. No compensation was available for the plaintiff if he obtained customers for Standard who bought directly from it. Nor does the contract obligate Standard to compensate him for sales made directly by Standard to plaintiff's customers. . . .

. . . . A condition must be implied that Standard would not solicit customers which had been obtained through plaintiff's efforts. The interpretation of the contract for which Standard contends would leave plaintiff and others in a position similar to his completely at the mercy of Standard. . . .

"We cannot accept [Standard's] construction of its meaning. An intention to make so one-sided an agreement is not readily to be inferred. . . .

"In every contract there is an implied covenant that neither party shall do anything that will have the effect of destroying or injuring the right of the other party to receive the fruits of the contract, which means that in every contract there exists a covenant of good faith and fair dealing." . . . 3 Corbin [on Contracts 278] 349–352 . . .

The implication of a condition finds support in many circumstances. . . . Plaintiff's only source of return on his substantial investments in the business was the sales he made to his customers. If Standard was at liberty to solicit his direct customers, as it contends, . . . plaintiff was in a state of economic servility; we do not believe that the parties intended such a result at the time the contract was signed. . . .

The contract before us is obviously a form contract prepared by Standard. It is a contract of "adhesion" in the sense that it is a take-it-or-leave-it whole. Such contracts are regarded by some authorities as anachronistic or inconsistent with real freedom of

contract. At least they should be construed with an awareness of the inequality of the bargainers. . . .
[Judgment reversed]

QUESTIONS

1. What created the problem in the *Perkins* case?
2. Could the problem in the *Perkins* case have been avoided?

8.   Joint, Several, and Joint and Several Contracts

The obligation of defendants bound by a contract may be several (separate), joint, or joint and several.[19] Printed forms will commonly specify that liability is joint and several.

B.   CONFLICT OF LAWS

When a lawsuit is brought on a contract, the court will seek to apply the law under which the contract was made. That is, a California court in many cases will not apply California law to a foreign (out-of-state) contract. The principles that determine when a court applies the law of its own state—the **law of the forum**—or some foreign law are called **conflict of laws.**

Because there are 50 state court systems and a federal court system, and a high degree of interstate activity, these conflict of laws questions arise frequently.

9.   State Courts

It is important to distinguish between the state in which the parties are **domiciled** or have their permanent home, the state in which the contract is made, and the state in which the contract is to be performed. The law of the state where the contract is made determines whether it is valid in substance and satisfies requirements as to form. Matters relating to the performance of the contract, excuse or liability for nonperformance, and the measure of

damages for nonperformance are generally governed by the law of the state where the contract is to be performed. Similar considerations apply to the interpretation of international contracts. Thus, a California court will apply Swiss law to a contract made in Switzerland that is to be performed in that country.

When a lawsuit is brought on a contract, the law of the forum determines the procedure and the rules of evidence.

(a) PLACE OF CONTRACTING. The state in which the contract is made is determined by finding the state in which the last act essential to the formation of the contract was performed. Thus, when an acceptance is mailed in one state to an offeror in another state, the state of formation of the contract is the state in which the acceptance is mailed if the acceptance becomes effective at that time.

If acceptance by telephone is otherwise proper, the acceptance takes effect at the place where the acceptance is spoken into the phone. Thus, an employment contract is made in the state in which the job applicant telephones an acceptance. Consequently, the law of that state governs a claim to workers' compensation, even though the injuries were sustained in another state.

If an action on a contract made in one state is brought in a court of another state, an initial question is whether that court will lend its aid to the enforcement of a foreign contract. Ordinarily, suit may be brought on a foreign contract. If there is a strong contrary local policy, however, recovery may be denied, even though the contract was valid in the state where it was made. But there is also authority that when a contract would be valid by the

---

[19]   Chun v Chun, 190 Cal App 3d 589, 235 Cal Rptr 553 (1987).

law of one state but invalid by the law of another, a court will apply the law of the state by which the contract is valid.[20]

The capacity of a natural person to make a contract is governed by the place of contracting. A corporation's capacity to make a contract is determined by the law of the state of incorporation.

(b) CENTER OF GRAVITY. It is common for contracts with interstate aspects to specify that they shall be governed by the law of a particular state. In the absence of a law-selecting provision in the contract, there is a growing acceptance of the rule that a contract should be governed by the law of the state that has the most significant contacts with the transaction. This is the state to which the contract may be said to gravitate.

For example, assume the buyer's place of business and the seller's factory are located in

state *A*, and the buyer is purchasing to resell to customers in state *A*. Many courts will hold that this is a contract governed by the law of state *A* in all respects. The fact that it is a state *B* contract by virtue of the chance circumstance that the seller's offer was accepted by the buyer in state *B* would not change this result. In determining which state has the most significant contacts, the court is to consider the place of contracting, negotiating, and performing; the location of the subject matter of the contract; and the domicile (residence) and states of incorporation and principal place of business of the parties.

When all states have the same rule of law, it is not important which state's law is followed. If, however, the law of the states involved is not the same, the choice of the state whose law is to govern will determine how the lawsuit will end. With the increasing interstate character of big business, the question of choice of law becomes increasingly important. Choice of law was at issue in the *Ashland Oil* case.

---

[20]   American Home Assurance Co. v Safway Steel Products Co., Inc. (Tex App) 743 SW2d 693 (1987).

ASHLAND OIL, INC. v TUCKER
(Mo App) 768 SW2d 595 (1989)

Tucker was employed by Ashland Oil. Tucker's contract prohibited him from working for a competitor after the termination of his employment. Tucker worked as a district manager of Ashland in Louisiana, Missouri, and Illinois. When his employment ended, he worked for a competitor in Missouri. This would be a breach of the anticompetitive covenant. However, Tucker claimed that the covenant did not bind him. He claimed that it was invalid by the law of Louisiana, where the contract of employment had originally been made. Suit was brought in Missouri to enforce the covenant. Under Missouri law the covenant was valid. Judgment was entered in favor of Ashland. Tucker appealed.

SIMON, J. . . . Tucker contends that the trial court erred in enforcing the non-competition agreement pursuant to Missouri law because Louisiana law should apply . . .

The service agreement of August 19, 1985 does not indicate the law governing its interpretation and enforcement . . . Under such circumstances, we follow the Restatement (Second) of Conflicts of Law (1971) . . .

Restatement (Second) of Conflicts § 6, Choice-of-Law provides:

(1) A court, subject to constitutional restrictions, will follow a statutory directive of its own state on choice of law.

(2) When there is no such directive, the factors relevant to the choice of the applicable rule of law include:

(a) the need of the interstate and international systems,
(b) the relevant policies of the forum,
(c) the relevant policies of other interested states and the relative interests of those states in the determination of the particular issue,
(d) the protection of justified expectations,
(e) the basic policies underlying the particular field of law,
(f) certainty, predictability and uniformity of result, and
(g) ease in determination and application of the law to be applied.

Restatements (Second) of Conflicts § 188 provides, in pertinent part:

(1) The rights and duties of the parties with respect to an issue in contract are determined by the local law of the state which, with respect to that issue, has the most significant relationship to the transaction and the parties under the principles stated in § 6,
(2) In the absence of an effective choice of law by the parties, the contacts to be taken into account in applying the principle of § 6 to determine the law applicable to an issue include:

(a) the place of the contracting;
(b) the place of negotiation of the contract;
(c) the place of performance;
(d) the location of the subject matter of the contract, and
(e) the domicile, residence, nationality, place of incorporation and place of the parties.

These contacts are to be evaluated according to their relative importance with respect to the particular issue.
(3) If the place of negotiating the contract and the place of performance are in the same state, the local law of this state will usually be applied. . . .

Here, the circumstances warrant application of Missouri law. . . . Tucker executed the service agreement in Louisiana and sent it to Ashland in Ohio. Negotiations occurred in Missouri and Ohio and Tucker's performance as District Manager occurred in Louisiana, Missouri and Illinois. Tucker resides in Missouri and Ashland has offices in Missouri. . . . The competition sought to be restrained would take place in Missouri. Thus, it is clear that Missouri has the most significant interest in the enforcement of this agreement. The interest of Louisiana is slight in comparison. . . .

[Judgment affirmed]

QUESTIONS

1. What was the basis for the court's decision in *Ashland Oil*?
2. What other rule of law could have been applied by the court?
3. The court in *Ashland Oil* made the choice of law that it did because of ethics. Appraise this statement.

10.   Federal Courts

When the parties to a contract reside in different states and the amount involved is $50,000 or more, an action may be brought in a federal court because of the parties' different citizenship. The federal court must apply the same rules of conflict of laws that would be applied by the courts of the state in which the federal court is sitting. Thus, a federal court in Chicago deciding a case involving parties from different states must apply the same rule of conflict of laws as would be applied by the state courts in Illinois. The state law must be followed by the federal court in such a case, whether or not the federal court agrees with the state law.

SUMMARY

Since a contract is based on the agreement of the parties, courts must give effect to the intent of the parties manifested thereby. The intent that is to be enforced is the intent as it reasonably appears to a third person. This objective intent is followed and the subjective or secret intent is ignored because the recognition of secret intention would undermine the stability of contracts and open the door to fraud.

In interpreting a contract, ordinary words are to be given their ordinary meanings. If trade or technical terms have been used, they are interpreted according to their technical meanings. The court must consider the whole contract and not read a particular part out of context. When different writings are executed as part of the same transaction, or one writing refers to or incorporates another, all the writings are to be read together as the contract of the parties. In some cases the reverse is done, and a contract is held divisible.

When provisions of a contract are contradictory, the court will try to reconcile or eliminate the conflict. If this cannot be done, the conclusion may be reached that there is no contract because the conflict makes the agreement indefinite as to a material matter. In some cases, conflict is solved by considering the form of the conflicting terms. Handwriting prevails over typing and printing, and typing prevails over printing. Ambiguity will be eliminated in some cases by the admission of parol evidence or by interpreting the provision strictly against the party preparing the contract, particularly when the party has significantly greater bargaining power.

In most cases the parties are held to their contract exactly as it has been written. In other cases the courts will imply certain terms to preserve the contract against the objection that essential terms are missing or to prevent hardship. The law will imply that performance be made within a reasonable time and that details of performance be reasonable when the contract fails to be specific on these points. Also, the law will imply an obligation to act in good faith.

When a contract has interstate aspects, it is necessary to determine which state's law governs the contract. The rules that govern that decision are called the law of conflict of laws. The parties may specify the jurisdiction whose law is to govern. If that jurisdiction bears a reasonable relationship to the contract, the choice will be given effect by the court. In the absence of such a provision, some courts will apply the older rule that the law of the state where the contract was made with respect to most matters and the law of the state where performance is to be made as to matters relating to performance. The modern, or center of gravity, view is to choose the jurisdiction that has the most significant relationship to the parties, the contract, and its performance. When an action is brought in a federal court because it involves citizens of different states (diversity of citizenship), the federal court must apply the conflict of laws principles that would be applied by the courts of the state in which the federal court is sitting.

QUESTIONS AND CASE PROBLEMS

1. What social forces are affected by the rule that a secret intention has no effect?

2. What is a condition precedent?

3. Harrison Builders made a contract to build a house for Kendall on the basis of cost plus 10 percent profit. The cost of the finished house was approximately $100,000. Kendall had expected that it would be $60,000 and claimed that Harrison was careless and extravagant in incurring costs of $100,000. Harrison asserted that as Kendall did not deny that the costs were $100,000, he could not dispute that they were proper. Is Harrison correct?

4. In letters between the two, Rita contracted to sell "my car" to Viola for $2,000. It is later shown that Rita owned two cars. Rita refused to deliver either car to Viola. Viola sued Rita for breach of contract. Rita raised the defense that the contract is too indefinite to be enforced because it cannot be determined from the writing which car is the subject matter of the contract. Is the contract too indefinite to be enforced?

5. Quinn of Ohio sues Norman of California in the federal district court for the southern district of New York. Quinn claims that the court should apply the conflicts of laws rules of Ohio because he is from Ohio and the plaintiff should have the choice of law. Norman claims that the federal court should apply federal law rather than the law of any particular state. Who is correct?

6. The Panasonic Industrial Company (PIC) made a contract making Manchester Equipment Company, Inc. (MECI) a "non-exclusive wholesale distributor" of its products. The contract stated that PIC "reserves the unrestricted right to solicit and make direct sales of the Products to anyone, anywhere." The contract also stated that it contained the entire agreement of the parties and that any prior agreement or statement was superseded by the contract. Thereafter PIC began to make direct sales to two of MECI's established customers. MECI claimed that this was a breach of the distribution contract and sued PIC for damages. Decide. What ethical values are involved? [Manchester Equipment Co., Inc. v Panasonic Industrial Co. 141 App Div 2d 616, 529 NYS2d 532]

7. Compare (a) the rule that a contract will be construed strictly against the person preparing it and (b) the rule that a typewritten provision prevails over a printed provision.

8. McGill and his grandson, Malo, made an agreement. McGill would live with Malo and receive support and maintenance in return for McGill's deeding his house to Malo. After a number of years McGill left the house because of the threats and physical violence of the grandson. There was no complaint of lack of support and maintenance. Had the grandson broken the contract? [McGill v Malo, 23 Conn Supp 447, 184 A2d 517]

9. A contract was made for the sale of a farm. The contract stated that the buyer's deposit would be returned "if for any reason the farm cannot be sold." Thereafter the seller stated that she had changed her mind, and would not sell, and offered to return the deposit. The buyer refused to take the deposit back and brought suit to enforce the contract. The seller defended on the ground that the "any reason" provision extended to anything, including the seller's changing her mind. Was the buyer entitled to recover? [Phillips v Rogers, 157 W Va 194, 200 SE2d 676]

10. Gerson Realty Co. rented an apartment to Casaly. The lease stated that it could be renewed on giving notice but declared that "such notice . . . shall be given or served and shall not be deemed to have been duly given or served unless in writing and forwarded by registered mail." Casaly sent a renewal notice by certified mail. Two years after receiving the notice, Gerson claimed that it was not effective because it had not been sent by registered mail. Was this notice effective? [Gerson Realty Inc. v Casaly, 2 Mass App 875, 316 NE2d 767]

11. The Norwest Bank had been lending money to Tresch to run a dairy farm. The balance due the bank after several years was $147,000. The loan agreement stated that Tresch would not buy any new equipment in excess of $500 without the express consent of the bank. Some time later, Tresch applied to the bank for a loan of $3,100 to purchase some equipment. The bank refused to make the loan because it did not believe that the new equipment would correct the condition for which it would be bought and would not result in significant additional income. Tresch then sued the bank claiming that its refusal to make the loan was a breach of the implied covenant of good faith and fair dealing. Decide. [Tresch v Norwest Bank of Lewistown, ___ Mont ___, 778 P2d 874]

12. Physicians Mutual Insurance Company issued a policy covering the life of Brown. The policy de-

clared that it did not cover any deaths resulting from "mental disorder, alcoholism, or drug addiction." Brown was killed when she fell while intoxicated. The insurance company refused to pay because of the quoted provision. Her executor, Savage, sued the insurance company. Did the insurance company have a defense? [Physicians Mut. Ins. Co. v Savage, 156 Ind App 283, 296 NE2d 165]

13. Buice was employed by the Gulf Oil Corporation as a driver. His contract of employment did not state that it was to continue for any specified time. Buice was fired because of excessive drinking. He was treated for alcoholism and was cured. He then applied to Gulf for reinstatement. Gulf refused to reinstate him. Buice then sued Gulf claiming that Gulf had followed the practice of reinstating addiction patients who were cured of their addictions, and it was his understanding that this was an implied term of his employment contract. Was Buice entitled to reinstatement? [Buice v Gulf Oil Corp. 172 Ga App 93, 322 SE2d 103]

14. On a Saturday morning the Boddifords purchased an automobile on credit from Budget Car Sales. The contract recited that the buyer acknowledged that the contract could be assigned to the Savannah Bank and Trust Company and the contract also declared that the contract should be "null and void" if the dealer "is unable to assign this contract" within a specified number of days. The contract was sent to the Savannah Bank by FAX, an electronic messaging device. Early Monday morning, Savannah phoned Budget that it accepted the assignment. Later that morning the Boddifords informed the bank that they did not want to go through with the sale and claimed that the contract was null and void because there was no acceptance of the assignment in writing. Decide. What ethical values are involved? [Budget Car Sales v Boddiford, 189 Ga App 316, 375 SE2d 632]

15. Carol and John were married. They separated and signed an agreement by which John promised to pay Carol $100 a month. A year later they were divorced, and John stopped making payments. Carol sued him for breach of the contract. John offered to testify that it was his intention that the payments would stop when the parties were divorced. Is this testimony admissible? [Grady v Grady, 29 NC App 402, 224 SE2d 282]

16

THIRD PERSONS AND CONTRACTS

When the economy was agrarian and the modern era of mass selling on credit had not begun, it was logical to regard a contract as a matter that concerned only the contracting parties. It was their private affair, and the relationship between them was described as privity of contract. Persons not in privity of contract had no rights with respect to contracts made by other persons. As time went by, society became aware that there were needs that could not be met by this concept of privity of contract. Life insurance would not be possible because the beneficiary, not being in privity of contract, would not have an enforce-able claim against the insurance company. Faced with such situations, society modified the rule of law so that third party beneficiaries could sue for breach of a contract to which they were strangers. This decision, however, led to another problem—that of defining third party beneficiaries so as to limit contract rights to those third parties that the original contracting parties sought to benefit. Society chose the policy of drawing a line so that those who are merely incidentally benefited cannot sue on a contract to which they are strangers.

The social decision of allowing strangers to get involved in a contract made by others also arose in connection with determining whether a party to a contract could transfer a right to receive money or to receive a performance or to delegate the duties imposed by the contract to another person. Subject to certain practical limitations, society gradually chose to allow the free transfer of rights and the free delegation of duties. Society has done this to provide the economy with greater flexibility in making financial and working arrangements. This has given rise to the body of law governing assignment of rights and delegation of duties.

FIGURE 16-1   CAN A THIRD PERSON SUE ON A CONTRACT?

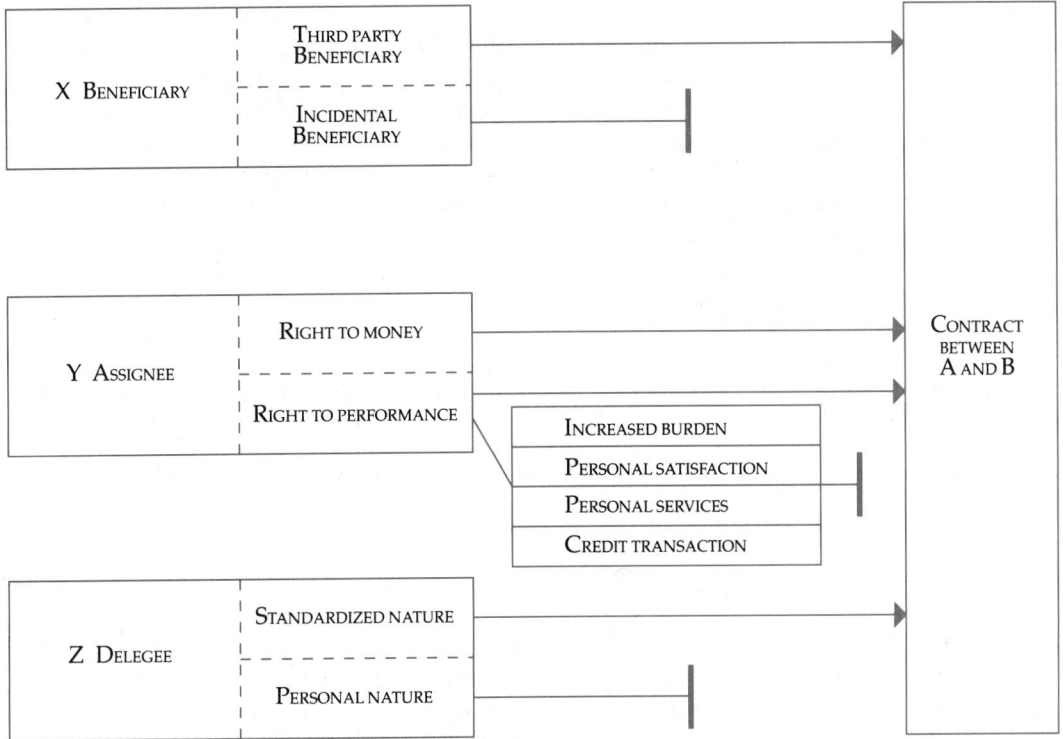

A. THIRD PARTY BENEFICIARY CONTRACTS

In some cases a third person who is not a party to the contract may sue on the contract.

1. Definition

When a contract is intended to benefit a third person, such person is a third party beneficiary and may bring suit on and enforce the contract. In some states, the right of the third party beneficiary to sue on the contract is declared by statute.

Ordinarily, *A* and *B* will make a contract that concerns only them. However, they may make a contract by which *B* promises *A* that *B* will make a payment of money to *C*. That is, the contracting parties intend to benefit *C*. Because of this intent, if *B* fails to perform that promise, *C*, who is not the original promisee, may enforce the contract against *B*, the promisor.[1] Such an agreement is a **third party beneficiary contract**. A life insurance contract is a third party beneficiary contract, as the insurance company promises the insured to make payment to the beneficiary. Such a contract entitles the beneficiary to sue the insurance com-

---

[1]   Glen L. Olson, Inc. v R.L. Thompson Enterprises, Inc. 88 Or App 309, 745 P2d 1227 (1987).

pany on the insured's death, even though the insurance company never made any agreement directly with the beneficiary.

It is not necessary that the third party beneficiary be identified by name. The beneficiary may be identified by class, with the result that any member of that class is a third party beneficiary.[2] For example, a contract between the promoter of an automobile stock car race and the owner of the race track contains a promise to pay specified sums of money to each driver racing a car in certain races. A person driving in one of the designated races is a third party beneficiary and can sue on the contract for the promised compensation.

At times it is difficult to decide whether a stranger to a contract should be called a third party beneficiary and therefore be entitled to sue on the contract. At other times the ques-

tion is easily answered, because one purpose dominates the entire transaction. In any case it is a question of intention whether the third person is an intended beneficiary.[3] If a contract expressly states that no third person may sue for its breach and that only the other contracting party may do so, it is obvious that there can be no third party beneficiary.

Parties to a contract are presumed to have contracted to benefit themselves. A stranger to the contract claiming to be a third party beneficiary has the burden of proving that the contracting parties had the intention to benefit the nonparty.[4]

In *Ron Case Roofing* the parties to a contract claimed that they never intended that a third person should have the rights of a third party beneficiary.

---

[2]   J.F. Inc. v S.M. Wilson & Co. 152 Ill App 3d 893, 105 Ill Dec 748, 504 NE2d 1266 (1987).

[3]   Hellenic Investment, Inc. v Kroger Co. (Tex App) 766 SW2d 861 (1989).
[4]   Bruner v Exxon Co. (Tex App) 752 SW2d 679 (1988).

RON CASE ROOFING & ASPHALT, INC. v BLOMQUIST
(Utah) 773 P2d 1382 (1989)

Blomquist, Panos, and the Vesper Financial Corporation (known collectively as the Vesper group) were engaged in developing real estate. They used the services of the Brooks Construction Company. Brooks would farm out or subcontract various phases of the work to other persons or subcontractors. Brooks subcontracted the roofing work on the Burton Plaza project to Ron Case Roofing. A dispute arose between Brooks and Ron Case. The dispute was finally settled by agreeing that a judgment be entered for $17,500 in favor of Ron Case and against Brooks. Thereafter a dispute arose between the Vesper and Brooks and others (collectively known as the Brooks group). This was settled by agreement. By this agreement, the Vesper group agreed to pay all claims against Brooks arising in connection with the Vesper projects. Ron Case sued the Vesper group, claiming that it was the third party beneficiary of that promise to pay the debts of Brooks, and that the Vesper group was required to pay to Ron Case the judgment owed to it by Brooks. Judgment was entered in favor of Ron Case. The Vesper group appealed.

ZIMMERMAN, J. . . . The Vesper group argues that it did not intend to assume any of Brooks Construction's liabilities to Ron Case and that the trial court should have permitted Vesper to introduce extrinsic evidence on that point.

The Vesper group's contention about what it really intended and its attempt to rely on extrinsic evidence in support of that contention ignores the settled rule that in interpreting a contract, we first look to the four corners of the agreement to determine the intentions of the parties. . . . The use of extrinsic evidence is permitted only if the document appears to incompletely express the parties' agreement or if it is ambiguous in expressing that agreement. . . . Neither of these tests is met here.

First, the document does not appear to incompletely express the parties' agreement. The settlement agreement . . . deals in a comprehensive fashion with the relationship between the Brooks group and the Vesper group, as it relates both to their various intercorporate dealings and to the Vesper projects. This indicates that the parties' whole agreement is contained in the document. . . . This impression is confirmed by the fact that the contract contains an integration clause in paragraph 19(c) which states that the "agreement sets forth the entire understanding among the parties and shall not be amended or terminated except by a written instrument duly executed by all the parties hereto." The trial court therefore properly precluded the Vesper group from introducing extrinsic evidence on the premise that the instrument is not complete. . . .

Second, the agreement is not ambiguous in expressing the parties' agreement regarding the debts incurred by Brooks in connection with the Vesper projects. Paragraph 4 states in pertinent part:

> Panos, Blomquist and Vesper, jointly and severally, agree to pay all indebtedness which is presently outstanding or in the future may arise which claims relate to the furnishing of labor, materials, equipment, tools, fuel, supplies and other items furnished to or incorporated into the Vesper Projects.

. . . The . . . question is whether, under the terms of the settlement agreement, Ron Case had a legal right to proceed against the Vesper group to recover Brooks Construction's unpaid judgment. We begin by reviewing the applicable principles of third-party beneficiary law. Section 302 of the Restatement (Second) of Contracts sets forth the governing principles for determining whether a nonparty is entitled to the rights of a third-party beneficiary under a contract . . . Section 302 provides:

> (1) Unless otherwise agreed between promisor and promisee, a beneficiary of a promise is an intended beneficiary if recognition of a right to performance in the beneficiary is appropriate to effectuate the intention of the parties and either
>   (a) the performance of the promise will satisfy an obligation of the promisee to pay money to the beneficiary; or
>   (b) the circumstances indicate that the promisee intends to give the beneficiary the benefit of the promised performance.
> (2) An incidental beneficiary is a beneficiary who is not an intended beneficiary.

For a third party to have enforceable rights under a contract, then, that party must be an "intended beneficiary" of the contract, and the intention of the parties is to be determined from the terms of the contract as well as the surrounding facts and circumstances. . . .

We now consider the terms of paragraph 4 . . . of the settlement agreement under these principles to determine whether Ron Case qualified as a third-party beneficiary. Paragraph 4 states quite clearly that the members of the Vesper group "agree to pay all indebtedness which is presently outstanding or in the future may arise which claims relate to the furnishing of labor, materials, equipment, tools, fuel, supplies and other items furnished to or incorporated into the Vesper Projects." Giving these words their "usual and ordinary meaning," . . . it is plain that the parties intended that the Vesper group would pay all obligations of Brooks due those furnishing labor and materials on any Vesper project, a description that includes Ron Case. Judged by the standards summarized in section 302 of the Restatement and followed by our cases, Ron Case is, therefore, a third-party beneficiary under the settlement agreement. . . .

[Judgment affirmed]

QUESTIONS

1. Did the court allow the Vesper group to testify as to its intention in entering into the settlement agreement with the Brooks group? What was the basis for the court's decision on this point?
2. Did the Vesper group agree to pay judgments entered against Brooks?
3. Of what importance is the Restatement of Contracts to the decision of the case?

2.   Modification or Termination of Third Party Beneficiary Contract

Can the parties to the contract modify or terminate it so as to destroy the right of the third party beneficiary? If the contract contains an express provision to change beneficiaries or to cancel the contract without the consent of the third party beneficiary, the parties to the contract may destroy the rights of the third party beneficiary by acting in accordance with such contract provision.[5]

In addition, the rights of a third party beneficiary are destroyed if the contract is discharged or ended by operation of law, as discussed in Chapter 17.

In the absence of a proper change or termination under a term of the contract or a discharge of the contract by operation of law, the parties to the contract cannot affect the rights of the third party beneficiary. However, if the third party beneficiary consents to the change or termination or acts in such a way as to mislead others, the beneficiary is barred or estopped from complaining.

3.   Limitations on Third Party Beneficiary

While the third party beneficiary rule gives the third person the right to enforce the contract, it obviously gives no greater rights than the contract provides. Otherwise stated, the third party beneficiary must take the contract as it is. If there is a time limitation or any other restriction in the contract, the third party beneficiary cannot ignore it but is bound thereby. Likewise, a third party beneficiary is required to arbitrate a dispute arising under the contract when the original parties to the contract were bound to arbitrate.[6]

4.   Incidental Beneficiaries

Not everyone who benefits from the performance of a contract between other persons is entitled to sue as a third party beneficiary. If the benefit was intended, the third person is a third party beneficiary with the rights described in the preceding sections. If the benefit was not intended, the third person is an incidental beneficiary. The fact that the contracting parties know that the performance of their contract will benefit a third person does not in itself make that person a third party beneficiary. In order for the third person to be such a beneficiary, the contract must clearly mani-

---

[5]   A common form of reservation is the life insurance policy provision by which the insured reserves the right to change the beneficiary. Section 142 of the Restatement of Contracts 2d provides that the promisor and promisee may modify their contract and affect the right of the third party beneficiary thereby unless the agreement expressly prohibits this or the third party beneficiary has changed position in reliance on the promise or has manifested assent to it.

[6]   Mayflower Ins. Co. v Pellegrino, 212 Cal App 3d 1326, 261 Cal Rptr 224 (1989).

fest an intent to confer a direct benefit on the third person.[7]

(a) DIRECT INCIDENTAL BENEFICIARY. When the performance of the contract will confer a direct, although not intended, benefit on the third person, that person is a **direct incidental beneficiary**. For example, when a private employer makes a contract with the U.S. government to employ and train disadvantaged unemployed persons, such persons are merely incidental beneficiaries. They cannot sue for damages if the contract with the government is broken by the employer. Such persons are direct incidental beneficiaries, as the performance of the contract would have directly benefited them.

The fact that a contract requires one of the parties to take steps that will protect or benefit a third person does not make such person a third party beneficiary. For example, when a city hired a contractor to do excavation work, the contract specified that the contractor should be careful of underground facilities. Such care benefited the electric power company that had underground facilities. However, that direct benefit did not make the power company a third party beneficiary to the contract. The power company was merely a direct incidental beneficiary.

Similarly, a security alarm company contracting to provide after-hours protection for the customer's store did not owe any duty to an employee held at gunpoint inside the store after it was closed. The employee could not sue the alarm company on the theory that she was a third party beneficiary of the contract to provide protection for the building.

Likewise, when the lease of a tenant prohibited it from disturbing other tenants, but the tenant used a punch press, a disturbed tenant could not sue the wrongdoing tenant for breach of its obligation to refrain from disturbing other tenants. The complaining tenant was merely an incidental beneficiary with respect to that obligation.

A contractor who has not been paid by the owner is not the third party beneficiary of the contract between the owner and the institution lending money to the owner for the construction project.[8]

(b) CONTINGENT INCIDENTAL BENEFICIARY. In contrast with the incidental beneficiary who is directly benefited by the performance of the contract, the situation may be such that the third party will benefit only if the obligee of the original contract takes some further action that will benefit the third person. For example, a landlord is not a third party beneficiary of the contract by which a bank agreed to lend money to the tenant, even though the tenant intended to use the money to make improvements to the rented premises. In effect, the landlord was an incidental beneficiary once removed. The landlord would benefit only (a) if the bank loaned the money to the tenant, and (b) if the tenant used the money to make the improvements. Thus, the bank could perform its duty by making the loan, but if the tenant never used the money to make the improvements, the landlord would never receive any benefit from that loan. The benefit to the landlord was therefore contingent on the tenant's using proceeds of the loan for making improvements.

(c) CONSEQUENCE OF INCIDENTAL BENEFICIARY STATUS. An incidental beneficiary cannot sue the parties to the contract that gave rise to the benefit or the possible benefit.

The importance in making the distinction between the direct and the contingent incidental beneficiary lies in the value of the distinction as proof of lack of intent to benefit the third person. For example, when the performance of a contract directly benefits the third person, it is necessary to go further and determine whether the parties to the contract had intended to confer that benefit on the third person. In contrast, in the case of a contingent incidental beneficiary it is obvious that the parties to the original contract did not intend to confer a benefit on that person who would only benefit if the obligee in turn

---

[7]   Baldwin v Leach (Idaho App) 769 P2d 590 (1989).

[8]   Fidelity Savings & Loan Ass'n v Morrison & Miller, Inc. (Tex App) 764 SW2d 385 (1989).

would *choose* to confer a benefit. Consequently, once it is established that the third party is, at best, a contingent incidental beneficiary, the lawsuit is ended, and there is no need to make further inquiry as to the intent of the original parties.

B.   ASSIGNMENTS

The parties to a contract have both rights and duties. Can rights be transferred or sold to another person? Can duties be transferred to another person?

5.   Definitions

An **assignment** is a transfer of rights. The party making the assignment is the **assignor**, and the person to whom the assignment is made is the **assignee**. An assignee of a contract may generally sue directly on the contract, rather than suing in the name of the assignor.

6.   Form of Assignment

Generally, an assignment may be in any form. Any words, whether written or spoken, that show an intention to transfer or assign will be given the effect of an assignment. Statutes, however, may require that certain kinds of assignments be in writing or be executed in particular form. This requirement is common in statutes limiting the assignment of claims to wages. It is not necessary to use the words *assign* or *transfer*. A statement that "you will be entitled to" a specific sum of money owed by a named person is sufficient to assign the right to that money.

Since no particular words are necessary to create an assignment, an authorization to the obligor (the other party to the original contract) to pay a third person is an assignment to such third person. For example, the printed forms supplied by the health insurer that read, "I hereby authorize payment directly to the below named dentist of the group insurance benefits otherwise payable to me," constitute an assignment to the dentist of such benefits.

Whether or not there is consideration for

the assignment does not affect the validity of the assignment. An assignment cannot be challenged by the obligor on the ground that there was no consideration. This is so because an assignment is not a contract. It is a transfer of a property right. An assignment may therefore be made as a gift, although it is usually part of a business transaction.

7.   Assignment of Right to Money

A person entitled to receive money, such as payment for the price of goods or for work done under a contract, may generally assign that right to another person. A claim or cause of action against another person may be assigned. A contractor entitled to receive payment from the owner can assign that right to the bank as security for a loan or can assign it to anyone else.

A partial assignment is valid, but it may be ignored by the debtor unless the owners of all parts of the claim in question demand payment or bring one lawsuit against the debtor.[9]

(a) FUTURE RIGHTS. By the modern rule, future and expected rights may be assigned. Thus, the contractor may assign money that is not yet due under the contract because the building has not yet been constructed. Likewise, an author may assign royalties that are expected to be received from contracts that the author expects to enter into in the future. The fact that there is nothing in existence now does not prohibit the assignment of what is expected to be existing in the future.

(b) CONSENT TO ASSIGNMENT OF RIGHTS. The party who is subject to the right of the other party, the obligor, may expressly consent to the assignment of the right. A provision that the contract should bind the successors to the parties constitutes consent to future assignments thereof.

(c) PROHIBITION OF ASSIGNMENT OF RIGHTS. A contract may prohibit the assignment of any rights arising thereunder. Some courts hold that such a prohibition is binding.

---

[9]   Space Coast Credit Union v Walt Disney World Co. (Fla App) 483 So 2d 35 (1986).

This means that an assignment made in violation of the prohibition has no effect. By the modern view a prohibition against assignment has no effect. Thus, an assignment is valid even though prohibited by the contract. By this view a provision in a construction contract that the contractor may not assign money to become due under the contract without the consent of the other contracting party is not binding. The assignee may recover the amounts due from the obligor. Under the Uniform Commercial Code, the assignment of accounts receivable cannot be prohibited by the parties.[10]

8. Assignment of Right to a Performance

When the contractual right of the obligee is that of receiving a performance by the other party, the obligee may ordinarily assign that right. However, if a transfer of a right to a performance would materially affect or alter a duty or the rights of the obligor, an assignment of the right to the performance is not permitted.[11] When an obligee is entitled to assign a right, the assignment may be done by unilateral act. There is no requirement that the obligor consent or agree. Likewise, the act of assigning does not constitute a breach of the contract, unless the contract specifically declares so.

When repairs or improvements are made to a building by one who guarantees the work to the owner, the owner, on selling the building, may assign the guarantee to the buyer.[12]

(a) ASSIGNMENT INCREASING BURDEN OF PERFORMANCE. When the assigning of a right would increase the burden of the obligor in performing, an assignment is ordinarily not permitted. To illustrate, if the assignor has the right to buy a certain quantity of a stated article and to take such property from the seller's warehouse, this right can be assigned. However, if the sales contract stipulated that the seller should deliver to the buyer's premises, and these premises were a substantial distance from the assignor's place of business, the assignment would not be given effect. In this case the seller would be required to give a different performance, by providing greater transportation, if the assignment were permitted.

(b) PERSONAL SATISFACTION. A similar problem arises when the goods to be furnished must be satisfactory to the personal judgment of the buyer. Since the seller only contracted that the performance would stand or fall according to the buyer's judgment, the buyer may not substitute the personal judgment of an assignee.

(c) PERSONAL SERVICES. An employer cannot assign to another the employer's right to have an employee work.[13] The relationship of employer and employee is so personal that the right cannot be assigned. The performance contracted by the employee was to work for a particular employer at a particular place and at a particular job.

To permit an assignee to claim the employee's services would be to change that contract.

(d) CREDIT TRANSACTION. When a transaction is based on extending credit, the person to whom credit is extended cannot assign any rights under the contract to another. For example, when land is sold on credit, the buyer cannot assign the contract unless the seller consents thereto. The making of an assignment is here prohibited because the assignee is a different credit risk. Whether the assignee is a better or worse credit risk is not considered.

9. Rights of Assignee

An assignee stands exactly in the position of the assignor.[14] The assignee's rights are no

---

[10] UCC § 9–318(4), although some cases still follow the contrary pre-Code law. See, for example, Cordis Corp. v Sonies International, Inc. (Fla App) 427 So 2d 782 (1983).

[11] Aslakson v Home Savings Ass'n (Minn App) 416 NW2d 786 (1987) (increase of credit risk).

[12] Decatur North Associates, Ltd. v Builders Glass, Inc. 180 Ga App 862, 350 SE2d 795 (1986).

[13] Escandar v Southern Management and Investment Corp. (Fla App) 534 So 2d 1203 (1988).

[14] Interfirst Bank Dallas v USF and G Co. (Tex App) 774 SW2d 391 (1989).

greater or less than those of the assignor. If the assigned right to payment is subject to a condition precedent, that same condition exists for the assignee. For example, when a contractor is not entitled to receive the balance of money due under the contract until all bills of suppliers of materials have been paid, the assignee to whom the contractor assigns the balance due under the contract is subject to the same condition.

10.   Delegation of Duties

A **delegation of duties** is a transfer of duties by a contracting party to another person who is to perform them. Under certain circumstances a contracting party may obtain someone else to do the work. When the performance is standardized and nonpersonal, so that it is not material who performs, the law will permit the delegation of the performance of the contract.[15] In such cases, however, the contracting party remains liable in the case of default of the person doing the work, just as though no delegation had been made.

[15]   Buckeye Ag-Center, Inc. v Babchuk (Ind App) 533 NE2d 179 (1989)

If performance involves a personal element, delegation is barred unless consented to by the person entitled to the performance.

(a) INTENTION TO DELEGATE DUTIES. In the absence of clear language in the assignment stating that duties are or are not delegated, all circumstances must be examined to determine whether there is a delegation. When the total picture is viewed, it may become clear what was intended. The fact that an assignment is made for security of the assignee is a strong indication that there was no intent to delegate to the assignee the performance of any duty resting on the assignor.[16]

A question of interpretation arises as to whether an assignment of "the contract" is only an assignment of the rights of the assignor or is both an assignment of those rights and a delegation of duties. The trend of authority is to regard such a general assignment as both a transfer of rights and a delegation of duties. The *Radley* case involved the effect of a blanket assignment of "the contract."

[16]   City National Bank of Fort Smith v First National Bank and Trust Co. of Rogers, 22 Ark App 5, 732 SW2d 489 (1987).

RADLEY v SMITH
6 Utah 2d 314, 313 P2d 465 (1957)

Smith, who owned the Avalon Apartments, a condominium, sold individual apartments under contracts that required each purchaser to pay $15 a month extra for hot and cold water, heat, refrigeration, taxes, and fire insurance. Smith assigned his interest in the apartment house under the various contracts to Roberts. She failed to pay the taxes on the building. Radley and other purchasers sued Smith and Roberts to compel them to pay the taxes. The action was dropped as to Smith. From a judgment against Roberts, she appealed.

CROCKETT, J. . . . The first of defendant's contentions is that the trial court erred in finding she had assumed any of the duties and obligations arising under the contracts between Smith and the plaintiffs. She maintains that in purchasing Smith's interest she was acquiring only the right to collect payments from the plaintiffs and that she had no intention of assuming the burdens of the contracts. While it is no doubt possible for a party to become the assignee of the rights under a contract without becoming responsible for the duties, the question whether a purported assignment of an entire contract includes such assumption depends upon its terms and the intent of the parties. Whenever uncertainty or ambiguity exists with respect thereto, it is proper for the court to consider all the facts and circumstances, including the words and actions of the parties forming the background of the transaction. . . .

It appears that the defendant had available Smith's contracts which set forth the corresponding rights and duties of the parties, and expressly stated that the provisions would bind the "successors and assigns." She, therefore, knew of the services required of the seller and in fact initially accepted and performed those responsibilities, and further, accepted the $15 per month which the contract recited was to pay for them, and for the payments of taxes. Applicable to this situation is the rule of construction stated in § 164 (1) of the Restatement of Contracts:

> Where a party to a bilateral contract, which is at the time wholly or partially executory on both sides, purports to assign the whole contract, his action is interpreted, in the absence of circumstances showing a contrary intention, as an assignment of the assignor's rights under the contract and a delegation of the performance of assignor's duties.

There is nothing in this case to affirmatively indicate anything other than that defendant was to assume the responsibilities of the seller under the contracts and the trial court's finding with respect to that issue must therefore be affirmed. . . .

[Judgment affirmed]

QUESTIONS

1. Was the intention of Roberts important in determining whether duties had been delegated to her?
2. Was it reasonable to believe the statement of Roberts that she did not intend to take over the performance of the duties?
3. What is the view of the Restatement of Contracts with respect to the assignment of a "contract"?

(b) DELEGATION OF DUTIES UNDER THE UCC. With respect to contracts for the sale of goods, "an assignment of 'the contract' or of 'all my rights under the contract' or an assignment in similar general terms is an assignment of rights and, unless the language or the circumstances (as in an assignment for security) indicate the contrary, it is a delegation of performance of the duties of the assignor, and its acceptance by the assignee constitutes a promise . . . to perform those duties. This promise is enforceable by either the assignor or the other party to the original contract."[17]

11.   Continuing Liability of Assignor

The making of an assignment does not relieve the assignor of any obligation of the contract.

In the absence of a contrary agreement, an assignor continues to be bound by the obligations of the original contract. Thus, the fact that a buyer assigns the right to goods under a contract does not terminate the buyer's liability to make payment to the seller. Likewise, when an independent contractor is hired to perform a party's obligations under a contract, that party is liable if the independent contractor does not properly perform the contract.

12.   Liability of Assignee

It is necessary to distinguish between the question of whether the obligor can assert a particular defense against the assignee and the question of whether any person can sue the assignee for failing to perform the contract.

[17]   UCC § 2–210(4).

Ordinarily, the assignee is not subject to suit by virtue of the fact that the assignment has been made. In the *Cuchine* case the buyer of a truck claimed that the dealer's assignee was liable for defects in the truck.

CUCHINE v H.O. BELL, INC.
_____ 210 _____ Mont 312, 682 P2d 723 (1984)

Cuchine purchased a pickup truck from H.O. Bell, Inc. The sale was made as a credit installment sale. Bell assigned the contract to the Ford Motor Credit Co. Cuchine brought the truck back to Bell for repairs. When it became apparent that the truck could not be repaired, Cuchine sued Bell and Ford. As to Ford, he claimed that by taking the assignment, Ford guaranteed that the truck would perform properly. Ford asserted that it was not liable for the truck because it was merely an assignee of the right to collect the money from Cuchine and was not a guarantor of the truck. Judgment was entered in favor of Ford, and Cuchine appealed.

SHEEHY, J. . . . Cuchine contends that the credit company assumed full contract liability when the assignment was accepted. Cuchine further contends that the credit company could not avoid this liability during the pendency of the action by reassigning the contract to H.O. Bell. Cuchine predicates the credit company's liability under the contract upon the following language which appears in the contract in bold, capital letters:

NOTICE—ANY HOLDER OF THIS CONSUMER CREDIT CONTRACT IS SUBJECT TO ALL CLAIMS AND DEFENSES WHICH THE DEBTOR COULD ASSERT AGAINST THE SELLER OF GOODS OR SERVICES OBTAINED PURSUANT HERETO OR WITH THE PROCEEDS HEREOF. RECOVERY HEREUNDER BY THE DEBTOR SHALL NOT EXCEED AMOUNTS PAID BY THE DEBTOR HEREUNDER.

This language is consistent with section 9–318 of the Uniform Commercial Code, adopted in Montana as section 30–9–318, MCA. That section reads in pertinent part:

Unless an account debtor has made an enforceable agreement not to assert defenses or claims arising out of a sale as provided in 30–9–206, the rights of an assignee are subject to:
   (a) all the terms of the contract between the account debtor and assignor and any defense or claim arising therefrom; . . .

At common law, it is a well established rule that a party to a contract cannot relieve himself of the obligations which the contract imposed upon him merely by assigning the contract to a third person. Therefore, we must determine whether, under the Uniform Commercial Code, the assignment of the contract to the credit company imposed full contract liability on the credit company as assignee.

The case law as to the effect of section 9–318 of the UCC on the liabilities of an assignee of contract rights is scant, but conclusive. In *Michelin Tires v. First National Bank of Boston* (1st Cir. 1981), 666 F.2d 673, the court examined section 9–318 and determined that:

The key statutory language is ambiguous. That 'the rights of an assignee are *subject to* . . . (a) all the terms of the contract' connotes only that the assignee's rights to recover are limited by the obligor's rights to assert contractual defenses as a set-off, implying that affirmative recovery against the assignee is not intended.

The court also noted that:

The words 'subject to,' used in their ordinary sense, mean 'subordinate to,' 'subservient to,' or 'limited by.' There is nothing in the use of the words 'subject to,' in their ordinary use, which would even hint at the creation of affirmative rights.

Such a conclusion is buttressed by the official comment to section 9–318. Official Comment 1 provides in pertinent part:

Subsection (1) makes no substantial change in prior law. An assignee has traditionally been subject to defenses or set-offs existing before an account debtor is notified of the assignment.

Under prior law, the assignee of a contract was generally not held liable for the assignor's breach of contract. . . . This rule has been carried into current law as well; where it is not clearly shown that the assignee under a contract expressly or impliedly assumed the assignor's liability under the contract the assignee is not subject to the contract liability imposed by the contract on the assignor.

We believe that the intent of section 9–318 of the Uniform Commercial Code and section 30-9-318, MCA, was to allow an account debtor to assert contractual defenses as a set-off; the provisions were not intended, generally, to place the assignee of a contract in the position of being held a guarantor of a product in place of the assignor. . . .

[Judgment affirmed]

QUESTIONS

1. What is the effect of the notice set forth in the first paragraph of the opinion?
2. Why is the assignee of a right not subject to the duties of the assignor?
3. Does the court recognize any exception to the rule of nonliability of the assignee?

(a) CONSUMER PROTECTION LIABILITY OF ASSIGNEE. The assignee of a right to money typically has no relationship to the original debtor, except with respect to receiving payments or collecting. Consumer protection laws, however, may subject the assignee to liability for the misconduct of the assignor. When the circumstances are such that the debtor could recover the money paid to the assignor, the debtor may recover that amount from the assignee by virtue of the Federal Trade Commission Regulation preserving consumer defenses.[18]

Some state statutes go beyond this and declare that the assignee must pay the debtor the same penalties that the seller-assignor would have been required to pay under a consumer protection law.[19]

(b) DEFENSES AND SETOFFS. The assignee's rights are no greater than those of the assignor. If the obligor could successfully defend against a suit brought by the assignor, the obligor will also prevail against the assignee.

The fact that the assignee has given value for the assignment does not give the assignee

---

[18]   See Section 13 of Chapter 29.

[19]   Home Savings Ass'n v Guerra (Tex App) 720 SW2d 636 (1986).

any immunity from defenses that the other party, the obligor, could have asserted against the assignor. The rights acquired by the assignee remain subject to any limitations imposed by the contract.

Modern contract forms commonly provide that the debtor waives or will not assert against an assignee of the contract exemptions and defenses that could have been raised against the assignor. Such waivers are generally valid, although consumer protection statutes often prohibit them. Some statutes take a modified position and permit barring a buyer if, when notified of the assignment, the buyer fails to inform the assignee of the defense against the seller.

Assignments of contracts are generally made to raise money. For example, an automobile dealer assigns a customer's credit contract to a finance company and receives cash for it. Sometimes assignments are made when an enterprise closes down and transfers its business to a new owner. The availability of defenses and setoffs is the same for both cases.

13. Notice of Assignment

An assignment, if otherwise valid, takes effect the moment it is made. It is not necessary that the assignee or the assignor give notice to the other party to the contract. As a practical matter, though, the assignee should give prompt notice of the assignment to prevent improper payment of the obligation.[20]

If the obligor is notified in any manner that there has been an assignment, and a demand is made that any money due must be paid to the assignee, the obligor's obligation can only be discharged by making payment to the assignee. Before the obligor knows that payment must be made to the assignee, any payment made by the obligor to the assignor reduces or cancels the debt, even though, as between the assignor and the assignee, it is the assignee who is entitled to the money. The only remedy of the assignee is to sue the assignor to recover the payments that were made by the obligor.

In the *First Trust and Savings* case the obligor on the assigned claim continued to make payments to the assignor after learning of the assignment. The assignee claimed that such payments did not discharge the obligor's liability.

[20] In some cases, an assignee will give notice of the assignment to the obligor in order to obtain priority over other persons who claim the same right or in order to limit the defenses that the obligor may raise against the assignee. UCC § 9-318.

FIRST TRUST AND SAVINGS BANK v SKOKIE SAVINGS AND LOAN ASS'N

126 Ill App 3d 432, 81 Ill Dec 246, 466 NE2d 1048 (1984)

Skokie Federal Savings and Loan Association made an agreement to lend money in installments to Spanish Court II for construction of a condominium. Spanish Court borrowed additional money from First Trust and Savings Bank and assigned to it the right to receive payments from Skokie. The assignment also authorized Skokie to make payments directly to First Trust. Skokie was given a copy of the assignment and authorization but continued to make payments directly to Spanish Court. Two and one-half years later, by which time all the money had been paid by Skokie to Spanish Court, First Trust sued Skokie claiming that it was liable for payments made to Spanish Court after Skokie had notice of the assignment made to First Trust. From a judgment for Skokie, First Trust appealed.

MCGLOON, J. . . . In October, 1978, Skokie Federal loaned Spanish Court II, Ltd. (Spanish Court) $2,400,000 to finance the construction of a 32-unit condominium in Highland Park, Illinois. Under the terms of the construction loan agreement, proceeds for the payment of "profit and overhead expenses" were to be disbursed to Spanish Court as various phases of the project were completed. An additional $100,000, needed to purchase labor and materials to commence construction, was obtained from First Trust. This loan was secured by the collateral assignment of the construction loan proceeds that Spanish Court was to receive from Skokie Federal. The language contained in the agreement read as follows:

> For value received, I hereby sell, assign, transfer and set unto The First Trust and Savings Bank, Glenview and Robert L. Munzer, their successors and assigns all rights to profit and overhead from a certain construction loan granted to Spanish Court II, Ltd. by Skokie Federal Savings and Loan Association per their Loan Commitment and Construction Loan Agreement dated October 16, 1978.
>
> Said Assignment is made to secure a loan in the amount of $100,000.00 to Spanish Court II, Ltd., which will be used for the start-up costs (labor and materials) prior to the opening of Skokie Federal Savings and Loan Association's Construction Loan.
>
> I hereby authorize Skokie Federal Savings and Loan Association to direct Pioneer National Title Insurance Company as Construction Payout Agent to make all payouts for profit and overhead payable to The First Trust and Savings Bank and Robert L. Munzer.

The assignment was accepted by First Trust and acknowledged by Skokie Federal on October 23, 1978. Between October, 1978 and May, 1981, First Trust did not receive any payments of profit and overhead. Although the owner of Spanish Court, Louis Frappier, occasionally discussed the $100,000 loan with a loan officer at First Trust, Stephen Miles, he never disclosed that Spanish Court was receiving disbursements of construction loan proceeds from Skokie Federal. On May 15, 1981, the final installment of the construction loan proceeds was made to Spanish Court. Thereafter, First Trust made a demand upon Skokie Federal for payment of the construction loan proceeds due under the assignment. Skokie Federal rejected the demand.

First Trust filed an action for declaratory judgment urging the court to determine that Skokie Federal had wrongfully paid funds directly to Spanish Court in derogation of First Trust's rights under the assignment. Thereafter, a motion for summary judgment was filed by Skokie Federal. After a hearing, the trial court granted summary judgment in favor of Skokie Federal based upon its finding that Skokie Federal did not receive an explicit direction to pay First Trust the assigned proceeds.

The sole issue presented for our determination is whether Skokie Federal, as the debtor of an account that had been assigned to First Trust, received sufficient notification that future payments should be made to the assignee to render it liable for continuing to disburse construction loan proceeds directly to Spanish Court.

Section 9–318(3) of the Uniform Commercial Code governs the situation in which a creditor has assigned its right to receive payments to another party. ... That section provides:

> The account debtor is authorized to pay the assignor until the account debtor receives notification that the amount due or to become due has been assigned and that payment is to be made to the assignee. A notification which does not reasonably identify the rights assigned is ineffective. If requested by the account debtor, the assignee must seasonably furnish reasonable proof that the assign-

ment has been made and unless he does so the account debtor may pay the assignor.

Section 9–318(3) has been interpreted as an express authorization for an account debtor to make payments to an assignor until the account debtor receives notification that the right to receive payments has been assigned and that the future payments are to be made to the assignee. Uniform Commercial Code Comment to section 9–318 further indicates that an account debtor may continue to pay the assignor even though the account debtor has knowledge of the assignment. The Illinois cases which rely on section 9–318(3) of the Code hold that enforcement of an assignee's rights under the assignment requires *both* notification of the assignment and a demand that future payments be made to the assignee. This holding is in accord with the plain language of the statute as clarified by Uniform Commercial Code Comment to section 9–318(3).

In the instant case, the assignment does not contain an explicit demand for Skokie Federal to make future disbursements of its construction loan proceeds to First Trust. The relevant language, which we have quoted above, merely "authorizes" Skokie Federal to direct the payout agent to make the disbursements to First Trust. Our review of the record supports the trial court's conclusion that, although Skokie Federal received notice of the existence of the assignment, it did not receive a demand that payments were to be made to First Trust. The uncontradicted affidavit of Steven Munson, an officer of Skokie Federal, states that Skokie Federal received no notification to pay any amount due under the assignment until after Skokie Federal made its final payment to Spanish Court.

Here . . . the trial court's conclusion that the assignment itself was not intended as a demand for payment directly to First Trust is fortified by the fact that First Trust acquiesced for so long in the payments to the assignor. . . . First Trust's failure in the present case to investigate whether and to whom payments were being made for over a 2 1/2 year period constituted a lack of common prudence. . . . Accordingly, we hold that First Trust, by its failure to demand direct payments, waived its rights to impose liability upon Skokie Federal.

[Judgment affirmed]

QUESTIONS

1. Was it not wrong for Skokie to pay Spanish Court when it knew that the money had been assigned to First Trust?
2. What remedy was available to First Trust?
3. Why was it important for the assignment agreement to authorize Skokie to pay First Trust?
4. What was the basis for the court's decision?

The Uniform Consumer Credit Code (UCC) restates the protection of the consumer-debtor making payment to the assignor without knowledge of the assignment. The UCC imposes a penalty for using a contract term that would destroy this protection of the consumer.

14.   Warranties of Assignor

When the assignment is made for a consider-ation, the assignor is regarded as impliedly warranting that the right assigned is valid. The assignor also warrants that the assignor is the owner of the claim or right assigned and that the assignor will not interfere with the assignee's enforcement of the obligation. The assignor does not warrant that the other party will pay or perform as required by the contract.

SUMMARY

Ordinarily, only the parties to contracts have rights and duties with respect to such contracts. Exceptions are made in the case of third party beneficiary contracts and assignments.

When a contract shows a clear intent to benefit a third person or class of persons, those persons are called third party beneficiaries, and they may sue for breach of the contract. A third party beneficiary is subject to any limitation or restriction found in the contract. A third party beneficiary loses all rights when the original contract is terminated by operation of law or if the contract reserves the right to change beneficiaries and such a change is made. In contrast, an incidental beneficiary benefits from the performance of a contract, but the conferring of this benefit was not intended by the contracting parties. An incidental beneficiary cannot sue on the contract.

An assignment is a transfer of a right; the assignor transfers a right to the assignee. In the absence of local statute, there are no formal requirements for an assignment. Any words manifesting the intent to transfer are sufficient to constitute an assignment. No consideration is required. Any right to money may be assigned, whether the assignor is entitled to the money at the time of the assignment or will be entitled or expects to be entitled at some time in the future. A contract term prohibiting the assignment of a right to money is invalid and does not prevent the making of an assignment.

A right to a performance may also be assigned except when it would increase the burden of performance, when performance under the contract is to be measured by the personal satisfaction of the obligee, or when it involves the performance of personal services or the credit of the person entitled to the performance.

When a valid assignment is made, the assignee has the same rights—and only the same rights—as the assignor. The assignee is also subject to the same defenses and setoffs as the assignor had been.

The performance of duties under a contract may be delegated to another person, except when a personal element of skill or judgment of the original contracting party is involved. The intent to delegate duties may be expressly stated. The intent may also be found in an "assignment" of "the contract," unless the circumstances make it clear that only the right to money was intended to be transferred. The fact that there has been a delegation of duties does not release the assignor from responsibility for performance. The assignor is liable for breach of the contract if the assignee does not properly perform the delegated duties. In the absence of an effective delegation or the formation of a third party beneficiary contract, an assignee of rights is not liable to the obligee of the contract for its performance by the assignor. Notice is not required to effect an assignment, but it has importance in terminating the ability of the obligor to assert defenses and setoffs not related to the assigned right. When notice of the assignment is given to the obligor together with a demand that future payments be made to the assignee, the obligor cannot discharge liability by payment to the assignor.

When an assignment is made for a consideration, the assignor makes implied warranties that the right assigned is valid and that the assignor owns that right and will not interfere with its enforcement by the assignee. The assignor does not warrant that the obligor on the assigned right will perform the obligation of the contract.

QUESTIONS AND CASE PROBLEMS

1. What social forces are affected by allowing an obligee to assign the right to obtain payment?
2. Give an example of a third party beneficiary contract.
3. A court order required John Baldassari to make specified payments for the support of his wife and child. His wife needed more money and applied for Pennsylvania welfare payments. In accordance with the law, she assigned to Pennsylvania her right to the support payments from

her husband. Pennsylvania then made greater payments to her. Pennsylvania obtained a court order directing John, in accordance with the terms of the assignment from his wife, to make the support order payments directly to the Pennsylvania Department of Public Welfare. John refused to pay on the ground that he had not been notified of the assignment or the hearing directing him to make payment to the assignee. Was he correct? [Pennsylvania v Baldassari, 279 Pa Super 491, 421 A2d 306]

4. Lee contracts to paint Sally's two-story house for $1,000. Sally realizes that she will not have sufficient money, so she transfers her rights under this agreement to her neighbor Karen, who has a three-story house. Karen notifies Lee that Sally's contract has been assigned to her and demands that Lee paint Karen's house for $1,000. Is Lee required to do so?

5. Assume that Lee agrees to the assignment of the house painting contract to Karen as stated in Question 4. Thereafter, Lee fails to perform the contract to paint Karen's house. Karen sues Sally for damages. Is Sally liable?

6. Jessie borrows $1,000 from Thomas and agrees to repay the money in 30 days. Thomas assigns the right to the $1,000 to the Douglas Finance Company. Douglas sues Jessie. Jessie raises the defense that she had only agreed to pay the money to Thomas and that when she and Thomas had entered into the transaction, there was no intention to benefit the Douglas Finance Company. Are these objections valid?

7. Classify the following as third party beneficiaries of an accident insurance policy obtained by an employer to cover accidents of the employees: (a) the employer, (b) the employee, (c) a hospital providing medical care for an injured employee, and (d) a doctor treating an injured employee for the injury after the employee is discharged from the hospital.

8. Oklahoma City made a contract with Hurst, operating under the name of Earth Products Co., giving him the right to remove sand from city property for five years. The contract provided that the city would measure the amount of sand removed and specify the price to be paid per cubic foot. The contract imposed certain limitations as to location of excavations, depth, and slopes. Hurst assigned the contract to Sand Products, Inc. Oklahoma City claimed that this assignment was a breach of the contract. Decide. What benefits accrue to each party from this decision? [Earth Products Co. v Oklahoma City (Okla) 441 P2d 399]

9. Lone Star Life Insurance Company agreed to make a long-term loan to Five Forty Three Land, Inc., whenever requested to do so by that corporation. Five Forty Three wanted this loan in order to pay off its short-term debts. The loan was never made, as it was never requested by Five Forty Three. That corporation owed the Exchange Bank & Trust Company on a short-term debt. Exchange Bank then sued Lone Star for breach of its promise on the theory that the Exchange Bank was a third party beneficiary of the contract to make the loan. Was the Exchange Bank correct? [Exchange Bank & Trust Co. v Loan Star Life Insurance Co. (Tex Civ App) 546 SW2d 948]

10. The New Rochelle Humane Society made a contract with the city of New Rochelle to capture and impound all dogs running at large. Spiegler, a minor, was bitten by some dogs while in the school yard. She sued the school district of New Rochelle and the Humane Society. With respect to the Humane Society, she claimed that she was a third party beneficiary of the contract that the Society had made with the city. She claims that she could therefore sue the Humane Society for its failure to capture the dogs by which she had been bitten. Was she entitled to recover? [Spiegler v School District of the City of New Rochelle, 39 Misc 2d 946, 242 NYS2d 430]

11. Helen left her job with the Clifton Co. Clifton then owned her about $300. Helen wanted Linda to have this money and assigned it to her. Linda then phoned Clifton that the money owed to Helen had been assigned to her and demanded that Clifton send her a check for the amount owed. Clifton refused to do so on the ground that the notice was not in writing. May Clifton refuse for this reason?

12. An electric power company made a contract for the construction of a dam to supply water power for the generation of electricity. The dam collapsed. Customers of the power company brought suit against the contractors who had constructed the dam and various persons who had inspected it, claiming that those persons had improperly performed their duties under their contracts and that the customers of the power company were third party beneficiaries of those contracts. Were the customers of the power company entitled to bring suit on the contract made by the power company with such inspectors and contractors? [Ziegler v Blount Bros. Constr. Co. (Ala) 364 So 2d 1163]

13. The Byron Chamber of Commerce hired Long,

an attorney, to petition the local court to put on the next election ballot the question as to whether the voters wanted to set up a park district. The petition was rejected by the court because the description of the park area was not adequate. Residents and taxpayers who lived in what would be the park area brought a lawsuit against Long on the theory that he had broken a contract of which they were third party beneficiaries. They claimed that they would have received the benefit of the creation of a park district. Were they entitled to recover damages from Long? [Byron Chamber of Commerce, Inc. v Long, 92 Ill App 3d 364, 48 Ill Dec 77, 415 NE2d 1361]

14. Brooks made a contract with Hayes by which Hayes agreed to construct a house for Brooks. Hayes made a contract with Marr to do the masonry work. The masonry work was defective.

Brooks sued Hayes for the damages. Hayes raised the defense that the work had been delegated to Marr and therefore was not Hayes' fault. Is this a valid defense? [Brooks v Hayes, 133 Wis 2d 228, 395 NW2d 167]

15. Kodiak Electric Association made a contract with DeLaval Turbine, Inc. to purchase a used generator unit. The contract required part of the unit to be repaired. DeLaval made a contract with Westinghouse Electric Corporation to do the repair work. After the repairs were made, the unit was delivered to Kodiak Electric Association. When in use, the part repaired by Westinghouse failed. Kodiak claimed that it was entitled to recover damages from Westinghouse as a third party beneficiary of the contract Westinghouse made to repair the unit. Was Kodiak correct? [Kodiak Electric Association, Inc. v DeLaval Turbine, Inc. (Alaska) 694 P2d 150]

17

DISCHARGE OF CONTRACTS

In the preceding chapters you have studied how a contract is formed, what it means, and who has rights under a contract. In this chapter attention is turned to how a contract is ended or discharged.

A. DISCHARGE BY PERFORMANCE

When it is claimed that a contract is discharged by performance, questions arise as to the nature, time, and sufficiency of the performance.

1. The Normal Discharge of Contracts

A contract is usually discharged by the performance of the terms of the agreement. In most cases the parties perform their promises and the contract ceases to exist or is thereby discharged. A contract is also discharged by the expiration of the time period specified in the contract.[1]

---

[1] Medical Oncology Hematology Group v Goldklang, 41 Ga App 183, 360 SE2d 41 (1987).

FIGURE 17-1   CAUSES OF CONTRACT DISCHARGE

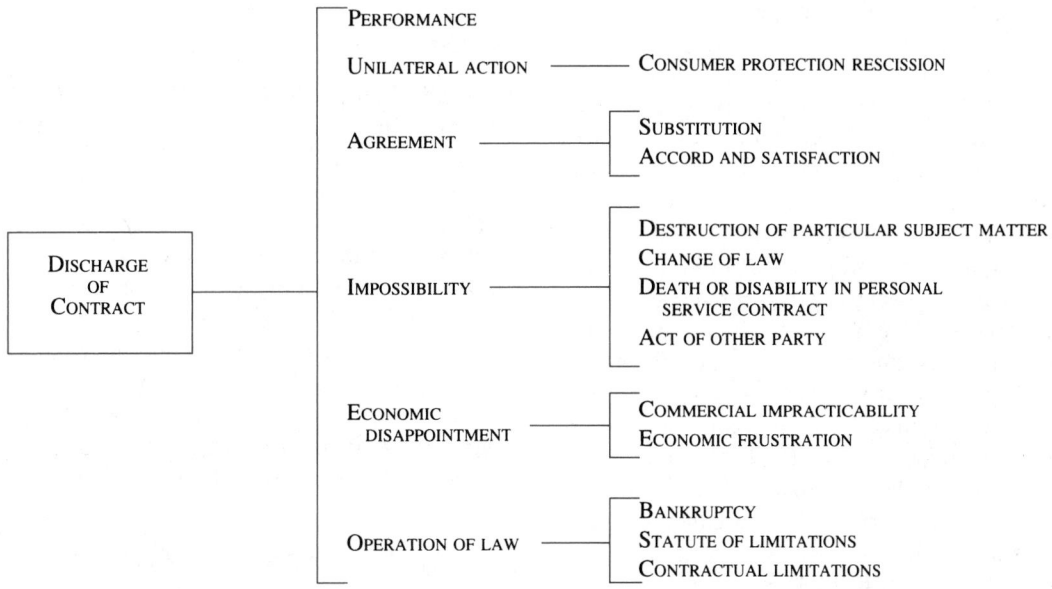

2.   Nature of Performance

Performance may be the doing of an act or the making of payment.

(a) TENDER. An offer to perform is known as a **tender**. If performance of the contract requires the doing of an act, a tender that is refused will discharge the party offering to perform. If performance requires the payment of a debt, however, a tender that is refused does not discharge the debt. It does stop the running of interest and does prevent the collection of court costs if the party is sued, providing the tender is kept open and the money is produced in court.

A valid **tender of payment** consists of an unconditional offer of the exact amount due on the date when due. A tender of payment is not just an expression of willingness to pay; it must be an actual offer to perform by making payment of the amount owed.[2] The debtor must offer **legal tender** or, in other words, such form of money as the law recognizes as lawful money and declares to be legal tender for the payment of debts. The offer of a check is not a valid tender of payment, as a check is

not legal tender (even when it is certified). A tender of part of the debt is not a valid tender. In addition to the amount owed, the debtor must tender all accrued interest and any costs to which the creditor is entitled. If the debtor tenders less than the amount due, the creditor may refuse the offer without affecting the right to collect the amount that is due. If the creditor accepts the smaller amount, the question arises as to whether it has been accepted as payment on account or as full payment of the balance that was due.

(b) PAYMENT. When payment is required by the contract, performance consists of the payment of money or, if accepted by the other party, the delivery of property or the rendering of services.

(1) Application of Payments. If a debtor owes more than one debt to the creditor and pays money, a question may arise as to which debt has been paid. If the debtor specifies the debt to which the payment is to be applied and the creditor accepts the money, the creditor is bound to apply the money as specified. Thus, if the debtor specifies that a payment is to be made for a current purchase, the creditor may not apply the payment to an older balance.

---

2   Graff v Burnett, 226 Neb 710, 414 NW2d 271 (1987).

If the debtor does not specify the application to be made, the creditor has the choice of deciding to which debt the payment should be applied. As between secured and unsecured claims, the creditor is free to apply the payment to the unsecured claim. The creditor, however, must apply the payment to a debt that is due as contrasted with one that is not yet due. The creditor cannot apply a payment to a claim that is illegal or invalid, but may apply the payment to a claim that cannot be enforced because it is barred by the statute of limitations. According to some authorities, the creditor may also apply the payment to a claim that cannot be enforced for lack of a writing required by the statute of frauds.

(2) No Application Specified. If neither the debtor nor the creditor has specified any application of the payment, application will be made by the court. There is a division of authority, however, as to whether the court is to make such application as will be more favorable to the creditor or to the debtor. Consumer protection statutes commonly require application to the oldest debt.

(3) Payment by Check. Payment by commercial paper, such as a check, is ordinarily a conditional payment. A check merely suspends the debt until the check is presented for payment.[3] If payment is then made, the debt is discharged; if not paid, the suspension terminates and suit may be brought on either the debt or the check. Frequently, payment must be made by a specified date. It is generally held that the payment is made on time if it is mailed on or before the final date for payment.

3.   Time of Performance

When the date or period of time for performance is specified in the contract, performance should be made on that date or within that time period.

(a) NO TIME SPECIFIED. When the time for performance is not specified in the contract, an obligation to perform within a reasonable time will be implied. The fact that no

time is stated neither impairs the contract on the ground that it is indefinite, nor allows an endless time in which to perform.

(b) WHEN TIME IS ESSENTIAL. If performance of the contract on or within the exact time specified is vital, it is said that "time is of the essence." Time is of the essence when the contract relates to property that is perishable or that is fluctuating rapidly in value.

An express statement in the contract that time is of the essence may not be controlling. When it is obvious that time is not important, such a statement will be ignored by the courts. It is the nature of the subject matter of the contract and the surrounding circumstances, rather than the declaration of the parties, that control.

(c) WHEN TIME IS NOT ESSENTIAL. Ordinarily, time is not of the essence, and performance within a reasonable time is sufficient. In the case of the sale of property, time will not be regarded as of the essence when there has not been any appreciable change in the market value or condition of the property and when the person who delayed does not appear to have done so for the purpose of speculating on a change in market price.

4.   Adequacy of Performance

When a party renders exactly the performance called for by the contract, no question arises as to whether the contract has been performed. In other cases there may not have been a perfect performance, or a question arises as to whether the performance made satisfies the standard set by the contract.

(a) SUBSTANTIAL PERFORMANCE. Perfect performance of a contract is not required. A party who in good faith has substantially performed the contract may sue to recover the payment specified in the contract. However, because the performance was not perfect, the performing party is subject to a counterclaim for the damages caused the other party. When a building contractor has substantially performed the contract to construct a building, the measure of damages is the cost of repair-

---

3   UCC § 3-802(1)(b).

ing or correcting the defects if that can be done at a reasonable cost.[4] If, however, the cost would be unreasonably disproportionate to the importance of the defect, as when a virtual rebuilding of the finished building would be required to make a minor correction, the measure of damages is the difference between the value of the building as completed and the value that the building would have had if the contract had been performed perfectly.

This rule of **substantial performance** applies only when departures from the contract or the defects were not made willfully. A contractor who willfully makes a substantial departure from the contract is in default and cannot recover any payment from the other party to the contract. In large construction contracts,

when the total value of the partial performance is large compared to the damages sustained through incomplete or imperfect performance, the courts tend to ignore whether or not the breach was intentional.

(1) What Constitutes Substantial Performance. There is no exact standard or test by which to determine whether a performance is substantial. A performance cannot be regarded as substantial if what has been done is of no use to the defendant. Thus, when a contractor failed to follow specifications for the construction of a swimming pool and the result was a pool that was so cracked that it would not hold water, the work of the contractor was not of any use to the other party. Therefore, the contractor could not recover on the ground of substantial performance.

The *Beeson* case raised the question of when is performance substantial.

[4]   Shreve v Biggerstaff (Ky App) 777 SW2d 616 (1989).

J.M. BEESON CO. v SARTORI
(Fla App) 553 So 2d 180 (1989)

The Beeson Company made a contract to construct a shopping center for Sartori. Before the work was fully completed, Sartori stopped making the payments to Beeson that were required by the contract. Beeson then stopped working and sued Sartori for the balance due under the contract, just as though it had been fully performed. Sartori defended on the ground that Beeson had not "substantially completed" the work, as that term was defined in the contract. Beeson proved that Sartori had been able to rent most of the stores in the center. Judgment was entered in favor of Sartori, and Beeson appealed.

WARNER, J. . . . Appellant contends that the trial court erred in finding that he did not substantially complete the work. In this case the contract provided that "substantial" completion occurred when "construction is sufficiently complete in accordance with the Contract Documents, so the owner can occupy or utilize the work or designated portion thereof for the use for which it is intended." The "work" under the contract "comprises the completed construction required by the contract documents." Under the contract in this case the work consisted of "construction and completion of a Shopping Center", including all of its component parts such as landscaping and paving. . . .

We agree with appellant's contention that the contractual definition of substantial completion in this case is similar to the well established doctrine of substantial performance, and the terms are interchangeable. . . .

Substantial performance is that performance of a contract which, while not full performance, is so nearly equivalent to what was bargained for that it would be unreasonable to deny the promisee the full contract price subject to the promisor's right to recover whatever damages have been occasioned him by the promisee's failure to render full performance. See 3A Corbin on Contracts, Section 702 et sequi.

To say that substantial performance is performance which is nearly equivalent to what was bargained for, as the case law defines the term, in essence means that the owner can use the property for the use for which it is intended. Furthermore, in defining substantial performance, one of the tests as enunciated by Corbin is the "degree of frustration of purpose":

> Extremely important factors in solving the present problem [of what is substantial performance] are the character of the performance that the plaintiff promised to render, the purposes and end that it was expected to serve in behalf of the defendant, and the extent to which the nonperformance by the plaintiff has defeated those purposes and ends, or would defeat them if the errors and omissions are corrected.

Corbin on Contracts, 3-A, Section 706. Thus, substantial completion as defined in the contract is the equivalent of substantial performance under the case law and authorities hereinbefore cited.

In the instant case . . . the owner was capable of having tenants occupy the spaces and collecting rents thereon, and he was already collecting substantial rents on many of the tenant spaces. . . .

When the owner was able to occupy . . . the constructed space, the construction was substantially completed. . . . At that point, the appellant was entitled to his full contract price, less the cost to complete.

[Judgment reversed and action remanded]

QUESTIONS

1. How does the court distinguish "substantial completion" from "substantial performance"?
2. What is the characteristic of a performance that is substantial?
3. Assume that a contractor makes a contract to build a house, digs a foundation, and then quits work. Has there been a substantial performance of the contract?

(2) *Limitations to substantial performance doctrine.* The doctrine of substantial performance will not be applied when the contract makes it clear that a literal and exact compliance is required.[5]

The doctrine of substantial performance does not apply to a condition precedent. Consequently, a lender, obligated to lend a specified amount for the purchase and renovation of an office building, was excused from making such loan when the duty to lend was subject to a condition precedent that a specific number of office space leases had to be signed,

but the required number was not obtained. The borrower's claim that the substantial performance rule should be applied to hold that there was a sufficient compliance with the rental condition was rejected.

(b) SATISFACTION OF PROMISEE OR THIRD PERSON. Sometimes an agreement requires that the promisor perform an act to the satisfaction, taste, or judgment of the other party to the contract. The courts are divided as to whether the promisor must so perform the contract as to satisfy the promisee or whether it is sufficient that the performance be such as would satisfy a reasonable person under the circumstances. When personal taste is an im-

---

[5]   Coastal Seafood Co., Inc. v Alcoa South Carolina, Inc. (SC App) 381 SE2d 502 (1989).

portant element, the courts generally hold that the performance is not sufficient unless the promisee is actually satisfied. In some instances, though, it is insisted upon that the dissatisfaction be shown to be in good faith and not merely to avoid paying for the work that has been done. The personal satisfaction of the promisee is generally required under this rule when one promises to make clothes or to paint a portrait to the satisfaction of the other party.

There is a similar division of authority when the subject matter involves the fitness or mechanical utility of property. With respect to things mechanical and to routine performances, however, the courts are more likely to hold that the promisor has satisfactorily performed if a reasonable person should be satisfied with what was done.[6]

[6]   Cranetex, Inc. v Precision Crane & Rigging of Houston, Inc. (Tex App) 760 SW2d 298 (1988).

When a building contract requires the contractor to perform the contract to the "satisfaction" of the owner, the owner generally is required to pay if a reasonable person would be satisfied with the work of the contractor.

When performance is to be approved by a third person, the tendency is to apply the reasonable-person test of satisfaction. This is true especially when the third person has wrongfully withheld approval or has become incapacitated.

When work is to be done subject to the approval of an architect, engineer, or other expert, the determination of that expert is ordinarily final and binding on the parties in the absence of fraud.

The *Forman* case raised the question of whether a seller should have been satisfied with the report as to the buyer's credit.

FORMAN v BENSON
112 Ill App 3d 1070, 68 Ill Dec 629, 446 NE2d 535 (1983)

Art Benson owned a tract of land. Eric Forman wanted to buy the land and to pay for it in ten annual installments. Benson was at first unwilling to extend such long credit but agreed to do so if the buyer agreed to include in the contract a provision "subject to the seller's approving buyer's credit report." The buyer agreed to this, and the provision was included in the contract. When the credit report was given to Benson, he stated that it "looked real good" and that he would give it to his attorney to examine. Thereafter Benson tried to get Forman to pay more for the land than stated in the contract. Forman refused to agree to the higher price. Benson then stated that he did not approve the credit report because Forman's liabilities were slightly more than four times his liquid assets. Forman sued to enforce the contract. From a decision in Forman's favor, Benson appealed.

HOPF, J. . . . We have discovered no case dealing with the interpretation of the specific clause in question. However, there is some Illinois case law regarding the interpretation of "satisfaction" clauses in general. In *Reeves & Co. v. Chandler* (1903), 113 Ill. App. 167, 170, the court found that satisfaction clauses generally fall into one of two classes. In one class, the decision as to whether a party is satisfied is completely reserved to the party for whose benefit the clause is inserted, and the reasons for his decision may not be inquired into and overhauled by either the other party or the courts. Cases falling into this class generally involve matters which are dependent upon the feelings, taste, or judgment of the party making the decision. The second class of cases are those in which the party to be satisfied is to base his determination on grounds which are just and reasonable. These cases generally involve matters which are capable of objective evaluation, or which involve considerations of operative fitness or mechanical utility. Matters of financial concern generally fall into this second category of cases. The adequacy of the grounds of a determination in this class are open to judicial scrutiny and are judged by a reasonable man standard.

However, the *Reeves* case also made it clear that the parties may agree to a reservation in one party of the absolute and unqualified freedom of choice on a matter not involving fancy, taste, or whim. . . .

It is apparent that under *Reeves* the fact that the clause was added as a concession or inducement to one of the parties is significant in determining whether the reasonableness standard should be applied. . . .

It seems clear from [other] cases that a reasonableness standard is favored by the law when the contract concerns matters capable of objective evaluation. However, where the circumstances are such that it is clear the provision was added as a personal concession to one of the contracting parties, the subjective, rather than the objective standard, should be applied.

In the present case, it is uncontroverted that the clause in question was inserted as a concession to the defendant and as an inducement to him to sign the contract, which he subsequently did. Ken Burnell testified that the addition of the provision indeed eased defendant's mind about the plaintiff's credit worthiness. In light of the fact that the relationship between the parties was to endure over a ten-year period of time, we think it is a reasonable construction of the provision that it was intended to allow defendant the freedom of making a personal and subjective evaluation of plaintiff's credit worthiness. . . .

The personal judgment standard, however, does not allow the defendant to exercise unbridled discretion in rejecting plaintiff's credit, but rather is subject to the requirement of good faith. . . . In the instant case the trial court made no specific finding whether defendant Benson rejected plaintiff's credit in good faith. However, the trial court did find that between the time the contract was executed and the time the offer was rejected, defendant attempted to renegotiate the purchase price of the building as well as the interest rate. Defendant has challenged this finding on appeal, claiming it was against the manifest weight of the evidence. We disagree. Both plaintiff and defendant testified that an increased purchase price was discussed. Thus, the trial court's finding in this regard was supported by the record and was not against the manifest weight of the evidence. Further, we hold that while defendant may have had a basis in his personal judgment for rejecting plaintiff's credit (*i.e.*, outstanding debts and a $2,000 loss reflected in an income tax return), his attempted renegotiation demonstrates that his rejection was based on reasons other than plaintiff's credit rating and was, therefore, in bad faith. . . .

[Judgment affirmed]

QUESTIONS

1. Did the contract specify that the credit report had to be satisfactory to the seller?
2. A satisfaction clause is governed by the objective standard. Comment on this statement and explain your answer.
3. What was the significance of the seller's seeking a higher price?

5.   Guarantee of Performance

It is common for an obligor to guarantee the performance. Thus, a builder may guarantee for one year that the work will be satisfactory.

The guarantee may be made by a third person. Thus, a surety company may guarantee to the owner that a contractor will perform the contract. In such case, it is clear that the obligation of the surety is in addition to the liability of the contractor and does not take the place of such liability.

B.   DISCHARGE BY ACTION OF PARTIES

Contracts may be discharged by the joint action of both contracting parties or, in some cases, by the action of one party alone.

6.   Discharge by Unilateral Action

Ordinarily, a contract cannot be discharged by the action of either party alone. In some cases the contract will give one or either party the right to cancel the contract by unilateral action, such as by notice to the other party. If the contract does not specify any duration, or it states a duration in such vague terms as "for life," the contract may be terminated by either party at will.

(a) CONSUMER PROTECTION RESCISSION. A basic principle of contract law is that a contract between competent persons is a binding obligation. Consumer protection legislation is introducing into the law a contrary concept—that of giving the consumer a chance to think things over and to rescind the contract. Thus, the federal Consumer Credit Protection Act (CCPA) gives the debtor the right to rescind a credit transaction within three days when the transaction would impose a lien on the debtor's home. A homeowner who mortgages the home to obtain a loan may cancel the transaction for any reason by notifying the lender before midnight of the third full business day after the loan is made.[7]

A Federal Trade Commission regulation gives the buyer three days in which to cancel a home-solicited sale of goods or services costing more than $25.[8]

7.   Discharge by Agreement

A contract may be discharged by the operation of one of its provisions or by a subsequent agreement. Thus, there may be a discharge by (a) terms of the original contract, as a provision that the contract should end on a specified date; (b) a mutual cancellation, in which the parties agree to end their contract; (c) a mutual **rescission,** in which the parties agree to annul the contract and return both parties to their original positions before the contract had been made; (d) substitution of a new contract between the same parties; (e) a **novation** or substitution of a new contract involving a new party;[9] (f) an accord and satisfaction; (g) a release; or (h) a waiver. To constitute a novation, it must be shown that an obligor to the original contract was released from liability, and that the new party to the second contract was accepted in substitution for the original obligor.[10]

(a) SUBSTITUTION. The parties may decide that their contract is not the one they want. They may then replace it with another contract. If they do so, the original contract is discharged by substitution.

It is not necessary for the parties to state expressly that they are making a substitution.

---

[7]   If the owner is not informed of this right to cancel, the three-day period does not begin until that information is given. In any case, however, the right to cancel is lost if the owner sells the house or three years elapse after the loan transaction. Consumer Credit Protection Act (CCPA) § 125, 15 USC § 1635 (a), (e), (f).

[8]   16 CFR § 429.1. This displaces state laws making similar provision for rescission, such as UCCC § 2.502

[9]   Wilson v Midstate Industries, Inc. (Mo App) 777 SW2d 310 (1989). In a few jurisdictions, the term *novation* is used generally to embrace the substitution of any new contract, whether between the original parties or not.

[10]   Whit-Log v Fibrex & Shipping Co., Inc. 90 Or App 237, 752 P2d 843 (1988).

Whenever they make a new contract that is clearly inconsistent with a former contract, the court will conclude that the earlier contract has been superseded by the later. Since the new contract must in itself be a binding agreement, it must be supported by consideration. Any suit brought thereafter must show a breach of the second or subsequent contract.

The fact that a second contract is entered into does not establish that the original contract is canceled. The later contract may merely add to or supplement the original contract, or it may merely modify part of the original contract. For the later contract to displace the first, the later contract must show the intent of the parties to substitute the later contract for the earlier contract. This intent may be shown by an express statement in the later contract that the parties thereby cancel or set aside the earlier contract, or the later contract may be so complete and so inconsistent with the earlier writing that the intent is clear that the later writing was a substitute for the earlier one.

The agreement modifying the original contract may be expressed in words or by conduct, but in any event it is essential that an agreement to modify be found.

A written contract may be modified by a subsequent oral agreement, even though the contract itself prohibits oral modification. However, the modification contract must be evidenced by a writing when the modified contract comes within the statute of frauds.

(b) ACCORD AND SATISFACTION. In lieu of the performance of an obligation specified by a contract, the parties may agree to a different performance. Such an agreement is called an **accord**. When the accord is performed or executed, there is an **accord and satisfaction**, which discharges the original obligation.[11] In order to constitute an accord and satisfaction, there must be a bona fide dispute, an agreement to settle the dispute, and performance of the agreement. To constitute a bona fide dispute, the parties must assert their respective positions in good faith. If one of the parties to the accord and satisfaction owes a fiduciary duty to the other party, such as an attorney to a client, there must be a full disclosure of all material facts by the party under the fiduciary duty.[12]

The accord that is the basis for the accord and satisfaction must be a binding agreement—that is, a contract. It must therefore meet the basic requirements of a simple contract.[13] If it is not a contract (for example, if it is not supported by consideration), there is no binding accord, and the prior contract is not discharged. The making of an accord does not by itself discharge the prior contract. It is not until the terms of the accord are carried out that there is a discharge of the earlier contract.

C.   DISCHARGE BY EXTERNAL CAUSES

Circumstances beyond the control of the contracting parties may discharge the contract.

8.   Discharge by Impossibility

Impossibility of performance refers to external or extrinsic conditions. This is contrasted with the obligor's personal inability to perform. Thus, the fact that a debtor does not have the money to pay and cannot pay a debt does not present a case of impossibility.

Riots, shortages of materials, and similar factors, even though external, usually do not excuse the promisor from performing a contract. A seller may have contracted to sell goods to a buyer. The fact that the seller cannot obtain these goods from any supplier does not excuse the seller from liability to the buyer, unless the inability to procure the goods was made a condition subsequent to the sales contract. Thus, the fact that the road contractor's contemplated gravel source cannot be used (and it is necessary to transport gravel from a more distant source, making performance more costly) does not discharge

---

[11]   Polin v Major, 150 Ill App 3d 988, 104 Ill Dec 122, 502 NE2d 355 (1986).

[12]   Ward v Richards & Rossano, Inc. 51 Wash App 423, 754 P2d 120 (1988).
[13]   Schroeder v Dy-Tronix, Inc. (Mo App) 723 SW2d 934 (1987).

the contractor from the obligation to construct a road. If there is nothing in the contract requiring that the gravel be obtained from the unavailable source, no question of impossibility of performance exists. A contract is not discharged merely because performance proves to be more burdensome than was originally contemplated.[14]

The fact that it will prove more costly to perform the contract than originally contemplated, or that the obligor has voluntarily gone out of business, does not constitute impossibility that excuses performance. No distinction is made in this connection between the acts of nature, people, or governments. For example, the adoption of a new government regulation made performance more costly. The contract was not discharged when the regulation was reasonably foreseeable because it was common in many parts of the country.[15]

(a) DESTRUCTION OF PARTICULAR SUBJECT MATTER. When parties contract expressly for or with reference to a particular subject matter, the contract is discharged if the subject matter is destroyed through no fault of either party. When a contract calls for the sale of a wheat crop growing on a specific parcel of land, the contract is discharged if that crop is destroyed by blight.

On the other hand, if there is merely a contract to sell a given quantity of a specified grade of wheat, the seller is not discharged when the seller's crop is destroyed by blight. The seller had made an unqualified undertaking to deliver wheat of a specified grade. No restrictions or qualifications were imposed as to the source. If the seller does not deliver the goods called for by the contract, the contract is broken, and the seller is liable for damages.

The parties may by their contract allocate the risk of loss. Thus, a contract for the sale of a building and land may specify that any loss from damage to the building should be borne by the seller.

(b) CHANGE OF LAW. A contract is discharged when its performance is made illegal by a subsequent change in the law. Thus, a contract to construct a nonfireproof building at a particular place is discharged by the adoption of a zoning law prohibiting such a building within that area. Mere inconvenience or temporary delay caused by the new law, however, does not excuse performance. Likewise, a change of law that merely increases the cost of the promisor is not a "change of law" that discharges the contract.[16] There is authority that the deregulating of an industry is not a change of law that discharges a contract entered into on the assumption of continuing regulation.

In the *N.C. Coastal Motor Line* case a buyer refused to make payments because of the effect of government deregulation of the trucking business.

---

[14] Heritage Life Ins. Co. v Heritage Group Holding Corp. (Tex App) 751 SW2d 299 (1988).
[15] Huffines v Swor Sand & Gravel Co., Inc. (Tex App) 750 SW2d 38 (1988).

[16] Central Controls Co., Inc. v AT & T Information Systems, Inc. (Mo App) 746 SW2d 150 (1988).

N.C. COASTAL MOTOR LINE, INC. v EVERETTE TRUCK LINE, INC.

77 NC App 149, 334 SE2d 499 (1985)

N.C. Coastal Motor Line was authorized by the Interstate Commerce Commission (ICC) to engage in interstate trucking operations. It made a contract to sell this authority to Everette Truck Line. Payment was to be made in eight annual installments. At the time of making the contract, it was unlawful to engage in interstate trucking without ICC authority. Everette made four annual payments. The trucking industry was then deregulated, and the authority of the ICC was no longer required to engage in interstate trucking. Everette refused to make any more payments on the ground that what it was paying for was worthless. N.C. Coastal sued Everette. Judgment was entered for Everette, and Coastal appealed.

JOHNSON, J. . . . Everette admits the signing of the contract, validity of the contract, and the sale price, which are the essential terms of any instrument. . . . Under section nine (9) entitled, SELLER'S WARRANTIES, it states in subsection (a) "There are *no proceedings pending* which adversely affect the operating rights proposed to be transferred." (emphasis added). Everette now argues that government deregulations in 1980, three years after the contract was entered into, rendered plaintiff's operating rights worthless, and thus breaches an "express but implied warranty" of permanent economic value. We find nothing . . . which gives rise to such an implied warranty. . . . Everette's attorney drafted the terms of the agreement whereby Coastal's warranty was expressly limited to no *pending* actions or proceedings which would affect the operating rights purchased by Everette. . . . Everette contends governmental deregulation was not foreseeable and that there were representations by Coastal to the effect that the operating authority would retain permanent value. Everette's pleadings and affidavits regarding the existence of an oral warranty through representations by Coastal do not establish a material issue of fact. "The obligation arising upon a warranty is that of an undertaking or promise that the goods shall be as represented or, more specifically, a *contract of indemnity* against loss by reason of defects therein." . . . In the agreement we find a written expression of Coastal's warranty which defendant in essence is seeking to expand. "The general rule is that when a written instrument is introduced into evidence, its terms may not be contradicted by parol or extrinsic evidence, and it is presumed that all prior negotiations are merged into the written instrument." . . . In the absence of allegations of fraud, mistake, duress or ambiguous terms, which Everette did not allege, any allegations of additional warranties or variation of the written agreement would not raise any issue of material fact and would be properly excludable.

Everette also raised lack of consideration as an affirmative defense. . . . At the time of purchase Coastal's operating rights were as represented, a valuable set of rights which Everette could not have otherwise acquired. Everette is without a legal defense to Coastal's claim.

[Judgment reversed and action remanded]

QUESTIONS

1. When the trucking industry was deregulated there was a change of law. What effect did that have on the contract of the parties? Explain.
2. What defenses were raised by the defendant?
3. How did the court dispose of the defenses of the defendant?

(c) DEATH OR DISABILITY. When the contract obligates a party to perform an act that requires personal skill or that contemplates a personal relationship with the obligee or some other person, the death or disability of the obligor, obligee, or other person (as the case may be) discharges the contract.[17] For ex-

---

[17]   Cazares v Saenz, 208 Cal App 3d 279, 256 Cal Rptr 209 (1989).

ample, the death of a newspaper cartoonist before the expiration of the contract discharges the contract. If the act called for by the contract can be performed by others or by the promisor's personal representative, however, the contract is not discharged.

The death of a person to whom personal services are to be rendered also terminates the contract when the death of that person makes impossible the rendition of the services contemplated. Thus, a contract to employ a person as the musical director for a singer terminates when the singer dies.

When the contract calls for the payment of money, the death of either party does not affect the obligation. If the obligor dies, the obligation is a liability of the obligor's estate. If the obligee dies, the right to collect the debt is an asset of the obligee's estate. The parties to a contract may agree, however, that the death of either the obligee or the obligor shall terminate the debt. In any case, the creditor can obtain insurance on the life of the debtor.

In the *Shutt* case it was claimed by the ex-husband that the agreement with his ex-wife to sell their home was discharged by her death.

SHUTT v BUTNER

62 NC App 701, 303 SE2d 399 (1983)

When Jean and Jerry Butner were divorced, their property settlement and divorce decree specified that when their son no longer needed their home, the home would be sold and the proceeds divided equally between Jean and Jerry. Jean died and Marie Shutt, her mother, was appointed her executrix. In a lawsuit between Shutt and Jerry, the court refused to order the sale of the home. Shutt appealed.

PHILLIPS, J. . . . The trial court erred in denying the plaintiff's motion for the sale of the marital homeplace. Though the defendant did become the *record* fee simple owner of the entirety held realty by operation of law upon the death of his wife, as the court concluded, he became so subject to his promise and agreement as follows:

(8) It is agreed that the wife shall have complete possession of the homeplace of the parties until the minor child TIMOTHY EUGENE BUTNER attains the age of 18 years or until the child respectively dies, marries, or is otherwise emancipated, at which time the homeplace of the parties will be sold and the proceeds will be divided equally among the parties. It is further agreed that the wife shall make monthly payments on the homeplace . . . and that the husband shall reimburse to the wife the amount by which her monthly mortgage payments have reduced the principal on the mortgage.

This agreement to sell their property and divide the proceeds between them, solemnly and deliberately made twice, was therefore doubly binding—first as an ordinary separation and settlement agreement . . . and second as a consent judgment in compromise and settlement of matters that were then being disputed in this litigation. . . .

Unlike the agreements involved in those cases, however, the agreement here requires little or no construction, only enforcement. The parties' obligation to sell the property and divide the proceeds was explicit and without ambiguity; nor was it contingent upon either party being alive when the time to sell came or anything else. The agreement to sell and divide was absolute and unequivocal; only the time was uncertain and that was clearly ascertainable from the terms used—no later than the boy's eighteenth birthday, then less than two years away, and sooner than that if the boy married, was otherwise emancipated, died, or stopped living there. Though the latter eventuality was not expressly provided for in the agreement as the others were, it is impliable from the obvious fact that the parties delayed the sale as they did only so that the boy could dwell there rent-free until his legally dependent status ended. Therefore, upon him ceasing to live there after his mother died, the reason for delaying the sale vanished, and the parties were obligated to go ahead with the sale if either so requested. That this is so, however, need not be demonstrated or even relied upon, since the son's eighteenth birthday has passed, and the property must be sold now in any event.

Nor were the defendant's obligations under the contract terminated by the death of the other contracting party. Few contracts are terminated by death in the absence of explicit provisions therein to the contrary. This is because all know that unexpected and untimely death is a constant possibility and are deemed to make their contracts in light thereof, and also because most contracts can be satisfactorily performed by personal representatives. The general rule is that "contracts bind the executor or administrator, though not named therein, and that death does not absolve a man from his engagements." . . . But in this instance it is unnecessary to resort to the general rule, because the parties themselves, leaving nothing to chance or the law's operation, had their agreement to provide that:

> . . . this Judgment shall be enforceable against the parties, their personal representatives, heirs and assigns.

Having so contracted, the defendant is bound thereby.

It is true, of course, for obvious reasons, that contracts of a personal nature or that require special talent—to marry, to draw a picture, write a book, perform on the stage, be one's companion, etc.—do come to an end upon the death of a party, unless the parties agree otherwise. . . . But selling a house and lot and dividing the proceeds does not depend upon talent or personality and the defendant's obligation with respect thereto still abides. . . .

[Judgment reversed]

QUESTIONS

1. How did the court classify the contract to sell the house?
2. Suppose that a contract is made between a real estate agent and the owner of an apartment house complex for the agent to sell the property. The agent dies before the sale is made. What effect does the death have on the contract?
3. As the ex-wife is no longer alive to receive one half of the proceeds from the sale of the property, the agreement to sell and divide the proceeds had failed; therefore, there was no reason to go through with the transaction. Appraise this statement and argument.

(d) ACT OF OTHER PARTY. There is in every contract "an implied covenant of good faith and fair dealing." In consequence of this covenant a promisee is under an obligation to do nothing that would interfere with performance by the promisor. When the promisee prevents performance or otherwise makes performance impossible, the promisor is discharged from the contract. Thus, a subcontractor is discharged from any obligation when unable to do the work because the principal contractor refuses to deliver the material, equipment, or money required by the subcontract. When the default of the other party consists of failing to supply goods or services, the duty may rest upon the party claiming a discharge of the contract to show that substitute goods or services could not be obtained elsewhere.

When the conduct of the other contracting party does not make performance impossible but merely causes delay or renders performance more expensive or difficult, the contract is not discharged. The injured party is, however, entitled to damages for the loss incurred.

A promisor is not excused from performing under the contract when it is the act of the promisor that has made performance impossible. Consequently, when a data service contracted with a bank to keypunch all its daily operations and to process the cards, the bank was not excused from its obligation under the contract by the fact that it converted to magnetic tapes and installed its own computers. The bank could not ignore its contract. It could only terminate the contract with the data service by giving the notice required by the contract.

9.   Economic Disappointment

The fact that the contract proves to be a bad bargain does not discharge the contract.[18] Some courts hold that a contract is discharged when, because of a change of circumstances, the performance of the contract has become such an economic disappointment that it would be unjust and oppressive to insist on performance.

(a) COMMERCIAL IMPRACTICABILITY.
At timees the cost of performance rises suddenly and so greatly that performance of the contract will result in a substantial loss. In this case some courts hold that the contract is discharged because it is **commercially impracti-** cable to perform. Although it is possible to perform, it has become such a bad bargain that the courts will not enforce it.

When future developments prove to be different than was assumed by the parties, there is a growing trend to find that there is an impossibility that discharges the contract. This doctrine is described as the doctrine of **supervening impracticability.**

After a contract is made, it may happen that a party's performance is made impracticable without his or her fault by the occurrence of an event the nonoccurrence of which was the basic assumption on which the contract was made. In such a case the duty to render that performance is discharged, unless the language or the circumstances indicates the contrary.[19]

(b) ECONOMIC FRUSTRATION.
Because of a change of circumstance, the performance of the contract may have no value to the party entitled to receive performance. For example, the holder of a franchise may make a contract for the construction of a building that will be used for the purpose of the franchise. If the franchise is terminated before the construction of the building begins, the former franchisee no longer has any use for the building. Some courts sympathize with the franchisee and hold that the construction contract has been discharged by **economic** or **commercial frustration.**

(c) THE MAJORITY RULE COMPARED.
The majority or traditional common law rule refuses to recognize commercial impracticability or economic frustration. By the common law rule the losses and disappointments against which commercial impracticability and economic frustration give protection are merely the risks that one takes in entering into a contract. Moreover, the situations could have been guarded against by including an appropriate condition subsequent in the contract. A condition subsequent declares that the contract will be void if a specified event occurs. Or the contract could have provided for a readjustment of compensation if there was a

---

18   Young v Tate, 232 Neb 915, 442 NW2d 865 (1989).

19   Restatement (2d) of Contracts, 261.

basic change of circumstances. The common law approach also rejects these two new concepts because they weaken the stability of a contract. The net result of these new concepts is that a contract ceases to be binding when there is a significant change in circumstances. That is, when a contract is most needed to give stability, the courts by these new concepts hold that there is no contract.

The common law rule is also opposed to the new concepts because they raise questions of measurement of matters that cannot be measured. How much change is needed in order to make a change "significant"?

In spite of the logical and practical objections to the new doctrines, it is likely that they will be given greater recognition by the courts in the future. The expanded recognition of the doctrine of unconscionability is developing a pattern of the judicial monitoring of contracts to prevent injustice. Further indication of a wider recognition of the concept that "extreme" change of circumstances can discharge a contract is found in the Uniform Commercial Code. The UCC provides for the discharge of a contract for the sale of goods when a condition that the parties assumed existed or would continue ceases to exist.[20]

If a contract clearly places upon one of the parties a particular risk, the contract is not discharged when that risk is realized and loss is sustained. Neither the concept of commercial impracticability nor economic frustration will be applied to cancel out provisions of a contract that allocate risk.

In the *Agosta* case it was claimed that economic frustration discharged a contract for the sale of stock of a corporation when the corporation went out of business.

---

[20] UCC § 2-615.

RE AGOSTA
122 Misc 2d 1091, 472 NYS2d 538 (1983)

John Agosta and his brother Salvatore each owned one half of the stock of Fontana D'Oro, Inc. The corporate business was the storing and wholesaling of food materials used in the pizza trade. The major asset was the warehouse where the corporation stored the food materials. Because of disputes, an action was brought to end the business. The action was settled by Salvatore's agreeing to sell his stock to John for $505,000. Shortly thereafter, a fire destroyed the warehouse, and the business had to shut down. John refused to go through with the settlement, and Salvatore brought an action for specific performance to compel him to perform his contract.

GOLDBERG, J. . . . This decision presents a novel question in this jurisdiction; whether an agreement for the sale of stock in a business corporation may be set aside when the underlying purpose of the sale is frustrated by unforeseeable circumstances. . . .

Concededly, the value of the stock has declined as a result of the fire. However, John could not be heard to complain on this account because of the well-known commercial policy which prevents one who has contracted to purchase securities from avoiding his obligation by reason of a decline, even a severe one, in the value of what he has agreed to buy. Additionally, the doctrine of impossibility of performance is inapplicable to the case at bar. In general, impossibility of performance may be equated with an inability to perform as promised due to intervening events, such as an act of state or destruction of the subject matter of the contract. When performance depends on the continued existence of a thing, and such continued existence was assumed as the basis of the agreement, the destruction of the thing puts an end to the obligation. Here, the subject matter, the shares of stock in the corporation, were not destroyed. The shares of stock are presently capable of being transferred. . . .

However, to consider the [settlement agreement] as merely a contract for the transfer of corporate stock as it might appear on its face would be to focus on one aspect of the agreement and to ignore the real intent of the parties. It would ignore the very context in which the agreement was entered into. It was contemplated that Fontana D'Oro Foods, Inc. would continue as a going business enterprise, changing merely from a company jointly owned and operated by John and Salvatore to one owned and operated by John alone. Transfer of the securities was a coincidental formality.

Analysis of the [settlement agreement] as a whole clearly demonstrates the accuracy of the foregoing conclusion. . . . It is clear that both parties were treating the underlying corporate assets and liabilities and, indeed, the operation of the corporation itself, as their own personal property and obligations and that the terminology of the [agreement] classifying the transaction as one for the sale of stock was an unfortunate misnomer not representing the true intent of the parties. While transfer of the corporate securities was most certainly contemplated it was but a minor ministerial act when viewed in the overall context of the transaction. . . .

To view this agreement as simply one for the sale of stock and not as one for the sale of a going business would be to exalt form over substance.

The Court now turns to the question of whether a supervening event has occurred of the type necessary to excuse non-performance.

Frustration of purpose is a corollary of the defense of impossibility of performance. . . .

In modern legal parlance, frustration of purpose refers to a situation where an unforeseen event has occurred, which, in the context of the entire transaction, destroys the underlying reasons for performing the contract, even though performance is possible, thus operating to discharge a party's duties of performance. . . .

We are faced with just such a set of circumstances in the instant case. As a result of the fire, performance by Salvatore Agosta would no longer give John Agosta a going business, which is what induced John Agosta to enter into the contract. Although some parts of the business still exist, for all practical purposes that business has been destroyed by the fire. As a result of that fire, the purpose of the contract has been frustrated since there is no longer a functioning business to purchase.

In order to succeed under the doctrine of frustration of purpose, the supervening event must be one which was not foreseeable by the parties. That the parties anticipated the possibility that a fire could destroy their warehouse and inventory is not in doubt. Both must have known, through their involvement in the company's affairs, of insurance coverage on these assets, as well as the existence of a policy covering business interruption. What could not have been foreseen, was the possibility (which has matured into a fact) that the insurance carrier would withhold payment of the corporation's claim based upon its arson investigation. Counsel has advised the Court that the present status of that investigation is not known, but it is not likely that the company will receive compensation for its losses in the foreseeable future, if at all. It is conceivable that the company will recover nothing, and also possible that due to the extended interruption in the company's operations, it may be difficult or impossible for the company ever to resume business, even if the insurance claim is paid in full.

When viewing the stipulation as one for the conveyance of an interest in an operating business it becomes apparent that this purpose has been frustrated by subsequent events that neither side could have reasonably anticipated.

The commercial policy which prevents a contract vendee of corporate stock from escaping his obligation to complete the purchase despite a diminution in value between the time of contract and the time of closing clearly applies when dealing with publicly traded securities or stock purchased primarily for investment purposes. Where, as here, the purpose of the contract to buy or sell corporate stock is to convey control of a functioning business, the Court has the equitable power to set aside the purchase agreement when the purpose has been frustrated by unforeseeable circumstances.

[Motion for specific performance denied]

[*The* Agosta *case was appealed several times and was reversed.* Re Fontana D'Oro, *65 NY2d 886, 493 NY2d 300, 428 NE2d 1216 (1985). The following memorandum opinion was filed by the court of last resort:*]

While the Appellate Division properly directed specific performance, both lower courts erroneously disregarded the form of the transaction—which was a stock transfer—and treated the transaction instead as a sale of a business or tangible assets. The well-settled rule is that "ownership of capital stock is by no means identical with or equivalent to ownership of corporate property." We recently reaffirmed this rule in *5303 Realty Corp. v. O & Y Equity Corp.*, 64 N.Y.2d 313, 486 N.Y.S.2d 877, 476 N.E.2d 276, in which we held that a notice of pendency was unavailable to a plaintiff in an action for specific performance of a contract to sell 100% of the stock in a corporation whose sole asset was an office building. Here, too, we cannot disregard the fact that the parties chose to structure their transaction as one involving stock, or that John agreed to pay $505,000 for Salvatore's stock. Given the form of their transaction, whether the parties might really have intended to transfer control of an ongoing business enterprise, rather than stock, can have no bearing on this conclusion. . . .

Since an agreement to convey stock in a close corporation may be enforced by specific performance, it was within the power of the Appellate Division to award such relief to Salvatore by directing Supreme Court to execute as nominee for John the various documents contemplated by the parties' stipulation.

[Specific performance ordered]

QUESTIONS

1. What social forces are advanced and what defeated by each of the two opinions in the *Agosta* case?
2. Does the appellate court opinion answer the basic question involved?

10.   Temporary Impossibility

Ordinarily, a temporary impossibility has either no effect on the performance obligation of a party, or at most suspends the duty to perform. If the obligation to perform is suspended, it is revived on the termination of the impossibility. If, however, performance at that later date would impose a substantially greater burden on the obligor, some courts discharge the obligor from the contract.

(a) WEATHER. Acts of God, such as tornadoes, lightning, and floods, usually do not terminate a contract, even though they make performance difficult or impossible. Thus, weather conditions constitute a risk that is assumed by a contracting party in the absence of a contrary agreement. Consequently, extra expense sustained by a contractor because of weather conditions is a risk that the contractor assumes in the absence of an express provision for additional compensation in such case.

(b) WEATHER CLAUSES. Modern contracts commonly contain a "weather" clause. This clause either expressly grants an extension for delays caused by weather conditions or expressly denies the right to any extension of time or additional compensation because of weather condition difficulties. Some courts hold that abnormal weather conditions excuse what would otherwise be a breach of contract. Thus, nondelivery of equipment has been excused when the early melting of a frozen river made it impossible to deliver.

11.   Discharge by Operation of Law

A contract is discharged by operation of law by (a) alteration or a material change made by a party; (b) destruction of the written contract with intent to discharge it; (c) merger when a judgment is obtained on the contract; (d) bankruptcy; (e) the operation of a statute of limitations; or (f) a contractual limitation.

(a) BANKRUPTCY. Most insolvent debtors may voluntarily enter into a federal court of bankruptcy or be compelled to do so by creditors. The trustee in bankruptcy then takes possession of the debtor's property and distributes it as far as it will go among the creditors. After this is done, the court grants the debtor a discharge in bankruptcy if it concludes that the debtor has acted honestly and has not attempted to defraud creditors.

Even though all creditors have not been paid in full, the discharge in bankruptcy discharges ordinary contract claims against the debtor.

(b) STATUTES OF LIMITATIONS. Statutes provide that after a certain number of years have passed, a contract claim is barred. The time limitation provided by state statutes of limitations varies widely. The period usually differs with the type of contract—ranging from a relatively short time for open accounts (ordinary customers' charge accounts) and other sales of goods (4 years),[21] to a somewhat longer period for written contracts (usually 5 to 10 years), to a maximum period for judgments of record (usually 10 to 20 years).

(c) CONTRACTUAL LIMITATIONS. Some contracts, particularly insurance contracts, contain a time limitation within which suit must be brought. This is in effect a private statute of limitations created by the agreement of the parties.

A contract may also require that notice of any claim be given within a specified time. A party who fails to give notice within the time specified by the contract is barred from suing thereon. A 12-month limitation in an insurance policy for the time for suit is not unconscionable, even though a person obtaining the insurance has virtually no chance of successfully negotiating for a change of the provision and must take it on a "take it or leave it" basis.[22]

---

[21]   UCC § 2-725(1).
[22]   Thomas v United Fire and Cas. Co. (Iowa) 426 NW2d 396 (1988).

SUMMARY

Most contracts are discharged by performance. An offer to perform is called a tender of performance. If a tender of performance is wrongfully refused, the duty of the tenderer to perform is terminated. If the performance required was the payment of money, the refusal of a proper tender does not discharge the debt. It does, however, prevent the creditor from recovering interest or costs if suit is thereafter brought against the tenderer to recover the amount owed. When the performance called for by the contract is the payment of money, it must be legal tender that is offered. In actual practice it is common to pay and to accept payment by checks or other commercial paper. When the debtor owes the creditor on several accounts and makes a payment, the debtor may specify which account is to be credited with the payment. If the debtor fails to do so, the creditor may choose which account to credit. If neither the creditor nor the debtor specifies, the court may do so. There is a conflict of authority as to whether a court's application of the payment should be made so as to favor the creditor or the debtor.

When a contract does not state when it is to be performed, it must be performed within a reasonable time. If time for performance is stated in the contract, the contract must be performed at the time specified if such time is essential (is of the essence). Performance within a reasonable time is sufficient if the specified time is not essential.

Ordinarily, a contract must be performed exactly in the manner specified by the contract. A less than perfect performance is allowed if it is a substantial performance and if damages are allowed the other party. The other contracting party or a third person may guarantee a perfect performance. Such a guarantor is then liable if the performance is less than perfect.

A contract cannot be discharged by unilateral action unless authorized by the contract itself or by statute, as in the case of consumer protection rescission.

As a contract arises from an agreement, it may also be terminated by an agreement. This may be a provision in the original contract or a subsequent agreement to rescind the contract. A contract may also be discharged by substitution of a new contract for the original contract; by a novation, or making a new con-tract with a new party; by accord and satisfaction; by release; or by waiver.

A contract is discharged when it is impossible to perform. Impossibility may result from the destruction of the subject matter of the contract, the adoption of a new law that prohibits performance, the death or disability of a party whose personal action was required for performance of the contract, or the act of the other party to the contract. Some courts will also hold that a contract is discharged when its performance is commercially impracticable or there is economic frustration. Although increased cost of performance ordinarily has no effect on a contract, if that increase is grossly disproportionate to the original performance cost, some courts will classify the situation as one of commercial impracticability and hold that the contract is discharged. In the case of economic frustration, the contract can be performed, but the performance has ceased to have any significant value to the party who originally contracted to obtain that performance. Temporary impossibility, such as a labor strike or bad weather, has no effect on a contract. It is common, though, to include protective clauses that excuse delay caused by temporary impossibility. A contract may be discharged by operation of law. This occurs when (1) the liability arising from the contract is discharged by bankruptcy, (2) suit on the contract is barred by the applicable statute of limitations, or (3) a time limitation is stated in the contract.

QUESTIONS AND CASE PROBLEMS

1. What social forces are affected by the doctrine of economic frustration?
2. Parties to a contract must perform their obligations entirely on the dates specified by the contract and will forfeit all rights if performance is not so made. Appraise this statement.
3. McMullen Contractors made a contract with Richardson to build an apartment house for a specific price. A number of serious apartment house fires broke out in the city, and an ordinance was adopted by the city council increasing the fire precautions that had to be taken in the construction of a new building. Compliance with these new requirements would make the construction of the apartment house for Richardson more expensive than McMullen had originally contemplated. Is McMullen discharged from the contract to build the apartment house?
4. Grattan contracted to build a house and garage for Boris for $50,000. The job was completed according to the specifications in all respects except that Grattan forgot to put a tool shed next to the garage, as was required by the contract

specifications. Boris refused to pay Grattan. Grattan sued Boris. Boris raised the defense that Grattan was not entitled to any money until the contract was completely performed and that the performance was incomplete because the tool shed had not been constructed. Was Boris correct?

5. Cotten was a real estate broker. Deasey owned property. He gave Cotten an exclusive right to sell the property for one year ending on January 30, 1986. The exclusive right provision meant that if Deasey or a broker other than Cotten were to sell the property, Cotten would still get his commission as though he had sold the property. On January 10, 1986, Deasey extended the contract with Cotten through April 30, 1986. The extension did not say anything as to whether the agency was exclusive. Unknown to Cotten, Deasey on February 3, 1986, made a contract to sell the property to Standley. The closing or settlement of the transaction was made on May 1, 1986, the day following the expiration of the extension date of the agreement with Cotten. Cotten sued Deasey to recover the commission on the sale to Standley. Deasey defended on the ground that the contract that had given Cotten an exclusive right had expired and that it had been superseded by the extension agreement that did not give Cotten any exclusive right. Decide. [Cotten v Deasey (Tex App) 766 SW2d 874]

6. Compare (a) the principle that time is generally not of the essence with (b) the right of a construction contractor to recover for a substantial performance of the contract.

7. Metalcrafters made a contract to design a new earth-moving vehicle for Lamar Highway Construction Company. Metalcrafters was depending on the genius of Samet, the head of its research department, to design a new product. Shortly after the contract was made between Metalcrafters and Lamar, Samet was killed in an automobile accident. Metalcrafters was not able to design the product without Samet. Lamar sued Metalcrafters for damages for breach of the contract. Metalcrafters claimed that the contract was discharged by Samet's death. Is it correct?

8. The Tinchers signed a contract to sell land to Creasy. The contract specified that the sales transaction was to be completed in 90 days. At the end of the 90 days Creasy requested an extension of time. The Tinchers refused to grant an extension and stated that the contract was ter-

minated. Creasy claimed that the 90-day clause was not binding because the contract did not state that time was of the essence. Was the contract terminated? [Creasy v Tincher, 154 W Va 18, 173 SE2d 332]

9. Kel Kim Corporation leased a vacant supermarket building from Central Markets. The lease ran for ten years, with the option to extend it for two five-year periods. The parties understood that Kel Kim would be using the building for a public roller skating rink, although the lease did not specify what use was to be made of the building. The lease required Kel Kim to maintain public liability insurance in the amount of one million dollars to protect Central Markets from any liability. Kel Kim obtained a policy for one-half million dollars. The lessor notified Kel Kim that the lease was terminated if proper insurance was not obtained in 30 days. Kel Kim claimed that it was not bound by the requirement of maintaining million-dollar insurance because it was impossible to obtain that much insurance on a roller skating rink. Was Kel Kim released from the million-dollar insurance clause? [Kel Kim Corp. v Central Markets, Inc. 70 NY2d 900, 524 NYS2d 384, 519 NE2d 295]

10. Dickson contracted to build a house for Moran. When it was approximately 25 to 40 percent completed, Moran would not let Dickson work any further because he was not following the building plans and specifications, and there were many defects. Moran hired another contractor to correct the defects and finish the building. Dickson sued Moran for breach of contract, claiming that he had substantially performed the contract up to the point where he had been discharged. Was Dickson correct? [Dickson v Moran (La App) 344 So 2d 102]

11. Compare a novation and a delegation of duties.

12. A leased a trailer park to B. At the time, sewage was disposed of by a septic tank system that was not connected with the public sewage system. B knew this, and the lease declared that B had examined the premises and that A made no representation or guarantee as to the condition of the premises. Some time thereafter, the septic tank system stopped working properly, and the county health department notified B that he was required to connect the sewage system with the public sewage system or else close the trailer park. B did not want to pay the additional cost involved in connecting with the public system. B claimed that he was released from the lease and was entitled to a refund of the deposit that

he had made. Was he correct? [Glen R. Sewell Sheet Metal v Loverde, 70 Cal 2d 666, 75 Cal Rptr 889, 451 P2d 721]

13. Oneal was a teacher employed by the Colton Consolidated School District. Because of a diabetic condition, his eyesight deteriorated so much that he offered to resign if he would be given pay for a specified number of "sick leave" days. The school district refused to do this and discharged Oneal for nonperformance of his contract. He appealed to remove the discharge from his record. Decide. What ethical values are involved? [Oneal v Colton Consolidated School District, 16 Wash App 2d 488, 557 P2d 11]

14. Northwest Construction, Inc. made a contract with the state of Washington for highway construction. Part of the work was turned over under a subcontract to the Yakima Asphalt Paving Company. The contract required that any claim be asserted within 180 days. Yakima brought an action for damages after the expiration of 180 days. The defense was raised that the claim was too late. Yakima replied that the action was brought within the time allowed by the statute of limitations and that the contractual limitation of 180 days was therefore not binding. Was Yakima correct? [Yakima Asphalt Paving Co. v Washington State Department of Transportation, 45 Wash App 663, 726 P2d 1021]

15. The Metropolitan Park District of Tacoma gave Griffith a concession to run its park. The agreement gave the right to occupy the parks and use any improvements found therein. The district later wished to set this agreement aside because it was not making sufficient money from the transaction. While it was seeking to do so, a boathouse and giftshop in one of the parks was destroyed by fire. The district then claimed that the concession contract with Griffith was discharged by impossibility of performance. Was it correct? [Metropolitan Park District of Tacoma v Griffith, 106 Wash 2d 5, 723 P2d 1093]

18

BREACH OF CONTRACT AND REMEDIES

When a party breaks a contract, society gives the other party—the injured party—a remedy against the defaulter. As seen in Chapter 16, sometimes the right to obtain a remedy for breach has been extended beyond the contracting parties to include third party beneficiaries and assignees.

Assume that the fact situation that constitutes a breach of contract is also a tort, as described in Chapter 8. Can an aggrieved party sue the defaulter for the tort? Society could have taken the position that, as the parties had made a contract, their respective rights must stand or fall as contract rights and that any other kind of liability was excluded. Instead, the aggrieved person is given the choice of seeking a remedy for breach of contract or for tort. This choice is given in the interest of putting the aggrieved person in as nearly as possible the same position that such person would have held had the contract been performed.

Once society decided to make a tort remedy available, it was necessary to decide who could seek such tort remedy. Could third person victims of the default be allowed to sue for the tort involved in the breach of the contract? Unlike the case of third party beneficiaries, there is often nothing in the contract that shows any intent to benefit such victims. Unlike the case of the assignee, there is no relationship between the third person tort victim and a party to the original contract. Society was thus faced with the necessity of deciding whether only a contracting party could sue the other contracting party for a tort, or whether anyone who could show injury could sue for such tort. The first choice seemed too narrow, and the second seemed too broad. Somewhere between the two extremes society has been struggling to develop a dividing line that will allow some third person victims to sue for tortious breach of contract but that will not allow too many to sue.

FIGURE 18-1   WHAT FOLLOWS THE BREACH?

A.   WHAT CONSTITUTES A BREACH OF CONTRACT

The question of remedies does not become important until it is first determined that there has been a breach of the contract.

1.   Definition of Breach

A **breach** is the failure to act or perform in the manner called for by the contract. When the contract calls for performance, such as the painting of the owner's house, the failure to paint or to paint properly is a breach of contract. If the contract calls for forbearance, the action of the creditor in bringing a lawsuit is a breach of the contract.

2.   Anticipatory Breach

When the contract calls for performance, the question of whether there has been a breach is determined by whether performance was made at the proper time. A party may make it clear before that time arrives that the contract will not be performed.

(a) ANTICIPATORY REPUDIATION. When a party expressly declares that performance will not be made when required, such declaration is called an **anticipatory repudiation** of the contract. To constitute such a repudiation, there must be a clear, absolute, unequivocal refusal to perform the contract according to its terms.

When a party insists that the contract has a meaning that it could not possibly have, such insistence is regarded as an anticipatory repudiation. This insistence clearly manifests that the declarant will not perform the contract according to its reasonable terms.

A party making an anticipatory repudiation may retract or take back the repudiation if the other party has not changed position in reliance on the repudiation. For example, if the buyer makes another purchase when the seller declares that the seller will not perform the contract, the buyer has acted in reliance on the seller's repudiation. The seller will therefore not be allowed to retract the repudiation.

(b) ANTICIPATORY REPUDIATION BY CONDUCT. The anticipatory repudiation may be expressed by conduct that makes it impossible for the repudiating party to perform thereafter. To illustrate, there is a repudiation by conduct if a farmer makes a contract to sell an identified mass of potatoes, then sells and delivers them to another buyer before the date specified for the delivery of the potatoes to the first buyer.

B.   WAIVER OF BREACH

The breach of a contract may have no importance because the other party to the contract waives the breach.

3.   Cure of Breach by Waiver

The fact that one party has broken a contract does not necessarily mean that there will be a lawsuit or a forfeiture of the contract. For practical business reasons one party may be willing to ignore or **waive** the breach. When it is established that there has been a waiver of a breach, the party waiving the breach cannot take any action on the theory that the contract was broken. The waiver, in effect, erases the past breach. The contract continues as though the breach had not existed.

Many times a tender of performance will be defective in some respect. There may be delays, or the product tendered may not be exactly what was ordered. The obligee will frequently accept the performance, although defective, without making any complaint as to the defect. Performance may be accepted because the obligee is not really troubled by the defect or because the obligee is in such a position that the defective performance must be accepted as better than none.

The waiver may be express, or it may be implied from the continued recognition of the existence of the contract by the aggrieved party.[1]

4.   Existence and Scope of Waiver

It is a question of fact whether there has been a waiver.

(a) EXISTENCE OF WAIVER. A party may express or declare that the breach of the contract is waived. A waiver of breach is more often the result of silence or failure to object in timely fashion than the result of an express forgiving of a breach. Thus, a party allowing the other party to continue performance without objecting that the performance is not satisfactory, waives the right to raise that objection when sued for payment by the performing party.[2]

(b) SCOPE OF WAIVER. The waiver of a breach of contract extends only to the matter waived. It does not show any intent to ignore other provisions of the contract. For example, a contractor may be late in completing the construction of a building. The owner could waive objection to the lateness and permit the contractor to finish the construction. Such waiver as to time does not waive the obligation of the contractor to complete the building

---

[1]   Creative Communications Consultants, Inc. v Gaylord (Minn App) 403 NW2d 654 (1987).
[2]   Old Mill Printers v Kruse (Minn App) 392 NW2d 621 (1986).

according to the plans and specifications. Only the time of performance requirement is waived.

5.   Waiver of Breach as Modification of Contract

When the contract calls for a continuing performance, such as making delivery of goods or paying an installment on the first of each month, the acceptance of a late delivery or a late payment may have more significance than merely waiving a claim for damages because of the lateness.

(a) REPEATED BREACHES AND WAIVERS. Repeated breaches and repeated waivers may show that the parties have modified their original contract. For example, the contract calling for performance on the first of the month may have been modified to permit performance in the first week of the month. When there is a modification of the contract, neither party can go back to the original contract without the consent of the other.

(b)   ANTI-MODIFICATION   CLAUSE. Modern contracts commonly specify that the terms of a contract shall not be deemed modified by waiver as to any breaches. This means that the original contract remains as agreed to. Either party may therefore return to and insist upon compliance with the original contract.

6.   Reservation of Right

It may be that a party is willing to accept a defective performance but does not wish to surrender any claim for damages for the breach. For example, the buyer of coal may need a shipment of coal so badly as to be forced to accept it although it is defective. At the same time the buyer does not wish to be required to pay the full purchase price for the defective shipment. The buyer wants to claim a deduction for damages because the shipment was defective. In such a case the buyer should accept the tendered performance with a **reservation of rights.** In the above illustration the buyer would state that the defective coal was accepted but that the right to damages for

nonconformity to the contract was reserved.[3] Frequently the buyer will express the same thought by stating that the coal is accepted without prejudice to a claim for damages for nonconformity, or that the shipment is accepted under protest.

The acceptance under reservation described above may be oral. It is preferable for practical reasons that it be in writing. In many cases the practical procedure is to make the declaration orally as soon as possible and then send a confirming letter. When the matter is sufficiently important, it is also desirable to have the wrongdoer countersign or make a written acknowledgment of the reservation letter.

C.   REMEDIES FOR BREACH OF CONTRACT

When a party has broken a contract, there are several remedies, one or more of which may be available to the injured party. The injured party may bring an action for damages, rescind the contract, bring a suit in equity to obtain specific performance, or commence a proceeding to obtain relief from an administrative agency of the government. There is also the possibility that arbitration or a streamlined procedure (discussed in Chapter 1) is available for the determination of the rights of the parties.

7.   Remedies upon Anticipatory Repudiation

When there has been an anticipatory repudiation of a contract, the aggrieved person has several options. The aggrieved party may (a) do nothing beyond stating that the performance at the proper time will be required, (b) regard the contract as having been definitively broken and bring a lawsuit against the repudiating party, without waiting to see if there will be a proper performance when the performance date arrives, or (c) regard the repudiation as an offer to cancel the contract, which

---

[3]   UCC § 1–207.

offer can be accepted or rejected. If accepted, there is a discharge of the original contract by the subsequent cancellation agreement of the parties.

8.   Action for Damages

When a breach of contract occurs, the injured party is entitled to bring an action for damages. The amount is such sum of money as will place the injured party in the same position that would have been attained if the contract had been performed.[4]

If the defendant has been negligent in performing the contract, the plaintiff may sue for the damages caused by the negligence. Thus, a person contracting to drill a well for drinking water can be sued for the damage caused by negligently drilling the well so as to cause the water to become contaminated. However, damages representing annoyance ordinarily may not be recovered for breach of contract. Likewise, the mere fact that the breaking of the contract causes the injured party to be emotionally upset does not ordinarily entitle that person to recover damages for such emotional distress.

(a) MEASURE OF DAMAGES. A plaintiff who has sustained actual loss is entitled to a sum of money that will, so far as possible, compensate for that loss. Such damages are called **compensatory damages.** An injured party who does not sustain an actual loss from the breach of a contract is entitled to a judgment of a small sum, such as $1, known as **nominal damages.** A party seeking to recover damages for breach of contract must produce

evidence that affords a reasonable basis for determining the monetary value of the damages with reasonable certainty. If the proof is uncertain, conjectural, or speculative, the plaintiff cannot recover compensatory damages.[5]

The fact that damages cannot be established with mathematical certainty is not a bar to their recovery. All that is required is reasonable certainty. The trier of fact is given a large degree of discretion in determining the damages.

(b) PUNITIVE DAMAGES. Damages in excess of actual loss, imposed for the purpose of punishing or making an example of the defendant, are known as **punitive damages** or **exemplary damages.** In contract actions punitive damages are not ordinarily awarded. In some consumer situations the recovery of punitive damages is allowed in order to discourage the defendant from breaking the law with others. For example, in cases in which the plaintiff is a consumer and the seller has acted wrongfully and stubbornly, there is an increasing trend to award punitive damages in order to prevent a repetition of such conduct.

The fact that the breaching party made prompt efforts to correct the situation when notified of the breach is strong evidence of the lack of the mental state justifying the imposition of punitive damages.[6]

In the *Morrow* case the plaintiff claimed the right to recover punitive damages because the defendant's breach of contract had been "wilful and wanton."

---

[4]   Adams v Orkin Exterminating Co. (Mo App) 763 SW2d 318 (1989).

[5]   Shadow Isle, Inc. v Granada Feeding Co. 226 Neb 325, 411 NW2d 331 (1987).
[6]   McDaniel v Bass-Smith Funeral Home, Inc. 80 NC App 629, 343 SE2d 228 (1986).

MORROW v L. A. GOLDSCHMIDT ASSOCIATES, INC.
112 Ill 2d 87, 96 Ill Dec 939, 492 NE2d 181 (1986)

L. A. Goldschmidt Associates constructed townhouses that were purchased by Morrow and others. The construction contracts were not properly performed, and Morrow and the other purchasers sued Goldschmidt for breach of the contract. In their complaint, they stated that the breach of the contract had been "wilful and wanton" and claimed punitive damages. Punitive damages were awarded the plaintiffs, and the defendant appealed.

MORAN, J. . . . As a general rule, punitive damages are not recoverable for breach of contract. . . . The sole purpose of contract damages is to compensate the nonbreaching party, and punitive damages are not available even for a "wilful" breach of contract. . . .

The rule against awarding punitive damages for breach of contract has been applied to situations, like the present case, where homeowners have sued builders or contractors for construction defects. Courts traditionally have refused to award punitive damages in such cases where the allegations against the builder or contractor amounted to nothing more than a breach of contract. . . .

An exception to the general rule that punitive damages are not recoverable for breach of contract is when the conduct causing the breach is also a tort for which punitive damages are recoverable. . . . That is, punitive damages are recoverable "where the breach amounts to an independent tort and there are proper allegations of malice, wantonness or oppression."

. . . Defendants, however, argue that plaintiffs have not alleged a separate tort for which punitive damages are available. They note that the complaint does not allege that the defects in workmanship and construction caused personal injury or damage to property other than to the townhouse units themselves. As such, they argue that plaintiffs have incurred only "economic losses" for which there is no tort recovery.

. . . Plaintiffs seek to recover only the costs of repairs to their homes caused by defendants' alleged faulty workmanship. . . . The plaintiffs here have not alleged a harm "above and beyond disappointed expectations." . . . They do not complain that the defects caused an accident which resulted in physical injury or damage to other property. Indeed, contrary to the findings of the appellate court, nowhere in plaintiffs' complaint is it alleged that the defects were a threat to health or safety. As such, the plaintiffs essentially are complaining that they did not receive the benefit of their bargain—a harm which is appropriately remedied by bringing an action for breach of contract.

Plaintiffs argue that the present case is distinguishable from [previous cases in which this court denied tort recovery to plaintiffs] because the defendants' conduct in those cases was merely negligent whereas the defendants' conduct here was allegedly "wilful and wanton." We disagree. Simply characterizing a breach of contract as "wilful and wanton" does not change the fact that plaintiffs are only seeking recovery for harm to a contract-like interest. We cannot agree that a breach of contract becomes a tort just because the breach was wilful and wanton. . . . Where the construction defects do not cause physical injuries or damage to other property, we are unwilling to impose tort liability on a builder for breach of his contract with the purchaser, even if the breach was wilful and wanton.

Moreover, we decline to adopt plaintiffs' alternative argument that punitive damages should be awarded for certain wilful and wanton breaches of contract, even though the breach is not accompanied by an independent tort. Although punitive damages appear to be recoverable in a few other jurisdictions for certain wilful breaches of contract . . ., we continue to adhere to the view that tort and contract law are founded on different policies which justify separate rules with respect to recovery of punitive damages. (See Corbin, Contracts sec. 1077, at 437–38 (1964).) We hold that counts VIII

> through XI of plaintiffs' complaint do not state a cause of action for the tort of wilful and wanton misconduct and punitive damages.
>
> [Judgment allowing punitive damages reversed]
>
> QUESTIONS
>
> 1. What did the court decide?
> 2. Did the court recognize any exception to the rule stated in its decision? Explain.
> 3. Under what circumstances could the plaintiffs in the *Morrow* case have recovered punitive damages in the action for breach of contract?

(c) DIRECT AND CONSEQUENTIAL DAMAGES. The breach of a contract may cause the other party direct and consequential loss. A **direct loss** is one that necessarily is caused by the breach of contract. A **consequential loss** is one that does not necessarily follow the breach of the contract but happens to do so in a particular case, because of the circumstances of the injured party. For example, if the seller breaks the contract to deliver a truck that operates properly, the buyer sustains the damages of receiving a truck that cannot be used. This is the direct loss. If the buyer of the truck needed the truck to take a harvest of ripe tomatoes to the cannery, the loss of the crop that could not be transported would be the consequential loss sustained by the farmer-buyer.

Consequential damages may be recovered if they were within the contemplation of the parties at the time they entered into their contract.[7] This does not mean that the parties must have actually thought of the consequential damage that would follow from a breach of the contract. It is sufficient that a reasonable person in the same position would have foreseen the probability of such damage.

In order to recover damages for a particular consequential loss, the plaintiff must show that it was within the defendant's contemplation—that is, it was foreseeable that the kind of loss in question could be sustained by the plaintiff if the contract was broken.

(d) MITIGATION OF DAMAGES. The injured party is under the duty to **mitigate the damages** if reasonably possible.[8] That is, damages must not be permitted to increase if this can be prevented by reasonable efforts. This means that the injured party must generally stop any performance under the contract in order to avoid running up a larger bill. It may require the injured party to buy or rent elsewhere the goods that the wrongdoer was obligated to deliver under the contract. In the case of the breach of an employment contract by the employer, the employee is required to seek other similar employment. The wages earned or that could have been earned from similar employment must be deducted from the damages claimed.

(1) Effect of Failure to Mitigate Damages. The effect of the requirement of mitigating damages is to limit the recovery by the injured party to the damages that would have been sustained had the injured party mitigated the damages. That is, recovery is limited to the direct loss, and damages for consequential loss are excluded. For example, assume that a commercial hauler makes a contract to buy a truck. Because the seller fails to deliver the truck, the buyer loses a hauling job on which a profit of $500 would have been made. Assume that the hauler could have rented a truck for $150 in time to do the hauling job. The hauler would then be under a duty to rent the truck so that the $500 profit would not be lost. By failing to do this, the hauler permitted the

[7]   Fairfax County Redevelopment and Housing Authority v Hurst and Associates Consulting Engineers, Inc. 231 Va 164, 343 SE2d 294 (1986).

[8]   Davis v First Interstate Bank of Idaho (Idaho) 765 P2d 680 (1988).

damages to grow from a rental cost of $150 to a loss of profit of $500. When the hauler sues the seller for breach of the sales contract, the rule of mitigation of damages will limit the hauler to recovering only $150, because the additional $350 loss was unnecessarily sustained. If in fact the hauler had rented a truck, the rental of $150 would be recoverable as damages from the seller. Thus, the hauler will only receive $150 damages whether or not a truck is rented in order to mitigate the damages.

(2) Excuse for Failure to Mitigate Damages. If there is nothing that the injured party can reasonably do to reduce damages, there is, by definition, no duty to mitigate damages. For example, a leasing company broke its contract to supply a specified computer and auxiliary equipment by delivering a less desirable computer. The specified computer and equipment could not be obtained elsewhere by the customer. Therefore, the customer was entitled to recover full damages.

When the cost of mitigating, as by purchasing elsewhere the goods that the seller failed to deliver, is unreasonably great, there is no duty to mitigate damages.

(e) CONVERSION OF FOREIGN CURRENCY. Judgments entered in state and United States federal courts must be stated in terms of United States currency—that is, American dollars. This raises a problem when an international contract is involved, and the plaintiff's damages are measured in terms of a foreign currency. The earlier American rule was to award the plaintiff the number of American dollars that the amount of the foreign currency would buy as of the rate of exchange on the day of the defendant's breach. In view of the present fluctuations in world currencies, the modern trend is to award the foreign plaintiff the number of American dollars determined by the rate of exchange on the date of the judgment when the use of that date will produce a more equitable result.[9]

9. Rescission

When there has been a material breach of the contract, the aggrieved party may rescind the contract. If the wrongdoing party objects, the aggrieved party may bring an action for rescission.

(a) RIGHT TO RESCIND. When one party commits a material breach of the contract, the other party may rescind the contract because of such breach. In some situations the right to rescind may be governed or controlled by civil service statutes or similar regulations, or by an obligation to submit the matter to arbitration or to a grievance procedure.

An injured party who rescinds after having performed or paid money under the contract may recover the reasonable value of the performance rendered or the money paid. This recovery is not based on the contract that has been rescinded but on a quasi contract that the law implies to prevent the defaulter from keeping the benefit received and thus being unjustly enriched. When a contract for the sale of land is rescinded, the buyer is entitled to the return of the purchase price and to compensation for any improvements made to the land. A deduction will be made from such sums for the reasonable rental value of the property during the time that the buyer was in possession.

The rescinding party must restore the other party to that party's original position.[10] If the rescinding party's own acts make this impossible, the contract cannot be rescinded. Thus, a buyer who has placed a mortgage on property purchased cannot rescind the sales contract because the property cannot be returned to the seller in its original, unmortgaged condition.

Care must be exercised in deciding to rescind a contract. If proper ground for rescission does not exist, the party who rescinds is guilty of repudiating the contract and is liable for damages for its breach.[11] Rescission and recovery of monetary damages are alternative

[9] Teca-Print A. G. v Amacoil Machinery, Inc. 525 NYS2d 535 (1988).

[10] Puskar v Hughes, 179 Ill App 3d 522, 127 Ill Dec 880, 533 NE2d 962 (1989).
[11] Joshua v McBride, 19 Ark App 31, 716 SW2d 215 (1986).

remedies, except in a contract for the sale of goods, in which case both remedies are available.

(b) JUDICIAL RESCISSION. If the party breaking the contract does not recognize the right of the aggrieved party to rescind the contract, the aggrieved party may bring an action in which the court will declare that the contract has been rescinded. In that action the court will also specify what payments or exchanges of property are to be made by the parties in order to return matters to the conditions existing before the contract was made.

10.   Action for Specific Performance

Under special circumstances the injured party may obtain the equitable remedy of specific performance that compels the other party to carry out the terms of a contract. Specific performance is ordinarily granted only if the subject matter of the contract is unique, thereby making a monetary award of damages an inadequate remedy. Monetary damages may be inadequate because it is not possible to make a reasonable determination of the damages the plaintiff will sustain by the breach of the contract. Monetary damages may be inadequate because a replacement or substitute performance cannot be obtained in the marketplace. Contracts for the purchase of land[12] will

---

[12]   Gordon v Bauer, 177 Ill App 3d 1073, 127 Ill Dec 26, 532 NE2d 855 (1988).

be specifically enforced, as will contracts for the sale of a business and the franchise held by the business.

Specific performance of a contract to sell personal property can generally be obtained only if the article is of unusual age, beauty, unique history, or other distinction. In the case of heirlooms, original paintings, old editions of books, or relics, identical articles could not be obtained in the market. Specific performance is also allowed a buyer in the case of a contract to buy shares of stock essential for control of a close corporation when those shares have no fixed or market value and are not quoted in the commercial reports or sold on a stock exchange.

The granting of specific performance is discretionary with the court. This relief will be refused (a) when the contract is not definite; (b) when there is an adequate legal remedy (usually a monetary award); (c) when it works an undue hardship or an injustice on the defaulting party or the consideration is inadequate; (d) when the agreement is illegal, fraudulent, or unconscionable; (e) when the court is unable to supervise the performance of such acts, as when services of a technical nature are to be rendered; or (f) when there has been unreasonable delay in bringing suit.

If the subject matter of the contract lacks uniqueness, specific performance cannot be obtained when the contract is broken.

The *Van Wagner Advertising* case turned on what constituted being "unique."

VAN WAGNER ADVERTISING CORP. v S & M ENTERPRISES
67 NY2d 177, 501 NYS2d 628, 492 NE2d 756 (1986)

Michaels owned a building. She made a lease with Van Wagner Advertising Corporation, giving it the right to erect a sign on one of the walls of the building facing automobile traffic entering Manhattan through the Midtown Tunnel. The lease ran for three years with options to renew up to ten years. Van Wagner erected an illuminated billboard and then leased it to Asch Advertising. Michaels later sold the building to S & M Enterprises. S & M was buying up the property on the block in order to construct a residential-commercial complex. S & M notified Van Wagner that it was terminating the lease. Van Wagner sued S & M for specific performance to make it adhere to the terms of the lease. The court held that the lease was improperly broken but refused to grant specific performance to compel obedience to the lease terms. Van Wagner appealed.

KAYE, J. . . . Whether or not to award specific performance is a decision that rests in the sound discretion of the trial court, and here that discretion was not abused. Considering first the nature of the transaction, specific performance has been imposed as the remedy for breach of contracts for the sale of real property . . . , but the contract here is to lease rather than sell an interest in real property. While specific performance is available, in appropriate circumstances, for breach of a commercial or residential lease, specific performance of real property leases is not in this State awarded as a matter of course. . . .

Van Wagner argues that specific performance must be granted in light of the trial court's finding that the "demised space is unique as to location for the particular advertising purpose intended". The word "uniqueness" is not, however, a magic door to specific performance. . . . Putting aside contracts for the sale of real property, where specific performance has traditionally been the remedy for breach, uniqueness in the sense of physical difference does not itself dictate the propriety of equitable relief. . . .

The point at which breach of a contract will be redressable by specific performance . . . must lie . . . in the uncertainty of valuing it: "What matters, in measuring money damages, is the volume, refinement, and reliability of the available information about substitutes for the subject matter of the breached contract. When the relevant information is thin and unreliable, there is a substantial risk that an award of money damages will either exceed or fall short of the promisee's actual loss. Of course this risk can always be reduced—but only at great cost when reliable information is difficult to obtain. Conversely, when there is a great deal of consumer behavior generating abundant and highly dependable information about substitutes, the risk of error in measuring the promisee's loss may be reduced at much smaller cost. In asserting that the subject matter of a particular contract is unique and has no established market value, a court is really saying that it cannot obtain, at reasonable cost, enough information about substitutes to permit it to calculate an award of money damages without imposing an unacceptably high risk of undercompensation on the injured promisee. Conceived in this way, the uniqueness test seems economically sound." (45 U Chi L Rev, at 362.) This principle is reflected in the case law . . . , and is essentially the position of the Restatement (Second) of Contracts, which lists "the difficulty of proving damages with reasonable certainty" as the first factor affecting adequacy of damages (Restatement [Second] of Contracts § 360[a]).

Thus, the fact that the subject of the contract may be "unique as to location for the particular advertising purpose intended" by the parties does not entitle a plaintiff to the remedy of specific performance.

Here, the trial court correctly concluded that the value of the "unique qualities" of the demised space could be fixed with reasonable certainty and without imposing an unacceptably high risk of undercompensating the injured tenant. Both parties complain: Van Wagner asserts that while lost revenues on the Asch contract may be adequate compensation, that contract expired February 28, 1985, its lease with S & M continues until 1992, and the value of the demised space cannot reasonably be fixed for the balance of the term. S & M urges that future rents and continuing damages are necessarily conjectural, both during and after the Asch contract, and that Van Wagner's damages must be limited to 60 days—the period during which Van Wagner could cancel Asch's contract without consequence in the event Van Wagner lost the demised space. S & M points out that Van Wagner's lease could remain in effect for the full 10-year term, or it could legitimately be extinguished immediately, either in conjunction with a bona fide sale of the property by S & M, or by a reletting of the building if the new tenant required use of the billboard space for its own purposes. Both parties' contentions were properly rejected.

First, it is hardly novel in the law for damages to be projected into the future. Particularly where the value of commercial billboard space can be readily determined by comparisons with similar uses—Van Wagner itself has more than 400 leases—the value of this property between 1985 and 1992 cannot be regarded as speculative. Second, S & M having successfully resisted specific performance on the ground that there is an adequate remedy at law, cannot at the same time be heard to contend that damages beyond 60 days must be denied because they are conjectural. If damages for breach of this lease are indeed conjectural, and cannot be calculated with reasonable certainty, then S & M should be compelled to perform its contractual obligation by restoring Van Wagner to the premises. Moreover, the contingencies to which S & M points do not, as a practical matter, render the calculation of damages speculative. While S & M could terminate the Van Wagner lease in the event of a sale of the building, this building has been sold only once in 40 years; S & M paid several million dollars, and purchased the building in connection with its plan for major development of the block. The theoretical termination right of a future tenant of the existing building also must be viewed in light of these circumstances. If any uncertainty is generated by the two contingencies, then the benefit of that doubt must go to Van Wagner and not the contract violator. Neither contingency allegedly affecting Van Wagner's continued contractual right to the space for the balance of the lease term is within its own control; on the contrary, both are in the interest of S & M. Thus, neither the need to project into the future nor the contingencies allegedly affecting the length of Van Wagner's term render inadequate the remedy of damages for S & M's breach of its lease with Van Wagner.

The trial court, additionally, correctly concluded that specific performance should be denied on the ground that such relief "would be inequitable in that its effect would be disproportionate in its harm to defendant and its assistance to plaintiff." It is well settled that the imposition of an equitable remedy must not itself work an inequity, and that specific performance should not be an undue hardship. . . .

[Judgment affirmed as to denial of specific performance]

QUESTIONS

1. What did the court hold and why?
2. How would the case have been decided if the action for specific performance had been brought by Asch Advertising?
3. Could the damages in the *Van Wagner* case be proven with mathematical certainty?

Ordinarily, contracts for the performance of personal services will not be specifically ordered. This is because of the difficulty of supervision by the court and because of the restriction of the Thirteenth Amendment of the federal Constitution prohibiting involuntary servitude except as criminal punishment. In some instances a court will issue a negative injunction that prohibits the defendant from rendering a similar service for anyone else.

This may indirectly have the effect of compelling the defendant to work for the plaintiff.

In order to do complete justice, the court in awarding specific performance can also award damages to compensate for the direct and consequential loss caused by the defendant's refusal to perform the contract.

D.   CONTRACT PROVISIONS AFFECTING REMEDIES AND DAMAGES

The contract of the parties may contain provisions that affect the remedies available or the recovery of damages.

11.   Limitation of Remedies

The contract of the parties may limit the remedies of the aggrieved parties. For example, the contract may give one party the right to repair or replace a defective item sold or to refund the contract price. The contract may require both parties to submit any dispute to arbitration or other streamlined procedure.

12.   Liquidated Damages

The parties may stipulate in their contract that a certain amount should be paid in case of a breach. This amount is known as **liquidated damages.** Liquidated damages may be variously measured by the parties. When delay is in mind, liquidated damages may be a fixed sum, as $100 for each day of delay. When there is a total default, damages may be a percentage of the contract price or may be the amount of the down payment.

(a) EFFECT. When a liquidated damage clause is held valid, the injured party cannot collect more than the amount specified by the clause. The defaulting party is bound to pay such damages once the fact is established that there has been a default.[13] The injured party is not required to make any proof as to damages sustained, and the defendant is not permitted to show that the damages were not as great as the liquidated sum.

(b) VALIDITY. In order to be valid, a liquidated damage clause must satisfy two requirements: (1) the situation must be one in which it is difficult or impossible to determine the actual damages, and (2) the amount specified must not be excessive when compared with the probable damages that would be sustained.

If the liquidated damages clause calls for the payment of a sum that is clearly unreasonably large and unrelated to the possible actual damages that might be sustained, the clause will be held to be void as a **penalty.** A liquidated damage provision tries to measure the compensation for a breach of the contract. In contrast, a penalty provision punishes the breach. When a liquidated damage clause is held invalid, the effect is merely to erase the clause from the contract. A party injured by breach of the contract may proceed to recover damages for its breach. Instead of recovering the liquidated damage amount, the injured party will recover such damages as are established by the evidence.

In the *Walter Implement* case the validity of a liquidated damage clause was challenged.

[13]   Burst v R. W. Beal & Co., Inc. (Mo App) 771 SW2d 87 (1989).

WALTER IMPLEMENT, INC. v FOCHT
107 Wash 2d 533, 730 P2d 1340 (1987)

Walter Implement, Inc. was a dealer for farm equipment. It leased five pieces of farm equipment to Focht and his wife for five years. The lease provided that if annual rental payments were not made, Walter could take back the equipment, resell it, and then sue Focht for any unpaid balance. The lease also required Focht to pay Walter liquidated damages in such case. These damages were to be "20 percent of the aggregate minimum rental charges for the unexpired portion of the term [of the lease]." Focht could not make the second annual payment and returned the equipment to Walter. It sold the equipment and then sued Focht for the liquidated damages. The court entered judgment for Walter for the liquidated damages, computing them by the formula contained in the lease. Focht appealed. The court of appeals held the liquidated damage clause void. Walter then appealed to the state supreme court.

GOODLOE, J. . . . The . . . issue we must decide is whether the liquidated damages clause in the resell remedy provision is enforceable. The clause provides for "an amount equal to twenty (20) percent of the aggregate minimum rental charges for the unexpired portion of the term of this agreement, not as a penalty, but as and for liquidated damages." Exhibit 1. The trial court enforced this clause. The court calculated that Focht, having made only one of the five annual payments, had an unexpired portion of $43,255.28 (four payments at $10,806.32) which was multiplied by 20 percent to get the liquidated damages figure of $8,645.06. The Court of Appeals reversed. It held the clause was unenforceable because it was not a product of the parties' negotiations, was inherently unfair, and bore no relation to the anticipated actual damages.

True liquidated damages clauses, those that are not penalties, are favored and will be upheld. This court follows the United States Supreme Court view that liquidated damages agreements fairly and understandingly entered into by experienced, equal parties with a view to just compensation for the anticipated loss should be enforced. The fact that the contracting parties designate a sum as liquidated damages is a circumstance given serious consideration, but it is not necessarily controlling or conclusive. The designation in this contract that the additional amount is not a penalty but is liquidated damages, therefore, does not decide the issue. Courts will look to the intention of the parties to make an accurate assessment of the clause's purpose. "A provision in a contract which bears no reasonable relation to actual damages will be construed as a penalty." *Enders*, 74 Wash. 2d at 594, 446 P.2d 200.

This court has adopted and applied a 2-part test to determine whether a liquidated damages clause is enforceable. First, the amount fixed must be a reasonable forecast of just compensation for the harm that is caused by the breach. Second, the harm must be such that it is incapable or very difficult of ascertainment. Reasonableness of the forecast will be judged as of the time the contract was entered. Determination of whether the test is met depends upon the facts and circumstances of each case. . . .

First, we look at the amount fixed to see if it is a reasonable forecast of just compensation for the harm caused by the breach. The involved liquidated damages clause which does not require a fixed amount but instead requires 20 percent of the outstanding rental payments does not appear to have any relation, reasonable or not, to an estimation of damages. A fixed amount of 20 percent of the full lease figure may be a reasonable forecast. In fact, the parties orally agreed that if Focht wished to buy the equipment at the end of the lease term, the cost would be 20 percent of the entire lease figure. This liquidated damages clause by containing a variable makes the amount of liquidated damages depend upon when the default occurs. Even this could be acceptable if . . . the variable was reasonably related to the damages. Here, the liquidated damages could vary from $2161.26 (default in the 4th year) to $8645.06 (default in the first year). No reasoning has been offered explaining how the variation reflects a reasonable forecast of the harm that is caused by the breach. For example, using this formula, the earlier the default the greater the penalty although the equipment is returned sooner resulting in less depreciation of the equipment.

Besides the formula not appearing to have any relation to the anticipated actual damages, such damages are not difficult to ascertain. *American Fin. Leasing & Servs. Co. v. Miller*, 41 Ohio App.2d 69, 322 N.E.2d 149 (1974), which uses the same 2-part test to evaluate liquidated damages clauses, involved a similar equipment lease provision. The *Miller* lease contained several optional remedies, one of which included a recovery of 10 percent of the actual cost to lessor of equipment sold in the event of a default. The court held that actual damages could be easily ascertained. Because of recoupment of the actual damages, the court determined the 10 percent figure

> neither bears a reasonable relationship to such damage, nor is in a reasonable proportion thereto.
>
> Such amount is patently in excess of the actual damage which could be suffered by the lessor, and therefore must be considered as a "penalty" rather than a stipulated "liquidated damage."

Miller, at 75, 322 N.E.2d 149. Using the same reasoning, the liquidated damages clause in this case fails. . . .

The consequence of the preceding analysis is that Walter Implement is entitled to a deficiency judgment. The deficiency judgment is based on actual damages. . . . In a true lease situation, the lessor has a right not only to the contract price but also to the return of the leased goods. The lessor is thus entitled at breach to the value the goods would have had at the expiration of the lease term in addition to the unpaid portion of the contract price. . . .

Evidence presented at trial suggested that the equipment was expected to be worth about 20 percent of the total lease price at the end of the lease, or about $10,000. If that forecast was reasonable, then Walter Implement's damages are the unpaid rents ($43,225.28) plus about $10,000, both reduced to present value, minus the value of the recovered equipment (about $35,000). We affirm the Court of Appeals and find the liquidated damages clause is a penalty and unenforceable. We remand to the trial court to determine how much the equipment reasonably could have been expected to be worth at the end of the lease term. That value should be included in the Fochts' debt and the deficiency adjusted accordingly.

[Judgment affirmed and action remanded]

QUESTIONS

1. Did the court hold that the lease arrangement for damages was illegal?
2. In view of the fact that the Washington supreme court affirmed the judgment of the court of appeals, why did it remand the action?
3. What was the basis for the court's decision?

---

13. Limitation of Liability

A contract may contain a provision stating that one of the parties shall not be liable for damages in case of breach. Such a provision is called an **exculpatory clause** or a **limitation of liability clause.** As an example of such a provision, a construction contract may state that the contractor shall not be liable for damages from delay caused by third persons.

(a) CONTENT AND CONSTRUCTION. An exculpatory clause must be clear and unambiguous. Moreover, such a clause is strictly construed.[14] For example, a limitation of liability for negligence does not bar liability for violation of a consumer protection statute.

(b) VALIDITY. Exculpatory clauses are generally valid, particularly between experienced business persons. Thus, a telephone company may limit its liability to a nominal amount for the omission of a customer's name and number from the yellow page directory where the limitation is conspicuous, the customer is experienced in business, and the omission was merely the result of simple negligence.[15] Release forms signed by participants in athletic and sporting events declaring that the sponsor, proprietor, or operator of the event shall not be liable for injuries sustained by the participants are binding.[16]

There is a growing trend to hold exculpatory provisions invalid when it is felt that they are oppressive or unconscionable because of the superior bargaining power of the party protected thereby. This is particularly likely to be the result when the party in question is a public utility. Such an enterprise is under the duty to provide the service to the public in a nonnegligent way.

In recent years the concept has developed that a limitation of liability is invalid when persons in an inferior bargaining position are involved. In any case, a limitation of liability is not binding if obtained by misconduct or deception.

In the *Madison* case it was claimed that a release did not bar suit for breach of a teaching contract that resulted in the death of a student.

---

[14]   Falkner v Hinckley Parachute Center, Inc. 178 Ill App 3d 597, 127 Ill Dec 859, 533 NE2d 941 (1989).
[15]   Soileau Coreil v Trans-Western Publishing (La App) 542 So 2d 198 (1989).

[16]   Milligan v Big Valley Corp. (Wyo) 754 P2d 1063 (1988).

MADISON v SUPERIOR COURT
203 Cal App 3d 589, 250 Cal Rptr 299 (1988)

Ken Sulejmanagic, aged 19, signed up for a course in scuba diving taught by Madison at the local YMCA. Before the instruction began, Ken was required to sign a form releasing Madison and the YMCA from liability for any harm that might occur. At the end of the course, Madison, Ken, and another student went out into deep water. Ken made the final dive required by the course program. Madison left Ken alone in the water while he took the other student for a dive. When Madison returned, Ken could not be found. It was later determined that he had drowned. The parents of Ken sued Madison and the YMCA for negligence in the performance of the teaching contract. The defendants raised the defense that the release signed by Ken shielded them from liability. The court held that the release was void. The defendants then filed a petition in the higher court requesting it to order the lower court to give effect to the release and to enter summary judgment in their favor.

CROSKEY, J. . . . The relevant portions of the agreement provide as follows:

"For and in consideration of permitting (1) *Ken Salejmanagie [sic]* to enroll in and participate in diving activities and class instruction of skin and/or scuba diving given by (2) *Norman Madison/Westchester YMCA* . . . the Undersigned hereby voluntarily releases, discharges, waives and relinquishes any and all actions or causes of action for personal injury, property damage or wrongful death occurring to him/herself arising as a result of engaging or receiving instructions in said activity or any activities incidental thereto wherever or however the same may occur and for whatever period said activities or instructions may continue, and the Undersigned does for him/herself, his/her heirs, executors, administrators and assigns hereby release, waive, discharge and relinquish any action or causes of action, aforesaid, which may hereafter arise for him/herself and for his/her estate, and agrees that under no circumstances will he/she or his/her heirs, executors, administrators and assigns prosecute, present any claim for personal injury, property damage or wrongful death against (2) *Norman Madison/Westchester YMCA* or any of its officers, agents, servants or employees for any of said causes of action, whether the same shall arise by the negligence of any of said persons, or otherwise. **IT IS [MY] INTENTION TO EXEMPT AND RELIEVE** *Norman Madison/Westchester YMCA* **FROM LIABILITY FOR PERSONAL INJURY, PROPERTY DAMAGE OR WRONGFUL DEATH CAUSED BY NEGLIGENCE."**

The agreement concludes with the following acknowledgment:

> The Undersigned acknowledges that he/she has read the foregoing two paragraphs, has been fully and completely advised of the potential dangers incidental to engaging in the activity and instructing of skin and/or scuba diving, and is fully aware of the legal consequences of signing the within instrument.

. . . The record does not disclose precisely how or why Ken lost his life . . . The critical question, however, is whether the agreement absolves defendants, in spite of their actions, from any liability to the plaintiffs. . . .

A plaintiff in a wrongful death action is subject to any defenses which could have been asserted against the decedent, including an express agreement by the decedent to waive the defendant's negligence and assume all risks. . . .

Although the words "assumption of the risk" are not specifically used [in Ken's release], it is clear that Ken expressly acknowledged his intent to do just that. In heavy bold type the release expressly states that it was Ken's intent to exempt and relieve the defendants from any liability for their *negligence*. By this language Ken expressly manifested his intent to relieve the defendants of any duty to him and to assume the entire risk of any injury. . . . The result is that the defendant is relieved of legal duty to the plaintiff; and being under no duty, he cannot be charged with negligence. . . .

Our examination of the agreement compels the conclusion that it was clear and free from ambiguity. It would be difficult to imagine language more clearly designed to put a layperson on notice of the significance and legal effect of subscribing to it. The emphasized references to the exemption and relief from "liability for personal injury, property damage or wrongful death caused by negligence" could not be more explicit.

Moreover, we perceive of no reason why Ken could not validly execute such a broad agreement. "No public policy opposes private, voluntary transactions in which one party, for a consideration, agrees to shoulder a risk which the law would otherwise have placed upon the other party. . . ."

. . . The court in *Kurashige v. Indian Dunes, Inc.* (1988) 200 Cal.App.3d 606, 246 Cal.Rptr. 310, concluded that a release signed by motorcycle dirtbike riders did not involve a public interest. The court, in language equally applicable here, stated that the release ". . . agreement used here was printed legibly, contained adequate, clear and explicit exculpatory language and indicated defendants were to be absolved from the consequences of their own negligence. . . . Furthermore, it did not involve the public interest: defendants' business was not generally thought to be suitable for public regulation; defendants did not perform a service of great importance to the public, and the business was not a matter of practical necessity for members of the public; and defendants' customers did not place their persons under defendants' control. . . .

Here, Ken certainly had the option of not taking the class. There was no practical necessity that he do so. In view of the dangerous nature of this particular activity defendants could reasonably require the execution of the release as a condition of enrollment. Ken entered into a private and voluntary transaction in which, in exchange for an enrollment in a class which he desired to take, he freely agreed to waive any claim against the defendants for a negligent act by them. This case involves no more a question of public interest than does motorcross racing . . . sky diving . . . or motorcycle dirtbike riding. . . .

Therefore, we conclude that the agreement is enforceable and, as against any action brought by Ken, would have served as *a complete defense."* It had the obviously intended legal effect of shifting the responsibility for any negligence by the defendants from the defendants to Ken. By this agreement, Ken effectively assumed all of the risks of any injury he might suffer as a result of defendants' negligence during the training course. . . .

We therefore determine that the legal effect of the release and waiver provisions of the agreement is to provide to defendants "a complete defense" to plaintiffs' action. . . .

[Judgment reversed]

QUESTIONS

1. Was it important whether Ken's release expressly declared that he "assumed the risk" of scuba diving?
2. What social force is furthered by the decision of the court?
3. Should the court in the *Madison* case have decided specifically whether the defendants were or were not negligent?

Some courts refuse to recognize provisions releasing a party from liability for negligence when the provisions are so inconspicuous as to raise a question of whether they were knowingly agreed to.[17]

14. Invalidity of Contract Provision Relating to Remedies or Damages

When a contract contains a valid provision governing remedies or damages, the parties are bound thereby. That means that they must follow the procedures specified or the aggrieved person is bound by the provision as to damages. What happens if the provision in question is invalid? The provision is merely ignored. The balance of the contract remains valid. This means that if the limitation of remedies is not valid, an aggrieved person may follow any remedy that would otherwise be available. If a liquidated damages or a limitation of damages clause is invalid, the aggrieved person may sue for the damages sustained, but must actually prove what those damages were.

[17]   Conradt v Four Star Promotions, Inc. 45 Wash App 847, 728 P2d 617 (1986).

SUMMARY

When a party fails to perform a contract or performs improperly, the other contracting party may sue for damages caused by the breach. What may be recovered by the aggrieved person is stated in terms of being direct or consequential damages. Direct damages are those that ordinarily will result from the breach. Consequential damages are those that are in fact caused by the breach but do not ordinarily or necessarily result from every breach of the particular kind of contract. Direct damages may be recovered on proof of causation and amount. Consequential damages can only be recovered if, in addition to proving causation and amount, it is shown that they were reasonably within the contemplation of the contracting parties as a probable result of a breach of the contract. The right to recover consequential damages is lost if the aggrieved party could reasonably have taken steps to avoid such damages. That is, the aggrieved person has a duty to mitigate or reduce damages by reasonable means.

In any case the damages recoverable for breach of contract may be limited to a specific amount by a liquidated damage clause or may be canceled out completely by a limitation of liability clause.

In a limited number of situations the aggrieved party may bring an action for specific performance to compel the other contracting party to perform the acts called for by the contract. Specific performance is always obtainable of a contract to sell land or real estate, on the theory that such property has a unique value. With respect to other contracts, specific performance will not be ordered unless it is shown that there was some unique element present, so that the aggrieved person would suffer a damage that could not be compensated for by the payment of money damages.

The aggrieved person also has the option of rescinding the contract if (1) the breach has been as to a material term and (2) the aggrieved party returns everything to the way that it was before the contract was made. Rescission and recovery of monetary damages are alternative remedies, except when the contract relates to the sale of goods. In the latter case, the aggrieved party may both rescind and obtain money damages.

Although there has been a breach of the contract, the effect of this breach is nullified if the aggrieved person by word or conduct waives the right to object to the breach. Conversely, an aggrieved party may accept a defective performance without thereby waiving a claim for breach if the party makes a reservation of rights. A reservation of rights can be made by stating that the defective performance is accepted without prejudice, under protest, or with reservation of rights.

The continued waiver of a breach of a particular clause may indicate that the parties have modified their contract by abandoning the clause to which the waiver relates. To guard against the unintended modification of a contract by waiver, the contract may contain a clause stating that nothing shall constitute a modification of the contract unless stated in writing.

QUESTIONS AND CASE PROBLEMS

1. What social forces are affected by the rule governing the mitigation of damages?
2. When must a party to a contract mitigate damages caused by the breach of the contract by the other party?
3. Anthony makes a contract to sell a rare painting to Laura for $100,000. The written contract specifies that if Anthony should fail to perform the contract, he will pay Laura $50,000 as liquidated damages. Anthony fails to deliver the painting and is sued by Laura for $50,000. Can she recover this amount?
4. Rogers owned land. He made a contract with Salisbury Brick Corporation that allowed it to remove earth and sand from his land. The contract ran for four years, with provision to renew it for additional 4-year terms up to a total of 96 years. The contract provided for compensation to Rogers based on the amount of earth and sand removed. By an unintentional mistake Salisbury underpaid Rogers the amount of $863 for the months of November and December of 1986. Salisbury offered this amount to Rogers, but he refused to accept it and claimed that he had been underpaid in other months. Rogers claimed that he was entitled to rescind the contract. Was he correct? [Rogers v Salisbury Brick Corp. (SC) 382 SE2d 915]
5. A, who had contracted to build a house for B, departed from the specifications at a number of points. It would cost approximately $1,000 to put the house in the condition called for by the

contract. *B* sued *A* for $5,000 for breach of contract and emotional disturbance caused by the breach. Decide.

6. Protein Blenders, Inc., made a contract with Gingerich to buy from him the shares of stock of a small corporation. When the buyer refused to take and pay for the stock, Gingerich sued for specific performance of the contract on the ground that the value of the stock was unknown and could not be readily ascertained because it was not sold on the general market. Was he entitled to specific performance? [Gingerich v Protein Blenders, Inc. 250 Iowa 646, 95 NW2d 522]

7. The buyer of real estate made a down payment. In the contract it was stated that the buyer would be liable for damages in an amount equal to the down payment if the buyer broke the contract. The buyer refused to go through with the contract and demanded his down payment back. The seller refused to return it and claimed that he was entitled to additional damages from the buyer because the damages that he had suffered were greater than the amount of the down payment. Decide. [Waters v Key Colony East, Inc. (Fla App) 345 So 2d 367]

8. Kuznicki made a contract for the installation of a fire detection system by Security Safety Corp. for $498. The contract was made one night and canceled at 9:00 a.m. the next morning. Security then claimed one-third of the purchase price from Kuznicki by virtue of a provision in the contract that "in the event of cancellation of this agreement ... the owner agrees to pay $33\frac{1}{3}$ percent of the contract price, as liquidated damages." Was Security Safety entitled to recover the amount claimed? [Security Safety Corp. v Kuznicki, 350 Mass 157, 213 NE2d 866]

9. Stabler was under contract to play professional football for Alabama Football, Inc. The corporation was not able to pay Stabler the amount due him under the contract. He sued for rescission. The club defended on the theory that nonpayment was not a sufficiently substantial breach of the contract to justify rescission. Was the club correct? [Alabama Football, Inc. v Stabler, 294 Ala 551, 319 So 2d 678]

10. Melodee Lane Lingerie Co. was a tenant in a building that was protected against fire by a sprinkler and alarm system maintained by the American District Telegraph Co. Because of the latter's fault, the controls on the system were defective and allowed the discharge of water into the building, which damaged Melodee's property. When Melodee sued A.D.T., it raised the defense that its service contract limited its liability to 10 percent of the annual service charge made to the customer. Was this limitation valid? [Melodee Lane Lingerie Co. v American District Telegraph Co. 18 NY2d 57, 271 NYS2d 937, 218 NE2d 661]

11. *A* owned a house. In May he made a contract with *B*, a roofer, to repair the roof on the house by July 1. *B* never came to repair the roof and heavy rains in the fall damaged the interior of *A*'s house. *A* sues *B* for breach of contract and claims damages for the harm done to the interior of the house. Is *A* entitled to recover such damages?

12. A subcontractor made a contract to do certain construction work on land owned by K-Mart Corporation. The subcontractor's contract required him to obtain insurance to protect the general contractor and K-Mart from any liability from third persons, and to deliver to the contractor written proof of such insurance before the subcontractor began any work. The subcontractor began work although he had not obtained the required insurance. Both K-Mart and the general contractor knew that the subcontractor had not obtained the insurance and that he had begun work without furnishing written proof of insurance. Whalen was injured in the course of the construction work and sued K-Mart and the contractor. They claimed that the subcontractor was liable because the subcontractor had not obtained insurance against such claims, as was required by the subcontract. Decide. [Whalen v K-Mart Corp. 166 Ill App 3d 339, 116 Ill Dec 776, 519 NE2d 991]

13. Lowell Prentice wanted to sell his farm, house, and land. After negotiation with Charles Classen, who wanted the property to operate a dairy, the price was agreed to as $45,000. Classen signed a contract for the purchase of the land. Under the contract, Classen made an initial deposit of 10 percent of the purchase price, and he was required to pay the balance in specified installments with 8 percent interest. The contract stated that if the buyer broke the contract, the seller could retain the initial payment of 10 percent and all improvements that had been made to the property by the buyer. Classen moved into the farmhouse with his family and lived there for the next year, during which time he improved the property by adding dairy equipment, a bulk tank, and cement floors in the dairy building. After a year, Classen failed to make necessary payments, and Prentice declared him in default. Classen claimed he was entitled to a refund of the initial 10 percent pay-

ment. He claimed that the contract provision allowing Prentice to retain this amount was unconscionable and void. Was he correct? [Prentice v Classen (SD) 355 NW2d 352]

14. Hembree, a contractor, wanted to borrow $40,000. He discussed borrowing that amount from Bradley. They agreed that vacant land owned by Hembree would be used as collateral. The parties then executed a contract by which Hembree contracted to sell the vacant land to Bradley for $40,000 and agreed to repurchase the land after one year for $50,000. The contract also required Hembree to pay a penalty of $1,000 a month if he failed to repurchase the land. If this transaction constituted a loan of $40,000, it was usurious. Under the applicable law, that would result only in the forfeiting of the right to any interest. It would not affect the right to collect the $40,000. Hembree did not transfer the title to Bradley as required by the contract. Bradley brought an action to obtain specific performance of the contract. Decide. [Hembree v Bradley (Fla App) 528 So 2d 116]

15. Wassenaar worked for Panos under a three-year contract that stated that if the contract was terminated wrongfully by Panos before the end of the three years, he would pay as damages the salary for the remaining time that the contract had to run. After three months Panos terminated the contract, and Wassenaar sued him for 21 months' pay. Panos claimed that this amount could not be recovered because the contract provision for the payment of such amount was a void penalty. Was this provision valid? [Wassenaar v Panos, 111 Wis 2d 518, 331 NW2d 357]

19

ACCOUNTANTS' LIABILITY AND MALPRACTICE

When is a professional, such as an accountant, an attorney, or a physician, liable for harm caused by improper performance? Under what circumstances can third persons sue for harm?

A. GENERAL PRINCIPLES

The liability of a contracting party for malpractice raises questions of what constitutes malpractice, what remedies are available to enforce liability for malpractice, and the effect of conduct of the plaintiff and of limitations of liability.

1.   What Constitutes Malpractice

When an accountant, a physician, or an attorney makes a contract to perform services, there is a duty to exercise such skill and care as is common within the community for persons performing similar services. If the services are not properly rendered in accordance with those standards, there is an improper practicing of the particular profession or, as it is commonly called, **malpractice.**

2.   Choice of Remedy

Because in cases of malpractice performance falls below the proper standard, malpractice is classified as negligence and constitutes a tort. In addition, because the services called for by the contract have not been rendered, malpractice is also a breach of the contract.

(a) BREACH OF CONTRACT OR TORT ACTION. As malpractice is both a breach of the contract and an independent tort, the client or patient who is harmed has the choice of suing for breach of contract or for the particular tort that is involved. Generally, the client or patient will bring a tort action when justified by the facts. This is so because the tort claimant may recover greater damages than the breach-of-contract plaintiff. Moreover, the tort claimant may have a longer period of time in which to sue. The statute of limitations runs on the tort claim from the date when the harm was discovered. In a contract action the statute of limitations runs from the date when the contract was broken. This may be very important, because in some cases the plaintiff does not realize that any harm has been sustained until a substantially long period of time after there was a breach of the contract.

The plaintiff does not have a choice of action when the only misconduct of the defendant is a breach of contract. In order to sue for a tort, the plaintiff must show that the defendant's breach was negligent or willful so that

it was tortious, as well as being a breach of contract.[1]

(b) ACTION BY THIRD PERSON. When the malpractice claim is brought by a third person rather than a client or patient of the defendant, the malpractice action will be brought on the tort theory. Suit cannot be brought by the third person on the original contract. The third person is not a party to that contract and ordinarily cannot be classified as a third party beneficiary of that contract.

3.   The Environment of Accountants' Malpractice Liability

In the course of this century there have been several changes that have influenced the law of malpractice liability as it relates to accountants.

First, the accountant has in many cases moved from being merely a clerical employee to being an essential participant in the planning of business strategies. In addition, the accountant in many instances has moved from being an employee of one employer to being an independent contractor performing accounting services for many clients. Also, the accountant is now employed in many cases for the purpose of producing data on which third persons will rely. For example, the accountant will prepare statements that will be submitted to banks to induce them to lend to the accountant's client. Likewise, such information may be supplied to prospective purchasers of stock of the client corporation.

As the above changes took place, it became natural for courts to allow third persons relying on the work product of the accountant to sue the accountant when malpractice caused loss to the third person.

At the same time that the changes noted above were taking place in the economy and in the legal status of the accountant, changes were taking place in other areas of the law. As will be seen in Chapter 27, manufacturers and remote sellers became liable to the ultimate

---

[1]   Computerized Design and Manufacturing, Inc. v Genrad Inc. 84 Or App 189, 733 P2d 485 (1987).

users for damages caused by defective products. Technicians became liable to third persons harmed by their negligence. Thus, this century brings a rising tide of liability to third persons. This background of liability to third persons in other areas has naturally influenced the law with respect to accountants.[2]

A word of caution is necessary. Just as the ocean moving up the shore does not move in a straight line but runs higher up the coast at some points, so the law did not change in all states at the same time. For example, some states limit recovery by third persons to cases where personal injuries are sustained. Other courts impose liability if third persons have suffered economic loss. It is this latter wave that is important to accountants, because negligence or false accounting inflict economic loss. States that recognize the right of third persons to sue for economic loss will naturally tend to permit third persons to sue accountants for malpractice. This will be considered in greater detail in Part C of this chapter.

4.   Assignment of Claim

Much of this chapter is concerned with the right of third persons to recover damages from accountants for malpractice. Distinct from the right of the third person to sue as a "third person" is the right of such person to sue as assignee of the client. The client with a malpractice claim against the accountant may assign this claim to a third person who can then sue the accountant for malpractice.

The same is true of malpractice claims against a technician. For example, an owner of

land hired a surveyor to survey the land. Then the owner sold it to a buyer, who resold it to another buyer.

The court held that a subsequent buyer could not sue the surveyor for negligence in preparing a defective survey. The court then held that the owner who hired the surveyor could assign to the subsequent buyer the owner's right under the survey contract. As a consequence, the subsequent buyer could sue the surveyor as assignee of the owner. The net result was the same as though the subsequent buyer had been allowed to sue the surveyor as a third person injured by the surveyor's negligence.

The rule that a client may assign a claim to a third person who can then sue is subject to certain restrictions. In some states, such an assignment will not be recognized because the claim is an unliquidated tort claim.[3] Assuming that the claim can be assigned, it is merely the claim of the client and does not extend to damages sustained by the third person. Because of these limitations, third persons will seek to recover in their own right, rather than as assignees of clients.

5.   Limitation of Liability

Can accountants protect themselves from liability for malpractice with respect to their clients and third persons? As the law generally permits any contracting party to limit or disclaim liability for negligence, an accountant may exclude liability for malpractice based on the theory of negligence. Influenced by the consumer protection movement and by the law as to product liability, courts will require such disclaimers to be (1) clear and unambiguous and (2) conspicuous. If these requirements are not met, the disclaimers will not be held effective.

(a) SCOPE OF LIMITATION. Disclaimers are valid when the circumstances are such that it is not reasonable to expect the accountant to stand behind particular data. For example,

---

[2]   The interplay between the various areas of malpractice liability and that of accountants is further seen in the fact that the Restatement of Torts, 2d, does not contain a separate provision applicable only to accountants, but deals with the subject of malpractice liability of accountants to third persons in a general section, 552. Section 552 declares that "one who in the course of his business, profession or employment, or in any other transaction in which he has a pecuniary interest, supplies false information for the guidance of others in their business transactions, is subject to liability for pecuniary loss caused to them by their justifiable reliance on the information, if he fails to exercise reasonable care or competence in obtaining or communicating the information." The section then continues to define what persons can enforce this liability.

[3]   Jackson v Rogers & Wells, 210 Cal App 3d 336, 258 Cal Rptr 454 (1989).

when the client owns land in a foreign country, it is reasonable for the accountant to accept the valuation placed on the land by someone in that foreign country. If the accountant includes in the financial statement prepared for the client a statement that the valuation of that land was obtained from an identified person in the foreign country and that the accountant assumes no responsibility for the accuracy of that valuation, the accountant is protected from the falsity of that information. Likewise, if the accountant's examination has been restricted, the accountant is protected from claims of third persons when the accountant makes a certification or statement that certain assets were not examined and that the figures relating thereto had not been verified. For example, when the accountant was restricted from examining accounts receivable and the certificate stated that no opinion was expressed as to accounts receivable, the accountant could not be held liable because the information relating to accounts receivable was not accurate.[4]

(b) LIMITATIONS ON EXCULPATORY PROVISIONS. A disclaimer based on lack of knowledge does not protect the accountant from liability if the accountant had knowledge or reason to know that the statements so made were in fact false. In such a case a court would hold that the disclaimer was not binding. The theory would be that when the accountant stated that personal knowledge was lacking, the accountant impliedly represented that the accountant did not have any knowledge or reason to know that the statements were not correct.

In some states, a limitation of liability or exculpatory clause will only protect the accountant from a malpractice suit brought by the client, not from a suit brought by a third person. In such cases the court applies the general rule of contract law that only a party to a contract is bound by an exculpatory or limitation of liability clause of the contract.[5]

When the malpractice liability of the accountant is based on intentional falsification of data, a limitation of liability will not be binding. This follows from the general rule of law that it is against public policy to permit a limitation of liability to immunize an intentional tort.

6. Contributory Negligence of Plaintiff

When suit is brought by a third person for malpractice, the defendant accountant may raise the defense of the contributory negligence of the plaintiff. If the plaintiff acted negligently in relying on a financial statement, the plaintiff cannot sue the accountant negligently preparing the statement.

For example, when the statement recites that it is merely a working examination and is not certified by the accountant, the third person is negligent if reliance is placed on the statement. In harmony with general principles of negligence law, the plaintiff is then barred by such contributory negligence.

In some cases it may be apparent from the face of the financial statement that the business represented therein is in poor financial condition. When a prudent person would see danger in the financial statement, the plaintiff not perceiving such danger cannot sue the accountant on the ground that the statement was negligently prepared.[6]

B.   MALPRACTICE LIABILITY OF NONACCOUNTANTS

The law governing the accountant's liability for malpractice has developed against the background of general principles governing the liability for improper performance of contract by technicians, surveyors, inspectors, and professionals other than accountants.

7. Standard of Care

When is a contracting party guilty of such

4   Stephans Industries Inc. v Haskins & Sells (CA10 Colo) 438 F2d 357 (1971).
5   American Centennial Ins. Co. v Wells Fargo Alarm Service, 152 Ill App 3d 503, 105 Ill Dec 457, 504 NE2d 742 (1986).
6   Hasbro Bradley, Inc. v Coopers & Lybrand, 128 App Div 2d 218, 515 NYS2d 461 (1987).

poor performance that the conduct may be called *malpractice*? Historically, the term *malpractice* was applied only to persons engaged in the practice of medicine or law. In the last half century the concepts of liability for poor performance of a professional have been extended to technicians, surveyors, and safety inspectors. All of these, as well as the lawyer and the doctor, must exercise that degree of care and skill commonly exercised by others following the same calling within the same community.

The standard just described is a variable standard, affected by time and place. As new knowledge develops and is accepted within the community, it is malpractice to fail to keep in step with the changing times. With respect to place, the community standards of one geographic area may differ from those of another. With modern methods of transportation and communication the geographic differential becomes less significant as there is a greater degree of exchange of knowledge and skills between different parts of the country.

8.   Persons Entitled to Damages

Once it is shown that a contracting party is guilty of malpractice, the next step is to determine who may recover damages for such improper conduct.

(a) OTHER CONTRACTING PARTY. When a party is guilty of malpractice, there is a breach of contract, and the other contracting party can sue for the damages caused by such breach.

(b) THIRD PERSONS. Prior to this century there was no malpractice liability to third persons. In this century liability to third persons is recognized to some extent.

(1) Privity of Contract Rule. The rule of law that bars a third person from suing for malpractice is called the **privity of contract rule**. According to this rule, a third person could not sue for breach of a contract, because there was no privity of contract between the third person and the defendant. This is the same concept that for several centuries barred a third person from claiming the right to sue on a contract as a third party beneficiary. The

privity of contract rule also barred the stranger to the contract from suing one of the contracting parties for malpractice. Many courts continue to follow this rule today. They fear that by abandoning the requirement of privity they may be subjecting the defendant to an endless number of lawsuits that in effect would cause the defendant's economic death. In some states the nonprivity plaintiff is barred from suing a remote defendant for malpractice negligence when the only damage sustained by the plaintiff is economic, as distinguished from personal injury or damage to other property.[7]

(2) Abandonment of Privity of Contract Rule. In this century a number of courts have abandoned the privity of contract rule. In some cases the court felt that no evil would follow the abandonment of the rule. The number of persons who might be affected would be small, so there was no danger of a flood of litigation. The defendant would not be economically destroyed, because insurance was available or the burden of liability could be passed on to other customers and clients by the defendant's raising fees and charges.

In one case in which the privity of contract rule was rejected, an insurance company was negligent in making a safety examination of the boiler in the insured building. Because of that negligence an employee was scalded from a bursting boiler. The court held that suit could be brought against the insurance company by the widow of the employee who died from the burn.[8] Likewise, the repairer of an automobile who negligently repairs the brakes is liable to a pedestrian injured when the brakes fail. A surveyor making a negligent survey for a real estate developer is liable to a subsequent purchaser of the land for loss caused by a mistake in the survey.[9] An owner, seeking to sell a building, may have an architect make an inspection and prepare a report

[7]   Sensenbrenner v Rust, Orling & Neale, Architects, Inc., 236 Va 419, 374 SE2d 55 (1988) (plaintiff denied right to sue remote architect and installer of swimming pool when negligence caused leaking of pool that damaged house).

[8]   Seay v Travelers Indemnity Co. (Tex App) 730 SW2d 774 (1987).

[9]   Cook Consultants, Inc. v Larson (Tex App) 700 SW2d 231 (1985).

as to its condition. The architect may be careless and report that the building condition was good when in fact it was poor. When a buyer buys the building in reliance on the false report, the buyer may sue the architect for the damages sustained. The negligence of an attorney in preparing a will may result in the exclusion of an intended beneficiary. Courts differ as to whether the intended beneficiary may sue the attorney. Some courts refuse to allow recovery because there was no privity of contract between the intended ben-

eficiary and the attorney. Others allow recovery on the theory that negligence malpractice liability may be imposed without privity of contract or on the theory that the intended beneficiary of the will was a third party beneficiary of the contract between the attorney and the client.[10]

In the *A. E. Investment Corporation* case the third person sued the architect for economic loss.

[10]   Hale v Groce, 304 Or 281, 744 P2d 1289 (1987).

A. E. INVESTMENT CORP. v LINK BUILDERS, INC.
62 Wis 2d 479, 214 NW2d 764 (1974)

The More-Way Development Company contracted with Link to construct a building. DeQuardo, Robinson, Crouch & Associates, Inc., were the architects who designed the building. After the building was constructed, A. E. Investment Corporation rented a part of the building. Because of the negligence of the architects, the building settled. A. E. Investment Corporation was forced to leave the building because of this condition. It then sued the architects for the economic loss sustained thereby. The architects filed a demurrer to the complaint. The lower court overruled the demurrer. The defendant architects appealed.

HEFFERNAN, J. . . . It was alleged that the architect was negligent in its failure to adequately supervise the construction, in that it failed to determine the nature and condition of the subsoil prior to and during construction. It was also alleged that, in view of the subsoil conditions, the plans were negligently drawn because they did not provide for the construction of a floor that was necessary to accommodate the plaintiff's business enterprise.

It was alleged that the defendant knew that the building would be used as a commercial store and the plaintiff would therein operate a supermarket. It was alleged that, as the direct and proximate result of the negligence, the floor space leased to the plaintiff began to settle, damage was caused to the walls, the floor became uneven, and eventually the premises became untenantable. . . .

The defendant defines the question . . . as being whether the defendant had a "duty to protect the subtenant plaintiff's future economic interests from loss allegedly resulting from a condition of the building." It responds to that question only by attempting to show that an architect owes no duty to a person with whom he is not in privity of contract. As a consequence, the defendant relies on the narrow argument that it has no responsibility for any economic loss to the plaintiff because it has no duty to the plaintiff at all and no responsibility to be answerable for any damages, irrespective of the nature of the loss. . . .

We believe that the narrow concept of duty relied on by the defendant architect has long been discarded in Wisconsin law. The duty of any person is the obligation of due care to refrain from any act which will cause foreseeable harm to others even though the nature of that harm and the identity of the harmed person or harmed interest is unknown at the time of the act. . . . ". . . Once an act has been found to be negligent, we no longer look to see if there was a duty to the one who was in fact injured." . . .

In the instant case . . . the defendant's alleged failure to properly take into account the condition of the subsoil when designing and supervising the construction of the building was an act or omission that would foreseeably cause some harm to someone. The duty was to refrain from such act or omission. Where, as here, it is alleged that the architect knew the purpose for which the building was being constructed, it was clearly foreseeable that a future tenant of the building was within the ambit of the harm. Hence, the harm to the particular plaintiff was foreseeable, although under the methodology of this court, it is not necessary that either the person harmed or the type of harm that would result be foreseeable. The act or omission in the face of foreseeable harm was negligence. . . .

Under Wisconsin negligence law, architects may be liable to third parties with whom they are not in privity of contract. The lack of privity does not constitute a policy reason for not imposing liability where negligence is shown to be a substantial factor in occasioning the harm.

The defendant also argues that, since an architect is a professional, his paramount duty is to his client, and that, if no duty is breached in connection with the architect-client relationship, there is no responsibility to third parties. We disagree with the argument that a professional can exonerate himself from liability for a negligent act which will foreseeably cause harm to third parties, merely because his client does not object. The very essence of a profession is that the services are rendered with the understanding that the duties of the profession cannot be undertaken on behalf of a client without an awareness and a responsibility to the public welfare. The entire ambit of state regulations as they apply to the profession of architecture is intended, not solely for the protection of the person with whom the architect deals, but for the protection of the world at large. Professionalism is the very antithesis to irresponsibility to all interests other than those of an immediate employer.

In the instant case, however, if, as it is alleged, the defendant architect negligently designed or permitted the erection of an unsuitable or unstable structure, it was hardly acting in the interests of its client, whether that client has seen fit to complain or not. . . .

[Judgment affirmed]

QUESTIONS

1. Was there a contract between the architect and the tenants of the building?
2. Were the tenants third party beneficiaries of the contract between the building owner and the architect?
3. Only a party to a contract or a third party beneficiary of a contract can sue for harm caused by the improper performance of a contract. Appraise this statement.

(3) Relaxation of Privity of Contract Rule. Some courts have been unwilling to follow the privity rule and yet have been faced with a case in which they were reluctant to abandon that rule. At times such a court has escaped from this dilemma by reaching the conclusion that the facts presented a situation that could be described as presenting the equivalent of

privity or substantially the same as privity of contract.

Such a court will allow the recovery of malpractice damages by a stranger to the contract when there is a sufficiently close connection of the stranger to the transaction or sufficient contact with the defendant that it appears proper to allow suit by the stranger.

C. ACCOUNTANTS' MALPRACTICE LIABILITY

There is not much litigation on the subject of what standards of conduct accountants should observe. Most of the litigation involves the question as to whether third persons may sue an accountant for malpractice.

FIGURE 19-1   SUING THE ACCOUNTANT

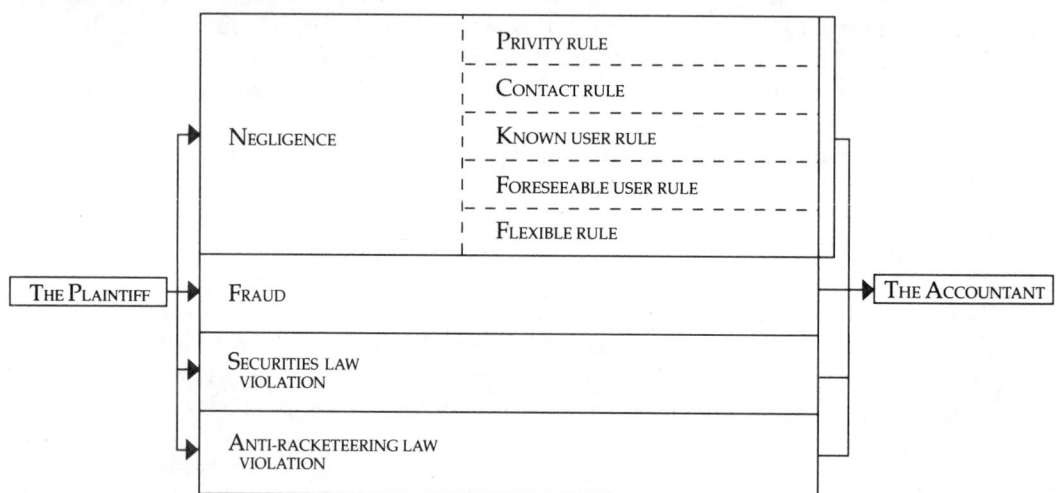

9.   Standards of Conduct for Accountants

Accountants are liable to their clients when loss is caused the clients because the accountants failed to observe the standards of sound accounting practices. Accountants are also liable if their failure to call attention to a condition causes a client to fail to take preventive steps and to thereby sustain a loss.

"Certified public accountants are liable for damages proximately caused by their negligence just like other skilled professions. . . . Accordingly they owe their clients a duty to exercise the degree of care, skill, and competence that reasonably competent members of their profession would exercise under similar circumstances."[11] Basically, the concept is the same as the one applied to doctors and attorneys.

[11]   Greenstein, Logan & Co. v Burgess Marketing, Inc. (Tex App) 744 SW2d 170 (1987).

An accountant is liable to the client when the accountant negligently fails to detect or fraudulently conceals signs that an employee of the client is embezzling from the client, or that the internal audit controls of the client's business are not being observed. An accountant who prepares tax returns and acts as tax manager for the client will be liable when additional taxes or penalties are assessed against the client as a result of negligently given advice.

10.   Nonliability to the Interloper

No court imposes liability on the accountant to a total stranger who gets possession of the accountant's work and then sustains a loss because of a false statement in the work. This applies regardless of whether such statement was negligent or intentional. For example, assume that a negligently prepared financial statement of a corporation is thrown in the wastepaper basket. It is then retrieved by a security guard. If the guard thinks that the statement is a "hot tip" and invests in the stock of the corporation on the basis of the statement, the guard cannot sue the accountant for negligence in preparing the statement. The courts have struggled to form a rule that will exclude what the court regards as interlopers but permit suits by those the courts regard as proper plaintiffs.

11. Nonliability to Person Affected by the Decision of Accountant's Client

On the basis of information furnished by the accountant to the client, the client may make a decision that affects a third person. For example, the report of the independent auditor may indicate that a fiscal officer of the client has not handled funds properly. The report may indicate that it is economically unsound to enter into a contract with a third person. Assume that the client relies on the accountant's report and fires the employee or refuses to make a contract with the third person. If the report of the accountant was negligently made, and the true facts would not have justified the action taken by the client, the question arises as to whether the third person or the discharged employee may sue the negligent accountant. It has been held that such a suit may not be brought.[12]

12. Accountants' Negligence Malpractice Liability to Third Persons

In the last century the negligence of the accountant would impose liability only to the client of the accountant. Today many states permit third persons to recover damages from the accountant.

(a) STATUS OF ACCOUNTANT. The accountant sued by the third person for malpractice may be an in-house accountant work-ing full-time for the particular employer. The accountant may be an independent contractor who regularly does accounting-related work, such as preparing financial statements and tax returns for different clients. The accountant may be an independent auditor.

What constitutes negligence is the same for all three types of accountants. As a practical matter a third person would not ordinarily sue the employee-accountant, because the claim would probably be much more than the employee could pay.

It is the independent contractor accountant and the independent auditor accountant who are more likely to be sued by third persons for negligent malpractice. The very fact that the accountant is an independent auditor indicates an intention and an awareness that the accountant prepares something on which third persons would rely.

(b) CONFLICTING THEORIES. A number of theories have been developed in this century to determine whether a third person sustaining a loss because of the accountant's negligence can sue the accountant for loss or whether such person is an interloper who cannot sue. These views may be identified as (1) the privity rule, (2) the contact rule, (3) the known user rule, and (4) the foreseeable user rule. In addition, some courts follow (5) a flexible rule, deciding each case as it arises.

Each of these views represents an attempt to draw a boundary line between the interloper and the "proper" plaintiff. Each view is supported by honest judges seeking to do justice. They have the same goal and are all guided by ethics, but the resultant rules of law are different.

(1) The Privity Rule. The privity rule excludes a negligence malpractice suit by a third person. This rule holds that only the person in privity with the accountant—that is, the client of the accountant—may sue the accountant.[13]

When the privity rule is applied, a bank

---

[12]   Harper v Inkster Public Schools and Arthur Andersen & Co. 158 Mich App 456, 404 NW2d 776 (1987).

[13]   This rule was originally known as the New York rule (Ultramares Corp. v Touche, 255 NY 170, 174 NE 441 (1931)), although it has been replaced in New York by the contact rule. The privity rule is still the law in many jurisdictions, although many have departed from it.

lending money to the client of the accountant cannot sue the accountant for malpractice.[14]

(2) The Contact Rule. As a relaxation of the privity requirement, New York now holds that a third person may sue a negligent accountant when there was some contact between the third person and the accountant. For example, an accountant may go to a bank to see what information the bank requires in order for the accountant's client to obtain a loan. In this case there is a sufficient "link" or "contact" between the bank and the accountant to allow the bank to sue the accountant if it sustains loss because of the accountant's negligence.[15] It appears that the New York contact rule requires that the accountant meet or communicate with the nonprivity plaintiff in order to establish a relationship equivalent to privity.[16]

Thus, there must be such contact with or dealings between the plaintiff and the accountant as to give the accountant reason to know that the plaintiff was relying for a particular purpose on the financial statements prepared by the accountant.

The contact rule applies to malpractice defendants generally. It not limited to suits against accountants.[17]

(3) The Known User Rule. By this rule the accountant is liable for a third person's negligently caused loss when the accountant knew that the third person would be using the accountant's work product. By this view the fact that the nonprivity plaintiff's reliance on a financial statement was foreseeable does not entitle such plaintiff to sue the accountant for negligent preparation of the statement. It must be shown that the accountant knew that the statement would be furnished to that plaintiff. The plaintiff's reliance must thus be actually foreseen and not merely reasonably foreseeable.[18]

In the *First Florida Bank* case the accountant claimed that the bank that had loaned money to the accountant's client was barred from suing the accountant because of lack of privity.

[14] Citizens National Bank v Kennedy and Coe, 432 Neb 477, 441 NW2d 180 (1989).

[15] Credit Alliance Corp. v Arthur Andersen & Co. 65 NY2d 536, 483 NE2d 110 (1985). Some courts are reluctant to turn their backs on the requirement of privity and describe the contact rule not as a different rule but as requiring "a relationship sufficiently intimate to be equated with privity." Empire of America v Arthur Andersen & Co. 129 App Div 2d 990, 514 NYS2d 578 (1987). A further attempt to define the New York rule was made in William Iselin & Co., Inc. v Landau, 71 NY2d 420, 527 NYS2d 176, 522 NE2d 21 (1988) (involving a review report), in which the court declared that it was necessary for a nonprivity plaintiff suing an accountant for negligent misrepresentation to establish "a nexus between them sufficiently approaching privity (Credit Alliance Corp. . . .)."

[16] In Franko v Mitchell (App) 158 Ariz 391, 762 P2d 1345 (1988), the court held that when the borrower's attorney met and discussed the proposed loan details with both the lender and the borrower, it could be found that there was an implied contract of employment between the borrower's attorney and the creditor, so as to permit the creditor to bring a malpractice action against the attorney. This would have been classified as "equivalent to privity" if the court had followed the New York terminology.

[17] Ossining Union Free School District v Anderson, 73 NY2d 417, 539 NE2d 91 (1989): "The long-standing rule is that recovery may be had for pecuniary loss arising from negligent representations where there is actual privity of contract between the parties or a relationship so close as to approach that of privity. Nor does the rule apply only to accountants. We have never drawn that categorical distinction, and see no basis for establishing such an arbitrary limitation now."

[18] Bancohio National Bank v Schiesswohl, 33 Ohio App 3d 329, 515 NE2d 997 (1986). The rule that the nonprivity plaintiff may recover from the accountant for malpractice negligence only if the accountant's statement was furnished to that plaintiff or the accountant knew that the client who was given the statement would in turn give the statement to the plaintiff, is often identified as "the Restatement rule," as based on Restatement (Second) Torts (1977) § 522(2). There is, however, some uncertainty as to the exact boundaries of the Restatement rule. See Selden v Burnett (Alaska) 754 P2d 256 (1988), Raritan River Steel Co. v Cherry, Bekaert & Holland, 322 NC 200, 367 SE2d 609 (1988).

FIRST FLORIDA BANK v MAX MITCHELL & CO.

(Fla) 558 So 2d (1990)

Maxwell was a CPA and president of the accounting firm of Max Mitchell & Co. He went to the first Florida Bank to negotiate a loan on behalf of a client, C.M.

Systems. The bank was induced to make the requested loan because the audit statements for several years showed that the client was in good financial condition. In reply to questions of the bank official, Maxwell stated that there was no change in the financial condition of the client from that shown in the audit statements and that the client did not owe any money to any bank. First Florida Bank loaned the money to the client. The money was never repaid. It was then discovered that the audit statements were seriously inaccurate and that the client owed a substantial sum to another bank. First Florida sued Max Mitchell & Co., claiming that the accounting firm had been negligent in the preparation of the financial statements. The defendant raised the defense that it could not be sued because it was not in privity with the bank.

Judgment was entered for the accounting firm. The bank appealed.

GRIMES, J. . . . The doctrine of privity has undergone substantial erosion in Florida. Indeed, in cases involving injuries caused by neligently manufactured products the requirement that there be privity between the plaintiff and the manufacturer has been abolished. . . . Further, this Court . . . held that a general contractor could sue an architect or engineer for damages proximately caused by their negligence on a building project despite the absence of privity of contract between the parties. The liability of a lawyer in the absence of privity has been limited to cases where the legal service neligently performed was apparently initiated by the lawyer's client to benefit a third party, such as in the drafting of a will. . . .

Most significant, however, to the instant case is this Court's decision in *First American Title Insurance Co. v. First Title Service Co.*, 457 So.2d 467 (Fla. 1984). . . .

Where the abstracter knows, or should know, that his customer wants the abstract for the use of a prospective purchaser, and the prospect purchases the land relying on the abstract, the abstracter's duty of care runs . . . not only to his customer but to the purchaser. Moreover, others involved in the transaction through their relationship to the purchaser—such as lender-mortgagees, tenants and title insurers—will also be protected where the purchaser's reliance was known or should have been known to the abstracter. But a party into whose hands the abstract falls in connection with a subsequent transaction is not among those to whome the abstracter owes a duty of care.

. . . The opinion in *First American Title Insurance* is also important for the arguments which this Court rejected. We declined to approve the principle that an abstracter is liable in negligence to all persons who might foreseeably use and rely on the abstract. . .

Some of the competing interests involved in selecting the proper standard for accountants' liability to third parties are set forth in Annotation, *Liability of Public Accountant to Third Parties*, 46 A.L.R.3d 979, 984 (1972):

It is contended by those favoring such liability that accountants, due to their professional status and the respect they command, invite reliance on their work by the business community, and that investors and creditors do, in fact, rely upon their accuracy and integrity; on the other hand, it is pointed out that unlike members of other professions, accountants have no control over the identity or number of those who rely on their work, and that imposition of liability, in negligence, to third parties would place an enormous potential burden on the profession. Those in favor of expanding liability argue that the accounting profession no longer needs the protection of nonliability in this area, due to its wealth, and contend that the cost of insurance protection could be passed on to the client, stating that the innocent relier should not be damaged because of the error of the negligent accountant. In reply, it is observed that the cost of such insurance protection is prohibitive and, in many cases, that such coverage is not available at any price; furthermore, it is said, such higher costs would tend to lead dominance of the profession by the large national accounting firms and to a curtailment of the availability of accountancy services to small businesses. Nor, it is contended, does the argument for extended liability take into consideration the ever more acute shortage of qualified public accountants in private practice. Those in favor of expanding liability argue that liability could easily be limited by the increased use of disclaimers and limited certifications, pointing to the success of the British experience in this area. Opponents, however, observe that the use of such devices is a commercial impossibility unless all accountants follow this practice, since it tends to dissatisfy the client, who will then turn to the use of other accountants not following this practice. . . .

Because of the heavy reliance upon audited financial statements in the contemporary financial world, we believe permitting recovery only from those in privity or near privity is unduly restrictive. On the other hand, we are persuaded by the wisdom of the rule which limits liability to those persons or classes of persons whom an accountant "knows" will rely on his opinion rather than those he "should have known" would do so because it takes into account the fact that an accountant controls neither his client's accounting records nor the distribution of his reports. . . .

There remains the need to apply this rule to the facts at hand. At the time Mitchell prepared the audits for C.M. Systems, it was unknown that they would be used to induce the reliance of First Florida Bank to approve a line of credit for C.M. Systems. Therefore, except for the unusual facts of this case, Mitchell could not be held liable to the bank for any negligence in preparing the audit. However, Mitchell actually negotiated the loan on behalf of his client. He personally delivered the financial statements to the bank with the knowledge that it would rely upon them in considering whether or not to make the loan. Under this unique set of facts, we believe that Mitchell vouched for the integrity of the audits and that his conduct in dealing with the bank sufficed to meet the requirements of the rule which we have adopted in this opinion.

[Judgment vacated and action remanded]

QUESTIONS

1. Did the availability of malpractice insurance affect the decision in the *First Florida* Bank case?
2. How would the court have decided the *First Florida Bank* case if the client, C.M. Systems, had taken the audit statements to the bank and negotiated directly with the bank to obtain the loan?
3. How can a bank protect itself when the applicant for a loan submits financial statements prepared by an accountant?

Under the known user rule it is sufficient if the user is a member of a known class even though the identity of the particular user is not known to the accountant. However, there is authority that when the identity of the intended user is known to the accountant, another person coming within the same class as the known user cannot sue the accountant.[19] For example, an accountant prepares a financial statement for the client with the knowledge that it will be taken by the client to the First National Bank in order to obtain a loan. The First National Bank may sue the accountant for negligent loss, even though the bank never had any direct contact or dealings with the accountant and was not in privity with the accountant. However, no one other than First National may sue the accountant for negligence. The fact that the plaintiff was a foreseeable user does not give the right to sue in a "known user" state. Accordingly, when the accountant prepared a financial statement for the client and nothing was said as to what further use of the statement would be made, creditors of the client could not sue the accountant for negligent preparation of the statement. It was the client who was the known user.[20]

If the court follows the privity rule or the contact rule described in the two preceding sections, the known user cannot sue the accountant for negligent malpractice. Moreover, some courts that follow the known user rule apply it so strictly that a substitute foreseeable

user is not allowed to sue. To illustrate, assume that in the case just stated the client was refused the loan by the First National Bank. The client might then make an application for a loan to the Second National Bank. It has been held that the Second National Bank could not sue the accountant, because the Second National Bank was not a known user. However, the Second National Bank would be allowed to sue under the views discussed in the sections that follow.

(4) The Foreseeable User Rule. The accountant may foresee that a particular class of unknown persons will rely on the accountant's work. For example, when the accountant prepares a financial statement, knowing that the client is going to use it to borrow money from some bank or finance company, the accountant foresees that there is a class of lenders. Likewise, the accountant may know that the financial statement will be used to sell the stock of the client corporation. Here again there is a class consisting of unknown persons.

When it is reasonable to foresee that there will be persons who will rely on the statement of the accountant, the foreseeable user rule imposes liability on the accountant for negligent malpractice. The foreseeable user rule allows such third persons to sue for their loss without regard to the lack of privity of contract between the third persons and the accountants.[21]

In the *Spherex* case, the lawsuit turned on whether the plaintiff could recover from the accountant hired by the plaintiff's customer.

---

[19] Blue Bell, Inc. v Peat, Marwich, Mitchell & Co. (Tex App) 715 SW2d 408 (1986) ("If under current business practice and the circumstances of that case, an accountant preparing audited financial statements knows *or should know* that such statements will be relied upon by a limited class of persons, the accountant may be liable for injuries to members of that class relying on his certification of the audited reports.") Note that to the extent that a court speaks in terms of "should know," there is the inference that the court is embracing "foreseeability" and is thus moving from the known user rule to the foreseeable user rule.

[20] Badische Corp. v Caylor, 257 Ga 131, 356 SE2d 198 (1987).

[21] Touche Ross & Co. v Commercial Union Ins. Co. (Miss) 514 So 2d 315 (1987). This rule is regarded by some courts as representing the majority view. The foreseeable user rule brings the law as to accountants into harmony with the tort law relating to other persons and activities.

SPHEREX, INC. v ALEXANDER GRANT & CO.
122 NH 898, 451 A2d 1308 (1982)

General Home Products (GHP) hired the accounting firm of Alexander Grant & Company to prepare an unaudited financial statement of GHP. The statement was to be based on financial information provided by GHP. GHP submitted the financial statement to Spherex so that GHP could buy on credit. The financial statement had been negligently prepared, and Spherex lost money by selling to GHP on credit. Spherex sued Alexander Grant on the ground that it knew that the financial statement prepared by it would be submitted to Spherex to obtain credit, but Grant was negligent in preparing it. Grant raised the defense that its potential liability did not extend to a party with whom it was not in privity. Grant also asserted that it is unreasonable, as a matter of law, for a third party to rely on an unaudited financial statement.

DOUGLAS, J. . . . It should be noted at the outset that the question before this court is not Alexander Grant's liability to Spherex for intentional misrepresentation, or fraud. *Ultramares Corp. v. Touche*, 255 N.Y. 170, 174 N.E. 441 (1931), the seminal case on an accountant's liability to third parties, from which Alexander Grant's privity defense stems, distinguished intentional from negligent misrepresentation, and held that an accountant could be liable to a non-client whom he intentionally deceived. Justice Cardozo, writing for the New York Court of Appeals, took note of the defendant accountant's liability in that case to a plaintiff who detrimentally relied on *intentional* material misstatements:

> The defendants owed to their employer a duty imposed by law to make their certificate without fraud, and a duty growing out of contract to make it with the care and caution proper to their calling. Fraud includes the pretense of knowledge when knowledge there is none. To creditors and investors to whom the employer exhibited the certificate, the defendants owed a like duty to make it without fraud, since there was notice in the circumstances of its making that the employer did not intend to keep it to himself.

In other words, where an accountant or other supplier of information knows that a materially false statement is to be conveyed to some party other than to whom it is made, public policy is served by holding the intentional wrongdoer accountable to the one who relies to his detriment on the misstatement of fact.

The considerations are different when the misrepresentation is *negligently* made. "If liability for negligence exists, a thoughtless slip or blunder, the failure to detect a theft or forgery beneath the cover of deceptive entries, may expose accountants to a liability in an indeterminate amount for an indeterminate time to an indeterminate class." Courts have read this language in *Ultramares* as requiring privity between a defendant-accountant and a plaintiff before liability for negligent misrepresentation can attach. . . .

Counsel for both parties agree, and our research has revealed no cases to the contrary, that this question is unsettled in New Hampshire. Yet, we have expressed our disfavor for the privity doctrine in personal injury cases. Our reluctance to apply the privity rule has extended to allowing a proper plaintiff to recover for mere financial loss resulting from the negligent performance of services. The duty that Spherex alleges it was owed by Alexander Grant is not entirely dissimilar to the duty we have held a promisor owes to an intended third-party beneficiary. In *Tamposi Associates v. Star Mkt. Co.*, 119 N.H. 630, 406 A.2d 132 (1979), we said "[a] third-party beneficiary relationship exists if . . . the contract is so expressed as to give the promisor reason to know that a benefit to a third party is contemplated by the promisee as one of the motivating causes of his making the contract." In the instant case, Spherex claims Alexander Grant's duty to produce an unaudited financial statement in a non-negligent manner grew out of Alexander Grant's engagement contract with GHP. Spherex's status as a third-party user of the financial statement prepared by Alexander Grant, if proved at trial, would be akin to an intended third-party beneficiary to whom Alexander Grant owed a duty of due care.

The *Ultramares* holding, and its apparent privity requirement, has been distinguished primarily on two bases. First, courts have sought to link the privity doctrine with Justice Cardozo's "social utility" rationale of protecting professionals from the specter of unlimited liability to a virtually limitless class of plaintiffs. Thus, judges have not hesitated to permit recovery where the plaintiff's identity was specifically known to the negligent defendant. . . . Beyond that, courts have been less willing to expand the frontier of liability. The question is "whether the defendant has some special reason to anticipate the reliance of the plaintiff."

Second, *Ultramares* has been distinguished as a relic of a bygone economic era. Both the sophistication of modern accounting procedures and the accountant's central role in the financing and investment industry are a far cry from the fledgling profession in need of judicial protection that existed at the time of *Ultramares*. One commentator has stated:

> The accountant today has a role of central responsibility in the business community. . . . This new circumstance, not present when *Ultramares* was decided, makes it clear that 'between the innocent reliant party and the negligent public accountant, the accountant should bear the burden of his negligence.' The accountant then must accept the burdens of legal responsibility that go along with the benefits derived from his important role in the modern business community.

The Restatement (Second) of Torts § 552 has sought to harmonize the accountant's contemporary role and his potential liability by holding him accountable to a "person or one of a limited group of persons for whose benefit and guidance he intends to supply the information or knows that the recipient intends to supply it. . . . " In effect, an accountant who negligently misrepresents information is held liable not only to known third parties but to an actually foreseeable class of third persons. As comment *a* to section 552 explains, extending an accountant's liability to an intended recipient of information "promotes the important social policy of encouraging the flow of commercial information upon which the operation of the economy rests." Furthermore, an accountant, like the manufacturer under products liability law, is in the best position to regulate the effects of his conduct by controlling the degree of care exercised during the performance of his professional duties. The accountant, through the fee structure, can pass along to his clients the cost of insuring against financial loss sustained by them through reliance upon his negligent misstatement of fact.

We believe section 552 of the Restatement represents a reasoned approach to the issue of professional liability for negligent misrepresentation. . . .

Nevertheless, we acknowledge that an accountant's potential liability is not boundless. "It is not enough that the maker merely knows of the ever-present possibility of repetition [of information supplied by him] to anyone, and the possibility of action in reliance upon it, on the part of anyone to whom it may be repeated." Restatement (Second) of Torts § 552 comment *h*, at 133. The plaintiff's relationship to the accountant becomes crucial because the risk of liability to which the supplier subjects himself by undertaking to give the information, while it may not be affected by the identity of the person for whose guidance the information is given, is vitally affected by the number and character of the persons, and particularly the nature and extent of the proposed transaction.

Therefore, while an accountant is to employ a sufficient degree of care in the performance of professional activities in order to protect himself from liability, the law must not arbitrarily extend that liability beyond his reasonable expectations as to whom the information will reach. "The risk reasonably to be perceived defines the duty to be obeyed. . . . " *Palsgraf v. Long Island R. Co.*, 248 N.Y. 339, 162 N.E. 99 (1928). We believe section 552 of the Restatement preserves such reasonable boundaries of liability.

We are unable, as a matter of law, to consider it unreasonable for a third party to rely upon information presented in an unaudited financial statement prepared by the defendant accountant, or to rely upon an accountant to verify the substantive accuracy of the information presented in an unaudited financial statement. It is for Spherex at trial to adduce evidence as to any duty undertaken by the accounting firm in its engagement contract with the client, irrespective of the unaudited nature of the financial statement it prepared.

[Action remanded]

QUESTIONS

1. Why does the court begin the discussion of the case with the statement that the case did not involve liability for intentional misrepresentation or fraud?
2. Was the court influenced by a change in the role of accountants? Explain your answer.
3. What standard is adopted by the Restatement of Torts for determining the negligence liability of accountants to third persons?

(5) The Flexible Rule. Some courts have rejected the requirement of privity in malpractice suits against accountants but have not adopted any one of the rules discussed in the preceding sections. These courts prefer to keep the question open and to decide each case as it arises.

When the malpractice claim relates to advice given to a client, there are strong arguments for retaining the privity rule. Thus, it has been held that when the accountant orally recommended to the client the making of an investment as a tax shelter, third persons to whom the client repeated the advice cannot sue the accountant for malpractice.[22]

(c) STATUTE OF LIMITATIONS. In a malpractice action against an accountant the statute of limitations runs from the date of the accountant's breach of duty. The date of the breach is used even though the occurrence of the breach or the extent of the harm caused thereby are not discovered by the client until a later date.[23] However, when the relationship between the client and the accountant with respect to the same matter is an ongoing relationship, there is authority that the statute of limitations does not begin to run until the conclusion of the IRS audit of the client's tax return.

In some states a claim for malpractice of an accountant is subject to a "professional malpractice" statute of limitations. In other states

---

[22]   Selden v Burnett (Alaska) 754 P2d 256 (1988).

[23]   Ford's Inc. v Russell Brown & Co. 299 Ark 426, 773 SW2d 90 (1989).

it is subject to the general statute of limitations applicable to negligence claims.[24]

13.   Accountants' Fraud Malpractice Liability to Third Persons

Society in general condemns fraud more strongly than it does negligence. This is seen in the greater liability of accountants for fraudulent malpractice.

(a) WHAT CONSTITUTES FRAUD WITH RESPECT TO ACCOUNTANTS. In Chapter 11, fraud was defined as a false statement made with knowledge that it was false or with reckless indifference as to whether it was true or not. This statement was made with the intent that the listener rely thereon, and the listener did so rely and sustained loss. In the field of accounting the false statement will typically be one of accounting in such manner as to make the client appear to be in a better financial position than is actually the case. For example, the client may own assets that are worthless, but the accountant retains them on the financial statement at cost or some other unreasonable value.

At times the falsification of the financial statement may be designed to downgrade the financial condition of the corporation. This has been done when the object was to induce shareholders to sell their stock to a dominant group of shareholders. The false financial statement purposely undervalued the assets of the corporation to make the stockholders believe that their stock had little value and that, therefore, they should sell at the low price offered by the dominant group.

(b) FRAUD LIABILITY OF ACCOUNTANTS TO INTENDED VICTIMS. When an accountant commits fraud, it is typically aimed to mislead a third person whose identity is known to the accountant or to a class of persons whose identity is known to the accountant. Any such victim, whether an identified person or the member of a contemplated class of potential victims, may sue the accountant

for loss caused by fraud. The problem of privity (relating to liability for negligence) is ignored when the basis of the malpractice suit is fraud. The social force of preventing fraud overrides the concern for creating a hardship on the accountant by allowing third persons to bring suit.

An accountant might make a false financial statement for a corporate client, with knowledge that it will be used in selling securities of the corporation to third persons. If so, such third persons may sue the accountant for the damages sustained. Thus, the accountant has been held liable for disguising the true character of a hoped-for profit from the sale and resale of real estate. The accountant described it as "deferred income," although there was little reason to believe that the transaction could ever be completed. In this case, the buyer, who was obligated to pay $5 million for the property, had assets of only $100,000. The financial statement would have shown a loss instead of a substantial profit if the true character of the transaction had been disclosed.

14.   Accountants' Malpractice Liability under Statutes

Statutes, particularly those relating to the sale of securities, may impose liability upon accountants to third persons not in privity.

(a) FEDERAL SECURITIES STATUTES. Federal statutes regulate the sale of stocks and bonds. This is described in detail in Chapter 48, Sections 3 through 10. Accountants involved in the issuance and sale of securities may be liable to investors under a number of provisions of the Securities Act of 1933 and the Securities Exchange Act of 1934.

(1) Securities Act of 1933. The Securities Act of 1933 deals with original distribution of securities. The Act requires disclosure of specific financial information in a **registration statement** filed with the Securities and Exchange Commission. Under Section 11 of the Act, accountants, lawyers, engineers, and appraisers who consent to being named in the registration statement as preparing any part of that statement are liable to purchasers of the securities for any untrue statement or omis-

---

[24]   Investors Reit One v Jacobs, 46 Ohio 176, 546 NE2d 206 (1989).

sion of material fact made in the registration statement. "Due diligence" is a defense for these professionals.

Section 12 of the 1933 Act applies to those who "offer or sell" securities and employ any device or scheme to defraud and obtain money by means of any untrue statement of material fact. Liability may be imposed on accountants whose conduct is a substantial factor in bringing about the fraudulent sale of a security. The more extensive the involvement or control of an accountant over a sale, the more likely the accountant is to be considered a seller under Section 12. Accountants who, in conjunction with clients, prepare fraudulent registration statements may be subject to civil liability as "aiders and abettors" under Section 12(2) of the 1933 Act. They may also be subject to criminal liability under Section 17(a) of the 1933 Act.

(2) Securities Exchange Act of 1934. The Securities Exchange Act of 1934 regulates secondary distribution of securities. Section 10(b) of the 1934 Act and SEC Rule 10b-5 impose liability on any person who employs any device, scheme, or artifice to defraud in connection with the purchase or sale of any security. Section 10(b) and Rule 10b-5 are the most effective federal security law provisions against accountants who participate in a fraudulent securities transaction. Under Section 10(b) and Rule 10b-5 a civil action for damages may be brought by any injured party who purchased or sold securities because of false, misleading, or undisclosed information. However, proof of *scienter*—proof that the accountant acted with guilty knowledge or intent to deceive—

is required. Liability cannot be based on negligence. Because fraudulent intent is required, an accountant is not liable to the purchaser of corporate securities when the accountant was negligent in failing to use appropriate auditing procedures and thereby failed to discover internal accounting practices of the corporate client that prevented the making of an effective audit.[25] However, a showing of shady accounting practices amounting to a "pretended audit" or of grounds supporting a representation so flimsy as to lead to the conclusion that there was no genuine belief behind it have supported findings of liability.[26]

(b) LIABILITY OF ACCOUNTANTS UNDER ANTI-RACKETEERING STATUTES. The federal Racketeer Influenced and Corrupt Organizations Act (RICO) authorizes the victim of a pattern of racketeering practices to sue for treble damages. Many states have similar laws.[27] When an accountant's conduct that constitutes malpractice aids or furthers a pattern of racketeering practices, the person injured may bring suit under RICO.[28]

---

[25]   Ernst & Ernst v Hochfelder, 425 US 185 (1976).
[26]   McLean v Alexander (CA3) 599 F2d 1190, 1198 (1979).
[27]   See Sections 7(b) and 8(c) of Chapter 7.
[28]   Bank of America v Touche Ross & Co. (CA11 Ga) 782 F2d 966 (1986); Equitable Life Assurance Society v Alexander Grant & Co. (DC NY) 627 F Supp 1023 (1985); First Fed. S. & L. Ass'n v Oppenheim, Appel, Dixon & Co. (SC NY) 629 F Supp 427 (1986). Criminal liability is also imposed by the antiracketeering statutes. If the accountant has the intent to defraud, there may be federal criminal liability for using the mail, a wire, radio, or television with intent to defraud, or for defrauding a bank, 18 USC §§ 1341 et seq. Most states have similar anti-fraud laws.

SUMMARY

When a contract requires a party to perform services, the party must perform with the care exercised by persons performing similar services within the same community. If the party negligently fails to observe those standards, there is both a breach of contract and a tort. This tort of negligent breach of contract constitutes malpractice, and the other party to the contract can sue the wrongdoer for either breach of contract or for the tort involved.

By the modern view third persons may also sue the wrongdoer for malpractice. In states that follow the older law the third person is barred from suing because of lack of privity. The rules governing the right of the third person to sue are applied in suits against technicians, architects, attorneys, and physicians.

When the malpractice suit is brought against an accountant for negligence, courts differ as to when a third person may sue. Some courts refuse to let the third person sue; these courts require privity of contract between the parties. Most courts allow suit by the third person against the wrongdoer but differ as to what the plaintiff must show in order to bring such a suit. In New York the plaintiff must show as a minimum that there was a "contact" with the accountant. In some states it is sufficient that the third person was a known user of the accountant's information. Other courts go further and allow the third person to sue if it was reasonable to foresee that the third person would make use of the accountant's information.

When the accountant is guilty of fraud, the intended victim of the fraud may sue the accountant, even though privity of contract is lacking.

In a suit brought under federal securities statutes, lack of privity is not a defense for an accountant.

To a limited degree an accountant is protected from malpractice liability by a disclaimer of liability or by the contributory negligence of the plaintiff.

When the malpractice of the accountant involves or promotes racketeering activity or fraud, the accountant is subject to civil and criminal liability under RICO and similar state laws.

QUESTIONS AND CASE PROBLEMS

1. What social forces are affected by allowing a stranger to a contract to sue for the harm caused by the negligent performance of the contract?

2. The president of Jones Corporation was concerned as to whether it would be necessary to borrow money to pay taxes. The corporation employed Roanne to prepare a financial statement of the corporation. When the president saw this statement, he decided that money should be borrowed. The lending bank required that the corporation submit a financial statement. The statement prepared by Roanne was submitted. It contained a number of negligent mistakes that misled the bank into lending the money to Jones. Jones went into bankruptcy shortly thereafter, and the bank recovered only a small percentage of the loan. The bank sued Roanne for the amount it could not collect. Was she liable in a state that followed the known user rule?

3. Thomas & Sons, certified public accountants, prepared a financial statement of the Continental Land Development Company. Much of the assets of the company consisted of land in foreign countries. Some of the land had been confiscated by the local governments. The financial statement prepared by Thomas stated that, based on the best information available, the land described therein was owned by Continental and had not been confiscated. The financial statement further recited that Thomas was entirely dependent on foreign sources for the information relating to the foreign land and had no knowledge of its accuracy. On the strength of this financial statement, the Fifth National Bank loaned money to Continental. The recitals as to the land owned by Continental and its value proved false, and the bank could not get back its loan. The bank sued Thomas. Was Thomas liable?

4. Compare the right of a third party beneficiary and the right of a third person to sue for a negligent breach of a contract.

5. Matthew is a certified public accountant. He prepared a balance sheet statement for the Stanley Corporation that he knew would be used by Stanley to obtain a loan from the Third National Bank. In order to satisfy Stanley, Matthew prepared the statement in such a way that the false impression was created that Stanley was a thriving, prosperous corporation. If the statement had been prepared in accordance with standard accounting procedures, it would have shown that Stanley was just about to become insolvent. The Third National Bank, relying on this financial statement, loaned money to Stanley. Shortly thereafter, Stanley went into bankruptcy, and the Third National Bank lost virtually the full amount of the loan. The bank sued Matthew for the loss. Matthew asserted that he could not be sued by a third person, as his only duty was to his client, the Stanley Corporation. Is this a valid defense?

6. Samari Brothers built an office building for the Pierce Corporation. Pierce rented one of the first-floor stores of the building to Byron. Because of defective construction work, there were water leaks into Byron's store. Byron sued Sa-

mari for the damage caused to his inventory by the leaks. Samari denied liability, on the ground that the building had been approved by the architect and accepted by the Pierce Corporation, so a third person, such as Byron, could not bring suit against Samari. Samari claimed Byron was merely an incidental beneficiary of the contract between Samari and Pierce. Is this a valid defense?

7. The First National Bank loaned money to the Erps Construction Company on the basis of financial statements of Erps prepared by Crawford, a CPA. The loan was not repaid, and the bank sued Crawford, claiming that because of his negligence the financial statements of Erps did not give a true picture of the contractor's financial condition. Crawford raised the defense that there was no privity of contract between him and the bank. Was this defense valid? [First National Bank v Crawford (W Va App) 386 SE2d 310]

8. Air-Speed, Inc. retained Hansman to obtain insurance to cover workers' compensation payments for its employees. Hansman notified Air-Speed that the insurance had been obtained. In fact it had not been, because Hansman negligently failed to forward the premiums to the insurance company to pay for the insurance. Thomas Rae was an employee of Air-Speed. He was killed in the course of his employment. His wife Christine was appointed as administratrix of his estate. She sued Air-Speed and Hansman for the payments that would have been received under a workers' compensation insurance policy if one had been obtained. Hansman denied liability on the ground that he had not made any contract with Christine to obtain insurance. Was this defense valid? [Rae v Air-Speed, Inc. 386 Mass 167, 435 NE2d 628]

9. Johnson was a notary public. Albin, pretending to be Werner, showed Johnson a deed signed with the name of Werner. Johnson did not do anything to determine the true identity of Albin as required by law. Instead he assumed that the signature was genuine and filled in the acknowledgment form on the deed, falsely reciting that Werner had appeared before him and that Werner had acknowledged the deed as being his deed. Actually, the deed was a forgery. Suit was brought by a member of the Werner family who had relied on the forged deed and thereby sustained damage when the true owner reclaimed the land. Decide. [Werner v Werner, 84 Wash 2d 360, 526 P2d 370]

10. The certified public accounting partnership of James, Guinn and Head prepared a certified audit report of four corporations, known as the Paschal Enterprises, with knowledge that their report would be used to induce Shatterproof Glass Corporation to lend money to those corporations. The report showed the corporations to be solvent when in fact they were insolvent. Shatterproof relied on the audit report; loaned approximately $500,000 to the four corporations, and lost almost all of it because the liabilities of the companies were in excess of their assets. Shatterproof claimed that James and other accountants had been negligent in preparing the report and sued them to recover the loss on the loan. The accountants raised the defense that they had not been retained by the plaintiff but rather by Paschal. Was this defense valid? [Shatterproof Glass Corporation v James (Tex Civ App) 466 SW2d 873]

11. The Milwaukee Sanitary Drain Commission made a contract with Nagel Construction, Inc. to construct drains according to the plans prepared by Progressive Engineering, Inc. Nagel made a subcontract with National Sand to perform part of the work. Because of the negligence of Progressive Engineering, a poor site was selected for the work of National Sand, and National Sand was subjected to additional costs. National Sand sued all parties involved. Progressive Engineering raised the defense that it could not be sued by National Sand because there was no privity of contract between them. Was this defense valid? [National Sand, Inc. v Nagel Construction, Inc. 132 Mich App 327, 451 NW2d 618]

12. Copenhaver made a will. It was prepared by his attorney, Rogers. The will attempted to create a trust that would benefit the grandchildren of Copenhaver. Because of the negligence of Rogers, the trust was void. The grandchildren sued him for malpractice. Was he liable? The court followed the common law. [Copenhaver v Rogers, 238 Va 361, 384 SE2d 593]

13. Suits Galore, Inc. was a clothing manufacturer. Landau made an audit and a financial report of Suits Galore. The statement prepared by Landau was not certified. It stated that it was a review report only and that no opinion was expressly stated by the accountant. On the basis of this report, William Iselin & Co., Inc. extended credit to Suits Galore. Shortly thereafter, Suits Galore went into bankruptcy. Iselin was not repaid the money it had loaned. Iselin sued Landau on the ground that the financial report had been negligently prepared and that Iselin could

sue Landau for the loss sustained. Was it correct? [William Iselin & Co., Inc. v Landau, 128 App Div 2d 453, 513 NYS2d 3]

14. Alton Packaging owned an airplane that was serviced by Garrett. Garrett found corrosion in the fuel tanks and replaced some of the tanks. Garrett did not enter into the logbook of the plane the making of the repairs or the existence of the corrosion problem. Alton sold the plane to B.L. Jet Sales, Inc. Difficulties developed because of the corrosion problem. B.L. sued Alton and Garrett. The claim against Garrett was the negligent failure to make the proper repair entry in the logbook of the plane so that subsequent purchasers would be aware of the problem. Garrett raised the defense that there was no privity of contract between him and the plaintiff and that the plaintiff was seeking to recover only for economic loss. Was this defense valid? [B.L. Jet Sales, Inc. v Alton Packaging Corp. (Mo App) 724 SW2d 669]

15. The U.S.F.&G. Co. issued policies of fire and public liability insurance to the Roosevelt Hotel and agreed to make periodic inspections of the premises for fire hazards and conditions dangerous to guests. Marie Hill and her husband were guests at the hotel. The insurer negligently failed to find a hazard that resulted in a fire that injured Marie Hill and killed her husband. She sued the insurer for damages for her injuries and for the wrongful death of her husband. The insurer denied liability because there was no privity of contract between the plaintiff and the insurer. Was this defense valid? [Hill v U.S.F. & G. Co. (CA5 Fla) 428 F2d 112]

PART THREE

PERSONAL PROPERTY
AND BAILMENTS

20

PERSONAL PROPERTY

Property includes the rights of any person to possess, use, enjoy, and dispose of a thing or object of value. Property is classified as real property and personal property. **Real property** means land and things permanently affixed to land, such as trees or buildings. **Personal property** includes all other property. This chapter develops the law of personal property, setting forth (1) the basic legal principles of personal property, (2) how title to personal property is acquired, (3) how rights in personal property are protected, and (4) the law concerning multiple owners of specific personal property.

A.   GENERAL PRINCIPLES

In common usage, the term *property* refers to a piece of land or a thing or an object. As a legal concept, however, *property* refers to the rights that an individual may possess in that piece of land or that thing or that object.[1] A right in a thing is property, without regard as to whether such right is absolute or conditional, perfect or imperfect, legal or equitable.

1.   Personal Property

Personal property consists of: (a) whole or fractional rights in things that are tangible and movable, such as furniture and books; (b) claims and debts, which are called **choses in action**; and (c) intangible proprietary rights, such as trademarks, copyrights, and patents.

The concept of personal property is expanding. For example, courts now generally include gas and water within the definition of *property*. Thus, persons who tap water mains and gas pipes to obtain water and gas without paying are guilty of taking property.

The modern techniques of sound and image recording have led to the necessity of giving protection against copying. Federal and state statutes provide for the copyright protection of compositions and create crimes of record and tape piracy. [2]

The theft of personal property that relates to computers is covered in Chapter 21.

2.   Limitations on Ownership

A person who has all possible rights in and over a thing is said to have **absolute ownership** of it. The term *absolute*, however, is somewhat misleading, for one's rights with respect to the use, enjoyment, and disposal of things are subject to certain restrictions. An owner's property is subject to the government's powers to tax, to regulate under the police power, and to take by eminent domain. It is subject to the creditors of the owner. Above all, the owner may not use property in a way that will unreasonably injure others.

---

[1]   Presley Memorial Foundation v Crowell (Tenn App) 733 SW2d 89 (1987).
[2]   PL 92-140, 85 Stat 391, 17 USC §§ 1, 5, 20, 101; Wyo Stat Anno § 40-13-205 (1989).

B.   ACQUISITION OF TITLE TO PERSONAL PROPERTY

Title to personal property may be acquired in different ways. For example, property is commonly purchased. The purchase and sale of goods is governed by the law of sales, covered in Part 4 of this book. In this chapter the following methods of acquiring personal property will be discussed: gift, the finding of lost property, transfer by a nonowner, occupation, and escheat.

3.   Gifts

Title to personal property may be transferred by the voluntary act of the owner without receiving anything in exchange—that is, by **gift**. The person making the gift, the **donor**, may do so because of things that the recipient of the gift, the **donee**, had done in the past or is expected to do in the future. However, such matters of inducement are not deemed consideration and thus do not alter the "free" character of the gift.

(a) *INTER VIVOS* GIFTS. The ordinary gift that is made between two living persons is an ***inter vivos gift.*** For practical purposes such a gift takes effect upon the donor's expressing an intent to transfer title and making delivery, subject to the right of the donee to disclaim the gift within a reasonable time after learning that it has been made.[3] As there is no consideration for a gift, there is no enforceable contract, and an intended donee cannot sue for breach of contract if the donor fails to complete the gift.

(1) Intent. The intent to make a gift requires an intent to transfer title at that time. In contrast, an intent to confer a benefit at a future date is not a sufficient intent to create any right in the intended donee. A delivery of property without the intent to make a gift does not transfer title.

(2) Delivery. Ordinarily, the delivery required to make a gift will be an actual handing over to the donee of the thing that is given.

The delivery of a gift may also be made by a **symbolic delivery**, as by the delivery of

---

[3]   Owen v Owen (SD) 351 NW2d 139 (1984).

means of control of property. Such means of control might be keys to a lock or keys to an automobile, or papers that are essential to or closely associated with the ownership of the property, such as documents of title or a ship's papers. The delivery of a symbol is effective as a gift if the intent to make a gift is established. This is in contrast to merely giving the recipient of the token temporary access to the property, as for example, until the deliverer comes back from the hospital.

A gift may be made by depositing money in the bank account of an intended donee. If the account is a joint account in the names of two persons, a deposit of money in the account by one person may or may not be a gift to the other. Parol evidence is generally admissible to show whether there was an intention to make a gift.

When a savings account passbook is essential to the withdrawal of money from a savings account, parents do not make a gift to a minor child when they open a savings account in the child's name but keep possession of the passbook.

FIGURE 20-1   *INTER VIVOS* GIFT

INTER VIVOS GIFT

LAW:	DONOR	1. INTENT AND 2. DELIVERY	UNLESS THE GIFT IS DISCLAIMED, TITLE PASSES TO DONEE
APPLICATION:	SMITH OWNS THE VAN GOGH PAINTING "THE IRISES"	1. HE STATES, "THIS IS FOR YOU MICHAEL," AND 2. PERSONALLY PRESENTS THE PAINTING TO HIS SON MICHAEL	MICHAEL BECOMES THE OWNER

(3) Donor's Death. If the donor dies before doing what is needed to make an effective gift, the gift fails. An agent or the executor or administrator of the estate cannot thereafter perform the missing step on behalf of the decedent. For example, in a state where a transfer of title to a motor vehicle could not be made without a transfer of the title certificate, that transfer must be made while the donor is living and cannot be made after the donor's death by the executor of the estate.

(b) GIFTS *CAUSA MORTIS*. A **gift** *causa mortis* is made when the donor, contemplating imminent and impending death, delivers personal property to the donee with the intent that the donee shall own it if the donor dies.[4] This is a conditional gift, and the donor is entitled to take the property back if (1) the donor

does not die; (2) the donor revokes the gift before dying; or (3) the donee dies before the donor.

(c) GIFTS AND TRANSFERS TO MINORS. The Uniform Gifts to Minors Act (UGMA), provides an additional method for making gifts of money and of registered and unregistered securities to minors.[5] Under the UGMA, a gift of money may be made by an adult to a minor by depositing it with a broker or a bank in an account in the name of the donor or another adult or a bank with trust powers "as a

---

[4]   Pina v Flaglore (SD) 443 NW2d 627 (1989).

[5]   The Uniform Gifts to Minors Act (UGMA) was originally proposed in 1956. It was revised in 1965 and again in 1966. One of these versions is in effect in the following states: Alaska, Connecticut, Delaware, Georgia, Indiana, Maryland, Mississippi, Nebraska, New Jersey, New Mexico, New York, Pennsylvania, South Carolina, Tennessee, Texas, Utah, Vermont, and Washington. It has been adopted for the U.S. Virgin Islands.

custodian for [*name of minor*] under the [*name of state*] Uniform Gifts to Minors Act." If the gift is a registered security, the donor registers the security in a similar manner.

The Uniform Transfers to Minors Act (UTMA)[6] revises and restates the UGMA. The UTMA not only allows for gifts of money and securities, but also expands the kinds of property that may be made the subject of a gift. It allows any kind of property, real or personal, tangible or intangible, to be made the subject of a transfer to a custodian for the benefit of a minor.[7] Real estate, automobiles, partnership interests, and business proprietorships may be so transferred under the Act. The UTMA permits transfers from parties other than donors, such as parties against whom a minor

has a tort claim or judgment. It is for this reason that the title of the revised act has been changed to the broader term "Transfers" rather than the narrower term "Gifts."

When property is held by a custodian for the benefit of a minor under the UGMA or the UTMA, the custodian has discretionary power to use the property for the "support, maintenance, education, and benefit" of the minor, but the custodian may not use the custodial property for the custodian's own personal benefit. The gift is final and irrevocable for tax and all other purposes upon complying with the procedure of the Act.

Under the UTMA as well as the UGMA, custodianships terminate and the property is distributed when the minor reaches age 21.

The *Heath* case involved a dispute over the ownership of two bank accounts established under the UGMA. The court was faced with deciding whether the donative intent and delivery, the two basic elements of every *inter vivos* gift of personal property, were present.

---

[6]   The Uniform Transfers to Minors Act was originally proposed in 1983. It has been adopted, often with minor variations, in the following states: Alabama, Arizona, Arkansas, California, Colorado, Florida, Hawaii, Idaho, Illinois, Iowa, Kansas, Kentucky, Louisiana, Maine, Massachusetts, Minnesota, Missouri, Montana, Nevada, New Hampshire, North Carolina, North Dakota, Ohio, Oklahoma, Oregon, Rhode Island, South Dakota, Virginia, West Virginia, Wisconsin, and Wyoming. It has also been adopted by the District of Columbia.

[7]   UTMA § 1(6).

HEATH v HEATH
143 Ill App 3d 390, 97 Ill Dec 615, 493 NE2d 97 (1986)

In 1980 Larry Heath received $10,000 from his father. These funds grew to $13,381 by 1983, and in March he used this money to establish two custodian bank accounts for his minor children under the Uniform Gifts to Minors Act. Larry was listed as custodian on each account. In August of 1984 Larry closed both accounts and returned the proceeds to his mother, because his father was in Europe. The childrens' mother, Pamela, brought suit to recover the funds, contending that the deposits were irrevocable gifts. Larry Heath contended that the money was his father's and it was never intended as a gift. From a judgment for the children, Larry Heath appealed.

HOPF, J. . . . In the instant case, sections 2 and 3 of the Illinois Uniform Gifts to Minors Act (the Act) are particularly relevant to a determination whether an irrevocable gift was created. These sections provide in part:

An adult may, during his lifetime make or provide for a gift of custodial property to a person who is a minor on the date of the gift or distribution: . . .
(2) if the subject of the gift is money, by paying or delivering it to a broker or

domestic financial institution for credit to an account in the name of the donor, another adult or a trust company, followed, in substance, by the words: "as custodian for . . . (name of minor) under the Illinois Uniform Gifts to Minors Act."

. . .

A gift made in a manner prescribed in this Act is irrevocable and conveys to the minor indefeasibly vested legal title to the custodial property given, but no guardian of the minor has any right, power, duty or authority with respect to the custodial property except as provided in this Act. Ill. Rev. Stat. 1983, ch. 110 1/2, pars. 202(a)(2), 203(a).

The Act is designed to make an *inter vivos* gift to a minor in a relatively simplified manner. By conveying the gift in the manner presented by the Act, the minor obtains indefeasibly vested legal title to the property which is gifted, and once the gift is made, it is irrevocable. A valid *inter vivos* gift requires proof of donative intent and delivery of the subject matter. As noted in section 2 above, the Act expressly addresses the element of delivery by providing that such element shall be satisfied by following the procedures set forth in the statute. However, the Act contains no provision regarding the element of donative intent and that element is the one at issue in the case at bar.

. . . Defendant has presented this court with three cases from other jurisdictions which have dealt with this issue and we find the holdings reached therein both persuasive and applicable to the instant case.

All three cases . . . held that, although establishing a bank account in a minor's name in compliance with the provisions of the Uniform Gifts to Minors Act is highly probative on the issue of donative intent, it did not create an irrebutable presumption of intent. Thus, documentary compliance with the statutory mechanisms of the Act constitutes *prima facie* evidence that a gift was made and intended. But, in appropriate circumstances, extrinsic evidence may be introduced to rebut the *prima facie* showing provided by the prescribed documentation of the Act. . . .

In the instant case the documentary evidence, in particular, the account signature cards signed by the defendant, clearly constituted a *prima facie* showing that the bank accounts . . . were intended to be irrevocable gifts to the named minors under the Act. . . . However, defendant argues in this court that his testimony was sufficient to rebut this documentary showing of donative intent. . . .

Defendant maintains that his testimony at the hearing shows he was unaware of the legal effect the account signature cards acquired upon his signing of them. Defendant attempts to pass himself off as a mere "factory worker" with apparently little knowledge of such matters. However, it is a matter of common knowledge that one should always read any document before signing it. Moreover, even a casual glance at the signature cards would have warned defendant that he was making a gift to a minor. At the top of the signature cards it clearly stated in capital letters "GIFT TRANSFERRED TO MINOR." On both sides of the signature cards it indicates that defendant is opening savings accounts for the children "as Custodian for" them under the Illinois Uniform Gifts to Minors Act. Additionally, directly above defendant's signature it states:

> This gift of money to the minor named, which gift shall be deemed to include all earnings thereon and any future earnings thereto, is irrevocable and is made in accordance with and to include all the provisions of the said Statute of this state as it is now or hereafter may be amended.

Underneath defendant's signature appear the words "Signature of Donor." This court finds defendant's claim of ignorance, regarding the legal effect of what he was signing, unworthy of belief.

Consequently, in our view, defendant's testimony regarding his alleged ignorance regarding the opening of the bank accounts in the names of his minor children was insufficient to rebut plaintiff's strong documentary showing that defendant had created irrevocable gifts. Additionally, although defendant testified the monies used for the accounts in question constituted a loan from his father which had to be repaid, defendant offered no other evidence to substantiate this contention.

... In our opinion, the trial court was correct in concluding that irrevocable gifts were created at the time defendant opened the bank accounts in the names of the minors under the Illinois Uniform Gifts to Minors Act.

[Judgment affirmed]

QUESTIONS

1. What are the two basic elements of every *inter vivos* gift of personal property?
2. Was the court influenced by the documentary compliance with the UGMA in reaching the determination on whether or not there was a "gift"?
3. After Larry Heath had opened the UGMA accounts, could he change his mind and revoke the transfer?

(d) CONDITIONAL GIFTS. A gift may be made on condition, such as "This car is yours when you graduate," or "This car is yours unless you drop out of school." The former gift is subject to a condition precedent, and the latter to a condition subsequent. The condition to the first gift must be satisfied before any gift or transfer takes place. The satisfaction of the second condition operates to destroy or divest a title that had already been transferred. Ordinarily no condition is recognized unless it is expressly stated. However, most courts regard an engagement ring as a conditional gift subject to the condition subsequent of a failure to marry. The inherent symbolism of the gift itself is deemed to foreclose the need to establish an express condition that the marriage will ensue. Most jurisdictions allow recovery of conditional engagement gifts only if the party seeking recovery has not unjustifiably broken off the engagement. The *Harris* case illustrates the application of this rule. However, a few states reject considerations of "fault" as to the breaking of an engagement and always require the return of the ring to the donor where there is a broken engagement on the theory that in most cases there is no real fault as such, but rather a change of mind.[8]

[8]   Brown v Thomas (App) 127 Wis 2d 318, 37 NW2d 868 (1985).

HARRIS v DAVIS
139 Ill App 3d 1046, 94 Ill Dec 326, 487 NE2d 1204 (1986)

Chip Harris gave Rebecca Davis a diamond ring upon their engagement to be married. Some time later Davis informed Harris that she no longer wanted to see him and that she had thrown the ring into a drainage ditch near her mother's home. Harris rented a metal detector and searched the area to no avail. He sued Davis for the value of the ring. From a judgment for Davis, Harris appealed.

JONES, J. . . . On appeal, the plaintiff argues that under Illinois law, the party failing to comply with an engagement or a contract to be married has no right to property acquired in contemplation of the marriage. (*Urbanus v. Burns* (1939), 300 Ill.App. 207, 20 N.E.2d 869; *Rockafellow v. Newcomb* (1870), 57 Ill. 186.) Plaintiff further argues that where an engagement is terminated because of the fault of the woman, the man is ordinarily entitled to the return of gifts made in contemplation of the marriage. (20 Ill.L. & Prac. § 22 (1968).) We agree.

The law in Illinois appears established that a gift given in contemplation of marriage is deemed to be conditional on the subsequent marriage of the parties, and the party who fails to perform on the condition of the gift has no right to property acquired under such pretenses.

A Pennsylvania court said: "A gift given by a man to a woman on condition that she embark on the sea of matrimony with him is no different from a gift based on the condition that the donee sail on any other sea", and "if, after receiving the provisional gift, the donee refuses to leave the harbor,—if the anchor of contractual performance sticks in the sands of irresolution and procrastination—the gift must be restored to the donor". *Pavlicic v. Vogtsberger* (1957), 390 Pa. 502, 507–09, 136 A.2d 127, 130.

There can be no question that the ring in the instant case was given by the plaintiff to the defendant in contemplation of marriage. Neither party disputes that fact. Neither is there any question that it was the defendant fiancée who broke the engagement. There is no allegation that plaintiff's acts caused the defendant to break the engagement. The record does not reveal the cause of the break-up. At any rate, the defendant failed to perform on the condition of the gift and, therefore, had no right either to retain the ring or to dispose of it. We, therefore, reverse the judgment of the trial court and hold that the defendant is liable to the plaintiff for the $1,390 value of the engagement ring.

[Judgment reversed]

QUESTIONS

1. State the rule of law set forth in this decision.
2. If Chip Harris had broken off the engagement, would he have been entitled to the return of the ring?

(e) ANATOMICAL GIFTS. The Uniform Anatomical Gift Act[9] permits persons eighteen years or older to make gifts of their bodies or any part or an organ. The gift would take effect upon the death of the donor. The gift may be made to a school, a hospital, an organ bank, or to a named patient. Such a gift may also be made, subject to certain restrictions, by the spouse, adult child, parent, adult brother or sister, or guardian of a deceased person.[10] Independently of the Act, living persons may make gifts of part of their bodies, as in the case of a blood transfusion or a kidney transplant.

4. Lost Property

Personal property is *lost* when the owner does not know where it is located but intends to retain title or ownership to it. The person find-

[9] This Act has been adopted in every state.

[10] Uniform Anatomical Gift Act (UAGA) §§ 2,3.

406 Part 3 Personal Property and Bailments

ing lost property does not acquire title but only possession. Ordinarily the finder of lost property is required to surrender the property to the true owner when the latter establishes ownership. Meanwhile the finder is entitled to retain possession as against everyone else.

Without a contract with the owner or a statute so providing, the finder of lost property is not entitled to a reward or to compensation for finding or caring for the property.

(a) FINDING IN PUBLIC PLACE. If the lost property is found in a public place, such as a hotel, under such circumstances that to a reasonable person it would appear that the property had been intentionally placed there by the owner and that the owner would be likely to recall where the property had been left and to return for it, the finder is not entitled to possession of the property. The finder must give it to the proprietor or manager of the public place to keep it for the owner. This exception does not apply if it appears that the property was not intentionally placed where it was found. In that case it is not likely that the owner will recall having left it there.

(b) STATUTORY CHANGE. In some states statutes have been adopted permitting the finder to sell the property or keep it if the owner does not appear within a stated period of time. In such a case, the finder is required to give notice, as by newspaper publication, in order to attempt to reach the owner.

5. Transfer by Nonowner

Ordinarily, a sale or other transfer by one who does not own the property will pass no title. No title is acquired by theft. The thief acquires possession only; and if the thief makes a sale or gift of the property to another, the latter only acquires possession of the property. The true owner may reclaim the property from the thief or from the thief's transferee.[11]

(a) AUTOMOBILES. In some states the general rule stated above is fortified by statutes that declare that the title to an automobile

cannot be transferred, even by the true owner, without a delivery of a properly endorsed title certificate. The states that follow the common law do not make the holding of a title certificate essential to the ownership of an automobile, although as a matter of police regulation the owner must obtain such a certificate.

(b) EXCEPTIONS. As an exception to the rule that a nonowner cannot transfer title, an agent, who does not own the property but who is authorized to sell it, may transfer the title of the agent's principal. Likewise, certain relationships, such as a pledge or an entrustment, create a power to sell and to transfer title. Likewise, an owner of property may be barred or estopped from claiming ownership when the owner has acted to deceive an innocent buyer into believing that someone else was the owner or had authority to sell.

6. Occupation of Personal Property

In some cases title to personal property may be acquired by occupation—that is, by taking and retaining possession of the property.

(a) WILD ANIMALS. Wild animals, living in a state of nature, are not owned by any individual. In the absence of restrictions imposed by game laws, the person who acquires dominion or control over a wild animal becomes its owner. What constitutes sufficient dominion or control varies with the nature of the animal and the surrounding circumstances. If the animal is killed, tied, imprisoned, or otherwise prevented from going at its will, the hunter exercises sufficient dominion or control over the animal and becomes its owner. If the wild animal, subsequent to its capture, should escape and return to its natural state, it resumes the status of a wild animal.[12]

As a qualification to the ordinary rule, the following exception developed. If an animal is killed or captured on the land of another while the hunter is on the land without permission of the landowner, the animal, when killed or captured, does not belong to the hunter but to the landowner.

---

[11] As to the right of the owner to sue for monetary damages see Section 12 of this chapter.

[12] Wiley v Baker (Tex Civ App) 597 SW2d 3 (1980).

(b) ABANDONED PERSONAL PROPER-
TY. Personal property is deemed abandoned
when the owner relinquishes possession of it
with the intention to disclaim title to it. Yester-
day's newspaper that is thrown out in the
trash is abandoned personal property. Title to
abandoned property may be acquired by the
first person who obtains possession and control of it. A person becomes the owner at the
moment of taking possession of the abandoned personal property.

When the owner of property flees in the
face of an approaching peril, property left behind is not abandoned. An abandonment occurs only when the owner voluntarily leaves
the property.

7.   Escheat

Who owns unclaimed property? In the case of
personal property, the practical answer is that
the property will probably "disappear" after
a period of time, or, if in the possession of a
carrier, hotel, or warehouse, it may be sold for
unpaid charges. A growing problem arises
with respect to unclaimed corporate dividends, bank deposits, insurance payments,
and refunds. Most states have a statute providing for the transfer of such unclaimed
property to the state government. This transfer to the government is often called by its feudal name of **escheat**. To provide for unclaimed
property, many states have adopted the Uniform Disposition of Unclaimed Property Act.[13]

In the *Presley* case, both Elvis Presley's estate and the state of Tennessee claimed the unrefunded ticket proceeds of a concert canceled
because of the singer's death.

[13]   The 1954 version of the Act has been adopted in Ar-
kansas. A 1966 version of the Act has been adopted in Alabama, Georgia, Indiana, Mississippi, Missouri, Nebraska,
Oklahoma, South Dakota, and the District of Columbia. A
1981 version of the Act has been adopted in Alaska, Ari-
zona, Colorado, Florida, Hawaii, Idaho, Illinois, Louisiana,
Maine, Montana, Nevada, New Hampshire, New Jersey,
New Mexico, North Dakota, Oregon, Rhode Island, South
Carolina, Utah, Virginia, Washington, Wisconsin, and the
Virgin Islands. Several states have adopted a composite of
an earlier version of the Act and the 1981 version: Iowa,
Maryland, Minnesota, Tennessee, and Vermont.

PRESLEY v CITY OF MEMPHIS
(Tenn App) 769 SW2d 221 (1988)

Elvis Presley contracted with Mid-South Coliseum Board (City of Memphis) for
the rental of the Coliseum and for personnel to sell tickets for concerts on August
27 and 28, 1977. $325,000 worth of tickets were sold. On August 16, 1977 Elvis
Presley died. Refunds were given to those who returned their tickets to the Coliseum Board. Ten years after his death, however, $152,279 worth of ticket proceeds
remained unclaimed in the custody of the Board. This fund had earned $223,760
in interest. Priscilla Presley and the co-executors of the estate of Elvis Presley
brought an action, claiming the unrefunded ticket proceeds for the canceled concerts. The state of Tennessee claimed that it was entitled to the proceeds under
the Uniform Disposition of Unclaimed Property Act. From a judgment for the co-
executors, the state appealed.

HIGHERS, J. . . . Although the ticket may have some value as memorabilia apart from its
intended function, such value was not the essence of the contract, had no bearing on
the original proceeds, and has none now.

When Presley died, performance of the concert became impossible, and the contract
was void. . . . The ticketholder was vested with a right to a refund of contract proceeds
from the Coliseum as Presley's agent. . . .

Tennessee's version of the UDUPA is codified at T.C.A. § 66-29-101 *et seq.*....§ 66-29-113 requires that the holder of the [abandoned] property report that property to the state treasurer. After notice is given . . . the property is to be delivered to the treasurer. . . .

The owner may recover at any time no matter how remote. . . .

The state has asserted that the definition in T.C.A. § 66-29-111 is applicable to the case at bar. That statute provides in pertinent part as follows:

> 66-29-111. Miscellaneous property held for another person.—All property, not otherwise covered by this chapter, including any income or increment thereon and deducting any lawful charges, that is held or owing in this state in the ordinary course of the holder's business and has remained unclaimed by the owner for more than seven (7) years after it became payable or distributable is presumed abandoned.

We agree with the state's assertion. The refunds in question have remained unclaimed in the more than seven years they have been held by the Coliseum in the ordinary course of its business. The ticketholder's right to a refund vested when the contract was voided. That right arose and the seven-year statutory period began when Elvis Presley died on August 16, 1977. Therefore, a presumption of abandonment as to unclaimed refunds matured on August 16, 1984. The present action . . . does not qualify as a claim under the statute because the plaintiffs have no legal right to the funds. Any right they might have had was lost when the contract was voided.

The presumption of abandonment under the UDUPA is statutory and therefore independent of common law principles of abandonment. . . . Intentional and voluntary relinquishment is not required under the statute. Statutory abandonment occurs when the conditions set out in the UDUPA exist. . . . Only statutorily abandoned property is disposed of under the UDUPA. . . .

We are well aware that this fund would not exist were it not for Elvis Presley's unique skills and talents while living and the legendary status he continues to hold in the years after his death. . . . These considerations might in the absence of the Tennessee statute merit granting the windfall to Presley's estate. But Presley's death voided the contract represented by each ticket sold, . . . and Presley's estate [has] no legal claim to the ticket proceeds. Granting the proceeds to either of them or to the Coliseum constitutes the type of windfall the drafters of UDUPA sought to address. . . . We believe the drafters of the UDUPA and our legislature intended such windfalls to benefit the public rather than individuals in precisely the manner we hold here. . . .

In summary, pursuant to the Tennessee UDUPA, we hold that the coliseum must deliver all of the unclaimed ticket refunds and all of the accumulated interest thereon to the treasurer. Further, the treasurer shall publish the existence of the unclaimed funds and hold those amounts until such time as they are claimed by the rightful owners, the ticketholders.

[Judgment reversed and action remanded]

QUESTIONS

1. On what basis did the Estate of Elvis Presley claim the unrefunded ticket proceeds and interest?
2. Present the state's legal position before the court.
3. Did the court think the intent of the drafters of the UDUPA would support the "windfall" in

> this case benefiting the estate of the individual whose legendary status generated the unclaimed funds? Explain.

C. PROTECTION OF PERSONAL PROPERTY

Property rights in trademarks, copyrights, and patents are acquired as provided by federal statutes, and the nature and extent of their legal protection will be covered in this chapter.

8. Trademarks and Service Marks

A *mark* is any word, name, symbol, or design, or a combination of these, used to identify a product or service.[14] If the mark identifies a product, such as an automobile or soap, it is called a **trademark**. If it identifies a service, such as a restaurant or dry cleaners, it is called a **service mark**.

The owner of a mark may obtain protection from its use by others by registering the mark in accordance with federal law.[15] In order to be registered, a mark must distinguish the goods or service of the applicant from those of others. Under the federal statute, a register, called the Principal Register, is maintained for the recording of such marks. Inclusion on the Principal Register grants the registrant the exclusive right to use the mark. Challenges may be made to the registrant's rights within five years of registration; but after five years the rights of the registrant are incontestable.

For many years businesses did not have the right to register marks until they were actually used. Thus, operators of new hotels or restaurants or others in the service industries could not register their names before opening their doors for business. A recent amendment to the federal trademark law allows a business to register a mark up to three years before using the name in business by filing an application certifying a bona fide "intent-to-use" and paying fees at six-month intervals until actual use begins.[16]

(a) REGISTRABLE MARKS. Marks that are coined, completely fanciful, or arbitrary are capable of registration on the Principal Register. The mark *Exxon*, for example, was coined by the owners. The name *Kodak* is also a creation of the owners of this trademark, has no other meaning in our language, and obviously serves to distinguish the goods of its owners from all others.

A suggestive term may also be registered. Such a term suggests rather than describes some characteristics of the goods to which it applies and requires the consumer to exercise some imagination to reach a conclusion as to the nature of the goods. For example, as a trademark for refrigerators, the term *Penguin* would be suggestive. As a trademark for paperback books, the term *Penguin* is arbitrary and fanciful.

Ordinarily, descriptive terms, surnames, and geographical terms are not registrable on the Principal Register.[17] A descriptive term identifies a characteristic or quality of an article or service, such as color, odor, function, or use. Thus, *Cough Calmers* was held not to be registrable on the Principal Register because it was merely descriptive of the goods normally called cough drops. However, an exception is made where a descriptive or geographic term or a surname has acquired a secondary meaning, and such a mark is registrable. A term or terms that have a primary meaning of their own acquire a **secondary meaning** when,

---

[14]   15 USC § 1127; Safeway Stores, Inc. v. Safeway Discount Drugs, Inc. (CA11 Fla) 675 F2d 1160 (1982). See also Trademark Clarification Act of 1984, PL 98-620, 98 Stat 333.
[15]   Lanham Act, 15 USC §§ 1050–1127.

[16]   PL 100-667, 15 USC § 1051 (1988); effective November 16, 1989.
[17]   A Supplemental Register exists for recording such marks. This recording does not give the registrant any protection, but it provides a source to which other persons designing a mark can go to make sure they are not duplicating an existing mark.

through long use in connection with a particular product, they have come to be known by the public at large as identifying the particular product or its origin. For example, the geographic term *Philadelphia* has acquired a secondary meaning as applied to cream cheese. It is widely accepted by the public as denoting a particular brand rather than any cream cheese made in Philadelphia. Factors considered by a court in determining whether a trademark has acquired secondary meaning are the amount and manner of advertising, volume of sales, length and manner of use, direct consumer testimony, and consumer surveys.

Generic terms that designate a kind or class of goods, such as *cola* or *rose' wine*, are never registrable.

(b) INJUNCTION AGAINST IMPROPER USE OF MARK. A person who has the right to use a mark may enjoin a competitor from imitating or duplicating the mark. The basic question in such litigation is whether the general public is likely to be confused by the mark of the defendant and to believe wrongly that it

identifies the plaintiff. If there is this danger of confusion, the court will enjoin the defendant from using the particular mark.

In some cases the fact that the products of the plaintiff and the defendant did not compete in the same market was held to entitle the defendant to use a mark that would have been prohibited as confusingly similar if the defendant manufactured the same product as the plaintiff. For example, it has been held that *Cadillac* as applied to boats is not confusingly similar to *Cadillac* as applied to automobiles; therefore, its use cannot be enjoined.[18]

In the *University of Georgia Athletic Association* case, the court was faced with the question of whether there was likelihood of confusion between the UGAA's service mark and athletic symbol *Bulldogs* and the trademark *Battlin' Bulldog Beer*.

[18]   General Motors Corporation v. Cadillac Marine and Boat Co., 140 USPQ 447 (1964). See also Amstar Corp. v Domino's Pizza Inc. (CA5 Ga) 615 F2d 252 (1980), where the mark *Domino* as applied to pizza was held not be confusingly similar to *Domino* as applied to sugar.

UNIVERSITY OF GEORGIA ATHLETIC ASS'N v LAITE
(CA11 Ga) 756 F2d 1535 (1985)

The University of Georgia Athletic Association (UGAA) brought suit against beer wholesaler Bill Laite for marketing Battlin' Bulldog Beer. The UGAA claimed that the cans infringed on its symbol for its athletic teams, which it had registered as a service mark and which depicted an English Bulldog wearing a sweater with a *G* and the word *BULLDOGS* on it. Soon after the beer appeared on the market, the university received telephone calls from friends of the university, who were concerned that Battlin' Bulldog Beer was not the sort of product that should in any way be related to the University of Georgia. The university's suit was based on the theory of false designation of origin in violation of the Lanham Act. Laite contended that the University of Georgia Bulldog was not a valid service mark; that his bulldog was different from the university's; and that his cans bore the disclaimer "Not associated with the University of Georgia." The district court permanently enjoined Laite from marketing the beer under the challenged label design. Laite appealed.

KRAVITCH, C.J.... Laite's first argument on appeal is that the "University of Georgia Bulldog" is not a valid trade or service mark worthy of protection. Laite cites *Universal City Studios, Inc. v. Nintendo Co.*, 578 F. Supp. 911 (S.D.N.Y. 1983), for the proposition that "[t]o make a successful claim of false designation of origin in violation of § 43(a) of the Lanham Act, 15 U.S.C. § 1125(a), [plaintiff] must demonstrate that its trademark possesses 'secondary meaning'—'the power of a name or other configuration to symbolize a particular business, product or company. . . .'" Laite contends that the record does not contain sufficient proof of secondary meaning, and that the vagueness of UGAA's mark, coupled with extensive third-party uses of the same or similar marks, demonstrates the absence of secondary meaning. . . . The general rule in this circuit is that proof of secondary meaning is required *only* when protection is sought for descriptive marks, as opposed to arbitrary or suggestive marks. We have long recognized that:

> Service marks fall into four categories. A strong mark is usually fictitious, arbitrary or fanciful and is generally inherently distinctive. It is afforded the widest ambit of protection. . . . A descriptive mark tells something about the product; it is protected only when secondary meaning is shown. . . . In contrast to the above is the suggestive mark, which subtly connotes something about the service or product. Although less distinctive than a fictitious, arbitrary or fanciful mark . . . a suggestive mark will be protected without proof of secondary meaning. . . . Lastly, there are generic terms, which communicate 'information about the nature or class of an article or service,' and therefore can never become a service or trademark.

Thus, secondary meaning is best characterized not as a general prerequisite for trade or service mark protection, but as a means by which otherwise unprotectable descriptive marks may obtain protection. As one commentator has explained:

> Secondary meaning converts a word originally incapable of serving as a mark into a full fledged trademark. . . . An arbitrary, fanciful, or otherwise distinctive word qualifies as a trademark immediately, because in the particular industry it has no primary meaning to overcome. Therefore it is initially registrable, and also protectable at common law. In the case of words with primary meaning, the reverse is true. Such words, be they descriptive or geographical, are initially non-registrable and unprotectable unless and until they have attained secondary meaning as trademarks.

We therefore hold that, . . . proof of secondary meaning is required in an action under section 43(a) *only* when protection is sought for a descriptive mark, as opposed to an arbitrary or suggestive mark. Turning to the mark at issue in the instant case, we are convinced beyond a shadow of a doubt that the "University of Georgia Bulldog" is not a descriptive mark. In our view, the portrayal of an English bulldog chosen by the university as a symbol for its athletic teams is, at best, "suggestive," if not downright "arbitrary." Thus, contrary to Laite's assertion, UGAA was not required to prove secondary meaning in order to prevail on its Lanham Act claim, and the district court did not err in granting injunctive relief to UGAA under section 43(a) despite the absence of proof of secondary meaning.

Laite's next argument is that the district court used the wrong factors in comparing the "Battlin' Bulldog" with the "University of Georgia Bulldog." Laite correctly points out that this circuit has recognized seven factors as relevant to the determination of a "likelihood of confusion" between two trade or service marks: (1) the type of mark at issue, (2) the similarity of design between the two marks, (3) the similarity of product, (4) the identity of retail outlets and purchasers, (5) the identity of advertising media utilized, (6) the defendant's intent, and (7) actual confusion between the two marks.

According to Laite, the court below erred by failing to consider all seven of the relevant factors before deciding that the sale of "Battlin' Bulldog Beer" created a "likelihood of confusion."

. . . [W]e are not convinced, after examining the record and the orders entered by the district court, that the court failed to consider all seven of the relevant factors. At the preliminary injunction hearing, counsel for Laite discussed at length the seven factors, as set out in the *Amstar Corp.* case. Moreover, in the order granting the preliminary injunction, the district court cited *Amstar Corp.* and specifically mentioned two of the seven factors, namely, the similarity of design and the defendant's intent. The fact that the court did not discuss the other five factors may indicate only that the court found those factors insignificant under the circumstances. . . .

As the district court pointed out, it is the combination of similar design elements, rather than any individual element, that compels the conclusion that the two bulldogs are similar. Had the cans of "Battlin' Bulldog Beer" been printed in different colors, or had the "Battlin' Bulldog" worn a different monogram on its sweater, we might have a different case. Instead, the cans are red and black, the colors of the University of Georgia, and the "Battlin' Bulldog" wears the letter "G." To be sure, the "Battlin' Bulldog" is not an exact reproduction of the "University of Georgia Bulldog." Nevertheless, we find the differences between the two so minor as to be legally, if not factually, nonexistent.

. . . Laite candidly admitted in the court below, and at oral argument in this court, that "Battlin' Bulldog Beer" was intended to capitalize on the popularity of the University of Georgia football program. In short, there can be no doubt that Laite hoped to sell "Battlin' Bulldog Beer" not because the beer tastes great, but because the cans would catch the attention of University of Georgia football fans.

Although we find the defendant's intent and the similarity of design between the two marks sufficient to support the district court's finding of a "likelihood of confusion," we also note that the remaining five factors either support the same conclusion or, at least, do not undermine it. For example, as we previously noted, the type of mark at issue in this case is at best "suggestive," if not downright "arbitrary." Such marks traditionally have been characterized as "strong." The fact that many other colleges, junior colleges, and high schools use an English bulldog as a symbol does not significantly diminish the strength of UGAA's mark, since almost all of the other schools (1) are geographically remote, (2) use a different color scheme, or (3) have names that begin with a letter other than "G." . . .

The "Battlin' Bulldog's" football career thus comes to an abrupt end. Laite devised a clever entrepreneurial "game plan," but failed to take into account the strength of UGAA's mark and the tenacity with which UGAA was willing to defend that mark. Like the University of Georgia's famed "Junkyard Dog" defense, UGAA was able to hold its opponent to little or no gain. . . . [W]e find that the district court did not err, in fact or in law, when it granted permanent injunctive relief to UGAA. . . .

[Judgment affirmed]

QUESTIONS

1. When is proof of secondary meaning required in a trademark or service mark infringement lawsuit?
2. In what category of service mark is the University of Georgia Bulldog?
3. What are the seven factors considered by this circuit court in determining whether "likelihood of confusion" exists between two marks?

(c) ABANDONMENT OF EXCLUSIVE RIGHTS TO MARK. An owner who has an exclusive right to use a mark may lose that right. If other persons are permitted to use the mark, it loses its exclusive character and is said to pass into the English language and become generic. Examples of formerly enforceable marks that have made this transition into the general language are *aspirin*, *thermos*, *cellophane*, and *shredded wheat*.

9. Copyrights

A **copyright** is the exclusive right given by federal statute to the creator of a literary or artistic work to use, reproduce, or display the work. By international treaties, copyrights given under the laws of one nation are generally recognized in another. Under the international treaty called the *Berne Convention*, copyright in the works of all U.S. authors are protected automatically in all Berne Convention nations. Berne Convention nations agreed in the treaty to treat nationals of other member countries like their own nationals.

A copyright does not prevent the copying of an idea but only the copying of the way the idea is expressed. That is, the copyright is violated when there is a duplicating of the words or the pictures of the creator but not when there is merely a copying of the idea those words or pictures express.

(a) WHAT IS COPYRIGHTABLE. Copyrights protect literary, musical, dramatic, and artistic work. Protected are books and periodicals; musical and dramatic compositions; choreographic works; maps; works of art such as paintings, sculptures, and photographs; motion pictures and other audiovisual works; sound recordings; and computer programs, discussed in Section 19 of Chapter 21.

(b) UNPUBLISHED WORK. As long as a work is not made public, it has the same protection as though it had been copyrighted.

(c) SECURING A COPYRIGHT. A copyright owner may sue for copyright infringement of a published work if the work has been registered with the Copyright Office in Washington, D.C. A registration application must be accompanied by two copies of the work for deposit in the Library of Congress. Each copy of the published work may contain (1) a copyright notice, such as "copyright" or "©," (2) the date of first publication, and (3) the name of the copyright owner.[19]

(d) DURATION OF COPYRIGHT. For works created after January 1, 1978, a copyright lasts for the creator's lifetime plus 50 years.[20] After a copyright has expired, the work is in the public domain and may be used by anyone without cost.

(e) LIMITATIONS ON EXCLUSIVE CHARACTER OF COPYRIGHT. A limitation on the exclusive rights of copyright owners exists under the principle of "fair use," which allows for the limited usage of copyrighted material in connection with criticism, news reporting, teaching, and research. Two important factors in judging if the usage is fair are: (1) the amount of text used in relation to the copyrighted work as a whole and (2) the effect of the use on the value of the work.[21]

10. Patents

A **patent** is the exclusive right that the inventor of a device can obtain under federal law. The patent gives the inventor an exclusive 17-year right to make, use, and sell the thing invented. At the end of 17 years the patent expires and cannot be renewed. Patents cannot be defeated by the combination of components outside the United States for sale in global markets. U.S. suppliers of components of a patented invention who actively induce the combination of components outside the United States in a manner that would infringe

---

[19] Under the Berne Convention Implementation Act, PL 100–568, 102 Stat 2854, 17 USC § 101, a law which adjusts U.S. copyright law to conform to the Berne Convention, it is no longer mandatory that works published after March 1, 1989 contain a notice of copyright. However, placing a notice of copyright on published works is strongly recommended. This notice prevents an infringer from claiming "innocent infringement" of the work, which would reduce the amount of damages owed. In order to bring a copyright infringement suit for a work of U.S. origins, the owner must have submitted two copies of the work to the Copyright Office for registration.

[20] Copyright Act of 1976, § 302(a), 17 USC § 302(a).

[21] Copyright Act of 1976, § 107, 17 USC § 107.

the patent if the activity occurred in the United States are liable as infringers under the Patent Law Amendments Act of 1984.[22]

If a patent is not obtained, or if the patent has expired, anyone may make, use, or sell the invention without permission of the inventor and without making any payment therefor.

(a) WHAT IS PATENTABLE. In order to be patentable, the invention must be something that is new and useful and must be something that would not have been obvious to a person of ordinary skill or knowledge in the art or technology to which the invention is related.[23]

The invention is the thing that is patented, whether it be a machine, a process, or a particular chemical composition of matter. The idea or inspiration, ways of doing business, and scientific principles cannot be patented unless there is some physical thing upon which they are based. Patent law has been interpreted to permit the patenting of human-made life forms.

(b) CONTRACTUAL PROTECTION OF INVENTIONS. Frequently an employee will invent a patentable device during working hours or use the employer's equipment and materials. To protect the employer in such situations, employment contracts commonly provide that any invention relating to the employer's business that is discovered by the employee while still an employee or during the first one or two years after leaving the employment shall be assigned to the employer. Such provisions are generally held valid, although a provision requiring the assignment of all inventions, whether or not related to the employer's business, has been held contrary to public policy and therefore invalid.

11. Secret Business Information

A business may have developed information that is not generally known but that cannot be properly protected under federal law. As long as such information is kept secret, it will be protected under state law relating to trade se-

crets.[24] The protection of trade secrets is necessary to encourage and protect invention and commercial enterprise, and to maintain standards of commercial ethics in the marketplace.

(a) TRADE SECRETS. A trade secret may consist of any formula, device, or compilation of information that is used in one's business and that is of such a nature that it gives an advantage over competitors who do not have such information. It may be a formula for a chemical compound; a process of manufacturing, treating, or preserving materials; and, to a limited extent, certain confidential customer lists.[25]

The courts in some states will not protect customer lists where customer identities are readily ascertainable from industry or public sources or where products or services are sold to a wide group of purchasers based on their individual needs.[26]

(b) LOSS OF PROTECTION. When secret business information is made public, it loses the protection it had while secret. Such loss of protection by publication occurs when the information is made known without any restrictions. In contrast, there is no loss of protection when secret information is shared or communicated for a special purpose and the person receiving the information knows that it is not to be made public.

When an article is unprotected by a patent or a copyright and is sold in significant numbers to the public who are free to resell to whomever they choose, competitors are free

---

[22] PL 98-622, 98 Stat 3383, 35 USC § 361.

[23] 35 USC §§ 101, 102, 103; Nitto Boseki Co. Ltd. v Owens Corning Corp. (DC Del) 597 F Supp 248 (1984).

[24] The Uniform Trade Secrets Act was officially amended in 1985. In either its original or amended form it is now in force in Alabama, Alaska, Arizona, California, Colorado, Connecticut, Delaware, Florida, Hawaii, Idaho, Illinois, Indiana, Kansas, Louisiana, Maine, Minnesota, Montana, Nevada, New Hampshire, New Mexico, North Dakota, Oklahoma, Oregon, Rhode Island, South Dakota, Utah, Virginia, Washington, West Virginia, and Wisconsin. Trade secrets are protected in all states either under theh Uniform Act or the common law and under both criminal and civil statutes.

[25] Restatement of Torts § 757, Comment b. See also American Credit Indemnity Co. v Sacks, 213 Cal App 3d 622, 262 Cal Rptr 92 (1989).

[26] American Paper & Packaging Products v Kirgan, 183 Cal App 3d 1318, 228 Cal Rptr 713 (1986); Steenhoven v College Life Insurance Co. (Ind App) 48 NE2d 661 (1984). Buffalo Imprints Inc. v Scinta, 534 NYS2d 55 (1988).

to "reverse engineer" (start with the known product and work backwards to devine the process) or copy the article. To illustrate, boatbuilder A develops a successful hull design which is not patented. Boatbuilder B purchases one of A's boats and copies A's hull by creating a mold from the boat it purchased. Boatbuilder B is free to build and sell boats utilizing the copied hull.[27]

In the *Acuson* case, an American manufacturer sued a Japanese company that had purchased one of its machines for reverse engineering purposes. The American company claimed that the Japanese firm had unlawfully acquired its trade secrets.

[27] Bonito Boats, Inc. v. Thunder Craft Boats, Inc. 103 L Ed 2d 118 (1989).

ACUSON CORP. v ALOKA CO. LTD.

209 Cal App 3d 425, 257 Cal Rptr 368 (1989)

Acuson Corporation manufactures ultrasonic imaging equipment in California. Aloka Co. Ltd., a Japanese company, also manufactures ultrasonic equipment. Aloka asked its American distributor, Johnson & Johnson Ultrasound to purchase an "Acuson 128" machine. Johnson & Johnson did so through a distributor without identifying Aloka as the ultimate purchaser. After the machine was delivered to Aloka's Tokyo plant, nine of its engineers spent eleven days reverse engineering the Acuson machine. Acuson later discovered that Aloka had indirectly purchased the machine, and it brought suit against Aloka alleging exploitation of its trade secrets. Aloka defended that it was free to examine and even copy the machine, since it was in the public domain. From a judgment for Acuson, Aloka appealed.

BRAUER, APJ. . . . Aloka's main contention is that the Acuson 128 cannot contain trade secrets since hundreds of the machine have been sold. The argument rests on two well-established principles. First, a trade secret loses its secrecy, and thus its protection under state law, after being disclosed to the public. . . . Second, state law may not prohibit the copying of objects in the public domain.

. . . While the point may be obvious, it bears emphasis that the term "secret" has a literal meaning in the context of trade secret law. "The character of the secret if important to the business is not material but it must, as the term implies, be kept secret by the one who claims it." . . . In particular, information and goods publicly disclosed cannot be trade secrets. . . .

The other important principle that affects this case derives from federal law. Patent and copyright law provide the exclusive means of obtaining a monopoly on a product that has been disclosed to the public. In contrast, "ownership of a trade secret does not give the owner a monopoly in its use, but merely a proprietary right which equity protects against usurpation by unfair means." . . . If federal law leaves an object in the public domain, state law may not prohibit its copying. . . .

Uncontradicted evidence shows that the Acuson 128 has been disclosed to the public. At least hundreds of the product have been sold since it was introduced in 1983. . . .

In the case of the Acuson 128, it is . . . physicians and hospitals who have an economic interest in the product and whose demand for the product encourages manufacturers to supply it. Disclosure to them is, for all relevant purposes, disclosure to the world. . . .

Federal patent law grants an inventor the right of exclusive use for a limited time in exchange for detailed disclosure and substantial creative effort, measured by the requirements of novelty, nonobviousness, and utility. These statutory prerequisites for patent protection reflect a "careful balance between public right and private monopoly to promote certain creative activity" and occur in a "'scheme of federal regulation ... so pervasive as to make reasonable the inference that Congress left no room for the States to supplement it.'" . . .

The likelihood that unpatented objects will be reverse engineered is part of the federal balance. . . . "The competitive reality of reverse engineering may act as a spur to the inventor, creating an incentive to develop inventions which meet the rigorous requirements of patentability." . . . State law prohibitions against reverse engineering disturb the federal scheme by "reduc[ing] th[e] competitive incentive, thus eroding the general rule of free competition upon which the attractiveness of the federal patent bargain depends." . . .

Trade secret law cannot confer monopoly rights to objects in the public domain. Trade secret law only gives protection against the misuse of confidential information when the owner has made reasonable efforts to maintain secrecy. . . .

Acuson is completely wrong when it argues that the law prohibits lengthy and expensive reverse engineering. To the contrary, state law encourages such efforts by giving to the competitor who invests substantial resources in reverse engineering the opportunity to hold in legally protected confidence the results of its labor. In other words, both the original inventor and the reverse engineer may claim protection for their labors. . . .

Even if a competitor is free to examine a publicly available machine, Acuson argues, the law nevertheless prohibits reverse engineering if the competitor obtains the product through improper means. The official comment to the Uniform Trade Secrets Act appears—but only at first glance—to support Acuson's argument: "The acquisition of the known product must of course, also be by a fair and honest means, such as purchase of the item on the open market for reverse engineering to be lawful. . . ." . . .

"[F]air and honest means" are the converse of "improper means"—the statutory term that the Uniform Act's drafters chose to encompass an unforeseeably broad range of ethically objectionable behavior. As the drafters noted, "[o]ne of the broadly stated policies behind trade secret law is 'the maintenance of standards of commercial ethics'" and that "'[a] complete catalogue of improper means is not possible.'" . . .

But unless a defendant has harmed the plaintiff's interest in a trade secret there is no basis for liability under trade secret law. It is this principle that makes sense of the Uniform Act's comment that lawful reverse engineering is predicated upon acquisition of a product by "fair and honest means." . . . Someone who, for example, knowingly uses the stolen design for a yet-unreleased product will be liable under trade secret law even though the product is later sold to the public. There is liability because the product was still secret at the time; actual trade secrets were compromised by unethical behavior. . . .

But to obtain a product by ethically questionable means will not create secrets where there were none in the first place. To illustrate, one who obtains a shipment of ordinary paper clips by fraudulently promising to pay may be liable for their value, but trade secret law will not prevent him from copying the paper clips.

Acuson has not cited any case—and we have found none—holding that a competitor's concealment of its identity to obtain a publicly available product will create liability under trade secret law. . . .

[O]ne need not deny that Acuson's "improper means" argument appeals to ethical sensibilities: perhaps a company should not conceal its identity to obtain a sample of its competitor's product. But trade secret law does not create an open-ended cause of action for every arguable breach of commercial ethics. Only when an ethical breach results in a compromise of actual trade secrets does that body of law have something to say.

[Judgment for Aloka].

QUESTIONS

1. What is the legal effect of the fact that hundreds of Acuson machines had been sold on the open market?
2. Is a business free to copy an article that is not protected by a patent or copyright?
3. Did the court find that Aloka used unethical means to obtain the Acuson 128?

(c) DEFENSIVE MEASURES. Employers have adopted measures to avoid the expense of trade secret litigation by limiting disclosure of trade secrets to only those employees with a "need to know," having employees sign nondisclosure agreements, and conducting exit interviews when an employee with confidential information terminates employment with the business, reminding the employee of the intent to enforce the nondisclosure agreement.

Employers have also adopted industrial security plans to protect their unique knowledge and competitive advantages from "outsiders," who may engage in theft, trespass, wiretapping, or other forms of commercial espionage.

12. Remedies for Violation of Property Rights

The remedy most commonly used by the owner of personal property for violations of property rights is an action for monetary damages when the property is negligently or willfully harmed, taken, or destroyed by the act of another. When the owner's property is taken under circumstances that would constitute larceny, the owner may sue for the wrong, called *conversion*, and will recover the monetary value of the property at the time of the unlawful taking, or may recover the property itself by an action at law.

The owner's right to recover damages for conversion may also be asserted against an innocent wrongdoer—that is, a person who in good faith has exercised dominion over the property of the plaintiff. For example, although the buyer of a stolen television set gave value and acted in good faith in the belief that the seller was the owner of the set, the conduct of the innocent buyer in taking possession of the set and exercising control over it is a conversion for which the innocent buyer is liable to the true owner.

If the defendant has infringed copyrights, patents, or marks of the plaintiff, the plaintiff may obtain an injunction ordering the defendant to stop such practices. If the infringement was intentional, the plaintiff may also recover from the defendant any profits obtained by the defendant from such infringement. If the infringement conduct is such as to constitute an unfair trade practice, the plaintiff may obtain a cease and desist order against the defendant from the Federal Trade Commission.

D. MULTIPLE OWNERSHIP OF PERSONAL PROPERTY

When all rights in a particular object of property are held by one person, that property is held in **severalty.** However, two or more persons may hold concurrent rights and interests in the same property. In that case, the property is said to be held in **cotenancy.** The various forms of cotenancy include (1) tenancy in common, (2) joint tenancy, (3) tenancy by entirety, and (4) community property.

13.   Tenancy in Common

A tenancy in common is a form of ownership by two or more persons. The interest of a tenant in common may be transferred or inherited, in which case the taker becomes a tenant in common with the others. This tenancy is terminated only when there is a partition or division, giving each a specific portion, or when one person acquires all of the interests of the co-owners.

14.   Joint Tenancy

A joint tenancy is another form of ownership by two or more persons. A joint tenant's interest may be transferred to a third person, but this destroys the joint tenancy. If one of two joint tenants transfers interest to a third person, the remaining joint tenant becomes a tenant in common with the third person.

Upon the death of a joint tenant, the remaining tenants take the share of the deceased tenant. The last surviving joint tenant takes the property as a holder in severalty.

(a) STATUTORY CHANGE. Statutes in many states have modified the common law by adding a formal requirement to the creation of a joint tenancy with survivorship. At common law such an estate would be created by a transfer of property to "*A* and *B* as joint tenants." Under these statutes, it is necessary to add the words *with right of survivorship,* or other similar words, if it is desired to create a right of survivorship. If no words of survivorship are used, the transfer of property to two or more persons will be construed as creating a tenancy in common. Under such a statute, a certificate of deposit issued only in the name of "*A* or *B*" does not create a joint tenancy, because it does not add words of survivorship.

(b) BANK ACCOUNTS. The deposit of money in a joint account constitutes a gift of a joint ownership interest in the money when that is the intent of the depositor.[28] The mere fact that money is deposited in a joint account does not in itself establish that there was such a gift, particularly when it can be shown by clear and convincing evidence that the deposits were made in the joint account "solely for the convenience of enabling either of the parties to draw therefrom for family purposes." When the joint account is merely an agency device, the account agent is not entitled to use any part of the account for personal purposes.

15.   Tenancy by Entirety

At common law a **tenancy by entirety** or **tenancy by the entireties** was created when property was transferred to both husband and wife. It differs from joint tenancy in that it requires a transfer to husband and wife. Also, the right of survivorship cannot be extinguished, and one spouse's interest cannot be transferred to a third person, although in some jurisdictions a spouse's right to share the possession and the profits may be transferred. This form of property holding is popular in common law jurisdictions because creditors of one of the spouses cannot reach the property while both are living. Only a creditor of both the husband and wife under the same obligation can obtain execution against the property. Moreover, the tenancy by entirety is, in effect, a substitute for a will since the surviving spouse acquires the complete property interest on the death of the other. There are usually other reasons, however, why each spouse should make a will.

In many states the granting of an absolute divorce converts a tenancy by the entireties into a tenancy in common.

16.   Community Property

In some states property acquired during the period of marriage is the community property of the husband and wife. Some statutes provide for the right of survivorship; others provide that half of the property of the deceased husband or wife shall go to the heirs or permit

---

28   In the Matter of Giacalone, 533 NYS 2d 457 (1988).

such half to be disposed of by will. It is commonly provided that property acquired by either spouse during the marriage is *prima facie* community property, even though title is taken in the spouse's individual name, unless it can be shown that it was obtained with property possessed by the spouse prior to the marriage.

SUMMARY

Personal property consists of whole or fractional ownership rights in things that are tangible and movable, as well as rights in things that are intangible.

Personal property may be acquired by purchase. Personal property may also be acquired by gift where the donor has present intent to make a gift and delivers possession to the donee. Personal property may also be acquired by finding lost property and by occupation.

Property rights in trademarks, copyrights, and patents are acquired as provided in federal statutes. A trademark or service mark is any word, symbol, or design, or a combination of these used to identify a product (in the case of a trademark) or a service (in the case of service mark). Terms for which protection is claimed will fall into one of four categories: (1) generic, (2) descriptive, (3) suggestive, or (4) arbitrary or fanciful. Generic terms are never registrable. Ordinarily, descriptive terms are not registrable. However, if a descriptive term has acquired a "secondary meaning" it is registrable. Suggestive and arbitrary marks are registrable. If there is likelihood of confusion, a court will enjoin the second user from using a particular mark.

A copyright is the exclusive right given by federal statute to the creator of a literary or artistic work to use, reproduce, or display the work for the life of the creator and 50 years after the creator's death. A patent gives the inventor an exclusive right for 17 years to make, use, and sell an invention that is new and useful and not obvious to those in the business to which the invention is related. Trade secrets that give an owner an advantage over competitors are protected under state law for an unlimited period so long as they are not made public.

All rights in a particular object of property can be held by one individual, in which case it is said to be held in severalty. Ownership rights may be held concurrently by two or more individuals, in which case it is said to be held in cotenancy. The major forms of cotenancy include (1) tenancy in common, (2) joint tenancy, (3) tenancy by entirety, and (4) community property.

QUESTIONS AND CASE PROBLEMS

1. What social forces give rise to the rule of law requiring that there be an actual or symbolic delivery in order to make a gift?
2. What qualities must an invention possess in order to be patentable?
3. Compare the protection afforded by a patent and the protection afforded by a trademark registration.
4. How does capturing a wild animal on unrestricted land during the hunting season compare with finding lost property?
5. Sullivan sold T-shirts with the name "Boston Marathon" and the year of the race imprinted on them. The Boston Athletic Association (BAA) sponsors and administers the Boston Marathon and has used the name "Boston Marathon" since 1917. The BAA registered the name "Boston Marathon" on the Principal Register. In 1986 the BAA entered into an exclusive license with Image, Inc. to use its service mark on shirts and other apparel. Thereafter when Sullivan continued to sell shirts imprinted with the name "Boston Marathon", the BAA sought an injunction. Sullivan's defense was that the general public was not being misled into thinking that his shirts were officially sponsored by the BAA. Without this confusion of source, he contended, no injunction should be issued. Decide. [Boston

Athletic Ass'n v Sullivan (CA1 Mass) 867 F2d 22]

6. The New York Banking Law provides that a presumption arises that a joint tenancy has been created when a bank account is opened in the names of two persons "payable to either or the survivor." While he was still single, Richard Coddington opened a savings account with his mother, Amelia. The signature card they signed stated that the account was owned by them as joint tenants with the right of survivorship. No statement as to survivorship was made on the passbook. Richard later married Margaret. On his death, Margaret claimed a share of the account on the ground that it was not held in joint tenancy, because the passbook did not contain words of survivorship and because the statutory presumption of a joint tenancy was overcome by the fact that Richard had withdrawn substantial sums from the account during his life. Decide. [Coddington v Coddington, 56 App Div 2d 697, 391 NYS2d 760]

7. Sony Corporation manufactured video cassette recorders (VCRs) that could be used to tape television shows for later home viewing. Sony sold them under the trade name Betamax through retail establishments throughout the country. Universal City Studios and Walt Disney Productions owned the copyrights on some of the television programs that were broadcast on public airwaves. Universal and Disney brought an action against Sony and certain large retailers contending that VCR consumers recorded some of their copyrighted works that had been shown on commercially sponsored television and thereby infringed on these copyrights. These plaintiffs sought damages and an injunction against the manufacture and marketing of VCRs. Sony contended that the noncommercial, home-use recording of material broadcast over public airwaves is a "fair use" of copyrighted works. Decide. [Sony Corp. v Universal Studios, 464 US 417]

8. Ruth and Stella were sisters. They owned a house as joint tenants with right of survivorship. Ruth sold her half interest to Roy. Thereafter, Stella died and Roy claimed the entire property by survivorship. Was he entitled thereto?

9. Mona found a wallet on the floor of an elevator in the office building in which she works. She posted several notices in the building informing of the finding of the wallet, but no one appeared to claim it. She waited for six months and then spent the money in the wallet in the belief that she owned it. Thereafter Jason, the person who lost the wallet, brought suit to recover the money. Mona's defense was that the money was hers, since Jason did not claim it within a reasonable time after she posted the notice. Is she correct? (Assume that the common law applies.)

10. In 1971 Harry Gordon turned over $40,000 to his son, Murray Gordon. Murray opened two $20,000 custodian bank accounts under the Uniform Gifts to Minors Acts for his minor children, Eden and Alexander. Murray was listed as the custodian of both accounts. On January 9, 1976 both accounts were closed, and a single bank check representing the principal of the accounts was drawn to the order of Harry Gordon. In April of 1976 Murray and his wife, Joan, entered into a separation agreement and were later divorced. Thereafter, Joan, on behalf of her children Eden and Alexander, brought suit against Murray to recover the funds withdrawn in January of 1976, contending that the deposits in both accounts were irrevocable gifts. Murray contended that the money was his father's, and it was never intended as a gift but was merely a means of avoiding taxes. Decide. [Gordon v Gordon, 419 NYS2d 684, 70 App Div 2d 86 (1979)]

11. Carol and Robert, both over twenty-one, became engaged. Robert gave Carol an engagement ring. He was killed in an automobile crash before they were married. His estate demanded that Carol return the ring. Was she entitled to keep it? [Cohen v Bayside Federal Savings and Loan Ass'n, 62 Misc 2d 738, 309 NYS2d 980]

12. The plaintiff, Herbert Rosenthal Jewelry Corporation, and the defendant, Kalpakian, manufactured jewelry. The plaintiff obtained a copyright registration of a jeweled pin in the shape of a bee. Kalpakian made a similar pin. Rosenthal sued Kalpakian for infringement of copyright registration. Kalpakian raised the defense that he was only copying the idea, not the way the idea was expressed. Was he liable for infringement of the plaintiff's copyright? [Herbert Rosenthal Jewelry Corp. v Kalpakian (CA9 Cal) 446 F2d 738]

13. Mineral Deposits Ltd. (MD Ltd.), an Australian company, manufactures the Reichert Spiral, a device used for recovering gold particles from sand and gravel. The spiral was patented in Australia, and MD Ltd. had applied for a patent in the U.S. Theodore Zigan contacted MD Ltd., stating he was interested in purchasing up to

200 devices for use in his gravel pit. MD Ltd. agreed to lend Zigan a spiral for the purpose of testing its efficiency. Zigan and Zbikowski made molds of the spiral's components and proceeded to manufacture 170 copies of the device. When MD Ltd. found out that copies were being made, it demanded the return of the spiral. MD Ltd. also sought lost profits for the 170 spirals manufactured by Zigan. Recovery was sought on a theory of misappropriation of trade secrets. Zigan offered to pay for the spiral lent him by MD Ltd. He argued that trade secrecy protection was lost by the public sale of the spiral. What ethical values are involved? Was Zigan's conduct a violation of trade secrecy law? [Mineral Deposits Ltd. v Zigan (Colo App) 773 P2d 609]

14. From October, 1965, through July, 1967, Union Carbide Corporation sold certain bulbs for high-intensity reading lamps under its trademark, EVEREADY. Carbide's sales of electrical products under the EVEREADY mark exceeded $100 million for every year after 1963; from 1963–1967 Carbide spent $50 million in advertising these products. In 1969 the defendant, Ever-Ready, Inc., imported miniature lamp bulbs for high-intensity lamps with "Ever-Ready" stamped on their base. In two surveys conducted by Carbide, 50 percent of those interviewed associated Carbide products with the marks used by Ever-Ready, Inc. Carbide sought an injunction against Ever-Ready's use of the name *Ever-Ready* on or in connection with the sale of electrical products. No monetary damages were sought. Ever-Ready, Inc. defended that Carbide's trademark EVEREADY was descriptive, and therefore the registration of the mark was improper and invalid. Carbide responded that its mark had acquired secondary meaning. Decide. [Union Carbide Corp. v Ever-Ready Inc. (CA7 Ill) 531 F2d 366.]

15. Anheuser-Busch had been interested in producing a low-alcohol beer, both because of its need to develop new markets for growth and because of growing public concern over the health aspects of beer consumption and the problem of drunken driving. Other breweries had similar interests; in fact, two smaller companies, Hudepohl Brewery and Christian Schmidt Brewing Company, had marketed reduced alcohol beers under the brand names of Pace and Break. Anheuser-Busch made an application for registration of the trademark LA and soon thereafter began marketing its low-alcohol product under the LA label. Following Anheuser-Busch's introduction of its product, the Stroh Brewery Company introduced "Schaefer LA," also a low-alcohol beer. An action to enjoin Stroh's use of LA followed. Anheuser-Busch contended that the term LA was suggestive in that it required some imagination to connect it with the product and, accordingly, was a protectable trademark. Stroh argued that LA was generic or descriptive in nature, since the term is comprised of the initials of the phrase *low alcohol*. Decide. [Anheuser-Busch Inc. v The Stroh Brewery Company (CA8 Mo) 750 F2d 631]

21

COMPUTERS AND THE LAW

Traditional rules of law drawn from contract law, tort law, and criminal law may be applied to computers. Also, in the last few years, many statutes that apply only to computers have been adopted.

A. GENERAL PRINCIPLES

The modern electronic computer has been in use for little over one-third of a century. In that time, changes in the design, size, and capacity of computers have resulted in their widespread use.

1.   Computers and the Environment of the Law

Computers are now part of the business environment. They have created new situations for which no prior law exists or the prior law is not adequate. In the last three decades, judges and lawmakers have been making new law to govern the new computer situations.[1]

(a) TERMINOLOGY. In this chapter the word *computer*, unless otherwise indicated, is used to refer collectively to hardware, software, and data. *Hardware* refers to the tangible objects, including the piece of equipment commonly known as the computer and all auxiliary attachments, such as disk and tape drives, monitors, printers, and terminals. *Software* describes the programs or instructions that control the operation of the hardware. *Data* refers to information, other than operating software, that is contained within the memory of the computer during processing or stored on some magnetic medium.

(b) COMPUTERS AND TAXATION. Computer hardware is subject to the same property and sales taxes as any other tangible personal property. Software is generally classified for tax purposes as intangible property. There is some authority, however, that makes a distinction between operational software and application software. The former consists of those programs without which a computer will not operate and which are therefore regarded as part of the value of the hardware and are classified as tangible personal property. In contrast, the application software consists of those programs designed to meet particular needs of a particular computer user and which may therefore be regarded as distinct from the computer and as constituting intangible personal property.

---

[1]   See Chapter 34 as to computers and bank collections and the transfer of funds.

FIGURE 21-1   LAW AND THE COMPUTER

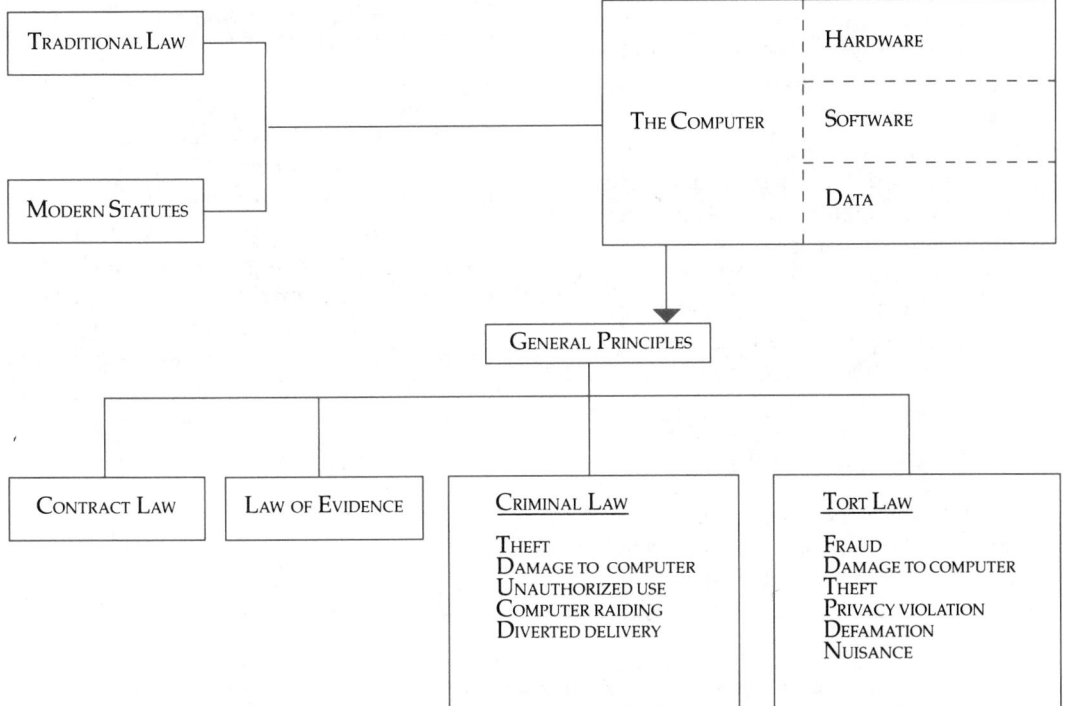

2. Management and the Computer

The law of computers relating to management is merely an extension of prior principles to new situations.

(a) NEGLIGENT USE OF THE COMPUTER. Management may be liable under ordinary negligence principles because of careless use of the computer. If management knows that its computer is not working properly but continues to use it without attempting to correct it, management may be held liable to third persons who are harmed by computer error.[2] Here the rules of law are the same as when management knowingly uses any other defective equipment. For example, a store making deliveries in a truck that is known to have bad brakes would be liable for negligence if the bad brakes led to a collision causing harm.

(b) PROTECTION OF THE COMPUTER. If the enterprise has a computer, management must take reasonable steps to maintain, protect, and ensure the accuracy of the computer. The duty to maintain is the same as the duty to maintain the building or any other equipment of the enterprise. Management must exercise care in the selection of personnel operating the computer, for the purpose of protecting against computer crimes and torts and protecting customers of the enterprise from inaccuracy.

Under general principles of law, a breach of the foregoing duties can cause a court to impose liability on management. Again, there is the limitation that management has discretion to make choices. Liability will not be imposed if the choice made by management with respect to the computer personnel or computer protection appeared reasonable under the circumstances.

3. Contract Law and the Computer

Contract law has not been affected by the computer, although contracts have been developed to govern computer-related transactions. Thus, the law for the sale of a computer is the same as the law governing the sale of a television set. When the customer asks the dealer for computer equipment that is compatible with an existing system, the law is the same as in any other case in which the buyer asks the seller to provide goods that will meet the particular needs of the buyer. For example, when a government representative asked a seller for a tape suitable for use in the government's NCR-304 computer system, there arose an implied warranty, unless otherwise excluded, that the tape furnished by the seller was fit for that purpose.[3] When the seller knows that the buyer is purchasing a computer in order to produce a payroll on time and with reduced work hours, an implied warranty arises that the machine will perform as desired by the buyer.[4]

Because of the subject matter involved, contracts will apply to the sale or lease of computers, the sale or lease of software, the development of customized software, and the providing of services for maintenance and repair. There may be a contract for an outside organization to provide the computer services needed by the enterprise. In connection with software there will probably be special contract provisions imposing restrictions as to matters that are trade secrets or otherwise protected.

There is some indication that when experienced business enterprises make a computer-related contract, the contract will be interpreted very strictly. In such a case it has been held that the customer was bound by fine-print provision of the contract on the theory that the customer knew from experience that such a clause would probably be in the contract.[5] Because of the consumer protection movement, it is unlikely that a court will take this approach with a small business purchasing its first computer or a person purchasing a computer for home use.

---

[2]   Swiss Air Transportation Co. v Benn, 467 NYS2d 341 (1983).

[3]   Appeals of Reeves v Soundcraft Corp. (ASBCA) 2 UCCRS 210 (1984).

[4]   Sperry Rand Corp. v Industrial Supply Corp. (CA5 Fla) 337 F2d 363 (1964); National Cash Register Co. v Adell Industries Inc. 57 Mich App 413, 225 NW2d 785 (1975).

[5]   AMF, Inc. v Computer Automation (SD Ohio) 573 F Supp 924 (1983).

4. The Computer and the Law of Evidence

The law of evidence has changed drastically in order to make it possible to admit evidence produced by the computer.

Computer printouts of "business records stored on electronic computing equipment are admissible in evidence if relevant and material, without the necessity of identifying, locating, and producing as witnesses the individuals who made the entries in the regular course of business if it is shown (1) that the electronic computing equipment is recognized as standard equipment, (2) the entries are made in the regular course of business at or reasonably near the time of the happening of the event recorded, and (3) the foundation testimony satisfies the court that the sources of information, method and time of preparation were such as to indicate its trustworthiness and justify its admission."[6]

(a) COMPUTER EVIDENCE FROM A PARTY TO LITIGATION. When a store sues its customer, can it prove what the customer owed by what the store's computer says? This question can arise in any contract setting, such as a suit for wages, commissions, or refunds.

In the *Victory Memorial Hospital* case the defendant objected to the admission of the hospital computer's printout on the ground that the information that had been supplied to the computer as input was wrong.

---

[6] Prudential Ins Co. v Kinney Plantation, Inc. (La App) 496 So 2d 1211 (1986); Federal Rules of Evidence, Rule 1001(1); (3); 803(5); 804(b)(5); 901(b)(9).

VICTORY MEMORIAL HOSPITAL v RICE

143 Ill App 3d 621, 97 Ill Dec 635, 493 NE2d 117 (1986)

Michael Rice was treated for gunshot wounds at the Victory Memorial Hospital. He refused to pay the hospital bill because he claimed it was not correct. As proof of the amount owed to it, the hospital offered in evidence a computer printout of the services rendered the defendant and the amounts owed for them. The court refused to admit the printout on the ground that there was no proof that the printout represented what the defendant owed. Judgment was entered against the hospital, and the hospital appealed.

LINDBERG, J. . . . Plaintiff . . . argues that the trial court erred when it refused to admit the computerized bills into evidence as business records. In Illinois, business records supplied by a computer are admissible in evidence without testimony of the persons who made the entries in the regular course of business if it is shown that (1) the electronic computing equipment is recognized as standard; (2) the entries are made in the regular course of business at or reasonably near the time of the happening of the event recorded; and (3) the foundation testimony satisfies the court that the sources of information, method and time of preparation were such as to indicate its trustworthiness and justify its admission.

In the present case the court stated that there was insufficient proof that the items listed on the bills represented services actually performed on defendant. In other words, the court questioned the reliability and trustworthiness of the data before its entrance into the computer. The only method of verifying such information would have been to match the computerized bill against the original entry data. There was testimony that in order for the hospital to have produced all of the documents of original entry in the present case it would have been forced to inaugurate an extremely involved and time consuming retrieval process, especially since defendant had been hospitalized on several occasions and had been treated on an outpatient basis also. The record indicates that a hospital witness produced approximately 30 slips indicating certain laboratory tests that were done on defendant and the results of those tests. She matched them to the corresponding date and charge on the bill. The original slips in question were in five parts, the last part of which went to the data processing department to be entered into the computer by code number. In contrast to the other four portions of the slip, the part which went to the billing department contained only numbers which were fed into the computer by trained personnel. The trial court questioned the verification testimony because the slips produced by the witness were not the actual number coded slips which were used to enter the data. Since the five slips in each packet contained the same information, however, and since the slips produced could be matched to the corresponding date and charge on the bill, as to those tests, the supporting documentation verifying the trustworthiness of the input information was sufficient in our opinion to show that defendant had been given the service for which he was charged.

In view of the rationale supporting prior decisions in Illinois regarding the admissibility of computerized evidence, we also conclude that the proper foundation was presented to establish that the source of information and method of preparation indicated trustworthiness and supported admission of the entire computerized bill. In *People v. Gauer* (1972), 7 Ill.App.3d 512, 514, 288 N.E.2d 24 this court stated that considering the general use of electronic computing and recording equipment in the business world and the business world's reliance on the equipment, the scientific reliability of such machines can scarcely be questioned. The Illinois Supreme Court held in *Grand Liquor Co., Inc. v. Department of Revenue* (1977), 67 Ill.2d 195, 10 Ill.Dec. 472, 367 N.E.2d 1238 that computer printouts are admissible pursuant to Supreme Court Rule 238 (87 Ill.2d R. 238) as long as the foundational tests . . . were met. Although . . . the trial court must be satisfied from the foundation testimony that the sources of information, method, and time of preparation were such as to indicate trustworthiness and justify admission, we are of the opinion that in the present case the trial court erred in not admitting the computerized bill into evidence as a business record based on the foundational evidence offered. The jury would still be free to accord the bills as much weight as in their opinion they deserved.

[Judgment reversed and action remanded]

QUESTIONS

1. Before the printout of a computer will be admitted in evidence, what must be shown?
2. What had been done by the hospital to support the admission of the computer printout into evidence?
3. Does the computer printout establish that the defendant owed the amount claimed by the plaintiff?

(b) COMPUTER EVIDENCE FROM A THIRD PERSON. Can the computer evidence generated by a third person be used to establish such facts as are shown thereby? This arises most frequently in a criminal prosecution in which a link in the chain of evidence against the defendant is the fact that a phone call was made from one particular place to another at a particular time. The computer-generated records of the telephone company have been admitted in evidence in such case to prove the making of the phone call.

(c) WEIGHT OF COMPUTER EVIDENCE.
In all matters relating to evidence there are basically two steps: (1) Can the particular evidence be admitted in court and considered in deciding the case? (2) Assuming that the evidence can be admitted and considered, what weight is to be given to it? Must it be believed, or can it be contradicted?

Computer evidence must meet these two challenges. Thus, the proper foundation must be established before the computer printout is admissible in court. After that, it is for the trier of fact to decide if the computer printout should be regarded as conclusive or inconclusive, or if it should be ignored.

(d) LIMITATIONS ON COMPUTER EVIDENCE.
In some cases computer evidence was excluded because the court believed the circumstances were such as to require greater proof of the reliability of the evidence. In other cases the evidence was excluded because the court did not believe that the computer could do what was required to make the evidence reliable.

When a computer is used for the purpose of gathering evidence against a suspected criminal, it may be necessary to go beyond proving the general reliability of the kind of equipment used. It may be necessary to prove the reliability of the specific equipment that was used.

The mere fact that a computer states a conclusion does not make the conclusion admissible in evidence.

B.   CRIMINAL LAW AND THE COMPUTER

In some situations the ordinary law of crimes fits the computer crime situation. In other situations new law is required.

5.   What is a Computer Crime?

The term *computer crime* is frequently used. It has no established definition. Generally, the phrase is used to refer to a crime that can only be committed by a person having some knowledge of the operation of a computer. Just as stealing an automobile requires knowledge of how to operate and drive a car, so the typical computer crime requires knowledge of how the computer works. This concept of a computer crime is satisfactory for the purpose of setting the stage, but it fails to tell us what law will be applied: the law of crimes or a new law relating to computers.

Some crimes may involve a computer without making direct use of one. In such case the ordinary law of crimes will apply. For example, a person using the mail to falsely advertise a service as computerized is guilty of committing the federal crime of using the mails to defraud.

A person dealing with the computer user may be guilty of a crime when the computer makes a mistake and such person takes advantage of the mistake without telling the computer user what has happened.

The more serious and costly wrongs relating to computers do not fit into the ordinary definitions of crime. There is a definite trend of adopting statutes to declare new computer crimes. These statutes are strictly construed. Only that conduct that is covered by the statute in question can be punished as the crime.

A criminal law statute must be sufficiently clear to be understood by ordinary persons of ordinary intelligence. In some cases the computer crimes statute was held unconstitutional as being too vague. A statute was held unconstitutionally too vague when it prohibited obtaining money by "alteration, deletion, or insertion of programs or data" into a computer.[7]

6.   The Computer as the Victim

A traditional crime may be committed by stealing or intentionally damaging the computer.

(a) THEFT OF HARDWARE.
When the computer itself is stolen, the ordinary law relating to theft crimes should apply. No reason

---

[7]   Louisiana v Azar (La) 539 So 2d 1222 (1989).

can be found why a theft of a computer should not be subject to the same law as the theft of a typewriter or a desk. Whatever the crime would be by statute in the case of these other objects, the same crime is committed when a computer is the subject matter of the theft.

(b) THEFT OF SOFTWARE. When a thief takes software, whether in the form of a program written on paper or a program on a disk or tape, a situation arises that does not fit into the common law definition of larceny. This is so because larceny at common law was confined to the taking of tangible property. The value of stolen software would be determined by the value of the tangible substance on which the program was recorded. Thus, under a traditional concept of property, which would ignore the value of the intangible program, the theft would only be petty larceny. Now, however, virtually every state has amended its definition of larceny or theft so that the stealing of software is a crime. In some states, the unauthorized taking of information may constitute a crime under a trade secrets protection statute.

(c) INTENTIONAL DAMAGE. The computer may be the "victim" of a crime when it is intentionally destroyed or harmed. In the most elementary form of damage, it could be harmed if smashed with an ax or destroyed in an explosion or a fire. In such cases, the wrongdoer may be seeking to do more than merely destroy or harm the computer. The intent may be to cause the computer's owner the financial loss of the computer and the destruction of the information that is stored in it.

When the wrongdoer has the purpose of destroying the software or the stored information, it is more likely that a more subtle way of committing the crime will be employed. In such case, the wrongdoer might gain access to the computer and then erase or alter the data in question. The wrongdoer might also achieve the desired purpose by interfering with the air-conditioning required by the computer, thereby causing it to malfunction. Or the wrongdoer may intentionally plant a "bug" or "virus" in software, causing the program to malfunction or to give incor-

rect output. Such damage may be the work of an angry employee or ex-employee, or it may be the work of a competitor. In the area of criminal law it might be a person destroying the record of prior convictions.

In earlier years, the criminal was probably only guilty of the crime of malicious destruction of or damage to property.[8] Again, the lawmakers have filled the gap between the technological environment and the law. Statutes adopted in many states now make it a crime to damage software or computer-stored information.

7. Unauthorized Use of Computer

In contrast with conduct intended to harm the computer or its rightful user or to acquire secret information, the least serious of computer crimes is the unlawful use of someone else's computer. In some states the unlawful use of a computer is not a crime. Although the user is stealing the time of the computer, the wrongdoer is not regarded as committing the crime of larceny because the wrongdoer has no intent to deprive the owner permanently of the computer.

In some states the borrowing of another's automobile without the owner's permission is not a crime where there is no intention to deprive the owner permanently thereof. If following the common law, states would undoubtedly use the same approach in the case of the unauthorized use of a computer.[9] The unauthorized taking of information from a computer is more serious, however. This computer crime has been widely regulated by recent statutes, noted in Section 8 of this chapter.

In the *Evans* case a statute creating crimes of larceny, embezzlement, and false pretenses in connection with computer time, services, or stored information was applied.

---

[8]   The crime of maliciously damaging or destroying property is ordinarily a misdemeanor and as such is subject only to a relatively small fine or short imprisonment.
[9]   The court in Indiana v McGraw (Ind) 480 NE2d 552 (1985) followed this approach.

EVANS v VIRGINIA

226 Va 292, 308 SE2d 126 (1983)

The Central Fidelity Bank had a department that sold stocks and bonds, primarily to large institutions. Evans and Smith worked in this department as salesmen. At intervals the bank would make computer printouts of the names and addresses of its customers and maturity dates of their investments. Smith asked that an extra copy of this printout be made for him. Smith was given two extra copies. He gave one to Evans. Thereafter Evans and Smith resigned from the bank and went to work for a competing bank. Smith gave the computer printout of customers to the new employer. Evans and Smith were then prosecuted for petit (petty) larceny by embezzlement. They appealed.

GORDON, J. . . . According to an officer of Central Fidelity, a customer security list would be useful for many years to come, an invaluable sales tool to produce profits. Another officer testified that if a competitor obtained the information on a list, the competitor would be given an edge in the business.

Central Fidelity brought a civil suit under Code § 18.2–500 for injury to its trade or business, resulting in a favorable decree. The indictments involved in this appeal followed.

In *Lund v. Commonwealth*, 217 Va. 688, 232 S.E.2d 745 (1977), this Court held that the taking of computer time and services in the form of printouts could not constitute larceny because the subject matter of larceny must be goods and chattels. Computer time and services, reasoned the Court, were not goods or chattels.

In 1978 the General Assembly enacted Code § 18.2–98.1:

Computer time or services or data processing services or information or data stored in connection therewith is hereby defined to be property which may be the subject of larceny under §§ 18.2–95 or 18.2–96, or embezzlement under § 18.2–111, or false pretenses under § 18.2–178.

Code § 18.2–111, under which Evans and Smith were prosecuted, makes a person guilty of larceny if he [does] "wrongfully and fraudulently use, dispose of, conceal or embezzle any . . . personal property, tangible or intangible, which he shall have received . . . by virtue of his . . . employment. . . ."

The indictments charged that Evans and Smith "unlawfully and feloniously did steal computer information or data stored in connection therewith, to-wit: a customer securities list."* . . .

The trial court instructed the jury that to convict it must find that the customer security list "was of some value." Code § 18.2–96 makes "simple larceny not from the person of another of goods and chattels of the value of less than $200" punishable as a misdemeanor.

The Commonwealth adduced no proof, says counsel, of the value of the list. Counsel therefore concludes that the evidence does not support the giving of the instruction. . . .

---

*   The trial did not proceed on the theory that the defendants embezzled a piece of paper. As observed by the trial judge, "there was never any indication, any observation, any allegation that this was a case involving the theft of paper."

The petit larceny statute, Code § 18.2–96, does not require proof of any minimum value.

"At the common law, an article to be the subject of larceny must be of some value. It is sufficient, however, it is said, if it be worth less than the smallest coin known to the law." *Wolverton v. Commonwealth*, 75 Va. 909, 913 (1881). Under settled Virginia law, no proof need be adduced to show that the subject of petit larceny has a specific value.

The evidence respecting the nature and use of the customer security list supplied proof that the list had value. The proof was augmented by testimony that the list was an invaluable sales tool, giving a competitor a valuable edge if the list fell into the competitor's hands. . . .

This Court in a recent case . . . described the elements of embezzlement:

A person entrusted with possession of another's personalty who converts such property to his own use or benefit is guilty of the statutory offense of embezzlement. Code § 18.2–111.

C.D. Smith v. Commonwealth, 222 Va. 646, 649, 283 S.E.2d 209, 210 (1981). And Black's Law Dictionary 300 (5th ed. 1979), . . . gives this definition of the noun form of *to convert:*

Unauthorized and wrongful exercise of dominion and control over another's personal property, to exclusion of or inconsistent with rights of the owner.

Proof was adduced that Evans and Smith converted the customer security list by exercising dominion and control inconsistent with the rights of Central Fidelity, the owner. The proof therefore justified the conviction of statutory embezzlement. . . .

[Conviction affirmed]

QUESTIONS

1. Is the decision in the *Evans* case in harmony with the common law?
2. Why was the prosecution for embezzlement?
3. Which of the two statutes quoted in the *Evans* case was the more essential to the prosecution?

8.   Computer Raiding

A serious computer crime involves taking information from a computer without the consent of the owner of the information. Whether this is done by having the computer make a printout of stored information or by tapping into the data bank of the computer by some electronic means is not important. In many instances the taking of information from the computer constitutes a crime of stealing trade secrets.

Both Congress and state legislatures have adopted statutes that declare it a crime to make any unauthorized use of a computer or to gain unauthorized access to a computer or the information stored in its database in order to cause harm to the computer or its rightful user.[10]

[10]   The Counterfeit Access Device and Computer Fraud Act of 1984, § 2102, PL 98-473, 98 Stat 2190, 18 USC §§ 1030 et seq.; Computer Fraud and Abuse Act of 1986, Act of Oct 16, 1986, PL 99-474, 100 Stat 1213, 18 USC § 1001, as amended; Electronic Communications Privacy Act of 1986, Act of Oct 21, 1986, PL 99-508, 100 Stat 1848, 18 USC § 2510; Computer Fraud Act of 1987, Act of Jan 8, 1988, PL 100-235, 101 Stat 1724, 15 USC § 272, 278, 40 USC § 759. Provision is made for training small businesses in the use and security of computers by the Small Business and Computer Security and Education Act of July 16, 1984, PL 98-362, 98 Stat 431, 15 USC §§ 633 et seq.

9. Diverted Delivery by Computer

In many industries deliveries are controlled by a computer. The person in charge of that computer or a criminal gaining access unlawfully to the computer may cause the computer to direct delivery to an improper place. That is, instead of shipping goods to the customers to whom they should go, the wrongdoer diverts the goods to a different place, where they will be received by the wrongdoer or by a confederate.

In precomputer days, written orders were sent from the sales department to the shipping department. The shipping department would then send the ordered goods to the proper places. If the person in the sales department or the person in the shipping department were dishonest, either one of them could divert the goods from the proper destination. Today this fraudulent diversion of goods may be effected by causing the computer to give false directions. Basically, the crime has not changed. The computer is merely the new instrument by which the old crime is committed. This old crime has taken on a new social significance because the amazingly large dollar value of the theft accomplished by means of it. In one case several hundred loaded freight cars were made to disappear. In another case a loaded oil tanker was diverted to unload into a fleet of tank trucks operated by an accomplice of the computer operator.

The crime of diverted delivery is not limited to goods. It has embraced transferring money from a proper account to a wrong account. Here millions of dollars have been involved in a single crime.

The case of diverted delivery by computer does not require any new law, because the appropriation of goods or money improperly delivered comes within the larceny-theft-embezzlement spectrum of crime. However, when a diverted delivery crime is effected by means of a computer, future statutes may classify the crime as aggravated larceny or the like, in order to impose the more severe penalty that society feels is called for by the huge dollar values involved. This feeling of society has led to the Electronic Fund Transfers Act described in the following section.

10. Electronic Fund Transfer Crimes

The Electronic Fund Transfers Act (EFTA)[11] makes it a crime to use any counterfeit, stolen, or fraudulently obtained card, code, or other device to obtain money or goods in excess of a specified amount through an electronic fund transfer system. The EFTA also makes it a crime to ship such devices or goods so obtained in interstate commerce, or knowingly to receive goods that have been obtained by means of the fraudulent use of the transfer system.

C. TORT LAW AND THE COMPUTER

Tort law applies to the computer with respect to damage to the computer, fraud, theft, the protection of privacy, defamation, and nuisance.

11. Fraud

The basic principles of tort law for fraud are applicable in computer situations. For example, if false statements are knowingly made to induce the sale of a computer, the seller is liable for fraud damages to the same extent as though any other kind of goods were the subject of the sale.[12] If the wrongdoer feeds false information to the computer and then uses the printout to deceive the victim, the wrongdoer is subject to the ordinary tort law governing fraud.

12. Damage to the Computer

Tort liability for damage to the computer arises in connection with damage to hardware and software.

(a) DAMAGE TO HARDWARE. Damage to hardware, including its destruction, will impose tort liability under the same principles of law as would apply if a typewriter, a car, a

---

[11] Act of November 10, 1978, § 916(n), PL 95-630, 92 Stat 3738, 15 USC § 1693n. See Chapter 34, Section 16 et seq.
[12] Computer Systems Engineering, Inc. v Qantel Corp. (CA1 Mass) 740 F2d 59 (1984).

desk, or any other tangible property were damaged or destroyed. The fact that the damage to the computer may cause a shutdown of the activities of the computer owner is significant in determining whether the defendant's act was done with such wantonness or reckless indifference to consequences as to authorize imposing punitive or exemplary damages upon the wrongdoer. Punitive or exemplary damages are those in excess of the amount needed to compensate the plaintiff for loss. Such damages are imposed to punish or make an example of the defendant.

(b) DAMAGE TO SOFTWARE. The defen-

dant may have damaged the software, for example, by erasing a part of the computer's memory. Here the tort law aspect of liability and of recovery of punitive damages is the same as for any other kind of property. In addition, many recently adopted statutes expressly impose tort liability for such misconduct.

(c) INSURANCE. When an insurance policy does not expressly state that it covers computer property, a question may arise as to whether hardware, software, and a database are protected by such a policy. The *Magnetic Data* case raised this question.

MAGNETIC DATA, INC. v ST. PAUL FIRE AND MARINE INS. CO.

(Minn App) 430 NW2d 483 (1988)

Magnetic Data, Inc. (MDI) is in the business of inspecting and repairing computer cartridges. A cartridge may be inspected by visual examination, a gauge measurement, or an electronic inspection. When an electronic inspection is made, all data that is stored in the cartridge is erased. The Sanger Corporation sent 22 cartridges to MDI for examination. Twelve of these were not to be inspected electronically because the cartridges were the only copy of the stored information. Through a mistake of MDI employees, all 22 cartridges were erased. Sanger sued MDI for the loss caused by such erasing. MDI claimed that the loss was covered by its comprehensive general liability policy (CGL) issued by the St. Paul Fire and Marine Insurance Company. MDI sued on the policy. Judgment was entered in its favor, and the insurance company appealed.

NIERENGARTEN, J. . . . [The inspection] of the twelve critical cartridges was an "accidental event" within the meaning of MDI's CGL policy because the loss of Sanger's data on the critical cartridges was "an unexpected, unforeseen, or undesigned happening or consequence." . . . The record does not indicate MDI's employees realized the erasure would result in loss of unduplicated information. While the technical task of erasing the data from the disks was performed intentionally, the electronic process itself was accidentally or mistakenly employed, and the loss of the computer data was the type of accidental loss intended to be covered by MDI's CGL policy. . . .

We conclude the erasure of the data on the critical cartridges was an "accidental event" within the meaning of the CGL policy. . . .

The parties dispute whether the erasure of the magnetically encoded data resulted in damage to "tangible" property. MDI states "it is the information stored on the disk cartridges which is of value to MDI's customers" and contends erasure of the information caused rearrangement of the subatomic particles on the cartridge disks. MDI submitted affidavits from two computer experts who suggest the subatomic particles on the surface of a magnetic disk are tangible property. St. Paul Fire claims erasure did not result in damage to tangible property and asserts the CGL policy does not cover any loss unless some damage to "tangible" property occurs.

    ... The policy does not limit coverage to claims arising from damage to tangible property. So long as an accidental event occurred which resulted in unexpected or unintended "property damage," including "loss of use of others' property that hasn't been physically damaged," the property damage is covered.... Even if magnetically encoded computer data is not tangible property, the computer information encoded on the critical cartridge disks was property of Sanger and its clients.... Since the computer information encoded on the critical cartridge disks was property and was unexpectedly or unintentionally destroyed during the [electronic] process, Sanger's loss of use of that property constitutes "property damage" within the meaning of MDI's CGL policy because the erasure was "caused by an accidental event." ... The CGL policy ... excludes coverage of damage to "property on MDI's premises ... for the purposes of being worked on by MDI's behalf." ... We distinguish between the physical components of the disk cartridges and the information encoded on the cartridge disks. Even though ... the disk cartridges were "located at the business premises of MDI" and the "disk cartridges were ... in the care, custody and control of MDI," we do not believe coverage necessarily is precluded ... because the damaged property—Sanger's computer information—was not on MDI's premises "for the purposes of being worked on." Sanger suspected certain computer disk cartridges were defective and that the cartridges may have caused Sanger's computer system to malfunction. However, there is no evidence in the record indicating the information encoded on the magnetic disks was the source of the suspected defects; nor is there any indication in the record that MDI was authorized or expected to perform any inspection processes that would affect Sanger's computer information.

    Our distinction between the physical computer disk cartridges and the magnetically encoded information stored on the disks may be technical because the computer disks and the magnetically encoded information contained on those disks are intimately related. However, we do not believe the distinction is artificial given the unique characteristics of the property involved. Sanger's information apparently was readily transferable and could have existed independent of the specific disks upon which it was encoded, and its existence on the critical cartridge disks apparently was fortuitous. Sanger's expectations about the type of work which would be performed on the critical cartridges also supports our conclusion that the disk cartridges and the information encoded on the disks were separate property. Sanger authorized only visual inspection and gauge testing of the critical cartridges and did not authorize electronic inspection because that process necessarily would erase unduplicated information stored in the critical cartridges. We only can conclude therefore that while the critical cartridges were on MDI's premises for the purposes of being worked on, the information encoded on the critical cartridge disks was separate property and not on MDI's premises for the purposes of being worked on....

    [Judgment affirmed]

QUESTIONS

1. What kind of property was involved in the *Magnetic Data* case?
2. Was the court in the *Magnetic Data* case concerned about damage to Sanger's program, by which Sanger stored information on the disks?

3. How would the case have been decided if MDI had been retained to verify the information on the disks, and that information was accidentally erased in the process of verification?

13. Theft of the Computer

The civil or tort liability for the theft of a computer parallels the criminal law with respect to such theft. Thus, an actual taking away of the hardware constitutes the tort of conversion.

14. The Computer and the Protection of Privacy

The law relating to the protection of privacy applies whether or not a computer is involved. That is, there is no change made or needed in the law of privacy because a computer had been used to invade the privacy in question. Statutes have been adopted to protect against such invasion as to computer-stored data.[13]

(a) WHY IS THERE CONCERN OVER PROTECTION OF PRIVACY? There is much public concern over protection of privacy, because of the efficiency of the computer. Consider the number of places that have some information about you. Every school you ever attended has some of your personal history. If you have applied for any kind of license, purchased goods on credit, obtained insurance, applied for a job, been treated by a doctor, or been admitted to a hospital, more of your life story is on paper. But this has never bothered you because, assuming that you had thought about it, you would have recognized that it would be practically impossible for anyone to assemble all the information about you from all the places where it is kept. Even assuming that the prying stranger would know where to

inquire, the cost of going back into old files to dig up information would be prohibitive.

In the computer age, by connecting separate computers into a network, it is possible to print out the story of your life within a matter of seconds. Thus, nothing that you did lies hidden away in dusty filing cabinets. Everything can be brought into the light within seconds.

To this danger of efficiency we add the ability of an outsider to invade a computer by computer raiding and acquire its information, even without anyone knowing that this has been done. We then have a terrifying product of: *A* [efficiency of the computer] times *B* [availability of information to unauthorized outsiders].

(b) WHO IS LIABLE FOR COMPUTER INVASION OF PRIVACY? The person making public the information stored in the computer may be an authorized user of the computer. The person may be an outsider without authority, who invades the computer and then makes public the private information obtained from the computer. In either case there is no problem in applying ordinary tort law to hold such person liable for tort damages for invasion of privacy.

Can management be held liable for the invasion of privacy? If the wrongdoer is an employee, it is possible that management will be liable for the employee's misconduct, on the theory that management had not properly screened job applicants, or was negligent in supervising employees, or is liable for employee misconduct under the circumstances.[14] If the wrongdoer is an outsider, can management be held liable for the invasion of privacy? It may be argued that management could have prevented the invasion of privacy by maintaining a better security system over the computer. It can be claimed that because of the

---

[13]   The federal Electronic Communications Privacy Act of October 21, 1986, PL 99-508, 100 Stat 1848, 18 USC § 2510 note. Protection from the invasion of privacy by the improper release of data stored in the federal government computers is made by the Computer Security Act of 1987, Act of January 8, 1988, PL 100-235, 101 Stat 899, 15 USC §§ 272, 278, 40 USC 159, and the Computer Matching and Privacy Protection Act of October 18, 1988, PL 100-503, 102 Stat 2507, 5 USC § 552a note.

[14]   The subject of employer liability for employee misconduct is discussed in Chapter 41 of this book.

negligence of management, it was possible for the outsider to raid the computer and obtain the information that was thereafter made public.

As an analogy, in some states, if the owner of an automobile leaves it parked on the street with the ignition key in the car and a thief steals the car and runs into a third person, the third person may sue the car owner for the injury caused by the thief who drove the car. Other courts refuse to impose liability in such a case. A court that would impose liability on the negligent car owner could impose liability on the negligent protector of the computer. This liability would be for the harm caused by the thief who raided the computer and then injured the plaintiff by making public information that had been private up to that point. The area is one in which statutory regulation can be expected.

15. Defamation by Computer

A person's credit standing or reputation may be damaged because a computer contains erroneous information that is supplied to third persons. Will the data bank operator or service company be held liable to the person who is harmed? If the operator or the company had exercised reasonable care to prevent errors and to correct errors, it is probable that there will not be liability on either the employee operating the equipment or the management providing the computer service.

The supplier of the wrong information is liable for the damages caused thereby when the error was caused by its negligence. Since the supplier is furnishing information to a limited group of subscribers, it is not protected by the guarantee of free speech.[15]

When negligence or an intent to harm is shown, the wrongdoer could be held liable for what may be called defamation by computer. It is likely that liability could be avoided by supplying the person to whom the information relates with a copy of any printout of information that the data bank supplies the third person. This would tend to show good faith and due care on the part of the management of the data bank operation and a reasonable effort to keep the information accurate.

Liability for defamation by computer may arise under the federal Fair Credit Reporting Act of 1970 when the person affected is a consumer. The federal Credit Card Act of 1970 further protects from defamation by computer. These acts, which are not limited to situations involving computers, are discussed in Chapter 29 on consumer protection.

16. The Computer as a Nuisance

The modern world generally looks upon the computer as a blessing. At times it may be a nuisance. This was the claim made in the *Page County Appliance* case.

[15] Dunn & Bradstreet, Inc. v Greenmoss Builders, 472 US 749 (1985).

PAGE COUNTY APPLIANCE CENTER, INC. v HONEYWELL, INC.
(Iowa) 347 NW2d 171 (1984)

ITT Electronic Services, Inc. (ITT), a subsidiary of Honeywell, Inc., leased a Honeywell computer to the Central Travel Service. A nearby enterprise, the Page County Appliance Center, Inc. claimed that there was a radiation leakage from the computer that interfered with the reception of the display televisions in the store and that this caused a loss of sales. Appliance Center sued the travel agency, Honeywell, and ITT. The defendants moved the trial court to enter a verdict in their favor. The court refused to do so. They appealed.

REYNOLDSON, C. J. . . . Appliance Center has owned and operated an appliance store in Shenandoah, Iowa, since 1953. In 1975 the store was acquired from his father by John Pearson, who sold televisions, stereos, and a variety of appliances. Before 1980 Pearson had no reception trouble with his display televisions. In early January 1980, however, ITT placed one of its computers with Central Travel Service in Shenandoah as part of a nationwide plan to lease computers to retail travel agents. Central Travel was separated by only one other business from the Appliance Center. [The] ITT computer was manufactured, installed, and maintained by Honeywell.

Thereafter many of Pearson's customers told him his display television pictures were bad; on two of the three channels available in Shenandoah he had a difficult time "getting a picture that was fit to watch." After unsuccessfully attempting several remedial measures, in late January 1980, he finally traced the interference to the operations of Central Travel's computer. Both defendants concede Pearson's problems were caused by radiation leaking from the Honeywell computer.

Appliance Center is alleging a "private nuisance," that is, an actionable interference with a person's interest in the private use and enjoyment of his or her property. . . .

Principles governing our consideration of nuisance claims are well established. One's use of property should not unreasonably interfere with or disturb a neighbor's comfortable and reasonable use and enjoyment of his or her estate. A fair test of whether the operation of a lawful trade or industry constitutes a nuisance is the reasonableness of conducting it in the manner, at the place, and under the circumstances shown by the evidence. Each case turns on its own facts. . . . The existence of a nuisance is not affected by the intention of its creator not to injure anyone. . . .

When the alleged nuisance is claimed to be offensive to the person, courts apply the standard of "normal persons in a particular locality" to measure the existence of a nuisance. This normalcy standard also is applied where the use of property is claimed to be affected. "The plaintiff cannot, by devoting his own land to an unusually sensitive use, . . . make a nuisance out of conduct of the adjoining defendant which would otherwise be harmless." W. Prosser, *The Law of Torts* § 87, at 579 (4th ed. 1971).

In the case before us, ITT asserts the Appliance Center's display televisions constituted a hypersensitive use of its premises. . . .

Clearly, the presence of televisions on any premises is not such an abnormal condition that we can say, as a matter of law, that the owner has engaged in a *peculiarly* sensitive use of the property.

ITT's second contention asserts trial court should have directed a verdict in its favor because it did not participate in the creation or maintenance of the alleged nuisance. We have noted ITT was engaged in a multimillion dollar, national program to lease computers to travel agencies. It owned this computer and leased it to Central Travel. It was to ITT that the agency first turned when the effect of the computer radiation became apparent. ITT continued to collect its lease payments; the computer did not operate for the benefit of Crowell [owner of Central Travel Service] alone. The jury could have found ITT evidenced some measure of its responsibility, as owner of the computer, in contacting Honeywell and making belated inquiries regarding Appliance Center's problems both to Pearson and Crowell.

It is no ground for directed verdict that the computer was leased to Central Travel. "One is subject to liability for a nuisance caused by an activity, not only when he carries on the activity but also when he participates to a substantial extent in carrying it on." Restatement (Second) of Torts § 834 (1979). Even one who contracts out nuisance-causing work to independent contractors may have the duty, upon notice, "to take reasonably prompt and efficient means to suppress the nuisance." . . . A failure to act under circumstances in which one is under a duty to take positive action to prevent or abate the invasion of the private interest may make one liable, Restatement (Second) of Torts § 824, and this may include a lessor or licensor. *Id.* comment d.

An action for damages for nuisance need not be predicated on negligence. Nuisance ordinarily is considered as a condition, and not as an act or failure to act on the part of the responsible party. A person responsible for a harmful condition found to be a nuisance may be liable even though that person has used the highest possible degree of care to prevent or minimize the effect.

Where there is reasonable doubt whether one of several persons is substantially participating in carrying on an activity, the question is for the trier of fact. . . . We hold such reasonable doubt existed on the record made in this case, and trial court did not err in refusing to direct a verdict on this ground.

[Judgment affirmed as to the matters set forth in the above excerpt from the opinion]

QUESTIONS

1. In the *Page County Appliance* case, who was negligent?
2. How does your answer to Question 1 affect the decision in the case?
3. Did the fact that the computer was leased have any significance?

D. PROTECTION OF PROGRAMS, CHIPS, AND MASK WORKS

Computer programs, chip designs, and mask works are protected from piracy, with varying degrees of success, by secrecy, restrictive licensing, or federal statutes.

17. Trade Secrets

Whenever practical, industry will employ trade secrecy to protect computer programs. This gives complete protection to the program owner. When computer tapes containing trade secrets are unlawfully taken away by an employee, the employee is guilty of the crime of theft of trade secrets.[16]

18. Restrictive Licensing

In order to retain greater control over software, it is common for the creator of software to license its use to others rather than to sell it to them. Such licensing agreements typically include restrictions on the use of the software by the licensee and give the licensor greater protection than given by the copyright law. These restrictions will commonly prohibit the licensee from renting copies of the software to third persons or from subjecting the software to reverse engineering.[17]

(a) ANTI-REVERSE ENGINEERING. A license will commonly prohibit the licensee from engaging in reverse engineering to discover the details of the structure of the licensed program. Existing statutes do not give this protection.

(b) ANTI-RENTING. A license to use a computer program will commonly prohibit the licensee from renting or relicensing the program to third persons. This is done to pro-

---

[16] Leonard v Texas (Tex App) 267 SW2d 171 (1988).

[17] Such provisions in a licensing agreement are not to be confused with the anticompetitive provisions in the employment contracts between the owner and its employees, by which they agree that after their employment is ended, they will not compete with the owner or work for a competitor of the owner for a stated period of time or within a stated geographic area. See Chapter 13, Section 19.

tect the program owner from the loss of such third persons as customers. Of greater importance, it removes the danger that such third persons will make copies of the program and then compete with the original program owner.

(c) VALIDITY. The validity of the restrictions noted above is uncertain.[18] It may be held that such license terms are displaced by federal law. An additional problem arises with respect to anti-reverse engineering provisions in those states that have adopted the Uniform Trade Secrets Act.[19] Although the Act does not contain any provision as to reverse engineering, the Official Comment of the Commissioners on Uniform Laws to § 1 of the Act expressly approves "reverse engineering" as a proper means of breaking a trade secret. While the comments of the commissioners are not adopted by the states, a court could hold that such comments manifested a local public policy that was violated by an anti-reverse engineering provision in a software license.

19.   Copyright Protection of Written Programs

Under the Computer Software Copyright Act of 1980[20] a written program is given the same protection as any other copyrighted material. This is so whether the program is written in source code (ordinary language) or object code (machine language). In determining whether there is a copyright violation under this statute, courts will examine the two programs in question to compare their structure, flow sequence, and organization. Moreover, the courts in their infringement analysis look to see if the most significant steps of the program are similar, rather than whether most of the program's steps are similar. To illustrate a

copyright violation, substantial similarity in structure of two computer programs for recordkeeping was found, even though the programs were dissimilar in a number of respects, where five particularly important subroutines within both programs performed almost identically.[21]

20.   Patent Protection of Written Programs

The extent to which computer programs can be patented is not settled. Many programs are not patentable because they contain mathematical formulas, and the courts are reluctant to grant a monopoly on a method of solving a mathematical problem, since such methods are the basic tools of scientific work.[22] Patents have been granted for computer programs, however. For example, a method of using a computer to carry out translations from one language to another was held to be patentable.

The patenting of a program has the disadvantage that the program is placed in the public records. It may be examined by anyone. This has the potential danger that the program will be copied. To detect patent violators and bring legal action is difficult and costly.

21.   Copyright Protection of Chip Design and Mask Works

The operations of a computer are controlled by electric current passing through its circuitry and activating transistors that work as switches. These transistors and connecting metallic tape are mounted on a small laminated base. The base is generally 1/4" square or smaller. Because of this small size, the base is called a chip. The chip is made of substances that are medium conductors of electricity— medium as contrasted with substances that

---

[18]   Vault Corp. v Quaid Software (DC Cal) 655 F Supp 750 (1987).
[19]   This Act has been adopted in Alabama, Alaska, Florida, California, Colorado, Connecticut, Delaware, Illinois, Indiana, Kansas, Louisiana, Maine, Minnesota, Montana, Nevada, North Dakota, Oklahoma, Oregon, Rhode Island, South Dakota, Virginia, Washington, West Virginia, and Wisconsin.
[20]   Act of Dec 12, 1980, PL 96-517, 17 USC §§ 101, 117, 94 Stat 3015.

[21]   Whelan Associates v Jaslow Dental Laboratory (CA3 Pa) 797 F2d 1222 (1986).
[22]   Gottschalk v Benson, 409 US 63 (1972); Parker v Flook, 437 US 584 (1978). But see Diamond v Diehr, 450 US 175 (1981), where a computerized process for curing rubber was held to be patentable, even though the process was based on a mathematical formula, since the inventor did not seek to prevent all others from using the formula, but only to prevent the use of the formula in conjunction with the other steps in his rubber-curing process.

are good conductors, such as copper, or with substances that are insulators, such as glass. Hence, the chip is called a semiconductor chip. In making the finished chip, some of the chip is eaten or etched away, and up to thousands of transistors are attached to the chip. This process is guided and controlled by a set of stencils or masks.[23] The making of the mask changes to a chip takes the program from the drawing board and incorporates it into the chip, which, when added to the computer as a component part, can make the computer perform according to the program. It is relatively easy for anyone with a set of masks (mask work) to mass-produce the chip. Mask works piracy is very profitable; huge sums, even up to millions of dollars, may have been spent in designing and manufacturing a mask work.

(a) THE SEMICONDUCTOR CHIP PROTECTION ACT. This Act (SCPA) gives copyright protection to mask works.[24]

The Act gives the mask work owner the exclusive right to use and exploit the work for ten years. Such privilege cannot be obtained if the mask work deals with matter that is ordinarily, generally known in the computer chip

---

[23]   This process is not to be confused with the printing of circuits, in which there is merely the pressing of a conducting wire or circuit on a nonconductor base.
[24]   Act of Nov. 8, 1984, as amended, PL 98-620, 98 Stat 3347, 17 USC §§ 901 et seq.

industry. When the privilege is granted, the mask work is marked with the symbol *M* or Ⓜ. This gives the public notice that the exclusive right under the Act has been obtained.

The Act does not protect from reverse engineering, provided the alleged infringer can show that substantial time and money was devoted to reverse engineering, as against the contention that the infringer merely copied the original.

(b) APPLICATION FOR PROTECTION. In order to obtain protection under SCPA, application must be made to the Register of Copyrights within two years after the first commercial exploitation of the mask work.

(c) PENALTY FOR VIOLATION OF SCPA. A person knowingly infringing the copyright created by SCPA is liable to the mask work owner for damages sustained by the owner. The wrongdoer can be required to forfeit to the owner any profits made by the infringement. As an alternative, the owner may elect to receive statutory damages of up to $250,000 as determined by the court.[25] The court may also order destruction or other disposition of the products and the equipment used to make the products. SCPA remedies include temporary restraining orders and injunctions against infringement.

---

[25]   17 USC § 911(c).

SUMMARY

The law applicable to computers may be traditional rules of law, or it may be new rules that apply only to computers. The law of contracts has not been changed by the computer. In contrast, the law of evidence has changed to allow computer printouts to be admitted in evidence when the proper foundation is laid. That is, before printouts may be admitted in favor of the computer user, it is necessary to establish that they were properly made, by standard procedures, using a standard computer. The law of torts has remained unchanged with respect to fraud, property damage, theft, defamation, privacy, and nuisance. Statutes have expanded the area of criminal law to meet situations in which computers are involved. The unauthorized use is made a crime by federal law and by many state statutes. The unauthorized taking of information from a computer is also a crime under federal and state statutes. Criminal conduct of diverting deliveries of goods and the transfer of funds, the theft of software, and computer raiding are made crimes to some extent by the federal Computer Access Device and Computer Fraud and Abuse Act of 1984 and the

Electronic Fund Transfers Act of 1978. Protection of computer programs and the design of computer chips and mask works is commonly obtained, subject to certain limitations, under the law of trade secrets, by restrictive licensing agreements, and by complying with federal statutes.

QUESTIONS AND CASE PROBLEMS

1. What social forces are affected by allowing computer printouts to be introduced as evidence?
2. The Metro Supply Store sued Connors for the bill owed to it. At the trial Metro offers as evidence of the debt its computer printout showing the various purchases made by Connors and the balance due. Connors objects that this printout cannot be admitted in court. Is he correct?
3. The town of Janesville sues Leonard for back taxes. The town produces a computer printout showing the taxes that are due. Leonard claimed that he had paid the amounts shown to be due with money orders, but that over the course of time he has lost the money order receipts. The town objects to Leonard's testimony on the ground that it contradicts what the computer says, and the computer cannot be contradicted. Is Leonard's testimony admissible?
4. The Sixth Amendment of the United States Constitution guarantees that "in all criminal prosecutions, the accused shall enjoy the right . . . to be confronted with the witnesses against him . . ." Rankin is prosecuted for a criminal conspiracy. Part of the evidence offered against him is the computer records of the telephone company showing a number of calls made from Rankin's home to the meeting place of the other accused conspirators. Rankin claimed that the Sixth Amendment of the Constitution requires that the prosecution produce in court a witness who can testify on the basis of the witness's own observation that the phone calls in question were made as stated by the computer printout. Is he correct?
5. Eastman needed public aid. The Department of Public Aid claimed that she had received more food stamps than the amount to which she was entitled. A hearing was held to determine whether this was so. On the basis of the computer printout showing distribution of food stamps, it was held that Eastman had received more than she should have. There was no other evidence on this point. Were these proceedings proper? [Eastman v Department of Public Aid, 178 Ill App 3d 993, 128 Ill Dec 276, 534 NE2d 458]
6. In a common law state, Hinkin steals a computer chip on which is stored information having commercial value of a million dollars. He is prosecuted for grand larceny. He raises the defense that he only committed petty larceny because the chip only costs $10, and by statute a larceny under $100 is petty larceny. Is he correct?
7. The Clayton factory controls a series of manufacturing operations by computers. The large number of computers, concentrated in a small area, set up an electromagnetic field that interfered with the fine instruments used by the Scientific Testing Laboratories, housed in a neighboring building. Scientific sues Clayton, claiming that the operation of Clayton's computers constitutes a nuisance. Clayton replies that it cannot be responsible for any side effects, because it was not negligent. Clayton states that, therefore, there cannot be a nuisance. Is Clayton correct?
8. Taylor was employed by Hopkins Company. After he was fired, he sought revenge against his former employer. He turned off the air conditioning in the computer room. It was midsummer, and the heat during the night ruined the memory bank of the computer. Hopkins asked the district attorney to prosecute Taylor. For what crimes could Taylor be prosecuted?
9. Lund was a graduate student at a university. In working on his doctoral dissertation, he made use of the university computer and was assisted by the personnel of the computer facility. The value of the information he thus obtained was about $30,000. Lund had not been authorized to use the computer, and he was prosecuted for common law grand larceny. Was he guilty? [Lund v Virginia, 217 Va 688, 232 SE2d 745]
10. Sallis was injured in an automobile collision with Lamansky. When he sued for damages, a psychiatrist testified on behalf of the defendant that the plaintiff's claim for pain and suffering was exaggerated. The psychiatrist said that the plaintiff had a hysterical personality with hypochondriacal tendencies and tended to exaggerate pain. In support of this testimony, the

psychiatrist offered in evidence the analysis made by a computer of tests conducted by the psychiatrist, the computer analysis reached the same result as the psychiatrist. The computer evidence was objected to by the plaintiff. The trial judge excluded the evidence and held that it could not be admitted. Was he correct? [Sallis v Lamansky (Iowa) 420 NW2d 795]

11. Pompeii Estates was a builder. It constructed a house to which the Consolidated Edison Company supplied electricity. Since it was a newly constructed, unoccupied house, Pompeii wrote Consolidated Edison, giving it an address where Pompeii could be reached. This address was never fed into the computer of Consolidated Edison. Consolidated Edison used the computer to determine when bills were not paid. When the bill for the empty Pompeii house was not paid, the computer directed the mailing of a notice to the empty house that the electricity would be shut off if the bill was not paid. Consolidated Edison did not send any notice to the address of Pompeii that it had in its files. Thereafter, Consolidated shut off the electricity, which in turn shut off the heating system. Consequently, the pipes froze and burst, causing extensive damage to the house. Pompeii sued Consolidated Edison for the damage. Was Consolidated Edison liable? [Pompeii Estates, Inc. v Consolidated Edison Co. 91 Misc 2d 233, 397 NYS2d 577]

12. Schlicht had a bank account. The bank's computer made a mistake and showed that he had a balance of $9,000 more than he really had in his account. He withdrew the $9,000. When the bank learned of the mistake, he was prosecuted for the crime of theft. Was he guilty? [Colorado v Schlicht (Colo App) 709 P2d 94].

13. Dorothy Judd had a bank account in Citibank. Withdrawals could be made from a cash machine by use of a plastic card. She claimed that the bank had charged her account for $800 more than she had actually removed from it. She sued the bank for this amount. The bank defended by proving that its computers showed withdrawals on her account from a cash machine in the amount of $800. She produced evidence that at the times shown on the bank's computer printouts, she was at work and could not have made the withdrawals. The bank claimed that its computer printouts could not be contradicted. Was it correct? [Judd v Citibank, 435 NYS2d 210]

14. Electric Supply Co. (ESCO) supplied Kitchens Construction, Inc. with materials that Kitchens used in constructing a building for the state of New Mexico. When ESCO was not paid, it brought suit for its unpaid bill. In support of its claim it offered in evidence a computer printout of the invoices for goods for which payment had not been made. Two ESCO employees testified how the original invoices had been prepared and that the database from which the computer printout was made was a compilation of the original records. Were the computer printouts admissible in evidence? [New Mexico for the use of Electric Supply Co., Inc. v Kitchens Construction, Inc. 106 NM 753, 750 P2d 114]

15. Hodgeson was prosecuted for manslaughter. The district attorney wanted to show that a phone call had been made from a certain telephone. In order to do this, the records of the telephone company were offered in evidence. The records consisted of a computer printout. Hodgeson objected to admitting this printout in evidence without producing in court the persons who had supplied the information that was stored in the computer. Should the printout be admitted? [Louisiana v Hodgeson (La) 305 So 2d 421]

22

BAILMENTS

Many instances arise in which the owner of personal property entrusts it to another—a person checks a coat at a restaurant, delivers a watch to a jeweler for repairs, or loans hedge clippers to a neighbor; or a company rents a car to a tourist for a weekend. The delivery of property to another under such circumstances is a bailment.

A. GENERAL PRINCIPLES

A **bailment** is the legal relationship that arises whenever one person delivers possession of personal property to another under an agreement by which the latter is under a duty to return the identical property to the former or to deliver it or dispose of it as agreed. The person who turns over the possession of the property is the **bailor**. The person who accepts possession is the **bailee**.

1. Elements of Bailment

A bailment is created when the following elements are present.

(a) AGREEMENT. The bailment is based on an agreement. This agreement may be express or implied. Generally it will contain all the elements of a contract. Thus, the bailment transaction in fact consists of (1) a contract to bail and (2) the actual bailing of the property.

442

Ordinarily, there is no requirement that the contract of bailment be in writing. The subject of a bailment may be any personal property of which possession may be given. Real property cannot be bailed.

(b) DELIVERY AND ACCEPTANCE. The bailment arises when, pursuant to the agreement of the parties, the property is delivered to the bailee and accepted by the bailee as subject to the bailment agreement.[1]

Delivery may be **actual,** as when the bailor physically hands a book to the bailee, or it may be **constructive,** as when the bailor points out a package to the bailee, who then takes possession of it. In the absence of a prior

---

[1]   Merrit v Nationwide Warehouse Co., Ltd. (Tenn App) 605 SW2d 250 (1980).

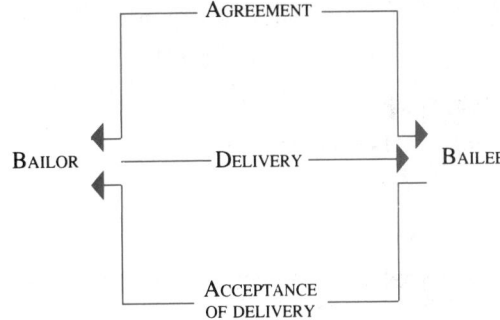

FIGURE 22-1   BAILMENT OF PERSONAL PROPERTY

agreement to the contrary, a valid delivery and acceptance generally requires that the bailee be aware that goods have been placed within the bailee's exclusive possession or control. The *Berglund* case illustrates a situation in which this element was not present.

BERGLUND v ROOSEVELT UNIVERSITY
18 Ill App 3d 842, 310 NE2d 773 (1974)

Richard Berglund, the plaintiff, was a full-time student at Roosevelt University. He was also the editor and photographer of the student newspaper. The university was unaware that Richard kept his own photographic equipment in the rooms it had assigned to the newspaper. One night this equipment was stolen from the newspaper office. Richard sued the university, on the theory that it had breached its duty as a bailee. He showed that former editors had also left their equipment in the university rooms. The university denied that it was a bailee. The trial court awarded $1,789.15 to Richard on the theory of an implied bailment, and the university appealed.

McNAMARA, J. . . . The characteristics common to every bailment are the intent to create a bailment, delivery of possession of the bailed items, and the acceptance of the items by the bailee. . . . A bailment can be established by express contract or by implication. . . . In determining the existence of an implied-in-fact bailment, one must analyze the facts surrounding the transaction, such as the benefits to be received by the parties, their intentions, the kind of property involved, and the opportunity of each to exercise control over the property. . . .

In the present case, plaintiff attempted to show that an implied-in-fact bailment had arisen between the parties. It is clear, however, that the failure of the plaintiff to prove any knowledge on the part of the defendant of the storage of the items doomed this attempt.

Knowledge on the part of the bailee is essential to prove proper delivery and acceptance. Physical control over the property allegedly bailed and an intention to exercise that control are needed to show that one is in possession of the bailed item. . . . And before acceptance can be inferred on the part of the alleged bailee of the goods purportedly bailed, there must be evidence to show notice or knowledge on the part of the bailee that the goods are in fact in his possession. . . . Yet in the present case defendant's consistent denial of having any knowledge that plaintiff had stored his camera equipment on the premises is supported by plaintiff's own testimony. Although normal procedure required plaintiff to seek permission of certain agents of defendant to store his property on the premises, plaintiff never bothered to do so. . . . Nor does the fact that prior student paper photographers may have similarly stored their equipment in the darkroom, without more, prove knowledge on the part of defendant. The record also reveals that defendant's security officers never exercised any degree of intentional control over plaintiff's goods. We conclude that plaintiff's failure to prove knowledge on the part of defendant of the goods stored resulted in his inability to prove a valid delivery of the camera equipment and a true acceptance of the goods by defendant. . . . Our holding on this issue obviates the necessity of considering whether defendant was negligent in its capacity as bailee.

[Judgment reversed]

QUESTIONS

1. What did the plaintiff claim?
2. Was it essential for the plaintiff to prove that the defendant had knowledge of the storage of the items in order to prove proper delivery and acceptance in this case?
3. Did the court find that there was a bailment?

2.   Nature of the Parties' Interests

The bailor and bailee have different legal interests in the bailed property.

(a) BAILOR'S INTEREST. The bailor is usually the owner, but ownership by the bailor is not required. It is sufficient that the bailor have physical possession.[2]

In the *Magee* case the defendant contended that it was not liable for a fur jacket it lost during summer storage because the customer did not prove that she owned the fur jacket in question.

---

[2]   Williams v Boswell (Minn App) 444 NW2d 887 (1989).

MAGEE v WALBRO, INC.
171 Ill App 3d 774, 121 Ill Dec 668, 525 NE2d 975 (1988)

Crella Magee delivered a blue fox jacket for summer storage to Walbro, Inc. (dba Mysel's Furs). When it was not returned, she sued Walbro for the fur's replacement cost of $3,400. Magee testified that she bought the jacket from Evans' Furs. Evans' Furs, however, showed no record of having made the sale. Walbro contended that since Magee had not proven that she owned the jacket, Walbro could not be held liable. Moreover, it contended that its liability was limited to $100, the amount on the receipt it sent Magee six weeks after the jacket was received for storage.

O'CONNOR, J. . . . In the instant case, the trial court ruled that the evidence established a bailment between Magee and defendants Walbro and Mysel. . . . Walbro and Mysel produced no evidence, however, to rebut the presumption of [their] negligence. Instead, they attacked Magee's assertion of ownership, a fact irrelevant to bailment, and maintained that Mysel's never received the fur jacket.

The evidence shows that a fur jacket was delivered to Mysel's. . . .

We now address whether the liability of defendants Walbro and Mysel may be limited to $100.00, as stated on the receipt that Magee received in July, 1982. . . .

In the instant case, Magee testified that she was not told of the limitation until after the fur was lost. . . . Magee should have known of the limitation after she received the receipt in July, but by that time her furs had been at Mysel's for six weeks.

Although the liability of Walbro and Mysel appears to be limited to $100, the limitation does not apply in the instant case because Magee had no knowledge of the limitation before agreeing to store her furs. . . . In the instant case, it would be unjust to permit Mysel and Walbro to assert a limitation that was not made clear at the time that the bailment contract was made because the coat was lost. We therefore hold that the $100 limitation of liability is inapplicable in this case.

For the foregoing reasons, judgment in favor of the defendants is reversed, and this case is remanded to the trial court to enter a judgment against defendants Walbro, Inc. and Mysel Furs and in favor of plaintiff Crella Magee in the amount of $3,400.00.

[Reversed and remanded]

QUESTIONS

1. Was it necessary for the bailor, Magee, to prove that she owned the fur in order to recover for its loss?
2. Did Walbro effectively limit its liability for the loss of the item to $100?
3. Did Walbro rebut the presumption of negligence in this case?

(b) BAILEE'S INTEREST. The bailee has only possession of the property. Title to the property does not pass to the bailee, and the bailee cannot sell the property to a third person unless the bailee is also an agent authorized to make such a sale. If the bailee attempts to sell the property, such sale transfers only possession, and the owner may recover the property from the buyer.

The bailor may cause third persons to believe that the bailee is the owner of the bailed property. If the bailor does so, the bailor is estopped from denying that the bailee is the owner as against persons who have relied on the bailor's representations. As a further exception, if the bailee is a dealer in goods of the kind entrusted to the bailee by the bailor, a sale by the bailee to a buyer in the ordinary course of business will pass the bailor's title to the buyer.

3.   Classification of Bailments

Bailments are classified as ordinary and extraordinary (or special). **Extraordinary bailments** are those in which the bailee is under unusual duties and liabilities by law, as in the case of bailments in which a motel or a common carrier is involved. **Ordinary bailments** include all other bailments.

Bailments may or may not provide for compensation to the bailee. On that basis they may be classified as **contract bailments** and **gratuitous bailments**. The fact that no charge is made by the bailor does not necessarily make the transaction a gratuitous bailment. If the bailment is made to further a business interest of the bailor, as when something is loaned free to a customer, the bailment is not gratuitous.

Bailments may also be classified in terms of benefit. A bailment may be for the sole benefit of the bailor, as when a farmer gratuitously transports another's produce to the city. A bailment may be for the sole benefit of the bailee, as when a person borrows a friend's automobile. A bailment may be for the benefit of both parties (mutual benefit bailment), as when someone rents a power tool. A mutual benefit bailment also arises when a prospective buyer of an automobile leaves the automobile that is to be traded in with the dealer so that the latter may test it and appraise it.

4.   Constructive Bailments

When one person comes into possession of personal property of another without the owner's consent, the law treats the possessor as a bailee and calls the relationship a **constructive bailment**. It is thus held that the finder of lost property is a bailee of that property.

When a city impounds an automobile, a bailment arises as to the vehicle and its contents. A seller who has not yet delivered the goods to the buyer is treated as bailee of the goods if title has passed to the buyer. Similarly, a buyer who is in possession of goods, the title to which has not yet passed from the seller, is a bailee.

5.   Renting of Space Distinguished

When a person rents space in a locker or building under an agreement that gives the renter the exclusive right to use that space, the placing of goods by the renter in that space does not create a bailment.[3] In such a case, putting property into the space does not constitute a delivery of goods into the possession of the owner of the space. On this basis, there is no bailment in a self-service parking lot when the owner of a car parks it and retains the key, and the owner's only contact with any parking lot employee is on making a payment when leaving the lot. In such situations the car owner merely rents the space for parking. The practical consequence of this conclusion is that if the car is damaged or stolen, the car owner cannot recover damages from the parking lot management unless the owner can show some fault on the part of the parking lot management. If the transaction were a bailment, the owner of the car would establish a *prima facie* right to recover by proving the fact of the bailment and the fact that there was a loss.

If the parking lot is a locked enclosure with a guard to whom the patron must surrender a parking ticket received on entering the lot in order to regain possession of the car, a modern trend regards the transaction as a bailment. The theoretical objection to this view is that the lot does not have full dominion and control over the car, since it cannot move the car because the patron has retained possession of the key. At the same time, as the lot has the power to exclude others from the car, courts have found it "realistic" to treat the parking lot as a bailee and hold it to a bailee's standard of care.

6.   Bailment of Contents of Container

It is a question of the intention of the parties, as that appears to a reasonable person, whether a bailment of a container also constitutes a bailment of articles contained in it—for example, whether a bailment of a coat is a bailment of articles in the coat. When the contained articles are of a class that is reasonably or normally to be found in the container, they

---

[3]   Magliocco v American Locker Co. 239 Cal Rptr 497 (1987).

may be regarded as bailed in the absence of an express disclaimer. If the articles are not of such a nature and their presence in the container is unknown to the bailee, there is no bailment of such articles. Consequently, although the circumstances are such that the parking of a car constitutes a bailment, there is no bailment of valuable drawings and sporting equipment that are on the back seat but not visible from the outside of the car. However, there is ordinarily a bailment of whatever is locked in the trunk.

B.   RIGHTS AND DUTIES OF THE PARTIES

A bailment creates certain rights and imposes certain duties on each party. These may be increased or modified by statute, by custom, or by the express agreement of the parties.

7.   Duties of the Bailee

The bailee has certain duties concerning performance, care, maintenance, and return of the bailed property. A bailee's lien allows for the retention of goods until charges are paid. Unauthorized use of the bailed property is forbidden.

(a) PERFORMANCE. If the bailment is based on a contract, the bailee must perform the bailee's part of the contract and is liable to the bailor for ordinary contract damages arising out of the failure to perform the contract.[4] Thus, if the bailment is for repair, the bailee is under the duty to make the repairs properly. The fact that the bailee used due care in attempting to perform the contract does not excuse the bailee from liability for failing to perform the contract.

(b) CARE OF PROPERTY. The bailee is under a duty to care for the bailed property. If the property is damaged or destroyed, the bailee is liable for the loss (1) if the harm was caused in whole or in part by the bailee's failure to use reasonable care under the circumstances, or (2) if the harm was sustained during the unauthorized use of the property by the bailee. Otherwise, the bailor bears the loss. Thus, if the bailee was exercising due care and was making an authorized use of the property, the bailor must bear the loss of or damage to the property caused by an act of a third person, whether willful or negligent; by an accident or occurrence for which no one was at fault; or by an act of God.[5] In this connection, the term *act of God* means a natural phenomenon that is not reasonably foreseeable, such as a sudden flood or lightning.

(1) Standard of Care. The standard for ordinary bailments is reasonable care under the circumstances—that is, the degree of care that a reasonable person would exercise in the situation in order to prevent reasonably foreseeable harm. The significant factors in determining what constitutes reasonable care in a bailment are the time and place of making the bailment, the facilities for taking care of the bailed property, the nature of the bailed property, the bailee's knowledge of its nature, and the extent of the bailee's skills and experience in taking care of goods of that kind.

Some courts state the standard of care in terms of the benefit characteristic of the bailment. Thus, when the bailment is for the sole benefit of the bailee, the bailee is held liable for the slightest negligence. When the bailment is for the mutual benefit of the parties, the bailee is held liable for ordinary negligence. In contrast, if the benefit is for the sole benefit of the bailor, the bailee is only required to exercise slight care and will only be liable for gross negligence.

(2) Contract Modification of Liability. A bailee's liability may be expanded by contract. A provision that the bailee assumes absolute liability for the property is binding, but there is a difference of opinion as to whether a stipulation to return the property "in good condi-

---

[4]   Computer Systems v Western Reserve Life, 19 Mass App 430, 475 NE2d 745 (1985).

[5]   Andrews v Allen (Tex Civ App) 724 SW2d 893 (1987).

tion" or "in as good condition as received" has the effect of imposing such absolute liability.

An ordinary bailee may limit liability, except for willful misconduct, by agreement or contract.[6] However, in some states statutes prohibit certain kinds of paid bailees, such as automobile parking garages, from limiting their liability for negligence.

Also, statutes in some states declare that a party cannot bar liability for negligent violations of common law standards of care where a public interest is involved. In the *Gardner* case the court was faced with the problem of whether an automobile repair business could exempt itself from liability for ordinary negligence by a clause in its service order contract where the service it performed affects the public interest.

---

[6]   State Farm Fire and Casualty Co. v B&F Marine Inc. (Fla App) 520 So 2d 649 (1988).

GARDNER v DOWNTOWN PORSCHE AUDI

180 Cal App 3d 713, 225 Cal Rptr 757 (1986)

In June, 1978, Bruce Gardner took his 1976 Porsche 911 automobile to be repaired at Downtown Porsche Audi (Downtown). Gardner signed a repair order bearing the disclaimer "not responsible for loss (of) cars . . . in case of . . . theft." While Gardner's car was parked in the repair garage, the car was stolen because of Downtown's negligence. Gardner sued Downtown for failing to redeliver his car. Downtown defended that the disclaimer absolved it of liability for its negligence. From a judgment in favor of Gardner for $16,000, Downtown appealed.

JOHNSON, J. . . . Downtown concedes negligence but argues the disclaimer absolves it of liability for this failure to exercise due care. Assuming the truth of Downtown's contention Gardner signed a repair slip containing this exculpatory language, and even assuming he read and understood it, we find the attempted exemption from liability to be against public policy and thus ineffective to excuse Downtown's negligence.

In the absence of a disclaimer the duties and liabilities of a bailee for hire—such as Downtown—are clear. Unless it can redeliver the subject of the bailment—in this instance, the 1976 Porsche—the bailee must prove it exercised due care in its care and custody of this property. If it fails to establish the absence of negligence the bailee is liable to the bailor for any damages suffered due to the failure to redeliver the bailed property. . . .

Traditionally the law has looked carefully and with some skepticism at those who attempt to contract away their legal liabilities for the commission of torts. (Prosser and Keeton, *Torts, Fifth Edition* (1984) pp. 482–483.) This general policy of the common law found legislative expression early in California's history with the enactment of Civil Code section 1668. This 1872 statute reads:

CERTAIN CONTRACTS UNLAWFUL. All contracts which have for their object, directly or indirectly, to exempt any one from responsibility for his own fraud, or willful injury to the person or property of another, or violation of law, *whether willful or negligent*, are against the policy of the law.

(Civ. Code § 1668, italics added.)

This section made it clear a party could not contract away liability for his fraudulent or intentional acts or for his negligent violations of *statutory* law. Less clear was the status of negligent violations of *common law* standards of care. While acknowledging some conflict in the cases, Witkin concludes California now follows the modern view of the Restatement of Contracts—"a contract exempting from liability for *ordinary* negligence is valid where *no public interest* is involved . . . and no statute expressly prohibits it. . . ."

The converse is also true, however. Under Civil Code section 1668 an automobile repair garage cannot exempt itself from liability even for ordinary negligence if the service it provides implicates the public interest. In a leading case striking down exculpatory clauses in hospital admission forms, *Tunkl v. Regents of University of California* (1963) 60 Cal.2d 92, the Supreme Court set forth six characteristics typical of contracts affecting the public interest.

(1) It concerns a business of a type generally thought suitable for public regulation. (2) The party seeking exculpation is engaged in performing a service of great importance to the public, which is often a matter of practical necessity for some members of the public. (3) The party holds himself out as willing to perform this service for any member of the public who seeks it, or at least any member coming within certain established standards. (4) As a result of the essential nature of the service, in the economic setting of the transaction, the party invoking exculpation possesses a decisive advantage of bargaining strength against any member of the public who seeks his services. (5) In exercising a superior bargaining power the party confronts the public with a standardized adhesion contract of exculpation, and makes no provision whereby a purchaser may pay additional fees and obtain protection against negligence. (6) Finally, as a result of the transaction, the person or property of the purchaser is placed under the control of the seller, subject to the risk of carelessness by the seller or his agents. . . .

To begin with, automobile repair shops are in a "business of a type . . . thought suitable for public regulation" in the state of California. They are licensed by the state and their performance is regulated by the Bureau of Automotive Repair of the State Department of Consumer Affairs.

Secondly, these repair shops are most definitely engaged in "performing a service of great importance to the public, . . ." and, moreover, one which is a "matter of practical *necessity*" for nearly *all* not just *"some* members of the public." . . .

The modern citizen lives—and all too frequently dies—by the automobile. Members of the general public need cars not merely for discretionary recreational purposes but to get to and from their places of employment, to reach the stores where they can purchase the necessities—as well as the frivolities—of life, and the like. An out of repair automobile is an unreliable means of transportation. Moreover, it is a dangerous one as well—to pedestrians and other drivers not just the owner. What is true of modern society in general is doubly true in Southern California, the capital of the motor vehicle. Indeed it is virtually impossible to exist in the Los Angeles area without a fully operational automobile. Thus, except for the few who can afford to buy a new car every time the ash trays fill up, people in this area find the automobile repair business a "service of great importance" and a "practical necessity."

Thirdly, Downtown held itself "out as willing to perform" this important service "for any member of the public" or at least for any member of the public who fell within the "established standard" of owning an automobile of the type it was equipped to repair, in this case a Porsche.

Fourthly, Downtown indisputably "possesses a decisive advantage of bargaining strength against" Gardner or almost "any member of the public who seeks [its] services." Like the hospital in *Tunkl* it is one of a relatively small number of entities dispensing a service which is a "practical necessity" to a large number of consumers.

Fifthly, it is apparent Downtown "confronts the public with a standardized adhesion contract of exculpation." The exculpatory language is incorporated in the printed form "repair order" all customers are expected to sign before Downtown will begin work on the car.

Finally, Gardner's Porsche was "placed under the control of" Downtown, "subject to the risk of carelessness by" Downtown and its employees. In order to make the repairs on Gardner's vehicle, Downtown took possession of the car and keys to the car. During this period, the security of the automobile was entirely in Downtown's hands. If this dealer were careless in storing the vehicle or the keys, the Porsche would become an easy target for theft and there would be little the owner could do about it.

Based on application of the *Tunkl* criteria, we therefore conclude automobile repair contracts "affect the public interest." It follows that clauses which exculpate repair firms for ordinary negligence in handling and securing vehicles under repair run afoul of Civil Code section 1668 and are "invalid as contrary to public policy."

Downtown concedes it was negligent. We hold its attempt to avoid legal responsibility for this negligence is unavailing. It follows Downtown is liable for non-delivery of the subject of the bailment, Gardner's Porsche.

[Judgment affirmed]

QUESTIONS

1. Was Gardner bound by the clear language of the repair order that he signed that said that Downtown was "not responsible for loss (of) cars . . . in case of . . . theft"?
2. Did Downtown admit it was negligent in taking care of the automobile during the bailment?
3. What characteristics are typical of contracts affecting the public interest?

By definition, a limitation of liability must be a term of the bailment contract before any question arises as to whether it is binding. Thus, a limitation contained in a receipt mailed by a bailee after receiving a coat for storage is not effective to alter the terms of the bailment as originally made. Likewise, a bailor is not bound by a limitation of liability that was not known at the time the bailment was made. In the *Allright* case the court had to decide whether a parking lot had given notice to a customer concerning its intention to limit liability.

ALLRIGHT, INC. v SCHROEDER
(Tex Civ App) 551 SW2d 745 (1977)

Schroeder parked his car on a parking lot operated by Allright, Inc. It was stolen from the lot. The lot denied liability to Schroeder on the ground that the parking ticket given stated there was no liability for theft and that the parking lot closed at 6 p.m. Also, a sign stated that after 6 p.m. patrons of the lot could obtain the keys of their cars at another location. From a judgment for Schroeder, Allright appealed.

COLEMAN, C.J. . . . Where parking lot owners attempt to limit liability by posting notices on the wall or by printing such a limitation on the claim check, the limitation must be called to the attention of the bailor before it may become part of the bailment contract. *Allright, Inc. v Elledge*, 515 SW2d 266 (Tex 1974). These provisions are strictly construed against the bailee. . . . In *Elledge* the Supreme Court of Texas held that a provision limiting liability of the parking lot owner to a maximum of $100.00 for loss of the bailor's automobile due to theft occasioned by the ordinary negligence of the parking lot owner was enforceable where this provision was inserted in a written contract signed by the bailor.

In this case the limitation provision printed on the claim check was not specifically called to the attention of the bailor at the time he left his automobile at the parking lot. Plaintiff testified that at the time he left his automobile with the defendant he knew that the claim check stated that the lot closed at 6 o'clock. The defendant asserts that this evidence also raises an issue of fact as to whether or not the plaintiff had read the provision limiting liability printed on the check.

There is no evidence that the plaintiff read the material appearing on the claim check which was given him on September 8. . . .

Notice that a lot will "close at 6 o'clock p.m." does not give notice that cars left after such time will be at the owner's risk. Such a sign might be construed to mean that no automobile would be accepted after 6 o'clock p.m. The fact that the closing time of the lot was posted on signs and was printed on the claim ticket does not exempt the operator of the lot from the exercise of ordinary care with respect to the safety of the property. . . .

ALLRIGHT, INC.
320 TRAVIS
WE CLOSE AT 6:00 P.M.
IMPORTANT — READ CAREFULLY

In consideration of low rates charged for parking, customer agrees that parking operator won't be responsible for loss by fire, misdelivery or theft, except such loss be occasioned by negligence of operator, and then only up to a maximum value of $100. Proportionately greater rates must be paid in advance if customer sets larger limits of liability.

**Articles
Left In
Car At
Own Risk**

**ALLRIGHT
AUTO PARKS**

191

The evidence does not establish whether the automobile was stolen before or after the lot had closed for the day on September 8, 1969. There was testimony that on special occasions the lot stayed open to a later hour. The plaintiff testified that he knew that the lot had been open after 6 o'clock closing time on previous occasions and that he inquired of the attendant whether or not the lot would be open later on this night. He testified that he was told that it would be open later. There was testimony that it closed at 6:00 p.m. on September 8, 1969. When his car was recovered the trunk was open, his spare tire was missing, and the keys were found in the trunk. The defendant represented that the keys to the car would be in its custody until returned to the owner.

The requested issue related to an immaterial fact. The operator had a duty to remove the keys from the car at closing time and to transport them to the place mentioned in their sign. The trial court submitted a general negligence issue and the jury found that the defendant's negligence proximately caused plaintiff's automobile to be stolen. . . .

Here the sign clearly represented to the patrons that some degree of care would be exercised for the safety of their automobiles after the closing time by reason of the notice that the car keys could be picked up after closing time at another location. No agreement that the bailment would expire at 6 o'clock p.m. will be implied from the fact that the plaintiff knew the signs stated that the lot would close at 6 o'clock p.m. under these circumstances.

[Judgment affirmed]

QUESTIONS

1. What did Allright contend?
2. What rule of construction is generally applied in interpreting limitation of liability provisions posted on walls or contained in claim checks?
3. On what basis did court decide the case?

---

(3) Insurance. In the absence of a statute or contract provision, a bailee is not under any duty to insure for the benefit of the bailor the property entrusted to the bailee.

(c) MAINTENANCE OF PROPERTY. In the situation of a bailment for hire, such as when a business rents an office copier from a leasing firm, the bailee, in the absence of a contrary contract provision, must bear the expense of repairs that are ordinary and incidental to the use of the machine. If, however, the repairs required are of an unusual nature or if the bailment is for a short period of time, the bailor is required to make the repairs unless the need for the repairs arose from the fault of the bailee.

(d) UNAUTHORIZED USE. The bailee is liable for conversion, just as though the bailee stole the property, if the bailee uses the property without authority or uses it in any manner to which the bailor had not agreed. Ordinarily, the bailee will be required to pay compensatory damages, although punitive damages may be imposed when the improper use was deliberate and when the bailee was recklessly indifferent to the effect of the use on the property.

(e) RETURN OF PROPERTY. The bailee is under a duty to return the identical property that is the subject of the bailment or to deliver it as directed by the bailment agreement. An exception exists for **fungible goods**, which are those goods of a homogeneous nature of which any unit is the equivalent of any other like unit. Examples of fungible goods are grain, potatoes (within the same grade), and petroleum (within the same grade). In the case of fungible goods, if the bailee contracts to return an equal amount of the same kind and quality, the transaction is a bailment. If the bailee has the option of paying an amount of money or returning property other than that which was delivered by the bailor, there is generally no bailment, but rather a "sale." Thus, when a farmer delivers wheat to a grain elevator that gives the farmer a receipt that promises to return either a similar amount of wheat or a certain sum of money on presentment of the receipt, the relationship is generally not a bailment.

The redelivery to the bailor or delivery to a third person must be made in accordance with the terms of the bailment contract as to time, place, and manner. When the agreement between the parties does not control these matters, the customs of the community govern.

(f) BAILEE'S LIEN. By common law or statute, a bailee is given a **lien** or the right to retain possession of the bailed property until the bailee has been paid for any charges for storage or repairs.[7] The lien is lost if the property is voluntarily returned to the bailor. If the bailor is guilty of any misconduct in regaining possession of the property, there is no loss of lien, and the bailee may retain possession if possession can be reacquired.[8]

A bailee who is authorized by statute to sell the bailed property to enforce a charge or claim against the bailor must give such notice as is required by the statute. A bailee who sells without giving the required notice is liable for conversion of the property.

In some states a bailee's lien may be extinguished where the bailee intentionally claims an amount greater than that to which the bailee is entitled. Thus, a car stereo seller's lien was extinguished when he knowingly demanded in his lien statement an additional charge of $50 per day for storage of the bailor's truck.[9] This charge was clearly excessive and an intentional demand for an amount in excess of that due the bailee.

8. Burden of Proof

When the bailor sues the bailee for damages to the bailed property, the bailor has the burden of proving that the bailee was at fault and that such fault was the proximate cause of the loss. A *prima facie* right of the bailor to recover is established, however, by proof that the property was delivered by the bailor to the bailee and thereafter could not be returned or was returned in a damaged condition. When this is done, the bailee has the burden of proving that the loss or damage was not caused by the bailee's failure to exercise the care required by law or by an unauthorized use of the property.[10]

9. Rights of the Bailor

The typical commercial bailment is a mutual benefit bailment. Under such a bailment the bailor has the right to compensation, commonly called rent, for the bailee's use of the property. If the bailor is obligated to render a service to the bailee, such as maintenance of the rented property, the bailor's failure to do so will ordinarily bar the bailor from recovering compensation from the bailee.

(a) RIGHTS AGAINST THE BAILEE. The bailor may sue the bailee for breach of contract if the goods are not redelivered to the bailor or delivered to a third person as specified by the bailment agreement. The bailor may also maintain an action against a bailee for negligence, willful destruction, and unlawful retention or conversion of the goods.

(b) RIGHTS AGAINST THIRD PERSONS. The bailor may sue third persons who damage or take the bailed property from the bailee's possession, even though the bailment is for a fixed period that has not yet expired. In such a case the bailor is said to recover damages for injury to the bailor's **reversionary interest**— that is, the right that the bailor has to regain

---

[7] Boyd v Panama City Boatyard Inc. (Fla App) 522 So 2d 1058 (1988).

[8] Smith v Cooper Chevrolet, Inc. (Ala) 404 So 2d 49 (1981).

[9] First Bank Southdale v Kinney (Minn App) 392 NW2d 740 (1986).

[10] Kinder v Fantasy Coachworks Ltd. (Mo App) 762 SW2d 533 (1989).

the property on the expiration of the period of the bailment.

10. Duties of the Bailor

The bailor has certain duties concerning the condition of the property bailed. Sometimes the duty concerning goods furnished by the bailor is described as an implied warranty.

(a) CONDITION OF THE PROPERTY. In a mutual benefit bailment, as a bailment for hire, the bailor is under a duty to furnish goods reasonably fit for the purpose contemplated by the parties. If the bailee is injured or the bailee's property is damaged because of the defective condition of the bailed property, the bailor may be held liable.[11] If the bailment is for the sole benefit of the bailee, the bailor is under a duty to inform the bailee of known defects. If the bailee is harmed by a defect that was known by the bailor, the bailor is liable for damages.[12] If the bailor receives a benefit from the bailment, the bailor must not only inform the bailee of known defects, but must also make a reasonable investigation to discover defects. The bailor is liable for the harm resulting from those defects that would have been disclosed had the bailor made such an examination, in addition to those defects that were known to the bailor.

If the defect would not have been revealed by a reasonable examination, the bailor, regardless of classification of the bailment, is not liable for the harm that results.

In any case a bailee who is aware of a defective condition of the bailed property but makes use of the property and sustains injury because of its condition is barred by contributory negligence or assumption of risk from collecting damages from the bailor.

(b) BAILOR'S IMPLIED WARRANTY. In many cases the duty of the bailor is described as an implied warranty that the goods will be reasonably fit for their intended use. Apart from an implied warranty, the bailor may ex-

pressly warrant the condition of the property. In this event the bailor will be liable for breach of the warranty to the same extent as though the bailor had made a sale rather than a bailment of the property.

With the increase in car and equipment leasing, a new trend in the cases is beginning to appear. This trend extends to the bailee and third persons the benefit of an implied warranty by the bailor that the article is fit for its intended use and will remain so. This is distinguished from the warranty that the article was merely reasonably fit, or that it was fit at the beginning of the bailment, or that the property was free from defects known to the bailor or that a reasonable investigation would disclose. The significance of an analysis on the basis of warranty lies in the fact that warranty liability may exist even though the bailor was not negligent.[13]

11. Liability to Third Persons

When injuries are sustained by third persons resulting from the use of bailed property, liability may, under certain circumstances, be imposed on the bailee or the bailor.

(a) LIABILITY OF BAILEE. When the bailee injures a third person with the bailed property, as when the bailee runs into a third person while driving a rented automobile, the bailee is liable to the third person to the same extent as though the bailee were the owner of the property. When the bailee repairs bailed property, the bailee is liable to a third person who is injured as a result of the negligent way in which the repairs were made.

(b) LIABILITY OF BAILOR. The bailor is ordinarily not liable to a third person injured by the bailee while using the bailed property. In states that follow the common law, a person lending an automobile to another is not liable to a third person injured by the bailee when the lender did not know or have reason to know that the bailee was not a fit driver.

The bailor is liable, however, to the injured

[11] Hall v Skate Escape, Ltd. 171 Ga App 178, 319 SE2d 67 (1984).
[12] Burke Enterprises Inc. v Mitchell (Ky) 700 SW2d 789 (1987).

[13] Goldman v Phantom Freight, Inc. 162 Mich App 472, 413 NW2d 433 (1987).

third person: (a) if the bailor has entrusted a dangerous instrumentality to one known to the bailor to be ignorant of its dangerous character; (b) if the bailor has entrusted an instrumentality, such as an automobile, to one known to the bailor to be so incompetent or reckless that injury of third persons is a foreseeable consequence; (c) if the bailor has entrusted property with a defect that causes harm to the third person when the circumstances are such that the bailor would be liable to the bailee if the bailee were injured by the defect; or (d) if the bailee is using the bailed article, such as driving an automobile, as the bailor's employee in the course of employment.

(c) TEST DRIVES. When a prospective pur-

chaser takes an automobile for a test drive, unaccompanied by the dealer, the law of bailments applies. A prospective purchaser (bailee) who promises to return the car in good condition after a test drive is responsible for damage to the car during the test drive.[14] Third persons injured by the negligence of a prospective purchaser during a test drive unaccompanied by the dealer ordinarily have no recourse against the dealer. In the *Blackburn* case the plaintiff claimed that the dealer should be held responsible for the negligence of a prospective purchaser during a test drive.

[14]   Universal Ins. Co. v Vallejo, ___ Mich App ___, 446 NW2d 510 (1989).

BLACKBURN v EVERGREEN CHRYSLER PLYMOUTH
53 Wash App 146, 765 P2d 922 (1989)

Donald Lougee was considering the purchase of a used Chrysler "Lazer" from Evergreen Chrysler Plymouth. After a brief test drive Donald was undecided about buying the car. The salesman suggested that he take it home overnight for an extended test drive. Later that night Donald asked his best friend Bret Blackburn, a mechanic, to accompany him on a test drive. During that drive, Lougee struck a power pole. Blackburn was seriously injured. Blackburn sued Lougee and Evergreen for damages. Evergreen denied liability for the damage caused during the test drive. The court directed a verdict in favor of Evergreen, and Blackburn appealed.

REED, C.J. . . . The sole issue is whether the owner of a car can be held vicariously liable for its negligent operation by a prospective purchaser during a test drive. The Washington Supreme Court twice has considered this issue, in *Hamp v Universal Auto Co.* . . . and *Robbins v Greene* . . . The rule set forth in those cases, and followed in the overwhelming majority of jurisdictions, is that the owner of a car is not liable for a prospective purchaser's negligence, because the purchaser usually is regarded as a bailee, and not as an agent of the owner. The exception to this rule applies only when the prospective purchaser is accompanied by the owner or his agent, *who retains the right to direct the operation of the car*; the question is not decided by the owner's mere presence in the car, but is a function of the degree of control exercised, and is a question for the jury. . . .

The Blackburns presented no evidence at trial that would support a verdict in their favor under the rule of *Hamp* and *Robbins*. It was undisputed that no Evergreen representative was present at the time of the accident. When the owner does not accompany the prospective purchaser on the test drive, he loses any right he had to control physical actions of the prospective purchaser. He has wholly surrendered the operation and control of the car to the test driver. . . . We find no meaningful factual distinctions between this case and *Hamp*.

We note that the majority of those courts that have considered this issue have concluded that an agency relationship is *not* present in situations such as that presented by this case. . . .

In conclusion, we hold that the evidence presented in this case could support only the conclusion that Lougee was a bailee as a matter of law. As such, Evergreen has no liability for Lougee's actions, and Evergreen was entitled to [a] directed verdict.

[Judgment affirmed]

QUESTIONS

1. State the issue before the court.
2. What was the legal relationship between Lougee, the driver, and Evergreen, the dealer?
3. On what basis did the court decide the case?

(d) FAMILY PURPOSE DOCTRINE. Under what is called the **family purpose doctrine**, some courts hold that when the bailor supplies a car for the use of members of the bailor's family, the bailor is liable for harm caused by a member of the family while negligently driving the car. Other jurisdictions reject this doctrine and refuse to impose liability on the bailor of the automobile unless there is an agency relationship between the bailor and the driver.

SUMMARY

A bailment is the legal relationship that exists when personal property is delivered by the bailor into the possession of the bailee under an agreement, express or implied, that the identical property will be returned or delivered in accordance with the agreement. In a bailment the title remains with the bailor (or the principal or employer of the bailor) while the bailee has the right of possession. When a person comes into the possession of the personal property of another without the owner's consent, the law refers to the relationship as a constructive bailment.

Bailments may be classified in terms of benefit as for the (a) sole benefit of the bailor, (b) sole benefit of the bailee, or (c) benefit of both parties (mutual benefit bailment). Some courts state the standard of care required of a bailee in terms of the class of bailment. Thus, if the bailment is for the sole benefit of the bailor, the bailee is only required to exercise slight care and is only liable for gross negligence. When the bailment is for the sole benefit of the bailee, the bailee is liable for the slightest negligence. When the bailment is for the mutual benefit of the parties, which is the typical commercial bailment, the bailee is liable for ordinary negligence. In other states the courts do not make the above distinctions based on the class of bailment but apply a "reasonable care under the circumstances" standard. An ordinary bailee may limit liability, except for willful misconduct or where prohibited by statute or by a provision in the bailment contract. A bailee (1) must perform the bailee's part of the contract; (2) unless otherwise agreed, must bear the repair expenses incidental to the use of a machine in a bailment for hire situation; and (3) must return the identical property. The bailee has a lien on the bailed property until paid for storage or repair charges.

In a bailment for hire situation, such as the renting of a motor vehicle or a tool, the bailor is under a duty to furnish goods reasonably fit for the purposes contemplated by the parties. The bailor may be held liable for damages or injury caused by the defective condition of the bailed property. Should a bailee injure a third person while driving a rented motor vehicle, the bailee is liable to the third person as though the bailee were the owner of the vehicle.

QUESTIONS AND CASE PROBLEMS

1. What social forces are affected by the recognition of a bailment relationship?
2. Mercedes is employed by Park Lane Supply Company to sell its merchandise. In the course of the day she stops and leaves the company car she is driving on a parking lot operated by Simms Garage. The car is stolen from the lot. In a lawsuit brought against Simms on the theory that Simms was a negligent bailee, Simms raises the defense that there was no bailment because Mercedes did not own the car that was left with Simms. Is Simms correct?
3. What is a bailee's lien?
4. Compare a gift with a bailment.
5. Lillian loaned her automobile to Harry. Harry negligently drove the automobile and hit Mark. Mark sued Lillian for damages. Is Lillian liable?
6. Compare a bailment with a constructive bailment.
7. John Hayes and Lynn Magosian, auditors for a public accounting firm, went to lunch at the Bay View Restaurant in San Francisco. John left his raincoat with a coatroom attendant, while Lynn chose to bring her new raincoat with her to the dining room, where she hung it on a coat hook near her booth. When leaving the restaurant, Lynn discovered that an individual had taken her new, expensive raincoat and left behind a coat of little value. When John sought to claim his raincoat at the coatroom, it could not be found. The attendant advised that it might have been taken while he was on his break. John and Lynn sue the restaurant claiming that the restaurant was a bailee of the raincoats and had a duty to return them. Are both John and Lynn correct?
8. When Todd left for college in late August, he left his Boston Whaler motor boat at Terry's Low Tide Marina for land storage during the fall and winter months. Terry rented the boat to his customers on a daily basis for the entire month of September. When Todd discovered this, he sued Terry for conversion. Terry contends that he has the legal status of bailee, had proper possession of the boat, and that he cannot be held liable for conversion. Decide.
9. Rhodes parked his car on the self-service, park-and-lock lot of Pioneer Parking Lot, Inc. The ticket that he received from the ticket meter stated the following, "NOTICE. THIS CONTRACT LIMITS OUR LIABILITY—READ IT. WE RENT SPACE ONLY. NO BAILMENT IS CREATED. . . ." Rhodes parked the car himself and kept the keys. There was no attendant at the lot. The car was stolen from the lot. Rhodes sued the parking lot on the theory it had breached its duty as a bailee. Was there a bailment? [Rhodes v Pioneer Parking Lot, Inc. (Tenn) 501 SW2d 569]
10. Lewis put a paper bag containing $3,000 in cash in a railroad station coin-operated locker. After the period of the coin rental expired, a locker company employee opened the locker, removed the money, and because of the amount, surrendered it to police authorities, as was required by the local law. When Lewis demanded the return of the money from Aderholdt, the police property clerk, the latter required Lewis to prove his ownership to the funds because there were circumstances leading to the belief that the money had been stolen by Lewis. He sued the police property clerk and the locker company. Was the locker company liable for breach of duty as a bailee? [Lewis v Aderholdt (Dist Col App) 203 A2d 919]
11. Rhoda Newman underwent physical therapy at PTAR Inc. in Rome, Georgia for injuries sustained in an auto accident. At a therapy session on February 6, it was necessary for Newman to take off two necklaces. Newman placed one of the necklaces on a peg on the wall in the therapy room, and the therapist placed the other necklace on the peg. After the session Newman forgot to retrieve her jewelry from the wall pegs. When she called the next day for the forgotten jewelry, it could not be found. She sued PTAR Inc. for the value of the jewelry on a bailment theory. PTAR Inc. responded that there was no

bailment relationship established, since Newman retained the right to remove the jewelry from the wall pegs. Decide. [Newman v Physical Therapy Associates of Rome, Inc. 89 Ga App 211, 375 SE2d 253]

12. Contract Packers rented a truck from Hertz Truck Leasing. Packers' employee, Cintrone, was injured while riding in the truck being driven by his helper when the brakes of the truck did not function properly. Cintrone sued Hertz for breach of the implied warranty that the truck was fit for normal use on public highways. Hertz defended that implied warranties apply only to sales and not to bailments for hire. [Cintrone v Hertz Truck Leasing & Rental Service, 45 NJ 434, 212 A2d 769]

13. Herbert Pellegrini and Hardie Maloney traveled together to the Georgia Numismatic Association coin show in Atlanta. After the show Pellegrini suggested that Maloney get the car, while Pellegrini checked out of the Waverly Hotel. Maloney agreed to do so, after being assured by Pellegrini that he would watch Maloney's briefcase containing $31,000 in coins. Pellegrini watched as Maloney set the briefcase down beside Pellegrini's three bags. When Maloney returned with the car, Pellegrini walked up to the vehicle carrying all three pieces of his luggage, but he had left Maloney's briefcase in front of the hotel. When they returned for the briefcase, it was gone. Maloney sued Pellegrini, who defended that he was not liable for the criminal acts of some unknown person. Decide. [Simon v Maloney (La App) 579 So 2d 925.]

14. June Southard was employed in the Sporting Goods Department of K-Mart. While at work, she was struck by a mounted fish that fell from the wall. The fish was owned by taxidermist Marty Hansen. The fish had been delivered to K-Mart as a sample of Hansen's work should the public wish to contact him directly. Southard sued Hansen for her injuries, on the basis that Hansen was vicariously liable for the negligence of his agent, K-Mart, in improperly hanging the fish. Hansen contended that his legal relationship with K-Mart was that of bailor and bailee respectively, and that as the bailor he was not liable to Southard. Decide. [Southard v Hansen (SD) 376 NW2d 56]

15. Welge owned a sofa and chair that Baena Brothers agreed to reupholster and to reduce the size of the arms. The work was not done according to the contract, and the furniture when finished had no value to Welge and was not accepted by him. Baena sued him for the contract price. Welge counterclaimed for the value of the furniture. Decide. [Baena Brothers v Welge, 3 Conn Cir 67, 207 A2d 749]

23

SPECIAL BAILMENTS AND DOCUMENTS OF TITLE

Because of the nature of the property involved or because of the circumstances under which possession of that property is transferred, some bailments have a particularly strong effect on the public interest. These bailments are called **special bailments.** They include the storage of goods in a warehouse as well as the transportation of goods by a carrier. The warehouses may be general warehouses, refrigerated or cold-storage warehouses, farm-products warehouses, or special-purpose warehouses. The carriers may be motor, rail, or air carriers; water carriers utilizing boats or barges on the coastal waters, the Great Lakes, or the inland waterways; or pipeline companies transporting oil and gas.

The storage and transportation of goods, as well as the documents used to evidence their ownership, are vital to American commerce. For this reason the law has imposed on the special bailee a liability more stringent than that imposed on ordinary bailees.

Because of the public interest in protecting the property of travelers, hotelkeepers were absolutely liable for loss or damage to their guests' property at common law. Most states, however, have reduced this liability by statute for the benefit of hotelkeepers. Statutes allow for the limitation of liability where notices inform guests of the existence of a safe where valuables may be deposited.

A. WAREHOUSERS

The storage of goods with a warehouser is a special bailment. The rights and duties of warehousers are defined by the common law and Article 7 of the Uniform Commercial Code.

1. Definitions

A **warehouser** is a person engaged in the business of storing the goods of others for compensation. **Public warehousers** hold themselves out to serve the public generally without discrimination.

A building is not essential to warehousing. Thus, an enterprise that stores boats outdoors on land is engaged in warehousing, since it is engaged in the business of storing goods for hire.

2. Rights and Duties of Warehousers

The rights and duties of a warehouser are for the most part the same as those of a bailee under a mutual benefit bailment.[1] A warehouser is not an insurer of goods. A warehouser is, however, responsible for loss or damage to goods stored in its warehouse where the warehouser was negligent.[2]

(a) STATUTORY REGULATION. Most states have passed warehouse acts defining the rights and duties of warehousers and imposing regulations. Regulations affect charges and liens, bonds for the protection of patrons, maintenance of storage facilities in a suitable and safe condition, inspections, and general methods of transacting business.

(b) LIEN OF WAREHOUSER. The public warehouser has a lien against the goods for reasonable storage charges.[3] It is a **specific lien** in that it attaches only to the property with respect to which the charges arose and cannot be asserted against any other property of the same owner in the possession of the warehouser. However, the warehouser may make a lien carry over to the other goods by noting on the receipt for one lot of goods that a lien is also claimed thereon for charges as to the other goods. The warehouser's lien for storage charges may be enforced by sale after due notice has been given to all persons who claim any interest in the property stored.[4]

In the *Tate* case the warehouser contended that the sale of the stored property to pay for storage and other charges was proper under Article 7.

---

[1]   UCC § 7-204.
[2]   See Chapter 22, Section 8 of the text for a discussion of the burden of proof in such cases.
[3]   UCC § 7-209 (1). The warehouser's lien provision of the UCC is constitutional as a continuation of the common law lien.
[4]   UCC § 7-210.

TATE v ACTION MOVING & STORAGE, INC.
95 NC App 541, 383 SE2d 229 (1989)

On March 24, 1984, Joseph Tate requested Action-Mayflower Moving & Storage Co. (Action) to ship his household belongings from Charlotte, North Carolina to Monrovia, Liberia. On March 26, 1984, Action prepared a detailed inventory of

> Tate's belongings, loaded them on its truck and received the belongings at its warehouse. It was paid $1,000 down, with the balance to be paid prior to shipping. On September 26, 1984, Tate sent a check for $3,800 and requested that his goods be shipped to Monrovia. A dispute arose over the total cost to be paid. On October 24, 1984, Tate advised Action to deduct $2,708.20 from the $4,800 already paid to cover Action's charges, and to allow Tate to have a different carrier pick up the goods. Action did not accept this offer. Thereafter, Action sought payment for its charges. Fifteen months later, after due notice to Tate and after publishing a notice of public sale in the newspaper, Action sold Tate's goods at a public sale. Tate brought suit for conversion. Action defended that it was entitled to sell the goods to satisfy what was owed for storage and other charges.

BECTON, J. . . . It is well settled that "[a] warehouseman has a lien against the bailor on the goods covered by a warehouse receipt." [UCC §] 7-209(1). The trial court found as fact that Action never issued a warehouse receipt or any document which it intended to serve as one. Action excepted to this finding. We conclude that this finding is unsupported by the evidence.

We first note that a warehouse receipt is defined by the U.C.C. as simply "a receipt issued by a person engaged in the business of storing goods for hire." [UCC §] 1-201(45). Further, "[a] warehouse receipt need not be in any particular form." [UCC §] 7-201. Action's admission in its answer that it agreed to store plaintiff's goods for up to six months supports the contention that the "Household Goods Descriptive Inventory" which was given to plaintiff when his goods were loaded was intended by Action to serve as a warehouse receipt. We also believe it was sufficient to constitute a warehouse receipt for purposes of holding Action responsible under Article Seven for its actions as a warehouseman. This document issued by Action listed each item picked up, its condition, the owner's name, the origin loading address, and was signed and dated by Action's authorized agent and driver. . . .

Even in the case of an irregular warehouse receipt, defendant had the obligation to act as a reasonably careful person in relation to plaintiff's goods. [UCC §] 7-204(1). Also, in enforcing any lien against plaintiff, defendant had the duty to comply with [UCC §] 7-210, "Enforcement of warehouseman's lien." [UCC §] 7-210(3) provides the following:

> Before any sale pursuant to this section any person claiming a right in the goods may pay the amount necessary to satisfy the lien and the reasonable expenses incurred under this section. In that event the goods must not be sold, but must be retained by the warehouseman subject to the terms of the receipt and this article.

The record shows, as quoted above, that on 24 October 1984 plaintiff wrote a letter to defendant instructing defendant to deduct from the $4800.00 which defendant was holding, $2708.20 to cover defendant's charges to date, and that plaintiff would arrange to have a different carrier pick up his goods from defendant. Defendant admitted receiving this letter. In its letter of 29 October 1984, defendant stated that the charges incurred thus far for storage and origin charges amounted to $2010.70 ($709.80 storage plus $1300.90 origin charges). Therefore, plaintiff's offer of $2708.20 was far more than adequate to cover the amount owed to defendant.

Defendant's president, Jack Taylor, was questioned in his deposition about plaintiff's letter of 24 October 1984:

> Q. But you remember getting this letter? And I'll represent to you that I've been furnished with a copy from your attorney, so it was in your file.
>
> A. I don't remember when I got it. I remember reading it, but, yes, I remember reading it. I don't remember when I got it.
>
> Q. And it contains the language that I just read to you?
>
> A. Yes.
>
> Q. And you still refused to do that at that time?
>
> A. We didn't ship his goods.
>
> Q. You didn't deduct the amount that he said you could and release his goods so he could make other arrangements for shipment, did you?
>
> A. Huh-uh (no), I did not. We returned the entire amount of money to him.
>
> Q. Months later?
>
> A. (Witness nods head affirmatively.)

Defendant's admission by Jack Taylor that he refused to accept payment by plaintiff, but instead continued to hold the goods, mounting up storage fees, was a clear violation of [UCC §] 7-210(3). Plaintiff effectively satisfied the lien on his goods by giving defendant $4800.00 and instructing him to take out of that amount even more than defendant needed to satisfy the debt. After this payment, defendant then had no right to sell the goods.

[UCC §] 7-210(9) states that "[t]he warehouseman is liable for damages caused by failure to comply with the requirements for sale under this section and in case of willful violation is liable for conversion." We believe defendant's failure to comply with the requirements of [UCC §] 7-210(3) as stated above, constituted a willful violation of the requirements for sale and that the defendant was properly held liable for conversion of plaintiff's goods. . . .

[Judgment affirmed]

QUESTIONS

1. Did Action issue a warehouse receipt to Tate?
2. What is the significance of the warehouser's issuing a warehouse receipt?
3. In this case did Action have the right to sell the goods to cover its storage and other charges?

3.   Warehouse Receipts

A **warehouse receipt** is a written acknowledgment by a warehouser (bailee) that certain property has been received for storage from a named person called a **depositor** (bailor). The warehouse receipt is a memorandum of a contract between the **issuer**, the warehouse that prepares the receipt, and the depositor. It sets forth the terms of the contract for storage. No particular form is required, but usually the receipt will state (a) the location of the warehouse where the goods are stored, (b) date of issuance of the receipt, (c) the number of the receipt, (d) information on negotiability or nonnegotiability of the receipt, (e) the rate of storage and handling charges, (f) a description of the goods or the packages containing them, and (g) a statement of any liabilities incurred for which the warehouser claims a lien or security interest.[5]

The warehouse receipt is also a **document of title**—that is, a document that in the regular course of business or financing is treated as adequately evidencing that the person in possession of it is entitled to receive, hold, and dispose of the document and the goods it cov-

---

[5]   UCC § 7-202(2).

ers.[6] The person lawfully holding this receipt is then entitled to the goods represented by the receipt. A warehouse receipt as a document of title is a symbol representing the goods. This receipt can be bought or sold and can be used as security to obtain credit from a financial institution.

4. Rights of Holders of Warehouse Receipts

The rights of the holders of warehouse receipts differ, depending on whether the receipts are nonnegotiable or negotiable.

(a) NONNEGOTIABLE WAREHOUSE RECEIPTS. A warehouse receipt in which it is stated that the goods received will be delivered to a specified person is a **nonnegotiable warehouse receipt**. A transferee of a nonnegotiable receipt acquires only the title and rights that the transferor had actual authority to transfer.[7] Therefore, the transferee's rights may be defeated by a good faith purchaser of the goods from the transferor of the receipt.[8]

(b) NEGOTIABLE WAREHOUSE RECEIPTS. A warehouse receipt stating that the goods will be delivered to the "bearer," or "to the order of" any named person is a **negotiable warehouse receipt**. If such a receipt is duly negotiated, the person to whom it is negotiated may acquire rights superior to those of the transferor.

(1) Negotiation. If the receipt provides for the delivery of the goods "to the bearer," the receipt may be negotiated by transfer of the document. If the receipt provides for delivery of the goods "to the order of" a named individual, the document must be endorsed by that person and delivered.

(2) Due Negotiation. A warehouse receipt is "duly negotiated" when the holder purchases the document in good faith, without notice of any defense to it, for value, in the regular course of business or financing.[9] The holder of such a duly negotiated document ac-

quires title to the document and title to the goods.[10] The holder also acquires the direct obligation of the issuer to hold or deliver the goods according to the terms of the warehouse receipt.

The holder's rights cannot be defeated by the surrender of the goods by the warehouser to the depositor. Indeed, it is the duty of the warehouser to deliver the goods only to the holder of the negotiable receipt and to cancel such receipt on surrendering the goods.[11]

The rights of a purchaser of a warehouse receipt by due negotiation are not cut off, for example, by the claim (a) that an original owner was deprived of the receipt in "bearer" form by misrepresentation, fraud, mistake, loss, theft, or conversion; or (b) that a bona fide purchaser bought the goods from the warehouser.

A purchaser of a warehouse receipt who takes by due negotiation does not cut off all prior claims, however. If the person who deposited the goods with the warehouser did not own the goods or did not have power to transfer title to them, the purchaser of the receipt is subject to the title of the true owner.[12] Accordingly, when goods are stolen and delivered to a warehouse, and a warehouse receipt is issued for them, the owner prevails over the purchaser by due negotiation.

(c) WARRANTIES. The transferor of a negotiable or nonnegotiable warehouse receipt makes certain implied warranties for the protection of the transferee. These warranties are that (1) the receipt is genuine, (2) its transfer is rightful and effective, and (3) the transferor has no knowledge of any facts that impair the validity or worth of the receipt.[13]

5. Field Warehousing

Ordinarily, stored goods are placed in a ware-

---

[6] UCC § 1-201(15); § 7-102(1)(e).
[7] UCC § 7-504(1).
[8] UCC § 7-504(2)(b).
[9] UCC § 7-501(4).

[10] UCC § 7-502(1).
[11] UCC § 7-403(3).
[12] UCC § 7-503(1).
[13] UCC § 7-507. These warranties are in addition to any that may arise between the parties by virtue of the fact that the transferor is selling the goods represented by the receipt to the transferee. See Chapter 27 as to seller's warranties.

FIGURE 23–1   NEGOTIABLE WAREHOUSE RECEIPT
(1) warehouser, (2) depositor, (3) goods, (4) warehouser's lien, (5) negotiable delivery terms, (6) warehouser's authorized agent. A negotiable warehouse receipt contains a promise to deliver to bearer or to depositor's order, unlike a nonnegotiable warehouse receipt that promises only to deliver to depositor. End-of-chapter Question 6 presents a problem related to the following document.

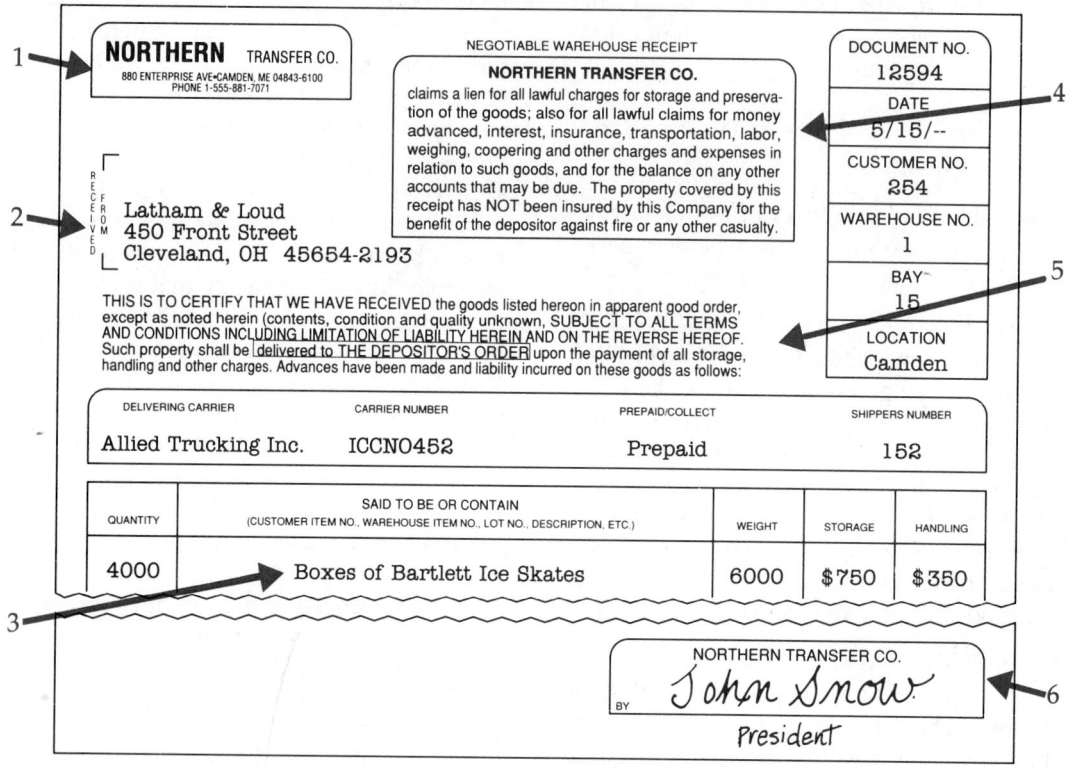

Front of receipt

Reverse side

house belonging to the warehouser. The owner of goods, such as a manufacturer, may keep the goods in the owner's own storage room or building. The warehouser may then take exclusive control over the room or the area in which the goods are stored and issue a receipt for the goods just as though they were in the warehouse. Such a transaction has the same legal effect with respect to other persons and purchasers of the warehouse receipts as though the property were in fact in the warehouse of the warehouser. This practice is called **field warehousing,** since the goods are not taken to the warehouse but remain "in the field."

The purpose of field warehousing is to create warehouse receipts that the owner of the goods is able to pledge as security for loans. The owner could, of course, have done this by actually placing the goods in a warehouse, but this would have involved the expense of transportation and storage.

6. Limitation of Liability of Warehouser

A warehouser may limit liability by a provision in the warehouse receipt specifying the maximum amount for which the warehouser can be held liable. This privilege is subject to two qualifications. First, the customer must be given the choice of storing the goods without such limitation if the customer pays a higher storage rate, and second, the limitation must be stated as to each item or as to each unit of weight. A limitation is proper when it states that the maximum liability for a piano is $1,000 or that the maximum liability per bushel of wheat is a stated amount. Conversely, there cannot be a blanket limitation of liability, such as "maximum liability $50," when the receipt covers more than one item.

General contract law determines whether a limitation clause is a part of the contract between the warehouser and the customer. A limitation in a warehouse receipt is not part of the contract when the receipt is delivered to the customer a substantial period of time after the goods have been left for storage.

B. COMMON CARRIERS

The purpose of a bailment may be transportation, not storage. In such case the bailee may be a common carrier.

7. Definitions

A **carrier** of goods is an individual or organization undertaking the transportation of goods, regardless of the method of transportation or the distance covered. The **consignor** or shipper is the person who delivers goods to the carrier for shipment. The **consignee** is the person to whom the goods are shipped and to whom the carrier should deliver the goods.

A carrier may be classified as (a) a **common carrier**, which holds itself out as willing to furnish transportation for compensation

without discrimination to all members of the public who apply, assuming that the goods to be carried are proper and the facilities of the carrier are available;[14] (b) a **contract carrier**, which transports goods under individual contracts; or (c) a **private carrier**, which is owned and operated by the firm transporting goods by it, such as a truck fleet owned and operated by an industrial firm. The common carrier law applies to the first class, the bailment law to the second, and the law of employment to the third.

8. Bills of Lading

When the carrier accepts goods for shipment or forwarding, the carrier ordinarily issues to the shipper a **bill of lading** in the case of land or water transportation or an **airbill** for air transportation.[15] This instrument is a document of title and provides rights similar to those provided by a warehouse receipt. A bill of lading is both a receipt for the goods and a memorandum of a contract stating the terms of carriage. Title to the goods may be transferred by transfer of the bill of lading made with that intention.

With respect to intrastate shipments, bills of lading are governed by the Uniform Commercial Code. As to interstate shipments, bills of lading are regulated by the Federal Bills of Lading Act.[16]

(a) CONTENTS OF BILL OF LADING. The form of the bill of lading is regulated in varying degrees by administrative agencies.[17] For example, the Interstate Commerce Commission requires that negotiable bills of lading be printed on yellow paper, and nonnegotiable or straight bills of lading be printed on white paper.[18]

As against the bona fide transferee of the bill of lading, a carrier is bound by the recitals

---

[14] Market Transport Ltd. v Maudlin, 301 Or 727, 725, P2d 914 (1986).

[15] Imitiaz v Emery Airfreight, Inc. (Tex Civ App) 728 SW2d 897 (1987).

[16] Title 49, USC § 81 et seq.

[17] The UCC contains no provision regulating the form of the bill of lading.

[18] Bill of Lading, 55 ICC 671.

in the bill as to the contents, quantity, or weight of goods.[19] This means that the carrier must produce the goods that are described or pay damages for failing to do so. This rule is not applied if facts appear on the face of the bill that should keep the transferee from relying on the recital.

(b) NEGOTIATION. A bill of lading is a **negotiable bill of lading** when by its terms the goods are to be delivered "to bearer" or "to the order of" a named person.[20] Any other bill of lading, such as one that consigns the goods to a named person, is a **nonnegotiable** or **straight bill of lading**. Like transferees of warehouse receipts who take by due negotiation, holders of bills of lading who take by due negotiation ordinarily also acquire the title to the bills and title to the goods represented by them. These rights are not affected by the fact that (1) the original owner had been somehow deprived of the bill in bearer form, (2) the goods had already been surrendered by the carrier, or (3) the goods had been stopped in transit.[21] The rights are defeated by the true owner, however, when a thief delivers the goods to the carrier and then negotiates the bill of lading.[22]

(c) WARRANTIES. By transferring for value a bill of lading, whether negotiable or nonnegotiable, the transferor makes certain implied warranties to the transferee. The transferor impliedly warrants that (1) the bill of lading is genuine, (2) its transfer is rightful and is effective to transfer the goods represented thereby, and (3) the transferor has no knowledge of facts that would impair the validity or worth of the bill of lading.[23]

9.   Rights of Common Carrier

A common carrier of goods has the right to make reasonable and necessary rules for the conduct of its business. It has the right to charge such rates for its services as yield it a fair return on the property devoted to the business of transportation, but the exact rates charged are regulated by the Interstate Commerce Commission in the case of interstate carriers and by state commissions in the case of intrastate carriers.[24] As an incident of the right to charge for its services, a carrier may charge **demurrage**—a charge for the detention of its cars or equipment for an unreasonable length of time by either the consignor or consignee.[25]

As security for unpaid transportation and service charges, a common carrier has a lien on goods that it transports. The carrier's lien also secures demurrage charges, the costs of preservation of the goods, and the costs of sale to enforce the lien.[26] The lien of a carrier is a specific lien. It attaches only to goods shipped under the particular contract, but includes all of the shipment even if it is sent in installments. When part of the shipment is delivered to the consignee, the lien attaches to the portion remaining in possession of the carrier.

10.   Duties of Common Carrier

A common carrier is generally required (a) to receive and carry proper and lawful goods of all persons who offer them for shipment so long as the carrier has room; (b) to furnish facilities that are adequate for the transportation of freight in the usual course of business, and to furnish proper storage facilities for goods awaiting shipment or awaiting delivery after shipment;[27] (c) to follow the directions given by the shipper; (d) to load and unload goods delivered to it for shipment (in less-than-carload lots in the case of railroads), but the shipper or consignee may assume this duty by contract or custom; and (e) to deliver the

---

[19]   UCC § 7-301(1).
[20]   UCC § 7-104(1)(a).
[21]   UCC § 7-502(2).
[22]   UCC § 7-503(1).
[23]   UCC § 7-507; Federal Bills of Lading Act (FBLA), 49 USC § 114, 116. When the transfer of the bill of lading is part of a transaction by which the transferor sells the goods represented thereby to the transferee, there will also arise the warranties that are found in other sales of goods.

[24]   GMW, Inc. v Certified Parts Corp. 135 Wis 2d 503, 400 NW2d 512 (1986).
[25]   Betsy Ross Foods v A, C & Y Railway Co. 17 Ohio App 3d 145, 468 NE2d 338 (1983).
[26]   UCC § 7-307(1); FBLA, 49 USC § 105.
[27]   Exquisite Form Industries v Transporters Ragat (DC Tex) 585 F Supp 473 (1984).

goods in accordance with the shipment contract.

Goods must be delivered at the usual place of delivery at the specified destination. When goods are shipped under a negotiable bill of lading, the carrier must not deliver the goods without obtaining possession of the bill, properly indorsed. When goods are shipped under a straight bill of lading, the carrier is justified in delivering the goods to the consignee or the consignee's agent without receiving the bill of lading, unless notified by the shipper to deliver the goods to someone else. If the carrier delivers the goods to the wrong person, the carrier is liable for breach of contract and for the tort of conversion.

11. Liabilities of Common Carrier

When goods are delivered to a common carrier for immediate shipment and while they are in transit, the carrier is absolutely liable for any loss or damage to the goods unless it can prove that the loss or damage was due solely to one or more of the following excepted causes: (a) act of God, meaning a natural phenomenon that is not reasonably foreseeable;[28] (b) act of public enemy, such as the military forces of an opposing government, as distinguished from ordinary robbers; (c) act of public authority, such as a health officer removing goods from a truck; (d) act of the shipper, such as fraudulent labeling or defective packing; or (e) inherent nature of the goods, such as those naturally tending to spoil or deteriorate.

The *Smith* case illustrates the extent of a common carrier's liability for damages to goods in transit.

---

[28] Utilities Pipeline Co. v American Petrofina (Tex Civ App) 760 SW2d 719 (1988).

SMITH v WATSON
(ND) 406 NW2d 685 (1987)

Glen Smith contracted with Dave Watson, a common carrier, to transport 720 hives of live bees along with associated equipment from Idabel, Oklahoma to Mandan, North Dakota. At 9:00 a.m. on May 24, 1984, while en route, Watson's truck skidded off the road and tipped over, severely damaging the cargo. Watson notified Smith of what had happened, and Smith immediately set out for the scene of the accident. He arrived at 6:00 p.m. with two bee experts and a Bobcat loader. They were hindered by the turned-over truck on top of the cargo, and they determined that they could not safely salvage the cargo that evening. The next day an insurance adjuster determined that the cargo was a total loss. The adjuster directed a bee expert, Dr. Moffat, to conduct the cleanup. Smith sued Watson for damages. The trial court found in favor of Smith but reduced his damages by $12,326.98 for failure to mitigate damages. Both Smith and Watson appealed.

VANDE WALLE, J. . . . A plaintiff seeking to recover damages has a duty to minimize or mitigate his damages and may not recover for damages which could have been avoided by reasonable efforts under the existing circumstances. However, the duty of a plaintiff to mitigate damages is not applicable where the defendant, who by breach of contract has caused injury to the plaintiff, has equal knowledge and opportunity to minimize the damages by performing the contract as he has obligated himself to do. . . .

Pursuant to Section 8-09-01, N.D.C.C., a common carrier is liable for loss or injury to property for any cause whatever, except for specified causes not relevant to this case, from the time the carrier accepts the property until proper delivery. Even when goods being transported by common carrier are initially damaged by an act of God or other cause for which the carrier is exempt from liability, the common carrier has a duty to minimize or mitigate damages to the property and is liable for failure to do so.

In this case the damage to Smith's bees, hives, and equipment resulted from a highway accident involving Watson's driver for which, the trial court determined, Smith was not responsible. It is undisputed that the cleanup and salvage operation for the accident was conducted through the efforts of Watson's insurance company. It is also undisputed that whatever cargo was salvageable was used as payment for the cleanup operation. Although Smith happened to be in the vicinity of the accident [after] it occurred, Watson had the primary responsibility to retain the necessary personnel and machinery to effectuate a cleanup and salvage operation to minimize loss of or damage to the cargo. Watson, as the carrier responsible for the accident, was liable for the cost of the cleanup operation. Therefore, Watson was the beneficiary of the salvaged cargo which was used as payment for those cleanup costs. We hold that, under these circumstances, Watson had a duty to mitigate the damages to Smith's property as a result of the accident occurring during Watson's transport of the property and that Watson cannot assert a failure by Smith to minimize damages where Watson had the primary responsibility as well as equal opportunity and knowledge to mitigate damages. . . .

[The district court judgment is increased by $12,096 and, as so modified, is affirmed]

QUESTIONS

1. State the rule that governs the liability of a common carrier for loss or damage to goods occurring after the carrier has accepted the goods and before proper delivery of the goods has been made.
2. Does the shipper have an obligation to mitigate damages when goods being transported by a common carrier are initially damaged by an "act of God"?
3. Which party, the shipper or carrier, was responsible for the cost of the cleanup operation required after Watson's accident?

(a) CARRIER'S LIABILITY FOR DELAY. A carrier is liable for losses caused by its failure to deliver goods within a reasonable time. Thus, the carrier is liable for losses arising from a fall in price or a deterioration of the goods caused by the carrier's unreasonable delay. The carrier, however, is not liable for every delay. The risk of ordinary delays incidental to transporting goods is assumed by the shipper.

(b) LIABILITY OF INITIAL AND CONNECTING CARRIERS. When goods are carried over the lines of several carriers, the initial and the final carrier, as well as the carrier on whose lines the loss is sustained, may be liable to the shipper or the owner of the goods.

Only one payment, however, may be obtained by the shipper.

(c) LIMITATION OF LIABILITY OF CARRIER. In the absence of a constitutional or statutory prohibition, a carrier generally has the right to limit its liability by contract.[29]

Nonrail common carriers operating within the jurisdiction of the Interstate Commerce Commission (ICC) may limit their liability to consignees for the negligent loss of consigned items to a certain stated dollar amount, such as $100 per package, provided that such limitations are filed and approved by the ICC as

[29]   Star-kist Foods v Chicago, Rock Island & Pacific R.R. (DC Ill) 586 F Supp 252 (1984).

part of the carriers' tariffs (rate schedules). Additionally, shippers must be allowed the option of selecting a higher value for the shipment, with payment of higher freight charges. The ICC has been barred from approving tariffs limiting the common law liability of rail common carriers for losses to property transported by rail in interstate commerce.[30]

(d) NOTICE OF CLAIM. The bill of lading and applicable government regulations may require that a carrier be given notice of any claim for damages or loss of goods within a specified time, generally within nine months.

(e) C.O.D. SHIPMENT. A common carrier transporting goods under a C.O.D. (cash on delivery) shipment may not make delivery of the goods without first receiving payment. If it does so, it is liable to the shipper for any loss resulting therefrom. If the carrier accepts a check from the consignee and the check is not honored by the bank on which it is drawn, the carrier is liable to the shipper for the amount thereof.

(f) REJECTED SHIPMENTS. When a common carrier tenders delivery of consigned goods to a consignee that refuses to accept the delivery, the carrier is no longer a common carrier, but becomes a warehouser. When the carrier-turned-warehouser receives new shipping instructions from the owner, its status again changes to that of a common carrier.

In the *Fisher* case the status of the trucking firm, and therefore its liability, was in question.

---

[30]   49 USC § 20 (11).

FISHER CORPORATION v CONSOLIDATED FREIGHTWAYS, INC.

230 Neb 832, 434 NW2d 17 (1989)

In June of 1984 Fisher Corporation delivered 132 VCRs (recorders) to Consolidated Freightways, Inc. at its California warehouse for shipment to World Radio, Inc. at Council Bluffs, Iowa. On July 6, 1984, World Radio rejected the shipment as duplicative of earlier shipments. On July 7, Consolidated loaded all of the VCRs onto a trailer, sealed it, and placed the trailer at the south end of its terminal. Also on July 7, it sent a letter to Fisher notifying it of World Radio's rejection and seeking disposition instructions. Testimony showed that Consolidated's security measures were reasonable and equal to those of other trucking companies in the area. On July 17, Consolidated discovered that a 5-foot hole had been cut in the chain link fence and that fifty-four recorders were missing. After the theft had occurred, but before Consolidated had discovered the theft, Fisher notified Consolidated to return the recorders to its California warehouse. When Consolidated did not return the stolen recorders, Fisher sued Consolidated for their value. The district court dismissed the suit, and Fisher appealed.

CAPORALE, J. . . . In its original petition, Fisher pled that it was entitled to recover on the theory that at the time of the theft, Consolidated was serving as a warehouser, or alternatively, on the theory that at the relevant time, Consolidated was serving as a common carrier. A warehouser, that is, one "engaged in the business of storing goods for hire," U.C.C. § 7-102(1)(h), is, in the absence of a contrary agreement, liable for goods lost while in its possession only if . . . the loss occurred through its negligence.

See U.C.C. § 7-204. A common carrier, on the other hand, is an insurer against loss from whatever cause, except an act of nature, of the public enemy, or of the owner of the goods. . . .

The bill of lading under which the recorders came into Consolidated's possession stated nothing about Consolidated's liability for loss should it find itself unable to deliver the recorders to World Radio as Fisher had directed. Under such a circumstance, once a common carrier tenders delivery of the consigned goods to a consignee which refuses delivery, the carrier loses its status as a common carrier and becomes a warehouser. . . . Where a common carrier turned warehouser, acting as a bailee, accepts instructions from the bailor to ship goods to a specified location, its status as a warehouser again changes to that of common carrier. . . .

The evidence is sufficient to sustain the jury's special finding that Consolidated did not receive Fisher's return authorization until after the theft had taken place, thereby making Consolidated a warehouser at the time of the loss rather than a common carrier. Moreover, the evidence concerning the manner in which Consolidated stored the recorders does not compel but does support the finding implicit in the general verdict that Consolidated had not been negligent. . . .

[Judgment affirmed]

QUESTIONS

1. When does a common carrier's warehouse status change back to that of a common carrier?
2. Was Consolidated a common carrier at the time the recorders were stolen from the trailer?
3. Was Consolidated negligent in the manner in which it stored the recorders? Why is this significant?

C.   FACTORS

A **factor** is a special type of bailee who sells consigned goods as though the factor were the owner of those goods.

12.   Definitions

Entrusting a person with the possession of property for the purpose of sale is commonly called **selling on consignment**.[31] The owner who consigns the goods for sale is the **consignor**. The person or agent to whom they are consigned is the factor or **consignee**; this individual may also be known as a commission merchant. A consignee's compensation is known as a **commission** or **factorage**. In a sale on consignment the property remains the property of the owner or consignor, and the consignee acts as the agent of the owner to pass the owner's title to the buyer.

13.   Effect of Factor Transaction

Since a factor is by definition authorized by the consignor to sell the goods entrusted to the factor, such a sale will pass the title of the consignor to the purchaser. Before the factor makes the sale, the goods belong to the consignor, but in some instances creditors of the factor may ignore the consignor and treat the goods as though they belonged to the consignee.[32] If the consignor is not the owner, as when a thief delivers stolen goods to the factor, a sale by the factor is an unlawful conversion. It is constitutional, however, to provide by statute that the factor who sells in good faith in ignorance of the rights of other persons in the

---

[31]   Amoco Oil Co. v DZ Enterprises Inc. (DC NY) 607 F Supp 595 (1985).

[32]   UCC § 2-326.

goods is protected from liability and cannot be treated as a converter of the goods.

D.   HOTELKEEPERS

A hotelkeeper has a bailee's liability with respect to property specifically entrusted to the hotelkeeper's care. In addition, the hotelkeeper has special duties with respect to a guest's property brought into the hotel.

14.   Definitions

The rules governing the special relationship between a hotelkeeper and guest arose in part because of the special needs of travelers. The legal definitions of *hotelkeeper* and *guest* are meant to exclude lodging of a more permanent character, such as that provided by boardinghouse keepers to boarders.

(a) HOTELKEEPER. The term **hotelkeeper** is used by law to refer to an operator of a hotel, motel, or tourist home, or to anyone who is regularly engaged in the business of offering living accommodations to all transient persons. In the early law the hotelkeeper was called an innkeeper or a tavernkeeper.

(b) GUEST. The essential element in the definition of a **guest** is that the guest is a transient. The guest need not be a traveler or come from a distance. A person living within a short distance of a hotel who engages a room at the hotel and remains there overnight is a guest.

A person who enters a hotel at the invitation of a guest or attends a dance or a banquet given at the hotel is not a guest. Similarly, the guest of a registered occupant of a motel room who shares the room with the occupant without the knowledge or consent of the management is not a guest of the motel, since there is no relationship between that person and the motel.

15.   Duration of Guest Relationship

The relationship of guest and hotelkeeper does not begin until a person is received as a guest by the hotelkeeper. The relationship terminates when the guest leaves or when the guest ceases to be a transient, as when the guest arranges for a more or less permanent residence at the hotel. The transition from the status of guest to the status of boarder or lodger must be clearly indicated. It is not established by the mere fact that one remains at the hotel for a long period, even though it runs into months.

16.   Hotelkeeper's Liability for Guest's Property

As to property expressly entrusted to the hotelkeeper's care, the hotelkeeper has a bailee's liability. At common law the hotelkeeper was an insurer of any other property of a guest.[33] As exceptions to this absolute liability at common law, the hotelkeeper is not liable for loss caused by an act of God, public enemy, act of public authority, the inherent nature of the property, or the fault of the guest.

In most states statutes limit or provide a method of limiting the common law liability of a hotelkeeper. The statutes may limit the extent of liability, reduce the liability of a hotelkeeper to that of an ordinary bailee, or permit the hotelkeeper to limit liability by contract or by posting a notice of the limitation. Some statutes relieve the hotelkeeper from liability when directions for depositing valuables with the hotelkeeper are posted on the doors of the rooms occupied, and the guest fails to comply with the directions. When a statute permits a hotel receiving valuables for deposit in its safe deposit box to limit its liability to the amount specified in the agreement signed by the guest, such limitation binds the guest even though the loss was caused by negligence on the part of the hotel. A hotelkeeper must substantially comply with such a statute in order to obtain its protection.[34]

In the *Hicks* case the court considered the question of whether a statute limiting a hotelkeeper's liability for the loss of a guest's property applies to a situation in which the hotel's negligence caused the loss.

[33]   Shepherd Fleets Inc. v Opryland Hotel Inc. (Tenn App) 759 SW2d 914 (1988).
[34]   H.D. Grimes v M. H. M. Inc. 299 Ark 560, 776 SW2d 336 (1989).

HICKS v DAYS INNS OF AMERICA INC.
183 Ga App 4, 357 SE2d 847 (1987)

The Hicks family, thinking that their room at the Days Inn was secure against theft, left several hundred dollars and a valuable antique pistol there for a short period of time. When they returned to their room, they discovered that the money and pistol had been stolen. They sued the hotelkeeper, contending that it was responsible for the loss of the money and the valuable pistol, due to its negligence in not providing better security for the room. They further asserted that the limitation of liability under state law does not apply to limit a hotelkeeper's liability for its own negligent acts. Days Inn disagreed. The court held that under state law the hotelkeeper's liability for negligence in the loss of a guest's property was limited to $100. The Hicks family appealed.

CARLEY, J. The evidence of record is undisputed that appellee had posted, on the inside of the door to appellants' motel room, a notice which required guests to store their valuables in the motel's safe and which otherwise limited appellee's liability for the loss of a guest's property to $100 unless the guest had made prior written notification that the value of his property exceeded that amount. See OCGA § 43-21-10; former OCGA § 43-21-12. This was a sufficient disclosure of the security measures that were made available by appellee for its guests' property and of the limitation on its liability as provided by the applicable statutes. . . .

In support of its motion for summary judgment as to appellants' negligence claim, appellee did not rely upon its publication of the notice authorized by OCGA § 43-21-10, pursuant to which it would "be relieved from responsibility" for appellants' "valuable articles" which were not placed in appellee's safe. Instead, appellee relied only upon its publication of the notice that is authorized by OCGA § 43-21-12 and which applies to the loss of property "other than valuable articles." The evidence is undisputed that appellee had posted, on the inside of the door to appellants' room, the notice authorized by OCGA § 43-21-12. Appellants assert only that they did not read the entire notice. They did not notify appellee in writing that their property's value was in excess of $100. Under these circumstances and OCGA § 43-21-12 as it existed at the time of appellants' loss, appellee's liability for their property damage was limited to $100. Accordingly, the trial court was correct in granting summary judgment limiting appellee's liability for its alleged negligence to a recovery of this amount. "The General Assembly by [enacting OCGA § 43-21-12] authorizing a limitation of liability has preempted the field on that subject." *Ellerman v. Atlanta American Hotel Corp.*, 126 Ga. App. 194, 196 (2), 191 S.E.2d 295 (1972).

[Judgment affirmed]

QUESTIONS

1. Did Days Inns comply with the state law limiting the common law liability of hotelkeepers?
2. Does the statutory limitation of liability for loss of a guest's property to $100 apply to situations where it is proven that the hotel's negligence caused the loss?

17.   Hotelkeeper's Lien

The hotelkeeper has a lien on the baggage of guests for the agreed charges or, if no express agreement was made, for the reasonable value of the accommodations furnished. Statutes permit the hotelkeeper to enforce this lien by selling the goods of the guests at a public sale. The lien of the hotelkeeper is terminated by (a) the guest's payment of the hotel charges, (b) any conversion of the guest's goods by the hotelkeeper, and (c) surrender of the goods to the guest. In the last situation an exception is made when the goods are given to the guest for temporary use.

18.   Boarders or Lodgers

To those persons who are permanent boarders or lodgers rather than transient guests, the hotelkeeper owes only the duty of an ordinary bailee of personal property under a mutual benefit bailment.

A hotelkeeper has no common law right of lien on property of boarders or lodgers, as distinguished from guests, in the absence of an express agreement creating such a lien. In a number of states, however, legislation giving a lien to a boarding house or a lodging housekeeper has been adopted.

SUMMARY

A warehouser stores the goods of others for compensation and, for the most part, has the rights and duties of a bailee in an ordinary mutual benefit bailment. A warehouser issues a warehouse receipt to the depositor of the goods. This receipt is a document of title that may entitle the person in possession of the receipt to receive the goods. The warehouse receipt can be bought, sold, or used as security to obtain financing from banks. A nonnegotiable warehouse receipt states that the goods received will be delivered to a specified person. A negotiable warehouse receipt states that the goods will be delivered to the "bearer," or "to the order of" a named person. If a negotiable warehouse receipt is duly negotiated, the transferee may acquire rights superior to the transferor. A warehouser may limit its liability for loss or damage to goods due to its own negligence to an agreed valuation of the property stated in the warehouse receipt, provided the depositor is given the right to store the goods without the limitation, at a higher storage rate.

A common carrier is in the business of accepting goods from the public for transportation to a designated destination for compensation. It issues to the shipper a bill of lading or an airbill. Both of these are documents of title and provide rights similar to those provided by a warehouse receipt. A common carrier is absolutely liable for any loss or damage to the goods unless the carrier can show that the loss was caused by an act of God, an act of a public enemy, an act of a public authority, an act of the shipper, or the inherent nature of the goods. Subject to certain limitations, the carrier may limit its liability by contract.

A factor is a special type of bailee, who has possession of the owner's property for the purpose of sale. The factor or consignee receives a commission on the sale.

A hotelkeeper is in the business of providing living accommodations to transient persons. These persons are called guests. Subject to exceptions, hotelkeepers were absolutely liable for loss or damage to their guests' property at common law. Most states, however, provide a method of limiting the common law liability of a hotelkeeper. A hotelkeeper has a lien on the property of the guest for the agreed charges.

QUESTIONS AND CASE PROBLEMS

1. What social forces are involved in the rule of law governing the liability of a common carrier for loss of freight?

2. Gowan sent goods by the Southern Mississippi Railroad to Robert in New Orleans. Fulton appeared in the New Orleans freight office of the

railroad and stated that he was Robert's employee, sent to pick up the shipment. The shipment was given to Fulton without any proof of his authority from Robert. Robert later demanded the goods, and it was then learned that Fulton did not have any authority from Robert and had disappeared with the shipment. Is the railroad liable to Robert?

3. Compare the liens of carriers, warehousers, and hotels in terms of being specific.

4. Compare the limitation of the liability of a warehouser and of a hotel.

5. Compare warehouse receipts and bills of lading as to negotiability.

6. Latham and Loud, sporting goods manufacturers' representatives in Cleveland, Ohio, hijacked a truckload of ice skates from the Bartlett Shoe and Skate Company of Bangor, Maine. Latham and Loud warehoused the skates at the Northern Transfer Company's warehouse and received a negotiable warehouse receipt. Preston, a lender who had previous business dealings with Latham and Loud and believed them to be honest individuals, made a bona fide purchase of the receipt. Bartlett discovered that the skates were at Northern's Warehouse and informed Northern of the hijacking. Northern delivered the skates to Bartlett. Latham and Loud fled the state. Preston, claiming that he was entitled to delivery of the skates, brought an action against Northern, since he acquired the negotiable receipt by due negotiation. Was Preston entitled to the skates?

7. Welch Brothers Trucking, Inc., a common carrier, made an agreement with B & L Export and Import Co. of San Francisco to transport a shipment of freshly harvested bluefin tuna from Calais, Maine to the Japan Air Lines freight terminal at New York's Kennedy Airport. The bluefin had been packed in ice and were to be shipped by Japan Air to Tokyo. Fresh bluefin at the peak of their autumnal fattening are used in the traditional Japanese raw fish dish *sashimi* and command very high prices. When transportation charges were not paid by B & L's representative in New York, Welch Brothers refused to release the shipment to Japan Air Lines. B & L's representative in New York explained that he had no check-writing authority, but assured Welch that it would be paid and pleaded for the release of the cargo because of its perishable nature. Transportation charges were not paid in the next 12-hour period because the principals of B & L were on a business trip to the Far East and could not be contacted. After waiting the 12-

hour period, Welch sent a telegram to B & L's offices in San Francisco stating the amount due and that it intended to auction the cargo in 24 hours if transportation charges were not paid. Welch also sent telegrams to all fish wholesalers listed in the New York City Yellow Pages seeking bidders after advising that the cargo would be sold at auction in 24 hours if the charges were not paid. Welch sold the shipment to the highest bidder at the appointed time for an amount just in excess of the transportation charges plus a demurrage charge for the 36-hour waiting period. When the principals of B & L were later informed of what happened, they were outraged and initiated suit against Welch for the profits they would have earned had the cargo been shipped and sold in Japan. Decide.

8. Richard Schewe and others placed personal property in a building occupied by the Winnebago County Fair Association, Inc. The property was destroyed by fire. Prior to placing their property in the building they signed a "Storage Rental Agreement" prepared by the County Fair Association, which stated in part that "No liability exists for damage or loss to the stored equipment from the perils of fire. . . ." The individuals brought suit against the County Fair Association to recover damages for the losses on the theory of negligence of a warehouser. The County Fair Association defended that the language in the storage agreement relieved it of all liability. [Allstate v Winnebago County Fair Association, Inc. 131 Ill App 3d 225, 86 Ill Dec 233, 475 NE2d 230]

9. Buffett sent a violin to Strotokowsky by International Parcel Service (IPS), a common carrier. Buffet declared the value of the parcel at $500 on the pick-up receipt given him by the IPS driver. The receipt also stated:

Unless a greater value is declared in writing on this receipt, the shipper hereby declares and agrees that the released value of each package covered by this receipt is $100.00, which is a reasonable value under the circumstance surrounding the transportation.

When the parcel was not received by Strotokowsky, he sued IPS for the full retail value of the violin—$2,000. IPS raised the defense that it was liable for just $100. Decide.

10. Dovax Fabrics, Inc. had been shipping goods by a common carrier, G & A Delivery Corp., for over a year, during which all of G & A's bills to Dovax bore the notation, "Liability limited to $50 unless value is declared and paid for. . . ."

Dovax gave G & A three lots of goods, having a total value of $1,799.95. A truck containing all three was stolen that night, without negligence on the part of G & A. Should Dovax recover from G & A (a) $1,799.95, (b) $150 for three shipments, or (c) nothing? [Dovax Fabrics, Inc. v G & A Delivery Corp. (NY Civ Ct) 4 UCCRS 492]

11. A guest in a motel opened the bedroom window at night and went to sleep. During the night a prowler pried open the screen, entered the room, and stole property of the guest. The guest sued the motel. The motel asserted that it was not responsible for property in the possession of the guest and that the guest had been contributorily negligent in opening the window. Could the guest recover damages? [Buck v Hankin, 217 Pa Super 262, 269 A2d 344]

12. On March 30, Emery Air Freight Corp. picked up a shipment of furs from Hopper Furs, Inc. Hopper's chief of security filled in certain items in the airbill. In the box entitled ZIP Code, he mistakenly placed the figure "61,045," which was the value of the furs. The ZIP Code box is immediately above the "declared value" box. The airbill contained a clause limiting liability to $10 per pound of cargo lost or damaged, unless the shipper makes a declaration of value in excess of the amount and pays a higher fee. A higher fee was not charged in this case, and Gerald Doane signed the airbill for the carrier and took possession of the furs. The furs were lost in transit by Emery, and Hopper sued for the value of the furs, $61,045. Emery's offer to pay $2,150, the $10 per pound rate set forth in the airbill, was rejected. Hopper claims that the amount $61,045, which was mistakenly placed in the ZIP Code box, was in fact part of the contract set forth in the airbill and that Emery, on reviewing the contract, must have realized a mistake was made. Decide. [Hopper Furs, Inc. v. Emery Air Freight Corp. (CA8 Mo) 749 F2d 1261]

13. Jose Maria Berga de Lema, a Brazilian resident, arrived in New York City. His luggage consisted of three suitcases, an attache case, and a cylindrical bag. The attache case and the cylindrical bag contained jewels, valued at $300,000. Mr. de Lema went from JFK Airport to the Waldorf Astoria Hotel, where he gave the three suitcases to hotel staff in the garage, and then he went to the lobby to register. The assistant manager, Mr. Baez, summoned room clerk Mr. Tamburino to assist him. Mr. de Lema stated, "The room clerk asked me if I had a reservation. I said, 'Yes. The name is Jose Berga de Lema.' And I said, 'I want a safety deposit box.' He said, 'Please fill out

your registration.' " While de Lema was filling out the reservation form, paying $300 in cash as an advance, and Tamburino was filling out a receipt for that amount, de Lema had placed the attache case and the cylindrical bag on the floor. A blond woman jostled de Lema, apparently creating a diversion, and when he next looked down, he discovered that the attache case was gone. Mr. de Lema brought suit against the hotel for the value of the jewels stolen in the hotel's lobby. The hotel maintained a safe for valuables and posted notices in the lobby, garage, and rooms, as required by the New York law that modifies a hotelkeeper's common law liability. The notices stated in part that the hotel is not liable for the loss of valuables that a guest neglects to deliver to the hotel for safekeeping. The hotel defends that de Lema neglected to inform it of the presence of the jewels and to deliver the jewels to the hotel. It states that it is not liable. Decide. [De Lema v Waldorf Astoria Hotel, Inc. (SDNY) 588 F Supp 19]

14. Frosty Land Foods shipped a load of beef from its plant in Montgomery, Alabama, to Scott Meat Company in Los Angeles via the Refrigerated Transport Co. (RTC), a common carrier. Early Wednesday morning, December 7, at 12:55 a.m., two of RTC's drivers departed from the Frosty Land facility with the load of beef. The bill of lading called for delivery at Scott Meat Company on Friday, December 9, at 6:00 a.m. The RTC drivers arrived in Los Angeles at approximately 3:30 p.m. on Friday, December 9. Scott notified the drivers that it could not process the meat at that time. The drivers checked into a motel for the weekend, and the load was delivered to Scott on Monday, December 12. After inspecting 65 of the 308 carcasses, Scott determined that the meat was in "off condition" and refused the shipment. On Tuesday, December 13, Frosty Land sold the meat, after extensive trimming, at a loss of $13,529. Frosty Land brought suit against RTC for its loss. Decide. [Frosty Land Foods v Refrigerated Transport Co. (CA5) 613 F2d 1344]

15. The Singer Corporation had been storing air conditioners in Stoda warehouses for several years. In May of 1974 Singer's transportation manager, Guy Bataglia, went to Stoda's "Hoffman Plant" warehouse, accompanied by Stoda's president, Larry Ellis. While looking over the building, Bataglia noticed the sprinkler system and inquired about it. Ellis, who knew the system had been turned off, said the system was active. Singer had 133 cartons of air condition-

ing units stored at the Hoffman Plant as of that day. On July 7, 1974, a fire broke out in the Hoffman Plant, totally destroying Singer's goods. Singer claimed that it was entitled to recover the value of the destroyed air conditioners from Stoda, since it made out a *prima facie* case of negligence, which was not rebutted. Stoda defended that it was not an insurer of the goods. Decide. [Singer Co. v Stoda, 79 App Div 2d 227, 435 NYS2d 508]

PART FOUR

SALES

24

NATURE AND FORM OF SALES

The most common business transaction is the sale of goods. The law of sales is a combination of the law merchant, the common law of England, and former statutes as modified and codified by Article 2 of the Uniform Commercial Code.

A. NATURE AND LEGALITY

A **sale of goods** is a present transfer of title to movable property for a price. This price may be a payment of money, an exchange of other property, or the performance of services.[1] When a free item is given with the purchase of other goods, it is the purchasing of the other goods that is the price for the "free" goods; hence, the transaction as to the free goods is a sale.

The parties to a sale are the person who owns the goods and the person to whom the

---

[1]   Uniform Commercial Code § 2-304(1). O'Keefe Elevator Co. v Second Ave. Properties, Ltd. 216 Neb 170, 343 NW2d 54 (1984).

title is transferred. The transferor is the seller or vendor, and the transferee is the buyer or vendee.

1.   Subject Matter of Sales

Goods, the subject matter of a sale under Article 2 of the Uniform Commercial Code, include anything movable at the time it is identified as the subject of the transaction.[2] The subject matter may not be (a) investment securities, such as stocks and bonds, the sale of which is regulated by Article 8 of the UCC; (b) choses in action, such as insurance policies and promissory notes, since they are assigned or negotiated rather than sold, or which, because of their personal nature, are not transferable in any case; or (c) real estate, such as a house, factory, or farm.

(a) NATURE OF GOODS. Most goods are tangible and solid, such as an automobile or a chair. But goods may also be fluid, such as oil or gasoline. Goods may also be intangible, such as natural gas and electricity. The UCC is applicable to both new and used goods.[3]

(b) EXISTING AND FUTURE GOODS. Goods physically existing and owned by the seller at the time of the transaction are called **existing goods**. All other goods are called **future goods**. Future goods include both goods that are physically existing but not owned by the seller and goods that have not yet been manufactured.

A person can make a contract to sell goods at a future date. No sale can be made of future goods. Since the "seller" does not have any title to future goods, there can be no transfer of that title now, and hence no sale. For example, an agreement made today that all fish caught on a fishing trip tomorrow shall belong to a particular person does not make that person the owner of any fish today.

When the parties attempt to effect a present sale of future goods, the agreement operates only as a contract to sell the goods. Thus, a farmer purporting to transfer the title today to a future crop would be held subject to a duty to transfer the crop when it came into existence. The contract itself does not pass the title to the crop.

2.   Sale Distinguished from Other Transactions

A sale is an actual present transfer of title. If there is a transfer of a lesser interest than title, the transaction is not a sale.

(a) BAILMENT. A bailment is not a sale because only possession is transferred to a bailee. Title to the property is not transferred. A lease of goods, such as a lease of an automobile, is a bailment.[4]

Although a bailment is not a sale, there is a trend in the law to hold the commercial bailor to the same responsibilities as a seller.

(b) GIFT. There can be no sale without a price. A **gift** is a gratuitous or free transfer of the title to property.

(c) CONTRACT TO SELL. When the parties intend that title to goods will pass at a future time and they make a contract so providing, a **contract to sell** is created.

(d) OPTION TO PURCHASE. A sale, a present transfer of title, differs from an **option to purchase**. The latter is neither a transfer of title nor a contract to transfer title, but a power to make a contract to sell.

(e) CONDITIONAL SALE. A **conditional sale** customarily refers to a "condition precedent" transaction, by which title does not vest in the purchaser until payment in full has

---

[2]   It may also include things that are attached to the land, such as (a) minerals or buildings or materials forming part of buildings if they are to be removed or severed by the seller, and (b) other things attached to the land to be removed by either party. UCC § 2-107.

[3]   Morrison v Sears Roebuck, 319 NC 298, 354 SE2d 495 (1987).

[4]   Under Article 2A of the UCC, there has been a codification of the law of leases. Article 2A applies to any transaction, regardless of form, that creates a lease of personal property or fixtures. Many of the provisions of the law of sales were carried over and changed to reflect differences in style, leasing terminology, or leasing practices. These include, among others, statute of frauds provisions, rules relating to offer and acceptance, and warranties. See the first page of Appendix 3, footnote *, for states that have adopted Article 2A as of the printing of this book.

FIGURE 24-1   COMPARISON OF SALES WITH OTHER TRANSACTIONS

TRANSACTION	TYPE OF PROPERTY	ESSENTIAL CHARACTERISTIC
SALE	PERSONAL OR REAL	PRESENT TRANSFER OF TITLE FOR A PRICE
BAILMENT	GOODS	TRANSFER OF POSSESSION WHILE RETAINING TITLE
GIFT	PERSONAL OR REAL	GRATUITOUS TRANSFER OF TITLE
CONTRACT TO SELL	PERSONAL OR REAL	TRANSFER OF TITLE AT A FUTURE DATE
OPTION TO PURCHASE	PERSONAL OR REAL	POWER TO MAKE A CONTRACT TO SELL
CONDITIONAL SALE	PERSONAL OR REAL	TITLE PASSES TO PURCHASER WHEN CONDITION IS SATISFIED

been made for the property purchased. This was formerly a common type of sale, used when the purchase was made on credit and payment was to be made in installments. The conditional sale has been replaced by a secured transaction under Article 9 of the UCC.

(f) CONTRACT FOR SERVICES. A contract for services is an ordinary contract and is not governed by the UCC.[5]

(g) CONTRACT FOR GOODS AND SERVICES. If a contract calls for both the rendering of services and the supplying of materials to be used in performing the services, the contract is classified according to its dominant element. If the sale of goods is dominant, it is a sales contract. If the service element is dominant, it is a service contract. For example, the contract of a repairer is a contract for services, even though parts are supplied to perform the task. The supplying of such parts is not regarded as a sale but is merely incidental to the primary contract of making repairs. In contrast, the purchase of a television set, with incidental service of installation, is a sale of goods because the purchase of the set is the dominant element.

In the *Meyers* case the court was faced with deciding whether a person assembling and installing prefabricated items was making a sale of goods or was rendering a service.

[5]   Professional Recruiters, Inc. v Oliver, 226 Neb 16, 409 NW2d 304 (1987).

MEYERS v HENDERSON CONSTRUCTION CO.
147 NJ Super 77, 370 A2d 547 (1977)

The Henderson Construction Co. was building a factory. Cyril Meyers contracted to install overhead doors in the factory. Meyers obtained the prefabricated but disassembled doors from the manufacturer. His contract with Henderson required Meyers to "furnish all labor, materials, tools and equipment to satisfactorily complete the installation of all overhead doors." Five years later, when Meyers sued Henderson for breach of contract, Henderson raised the defense that the contract was for the sale of goods, in which case it would be barred by the UCC's four-year statute of limitations. Meyers claimed that it was a contract for services, for which the UCC's statute of limitations was not applicable, and suit could be brought within six years.

WEISS, J. . . . Which statute properly applies depends upon how the contract may be most accurately characterized—as one for the sale of goods (as defined in [UCC §] 2-105(1)) plus incidental services, or as one for construction services with the subcontractor furnishing materials as well as labor. . . .

[UCC §] 2-105 requires that, in order to be classified as goods, the subject matter of a contract must be "movable at the time of identification to the contract." This definitional section continues, excluding some "things" from UCC coverage. But there is no exception for goods which require servicing before they can be used. . . . Some courts have characterized contracts as involving primarily services, with the transfer of materials being so incidental to the services as to exclude coverage by the UCC, . . . [when those contracts involved] the sale and installation of blacktop, construction of a house with a builder furnishing all materials and labor, construction of electrical equipment, construction and sale of a house, and finally sale and erection of structural steel in the construction of a bridge.

It is apparent that at some point the service element may so dominate the subject matter of a contract as to bring it outside UCC coverage. An agreement to paint a house is a classic example of this situation. In *Bonebrake v Cox*, [(CA8 Iowa) 499 F2d 951] the Eighth Circuit was faced with the task of enunciating a test to cover borderline cases. There the issue was whether the four-year UCC limitation period barred an action of allegedly defective used bowling equipment which had been supplied and installed by defendant. . . .

As is the case here, *Bonebrake* involved the purchase of manufactured goods which were useless without a substantial amount of labor. One lump sum was charged for the equipment and its installation. . . .

The cases presenting mixed contracts of this type are legion. The test for inclusion or exclusion is not whether they are mixed, but, granting that they are mixed, whether their predominant factor, their thrust, their purpose, reasonably stated, is the rendition of service, with goods incidentally involved (e.g., contract with artist for painting) or is a transaction of sale, with labor incidentally involved (e.g., installation of a water heater in a bathroom). . . . See also *Cleveland Lumber Co. v Proctor and Schwartz, Inc.* 397 F Supp 1088 (ND Ga 1975).

It cannot be denied that the overhead doors were useless without the performance of installation services. . . .

When presented with two elements of a contract, each absolutely necessary if the subject matter is to be of any significant value to the purchaser, it is a futile task to attempt to determine which component is "more necessary." Thus the *Bonebrake* test looks to the predominant purpose, the thrust of the contract as it would exist in the minds of reasonable parties. There is no surer way to provide for predictable results in the face of a highly artificial classification system.

Applying the test here, we find the predominant reason for the agreement to have been the procurement of overhead doors, with the installation services being incidental. The contract is, therefore, governed by the UCC, and the four-year limitation period of [UCC §] 2-725 is properly applicable. . . .

[Judgment for defendant]

QUESTIONS

1.   What was the importance of determining whether Meyers was selling services or goods?

> 2. What provision does the UCC make with respect to goods that require servicing by the supplier before they can be used by the customer?
> 3. Would it have affected the decision if Meyers had constructed the doors from building materials rather than having assembled and installed prefabricated doors?

3.   Law of Contracts Applicable

A sale is a voluntary transaction between two persons. Accordingly, most of the principles that apply to contractual agreements in general are equally applicable to a sale of goods.

Modern marketing practices have modified the strict principles of contract law, and this modified approach is carried into the UCC. Thus, the requirements for a sales contract are not as strict as the requirements for other types of contracts. For a sales contract it is sufficient that the parties by their conduct recognize the existence of a contract, even though it cannot be determined when the contract was made, and (generally) even though one or more terms are left open.[6]

In most instances the UCC treats all buyers and sellers alike. In some it treats merchants differently than it does the occasional or casual buyer or seller. In this way the UCC recognizes that the merchant is experienced and has a special knowledge of the relevant commercial practices.

(a) OFFER. Contract law as to offers is applicable to a sales contract, with the following exception. A **firm offer** by a merchant cannot be revoked if the offer (1) expresses an intention that it will not be revoked, (2) is in a writing, and (3) is signed by the merchant. An express period of irrevocability in the offer cannot exceed three months. If nothing is said as to the duration of the offer, irrevocability continues only for a reasonable time. A firm offer is effective regardless of whether the merchant received any consideration to keep the offer open.

(b) ACCEPTANCE. An offer to buy or sell goods may be accepted in any manner and by any medium that is reasonable under the circumstances.[7] However, if a specific manner or medium is clearly indicated by the terms of the offer or the circumstances of the case, the offer can only be accepted in that manner.

Unless it is expressly specified that an offer to buy or sell goods must be accepted just as made, the offeree may accept an offer and at the same time propose an additional term. Contrary to the general contract law rule, the new term does not reject the original offer. A contract arises on the terms of the original offer, and the new term is a counteroffer. If, however, the offer states that it must be accepted exactly as made, the ordinary contract law rules apply. If the additional term is treated as a counteroffer, that term does not become binding until accepted by the original offeror.

In a transaction between merchants, the additional term becomes part of the contract if that term does not materially alter the offer and no objection is made to it. However, if such an additional term in the seller's form of acknowledgment operates solely to the seller's advantage, it is a material term and must be accepted to be effective.

In the *Herzog Oil* case the seller sued the buyer for interest and attorney's fees, pursuant to terms contained in a written confirmation of an oral contract between the parties. The confirmation was sent after delivery of the goods.

---

[6]   UCC § 2-204. This provision is limited by requiring that there be "a reasonably certain basis for giving an appropriate remedy."

[7]   UCC § 2-206(1). An order or other offer to buy goods that are to be sent promptly or currently can be accepted by the seller by actually shipping the goods.

HERZOG OIL FIELD SERVICE v OTTO TORPEDO COMPANY
—— Pa Super ——, 570 A2d 549 (1990)

> Herzog delivered 2,000 feet of pipe-drilling equipment to Otto. The delivery of the materials was accompanied by the delivery of a "pipe tally report," a type of invoice used in the business, which stated that a finance charge of 1.5 percent per month of the unpaid balance would be added after 30 days. On the same day, a written invoice was sent, listing the materials delivered, the price, the terms (net 30 days) and indicating that balances over 30 days would carry a 1.5 percent monthly finance charge. It also stated that if an account were turned over for collection, attorney's fees in the amount of 25 percent of the balance would be added. No objection to the terms of the invoice was made by Otto to Herzog. Subsequently, Otto refused to pay on the invoice. The trial court held that there was a breach of contract but refused to grant any interest or attorney's fees. Herzog appealed.

BRODSKY, J. . . . There seems to be little dispute that the invoice sent by Herzog on the day of delivery is a written confirmation within the meaning of § 2-207. The question appears to be whether a confirmation sent *after delivery* of the goods falls within the scope of § 2-207. We conclude that it does.

. . . The "general rule" portion of § 2-207 states "a written confirmation which is sent within a reasonable time operates as an acceptance even though it states terms additional to or different from those offered or agreed upon. . . ." Subsection (b) indicates that these additional terms are to be construed as proposals for addition which, between merchants, become part of the contract if they are not objected to and if they do not materially alter the agreement. No objection to the terms in question was lodged and, at least as to the interest term, the court indicated that they did not constitute a material alteration of the contract. Thus, initially it would seem that there is no requirement that the written documents be sent prior to a delivery of the goods.

. . . The first comment states "this section is intended to deal with two typical situations. The one is the written confirmation, where *an agreement has been reached* either orally or by informal correspondence between the parties *and is followed* by one or both of the parties sending formal memoranda embodying the terms so far as agreed upon and adding terms not discussed." (emphasis added). The second comment adds: "Under this Article a proposed deal which in commercial understanding has in fact been closed is recognized as a contract. Therefore, any additional matter contained in the confirmation or in the acceptance falls within subsection (2) and must be regarded as a proposal for an added term. . . ." Comment three states: "[w]hether or not additional or different terms will become part of the agreement depends upon the provision of subsection (2). If they are such as materially to alter the original bargain, they will not be included unless expressly agreed to by the other party. If, however, they are terms which would not so change the bargain they will be incorporated unless notice of objection to them has already been given or is given within a reasonable time." . . .

The above material conclusively establishes that confirming memoranda of a previously reached agreement are subject to § 2-207. The only possible distinguishing feature of the present case is that the confirmation was sent after delivery, rather than before. However, from a standpoint of legal principle, this would seem to be an imma-terial distinction. All of the above references indicate that the confirming memoranda can effectuate terms in the agreement even when submitted after a commercially acceptable and legally binding contract has been formed. The point of importance is the recognition that a contract can be formed even if many of the particulars or specifics have not been discussed or agreed upon.

Under the Code, there are many ways in which parties can enter into a legal con-tractual relationship. . . . And certainly upon shipment or acceptance of the goods at the drilling site. . . .

We have little difficulty in determining that the interest charge term is not one that materially alters the agreement. The trial court reached that conclusion, and comment 5 to § 2-207 states, as an example of a term that does not materially alter the contract, "a clause providing for interest on overdue invoices . . . where they are within the range of trade practice . . . ." Furthermore, it is common in commercial circles, includ-ing transactions with nonmerchants, for balances to be subjected to interest charges. As such, and since no objection to the term was lodged, we find that the trial court erred in not allowing appellant interest as provided in the written confirmation. Under oper-ation of § 2-207 the term must be considered as part of the agreement. . . .

In contrast, however, we find that the provision calling for the addition of an attor-ney's fee of 25% of the balance due is a material alteration and, therefore, did not become part of the agreement. We come to this conclusion for a few reasons. First, in common experience an attorney's fee provision is considerably less common than an interest rate provision; thus, it would not be as readily expected or anticipated.

Secondly, when found, such clauses are usually less than 25% of the balance, often 10 or 15%, thus bringing the reasonableness of this particular clause into question. Thirdly, a lump sum addition of 25% changes the obligor's financial obligation under the contract to, what must be considered, a material degree. Fourthly, we choose to follow the precedent of *Johnson Tire Service, Inc. v. Thorn, Inc.,* 613 P.2d 521, 529 (Utah, 1980), where this conclusion was also reached. There, the Utah court disallowed a clause, purportedly added under operation of § 2-207, which called for the buyer to pay costs of collection including "reasonable attorney's fees", because it found that such a clause constituted a material alteration. Thus, we conclude that the attorney's fee provision constitutes a material alteration of the agreement under § 2-207 and that the trial court correctly refused to enforce it. . . .

[Reversed as to interest, affirmed as to attorney's fee]

QUESTIONS

1. When will additional or different terms to a paper described by UCC § 2-207 become part of an agreement?
2. Did the provision for interest and the provision for attorney's fees materially alter the agreement?
3. State the decision of the court and the basis for the decision.

A buyer may expressly or by conduct agree to a term added by the seller to the ac-ceptance of the buyer's offer. The buyer may agree orally or in writing to the additional term. There is an acceptance by conduct if the buyer accepts the goods with knowledge that the term has been added by the seller.

When a term of an acceptance conflicts

with a term of an offer, but it is clear that the parties intended to be bound by a contract, the UCC recognizes the formation of a contract. The terms that are conflicting cancel out and are ignored. The contract then consists of the terms of the offer and acceptance that agree, together with those terms that the UCC or contract law implies into a contract.

(c) DETERMINATION OF PRICE. The price for goods may be expressly fixed by the contract. If not fixed by the contract, the price may be an open term, whereby the parties merely indicate how the price should be determined at a later time or make no provision whatever as to the price.

When persons experienced in a particular industry make a contract for goods without specifying the price to be paid, the price will be determined by the manner that is customary in the industry. Ordinarily, if nothing is said as to price, the buyer is required to pay the reasonable value of the goods, which is generally the market price.

In recent years there has been an increase in the use of the "cost plus" formula for determining price. Under this formula, the buyer pays the seller a sum equal to the cost to the seller of obtaining the goods plus a specified percentage of that cost. The percentage represents the seller's profit.

The contract may expressly provide that one of the parties may determine the price. In such a case that party must act in good faith.[8] The contract may specify that the price shall be determined by some standard or by a third person.

(d) OUTPUT AND REQUIREMENTS CONTRACTS. Somewhat related to the open term concept concerning price is the concept involved in the output and requirements contracts that the quantity to be sold or purchased is not a specific quantity. Instead it is such amount as the seller should produce or the buyer should require. Although this intro-duces an element of uncertainty, such sales contracts are valid. To prevent oppression, they are subject to two limitations: (1) the parties must act in good faith, and (2) the quantity offered or demanded must not be unreasonably disproportionate to prior output or requirements or to a stated estimate.

When the sales contract is a continuing contract, as one calling for periodic delivery of fuel, but no time is set for the life of the contract, the contract runs for a reasonable time. It may be terminated on notice by either party.

(e) SEALS. A seal on a sales contract or on an offer of sale has no effect. Thus, in determining whether there is consideration or whether the statute of limitations is applicable, the fact that there is a seal on the sales contract is ignored.

(f) IMPLIED CONDITIONS. The field of implied conditions under contract law is broadened by the UCC. The UCC permits the release of a party from any obligation under a sales contract when performance has been made commercially impracticable, as distinguished from "impossible,": (1) by the occurrence of a contingency, the nonoccurrence of which was a basic assumption on which the contract was made; or (2) by compliance in good faith with any applicable governmental regulation or order. "A severe shortage of raw materials or of supplies due to a contingency such as war, embargo, local crop failure, unforeseen shutdown of major sources of supply or the like, which either causes a marked increase in cost or altogether prevents the seller from securing supplies necessary to his performance, is within the contemplation" of this provision of the Code.[9]

(g) MODIFICATION OF CONTRACT. An agreement to modify a contract for the sale of goods is binding even though the modification is not supported by consideration.[10]

(h) PAROL EVIDENCE RULE. The parol evidence rule applies to the sale of goods with

---

[8] Good faith requires that the party act honestly and, in the case of a merchant, also requires the party to follow reasonable commercial standards of fair dealing that are recognized in the trade. UCC §§ 1-201(19), 2-103(1)(b).

[9] UCC § 2-615, Official Comment, point 4.
[10] UCC § 2-209(1).

the slight modification that a writing is not presumed to represent the entire contract of the parties unless the court specifically decides that it does. If the court so decides, parol evidence is admissible to show what the parties meant by their words. Additional terms cannot be added to the writing by parol evidence.

If the court decides that the writing was not intended to represent the entire contract, the writing may be supplemented by parol proof of additional terms, as long as such terms are not inconsistent with the original written terms.

(i) USAGE OF TRADE AND COURSE OF DEALING.

The patterns of doing business as shown by the prior dealings of the parties and the usages of the trade enter into and form part of their contract. These patterns may be looked to in order to find what was intended by the express provisions and to supply otherwise missing terms.

(j) FRAUD AND OTHER DEFENSES.

The defenses that may be raised in a suit on a sales contract are in general the same as those that may be raised in a suit on any other contract. A defrauded party may cancel the transaction and recover what was paid or the goods that were delivered, together with damages for any loss sustained. If title was obtained by the buyer by means of fraud, the title is voidable by an innocent seller.

If the sales contract or any clause in it was unconscionable when made, a court may refuse to enforce it.

4. Illegal Sales

At common law a sale was illegal if the subject matter itself was illegal. A transaction may also be illegal even though the subject matter of the sale is unobjectionable, if the agreement provides that the goods sold shall be employed for some unlawful purpose or if the seller assists the buyer in an unlawful act. To illustrate, when the seller falsely labels domestic goods, representing them to be imported, to assist the buyer in perpetrating a fraud

on the buyer's customers, the sale is illegal. However, the mere fact that the seller has knowledge of the buyer's unlawful purpose does not, under the general rule, make the sale illegal unless the purpose is the commission of a serious crime.

(a) ILLEGALITY UNDER STATUTES.

Every state has legislation prohibiting certain sales when they are not conducted according to the requirements of the statutes. Statutes commonly regulate sales by establishing standards as to grading, size, weight, and measure, and by prohibiting adulteration.

Statutes may regulate the sale of "secondhand" goods. Such a statute does not apply to a casual seller, but only to one whose regular business consists of selling goods of the kind covered by the statute.

States may prohibit the making of sales on Sunday. This may apply either to sales generally or to particular classes of commodities or stores.

The federal Food, Drug, and Cosmetic Act prohibits the interstate shipment of misbranded or adulterated foods, drugs, cosmetics, and therapeutic devices. A product that does not carry adequate use instructions and warnings is deemed "misbranded."

(b) EFFECT OF ILLEGAL SALE.

An illegal sale or contract to sell cannot be enforced. As a general rule, courts will not aid either party in recovering money or property transferred pursuant to an illegal agreement. Here, the ordinary contract law rule as to illegality is applied. However, if a sale is made illegal by statute, a seller who violates the law may be held liable for the damage caused.

5. Bulk Transfers

When a merchant is about to transfer a major part of the merchant's materials, supplies, merchandise, or other inventory, not in the ordinary course of business, advance notice of the transfer should be given to creditors. This notice should be given by the transferee in accordance with Article 6 of the Uniform Commercial Code.[11] The essential characteristic of businesses subject to Article 6 is that they sell from inventory or a stock of goods, as contrasted with businesses that render services.[12] Thus, a beauty salon is ordinarily a service enterprise and is not subject to the bulk transfer article. This is contrasted with a store selling cosmetics, which is subject to Article 6.

(a) EFFECT OF NONCOMPLIANCE WITH ARTICLE 6. If the notice required by Article 6 is not given, the creditors of the seller may reach the sold property in the hands of the buyer. Creditors may also reach the property in the hands of any subsequent transferee who knew that there had not been compliance with the UCC or who did not pay value. This provision is designed to protect the creditors of a merchant from the merchant's selling all the inventory, pocketing the money, and then disappearing, leaving the creditors unpaid. The protection given to creditors by the bulk transfer legislation is in addition to the protection that they have against their debtor for fraudulent transfers and the remedies that can be employed in bankruptcy proceedings.

The fact that there has been noncompliance with Article 6 of the UCC regulating bulk transfers, however, does not affect the validity of a bulk sale of goods between the immediate parties to the transfer. Article 6 governs only the rights of creditors of the transferor.

(b) LIABILITY OF BULK PURCHASER. Ordinarily, the bulk purchaser who receives the goods does not become liable for the debts of the bulk seller merely because the requirements of Article 6 have not been satisfied. In contrast, if the buyer mixes the transferred goods with other goods so that it is not possible for the creditor to identify the transferred goods that are subject to the creditor's claim, the bulk buyer is personally liable for the debts of the bulk seller. The liability of the bulk buyer will not exceed the value of the goods transferred, however.

B.   FORM OF SALES CONTRACT

A contract for the sale of goods may be oral or written. In some cases, it must be evidenced by a writing or it cannot be enforced in court.

6.   Amount

Whenever the sales price of goods is $500 or more, the sales contract must be evidenced by a writing to be enforceable.[13] The section of the UCC setting forth this requirement is known as the statute of frauds.

7.   Nature of the Writing Required

The writing evidencing the sales contract may be either (1) a complete written contract signed by both parties or (2) a memorandum signed by the defendant. In any case it must meet the following requirements.

(a) TERMS. The writing must indicate that there has been a completed transaction as to certain goods. Specifically, it need only (1) indicate that a sale or contract to sell has been made[14] and (2) state the quantity of goods involved. Any other missing terms may be shown by parol evidence.

(b) SIGNATURE. The writing must be signed by the person who is being sued or by the authorized agent of that person. The signature must be placed on the paper with the intention of authenticating the writing. The signature may consist of initials or may be printed, stamped, or typewritten, as long as it is made with the necessary intent.

When the transaction is between merchants, an exception is made to the requirement of signing. The failure of a merchant to

---

[11]   In 1989 the National Conference of Commissioners on Uniform State Laws recommended that Article 6 be repealed on the ground that it was obsolete and had little value in the modern business world. At the same time, the commissioners adopted a revised version of Article 6 (Alternative B) for adoption by those states that desired to retain the concept with respect to bulk sales. See Appendix 3, footnote *, of this text for a list of states that have adopted revised Article 6.

[12]   J.I. Hass Co. Inc. v Frank A. Kristal Associates, Inc. 127 App Div 2d 541, 512 NYS2d 104 (1987).

[13]   UCC § 2-201.

[14]   Martco, Inc. v Doran Chevrolet, Inc. (Tex Civ App) 632 SW2d 927 (1982).

repudiate a confirming letter sent by another merchant within ten days of receiving such a letter binds the nonsigner, just as if the receiving merchant had signed the letter. This makes it necessary for a merchant seller to watch the mail and to act within ten days of receiving a mailed confirmation. This was the problem that arose in the *Thomson Printing* case.

THOMSON PRINTING MACHINERY CO. v B. F. GOODRICH CO.

(CA7 Ill) 714 F2d 744 (1983)

Thomson Printing buys and sells used printing machinery. Thomson brought suit on an oral contract for the purchase from B.F. Goodrich Company of printing machinery. Goodrich defended on the basis that the Statute of Frauds required a writing. Thomson argued that the statute had been satisfied when Goodrich failed to object to a memorandum of the sale that had been sent within four days after the oral agreement had been made. Goodrich alleged that Thomson had not sufficiently addressed the envelope containing the memorandum and that, consequently, it had never been received by anyone who had reason to know what it concerned. The court sustained these objections and held that the "between merchants" provision had not been satisfied and that accordingly any oral contract between the parties could not be enforced. From a judgment in favor of the defendant, Thomson appealed.

CUDAHY, C. J. . . . A modern exception to the usual writing requirement is the "merchants" exception of the Uniform Commercial Code, § 2-201(2), which provides:

Between merchants if within a reasonable time a writing in confirmation of the contract and sufficient against the sender is received and the party receiving it has reason to know its contents, it satisfies the [writing requirement] against such party unless written notice of objection to its contents is given within 10 days after it is received.

We must emphasize that the only effect of this exception is to take away from a merchant who receives a writing in confirmation of a contract the Statute of Frauds defense if the merchant does not object. The sender must still persuade the trier of fact that a contract was in fact made orally, to which the written confirmation applies.

In the instant case, James Thomson sent a "writing in confirmation" to Goodrich four days after his meeting with Ingram Meyers, a Goodrich employee and agent. The purchase order contained Thomson Printing's name, address, telephone number and certain information about the machinery purchase. The check James Thomson sent to Goodrich with the purchase order also had on it Thomson Printing's name and address, and the check carried notations that connected the check with the purchase order.

Goodrich argues, however, that Thomson's writing in confirmation cannot qualify for the 2-201(2) exception because it was not received by anyone at Goodrich who had reason to know its contents. Goodrich claims that Thomson erred in not specifically designating on the envelope, check or purchase order that the items were intended for Ingram Meyers or the surplus equipment department. Consequently, Goodrich contends, it was unable to "find a home" for the check and purchase order despite attempts to do so, in accordance with its regular procedures, by sending copies of the documents to several of its various divisions. Ingram Meyers testified that he never learned of the purchase order until weeks later when James Thomson called to arrange for removal of the machines. By then, however, the machines had long been sold to someone else.

We think Goodrich misreads the requirements of 2-201(2). First, the literal requirements of 2-201(2), as they apply here, are that a writing "is received" and that Goodrich "has reason to know its contents." There is no dispute that the purchase order and check were received by Goodrich, and there is at least no specific or express requirement that the "receipt" referred to in 2-201(2) be by any Goodrich agent in particular.

These issues are not resolved by [2-201(2)], but it is probably a reasonable projection that a delivery at either the recipient's principal place of business, a place of business from which negotiations were conducted, or to which the sender may have transmitted previous communications, will be an adequate receipt.

As for the "reason to know its contents" requirement, this element "is best understood to mean that the confirmation was an instrument which should have been anticipated and therefore should have received the attention of appropriate parties. The receipt of a spurious document would not burden the recipient with a risk of losing the [Statute of Frauds] defense. . . ." In the case before us there is no doubt that the confirmatory writings were based on actual negotiations (although the legal effect of the negotiations was disputed), and therefore the documents were not "spurious" but could have been anticipated and appropriately handled.

. . . Section 1-201, the definitional section of the U.C.C., provides that notice received by an organization

> is effective for a particular transaction . . . from the time when it would have been brought to [the attention of the individual conducting that transaction] if the organization had exercised *due diligence.*

The Official Comment states:

> reason to know, knowledge, or a notification, although "received" for instance by a clerk in Department A of an organization, is effective for a transaction conducted in Department B only from the time when it was *or should have been* communicated to the individual conducting that transaction.

Thus, the question comes down to whether Goodrich's mailroom, given the information it had, should have notified the surplus equipment manager, Ingram Meyers, of Thomson's confirmatory writing. At whatever point Meyers should have been so notified, then at that point Thomson's writing was effective even though Meyers did not see it.

The definitional section of the U.C.C. also sets the general standard for what mailrooms "should do":

> An organization exercises due diligence if it maintains reasonable routines for communicating significant information to the person conducting the transaction and there is reasonable compliance with the routines.

One cannot say that Goodrich's mailroom procedures were reasonable as a matter of law: if Goodrich had exercised due diligence in handling Thomson Printing's purchase order and check, these items would have reasonably promptly come to Ingram Meyers' attention. First, the purchase order on its face should have alerted the mailroom that the documents referred to a purchase of used printing equipment. Since Goodrich had only one surplus machinery department, the documents' "home" should not have been difficult to find. Second, even if the mailroom would have had difficulty in immediately identifying the kind of transaction involved, the purchase order had Thomson Printing's phone number printed on it and we think a "reasonable routine" in these particular circumstances would have involved at some point in the process a simple phone call to Thomson Printing. Thus, we think Goodrich's mailroom mishandled the confirmatory writings. This failure should not permit Goodrich to escape liability by pleading nonreceipt.

We note that the jury verdict for Thomson Printing indicates that the jury found as a fact that the contract had in fact been made and that the Statute of Frauds had been satisfied. Also, Goodrich acknowledges those facts about the handling of the purchase order which we regard as determinative of the "merchants" exception question. We think that there is ample evidence to support the jury findings both of the existence of the contract and of the satisfaction of the Statute.

The district court, in holding as a matter of law that the circumstances failed to satisfy the Statute of Frauds, was impressed by James Thomson's dereliction in failing to specifically direct the purchase order and check to the attention of Ingram Meyers or the surplus equipment department. We agree that Thomson erred in this respect, but, for the reasons we have suggested, Goodrich was at least equally derelict in failing to find a "home" for the well-identified documents. Goodrich argues that in the "vast majority" of cases it can identify checks within a week without contacting an outside party; in the instant case, therefore, if Goodrich correctly states its experience under its procedures, it should presumably have checked with Thomson Printing promptly after the time it normally identified checks by other means—in this case, by its own calculation, a week at most. Under the particular circumstances of this case, we therefore think it inappropriate to set aside a jury verdict on Statute of Frauds grounds. . . .

[Reversed and remanded]

QUESTIONS

1.   What does the UCC provide when a merchant sends to another merchant a signed, written confirmation of their oral contract?
2.   Does a signed confirmation have to be actually received at the seller's principal place of business?
3.   How did the court decide the contention of Goodrich that the confirmation was not received by anyone who had reason to know its contents?

(c) PURPOSE OF EXECUTION. A writing can satisfy a statute of frauds, even though it was not made for that purpose. Accordingly, when the buyer writes to the seller, after a 45-day delay, and merely criticizes the quality of the goods, the letter satisfies the statute, as it indicates that there was a sale of those goods.

(d) PARTICULAR WRITINGS. Formal contracts, bills of sale, letters, and telegrams are common forms of writings that satisfy the requirement. Purchase orders, cash register receipts, sales tickets, invoices, and similar papers generally do not satisfy the requirement as to a signature, and sometimes they do not specify any quantity or commodity.

Two or more writings may constitute the "writing" that satisfies the statute of frauds.[15]

8.   Effect of Noncompliance

A sales agreement that does not satisfy the statute of frauds cannot be enforced. However, the oral contract itself is not unlawful and may be voluntarily performed by the parties.

9.   Exceptions to Requirement of a Writing

The absence of a writing does not always bar proof of a sales contract.

(a) NONRESELLABLE GOODS. No writing is required when the goods are specially made for the buyer and are of such an unusual nature that they are not suitable for sale in the ordinary course of the seller's business. For example, 14 steel doors were tailor-made by the seller for the buyer's building. The doors were not suitable for sale to anyone else in the ordinary course of the seller's business, and they could only be sold as scrap. In this case the oral contract of sale could be enforced.

In order for the nonresellable goods exception to apply, the seller must have made a substantial beginning in manufacturing the goods or, if a distributor, in procuring them, before notice of repudiation by the buyer is received.

(b) RECEIPT AND ACCEPTANCE. An oral sales contract may be enforced if it can be shown that the goods were delivered by the seller and were received and accepted by the buyer. Thus, if the buyer receives and accepts goods on credit, the seller may sue for the purchase price, even if it is over $500 and there is no writing. The receipt and acceptance of the goods by the buyer took the contract out of the statute of frauds. Both a receipt and an acceptance by the buyer must be shown. If only part of the goods had been received and accepted, the contract may be enforced only insofar as it relates to those goods received and accepted.[16]

(c) PAYMENT. An oral contract may be enforced if the buyer has made full payment. In the case of part payment for divisible units of goods, a contract may be enforced only with respect to the goods for which payment has been made and accepted. If part payment is made for indivisible goods, such as an automobile, a part payment avoids the statute of frauds and permits proof of the entire oral contract.

(d) ADMISSION. An oral contract may be enforced if the party against whom enforcement is sought admits in pleadings, testimony, or otherwise in court that a contract for sale was made. The contract, however, is not enforceable beyond the quantity of goods admitted.[17]

10.   Non-Code Requirements

In addition to the UCC requirement as to a writing, other statutes may impose requirements. For example, state consumer protection legislation commonly requires the execution of a detailed contract and the giving of a copy thereof to the consumer. The result is that even though the UCC requirements have been satisfied, the buyer may still be able to avoid the transaction because of noncompliance with the requirements of other statutes.

11.   Bill of Sale

Regardless of the requirement of the statute of frauds, the parties may wish to execute a writing as evidence or proof of the sale. Through custom this writing has become known as a **bill of sale**, but it is neither a bill nor a contract. It is merely a receipt or writing signed by the seller reciting the transfer to the buyer of the title to the described property. The only effect of the bill of sale is to bar the seller from later denying the making of the sale. If the seller did not have title to the goods, the bill of sale does not give the buyer any title.

In some states, provision is made for the public recording of bills of sale when goods

---

[15]   West Central Packing, Inc. v A.F. Murch Co. 109 Mich App 493, 311 NW2d 404 (1981).
[16]   Allied Grape Growers v Bronco Wine Co. 203 Cal App 3d 432, 249 Cal Rptr 872 (1988).

[17]   Gooch v Farmers Marketing Ass'n (Miss) 519 So 2d 1214 (1988).

are left in the seller's possession. Some states require the production of the bill of sale before the title to any automobile will be registered in the name of the purchaser.

Although the bill of sale states that the full purchase price has been paid, the seller may show that in fact it has not been so paid.

C.   UNIFORM LAW FOR INTERNATIONAL SALES

The United Nations Convention on Contracts for the International Sale of Goods (CISG) applies to contracts between parties in the United States and parties in the other nations that have ratified the convention.[18] The provisions of this convention or international agreement have been strongly influenced by Article 2 of the Uniform Commercial Code. The international rules of the convention automatically apply to contracts for the sale of goods if the buyer and seller have places of business in different countries that have ratified the convention. The sales contract, however, may exclude the convention provisions.

---

[18]   52 Fed Reg. 6262 (1987).

12.   Scope of the CISG

The CISG does not govern all contracts between parties in the countries that have ratified it. The CISG does not apply to goods bought for personal, family, or household use. The CISG does not apply to contracts in which the preponderant part of the obligations of the party who furnishes the goods consists of the supply of labor or other services. In addition, it does not apply to the liability of the seller to any person for death or personal injury caused by the goods.

The CISG governs the formation of the contract of sale and the rights and obligations of the seller and the buyer arising from such a contract. The CISG provides a basis for answering questions and settling issues the parties failed to deal with in their contracts.

13.   Statute of Frauds

Under the CISG a contract for the sale of goods need not be in any particular form and can be proved by any means. The convention, by this provision, has abolished the statute of frauds requirement of a writing. Countries may, however, retain the UCC requirements of the statute of frauds by requiring certain contracts to be evidenced by a writing.

SUMMARY

A sale of goods, governed by Article 2 of the UCC, is a present transfer of title to movable property for a price. Goods, the subject matter of a sale, include anything movable at the time it is identified as the subject of the transaction. Goods physically existing and owned by the seller at the time of the transaction are existing goods. Goods that are not existing goods are known as future goods. There can be no present sale of future goods, and any agreement to sell such goods operates as a contract to sell.

A bailment is not a sale because no title is transferred. A gift is not a sale since there is no price paid for the gift. A contract for services is an ordinary contract and is not governed by the UCC. If a contract calls for both the rendering of services and the supplying of goods, the

contract is classified according to its dominant element.

The law of contracts is applicable to a sale of goods. Contract law as to offers is applicable to a sale of goods, except for rules concerning a firm offer and an acceptance with new terms. In sales contracts a contract arises on the terms of the original offer and the new terms are considered counteroffers. If the transaction is between merchants, the additional terms become part of the contract if those terms do not materially alter the offer and no objection is made to them.

The price term may be expressly fixed by the parties. The parties may make no provision as to price, or they may indicate how the price should be determined later. In output or requirements contracts, the quantity that is to be sold or purchased is not specified, but such contracts are nevertheless valid. Output and requirements contracts are contracts to sell, and the specific quantities are identified at the time of the sale. A seal has no effect on a contract. A contract relating to a sale of goods may be modified even though the modification is not supported by consideration. The parol evidence rule applies to a sale of goods in much the same manner as to ordinary contracts that are not for sale of goods. There is the slight modification that a writing is not presumed to represent the entire contract of the parties unless the court specifically decides that it does. Most contract defenses may be raised in a suit on a sales contract. An illegal sale or contract to sell cannot be enforced.

A merchant who transfers a major part of the merchant's merchandise or inventory not in the ordinary course of business must comply with the bulk transfer provisions of the UCC.

A sales contract for $500 or more must be evidenced by a writing. Several exceptions exist: the goods are specially made for the buyer and are nonresellable in the seller's ordinary market; the buyer received and accepted the goods; the buyer has made either full or part payment; or the party against whom enforcement is sought admits in court pleadings or testimony that a contract for sale was made.

Uniform rules for international sales are applicable to contracts for sales among parties in countries that have ratified the CISG. Under the CISG a contract for the sale of goods need not be in any particular form and can be proved by any means.

QUESTIONS AND CASE PROBLEMS

1. What social forces are affected by the rule that consideration is not required for a modification of a contract for the sale of goods?

2. On Monday Nancy sells her sewing machine to Irma. It is agreed that Irma will pay for the sewing machine on the next Friday, payday, and that Nancy will retain title and possession until such payment is made. Is there a sale of the sewing machine on Monday?

3. Ethel wrote to Lasco Dealers, inquiring as to the price of a certain freezer. Lasco wrote her a letter signed by its credit manager stating that Ethel could purchase the freezer in question during the next 30 days at the price of $400. Ethel wrote back the next day ordering a freezer at that price. Ethel's letter was received by Lasco the following day, but Lasco wrote an answering letter stating that it had changed the price to $450. Ethel claims that Lasco could not change its price. Is Ethel correct?

4. Emily purchases a refrigerator-freezer from the Elton Appliance Shop for $600. The purchase is made over the phone. Thereafter, Elton sends Emily a letter thanking her for the purchase of the refrigerator-freezer. Before the refrigerator-freezer is delivered to Emily, she telephones Elton and cancels the purchase. Elton then sues her for damages. She raises the defense of the statute of frauds. Elton produces a copy of the letter that it sent to Emily. Does this letter avoid the defense of the statute of frauds?

5. Danfie Company of New York owns leather hides stored in a warehouse in the south of France. Danfie sells some of these hides to the Haldane Company of Chicago. Danfie and Haldane agree that the price shall be determined by Rumfort, who lives in the south of France and is recognized in the trade as an expert in leather. Haldane becomes dissatisfied with the contract and claims that it is not binding because it is too indefinite in that it does not state the price to be paid for the leather. Is Haldane correct?

6. Valley Trout Farms ordered fish food from Rangen. Both parties were merchants. The invoice that was sent with the order stated that a specified charge would be added to any unpaid bills. This was a percentage that was common in the industry. Valley Farms did not pay for the food and did not make any objection to the late charge stated in the invoice. When sued by Rangen, Valley Trout claimed that it had never agreed to the late charge and therefore was not required to pay it. Is Valley Farms correct? [Rangen, Inc. v Valley Trout Farms, Inc. 104 Idaho 284, 658 P2d 955]

7. The Tober Foreign Motors, Inc. sold an airplane

to Skinner on installments. Later it was agreed that the amount of the monthly installments should be reduced by one-half. Thereafter, Tober claimed that the reduction agreement was not binding because it was not supported by consideration. Was this claim correct? [Skinner v Tober Foreign Motors, Inc. 345 Mass 429, 187 NE2d 669]

8. The LTV Aerospace Corporation manufactured all-terrain vehicles for use in Southeast Asia. LTV made an oral contract with Bateman under which Bateman would supply the packing cases needed for their overseas shipment. Bateman made substantial beginnings in the production of packing cases following LTV's specifications. LTV thereafter stopped production of its vehicles and refused to take delivery of any cases. When sued by Bateman for breach of contract, LTV raised the defense that the contract could not be enforced because there was no writing that satisfied the statute of frauds. Was this a valid defense? [LTV Aerospace Corp. v Bateman (Tex Civ App) 492 SW2d 703]

9. Suburban Gas Heat of Kennewick sold propane gas for domestic consumption. As the result of its negligence in supplying propane gas mixed with water, there was an explosion that caused damage to Kasey. When Kasey sued to enforce the liability of Suburban Gas Heat as a seller, Suburban raised the defense that it was engaged in furnishing a public service, not in the sale of goods. Was Suburban correct? [Kasey v Suburban Gas Heat of Kennewick, Inc. 60 Wash 2d 468, 374 P2d 549]

10. Members of the Colonial Club purchased beer from outside the state and ordered it sent to the Colonial Club. The club then kept it in the club refrigerator and served the beer to its respective owners on demand. The club received no compensation or profit from the transaction. The club was indicted for selling liquor. Was it guilty? [North Carolina v Colonial Club, 154 NC 177, 69 SE 771]

11. Fastener Corporation sent a letter to Renzo Box Company. The letter, signed by Ronald Lee, Fastener's sales manager, read as follows: "We hereby offer you 200 type #14 Fastener bolts at $5 per bolt. This offer will be irrevocable for 10 days." On the fifth day, Fastener informed Renzo it was revoking the offer, alleging that there was no consideration for the offer. Could Fastener revoke? Explain.

12. Baker and Smith entered into an oral contract for the purchase and sale of certain goods for the amount of $5,000. Smith admitted in his testimony that he entered into a contract but contended that the amount was only $4,500 and that the oral contract was unenforceable because of the Statute of Frauds. Do you agree with this contention? Why?

13. Frey ordered a unique cabinet from Stull, a cabinetmaker. The cabinet had to be specially made by Stull to meet Frey's requirements. The price of the cabinet was $1,500. The contract was made over the telephone by Frey and Stull. Stull completed the cabinet and tendered delivery to Frey. Frey refused to accept it or pay for it, even though the work was completed on time. Stull could not sell the cabinet to anyone else in the course of her business. Stull sued Frey for breach of the oral contract. Will Stull recover? Explain.

14. Lawrence Fashions, a retail dress merchant, placed a telephone order with Bentley Company for 240 dresses for a total price of $5,000. The next week Lawrence Fashions received, inspected, and accepted 120 dresses. Lawrence Fashions refused to accept the balance when tendered and sought to return the other 120 dresses, claiming it was not obligated to keep and pay for them. Decide.

15. Compare a sale, a bailment, and a gift.

25

RISK AND PROPERTY RIGHTS

In most sales the buyer receives the proper goods and makes payment, and the transaction is thus completed. However, problems may arise. If the parties can foresee potential problems, they can state in their contract what results they desire if such problems do in fact occur. If the parties do not provide in their contract for potential problems, the rules in this chapter apply.

A. TYPES OF TRANSACTIONS AND POTENTIAL PROBLEMS

The solutions to problems of risk and property

rights vary with the kind and terms of the transaction between the seller and the buyer.

1. Types of Problems

Problems involving risk and property rights in sales transactions often relate to damage to the goods, the claims of creditors of the parties to the sales contract, or the obtaining of insurance by those parties.

(a) DAMAGE TO GOODS. If the goods are damaged or totally destroyed without any fault of either the buyer or the seller, must the seller bear the loss and supply new goods to the buyer? Or is it the buyer's loss, so that the

496

buyer must pay the seller the purchase price even though the goods are damaged or destroyed?[1] The fact that there may be insurance does not avoid this question, for the answer to it determines whose insurer is liable and the extent of that insurer's liability.

(b) CREDITORS' CLAIMS. Creditors of a seller may seize the goods as belonging to the seller. The buyer's creditors may seize them on the theory that they belong to the buyer. In such cases the question arises as to whether the creditors are correct as to who owns the goods. The question of ownership is also important in connection with the consequence of a resale by the buyer, or the liability for or the computation of certain kinds of taxes, and the liability under certain registration and criminal law statutes.[2]

(c) INSURANCE. Until the buyer has received the goods and the seller has been paid, both the seller and buyer have an economic interest in the sales transaction.[3] The question arises as to whether either or both have enough interest to entitle them to insure the property involved; that is, whether they have an insurable interest.[4]

2.   Nature of the Transaction

The answer to be given to each of the questions noted in the preceding section depends upon the nature of the transaction between the seller and the buyer. Sales transactions may be classified according to the nature of the goods and the terms of the transaction.

(a) EXISTING AND IDENTIFIED GOODS. Existing goods are physically in existence and owned by the seller. When particular goods have been selected by either the buyer or the seller, or both of them, as being the goods called for by the sales contract, the goods are called **identified goods**. Thus, when you go into a store, point at a particular item, and tell the clerk, "I'll take that one," the sales transaction relates to existing and identified goods.

(b) FUTURE AND UNIDENTIFIED GOODS. Goods are future goods when they are not yet owned by the seller, or when they are not yet in existence. Before goods have been identified to the contract, they are unidentified. Consequently, when you tell the clerk in the store you want one of the items advertised in the paper, the transaction relates to unidentified goods. Your reference to the newspaper ad describes the thing you want, but it does not identify any particular item as the one the seller is to deliver. Future goods are involved if a store tells you that it is out of the advertised item but can order it from the factory or that the factory is going to make a new run of the item and that it will arrive next month.

(c) TERMS OF THE TRANSACTION. Ordinarily, the seller is only required to make the goods available to the buyer. If transportation is provided, the seller is normally only required to make shipment, and the seller's part of the contract is performed by handing the goods over to a carrier for shipment to the buyer. However, the terms of the contract may obligate the seller to deliver the goods at a particular place—for example, to make delivery at the buyer's warehouse. The seller's part of the contract is then not completed until the goods are brought to the destination point and there tendered to the buyer. If the transaction calls for sending the goods to the buyer, it is ordinarily required that the seller deliver the goods to a carrier under a proper contract for shipment to the buyer. Actual physical delivery at destination is required only when the contract expressly so states.

Instead of calling for the actual delivery of goods, the sales transaction may relate to a transfer of the document of title representing the goods. For example, the goods may be stored in a warehouse, and the seller and the buyer have no intention of moving the goods. The parties intend that there shall be a sale and a delivery of the warehouse receipt that

---

[1]   The subject is regulated by UCC § 2-509.
[2]   UCC § 2-401.
[3]   See UCC § 2-501(1)(a).
[4]   In order to insure property, a person must have such a right or interest in the property that its damage or destruction would cause financial loss. This is called an *insurable interest* in the property. The ownership of goods that are the subject of a sales transaction is determined by the UCC for the purpose of insurance.

stands for the goods. Here the obligation of the seller is to produce the proper paper, as distinguished from the goods themselves. The same is true when the goods are represented by any other document of title, such as a bill of lading issued by a carrier.

3.   Existing Goods Identified at Time of Contracting

In a transaction relating to existing and identified goods, where there is no document of title, such as a warehouse receipt or a bill of lading, the title to the goods passes to the buyer at the time the parties agree to the transaction. They may, however, state in the contract that the title shall not pass to the buyer until the full purchase price has been paid.

When the buyer becomes the owner of the goods in the situation here considered, the buyer has an insurable interest in them. The seller has an insurable interest in the goods be-

fore title passes to the buyer. The insurable interest of the seller terminates when title passes to the buyer unless the seller has a lien or a security interest to protect any balance due.

As to risk of loss, a distinction must be made between a merchant seller and a non-merchant seller. If the seller is a merchant, the risk of loss passes to the buyer on receiving the goods from the merchant. If the seller is a nonmerchant, the risk of loss passes when the seller makes the goods available to the buyer. The risk thus remains longer on the merchant seller. Receiving the goods from a merchant means that the buyer takes actual physical possession of the goods.[5]

When the buyer leaves the purchased goods with the seller, who bears the risk of loss if the goods are destroyed? In the *Schock* case the buyer claimed that the seller bore the risk of loss.

---

[5]   Spikes v Baier, 6 Kan App 2d 45, 626 P2d 816 (1981).

SCHOCK v RONDEROS
(ND) 394 NW2d 697 (1986)

Schock negotiated to purchase a mobile home that was owned by and located on the sellers' property. On April 15, buyer appeared at sellers' home and paid them the agreed-upon purchase price of $3,900. Schock received a bill of sale and an assurance from sellers that the title certificate would be delivered soon. On that date, with the permission of sellers, Schock prepared the mobile home for removal. His preparations included the removal of skirting around the mobile home's foundation, removal of the tie-downs, and removal of the foundation blocks, causing the mobile home to rest on the wheels of its chassis. Schock intended to remove the mobile home from the sellers' property a week later, and sellers had no objection to having the mobile home remain on their premises until that time. Sellers also promised to have the electricity and natural gas disconnected by that time. Two days later, the mobile home was destroyed by high winds as it sat on sellers' property. Schock received in the mail a clear certificate of title to the mobile home. Thereafter, Schock sued the sellers for return of his money on the ground that when the mobile home was destroyed, the risk of loss was on the sellers. From a judgment in favor of the sellers, Schock appealed.

ERICKSTAD, J. . . . The issue of which party in this case must bear the loss of the mobile home is determined by the risk of loss provisions under [UCC § 2-509], which provide in relevant part:

3. In any case not within subsection 1 or 2, the risk of loss passes to the buyer on

his receipt of the goods if the seller is a merchant; otherwise the risk passes to the buyer on tender of delivery.

It is undisputed that the Sellers are not merchants; therefore, the risk of loss was on them until they made a "tender of delivery" of the mobile home at which time the risk of loss passed to Buyer. The location or status of the title is not a relevant consideration in determining which party must bear the loss of the mobile home. *Martin v Melland's Inc.*, 283 N.W.2d 76 (N.D.1979).

Pursuant to [UCC § 2-503], tender of delivery requires that the seller "put and hold conforming goods at the buyer's disposition. . . ." The trial court determined that there had been payment for and acceptance of the mobile home by Buyer. Within that conclusion is an implicit determination that there was a completed tender of delivery by Sellers.

The Sellers disconnected the electricity and natural gas to the mobile home prior to its destruction, and nothing remained for them to do as a prerequisite to Buyer's taking possession of the home. . . . The Sellers testified that following Buyer's payment for the home on April 15, 1985, Buyer could have removed the home from their premises at any time. . . . The Sellers, consistent with a completed tender of delivery, acquiesced in Buyer's decision to prepare, on April 15, 1985, the mobile home for removal. As part of those preparations Buyer removed the skirting, the tie downs, and the blocks. He also removed and took with him a set of steps to the mobile home. We believe those actions by Buyer constituted an exercise of possession which is consistent with our conclusion that Sellers had tendered delivery of the mobile home to him on that date. Thus, we hold that on April 15, 1985, the Sellers tendered delivery of the mobile home and the risk of loss passed to Buyer. Accordingly, we further hold that the trial court did not err in denying Buyer's claim for return of the $3,900 purchase money. . . .

[Judgment affirmed]

QUESTIONS

1. Did the title certificate have any bearing on who had risk of loss?
2. Was there a tender of delivery of the mobile home?
3. Would the result have been different if the sellers had been merchants?

4.   Goods Represented by Negotiable Document of Title

Merchants dealing in large quantities of goods often prefer to deal with negotiable documents of title to the goods instead of making a physical delivery of the goods. In such a transaction the buyer acquires an insurable interest in the goods at the time and place of contracting. Unless otherwise provided in the contract, however, the buyer does not become subject to the risk of loss or acquire the title until delivery of the document is made.[6]

[6]   Express provision is made for the case of a nonnegotiable document and other factual variations. UCC § 2-509(2)(c), § 2-503(4).

5.   Future and Unidentified Goods

If the goods either are future goods or have not been identified by the time the transaction is agreed to, the rules stated in Sections 3 and 4 of this chapter do not apply. Instead, the following rules govern the transaction if the parties do not state otherwise.

(a) MARKING FOR BUYER. A buyer may send an order for goods to be manufactured by the seller or to be filled from inventory or by purchases from third persons. If so, one step in the process of filling the order is the seller's act of marking, tagging, labeling, or in some way indicating to the shipping department that certain goods are the ones to be sent or delivered to the buyer under the order. This act of unilateral identification of the goods is enough to give the buyer a property interest in the goods, and it entitles the buyer to insure them. Neither risk of loss nor title passes to the buyer at that time, however. Risk of loss and title remain with the seller, who, as the continuing owner, also has an insurable interest in the goods. Thus, neither title nor risk of loss passes to the buyer until some later event, such as a shipment or delivery, occurs.

(b) CONTRACT FOR SHIPMENT TO BUYER. In a contract for shipment of future goods to a buyer, the contract is performed by the seller by delivering the goods to a carrier for shipment to the buyer. Under such a contract the risk of loss and the title pass to the buyer when the goods are delivered to the carrier—that is, at the time and place of shipment. After the goods are delivered to the carrier, the seller has no insurable interest unless the seller has reserved a security interest in the goods.

The fact that a shipment of goods is represented by a bill of lading or an airbill issued by the carrier, and that in order to complete the transaction it will be necessary to transfer that bill to the buyer, does not affect these rules or bring the transaction within Section 4 of this chapter.

(c) CONTRACT FOR DELIVERY AT DESTINATION. When the contract requires the seller to make delivery of future goods at a particular destination, the buyer acquires a property right and an insurable interest in the goods at the time and place they are marked or shipped. However, the risk of loss and the title do not pass until the carrier tenders or makes the goods available at the destination. The seller retains an insurable interest until that time.

A provision in the contract directing the seller to "ship to" the buyer does not convert the contract into a contract calling for delivery at destination.

6. Damage to or Destruction of Goods

In the absence of a contrary agreement, dam-

FIGURE 25-1   RISK AND PROPERTY RIGHTS IN SALES CONTRACTS

Nature of Goods	Terms of Transaction	Transfer of Risk of Loss to Buyer	Transfer of Title to Buyer	Acquisition of Insurable Interest by Buyer *
Existing Goods Identified at Time of Contracting	1. Without Document of Title	Buyer's receipt of goods from merchant seller, tender of delivery by nonmerchant seller § 2-509(3)	Time and place of contracting § 2-401(3)(b)	Time and place of contracting § 2-501(1)(a)
	2. Delivery of Document of Title Only	Buyer's receipt of negotiable document of title § 2-509(2)(a)	Time and place of delivery of documents by seller § 2-401(3)(a)	Time and place of contracting § 2-501(1)(a)
Future Goods	3. Marking for Buyer	No transfer until a later event	No transfer until a later event	At time of marking § 2-501(1)(b)
	4. Contract for Shipment to Buyer	Delivery of goods to carrier § 2-509(1)(a)	Delivery of goods to carrier § 2-401(2)(a)	Delivery to carrier or marking for buyer § 2-501(1)(b)
	5. Contract for Delivery at Destination	Tender of goods at destination § 2-509(1)(b)	Tender of goods at destination § 2-401(2)(b)	Delivery to carrier or marking for buyer § 2-501(1)(b)

* The seller retains an insurable interest in the goods as long as the seller has a security interest in them. When the buyer acquires an insurable interest, the buyer also acquires a special property in the goods, less than title, which entitles the buyer to assert certain remedies against the seller.

age to or destruction of the goods affects the transaction as follows.

(a) DAMAGE TO IDENTIFIED GOODS BEFORE RISK OF LOSS PASSES. Goods that were identified at the time the contract was made may be damaged or destroyed without the fault of either party before the risk of loss has passed. If so, the contract is avoided if the loss is total. The loss may be partial or the goods may have so deteriorated that they do not conform to the contract. In this case the buyer has the option, after inspection of the goods, to either avoid the contract or accept the goods subject to an allowance or deduction from the contract price. In either case, the buyer cannot assert any claim against the seller for breach of contract.[7]

(b) DAMAGE TO IDENTIFIED GOODS AFTER RISK OF LOSS PASSES. If partial damage or total destruction occurs after the risk of loss has passed to the buyer, it is the buyer's loss. The buyer may be able to recover the amount of the damages from the person in possession of the goods or from a third person causing the loss.

(c) DAMAGE TO UNIDENTIFIED GOODS. As long as the goods are unidentified, no risk of loss passes to the buyer. If any goods are damaged or destroyed during this period, the loss is the seller's. The buyer is still entitled to receive the goods described by the contract. The seller is therefore liable for breach of contract if the proper goods are not delivered.

The only exception arises when the parties have expressly provided in the contract that the destruction of the seller's supply shall release the seller from liability or when it is clear that the parties contracted for the purchase and sale of part of the seller's supply to the exclusion of any other possible source of such goods. In such case, the destruction of or damage to the seller's supply is a condition subsequent that discharges the contract.

(d) RESERVATION OF TITLE OR POSSESSION. When the seller reserves title or possession solely as security to make certain that the buyer will pay the purchase price, the risk of loss is borne by the buyer if the circumstances are such that the loss would be on the buyer in the absence of such a reservation.

7.   Effect of Seller's Breach

When the seller breaches the contract by sending the buyer goods that do not conform to the contract and the buyer rejects the goods, the risk of loss does not pass to the buyer.[8] This means that the risk of loss remains on the seller even though the risk would ordinarily have passed to the buyer. If, because of the nature of the transaction, the risk of loss had already passed to the buyer before there was the opportunity to inspect the goods, the buyer's rejection of the goods returns the risk of loss to the seller.

In the *Graybar* case the seller claimed that the buyer should bear the loss of rejected goods when the loss occurred before the seller took the goods back.

[7]   UCC § 2-613.

[8]   United Air Lines, Inc. v Conductron Corp. 69 Ill App 3d 847, 26 Ill Dec 344, 387 NE2d 1272 (1979).

GRAYBAR ELECTRIC CO. v SHOOK
283 NC 213, 195 SE2d 514 (1973)

Harold Shook ordered three reels of burial cable from Graybar Company for use in construction work. By mistake, two of the three reels that were sent were aerial cable, although each carton was marked "burial cable." Shook accepted the one reel of proper cable and rejected the two nonconforming reels. Because of their size they were left on the ground at the construction site, Six Run Grocery Store, in a rural community. Graybar was notified of the rejection. Graybar did not collect the cable. Shook attempted to return the cable but could not do so because there was a strike of truck drivers. About four months later the two reels of cable were stolen by unidentified persons. Graybar sued Shook for the purchase price. From a judgment for Shook, Graybar appealed.

HIGGINS, J. . . . The plaintiff contends the defendant contracted to [return the nonconforming cable.] The defendant contends he agreed to contact a trucking company and request that it pick up and return the nonconforming reels. The defendant's request was turned down by three different trucking concerns on account of a strike in the trucking industry.

As the defendant's underground cable work progressed beyond the Six Run Grocery Store, the defendant left the nonconforming cable at the store and so notified the plaintiff. The evidence discloses that the cable was stored directly beside the grocery store building near the owner's dwelling in a space which the defendant rented for storage purposes. "The area where the cable was stored was well lighted at all times."

On July 20, 1970, the defendant discovered that one of the reels had been stolen and the following day notified the plaintiff. On that day, also, the defendant contacted a garage operator who promised to pick up the remaining reel and store it in his garage some distance from Six Run. However, before the transfer, the second reel was stolen. The defendant so notified the plaintiff.

The court, upon the disputed facts, found the defendant had not entered into a contract to return the nonconforming cable. . . .

The plaintiff, having made the error of delivering the nonconforming goods on a moving job in the country, was entitled to notice of the nonconformity sufficient to enable it to repossess the nonconforming goods. The plaintiff was given prompt notice but delayed action for more than three months. The cable was stolen from the defendant's regular storage space where the plaintiff had delivered it. Evidence is lacking that a safer storage space was available. The defendant's workmen moved on, leaving the cable and the responsibility for its safety on the owner.

The plaintiff, failing in its efforts to establish a contract on the part of the defendant to return the shipment, however, contends in the alternative that [UCC §] 2-602(2)(b) . . . required the defendant to exercise reasonable care in holding the rejected goods pending the plaintiff's repossession and removal and that the defendant failed to exercise the required care in storage.

Actually, the plaintiff made an on the spot delivery at a store and dwelling in the country. The defendant's work force was stringing underground cable along the highway and the crew was in continual movement. Obviously the crew could not be expected to carry with it two thousand pounds of useless cable and was within its rights placing the cable in its regular storage space and notifying the plaintiff of the place of storage. Both parties realized that cable weighing almost a ton would require men and a truck to remove it. Also both parties assumed that the danger of theft from a well lighted store area was a minimal risk. The property itself was a poor candidate for larceny. The cable was permitted to remain where the plaintiff knew it was located for more than three months. The plaintiff, therefore, had ample opportunity to repossess its property.

The Uniform Commercial Code emphasizes promptness and good faith. The prospective purchaser may exercise a valid right to reject and even if he takes possession, responsibility expires after a reasonable time in which the owner has opportunity to repossess. "Where a tender or delivery of goods so fails to conform to the contract as to give a right of rejection the risk of their loss remains on the seller until cure or acceptance." [UCC §] 2-510(1). The defendant did not accept the aerial cable. According to the evidence and the court's findings, the defendant acted in accordance with the request of the owner in attempting to facilitate the return of that which the defendant rejected. The plaintiff with full notice of the place of storage which was at the place of delivery did nothing but sleep on its rights for more than three months.

The superior court was fully justified in the findings of fact, conclusions of law, and in the judgment dismissing the action. The judgment of the Court of Appeals affirming the superior court was correct. . . .

[Judgment affirmed]

QUESTIONS

1. What was the theory of the plaintiff seller?
2. Did the court agree with the seller's theory? Explain.
3. What decision would the court have made if the cable had been stolen within twenty-four hours after the seller was notified of the buyer's rejection?

8.   Returnable Goods Transactions

The parties may agree that conforming goods can be returned to the seller. This may be (a) a sale on approval, (b) a sale or return, or (c) a consignment sale. In the first two types of transactions the buyer is allowed to return the goods as an added inducement to purchase. The consignment sale is used when the seller is actually the owner's agent for the purpose of selling goods.

Classifying the transaction is the first step in determining the rights of the parties when the buyer may return the goods to the seller. A consignment sale is easily recognized because of its agency characteristics. The agreement of the parties may expressly state that the transaction is a sale on approval or a sale or return. If the agreement of the parties is not clear on this point, and the transaction is not an agency or consignment, classification of the transaction is controlled by the use the buyer will make of the goods. It is a **sale on approval** if the goods are purchased for use by a consum-

er. It is a **sale or return** if purchased for resale—that is, by a merchant.[9]

If the transaction does not give the buyer the right to return the goods, the buyer cannot return goods that conform to the contract if the seller refuses to take them back.

(a) SALE ON APPROVAL. In a sale on approval, no sale takes place (meaning there is no transfer of title) until the buyer approves. Title and risk of loss remain with the seller until there is an approval. Since the buyer is not the "owner" of the goods before approval, the buyer's creditors cannot reach the goods.

The buyer's approval may be shown by (1) express words, (2) conduct, or (3) the lapse of time. Use of the goods that is merely a trying out or testing does not constitute approval. Any use that goes beyond trying out or test-

9   UCC § 2-326(1). An "or return" provision is treated as a sales contract for the purpose of applying the statute of frauds; it cannot be established by parol evidence when it would contradict a sales contract indicating an absolute sale. UCC § 2-326(4).

ing, such as repairing or giving away as a present, is inconsistent with the continued ownership of the seller. Therefore, such use shows approval by the buyer. The contract may give the buyer a fixed number of days for approval. The expiration of that period of time, without any action by the buyer, constitutes an approval. If no time is stated in the contract, the lapse of a reasonable time without action by the buyer constitutes an approval. If the buyer gives the seller notice of disapproval, the lapse of time thereafter has no effect.

If the goods are returned by the buyer, the seller bears the risk and expense of the return.[10]

(b) SALE OR RETURN. A sale or return is a completed sale with an option for the buyer to return the goods. The buyer thereby sells or transfers back to the seller the title that had already passed to the buyer. As to the original sale, title and risk of loss pass to the buyer as in the case of the ordinary or absolute sale. Until the actual return of the goods is made, the title and risk of loss remain with the buyer. The expense and risk of return is on the buyer.

As long as the goods remain in the buyer's possession, the buyer's creditors may treat the goods as belonging to the buyer. The buyer under a sale or return may return all of the goods or any commercial unit thereof. A **commercial unit** is any article, group of articles, or quantity that is regarded commercially as a separate unit or item, such as a particular machine, a suite of furniture, or a carload lot. In order to exercise the right to return the goods, they must be substantially in their original condition. Also, the option to return must be exercised within the time specified by the contract, or within a reasonable time if none is specified.

(c) CONSIGNMENT SALE. By a consignment or sale on consignment, the owner of goods sends them to a dealer to sell. As between the owner (consignor) and the dealer, there is no transfer of title. The relationship is merely an agency relationship. A consignee is

of course required to return any goods not sold, but this does not make it either a sale on approval or a sale or return. When a sale is made by the consignee to a third person, the title of the consignor passes from the consignor directly to the third person.

At no time is the consignee the owner of the goods. In some instances, however, the creditors of the consignee may treat the goods held on consignment as though they belonged to the consignee, thereby ignoring and destroying the consignor's ownership.[11]

9.   Reservation of a Security Interest

The seller may fear that the buyer will not pay for the goods. The seller could protect against this danger by insisting that the buyer pay cash immediately. This may not be practical, for geographic or business reasons. The seller may then give credit to the buyer, but obtain protection by retaining a security interest in the goods. When goods are shipped to the buyer, the creditor may create a temporary security interest so that the buyer must make payment before obtaining the goods from the carrier. Between merchants this is done by various ways of handling the bill of lading issued by the carrier. In the case of a consumer buyer, it is customary for the seller to make the shipment C.O.D. In a C.O.D. shipment, the consumer must pay for the goods before taking possession from the carrier. Under the bill of lading or the C.O.D. shipment, the security interest of the seller ends when the goods are delivered to the buyer. If a seller desires a security interest that will continue as long as the purchase price remains unpaid, a secured transaction under Article 9 of the Uniform Commercial Code will be created.

The fact that a seller has a security interest in the goods, by virtue of a C.O.D. provision or any other device, has no effect on the question of whether title or risk of loss has passed to the buyer. These questions are answered just as though there were no security interest. For example, under a shipment contract of fu-

---

[10]   UCC § 2-327(1).

[11]   Escrow Connection v Haas, 189 Cal App 3d 1640, 235 Cal Rptr 200 (1987).

ture goods from a distant seller, the risk of loss and the title pass to the buyer on delivery to the carrier. The result is the same even though such shipment is made C.O.D.

10.   Effect of Sale on Title

As a general rule, a seller can sell only what the seller owns. If a person in possession of goods is not the owner, as in the case of a finder, thief, or a bailee, a sale by such possessor passes only possession. It is immaterial that the buyer from the possessor had purchased in good faith and had given value. The attempted sale does not pass any title. Consequently, the buyer of stolen goods must surrender them to the true owner and can be sued by the true owner for damages for conversion of the goods. The fact that the negligence of the owner made the theft possible or contributed to the losing of the goods does not bar the owner from recovering the goods or money damages from the thief, the finder, or the purchaser from either of them.[12]

In some instances, however, either because of the conduct of the owner or the desire of society to protect the bona fide purchaser for value, the law permits a greater title to be transferred than the seller possessed.

(a) CONSIGNMENT SALE. A manufacturer or distributor may send goods to a dealer for sale to the public with the understanding that the manufacturer or distributor is to remain the owner, and the dealer in effect is to act as selling agent. When the dealer maintains a place of business at which the dealer sells goods of the kind in question under a name other than that of the consigning manufacturer or distributor, the creditors of the dealer may reach the goods as though they were owned by the dealer. Such goods are deemed to be on sale or return, with title and risk of loss passing to the dealer as in the case of an ordinary sale or return. The consignor can avoid this result by complying with an applicable law providing for the consignor's interest to be evidenced by a sign, by showing

that the person conducting the business is generally known by the creditors to be substantially engaged in selling goods of others, or by complying with the filing provisions of Article 9.[13]

(b) ESTOPPEL. The owner of property may be estopped from asserting ownership and thus be barred from denying the right of another person to sell the property. A person may purchase something and have the bill of sale made out in the name of a friend to whom possession of the property and the bill of sale are given. This might be done in order to deceive creditors of the true owner or to keep other persons from knowing that the purchase was made. If the friend should sell the property to a bona fide purchaser who relies on the bill of sale as showing that the friend is the owner, the true owner is estopped or barred from denying the friend's apparent ownership and right to sell.

(c) POWERS. In certain circumstances, persons in possession of someone else's property may sell the property. This is true in the case of pledgees, lienholders, and some finders who, by statute, may have authority to sell the property either to enforce their claim or when the owner cannot be found.

(d) NEGOTIABLE DOCUMENTS OF TITLE. By statute, certain documents of title, such as bills of lading and warehouse receipts, are negotiable when executed in proper form. By virtue of such provisions the holder of a negotiable document of title may transfer to a good faith purchaser for value such title as was possessed by the person leaving the property with the issuer of the document. In such cases it is immaterial that the holder had not acquired the document in a lawful manner.

(e) VOIDABLE TITLE. If the buyer has a voidable title, as when the goods were obtained by fraud, the seller can rescind the sale. However, if the buyer resells the property to a bona fide purchaser before the seller has rescinded the transaction, the subsequent purchaser acquires valid title. It is immaterial

---

[12]   Pate v Elliott, 61 Ohio App 2d 144, 400 NE2d 910 (1978) (theft).

[13]   UCC § 2-326(3).

whether the buyer having the voidable title had obtained title by fraud as to identity or by larceny by trick, or had paid for the goods with a bad check, or that the transaction was a cash sale and the purchase price had not been paid.[14]

If the transferee from the holder of the voidable title is not a good faith purchaser, the title remains voidable. The true owner may reclaim the goods.[15]

(f) SALE BY ENTRUSTEE. If the owner entrusts goods to a merchant who deals in goods of that kind, the latter has the power to transfer the entruster's title to anyone who buys from the entrustee in the ordinary course of business.

It is immaterial why the goods were entrusted to the merchant. Hence, the leaving of a watch for repair with a jeweler who sells new and second-hand watches gives the jeweler the power to pass the title of the repair customer to a buyer in the ordinary course of business. Goods in inventory thus have a de-gree of "negotiability." The ordinary buyer, whether a consumer or another merchant, buys the goods free of the ownership interest of the person entrusting the goods to the seller.[16] The entrustee is, of course, liable to the owner for damages caused by the entrustee's sale of the goods. The entrustee is also guilty of some form of statutory offense of embezzlement.

In the case of an entrustee who is not a merchant, such as a prospective customer trying out an automobile, there is no transfer of title to the buyer from the entrustee. Likewise, there is no transfer of title when a mere bailee, such as a repairer, who is not a seller of goods of that kind, sells the property of a customer.

If a third person has a claim to the goods, and the claim is superior to that of the entruster, a sale by the entrustee does not destroy that claim but passes the title of the entruster subject to such claim.[17]

The *Kahr* case involved a mistaken delivery of goods to an entrustee who resold the goods to a third party.

---

[14]   Ledbetter v Darwin Dobbs Co., Inc. (Ala) 473 So 2d 197 (1985).
[15]   Kimberly & European Diamonds, Inc. (CA6 Ky) 684 F2d 363 (1982).

[16]   Canterra Petroleum, Inc. v Western Drilling & Mining Supply (ND) 418 NW2d 267 (1987).
[17]   Commercial Credit Equipment Corp. v Bates, 154 Ga App 71, 267 SE2d 469 (1980).

KAHR v MARKLAND
(Ill App) 543 NE2d 579 (1989)

The Kahrs were owners of 28 pieces of valuable sterling silver. They brought sacks of used clothing for donation to Goodwill. Unknown to the Kahrs, the sterling silver was included in the sacks given to Goodwill. At the time of the donation, the Kahrs informed Goodwill that the donation was used clothing. Later on the same day, Goodwill sold the sterling silver to Markland for $15. The Kahrs alleged that the sale of the silver to Markland was without their consent and that Goodwill had therefore transferred void title to the silver to Markland. Markland alleged an entrusting of possession and that valid title was transferred. From a judgment in favor of the Kahrs, Markland appealed.

McCULLOUGH, J. . . . Sections 2-403(2) and (3) of the UCC provide:

(2) Any entrusting of possession of goods to a merchant who deals in goods of

that kind gives power to transfer all rights of the entruster to a buyer in ordinary course of business.

(3) "Entrusting" includes any delivery and any acquiescence in retention of possession regardless of any condition expressed between the parties to the delivery or acquiescence and regardless of whether the procurement of the entrusting or the possessor's disposition of the goods have been such as to be larcenous under the criminal law. . . .

The UCC defines "delivery" as follows:

"Delivery" with respect to instruments, document of title, chattel paper or certificated securities means voluntary transfer of possession. . . . (§ 1-201(14).)

The above definition does not extend to goods. However, the comments on subsection (3) of section 2-403, as adopted in Illinois, state:

. . . [Entrusting] includes *any voluntary transfer of possession by or with the consent of the entruster.* (Emphasis added.)

An entrustment requires four essential elements: (1) an actual entrustment of the goods by the delivery of possession of those goods to a merchant; (2) the party receiving the goods must be a merchant who deals in goods of that kind; (3) the merchant must sell the entrusted goods; and (4) the sale must be to a buyer in the ordinary course of business. . . . The record establishes there was no delivery or voluntary transfer of the sterling silver because plaintiffs were unaware of its place in the bags of clothes. Markland does not dispute this fact but dismisses it as immaterial.

Before the entrustment provisions of the UCC can be applied, a delivery is required. Plaintiff's act of unknowingly leaving the sterling silver with Goodwill is not equivalent to a voluntary transfer. The term "voluntary" is defined as: "proceeding from the will or from one's own choice or consent" and "done by design or intention." (Webster's Third New International Dictionary 2564 (1981).) We conclude the entrustment provisions of the UCC do not apply to this case.

We agree with the trial court that the silver was lost property. Property is lost when it is unintentionally separated from the dominion of its owner. . . . The general rule is that the finder is entitled to possession of lost property against everyone except the true owner. . . . We find this case is similar to *Michael*. There, file cabinets were sold "as is" by First Chicago to a second-hand office supply dealer. Several drawers in the cabinets were locked. The dealer gave the cabinets to an individual at a parking lot sale. Some of the file cabinets were still locked. The buyer from the dealer gave one locked cabinet without any keys to the plaintiff, Michael. Six weeks later, the cabinet fell over, the drawers opened, and Michael found over 1,600 negotiable certificates of deposit payable to "bearer" worth over $6 million dollars. Testimony at trial revealed First Chicago was unaware the certificates were in the file cabinet it sold to the dealer. The plaintiff argued the certificates were abandoned property and therefore, he was entitled to possession. The trial court entered judgment for First Chicago, reasoning that the plaintiff had not proved the certificates were abandoned. The appellate court affirmed and noted that the evidence clearly established that First Chicago intended only to sell used furniture to the dealer. Moreover, the evidence failed to establish that First Chicago intended to permanently give up all rights to the certificates. Thus, possession belonged to First Chicago.

As in *Michael,* plaintiffs here intended to donate only clothes to Goodwill and testified that Goodwill was advised the donation was clothes. The Goodwill employee who received the donation testified she did not recall being advised of the contents of the donation. Plaintiffs' testimony and prompt action remains unrebutted. We note a treatise on the UCC supports our conclusion:

> The Code does not alter the basic pre-Code concept that a possessor cannot pass title. Thus, in the absence of circumstances bringing the case within the scope of UCC § 2-403, it follows that where the owner loses or is robbed of his property and the finder or thief, or anyone who has a temporary right to use it, attempts to sell or pledge it without consent, the owner may follow and reclaim it no matter in whose possession it may be found. That is to say, if the possession of the seller or pledgor is that of a bailee or a trespasser, the loss must fall on him whose act made the loss possible so as not to benefit the pledgee or vendee, for the latter stands in no better position than a person who innocently buys, leases, or acquires property that has been stolen.

3 R. Anderson, Uniform Commercial Code, Section 2-403:26, at 584 (3d ed. 1983). . . . [Judgment affirmed]

QUESTIONS

1. What is meant by an entrustment under the UCC?
2. Was there an entrustment by the Kahrs?
3. What was the basis for the court's decision?

B. SPECIAL SITUATIONS

Risk and property rights in the case of goods in self-service stores and goods sold at auction will be discussed in the following sections.

11. Self-Service Stores

In the case of goods in a self-service store, the reasonable interpretation of the circumstances is that the store, by its act of putting the goods on display on the shelves, makes an offer to sell such goods for cash and confers on a prospective customer a license to carry the goods to the cashier in order to make payment. Most courts hold that there is no transfer of title until the buyer makes payment to the cashier.

A contrary rule adopts the view that "a contract to sell" is formed when the customer "accepts" the seller's offer by taking the item from the shelf.

By another contrary view, a sale actually occurs when the buyer takes the item from the shelf. That is, title passes at that moment to the buyer, even though the goods have not yet been paid for. Under this view, if the buyer places the item back on the shelf, this is merely a "return" by the buyer. By this return the buyer transfers back to the seller the title that had already passed to the buyer when the item was removed from the shelf.

In the *Fender* case a customer in a self-service store was injured by an item that she was about to pay for. This raised the question of whether she had the status of a buyer under a sales contract.

FENDER v COLONIAL STORES, INC.

138 Ga App 138, 225 SE2d 691 (1976)

> Fender was a customer in the Big Star self-service store owned by Colonial Stores, Inc. She placed her selections on the cashier's counter. While lifting a six-pack of Coca Cola from her cart to the counter, one of the bottles exploded, and she was injured by the flying glass. She sued Colonial Stores. She claimed that the defendant was liable for breach of warranty. The defendant denied this liability on the ground that there could be no warranty liability until there was a sale and that the Coca Cola had not been sold to Fender, because she had not yet paid for it. From a judgment for Colonial, Fender appealed.

DEEN, P. J. . . . An action based on breach of warranty necessitates a showing of the existence of the warranty, the fact that the warranty was broken and that the breach of the warranty was the proximate cause of the loss sustained. . . . The defendant-retailer contends that the plaintiff's evidence failed to establish the existence of a warranty. [UCC §] 2-314(1) provides . . . a warranty that the goods shall be merchantable is implied in a *contract for their sale* if the seller is a merchant with respect to goods of that kind . . . " (Emphasis supplied.) The retailer urges there was no warranty because at the moment of explosion the plaintiff had as yet not paid for the bottle.

The retailer argues that no title had passed on the goods; this ignores, however, the clear language of [UCC §] 2-314 that a warranty is implied upon a contract for sale and not solely upon the execution of the sale itself. [UCC §] 2-106(1) defined "contract for sale" as "both a present sale of goods and a contract to sell goods at a future time . . ." We therefore see this issue as not one of title passing from the retailer to the consumer but one of the existence of a contract between the parties to sell goods at a future time. A contract is of course "an agreement between two or more parties for the doing or not doing of some specified thing" and requires "parties able to contract, a consideration moving to the contract, the assent of the parties to the terms of the contract, and a subject-matter upon which it can operate." . . . The plaintiff has the burden of showing the existence of the warranty by establishing that at the time the bottle exploded there was a contract for its sale existing between herself and the retailer.

The plaintiff's evidence in this case showed that the retailer's store was of the usual "self-service" type, in which customers were supplied with carts and allowed to roam the aisles at will, selecting items from the shelves and cases and then negotiating the check-out line where the purchases are rung up on the register and the total price is paid. The plaintiff testified that she had finished her shopping and was in the physical act of placing the bottles on the counter for payment when the explosion occurred; she further testified that she was at the check-out counter to pay for her purchases.

We think this evidence sufficient to show that the retailer's act of placing the bottles on the shelf with the price stamped upon them manifested an intent to offer them for sale, the terms of the offer being that it would pass title to the customer when they were presented at the check-out counter and paid for. Likewise we think that the evidence shows that the plaintiff's act of taking physical possession of the goods with the intent to purchase them manifested an intent to accept the offer and a promise to take them to the check-out counter and to there pay for them. . . . Placing the goods on the shelf for customer inspection and selection was clearly an offer to sell them at the stated price; the retailer did not indicate by language or circumstances that acceptance of this offer could not be accomplished by taking possession of the goods with an implied *promise* to pay for them upon check-out rather than by the actual act of exchanging money. It is equally reasonable under the terms of the offer that acceptance could occur in any one of three ways: (1) by delivering the goods to the check-out counter and paying for them; (2) by the promise to pay for the goods as evidenced by their physical delivery to the check-out counter; and (3) by the promise to deliver the goods to the check-out counter and to pay for them there as evidenced by taking physical possession of the goods by their removal from the shelf. Under the circumstances surrounding this transaction we believe reasonable men could conclude that the plaintiff's act of taking physical possession of the goods with the intent to pay for them constituted a reasonable mode of acceptance; that by taking physical possession and delivering to the check-out counter the plaintiff promised to pay for them at the stated price and that this promise is sufficient consideration to support a contract . . . ; that a contract for the sale of the goods came into being when the plaintiff accepted the offer by taking physical possession thereof with the intent to pay for them; and that from that moment forward the implied warranties of [UCC §] 2-314 were applicable. See *Seigel v Giant Food, Inc.* 20 Md App 611, 318 A2d 874. "A contract for sale of goods may be made in any manner sufficient to show agreement, including conduct by both parties which recognizes the existence of such a contract. An agreement sufficient to constitute a contract for sale may be found even though the moment of its making is undetermined." . . .

Nor do we believe that the fact that the customer in a "self-service" store has the right to return merchandise to the shelves at any time before payment is made militates against a finding that a contract for the sale of goods has come into being before such payment. " 'Termination' occurs when either party pursuant to a power created by agreement or law puts an end to the contract otherwise than for its breach . . . " [UCC §] 2-106(3). We believe that the fact that the retailer permits the customer to "change his mind" indicates only an agreement between the parties to allow the customer to end his contract with the retailer irrespective of a breach of the agreement by the retailer. . . .

In reaching this decision that in the context of a self-service store a contract for sale of goods may arise before payment is actually made for the goods, we are not unaware of decisions in other jurisdictions to the contrary. *Loch v Confair,* 361 Pa 158, 63 A2d 24; *Lasky v Economy Grocery Stores,* 319 Mass 224, 65 NE2d 305; *Day v Grand Union Co.,* 280 AppDiv 253, 113 NYS2d 436. These cases were all decided prior to the adoption in their jurisdictions of the Uniform Commercial Code with its liberalized concept of contract formation and at a time when passage of "title" was the relevant legal prerequisite to a warranty action. It is true that the Court of Appeals of our sister state of North Carolina by discussion of the "passage of title" in a recent decision reached a similar result to that we have reached here. *Gillispie v The Great Atlantic and Pacific Tea Co.,* 14 NCApp 1, 187 SE2d 441. While we agree with the result reached in the *Gillispie* decision we do not agree that the question of whether a contract for sale exists is dependent upon the passage of title. We embrace rather the well-reasoned opinions . . . to the effect that a contract of sale of goods in the self-service supermarket context may arise before payment is actually made for the goods and title passes.

The retailer urges that even if we find a warranty has arisen in this case, as we have in fact so found, that the plaintiff's evidence fails to show a breach thereof. The testimony was that the goods selected were normal in appearance, that the bottles had not struck or touched the carton or any of the bottles against any object at any time after they were removed from the shelf, but that the bottle exploded as it was being placed on the counter for check-out and that the plaintiff was injured by flying glass. "It is obvious that Coca Cola bottles which would break under normal handling are not fit for the ordinary use for which they were intended and that the relinquishment of physical control of such a defective bottle to a consumer constitutes a breach of warranty. Thus the evidence was sufficient to show that when the bottles left the retailer's control they did not conform to the representations of the warranty of merchantability, and that this breach of the warranty was the cause of the loss sustained. Having made this *prima facie* showing appellant was entitled to have the jury pass upon the questions of whether the warranty was breached, and if so, whether the breach caused [her] injury."

. . .

[Judgment reversed]

QUESTIONS

1. Did the customer own the six-pack at the time one of the bottles exploded?
2. Was the case affected by your answer to Question 1?
3. The fact that the customer in a self-service store may return a selected item to the shelf means that the customer does not have any contract of purchase with the store. Appraise this statement.

12.   Auction Sales

When goods are sold at an auction in separate lots, each lot is a separate transaction, and title to each passes independently of the other lots. Title to each lot passes when the auctioneer announces by the fall of the hammer or in any other customary manner that the lot in question has been sold to the bidder.[18]

[18]   UCC § 2-328.

SUMMARY

Problems relating to risk and property rights in sales transactions often involve damage to the goods, the claims of creditors, and insurance. The solution to these problems often depends on the nature of the transaction between the seller and the buyer. Sales transactions may be classified according to the nature of the goods and the terms of the transactions.

Existing goods are physically in existence and owned by the seller. Future goods are not yet owned by the seller or are not yet in existence. The title to existing goods that are identified at the time of the contract passes to the buyer at the time the parties agree to the transaction. Once the goods are identified, both the buyer and the seller have an insurable interest in the goods. If the goods are damaged after the sales agreement has been made, a merchant seller bears the loss occurring until the time the buyer receives the goods. If the seller is not a merchant, the risk of loss passes to the buyer when the goods are tendered or made available to the buyer. In a shipment contract, title and risk of loss pass at the time and place of shipment; in a destination contract, title and risk pass when the goods are made available at the destination. As long as the goods are unidentified, neither title nor risk of loss passes to the buyer.

In cases where the risk of loss would ordinarily pass to the buyer, the risk nevertheless remains with the seller if the goods do not conform to the contract. Even when the goods do conform to the contract, the buyer and seller could have agreed in their contract that the goods may be returned. The nature of their agreement, as a sale on approval, sale or return, or consignment sale, determines who has title and who bears the risk of loss.

The reservation of a security interest in goods does not affect the question of whether title or risk of loss has passed to the buyer.

Ordinarily, sellers cannot pass any better title than they possess. In some cases, however, the law permits a greater title to be transferred.

In an auction sale, title passes when the auctioneer accepts the bidder's offer.

QUESTIONS AND CASE PROBLEMS

1. What social forces are affected by the rule that the buyer has an insurable interest when future goods are marked for shipment to the buyer?

2. By letter, Felicia in Oklahoma orders a sewing machine from the Jakoby Sewing Machine Company in Chicago. The order of Felicia is accepted, but nothing is said as to whether the sale is for cash or on credit. How can Jakoby be sure that payment is made before Felicia gets possession of the sewing machine?

3. Kirk buys a television set from the Janess Television Store. At the time of the sale Kirk gives Janess a check for the purchase price and obtains a receipt marked "paid in full." The check is a bad check as it is drawn on an account in which the balance is not sufficient to cover the amount of the check. Kirk knows this but hopes to leave town with the television set before Janess learns that the check is bad. Is Kirk the owner of the television set?

4. Lotus Corporation sold and delivered a photocopier to Smith, for use in Smith's business. According to their agreement, Smith may return the copier within 30 days. During the 30-day period, Smith's place of business burns to the ground. Who has title to the photocopier? Who has risk of loss? Explain.

5. Jamison wants to buy a new truck. Kenton, a dealer, tries to sell him a particular truck. Jamison is not certain that this is the truck he wants. To encourage him to buy, Kenton sells the truck to him on "30-day approval." Jamison owes the First National Bank on an overdue debt, and 25 days later the bank has the sheriff seize the truck in order to sell it to pay off the debt owed by Jamison. Both Kenton and Jamison object that the bank cannot do this. Are they correct?

6. O owned a television set. T stole the set and sold it to A, who purchased for value and in good faith. A resold the set to B who also purchased in good faith and for value. O sued B for the set. B raised the defense that he had purchased it in good faith from a seller who had sold in good faith. Was this defense valid? [Johnny Dell, Inc. v New York State Police, 84 Misc 2d 360, 375 NYS2d 545]

7. B purchased a used automobile from A with a bad check. A then took the automobile to an auction, in which the automobile was sold to C, who had no knowledge of its prior history. When B's check was dishonored, A brought suit against C to reclaim the automobile. Was he entitled to do so? [Greater Louisville Auto Auction, Inc. v Ogle Buick, Inc. (Ky) 387 SW2d 17]

8. Coppola collected coins. He joined a coin club, First Coinvestors, Inc. The club would send coins to its members, who were to pay for them or return them within ten days. What was the nature of the transaction? [First Coinvestors, Inc. v Coppola, 88 Misc 2d 495, 388 NYS2d 833]

9. Sandford signed an agreement to purchase a used calculator from Roberts. Andrews agreed to pick it up the next day. The Roberts salesperson marked the calculator "sold," placed Sandford's name on it, and moved it to the storeroom. That night thieves broke into the storeroom and took everything, including the calculator. This was in no way caused by the negligence of Roberts. Sandford refuses to pay unless he receives his calculator. Who bears the risk of loss? Why?

10. A manufacturer of knitwear loaded a trailer with goods ordered by the buyer. The loaded trailer was to be hauled away by a carrier. After the trailer was loaded but before it was taken away, it was damaged by fire. The manufacturer claimed that the buyer must bear the risk of loss because the goods were future goods covered by a shipment contract. Was the manufacturer correct? [A. M. Knitwear Corp. v All America

Export-Import Corp. 50 App Div 2d 558, 375 NYS2d 23]

11. Compare the effect upon title of a repair shop's unauthorized sale of a customer's television set when (a) the repair shop only makes repairs, and (b) the repair shop also sells new and used television sets.

12. The Leton Wholesale Company sold and delivered ten executive desks on consignment to Lois, the owner and manager of the Handy Office Supply Company. Lois had severe financial problems, and her creditors petitioned the court to allow attachment of her inventory. A marshal seized the entire inventory of the Handy Office Supply Company, including the ten executive desks. Explain how the Leton Wholesale Company could have prevented the desks from becoming subject to the claim of the creditors of Lois.

13. Smith operated a marina and sold and repaired boats. Gallagher rented a stall at the marina, where he kept his vessel, the River Queen. Without any authorization, Smith sold the vessel to Courtesy Ford. Gallagher sued Courtesy Ford for the vessel. What was the result? [Gallagher v Unenrolled Motor Vessel River Queen (CA5 Tex) 475 F2d 117]

14. Without permission, Grissom entered onto land owned by another. He then proceeded to cut and sell the timber from the land. On learning that the timber had been sold, the owner of the land brought an action to recover the timber from the purchaser. The purchaser argued that he was a good faith purchaser who had paid value and therefore was entitled to keep the timber. Decide. [Baysprings Forest Products, Inc. v Wade (Miss) 435 So 2d 690]

15. On October 1, by written contract, Donnely sold a pile of lumber in his yard to Dean. Dean was to pick up the lumber on October 15 and pay for it at that time. On October 7, Lawrence, who had a judgment against Donnely, had a sheriff seize the lumber by writ of execution. Both Donnely and Dean claimed that the seizure was illegal, because Donnely no longer owned the lumber. Were they correct? Explain.

26

OBLIGATIONS AND PERFORMANCE

Each party to a sales contract must perform according to its terms. Each is likewise under the duty to act with good faith in its performance and to do nothing to impair the other party's expectation that the contract will be performed.

A. GENERAL PRINCIPLES

Contracts for the sale of goods impose certain obligations on the parties to the contracts.

1. Obligation of Good Faith

"Every contract or duty within [the UCC] imposes an obligation of good faith in its performance or enforcement."[1] The UCC defines good faith as meaning "honesty in fact in the conduct or transaction concerned."[2] In the case of a merchant seller or buyer of goods, the UCC carries the concept of good faith further. The UCC imposes the additional requirement that the merchant seller or buyer observe "reasonable commercial standards of fair dealing in the trade."[3]

---

[1] UCC § 1-203. Servbest Foods, Inc. v Emessee Industries, Inc. 82 Ill App 3d 662, 37 Ill Dec 945, 403 NE2d 1 (1980).
[2] UCC § 1-201(19); Chemical Bank of Rochester v Haskell, 51 NY2d 85, 432 NYS2d 478, 411 NE2d 1339 (1980).
[3] UCC § 2-103(1)(b).

In the *Umlas* case the owner of a car wanted to trade it in on the purchase of a new car. He claimed that the dealer did not observe good faith in making a reappraisal of the used car.

UMLAS v ACEY OLDSMOBILE, INC.
(NY Civil Court) 62 Misc 2d 819, 310 NYS2d 147 (1970)

Harry Umlas made a contract to buy a new automobile from Acey Oldsmobile. He was allowed to keep his old car until the new car was delivered. The sales contract gave him a trade-in value of $650 on the old car, but specified that it would be reappraised when it was actually brought in to the dealer. When Umlas brought the trade-in to the dealer, an employee of Acey took it for a test drive and told Acey that it was worth from $300 to $400. Acey stated to Umlas that the trade-in would be appraised at $50. Umlas refused to buy from Acey and purchased from another dealer who appraised the trade-in at $400. Umlas sued Acey for breach of contract. Acey defended on the ground that its conduct was authorized by the reappraisal clause.

SANDLER, J. . . . Underlying plaintiff's lawsuit is the charge . . . that the reappraisal was not done in good faith.

The defendant interposed a counterclaim for an amount just in excess of $300.00 that is totally without any semblance of merit, and that was obviously designed to harass the plaintiff by removing the case from the Small Claims Part of this Court.

I find as a fact that defendant's employee did state to plaintiff that he had reappraised plaintiff's car in the amount of $50.00 . . . and that this valuation was not made in good faith.

The critical legal question thus becomes whether the provision of the form order, under which defendant reserved the right to reappraise the used car allowance at the time of delivery where delivery is deferred, implies that the right of reappraisal is to be exercised in good faith. I conclude as a matter of law that good faith is an essential implied condition for the exercise of the right of reappraisal. See Uniform Commercial Code, 1–201, 2–103; c.f. 2–305.

To hold otherwise would mean that the order agreement, and the promises exchanged therein, was intended to be wholly illusory until delivery had been completed. Such a construction would make a travesty of an agreement that evoked from the plaintiff, as it was intended to, the following substantial reliance: a down payment, suspension for a period of his right to acquire a car elsewhere, and the securing of a bank loan. . . .

In reaching the above conclusion, I do not wish to be understood as doubting the legitimate considerations prompting the provision in question when the delivery of the car is to be deferred. Obviously, the buyer's car may suffer some deterioration during the intervening period. . . .

But the fact that the clause represents a reasonable response to a practical problem does not obscure the reality that it is open to, and indeed lends itself to, serious and recurrent abuse. In the presence of a potential buyer, searching for the optimum price for his used car, a dealer may well be disposed to place a generous value on the used car, realizing that he could later renegotiate the figure when his bargaining position was immensely strengthened.

For it is surely clear that when a buyer has signed an order for a particular car of a certain color and with special accessories, has made a cash down payment, has secured a bank loan, and has arrived in his somewhat worn old car ready to receive a resplendent new vehicle, his ability to resist a new less-favorable deal is at a very low ebb indeed.

Surely, it is no surprise that defendant's witness acknowledged that used car allowances are often lowered at the delivery date. And although no testimony was presented directly, it is surely a fair surmise that instances in which used cars are found to have a higher value at the delivery date would represent extraordinary phenomena in the annals of any car dealer.

... The plaintiff, like any purchaser under the circumstances, was entitled to a good faith valuation of his car on the delivery date.

In the absence of any good faith reappraisal by the defendant, the only valuation by the defendant is that fixed at the time of the original order, and I find that to be controlling.

Accordingly, I find for the plaintiff. . . .

QUESTIONS

1. What part of the contract between Umlas and Acey was violated?
2. What could Umlas have done for his protection?
3. Compare the *Umlas* decision and the common law concept of "let the buyer beware."

2.   Time Requirements of Obligations

In the case of a cash sale not requiring the physical moving of the goods, the duties of the seller and buyer are concurrent. Each one has the right to demand that the other perform at the same time. That is, as the seller hands over the goods, the buyer theoretically must hand over the purchase money. If either party refuses to act, the other party has the right to withhold performance. In the case of a shipment contract there is a time interval between the performance of the parties; the seller will have performed by delivering the goods to the carrier, but the buyer's obligation will not begin until the goods have been received and accepted by the buyer.

3.   Repudiation of the Contract

The seller or the buyer may refuse to perform the contract when the time for performance arises. This is a **repudiation** of the contract.[4] Likewise, before that time arrives, one party may inform the other that the contract will never be performed. This repudiation made in advance of the time for performance is called an **anticipatory repudiation**.

(a) ACTION OF AGGRIEVED PARTY. If there is a clear anticipatory repudiation of the contract and the loss of the repudiated performance substantially impairs the value of the contract to the other party, the aggrieved party may request the repudiating party to retract or take back the repudiation. While waiting to see what happens, the aggrieved party may hold up rendering any further performance under the contract. In any case the aggrieved party may assert that the contract has been broken and utilize any of the remedies available for breach.

---

[4]   Unique Systems, Inc. v Zotos International, Inc. (CA8 Minn) 622 F2d 373 (1980).

An aggrieved party may act without sufficient justification; that is, in fact there may have been no anticipatory repudiation. In such a case the aggrieved party who withholds performance is the one who is breaking the contract and is liable for damages for breach.

(b) RETRACTION OF ANTICIPATORY REPUDIATION. Prior to the time when performance is due, the party who made the anticipatory repudiation may retract it or take it back. This cannot be done if the other party has (1) canceled the contract because of the repudiation, (2) materially changed position, as by making other sales or purchases, or (3) expressly accepted the repudiation as final.

4.   Adequate Assurance of Performance

A party to a sales contract may think that the other party will not perform the contract. For example, the seller's warehouse is destroyed by fire. The buyer could fear that the seller will not be able to make a delivery scheduled for the following month. Whenever a party to a sales contract has reasonable grounds for being concerned about the future performance of the other party, a written demand may be made on such other party for assurance that the contract will be performed.[5]

(a) FORM OF ASSURANCE. The person on whom demand for assurance is made must give "such assurance of due performance as is adequate under the circumstances of the particular case." The exact form of assurance is not specified by the UCC. If the party on whom demand is made has an established reputation, a reaffirmation of the contract obligation and a statement that it will be performed may be sufficient to assure a reasonable person that it will be performed. In contrast, the person's reputation or economic position at the time may be such that mere words and promises would not give any real assurance. In such case it may be necessary to have a third person (or an insurance compa-

ny) guarantee performance or to put up property as security for performance.

(b) FAILURE TO GIVE ASSURANCE. If adequate assurance is not given, the demanding party may treat the contract as repudiated.[6] The demanding party is then free to make a substitute contract with a third person to replace the repudiated contract.

B.   DUTIES OF THE PARTIES

The obligations of the parties to a sales contract include (1) the seller's duty to deliver the goods, (2) the buyer's duty to accept the goods, and (3) the buyer's duty to pay for the goods. In addition, special terms may give rise to other duties of the parties.

5.   Seller's Duty to Deliver

The seller has the duty to deliver the goods in accordance with the terms of the contract. This duty to make "delivery" does not require physical transportation but merely means that the seller must permit the transfer of possession of the goods to the buyer. That is, the seller makes the goods available to the buyer. The delivery is sufficient if it is made in accordance with the terms of the sale or contract to sell.

(a) PLACE, TIME, AND MANNER OF DELIVERY. The terms of the contract determine whether the seller is to send the goods or the buyer is to call for them, whether the goods must be transported by the seller to the buyer, or whether the transaction is to be completed by the delivery of documents without the movement of the goods. In the absence of a provision in the contract or a contrary course of performance or usage of trade, the place of delivery is the seller's place of business, if the seller has one; otherwise it is the seller's residence. However, if the subject matter of the contract consists of identified goods that are known by the parties to be in some other place, that place is the place of delivery. Doc-

---

[5]   UCC § 2-610; Scott v Crown Co. (Colo App) 765 P2d 1043 (1988).

[6]   UCC § 2-609(4). This assurance must be given within 30 days.

uments of title may be delivered through customary banking channels.[7] If no time for shipment or delivery is stated, delivery or shipment is required within a reasonable time.[8]

When a method of transportation called for by the contract becomes unavailable or commercially unreasonable, the seller must make delivery by means of a commercially reasonable substitute if available. The buyer must accept such substitute.[9] This provision is applicable when a shipping strike makes impossible the use of the method of transportation specified in the contract of sale.

(b) QUANTITY DELIVERED. The buyer has the right to insist that all the goods be delivered at one time. If the seller delivers a smaller or larger quantity than that stipulated in the contract, the buyer may refuse to accept the goods.

(c) CURE OF DEFECTIVE TENDER OR DELIVERY. If the seller tenders or delivers

nonconforming goods, the buyer may reject them. This does not end the transaction. The seller is given a second chance to make a proper or **curative tender** of conforming goods.[10]

This right is restricted in terms of whether the second tender can be made within the time called for by the contract. If the time for making delivery under the contract has not expired, the seller need only give the buyer **seasonable** (timely) notice of the intention to make a proper delivery within the time allowed by the contract. The seller may then do so. If the time for making the delivery has expired, the seller may be given an additional reasonable time in which to make a substitute conforming tender. Additional time is allowed if (1) the seller so notifies the buyer, and (2) the seller had acted reasonably in making the original tender, believing that it would be acceptable to the buyer.

The *Worldwide* case deals with the right of the seller to cure a tender of goods that did not conform to the contract specifications.

---

[7]   UCC § 2-308.
[8]   UCC § 2-309.
[9]   UCC § 2-614(1).

[10]   UCC § 2-508. Stephenson v Frazier (Ind App) 399 NE2d 794 (1980).

WORLDWIDE RV SALES & SERVICE, INC. v BROOKS
(Ind App) 534 NE2d 1132 (1989)

Brooks agreed to buy a motor home with dual air conditioners from Worldwide. Brooks discovered that the motor home had only one air conditioner. Brooks rejected the motor home. Worldwide offered to put in the two air conditioners originally requested and remove the other one, leaving a hole in the roof. Brooks refused the offer. Worldwide refused to refund his down payment. From a judgment in favor of Brooks, Worldwide appealed.

STATION, J. . . . This matter falls under the Uniform Commercial Code Sales, [Section] 2-101 et seq. Worldwide argues that [UCC §] 2-508 entitled it to cure the problem and prevent cancellation of the contract. That section states that:

(1) Where any tender or delivery by the seller is rejected because non-conforming and the time for performance has not yet expired, the seller may seasonably notify the buyer of his intention to cure and may then within the contract time make a conforming delivery.
(2) Where the buyer rejects a non-conforming tender which the seller had reasonable grounds to believe would be acceptable with or without money allowance

the seller may if he seasonably notifies the buyer have a further reasonable time to substitute a conforming tender.

Worldwide claims that on the same day Brooks rejected the motorhome Worldwide offered to install a second roof air conditioner at no extra charge. Our examination of the record reveals that Worldwide's representative asked if the deal could be saved if they installed a second roof air conditioner. This "offer to cure" was accompanied with the warning that this alteration would result in a hole in the center of the motorhome. To benefit from the remedial effect of [UCC §] 2-508 the seller must "make a conforming delivery" or "substitute a conforming tender." Worldwide did not fulfill this statutory requirement.

Worldwide's brief states that Worldwide tendered conforming goods on the same day Brooks rejected them. The facts do not substantiate this claim. [UCC §] 2-503 states in pertinent part that "tender of delivery requires that the seller put and hold conforming goods at the buyer's disposition and give the buyer any notification reasonably necessary to enable him to take delivery." We have already determined that Brooks rejected the goods because they were non-conforming and that Worldwide's offer to cure was inadequate.

[Judgment affirmed]

QUESTIONS

1. Was the buyer's rejection proper?
2. What are the requirements for the seller's right to cure?
3. Did the seller act properly in exercising the right to cure?

6.   Buyer's Duty to Accept Goods

The buyer must accept goods that conform to the contract. Refusal to do so is a breach of the contract.

(a) RIGHT TO EXAMINE GOODS. In order to see if the goods in fact conform to the contract, the buyer has the right to examine the goods when tendered by the seller. As an exception to this rule, the buyer has no right to examine goods sent C.O.D. until payment is made.

(b) WHAT CONSTITUTES ACCEPTANCE OF GOODS. Acceptance of goods means that the buyer, pursuant to a contract, takes goods as the buyer's own. This may be done by an express statement of approval. Acceptance can also be shown by conduct inconsistent with rejection, as illustrated in the *Fram* case. A third way of accepting goods is by lapse of time.[11]

[11]   UCC §§ 2-602(1) and § 2-606(1). Tonka Tours, Inc. v Chadima (Minn) 372 NW2d 723 (1985).

UNITED STATES FOR THE USE OF FRAM CORP. v CRAWFORD
(CA5 Ga) 443 F2d 611 (1971)

Floyd Crawford, who was constructing a building for the United States Navy, purchased fuel equipment from Fram Corp. and installed the equipment in the building. Fram sued for the purchase price. Crawford claimed that he had not accepted the equipment because it was defective. From a judgment for Crawford, Fram appealed.

AINSWORTH, C.J.... The contract price for the fuel filter/separator units was $55,564.20. Floyd Crawford admitted at the trial that of that sum, $6,298.50 had not been paid. There was no testimony to the contrary. The appellees maintain that they are excused from further payment by the deficiencies in Fram's performance on the contract. Fram contends, to the contrary, that the Trial Judge should have directed a verdict in its favor on its claim for the $6,298.50. We sustain Fram's contention.

It is undisputed that Fram furnished the eighteen fuel filter/separator units called for by the contract, and that Crawford received and installed all eighteen units. Section 2–607 of the Uniform Commercial Code ... provides ... "The buyer must pay at the contract rate for any goods accepted." Acceptance of goods occurs when the buyer "does any act inconsistent with the seller's ownership." Georgia UCC § 2-606(1)(c). No case is reported in which the Georgia courts have had occasion to interpret section 2-606(1)(c). Courts in other jurisdictions, interpreting the same section of the Uniform Commercial Code, have held that installation by the buyer of heavy equipment supplied by the seller is an act inconsistent with the seller's ownership. See *Marbelite Company v City of Philadelphia*, 208 Pa Super 256, 222 A2d 443 (1966) (traffic signal equipment); *Park County Implement Co. v Craig* (Wyo) 397 P2d 800 (1964) (hoist and dump bed on vehicle). We believe that the Georgia courts, confronted with the same issue in the instant case, would give section 2-606(1)(c) the same construction. A buyer who has accepted goods may under certain conditions revoke his acceptance. Georgia UCC § 2-608. However, once Crawford had accepted and installed the units supplied in place on the Albany site, any subsequent attempt at revocation was ineffective....

[Judgment reversed and action remanded]

QUESTIONS

1. Who was the plaintiff?
2. Was it important whether the buyer had accepted the equipment? Explain.
3. Did Crawford ever inform Fram Corporation that the equipment was accepted?

A buyer accepts the goods by making continued use of them and by not attempting to return the goods. A buyer, of course, accepts the goods by modifying them, because such action is inconsistent with a rejection or with the continued ownership of the goods by the seller. Consequently, when the purchaser of a truck installs a hoist and a dump bed on it, such action constitutes an acceptance by conduct. The buyer therefore becomes liable for the contract price of the truck.

7.   Buyer's Duty to Pay

The buyer must pay for goods accepted and must pay the amount stated in the sales contract.

(a) TIME OF PAYMENT. The sales contract may require payment in advance or may give the buyer credit by postponing the time for payment.[12]

(b) FORM OF PAYMENT. Unless otherwise agreed, payment by the buyer requires payment in cash.

---

[12]   UCC § 2-310(a). If delivery under the contract is to be made by delivery of a document of title, payment is due at the time and place at which the buyer is to receive the document, regardless of where the goods are to be received. § 2-310(c).

The seller may accept a check or a promissory note from the buyer. If the check is not paid by the bank, the purchase price remains unpaid. A promissory note payable at a future date gives the buyer credit by postponing the time for payment.

The seller may refuse to accept a check or promissory note. When the seller does so, the seller must give the buyer reasonable time in which to obtain legal tender with which to make payment.

8.   Duties under Particular Terms

A sale may be as simple as a face-to-face exchange of money and goods. It frequently involves a more complicated pattern, with some element of transportation, generally by a common carrier. This, in turn, generally results in the addition of certain special terms to the sales transaction.

(a) C.I.F., C. & F. Under a **C.I.F.** contract the buyer pays the seller a lump sum covering the cost (selling price) of the goods, insurance on the goods, and freight to the specified destination. **C. & F.** contracts are similar except that under such contracts the seller is not obligated to insure the goods for the buyer's benefit. Under both these terms the risk of loss and

title to the goods pass to the buyer after the goods have been delivered to the carrier.

(b) F.O.B. The term **F.O.B.** (free on board) is a condensed way of saying that the seller has the obligation of (1) putting the goods on board a named vessel, truck, or other carrier, or (2) making tender at a named geographical point. When used to specify a geographical point, it may be F.O.B. the seller's city, the buyer's city, or an intermediate point. For example, the F.O.B. point may be the Port of New York for goods that are to be sent by land to New York and by water to a foreign country. Under the F.O.B. term, risk of loss and title pass to the buyer at the F.O.B. point. This is so even though such transfer would have occurred at a different point if the shipment had not been F.O.B. The seller pays the cost of transporting the goods to the F.O.B. point.[13] The buyer pays transportation costs from that point on.

(c) F.A.S., EX-SHIP. The term **F.A.S.** means free alongside the named vessel. The seller, at the seller's own expense and risk, must deliver the goods alongside a named vessel. Risk of loss and title pass to the buyer at the shipping point.

---

[13]   Buenger v Pruden (Wyo) 713 P2d 771 (1986).

FIGURE 26-1   OBLIGATIONS AND PERFORMANCE

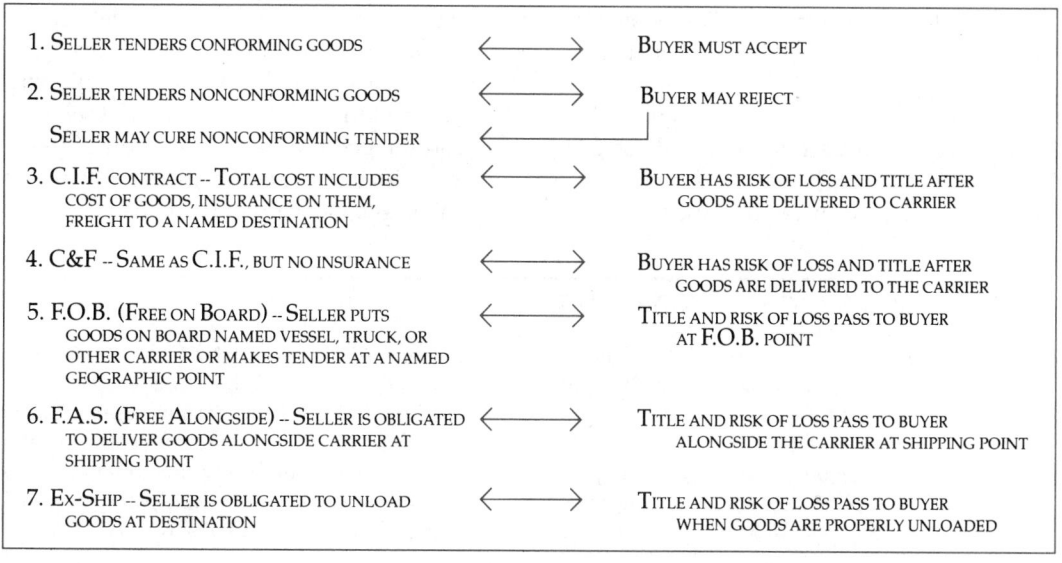

The term *ex-ship* obligates the seller to deliver or unload the goods from a ship that has reached a place at the named port of destination where goods of the kind are usually discharged. Risk of loss and title pass to the buyer when the goods leave the ship's tackle or are otherwise properly unloaded.

SUMMARY

Every sales contract imposes an obligation of good faith in its performance or enforcement. Good faith means honesty in fact in the conduct or transaction concerned. For merchants, the UCC imposes the additional requirement of observing "reasonable commercial standards of fair dealing in the trade."

In the case of a cash sale where no transportation of the goods is required, both the buyer and the seller may demand concurrent performance.

If a buyer or seller refuses to perform a contract, it is called a repudiation. A repudiation made in advance of the time for performance is called an anticipatory repudiation. If either party to a contract feels insecure about the performance of the other, that party may demand adequate assurance of performance. If that assurance is not given, the demanding party may treat the contract as repudiated.

The seller has the duty to deliver the goods in accordance with the terms of the contract. This duty does not require physical transportation; it requires that the seller permit the transfer of possession of the goods to the buyer. If the seller tenders nonconforming goods, the buyer may reject them. Subject to certain limitations, the seller may then make a curative tender.

The buyer has a duty to accept goods that conform to the contract. Refusal to do so is a breach of contract. The buyer is deemed to have accepted goods when the buyer express-es acceptance or does something inconsistent with rejection. A buyer is also deemed to have accepted goods if the buyer fails to reject the goods after having a reasonable opportunity to inspect them, or if a reasonable time has elapsed after the buyer inspected the goods or had the opportunity to inspect them. The buyer must pay for accepted goods in accordance with the terms of the contract.

The parties to a sales contract assume certain duties where goods are shipped under particular shipping terms. In a C.I.F. contract the buyer pays the seller the cost of the goods, insurance, and freight to the specified destination. In a C. & F. contract the seller is not obligated to insure the goods for the buyer's benefit. Under both these terms the risk of loss and title to the goods pass to the buyer after the goods have been delivered to the carrier.

In an F.O.B. (free on board) contract the seller has the obligation of putting the goods on board a named carrier or making delivery at a particular destination. The risk of loss and title to the goods pass to the buyer at the F.O.B. point.

In an F.A.S. contract the seller, at the seller's own expense and risk, must deliver the goods alongside a named vessel. Risk of loss and title pass to the buyer at the shipping point. The term *ex-ship* obligates the seller to unload the goods at the named port of destination. Risk of loss and title pass to the buyer when the goods are properly unloaded.

QUESTIONS AND CASE PROBLEMS

1. What social forces are involved in the rule of law governing the substitution of a different method of transportation to replace the method specified in the contract of sale?

2. Elkins Appliance Store makes a contract to purchase 100 electric toasters from the Greystone Electric Company, with delivery to be made on November 1. A week later Greystone informs Elkins that its factory has been severely damaged by fire and that Greystone is uncertain as to whether it will be able to deliver the toasters by November 1 or at any time. Elkins claims that this statement is an anticipatory repudiation of the contract. Is Elkins correct?

3. Cameron ordered a new mobile home from Mobile Homes, Inc., but the mobile home delivered was smaller than the one he ordered. Cameron expressed his dissatisfaction with the discrepancies but nevertheless made a partial payment. Cameron also had a gas line installed in the new mobile home. Cameron then brought an action to rescind the contract because the mobile home failed to conform to the contract. Is Cameron entitled to rescind? Why?

4. Louise in St. Louis orders a set of kitchen knives by mail from Grant Company in Seattle. They are sent C.O.D. to Louise. In order to be sure that there has been no mistake, Louise wants to examine the knives before she pays the carrier. Can she do so?

5. The Melvin Electric Motor Corporation makes a contract with the Raskob Gear Company for the latter to supply 10,000 sets of reduction gears according to specifications supplied by Melvin. The president of Melvin reads in the newspaper that there is a strike in the Raskob plant. The president of Melvin telephones the president of Raskob to express concern over whether Raskob will be able to perform the contract. The conversation does not lessen the fears of the president of Melvin, and the conversation concludes with Melvin's president demanding assurance from Raskob that performance will be made. The president of Melvin does not hear anything further from Raskob during the next 30 days. Can Melvin treat the contract as repudiated by Raskob?

6. International Minerals and Metals Corporation contracted to sell Weinstein scrap metal, to be delivered within 30 days. Later the seller informed the buyer that it could not make delivery within that time. The buyer agreed to an extension of time, but no limiting date was set. Within what time must the seller perform? [International Minerals and Metals Corp. v Weinstein, 236 NC 558, 73 SE2d 472]

7. Carlson ordered equipment from the Ventresca Foundry in St. Louis, Missouri, to be sent "F.O.B. Chicago, Illinois." The equipment was placed on a motor freight truck under a proper shipment contract. The truck was wrecked before it reached Chicago. Ventresca demanded payment of the purchase price from Carlson on the theory that the contract was a shipment contract and that the risk of loss passed to Carlson when the equipment was delivered to the carrier in St. Louis. Was Ventresca correct?

8. The Spaulding & Kimball Co. ordered from the Aetna Chemical Co. 75 cartons of window washers. The buyer received them and sold about a third to its customers. The buyer later refused to pay for them, claiming that the quality was poor. The seller sued for the price. Decide. [Aetna Chemical Co. v Spaulding & Kimball Co. 98 Vt 51, 126 A 582]

9. A computer manufacturer promoted the sale of a digital computer as a "revolutionary breakthrough." It made a contract to deliver one of these computers to a buyer. It failed to deliver the computer and explained that its failure was caused by unanticipated technological difficulties. Was this an excuse for nonperformance by the seller? [United States v Wegematic Corp. (CA2 NY) 360 F2d 674]

10. Ellis entered into a contract on April 4 to sell to Bound Brook Stove Works a stated quantity of pig iron, which it needed to manufacture stoves for its customers. No time was specified for deliveries, and nothing was specified beyond authorizing deliveries by installments. Several installments were delivered between the date of the contract and October 28. On November 23 Ellis tendered a substantial installment, which was refused on the ground that it was too late. Was the buyer correct in refusing on this ground? Why?

11. Teeman made a contract to purchase lumber from the Oakhill Mill. The contract called for payment to be made on delivery to Teeman. When the truck from the mill arrived to deliver the lumber, Teeman gave the driver a check for the purchase price. The driver refused to take the check, returned to the mill, and the mill then notified Teeman that the contract was canceled. Was the mill entitled to cancel the contract?

12. Lury has a contract to sell with Burns, with whom he has not previously dealt, to make four quarterly deliveries of product Z on 30 days' credit. Two months after the first delivery under the contract, Burns has not yet paid. May Lury demand adequate assurance of performance?

13. Francine Moss was in the process of furnishing her apartment. She purchased a leather sofa and three leather chairs from Davenport Furniture, Inc. These items were to be delivered in 20 days. She paid part of the purchase price upon executing the order and agreed to pay the balance on delivery. Davenport delivered the sofa and the chairs a week later, but the leather chairs did not match the sofa. Francine thereupon rejected the sofa and the chairs. She also demanded the return of her money. What rights, if any, does Davenport have?

14. The Singer Appliance Co. purchased refrigera-

tors from the Specialty Refrigerator Co. It used them as demonstrators for eight and a half months and then notified Specialty Refrigerator Co. that the refrigerators did not work. Singer Appliance offered to return the refrigerators.

Was Specialty Refrigerator required to take back the goods?

15. Compare or contrast an F.O.B. shipping term with an F.O.B. destination term with respect to when the risk of loss and title pass to the buyer.

27

WARRANTIES AND OTHER PRODUCT LIABILITY THEORIES

When goods are defective and cause injury or loss, the person harmed has a claim for product liability.

A. GENERAL PRINCIPLES

The remedy of the harmed person may be

governed by the common law, by the UCC, or by the newly emerging case law.

1.   Theories of Liability

Two centuries ago a buyer was limited to suing a seller for breach of an express guarantee or for negligence or fraud. After the onset of mass production and distribution, however, these remedies had little value. A guarantee was good, but in the ordinary sales transaction no one stopped to get a guarantee. One never asked the manager of the supermarket to give a guarantee that the loaf of bread purchased was fit to eat. Further, negligence and fraud have become generally impossible to prove in a mass-production world. How can one prove how a can of soup was prepared months earlier? The making of fraudulent statements by the seller is rather rare.

In order to give protection from harm-causing products, the law developed the concept of warranty liability. Warranties are either express or implied and are governed by the UCC. More recently, many courts have decided that still broader protection was required and created an additional concept of strict tort liability.

There are accordingly six theories in the law to protect from harm caused by defective products: guarantee, negligence, fraud, express warranty, implied warranty, and strict tort liability. If the plaintiff is a consumer or an employee, there might also be consumer protection liability or employee protection liability. In every case the plaintiff does not have a choice of all theories. The facts of the case will ordinarily exclude some theories. In some situations the plaintiff will have the choice of two or more theories.

2.   Nature of Harm

When a product is defective, harm may be caused to (a) a person, (b) property, or (c) economic or commercial interests. The buyer of a truck may be injured when it goes out of control and plunges down the side of a hill. Third persons, such as passengers in the truck, bystanders, or the driver of a car hit by the truck, may also be injured. The defective truck may also cause injury to a total stranger who seeks to rescue one of the victims. Property damage is sustained when the buyer's truck is damaged when it plunges down the slope. The car of another driver may be damaged, or a building into which the runaway truck careens may be damaged. Commercial and economic interests of the buyer are affected by the fact that the truck is defective. Even if no physical harm is sustained, the fact remains that the truck is not as valuable as it would have been. The buyer who has paid for the truck on the basis of the value it should have had has sustained an economic loss. If the buyer is required to rent a truck from someone else or loses an opportunity to haul freight for compensation, the fact that the truck was defective also causes economic or commercial loss.

3.   Who May Sue and Be Sued

Until the early part of this century only the parties to the sales contract could sue each other. Thus, a seller could be sued by the buyer, but other persons could not sue, because they were not in privity of contract.

This requirement of privity of contract has been widely rejected. The law is moving toward the conclusion that persons harmed because of an "improper" product may sue anyone who is in any way responsible.

(a) THE PLAINTIFF. By the modern view, not only the buyer, but also customers and employees of the buyer and even third persons or bystanders may sue because of harm caused by an improper product. The UCC expressly abolishes the requirement of privity when the plaintiff is a member of the buyer's family or household or a guest of the buyer and has sustained personal injury because of the product.[1]

Some states require privity of contract, particularly when the plaintiff does not sustain personal injury or property damage and seeks to recover only economic loss. However, a manufacturer making an express warranty as to a consumer product costing over $15

---

[1]   UCC § 2-318.

may be sued for the economic loss sustained by the buyer.

(b) THE DEFENDANT. The plaintiff who is entitled to sue may sue the seller, a remote seller, a manufacturer, and generally even the manufacturer of the component part of the product that caused the harm.[2] For example, when a person is struck by an automobile because of its defective brakes, the victim may sue the seller and the manufacturer of the car. The maker of the brake assembly or system that the car manufacturer installed in the car could also be sued.

(c) DIRECT SALES CONTACT. In many instances recovery is allowed by a buyer against a manufacturer because there have been direct dealings between them. These dealings justify regarding the buyer and the manufacturer as being in privity, as against the contention that the buyer was only in priv-

ity with the local dealer from whom the product was bought.[3] When the manufacturer enters into direct negotiations with the ultimate buyer with respect to any phase of the manufacturing or financing of the transaction, the sale will probably be treated as though it were made directly by the manufacturer to the ultimate purchaser. This is so even though, for the purpose of recordkeeping, the transaction is treated as a sale by the manufacturer to the dealer and by that dealer to the ultimate purchaser. Likewise, recovery may be allowed when the consumer mails to the manufacturer a warranty registration card that the manufacturer packed with the manufactured article.

In the *Nobility Homes* case the purchaser of a mobile home sued the manufacturer for breach of warranty. The manufacturer claimed that the purchaser could sue only the dealer from whom the home had been purchased.

[2]   Mendelson v General Motors Corp. 432 NYS2d 132 (1980).

[3]   Richards v Goerg Boat & Motors, Inc. (Ind App) 384 NE2d 1084 (1979).

NOBILITY HOMES OF TEXAS v SHIVERS
(Tex Civ App) 539 SW2d 190 (1976)

John Shivers and his wife purchased a mobile home from Marvin Hurley. Because of many defects, the home had a market value of approximately $9,000 less than the contract price. The buyers sued the manufacturer, Nobility Homes of Texas, for this amount. From a judgment in favor of the plaintiffs, Nobility Homes appealed.

DIES, C.J. . . . Hurley had previously purchased this unit from the defendant, the manufacturer thereof. Hurley was not an agent for the defendant. . . .

Defendant . . . asserts that it could not be liable for any damages to plaintiffs because there was no privity of contract between them, and plaintiffs are only seeking economic loss. . . . The generally recognized landmark case for support of the principle that privity is not required in pure economic loss cases is *Santor v A & M Karagheusian, Inc.* 44 NJ 52, 207 A2d 305 (1965). There, Santor brought suit against the manufacturer of a carpet which he had purchased from one of its distributors. The only contract was between Santor and the distributor, which had subsequently gone out of business. Santor sought recovery only for the loss of value of the carpeting.

After a thorough discussion of the positions of the various states and the concomitant rationale of the divergent views, the New Jersey Supreme Court held that privity was not necessary to maintain an action by a consumer against the manufacturer for redress of an economic loss. The Court restated the holdings which do not require privity for recovery in instances of personal injury and said:

> But we see no just cause for recognition of the existence of an implied warranty of merchantability and a right to recovery for breach thereof regardless of lack of privity of the claimant in the one case [as in personal injury] and the exclusion of recovery in the other simply because loss of value of the article sold is the only damage resulting from the breach. . . .
>
> From the standpoint of principle, we perceive no sound reason why the implication of reasonable fitness should be attached to the transaction and be actionable against the manufacturer where the defectively made product has caused personal injury, and not actionable when inadequate manufacture has put a worthless article in the hands of an innocent purchaser who has paid the required price for it. In such situations considerations of justice require a court to interest itself in originating causes and to apply the principle of implied warranty on that basis, rather than to test its application by whether personal injury or simply loss of bargain resulted from the breach of the warranty. True, the rule of implied warranty had its gestative stirrings because of the greater appeal of personal injury claim. But, once in existence, the field of operation of the remedy should not be fenced in by such a factor.

The court accepted these logical principles of equity and incorporated with them the substantive law of strict liability in tort. It again refused to accept the personal injury/economic loss dichotomy and held that only through tort liability would the burden of the injury be placed where it should be—on the maker of the product. This is because, though the breach arose initially from the sales contract, it was a " 'tortious wrong suable by a noncontracting party . . .' "

It is our opinion that the interests of equity and justice will best be served by accepting the view that privity in cases now under consideration should not be required. Matters of public policy dictate that no different treatment should be accorded in instances where a consumer suffers personal injury or damage to other property, and situations where the harm is the diminution of value of the product itself and the resulting economic loss. In both circumstances there is an "injury" to the public sector, whose only action in the commercial transaction is to purchase goods placed in the stream of commerce by the manufacturer. To insulate the maker of the goods under these conditions can result only by resort to reasoning which is no longer viable in our current economic practices and present sense of justice. . . .

A practical consideration also supports the position advanced by this Court today; the problem of wasteful litigation. In quoting from *Randy Knitwear, Inc. v American Cyanamid Company* (226 NYS2d 363, 181 NE2d 399) the Court in *Santor* restated:

> It is true that in many cases the manufacturer will ultimately be held accountable for the falsity of his representations, but only after an unduly wasteful process of litigation. Thus, if the consumer or ultimate business user sues and recovers, for breach of warranty, from his immediate seller and if the latter, in turn, sues and recovers against his supplier in recoupment of his damages and costs, eventually, after several separate actions by those in the chain of distribution, the manufacturer may finally be obliged to shoulder the responsibility which should have been his in the first instance.

... The pursuit of such wasteful litigation which is often inadequate should not be required in this State.

This jurisdiction should refrain from the "narrow legalistic view" that privity is necessary before the public may recover for damages suffered when the product diminishes in value and/or becomes worthless because of the defective workmanship of the manufacturer. ...

[Judgment affirmed]

QUESTIONS

1. What was the theory on which the plaintiff sued the defendant?
2. What kind of loss was sustained by the plaintiff?
3. Was the court in the *Nobility Homes* case influenced by the nature of the plaintiff's loss?

B.   EXPRESS WARRANTIES

A warranty may be express or implied. Both have the same effect and operate as though the defendant had made an express guarantee. An express guarantee is governed by the common law of contracts. Warranties are governed primarily by the UCC.

4.   Definition of Express Warranty

An **express warranty** is a statement by the defendant relating to the goods, which statement is part of the basis of the bargain. That is, the statement is part of the basis of the sale. This means that the buyer has purchased the goods on the reasonable assumption that they were as stated by the seller. Thus, a statement by the seller with respect to the quality, capacity, or other characteristic of the goods is an express warranty. To illustrate, the seller may say: "This cloth is all wool," "This paint is for household woodwork," or "This engine can produce 50 horsepower."

A representation that an airplane is a 1988 model is an express warranty. A statement that a product was particularly developed for a special purpose is an express warranty that it will achieve that purpose.[4]

There is no requirement of reliance on an express warranty. The question is merely whether the statement of the seller became part of the bargain of the parties.

5.   Form of Express Warranty

No particular form of words is necessary to constitute an express warranty. A seller need not state that a warranty is being made or that one is intended. It is sufficient that the seller assert a fact that becomes a part or term of the bargain or transaction between the parties.

It is not necessary that the seller make an express statement, for the express warranty may be found in conduct. Accordingly, if the buyer asks for a can of outside house paint and the seller hands over a can of paint, the seller's conduct expresses a warranty that the can contains outside house paint.

The seller's statement may be written or printed as well as oral. The words on the label of a can and in a newspaper ad for "boned chicken" constitute an express warranty that the can contains chicken that is free of bones.

The illustrations in a seller's catalog are descriptions of the goods. Therefore an express warranty arises that the goods will conform to a catalog illustration.

6.   Time of Making Express Warranty

It is immaterial whether the express warranty is made at the time of or after the sale. No separate consideration is required for the warran-

___
[4]   Crickett Alley Corp. v Data Terminal Systems, Inc. 240 Kan 661, 732 P2d 719 (1987).

ty when it is a part of a sale. If a warranty is made after the sale, no consideration is required, since it is regarded as a modification of the sales contract.

In the *Werner* case the buyer claimed that oral statements made by the seller before the sale were express warranties as to the future performance of the goods.

WERNER v MONTANA
117 NH 721, 378 A2d 1130 (1977)

Peter Werner purchased the White Eagle, a wooden sailing sloop, from Robert Montana. The sloop leaked, and Werner brought an action to cancel the sale on the ground that there had been an express oral warranty that it would not leak. Montana contended that no warranty was stated in any of the writings involved in the transaction, that the parol evidence rule prevented proof of statements made in the course of negotiations, and that accordingly there was no express warranty. The case was heard by a master, who recommended that judgment be entered for Werner. Montana appealed.

LAMPRON, J. . . . Plaintiff put the White Eagle into the water. After allowing ordinarily sufficient time for the planking to swell, or "make up," to form a watertight hull, plaintiff found that the White Eagle still leaked and could not be sailed. Plaintiff then discovered that there was extensive dry rot in the hull and that the cost of repairs would be substantial. After some discussions with defendant in the course of the summer concerning the problem, on September 8, 1972, plaintiff wrote defendant a letter complaining about the dry rot and unseaworthiness of the White Eagle and demanding that defendant take back the White Eagle and refund the purchase price. Defendant refused and plaintiff brought this action.

The basis for plaintiff's action is that there was a breach of an express warranty. [UCC §] 2-313. Plaintiff alleged that defendant, in the course of negotiations prior to sale, made certain statements to the effect that the White Eagle would "make up" when placed in the water and become watertight and that such statements amounted to an express warranty as to the sloop's condition. Defendant argues that any statements made by the defendant prior to sale could not be admitted or considered as constituting an express warranty by virtue of [UCC §] 2-202 (Parol or Extrinsic Evidence Rule). . . .

Under the Uniform Commercial Code an express warranty may be created by a seller who makes "any affirmation of fact or promise . . . to the buyer which relates to the goods and becomes part of the basis of the bargain." [UCC §] 2-313(1)(a). In addition, "any description of the goods which is made part of the basis of the bargain creates an express warranty that the goods shall conform to the description." [UCC §] 2-313(1)(b).

In general, affirmations of fact made by a seller about the goods being sold are considered a part of the description of the goods and are regarded as forming a part of the sales agreement. Uniform Laws Comment 3 to [UCC §] 2-313; 1 R. Anderson, Uniform Commercial Code § 2-313:45 (2d ed 1970). There was evidence that during the course of negotiations the parties had discussed the ship's watertightness and that defendant had told plaintiff that the White Eagle would become watertight once placed in water and allowed sufficient time to "make up." Considering the negotiations of the parties as a whole, particularly plaintiff's concern with whether the White Eagle was watertight, and considering the importance of watertightness for a ship, these assurances by defendant regarding the condition of the White Eagle could properly be considered as making part of the basis of the bargain. *See* 1 R. Anderson, *supra* § 2-313:7. Therefore, . . . the master did not err in ruling that these affirmations or descriptions of the White Eagle by the defendant created an express warranty under both [UCC §] 2-313(1)(a) and (b).

[UCC §] 2-202 excludes evidence of any additional oral agreement or terms when a written agreement is intended by the parties to be a final expression of their agreement. However, unless the writing was intended as a complete and exclusive statement of the terms of the agreement, evidence of consistent additional terms are admissible. [UCC §] 2-202(b). There was no evidence that the writings in this case, the notice of intent to purchase, the bill of sale, and the advertisement incorporated therein by reference, were intended by the parties as constituting a complete and exclusive statement of the terms of their agreement. The master therefore could properly find defendant's statements regarding the White Eagle's watertightness as being an express warranty which was a consistent additional term of the agreement . . . 1 R. Anderson, Uniform Commercial Code § 2-313:22; R. Nordstrom, Sales § 53 (1970). . . .

Defendant argues that plaintiff failed to prove a breach of warranty because the evidence did not establish that the leaking of the White Eagle was caused by the dry rot, or by any other cause, and therefore did not establish that the leaking constituted a breach of the alleged warranty. It is true that the master found there was no evidence to connect the leaking with the dry rot in the hull. However, the master did not find that defendant had made any warranty that the White Eagle was free from dry rot. Rather, the master found that defendant had told plaintiff that the White Eagle was suitable for sailing, and that defendant's statements which created the warranty were to the effect that the White Eagle had not leaked and would not leak after a sufficient swelling period was allowed. The master found that the White Eagle's "inability to 'make up' " created a breach of this warranty. While it is true that there was no evidence to establish the cause of the leaking, such evidence was not necessary. The plaintiff was required only to establish the existence of an express warranty and to establish that the White Eagle was defective in that its condition did not comply with the condition warranted by defendant. . . . The evidence was undisputed that the White Eagle continued to leak and was not seaworthy despite being allowed to soak for over six weeks. Plaintiff therefore met his burden establishing the boat's defective condition.

Defendant also argues that any warranty made related only to the condition of the White Eagle at the time of sale and that plaintiff failed to prove that the White Eagle was not as warranted at that time. While an express warranty generally relates only to the condition of the goods at the time of sale, a warranty may relate to another point in time if so specified. 1 R. Anderson, supra § 2-313:12. The warranty found by the master to have been made by defendant was that the White Eagle would not leak; that it would be tight after a two-week swelling period. The discussions between the parties prior to sale occurred after September 1, 1971, and the bill of sale was dated January 1, 1972. It would not be until the following spring or summer that plaintiff would have the first occasion to put the White Eagle in the water and allow for the swelling defendant indicated would occur. The warranty as to tightness therefore did not relate simply to the condition of the White Eagle as of the date of sale, but necessarily related to the time when the boat would be put in the water and prepared for sailing. Under these circumstances defendant's statement amounted to an express warranty.

Although reliance on the part of the buyer is not necessary for the creation of an express warranty, the master properly found that plaintiff did in fact rely on defendant's affirmation that the boat would not leak and it became part of the bargain. . . .

[Judgment affirmed]

QUESTIONS

1. Why did the plaintiff sue the defendant?
2. Did the seller guarantee that the sloop would not leak?
3. Did the seller say that he warranted that the sloop would not leak after being placed in the water?

7.   Seller's Opinion or Statement of Value

"An affirmation merely of the value of goods or a statement purporting to be merely the seller's opinion or commendation of the goods does not create a warranty."[5] A purchaser, as a reasonable person, should not believe such statements implicitly. Therefore, the buyer cannot hold the seller to them should they prove false. Thus, "sales talk" by a seller that "this is the best piece of cloth in the market" or that glassware "is as good as anyone else's" is merely an opinion that the buyer cannot ordinarily treat as a warranty.

Statements made by the seller of cosmetics that its products were "the future of beauty" and that they were "just the product for you [the plaintiff]" were "sales talk" arising "in the ordinary course of merchandising." They did not constitute warranties.

It is probable, however, that the UCC will permit an exception to be made, as under the prior law, when the circumstances are such that a reasonable person would rely on such a statement. If the buyer has reason to believe that the seller has expert knowledge of the conditions of the market and the buyer requests the seller's opinion as an expert, the buyer would be entitled to accept as a fact the

seller's statement as to whether a given article was the best obtainable. The statement could be reasonably regarded as forming part of the basis of the bargain. Thus, a statement by a florist that bulbs are of first-grade quality may be a warranty.

8.   Warranty of Conformity to Description, Sample, or Model

When the contract is based in part on the understanding that the seller will supply goods according to a particular description or that the goods will be the same as the sample or a model, the seller is bound by an express warranty that the goods shall conform to the description, sample, or model.[6] Ordinarily, a **sample** is a portion of the whole mass that is the subject of the transaction. A **model** is a replica of the article in question.

9.   Federal Regulation of Express Warranties

A seller who makes an express warranty as to a consumer product costing more than $15 must conform to certain standards imposed by federal statute[7] and by regulations of the Federal Trade Commission.[8] The seller is not required to make any express warranty. If one

---

5   UCC § 2-313(2); Pell City Wood, Inc. v Forke Bros, Auctioneers, Inc. (Ala) 474 So 2d 694 (1985).

6   Curry Motor Co. v Hasty (Ala) 505 So 2d 347 (1987).
7   PL 93-637, 15 USC §§ 2301 et seq.
8   16 CFR § 700.1 et seq.

is made, it must be stated in ordinary, understandable language and must be made available for inspection before purchasing so that the consumer may comparison shop.

(a) FULL WARRANTIES. If the seller or the label states that a **full warranty** is made, the seller is obligated to fix or replace a defective product within a reasonable time, without cost to the buyer. If the product cannot be fixed or if a reasonable number of repair attempts are unsuccessful, the buyer has the choice of a cash refund or a free replacement. No unreasonable burden may be placed on a buyer seeking to obtain warranty service. A full warranty runs for its specified life without regard to the ownership of the product.

(b) LIMITED WARRANTIES. Any warranty that does not provide the complete protection of a full warranty is a **limited warranty**. For example, a warranty is limited if the buyer must pay any cost for repair or replacement of a defective product, if only the first buyer is covered by the warranty, or if the warranty only covers part of the product. A warrantor making a full warranty cannot require that the buyer pay the cost of sending the product to or from a warranty service point. A warrantor making a full warranty cannot require the buyer to return the product to such a point if it weighs over 35 pounds, to return a part for service unless it can be easily removed, or to fill out and return a warranty registration card shortly after purchase in order to make the warranty effective. If the warrantor imposes any of these burdens, the warranty must be called a limited warranty. A limited warranty must be conspicuously described as such by the seller.

10.   Effect of Breach of Express Warranty

If the express warranty is false, there is a breach of the warranty. The warrantor is then liable just as though the truth of the warranty had been guaranteed. It is no defense that the defendant honestly believed that the warranty was true, had exercised due care in manufac-turing or handling the product, or had no reason to believe that the warranty was false.

C.   IMPLIED WARRANTIES

Whenever a sale of goods is made, certain warranties are implied unless they are expressly excluded. The scope of these warranties may differ, depending on whether the seller is a merchant or a casual seller.

11.   Definition of Implied Warranty

An **implied warranty** is one that was not made by the seller but is implied by law. In certain instances the law implies or reads a warranty into a sale although the seller did not make it. That is, the implied warranty arises automatically from the fact that a sale has been made. Express warranties arise because they form part of the basis on which the sale has been made.

The fact that express warranties are made does not exclude implied warranties. When both express and implied warranties exist, they should be construed as being consistent with each other and cumulative if such construction is reasonable. In case it is unreasonable to construe them as consistent and cumulative, an express warranty prevails over an implied warranty as to the subject matter, except in the case of an implied warranty of fitness for a particular purpose. When there is an express warranty as to a particular matter, it is unnecessary to find an implied warranty relating thereto.

12.   Implied Warranties of All Sellers

A distinction is made between a merchant seller and the casual seller. There is a greater range of warranties in the case of the merchant seller.

(a) WARRANTY OF TITLE. Every seller, by the mere act of selling, makes a warranty that the seller's title is good and that the transfer is rightful.

A warranty of title may be specifically excluded, or the circumstances may be such as to prevent the warranty from arising. The latter situation is found when the buyer has reason to know that the seller does not claim to hold the title or that the seller is purporting to sell only such right or title as the seller or a third person may have. For example, no warranty of title arises when the seller makes the sale in a representative capacity, such as a sheriff, an auctioneer, or an administrator of a decedent's estate. Likewise, no warranty arises when the seller makes the sale as a pledgee or mortgagee.

(b) WARRANTY AGAINST ENCUMBRANCES. Every seller, by the mere act of selling, makes a warranty that the goods shall be delivered free from any security interest or any other lien or encumbrance of which the buyer at the time of the sales transaction had no knowledge. Thus, there is a breach of warranty if the automobile sold to the buyer is delivered subject to an outstanding encumbrance placed on it by the original owner and unknown to the buyer at the time of the sale.

This warranty refers to the goods only at the time they are delivered to the buyer. It is not concerned with an encumbrance that existed before or at the time the sale was made. For example, a seller may not have paid in full for the goods, and the original supplier may have a lien on them. The seller may resell the goods while that lien is still on them. The seller's duty is to pay off the lien before delivering the goods to the buyer.

(c) WARRANTY OF FITNESS FOR A PARTICULAR PURPOSE. A buyer may intend to use the goods for a particular or unusual purpose, as contrasted with the ordinary use for which they are customarily sold. If so, the seller makes an implied warranty that the goods will be fit for the purpose when the buyer relies on the seller's skill or judgment to select or furnish suitable goods, and when the seller at the time of contracting knows or has reason to know the buyer's particular purpose and the buyer's reliance on the seller's judgment.[9]

When the seller knows that the buyer is purchasing an accounting machine in order to produce a payroll on time and with reduced work hours, an implied warranty arises that the machine will perform as desired by the buyer.

When the buyer makes the purchase without relying on the seller's skill and judgment, no warranty of fitness for a particular purpose arises.[10]

13.   Additional Implied Warranties of Merchant Seller

A seller who deals in goods of the kind in question is classified as a **merchant** by the UCC and is held to a higher degree of responsibility for the product than one who is merely making a casual sale.

(a) WARRANTY AGAINST INFRINGEMENT. Unless otherwise agreed, every merchant seller warrants that the goods will be delivered free of the rightful claim of any third person by way of patent or trademark infringement or the like.

(b) WARRANTY OF MERCHANTABILITY OR FITNESS FOR NORMAL USE. A merchant seller makes an implied warranty of the merchantability of the goods sold.[11] This warranty is in fact a group of warranties, the most important of which is that the goods are fit for the ordinary purposes for which they are sold.

A merchant is not protected from warranty liability by the fact that every possible step was taken to make the product safe. Similarly, it is no defense that the defendant could not have known of or discovered the defective character of the product. Warranty liability is not merely an assurance that the defendant has exercised due care but is an undertaking or guarantee that the product is fit for use.

In the *Shell* case the plaintiff alleged a breach of warranty of merchantability and a breach of the warranty of fitness for a particular purpose.

---

[9]   UCC § 2-315. This warranty applies to every seller, but as a matter of fact it will probably always be a merchant seller who has such skill and judgment that the UCC provision would be applicable.

[10]   B. W. Feed Co., Inc. v General Equipment Co. 44 Or App 467, 605 P2d 1205 (1980).

[11]   Miller v Badgley, 51 Wash App 285, 753 P2d 530 (1988).

SHELL v UNION OIL CO.
(Ala) 489 So 2d 569 (1986)

John Shell, an employee of the Goodyear Tire and Rubber Company, came into contact with a naphtha product supplied by Union Oil. The product contained benzene, a carcinogen known to cause leukemia. The product complied with specifications established by Goodyear that limited the amount of benzene any shipment could contain. In addition, Union supplied Goodyear with safety data sheets setting forth precautions that should be taken to prevent exposure when using benzene. Shell brought an action against the suppliers of the chemical compound alleging breach of warranties. From a judgment in favor of the suppliers, Shell appealed.

JONES, J. . . . In its simplest terms, the questions presented are:

1. Was there a duty owed, i.e., was there an implied promise?
2. If so, was that duty breached, i.e., was the promise unperformed? and
3. Did that duty extend to this Plaintiff, i.e., was the obligation of performance intended for Shell's protection? Shell can prevail, of course, only if the answer to *all* three questions is "yes."

If we assume a "yes" answer to each of the first two questions, then the third question must be answered in the affirmative, in light of Code 1975, § 2-318:

Third-party beneficiaries of warranties express or implied.
    A seller's warranty, whether express or implied, extends to any natural person if it is reasonable to expect that such person may use, consume or be affected by the goods and who is injured in person by breach of the warranty. A seller may not exclude or limit the operation of this section.

Therefore, we will concentrate on the first two questions.

I

Plaintiff's first theory is based upon breach of warranty of merchantability, and he relies on [UCC] § 2-314, which reads in part:

Implied warranty: Merchantability.
    (1) Unless excluded or modified (section 2-316), a warranty that the goods shall be merchantable is implied in a contract for their sale if the seller is a merchant with respect to goods of that kind. Under this section the serving for value of food or drink to be consumed either on the premises or elsewhere is a sale.
    (2) Goods to be merchantable must be at least such as:

        (a) Pass without objection in the trade under the contract description; and
        (b) In the case of fungible goods, are of fair average quality within the description; and
        (c) Are fit for the ordinary purposes for which such goods are used; and
        (d) Run, within the variations permitted by the agreement, of even kind, quality and quantity within each unit and among all units involved; and

(e) Are adequately contained, packaged, and labeled as the agreement may require; and

(f) Conform to the promises or affirmations of fact made on the container or label if any.

Plaintiff's implied warranty of merchantability theory, as we understand it, is to the effect that, because the substance supplied by Defendants caused cancer, it could not be "fit for ordinary purposes for which such goods are used"; that is, because this is a cancer-causing substance, it is unreasonably dangerous, and, therefore, cannot be merchantable. Such an argument ignores the clear distinction between causes of action arising under tort law and those arising under the U.C.C. as adopted in Alabama. A Texas court recognized that distinction in *Mid Continent Aircraft Corp. v. Curry County Spraying Service, Inc.,* 553 S.W.2d 935 (Tex.Civ.App. 1977):

> [U.C.C.] law, whose statutory language makes no reference to tort law in connection with products liability, concerns itself with the quality of the product by establishing standards of merchantability for a particular purpose . . . [while the tort law] concerns itself with safety standards by imposing strict liability upon one who sells an unreasonably dangerous product which causes physical harm. The considerations supporting either of the principles are not affected by the considerations underlying the other, and the standards of quality of a product, with the attendant risk of the bargain, are entirely distinct from its standards of safety, with a possible unreasonable risk of harm. It follows that a violation of the standards of safety which results in physical harm to the unreasonably dangerous product itself subjects the seller to the tort rule of strict liability.

553 S.W.2d at 940.

Whether this product was unreasonably dangerous, therefore, is not a question properly addressed in an action brought under the provisions of the U.C.C.

To cover the initial bare bones question (Was there a duty owed?) with flesh, we should reask the question: Did the sale of the subject product give rise to an implied warranty of merchantability in the sense that these two manufacturers promised the employee that he would not be injured by his use of or contact with their product? The answer must be made in the context of § 2-314: "[Whether this product was] fit for the ordinary purposes for which such goods are used." In this instance, the product—made to Goodyear's specifications—performed the job it was intended to do; and the manufacturers' warnings and precautions, accompanying the products, were in keeping with their knowledge of its inherent dangers. Thus, any duty arising under this section of the Code was not breached. Indeed, more precisely, these undisputed facts do not give rise to a warranty of merchantability, as contended by Shell.

The implied warranty mandated by this section of the U.C.C. is one of *commercial* fitness and suitability, and a private right of action is afforded only where the user or consumer is injured by the breach of *that* warranty. That is to say, the U.C.C. does not impose upon the seller the broader obligation to warrant against health hazards inherent in the use of the product when the warranty of commercial fitness has been complied with. Those injured by the use of or contact with such a product, under these circumstances, must find their remedy outside the warranty remedies afforded by the U.C.C. . . . The Defendants were entitled to judgment as a matter of law.

II

The second action was brought under the theory of breach of the warranty of fitness for a particular purpose provided for in the Code as follows:

§ 2-315. Implied warranty: Fitness for particular purpose.

Where the seller at the time of contracting has reason to know any particular purpose for which the goods are required and that the buyer is relying on the seller's skill or judgment to select or furnish suitable goods, there is unless excluded or modified under section 2-316 an implied warranty that the goods shall be fit for such purpose.

While privity is not a requirement, the injured third party beneficiary can have no more interest than the principal parties. Because Goodyear set the specifications for this product, it did not rely on "the seller's skill or judgment to select or furnish suitable goods." Goodyear was well aware of the connection between benzene and leukemia at the time it set the standards which these Defendants were required to meet. Because Goodyear, the buyer, did not rely on the seller's skill or expertise, as required by § 2-315, no duty on the part of Defendants arose under this section of the Code.

[Judgment affirmed]

QUESTIONS

1. Why did Shell allege a breach of warranty of merchantability?
2. Was there a breach of warranty of fitness for a particular purpose?
3. What disposition did the court make of the claim that there was a breach of warranty of merchantability?

14.   Warranties in Particular Sales

Particular types of sales may involve special considerations.

(a) SALE ON BUYER'S SPECIFICATIONS. When the buyer furnishes the seller with exact specifications for the preparation or manufacture of goods, the same warranties arise as in the case of any other sale of such goods by the particular seller. No warranty of fitness for a particular purpose can arise, however. It is clear that the buyer is purchasing on the basis of the buyer's own decision and is not relying on the seller's skill and judgment. Likewise, the manufacturer is not liable for loss caused by a design defect.[12]

(b) SALE OF SECONDHAND OR USED GOODS. As far as the UCC is concerned, there is no difference between the warranties arising in the sale of used or secondhand goods and those arising in the sale of new goods.[13]

As to ordinary goods, what is "fit for normal use" will be a lower standard for used than for new goods. Some courts still follow their pre-Code law, under which no warranties of fitness arose in the sale of used goods.

(c) SALE OF FOOD OR DRINK. The sale of food or drink, whether to be consumed on or off the seller's premises, is a sale. When made by a merchant, a sale of food or drink carries the implied warranty that the food is fit for its ordinary purpose, that is, for human consumption.[14]

Thus, the seller of canned crabmeat has broken this warranty when the can contains a nail. Does it make any difference if the thing which harms the buyer is a crabshell? Some courts refuse to impose warranty liability if the thing in the food which causes the harm was naturally present, as the crabshell in crabmeat, prune stones in stewed prunes, or bones in canned fish. Other courts reject this "natural substance" exception. They hold that there

---

[12]   Wisconsin Electric Power Co. v Zallea Brothers, Inc. (CA7 Wis) 606 F2d 697 (1979).
[13]   Hargett v Midas Intern'l. Corp. (Miss) 508 So 2d 663 (1987).

[14]   Fernandes v Union Bookbinding Co. Inc. 400 Mass 27, 507 NE2d 728 (1987).

is liability if the seller does not deliver to the buyer goods of the character that the buyer reasonably expected. Thus, there is a breach of the implied warranty of fitness for normal use if the buyer reasonably expected the food to be free of harm-causing natural things, such as shells and bones.

This was the situation in the *Phillips* case.

PHILLIPS v WEST SPRINGFIELD
405 Mass 411, 540 NE2d 1331 (1989)

Phillips, a high school senior, was eating in the high school cafeteria. He bit into a cube of turkey, which contained a bone that injured him. He sued the city for breach of warranty. From a judgment in favor of the city, Phillips appealed.

WILKINS, J. . . . Twenty-five years ago Justice Reardon wrote for this court a much cited opinion holding that a restaurant was not liable for breach of warranty under [UCC] § 2-314(2)(*c*), for injuries caused by a fish bone in fish chowder. *Webster v Blue Ship Tea Room, Inc.*, 347 Mass. 421, 198 N.E.2d (1964). In this appeal, which we transferred here on our own motion, we decide a somewhat similar case. This one involves not a fish bone in fish chowder served in a quaint restaurant on a wharf overlooking Boston Harbor, but rather a turkey bone in a bite-sized cube of white turkey meat ladled, along with gravy and peas, onto a mount of mashed potatoes in a high school cafeteria in West Springfield. The plaintiff, a high school senior, bit into one of the turkey cubes, felt something in his throat, and after some effort expelled "a small, 1½-inch hooked bone." He sustained injury to his esophagus and was hospitalized for four days.

The plaintiff argues that the judge, who heard the case without a jury, erred in deciding the breach of warranty claim against him because she applied the "foreign substance–natural substance" test rather than the consumer's "reasonable expectations" test. When the foreign substance–natural substance test is applied, there is no liability as a matter of law for breach of warranty if the injury-causing substance is natural to the food, and liability is automatic if the offending item is foreign to the food. . . . 3 R. A. Anderson, Uniform Commercial Code 2-314:183- 2-314:185 (1983 & Supp. 1988). The reasonable expectations test, on the other hand, considers whether the consumer reasonably should have expected to find the injury-causing substance in the food. . . .

The reasonable expectations test has been generally recognized as preferable to the foreign substance–natural substance test. The foreign substance–natural substance test exonerates a seller of food from liability for the lack of fitness of the food for ordinary purposes simply because the injury causing substance was natural to the food. It fails to focus the seller's attention on the consumer's reasonable beliefs and to recognize that sellers may fairly be held responsible in some instances for natural substances in food that cause injury. This court's discussion in its *Webster* opinion focused on the reasonable expectations of a consumer of fish chowder and concluded, as a matter of law, that bones in fish chowder should reasonably be expected. *Webster v. Blue Ship Tea Room, Inc., supra*, 347 Mass. at 426, 198 N.E.2d 309. In our view, the reasonable expectations test is the appropriate one to apply in determining liability for breach of warranty of merchantability under [UCC] § 2-314(2)(*c*), by reason of a bone or other substance in food that caused harm to a consumer.

We turn to the judge's findings and rulings. The judge found that "[t]he plaintiff reasonably expected that the turkey meat was boneless based on its being white meat, the fact that it was cut into bite size pieces and the manner in which it was served, i.e., ladled with gravy onto potatoes." She ruled as a matter of law, however, that the plaintiff had failed to prove that the defendant breached its warranty of merchantability. She noted that "[t]he bone in the turkey was not a foreign substance and did not render the meal unwholesome," citing the *Webster* case. She ruled further that "[t]he plaintiff as an ordinary consumer of the turkey meal should have reasonably expected the likelihood of a bone in the turkey meat." . . .

We disagree with the plaintiff's claim that the judge decided the case against him solely on the ground that a turkey bone in a piece of turkey is not a foreign substance. Her discussion of reasonable expectations would have been unnecessary if she had decided the case by applying the foreign substance–natural substance test.

The trial judge's finding of fact that the plaintiff reasonably expected that the turkey meat was boneless contrasts with her ruling of law that an ordinary consumer of the turkey meal should have reasonably expected the likelihood of a bone in the turkey meat. The plaintiff's subjective expectations may not have been those of an ordinary objective consumer of the meal, and thus the judge's findings and rulings are not necessarily inconsistent. . . . On the other hand, the reasons she provided for the reasonableness of the plaintiff's expectation that there would be no bones (the bite size pieces of only white meat served on top of mashed potatoes) seem to be objective, and not subjective, criteria.

The plaintiff is entitled to a clarification of the judge's findings of fact and rulings of law. Although we recognize that in particular circumstances no consumer could reasonably expect not to find the injury-causing object and thus a directed verdict for a defendant would be proper, on the facts found in this case, the defendant was not entitled to prevail as a matter of law. The answer depends on what the reasonable expectations of an ordinary high school student would be concerning the likely presence of a bone in this meal. As the trier of fact, the judge has not made and should make a finding on that dispositive question.

[Judgment vacated and case remanded to the Superior Court for further consideration]

QUESTIONS

1. What did the plaintiff argue?
2. What is the difference in result if the foreign–natural substance test is applied as opposed to the reasonable expectations test?
3. Why was this case sent back to the lower court for further action?

15.   Necessity of Defect

In order to impose liability for breach of an implied warranty, it is ordinarily necessary to show that there was a defect in the product and that this defect was the cause of the plaintiff's harm. A product may be defective because there is (a) a manufacturing defect, (b) a design defect, (c) inadequate instruction on how to use the product, or (d) inadequate warning against dangers involved in using the product.

If the manufacturer's blueprint shows that there should be two bolts at a particular place and the factory puts in only one bolt, there is a manufacturing defect. If the two bolts are put in but the product breaks because four bolts are required to provide sufficient strength, there is no manufacturing defect, but there is a design defect. A product that is properly designed and properly manufactured may be dangerous because the user is not given sufficient instructions on how to use the product. Also a product is defective if there is a danger that is not obvious, and there is no warning at all or a warning that does not describe the full danger. For example, a can of adhesive used to cement tiles to a floor is defective when the label on the can merely states that the cement should not be used near an open flame, but does not state that a newly cemented floor would throw off vapor that would stay in the room for several hours and would explode if any spark or flame were present.

Many courts are relaxing the requirement of proving the existence of a specific defect. These courts impose liability when the goods are in fact not fit for their normal purpose. These courts allow the buyer to prove goods are not fit for their normal purpose by evidence that the goods do not function properly, even though the buyer does not establish the specific defect.

In contrast with the suit for breach of an implied warranty, when the plaintiff sues for breach of an express warranty or a guarantee, it is not necessary to show that there was a defect that caused the breach. It is sufficient to show that the goods did not conform to the guarantee or to the express warranty. Why they did not is immaterial.

16. Warranties in the International Sale of Goods

Both the warranties of merchantability and fitness for a particular purpose exist under the Convention on Contracts for the International Sale of Goods (CISG). (See Part C, Chapter 24.) In most cases the provisions are identical to those of the UCC. Sellers, however, can expressly disclaim the convention's warranties without mentioning merchantability or making the disclaimer conspicuous.

D. DISCLAIMER OF WARRANTIES

The seller and the buyer may agree that there shall be no warranties. In some states this option is limited for reasons of public policy or consumer protection.

17. Validity of Disclaimer

Warranties may be disclaimed by agreement of the parties, subject to the limitation that such a provision must not be unconscionable.[15]

If a warranty of fitness[16] is excluded or if it is modified in writing, the exclusion or modification must be conspicuous in order to make certain that the buyer will be aware of its presence. If the implied warranty of merchantability is excluded, the exclusion clause must expressly mention the word *merchantability*. The exclusion must be conspicuous if written.

(a) CONSPICUOUSNESS. A disclaimer provision is made conspicuous by printing it under a conspicuous heading, but in such case the heading must indicate that there is an exclusion or modification of warranties. Conversely, a heading cannot be relied on to make such a provision "conspicuous" when the heading is misleading and wrongfully gives the impression that there is a warranty. For example, the heading "Vehicle Warranty" is misleading if the provision that follows contains a limitation of warranties. A disclaimer that is hidden in a mass of printed material handed to the buyer is not conspicuous and is not effective to exclude warranties. Similarly, an inconspicuous disclaimer of warranties under a

---

[15] UCC §§ 2-316(1), 2-302(1). A distinction must be made between holding that the circumstances do not give rise to a warranty, thus precluding warranty liability, and holding that the warranty that would otherwise arise was excluded or surrendered by the contract of the parties. Dubbe v A.O. Smith Harvestore Products (Minn App) 399 NW2d 644 (1987).

[16] By the letter of the Code, the text statement is applicable to any warranty of fitness (see UCC § 2-316(2)), although by the Official Comment to § 2-316, point 4, it would appear to be only the warranty of fitness for a particular purpose.

heading of "Notice to retail buyers" has no effect.

When a waiver of warranties fails to be effective because it is not conspicuous, the implied warranties that would arise in the absence of any waiver are operative.

(b) UNCONSCIONABILITY AND PUBLIC POLICY. An exclusion of warranties made in the manner specified by the UCC is not unconscionable. There is also authority that when the breach of warranty is the result of negligence of the seller, the disclaimer of warranty liability and a limitation of remedies to refunding the purchase price is not binding. Such a limitation is unreasonable, unconscionable, and against sound public policy. In some states, warranty disclaimers are invalid as contrary to public policy or because they are prohibited by consumer protection laws.

If a seller makes any written warranty of a consumer product costing more than $15, the seller is barred from excluding any implied warranty that would be implied under the law of sales.

18.   Particular Provisions

A statement such as "There are no warranties that extend beyond the description on the face hereof" excludes all implied warranties of fitness. Implied warranties (other than the warranty of title and the warranty against encumbrances) are excluded by the statement "as is," "with all faults," or other language that in normal, common speech calls attention to the warranty exclusion and makes it clear that there is no implied warranty.

In order for a disclaimer of warranties to be a binding part of an oral sales contract, the disclaimer must be called to the attention of the buyer.

Provisions in a sales contract excluding warranties have only that effect. They do not bar the buyer from recovering damages for fraud, negligence, or strict tort liability.

19.   Exclusion of Warranties by Examination of Goods

There is no implied warranty with respect to

defects in goods that an examination should have revealed when the buyer, before making the final contract, has examined the goods, or model or sample, or has refused to make such examination.

The examination of the goods by the buyer does not ordinarily exclude the existence of an express warranty. It may, however, if it can be concluded that the buyer, by the examination, learned of the falsity of the statement claimed to be a warranty. As a consequence, such statement did not in fact form part of the basis of the bargain.

FIGURE 27-1   WARRANTIES

WARRANTIES

1. EXPRESS
      A. MAY BE ORAL OR WRITTEN
      B. FORM PART OF BASIS OF BARGAIN
      C. STATEMENT OF FACT
2. IMPLIED
      A. GOOD TITLE
      B. NO ENCUMBRANCES
      C. FITNESS FOR PARTICULAR PURPOSE
      D. NO INFRINGEMENT OF PATENT OR
            TRADEMARK
      E. MERCHANTABILITY
3. DISCLAIMERS
      A. MUST NOT BE UNCONSCIONABLE
      B. IF WRITTEN, MUST BE CONSPICUOUS
      C. IF DISCLAIM WARRANTY OF MERCHANT-
            ABILITY, MUST EXPRESSLY MENTION
            MERCHANTABILITY
      D. NO IMPLIED WARRANTIES WHERE
            GOODS SOLD "AS IS" OR "WITH ALL
            FAULTS"

20.   Post-Sale Disclaimer

Frequently the statement purporting to exclude or modify warranties appears for the first time in a written contract sent to confirm or memorialize the oral contract made earlier. The exclusion or modification may likewise appear in an invoice, a bill, or an instruction manual delivered to the buyer at or after the time the goods are received. Such post-sale disclaimers have no effect on warranties that arose at the time of the sale.

An exclusion of warranties in a manufacturer's manual given to the buyer after the sale is not binding on a buyer, because it is not a term of the sales contract.

If the buyer assents to the post-sale disclaimer, however, it is effective as a modification of the sales contract.

E.   OTHER THEORIES OF PRODUCT LIABILITY

In addition to suit for breach of an express guarantee, an express warranty, or an implied warranty, a plaintiff in a given product liability case may be able to sue for negligence, fraud, or strict tort liability.

21.   Negligence

A person injured because of the defective condition of a product may be entitled to sue the seller or manufacturer for the damages for negligence. The injured person must be able to show that the defendant was negligent in the preparation or manufacture of the article or failed to provide proper instructions and warnings as to dangers. An action for negligence rests on common law tort principles. It does not require privity of contract.

22.   Fraud

The UCC expressly preserves the pre-Code law as to fraud. Thus, a person defrauded by false statements as to a product obtained from a distributor or manufacturer will generally be able to recover damages for the harm sustained because of such misrepresentations. Fraudulent statements are made with knowledge that they are false or with reckless indifference as to whether they are true.

23.   Strict Tort Liability

Independently of the UCC, a manufacturer or distributor of a defective product is liable under strict liability to a person who is injured by the product. This liability exists without regard to whether the person injured is a purchaser, a consumer, or a third person, such as a bystander.[17] It is no defense that privity of contract does not exist between the injured party and the seller. Likewise, it is no defense that the defect was found in a component part purchased from another manufacturer.[18] This concept is not one of absolute liability; that is, it must first be shown that there was a defect in the product at the time it left the control of the seller.[19] The seller is liable if the product is defective and unreasonably dangerous and has caused harm. It is immaterial whether or not the seller was negligent or whether the user was guilty of contributory negligence. Assumption of risk by the injured party, on the other hand, is a defense available to the seller.[20]

24.   Cumulative Theories of Liability

The theories of product liability are not mutually exclusive. Thus, a given set of facts may give rise to two or more theories of liability, as in the *Shaw* case.

---

[17]   Walker v Clark Equipment Co. (Iowa) 320 NW2d 561 (1982).
[18]   The concept of strict tort liability was judicially declared in Greenman v Yuba Power Products, 59 Cal 2d 57, 27 Cal Rptr 697, 377 P2d 897 (1963). This concept has been incorporated in the Restatement of Torts 2d as § 402A.
[19]   McLaughlin v Michelin Tire Corp. (Wyo) 778 NW2d 59 (1989).
[20]   Central Telephone Co. v Fixtures Mfg. _____Nev _____, 738 P2d 510 (1987).

SHAW v GENERAL MOTORS
(Colo App) 727 P2d 387 (1986)

General Motors (GM) manufactured the cab and chassis of a truck that was sold unchanged by Daniels Motors (DM) to the city of Colorado Springs. Fontaine Truck Equipment Co.(FTE) manufactured a dump bed and hoist that was sold by another equipment company to the City of Colorado Springs. Fontaine installed the dump bed and hoist on the General Motors truck and made further modifications as specified by the city, so that the truck would be usable as a pothole repair truck by the city. Shaw, while in the city's employ, was injured when his co-worker backed the pothole repair truck over him. Shaw brought suit against GM, DM, and FTE. Shaw argued that the truck was defective and unreasonably dangerous to its user because of defendants' failure to warn of the necessity of installing a back-up alarm, and because of defendants' alleged failure to fulfill their duty in installing such a back-up alarm. He claimed liability because of (1) strict liability, (2) negligence, (3) breach of implied warranties of fitness and merchantability, and (4) breach of express warranties. From a judgment in favor of defendants, Shaw appealed.

PIERCE, J. . . .

I. Strict Liability
General Motors

A manufacturer of component parts, such as GM here, may be held strictly liable for injuries as a result of design defects in the component when it is expected to and does reach the consumer without substantial change in condition. While it may be arguable whether GM's cab and chassis underwent "substantial change in condition" because of the modifications made by the City, other issues regarding strict liability must be considered as to GM.

The critical questions as concerns GM are whether the condition of the truck at the time of its delivery to DM was defective and unreasonably dangerous without a back-up alarm or unreasonably dangerous as a result of a failure to warn. Based on the pleadings and other materials submitted, the truck was not in such a defective condition so as to impose strict liability upon GM.

The record here shows that the GM cab and chassis could be equipped for numerous different uses; that, at the time of assembly by GM, there was no restriction of rear vision; and that it was assembled by GM with two rear-view mirrors for visibility around most body installations. In rebuttal, plaintiff points to deposition testimony by a GM engineer who admitted that a back-up alarm system would be "desirable" given the City's use of the truck as a pothole repair truck. This testimony, however, does not show that a defective condition existed at the time of the truck's delivery to DM.

As a result, at the time that the truck left GM's control, it had no "inherent dangers" such as would expose GM to liability for failure to warn of an unreasonably dangerous condition. Based on the record, the likelihood of an accident resulting from the GM truck in the condition in which it was delivered was not such as to require warnings.

Plaintiff argues that GM should have foreseen that its truck would be transformed into a pothole filling truck which had visual impairment. Under the circumstances of this case, to require such foreseeability would be tantamount to making GM an insurer against all accidents. The principle of strict liability does not impose such absolute liability.

Thus, plaintiff could not have prevailed against GM on a theory of strict liability. Accordingly, judgment was proper.

Fontaine

The critical questions as to FTE are whether the dump bed and hoist were in such a condition at the time of their delivery to the equipment company as to be defective and unreasonably dangerous without a back-up alarm or unreasonably dangerous as a result of a failure to warn. . . .

The fundamental bases for plaintiff's allegations that the dump bed and hoist are defective are that: (1) it lacked a back-up alarm and (2) FTE failed to warn that lack of a back-up alarm constituted an inherent danger. The lack of a back-up alarm cannot be considered an unreasonably dangerous or defective condition until final assembly of all components, because, until assembled, there can be no need for the back-up device.

. . . With respect to plaintiff's allegation that FTE failed to warn, considering the unlikelihood of the dump bed and hoist backing up by themselves, we conclude there is no reasonable likelihood of an accident as a result of FTE's failure to warn. The condition of FTE's product was not, therefore, defective and unreasonably dangerous without a warning. Thus, liability could not attach to FTE. Strict liability does not equate to absolute liability.

Therefore, plaintiff's allegations did not provide a valid basis for relief, and judgment was proper in favor of FTE.

II. Negligence

Before liability can be found in a negligence action, the existence of a duty of care must be determined. This is a question of law. Whether the law should impose a duty requires consideration of the risk involved, the foreseeability and likelihood of injury as weighed against the social utility of the actor's conduct, the magnitude of the burden of guarding against injury or harm, and the consequences of placing the burden upon the actor.

Based on these considerations, there may be a duty to install an alarm system, but it does not lie with the defendants here.

We rule that defendants here owed no duty to the class to which plaintiff belongs. GM, DM, and FTE, as manufacturers and sellers of component parts that were assembled by the City, could not properly evaluate, or likely foresee, the risks arising from not installing a specific safety feature such as a back-up alarm. The burden of guarding against the injury suffered here should appropriately be placed upon the entity that designed the final product, arranged for acquisition of all the component parts, and directed their assembly. We find little social utility in placing this burden upon the manufacturers and sellers of the component parts, who did not partake in the designing or assembling of the final product.

Thus, absent a duty of care, plaintiff's claims of negligence were properly dismissed against GM, DM, and FTE.

III. Implied Warranties

Implied warranty liability can extend to the manufacturer of component parts. Such liability can also extend to sellers of component parts. However, the lack of fitness for ordinary purposes as well as for particular purposes must be found in the component parts before they leave the component parts manufacturers or sellers.

Plaintiff claims that the GM cab and chassis were not safe and fit for this use and application. However, as was discussed in Part I herein, the record does not show that a defective condition existed at the time that the truck left GM and DM. The documentation presented here unrebuttably shows that the GM truck was safe and fit for ordinary use and for its particular purpose, as that particular purpose was identifiable prior to assembly by the City. Therefore, based on the record, plaintiff could not prevail on his claims of breach of implied warranties against GM and DM.

Moreover, the record shows that DM sold to the City a truck which met the specifications set forth in the City's bidding form. DM, having substantially complied with the specifications will not be held to have extended a warranty of fitness.

The record also supports FTE's substantial compliance with the City's specifications. Therefore, it too cannot be held liable on implied warranties of fitness for particular or ordinary purposes.

IV. Express Warranties

In their pleadings, plaintiff alleges that GM, DM, and FTE breached express warranties of safety and fitness, and other express warranties set forth in their publications. On appeal, plaintiff specifically argues that deposition testimony stating that "Chevy's business is providing the right truck for your business" represents an express warranty to which the GM truck did not conform. This language does not constitute an affirmation of fact or a promise; it is "merely the sellers' opinion or commendation of the goods." See [UCC §] 2-313(2). . . . Thus, no warranty was created. . . .

[Judgments affirmed]

QUESTIONS

1. How did the court decide the question of strict liability against the defendants?
2. How did the court decide the issue of negligence?
3. Was there a breach of either express or implied warranties?

SUMMARY

There are six theories in the law to protect from harm caused by defective products. They are (1) guarantee, (2) negligence, (3) fraud, (4) express warranty, (5) implied warranty, and (6) strict tort liability.

Theories of product liability are not mutually exclusive. A given set of facts may give rise to liability under two or more theories of product liability.

The requirement of privity of contract (that is, that only the parties to the sales contract could sue each other) has been widely rejected. The law is moving toward the conclusion that persons harmed because of an improper product may sue anyone who is in any way responsible. The requirement of privity has been abolished by the UCC in cases where the plaintiff is a member of the buyer's family or household or a guest in the buyer's home and has sustained personal injury because of the product.

Warranties may be express or implied. Both have the same effect and operate as though the defendant had made an express guarantee.

A warranty made after a sale does not require consideration. It is regarded as a modification of the sales contract.

Express warranties are regulated by federal statute and the FTC. These warranties are labeled as full or limited warranties and must conform to certain standards.

A distinction is made between a merchant seller and the casual seller. There is a greater range of warranties in the case of the merchant seller.

A seller makes a warranty of good title unless such warranty is excluded. Warranties that the goods shall conform to the description, sample, or model are express warranties, while warranties of fitness for a particular purpose and merchantability are implied warranties.

Warranties may be disclaimed by agreement of the parties, provided the disclaimer is not unconscionable. A written disclaimer to exclude warranties must be conspicuous. Post-sale disclaimers have no effect on warranties that arose at the time of the sale.

The warranties of merchantability and fitness exist under the CISG. Under CISG, disclaimers need not mention merchantability, nor must the disclaimer be conspicuous.

The strict tort liability plaintiff must show that there was a defect in the product at the time it left the control of the defendant. No negligence need be established on the part of the defendant, nor is contributory negligence of the plaintiff a defense. The defendant may show that the injured party assumed the risk.

QUESTIONS AND CASE PROBLEMS

1. What social forces are affected by the abolition of the requirement of privity in product liability suits?

2. Norma purchases a wool dress from the Borolsky Dress Shop. After she gets the dress home, she is doubtful as to the quality of the cloth. When she complains, Borolsky assures her that the cloth is 100 percent wool. Later, Norma proves that the dress is only 60 percent wool. Can she hold Borolsky liable on the statement that it was 100 percent wool?

3. Webster purchased a used automobile from an automobile dealer, and the contract of sale provided: "This automobile is sold 'AS IS.' " Have the warranties (1) of title, or (2) against encumbrances been disclaimed?

4. Steve purchases an electric kitchen range from the Shermack Electric Appliance Company. In the instruction manual that is enclosed in the crate in which the range is delivered to Steve's home, there is a statement that Shermack makes no warranty, express or implied, with respect to the range. The range works properly for two weeks and then ceases to function. When Steve demands his money back from Shermack, it raises the defense that all warranties, including that of fitness for normal use, were excluded by the statement in the manual. Is Shermack correct?

5. Edgmore has a class reunion at his house. There is a substantial amount of food left over. He sells the surplus food to his neighbor Hartranft for a fraction of its price. In eating this food, Hartranft is injured from a piece of glass that was contained in a can of salmon. Hartranft sues Edgmore for the injuries sustained. Is Edgmore liable?

6. A buyer purchased a new car wash from a dealer. It washed the cars effectively, but it would knock off external accessories such as mirrors and radio antennas. When the buyer complained, the seller stated that the contract made no provision with respect to such matters. Was this a valid defense?

7. A purchased a refrigerator from the B store. The written contract stated that the refrigerator was sold "as is" and that the warranty of merchantability and all warranties of fitness were excluded. This was stated in large capital letters printed just above the line on which A signed her name. The refrigerator worked properly for a few weeks and then stopped. B refused to do anything about it because of the exclusion of the warranties made by the contract. A claimed that this exclusion was not binding because it was unconscionable. Was A correct? [Avery v Aladdin Products Div., Nat'l. Service Industries, Inc. 128 Ga App 266, 196 SE2d 357]

8. A manufacturer advertised its product in national magazines. The advertisement induced a buyer to purchase the product. The product did not live up to the statements in the advertisement. The buyer claimed that there was a breach of warranty. The manufacturer contended that the statements in the advertisement were obviously sales talk and therefore could not constitute a warranty. Was this a valid defense? [Westrie Battery Co. v Standard Electric Co. (CA10 Colo) 482 F2d 1307]

9. Clark suffered an injury due to a defect in a chain saw he had purchased from Grey Hardware. The saw was manufactured by Lee Tool Corp. Clark commences an action against Lee Tool Corp., based upon strict liability. Lee Tool Corp. argues that absent privity, the suit will be dismissed. Is Lee Tool Corp. correct? Why?

10. The defendant, Zogarts, manufactured and sold a practice device for beginning golfers. The statements on the package stated that the device was completely safe and that a player could never be struck by the golf ball of the device. Hauter was hit by the ball when practicing with the device. He sued Zogarts. Zogarts denied liability on the ground that the statements were merely matters of opinion, so liability could not be based on them. Was this a valid defense? [Hauter v Zogarts, 14 Cal 104, 120 Cal Rptr 681, 534 P2d 377]

11. A buyer purchased an engine to operate an irrigation pump. The buyer selected the engine from a large number that were standing on the floor of the seller's stockroom. A label on the en-

gine stated that it would produce 100 horsepower. The buyer needed an engine that would generate at least 80 horsepower. In actual use in the buyer's irrigation system, the engine generated only 60 horsepower. The buyer sued the seller for damages. The seller raised the defense that no warranty of fitness for the buyer's particular purpose of operating an irrigation pump had arisen, because the seller did not know of the use to which the buyer intended to put the engine, and the buyer had not relied on the seller's skill and judgment in selecting the particular engine. Was the seller liable? [Potter v Ryndall, 22 NC App 129, 205 SE2d 808, cert den 285 NC 661, 207 SE2d 762]

12. Roberts, a certified public accountant, explained to Haynes, a sales agent for a manufacturer of calculating machines, a certain kind of accounting work for which he needed a machine. He asked Haynes to select a machine from his principal's stock and deliver it. Haynes had his firm deliver to Roberts a machine, for which Roberts paid cash. Later Roberts discovered that the machine would not do the required work. What warranty, if any, was breached?

13. Brady Co. made toys for children. One of their toys was a ball with a hard surface, which was designed to be bounced on the ground and to make a loud noise. Jean, a young girl, and her friends were playing with the toy. One of the friends bounced it on the ground. It struck Jean in the eye, causing her to lose sight in her left eye. She sued the toy company on the ground that it had made a dangerous instrumentality and was therefore liable for the resulting harm. Was it liable? Why?

14. A strict tort liability defendant may raise the defense that there was no negligence involved and that, even if there was negligence, the plaintiff cannot recover because the plaintiff was guilty of contributory negligence. Appraise this statement.

15. Mark went to the Happy Hour Cafe to eat breakfast. He ordered grapefruit juice, French toast, and milk. While drinking the milk, his throat was cut because the milk contained a piece of glass. Mark thereupon brought an action against Happy Hour to recover damages for personal injuries resulting from an implied breach of warranty. Will he be successful?

28

REMEDIES FOR BREACH OF SALES CONTRACTS

If one of the parties to a sale fails to perform the contract duties, the law makes several remedies available to the other party. In addition, the parties may have included provisions pertaining to remedies in their contract.

A. STATUTE OF LIMITATIONS

Judicial remedies are ordinarily subject to a time limitation that bars resort to the courts after the expiration of a particular period of time. The UCC supplies the statute of limitations for sales of goods except when suit is brought on a theory of tort, such as negligence, fraud, or strict tort.

1.   Code Claim

An action for a breach of a sales contract must be commenced within four years after the cause of action arises. This time limit applies regardless of when the aggrieved party learned that there was a cause of action. In the case of a warranty, the breach occurs when tender of delivery is made to the buyer, even though no defect then appears and no harm is sustained until a later date.[1]

(a) FUTURE PERFORMANCE WARRANTY. When an express warranty is made as to future performance, the statute of limitations does not run from the time of the tender but from the date when the future performance begins.[2]

(b) NOTICE OF DEFECT. The buyer who sues the seller for damages claimed because of a breach of the sales contract must give the seller notice of such breach within a reasonable time after the buyer discovers or should have discovered the breach.[3]

2.   Non-Code Claim

When the plaintiff sues on a non-Code theory, even though it relates to goods, the UCC statute of limitations does not apply. Thus, when the plaintiff sues on the basis of strict tort, fraud, or negligence, the action is subject to the tort statutes of limitations. When the plaintiff sues on the basis of an express guarantee, the action is governed by the contract statute of limitations.

B.   REMEDIES OF THE SELLER

When a sales contract is broken by the buyer, the seller has a number of remedies available. The more common ones are discussed in the following sections.[4]

3.   Seller's Lien

In the absence of an agreement for the extension of credit to the purchaser, the seller has a lien on the goods. That is, the seller has the right to retain possession of the goods until the buyer pays for them. Even when the goods are sold on credit, the seller has a lien on the goods if the buyer becomes insolvent or if the credit period expires while the goods are in the seller's possession.

The seller's lien may be lost by (a) waiver, as by a later extension of credit, (b) delivery of the goods to a carrier or other bailee, without a reservation of title or possession, for the purpose of delivery to the buyer, (c) acquisition of the property by the buyer or an agent by lawful means, or (d) payment or tender of the price by the buyer.

4.   Resale by Seller

When the buyer has broken the contract by wrongfully rejecting the goods, wrongfully revoking acceptance, failing to pay, or repudiating the contract, the seller may resell the goods or the balance of them in the seller's possession. After the resale, the seller is not liable to the original buyer on the contract or for any profit obtained on the resale. On the other hand, if the proceeds are less than the contract price, the seller may recover the loss from the original buyer.[5]

Reasonable notice must be given to the original buyer of the intention to make a private sale. Such notice must also be given of a public sale unless the goods are perishable in nature or threaten to decline rapidly in value.

---

[1]   Nelson v International Harvester Corp. (Minn App) 394 NW2d 578 (1986).
[2]   Safeway Stores, Inc. v Certain-Teed Corp. (Tex App) 710 SW2d 544 (1986).
[3]   UCC § 2-607(3)(a).

[4]   When the goods purchased by the buyer are being shipped to the buyer or are held in a warehouse, an unpaid seller has a limited right to prevent delivery of the goods to the buyer. UCC § 2-705. If the buyer repudiates the contract while the goods are being manufactured, the seller-manufacturer may stop further production or may complete the manufacturing of the goods. UCC § 2-704(2). An unpaid seller who sold on credit has a limited right to take the goods back if the buyer was insolvent. UCC § 2-702.
[5]   UCC § 2-706(1), (6).

Notice of a public sale must also be given to the general public in such manner as is commercially reasonable under the circumstances.

5.   Cancellation by Seller

When the buyer wrongfully rejects the goods, wrongfully revokes an acceptance of the goods, repudiates the contract, or fails to make a payment due on or before delivery, the seller may cancel the contract. Such action puts an end to the contract, discharging all obligations on both sides that are still unperformed. The seller retains any remedy with respect to the breach by the buyer. Cancellation revests the seller with title to the goods.

A seller may cancel the contract only if the buyer's breach substantially impairs the value of the contract to the seller.

6.   Seller's Action for Damages

If the buyer wrongfully refuses to accept the goods or repudiates the contract, the seller may sue for the damages that the seller sustains. In the ordinary case the amount of damages is to be measured by the difference between the market price at the time and place of the tender of the goods and the contract price.

If this measure of damages does not place the seller in the position in which the seller would have been placed by the buyer's performance, recovery may be permitted of lost profits, together with an allowance for overhead. The seller may in any case recover, as incidental damages, any commercially reasonable charges, expenses, or commissions incurred in enforcing that remedy. For example, the seller may recover expenses sustained in the transportation, care, and custody of the goods after the buyer's breach and may recover costs incurred in the return or resale of the goods. Such additional damages are recovered in addition to any other damages that may be recovered by the seller.

The seller is not entitled to recover the contract or purchase price except as stated in the next section of text.

7.   Seller's Action for the Purchase Price

The right to sue for the contract price, as distinguished from a suit for damages for breach of contract, is a remedy that is not ordinarily available to the seller. The seller may bring an action to recover the purchase price, together with incidental damages as described in connection with the action for damages, if (a) the goods have been accepted, and there has not been any rightful revocation of acceptance; (b) conforming goods were damaged or destroyed after the risk of loss passed to the buyer; or (c) the seller has identified proper goods to the contract but, after the buyer's breach, has been or will be unable to resell them at a reasonable price.

C.   REMEDIES OF THE BUYER

When a sales contract is broken by the seller, the buyer has a number of remedies provided by Article 2 of the UCC.

8.   Rejection of Improper Tender or Delivery

If the tender made by the seller or the goods do not conform to the contract in any respect, the buyer may reject the goods. For example, the buyer may reject a mobile home when it does not contain an air conditioner with the capacity specified by the contract.

The buyer may reject a tender that is not perfect, as against the contention that a substantial performance is sufficient.

Goods tendered may consist of different units, some of which conform to the contract and some of which do not. In such a case the buyer has the choice of (a) rejecting the entire quantity tendered, (b) accepting the entire tender, or (c) accepting any one or more commercial units and rejecting the rest.[6]

---

[6]   McClure Oil v Murray Equipment, Inc. (Ind App) 515 NE2d 546 (1987).

The rejection must be made within a reasonable time after the delivery or tender, and the buyer must notify the seller of the choice made.[7]

After rejecting the goods, the buyer may not exercise any right of ownership as to the goods. The buyer but must hold the goods, awaiting instructions from the seller.

9.   Revocation of Acceptance

The buyer may revoke acceptance of the goods when they do not conform to the contract and the defect substantially impairs the value of the contract to the buyer. For example, a buyer purchased an emergency electric power plant. The plant produced only about 65 percent of the power called for by the contract. This was not sufficient to operate the buyer's equipment. Repeated attempts to improve the system failed. There was such a nonconformity as substantially impaired the value of the contract to the buyer, and the buyer was entitled to revoke acceptance.

Proof of substantial impairment is required to justify revocation of acceptance. The mere fact that the goods do not conform to the contract does not entitle the buyer to revoke acceptance. On the other hand, it is not necessary that the buyer show that the goods are worthless. The revocation of acceptance does no more than revoke the acceptance. In itself, it does not cancel the contract with the seller. After revoking acceptance, the buyer has the choice of canceling that contract or insisting that the seller deliver conforming goods in place of the goods originally delivered.

In the *Asciolla* case the court faced the question of whether the seller could prevent the buyer from revoking acceptance by offering to repair the defects.

---

[7]   UCC § 2-602(1).

ASCIOLLA v MANTER OLDSMOBILE-PONTIAC, INC.
8 NH 91, 370 A2d 270 (1977)

Angello Asciolla purchased a new automobile in December. The car was waterproofed and then delivered to the buyer. He drove it to Wisconsin the following January. The car stood outside overnight. The next day the car would not run because the transmission was inoperable. There was ice in the transmission and substantial rust. These facts seemed to confirm the statement that was later made to the buyer that the car had been flooded before it had been sold to him. The dealer offered to repair the car. The buyer refused to accept repairs and insisted that he could revoke his acceptance. He demanded a new car. He sued the dealer and the manufacturer. The case was referred to a master, who recommended that damages be awarded to the buyer. However, the master decided that the buyer should not be allowed to revoke the acceptance, because a reasonable person would have been satisfied with the repairs that were offered by the seller. From this judgment, the plaintiff appealed.

DOUGLAS, J. . . . The question . . . is whether the inoperable transmission of the plaintiff's car was a defect that substantially impaired the value of the product to him. [UCC §] 2-608, Comment 2 states that the test of "substantial impairment" is "whether the non-conformity is such as will *in fact* cause a substantial impairment of value *to the buyer* . . ." (Emphasis added). This section, therefore, creates a subjective test in the sense that the needs and circumstances of the particular buyer must be examined. . . . The trier of fact must make an objective determination that the value of the goods to the buyer has in fact been substantially impaired. . . . *Tiger Motor Co. v McMurtry,* 284 Ala 283, 224 So 2d 638 (1969). . . .

We find . . . that the value of the subject automobile to [the buyer] was substantially impaired. In purchasing a new car the plaintiff was making a major investment. Few items which are considered necessities occupy such a significant portion of an individual consumer's income as does a new automobile. Few purchases are made with more care and deliberation. The record indicates that the plaintiff was a particularly prudent and painstaking car buyer and that he had indeed once before refused to accept an automobile from the defendants which merely had a dented fender which had been repaired. Within three weeks of the purchase of the car at issue in this case he found it to be totally inoperable. He was informed by franchised representatives of the manufacturer that the car had been flooded or submerged. While the master found that the evidence presented at the hearing did not support such a conclusion, no satisfactory reason was ever presented to the plaintiff to otherwise explain the presence of ice in his transmission. Nor was [the buyer] offered any guarantees concerning other deficiencies, caused by the same mysterious condition, which he very reasonably apprehended might arise in the future.

Under these facts, we think it clear that the plaintiff's confidence in the reliability and integrity of his new automobile was severely undermined. He had bargained for a new car, expecting to receive a vehicle upon whose dependability and safety he could comfortably rely. Instead he received a product which he understandably feared was what is known in popular parlance as "a lemon." The plaintiff is correct in his assertion that a new automobile is more than the sum of its various components. It is the integrity of the vehicle as a whole which is the essence of the consumer's bargain. As the Superior Court of New Jersey said in a markedly similar case concerning a new car with a defective transmission "[the buyer] assumed what every new car buyer has a right to assume and, indeed, has been led to assume by the high powered advertising techniques of the auto industry—that his new car, with the exception of very minor adjustments, would be mechanically new and factory-furnished, operate perfectly, and be free of substantial defects." *Zabriskie Chevrolet, Inc. v Smith,* 99 NJ Super 441, 240 A2d 195 (1968). The plaintiff's situation cannot be accurately compared to cases . . . in which the cars presented defects which were trivial and readily repaired. The new car in the instant case was rendered wholly inoperable by a defective condition which permeated one of its most essential systems. Under such circumstances, his revocation of acceptance is justified. . . .

The defendants contend that they are entitled to cure the nonconformity in the tendered goods. Although a seller is given the right to cure under [UCC §] 2-508 in the context of rejection of goods, no such right is granted by [UCC §] 2-608(1)(b) when acceptance is being revoked. Whether a seller's right to cure may be implied under this section has been the subject of considerable dispute. . . . We need not decide the question in this case, however. For the reasons set forth above, any cure other than replacement of the automobile with a new one would, under the facts of this case, be insufficient to accomplish a conforming tender. See *Zabriskie Chevrolet, Inc. v Smith, supra;* 2 R. Anderson, Uniform Commercial Code § 2-608:10 (2d ed. 1971). . . .

[Judgment reversed and action remanded]

QUESTIONS

1. What remedy did the buyer exercise?
2. Was he entitled to do so?
3. Was it important that the seller offered to repair the defects?

10. Procedure for Revoking Acceptance

In order to revoke acceptance of the goods, the buyer must take certain steps.

(a) NOTICE OF REVOCATION. The acceptance of goods cannot be revoked unless the buyer gives the seller a notice of revocation. The revocation of acceptance is effective when the buyer notifies the seller. It is not necessary that the buyer make an actual return of the goods in order to make the revocation effective.

(b) TIME FOR REVOCATION. The notice of revocation must be given within a reasonable time after the buyer discovers that the goods do not conform or after the buyer should have discovered such nonconformity. A buyer is not required to notify the seller of the revocation of acceptance until the buyer is reasonably certain that the nonconformity of the goods substantially impairs the value of the contract. Thus, the mere fact that the buyer suspects that the goods do not conform and that such nonconformity may substantially impair the value of the contract does not itself require that the buyer immediately give notice to the seller.

In the *Cato* case the buyer claimed that he had revoked his acceptance within a reasonable time.

CATO EQUIPMENT CO. INC. v MATTHEWS
91 NC App 546, 372 SE2d 872 (1988)

Matthews purchased a crankshaft for installation in a rebuilt engine. He returned the first crankshaft, in the belief that it was too small. Cato assured Matthews that it would stand behind its product. Relying on this assurance, Matthews requested and installed a second crankshaft. It was used for several months, during which time it was discovered that the second crankshaft had cracks that caused damage to other engine parts. Matthews promptly notified Cato of the defect, requesting a further replacement. Cato sued for the purchase price when Matthews refused to pay for the second crankshaft. Matthews counterclaimed on the ground of breach of implied warranty and revoked his acceptance. From a judgment in favor of Matthews, Cato appealed.

ARNOLD, J. . . . Under U.C.C. 2–608, a buyer

may revoke his acceptance of a lot or commercial unit whose nonconformity substantially impairs its value to him if he has accepted it . . . without discovery of such nonconformity if his acceptance was reasonably induced either by the difficulty of discovery before acceptance or by the seller's assurances. [UCC §] 2-608(1)(b).

The trial court found that cracks existed in the crankshaft at the time defendant received it. It also concluded that the plaintifff had breached its implied warranties to defendant and allowed a set-off by defendant of the purchase price. By implication, the trial court determined that defendant revoked his acceptance and was entitled to damages for the defective crankshaft.

In order for a buyer to show that his revocation was justifiable, the following four elements must be proved: (1) that the goods contained a nonconformity that substantially impaired their value to him; (2) that he either accepted the goods knowing of the nonconformity but reasonably assuming that it would be cured, or that he accepted the goods not knowing of the nonconformity due to the difficulty of the discovery or reasonable assurances from the seller that the goods were conforming; (3) that revocation occurred within a reasonable time after he discovered or should have discovered the defect; and (4) that he has notified the seller of his revocation. . . .

The trial court determined that the crankshaft was cracked when defendant installed it in the engine. It also found that the crack caused damage to the rod bearing. Obviously a crankshaft which was cracked and caused damage to other parts of the engine substantially impaired its value to defendant.

From the record and the trial court's findings of fact, it is apparent that the cracks were impossible to discover prior to their use in the engine. Only when the crankshaft was removed from the engine and cleaned up did defendant discover the cracks.

What is a reasonable time for a buyer to revoke his acceptance is ordinarily a question of fact for the jury. . . . In determining what is a reasonable time, it is proper to consider all the surrounding circumstances, including the nature of the defect, the complexity of the goods involved, the sophistication of the buyer, and the difficulty of the discovery.

Defendant was not able to discover the hairline cracks in the crankshaft until after its use in the engine when they became more severe and apparent. . . . There was no reasonable delay in defendant's revocation.

Defendant notified plaintiff of his revocation as soon as he learned of the damage to the crankshaft and bearings. He ordered a new crankshaft under the impression that [Cato] would replace the first crankshaft if it were defective.

Under [UCC §] 2-608(3), a buyer who revoked his acceptance has the same rights and duties with regard to the goods involved as if he had rejected them. The measure of damages for breach of warranty is the difference at the time of acceptance between the value of the goods accepted and the value they would have had if they had been warranted. [UCC §] 714(2). The crankshaft had no value as delivered and the damages were the purchase price. We find error neither in the trial court's implicit determination of revocation and damages, nor in its set-off of defendant's damages against the purchase price owed to plaintiff. . . .

[Judgment affirmed]

Questions

1. When must revocation of acceptance occur?
2. Did Matthews make a timely revocation? Explain.
3. Could Matthews have sued for breach of warranty?

A buyer is not barred from revoking acceptance of the goods because the buyer has delayed until attempts of the seller to correct the defects proved unsuccessful. For example, the lapse of even a year does not bar revocation of acceptance where the goods are of a complex nature, such as a computer, and the seller was continuously experimenting and assuring the buyer that the goods would be made to work.

(c) DISPOSITION OF GOODS AFTER REVOCATION. After making a revocation of acceptance, the buyer must hold the goods awaiting instructions from the seller. If the buyer has paid the seller in advance, the buyer may retain possession of the goods after revoking acceptance as security for the refund of the money that has been paid. Post-revocation use of the goods does not nullify the prior revocation of acceptance when such use is reasonable under the circumstances.[8]

11. Buyer's Action for Damages for Nondelivery

If the seller fails to deliver as required by the contract or repudiates the contract, the buyer is entitled to sue the seller for damages for breach of contract. The buyer may also sue for damages if the buyer properly rejects tendered goods or revokes acceptance of nonconforming goods. The buyer is entitled to recover the difference between the market price at the time the buyer learned of the breach and the contract price.

Within a reasonable time after the seller's breach, the buyer may cover—procure the same or similar goods elsewhere.[9] If the buyer acts in good faith, the measure of damages for the seller's nondelivery or repudiation is then the difference between the cost of cover and the contract price.

12. Action for Breach of Warranty

One remedy that may be available to a buyer is an action for breach of warranty.

(a) NOTICE OF BREACH. If the buyer has accepted goods that do not conform to the contract or as to which there is a breach of warranty, the buyer must notify the seller of the breach within a reasonable time after the breach is discovered or should have been discovered. Otherwise the buyer is not entitled to complain.[10]

(b) MEASURE OF DAMAGES. If the buyer has given the necessary notice of breach, the buyer may recover damages measured by the loss resulting in the normal course of events from the breach. If suit is brought for breach of warranty, the measure of damages is the difference between the value of the goods as they were when accepted and the value that they would have had if they had been as warranted.

In other cases the buyer may recover the difference between the contract price and the actual value of the goods.

The buyer may also recover as damages the loss directly and naturally resulting from that breach. In other words, the buyer may recover for the loss proximately resulting from the failure to deliver the goods as warranted. Thus, a buyer may recover the cost of renting other equipment when the equipment sold by the defendant did not work because of its defective condition. When the buyer resells the goods and then, because of their defective condition, is required to indemnify customers of the buyer, the original buyer may recover such loss from the original seller as consequential damages.

Where the condition that breaches the warranty induces fright that causes illness, the warranty liability includes damages for such illness.

A buyer who is entitled to recover damages from the seller may deduct the amount of such damages from any balance remaining due on the purchase price, provided the seller is notified of the buyer's intention to do so.[11]

8   Barco Auto Leasing House, 202 Conn 106, 250 A2d 162 (1987).
9   Banner Iron Works, Inc. v Amax Zinc Co. (CA8 Mo) 621 F2d 883 (1980).

10   Armco Steel Corp. v Isaacson Structural Steel Co. (Alaska) 611 P2d 507 (1980).
11   UCC § 2-717.

(c) NOTICE OF THIRD PARTY ACTION AGAINST BUYER. The buyer may be sued in consequence of the seller's breach of warranty. For example, the buyer's customers may sue because of the condition of the goods that the buyer has resold to them. In such a case it is optional with the buyer whether or not to give the seller notice of the action and to request the seller to defend that action.

The buyer may also be sued by a third person because of patent infringement. In this case, however, the buyer must give notice of the action to the seller. Moreover, the seller can demand control over the defense of that action.[12]

13.   Cancellation by Buyer

The buyer may cancel or rescind the contract if the seller fails to deliver the goods or repudiates the contract or if the buyer has rightfully rejected tender of the goods or rightfully revoked acceptance of them. A buyer who cancels the contract is entitled to recover as much of the purchase price as has been paid, including the value of any property given as a trade-in as part of the purchase price. The fact that the buyer cancels the contract does not destroy the buyer's cause of action against the seller for breach of that contract. The buyer may therefore recover from the seller not only any payment made on the purchase price, but also damages for the breach of the contract. The damages represent the difference between the contract price and the cost of cover.[13]

The right of the buyer to cancel or rescind the sales contract may be lost by a delay in exercising the right. A buyer who, with full knowledge of the defects in the goods, makes partial payments or performs acts of dominion inconsistent with any intent to cancel cannot thereafter cancel the contract.

14.   Buyer's Resale of Goods

When the buyer has possession of the goods after rightfully rejecting them or after rightfully revoking acceptance, the buyer is treated the same as a seller in possession of goods after the default of a buyer. That is, the aggrieved buyer has a security interest in the goods to protect the claim against the seller and may resell the goods. From the proceeds of the sale, the aggrieved buyer is entitled to deduct any payments made on the price and any expenses reasonably incurred in the inspection, receipt, transportation, care and custody, and resale of the goods.[14]

15.   Action for Conversion or Recovery of Goods

When, as a result of the sales agreement, ownership passes to the buyer and the seller wrongfully refuses or neglects to deliver the goods, the buyer may maintain any action allowed by law to the owner of goods wrongfully converted or withheld. The obligation of the seller to deliver proper goods may be enforced by an order for specific performance when the goods are "unique or in other proper circumstances."[15] Distributors have been granted specific performance against suppliers to deliver the goods covered by supply contracts. Specific performance will not be granted, however, merely because the price of the goods purchased from the seller has gone up. In such a case the buyer can still purchase the goods in the open market. The fact that it will cost more to cover can be compensated for by allowing the buyer to recover greater damages from the seller.

16.   Remedies for Fraud of Seller

Independently of the preceding remedies, the buyer has the right to sue the seller for damages for the latter's fraud and to cancel the transaction on that ground.[16]

Because these remedies for fraud exist independently of the provisions of the UCC, the buyer may assert such remedies even though barred by the UCC from exercising any remedy for a breach of warranty. Likewise, a limi-

---

[12]   UCC § 2-607.
[13]   UCC § 2-712(1), (2).

[14]   UCC § 2-715(1).
[15]   UCC § 2-716(1).
[16]   Stephenson v Frazier (Ind App) 399 NE2d (1980).

FIGURE 28-1   REMEDIES FOR BREACH OF SALES CONTRACT

Remedies of Seller	Remedies of Buyer
Lien Resale Cancellation Action for damages Action for price	Rejection of improper tender or delivery Revocation of acceptance Action for damages for nondelivery Action for damages for breach of warranty Cancellation Resale Action for conversion or recovery Action for fraud

tation on remedies or exclusion of warranty liability has no effect on the buyer's claim for damages for fraud.

D.   CONTRACT PROVISIONS ON REMEDIES

The UCC permits the parties to modify or limit by their contract the remedies that they otherwise possess.

17.   Limitation of Damages

The parties to the sales contract may seek to limit or exclude the recovery of damages in case of breach.

(a) LIQUIDATION OF DAMAGES. The parties may specify the exact amount of damages that may be recovered in case of breach. Such a **liquidation of damages clause** is valid if the amount so specified is reasonable in the light of the actual harm that would be caused by the breach, the difficulty of proving the amount of such loss, and the inconvenience and impracticality of suing for damages or enforcing other remedies for breach.

(b) EXCLUSION OF DAMAGES. The sales contract may provide that in case of breach no damages may be recovered, or that no consequential damages may be recovered. Such total exclusions are *prima facie* unconscionable, and therefore *prima facie* not binding, when

goods are sold for consumer use and personal injuries are sustained. Thus, a defendant in such a case cannot rely on the contract limitation unless the defendant is able to prove that the limitation of liability was commercially reasonable and fair, rather than oppressive and surprising. Moreover, when the seller would be liable to the buyer for damages, the seller cannot exclude liability for personal injuries to members of the buyer's family or household or to guests of the buyer.

In cases not involving consumer goods and personal injuries, the plaintiff has the burden of proving that a limitation on damages is not binding because unconscionable. When the seller knows that the failure of the product, such as a harvester, to perform will cause serious economic loss, a limitation of damages to the return of the purchase price is void as unconscionable.

A limitation of damages that is hidden in a paragraph headed *guarantee* is misleading and unconscionable.[17]

18.   Down Payments and Deposits

The buyer may have made a deposit with the seller or an initial or down payment at the time of making the contract. If the contract contains a valid provision for liquidation of damages and the buyer defaults, the seller

---

[17]   Jutta's Incorporated v Fireco Equipment Co. 150 NJ Super 301, 375 A2d 687 (1977).

must return any part of the down payment or deposit in excess of the amount specified by the liquidated damages clause. In the absence of such a clause and in the absence of proof of greater damages sustained, the seller's damages are computed as 20 percent of the purchase price or $500, whichever is smaller. The extent to which the down payment exceeds such amount must be returned to the buyer.

19.   Limitation of Remedies

The parties may validly limit the remedies that are provided by the Code in the case of breach of contract. Thus, a seller may specify that the only remedy of the buyer for breach of warranty shall be the repair or replacement of the goods, or that the buyer shall be limited to returning the goods and obtaining a refund of the purchase price. A limitation of remedies need not be conspicuous.

(a) CONSTRUCTION FAVORING CU-MULATIVE REMEDIES. When the sales contract specifies a remedy to which a party will be entitled, a question arises as to whether the parties intended a sole or exclusive remedy. It must be clearly stated that the remedy was to be the exclusive remedy. If it is not clearly stated, the remedy stated will be regarded as being in addition or cumulative to the remedies already existing under the Code.[18]

(b) FAILURE OF LIMITED REMEDY. A provision limiting the seller's obligation to the repair of the goods or the replacement of defective parts fails in its essential purpose and is not binding when the seller is unable or refuses to make the goods function properly within a reasonable time. The buyer is entitled to goods that will be fit to the extent required by the express or implied warranties. When there is such a failure to correct the defect, the buyer may use any remedy authorized by the Code, just as though the contract had not contained any limitation on remedies.

In the *Osburn* case the dealer and the manufacturer of a mobile home claimed that their only obligation was to make repairs and that it did not matter if the repairs were unsuccessful.

---

[18]   V. Zappala & Co. v Pyramid Co. 81 App Div 2d 983, 39 NYS2d 765 (1981).

OSBURN v BENDIX HOME SYSTEMS, INC.
(Okla) 613 P2d 445 (1980)

Vernon and Phyllis Osburn purchased a mobile home from Bendix Home Systems, Inc. The "warranty" of the dealer and of the manufacturer stated that the liability for breach of warranty was limited to repairing any defects. The Osburns' home had numerous defects. After repeated repairs the home was still defective. The Osburns sued the dealer and the manufacturer for breach of warranty. The defendants asserted that their only obligation was to make repairs. From a judgment for the Osburns, the defendants appealed.

OPALA, J. . . . Was the evidence with respect to the existence of defects sufficient to sustain a legal claim for breach of warranty? Did the limitation-of-remedy clause in [the] manufacturer's warranty "fail of its essential purpose" so as to make expanded UCC remedies available to the buyer under [UCC §] 2-719(2)? . . .

The proof here amply shows that, in addition to the substantial water leakage, numerous other defects and deficiencies existed. These consisted of (a) leaking water faucets, (b) buckled wall paneling, (c) missing interior trim, (d) insecurely fastened kitchen cabinets, (e) torn carpet and (f) a roof that made rumbling noises. All of these defects came to be discovered by the buyer shortly after he had moved into the home and all were promptly reported to the dealer pursuant to the warranty requirements. . . .

The warranty here in suit restricts the buyer's right of recovery for its breach to "repair or replacement of defective parts." The limitation so imposed is not, on its face, unconscionable. In fact, § 2-719(1)(a) expressly sanctions its employment. Limiting the buyer to the remedy of repair or replacement does not appear unfair because the warranty clause amply assures him of receiving the goods which either do or will conform to the contract. The purpose of the clause, as applied to this case, was hence to provide the buyer with a mobile home substantially free of defects. Implicit in the warranty-imposed obligation to repair or replace is the duty of providing conformable goods within a reasonable time after a defect in the original delivery is discovered.* Where the seller is afforded a reasonable opportunity to correct the defect and fails timely to respond or is repeatedly unsuccessful in the efforts to meet the warranty-imposed obligation, the limitation of remedy is deemed to have failed of its essential purpose *eo instante* and without the necessity of a prior judicial declaration.** The buyer is then free to invoke any of the broader remedies available under the Code.

Neither the seller nor the manufacturer was successful in the effort of rectifying the faulty conditions before the home was severely damaged by water leakage. When the home was not made to conform to the warranty within a reasonable time, the buyer—then left without the substantial value of his bargain—was relieved by the Code of the warranty-imposed limitation and hence able to seek broader recovery.

Manufacturer next complains that the trial court gave improper instructions upon the measure of damages for the breach in suit. The charge given called upon the jury to apply the difference—at the time and place of acceptance—between the actual value of the goods accepted and the value they would have had if they had been as warranted. This measure is, of course, proper when the evidence shows, as it did here, that the warranty-imposed limited-recovery clause "failed of its essential purpose."

[Judgment affirmed]

QUESTIONS

1. What defense did the defendants raise?
2. How did the plaintiffs meet this argument?
3. Is there any relationship between the implied warranty provisions of the Code and the Code's provision as to the failure of a limited remedy?

---

* What is a "reasonable time" for taking any action under the UCC depends on the nature, purpose, and circumstance of such action. . . . The terms of § 2-719(1) permit parties to tailor the outer limit of allowable recovery to their particular requirements, giving effect to reasonable agreements limiting or modifying existing remedies. They are designed to facilitate a fair recompense for breach of the contractual obligations. UCC § 2-719, Official Comment No. 1. *Conte v Dwan Lincoln-Mercury*, 172 Conn 112, 374 A2d 144 [1976]; . . . "The purpose of an exclusive remedy of replacement or repair of defective parts, whose presence constitute a breach of an express warranty, is to give the seller an opportunity to make the goods conforming while limiting the risks to which he is subject by excluding direct and consequential damages that might otherwise arise." *Beal v General Motors Corp.* 354 F Supp 423, 426 [D Del 1973].

** When a manufacturer limits its obligation to repair and replacement of defective parts, and repeatedly fails to correct the defect as promised within a reasonable time, it is liable for the breach of that promise as a breach of warranty. *Matthews v Ford Motor Co.*, 479 F.2d 399 [4th Cir. 1973]. . . . The fact that a manufacturer in good faith attempts to repair the defect whenever requested to do so is not a fulfillment of the warranty; he must demonstrate that the defect is permanently remedied as promised in the express warranty. . . . He can be liable for failure to fulfill the warranty obligation even if his failure to repair is neither wilful nor negligent. *Soo Line R. Co. v Fruehauf Corp.*, 547 F.2d 1365 [8th Cir. 1977].

20.   Waiver of Defenses

A buyer may be barred from objecting to a breach of the contract by the seller because the buyer has waived the right to do so.

(a) EXPRESS WAIVER. When sales are made on credit, the seller will ordinarily plan to assign the sales contract to a bank or other financer. The seller thereby converts into immediate cash the customer's obligation to pay in the future. To make the transaction more attractive to banks and financers, the credit seller will generally include in the sales contract with each buyer a **waiver of defenses** clause. By this clause the buyer agrees not to assert against the seller's assignee any defense held against the seller. For example, if the computer system does not work properly, the buyer agrees to complain only to the seller. The buyer agrees not to complain to the seller's assignee but will continue to pay the assignee just as though everything were satisfactory.

(b) IMPLIED WAIVER. When the buyer executes a promissory note as part of the credit transaction described above, the buyer automatically waives with respect to the seller's assignee any defense that could not be raised against a holder in due course of the note. This will be considered in greater detail in Chapter 32. What it means in the ordinary situation is that when the buyer signs a promissory note for the balance due, the buyer cannot assert against the finance company or the bank the defense that the buyer never got the goods called for by the contract, that the goods were defective and did not work, or that the contract had been entered into because of the fraudulent misstatements of the seller.

21.   Preservation of Defenses

Consumer protection laws and regulations seek to protect consumers by preserving defenses. In such cases there is no waiver of defenses as described in Section 20 of this chapter. If the basis for the defense to a home-solicited sale becomes apparent within time to cancel the sale, it is possible that the consumer may assert the defense by exercising the right of cancellation as described in Section 6(a) of Chapter 17.

(a) PRESERVATION NOTICE. Consumer defenses will be preserved by the Federal Trade Commission regulation requiring that the papers signed by a consumer contain a provision that expressly states that the consumer is reserving any defense arising from the transaction.[19] A defense of the consumer arising from the original transaction may therefore be asserted against a third person acquiring such paper.

(b) PROHIBITION OF WAIVER. When the Federal Trade Commission preservation notice is included in the paper that is received by the third person, it is unnecessary to consider whether a waiver of defenses could be validly made. If the preservation notice is not included, the seller has committed an unfair trade practice. The question then arises as to whether the buyer may assert against an assignee a defense that could have been asserted against the seller. The answer to this question depends on state law. In many states consumer protection statutes nullify a waiver of defenses by expressly providing that the buyer may assert against the seller's transferee any defense that might have been raised against the seller. Under some statutes, the buyer must give notice of any defense within a specified number of days after being notified of the assignment. Some courts extend consumer protection beyond the scope of the statute by ignoring a time limitation on the giving of notice of defenses and allow consumers to give late notice of defenses.

E.   REMEDIES IN THE INTERNATIONAL SALE OF GOODS

The United Nations Convention on Contracts for the International Sale of Goods (CISG) provides remedies for breach of a sales contract between parties from nations that have approved the CISG.

---

[19]   16 CFR § 433.1. It is an unfair or deceptive trade practice to take or receive a consumer credit contract that fails to contain such a preservation notice. See Chapter 32, Section 7 of this text.

22. Remedies of the Seller

Under the CISG, if the buyer fails to perform any obligations under the contract, the seller is given various remedies. The seller may require the buyer to pay the price, take delivery, and perform other obligations under the contract. The seller may also declare the contract avoided if the failure of the buyer to perform obligations under the contract amounts to a fundamental breach of contract.

23. Remedies of the Buyer

Under the CISG a buyer may reject goods only if the tender is a fundamental breach of the contract. This is in contrast to the UCC requirement of perfect tender. Under the CISG a buyer may also reduce the price when nonconforming goods are delivered, even though no notice of nonconformity is given. The buyer in this case must have a reasonable excuse for failure to give notice.

SUMMARY

The law provides a number of remedies for the breach of a sales contract. Remedies based on UCC theories are subject to a four-year statute of limitations. If the remedy sought is based on a non-UCC theory, the four-year limitation does not apply. A tort or contract statute of limitations will apply.

Remedies of the seller may include (1) a lien on the goods until the seller is paid, (2) the right to resell goods, (3) the right to cancel the sales contract, and (4) the right to bring an action for damages or, in some cases, for the purchase price.

Remedies of the buyer may include (1) rejection of nonconforming goods, (2) revocation of acceptance, (3) an action for damages for nondelivery of conforming goods, (4) an action for breach of warranty, (5) cancellation of the sales contract, (6) the right to resell the goods, (7) the right to bring an action for conversion, recovery of goods, or specific performance, and (8) the right to sue for damages and cancel the transaction because of the seller's fraud.

The parties may modify their remedies by contractual provision for liquidated damages, limitations on statutory remedies, or waiver of defenses. Legislative and administrative regulations restrict this freedom of contract to some extent, for the benefit of consumers.

Under the CISG the seller may require the buyer to pay the price, take delivery, and perform obligations under the contract, or may declare the contract avoided if there is a fundamental breach of contract.

Under the CISG a buyer may reject goods only if there is a fundamental breach of contract. The buyer may also reduce the price of goods if nonconforming, even without notice to the seller of nonconformity. The buyer must, however, have a reasonable excuse for failure to give notice.

QUESTIONS AND CASE PROBLEMS

1. What social forces are involved in the rule of law allowing the buyer to cover on the seller's breach?

2. Donna purchased a snowmobile from the Park Manufacturing Company. Three years later it rolled over and injured her. She sued Park two years after her accident, alleging that Park had breached its implied warranty of merchantability. The suit was based on the theory that the snowmobile had rolled over because of a design defect and that this defect showed that the snowmobile was not fit for its normal use. Is Park liable for the injuries sustained by Donna?

3. Gwendolyn purchased a washing machine from the Melvin Appliance Center. She did not notice that on the back of the contract that she signed there was a statement in fine print that in the event of any defects, Melvin's liability was limited to repairing or replacing the defective parts. There was a defective switch in the washing machine. The switch caused the machine to overheat and set fire to the laundry

room of Gwendolyn's house. She demanded that Melvin pay her for the damage caused to the laundry room. Melvin offered to repair the washing machine free of charge and insisted that it had no greater liability because of the limitation of liability in the contract. Gwendolyn claimed that the limitation clause was not binding because it was not conspicuous. Was she correct?

4. Ward ordered a $500 television set from Greyline Markets Inc. Greyline wrote Ward an acceptance of his order. The next day Ward found a store selling the same set for $400. He notified Greyline that he was canceling his order of the day before. Greyline insisted that he could not do this and that he must pay $500 for the set. Was Greyline correct?

5. Under what circumstances may the seller sue the buyer for the price?

6. The goods purchased by the buyer were defective. The seller made repeated attempts to correct the defect. It became apparent that it was impossible to correct the defect. The buyer notified the seller that the buyer was revoking acceptance of the goods. The seller offered to try again to repair the goods. The buyer rejected this offer and repeated that acceptance of the goods was being revoked. The seller claimed that the buyer could not revoke acceptance as long as the seller offered to repair the goods. Was the seller correct? [See Fenton v Contemporary Development Co. 12 Wash App 345, 529 P2d 883]

7. After a sales contract was made, the seller's factory was destroyed by fire. The seller and the buyer then agreed to cancel the contract. Thereafter, the seller's factory was rebuilt, and the buyer demanded that the seller perform the contract. Was the seller required to do so? [Goddard v Ishikawajima-Harima Heavy Industries Co. 29 App Div 2d 754, 287 NYS2d 901]

8. Sam wants to buy a car on credit from Henry Motors. He is afraid, however, that Henry will assign his contract to a finance company and that the finance company will be able to collect the balance due on the car even if the car does not run properly. Sam wants to be able to defend against the finance company by showing that there are defects in the car. Is this possible?

9. Wolosin purchased a vegetable and dairy refrigerator case from the Evans Manufacturing Corp. Evans sued Wolosin for the purchase price. Wolosin raised as a defense a claim for damages for breach of warranty. The sales contract provided that Evans would replace defec-

tive parts free of charge for one year and that "This warranty is in lieu of any and all other warranties stated or inferred, and of all other obligations on the part of the manufacturer, which neither assumes nor authorizes anyone to assume for it any other obligations or liability in connection with the sale of its products." Evans claimed that it was only liable for replacement of parts. Wolosin claimed that the quoted clause was not sufficiently specific to satisfy the limitation of remedies requirement of UCC § 2-719. Decide. [Evans Mfg. Corp. v Wolosin (Pa) 47 Luzerne County Leg Reg 238]

10. McInnis purchased a tractor and scraper as new equipment of current model from the Western Tractor & Equipment Co. The written contract stated that the seller disclaimed all warranties and that no warranties existed except as were stated in the contract. Actually, the equipment was not the current model but that of the prior year. Likewise, the equipment was not new but had been used for 68 hours as a demonstrator model, after which the hour meter had been reset to zero. The buyer sued the seller for damages. The latter defended on the ground that all liability for warranties had been disclaimed. Was this defense valid? [McInnis v Western Tractor & Equipment Co. 63 Wash 2d 652, 388 P2d 562]

11. Compare or contrast the statute of limitations for a breach of warranty on tender of delivery of goods with the statute of limitations for breach of an express warranty as to future performance.

12. Keenan rejected nonconforming goods delivered to him by Ross. After the rejection, but before Ross had been allowed a reasonable time to give instructions for the disposition of the goods, Keenan arranged a sale of the goods at a substantially reduced price. Ross in the meantime had sold the goods to another of his customers. What rights, if any, does Ross have against Keenan?

13. Peters, the buyer, received merchandise from Hadley, the seller. On looking over the goods, Peters noticed that certain of the goods did not conform to the contract. He therefore called Hadley, who stated, "We always take care of our customers." Peters then accepted the goods. The nonconformity not being remedied within a reasonable time, Peters informed Hadley that he revoked his acceptance. Hadley refused to take back the goods. Who will prevail?

14. A buyer purchased goods from a seller. He telephoned the seller that he revoked his accep-

tance of the goods. The seller claimed that the revocation of acceptance was not effective because it was not accompanied by a return or offer to return the goods. Was the seller correct?

15. Landry purchased a television set from the Montgomery Music Co. for $800. He paid $100 down, and five weeks later he paid $200. After having the set for over 15 months, he sued to rescind the sale and recover the $300 on the ground that the set had been guaranteed to his personal satisfaction and that from the time he received it, it had been unsatisfactory. Was he entitled to recover? Why?

29

CONSUMER PROTECTION

In the last few decades the consumer protection movement has made a substantial number of changes to traditional law.

A. GENERAL PRINCIPLES

Consumer protection began with the aim of protecting the person of limited means and limited knowledge. This was the opening wedge, but the movement has expanded so that today the objective is protecting everyone from being victimized. This is in keeping with the American concept of equality before the law. If protection is needed, it should be extended to everyone who needs it.

1. Expansion of Protection

The consumer protection movement was started to protect poor, ignorant individuals. The social forces of protecting the person and protecting from fraud, exploitation, and oppression have expanded the category of protected consumers. Many consumer protection statutes now define *consumer* as any person, partnership, corporation, bank, or government that uses goods or services. Thus, it has been held that the word *consumer* includes a collector paying nearly $100,000 for jade art objects, a glass manufacturer purchasing 3 million gallons of diesel oil fuel, or the city of Boston purchasing insurance. In Texas the protected group of buyers of goods and services includes the state of Texas, its governmental agencies, and businesses with assets under $25 million.[1]

In a few states a limitation is imposed that a suit involving the consumer be of public interest or concern. Thus, a dispute between real estate brokers could not be brought within the consumer protection statute when the facts were so unusual that there was no general public interest in the outcome of the case. That is, it was not a situation that was likely to occur with many other consumers. Note that the fact that both the plaintiff and the defendant in the broker case were experienced business persons did not exclude either of them from the protection of the consumer protection statute.

Consumer protection statutes are drawn in very general terms. For example, under the Louisiana statute "a practice is unfair when it offends established public policy and when the practice is immoral, unethical, oppressive, unscrupulous, or substantially injurious to consumers."

A person violating the provisions of a consumer protection statute is liable even though there was no intention to violate the law and even though the breach was a single occurrence rather than a pattern of repeated conduct.[2]

2.   Proof of Consumer Status

A consumer claiming that there has been a violation of the consumer protection statute has the burden of proving that the statutory definition of *consumer* has been satisfied.[3] However, the consumer is not required to prove that none of the statutory exceptions or defenses are available to the defendant. If the defendant produces evidence showing the applicability of an exception or defense, the consumer must produce opposing evidence. If a dispute of fact is thus raised, the defendant has the ultimate burden of convincing the trier of fact that the exception is applicable or that the defense may be raised.

3.   Who Is a Defendant in a Consumer Protection Suit?

The defendant in consumer protection situations is a person or an enterprise that regularly enters into the kind of transaction in which the injured consumer was involved. For example, it is the merchant seller, the finance company, the bank, the leasing company, the home repairer, and any others who enter regularly into a particular kind of transaction.

Society feels that such a business or enterprise, familiar with all the procedures and practices of that business, is likely to be able to victimize the consumer. Of course, this argument is less convincing as we move away from the original image of the helpless consumer. Nevertheless, there is still the sound basis that the purpose of consumer protection is to clean up the business world. Therefore, it is the defendant in business with which consumer protection is concerned.

4.   Consumer Negligence

Consumer protection law is directed at protecting the consumer from the misconduct of others. Disclosure provisions are frequently imposed. These provisions give the consumer the information that the consumer would lack and would not have enough experience or bargaining power to demand. In a limited number of situations the consumer is given the power to rescind a transaction if hindsight makes the consumer unhappy with the deal that had been made.

Consumer protection, however, does not protect a consumer from the consumer's own negligence. Thus, a consumer is bound by a contract even though the consumer signed

---

[1]   Statutes that broaden the protected group to protect buyers of goods and services generally are often called deceptive trade practices statutes, instead of the earlier name of consumer protection statutes.

[2]   Ashlock v Sunwest Bank of Roswell, 107 NM 100, 753 P2d 346 (1988).

[3]   Eckman v Centennial Savings Bank (Tex App) 742 SW2d 826 (1988).

without reading or understanding what it meant. Moreover, when the contract signed by the consumer clearly states one thing, the consumer cannot prove that the other contracting party had made statements contradicting what was stated in the signed contract.[4]

Consumers should exercise reasonable care and not blindly trust consumer protection law to rescue them from their own blunders.

5.   Consumer Remedies

The theoretical right of the consumer to sue or to assert a defense is often of little practical value to the consumer. The amount involved may be small compared with the cost of litigation. Consumer protection legislation provides special remedies.

(a) GOVERNMENT AGENCY ACTION. The Uniform Consumer Credit Code (UCCC) provides for an administrator who will, in a sense, police business practices to ensure conformity with the law. This is not regarded by some as an improvement. It has been criticized because of the danger that the administrator may be creditor-oriented. As a consequence, the debtor might be deprived of protection in many cases when it is a question of policy or discretion as to what action, if any, should be taken by the administrator.

(b) ACTION BY ATTORNEY GENERAL. A number of states provide that the state attorney general may bring an action on behalf of a particular group of consumers. In these actions the attorney general sues to obtain cancellation of the consumers' contracts and restitution of whatever they had paid.

Many states permit the attorney general to bring an action to enjoin violation of the consumer protection statute. Consumer protection statutes commonly give the attorney general the authority to seek a voluntary stopping of improper practices before seeking an injunction from a court.

(c) ACTION BY CONSUMER. Some consumer protection statutes provide that a consumer who is harmed by a violation of the statutes may sue the enterprise that acted improperly. The consumer may sue to recover a specified penalty or may bring an action on behalf of consumers as a class. Consumer protection statutes are often designed to rely on private litigation as an aid to enforcement of the statutory provisions. The Consumer Product Safety Act of 1972 authorizes "any interested person" to bring a civil action to enforce a consumer product safety rule and certain orders of the Consumer Product Safety Commission. In other cases, however, the individual consumer cannot bring any action, and enforcement of the law is entrusted exclusively to an administrative agency.

In any case, a consumer who shows only that the defendant had broken a contract is not entitled to recover under a fair business practices or deceptive trade practices act. In addition, the plaintiff must show misconduct of the kind prohibited by the statutes.[5]

The *Varady* case illustrates the use of a statutory penalty in the Uniform Consumer Credit Code to induce private litigation as an enforcement aid.

---

[4]   Heidt v Potamkin Chrysler-Plymouth, Inc. 181 Ga App 903, 354 SE2d 440 (1987).

[5]   Gross v Ideal Pool Corp. 181 Ga App 483, 352 SE2d 806 (1987).

VARADY v WHITE
42 Colo App 389, 661 P2d 284 (1982)

Robert White was an electronic technician. His wife Marilyn was a homemaker. The Whites owned a 90-acre tract of land, which they subdivided and sold as unimproved lots. The sixth lot was sold to Kenneth Varady. All sales were made partly on credit, with an unpaid balance being secured by some form of collateral agreement. The Whites failed to inform Varady of certain matters that the UCCC required them to disclose. Within three days after the transfer of ownership of the land to Varady, Varady notified the Whites that he was rescinding the transaction. The Whites refused to return Varady's money to him or to take back the land. Varady brought an action against the Whites. From a judgment in their favor, he appealed.

KELLY, J. . . . [UCCC] Section 5-2-104(1)(a) provides that a "consumer credit sale" is a sale of an interest in land in which "credit is granted . . . by a person who *regularly* engages as a seller in *credit transactions of the same kind . . .*" (emphasis added). Thus, in order to determine whether the disputed transaction is subject to the disclosure requirements of the UCCC, we must consider whether, as a matter of law, the prior transactions constituted "regular" credit transactions and whether they were of "the same kind" as the subject transaction.

Colorado's UCCC is based on the Federal Consumer Credit Protection Act (CCPA), 15 U.S.C.A. § 1601, et seq., and the intent of the CCPA "seems to have been to except from the Act only those lenders whose extensions of credit are an occasional, isolated, and incidental portion of their business." *Eby v Reb Realty, Inc.*, 495 F2d 646 (9th Cir. 1974). Thus, private homeowners who take back second mortgages upon selling their homes would normally not be required to comply with the disclosure requirements of the Act.

Although the Whites sold their own home and took a second mortgage, they had subdivided their 90-acre property and sold five unimproved lots in their subdivision prior to the sale to plaintiffs. Neither defendant had a real estate license or worked full time in the real estate business: Robert White was an electronic technician and Marilyn White was a housewife. However, the subdivision and the sale of lots is itself a business venture. After five separate sales of lots from a 90-acre tract, the Whites cannot claim ignorance of real estate transactions. Moreover, they sold more unimproved lots after the sale to plaintiffs. In *Eby, supra,* the realty firm was held to have engaged in "regular" credit transactions although it had sold only three parcels on credit within a time span of nineteen months. The Whites sold lots in September and October of 1974, and April, June, and July of 1976 before the sale to the Varadys. This constitutes "regular" credit transactions for purposes of § 5-2-104(1)(a), C.R.S. 1973.

Since the phrase "credit transactions of the same kind" is not included in the definition of a credit transaction under the CCPA, we must interpret this phrase without the aid of federal guidelines. While the Whites sold the Varadys improved land and the prior sales conveyed unimproved lots, the presence or absence of improvements is not a critical factor in determining whether transactions are of the same kind. All the sales consisted of an "interest in land" purchased primarily for a personal, family, or household use under § 5-2-104(1)(c), C.R.S. 1973.

The two sales in 1974 and the sale to the Varadys in 1976 involved second deeds of trust, while the other three sales in 1976 involved first deeds of trust. However, the Whites were the creditors in each of the transactions, so the form of the security interest is not determinative of this issue. Although these six transactions were not identical in each minute detail, we conclude, as a matter of law, that they were "credit transactions of the same kind." Therefore, since the Whites regularly engaged in credit transactions of the same kind, their sale to the Varadys was a "consumer credit sale" under § 5-2-104(1)(a), C.R.S. 1973.

Since the Varady-White transaction was a consumer credit sale of an interest in land, the debtors have rescission rights under § 5-5-204, C.R.S. 1973. This section permits the debtor to rescind the transaction "until midnight of the third business day following the consummation of the transaction or the delivery of the disclosures required under this section . . . whichever is later. . . ." When a debtor rescinds, § 5-5-204(2), C.R.S. 1973, affords him a number of rights. First, he is not liable for any credit service charge, and any security interest given by the debtor becomes void upon the rescission. Second, within ten days after receipt of a notice of rescission, the creditor must return to the debtor "the money or property given as earnest money, down payment, or otherwise," and must terminate any security interest created under the transaction. And third, upon the performance of the creditor's obligations, the debtor must tender the property to the creditor, and unless the creditor takes possession of the property within ten days after the tender by the debtor, the debtor may keep the property without paying for it.

Where, as here, the creditors have not made the disclosures required by the UCCC, the debtors are at liberty to rescind the contract at their pleasure. . . . Since the Varadys gave the Whites notice of their intent to rescind within three days of closing, and the Whites did not return the Varadys' payments and terminate their security interest within ten days of the notice of rescission, the Whites must return all money paid to them by the Varadys, and ownership of the property vests in the Varadys without their obligation to pay for it.

The Whites were subject to a statutory duty to inform the Varadys of their right to rescind the transaction. . . . Although the Whites did not act purposefully to deprive the Varadys of their rights, it is up to the creditor to avoid forfeiture by complying with the UCCC. . . .

[Judgment reversed]

QUESTIONS

1. Why did the court hold that the UCCC was applicable?
2. Was the answer to the first question inevitable?
3. What social forces are affected by this decision?

SCOPE OF RELIEF. The consumer protection statutes only provide relief as to conduct condemned by such statutes. They afford no protection to a consumer against a mere breach of contract. Thus, the fact that the seller never delivers the goods purchased by the buyer does not by itself constitute a violation of a consumer protection statute. However, there may be other circumstances that, when combined with the nondelivery of the goods, will show that the seller has violated a consumer protection statute.

6.   Civil and Criminal Penalties

The seller or lender engaging in improper consumer practices may be subject to civil penalties and criminal punishment. In some instances the laws in question are the general laws applicable to improper conduct, while in other cases the laws are specifically aimed at the particular consumer practices.

An example of a violation of the general law is a contractor who falsely stated to a homeowner that certain repairs needed on the roof cost, with labor and materials, $650. In fact, they cost only $200, and the contractor was guilty of the crime of obtaining money by false pretenses.

Illustrative of specific consumer protection statutes, the Truth in Lending Act subjects the creditor to a separate claim for damages for each periodic statement that violates the disclosure requirements. Furthermore, consumer protection statutes of the disclosure type generally provide that the creditor cannot enforce the obligation of the debtor if the required information is not set forth in the contract.

B. AREAS OF CONSUMER PROTECTION

The following sections discuss the more important areas of consumer protection.

7. Advertising

Statutes commonly prohibit fraudulent advertising. Most advertising regulations are entrusted to an administrative agency, such as the Federal Trade Commission (FTC). The FTC is authorized to issue orders to stop false or misleading advertising. Statutes prohibiting false advertising are liberally interpreted.

(a) DECEPTION. Under consumer protection statutes deception, rather than fraud, is the significant element. There is a breach of such statutes even though there is no proof that the wrongdoer intended to defraud or deceive anyone.[6]

This is a shift of social point of view. That is, instead of basing the law in terms of fault of the actor, the law is concerned with the problem of the buyer who is likely to be misled. The good faith of an advertiser or the absence of intent to deceive is immaterial. The purpose of false advertising legislation is to protect the consumer rather than to examine the advertiser's motives.

The net effect of the truth in advertising legislation is that a seller must make an accurate and substantially complete description of the product and the terms on which it is sold. The seller must do so in a way that the buyer can be expected to understand.

At common law a seller was not liable when the product did not live up to the opinion expressed by the seller to the buyer. The theory of the common law was that the buyer should recognize that the statement was merely the opinion of the seller and that the buyer should not rely thereon. In the realities of the marketplace, buyers do rely on sellers' opinions. Therefore, the unfair trade practices laws condemn false opinions of sellers that mislead buyers.

The FTC requires that an advertiser maintain a file containing the data claimed to support an advertising statement as to safety, performance, efficacy, quality, or comparative price of an advertised product. The FTC can require the advertiser to produce this material. If it is in the interest of the consumer, the FTC can make this information public, except to the extent that it contains trade secrets or material that is privileged.

In the *Colgate-Palmolive* case, advertising that was attacked as deceptive was defended on the ground that it was not fraudulent.

---

[6]   Haag v Dry Basement, Inc. 11 Kan App 2d 649, 732 P2d 392 (1987).

FTC v COLGATE-PALMOLIVE CO.
380 US 374 (1965)

The Colgate-Palmolive Co. sells a shaving cream, Rapid Shave. To test the effectiveness of the cream, the company put it on sandpaper and then shaved the sandpaper. The company then wanted to run a commercial on television showing this test as proof that the product could soften even the toughness of sandpaper. When the actual test was telecast, the sandpaper looked like ordinary colored paper. In order to have something that really looked like sandpaper, the advertiser used a sheet of Plexiglass on which sand had been sprinkled. The Federal

Trade Commission prohibited this commercial on the ground that it deceived the viewer. The advertiser claimed that there was no deception because the viewer was merely being given an accurate visual representation of the test that had actually been made. The FTC issued an order to stop the commercial. The court of appeals reversed this order. The case was then appealed to the U.S. Supreme Court.

WARREN, C.J. . . . The Commission found that the undisclosed use of a plexiglass substitute for sandpaper was [a] material misrepresentation that was a deceptive act separate and distinct from [any] misrepresentation concerning Rapid Shave's underlying qualities. Even if the sandpaper could be shaved just as depicted in the commercials, the Commission found that viewers had been misled into believing they had seen it done with their own eyes. As a result of these findings the Commission entered a cease-and-desist order against the respondents [Colgate and the advertiser]. . . .

. . . The Commission expressed the view that without this visible proof of Rapid Shave's moisturizing ability some viewers might not have been persuaded to buy the product. . . .

. . . When the Commission was created by Congress in 1914, it was directed by § 5 to prevent "unfair methods of competition in commerce." Congress amended the Act in 1938 to extend the Commission's jurisdiction to include "unfair or deceptive acts or practices in commerce"—a significant amendment showing Congress' concern for consumers as well as for competitors. It is important to note the generality of these standards of illegality. . . .

This statutory scheme necessarily gives the Commission an influential role in interpreting § 5 and in applying it to the facts of particular cases arising out of unprecedented situations. Moreover, as an administrative agency which deals continually with cases in the area, the Commission is often in a better position than are courts to determine when a practice is "deceptive" within the meaning of the Act. . . .

We accept the Commission's determination that the commercials involved in this case contained three representations to the public: (1) that sandpaper could be shaved by Rapid Shave; (2) that an experiment had been conducted which verified this claim; and (3) that the viewer was seeing this experiment. . . . For the purposes of our review, we can assume that the first two representations were true; the focus of our consideration is on the third, which was clearly false. The parties agree that § 5 prohibits the intentional misrepresentation of any fact which would constitute a material factor in a purchaser's decision whether to buy. They differ, however, in their conception of what "facts" constitute a "material factor" in a purchaser's decision to buy. Respondents submit, in effect, that the only material facts are those which deal with the substantive qualities of a product. The Commission, on the other hand, submits that the misrepresentation of *any* fact so long as it materially induces a purchaser's decision to buy is a deception prohibited by § 5.

The Commission's interpretation of what is a deceptive practice seems more in line with the decided cases than that of respondents. . . .

We agree with the Commission . . . that the undisclosed use of plexiglass in the present commercials was a material deceptive practice. . . . Respondents claim that it will be impractical to inform the viewing public that it is not seeing an actual test, experiment or demonstration, but we think it inconceivable that the ingenious advertising world will be unable, if it so desires, to conform to the Commission's insistence that the public be not misinformed. If, however, it becomes impossible or impractical to show simulated demonstrations on television in a truthful manner, this indicates that television is not a medium that lends itself to this type of commercial, not that the commercial must survive at all costs. . . .

[Judgment reversed]

QUESTIONS

1. Was Colgate-Palmolive being sued for damages for fraud?
2. Who was harmed by the commercial for Rapid Shave?
3. Was Colgate-Palmolive guilty of fraudulent selling practices?

(b) CORRECTIVE ADVERTISING. When an enterprise has made false and deceptive statements in advertising, the Federal Trade Commission may require that new advertising be made in which the former statements are contradicted and the truth stated. This corrective advertising required by the Federal Trade Commission is also called **retractive advertising**.

8. Seals of Approval

Many commodities are sold or advertised with a sticker or tag stating that the article has been approved or is guaranteed by some association or organization. Ordinarily, when a product is thus sold, it will in fact have been approved by some testing laboratory and will probably have proven adequate to meet ordinary consumer needs. Selling with a seal of approval of a third person makes, in effect, a guarantee that the product has been so approved. Such a seller is liable if the product was, in fact, not approved. In addition, the seller is ordinarily liable for fraud if the statement is not true.

9. Labeling

Closely related to the regulation of advertising is the regulation of label and marking of products. Various federal statutes are designed to give the consumer accurate information about the product, while others require warnings as to dangers of use or misuse. Consumer protection regulations prohibit the use in the labeling or marking of products of such terms as

jumbo, giant, or *full,* which tend to exaggerate and mislead.

10. Selling Methods

Consumer protection statutes prohibit the use of improper and deceptive selling methods.[7] These statutes are liberally construed to protect consumers from improper practices.

(a) DECEPTIVE PRACTICES. Consumer protection statutes and deceptive trade practice acts are violated when the statements or the business methods of the defendant are deceptive. It is not necessary to prove that the defendant was guilty of fraud. Hence it is immaterial that the defendant who misrepresented the facts did not intentionally do so.[8]

(b) DISCLOSURE OF TRANSACTION TERMS. The federal law requires the disclosure of all interest charges, points or fees for granting loans, and similar charges. These

---

[7] As to states adopting the UCCC, see Chapter 1, Section 30. The Uniform Consumer Sales Practices Act has been adopted in Kansas, Ohio, and Utah; a Uniform Deceptive Trade Practices Act (1966 revision) has been adopted in Colorado, Georgia, Hawaii, Minnesota, Nebraska, New Mexico, Ohio, and Oregon; the 1964 version of the Uniform Deceptive Trade Practices Act was adopted in Delaware, Illinois, Maine, and Oklahoma; and a Model Land Sales Practice Act has been adopted in Alaska, Connecticut, Florida, Hawaii, Idaho, Kansas, Minnesota, Montana, South Dakota, and Utah. The federal government has expanded the protection of the consumer's food supply by the Nutrition Labeling and Education Act of 1990, Act of November 8, 1990, PL 101-535, 104 Stat 2353, ____USC § ____; and the Sanitary Food Transportation Act of 1990, Act of November 3, 1990, PL 101-500, 104 Stat 1213, ____USC § ____.

[8] RRTM Restaurant Corp. v Keeping (Tex App) 766 SW2d 804 (1989).

charges must be set forth as an annual percentage rate so that the consumer can see just how much the transaction costs a year and can compare alternatives.[9]

If sellers advertise that they will sell or lease on credit, they cannot state merely the monthly installments that will be due. They must give the consumer additional information: (1) the total cash price; (2) the amount of the down payment required; (3) the number, amounts, and due dates of payments; and (4) the annual percentage rate of the credit charges.[10]

In various ways, consumer protection statutes seek to protect the consumer from surprise or unbargained-for terms and from unwanted contracts. Under consumer protection statutes it is commonly a deceptive trade practice to fail to disclose to a consumer information that would have prevented the consumer from entering into the transaction if the disclosure had been made.[11]

(1) More-Than-Four-Installments Rule. Whenever a consumer sale or contract provides for payment in more than four installments, it is subject to the Truth in Lending Act. This is so even though no service or finance charge is expressly added because of the installment pattern of paying.

When consumer credit is advertised as repayable in more than four installments and no finance charge is expressly imposed, the advertisement must "clearly and conspicuously" state that "the cost of credit is included in the price" quoted for the goods and services.

(2) Contract on Two Sides. In order to be sure that disclosures required by federal law are seen by the consumer, special provision is made for the case when the terms of the transaction are printed on both the front and back of a sheet or contract. In such case, (a) both sides of the sheet must carry the warning: "NOTICE: see other side for important information," and (b) the page must be signed at the end of the second side. Conversely, the requirements of the federal law are not satisfied when there is no warning of "see other side" and the parties sign the contract only on the face, or the first side, of the paper.

(3) Particular Sales and Leases. The Motor Vehicle Information and Cost Savings Act requires the disclosure to the buyer of various elements in the cost of an automobile. The Act prohibits selling an automobile without informing the buyer that the odometer has been reset below the true mileage. A buyer who is caused actual loss by odometer fraud may recover from the seller three times the actual loss or $1,500, whichever is greater.[12] There is a breach of the federal statute when the seller has knowledge that the odometer has turned itself at 100,000 miles but the seller then states that the mileage is 20,073 miles instead of 120,073. The Consumer Leasing Act of 1976 requires that persons leasing automobiles and other durable goods to consumers make a full disclosure to the consumer of the details of the transaction.

Although the federal statute imposes liability only when the seller "knowingly" violates the statute, it is not necessary to prove actual knowledge. An experienced auto dealer cannot claim lack of knowledge that the odometer was false when that conclusion was reasonably apparent from the condition of the car.[13]

(c) HOME-SOLICITED SALES. A sale of goods or services for $25 or more made to a buyer at home may be set aside within three days. This right may be exercised merely because the buyer does not want to go through with the contract. There is no requirement of

---

[9]   Consumer Credit Protection Act (CCPA), 15 USC § § 1605, 1606, 1636; Regulation Z adopted by the Federal Reserve Board of Governors, § 226.5.
The obligation of disclosure has been further extended by the Fair Credit and Charge Card Disclosure Act of 1988. Act of Nov. 3, 1988, PL 100-583, 102 Stat 2960, 15 USC § § 1601 note, et seq. and by the Home Equity Loan Consumer Protection Act of Nov. 23, 1988, PL 100-709, 102 Stat 4729, 15 USC § § 1601 note, et seq.
[10]   Regulation Z, § 1210, Consumer Leasing Act of 1976, 15 USC § 1667.
[11]   Pfeiffer v Ebby Halliday Real Estate, Inc. (Tex App) 747 SW2d 887 (1988).

[12]   Act of October 20, 1972, § § 403, 409, PL 92-513, 86 Stat 947, 15 USC § § 1901 et seq., as amended.
[13]   Denmon v Nick's Auto Sales (La App) 537 So 2d 796 (1989).

proving any misconduct of the seller or any defect in the goods or services.[14]

(d) REFERRAL SALES. The technique of giving the buyer a price reduction for customers referred to the seller is theoretically lawful. In effect, it is merely paying the buyer a commission for the promotion of other sales. In actual practice, however, the referral sales technique is often accompanied by fraud or by exorbitant pricing, so that consumer protection laws variously condemn referral selling. As a result, the referral system of selling has been condemned as unconscionable under the UCC and is expressly prohibited by the UCCC.

11.   The Consumer Contract

There are several ways in which consumer contracts are affected by consumer protection legislation.

(a) FORM OF CONTRACT. Consumer protection laws commonly regulate the form of the contract, requiring that certain items be specifically listed, that payments under the contract be itemized, and that the allocation to such items as principal, interest, and insurance be indicated. Generally, certain portions of the contract or all of the contract must be printed in type of a certain size, and a copy must be furnished to the buyer. Such statutory requirements are more demanding than the statute of frauds section of the UCC. It is frequently provided that the copy furnished the consumer must be completely filled in. Back-page disclaimers are void if the front page of the contract does not call attention to the presence of such terms.

(b) CONTRACT TERMS. Consumer protection legislation does not ordinarily affect the right of the parties to make a contract on such terms as they choose. It is customary, however, to prohibit the use of certain clauses that are believed to bear too harshly on the debtor or that have too great a potential for exploitive abuse by a creditor. For example,

the UCCC prohibits provisions permitting a creditor to enter a judgment against a debtor without giving the debtor any chance to make a defense.[15]

The federal Warranty Disclosure Act of 1974 establishes disclosure standards for consumer goods warranties, in order to make them understood by the consumer.[16]

The parties to a credit transaction may agree that payments should be made in installments but that if there is a default as to any installment, the creditor may declare the entire balance due at once. This cancels or destroys the schedule for payments by making the entire balance immediately due. Such *acceleration* of the debt can cause the debtor great hardship. Because of this, some statutes limit or prohibit the use of acceleration clauses.

(c) LIMITATION OF CREDIT. Various laws may limit the ability to borrow money or purchase on credit. In some states, it is prohibited to make **open-end mortgages**, by which the mortgage secures a specified debt and such additional loans as may thereafter be made. Consumer protection is also afforded in some states by placing a time limit on smaller loans.

A Federal Trade Commission regulation declares it an unfair trade practice to require a consumer borrowing or buying on credit to give the lender or seller as collateral a security interest in all of the consumer's household goods.[17]

(d) UNCONSCIONABILITY. To some extent consumer protection has been provided under the UCC by those courts that hold that the "unconscionability" provision protects from "excessive" or "exorbitant" prices when goods are sold on credit.[18]

Some statutes are aimed at preventing price gouging as to goods or services for which the demand is abnormally greater than the supply. The New York statute provides:

---

[14]   Federal Trade Commission Regulation, 16 CFR § 429.1.

[15]   UCCC § § 2.415, 3.407.
[16]   Act of January 4, 1975, PL 93-637, 88 Stat 2183, 15 USC § 2301.
[17]   16 CFR § 444.2(4)(1988).
[18]   UCC § 2-302(1).

"During any abnormal disruption of the market for consumer goods and services vital and necessary for the health, safety and welfare of consumers, resulting from stress of weather, convulsion of nature, failure or shortage of electric power or other source of energy . . . no merchant shall sell or offer to sell any such consumer goods or services for an amount which represents an unconscionably excessive price." Consumer goods and services are defined as "those used, bought or rendered primarily for personal, family or household purposes." Such a statute protects purchasers of electric generators for home use during a hurricane-caused blackout.[19]

12.   Credit Cards

Today's credit card may be designed for a specific use, such as for travel and entertainment or for a particular group of commodities; or it may be a general-purpose card, covering the purchase of any kind of goods and services.

(a) UNSOLICITED CREDIT CARD. The unsolicited distribution of credit cards to persons who have not applied for them is prohibited.

(b) SURCHARGE PROHIBITED. By some statutes a seller cannot add any charge to the purchase price because the buyer uses a credit card instead of paying with cash or a check.[20]

(c) UNAUTHORIZED USE. A cardholder is not liable for more than $50 for the unauthorized use of a credit card. In order to impose liability up to that amount, the issuer must show that (1) the credit card was an accepted card,[21] (2) the issuer had given the holder adequate notice of possible liability in such case, (3) the issuer had furnished the

holder with a self-addressed, prestamped notification form to be mailed by the holder in the event of the loss or theft of the credit card, (4) the issuer had provided a method by which the user of the card could be identified as the person authorized to use it,[22] and (5) unauthorized use of the card had occurred or might occur as a result of loss, theft, or some other event.

(d) UNAUTHORIZED PURPOSE DISTINGUISHED. There is an unauthorized use of a credit card only when it is used without the permission or approval of the cardholder. In contrast, the holder may authorize another person to use the card but to use it for a particular purpose, such as to buy a particular item. If the person uses the card for a purpose other than the one specified by the holder, there is still an authorized use of the card, even though it is for an unauthorized purpose. In such a case the cardholder is liable for all charges made on the card, even though they were not intended by the cardholder when the card was loaned.[23] The same rule is applied when an employer has cards issued to employees for making employment-related purchases, but one of the employees uses the card for personal purposes.

13.   Payments

Consumer legislation may provide that when a consumer makes a payment on an open charge account, the payment must be applied toward payment of the earliest charges. The result is that, should there be a default at a later date, any right of repossession of the creditor is limited to the later, unpaid items. This outlaws a contract provision by which, upon the default of the buyer, the seller could assert the right to repossess all purchases that had been made at any prior time. Such a provision is outlawed by the UCCC and probably

---

[19]   New York v Two Wheel Corp. 71 NY2d 693, 530 NYS2d 46, 523 NE2d 692 (1988).

[20]   In contrast, the Truth in Lending Act Amendment of 1976, 15 USC § 1666f, permits a merchant to offer a discount to cash-paying customers but not customers using a credit card.

[21]   A credit card is "accepted" when "the cardholder has requested and received or has signed or has used, or authorized another to use [it], for the purpose of obtaining money, property, labor, or services on credit." CCPA § 103(l).

[22]   Regulation Z of the Board of Governors of the Federal Reserve, § 226.13(d), as amended, provides that the identification may be "signature, photograph, or fingerprint on the credit card or by electronic or mechanical confirmation."

[23]   Michigan National Bank v Olson, 44 Wash App 898, 723 P2d 438 (1986).

would be found unconscionable under the UCC.

14.   Preservation of Consumer Defenses

Consumer protection laws generally prohibit a consumer from waiving or giving up any defense provided by law.

In the ordinary contract situation, when goods or services purchased or leased by a consumer are not proper or are defective, the consumer is not required to pay the seller or lessor or is only required to pay a reduced amount. With the modern expansion of credit transactions, sellers and lessors have used several techniques for getting paid without regard to whether the consumer had any complaint against them. To prevent this, the Federal Trade Commission has adopted a regulation that requires that in every sale or lease of goods or services to a consumer, the contract of the consumer contain a clause giving the consumer the right to assert defenses. These defenses may be asserted not only against the seller or lessor but also against a third person, such as a bank or finance company, to which the seller or lessor transfers the collection rights. The FTC regulation requires that the following notice be included in bold-face type at least ten points in size:

NOTICE

ANY HOLDER OF THIS CONSUMER CREDIT CONTRACT IS SUBJECT TO ALL CLAIMS AND DEFENSES WHICH THE DEBTOR COULD ASSERT AGAINST THE SELLER OF GOODS OR SERVICES OBTAINED PURSUANT HERETO OR WITH THE PROCEEDS HEREOF. RECOVERY HEREUNDER BY THE DEBTOR SHALL NOT EXCEED AMOUNTS PAID BY THE DEBTOR HEREUNDER.

15.   Product Safety

The health and well-being of consumers is protected by a variety of statutes and rules of law, some of which antedate the modern consumer protection era.

Most states have laws governing the manufacture of various products and establishing product safety standards. The federal Consumer Product Safety Act provides for research and the setting of uniform standards for products in order to reduce health hazards. This Act also establishes civil and criminal penalties for the distribution of unsafe products, recognizes the right of an aggrieved person to sue for monetary damages and to obtain an injunction against the distribution of unsafe products, and creates a Consumer Product Safety Commission to administer the Act.[24]

A consumer, as well as various nonconsumers, may hold a seller or manufacturer liable for damages when the product causes harm, as was discussed in Chapter 27 of this book.

The federal Anti-Tampering Act[25] makes it a federal crime to tamper with consumer products.

16.   Credit, Collection, and Billing Methods

Various provisions have been made to protect consumers from discriminatory and improper credit and collection practices.

(a) CREDIT DISCRIMINATION. It is unlawful to discriminate against an applicant for credit on the basis of race, color, religion, national origin, sex, marital status, or age; because all or part of the applicant's income is obtained from a public assistance program; or because the applicant has in good faith exercised any right under the Consumer Credit Protection Act (CCPA). When a credit application is refused, the applicant must be furnished with a written explanation as to why the application was rejected.

(b) CORRECTION OF ERRORS. When the consumer believes that an error has been made in billing by the issuer of a credit card,

---

[24]   Act of October 27, 1972, PL 92-573, 86 Stat 1207, 15 USC § 2051-2081; as amended by the Consumer Product Safety Improvements Act of 1990, Act of November 16, 1990, PL 101-608, 104 Stat 3110, ___USC § ___.

[25]   Act of October 13, 1983, PL 98-127, 97 Stat 831, 13 USC § 1365.

the consumer should send the creditor a written statement and explanation of the error. The creditor or card issuer must investigate and make a prompt written reply to the consumer.[26]

(c) IMPROPER COLLECTION METHODS. Unreasonable methods of debt collection are often expressly prohibited by statute or are held by courts to constitute an unreasonable invasion of privacy.[27] Statutes generally prohibit sending bills in such a form that they give the impression that a lawsuit has been begun against the consumer and that the bill is legal process or a warrant issued by the court. The CCPA prohibits the use of extortionate methods of loan collection. A creditor may be prohibited from informing the employer of the debtor that the latter owes money.

When a seller made telephone calls to the buyer and the buyer's relatives and made obscene, threatening, and malicious statements that caused the buyer to become physically ill, the seller was liable for the tort of intentional mental disturbance. In order to give rise to

such liability, the statements made must be more than mere insults, indignities, threats, and annoyances, and must be so shocking and outrageous as to exceed all reasonable bounds of decency.

A creditor is liable for unreasonably attempting to collect a bill that in fact has been paid. This liability can arise under general principles of tort law, as distinguished from special consumer protection legislation.

A debt collection letter sent to the debtor's place of employment was found to be a violation of the Fair Debt Collection Practices Act. The words "final demand for payment" could be read through the envelope. The fact that it was likely that the debtor would be embarrassed by the delivery of such a letter to the employer's address affected the outcome of the case. In another case a bank's threat to prosecute the depositors if they did not return to the bank money that had been paid to them by mistake violated a state debt collection law. No criminal statute prohibited the depositors' conduct.

When a collection agency violates the Fair Debt Collection Practices Act, it is liable to the debtor for damages. It is no defense that the debtor in fact owed the money that the agency was seeking to collect.

In the *Johnson* case the consumer sued the collection agency for trying to collect a debt that was admittedly owed.

---

[26] Fair Credit Billing Act, Act of October 18, 1974, PL 93-495, 15 USC § 1601.

[27] Fair Debt Collection Practices Act, Act of September 20, 1977, PL 95-109, 91 Stat 874, 15 USC § § 1692 et seq.; Federal Trade Commission Regulation, 16 CFR Part 237.

JOHNSON v STATEWIDE COLLECTIONS, INC.
(Wyo) 778 P2d 93 (1989)

Johnson purchased a shotgun and paid with a check. He returned the gun the next day. He could not get his money back from the store, so he stopped payment on his check. The store claimed that it was not required to make a refund of the purchase price and gave its claim for the purchase price to the Statewide Collection Agency (also doing business as CheckRite). CheckRite sent a demand for payment to Johnson. This was answered by Johnson's attorney by a letter sent to CheckRite by certified mail. CheckRite ignored the attorney and made another demand on Johnson for payment. Johnson sued Statewide for damages, claiming that it violated the Fair Debt Collection Practices Act (FDCPA) because it had not obtained a verification of the debt from the creditor nor sent such a verification to Johnson, that it demanded from the debtor more money than was due, and that it ignored the debtor's attorney. Judgment was entered in favor of Johnson, and Statewide appealed.

THOMAS, J. . . . We . . . consider the merits of the several asserted grounds for recovery under the FDCPA. Congress adopted this legislation in 1977 to protect consumers from abusive, deceptive, and unfair debt collection activities by eliminating certain offensive and unethical practices in vogue with many third-party debt collectors. . . . The objectionable practices, still prevalent even after the adoption of the FDCPA, often are exacerbated because independent collectors generally are unconcerned with the consumer's opinion of them, or their own reputations in the eyes of the public, and they proceed accordingly. This attitude is different from that of the direct creditor who often wishes to maintain some good will as well as some prospect of salvaging future business from their effort. . . . Some of the objectionable practices, more blatant and egregious than others, that transgress the FDCPA include obscene and profane language, direct threats of violence, harassing phone calls made at any and all hours of the day or night, disclosure of the debtor's personal affairs to friends and employers, attempts to collect more than is owed, intentional misrepresentation of legal rights and obligations, and impersonation of public officials and attorneys. . . .

Because the goal of the FDCPA is to eliminate abusive collection practices, it is applicable whether or not a valid debt exists. . . . A violation of the FDCPA cannot be defended even by establishing that the debt was long overdue and difficult to collect. Standing is afforded an aggrieved consumer to proceed under the act as long as the collector was purporting to attempt to collect an alleged debt. In a report from the subcommittee, its chairman said, "every individual, *whether or not he owes the debt*, has the right to be treated in a reasonable and civil manner." . . .

Administrative enforcement of the FDCPA is assigned to the Federal Trade Commission, 15 U.S.C. § 1692*l*, but the primary enforcement, in order to eliminate the objectionable practices, is self enforcement by the aggrieved debtor acting as a "private attorney general" through a civil action like that initiated by Johnson. . . . The incentive provided by the FDCPA for private enforcement is the recovery of attorney fees and costs, plus a civil penalty of up to $1000, in addition to actual damages when the debtor is successful in the civil action. . . .

Against this general background, we address the several claimed violations of the FDCPA that Johnson contends support the judgment awarded by the county court. The first of those arises under 15 U.S.C. § 1692g(b) which provides:

(b) Disputed debts. If the consumer notifies the debt collector in writing within the thirty-day period described in subsection (a) of this section that the debt, or any portion thereof, is disputed, or that the consumer requests the name and address of the original creditor, the debt collector shall cease collection of the debt, or any disputed portion thereof, until the debt collector obtains verification of the debt or a copy of a judgment, or the name and address of the original creditor, and a copy of such verification or judgment, or name and address of the original creditor, is mailed to the consumer by the debt collector.

This provision of the FDCPA requires the verification, or validation, of the alleged debt in order to prevent collection activities from being directed against the wrong person or against a debtor who has paid. . . .

CheckRite did not send verification of the debt to either Johnson or Johnson's attorney. The manager testified that he had communicated with the retail store on several other occasions on each of which the debt was verified to him.

It was CheckRite's duty, under the statute, to cease collection activities on the date it received the letter from Johnson's counsel until it sent Johnson, through his counsel, verification of the alleged debt. . . .

. . . CheckRite had failed to comply with 15 U.S.C. § 1692g because it had not received a verification or validation from the retail store that it could mail to Johnson. . . . CheckRite made no attempt to comply with the mailing requirement. The burden is upon the debt collector to demand adequate verification so that it can comply with the mailing requirement of the statute. The failure to do so by CheckRite, in this instance, subjects it to the sanctions provided under 15 U.S.C. § 1692k.

The next basis for liability raises the issue of whether CheckRite violated the provisions of 15 U.S.C. § 1692f(1) by attempting to collect more from Johnson than was permitted either by agreement or by law. . . . CheckRite agrees that this is true, but defends it conduct as not a violation of the FDCPA by contending that the improper claim was the product of an inadvertent clerical error. . . .

The . . . FDCPA provides:

A debt collector may not use unfair or unconscionable means to collect or attempt to collect any debt. Without limiting the general application of the foregoing, the following conduct is in violation of this section:

(1) The collection of any amount (including any interest, fee, charge, or expense incidental to the principal obligation) unless such amount is expressly authorized by the agreement creating the debt or permitted by law. 15 U.S.C. § 1692f.

The concession by CheckRite that the demand encompassed an overcharge manifests a prima facie violation of the FDCPA. . . . In submitting its argument that the overcharge was the result of an inadvertent clerical error, CheckRite invokes . . . 15 U.S.C. § 1692k(c) that provides:

(c) Intent. A debt collector may not be held liable in any action brought under this subchapter if the debt collector shows by a preponderance of evidence that the violation was not intentional and resulted from a bona fide error notwithstanding the maintenance of procedures reasonably adapted to avoid any such error.

. . . While CheckRite's explanation is plausible . . . the record is silent with respect to any procedures reasonably adopted by CheckRite to preclude just such an error. . . . The collector is liable under the act without regard to whether the overcharge was intentional or not unless proper procedures to preclude the error are maintained. . . .

CheckRite also violated the FDCPA by sending a demand letter directly to him after it had been advised that he was represented by counsel. The pertinent provision is 15 U.S.C. § 1692c(a)(2) that provides:

(a) Communication with the consumer generally—Without the prior consent of the consumer given directly to the debt collector or the express permission of a court of competent jurisdiction, a debt collector may not communicate with a consumer in connection with the collection of any debt— . . .

(2) if the debt collector knows the consumer is represented by an attorney with respect to such debt and has knowledge of, or can readily ascertain, such attorney's name and address, unless the attorney fails to respond within a reasonable period of time to a communication from the debt collector or unless the attorney consents to direct communication with the consumer. . . .

CheckRite admits that it sent an additional communication to Johnson after receiving the advice that he was represented by counsel. . . . The communication directly with Johnson . . . was an additional violation of the FDCPA. . . .

[Judgment affirmed]

QUESTIONS

1. Can a debt collection agency defend against the claim for violating the FDCPA by proving that the debt in fact was owed and that the debtor knew that it was owed?
2. What must a collection agency do when a consumer notifies it in writing within a 30-day period that a debt assigned to it for collection is disputed?
3. Assume that a collection agency knows that the debtor's affairs are frequently handled by the attorney John Jones, Esq. To whom should the agency send the verification of the debt?

17.   Protection of Credit Standing and Reputation

In many instances one party to a transaction wishes to know certain things about the other party. This situation arises when a person purchases on credit or applies for a loan, a job, or a policy of insurance. Between two and three thousand private credit bureaus gather such information on borrowers, buyers, and applicants and sell such information to interested persons.

The Fair Credit Reporting Act (FCRA) of 1970[28] seeks to protect consumers from various abuses that may arise. FCRA applies only to **consumer credit**, which is defined as credit for "personal, family, and household" use; it does not apply to business or commercial transactions.

The Act does not apply to the investigation report made by an insurance company of a policy claim.[29]

(a) PRIVACY. A report on a person based on personal investigation and interviews is called an **investigative consumer report**. It may not be made without informing the person investigated of the right to discover the results of the investigation. Bureaus are not permitted to disclose information to persons not having a legitimate use for it. It is a federal crime to obtain or to furnish a bureau report for an improper purpose.

On request, a bureau must tell a consumer the names and addresses of persons to whom it has made a credit report during the previous six months. It must also tell, when requested, which employers were given such a report during the previous two years.

A store may not publicly display a list of named customers from whom it will not accept checks; such action is an invasion of the privacy of those persons.

(b) PROTECTION FROM FALSE INFORMATION. Much of the information obtained by credit bureaus is based on statements made by persons, such as neighbors, when interviewed by the bureau's investigator. Sometimes the statements are incorrect. Quite often they are hearsay evidence and would not be admissible in a legal proceeding. Nevertheless, such statements may go on the records of the bureau without further verification and be furnished to a client of the bureau, who will tend to regard them as accurate and true.

---

[28]   Act of October 26, 1970, PL 91-508, 84 Stat 1128, 15 USC §§ 1681 et seq.
[29]   Kemp v County of Orange, 211 Cal App 3d 1422, 260 Cal Rptr 131 (1989).

A person has a limited right to request that a credit bureau disclose the nature and substance of the information it possesses. The right to know does not extend to medical information. It is not required that the bureau identify the persons giving information to its investigators. The bureau is not required to give the applicant a copy of, or to permit the applicant to see, any file.

When a person claims that the information of the bureau is erroneous, the bureau must take steps within a reasonable time to determine the accuracy of the disputed item.

Adverse information obtained by investi-gation cannot be given to a client after three months unless verified to determine that it is still valid. Most legal proceedings cannot be reported by a bureau after seven years. A bankruptcy proceeding cannot be reported after ten years.

In the *Thompson* case a person who was denied credit because of the mistake of a credit reporting agency brought suit against the agency. Was it liable? The court was faced with determining what standard of care should be required of a credit reporting agency.

THOMPSON v SAN ANTONIO RETAIL MERCHANTS ASS'N

(CA5 Tex) 682 F2d 509 (1982)

The San Antonio Retail Merchants Association (SARMA) was a credit reporting agency. It was asked by one of its members to furnish information on William Douglas Thompson, III. It supplied information from a file that contained data on William III and also on William Daniel Thompson, Jr. The agency had jumbled information related to William Jr. into the file relating to William III, so that all information appeared to relate to William III. William Jr. had a bad credit standing, and SARMA gave a bad report on William III. Because of this report, he was denied credit by several enterprises. He then sued SARMA for its negligence in confusing him with William Jr. From a judgment in Williams's favor, SARMA appealed.

PER CURIAM. SARMA provides a computerized credit reporting service to local business subscribers. This service depends heavily upon credit history information fed into SARMA's files by subscribers. A key mechanism used by SARMA to update its files is a computerized "automatic capturing" feature. A subscriber must feed certain identifying information from its own computer terminal into SARMA's central computer in order to gain access to the credit history of a particular consumer. When presented with this identifying information, SARMA's computer searches its records and displays on the subscriber's terminal the credit history file that most nearly matches the consumer. The decision whether to accept a given file as being that of a particular consumer is left completely to the terminal operator. When a subscriber does accept a given file as pertaining to a particular consumer, however, the computer automatically captures into the file any information input from the subscriber's terminal that the central file did not already have.

A disadvantage of an automatic capturing feature is that it may accept erroneous information fed in by subscribers, unless special auditing procedures are built into the system. In the instant case, SARMA failed to check the accuracy of a social security number obtained by its automatic capturing feature. The social security number is the single most important identifying factor for credit-reference purposes. As a result, the computer erroneously began to report the bad credit history of "William Daniel Thompson, Jr.," to subscribers inquiring about "William Douglas Thompson, III."

Under 15 U.S.C. § 1681o of the Fair Credit Reporting Act (Act), a "consumer reporting agency" is liable to "any consumer" for negligent failure to comply with "any requirement imposed" by the Act. In the instant case, the district court determined that SARMA was liable under section 1681o for negligent failure to comply with section 1681e(b) of the Act, which provides:

> When a consumer reporting agency *prepares* a consumer report, it shall follow *reasonable procedures* to assure *maximum possible accuracy* of information concerning the individual about whom the report relates.

15 U.S.C. § 1681e(b) (emphasis added).

Section 1681e(b) does not impose strict liability for any inaccurate credit report, but only a duty of reasonable care in preparation of the report. That duty extends to updating procedures, because "preparation" of a consumer report should be viewed as a continuing process and the obligation to insure accuracy arises with every addition of information. The standard of conduct by which the trier of fact must judge the adequacy of agency procedures is what a reasonably prudent person would do under the circumstances.

Applying the reasonable-person standard, the district court found two acts of negligence in SARMA's updating procedures. First, SARMA failed to exercise reasonable care in programming its computer to automatically capture information into a file without requiring any minimum number of "points of correspondence" between the consumer and the file or having an adequate auditing procedure to foster accuracy. Second, SARMA failed to employ reasonable procedures designed to learn the disparity in social security numbers for the two Thompsons. . . .

With respect to the first act of negligence, George Zepeda, SARMA's manager, testified that SARMA's computer had no minimum number of points of correspondence to be satisfied before an inquiring subscriber could accept credit information. Moreover, SARMA had no way of knowing if the information supplied by the subscriber was correct. Although SARMA did conduct spot audits to verify social security numbers, it did not audit all subscribers. With respect to the second act of negligence, SARMA's verification process failed to uncover the erroneous social security number even though. . . . a specific request [had been made] for a "revision" to check the adverse credit history ascribed to the plaintiff. SARMA's manager, Mr. Zepeda, testified that what should have been done upon the request for a revision, was to pick up the phone and . . . learn, among other things, the social security number for William Daniel Thompson, Jr. It was the manager's further testimony that the social security number is the single most important information in a consumer's credit file. In light of this evidence, this Court cannot conclude that the district court was clearly erroneous in finding negligent violation of section 1681e(b). . . .

The district court's award of $10,000 in actual damages was based on humiliation and mental distress to the plaintiff. Even when there are no out-of-pocket expenses, humiliation and mental distress do constitute recoverable elements of damage under the Act. In the instant case, the amount of damages is a question of fact which may be reversed by this Court only if the district court's findings are clearly erroneous. . . .

[Judgment affirmed]

On general principles of agency law, a creditor hiring someone or a collection agency to collect a debt is liable to the debtor for damages for unlawful conduct of the collector. It is no defense that the creditor did not intend nor have any knowledge of such conduct.

18.   Expansion of Consumer Protection

Various state laws aimed at preventing fraudulent sales of corporate securities, commonly called **blue sky laws**, have been adopted. These statutes are discussed in Chapter 48 on corporate stock. Other statutes have been adopted to protect purchasers of real estate and buyers of services.

(a) REAL ESTATE DEVELOPMENT SALES. Anyone promoting the sale of a real estate development that is divided into 50 or more parcels of less than five acres each must file with the secretary of Housing and Urban Development (HUD) a **development statement**. This statement must set forth significant details of the development, as required by the federal Land Sales Act.[30]

Anyone buying or renting one of the parcels in the subdivision must be given a **property report**. This is a condensed version of the development statement filed with the secretary of HUD. This report must be given to the prospective customer more than 48 hours before the signing of the contract to buy or lease.

If the development statement is not filed with the secretary, the sale or rental of the real estate development may not be promoted through the channels of interstate commerce or by the use of the mail.

If the property report is given to the prospective buyer or tenant less than 48 hours before the signing of a contract to buy or lease, or after it has been signed, the contract may be avoided within 48 hours. If the property report is never received, the contract may be avoided, and there is no statutory limitation on the time in which this may be done.

The federal statute prohibits imposing or receiving unauthorized payments in connection with a real estate settlement.

State statutes frequently require that particular enterprises selling property tell or disclose certain information to prospective buyers.[31]

(b) SERVICE CONTRACTS. The UCCC treats a consumer service contract the same as a consumer sale of goods if (1) payment is made in installments or a credit charge is made, and (2) the amount financed does not exceed $25,000. It defines *services* broadly as embracing work, specified privileges, and insurance provided by a noninsurer. The inclusion of *privileges* makes the UCCC apply to contracts calling for payment on the installment plan or including a financing charge for transportation, hotel and restaurant accommodations, education, entertainment, recreation, physical culture (such as athletic clubs or bodybuilding schools), hospital accommodations, cemetery accommodations, and funerals.

In some states, it is unlawful for a repair shop to make unauthorized repairs to an automobile and then to refuse to return the automobile to the customer until paid for such repairs.

---

[30]   Act of August 1, 1968, as amended, PL 90-448, 82 Stat 590, 15 USC §§ 1701-1720.

[31]   Tara Hills Condominium Ass'n v Gaughan (Minn App) 399 NW2d 638 (1987).

(c) FRANCHISES. A franchisee is a consumer entitled to sue the franchisor for violation of a state deceptive practices act. In order to protect a prospective franchisee from deception, a Federal Trade Commission regulation requires that the franchisor give a prospective franchisee a disclosure statement ten days before the franchisee signs a contract or pays any money for a franchise. The disclosure statement provides detailed information relating to the franchisor's finances, experience, size of operation, and involvement in litigation. The statement must set forth any restrictions imposed on the franchisee; any costs that must be paid initially or in the future; and the provisions for termination, cancellation, and renewal of the franchise. False statements as to sales, income, or profits are prohibited. Violation of the regulation is subject to a fine of $10,000.

In the *Morris* case the franchisees claimed that they were misled by the concealment of a material fact by the franchisor.

MORRIS v INTERNATIONAL YOGURT CO.
107 Wash 2d 314, 729 P2d 33 (1986)

The International Yogurt Company (IYC) had developed a unique mix for making frozen yogurt and related products. Morris and his wife purchased a franchise from the company. They were not told that a franchise was not required to obtain the mix—that the company would sell its yogurt mix to anyone. The franchise business of the Morrises was a failure, and they sold it at a loss after three years. They then sued the company for fraud and for violation of the state Franchise Investment Protection Act (FIPA) and the state Consumer Protection Act. From a decision against them, they appealed.

DURHAM, J. . . . The next issue we must consider is if IYC violated FIPA by failing to disclose to the Morrises that the yogurt mix was available to nonfranchisees. [The statute] provides in part:

It is unlawful for any person in connection with the offer, sale, or purchase of any franchise directly or indirectly: (2) To sell or offer to sell a franchise in this state by means of any written or oral communication which includes an untrue statement of a material fact or omits to state a material fact necessary in order to make the statements made in light of the circumstances under which they were made not misleading.

. . . Initially, we must determine when a fact is material under [the FIPA]. This provision is essentially the same as the antifraud provision in the Securities Act of Washington. . . . For purposes of the latter provision, a "material fact" is "'a fact to which a reasonable man would attach importance in determining his choice of action in the transaction in question.'" . . .

The next question is if IYC's failure to disclose to the Morrises that the yogurt mix was available to nonfranchisees was an omission of a material fact. In order to determine if a reasonable person would consider this fact important in purchasing the franchise, it is necessary to consider initially the importance of the yogurt mix itself to the potential franchisee.

The evidence in the record indicates that the yogurt mix was an essential element of the franchise. First, the franchise agreement placed particular emphasis on the fact that, in exchange for purchasing an IYC franchise, the franchisee would obtain the right to purchase and use a special yogurt mix. The agreement goes to considerable length in discussing the yogurt mix. Section 9 of the agreement states in part:

> The yogurt mix to be used in the preparation of all frozen yogurt sold at the Franchised Location is unique, and its formula and process for manufacture may be regarded as a trade secret. The right to purchase and use the mix is granted to Franchisee pursuant to this Agreement.

Thus, the agreement clearly indicates that the right to purchase this one-of-a-kind yogurt mix is a key feature of the franchise.

Section 9 of the agreement further provides that the franchisor will make the formula for the manufacture of the mix available to certain dairy manufacturers, which shall be regarded as approved sources from which the franchisee will purchase the mix. If the franchisee wishes to purchase the mix from a different manufacturer, he must request in writing that the franchisor disclose the formula and process for manufacture to that manufacturer. The agreement further states:

> Franchisor shall exercise its reasonable good business judgment in determing whether the formula and process should be disclosed to that manufacturer, *taking into consideration such factors as that manufacturer's ability to produce a mix of satisfactory quality, and that manufacturer's ability to adequately protect the formula and process from disclosure to unauthorized persons.*

(Italics ours.) By suggesting that IYC will limit access to the formula for the yogurt mix, this provision reinforces the fact that the mix is significant to IYC's product.

. . . In summary, the evidence as a whole indicates that the yogurt mix as well as the flavoring contributed to the distinctiveness of IYC's final product. . . . This yogurt mix was a major, essential element of IYC yogurt.

. . . IYC's failure to disclose to the Morrises the availability of the yogurt mix to nonfranchisees was an omission of a material fact. In deciding whether to purchase the franchise, a reasonable person reading the franchise agreement would have considered it important that the same yogurt mix was available to persons not purchasing the franchise. The fact that an essential component of the franchise's major product is unique and considered a trade secret is a far less value to the potential franchisee if that ingredient is generally available to all persons whether or not they have purchased the franchise. A person might not consider it worthwhile to invest in the franchise if he knew he could obtain the mix without paying the franchise fee. For these reasons, we conclude that IYC's failure to disclose to the Morrises the availability of the yogurt mix to nonfranchisees was an omission of a material fact necessary to make the statements IYC made not misleading, and therefore, was a violation of [the FIPA].

. . . FIPA's provision on damages states that a person who sells a franchise in violation of the statute "shall be liable to the franchisee . . . who may sue at law or in equity for damages caused thereby."

We hold . . . that in an action alleging the omission of a material fact in violation of [FIPA], proof of nondisclosure of a material fact establishes a presumption of reliance which the defendant may rebut by proving that the plaintiff would still have purchased the franchise even if the material fact had been disclosed. This case is remanded to the trial court to determine, in a manner consistent with this opinion, if IYC's failure to disclose to the Morrises the availability of the mix to nonfranchisees cause the Morrises to suffer damages.

... We reverse the Court of Appeals decision that IYC did not omit a material fact in violation of [FIPA] when it failed to disclose to the Morrises the availability of the yogurt mix to nonfranchisees. We remand the case to the trial court to decide if the Morrises may recover damages for IYC's violation . . . , according to the principles in this opinion.

[Reversed on the issue of the effect of the omission and action remanded to determine damages]

QUESTIONS

1. Did the company expressly state that its unique yogurt mix would be sold only to franchisees?
2. Why does the court describe the availability of the yogurt mix to nonfranchisees as a material fact?
3. Why is the court concerned with "reliance" by the prospective franchise buyer?

FIGURE 29-1   THE LEGAL ENVIRONMENT OF THE CONSUMER

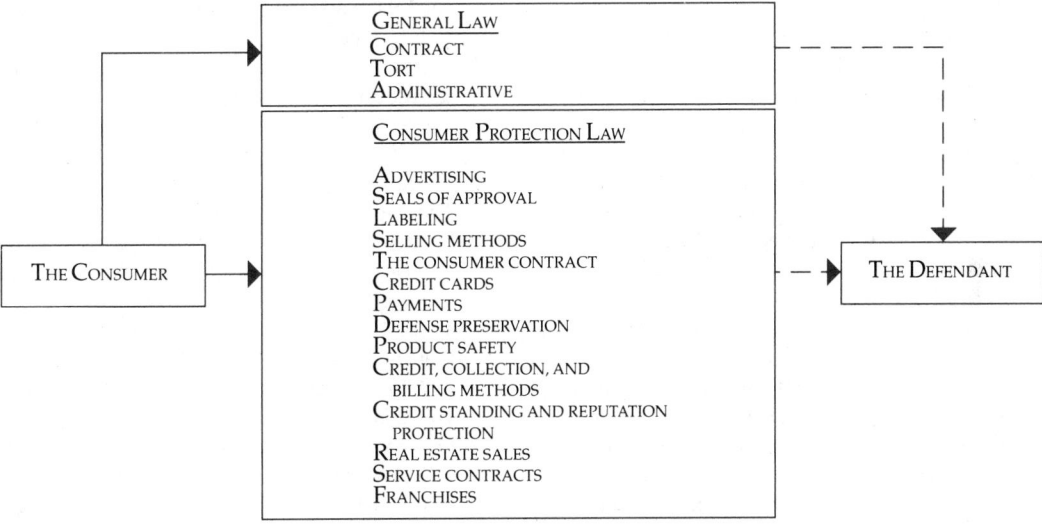

SUMMARY

With the modern era of consumer protection, society has accepted the premise that equality before the law is not appropriate to the marketplace, where modern methods of marketing, packaging, and financing have reduced the ordinary consumer to a subordinate position. In order to protect the consumer from the hardship, fraud, and oppression that could result from being in such an inferior position, the law has, at many points, limited the freedom of action of the enterprise with which the consumer deals.

Consumer protection laws are directed at false and misleading advertising; misleading or false use of seals of approval and labels; the methods of selling—requiring the disclosure of terms, permitting consumer cancellation of home-solicited sales, and, in some states, prohibiting referral sales. The consumer is protected in a contract agreement by regulation of its form, prohibition of unconscionable terms, and limitation of the credit that can be extended to a consumer. Credit card protections include the prohibition of the unauthorized distribution of such cards and limited liability of the cardholder for the unauthorized use of a credit card. The application of payments; the preservation of consumer defenses as against a transferee of the consumer's contract; product safety; the protection of credit standing and reputation; and (to some extent) real estate development sales, franchises, and service contracts are all included in consumer protection laws.

When a consumer protection statute is violated, an action may sometimes be brought by the consumer against the wrongdoer. More commonly, such action is brought by an administrative agency or by the attorney general of the state.

QUESTIONS AND CASE PROBLEMS

1. What is the object of each of the following rules of law?
   (a) Back-page disclaimers are void if the front page of the contract does not call attention to the presence of such terms.
   (b) A consumer's waiver of a statute designed for consumer protection is void, but the transaction otherwise binds the consumer.
2. Neil purchased a printing press from Guardian Press Company for $12,000, payment to be made in three installments of $4,000 each. Neil later sued Guardian for failing to make the disclosures specified by the federal Truth in Lending Act. Was Guardian required to make disclosures under the Act?
3. Cora telephoned from her home to the Nowlin Music Supply Company and ordered an electric guitar. The employee of Nowlin answering the phone stated that Cora's order was accepted and that the guitar would be sent to Cora within a few days. That night Cora saw an ad in the newspaper for the same guitar for $100 less than the Nowlin price. Cora wrote and mailed a letter the next day to the Nowlin Company stating that she canceled her order. May Cora do so?
4. Ward purchased an ice-making machine from Kold-Serve Corp. The machine had been sold by Kold-Serve to another buyer but was returned to Kold-Serve. The president of Kold-Serve sold this machine as a "demonstrator model." He did not inform Ward of its prior sale and return. Later Ward sued Kold-Serve, claiming that it had "knowingly" committed an unfair trade practice in the sale of the machine to him. Was Ward correct? [Kold-Serve Corp. v Ward (Tex App) 736 SW2d 750]

5. The California consumer protection statute prohibits the use of false or misleading representations in the sale of goods or services. Mayne borrowed money from the Bank of America National Trust and Savings Association. He later sued the bank, claiming that it had violated the statute. The bank asserted that Mayne was required to prove that he had been deceived by the information furnished by the bank. Was the bank correct? [Mayne v Bank of America National Trust and Savings Ass'n (Cal App) 242 Cal Rptr 357]
6. The Merit Breakfast Food Company sold its breakfast cereal in ordinary-sized packages, but the packages were labeled *jumbo* size. Merit was ordered to stop using this term by the Federal Trade Commission. Merit raised the defense that the term *jumbo* was not used with any intent to defraud, so its use was not improper. Was this a valid defense?
7. Compare the disclosure requirements for the sale of a television by a dealer for $400 payable in (a) cash, (b) two installments, and (c) eight installments.
8. Thomas was sent a credit card through the mail by a company that had taken his name and address from the telephone book. Because he never requested the card, Thomas left the card lying on his desk. A thief stole the card and used it to purchase merchandise in several stores in the name of Thomas. The issuer of the credit card claimed that Thomas was liable for the total amount of the purchases made by the thief. Thomas claimed that he was not liable for any amount. The court decided that Thomas was liable for $50. Who is correct?

9. A federal statute prohibits the interstate shipment of deceptively or fraudulently labeled goods. Acting under the authority of this statute, federal officers seized a shipment of 95 barrels that were labeled *apple cider vinegar*. This vinegar had been made from dried apples that had been soaked in water. The government claimed that the label was false, because apple cider vinegar meant to the average person that the vinegar had been made from fresh apples. The shipper claimed that since the barrels in fact contained vinegar that had been made from cider produced from apples, the labels were truthful in calling the contents by the name of *apple cider vinegar*. Was the shipper correct? [United States v 95 Barrels of Alleged Apple Cider Vinegar, 265 US 438]

10. Wilke was contemplating retiring. In response to an advertisement he purchased from Coinway 30 coin-operated testing machines. He purchased these because Coinway's representative stated that by placing these machines at different public places, Wilke could obtain supplemental income. This statement was made by the representative although he had no experience as to the cost of servicing such machines or their income-producing potential. The operational costs of the machines by Wilke exceeded the income. Wilke sued Coinway to rescind the contract, alleging that it was fraudulent. Coinway defended on the ground that the statements made were merely matters of opinion and did not constitute fraud. Was Wilke entitled to rescission? [Wilke v Coinway, Inc., 257 Cal App 2d 126, 64 Cal Rptr 845]

11. Greif obtained credit cards from Socony Mobil Oil Co. for himself and his wife. The card specified, "This card is valid unless expired or revoked. Named holder's approval of all purchases is presumed unless written notice of loss or theft is received." Later Greif returned his card to the company, stating that he was canceling it, but that he could not return the card in his wife's possession because they had separated. Subsequently, Socony sued Greif for purchases made by the wife on the credit card in her possession. He defended on the ground that he had canceled the credit card contract. Decide. [Socony Mobil Oil Co. v Greif, 10 App Div 2d 119, 197 NYS2d 522]

12. The Southwestern Bell Telephone Company held a judgment against Wilson for $9,500. It instructed two attorneys and some of its employees to collect the judgment. In their attempts to do so, they allegedly committed various torts and harassed Wilson. He sued Southwestern. It denied liability for the conduct of the attorneys and the employees because it had not authorized any improper collection practices. Was this defense valid? [Southwestern Bell Tele. Co. v Wilson (Tex App) 768 SW2d 755]

13. A suit was brought against General Foods on the ground that it was violating the state law prohibiting false and deceptive advertising. It raised the defense that the plaintiffs had failed to show that the public had been deceived by the advertising, that the public in fact had not relied on the advertising, and that there was no proof that anyone had sustained any damage because of the advertising. Were these valid defenses? [Committee on Children's Television, Inc. v General Foods Corp. 35 Cal 3d 197, 197 Cal Rptr 783, 673 P2d 660]

14. The McNeils ran Hangman Ridge Training Stables, Inc. They owned all the stock in the corporation. They needed money, and the Farmers Home Loan Administration agreed to give them a loan if property owned by the corporation was transferred to the McNeils as individuals and they gave the lender the mortgage on that land. The Safeco Title Insurance Company handled the transaction. The employee in charge told the parties that she was not an attorney. About a year later it was learned that the McNeils owed $3,500 in taxes because of the transaction. They claimed that the Safeco employee should have informed them that they should have obtained independent legal and tax advice. They claimed that because of this Safeco had violated the state consumer protection act. Were they correct? [Hangman Ridge Training Stables, Inc. v Safeco Ins. Co. 105 Wash 2d 778, 719 P2d 531]

15. The town of Newport obtained a corporate MasterCard. The card was given to the town clerk to use in purchasing fuel for the town hall. The town clerk used the card for personal restaurant, hotel, and gift shop debts. The town refused to pay the card charges on the ground that they were unauthorized. Was the town correct? [MasterCard v Town of Newport, 133 Wis App 2d 328, 396 NW2d 345]

PART FIVE

COMMERCIAL PAPER

30

KINDS OF PAPER, PARTIES, AND NEGOTIABILITY

Under the law of contracts a promise, when supported by consideration, creates certain legal rights that may be assigned to another person. Even before these common law rules relating to contracts were developing, another body of law, the law merchant, was creating principles relating to a different type of obligation and the transfer of rights arising therefrom. In the course of time this obligation became the bill of exchange, also known today as a draft, a trade acceptance, or, with certain modification, a check. In time, another type of instrument, the promissory note, appeared. Both drafts and promissory notes may have the quality of negotiability. This is a quality that distinguishes them from contracts. The rights drafts and notes represent can be trans-ferred in such a way that the transferee may be immune from certain contract defenses. As a group, these instruments are known as commercial paper or negotiable instruments.

A. KINDS OF COMMERCIAL PAPER AND PARTIES

Commercial paper, such as checks and promissory notes, is a substitute for money and can be used as a means of providing credit.

1. Definition

Commercial paper includes written promises (such as promissory notes) or orders (such as checks or drafts) to pay money, and it may be transferred by the process of negotiation. **Negotiation** is the transferring of commercial paper in such a way as to make the transferee the holder of the paper. Much of the importance of commercial paper lies in the fact that it is more readily transferred than ordinary contract rights and that the transferee of commercial paper may acquire greater rights than would an assignee of a contract. A person who acquires a commercial paper may therefore be subject to less risk.

2. Kinds of Commercial Paper

Commercial paper falls into four categories: (1) promissory notes, (2) drafts or bills of exchange, (3) checks, and (4) certificates of deposit.

(a) PROMISSORY NOTES. A **negotiable promissory note** is an unconditional promise in writing made by one person to another, signed by the maker, engaging to pay on demand or at a definite time a sum certain in money to order or to bearer.[1] (See Figure 30-1.)

(b) DRAFTS. A **negotiable draft** or **bill of exchange** is an unconditional order in writing addressed by one person to another, signed by the person giving it, requiring the person to whom it is addressed to pay on demand, or at a definite time, a sum certain in money to order or to bearer.[2] (See Figure 30-2) In effect, it is an order by one person on a second person to pay a sum of money. The person who gives the order is called the **drawer** and is said to draw the bill. The person on whom the order to pay is drawn is the **drawee**. The person to whom payment is to be made is the **payee**. The drawer may also be named as the drawee.

The drawee who is ordered to pay the paper is not bound to do so. However, the drawee may agree to pay the paper, in which case the drawee is called an **acceptor**.

(c) CHECKS. A **check** is a draft drawn on a bank and is payable on demand.[3] It is an order by a depositor (the drawer) on a bank (the drawee) to pay a sum of money to the order of another person (the payee). A check is always drawn on a bank as drawee and is always payable on demand.

(d) CERTIFICATES OF DEPOSIT. A **certificate of deposit** (CD) is an instrument issued by a bank. A CD acknowledges the deposit of a specific sum of money and promises to pay the holder of the certificate that amount, usu-

---

[1] UCC § 3-104(1). See Appendices 5 and 7 for a table of sections and for provisions of the 1990 revision of Article 3 that affect the law stated in this chapter.

[2] UCC § 3-104(1).
[3] UCC § 104(2)(b).

FIGURE 30-1   PROMISSORY NOTE
Parties: maker (buyer, borrower, or debtor)—Linda S. Robinson; payee (seller, lender, or creditor)—Paul Garcia.

$650.00 _____ Albany, New York _August 15_____ 19 --

_Three months_____ after date _I__ promise to pay to

the order of _Paul Garcia_____

_Six hundred fifty_____ Dollars

Payable at _Citizens State Bank_____

with interest at _14_ %

No. _36_   Due _November 15, 19--_   _Linda S. Robinson_

FIGURE 30-2   DRAFT (BILL OF EXCHANGE)
Parties: drawer (seller or creditor)—David E. Bowman; drawee (buyer or debtor)—Susan Miller; payee (seller's or creditor's bank)—Security National Bank.

ally with interest, when the certificate is surrendered.[4]

3.   Parties to Commercial Paper

A note has two original parties—the maker and the payee. A draft or a check has three original parties—the drawer, the drawee, and the payee. In addition to these original parties, a commercial paper may have one or more of the parties described under (e) through (k) of this section.

(a) MAKER. The **maker** is the person who writes out and creates a promissory note. If the paper is not a promissory note, the creator has a different name, as the drawer of a check.

(b) DRAWER. The **drawer** is the person who writes out and creates a draft. This includes bills of exchange, trade acceptances, and checks. It is essential to bear in mind the distinction between a maker and a drawer; the liability of the maker is primary, while that of a drawer is secondary.

(c) DRAWEE. The **drawee** is the person to whom the draft is addressed and who is ordered to pay the amount of money specified in the draft.

(d) PAYEE. The **payee** is the person named on the face of the paper to receive payment. In a check stating "pay to the order of John Jones," the named person, John Jones, is the payee.

A payee has no rights in the paper until it has been delivered by the drawer or the maker. Likewise, the payee is not liable on the paper in any way until the payee transfers the paper to someone else or receives payment of it.

(e) ACCEPTOR. When the drawee has signified in writing on the draft the willingness to make the specified payment, the drawee is called the **acceptor.**

(f) INDORSER.[5] The owner of commercial paper who signs on the back of the paper is an **indorser.** Thus, if a check is made payable to the order of P, P may indorse it to E to pay a debt that P owes E. In such a case, P, who is the payee of the check, is now also an indorser.

(g) INDORSEE. The person to whom an indorsement is made payable is called an **indorsee.** The indorsee may in turn indorse the instrument and then is also an indorser.

(h) BEARER. The person in physical possession of a commercial paper that is payable to bearer is called a **bearer.**

[4]   A certificate of deposit "is an acknowledgment by a bank of receipt of money with an engagement to repay it," as distinguished from a note, which "is a promise other than a certificate of deposit." UCC § 3-104(2)(c), (d).

[5]   The spelling "endorse" is commonly used in business. The spelling "indorse" is used in the UCC.

(i) HOLDER. A **holder** is a person in possession of commercial paper that is payable at that time either to the order of such person, as payee or indorsee, or to bearer. For example, if *H* has possession of a check made payable to the order of *H*, *H* is a holder.

A person who takes the paper for value, in good faith, and without notice that it is overdue or has been dishonored or that there are defenses against or claims to it is called a **holder in due course**. The law gives a holder in due course preferred status. A holder in due course is immune from certain defenses when such a holder brings suit on the paper. (See Chapter 32 for rights and defenses of holders.) A person becoming the holder of an instrument at any time after it was once held by a holder in due course is described as a **holder through a holder in due course**. Ordinarily, a holder through a holder in due course is given the same special rights as a holder in due course.

(j) ACCOMMODATION PARTY. A person who becomes a party to a commercial paper in order to add strength to the paper for the benefit of another party to the paper is called an **accommodation party**.

(k) GUARANTOR. A **guarantor** is a person who signs a commercial paper and adds a promise to pay the instrument under certain circumstances. Ordinarily, this is done by merely adding *payment guaranteed* or *collection guaranteed* to the signature of the guarantor on the paper.

The addition of *payment guaranteed* or similar words means that the guarantor will pay the instrument when due. *Collection guaranteed* or similar words means that the guarantor will not pay the paper until after the holder has sought to collect payment from the maker or acceptor and has been unable to do so.

If the meaning of the guaranty is not clear, it is construed as a guaranty of payment. For example, when an indorser adds a statement that the paper is *guaranteed* or adds the word *guarantor* to the indorsement, without specifying whether it is payment or collection that is guaranteed, the indorser is deemed to be a guarantor of payment. As a consequence, the

holder of the paper may proceed directly against such a guarantor without first proceeding against any other party on the paper.

The liability of a guarantor of payment is as extensive as that of the original debtor.

4.   Liability of Parties

A person who by the terms of the instrument is absolutely required to pay is **primarily liable**. For a note, the maker is primarily liable; for a draft, the acceptor (the drawee who has accepted) is primarily liable. A guarantor of payment is primarily liable in any case. Other parties are either secondarily or conditionally liable, as in the case of an indorser, or they are not liable in any capacity. A person who transfers the paper and indorses without recourse or does not sign it is not liable for its payment.[6]

(a) ACCOMMODATION PARTIES. An accommodation party is liable on the paper regardless of whether the paper is signed merely as a matter of friendship or in return for payment. When suit is brought against an accommodation party by a plaintiff who gave value for the paper, the accommodation party cannot avoid liability on the ground that the plaintiff knew of the accommodation character.

The accommodation party is not liable to the party accommodated.[7] If the accommodation party is required to pay the paper, that party has a right to recover the payment from the person accommodated. Parol evidence may be admitted to show that a party to the paper had signed to accommodate another party.[8]

(b) GUARANTORS. A **guarantor of payment** has primary liability. The guarantor of payment is liable for payment of the paper even though the holder has not sought to obtain payment from any other party. It is immaterial that payment was not demanded

---

6   Pike Burden Printing, Inc. v Pike Burden, Inc. (La App) 396 So 2d 361 (1981).

7   UCC § 3-415(5).

8   Citizens Savings Bank and Trust Co. v Hardaway (Tenn App) 724 SW2d 352 (1986).

from the primary party or that the primary party had sufficient assets to pay the paper.

The **guarantor of collection** is not required to pay the paper until collection has been attempted and has failed, or unless an attempt to collect would obviously be useless.

B.   NEGOTIABILITY

As noted early in this chapter, one of the important qualities of commercial paper is its negotiability. It is this quality of negotiability that makes commercial paper acceptable as a circulating medium of exchange (that is, a substitute for money or credit) in commercial transactions.

5.   Requirements of Negotiability

In order to be negotiable an instrument must be (a) in writing and (b) signed by the maker or drawer; it must contain (c) a promise or order (d) of an unconditional character (e) to pay in money (f) a sum certain; (g) it must be

payable on demand or at a definite time; (h) it must be payable to order or bearer;[9] and (i) a party who is a drawee must be identified with reasonable certainty.

In addition to these formal requirements, the instrument must be delivered or issued by the maker or drawer to the payee or the latter's agent with the intent that it be effective and create a legal obligation.

If an instrument is not negotiable, the rights of the parties are governed by the general body of contract law.[10] If there is any uncertainty as to whether a paper is negotiable, it is deemed nonnegotiable.

Sometimes, as in the *Frank* case, what appears to be a negotiable instrument may contain a provision that impairs its negotiability and converts it to a simple contract.

---

[9]   Smith v Rushing Construction Co., 84 NC App 692, 353 SE2d 692 (1987).

[10]   First Investment Co. v Andersen (Utah) 621 P2d 683 (1980). Note, however, that if the nonnegotiability results from the fact that the instrument is not payable to order or to bearer, it is governed by Article 3 of the Code ("Commercial Paper") with the limitation that there cannot be a holder in due course of such paper. UCC § 3-805.

FRANK v HERSHEY NATIONAL BANK
269 Md App 138, 306 A2d 207 (1973)

East Penn Broadcasting Company borrowed money from the Hershey National Bank. The promissory note representing the loan was made payable "to the Hershey National Bank." It also contained a provision authorizing confession of judgment against the borrower at any time. This provision allowed a judgment to be entered against East Penn without the formality involved in an ordinary action or proceeding. The note was signed with the typewritten name of the borrowing corporation and the handwritten signature of three individuals including the defendant, Frank. The loan was not paid. Frank and the others were sued on the note by the bank. Frank and the other individuals raised defenses under the UCC. The bank claimed that the UCC was not applicable. From a judgment in favor of the bank, Frank and the others appealed.

DIGGES, J. . . . We find the notes to be nonnegotiable and the UCC to be inapplicable. Therefore, the liability of the parties is determined as a matter of simple contract law. . . .

To be negotiable, an instrument must, among other requirements, "be payable to order or to bearer." (§ 3-104(1)(d)) The absence of these magic words renders a note nonnegotiable. Here, the notes in question contain just a "promise to pay to the Hershey National Bank" the amount due. However, § 3-805 entitled "instruments not payable to order or to bearer" specifies that: "This subtitle *applies* to any instrument whose terms do not preclude transfer and *which is otherwise negotiable within this subtitle* but which is not payable to order or to bearer, except that there can be no holder in due course of such an instrument." ... The official comments to this section indicate that: "This section covers the 'nonnegotiable instrument.' As it has been used by most courts, this term has been a technical one of art. It does not refer to a writing, such as a note containing an express condition, which is not negotiable and is entirely outside of the scope of this Subtitle and to be treated as a simple contract. It refers to a particular type of instrument which meets all requirements as to form of a negotiable instrument except that it is not payable to order or to bearer."

Thus, while these notes could still be governed by the Code even though they lack words of negotiability, they must meet all other "requirements as to form of a negotiable instrument" except for that. The notes here do not conform to this standard. The UCC § 3-112(1)(d) provides that the negotiability of an instrument is not affected by "a term authorizing confession of judgment on the instrument if it is not paid when due." We held in *Stankovich v Lehman*, 230 Md 426, 187 A2d 309 (1963), a case decided under the Negotiable Instruments Act, that the authorization to confess judgment "as of any term" permitted entry of judgment at any time prior to the maturity of the note and therefore destroyed negotiability. ... "It would seem logical that if the statute, as it does, preserves negotiability only if the confession of judgment is at or after maturity, the warrant to confess must expressly, or by necessary implication, restrict its exercise to that time if the note is to be negotiable, and that if the warrant is silent as to the time when it can be exercised, the reasonable implication must be that it can be done at any time. Most of the cases involving this general area of the law have arisen in Pennsylvania, and the Courts of that State have held that notes containing stipulations for confession of judgment without specification or limitation as to time are, like those expressly authorizing judgment prior to maturity, nonnegotiable." ...

Since these nonnegotiable notes are not governed by the UCC, their effect is, as already noted, determined under principles of simple contract law.

[Judgment affirmed]

QUESTIONS

1. What made the instrument nonnegotiable? Explain.
2. Why was the issue of negotiability important?

(a) WRITING. A commercial paper must be in writing. "Writing" includes handwriting, typing, printing, and any other method of setting words down in a permanent form. The use of a pencil is not wise, because such writing is not as durable as ink, and the instrument may be more easily altered. A commercial paper may be partly printed and partly typewritten.

Since the commercial paper is a writing, the parol evidence rule applies. This rule prohibits modifying the instrument by proving the existence of a conflicting oral agreement alleged to have been made before or at the time of the execution of the commercial paper.

(b) SIGNATURE. The instrument must be signed by the maker or drawer. The signature usually appears at the lower right-hand corner of the face of the instrument, but it is immaterial whether the signature is so placed.

However, if the signature is placed on the instrument in such a manner that it does not in itself clearly indicate that the signer was the maker, drawer, or acceptor, the signer is held to be only an indorser.

The signature itself may consist of the full name or of any symbol adopted for that purpose. It may consist of initials, figures, or a mark. A person signing a trade or an assumed name is liable to the same extent as though the signer's own name had been used.

(1) Agent. A signature may be made by the drawer or maker or by an authorized agent. No particular form of authorization to an agent to execute or sign a commercial paper is required.

An agent signing commercial paper should disclose on the paper (a) the identity of the principal and (b) the fact that the signing is made in a representative capacity. When both are done, an authorized agent is not liable on the paper. The representative capacity of an officer of an organization is sufficiently shown by the signature of the officer preceded or followed by the title of the office and the organization name.

(2) Nondisclosure of Agency or Principal. If a person who signs a commercial paper in a representative capacity, such as an agent or an officer of a corporation, executes the paper without disclosing both the identity of the principal and the existence of the representative capacity, the agent appears to be signing the paper as a personal obligation. Under these circumstances the agent is personally bound by the paper with respect to subsequent holders. This is so regardless of whether the agent had intended to be personally bound or to act in a representative capacity.[11]

In the *First National Bank* case the question was whether corporate officers were personally liable on the notes of the corporation where there was no indication of signing in a representative capacity.

---

[11] St. Francois County Service v Gelert (Mo App) 768 SW2d 636 (1989).

FIRST NATIONAL BANK v BLACKHURST
(W Va) 345 SE2d 567 (1986)

Long, Blackhurst, and Sheets formed a corporation to own and operate a ski apparel shop. They served as president, vice president, and secretary-treasurer, respectively, of the corporation, Josh, Inc. Before opening the store the three officers established a line of credit with the First National Bank. This line of credit was to be used to finance the purchase of inventory. On different dates they executed eight notes of varying amounts, totaling $94,190. The shop failed and filed for bankruptcy. It was unable to pay its debt to the bank. The bank instituted an action against the officers, claiming that the notes were personal obligations of the defendants rather than exclusively the corporate obligations of Josh, Inc. The defendants argued that at all times they were acting in a representative capacity as officers of Josh, Inc., that the loans were made to the corporation, and that they were not personally liable. From a judgment in favor of the bank, the officers appealed.

NEELY, J. . . . In this case we decide whether the defendants, Jo Debra Long, A. A. Blackhurst, and Robert A. Sheets, are personally liable on notes they executed in favor of the plaintiff, First National Bank in Marlinton. . . .

Commercial paper's value lies largely in its negotiability. Accordingly, Article Three of the *Uniform Commercial Code*, which governs commercial paper, was designed to avoid situations where it would be unclear whether a representative signing a negotiable instrument obligated his principal or himself. [UCC §] 3-403 . . . establishes rules to enable subsequent holders to determine, by reference solely to the instrument itself, which party is liable on the instrument. In general, representative capacity must be shown on the face of the instrument if a representative signs his own name to an instrument but wishes to avoid personal liability. On each of the notes in this case the three defendants' signatures are affixed in the bottom right hand corner under a typewritten legend stating "Josh, Inc." The defendants argue that the legend indicates that they were signing in their corporate capacity rather than as individuals. The legend alone is not enough to free the defendants of personal liability. . . .

[Judgment affirmed]

QUESTIONS

1. Did the notes show the name of the principal?
2. How should officers of a corporation sign notes of the corporation to avoid personal liability?
3. What was the basis for the court's decision?

(c) PROMISE OR ORDER TO PAY. A promissory note must contain a promise to pay money. No particular form of promise is required; the intention as gathered from the face of the instrument controls.[12] If the maker uses such a phrase as, "I certify to pay," a promise is implied. A mere acknowledgment of a debt, such as a writing stating "I.O.U.," is not a commercial paper.

A draft or check must contain an order or command to pay money.[13] As in the case of a promise in a note, no particular form of order is required.

(d) UNCONDITIONAL PROMISE OR ORDER. For an instrument to be negotiable, the promise or order to pay must be unconditional. For example, when an instrument makes the duty to pay dependent on the completion of the construction of a building, the promise is conditional, and the instrument is nonnegotiable. Also, the promise or order is conditional, and the instrument is nonnegotiable, if the instrument states that it is subject

to another agreement. In such a case the paper is not negotiable because the obligation of the paper is dependent on the performance of the other agreement.

An order for the payment of money out of a particular fund, such as $10 from next week's salary, is conditional.[14] If, however, the instrument is based on the general credit of the drawer and the reference to a particular fund is merely to indicate a source of reimbursement for the drawee, such as "charge my expense account," the order is considered unconditional.[15]

(e) PAYMENT IN MONEY. A commercial paper must call for payment in *money*—that is, any circulating medium of exchange that is legal tender at the place of payment. If the order or promise is not for money, the instrument is not negotiable. For example, an instrument that requires the holder to take stock or goods in place of money is nonnegotiable.

(f) SUM CERTAIN. This means an exact amount. Unless the instrument is definite on

---

[12]   Fejta v Werner Enterprises (La App) 412 So 2d 155 (1982).
[13]   UCC § 3-104(1)(b).

[14]   UCC 3-105(2)(b).
[15]   Rogers v Willard (Fla App) 453 So 2d 1175 (1984).

its face as to how much is to be paid, there is no way of determining how much the instrument is worth.

Minor variations from the above rule are allowed in certain cases. Thus, commercial paper is not made nonnegotiable because the interest rate changes at maturity or because certain costs and attorney's fees may be recovered by the holder.[16] There is a conflict of authority as to whether an instrument providing for floating or variable interest is negotiable.

(g) TIME OF PAYMENT. A commercial paper must be payable on demand or at a definite time. If it is payable "when convenient," the instrument is nonnegotiable, because the day of payment may never arrive. An instrument payable only upon the happening of a particular event that may never happen is not negotiable. For example, a provision to pay when a person marries is not payable at a definite time, since that particular event may never occur. It is immaterial whether the contingency in fact has happened, because from an examination of the instrument alone it still appears to be subject to a condition that may never happen.

(1) Demand. An instrument is payable on **demand** when it is expressly specified to be payable "on demand," or at sight, or upon presentation. Presentation occurs when the holder presents the instrument to the party required to pay and demands payment. Commercial paper is also payable on demand when no time for payment is stated in the instrument.[17]

(2) Definite Time. The time of payment is **definite** if the instrument is payable (a) on or before a stated date, (b) at a fixed period after a stated date, (c) at a fixed period after sight, (d) at a definite time subject to any acceleration, (e) at a definite time subject to extension at the option of the holder, (f) at a definite time subject to extension to a further definite date at the option of the maker or acceptor, or (g) at a definite time subject to an extension to a fur-

ther definite date automatically on or after the occurrence of a specified act or event.[18]

(3) Missing or Incorrect Date. Paper that is not dated is deemed dated on the day it is issued to the payee. Any holder may add the correct date to the paper.

When a commercial paper is dated, the date is deemed *prima facie* to be the true date, whether the date was originally inserted or was thereafter added.[19] A commercial paper may be antedated or postdated, provided that it is not done to defraud anyone. The holder acquires title as of the date of delivery, without regard to whether this is the date stated in the instrument.

(h) ORDER OR BEARER. A commercial paper must be payable to order or to bearer.[20] This requirement is met by such expressions as "Pay to the order of John Jones," "Pay to John Jones or order," "Pay to bearer," and "Pay to John Jones or bearer." The use of the phrase "to the order of John Jones" or to "John Jones or order" is important in showing that the person executing the instrument is indicating that there is no intention to restrict payment of the instrument to John Jones only. These phrases indicate that there is no objection to paying anyone to whom John Jones orders the paper to be paid. Similarly, if the person executing the instrument originally states that it will be paid to "bearer" or "to John Jones or bearer," there is no restricting of payment of the paper to the original payee. If the instrument is payable on its face "to John Jones," however, the instrument is not negotiable, and there cannot be a holder in due course.

(1) Order Paper. An instrument is **payable to order** when by its terms it is payable to the order of any person described therein with reasonable certainty ("pay to the order of K.

---

16   Means v Clardy (Mo App) 735 SW2d 6 (1987).
17   UCC § 3-108.

18   UCC § 3-109(1).
19   UCC § 3-114(3). If the wrong date is inserted, the true date can be proved unless the holder is a holder in due course or a holder through a holder in due course, in which case the date, even though wrong, cannot be contradicted.
20   Beyer v First National Bank (Mont) 612 P2d 1285 (1980).

FIGURE 30-3   REQUIREMENTS OF NEGOTIABILITY

In writing and signed by maker—Donald C. Rich; containing an unconditional promise or order to pay--"I promise to pay"; sum certain in money—"ten thousand and no/100 dollars"; payable on demand or at a definite time--"six months after date"; payable to order or to bearer—"pay to the order of Sally Kase."

$10,000.00   September 1, 19--

Six months after date I promise to pay to the order of

Sally Kase ten thousand and no/100 dollars with interest

at 12 percent.

Donald C. Rich

Read"), or to a person so described or order ("pay to K. Read or order").

(2) Bearer Paper. An instrument is **payable to bearer** when by its terms it is payable (a) to bearer or the order of bearer, (b) to a specified person or bearer, (c) to "cash," or "the order of cash," or any other designation that does not purport to identify a person, or (d) if the last or only indorsement is a blank indorsement (an indorsement that does not name the person to whom the paper is negotiated).

Whether an instrument was negotiable was the issue in the *Sunrizon Homes* case.

SUNRIZON HOMES v AMERICAN GUARANTY INVESTMENTS

(Okla) 782 P2d 103 (1988)

Apple Homes sold a mobile home to the Renaults. The Renaults executed an installment sales contract and a security agreement in favor of Apple. Thereafter, Apple assigned its contractual rights in the contract to American Guaranty. American Guaranty issued a check to Apple for $39,000. Continental Federal purchased an assignment of American Guaranty's rights in the installment sales contract for $40,000. The installment sales contract stated that the buyer promised to pay to the seller monthly installments for a period of 15 years. Continental notified the buyers that their loan payments were to be made to Continental. American Guaranty's check to Apple was returned for insufficient funds. Apple, unable to collect on the check, filed an action for rescission of the assignment from American Guaranty to Continental Federal. Apple asserted that the sales contract was a nonnegotiable instrument and that Continental Federal had no better rights than its assignor, American Guaranty. Continental Federal argued that it was a holder in due course. From a judgment in favor of Continental Federal, Apple appealed.

KAUGER, J. . . . The nature of the instrument, i.e., negotiable or nonnegotiable, is essential to determine what rights Continental received under its assignment from American Guaranty. If the contract for sale is a negotiable instrument, Continental may qualify as a holder in due course taking the assignment free of any claim or defense. If the contract for sale is not a negotiable document, Continental stands in the shoes of its assignor, American Guaranty, and the instrument is subject to the defense of failure of consideration—the bad check. Continental asserts that it took the assignment for value, in good faith, without knowledge of any claims or defenses, and that it qualifies as a holder in due course.

Pursuant to [UCC] § 3-302, before one may be a holder in due course, the holder must take an "instrument." Instrument is defined by § 3-102 (1)(e) as a *negotiable* instrument. Section 3–104 provides that a negotiable instrument must be signed by the maker or drawer, contain an unconditional promise to pay a sum certain in money, and be made payable to order or to bearer.

It is undisputed that the sales contract meets the first two requirements of a negotiable instrument. It is signed by the maker or drawer, and it contains an unconditional promise to pay a sum certain in money. Nevertheless, Apple argues that because the contract does not contain the indispensable words of negotiability, "pay to order or to bearer," Continental is not a holder in due course. The installment sales contract states that the buyer promises "to pay to the Seller" monthly installments for a period of 15 years. Continental argues that this language meets the requirement that the instrument be payable to bearer under § 3-111 which defines an instrument as payable to bearer when it is payable to bearer or the order of bearer, a specified person or bearer, cash or order of cash, or any indication not purporting to designate a specific payee.

The words—order and bearer—place a party on notice that the assignment is negotiable. The general rule in jurisdictions which have considered this question, is that a note payable to a specific person, rather than to order or bearer is nonnegotiable. *The sales contract fails to meet the criteria of § 3-104 that a negotiable instrument be made payable to order or bearer.* Continental is not a holder in due course of a negotiable instrument, and it is subject to the defense of failure of consideration.

[Judgment reversed]

QUESTIONS

1. What is the significance of the words *order* and *bearer*?
2. Was Continental Federal a holder in due course?
3. If an instrument is not negotiable, may it still be enforced?

---

6. Effect of Provisions for Additional Powers or Benefits

Certain provisions in an instrument that give the holder additional powers and benefits may or may not affect negotiability.

(a) COLLATERAL. The inclusion of a power to sell collateral security, such as corporate stocks and bonds, on default does not impair negotiability. An instrument secured by collateral contains as absolute a promise or order as an unsecured instrument. Negotiability is not affected by a promise or power to maintain or protect collateral or to give additional collateral or to make the entire debt due if the additional collateral is not supplied according to the terms of the promise.

(b) ACCELERATION. A power to accelerate the due date of an instrument on a default

in the payment of interest or of any installment of the principal, or on the failure to
maintain or provide collateral, does not affect
the negotiability of an instrument. However, a
holder's power to accelerate the due date "at
will" or when a person "deems himself insecure" must be exercised in good faith.[21]

(c) REQUIREMENT OF ANOTHER ACT.
A provision authorizing the holder to require
an act other than the payment of money, such
as the delivery of goods, makes the instrument nonnegotiable.[22]

---

[21]   UCC § 1-208.
[22]   UCC § 3-104(1)(b).

7.   Additional Documents

The fact that a separate document is executed
that gives the holder additional protection, as
a mortgage on real estate, or the right to repossess goods sold to the maker of the instrument, does not impair the negotiability of the
commercial paper.

As between the parties to the original
paper, the liability on the paper will be controlled by the terms of any other documents as
well as the commercial paper. In contrast, subsequent holders of the commercial paper can
rely on the face of the paper and are not affected by the terms of any additional separate
document.

SUMMARY

Commercial paper includes written promises
or orders to pay money and may be transferred by negotiation. A transferee of commercial paper may be immune from certain contract defenses. Because of this, commercial
paper is more acceptable than ordinary contracts to transferees.

There are four categories of commercial
paper: (1) promissory notes, (2) drafts or bills
of exchange, (3) checks, and (4) certificates of
deposit.

A negotiable promissory note is an unconditional promise in writing, made by one person to another, signed by the maker, promising to pay on demand or at a definite time a
sum certain in money, to order or to bearer. A
negotiable draft or bill of exchange is an unconditional order in writing, addressed by one
person to another, signed by the one giving it,
requiring the person to whom it is addressed
to pay on demand or at a definite time a sum
certain in money, to order or to bearer. A check
is a draft drawn on a bank and payable on demand. A certificate of deposit is an instrument
issued by a bank that acknowledges the deposit of a specified sum of money and promises to pay the holder of the certificate that

amount, usually with interest, upon surrender
of the certificate.

The original parties to a note are the maker
and payee. The original parties to a draft are
the drawer, the drawee, and the payee. One
who signs on the back of the paper is called an
indorser. The person to whom an indorsement
is made payable is called an indorsee. A person in physical possession of a commercial
paper that is payable to bearer is called a bearer and a holder. If the paper is payable to the
order of the possessor, or the possessor is the
indorsee of the last indorsement, the possessor is a holder.

A holder in due course is a favored holder
of commercial paper. A person taking commercial paper through a holder in due course
is a holder through a holder in due course and
is immune from certain defenses.

The requirements of negotiability are that
the instrument (1) must be in writing, (2) be
signed by the maker or drawer, (3) contain an
unconditional promise or order, (4) to pay a
sum certain in money, (5) on demand or at a
definite time, (6) to order or to bearer. If an instrument is not negotiable, it is governed by
the rules of contract law.

QUESTIONS AND CASE PROBLEMS

1. What social forces are affected by the rule of law governing the nature of a signature on commercial paper?

2. Name the four kinds of commercial paper.

3. Dorothy purchased a power mower from Reilly Brothers on credit. She gave Reilly a promissory note for the balance due. To induce Reilly to accept this note, Jeanette wrote on the back *guaranteed* and then signed her name. Dorothy promised Jeanette that Jeanette would never be required to pay this note. Dorothy did not pay the note to Reilly, and Reilly sued Jeanette. Jeanette claimed that Reilly could not sue her because of Dorothy's promise and that, in any case, Reilly could not sue Jeanette until Reilly had attempted to collect the money from Dorothy. On the facts stated, is Jeanette liable?

4. Hampton purchased cloth from Regal Fibres, Inc., on behalf of Twentieth Century Clothing Company, by whom Hampton was employed. Hampton informed Regal that she was acting for Twentieth Century and signed a promissory note for the purchase price of the cloth. The note stated, "I promise to pay . . . " and was signed "Gertrude Hampton." Regal sold the note to the Commercial Finance Company. Commercial sued Hampton on the note. She claimed that she was not liable, because she had acted as agent for Twentieth Century and had so informed Regal Fibres. Is this a valid defense?

5. A Republican delivered his promissory note to a friend, a Democrat, promising to pay a thousand dollars "30 days after the Republican candidate for Governor shall be defeated in the November election." Give your opinion as to whether or not the expression of time of payment is proper for a negotiable instrument.

6. A note, in addition to the ordinary provisions of such an instrument, states on its face that it is secured by stated collateral. Discuss the effect, if any, that the specification of such collateral has upon negotiability of the instrument.

7. Nelson gave Buchert the following instrument, dated July 6, 1988:
   One year after date I promise to pay to the order of Dale Buchert one thousand dollars in United States Savings Bonds payable at Last Mortgage Bank. (signed) Ronald K. Nelson
   Does this instrument qualify as a negotiable instrument?

8. Compare the liability of the acceptor of a draft with the liability of the maker of a note.

9. Money was borrowed from a bank by a corporation. The president of the corporation negotiated the loan and signed the promissory note. On the first line he wrote the name of the corporation. On the second line he signed his own name. The note was negotiated by the lending bank to the Federal Reserve Bank. The note was not paid when due, and the Federal Reserve Bank sued the corporation and the president. The president raised the defense that he was not bound on the note because he did not intend to bind himself and because the money obtained by the loan was used by the corporation. Is the president liable on the note? [See Talley v Blake (La App) 322 So 2d 877 (non-Code); Geer v Farquhar, 270 Or 642, 528 P2d 1335]

10. Rinehart issues a check that satisfies all the requirements of negotiability. It is payable to the order of cash. Is the instrument payable to order or to bearer?

11. Is the following instrument negotiable?
    I, Richard Bell, hereby promise to pay to the order of Lorry Motors Ten Thousand Dollars ($10,000) upon the receipt of the final distribution from the estate of my deceased aunt, Rita Dorn. This negotiable instrument is given by me as the down payment on my purchase of a 1986 Buick to be delivered in three weeks.
    Richard Bell (signature)

12. Smith has in his possession the following instrument:
    September 1, 1986
    I, Selma Ray, hereby promise to pay Helen Savit One Thousand Dollars ($1,000) one year after date. This instrument was given for the purchase of Two Hundred (200) shares of Redding Mining Corporation, Interest 6%.
    Selma Ray (signature)
    Smith purchased the instrument from Helen Savit at a substantial discount. Savit specializes in the sale of counterfeit stock. Selma Ray was one of her innocent victims. Smith is seeking to collect on the instrument. What are the rights of Smith against Ray on the instrument?

13. Master Homecraft Company received a promissory note with a stated face value from Mr. and Mrs. Zimmerman. The note was payment for remodeling of their home. The note contained unused blanks for installment payments.

There was no maturity date. Master Homecraft sued the Zimmermans on the note. They argue that they should not be liable on the note because it is impossible to determine from its face the amount due or the date of maturity. Decide. [Master Homecraft Co. v Zimmerman, 208 Pa 401, 22 A2d 440]

14. On July 1, 1989, Ralph Golde signed a promissory note that was made payable to the order of Williams, Inc. for $20,000 plus 6 percent interest, payable 90 days from date. On the front of the note above his signature Golde wrote: "Subject to satisfactory delivery of goods purchased this date. Delivery to be made not later than July 31, 1989." Is the note negotiable commercial paper? Explain.

15. Indicate whether an instrument is payable (1) to order, (2) to bearer, or (3) neither to order nor bearer if the instrument states:
    (a) Pay to cash.
    (b) Pay to the order of bearer.
    (c) Pay to the order of John Jones.
    (d) Pay to John Jones.
    (e) Pay to bills payable.

31

TRANSFER OF COMMERCIAL PAPER

Commercial paper may be transferred by negotiation or assignment. If the transfer is made in the manner required by the UCC,[1] the transfer is called a negotiation and the transferee becomes a holder. If there is no negotiation, the transferee is merely an assignee. When the transfer is made by negotiation, the rights of the transferee may rise higher than those of the transferor, depending on the circumstances attending the negotiation. When the transfer is made by assignment, the assignee has only those rights that the assignor possessed.

The transfer of ownership of commercial paper may be made as a gift. In most cases, however, it will be made for value.[2]

[1]   See Appendices 5 and 7 for a table of sections and provisions of the 1990 revision of UCC Article 3 that affect the law stated in this chapter.

[2]   Brown v Bell, 291 Ark 116, 722 SW2d 592 (1987).

A.   NEGOTIATION OF COMMERCIAL PAPER

Negotiation is the transferring of commercial paper in such a way as to make the transferee the holder of the paper. This, in turn, is controlled by whether the paper is order paper or bearer paper.

1.   Time for Determining Order or Bearer Character of Paper

The order or bearer character of the paper is determined as of the time when the negotiation is about to take place, without regard to the character of the paper originally or at any intermediate time. Accordingly, when the last indorsement specifies the person to whom the indorser makes the instrument payable, the paper is order paper, without regard as to whether it was bearer paper originally or at any intermediate time. The holder cannot treat the paper as bearer paper merely because it had once been bearer paper.

2.   Negotiation of Order Paper

An instrument payable to order may be negotiated only by indorsement and delivery of the paper. Indorsement and delivery may be made by the person to whom the paper is then payable or by an authorized agent of that person.

(a) MULTIPLE PAYEES AND INDORSEES. Ordinarily, one person is named as the payee in the instrument, but two or more payees may be named. In that case the instrument may specify that it is payable to any one or more of them or that it is payable to all jointly. If nothing is specified, the instrument is payable to all of the payees, and they are **joint payees**. For example, if the instrument is made payable "to the order of A and B," the two persons named are joint payees. The indorsements of both A and B are required to negotiate the instrument.

If the instrument is payable to **alternate payees** or if it has been negotiated to alternate indorsees, as "A or B," it may be indorsed and delivered by either of them.

(b) AGENT OR OFFICER AS PAYEE. The instrument may be made payable to the order of an officeholder. For example, a check may read "Pay to the order of Receiver of Taxes." Such a check may be received and negotiated by the person who at the time is the Receiver of Taxes. This is a matter of convenience, since the person writing the check is not required to find out the actual name of the Receiver of Taxes at that time.

If the instrument is drawn in favor of a person as "Cashier" or some other fiscal officer of a bank or corporation, it is *prima facie* payable to the bank or corporation of which such person is an officer. The instrument may be negotiated by the indorsement of either the bank or the corporation, or of the specified officer. If drawn in favor of an agent, it may similarly be negotiated by the agent or the agent's principal.[3]

(c) MISSING INDORSEMENT. Although order paper cannot be negotiated without indorsement, it can be assigned to another without indorsement. In such a case, the transferee has the same rights as the transferor. If the transferee gave value for the paper, the transferee also has the right to require that the transferor indorse the instrument unqualifiedly and thereby effect a negotiation of the instrument.

The transferee of order paper that the transferor has not indorsed may bring suit as an assignee. It is no defense to the obligor that there was no indorsement.

3.   Negotiation of Bearer Paper

Any commercial paper payable to bearer may be negotiated by a mere transfer of possession. Thus, bearer paper is negotiated to a person taking possession of it, without regard to whether such taking of possession was done with the consent of the owner of the paper.

The paper may be negotiated by a mere transfer of possession not only when the instrument expressly states that it is payable to bearer, but also when the law interprets it as being payable to bearer. For example, a check

---

[3]   UCC § 3-117.

payable to the order of "Cash" is declared to be bearer paper and may be negotiated by a transfer of possession.

Although bearer paper may be negotiated by a mere transfer of possession, the one to whom it is delivered may insist that the bearer indorse the paper. This will impose the liability of an indorser upon the one negotiating the paper. This situation most commonly arises when a check payable to "Cash" is presented to a bank for payment.

4. Forged and Unauthorized Indorsements

A forged or unauthorized indorsement is by definition no indorsement of the person by whom it appears to have been made. Accordingly, the possessor of the paper is not the holder when the indorsement of the person whose signature was forged was necessary for effective negotiation of the paper to the possessor.

If payment of commercial paper is made to one claiming under or through a forged indorsement, the payor is ordinarily liable to the person who is the rightful owner of the paper, unless such person is estopped or barred by negligence or other conduct from asserting any claim against the payor.

A forged or unauthorized indorsement may be ratified.[4] In that case it is effective as though it had been genuine and authorized.

The *Mott* case deals with the question of whether a bank should be held liable for allowing the manager of a corporation to deposit in his own account checks that were payable to the corporation.

---

[4]   Bank of Hoven v Rausch (SD) 382 NW2d 39 (1986).

MOTT GRAIN CO. v FIRST NATIONAL BANK & TRUST CO.
(ND) 259 NW2d 667 (1977)

Baszler was a manager of the grain elevator of the Mott Company and an officer of the company. He had expensive tastes and always needed money for his lifestyle. A corporate resolution executed by the Mott Company with the bank authorized officers to indorse or deposit in the corporate account checks payable to the corporation. Baszler took seventeen checks payable to the company and, instead of depositing them in the company account, indorsed and deposited them in his own account with the bank. The Mott Company claimed that the bank was liable for the amount of these checks that were improperly deposited. From a judgment in favor of the Mott Company, the bank appealed.

VOGEL, J. . . . This case is governed by the Uniform Commercial Code.

Leaving aside for the moment questions raised by the "Corporate Authorization Resolution" . . ., there can be little doubt that the bank is liable to the payee of checks which are negotiated upon indorsements which are forged or unauthorized.

Under UCC § 3-404, a payee of a check may recover from a bank which cashes a check on which the payee's signature is unauthorized.

An unauthorized signature is one which is either forged or made without actual, apparent, or implied authority. [UCC § 1-201 (43)].

Forged indorsements are inoperative as signatures of the payee, whether they are indorsements for deposit UCC § 3-205 or in blank UCC § 3-204, unless ratified or unless the owner is precluded from denying authority. [UCC § 3-404].

A bank which negotiates checks bearing forged or unauthorized indorsements is therefore liable in conversion to the true owner of the checks.

The bank asserts that the general law stated above does not apply because of the terms of the "Corporate Authorization Resolution." It points in particular to the language [of the resolution] authorizing any of the three owner-officers of the grain company to sign "checks, drafts and other withdrawal orders and any and all other directions and instructions of any character with respect to funds of this corporation now or hereafter with said Bank" and that the bank is authorized to "pay and charge to such account or accounts any checks, drafts and other withdrawal orders so signed, and to honor any directions or instructions so signed, whether or not payable to the individual order of or deposited to the individual account of or inuring to the individual benefit of any of the foregoing officers or persons."

Since the meaning of this terminology is unclear, we could simply hold that it is ambiguous and construe it against the party which drew it and submitted it to the grain company.

However, we believe that accepted methods of construing contractual language require us to hold that the language in question does not authorize the bank to negotiate checks payable to the grain company but indorsed by one of the officers and either cashed or deposited to his own account. The quoted language authorizes the bank to honor checks, drafts, and other withdrawal orders and directions and instructions of any character "with respect to funds of this corporation now or hereafter *with* said Bank. . . ." While the use of the word "with" is unfortunate and less than clear, we understand the language to mean that money of the corporation on deposit with the bank is subject to being withdrawn by checks, drafts, or other withdrawal orders, or transferred as directed or instructed by any one of the officers. However, the language does not cover money which is not deposited with the bank or in its hands. When the improperly indorsed checks involved in this appeal were presented to the bank, they were not presented as funds of the corporation, but as funds of the individual officer indorsing them. The bank did not treat them as funds of the corporation, but treated them as funds of the individual. The checks therefore were not "funds of this corporation now or hereafter with said Bank" and were not within the description of the language quoted above in the "Corporate Authorization Resolution."

[Judgment affirmed]

QUESTIONS

1. What is the liability of a bank that negotiates a check bearing a forged or unauthorized indorsement?
2. What was the argument of the bank?
3. Was the bank correct?

5.   Impostor Rule

Ordinarily, when the name of the payee is indorsed on commercial paper by a person who is not the payee or the agent of the payee, such indorsement is not effective to negotiate the paper. This signature is ineffective to negotiate the paper because the paper has not been indorsed and delivered by the person to whom it was then payable (namely, the payee) or by his authorized agent.

The UCC makes exceptions to this general rule in three situations, which are covered by the **impostor rule.**[5] In these situations the unauthorized or forged character of the payee's signature is ignored as far as negotiation is concerned. The signature is given the same effect as though it had been authorized by the named payee. One exception is made by the rule when an impostor has induced the maker or drawer to issue the instrument to the person whose identity has been assumed by the impostor, or to a confederate, in the name of that payee. For example, a person impersonates the holder of a savings account and, by presenting a forged withdrawal slip to the savings bank, gets the bank to issue a check payable to the bank's customer. The bank then hands the check to the impersonator in the belief that the impersonator is the customer.

A second exception is made by the rule when the person signing as, or on behalf of, the drawer or maker intends the named payee to have no interest in the paper. This situation arises when the owner of a checking account wishes to conceal the true purpose of taking money from the bank. The account owner makes out a check purportedly in payment of a debt that in fact does not exist.

[5] UCC § 3-405.

The third exception is made by the rule when an agent or employee of the maker or drawer has supplied the name used for the payee, intending that the payee should not have any interest in the paper. The last situation is illustrated by the case of an employee who fraudulently causes an employer to sign a check made to a customer or another person, whether existing or not. The employee does not intend to send it to that person but rather intends to forge the latter's indorsement, to cash the check, and to keep the money.

The impostor rule does not apply when there is a valid check to an actual creditor for a correct amount owed by the drawer, and someone thereafter forges the payee's name, even though the forger is an employee of the drawer.

Even when the unauthorized indorsement of the payee's name is effective by virtue of the impostor rule, a person forging the payee's name is subject to civil and criminal liability for making such an indorsement.

The impostor rule applies without regard to whether or not the drawee acted with reasonable care. The *Northbrook Property* case deals with the question of negligence of a drawee bank in accepting forged checks.

NORTHBROOK PROPERTY AND CAS. CO. v CITIZENS & SOUTHERN NATIONAL BANK

184 Ga App 326, 361 SE2d 531 (1987)

Northbrook Property and Casualty Insurance Company, as subrogee of Devin Management Company, Inc., brought suit against the Citizens and Southern National Bank (C & S), seeking damages in the amount of $75,805.89. Northbrook alleged, as insurer of Devin, that Devin's employee, Patricia Ferguson, cashed numerous unauthorized checks drawn by her on Devin's account and payable to fictitious individuals. She then indorsed these checks and presented them to C & S. Northbrook further alleged that C & S negligently accepted the checks and, without further inquiry or authorization, paid the funds to Patricia Ferguson in contravention of accepted banking practices and in violation of its contractual obligation to its depositors. From a judgment in favor of Citizens & Southern, Northbrook Property appealed.

BEASLEY, J. . . . Patricia Ferguson, Devin's office manager and bookkeeper, was authorized to sign the checks on behalf of the maker, Devin, and all checks for which recovery is sought were signed on Devin's behalf by her. . . . The controversy centers on checks . . . which were made payable to fictitious persons or to actual persons who were not intended by Patricia Ferguson to have any interest in the items. During the time in question 369 checks were presented to branches of C & S for cashing, only 11 of which bore Patricia Ferguson's indorsement (the others were indorsed in the payee's name). C & S was informed of Devin's claim in February 1983.

The trial court granted C & S's partial motion for summary judgment finding [UCC §] 3-405 to be controlling. Northbrook appeals to this court and contends that although [UCC §] 3-405 is applicable, the fictitious payee/padded payroll defense contained therein is not absolute but should further involve the issue of whether the drawee bank was negligent in accepting forged items from an employee of the drawer.

As stated in the briefs, this is a question of first impression in Georgia. [UCC §] 3-405(1)(b) and (c) . . . states: "An indorsement by any person in the name of a named payee is effective if: . . . A person signing as or on behalf of a maker or drawer intends the payee to have no interest in the instrument; . . . or an agent or employee of the maker or drawer has supplied him with the name of the payee intending the latter to have no such interest."

Anderson, Uniform Commercial Code, p. 163 § 3-405.3 points out that Code § 3-405 "permits anyone to indorse paper made payable to a fictitious person or to one who was not intended to acquire any interest in the paper. The purpose of § 3-405 is to promote negotiability and foster the commercial reliability of paper. The rationale of UCC § 3-405 is that the employer-drawer should bear the loss caused by his dishonest employee rather than thrusting it upon the drawee bank."

The Official Code Comment to U.C.C. § 3-405 explains that the test of subsection (1)(b) "is not whether the named payee is 'fictitious,' but whether the signer intends that he shall have no interest in the instrument. The following situations illustrate the application of the subsection. (a) The drawer of a check, for his own reasons, makes it payable to P knowing that P does not exist. . . . (c) The drawer makes the check payable to P, an existing person whom he knows, intending to receive the money himself and that P shall have no interest in the check. (d) The treasurer of a corporation draws its check payable to P, who to the knowledge of the treasurer does not exist. (e) The treasurer of a corporation draws its check payable to P. P exists but the treasurer has fraudulently added his name to the payroll intending that he shall not receive the check."

Thus, a loss from the activities of a faithless employee must be borne by the employer rather than the drawee bank. This is accomplished by making the indorsement effective even though it is unauthorized. "The principle followed is that the loss should fall upon the employer as a risk of his business enterprise rather than upon the subsequent holder or drawee. The reasons are that the employer is normally in a better position to prevent such forgeries by reasonable care in the selection or supervision of his employees, or, if he is not, is at least in a better position to cover the loss by fidelity insurance, and that the cost of such insurance is properly an expense of his business rather than of the business of the holder or drawee." Official Code Comment, U.C.C. § 3-405.

An overwhelming majority of the jurisdictions confronted with this issue have recognized the import of the code section to be that any loss arising from situations provided for therein should fall upon the employer and negligence on the part of the bank is irrelevant. Only bad faith by a bank prevents invoking the code section to defeat a claim.

Northbrook asks that we choose the minority position which is now viable in only one jurisdiction, California. Some strong policy arguments have been proffered in support of this position. . . . But these policy considerations are for the legislature. We are charged solely with construing the statutory language. We come to the . . . result . . . that the code section makes no provision for negligence by the bank. Fortification for this plain meaning construction is implicit from the tenor of the U.C.C. In those situations where negligence is a factor, it invariably expressly appears in the section involved.

We therefore adopt the construction called for by the official comment and recognized by the near unanimous majority of other states which have considered the issue. Northbrook cannot recover because of mere negligence on the part of C & S.

[Judgment affirmed]

QUESTIONS

1. What was the argument of Northbrook Property?
2. What was the basis for the court's decision?

6.   Effect of Incapacity or Misconduct on Negotiation

A negotiation is effective even though (a) it was made by a minor or any other person lacking capacity; (b) it was an act beyond the powers of a corporation; (c) it was obtained by fraud, duress, or mistake of any kind; or (d) the negotiation was part of an illegal transaction or was made in breach of duty. Under general principles of law apart from the UCC, the transferor in such cases may be able to set aside the negotiation or to obtain some other form of legal relief. If, however, the instrument has in the meantime been acquired by a holder in due course, the negotiation can no longer be set aside.

7.   Lost Paper

The effect of losing commercial paper depends on who is suing or demanding payment from whom and whether the paper was order paper or bearer paper when it was lost. If the paper is order paper, the finder does not become the holder, because the paper, by definition, is not indorsed and delivered by the person to whom it was then payable. The for-

mer holder who lost it is still the rightful owner of the paper, although technically not the holder because not in possession of the paper.

When a commercial paper is lost, it may be possible to have a new paper issued in its place. Thus, an employer may issue a new paycheck to replace a check lost by an employee. If the lost paper is a promissory note, it is less likely that the maker will oblige by executing a new promissory note. In any event, the owner of the lost paper may bring suit on it against any party liable thereon.

There is, of course, the practical difficulty of proving just what the lost paper provided and explaining the loss of the paper. The court may also require that the plaintiff suing on the lost instrument furnish the defendant with security to indemnify the defendant against loss by reason of any claim that might thereafter be made on the lost instrument.[6]

If the paper is in bearer form when it is lost, the finder, as the possessor of bearer paper, is the holder and is entitled to enforce payment.

---

[6]   UCC § 3-804.

B.   KINDS OF INDORSEMENTS

Some commercial paper may be transferred without an indorsement. An indorsement is required in other cases.

The person to whom an instrument is payable, either on its face or by indorsement, or the person in possession of bearer paper may indorse it for the purpose of negotiating it by merely signing it. The person may add certain words or statements as part of the indorsement. By definition an indorsement is written on the back of an instrument.

8.   Blank Indorsement

When the indorser merely signs the paper, the indorsement is called a **blank indorsement**. (See Figure 31-1.) A blank indorsement does not indicate the person to whom the instrument is to be paid, that is, the transferee. A person who is in possession of paper on which the last indorsement is blank is the holder.

FIGURE 31-1   BLANK INDORSEMENT

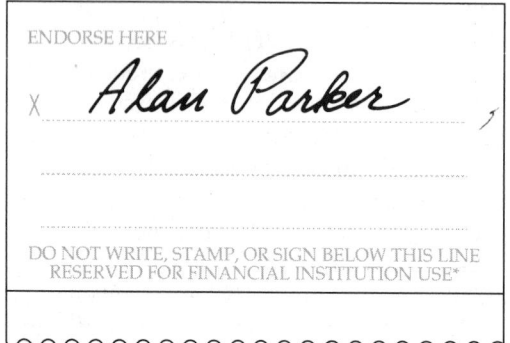

(a) CONVERTING THE BLANK INDORSEMENT. The holder of an instrument on which the last indorsement is blank may write above the blank indorsement a statement that the instrument is payable to that particular holder.[7] This is called *completing* the indorsement or *converting* the blank indorsement to a special indorsement by specifying the identity of the indorsee. It protects the holder, because the paper cannot be negotiat-

---

7   UCC § 3-204(3).

ed thereafter without the indorsement and delivery of such holder.

(b) EFFECT OF BLANK INDORSEMENT. Negotiation by a blank indorsement does four things: (1) it passes the ownership of the instrument; (2) it gives rise to certain implied warranties; (3) it imposes upon the indorser secondary liability for payment of the paper; and (4) it changes the paper to bearer paper, which may be negotiated by transfer of possession alone.

9.   Special Indorsement

A **special indorsement** consists of the signature of the indorser and words specifying the person to whom the indorser makes the instrument payable, that is, the indorsee. (See Figure 31-2.) Common forms of this kind of indorsement are "Pay to the order of Roberta Hicks, E.S. Flynn" and "Pay to Roberta Hicks or order, E.S. Flynn." It is not necessary that the indorsement contain the words "order" or "bearer." Thus, a commercial paper indorsed in the form "Pay to Roberta Hicks, E.S. Flynn" continues to be negotiable and may be negotiated further. In contrast, an instrument that on its face reads "Pay to E.S. Flynn" is not negotiable.

FIGURE 31-2   SPECIAL INDORSEMENT

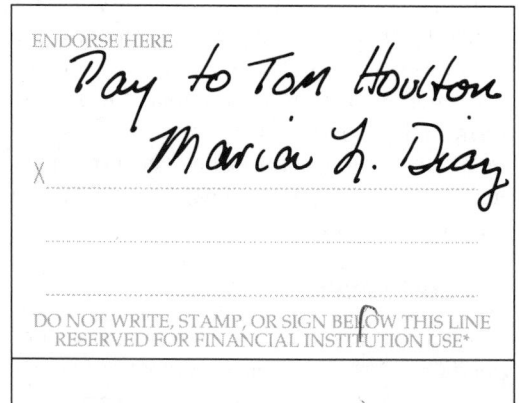

As in the case of the blank indorsement, a special indorsement transfers title to the instrument. It also results in the indorser making certain warranties about the instrument and imposes on the indorser a secondary liability to pay the amount of the instrument when certain requirements are satisfied. When a special indorsement is made, the paper becomes order paper and may only be negotiated by an indorsement and delivery.

10.   Qualified Indorsement

A **qualified indorsement** is one that qualifies the effect of a blank or a special indorsement by disclaiming or destroying the liability of the indorser to answer for dishonor by the maker or drawee. This may be done by including the words "without recourse" in the body of the indorsement or by using any other words that indicate an intention to destroy the indorser's secondary liability for dishonor by the maker or drawee.[8] (See Figure 31-3.)

FIGURE 31-3   QUALIFIED INDORSEMENT

The qualification of an indorsement does not affect the passage of title or the negotiable character of the paper. It merely disclaims the indorser's secondary liability for payment of the paper.

This form of indorsement is most commonly used when the qualified indorser is known to be a person who has no personal interest in the transaction. For example, an agent or an attorney who is merely indorsing to a principal or client a check of a third person made payable to the agent or attorney might make a qualified indorsement. Here the transferee recognizes that the transferor is not a party to the transaction and therefore should not be asked to vouch for the payment of the paper.

11.   Restrictive Indorsement

A **restrictive indorsement** specifies the purpose of the indorsement or the use to be made of the paper. (See Figure 31-4.) An indorsement is restrictive when it includes words showing that the paper is to be deposited (as "for deposit") or is negotiated for collection, or to an agent or trustee, or the negotiation is conditional.[9]

FIGURE 31-4   RESTRICTIVE INDORSEMENT

A restrictive indorsement does not prevent transfer or negotiation of the paper, even when it expressly states that transfer or negotiation is prohibited.

If the restriction is in the form of a conditional indorsement, the holder may be a holder in due course—subject only to the requirement that the maker must pay only if the condition is fulfilled. For example, an instrument payable to the order of P is indorsed by P, "Pay Allen Weber if X ship arrives at port before October 1." Weber indorsed the instrument to Byrd. Byrd cannot collect from the maker unless the X ship arrives at port before October 1. If the maker pays Byrd, the maker may have to pay again to P, who indorsed restrictively.

8   Florida Coast Bank v Monarch Dodge (Fla App) 430 So 2d 607 (1983).

9   UCC § 3-205. Walcott v Manufacturers Hanover Trust, 133 Misc 2d 725, 507 NYS 2d 961 (1986).

A bank may ignore and is not affected by the restrictive indorsement of any person except the holder transferring the instrument to the bank or the person presenting it to the bank for payment. However, a **depositary bank** (that is, the one in which the customer deposits the item) and persons not in the bank collection process must recognize the restrictive indorsement to the extent of applying any value given in a manner consistent with the indorsement.[10]

The distinction between a blank, special, and restrictive indorsement is illustrated by the *Walcott* case.

[10]   Marine Midland Bank, N.A. v Prince, 157 NYS2d 220, 443 NE2d 932 (1982).

WALCOTT v MANUFACTURERS HANOVER TRUST
133 Misc 2d 725, 507 NYS 2d 961 (1986)

Walcott sent his October paycheck, together with a money order, to Midatlantic Mortgage Company in payment of his November mortgage. Walcott alleged that he signed his name to the back of the check and placed his mortgage number and the Midatlantic mailing sticker on the back of the check. He then placed the check and money order in an envelope directed to Midatlantic Mortgage Company and dropped the envelope into a United States Postal box. Some time later Walcott was notified that he was late with the November payment. Walcott learned that his check had been cashed by Bilko Check Cashing and deposited in Bilko's account with Manufacturers Hanover. The check was finally cleared through Citibank and charged to the account of the original payor, the New York City Transit Authority. Walcott claimed that the check was stolen and Manufacturer's Hanover had wrongfully credited it to Bilko's account. Walcott sued Manufacturers and Bilko for the amount of the check. Walcott claimed that his indorsement was either a special or restrictive indorsement, which should have prevented a thief from cashing the check.

HARKAVY, J. . . .

SPECIAL INDORSEMENT

Uniform Commercial Code § 3-204 subdivision (1) defines a special indorsement as being one that ". . . specifies the person to whom or to whose order it makes the instrument payable. Any instrument specially indorsed becomes payable to the order of the special indorsee and may be further negotiated only by his indorsement."

Examination of the back of the check, reveals that Mr. Walcott did not specify any particular indorsee. In order for the alleged attached sticker to have served that purpose it must have also complied with UCC § 3-202 subdivision (2): "An indorsement must be written by or on behalf of the holder and on the instrument or a paper so firmly affixed thereto as to become a part thereof." The back of the check shows no sticker attached at all. Even if it had originally been affixed thereto, as plaintiff claims, it obviously became detached easily, thus failing to meet the indorsement requirements under the UCC to constitute a special indorsement.

RESTRICTIVE INDORSEMENT

As to the numbers written underneath plaintiff's signature, they did not have the effect of restricting plaintiff's indorsement. "An indorsement is restrictive which either

(a) is conditional; or
(b) purports to prohibit further transfer of the instrument; or
(c) includes the words 'for collection,' 'for deposit,' 'pay any bank,' or like terms signifying a purpose of deposit or collection; or
(d) otherwise states that it is for the benefit or use of the indorser or of another person." UCC § 3-205.

This section of the Uniform Commercial Code is very specific. The series of numbers representing plaintiff's mortgage account was insufficient to restrict negotiation of plaintiff's check.

BLANK INDORSEMENT

Plaintiff's indorsement had the effect of converting the check into a bearer instrument. The series of numbers having no restrictive effect, Mr. Walcott indorsed the check in blank, or otherwise stated, he simply signed his name. A blank indorsement under UCC § 3-204 subdivision (2) ". . .specifies no particular indorsee and may consist of a mere signature." Additionally, "An instrument payable to order and indorsed in blank becomes payable to bearer and may be negotiated by delivery alone. . . ." Consequently, since plaintiff failed to limit his blank indorsement, the check was properly negotiated by delivery to third party defendant Bilko and properly cashed by them.

[Judgment for defendants]

QUESTIONS

1. Was Walcott's indorsement either special or restrictive?
2. What was the nature and effect of Walcott's indorsement?
3. What was the basis for the decision of the court?

12. Correction of Name by Indorsement

Sometimes the name of the payee or indorsee of a commercial paper is improperly spelled. Thus, H.A. Price may receive a paycheck that improperly is payable to the order of "H.O. Price." If this was a clerical error and the check is intended for H.A. Price, the employee may ask the employer to write a new check payable in the proper name. Instead of doing this, the payee or indorsee whose name is misspelled may indorse the wrong name, the correct name, or both. A person giving or paying value for the instrument may require both.[11]

This correction of name by indorsement may be used only when it was intended that the instrument should be payable to the person making the corrective indorsement. If there were in fact two employees, one named H.A. Price and the other H.O. Price, it would be illegal as a forgery for one to take the check intended for the other and by indorsing it obtain the benefit of the proceeds of the check.

13. Bank Indorsement

In order to simplify the transfer of commercial paper from one bank to another in the process of collecting items, "any agreed method which identifies the transferor bank is sufficient for the item's further transfer to another

[11]   UCC § 3-203.

bank."[12] Thus, a bank may indorse with its Federal Reserve System number instead of using its name.

Likewise, when a customer has deposited an instrument with a bank but has failed to indorse it, the bank may make an indorsement for the customer unless the instrument expressly requires the payee's personal indorsement. Furthermore, the mere stamping or marking on the item of any notation showing that it was deposited by the customer or credited to the customer's account is declared to be effective as an indorsement by the customer.[13]

C.   WARRANTIES OF TRANSFEROR BY NEGOTIATION

When commercial paper is transferred, certain implied warranties are imposed by law on the transferor. When an instrument is transferred in exchange for value, the transaction is similar in some respects to a sale of goods. In the case of a sale of goods, certain warranties as to title, description, and quality arise, which, if breached, give the buyer a cause of action against the seller. The transferor of commercial paper, by the act of making the transfer, warrants the existence of certain facts. These warranties vary according to whether the instrument is transferred with or without an indorsement and according to the nature of the indorsement.

14.   Warranties of Unqualified Indorser

When the holder of a commercial paper negotiates it by an unqualified indorsement, and receives consideration, the transferor warrants the following.

(a) Ownership of good title, which includes the genuineness of all indorsements necessary to title to the instrument or authorization to act for one who has good title. For example, Rita makes a note payable to the order of Jorge. The note is stolen, and the thief forges Jorge's signature on the back of the note, making it payable to the order of Lawten. Lawten, without knowledge of the forged indorsement, transfers and indorses the note to Selma for value. Selma could not recover from the maker, since she did not have good title. Selma, however, can sue Lawten for breach of warranty of good title, because a necessary signature (Jorge's) was not genuine.

(b) The act of transferring the instrument is rightful, independent of the question of title or authority to act. For example, if a payee of a note breaches a contract with the maker to hold the note until certain goods are shipped by transferring the note before the goods are shipped, the transfer is not rightful. This payee becomes liable to the transferee for any loss occasioned by the early transfer of the note.

(c) The signatures on the instrument are genuine or executed by authorized agents.

(d) The instrument has not been materially altered.

(e) The indorser has no knowledge of the existence or commencement of any insolvency proceeding against the maker or acceptor of the instrument, or against the drawer of an unaccepted draft or bill of exchange.

(f) No defense of any party is good against the indorser.

These warranties made by the unqualified indorser pass to the transferee and to any subsequent holder who acquires the instrument in good faith.[14]

The holder's indorsement of the check does not give rise to any warranty that the account of the drawer in the drawee bank contains funds sufficient to cover the check.

15.   Warranties of Other Parties

Warranties are also made by the indorser who indorses "without recourse" and by one who transfers by delivery only.

---

[12]   UCC § 4-206.
[13]   UCC § 4-205(1).

[14]   UCC § 3-417(2).

(a) QUALIFIED INDORSER. The warranty liability of the indorser who indorses "without recourse" is the same as that of the unqualified indorser, with one difference. The warranty as to "no defenses" is limited to a warranty that the indorser does not have knowledge of any defense, rather than that no defense exists.[15] The warranties of a qualified indorser run to the same persons as those of an unqualified indorser.

(b) TRANSFEROR BY DELIVERY. The warranties made by one who transfers a commercial paper by delivery are the same as those made by an unqualified indorser, except that they run only to the immediate transferee, and then only if consideration has been given for the transfer.[16] Subsequent holders cannot enforce such warranties against this prior

transferor by delivery, regardless of the character of such holders.

D.   ASSIGNMENT OF COMMERCIAL PAPER

Although commercial paper may be negotiated, it may also be assigned. The assignment may result from the act of the parties or by operation of law.

16.   Assignment by Act of the Parties

Commercial paper may be assigned in the same manner as any other contract right, by the express act of the holder. A commercial paper is also regarded as assigned when a person whose indorsement is required to negotiate the instrument transfers it without indorsing it.

In the *Duxbury* case the court dealt with a promissory note that was transferred without indorsement.

---

[15]   UCC § 3-417(3). The qualified indorsement does not exclude other warranties unless it is specified to be "without warranties."

[16]   UCC § 3-471(2).

DUXBURY v ROBERTS
338 Mass 385, 446 NE2d 401 (1983)

Roberts issued a promissory note payable to the order of Baines. Baines handed this note over to Duxbury without indorsing it. Baines also gave him a separate paper, in which Baines stated that the note was being transferred to Duxbury. When Duxbury sued Roberts on the note, Roberts contended that he was not liable, because Duxbury was not a holder in due course of the paper. From a judgment in favor of Duxbury, Roberts appealed.

HENNESSEY, C. J. . . . The defendants argue that the trial judge improperly determined that Duxbury was a holder in due course. The Appellate Division found the trial judge to be in error on this issue because the note was not negotiated properly to Duxbury. We agree with the Appellate Division. One does not become a holder of a negotiable instrument unless there is a negotiation of that instrument as required under the Uniform Commercial Code, § 3-202(1). To have a negotiation of an instrument payable to order, the instrument must be delivered with any necessary indorsement. "An indorsement must be written by or on behalf of the holder and on the instrument or on a paper so firmly affixed thereto as to become a part thereof." In this case Baines did not sign the note when he transferred it to Duxbury. Rather, he signed only the document entitled, "Partial Assignment of Note and Mortgage." His signing of this document does not constitute an indorsement of the note because it was not "so firmly affixed thereto as to become a part thereof." Therefore, Duxbury did not become a holder or a holder in due course. We agree, however, with the Appellate Division which determined further that notwithstanding the trial judge's improper resolution of the holder in due course issue, the plaintiff was properly entitled to judgment on the merits.

We, thus, reject the defendants' final contention that the assignment to Duxbury was not valid. Under [UCC] § 3-201(1), even though the instrument was not negotiated, Duxbury acquired the rights of his transferor, Baines, subject to all defenses available against Baines. . . .

[Judgment affirmed]

QUESTIONS

1. How is order paper negotiated?
2. Was there a negotiation by Baines to Duxbury?
3. What rights did Duxbury have on the note?

When a necessary indorsement is missing, the transferee has only the rights of an assignee. If the transferee acquires the paper for value, the transferee is entitled, however, to require that the transferor indorse the instrument.[17] If the indorsement is obtained, then the transferee is deemed a holder, but only as of the time when the indorsement is made.

---

[17]   UCC § 3-201(3).

17.   Assignment by Operation of Law

An assignment by operation of law occurs when by virtue of the law one person's title to commercial paper is vested in another. For example, if the holder of a commercial paper becomes a debtor under the Bankruptcy Code or dies, the title to the instrument vests automatically in the trustee in bankruptcy or in the personal representative of the decedent's estate, respectively.

SUMMARY

Commercial paper may be transferred by negotiation or assignment. If an instrument is negotiated, the rights of the transferee may rise higher than those of the transferor. If an instrument is assigned, the assignee has only those rights that the assignor had.

Negotiation is the transfer of commercial paper in such a way as to make the transferee the holder of the paper. Order paper is negotiated by an indorsement and a delivery by the person to whom it is then payable. Bearer paper is negotiated by a transfer of possession. The order or bearer character of paper is determined by the face of the paper, as long as

the paper is not indorsed. If the paper has been indorsed, the character is determined by the last genuine indorsement.

A forged or unauthorized indorsement is no indorsement, and the possessor of the paper cannot be a holder. The UCC makes exceptions to this general rule in three situations, in which the indorsement is given the same effect as though it had been authorized by the named payee. One exception is when an impostor has induced the maker or drawer to issue the instrument to the person whose identity has been assumed by the impostor. The second exception is when the person signing as or on behalf of the drawer intends that the named payee shall have no interest in the paper. The third exception is when an agent or employee of the drawer has given the drawer the name used as the payee, intending that the payee should not have any interest in the paper.

A negotiation is effective even though (1) it is made by a minor, (2) it is an act beyond the powers of a corporation, (3) it is obtained by fraud, or (4) the negotiation is part of an illegal transaction. However, the transferor may be able to set aside the negotiation under general legal principles apart from the UCC.

There are a number of different kinds of indorsements that can be made on commercial paper. When an indorser merely signs the paper, the indorsement is called a blank indorsement. If the last indorsement is a blank indorsement, the paper is bearer paper, which may be negotiated by transfer of possession alone. A special indorsement consists of the signature of the indorser and words specifying the person to whom the indorser makes the instrument payable. If the last indorse-

ment is a special indorsement, the paper is order paper and may be negotiated only by an indorsement and delivery. A qualified indorsement destroys the liability of the indorser to answer for dishonor of the paper by the maker or drawee. A restrictive indorsement specifies the purpose of the indorsement or the use to be made of the paper.

An indorser who negotiates by an unqualified indorsement and receives consideration makes the following warranties: (1) title is good, (2) all the signatures are genuine, (3) the instrument has not been materially altered, (4) the indorser has no knowledge of any insolvency proceeding against the maker or drawer, and (5) no defense of any party is good against the indorser. A transferor indorsing with a qualified indorsement warrants only that the transferor has no knowledge of any defense, rather than that no defense exists. Otherwise the qualified indorser makes the same warranties as an unqualified indorser. A transferor who does not indorse the instrument makes these warranties only to the immediate transferee.

QUESTIONS AND CASE PROBLEMS

1. What social forces are affected by the law as to qualified indorsements?
2. As soon as Bertha gets her weekly paycheck, she carefully writes her name on the back so that everyone will know that it is her check. Is Bertha protected by doing this?
3. Allan pays Bestor $100, which Allan owes Bestor, with a check stating "pay to the order of Dale Bestor $100." How can Bestor transfer this check to Wickard in such a way as to make Wickard the holder of the check?
4. Higgins owes the Packard Appliance store $100. He mails a check to Packard. The check is drawn on the First National Bank and states "pay to the order of cash $100." This check is stapled to a letter stating that the $100 is in payment of the debt owed by Higgins. Edwards is employed by Packard in the mailroom. Edwards removes the letter from its envelope, detaches the check, and disappears. No one knows what becomes of the check until it is presented at the First National Bank by a person identifying himself as Gene Howard. The bank pays

this person $100 and debits that amount against the account of Higgins. Higgins protests that this cannot be done because the check was lost and never belonged to Howard. Is Higgins correct?

5. A thief steals a blank promissory note from Roger, makes it payable to Dodd, and forges Roger's name to it as maker. Dodd gives value for the note and indorses it to Nell, who in turn indorses it to Robert, a holder in due course. Robert attempts to collect against Roger, who proves that his signature was a forgery. Does Robert have any rights against Dodd or Nell? Why?
6. Huff, the assistant to the controller of a general partnership, told the controller that the firm owed Janet Richards $250. Richards was a fictitious person, but relying on Huff's statement, the controller signed the partnership's name to a check. Huff indorsed the check on its back, signing the name "Janet Richards," and cashed it at a liquor store. Hudson Bank charged the partnership's account for the $250 and returned

it with the rest of the checks for the month. Subsequently, the fraudulent conduct of Huff was discovered by the partnership's auditors. Must the Hudson Bank recredit the partnership's account with $250?

7. Gellert pays her rent by indorsing to Parker, her landlord, a check payable to the order of Gellert. The check appears to have been drawn by McCoy. Actually, the signature of McCoy is a forgery. The check is indorsed by Parker with only his name and delivered by him to Tipton, a roofer who repaired the roof. Tipton delivers the check without any indorsement to the Ruane Supply Company, the supply house from which he purchased the roofing materials. Ruane transfers the check without indorsement to the Metropolitan Manufacturing Company, which manufactured the supplies sold to the supply house. Metropolitan presents the check to the bank. The bank refuses to pay the check. Metropolitan demands payment from McCoy. McCoy refuses to pay because the check is a forgery. Metropolitan then sues Tipton for breach of warranty. Is Tipton liable?

8. Benton, as agent for Savidge, received an insurance settlement check from the Metropolitan Life Insurance Co. He indorsed it "For deposit" and deposited it in the Bryn Mawr Trust Company in the account of Savidge. What was the nature and effect of this indorsement? [Savidge v Metropolitan Life Insurance Co. 380 Pa 205, 110 A2d 730]

9. Humphrey drew a check for $100. It was stolen and the payee's name forged as an indorser. The check was then negotiated to Miller, who had no knowledge of these facts. Miller indorsed the check to the Citizens Bank. Payment of the check was voided on the ground of the forgery. The Citizens Bank then sued Miller as indorser. Decide. [Citizens Bank of Hattiesburg v Miller, 194 Miss 557, 11 So 2d 457]

10. When claims filed with the insurance company were approved for payment, they were given to the claims clerk, who would prepare checks to pay those claims and then give the checks to the treasurer to sign. The claims clerk of the insurance company made a number of checks payable to persons who did not have any claims and gave them to the treasurer together with the checks for valid claims, and the treasurer signed all the checks. The claims clerk then removed the false checks, indorsed them with the names of their respective payees, and cashed them at the bank where the insurance company had its account. The bank debited the account of the insurance company with the amount of these checks. The insurance company claimed that the bank could not do this because the indorsements on the checks were forgeries. Is the insurance company correct? [General Acci. Fire & Life Assur. Corp. v Citizens Fidelity Bank & Trust Co. (Ky) 519 SW2d 817]

11. Compare or contrast the warranties of an unqualified indorser with those of a qualified indorser.

12. Charles made an instrument payable to Larry, a minor. Larry indorsed and delivered the instrument to Quest, a holder in due course. When Quest sued Charles on the instrument, he claimed that he was not liable, since the instrument was negotiated by a minor. Decide.

13. Fisher wanted to have his house painted. His father wrote out a check to the order of Fisher for $200 as a down payment for the painting. Fisher then made a contract with Denny to paint the house. For the down payment on this contract he took his father's check and indorsed on it "Pay to Denny upon condition of the proper painting of my home at 510 N. Maine St., Jonesville." He then delivered the check to Denny. Could Denny cash the check before he completed the painting work?

14. A note was indorsed "without recourse" to the Hudson Bank by Starlit Equipment. When the bank tried to collect on the note, the maker of the note alleged that his signature was forged. The bank then sued Starlit. Starlit defended the action on the basis that the instrument was signed "without recourse." Decide.

15. Two employees of the state of New Mexico fraudulently procured and indorsed a warrant (that is, a draft drawn against funds of the state) made out to the Greater Mesilla Valley Sanitation District. There was no such sanitation district. The employees obtained payment from the Citizens Bank. Western Casualty, the state's insurer, reimbursed the state for its loss and then brought suit against the bank for negligently paying the warrant. Decide. [Western Casualty & Surety Co. v Citizens Bank of Las Cruces (CA10 NM) 676 F2d 1344]

32

RIGHTS OF HOLDERS
AND DEFENSES

Commercial paper litigation may arise between the original parties to the instrument or, where commercial paper has been negotiated, between the maker or drawer and a holder or between subsequent holders. When the original parties are involved, ordinary contract defenses, such as failure of consideration, may be asserted. When the instrument has left the hands of the payee and has been negotiated to a holder in due course, such a holder will take the instrument free from many kinds of claims that might be asserted by a party to the instrument.

A. KINDS OF HOLDERS

When a commercial paper is negotiated to a person, that person is the holder—either an ordinary holder or a favored holder.

1. Ordinary Holders and Assignees

Any holder has all the rights relating to the paper. The holder, although an ordinary holder, is the only person who may demand payment, bring suit for the collection of the paper, give a discharge or release from liability on the paper, or cancel the liability of another party to the paper.

When the holder sues on the paper, the holder is only required to produce the paper in court and show that the signature of the defendant is genuine. If that is done and there is no evidence of a defense, the holder is entitled to a judgment for the full face amount of the paper.

The holder may generally sue any one or more prior parties on the paper without regard to the order in which such persons signed the paper or the order in which such persons may be liable to each other.

The fact that the holder is merely an ordinary holder has no significance if the defendant does not have any defense.

The assignee of a commercial paper is in the same position and has the same rights as an ordinary holder. It is immaterial whether the person is an assignee by express assignment, by operation of law, or in consequence of the omission of an essential indorsement.

2. Favored Holders

The law gives certain holders of commercial paper a preferred standing by protecting them from certain defenses when they sue to collect payment. This protection is given in order to make commercial paper more attractive by giving the favored holder an immunity not possessed by an ordinary holder or an assignee. The favored holders are known as the *holder in due course* and the *holder through a holder in due course.*

(a) HOLDER IN DUE COURSE. In order to have the preferred status of a holder in due course, a person must first be a holder. This means that the possessor of the paper must have acquired it by proper negotiation. That is, the person in question must be the possessor of bearer paper or must be the possessor of order paper payable to that person as payee or indorsee.[1] The concept of due course may be understood better if modern terminology is substituted and "due course" is thought of as an ordinary transaction.

In addition to being a holder, the holder in due course must meet certain conditions that pertain to (1) value, (2) good faith, (3) ignorance of paper's being overdue or dishonored, and (4) ignorance of defenses and adverse claims.[2]

1. Value. Since the law of commercial paper is fundamentally a merchant's or business person's law, it favors only the holders who have given value for the paper. For example, since a legatee under a will does not give value, a person receiving bonds as a legacy is not a holder in due course.

A person takes an instrument for value (a) by performing the act for which the instrument was given, such as delivering the goods for which the check was sent in payment, (b) by acquiring a security interest in the paper, as when it has been pledged as security for another obligation, or (c) by taking the instrument in payment of, or as security for, a debt.[3] When value is given, the courts do not measure or appraise the value given.

A promise not yet performed, although sufficient as consideration for a contract, does not constitute value to satisfy this requirement for a holder in due course.[4]

A bank does not give value for a deposited check when it credits the depositor's account with the amount of the deposit. The bank gives value to the extent that the depositor withdraws money against that credit.

In the *Trail Leasing* case a bank alleged it paid value, thus making it a holder in due course.

---

[1]   Although it is an uncommon occurrence, the original payee may also be a holder in due course, provided the necessary elements are satisfied. UCC § 3–302(2). Hartford Accident & Indemnity v American Express, 136 Misc 2d 62, 518 NYS2d 93 (1987). See Appendices 5 and 7 for a table of sections and provisions of the 1990 revision of Article 3 that affect the law stated in this chapter.

[2]   In a few special cases, a purchaser of commercial paper is not considered a holder in due course even though all these elements have been satisfied. This is true when the sales are not of an ordinary commercial nature, such as when paper is acquired by judicial sale, sale of the assets of an estate, or a bulk sale not in the regular course of business of the transferor. UCC § 3–302(3).

[3]   UCC § 3–303. It is also provided that there is a taking for value when another commercial paper is given in exchange or when the taker makes an irrevocable commitment to a third person, as by providing a letter of credit. UCC § 3–303(c).

[4]   Sea Air Support, Inc. v Herrmann, 96 Nev 574, 613 P2d 413 (1980).

TRAIL LEASING, INC. v DROVERS FIRST AMERICAN BANK

(Minn) 447 NW2d 190 (1989)

> Over a period of about two years, Pamela Haas, employed as assistant book-keeper by Trail Leasing, embezzled funds from her employer. Haas got corporate officers to sign checks payable to Drovers Bank, that she would then cash for herself. Trail Leasing alleged that the bank should not have allowed Haas, who was not authorized to write checks, to obtain funds in this manner. The bank claimed that it was a holder in due course, protected from liability. Trail Leasing agreed that the bank took the checks in good faith and without notice of the embezzlement scheme, but contended that the bank never gave value. From a judgment in favor of Trail Leasing, the bank appealed.

SIMONETT, J . . . . Under [UCC §]3–302, a holder in due course is anyone who takes the instrument "(a) for value; and (b) in good faith; and (c) without notice that it is overdue or has been dishonored or of any defense against or claim to it on the part of any person." Here it has been stipulated that Drovers took the Haas checks in good faith and without notice of any claims. The issue then becomes, as it did for the appeals panel, whether Drovers meets the third requirement of taking the checks "for value." This, too, is the issue raised in the petition for further review by Drovers.

We conclude that Drovers took the Haas checks "for value" and, therefore, was a holder in due course.

"A holder takes the instrument for value," says [UCC §]3–303(a), "to the extent that the agreed consideration has been performed or that he acquires a security interest in or lien on the instrument otherwise than by legal process." This provision eliminated a conflict in prior law by making clear that merely a promise to the transferor is not value until the promise has been performed. Here Drovers performed; it paid cash for the checks. Trail Leasing argues that at best Drovers gave only "conditional value" because it retained and exercised the right to debit Trail Leasing's commercial account. But even so, the bank first had to pay out its money before debiting Trail Leasing's account. As the comment to [UCC §]3–303 says, "Where an agreed sum of money is actually paid for an instrument . . . as the purchase price for it . . . the instrument is clearly taken 'for value' . . . ." *Roland v. Republic Nat'l Bank of Dallas*, 463 S.W.2d 747, 749 (Tex.Civ.App.1971) (bank becomes a holder in due course when bank paid face value for checks presented by payee and drawn on an account at bank and thus had right to reimburse itself from customer's account.) Cases cited by Trail Leasing where a bank takes a check, credits the depositor's account, but never issues cash against the check, are not on point. This is not a case, either, where Haas withdrew money from Trail Leasing's account with a simple withdrawal slip. Here she used a valid negotiable instrument.

[Judgment reversed]

QUESTIONS

1. When does a person take an instrument for value?

2. What was the argument of Trail Leasing?
3. Did Drovers take the Haas checks for value?

2. Good Faith. The element of good faith requires that the taker of commercial paper act honestly in the acquisition of the instrument. Bad faith may sometimes be indicated by the small value given. This does not mean that the transferee must give full value, but it does mean that a gross inadequacy of value may be evidence of bad faith. Bad faith is established by proof that the transferee had knowledge of such facts as rendered it improper to acquire the instrument under the circumstances.

The fact that a transferee acted carelessly does not establish bad faith.[5] If the transferee takes the instrument in good faith, it is immaterial whether the transferor acted in good faith.

3. Ignorance of Paper's Being Overdue or Dishonored. Commercial paper may be negotiated even though (a) it has been dishonored, whether by nonacceptance or nonpayment; (b) the paper is overdue, whether because of lapse of time or the acceleration of the due date; or (c) it is demand paper that has been outstanding more than a reasonable time. In other words, ownership may still be transferred. Nevertheless, the fact that the paper is circulating at a late date or after it has been dishonored is a suspicious circumstance that is deemed to put the person acquiring the paper on notice that there is some adverse claim or defense. A person who acquires title to the paper under such circumstances, therefore, cannot be a holder in due course.

4. Ignorance of Defenses and Adverse Claims. Prior parties on the paper may have defenses that they could raise if sued by the person with whom they dealt. For example, the drawer of a check, if sued by the payee, might have the defense that the merchandise delivered by the payee was defective. In addition, third persons, whether prior parties or not, may be able to assert that the instrument

belongs to them and not to the possessor. A person who acquires the commercial paper with notice or knowledge that any party might have a defense or that there is any adverse claim to the ownership of the instrument cannot be a holder in due course. Thus, the holder of commercial paper cannot be a holder in due course when the holder acquired the paper with knowledge that there had been a failure of consideration with respect to the contract for which the paper had been given.

Knowledge acquired by the taker after acquiring the paper does not prevent the taker from being a holder in due course. Consequently, the fact that the taker, after acquiring the paper, learns of a defense does not operate retroactively to destroy the taker's character as a holder in due course.

Knowledge of certain facts constitutes notice to the person acquiring a commercial paper that there is a defense or an adverse claim. The holder or purchaser of the paper is deemed to have notice of a claim or defense in the following situations.[6] If the instrument is so incomplete, bears such visible evidence of forgery or alteration, or is otherwise so irregular as to call into question its validity, terms, or ownership, or to create an ambiguity as to the party who is required to pay, the person acquiring the paper is on notice of a claim or defense. The purchaser also has notice of a claim or defense if the purchaser has notice that the obligation of any party is voidable in whole or in part, or that all parties to the paper have been discharged. For example, the subsequent holder may know that a note given for home improvement work in fact covers both the improvements and a loan. The holder also knows that the transaction is usurious because excessive costs were charged for the work to conceal the usurious interest. Such a holder is not a holder in due course.

---

[5]   Funding Consultants, Inc. v Aetna Casualty and Surety Co. 187 Conn 637, 447 A2d 1163 (1982).

[6]   UCC § 3–304(1).

In general, a holder who has knowledge of such facts as would put a reasonable person on inquiry is deemed to have knowledge of the facts that would be learned if such inquiry were made.

The purchaser of commercial paper does not have notice of a defense that bars such a purchaser from being a holder in due course merely because of the following situations.[7] The purchaser may know that the instrument is antedated or postdated or that a person has signed for accommodation. Likewise, a purchaser of commercial paper may be a holder in due course even if the purchaser knows that an incomplete instrument has been completed, unless the purchaser has notice of any improper completion. A purchaser of commercial paper is not barred from holder in due course status because the purchaser knows that there was a negotiation by a fiduciary, unless the purchaser has knowledge that the fiduciary is breaching a duty. Holder in due course status is not affected by knowledge that there is a default in payment of interest on the instrument.

In the *Money Mart* case the drawer of a payroll check argued that the purchaser of that check should have inquired as to whether the check would be honored before cashing it.

---

[7] First Federal Savings & Loan Ass'n v Gump & Ayers Real Estate (Utah App) 791 P2d 1096 (1989).

MONEY MART CHECK CASHING CENTER INC. v EPICYCLE CORPORATION
(Colo) 667 P2d 1372 (1983)

An employee of Epicycle cashed his final payroll check at Money Mart Check Cashing Center. Epicycle had issued a stop payment order on the check. Money Mart deposited the check through normal banking channels. The check was returned to Money Mart marked "Payment Stopped." Money Mart brought an action against Epicycle claiming that, as a holder in due course, it was entitled to recover against Epicycle. Epicycle argued that Money Mart could not be a holder in due course because it failed to verify the check as good prior to cashing it. From a judgment in favor of Epicycle, Money Mart appealed.

ROVIRA, J. . . . The question before us is whether Money Mart is a holder in due course. If it is, it takes the check free of any of Epicycle's claims to the check or defenses against [its employee. UCC § 3–302(1)] provides:

(1) A holder in due course is a holder who takes the instrument:
   (a) For value; and
   (b) In good faith; and
   (c) Without notice that it is overdue or has been dishonored or of any defense against or claim to it on the part of any person.

That Money Mart took the check for value is undisputed, leaving the questions of "good faith" and "notice."

"Good faith" is defined as "honesty in fact in the conduct or transaction concerned." The drafters of the Uniform Commercial Code intended that this standard be a subjective one. Thus, the question is: "Was this alleged holder in due course acting in good faith, however stupid and negligent his behavior might have been?"

The only testimony on the question of good faith is that Money Mart cashed the check without knowing that a stop payment order had been issued on it. The Superior Court concluded that Money Mart was not a holder in due course because it "did not inquire as to the check itself and had no knowledge as to whether the check was stolen, incomplete, or secured by fraud." Under a subjective standard, an absence of knowledge is not equivalent to a lack of good faith.

We now consider whether Money Mart had "notice" of the fact that payment had been stopped on the check or that Cronin had obtained the check improperly. A person has "notice" of a fact when:

(a) He has actual knowledge of it; or
(b) He has received a notice or notification of it; or
(c) From all the facts and circumstances known to him at the time in question he has reason to know that it exists.

As can be seen, tests other than "actual knowledge" may be used in determining whether a person is a holder in due course. There is no allegation that Money Mart had received notification of the defenses, so we must now determine whether Money Mart had "reason to know" of them. . . .

The Superior Court held that Money Mart's failure to inquire about the validity of the check constituted negligence. However, there is nothing in the Uniform Commercial Code and nothing in the record to support such a conclusion.

A determination of whether a holder has "reason to know" is based upon "all the facts and circumstances known to him." A person "knows" of a fact when he has "actual knowledge" of it. The question therefore is whether Money Mart had actual knowledge of facts giving it reason to know that a defense existed. There is nothing to distinguish the facts of this case from any other of the thousands of checks that Money Mart and others cash each year: A man came to Money Mart to cash his paycheck; Money Mart is in the business of cashing paychecks; the face of the check disclosed nothing to raise even a suspicion that there was something wrong with it.

It has often been held that where an instrument is regular on its face there is no duty to inquire as to possible defenses unless the circumstances of which the holder has knowledge are of such a nature that failure to inquire reveals a deliberate desire to evade knowledge because of a fear that investigation would disclose the existence of a defense. There is nothing in using a check-cashing service instead of a bank that would lead to a rule imposing different standards on the two kinds of institutions.

Accordingly, we hold that Money Mart is a holder in due course and, as such, is not subject to the defenses Epicycle may have against Cronin.

[Judgment reversed]

QUESTIONS

1. Did Money Mart take the check for value?
2. Did Money Mart take the check in good faith and without notice that payment had been stopped or that Cronin had obtained the check improperly?
3. What was the basis for the court's decision?

(b) HOLDER THROUGH A HOLDER IN DUE COURSE. Those persons who become holders of the instrument after a holder in due course are given the same protection as the holder in due course, provided they are not parties to fraud or illegality that affects the instrument.

This means that if an instrument is negotiated from A to B to C to D, and B is a holder in due course, both C and D will enjoy the same rights as B. If C received the instrument as a gift or with knowledge of failure of consideration or other defense, or if D took the instrument after maturity, they could not themselves be holders in due course. Nevertheless, they are given the same protection as a holder in due course because they took the instrument through such a holder, namely B. It is not only C, the person taking directly from B, but also D, who is given this extra protection.

B.   DEFENSES

The importance of being a holder in due course or a holder through a holder in due course is that those holders are not subject to certain defenses when they demand payment or bring suit on a commercial paper. These defenses may be described as **limited defenses.** Another class of defenses, **universal defenses,** may be asserted against any plaintiff, whether the party is an assignee, an ordinary holder, a holder in due course, or a holder through a holder in due course.

3.   Defenses Against an Ordinary Holder or Assignee

A holder who is neither a holder in due course nor a holder through a holder in due course is subject to every defense, just as though the instrument were not negotiable. Thus, an ordinary holder suing on the promissory note of a buyer is subject to the latter's defense of breach of warranty.[8]

4.   Limited Defenses Not Available Against a Holder in Due Course

Neither a holder in due course nor one having the rights of such a holder is subject to any of

the following defenses.[9] They are limited defenses. These defenses are also barred with respect to any instrument that is executed to renew or extend the original instrument.

(a) ORDINARY CONTRACT DEFENSES. In general terms, the defenses that could be raised against a suit on an ordinary contract cannot be raised against a holder in due course. Accordingly, the defendant cannot assert against the holder in due course the defense of lack, failure, or illegality of consideration with respect to the transaction between the defendant and the person with whom the defendant dealt.

(b) INCAPACITY OF DEFENDANT. Ordinarily, the incapacity of the defendant, other than that of minority, may not be raised against a holder in due course. Such incapacity is a defense, however, if by general principles of law that incapacity, such as insanity of a person for whom a guardian has been appointed by a court, makes the instrument a nullity.[10]

(c) FRAUD IN THE INDUCEMENT. When a person knowingly executes commercial paper and knows its essential terms but is persuaded or induced to execute it because of fraudulent statements, such fraud cannot be raised against a holder in due course or a holder through a holder in due course. As an illustration, M is persuaded to purchase an automobile because of P's statements concerning its condition. M gives P a note, which is negotiated until it reaches H, who is a holder in due course. M meanwhile learns that the car is not as represented and that P's statements were fraudulent. When H demands payment of the note, M cannot refuse to pay on the ground of P's fraud. M must pay the note. M may then sue P for damages for fraud.

(d) PRIOR PAYMENT OR CANCELLATION. When a commercial paper is paid, the person making the payment should demand the surrender of the instrument. If this is not done, it is possible for the holder to continue

---

[8]   Pascal v Tardera, 123 App Div 2d 752, 507 NYS2d 225 (1986).

[9]   UCC § 3–305.
[10]   UCC § 3–305(2)(b).

to negotiate it. Another person may thus become the holder of the instrument. When the new holder demands payment of the instrument, the defense cannot be raised that payment had been made to a former holder if the new holder is a holder in due course. The fact that the person making the payment obtained a receipt from the former holder does not affect the application of this principle. The fact that payment had been made could not be ascertained from the instrument itself.

When the holder and the party primarily liable have agreed to cancel the instrument but the face of the instrument does not show any sign of cancellation, the defense of cancellation cannot be asserted against a holder in due course. Similarly, an order to stop payment of a check cannot be raised as a defense by the drawer of a check against a holder in due course.

(e) NONDELIVERY OF AN INSTRUMENT. A person may write out a commercial paper or indorse an existing paper and leave it on a desk for future delivery. At that moment, the instrument or the indorsement is not effective, because there has been no delivery.

Assume that through the negligence of an employee or through the theft of the instrument, it comes into the hands of another person. If the instrument is in such a form that it can be negotiated, as when it is payable to bearer, a subsequent receiver of the instrument may be a holder in due course or a holder through a holder in due course. As against that holder, the person who wrote the instrument or indorsed it cannot defend on the ground that there had been no delivery.

(f) CONDITIONAL OR SPECIFIED PURPOSE DELIVERY. As against a favored holder, a person who would be liable on the instrument cannot show that the instrument, unconditional on its face, was in fact delivered subject to a condition that had not been satisfied or that it was delivered for a particular purpose but was not so used. Assume that A makes out a check to the order of B and hands it to C with the understanding that C shall not deliver the check to B until B delivers certain merchandise. If C should deliver the check to B before the condition is satisfied and B then negotiates the check, a holder in due course or a holder through a holder in due course may enforce the instrument.

(g) DURESS CONSISTING OF THREATS. The defense that a person signed or executed a commercial paper under threats of harm or violence may not be raised as a defense against a holder in due course when the effect of such duress is merely to make the contract voidable at the election of the victim of the duress.

(h) UNAUTHORIZED COMPLETION. A maker or drawer may sign a commercial paper and leave blank the name of the payee, the amount, or any other term and then hand the instrument to another to be completed. If so, the defense of an improper completion cannot be raised when payment is demanded or suit brought by a subsequent holder in due course or a holder through a holder in due course. For example, Fulton gave Perry a note duly executed except for the amount. Fulton gave Perry authority to fill in an amount not to exceed $300. Perry filled in the note for $500. If Perry had negotiated the instrument to a holder in due course, the instrument could have been enforced as completed.[11]

(i) THEFT. As a matter of definition, a holder in due course will not have acquired the paper through theft, and any defense of theft therefore must relate to the conduct of a prior party. Assuming that the theft of the paper does not result in a defect in the chain of necessary indorsements, the defense that the instrument has been stolen cannot be raised against a holder in due course or a holder through a holder in due course.[12]

5.   Universal Defenses Available Against All Holders

Certain defenses are regarded as so basic that the social interest in preserving them outweighs the social interest of giving commer-

[11]   UCC § 3–407(3). Virginia Capital Bank v Aetna Casualty and Surety Co. 231 Va 283, 343 SE2d 81 (1986).
[12]   UCC § 3–305(1).

cial paper the free-passing qualities of money. Accordingly, such defenses are given universal effect and may be raised against all holders, whether ordinary holders, holders in due course, or holders through a holder in due course. Such defenses are therefore appropriately called *universal defenses*.

(a) FRAUD AS TO THE NATURE OR ESSENTIAL TERMS OF THE PAPER. The fact that a person signs a commercial paper because the person is fraudulently deceived as to its nature or essential terms is a defense available against all holders. This is the situation when an experienced business person induces an illiterate person to sign a note by falsely representing that, for example, it is a contract for repairs or that it is a character reference. This defense, however, cannot be raised when it is the negligence of the defending party that prevented learning the true nature and terms of the instrument.

(b) FORGERY OR LACK OF AUTHORITY. The defense that a signature was forged or signed without authority may be raised against any holder, unless the person whose name was signed has ratified it or is estopped by conduct or negligence from denying it.[13]

The fact that the negligence of the drawer helped the wrongdoer does not bar the drawer from raising the defense of forgery.

(c) DURESS DEPRIVING CONTROL. A person may execute or indorse a commercial paper in response to a force of such a nature that, under general principles of law, there is duress that makes the transaction a nullity rather than merely voidable. If so, such duress may be raised as a defense against any holder.

(d) INCAPACITY. The fact that the defendant is a minor, who under general principles of contract law may avoid the obligation, is a matter that may be raised against any kind of holder. Other kinds of incapacity may only be raised as a defense if the effect of the incapacity is to make the instrument a nullity.

(e) ILLEGALITY. If the law declares that an instrument is void when executed in connection with certain conduct, such as gambling or usury, that defense may be raised against any holder. Similarly, when contracts of a corporate seller are a nullity because its charter has been forfeited, a promissory note given to it by a buyer is void. That defense may be raised as against a holder in due course. If the law merely makes the transaction illegal but does not make the instrument void, the defense cannot be asserted against a holder in due course or a holder through a holder in due course.

(f) ALTERATION. An **alteration** is a change to an instrument that is both material and fraudulently made by a party to the instrument. An alteration is material when it changes the contract of any party, as by changing the date, place of payment, rate of interest, or any other important term.[14] Material alterations also include any modification that changes the number or the relationship of the parties to the paper, by adding new terms or by cutting off a part of the paper itself.

An alteration must be made to the instrument itself. An oral or a collateral written agreement between the holder and one of the parties that modifies the obligation of the party is not an "alteration" within the sense just discussed. This is true even though the obligation of a party is changed or altered thereby.

1. Person Making Alteration. By definition an alteration is a change made by a party to the instrument. A change of the instrument made by a nonparty has no effect. Recovery may be had on the instrument as though the change had not been made, provided it can be proved what the instrument had been in its original form.

2. Effect of Alteration. The fact that an instrument has been altered may be raised against any holder. Unlike other defenses, however, it is only a partial defense against a favored holder. That is, a holder in due course

---

[13]   UCC § 3–404(1); Bank of Hoven v Rausch (SD) 382 NW2d 39 (1986).

[14]   Kramer v Exchange Natl. Bank of Chicago, 118 Ill 277, --- Ill Dec ---, 515 NE2d 57 (1987).

or a holder through a holder in due course may enforce the instrument according to its original terms prior to its alteration.

For example, Ryan signed a negotiable demand note for $100, made payable to Long. A subsequent holder changed the amount from $100 to $700. A later holder in due course presented the note to Ryan for payment. Ryan would still be liable for the original amount, $100. However, if the person sued by the holder in due course has by negligence substantially contributed to making the alteration possible, that defendant is precluded or barred from asserting the defense of alteration.

6.   Adverse Claims to the Paper

Distinct from a defense that a defendant may raise against the plaintiff as a reason against paying the instrument is a claim of a third person to be the owner of the paper. Assume that a check was made payable to the order of *B*; that thereafter blank indorsements are made by *B*, *C*, and *D*; and that *E* in possession of the check appears to be the holder. *B* might then claim and show, if such be the case, that *C* had fraudulently deceived *B* into indorsing the check; that *B* therefore avoids the indorsement because of such fraud; and that accordingly the check still belongs to *B*. *B* in such a case is making an adverse claim to the instrument.

(a) EFFECT OF ADVERSE CLAIM. A holder in due course holds commercial paper free and clear from all adverse claims of any other person to the paper. This includes both equitable and legal interests of third persons and the right of a former holder to rescind negotiation.[15]

In contrast, such adverse claims may be asserted against a holder who is not a holder in due course. This means that the adverse claimant may bring an action against the holder to obtain the paper, since the law generally provides for the recovery of property by the owner from anyone else.

(b) DEFENDANT'S ASSERTION OF ADVERSE CLAIM. Ordinarily, a defendant when sued by a holder cannot raise against the holder the defense that the holder's ownership is subject to an adverse claim. This may be done only when the adverse claimant has also become a party to the action or is defending the action on behalf of the defendant.

This limitation is imposed to protect the adverse claimant from a decision in an action to which the adverse claimant was not a party. It is also imposed to prevent opening the door to perjury by giving any defendant the opportunity of beclouding the issues by raising a false claim that a third person has an adverse interest.

7.   Avoidance of Holder in Due Course Protection

In certain situations the taker of a commercial paper is denied the status of a holder in due course or is denied the protection of a holder in due course.

(a) PARTICIPATING TRANSFEREE. The seller of goods on credit frequently assigns the sales contract and buyer's promissory note to the manufacturer who made the goods, to a finance company, or to a bank. In such a case, the assignee of the seller will be a holder in due course of the buyer's commercial paper if the paper is properly negotiated and the transferee satisfies all the elements of being a holder in due course. The transferee, however, may take such an active part in the sale to the seller's customer or may be so related to the seller that it is proper to conclude that the transferee was in fact a party to the original transaction and had notice or knowledge of any defense of the buyer against the seller. This conclusion automatically bars holding that the transferee is a holder in due course.

In the *Cessna Finance* case a transferee of a promissory note and installment contract claimed holder in due course status.

---

[15]   UCC § 3–305(1), 3–207(2).

CESSNA FINANCE CORP. v WARMUS

159 Mich App 706, 407 NW2d 66 (1987)

> Warmus purchased an airplane from Cessna Aircraft. He executed an installment sales contract and promissory note. The sales contract named Cessna Finance as assignee.* After allegedly encountering mechanical difficulties with the plane, Warmus ceased payments on the installment contract. Assignee Cessna Finance, claiming holder in due course status, sued Warmus. Warmus defended on the ground that the sole consideration for the execution of the installment contract failed. Warmus also claimed that assignee financing company was so closely connected with the sales transaction that it could not be a holder in due course. From a judgment in favor of Cessna Finance Corporation, Warmus appealed.

CARNOVALE, J. . . . Warmus requested a ruling that Cessna Finance was not a holder in due course of the promissory note and installment sales contract it took by assignment from Cessna Aircraft. To support his motion, Warmus submitted: (1) Cessna Finance's admissions that it drafted the installment sales contract form used by Cessna Aircraft in defendant's purchase transaction and that its own name was preprinted thereon under "assignments"; (2) Cessna Finance's admission that it drafted the promissory note form that was used by Cessna Aircraft; (3) Cessna Finance's admission that it performed a credit check on defendant before he purchased the airplane from Cessna Aircraft; (4) the deposition testimony of Cessna Finance's administrative manager, David Carl Peaden, that more than fifty percent of Cessna Finance's income derives from the sale of aircraft manufactured by Cessna Aircraft; (5) interrogatory answers that five persons from Cessna Finance's seven-member board were on Cessna Aircraft's board at the time Warmus executed the contract, three of whom were corporate officers of Cessna Aircraft.

Cessna Finance replied with its own motion . . . predicated upon a waiver of defenses clause which provided for assignment of the contract and stated "when so assigned the contract shall be free from any claims whatsoever which buyer might have against seller."

. . . Warmus contends he may assert the defense of failure of consideration against Cessna Finance because Warmus is a party with whom the holder, Cessna Finance, has dealt. To avoid Cessna Finance's argument that only Cessna Aircraft owed a duty to Warmus under the installment sales contract, Warmus urges this Court to adopt the "close-connections" or "close-connectedness" doctrine. Under that doctrine, if the assignee financing company is closely connected with the sales transaction, it cannot claim that it is a holder in due course.

The trial court rejected Warmus' reliance on the close-connections doctrine, reasoning that the majority of states which have adopted the doctrine apply it only to consumer transactions. The court further relied on M.C.L. § 445.865(d); M.S.A. § 19.416(115)(d), which provides that holders of retail installment contracts are subject to all claims and defenses of a buyer of *consumer goods* arising out of the retail transaction, notwithstanding any other provision of law. By negative implication, the court rea-

---

* Authors' Note: In the trade, "assignment of the note and contract" is used to mean negotiation of the note and assignment of the contract.

soned that the Legislature intended no similar protection for persons such as Warmus, who enter into business transactions.

We believe that the trial judge has erred . . . because a question of fact existed as to whether Cessna Finance was a holder in due course.

[UCC §9-206] provides:

> Subject to any statute or decision which establishes a different rule for buyers or lessees of consumer goods, an agreement by a buyer or a lessee that he will not assert against an assignee any claim or defense which he may have against the seller or lessor is enforceable by an assignee who takes his assignment for value, in good faith and without notice of a claim or defense, except as to defenses of a type which may be asserted against a holder in due course of a negotiable instrument under the article on commercial paper (article 3). A buyer who as part of one transaction signs both a negotiable instrument and a security agreement makes such an agreement.

Pursuant to the above statute, an assignee may rely on an agreement precluding an assertion of certain defenses against an assignee only if the assignee is a holder in due course.

A holder in due course of an instrument is one who takes the instrument (1) for value, (2) in good faith, and (3) without notice that it is overdue or has been dishonored, or of any defenses or claims to it. [UCC § 3-302]. Holder-in-due-course status operates to insulate the holder from certain defenses to the instrument of any party with whom the holder has not dealt. However, a holder is subject to all defenses of a party with whom the holder has dealt. [UCC § 3-305]. . . .

We believe issues of material fact remain in the instant case, and thus that the question of good faith and notice should properly be submitted to the trier of fact. Evidence exists that Cessna Finance's name, as assignee, was on the preprinted form at the time of the execution of the lease agreement. Evidence exists that Cessna Finance made an independent check of Warmus' credit. Evidence exists that management of Cessna Finance and Cessna Aircraft was related by common members of their boards of directors and corporate officers. . . .

Under our disposition, it is unnecessary to adopt the close-connectedness doctrine. We believe that the doctrine is only a substitute for a proper analysis under existing law. Stated otherwise, it is unnecessary to adopt the doctrine when the issue can be properly addressed under existing law. To the extent that the factors relied on by other courts as indicative of close-connectedness are within the totality of the circumstances of a particular case, the parties may rely on them to establish that an assignee is not a holder in due course.

[Judgment reversed]

QUESTIONS

1. What is meant by the close-connections doctrine?
2. Did court adopt the doctrine?
3. What was the basis for the court's decision?

(b) THE FEDERAL TRADE COMMIS-SION RULE. In 1976, the FTC adopted a rule that to some extent limits the rights of a holder in due course in a **consumer credit transaction.** The rule protects consumers who purchase goods or services for personal, family, or household use.[16] When the buyer is sued by a finance company on the note given to the seller, the buyer may raise any defense that could have been raised against the seller if the con-

sumer's contract contains the notice required by the FTC regulation. The FTC regulation requires that the following notice be included in boldface type at least ten points in size:

NOTICE

ANY HOLDER OF THIS CONSUMER CREDIT CONTRACT IS SUBJECT TO ALL CLAIMS AND DEFENSES WHICH THE DEBTOR COULD ASSERT AGAINST THE SELLER OF GOODS OR SERVICES OBTAINED WITH THE PROCEEDS HEREOF. RECOVERY HEREUNDER BY THE DEBTOR SHALL NOT EXCEED AMOUNTS PAID BY THE DEBTOR HEREUNDER.

[16]   The regulation does not cover purchases of real estate, securities, or consumer goods or services of which the purchase price is more than $25,000. Roosevelt Federal Sav. & Loan Ass'n v Crider (Mo App) 722 SW2d 325 (1986).

SUMMARY

A holder of commercial paper can be either an ordinary holder or a favored holder. The ordinary holder has the same rights that an assignee would have. Favored holders are protected from certain defenses. Favored holders are (1) holders in due course and (2) holders through holders in due course. To be a holder in due course, a person must first be a holder; that is, the person must have acquired the paper by a proper negotiation. The holder must meet certain requirements to be a holder in due course. The holder must take for value, in good faith, without notice of paper overdue or dishonored, and without notice of defenses and adverse claims. Those persons who become holders of the instrument after a holder in due course are given the same protection as the holder in due course, provided they are not parties to any fraud or illegality affecting the instrument.

The importance of being a holder in due course or a holder through a holder in due course is that those holders are not subject to certain defenses when they demand payment or bring suit on commercial paper. These defenses are limited defenses and include ordi-

nary contract defenses, incapacity unless it makes the instrument a nullity, fraud in the inducement, prior payment or cancellation, nondelivery of an instrument, duress consisting of threats, unauthorized completion, and theft of the paper that does not result in a defect in the chain of necessary indorsements. Universal defenses may be asserted against any plaintiff, whether that party is an assignee, an ordinary holder, a holder in due course, or a holder through a holder in due course. Universal defenses include fraud as to the nature or essential terms of the paper, forgery or lack of authority, duress depriving control, infancy, illegality, and alteration. Alteration is only a partial defense; the favored holder may enforce the instrument according to its original terms.

The Federal Trade Commission provides for limiting the immunity of a holder in due course from defenses of consumer buyers against their sellers. Immunity is limited in consumer credit transactions if the notice specified by the FTC regulation is included in a sales contract.

QUESTIONS AND CASE PROBLEMS

1. What social forces are affected by the holder in due course rule?

2. Holton owes Zeigler $100. Holton draws a check on her bank payable to the order of Zeigler for $100 and delivers the check to Zeigler. The question arises as to whether Zeigler has taken the check for value. The argument is made that Zeigler did not give anything in return for the check and therefore has not given value. Is this argument correct?

3. Bushnell purchased an automobile from Gable because of the latter's fraudulent statements as to the condition of the car. Bushnell gave Gable a check drawn on the Exchange Bank for the purchase price. Gable cashed the check at the Industrial Bank. When Bushnell learned that he had been defrauded, he stopped payment on the check. Bushnell also informed the Exchange Bank and the Industrial Bank of Gable's misconduct. Industrial Bank claimed that Bushnell was liable to it on the dishonored check. Bushnell claimed that the Industrial Bank was subject to the defense of fraud in the inducement. Industrial Bank denied this, on the ground that it was a holder in due course. Bushnell claimed that Industrial Bank was not a holder in due course, because it knew of Gable's fraud. Was Bushnell correct?

4. Johnson issued an order promissory note to James. However, Johnson did not fill in James' name. Henry knew this, but nevertheless took the note from James for value, after James inserted his name and indorsed the note. Johnson did not pay on the due date, alleging lack of consideration, which was a fact. Henry brings suit. Will he recover? Why?

5. What is the underlying reasoning behind making universal defenses available against all holders?

6. Compare (a) an assignee, (b) a holder, (c) a holder in due course, and (d) a holder through a holder in due course, with respect to the defense that the defendant is seventeen years of age.

7. How does fraud as a limited defense differ from fraud as a universal defense?

8. Elliot, an officer of Impact Marketing, drew six postdated checks on Impact's account. The checks were payable to Bell for legal services to be subsequently performed for Marketing. Financial Associates purchased them from Bell. Financial collected on four of the checks. Payment was stopped on the last two when Bell's services were terminated. Financial argues that it was a holder in due course and had the right to collect on the checks. Marketing claims that since the checks were postdated and issued for an executory promise, Financial could not be a holder in due course. Who is correct? Why? [Financial Associates v Impact Marketing, 90 Misc 2d 545, 394 NYS2d 814]

9. D drew a check to the order of P. It was later claimed that P was not a holder in due course, because the check was postdated and because P knew that D was having financial difficulties and that the particular checking account on which this check was drawn had been frequently overdrawn. Do these circumstances prevent P from being a holder in due course? [Citizens Bank, Booneville v National Bank of Commerce (CA10 Okla) 334 F2d 257; Franklin National Bank v Sidney Gotowner (NY Sup Ct) 4 UCCRS 953]

10. H acquired a check by indorsement. At the time that H acquired the check, he knew of all the circumstances surrounding the original issue of the check. If H had known the legal significance of those circumstances, he would have realized that the drawer of the check had a valid defense. Because H did not know the law, he did not realize that the drawer had a defense. He took the check in good faith, believing that everything was proper. In a subsequent lawsuit on the check the question arose as to whether H was a holder in due course. The defendant claimed that H was not, because H knew of the defense based on the surrounding circumstances, and H's ignorance of the law did not excuse him from the consequence of that knowledge, because ignorance of the law is no excuse. Was H a holder in due course? [Hartford Life Ins. Co. v Title Guarantee Co., 172 App DC 156, 520 F2d 1170]

11. A customer of a bank purchased a bank money order and paid for it with a forged check. The money order was negotiable and was acquired by N, who was a holder in due course. When N sued the bank on the money order, it raised the defense that its customer had paid with a bad check. Could this defense be raised against N? [Bank of Niles v American State Bank, 14 Ill App 3d 729, 303 NE2d 186]

12. Statham drew a check. The payee indorsed it to the Kemp Motor Sales Co. Statham then stopped payment on the check on the ground

that there was a failure of consideration for the check. Kemp sued Statham on the check. When Statham raised the defense of failure of consideration, Kemp replied that it was a holder in due course. Statham claimed that Kemp could not recover because it learned of his defense before it deposited the check in its bank account. Decide. [Kemp Motor Sales v Statham, 120 Ga App 515, 171 SE2d 389]

13. Layton wished to make a gift of $2,000 to his niece, but he did not have the cash. Layton therefore executed a demand negotiable promissory note for $2,000 payable to the order of his niece, delivered the note to his niece, and stated: "You can present this note as a claim against my estate if the note is not paid before my death." The niece immediately sold the note to Richards, a holder in due course. Richards presented the note to Layton for payment, and Layton refused payment. What defense is available to Layton?

14. Shade asked Dow to give him a check for $100 in return for Shade's delivery the next day of a television set. Dow gave the check, but Shade never delivered the television set. Does Dow have a defense if sued on the instrument: (a) by Shade; (b) by Shade's brother, to whom Shade gave the check as a gift, without indorsement; (c) by a grocer to whom Shade's brother negotiated the instrument for value in the ordinary course of business the next day (the grocer took the check without knowledge of the defense and while acting in good faith)? Explain your answer.

15. Dorsey was negligent in not determining that the paper he was signing was actually a promissory note. The note was negotiated by proper indorsement and delivery to the New Jersey Mortgage and Investment Co. The evidence established that New Jersey Mortgage and Investment was a holder in due course. Dorsey refused to pay, alleging fraud as to the nature of essential terms. Decide. [New Jersey Mortgage and Investment Co. v Dorsey, 33 NJ 448, 165 A2d 297]

33

LIABILITIES OF THE PARTIES AND DISCHARGE FROM LIABILITY

The law of commercial paper relating to presentment, dishonor, and discharge is regulated by Part 5 of Article 3 of the UCC.[1] Much of this law, however, does not have practical importance because it relates to situations that rarely occur in the world of business. The following discussion is, therefore, a simplified presentation of the subject, aimed at basic requirements and the points that have given rise to litigation.

[1] See Appendices 5 and 7 for a table of sections and provisions of the 1990 revision of Article 3 that affect the law stated in this chapter.

A. PARTIES TO AN INSTRUMENT

Parties to an instrument may be classified as primary or secondary.

1. Primary Parties

Primary parties are the parties required to pay the instruments when they are due. The maker in the case of a promissory note and the drawee-acceptor in the case of a draft are primary parties. A drawee is not liable for payment of a draft before acceptance. An **acceptance** is the drawee's written and signed assent to the order of the drawer. An acceptance must be written on the draft. A drawee's refusal to accept the draft does not give the holder any right to sue the drawee on the paper. The draft does not operate as an assignment of money, even though the drawee has possession of funds of the drawer.

The liability of a primary party on an instrument continues for the period of the statute of limitations. The holder need not give the primary party any advance notice of demand.

2.   Secondary Parties

Secondary parties have conditional liability that may be enforced if the primary parties fail to pay. Secondary parties include the drawer of a draft and the unqualified indorser of a draft or a note.

B.   PRESENTMENT AND DISHONOR

The conditional liability of secondary parties cannot be enforced until three conditions precedent are met—presentment of the instrument for payment or acceptance, dishonor, and notice of dishonor.[2]

3.   Presentment

Presentment is a demand upon a drawee for acceptance or a demand upon a maker, acceptor, or indorser for payment.[3] Commercial paper should be presented to any primary party for payment at the time of maturity. However, a failure to make a presentment for payment will not discharge primary parties from their obligation. Liability continues until barred by the statute of limitations. Failure to make presentment when the paper is due will discharge all secondary parties.

(a) HOW PRESENTMENT IS MADE. Presentment must be made by or on behalf of the holder to the party primarily liable at the place specified in the instrument. The presentment must be made at a reasonable time and, if made at a bank, must be made during its banking day. It is not necessary that there be actual physical presentation of the paper, although the person to whom presentment is made usually will ask that the instrument be shown. Once the paper is paid, the holder must surrender the instrument.[4]

(b) WHEN PRESENTMENT IS EXCUSED OR UNNECESSARY. Presentment for payment may not be made for various reasons. It will be excused or unnecessary (1) if presentment has been waived by the party being charged, (2) if presentment cannot be made in spite of due diligence, (3) if the primary party has died, or (4) if the secondary party has no reason to expect that the instrument will be paid.[5]

4.   Dishonor

Dishonor occurs when an instrument has been duly presented for acceptance or payment, but acceptance or payment cannot be obtained or is refused. If proper notice has been given to the secondary parties—the drawer and the indorsers—the holder has an immediate right of recourse against them.[6]

5.   Notice of Dishonor

If commercial paper is dishonored, any secondary party who is not given proper notice thereof is released from liability, unless the giving of notice is excused.

It was a failure to give proper notice of dishonor that caused problems for the holder in the *Hane* case.

[2]   Binford v Lichtenberger Estate, 62 Or App 439, 660 P2d 1077 (1983).
[3]   UCC § 3–504(1).
[4]   UCC §§ 3–503, 3–504, 3–505.
[5]   UCC § 3–511.
[6]   UCC § 3–507.

HANE v EXTEN
255 Md 668, 259 A2d 290 (1969)

Theta Electronic Laboratories executed a promissory note payable to Thomson and his wife. The note was indorsed by Exten, O'Neil, and James Hane, and their wives. The Thomsons assigned the note to John Hane. The note was not paid when due. John Hane took judgment by confession against the maker and the Extens. Upon learning of the judgment, the Extens moved that the judgment be vacated as to them, and their motion was granted. John Hane appealed.

SINGLEY, J. . . . John B. Hane is the assignee of the note of Theta Electronic Laboratories, Inc. (Theta) in the stated amount of $15,377.07. . . . [The note provided] that "In the event of the failure to pay the interest or principal, as the same becomes due on this Note, the entire debt represented hereby shall at the end of thirty (30) days become due and demandable. . . ." The note was assigned without recourse to Hane by George B. and Marguerite F. Thomson, the original payees, on 26 November 1965. A default having occurred in the making of the monthly payments, Hane took judgments by confession in the Circuit Court for Montgomery County on 7 June 1967 against Theta and three individuals, Gerald M. Exten, Emil L. O'Neil, and James W. Hane, and their wives, who had indorsed Theta's note. On motion of the Extens, the judgment was vacated as to them. . . . From a judgment for the Extens, Hane has appealed.

This case raises the familiar question: Must Hane show that the Extens were given notice of presentment and dishonor before he can hold them on their indorsement?

The court below, in finding for the Extens, relied on the provisions of Uniform Commercial Code. . . . Section 3–414(1) provides:

Unless the indorsement otherwise specifies (as by such words as "without recourse") every indorser engages that upon dishonor and any necessary notice of dishonor and protest he will pay the instrument according to its tenor at the time of his indorsement to the holder or to any subsequent indorser who takes it up, even though the indorser who takes it up was not obligated to do so.

§ 3–501(1)(b) provides that "Presentment for payment is necessary to charge any indorser" and § 3–501(2)(a) that "Notice of any dishonor is necessary to charge any indorser," in each case subject, however, to the provisions of § 3–511 which recite the circumstances under which notice of dishonor may be waived or excused, none of which is here present. § 3–502(1)(a) makes it clear that unless presentment or notice of dishonor is waived or excused, unreasonable delay will discharge an indorser.

There was testimony from which the trier of facts could find as he did that presentment and notice of dishonor were unduly delayed.

It is clear that Hane held the note from November 1965, until some time in April, 1967, before he made demand for payment. UCC § 3–503(1)(d) provides that "Where an instrument is accelerated, presentment for payment is due within a reasonable time after the acceleration." "Reasonable time" is not defined in § 3–503, except that § 3–503(2) provides, "A reasonable time for presentment is determined by the nature of the instrument, any usage of banking or trade, and the facts of the particular case." But § 1–204(2) characterizes it: "What is a reasonable time for taking any action depends on the nature, purpose, and circumstances of such action."

Reasonableness is primarily a question for the fact finder . . . 1 Anderson's Uniform Commercial Code, Commentary, § 1–204:3. . . . We see no reason to disturb the lower court's finding that Hane's delay of almost 18 months in presenting the note "was unreasonable from any viewpoint." . . .

As regards notice of dishonor, § 3–508(2) requires that notice be given by persons other than banks "before midnight of the third business day after dishonor or receipt of notice of dishonor." Exten, called as an adverse witness by Hane, testified that his first notice that the note had not been paid was the entry of the confessed judgment on 7 June 1967. Hane's brother testified that demand had been made about 15 April 1967. He was uncertain as to when he had given Exten notice of dishonor, but finally conceded that it was "within a week." The lower court found that the ambiguity of this testimony, coupled with Exten's denial that he had received *any* notice before 7 June fell short of meeting the three-day notice requirement of the UCC. The date of giving notice of dishonor is a question of fact, solely for determination by the trier of facts. . . . We cannot say that the court erred in its finding.

In the absence of evidence that presentment and notice of dishonor were waived or excused, Hane's unreasonable delay discharged the Extens, § 3–502(1)(a). . . .

[Judgment affirmed]

QUESTIONS

1. Within what time must notice of dishonor be given?
2. Within what time must a holder in due course give notice of dishonor?

(a) HOW NOTICE IS GIVEN. Notice is ordinarily given by the holder who has been refused payment. Notice may be given in any reasonable manner, oral or written. It may have any terms, as long as it identifies the instrument and states that it has been dishonored. Any necessary notice must be given by a bank before midnight of the next banking day following the business day on which the bank receives the instrument or notice. By a nonbank, notice must be given before midnight of the third full business day following the dishonor or receipt of notice of dishonor. Written notice is effective when sent, even if it is not received.

In the *Greer* case a bank claimed that it had acted promptly in giving notice.

GREER v WHITE OAK STATE BANK
(Tex App) 673 SW2d 326 (1984)

Jack Greer and Donald Biesel owned a bowling alley. George Ford and Bowling and Billiard Supply of Dallas (B & B) had outstanding liens on the alley. Greer, Biesel, Ford, and B & B were named as beneficiaries of an insurance policy on the bowling alley. The bowling complex burned, and a check from the insurance company was issued to Greer, Biesel, Ford, and B & B. All the parties indorsed the check. The insurance check was deposited in Greer's account at the White Oak State Bank. Greer then issued checks drawn on that account to Ford and B &

B in payment of their claims. The insurance company was insolvent; therefore, the drawee bank dishonored the insurance check on August 3, 1981, and notified the White Oak Bank that same day by telephone. The oral notification was followed by written notice of dishonor, which was received by the White Oak Bank ten days later, on August 13, 1981. White Oak then notified the indorsers of the dishonor on August 14, 1981. White Oak brought suit against the indorsers on the dishonored check. They denied liability because of White Oak's failure to notify them promptly of the dishonor. From a judgment in favor of White Oak, the indorsers appealed.

CORNELIUS, C. J. . . . [UCC §§ 3–501, 3–503, and 3–502], respectively, provide that unless excused, notice of dishonor is necessary to charge any indorser of an item; notice must be given by a bank before its midnight deadline (the next banking day after the banking day it received the item); and that any unexcused delay in giving notice of dishonor discharges any indorser. The bank argues that these code provisions do not apply to Greer, Ford and B & B because (1) oral notice of dishonor is not effective and the indorsers were promptly notified after the bank received written notice of the check's dishonor on August 14, 1981, and (2) the telephone notice from the bank in Dallas did not specify that Ford and B & B were indorsers, so in any event it did not receive notice of dishonor *as to them* until August 13, 1981. We cannot agree with either of these propositions.

Section 3–508 expressly provides that notice of dishonor may be oral. The bank contends that Section 4–202(1)(b) supersedes Section 3–508 with respect to notice from a collecting bank, and because that section refers to "sending" notice of dishonor, only a written notice is contemplated. We disagree. The adequacy of oral notice is confirmed by Section 4–104(3) which specifically makes the notice of dishonor provisions of Section 3–508 applicable to transactions under Article 4. Moreover, the jury found upon sufficient evidence that White Oak State Bank and the First National Bank in Dallas had agreed prior to August 3, 1981, that notice of returned items could be sent by telephone. The requirements of Article 4 may be modified by agreement.

The failure of the telephone notice to name Ford and B & B as indorsers did not render the notice ineffective as to them. Section 3–502(1)(a) provides that if notice of dishonor is not given when due, *any* indorser is discharged. Delay in giving notice may be excused when a party does not know it is due or when the delay is caused by circumstances beyond his control. But there was no jury finding here that any circumstance existed which would excuse the Bank from notifying Ford and B & B. In fact, the employee who received the telephone notice testified that the information she received was sufficient to enable her to identify the check and all parties to it.

As indicated, Greer, Ford and B & B were all discharged, *as indorsers*, from any obligation on the check. . . .

[Judgment reversed]

QUESTIONS

1. What was the argument of White Oak Bank?
2. Why is it important for indorsers to receive timely notice of dishonor?
3. State the decision of the court and the basis for the decision.

(b) EXCUSE FOR DELAY OR ABSENCE OF NOTICE OF DISHONOR. Delay in giving notice of dishonor is excused under the same circumstances as delay in making presentment for payment. It is excused for any of the following: (1) waiver, (2) inability to give notice in spite of due diligence, and (3) the fact that the party notified did not have any reason to believe that the instrument would be paid.[7]

[7] UCC § 3–511.

FIGURE 33–1   LIABILITIES OF PARTIES FOR PAYMENT

PARTY	PRIMARY LIABILITY	SECONDARY LIABILITY
ACCEPTOR	X	
DRAWEE		
DRAWER		X
GUARANTOR OF PAYMENT	X	
MAKER OF NOTE	X	
UNQUALIFIED INDORSER		X

C.   DISCHARGE FROM LIABILITY

A party may be discharged individually or by some act that discharges all parties to the paper at one time.

6.   Discharge of Individual Parties

A party to a commercial paper, just as a party to an ordinary contract, is usually discharged from liability when payment is made to the proper person. The discharge from liability may also be effected in a number of other ways.

(a) THE LAW OF CONTRACTS. Commercial paper may be discharged in the same manner as an ordinary contract for the payment of money. Accordingly, there may be a discharge by accord and satisfaction, by a novation, or by operation of law, such as a discharge in bankruptcy and the operation of the statute of limitations.[8]

(b) PAYMENT. The obligation of a particular party on commercial paper is discharged by payment of the amount of the instrument to the holder or to the holder's authorized agent.[9] Payment to anyone else is not effective to discharge the liability of the payor.

(c) CANCELLATION AND RENUNCIATION. The holder of an instrument may discharge the liability of a party by placing something indicative of discharge on the paper. For example, the holder may intentionally mark the instrument canceled or may destroy or mutilate the instrument or a party's signature. There is no cancellation when the paper is destroyed by accident or mistake.

A holder can also discharge a party's liability by renouncing the holder's rights against the party in a written paper to that effect, delivered with the instrument or by surrendering the instrument to the party to be discharged.[10]

[8] Duke v Young (Ala) 496 So 2d 37 (1986).

[9] UCC § 3–603(1).
[10] UCC § 3–605.

No consideration is needed for a discharge by cancellation or renunciation.

In the *Ohio Casualty* case a maker of a promissory note claimed a discharge by cancellation.

OHIO CAS. INS. CO. v YAKLICH
(Colo App) 768 P2d 1274 (1989)

West was indebted to Midtown National Bank up to his maximum allowable credit limit. Because West could not borrow additional funds from the Midtown National Bank, Yaklich borrowed $16,000 from the Midtown National Bank for West and executed a promissory note to the bank in that amount. The due date of the note was extended twice by agreements signed by Yaklich. Yaklich made no payments on the note. Some time thereafter, the note was stamped "Paid" by Vergo, then president of the bank, and the note was surrendered to West, who delivered it to Yaklich. Vergo's actions in this regard were done in connection with an extensive fraud scheme being perpetrated by him. Because of many problems, the bank was liquidated by the FDIC. FDIC made demand upon Ohio Casualty for payment of the note. Ohio Casualty had issued its own bond covering the bank for misdeeds of its officers and employees, including Vergo. Under the bond provisions, Ohio Casualty paid FDIC the amount due on Yaklich's note and received an assignment of the right to attempt collection on the note. Yaklich failed to pay the note, and Ohio Casualty sued. From a judgment in favor of Ohio Casualty, Yaklich appealed.

JONES, J. . . . We disagree with Yaklich's contention that the trial court erred in not applying [UCC § 3-605], which provides for discharge if the holder, by any means, cancels the instrument.

The trial court found that Yaklich's liability was not discharged under [UCC § 3-605], notwithstanding the fact that the note was stamped "Paid" and returned to Yaklich, because the act of Vergo in taking such illegal action was clearly beyond his authority and is not binding on the Bank.

Section 3-605(1) . . . provides:

The holder of an instrument may even without consideration discharge any party:

(a) In any manner apparent on the face of the instrument or the indorsement, as by intentionally cancelling the instrument or the party's signature by destruction or mutilation, or by striking out the party's signature; or

(b) By renouncing his rights by a writing signed and delivered or by surrender of the instrument to the party to be discharged.

Despite the language of § 3-605, a cancellation or renunciation has no effect when made by a person without authority from the holder. . . . The same is true if cancellation or renunciation is made unintentionally or by mistake. . . .

Moreover, a cancellation induced through fraud does not act to discharge the parties. . . .

We agree with the trial court that, inasmuch as the note had not been paid, Vergo was without authority to indicate otherwise or to surrender it to Yaklich. . . .

Yaklich's reliance on *First National Bank v. Wich*, 62 Colo. 119, 160 P. 1036 (1916) is misplaced. In that case, the bank's cashier signed a memorandum which promised to deliver shares of capital stock to a borrower in exchange for the borrower's note in the amount of $570, payable to the bank. The cashier failed to secure the stock so that the borrower received no consideration for the note. That case is distinguishable from the present case in that there the cashier acted to benefit the bank, not himself. Here, Yaklich received consideration for the note, and Vergo's acts were for his own benefit, and to the detriment of the bank, and also defrauded third-party customers of the bank.

[Judgment affirmed]

QUESTIONS

1. What is the difference between cancellation and renunciation?
2. What was the argument of Yaklich?
3. What was the basis for the decision of the court?

(d) IMPAIRMENT OF RIGHT OF RECOURSE OR OF COLLATERAL. A holder may, in some cases, extend the time of payment, release the principal debtor, or impair collateral security furnished as security for the payment of the instrument. Such actions discharge any party whose rights are affected by such impairment.[11]

(e) ALTERATION. When an instrument is altered (that is, materially and fraudulently changed by the holder), any party whose obligation is changed thereby is discharged. Exceptions exist if such party has assented to the alteration or is barred by conduct from asserting a discharge. The effect of the discharge is limited, however, for a holder in due course may enforce the paper according to its original terms.[12]

7.   Discharge of all Parties

The primary party on an instrument—that is, the maker of a note or the acceptor of a draft—has no right of recourse against any party to the paper. Conversely, every other party who may be liable on the paper has a right of recourse against the party primarily liable. If the holder discharges in any way a party who is primarily liable, all parties to the instrument are discharged.[13]

When a party primarily liable on the paper reacquires it as owner at any time, the instrument is then held by the one who has no right to sue any other party on the instrument. Such reacquisition therefore discharges the liability of all intervening parties to the instrument.

No discharge is effective against a holder in due course unless such holder has notice of the discharge when taking the instrument.[14]

[13]   Heintz v Woodson (Mo App) 714 SW2d 782 (1986).
[14]   UCC § 3–602. As an exception to this rule, a holder in due course is subject to a discharge in insolvency proceedings of any party, even though the paper was taken without notice or knowledge of such discharge. UCC § 3–305(2)(e).

[11]   Valley Bank & Trust v Rite Way Concrete (Utah App) 742 P2d 105 (1987).
[12]   UCC § 3–407.

SUMMARY

The maker of a promissory note and the acceptor of a draft are primarily liable for paying the face of the instrument. Payment may be demanded from the maker or acceptor as soon as the paper is due.

Secondary parties are required to pay the

paper if the primary party failed to do so after proper presentment and if proper notice of default was given to the secondary party.

Presentment and notice of dishonor may be excused under certain circumstances.

Dishonor occurs when an instrument has been duly presented for acceptance or payment but such acceptance or payment cannot be obtained or is refused. Upon proper notice to the secondary parties of such refusal or inability to obtain acceptance or payment, the holder has an immediate right of recourse against them. Any secondary party not given proper notice will be discharged from liability on the instrument. Notice of dishonor is excused under the same circumstances as delay in making presentment for payment. Notice may be given in any reasonable manner; it may be oral or written; and it must be given (if the holder is not a bank) before midnight of the third full business day after dishonor.

A party may be discharged individually or by some act that has discharged all parties to the paper at one time. There may be a discharge by accord and satisfaction, novation, or operation of law. There may be a discharge by payment of the instrument to the holder or the holder's authorized agent by cancellation, renunciation, impairment of right of recourse or of collateral, or by an alteration.

A discharge of the party primarily liable discharges all persons who had a right of recourse against the primary party. No discharge is effective against a holder in due course, unless such holder has notice of the discharge when taking the instrument.

QUESTIONS AND CASE PROBLEMS

1. What social forces are affected by the rule that giving notice of dishonor to a secondary party before midnight of the third business day following dishonor is sufficient?

2. Ragno borrows money from the Main Street Bank and gives a promissory note for the amount of the loan. The note is due in 60 days. Main Street indorses and delivers the note to the Third National Bank. Ragno fails to pay the note when it is due. A month after it is due, the Third National Bank sues the Main Street Bank for the amount of the note. Is it liable?

3. Henri draws a draft on Marchamp, directing Marchamp to pay $1,000 on demand to the order of Clara. Marchamp is indebted to Henri for $10,000. When Clara presents the draft of Henri, Marchamp refuses to make any payments to Clara. Clara sues Marchamp. Can she recover?

4. Compare a note and draft both payable at a definite time with regard to the need of presentment for payment with respect to (a) the maker, (b) an acceptor, and (c) an unqualified indorser.

5. Charles executed a promissory note payable to Smith. The payee indorsed the note to the Standard Sewing Machine Company. When the maker refused to pay the instrument, Smith was orally notified of the dishonor. The note was described so that Smith could identify it. Did this constitute sufficient notice? Explain.

6. Four promissory notes were executed by Continental Diamond Mines, Inc., payable to the order of M. Kopp. The notes were thereafter indorsed to M. Kopp, Inc., and then to Rafkin. Rafkin was the holder on the due date. Was it necessary for him to make a presentment of the notes to Continental Diamond Mines in order to hold it liable on the notes? [Rafkin v Continental Diamond Mines, Inc. 33 Misc 2d 156, 228 NYS2d 317]

7. A indorsed a promissory note on the back. At the top of the back, above all indorsements, there were printed the words "Notice of protest waived." The note was not paid when due. The holder sent A notice that the note was not paid, but A did not receive the notice because it was sent to a former address at which he no longer lived. A denied liability because he had not been properly notified. Decide. [Lizza Asphalt Construction Co. v Greenvale Construction Co. (NY Sup Ct) 4 UCCRS 954]

8. Mellen-Wright Lumber Co., the holder of a note, sued McNett, as maker, and Kendall, as indorser. The latter claimed that he had not received notice of the dishonor of the note by the maker. The holder proved that he had sent the following letter, dated June 10, to Kendall.

Dear Sir: We hold note for $2,000 with interest at 7 percent signed by Earl P. McNett and

Anna J. McNett, his wife, on which you indorsed guaranteeing payment.

This note will be due June 12 and we are going to ask that you arrange to pay same promptly. We would appreciate this being paid by not later than Friday, June 18.

Kindly advise if you wish to make payment at our office or at one of our local banks.

We are enclosing a stamped self-addressed envelope for reply.

Was Kendall liable? [Mellen-Wright Lumber Co. v McNett, 242 Mich 369, 218 NW 709]

9. On August 15 Janet borrowed $3,000 from Richard, giving Richard in return a negotiable promissory note for $3,000, payable to the order of Richard. The note was due in 30 days. On September 10th Richard indorsed the note to the Alden Car Co. On September 12th, Alden Car Co. learned that Janet was seriously ill. Alden Car Co. wrote Janet that they were discharging her from liability on the instrument. On the due date, Alden Car Co. asked Richard to pay the note as an indorser, explaining why they did not collect from Janet. Is Richard obligated to pay?

10. As part of a business plan, Schwald executed and delivered a note to Montgomery. The parties then made a new business arrangement, and Montgomery intentionally tore up the note and threw it into the wastebasket. It was subsequently contended that this note had been cancelled. Do you agree? [Montgomery v Schwald, 117 Mo App 75, 166 SW 831]

11. Gorman executed and delivered to the First National Bank a negotiable promissory note payable to its order. The note was stolen from the bank. Some time later, Richardson, a former employee of the bank, delivered the note to Gorman in return for Gorman's payment of the balance then due. The note was returned to Gorman, marked "paid." First National Bank sued Gorman for the balance of the loan. He raised the defense that the note had been discharged by payment. Decide. [First National Bank v Gorman, 45 Wyo 519, 21 P2d 549]

12. Paul Heyman indorsed a note executed by his son as maker. His son defaulted on the note. When Heyman was sued as indorser, he claimed that he was discharged, since a proper presentment on his son had not been made. The holder replied that the son had disappeared and, after reasonable diligence, such a presentment could not be made and was therefore excused. Decide. [Gaffin v Heyman (RI) 428 A2d 1066]

13. The Citizens State Bank issued a cashier's check payable to the order of Donovan. He indorsed it to Denny, who did business as the Houston Aircraft Co., and included in the indorsement a recital that it was "in full satisfaction of any and all claims of any character whatever." Denny crossed out this quoted phrase and wrote Donovan and the bank that he had done so. The Houston Aircraft Co. sued the Citizens National Bank on the check. Was the bank liable? [Houston Aircraft v Citizens State Bank (Tex Civ App) 184 SW2d 335]

14. The holder of a note failed to present it to the maker for payment. The maker proves that he had the money ready for payment on the due date. Since that time, however, he has had some disastrous business losses. He now contends that he need not pay. Is the maker liable? Why?

15. First Properties, Inc. issued a promissory note to the order of Fletcher. Fletcher indorsed the note to Dannon, who in turn took the note to his bank for collection. The teller at the bank mistakenly stamped the note "paid," although payment had not yet been received. Dannon had no knowledge that the note was so stamped. The creditors of First Properties, Inc. raised the question of whether the note had been canceled. Decide.

34

CHECKS AND FUNDS TRANSFERS

A deposit of money to the depositor's credit in a bank creates the relationship of debtor and creditor between the bank and depositor. This deposit creates a liability on the bank to repay upon demand, on the written order of the depositor, the credit established. This written order is known as a *check*.

A. CHECKS

In business the majority of money obligations are settled by means of checks. By using checks it is possible to make payment safely and conveniently, without the need for safeguarding a shipment of money. The checkbook stub and the canceled check make a written record that may be used at a later date to show that payment was made.

1. Nature of a Check

A **check** is a particular kind of draft. The first three of the following features of a check distinguish it from other drafts or bills of exchange.[1]

(a) DRAWEE. The drawee of a check is always a bank.

(b) SUFFICIENT FUNDS ON DEPOSIT. As a practical matter, the check is drawn on the assumption that the bank has on deposit in the drawer's account an amount sufficient to pay the check. In the case of a draft there is no assumption that the drawee has any of the drawer's money with which to pay the instrument. Actually, the rights of the parties are not affected by the fact that the depositor does not have sufficient funds on deposit with the bank to pay the check.

If a draft is dishonored, the drawer is civilly liable. If a check is drawn with intent to defraud the person to whom it is delivered, the drawer is also subject to criminal prosecution in most states under what are known as *bad check laws*. Most states provide that if the check is not made good within a stated period, such as ten days, it will be presumed that the check was originally issued with the intent to defraud.

(c) DEMAND PAPER. A check is demand paper. A draft may be payable either on demand or at a future date. The standard form of check does not specify when it is payable, and it is therefore automatically payable on demand. This eliminates the need for an acceptance, since the holder of the check will merely present it for payment.

One exception arises when a check is postdated, that is, when the check shows a date later than the actual date of execution. Here the check is not payable until the date arrives.[2] This, in effect, changes the check from demand paper to time paper without expressly stating so.

While it is customary for banks to supply depositors with printed forms of checks, a check may be any writing.[3] A card, given to a computer terminal located away from a bank for the purpose of withdrawing money from the bank or making a repayment on a loan, is also a check.[4]

(d) DELIVERY NOT ASSIGNMENT. The delivery of a check is not an assignment of the money on deposit. Therefore, it does not automatically transfer the rights of the depositor against the bank to the holder of the check. There is no duty on the part of the drawee bank to the holder to pay the holder the amount of the check.[5]

---

[1] Checks are governed by both Article 3 of the UCC relating to commercial paper and Article 4 governing bank deposits and collections. See Appendices 5 to 8 for table of sections and for provisions of the 1990 revisions of Articles 3 and 4 that affect the law stated in this chapter.

[2] Howells, Inc. v Nelson (Utah) 565 P2d 1147 (1977).
[3] The printed bank check is preferable because it generally carries magnetic ink figures that facilitate sorting and posting.
[4] Illinois v Continental Illinois National Bank (CA7 Ill) 536 F2d 176 (1976).
[5] UCC § 3–409(1). Galaxy Boat Mfg. Co. v East End State Bank (Tex App) 641 SW2d 594 (1982).

FIGURE 34–1   DIFFERENCES BETWEEN A CHECK AND A DRAFT

CHECK	DRAFT
1. DRAWEE IS ALWAYS A BANK 2. CHECK IS DRAWN ON ASSUMPTION MONEY IN BANK TO COVER CHECK 3. CHECK IS PAYABLE ON DEMAND (UNLESS POSTDATED)	1. DRAWEE IS NOT NECESSARILY A BANK 2. NO ASSUMPTION DRAWEE HAS ANY OF DRAWER'S MONEY TO PAY INSTRUMENT 3. DRAFT MAY BE PAYABLE ON DEMAND OR AT FUTURE DATE

2.   Certified Checks

The drawee bank may certify or accept a check drawn on it. The certification must be written on the check and signed by an authorized representative of the bank.

When a bank certifies a check, it will set aside in a special account maintained by the bank as much of the depositor's account as is needed to pay the certified check. With respect to the holder of the check, the certification is an undertaking by the bank that when the check is presented for payment, the bank will make payment according to the terms of the check. Payment is without regard to the standing of the depositor's account at that time.

A check may be certified by a bank upon the request of the drawer or the holder. In the latter case all prior indorsers and the drawer are released from liability.[6] Since the holder could have received payment, as the bank was willing to certify the check, and since the holder did not take the payment but chose to take the certification, the prior secondary parties are released from liability. When the certification is obtained by the drawer, there is no release of the secondary parties.

3.   Liability of Drawer

If the check is presented for payment and paid, no liability of the drawer arises. If the bank refuses to make payment, the drawer is then subject to the same liability as in the case of the nonpayment of an ordinary draft. If proper notice of dishonor is not given the drawer of the check,[7] the drawer will be discharged from liability to the same extent as the drawer of an ordinary draft.

4.   The Depositor-Bank Relationship

The depositor-bank relationship imposes duties upon the bank.

(a) PRIVACY. The bank owes the depositor the duty of maintaining secrecy concerning information that the bank acquires in connection with the depositor-bank relationship. Law enforcement officers and administrative agencies cannot require the disclosure of information relating to a depositor's account without obtaining the depositor's consent or a search warrant, or following the statutory procedures designed to protect depositors from unreasonable invasions of privacy.[8]

(b) PAYMENT. A bank is under a general contractual duty to its depositor to pay on demand all checks to the extent of the funds in the depositor's account. When the bank breaches this contract, the bank is liable to the drawer for damages. As in the case of an unaccepted draft, in the absence of an independent contractual duty, the bank owes no duty to the holder to accept or pay a check.

1. Stale Checks. A bank acting in good faith may pay a check presented more than six months after its date (commonly known as a **stale check**), but unless the check is certified, the bank is not required to do so. The fact that a bank may refuse to pay a check that is more than six months old does not mean that it must pay a check that is less than six months old or that it is not required to exercise reasonable care in making payment of any check.

2. Payment After Depositor's Death. Subject to certain exceptions, the authority of a bank to act with respect to its depositor's check terminates with the death of the depositor. As an exception to this general rule, the drawee bank's power continues for some time after the death of the depositor. For the first ten days after the depositor's death, the bank may continue to pay or certify checks of the depositor even though it knows of the depositor's death, unless ordered to stop payment by a person claiming an interest in the account.[9] If the bank does not know of the death of the drawer, its power to pay and certify checks of the depositor continues for ten days after being notified of the death.

---

[6]   UCC § 3–411(1). Sherwin-Williams Co. v Sarrett (Miss) 405 So 2d 842 (1981).

[7]   Under Federal Reserve regulations notice of dishonor may be given by telephone. Security Bank and Trust Co. v Federal Nat. Bank (Okla App) 554 P2d 119 (1976).

[8]   Right to Financial Privacy Act of 1978, PL 95–630, 92 Stat 3697, 12 USC § 3401 et seq.

[9]   UCC § 4–405.

5. Stopping Payment of Check

The drawer may **stop payment** of a check by notifying the drawee bank not to pay it when it is presented for payment. This procedure is useful when a check is lost or mislaid. A duplicate check can be written, and, to make sure that the payee does not receive payment twice or that an improper person does not receive payment on the first check, payment on the first check can be stopped. Likewise, if payment is made by check and then the payee de-faults on the contract, so that the drawer would have a claim for breach of contract, payment on the check can be stopped, provided the check has not been paid.

The drawer cannot stop payment of a certified check. A bank customer cannot stop payment of a cashier's check.

The *First Financial* case involved the question of whether payment could be stopped on a cashier's check.

FIRST FINANCIAL BANK v FIRST AMERICAN BANK
(La App) 489 So 2d 388 (1986)

First Financial filed suit against First American Bank, seeking payment of a cashier's check issued by First American to First Financial in the amount of eighteen hundred dollars ($1,800). First American had issued its cashier's check in exchange for a personal check on which a stop payment order had been issued. From a judgment in favor of First Financial, First American appealed.

WICKER, J. . . . On Friday, May 3, 1985, Mrs. Tommy Marzoni, a customer of First American, deposited a personal check in the amount of Eighteen Hundred Dollars ($1,800.00) into First Financial. The check was drawn on her account at First American. On that same date, she spoke to Cindy Pilgram, an employee at First American, and informed her that she wished to stop payment on her personal check. She was informed, however, that she would have to place her request in writing. Consequently, she appeared at First American on Monday, May 6, 1985 at 9:00 a.m. to institute the stop payment order. On that same date, subsequent to her written request, but prior to the time at which all window tellers could be informed of the order, one of First Financial's employees appeared at First American and presented the personal check to Gloria Detillier, a cashier at First American, and requested a cashier's check in exchange. Such a check in the amount of Eighteen Hundred Dollars ($1,800.00) was issued by First American in exchange for Mrs. Marzoni's personal check.

Shortly thereafter, the employees of First American learned of the stop payment order on the personal check and immediately notified First Financial that the bank would not honor the cashier's check. On Tuesday, May 7, 1985, First American issued a stop payment order on its cashier's check. Prior to that order reaching First Financial, it credited the amount to pay off a loan in the name of Mr. Tommy Marzoni and to credit the account of Mrs. Marzoni with the remaining funds. The amount so credited to the account was subsequently withdrawn prior to the stop payment order on the cashier's check reaching First Financial. . . .

This appeal presents questions of first impression in this jurisdiction, namely, whether a bank can stop payment on its cashier's check and whether it can assert a defense of failure of consideration in that payment on the personal check accepted in exchange for the cashier's check had been stopped. . . .

Louisiana's version of Articles 1, 3, 4 and 5 of the Uniform Commercial Code (U.C.C.) and Articles 7 and 8 is contained in L.S.A.- R.S. 10:1-101 et seq. Our version is similar to that of the U.C.C. in that it also has only one reference to cashier's checks. L.S.A.-R.S. 10:4-211 provides in pertinent part that:

> 1) A collecting bank may take in settlement of an item . . .
>
> (b) a *cashier's check* or similar primary obligation of a remitting bank which is a member of or clears through a member of the same clearing house or group as the collecting bank. . . .

A review of our Louisiana jurisprudence reveals that no court has specifically addressed the issue of whether a bank can stop payment on its own cashier's check. . . .

Since Louisiana law does not address the issue of whether a bank can stop payment on its cashier's check or whether it can assert the defense of failure of consideration, we now turn to a view of other jurisdictions to determine their treatment of such a check.

The majority of jurisdictions define a cashier's check as a substitute for cash.

Most of the courts which follow the majority view disallow defenses on the part of the issuing bank.

New York courts in particular have favored a rule which opposes the stopping of payment of a cashier's check. In *Kaufman [v Chase Manhattan Bank*, 370 F Supp 276 (SDNY 1973)] the court summarized New York law as having accorded a special status to a cashier's check as follows:

> An ordinary check is an order by one party (drawer) directing a second party (drawee) to pay, on demand, a fixed sum of money to a third party (payee). The drawer is primarily liable to the payee for the amount of the check until that check has been accepted by the drawee. Payment on the check may be stopped by the drawer only if the drawee receives notice prior to acceptance. . . .
>
> *A cashier's check, however, is a check drawn by the bank upon itself, payable to another person, and issued by an authorized officer of the bank. The bank, therefore, becomes both the drawer and drawee; and the check becomes a promise by the bank to draw the amount of the check from its own resources and to pay the check upon demand. Thus, the issuance of the cashier's check constitutes an acceptance by the issuing bank; and the cashier's check becomes the primary obligation of the bank. . . .*

. . . The *Kaufman* court looked to the public policy regarding the nature and usage of cashier's checks in the commercial world and the fact that such a policy would favor a rule which prohibits the stop payment of a cashier's check.

The rationale behind an approach which treats cashier's checks as cash equivalents is explained in the leading case of *National Newark & Essex Bank [v Giordano*, III NJ Super 347, 268 A2d 327 (1970)] as follows:

> a cashier's check circulates in the commercial world as the equivalent of cash. . . . People accept a cashier's check as a substitute for cash because the bank stands behind it, rather than an individual. In effect the bank becomes a guarantor of the value of the check and pledges its resources to the payment of the amount represented upon presentation. To allow the bank to stop payment on such an instrument would be inconsistent with the representation it makes in issuing the check.

Such a rule would undermine the public confidence in the bank and its checks and thereby deprive the cashier's check of the essential incident which makes it useful. People would no longer be willing to accept it as a substitute for cash if they could not be sure that there would be no difficulty in converting it into cash. . . .

In contrast, a minority of the jurisdictions look to the status of the instrument and view the cashier's check as a negotiable instrument. Of this minority, most of these courts view it as a bank draft, the others view it as a negotiable promissory note.

These courts, however, do recognize the validity of certain defenses to payment. In the instant case, appellant raises the defense of lack of consideration. It contends that since it issued a cashier's check for a personal check which it subsequently learned had a stop payment order, it received no consideration and thus can assert this defense. It relies on the legal analysis which treats the cashier's check as a negotiable instrument subject to the defenses relative to a holder or a holder in due course.

We adhere to the majority view that a cashier's check is a substitute for cash or a cash equivalent. Moreover, we adopt the analysis used by several courts of applying U.C.C. Section 4-303(1)(a) to prohibit a bank from asserting a defense to payment of a cashier's check.

In *Kaufman, supra*, the court held that:

> Since a cashier's check is a bank's primary obligation, a cashier's check is presumed to have been issued for value. This presumption cannot be overcome by evidence that the bank did not receive consideration for the cashier's check from the payee. Such proof is irrelevant and provides no defense.

By its act of issuing the cashier's check, the bank undertakes a primary obligation to pay the amount when presented. In particular, it undertakes the obligation to pay the amount from its own resources.

The applicable section in our statute is L.S.A.-R.S. 10:4-303(1)(a) which provides that:

> (1) Any knowledge, notice or stop-order received by, legal process served upon or setoff exercised by a payor bank, whether or not effective under other rules of law to terminate, suspend or modify the bank's right or duty to pay an item or to charge its customer's account for the item, comes too late to so terminate, suspend or modify such right or duty if the knowledge, notice, stop-order or legal process is received or served and a reasonable time for the bank to act thereon expires or the setoff is exercised after the bank has done any of the following:
>   (a) accepted or certified the item. . . .

Accordingly, since L.S.A.-R.S. 10:4-303(1)(a) disallows stop payment orders on accepted items, the bank cannot issue a stop payment order on its cashier's check. Thus, any defenses allowed in L.S.A.-R.S. 10:3-305 and 306 relative to the status of holder or holder in due course do not apply. Moreover, the court in *Kaufman, supra*, felt that the bank could have protected itself by ensuring that it had received payment before issuing.

Considering the law and the views expressed, we hold that a cashier's check is a cash equivalent and therefore a bank is prohibited from issuing a stop payment order on its own cashier's check for failure of consideration.

QUESTIONS

1. What is meant by a cashier's check?
2. What was the argument of the appellant, First American?
3. What reason did the court give for rejecting the argument of the appellant?

(a) FORM OF STOP PAYMENT ORDER. The stop payment order may be either oral or written. If oral, however, it is only binding on the bank for 14 calendar days unless confirmed in writing within that time. A written stop payment order or confirmation is effective for six months.

(b) LIABILITY TO HOLDER FOR STOPPING PAYMENT. The act of stopping payment may in some cases make the depositor liable to the holder of the check. If the depositor has no proper ground for stopping payment, the depositor is liable to the holder of the check. In any case the depositor is liable for stopping payment with respect to any holder in due course or other party having the rights of a holder in due course, unless payment was stopped for a reason that may be asserted against such a holder as a defense. The fact that payment of a check has been stopped does not affect its negotiable character.[10]

6. Time of Presentment of Check for Payment

In order to charge a secondary party to demand paper, presentment for payment must generally be made on the primary party to the instrument within a reasonable time after that secondary party has signed it. Reasonable time is determined by the nature of the instrument, by commercial usage, and by the facts of the particular case.[11]

Failure to make timely presentment discharges all prior indorsers of the instrument. It also discharges the drawer, if the draft was payable at a bank, to the extent that the drawer has lost, through the bank's failure, money that was on deposit at the bank to meet the payment of the instrument.[12]

The UCC establishes two presumptions as to what is a reasonable time in which to present a check for payment.[13] If the check is not certified and is both drawn and payable within the United States, it is presumed as to the drawer that 30 days after the date of the check or the date of its issuance, whichever is later, is the reasonable period in which to make presentment for payment. With respect to the liability of an indorser, seven days after indorsing is presumed to be a reasonable time.[14]

7. Dishonor of Check

When a check is dishonored by nonpayment, the holder must follow the same procedure of notice to the secondary parties as in the case of a draft or bill of exchange in order to hold them liable for payment. As in the case of any drawer of a draft or bill of exchange who countermands payment, notice of dishonor need not be given to the drawer who has stopped payment on a check. Notice is also excused under any circumstances that would excuse notice in the case of a promissory note. For example, no notice need be given a drawer or an indorser who knows that insufficient funds to cover the check are on deposit, since such party has no reason to expect that the check will be paid by the bank.[15]

---

[10] Runkel v First Nat. Bank of Devils Lake (ND) 393 NW2d 265 (1986).
[11] UCC § 3–503(1)(e),(2).

[12] UCC § 3–502(1).
[13] A presumption means that, in the absence of evidence that supports a contrary conclusion, the trier of fact must find the existence of the fact presumed. UCC § 1–201(31).
[14] UCC § 3–503(2).
[15] UCC § 3–511(2)(b).

When a check is sent in the course of the collection process to the bank on which it is drawn, that bank must either pay or promptly return the check as unpaid, or send notice of its dishonor, as by returning the check unpaid for "insufficient funds." If the drawee bank does not act before its midnight deadline, it automatically becomes liable for the face of the instrument.[16] Oral notice of dishonor is sufficient.

(a) BANK'S LIABILITY TO DRAWER OF CHECK. The contract between the depositor (drawer) and the bank (drawee) obligates the latter to pay in accordance with the orders of its depositor as long as there is sufficient money on deposit to make such payment. If the bank improperly refuses to make payments, it is liable to the drawer for damages sustained by the drawer in consequence of such dishonor.

(b) BANK'S LIABILITY TO HOLDER. If the check has not been certified, the holder has no claim against the bank for the dishonor of the check, regardless of the fact that the bank acted in breach of its contract with its depositor. A bank that certified the check is liable to the holder when it dishonors the check. The certification imposes on the bank a primary liability to pay the face amount of the check.

The liability of secondary parties on the check is not affected by whether the holder has any right against the drawee bank.

8.   Agency Status of Collecting Bank

When a person deposits a commercial paper in a bank, the bank is ordinarily thereby made an agent to collect or obtain the payment of the paper. Unless the contrary intent clearly appears, a bank receiving an item is deemed to take it as agent for the depositor rather than as purchaser of the paper. This presumption is not affected by the form of the indorsement or by the absence of any indorsement. The bank is also regarded as being merely an agent even though the depositor has the right to make immediate withdrawals against the deposited item.[17] In consequence of the agency status, the depositor remains the owner of the item and is therefore subject to the risks of ownership involved in its collection, in the absence of fault on the part of any collecting bank.[18]

When a bank cashes a check deposited by its customer or cashes a check drawn by its customer on the strength of a deposited check, it is a holder of the check deposited by its customer. The bank may sue the parties thereon, even though as between the customer and the bank the latter is an agent for collection and has the right to charge back the amount of the deposited check if it cannot be collected. When the bank receives final settlement for an item taken for collection, the agency status ends, and the bank is merely a debtor of its customer, just as though the customer had made an ordinary cash deposit in the bank.[19]

B.   LIABILITY OF BANK FOR IMPROPER PAYMENT AND COLLECTION

The drawee bank may be liable for paying a check contrary to a stop payment order or when there has been a forgery or alteration.

9.   Payment over a Stop Payment Order

A bank must be given a reasonable time to put a stop payment order into effect. However, if the bank makes payment of a check after it has been properly notified to stop payment, it is liable to the depositor for the loss the depositor sustains, in the absence of a valid limitation of the bank's liability.[20] The burden of establishing the loss resulting in such case rests upon the depositor. In the *Tusso* case the court found that one and one-half hours was a reasonable time to put the stop payment order into effect.

---

[16]   UCC § 4–302, 4–104(1)(h). Southwest Nat. Bank v ATG Const. 241 Kan 257, 736 P2d 894 (1987).

[17]   UCC § 4–201(1).
[18]   UCC § 4–202.
[19]   Cooper v Union Bank, 9 Cal 3d 123, 107 Cal Rptr 1, 507 P2d 609 (1973).
[20]   UCC § 4–403(2).

TUSSO v SECURITY NATIONAL BANK
349 NYS2d 914 (1973)

Tusso sent a check for $600, drawn on the Security National Bank, to the Adamson Company. He then realized that he had already paid Adamson. Tusso was at the bank the next morning at 9:00 a.m. when it opened. He notified the bank to stop payment on the $600 check he had written the day before. At 10:40 a.m., about an hour and a half later, the payee arrived at the bank with the check. The bank certified the check and charged it to Tusso's account. Tusso sued the bank to recover the amount so charged. The bank claimed that he was required to prove that the bank was negligent.

COLANERI, J. . . . The bank's . . . defense is incorrect. [UCC §] 4–403(1) entitles a bank customer to stop payment on his check by giving notice to that effect "at such time and in such manner as to afford the bank a reasonable opportunity to act on it prior to any action by the bank with respect to the item. . . . " The statute does not place any other affirmative burden of proof upon the plaintiff with respect to the stop payment order other than the "burden of establishing the fact and amount of loss resulting from the payment of an item contrary to a binding stop payment order. . . . " (UCC § 4–403(3)). . . .

To read into this statute the additional requirement that the drawer prove the commission of a negligent act by the bank in order to recover would, in effect, alter the statute in a manner not intended by the legislature. . . . A valid stop payment order received by the bank prior to payment or certification renders subsequent payment wrongful, whether or not the bank was shown to be negligent in making such payment. . . .

The plaintiff in this case has the burden of proving that the stop payment order was received by the bank at such time as to afford it a reasonable opportunity to act on such order. . . . The facts as presented support this contention and therefore the court finds in favor of the plaintiff and against the defendant bank.

It has been held that a bank which improperly paid a check on which payment had been stopped may recover from the one who received payment, if such payee was not a holder for value. . . . The facts developed in this case indicate that the defendant construction corporation was already fully paid for its services. Therefore the construction corporation has no right to retain the additional funds improperly paid by the bank, and the court finds that the bank is entitled to judgment against the third party defendant for the amount of the improperly certified check.

Accordingly, judgment for the plaintiff against the defendant (Security National Bank) in the sum of $600.00 with interest thereon from July 25, 1972, together with the costs and disbursements of this action, and, further, the defendant and third-party plaintiff (Security National Bank) may have judgment over and against the third party defendant (Adamson Construction Corporation) in the sum of $600.00 with interest thereon from July 25, 1972, together with the costs and disbursements of this action.

QUESTIONS

1. What would the result have been if the check issued by Tusso had been certified when it was sent to the Adamson Company?

2. When a bank makes payment of check in violation of a proper stop payment order, is the bank protected from liability if it has exercised reasonable care?
3. Was the drawer required to prove that the bank was negligent in paying the check over the stop payment order?

10. Payment on Forged Signature of Drawer

A **forgery** of the signature occurs when the name of the depositor has been signed by another person without authority to do so and with the intent to defraud by making it appear that the check was signed by the depositor. The bank is liable to the depositor (drawer) if it pays a check on which the drawer's signature has been forged, since a forgery ordinarily has no effect as a signature. The risk of loss caused by the forged signature of the drawer is thus placed on the bank, without regard to whether the bank could have detected the forgery.[21]

Although the bank has no right to pay a check on which the drawer's signature is forged, the drawer may be barred from objecting that the signature was a forgery. If the drawer's negligence contributed substantially to the forging of the signature, the drawer cannot assert that it was forged when the drawee bank makes payment of the check while acting in good faith and conforming to reasonable commercial standards. For example, if the drawer signs checks with a mechanical writer, reasonable care must be exercised to prevent unauthorized persons from making use of it to forge or "sign" the drawer's name with such device. If the depositor's negligence enables a third person to make such improper use of the device, the depositor is barred from objecting to the payment of the check by the bank.

When a check is presented to the drawee bank for payment, the drawee alone is responsible for determining whether the signature of the drawer, its customer, is a forgery. Prior indorsers (those who indorsed prior to the plaintiff-holder) do not warrant that the signature of the drawer is genuine, and if the bank pays money or gives a cashier's check in payment of the depositor's check, the drawee cannot thereafter recover the money paid or defend against payment on the cashier's check on the ground that the drawer's signature had been forged.

11. Payment on Forged or Missing Indorsement

A drawee bank that honors a depositor's check bearing a forged indorsement must recredit the drawer's account upon the drawer's discovery of the forgery and notification to the bank. Since the bank paid out the money to a person who was not the holder of the instrument, the drawer could bring an action against the bank in conversion if the bank should fail to recredit the drawer's account.[22]

A drawee bank is liable for the loss when it pays a check that lacks an essential indorsement. In such a case the instrument is not properly payable. By definition the person presenting the check for payment is not the holder of the instrument and is not entitled to demand or receive payment.

When a person deposits a check but does not indorse it, the depositor's bank may make an indorsement on behalf of the depositor unless the check expressly requires the customer's indorsement. A bank cannot add the missing indorsement of a person who is not its customer depositing the item in the customer's account in the bank.[23]

12. Alteration of Check

If the face of the check has been altered so that the amount to be paid has been increased, the

---

[21] Perini Corp. v First Nat. Bank (CA5 Ga) 553 F2d 398 (1977).

[22] UCC § 3–419(1)(c).
[23] Krump Constr. Co., Inc. v First Nat. Bank, 98 Nev 570, 655 P2d 524 (1982).

bank is liable to the drawer for the amount of the increase when it makes payment for the greater amount.

The drawer may be barred from claiming that there was an alteration because of conduct with respect to writing the check or conduct after receiving the canceled check from the bank. As to the former, the drawer is barred if the check was carelessly written, the negligence substantially contributed to the making of the material alteration, and the bank honored the check in good faith and observed reasonable commercial standards in so doing.[24]

For example, the drawer is barred when the check was written with blank spaces so that it was readily possible to change "four" to "four hundred," and the drawee bank paid out the latter sum without any cause to know that there was an alteration. Therefore, a careful person will write figures and words close together and run a line through or cross out any blank spaces.

13.   Unauthorized Collection of Check

Although a bank acts as agent for its customer in obtaining payment of a check deposited with it by its customer, it may be liable to a third person when the act of its customer is unauthorized or unlawful with respect to the third person. That is, if the customer has no authority to deposit the check, the bank, in obtaining payment from the drawee of the check and thereafter depositing the proceeds of the check in the account of its customer, may be liable for conversion of the check to the person lawfully entitled to the check and its proceeds.

14.   Indemnity Right of Bank

When a bank is held liable to a drawer or a depositor for a payment or collection that is improper because a signature on the check is a forgery, the bank will in many instances be able to recover its loss from a prior party to the

paper who has made either an express or implied warranty that signatures are genuine.

15.   Time Limitations

The liability of the bank to its depositor is subject to certain time limitations.

(a) NON-CODE STATUTE OF LIMITATIONS. A local non-Code statute of limitations will fix the maximum time for asserting a claim against a bank for the breach of the customer-bank deposit contract, an action against any bank for conversion of an item of commercial paper, or an action by one bank against another bank or party to paper to obtain indemnity or contribution.

(b) FORGERY AND ALTERATION REPORTING TIME. A depositor must examine with reasonable care and promptness a bank statement and relevant checks that are paid in good faith and sent to the depositor by the bank, and to discover any unauthorized signature or alteration on the checks. The depositor must notify the bank promptly after discovering either of the foregoing. If the bank exercises ordinary care in paying a forged or altered check and suffers a loss because the depositor fails to discover and notify the bank of the forgery or alteration, the depositor cannot assert the unauthorized signature or the alteration against the bank.[25]

Regardless of the care or lack of care of either the depositor or the bank, the depositor is precluded from asserting the depositor's unauthorized signature or any alteration if the depositor does not report it within one year from the time the bank statement is received. A forged indorsement must be reported within three years.[26]

In the *Southern Guaranty Insurance* case a customer alleged that the drawee bank failed to exercise reasonable care by honoring checks with forged signatures and indorsements.

---

[24]   UCC § 3–406.

[25]   Vending Chattanooga v American Nat. Bank and Trust (Tenn) 730 SW2d 624 (1987).
[26]   UCC § 4–406(4).

SOUTHERN GUARANTY INSURANCE COMPANY v FIRST ALABAMA BANK

(Ala) 540 So 2d 732 (1989)

Southern issued an insurance policy to Bay Paper, insuring it against losses from employee dishonesty. Bay Paper's president hired Sue Russell as Paper's book-keeper. Russell was solely responsible for Paper's payroll and check procedures, and she was solely responsible for reviewing the company's bank statements and canceled checks. She was also the only Paper employee responsible for reconciling the company's bank statements with the checking and payroll records. Paper maintained a payroll checking account at First Alabama Bank (FAB). Soon after being hired, Russell embarked upon a scheme of writing duplicate payroll checks drawn on Bay Paper's payroll account at FAB and made payable to existing Bay Paper employees. She forged the signature of the president of Bay Paper and then forged the indorsements of the payees. She then deposited the checks into her personal checking account. Only one of the 25 checks that FAB tellers accepted for deposit into Russell's account bore her indorsement. Some of the checks bore restrictive indorsements restricting the checks to deposit for credit of the named payee; nevertheless, FAB accepted these checks for deposit into Russell's account. Southern sued FAB, claiming that they were negligent in failing to follow established banking practices, failing to act in a commercially reasonable manner, failing to detect the forged signatures on Bay Paper's checks, and failing to detect forged indorsements. Southern also claimed that the bank's negligence had proximately caused Southern to sustain damages. From a judgment in favor of the bank, Southern appealed.

SHORES, J. . . . Under [the UCC], a bank may charge a customer's account only when an item is deemed "properly payable." [UCC §] 4-401. Thus, by negative implication, 4-401 imposes liability on a drawee bank that charges a customer's account for items not properly payable. . . . The crux of the plaintiff's claim is that FAB improperly paid those items forged by Ms. Russell, and, therefore, that Southern is entitled to recover from FAB the funds that it reimbursed Bay Paper.

[The UCC] however, imposes certain duties not only upon the bank, but upon the bank customer as well. Section 4-406(1) provides:

> When a bank sends to its customer a statement of account accompanied by items paid in good faith in support of the debit entries or holds the statement and items pursuant to a request or instructions of its customer or otherwise in a reasonable manner makes the statement and items available to the customer, the customer must exercise reasonable care and promptness to examine the statement and items to discover his unauthorized signature or any alteration on an item and must notify the bank promptly after discovery thereof.

The record reflects, without contradiction, that Bay Paper's bookkeeper, Ms. Russell, worked on Bay Paper's payroll account, kept the general ledger, and maintained Bay Paper's payables checkbook. She was solely responsible for Bay Paper's payroll and checking procedures, and she was solely responsible for reviewing the company's bank statements and canceled checks. Moreover, she was the only Bay Paper employee responsible for reconciling the company's bank statements with the checking and pay-roll records. This evidence is sufficient to warrant the conclusion that Bay Paper failed to exercise reasonable care as required under § 4-406(1). . . .

A customer's failure to comply with [UCC §] 4-406(1) is dealt with by § 4-406(2):

> If the bank establishes that the customer failed with respect to an item to comply with the duties imposed on the customer by subsection (1) the customer is pre-cluded from asserting against the bank:
>
> (a) His unauthorized signature or any alteration on the item if the bank also establishes that it suffered a loss by reason of such failure. . . .

A third subsection, however, also bears upon the issue in this case. Section 4-406(3) states that "[t]he preclusion under subsection (2) does not apply if the customer estab-lishes lack of ordinary care on the part of the bank in paying the item(s)." Our Court of Civil Appeals has held that under this section the bank is not required to establish that it exercised ordinary care, but that the plaintiff has the burden of establishing the bank's lack of ordinary care. . . . We agree. Thus, we now look to determine whether the plaintiff adduced any evidence that would permit a finding that the bank failed to exercise ordinary care when it deposited forged checks into Ms. Russell's account.

FAB's failure to require Ms. Russell to indorse the checks she presented for deposit, and FAB's acceptance of checks for deposit into Ms. Russell's account despite the pres-ence of restrictive indorsements constitutes some evidence from which the jury could find that FAB failed to exercise ordinary care in paying forged Bay Paper checks.

FAB argues, however, that checks involving "double forgeries," that is, cases where both the drawer's signature and the indorsement are forged, are regarded as forged checks only, and that, therefore, any negligence of the drawee bank with regard to indorsements is irrelevant. See *Perini Corp. v. First Nat'l Bank*, 553 F.2d 398 (5th Cir.1977).

We do not believe the "double forgery" issue as addressed in *Perini* is implicated under the present facts, and, therefore, we neither adopt nor reject the view repre-sented by that case. The *Perini* court dealt with the question of where to allocate loss as between a drawee bank and a depository bank; the question before this Court addresses where to allocate loss as between the drawee bank and the customer. We further note that, under the present facts, FAB acted as both the drawee bank and the depository bank; thus, there can be no question as to where the loss will be allocated as between the drawee bank and the depository bank.

It is true that other courts have held that, where a "double forgery" exists, the cus-tomer's cause of action against the drawee bank is based upon the forged drawer's signature, and not upon the forged indorsement. *Id.* However, the fact that the cus-tomer does not have a cause of action based upon the forged indorsement when there is a "double forgery" does not mean that the drawee bank's failure to exercise ordinary care with regard to indorsements is irrelevant for purposes of imposing liability on the drawee bank based upon its payment of a check with a forged drawer's signature. Section 4-406(3) requires the bank to exercise ordinary care in paying items. The lan-guage of § 4-406(3) is unqualified. The statute does not distinguish between items bear-ing forged drawer's signatures and items bearing forged indorsements, but requires the exercise of ordinary care as to all items. Therefore, one can not, as FAB suggests, selectively exercise ordinary care with regard to the drawer's signature and remain true to the clear mandate of the statute; rather, the statute requires the exercise of ordinary care with regard to the item as a whole. To rule otherwise, we believe, would narrow the scope of the provision beyond what we think the drafters intended.

We are impressed with the reasoning of the Supreme Court of North Dakota in a case involving the exact issue before us. There, the plaintiff customer brought suit against the drawee bank for payment of checks drawn on the customer's account which bore forged drawer's signatures. The drawee bank asserted that the customer was precluded from recovering on these checks under § 4–406(2) of the UCC. The customer contended that the preclusion of § 4–406(2) did not apply because the drawee bank, in paying the checks, had failed to exercise "ordinary care" within the meaning of § 4–406(3) because the indorsements of the checks were defective. The issue before the court was whether the drawee bank, in making payment on the forged checks, had failed to exercise ordinary care within the meaning of § 4–406(3) of the UCC. The Supreme Court of North Dakota stated:

> Each of the nine forged checks at issue on this appeal has Wayne Anderson's signature forged as drawer of the check by Averill Anderson. All nine checks are payable to the order of Wayne Anderson as payee; however, none of the checks is endorsed with Wayne Anderson's signature, either genuine or forged. In our determination of whether or not the trial court erred in finding that Citizens failed to exercise ordinary care in making payment on the forged checks we must scrutinize Citizens' payment of each check with respect to:
> (1) the drawer's signature on the check, and
> (2) *the endorsement(s) on the check.*

Thoreson v. Citizens State Bank, 294 N.W.2d 397, 400 (N.D. 1980).

We hold, therefore, that the drawee bank's negligence with regard to the indorsements on checks is relevant for purposes of § 4-406(3).

Because material evidence exists supporting the position of the non-moving party, we must reverse FAB's summary judgment.

[Reversed and remanded]

QUESTIONS

1. What was the argument of Southern?
2. Did Bay Paper exercise reasonable care?
3. What did the court decide?

(c) UNAUTHORIZED SIGNATURE OR ALTERATION BY SAME WRONGDOER. Often the same wrongdoer perpetrates a series of forgeries or alterations. The depositor must warn the bank as soon as possible of the first forgery or altered item so that the bank can protect itself from a repetition of the misconduct. A failure by the depositor to notify the bank within 14 days after a statement of account with the paid items is available to the depositor bars the depositor from holding the bank liable for the loss on additional checks forged or altered by the same wrongdoer that are thereafter paid in good faith by the bank.[27]

C.   ELECTRONIC FUND TRANSFERS ACT

The primary objective of the **Electronic Fund**

---

[27]   UCC § 4–406(2)(b).

Transfers Act (EFTA) is to provide for individual consumer rights when participating in electronic fund transfer systems.[28] The term **electronic fund transfer** means any transfer of funds (other than a transaction originated by check, draft, or similar paper instrument) that is initiated through an electronic terminal, telephone, computer, or magnetic tape so as to authorize a financial institution to debit or credit an account. The service available from an automated teller machine is a common form of EFT.

16.   Kinds of Electronic Fund Transfer Systems

There are currently four common kinds of EFT systems in use. In some of these systems the consumer has a card giving him or her access to the machine. The consumer usually has a private code that prevents others from using the card if they obtain possession of it.

(a) AUTOMATED TELLER MACHINE. The automated teller machine (ATM) performs many of the tasks of human bank tellers. Once an individual activates the ATM, it allows the user to deposit and withdraw funds from his or her account, to transfer funds between accounts, to make payment on loan accounts, and to obtain cash advances from bank credit cards.

(b) PAY-BY-PHONE SYSTEM. This system facilitates the paying of bills without writing checks. The consumer calls the bank and directs the transfer of funds to a designated third party.

(c) DIRECT DEPOSIT AND WITHDRAWAL. An employee may authorize an employer to deposit the former's wages directly to the employee's account. A consumer who has just purchased an automobile on credit may elect to have monthly payments withdrawn from the consumer's bank account and paid directly to the seller.

(d) POINT-OF-SALE-TERMINAL. This device allows a business with such a terminal

to transfer funds from the consumer's account to the store account.

17.   Responsibility and Liability of Financial Institution

The consumer must be furnished in advance with the prescribed terms and conditions of all EFT services and must be given periodic statements covering account activity. Any automatic EFT from an individual's account must be authorized in writing in advance.

The financial institution is liable to a consumer for all damages proximately caused by its failure to make an EFT in accordance with the terms and conditions of an account, unless the consumer's account has insufficient funds, the funds are subject to legal process, the transfer would exceed an established credit limit, or insufficient cash is available in an ATM.

18.   Consumer Liability

A consumer who notifies the issuer of the EFT card within two days after learning of a loss or theft of the card is limited to a maximum liability of $50 for unauthorized use of the card. Failure to notify within this time will increase the consumer's liability for losses to a maximum of $500.

The consumer has a responsibility to examine periodic statements provided by the financial institution. If it is established that a loss would not have occurred if the consumer had reported within 60 days of the transmittal of the statement any unauthorized transfer, the loss is borne by the consumer.

D.   FUNDS TRANSFERS

In states that have adopted Article 4A of the Uniform Commercial Code, funds transfers by big business are governed by that Article.[29]

---

[28]   15 USC §§ 1693 et seq.

[29]   An exhaustive, professional-level analysis of Article 4A appears in Anderson on the Uniform Commercial Code (Lawyers Co-operative Publishing Co., 3rd Edition), Supplement to Volume 7. See Appendix 3, note 1, of this text for states adopting Article 4A.

19. Characteristics of Funds Transfers

The transfers regulated by Article 4A have the characteristics of being made between highly sophisticated parties who are dealing with large sums of money. Speed of transfer is often an essential characteristic. An individual transfer may involve many millions of dollars, and the national total of transfers on a business day can amount to trillions of dollars.

20. Pattern of Funds Transfers

In the most simple form of funds transfer both the debtor and the creditor have a separate account in the same bank.[30]

In such a situation the debtor can instruct the bank to pay the creditor a specified sum of money by subtracting that amount from the debtor's account and adding it to the creditor's account. As a practical matter, the debtor will merely instruct the bank to make the transfer and the bank on making the transfer will debit the debtor's account.

A more complex situation is involved if each party has an account in a different bank. In such case the funds transfer could involve only these two banks and no clearing house. Thus, the buyer could instruct the buyer's bank to direct the seller's bank to make payment to the seller. Here there would be direct communication between the two banks. In a more complex situation the buyer's bank may relay the payment order to another bank, called an *intermediary bank,* and that bank in turn would transmit it to the seller's bank.

Further complexity is found when there are two or more intermediary banks, or a clearing house is involved.

21. Scope of UCC Article 4A

Article 4A applies to all funds transfers except as expressly excluded by its own terms, by federal preemption, or by agreement of the parties or clearing house rules.

Some funds transfers are excluded from Article 4A because of their nature or because of the parties involved.

(a) EFTA AND CONSUMER TRANSACTIONS. By the express provision of Article 4A, it does not apply to consumer transactions payments to which EFTA applies. If any part of the funds transfer is subject to EFTA, the entire transfer is expressly excluded from the scope of UCC Article 4A.[31]

(b) DEBIT TRANSFERS. When the person making payment, such as the buyer, makes the request that payment be made to the beneficiary's bank, the transaction is called a *credit transfer.* If the beneficiary entitled to money goes to the bank, pursuant to prior agreement, and requests payment to it, the transaction is called a *debit transfer.* The latter kind of transfer is not regulated by Article 4A. That article applies only to transfers begun by the person desiring to make payment to the beneficiary.

(c) NONBANK TRANSFERS. In order for Article 4A to apply to a money transfer, it is necessary that once the transfer is begun, all communication is between banks. Thus, sending money by Western Union does not come under 4A, because there is no bank-to-bank communication. Payment by check is also not covered, because the drawer of the check sends the check directly to the payee. There is no involvement of banks until the payee deposits the check or presents it to cash it. Likewise excluded from Article 4A by the bank-to-bank requirement is payment by use of a credit card even when the transaction would not come within the scope of EFTA.

22. Definitions

Article 4A employs a number of terms that are peculiar to Article 4A or that are used in that Article in a particular context.

---

[30]   The text refers to "debtor" and "creditor" in the interest of simplicity and because that situation is the most common in the business world. However, a gift may be made by a funds transfer. Likewise, a person having separate accounts in two different banks may transfer funds from one bank to another.

[31]   UCC § 4A-108. This exclusion applies when any part is subject to Regulation E adopted under the authority of that statute.

(a) FUNDS TRANSFER. A **funds transfer** is more accurately described as a communication of instructions or requests to pay a specific sum of money to or to the credit of a specified account or person.[32] There is no actual physical transfer or passing of money or precious metal.

(b) ORIGINATOR. The person starting the funds transfer is called the **originator** of the funds transfer.[33]

(c) BENEFICIARY. The **beneficiary** is the ultimate recipient of the benefit of the funds transfer. Whether it is the beneficiary personally, an account owned by the beneficiary, or a third person to whom the beneficiary owes money is determined by the payment order.

(d) BENEFICIARY'S BANK. The **beneficiary's bank** is the final bank in the chain of transfer, which carries out the transfer by making payment or application as directed by the payment order.

(e) PAYMENT ORDER. The **payment order** is the direction given by the originator to the originator's bank or by any bank to a subsequent bank to make the specified funds transfer. Although called an *order,* it is in fact a request. No bank is required or obligated to accept a payment order unless it is so bound by a contract or clearing house rule that operates outside of Article 4A.

(f) ACCEPTANCE OF PAYMENT ORDER. When a receiving bank other than the beneficiary's bank receives a payment order, it accepts or executes that order by issuing a payment order to the next bank in the transfer chain. When the beneficiary's bank agrees to or actually makes the application of funds as directed by the payment order, the order is termed accepted by that bank.

23.   Form of Payment Order

There is no regulation of any kind of the form of the payment order. There is no requirement that there be any writing as to any matter relating to a funds transfer. As a practical matter it is probable that there will be a written contract between an originator and the originator's bank. There may be agreements between parties and banks, and also clearing house and funds transfer system rules that require a writing.

24.   Manner of Transmitting Payment Order

Article 4A makes no regulation of the manner of transmitting a payment order. As a practical matter most funds transfers coming under Article 4A are controlled by computers, and payment orders will be electronically transmitted. Article 4A, however, applies to any funds transfer payment order, even though made orally, as by telephone, or in a writing, as by a letter.

Again, the agreement of the parties or clearing house and funds transfer system rules may impose some restrictions as to the method of communicating orders.

25.   Security Procedure

Because there is no writing and no face-to-face dealing in the typical funds transfer, Article 4A contemplates that the banks in the transfer chain will agree upon a commercially reasonable security procedure. Under such a procedure a bank receiving a payment order should be able to verify that the payment order was authorized by the purported sender and that it is free from error.[34]

A bank that receives a payment order that passes the security procedure may act on the basis of the order. It is immaterial that in fact the order was not authorized or was fraudulent.

26.   Regulation by Agreement and Funds Transfer System Rule

Article 4A, with minor limitations, permits the parties to make agreements that modify or change the provisions of Article 4A that

---

[32]   UCC § 4A-103(a)(1), 4A-104(a).
[33]   In some cases the originator is a bank, as in the case when a bank has funds held for it on deposit in another bank and wishes to move funds from that account.

[34]   UCC § 4A-201.

would otherwise govern. Likewise, the rules of a clearing house or a funds transfer system through which the banks operate may change the provisions of the Code.

(a) CHOICE OF LAW. When the parties enter into an agreement governing a funds transfer, they may designate the jurisdiction whose law is to apply in interpreting the agreement. The parties are given a free hand to select any jurisdiction they choose. Contrary to the rule applicable in other Code transactions, there is no requirement that the jurisdiction selected bear any relationship to the transaction.[35]

(b) CLEARING HOUSE RULES. The banks involved in a particular funds transfer may be members of the same clearing house. In such case they will be bound by the lawful rules and regulations of the house. Thus, the rights of the parties may be determined by the rules of FedWire, a clearing house system operated by the Federal Reserve System, or by CHIPS, which is a similar system operated by the New York clearing house.

27.   Acceptance of Payment Order

A bank receiving a payment order accepts the order when the bank complies with its terms. What this means depends on whether the receiving bank is an intermediary bank or is the beneficiary's bank.

(a) INTERMEDIARY BANK. An intermediary bank accepts a payment order when it carries out or executes the order by transmitting a similar payment order to the next bank in the transfer chain. Unlike a check that is sent through bank collection channels, the original payment order is not transferred, but a new payment order by the intermediary bank is dispatched.

(b) BENEFICIARY'S BANK. The beneficiary's bank accepts a payment order when it notifies the beneficiary that the beneficiary's bank holds the amount of the payment order at the disposal of the beneficiary. The payment order may require the beneficiary's bank to credit the amount to an account or to a named person. The person so named may be the beneficiary, as when a buyer uses a funds transfer to pay the purchase price to the seller. It may also be a designated third person. This would be the case when the buyer directs the crediting of the bank account of a manufacturer in order to discharge or reduce the debt of the seller to the manufacturer. The transfer to the manufacturer would of course also reduce or discharge the debt of the buyer to the seller.

When the beneficiary's bank acts as directed by the payment order, it accepts the order. When it does so, it takes the place of the originator as the debtor owing the beneficiary. In such a case the originator no longer owes the beneficiary, and the debt to the beneficiary is discharged or reduced by the amount of the payment order.[36]

28.   Reimbursement of Bank

After the beneficiary's bank accepts the payment order, it, and every bank ahead of it in the funds transfer chain, is entitled to reimbursement of the amount paid to or for the beneficiary. This reimbursement is due from the preceding bank. By going back along the funds transfer chain, the originator's bank, and ultimately the originator, makes payment of this reimbursement amount.

29.   Refund on Noncompletion of Transfer

If the funds transfer is not completed for any reason, the sender or originator is entitled to a refund of any payment that has been made in advance to the originator's bank. The sender or originator is not required to reimburse any bank for payment made by it.[37]

30.   Error in Funds Transfer

There may be an error in a payment order. The effect of an error depends upon its nature.

---

[35]   UCC § 4A-507.

[36]   UCC § 4A-406.
[37]   UCC § 4A-402.

(a) KIND OF ERROR. The error in a payment order may consist of a wrong identification or a wrong amount.

1. Wrong Beneficiary or Account Number. The payment order received by the beneficiary's bank may contain an error in the designation of the beneficiary or in the account number. This error may result in payment being made to or for the wrong person or account.

2. Excessive Amount. The payment order may call for the payment of an amount that is greater than it should be. For example, the order may wrongly add an additional zero to the specified amount.

3. Duplicating Amount. The payment order may be issued overlooking the fact that a similar payment order has already been transferred, so that the second order duplicates the first. This duplication would result in double the proper amount's being paid by the beneficiary's bank.

4. Underpayment. The payment order may call for the payment of a smaller sum than was ordered. For example, the order may drop off one of the zeros from the amount ordered by the originator.

(b) EFFECT OF ERROR. When the error is one of the first three classes noted above, the bank committing the error will bear the loss because it will not be allowed reimbursement for any amount that it caused to be wrongfully paid. In contrast, when the error is merely underpayment, the bank making the mistake can cure the fault by making a supplementary order for the amount of the underpayment. If verification by agreed security procedure would disclose an error in the payment order, a bank is liable for any loss caused by the error if it failed to verify the payment order by such a procedure. In contrast, if the security procedure was followed but did not reveal any error, there is no liability for accepting the payment order.

When an error of any kind is made, there is also the possibility that there may be liability arising by virtue of a collateral agreement of the parties, a clearing house or funds transfer system rule, or general principles of contract law. However, the right of the originator to complain that there is an error may be lost in certain cases by failing to notify the involved bank that the mistake had been made.[38]

31. Liability For Loss

Unless otherwise regulated by agreement or clearing house rule, there is very slight liability imposed on a bank in the funds transfer chain that follows the agreed security procedure.

(a) UNAUTHORIZED ORDER. If a bank executes or accepts an unauthorized payment order, it is liable to any prior party in the transfer chain for the loss caused thereby. However, as a practical matter such loss will rarely be imposed, because the transfer is typically made under an agreement establishing a security procedure. If a bank acts on the basis of an unauthorized order that nevertheless is verified by the security procedure, the bank is not liable for the loss caused thereby.

The customer, however, can avoid this effect of verification by a security procedure by proving that the security procedure was not commercially reasonable or that the payment order was initiated by a total stranger. The latter requires that the customer show that the initiator was not an employee or agent of the customer having access to confidential security information or a person who obtained that information from a source controlled by the customer. However, it is immaterial whether the customer was at fault.[39]

(b) FAILURE TO ACT. In most cases a bank that fails to carry out a payment order is liable at the most for interest loss and expenses. There is no liability for the loss sustained by the originator or for consequential damages suffered because payment was not made to satisfy the originator's obligation to the beneficiary.[40] Thus, a person seeking to exercise an option by forwarding money to the optionor

---

38 UCC § 4A-304.
39 UCC § 4A-203.
40 UCC § 4A-305.

cannot recover for the loss of the option when the failure of a bank to act results in the optionor's not receiving the money in time. Likewise, an originator cannot sue any bank for the lost profit that the originator would have made in reselling goods in the following situation. The resale was prevented by the fact that the funds transfer was not made to the seller in time, whereupon the seller declared the buyer in default. The seller then refused to deliver the goods needed by the originator for resale.

SUMMARY

A check is a particular kind of draft; it is drawn on a bank and payable on demand. A delivery of a check is not an assignment of money on deposit with the bank on which it is drawn. Therefore, it does not automatically transfer the rights of the depositor against the bank to the holder of the check, and there is no duty on the part of the drawee bank to the holder to pay the holder the amount of the check.

Certification of a check by the bank is the acceptance of the draft—the bank becomes the primary party. Certification may be at the request of the drawee or the holder. On certification by the holder all prior indorsers and the drawer are released from liability. Notice of nonpayment of a check must be given to the drawer of a check. If no notice is given, the drawer will be discharged from liability to the same extent as the drawer of an ordinary draft. The drawee bank owes the depositor certain duties, such as not disclosing information relating to the depositor's account and paying on demand all checks issued by the depositor.

A depositor may stop payment on a check. However, the depositor may become liable to a holder in due course unless such stopping of payment was for a reason that may be raised against a holder in due course. The stop payment order may be oral (binding for 14 calendar days) or written (effective for six months).

Liability of a secondary party cannot be enforced unless that party was given proper notice of the dishonor.

The depositary bank is the agent of the depositor for the purpose of collecting the deposited item. The bank may become liable for paying a check contrary to a stop payment order or when there has been a forgery or alteration. The bank is not liable, however, if the drawer's negligence has substantially contributed to the forgery. A bank that pays on a forged signature must recredit the drawer's account. A depositor is subject to certain time limitations in order to enforce liability on the bank.

An electronic fund transfer is a transfer of funds (other than a transaction originated by check, draft, or other commercial paper) that is initiated through an electronic terminal, telephone, computer, or magnetic tape so as to authorize a financial institution to debit or credit an account. The Electronic Fund Transfers Act requires that a financial institution furnish consumers with specific information containing all the terms and conditions of all EFT services. Under certain conditions the financial institution will bear the loss for unauthorized transfers. Under other circumstances, the loss will be borne by the consumer.

Funds transfers regulated by UCC, Article 4A, are those made between highly sophisticated parties who deal with large sums of money. If any part of the funds transfer is subject to EFTA, such as consumer transactions, the entire transfer is expressly excluded from the scope of UCC Article 4A. A funds transfer is simply a communicating of instructions or requests to pay a specific sum of money to or to the credit of a specified person. The person starting the funds transfer is called the *originator* of the funds transfer. The *beneficiary* is the ultimate recipient of the funds transfer.

QUESTIONS AND CASE PROBLEMS

1. What social forces are involved in the common statutory provision that it will be presumed that a check was issued with intent to defraud if the drawer does not pay the amount of the check within ten days after its dishonor?

2. When a bank certifies a check, what does it undertake to do with respect to the holder of the check?

3. Shirley drew a check on her account in the First Central Bank. She later telephoned the bank to stop payment on the check. The bank agreed to do so. Sixteen days thereafter, the check was presented to the bank for payment and was paid by the bank. Shirley sued the bank for violating the stop payment order. The bank claimed it was not liable. Is Shirley entitled to recover?

4. Tom had a checking account with the Farmers National Bank. A check was written by an unknown person, who forged the signature of Tom as a drawer of the check and then presented the check to the Farmers National Bank for payment. The bank paid the check and debited Tom's account for the amount of the check. When Tom received the monthly statement from the bank, he demanded that the bank restore the amount of this debit. Was he correct?

5. Shipper was ill for 14 months. His wife did not take care of his affairs carefully, nor did she examine his bank statements as they arrived each month. One of Shipper's friends had forged his name to a check in favor of himself for $10,000. The drawee bank paid the check and charged Shipper's account. Shipper did not notify the bank for 13 months after he received the statement and the forged check. Can he compel the bank to reverse the charge? Why?

6. Gloria maintains a checking account at the First Bank. On the third day of January the bank sent Gloria a statement of her account for December, accompanied by the checks that the bank had paid. One of the checks had her forged signature, which Gloria discovered on the 25th of the month, when she prepared a bank reconciliation. Upon this discovery, Gloria immediately notified the bank. On January 21 the bank paid another check forged by the same party who had forged the December item. Who must bear the loss on the forged January check?

7. Dean bought a car from Cannon. In payment, Dean gave him a check drawn on the South Dorchester Bank of the Eastern Shore Trust Company. The payee, Cannon, cashed the check at the Cambridge Bank of the Eastern Shore Trust Company. The drawee bank refused payment when the check was presented on the ground that Dean had stopped payment because of certain misrepresentations made by Cannon. Will the Eastern Shore Trust Company succeed in an action against Dean for payment? [Dean v Eastern Shore Trust Co. 159 Md 213, 150 A 797]

8. A depositor drew a check and delivered it to the payee. Fourteen months later the check was presented to the drawee bank for payment. The bank did not have any knowledge that anything was wrong and paid the check. The depositor then sued the person receiving the money and the bank. The depositor claimed that the bank could not pay a stale check without asking the depositor whether payment should be made. Was the depositor correct? [Advanced Alloys, Inc. v Sergeant Steel Corp. 340 NYS2d 266]

9. Siniscalchi drew a check on his account in the Valley Bank of New York. About a week later the holder cashed the check at the bank on a Saturday morning. The following Monday morning Siniscalchi gave the bank a stop payment order on the check. The Saturday morning transactions had not yet been recorded, and neither the bank nor Siniscalchi knew that the check had been cashed. When that fact was learned, the bank debited Siniscalchi's account for the amount of the check. He claimed that the bank was liable because the stop payment order had been violated. Was the bank liable? [Siniscalchi v Valley Bank of New York, 359 NYS2d 173]

10. Bogash drew a check on the National Safety Bank and Trust Co., payable to the order of the Fiss Corp. At the request of the Fiss Corp. the bank certified the check. The bank later refused to make payment on the check because there was a dispute between Bogash and the corporation as to the amount due to the corporation. The corporation sued the bank on the check. Decide. [Fiss Corp. v National Safety Bank and Trust Co. 191 Misc 397, 77 NYS2d 293]

11. Compare or contrast the legal differences between certification of a check by a bank at the request of the depositor and at the request of a holder.

12. Steinbaum executed and delivered a check to the order of the White Way Motors, the name

under which DiFranco was doing business. Before the check was paid, Steinbaum stopped payment on the check. DiFranco sued Steinbaum on the check. Decide. [DiFranco v Steinbaum (Mo App) 177 SW2d 697]

13. Paradine drew a check on the Citizen's National Bank and gave it to Davis in payment of a debt. Davis asked an assistant teller at the bank whether Paradine had sufficient funds on deposit to cover the check. He was informed that he had. Instead of presenting the check for payment at the bank, Davis deposited the check at his own bank, which then took steps toward collecting from Paradine's bank. Before this collection was completed, Paradine had withdrawn his entire balance from Citizen's National Bank. Davis sued the Citizen's National Bank for the amount of the check. Will he recover? Why?

14. Shortly before the close of banking hours on Friday, a creditor receives from his debtor two checks, one of which has been certified before its delivery to the creditor. Certification of the other check is secured by the creditor, but too late for the deposit of either check in the creditor's bank until Monday. On Monday, the bank on which both checks were drawn does not open for business; it has been taken over by the State Banking Department. What is the position of the creditor with respect to each check? Give reasons.

15. Stanley Salton delivered a $50 check to Doris Dean. Dean wrongfully raised the amount to $250, using spaces that Salton negligently had left blank. Dean then indorsed and delivered the check to Watkins, who took it for value, in good faith, and without notice of the alteration. In due course the check was presented for payment to Salton's bank, which paid it in good faith and in accordance with reasonable commercial standards. Salton protested when the bank charged his account for $250. What is the argument of the bank?

PART SIX

DEBTOR-CREDITOR
RELATIONS AND
RISK MANAGEMENT

35

SECURED TRANSACTIONS UNDER ARTICLE 9

A person selling goods on credit or lending money has a right, grounded in contract, to receive from the debtor the amount due under the terms of the agreement. If the debtor defaults, the creditor has the right to sue for damages. However, the creditor may want more protection than is afforded by this right to sue on the debt.

Prior to the adoption of the Uniform Commercial Code (UCC) there were a number of devices designed to give the lender/seller an interest in specific property of the borrower/buyer. This interest could be used to satisfy any claims of the creditor resulting from the debtor's breach. These devices included (1) conditional sales, wherein the seller retained title until the condition of payment in full had been satisfied; (2) bailment leases, by which the buyer rented the property and could acquire title only after the payment of sufficient rentals to equal the purchase price; (3) chattel mortgages, by which the buyer, upon taking title from the seller, gave the seller a mortgage on the property for the amount of the purchase price; and (4) trust receipts, by which the borrower/buyer agreed to hold the goods in trust for the lender.

A.   GENERAL PRINCIPLES

Article 9 of the UCC consolidates this fragmented field of security devices into one device, called a **secured transaction.**[1] A creditor who complies with the requirements of Article 9 may create a security interest that protects the creditor against the debtor's default by allowing the creditor to recover the goods in the debtor's possession. Any transaction intended to create such an interest (regardless of its form) is subject to the requirements of Article 9.

1.   Creation of a Security Interest

A **security interest** is an interest in personal property or fixtures that secures payment or performance of an obligation.[2] The property in which the interest is held is called the **collateral.** The party holding the interest is termed the **secured party.**[3] The interest may be possessory, wherein the collateral is in the possession of the secured party; or it may be nonpossessory, wherein the debtor is in possession of the collateral.

A security interest is said to **attach** when the following three prerequisites are met. There must be a security agreement. Value must be given. The debtor must have rights in the collateral.[4]

(a) SECURITY AGREEMENT. The agreement of the creditor and the debtor that the creditor shall have a security interest in the goods must be evidenced by a written **security agreement,** unless the creditor retains a possessory security interest by taking possession of the collateral. The agreement must be signed by the debtor and must reasonably describe the collateral.

(b) VALUE. To be effective for the attaching of a security interest, value is given when the secured party lends money to the debtor or agrees to lend money to the debtor. In most cases value is any consideration that supports a simple contract.

(c) DEBTOR HAS RIGHTS IN THE COLLATERAL. The debtor must have rights in the collateral. That is, the debtor must either own or have the right to possession of the collateral.

(d) FUTURE TRANSACTIONS. The security agreement may contemplate future action by extending to **future advances** if money is lent or to **after-acquired goods,** that is, goods to be acquired and delivered to the buyer at a future date. In general the security interest does not attach to future goods until the buyer has rights in such goods.[5]

In order to protect consumers a limit is placed upon the extent to which after-acquired property may be bound by a security interest. In order to be collateral for a consumer obligation the consumer must acquire the later property within ten days after the creditor gave value to the consumer. That is, the creditor cannot bind all property acquired at any time in the future but only that which is acquired within ten days after the creditor

---

[1]   This chapter is based on the UCC, including the 1972 amendments, excerpts of which are set forth in Appendix 3. The changes made by the 1972 amendments are confined mainly to Article 9 on secured transactions.

[2]   UCC § 1-201(37).

[3]   UCC § 9-105(1).

[4]   UCC § 9-203(1),(2). Louis & Diederich v Cambridge European Imports, 189 Cal App 3d 1574, 234 Cal Rptr 889 (1987).

[5]   UCC § 9-204.

sells the goods or lends the money to the consumer.

(e) PERFECTION. When a security interest in property is superior to other interests and claims to the property, it is said to be **perfected.** Perfection may generally be obtained by filing a financing statement in the proper governmental office. If the collateral is tangible personal property, the creditor has the alternative of perfecting the security interest by taking possession of the collateral. If the collateral is consumer goods, neither filing nor taking possession is required to perfect a purchase money security interest in the goods, because such an interest is perfected as soon as it attaches. A creditor who has a security agreement and either sells goods to a consumer on credit or lends money to enable the debtor to purchase goods has a **purchase money security interest.**[6] Perfection of a purchase money security interest is more readily lost than perfection based upon filing or possession.

2. Classification of Collateral

The UCC divides tangible personal property or goods into four different classes: consumer goods, equipment, inventory, and farm products.[7] These goods are classified by the debtor's intended use, not their physical characteristics. For example, a television set in the hands of a manufacturer or retailer would be inventory. However, in the hands of the borrower or buyer for personal use, it is a consumer good.

(a) CONSUMER GOODS. Goods are **consumer goods** if they are used or bought primarily for personal, family, or household use (e.g., a family's car).

(b) EQUIPMENT. Goods are classified as **equipment** if they are used or bought primarily for use in a business (e.g., a musical instrument used by a nightclub entertainer).

(c) INVENTORY. Goods are classified as **inventory** if they are held by the debtor primarily for sale or lease to others (for example, a refrigerator bought by a dealer) or if they are raw materials, work in process, or materials consumed in a business.

(d) FARM PRODUCTS. Goods are **farm products** if they are crops, livestock, or supplies used or produced in farming operations.

B. SECURED CREDIT SALES OF CONSUMER GOODS

Consumer credit sales are treated differently from secured credit sales of inventory. Perfection by filing in a public office is not required for consumer goods. For most consumer transactions the amount involved would not warrant the filing expense.

3. Rights of the Seller of Consumer Goods Independent of Default

The seller stands in a dual position of being both a seller, having rights under Article 2 of the UCC governing sales, and a secured creditor, having rights under Article 9 of the UCC regulating secured transactions.[8]

The secured credit seller of consumer goods has rights that are effective not only against the buyer but also against purchasers of the property from the buyer, as soon as the security agreement is executed with respect to goods in which the buyer has acquired an interest. From that moment on, the seller's interest is generally effective against third persons[9] and is described as a **perfected security interest.**

(a) FILING NOT REQUIRED. In an ordinary intrastate sale of consumer goods under a secured transaction, no filing in any state or government office is required in order to perfect the secured seller's interest. The security agreement will protect the seller against creditors of the buyer and most third parties who thereafter buy the property from the buyer.[10]

---

6   Borg-Warner Acceptance v Tascosa Nat'l Bank (Tex Ct App) 784 SW2d 129 (1990).
7   UCC § 9-109.

8   UCC § 9-113.
9   UCC § 9-201.
10 Howell State Bank v Jericho Boats, Inc. 533 NYS 2d 363 (1988).

(b) INTERSTATE SECURITY INTERESTS. The UCC regulates not only transactions within the state but also the effect to be given security interests in property brought into the state from another state. If the interest of the secured party was perfected in the other state, that interest is regarded as perfected by the state into which the property is brought. Within the second state, however, it is necessary to file within four months in order to keep the security interest continuously perfected.

If title to the property, such as an automobile, is represented by a title certificate, the law of the state that issued the certificate determines whether an interest is perfected. Accordingly, if the law of the certificate-issuing state requires that a security interest be noted on the title certificate in order to be perfected, that requirement is the exclusive means of perfecting the interest of the secured creditor.[11]

(c) REPAIR AND STORAGE LIEN. In most states persons making repairs to or storing property have a right to assert a lien against the property for the amount of their charges. If there is an outstanding security interest in the goods when the customer brings them for repair or storage, the lien for repairs or storage charges has priority over the outstanding security interest.[12]

In the *National Bank* case a car dealer who had repaired a new Cadillac claimed priority to the car over a bank that had financed the debtor's purchase.

---

[11]   UCC § 9-103(2).
[12]   UCC § 9-310.

NATIONAL BANK v BERGERON CADILLAC, INC.

66 Ill 2d 140, 361 NE2d 1116 (1977)

In order to finance the purchase of a new automobile, Gladys Schmidt obtained a loan from the National Bank and gave the bank a security interest in the new automobile to protect its loan. The bank perfected the security interest in accordance with the UCC. Gladys later took the automobile to Bergeron Cadillac for repairs. Thereafter, she stopped paying installments to the bank and the bank sought to repossess the automobile from Bergeron Cadillac. The latter refused to surrender the automobile until paid for the repairs. The bank claimed that it was entitled to the automobile because it had perfected its security interest. The bank brought an action against Bergeron to recover the automobile. From a decision in favor of Bergeron, National Bank appealed.

WARD, C.J. . . . The trial court entered judgment for the defendant, holding that its common law possessory lien based on repairs it had made on the auto had priority over the plaintiff's prior security interest under section 9-310 of the Uniform Commercial Code. . . .

In February of 1973 the plaintiff loaned Gladys Schmidt $4,120 to enable her to purchase the automobile, taking a security interest in the automobile to secure the loan. This security interest was perfected by filing in the office of the Secretary of State. . . . In August of 1973 Schmidt brought the auto to the defendant's shop for repairs. The cost of the materials and service was approximately $2,000, and, when Schmidt failed to pay, the defendant, through an inquiry to the Secretary of State, learned of the plaintiff's security interest. The defendant exercised its right of lien for the unpaid charges and retained possession of the auto. In September, Schmidt defaulted on her loan payments, and in October the plaintiff ascertained that the Cadillac was in the defendant's possession. The plaintiff's demand on the defendant for the Cadillac under its security interest was refused, and the plaintiff [brought this action].

The plaintiff contends that the right to a common law possessory lien has been superseded in Illinois by two statutes which provide for repairmen's liens. Ill Rev Stat 1973, ch. 82, pars. 40 through 47 and 47a through 47f.

Section 9-310 of the Uniform Commercial Code . . . provides:

> When a person in the ordinary course of his business furnishes services or materials with respect to goods subject to a security interest, a lien upon goods in the possession of such person given by statute or rule of law for such materials or services takes priority over a perfected security interest unless the lien is statutory and the statute expressly provided otherwise. . . .

The plain language of section 9-310 gives the lien of persons furnishing services or materials upon goods in their possession priority over a perfected security interest unless the lien is created by statute and the statute expressly provides otherwise.

The comment of Anderson (Anderson, Uniform Commercial Code) is:

> Code section 9-310 declares the priority of the lien of persons furnishing services or materials with respect to goods in their possession. Such a lien is, basically, the artisan's lien of the common law. Whether such a lien is based upon decision or statute law, Code section 9-310 gives it priority, with one exception, over a pre-existing security interest in the goods. . . .
>
> The single exception relates to a lien created by statute; such a lien does not have such priority if the statute expressly provides otherwise. Accordingly, the lien has priority when it is based upon the common law or decision, or when it is based upon a statute which is silent as to priorities or which gives the lien priority. The lien is subordinated to the security interest only when the lien statute expressly so declares. 4 Anderson, Uniform Commercial Code sec. 9-310, at 341-42(2 ed. 1971). . . .

The artisan's possessory lien of the common law is recognized in Illinois. . . .

We cannot accept the plaintiff's contention that the General Assembly's enactment of the two statutes creating liens in favor of repairmen with respect to personal property . . . evidenced an intent to supersede the artisan's common law lien. Both of the statutes expressly provide that the liens created shall be in addition to, and shall not exclude, any lien existing by virtue of the common law. . . .

As the defendant had a common law possessory lien for services and materials in connection with the repairs it made, its lien takes priority over the plaintiff's earlier perfected security interest under the provisions of section 9–310 of the Uniform Commercial Code. . . .

[Judgment affirmed]

QUESTIONS

1. Did the repairer have a common law lien?
2. Would the decision have been changed if the lien of the repairer had been created by statute?

4.   Rights of the Buyer of Consumer Goods Independent of Default

In a secured transaction the buyer, like the seller, has a double status under the UCC. By virtue of Article 2 the buyer has certain rights as a buyer, and by virtue of Article 9 the buyer has certain rights as a debtor in a secured transaction.

(a) RIGHTS AS A BUYER. The buyer has certain rights of ownership in the collateral. It is not material whether technically the buyer is the owner of the title. The buyer may voluntarily transfer whatever interest is owned by the buyer, and the creditors of the buyer may reach that interest by the process of law as fully as though there were no security agreement. Such third persons generally cannot acquire any greater rights than the buyer; therefore, they hold the property subject to the security interest of the seller.

(b) RIGHTS AS A DEBTOR. The secured transaction buyer is a debtor to the extent that there is a balance due on the purchase price. In order for the buyer to know just how much is owed and to check what the seller claims is due, the buyer has the right to compel the seller to state what balance is owed and also to specify in which collateral the seller claims a security interest. This is done by the buyer's sending the seller a statement of the amount believed to be due, or a statement of the collateral believed to be subject to the security agreement, with the request that the seller approve or correct the statement. The seller must so indicate; and if there has been an assignment of the contract and the security interest

to a third person, the seller must furnish the buyer with the name and address of such successor in interest.

5.   Protection of Subpurchaser

When the seller of consumer goods sells on credit, filing of a financing statement is not necessary to protect the seller's security interest in the goods against other creditors of the buyer. A security interest in the goods is perfected or arises by attachment alone, even though the seller gives the buyer possession of the goods. This rule relieves retail merchants who sell many articles on installment plans of the burdens of filing and paying filing fees.

When no financing statement is filed, however, a resale by the consumer to another consumer will destroy the seller's security interest if the second purchaser does not have knowledge of the security interest of the original party and buys for personal, family, or household use.[13] For example, a consumer buys a refrigerator under an installment contract whereby the appliance store retains a security interest in the refrigerator. The appliance store does not file a financing statement, though its interest is perfected by attachment. Some time later the consumer sells the refrigerator to a neighbor, who is unaware of the prior security interest. The neighbor takes free of the security interest.

The *Balon* case illustrates the rights of subpurchasers of consumer goods who purchased the goods from a consumer-purchaser.

---

[13]   UCC § 9-307(2).

BALON v CADILLAC AUTOMOBILE CO.
113 NH 108, 303 A2d 194 (1973)

Balon and Gibert each purchased a Cadillac for personal use from Russell Saia, a private owner. They did not know that each car was subject to an unfiled security interest in favor of the original seller, the Cadillac Automobile Company of Boston. Balon and Gibert claimed that they owned their cars free of the security interest of Cadillac. Cadillac contended that Balon and Gibert did not believe that they were purchasing a clear title and that they were subject to its unfiled security interests. Cadillac repossessed the cars. Balon and Gibert sued Cadillac. From a judgment in favor of Balon and Gibert, Cadillac appealed.

LAMPRON, J. . . . The issue to be decided is whether the trial court properly found and ruled that Balon and Gibert each had clear title to his automobile by virtue of § 9-307 of the [UCC]. . . .

On September 28, 1965, Charles Pernokas was a salesman for Cadillac Automobile in Boston, Massachusetts. He had previously worked for another employer as a car salesman with Russell Saia. On that day Saia came to Cadillac Automobile looking for a convertible for a customer. Pernokas showed him two cars and Saia said he would hear from him shortly. He telephoned soon thereafter saying that his customer, Peter J. Russell, would take one of the Cadillac convertibles and gave the required credit information and references. On the next day, Saia telephoned Pernokas again and told him another customer, Joseph P. DeLuca, would take the other convertible and gave credit information on him.

Pernokas testified that in each instance he delivered the car to Saia's place and that Saia and another person, supposedly Russell in one instance and DeLuca in the other, identified himself and signed the security agreements. The selling price, $5300 for each car, was paid by a $1000 cash down payment on each and the balance financed on a conditional sale agreement.

At about that time, an individual named Arthur Freije told Balon in Manchester that "somebody" had "a friend" who could get a good deal on Cadillacs. "Somebody" was Fred Sarno who had accompanied Saia on his visit to the Cadillac garage after which the two cars in question were bought. The "friend" was Russell Saia. Balon passed the information along to his stepfather, Gibert, and eventually both Balon and Gibert purchased a Cadillac convertible through Freije for $4300 each.

The October and November payments on these Cadillacs were not made to Cadillac Automobile. As a result of these defaults, Simons, its credit manager, made an investigation and concluded that Peter J. Russell and Joseph P. DeLuca, the apparent purchasers, did not exist and decided that "both of these were two straw deals." The trial court properly found on the evidence that the two Cadillac automobiles in question were purchased by Russell Saia and that he was the principal in their sale to Balon and Gibert.

[UCC §] 9-307 . . . reads as follows:

(1) A buyer in the ordinary course of business . . . takes free of a security interest created by his seller even though the security interest is perfected and even though the buyer knows of its existence.

(2) In the case of consumer goods . . . a buyer takes free of a security interest even though perfected if he buys without knowledge of the security interest, for value and for his own personal, family or household purposes . . . unless prior to the purchase the secured party has filed a financing statement covering such goods.

The secured interest of Cadillac Automobile was perfected when the agreement of the parties was executed. . . . However the security agreements covering these two automobiles were never filed. . . .

The buyer protected by § 9-307(1) is one who purchases in the ordinary course of business from a person in the business of selling goods of the kind involved. § 1-201(9).

Hence § 9-307(1) applies primarily to purchases from the inventory of a dealer in the type of goods sold. 4 Anderson, Uniform Commercial Code 323:24 (2d ed. 1971); *see National Shawmut Bank v Jones*, 108 NH 386, 236 A2d 484 (1967). The buyer protected under § 9-307(2) is one who purchases goods for consumer use, that is, for personal, family or household purposes, from a consumer seller. In order to fall within the protection of this section the goods must be consumer goods in the hands of both the buyer and the seller. . . .

The categorization of these automobiles at the time of the execution of the security agreement with Cadillac Automobile is an important factor in determining whether they were inventory or consumer goods in the hands of Saia when he sold them. . . . This classification of the goods remains unchanged in the controversy between Balon, Gibert, and Cadillac Automobile when it seeks to enforce its security agreement. Simon, Cadillac's credit manager, testified that it is company policy to record security agreements except when the buyer is an individual consumer as determined by the contract. Their security agreement provides that if the car is purchased for business purposes the address of the buyer's place of business must appear as the address on the front of the contract. There was evidence that the address on the front of the Peter Russell contract was listed in the Boston directory as the residence of Mrs. Jean Saia. Simon also testified that as far as the seller was concerned these sales were made to two private consumers for their personal, family and household use. Accordingly, following its policy with respect to consumer purchasers, the security agreements were not filed.

We hold that the trial court properly found and ruled that Russell Saia was a dishonest consumer purchaser of these automobiles. We further hold that these cars remained consumer goods in his hands at the time of the sales to Balon and Gibert who are protected by [UCC §] 9-307(2) if they were good faith consumer buyers for value without knowledge of Cadillac's security interest.

The company maintains, however, that the only conclusion which can be reached on the evidence is that Balon and Gibert "could not have conceivably held honest convictions that these transactions were legitimate." In support it cites § 1-201(19) which provides: " 'Good faith' means honesty in fact in the conduct or transaction concerned." By its terms this is a subjective standard of good faith, that is, whether the particular purchaser believed he was in good faith, not whether anyone else would have held the same belief. The test is what the particular person did or thought in the given situation and whether or not he was honest in what he did. . . .

There was evidence that Gibert had known Freije, who made the approaches which culminated in these sales, in a social way for about fifteen years. His wife had known him all her life. Balon knew him also and had purchased a 1963 Cadillac from him without any untoward incidents. Balon and Gibert learned from inquiries made to dealers known to them that the asking price of $4300 was consistent with prices at which such cars could be bought. The explanation advanced that these convertibles sold in September, when the new models were due, could be found by them plausible reasons for the price quoted. Simon testified that when Balon and Gibert came to Boston after their cars were taken they seemed genuinely concerned [in] trying to figure out what happened. There was no evidence that they had actual knowledge of the status of the title to these cars. The fact that others might have acted differently, made more inquiries, or been more suspicious does not require a conclusion that they lacked good faith when they purchased these cars. . . . The evidence is clear that they paid value and bought for personal, family, or household purposes.

> We hold that the trial court properly found and ruled that Balon and Gibert were good faith consumer buyers for value from a consumer seller without knowledge of Cadillac Automobile's security interest which had not been filed. . . . Consequently they were entitled to the protection of [UCC §] 9-307(2). . . .
>
> [Judgment affirmed]

QUESTIONS

1. Classify the collateral in the hands of Russell Saia.
2. Why did Cadillac Automobile not file a financing statement?
3. Did Balon and Gibert acquire title clear of any prior security interest?

C. SECURED CREDIT SALES OF INVENTORY

In contrast with one who buys goods for personal use, the buyer may be a merchant or dealer who intends to resell the goods. The goods that such a merchant or dealer buys are classified as inventory. The financing of the purchase of inventory may involve a third person, rather than the seller, as creditor. For example, a third person, such as a bank or finance company, may lend the dealer the money with which to make the purchase and to pay the seller in full. In such a case the security interest in the goods may be given by the buyer to the third person rather than to the seller. Accordingly, the terms *creditor* and *secured party* may refer to a seller who sells on credit or to a third person who finances the purchase of goods.

In general, the provisions regulating a secured transaction in inventory follow the same pattern as is applicable to the secured credit sale of consumer goods. Variations recognize the differences in the commercial settings of the two transactions.

Initially there must be possession of the goods or there must be a written security agreement to give rise to the security interest. If perfection of the interest is desired, there must also be a filing of a financing statement, or the creditor must hold possession of the collateral.

6. Use of Property and Extent of Security Interest

A secured transaction relating to inventory generally gives the buyer full freedom to deal with the collateral goods as though the goods were not subject to a security interest. Thus, the parties may agree that the buyer-dealer may mingle the goods with existing inventory, resell the goods, take goods back and make exchanges, and so on, without being required to keep any records of just what became of the goods covered by the security agreement, or to replace the goods sold with other goods, or to account for the proceeds from the sale of the original goods.

(a) AFTER-ACQUIRED PROPERTY. The security agreement may expressly provide that the security interest of the creditor shall bind after-acquired property. **After-acquired property** means other goods thereafter obtained by the buyer. The combination of the buyer's freedom to use and dispose of the collateral and the subjecting of after-acquired goods to the interest of the secured creditor permits the latter to have a floating lien. A **floating lien** is a claim in a changing or shifting stock of goods of the buyer. Conversely stated, the UCC rejects the common law concept that the security interest was lost if the collateral was not maintained and accounted for separately. Under the common law a floating lien on the buyer's property was held void as a fraud against the latter's creditors.

The security interest in inventory covered as after-acquired property has priority over claims of subsequent creditors and third persons. Exceptions are made in the case of buyers in the ordinary course of business and sellers to the debtor holding perfected purchase money security interests in the goods sold to the debtor.

(b) PROCEEDS OF COLLATERAL. The secured transaction covers proceeds from the collateral, unless such interest is expressly excluded. **Proceeds** include cash, checks, and accounts receivable arising on a sale of the collateral and also indemnification from an insurer for damage to the collateral.[14]

7.   Filing of Financing Statement

Filing is usually required to perfect the creditor's interest in inventory or the proceeds therefrom. An exception is made when a statute requires the security interest to be noted on the title certificate issued for the property. A security interest in a motor vehicle that is inventory is perfected by filing under the UCC, but a privately owned vehicle is perfected by a notation on the title registration certificate.

An unperfected security interest is valid against anyone standing in the position of the debtor.

(a) FINANCING STATEMENT. The paper that is filed is a financing statement (see Figure 35-1) and is distinct from the security agreement that was executed by the parties to give rise to the secured transaction.[15] The **financing statement** must be signed by the debtor. It must give an address of the secured party from which information concerning the security interest may be obtained. The financing statement must give a mailing address of the debtor, and it must contain a statement in-

dicating the kinds, or describing the items, of collateral.

The financing statement does not set forth the terms of the agreement between the parties. This is done in the security agreement. The financing statement gives notice that the secured creditor who has filed may have a security interest in the collateral described in the statement.

A financing statement signed by a debtor can extend the security interest of the creditor to collateral not described in an underlying security agreement if the security agreement so provides.

(b) ERRORS IN THE FINANCING STATEMENT. Errors in the financing statement have no effect unless they are seriously misleading. If they are seriously misleading, the filing has no effect and does not perfect the security interest. For example, a description of the collateral in the financing statement as "all personal property" is not sufficient, and therefore, the filing of the statement does not perfect the security interest.

(c) PLACE OF FILING. The UCC gives each state the option to provide for the filing of the financing statement under (1) **local filing,** as in the county of residence or place of business of the debtor, (2) **central filing,** as in a particular office in the state capital, or (3) **dual filing,** a combination of both local and central filing.

(d) DEFECTIVE FILING. When the filing of the statement is defective, either because the statement is so erroneous as to be seriously misleading or the filing is made in a wrong county or office, the filing fails to perfect the security interest. This means that other creditors who have liens on the collateral and the trustee in bankruptcy of the debtor have a right to the collateral superior to that of the original secured creditor.

8.   Duration and Continuation of Filing

The filing of the financing statement is effective for five years. At the expiration thereof, the perfection of the security interest termi-

---

[14]   UCC § 9-306(1). C. O. Funk & Son Inc. v Sullivan Equipment, Inc., 89 Ill 2d 27, 431 NE2d 370 (1982).
[15]   UCC § 9-402. However, the security agreement may be filed as a financing statement if it contains the required information.

FIGURE 35-1   FINANCING STATEMENT

Uniform Commercial Code — FINANCING STATEMENT

This FINANCING STATEMENT is presented to a Filing Officer for filing pursuant to the Uniform Commercial Code.	No. of Additional Sheets Presented:	3. ☐ The Debtor is a transmitting utility.
1. Debtor(s) (Last Name First) and Address(es):	2. Secured Party(ies) Name(s) and Address(es)	4. For Filing Officer: Date, Time, No. Filing Office

5. This Financing Statement covers the following types (or items) of property:

6. Assignee(s) of Secured Party and Address(es)

7. ☐ The described crops are a growing or to be grown on:*
☐ The described goods are or are to be affixed to:*
☐ The lumber to be cut or minerals or the like (including oil and gas) is on:*
*(Describe Real Estate Below)

☐ Products of the Collateral are also covered.

8. Describe Real Estate Here: ☐ This statement is to be indexed in the Real Estate Records: 9. Name of a Record Owner

No. & Street	Town or City	County	Section	Block	Lot

10. This statement is filed without the debtor's signature to perfect a security interest in collateral (check appropriate box)
☐ under a security agreement signed by debtor authorizing secured party to file this statement, or
☐ which is proceeds of the original collateral described above in which a security interest was perfected, or
☐ acquired after a change of name, identity or corporate structure of the debtor, or ☐ as to which the filing has lapsed, or already subject to a security interest in another jurisdiction:
☐ when the collateral was brought into the state, or ☐ when the debtor's location was changed to this state.

By _____   By _____
          Signature(s) of Debtor(s)   Signature(s) of Secured Party(ies)

(1) Filing Officer Copy-Numerical

---

nates unless a continuation statement has been filed prior thereto. The **continuation statement** is merely a written declaration by the secured party that identifies the original filing statement by its file number and declares that it is still effective. The filing of the continuation statement continues perfection of the security for a period of five years after the last date upon which the original filing was effective. The filing of successive continuation statements will continue the perfection indefinitely.[16]

9.   Termination of the Buyer's Obligation

A buyer who has paid the debt in full may make a written demand on the secured party,

or the latter's assignee if the security interest has been assigned, to send the buyer a termination statement. A **termination statement** indicates a security interest is no longer claimed under the specified financing statement. The buyer may then present this statement to the filing officer who marks the record "terminated" and returns to the secured party the various papers that had been filed. Public notice is thereby given that the secured obligation is discharged and the financing transaction terminated.[17]

10.   Protection of Customers of the Buyer

The customer of the dealer selling from inventory takes the goods free from the security in-

---

[16]   UCC § 9-403(3).

[17]   UCC § 9-404.

terest of the dealer's supplier. That is, one who buys in the ordinary course of business items of property taken from the original buyer's inventory is free of the secured party's interest. This is so even though the interest was perfected by filing and even though such ultimate customer knew of the secured party's interest.[18] For example, a finance company lends money to a retailer to finance the retailer's inventory of new refrigerators. It takes a security interest in the inventory and files a financing statement. The retailer then sells a refrigerator to a customer. The customer takes the refrigerator free of the finance company's security interest, even though the dealer may be in default on its loan to the finance company. If this were not so, buyers would be reluctant to buy goods. The sale to the consumer was obviously contemplated by the parties. The finance company really expected to be paid from the proceeds of the sale of the collateral.

D. SECURED CREDIT SALES OF EQUIPMENT

In general, secured credit sales of equipment are treated the same as secured transactions with regard to inventory. However, the various provisions relating to resale by the buyer and the creditor's rights in proceeds have no practical application. The buyer does not resell the property but makes the purchase with the intention of keeping and using or operating it.

11.   Use of Collateral

For the purpose of secured transactions a distinction is made as to the purpose for which the buyer procures the goods. If an ultimate consumer purchases primarily for personal, family, or household use, the goods are de-

scribed as consumer goods. However, the consumer's purchase is described as equipment if used or purchased for use primarily in a business, in farming, or in a profession.

12.   Filing

In the ordinary sale of consumer goods, filing of a financing statement is not required. In contrast, filing is required to perfect a security interest in equipment.

E. RIGHTS OF PARTIES AFTER DEFAULT

When a debtor defaults on an obligation in a secured transaction, the secured party has certain rights with respect to the enforcement of the claim against the collateral.[19] These rights can be spelled out by the security agreement itself. The UCC also provides for procedures that the secured party can follow in the event the security agreement does not itself make provision for them.

13.   Secured Seller's Repossession and Resale of Collateral

Upon the buyer's default, the secured party is entitled to take the collateral or purchased property from the buyer. Self-help repossession is allowed if this can be done without causing a breach of the peace. If a breach of the peace might occur, the seller must use court action to regain the collateral.

In the *Ragde* case the debtor alleged a breach of the peace by a repossession at 5 a.m.

---

[18]   UCC § 9-307(1). Central Finance Loan v Bank of Illinois, 149 Ill App 3d 724, 102 Ill Dec 965, 500 NE2d 1066 (1986).

[19]   The term *default* is not defined in Article 9. The parties to a secured transaction may specify in their agreement what constitutes a default. If they say nothing, default means the failure to perform the obligation underlying the transaction.

RAGDE v PEOPLES BANK

53 Wash App_____, 767 P2d 949 (1989)

Ragde executed a note in favor of Peoples Bank. His 1974 Mercedes automobiles were collateral for the note. When Ragde defaulted on the note, Peoples hired a towing company to repossess the cars in which it held a security interest. At 5 a.m. two tow trucks under contract with the bank retrieved the cars from Ragde's driveway. The repossession was uneventful, and no confrontation or verbal exchange took place. Ragde alleged that the repossession caused a tremendous ruckus, awakening him and causing him to leap out of bed, fall onto some furniture, and hurt his back. He also alleged that the noise caused him severe emotional and mental shock. Ragde filed a complaint against the bank and the towing company, alleging breach of the peace. From summary judgment in favor of the bank and the towing company, Ragde appealed.

WINSOR, J.... [UCC §] 9-503 empowers a secured creditor to take possession of collateral upon default by the debtor, provided the creditor can do so without a "breach of the peace." When a repossession results in a "breach of the peace," the creditor is liable for resultant damages, including damages for personal injuries sustained by the debtor in resisting the repossession....

Ragde contends that because the repossession at issue here was conducted at night, in his driveway, in a remote and private area, it breached the peace. He argues that a breach of the peace need not involve a physical confrontation, but includes acts likely to provoke disturbance. According to Ragde, a "night raid" that causes a "tremendous ruckus" in a secluded residential neighborhood has potential for provoking a disturbance, and therefore it should be a jury question as to whether such a repossession is in fact a breach of the peace.

We agree that a breach of the peace does not necessarily require a physical confrontation. In *Stone Mach. Co. v. Kessler*, 1 Wash.App. 750, 463 P.2d 651 (1970), the court quoted with approval the following definitions of breach of the peace:

A breach of the peace is a public offense done by violence, or one causing or likely to cause an immediate disturbance of public order.

To constitute a "breach of the peace" it is not necessary that the peace be actually broken, and if what is done is unjustifiable and unlawful, tending with sufficient directness to break the peace, no more is required, nor is actual personal violence an essential element of the offense.

... We do not agree, however, that the repossession here breached the peace. First, Ragde offers no support for his conclusory statement that the repossession caused a "tremendous ruckus." Conclusory statements do not create a question of fact sufficient to defeat a motion for summary judgment.... In any event, Ragde offers no legal authority for his position that noise alone can be a breach of the peace for purposes of [UCC §] 9-503. Without such authority, we are unwilling to hold that making noise is an act likely to break the peace....

Second, Ragde's argument that a "night raid" is a breach of the peace is without legal basis. Although there is little case law on the "night raid" issue, the Arkansas

Supreme Court recently held that a 4 a.m. repossession from the debtor's driveway was not a breach of the peace, reasoning:

> There is no evidence that McClendon entered any gates, doors, or other barricades to reach the truck. He just attached the truck to his wrecker in the dead of the night and drove away. There was no confrontation with Baldwin. He was asleep when the truck was repossessed. The repossession was accomplished without breaching the peace according to our cases.

. . . So long as the law permits automobiles to be repossessed from residential property, it is reasonable to allow the repossession to occur in the early morning hours. At that hour, a confrontation with the debtor is likely avoided, and the debtor is not subjected to the humiliation of having his or her automobile repossessed from a public place. Moreover,

> the business community must be given some latitude to pursue reasonable methods of collecting debts even though such methods often might result in some inconvenience or embarrassment to the debtor.

. . . We hold that the circumstances of the Ragde repossession did not amount to a breach of the peace.

[Judgment affirmed]

QUESTIONS

1. What was the argument of Ragde?
2. Did the bank have a right to repossess the cars?
3. What determines the rights of parties after a default?
4. Was there a breach of the peace?

If the debtor defaults, the secured creditor may sell the collateral. The sale may be private or public, at any time and place, and on any terms, provided such sale is done in a manner that is commercially reasonable.[20] The seller's resale destroys all interest of the debtor in the goods.

(a) COMPULSORY RESALE. If the buyer has paid 60 percent or more of the cash price of the consumer goods, the seller must resell them within 90 days after repossession. There is an exception if the buyer, after default, has signed a written statement surrendering the right to require the resale. If the seller does not resell within the time specified, the buyer may

sue for conversion of the collateral or proceed under the UCC provision applicable to failure to comply with the UCC.[21]

(b) NOTICE. Ordinarily, notice must be given of the sale of collateral. The UCC does not specify the form of notice, and any form of notice that is reasonable is sufficient. A letter to the debtor can satisfy this requirement. If a public sale is made, the notice must give the time and place of the sale. If a private sale is made, it is sufficient to give reasonable notice of the time after which the private sale will be made. No notice is required when the collateral is perishable, is threatening to decline rapidly in value, or is sold on a recognized market or exchange.

---

[20]   UCC § 9-504. John Deere Leasing Co. v Fraken (Iowa) 395 NW2d 885 (1986).

[21]   UCC § 9-507.

14. Debtor's Right of Redemption

The debtor may exercise the right to redeem the collateral at any time prior to the time the secured party has disposed of the collateral or entered into a binding contract for resale. To redeem, the debtor must tender the entire obligation that is owed, plus any legal costs and expenses incurred by the secured party.[22]

15. Disposition of Collateral by Sale

Upon the debtor's default, the creditor may sell the collateral at public or private sale or may lease it to a third party, as long as the creditor acts in a commercially reasonable manner. The proceeds of the sale are applied in the following order: (a) to pay the expenses of the secured party in connection with the default; (b) to pay the debt owed the secured party; and (c) to pay the indebtedness owed other secured parties in the collateral.

F. PRIORITIES

Two or more parties may have conflicting interests in the same collateral.

16. Rights of Parties with Conflicting Interests

The UCC sets forth certain rules relative to these rights.

When there are two secured parties and neither party perfected the security interest, then the first attaching interest prevails.

If one party has an unperfected interest and the second party has a perfected interest, the second party prevails.

If both parties have perfected interests, the general rule is that the first to file or perfect will prevail. For example, Robinson borrows $20,000 from First Bank using her jewelry as collateral. She signs a security agreement and financing statement in First Bank's favor. The bank files on October 1 and loans Mrs. Robin-

son the $20,000 on October 5. On October 3, while awaiting the bank loan, Mrs. Robinson borrows $10,000 from Best Credit and uses the same jewelry as collateral by giving it to Best Credit. Mrs. Robinson fails to pay either debt. The First Bank will have priority since it filed first. If Easy Credit had taken possession before the bank filed, then Easy Credit would have priority under the first to either file or perfect rule.

There are two special rules that apply to purchase money security interests vs. nonpurchase money security interests.

(1) If the collateral is inventory, the purchase money secured creditor must do two things to prevail. The creditor must perfect before the debtor receives possession of the goods. The creditor must also give prior written notice to any other secured party who has previously filed a financing statement with respect to that inventory.

(2) If the collateral is noninventory collateral, such as equipment, the purchase money secured creditor will prevail over all others in the same collateral if perfection is made within ten (10) days after the giving of possession.

G. SECURED LOAN TRANSACTIONS

A secured transaction may be employed to protect one who lends on credit. The secured transaction may be one in which the collateral is delivered to or pledged with the creditor, or it may be one in which the borrower retains possession of the collateral.

17. Pledges

A *pledge* is a secured transaction in which the lender is given possession of the personal property or collateral subject to the security interest. Because it is an interest in personal property which secures payment or performance of an obligation, a pledge is a security interest subject to the provisions of UCC Article 9. A pledge is a bailment created as security for the payment of a debt. Under a pledge,

---

[22] UCC § 9-506.

specific property is delivered into the possession of a bailee-creditor with the authority, express or implied, that in the event that the debt is not paid, the property may be sold and the proceeds of the sale applied to discharge the debt secured by the pledge. For example, a person borrowing $1,000 may give the creditor property worth $1,000 or more to hold as security. In contrast, the mere recital that a debt is "secured by a pledge" of specified property, does not create a pledge when the creditor does not have possession of that property.

If the borrower repays the loan, the property which is pledged is returned by the creditor. If the loan is not repaid, the creditor may sell the property and reduce the debt by the amount of the net proceeds of the sale.

(a) CREATION AND PERFECTION. The pledge relation arises as soon as it is agreed that the pledgee shall have a security interest in the property which is delivered to the pledgee and on the basis thereof the pledgee gives value, such as lending money.

Perfection arises from the fact that the collateral is in the possession of the creditor. Filing is not required.

If the creditor returns the pledged property to the debtor, the pledge is terminated.

(b) DUTIES OF PLEDGEE. Because the secured party or pledgee is in possession of the property or collateral, reasonable care must be exercised in preserving the property and the creditor is liable for damage which results from failing to do so.

SUMMARY

A security interest is an interest in personal property or fixtures that secures payment or performance of an obligation. The property that is subject to the interest is called the *collateral*, and the party holding the interest is called the *secured party*. *Attachment* is the creation of a security interest. To secure protection against third parties' claims to the collateral, the secured party must perfect the security interest.

Tangible collateral is divided into four classes: consumer goods, equipment, inventory, and farm products. These goods classifications are based on the debtor's intended use, not on the physical characteristics of the goods.

In the ordinary credit sale of consumer goods, no filing in any state or government office is required in order to perfect the secured party's interest. The secured party who does not file will still have priority over other creditors of the buyer but will not have priority over a subpurchaser of the debtor who buys for personal, family, or household use without knowledge of the security interest. If the secured party wants to be protected against the subpurchaser, a financing statement must be filed.

In the case of goods classified as inventory, unless the secured party holds possession of the collateral, the secured party must file a financing statement to perfect the interest. A financing statement must be signed by the debtor, must have the names and addresses of the parties, and must describe the collateral. A security interest covers proceeds from the sale of the collateral unless such interest is expressly excluded. Any customer of the dealer selling from inventory will take the goods free from the security interest of the dealer's supplier, even though the customer knows that the goods are subject to a perfected security interest. The filing, however, will protect the secured creditor from certain other creditors.

A secured credit sale of equipment is treated the same as a secured credit sale of inventory, except that the provisions relating to resale by the buyer have no practical application.

Upon default a secured party may repossess the collateral from the buyer if this can be done without a breach of the peace. If a breach of the peace might occur, the secured party must use court action to regain the collateral. If the buyer has paid 60 percent or more of the cash price of the consumer goods, the seller must resell them within 90 days after repossession unless the buyer, after default, has waived this right in writing. Notice to the debtor of the sale of the collateral is usually required. A debtor may redeem the collateral prior to the time the secured party disposes of it or contracts to resell it.

If two or more parties have conflicting interests in the same collateral, priorities are determined according to UCC Article 9 rules.

A secured loan transaction may be a *pledge*, in which the collateral is held by the creditor, or it may be a transaction in which the borrower retains possession of the collateral. A filing is not required to perfect a security interest for a pledge.

QUESTIONS AND CASE PROBLEMS

1. What social forces are affected by the destruction of a security interest in consumer goods when a consumer/debtor resells the goods to another consumer who does not know of the security interest?

2. List three ways for a secured party to perfect a security interest.

3. Wayne Smith purchased a computer from Lee Sounds, Inc., for personal use. Smith signed an installment purchase note and a security agreement. Under the terms of the note Smith was to pay $100 down and $50 a month for 20 months. The security agreement included a description of the computer. However, Lee did not file a financing statement. Did Lee fulfill the requirements necessary for the attachment and perfection of its security interest in the computer? Why?

4. Thompson Home Appliance Store purchased refrigerator-freezers from the Henson Manufacturing Company and financed the purchase by obtaining a loan from the First National Bank. Thompson signed an agreement giving the bank a security interest in its inventory of refrigerator-freezers. Erhart purchased a refrigerator-freezer from Thompson on credit. The bank claimed that its security interest extended to the down payment that Erhart had made and to the unpaid balance that she owed Thompson. Was the bank correct?

5. Murray purchased an air conditioner from the Electric Company, to be used in his residence. Classify the air conditioner as collateral when in the possession of (a) the Electric Company and (b) Murray.

6. Compare or contrast attachment of a security interest with perfection of a security interest.

7. Rawlings purchased a typewriter from the Kroll Typewriter Co. for $600. At the time of the purchase he made an initial payment of $75 and agreed to pay the balance in monthly installments. A security agreement was prepared that complied with the UCC. However, the agreement was never filed. Rawlings, at a time when he still owed a balance on the typewriter and without the consent of Kroll, sold the typewriter to a neighbor. The neighbor, who had no knowledge of the security interest, used the typewriter in her home. Can Kroll repossess the typewriter from the neighbor?

8. Compare or contrast a financing statement, a continuation statement, and a termination statement.

9. Benson purchased a new Ford Thunderbird automobile. She traded in her old car and used the Magnavox Employees Credit Union to finance the balance. The credit union took a security interest in the Ford. Subsequently, the Ford was involved in a number of accidents. It was taken to a dealer for repairs. Benson was unable to pay for the work done. The dealer claimed a lien on the car for services and materials furnished. The Magnavox Employees Credit Union also claimed priority. Which claim has priority? [Magnavox Employees Credit Union v Benson, 165 Ind App 155, 331 NE2d 46]

10. *A* owned a store. He borrowed from the *B* bank and gave the bank a security interest in the "inventory" of the store. The security agreement described the collateral as inventory but did not contain any provision as to after-acquired property. *A* later became subject to bankruptcy proceedings, and his trustee in bankruptcy claimed that the secured transaction did not bind after-acquired property because the security agreement did not expressly state that it did. Was the trustee correct? [Re Fibre Glass Boat Corp. (DC Fla) 324 F Supp 1054, aff'd (CA5 Fla) 448 F2d 781]

11. Hull-Dobbs sold an automobile to Mallicoat and then assigned the sales contract to the Volunteer Finance & Loan Corp. Later Volunteer re-

possessed the automobile and sold it. When Volunteer sued Mallicoat for the deficiency between the contract price and the proceeds on resale, Mallicoat raised the defense that he had not been properly notified of the resale. The loan manager of the finance company testified that Mallicoat had been sent a registered letter stating that the car would be sold. He did not state whether the letter merely declared in general terms that the car would be sold or specified a date for its resale. He admitted that the letter never was delivered to Mallicoat and was returned to the finance company "unclaimed." The loan manager also testified that the sale was advertised by posters, but on cross examination he admitted that he was not able to state when or where it was thus advertised. It was shown that Volunteer knew where Mallicoat and his father lived and where Mallicoat was employed. Mallicoat claimed that he had not been properly notified. Volunteer asserted that sufficient notice had been given. Was the notice of the resale sufficient? [Mallicoat v Volunteer Finance & Loan Corp. 57 Tenn App 106, 415 SW2d 347]

12. *A* borrowed money from *B*. He orally agreed that *B* should have a security interest in certain equipment that was standing in *A*'s yard. There was nothing in writing, and no filing of any kind was made. Nine days later *B* took possession of the equipment. What kind of interest did *B* have in the equipment? [Transport Equipment Co. v Guaranty State Bank (CA10 Kan) 518]

13. Cook sold Martin a new tractor truck for approximately $13,000, with a down payment of approximately $3,000 and the balance to be paid in 30 monthly installments. The sales agreement provided that upon default in any payment Cook could take "immediate possession of the property . . . without notice or demand. For this purpose vendor may enter upon any premises

the property may be." Martin failed to pay the installments when due, and Cook notified him that the truck would be repossessed. Martin had the tractor truck, attached to a loaded trailer, locked on the premises of a company in Memphis. Martin intended to drive to the West Coast with the trailer. When Cook located the tractor truck, no one was around. In order to disconnect the trailer from the truck (as Cook had no right to the trailer) Cook removed the wire screen over a ventilator hole by unscrewing it from the outside with his penknife. He next reached through the ventilator hole with a stick and unlocked the door of the tractor truck. He then disconnected the trailer and had the truck towed away. Martin sued Cook for unlawfully repossessing the truck by committing a breach of the peace. Decide. [Martin v Cook, 237 Miss 267, 114 So 2d 669]

14. Muska borrowed money from the Bank of California. He secured the loan by giving the bank a security interest in equipment and machinery that he had at his place of business. The bank filed a financing statement to perfect the interest. The statement contained all the information required by the Code, except that it failed to state the residence address of the debtor. Muska filed for bankruptcy. The trustee in bankruptcy claimed that the security interest of the bank was not perfected on the theory that the omission of the residence address from the financing statement made it defective. Decide. [Lines v Bank of California (CA9 Cal) 467 F2d 1274]

15. O'Donnell sells a refrigerator to Garnet on credit and obtains a proper security agreement so that the refrigerator may serve as collateral for the payment of the amount due. Does O'Donnell have a purchase money security interest? Why or why not?

36

OTHER SECURITY DEVICES

Subject to certain exceptions, Article 9 of the UCC regulates all secured transactions dealing with personal property. The secured credit sales of consumer goods, inventory, and equipment were discussed in Chapter 35. This chapter considers other common forms of security devices.

A.   SURETYSHIP AND GUARANTY

Parties may make a contract by which one party agrees to pay if another party does not pay or defaults in the performance of an obligation. The relationship by which one person becomes responsible for the debt or undertaking of another person is used most commonly to ensure that a debt will be paid or that a contractor will perform the work called for by a contract.

1.   Definitions

One kind of agreement to answer for the debt or default of another is called a contract or undertaking of **suretyship,** and the third person is called a **surety.** The other kind of agreement is called a contract or undertaking of **guaranty,** and the third person is called a **guarantor.** In both cases the person who owes the money or is under the original obligation to pay or perform is called the **principal,** the principal debtor, or debtor.[1] The person to whom the debt or obligation is owed is known as the **creditor.**

Suretyship and guaranty undertakings have the common feature of a promise to answer for the debt or default of another, but they have a basic difference. The surety is pri-

marily liable for the debt or obligation of the principal; ordinarily the guarantor is only secondarily liable. This means that the moment the principal is in default, the creditor may demand performance or payment from the surety. The creditor generally cannot do so in the case of the guarantor and must first attempt to collect from the principal. An exception is an **absolute guaranty,** which creates the same obligation as a suretyship. A guaranty of payment creates an absolute guaranty.

The *General Motors Acceptance* case illustrates the difference between a surety and a guarantor.

---

[1]   Unless otherwise stated, *surety* as used in the text includes guarantor as well as surety, and *guaranty* is limited to a conditional guaranty. The word *principal* is also used by the law to identify the person who employs an agent. The *principal* in suretyship must be distinguished from the agent's *principal*.

GENERAL MOTORS ACCEPTANCE CORP. v DANIELS
303 Md 254, 492 A2d 1306 (1985)

In June, 1981, John Daniels agreed to purchase a used automobile from Lindsay Cadillac Company. Because John had a poor credit rating, his brother Seymoure agreed to cosign the installment sales contract. On June 23, 1981, Seymoure accompanied John to Lindsay Cadillac and signed the contract on the line designated *Buyer.* John signed the contract on the line designated *Co-Buyer.* Lindsay Cadillac then assigned the contract to General Motors Acceptance Corporation (GMAC), a company engaged in the business of financing automobiles. Installment payments were not made, and GMAC then sued Seymoure to collect the amount due. No suit was brought against John because he could not be served with process. Seymoure claimed that he was simply a guarantor, not a surety, and therefore could not be sued until GMAC had brought suit against John. From a judgment in favor of Seymoure, GMAC appealed.

COLE, J. . . . GMAC marshals several alternative arguments in support of its position that the District Court was clearly erroneous in finding that Seymoure was a guarantor of the contract between John and itself. In particular, GMAC argues that Seymoure was a surety for his brother in this transaction. We agree.

Maryland law has consistently maintained a distinction between a contract of suretyship and a contract of guaranty. A review of the distinguishing characteristics of each of these contracts, together with a summary of the relevant principles governing the interpretation and construction of contracts, provides a useful, if not necessary, predicate to the resolution of the issue presented in this case.

A contract of suretyship is a tripartite agreement among a principal obligor, his obligee, and a surety. This contract is a direct and original undertaking under which the surety is primarily or jointly liable with the principal obligor, and therefore is responsible at once if the principal obligor fails to perform. A surety is usually bound with his principal by the same instrument, executed at the same time, and on the same consideration. As Judge Rodowsky explained in *Rosenbloom v. Feiler,* 290 Md. 598, 604,

431 A.2d 102, 106 (1981) (quoting L. Simpson, *Handbook on the Law of Suretyship* § 17, at 28 (1950)), "[i]n suretyship the [obligee] has or is about to extend credit to [the principal obligor], and the promise is made to protect the [obligee] in case the principal fails to perform."

Ultimate liability rests upon the principal obligor rather than the surety, but the obligee has remedy against both. The surety, however, becomes subrogated to the rights of the obligee when the surety pays the debt for the principal obligor. With respect to notice of default, the surety is ordinarily held to know every default of his principal because he is under a duty to make inquiry and ascertain whether the principal obligor is discharging the obligation resting on him. *See* L. Simpson, *supra*, § 41 ("[I]t is generally not necessary for the creditor to notify the surety of the fact that the principal debtor is in default on his promise. It is the duty of the surety to the creditor to see that the debt is paid."). Consequently, the surety is ordinarily liable without notice.

A contract of guaranty, similar to a contract of suretyship, is an accessory contract. Despite this similarity, a contract of guaranty has several distinguishing characteristics. First, this particular contract is collateral to and independent of the principal contract that is guaranteed and, as a result, the guarantor is not a party to the principal obligation. A guarantor is therefore secondarily liable to the creditor on his contract and his promise to answer for the debt, default, or miscarriage of another becomes absolute upon default of the principal debtor and the satisfaction of the conditions precedent to liability. Second, the original contract of the principal is not the guarantor's contract, and the guarantor is not bound to take notice of its nonperformance. Rather, the guarantor agrees that the principal is able to and will perform a contract that he has made or is about to make, and that if he defaults the guarantor will pay the resulting damages provided the guarantor is notified of the principal's default. As such, the guarantor insures the ability or solvency of the principal. Third, the contract of guaranty is often founded upon a separate consideration from that supporting the contract of the principal and, consequently, the consideration for the guarantor's promise moves wholly or in part to him. Fourth, and in sum, the guarantor promises to perform if the principal does not. By contrast, a surety promises to do the same thing that the principal undertakes. . . .

Our review of the evidence in this case convinces us that the District Court erred in finding that Seymoure was a guarantor rather than a surety with respect to the installment sales contract. In our judgment the indicia for determining whether a contract is one for suretyship or one for guaranty all point to the existence of a suretyship agreement.

Initially, we note that because the contractual language is clear and unambiguous on its face, we confine our review to the contract itself. Seymoure agreed to purchase the subject automobile by affixing his signature to the installment sales contract on the line designated "Buyer."

The contract clearly stated that all buyers agreed to be jointly and severally liable for the purchase of that vehicle. Therefore, under the objective law of contracts, a reasonable person knew or should have known that he was subjecting himself to primary liability for the purchase of the automobile. In short, although uncompensated sureties are favorites of the law, Seymoure's careless indifference does not insulate him from primary liability on that agreement.

Seymoure executed the same contract as his brother, thereby making himself a party to the original contract. There is no evidence that Seymoure executed an agreement collateral to and independent of this contract. This fact, standing alone, ordinarily negates the existence of a guaranty. As one court observed, "[i]t is certain that in most cases 'the joint execution of a contract by the principal and another operates to exclude the idea of a guaranty and that in all cases such fact is an index pointing to suretyship.'" *Phoenix Insurance Co. v. Lester Bros.*, 203 Va. 802, 807, 127 S.E.2d 432, 436 (1962).

Both Seymoure and John signed the contract at the same time. Although not dispositive, this fact tends to establish the existence of a contract of suretyship rather than a contract of guaranty. Furthermore, there are no competent facts indicating that Seymoure expressly agreed to pay for the automobile only upon the default of John. Seymoure also did not qualify his signature in any manner. Thus, by the terms of the contract Seymoure agreed to be primarily and jointly liable with John for the purchase of the automobile. GMAC was therefore not required to proceed against John in the first instance, and the failure of GMAC promptly to notify Seymoure of the default in payments and of the lapse in physical damage insurance coverage does not constitute a discharge.

Finally, on the facts of this case it is immaterial that the contract did not expressly designate Seymoure as a "surety." Whether a party has entered into a contract of suretyship or guaranty is to be determined by the substance of the agreement and not by its nomenclature.

[Judgment reversed]

QUESTIONS

1. What is the principal difference between a surety and a guarantor?
2. Was Seymoure a surety or a guarantor?
3. What was the basis for the court's decision?

2. Indemnity Contract Distinguished

Both suretyship and guaranty differ from an **indemnity contract,** which is an undertaking by one person, for a consideration, to pay another person a sum of money in the event that the other person sustains a specified loss. A fire insurance policy is an example of an indemnity contract.

3. Creation of the Relation

The suretyship and guaranty relationships are based upon contract. The principles relating to capacity, formation, validity, and interpretation of contracts are applicable. Generally, the ordinary rules of offer and acceptance apply. Notice of acceptance must usually be given by the creditor to the guarantor.

In most states the statute of frauds requires that contracts of guaranty be in writing in order to be enforceable, subject to the exception that no writing is required when the promise is made primarily for the promisor's benefit.

In the absence of a special statute, no writing is required for contracts of suretyship or indemnity, because they impose primary liability and not a secondary liability to answer for the debt or default of another. Special statutes or sound business practice, however, commonly require the use of written contracts for both suretyship and indemnity.

When the contract of guaranty is made at the same time as the original transaction, the consideration for the original promise that is covered by the guaranty is also consideration for the performance of the guarantor. When the guaranty contract is entered into as a separate, subsequent transaction, there must be new consideration for the promise of the guarantor.

4.   Rights of Sureties

Sureties have a number of rights to protect them from sustaining loss, to obtain their discharge because of the conduct of others that would be harmful to them, or to recover money that they were required to pay because of the debtor's breach.

(a) EXONERATION. If the position of the surety becomes endangered, as when the debtor is about to leave the state, the surety may call upon the creditor to take action against the debtor. If at that time the creditor could proceed against the debtor and fails to do so, the surety is released or exonerated from liability to the extent that the surety has been harmed by such failure.

(b) SUBROGATION. When a surety pays a debt that it is obligated to pay, it automatically acquires the claim and the rights of the creditor. This is known as **subrogation.** That is, once the creditor is paid in full, the surety

stands in the same position as the creditor and may sue the debtor or enforce any security that was available to the creditor in order to recover the amount it has paid. The effect is the same as if the creditor, upon being paid, made an express assignment of all rights to the surety.

(c) INDEMNITY. A surety that has made payment of a claim for which it was liable as surety is entitled to indemnity from the principal; that is, it is entitled to demand from the principal reimbursement of the amount that it has paid.

(d) CONTRIBUTION. If there are two or more sureties, each is liable to the creditor for the full amount of the debt, until the creditor has been paid in full. As between themselves, however, each is liable only for a proportionate share of the debt. Accordingly, if a surety has paid more than its share of the debt, it is entitled to demand that its co-sureties contribute to it in order to share the burden that, in the absence of a contrary agreement, must be borne equally.

In the *Collins* case a person paying a debt claimed that he was entitled to contribution.

COLLINS v THROCKMORTON
(Del App) 425 A2d 146 (1981)

Throckmorton and Collins were the sole stockholders as well as officers and directors in Central Ceilings Inc. Central borrowed money from the Wilmington Trust Co. A demand note was executed by the corporate officers. Throckmorton, and his wife, and Collins, and his wife, signed as unconditional guarantors of the note on behalf of Central. Central eventually went out of business. Throckmorton and his wife took out a bank loan to satisfy the demand note. The bank then assigned the original demand note with all its rights to Throckmorton. He claimed contribution from the Collinses for half of the amounts paid by him. From a judgment in favor of the plaintiff, the defendants appealed.

MCNEILLY, J. . . . The right of a surety or guarantor, upon being compelled to pay more than his just proportion of the principal's debt, to be reimbursed by his fellow guarantors for the excess is grounded on equitable principles. . . .

The Restatement of the Law of Security provides in pertinent part:

(1) A surety who has discharged more than his proportionate share of the principal's duty is entitled to contribution from a co-surety.

(a) who has consented to the surety's becoming bound, in the proportionate amount of the net outlay properly expended. . . .

The undisputed facts show that the 1973 note was guaranteed by four persons. Consequently, each was potentially liable for one-quarter of Central's default on the note. Although the complaint alleged the plaintiff [Throckmorton] personally satisfied Central's default by paying the entirety of the principal and interest owed on the note in May, 1975, the defendants argue that the trial proofs show that the plaintiff's wife, the fourth co-guarantor, contributed equally with the plaintiff to this satisfaction. Thus, of the $9,668.73 paid to satisfy the 1973 note, the defendants claim the plaintiff contributed only half ($4,834.36). Of that amount the plaintiff was personally liable for half, which constituted one-quarter of Central's total default ($2,417.18). Thus argue the defendants, the maximum amount of contribution which the plaintiff could recover from the two defendants was $2,417.18, *i.e.*, the amount in excess of his share of Central's default which the plaintiff personally paid to satisfy the 1973 note. Therefore, the defendants argue that the Trial Court's decision, which was premised on the assumption that the plaintiff satisfied the entire default by Central (or at least three-quarters thereof), erroneously awarded judgment against each defendant in the amount of $2,417.18, double the excess amount which the plaintiff allegedly paid in satisfaction of the note and, thus, double the total amount of contribution which he was entitled to recover from the defendants collectively. . . .

Although there was no direct testimony concerning the respective amounts which the plaintiff and his wife contributed to satisfaction of the 1973 note, the bank's assignment of the note to the plaintiff, individually, gives rise to a reasonable inference that, as between the plaintiff and his wife, the plaintiff alone was entitled to seek contribution from the defendants. While it would obviously be desired to have a more detailed and explicit factual record on this point, the failure to so develop the record must be laid at the defendants' doorstep. Therefore, we will not disturb that portion of the Trial Court's judgment which requires each defendant to pay the plaintiff $2,417.18 for their contributive shares on the demand note as satisfied. . . .

[Judgment affirmed]

QUESTIONS

1. What was the basis for the court's decision?
2. When there is more than one surety, can the creditor hold one surety liable for the full amount of the debt?

5.   Defenses of Sureties

The surety's defenses include not only those that may be raised by a party to any contract but also the special defenses that are peculiar to the suretyship relation.

(a) ORDINARY CONTRACT DEFENSES. Since the relationship of suretyship is based upon a contract, the surety may raise any defense that a party to an ordinary contract may raise, such as lack of capacity of parties, absence of consideration, fraud, or mistake.

Fraud and concealment are common defenses. Since the risk of the principal's default is thrown upon the surety, it is unfair for the creditor to conceal from the surety facts that are material to the surety's risk.

Fraud on the part of the principal that is unknown to the creditor and in which the creditor has not taken part does not ordinarily release the surety.

By common law the creditor was not required to volunteer information to the surety and was not required to disclose that the principal was insolvent. There is a growing modern view that the creditor should be required to inform the surety of matters material to the risk when the creditor has reason to believe that the surety does not possess such information.

(b) SURETYSHIP DEFENSES. In addition to the ordinary defenses that can be raised against any contract, the following defenses are peculiar to the suretyship relation.

1. The original obligation was invalid.
2. The principal was discharged by payment or some other means.
3. The original contract was modified without the surety's consent.

In the *C.I.I.S.* case the guarantors argued that they were not liable on the guaranty because a new agreement was entered into and they did not guarantee the new contract.

C.I.I.S. PARTNERS v MILLER
(Colo App) 762 P2d 700 (1988)

U-Plumb-It Corporation (tenant) leased spaces 5 & 6 in landlords' shopping center. Miller and Moses were officers, shareholders, and directors of tenant. Since the landlords were unfamiliar with Miller and the tenant had no history as an ongoing business, the landlords required Moses to guarantee payments under the lease. The guaranty provided: "To accept lessee's corporate signature lessor has required and undersigned hereby personally guarantees all of lessee's obligation contained in this lease." The guaranty was an addendum to the lease. Tenant decided to move to a different location in the shopping center. Moses, as secretary of tenant corporation, negotiated an addendum to the lease with the landlords, which released spaces 5 & 6 and substituted spaces 2 & 3. The addendum also raised the monthly rent by about $100. Tenant moved to the new location and then defaulted on the lease and vacated the premises. The landlords sued tenant and guarantors to enforce the lease and guaranty. The landlords maintained that when the parties executed the second lease addendum, they intended to amend the old lease and did not intend to create a new lease. From a judgment in favor of the guarantors, the landlords appealed.

TURSI, J. . . . Guarantors cited *Green Shoe Manufacturing Co. v. Farber,* 712 P.2d 1014 (Colo. 1986) and asserted that, as a matter of law, the surrender of the demised premises and leasing of new premises was not a modification of an existing lease, but rather was a new lease and that guarantors did not guarantee the new lease. . . .

The trial court, relying on *Green Shoe Manufacturing Co. v. Farber, supra,* determined that the addendum created a new lease by completely changing the leased premises. It concluded that guarantors were not liable under the new lease and granted summary judgment in their favor.

It later appeared that tenant had become a defunct corporation. Accordingly, the trial court dismissed the claim against tenant on landlords' motion and entered final judgment.

Landlords assert that a change of premises within the shopping center alone was not enough to discharge guarantors' liability on the theory that a new lease had been formed. They maintain that in *Green Shoe Manufacturing Co. v. Farber, supra,* there were three factors that combined to transform the modification into a new lease.

While the court in *Green Shoe* discussed three factors that worked in combination, it primarily stated:

> Since the demised premises are basic elements of a lease, a change in those premises, at some point, must result in the creation of a new lease. While we do not attempt to draw that line here, it is clear that where no part of the original premises is covered by the new agreement, that new agreement goes beyond a mere modification of the original. . . .

Here, no part of the original premises remained as part of the agreement pursuant to the addendum. Therefore, we agree with the trial court that a new lease was created by the addendum.

. . . In general, when the principal obligation is materially altered to the detriment of the guarantor, without the guarantor's consent, that alteration discharges the guarantor's liability. . . . However, the consent of the guarantor to alterations is binding whether it is expressed as a part of the initial obligation or is given later either before or subsequent to the alteration. . . .

In order to determine the scope of a guarantor's liability, the guaranty must be "reasonably interpreted according to the intention of the parties as disclosed by the surrounding circumstances." . . .

Here, Moses, as secretary of the corporation, initiated the change in the premises underlying the lease, then negotiated, and executed the lease addendum. Moses' central involvement in the change in location and execution of the addendum raises a question regarding his intention to consent to the alterations as guarantor.

Since the parties' intent is a factual question . . . there remains a genuine issue of material fact to be resolved. . . .

We distinguish this case from *Green Shoe Manufacturing Co. v. Farber, supra,* in that *Green Shoe* concerned a landlord who sought to hold the guarantor of the lease liable based on a broad consent-for-modification clause in the original lease. Here, landlords do not rely on such a clause, but rather maintain that Moses consented to the alteration of his obligation by negotiating and executing the addendum. This issue of the guarantor's consent to the alteration of the obligation subsequent to the original guaranty agreement was not addressed in *Green Shoe.* . . .

[Judgment Reversed]

QUESTIONS

1. What was the argument of the tenants?
2. What was the argument of the landlords?
3. What was the court's decision?

B.   LETTERS OF CREDIT

A letter of credit is a form of agreement that the issuer of the letter will pay drafts drawn by the creditor. It is thus a form of advance arrangement for financing, in that it is known in advance how much money may be obtained from the issuer of the letter. It is likewise a security device, because the creditor knows that the drafts that the creditor draws will be accepted or paid by the issuer of the letter.

The use of letters of credit arose in international trade. While this continues to be the

FIGURE 36-1   LETTER OF CREDIT
While there are few formal requirements for creating a letter of credit, banks often use a standard form similar to the one pictured here.

THE NATIONAL BANK OF COMMERCE
St. Louis, MO

To: DATE _____

                                                 BRANCH _____

LADIES and GENTLEMEN,

We open an IRREVOCABLE DOCUMENTARY CREDIT NO

in favor of _____

_____

For account of _____

_____

For an amount not exceeding _____

Valid until _____ Available by beneficiary's draft in duplicate on accountees at _____
_____ drawn to the order of negotiating Bank (without recourse) for 100% of net invoice value bearing
date, credit number and accompanied by documents (marked X below) at least in duplicate, unless otherwise specified.

☐   Full set of CLEAN ON BOARD OCEAN BILLS OF LADING to order endorsed in blank, marked "freight paid/ payable at
     destination" and notify accreditors.

☐   INSURANCE POLICY OR UNDERWRITERS' CERTIFICATE in duplicate, blank endorsed in currency of credit for at least
     _____ % of invoice value against Marine, War and Strike risks.

☐   PACKING SPECIFICATION in quadruplicate.

☐   INVOICE in sextuplicate in English duly signed by beneficiaries certifying that the goods shipped are in accordance with
     order / indent/pro-forma Invoice No. _____ dated _____
     showing Import Licence No. _____

Documents to cover shipment of:				
From:	To:	Shipment not later than	Partshipment	Transhipment

All bank charges, including postage s for beneficiaries account.

Original draft and one set of documents to be sent to us by registered airmail and the duplicate draft with the remaining
documents by subsequent registered air-mail.

REIMBURSEMENT INSTRUCTIONS.

Yours faithfully,
THE NATIONAL BANK OF COMMERCE,

_____   _____
ACCOUNTANT   MANAGER

No. 4355610

primary area of use, there is a growing use of letters in domestic sales and in transactions in which the letter of credit takes the place of a surety bond. Thus, a letter of credit has been used to assure that a borrower would repay a loan, that a tenant would pay the rent due under a lease, and that a contractor would properly perform a construction contract.[2]

6.   Definition

A **letter of credit** is an engagement by its issuer that it will pay or accept drafts when the conditions specified in the letter are satisfied. The issuer is usually a bank.

Three contracts are involved in letter-of-

credit transactions: (1) the contract between the issuer and the customer of the issuer; (2) the letter of credit itself; and (3) the underlying agreement, often a contract of sale, between the beneficiary and the customer of the issuer of the letter of credit. The letter of credit is completely independent from the other two contracts.

The issuer of the letter of credit is not a surety that is underwriting payment by its customer. The issuer of the letter is in effect the obligor on a third party beneficiary contract made for the benefit of the beneficiary of the letter.

The *Travelers'* case is an illustration of the use of a letter of credit and how it differs from a contract of suretyship. The case also illustrates the contractual commitment of a bank to make payment under specified conditions.

---

[2]   Barclays Bank D.C.O. v The Mercantile National Bank (CA5 Ga) 481 F2d 1224 (1973).

TRAVELERS INDEMNITY CO. v FLUSHING NAT'L. BANK
90 Misc 2d 964, 396 NYS2d 754 (1977)

Berley was a party to a lawsuit. The court required him to file a $40,000 bond. The Travelers Indemnity Company issued the bond but required Berley to give it a certified check for $40,000 as security. Subsequently, Berley obtained a letter of credit for $40,000 from the Flushing National Bank. By this letter of credit the bank agreed to honor drafts drawn upon it by the indemnity company when it incurred liability on the Berley bond. Berley gave this letter of credit to the indemnity company and took back his certified check. Thereafter, a claim was made on the Berley bond. The indemnity company then drew a draft upon the bank pursuant to the letter of credit. The bank refused to pay the draft, on the grounds that the indemnity company had not given any consideration for the letter of credit and that the bank was released from liability because the indemnity company's release of the certified check constituted an impairment of collateral.

FINZ, J.... The defendant bank now claims that it should be released from the terms of the letter of credit....

It claims, first of all, that there was no consideration for the issuance of the letter of credit.... In addition, it asserts that the credit is unenforceable by reason of the fact that the plaintiff, having in its hands a certified check in the sum of $40,000, released the check and thereby released the defendant since the defendant was, in effect, a guarantor or a surety to the plaintiff. Lastly, the defendant bank alleges that it was the plaintiff's fraud and concealment of facts which have rendered the letter of credit unenforceable.

Before proceeding in any direction it is necessary to make clear the nature of a letter of credit.

"Credit" or "letter of credit" means an engagement by a bank or other person made at the request of a customer and of a kind within the scope of this Article (UCC Section 5-102) that the issuer will honor drafts or other demands for payment upon compliance with the conditions specified in the credit. . . .

A letter of credit is a contract. It is distinguished by the fact that it is inevitably linked to another understanding, usually also a contract, but is independent of that other understanding or contract. Appreciation of these two simple concepts: that a letter of credit is a contract, and that the letter of credit contract stands alone to be construed within its own four corners, is sufficient to provide understanding, it is indispensable to avoid confusion.

Confining ourselves, as noted above, to bank letters of credit, the first fundamental is that the bank engage itself as a principal in the letter of credit transaction but is neither engaged in nor . . . in any way concerned with the understanding, contract, or transaction which may have made the letter of credit necessary or convenient.

The purpose of the letter of credit is to provide a method of payment, through banking channels, which defines the terms and conditions upon which *and only upon which the payment will be made*, and which, within the strict limits of those terms and conditions, engages the full *primary* responsibility of the bank to make the payment, in addition to whatever obligation may lie upon the party for whose account the bank has issued or confirmed the letter of credit. This is the only role which the bank undertakes, and its only engagement, legal, commercial, or moral. This is, in short, the limitation of the letter of credit. If the limitation is recognized at all times by all interested parties, there is room neither for dispute nor for disappointment. Disappointment, disputes, and litigation arise only when one or another of the parties overlooks the functional limitation and takes the bank's letter of credit to be a guaranty of performance of some related but separate mercantile contract. (McKinney's Consolidated Laws Uniform Commercial Code, Practice Commentary p. 642.)

The letter of credit, probably because of its simple structure and its unqualified agreement to pay, notwithstanding any condition outside of its own terms, has become a principal instrument of international trade and, increasingly, of domestic transactions. It is in this framework that the defenses raised by the defendant should be considered.

The fact that plaintiff did not rely on the letter of credit when it issued its bond is not relevant to the question of consideration for the issuance of the letter of credit. If this were an issue at all, the question of consideration only arises as between the issuers of the credit and its customer. The beneficiary . . . would not in any event give consideration to the issuer.

The problem of consideration does not arise, however, in view of UCC § 5-105, which states: "No consideration is necessary to establish a credit or to enlarge or otherwise modify its terms. . . ."

A letter of credit, insofar as it is a contract, partakes of the rules of construction generally applicable to contracts. . . . Since there were no special rules adopted with regard to interpretation of the terms of a letter of credit, the ordinary rules of law apply (UCC § 1-103). "The same general principles which apply to other contracts in writing govern letters of credit. . . . Moreover, as between the beneficiary of a letter of credit and the issuer . . . if ambiguity exists, the words are taken as strongly against the issuer as a reasonable reading will justify. . . ."

In addition, the beneficiary, when it presents a demand for payment or a draft, warrants that there has been compliance with the necessary conditions of the letter of credit (UCC § 5-111[1]).

The claim that the release of the collateral without knowledge or consent of the defendant, discharged the defendant's obligation as a surety, depends upon the relationship of the defendant and plaintiff.

> The issuer of a letter of credit does not have the status of a surety or guarantor. A surety is generally not liable on his undertaking unless his principal is liable and in default on the underlying liability. The defenses of the principal are available to the surety and, if the underlying debt is canceled, the surety's obligation ceases. (*Association de Axucareros de Guatemala v United States Nat. Bank* (CA9 Or) 423 F2d 638). The letter of credit, unlike the classic surety undertaking, is a primary obligation between the issuer and the beneficiary. (See UCC § 5-114:1, pt 1,) [(Anderson Uniform Commercial Code, Second Edition, § 5-114:7.)]

Undoubtedly, a guarantor or a surety has the right to expect that the terms upon which the guarantee was made would remain unchanged, absent the knowledge and consent to such change by the guarantor. A release of collateral or a change in the terms would certainly operate to release the surety or guarantor. . . .

In this case, the letter was not issued on the strength of any collateral held by the plaintiff. It is admitted in the affidavit in opposition that defendant had no knowledge that the bond was issued or how it was collateralized. It offered no guarantee to the plaintiff. It dealt entirely with its own customer. It had dealt with him on previous occasions and it knew that he had obligations which "were very substantial" and "the Bank was becoming concerned about Berley's ability to pay the loans. . . . Berley owed the Bank nearly $300,000 when the letter of credit was issued." They had nearly five weeks, after being informed of all the circumstances, to inquire of the defendant as to the status of the bond. They questioned Berley as to the wording of the letter of credit and then, finally, accepted it, issuing the letter in the form suggested.

[Judgment for Travelers Indemnity Company]

QUESTIONS

1. Must the customer or the beneficiary give consideration for a letter of credit?
2. Why was the issuer of the letter not discharged when the certified check was given back to the customer?

7.   Parties

The parties to a letter of credit are (a) the issuer, (b) the customer who makes the arrangements with the issuer, and (c) the beneficiary who will be the drawer of the drafts that will be drawn under the letter of credit. There may also be (d) an advising bank,[3] if the local issuer of the letter of credit requests its correspondent bank where the beneficiary is located to

---

[3]   Artoc Bank & Trust v Sun Marine Terminals (Tex App) 760 SW 2d 311 (1988).

notify or advise the beneficiary that the letter has been issued.

As an illustration of the above definitions, an American merchant may buy goods from a Spanish merchant. There may be a prior course of dealings between the parties, so that the seller is willing to accept the buyer's commercial paper as payment or to accept trade acceptances drawn on the buyer. If the foreign seller is not willing to do this, the American buyer, as customer, may go to a bank, the issuer, and obtain a letter of credit naming the Spanish seller as beneficiary. The American bank's correspondent or advising bank in Spain notifies the Spanish seller that this has been done. The Spanish seller will then draw drafts on the American buyer. By the letter of credit, the issuer is required to accept or pay these drafts.

8.   Duration

A letter of credit continues for any time specified therein. Generally, a maximum money amount is stated in the letter, so that the letter is exhausted or used up when drafts aggregating that maximum have been accepted or paid by the issuer. A letter of credit may be used in installments as the beneficiary chooses. A letter of credit cannot be revoked or modified by the issuer or the customer without the consent of the beneficiary unless that right is expressly reserved in the letter.

9.   Form

A letter of credit must be in writing and signed by the issuer. If the credit is issued by a bank and requires a documentary draft or a documentary demand for payment,[4] or if the credit is issued by a nonbank and requires that the draft or demand for payment be accompanied by a document of title, the instrument is presumed to be a letter of credit (rather than a contract of guaranty). Otherwise, the instrument must conspicuously state that it is a letter of credit.[5] Consideration is not required to establish or modify a letter of credit.

10.   Duty of Issuer

The issuer is obligated to honor drafts drawn under the letter of credit if the conditions specified in the letter have been satisfied. Generally, this means that the bank must assure itself that all specified papers have been submitted. The issuer has no duty to verify that the papers are properly supported by facts or that the underlying transaction has been performed. It is thus immaterial that the goods sold by the seller in fact do not conform to the contract, as long as the seller tenders the documents specified by the letter of credit.[6] If the issuer dishonors a draft without justification, it is liable to its customer for breach of contract.

---

[4]   A documentary draft or a documentary demand for payment is one the honor of which is conditioned upon the presentation of one or more documents. A document could be a document of title, security, invoice, certificate, notice of default, or other similar paper. UCC § 5-103(1)(b).
[5]   Commercial Corp. v Hynutek, Inc. 705 SW2d 713 (1986).
[6]   Intraworld Industries, Inc. v Girard Trust Bank, 461 Pa 343, 336 A2d 316 (1975).

SUMMARY

Suretyship and guaranty undertakings have the common feature of a promise to answer for the debt or default of another. A surety is primarily liable for the debt or obligation of the principal debtor. The guarantor is ordinarily only secondarily liable, unless the guarantor has made an absolute guaranty. The surety and guaranty relationships are based upon contract. Sureties have a number of rights to protect them. They are exoneration, subrogation, indemnity, and contribution. In addition to those rights, sureties also have certain defenses. They include ordinary contract defenses as well as some defenses peculiar to the suretyship relationship, such as the original contract was invalid, the principal obligation was discharged, or the original contract was modified without the surety's consent.

A letter of credit is an agreement that the issuer of the letter will pay drafts drawn on the issuer by the beneficiary of the letter. The issuer of the letter of credit is usually a bank. There are three contracts involved in letter-of-credit transactions: (1) the contract between the issuer and the customer of the issuer, (2) the letter of credit itself, and (3) the underlying agreement between the beneficiary and the customer of the issuer of the letter of credit. The parties to a letter of credit are the issuer, the customer who makes the arrangement with the issuer, and the beneficiary who will be the drawer of the drafts to be drawn under the letter of credit. The letter of credit continues for any time specified therein. The letter of credit must be in writing and signed by the issuer. Consideration is not required to establish or modify a letter of credit. If the conditions in the letter of credit have been complied with, the issuer is then obligated to honor drafts drawn under the letter of credit.

QUESTIONS AND CASE PROBLEMS

1. What social forces are affected by the use of a letter of credit?
2. Kiernan Construction Company makes a contract with Jackson to build a house for her. The Century Surety Company executes a bond to protect Jackson from loss should Kiernan fail to construct the house or pay labor and material bills. Kiernan fails to build the house. Jackson sues the Century Surety Company. It raises the defense that Jackson must first sue Kiernan. Is it correct?
3. Identify the parties to a letter of credit.
4. What is the duration of a letter of credit?
5. The surety's right of subrogation arises as soon as the surety pays any part of the debt that the surety is obligated to pay. Appraise this statement.
6. Eberstadt owed Terence $500. He gave his note for that amount to Terence. At the same time an agreement signed by Reid and given to Terence was as follows: "I agree to be surety for the payment of Eberstadt's note for $500." On maturity of the note, Eberstadt paid $200 on account and gave a new note for $300 due in three months. Reid was not informed of this transaction. The new note was not paid at maturity. Terence sues Reid. Does Reid have any defense?
7. How does a contract of suretyship and guaranty differ from an indemnity contract?
8. A made a contract to purchase goods from B. In order to assure B that he would be paid, A obtained a letter of credit from the C bank. The letter was irrevocable and provided that C would honor drafts for the purchase price of goods shipped to A upon presentment to the bank of the drafts, the bill of lading showing shipment to A, and the invoice showing the nature and price of the goods shipped. Because of financial difficulties, A did not want to receive the goods under the contract and made an agreement with C that no drafts would be honored pursuant to the letter of credit. B shipped goods to A under the contract and presented drafts, the proper bills of lading, and invoices to C. C refused to honor the drafts. B sued C. It claimed that it was not liable because the letter of credit that had obligated it to accept the drafts had been terminated by the agreement of its customer. Was this a valid defense?

9. The Kitsap County Credit Bureau held against Alderman a claim, the payment of which had been guaranteed by Richards. When Richards was sued on his guaranty, he proved that the claim against Alderman had been settled by compromise upon Alderman's paying $100 to the creditor. What was the result? [Kitsap County Credit Bureau v Richards, 52 Wash 381, 325 P2d 292]

10. Hugill agreed to deliver shingles to the W. I. Carpenter Lumber Co. He furnished a surety bond to secure the faithful performance of the contract on his part. After a breach of the contract by Hugill, the lumber company brought an action to recover its loss from the surety, the Fidelity & Deposit Co. of Maryland. The surety denied liability, on the grounds that there was concealment of (a) the price to be paid for the shingles and (b) the fact that a material advance had been made to the contractor equal to the amount of the profit that he would make by performing the contract. Decide. [W. I. Carpenter Lumber Co. v Hugill, 149 Wash 45, 270 P 94]

11. Donaldson sold plumbing supplies. The St. Paul-Mercury Indemnity Co., as surety for him, executed and delivered a bond to the State of California for the payment of all sales taxes.

Donaldson failed to pay, and the company paid the taxes that he owed. The company then sued him for the taxes. What was the result? [St. Paul-Mercury Indemnity Co. v Donaldson, 225 SC 476, 83 SE2d 159]

12. Paul owed Charles a $1,000 debt, due September 1. On August 15, George, for consideration, orally promised Charles to pay the debt if Paul didn't. On September 1, Paul didn't pay, so Charles demanded $1,000 from George. Is George liable? Why?

13. First National Bank hired Longdon as a secretary and obtained a surety bond from Belton covering the bank against losses up to $100,000 resulting from Longdon's improper conduct in the performance of his duties. Both Longdon and the bank signed the application for the bond. After one year of service Longdon was promoted to the position of teller in the bank, and the original bond remained in effect. Shortly after Longdon's promotion a surprise examination revealed that Longdon had taken advantage of his new position and had stolen $50,000 from the bank. He was arrested and charged with embezzlement. Longdon had only $5,000 in assets at the time of his arrest. (a) If the bank demands a payment of $50,000 from Belton, what defense, if any, might Belton raise to deny any obligation to the bank? (b) If Belton fully reimburses the bank for its loss, under what theory or theories, if any, may Belton attempt to recover from Longdon?

14. List and explain the rights of a surety.

15. Partridge lends $1,000 to Fazio, who agrees to repay the amount in three months. A month after the loan Partridge requests security, and Shank, without asking for or receiving payment for so doing, gives Partridge a written promise to answer in the event of default by Fazio. Fazio defaults. Partridge sues Fazio and obtains judgment; execution is issued and returned unsatisfied. Partridge then sues Shank, who claims there is no consideration for her promise. Is this defense valid? Explain.

37

BANKRUPTCY

Our society has provided a system by which the honest but financially overburdened debtor can pay into court whatever property the debtor possesses, be relieved of most obligations, and begin economic life anew. This system is called **bankruptcy.**

Historically, the bankruptcy law was not concerned with benefiting the debtor as much as it was with benefiting the debtor's creditors. In its origin, the law was designed to compel fraudulent debtors to bring their property into court and to pay it to their creditors, thus preventing them from concealing their property or from paying it to only some of their creditors. Today, a bankruptcy proceeding is concerned with benefiting both debtor and creditors, as can be seen from the fact that a case in bankruptcy may be initiated by the debtor (a voluntary case) or by creditors (an involuntary case).

A.   BANKRUPTCY LAW

Congress, under the power granted to it by the Constitution, enacted the Bankruptcy Act in 1898. This legislation was subsequently amended by the Chandler Act of 1938. However, the Bankruptcy Reform Act of 1978 (the Bankruptcy Code) was the first comprehensive revision to modernize the bankruptcy laws by making both substantive and procedural changes. The Bankruptcy Amendments Act of 1984 and Supreme Court Bankruptcy Rules supplement the 1978 Act.

1.   Bankruptcy Courts

The 1978 Act established a United States Bankruptcy Court as an adjunct to the federal district court in each judicial district. This measure greatly expanded the jurisdiction of the bankruptcy courts. Under the 1978 Act the bankruptcy courts could not only hear and decide all bankruptcy cases but were also granted nonexclusive jurisdiction to hear and decide all civil proceedings arising under the bankruptcy law or relating to cases under the bankruptcy law. However, this expansion of bankruptcy court jurisdiction was held by the United States Supreme Court to violate Article III of the U.S. Constitution.[1] The 1978 Act had given bankruptcy judges most of the authority of federal district court judges, but none of their tenure or salary protection.

The Bankruptcy Amendments Act of 1984 restructured the bankruptcy court system, limiting the powers of bankruptcy judges. The amendments removed the authority of bank-

ruptcy judges over nonbankruptcy issues. In effect, the amendments vested all jurisdiction over bankruptcy cases in the United States District Courts, which may refer all cases and related proceedings to adjunct bankruptcy courts.

2.   Kinds of Bankruptcy Proceedings

Under the 1978 Act, three kinds of bankruptcy proceedings are available to individuals and businesses:

1. liquidation, sometimes called a "Chapter 7" bankruptcy;
2. reorganization, sometimes called a "Chapter 11" bankruptcy; and
3. extended time payment, sometimes called a "Chapter 13" bankruptcy.

B.   LIQUIDATION UNDER CHAPTER 7

In liquidation proceedings, the debtor's nonexempt assets are collected by the trustee representing the creditors. The trustee liquidates the assets and distributes the proceeds to the creditors. The debtor is then discharged from most debts. A liquidation can be voluntary or involuntary.

3.   Commencement of the Case

A bankruptcy case refers to the proceeding in the bankruptcy court. The principal difference between a voluntary case and an involuntary case lies in the manner in which the proceedings are initiated.

(a) VOLUNTARY. A **voluntary case** is commenced by the debtor's filing a petition with the bankruptcy court. A joint petition may be filed by a husband and wife. The commencement of a voluntary case constitutes an order for relief; no formal adjudication is needed.[2] Unless the court orders otherwise, a debtor must also file a schedule of current income and current expenditures.

---

[1]   Northern Pipeline Constr. Co. v Marathon Pipe Line Co. 458 US 50 (1982).

[2]   11 USC § 301.

Individuals, partnerships, and corporations, except railroads, banks, insurance companies, savings and loan associations, and credit unions, may file a voluntary petition.[3]

(b) INVOLUNTARY. An **involuntary case** is commenced by the creditors by filing a petition with the bankruptcy court.

An involuntary case may be commenced against any individual, partnership or corporation, except those excluded from filing voluntary petitions, as well as farmers and nonprofit corporations, who may not be subject to an involuntary case.[4]

4.   Number and Claims of Petitioning Creditors

If there are 12 or more creditors, at least three, whose unsecured claims total $5,000 or more, must sign the involuntary petition. If there are fewer than 12 creditors, excluding employees or insiders, any creditor whose unsecured claim is at least $5,000 may sign the petition.

If the creditor holds security for the claim,

only the amount of the claim in excess of the value of the security is counted. The holder of a claim that is the subject of a bona fide dispute may not be counted as a petitioning creditor.[5]

5.   Grounds for Relief for Involuntary Case

The mere filing of an involuntary case petition does not constitute an order for relief. The debtor may contest the bankruptcy petition. If the debtor does not contest the petition, the court will enter an order for relief if at least one of the following grounds exists: (a) the debtor is generally not paying debts as they become due, or (b) within 120 days before the filing of the petition, a custodian has been appointed for the debtor's property. No act of misconduct on the part of the debtor need be shown.[6]

In the *Arker* case the court was faced with the problem of whether a failure to pay a debt to a single creditor should be grounds for relief in an involuntary case.

---

[3]   11 USC § 109(b).
[4]   11 USC § 303(a).

[5]   11 USC § 303(b)(1).
[6]   11 USC § 303(h)(1) and (2).

IN RE SOL ARKER
6 BR 632 (ED NY 1980)

Bank Leumi Trust Company commenced an involuntary case in bankruptcy against Sol Arker. The bank claimed that Arker was generally not paying his debts, since the bank had been unable to collect on a $190,000 judgment that it held against Arker. Arker denied that he was generally not paying his debts and asserted further that he had no assets that could be used to satisfy the bank's claim.

PARENTE, B.J. . . . The alleged debtor denies that he is generally not paying his debts as they become due.

Whether the Court should grant an order for relief against the alleged debtor rests on the resolution of the following:

Should the Court grant an order for relief where the petitioning creditor contends that the alleged debtor has failed to pay one creditor and where the alleged debtor has no assets for the Bankruptcy Court to administer.

As set forth in 11 U.S.C. § 303 and as is relevant to the case now before the Court, an involuntary case may be commenced under Chapter 7 or Chapter 11 of the Bankruptcy Code against any person that may be a debtor under those chapters. In cases such as the case at bar, where the debtor has fewer than twelve creditors, § 303(b)(2) provides that a petition may be brought by a single entity which is a holder of a claim against the alleged debtor that is not contingent as to liability. . . .

Subsection (h) of § 303 enunciates the standard for an order for relief on an involuntary petition.

Section 303(h) provides in relevant part:

> (h) If the petition is not timely controverted, the court shall order relief against the debtor in an involuntary case under the chapter under which the petition was filed. Otherwise, after trial, the court shall order relief against the debtor in an involuntary case under the chapter which the petition was filed, only if
> (1) The debtor is generally not paying such debtor's debts as such debts become due: or. . . .

The phrase "the debtor is generally not paying such debtor's debts as such debts become due" is not defined in the Bankruptcy Code.

However, when faced with this issue, the bankruptcy courts have consistently held that in order to determine whether the alleged debtor is generally paying his debts as they become due, the amount of the debts not being paid and the number of creditors not being paid are significant factors. . . .

Specifically, in the *Matter of 7H Land & Cattle Co.*, 2 CBC 2d 554 (D Nev. 1980), the bankruptcy court was faced with the following issue:

Does an allegation that the alleged debtors have failed to pay one creditor constitute "generally not paying such debtors' debts as they become due"?

The Court stated that as a general rule:

> It may be assumed that in the ordinary case there can be no order for relief with no more proof than mere failure to meet liability to a single creditor.

However, the Court further states that there should be two exceptions to this general rule:

> First: An order for relief should be granted in the exceptional case of an alleged debtor with a sole creditor who would otherwise be without an adequate remedy under non-bankruptcy law.
> Second: If the petitioning creditor makes a showing of special circumstances amounting to fraud, trick, artifice, or scam, then an order for relief should be granted.

This Court agrees with the principle of law enunciated in the *Matter of 7H Land and Cattle Co.* Thus, given the facts of the case at bar, unless one of the exceptions to the general rule stated in said case applies, the petitioning creditor's request for an order for relief should be denied.

The petitioning creditor did not put before this Court a claim that there were circumstances surrounding the petitioning creditor which bear closely upon trick, artifice, scam or fraud by the alleged debtor. Therefore, the second exception to the general rule does not apply to the case at bar.

With respect to the first exception, i.e., an alleged debtor with a sole creditor who would otherwise be without an adequate remedy under non-bankruptcy law, although there is ample evidence in the record to support the Court's finding that the petitioning creditor has exhausted all possible nonbankruptcy remedies, there is an additional factor in this case which was not present in the *Matter of 7H Land and Cattle Co.*

The Court in the case at bar is faced with the following situation: an involuntary petition has been filed against an alleged debtor who has no free assets which could be liquidated for the benefit of his creditors and who has only one creditor which has yet to be paid. It is manifest that the alleged debtor has no free assets to be liquidated which is decisive to this Court's conclusion that an order for relief should not be granted in the case at bar. This conclusion is predicated on the purpose of an involuntary proceeding which is to secure an equitable distribution of the assets of the alleged debtor among all his creditors. . . . To grant an order for relief in a case where there are no assets to be liquidated for the benefit of creditors would not be in comport with this long standing policy underlying involuntary proceedings.

Further support for this precept is found in the *Matter of Oak Winds*, 2 CBC 2d 417 (ND Fla 1980). In that case . . . the court stated in relevant part:

> In sum, it is evident and this Court is satisfied that there would not be any useful purpose to retain jurisdiction of this case either as a reorganization case under Chapter 11 of the Code since there is obviously no desire by the debtor to effectuate any involuntary reorganization *nor would it serve any useful purpose to consider a conversion of this case into a liquidating case under Chapter 7 simply because there are no free assets which could be liquidated for the benefit of the general unsecured creditors or, the only one in this instance.* (emphasis added)

Just as the court in the *Matter of Oak Winds* refused to convert the involuntary Chapter 11 case to a Chapter 7 case on the ground that there were no free assets to liquidate, this Court is constrained to deny the granting of an order for relief in the case at bar. To grant an order for relief in the case at bar would serve no purpose since there are not assets for this Court to administer.

[Petition denied]

QUESTIONS

1. What are the requirements for the commencement of an involuntary case?
2. How many creditors signed the petition in this case?
3. Did the court grant the relief requested?

6.   Automatic Stay

The filing of either a voluntary or involuntary petition operates as an **automatic stay**, which prevents creditors from taking action such as filing suits or foreclosure actions against the debtor.[7] The stay freezes all creditors in their filing date position, so that no one creditor gets an advantage over the others. This automatic stay ends when the bankruptcy case is closed or dismissed or when the debtor is granted a discharge.

7.   Rights of Debtor in Involuntary Case

If an involuntary petition is dismissed other than by consent of all petitioning creditors and the debtor, the court may award costs, reasonable attorney's fees, or damages to the debtor. The damages are those that may be caused by the taking of possession of the debtor's property. The debtor may also recover damages against any creditor who filed the petition in bad faith.[8]

---

[7]   11 USC § 362.

[8]   11 USC § 303(i).

8.   Trustee in Bankruptcy

The trustee in bankruptcy is elected by the creditors. An interim trustee will be appointed by the court or by the United States Trustee if a trustee is not elected by the creditors.

(a) STATUS OF THE TRUSTEE. The trustee is deemed to be the successor to and stand in the shoes of the debtor. By operation of law the trustee automatically becomes the owner of all the property of the debtor in excess of the property to which the debtor is entitled under exemption laws. Property inherited by the debtor within six months after the filing of the petition also passes to the trustee.

(b) RIGHTS OF THE TRUSTEE. The bankruptcy trustee possesses the rights and the powers of the most favored creditor of the debtor. This means that the trustee can avoid (1) transfers by the debtor that a creditor holding a valid claim under state law could have avoided at the commencement of the bankruptcy case, (2) **preferences,** that is, transfers of property by the debtor to a creditor, the effect of which enables the creditor to obtain a greater percentage of the creditor's claim than the creditor would have received had the debtor's assets been liquidated in bankruptcy, and (3) statutory liens that became effective against the debtor at the commencement of the bankruptcy.

9.   Voidable Transfers

A debtor may not transfer property to prevent creditors from satisfying their legal claims. The trustee may avoid any such transfer made or obligation incurred by the debtor within one year of bankruptcy when the debtor's actual intent was to hinder, delay, or defraud creditors by so doing.

The trustee may also avoid certain transfers of property made by a debtor merely because their effect is to make the debtor insolvent or to reduce the debtor's assets to an unreasonably low amount.[9]

(a) THE INSOLVENT DEBTOR. A debtor is insolvent when the total fair value of all the debtor's assets does not exceed the debts owed by the debtor. This is commonly called the **balance sheet test,** because it is merely a comparison of assets to liabilities, without considering whether the debtor will be able to meet future obligations as they become due.

(b) PREFERENTIAL TRANSFERS. A transfer of property by the debtor to a creditor may be set aside and the property recovered by the debtor's trustee in bankruptcy if (1) the transfer was to pay a debt incurred at some earlier time, (2) the transfer was made when the debtor was insolvent and within 90 days before the filing of the bankruptcy petition, and (3) by the transfer the creditor received more than such creditor would have received in a liquidation of the debtor's estate. A debtor is presumed to be insolvent on and during the 90 days immediately preceding the date of the filing of the bankruptcy petition.[10]

Transfers made to **insiders**—that is, the debtor's relatives, partners, directors, and controlling persons—within the 12 months prior to the filing of the petition may be set aside.[11]

Certain transfers by a debtor may not be attacked by the trustee as preferences. A transaction for a present consideration, such as a cash sale, is not subject to attack. A payment by a debtor in the ordinary course of business, such as the payment of a utility bill, is not subject to attack. A payment by an individual debtor whose debts are primarily consumer debts is not subject to attack if the aggregate value of the transfer is less than $600.[12]

In the *Jaggers* case a trustee objected to a debtor's payments on a promissory note on the grounds that these payments were preferences.

---

[9]   11 USC § 548.

[10]   11 USC § 547(f).
[11]   11 USC § 547(b)(4)(B).
[12]   11 USC § 547(c)(7).

IN RE JAGGERS

48 BR 33 (WD Tex 1985)

On May 7, 1981, Joseph Jaggers filed a petition under Chapter 7 of the Bankruptcy Code. At the time the petition was filed, he was indebted to the Cove State Bank on a promissory note. The principal amount of the note had originally been in excess of $68,000. Two payments had been made on the note. One payment was made on February 23, 1981, in the form of a check drawn on the account of T-Vest Corporation and signed by Dorothea M. Kerr, an authorized signatory on the T-Vest account. Another payment was made on March 23, 1981, in the form of a check drawn on the account of J. & D. Finance and signed by Jaggers, an authorized signatory on the J. & D. account. The trustee in bankruptcy claimed that these payments were preferential transfers.

THOMPSON, C.J. . . . The T-Vest Corporation is a Texas Corporation. The Debtor and his wife were directors of the corporation. The Debtor was the Chairman of the Board of Directors and his wife was the secretary of the corporation. One Hundred percent of the stock of T-Vest Corporation was owned by the Debtor and his wife. The Debtor controlled and directed the disbursement of the funds from the T-Vest Corporation account. At the direction of the Debtor, payments of both personal and business expenses were made as well as payments to the Debtor and his associates for consulting fees.

[The account] maintained by the T-Vest Corporation and controlled by the Debtor was a "conduit" or depository account for funds received by the T-Vest Corporation from Astroglass Boat Company, Star Custom Trailers, and other entities with which the Debtor was associated. Funds belonging to the various entities and funds belonging to the Debtor were commingled in the T-Vest account. At the time of the payments in question the Debtor exercised effective control over Astroglass Boat Company and Star Custom Trailers. The T-Vest account was also used for the receipt of consulting fees earned by the Debtor, Monty Tounsend, and other associates of the Debtor. . . .

J. & D. Finance Co. was not a corporation. The account in the name of J. & D. Finance was used for both personal and business purposes of the Debtor. All disbursements from this account were controlled by the Debtor. Funds from Astroglass Boat Company and Maiden-Craft, a Tennessee Corporation wholly owned and controlled by the Debtor and his wife, were funneled through the J. & D. Finance Co. account for payment of various operating and business expenses. The J. & D. Finance Co. account was used as a depository account for funds from Astroglass Boat Co., Maiden-Craft and the T-Vest Corporation. Funds belonging to these entities and the Debtor were commingled in the account. . . .

The payments to Cove State Bank from the T-Vest and J. & D. Finance Co. accounts directly benefited the Debtor because Joseph N. Jaggers was personally liable on the debt to Cove State Bank. The disbursements from these funds were credited on the general ledgers of Joseph Jaggers as salary fulfillments.

The threshold question before the Court is whether the payments . . . by the Debtor to Cove State Bank constituted a preferential transfer in violation of 11 U.S.C. Section 547(b).

In order to avoid a transfer, the trustee must establish by a fair preponderance of the evidence each controverted element of a voidable preference. The six elements which must be present for this Court to find that a preference exists under 11 U.S.C. Section 547(b) are:

(1) The property transferred was the property of the Debtor;
(2) The transfer was "to or for the benefit of a creditor;"
(3) The payment was made "for or on account of an antecedent debt owed by the debtor before such transfer was made;"
(4) The transfer was made while the Debtor was insolvent;
(5) The transfer was made on or within 90 days before the date of the filing of the petitions; and
(6) The transfer enabled the creditor to receive more than such creditor would have received if the transfer had not been made, and the creditor received payment of the debt to the extent provided under the bankruptcy code.

The parties have stipulated that the payments . . . were for the benefit of Cove State Bank, that they were made on or before 90 days before the date of the filing of the Debtor's petition, that the payments were made while the debtor was insolvent, and that these payments enabled Cove State Bank to receive more than it would otherwise have received in the Debtor's Chapter 7 case. The only issue then before the Court is whether the funds transferred constituted "property of the estate" within the meaning of 11 U.S.C. Section 547(b).

In order to ascertain whether certain monies constitute property of the debtor the Court must determine whether the debtor had an interest in the funds such that a transfer thereof would result in a diminution of the estate.

In the case at bar, though the Debtor did have ownership rights in the accounts from which the payments to Cove State Bank were made, it is apparent that he did not own the funds in their entirety. The Debtor shared ownership interests in the accounts in question with Astroglass Boat Co., Star Custom Trailers and Mr. Monty Tounsend. It is clear, therefore, that the funds which the debtor used to pay Cove State Bank were, in part, the property of a third party.

When a debtor uses the funds of a third party to pay an obligation of the debtor the Court must look to the source of the control over the disposition of the funds in order to determine whether a preference exists. If the debtor controls the disposition of the funds and designates the creditor to whom the monies will be paid independent of the third party whose funds are being used in partial payment of the debt, then the payments made by the debtor to the creditor constitute a preferential transfer. Hence, if the funds are available for payment to the creditors of the debtor generally the funds are an asset of the estate and payment thereof constitutes a diminution of the estate.

The question the Court must ask is whether the funds of the third party were available for use by the debtor generally or were the funds solely available for the purpose of discharging a particular debt to a particular creditor. . . .

In the case at bar, the Debtor made two payments to Cove State Bank in check form in the amounts of $7,900.43 and $5,000.00 respectively. The $5,000.00 check on the account of J. & D. Finance Company was signed by the Debtor and the Debtor directed that payment be made to Cove State Bank. This transfer, on its face, was directed solely by the Debtor. By virtue of the Debtor's exclusive control over the disposition of the funds in payment of a personal obligation of the Debtor, the funds were available for payment to creditors of the Debtor generally and constituted an asset of the estate. The $7,900.43 check on the T-Vest Corporation account was tendered to Cove State Bank for the purpose of reducing the balance on the promissory note owed by the Debtor to

Cove State Bank. Though the check was not signed by the Debtor, there is no evidence that the use of the funds in the T-Vest account by the Debtor was conditioned upon payment of those funds to Cove State Bank. It is apparent that the Debtor controlled the distribution of funds from the T-Vest Corporation account. As a result of that control, the funds used by the Debtor for the payment of Cove State Bank were available to the creditors of the Debtor generally and constituted assets of the estate. The payments to Cove State Bank, therefore, were made with property of the estate. The payments resulted in a diminution of the estate and thereby constituted a preferential transfer of the property of the estate. . . .

[Judgment for the trustee]

QUESTIONS

1. When does payment to a creditor constitute a voidable preference?
2. Did Jaggers intend to prefer Cove State Bank over other creditors?
3. Did the court agree with the trustee?

C.   ADMINISTRATION OF DEBTOR'S ESTATE

Bankruptcy law regulates the manner in which creditors present their claims and how the assets of the debtor are to be distributed in payment of such claims.

10.   Proof of Claim

In a bankruptcy case the debtor will file a list of creditors. The court will then send a notice of the case to listed creditors. The creditors that wish to participate in distribution of the proceeds of the liquidation of the debtor's estate must file a proof of claim. A **proof of claim** is a written statement, signed by the creditor or an authorized representative, setting forth any claim made against the debtor and the basis thereof. It must ordinarily be filed within 90 days after the first meeting of creditors.[13] A creditor is not excused from filing within that time even though the trustee in bankruptcy in fact knew of the existence of the creditor's claim. A **claim** is a right to payment, whether liquidated (certain and not disputed), unliquidated, contingent, unmatured, disputed, legal, or equitable.

11.   Priority of Claims

Creditors who hold security for payment, such as a lien or a mortgage on the debtor's property, are not affected by the debtor's bankruptcy. Secured creditors may enforce their security in order to obtain payment of their claims. The unsecured creditors share in the remaining assets of the debtor. Some have priority over others. Any balance remaining after all creditors have been paid is turned over to the debtor.

The unsecured debts that have priority and the order of priority are[14]

(a) Costs and expenses of administration of the bankruptcy case, including fees to trustees, attorneys, and accountants, and the reasonable expenses of creditors in recovering property transferred or concealed by the debtor.

(b) Claims arising in the ordinary course of a debtor's business or financial affairs after the commencement of the case and before the appointment of a trustee.

(c) Claims for wages, salaries, or commissions, including vacation, severance, or sick leave pay earned within 90 days before the filing of the petition or the date of

---

[13]   Bankruptcy Rule 3002(c).

[14]   11 USC § 507(1) to (6).

cessation of the debtor's business, whichever occurred first. The amount of such
claims is limited, however, to $2,000 for
each person.

(d) Claims arising for contributions to employee benefit plans. The amount is limited by the Code, and services must have
been rendered within 180 days before the
filing of the petition or when the debtor
ceased doing business, whichever occurred first.

(e) Claims by consumer creditors, not to exceed $900 for each claimant, arising from
the purchase of consumer goods or services, where such property or services
were not delivered or provided.

(f) Federal and state income taxes due within
three years of the filing of the petition.

D.   DEBTOR'S DUTIES AND EXEMPTIONS

The Bankruptcy Code imposes certain duties
upon the debtor and provides for specific exemptions of some of the debtor's estate from
the claims of creditors.

12.   Debtor's Duties

The debtor must file with the court a list of
creditors, a schedule of assets and liabilities,
and a statement of the debtor's financial affairs. The debtor must also appear for examination under oath at the first meeting of
creditors.

13.   Debtor's Exemptions

The debtor is permitted to claim certain property of the estate in the trustee's possession
and keep it free from claims of creditors. Unless state law forbids the choice, the debtor
may elect either the exemptions permitted by
the laws of his or her state of domicile or those
set forth in the Bankruptcy Code. If a husband
and wife file a joint petition, they must elect
together to use either the state or federal exemptions. If they cannot agree on which to
elect, they will be deemed to have chosen the
federal exemptions. The Bankruptcy Code

provides for the following exemptions, among
others: the debtor's interest in real or personal
property used as a residence to the extent of
$7,500; the debtor's interest in a motor vehicle
to the extent of $1,200; household furnishings
of the debtor or the debtor's dependents, not
to exceed $200 per item, or $4,000 in aggregate
value; payments under a life insurance contract; alimony and child support payments;
and awards from personal injury causes of
action.[15]

E.   DISCHARGE IN BANKRUPTCY

The main objectives of a bankruptcy proceeding are the collection and distribution of the
debtor's assets and the discharge of the debtor
from obligations. The decree terminating the
bankruptcy proceeding is generally a **discharge** that releases the debtor from debts.

14.   Denial of Discharge

The court will refuse to grant a discharge if the
debtor has (a) within one year of the filing of
the petition fraudulently transferred or concealed property with intent to hinder, delay, or
defraud creditors, (b) failed to keep proper financial records, (c) made a false oath or account, (d) failed to explain satisfactorily any
loss of assets, (e) refused to obey any lawful
order of the court or refused to testify after
having been granted immunity, (f) obtained a
discharge within the last six years, or (g) filed
a written waiver of discharge that is approved
by the court.[16]

15.   Effect of Discharge

A discharge releases the debtor from the unpaid balance of most debts. However, a discharge does not release a person from (a) a tax,
customs duty, or tax penalty, (b) student loans,
unless the loan first became due more than
five years before bankruptcy or unless excepting the loan from discharge would impose
undue hardship upon the debtor, (c) loans ob-

---

[15]   11 USC § 522.
[16]   11 USC § 727.

FIGURE 37-1   DEBTS FROM WHICH A DEBTOR IS NOT DISCHARGED

NONDISCHARGEABLE DEBTS
A.   TAX PENALTY
B.   STUDENT LOANS RECEIVED WITHIN FIVE YEARS OF BANKRUPTCY UNLESS UNDUE HARDSHIP WILL RESULT
C.   LOANS OBTAINED BY USE OF FALSE FINANCIAL STATEMENT
D.   UNSCHEDULED DEBTS
E.   LIABILITY FOR FRAUD WHILE ACTING AS FIDUCIARY; EMBEZZLEMENT; LARCENY
F.   ALIMONY AND CHILD SUPPORT
G.   LIABILITY FOR WILLFUL AND MALICIOUS INJURY TO PROPERTY
H.   JUDGMENTS BASED UPON DRIVING WHILE INTOXICATED
I.   CONSUMER DEBTS FOR LUXURY GOODS
J.   CASH ADVANCES

tained by use of a false financial statement, made with intent to deceive, and upon which the creditor reasonably relied, (d) debts not duly scheduled in time for allowance, (e) liability for fraud while acting in a fiduciary capacity or by reason of embezzlement or larceny, (f) liability for alimony and child support, (g) liability for willful and malicious injury to property, (h) judgments against the debtor for liability for driving while intoxicated, (i) a consumer debt to a single creditor aggregating more than $500 for luxury goods or services, and (j) cash advances based on consumer credit exceeding $1,000.[17]

The debt for luxury goods must be incurred within 40 days of the order for relief; the cash advances must be incurred within 20 days of the order for relief.

In the *Reilly* case a student requested a discharge of her student loan, based upon undue hardship.

[17]   11 USC § 523.

IN RE REILLY
118 BR 38 (D Md 1990)

Reilly is a divorced mother of three young children. Her former husband is incurably ill and is unable to contribute significantly to their support. The family house was sold at foreclosure, and Reilly and her children were forced to move in with her parents, where she pays rent of $250 per month. Reilly works, sometimes full-time and sometimes part-time. Her monthly income cannot meet the necessary family expenses. Reilly's monthly income is only slightly above poverty guidelines for a family of four. There is a monthly deficit because expenses are greater than income. Reilly requires 24 credits in order to obtain her college degree. Until it is completed, she is not in a position to advance in her employment. Reilly's student loan is $2,762. Reilly filed a complaint to discharge her student loan because paying it would impose an inordinate burden upon her.

SCHNEIDER, B.J. . . . Paragraph (B) of Bankruptcy Code Section 523(a)(8) permits an exception to the nondischargeability of student loans. The exception exists when repayment of the student loan would impose an undue hardship on the debtor. The "hardship" provision of § 523(a)(8)(B) is

> discretionary with the bankruptcy judge who will have to determine whether payment of the debt will cause undue hardship on the debtor and his dependents thus defeating the "fresh start" concept of the bankruptcy laws. There may well be circumstances that justify failure to repay a student loan such as illness, incapacity or other extenuating circumstances. When the court finds that such circumstances exist, it may order the debt discharged. . . .

Courts have developed a number of tests to determine if a debtor's student loan should be discharged under § 523(a)(8)(B). In *Andrews v. South Dakota Student Loan Assistance Corporation*, 661 F.2d 702 (8th Cir.1981), the court considered whether the debtor's present and anticipated future income was sufficient to cover the debtor's reasonable living expenses. The court held that if the debtor's income is adequate to support the debtor and the debtor's dependents at a "minimal standard of living," as well as to repay the student loan, the debt cannot be discharged.

In *Andrews*, even though debtor was a 36 year old with Hodgkins disease, divorced, and receiving no alimony, the court vacated and remanded the bankruptcy court's discharge of the debtor's student loan debts on the grounds that the determination of undue hardship required the bankruptcy court to examine the debtor's "necessary living expenses." Thus, the court required a subjective evaluation of the debtor's reasonable living expenses and then a determination as to whether the debtor could repay her loan out of the balance of her estimated income less reasonable living expenses.

In denying a discharge based on undue hardship, the court in *Brunner v. New York State Higher Education Services Corporation*, 46 B.R. 752 (S.D.N.Y.1985) held that

> obtaining a discharge of student loans in bankruptcy prior to five years after they first come due requires a three-part showing: (1) that the debtor cannot, based on current income and expenses, maintain a "minimal" standard of living for himself or herself and his or her dependents if forced to repay the loans, (2) that this state of affairs is likely to persist for a significant portion of the repayment period of the student loan, and (3) that the debtor has made good faith efforts to repay the loans.

In *Brunner*, the court did not allow discharge because the debtor's master's degree in social work made it quite possible that she would get a higher paying job in the near future, enabling her to pay off her student loan while still maintaining a "minimal" standard of living for herself and because by filing for discharge within a month of when her first loan payment was due, she did not adequately demonstrate good faith in attempting to pay off her student loans.

In *Conner v. Illinois State Scholarship Commission*, 89 B.R. 744 (Bankr.N.D.Ill.1988) the court applied a test which considered (1) whether the debtor had the ability to pay off the student debt and still maintain a minimal standard of living, (2) whether the debtor had made a good faith effort to pay off the loan by minimizing expenses, renegotiating the terms of the loan or finding a better job and (3) whether discharge would frustrate the legislative intent to prevent abuse of student loans under § 523(a)(8)(B).

The court suggested that discharge of student loans should be denied if the debtor's motivation in filing bankruptcy was solely to discharge student loan obligations. Such motivation is to be discovered by determining the percentage of debt attributable to the student loan.

Finally, in *Bryant v. Pennsylvania Higher Education Assistance Agency*, 72 B.R. 913 (Bankr.E.D.Pa.1987), the court developed its own test by studying the purpose of Section 523(a)(8)(B) as indicated in the Report of the Commission on the Bankruptcy Laws of the United States:

> In order to determine ... "undue hardship"; ... the rate and amount of [the debtor's] future resources should be estimated reasonably in terms of ability to obtain, retain, and continue employment and the rate of pay that can be expected. Any unearned income or other wealth which the debtor can be expected to receive should also be taken into account. The total amount of income, its reliability, and the periodicity of its receipt should be adequate to maintain the debtor and his dependents at a minimal standard of living within their management capacity as well as to pay the education debt.

... Unusual responsibilities arising from the needs of dependents can be a circumstance supporting discharge. If the debtor's net annual income is near the poverty line, then discharge may be in order. Further, if the debtor's net annual income is below the federal poverty level, then the creditor must show that some "unique" or "extraordinary" circumstance exists to exclude the debt from discharge. Without this showing of a special circumstance, the loan should be discharged because repayment would likely cause the debtor an undue hardship.

The *Bryant* court discharged student loans in two Chapter 7 cases based on undue hardship, while denying a discharge in a third case. In applying its objective test, the court held that the obligation of a debtor whose annual *gross* income was beneath the federal poverty guideline should be discharged because the debtor could not afford to repay her debt and still maintain a minimal standard of living; the obligation of a debtor whose income was "significantly more" than the poverty income guideline should not be discharged because the debtor had no "unique" or "extraordinary" circumstances that would support a determination of undue hardship, and the obligation of a debtor whose net annual income was approximately at federal poverty guidelines should be discharged because the likelihood of a higher income and better circumstances was not so clear as to constitute "unique" or "extraordinary" circumstances.

Applying any one of the foregoing tests in the instant case, there is no question that the repayment of the student loans will impose an undue hardship upon this debtor....

The Court is satisfied that this debtor would have made all such payments if she were financially able to do so, which clearly she is not. Therefore, the student loans in this case will be discharged.

[Discharge granted]

F.   REORGANIZATIONS AND PAYMENT PLANS UNDER CHAPTERS 11 AND 13

In addition to liquidation under Chapter 7, the Bankruptcy Code permits the debtors to restructure the organization and finances of their businesses so that they may continue to operate. In these so-called rehabilitation plans, the debtor keeps all the assets (exempt and nonexempt), remains in business, and makes a settlement that is acceptable to the majority of the creditors, whose decision is binding upon the minority.

The Code also provides for the adoption of extended time payment plans for individual debtors who have regular income and who owe unsecured debts of less than $100,000 and secured debts of less than $350,000.

16.   Business Reorganizations under Chapter 11

Individuals, partnerships, and corporations in business may be reorganized under the Bankruptcy Code. The first step is to file a plan for the reorganization of the debtor. This plan may be filed by the debtor or by any party in interest or committee of creditors.

(a) CONTENTS OF PLAN. The plan divides ownership interests and debts into those that will be affected by the adoption of the plan and those that will not. It then specifies what will be done to those interests and claims that are affected. For example, where mortgage payments are too high for the income of the enterprise, a possible plan would be to reduce the mortgage payments and give the mortgage holder preferred stock to compensate for the loss sustained.

Persons within a particular class must all be treated the same way. For example, the holders of first mortgage bonds must all be treated similarly.

A plan may also provide for the assumption, rejection, or assignment of executory contracts. Thus, the trustee or debtor may under certain circumstances suspend performance of a contract not yet fully performed. Collective bargaining agreements may be rejected in this manner, with the approval of the bankruptcy court.[18]

(b) CONFIRMATION OF PLAN. When the plan is prepared, it must be approved or **confirmed** by the court. This confirmation will be realized if the plan has been submitted in good faith and if its provisions are reasonable.[19]

After the plan is confirmed, the owners and creditors of the enterprise have only such rights as are specified in the plan and cannot go back to their original positions.

17.   Extended Time Payment Plans under Chapter 13

An individual debtor who has a regular income may submit a plan for the installment payment of outstanding debts. If approved by the court, the debtor may then pay the debts in the installments specified by the plan, even if the creditors had not originally agreed to such installment payments.

(a) CONTENTS OF PLAN. The individual debtor plan is, in effect, a budget of the deb-

---

[18]   11 USC § 1113, modifying the holding of the U.S. Supreme Court in NLRB v Bildisco, 465 US 513 (1984).
[19]   11 USC § 1129.

tor's future income with respect to outstanding debts. The plan must provide for the eventual payment in full of all claims entitled to priority under the Bankruptcy Code. Creditors holding the same kind or class of claim must all be treated the same way.

(b) CONFIRMATION OF PLAN. The plan has no effect until it is approved or confirmed by the court. This confirmation will be realized if the plan was submitted in good faith and is in the best interests of the creditors.[20]

When the plan is confirmed, debts are payable in the manner specified in the plan.

(c) DISCHARGE OF DEBTOR. After all the payments called for by the plan have been made, the debtor is given a discharge that releases the debtor from liability for all debts except those that would not be discharged by an ordinary bankruptcy discharge.[21]

18.   Protection against Discrimination

Federal, state, or local law may not discriminate against anyone on the basis of a discharge in bankruptcy.[22] This principle is illustrated in the *Young* case.

---

[20]   11 USC § 1325.

[21]   11 USC § 1328. See Chapter 37, Section 15 of this book.
[22]   11 USC § 525.

IN RE YOUNG, DEBTOR
10 BR 17 (SD Cal 1980)

Marion Young, the debtor, filed her extended time payment plan with the court. Subsequent to the filing of the petition, she was issued a citation for a traffic violation. In her confirmed plan, she proposed to pay 100 percent of her debts. Her application for renewal of her driver's license was denied because of her failure to pay a fine for not appearing in court on the traffic violation. She moved to have the bankruptcy court order the state to renew her license.

KATZ, B.J. . . . After hearing arguments presented by counsel, the court hereby makes the following findings of fact and conclusions of law:

Findings of Fact

1. Plaintiff filed her voluntary petition on May 19, 1980 under the provisions of Chapter 13 of Title 11 of the United States Code. The debtor's plan filed in the case provides for payment of 100% of creditor's claims as allowed, and was confirmed on July 8, 1980.
2. Plaintiff was issued a citation on May 31, 1979 for a traffic violation and executed a written promise to appear or post bail with the Municipal Court, West Orange County Judicial District. This obligation was listed in plaintiff's bankruptcy schedules for payment under her Chapter 13 plan. Plaintiff has not appeared in court on the offense nor posted bail in lieu of her appearance, and a bench warrant has been issued for her arrest.
3. Plaintiff's application for renewal of her California driver's license has been denied by defendant Department of Motor Vehicles under the authority of sections 12807(c) and 40508(a) of the California Vehicle Code, stating as grounds therefor plaintiff's failure to appear on the traffic violation.

Conclusions of Law

1. Section 525 of the Code provides in pertinent part that "A governmental unit may not deny, revoke, suspend, or refuse to renew a license . . . solely because the bankrupt or debtor . . . has not paid a debt that is dischargeable in the case under this Title or that was discharged under the Bankruptcy Act." *11 USC § 525.*
2. Plaintiff's obligation on account of the traffic citation is a criminal fine that is not dischargeable under section 523(a)(7) of the Code. *11 USC § 523(a)(7). . . .*
4. Section 1328(a) provides that after completion by the debtor of all payments under the plan, the court shall grant the debtor a discharge of all debts provided for by the plan or disallowed under section 502 except for certain debts and obligations on account of support excepted from discharge. Other obligations, including fines excepted from discharge under section 523(a)(7) of the Code, are dischargeable in a Chapter 13 case. *11 USC § 1328(a).*
5. A criminal fine dischargeable in a Chapter 13 case is a dischargeable debt within the provisions of section 525 of the Code, and defendant Department of Motor Vehicles is a governmental unit subject to the provisions of that section. *11 USC §§ 1328(a)(2), 525.*
6. Defendant's action in denying plaintiff's application for a renewal license is in violation of the anti-discrimination provisions of the Bankruptcy Code. *11 USC § 525.*
7. Plaintiff is entitled to a renewal license during the pendency of her Chapter 13 case, and discharge of her obligations upon completion of the payments provided for in her Chapter 13 plan. Should plaintiff convert to a liquidation case . . . the obligation for the traffic fine would not be dischargeable, and the Department of Motor Vehicles would be justified in revoking plaintiff's license. Likewise if plaintiff receives a hardship discharge under the provisions of section 1328(b), the Department could revoke plaintiff's license.

For the reasons stated above, plaintiff's motion for partial summary judgment shall be *Granted,* and defendant's crossmotion for summary judgment *Denied.* On stipulation of the parties, plaintiff's complaint in this action shall be dismissed as to all defendants without prejudice. Counsel for plaintiff shall prepare an order directing the Department of Motor Vehicles to issue plaintiff a renewal California driver's license.

QUESTIONS

1. What are the requirements for an extended time payment plan?
2. Was the Department of Motor Vehicles required to issue a license to Young? Why or why not?

SUMMARY

Jurisdiction over bankruptcy cases is in the United States District Courts, which may refer all cases and related proceedings to adjunct bankruptcy courts.

Three bankruptcy proceedings are available to individuals and businesses. They are liquidation, reorganization, and extended time payment.

A liquidation proceeding under Chapter 7 may be either voluntary or involuntary. A voluntary case is commenced by the debtor by filing a petition with the bankruptcy court. An involuntary case is commenced by the creditors by filing a petition with the bankruptcy court. If there are 12 or more creditors, at least three, whose unsecured claims total $5,000 or more, must sign the involuntary petition. If there are fewer than 12 such creditors, any creditor whose unsecured claim is at least $5,000 may sign the petition. If the debtor contests the bankruptcy petition, it must be shown that the debtor is not paying debts as they become due, or that within 120 days before the date of the filing of the petition a custodian had been appointed for the debtor's property.

An automatic stay prevents creditors from taking action against the debtor after a bankruptcy petition is filed.

The trustee in bankruptcy is elected by the creditors and is the successor to and stands in the place of the debtor. The trustee can avoid transfers of property to prevent creditors from satisfying their legal claims. Preferential transfers to creditors and to insiders may be set aside. A transaction for a present consideration such as a cash sale is not a preference.

Bankruptcy law regulates the manner in which creditors present their claims and how the assets of the debtor are to be distributed in payment of the claims.

Claims are paid in the following order of priority: (a) secured debts, (b) administrative expenses, (c) claims arising in the ordinary course of the debtor's business, (d) wage claims limited to $2,000 for each claimant and to wages earned within 90 days before the filing of the petition, (e) claims for contributions to employee benefit plans, (f) claims by consumer creditors, (g) taxes, and (h) general creditors. Certain property of the debtor is exempt from the claims of creditors.

The decree terminating the bankruptcy proceedings is generally a discharge that releases the debtor from most debts. If the debtor is a dishonest debtor, no discharge will be given. Dishonesty exists when the debtor has fraudulently transferred property, failed to keep proper records, or failed to obey a court order, among other things. Certain debts, such as taxes, student loans, loans obtained by use of a false financial statement, alimony, and debts not duly scheduled, are not dischargeable.

Individuals, partnerships, and corporations in business may be reorganized so that a business may continue to operate. A plan for reorganization must be approved by the court. Individual debtors with a regular income may adopt extended time payment plans for the payment of debts. A plan for extended time payment must also be confirmed by the court.

Federal, state, or local law may not discriminate against anyone on the basis of a discharge in bankruptcy.

QUESTIONS AND CASE PROBLEMS

1. What social forces are affected by permitting a debtor to avoid paying debts by going into bankruptcy?
2. What is meant by the term "insider," as used in preferential transfers?
3. Barron sold goods on credit to Charles by relying on a false financial statement issued by Charles. Charles later filed for voluntary bankruptcy, still owing this debt to Barron. Barron claimed that Charles was not entitled to a discharge from this particular debt because of the fraud. Was Barron correct?
4. Ruth commenced a voluntary case with the bankruptcy court. After her assets subject to the claims of creditors were liquidated, her trustee had possession of $2,000 in cash. Various creditors had filed claims for $20,000. Ruth's trustee claimed that the $2,000 should be used to pay the fee of the trustee, the fee of Ruth's accountant, and other administrative expenses of the bankruptcy case. The other creditors claimed that they were entitled to a portion of the $2,000. Were the other creditors correct?
5. Anita knows Jean to be insolvent. She sells Jean her auto for $500 and receives cash in payment for the car. An involuntary bankruptcy case is commenced against Jean by the creditors some time later. The trustee in bankruptcy attempts to

recover the $500 on the ground that it was a preferential transfer. Will the trustee be successful?

6. Smith has 20 creditors. Three creditors with unsecured claims that total $10,000 signed an involuntary bankruptcy petition against Smith. Smith has been unable to pay debts as they become due. Smith objects to the petition's being filed, since the creditors have failed to allege that Smith has engaged in any misconduct. Will the creditors be successful?

7. Which of the following, if any, survive Rogers' discharge in bankruptcy? a. Wages amounting to $400 to three employees, earned within 60 days of the bankruptcy. b. A judgment against Rogers for injuries received because of Rogers' negligent operation of an automobile. c. A judgment against Rogers by Landers for breach of contract. d. Rogers' obligation for alimony and child support.

8. Kentile sold goods over an extended period of time to Winham. The credit relationship began without Winham's being required to furnish any financial statement. After some time, payments were not made regularly. Kentile requested a financial statement. Winham submitted a statement for the year that had just ended. Thereafter, Kentile requested a second statement. The second statement was false. Kentile objected to Winham's discharge in bankruptcy, because of the false financial statement. Should the discharge be granted? Why or why not?

9. Essex is in serious financial difficulty and is unable to meet current unsecured obligations of $40,000 to some 20 creditors, who are demanding immediate payment. Essex owes Stevens $5,000, and Stevens has decided to file an involuntary petition against Essex. Can Stevens file the petition?

10. Sonia, a retailer, has the following assets: a factory worth $100,000; accounts receivable amounting to $75,000, which fall due in from four to six months; and $2,000 cash in the bank.

Sonia's sole liability is a $20,000 note falling due today, which Sonia is unable to pay. May Sonia be forced into involuntary bankruptcy under the Bankruptcy Code?

11. Samson Industries, Inc. ceased doing business and is in bankruptcy proceedings. Among the claimants are five employees seeking unpaid wages. Three of the employees are owed $3,500, and two are owed $1,500. These amounts became due within 90 days preceding the filing of the petition. How much, if anything, will the employees receive?

12. The First Bank of Harris was in financial difficulty. The bank wanted to file a voluntary bankruptcy petition. Shareholders of the bank objected. Were they correct in objecting? Explain.

13. Carol Cott, doing business as Carol Cott Fashions, is worried about an involuntary bankruptcy proceeding being filed by her creditors. Her net worth using a balance-sheet approach is $8,000 ($108,000 assets minus $100,000 liabilities). However, her cash flow is negative, and she has been hard pressed to meet current obligations as they mature. She is, in fact, some $12,500 in arrears in payments to her creditors on bills submitted during the past two months. Will the fact that Carol is solvent in the bankruptcy sense result in the court's dismissing the creditors' petition if Carol contests the propriety of the filing of the petition? Explain.

14. A trustee, the United States government, and wage earners all claim first priority in bankruptcy for their claims. Who will be paid first? Explain.

15. On July 1, Roger Walsh, a sole proprietor operating a grocery, was involuntarily petitioned into bankruptcy by his creditors. At that time, and for at least 90 days prior thereto, Walsh was unable to pay current obligations. On June 16, Walsh paid the May electric bill that was incurred in his business. The trustee in bankruptcy claims that this payment was a voidable preference. Is the trustee correct? Explain.

38

INSURANCE

The function of insurance is to distribute the risk of substantial, individual loss over a large group of individuals who are exposed to similar risks. Insurance companies, through actuarial and other data-collecting devices, measure the risks of loss from the perils covered and set a premium or price for the insurance protection provided.

Insurance companies perform a wide range of services such as training businesses in loss prevention, investigating and apprais-ing losses, and managing the vast sums of money they collect as premiums. However, the cornerstone on which the insurance industry is built is the contract.

A. INTRODUCTION TO THE INSURANCE CONTRACT

Insurance is a contract by which one party for a stipulated consideration promises to pay another party a sum of money upon the destruction of, loss of, or injury to something in which the other party has an interest.

1.   The Parties

The promisor in an insurance contract is called the **insurer** or **underwriter**. The person to whom the promise is made is the **insured**, the assured, or the policyholder. The promise of the insurer is generally set forth in a written contract called a **policy**.

Insurance contracts are ordinarily made through an agent or broker. The **insurance agent** is an agent of the insurance company, generally working exclusively for one company. For the most part, the ordinary rules of agency law govern the dealings between this agent and the applicant for insurance.[1]

The **insurance broker** is generally an independent contractor who is not employed by any one insurance company. When a broker obtains a policy for a customer, the broker is the agent of the customer for the purpose of that transaction. Under some statutes the broker is made an agent of the insurer with respect to transmitting the applicant's payments to the insurer.

2.   Insurable Interest

A person obtaining insurance must have an insurable interest in the subject matter insured. If not, the insurance contract cannot be enforced.

(a) INSURABLE INTEREST IN PROPERTY. A person has an insurable interest in property whenever the destruction of the property will cause a direct pecuniary loss to that person.[2]

It is immaterial whether the insured is the owner of the legal or equitable title, a lien holder, or merely a person in possession of the property.[3] Thus, a contractor remodeling a building has an insurable interest in the build-

ing to the extent of the money that will be paid under the contract, because the contractor would not be able to receive that money if the building were destroyed by fire.

In order to collect on property insurance, the insured must have an insurable interest at the time the loss occurs.

(b) INSURABLE INTEREST IN LIFE. A person who obtains life insurance can generally name anyone as beneficiary, regardless of whether that beneficiary has an insurable interest in the life of the insured. If the beneficiary obtains the policy, however, he or she must have an insurable interest in the life of the insured. Such an interest exists if the beneficiary can reasonably expect to receive pecuniary gain from the continued life of the other person and, conversely, would suffer financial loss from the latter's death. Thus, a creditor has an insurable interest in the life of the debtor since the death of the debtor may mean that the creditor will not be paid the amount owed.

A partner or partnership has an insurable interest in the life of each of the partners, because the death of any one of them will dissolve the firm and cause some degree of loss to the partnership. A business enterprise has an insurable interest in the life of an executive or a key employee, because that person's death would inflict a financial loss upon the business to the extent that a replacement might not be readily available or could not be found.

In the case of life insurance the insurable interest must exist at the time the policy is obtained. It is immaterial that the interest no longer exists when the loss is actually sustained. Thus, the fact that a husband (insured) and wife (beneficiary) are divorced after the life insurance policy was procured does not affect the validity of the policy.

In the *Graves* case the court was faced with two questions: (1) Does a partner have an insurable interest in the life of another partner? (2) Was the surviving partner required to remit the proceeds to the estate of the deceased partner as a payment for the deceased partner's interest?

[1]   Tidelands Life Insurance Co. v France (Tex Civ App) 711 So 2d 728 (1986).
[2]   De Witt v American Family Mutual Ins. Co. (Mo) 667 SW2d 700 (1984).
[3]   Hunter v State Farm Fire & Casualty Co. (Ala) 543 So 2d 679 (1989).

GRAVES v NORRED
(Ala) 510 So 2d 816 (1987)

Jewell Norred's husband, James Norred, was the business partner of Clyde Graves for some ten years. On May 7, 1979, Graves and Norred took out term life insurance policies, with Graves being the beneficiary of Norred's policy and Norred being the beneficiary of Graves' policy. Premiums were paid out of partnership funds. On February 28, 1983, Graves and Norred divided the partnership assets but did not perform the customary steps of dissolving the partnership. Graves became the sole owner of the business and continued to pay the premiums on both insurance policies until James Norred died on December 5, 1983. Jewell Norred sued Graves seeking the proceeds of the insurance policy for herself, alleging that Graves had no insurable interest in the life of James Norred at the time of his death. She also contended that the proceeds should go to the estate as a payment for Norred's interest in the partnership. From a judgment on behalf of the estate, Graves appealed.

ADAMS, J. . . . Jewell Norred argues that she should receive the benefits of the insurance policy because she alone had an insurable interest in the insurance contract. . . . The prevailing rule among the states is that a partner or partnership has an insurable interest in the life of one of the partners. 43 Am.Jur.2d *Insurance* § 989 (1982). It is not the mere existence of the partnership which provides the basis for the insurable interest. It is the insuring partner's "reasonable expectation of pecuniary benefit from the continuance of the insured's life." *Id.*, at 1000. This interest continues even if the partnership is discontinued prior to death of one of the partners, *Id.* . . .

In the instant case each partner took out a life insurance policy on the other. Both sides testified that the purpose was to provide for one partner at the other partner's death. The manner of providing for the surviving partner is in dispute between the parties. However, there is not legal uncertainty that both partners had an insurable interest in the life of the other partner.

We next turn our analysis to the designation of the beneficiary in order to determine who should be entitled to the proceeds of the life insurance policy. In the case of *Williams v Williams*, 438 So.2d 735 (Ala. 1983), a partner designated the other partners (his brothers), as the beneficiaries of his life insurance policy. Pursuant to the partnership's dissolution agreement, the surviving partners were to receive the insurance proceeds and then use those proceeds to purchase the deceased partner's interest. Although it was written in an awkward manner, the dissolution agreement was held to be valid and enforceable. . . . Unlike the present case, in *Williams* a written partnership agreement and a dissolution agreement existed. However, both agreements involved the designation of the partners as beneficiaries instead of the spouse or estate. As stated by Chief Justice Torbert, "The fact that the decedent selected his partners, as opposed to his spouse or estate, as beneficiaries of the life insurance . . . is unquestionably permissible. Partners continue to be free to select whomever they wish to benefit from insurance on their lives." *Williams*, 438 So.2d at 739. In this case, the plaintiff's evidence that the decedent intended for the proceeds to go to his estate consisted solely of oral testimony from the plaintiff's brother (the insurance agent), and an ambiguous statement from a mutual friend of both partners. No ambiguity existed in the designation of the beneficiary. There was no written agreement like the dissolution agreement in *Williams*, supra, which provided that the surviving partners were to use the proceeds to purchase the deceased partner's interest. We require more than oral testimony, like the testimony presented here, in order to show that it was not the intention of the decedent that the designated beneficiary retain the proceeds. Therefore, we reverse the trial court's judgment designating Norred's estate as the rightful recipient of the proceeds instead of the designated beneficiary.

[Reversed and remanded]

QUESTIONS

1. Did Graves have an insurable interest in the life of Norred following the discontinuance of the partnership?
2. Was Graves required to remit the proceeds of the insurance to Norred's estate as payment for Mr. Norred's partnership interest, subject to set-offs due Graves?
3. Can a partner select his or her partner, as opposed to his or her spouse or estate, as beneficiary under a life insurance policy?

3. The Insurance Contract

The formation of a contract of insurance is governed by the general principles applicable to contracts.[4] Frequently, a question arises as to whether advertising material, estimates, and statistical projections constitute a part of the contract.

By statute it is now commonly provided that an insurance policy must be written. In order to avoid deception, many statutes also specify the content of certain policies, in whole or in part. Some statutes specify the size and style of type to be used in printing the policies. Provisions in a policy that conflict with statutory requirements are generally void.

(a) THE APPLICATION AS PART OF THE CONTRACT. The application for insurance is generally attached to the policy when issued and is made part of the contract of insurance by express stipulation of the policy.

The insured should examine the policy and an attached application. Any false statement in the application binds the insured, if the policy and the attached application are retained without objection to such statement.

(b) STATUTORY PROVISIONS AS PART OF THE CONTRACT. When a statute requires that insurance contracts contain certain provisions or cover certain specified losses, a contract of insurance that does not comply with the statute will be interpreted as though it contained all the provisions required by the statute.[5] When a statute requires that the insurance contract include any exceptions, limitations, or restrictions, the insurer may not rely upon an exception, limitation, or restriction not stated in the contract to defeat an insured's claim.

4. Antilapse and Cancellation Statutes and Provisions

If the premiums are not paid on time, the policy under ordinary contract law would lapse because of nonpayment. However, as to life insurance policies, either by policy provision or statute, the insured is allowed a grace period of 30 to 31 days in which to make payment of the premium due.[6] When there is a default in the payment of a premium by the insured, the insurer may be required by statute (1) to

---

[4] Employers Mutual Casualty Co. v Pigeon Creek Corp. 1 Ark App 179, 614 SW2d 516 (1981).

[5] Samson v Transamerica Ins. Co. 30 Cal App 3d 220, 178 Cal Rptr 343, 636 P2d 32 (1981).

[6] Flowers v Provident Life and Acc. Ins. Co. (Tenn) 713 SW2d 69 (1986).

issue a paid-up policy in a smaller amount, (2) to provide extended insurance for a period of time, or (3) to pay the cash surrender value of the policy.

The contract of insurance may expressly declare that it may or may not be canceled by the insurer's unilateral act. By statute or policy provision, the insurer is commonly required to give a specific number of days' written notice of cancellation.

5.   Modification of Contract

As is the case with most contracts, a contract of insurance can be modified if both insurer and insured agree to the change. The insurer cannot modify the contract without the consent of the insured when the right to do so is not reserved in the insurance contract.[7]

In order to make changes or corrections to the policy, it is not necessary to issue a new policy. An endorsement on the policy or the execution of a separate rider is effective for the purpose of changing the policy.

When a provision of an endorsement conflicts with a provision of the policy, the endorsement controls, because it is the later document.

6.   Interpretation of Contract

A contract of insurance is interpreted by the same rules that govern the interpretation of ordinary contracts. Words are to be given their ordinary meaning and interpreted in light of the nature of the coverage intended. Thus, an employee who has been killed is not regarded as disabled within the meaning of a group policy covering employees.

The courts are increasingly recognizing the fact that most persons obtaining insurance are not specially trained. Therefore, the contract of insurance is to be read as it would be understood by the average person or by the average person in business, rather than by one with technical knowledge of the law or of insurance.[8]

7.   Coverage of Policy

When an insurance claim is disputed by the insurer, the person bringing suit has the burden of proving that there was a loss, that it occurred while the policy was in force, and that the loss was of a kind that was within the coverage or scope of the policy.

A policy will contain exceptions to the coverage. This means that the policy is not applicable when an exception applies to the situation.[9] Exceptions to coverage are generally strictly interpreted against the insurer. The insurer has the burden of proving that the facts were such that there was no coverage because an exception applied. Also, a modern trend holds that although an exception is literally applicable to the situation, it will be ignored and coverage sustained when there is no cause-and-effect relationship between the loss and the conduct that was the violation of the exception.

8.   Insurer Bad Faith

When it is the insurer's duty to defend the insured and the insurer wrongfully refuses to do so, the insurer is guilty of breach of contract and is liable for all consequential damages resulting from the breach. In some jurisdictions an insured can recover for an excess judgment rendered against the insured when it is proven that the insurer was guilty of negligence or bad faith in failing to defend the action or settle the matter within policy limits.

In some states laws have been enacted making an insurer liable for a statutory penalty and attorneys' fees in case of a failure or delay, in bad faith, to pay a valid claim within a specified period of time. A bad faith refusal is generally considered to be any frivolous or unfounded refusal to comply with the demand of a policyholder to pay according to the policy.[10] Penalties are improper when the insurer has any reasonable ground to contest the claim or when there is a bona fide dispute

---

[7]   Krebs v Strange (Miss) 419 So 2d 178 (1982).
[8]   Coconio County v Fund Administrators Assn. Inc. 49 Ariz 42, 719 P2d 693 (1986).

[9]   Fireman's Fund Ins. v Fibreboard Corp. 182 Cal App 3d 462, 227 Cal Rptr 203 (1986).
[10]   American Family Life Insurance Co. v U.S. Fire Co. (CA11 Ga) 855 F2d 826 (1989).

as to a material fact relevant to whether the insurer is liable.[11]

In the *Filasky* case the court was faced with the questions of whether, in addition to the benefits due the insured under her policies, she was entitled to compensatory and punitive damages for bad faith failure to investigate and pay her claims.

[11]   Shipes v Hanover Ins. Co. (CA11 Ga) 884 F2d 1357 (1989).

FILASKY v PREFERRED RISK MUTUAL INS. CO.
152 Ariz 591, 734 P2d 76 (1987)

Linda Filasky was insured by Preferred Risk Mutual Insurance Company under automobile and homeowner's insurance policies. On June 17, 1982, while working, she was injured in an automobile accident and was hospitalized for two weeks. While she was in the hospital, her home was burglarized, and many valuable items were stolen. On July 7, 1982, a rainstorm damaged her roof and family room. She filed a claim for lost income benefits under her automobile policy and filed claims for theft loss and water damage under her homeowners policy. Filasky sued Preferred Risk for the bad faith delay in settling claims under her two policies, contending that it took groundless positions and failed to investigate her claims adequately. Ultimately, all benefits due Filasky were paid by January 25, 1984. From a judgment for Filasky for $100,000 compensatory damages and $1,000,000 in punitive damages, Preferred Risk appealed.

GORDON, C.J. . . . In 1981 we recognized that an insurer has a legal duty to act in good faith when settling its policyholders' claims; violation of that duty constitutes a tort. An insurer can challenge claims that are "fairly debatable"; however, it breaches its legal duty when it "intentionally denies or fails to process or pay a claim without a reasonable basis for such action." *Linthicum v. Nationwide Life Insurance Company*, 150 Ariz. 354, 362 (App. 1985); aff'd, 150 Ariz. 36 (1986). We recently wrote:

To be liable for tort damages, it [the insurer] need only to have intended its act or omission [of denying or failing to provide the insured with the security and protection from calamity which is the object of the relationship], lacking a founded belief that such conduct was permitted by the policy.

The founded belief is absent when the insurer either knows that its position is groundless or when it fails to undertake an investigation adequate to determine whether its position is tenable. In either event, its position is without reasonable basis and subjects it to payment of damages in addition to those traditionally recoverable in a breach of contract action.

Rawlings v. Apodaca, 151 Ariz. 149, 160, 726 P.2d 565, 576 (1986).

. . . All of the evidence clearly suggests that reasons given by Preferred Risk for delaying settlement of Filasky's three claims were groundless or inadequately investigated and supports the jury's conclusion that Preferred Risk breached its duty to deal with Filasky in good faith.

Compensatory Damages

The jury awarded compensatory damages of $100,000 to Filasky for her emotional distress and attorneys' fees. To recover damages for emotional distress caused by the insurer's bad faith, the insured must demonstrate that the insurer's bad faith resulted in an invasion of property rights. . . . Damages for pain, humiliation, or inconvenience, as well as pecuniary losses for expenses such as attorney's fees, trigger an invasion of protected property rights.

Evidence supports the jury's $100,000 compensatory damage award. Not only did Filasky incur economic losses of approximately $4000 in attorney's fees and the lost time value of her insurance proceeds, she also endured months of overwhelming inconvenience and frustration caused by Preferred Risk's callous disregard for her plight. The record indicates that Filasky may have been able to maintain her house payments if Preferred Risk had paid her lost wages claim on a timely basis. The record also indicates that Preferred Risk frustrated Filasky's attempts at resolving her claims by engaging in such dilatory tactics as not returning her telephone calls, ignoring her pleas for personal assistance in completing forms, repeating requests with which Filasky had already complied, and rejecting her claims but providing no reasons for doing so.

We do not believe the jury's compensatory damage award of $100,000 was motivated by passion or prejudice; nor do we believe the amount is excessive or grossly disproportionate to the damage incurred. The evidence reveals that Filasky suffered pecuniary losses and damages for frustration, inconvenience, and humiliation. In our opinion, the record fully justifies the jury's award of $100,000 in compensatory damages for emotional distress and attorneys' fees.

Punitive Damages

Punitive damages may be awarded in a bad faith insurance case. However, punitive damages may not be awarded in a bad faith insurance case absent evidence reflecting "something more" than conduct necessary to establish the tort. We recently articulated a standard for determining whether the requisite "something more" exists:

> To obtain punitive damages, plaintiff must also show that the evil hand that unjustifiably damaged the objectives sought to be reached by the insurance contract was guided by an evil mind which either consciously sought to damage the insured or acted intentionally, knowing that its conduct was likely to cause unjustified, significant damage to the insured. When defendant's motives are shown to be so improper, *or* its conduct so oppressive, outrageous or intolerable that such an "evil mind" may be inferred, punitive damages may be awarded.

Rawlings, 151 Ariz. at 162–63, 726 P.2d at 578–79. . . .

Preferred Risk's reasons for its dilatory settlement of Filasky's three claims were either groundless or inadequately investigated. This conduct supported the jury's conclusion that Preferred Risk acted in bad faith. However, evidence of "something more" than indifference to facts and failure to properly and timely investigate an insurance claim must exist before the trial court can instruct the jury on punitive damages. We have read the record and conclude that evidence that Preferred Risk acted toward Filasky in an aggravated, outrageous, malicious, or fraudulent manner, that Preferred Risk was guided by an evil mind which either consciously sought to injure Filasky or acted intentionally, knowing that its conduct was likely to cause unjustified, significant damage to Filasky, is slight and inconclusive at best. Therefore, the trial judge erred in submitting the issue of punitive damages to the jury.

Conclusion

We affirm the jury's finding of bad faith and its compensatory damage award of $100,000. We reverse its punitive damage award of $1,000,000 and remand this case to the trial court for entry of judgment consistent with this opinion.

[Affirmed in part; reversed in part]

QUESTIONS

1. Does an insurer's failure to settle the insured's claims in good faith constitute a tort?
2. Did the appeals court allow a compensatory award for pecuniary losses and damages for frustration, inconvenience, and humiliation in addition to the insurance benefits due the insured under the two policies?
3. What must an insured prove in order to be entitled to recover punitive damages in an action claiming that the insurer had failed to act in good faith?

9. Time Limitations on Insured

The insured must comply with a number of time limitations in making a claim. For example, the insured must promptly notify the insurer of any claim that may arise, submit a proof of loss statement within the time set forth in the policy, and bring any court actions based on the policy within a specified time period.

10. Subrogation of Insurer

In some instances the insured has a claim against a third person for the harm covered by the insurance policy. For example, the insured (who has an automobile collision insurance policy) who is in a collision may have a claim against the other driver. If the insurer pays the insured the full amount of the insured's claim, the insurer is then subrogated to the insured's claim against the third person who caused the harm. This means that the insurer acquires the claim of the insured against the third person, just as though the insured had assigned the claim to the insurer. When the insurer is subrogated to the insured's claim, the insurer may enforce that claim against the third person.[12]

From the money recovered from the third person, the insurer is entitled to keep an amount equal to the payment made by the insurer to the insured, together with interest and costs.

B. KINDS OF INSURANCE

The insurance industry offers a wide range of insurance plans, to provide protection suited to the variety of needs faced by businesses and individuals.

Businesses today have specialized risk managers, who identify the risks to which individual businesses are exposed, measure those risks, and purchase insurance to cover those risks (or decide to self-insure in whole or in part). Businesses may purchase comprehensive "all risk" business liability and indemnity policies. Businesses may also purchase policies providing liability insurance for their directors and officers. Because of recent adverse court decisions against corporate directors and officers, premiums and deductibles for this kind of insurance have increased, and availability has decreased.

Insurance policies can be grouped into certain categories. Four major categories of insurance are considered below: (1) marine and

---

[12] Fincher v J.C. Penney Cas. Ins. Co. (Ala App) 522 So 2d 532 (1988).

FIGURE 38-1   SUBROGATION

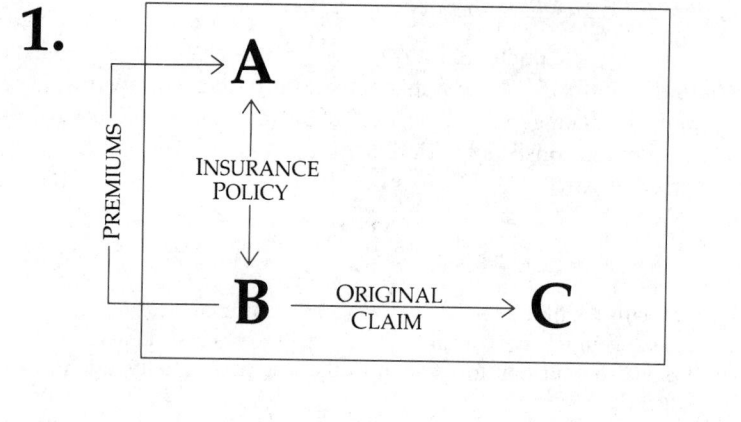

A = INSURER

B = INSURED

C = THIRD PARTY
    WHO CAUSED
    B TO
    SUSTAIN
    LOSS

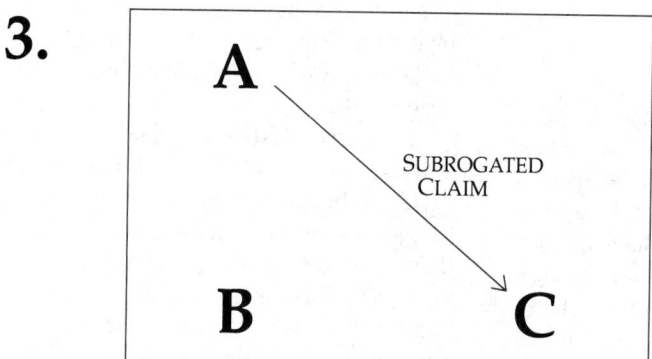

inland marine insurance, (2) fire and home-owners insurance, (3) automobile insurance, and (4) life insurance.

11.   Marine Insurance

Marine insurance policies involve perils relating to the transportation of goods. Ocean marine insurance policies cover the transporta-

tion of goods in vessels in international trade. Inland marine insurance principally covers domestic shipments of goods over land and inland waterways.

(a) OCEAN MARINE. Ocean marine insurance is a form of insurance that covers ships and their cargoes against "perils of the sea." Four classes of ocean marine insurance are generally available: (1) hull, (2) cargo, (3) liability, and (4) freight. **Hull insurance** covers physical damage to the vessel.[13] **Cargo insurance** protects the cargo owner against financial loss if the goods being shipped are lost or damaged at sea. **Liability insurance** covers the shipowner's liability if the ship causes damage to another ship or its cargo. **Freight insurance** insures that the shipowner will receive payment for the transportation charges.

In the *Commodities Reserve Co.* case a cargo owner sued the insurer for breach of an ocean marine cargo policy.

---

[13]   Employers Insurance of Wausau v International Marine Towing (CA5 La) 864 F2d 1225 (1989).

COMMODITIES RESERVE CO. v ST. PAUL FIRE & MARINE INS. CO.
(CA9 Cal) 879 F2d 640 (1989)

Commodities Reserve Co. (CRC) contracted to sell 1,008 tons of beans and 50 tons of seeds to purchasers in Venezuela. CRC purchased the beans and seeds in Turkey and chartered space on the ship MV West Lion. The cargo was insured under an ocean marine policy issued by St. Paul Fire & Marine Insurance Co. (St. Paul). While the ship was sailing through Greek waters, Greek authorities seized the vessel for carrying munitions. CRC had to go to the expense of obtaining an order from a court in Crete to release the cargo. When St. Paul refused to pay the costs of the Cretan litigation to release the cargo, CRC brought suit against St. Paul. Judgment was entered for St. Paul. CRC appealed.

FARRIS, C.J. . . . Commodities Reserve primarily seeks recovery under the Sue & Labor Clause of its insurance contract with St. Paul, which provides:

In case of any loss or misfortune, it shall be lawful and necessary to and for the Assured...to sue, labor and travel for, in and about the defense, safeguard and recovery of the said goods and merchandise . . . to the charges whereof, the [insurer] will contribute according to the rate and quantity of the sum hereby insured.

This standard provision requires the insurer to reimburse the assured for expenses incurred in preventing a loss for which, if it had occurred, the insurer would be liable. . . .

The Average Clause is the general basis for liability. It provides that the policy covers "all risks of physical loss or damage from any external cause excepting those risks excluded by the F.C. & S. [Free of Capture & Seizure] and S.R. & C.C. [Strikes, Riots & Civil Commotions] Clauses. . . ."

The F.C. & S. Clause, one of the Paramount Warranties, declares that:

Notwithstanding anything herein contained to the contrary, this insurance is warranted free from: (a) capture, seizure, arrest, restraint, detainment, confiscation, preemption, requisition or nationalization, and the consequences thereof or any attempt thereat, whether in time of peace or war and whether lawful or otherwise. . . .

St. Paul argues that the F.C. & S. Clause . . . excuses it from liability. . .

When the Greek authorities detained the ship, they did not claim jurisdiction over Commodities Reserve's cargo. . . . Instead, the captain refused to release the cargo. Due to the captain's conduct, Commodities Reserve had to secure a court order compelling the release of its cargo. The litigation expenses incurred to release the cargo are recoverable under the Average Clause, which covers "all risks of physical loss or damage from any external cause." *See Champion Int'l Corp. v. Arkwright-Boston Mfr. Mutual Ins. Co.*, 1982 AMC 2496 (S.D.N.Y.), aff'd, 714 F.2d 112 (2d Cir.1982) (insured entitled to recover for expenses, including litigation, incurred to recover cargo after carrier converted it under policy insuring plaintiff against "all risk of physical loss or damage to its cargo from an external source"). The Sue and Labor Clause required Commodities Reserve to "sue . . . for . . . recovery of said goods and merchandise" in case of loss or misfortune, and mandates payment of the charges by the insurer.

The detention by Greek authorities was not the proximate cause of the litigation expenses. The detention did not necessitate the suit in Crete. The litigation expenses were incurred solely because of the captain's refusal to release the cargo. Consequently, the Free of Capture and Seizure Clause does not preclude recovery of these expenses.

The district court erred in granting St. Paul summary judgment on this issue. Summary judgment for the litigation expenses should be awarded to Commodities Reserve on its cross-motion for summary judgment.

[Reversed and remanded]

QUESTIONS

1. What defense did the insurer raise?
2. Were the litigation expenses incurred because of the seizure of the vessel by Greek authorities?
3. Under the ocean marine policy in effect, was the insurer held liable for the litigation expenses?

(b) INLAND MARINE. The extension of ocean marine insurance coverage to inland risks was inevitable. Transportation of goods from Amsterdam to Philadelphia involved some nonoceanic travel. The goods had to be moved from the warehouse to the vessel and from the vessel to a form of "over land" transportation for movement to a warehouse in Philadelphia. Since these "over land" risks were not covered by the ocean marine policies, a new form of insurance had to be devised.

Inland marine insurance is used to insure domestic goods in transit. These goods may be shipped by a common carrier, such as a trucking company, railroad or airline, or shipped on coastal or river barges, or by the shipper's own trucks. Inland marine insurance can be used to insure property held by a bailee. Moreover, it is common for institutions financ-ing automobile dealers' new car inventories to purchase inland marine insurance policies to insure against damage to the automobiles while in inventory.[14]

12.   Fire and Homeowners Insurance

A **fire insurance** policy is a contract to indemnify the insured for destruction of or damage to property caused by fire. In almost every state the New York standard fire insurance form is the standard policy. A **homeowners insurance** policy is a combination of the standard fire insurance policy and comprehensive personal liability insurance. It thus provides fire, theft, and certain liability protection in a single insurance contract.

---

[14]   Boyd Motors Inc. v Employers Insurance of Wausau (CA10 Okla) 880 F2d 270 (1989).

(a) FIRE INSURANCE. In order for fire loss to be covered by fire insurance, there must be an actual, hostile fire that is the immediate or proximate cause of the loss. A **hostile fire** is one that to some extent becomes uncontrollable, burns with excessive heat, or escapes from the place where it is intended to be.[15] To illustrate, when soot is ignited and causes a fire in the chimney, the fire is hostile. On the other hand, if a loss is caused by the smoke or heat of a fire that has not broken out of its ordinary container or become uncontrollable, it results from a friendly fire and is not covered by the policy.

(1) Coinsurance. The insurer is liable for the actual amount of the loss sustained, up to the maximum amount stated in the policy. An exception exists when the policy contains a coinsurance clause. A **coinsurance** clause requires the insured to maintain insurance on the covered property up to a certain amount or a certain percent of the value (generally 80 percent). Under such a provision, if the policyholder insures the property for less than the required amount, the insurer is liable only for the proportionate share of the amount of insurance required to be carried. To illustrate, suppose the owner of a building with a value of $200,000 insures it against loss to the extent of $120,000. The policy contains a coinsurance clause requiring that insurance of 80 percent of the value of the property be carried (in this case, $160,000). Assume that an $80,000 loss is then sustained. The insured would not receive $80,000 from the insurer. The insured would receive only three-fourths of that amount, which is $60,000, because the amount of the insurance carried ($120,000) is only three-fourths of the amount required ($160,000).

In some states use of a coinsurance clause is prohibited or is permitted only with the consent of the insured.

(2) Assignment. Fire insurance is a personal contract, and in the absence of statute or contractual authorization it cannot be assigned before a loss is sustained, without the consent of the insurer.

(3) Occupancy. Provisions in a policy of fire insurance relating to the use and occupancy of the property are generally strictly construed, because they relate to the hazards involved.

(b) HOMEOWNERS INSURANCE. In addition to providing protection against losses resulting from fire, the homeowners policy provides liability coverage for accidents or injuries that occur on the premises of the insured. Moreover, the liability provisions provide coverage for unintentional injuries to others away from home for which the insured or any member of the resident family is held responsible, such as injuries caused others by golfing, hunting, or fishing accidents. Generally, motor vehicles, including mopeds and recreation vehicles, are excluded from such personal liability coverage.[16]

A homeowners policy also provides protection from losses caused by theft.

A homeowners policy provides protection for all permanent residents of the household, including all family members living with the insured. Thus, a son of the insured who lives at home has the right to bring suit against the insurer, under the homeowner's policy, for the value of personal property lost when the home is destroyed by fire.[17]

13.   Automobile Insurance

Associations of insurers, such as the National Bureau of Casualty Underwriters and the National Automobile Underwriters Association, have proposed standard forms of automobile insurance policies. These forms have been approved by the association members in virtually all states. The form used today by most insurers is the Personal Auto Policy (PAP).

(a) PERILS COVERED. **Liability insurance** protects the insured driver or owner from the claims of others for bodily injuries or damage to their property. Part A of the PAP contains the liability coverages. Part B of the policy provides the coverage for medical ex-

---

[15]   Perkins Hardwood Lumber Co. v Bituminous Casualty Corp. 190 Ga App 231, 378 SE2d 407 (1989).

[16]   Western v Home Owners Insurance Co. 157 Mich App 261, 403 NW2d 115 (1987).

[17]   Gulf Insurance Co. v Mathis, 183 Ga App 323, 358 SE2d 307 (1987).

penses sustained by a covered person or persons in an accident. Part C of the PAP provides coverage for damages the insured is entitled to recover from an **uninsured motorist.** Part D provides coverage for loss or damage to the covered automobile. Coverage under Part D includes collision coverage and coverage of "other than collision" losses, such as fire and theft.

(b) COVERED PERSONS. Covered persons include the named insured or any family member (a person related by blood, marriage or adoption or a ward or foster child who is a resident of the household). If an individual is driving with the permission of the insured, that individual is also covered.

(c) USE AND OPERATION. The terms *use* and *operation* as found in a policy are liberally interpreted to include events in which there is some involvement of the automobile, even though not for the purpose of transportation.[18] For example, the insured *uses* the automobile when packages are being loaded into it.

(d) NOTICE AND COOPERATION. The insured is under a duty to give notice, to inform, and to cooperate with the insurer. Notice and cooperation are conditions precedent to the liability of the insurer.

(e) NO-FAULT INSURANCE. Traditional tort law (automobile negligence law) placed the economic losses resulting from an automobile accident on the one at fault. The purpose of automobile liability insurance is to relieve the wrongdoer from the consequences of a negligent act by paying defense costs and the damages assessed. Under no-fault laws, injured persons are barred from suing the party at fault for ordinary claims. When the insured is injured while using the insured automobile, the insurer will make a payment without regard to whose fault caused the harm.[19] However, if the automobile collision results in a permanent serious disablement or

disfigurement, or death, or if the medical bills and lost wages of the plaintiff exceed a specified amount, suit may be brought against the party who was at fault.

14.   Life Insurance

There are three basic types of life insurance: term insurance, whole life insurance, and endowment insurance.

Term insurance is written for a specified number of years and terminates at the end of that period. If the insured dies within the time period covered by the policy, the face amount is paid to the beneficiary. If the insured is still alive at the end of the time period, the contract expires and the insurer has no further obligations. Term policies have little or no cash value.

Whole life insurance (which is sometimes called *ordinary* life insurance) provides lifetime insurance protection. It also has an investment element. Part of every premium covers the cost of insurance, and the remainder of the premium is devoted to the investment component of the policy, which builds up over time to its **cash surrender value**.

An **endowment insurance** policy is one that pays the face amount of the policy if the insured dies within the policy period. If the insured lives to the end of the policy period, the face amount is paid to the insured at the end of the period.

(a) EXCLUSIONS. Life insurance policies frequently provide that death shall not be within the protection of the policy or that a double indemnity provision shall not be applicable when death is caused by (1) suicide,[20] (2) narcotics, (3) the intentional act of another, (4) execution for a crime, (5) war activities, or (6) operation of aircraft.

(b) THE BENEFICIARY. The recipient of proceeds of a life insurance policy that are payable upon the death of the insured is called the **beneficiary**. The beneficiary may be a

---

[18]   State Farm Ins. v Whithead (Mo App) 711 SW2d 198 (1986).
[19]   Brehm v Illinois Farmers Insurance (Minn) 390 NW2d 475 (1986).

[20]   Southern Farm Bureau Life Ins. Co. v Dettle (Tex Civ App) 707 SW2d 271 (1986).

third person or the estate of the insured. There may be more than one beneficiary.

The beneficiary named in the policy may be barred from claiming the proceeds of the policy. It is generally provided by statute or stated by court decision that a beneficiary who has feloniously killed the insured is not entitled to receive the proceeds of the policy.[21]

The customary policy provides that the insured reserves the right to change the beneficiary without the latter's consent. When the policy contains such a provision, the beneficiary cannot object to a change that destroys all of that beneficiary's rights under the policy and that names another person as beneficiary.

The insurance policy will ordinarily state that in order to change the beneficiary, the insurer must be so instructed in writing by the insured, and the policy must then be endorsed by the company with the change of the beneficiary. These provisions are generally construed liberally. If the insured has notified the insurer but dies before the endorsement of the change by the company, the change of beneficiary is effective. However, if the insured has not taken any steps to comply with the policy

requirements, a change of beneficiary is not effective, even though a change was intended.

(c) INCONTESTABILITY CLAUSE. Statutes commonly require the inclusion of an **incontestability clause** in life insurance policies. Ordinarily, this clause states that after the lapse of two years the policy cannot be contested by the insurance company. The insurer is free to contest the validity of the policy at any time during the contestability period. Once the period has expired, the insurer must pay the stipulated sum upon the death of the insured and cannot claim that in obtaining the policy the insured had been guilty of misrepresentation, fraud, or any other conduct that would entitle it to avoid the contract of insurance.[22]

In the *Kane* case the insurer claimed that there should be an exception to the incontestability period. The criminal history of the insured was not discoverable in a background check because the insured was given a new identity under the federal witness protection program.

---

[21]   Johnson v State Farm Fire and Casualty Co. 151 Ill App 3d 879, 104 Ill Dec 890, 503 NE2d 602 (1987).

[22]   Chavis v Southern Life Ins. Co. 318 NC 259, 347 SE2d 425 (1986).

BANKERS SECURITY LIFE INSURANCE SOCIETY v KANE
(CA11 Fla) 885 F2d 820 (1989)

In 1976 Arthur Katz testified for the U.S. government in a stock manipulation case. He also pled guilty and testified against three of his law partners in an insurance fraud case. He received a six-month sentence in a halfway house and a $5,000 fine. Katz was placed in the Federal Witness Protection Program. Katz and his wife changed their names to Kane and moved to Florida under the program. Both he and his wife obtained new driver's licenses and social security numbers. Using his new identity, "Kane" obtained two life insurance policies totaling $1.5 million and named his wife beneficiary. A routine criminal background check on Kane found no criminal history. From 1984 to 1987 Kane invested heavily in the stock market. On October 17, 1987, the day the stock market crashed, Kane shot and wounded his stockbroker, shot and killed the office manager, and then committed suicide. The insurers refused to pay on the policies, claiming that they never insure persons with criminal records. Mrs. Kane contended that the policies were incontestable after they had been in effect for two years. From a judgment for Mrs. Kane, the insurers appealed.

SHOOB, D.J. . . . Essentially, appellants seek a court-created exception to the Florida rule that insurance policies are incontestable after they have been in effect for two years. Fla.Stat. § 627.455 (1984). Appellants correctly argue that the purpose of this statute is to create a reasonable time period during which insurance companies can investigate applicants and void policies issued in error, while protecting consumers from untimely efforts to void policies. . . . Appellants maintain that this purpose is not served, however, by enforcing the incontestability clauses at issue here.

Appellants urge the Court to adopt the reasoning of several Pennsylvania cases that have created an "imposter" exception where the insurance company, through reasonable investigation, could not have discovered fraud in the issuance of a policy. . . . See *Unity Mutual Life Insurance Co. v. Moses*, 621 F. Supp. 13 (E.D.Pa. 1985). Appellants maintain that in such cases no contract exists (and no incontestability clause) because there is no meeting of the minds as to the identity of the insured.

Although appellants present a novel argument, it must fail based on the strict construction of the incontestability clauses under Florida law. . . .

We will not create exceptions to Florida law or void insurance policies *ab initio* in a manner that would undermine the intent of the Florida legislature and the practice in the Florida courts.

We also reject appellants' argument that the district court should not have dismissed their complaints without leave to amend. Any amendments to the complaints would have been futile. There is no set of facts upon which appellants could succeed because the district court correctly held that appellants are not entitled to an exception to Florida's incontestability statute.

. . . Finally, appellants cannot bring a separate tort suit for fraud. . . .

In this case a fraud suit would merely provide a different means to challenge the validity of the insurance contract. The district court properly rebuffed appellants' efforts to evade the Florida incontestability statute in this manner. . . .

[Judgment affirmed]

QUESTIONS

1. What is the purpose of the statute requiring the inclusion of incontestability clauses in life insurance policies?
2. How are incontestability clauses construed?
3. Did the court leave the insurer other legal means to challenge the enforceability of the policy?

SUMMARY

Insurance is a contract, called a *policy*. By an insurance policy provision is made by the insurer, in consideration of premium payments made by the insured, to pay the insured or beneficiary a sum of money if the insured sustains a specified loss. These contracts are made through an insurance agent, who is an agent for the insurance company, or through an insurance broker. An insurance broker is the agent of the insured when obtaining a policy for the latter.

The person purchasing an insurance contract must have an insurable interest in the subject matter insured, be it life or property. An insurable interest in property exists when the damage or destruction of the property will cause a direct monetary loss to the insured. To collect on a property insurance policy, the insured must have an insurable interest at the time of loss. An insurable interest in the life of the insured exists if the purchaser would suffer a financial loss from the insured's death. This interest must exist as of the time the policy is obtained.

Ocean marine policies insure ships and their cargoes against the perils of the sea. Inland marine policies insure domestic goods in transit, including goods transported by truck, rail, air, and barge.

In order for a fire loss to be covered by fire insurance there must be an actual, hostile fire that is the immediate or proximate cause of the loss. The insurer is liable for the actual amount of the loss sustained up to the maximum amount stated in the policy. An exception exists when the policy contains a coinsurance clause requiring the insured to maintain insurance up to a certain percentage of the value of the property. To the extent this is not done, the insured is deemed a coinsurer with the insurer, and the insurer is liable for only its proportional share of the amount of insurance required to be carried. A homeowners insurance policy provides fire, theft, and liability protection in a single contract.

The owner or operator of a motor vehicle may purchase liability insurance for protection from claims made by third persons for their bodily injuries or the damage to their property caused by the operation or use of the motor vehicle. The owner may also purchase coverage for damage to the owner's property, regardless of whether the owner was at fault. This is called *collision* coverage. Additionally, the owner may purchase fire and theft coverage. Special limited coverage is required by law in most states to cover personal injuries caused by uninsured motorists.

A life insurance policy requires the insurer to pay a stipulated sum of money to a named beneficiary upon the death of the insured. It may be a term insurance policy, a whole life policy, or an endowment policy. State law commonly requires the inclusion of an incontestability clause, whereby at the conclusion of a two-year period the insurer cannot contest the validity of the policy based on misstatements or misrepresentations of the insured in the application for insurance.

QUESTIONS AND CASE PROBLEMS

1. What social forces are affected by imposing the requirement of insurable interest?
2. Compare (a) a contract of insurance and (b) an ordinary contract.
3. What time limits may bar an insured from recovering on the policy questioned?
4. James Butler purchased a stolen automobile without knowing that it had been stolen. He insured it with Farmers Insurance Company. The policy covered loss by accidental means. The automobile was seized by the local police and returned to its true owner. Butler then sued on his insurance policy, claiming that there had been a loss by accidental means. The insurer raised the defense that Butler did not have an insurable interest in the automobile, because it was a stolen car. Was this defense valid? [Butler v Farmers Insurance Co. 126 Ariz 377, 616 P2d 46]

5. From the United Insurance Co., Rebecca Foster obtained a policy insuring the life of Lucille McClurkin and naming herself as beneficiary. Lucille did not live with Rebecca, and Rebecca did not inform Lucille of the existence of the policy. Rebecca paid the premiums on the policy and, upon the death of Lucille, sued the United Insurance Co. for the amount of the insurance. At the trial, Rebecca testified vaguely that her father had told her that Lucille was her second cousin on his side of the family. Was Rebecca entitled to recover on the policy? [Foster v United Insurance Co. 250 SC 423, 158 SE2d 201]
6. Mike Edwards insured his car against theft with the State Farm Mutual Automobile Insurance Company. He later sold the car to Steven Davis, who paid for the car with a bad check that the bank refused to honor because of insufficient funds. Neither Steven nor the car were ever

seen again. Mike claimed that his insurance company was liable for the loss, on the ground that the policy covered theft, and there had been a theft of his car. The insurance company answered that Edwards had been defrauded by use of a bad check but that this was not a theft of the car. Decide. [Edwards v State Farm Automobile Ins. Co. (Iowa) 296 NW2d 804]

7. Assistant manager trainee R. G. Smith suspected Bowen of shoplifting at Broad & Marshall Department Store. After getting permission from the store manager to follow her, he observed Bowen driving out of the store's parking lot. Smith followed her in his car and forced her into a ditch, where her car overturned and was destroyed. Bowen received the fair market value for her car from her insurance company, General National Mutual (GNM), and executed a subrogation agreement in connection with this payment. Bowen is planning on bringing suit against Smith and the store for actual and punitive damages for the injury and indignity suffered. GNM brings suit against Smith and the store for damage to the car. They defend that GNM is not the proper party plaintiff. Decide.

8. Stefan Etterle and his wife, Justyna, insured their house with Excelsior Insurance Co. The policy protected them from damage to the dwelling by fire. Some time later they transferred the title of the house to their son Stephen, as a matter of convenience because of their ill health. Two months later, the house was damaged by fire. The parents and the son demanded payment on the policy for the loss sustained. Excelsior refused to make payment on the ground that the parents did not have any insurable interest in the property and that the son was not named on the policy. Decide. [Etterle v Excelsior Ins. Co. 74 App Div 2d 436, 428 NYS2d 95]

9. Collins owned a Piper Colt airplane. He obtained from the South Carolina Insurance Company a liability policy covering the plane. The policy provided that it did not cover loss sustained while the plane was being piloted by a person who did not have a valid pilot's certificate and a valid medical examination certificate. Collins held a valid pilot's certificate, but his medical examination certificate had expired three months before. Collins was piloting the plane when it crashed, and he was killed. The insurer denied liability because Collins did not have a valid medical certificate. It was stipulated by both parties that the crash was in no way caused by the absence of the medical certificate. Decide. [South Carolina Ins. Co. v Collins (SC) 237 SE2d 358]

10. Marshall Produce Co. insured its milk and egg processing plant against fire. Smoke from a fire near its plant was absorbed by its egg powder. Cans of the powder delivered to the U.S. government were rejected as contaminated. Marshall Produce sued the insurance company for a total loss. The insurer contended that there had been no fire involving the insured property and no total loss. Decide. [Marshall Produce Co. v St. Paul Fire & Marine Ins. Co. 256 Minn 404, 98 NW2d 280]

11. Amador Pena had three insurance policies on his life. He wrote a will in which he specified that the proceeds from the insurance policies should go to his children instead of to Leticia Pena Salinas and other beneficiaries named in the policies. He died the next day. The insurance companies paid the proceeds of the policies to the named beneficiaries. The executor of Pena's estate sued Salinas and the other beneficiaries for the insurance money. Decide. [Pena v Salinas (Tex Civ App) 536 SW2d 671]

12. Spector owned a small automobile repair garage in rural Kansas, valued at $40,000. He purchased fire insurance coverage against loss to the extent of $24,000. The policy contained an 80 percent coinsurance clause. A fire destroyed a portion of his parts room, causing a loss of $16,000. Spector believes he is entitled to be fully compensated for this loss, since it is less than the $24,000 of fire protection that he purchased and paid for. Is Spector correct?

13. Carman Tool & Abrasives, Inc. (Carman) purchased two milling machines, F.O.B. Taiwan, from the Dah Lih Machinery Co. Carman purchased ocean marine cargo insurance on the machines from St. Paul Fire and Marine Insurance Co. Carman authorized Dah Lih to arrange for the shipment of the two machines to Los Angeles, using the services of Evergreen Lines. Dah Lih booked the machinery for shipment on board Evergreen's container ship, the M/V Ever Giant, arranged for the delivery of the cargo to the ship, provided all the relevant shipping information for the bill of lading, and was the party to whom the bill was issued. Dah Lih then delivered the bill of lading to its bank, which in turn negotiated it to Carman's bank in exchange for a letter of credit authorizing payment to Dah Lih. After the cargo was removed from the vessel in Los Angeles but before it was delivered to

Carman, the milling machines were damaged to the extent of $115,000. Is the insurer liable to Carman? Can the insurer recover from Evergreen? [Carman Tool & Abrasives, Inc. v Evergreen Lines (CA9 Cal) 871 F2d 897]

14. Vallot was driving his farm tractor on the highway. It was struck from the rear by a truck, overturned, exploded, and burned. Vallot was killed, and a death claim was made against All American Insurance Company. The death of Vallot was covered by the company's policy if Vallot had died from "being struck or run over by" the truck. The insurance company claimed that the policy was not applicable because Vallot had not been struck, in that the farm tractor had been struck and Vallot's death occurred when the overturned tractor exploded and burned. The insurance company also claimed that it was necessary that the insured be both struck and run over by another vehicle. Decide. [Vallot v All American Insurance Co. (La App) 302 So 2d 625]

15. When Jorge de Guerrero applied for a $200,000 life insurance policy with John Hancock Insurance Co., he stated on the insurance application that he had not seen a physician within the past five years. In fact he had several consultations with his physician, who three weeks prior to the application had diagnosed him as overweight and suffering from goiter. His response to the question on drug and alcohol use was that he was not an alcoholic or user of drugs. In fact he had been an active alcoholic since age sixteen and was a marijuana user. De Guerrero died within the two-year contestability period included in the policy, and John Hancock refused to pay. The beneficiary contended that all premiums were fully paid on the policy, and any misstatements in the application were unintentional. John Hancock contended that if the deceased had given the true facts, the policy would not have been issued. Decide. [de Guerrero v John Hancock Mutual Life Insurance Co. (Fla App) 522 So 2d 1032]

PART SEVEN

AGENCY AND EMPLOYMENT

39

AGENCY—CREATION AND TERMINATION

One of the most common legal relationships is that of agency. By virtue of the agency device, one person can make contracts at numerous places with many different parties at the same time. A principal or employer can sometimes be held liable in tort when an agent or employee injures a third person while performing business-related tasks directed by the principal or employer. Thus, disputes based upon contract law and tort law may arise out of transactions or work done for others. The rights and liabilities of the parties to the dispute may turn not only on the point of contract or tort law, but also on whether or not an agency relationship existed.

A. NATURE OF THE AGENCY RELATIONSHIP

Agency is based on the consent of the parties and for that reason is called a *consensual* relationship. If consideration is present, the relationship is also contractual. The law sometimes imposes an agency relationship.

1.   Definitions and Distinctions

Agency is a relationship based on an express or implied agreement by which one person, the **agent**, is authorized to act under the control of and for another, the **principal**, in negotiating and making contracts with third persons.[1] The acts of the agent obligate the principal to third persons and give the principal rights against third persons.

The term *agency* is frequently used with other meanings. It is sometimes used to denote the fact that one has the right to sell certain products, such as when a dealer is said to possess an automobile agency. In other instances the term is used to mean an exclusive right to sell certain articles within a given territory. In these cases, however, the dealer is not an agent in the sense of representing the manufacturer.[2] Courts are sometimes called on to determine if an agency relationship existed although the term *agent* had not been used.

Because the agency relationship creates certain rights and liabilities not present in other associations, it is important to be able to distinguish agencies from other similar relationships.

(a) EMPLOYEES AND INDEPENDENT CONTRACTORS. Control and authority are characteristics that distinguish ordinary employees and independent contractors from agents.

---

[1]   Restatement, Agency, 2d §1; Union Miniere, S.A. v Parday Corp. (Ind App) 521 NE2d 200 (1988).

[2]   Professional Lens Plan, Inc. v Polaris Leasing Corp. 238 Kan 384, 710 P2d 1297 (1985).

FIGURE 39-1   AGENCY RELATIONSHIP

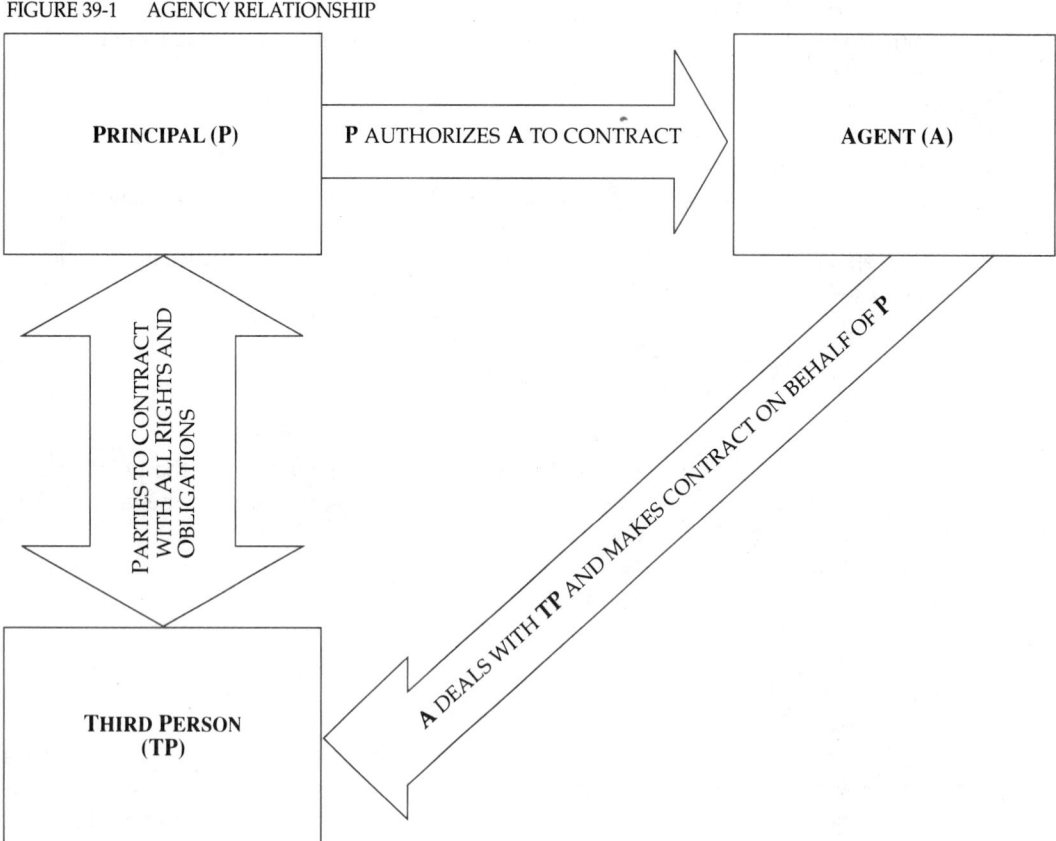

(1) Employees. An agent is distinguished from an ordinary employee, who is not hired to represent the employer in dealings with third persons. It is possible, however, for the same person to be both an agent and an employee. For example, the driver of a milk delivery truck is an agent, as well as an employee, in making contracts between the milk company and its customers but is only an employee with respect to the work of delivering milk.

(2) Independent Contractors. An agent or employee differs from an independent contractor in that the principal or employer has control over and can direct the agent or an employee but does not have control over the performance of work by an independent contractor.[3]

In the *Yelverton* case the application of the "right to control" test determined whether an individual was an agent, an employee, or an independent contractor.

[3]   Noonan v Texaco, Inc. (Wyo) 713 P2d 160 (1986).

YELVERTON v LAMM
__ NC App __, 380 SE2d 621 (1989)

Patricia Yelverton died as a result of injuries sustained when an automobile owned and driven by Joseph Lamm crossed the center line of a roadway and struck the automobile driven by Yelverton. Yelverton's executor brought suit against Lamm and Lamm's alleged employer Premier Industrial Products Inc. The executor contended that Premier was vicariously liable for the negligence of Lamm. Premier defended that Lamm was not its agent or employee, but was an independent contractor. From a judgment for Premier, Yelverton appealed.

COZORT, J. . . . An independent contractor, as distinguished from an employee, is "one who exercises an independent employment and contracts to do certain work according to his own judgment and method, without being subject to his employer except as to the result of his work." *Cooper v. Asheville-Citizen Times Publishing Co.*, 258 N.C. 578, 587, 129 S.E.2d 107, 113 (1963). . . . The test in determining a worker's status is whether the employer has the right to control the worker with respect to the manner or methods of doing the work or the agents to be employed in it, or has the right merely to require certain results according to the parties' contract. . . . If the requisite right to control is found to exist, then an employer is held liable, albeit vicariously, for the negligent acts of its agents, servants, or employees which cause injuries to third persons; but an employer is not liable to third parties for the negligence of an independent contractor. . . .

. . . The evidence before the trial court was that, since 1963, Lamm had represented Premier as a sales agent who took orders from customers for a certain line of Premier's products. The relationship between Lamm and Premier was governed by a written contract entitled "Independent Agent Agreement" wherein Lamm, as "Independent Agent," was given a nonexclusive right to sell Premier's products in a designated territory. The Agreement provided that all orders were subject to acceptance by Premier and were not binding upon Premier until so accepted.

Pursuant to the contract, Lamm was paid by commission only and did not receive a commission for any order which was rejected by Premier. All expenses incurred by Lamm in his business as sales agent for Premier were to be borne by Lamm. Lamm was allowed to work on a self-determined schedule, retain assistants at his own expense, and render services to or sell the products of other companies not in competition with Premier. The Agreement could be terminated by either party "with or without cause." In addition, the Agreement contained the following provision:

> Independent Agent and the Company recognize that the Company has no right to control Independent Agent in the manner in which he or she performs his or her obligations under this Agreement and that Independent Agent is free to perform such obligations in the manner he or she sees fit.

Uncontradicted testimony given by affidavit and depositions confirms that the parties conducted their relationship as delineated in the Independent Agent Agreement. Plaintiff does not appear to dispute testimony that Lamm worked when, in his judgment, he felt he needed to, was paid solely on a commission basis, was not reimbursed for his expenses, and operated his business as he saw fit. Premier's sales manager stated in his affidavit that Lamm was "among the most independent of independent contractors taking orders for Premier"; that he "did not want, or accept, any guidance or suggestions as to how he should operate his business"; and that he "was not required to, and generally did not, follow any suggestions I made but instead adopted his own methods, and he was perfectly entitled to do this." Affiant also stated that from time to time he had gone with Lamm to make calls and on one occasion had seen in the trunk of Lamm's car "hundreds of pairs" of men's socks which Lamm said he was selling to customers, as he was entitled to do under the terms of the parties' Agreement.

In addition, Premier deducted no income taxes from Lamm's commissions and made no deductions or payments for social security for Lamm. Premier filed Forms 1099 rather than W-2 forms with the Internal Revenue Service; payments to Lamm were designated "nonemployee compensation." . . .

It is true that "a mere contractual declaration is not determinative of the relationship and the rights of the parties." *Watkins v. Murrow*, 253 N.C. 652, 657, 118 S.E.2d 5, 8 (1961). But this is simply to say that the court will not ignore the true relationship existing between the parties, and that an employer who exercises control in spite of a contractual declaration to the contrary may be held vicariously liable. *See id.* The undisputed evidence in the case before us, however, establishes more than a "mere contractual declaration"; it clearly shows that the parties intended Lamm's status to be that of an independent contractor and in fact conducted their dealings according to those express intentions. . . .

We therefore affirm the trial court's ruling that Premier was entitled to judgment in its favor as a matter of law.

[Judgment affirmed]

QUESTIONS

1. Was Lamm Premier's agent?
2. Was Lamm an employee of Premier?
3. Was Lamm an independent contractor?
4. Can an employer avoid liability for the acts of employees under its control by having the workers sign contracts stating that they are independent contractors?

A person who appears to be an independent contractor may in fact be so controlled by the other party that the contractor is regarded as an agent of, or employee of, the controlling person.

The separate identity of an independent

contractor may be concealed so that the public believes that it is dealing with the principal. When this situation occurs, the principal is liable for the negligence of the independent contractor.

A person may be an independent contractor generally but an agent with respect to a particular transaction.[4] Thus, an "agency" or a "broker" rendering personal services to customers is ordinarily an independent contractor but will be the agent of a customer when the rendering of a service involves making a contract on behalf of the customer with a third person.

(b) REAL ESTATE BROKERS. A real estate broker is generally not an agent with authority to make a contract with a third person that will bind the broker's client. Typically, the broker's authority is limited to locating a seller or buyer and bringing the parties together. Even when the third person and the broker sign a "contract," it is generally only an offer by the third person, and it does not become a binding contract until accepted by the client of the broker.

(c) BAILEES. When personal property is delivered to another under an agreement that the property will be returned to the deliverer or transferred to a third person, a bailment arises. The person to whom the property is delivered, the bailee, is not an agent, because the bailee has no authority to act for or make any contract on behalf of the bailor.

Situations commonly arise, however, in which the same person is both an agent and a bailee. A salesperson who is lent a company car is a bailee with respect to the car, but with respect to making sales contracts the same person is an agent.

(d) REQUIRED ACT. The mere fact that one person requires another person to perform an act does not make the latter person the agent of the former. For example, when a bank directs a borrower to obtain the signature of another person in order to secure a bank loan, the borrower is not the agent of the bank in making contact with the other person and procuring the required signature.

2.   Purpose of Agency

An agency may be created to perform almost any act that the principal could lawfully do. The object of the agency must not be criminal, nor may it be contrary to public policy. Some acts must be performed in person and cannot be entrusted or delegated to an agent. Voting, swearing to the truth of documents, testifying in court, and making a will are instances where personal action is required. In the preparation of a document, however, it is proper to employ someone else to prepare the paper that is then signed or sworn to by the employing party. Various forms that are required by statute, such as applications for licenses and tax returns, in some instances expressly authorize the execution of such forms by an agent, as long as the identities of both principal and agent and the latter's representative capacity are clearly shown.

3.   Who May Be a Principal

Any person who is competent to act may act through an agent. The appointment of an agent by a person lacking capacity is generally void or voidable to the same extent that a contract made by such person would be. Thus, a minor acting through an agent will effect a contract that will be voidable to the same extent as though made by the minor.

4.   Who May Be an Agent

Since a contract made by an agent is, in law, the contract of the principal, it is immaterial whether the agent has legal capacity to make a contract. Therefore, it is permissible to employ as agents persons who are aliens, minors, and others who are under a natural or legal disability.

Ordinarily, an agent is one person acting for another, but an agent may be a partnership or a corporation.

5.   Classification of Agents

A **special agent** is authorized by the principal

---

[4]   Kight v Sheppard Building Supply Co. (Miss) 537 So 2d 1355 (1989).

to handle a definite business transaction or to do a specific act. One who is authorized by another to purchase a particular house is a special agent.

A **general agent** is authorized by the principal to transact all affairs in connection with a particular kind of business or trade, or to transact all business at a certain place.[5] To illustrate, a person who is appointed as manager by the owner of a store is a general agent.

A **universal agent** is authorized by the principal to do all acts that can be delegated lawfully to a representative. This form of agency arises when a person absent by virtue of being in the military service gives another person a blanket power of attorney to do anything that must be done during such absence.

6.   Agency Coupled with an Interest

An agent has an **interest in the authority** when consideration has been given or paid for the right to exercise the authority. To illustrate, when a lender, in return for making a loan of money, is given, as security, authority to collect rents due to the borrower and to apply those rents to the payment of the debt, the lender becomes the borrower's agent with an interest in the authority given to collect the rents.

An agent has an **interest in the subject matter** when, for a consideration, the agent is given an interest in the property with which the agent is dealing. Hence, when the agent is authorized to sell property of the principal and is given a lien on such property as security for a debt owed to the agent by the principal, the agent has an interest in the subject matter.

B.   CREATING THE AGENCY

An agency may arise by appointment, conduct, ratification, or operation of law.

7.   Authorization by Appointment

The usual method of creating an agency is by

express authorization; that is, a person is appointed to act for or on behalf of another.

In most instances the authorization of the agent may be oral. However, some appointments must be made in a particular way. A majority of the states, by statute, require the appointment of an agent to be in writing when the agency is created to acquire or dispose of any interest in land. A written authorization of agency is called a **power of attorney**. An agent acting under a power of attorney is referred to as an **attorney in fact**.[6]

Ordinarily, no agency arises from the fact that two people are married to each other or that they are co-owners of property. Consequently, when a check is made payable to the order of husband and wife, it is necessary for each to indorse the check. The fact that both names are on the check does not create an agency by which the husband can indorse the wife's name and deposit the money into the husband's own bank account.

8.   Authorization by Conduct

Conduct consistent with the existence of an agency relationship may be sufficient to bind the principal.

(a) PRINCIPAL'S CONDUCT AS TO AGENT. An agency is created by the consent of the parties. Therefore, any conduct of the principal, including words, that gives a person reason to believe that the principal consents to that person's acting as agent is sufficient to create an agency. Likewise, if one person, knowingly and without objection, permits another to act as agent, the law will find in such conduct an expression of authorization to the agent, and the principal will not be permitted to deny that the agent was in fact authorized. Thus, if the owner of a hotel allows another person to assume the duties of hotel clerk, that person may infer from the owner's conduct an authority to act as the hotel clerk.

(b) PRINCIPAL'S CONDUCT AS TO THIRD PERSONS. The principal may have such dealings with third persons as to cause

5   Washington National Ins. Co. v Strictland (Ala) 491 So 2d 872 (1986).

6   DeBueno v Castro (Fla App) 543 So 2d 393 (1989).

them to believe that the "agent" has authority. Thus, if the owner of a store places another person in charge, third persons may assume that the person in charge is the agent for the owner in that respect. The "agent" then appears to be authorized and is said to have **apparent authority**, and the principal is estopped from contradicting the appearance that has been created.[7]

The term *apparent authority* is used when there is only the appearance of authority, but no actual authority, and that appearance of authority was created by the principal.[8] The test for the existence of apparent authority is an objective test determined by the principal's outward manifestations through words or conduct that lead a third person reasonably to

believe that the "agent" has authority. A principal's express restriction on authority not made known to a third person is no defense. Apparent authority extends to all acts that a person of ordinary prudence, familiar with business usages and the particular business, would be justified in believing that the agent has authority to perform.

The mere placing of property in the possession of another does not give that person either actual or apparent authority to sell the property.

It is essential to the concept of apparent authority that the third person reasonably believe that the agent has authority. If the basis for such belief is not reasonable, no apparent authority arises. In the *Lundberg* case, the court was faced with deciding whether a third party was justified in believing that a breeding farm manager had authority to contract on behalf of the owner of the farm.

---

[7]   Foote & Davis, Inc. v Arnold Craven, Inc. 72 NC App 591, 324 SE2d 889 (1985).
[8]   Foley v Allard (Minn App) 405 NW2d 503 (1987).

LUNDBERG v CHURCH FARMS, INC.
151 Ill App 3d 452, 104 Ill Dec 309, 502 NE2d 806 (1986)

Gilbert Church owned Church Farms, Inc. in Manteno, Illinois, and he advertised its well-bred stallion Imperial Guard for breeding rights at $50,000, directing all inquiries to "Herb Bagley, Manager." Herb Bagley lived at Church Farms and was the only person available to visitors. Vern Lundberg responded to the advertisement. After discussions with Bagley, wherein Bagley stated that Imperial Guard would remain in Illinois for at least a two-year period, Lundberg and Bagley executed a two-year breeding rights and syndication agreement, which was signed by Lundberg and by Bagley as "Church Farms Inc., H. Bagley, Mgr." When Gil Church moved Imperial Guard to Oklahoma prior to the second year of the contract, Lundberg brought suit for breach of contract. Church testified that Bagley had no authority to sign contracts for Church Farms or to change or add terms. From a judgment for Lundberg, Church appealed.

UNVERZAGI, J. . . . Defendant . . . [contends] that the jury's verdict and the size of its award were contrary to the manifest weight of the evidence. Specifically, defendant contends that plaintiffs have failed to establish that Bagley had apparent authority to negotiate and sign the Lundberg contract for Church Farm. . . .

The party asserting an agency has the burden of proving its existence, but may do so by inference and circumstantial evidence. Additionally, an agent may bind his principal by acts which the principal has not given him *actual* authority to perform, but which he *appears* authorized to perform. An agent's apparent authority is that authority which "the principal knowingly permits the agent to assume or which he holds his agent out as possessing. It is the authority that a reasonably prudent man, exercising diligence and discretion, in view of the principal's conduct, would naturally suppose the agent to possess." The agent's authority must be derived from some act or statement of the *principal*. Defendant argues that plaintiffs' proof is based on Bagley's own assertions of authority rather than the acts or statements of Church Farm or Gil Church. We disagree.

Plaintiffs produced evidence at trial that Gil Church approved the Imperial Guard advertisement listing Herb Bagley as Church Farm's manager, and directing all inquiries to him. Church also permitted Bagley to live on the farm and to handle its daily operations. Bagley was the only person available to visitors to the farm. Bagley answered Church Farm's phone calls, and there was a preprinted signature line for him on the breeding rights package.

The conclusion is inescapable that Gil Church affirmatively placed Bagley in a managerial position giving him complete control of Church Farm and its dealings with the public. We believe that this is just the sort of "holding out" of an agent by a principal that justifies a third person's reliance on the agent's authority. See *Scholenberger v. Chicago Transit Authority* (1980), 84 Ill.App.3d 1132, 1138 (noting that apparent authority exists when principal allows public to deal exclusively with agent).

We cannot accept defendant's contention that the Lundbergs were affirmatively obligated to seek out Church to ascertain the actual extent of Bagley's authority. Where an agent has apparent authority to act, the principal will be liable in spite of any undisclosed limitations the principal has placed on that authority.

[Judgment affirmed]

QUESTIONS

1. Did the court find that Bagley had authority to bind Church Farms, Inc.? Explain.
2. What could Gil Church have done to prevent the dispute in this case?

(c) ACQUIESCENCE BY PRINCIPAL. The conduct of the principal that gives rise to the agent's authority may be acquiescence in or failing to object to acts done by the purported or apparent agent over a period of time.[9] For example, a person collecting payments on a note and remitting the proper amounts to the holder of the note will be regarded as the latter's agent for collection when this conduct has been followed over a period of years without objection.

9.   Agency by Ratification

An agent may attempt, on behalf of the principal, to do an act that was not authorized, or a person who is not the agent of another may attempt to act as such an agent. Generally, in such cases, the principal for whom the agent claimed to act has the choice of ignoring the transaction or of ratifying it. Ordinarily, any unauthorized act may be ratified.

(a) INTENTION TO RATIFY. Initially, ratification is a question of intention. Just as in the case of authorization, when there is a question of whether or not the principal authorized the agent, so there is a question of whether or not the principal intended to approve or ratify the action of the unauthorized agent.[10]

The intention to ratify may be expressed in words, or it may be found in conduct indicat-

---

[9]   Vacura v Haar's Equipment Co. (Minn) 364 NW2d 387 (1985).

[10]   Miles v Plumbing Services of Houston, Inc. (Tex Civ App) 668 SW2d 509 (1984).

ing an intention to ratify. As examples, the principal may pay for goods ordered by the agent or perform the contract that the agent had made and accept payments for such performance.

In the *Werlein* case it was asserted that the defendant's conduct manifested a clear intent to ratify another person's unauthorized act of signing defendant's name.

PHILIP WERLEIN, LTD. v DANIELS
(La App) 538 So 2d 722 (1989)

Vera Daniels and Fredrine Julian were employed by the Marriott Hotel in New Orleans and were close personal friends. One day after work Daniels and Julian went to Werlein's music store to open up a credit account. Julian, with Daniels' authorization and in her presence, applied for credit using Daniels' name and credit history. Later, Julian went to Werlien's without Daniels and charged the purchase of a television set to Daniels' account, executing a retail installment contract by signing Daniels' name. When the payments were not made, Werlien's sued Daniels for the unpaid balance. Daniels denied that she authorized or ratified the purchase of the television. From a judgment for Werlein's, Daniels appealed.

WARD, J. . . . Julian testified that Daniels saw the television at her home on the day it was delivered [in late December 1986], and that when she told Daniels she charged the television to the Werlein's account, Daniels merely told her to continue making payments on the account. After Werlein's presented [Julian's] check [in payment of the account] to the bank, the bank returned the check with the notation that the checking account was closed.

Werlein's managers testified that Daniels expressed no surprise or concern when first contacted about the delinquency of the account. Instead, she responded to the first call by claiming that a money order for the television deposit was in the mail. When contacted a second time, she asked for a "payout balance" on the account. Not until April 1987 did Daniels make any effort to object to the account or inform Werlein's that she would not pay for the purchases. This evidence shows that Daniels, rather than repudiating the purchases, remained silent and essentially acknowledged the debt when confronted by Werlein's. . . .

A person is bound by her signature being executed by another person when done in her presence and under her authority. *Nationwide Finance Co. of Gretna, Inc. v. Pitre,* 243 So.2d 326 (La.App. 4th Cir.1971). The Trial Judge found, and the evidence clearly shows, that Daniels accompanied Julian to Werlein's to open the account . . .

The evidence, however, neither indicates that Daniels accompanied Julian to Werlein's for the purchase of the television nor that Daniels authorized or even knew about Julian's plan to purchase the television. When a person's signature is executed by another person outside of her presence or without her knowledge or authority, the person must be proven to have ratified the unauthorized act to be bound by her signature. *Nationwide, supra.* The facts must indicate a clear and absolute intent to ratify the act. . . . In this case, Daniels's conduct displays her clear intent to ratify Julian's unauthorized act of signing her name to the contract for the purchase of the television.

Applying principles of agency law in this case, we find that the Trial Judge did not err in finding Daniels liable to Werlein's. . . .
[Judgment affirmed]

QUESTIONS

1. Did Daniels authorize Julian to purchase the television set?
2. State the applicable rule of law regarding responsibility for unauthorized signatures.
3. What actions of Daniels support the conclusion that Daniels ratified the unauthorized signing of her name to the contract for the purchase of the television by Julian?

If the conditions of ratification are satisfied, a principal ratifies an agent's act when, with knowledge of the act, the principal accepts or retains the benefit of the act,[11] or brings an action to enforce legal rights based upon the act, or defends an action by asserting the existence of a right based on the unauthorized transaction, or fails to repudiate the agent's act within a reasonable time. The receipt, acceptance, and deposit of a check by the principal with knowledge that it arises from an unauthorized transaction is a common illustration of ratification of the unauthorized transaction by conduct.

(b) CONDITIONS FOR RATIFICATION. In addition to the intent to ratify, expressed in some instances with certain formality, the following conditions must be satisfied in order that the intention take effect as a ratification:

1. The agent must have purported to act on behalf of or as agent for the identified principal.
2. The principal must have been capable of authorizing the act both at the time of the act and at the time when it was ratified.
3. The principal must ratify the act before the third person withdraws.
4. The act to be ratified must generally be legal.
5. The principal must have full knowledge of all material facts. If the agent conceals a material fact, the ratification of the principal that is made in ignorance of such fact is

not binding. Of course, there can be no ratification when the principal does not know of the making of the contract by the alleged agent. Consequently, when the owner's agent and a contractor make unauthorized major changes to an installation contract without knowledge of the owner, the fact that the owner had no knowledge of the matter bars any claim of ratification of the agent's act.

It is not always necessary, however, to show that the principal had actual knowledge. Knowledge will be imputed if a principal knows of such other facts as would put a prudent person on inquiry, or if that knowledge can be inferred from the knowledge of other facts or from a course of business. Knowledge is likewise not an essential factor when the principal does not care to know the details and is willing to ratify the contract regardless of such lack of knowledge.

(c) FORM OF RATIFICATION. An agreement that is binding although oral may be ratified orally or by conduct. If a contract cannot be enforced unless evidenced by a writing, it is generally held that a ratification of the contract must be in writing.[12]

(d) EFFECT OF RATIFICATION. When an unauthorized act is ratified, the effect is the same as though the act had been originally authorized. Ordinarily, this means that the prin-

---

[11]   MSP Industries Inc. v Diversified Mortgage Services Inc. (Colo App) 777 P2d 237 (1989).

[12]   Monti v Tangora, 99 Ill App 3d 575, 54 Ill Dec 732, 425 NE2d 597 (1981).

cipal and the third party are bound by the contract made by the agent.[13] When the principal ratifies the act of the unauthorized person, such ratification releases that person from the liability that would otherwise be imposed for having acted without authority.

10.   Agency by Operation of Law

In certain instances the courts, influenced by necessity or social desirability, create or find an agency when there is none. For example, a married dependent may purchase necessaries and charge them to the spouse's account when the spouse does not supply them. Here the social policy is the furtherance of the welfare of the neglected dependent spouse. As another example of agency by operation of law, a minor may purchase necessaries on the parent's credit when the latter fails to supply them.

An emergency power of an agent to act under unusual circumstances not covered by the agent's authority is recognized when the agent is unable to communicate with the principal and when failure to act would cause the principal substantial loss.

11.   Proving the Agency Relationship

The burden of proving the existence of an agency relationship rests upon the person who seeks to benefit by such proof. The third person who desires to bind the principal because of the act of an alleged agent has the burden of proving that the latter person was in fact the authorized agent of the principal and possessed the authority to do the act in question.[14] For example, when the buyer asserts that there has been a breach of an express warranty made by the seller's agent, the buyer must establish that there was an actual or apparent authority to make the warranty. In the absence of sufficient proof, the jury must find that there is no agency. The authority of the agent may be established by circumstantial evidence.

---

[13]   Taylor v Roy (La App) 499 So 2d 595 (1986).
[14]   Fleck v. Jaques Seed Co. (ND) 445 NW2d 649 (1989).

C.   TERMINATION OF AGENCY

An agency may be terminated by the act of one or both of the parties to the agency agreement or by operation of law. When the authority of an agent is terminated, the agent loses all right to act for the principal.

12.   Termination by Act of Parties

In most cases, either party to an agency relationship has the power to terminate that relationship at any time. In some cases, however, the terminating party may be liable to the other party for damages.

(a) EXPIRATION OF AGENCY CONTRACT. The ordinary agency may expire by the terms of the contract creating it. Thus, the contract may provide that it shall last for a stated period, such as five years; or until a particular date arrives; or until the happening of a particular event, such as the sale of certain property. In such a case the agency is automatically terminated when the specified date arrives or the event at which it is to end occurs.

When it is provided that the agency shall last for a stated period of time, it terminates upon the expiration of that period, without regard to whether the acts contemplated by the creation of the agency have been performed. If no period is stated, the agency continues for a reasonable time, but it may be terminated at the will of either party.

(b) AGREEMENT. Since the agency relationship is based on consent, it can be terminated by the consent of the principal and agent.

(c) OPTION OF A PARTY. An agency agreement may provide that upon the giving of notice or the payment of a specified sum of money, one party may terminate the relationship.

(d) REVOCATION BY PRINCIPAL. The relationship between principal and agent is terminated whenever the principal discharges the agent, even if the agency was stated to be "irrevocable." If the agency was not created for a specified time but was to exist only at will, or if the agent has been guilty of miscon- duct, the principal may discharge the agent without liability. The intent to revoke must be clearly and unequivocally expressed.

In the *Kinmon* case the court was called upon to determine whether the principal had revoked his agent's authority to sell a summer estate at auction.

KINMON v J. P. KING AUCTION CO., INC.
290 Ala 323, 276 So 2d 569 (1973)

Kinmon owned a summer home that he wanted to sell at auction. He employed the J. P. King Auction Company (King) to make the sale. King sold the property to the highest bidder for $35,000. Kinmon had expected twice that much and refused to convey title to the buyer or to pay commissions to King. King sued Kinmon to collect the commissions. Kinmon raised the defense that he had revoked King's authority to sell the property. From a judgment for King, Kinmon appealed.

FAULKNER, J. . . . "Bittersweet" is a home in Perdido Beach, Alabama. . . .

On July 29, 1971, George H. Kinmon, the owner, signed a contract with J. P. King Auction Company (King) to sell the property "for the highest price obtainable." Kin- mon testified to having "conveyed" to the representatives of King that he expected to realize $103,500 for the property. The latter told Kinmon that Bittersweet would bring what it was worth the day of the sale. The written contract did not incorporate any guaranteed minimum price, referring merely to "the highest price obtainable."

King prepared and distributed a brochure announcing the "absolute auction" of Bittersweet:

This is the place for your Vacation Home or Company Lodge, plenty of room for sleeping and entertaining on Beautiful Soldier Creek just a few minutes by boat to Alabama Point and on out into the Gulf for some of the best fishing in the world. Enjoy swimming and skiing from your own boathouse or just plain fish- ing from the pier. There is everything to enjoy at "Bittersweet."

Let Today's Investment Be Tomorrow's Security.

"YOUR PRICE IS OUR PRICE."

Kinmon, concerned about the possibility of not realizing an adequate price for his property, protested against the inclusion of the terms "Your Price is Our Price" and "absolute auction." However, preparations for the auction continued. Signs announc- ing the forthcoming auction and stating "Your Price is Our Price" remained undis- turbed by Kinmon.

On August 21, 1971, the day of the auction, Kinmon was "upset." He told King's secretary that he wasn't signing anything. At one point during the bidding, Kinmon went up to King and stated that if Bittersweet did not bring $70,000, "I will take you to Supreme Court." King went ahead with the bidding and sold the property to the high- est bidder for $35,000. Kinmon subsequently refused to convey the property or pay King's commission. King sued, and the Circuit Court of Baldwin County held that he was entitled to his commission. Kinmon appealed from this decree.

... There is no doubt Kinmon and King could have written a $50,000, $70,000, or $100,000 minimum price for Bittersweet into their auction sale contract. They did not do so. The contract recites that Bittersweet would be sold "for the highest price obtainable." Kinmon may have wished or hoped that the sale would realize $100,000. However, it is elementary that it is the terms of the written contract, not the mental operations of one of the parties, that control its interpretation. ...

Contracting parties are free to modify their contract by mutual assent. ... After expressing discontent with the advertised slogan "Your Price is Our Price," Kinmon could have asked King to insert a minimum price guarantee into the contract. He did not do so. Unilateral grumbling cannot modify a bilateral contract.

It is the general rule that the agency to sell at auction, whether such auction be "with reserve" or "absolute," may be withdrawn at any time prior to the opening of bids. ... This withdrawal of authority must be clear and unequivocal. Nowhere in the record is there evidence that Kinmon clearly and unequivocally stated that he no longer wished King to sell his property, that he was revoking King's authority, that he was withdrawing Bittersweet from sale. Being "upset" is not enough; threatening to take King to court if $70,000 were not realized is not enough.

[Judgment affirmed]

QUESTIONS

1. What did Kinmon contend?
2. Did the court agree with Kinmon's contentions?
3. What could the principal have done to avoid liability?

Any conduct that manifests an intent to revoke the authority is sufficient. For example, a principal may take back from the agent the property that had been entrusted to the agent for the purpose of the agency, or the principal may retain another agent to do what the original agent had been authorized to do. When the agency is based on a contract to employ the agent for a specified period of time, the principal is liable for damages if the principal wrongfully discharges the agent. The fact that the principal is liable for damages does not, however, prevent the principal from terminating the agency by discharging the agent. In such a case, it is said that the principal has the *power* to terminate the agency by discharging the agent but does not have the *right* to do so.

(e) RENUNCIATION BY AGENT The agency relationship is terminated if the agent refuses to continue to act as agent. For instance, the agent may abandon the object of the agency and act in self-interest by committing a fraud upon the principal.

If the relationship is an agency at will, the agent has the right, as well as the power, to renounce or abandon the agency at any time. The agent has the right of renunciation of the relationship in any case if the principal is guilty of making wrongful demands or of other misconduct.

If, however, the agency is based on a contract calling for the continuation of the relationship for a specified or determinable period (that is, until a particular date arrives or a certain event occurs), the agent has no right to abandon or renounce the relationship if the principal is not guilty of wrongdoing.

When the renunciation by the agent is wrongful, the agent is liable to the principal for the damages that the principal sustains.

(f) RESCISSION. The agency contract may be terminated by rescission to the same extent that any other contract may be so terminated.

13.   Termination by Operation of Law

The agency relationship is a personal one, and anything that renders one of the parties incapable of performing will result in the termination of the relationship by operation of law.

(a) DEATH. The death of either the principal or agent ordinarily terminates the authority of an agent automatically, even if the death is unknown to the other.[15] Some state statutes provide that the death of the principal is not a revocation until the agent has notice or that the death is not a revocation as to third persons who deal with the agent in good faith and are ignorant of the death. Generally, however, these statutes are limited to principals who are members of the armed forces.

In an attorney-client relationship the death of the client does not terminate the agency if the client has expressly agreed that the attorney should conduct the proceeding to its conclusion.

(b) INSANITY. The insanity of either the principal or the agent ordinarily terminates the agent's authority. If the incapacity of the principal is only temporary, the agent's authority may be merely suspended rather than terminated.

(c) BANKRUPTCY. Bankruptcy of the principal or agent usually terminates the relationship. It is generally held, however, that the bankruptcy of an agent does not terminate the agent's power to deal with goods of the principal held by the agent.

Insolvency, as distinguished from a formal adjudication of bankruptcy, usually does not terminate the agency. In most states, accordingly, the authority of an agent is not terminated by the appointment of a receiver for the principal.

(d) IMPOSSIBILITY. The authority of an agent is terminated when it is impossible to perform the agency for any reason. Examples are the destruction of the subject matter of the agency, the death or loss of capacity of the third person with whom the agent is to contract, or a change in law that makes it impossible to perform the agency lawfully.

(e) WAR. When the country of the principal is at war with that of the agent, the authority of the agent is usually terminated or at least suspended until peace is restored. When the war has the effect of making performance impossible, the agency is, of course, terminated. For example, the authority of an agent who is a nonresident enemy alien to sue is terminated, because such an alien is not permitted to sue.

(f) UNUSUAL EVENTS OR CHANGES OF CIRCUMSTANCES. The authority of an agent is also terminated by the occurrence of an unusual event or a change in value or business conditions of such a nature that the agent should reasonably infer that the principal would not desire the agent to continue to act under the changed circumstances. For example, an agent employed to sell land at a specified price should regard the authority to sell at that price as terminated when the value of the land increases greatly because of the discovery of oil on the land.

14.   Disability of the Principal Under the UDPAA

The Uniform Durable Power of Attorney Act (UDPAA) permits the creation of an agency by a writing that specifies that "this power of attorney shall not be affected by subsequent disability or incapacity of the principal." Alternatively, the UDPAA permits the agency to come into existence upon the "disability or incapacity of the principal." To be effective the principal must designate the attorney in fact in writing, and the writing must contain words showing the intent of the principal that the authority conferred shall continue notwithstanding the disability or incapacity of the principal. The UDPAA, which is being

---

[15]   New York Life Ins. Co. v Estate of Haelen, 521 NYS2d 970 (1987).

rapidly adopted by the states,[16] changes the common law and the general rule that insanity of the principal terminates the agent's authority to act for the principal. Society today recognizes that it may be in the best interest of a principal and good for the business environment for a principal to designate another as an attorney in fact to act for the principal when the principal becomes incapacitated.[17]

15. Termination of Agency Coupled with an Interest

An agency coupled with an interest is an exception to the general rule as to the termination of an agency. Such an agency cannot be revoked by the principal before the expiration of the interest. It is not terminated by the death or insanity of either the principal or the agent.

16. Effect of Termination of Authority

If the agency is revoked by the principal, the authority to act for the principal is not terminated until notice of revocation is received by the agent. As between the principal and the agent, the *right* of the agent to bind the principal to third persons generally ends immediately upon the termination of the agent's authority. Such termination is effective without the giving of notice to third persons.

When the agency is terminated by the act of the principal, notice must be given to third persons. If such notice is not given, the agent may have the *power* to make contracts that will bind the principal and third persons. This rule is predicated on the theory that a known agent will have the appearance of still being the agent unless notice to the contrary is given to third persons. This situation arose in the *Record* case.

---

[16] The Uniform Durable Power of Attorney Act has been adopted in Alabama, Arizona, California, Colorado, Delaware, District of Columbia, Hawaii, Idaho, Indiana, Kansas, Kentucky, Maine, Massachusetts, Michigan, Minnesota, Missouri, Montana, Nebraska, New Mexico, North Dakota, Oklahoma, Pennsylvania, South Carolina, Tennessee, Utah, West Virginia, and Wisconsin.

[17] The Uniform Probate Code and the Uniform Durable Power of Attorney Act provide for the coexistence of durable powers and guardians or conservators. These acts allow the attorney in fact to continue to manage the principal's financial affairs, while the court-appointed fiduciary would take the place of the principal in overseeing the actions of the attorney in fact. See Rice v Flood (Ky) 768 SW2d 57 (1989).

RECORD v WAGNER
100 NH 419, 128 A2d 921 (1957)

Donald Record owned a farm that was operated by his agent, David Berry, who lived on the property. The latter hired Fred Wagner to bale the hay in 1953 and told him to bill Record for this work. He did so and was paid by Record. By the summer of 1954 the agency had been terminated by Record, but Berry remained in possession as tenant of the farm, and nothing appeared changed. Later in the same year Berry asked Wagner to bale the hay the same as in the prior year and bill Record for the work. Wagner did so, but Record refused to pay on the ground that Berry was not then his agent. When Wagner sued Record and recovered a judgment against him, Record appealed.

DUNCAN, J. . . . "It is a familiar principle of law that the authority of the agent to bind his principal continues, even after an actual revocation, until notice of the revocation is given." *Claflin v Lenheim*, 66 NY 301.

By paying the 1953 bill, the defendant recognized Berry's authority to hire the plaintiff on the former's credit. Berry then resided on the defendant's farm, and was properly found the defendant's agent at that time. In 1954, Berry continued to reside on the main farm, and to all appearances was operating it in the same manner and in the same capacity. If in fact he had ceased to occupy the farm as agent, but did so as a tenant, the defendant made no effort to notify the plaintiff of the change in Berry's status.

It could be found that in the exercise of reasonable diligence the plaintiff was justified as a result of the defendant's conduct in believing that Berry had authority to pledge the defendant's credit in 1954 for the same services which the defendant recognized as a proper charge against himself in 1953. . . . The important fact is that the defendant permitted the outward appearances of Berry's authority to remain unchanged in 1954 from what they were in 1953, and by not notifying the plaintiff of the termination of the agency permitted the plaintiff to be misled. Having done so, he rather than the plaintiff should bear the loss. . . . We do not consider the circumstance that Berry had previously pledged the defendant's credit upon only one occasion . . . to be of controlling importance. . . . The evidence that no question of the agent's authority was raised on the occasion, coupled with the evidence of the misleading circumstances of his continued occupancy and management of the farms and the cattle in the defendant's continued absence, was sufficient to warrant the verdict.

[Judgment for Wagner]

QUESTIONS

1. Was Berry the agent of Record in 1954 when Berry asked Wagner to bale hay and bill Record for the work?
2. After termination of the agency by Record, did Berry continue to have the power to bind Record?
3. Of what significance was the fact that Berry had pledged Record's credit in only one prior transaction?

When the law requires the giving of notice in order to end the power of the agent to bind the principal, individual notice must be given or mailed to all persons who had prior dealings with the agent. In addition, notice to the general public can be given by publishing a statement that the agency has been terminated in a newspaper of general circulation in the affected geographical area.

If a notice is actually received, the power of the agent is terminated, without regard to whether the method of giving notice was proper. Conversely, if proper notice is given, it is immaterial that it does not actually come to the attention of the party notified. Thus, a member of the general public cannot claim that the principal is bound on the ground that the third person did not see the newspaper notice stating that the agent's authority had been terminated.

SUMMARY

An agency relationship is created by an express or implied agreement whereby one person, the agent, is authorized to act on behalf of and subject to the control of another person, the principal. When an agency relationship exists, the acts of the agent obligate the principal to a third person and give the principal rights against the third person. An agent differs from an independent contractor in that the principal, who controls the acts of an agent, does not have control over the details of performance of work by the independent contractor.

A special agent is authorized by the principal to handle a specific business transaction. A general agent is authorized by the principal to transact all business affairs of the principal at a certain place. A universal agent is authorized to perform all acts that can be lawfully delegated to a representative.

The usual method of creating an agency is by express authorization. However, an agency relationship may be found to exist when the principal causes or permits a third person reasonably to believe that an agency relationship exists. The "agent" appears to be authorized and is said to have apparent authority.

An unauthorized transaction by an agent for a principal may be ratified by the principal when the principal, with knowledge of all material facts, accepts the benefits of the act.

The duration of the agency relationship is commonly stated in the contract creating the relationship. In most cases either party has the power to terminate the agency relationship at any time. However, the terminating party may be liable for damages to the other if the termi-

nation is in violation of the agency contract. When a principal terminates an agent's authority, it is not effective until the notice is received by the agent. Since a known agent will have the appearance of still being an agent, notice must be given to third persons of the termination, and the agent may have the power to bind the principal and third persons until such notice is given. An agency is terminated by operation of law on (1) the death of the principal or agent; (2) insanity of the principal or agent; (3) bankruptcy of the principal or agent; (4) impossibility of performance, such as the destruction of the subject matter; (5) war; or (6) the occurrence of unusual events or changes of circumstances. An agency coupled with an interest is an exception to the above stated rules on termination; it cannot be revoked by the principal prior to the expiration of the interest.

In states that have adopted the Uniform Durable Power of Attorney Act (UDPAA), an agency that is not affected by subsequent disability or incapacity of the principal may be created. In UDPAA states an agency may also be designated to come into existence upon the "disability or incapacity of the principal." The designation of an attorney in fact under the UDPAA must be in writing.

QUESTIONS AND CASE PROBLEMS

1. What social forces are affected by allowing an agent to make a contract that will bind the agent's principal and a third person?
2. How does an agent differ from an independent contractor?
3. Compare authorization of an agent by (a) appointment and (b) ratification.
4. Bryan Bruno, while a loan officer of Anchor Equities Ltd., a mortgage banking firm, deposited funds into the bank accounts of certain loan applicants and then received bank verification statements that the applicants had the required 20 percent cash down payments in their accounts. The funds were withdrawn from each bank account once the statement was received. On the basis of these verification statements, the loan applications were approved by Anchor. Tristan Joya was part owner of the corporation

that built the homes for which the mortgage loan applications were submitted. Bruno received commissions as the originator on all loans approved. Bruno told Joya that there was nothing wrong with facilitating the applications as he had been doing. Joya's corporation received the loan proceeds. The loans went into default. Anchor sued Joya and others for fraud. Joya contends that Anchor clothed its loan officer Bruno with apparent authority to complete the applications as he did, and Anchor therefore cannot recover from Joya. Decide. [Anchor Equities Ltd. v Joya (App) ___ Ariz ___, 773 P2d 1022]
5. Crawford was the agent for Kolb. Kolb mailed Crawford a letter informing her that she was discharged. Crawford made a contract as agent for Kolb prior to receipt of the letter. Was Craw-

ford Kolb's agent when she made this contract, so as to bind Kolb?

6. Compare (a) the termination of an agency with (b) the discharge of a contract.

7. Ken Jones, the number-one-ranked prizefighter in his weight class, signed a two-year contract with Howard Stayword, with Stayword being obligated to represent and promote Jones in all business and professional matters, including the arrangement of fights. For these services Jones contracted to pay Stayword 10 percent of gross earnings. After a year, when Stayword proved unsuccessful in arranging a title match with the champion, Jones fired Stayword. During the following year Jones earned $4 million. Stayword sued Jones for $400,000. Jones defended himself on the basis that a principal has the absolute power at any time to terminate an agency relationship by discharging the agent, so he was not liable to Stayword. Was Jones correct?

8. Paul Strich did business as an optician in Duluth, Minnesota. Paul used only the products of the Plymouth Optical Company, a national manufacturer of optical products and supplies with numerous retail outlets and some franchise arrangements in areas other than Duluth. In order to increase business, Paul renovated his office and changed the sign on his office to read "Plymouth Optical Co." Paul did business in this manner for more than three years—advertised under that name, paid bills with checks bearing the name of Plymouth Optical Co., and listed himself in the telephone and city directories by that name. Plymouth immediately became aware of what Paul was doing. However, since Paul used only Plymouth products, it saw no advantage at that time in prohibiting Paul from using the name and losing him as a customer, since Plymouth did not have a franchisee in Duluth. Paul contracted with the Duluth Tribune for advertising, making the contract in the name of Plymouth Optical Co. When the advertising bill was not paid, the Duluth Tribune sued Plymouth Optical Company for payment. Plymouth defended that it had never authorized Paul to do business under the name, nor had it authorized him to make a contract with the newspaper. Decide.

9. Phyllis Thropp opened a margin trading account with Bache broker R. Gregory, placing in his care securities valued at $40,000. Subsequently, her husband, a friend of the broker, forged his wife's signature on a completely blank power of attorney form and sent it to the broker. Mr. Thropp then ordered Gregory to sell his wife's securities for cash and ordered Bache to issue seven checks in his wife's name. Mr. Thropp later forged and cashed the checks. Mrs. Thropp and her husband saw the broker socially, and her frequent questions about her account brought vague answers about the condition of the market, but he never mentioned the numerous sales for cash. In December, 1972, Mr. Thropp confessed that he had stolen the money to pay gambling debts and assured her that the broker was not involved in depleting her account. Mrs. Thropp, being seven months pregnant at the time, took no action. In 1975 she filed for a divorce, and in a deposition from the broker relating to the divorce she learned that he might have mishandled her account. An assistant manager of the firm testified that a broker would not be authorized to take directions to trade in an account from one who held a power of attorney similar to the document forged by Mr. Thropp. Mrs. Thropp brought suit against Bache. Bache contended that Mrs. Thropp ratified the actions of Mr. Thropp and Bache. Decide. [Thropp v Bache Halsey Stuart Shields, Inc. (CA6 Ohio) 650 F2d 817 (1981)]

10. Anita Beck Bosiger, president of Anita Beck Cards & Such Inc. (Beck), and Shirley Hutton, a national sales director for Mary Kay Cosmetics, agreed that Beck would manufacture calendars and stationery to be sold at Mary Kay conventions. To finance the project, Hutton gave $20,000 to Beck. They prepared and signed a document to reflect the quantity and prices of goods shipped from Beck to the Dallas convention for sale under Hutton's supervision. The document stated, "Commission is 15% on all but calendars." The unsold goods were shipped back to Beck's business at Beck's expense. The undertaking proved to be a substantial failure. Hutton sued Beck for the return of the $20,000, claiming that she was Beck's agent and that the money had been a loan. Beck claimed that the money was the down payment on the actual purchase of the goods by Hutton. Decide. [Hutton v Anita Beck Cards and Such, Inc. (Minn App) 366 NW2d 358 (1985)]

11. Walker owned a trailer that he wished to sell. He took it to the business premises of Pacific Mobile Homes. The only person on the premises at that time, and several other times when Walker was there, was Stewart, who identified himself as a salesman of Pacific and agreed to

take possession of Walker's trailer and to attempt to sell it for him. Stewart made out some forms of Pacific Mobile Homes and thereafter wrote some letters to Walker on the letterhead of Pacific. Walker's trailer was sold, but the salesman disappeared with most of the money. Walker sued Pacific for the proceeds of the sale. It denied liability, on the ground that Stewart lacked authority to make any sales agreement and that all salesmen of Pacific were expressly forbidden to take used trailers to sell for their owners. Is this defense valid? [Walker v Pacific Mobile Homes, 68 Wash 2d 347, 413 P2d 3]

12. Hill purchased furniture from Grant Furniture. When she complained that it was damaged, she was told that they would send someone to repair the damage. An independent contractor, Newman, was sent to mend the furniture. He identified himself as the man from Grant's. The lacquer he put on the furniture exploded and caused serious injury to Hill. She sued both Newman and Grant. Grant claimed that Newman was an independent contractor and that it was therefore not liable for his conduct. Was Grant correct? [Hill v Newman, 126 NJ Super 557, 316 A2d 8]

13. Mrs. Bird, a woman of means, was living in deplorable conditions. Because of her bizarre behavior, neighbors got in contact with her cousin, Logan Ledbetter, who in turn had Mrs. Bird examined by Dr. Phillips, a psychiatrist. Dr. Phillips determined that Mrs. Bird was suffering from "an organic brain syndrome, chronic, probably secondary to cerebral arteriosclerosis," that "her mental function was very impaired," and that in his opinion Mrs. Bird was "mentally incompetent at the time of the examination." Ledbetter planned to deal with the situation by selling off a number of valuable real estate holdings owned by Mrs. Bird and using the proceeds to pay for proper care for Mrs. Bird. Soon thereafter Mrs. Bird executed a power of attorney designating Logan Ledbetter as her attorney in fact, and Ledbetter entered into a contract to sell a large parcel of land to Andleman Associates. Mrs. Bird's niece, Barbara, who disliked Ledbetter, filed a petition seeking to have Mrs. Bird declared incompetent and herself named guardian of her estate. The court appointed Barbara as guardian, and she refused to allow the sale of the land to Andleman. In the complicated lawsuit that resulted, Ledbetter and Andleman contended that Ledbetter acted in good faith and had a properly executed power of attorney, and therefore, his signing the sales contract with Andleman was binding on Mrs. Bird (the principal). Atkins (the real estate agent who produced the ready, willing, and able buyer) sought his 10 percent commission under the listing agreement signed by Ledbetter as agent for Mrs. Bird. Barbara contended that the power of attorney was void and that Ledbetter owed the real estate commission since he breached his implied warranty that he had a principal with capacity. Decide.

14. Guy Hunt was a Republican candidate for governor. Jim Hooley, who served as paid campaign manager, made a fund-raising proposal to Hunt, which consisted of a mass mailing of literature requesting contributions to be used in the campaign. Hunt expressly told Hooley that the campaign could not afford to finance this particular fund-raising plan and that loans and the proceeds from the fund-raising would have to cover all expenses connected with the plan. Hooley raised some $15,000 in loans and deposited these funds in a special account. Mailing brochures were designed and proofs shown to Hunt. At the bottom of the brochures, the following appeared: "Pd. Pol. Adv. by Guy Hunt Campaign." Hooley then got in contact with Oscar Davis, telling Davis he represented the Guy Hunt Campaign. Davis, who had previously done printing for the campaign, printed and mailed the materials. The fund-raising plan did not produce enough contributions to pay Davis, and he sued Hunt for the balance due. Hunt refused to pay, contending that Hooley did not have authority to obtain credit in Hunt's name. Decide. [Hunt v Davis (Ala Civ App) 387 So 2d 209]

15. Morris Lew owns a store on Canal Street in New Orleans. He paid a person named Mike and other individuals commissions for customers brought into the store. Lew testified that he had known Mike for less than a week. Sherif Boulos and Paul Durso, partners in a wholesale jewelry business, were visiting New Orleans on a business trip when Mike brought them into the store to buy a stereo. While Durso finalized the stereo transaction with the store's manager, Boulos and Mike negotiated to buy 2 cameras, 3 videos, and 20 gold Dupont lighters. Unknown to the store's manager, Mike was given $8,250 cash and was to deliver the merchandise later that evening to the Marriott Hotel where Boulos and Durso were staying. Mike gave a receipt for the cash, but it showed no sales tax or indication

that the goods were to be delivered. Boulos testified that he believed Mike was the store's owner. Mike never delivered the merchandise, and no one has seen or heard from him since. Boulos and Durso contend that Lew is liable for the acts of his agent, Miguel "Mike" Felberg or Feldberg. Lew denied that Mike was his agent, and the testimony showed that Mike had no actual authority to make a sale, to use a cash register, or even to go behind a sales counter. Decide. [Boulos v Morrison (La) 503 So 2d 1]

40

PRINCIPAL AND AGENT

The principal, the person who permits or directs another to act for the principal's benefit, may under certain circumstances be held liable by courts for the dealings of the agent, the active participant in a transaction. Clearly, the principal should be liable for the acts of the agent when the principal has given the agent express authority to so act. Should the principal be bound by an agent when the agent acts beyond authority or when the agent misrepresents authority? The principal may be held liable on one of the *authority* theories set forth in this chapter, if justice requires it. The courts are concerned with protecting the property of the principal, but they recognize that third persons have to be able to rely on the reasonable appearance of authority of agents if our commercial markets are to function effectively.

The nature of the agency relationship is better understood when the duties and liabilities of the agent and principal to each other are studied.

A. AGENT'S AUTHORITY

The fact that one person is the agent of another does not dispose of all questions. It is necessary to determine the scope of the agent's authority.

1.   Scope of Agent's Authority

The scope of an agent's authority may be determined from the express words of the principal to the agent, or it may be implied from the principal's words or deeds or from the customs of the trade or business.

(a) EXPRESS AUTHORITY. If the principal tells the agent to perform a certain act, the agent has **express authority** to do so. Express authority can be indicated orally or in writing.

(b) INCIDENTAL AUTHORITY. An agent has implied **incidental authority** to perform any act reasonably necessary to execute the express authority given to the agent. To illustrate, if the principal authorizes the agent to purchase goods without furnishing funds to the agent to pay for them, the agent has implied incidental authority to purchase the goods on credit.

(c) CUSTOMARY AUTHORITY. An agent has implied **customary authority** to do any act that, according to the custom of the community, usually accompanies the transaction for which the agent is authorized to act. For example, an agent who has express authority to receive payments from third persons has implied authority to issue receipts.

One authorized to act as a general manager has the power to make any contract necessary for the usual and ordinary conduct of business. Likewise, an agent authorized to obtain advertising may contract for television time, because the use of television as an advertising medium is customary. Authorization to contract for television time can also be regarded as incidental to a general, unrestricted authorization to advertise.[1]

(d) APPARENT AUTHORITY. A person has apparent authority as an agent when the principal, by words or conduct, leads a third person reasonably to believe that such person has that authority and the third person relies on that appearance.[2]

2.   Effect of Proper Exercise of Authority

When an agent with authority properly makes a contract with a third person that purports to bind the principal, there is by definition a binding contract between the principal and the third person. The agent is not a party to this contract. Consequently, when the owner of goods is the principal, the owner's agent is not liable for breach of warranty with respect to the goods "sold" by the agent because the owner-principal, not the agent, was the "seller" in the sales transaction.[3]

3.   Duty to Ascertain Extent of Agent's Authority

A third person who deals with a person claiming to be an agent cannot rely upon the statements made by the agent concerning the extent of authority. If the agent is not authorized to perform the act or is not even the agent of the principal, the transaction between the alleged agent and the third person will have no legal effect between the principal and the third person.

Third persons who deal with an agent whose authority is limited to a special purpose are bound at their peril to find out the extent of the agent's authority. An attorney is such an agent. Unless the client holds the attorney out as having greater authority than usual, the attorney has no authority to settle a claim without approval from a client.

The extent of an attorney's authority to settle a claim was disputed in the *Miotk* case.

---

[1]   Columbia Broadcasting System v Stokely-Van Camp, Inc. (CA2 NY) 522 F2d 369 (1975).

[2]   Draemel v Rufenacht, Dromagen & Hertz, Inc. 223 Neb 645, 392 NW2d 759 (1986).

[3]   Wright Waterproofing Co. v Allied Polymers (Tex Civ App) 602 SW2d 67 (1980).

MIOTK v RUDY
227 Kan 296, 605 P2d 587 (1980)

Irene Miotk was a passenger in a car when it was struck by another car driven by Vernon Rudy. Miotk retained attorney John D. Logsdon to represent her in a personal injury action against Rudy. Logsdon filed suit on behalf of Miotk and later entered negotiations with Rudy's attorney to settle the case. As an offer of settlement, Rudy's attorney sent Logsdon a check made out to "Irene Miotk and John D. Logsdon, her attorney" along with a release for Ms. Miotk to sign. Logsdon failed to return the signed release by the day the case was set for trial, but he advised Rudy's attorney that the settlement was agreed to; the court approved the settlement and dismissed the case. Unknown to all parties and the court, Logsdon had apparently forged Irene Miotk's indorsement to the check and had retained the proceeds. Miotk hired new counsel, who filed a motion to set aside the dismissal of her action. In an accompanying affidavit, Miotk stated that she at no time authorized the settlement of the case, nor was she ever offered any sum of money by Logsdon. The trial court denied the motion to set aside the dismissal, and Miotk appealed.

SWINEHART, J. . . . It has been recognized generally that a client is bound by the appearance, admissions, and actions of counsel acting on behalf of his client. The client has control over the subject matter of litigation. An attorney has no authority to compromise or settle his client's claim without his client's approval. . . .

Defendant, while recognizing [this] rule . . . characterizes it as "idealistic in concept, but extremely difficult . . . to follow." He points out that he clearly relied on the representations of plaintiff's attorney and that the dismissal was entered pursuant to the express representation of plaintiff's attorney to the court and defense counsel that the settlement was authorized. Defendant urges as matter of public policy that the dismissal should not be set aside.

Defendant's argument is essentially that an attorney should be held to have apparent authority to settle an action. This appears to be the rationale of the trial court's denial of the plaintiff's motion. This argument is at first glance appealing. It is clear that the relation of attorney and client is one of agency and the general rules of law that apply to agency apply to that relation. . . . The law recognizes two distinct types of agency, actual and ostensible or apparent. . . . The evidence is uncontradicted that Logsdon lacked actual authority to settle plaintiff's case and there is no issue in that regard. However, the liability of the principal for the acts and contracts of his agent is not limited to such acts and contracts of the agent as are expressly authorized, necessarily implied from express authority, or otherwise actually conferred by implication from the acts and conduct of the principal. . . .

The difficulty in the present case is that there is no evidence of apparent authority on the part of Logsdon to settle plaintiff's case other than his retention as her attorney. . . .

Kansas law is in accord on the general agency principle that those who deal with an agent whose authority is limited to special purposes are bound at their peril to know the extent of his authority. . . . [A]n attorney as agent for his client, is limited to control over procedural matters incident to litigation. . . . An attorney ordinarily has no apparent authority to settle his client's action without the client's consent.

There being no evidence other than Logsdon's employment as plaintiff's attorney of Logsdon's apparent authority to settle plaintiff's action, we hold that the trial court abused its discretion in denying plaintiff's motion pursuant to K.S.A. 60–260(b) to set aside the judgment of dismissal. The case is remanded with directions to grant plaintiff's motion and proceed with trial of the issues on the merits.

[Judgment reversed and action remanded]

QUESTIONS

1. What did the defendant contend?
2. Did the court sustain the defendant's contention?
3. Was Irene Miotk bound by the representation of attorney Logsdon to the court that she had authorized the settlement of the case?

(a) AGENT'S ACTS ADVERSE TO PRINCIPAL. The third person who deals with an agent is required to take notice of any acts that are clearly adverse to the interest of the principal. Thus, if the agent is obviously making use of funds of the principal for the agent's personal benefit, persons dealing with the agent should recognize that the agent may be acting without authority and that they are dealing with the agent at their peril.

The only certain way that third persons can protect themselves is to inquire of the principal whether the agent is in fact the agent of the principal and has the necessary authority. If the principal states that the agent has the authority, the principal cannot later deny this authorization unless the subject matter is such that an authorization must be in writing in order to be binding.

(b) DEATH OF THIRD PERSON. The extent of the agent's authority becomes particularly significant when the third person dies after the transaction with the agent but before any action has been taken by the principal. If the agent had authority to contract on behalf of the principal, the agent's agreement with the third person would give rise immediately to a binding contract. The third person's subsequent death would ordinarily not affect that contract. In contrast, if the agent did not have authority to contract but only to transmit an offer from the third person, the death of the

third person before the principal had accepted the offer would work a revocation of the offer. The principal could not create a contract by purporting to accept after the death of the third person.

4.   Limitations of Agent's Authority

A person who has knowledge of a limitation on the agent's authority cannot disregard that limitation. When the third person knows that the authority of the agent depends on whether financing has been obtained, the principal is not bound by the act of the agent if the financing in fact was not obtained. If the authority of the agent is based on a writing, and the third person knows that there is such a writing, the third person is charged with knowledge of the limitations contained in it.

(a) APPARENT LIMITATIONS. In some situations it will be apparent to third persons that they are dealing with an agent whose authority is limited. When third persons know that they are dealing with an officer of a private corporation or a representative of a government agency, they should recognize that such a person will ordinarily not have unlimited authority and that a contract made with the officer or representative may not be binding unless ratified by the principal.

(b) SECRET LIMITATIONS. If the principal has clothed an agent with authority to perform certain acts but the principal gives secret instructions that limit the agent's authority, the third person is allowed to take the authority of the agent at its face value. The third person is not bound by the secret limitations of which the third person has no knowledge.

5.   Delegation of Authority by Agent

As a general rule, an agent cannot delegate to another the authority obtained from the principal. In other words, unless the principal expressly or in an implied manner consents, an agent cannot appoint *subagents* to carry out the agent's duties. The reason for this rule is that since an agent is usually selected because of some personal qualifications, it would be unfair and possibly injurious to the principal if the authority to act could be shifted by the agent to another—particularly when the agent was originally appointed for the performance of a task requiring discretion or judgment. For example, an agent who is appointed to adjust claims against an insurance company cannot delegate the performance of that duty to another. The *Bucholtz* case sets forth reasons for the general rule that an agent cannot avoid responsibility for the carrying out of the tasks of the agency by delegating the tasks to a subagent.

BUCHOLTZ v SIROTKIN TRAVEL LTD.
74 Misc 2d 180, 343 NYS2d 438 (1973)

Helen Bucholtz made reservations through the Sirotkin Travel Agency for a three-day trip to Las Vegas. The reservations were in fact not made by the agency, and Bucholtz sued the agency for damages for breach of its contract. The agency raised the defense that the mistake was the fault of another travel agency or "wholesaler" through which the agency made reservations on behalf of its client.

DONOVAN, J. . . . This small claim proceeding involves a matter of increasing importance to the traveling public, namely, the responsibility of a travel agency in connection with the sale of a tour.

Claimant engaged the defendant travel agency to make reservations for a three day trip for herself and her husband to Las Vegas. The agency advised the claimant that they would stay at the Aladdin Hotel. Changes were made in the arrival and departure time of their flight from that originally stated. At the airport tags on the plaintiff's baggage were switched so that the baggage was not directed to the Aladdin Hotel. On arrival in Las Vegas the claimant learned that no reservations had been made for herself or her husband at the Aladdin Hotel. They were required to take alternative accommodations at a motel. The motel was a half mile out of town. This created additional expense and inconvenience for the claimant and her husband in traveling to the places of interest in the town. . . .

In this case nothing was done by the travel agency to verify or confirm either the plane reservations or the hotel reservations. If this duty is the responsibility of the travel agency, then the travel agency is liable in negligence for its failure to exercise reasonable care in making the reservations.

It may be urged that the default in this respect is that of the remote "wholesaler."

Where, as here, the agent is selected because he is supposed to have some special fitness for the performance of the duties to be undertaken, the traveler is entitled to rely on the judgment and discretion of that agent as well as his honesty and financial responsibility. The agent may not evade responsibility by delegating to a subagent the carrying out of the task which has been committed to him. . . . Travel agencies may find it convenient, in the course of transacting their business, to deal with wholesalers. The news reports are so voluminous that we may take judicial notice of the vice inherent in conducting business in so loose a fashion. The wholesaler may fail to pay for accommodations or may even fail to book the accommodations and the traveler is left in a helpless situation. He either has no recourse because of financial insufficiency or he may be required to travel to a distant jurisdiction in order to maintain a suit.

Unless the principal, here the traveler, has expressly or impliedly authorized the travel agency to delegate responsibility to a second agency or "wholesaler," the responsibility must remain on the defendant travel agency. In an area so fraught with danger to the traveler, public policy demands that the travel agency be held responsible to: (a) verify or confirm the reservations and (b) use reasonable diligence in ascertaining the responsibility of any intervening "wholesaler" or tour organizer. . . .

Claimant here did not consent to any delegation of the duty owed to her by the defendant travel agency.

The defendant is liable to the claimant for the breach of its fiduciary responsibility in failing to use reasonable care to confirm the reservations. . . .

[Judgment for plaintiff]

QUESTIONS

1. What was the factual basis of the lawsuit?
2. "An agent may avoid responsibility by delegating to another person the carrying out of the task of the agency." Does the court agree with this statement?
3. State the decision of the court and the basis for the decision.

Agents, however, may authorize others to perform their work for them in the following instances:

1. When the acts to be done involve only mechanical or ministerial duties. Thus, an agent to make application for hail insurance on wheat may delegate to another the clerical act of writing the application. Also, it may be shown that there is customary authority for a clerk in the office of the insurance agent to sign the agent's name so as to have the effect of a signing by the agent and be binding upon the insurance company, the agent's principal.
2. When a well-known custom recognizes such appointment. To illustrate, if one is authorized to buy from or sell to a grain elevator, one may do so through a broker when that is the customary method.
3. When the appointment is justified by necessity or sudden emergency and it is impractical to communicate with the principal, and the appointment of a subagent is reasonably necessary for the protection of the interests of the principal entrusted to the agent.
4. When it is contemplated by the parties that subagents would be employed. For example, a bank may now generally use subagents to receive payments of notes that have been left for collection, since the parties contemplate that this will be done. Also, the authority to appoint subagents can be inferred where the principal knows or has reason to know that the agent employs subagents. Thus, an agent may grant subagents power to bind a principal fire insurance company when the agent had a long-standing practice of appointing sub-

agents, and this was known to the principal.[4]

B.   DUTIES AND LIABILITIES OF PRINCIPAL AND AGENT

The creation of the principal-agent relationship gives rise not only to powers but also to duties and liabilities.

6.   Duties and Liabilities of Agent During Agency

While the agency relationship exists, the agent owes certain duties to the principal.

(a) LOYALTY. An agent must be loyal or faithful to the principal. The agent must not obtain any secret benefit from the agency.[5] If

the principal is seeking to buy or rent property, the agent cannot secretly obtain the property and then sell or lease it to the principal at a profit.

An agent who owns property cannot sell it to the principal without disclosing that ownership to the principal. If disclosure is not made, the principal may avoid the contract, even if the agent's conduct did not cause the principal any financial loss. Alternatively, the principal can approve the transaction and sue the agent for any secret profit obtained by the agent.

A contract is voidable by the principal if the agent who was employed to sell the property purchases the property either directly or indirectly without full disclosure to the principal. In the *Johnson* case the agent believed he could purchase his principal's property in his father-in-law's name, so long as the principal was paid the specified net amount sought by the principal.

---

[4]   Bloom v Wolfe, 37 Colo App 407, 547 P2d 934 (1976).
[5]   Nguyen v Scott, 206 Cal App 3d 725, 253 Cal Rptr 800 (1988).

JOHNSON v HAND
189 Ga App 706, 377 SE2d 176 (1988)

Michael Johnson was employed as a real estate agent. He inquired of Byron Hand whether he wished to sell certain property. Hand responded that he would be willing to sell the property for a specified net price. Shortly thereafter, Johnson returned with a sales contract, which he presented for Hand's acceptance. The sale price was sufficient to net Hand the amount that he had specified. Johnson did not disclose, however, that the purchaser who was named in the sales contract was his own father-in-law. Hand signed the contract. At the closing, Johnson's wife Rae "sat in" for the absent purchaser. Shortly after title to the property had been transferred to his wife and then to his father-in-law, Johnson sold the property to a third party for a price that was significantly greater than that which Hand had been paid. A large part, if not all, of the profit from this sale went to Michael Johnson, rather than to his father-in-law. When Hand learned that the property had been resold for a price greater than he had been paid, he brought this action against Johnson, claiming that Johnson had breached his duty to Hand. From a judgment for Hand, Johnson appealed.

CARLEY, J. . . . The relationship of principal and agent is confidential and fiduciary, and demands of the agent loyalty and good faith to the principal. . . . [A Georgia statute] provides that "The agent shall not make a personal profit from his principal's property;

for all such he is bound to account." . . . The rule forbidding an agent . . . from purchasing his principal's property, without the express consent and knowledge of the principal, is not made inapplicable because the property was listed for sale with the agency at a fixed or minimum price. When (Hand), the owner, named the minimum price that (he) would accept for (his) property, it was manifestly intended as a guide to (his) agent in negotiating the sale, and implied a just expectation on (his) part and an engagement on (his) agent's part that he would make an honest endeavor to obtain a higher price. . . .

The original sales contract was clearly relevant to show the initiation by Michael Johnson of an undisclosed effort on his part to earn a secret personal profit on the eventual resale of Hand's property by first attempting to purchase it indirectly through his father-in-law. An agent owes to his principal a loyal adherence to his interests, and it would be a fraud upon the principal, and would contravene the public policy, to permit an agent, *without the full knowledge* and consent of his principal, to enter into a relation involving such a duty, when his allegiance had been already pledged to one having adverse interests, or when his own personal interests would be antagonistic to those of his principal. The rule has also been thus stated: An agent will not be allowed to place himself in a position in which his duty and interest conflict, or be permitted to make a *secret profit* out of his agency. . . .

[Judgment affirmed]

QUESTIONS

1. Isn't the seller's right to a remedy defeated because Johnson obtained a purchaser at the net price sought by the seller?
2. May an agent ever buy a principal's property?
3. Did Johnson act contrary to any of the ethical principles set forth in Figure 1 of the "Analysis of Court Opinions" in the introductory pages of this textbook?

An agent cannot act as agent for both parties to a transaction unless both know of the dual capacity and agree to it. If the agent does so act without the consent of both parties, the transaction is voidable at the election of any principal who did not know of the agent's double status.

An agent must not accept secret gifts or commissions from third persons in connection with the agency. If the agent does so, the principal may sue the agent for those gifts or commissions. Such practices are condemned because the judgment of the agent may be influenced by the receipt of gifts or commissions.

It is a violation of an agent's duty of loyalty to make and retain secret profits.

An agent is, of course, prohibited from aiding the competitors of a principal or disclosing to them information relating to the business of the principal. It is also a breach of duty for the agent knowingly to deceive a principal.

(b) OBEDIENCE AND PERFORMANCE. An agent is under a duty to obey all lawful instructions.[6] The agent is required to perform the services specified for the period and in the way specified. An agent who does not is liable to the principal for any harm caused. For example, if an agent is instructed to take cash payments only but accepts a check in payment, the agent is liable for the loss caused the principal if the check is dishonored by nonpayment. Likewise, when an insurance broker undertakes to obtain a policy of insurance giv-

---

[6]   Stanford v Neiderer, 178 Ga 56, 341 SE2d 892 (1986).

ing a principal a specified coverage but fails to obtain a policy with the proper coverage, the broker, as agent of the principal, is liable to the principal for the loss thereby caused.

If the agent violates instructions, it is immaterial that the agent acted in good faith or intended to benefit the principal. It is the fact that the agent violated the instructions and thereby caused the principal a loss that imposes a liability on the agent. In determining whether the agent has obeyed instructions, they must be interpreted in a way that a reasonable person would interpret them.

(c) REASONABLE CARE. It is the duty of an agent to act with the care that a reasonable person would exercise under the circumstances. In addition, if the agent possesses a special skill, as in the case of a broker or an attorney, the agent must exercise that skill.

(d) ACCOUNTING. An agent must account to the principal for all property or money belonging to the principal that comes into the agent's possession. The agent should, within a reasonable time, give notice of collections made and render an accurate account of all receipts and expenditures. The agency

agreement may state at what intervals or on what dates such accountings are to be made.

An agent should keep the principal's property and money separate and distinct from that of the agent. If property of the agent is mingled with property of the principal so that the two cannot be identified or separated, the principal may claim all of the commingled mass. Furthermore, when funds of the principal and the agent are mixed, any loss that occurs must be borne by the agent.

(e) INFORMATION. It is the duty of an agent to keep the principal informed of all facts relating to the agency that are relevant to protecting the principal's interests.[7]

The *Allen Industries* decision illustrates the rule that an agent has a duty to disclose to the principal every material fact, circumstance, and advantage in relation to a sale. Moreover, the case points out that an agent's attempt to receive a higher commission is a violation of the duty of honesty and loyalty to the principal.

[7]   Restatement, Agency 2d § 381; Owen v Shelton, 221 Va 1047, 277 SE2d 189 (1981).

ALLEN INDUSTRIES INC. v SHELDON GOOD CO.
153 Ill App 3d 120, 106 Ill Dec 313, 505 NE2d 1104 (1987)

Joan Kulwin owned Allen Industries Inc., which owned a commercial building in Evanston, Illinois. She granted the Sheldon Co. the exclusive right to sell the building and agreed to pay a commission to Sheldon upon the sale. This commission was to be divided in half between Sheldon and a cooperating broker, should a cooperating broker secure the purchaser. On August 21, 1985, Sheldon Co. presented Kulwin a written offer in final contract form from J.W. Collier. She rejected this offer of $335,000 and made a counteroffer of $350,000. On August 22 Collier accepted the counteroffer. The contract called for the seller to take back a mortgage for $249,000. At the closing Sheldon Co. received a $18,000 commission. Kulwin later found out that Maurice Leviton, President of TLC, on his third inspection of the property on August 16, 1985, advised Sheldon Co. that he was preparing an all-cash offer on the property. He made this offer to Sheldon Co. on August 22, 1985, and it was rejected by Sheldon Co. because Kulwin had accepted Collier's offer at that point. Kulwin sued Sheldon Co. for breach of the fiduciary duty in failing to inform her of all facts material to the sale. She asserted that Sheldon Co. failed to do so to avoid sharing half the commission with the cooperating broker who showed TLC the property. Sheldon Co. denied that it had a duty to report conversations of a speculative nature to the seller. From a judgment for Sheldon Co., Kulwin appealed.

STAMOS, J. . . . The relationship between principal and agent for the purchase or sale of property is a fiduciary one, and the agent in the exercise of good faith must make known to his principal all material facts within his knowledge which in any way affect the transaction and the subject matter of his agency. Material facts are those facts which the agent should realize have or are likely to have a bearing upon the desirability of the transaction from the viewpoint of the principal.

If a party employs an agent to make a sale of land he is entitled to all the skill, ability and industry of such agent to make the sale on the best terms that can be had. An agent cannot deal for his own advantage with things to be sold because of his confidential relationship with his principal and because of his duty to disclose to his principal every fact, circumstance or advantage in relation to a sale, which may come to his knowledge. . . .

[A] purchaser's expressions of interest in property to be sold and his statements that he is preparing an offer for said property are material facts which a real estate broker has a duty to convey to his client. It is evident that plaintiffs would have been in an improved position to gain a better price or more favorable terms had they known that there was more than one purchaser interested in their property. Plaintiffs would have benefited from the heightened demand for their property by allowing each prospective purchaser to compete against the other for plaintiffs' property. In fact, TLC's offer included more favorable terms than the contract made with the ultimate purchaser, J.W. Collier. . . . It is possible that plaintiffs would have found TLC's cash offer to have been more favorable than Collier's. In any event, defendants had a duty to inform the seller of all facts that might influence him in accepting or rejecting the offer. It cannot be said that plaintiffs would not have been influenced by TLC's offer in accepting or rejecting Collier's offer. Therefore, we hold that the dismissed counts sufficiently allege the breach of a fiduciary duty to plaintiffs by failing to disclose material facts to them regarding the sale of their property.

Plaintiffs allege, additionally, that defendants' failure to inform plaintiffs of TLC's offer was an attempt to make personal gain by receiving a higher commission. Such conduct, if proven, is strictly prohibited in this state because it violates an agent's duty of honesty and loyalty toward his principal. This obligation toward a principal prohibits an agent from dealing independently of the interests of his principal to his personal gain in the subject matter of the agency, on the grounds that such activities will necessarily tempt that agent to abandon the interests of his principal in favor of his own interests. In fact, an agent who deals independently of the interests of his principal breaches his fiduciary duty and is therefore barred from any recovery for his services. (When a broker breaches his duties toward his employer he will, in almost every case, lose his commission.) In this instance, defendants allegedly received an $18,000 commission from the sale of plaintiffs' property to J.W. Collier, a client brought in by defendants. Under the listing agreement, defendants would have received only 1/2 of that commission or $9,000 and advertising expenses up to $5,000 if the property was sold to TLC, a prospective purchaser not brought in by defendants.

[Reversed and remanded with directions]

QUESTIONS

1. Did Sheldon Co. have an obligation to report each conversation of a speculative nature that the agent had with a prospective purchaser concerning offers that might be made in the indeterminate future?
2. Did Sheldon Co. have a right to protect its full commission by preserving the sale for its purchaser, as opposed to the purchaser produced by another broker?
3. Is a real estate agent who breaches a duty owed the seller entitled to the full commission when the property is sold?

7.   Duties and Liabilities of Agent after Termination of Agency

When the agency relationship ends, the duties of the agent continue only to the extent necessary to perform prior obligations. For example, the agent must return to the former principal any property that had been entrusted to the agent for the purpose of the agency. With the exception of such "winding up" duties, the agency relationship is terminated, and the former agent can deal with the principal as freely as with a stranger.[8]

8.   Enforcement of Liability of Agent

When the agent's breach of duty causes harm to the principal, the amount of the loss may be deducted from any compensation due the agent or may be recovered in an ordinary lawsuit.

When the agent handles money for the principal, the contract of employment may provide that the amount of any shortages in the agent's account may be deducted from the compensation to which the agent would otherwise be entitled.

If the agent has made a secret profit, the principal may recover that profit from the agent. In addition, the agent may forfeit the right to all compensation, without regard to whether the principal benefited from some of the actions of the agent and without regard to whether the principal had actually been harmed.

9.   Duties and Liabilities of Principal to Agent

The principal is under certain duties to the agent. The principal must perform the contract, compensate the agent for services, make reimbursement for proper expenditures, and under certain circumstances must indemnify the agent for loss.

(a) EMPLOYMENT ACCORDING TO TERMS OF CONTRACT. When the contract is for a specified time, the principal is under the obligation to permit the agent to act as such for the term of the contract. Exceptions are made for just cause or contract provisions that permit the principal to terminate the agency sooner. If the principal gives the agent an exclusive right to act as such, the principal cannot give anyone else the authority to act as agent, nor may the principal do the act to which the exclusive agent's authority relates. If the principal or another agent does so, the exclusive agent is entitled to full compensation, just as though the act had been performed by the exclusive agent.

(b) COMPENSATION. The principal must pay the agent the compensation agreed on.[9] If the parties have not fixed the amount of the compensation by their agreement but intended that the agent should be paid, the agent may recover the customary compensation for such services. If there is no established compensation, the agent may recover the reasonable value of the services rendered.[10]

---

[8]   Corron & Black of Illinois, Inc. v Magner, 145 Ill App 3d 151, 98 Ill Dec 663, 494 NE2d 785 (1986).

[9]   Olsen v Bondurant Co. (Colo App) 759 P2d 861 (1988).
[10]   Lone Star Steel Co. v Scott (Tex Civ App) 759 SW2d 144 (1988).

FIGURE 40–1   DUTIES OF PRINCIPALS AND AGENTS

Agent's Duties to Principal	Principal's Duties to Agent
Loyalty Obedience and performance according to terms of contract Reasonable care Information Accounting	Employment according to terms of contract Compensation Reimbursement Indemnity

1. Repeating Transactions. In certain industries third persons make repeated transactions with the principal. In such cases, the agent who made the original contract with the third person commonly receives a certain compensation or percentage of commissions on all subsequent renewal or additional contracts. In the insurance business, for example, the insurance agent obtaining the policyholder for the insurer receives a substantial portion of the first year's premium and then receives a smaller percentage of the premiums paid by the policyholder in subsequent years.

Whether an agent or an agent's estate is entitled to receive compensation on repeating transactions, either after the termination of the agent's employment or after the agent's death, depends on the terms of the agency contract. Frequently it is provided that the right to receive compensation on repeating transactions terminates upon the termination of the agent's authority or employment by the principal.

2. Post-Agency Transactions. An agent is not entitled to compensation in connection with transactions, such as sales or renewals of insurance policies, occurring after the termination of the agency, even if the post-agency transactions are the result of the agent's former activities. However, some contracts between a principal and an agent expressly state whether the agent has the right to post-termination compensation.

(c) REIMBURSEMENT. The principal is under a duty to reimburse the agent for all disbursements made at the request of the principal and for all expenses necessarily incurred in the lawful discharge of the agency for the benefit of the principal. The agent cannot recover, however, for expenses caused by the agent's own misconduct or negligence. By way of illustration, if the agent transfers title to the wrong person, the agent cannot recover from the principal the expense incurred in correcting the error.

(d) INDEMNITY. It is the duty of the principal to indemnify the agent for any losses or damages suffered on account of the agency that were not caused by the agent's fault.

When the loss sustained is not the result of obedience to the principal's instructions but of the agent's misconduct or of an obviously illegal act, the principal is not liable for indemnification.

SUMMARY

The scope of an agent's authority is important, since an agent acting with authority has the power to bind the principal. The scope of an agent's authority may be determined from the express words of the principal to the agent; this is called *express authority*. An agent has incidental authority to perform any act reasonably necessary to execute the express authority given the agent. An agent's authority may be implied so as to enable the agent to perform any act in accordance with the general customs or usages in the business or industry. This authority is often referred to as *customary authority*. An individual is clothed with apparent authority where the principal, by words or conduct, leads a third person reasonably to believe that the individual has the authority of an agent.

The effect of a proper exercise of authority by an agent is to bind the principal and third person to a contract. The agent, not being a party to the contract, is not liable in any respect under the contract. A third person dealing with a person claiming to be an agent has a duty to ascertain the extent of the agent's authority and has a duty to take notice of any acts that are clearly adverse to the principal's interests. The third person cannot claim that apparent authority existed when the person has notice that the agent's conduct is adverse to the interests of the principal. A third person who has knowledge of limitations on an agent's authority is bound by those limitations. A third person is not bound by secret limitations.

An agent cannot appoint subagents to do the agent's duties unless (a) the duties are ministerial; (b) to do so is a well-established custom in the industry in question; (c) to do so is justified by emergency conditions; or (d) it was contemplated by the parties that subagents would be employed.

While the agency relationship exists, the agent owes the principal the duties of (a) being loyal; (b) obeying all lawful instructions; (c) exercising reasonable care; (d) accounting for all property or money belonging to the principal; and (e) informing the principal of all facts relating to the agency that are relevant to the principal's interests. The duties of an agent continue after termination of the agency only to the extent necessary to perform prior obligations, such as return of the former principal's property. After termination of the agency, the agent may deal with the principal as freely as with a stranger.

The principal owes certain duties to the agent, including (a) fulfilling all terms of their contract; (b) paying the agreed compensation for services of the agent; (c) reimbursing the agent for proper expenditures; and (d) indemnifying the agent for losses suffered on account of the agency through no fault of the agent.

QUESTIONS AND CASE PROBLEMS

1. What social forces are affected by the rule that a third person must ascertain the extent of an agent's authority?

2. Harvey Marks was agent for the Trojian Sportswear Co., covering the company's Midwest territory. He contracted on behalf of Trojian to provide the Lynnfield High School football team with sixty "game" football jerseys. The jerseys delivered to the school were of such poor quality that they were clearly not fit for the intended purpose of serving as "game" jerseys. The Lynnfield School Department sued Marks, the person who sold them the jerseys, for breach of warranty. Decide.

3. Can a person act as agent for both parties to a transaction?

4. Compare (a) secret limitations on authority of an agent with (b) apparent authority of an agent.

5. After an agency has been terminated, the agent is not entitled to further compensation. Appraise this statement.

6. Martha Christiansen owns women's apparel stores bearing her name in New Seabury, Massachusetts; Lake Placid, New York; Palm Beach, Florida; and Palm Springs, California. At a meeting with her four store managers she discussed styles she thought appropriate for the forthcoming season, advised them as always to use their best judgment in the goods they purchased for each of their respective stores, and cautioned, "but no blue jeans." Later, Jane Farley, the manager of the Lake Placid store, purchased a line of high-quality blue denim outfits

(designer jeans with jacket and vest options) from Women's Wear, Inc. for the summer season. The outfits did not sell. Martha refused to pay for them, contending that she told all of her managers "no blue jeans," and that if it came to a lawsuit, she would fly in three managers to testify that Jane Farley had absolutely no authority to purchase denim outfits and was, in fact, expressly forbidden to do so. Women's Wear sued Martha, and the three managers testified for Martha. Is the fact that Martha had explicitly forbidden Farley to purchase the outfits in question sufficient to relieve her from liability for the purchases made by Farley?

7. The Taylors were depositors of the Equitable Trust Company of Maryland. Equitable issued them a treasurer's check for $20,000. Mr. Vittetoe, a loan officer of the bank, received a long-distance telephone call from a person who identified himself as Mr. Taylor and requested that the $20,000 represented by the treasurer's check be transferred to the account of Jody Associates at Irving Trust Company in New York. Mr. Vittetoe did not know Mr. Taylor personally and replied that written instructions from Taylor would be required. Some time later, Frank Terranova appeared at the bank and stated that he was Taylor's agent, surrendered the treasurer's check, which had not been indorsed, and requested that the money represented thereby be transferred to the account of Jody Associates in the Irving Trust Company. Terranova also presented a letter that he had signed in his own name, in which was repeated the request to transfer the $20,000. Equitable verified Mr. Terranova's signature by checking his driver's license and a major credit card and thereafter made the transfer as requested. Taylor denied that Terranova had the authority to request the transfer and sued Equitable for damages. The bank contends that it was entitled to rely on the written instructions submitted to the bank by Terranova. Decide.

8. Regional Broadcasters of Michigan, Inc. owned and operated radio station WTRU. Moreschini supplied advertising material to WTRU under contract made with the station manager. When Moreschini sued Regional Broadcasters, it raised the defense that the manager had been instructed not to make any contracts on behalf of the station. Was Regional bound? [Moreschini v Regional Broadcasters, 373 Mich 496, 129 NW2d 859]

9. Barbara Fox was the agent of Burt Hollander, a well-known athlete. She discovered that Tom

Lanceford owned a '57 Chevrolet convertible, which had been stored in a garage for the past fifteen years. After demonstrating to Lanceford that she was the authorized agent of Hollander, she made a contract with Lanceford on behalf of Hollander to purchase the Chevrolet. Lanceford later discovered that the car was much more valuable than he originally believed, and he refused to deliver the car to Fox. Fox sued Lanceford for breach of contract. Can she recover?

10. Mallas was the real estate agent of Boyne U.S.A. Inc., and was responsible to seek buyers for Boyne's Big Sky resort properties in Bozeman, Montana. Mallas and Frank made an offer to Boyne's General Manager John Kircher to purchase the entire Big Sky resort properties for $7 million down and a $13 million note. John relayed the offer to Boyne and was told that the price was acceptable. Mallas and Frank made a written offer, which paid Mallas a commission on the sale and subordinated Boyne's note "to any bank financing required by the buyer." After being assured by Mallas that the document was merely a "letter of intent" needed by Mallas for his financial backers, John Kircher signed the document. Thereafter, Mallas and Frank sought to specifically enforce the document. Boyne U.S.A. Inc. sought to void the contract. Decide. [Boyne U.S.A. Inc. v Mallas, 236 Mont 305, 769 P2d 1235]

11. An attorney received a check made payable to the order of his client. The attorney indorsed the client's name and cashed the check at the bank on which it was drawn. The client then sued the bank for the amount that had been paid the attorney. The bank raised the defense that the attorney had authority to sign for the client and to receive payment on the client's behalf. Was this a valid defense? [Aetna Casualty & Surety Co. v Traders Nat'l. Bank & Trust Co. (Mo App) 514 SW2d 860]

12. Kribbs owned real estate that had been leased through his agent, Jackson, at a monthly rental of $275. When this lease terminated, Jackson and a third person, Solomon, made an agreement that if the latter obtained a new tenant for a rental of $500 a month, Jackson would pay Solomon $100 a month. The latter obtained a new tenant, who paid a monthly rental of $550. Jackson continued to send Kribbs $275 a month, less his commissions and janitor and utility costs; paid Solomon $100 a month; and kept the balance of the rental for himself. When Kribbs learned of these facts three years later, he sued Jackson for the money he had kept for himself

and that which he had paid Solomon. Jackson defended that Kribbs accepted and was satisfied with the $275 per month, that the additional funds were the sole result of Jackson's own entrepreneurship, and that the funds should accrue solely to Jackson's benefit. Was he correct? [Kribbs v Jackson, 387 Pa 611, 129 A2d 490]

13. DSG is in the government food service contracting business. Fredrick Anderson was employed by DSG to survey contracts in preparation for bids. Edward Mitura served as manager of DSG's Fort Riley, Kansas, contract. In early November, 1982, the food service contract at Fort Campbell, Kentucky, became available for bidding. On November 8, Anderson and Mitura toured the Fort Campbell facility with other prospective bidders, and Mitura informed Anderson of his intention to bid personally on the contract. Anderson hired an accountant, Larry Golden, concerning the cost per hour to be used in a bid, and it was determined to be $7.78. Anderson provided Mitura with this figure, and Mitura paid Golden's bill. On November 16, DSG submitted a bid. DSG was not notified by Anderson that Mitura was going to submit a bid. On November 22, Mitura, through his wife, submitted a bid. On November 23, Mitura notified DSG that he had submitted a bid on the Fort Campbell contract and quit his job. On November 24, the bids were opened, and Mitura's bid turned out to be the lowest. On December 12, Anderson resigned from DSG to work with Mitura, and the Fort Campbell contract was subsequently awarded to Mitura. DSG sued Mitura and Anderson for breach of their fiduciary duty to DSG by competing with it while employed by DSG. Mitura and Anderson contend that they were free to compete with their former employer once their employment relationship was terminated. They point out that their contract at Fort Campbell did not begin until well after both had terminated their work for DSG. Decide. [DSG Corp v Anderson (CA6 Ky) 754 F2d 678]

14. Cristallina S.A., a Panamanian corporation engaged in the purchase and sale of works of art, employed Christie's International to sell eight paintings at a May 19 auction. Based on the assessment of its experts, Christie's notified the press on May 12 that it expected to receive between $5 million and $9 million for the paintings. On the day before the auction, Christie's president David Bathurst recommended that the "reserves"—the private agreement between the seller and auctioneer on the prices below which an item may not be sold—be set at $9,250,000. The auction was a conceded failure, with just one of the eight paintings being sold. Cristallina sued Christie's, contending that as its agent Christie's failed to inform it of the information released to the press on May 12 and the underlying information on which the press estimates were made; and that the released estimates made it virtually impossible to sell the paintings unless the reserves were lowered. Christie's contended that as an auctioneer it cannot guarantee the results of a sale. Decide. [Cristallina S.A. v Christie, Manson & Woods, 117 App Div 2d 284, 502 NYS2d 165]

15. Bankerd and his wife Virginia owned a home in Maryland, as tenants by the entirety. They lived there until 1966, when Mrs. Bankerd moved out as a result of marital problems. Mr. Bankerd continued to live in the house until July, 1968, when he "left for the west." Mrs. Bankerd thereupon resumed residency and assumed all expenses for the home. Before Mr. Bankerd's departure, he executed a power of attorney to King. The power of attorney was later updated to authorize King to sell the property "on such terms as to him seem best." In 1977 Mrs. Bankerd asked King to exercise the power of attorney and to transfer Mr. Bankerd's interest in the property to her so that she could sell the property and retire. King wrote to Mr. Bankerd on three occasions at various addresses, but was unsuccessful in reaching him. King believed that Mr. Bankerd didn't care about the property and that he had abandoned his interest in it. King therefore conveyed Mr. Bankerd's interest in the property to Mrs. Bankerd. Mrs. Bankerd paid no consideration for the transfer, and King received no compensation. Later, Mr. Bankerd sued King, claiming that King had breached his duty of loyalty in connection with the conveyance of the property. King defended that under the broad language of the power of attorney, he had acted within his authority. [King v Bankerd, 303 Md 98 492 A2d 608]

41

THIRD PERSONS IN AGENCY

In agency transactions the third person has certain rights and liabilities with respect to the agent and the principal. Many of these rights and liabilities are contractual in nature. How-ever, the agency transaction can also produce tort and criminal liability for the agent and, under certain circumstances, for the principal as well.

A.   LIABILITY OF AGENT TO THIRD PERSON

The liability of the agent to the third person depends on the existence of authority and the manner of executing the contract.

1.   Action of Authorized Agent of Disclosed Principal

If an agent makes a contract with a third person on behalf of a disclosed principal and has proper authority to do so, and if the contract is executed properly, the agent has no personal liability on the contract. Whether the principal performs the contract or not, the agent cannot be held liable by the third party. Thus, an insurance agency arranging for the insuring of a customer with a named company is not liable on the policy that the company issues to the insured. If the agent lacks authority, however, or if certain other circumstances exist, the agent may be liable.

In speaking of an agent's action as authorized or unauthorized, it must be remembered that "authorized" includes action that, though originally unauthorized, was subsequently ratified by the principal. Once there is an effective ratification, the original action of the agent is no longer treated as unauthorized.

2.   Unauthorized Action

If a person makes a contract as agent for another but lacks authority to do so, the contract does not bind the principal. When a person purports to act as agent for a principal, an implied warranty arises that such person has authority to do so.[1] If the agent lacks authority, there is a breach of this warranty. If the agent's act causes loss to the third person, that third person may generally hold the agent liable for the loss. It is no defense for the agent in such case that the agent acted in good faith or misunderstood the scope of authority. The purported agent is not liable for conduct in excess of authority when the third person knows that the agent is acting beyond the authority given by the principal.

An agent with a written authorization may avoid liability on the implied warranty of authority by showing the written authorization to the third person and permitting the third person to determine the scope of the agent's authority.

3.   No Principal with Capacity

A person purporting to act as agent warrants by implication that there is an existing principal and that the principal has legal capacity. If there is no principal, or if the principal lacks capacity, the person acting as an agent is liable for any loss caused the third person.

The agent can avoid liability on the implied warranty of the existence of a principal with capacity by making known to the third person all material facts or by obtaining the agreement of the third person that the agent shall not be liable.

4.   Disclosure of Principal

There are three degrees to which the existence and identity of the principal may be disclosed or not disclosed. An agent's liability as a party to a contract with a third person is affected by the degree of disclosure.

(a) DISCLOSED PRINCIPAL. When the agent makes known the identity of the principal and the fact that the agent is acting on behalf of that principal, the principal is called a **disclosed principal.** The third person dealing with an agent of a disclosed principal ordinarily intends to make a contract with the principal, not with the agent. Consequently, the agent is not a party to and is not bound by the contract that is made.[2]

(b) PARTIALLY DISCLOSED PRINCIPAL. When the agent makes known the existence of a principal but not the principal's identity, the principal is a **partially disclosed principal.** As the third party does not know the identity of

---

[1]   Moore v Lewis, 51 Ill 3d 388, 9 Ill Dec 337, 366 NE2d 594 (1977).

[2]   New York Times v Glynn-Palmer Inc. 525 NYS2d 565 (1988).

the principal, the third person is making the contract with the agent, and the agent is therefore a party to the contract.

(c) UNDISCLOSED PRINCIPAL. When the third person is not told or does not know that the agent is acting as an agent for anyone else, the unknown principal is called an **undisclosed principal**.[3] In such case the third person is making the contract with the agent, and the agent is a party to that contract. For

³   Crown Controls Inc. v Smiley, 47 Wash App 832, 737 P2d 709 (1987).

example, an agent selling the goods of an undisclosed principal is the "seller" in the sales contract. The agent is liable for breach of the implied warranty of title if the principal in fact was not the owner of the goods sold by the agent.

In the *Rothschild* case the court was faced with deciding whether an agent was liable under contracts made on behalf of a principal. The agent did not disclose the name of the principal at the time the contracts were made, but the identity of the principal was later made known to the other contracting party.

ROTHSCHILD SUNSYSTEMS INC. v PAWLUS
514 NYS2d 572 (1987)

Richard Pawlus was an owner of Dutch City Wood Products Inc., which did business as "Dutch City Marketing." Pawlus believed he was acting on behalf of the corporation and purchased merchandise from Rothschild Sunsystems Inc. from April 24, 1985 to June 24, 1985, using the designation "Richard Pawlus Dutch Marketing" on orders and correspondence. In October, when a balance of $9,882.34 was owed Rothschild, the seller was notified by Pawlus' attorney that Pawlus was acting on behalf of the corporation when the merchandise was purchased. Rothschild sued Pawlus for payment for the merchandise and obtained a summary judgment. Pawlus contended that he was an agent of the corporation and therefore not personally liable. Pawlus appealed.

MURPHY, J. . . . The inquiry here is whether there exist any triable issues of fact. Plaintiff's complaint alleges that it shipped goods to Pawlus at his request, that Pawlus accepted the goods without objection and that the balance due on the account had not been paid despite reasonable demand having been made. Invoices to establish the allegations were submitted. Plaintiff also alleged that Pawlus never stated that he was acting on behalf of a corporation. Thus, plaintiff made out a cause of action on an account. It was then incumbent on Pawlus to demonstrate in acceptable evidentiary form that issues of fact existed. Pawlus, in his opposing papers, did not deny that he placed the orders or received the merchandise. Nor did he dispute any of the items in the account. He simply alleged that he acted on behalf of the corporation, Dutch City Wood Products, Inc., which was doing business as Dutch City Marketing. Further, he stated that plaintiff was made aware of this fact on October 17, 1985. However, this was well after the orders were placed and filled. The record also includes a letter from Pawlus dated September 12, 1985 which he signed "Richard Pawlus Dutch City Marketing" and which bears a letterhead "Dutch City Marketing." No mention of a corporation is made.

An agent will be liable as a principal if the fact of the agency relationship is not known by the person with whom the agent deals. Such disclosure must be made at the time of the contract. Here, Pawlus has failed to even allege that the existence of an agency was made known to plaintiff. Thus, summary judgment was properly granted to plaintiff.

[Judgment affirmed]

QUESTIONS

1. Was Dutch City Wood Products Inc. a partially disclosed principal?
2. Did the fact that Rothschild was notified that Pawlus was acting as an agent prior to the lawsuit relieve Pawlus from liability?
3. State the rule of the case.

5.   Wrongful Receipt of Money

If an agent obtains a payment of money from a third person by use of illegal methods, the agent is liable to the third person.

If the third person makes an overpayment to the agent or a payment when none is due, the agent is also usually liable to the third person for the amount of such overpayment or payment. If the agent has acted in good faith and does not know that the payment was improperly made, however, the agent is liable to the third person only so long as the agent has possession or control of the overpayment. If the agent has remitted the overpayment to the principal before its return is demanded by the third person, the agent is not liable to the third person. In the latter case, the third person's right of action, if one exists, is only against the principal. But payment to the principal does not relieve the agent of liability when the agent knows that the payment was not proper.

6.   Assumption of Liability

Agents may intentionally make themselves liable on contracts with third persons.[4] This situation frequently occurs when the agent is a well-established local brokerage house or other agency and when the principal is located out of town and is not known locally.

In some situations the agent will make a contract that will be personally binding. If the principal is not disclosed, the agent is necessarily the other contracting party and is bound by the contract. Even when the principal is disclosed, the agent may be personally bound if it was the intention of the parties that the agent assume a personal obligation, even though this was done in order to further the business of the principal. To illustrate, if an attorney hires an expert witness to testify on behalf of a client, the attorney is an agent acting on behalf of a disclosed principal and is not personally liable for an expert witness fee. However, where an expert witness asks the attorney about payment, and the attorney states, "Don't worry, I will take care of it," the attorney (agent) has assumed a personal obligation and is liable for the fee.[5]

7.   Execution of Contract

A simple contract that would appear to be the contract of the agent can be shown by other evidence, if believed, to have been intended as a contract between the principal and the third party. If the intention is established, it will be permitted to contradict the face of the written contract, and the contract as thus modified will be enforced.

In the *Memorial Hospital* case, where a daughter signed a guarantee of payment form upon bringing her incapacitated mother to a hospital, the court considered the daughter's defense that she had signed the guarantee form only as agent for her mother and thus could not be held personally responsible for unpaid charges.

[4]   Forbes Homes Inc. v Trimpi, 70 NC App 614, 320 SE2d 328 (1984).

[5]   Boros v Carter (Fla App) 537 So 2d 1134 (1989).

MEMORIAL HOSPITAL v BAUMANN

475 NYS2d 636 (1984)

During the early morning hours of January 10, 1981, Beverly Baumann accompanied her mother to Memorial Hospital, where her mother was placed in intensive care for symptoms of heart ailment. Baumann signed various documents, including one that authorized the hospital to release medical information and to receive directly the mother's insurance benefits. This form stated, "I understand I am financially responsible to the hospital for charges not covered by this authorization." Baumann's mother died during the course of her hospitalization. Thereafter, the hospital commenced suit to recover $19,013.42 in unpaid hospital charges based upon the form, signed by Baumann, that the hospital called a "guarantee of payment." Baumann contended that she signed the document as an agent for a disclosed principal and was thus not personally liable. From a judgment for Baumann, the hospital appealed.

MEMORANDUM DECISION. . . . Defendant's affidavit clearly states that she "signed [the] documents understanding that it was on behalf of [her] mother", thereby giving notice of an agency claim in this case. Plaintiff made no attempt to refute this assertion and does not claim on this appeal that it was surprised or prejudiced by defendant's reliance on the agency defense. Accordingly, we conclude that the agency defense was properly considered by Special Term.

On the merits, we recognize as well settled the proposition that an agent assumes no personal liability in executing a contract for a disclosed principal, unless it is clear that the agent intends to be bound personally. Defendant's unrefuted affidavit establishes that she did not intend to be bound personally because she signed the forms on behalf of her incapacitated mother who was clearly, as the patient to whom services were to be rendered in an emergency situation, the principal. Thus, Special Term's conclusions that defendant was acting as an agent for a disclosed principal and could not be personally liable to the hospital were correct.

[Judgment affirmed]

QUESTIONS

1. On what basis did the hospital claim Baumann was responsible for the unpaid bills?
2. What was Baumann's defense?
3. What action could Baumann have taken at the hospital that would have avoided any question as to her responsibility for unpaid charges?

To avoid any question of interpretation, an agent should execute an instrument by signing the principal's name and either "by" or "per" and the agent's name. For example, if Jane R. Craig is an agent for B. G. Gray, Craig should execute instruments by signing either "B. G. Gray, by Jane R. Craig" or "B. G. Gray, per Jane R. Craig." Such a signing is in law a signing by *Gray*, and the agent is therefore not a party to the contract.[6] The signing of the principal's name by an authorized agent without indicating the agent's name or identity is likewise in law the signature of the principal.

If the instrument is ambiguous as to

6 Barnes v Sadler, 95 NM 334, 622 P2d 239 (1981).

whether the agent has signed in a representative or an individual capacity, parol evidence is admissible, as between the original parties to the transaction, to establish the character in which the agent was acting. If the body of the contract states an obligation that clearly refers only to the principal, the agent is not bound by the contract even though it is signed in the agent's individual name without indicating any agency.

8.   Failure to Obtain Commitment of Principal

In some situations the agent is in effect an intermediary, or go-between, who has the duty to the third person to see to it that the principal is bound to the third person. For example, an insurance agent has authority to write policies of insurance. The agent tells a policyholder whose fire policy has been canceled that the agent will look into the matter and that the insured should forget about it unless notified by the agent. In such a case, the latter is under an obligation to make reasonable efforts to obtain the reinstatement of the policy or to notify the insured that it is not possible to do so. The agent is liable to the insured for the latter's fire loss if the agent does not obtain the reinstatement of the policy and fails to so inform the insured.

9.   Torts and Crimes

Agents are liable for harm caused third persons by the agents' fraudulent, intentional, or negligent acts. The fact that they were acting as agents at the time or that they acted in good faith under the directions of a principal does not relieve them of liability if their conduct would impose liability on them were they acting for themselves. With respect to liability for torts and crimes, no distinction is made as to whether the person causing harm is an agent or an employee.[7]

If an agent commits a crime, such as stealing from a third person or shooting the third person, the agent is liable for the crime, without regard to the fact of acting as an agent. The

agent is liable, without regard to whether the agent acted in self-interest or sought to advance the interest of the principal.

B.   LIABILITY OF THIRD PERSON TO AGENT

A third party may be liable to an agent because of the manner in which the transaction was conducted or because of acts causing harm to the agent.

10.   Action of Authorized Agent of Disclosed Principal

Ordinarily, the third person is not liable to the agent for a breach of contract that the agent has made with the third person on behalf of a disclosed principal. In certain instances, however, the third person may be liable to the agent.

11.   Undisclosed and Partially Disclosed Principal

If the agent executed the contract without the third party's knowing both of the existence of the agency and the identity of the principal, and the third party breaches the contract, the agent may sue the third party for the breach.

In such instances, if the contract is a simple contract, the principal may also sue the third person even though the third person thought the contract was only with the agent.

If the contract is a commercial paper, the undisclosed principal not appearing on the instrument as a party may not bring an action to enforce the contract.

12.   Agent Intending to Be Bound

If the third person knew that the agent was acting as an agent but nevertheless the parties intended that the agent should be personally bound by the contract, the agent may sue the third person for breach of contract.

13.   Execution of Contract

The principles that determine when an agent is liable to the third person because of the way

---

[7]   Mannish v Lacayo (Fla App) 496 So 2d 242 (1986).

in which a written contract was executed apply equally in determining when the third person is liable to the agent because of the way in which the contract is executed. If the agent could be sued by the third person, the third person can be sued by the agent. Thus, if the agent executes a commercial paper in the agent's own name, only the agent can sue the third person on that instrument.

14.   Agent as Transferee

The agent may sue the third person for breach of the latter's obligation to the principal when the principal has assigned or otherwise transferred a claim or right to the agent, whether absolutely for the agent's own benefit or for the purpose of collecting the money and remitting it to the principal.

C.   LIABILITY OF PRINCIPAL TO THIRD PERSON

The principal is liable to the third person for the properly authorized and executed contracts of the agent and, in certain circumstances, for the agent's unauthorized contracts.

15.   Agent's Contracts

The liability of a principal to a third person on a contract made by an agent depends on the extent of disclosure of the principal and the form of the contract that is executed.

(a) SIMPLE CONTRACT WITH PRINCIPAL DISCLOSED. When a disclosed principal with contractual capacity authorizes or ratifies an agent's transaction with a third person, and when the agent properly executes a contract with the third person as an agency transaction, a binding contract exists between the principal and the third person. The principal and the third person may each sue the other in the event of a breach of the contract. The agent is not a party to the contract, is not liable for its performance, and cannot sue for its breach.[8]

The liability of a disclosed principal to a third person is not discharged by the fact that the principal gives the agent money with which to pay the third person. Consequently, the liability of a buyer for the purchase price of goods is not terminated by the fact that the buyer paid the buyer's agent the purchase price to remit to the seller.

(b) SIMPLE CONTRACT WITH PRINCIPAL UNDISCLOSED. An undisclosed principal is liable for a simple contract made by an authorized agent. Although the third person initially contracted with the agent alone, the third person upon learning of the existence of the undisclosed principal, may sue that principal. In some states the third person must elect whether to hold the agent or the previously undisclosed principal liable for the debt. Under this "election of remedies rule," if the third person elects to hold the principal liable, and the principal turns out to be insolvent, the third person may not collect from the agent. The trend in the development of the law is to reject this rule. The modern rule allows judgments to be entered simultaneously against the agent and the undisclosed principal. It allows a third person to collect from the agent, the principal, or both until the judgment is fully satisfied (joint and several liability).[9]

(c) SIMPLE CONTRACT WITH PRINCIPAL PARTIALLY DISCLOSED. A partially disclosed principal is liable for a simple contract made by an authorized agent. The right of the third person is alternative as against either the agent or the principal.[10]

An undisclosed principal whose name or description does not appear on commercial paper is not liable as a party thereto.[11] Thus, an undisclosed principal is not liable on commercial paper executed by an agent in the agent's own name.

16.   Payment to Agent

When the third person makes payment to an authorized agent, the payment is deemed

[8]   Levy v Gold & Co. Inc. 141 App Div 2d 511, 529 NYS2d 133 (1988).

[9]   Crown Controls Inc. v Smiley, 110 Wash 2d 695, 756 P26 717 (1988).
[10]   James C. Smith & Associates, Inc. v Everett, 1 Ohio App 3d 118, 439 NE2d 932 (1981).
[11]   UCC §§ 3–401, 3–403.

made to the principal. The principal must give the third person full credit for the payment made to the agent, even if the agent never remits or delivers the payment to the principal, as long as the third person made the payment in good faith and had no reason to know that the agent would be guilty of misconduct.[12]

As apparent authority has the same legal consequence as actual authority, a payment made to a person with apparent authority to receive the payment is deemed a payment to the apparent principal. When payment by a debtor is made to a person who is not the actual or apparent agent of the creditor, such a payment does not discharge the debt unless that person in fact pays the money over to the creditor.

17.   Agent's Statements

A principal is bound by a statement made by an agent while transacting business within the scope of authority.[13] This means that the principal cannot thereafter contradict the statement of the agent and show that it is not true. Statements or declarations of an agent, in order to bind the principal, must be made at the time of performing the act to which they relate, or shortly thereafter.

18.   Agent's Knowledge

The principal is bound by knowledge or notice of any fact that is acquired by an agent while acting within the scope of actual or apparent authority.[14]

When a commercial paper is indorsed to the principal, and the agent acting for the principal has a knowledge of a matter that would be a defense to the paper, such knowledge of the agent is imputed to the principal and bars the principal from being a holder in due course. When a fact is known to the agent

of the seller, the sale is deemed made by the seller with knowledge of that fact. For example, where the agent recommending and selling weed eradicator to the buyer knew that it would be used in a drainage ditch in the Mississippi River delta, a warranty of fitness for that particular purpose arose because the seller was deemed to know what the agent knew. Likewise, when an employee knows that there has been a pollution of water contrary to law, such knowledge is imputed to the corporate employer, even if no officer or director had in fact any knowledge thereof.

The rule that the agent's knowledge is imputed to the principal is extended in some cases to knowledge gained prior to the creation of the agency relationship. The notice and knowledge in any case must be based on reliable information. Thus, when the agent hears only rumors, the principal is not charged with notice.

(a) EXCEPTIONS. If the subject matter is outside the scope of the agent's authority, the agent is under no duty to inform the principal of the knowledge, and the principal is not bound thereby.

The principal is not charged with knowledge of an agent under the following circumstances: (1) when the agent is under a duty to another person to conceal such knowledge; (2) when the agent is acting adversely to the principal's interest; or (3) when the third party acts in collusion with the agent for the purpose of cheating the principal. In such cases it is not likely that the agent would communicate knowledge to the principal. The principal is therefore not bound by the knowledge of the agent.

(b) COMMUNICATION TO PRINCIPAL. As a consequence of regarding the principal as possessing the knowledge of the agent, when the law requires that a third person communicate with the principal, that duty may be satisfied by communicating with the agent. Thus, an offeree effectively communicates the acceptance of an offer to the offeror when the offeree makes such communication to the offeror's agent. An offeror effectively communicates the revocation of an offer to the offeree by

[12]   This general rule of law is restated in some states by § 2 of the Uniform Fiduciaries Act, which is expressly extended by § 1 thereof to agents, partners, and corporate officers. Similar statutory provisions are found in a number of other states.
[13]   Potomac Leasing Co. v Bulger (Ala) 531 So 2d 307 (1988).
[14]   Baldinger Baking Co. v Stepan (Minn App) 354 NW2d 569 (1984).

communicating the revocation to the offeree's agent.

D.   LIABILITY OF PRINCIPAL FOR TORTS AND CRIMES OF AGENT

Under certain circumstances the principal may be liable to the third person for the torts or crimes of the agent or employee.

19.   Vicarious Liability for Torts and Crimes

Assume that an agent or an employee causes harm to a third person. Is the principal or employer liable for this conduct? If the conduct constitutes a crime, can the principal or employer be criminally prosecuted? The answer is that in many instances the principal or employer is liable civilly and may be prosecuted criminally. That is, the principal or employer is liable although personally free from fault and not guilty of any wrong. This concept of imposing liability for the fault of another is known as **vicarious liability.**

The situation arises both when an employer has an employee and a principal has an agent who commits the wrong. The rules of law governing the vicarious liability of the principal and the employer are the same. In the interest of simplicity, this section will be stated in terms of employees acting in the course of employment. It is to be remembered that these rules are equally applicable to agents acting within the scope of their authority. As a practical matter, some situations will arise only with agents. For example, the vicarious liability of a seller for the misrepresentations made by a salesperson will arise only when the seller appointed an agent to sell. In contrast, both the employee hired to drive a truck and the agent being sent to visit a customer could negligently run over a third person. In many situations a person employed by another is both an employee and an agent, and the tort is committed within the phase of "employee" work.

The rule of law imposing vicarious liability on an innocent employer for the wrong of an employee is also known as the doctrine of **respondeat superior.** In modern times this doctrine can be justified on the grounds that the business should pay for the harm caused in the doing of the business, that the employer will be more careful in the selection of employees if made responsible for their actions, and that the employer may obtain liability insurance to protect against claims of third persons.

(a) NATURE OF ACT. The wrongful act committed by the employee may be a negligent act, an intentional act, a fraudulent act, or a violation of a government regulation. It may give rise only to civil liability of the employer, or it may also subject the employer to prosecution for crime.

(1) Negligent Act. Historically, the act for which liability would be imposed under the doctrine of *respondeat superior* was a negligent act committed within the scope of employment.

(2) Intentional Act. Under the common law a master was not liable for an intentional tort committed by a servant. The modern law holds that an employer is liable for an intentional tort committed by an employee for the purpose of furthering the employer's business.[15] Thus, an employer is not liable for an intentional, unprovoked assault committed by an employee on a third person or customer of the employer because of a personal grudge or for no reason. However, the employer will be held liable by the modern view when the employee's assault was committed in the belief that the employee was thereby advancing the employer's interest.[16] For example, an employee may be hired to retake property, as in the case of an employee of a finance company hired to repossess automobiles on which installment payments have not been made. In such a case the employer is generally liable for any unlawful force used by the employee in retaking the property or in committing an assault on a debtor.

---

[15]   Bourk v Iseman Mobile Homes (SD) 316 NW2d 343 (1982).
[16]   Restatement, 2d Agency § 231; Carrero v NYC Housing Authority (DC NY) 668 F Supp 196 (1987).

(3) Fraud. The modern decisions hold the employer liable for fraudulent acts or misrepresentations. The rule is commonly applied to a principal-agent relationship. To illustrate, when an agent makes fraudulent statements in selling stock, the principal is liable for the buyer's loss. In states that follow the common law rule of no liability for intentional torts, the principal is not liable for the agent's fraud when the principal did not authorize or know of the fraud of the agent.

(4) Governmental Regulation. The principal may be liable because of the agent's violation of a governmental regulation. Such regulations are most common in the areas of business and of protection of the environment. In such a case the employer may be held liable for a penalty imposed by the government. In some cases the breach of the regulation will impose liability on the principal in favor of a third person who is injured in consequence of the violation.

(b) COURSE OF EMPLOYMENT. The mere fact that a tort or crime is committed by an employee does not necessarily impose vicarious liability on the employer. It must also be shown that the employee was acting within the scope of the authority if an agent, or in the course of employment if an employee.[17] If the agent or employee was not so acting, there is no vicarious liability.

The *Frito-Lay* case turned on whether the employee was acting within the course of his employment when he assaulted a third person in an attempt to retake certain company property.

[17]   Rubin v Yellow Cab Co. 154 Ill App 3d 336, 107 Ill Dec 450, 507 NE2d 114 (1987).

FRITO-LAY INC. v RAMOS
(Tex Civ App) 770 SW2d 887 (1989)

On July 11, 1984, Jose Padilla was working as a vacation-relief route salesman for Frito-Lay. He testified that he made a route stop at Sal's Beverage Shop. He was told by Mrs. Ramos that she was dissatisifed with Frito-Lay service and no longer wanted their products in the store. He asked if there was anything he could do to change her mind. She said, "No," and told him to pick up his merchandise. He took one company-owned merchandise rack to his van and was about to pick up another rack when Mr. Ramos said that rack had been given to him by the regular route salesman. Mr. Padilla said the route salesman had no authority to give away Frito-Lay racks. A confrontation occurred over the rack, and Padilla pushed Mr. Ramos against the cash register, injuring Ramos's back. Frito-Lay had a company policy, clearly communicated to all employees, which prohibited them from getting involved in any type of physical confrontation with a customer. Frito-Lay contended that Padilla was not acting within the course and scope of his employment when the pushing incident took place, and that the company was therefore not liable to Ramos. Ramos contended that Frito-Lay was responsible for the acts of its employee Padilla. From a judgment for Ramos, Frito-Lay appealed.

OSBORN, C.J. . . . Much has been written about whether an attack by an employee normally results from a personal animosity and is outside the master's business, which usually is the case, or whether the employer placed the employee in a position which involved the use of force, and his conduct is within the course and scope of his employment. . . .

Clearly, an attack based primarily upon a confrontation or ill will between an employee and a third party will be found to be outside the normal course and scope of employment. *Kendall v. Whataburger, Inc.*, 759 S.W. 2d 751 (Tex. App.—Houston [1st Dist.] 1988, no writ). . . .

In our case, the issue is not just over an exchange of words about the type of service the customer was receiving. It involved the right to certain personal property. Mr. Padilla knew the rack was custom made for Frito-Lay. He concluded the route salesman had no right to give that property to a customer. Thus, he concluded that as a company employee, he was obligated to remove all company equipment if the customer no longer was going to sell its merchandise. Under those circumstances of being responsible for what he thought was company equipment, he was acting within the course and scope of his employment. The evidence supports the jury's answer and it is not against the great weight and preponderance of the evidence.

[Judgment affirmed]

QUESTIONS

1. Was Padilla acting within the scope of his employment as a route salesman when he sought to retake the merchandise rack?
2. What is the significance of a determination that an employee was acting within the scope of employment when the unlawful act was committed?
3. Can an employer avoid liability for an intentional tort of an employee by promulgating a company rule prohibiting all employees from using unlawful force in retaking company property?

(c) EMPLOYEE OF THE UNITED STATES. The Federal Tort Claims Act declares that the United States shall be liable vicariously whenever a federal employee driving a motor vehicle in the course of employment causes harm under such circumstances that a private employer would be liable. Contrary to the general rule, the statute exempts the employee driver from liability.

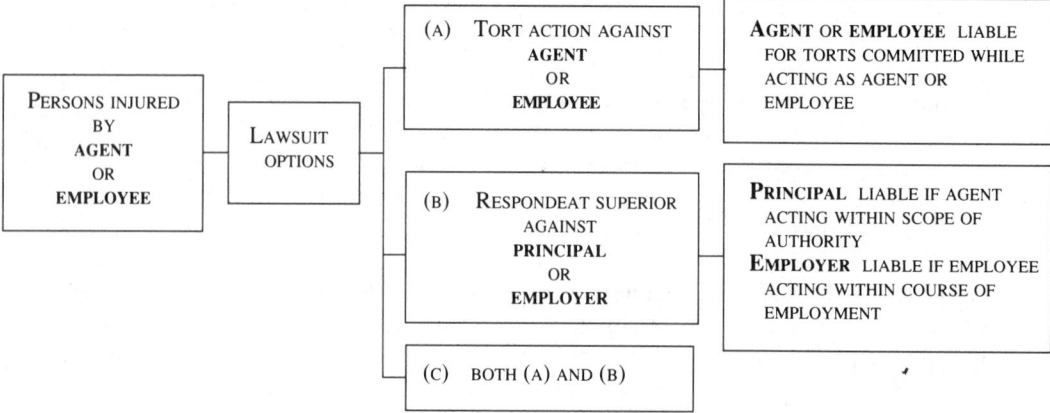

FIGURE 41-1   LIABILITY FOR TORTS OF AGENT OR EMPLOYEE

20.   Other Theories of Liability

If an employee is not acting within the course of employment, the employer cannot be held liable on the theory of *respondeat superior*. This does not mean, however, that the employer will necessarily not be liable. In some cases the employer will be liable without regard to the nature of the act or whether the employee was acting in the course of employment. For example, the employer may be held liable as a bailor for lending an automobile to a bailee-employee.

An employer is liable for the tortious and criminal consequences of acts expressly authorized. For example, if the employer instructs an employee to hijack a competitor's truck, the employer is both civilly and criminally liable, without any consideration being given to the question of whether such activity is within the course of employment of the employee. An employer is also liable upon giving defective equipment to an employee when the defect causes harm, or upon giving control of proper equipment to an unfit employee when, because of the latter's lack of qualifications, harm is caused a third person.

21.   Agent's Crimes

The principal is liable for the crimes of the agent committed at the principal's direction. When not authorized, however, the principal is ordinarily not liable for the crime of an agent merely because it was committed while otherwise acting within the scope of the latter's authority or employment.

Some states impose liability on the employer when the employee has in the course of employment violated liquor sales laws, pure food laws, or laws regulating prices or prohibiting false weights. Thus, by some courts, an employer may be held criminally responsible for an employee's sale of liquor to a minor in violation of the liquor law, even though the sale was not known to the employer and violated instructions given to the employee.

22.   Owner's Liability for Acts of an Independent Contractor

If the work is done by an independent contractor rather than by an employee, the owner is not liable for harm caused by the contractor to third persons or their property. Likewise, the owner is not bound by the contracts made by the independent contractor.[18] The owner is ordinarily not liable for harm caused to third persons by the negligence of the employees of the independent contractor.

In the *Guillory* case the plaintiff sought to avoid the application of the general rule that the owner is not liable for harm caused by an independent contractor by arguing that (1) the owner had control over the conduct of the contractors in question, and (2) the owner should be liable under the exception for inherently dangerous work.

---

[18]   Spivey v Brown, 150 Ill App 3d 139, 103 Ill Dec 876, 502 NE2d 23 (1986).

GUILLORY v CONOCO, INC.
(La App) 521 So 2d 1220 (1988)

Conoco contracted with Daniel Construction Company to build a "sour crude" oil refinery. Under the contract Daniel Co. was to award and manage all subcontracts, provide field supervisory personnel, enforce safety rules on its employees and subcontractors, and control and manage the entire project. Daniel subcontracted the roofing work to Morgan Roofing Co. Charles Guillory, a Morgan employee, while working on the roof of a 48-foot high tank without fall protection, fell from the roof and was seriously injured. Two weeks prior to the fall a Conoco supervisor visiting the work site observed that Morgan Roofing employees were working without fall protection, in violation of safety rules. He immediately notifed Daniel Co. Guillory brought suit against Conoco claiming Conoco was liable for the torts of Morgan and David Co. because it had control over their conduct. Guillory also contended that the owner, Conoco, was liable under the "inherently dangerous work" doctrine. Conoco contended that it was not liable for the harm caused by an independent contractor or a subcontractor working under the control of the independent contractor.

CULPEPPER, J. . . . In *Hickman v. Southern Pacific Transport Co.*, 262 La. 102, 262 So.2d 385 (1972), the court held that the relationship of principal and independent contractor exists when the following conditions are met:

1. There is a valid contract between the parties;
2. The work being done is of an independent nature such that the contractor may employ non-exclusive means in accomplishing it;
3. The contract calls for specific piecework as a unit to be done according to the independent contractor's own methods without being subject to the control and direction of the principal, except as to the result or the services to be rendered;
4. There is a specific price for the overall undertaking; and
5. Specific time or duration is agreed upon and not subject to termination at the will of either side without liability for breach.

. . . In the present case the contract between Conoco and Daniel meets all of the *Hickman* criteria, including the right to control the work was reserved by Daniel. Daniel was to provide field supervisory personnel, prepare the work plans and schedules, manage the work progress, prepare and implement the budget, plan and maintain a field quality control program, plan and maintain a labor relations program, award and manage subcontractors, and provide construction equipment, tools and sanitary facilities. Conoco imposed its own plant safety program on the jobsite workers through Article 10.1 of the contract. However, Daniel was responsible for enforcing the safety rules on its employees and subcontractors. (Contract Articles 3.2 and 10.1) Although Conoco personnel monitored the work progress and ran field tests, they did not exercise direct supervision over the step-by-step process of accomplishing the work. . . . Daniel Construction Company was clearly an independent contractor, as stipulated in Contract Article 3.1. Therefore, the trial judge did not err in finding that the contract gave Conoco no operational control over Morgan Roofing Company's work area.

Nor did the trial judge err in not instructing the jury that Conoco could be independently negligent for the action or inaction of Daniel's employees. The law is settled that a principal is not liable to third parties for the torts of an independent contractor. . . . An independent contractor is responsible for the torts of its employees. LSA-C.C. art. 2320. The Contract Articles 3.2 and 3.3 stipulated that Daniel was to be fully responsible to Conoco for the acts, errors and omissions of Daniel's subcontractors. It was Daniel's duty to manage the subcontracts. Therefore, Conoco's personnel were not responsible for enforcement of the safety rules on the jobsite. In accordance with Contract Article 2.1, Conoco correctly pointed out the safety violations to Daniel Construction, who was responsible to Conoco for correcting the situation. Conoco was not independently negligent.

Plaintiff also contends that Conoco owed a duty of care to plaintiff, as an employee of an independent contractor, because the work to be performed was inherently or intrinsically dangerous. The rule as to inherently or intrinsically dangerous work was set forth in *Montgomery v Gulf Refining Co.*, 168 La. 73, 121 So. 578 (1929):

> Ordinarily, an employer is not liable for offenses of an independent contractor committed in the course of performing his duties under the contract. An important exception to this rule, which has been recognized in this state, is that if the work is inherently or intrinsically dangerous unless proper precautions are taken to avoid injury, the employer cannot avoid liability by letting the work out to an independent contractor.

> . . . Ultrahazardous activities were defined in *Kent v. Gulf States Utilities Co.*, 418 So.2d 493, 498 (La. 1982), as activities which can cause injuries to others even when conducted with the greatest prudence and care. Therefore the critical inquiry in determining whether an activity is inherently or intrinsically dangerous is whether it can be made safe when it is performed in a proper and workmanlike manner. . . . Evidence presented at trial established that the use of fall protection, as required by Conoco safety rules, OSHA, and common sense, would have made the work safe. In this case, the plaintiff was not injured by an ultrahazardous activity, but by unsafe work methods. . . .

[Judgment affirmed]

QUESTIONS

1. Did the owner, Conoco, have operational control over the work area where Guillory was injured, so as to make it liable to Guillory?
2. What is the test used to determine whether an activity is inherently dangerous?
3. Was Conoco found liable under the "inherently dangerous work" exception?

(a) EXCEPTIONS TO OWNER'S IMMUNITY. There is a trend toward imposing liability on the owner when the work undertaken by the independent contractor is inherently dangerous. That is, the law is taking the position that if the owner wishes to engage in a particular activity, the owner must be responsible for the harm it causes. The owner cannot be insulated from such liability by the device of hiring an independent contractor to do the work. In such cases, the courts regard the activity as having such a high potential of harm that the owner is not permitted to delegate to another the duty to protect the public from harm.

Regardless of the nature of the activity, the owner may be liable for the torts and contracts of the independent contractor when the owner controls the conduct of the independent contractor. For example, when the franchisor ex-

ercises a high degree of control over the franchisee, the relationship will be recognized as an agency relationship, and the franchisor is bound by the action of the franchisee.

In certain circumstances, such as providing security for a business, bill collecting, and repossessing collateral, there is an increased risk that torts may be committed by the individuals performing such duties. The trend of the law is not to allow the employment of an independent contractor for such work to insulate the employer.[19]

(b) UNDISCLOSED INDEPENDENT CONTRACTOR. In some situations the owner appears to be doing the act in question be-

---

[19]   General Finance Corp. v Smith (Ala) 505 So 2d 1045 (1987).

cause the existence of the independent contractor is not disclosed or apparent. This situation occurs most commonly when a franchisee does business under the name of the franchisor; when a concessionaire, such as a restaurant in a hotel, appears to be the hotel restaurant, although in fact it is operated by an independent concessionaire; or when the buyer of a business continues to run the business in the name of the seller. In such cases of an undisclosed independent contractor, it is generally held that the ostensible owner (that is, the franchisor, the grantor of the concession, or the seller) is liable for the torts and contracts of the undisclosed independent contractor.

23. Enforcement of Claim by Third Person

A lawsuit by a third person may be brought against the agent or the principal if each is liable. In most states and in the federal courts the plaintiff may sue either or both in one action when both are liable. If both are sued, the plaintiff may obtain a judgment against both, although the plaintiff is allowed to collect the full amount of the judgment only once.

E. TRANSACTIONS WITH SALES PERSONNEL

Many transactions with sales personnel do not result in a contract with the third person with whom the salesperson deals.

24. Soliciting Agent

The giving of an order to a salesperson ordinarily does not give rise to a contract. Ordinarily, a salesperson is an agent whose authority is limited to soliciting offers from third persons and transmitting them to the principal for acceptance or rejection. Such an agent does not have authority to make a contract that will bind the principal to the third person. The employer of the salesperson is not bound by a contract until the employer accepts the order.

(a) REASONS FOR LIMITATION ON AUTHORITY OF SALES PERSONNEL. The limitation on the authority of the salesperson is commonly based on the fact that credit may be involved in the transaction. The employer of the salesperson usually does not wish to permit its soliciting agent to make decisions as to the sufficiency of the credit standing of the buyer, but wishes all of these matters to be handled by the credit management department of the home office.

To avoid difficulties, it is common to limit the authority of a salesperson to that of merely a soliciting agent accepting and transmitting orders to the employer. To make this clear to buyers, order forms signed by the customer, who is given a copy, generally state that the salesperson's authority is limited in this manner and that there is no "contract" with the employer until the order is approved by the home office.

(b) WITHDRAWAL OF CUSTOMER. From the fact that the customer giving a salesperson an order does not ordinarily have a binding contract with the employer of the salesperson until the employer approves the order, it necessarily follows that the customer is not bound by any contract until the employer approves the order. Prior to that time the "buyer" may withdraw from the transaction. Withdrawal under such circumstances is not a breach of contract, because by definition there is no contract to be broken. Likewise, if the "buyer" has given the salesperson any money deposit, down payment, or part payment on the purchase price, the customer, on withdrawing from the transaction, is entitled to a refund of any such payment.

25. Contrast with Contracting Agent

In contrast with the consequences when the salesperson is only a soliciting agent, if the person with whom the buyer deals has authority to make contracts, there is by definition a binding contract between the principal and the customer from the moment that the agent agrees with the customer. That is, the contract arises when the agent accepts the customer's order. Should the customer seek to withdraw from the contract thereafter, the customer must base such action on a ground that justifies the unilateral repudiation or rejection of the contract. If the customer has no such justification, the action of withdrawing is a breach of contract. The customer is then liable for the seller's resulting damages. If the buyer has made any down payment, prepayment, or deposit, the seller may deduct damages from the amount thereof before refunding any excess to the buyer. When the transaction relates to the sale of goods, the seller is entitled to retain from such advance payment either $500 or 20 percent of the purchase price, whichever is less, unless the seller can show that greater damages were in fact sustained.[20]

---

[20]   UCC § 2–718(2)(b). See Chapter 29, Section 6(a) of this book as to consumer protection rescission.

SUMMARY

An agent of a disclosed principal who makes a contract within the scope of authority with a third person has no personal liability on the contract. It is the principal and third person who may each sue the other in the event of a breach. A person purporting to act as an agent for a principal warrants by implication that there is an existing principal with legal capacity and that the principal has authorized the agent to act. The person acting as an agent is liable for any loss caused the third person for breach of these warranties. An agent of a partially disclosed or an undisclosed principal is a party to the contract with the third person. The agent may enforce the contract against the third person and is liable for its breach. To avoid problems of interpretation, an agent should execute a contract "Principal, by Agent." Agents are liable for harm caused third persons by their fraudulent, malicious, or negligent acts.

An undisclosed or partially disclosed principal is liable to a third person on a simple contract made by an authorized agent. Exceptions exist if the principal has made a good faith settlement of the account with the agent or where satisfaction of the claim has been obtained from the agent. When a third person makes payment to an authorized agent, it is deemed paid to the principal.

A principal or employer is vicariously liable under the doctrine of *respondeat superior* for the torts of an agent or employee committed within the scope of authority or course of employment. However, a principal is not liable for the crimes of an agent merely because they were committed while otherwise acting within the scope of authority; rather, it is usually necessary to show that the principal authorized or directed the criminal conduct. An owner is not liable for torts caused by an independent contractor to third persons or their property, unless the work undertaken by the independent contractor is inherently hazardous.

A salesperson is ordinarily an agent whose authority is limited to soliciting offers (orders) from third persons and transmitting them to the principal. The principal is not bound until the principal accepts the order. The customer may withdraw an offer at any time prior to acceptance.

QUESTIONS AND CASE PROBLEMS

1. What social forces are affected by the rule that an agent receiving an overpayment is not liable for the amount thereof when the payment was received in ignorance of the mistake and has been remitted to the principal?

2. Myles Murphy was appointed by Cy Sinden, a famous developer, to purchase land for a shopping center near the intersection of I-95 and Route 1. Mary Mason, the property owner, contracted with Murphy for the sale of the property. Due to an economic downturn Sinden was unable to provide the planned behind-the-scenes financing for the venture, and the contract was not performed. Mason's real estate experts de-

termined that she lost $2 million because of the breach of contract. Mason also discovered that Sinden was "behind the deal." If Mason elects to sue Sinden, who turns out to be unable to pay the judgment because of the collapse of his business "empire," can she thereafter bring suit against Murphy?

3. Compare a third party beneficiary contract with a contract made by an agent on behalf of an undisclosed principal.

4. What is the justification for the doctrine of *respondeat superior*?

5. Compare the liability of an agent's undisclosed principal to a third person on (a) a promissory note, (b) a sealed contract, and (c) an oral contract.

6. Mills Electric Company signed a contract with S&S Horticulture Architects, a two-person landscaping partnership operated by Sullivan and Smyth, to maintain the grounds and flowers at the Mills Electric Company plant in Jacksonville, Florida. Mills checked references of S&S and found the company to be highly reputable. The contract set forth that S&S would select the flowers for each season and would determine when to maintain the lawns, so long as the lawns were properly maintained. The contract called for payments to be made to S&S on the first workday of each month, and the contract stipulated that "nothing herein shall make S&S an agent of the company." The contract also required that S&S personnel wear uniforms identifying them as employees of S&S. S&S had other accounts, but the large Mills Electric plant took up most of their time. While working on a terraced area near the visitors' entrance to the plant, Sullivan lost control of his large commercial mower, and the mower struck Gillespie, a plant visitor, causing serious injury to her. A witness heard Sullivan apologizing to Gillespie, saying "running that mower on the terrace is a two-person job." Gillespie brought suit against Mills Electric Co., contending Mills should be held vicariously liable for the negligence of Sullivan. Should Mills be held liable on this theory?

7. Anthony Perkins was admitted to Children's Hospital by a private pediatric surgeon, Dr. Green. On the evening of July 18, 1984, Dr. Green performed a tracheotomy to correct a congenital condition in the infant's windpipe. Thereafter, Dr. Green examined Anthony in the intensive care unit, where he had been taken after the surgery, and gave instructions as to his treatment. Dr. Green left the hospital at 11:00 p.m., and Anthony came under the exclusive care of the nurses and residents employed by the hospital. At about 3:55 a.m. Anthony stopped breathing, and during the five to seven minutes that elapsed before hospital personnel were able to restore his breathing and heartbeat, he suffered irreversible brain damage. Anthony and his parents brought suit against Children's for negligent post-operative care rendered by the hospital's residents. Expert testimony revealed that the residents who were employed and paid by the hospital had been negligent in failing to use adequate medical procedures in light of the symptoms that Anthony exhibited for almost two hours before the crisis occurred and in the resuscitation efforts employed after its onset. Children's contends that the residents were under the direction and control of Dr. Green so that he, rather than Children's, was responsible for their negligence. Decide.

8. Weisz purchased a painting at an auction sale in the Parke-Burnett Galleries. It was later shown that the painting was a forgery. When Weisz sued Parke-Burnett for breach of warranty, it raised the defense that it was making the sale for the owner, and therefore, any warranty suit must be brought against the owner. Was it correct? [Weisz v Parke-Burnett Galleries, Inc. 325 NYS2d 576]

9. Jason Lasseigne, a little league baseball player, was seriously injured at a practice session when he was struck on the head by a poorly thrown baseball from a team member, Todd Landry. The league was organized by American Legion Post 38. Claude Cassel and Billy Johnson were the volunteer coaches of the practice session. The Lasseignes brought suit on behalf of Jason against Post 38, contending that vicarious liability should attach to Post 38 for negligent coaching of Cassel and Johnson. They argued that since Post 38 is a nonprofit domestic corporation, it is liable for the acts of its agents or employees when the wrongful conduct occurred in furtherance of the corporation's activities. Post 38 contends that it had no right to control the details of the work of the volunteer coaches or the manner in which practices were conducted, and as a result should not be held vicariously liable for the actions of the coaches. Decide. [Lasseigne v American Legion Post 38 (La App) 543 So 2d 1111]

10. Moritz was a guest at the Pines Hotel. While she was sitting in the lobby, Brown, a hotel employee, dropped a heavy vacuum cleaner on her knee. When she complained, he insulted her and hit her with his fist, knocking her uncon-

scious. She sued the hotel for damages. Was the hotel liable? [Moritz v Pines Hotel, Inc. 53 App Div 2d 1020, 383 NYS2d 704]

11. E. I. duPont de Nemours & Co. licensed Enjay Chemical Company (now Exxon) and Johnson & Johnson to use certain chemical processes, in return for which royalty payments were to be made to duPont. By agreement between the companies, the royalty payments were to be made by check sent to a specified duPont employee, C.H.D., in its Control Division. These checks were sent during the next nine years. C.H.D. altered some of them so that he was named thereon as the payee. He then cashed them and used the money for his own purposes. Liberty Mutual Insurance Company, which insured the fidelity of duPont's employees, and duPont sued Enjay and Johnson & Johnson on the basis that they still owed the money represented by the checks that C.H.D. had converted. Did they still owe this money? [Liberty Mutual Insurance Co. v. Enjay Chemical Co. (Del Super) 316 A2d 219]

12. The Bay State Harness Horse Racing and Breeding Association conducted horse races. Music was supplied for the patrons by an independent contractor hired by the association. Some of the music played was subject to a copyright held by Famous Music Corporation. The playing of that music was a violation of the copyright unless royalties were paid to Famous Music. None were paid, and Famous Music sued the association. It raised the defense that the violation had been committed by an independent contractor that was specifically instructed not to play Famous Music's copyrighted material. Decide. [Famous Music Corporation v Bay State Harness Horse Racing and Breeding Association, Inc. (CA1 Mass) 554 F2d 1213]

13. On September 24, 1984, Bernie and Joanne Van Rossem made arrangements for a honeymoon trip to Jamaica with the Penney Travel Service, paying on that date $2,059 to Penney in advance of the scheduled departure date of November 10, 1984. On their wedding day they received a telephone call from Penney Travel, advising them that Lotus Tours, the wholesaler through which Penney had booked their travel reservations, had gone bankrupt. They were further informed that Lotus had paid their airfare prior to bankruptcy, but that their reservation at the Sandles Resort had not been paid by Lotus Tours. The Van Rossems booked new reservations at "Couples" resort, where they paid $1,312 for substitute accommodations. The Van Rossems were not told at any time prior to their wedding day of the fact that Penney was acting as agent for the wholesaler Lotus. Penney Travel contended that it is well known by the public that travel agents act as agents or wholesalers in the travel business. Penney could show conclusively that the $2,059 received from the Van Rossems was forwarded to Lotus Travel as of October 4, 1984, and that they had not received any commission because of the bankruptcy. The Van Rossems brought suit against Penney Travel for the cost of the substitute accommodations. On what theory or theories could the Van Rossems rely? What defense would Penney Travel raise? Decide. [Van Rossem v Penney Travel Service, 128 Misc 2d 50, 488 NYS 2d 595]

14. Neal Rubin, while driving his car in Chicago, inadvertently obstructed the path of a Yellow Cab Co. taxi driven by Robert Ball, causing the taxi to swerve and come in contact with Rubin's car. Angered by Rubin's driving, Ball got out of his cab and proceeded to hit Rubin over the head and shoulders with a metal pipe. Rubin sued the Yellow Cab Co. for the damages caused by this beating, contending that the employer was vicariously liable for the beating under the doctrine of *respondeat superior*, since the beating occurred in furtherance of the employer's business, which is to obtain fares without delay. The company defends that Ball's beating of Rubin was not an act undertaken to further the employer's business. Is the employer liable under *respondeat superior*? [Rubin v Yellow Cab Co. 154 Ill App 3d 336, 107 Ill Dec 450, 507 NE2d 114]

15. Brazilian & Columbian Co. (B&C), a food broker, ordered 40 barrels of olives from Mawer-Gulden-Annis, Inc. (MGA). MGA's shipping clerk was later told to make out the bill of lading to B&C's customer, Pantry Queen; the olives were shipped directly to Pantry Queen. Eight days after the delivery, the president of B&C wrote MGA to give it the name of its principal, Pantry Queen, and advised MGA to bill the principal directly. Pantry Queen was unable to pay for the olives, and MGA sued B&C for payment. B&C defended that it was well known to MGA that B&C was a food broker (agent), and the olives were shipped directly to the principal by MGA. It stated that as an agent it was not a party to the contract and was thus not liable. Decide. [Mawer-Gulden-Annis, Inc. v Brazilian & Columbian Coffee Co. 49 Ill App 2d 400, 199 NE2d 222]

42

EMPLOYMENT

The law of employment is based on the law of contracts. It is the role of the employer and an individual or group of employees to contract on terms for wages, hours, working conditions, and the duration of the employment relationship. The employment relationship is also regulated by statutes known as labor legislation. Labor legislation deals with such is-

sues as fair hiring practices, termination of employment for union activities, compensation for injured employees, compensation for the unemployed, the protection of the pension interests of employees, and the protection of the health and safety of employees.

In Chapter 4, "Government Regulation," employment-related law under the National

Labor Relations Act and Title VII of the Civil Rights Act was presented. Sections 6 and 7 of Chapter 4 should be reviewed before studying this chapter.

A. THE EMPLOYMENT RELATIONSHIP

The relationship of an employer and an employee exists when, pursuant to an express or implied agreement of the parties, one person, the **employee**, undertakes to perform services or to do work under the direction and control of another, the **employer**, for compensation. In the older cases this relationship was called the master-servant relationship.

1. Nature of Relationship

An employee without agency authority is hired only to work under the control of the employer. An employee differs from (a) an agent, who is to negotiate or make contracts with third persons on behalf of and under the control of a principal, and from (b) an independent contractor, who is to perform a contract independent of, or free from, control by the other party.[1]

2. Creation of Employment Relationship

The relationship of employer and employee can be created only with the consent of both parties. Generally, the agreement of the parties is a contract. It is therefore subject to all of the principles applicable to contracts. The contract will ordinarily be express. It may be implied, as when the employer accepts the rendering of services that a reasonable person would recognize as being rendered with the expectation of receiving compensation.

(a) INDIVIDUAL EMPLOYMENT CONTRACTS. As in contracts generally, both parties must assent to the terms of the employment contract. Subject to statutory restrictions, the parties are free to make a contract on any terms they wish. Historically, wages constituted the sole reward of labor. Today, additional benefits are usually granted employees, either by virtue of the contract of employment or by a federal or state statutory provision.

(b) COLLECTIVE BARGAINING CONTRACTS. Collective bargaining contracts govern the rights and obligations of employers and employees in many private and public sector employment relations. Under collective bargaining, representatives of the employees bargain with a single employer or a group of employers for an agreement on wages, hours, and working conditions for the employees. The agreement worked out by the representatives of the employees, usually union officials, is generally subject to a ratification vote by the employees. Terms usually found in collective bargaining contracts are: (1) identification of the work belonging exclusively to designated classes of employees; (2) wage and benefits clauses; (3) promotion and layoff clauses, which are generally tied in part to seniority; (4) a management's rights clause; and (5) a grievance procedure. A grievance procedure provides a means by which persons contending that the contract was violated or that they were disciplined or discharged without just cause may ultimately have their cases decided by impartial labor arbitrators.

When there is a collective bargaining contract, the "contract of employment" in effect consists of two contracts. One is the collective bargaining contract made by the employees' representative with the employer. The other is the individual employment contract made by each employee with the employer. Although the individual contracts are distinct, they must conform to the basic plan or terms established by the collective bargaining contract. Examples of two-contract employment situations are those involving professional athletes and those involving actors and writers working in the entertainment industries.

3. Duration and Termination of Employment Contract

In many instances the employment contract

---

[1]   Bill Rivers Trailers Inc. v Miller (Fla App) 489 So 2d 1139 (1986).

does not state any time or duration. In such a case it may be terminated at any time by either party. In contrast, the employment contract may expressly state that it shall last for a specified period of time, as a contract to work as general manager for five years. In some instances, a definite duration may be implied by the circumstances.

Ordinarily, a contract of employment may be terminated in the same manner as any other contract. If it is to run for a definite period of time, the employer cannot terminate the contract at an earlier date without justification for so doing. If the employment contract does not have a definite duration, it is terminable at will. Under the **employment-at-will doctrine** the employer has historically been allowed to terminate the employment contract at any time for any reason or for no reason.[2] Recent decisions, and in some in-

stances statutes, have changed the rule in numerous states by limiting the power of the employer to discharge the employee.

Court decisions in a majority of jurisdictions have carved out exceptions to the employment-at-will doctrine when the discharge violates an established public policy, such as discharging an employee in retaliation for insisting that the employer comply with the state's food and drug act[3] or for filing a workers' compensation claim.[4]

The *Del Mar* case illustrates an application of the public policy exception to the employment-at-will doctrine.

---

[2]   Elder v Ivey, 171 Ga App 496, 320 SE2d 217 (1984).

[3]   Sheets v Teddy's Frosted Foods, 179 Conn 471, 427 A2d 385 (1980).
[4]   Peru Daily Tribune v Shuler (Ind App) 544 NE2d 560 (1989); Niblo v Parr Mfg. Inc. (Iowa) 445 NW2d 351 (1989).

JOHNSTON v DEL MAR DISTRIBUTING CO. INC.
(Tex Civ App) 776 SW2d 768 (1989)

Nancy Johnston was employed by Del Mar Distributing Co. She was required to prepare shipping documents for goods being shipped from Del Mar's Corpus Christi warehouse to other Texas cities. Del Mar required her to package a semi-automatic weapon for delivery to a grocery store in Brownsville, Texas and to label the package "fishing gear." Concerned that her actions might be in violation of a federal regulation or law, she sought the advice of the federal Bureau of Alcohol, Tobacco & Firearms (Bureau). Soon after Del Mar discovered that Johnston had contacted the Bureau, her employment was terminated. She brought suit for wrongful discharge. Del Mar contended that since Johnston's employment was for an indefinite period of time, she was an employee at will, and it therefore had the absolute right to terminate her for any reason or no reason at all. From a judgment for Del Mar, Johnston appealed.

BENAVIDES, J. . . . In 1888, the Texas Supreme Court first enunciated the employment-at-will doctrine in the case of *Eastline & R.R.R. Co. v Scott*. The Texas Supreme Court held that absent a specific contractual provision to the contrary, either the employer or the employee may terminate their relationship at any time, for any reason. . . .

Today, the absolute employment-at-will doctrine is increasingly seen as a "relic of early industrial times" and a "harsh anachronism." *Sabine Pilot Service, Inc. v. Hauck*, 687 S.W.2d 733, 735 (Tex. 1985) (Kilgarlin, J., concurring). . . .

On appeal, appellant alleges that her petition did state a cause of action pursuant to the public policy exception announced in *Sabine Pilot*. In her brief, appellant contends that since Texas law currently provides that an employee has a cause of action when she is fired for refusing to perform an illegal act, it necessarily follows that an employee states a cause of action where she alleges that she is fired for simply inquiring into whether or not she is committing illegal acts. To hold otherwise, she argues, would have a chilling effect on the public policy exception announced in *Sabine Pilot*. We agree.

It is implicit that in order to refuse to do an illegal act, an employee must either know or suspect that the requested act is illegal. In some cases it will be patently obvious that the act is illegal (murder, robbery, theft, etc.); however, in other cases it may not be so apparent. Since ignorance of the law is no defense to a criminal prosecution, it is reasonable to expect that if an employee has a good faith belief that a required act might be illegal, she will try to find out whether the act is in fact illegal prior to deciding what course of action to take. If an employer is allowed to terminate the employee at this point, the public policy exception announced in *Sabine Pilot* would have little or no effect. To hold otherwise would force an employee, who suspects that a requested act might be illegal, to: (1) subject herself to possible discharge if she attempts to find out if the act is in fact illegal; or (2) remain ignorant, perform the act and, if it turns out to be illegal, face possible criminal sanctions.

We hold that since the law recognizes that it is against public policy to allow an employer to coerce its employee to commit a criminal act in furtherance of its own interest, then it is necessarily inferred that the same public policy prohibits the discharge of an employee who in good faith attempts to find out if the act is illegal. It is important to note that we are not creating a new exception to the employment-at-will doctrine. . . . Rather, we are merely enforcing the narrow public policy exception which was created in *Sabine Pilot*.

Therefore, we find the *Sabine Pilot* exception necessarily covers a situation where an employee has a good faith belief that her employer has requested her to perform an act which may subject her to criminal penalties. Public policy demands that she be allowed to investigate into whether such actions are legal so that she can determine what course of action to take (i.e., whether or not to perform the act).

Furthermore, it is the opinion of this Court, that the question of whether or not the requested act was in fact illegal is irrelevant to the determination of this case. We hold that where a plaintiff's employment is terminated for attempting to find out from a regulatory agency if a requested act is illegal, it is not necessary to prove that the requested act was in fact illegal. A plaintiff must, however, establish that she had a good faith belief that the requested act might be illegal, and that such belief was reasonable. Accordingly, we sustain appellant's third and fourth points of error. . . .

[Reversed and remanded]

QUESTIONS

1. Does an employee have a cause of action when fired for refusing to perform an illegal act?
2. Does an employee have a cause of action when fired for attempting to find out from a federal agency if a certain act is illegal?
3. Must the employee prove that the requested act is in fact illegal in order to recover damages for wrongful discharge?
4. Give your opinion why the absolute employment-at-will doctrine is seen as a "harsh anachronism."

The obligation to act in good faith and deal fairly has been held by some courts to bar the employer's terminating an at-will contract when this is done to benefit the employer financially at the expense of the employee. Examples are terminating an employee to save the payment of commissions or terminating an employee to save the payment of pension benefits.[5]

Courts may construe employers' statements concerning continued employment as a part of the employment contract. If so, good cause would then be required for the discharge of an at-will employee. Also, written personnel policies used as guidelines for the employer's supervisors have been interpreted as being contractual provisions. These policies have thus been held to restrict the employer's right to discharge at-will employees without proof of good or just cause.[6] Moreover, employee handbooks that provide for "proper notice and investigation" before termination may bar employers from terminating employees without providing such notice and an investigation.[7]

Some courts still follow the common law at-will rule because they believe that a court should not rewrite the contract of the parties to provide employee protection that was never intended. Some courts favor the view limiting the employer from making an at-will discharge but will not adopt such a rule by decision as it is felt that such a significant change should be made (if at all) by the legislature.[8]

If an employment contract provides that an employee can be fired only for "good cause" or "just cause," a lesser standard for discharge will not be allowed by a court.

(a) FEDERAL LAWS. As set forth in Chapter 4, the National Labor Relations Act prohibits dismissal for union activities. Title VII of the Civil Rights Act of 1964, as amended, prohibits terminating employment for a reason amounting to discrimination because of race, color, sex, religion, or national origin. Sexual harassment is also prohibited by Title VII. The Equal Pay Act provides for equal pay for men and women doing equal work. The Age Discrimination in Employment Act protects certain employees from discrimination and discharge based on age.[9] The Rehabilitation Act and the Americans with Disabilities Act protect disabled workers against discrimination.

(1) Sexual Harassment. Quid pro quo sexual harassment involves supervisors seeking sexual favors from their subordinates in return for job benefits such as continued employment, promotion, a raise, or a favorable performance evaluation.[10] In such a case, when a supervisor's actions affect job benefits, Title VII's prohibition against sex discrimination has been violated. The employer is then liable to the employee for lost wages because of the supervisor's misconduct.

A second form of sexual harassment is the so-called hostile working environment harassment. With this type of harassment an employee's economic benefits have not been affected by the supervisor's conduct, but the supervisor's sexually harassing conduct has nevertheless caused anxiety and "poisoned" the work environment. Such conduct may include unwelcome sexual flirtation, propositions, or other abuse of a sexual nature, including the use of degrading words or the display of sexually suggestive pictures. Although no compensatory or punitive damages are available for so-called pure hostile environment cases, an injunction against such conduct can be obtained and attorney's fees awarded. Moreover, if such conduct drives

[5]   Metcalf v Intermountain Gas Co. (Idaho) 778 P2d 744 (1989).
[6]   Bratton v Menard, Inc. (Minn App) 438 NW2d 116 (1989).
[7]   Duldulao v St. Mary Nazareth Hospital Center, 115 Ill 2d 482, 106 Ill Dec 8, 505 NE2d 314 (1987). *But see* Bankey v Storer Broadcasting Co., 149 Mich 401, 443 NW2d 112 (1989).
[8]   D'avino v Trachtenburg, 149 App Div 2d 401, 539 NYS2d 755 (1989).

[9]   29 USC §§ 621–34.
[10]   EEOC *Guidelines* § 1604.11(f) define sexual harassment as follows: Unwelcome sexual advances, requests for sexual favors, and other verbal or physical conduct of a sexual nature constitute sexual harassment when (1) submission to such conduct is made either explicitly or implicitly a term or condition of an individual's employment, (2) submission to or rejection of such conduct has the purpose or effect of unreasonably interfering with an individual's work performance or creating an intimidating, hostile, or offensive working environment.

FIGURE 42-1   EMPLOYER POLICY AND PROCEDURE TO AVOID LIABILITY FOR "HOSTILE ENVIRONMENT" SEXUAL HARASSMENT

EMPLOYER PROCEDURE
A. DEVELOP AND IMPLEMENT AN EQUAL EMPLOYMENT POLICY THAT SPECIFICALLY INCLUDES SEXUAL HARASSMENT AS A PROHIBITED ACTIVITY FOR WHICH DISCIPLINE UP TO AND INCLUDING DISCHARGE WILL BE IMPOSED.   B. DESIGNATE A RESPONSIBLE SENIOR OFFICIAL TO WHOM COMPLAINTS OF SEXUAL HARASSMENT CAN BE MADE. AVOID ANY PROCEDURE THAT REQUIRES AN EMPLOYEE TO FIRST COMPLAIN TO THE EMPLOYEE'S SUPERVISOR, SINCE THAT INDIVIDUAL MAY BE THE OFFENDING PERSON.   C. INVESTIGATE ALL COMPLAINTS THOROUGHLY AND EXPEDITIOUSLY.   D. IF A COMPLAINT HAS MERIT, THE EMPLOYER SHOULD IMPOSE APPROPRIATE AND CONSISTENT DISCIPLINE, DEPENDING UPON THE SERIOUSNESS OF THE OFFENSE.

the employee to quit the job, the employer may be responsible for the economic losses caused the employee.[11]

An employer is liable for the sexual harassment caused its employees by co-workers or its customers only when it fails to take remedial action after being informed of the misconduct. Employers may avoid liability for "hostile environment" sexual harassment by affirmatively raising the subject with all of the employees, expressing strong disapproval of such conduct, advising employees how to inform it of instances of sexual harassment, and taking disciplinary action against wrongdoers.

(2) Equal Pay Act. The Equal Pay Act prohibits employers from paying employees of one sex lower wages than the rate paid employees of the opposite sex for equal work or substantially equal work in the same establishment, on jobs that require substantially equal skill, effort, and responsibility and that are performed under similar working conditions.[12] The Equal Pay Act does not prohibit all variations in wage rates paid men and women, but only those variations based solely on sex. The Act sets forth four exceptions. Variances in wages are allowed pursuant to (1) a seniority system, (2) a merit system, (3) a system that measures earnings by quantity or quality of production, or (4) a differential based on any factor other than sex.

(3) Age Discrimination. The Age Discrimination in Employment Act (ADEA) forbids discrimination by employers, unions, and employment agencies against men and women over 40 years of age.[13] The ADEA prohibits mandatory retirement for age.[14]

(4) Discrimination Against Disabled Workers. Some 43 million people have one or more physical or mental disabilities. Some impairments are obvious, such as paraplegia or blindness. Others may not be readily noticeable, such as heart disease, high blood pressure, and diabetes. In some cases, persons have recovered from their disabilities but have encountered job discrimination because of their past medical records. Cancer and mental or emotional disorders are examples of

---

[11]   Meritor Savings Bank v Vinson, 477 US 57 (1986).
[12]   29 USC § 206(d)(1).

[13]   29 USC § 623.
[14]   PL 99-592 "Age Discrimination in Employment Act of 1986," 29 USC § 621. See the Act for exceptions.

past medical conditions that may be associated with job discrimination.

The right of disabled persons to enjoy equal employment opportunities was established on the federal level with the enactment of the Rehabilitation Act of 1973.[15] Although not designed specifically as an employment discrimination measure, but rather as a comprehensive plan to meet many of the needs of the disabled, the Act contains three sections that provide guarantees against discrimination in employment. Section 501 is applicable in the federal government itself; Section 503 applies to federal contractors; and Section 504 applies to the recipients of federal funds.

The Americans With Disabilities Act[16] extends protection beyond the federal level. This 1990 Act prohibits all private employers with 15 or more employees from discriminating against disabled individuals, who, with or without reasonable accommodations are qualified to perform the essential functions of the job. Enforcement agencies are required to coordinate and apply consistent standards in administering the Rehabilitation Act and the Disabilities Act.

An employer may make pre-employment inquiries into the ability of a job applicant to perform job-related functions. However, an employer is prohibited from making inquiries as to whether the applicant is an individual with a disability.

A person with a contagious disease may be protected under the Acts. The courts will determine if the employee can work based on individualized medical judgments about (1) how the disease is transmitted, (2) the duration of the risk, (3) the severity of the risk, (4) the probability that the disease will be transmitted, and (5) whether the individual is otherwise qualified.

AIDS victims are within the protection of both Acts and must be treated just as anyone else with a disability.[17]

(b) JUSTIFIABLE DISCHARGE. An employer may be justified in discharging an employee because of the employee's (1) nonperformance of duties, (2) misrepresentation or fraud in obtaining the employment, (3) disobedience to proper directions, (4) disloyalty, (5) theft or other dishonesty, (6) possession or use of drugs or intoxicants, (7) misconduct, or (8) incompetence.

Employees generally have the right to lay off employees because of economic conditions, including a lack of work. Such actions are sometimes referred to as reductions in force or RIFs. However, employers must be very careful not to make layoffs based on age, for that is a violation of the ADEA.

In some states a "service letter" statute requires an employer on request to furnish a discharged employee with a letter stating the reason for the discharge.

(c) REMEDIES. An employee who has been wrongfully discharged may bring against the employer an action to recover (1) wages, (2) damages for breach of contract, or (3) damages representing the value of services already performed. In certain instances the employee may also bring (4) an action to compel the employer to specifically perform the employment contract or (5) a proceeding under federal or state labor relations or antidiscrimination statutes, seeking reinstatement with back pay and the reinstatement of full seniority rights.

4.   Duties of the Employee

The duties of an employee are determined primarily by the contract of employment with the employer. The law also implies certain obligations.

(a) SERVICES. Employees are under the duty to perform or hold themselves in readiness to perform such services as may be required by the contract of employment. If employees hold themselves in readiness to comply with their employer's directions, they have discharged this obligation. They do not forfeit the right to compensation because the employer has withheld directions and has thus kept them idle.

---

[15]   29 USC §§ 701–794.
[16]   PL 101-336, 42 USC §§ 12101–12117.
[17]   Chalk v U.S. District Court (CA9 Cal) 840 F2d 701 (1988).

Employees agree by implication to serve their employer honestly and faithfully. They also agree by implication to serve the employer exclusively during the hours of employment. The employee may do other work, however, if the time and nature of such other employment are not inconsistent with the duties owed to the first employer and if the contract of employment with the first employer does not contain any provision against it.

An employee must obey reasonable regulations and requirements adopted by the employer.

Employees imply by acceptance of a job that, in performing their duties, they will exercise due care and ordinary diligence, according to the nature of the work. When skill is required, employees need exercise only ordinary skill, unless they have held themselves out as possessing special skills.

(b) TRADE SECRETS. An employee may be given confidential trade secrets by the employer. In such a case the employee must not disclose such knowledge to others. An agreement by the employee to refrain from disclosing trade secrets is binding. Even in the absence of such an agreement an employee is prohibited from disclosing the trade secrets of the employer. If the employee violates this obligation, the employer may enjoin the use of the information by the employee and by any person to whom it is disclosed by the employee.[18]

Former employees who are competing with their former employer may be enjoined from using information about suppliers and customers that they obtained while employees, when such information is of vital importance to the employer's business. Such relief is denied if the information is not important or not secret.[19]

(c) INVENTIONS. In the absence of an express or implied agreement to the contrary, the inventions of an employee belong to the employee. This is true even though the employee used the time and property of the employer in the discovery. An exception exists if the employee was employed for the express purpose of inventing the things or processes that were discovered.

If the invention is discovered during working hours and with the employer's materials and equipment, the employer has the right, called a **shop right**, to use the invention without charge in the running of the employer's business. If the employee has obtained a patent for the invention, the employee must grant the employer a nonexclusive license to use the invention without the payment of any royalty. The shop right of the employer does not give the right to make and sell machines that embody the employee's invention; it only entitles the employer to use the invention without cost in the operation of the employer's plant.

In contrast, when an employee is employed to secure certain results from experiments to be conducted in the course of employment, the inventions so discovered belong to the employer. The grounds are that there is a trust relationship or that there is an implied agreement by the employee to make an assignment of the inventions to the employer.

5.   Rights of the Employee

The rights of an employee are determined primarily by the contract of employment. As in the case of duties, the law also implies certain rights.

(a) COMPENSATION. The rights of an employee with respect to compensation are governed in general by the same principles that apply to the compensation of an agent. In the absence of an agreement to the contrary, when an employee is discharged, whether for cause or not, the employer must pay wages down to the expiration of the last pay period.[20] The express terms of employment, the terms of collective bargaining contracts, or custom frequently provide for payment of wages for

---

[18]   Henry Hope X-Ray Products, Inc. v Marron Carrel, Inc. (CA9 Ariz) 674 F2d 1336 (1982).

[19]   Headquarters Buick-Nissan v Michael Oldsmobile, 149 App Div 2d 302, 539 NYS2d 355 (1989).

[20]   Alexander v Brown Builders Inc. (La App) 490 So 2d 653 (1986).

fractional terminal periods, and they may even require a severance pay equal to the compensation for a full period of employment. Provisions relating to deferred compensation under a profit sharing trust for employees are liberally construed in favor of employees.

When an employer fails to pay past-due wages because of procedural pitfalls created by the employer or because of negligence or bad faith, most states have wage payment and collection laws that allow workers to file lawsuits to recover their just compensation. These laws authorize the assessment of penalty wages and the payment of attorney fees for employees who are successful in suits for unpaid wages. However, where there is a justifiable dispute as to the amount of wages owed, the courts have declined to award penalties. In addition to hourly wages, payments due for vacations and certain bonuses are considered "wages" under the state statutes.[21]

In the *Garrison* case the claim was made that the employer was responsible for unpaid vacation "wages," plus penalty wages and attorney fees.

---

[21]   Knutson v Snyder Industries, Inc. 221 Neb 374, 436 NW2d 496 (1989).

GARRISON v BURGER KING CORP
(La App) 537 So 2d 834 (1989)

Diane Garrison started her employment with Burger King on October 6, 1978. She resigned from this employment as of July 30, 1987. When her final paycheck did not contain payment for her accumulated vacation benefits, she made a formal demand for this pay and thereafter initiated a lawsuit. Burger King defended that Garrison had not worked the necessary "service year" qualifying time. From a judgment for Garrison, Burger King appealed.

DUFRESNE, J. . . . From reviewing the record, Garrison had satisfied the employment requirements for vacation wages prior to her termination.

She had worked for Burger King over eight years and had completed forty-one weeks of employment the year of her resignation. Burger King's employee handbook and a posted notice entitled "Your Vacation Benefits" clearly state that Burger King's vacation policy is applicable to an employee who has worked 40 of the 52 weeks of the year. These same publications indicate that any employee who has worked for Burger King for five to fourteen years will earn three weeks of vacation pay. The vacation policy does not require time be actually taken off from work. Rather, it is called a "bonus, in the form of vacation pay."

The policy does not require that the employee still be employed on her anniversary date in order to receive the vacation pay. Garrison worked over 40 weeks during the year which began October 16, 1986 (her last anniversary date) until the date she resigned on July 30, 1987.

On the date of Garrison's termination, she was earning $6.05 per hour as a production leader and averaged 31.22 hours per week. Pursuant to Burger King's handbook vacation policy, Garrison was entitled to $566.64 in vacation wages at the time of her resignation.

Our review of the jurisprudence reveals that vacation pay is equivalent to wages for purposes of LSA-R.S. 23:631 . . . and once an employee's right to vacation benefits has vested, an employer cannot force forfeiture of this beneficial right. . . .

Burger King argues that before receiving vacation pay, a full "Service Year" must be completed and the employee must have worked 40 weeks of that service year, or still be employed on the employment anniversary date. However, we find no mention of the "Service Year" requirement in any of the literature distributed to the employees which is made part of this record. At best, the language of the subject handbook has sufficient ambiguity to confuse even a careful and skillful reader, thus must be construed against Burger King.

It is clear that a company policy can have no adverse effect on the requirement of prompt payment of earned wages upon termination of an employee. . . .

Because Burger King failed to accurately compensate Garrison in vacation wages, we must determine whether the conduct was in bad faith and were there any valid equitable defenses. . . .

There are no statutory provisions on what constitutes an equitable defense. Generally, when there is a justifiable dispute as to the amount of wages owed, the courts have declined to award penalties. . . .

Burger King's defense for non-payment of the vacation wages is based on an alleged policy requiring completion of a "service year." There is no evidence in the record which would support this position. The record is void of evidence showing that employees were given notice of the alleged "service year" policy. The trial court correctly decided that Burger King failed to establish a lawful defense for withholding Garrison's vacation wages.

When an employer is arbitrary or sets out procedural pitfalls for its employees or is merely negligent in failing to pay past-due wages, penalty wages have been assessed. . . .

Garrison had eight years of employment and properly made demand for just compensation. Burger King's conduct constituted an impermissible forfeiture of earned wages. Penalty wages were properly, but inaccurately assessed against Burger King. Accordingly, the judgment relative to penalty wages is amended as follows: Pursuant to LSA-R.S. 23:632, penalties are to be equal to 90 days wages. Garrison would be entitled to \$2,427.12 (\$6.05 × 31.22 hours × 12.85 weeks (90 days)) in penalty wages together with her vacation wages of \$566.64 for a principal amount of \$2,993.76, and legal interest.

The trial court awarded \$750.00 in attorney's fees and Burger King argues such an amount as abusive. We disagree. Attorney fees are mandatory whenever an employee is successful in a suit for unpaid wages. . . .

The purpose of LSA-R.S. 23:632 is to encourage workers to file lawsuits when they have been unlawfully denied just compensation and to motivate attorneys to handle such suits.

Considering the record, the issues and time involved, we find no error with the award of \$750.00 in attorney's fees.

Because a lawyer's time is his stock in trade, and recognizing that answering an appeal is time consuming and will cost an attorney the utilization of his resources, we shall add \$250.00 to the attorney's fees for a total amount of \$1,000.00.

For the above assigned reasons the judgment of the trial court is affirmed and amended. . . .

[Affirmed and amended]

(b) EMPLOYEE'S LIEN OR PREFER-ENCE. Most states protect by statute an employee's claim for compensation. Protection may be by either a lien or preference over other claimants of payment out of proceeds from the sale of the employer's property. These statutes vary widely in their terms. They are usually called **laborers'** or **mechanics' lien laws**. Sometimes the statutes limit their protection to workers of a particular class, such as plasterers or bricklayers. Compensation for the use of materials or machinery is ordinarily not protected by such statutes.

6.   Pension Plans and Federal Regulation

Many employers have established pension plans as post-retirement benefits to their employees. The Employees Retirement Income Security Act (ERISA)[22] was adopted in 1974 to provide protection for the pension interests of employees.

(a) FIDUCIARY STANDARDS AND REPORTING. Persons administering a pension fund must handle it so as to protect the interest of the employees. The fact that an employer contributed all or part of the money does not entitle the employer to use the fund as though it were still owned by the employer. Persons administering pension plans must make detailed reports to the Secretary of Labor.

(b) VESTING. *Vesting* takes place when the right of an employee to pension benefits becomes fixed so that it cannot be altered. Prior to ERISA many pension plans did not vest accrued benefits until 20 to 25 years of service by an employee. Thus, an employee who was forced to terminate service after 18 years would not receive any pension rights or benefits whatsoever. Under ERISA, employees' rights must be fully vested within five or seven years in accordance with the two vesting options available under the law.

In the past it was common for pension plans to contain "break in service" clauses, whereby employees who left their employment for a period longer than one year, for any reason other than an on-the-job injury, lost valuable pension eligibility rights. Under the Retirement Equity Act of 1984,[23] which was designed to provide greater pension equity for women, an individual can leave the work force for up to five consecutive years and still retain eligibility for pension benefits.

(c) FUNDING. ERISA requires that contributions be made by employers to their pension funds on a basis that is actuarially determined so that the pension fund will be large enough to make the payments that will be required of it. The Treasury Department is authorized to issue regulations, opinions, variances, and waivers pertaining to funding.

(d) TERMINATION INSURANCE. ERISA establishes an insurance plan to protect employees when the employer goes out of business. To provide this protection, the statute creates a Pension Benefit Guaranty Corporation (PBGC). In effect, this corporation guar-

[22]   PL 93-406, 88 Stat 829, 29 USC §§ 1001–1381. A number of subsequent acts have also affected private pensions, notably the Tax Equity and Fiscal Responsibility Act of 1982, the Tax Reform Act of 1984, and the Tax Reform Act of 1986.

[23]   PL 98-397, 29 USC § 1001.

antees that the employee will receive benefits, in much the same way as the Federal Deposit Insurance Corporation protects bank depositors. The PBGC is financed by small payments made by employers for every employee covered by a pension plan.

(e) ENFORCEMENT. ERISA authorizes the Secretary of Labor and employees to bring court actions to compel the observance of the statutory requirements.

7.   Attachment and Garnishment of Wages

It is generally provided that a creditor may require a third person who owes money to a debtor of the creditor to pay such an amount to the creditor to satisfy the creditor's claim against the debtor. That is, if *A* has a valid claim for $100 against *B*, and if *C* owes *B* $100, *A* can require *C* to pay the $100 to *A*, thereby satisfying both *C*'s debt to *B* and *B*'s debt to *A*. The necessary legal procedure generally requires the third person to pay the money into court or to the sheriff rather than directly to the original creditor. The original creditor may also, by this process, reach the debtor's tangible property that is in the custody or possession of a third person. This procedure is commonly called **attachment**, and the third person is called a **garnishee**.

Under the federal Truth in Lending Act (Title I of the Federal Consumer Credit Protection Act), only a certain portion of an employee's pay can be garnished. Ordinarily, the amount that may be garnished may not exceed (a) 25 percent of the employee's weekly take-home pay or (b) the amount by which the weekly take-home pay exceeds 30 times the federal minimum hourly wage, whichever is less.[24] The federal statute also prohibits an employer from discharging an employee because wages have been garnished for any one in-

debtedness. The federal statute does not prevent the discharge of an employee because of several garnishments based on different debts.

B.   UNEMPLOYMENT BENEFITS

Generally, when employees are without work through no fault of their own, they are eligible for unemployment compensation benefits.

8.   Unemployment Compensation

Unemployment compensation today is provided primarily through a federal-state system under the unemployment insurance provisions of the Social Security Act of 1935. All of the states have laws that provide similar benefits, and the state agencies are loosely coordinated under the federal Act. Agricultural employees, domestic employees, and state and local government employees are not covered by this federal-state system. Federal programs of unemployment compensation exist for federal civilian workers and former service personnel. A separate federal unemployment program applies to railroad workers.

9.   Benefits and Eligibility

The states are largely free to prescribe the amount and duration of benefits and the conditions required for eligibility. In most states the unemployed person must be available for placement in a similar job and be willing to take such employment at a comparable rate of pay. Full-time students generally have difficulty proving that they are "available" for work once they become unemployed. If an employee quits a job without cause or is fired for misconduct, the employee is ordinarily disqualified from receiving unemployment compensation benefits.

An employee's stealing property from an employer constitutes misconduct for which benefits will be denied. Moreover, an employee's refusal to participate in random drug testing has been found to constitute misconduct

---

[24]   Consumer Credit Protection Act § 303. Under the Uniform Consumer Credit Code, where adopted, this second alternative has been increased to 40 times the federal hourly minimum pay. UCCC § 5.105(2)(b). Prejudgment attachment of wages without notice and hearing is invalid. Sniadach v Family Finance Corp. 395 US 337 (1969).

for which benefits can be denied.[25] Also, an employee's refusal to complete the aftercare portion of an alcohol treatment program has been found to be misconduct connected with work disqualifying the employee from benefits.[26]

C.   EMPLOYEE'S HEALTH AND SAFETY

The Occupational Safety and Health Act of 1970 (OSHA) was passed in order to assure every worker, so far as possible, safe and healthful working conditions and to preserve the country's human resources.[27] OSHA provides for (a) establishing safety and health standards and (b) effective enforcement of these standards and the other employer duties required by OSHA.

10.   Standards

The Secretary of Labor has been granted broad authority under OSHA to promulgate occupational safety and health standards. Except in emergency situations, public hearings and publication in the *Federal Register* are required before the Secretary can issue a new standard. Thereafter, any person adversely affected may challenge the validity of the standard in a U.S. court of appeals. The Secretary's standards will be upheld if they are reasonable and supported by substantial evidence. However, the Secretary does not have unbridled discretion to adopt costly standards to create an absolutely risk-free work place. Rather, the Secretary must demonstrate a need for a new standard by showing that it is reasonably necessary to protect employees against a "significant risk" of material health impairment.[28] The cost of compliance with new standards may run into billions of dollars. The Secretary is not required to do a cost-

benefit analysis for a new standard. However, the Secretary must show that the standard is economically feasible.[29]

11.   Employer Duties

Employers have a "general duty" to furnish to each employee a place of employment that is free from recognized hazards that are likely to cause death or serious physical injuries.[30]

Employers are required by OSHA to maintain records of occupational illness and injuries if they result in death, loss of consciousness, medical treatment other than first aid, or one or more lost workdays. Such records have proven to be a valuable aid in recognizing areas of risk. They have been especially helpful in identifying the presence of occupational illnesses.

12.   Enforcement

The Occupational Safety and Health Administration (also identified as OSHA), an agency within the Department of Labor, is the primary administrative agency under the Act. OSHA has authority to conduct inspections and to seek enforcement action where there has been noncompliance. Work site inspections are conducted when employer records indicate incidents involving fatalities or serious injuries. Such inspections may also result from employee complaints. Employees making such complaints are protected by the Act from possible employer retaliation.[31] Employers have the right to require that an OSHA inspector secure a warrant prior to inspection of the employer's plant.

If OSHA issues a citation against an employer, the employer may challenge it before the Occupational Safety and Health Review Commission. The Commission is fully independent of OSHA; its sole function is to adjudicate contested enforcement actions. Judicial review of a Commission ruling is obtained before a U.S. court of appeals.

[25]   Chiles Offshore, Inc. v Administrator, DES (La App) 551 So 2d 849 (1989).
[26]   Henson v Employment Security Department, 113 Wash 2d 374, 779 P2d 715 (1989).
[27]   29 USC §§ 651 et seq.
[28]   Industrial Union Department, AFL-CIO v American Petroleum Institute, 448 US 607 (1980).

[29]   American Textile Manufacturers Institute v Donovan, 452 US 490 (1981).
[30]   29 USC § 654(a). UAW v General Dynamics Land Systems Division (CA Dist Col) 815 F2d 1570 (1987).
[31]   29 USC § 660(C).

The Secretary of Labor is empowered to seek injunctive and other appropriate relief in a U.S. district court against an employer who discriminates against an employee for testifying or exercising "any right" under the Act. In the *Whirlpool* case the court was faced with the problems of whether two employees were exercising any right under the Act when they refused to perform work that they considered dangerous and whether the employer's disciplinary action against the employees was discriminatory.

WHIRLPOOL CORPORATION v MARSHALL
445 US 1 (1980)

Virgil Deemer and Thomas Cornwell, employees at the Whirlpool Corporation's plant in Marion, Ohio, refused to comply with a supervisor's order that they perform maintenance work on certain mesh screens located some 20 feet above the plant floor. Twelve days before this incident a fellow employee had fallen to his death from the screens. After the refusal, the men were ordered to punch out and leave the plant. They were not paid for the remaining six hours of their shift. Written reprimands for insubordination were placed in their employment files. Section II(C)(1) of the Occupational Safety and Health Act provides that no employer shall discharge or in any manner discriminate against an employee because the employee filed a complaint with OSHA, or testified in any OSHA proceeding, or exercised any right afforded by the Act. A regulation issued by the Secretary of Labor under the Act provides that an employee who, with no reasonable alternative, refuses in good faith to be exposed to a dangerous condition will be protected against subsequent discrimination. The Secretary of Labor filed suit in U.S. district court against Whirlpool, contending that Whirlpool's actions against Deemer and Cornwell constituted "discrimination" under the Secretary's regulation and Section II(C)(1) of the Act. Whirlpool contended that the regulation encouraged workers to engage in "self-help" and unlawfully permitted a "strike with pay." The court held that the Secretary's regulation was inconsistent with the Act and denied relief. The U.S. court of appeals reversed this decision, and Whirlpool appealed.

STEWART, J. . . . On June 28, 1974, a maintenance employee fell to his death through the guard screen in an area where the newer, stronger mesh had not yet been installed. Following this incident, the petitioner effectuated some repairs and issued an order strictly forbidding maintenance employees from stepping on either the screens or the angle-iron supporting structure. An alternative but somewhat more cumbersome and less satisfactory method was developed for removing objects from the screen. This procedure required employees to stand on power raised mobile platforms and use hooks to recover the material.

On July 7, 1974, two of the petitioner's maintenance employees, Virgil Deemer and Thomas Cornwell, met with the plant maintenance superintendent to voice their concern about the safety of the screen. The superintendent disagreed with their view, but permitted the two men to inspect the screen with their foreman and to point out dangerous areas needing repair. Unsatisfied with the petitioner's response to the results of this inspection, Deemer and Cornwell met on July 9 with the plant safety director. At that meeting, they requested the name, address, and telephone number of a representative of the local office of the Occupational Safety and Health Administration (OSHA). Although the safety director told the men that they "had better stop and think about what [they] were doing," he furnished the men with the information they requested. Later that same day, Deemer contacted an official of the regional OSHA office and discussed the guard screen.

The next day, Deemer and Cornwell reported for the night shift at 10:45 p.m. Their foreman, after himself walking on some of the angle-iron frames, directed the two men to perform their usual maintenance duties on a section of the old screen. Claiming that the screen was unsafe, they refused to carry out this directive. The foreman then sent them to the personnel office, where they were ordered to punch out without working or being paid for the remaining six hours of the shift. The two men subsequently received written reprimands, which were placed in their employment files. . . .

[C]ircumstances may sometimes exist in which the employee justifiably believes that the express statutory arrangement [OSHA] does not sufficiently protect him from death or serious injury. Such circumstances will probably not often occur, but such a situation may arise when (1) the employee is ordered by his employer to work under conditions that the employee reasonably believes pose an imminent risk of death or serious bodily injury, and (2) the employee has reason to believe that there is not sufficient time or opportunity either to seek effective redress from his employer or to apprise OSHA of the danger.

Nothing in the Act suggests that those few employees who have to face this dilemma must rely exclusively on the remedies expressly set forth in the Act at the risk of their own safety. But nothing in the Act explicitly provides otherwise. Against this background of legislative silence, the Secretary has exercised his rulemaking power under 29 USC § 657(g)(2) and has determined that, when an employee in good faith finds himself in such a predicament, he may refuse to expose himself to the dangerous condition, without being subjected to "subsequent discrimination" by the employer. . . .

The regulation clearly conforms to the fundamental objective of the Act—to prevent occupational deaths and serious injuries. The Act, in its preamble, declares that its purpose and policy is "to assure so far as possible every working man and woman in the Nation safe and healthful working conditions and to *preserve* our human resources." 29 USC § 651(b). (Emphasis added.)

To accomplish this basic purpose, the legislation's remedial orientation is prophylactic in nature. The Act does not wait for an employee to die or become injured. It authorizes the promulgation of health and safety standards and the issuance of citations in the hope that these will act to prevent deaths or injuries from ever occurring. It would seem anomalous to construe an Act so directed and constructed as prohibiting an employee, with no other reasonable alternative, the freedom to withdraw from a workplace environment that he reasonably believes is highly dangerous.

Moreover, the Secretary's regulation can be viewed as an appropriate aid to the full effectuation of the Act's "general duty" clause. That clause provides that "[e]ach employer . . . shall furnish to each of his employees employment and a place of employment which are free from recognized hazards that are causing or are likely to cause death or serious physical harm to his employees." 29 USC § 654(a)(1). As the legislative history of this provision reflects, it was intended itself to deter the occurrence of occupational deaths and serious injuries by placing on employers a mandatory obligation independent of the specific health and safety standards to be promulgated by the Secretary. Since OSHA inspectors cannot be present around the clock in every workplace, the Secretary's regulation ensures that employees will in all circumstances enjoy the rights afforded them by the "general duty" clause.

[The Court next considered and rejected Whirlpool's contention that the legislative history is contrary to the Secretary's regulation. The Court explained its view as follows:]

When it rejected the "strike with pay" concept, therefore, Congress very clearly meant to reject a law unconditionally imposing upon employers an obligation to continue to pay their employees their regular pay checks when they absented themselves from work for reasons of safety. But the regulation at issue here does not require employers to pay workers who refuse to perform their assigned tasks in the face of imminent danger. It simply provides that in such cases the employer may not "discriminate" against the employees involved. An employer "discriminates" against an employee only when he treats that employee less favorably than he treats others similarly situated.

[In a footnote to the decision, the Court applied the above principles to the situation of Deemer and Cornwell. The Court stated that the placing of reprimands in their personnel files clearly constituted discrimination. The Court stated that whether the denial of work and pay for the six-hour period also constituted discrimination was a question not before the Court.]

[Judgment of Court of Appeals affirmed]

QUESTIONS

1. Was the order of the foreman to perform maintenance duties on the old section of the screen contrary to the company's directive not to step on screens or the angle-iron supporting the structure?
2. Does the Secretary of Labor's regulation aid in giving full effect to OSHA's "general duty" clause?
3. Does the Secretary of Labor's regulation require the employer to pay employees who refuse to perform work in the face of imminent danger?

13.   State "Right to Know" Legislation

Laws that guarantee individual workers the "right to know" if there are hazardous substances in their workplaces have been enacted by many states in recent years. These laws commonly require an employer to make known to an employee's physician the chemical composition of certain substances in the workplace, in connection with the diagnosis and treatment of an employee by the physician. Further, local fire and public health officials, as well as local neighborhood residents, are granted the right to know if local employers are working with hazardous substances that could pose health or safety problems.

D.   COMPENSATION FOR EMPLOYEE'S INJURIES

For most kinds of employment, workers' compensation statutes govern compensation for injuries.[32] These statutes provide that the injured employee is entitled to compensation for accidents occurring in the course of employment from a risk involved in that employment.

---

[32]   Every state has some form of workers' compensation legislation, though the statutes vary widely from state to state. Some statutes apply only to employees engaged in manual or mechanical labor; others extend coverage to virtually all employees.

14. Common Law Status of Employer

In some employment situations the common law principles apply. This is so because workers' compensation statutes commonly do not apply to employers with fewer than a prescribed minimum number of employees or to agricultural, domestic, or casual employment. It is therefore necessary to consider the duties and defenses of employers apart from workers' compensation statutes.

(a) DUTIES. The employer is under the common law duty to furnish an employee with a reasonably safe place in which to work, reasonably safe tools and appliances, and a sufficient number of competent fellow employees for the work involved. The employer is also under the common law duty to warn the employee of any unusual dangers peculiar to the employer's business.

(b) DEFENSES. At common law the employer is not liable to an injured employee if the employee is harmed by the act of a fellow employee. Likewise, an employer is not liable at common law to an employee harmed by an ordinary hazard of the work, because the employee assumed such risks. If the employee is guilty of contributory negligence, regardless of the employer's negligence, the employer is not liable to an injured employee at common law.

15. Statutory Changes

The rising incidence of industrial accidents resulting from the increasing use of more powerful machinery and the growth of the industrial labor population led to a demand for statutory modification of common law rules relating to liability of employers for industrial accidents.

(a) MODIFICATION OF EMPLOYER'S COMMON LAW DEFENSES. One kind of change by statute was to modify the defenses that an employer could assert when sued by an employee for damages. For example, under the Federal Employer's Liability Act (FELA), which covers railroad workers, the injured employee must still bring an action in court and prove the negligence of the employer or other employees. However, the burden of proving the case is made lighter by limitations on employers' defenses. Under FELA, contributory negligence is a defense only in mitigation of damages; assumption of the risk is not a defense.[33]

(b) WORKERS' COMPENSATION. A more sweeping development was made by the adoption of workers' compensation statutes in every state. In addition, civil employees of the U.S. government are covered by the Federal Employees' Compensation Act. When an employee is covered by a workers' compensation statute, and when the injury is job-connected, the employee's remedy is limited to that provided in the workers' compensation statute.[34]

The *Halliman* case illustrates the exclusivity of the Workers' Compensation Act remedy.

---

[33]   Federal Employer's Liability Act, 45 USC §§ 1 et seq.
[34]   Arrow Uniform Rental, Inc. v Suter (Ind App) 545 NE2d 832 (1989).

HALLIMAN v LOS ANGELES UNIFIED SCHOOL DISTRICT
163 Cal App 3d 46, 209 Cal Rptr 175 (1984)

Robert Halliman was employed as a teacher by the Los Angeles Unified School District at Milliken Junior High School. On November 4, 1982, a minor student, Louis "R.," intentionally threw a rock at him, hitting him on the head and seriously injuring him. The same student had committed previous assaults on the school grounds, including an assault earlier that very day. Halliman and his wife brought suit against the Los Angeles Unified School District and the student's parents, seeking damages. Halliman contended that the defendants had the power and ability to prevent the student's conduct by appropriate disciplinary action but did not do so, ignoring their duty to protect students and teachers. The school district filed a motion for a summary judgment on the ground that the Workers' Compensation Act provided the exclusive remedy for Halliman's injury. From a summary judgment in favor of the school district, Halliman appealed.

ARGVELLES, A. J.... In this appeal from a judgment favoring a school district, we are called upon to determine whether workers' compensation is the exclusive remedy for a teacher's injuries caused by a student's unprovoked assault while the teacher is acting within the scope of his employment....

We find . . . that plaintiffs have failed to state facts negating application of the exclusive remedy provision of the workers' compensation laws in their complaint....

We disagree with plaintiffs' contention that *Meyer v. Graphic Arts International Union* (1979) 88 Cal. App. 3d 176, 151 Cal. Rptr. 597, is dispositive of the issue in their favor. *Meyer* involved injury by a coemployee of plaintiff, and there had been reported prior acts of aggression by that person against the complaining employee followed by the employer's ratification or acquiescence in failing to discipline, censure, criticize, suspend or discharge the offending coemployee. Here, as defendant correctly points out, the assailant was not a coemployee but a student for whom the plaintiff teacher, among other employees at the school, was responsible. The record before us discloses no reports of prior assaults upon plaintiff teacher by the same student. Additionally, the student's school records indicated that he had, indeed, been previously suspended and otherwise disciplined for prior assaults.

In *Adler v. Los Angeles Unified School Dist.* (1979) 98 Cal. App. 3d 280, 288, 159 Cal. Rptr. 528, though the case was decided on other grounds, the court presumed that where a teacher was injured in a classroom attack by a student, the available workers' compensation remedy barred a civil lawsuit for damages against the employer by virtue of Labor Code section 3601. Under the facts of this case, we so hold.

Plaintiffs argue that a student in this context is akin to an employer's agent or a coemployee who is "under the control" of the employer; and, therefore, the school district "employer" comes within the statutory exception to the exclusive remedy provisions of the workers' compensation laws for intentional acts of agents and coemployees. But, teacher and student are not equals, standing shoulder to shoulder in the classroom or on the playground, with the same status, rights, duties, responsibilities, maturity, judgment, knowledge and skill. If an analogy is to be drawn, a more appropriate one would liken the student to raw material which must be wrought by the employee into a finished product.

Thus, we find it helpful in addressing plaintiff's contentions to refer to those cases where the alleged intentional misconduct of the employer does not go beyond failure to assure a safe working environment. The California Supreme Court in *Johns-Manville Products Corp. v. Superior Court* (1980) 27 Cal. 3d 465, 165 Cal. Rptr. 858, 612 P.2d 948, reviewed cases where the employer concealed inherent dangers in the material its employees were required to handle, or made false representations in that regard, or allowed an employee to use a machine without proper instruction. Workers' compensation was held to be the exclusive remedy for any injuries thus suffered. The Supreme Court concluded that the workers' compensation laws provided "the sole remedy for additional compensation against an employer whose employee is injured in the first instance as the result of a deliberate failure to assure that the physical environment of the work place is safe."

The facts of the present case do not justify a departure from such precedent. [Judgment affirmed]

QUESTIONS

1. State the issue before the court.
2. Why did the Hallimans bring an action for damages in a court of law when Halliman was clearly entitled to benefits under the workers' compensation law?
3. When an employee is injured as a result of an employer's deliberate failure to provide a safe workplace, may the employee sue the employer for damages in a court of law?
4. Is there an exception to the exclusive remedy provisions of the workers' compensation laws for intentional acts of agents or "coemployees"?

For injuries arising within the course of the employee's work from a risk involved in that work, the workers' compensation statutes usually provide: (1) immediate medical benefits; (2) prompt periodic wage replacement, very often computed as a percentage of weekly wages (ranging from 50 percent to 80 percent of the injured employee's wage) for a specified number of weeks; and (3) a death benefit of a limited amount. In such cases compensation is paid without regard to whether the employer or the employee was negligent. However, no compensation is generally allowed for a willful, self-inflicted injury or one sustained while intoxicated.

There has been a gradual widening of the workers' compensation statutes, so compensation today is generally recoverable for both accident-inflicted injuries and occupational diseases. In some states compensation for occupational diseases is limited to those named in the statute, such as silicosis, lead poisoning, or injury to health from radioactivity. In other states any disease arising from an occupation is compensable.

Workers' compensation proceedings are brought before a special administrative agency or workers' compensation board. In contrast, a common law action for damages or an action for damages under an employer's liability statute is brought in a court of law.

E.   EMPLOYER-RELATED IMMIGRATION LAWS

The Immigration and Naturalization Act (INA), the Immigration Reform and Control Act of 1986 (IRCA), and the Immigration Act of 1990[35] are the principal employer-related immigration laws.

16.   Immigration Reform

IRCA[36] granted amnesty to illegal aliens who had lived in the United States since before January 1, 1982. IRCA also established a system for the legalization of the residency of certain foreign, seasonal agricultural workers (SAWs). IRCA sets forth criminal and civil penalties against employers who knowingly hire illegal aliens. The Immigration Marriage Fraud Amendments[37] to the INA became law in 1986, allowing aliens married to U.S. citi-

---

[35]   PL 101-649, 8 USC § 1101.
[36]   PL 99-603, also known as the Simpson-Rodino Act, 8 USC § 1101.
[37]   PL 99-639, 8 USC § 1186.

zens conditional permanent residence status. This status is reviewable at the end of a two-year period, at which time the condition will be lifted if the marriage has not been legally terminated. Criminal penalties of up to five years in prison and fines of up to $250,000 may be applied to those who knowingly arrange or participate in fraudulent marriage for immigration benefits.

17. Employer Sanctions and Verification Responsibilities

The availability of jobs and higher pay scales have been principal factors drawing illegal immigrants to the United States. The premise on which the IRCA is structured is that if employer sanctions are applied, and if employers are enlisted to help enforce the immigration laws, employment opportunities for illegal immigrants will be drastically diminished, and so will illegal immigration.

(a) EMPLOYER SANCTIONS. Section 101 of the IRCA makes it illegal to hire, recruit, or hire for a fee unauthorized aliens. The law also makes it illegal for an employer to employ a person in the United States if the employer knows that the person is (or has become) an unauthorized alien with respect to employment. An employer who violates the law is subject to pay civil penalties of $250 to $2,000 for each unauthorized alien. This penalty is increased to $2,000 to $5,000 for each alien for a second violation. Criminal penalties, when a "pattern or practice" of unlawful hiring exists, can include a fine of not more than $3,000 for each unauthorized alien, as well as imprisonment for up to six months.

(b) EMPLOYER VERIFICATION. The law requires employers to verify that each new employee hired after November 6, 1986, is authorized to work in the United States. The INS has designated Form I-9, "Immigration Eligibility Verification Form," as the official verification form to comply with the IRCA. The prospective employee must complete the initial portion of Form I-9, attesting under the penalty of perjury that he or she is a U.S. citi-

zen or is authorized to work in the United States by the INS and that the verification documents presented to the employer are genuine and relate to the signer. The employer must then review the documents that support the individual's right to work in the United States. Documents that both identify and support an individual's eligibility to work are a U.S. passport, a certificate of U.S. citizenship, a certificate of nationalization, an unexpired foreign passport with attached visa authorizing U.S. employment, or an Alien Registration Card. In lieu of the above documents the prospective employee may provide an individual document evidencing his or her identity and another document evidencing his or her right to employment. Thus, a state driver's license is sufficient to provide identity, and a social security card or official birth certificate issued by a municipal authority is sufficient to prove employment eligibility. There are numerous other documents that satisfy the identity and employment eligibility documentation requirements.

The employer, after examining all documents, signs the following certification:

I attest, under penalty of perjury, that I have examined the documents presented by the above individual, that they appear to be genuine, relate to the individual named, and that the individual, to the best of my knowledge, is authorized to work in the United States.

The employer has three days to complete the I-9s. I-9s must be completed for all employees hired after November 6, 1986, including employees who are U.S. citizens. The I-9s must be kept for three years after the date of hire.

Fines of between $100 and $1,000 may be imposed on the employer for each individual employee for failure to comply with the paperwork verification requirements.

(c) BURDEN OF PROOF AND AFFIRMATIVE DEFENSES. In an action against the employer under the IRCA, the government must establish that the employer had "actual knowledge" that the employee was unauthorized to work in the United States. This standard is one of the highest standards of proof under law.

The IRCA provides an affirmative defense for an employer if the employer, in good faith, simply complies with the verification requirements of the Act. This is accomplished "if the document reasonably appears on its face to be genuine."[38]

18.   Business Visas

The IRCA does not affect business visas. Non-immigrant B-1 business visas are issued by a U.S. consular office abroad after it has been shown that the visitor (a) has a foreign residence that has not been abandoned, (b) intends to enter the United States for a limited period of time, and (c) will engage solely in legitimate business activities for which he or she will not be paid in the United States.[39] Thus, aliens may qualify for a B-1 visa to perform after-sale warranty work on equipment sold by a foreign company to a U.S. purchaser.

Certain investors qualify for E-2 business visas. Principal foreign investors responsible for development and direction of an enterprise in the United States are granted such a visa. An E visa is very desirable, because it is usually issued for extended periods of time (often four to five years) and may be renewed indefinitely, so long as the alien maintains his or her role with respect to the investment.

L-1 visas allow qualifying multinational businesses to make intracompany transfers of foreign persons to the United States, if the individuals are employed in management or have "specialized knowledge." L-1 visas are good for an initial period of up to three years, with a possible extension not to exceed two years. The alien must then depart the country and live outside of it for a year before again being eligible for L-1 status.

H-1 classification visas allow aliens of "distinguished merit and ability" to enter and work in the United States for an initial period of up to three years, with extensions in increments of two years. These persons include architects, engineers, lawyers, physicians, surgeons, and teachers in elementary and secondary schools and in colleges.

Seasonal and temporary workers "performing skilled or unskilled labor" may obtain H-2 visas for an initial period of one year, with extensions allowing for a total length of stay not to exceed three years, if an employer demonstrates that qualified U.S. workers are not available.

---

[38]   IRCA § 101(a)(1); 8 USC § 1324 A(b)(1)(A).
[39]   Department of State, 9 Foreign Affairs Manual, § 41.25.

SUMMARY

The relationship of employer and employee is created by the agreement of the parties and is subject to all of the principles applicable to contracts. If the employment contract sets forth a specific duration, the employer cannot terminate the contract at an earlier date unless just cause exists. If no definite time period is set forth, the individual is an at-will employee. In those states where the employment-at-will doctrine is followed, an employer can terminate the contract of an at-will employee at any time, for any reason or for no reason. Courts in a majority of jurisdictions, however, have carved out exceptions to this doctrine when the discharge violates public policy or is contrary to good faith and fair dealing in the employment relationship. Also, federal laws prohibit termination of covered employees because of their union activities or because of their race, color, sex, religion, national origin, age, or handicap. However, employers may terminate employees for just cause.

The Employees Retirement Income Security Act (ERISA) was enacted to provide protection of the pension interests of employees by requiring (a) high standards of those administering the funds, (b) reasonable vesting of benefits, (c) adequate funding, and (d) an insurance program to guarantee payments of earned benefits.

Unemployment compensation benefits are provided to persons for a limited period of time if they are out of work through no fault of their own. Persons receiving unemployment compensation must be available for placement in a similar job at a comparable rate of pay.

In order to assure every working person safe and healthful working conditions, the Occupational Safety and Health Act provides for (a) the establishment of safety and health standards and (b) the effective enforcement of these standards. "Right-to-know" laws have been enacted by many states; these laws require employers to inform their employees of any hazardous substances present in the workplace.

Workers' compensation laws provide for the prompt payment of compensation and medical benefits to persons injured in the course of employment, without regard to fault. The injured employee's remedy is generally limited to that provided by the workers' compensation statute.

The Immigration Reform and Control Act was designed to discourage aliens from illegally entering the United States by eliminating job opportunities for them through employer sanctions. Business visas may be obtained from U.S. consular offices abroad by qualifying foreign persons.

QUESTIONS AND CASE PROBLEMS

1. What social forces are affected by the "shop right" rule applicable to inventions of an employee?
2. Compare the protection of trade secrets and the protection given an unpublished literary or artistic work (common-law copyright).
3. What remedies does an employee who has been wrongfully discharged have against an employer?
4. Michael Hauck claims that he was discharged by his employer, Sabine Pilot Service, Inc., because he refused his employer's direction to perform the illegal act of pumping the bilges of his employer's vessel into the waterways. Hauck was an employee at will, and Sabine contends that it therefore had the right to discharge him without having to show cause. Hauck brought a wrongful discharge action against Sabine. Decide. [Sabine Pilot Service Inc v Hauck (Tex) 687 SW2d 733]
5. Robert Evjen was a full-time employee for Boise Cascade Corp. At the same time, he was a full-time student at Chemeta Community College. He was laid off as part of a general economy move by the employer. He applied for unemployment compensation. The referee found that Evjen never missed work in order to go to classes, that Evjen could not afford to go to school without working, and that in case of any conflict between work and school, work came first. Boise Cascade believed that as a full-time student, Evjen was not eligible for benefits. Was Evjen entitled to unemployment compensation

benefits? [Evjen v Employment Agency, 22 Or App 372, 539 P2d 662]
6. A teenage, female, high school student named Salazar was employed part-time at Church's Fried Chicken restaurant. Salazar was hired and supervised by Simon Garza, the assistant manager of the restaurant. Garza had complete supervisory powers when the restaurant's manager, Garza's roommate, was absent. Salazar alleged that while she worked at the restaurant, Garza would refer to her and all other females by a Spanish term that she found objectionable. According to Salazar, Garza once made a lecherous comment about her body and repeatedly asked her about her personal life. On another occasion, Garza allegedly physically removed eye shadow from Salazar's face because he thought it looked ugly. Salazar also claimed that one night she was restrained in a back room of the restaurant while Garza and another employee fondled her. Later that night, when Salazar told a customer what had happened, she was fired. Salazar filed an action under Title VII against Garza and Church's Fried Chicken, Inc., alleging sexual harassment. Church's, the corporate defendant, maintains that it should not be held liable under Title VII for Garza's harassment. Church's bases its argument on the existence of a published "fair treatment policy." Decide. [Salazar v Church's Fried Chicken, Inc., 44 FEP 472 (SD Tex)]
7. Compare (a) an employee and (b) an independent contractor.

8. Juan Ortiz was regularly employed by Donegan Productions Co. as an actor on an afternoon television series. A dispute arose as to Donegan's financial obligations to Juan. Donegan claimed that the dispute must be resolved solely on the basis of the written individual employment contract that Juan and Donegan Productions had signed and that the past practice, usages of the profession, and an existing collective bargaining contract with AFTRA (American Federation of Television and Radio Artists) were not relevant. Was Donegan Productions correct?

9. Jane Richards was employed as the sole crane operator of the Gale Corporation. She also held the part-time union position of shop steward for the plant. On May 15, Richards complained to OSHA concerning what she contended were seven existing violations of the Occupational Safety and Health Act. These violations were brought to her attention by members of the bargaining unit. On May 21, she stated to the company's general manager at a negotiating session: "If we don't have a new contract by the time the present one expires on June 15, we will strike." On May 22, an OSHA inspector arrived at the plant, and Richards told her supervisor that "I blew the whistle." On May 23, the company rented and later purchased two large electric forklifts that were used to do the work formerly performed by the crane; consequently, the crane operator's job was abolished. Under the existing collective bargaining contract, the company had the right to lay off for lack of work. The contract also provided for arbitration and prohibited discipline or discharge without "just cause." On May 23, Richards was notified that she was being laid off "for lack of work" within her classification of crane operator. She was also advised that the company was not planning on using the crane in the future and that, if she were smart, she would get another job. Richards claims that her layoff was in violation of the National Labor Relations Act, the Occupational Safety and Health Act, and the collective bargaining agreement. Is she correct?

10. Samuel Sullivan, president of the Truck Drivers and Helpers International Union, also holds the position of president of the union's pension fund. The fund consists of both employer and employee contributions, which are forwarded quarterly to the fund's offices in New York City. Sullivan orders Mark Gilbert, the treasurer of the fund, not to give out any information to anyone at any time concerning the fund, because it is union money and because the union is entitled to take care of its own internal affairs. Is Sullivan correct?

11. John Chadbourne was hired by Raytheon on February 4, 1980. His job performance reviews were uniformly high. In December, 1983, Chadbourne was hospitalized and diagnosed as having AIDS. In January, 1984, his physician informed Raytheon that Chadbourne was able to return to work. On January 20, 1984, Chadbourne took a return-to-work physical examination required by Raytheon. The company's doctor wrote the County Communicable Disease Control Director, Dr. Juels, seeking a determination on the appropriateness of Chadbourne's returning to work. Dr. Juels informed the company that ". . . contact of employees to an AIDS patient appears to pose no risk from all evidence accumulated to date." Dr. Juels thereafter visited the plant and advised the company doctor that there was no medical risk to other employees at the plant if Chadbourne returned to work. Raytheon refused to reinstate Chadbourne to his position until July 19, 1984. Its basis for denying reinstatement was that coworkers might be at risk of contracting AIDS. Was Raytheon entitled to bar Chadbourne from work during the six-month period of January through July? [Raytheon v Fair Employment and Housing Commission, 212 Cal App 3d 1242, 261 Cal Rptr 197]

12. Buffo was employed by the Baltimore & Ohio Railroad Co. Along with a number of other workers, he was removing old brakes from railroad cars and replacing them with new brakes. In the course of the work, rivet heads and scrap from the brakes accumulated on the tracks under the cars. This debris was removed only occasionally, when the men had time. Buffo, while holding an air hammer in both arms, was crawling under a car when his foot slipped on scrap on the ground. This incident caused him to strike and injure his knee. He sued the railroad for damages under the Federal Employers' Liability Act. Decide. [Buffo v Baltimore & Ohio Railroad Co. 364 Pa 437, 72 A2d 593]

13. Mark Phipps was employed as a cashier at a Clark gas station. A customer drove into the station and asked him to pump leaded gasoline into her 1976 Chevrolet—an automobile equipped to receive only unleaded gasoline. The station manager told Phipps to comply with the request, but he refused, believing that his dispensing leaded gasoline into the gas tank

was a violation of law. Phipps stated that he was willing to pump unleaded gas into the tank, but the manager immediately fired him. Phipps sued Clark for wrongful termination. Clark contended that it was free to terminate Phipps, an employee at will, for any reason or no reason. Decide. [Phipps v Clark Oil & Refining Corp (Minn App) 396 NW2d 588]

14. Cream was an officer and employee of Leo Silfen, Inc. He was discharged and then went into business for himself, conducting a business similar to that of his former employer. He obtained lists of users of his products from enterprises publishing mailing and commercial lists. Out of the persons he solicited from these lists, 47 were customers of Silfen. Silfen brought an action to enjoin Cream from soliciting its customers. Cream showed that Silfen had approximately 1,100 customers. Decide. [Leo Silfen, Inc. v Cream, 29 NY2d 387, 328 NYS2d 423, 278 NE2d 636]

15. Michael Kittell was employed at Vermont Weatherboard Company. While operating a saw at the plant, Kittell was seriously injured when a splinter flew into his eye and penetrated his head. Kittell sued Vermont Weatherboard, seeking damages on a common law theory. His complaint alleged that he suffered severe injuries solely because of the employer's wanton and willful acts and omissions. The complaint stated that he was an inexperienced worker, set to work without instructions or warning on a saw from which the employer had stripped away all safety devices. Vermont Weatherboard made a motion to dismiss the complaint on the ground that the Workers' Compensation Act provided the exclusive remedy for his injury. Decide. [Kittell v Vermont Weatherboard, Inc. 138 Vt 439, 417 A2d 926]

PART EIGHT

BUSINESS ORGANIZATIONS

43

FORMS OF BUSINESS ORGANIZATIONS

Business ventures may be conducted under various forms of organization. The principal forms of business organizations are (1) individual or sole proprietorships, (2) partnerships, and (3) corporations. The particular form of business organization selected is determined by the nature of the proposed business and considerations of control, tax liability, and liability for debts of (and claims against) the business.

Certain forms of special venture organizations have evolved to meet modern business and investment needs. These include franchises, joint ventures, cooperatives, and unincorporated associations.

A. PRINCIPAL FORMS OF BUSINESS ORGANIZATIONS

The law of business organizations may be better understood if major advantages and disadvantages of proprietorships, partnerships, and corporations are first considered.

1. Individual Proprietorships

A **sole** or **individual proprietorship** is a form of business ownership in which one individual owns a business. The owner may be the sole worker of the business or may employ as many individuals as needed to run the concern. Individual proprietorships are commonly used in retail establishments, service businesses, and agriculture.

(a) ADVANTAGES. The proprietor or owner is not required to expend resources on organizational fees. The proprietor, as the sole owner, controls all of the decisions and receives all of the profits. The business's net earnings are not subject to the corporate income tax, but are taxed as personal income.

(b) DISADVANTAGES. The proprietor is subject to unlimited personal liability for the debts of the business, and the proprietor cannot effectively limit this risk. The investment capital in the business is limited by the resources of the sole proprietor; this limitation very often impedes the growth of the business. Since all contracts of the business are made by the owner or in the owner's name by agents of the owner, the authority to make contracts terminates upon the death of the owner, and the business is subject to disintegration.

2.   Partnerships

While an individual proprietorship relies on the capital investment and business skill of the sole owner, a **partnership** involves the pooling of capital resources and the business or professional talents of two or more individuals with the goal of making a profit. Law firms, medical associations, and architectural and engineering firms may operate under the partnership form, although there is a trend for such professional firms to incorporate. A wide range of retail and service businesses operate as partnerships.

(a) ADVANTAGES. The partnership form of business organization allows individuals to pool resources and then initiate and conduct their business without the requirement of a formal organizational structure and without the expense of organizational fees. As will be seen, partnership agreements are often informal and may even be unwritten.

(b) DISADVANTAGES. Major disadvantages of a partnership are the unlimited per-

sonal liability of each partner and the uncertain duration of the business because the partnership is dissolved by the death of a partner.

3.   Corporations

Business corporations exist to make a profit. They are created by government grant. The statute regulating the creation of corporations requires a corporate structure consisting of shareholders, directors, and officers. The shareholders, as the owners of the business, elect a board of directors, who are responsible for the management of the business. The directors employ officers, who serve as the agents of the business and who run the day-to-day operations. Corporations range in size from incorporated one-owner enterprises to large multinational concerns.

(a) ADVANTAGES. The major advantage to the shareholder, or investor, is that the shareholder's risk of loss from the business is limited to the amount of capital that the shareholder invested in the business. This factor, coupled with the free transferability of corporate shares, makes the corporate form of business organization an acceptable mechanism for many investors to contribute the capital assets needed to finance large business enterprises. As the capital needs of a business expand, the corporate form becomes more attractive.

A corporation is a separate legal entity capable of owning property, contracting, suing, and being sued in its own name. It may be established with a perpetual life. In contrast to the case of a partnership or proprietorship, the death of an owner has no legal effect on the entity.

(b) DISADVANTAGES. A corporation is required to pay corporate income taxes. Shareholders, when they receive a distribution of profits for the corporation, are required to pay personal income taxes on the amount received. This is a form of double taxation, which may weigh against incorporation.

The limited liability of shareholders may result in a limitation of the credit available to the corporation. Also, incorporation involves the expenditure of funds for organizational and operational expenses. Documents necessary for the formation of a corporation, which are required by state law, must be prepared, and certain filing fees must be paid. State corporation laws may also require the filing of an annual report and other reports.

B.   SPECIALIZED FORMS OF ORGANIZATIONS

Specialized forms of business organizations exist to meet modern business and investment needs. Thus, a fast-food enterprise may choose to expand its business by the use of franchises, whereby it is paid royalties from the gross receipts of restaurants owned and operated by franchisees. Or two construction companies may form a joint venture to construct a major project, when individually the companies lack sufficient resources to undertake the project. Each enterprise seeks to use the structure that will permit the attainment of its desired goals in the most efficient manner while protecting the enterprise and the participants from the risks that may arise.

4.   Franchises

The use of franchises has expanded rapidly in recent years. The franchise serves as a method of controlling and financing operations by the franchisor and as a method of investment and participation by the franchisee.

(a) DEFINITIONS. A **franchise** has been defined by the Federal Trade Commission as "an arrangement in which the owner of a trademark, trade name, or copyright licenses others, under specified conditions or limitations, to use the trademark, trade name, or copyright in purveying goods or services." The **franchisor** is the party granting the franchise, and the **franchisee** is the person to whom the franchise is granted.

(b) THE FRANCHISOR AND THE FRANCHISEE. Theoretically, the relationship between the franchisor and the franchisee is an arm's-length relationship between two independent contractors. Their respective rights are determined by the contract existing between them. A franchise, then, is not a business entity *per se*. Rather, a franchise is a business relationship between distinct business organizations, which is governed by the franchise contract.

(1) Duration and Termination. The franchise may last for as long as the parties agree. Commonly, it runs for a short period of time, such as a year, so the franchise holder is well aware that, to stay in business, the terms of the franchise contract must be followed. The laws in some states may require limited advance written notice of cancellation,[1] but franchising is basically contractual in nature.

The *McDonald's Corp.* case is an example of the basic contractual nature of franchising. Moreover, it demonstrates that the parties may expect the courts to apply franchise agreements as written.

---

[1]   See, for example, Mo Rev Stat § 407.405; Ridings v Thoele (Mo) 739 SW2d 547 (1987).

MCDONALD'S CORP. v ROBERT A. MAKIN, INC.
(DC NY) 653 F Supp 401 (1986)

McDonald's Corporation entered into a contract with Robert A. Makin, Inc., to franchise a McDonald's restaurant in Clarence, New York. The franchise agreement required Makin to make monthly payments of license and lease fees to McDonald's, and the agreement provided for the termination of the franchise if

Makin should fail to make all payments under the agreement. Makin failed to make monthly payments from October 1985 through February 10, 1986. McDonald's gave notice that it had terminated the franchise. Makin refused to terminate operations and surrender the premises. McDonald's sued Makin, individually and as a corporation, for the amount due and for a court order granting it the right to enter and take possession of the restaurant. Makin's defense was that McDonald's engaged in a coercive pricing policy in violation of the Sherman Antitrust Act.

CURTIN, D.J. . . . The franchise agreement obligates the defendants to pay monthly fees to plaintiff for the franchise. Nowhere do the defendants deny their failure to pay these fees since October, 1985. Yet, defendants have maintained possession and operation of the franchise property. At oral argument, counsel for defendants contended that McDonald's conduct . . . caused defendants' inability to make the payments. Defendants' counterclaims do not allege that McDonald's conduct caused the non-payment; moreover, defendants contend that most of McDonald's alleged illegal conduct began 7–14 years ago, over which time defendants regularly made the monthly fee payments. In any event, it should be clear to all concerned that

> it is against the law as well as sound morals to permit a party to a contract to repudiate the contract or his obligation under it, and at the same time retain the consideration that he has received. . . .

Defendants' counterclaims will, of course, be adjudicated in their own right; however, the alleged wrongs of plaintiff do not constitute affirmative defenses to defendants' non-payment of franchise fees. The defendants may not use their counterclaims to avoid judgment for the amounts already due under the franchise agreement. The failure of defendants to pay the monthly franchise fees is a breach of contract as to which there exists no genuine factual issue.

Accordingly, plaintiff's motion for summary judgment on Count III of the complaint is granted. . . .

[The] defendants' antitrust claim [will not] bar summary judgment with respect to the validity of the termination. In *Lewis v. Seanor Coal Company*, the United States Court of Appeals for the Third Circuit found that:

> [t]he company's claim that the agreement violates the Sherman Anti-Trust Act is not a defense to the trustees' action. It is now well established that the remedy for violation of the antitrust law is not avoidance of payments due under a contract, but rather the redress which the antitrust statute establishes,—a private treble damage action. 382 F.2d 437, 441 (3d Cir. 1967), cert. denied, 390 U.S. 947 (1968). . . .

Defendants have not alleged that the requirement that they pay fees for the use of the franchise is at all connected with the illegal price-fixing allegedly engaged in by McDonald's. The termination is a clear contractual result of the failure to pay the required fees. Thus, defendants' antitrust claim does not preclude summary judgment on this action.

. . . It is clear under basic contract principles that, absent an affirmative defense excusing the defendants' failure to pay, the Makins cannot refuse to meet their obligations under the contract while enjoying all of its benefits. Upon the Makins' refusal to

Chapter 43 Forms of Business Organizations

pay the amounts owed, McDonald's had a clear contractual right to terminate the franchise agreement.

Accordingly, plaintiff's motion for summary judgment on Count I of the complaint is granted.

I find that the franchise contract, consisting of the license and lease documents referenced herein, has been lawfully terminated as of February 10, 1986. In accordance with the provisions of the agreement, McDonald's has an immediate right to enter and take possession of the North Transit Road McDonald's and to require defendants to forthwith return all material containing McDonald's trade secrets, operating instructions, or business practices and to discontinue the use of the McDonald's System. In accordance with the provisions of the contract, McDonald's is also awarded the reasonable expenses of litigation in this action, including attorney's fees, with interest thereon at the legal rate.

[So ordered]

QUESTIONS

1. On what basis did McDonald's contend that it had a right to receive monthly payments and, when the payments were not made, the right to terminate the franchise and take possession of the restaurant?
2. Is an alleged antitrust violation a defense for a franchisee's failure to make monthly payments under a franchise agreement?
3. What was the proper procedure for Makin, Inc., to follow if it believed McDonald's violated the Sherman Antitrust Act?

Franchise contracts generally specify the causes for which the franchisor may terminate the franchise, such as the franchisee's death, bankruptcy, failure to make payments, or failure to meet sales quotas. Franchise contracts frequently contain an arbitration provision under which a neutral party is to make a final and binding determination as to whether or not there has been a breach of the contract sufficient to justify cancellation of the franchise. The arbitration provision may provide that the franchisor can appoint a trustee to run the business of the franchisee while the arbitration proceedings are pending.

Holders of automobile dealership franchises are protected from bad faith termination of their dealerships by the federal Automobile Dealers' Franchise Act.[2] When an automobile manufacturer makes arbitrary and unreasonable demands and thereafter ter-

minates the dealer's franchise for failure to comply with the demands, the manufacturer is liable for the damages caused thereby. However, a manufacturer is justified in terminating an automobile dealership if the dealership fails to maintain the required sales quota when the manufacturer has given the dealer repeated warnings, when the quota is reasonable, and when the quota has been reduced to reflect local economic conditions.

When the relationship between the franchisor and the franchisee is created primarily for the sale of products manufactured by the franchisor, the rights of the parties are governed by the law of sales of Article 2 the UCC. Also, it should be remembered from Chapter 4, "Government Regulation," that vertical price-fixing agreements between a franchisor-manufacturer and its franchisee-distributor are a violation of the federal antitrust laws. Thus, when a manufacturer of winches terminated one of the distributorships for discounting prices contrary to the manufacturer's

[2]   15 USC § 1222. A number of states have similar statutes.

resale price maintenance policy, the manufacturer was in violation of Section 1 of the Sherman Antitrust Act and was required to pay three times the actual damages caused by the termination.[3]

(2) Regulation. There continue to be statutory reform movements, both at the federal and state levels, to provide general protection for the franchise holder. Protective regulation of franchisees generally relates to problems of fraud in the sale of the franchise and to the protection of the franchisee from unreasonable demands and termination by the franchisor.[4]

The Petroleum Marketing Practices Act (PMPA) gives a gasoline franchisee the opportunity to continue in business by purchasing the entire premises used in selling motor fuel when the franchisor determines to sell the property and not to renew a lease.

The *Crone* case illustrates the application of a state retail franchising law to a case alleging the unlawful cancellation of a franchise without reasonable cause.

---

[3]   Pierce v Ramsey Winch Co. (CA5 Tex) CCH Bus Fran Rptr, ¶ 8318 (1985).

[4]   Wirkkula v Union Oil Co. of California, 98 Or App 282, 780 P2d 223 (1989).

CRONE v RICHMOND NEWSPAPERS, INC.
238 Va 262, 384 SE2d 77 (1989)

James Crone and other newspaper distributors brought actions against Richmond Newspapers, Inc. (RNI), under a state retail franchising act. The plaintiffs sought damages for the cancellation of their contracts to distribute newspapers for RNI. The distributors used racks in the sale of the newspaper and were required under their contract with RNI to paint and maintain the racks and display the RNI logo on each rack. In March of 1986, RNI canceled the contracts with their distributors and commenced using its own employees to perform the work in question. The distributors contended that the cancellations were without reasonable cause as defined in the retail franchising act. RNI contended that its contracts were not franchises within the meaning of the act. From a judgment ruling that the contracts were not franchises within the meaning of the act, Crone and the other distributors appealed.

COMPTON, J. . . . The policy of the Commonwealth, as declared in the Act, is "to regulate commerce partly or wholly within the Commonwealth of Virginia" in order to correct "such inequities as may exist in the franchise system so as to establish a more even balance of power between franchisors and franchisees; to require franchisors to deal fairly with their franchisees . . . and to provide franchisees more direct, simple, and complete judicial relief against franchisors who fail to deal in a lawful manner with them." Code § 13.1-558.

The Act further provides, as pertinent to this controversy, that a franchise is "a written contract or agreement . . . between two or more persons" in which a franchisee "is granted the right to engage in the business of offering, selling or distributing goods or services at retail under a marketing plan or system prescribed in substantial part by a franchisor," and the "operation of the franchisee's business pursuant to such plan or system is substantially associated with the franchisor's trademark, service mark, trade name, logotype, advertising or other commercial symbol designating the franchisor or its affiliate." § 13.1-559(b)(1) and (2).

The present dispute stems from the following sentence in § 13.1-559: "This chapter shall apply only to a franchise the performance of which contemplates or requires the franchisee to establish or maintain a place of business within the Commonwealth of Virginia."

The Act further provides: "It shall be unlawful for a franchisor to cancel a franchise without reasonable cause. . . ." § 13.1-564. Also, the Act permits a franchisee who has suffered damages as the result of any violation of the foregoing section to bring an action against its franchisor to recover such damages, as well as reasonable attorney's fees and costs. § 13.1-571(a).

. . . [T]he Act applies only to an agreement "the performance of which contemplates or requires the franchisee to establish or maintain a place of business within the Commonwealth of Virginia." A plain reading of that provision, in the context of the whole Act, demonstrates to us that it simply requires the business transacted under the franchise agreement to have a nexus to the Commonwealth. The proviso merely records the intention of the General Assembly to legislate constitutionally by regulating business within the State in a field which often involves transactions in interstate commerce.

In our view, the provision is not so restrictive, as RNI contends, as to place the burden upon a party seeking protection of the Act to show that a fixed physical site where business is transacted, such as a shop, office or warehouse, has been established. The franchisee need not prove, for example, that a freestanding, coin-operated newspaper rack, resting at a street corner unattended by any salesperson, meets some technical definition of "place of business." Rather, the party seeking coverage of the Act must show only a business connection or link with this State. The distributor in this case has alleged such a connection.

Here, a Virginia resident has agreed to distribute a product from a specified location within a designated Virginia [rack account] territory. In other words, the obligations of the contract require the distributor to perform business from "places" within the State. As we interpret the Act, the focus is not on whether a single vending machine, a [rack account] territory, or the distributor's residence qualify independently as a "place of business." So long as the places where the distributor operates under the contract, disseminating RNI's product, are within the State, the required nexus exists. . . .

[Reversed and remanded]

QUESTIONS

1. Why did the state pass the retail franchising act?
2. Can a business person avoid the application of the state franchising act by carefully avoiding all reference to the words "franchise," "franchising," "franchisor," and "franchisee" in its contract with each distributor?
3. Assess the validity of the following statement: "Because an unattended, coin-operated newspaper rack is not a 'place of business' within the state, the retail franchising law did not apply to the distributors."

In order to protect a prospective franchisee from deception, the Federal Trade Commission adopted a rule that requires the franchisor to give a prospective franchisee a disclosure statement. The statement sets forth the franchisee's financial and legal obligations. It must be given to the prospective franchisee ten days before the franchisee signs a contract or pays any money for a franchise. Under the FTC disclosure rule, a franchisor must pay a civil penalty of as much as $10,000 for each violation when it is shown that a "sale" relating to a franchise subject to the FTC rule was made, the franchisor "knew or should have known" of the disclosure rule, and no disclosure statement was given to the "buyer."[5]

(c) THE FRANCHISOR AND THIRD PERSONS. In theory, the franchisor is not liable to a third person dealing with or affected by the franchise holder. This freedom from liability is one of the reasons franchisors grant franchises. If the negligence of the franchisee causes harm to a third person, the franchisor is not liable, because the franchisee is an independent contractor.[6] However, franchisors continue to be subject to lawsuits based on the wrongful conduct of their franchisees, on a theory of apparent authority. When plaintiffs have succeeded against franchisors, they have alleged and proven conduct or representations by the franchisor of control over the franchisee, and reliance on such by the plaintiffs. In a recent case against the Shell Oil Company for damages for an injury caused by an employee of a franchisee, the plaintiff succeeded before the court, relying upon the following policy precedent:

Public policy may require that an oil company ostensibly holding itself out to the public as the owner and operator of a service station and advertising special care and good service should bear the responsibility for seeing that the station's services are dispensed reasonably and appropriately.[7]

In another case against Shell Oil Company by a customer injured at a Shell gas station, the court rejected the plaintiff's apparent-authority argument, noting that the oil company did not own or operate the station but merely sold petroleum products to the station.[8]

In order to insulate themselves from liability, franchisors often require that individual franchisees take steps to publicly maintain their own individual identity as a business. Thus, a gasoline service station may post a sign stating that it is "dealer owned and operated," or a real estate franchisee may list on its business sign the franchise name and the name of the local owner, such as "Century 21, L & K Realty Co."

When the franchisee makes a contract with a third person, the franchisor is not liable on the contract. The franchisee is not the agent of the franchisor and does not have any authority to bind the franchisor by contract.

(1) Actual Control. A franchisor is liable to third persons when the franchisor exercises such actual control over the operations of the franchisee that the latter is not to be regarded as an independent contractor but rather as an employee or agent of the franchisor. Moreover, a franchisor is liable for its own negligence in inspecting and recommending fixtures and equipment to be used by its franchisees.[9]

(2) Product Liability. Sometimes a franchise involves the resale of goods manufactured or obtained by the franchisor and supplied to the franchisee. If such a product causes harm to the franchisee's customer, the franchisor will be liable to the customer, on theories of product liability.[10]

(d) THE FRANCHISEE AND THIRD PERSONS. When the franchise holder has any contract relationship or contact with a third person, the contract or tort liability of the franchisee is the same as though there were no franchise. The fact that there is a franchise does not add to or subtract from the liability that the franchisee would have in the same situation had there been no franchise. For example, if the franchise is to operate a restaurant, the franchise holder is liable to a customer for breach of an implied warranty of the fitness of the food for human consumption to the same extent as though the franchise holder were running an independent restaurant. If the

[5]   US v TCI Inc. CCH Trade Cases, ¶ 62,058 (1987).
[6]   Frey v PepsiCo. 191 Ga App 385, 382 SE2d 648 (1989).
[7]   Shadel v Shell Oil Co. 195 NJ Super 311, 478 A2d 1262 (1984).
[8]   Albright v Parr, 126 Ill App 3d 464, 81 Ill Dec 648, 467 NE2d 348 (1984).

[9]   Papastathis v Southland Corp. (App) 150 Ariz 279, 723 P2d 97 (1986).
[10]   See Chapter 27 of this book.

franchise holder negligently causes harm to a third person, as by running over that person with a truck used in the enterprise, the tort liability of the franchise holder is determined by the principles that would be applicable if no franchise existed. The franchise holder is liable on a contract made in the franchise holder's own name.

5.   Joint Ventures

A **joint venture**, or joint adventure, is a relationship in which two or more persons combine their labor or property for a single business undertaking and share profits and losses equally, or as otherwise agreed.[11] When several contractors pool all their assets in order to construct one tunnel, the relationship is a joint venture.

A joint venture is similar in many respects to a partnership. It differs primarily in that the joint venture typically relates to the pursuit of a single enterprise or transaction, although its accomplishment may require several years. A partnership is generally a continuing business or activity. A partnership may, however, be expressly created for a single transaction. Because the distinction is so insubstantial, most courts hold that joint ventures are subject to the same principles of law as partnerships.[12] Thus, the duties owed by the joint venturers to each other are the same as those that partners owe to each other.

It is essential that there be a community of interest or purpose and that each co-adventurer have an equal right to control the operations or activities of the undertaking.[13] The actual control of the operations may be entrusted to one of the joint venturers. Thus, the fact that one joint adventurer is placed in control of the farming and livestock operations of the undertaking and appears to be the owner of the land does not destroy the joint adventure relationship.

(a) DURATION OF JOINT VENTURE. When a joint venture agreement states the time for which the venture is to last, such a specification will be given effect. In the absence of a fixed duration provision a joint venture is ordinarily terminable at the will of any participant. When the joint venture clearly relates to a particular transaction, such as the construction of a specified bridge, the joint venture ordinarily lasts until the particular transaction or project is completed or becomes impossible to complete.

(b) LIABILITY TO THIRD PERSONS. The conclusion that persons are joint venturers is important when a suit is brought by or against a third person for personal injuries or property damage. If there is a joint venture, the fault or negligence of one venturer will be imputed to the other venturer.[14]

6.   Unincorporated Associations

An **unincorporated association** is a combination of two or more persons for the furtherance of a common nonprofit purpose. No particular form of organization is required. Any conduct or agreement indicating an attempt to associate or work together for a common purpose is sufficient. Social clubs, fraternal associations, sororities, and political parties are common examples of unincorporated associations.

The authority of an unincorporated association over its members is governed by ordinary principles of contract law. An association cannot expel a member for a ground that is not expressly authorized by the contract between the association and the member.

Except when otherwise provided by statute, an unincorporated association does not have any legal existence apart from the members who compose it. Thus, an unincorporated association cannot sue or be sued in its own name.

Generally, the members of an unincorporated association are not liable for the debts or liabilities of the association by the mere fact that they are members. Generally, it must be

---

[11]   See Florida Trading and Investment Co. Inc. v River Construction Services Inc. (Fla App) 537 So 2d 599 (1988).

[12]   Burruss v Green Auction & Realty Co. Inc. 228 Va 6, 319 SE2d 725 (1984).

[13]   Dunbar v RKG Engineering, Inc. (Tex Civ App) 746 SW2d 314 (1988).

[14]   Kim v Chamberlain (Ala App) 504 So 2d 1213 (1987).

shown that they authorized or ratified the act in question. If either authorization or ratification by a particular member can be shown, that member has unlimited liability for the act.

"Authorization" may be found where the negligent act in question is within the scope of the association's purposes and there is tacit approval of the act, as in the *Ermert* case.

ERMERT v HARTFORD INSURANCE CO.
(La App) 531 So 2d 506(1988)

Karl F. Ermert, III, was spending the weekend as a guest of Russell Larrieu at a hunting camp. The camp was located on Bayou Bienvenue near Lake Borgne in the marshlands of St. Bernard Parish, Louisiana. Ermert, Russell Larrieu, and several other men were at the hunting camp to participate in the building of duck blinds to be used in the upcoming duck season. On the morning of November 14, one of the men, Kenneth Decareaux, saw a nutria outside of the hunting camp and began loading a shotgun for the purpose of shooting the nutria. As Decareaux was leaving the hunting camp with the loaded shotgun, the gun discharged and struck Ermert in his left foot. Ermert sued each of the individuals present. The evidence showed that the group of men constituted a loose unincorporated association formed solely for recreational and not business purposes. The club had no formal meetings, and any "rules" regarding hunting safety were common sense rules to which all hunters should adhere. From a judgment holding that members of the club not involved in the shooting were not personally liable, Ermert appealed.

PLOTKIN, J.... A review of the caselaw from other jurisdictions indicates that most states adhere to the "general agency principles" for applying liability to members of an unincorporated association.... Many courts which have considered the question have also applied a duty/risk analysis to determine whether the club itself and/or the non-tortfeasor members of the club should be held liable.

For example, in *Lyons v. American Legion Post No. 650*, 172 Ohio St. 331, 175 N.E.2d 733 (1961), the Ohio Supreme Court differentiated between unincorporated associations organized and functioning for business and commerce reasons from those organized and conducted for fraternal or social purposes on the following basis: the former are controlled by partnership principles, while the latter are controlled by agency principles. *Id*. 175 N.E.2d at 737. Using those principles, the court held that an action would lie only against those members of the club who authorize or subsequently ratify the injury-causing action. *Id*. ...

Applying the general agency principles ... we hold that the non-tortfeasor members of the hunting club in the instant case should be held liable for the defendant's injuries on the basis of the following findings. ...

The testimony concerning the events of the morning in question indicates that Decareaux's actions in attempting to shoot the nutria were within the scope of the purposes for which the organization was formed. ... The tortfeasor in this case was one of the "official" chefs when the club members met at the camp. He testified at trial that he intended to cook the nutria for the group to eat. Obviously, the action was taken for the good of the group as a whole.

Finally, the circumstances indicate that the action was taken with the "passive approval" of the other members of the club who were present at the club at the time the accident occurred. . . .

The uncontroverted evidence is that several other members of the club were present at the time the accidental shooting occurred and apparently no one objected to or tried to prevent Decareaux's actions. Therefore, the other members of the club should be found liable for plaintiff's injuries because they tacitly assented to Decareaux's actions, as well as for the other reasons discussed above. . . .

Although all the other defendants, who were members of the club and present at the camp when the accident occurred, must be held liable for the damages sustained by the plaintiff in this case, that liability should not extend to Alkaney Cummings, who was not present and whose testimony indicates that he had not been a member of the club in question for years. . . .

[Reversed and remanded]

QUESTIONS

1. Does mere membership in an unincorporated association make all members liable for the negligence of some of the members?
2. Was Cummings held liable for the shooting injury? Why or why not?
3. When are members of an unincorporated association held liable for the negligence of their associates?

7.   Cooperatives

A **cooperative** consists of a group of two or more independent persons or enterprises that cooperate with respect to a common objective or function. Thus, farmers may pool their farm products and sell them. Consumers may likewise pool their orders and purchase goods in bulk.

(a) INCORPORATED COOPERATIVES. Statutes commonly provide for the special incorporation of cooperative enterprises. Such statutes often provide that any excess of payments over cost of operation shall be refunded to each participant member in direct proportion to the volume of business that the member has done with the cooperative. This arrangement contrasts with the payment of a dividend by an ordinary business corporation, in which the payment of dividends is proportional to the number of shares held by the shareholder and is unrelated to the extent of the shareholder's business activities with the enterprise.

(b) ANTITRUST LAW EXEMPTION. The agreement by the members of sellers' cooperatives that all products shall be sold at a common price is an agreement to fix prices. Therefore, the sellers' cooperative is basically an agreement in restraint of trade and a violation of antitrust laws. The Capper-Volstead Act of 1922 expressly exempts normal selling activities of farmers' and dairy farmers' cooperatives from the operation of the federal Sherman Antitrust Act, as long as the cooperatives do not conspire with outsiders to fix prices.

SUMMARY

The three principal forms of business organizations are sole proprietorships, partnerships, and corporations. An individual proprietorship is a form of business organization in which one person owns the business, controls all decisions, receives all profits, and has unlimited liability for all obligations, liabilities, and losses (if any). A partnership involves the pooling of capital resources and talents of two or more persons with the goal of making a profit; the partners are subject to unlimited personal liability. A business corporation exists to make a profit. It is created by government grant, and its shareholders elect a board of directors, who are responsible for managing the business. A shareholder's liability is limited to the capital the shareholder invested in the business. The corporation continues without regard to the death of shareholders or the transfer of stock by them.

The selection of the form of organization is often determined by the nature of the business, tax considerations, the financial risk involved and the importance of limited liability, and the extent of control of management desired.

A franchise is an agreement or a contract by which the owner of a trademark, trade name, or copyright licenses others to use the mark or copyright in the selling of goods or services. In order to protect against fraud, the FTC requires that franchisors provide prospective franchisees with a disclosure statement ten days prior to any transaction. The Automobile Dealers' Franchise Act and the Petroleum Marketing Practices Act are federal laws that provide covered franchisees with protection from bad faith terminations. State laws also provide protection to franchisees in a wide range of businesses. In theory, the franchisor is not liable in any way to third persons dealing with the franchisee. However, litigation against franchisors for the torts of franchisees is common, with plaintiffs often alleging apparent authority. Such suits are successful only if the plaintiffs can demonstrate actual or apparent control over the operations of the franchisee by the franchisor.

A joint venture exists when two or more persons combine their labor or property for a single business undertaking and share profits and losses as agreed. An unincorporated association is a combination of two or more persons for the pursuit of a common, nonprofit purpose.

A cooperative consists of two or more persons or enterprises, such as farmers, who cooperate with respect to a common objective, such as the distribution of farm products.

QUESTIONS AND CASE PROBLEMS

1. What social forces are affected by the federal Automobile Dealers' Franchise Act?

2. Herbert buys Magda brand television sets directly from the factory and resells them to retail customers. He sells so many of the Magda sets that he does not carry any other make of set. Herbert advertises in the local newspaper as being "your Magda dealer." In a dispute with the factory over entitlement to a large commercial Magda sign given to all Magda franchisees, Herbert claims that he is a franchisee because he is selling under Magda name. Is he correct?

3. When is a franchisor held liable to a third person dealing with or affected by the franchisee?

4. Elizabeth, Josephine, and Florence entered into an agreement to purchase a tract of land, build houses on it, sell the houses, and then divide the net profit. What kind of business organization was intended?

5. Jerome, Sheila, Gary, and Ella agreed to purchase a tract of land and make it available for use as a free playground for neighborhood children. They called the enterprise the Meadowbrook Playground. One of the playground swings was improperly hung by Jerome and Gary, and a child was injured. Suit was brought against the Meadowbrook Playground. Can damages be recovered?

6. If a group of farmers agree among themselves to pool their products and set a common price for the sale of these products, would this be price fixing in violation of the federal antitrust laws?

7. Compare and contrast a franchise and a contract.

8. The Armory Committee was composed of officers from various National Guard units. They organized a New Year's Eve dance, at a charge of $2 per person to defray costs. Perry, along with others, was a member of the Armory Committee. Libby was a paying guest at the dance and was injured by slipping on frozen ruts in

the immediate approaches of the steps leading to the armory building where the dance was held. He sued Perry, Turner, and the other committee members. The evidence showed that every member of the committee had taken some part in planning or running the dance, with the exception of Turner. Was the Armory Committee an unincorporated association or a joint venture? Decide. [Libby v Perry (Me) 311 A2d 527]

9. The Kawasaki Shop of Aurora, Illinois (dealer) advised the Kawasaki Motor Corp. (manufacturer) that it intended to move the Kawasaki franchise from New York Street to Hill Avenue, which was in the same market area. The Hill Avenue location was also the site of a Honda franchise. The manufacturer's sales manager advised the dealer that he did not want the dealer to move in with Honda at the Hill Avenue site. In February, 1982, the dealer went ahead and moved to the Hill Avenue location. Effective May 1, 1982, the manufacturer terminated the dealer's franchise contract. The dealer brought suit against the manufacturer under the state motor vehicle franchise act, which made it unlawful to terminate franchises for site control (requiring that the dealer's site be used exclusively as a Kawasaki dealership). The manufacturer defended that it had a right to have its products sold by a new dealer who was not affiliated with a competitor. Decide. [Kawasaki Shop v Kawasaki Motors Corp. 188 Ill App 3d 664, 136 Ill Dec. 4, 544 NE2d 457]

10. Goodward, a newly hired newspaper reporter for the Cape Cod News, learned that the local cranberry growers had made an agreement under which they pooled their cranberry crops each year and sold the crops at what they determined to be a fair price. Goodward believes that such an agreement is in restraint of trade and a violation of the antitrust laws. Is he correct?

11. Food Caterers, Inc., of East Hartford, Connecticut, obtained a franchise from Chicken Delight, Inc., to use that name at its store and agreed to the product standards and controls specified by the franchisor. The franchise contract required the franchisee to maintain a free delivery service in order to deliver hot, freshly prepared food to customers. The franchisee used a delivery truck that bore no sign or name. Its employee Carfiro drove the truck in making a delivery of food. He negligently struck and killed McLaughlin. The victim's estate sued Chicken Delight, on the theory that Carfiro was its agent because he was doing work that Chicken Delight required to be done and that benefited Chicken Delight. Was

Carfiro the agent of Chicken Delight? [McLaughlin's Estate v Chicken Delight, Inc. 164 Conn 317, 321 A2d 456]

12. Groseth had the International Harvester (IH) truck franchise in Yankton, North Dakota. The franchise agreement Groseth signed required dealers to "cooperate with the Company by placing orders for goods in accordance with advance ordering programs announced by the Company." IH sought to terminate Groseth's franchise because Groseth refused to comply with IH's requirement that a computerized "dealer communication network" (DCN) be set up. Under the DCN each dealer was required to obtain a computer terminal, display screen, and software. The DCN was initially used for ordering parts. The DCN allowed IH to trim its payroll of employees previously needed for manual processing of "parts" orders. Groseth refused to set up the DCN because of the expense of the system. Moreover, it contended that the task of ordering parts was easily accomplished by telephone or written orders. Did IH have good cause to terminate Groseth's franchise? [Matter of Groseth International Harvester Inc. v International Harvester (SD) 442 NW2d 229].

13. Brenner was in the scrap iron business. Almost daily Plitt lent Brenner money with which to purchase scrap iron. The agreement of the parties was that when the scrap was sold, Plitt would be repaid and would receive an additional sum as compensation for making the loan. The loans were to be repaid in any case, without regard to whether Brenner made a profit. A dispute arose as to the nature of the relationship between the two men. Plitt claimed that it was a joint venture. Decide. [Brenner v Plitt, 182 Md 348, 34 A2d 853]

14. Donald Salisbury, William Roberts, and others purchased property from Laurel Chapman, a partner of Chapman Realty, a franchisee of Realty World, Inc. The purchasers made payments directly to Laurel Chapman at the Realty World office, and Chapman was supposed to make payments on the property's mortgage. However, Chapman did not make the payments and absconded with the funds. Salisbury and Roberts sued the franchisor, Realty World, contending that Realty World was liable for the wrongful acts of the apparent agent, Chapman. Realty World and Chapman Realty are parties to a franchise agreement that states that the parties are franchisor and franchisee. The agreement contains a clause that required Chapman to prominently display a certificate in the office

setting forth Chapman's status as an independent franchisee. Chapman displayed such a sign, but the plaintiffs do not recall seeing it. Chapman Realty hires, supervises, and sets the compensation for all of its employees. The plaintiffs point out that Chapman Realty used the service mark "Realty World" on its signs, both outside and inside its offices. They point out that a Realty World manual sets forth the general standards by which franchisees must run their businesses and that such is clear control over the franchise. They contend that, all things considered, Realty World held out Chapman Realty as having authority to bind Realty World. Realty World disagrees, stating that both are independent businesses. Decide. [Salisbury v Chapman and Realty World, Inc. 124 Ill App 3d 1057, 65 NE2d 127]

15. H.C. Blackwell Co. held a franchise from the Kenworth Truck Co. to sell its trucks. After 12 years the franchise was nearing expiration. Kenworth notified Blackwell that the franchise would not be renewed unless Blackwell sold more trucks and improved its building and bookkeeping systems within the next 90 days. Blackwell spent $90,000 in attempting to meet the demands of Kenworth but could not do so, because a year was required to make the specified changes. Kenworth refused to renew the franchise. Blackwell sued Kenworth for damages under the Federal Automobile Dealers' Franchise Act. Blackwell claimed that Kenworth had refused to renew in bad faith. Decide. [Blackwell v Kenworth Truck Co. (CA5 Ala) 620 F2d 104]

44

CREATION AND TERMINATION OF PARTNERSHIPS

Modern partnership law shows traces of Roman law, the law merchant, and the common law of England. A codification of partnership law is found in the Uniform Partnership Act (UPA), which has been adopted by 49 states.[1]

Partnerships are created by agreement. The UPA contains a set of rules on the creation of partnerships; these rules deal with the wide range of issues that may develop from an informal formation process.

Dissolution of a partnership may result from the acts of the partners. It may be by operation of law, as in the death of a partner. Dissolution may also be by court decree, when the dissension among the partners is so seri-

---

[1] The UPA has been adopted in all states except Louisiana, and it is in force in the District of Columbia, Guam, and the Virgin Islands.

ous that continuation of the business is impracticable.

A.   NATURE AND CREATION

A discussion of the creation of partnerships must be prefaced with a discussion of the nature of the partnership relation, including the characteristics of a partnership, the various classifications of partnerships and partners, and the nature of partnership property.

1.   Definition

A **partnership** is a relationship created by the voluntary "association of two or more persons to carry on as co-owners a business for profit."[2] The persons so associated are called **partners**. A partner is the agent of the partnership and of each partner with respect to partnership matters. A partner, however, is not an employee of the partnership, even when doing work that would ordinarily be done by an employee.

2.   Characteristics of a Partnership

A partnership can be described in terms of its characteristics.

a. A partnership is a voluntary, consensual relationship; it is not imposed by law. Because of the intimate and confidential nature of the partnership relation, courts do not attempt to thrust a partner on anyone.
b. A partnership usually involves partners' contributions of capital, services, or a combination of these.
c. The partners are associated as co-owners and principals to transact the business of the firm.
d. A partnership is organized for the profit of its members. If profit is not its object, the group will commonly be an unincorporated association.

The trend of the law is to treat a partnership as a separate legal person, although historically and technically it is merely a group of individuals, each of whom owns a fractional interest in the common enterprise.[3] The UPA does not make the partnership a separate entity, and therefore, suit cannot be brought by the firm in its name in the absence of a special statute or procedural rule so providing. Some courts regard a partnership as distinct from the individual partners, so a partnership cannot claim the benefit of a personal immunity possessed by an individual partner.

As a partnership is based on the agreement of the parties, the characteristics and attributes of the partnership relationship are initially a matter of the application of general principles of contract law. The principles of partnership are then added.

3.   Purposes of a Partnership

A partnership, whether it relates to the conduct of a business or a profession, may be formed for any lawful purpose. A partnership cannot be formed to carry out immoral or illegal acts, or acts that are contrary to public policy.

4.   Classification of Partnerships

Ordinary partnerships are classified as general and special partnerships, and as trading and nontrading partnerships. The ordinary partnership is distinguished from the limited partnership, which is created by statute.[4]

(a) GENERAL AND SPECIAL PARTNERSHIPS. A **general partnership** is created for the general conduct of a particular kind of business, such as a hardware business or a manufacturing business. A **special partnership** is formed for a single transaction, such as the purchase and resale of a certain building.

(b) TRADING AND NONTRADING PARTNERSHIPS. A **trading partnership** is organized for the purpose of buying and selling, such as a firm engaged in the retail grocery business. A **nontrading partnership** is one organized for a purpose other than engaging in

---

[2]   Uniform Partnership Act, § 6(1).

[3]   Decker Coal Co. v Commonwealth Edison Co. 714 P2d 155 (1986).
[4]   See Chapter 45.

commerce, for example, the practice of law or medicine.

Although the UPA does not expressly adopt this distinction, many cases decided under the UPA follow it, or rely on the basic soundness of the distinction to analyze whether or not partners exceeded their authority. The distinction between trading and nontrading partnerships was utilized in the *Patel* case.

PATEL v PATEL

212 Cal App 3d 6, 260 Cal Rptr 255 (1989)

L.G. and S.L. Patel, husband and wife, along with their son Rajeshkumar, ("R") formed a partnership in 1986 to own and operate the City Center Motel in Eureka, California. L.G. and S.L. decided to sell the motel and contracted with P.V. and Kirit Patel for its sale. Neither the broker nor the purchasers knew of "R"'s interest in the hotel. When L.G. and S.L. notified "R" of their plans, to their surprise he refused to sell his 35 percent interest in the motel. L.G. and S.L. therefore notified P.V. and Kirit that they wished to withdraw from the deal. P.V. and Kirit sued for specific performance. From a judgment for the hotel owners, P.V. and Kirit appealed.

CHANNELL, J. . . . Generally, every partner is an agent of the partnership for the purpose of its business, and the act of every partner to carry on the business of the partnership binds the partnership. [UPA § 9(1)] However, partners acting without the approval of the remaining partners may not do any act which would make it impossible to carry on the ordinary business of the partnership. [UPA § 9(3)(c)] These provisions distinguish between acts of a partner which bind the partnership without the express authority of the remaining partners and acts binding on the partnership only after express authorization by all partners. A contract executed by less than all of the partners to sell partnership real estate binds the other partners if the partnership *is in the business of buying or selling real estate* and the property covered by the contract is *part* of the stock held for sale. . . . Enforcement of the contract for sale of the motel, executed by L.G. and S.L. without the approval of their partner Rajeshkumar, would result in the sale of *all* of the partnership assets, making it impossible for the partnership to continue, in violation of subdivision (3)(c) of section [9].

Historically, partnerships were divided into two types: commercial or trading partnerships and noncommercial or nontrading partnerships. Although this distinction has been rejected in California, it remains a valuable tool in considering whether L.G. and S.L. exceeded their statutory authority by entering into the real estate sale contract, thus making it impossible to carry on the ordinary business of the partnership. . . . In the case of a commercial or trading partnership in which the usual partnership business is to hold and sell real property, a contract such as that involved in this case—to sell the sole partnership asset—would be enforceable. . . . By contrast, when—as in the present case—the usual partnership business is to run a business, rather than to hold it in anticipation of its eventual sale, the partnership is not bound by a contract selling that business without the approval of all partners. . . . Under these circumstances, the trial court properly denied specific performance of the unauthorized contract in order to prevent destruction of the partnership, in compliance with subdivision (3)(c) of section [9]. . . .

... To enforce the contract of sale without Rajeshkumar's approval would frustrate the purpose of subdivision (3)(c) of section [9] by making it impossible for the partnership to continue. As the purpose of the partnership is to operate a motel, rather than to hold it for eventual sale, we believe that the better result would be to preserve the partnership and hold the contract unenforceable. ...

[Judgment affirmed]

QUESTIONS

1. Does a contract for the sale of partnership real estate executed by fewer than all of the partners of a "trading partnership" that holds and sells real estate bind the other partners?
2. Was the City Center Motel partnership a real estate "trading partnership"?
3. Apply UPA § 9(3)(c) to the facts of this case.

5. Firm Name

In the absence of a statutory requirement, a partnership need not have a firm name, although it is customary to have one. The partners may, as a general rule, adopt any firm name they desire. They may use a fictitious name or even the name of a stranger. There are, however, certain limitations on the adoption of a firm name:

a. The name cannot be the same as or deceptively similar to the name of another firm for the purpose of attracting its patrons.
b. Some states prohibit the use of the words "and company" unless they indicate an additional partner.
c. Most states require the registration of a fictitious partnership name. For example, Ken and Steve Swain transact business under a partnership name, *The Berkshire Dairy Farm*. Since such a name does not reveal the names of the partners, a certificate stating the names and addresses of the partners must be filed at the public office designated by state law, usually a city or town clerk's office.

6. Classification of Partners

Partners may be general, nominal, silent, secret, or dormant.

a. **General partners** are those who publicly and actively engage in the transaction of firm business.
b. **Nominal partners** hold themselves out as partners or permit others to hold them out as such. They are not in fact partners, but in some instances they may be held liable as partners.
c. **Silent partners** are those who, although they may be known to the public as partners, take no active part in the business.
d. **Secret partners** are those who take an active part in the management of the firm but who are not known to the public as partners.
e. **Dormant partners** are ones who take no active part in transacting the business and who remain unknown to the public.

7. Who May Be Partners

In the absence of statutory provisions to the contrary, persons who are competent to contract may form a partnership. A minor may become a partner but may avoid the contract of partnership and withdraw.

In general, the capacity of an insane person to be a partner is similar to that of a minor, except that an adjudication of insanity usually makes subsequent agreements void rather than merely voidable. An enemy alien may not be a partner, but other aliens may enter into partnerships. A corporation, unless expressly authorized by statute or its certificate of incorporation, may not act as a partner. The modern statutory trend, however, is to permit corporations to become partners.

8.   Creation of Partnership

A partnership is a voluntary association; it exists because the parties agree to be in partnership.[5] If there is no agreement, there is no partnership. If the parties agree that the legal relationship between them shall be such that they in fact operate a business for profit as co-owners, a partnership is created, even though the parties may not have labeled their new relationship a partnership. The law is concerned with the substance of what is done rather than the name. Conversely, a partnership does not arise if the parties do not agree to the elements of a partnership, even though they call it a partnership.

The manner in which an enterprise is described in a tax return or an application for a license is significant in determining whether it is a partnership as against a person making the return or the application.[6] The mere fact that the enterprise is described as a partnership is not controlling or binding, however, as to a person named as a partner in the return or in the application if that person did not know of its preparation, did not sign it, and did not know what it said. When the parties are in fact employer and employee, there is no partnership, even though the employer files a partnership form of income tax return.

9.   Partnership Agreement

As a general rule, partnership agreements need not be in writing.[7] A partnership agreement must be in writing, however, if it is within the provision of the statute of frauds that a contract that cannot be performed within one year must be in writing. In some situations the agreement may come under the provision of the statute that requires a transfer of interest in land to be in writing. Generally, however, the agreement need not be written solely because the partnership is formed to engage in the business of buying and selling real estate.

Even when unnecessary, it is always desirable to have the partnership agreement in writing to avoid subsequent controversies as to respective rights and duties. The formal document that is prepared to evidence the contract of the parties is termed a **partnership agreement, articles of partnership**, or **articles of copartnership**. The partnership agreement will govern the partnership during its existence and may also contain provisions relating to dissolution. When matters arise that are not covered by the agreement, the rights of the parties will be determined by statute or court decision.

10.   Determining Existence of Partnership

Whether a partnership exists is basically a matter of proving the intention of the parties.

As in the case of agency, the burden of proving the existence of a partnership is on the person who claims that one exists.

When the parties have not clearly indicated the nature of their relationship, the law has developed the following guidelines to aid in determining whether the parties have created a partnership.

(a) CONTROL. The presence or absence of control of a business enterprise is significant in determining whether there is a partnership and whether a particular person is a partner.

(b) SHARING PROFITS AND LOSSES. The fact that the parties share profits and losses is strong evidence of a partnership.[8]

(c) SHARING PROFITS. An agreement that does not provide for sharing losses but does provide for sharing profits is evidence that the parties are partners, as it is assumed that they will also share losses. Sharing profits is *prima facie* evidence of a partnership. However, a partnership is not to be inferred when profits are received in payment of (1) a debt, (2) wages, (3) rent, (4) an annuity to a deceased partner's surviving spouse or representative, (5) interest, or (6) payment for the

5   Shain Investment Co., Inc. v Cohen, 15 Mass App 4, 443 NE2d 126 (1982).
6   Shinn v Vaughn, 83 Or App 251, 730 P2d 1290 (1986).
7   Stratman v. Dietrich (Colo App) 765 P2d 603 (1988); Beck v. Clarkson (SC App) 387 SE2d 681 (1989).

8   Boyarsky v Froccaro, 131 App Div 2d 710, 516 NYS2d 775 (1987).

FIGURE 44-1   PARTNERSHIP AGREEMENT

Ordinarily, the partnership agreement may be oral, but sound business practice requires that there be a detailed partnership agreement stating the rights and duties of all persons concerned.

PARTNERSHIP AGREEMENT

This is a partnership agreement executed at Cincinnati, Ohio, this 9th day of September, 1989 by and among Louis K. Hall, Sharon B. Young, and C. Lynn Mueller, individuals residing in Cincinnati, Ohio, hereinafter sometimes referred to individually as "Partner" and collectively as "Partners".

RECITALS

The Partners to this agreement desire to acquire a certain parcel of real estate and to develop such real estate for lease or sale, all for investment purposes. This agreement is being executed to delineate the basis of their relationship.

PROVISIONS

1. _Name: and Principal Offices_. The name of the partnership shall be: Hall, Young, and Mueller, Associates. Its principal place of business shall be at: 201 River Road, Cincinnati, Ohio 45238.

2. _Purpose_. The purpose of the partnership shall be to purchase and own for investment purposes, a certain parcel of real estate located at 602 Sixth Street, Cincinnati, Ohio, and to engage in any other type of investment activities that the partnership may from time to time hereinafter unanimously agree upon.

3. _Capital Contributions_. The capital of the partnership shall be the aggregate amount of cash and property contributed by the Partners. A capital account shall be maintained for each Partner.

A. _Capital Contributions_. Any additional capital which may be required by the partnership shall be contributed to the partnership by the Partners in the same ratio as that Partner's original contribution to capital as to the total of all original capital contributions to the partnership unless otherwise agreed by the Partners.

B. _Withdrawal of Capital_. Capital shall be withdrawn from the partnership by the Partners only pursuant to a mutual agreement of all Partners.

C. _Interest on Capital Contributions_. No interest shall be paid on any capital contributions by the Partners hereof.

4. _Shares of Profits and Losses_. The net profits and net losses of the partnership shall be divided equally among the four

-2-

...s, gains and losses of the partnership ...dance with generally accepted account... applied.

...his partnership shall begin upon the ...nd shall continue indefinitely unless ...er provided.

...tnership Business. Each of the three ...s to the management and control of ...: unless otherwise specifically pro... ...he affirmative vote of a majority ...'d before any such actions are taken ...stood and agreed between the Part... ...in or possess an interest in other ...; and description, independently or ...imited to real estate business in ...clude without limitation, owner... ...ation and development of real ...nor the Partners shall have any ...ventures or to the income or ...tnership may employ or transact ...anding the fact that any Partner ...of, or may have an interest in ...tities, and neither the part... ...have any rights in or to any

...account of the partnership ...the basis of the calender year. ...d at the end of each calender ...ership. They and all vouch... ...., papers and documents and ...ip or its affairs shall be ...tnership and shall be open ...pection of each Partner.

...shall maintain bank accounts ...ners from time to time may ...be drawn upon checks signed ...r as they may designate, or ...r shall agree upon by major-

...ests. No Partner shall sell, ...encumber or alienate his interest in ...the partnership in the event that a Partner wishes to sell his interest ...such interest to the remaining Partners, he must first offer to sell ...hereinafter set out, or any part thereof, at the price and on the terms ...ners of his desire to sell, and he shall give notice to the remaining Part... ...fourteen (14) days after receipt of such notice the remaining Partners shall have ...cise their option. The remaining Partners shall have the right to

19. _Ohio Law_ ...executed in the St... business of the p... books and records... State of Ohio, m... in the State of... ciled in the St... hereto that th... of the State of O... validity and interpre... ing to the rights and oblig... this agreement, shall be const... laws of the State of Ohio.

IN WITNESS WHEREOF, the parties hereto have agreement this 9th day September, 1989.

Louis K. Hall
Louis K. Hall

Sharon B. Young
Sharon B. Young

C. Lynn Mueller
C. Lynn Mueller

goodwill of the business. The fact that one doctor receives one-half of the net income does not establish that doctor as a partner of another doctor when the former was guaranteed a minimum annual amount and when federal income tax and social security contributions were deducted from the payments to him or her, thus indicating that the relationship was employer and employee.[9] If there is no evidence of the reason for receiving the profits, a partnership of the parties involved exists.

(d) GROSS RETURNS. The sharing of gross returns is itself very slight, if any, evidence of partnership. To illustrate, in a case in which one party owned a show that was exhibited on land owned by another under an agreement to divide the gross proceeds, no partnership was proven. There was no co-ownership or community of interest in the business. Similarly, it was not established that there was a partnership when it was shown that a farmer rented an airplane to a pilot to do aerial chemical spraying under an agreement by which the pilot would pay the farmer, as compensation for the use of the plane, a share of the fees that the pilot received.

(e) CO-OWNERSHIP. Neither the co-ownership of property nor the sharing of profits or rents from property that two or more persons own creates a partnership. Thus, the fact that a person acquires a 49 percent interest in a trailer park does not establish that such person is a partner. This in itself does not establish that the co-owners are together conducting the trailer park business for profit. Conversely, the mere fact that there is a sharing of the income from property by joint owners does not establish that they are partners.

(f) CONTRIBUTION OF PROPERTY. The fact that all persons have not contributed capital to the enterprise does not establish that the enterprise is not a partnership. A partnership may be formed even though some of its members furnish only skill or labor.

(g) FIXED PAYMENT. When a person who

performs continuing services for another receives a fixed payment for such services, not dependent upon the existence of profit and not affected by losses, that person is not a partner.

11. Partners as to Third Persons

In some instances persons who are in fact not partners may be held accountable to third persons as though they were partners. This liability arises when they conduct themselves in such a manner that others are reasonably led to believe that they are partners and to act in reliance on that belief, to their injury.[10] A person who is held liable as a partner under such circumstances is termed a *nominal partner*, a *partner by estoppel*, or an *ostensible partner*.

Partnership liability may arise by estoppel when a person who in fact is not a partner is described as a partner in a document filed with the government, provided the person so described has in some way participated in the filing of the document and the person claiming the benefit of the estoppel had knowledge of that document and relied on the statement. For example, suppose that the partnership of A and B, in registering its fictitious name, specifies A, B, and C as partners and that the registration certificate is signed by all of them. If a creditor who sees this registration statement extends credit to the firm in reliance in part on the fact that C is a partner, C has a partner's liability insofar as that creditor is concerned.

Conversely, no estoppel arises when the creditor does not know of the existence of the registration certificate and consequently does not rely thereon in extending credit to the partnership. Likewise, such liability does not arise when C does not know of the certificate.

12. Partnership Property

In general, partnership property consists of all the property contributed by the partners or ac-

---

[9]   UPA § 7(4).

[10]   UPA § 16(1); Johnson v Slusser, 33 Wash App 439, 655 P2d 261 (1982); Royal Bank and Trust Co. v Weintraub, Gold & Alper, 68 NY2d 124, 506 NYS2d 151 (1986).

quired for the firm or with its funds.[11] There is usually no limitation on the kind and amount of property that a partnership may acquire. The firm may own real as well as personal property, unless it is prohibited from doing so by statute or by the partnership agreement.

The parties may agree that real estate owned by one of the partners should become partnership property. When this intent exists, the particular property constitutes partnership property even if it is still in the name of the original owner.

In the *Mehl* case a dispute arose as to whether or not a bar purchased by one partner with checks written on the partnership bank account was a partnership asset.

[11]   UPA § 8.

MEHL v MEHL
(Mont) 786 P2d 1173 (1990)

Eugene and Marlowe Mehl are brothers. Since 1950 they have operated the family farm as a partnership known as "Mehl Brothers" or "Mehl Farms." The partnership operated without a written partnership agreement, and it had no definite term. Property held by the partnership consisted primarily of farming equipment and machinery. All proceeds were deposited in a checking account at a local bank, and expenses were paid from that account. The brothers had agreed to split all profits on a fifty-fifty basis. Whenever money was needed by either partner, the practice was that he would tell the other and withdraw such money. In 1973, Eugene Mehl withdrew $7,200 from the partnership account and bought the Dagmar Bar located in Dagmar, Montana. The warranty deed and the liquor license to the bar were held in the names of Eugene Mehl and his wife, Bonnie. In 1980, Eugene and Bonnie were divorced, and Bonnie received the bar and liquor license as part of the property settlement. The partnership was dissolved by written notice from Marlowe to Eugene in 1983. A complaint was filed in court over whether the Dagmar Bar was a partnership asset. From a decision that the bar was a partnership asset, Eugene appealed.

MCDONOUGH, J. . . . Eugene Mehl contends it was reversible error for the District Court to treat the Dagmar Bar as a partnership asset, and it was reversible error to assign a $50,000 value to the bar. We disagree. [UPA § 8(2)] states: "Unless a contrary intention appears, property acquired with partnership funds is partnership property."

The record shows that Eugene purchased the Dagmar Bar with two checks written on the partnership account. Therefore, the burden is on him to show that the bar did not belong to the partnership.

Documentation of ownership of the bar was submitted by both parties. Eugene Mehl submitted the warranty deed and liquor license to the bar which were in his and his wife's name. He also entered into evidence bank statements, employment registrations and other financial records which tended to indicate that he was the owner of the bar.

Marlowe Mehl submitted tax records and the property settlement between Eugene and his ex-wife Bonnie, which stated that the bar was partnership property. The lower court reviewed the evidence submitted by both parties and determined that the evidence submitted by Eugene did not overcome the presumption contained in [UPA § 8(2)].

We acknowledge, however, that the evidence on this issue is conflicting. In light of the presumption created by UPA § 8(2), and in light of the evidence of ownership contained within the tax records and property settlement, we find there is substantial evidence for the court's findings and there is no abuse of discretion. Accordingly, the District Court's findings must be affirmed. . . .

[Judgment affirmed]

QUESTIONS

1. Explain the underlying dispute in this case.
2. What rule of law was applied to resolve the dispute over the ownership of the bar?
3. How did the court decide the case?

13.   Tenancy in Partnership

Partners hold title to firm property by **tenancy in partnership**.[12] The characteristics of such a tenancy are:

a. Each partner has an equal right to use firm property for partnership purposes in the absence of a contrary agreement.

b. A partner possesses no divisible interest in any specific item of partnership property that can be voluntarily sold, assigned, or mortgaged by a partner.[13]

c. A creditor of a partner cannot proceed against any specific items of partnership property.[14] The creditor can proceed only against the partner's interest in the partnership. This is done by applying to a court for a **charging order**. By this procedure, the share of any profits that would be paid to the debtor-partner is paid to a receiver on behalf of the creditor, or the court may direct the sale of the interest of the debtor-partner in the partnership.

d. On the death of a partner, the partnership property vests in the surviving partners for partnership purposes and is not subject to the rights of the surviving spouse of the deceased partner.

14.   Assignment of Partner's Interest

Although a partner cannot transfer specific items of partnership property in the absence of authority to so act on behalf of the partnership, a partner's interest in the partnership may be voluntarily assigned by the partner. The assignee does not become a partner without the consent of the other partners.[15] Without this consent, the assignee is entitled to receive only the assignor's share of the profits during the continuance of the partnership and the assignor's interest upon the dissolution of the firm. The assignee has no right to participate in the management of the partnership, nor does the assignee have a right to inspect the books of the partnership.

B.   DISSOLUTION AND TERMINATION

Partnerships may be dissolved by the acts of the partners, by order of a court, or by operation of law. Dissolution changes the legal status of both the partnership and the individual partners.

---

[12]   UPA § 25(1).
[13]   Putnam v Shoaf (Tenn App) 620 SW2d 510 (1981).
[14]   UPA § 25(2) (c).

[15]   Bourgeois v Medical Center of E. New Orleans (La App) 482 So 2d 795 (1986).

15. Effect of Dissolution

Dissolution ends the right of the partnership to exist as a going concern, but it does not end the existence of the partnership.[16] It is followed by a winding-up period, upon the conclusion of which the partnership's legal existence terminates.

Dissolution reduces the authority of the partners. From the moment of dissolution, the partners lose authority to act for the firm, "except so far as may be necessary to wind up partnership affairs or to complete transactions begun but not then finished."[17] The vested rights of the partners are not extinguished by dissolving the firm, and the existing liabilities remain. Thus, when the partnership is dissolved by the death of a partner, the estate of the deceased partner is liable to the same extent as the deceased partner.

16. Dissolution by Act of Parties

A partnership may be dissolved by action of the parties.

(a) AGREEMENT. A partnership may be dissolved in accordance with the terms of the original agreement of the parties, as by the expiration of the period for which the relationship was to continue or by the performance of the object for which it was organized.[18] The relationship may also be dissolved by subsequent agreement. The partners may agree to dissolve the firm before the lapse of the time specified in the articles of partnership or before the attainment of the object for which the firm was created.

(b) EXPULSION. A partnership is dissolved by the expulsion of any partner from the business, whether or not authorized by the partnership agreement.[19]

(c) ALIENATION OF INTEREST. Neither a voluntary sale of a partner's interest nor an involuntary sale for the benefit of creditors works a dissolution of the partnership.

(d) WITHDRAWAL. A partner has the power to withdraw from the partnership at any time, but if the withdrawal violates the partnership agreement, the withdrawing partner becomes liable to the co-partners for damages for breach of contract. When the relationship is for no definite purpose or time, a partner may withdraw without liability at any time. Restrictive provisions on later employment are commonly found in partnership agreements, particularly in the accounting and medical professions and in marketing organizations. Lawyers may not participate in such restrictive provisions due to the strong public interest in allowing clients to retain counsel of their choice.[20]

The *Weeks* case raised the question of whether a partnership could be dissolved by a partner at any time because the partnership agreement did not state a definite period for its existence.

---

[16] Sheppard v Griffin (Tenn App) 776 SW2d 119 (1989).
[17] UPA § 33.
[18] UPA § 31(1) (a).

[19] Susman v Cypress Venture, 187 I11 App 3d 312, 134 Ill Dec 901, 543 NE2d 184 (1989).
[20] Meehan v Shaughnessy, 404 Mass App 419, 535 NE2d 1255 (1989).

WEEKS v MCMILLAN
(SC App) 353 SE2d 289 (1987)

William Weeks joined an established public accounting firm known as Harris, McMillan, Hudgins & Co. in 1974. In 1980, Sara Penn joined the firm as a partner, and a new partnership agreement was executed by all of the partners. In 1983, Hudgins and Harris retired, and the partners agreed to admit Robert Cooper and

Toni McKinley as partners, but no new partnership agreement was executed. Thereafter, Weeks became disgruntled and gave notice on July 31, 1984, that he elected to dissolve the partnership. After a short period of cooperation, the remaining partners denied Weeks access to the firm's records and files. Weeks commenced this action for a court-ordered confirmation of the dissolution and for an accounting. The partners counterclaimed for the enforcement of the 1980 partnership agreement that they claimed precluded dissolution. They also claimed that Weeks had violated the noncompetition clause in the 1980 agreement. From a judgment for Weeks, the partners appealed.

CURETON, J. . . . The threshold question in this appeal is whether the retirement of Hudgins and Harris and the admission of Cooper and McKinley effected a dissolution of the partnership. The master found that the change in the membership of the partnership resulted in a dissolution. We agree with the master. A dissolution is defined in [UPA § 29] as "the change in the relation of the partners caused by any partner ceasing to be associated in the carrying on as distinguished from the winding up of the business." The common law rule is that both the admission of a partner and the withdrawal of a partner will effect a dissolution. 60 Am.Jur.2d *Partnership* Sections 177 and 178 (1972).

While the authorities are not in total agreement on whether the Uniform Partnership Act changes the common law regarding the causes for dissolution, it is generally accepted that since the Uniform Act only incorporated in part the common law on dissolutions, other means of dissolution known to the common law are not precluded by the Act. We hold that the withdrawal of two partners and the admission of two other partners worked an ipso facto dissolution of the partnership represented by the 1980 agreement.

We agree with the master that after the change in membership of the partnership in 1983, there then existed between the parties to this action a partnership in fact of indefinite duration, and an at will partnership. A partnership at will is subject to dissolution by the act of one or more partners at any time.

The appellant partners also argue that the partnership existing after the change in membership adopted the provisions of the 1980 agreement and, thus, the partnership was not one at will. They further argue that because the partners adopted the 1980 agreement, Weeks is bound by the noncompetition clause in the agreement. We disagree. The 1980 agreement, even if adopted by the partners to this action, sets no definite time for termination of the partnership status and is, for all practical purposes, a partnership at will and subject to dissolution by Weeks. . . . Finally, we find that regardless of whether or not some portions of the agreement were adopted by all of the partners in the new partnership, the evidence is essentially uncontradicted that Weeks voiced objection to being bound by the noncompetition provision after the change in membership of the partnership, and never thereafter affirmatively agreed to be bound by the provision. Like any other contract, Weeks cannot be bound by partnership terms to which he did not agree. . . .

[Judgment affirmed]

QUESTIONS

1. May a partnership of indefinite duration be dissolved by the act of one partner at any time?

> 2. Was the dissolution in this case by "act of the parties" or by "decree of court"?
> 3. Was Weeks bound by the noncompetition clause in the 1980 agreement?

17.   Dissolution by Operation of Law

A partnership is dissolved by operation of law in the following instances.

(a) DEATH. An ordinary partnership is dissolved immediately upon the death of any partner. Thus, when the executor of a deceased partner carries on the business with the remaining partner, there is legally a new firm.

(b) BANKRUPTCY. Bankruptcy of the firm or of one of the partners causes the dissolution of the firm; insolvency alone does not.

(c) ILLEGALITY. A partnership is dissolved "by an event which makes it unlawful for the business of the partnership to be carried on or for the members to carry it on in partnership." To illustrate, when it is made unlawful by statute for judges to engage in the practice of law, a law firm is dissolved when one of its members becomes a judge.

(d) WAR. A partnership is ordinarily dissolved when there is war between the governments to which the different partners owe allegiance.

18.   Dissolution by Decree of Court

When a partnership is to continue for a specified time, there are several situations in which one partner is permitted to obtain its dissolution through a decree of court. A court will not order the dissolution for trifling causes or temporary grievances that do not involve a permanent harm or injury to the partnership.

The filing of a complaint seeking a judicial dissolution does not in itself cause a dissolution of the partnership; it is the decree of the court that has that effect.

A partner may obtain a decree of dissolution for any of the following reasons.

(a) INSANITY. A partner has been judicially declared insane or of unsound mind.

(b) INCAPACITY. One of the partners has become incapable of performing the terms of the partnership agreement.

(c) MISCONDUCT. One of the partners has been guilty of conduct that substantially tends to affect prejudicially the continuance of the business. The habitual drunkenness of a partner is a sufficient cause for judicial dissolution.

(d) IMPRACTICABILITY. One of the partners persistently or willfully acts in such a way that it is not reasonably practicable to carry on the partnership business. Dissolution will be granted when dissensions are so serious and persistent as to make continuance impracticable, or when all confidence and cooperation between the parties have been destroyed.

(e) LACK OF SUCCESS. The partnership cannot continue in business except at a loss.

(f) EQUITABLE CIRCUMSTANCES. A decree of dissolution will be granted under any other circumstances that equitably call for a dissolution. Such a situation exists when one partner has been induced by fraud to enter into the partnership.

19.   Notice of Dissolution

The statement that dissolution terminates the authority of the partners to act for the firm requires some modification. Under some circumstances, one partner may continue to possess the power to make a binding contract.

(a) NOTICE TO PARTNERS. When the firm is dissolved by the act of a partner, notice must be given to the other partners unless that partner's act clearly shows an intent to withdraw from or to dissolve the firm. If the withdrawing partner acts without notice to the other partners, that partner is bound as between them on contracts created for the firm.

Where the dissolution is caused by the act, death, or bankruptcy of a partner, each partner is liable to the co-partners for a share of any liability created by any partner acting for the partnership as if the partnership had not been dissolved unless (1) the dissolution being by act of any partner, the partner acting for the partnership had knowledge of the dissolution, or (2) the dissolution being by the death or bankruptcy of a partner, the partner acting for the partnership had knowledge or notice of the death or bankruptcy.

(b) NOTICE TO THIRD PERSONS. When dissolution is caused by the act of a partner or of the partners, notice must be given to third parties. A notice should expressly state that the partnership has been dissolved.[21] Circumstances from which a termination may be inferred are generally not sufficient notice. Thus, the fact that the partnership checks added "Inc." after the partnership name is not sufficient notice that the partnership does not exist and that the business has been incorporated.

Actual notice of dissolution must be given to persons who have dealt with the firm. To persons who have had no dealings with the firm, a publication of the fact is sufficient. Such notice may be by newspaper publication, by posting a placard in a public place, or by any similar method. Failure to give proper notice continues the power of each partner to bind the others in respect to third persons on contracts within the scope of the business.

When dissolution has been caused by operation of law, notice to third persons is not required. As between the partners, however, the UPA requires knowledge or notice of dissolution by death and bankruptcy. It has been held that when a third party dealing with the partnership is not informed of the death of a partner, the surviving partners and the firm are bound by a notice sent by the third person to the deceased partner.

20. Winding up Partnership Affairs

In the absence of an express agreement permitting continuation of the business by the surviving partners, they must wind up the business and account for the share of any partner who has withdrawn, has been expelled, or has died.[22] If the remaining partners continue the business and use the partner's distributive share in so doing, that partner is entitled to that share, together with interest or the profit earned thereon.

Although the partners have no authority after dissolution to create new obligations, they retain authority to do acts necessary to wind up the business.

The *King* decision illustrates the important distinction between the authority of a surviving partner to take actions appropriate for winding up the partnership business, as opposed to the continuation of the partnership business as usual.

---

[21]   Lemay Bank & Trust Co. v Lawrence (Mo App) 710 SW2d 318 (1986).

[22]   Ross v Walsh (Tex Civ App) 629 SW2d 823 (1982).

KING v STODDARD
28 Cal App 3d 708, 104 Cal Rptr 903 (1972)

The Stoddard family—father, mother, and son—formed a partnership that published a newspaper, the *Walnut Kernel*. The parents died, and the son continued to run the paper. King performed accounting services for the paper. When he was not paid, King sued the son and the executors of the estates of the deceased partners, claiming that his bill was a partnership liability for which each was liable. The executors defended on the ground that the son, as surviving partner, did not have authority to employ an accountant but was only authorized to wind up the partnership business. To this defense King answered that the newspaper was continued in order to preserve its asset value as a going concern, so that it could be sold. The running of the paper was therefore part of the winding-up process. If true, this would give the surviving partner the authority to employ the accountant. From a judgment in favor of the accountant, the executors appealed.

BROWN, J. . . . The estate's liability was predicated upon the court's finding that the services were rendered during the process of winding up the partnership operation of the Walnut Kernel newspaper. We have concluded that the trial court erred and that the continuation of the business was not a winding up of the affairs of the partnership.

The partnership was dissolved by operation of law upon the deaths of Alda and Lyman E. Stoddard, Sr. . . . "In general a dissolution operates only with respect to future transactions; as to everything past the partnership continues until all pre-existing matters are terminated.". . .

[UPA § 35] provides that "[a]fter dissolution a partner can bind the partnership. . . (a) By any act appropriate for winding up partnership affairs. . . ."

It is this latter provision upon which the court based its decision that the estates of the deceased partners were liable for the accounting services performed after dissolution. The court found that "LYMAN STODDARD, JR.'S continuation of the WALNUT KERNEL business was an appropriate act for winding up the partnership, since the assets of the business would have substantial value only if it was a going business. . . .

We disagree with this finding. It is probably true that there might have been advantages to the partnership to sell the business as a going business, but the indefinite continuation of the partnership business is contrary to the requirement for winding up of the affairs upon dissolution. In *Harvey v Harvey*, 90 Cal App 2d 549, 203 P2d 112, the court disapproved a finding that the business and assets of a partnership were of such character as to render its liquidation impracticable and inadvisable until a purchaser could be found. The court stated: "In effect it [the finding] authorizes the indefinite continuation of the partnership after the death of a partner, a procedure not in accordance with section 571 of the Probate Code. Respondents counter with the argument that the business is such that it cannot be wound up profitably, and the estate given its share. But this argument overlooks the distinction between winding up a business and winding up the partnership interest in that business.". . .

Even if we assume that a situation might exist where continuation of the business for a period would be appropriate to winding up the partnership interest, such a situation did not exist here. The record reflects the fact that the surviving partner was not taking action to wind up the partnership as was his duty . . . nor did the estates consent in any way to a delay. Rather, their insistence on winding up took the form of an effort to sell the business and a suit to require an accounting. There is nothing in the record upon which to base the argument made by respondent that appellants consented to his continued employment. The fact that they did not object is of no relevance. They had no right to direct and did not participate in the operation of the business. Therefore, the determination that the acts of the accountants were rendered during a winding up process is not based upon substantial evidence. . . .

We conclude that the services of respondents were rendered after the dissolution resulting from the deaths of the partners, Lyman, Sr., and Alda Stoddard, and do not constitute services during the "winding up" processes of the partnership. . . .

[Judgment reversed]

QUESTIONS

1. What did King contend?
2. Did the court agree with King?
3. Based upon the first sentence of Section 20 of this chapter, when would it be possible for a surviving partner to temporarily continue a business during the winding-up process?

When dissolution is obtained by court decree, the court may appoint a receiver to conduct the winding up of the partnership business. This may be done in the usual manner, or the receiver may sell the business as a going concern to those partners who wish to continue its operation.

With a few exceptions, all partners have the right to participate in the winding up of the business.[23]

When the firm is dissolved by the death of one partner, the partnership property vests in the surviving partners for the purpose of administration. They must collect and preserve the assets, pay the debts, and, with reasonable promptness, make an accounting to the representative of the deceased partner's estate. In connection with these duties, the law requires the highest degree of integrity. A partner cannot purchase any of the partnership property without the consent of the other partners.

21.   Distribution of Assets

Creditors of the firm have first claim on the assets of the partnership. Difficulty arises when there is a contest between the creditors of the firm and the creditors of the individual partners. The general rule is that firm creditors have first claim on assets of the firm. The individual creditors share in the remaining assets, if any.

Conversely, creditors of the individual partners have priority in the distribution of the individual assets. The claims of the firm creditors may be satisfied out of the individu-

al partner's assets only after claims of the creditors of the individuals are settled.

After the firm's liabilities to nonpartners have been paid, the assets of the partnership are distributed as follows: (1) each partner is entitled to a refund of advances made to or for the firm; (2) contributions to the capital of the firm are then returned; (3) the remaining assets, if any, are divided equally as profits among the partners unless there is some other agreement. If the partnership has sustained a loss, the partners share it equally in the absence of a contrary agreement.

Distribution of partnership assets must be made on the basis of actual value when it is clear that the book values are merely nominal or arbitrary amounts.

A provision in a partnership agreement that upon the death of a partner the interest of the partner shall pass to that partner's surviving spouse is valid and takes effect as against the contention that it is not valid because it does not satisfy the requirements applicable to wills.

22.   Continuation of Partnership Business

As a practical matter, the business of the partnership is commonly continued after dissolution and winding up. In all cases, however, there is a technical dissolution, winding up, and a termination of the life of the original partnership. If the business continues, either with the surviving partners or with them and additional partners, it is a new partnership. Again, as a practical matter, the liquidation of the old partnership may in effect be merely a

---

[23]   UPA § 37.

matter of bookkeeping entries, with all parties in interest contributing again or relending to the new business any payment to which they would be entitled from the liquidation of the original partnership.

SUMMARY

A partnership is a relationship created by the voluntary association of two or more persons to carry on as co-owners a business for profit. General partners are those who are publicly and actively engaged in the transaction of firm business. Nominal partners hold themselves out as partners or permit others to hold them out as such. Secret partners are those who take an active part in the management of the firm but are not known to the public as partners.

A partnership agreement governs the partnership during its existence and may also contain provisions relating to dissolution. The agreement need not be in writing, unless required by the statute of frauds. Proof of the existence of a partnership may be found from the presence of shared control in the running of the business and the fact that the parties share profits and losses. The sharing of gross returns, as opposed to profits, is very slight evidence of a partnership.

Partners hold title to firm property by tenancy in partnership. A creditor of a partner cannot proceed against any specific item of partnership property, but must obtain a charging order to seize the debtor-partner's share of the profits. An assignee of a partner's interest does not become a partner without the consent of the other partners, and is entitled only to a share of the profits and the assignor's interest upon dissolution.

Dissolution ends the right of the partnership to exist as a going concern. Dissolution is followed by a winding-up period and the distribution of assets. A partnership may be dissolved by the parties themselves in accordance with the terms of the partnership agreement, by expulsion of a partner, by withdrawal of a partner, or by the bankruptcy of the firm or one of the partners. A court may order dissolution of a partnership, on the petition of a partner, because of the insanity, incapacity, or major misconduct of a partner. Lack of success is also a basis for dissolution, as well as impracticability or other circumstances that equitably call for dissolution. Notice of dissolution, except dissolution by operation of law, must be given. Actual notice must be given to those who have dealt with the firm as a partnership. All partners generally have a right to participate in the winding up of the business. After the firm's liabilities to nonpartners have been paid, the assets are distributed among the partners as follows: (1) refund of advances, (2) return of contributions to capital, and (3) division of remaining assets in accordance with the partnership agreement or, if no agreement is expressed, division of net assets equally among the partners.

QUESTIONS AND CASE PROBLEMS

1. What social forces are affected by the rule that distribution of partnership assets must be made on the basis of actual value when it is clear that the book values are merely nominal or arbitrary amounts?
2. What is the effect of dissolution on a partnership?
3. In proving that *A* and *B* are partners, compare the effect of proof that they (a) share gross returns, (b) are co-owners of property used in or by a business, or (c) share profits.
4. Ray, Linda, and Nancy form a partnership. Ray and Linda contribute property and cash. Nancy contributes only services. Linda dies, and the partnership is liquidated. After all debts are paid, there is not sufficient surplus to pay back

Linda's estate and to pay Ray for the property and cash originally contributed by Ray and Linda. Nancy claims that the balance should be divided equally between Ray, Linda's estate, and Nancy. Is she correct?

5. Compare the requirement of notice to third persons when (a) an agency is terminated and (b) a partnership is dissolved.

6. Baxter, Bigelow, Owens, and Dailey were partners in a New York City advertising agency. Owens, who was in poor health and wanted to retire, advised the partners that she had assigned her full and complete interest in the partnership to her son Bartholomew, a highly qualified person with ten years of experience in the advertising business. Baxter, Bigelow, and Dailey refused to allow Bartholomew to attend management meetings and refused his request to inspect the books. Bartholomew points out that his mother had invested as much in the firm as any other partner. He believes, as assignee of his mother's full and complete partnership interest, that he is entitled to (a) inspect the books as he sees fit and (b) participate fully in the management of the firm. Is Bartholomew correct?

7. Amy Gargulo and Paula Frisken operated as a partnership "Kiddies Korner," an infants' and children's clothing store. They operated the business very successfully for three years, with both Paula and Amy doing the buying and Paula keeping the books and paying the bills. Amy and Paula decided to expand the business when an adjoining store became vacant. At the same time, they incorporated the business for protection against the business risks involved in the expansion. Children's Apparel, Inc., was a major supplier to the business before the expansion and allowed very liberal payment terms. After the expansion, business did not increase as anticipated, and when a nationally known manufacturer of children's apparel opened a factory outlet nearby, the business could no longer pay its bills. Children's Apparel, Inc., which supplied most of the store's stock after expansion, sues Amy and Paula as partners for past-due bills on expansion stock. Children's Apparel, Inc., did not know that Amy and Paula had incorporated. Amy and Paula defended that the business was incorporated and that they therefore may not be held personally liable for business debts occurring after incorporation. Are Amy and Paula correct?

8. Calvin Johnson and Rudi Basecke did business

as the Stockton Cheese Co., a partnership. The partnership owned a building and equipment. By agreement dated January 31, 1981, the partners agreed to dissolve the partnership but never got around to completing the winding-up process. Johnson continued to use the building. He paid the insurance on the building, eliminating Basecke's name in 1982. The building was destroyed by fire on January 6, 1986. Johnson claimed the proceeds of the fire insurance policy. He pointed out that he and his wife were the named insureds on the policy and that they had made the payments. Basecke claimed that although the partnership was dissolved in 1981, the winding up of the partnership was not completed at the time of the fire, and that he was therefore entitled to half of the net proceeds of the policy. Decide. [State Casualty v Johnson (Mo App) 766 SW2d 113]

9. Williams owned and operated a bakery business. His two sons were employed in the business and from time to time received a share of the profits as a bonus. The father and one of the sons died. The administrator of the son's estate, the First National Bank, then sued the estate of the father for an accounting, claiming that the father and the two sons were a partnership and that the deceased son's estate was therefore entitled to a one-third share. Decide. [First National Bank v Williams, 142 Or 648, 20 P2d 222]

10. Larson entered into a Special Manager Incentive Agreement (SMIA) with Tandy Corporation. Larson agreed to manage a Radio Shack store for compensation equal to one-half of the adjusted gross profit of the store as computed by a specific formula and to provide the company with a $20,000 "security deposit" on equipment used to set up the store. The agreement was for a period of two years, automatically renewable annually until either party gave notice of termination 30 days prior to the end of a fiscal year. After some eight and one half years of operating under renewed agreements Tandy gave Larson notice of his termination. Larson sued Tandy, claiming that the SMIA was a partnership agreement, since there were shared risks, expenses, profits, and losses. He sought an accounting for his reasonable share in the value of the store. Tandy defended that under the SMIA Larson was an employee-manager, not a partner, and that the ultimate decision making on all matters was Tandy's. Decide. [Larson v Tandy Corp. 187 Ga App 893, 371 SE2d 663]

11. Langdon, Hurdle, and Hoffman formed a part-

nership to practice medicine. The agreement provided that if any partner withdrew from the firm within five years, he could not practice within a specified geographic area for a specified time. Five years and one day later, Hoffman withdrew from the partnership. Langdon and Hurdle brought suit against Hoffman, claiming that Hoffman was liable for damages for withdrawing from the partnership. Decide. [Langdon v Hurdle, 17 NC App 530, 195 SE2d 71]

12. Bowen owned and operated the Havana Club in a rented building. He owned all the physical assets of the business. He made an agreement with Cutler, the bartender, that she would operate the club, purchase supplies, pay bills, keep the books, and hire and fire employees. Cutler and Bowen were each to receive $100 a week and to divide the net profits. A partnership form of income tax return was filed for the business. At a later date, the Redevelopment Agency took the building in which the Havana Club was operated. The club went out of business because it could not find a new location. The Redevelopment Agency paid the club $10,000 damages for disruption of business. Cutler sued Bowen for one-half of the sum paid by the Redevelopment Agency on the theory that they had been a partnership. Bowen claimed that he was the sole owner of the business because he was the owner of the physical assets. Decide. [Cutler v Bowen (Utah) 543 P2d 1349]

13. Chaiken and two others ran a barber shop. The Delaware Employment Security Commission claimed that the other two persons were employees of Chaiken and that Chaiken had failed to pay the unemployment compensation tax assessed against employers. He defended on the ground that he had not "employed" the other two and that all three were partners. The evidence showed that Chaiken owned the barber shop; he continued to do business in the same trade name as he had before he was joined by the two additional barbers; and he had a separate contract with each of the two, which specified the days for work and the days off. It was also shown that Chaiken had registered the partnership name and the names of the three partners and that federal tax returns used for partnership had been filed. Decide. [Chaiken v Employment Security Commission (Del Super) 274 A2d 707]

14. Gus Jebeles and his brother-in-law Gus Costellos entered into an oral partnership agreement on September 2, 1977, to conduct a business under the name of "Dino's Hot Dogs" at a location on the Montgomery Highway. Jebeles, who had expertise in this kind of business, arranged for the lease and furnished the logo used by the partnership. From the beginning, Costellos devoted himself to the business full-time, and Jebeles devoted relatively little time to the business. Marital difficulties developed between Jebeles and his wife, who was Costellos' sister. Divorce proceedings began in January of 1979. At that time Costellos ceased to remit any funds to Jebeles and changed the locks on the doors of the premises. Jebeles filed suit seeking a dissolution of the partnership and an accounting of all profits. As judge, you believe that it would be ill-advised to dissolve the partnership and lose the valuable lease to the business premises and the future profits of the business. Instead, you are considering ordering that the partnership continue, with Costellos as the sole active partner and Jebeles as a silent partner. You plan on ordering an accounting. Would your decision be upheld on appeal? [Jebeles v Costellos (Ala) 391 So 2d 1024]

15. On August 23, 1973, Friedman, the "O" Street Carpet Shop, Inc., and Langness formed a partnership known as NFL Associates. "O" Street Carpet's net contribution to capital was $5,004. Langness contributed $14,000 in cash. Friedman contributed his legal services, on which no value was placed by the articles of partnership. The articles stated that Friedman was entitled to 10 percent of the profits. The articles provided that Langness was to receive payments of $116.66 per month. The partnership's accountant treated the payments to Langness as a return to Langness of her capital. In October of 1978, the partnership sold the rental property owned by the partnership, and the partnership was wound up. Friedman claimed that he was entitled to 10 percent of the partnership capital upon dissolution. Langness claimed that Friedman was not entitled to a capital distribution and that the monthly payments to her should not have been treated as a return of capital. Decide. [Langness v "O" Street Carpet, Inc. 217 Neb 569, 353 NW2d 709]

45

POWERS AND DUTIES OF PARTNERS

The powers and duties of partners are governed by the partnership agreement in those situations for which the partners had the foresight to make express provision in the partnership agreement. In all situations not covered by a partnership agreement, partnership law applies.

A partner's authority to act for the firm is similar to an agent's authority to act for a principal. However, unlike an agent, a partner is a co-owner who has rights in the partnership property and liability for partnership losses. Because of each partner's power to make decisions that may bind the firm, high standards of fair dealing are necessary between the partners. Such high standards of conduct affect the duties, rights, and liabilities of the partners.

A limited partnership is a form of business organization created by law. This form allows individuals to invest in a firm and share in its profits, but such individuals have no right to manage the firm. Limited partners have no liability for firm debts beyond the amount of their investment.

A. AUTHORITY OF PARTNERS

The scope of a partner's authority is determined by the partnership agreement and by the nature of the partnership.

1. Authority of Majority of Partners

When there are more than two partners in a

firm, the decision of the majority prevails in matters involving how the ordinary functions of the business will be conducted. To illustrate, a majority of the partners of a firm decide to increase the firm's advertising. They subsequently enter into a contract for that purpose. The transaction is valid and binds the firm and all of the partners.

Majority action is not binding if it contravenes the partnership agreement. For such matters, unanimous action is required.[1] Thus, the majority of the members cannot change the nature of the business against the protests of the minority.

When there is an even number of partners, there is the possibility of an even division on a matter that requires majority approval. In such a case the partnership is deadlocked. When the partners are evenly divided on any question, one partner has no authority to act. If the division is over a basic issue and the partners persist in the deadlock, so that it is impossible to continue the business, any one of the partners may petition the court to order the dissolution of the firm.

2.   Express Authority of Individual Partners

An individual partner may have express authority to perform certain acts, either because the partnership agreement so declares or because a sufficient number of partners have agreed thereto.

A partner's authority to act for the firm is similar to that of an agent to act for a principal. Thus, in addition to express authority, a partner has the authority to do those acts that are customary for a member of a partnership conducting the particular business of that partnership.[2] As in the case of an agent, the acts of a partner in excess of authority do not ordinarily bind the partnership.

3.   Customary Authority of Individual Partners

A partner, by virtue of being a co-manager of the business, customarily has certain powers necessary and proper to carrying out that business. In the absence of express limitation, the law therefore will imply that a partner has such powers. The scope of such power varies with the nature of the partnership and also with the business customs and usages of the area in which the partnership operates.

The following are the more common of the customary or implied powers of individual partners.

(a) CONTRACTS. A partner may make any contract necessary to the transaction of the firm business.[3]

When a plaintiff sues on a promissory note or other contract executed by a partner who does not possess express authority to enter into such transaction, the plaintiff has the burden of proving that the making of the contract or the giving of commercial paper was "usual" for a business of the character of the partnership.

(b) SALES. A partner may sell the firm's goods in the regular course of business and make the usual warranties incidental to such sales. However, this authority is limited to the goods held for sale by the partnership.

(c) PURCHASES. A partner may purchase any kind of property within the scope of the business and for this purpose may pledge the credit of the firm. This authority is not affected by the fact that the partner subsequently misuses or keeps the property instead of turning it over to the firm.

(d) LOANS. A partner in a trading firm may borrow money for partnership purposes. In doing so the partner may execute commercial paper in the firm name or give security, such as a mortgage or a pledge of the personal property of the firm. If the third person acts in good faith, the transaction is binding even if the partner misappropriates the money. A partner in a nontrading partnership does not ordinarily possess the power to borrow in the name of the firm.

---

[1]   Uniform Partnership Act, § 18 (h).
[2]   Ball v Carlson (Colo App) 641 P2d 303 (1981).

[3]   Barnes v Campbell Chain Co., Inc. 47 NC App 488, 267 SE2d (1980).

(e) INSURANCE. A partner may insure the firm property, cancel an insurance policy, or make proof of loss and accept a settlement for the loss.

(f) EMPLOYMENT. A partner may hire such employees and agents as are necessary to carry out the purpose of the enterprise.

(g) CLAIMS AGAINST FIRM. A partner has the authority to compromise, adjust, and pay bona fide claims against the partnership. A partner may pay debts out of the firm funds or by transferring firm property.

(h) CLAIMS OF FIRM. A partner may adjust, receive payment of, and release debts and other claims of the firm. In so doing a partner may take money or commercial paper but, as a general rule, cannot accept goods in payment. One who makes a proper payment is protected even if the partner to whom the payment is made embezzles the money or fails to account to the firm for the payment.

(i) ADMISSIONS. A partner may bind the firm by admissions or statements that are adverse to the interests of the partnership if they are made in regard to firm affairs and in pursuance of firm business. For example, when a buyer takes a purchase back to the partnership's store, the admission by the partner then in the store that the product is defective binds the firm.

(j) NOTICE. A partner may receive notice of matters affecting the partnership affairs, and such notice, in the absence of fraud, is binding on the other partners.[4]

4.   Limitations on Authority

The partners may agree to limit the normal powers of each partner. When a partner, contrary to such an agreement, negotiates a contract for the firm with a third person, the firm is bound if the third person was unaware of the agreement. In such a case the partner violating the agreement is liable to the other partners for any loss caused by the breach of the limitation. If the third person knew of the limitation, the firm would not be bound.[5]

In the *Schnucks Markets* case the court was faced with deciding whether a partner whose authority was limited could bind the partnership contrary to the limitation.

---

[4]   Grayson v Wolfsey, Rosen, Kweskin & Kuriansky, 40 Conn Supp 1, 478 A2d 629 (1984).
[5]   UPA § 9(4).

SCHNUCKS MARKETS INC. v CASSILLY
(Mo App) 724 SW2d 664 (1987)

David Cassilly and Joseph Mason, doing business as Glen Park Properties, were partners in the real estate development business. Schnucks Markets brought an action against the partners for breach of contract. Schnucks testified that Cassilly and Schnucks agreed that Glen Park and the Market would split the cost of extending a sewer line to the market and that Glen Park did not pay its share of the $25,263.36 cost. Glen Park vigorously denied that Cassilly had authority to contract for Glen Park and to bind the partnership. From judgment for Schnucks, the partnership appealed.

PUDLOWSKI, P.J. . . . Glen Park . . . contends [that] the court erred in not directing a verdict for them as the evidence conclusively established that Cassilly did not have the authority to bind the partnership and that the trial court failed to include an instruction on the issues of Cassilly's authority. . . . In essence, Glen Park rests its defense on a statement made by Cassilly in a deposition that he did not have such authority. As it was "uncontradicted," Glen Park reasons that Schnucks failed its burden of proving authority

[UPA § 9(1)] states:

1. Every partner is an agent of the partnership for the purpose of its business, and the act of every partner, . . . for apparently carrying on in the usual way the business of the partnership of which he is a member binds the partnership, unless the partner so acting has in fact no authority to act for the partnership in the particular matter, and the person with whom he is dealing has knowledge of the fact that he has no such authority.

Cassilly and Mason conceded that Glen Park was a partnership, thus they are both agents of the partnership and of each other. As the statute notes, there are exceptions to this rule. First, the act of the partner must be "for the purpose of its business" and in "carrying on in the usual way the business of the partnership." Negotiating at conventions and elsewhere an oral contract to divide the costs of sewer installation necessary for development of property certainly fits these requirements. . . . Glen Park . . . contends that negotiating the installation of sewer lines is a one-time deal and thus not in the course of partnership business. This is clearly refuted by the record. Finally, Glen Park relies on *Boonville National Bank v. Thompson*, 99 S.W.2d 93, 102 (Mo.1936) which states that the doctrine of agency does not apply to a non-trading partnership. *Black's Law Dictionary* (5th ed.) defines "Trading partnership" as "a firm the nature of whose business, according to the usual modes of conducting it, imports the necessity of buying and selling." *Id.* at 1339. Thus, it appears that Glen Park qualifies as a trading partnership. More important, however, the Uniform Partnership Act, which Missouri adopted thirteen years after *Thompson*, defines "partnership" as "an association of two or more persons to carry on as co-owners of a business for profit." [UPA § 6(1)] This more expansive definition leads us to the conclusion that *Thompson's* distinction between trading and non-trading partnerships is no longer relevant to the issue of partner agency authority.

Glen Park urges error in the failure to include an instruction . . . on whether Cassilly served as Glen Park's agent. Glen Park argues that since Cassilly denied agency, there arose a disputed issue of material fact which required the court to give an instruction. . . . Cassilly's denial of agency did not elevate this to a legally material issue for even if Cassilly did not possess authority, Glen Park would still be bound. [UPA § 9(1)] requires that if the partner in fact has no authority, "the person with whom he is dealing must have knowledge that he has no such authority." Glen Park presented no evidence that Schnucks had knowledge of Cassilly's supposedly limited status. It thus became unnecessary for the trial court to submit on this issue. . . .

[Judgment affirmed]

QUESTIONS

1. Did Glen Park claim that the partnership was not liable because the plaintiff failed to prove that Cassilly had authority to bind the partnership?
2. How did the court dispose of Glen Park's contentions on the authority of Cassilly?
3. Can a partner whose authority is limited nevertheless bind the partnership contrary to the limitation?

A third person cannot assume that the partner has all the authority that the partner purports to have. If there is anything that would put a reasonable person on notice that the partner's powers are limited, the third person is bound by that limitation.

The third person must be on the alert for the following situations in particular, as they warn that the partner with whom the third person deals either has restricted authority or no authority at all.

(a) NATURE OF BUSINESS. A third person must take notice of limitations arising out of the nature of the business. A partnership may be organized for a particular kind of business, trade, or profession. Third persons are presumed to know the limitations commonly imposed on partners in such enterprises. An act of a partner that would ordinarily bind a commercial firm, such as the issuance of a note, would not bind a partnership engaged in a profession. A partner in a trading partnership has greater powers than one in a nontrading firm.

(b) SCOPE OF BUSINESS. A third person must recognize and act in accordance with limitations that arise from the scope of the business. A partner cannot bind the firm to a third person in a transaction not within the scope of the firm's business unless the partner had express authority to do so. Thus, when a partner in a dental firm speculates in land or when a partner in a firm dealing in automobiles buys television sets for resale, the third person, in the absence of estoppel or express authority, cannot hold the other partners liable on such a contract. The scope of the business is a question of fact to be determined by the jury from the circumstances of each case. In general, the scope comprises the activities commonly recognized as a part of a given business at a given place and time. However, the usual scope may be enlarged by agreement or by conduct.

(c) TERMINATION OF PARTNERSHIP. A third person should watch for the termination of the partnership, either when the partner-

ship is terminated under conditions requiring no notice or when notice of the termination has been properly given.

(d) ADVERSE INTEREST. A third person must take notice of an act of a partner that is obviously against the interest of the firm. To illustrate, if a partner issues a promissory note in the firm name and delivers it to a creditor in payment of a personal obligation, the creditor risks nonpayment. Such an act may be a fraud upon the firm.

5.   Prohibited Transactions

There are certain transactions into which a partner cannot enter on behalf of the partnership unless the partner is expressly authorized to do so. A third person entering into such a transaction does so at the risk that the partner has not been so authorized.

The following are prohibited transactions.

(a) CESSATION OF BUSINESS. A partner cannot bind the firm by a contract that would make it impossible for the firm to conduct its usual business.[6]

(b) SURETYSHIP. A partner has no implied authority to bind the firm by contracts of surety, guaranty, or indemnity for purposes other than the firm business.[7]

(c) ARBITRATION. A partner cannot submit controversies of the firm to arbitration "unless authorized by the other partners or unless they have abandoned the business."[8]

(d) CONFESSION OF JUDGMENT. All partners should have an opportunity to defend in court. Because of this, a partner cannot confess judgment against the firm on one of its obligations. Exceptions exist when the other partners consent or when they have abandoned the business.

(e) ASSIGNMENT FOR CREDITORS. A partner cannot ordinarily make a general as-

---

[6]   Wales v Roll (Wyo) 769 P2d 899 (1989).
[7]   First Interstate Bank of Oregon v Bergendahl, 80 Or App 479, 723 P2d 1005 (1986).
[8]   UPA § 9(3) (e).

signment of firm property for the benefit of creditors, unless authorized by the other partners or unless they have abandoned the business.

(f) PERSONAL OBLIGATIONS. A partner

cannot discharge personal obligations or claims of the firm by interchanging them in any way.[9]

[9] Slingerland v Hurley (Fla App) 288 So 2d 587 (1980).

FIGURE 45-1   LIMITATIONS ON AUTHORITY OF INDIVIDUAL PARTNER TO BIND PARTNERSHIP

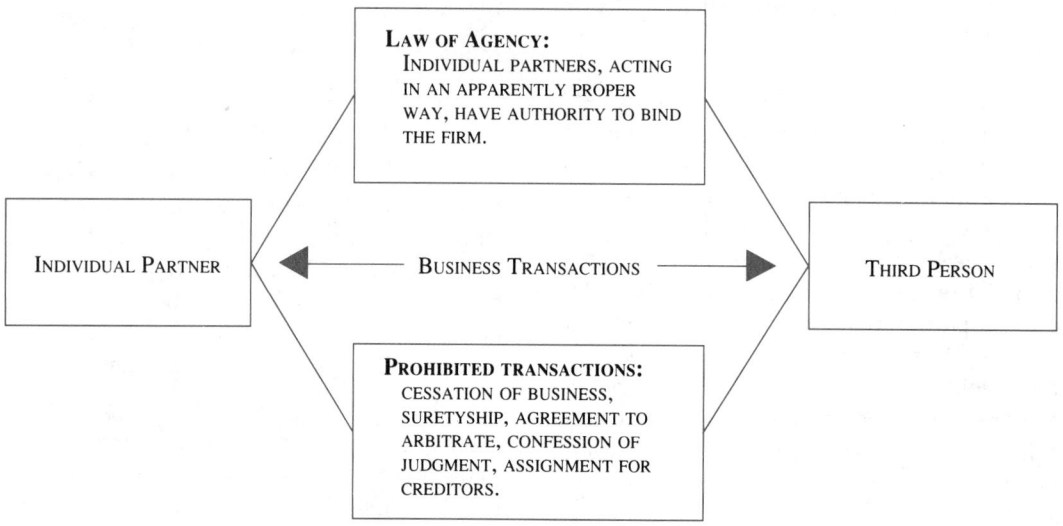

B. DUTIES, RIGHTS, REMEDIES, AND LIABILITIES OF PARTNERS

The duties, rights, remedies, and liabilities among the partners are influenced, to a large extent, by the high standards of fair dealing necessary for the successful operation of the partnership form of business.

6. Duties of Partners

In many respects, the duties of a partner are the same as those of an agent.

(a) LOYALTY AND GOOD FAITH. Each partner must act in good faith toward the other(s). One must not take any advantage over the other(s) by the slightest misrepresentation or concealment. Each partner owes a duty of loyalty to the firm. This duty requires a partner's devotion to the firm's business and bars the making of any secret profit at the ex-

pense of the firm, the use of the firm's property for personal benefit, or the exploitation for personal gain of a business opportunity of the partnership.[10] A partner's duties to the firm must be observed above the furtherance of the partner's own personal interest. To illustrate, when one partner renewed a lease of the building occupied by the firm but the lease was renewed in the name of that partner alone, that partner was compelled to hold the lease for the firm. The failure to renew the lease in the name of the firm was a breach of the duties of good faith and loyalty owed to the firm.

A partner, in the absence of an agreement to the contrary, is required to give undivided time and energy to the furtherance of the partnership business. In any case a partner cannot promote a competing business. If the partner

[10] Gilroy v Conway, 151 Mich App 628, 391 NW2d 419 (1986); Hooper v Yoder (Colo) 737 P2d 852 (1987).

does so, the partner is liable for damages sustained by the partnership.

A partner's fiduciary duty to other partners extends to any transaction connected with the formation, conduct, or liquidation of the partnership. In the *Steeby* case the court had to decide whether a partner violated his fiduciary duty to the other partner. One partner was secretly making new contracts with partnership clients on behalf of the partner's new firm after the partnership was dissolved, while the winding up of partnership affairs was being completed.

STEEBY v FIAL
(Colo App) 765 P2d 1081 (1988)

Roger Steeby and Charles Fial formed a partnership at will in January 1977 to perform auditing services. The partnership hired individuals on a contract basis to perform the actual auditing work. Steeby and Fial spent their time supervising the auditors' work and finding new business. Fial brought in 80 percent of the new business but was receiving 50 percent of the profits. He decided to dissolve the partnership and did so by notice to Steeby dated July 11, 1984. During the winding up of the partnership's affairs, Fial terminated contracts with partnership clients and negotiated new contracts with them on behalf of his new firm. From September 1984 through February 1985 he signed up the auditors to work for his new firm. The partnership was formally terminated on May 23, 1985. Steeby brought suit against Fial for breach of fiduciary duty. Fial contended that once the partnership was dissolved it was proper business judgment to start setting up his new business, by making new contracts with clients and signing up the auditors to perform work for the new firm. From a judgment for Steeby, Fial appealed.

PLANK, J. . . . Partners in a business enterprise owe to one another the highest duty of loyalty; they stand in a relationship of trust and confidence to each other and are bound by standards of good conduct and square dealing. . . . This principle is codified in [UPA § 21(1)] which provides that:

> Every partner must account to the partnership for any benefit and hold as trustee for it any profits derived by him without the consent of the other partners from any transaction connected with the formation, conduct, or liquidation of the partnership or from any use by him of his property.

Furthermore, each partner has the right to demand and expect from the other a full, fair, open, and honest disclosure of everything affecting the relationship. . . . *See* [UPA § 20].

Generally, a partnership proceeds through a three-step dismantling: dissolution, winding up, and termination. . . . The parties' relationship changes and their partnership dissolves when a partner ceases to be associated in the carrying on, as distinguished from the winding up, of the business. . . . That dissolution, however, does not terminate the partnership. Rather, the partnership continues until the winding up of partnership affairs is completed. Upon the completion of winding up, the partnership is thereby terminated.

Here, during the winding up period, Steeby and Fial agreed that the auditors would be told that the partnership was being dissolved but that they were to continue their work on partnership accounts. Thereafter, Fial unilaterally contracted with the auditors to do auditing for clients which had been clients of the partnership. Fial dealt individually with existing partnership clients and established new contractual relationships with them but on the behalf of his new firm. The trial court determined correctly that Fial had breached his fiduciary duty to Steeby by concealing the termination of the contracts with the auditors and partnership clients and subsequently renegotiating these contracts for his own personal gain.

Even after dissolution of a partnership, both partners continue to have a fiduciary duty to the other partner that continues until the partnership assets have been divided and the liabilities have been satisfied. . . . A partner is not entitled to take any action with respect to unfinished partnership business which leads to purely personal gain. . . . Further, a partner completing unfinished partnership business cannot cut off the rights of the other partners in the dissolved partnership by the tactic of entering into a "new" contract to complete such business. . . .

When a breach of fiduciary duty has been established, the injured party may recover his share of the partnership profits and property through the imposition of a constructive trust. . . . "Constructive trusts are raised by equity in respect of property which has been acquired by fraud, or where, though acquired originally without fraud, it is against equity that it should be retained by him who holds it." *Page v. Clark*, 197 Colo. 306, 592 P.2d 792 (1979).

Here, the trial court imposed a constructive trust on behalf of Steeby for one-half of all profits received by Fial as an equitable remedy for Fial's breach of duty. We conclude that, in doing so, the trial court properly exercised its equitable power. . . .

[Judgment affirmed]

QUESTIONS

1. When was the partnership dissolved?
2. Once the partnership was dissolved, was Fial free to set up a new business with clients and auditors from the partnership, without the consent of Steeby?
3. What was the measure of damages?

The obligation of a partner to refrain from competing with the partnership continues after the termination of the partnership if the partnership agreement contains a valid anti-competitive covenant.[11] In the absence of any such restriction, or if the restriction agreed on is held invalid, a partner is free to compete with the remaining partners, even though they continue the partnership business.

(b) OBEDIENCE. Each partner is under the obligation to perform all duties and to obey all restrictions imposed by the partnership agreement or by the vote of the requisite number of partners. Consequently, each partner must observe any limitation imposed by a majority of the partners with respect to the ordinary details of the partnership business. If a majority of the partners operating a retail store decide that no sales shall be made on credit, a partner who is placed in charge of the store must obey this limitation. If a third person does not know of the limitation, the managing partner has the power to make a binding sale on credit to such person. If the third person does not pay the bill and the firm thereby suffers loss, the partner who violated the no-credit limitation is liable to the firm for the loss caused by such disobedience.

[11]   Wright v Belt, 6 Kan App 2d 854, 636 P2d 188 (1981).

(c) REASONABLE CARE. A partner must use reasonable care in transacting the business of the firm and is liable for any loss resulting from a failure to do so. A partner is not liable, however, for honest mistakes or errors of judgment.

(d) INFORMATION. A partner has the duty to inform the partnership of matters relating to the partnership and must "render on demand true and full information of all things affecting the partnership to any partner or the legal representative of any deceased partner or partner under legal disability."[12]

The obligation to inform embraces matters relating to the purchase by one partner of the interest of another and to matters relating to the liquidation of the partnership.

(e) ACCOUNTING. A partner transacting any business for the firm must make and keep, or turn over to the proper person, correct records thereof. If the partners have delegated to one of the partners the task of keeping the books and accounts for all the business of the firm, that partner must keep proper records. If they are disputed, the recordkeeper has the burden of proving their accuracy. If it is not shown that the records are correct, the recordkeeper is held liable.

When an action is brought to compel a partner to account, the court may require the making of an audit by a disinterested third person.

When a partnership is organized for an illegal purpose or for conducting a lawful business in an unlawful manner, a wrongdoing partner cannot obtain an accounting by the partnership. For example, when the members of an engineering partnership did not have the license required for engineering work, one of the partners, an unlicensed engineer, could not require the other partners to account.

7.   Rights of Partners as Owners

Each partner, in the absence of a contrary agreement, has the following rights. These rights stem from the fact that the partner is a co-owner of the partnership business.

(a) MANAGEMENT. Each partner has a right to take an equal part in transacting the business of the firm. It is immaterial that one partner contributed more than another or that one contributed only services.

Incidental to the right to manage the partnership, each partner has the right to possession of the partnership property for the purposes of the partnership.

(b) INSPECTION OF BOOKS. All partners are equally entitled to inspect the books of the firm. "The partnership books shall be kept, subject to any agreement between the partners, at the principal place of business of the partnership, and every partner shall at all times have access to and may inspect and copy any of them."[13]

(c) SHARE OF PROFITS. Each partner is entitled to a share of the profits. The partners may provide, if they so wish, that profits shall be shared in unequal proportions. In the absence of such a provision in the partnership agreement, each partner is entitled to an equal share of the profits, without regard to the amount of capital contributed or services performed for the partnership.

The right to profits is regarded as personal property, regardless of the nature of the partnership business. Upon the death of a partner, the right to a share of the profits and an accounting passes to the deceased partner's executor or administrator.

(d) COMPENSATION. In the absence of a contrary agreement, a partner is not entitled to compensation for services performed for the partnership.[14] There is no entitlement even if the services are unusual or more extensive than the services rendered by other partners. Consequently, when one partner becomes seriously ill and the other partners transact all of the firm's business, they are not entitled to compensation for these services. The sickness of a partner is considered a risk assumed in the relationship. No agreement can be inferred that the active partners are to be compensated, even though the services rendered

---

[12]   UPA § 20.

[13]   UPA § 19.
[14]   Altman v Altman (CA3 Pa) 653 F2d 755 (1981).

by them are such that they would ordinarily be rendered in the expectation of receiving compensation. As an exception, "a surviving partner is entitled to reasonable compensation for services performed in winding up the partnership affairs."[15]

To illustrate the effect of an agreement of the partners, they may agree that one of the partners shall devote full time as manager of the business and that a salary shall be paid for such services in addition to the managing partner's share of the profits.

(e) REPAYMENT OF LOANS. A partner is entitled to the return of any money advanced to or for the firm. Such amounts must be separate and distinct from original or additional contributions to the capital of the firm.

(f) PAYMENT OF INTEREST. In the absence of an agreement to the contrary, contributions to capital do not draw interest. The theory is that the profits constitute sufficient compensation. Advances by a partner in the form of loans are treated as if they were made by a stranger and bear interest from the date the advance is made.

(g) CONTRIBUTION AND INDEMNITY. A partner who pays more than a proportionate share of the debts of the firm has a right to contribution from the other partners. Under this principle, if an employee of a partnership negligently injures a third person while acting within the scope of employment, and if the injured party collects damages from one partner, the latter may enforce contribution from the other partners in order to divide the loss equally between them.

The partnership must indemnify every partner for payments made and personal liabilities reasonably incurred in the ordinary and proper conduct of its business or for the preservation of its business or property. A partner has no right, however, to indemnity or reimbursement if the partner has (1) acted in bad faith, (2) negligently caused the necessity for payment, or (3) previously agreed to bear the expense alone.[16]

(h) DISTRIBUTION OF CAPITAL After the payment of all creditors and the repayment of loans made to the firm by partners, every partner is entitled to receive a share of the firm property upon dissolution. Unless otherwise stated in the partnership agreement, all partners are entitled to the return of their capital contributions.

After such distribution is made, each partner is the sole owner of the fractional part distributed to that partner, rather than a co-owner of all the property as during the existence of the partnership.

8. Liability of Partners and Partnership as to Particular Acts

The liability of a partnership and of the partners for the acts of individual partners and of employees is governed by the same principles as apply to the liability of an employer or a principal for the acts of an employee or agent.

(a) CONTRACTS. All members of the firm are liable on contracts made by a partner for the partnership and in its name if such contracts are made within the scope of the partner's real or apparent authority. Members are liable even though the partners may be unknown to the third person. Thus, a dormant partner, when discovered, can be held liable with the others.

When a partner acting on behalf of the partnership makes an authorized, simple contract but does so in the partner's own name, the firm and the other partners are liable as undisclosed principals.

When a partner with necessary authority executes commercial paper in the name of the firm, the firm and every partner is bound thereby. If a partner signs commercial paper in the partner's own name, the partnership and the other partners cannot sue or be sued thereon as undisclosed principals. Although partnership law determines the authority of a partner to enter into transactions on behalf of the firm, the UCC governs how commercial paper is to be executed by a partner.

When a borrowing partner gives the lender a promissory note for the partner's personal obligation, the partnership and the other partners cannot be liable thereon, even if the bor-

---

[15] UPA § 18(f).
[16] Gramacy Equities Corp. v DuMont, 72 NY2d 560, 531 NE2d 629 (1988).

rowing partner uses the money for the benefit of the partnership.

The fact that a partner has either express or implied authority to bind the partnership does not in itself establish that a contract made by the partner is a partnership contract, as distinguished from the individual contract of the partner. As in the case of agency situations generally, a contract between the third person and the principal, here the partnership, does not arise when that is not the intention of the parties. Consequently, where a third person and a partner make a contract intending to bind the partner individually, rather than the partnership, no contract liability of the partnership is created. Care must be taken to distinguish this situation from that in which the partnership is not disclosed and in which the third person has the intention of dealing with the partner only. In such cases the partnership and the other partners may be bound or have rights under the rules governing undisclosed principals who act through authorized agents.

(b) TORTS. All partners are liable for torts, such as fraud, trespass, negligence, and assaults committed by one partner while transacting firm business.[17] Accordingly, a partnership formed to manage real estate is liable for a battery inflicted by one partner on a tenant in collecting the rent. Each partner in a partnership formed for the general practice of medicine is liable for an injury to a patient resulting from the lack of skill or the negligence of any one of the partners.

(c) CRIMES. The partners of a firm and the partnership itself are liable for certain crimes committed by a partner in the course of the business, such as selling goods without obtaining a necessary vendor's license. A partnership, as distinct from the individual partners, may be fined for committing the crime of violating the federal law establishing regulations for the safe interstate transportation of explosives. If carrying on the firm business does not necessarily involve the commission of the act constituting a crime, the firm and the partners not participating in the commission of the crime or authorizing its commission generally are not criminally liable. This exception is not recognized in some cases, such as the making of prohibited sales to minors or sales of adulterated products.

9.   Nature of Partner's Liability

By virtue of the UPA, partners are jointly liable on all firm contracts.[18] They are jointly and severally liable for all torts committed by an employee or one of the partners in the scope of the partnership business. When partners are liable for the wrongful injury caused a third person, the latter may sue all or any of the members of the firm.

In the *Zuckerman* case the issue was whether the court could render a judgment against a doctor for malpractice committed by his partner, even though the summons did not name the partnership or designate the doctor as a partner.

---

[17]   UPA § 13. See Bergh v Mills (Wyo) 763 P2d 214 (1988).

[18]   Holt v Owen Electric Supply Inc. (Tex Civ App) 722 SW2d 22 (1986).

ZUCKERMAN V ANTENUCCI
478 NYS2d 578 (1984)

Daniel Zuckerman, an infant, and Elaine Zuckerman, his mother, brought a medical malpractice action against Dr. Joseph Antenucci and Dr. Jose Pena. Both had treated the mother during pregnancy. Although the summons did not state that the two defendants were partners, the undisputed, unopposed, and uncontradicted evidence at the trial established that relationship and the fact that the alleged acts of malpractice were done in the course of partnership business. The

> jury returned a verdict finding that Dr. Pena was guilty of malpractice but that Dr. Antenucci was not guilty of malpractice. The amount of the verdict totaled $4 million. The Zuckermans made a posttrial motion for judgment against the defendants, Joseph Antenucci and Jose Pena, in the sum of $4 million. Dr. Antenucci contends that he should not be held liable on a partnership theory for the act of his partner because the summons that commenced the action did not name the partnership as a defendant and did not identify Antenucci as a partner.

LEVISS, J.... The issue is whether this court has jurisdiction to render a judgment against defendant Antenucci on the basis of a tort committed by his partner, even though the summons served did not designate defendant Antenucci as a partner. ...

A party may be sued individually and directly for the tort of his partner. A partnership is liable for the tortious act of a partner, and a partner is jointly and severally liable for tortious acts chargeable to the partnership.

> Thus, if a partner, while acting in the course of the partnership business injures a third person, such third person would have the right to sue all of the partners together in one lawsuit, or any one or all of the partners individually, including even one who did not cause the injury. ...
>
> If it is a joint and several obligation of the partnership (based on a tort), any one (or some or all) of the individual partners may be sued personally *without suing the partnership itself.* ...
>
> When a tort is committed by the firm, the wrong is imputable to all of the partners jointly and severally, and an action may be brought against all or any of them in their individual capacities ... or against the partnership as an entity.

To illustrate how a plaintiff may proceed where a tort is chargeable to a partnership, Professor Beane supposes a partnership, the ABC Shoe Store, composed of Able, Baker, and Charles. A customer, Mrs. Jones, who is injured by Kit, an employee of the partnership, may elect to sue in several different ways:

> For example, Mrs. Jones may commence an action listing as defendants: "Able, Baker, and Charles individually and as partners, doing business under the name of ABC Shoe Store"; or she could commence an action listing "ABC Shoe Store" as the defendant; or she could sue any of the individual partners directly (without naming the partnership) as they are each jointly and severally liable for the tort. Therefore, she could commence an action against "Able" or she could commence an action against "Able and Baker", or against "Able and Charles", or "Baker and Charles." Since a person is liable for one's own tort, Mrs. Jones could also sue Kit, the employee; Kit could be named as a defendant in any of the preceding suggested actions. (Beane, *The Essentials of Partnership Law,* p 63.)

It may thus be seen that the plaintiffs herein did not have to sue a partnership entity and did not have to write "Joseph Antenucci, a partner" on the summons in order to hold him liable on a partnership theory for the act of defendant Pena. Jurisdiction over defendant Antenucci individually is sufficient for a judgment against him based on a tort committed by his partner.

Therefore, even though the jury found that defendant Antenucci was not guilty of any malpractice in his treatment of the patient, but that defendant Pena (his partner) was guilty of malpractice in his treatment of the patient, they were then both jointly and severally liable for the malpractice committed by defendant Pena by operation of law.

[Motion granted]

QUESTIONS

1. Was Dr. Antenucci found guilty of malpractice?
2. Were Dr. Pena's acts of malpractice done in the course of the Pena-Antenucci partnership business?
3. If the court had jurisdiction over Dr. Antenucci individually, could it render a judgment against him based on a tort committed by his partner?

10.   Extent of Partner's Liability

Each member of the firm has individual and unlimited liability for the debts of the partnership, regardless of the member's investment or interest in the firm.

In the *CCIC* case the court considered the question of whether one partner could be held liable for the full amount of a judgment against the partnership.

CCIC v MCELMURRY
102 Mich App 536, 302 NW2d 222 (1981)

The Inn Group, Inc. defaulted on a promissory note, loan agreement, and mortgage. MHS Enterprises, a Michigan partnership of which Leland McElmurry was one of three partners, guaranteed the Inn Group's performance to Commonwealth Capital Investment Corporation (CCIC). CCIC brought suit against both the partnership and the three partners for default on the loan agreement. Suit was brought at a time when the partnership had been dissolved and was in the winding up process. The court entered a judgment against the partnership. Five months later CCIC brought suit against Leland McElmurry, in his capacity as a partner of MHS, to satisfy the judgment against the partnership. Since McElmurry admitted that he was a partner of MHS, the court found him liable for the entire debt of $1,137,285. McElmurry appealed.

PER CURIAM. . . . Defendant first contends that since MHS was dissolved prior to the institution of plaintiff's suit, no judgment could be rendered against it and, as such, he could not be liable on the void judgment as a general partner.

. . . Section 30 of the Uniform Partnership Act, provides:

On dissolution the partnership is not terminated, but continues until the winding up of partnership affairs is completed.

In *Englestein v Mackie*, 35 Ill App 276, 182 NE2d 351 (1962), the Illinois Court of Appeals said the following about section 30 of the Uniform Partnership Act:

The terms "dissolution" and "termination", as employed in the Partnership Act are not synonyms and, as used, have different meanings. Dissolution does not terminate the partnership and does not end completely the authority of the partners. The order of events is: (1) dissolution; (2) winding up; and (3) termination.

Termination extinguishes their authority. It is the ultimate result of the winding up and occurs at the conclusion of the wind up.

The "winding up of partnership affairs" includes the satisfaction of debts against it. Consequently, it is our opinion that a partnership may be sued in its own name following dissolution, but prior to termination. . . .

Plaintiff properly sued the partnership as an entity. Consequently, the judgment entered against the partnership was not void, and defendant could be held liable as a general partner of the partnership.

Defendant further contends that there is no right to proceed against an individual partner based upon a judgment against the partnership. We disagree. UPA § 15 provides that all partners are jointly liable for the debts and obligations of the partnership. Furthermore, UPA § 36(1) provides that the dissolution of the partnership does not discharge the existing liability of any partner.

We agree with defendant that the judgment creditor of a partnership must first bring execution against the partnership assets before seeking to reach a general partner's individual assets. See, UPA § 18(a); and UPA § 40(d). However, defendant does not allege that partnership assets remain which might be used to satisfy the debt. An examination of the record suggests that, in fact, no such assets do continue to exist. Thus, the trial court's order was not improperly entered.

[Judgment affirmed]

QUESTIONS

1. Can a partnership be sued following dissolution of the partnership, when the partnership is in the winding-up process?
2. Can one of three partners be held liable for the entire debt of a partnership?
3. Does dissolution of the partnership discharge the existing liability of the partners?

(a) LIABILITY FOR BREACH OF DUTY. When a partner violates a duty owed to the partnership, the partner's liability is determined by the general principles of contract, tort, or agency law that may be applicable to such conduct.

When one partner commits a fraud upon another partner, the injured partner may recover compensatory and sometimes exemplary damages from the wrongdoing partner.

(b) LIABILITY OF NEW PARTNERS. A person admitted as a partner into an existing partnership has limited liability for all the obligations of the partnership arising before such admission. This is a limited liability, in that the preadmission claim may be satisfied only out of partnership property and does not extend to the individual property of the newly

admitted partner.[19] The incoming partner does not become personally liable for preadmission claims unless the incoming partner expressly promises to pay such claims.

(c) EFFECT OF DISSOLUTION ON PARTNER'S LIABILITY. A partner remains liable after dissolution of the partnership unless expressly released by the creditors or unless all claims against the partnership have been satisfied.[20] The dissolution of the partnership does not of itself discharge the existing liability of any partner. The individual property of a deceased partner is liable for the obligations of the partnership that were incurred while the deceased partner was alive. However, the in-

[19]   UPA § 17; see also UPA § 41 (1), (7).
[20]   Gjovik v Strope (Minn) 401 NW2d 664 (1987).

dividual creditors of the deceased partner have priority over the partnership creditors with respect to such property.[21]

11.   Enforcement and Satisfaction of Creditor's Claims

The firm may have been sued in the name of all the individual partners doing business as the partnership, as "Plaintiff v *A, B, C*, doing business as the Ajax Warehouse." In such case those partners named are bound by the judgment against the firm if they have been properly served in the suit. Partners either not named or not served are generally not bound by the judgment.

If a debt is contractual in origin, the common law requires that the partnership's assets be resorted to and exhausted before partnership creditors can reach a partner's individual assets.[22]

Personal creditors of a partner must first pursue the assets of that partner for satisfaction of their claims. After a partner's personal assets are exhausted, the creditor may enforce the unpaid portion of a judgment by obtaining a **charging order** against the partner's interest in the partnership. Under such an order a court requires that the partner's share of the profits be paid to the creditor until the debt is discharged.

C.   LIMITED PARTNERSHIPS

A common form of modified partnership is the limited partnership.

12.   Limited Partnership Principles

A limited partnership is solely a creature of statute. Some states have adopted the Uniform Limited Partnership Act (ULPA).[23] Others have adopted the Revised Uniform Limit-

ed Partnership Act (RULPA) or the RULPA as amended in 1985.[24]

In a limited partnership certain members contribute capital without liability for firm debts beyond the amount of their investment. These members are known as **limited partners.** The partners who manage the business and are personally liable for the firm debts are **general partners.**[25] A limited partnership can be formed by "one or more general partners and one or more limited partners."[26]

(a) FORMATION. Unlike a general partnership, this special form can be created only by executing a certificate of limited partnership. Under the ULPA the certificate must set forth the name and business address of each partner, specifying which partners are general partners and which are limited partners. The essential details of the partnership and the relative rights of the partners must also be specified. The certificate, when executed, must be recorded locally in the office of the official in charge of public records. This official might be the County Clerk or Recorder of Deeds of the county in which the principal place of business of the partnership is located.

Under the 1985 amendments to the RULPA, the certificate need only include (1) the limited partnership's name; (2) the address of the partnership's registered office and the name and business address of its agent for service of process; (3) the name and business address of each general partner; (4) its mailing address; and (5) the latest date upon which the limited partnership is to dissolve. The names of the limited partners (the investors) are not

---

[21]   UPA § 36.
[22]   McCune v Mountain Bell (Utah) 758 P2d 914 (1988); Midwood Development Corp. v K 12th Associates, 146 App Div 2d 754, 537 NYS2d 237 (1989).
[23]   The ULPA governs limited partnerships in Alaska, Maine, New York, Utah, and Vermont.

[24]   The 1976 RULPA has been adopted by Alabama, Arizona, Arkansas, California, Colorado, Connecticut, Delaware, Idaho, Iowa, Kansas, Maryland, Massachusetts, Michigan, Minnesota, Montana, Nebraska, New Jersey, North Dakota, Ohio, Oklahoma, Rhode Island, South Carolina, Virginia, Washington, West Virginia, Wisconsin and Wyoming. The RULPA with the 1985 amendments has been adopted by the District of Columbia, Florida, Georgia, Hawaii, Illinois, Indiana, Kentucky, Mississippi, Missouri, Nevada, New Hampshire, New Mexico, North Carolina, Oregon, Pennsylvania, South Dakota, Tennessee, Texas, and Virginia. Louisiana has not enacted either the ULPA or RULPA.
[25]   Brooke v Mt. Hood Meadows Ltd. 81 Or App 387, 725 P2d 925 (1986).
[26]   ULPA § 1; RULPA § 101(7).

required. This allows for the preservation of the confidentiality of the investors' names from competitors. Moreover, new investors may be admitted as limited partners without the significant administrative burden involved in amending the certificate as is required under the ULPA. The RULPA provides for filing of the certificate with the office of the secretary of state, as opposed to the local filing required under the ULPA.

When there is no filing of the limited partnership certificate, the participants have the status and liability of general partners in a general partnership. However, technical defects in the certificate do not prevent formation of a limited partnership if there has been substantial, good faith compliance with the filing requirements.[27]

In the *Brookwood Fund* case it was argued that since the newly admitted investors to a limited partnership were not timely recorded on the certificate of limited partnership as required by the ULPA, they were liable as general partners.

[27]   ULPA § 2(2); RULPA § 201(b).

---

8 BROOKWOOD FUND v BEAR STEARNS & CO., INC.
148 App Div 2d 661, 539 NYS2d 411 (1989)

8 Brookwood Fund was originally formed as a limited partnership on April 24, 1987. The certificate of limited partnership was filed with the Westchester County Clerk in April 1987. Between May and August of 1987 additional investors joined Brookwood as limited partners. On October 17, 1987, the stock market crashed. On October 19, 1987, Bear Stearns liquidated Brookwood's margin accounts. On October 23, 1987, a certificate amending the original certificate of limited partnership to reflect the newly admitted limited partners was filed with the Westchester County Clerk. In late October, Bear Stearns started arbitration proceedings against Brookwood, to recover $1,849,183, that was owed after the liquidation of the margin account. Brookwood sought an injunction to bar arbitration proceedings against the limited partners of Brookwood. From a judgment for the limited partners, Bear & Stearns appealed.

PER CURIAM. . . . The record indicates that Brookwood was originally formed as a limited partnership. The original certificate of limited partnership, filed with the Westchester County Clerk on April 24, 1987, listed Kenneth Stein as the "General Partner" and Barbara Stein as the "Original Limited Partner." Between May and August 1987, additional investors joined Brookwood as limited partners pursuant to Article 10 of the Agreement of Limited Partnership. . . .

Each of the additional investors signed a document entitled "Supplement to Agreement of Limited Partnership of 8 Brookwood Fund" and, pursuant thereto, each of the additional investors agreed to become an "Additional Limited Partner" in accordance with the terms of the original Agreement of Limited Partnership. In this regard, Article 8 of the Agreement of Limited Partnership provides as follows:

Article 8. Limitation on Liability of Limited Partners.

No Limited Partner . . . shall be liable for any debts, obligations or loss of the Partnership in excess of the amount of such Limited Partner's capital in the Partnership. The General Partner shall have unlimited liability for the debts of the Partnership.

Thereafter, these additional investors conducted themselves, at all times, as limited partners, *i.e.*, they did not participate in the management of the partnership. Finally, the record indicates that a certificate amending the original certificate of limited partnership, so as to reflect the newly added limited partners, was not filed with the Westchester County Clerk until October 23, 1987, six days after the October 19th 1987 liquidation of Brookwood's margin account.

On the instant appeal, the defendants argue that (1) pursuant to statutory mandate, (*see*, [ULPA § 8 and 25]) the certificate amending the original certificate of limited partnership, so as to reflect the newly added limited partners, had to be filed with the Westchester County Clerk, and (2) until October 23, 1987, when Brookwood complied with that statutory mandate, those investors who joined Brookwood after the filing of the original certificate of limited partnership were not limited partners, as they mistakenly believed, but rather were general partners, and therefore obligated to arbitrate any controversy arising out of the liquidation of Brookwood's margin account on October 19, 1987. However, even if we were to assume, arguendo, that there is merit to this argument . . . an affirmance would still be warranted. The record supports the finding of the Supreme Court that the additional investors and purported limited partners in Brookwood, upon receiving a notice of intention to arbitrate from Bear Stearns and Sloate Weisman dated October 26, 1987, concerning the "debit balance . . . in the amount of $1,849,183.00," "promptly renounced" their interests in the profits of the limited partnership, pursuant to [ULPA § 11]. Partnership Law [§ 11] provides as follows:

Status of person erroneously believing himself a limited partner.

"A person who has contributed to the capital of a business conducted by a person or partnership erroneously believing that he has become a limited partner in a limited partnership is not, by reason of his exercise of the rights of a limited partner, a general partner with the person or in the partnership carrying on the business, or bound by the obligations of such person or partnership; provided that on ascertaining the mistake he promptly renounces his interest in the profits of the business, or other compensation by way of income. . . .

Accordingly, the Supreme Court properly enjoined the [brokerage firm] from commencing "any action, proceeding or arbitration claim against Brookwood's limited partners.". . .

[Judgment affirmed]

QUESTIONS

1. Was the certificate amending the original certificate of limited partnership filed in time to protect the newly admitted "limited partners" from liability beyond their investments?
2. Did ULPA § 11 provide an escape from personal liability beyond their investment for the newly admitted "limited partners"?
3. Would the newly admitted "limited partners" have been subject to the same legal problems if the limited partnership had been formed in a RULPA state?

(b) CAPITAL CONTRIBUTIONS. Under the ULPA the limited partner contributes cash or property, but not services. Under the RULPA, however, the limited partner may contribute services.

(c) FIRM NAME. With certain exceptions, the limited partner's name cannot appear in the firm name. If improper use is made of the limited partner's name, giving the public the impression that the limited partner is an active partner, the limited partner loses the protection of limited liability and becomes liable without limit, as a general partner. Under the RULPA, the words *limited partnership* must appear without abbreviation in the firm name.

(d) MANAGEMENT AND CONTROL OF THE FIRM. The general partners manage the

business and are personally liable for firm debts. Limited partners (the investors) have the right to a share of the profits and a return of capital upon dissolution and have limited liability. The limitation of liability may be lost, however, should they participate in the control of the business.

The RULPA lists a number of "safe harbor" activities in which limited partners may engage without losing their protection from liability. These activities include:

1. being a contractor for or an agent or employee of the limited partnership or of a general partner;
2. consulting with and advising a general partner regarding the partnership business;

FIGURE 45-2   COMPARISON OF LIMITED PARTNERSHIP AND GENERAL PARTNERSHIP

	LIMITED PARTNERSHIP	GENERAL PARTNERSHIP
CREATION:	FILING A CERTIFICATE OF LIMITED PARTNERSHIP WITH APPROPRIATE STATE OFFICE	NO FORMALITY REQUIRED
LIABILITY:	GENERAL PARTNERS: UNLIMITED LIABILITY FOR FIRM DEBTS LIMITED PARTNERS: NO LIABILITY BEYOND LOSS OF INVESTMENT	UNLIMITED LIABILITY OF EACH PARTNER FOR FIRM DEBTS
MANAGEMENT:	GENERAL PARTNERS ACCORDING TO THEIR PARTNERSHIP AGREEMENT OR UNIFORM PARTNERSHIP ACT (UPA) LIMITED PARTNERS EXCLUDED	ALL PARTNERS ACCORDING TO THEIR PARTNERSHIP AGREEMENT OR UNIFORM PARTNERSHIP ACT (UPA)
DISSOLUTION:	AS SET FORTH IN THE PARTNERSHIP AGREEMENT OR THE ULPA OR RULPA	AS SET FORTH IN PARTNERSHIP AGREEMENT OR THE UPA

3. acting as a surety for the limited partnership; and
4. voting on partnership matters such as dissolution and winding up the limited partnership or the removal of a general partner.

(e) RIGHT TO SUE. A limited partner may bring an action on behalf of the limited partnership against outsiders for economic injury to the firm, when the general partners refuse to do so. Also, the limited partners may sue the general partners to protect the limited partners' interests.

(f) DISSOLUTION. The dissolution and winding up of limited partnerships is governed by the same principles applicable to general partnerships.

SUMMARY

When there are more than two partners in a firm, the decisions of the majority prevail on ordinary matters relating to the firm's business, unless they are contrary to the partnership agreement. A partner's authority to act for the firm is similar to that of an agent to act for a principal. A partner may have express authority to act as set forth in the partnership agreement or as agreed to by a sufficient number of partners. A partner has the customary or implied power to make contracts to transact the firm's business; to sell the firm's goods in the regular course of business; to make purchases within the scope of the business; and, in a trading partnership, to borrow money for firm purposes. Further, a partner may purchase insurance, hire employees, and adjust claims for and against the firm. However, a partner may not bind the firm by a contract that would make it impossible for the firm to conduct its business. In the absence of express authority from the firm, an individual partner cannot enter into a suretyship contract or an agreement to submit a partnership dispute to arbitration, confess judgment against the firm, make an assignment of the firm's assets for the benefit of its creditors, or discharge personal obligations of the partner by paying them with obligations of the firm.

A partner's duties are the same as those of an agent. These duties include loyalty and good faith, obedience, reasonable care, providing full information on all matters affecting the firm, and keeping proper and correct records. Absent a contrary agreement, each partner has the right to take an equal part in the management of the business, to inspect the books, to share in the profits, and after payment of all of the firm's debts and the return of capital, to share in the firm's property or surplus upon dissolution.

Partners are subject to unlimited personal liability to partnership claimants. Partners are jointly liable on all firm contracts. They are jointly and severally liable for all torts committed by one of the partners or by a firm employee within the scope of the partnership's business. A partner remains liable after dissolution, unless expressly released by creditors. Absent assumption, an incoming partner is not personally liable for existing partnership debts.

A limited partnership consists of one or more limited partners, who contribute cash, property, or services without liability for losses beyond their investment, and one or more general partners, who manage the business and have unlimited personal liability. Limited partnerships are created by statute. A certificate and public filing are required.

QUESTIONS AND CASE PROBLEMS

1. What social forces are affected by the rule governing the authority of a majority of the partners?

2. The Acorn Hardware Store is owned and operated by a partnership consisting of five partners. They disagree as to whether they should

have the building repainted. How many partners must agree to repaint?

3. Mark, Sylvia, and Lucy form and operate an automobile dealership as a partnership. Mark sells one of the automobiles of the partnership to Frances at a price below dealer cost, thinking that a profit could be made in servicing the vehicle. Sylvia and Lucy seek to avoid the sale to Frances on the ground that Mark was never authorized to make the sale to Frances. Is the sale binding on the partnership?

4. Compare the right of a partner to engage in a business that competes with the firm (a) while still a partner and (b) after leaving the partnership.

5. Ross, Marcos, and Albert are partners. Ross and Marcos each contributed $60,000 to the partnership. Albert contributed $30,000. At the end of the fiscal year, there are distributable profits totaling $150,000. Ross claims $60,000 as his share of the profits. Is he entitled thereto?

6. What is the effect of dissolution on a partner's liability?

7. Charles and Sonny Monin are brothers. They formed a partnership in 1967 for hauling milk for Dairymen Incorporated (DI), an organization of milk producers. The brothers had a falling out in 1984, and Sonny notified Charles that he was dissolving the partnership in July of 1984. The partnership's contract with DI expired on October 16, 1984. On September 24, 1984, the brothers executed an agreement to conclude their business arrangement, whereby they would hold a private auction between themselves for all the assets of the partnership, "including equipment and milk routes." The agreement contained a covenant not to compete. Charles was the successful bidder at $86,000. The value of the milk-hauling equipment was $22,000 and the milk routes $64,000. Sonny notifed DI that he wanted to apply for the right to haul milk after the expiration of the partnership's contract. Charles was the only other applicant for the milk routes. Sonny was selected over Charles for the new DI contract. Charles sued Sonny for breach of his fiduciary duty because Sonny failed to withdraw his application with DI for the milk routes after agreeing to allow Charles to buy his interest in those milk routes. Sonny contended that the partnership had no interest in the milk routes after the contract expired on October 16, 1984, and that he was therefore free to pursue the contract. Decide. [Monin v Monin (Ky App) 785 SW2d 499]

8. Compare the effect of a secret limitation on the authority of (a) an agent and (b) a partner.

9. George M. and James P. McCune did business as McCune & McCune, a general law partnership. Mountain Bell provided telephone service to McCune & McCune through November of 1983, when the partnership dissolved and its telephone service was discontinued. Mountain Bell transferred the unpaid balance of the partnership's account to the individual business account of George McCune. George brought suit against Mountain Bell to enjoin it from suspending his service, contending that partnership law requires that partnership assets be marshalled and exhausted before a partnership creditor can reach a partner's individual assets. Mountain Bell contended that it has the right to cross-bill customers' accounts for unpaid bills, and if the bill remains unpaid, it has a right to suspend service on the account to which the debt has been transferred. Decide. [McCune & McCune v Mountain Bell Tel. Co. (Utah) 758 P2d 914]

10. Mason and Phyllis Ledbetter operated a business in Northbrook, Illinois, as a partnership. This partnership, called Ledbetters' Nurseries, specialized in the sale of garden lilies. The grounds of the nurseries were planted with numerous species of garden lilies, and hundreds of people toured the Ledbetters' gardens each day. After a tour, Mrs. Shelia Clark invited Mason to Chicago to discuss the possible sale of the facilities at a "top-notch price." Mason felt he could not refuse the high offer made by Mrs. Clark on a take-it-or-leave-it basis, and he signed a contract to sell the entire facilities, including all flowers and the business name, to Mrs. Clark. When Phyllis refused to go along with the contract, Mrs. Clark brought suit against the Ledbetters' Nurseries partnership, seeking to obtain a decree of specific performance of the sales contract. Decide.

11. Holmes and Clay are partners in a medical partnership. Each had invested $25,000 in the practice; the total market value of all firm assets was $50,000. Marsh, a former patient of Holmes, sued Holmes and Clay for malpractice because of surgery performed by Holmes. Marsh's suit was successful, and a judgment was entered for $150,000 against the two partners. Holmes had suffered a prior financial setback, and he did not have funds or property other than partnership assets to pay the judgment. Arrangements were made by Holmes and Clay to pay $50,000 using the firm assets. Marsh now seeks to collect

$100,000 from Clay. Clay objects that it is absurd to seek payment from her out of her own personal assets when she was not at fault and, indeed, was not even at the hospital on the day the surgery was performed. Is Clay liable to Marsh for the unpaid balance of the judgment?

12. Hacienda Farms, Limited, was organized as a limited partnership, with Ricardo de Escamilla as the general partner and James L. Russell and H.W. Andrews as limited partners. The partnership raised vegetables and truck crops that were marketed principally through a produce concern controlled by Andrews. All three individuals decided which crops were to be planted. The general partner had no power to withdraw money from the partnership's two bank accounts without the signature of one of the limited partners. After operating for some seven and one-half months under these procedures, the limited partners required the general partner to resign as farm manager, which he did. Six weeks later the partnership went into bankruptcy. Laurance Holzman, as trustee in bankruptcy, brought an action against Russell and Andrews, claiming that they had become liable to the creditors of the partnership as general partners because they had taken part in the control of the partnership business. How would you decide the case under the ULPA? Would the outcome be different under the RULPA? [Holzman v de Escamilla, 86 Cal App 2d 858, 195 P2d 833]

13. The St. John Transportation Co., a corporation, made a contract with the partnership of Bilyeu & Herstel, contractors, by which the latter was to construct a ferryboat. Herstel, a member of the firm of contractors, executed a contract in the firm name with Benbow for certain materials and labor in connection with the construction of the ferryboat. In an action brought by Benbow to enforce a lien against the ferryboat, the *James Johns*, it was contended that all members of the firm were bound by the contract made by Herstel. Do you agree? [Benbow v The James Johns, 56 Or 554, 108 P 634]

14. William and Charlotte Davis operated the Davis Nursing Home as a partnership. William made a contract to sell the home and all its assets and goodwill to Feingold. Charlotte refused to recognize the contract. Feingold sued William and Charlotte to obtain a decree of specific performance of the sales contract. Decide. [Feingold v Davis, 444 Pa 339, 282 A2d 291]

15. Zemelman and others did business as a partnership under the name of Art Seating Company. The partnership obtained a fire insurance policy from the Boston Insurance Company. There was a fire loss, and a claim was filed under the policy. The claim was prepared by one of the partners, Irving Zemelman. The insurance company asserted that false statements were made by Zemelman and that the insurer was therefore not liable on the policy. The policy contained an express provision stating that it was void if a false claim were made. The partnership replied that it was not bound by any fraudulent statement of Zemelman, as the making of fraudulent statements was not within the scope of his authority. Is the partnership correct? [Zemelman v Boston Insurance Co. 4 Cal App 3d 15, 84 Cal Rptr 206]

46

INTRODUCTION TO CORPORATION LAW

The corporation is one of the most important forms of business organization. To the large-scale enterprise the corporate form makes financing easier by dividing the entity's ownership into many small units, or shares of stock, that can be sold to a wide range of investors. In addition to assisting the financing of operations, the corporate device offers a limited liability to the owners and a perpetual succession. A corporation's existence is not af-fected by the death of any particular owner or by the transfer of the shares of stock of any particular owner.

A.   NATURE AND CLASSES

A corporation is an artificial person that is cre-ated by governmental action. A number of dif-ferent kinds of corporations may be created.

1.   The Corporation as a Person

A **corporation** is an artificial being, created by government grant and endowed with certain powers. That is, the corporation exists in the eyes of the law as a person, separate and distinct from the persons who own the corporation.[1]

This concept means that property of the corporation is not owned by the persons who own shares in the corporation, but by the corporation. Debts of the corporation are debts of this artificial person, not of the persons running the corporation or owning shares of stock in it. The corporation can sue and be sued in its own name with respect to corporate rights and liabilities, but the shareholders cannot sue on behalf of the corporation unless the corporation refuses to sue. Shareholders cannot be sued as to corporate liabilities.

A corporation is formed by obtaining approval of a **certificate of incorporation, articles of incorporation,** or a **charter** from the state or national government.[2]

2.   Classifications of Corporations

Corporations may be classified in terms of their relationship to the public, the source of their authority, and the nature of their activities.

(a) PUBLIC, PRIVATE, AND QUASI-PUBLIC CORPORATIONS. A **public corporation** is one established for governmental purposes and for the administration of public affairs. A city is a public or municipal corporation acting under authority granted to it by the state.

A **private corporation** is one organized by persons, whether for charitable and benevolent purposes or for purposes of finance, industry, and commerce. Private corporations are often called "public" in business circles when the stock is sold to the public, that is, publicly traded on the stock exchanges.

A **quasi-public corporation,** also known as a public-service corporation or a public utility, is a private corporation furnishing services on which the public is particularly dependent. Examples of quasi-public corporations are railroads and gas and electric companies.

(b) PUBLIC AUTHORITIES. In the twentieth century, the public increasingly demands that government perform services. Some of these are performed directly by government. Others are performed by separate corporations or **authorities** that are created by government. For example, a city parking facility may be organized as a separate municipal parking authority. A public low-cost housing project may be operated as an independent housing authority.

(c) DOMESTIC AND FOREIGN CORPORATIONS. A corporation is called a **domestic corporation** with respect to the state under whose law it has been incorporated. Any other corporation going into that state is called a **foreign corporation.** Thus, a corporation holding a Texas charter is a domestic corporation in Texas but a foreign corporation in all other states.

(d) SPECIAL SERVICE CORPORATIONS. Corporations formed for transportation, banking, insurance, savings and loan operations, and similar specialized functions are subject to separate codes or statutes with regard to their organization. In addition, federal and state laws and administrative agencies regulate in detail the manner in which these businesses are conducted.

(e) CLOSE CORPORATIONS. A corporation whose shares are held by a single shareholder or a closely knit group of shareholders is known as a **close corporation.** The shares are not traded publicly. Many such corporations are small firms that in the past would

---

[1]   Macaluso v Jenkins, 96 Ill App 3d 254, 51 Ill Dec 743, 420 NE2d 251 (1981).

[2]   *Charter, certificate of incorporation,* and *articles of incorporation* are all terms used to refer to the documents that serve as evidence of a government's grant of corporate existence and powers. Most state incorporation statutes now provide for a certificate of incorporation issued by the secretary of state, but a Revised Model Business Corporation Act has done away with the certificate of incorporation in an attempt to reduce the volume of paperwork handled by the secretary of state. Under the RMBCA, corporate existence begins when articles of incorporation are filed with the secretary of state. An endorsed copy of the articles together with a fee, receipt, or acknowledgment replace the certificate of incorporation. See RMBCA §§ 1.25 and 2.03 and footnote 5 in this chapter.

have operated as proprietorships or partnerships but are incorporated to obtain either the advantages of limited liability or a tax benefit, or both.

Statutes have in many states liberalized the corporation law as it applies to close corporations. For example, some statutes permit incorporation by a smaller number of persons, allow a one-person board of directors, and eliminate the requirement of formal meetings.[3]

(f) "S CORPORATIONS." Under the Internal Revenue Code, if all of the shareholders of a qualifying close corporation consent, the shareholders may elect to be treated as partners for tax purposes and retain the benefit of limited liability under the corporate form. This device allows shareholders to avoid the double taxation of the corporate form of organization, where the corporation pays taxes on its income and then the shareholders pay taxes on dividends.

(g) PROFESSIONAL CORPORATIONS. A corporation may be organized for the purpose of conducting a profession.

(h) NONPROFIT CORPORATIONS. A **nonprofit corporation** (or an eleemosynary corporation) is one that is organized for charitable or benevolent purposes. Nonprofit corporations include certain hospitals, homes, and universities.[4] Special procedures for incorporation are sometimes prescribed, with provision for a detailed examination and hearing as to the purpose, function, and methods of raising money for the enterprise.

3.   Corporations and Governments

Problems between governments and corporations arise with respect to the power of governments to create and regulate corporations.

(a) POWER TO CREATE. Since by definition a corporation is created by government grant, the right to be a corporation must be obtained from the proper government. The federal government may create corporations whenever appropriate to carry out the powers granted to it.

Generally, a state by virtue of its police power may create any kind of corporation for any purpose. Most states have a **general corporation code** that lists certain requirements, and anyone who satisfies the requirements and files the necessary papers with the government may automatically become a corporation. In 1950, the American Bar Association published a Model Business Corporation Act (ABA MBCA) to assist legislative bodies in the modernization of state corporation laws. An updated version, incorporating numerous revisions made over the years, was published in 1969. Statutory language similar to that contained in the 1969 version of the MBCA has been adopted in whole or in part by 35 states. The 1984 revision of the Model Act (RMBCA) represents the first complete revision in more than 30 years.[5] Jurisdictions following the Model Act have made numerous modifications to reflect their differing views in the balancing of interests of public corporations, shareholders, and management. Caution must therefore be exercised in making generalizations about Model Act jurisdictions. There is no *uniform* corporation act.

(b) POWER TO REGULATE. The extent of

---

[3]   This distinction between large and small corporations is part of the same current of legal development that in the Uniform Commercial Code has given rise to the distinction between the merchant seller or buyer on the one hand and the casual seller or buyer on the other.

[4]   The Committee on Corporate Laws of the American Bar Association has prepared a Model Non-Profit Corporation Act. The Non-Profit Corporation Act has formed the basis for nonprofit corporation statutes in Alabama, Iowa, Nebraska, North Carolina, North Dakota, Ohio, Oregon, Texas, Virginia, Washington, Wisconsin, and the District of Columbia.

[5]   The Revised Model Business Corporation Act (1984) was approved by the Committee on Corporate Laws of the Section of Corporation, Banking and Business Law of the American Bar Association. The Committee approved revisions to Sections 6.40 and 8.33 on March 27, 1987. Excerpts of the 1984 Act, as revised, are presented in Appendix 8 to this book. Model Act citations are to the 1984 Revised Model Business Corporation Act (RMBCA) unless specifically designated otherwise.

the power of governments to regulate corporations is affected by whether a corporation is given the rights of a person and of a citizen.

(1) Protection of the corporation as a person. The Constitution of the United States prohibits the national government and the state governments from depriving any "person" of life, liberty, or property without due process of law. Many state constitutions contain a similar limitation on their respective state governments. A corporation is regarded as a "person" within the meaning of such provisions.

The federal Constitution prohibits a state from denying to any "person" within its jurisdiction the equal protection of the laws. No such express limitation is placed on the federal government, although the due process clause binding the federal government is liberally interpreted so that it prohibits substantial inequality of treatment.

(2) Protection of the corporation as a citizen. For certain purposes, such as determining the right to bring a lawsuit in a federal court, a corporation today is deemed a citizen of any state in which it has been incorporated and of the state where it has its principal place of business. The actual citizenship of the individual persons owning the stock of the corporation is ignored. Thus, the corporation incorporated in New York is a New York corporation even though its shareholders are citizens of many other states. Likewise, a Delaware corporation having its principal place of business in New York is deemed to be a citizen of New York as well as of Delaware.[6] An environmental protection law authorizing any citizen to bring suit to prevent pollution permits a corporation to bring such a suit.

The federal Constitution prohibits states from abridging "the privileges or immunities of citizens of the United States." A corporation, however, is not regarded as a citizen within this clause. Thus, with one exception, a foreign corporation has no constitutional right to do business in another state if that other state wishes to exclude it. For example, Penn-

sylvania can deny a New York corporation the right to come into Pennsylvania to do business. As a practical matter, most states do not exclude foreign corporations but seize on this power as justifying special regulation or taxation. On this basis it is commonly provided that a foreign corporation must register or even take out a domestic charter, file copies of its charter, pay certain taxes, or appoint a resident agent before it can do business within the state.

As an exception to the power of a state, a state cannot require a license or registration of a foreign interstate commerce corporation or impose a tax on the right to engage in such a business.

4.   Ignoring the Corporate Entity

Ordinarily, a corporation will be regarded and treated as a separate legal person, and the law will not look behind a corporation to see who owns or controls it.

The fact that two corporations have identical shareholders does not justify a court in regarding the two corporations as being one. Likewise, the fact that there is a close working relationship between two corporations does not in itself constitute any basis for ignoring their separate corporate entities when they in fact are separately run enterprises.[7]

(a) "PIERCING THE CORPORATE VEIL." A court may disregard the corporate entity, or figuratively "pierce the corporate veil," when exceptional circumstances warrant. The decision whether to disregard the corporate entity is made on a case-by-case basis, weighing all factors before the court. Factors that may lead to piercing the corporate veil and imposing liability on its owners (the shareholders) are (1) failure to maintain adequate corporate records and the commingling of corporate and other funds, (2) grossly inadequate capitalization, (3) diversion by shareholders of corpo-

---

[6]   28 USC § 1332(c).

[7]   Extra Energy Coal Co. v Diamond (Ind) 467 NE2d 439 (1984).

rate funds or assets, (4) the formation of the corporation to evade an existing obligation, (5) the formation of the corporation to perpetrate a fraud or conceal illegality,[8] and (6) a de-

---

[8]   Brock Builders Inc. v Dahlbeck, 223 Neb 493, 391 NW2d 110 (1986).

termination that injustice and inequitable consequences would result if the corporate entity were recognized.

The *Klein* case dealt with whether the corporate entity should be ignored.

KLEIN v SPORTING GOODS, INC.
(Tex Civ App) 772 SW2d 173 (1989)

In May 1985, Ed Klein was the sole shareholder, director, and chief executive officer of The Gun Exchange, Inc., a retail firearms dealership. The inventory of The Gun Exchange had been pledged as security for a $622,500 debt owed to InterFirst Bank. It also owed $231,484.60 to Sporting Goods, Inc.; this debt was unsecured. On May 20, 1985, InterFirst Bank notified Klein of its intention to foreclose on the inventory and sell it at public auction. InterFirst Bank further advised Klein that, pursuant to his personal guarantee, he would be responsible for any deficiency following the sale. Klein immediately incorporated "The Gun Store Inc." for the purpose of purchasing the assets of The Gun Exchange at the foreclosure sale. Before the foreclosure sale, Klein obtained a $650,000 line of credit from CharterBank on behalf of The Gun Store. At the sale Klein purchased the assets of The Gun Exchange for $650,000, even though the highest prior bid was $175,000. (Had the $175,000 bid been accepted, Klein would have been personally liable for the deficiency to InterFirst Bank). After the foreclosure sale no funds existed to pay the unsecured creditors of The Gun Exchange. Following the sale, The Gun Store began operating as a retail firearms dealer with the inventory purchased from the foreclosure sale, in the same location and with the same personnel as The Gun Exchange. Sporting Goods Inc. sued The Gun Exchange Inc. and Klein individually for the $231,484.60. A default judgment was rendered against The Gun Exchange. Sporting Goods Inc. proceeded against Klein personally under a constructive fraud theory, claiming that the corporate fiction should be disregarded and Klein held liable for the debts of The Gun Exchange. From a judgment for Sporting Goods Inc., Klein appealed.

MURPHY, J. . . . The corporate fiction normally insulates shareholders, officers, and directors from liability for corporate obligations, but will be disregarded, even though corporate formalities have been observed and individual property has been kept separate, when the corporate form has been used as part of a basically unfair device to achieve an inequitable result. . . . Neither fraud nor an intent to defraud need be shown as a prerequisite to disregarding the corporate entity; it is sufficient if recognizing the separate corporate existence would bring about an inequitable result. Constructive fraud is the breach of some legal or equitable duty which, irrespective of moral guilt, the law declares fraudulent because of the tendency to deceive others, to violate confidence, or to injure public interests. . . .

Under the facts in this case, there is some evidence to support the jury's finding of constructive fraud. In considering all the evidence, the jury's finding was not so against the great weight and preponderance of the evidence as to be manifestly unjust. The jury could well have concluded that The Gun Store was merely a continuation of The Gun Exchange, with the foreclosure sale being used as a method to avoid creditors. Therefore, the evidence was legally and factually sufficient to support the jury's finding of constructive fraud, allowing a judgment disregarding the corporate fiction, and holding appellant personally liable for the debts of The Gun Exchange. . . .

The jury found that appellant committed constructive fraud by using the corporate fiction as a sham to perpetrate a fraud on appellees. In doing so, the jury found that the corporate fiction should be disregarded. When the corporate fiction is disregarded, the individual, in this case appellant, becomes identical with the corporation, and the individual stands liable for the acts and obligations of the corporation. . . .

[Judgment affirmed]

QUESTIONS

1. Why did Klein bid $650,000 for the inventory of The Gun Exchange when the prior highest bid was $175,000?
2. Will courts ignore the corporate form where it has been used as part of a basically unfair device to achieve an inequitable result?
3. Summarize the evidence of constructive fraud in this case.

Some courts use different terminology when disregarding the corporate entity. When a person uses a corporation as a mask behind which to hide from a person being defrauded, the court will hold the wrongdoer liable for the acts of the corporation. The court may state that the corporation is the *alter ego* of the wrongdoer.[9]

(b) FUNCTIONAL REALITY. When a corporation is in effect merely a department of a large enterprise, as when a large manufacturer incorporates its marketing department while continuing to hold itself out to the public as a single enterprise, it is likely that the separate corporate character of the incorporated department will be ignored.

(c) OBTAINING ADVANTAGES OF CORPORATE EXISTENCE. The court will not go behind the corporate identity merely because the corporation has been formed to obtain tax savings or to obtain limited liability for its shareholders. Likewise, the corporate entity

will not be ignored merely because the corporation does not have sufficient assets to pay the claims against it.

One-person, family, and other closely held corporations are permissible and fully entitled to all of the advantages of corporate existence. The fact that the principal shareholder oversees the day-to-day operations does not justify setting aside the corporate entity. However, factors that lead to piercing the corporate veil—such as grossly inadequate capitalization, commingling of assets, and failure to maintain separate corporate books and accounts—are more common in these kinds of corporations.[10]

B.   CREATION OF THE CORPORATION

All states have general laws governing the creation of corporations by persons who comply with the provisions of the statutes.

---

[9]   El Paso Development Co. v Berryman (Tex Civ App) 769 SW2d 584 (1989).

[10]   Mac Chambers Co. v Iowa Tae Kwon Do Academy, Inc. (Iowa) 412 NW2d 593 (1987).

5. Promoters

Corporations frequently come into existence as the result of the activities of one or more persons known as *promoters*. However, there is no legal requirement for the services of a promoter in the formation of a corporation.

The **promoter** brings together persons interested in the enterprise, aids in obtaining subscriptions to stock, and sets in motion the machinery that leads to the formation of the corporation itself.

A corporation is not liable on a contract made by its promoter for its benefit unless it takes some affirmative action to adopt such contract. Such action may be express words of adoption or acceptance of the benefits of the contract. A corporation may also become bound by such contracts by assignment or by novation.

The promoter is personally liable for all contracts made on behalf of the corporation before its existence unless the promoter is exempted by the terms of the agreement or by the circumstances surrounding it.[11] When a promoter makes a contract on behalf of a corporation to be formed thereafter, the promoter is liable thereon if the corporation is not formed, in the absence of an agreement that the promoter should not be so liable.

In the *Clinton Investors* case the person executing a pre-incorporation lease in the name of a proposed corporation did not believe himself to be a promoter, nor did he contemplate that he could be personally liable for obligations incurred under the lease.

[11]   Pierson v Coffey (Ky App) 706 SW2d 409 (1985); Company Store Development Corp. v Pottery Warehouse (Tenn App) 733 SW2d 886 (1987).

CLINTON INVESTORS CO. v WATKINS
146 App Div 2d 861, 536 NYS2d 270 (1989)

Clinton Investors Co. (Clinton), as landlord, entered into a three-year lease with "The Clifton Park Learning Center" (learning center) as tenant. The lease was executed by Berne Watkins, who represented himself to be the treasurer of the learning center. On May 31, 1984, the day before the lease term commenced, Watkins signed a rider to the lease. He again signed as treasurer of the tenant, but identified the tenant as "the Clifton Park Learning Center, Inc." Watkins had not consulted an attorney regarding the formation of the corporation. He mistook the reservation of the business name with the Secretary of State for the filing of a certiciate of incorporation. On February 11, 1985, a certificate of incorporation was filed. By March 1986 the learning center had become delinquent in rental payments and other fees in the amount of $18,103. Clinton sued Watkins and the learning center for the amounts due. The court granted Watkins notice for dismissal of the complaint against him, and Clinton appealed.

VESAWICH, J. . . . Because no corporation existed when Watkins signed the lease with plaintiff, his legal status was that of a promoter of the learning center. . . . Generally, a promoter who executes a preincorporation contract in the name of a proposed corporation is himself personally liable on the contract unless the parties have otherwise agreed. Watkins asserts that because the learning center corporation subsequently adopted the lease he is therefore no longer liable on the lease. However, corporate adoption of a contract "gives rise to corporate liability in addition to any individual liability" (*Universal Inds. Corp. v. Lindstrom*, 92 A.D.2d 150, 152, 459, N.Y.S.2d 492) so that the promoter nevertheless remains obligated unless there has been a novation between the corporation and the plaintiff, which is not the situation here. Nor does the record disclose any explicit or implicit agreement by plaintiff not to hold Watkins personally liable on the lease. . . .

Watkins also argues that because the learning center conducted its affairs with plaintiff as a corporation it should be treated as a de facto corporation. A pivotal element of a de facto corporation is a colorable attempt to comply with the statutes governing incorporation. . . . In the instant case, the only activity approaching colorable compliance is an alleged name reservation on an undisclosed date. Moreover, the action of the subsequently formed corporation to adopt the lease is an acknowledgement that Watkins had signed as a promoter of a proposed corporation. In sum, Watkins has failed to proffer evidence sufficient to raise a triable factual issue respecting whether he is personally liable on the lease with plaintiff. . . .

[Judgment reversed and summary judgment entered against Watkins]

QUESTIONS

1. What was Watkins' legal status when he signed the lease?
2. Is it true that because the learning center corporation subsequently adopted the lease, Watkins was no longer liable on the lease?
3. Did the court find that the learning center was a de facto corporation, thus freeing Watkins from personal liability?

A promoter is liable for all torts committed in connection with the promoter's activities. The corporation is not ordinarily liable for the torts of the promoter, but it may become liable by its conduct after incorporation. Thus, when a corporation, with actual or implied notice of the fraud of the promoter, assumes the promoter's contract, the corporation is liable for the promoter's fraud that induced the other party to enter into the contract.

A promoter stands in a fiduciary relation to the corporation and to stock subscribers: The promoter cannot make secret profits at their expense. Accordingly, if a promoter makes a secret profit on a sale of land to the corporation, the promoter must surrender the profit to the corporation. The promoter may be held guilty of embezzlement if the promoter converts property that should have gone to the corporation.

The corporation is not liable in most states for the expenses and services of the promoter unless it subsequently promises to pay for them or unless the corporation's charter or a statute imposes such liability on it.

6.   Incorporation

One or more natural persons or corporations may act as **incorporators** of a corporation by signing and filing articles of incorporation with the designated government official.[12] These articles are filed in duplicate. The designated official (usually the secretary of state), upon being satisfied that the articles conform to the statutory requirements, stamps *filed* and the date on each copy. The official then retains one copy and returns the other copy, along with a filing fee receipt, to the corporation.[13]

Statutes may require the incorporators to give some form of public notice, as by advertising in a newspaper, of the intention to form the corporation.

7.   Application for Incorporation

The instrument by which a private corporation is formed in most jurisdictions is called the *articles of incorporation*. The instrument is

---

[12]   RMBCA § 2.01.
[13]   RMBCA § 1.25.

filed with the secretary of state and sets forth certain information about the new corporation. The articles of incorporation must contain (a) the name of the corporation, (b) the number of shares of stock the corporation is authorized to issue, (c) the street address of the corporation's initial registered office and the name of its initial registered agent, and (d) the name and address of each incorporator.[14] The articles of incorporation may contain optional provisions, such as the purpose or purposes for which the corporation is organized. If there is no "purpose clause," the corporation will automatically have the purpose of engaging in any lawful business.[15] Also, if no reference is made to the period of duration of the corporation in the articles of incorporation, it will automatically have perpetual duration.[16] If the articles of incorporation conform to the requirements of the state corporation law, the secretary of state will issue a certificate of incorporation in most states.

8.   The Certificate of Incorporation

Most state incorporation statutes now provide for a certificate of incorporation issued by the secretary of state, but the Revised Model Business Corporation Act has eliminated the certificate of incorporation in an effort to reduce the volume of paper work handled by the secretary of state. Under the RMBCA, corporate existence begins when the articles are filed with the secretary of state.[17] Under the older practice still followed by most states, corporate existence begins upon the issuance of the certificate of incorporation by the secretary of state.

9.   Proper and Defective Incorporation

If the procedure for incorporation has been followed, the corporation has a perfect legal right to exist. It is then called a **corporation de**

jure, meaning that it is a corporation by virtue of law.[18]

Assume that there is some defect in the corporation that is formed. If the defect is not a material one, the law usually will overlook the defect and hold that the corporation is a corporation *de jure.*

The RMBCA abolishes objections to irregularities and defects in incorporating. It provides that the "secretary of state's filing of the articles of incorporation is conclusive proof that the incorporators satisfied all conditions precedent to incorporation. . . ."[19] Many state statutes follow this pattern. Such an approach is based on the practical consideration that when countless persons are purchasing shares of stock and entering into business transactions with thousands of corporations, it becomes an absurdity to expect that anyone is going to make the detailed search that would be required to determine whether a given corporation is a *de jure* corporation.[20]

(a) DE FACTO CORPORATION. The defect in the incorporation may be so substantial that the law cannot ignore it and will not accept the corporation as a *de jure* corporation. Yet there may be sufficient compliance so that the law will recognize that there is a corporation. When this occurs, the association is called a *de facto* **corporation.**

Although there is conflict among the authorities, the traditional elements of a *de facto* corporation are that (1) a valid law exists under which the corporation could have been properly incorporated; (2) an attempt to organize the corporation has been made in good faith; (3) a genuine attempt to organize in compliance with the requirements of the statute has been made; and (4) there has been a use of the corporate powers.

(b) PARTNERSHIP VERSUS CORPORATION BY ESTOPPEL. The defect in incorpo-

---

[14]   RMBCA § 2.02.
[15]   RMBCA § 3.01.
[16]   RMBCA § 3.02.
[17]   RMBCA § 2.03(a).

[18]   Kansas v Construction Enterprises, Inc. 6 Kan App 2d 627, 631 P2d 1240 (1981).
[19]   RMBCA § 2.03(b).
[20]   This trend and the reasons therefor may be compared to those involved in the concept of the negotiability of commercial paper. Note the similar protection from defenses given to the person purchasing shares of stock for value and without notice. UCC § 8–202.

ration may be so great that the law will not accept the association as a *de facto* corporation. In such a case, in the absence of a statute making the incorporation conclusive, there is no corporation. If the individuals proceed to run the business in spite of such irregularity, they may be held liable as partners.[21]

The partnership liability rule is sometimes not applied when the third person dealt with the business as though it were a corporation.

In such instances it is stated that the third person is estopped from denying that the "corporation" with which the business was transacted has legal existence. In effect, there is a corporation by estoppel with respect to that creditor.

Several jurisdictions that follow the 1969 MBCA have expressly retained the doctrines of corporation by estoppel and *de facto* corporations.[22] However, courts interpreting the language of the 1969 MBCA have determined that the *de facto* corporation doctrine and the corporation by estoppel doctrine no longer exist.

---

[21]   In a minority of states the court will not hold the individuals liable as partners, but will hold liable the person who committed the act on behalf of the business on the theory that such person was an agent who acted without authority and is therefore liable for breach of the implied warranties of the existence of a principal possessing capacity and of proper authorization.

[22]   See Ga. Bus. Corp. Code § 22–5103; Minn. Bus. Corp. Act § 301:08. See also H. Rich Corp. v Feinberg (Fla App) 518 So 2d 377 (1987).

THOMPSON & GREEN MACHINERY CO. v MUSIC CITY LUMBER CO.

(Tenn App) 683 SW2d 340 (1984)

On January 27, 1982, Joe Walker purchased a wheel loader machine from the Thompson & Green Machinery Co. (T-G). Walker signed a promissory note for $37,886.30 on behalf of "Music City Sawmill, Inc. by Joe Walker, President." When Sawmill was unable to make payments on the loader, the machine was returned to T-G and later sold for $17,925. T-G brought suit against Sawmill on May 5, 1983 and thereafter discovered that Sawmill had not been incorporated on January 27, 1982, when the machine was sold, but rather had been incorporated on January 28, 1982. T-G then sued Walker individually. The lawsuit was Walker's first notice that Sawmill was not incorporated on the date of the sale. Walker insisted that T-G dealt with Sawmill as a corporation and did not intend to bind him personally on the note and that T-G was therefore estopped from denying Sawmill's corporate existence. T-G responded that under language virtually identical to Sections 56 and 146 of the 1969 MBCA the doctrines of *de facto* corporations and corporation by estoppel were no longer applicable in the state, and Walker was personally liable. From a judgment for Walker, T-G appealed.

LEWIS, J. . . . It is conceded that Sawmill did not have a corporate existence on January 27th. It therefore follows that Mr. Walker could not and did not have authority to act for Sawmill on January 27th when he executed the promissory note to plaintiff.

It is a general rule that one who deals with an apparent corporation as such and in such manner as to recognize its corporate existence de jure or de facto is thereby estopped to deny the fact thus admitted. . . . The estoppel extends as well to the privies as to the parties to such transactions. The general rule is applied in actions brought by either of the contracting parties against the other, and in actions by the persons dealing with the corporation, wherein the existence of the corporation is assailed for the purpose of establishing individual partnership liability on the part of its members.

Tennessee has long recognized the foregoing rule. Our Supreme Court, in *Ingle System Co. v. Norris & Hall*, 134 Tenn. 472, 178 S.W. 1113 (1915), stated:

> When a private person enters into a contract with a body purporting to be a corporation, in which that body is described by the corporate name which it has assumed, such private person thereby admits the existence of the corporation for the purpose of the suit brought to enforce the obligations, and will not be permitted to deny the corporate existence of the plaintiff.

However, in 1968 the Tennessee General Assembly enacted the "Tennessee General Corporations Act," Chapter 523, Pub. Acts of 1968.

Our research reveals no Tennessee decision which has addressed either de facto corporation or corporation by estoppel since the passage of the act in 1968.

Courts in other jurisdictions which have considered the question of de facto corporations under statutes similar to Tenn. Code Ann. §§ 48–1-204 and 48–1-1405 have held that under the act, de facto corporations no longer exist. . . .

Corporate existence does not begin until such time as "the charter is filed by the secretary of state." [See 1969 MBCA § 56]. . . .

[1969 MBCA § 146] mandates that "all persons who assume to act as a corporation without authority so to do shall be jointly and severally liable for all debts and liabilities incurred or arising as a result thereof."

The General Assembly, in enacting [MBCA § 146] saw fit to place statutory liability upon those who assume to act as a corporation without authority. [Section 146] does not contain an exception that one who assumes to act as a corporation without authority shall be jointly and severally liable for debts and liabilities *except* when the plaintiff thereafter dealt with the corporation as a corporation or when the plaintiff did not intend to bind one who assumed to act personally. No exceptions are contained in [§ 146]. For this Court to hold that under the circumstances here Mr. Walker is not liable, it would be necessary that this Court rewrite the Tennessee General Corporations Act and hold that the Act does not mean what it says. We are not at liberty to do so. We find nothing ambiguous in [§ 146]. It is clear that "all persons who assume to act as a corporation without authority so to do shall be jointly and severally liable for all debts and liabilities incurred or arising as a result thereof." We find no good faith exception in the act. To allow an estoppel would be to nullify [§ 146].

We are of the opinion that the doctrine of corporation by estoppel met its demise by the enactment of the Tennessee General Corporations Act of 1968.

[Judgment reversed and action remanded]

QUESTIONS

1. Did Walker make the contract on behalf of Sawmill, Inc., in the good faith belief that it was a corporation?
2. Did T-G intend to hold Walker individually liable on the promissory note when it was signed?
3. State the rule of the case.

The 1984 Model Act contains a more flexible standard than the 1969 version. The 1984 Act imposes liability for preincorporation debts only on persons who act as or on behalf of a corporation knowing that no corporation exists.[23]

10. Insolvency, Bankruptcy, and Reorganization

When a corporation has financial troubles that are so serious that it is insolvent, the best thing may be to go through bankruptcy or reorganization proceedings. The law as to bankruptcy and reorganizations is discussed in Chapter 37.

11. Forfeiture of Charter

Under the RMBCA the secretary of state may commence proceedings to administratively dissolve a corporation if (a) the corporation does not pay franchise taxes within 60 days after they are due, (b) the corporation does not file its annual report within 60 days after it is due, or (c) the corporation is without a registered agent or registered office for 60 days or more.[24] Owners and officers of a dissolved corporation are not shielded from personal liability by using the corporate name in making contracts.[25]

12. Judicial Dissolution

In some states provision is made for the judicial dissolution of a corporation when its management is deadlocked and the deadlock cannot be broken by the shareholders.[26] In some states a "custodian" may be appointed for a corporation when the shareholders are unable to break a deadlock in the board of directors and irreparable harm is threatened or sustained by the corporation because of the deadlock.

C. CORPORATE POWERS

All corporations do not have the same powers. For example, those that operate banks, insurance companies, and railroads generally have special powers and are subject to special restrictions.

Except for limitations in the federal Constitution or the state's own constitution, a state legislature may give corporations any lawful powers. The RMBCA contains a general provision on corporate powers granting the corporation "the same powers as an individual to do all things necessary or convenient to carry out its business and affairs."[27] State statutes generally contain broad catchall grants of powers.

13. Particular Powers

Modern corporation codes give corporations a wide range of powers.

(a) PERPETUAL SUCCESSION. One of the distinctive features of a corporation is its perpetual succession or continuous life—the power to continue as a unit forever or for a stated period of time, regardless of changes in stock ownership.

(b) CORPORATE NAME. A corporation must have a name to identify it. As a general rule, it may select any name for this purpose.

Most states require that the corporate name contain some word indicating the corporate character[28] and that it shall not be the same as or deceptively similar to the name of another corporation. Some statutes likewise prohibit the use of a name that is likely to mislead the public.

(c) CORPORATE SEAL. A corporation may have a distinctive seal. However, a corporation need not use a seal in the transaction of business unless such is required by statute or unless a natural person in transacting that business would be required to use a seal.

(d) BYLAWS. **Bylaws** are the rules and regulations enacted by a corporation to govern the affairs of the corporation and its shareholders, directors, and officers.

---

[23] RMBCA § 2.04.
[24] RMBCA § 14.20.
[25] Priceco, Inc. v Youngstrom (Idaho App) 786 P2d 606 (1990).
[26] RMBCA § 14.30 (2)(I).

[27] RMBCA § 3.02.
[28] RMBCA 4.01 (a) declares that the corporate name must contain the word "corporation," "company," "incorporated," "limited," or an abbreviation of one of these words.

Bylaws are adopted by shareholders, although in some states it may be provided that they are to be adopted by the directors of the corporation. Action by the state or an amendment of the corporate charter is not required to make the bylaws effective.

The bylaws are subordinate to the general law of the state, including the statute under which the corporation is formed, as well as to the charter of the corporation.[29] Bylaws that conflict with such superior authority or that are in themselves unreasonable are invalid. Bylaws that are valid are binding on all shareholders, regardless of whether they know of the existence of those bylaws or were among the majority that consented to their adoption. Bylaws are not binding upon third persons, however, unless they have notice or knowledge of them.

(e) STOCK. A corporation may issue certificates representing corporate stock.

(f) MAKING CONTRACTS. Corporation codes give corporations the power to make contracts.

(g) BORROWING MONEY. Corporations have the implied power to borrow money in carrying out their authorized business purposes.

(h) EXECUTING COMMERCIAL PAPER. The power to issue or indorse commercial paper, or to accept drafts, is implied when the corporation has the power to borrow money and when such means are appropriate and ordinarily used to further the authorized objectives of the corporation.

(i) ISSUING BONDS. A corporation may exercise its power to borrow money by issuing bonds. The bonds issued by a corporation are subject to Article 8 of the UCC, "Investment Securities."

(j) TRANSFERRING PROPERTY. The corporate property may be leased, assigned for the benefit of creditors, or sold. In many states, however, a solvent corporation may not trans-fer all of its property without the consent of all or a substantial majority of its shareholders. In any case the sale must be for a fair price.

A corporation, having power to incur debts, may mortgage or pledge its property as security for those debts. This rule does not apply to franchises of public service companies, such as street transit systems and gas and electric companies.

(k) ACQUIRING PROPERTY. Although the power to acquire and hold property is usually given in the charter, a corporation always has the implied power to acquire and hold such property as is reasonably necessary for carrying out its express powers.

(l) BUYING BACK STOCK. Generally, a corporation may purchase its own stock if it is solvent at the time and the purchase does not impair capital.[30] Stock that is reacquired by the corporation that issued it is commonly called **treasury stock.** Ordinarily, the treasury stock is regarded as still being issued or outstanding stock.[31] As such, the shares are not subject to the rule that original shares cannot be issued for less than par (the dollar amount listed on the face of the stock certificate). They can be sold by the corporation at any price.

The RMBCA eliminates the concept of par value and the technical distinctions between original shares and treasury shares that exist in conventional statutes. Thus, under the RMBCA, authorized but unissued shares may be issued on the same basis as treasury shares.[32]

Although treasury stock retains the character of outstanding stock, it has an inactive status while it is held by the corporation. Thus, the treasury shares cannot be voted, nor can dividends be declared on them.

(m) DOING BUSINESS IN ANOTHER STATE. A corporation has the inherent power,

[29]   Roach v Bynum (Ala) 403 So 2d 187 (1981).

[30]   See § RMBCA 6.31 (a) subject to the limitations of § 6.40.
[31]   When a corporation reacquires its own shares, it has the choice of "retiring" them and thus restoring them to the status of authorized but unissued shares or of treating them as still issued and available for transfer. It is the latter that are described as treasury shares.
[32]   See Official Comments to RMBCA § 6.21 and § 6.31.

and generally is expressly authorized, to engage in business in other states. However, this grant of power by the incorporating state does not exempt the corporation from satisfying the restrictions imposed by the foreign state in which it seeks to do business.

(n) PARTICIPATING IN ENTERPRISE. Corporations may generally participate in an enterprise to the same extent as individuals. They may enter into joint ventures. The modern statutory trend is to permit a corporation to be a member of a partnership. A corporation may be a limited partner. The RMBCA authorizes a corporation "to be a promoter, partner, member, associate, or manager of any partnership, joint venture, trust, or other entity."[33]

(o) PAYING EMPLOYEE BENEFITS. The RMBCA empowers a corporation "to pay pensions and establish pension plans, pension trusts, profit-sharing plans, share bonus plans, share option plans, and benefit or incentive plans for any or all of its current or former directors, officers, employees, and agents."[34]

(p) MAKING CHARITABLE CONTRIBUTIONS. The RMBCA authorizes a corporation, without any limitation, "to make donations for the public welfare or for charitable scientific, or educational purposes."[35] In some states limitation is imposed on the amount that can be donated for charitable purposes.

14.   *Ultra Vires* Acts

When a corporation acts in excess of or beyond the scope of the powers granted by its charter and the statute under which it was organized, the corporation's act is described as **ultra vires.** Such an action is improper in the same way that it is improper for an agent to act beyond the scope of the authority given by the principal. It is also improper with respect to shareholders and creditors of the corporation, because corporate funds have been diverted to unauthorized uses.

In the past, corporations were formed by obtaining a grant of a charter from the king or state legislature. Thus, a charter would be granted to build a turnpike or to run a bank. Typically, the charter would concentrate on the main point and specifically grant the powers needed to attain the objective of the corporation. There was no general listing of corporate powers. In this century, corporate existence begins by fulfilling the clerical matter of filing articles of incorporation that conform to the statute adopted by the legislature. Typically, this statute will state that every corporation formed under the statute will have certain powers unless the articles of incorporation expressly exclude some of the listed powers, and then the statute will list every possible power that is needed to run a business. In some states, the legislature makes a blanket grant of all the power that a natural person running the business would possess.[36] The net result is that the modern corporation possesses such a broad scope of powers that it is difficult to find an action that is *ultra vires.* If a mining corporation should begin to manufacture television sets, there might be an *ultra vires* transaction, but such an extreme departure rarely happens.

Nonprofit corporations have a more restricted range of powers than business corporations. Certain actions not authorized by the charters of nonprofit corporations may be found to be *ultra vires.*[37]

D.   CONSOLIDATIONS, MERGERS, AND CONGLOMERATES

Two or more corporations may be combined to form a new structure or enterprise. This combination may be a consolidation, a merger, or the formation of a conglomerate.

---

[33]   RMBCA § 3.02(9).
[34]   RMBCA § 3.02(12).
[35]   RMBCA § 3.02(13).

[36]   Note the broad powers granted under the RMBCA § 3.02; see also Cal. Corp. Code §§ 202(b), 207, 208 for all-purpose clause granting "all of the powers of a natural person in carrying out its business activities."
[37]   Lovering v Seabrook Island Property Owners Association 289 SC App 77, 344 SE2d 862 (1986). But see St. Louis v Institute of Med. Ed. & Res. (Mo App) 786 SW2d 885 (1990).

15.   Definitions

The form through which the combination is accomplished will affect the identity of the resulting corporation.

    (a) CONSOLIDATION. In a **consolidation** of two or more corporations, their separate existences cease, and a new corporation with the property and the assets of the old corporations comes into being.

    When a consolidation is effected, the new corporation ordinarily succeeds to the rights, powers, and immunities of its component parts. However, limitations may be prescribed by certificate of incorporation, constitution, or statute.

FIGURE 46–1   CONSOLIDATION

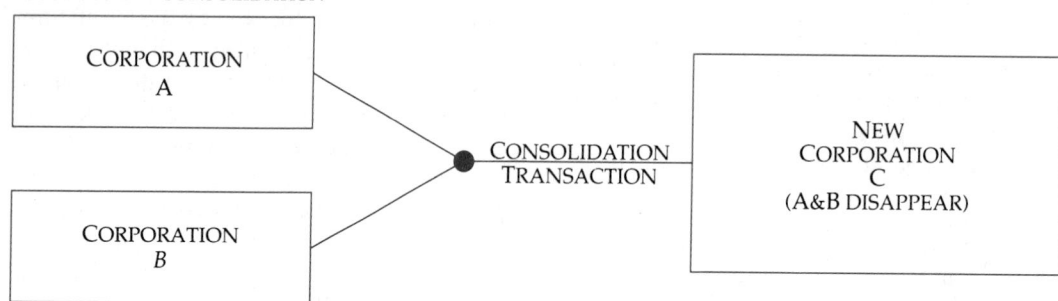

    (b) MERGER. Merger differs from consolidation in that, when two corporations merge, one absorbs the other. One corporation preserves its original charter and identity and continues to exist; the other disappears, and its corporate existence terminates.

FIGURE 46–2   MERGER

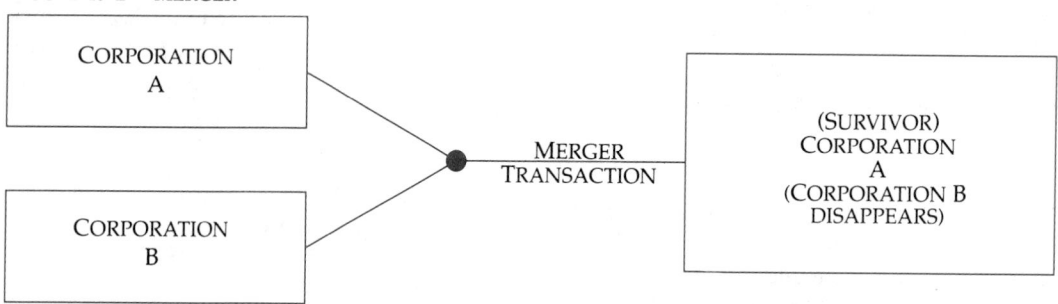

    Usually, if a stockholder dissents from a proposed consolidation or merger, or if a stockholder fails to convert existing shares into stock of the new or continuing corporation, the dissenting stockholder or the corporation may make application to the courts to appraise the value of the stock held. The new or continuing corporation is then required to pay the value of the stock to the stockholder, and the stockholder is required to transfer the stock to the new or continuing corporation. In effect, the court orders the new or continuing corporation to buy the stock from the dissenting stockholder.

    Complex transactions are often involved in the elimination of the ownership interests of minority shareholders. A "two-step merger" may take place. First, an outside investor purchases control of the majority shares of the target corporation by tender offer or through private negotiations. Then this newly acquired control is used to arrange for the target and a second corporation controlled by the outside investor to merge, with one condition being the "freeze-out" of the minority shareholders of the target corporation by the forced cancellation of their shares, generally through a cash purchase.

As set forth in *Alpert,* in reviewing a freeze-out merger the courts look to see if the merger was for a legitimate corporate purpose and, considering the transaction as a whole, whether it was fair to the minority shareholders.

ALPERT v 28 WILLIAMS STREET CORPORATION
63 NY2d 557, 473 NE2d 19 (1984)

Since 1955, a valuable 17-story office building located at 79 Madison Avenue in New York City had been owned by 79 Realty Corporation, which had no other substantial assets. About two-thirds of 79 Realty Corporation's outstanding shares were held by two couples, the Kimmelmans and the Zauderers, who were also the company's sole directors and officers. Jack Alpert and three others (the Alpert group) owned 26 percent of the outstanding shares. A consortium of investors formed a limited partnership known as Madison 28 Associates for the purpose of purchasing the building. In March of 1980, Madison Associates began negotiations with the Kimmelmans and Zauderers to purchase the controlling block of stock at a price equal to its proportion of the building's value—agreed in June 1980 to be $6,500,000. In addition, Madison Associates promised that it would offer to purchase the Alpert group's stock under the same terms within four months of the closing of the stock purchase agreement in September, 1980.

Upon selling their shares, the Kimmelmans and the Zauderers resigned their positions with the 79 Realty Corporation and were replaced by four partners of Madison Associates. Now acting as the controlling directors of 79 Realty Corporation on October 17, 1980, they approved a plan to merge the 79 Realty Corporation with Williams Street Realty Corporation, which Madison Associates owned. A shareholders meeting was called, and a statement of intention to merge was sent out to the shareholders prior to the meeting; the statement included the plan to dissolve 79 Realty Corporation after the merger. The merger was approved by two-thirds of the shareholders, and 79 Realty Corporation was thereafter dissolved. The Alpert group brought suit contending that the merger was unlawful because the sole purpose was to benefit the Madison Associates, which had a clear conflict of interest. The Madison Associates defended that the merger advanced certain proper business purposes such as the beneficial tax advantages through depreciation and the attraction of outside capital for needed renovations. From a judgment for the Madison Associates, the Alpert group appealed.

COOKE, C. J. . . . On this appeal, the principal task facing this court is to prescribe a standard for evaluating the validity of a corporate transaction that forcibly eliminates minority shareholders by means of a two-step merger. It is concluded that the analysis employed by the courts below was correct: the majority shareholders' exclusion of minority interests through a two-step merger does not violate the former's fiduciary obligations so long as the transaction viewed as a whole is fair to the minority shareholders and is justified by an independent corporate business purpose. Accordingly, this court now affirms.

In New York, two or more domestic corporations are authorized to "merge into a single corporation which shall be one of the constituent corporations," known as the "surviving corporation" (see Business Corporation Law, § 901). The statute does not delineate substantive justifications for mergers, but only requires compliance with certain procedures: the adoption by the boards of each corporation of a plan of merger setting forth, among other things, the terms and conditions of the merger, a statement of any changes in the certificate of incorporation of the surviving corporation; the submission of the plan to a vote of shareholders pursuant to notice to all shareholders; and adoption of the plan by a vote of two thirds of the shareholders entitled to vote on it.

Generally, the remedy of a shareholder dissenting from a merger and the offered "cash-out" price is to obtain the fair value of his or her stock through an appraisal proceeding. This protects the minority shareholder from being forced to sell at unfair prices imposed by those dominating the corporation while allowing the majority to proceed with its desired merger. . . . The pursuit of an appraisal proceeding generally constitutes the dissenting stockholder's exclusive remedy. An exception exists, however, when the merger is unlawful or fraudulent as to that shareholder, in which event an action for equitable relief is authorized. . . . Thus, technical compliance with the Business Corporation Law's requirements alone will not necessarily exempt a merger from further judicial review.

Because the power to manage the affairs of a corporation is vested in the directors and majority shareholders, they are cast in the fiduciary role of "guardians of the corporate welfare." . . . In this position of trust, they have an obligation to all shareholders to adhere to fiduciary standards of conduct and to exercise their responsibilities in good faith when undertaking any corporate action, including a merger. . . .

It has long been recognized in this State that, under certain circumstances, "the particular interest of the few must give way to the general interest of the many." . . . Thus, departure from precisely uniform treatment of stockholders may be justified, of course, where a bona fide business purpose indicates that the best interests of the corporation would be served by such departure." . . .

In the context of a freeze-out merger, variant treatment of the minority shareholders—i.e., causing their removal—will be justified when related to the advancement of a general corporate interest. The benefit need not be great, but it must be for the corporation. For example, if the sole purpose of the merger is reduction of the number of profit sharers—in contrast to increasing the corporation's capital or profits, or improving its management structure—there will exist no "independent corporate interest." . . . All of these purposes ultimately seek to increase the individual wealth of the remaining shareholders. What distinguishes a proper corporate purpose from an improper one is that, with the former, removal of the minority shareholders furthers the objective of conferring some general gain upon the corporation. Only then will the fiduciary duty of good and prudent management of the corporation serve to override the concurrent duty to treat all shareholders fairly. . . .

In sum, in entertaining an equitable action to review a freeze-out merger, a court should view the transaction as a whole to determine whether it was tainted with fraud, illegality, or self-dealing, and whether the minority shareholders were dealt with fairly, and whether there exists any independent corporate purpose for the merger.

Noting that defendants had not employed any neutral committees in negotiating the merger, Supreme Court conducted its own objective review of the transaction. There is evidence in the record to support its conclusion that, viewed as a whole, the transaction was fair. Full disclosure of material information was made in the statement of intent mailed to plaintiffs who also had access to Realty Corporation's books. The stock price was tied to the fair market value of the office building, the corporation's only substantial asset, which was determined in arm's length negotiations.

Without passing on all of the business purposes cited by the Supreme Court as underlying the merger, it is sufficient to note that at least one justified the exclusion of plaintiffs' interests: attracting additional capital to effect needed repairs of the building. There is proof that there was a good-faith belief that additional, outside capital was required. Moreover, this record supports the conclusion that this capital would not have been available through the merger had not plaintiffs' interest in the corporation been eliminated. Thus, the approval of the merger, which would extinguish plaintiffs' stock, was supported by a bona fide business purpose to advance this general corporate interest of obtaining increased capital.

[Judgment affirmed]

QUESTIONS

1. What is a freeze-out merger?
2. Did the defendants follow the statutory procedures for the merger of the two domestic corporations?
3. What protection does state law provide shareholders dissenting from a merger?

(c) CONGLOMERATE. *Conglomerate* is the term describing the relationship of a parent corporation to subsidiary corporations engaged in diversified fields of activity unrelated to the field of activity of the parent corporation. For example, a wire manufacturing corporation that owns all the stock of a newspaper corporation and of a drug manufacturing corporation would be described as a conglomerate. In contrast, if the wire manufacturing company owned a mill to produce the metal used in making the wire and owned a mine that produced the ore that was used by the mill, the relationship would probably be described as an *integrated industry* rather than as a conglomerate. This term is merely a matter of usage rather than of legal definition. Likewise, when the parent company is not engaged in production or the rendering of services, it is customary to call it a *holding company.*

Without regard to whether the enterprise is a holding company or whether the group of businesses constitute a conglomerate or an integrated industry, each part is a distinct corporation to which the ordinary corporation law applies. In some instances additional principles apply because of the nature of the relationship existing between the several corporations involved. In some instances the entity of one of the corporations in the conglomerate group may be ignored.

16. Legality

Consolidations, mergers, and asset acquisitions between enterprises are often prohibited by federal antitrust legislation on the ground that the effect is to lessen competition in interstate commerce. A business corporation may not merge with a charitable corporation because this combination would divert the assets of the respective corporations to purposes not intended by their shareholders.

17. Anti-takeover Laws

Corporate takeovers usually have a positive impact on shareholders of the target corporation because of the cash premiums offered to them to induce them to "tender" the number of shares necessary to gain control of the target corporation. However, takeovers may have an adverse impact on the target corporation's managers and employees and the local economy when the acquiring corporation puts into effect the economies and personnel cutbacks resulting from the merger. Political pressure by employees and local communities has caused most states to enact laws making it more difficult for corporate takeovers to succeed.

State anti-takeover laws commonly provide that the acquisition of "control shares" in a corporation will not include voting rights unless a majority of preexisting disinterested shareholders so agree at a meeting to be held within 50 days from the date the offer is first published.[38]

18.   Liability of Successor Corporations

When corporations are combined in any way, the question arises as to who is liable for the debts and obligations of the predecessor corporations.

(a) MERGERS. Generally, the enterprise engaging in or continuing the business after a merger or consolidation succeeds to all of the rights and property of the predecessor, or disappearing, corporations and is subject to all of the debts and liabilities of the predecessor corporations.[39] Thus, a successor corporation is liable for the contracts of a predecessor corporation, and it is no defense that the third party did not have a contract with the successor corporation.

(b) ASSET SALES. In contrast with a merger or consolidation, a corporation may merely purchase the assets of another business. In that case the purchaser does not become liable for the obligations of the predecessor business.[40]

Successor firms may seek to avoid the predecessor firm's liabilities by casting the transaction in the form of an asset sale while in actuality (but not in form) structuring a merger.

In the *Marks* case the court was faced with deciding whether the transactions were asset sales, which insulated the purchaser from liability, or *de facto* mergers, which made the purchaser liable for the obligations of the predecessor corporations.

---

[38]   See, for example, Indiana Control Share Acquisition Act, Ind Bus Corp Law § 23–1–17–1 (Supp 1990). The constitutionality of this law, including the 50-day maximum period as compared to the 20-day waiting period of the Williams Act, was upheld by the U.S. Supreme Court in CTS Corp. v Dynamics Corp. of America, 481 US 69 (1987).

[39]   Bernard v Kee Manufacturing Co. (Fla App) 394 So 2d 552 (1981).
[40]   Hamaker v Kenwel-Jackson Machine, Inc. (SD) 387 NW2d 515 (1986).

MARKS v MINNESOTA MINING AND MANUFACTURING CO.
187 Cal App 3d 1429, 232 Cal Rptr 594 (1986)

In June of 1977 McGhan/Cal. Inc., a manufacturer of prostheses used in breast augmentation surgery, was acquired by a wholly owned Delaware subsidiary of 3M, called McGhan/Del. Inc. In April 1977 Mary Marks had surgery; two McGhan implants were used. Because of defects in the McGhan implants, Marks underwent three additional operations, eventually having the McGhan products replaced with implants manufactured by another company. Beginning in 1976 McGhan/Cal. and, later, McGhan/Del. received numerous complaints about its implants and received inquiries from the FDA. McGhan/Del. removed the product from the market in April of 1979. On January 1, 1981, 3M's wholly owned subsidiary McGhan/Del. Inc. was reorganized as a division of 3M and dissolved. In January 1982, following her fourth surgery, Marks brought a product liability suit against 3M. 3M contended that it was not liable for the actions of the predecessor corporation. The jury returned a verdict of $25,850 in compensatory damages and $75,000 in punitive damages. The trial judge deleted the punitive damages, and both parties appealed.

NEWSOM, J. . . . While it is the general rule that a purchaser of assets for cash does not assume the seller's liabilities, there are several exceptions to that rule, one of which—where a de facto merger has occurred—we find applicable here. This exception applies where the assets of one corporation are transferred without consideration which can be made available to satisfy claims or "where the consideration consists wholly of shares of the purchaser's stock which are promptly distributed to the seller's shareholders in conjunction with the seller's liquidation. (*Shannon v. Samuel Langston Company* (W.D. Mich. 1974) 379 F.Supp 797, 801)."

Our analysis of the McGhan/Cal. to McGhan/Del. transfer reveals that the first transaction was carried out pursuant to an agreement, dated May 11, 1977, between 3M and McGhan/Cal. entitled "Agreement and Plan of Reorganization." Pursuant to its terms, McGhan/Cal. was to receive shares of 3M stock in exchange for all of its business, assets and goodwill, including the corporate name and the shares of stock of its foreign subsidiary. McGhan/Cal. was required by the agreement to change its name, distribute the 3M stock to its shareholders and dissolve as soon as practicable. All McGhan/Cal. employees, including the seven shareholders, were requested to sign employment agreements with 3M. All five founders of McGhan/Cal. continued to work for McGhan/Del. in substantially the same capacity after the reorganization. Thus, as described by Donald McGhan, the "operating board" (if not the formal board of directors) remained the same. All McGhan/Cal. shareholders became shareholders of 3M.

The agreement also provided for the assumption by 3M of specified liabilities shown on the balance sheets. . . .

We find *Shannon, supra,* particularly persuasive. There, Harris Intertype Corporation entered into an agreement with Samuel M. Langston Company to purchase assets in exchange for Harris stock. (*Shannon, supra,* 379 F.Supp. at p. 799.) Langston was required to change its name. It was subsequently dissolved and the Harris stock distributed to its shareholders. Harris assumed all obligations which were "necessary for the uninterrupted continuation of normal business operations. . . ." A Harris subsidiary took over and continued the operations of Langston under the name The Langston Company. The subsidiary was merged into Harris the year after the plaintiff was injured by a product manufactured by the first Langston corporation. The court characterized this transaction as a de facto merger, and on that basis found Harris liable for the damages due to the defective product. Reasoning from the premise that "a purchaser of corporate assets will be liable for the debts and liabilities of the transferor when the transaction amounts to a consolidation or merger of the seller and purchaser", the court concluded: "Public policy requires that Harris Intertype, having received the benefits of a going concern, should also assume the costs which all other going concerns must ordinarily bear." The court added that "solvent corporations, going concerns, should not be permitted to discharge their liabilities to injured persons simply by shuffling paper and manipulating corporate entities."

Here, as in *Shannon, supra,* the result of the transaction was exactly that which would have occurred had a statutory merger taken place, and we are accordingly convinced of the necessity and the fairness of transferring liability from McGhan/Cal. to McGhan/Del. . . .

With respect to the second reorganization, McGhan/Del., the wholly owned subsidiary of 3M which manufactured the defective product at issue, was "reorganized" into its parent company 11 months before plaintiff's injury. Evidence of the nature of these transactions is sparse, consisting of the declaration of a 3M officer that effective January 1, 1981, McGhan/Del. was reorganized as a division of 3M and then dissolved. Counsel for 3M refers to the transaction as a "merger."

. . . McGhan/Del. continued doing business after the reorganization as "McGhan/3M," a component of its corporate parent. And since 3M was the sole shareholder, it is highly unlikely that cash was paid for the business of McGhan/Del. We therefore find that the reorganization amounted to a continuation of a de facto merger. Thus, when McGhan/Del. became a part of its parent, as a matter of corporate law it carried with it all of its liabilities.

. . . The critical fact is that while there was more than one merger or reorganization, an analysis of each transaction discloses to us that its intrinsic structure and nature, unlike a sale of assets for cash, was of a type in which the corporate entity was continued and all liability was transferred. All the indicia of a merger are present. We accordingly conclude that the second reorganization, like the first, transferred all liabilities to the surviving corporation. 3M is therefore liable for all liabilities of its subsidiary, including the punitive damages awarded to plaintiff.

The judgment notwithstanding the verdict is reversed with instructions to reinstate the judgment entered on the jury's verdict which included the award of punitive damages.

Appellant Marks is entitled to costs on this appeal.

[Judgment reversed]

QUESTIONS

1. Did the court find that the result of the transaction between McGhan/Cal. and McGhan/Del. was exactly what would have occurred had a statutory merger taken place?
2. What is the basis for holding a successor corporation liable for the debts of a predecessor corporation when there is a *de facto* merger?
3. If 3M had purchased all of the assets of McGhan/Cal. for cash and used the former McGhan/Cal. plant and equipment to make tapes, would it have been held liable to Marks?

SUMMARY

A corporation is an artificial person, created by government action, that exists as a separate and distinct entity and is endowed with certain powers. In most states the corporation comes into existence when the secretary of state issues a certificate of incorporation. The most common forms of corporations are private business corporations whose stock is sold to the public (publicly held) and close corporations, which are business firms whose shares are not traded publicly. Corporations may be formed for purposes other than conducting a business. For example, there are nonprofit corporations, municipal corporations, and public authorities for governmental purposes.

Ordinarily, each corporation will be treated as a separate person, and the law will not look beyond the corporate identity merely because the corporation has been formed to obtain tax savings or limited liability. The fact that two corporations have the same shareholders does not justify disregarding the separate corporate entities. However, when a corporation is formed to perpetrate a fraud, a court will ignore the corporate form, or "pierce the corporate veil." The corporate form will also be ignored to prevent injustice or because of the functional reality that the two corporations in question are one.

A promoter is a person who brings together the persons interested in the enterprise and sets in motion all that must be done to form a corporation. A corporation is not liable on contracts made by its promoter for the corporation unless it adopts the contracts; the promoter is personally liable for contracts made for the corporation before its existence. A promoter stands in a fiduciary relation to the corporation and stock subscribers.

The procedures for incorporation are set forth in the statutes of each state. In most states the corporation comes into existence upon issuance of the certificate of incorporation. The business is then called a corporation *de jure.* When compliance with all statutory procedures for incorporation is lacking, a *de facto* corporation may be found to exist. Or, when sufficient compliance for a *de facto* corporation does not exist, a third person may be estopped from denying the legal existence of the "corporation" with which it did business (corporation by estoppel). However, the 1969

ABA MBCA has been construed as having abolished the *de facto* corporation and corporation by estoppel doctrines.

A corporation has the power to continue as a unit forever or for a stated period of time, regardless of changes in the ownership of the stock. It may make contracts, issue stocks and bonds, borrow money, execute commercial paper, transfer and acquire property, acquire its own stock if it is solvent and the purchase does not impair capital, and make charitable contributions. Subject to limitations, a corporation has power to do business in other states. A corporation also may participate in a business enterprise to the same extent as an individual. That is, it may be a partner in a partnership, or it may enter a joint venture or other enterprise. Special service corporations such as banks, insurance companies, and railroads are subject to separate statutes with regard to their organization and powers.

An *ultra vires* act occurs when a corporation acts beyond the scope of the powers granted by its charter and the statute under which it was organized. Because most states grant broad powers to corporations, it is unlikely that a modern corporation would act beyond the scope of its powers.

Two or more corporations may be combined to form a new enterprise. This combination may be a consolidation—with a new corporation coming into existence—or a merger—wherein one corporation absorbs the other.

QUESTIONS AND CASE PROBLEMS

1. What social forces are affected by the recognition of a corporation as a distinct legal entity?
2. The Karnak Chemical Company is incorporated in Utah. It wishes to do business in Oklahoma but is required to pay a tax assessed by Oklahoma against foreign corporations. Stephen owns shares in Karnak. He claims that it is not subject to the Oklahoma tax because Karnak is an American corporation and, therefore, is a domestic corporation to all states. Is he correct?
3. Susan sued the Mobile Construction Company. Philip was the only shareholder of the corpora-

tion. Susan obtained a judgment against the corporation. Philip then dissolved the corporation and took over all its assets. He agreed to pay all outstanding debts of the corporation except the judgment in favor of Susan. She sued Philip on the ground that he was liable for the judgment against the corporation. He claimed that the judgment was only the liability of the corporation and that he was not liable because he was merely a shareholder and had not assumed the liability for the judgment. Is Philip liable on the judgment?

4. Edwin Edwards and Karen Davis owned EEE, Inc., which owned three convenience stores all of which sold gasoline. Reid Ellis delivered to the three convenience stores $26,675.02 worth of gasoline, for which he was not paid. Ellis demonstrated that Edwards and Davis owned the business, ran it, and in fact personally ordered the gasoline. He contends that they are personally liable for the debt owed him by EEE, Inc. Decide. [Ellis v Edwards, 180 Ga App 301, 348 SE2d 764]

5. What are common grounds for forfeiture (administrative dissolution) of the corporate charter?

6. Compare and contrast consolidations, mergers, and conglomerates.

7. Norman was organizing a new corporation: the Collins Home Construction Company. Fairchild knew that the corporation was not yet formed but made a contract by which he agreed to sell certain goods to Collins. The corporation was later organized and ratified the contract that Norman had made with Fairchild. Fairchild, however, did not perform the contract and was sued by Collins. Fairchild raised the defense that he had never made any contract with Collins and that a corporation that did not exist could not have made a contract. Were these defenses valid?

8. In 1977 Morris Gray leased waterfront property on the Ross Barnett Reservoir to a restaurant, Edgewater Landing Inc., for a ten-year term. After a year and one-half, Edgewater's original shareholder, Billy Stegall, sold all of his shares in the corporation to Tom Bradley. Bradley transferred portions of his shares to others. As of 1986 Tom Bradley and Bradley's bookkeeper, Sandra Martin, owned all the shares in the restaurant. Sandra's husband Randy acted as its manager. Gray visited the property in September of 1986 and found many problems with the condition of the property. It took $102,342 to repair the run-down property. Gray sued Edgewater Landing Inc. and Tom Bradley and Sandra Martin individually for breach of the lease agreement. Bradley and Martin contend that they are not individually liable to the property owner. Decide. [Gray v Edgewater Landing, Inc. (Miss) 541 So 2d 1044]

9. Emmick was a director and shareholder of Colonial Manors, Inc. (CM). He organized another corporation named Oahe Enterprises, Inc. In order to obtain shares of the Oahe stock, Emmick transferred CM shares arbitrarily valued at $19 per share to Oahe Corporation. The CM shares had a book value of $.47 per share, but Emmick believed that the stock would increase to a value of $19. The board of Oahe approved Emmick's payment with the value of $19 per share. Golden sued Emmick on the ground that he had fraudulently deceived the Oahe Corporation as to the value of the CM shares and thus had made a secret profit when he received the Oahe shares that had a much greater value than the CM shares he gave in exchange. Emmick defended that it was his firm opinion that the future potential value of CM shares would surely reach $19 per share. Decide. [Golden v Oahe Enterprises, Inc. (SD) 295 NW2d 160]

10. The Branmar Theatre Co., a family corporation, leased a theater from Branmar, Inc. The lease prohibited it from assigning the lease. The holders of the stock of Branmar Theatre Co. sold their stock to the Schwartzes. The lessor, Branmar, Inc., claimed that this was a prohibited assignment and threatened to cancel the lease. Branmar Theatre Co. thereafter brought an action for a declaratory judgment to enjoin the cancellation of the lease. Should the court enjoin the cancellation of the lease? [Branmar Theatre Co. v Branmar, Inc. (Del Ch) 264 A2d 526]

11. Mulley was a promoter of a corporation not yet formed, Collier County Developers, Inc. He, as promoter, made a contract with Vodopich for services in selling certain real estate. Vodopich later sued Mulley for breach of the contract. Mulley claimed that he was not liable because Vodopich knew that the corporation had not yet been formed. Was he correct? [Vodopich v Collier County Developers, Inc. (Fla App) 319 So 2d 43]

12. The Seabrook Island Property Owners Association, Inc. (the association) is a nonprofit corporation organized under state law to maintain streets and open spaces owned by property owners. The Seabrook Island Company is the developer of Seabrook Island and has majority control of the board of directors of the association. The association's bylaws empower the board of directors to levy an annual maintenance charge. Neither the association's charter nor its bylaws authorize the board to assess any other charges. When the board levied, in addition to the annual maintenance charge, an "emergency budget assessment" on all members in order to rebuild certain bridges and to revitalize the beach, the Loverings and other property owners challenged in court the asso-

ciation's power to impose the assessment. Decide. [Lovering v Seabrook Island Property Owners Association, 289 SC App 77, 344 SE2d 862.]

13. Adams and two other persons were promoters for a new corporation, the Aldrehn Theaters Co. The promoters retained Kridelbaugh to perform legal services in connection with the incorporation of the new business and promised to pay him $1,500. Aldrehn was incorporated through Kridelbaugh's services, and the promoters became its only directors. Kridelbaugh attended a meeting of the board of directors at which he was told that he should obtain a permit for the corporation to sell stock, because the directors wished to pay him for his prior services. The promoters failed to pay Kridelbaugh, and he sued the corporation. Was the corporation liable? [Kridelbaugh v Aldrehn Theaters Co. 195 Iowa 147, 191 NW 803]

14. On August 19, 1980, the plaintiff, Joan Ioviero, injured her hand when she slipped and fell while leaving the dining room at the Hotel Excelsior in Venice, Italy. This hotel was owned by the Italian corporation "Cigahotels, S.p.A." In 1973 a firm called "Ciga Hotels, Inc." was incorporated in New York. Its certificate of incorporation was amended in 1979, changing its name to "Landia International Services, Inc." This New York corporation was employed by the Italian corporation, Cigahotels, S.p.A., to provide sales and promotional services in the United States and Canada. Ioviero sought to hold the New York corporation liable for her hand injury at the Venice hotel. She pointed to the similarity of the first corporate name used by the New York firm to the name Cigahotels, S.p.A., and the fact that the New York firm represented the interests of the Italian firm in the United States, as clear evidence that the two firms were the same, single legal entity. She asked that the court disregard the separate corporate entities. The New York corporation moved that the case be dismissed, because it was duly incorporated in New York and did not own the Excelsior Hotel in which Ioviero was injured. Decide. [Ioviero v CigaHotel, Inc. aka Landia I.S. Inc. 101 App Div 2d 852, 475 NYS2d 880].

15. William Sullivan was ousted from the presidency of the New England Patriots Football Club, Inc. Later, he borrowed $5,348,000 to buy 100 percent control of the voting shares of the corporation. A condition of the loan was that he reorganize the Patriots so that the income from the corporation could be devoted to repayment of the personal loan, and the team's assets could be used as collateral. Sullivan therefore arranged for a cash freeze-out merger of the holders of the 120,000 shares of nonvoting stock. David Coggins, who owned 10 shares of nonvoting stock and took special pride in the fact that he was an owner of the team, refused the $15-a-share buyout and challenged the merger in court. He contended that the merger was not for a legitimate corporate purpose but rather to enable Sullivan to satisfy his personal loan. Sullivan contended that legitimate business purposes were given in the merger proxy statement, such as the NFL policy of discouraging public ownership of teams. Coggins responded that before the merger Sullivan had 100 percent control of the voting stock and thus control of the franchise, and that no legal basis existed to eliminate public ownership. Decide. [Coggins v New England Patriots Football Club, 397 Mass 525, 492 NE2d 1112]

47

CORPORATE STOCK AND SECURITIES

The two most common instruments used to provide the capital structure of a corporation are stocks and bonds.

A share of stock is an ownership of equity interest in the corporation. A bond is a debt security; a bondholder is a creditor of the corporation rather than an owner. The combination of debt and equity securities is a firm's capital structure.

A. CORPORATE STOCK

A shareholder owns a share or portion of the

900

corporation. That fractional ownership is customarily represented by a share or stock certificate. *Share* and *stock* are synonymous.

1. Nature of Stock

Membership in a corporation is based on ownership of one or more shares of stock of the corporation. Each share represents a fractional interest in the total property possessed by the corporation. The shareholder does not own or have an interest in any specific property of the corporation; the corporation is the owner of all of its property.

(a) CAPITAL AND CAPITAL STOCK. **Capital** refers to the net assets of the corporation. Shares that have been issued to holders are said to be **outstanding. Capital stock** refers to the value received by the corporation for its outstanding stock.

(b) VALUATION OF STOCK. Corporate stock may have a specified **par value.** This means that the person subscribing to the stock and acquiring it from the corporation must pay that amount. When stock is issued by the corporation for a price greater than the par value, some statutes provide that only the par value amount is to be treated as stated capital, the excess being allocated to surplus.

Shares may be issued with no par value. In such a case no amount is stated in the certificate, and the amount that the subscriber pays the corporation is determined by the board of directors. The Revised Model Business Corporation Act eliminates the concept of par value, so stock issued by corporations in states following the RMBCA is always *no par.*

The value found by dividing the value of the corporate assets by the number of shares outstanding is the **book value** of the shares. The **market value** of a share of stock is the price at which that stock can be voluntarily bought or sold on the open market.

2. Certificate of Stock

The corporation ordinarily issues a **certificate of stock** or **share certificate** as evidence of the shareholder's ownership of stock. The issuance of such certificates is not essential either

to the existence of a corporation or to the ownership of its stock.[1] However, it is an almost universal practice since it is a convenient method of proving ownership and since it makes transfer of ownership easier.

3. Kinds of Stock

The stock of a corporation may be divided into two or more classes.

(a) CLASSIFICATION BY PREFERENCES. **Common stock** is ordinary stock that has no preferences. Each share usually entitles the holder to have one vote, to receive a share of the profits in the form of dividends when declared, and to participate in the distribution of capital upon dissolution of the corporation. **Preferred stock** has a priority over common stock. The priority may be with respect to dividends. Preferred stock may also have a priority over common stock in the distribution of capital upon dissolution of the corporation. Preferred stock is ordinarily nonvoting.

(1) Cumulative Preferred Stock. Ordinarily, the right to receive dividends is dependent on the declaration of dividends by the board of directors for that particular period of time. If there is no fund from which the dividends may be declared or if the directors do not declare them from an available fund, the shareholder has no right to dividends. The fact that a shareholder has not received dividends for the current year does not in itself give the right to accumulate or carry over into the next year a claim for those dividends.

In the absence of a statement that the right to dividends is noncumulative, it is frequently

---

[1]   Krosnar v Schmidt Krosnar McNaughton Garret Co., 282 Pa Super 526, 423 A2d 370 (1980). Amendments to Article 8 of the UCC adopted in 1977 give corporations the option of providing for the ownership of shares not represented by certificates. In substance, ownership is established by information stored in a data bank, but no share certificates are issued. These 1977 amendments have been adopted in Arkansas, California, Colorado, Connecticut, Delaware, Florida, Hawaii, Idaho, Illinois, Indiana, Iowa, Kansas, Kentucky, Louisiana, Maine, Maryland, Massachusetts, Michigan, Minnesota, Montana, Nebraska, Nevada, New Hampshire, New Mexico, New York, North Carolina, North Dakota, Ohio, Oklahoma, Oregon, Rhode Island, South Dakota, Tennessee, Texas, Utah, Virginia, Washington, West Virginia, Wisconsin, and Wyoming.

held that preferred stock has the right to accumulate dividends for each year in which there was a surplus available for dividend payment but dividends were not declared.

(2) Participating Preferred Stock. Sometimes the preferred stock is given the right of participation. If so, after the common shares receive dividends or a capital distribution equal to that first received by the preferred stock, both kinds participate or share equally in the balance.

(b) DURATION OF SHARES. Ordinarily, shares continue to exist for the life of the corporation. However, any kind of shares, whether common or preferred, may be made terminable at an earlier date.

Convertible shares entitle the shareholder to exchange owned shares for a different kind of share or for bonds of the corporation.

(c) FRACTIONAL SHARES. A corporation may issue fractional shares or scrip or certificates representing such fractional shares that can be sold or combined for the acquisition of whole shares.

B.   ACQUISITION OF SHARES

Shares of stock may be acquired by (1) subscription, either before or after the corporation is organized, or (2) transfer of existing shares from a shareholder or from the corporation.

4.   Statute of Frauds

A contract for the sale of corporate shares must be evidenced by a writing or it cannot be enforced.[2] The writing must show that there has been a contract for the sale of a stated quantity of described securities at a defined or stated price. The writing must be signed in the manner required of a writing for the sale of goods. No writing is required for a contract by which a broker agrees with a customer to buy or sell securities for the customer.

5.   Subscription

A **stock subscription** is a contract or an agreement to buy a specific number and kind of shares when they are issued. As in the case of any other contract, the agreement to subscribe to shares of a corporation is subject to avoidance for fraud.

(a) SUBSCRIPTION BEFORE INCORPORATION. In many states a preincorporation subscription of shares is regarded as an offer to the corporation. By this view, it is necessary for the corporation to accept the subscription offer either expressly or by conduct. A few states hold that such subscriptions automatically become binding contracts when the organization has been completed. In some states the preincorporation subscription is irrevocable for a stated period.[3] The RMBCA provides that "a subscription for shares entered into before incorporation is irrevocable for six months unless the subscription agreement provides a longer or shorter period or all the subscribers agree to revocation."[4]

(b) SUBSCRIPTION AFTER INCORPORATION. Subscriptions may be made after incorporation. In that event the transaction is like any other contract with the corporation. The offer of the subscription may come from the subscriber or from the corporation. In either case there must be an acceptance. Upon acceptance the subscriber immediately becomes a shareholder with all the rights, privileges, and liabilities of a shareholder, even though the subscriber has not paid any of the purchase price. However, the transaction may be only a contract for the future issue of shares rather than a present subscription.

6.   Transfer of Shares

In the absence of a valid restriction, a shareholder may transfer shares to anyone.

(a) RESTRICTIONS ON TRANSFER. Restrictions on the transfer of stock are valid provided they are not unreasonable. In order to

---

[2]   UCC § 8–319(a). Smith v Baker (Ky App) 715 SW2d 890 (1986).

[3]   Prejean v Commonwealth for Community Change, Inc. (La App) 503 So 2d 661 (1987).
[4]   RMBCA § 6.20(a).

prevent its stock from going into the hands of strangers, it is lawful to require that the corporation or other stockholders be given the first right to purchase stock before a shareholder may sell it to an outsider. Also, a provision giving a corporation the right to purchase a shareholder's shares upon death is valid.

A restriction on the right to transfer is not effective as against the purchaser of the certificate unless the restriction is conspicuously noted on the certificate or unless the transferee has actual knowledge of the restriction.

In the *Fought* case the court considered whether shares of stock were sold in violation of a stock redemption agreement.

FOUGHT v MORRIS
(Miss) 543 So 2d 167 (1989)

In 1974 Billy Fought, Brady Morris, Clayton Strong, and John Peyton organized Vicksburg Mold and Die, Inc., for the purpose of designing and manufacturing plastic and metal products. Each individual was issued twenty-five shares of stock. The shareholders entered into a stock redemption agreement requiring a stockholder wishing to sell his stock to offer proportionate shares to each stockholder. Morris was elected president and Fought vice president, and all four individuals worked at the plant. Strong retired in 1979 and sold his shares in accordance with the stock redemption plan. In 1983 Peyton decided to sell his shares and agreed to sell them all to Morris, thus giving Morris control of the corporation. Fought sued Morris for breach of his fiduciary duty to Fought and for the value of Fought's *pro rata* share of Peyton's stock. From a judgment for Morris, Fought appealed.

ANDERSON, J. . . . Dispute exists in the record as to whether Morris and Fought agreed that the corporation could not purchase Peyton's stock. More to the point, however, the record is clear that Fought offered to purchase his pro-rata share and that Morris offered to purchase all of Peyton's shares. The evidence indicates that Morris' intent in offering to purchase all Peyton's shares was to "freeze out" Fought.

As we discussed above, directors and officers of a corporation stand in a fiduciary relationship to the corporation and its stockholders. These duties include exercising the utmost good faith and loyalty in discharge of the corporate office. . . .

The chancellor found that Morris won in the scramble between Fought and Morris for Peyton's stock. However, at the inception of the corporation the four stockholders entered into a Stock Redemption Agreement to prevent such a scramble. Section 2 of the agreement provided in pertinent part that:

In the event that any stockholder should desire to dispose of any of his stock in the Company during his lifetime, he shall *first offer to sell all of this stock to the Company. . . . Any share not purchased by the Company within thirty days after receipt of such offer shall be offered to the other stockholders, each of whom shall have the right to purchase such portion of the stock offered for sale as the number of shares owned by him at such date shall bear to the total number of shares owned by all the other stockholders* provided, however, that if any stockholder does not purchase his full proportionate share of the stock, the unaccepted stock may be purchased by the other stockholders. . . . (Emphasis added).

This agreement insured that stock in the corporation always would be offered to the corporation, or in the alternative, each shareholder would have a right to purchase a pro-rata share.

A Stock Redemption Agreement is one guide for corporate policy, which may restrain the transferability of stock. Shareholders in a close corporation have an interest in maintaining a balance of power that frequently is protected by such agreements. . . .

Generally, a director violates no duty by dealing in his own stock on his own account. This rule is not applicable, however, when there is a . . . stock redemption agreement, in order to maintain proportionate control of the corporation. . . .

In [this case] the stockholders had entered into an agreement which constituted corporate policy. This policy was adhered to when Strong sold his stock. However, the record reveals that Morris was unhappy with Fought. When Peyton decided to sell his stock, Morris saw a way to take control, as evidenced by his statement that he would undertake to relieve Peyton from liability on the bank note only if he could purchase all of Peyton's stock.

The court below failed to perceive Morris' fiduciary duty, as an officer and director of Vicksburg Mold and Die, Inc., to conduct his office with prudence and all good fidelity. Morris' intended exclusion of Fought from the purchase of Peyton's shares was a breach of the Stock Redemption Agreement and bylaws, and, therefore, a breach of his fiduciary duty as an officer, a director and a stockholder under the good faith standard we adopt today. . . . We hold, therefore, that Morris breached his fiduciary duty in purchasing all of Peyton's stock, contrary to the Stock Redemption Agreement. . . .

We find: (1) Morris breached his fiduciary duty as director, an officer and stockholder by purchasing Peyton's total shares of stock in violation of the stockholders' purchase redemption agreement, (2) the Foughts are entitled to the fair market value of the stock in accordance with paragraph 6 of the stock redemption agreement.

[Reversed and remanded]

QUESTIONS

1. What was Section 2 of the stock redemption agreement devised to achieve?
2. What did Morris expect to achieve by purchasing all of Peyton's stock?
3. Did Morris breach any fiduciary duty to Fought?

A restriction on the transfer of stock is strictly interpreted. For example, a restriction on the sale of stock is not applicable to a gift of stock.

(b) INTEREST TRANSFERRED. The transfer of shares may be absolute; that is, it may divest all ownership and make the transferee the full owner. Alternatively, the transfer may be merely for security, as when stock is pledged to secure the repayment of a loan.

7.   Mechanics of Transfer

The ownership of shares is transferred by the delivery of the certificate of stock, indorsed by its owner in blank or to a specified person. Ownership may also be transferred by the delivery of the certificate accompanied by a separate assignment or power of attorney executed by the owner.[5]

A delivery from the owner of the shares directly to the transferee is not required. It can be made to an intermediary. When there is no

---

[5]   UCC § 8–309. The second alternative of a delivery of an unindorsed certificate is designed to keep the certificate "clean," as when the transfer is for a temporary or special purpose, as in the case of a pledge of the certificate as security for a loan.

delivery of the share certificate to anyone, however, there is no transfer of ownership of the shares.

A physical transfer of the certificate without a necessary indorsement is effective as between the parties, because indorsement is necessary only to make a transferee a bona fide purchaser as against third parties. Thus, a gift of shares is binding even though the above rules have not been satisfied.[6]

8.   Effect of Transfer

The transfer of existing shares of stock raises questions as to the validity and effect of the transfer as between the parties to the transfer and between them and the corporation.

(a) VALIDITY OF TRANSFER. Since a transfer of shares is a transfer of ownership, the transfer must in general satisfy the requirements governing any other transfer of property or agreement to transfer property. As between the parties, a transfer may be set aside for any ground that would warrant similar relief under property law. If the transfer of stock has been obtained by duress, the transferor may obtain a rescission of the transfer.

(b) NEGOTIABILITY. Under the common law the transferee of shares of stock had no greater right than the transferor because the certificate and the shares represented by the certificate were nonnegotiable. By statute, the common law rule has been changed by imparting negotiability to the certificate. Just as various defenses cannot be asserted against the holder in due course of a commercial paper, it is provided that similar defenses cannot be raised against the person acquiring the certificate in good faith and for value. As against such a person, the defenses cannot be raised that the transferor did not own the shares or did not have authority to deliver the certificate, or that the transfer was made in violation of a restriction on transfer not known to the person and not noted conspicuously on the certificate.

The fact that corporate stock has the quality of negotiability does not make it commercial paper within Article 3 of the UCC. Shares of stock are classified under the UCC as investment securities. Article 8, as supplemented by the non-Code law that has not been displaced, is the source of the law governing the rights of the parties to the transaction involving such securities. Nevertheless, courts may look to Article 3 for guidance when a question regarding an investment security cannot be resolved on the basis of the language in Article 8 alone.

(c) SECURED TRANSACTION. Corporate stock is frequently delivered to a creditor as security for a debt owed by the shareholder. Thus, a debtor borrowing money from a bank may deliver shares of stock to the bank as collateral security for the repayment of the loan. A broker's customer purchasing stock on margin may leave the stock in the possession of the broker as security for the payment of any balance due. The delivery of the security to the creditor gives rise to a perfected security interest without any filing by the creditor. In itself, the pledge does not make the pledgee of the corporate stock the owner of the stock.

(d) EFFECT OF TRANSFER ON CORPORATION. Until there is a transfer on its books, the corporation is entitled to treat as the owner the person whose name is on the books. The corporation may properly refuse to recognize the transferee when the corporation is given notice or has knowledge that the transfer is void or in breach of trust. In such a case the corporation properly refuses to register a transfer until the rights of the parties have been determined.

The corporation may also refuse to register the transfer of shares when the outstanding certificate is not surrendered to it, in the absence of satisfactory proof that it has been lost, destroyed, or stolen.

9.   Lost, Destroyed, and Stolen Securities

The owner of a lost, destroyed, or stolen security is entitled to a replacement security if the owner files a sufficient indemnity bond and

---

[6]   Ross' Estate (Utah) 626 P2d 489 (1981).

requests the new security within a reasonable time before the issuer has notice that the original certificate has been acquired by a bona fide purchaser. If, after the issue of the new security, a bona fide purchaser appears with the original security, the corporation must register a transfer of the security to that person and accept such person as the owner of the shares.[7]

C.   RIGHTS OF SHAREHOLDERS

The control of the shareholders over the corporation is indirect. Periodically (ordinarily, once a year) the shareholders elect directors and by this means can control the corporation. At other times, however, the shareholders have no right or power to control the corporate activity so long as it is conducted within lawful channels.

10.   Ownership Rights

Ownership rights in a corporation are generally represented by shares of stock and are generally freely transferable.

(a) CERTIFICATES OF STOCK. A shareholder generally has the right to have a properly executed certificate as evidence of ownership of shares.[8]

(b) TRANSFER OF SHARES. Subject to certain valid restrictions, as discussed previously in this chapter,[9] a shareholder has the right to transfer the shares and may sell the shares at any price the marketplace dictates or transfer them as a gift. In the *Shoaf* case the court considered whether a shareholder who controlled a majority of the corporation's shares had a duty to refrain from receiving a premium upon the sale of his controlling stock.

---

[8]   As to shares without certificates under the 1977 version of the Uniform Commercial Code, see footnote 2 of this chapter.
[9]   Section 6.

[7]   UCC § 8–405.

SHOAF v WARLICK
(SC App) 380 SE2d 865 (1989)

Paul Warlick, Jr. was the president and chief executive officer and a stockholder of Coca-Cola Bottling Co. of Anderson S.C. (Coke-Anderson). He controlled 273.5 shares of stock of the total of 480 shares of stock outstanding, including the stock of his mother, uncle, and aunt. Warlick agreed to sell this controlling interest in Coke-Anderson to Coke-Ashville for $4 million, which included a premium to be paid him for his controlling interest. Wayne Shoaf, a minority shareholder, brought suit against Warlick, contending that Warlick had violated his fiduciary duty to the corporation and had received an unlawful premium for the sale of the majority interest in Coke-Anderson. From a judgment for Warlick, Shoaf appealed.

SHAW, J. . . . The issues we are asked to consider are whether Mr. Warlick had a fiduciary duty owed to the other stockholders and whether he breached this duty, and, whether Mr. Warlick has a basis to claim appellants are equitably estopped from attacking his premium received for his stock.

South Carolina has long followed the general rule that corporate stock is personal property which the owner may "dispose of . . . as he sees fit." . . . Concomitantly, when selling stock, stockholders must "necessarily act for themselves, and not as trustees for other stockholders." . . . This general rule applies as well to majority shareholders:

> A dominant or majority shareholder is generally under no duty to the minority stockholders to refrain from receiving a premium upon the sale of his controlling stock.

12B W. Fletcher, *Cyclopedia of the Law of Private Corporations*, § 5805.10, at 139 (rev. perm. ed. 1980).

This issue was more specifically framed and decided by the Florida Court of Appeals. Its analysis of the law speaks equally to the case at hand:

> The law of the marketplace dictates that a shareholder who has a controlling interest in a corporation will likely be able to receive a higher price per share than a minority shareholder. *As a general rule, nothing in the law of the courthouse prevents a majority shareholder from retaining this "control premium." . . . This is so even if, as is so frequently the case, the controlling shareholder is an officer or director of the corporation. . . . Officers and Directors § 5:01, at 5-2 (1984).* While some decades ago this general rule was under persistent attack in academia, it is clear that the rule survived unscathed in the courts and, indeed, now finds itself in fashion in a significant segment of academia. This debate aside, *courts have generally held firm to the rule*:
>
> "The thoughtful and scholarly writings of the academic commentators on the sale of control have had surprisingly little influence on the way courts decide cases. With only infrequent and relatively minor exceptions, *the courts still adhere to the traditional view that a shareholder, irrespective of whether he is also a director, officer, or both, may sell his shares, just as he may sell other kinds of personal property, for whatever price he can obtain, even if his shares constitute a controlling block and the price per share is enhanced by that fact.* Further, the courts generally hold that neither the selling shareholder nor his purchaser is under an obligation to see that other shareholders are provided opportunities to sell their shares on the same favorable terms as the controlling shareholder or even to inform minority shareholders of the price and other terms of the sale of the controlling interest." O'Neal, *Symposium: Sale of Control—Introduction*, 4 J. Corp. L. 239, 239 (1979). (emphasis added, footnote omitted)

Martin v. Martin, 529 So.2d 1174 (Fla. 3d Dist.Ct.App.1988)
   [Judgment affirmed]

QUESTIONS

1. What did the plaintiff contend?
2. Can a shareholder who is also an officer and director of the corporation lawfully obtain a premium for selling the controlling interest in a corporation?
3. State the general rule of law applicable to this case.

11.   Right to Vote

The right to vote means the right to vote at shareholders' meetings for the election of directors and on such other special matters as must be passed upon by the shareholders. As an illustration of the latter, a proposal to change the capital structure of the corporation or a proposal to sell all or substantially all the assets of the corporation must be approved by the shareholders.

(a) WHO MAY VOTE. Ordinarily, only **shareholders of record**—those common shareholders in whose name the stock appears on the books of the corporation—are entitled to vote. The board of directors may fix a date for closing the corporate books for this purpose.[10]

(b) NUMBER OF VOTES. Absent a provision to the contrary, for each share owned each shareholder is entitled to one vote on each matter to be voted. This procedure is called **straight voting,** and it is the normal method for shareholder voting on corporate matters. However, in the case of voting to elect directors only, cumulative voting is mandatory in nearly half of the states, being imposed either by constitution or by statute. Cumulative voting is permitted by law in other states when cumulative voting rights are provided for in the articles of incorporation or bylaws. **Cumulative voting** is a form of voting that is designed to give proportional representation on the board of directors to minority shareholders. Under a cumulative voting plan, each shareholder has as many votes as the number of shares owned multiplied by the number of directors to be elected. Minority shareholders may then cast all of their votes for a candidate who will represent their interests on the board of directors. Under straight voting, minority shareholders would always be outvoted. For example, assume that minority shareholder Susan Jones owned 350 shares of stock, and a majority interest controlled the remaining 650 shares. Also assume that nine directors are to be elected to the board. If straight voting were used for the election of directors, the majority shareholder with 650 shares would always outvote Susan's 350 shares. However, under cumulative voting, Susan would be allowed 3,150 votes (350 shares times 9 directors). This number of votes would guarantee her ability to elect three directors to represent her inter-

ests on the board. Susan, who owns 35 percent of the stock, is thus able to elect one-third of the board.

(c) VOTING BY PROXY. A shareholder has the right to authorize another to vote the shares owned by the shareholder. This procedure is known as **voting by proxy.** In the absence of restrictions to the contrary, any person, even one not a shareholder, may act as a proxy. Ordinarily, authority to act as a proxy may be conferred by an informal written instrument.[11]

(d) VOTING AGREEMENTS AND TRUSTS. Shareholders, as a general rule, are allowed to enter into an agreement by which they concentrate their voting strength for the purpose of electing directors.

A **voting trust** exists when by agreement a group of shareholders or all of the shareholders transfer their shares in trust to one or more persons as trustees, who are authorized to vote the stock during the life of the trust agreement.[12] In general, such agreements have been upheld if their object is lawful. In some jurisdictions such trusts cannot run beyond a specific number of years. There are some signs of a relaxation as to this matter. Several states have abandoned all time limitations, several have extended the time limitation, and many states provide for an extension or renewal of the agreement.

12. Preemptive Offer of Shares

If the capital stock of a corporation is increased, shareholders ordinarily have the **preemptive right** to subscribe to such percentage of the new shares as their old shares bore to the former total of capital stock. This right is given in order to enable shareholders to maintain their relative interests in the corporation.

The existence of a preemptive right may make impossible the concluding of a transaction in which the corporation is to transfer a block of stock as consideration. Moreover, practical difficulties arise as to how stock

---

[10] RMBCA § 7.07.

[11] See, for example, the regulations of the Securities and Exchange Commission, Rule X-14A-4.

[12] Bettner Trust v Bettner (Ind App) 495 NE2d 194 (1986).

should be allocated among shareholders of different classes.

The RMBCA provides that shareholders do not have preemptive rights unless the articles of incorporation so provide.[13] When the corporation elects to have preemptive rights by so stating in its articles of incorporation, the RMBCA sets forth rules dealing with most of the problems involving preemptive rights.[14] Under this model provision there is no preemptive right with respect to the transfer of a block of stock as consideration. Also, the model provision deals with how stock should be allocated among shareholders of different classes.

13.   Inspection of Books

A shareholder has the right to inspect the books of the shareholder's corporation. The request for inspection must be made in good faith, for proper motives, and at a reasonable time and place. The RMBCA authorizes inspection of corporate records "if the demand is made in good faith and for proper purpose."[15]

The purpose of inspection must be reasonably related to the shareholder's interest as a shareholder. A shareholder is entitled to inspect the records to determine the financial condition of the corporation, the quality of its management, and any matters relating to rights or interests in the corporate business, such as the value of stock.

Whether a stockholder who became part owner and employee of a competing business could inspect the books was the issue in the *Carter* case.

---

[13]   RMBCA § 6.30(a).
[14]   RMBCA § 6.30(b).

[15]   RMBCA § 16.02(c).

CARTER v WILSON CONSTRUCTION CO., INC.
(NC App) 348 SE2d 830 (1986)

William Carter, a former officer and employee of Wilson Construction Co. Inc., owned 317 shares of stock in the corporation. He left the Wilson corporation to become part owner and employee of C & L Contracting Co., which was a direct competitor of the Wilson corporation. Carter requested access to the Wilson corporate books in order to determine the value of his shares. The corporation refused, not wanting to divulge its business practices to a direct competitor. From a decision for Carter, which also assessed a $500 penalty against both the corporation's president and the corporation, the Wilson corporation and its president appealed.

JOHNSON, J. . . . Defendants contend in their first Assignment of Error that the court erred in finding that plaintiff had a proper purpose for obtaining access to the corporate information he requested. Defendants further contend that plaintiff's stated purpose was "a mask for more illegitimate purposes that would damage [defendant corporation's] ability to compete." Defendants characterize plaintiff as a "disgruntled minority shareholder" who "left his position without notice," leaving both companies "in pretty bad shape" in order to start his own competing business. . . .

The pertinent portion of G. S. § 55–38 provides as follows:

(b) A qualified shareholder, upon written demand stating the purpose thereof, shall have the right, in person, or by attorney, accountant or other agent, at any reasonable time or times, *for any proper purpose,* to examine at the place where they are kept and make extracts from, the books and records of account, minutes and record of shareholders of a domestic corporation or those of a foreign corporation actually or customarily kept by it within this State. . . . A shareholder's rights under this subsection may be enforced by an action in the nature of mandamus.

(Emphasis added.)

It is undisputed by the parties that plaintiff is a qualified shareholder. The issue is whether plaintiff's request to examine the corporate records was for "any proper purpose." Absent a statutory restriction, a shareholder has a common law right to inspect and examine the books and records of the corporation, given to him for the protection of his interests. G.S. § 55-38(b) does not give a qualified shareholder an absolute right of inspection and examination for a mere fishing expedition, or for a purpose not germane to the protection of his economic interest as a shareholder in the corporation. For a shareholder to have the right to actually visit a corporation's office and possibly disrupt its normal operation in order to inspect corporate books and records of account, our legislature has correctly decided that his motives must be "proper." Purposes which previously have been deemed proper are the shareholder's good faith desire to (1) determine the value of his stock; (2) investigate the conduct of the management; and (3) determine the financial condition of the corporation. The burden of proof rests upon the defendants, if they wish to defeat the shareholder's demand, to allege and show by facts, if they can, that the shareholder is motivated by some improper purpose. "In issuing the writ of mandamus the court will exercise a sound discretion, and grant the right under proper safeguards to protect the interests of all concerned." [*Cooke v. Outland,* 265 N.C. 601,] 613, 144 S.E.2d 843, *quoting Guthrie v. Harkness,* 199 U.S. 148, 156 (1905).

Here, plaintiff stated a proper purpose in his complaint. Defendants must overcome the presumption of good faith in plaintiff's favor by showing that plaintiff's purpose is improper. The evidence adduced at trial by plaintiff tended to show: that plaintiff tried to sell his stock in defendant corporation to defendant corporation, who declined plaintiff's offer to sell; . . . and that the net worth of defendant corporation decreased from August 1983 to August 1984. This evidence supports plaintiff's allegation of a proper purpose.

The evidence adduced at trial by defendants showed that plaintiff is currently part owner and employee of a business, C & L Contracting. According to the testimony of defendant Wilson, "We are in direct competition on all work in the [P]iedmont, North Carolina, that is bridge work" and that to allow plaintiff access to the books and records of accounts of defendant corporation "would put us at a disadvantage."

This evidence is insufficient to override the presumption that plaintiff is acting in good faith. . . . The mere possibility that a shareholder may abuse his right to gain access to corporate information will not be held to justify a denial of a legal right, if such right exists in the shareholder. . . .

[Judgment affirmed]

QUESTIONS

1. Is the state statute applicable in this case similar to the RMBCA provision authorizing inspection of corporate records?

2. Did the court agree with the Wilson corporation that its refusal was justified because Carter, now a direct competitor for bridge work in the state, would gain an unfair competitive advantage?

3. Who has the burden of proving that a shareholder's purpose in inspecting a corporation's books is "proper"?

A shareholder is entitled to inspect the books to obtain information needed for a lawsuit against the corporation or its directors or officers, to organize the other shareholders into an "opposition" party to remove the board of directors at the next election, or to buy the shares of other shareholders.

Inspection has frequently been refused when it was sought merely from idle curiosity or for "speculative purposes." Inspection has sometimes been denied on the ground that it was merely sought to obtain a mailing list of persons who would be solicited to buy products of another enterprise. Inspection has also been refused when the object of the shareholder was to advance political or social beliefs without regard to the welfare of the corporation.

Many cases deny the right of inspection when it would be harmful to the corporation or is sought only for the purpose of annoying, harassing, or causing vexation, or for the purpose of aiding competitors of the corporation. In contrast, the right of inspection is so broadly recognized in some states that the fact that the shareholder may possibly make an improper use of the information obtained does not bar inspection.

(a) FORM OF BOOKS. There are generally no legal requirements as to the form of corporate books and records. The RMBCA recognizes that corporate books and records may be stored in modern data storage systems. "A corporation shall maintain its records in written form or in any other form capable of conversion into written form within a reasonable time."[16]

(b) FINANCIAL STATEMENTS. In recognition of the widespread practice of corpora-tions to prepare formal financial statements, the RMBCA requires a corporation to furnish annual financial statements. These statements include a balance sheet as of the end of the fiscal year, an income statement for that year, and a statement of changes in shareholders' equity for that year.[17] A number of state statutes contain similar provisions.

14.   Dividends

A shareholder has the right to receive a proportion of dividends as they are declared, subject to the relative rights of other shareholders to preferences, accumulation of dividends, and participation. There is no absolute right that dividends be declared but only that dividends, when declared, must be paid in the manner indicated.

(a) FUNDS AVAILABLE FOR DECLARATION OF DIVIDENDS. Statutes commonly provide that no dividends may be declared unless there is a "surplus" for their payment. This surplus is generally calculated as the amount of the corporate assets in excess of the outstanding liabilities and paid-in capital of the corporation.

As an exception to these rules, a wasting assets corporation may pay dividends out of current net profits without regard to the preservation of the corporate assets. **Wasting assets corporations** are those designed to exhaust or use up the assets of the corporation (as by extracting oil, coal, iron, and other ores), as compared with manufacturing plants, wherein the object is to preserve the plant as well as to continue to manufacture. A wasting assets corporation may also be formed for the purpose of buying and liquidating a stock of

---

[16]   RMBCA § 16.01(d).

[17]   RMBCA § 16.20.

merchandise from a company that has received a discharge in bankruptcy court.

In some states statutes provide that dividends may be declared from current net profits, without regard to the existence of a deficit from former years, or from surplus.

(b) DISCRETION OF DIRECTORS. Assuming that a fund is available for the declaration of dividends, it is then a matter primarily within the discretion of the board of directors whether a dividend shall be declared. The fact that there is a surplus that could be used for dividends does not determine that they must be declared. This rule is not affected by the nature of the shares. Thus, the fact that the shareholders hold cumulative preferred shares does not give them any right to demand a declaration of dividends or to interfere with an honest exercise of discretion by the directors.

In general, a court will refuse to substitute its judgment for the judgment of the directors of the corporation and will interfere with their decision as to dividend declaration only when it is shown that their conduct is harmful to the welfare of the corporation or its shareholders.[18] The courts, however, will compel the declaration of a dividend when it is apparent that the directors have amassed a surplus beyond any practical business need.

(c) FORM OF DIVIDENDS. Customarily, a dividend is paid in money. However, it may be paid in property, such as a product manufactured by the corporation, in shares of other corporations held by the corporation, or in shares of the corporation itself.

(d) EFFECT OF TRANSFER OF SHARES. In determining who is entitled to dividends, it is immaterial when the surplus from which the distribution is made was earned. As between the transferor and the transferee, if the dividend is in cash or property other than the shares of the corporation declaring the dividend, the person who was the owner on the date the dividend was declared, the **record**

date, is entitled to the dividend. Thus, if a cash dividend is declared before a transfer is made, the transferor is entitled to it. In applying this rule, it is immaterial when distribution of the dividend is made.

The rule that the date of declaration determines the right to a cash dividend is subject to modification by the corporation. The board of directors, in declaring the dividend, may state that it will be payable to those who will be the holders of record on a later specified date, which then becomes the record date.

If the dividend consists of shares in the corporation declaring the dividend, ownership is determined by the date of distribution. Whichever party is the owner of the shares when the stock dividend is distributed is entitled to the stock dividend. The reason for this variation from the cash dividend rule lies in the fact that the declaration of a stock dividend has the effect of diluting the existing corporate assets among a larger number of shares. The value of the holding represented by each share is accordingly diminished. Unless the person who owns the stock on the distribution date receives a proportionate share of the stock dividend, the net effect will be to lessen that person's holding.

The transferor and transferee may enter into any agreement they choose with respect to dividends.

These rules determine the right to dividends as between transferor and transferee. Regardless of what those rights may be, the corporation is generally entitled to continue to recognize the transferor as a shareholder until it has been notified that a transfer has been made and the corporate records are accordingly changed. If the corporation, believing that the transferor is still the owner of the shares, sends the transferor a dividend to which the transferee is entitled, the transferee cannot sue the corporation. In that case, the remedy of the transferee is to sue the transferor for the dividend that the latter has received.

15. Capital Distribution

Upon the dissolution of the corporation, the shareholders are entitled to receive any bal-

---

[18]   Gabelli & Co. v Liggett Group, Inc. (Del Sup) 479 A2d 276 (1984).

ance of the corporate assets that remains after the payment of all creditors. Certain classes of stock may have a preference or priority in this distribution.

16.   Shareholders' Actions

When the corporation has the right to sue its directors or officers or third persons for damages caused by them to the corporation or for breach of contract, one or more shareholders may bring such action if the corporation refuses to do so. This is a **derivative** (secondary) **action,** in that the shareholder enforces only the cause of action of the corporation, and any money recovery is paid into the corporate treasury.[19]

In a derivative action, when a corporation has failed to enforce a right, a shareholder bringing such a suit must show that a demand was made on the directors to enforce the right in question and that the directors refused to do so.[20] The Investment Company Act of 1940 (ICA) authorizes shareholders to sue investment advisors to recover excessive fees paid the advisors by the corporation. The shareholders may bring such action without any prior demand on the directors of the corporation.[21]

An action cannot be brought by minority shareholders, however, if the action of the corporate directors or officers has been ratified by a majority of the shareholders acting in good faith and if the matter is of such a nature that had such majority originally authorized the acts of the directors or officers, there would not have been any wrong.

Shareholders may also intervene or join in an action brought against the corporation when the corporation refuses to defend the action against it or is not doing so in good faith. Otherwise, the shareholders may take no part in an action by or against the corporation.

Lawsuits may be brought by minority shareholders against majority shareholders who are "oppressive" toward minority shareholders.[22] Oppressive conduct may include payment of grossly excessive salaries and fringe benefits to the majority stockholders who are also serving as officers of the corporation.[23] Suits for dissolution for oppressive conduct commonly involve *close* or *closely held* corporations, where shares are owned by a small group of shareholders and shareholders actively serve as both directors and officers of the corporation. When oppressive conduct is found, courts may order the majority shareholders to buy the shares of the minority or require the liquidation of the corporation.

Shareholders in a deadlocked corporation may bring an action to obtain a dissolution of the corporation.

D.   LIABILITY OF SHAREHOLDERS

The shareholder is ordinarily protected from liability for the acts of the corporation. Some exceptions are made by statute.

17.   Limited Liability

The liability of a shareholder is generally limited. This means that the shareholder is not personally responsible for the debts and liabilities of the corporation. The capital contributed by the shareholders may be exhausted by the claims of creditors, but there is no personal liability for any unpaid balance.[24]

18.   Exceptions to Limited Liability

Liability may be imposed on a shareholder as though there were no corporation when the court ignores the corporate entity, either because of the particular circumstances of the case or because the corporation is so defectively organized that it is deemed not to exist.

(a) WAGE CLAIMS. Statutes sometimes

---

[19]   Brown v Tenny, 125 Ill App 3d 348, 532 NE2d 230 (1988).
[20]   Greenfield v Hamilton Oil Corp (Colo App) 760 P2d 664 (1988).
[21]   Daily Income Fund, Inc. v Fox, 464 US 523 (1984).

[22]   RMBCA § 14:30(2)(ii).
[23]   Maschmeier v Southside Press Ltd. (Iowa App) 435 NW 2d 377 (1988).
[24]   Salem Tent & Awning Co. v Schmidt, 79 Or App 475, 719 P2d 899 (1986).

provide that the shareholders shall have unlimited liability for the wage claims of corporate employees. This principle has been abandoned in some states in recent years or has
been confined to the major shareholders of
corporations of which the stock is not sold
publicly.

(b) UNPAID SUBSCRIPTIONS. Most
states prohibit the issuance of par value shares
for less than par or except for "money, labor
done, or property actually received." Whenever shares issued by a corporation are not
fully paid for, the original subscriber receiving
the shares, or any transferee who does not
give value or who knows that the shares were
not fully paid, may be liable for the unpaid
balance if the corporation is insolvent and the
money is required to pay the creditors.[25]

If the corporation has issued the shares as
fully paid, or has given them as a bonus, or
has agreed to release the subscriber for the unpaid balance, the corporation cannot recover
that balance. The fact that the corporation is
thus barred does not prevent the creditors of
the corporation from bringing an action to
compel payment of the balance. The same
rules are applied when stock is issued as fully
paid in return for property or services that
were overvalued so that the stock is not actually paid for in full. There is a conflict of authority, however, as to whether the shareholder is liable from the mere fact that the property
or service given for the shares was in fact
overvalued by the directors or whether it
must also be shown that the directors had
acted in bad faith in making the erroneous
valuation. The trend of modern statutes is, in
the absence of proof of fraud, to prohibit disputing the valuation placed by the corporation on services or property.

If a statute makes void the shares issued
for less than par, they may be canceled in a
suit brought by the corporation.

(c) UNAUTHORIZED DIVIDENDS. If dividends are improperly paid out of capital, the
shareholders are generally liable to creditors
to the extent of such depletion of capital. In
some states the liability of the shareholder depends on whether the corporation was insolvent at the time and whether debts were existing at the time.

19.   The Professional Corporation

The liability of a shareholder in a professional
corporation is limited to the same degree as
that of a shareholder in an ordinary business
corporation.[26] Several fact situations may
arise.

(a) ACT OF SHAREHOLDER IN CREAT-
ING LIABILITY. The statutes that authorize
the formation of professional corporations
usually require that share ownership be limited to duly licensed professionals. If a shareholder in a professional corporation, such as a
corporation of physicians, negligently drives
the professional corporation's automobile in
going to attend a patient, or is personally obligated on a contract made for the corporation,
or is guilty of malpractice, the physician-
shareholder is liable without limit for the liability that has been created. This is the same
rule of law that applies in the case of the ordinary business corporation. Professional corporation statutes generally repeat the rule
with respect to malpractice liability by stating
that the liability of a shareholder for malpractice is not affected by the fact of incorporation.

(b) MALPRACTICE LIABILITY OF AN
ASSOCIATE. The liability of a shareholder in
a professional corporation for the malpractice
of an associate varies from state to state, depending on the language of the professional
corporation statute in effect and on the court
decisions under the statute.[27]

If the statute provides for limited liability,

---

[25]   Frasier v Trans-western Land Corp. 210 Neb 681, 316
NW2d 612 (1982). But see Brunfield v Horn (Ala) 547 S 2d
415 (1989).

[26]   Jones v Teilberg (App) 151 Ariz 240, 727 P2d 18 (1986).
[27]   ABA Model Professional Corporation Amendments
(1984) § 34 offers three alternative positions as to liability
of shareholders: (1) limited liability, as in a business corporation, (2) vicarious personal liability, as in a partnership, and (3) personal liability limited in amount conditioned on financial responsibility in the form of insurance
or a surety bond.

as in a business corporation, then where doctors *A*, *B*, and *C* are a professional corporation, *B* will not be liable for the malpractice of *C*. If the statute provides for vicarious personal liability, as in a partnership, and doctors *A*, *B*, and *C* are a professional corporation, each will have unlimited liability for any malpractice liability incurred by the other. Often the statutory reference to malpractice liability is not very clear, and the courts are called on to resolve the question of the liability of a shareholder-professional for the malpractice of an associate.

E.   BONDS

Bonds are certificates issued by a corporation to persons lending money to it. The relationship between the bondholder and the issuing corporation is that of creditor and debtor.

20.   Characteristics of Bonds

A **bond** represents a loan of funds to a corporation by an investor for a relatively long period of time, generally five years or longer. A bond obligates the corporation to pay the bondholder the amount of the loan, called the **principal,** at a stated time, called the **maturity date;** and to pay a fixed amount of interest at regular intervals, commonly every six months.

A bond may be secured by a mortgage or lien on corporate property. A **debenture** is an unsecured bond of the corporation, with no specific corporate assets pledged as security for payment.

Bonds are negotiable securities,[28] which are readily transferable to buyers on the "bond market." Bonds held by owners whose names and addresses are registered on the books of the corporation are called *registered bonds.*

21.   Terms and Control

The contractual terms of a particular bond issue are set forth in an agreement called a **bond indenture.** An **indenture trustee,** usually a commercial banking institution, represents the best interests of the bondholders in making sure that the terms and covenants of the bond issue are met by the corporation.[29] For example, the terms of the bond indenture may require a **sinking fund,** by which the borrowing corporation is required to set aside a fixed amount of money each year toward the ultimate redemption of the bonds. The indenture trustee makes certain that such terms are complied with in accordance with its responsibilities set forth in the bond indenture.

Bondholders do not vote for directors or have the right to vote on matters on which shareholders vote. However, where the debt is risky, it is highly likely that there will be significant restraints on the corporation's freedom of action, imposed by the terms of the indenture. For example, high-yield, high-risk bonds used for raising capital for mergers, acquisitions and leveraged buyouts (so-called "junk bonds") commonly contain many restrictions on the corporation.

---

[28]   UCC § 8–105.
[29]   Lorenc v CSX Corp. (DC Pa) CCH Sec L Rpts ¶¶ 95298 (1990).

SUMMARY

The ownership of a corporation is evidenced by a holder's shares of stock that have been issued by the corporation. Common stock is ordinary stock that has no preferences but entitles the holder to (1) participate in the control of the corporation by exercising one vote per share of record, (2) share in the profits in the form of dividends, and (3) participate, upon dissolution, in the distribution of net assets, after the satisfaction of all creditors (including bondholders). Other classes of stock exist, such as preferred stock, which has priority over common stock as to dividends and/or distributions of net assets upon dissolution. Shares may be acquired by subscription of an original issue or by transfer of existing shares.

Shareholders control the corporation, but this control is indirect. Through their voting rights they elect directors, and by this means they can control the corporation. Preemptive rights allow shareholders to maintain their voting percentage and control when the corporation issues additional shares of stock. Shareholders have the right to inspect the books of the corporation, unless it would be harmful to the corporation. Shareholders also have the right to receive dividends at the discretion of the directors. Shareholders may bring a derivative action on behalf of the corporation for damages to the corporation if, on demand, the corporation refuses to do so. Shareholders are ordinarily protected from liability for the acts of the corporation.

Bonds are debt securities, and a bondholder is a creditor rather than an owner of the corporation. Bondholders' interests are represented by an indenture trustee, who is responsible for ensuring that the corporation complies with the terms of the bond indenture.

QUESTIONS AND CASE PROBLEMS

1. What social forces are affected by the rule requiring that a transfer restriction be known to the transferee or conspicuously noted on the share certificate?

2. What is the distinction between capital and capital stock?

3. Barbara, Joel, and Edna each own less than 5 percent of the stock of the Enrico Storm Door Corporation. Individually, their holdings are too small to be significant in any stockholders' election. Barbara suggests that they and other small shareholders combine their votes by transferring their shares to trustees who will vote the aggregate of their shares as a block. Joel agrees with the idea but says he is afraid that this is an illegal conspiracy. Is he correct?

4. Compare the effect of an oral contract (a) by A to sell 100 shares of X corporation stock to B and (b) by stockbroker C to sell A's stock in the X corporation when the market price reaches $10 a share.

5. The stock of the West End Development Company was subject to a transfer restriction. This restriction required that any shareholder selling shares must first offer every other shareholder the right to purchase a proportion of the shares being sold. The proportion was to be the same as the percentage of the outstanding shares that the other shareholders already owned. This restriction was stated in the articles of incorporation but was not stated on the stock certificate of the corporation. The Taylors owned stock in the company. They sold their stock to Vroom, an officer of the corporation, without first offering any stock to the other shareholders, as required by the restriction. The other shareholders brought an action against Vroom to recover from him the percentages of the shares to which they would have been entitled had the Taylors followed the transfer restriction. Decide. [Irwin v West End Development Co. (CA10 Colo) 481 F2d 34]

6. Siebrecht organized a corporation called the Siebrecht Realty Co. and then transferred his building to the corporation in exchange for its stock. The corporation rented different parts of the building to different tenants. Elenkrieg, an employee of one of the tenants, fell and was injured because of the defective condition of a stairway. She sued Siebrecht individually on the ground that the corporation had been formed by him for the purpose of securing limited liability. Decide. [Elenkrieg v Siebrecht, 238 NY 254, 144 NE 519]

7. Dixon requests an inspection of the books of G. S. & M. Company. The objection was raised that he did not own 5 percent or more of the corporate stock. If this is true, is Dixon barred from inspecting the books?

8. Ken and Charlotte Maschmeier were the majority shareholders of the Southside Press. Ken and Charlotte each owned 1,300 shares. Marty and Larry Maschmeier each owned 1,200 shares of the corporation. Marty and Larry had a falling-out with Ken and Charlotte and were terminated as employees of the business in the summer of 1985. Ken and Charlotte started a new corporation, which employed most of the employees of the old corporation and which took most of the former customers of the old corporation. Gross receipts of the Southside Press went from $613,258 in 1985 to $18,172 in 1987. The $18,172

figure was from the lease of equipment. Ken and Charlotte continued to draw from Southside annual salaries of $20,000, which were in excess of the gross receipts of the business. Marty and Larry brought suit against Ken and Charlotte alleging "oppressive" conduct. Ken and Charlotte stated that they paid Marty and Larry excellent salaries when they were employed by the corporation. Ken and Charlotte contended they had a right to start a new corporation as they saw fit. Decide. [Maschmeier v Southside Press Inc. (Iowa App) 435 NW2d 377].

9. *A* owned corporate stock. He told *B* that he was going to give the stock to *B* and handed the stock certificate to *B*. *B* requested that *A* indorse the certificate. *A* refused to do so. Who was the owner of the stock? [Smith v Augustine, 82 Misc 2d 326, 368 NYS2d 675]

10. Shares of stock represent debts owed by the corporation to the shareholders. Is this statement correct?

11. *K* owned shares of stock in the *J* corporation. He left the shares of stock lying on top of his desk in his office. Many persons continually passed through the office, and one day *K* realized that someone had taken the shares of stock from the top of his desk. *K* applied to the *J* corporation for the issuance of a duplicate stock certificate. The corporation refused to issue a duplicate, on the ground that it was *K*'s own fault that the original certificate had been stolen. *K* claimed that he was entitled to a new certificate even though he had been at fault. Was he correct? [Ibanez v Farmers Underwriters Ass'n, 14 Cal 3d 390, 121 Cal Rptr 256, 534 P2d 1336]

12. Corporation *A* wished to employ *B*. Negotiations were conducted by telephone. In order to induce *B* to accept employment, the proper representative of Corporation *A* promised *B* that in addition to a money salary, *B* would receive a specified number of shares of stock of Corporation *A* for each year of employment. *B* went to work for Corporation *A* and received his money salary, but three years went by with no stock being delivered to him. *B* then sued Corporation *A* to compel it to issue the stock. It raised the defense that the agreement to give *B* stock could not be enforced because it was not evidenced by writing as required by UCC § 8–319. Was this a valid defense? [Bingham v Wells, Rich, Greene, Inc. 34 App Div 2d 924, 311 NYS2d 508; Butcher v United States Invest. Corp. 236 Pa Super 8, 344 A2d 583]

13. Linhart owned shares of stock in the First National Bank. She borrowed money from the bank and pledged the stock as security. She thereafter decided to transfer 70 head of cattle and the shares of stock to her son. She could not deliver the share certificate to him because it was held by the bank. She therefore executed a bill of sale reciting the transfer of the cattle and the stock to the son. She gave him the bill of sale, and he had the bill recorded. After her death, the son brought an action to determine the ownership of the stock. Was the son the owner of the shares?

14. Birt was a patient in the hospital. The doctor who treated him was a shareholder of a professional corporation organized under the Indiana Medical Professional Corporation Act. Birt claimed that the doctor who treated him was guilty of malpractice and sued the doctor. He also sued the professional corporation and all of the officers, directors, and shareholders of the professional corporation. These other defendants asserted that they were not liable because the corporate entity shielded them. The plaintiff claimed that the corporation was not a shield, because in fact all the persons were rendering medical services and should therefore be held liable as in a partnership. The statute did not expressly regulate the matter beyond declaring that it did not change the law between a person supplying medical services and the patient. Decide. [Birt v St. Mary Mercy Hospital, 175 Ind App 32, 370 NE2d 379].

15. Ronald Naquin, an employee of Air Engineered Systems & Services, Inc. (Air Engineered), owned one-third of its outstanding shares. After six years he was fired, and an offer was made to buy out his interest in Air Engineered at a price that Naquin thought inadequate. He then formed a competing business and made a written request to examine the corporate records of Air Engineered. This request was denied. Naquin filed suit to require Air Engineered to allow him to examine the books. Air Engineered raised the defense that he was a competitor seeking to gain unfair competitive advantage. Decide. [Naquin v Air Engineered Systems & Services, Inc. (La App) 463 So 2d 992]

48

SECURITIES REGULATION

After the stock market crash of 1929, Congress investigated the buying and selling practices that existed in the securities markets and determined that federal regulation was necessary to prevent the fraudulent, deceptive, and manipulative practices found to exist. Various federal statutes administered by the Securities and Exchange Commission (SEC) were then enacted to regulate the sale of securities for the benefit of investors. Such laws protect investors through disclosure requirements and prohibitions against fraud and manipulation.

States also have laws regulating the intrastate sale of securities.

A. STATE REGULATION

In order to protect the public from the sale of fraudulent securities, many states have adopted statutes regulating the intrastate sale of securities.

1. State Blue Sky Laws

State laws regulating securities are called **blue sky laws.** The term *blue sky* is derived from the purpose of such laws, which is to prevent the sale of speculative schemes that have no more value than a small area of blue sky. The state statutes vary in detail. They commonly contain (1) an antifraud provision prohibiting fraudulent practices and imposing criminal penalties for violations; (2) broker-dealer licensing provisions regulating the persons engaged in the securities business; and (3) provisions for the registration of securities, including disclosure requirements, with a designated governmental official.

State blue sky laws are subject to the very important limitation that they can apply only to intrastate transactions, not to sales made in interstate commerce.

2.   Uniform Securities Act

A Uniform Securities Act,[1] covering the foregoing three categories of regulations, exists to provide guidance to states in updating their securities laws. This Act contains alternative regulations, which can be adopted by states with different regulatory philosophies.

In the *Taylor* case the court was called upon to interpret a state law patterned after the Uniform Securities Act.

---

[1]   7B Uniform Laws Annotated 515.

TAYLOR v PERDITION MINERALS GROUP, LTD.
(Kan) 766 P2d 805 (1988)

W. W. Taylor purchased 400,000 shares of stock in the Perdition Minerals Group Ltd., Inc. (Perdition) for $200,000. The shares were never registered in accordance with the Kansas Securities Act (KSA). The corporation became insolvent, and Taylor sued the corporation's four directors to rescind the purchase and recover the purchase price because of misrepresentations that were made to induce the sale. The trial court held that under state law an innocent director, to be liable, must be shown to have materially aided in the sale of securities. The trial court entered judgment in favor of the four directors. Taylor appealed.

SIX, J. . . . The statute K.S.A.1987 Supp. 17–1268(a) establishes the liability of any person who sells a security which is required to be registered under K.S.A. 17–1255 but is not registered, or any person who sells a security by means of untrue statements of material facts. Such a person may be liable to the person buying the security for the consideration paid for the security plus interest, costs, and attorney fees.

The alleged liability of the director defendants is based on K.S.A.1987 Supp. 17–1268(b), which provides:

> Every person who directly or indirectly controls a seller liable under subsection (a), *every partner, officer, or director (or person occupying a similar status or performing similar functions) or employee of such a seller who materially aids in the sale*, and every broker-dealer or agent who materially aids in the sale is also liable jointly and severally with and to the same extent as the seller, unless the nonseller who is so liable sustains the burden of proof that such nonseller did not know, and in the exercise of reasonable care could not have known, of the existence of the facts by reason which the liability is alleged to exist. There is contribution as in cases of contract among the several persons so liable. (Emphasis added.)

The Taylors contend that the Kansas statute is a "substantially verbatim" enactment of § 410(b) of the 1956 Uniform Securities Act as amended in 1958. A comparison of the two reveals minor differences in punctuation and phrasing. These differences, the director defendants assert, give the statute a different meaning from the corresponding section of the Uniform Securities Act....

The National Conference of Commissioners on Uniform State Laws approved the Uniform Securities Act in 1956. In 1957, Kansas, using the Uniform Act as a model, enacted the Kansas Securities Act....

The changes in punctuation and phrasing effected by the legislature in transforming § 410(b) of the Uniform Act into K.S.A. 1987 Supp. 17–1268(b) do not insulate directors from strict liability when unregistered securities are sold.

The states that have passed § 410(b) of the Uniform Securities Act have consistently interpreted the statute to impose strict liability on partners, officers, and directors unless the statutory defense of lack of knowledge is proven....

K.S.A.1987 Supp. 17–1268(b) does not require that a director materially aid in the illegal sale of securities in order to be held jointly and severally liable for the sale.

Our analysis of legislative intent commences with the observation that "Blue Sky" provisions are to be liberally interpreted in favor of purchasers to prevent fraud....

Kansas has required registration of securities since 1911....

The first securities statute with teeth was passed in Kansas. Loss, Fundamentals of Securities Regulation 8 (2d ed. 1988). According to Professor Louis Loss, Kansas had been a "stronghold" of populist philosphy. The resulting carryover today is to be found in the relative strictness of Midwestern securities statutes. "Indeed, it was in Kansas, apparently that the term 'blue sky law' first came into general use to describe legislation aimed at promoters who 'would sell building lots in the blue sky in fee simple.'" Loss, Fundamentals of Securities Regulation 8.

The drafters comment to § 410(b) of the Uniform Securities Act observes, "This section is now in the Kansas act substantially verbatim, and Virginia has adopted it with modifications." Loss and Cowett, Blue Sky Law 393 (1958)....

What did the legislature intend the phrase, "of such a seller who materially aids in the sale" following the word "employee" to modify? Was the phrase intended to modify only an "employee" of such seller, or was it intended to reach back further into the language of the statute and also modify "every partner, officer, or director"? We are persuaded the critical phrase modifies only "employee" of such seller.

If the legislature had intended to make directors liable only in the event they had materially aided in the sale, the Kansas language could easily have read, "every partner, officer, or director *of such a seller who materially aids in the sale.*" (Emphasis added.)...

Prior to the adoption of K.S.A.1987 Supp. 17–1268(b), a director of a seller was liable only if he or she "participated or aided in any way in making such sale."

Section 410(b) of the Uniform Act altered a director's liability status. Strict director liability was imposed by § 410(b) unless the statutory defense of lack of knowledge was proven. If the Kansas Legislature in 1957 had intended to continue to provide the "materially aids in the sale" shield to Kansas directors it could easily have used the G.S.1949, 17–1240 concept that had been in place since 1929....

We remand the case for trial. The Taylors have established a prima facie case. The statutory defense issue will be determined by the trier of fact.

[Reversed and remanded]

QUESTIONS

1. Explain the origin of the term "blue sky law."

2. Does Taylor have to prove that the directors materially aided in the sale of the securities to him in order for them to be liable under KSA 17–1268(b) and § 410(b) of the Uniform Securities Act?

3. To what liability are the directors exposed in this case?

B.   FEDERAL REGULATION

The stock market crash of 1929 and the Great Depression that followed led to the enactment of legislation to regulate the securities industry.

3.   Federal Laws Regulating the Securities Industry

Six federal securities regulation laws were passed in the period between 1933 and 1940. The two principal laws that provide the basic framework for the federal regulation of the sale of securities in interstate commerce are the Securities Act of 1933 and the Securities Exchange Act of 1934. The 1933 Act deals with the original distribution of securities by the issuing corporations. The 1934 Act is concerned with the secondary distribution of securities in the national securities markets and in the over-the-counter markets.

Four other federal laws deal with specific aspects of the securities industry. The Public Utility Holding Company Act of 1935[2] provides comprehensive regulation of holding companies and their subsidiaries in the interstate gas and electric utilities businesses. The Trust Indenture Act of 1939[3] was enacted to protect the interests of the holders of bonds and other debt securities offered to the public in interstate commerce, by requiring the appointment of independent institutional trustees. The Investment Company Act of 1940[4] provides for the registration and comprehensive regulation of mutual funds and all other investment companies. The Investment Advisors Act of 1940[5] requires registration with the SEC of all persons engaged in the business of providing investment advice in interstate commerce. In 1970 the Securities Investors Protection Act was enacted to protect investors from the business failures of brokers and dealers.

The Securities Enforcement Remedies and Penny Stock Reform Act of 1990[6] (Remedies Act) was enacted to provide the SEC with new enforcement remedies to reduce the incidence of fraudulent financial reporting and to deter financial fraud. Under the 1990 Remedies Act the SEC may initiate administrative proceedings against any person or entity, whether regulated by the SEC or not, to *cease and desist* from committing or causing a violation of federal securities law. Where the SEC determines a notice and hearing would be contrary to the public interest because of the likelihood of dissipation of assets or significant harm to investors, it may issue a *temporary cease and desist order* prior to notice and a hearing. The SEC may also order an accounting and disgorgement of ill-gotten gains. And, it may seek a civil injunction in federal court with a monetary penalty up to the amount of the gross pecuniary gain or up to $100,000 for an individual and $500,000 for an entity. The Remedies Act also expressly authorizes courts to bar individuals who have engaged in fraudulent activities from serving as officers and directors of public corporations.

The Securities Acts Amendments of 1990[7] authorizes sanctions against SEC-regulated persons for violation of foreign laws, and facilitates the ability of the SEC and foreign regulators to exchange information and cooperate in international securities law enforcement.

---

[2]   15 USC §§ 79–792–6.
[3]   15 USC §§ 77aaa to 77bbb.
[4]   15 USC §§ 80a-1 to 80a-52.
[5]   15 USC §§ 80b-1 to 80b-21.

[6]   PL 101-429, 104 Stat 931, 15 USC § 77g.
[7]   PL 101-550, 104 Stat 2713, 15 USC § 78a.

The Market Reform Act of 1990[8] was enacted to provide the SEC with powers to deal with market volatility. Under the law the SEC has the power to suspend all trading when markets are excessively volatile. Also the SEC may require "large traders" to identify themselves and provide information concerning their trading.

4.   Definition of "Security"

In order for the Securities Acts to apply to a given transaction, the transaction must involve a "security" within the meaning of the Acts.[9] Congress recognized the virtually limitless scope of human ingenuity and the countless and variable schemes that could be devised by those who seek the use of the money of others on the promise of profits. It therefore enacted a definition of "security" sufficiently broad to encompass virtually any instrument that might be sold as an investment.

The definition of security includes not only investment instruments such as stocks and bonds but also "investment contracts." The definition of an "investment contract" developed by the Supreme Court is sufficiently broad to allow the Securities Acts to apply to a wide range of investment transactions or schemes, including the sale of bottled whiskey, the sale of cattle breeding programs, and limited partnerships for oil and gas exploration. Under the Supreme Court's definition, an investment contract exists if the following essential elements are present: (1) an investment of money, (2) a common enterprise, (3) an expectation of future profits, (4) from the efforts of others.[10] Thus, the sale of citrus groves to investors, coupled with the execution of service contracts to plant, harvest, sell the fruit and distribute the profits of the venture to the investors, is an investment contract.

In the *Reves* case, which contains the statutory definition of a security, the Supreme Court had to decide whether a note issued by an agricultural cooperative was a "security" within the meaning of the 1934 Act.

---

[8]   PL 101-432, 104 Stat 963, 15 USC § 78a.

[9]   The Supreme Court consistently has held that the definition of a security set forth in § 3(a)(10) of the 1934 Act is identical to the definition set forth in § 2(1) of the 1933 Act.

[10]   SEC v W.J. Howey Co., 328 US 293 (1946), as restated by United Housing Foundation Inc. v Forman, 421 US 837 (1975).

REVES v ERNST & YOUNG
494 US ___, 108 L Ed 2d 47 (1990)

In order to raise money to support its general business operations, the Farmer's Cooperative of Arkansas and Oklahoma (Co-Op) sold uncollateralized and uninsured promissory notes, payable on demand by the holder. Offered to both Co-Op members and nonmembers and marketed as an "Investment Program," the notes paid a variable interest rate higher than that of local financial institutions. After the Co-Op filed for bankruptcy, Bob Reves and the other holders of the notes filed suit in the U.S. district court against the Co-Op's auditor, Arthur Young Co., the predecessor firm to Ernst & Young. They alleged that it had violated the antifraud provisions of the Securities Exchange Act of 1934—which regulates certain specified instruments, including "any note[s]"—by intentionally failing to follow generally accepted accounting principles that would have made the Co-Op's insolvency apparent to potential note purchasers. Ernst & Young defended that the notes were not "securities" under the 1934 Act. The noteholders prevailed at trial, but the Court of Appeals reversed. The noteholders appealed to the U.S. Supreme Court.

MARSHALL, J. . . . This case requires us to decide whether the note issued by the Co-Op is a "security" within the meaning of the 1934 Act. Section 3(a)(10) of that Act is our starting point:

> "The term "security" means any note, stock, treasury stock, bond, debenture, certificate of interest or participation in any profit-sharing agreement or in any oil, gas, or other mineral royalty or lease, any collateral-trust certificate, preorganization certificate or subscription, transferable share, investment contract, voting-trust certificate, certificate of deposit . . . or in general, any instrument commonly known as a "security"; or any certificate of interest or participation in, temporary or interim certificate for, receipt for, or warrant or right to subscribe to or purchase, any of the foregoing; but shall not include currency or any note, draft, bill of exchange, or banker's acceptance which has a maturity at the time of issuance of not exceeding nine months, exclusive of days of grace, or any renewal thereof the maturity of which is likewise limited. 48 Stat. 884, as amended, 15 U.S.C. § 78c(a)(10).

. . . Congress' purpose in enacting the securities laws was to regulate *investments*, in whatever form they are made and by whatever name they are called. . . . Some instruments are obviously within the class Congress intended to regulate because they are by their nature investments. In *Landreth Timber Co. v. Landreth*, 471 U.S. 681, 105 S.Ct. 2297, 85 L.Ed.2d 692 (1985), we held that an instrument bearing the name "stock" that, among other things, is negotiable, offers the possibility of capital appreciation, and carries the right to dividends contingent on the profits of a business enterprise is plainly within the class of instruments Congress intended the securities laws to cover. *Landreth Timber* does not signify a lack of concern with economic reality; rather, it signals a recognition that stock is, as a practical matter, always an investment if it has the economic characteristics traditionally associated with stock. Even if sparse exceptions to this generalization can be found, the public perception of common stock as the paradigm of a security suggests that stock, in whatever context it is sold, should be treated as within the ambit of the Acts. . . .

We made clear in *Landreth Timber* that stock was a special case, explicitly limiting our holding to that sort of instrument. . . . Although we refused finally to rule out a similar *per se* rule for notes, we intimated that such a rule would be unjustified. Unlike "stock," we said, " 'note' may now be viewed as a relatively broad term that encompasses instruments with widely varying characteristics, depending on whether issued in a consumer context, as commercial paper, or in some other investment context." . . .

The Second Circuit's "family resemblance" approach begins with a presumption that *any* note with a term of more than nine months is a "security." See, *e.g., Exchange Nat'l Bank of Chicago v. Touche Ross & Co.*, 544 F.2d 1126, 1137 (CA2 1976). Recognizing that not all notes are securities, however, the Second Circuit has also devised a list of notes that it has decided are obviously not securities. Accordingly, the "family resemblance" test permits an issuer to rebut the presumption that a note is a security if it can show that the note in question "bear[s] a strong family resemblance" to an item on the judically crafted list of exceptions or convinces the court to add a new instrument to the list. . . .

In contrast, the Eighth and District of Columbia Circuits apply the test we created in *SEC v. W.J. Howey Co.*, 328 U.S. 293, 66 S.Ct. 1100, 90 L.Ed. 1244 (1946), to determine whether an instrument is an "investment contract" to the determination whether an instrument is a "note." Under this test, a note is a security only if it evidences "(1) an investment; (2) in a common enterprise; (3) with a reasonable expectation of profits; (4) to be derived from the entrepreneurial or managerial efforts of others." . . .

The . . . two contenders—the "family resemblance" and "investment versus commercial" tests—are really two ways of formulating the same general approach. Because we think the "family resemblance" test provides a more promising framework for analysis, however, we adopt it. The test begins with the language of the statute; because the Securities Acts define "security" to include "any note," we begin with a presumption that every note is a security. We nonetheless recognize that this presumption cannot be irrebuttable. . . . Congress was concerned with regulating the investment market, not with creating a general federal cause of action for fraud. In an attempt to give more content to that dividing line, the Second Circuit has identified a list of instruments commonly denominated "notes" that nonetheless fall without the "security" category. See *Exchange Nat. Bank, supra,* at 1138 (types of notes that are not "securities" include "the note delivered in consumer financing, the note secured by a mortgage on a home, the short-term note secured by a lien on a small business or some of its assets, the note evidencing a 'character' loan to a bank customer, short-term notes secured by an assignment of accounts receivable, or a note which simply formalizes an open-account debt incurred in the ordinary course of business (particularly if, as in the case of the customer of a broker, it is collateralized)"); . . . (adding to list "notes evidencing loans by commercial banks for current operations").

We agree that the items identified by the Second Circuit are not properly viewed as "securities." More guidance, though, is needed. It is impossible to make any meaningful inquiry into whether an instrument bears a "resemblance" to one of the instruments identified by the Second Circuit without specifying what it is about *those* instruments that makes *them* non-"securities." Moreover, as the Second Circuit itself has noted, its list is "not graven in stone," . . . and is therefore capable of expansion. Thus, some standards must be developed for determining when an item should be added to the list.

An examination of the list itself makes clear what those standards should be. In creating its list, the Second Circuit was applying the same factors that this Court has held apply in deciding whether a transaction involves a "security." First, we examine the transaction to assess the motivations that would prompt a reasonable seller and buyer to enter into it. If the seller's purpose is to raise money for the general use of a business enterprise or to finance substantial investments and the buyer is interested primarily in the profit the note is expected to generate, the instrument is likely to be a "security." If the note is exchanged to facilitate the purchase and sale of a minor asset or consumer good, to correct for the seller's cash-flow difficulties, or to advance some other commercial or consumer purpose, on the other hand, the note is less sensibly described as a "security." . . . Second, we examine the "plan of distribution" of the instrument . . . to determine whether it is an instrument in where there is "common trading for speculation or investment." . . . Third, we examine the reasonable expectations of the investing public: The Court will consider instruments to be "securities" on the basis of such public expectations, even where an economic analysis of the circumstances of the particular transaction might suggest that the instruments are not "securities" as used in that transaction. . . . Finally, we examine whether some factor such as the existence of another regulatory scheme significantly reduces the risk of instrument, thereby rendering application of the Securities Acts unnecessary. . . .

We conclude, then, that in determining whether an instrument denominated a "note" is a "security," courts are to apply the version of the "family resemblance" test that we have articulated here: a note is presumed to be a "security," and that presumption may be rebutted only by a showing that the note bears a strong resemblance (in terms of the four factors we have identified) to one of the enumerated categories of instrument. If an instrument is not sufficiently similar to an item on the list, the decision whether another category should be added is to be made by examining the same factors.

Applying the family resemblance approach to this case, we have little difficulty in concluding that the notes at issue here are "securities." Ernst & Young admits that "a demand note does not closely resemble any of the Second Circuit's family resemblance examples." . . . Nor does an examination of the four factors we have identified as being relevant to our inquiry suggest that the demand notes here are not "securities" despite their lack of similarity to any of the enumerated categories. The Co-Op sold the notes in an effort to raise capital for its general business operations, and purchasers bought them in order to earn a profit in the form of interest. Indeed, one of the primary inducements offered purchasers was an interest rate constantly revised to keep it slightly above the rate paid by local banks and savings and loans. From both sides, then, the transaction is most naturally conceived as an investment in a business enterprise rather than as a purely commercial or consumer transaction.

As to the plan of distribution, the Co-Op offered the notes over an extended period to its 23,000 members, as well as to nonmembers, and more than 1,600 people held notes when the Co-Op filed for bankruptcy. To be sure, the notes were not traded on an exchange. They were, however, offered and sold to a broad segment of the public, and that is all we have held to be necessary to establish the requisite "common trading" in an instrument. . . .

The third factor—the public's reasonable perceptions—also supports a finding that the notes in this case are "securities." We have consistently identified the fundamental essence of a "security" to be its character as an "investment." . . . The advertisements for the notes here characterized them as "investments," and there were no countervailing factors that would have led a reasonable person to question this characterization. In these circumstances, it would be reasonable for a prospective purchaser to take the Co-Op at its word.

Finally, we find no risk-reducing factor to suggest that these instruments are not in fact securities. The notes are uncollateralized and uninsured. . . . The notes here would escape federal regulation entirely if the Acts were held not to apply.

The court below found that "[t]he demand nature of the notes is very uncharacteristic of a security" . . . on the theory that the virtually instant liquidity associated with demand notes is inconsistent with the risk ordinarily associated with "securities." This argument is unpersuasive. Common stock traded on a national exchange is the paradigm of a security, and it is as readily convertible into cash as is a demand note. The same is true of publicly traded corporate bonds, debentures, and any number of other instruments that are plainly within the purview of the Acts. The demand feature of a note does permit a holder to eliminate risk quickly by making a demand, but just as with publicly traded stock, the liquidity of the instrument does not eliminate risk all together. Indeed, publicly traded stock is even more readily liquid than are demand notes, in that a demand only eliminates risk when and if payment is made, whereas the sale of a share of stock through a national exchange and the receipt of the proceeds usually occur simultaneously.

We therefore hold that the notes at issue here are within the term "note" in § 3(a)(10).

Relying on the exception in the statute for "any note . . . which has a maturity at the time of issuance of not exceeding nine months," 15 U.S.C. § 78c(a)(10), respondent contends that the notes here are not "securities," even if they would otherwise qualify. . . .

Neither the law of Arkansas nor that of any other State provides an answer to the federal question, and as a matter of federal law, the words of the statute are far from "plain" with regard to whether demand notes fall within the exclusion. If it is plausible to regard a demand note as having an immediate maturity because demand *could* be made immediately, it is also plausible to regard the maturity of a demand note as being in excess of nine months because demand *could* be made many years or decades into the future. Given this ambiguity, the exclusion must be interpreted in accordance with its purpose. . . . In light of Congress' broader purpose in the Acts of ensuring that investments of all descriptions be regulated to prevent fraud and abuse, we interpret the exception not to cover the demand notes at issue here. Although the result might be different if the design of the transaction suggested that both parties contemplated that demand would be made within the statutory period, that is not the case before us.

For the foregoing reasons, we conclude that the demand notes at issue here fall under the "note" category of instruments that are "securities" under the 1933 and 1934 Acts. . . .

[Judgment reversed and action remanded]

QUESTIONS

1. What was Congress' purpose in enacting the securities laws?
2. List the type of notes that are not "securities."
3. What factors did the Supreme Court consider in deciding whether a transaction involved a security?
4. Apply the factors identified in the answer to Question 3 to the facts of the *Reves* case.

5. Securities Act of 1933

The 1933 Act deals with the original distribution of securities. It prohibits the offer or sale of securities to the public in interstate commerce before a **registration statement** containing disclosure of specific financial information regarding the security, the issuer, and the underwriter has been filed with the SEC. The seller must also provide a prospectus to each potential purchaser of the securities. The **prospectus** sets forth the key information contained in the registration statement. The object is to provide the interested investor with detailed information about the security and the enterprise. The SEC does not approve or disapprove the securities as being good or bad investments but only reviews the form and content of the registration statement and the prospectus to ensure full disclosure. The requirements of advance disclosure to the public through the filing of the registration statement with the SEC and the sending of a prospectus to each potential purchaser are commonly referred to as the **registration requirements** of the 1933 Act.

(a) APPLICABILITY. The Act applies to (1) stocks, (2) corporate bonds, and (3) any conceivable kind of corporate interest or instrument that has the characteristics of an investment security. Numerous other instruments have been created to provide the capital structure of business, including convertible securities and variable annuities. The Act applies to all such instruments that have investment characteristics.

(b) THE REGISTRATION PROCESS. Section 5 of the 1933 Act provides for the division of the registration process into three time periods: (1) the *prefiling period*, filing the registration statement with the SEC; (2) the *waiting pe-riod,* from the date of filing with the SEC to the date the registration statement becomes effective (a minimum of 20 days, but commonly extended for additional 20-day periods after each amendment by the issuer in compliance with SEC requirements for additional information); and (3) the *post-effective period.* The time divisions allow the public an opportunity to study the information disclosed in the reg-

istration process before a final sale can be consummated. Permissible, required, and prohibited activities during the time periods are set forth in Figure 48–1. Under SEC Regulation A, a simplified registration process is available for small issues of securities (under $1.5 million).[11]

[11]   Securities Act, § 3(b), 15 USC § 77bb. Securities Act Rules 251–264.

FIGURE 48-1   REGISTRATION PERIODS

	PROHIBITED OR REQUIRED ACTIVITIES	PERMITTED ACTIVITIES
PREFILING PERIOD	ISSUER MUST NOT SELL OR OFFER FOR SALE A SECURITY BEFORE REGISTRATION STATEMENT IS FILED.	ISSUER MAY PLAN WITH UNDERWRITERS THE DISTRIBUTION OF THE SECURITY.
WAITING PERIOD	NO FINAL SALE OF A SECURITY PERMITTED DURING THIS PERIOD.	PRELIMINARY PROSPECTUS* CONTAINING INFORMATION FROM THE REGISTRATION STATEMENT BEING REVIEWED BY THE SEC MAY BE DISTRIBUTED TO INVESTORS, WHO MAY MAKE OFFERS. ADVERTISEMENTS MAY BE PLACED IN FINANCIAL PUBLICATIONS, IDENTIFYING PARTICULARS OF THE SECURITY, FROM WHOM A PROSPECTUS CAN BE OBTAINED, AND BY WHOM ORDERS WILL BE EXECUTED.**
POST-EFFECTIVE PERIOD	MUST PROVIDE A COPY OF FINAL PROSPECTUS WITH EVERY WRITTEN OFFER, CONFIRMATION OF SALE, OR DELIVERY OF SECURITY. MUST UPDATE PROSPECTUS WHENEVER IMPORTANT NEW DEVELOPMENTS OCCUR, OR AFTER NINE MONTHS.	SALES OF THE SECURITY MAY BE COMPLETED.

  * THE PRELIMINARY PROSPECTUS IS COMMONLY CALLED THE "RED HERRING" PROSPECTUS BECAUSE OF THE RED INK CAPTION REQUIRED BY THE SEC, INFORMING THE PUBLIC THAT A REGISTRATION STATEMENT HAS BEEN FILED BUT IS NOT YET EFFECTIVE, AND THAT NO FINAL SALE CAN BE MADE UNTIL AFTER THE EFFECTIVE DATE.

 ** THESE ADVERTISEMENTS ARE SOMETIMES CALLED "TOMBSTONE ADS" BECAUSE THEY ARE COMMONLY FRAMED BY A BLACK INK BORDER.

(c) REGISTRATION EXEMPTIONS. Certain private and limited offerings of securities are exempt from the registration requirements of the Act. Under SEC Regulation D, offerings of any amount made solely to accredited investors, such as banks, insurance companies, investment companies, or directors and executive officers of the issuing corporation, are exempt from the registration requirements of the Act. These accredited investors generally have access to the kinds of information dis-

closed in a registration statement and prospectus.

Offerings of securities restricted to residents of the state in which the issuing corporation is organized and doing business are exempt from federal regulation. This "intrastate offering" exemption is applied very narrowly by the SEC and the courts, and such offerings are subject to state laws.

1. Rule 505 Exemption. SEC Rule 505, promulgated under Regulation D, exempts

from registration offerings of less than $5 million to fewer than 35 nonaccredited purchasers (not offerees) over a 12-month period. No limit exists on the number of accredited investors who may participate. No general solicitation or general advertising is permitted under Rule 505. If any prospective investors are nonaccredited, the issuer must furnish all investors with specific information on the issuer, its business, and the securities offered for sale.

2. Rule 504 Exemption. Under SEC Rule 504 of Regulation D, an issuer is permitted to sell securities for an aggregate price of up to $1 million in a one-year period to any number of investors without furnishing any explanation to the purchasers, provided no more than $500,000 worth of securities are sold without registration under a state's securities law. This rule was fashioned to provide an exception for small offerings by small issuers.

3. Rule 506 Exemption. As opposed to Rules 505 and 504, which exempt offerings limited to $5 million and $1 million, respectively, SEC Rule 506, the so-called private placement exemption, has no limitation on the amount that may be raised by the offering. As in Rule 505, specific information must be provided to all buyers if any buyers are nonaccredited investors, and the number of nonaccredited investors is limited to fewer than 35. Further, the rule requires that the issuer shall reasonably believe that each nonaccredited investor has sufficient experience in investments as to be capable of evaluating the merits and risks of the investment.

4. Restrictions. Securities acquired under a Regulation D exemption from registration are considered **restricted securities.** Their resale may require registration. Rules requiring registration of Regulation D securities prior to resale are promulgated to ensure that investors purchase these securities as an investment rather than for public distribution. When there is no attempt to make public distributions, investors ordinarily fit within one of several exemptions to registration upon resale.

(d) LIABILITY. Issuers, sellers and "aiders and abettors" may be subject to civil and criminal liability under the 1933 Act.

1. Issuers' Liability for False or Misleading Statements. The Securities Act of 1933 imposes civil liability under Section 11 for making materially false or misleading statements in a registration statement and for the omission of any required material fact. Any investor who sustains a loss because of the false statements or omissions of the registration statement may sue to recover damages under Section 11. An issuing company has virtually no defense in such an action if there has been a false statement and a loss. However, individual defendants, such as accountants who helped prepare portions of the registration statement, may defend by proving they acted in good faith and with due diligence.

2. Liability of Sellers of Securities. Section 12 of the 1933 Act applies to those who "offer or sell" securities and employ any device or scheme to defraud or obtain money by means of untrue statements of material facts. This section makes such individuals or firms liable to purchasers for damages sustained.

Where there are untrue statements of material facts, purchasers may recover under § 12(2), unless they have actual knowledge of the untruth or omission.[12] Constructive knowledge, which the plaintiff might have acquired by exercising ordinary care (such as reading the documents supplied by the seller), will not preclude recovery when there is no actual knowledge.[13]

(3) Others That Are Liable. Section 24 of the 1933 Act imposes criminal penalties on anyone who willfully makes untrue statements of material facts or omits required material facts

---

[12] As codified, § 12(2) provides in part: "Any person who . . . (2) offers or sells a security . . . by means of a prospectus or oral communication, which includes an untrue statement of a material fact or omits to state a material fact necessary in order to make the statements, in the light of circumstances under which they were made, not misleading (the purchaser now knowing of such untruth or omission), and who shall not sustain the burden of proof that he did not know, and in the exercise of reasonable care could not have known, of such untruth or omissions, shall be liable to the person purchasing such security from him, who may sue either at law or in equity in any court of competent jurisdiction, to recover the consideration paid for such security with interest thereon, less the amount of any income received thereon, upon the tender of such security, or for damages if he no longer owns the security." 15 USC § 771(2).

[13] Caselz v Weff (CA9 Cal) 883 F2d 805 (1989).

in a registration statement. Section 17 of the Act makes it unlawful for any person to employ any device, scheme, or artifice to defraud in the offer or sale of securities. Law firms and public accounting firms that prepare fraudulent registration statements in conjunction with clients may be subject to civil liability as "aiders and abettors" under Section 12(2) of the Act and may be subject to criminal liability under Section 17(a) of the Act. Even if a security is exempt from registration, the civil and criminal liabilities just discussed still apply if interstate commerce or the mails are involved in the offer or sale of the security.

Prior to the passing of the 1990 Remedies Act, the SEC could proceed against individuals only if they directly violated or aided and abetted a violation of securities law. Under the 1990 Remedies Act liability hinges on whether the person "knew or should have known" that the act as omission "would contribute" to the violation. This standard increases the potential liability of corporate officers, directors, attorneys, and accountants for violations committed by the corporation.

6.   Securities Exchange Act of 1934

The 1934 Act deals with the secondary distribution of securities. It was designed to prevent fraudulent and manipulative practices on the security exchanges and in over-the-counter markets. The Act also seeks to provide for fair and honest markets for securities by requiring disclosure of information to buyers and sellers of the securities. Furthermore, the Act controls credit in these markets.

(a) REGISTRATION REQUIREMENTS. Exchanges, brokers, and dealers who deal in securities traded in interstate commerce or on any national security exchange must register with the SEC unless exempted by it.

Companies whose securities are listed on a national securities exchange, and unlisted companies that have assets in excess of $3 million and have 500 or more shareholders, are subject to the reporting requirements of the Act.[14]

Form 10-K is the principal annual report form used by commercial and industrial companies required to file under the 1934 Act. The reports require nonfinancial information about the registrant's activities during the year, such as the nature of the firm's business, the property or businesses it owns, and a statement concerning legal proceedings by or against the company. The report requires the submission of financial statements, with management's analysis of the financial condition of the company, and a report and analysis of the performance of corporate shares. It requires a listing of all directors and executive officers and disclosure of executive compensation information.

Registrants who are required to file 10-K reports must also file quarterly reports, called 10-Q reports. The 10-Q reports are principally concerned with financial information relevant to the quarterly period.

The SEC requires that annual shareholder reports be submitted to shareholders in any proxy solicitation on behalf of management. These reports contain essentially the same information provided in the 10-K.

(b) ANTIFRAUD PROVISION. Section 10(b) of the 1934 Act makes it unlawful for any person to use any manipulative or deceptive device in contravention of SEC rules.[15] Under the authority of Section 10(b) of the 1934 Act, the SEC has promulgated Rule 10b-5. This rule is the principal antifraud rule relating to the secondary distribution of securities. The rule states:

It shall be unlawful for any person, directly or indirectly, by use of any means or instrumentality of interstate commerce, or of the mails or of any facility of any national securities exchange,

(a) To employ any device, scheme, or artifice to defraud.

(b) To make any untrue statement of a material fact or to omit to state a material fact necessary in order to make the statements made, in the light of the circumstances under which they were made, not misleading, or

---

[14]   SEC Release No. 34–18647 (April 15, 1982).

[15]   15 USC § 78j(b).

(c) To engage in any act, practice, or course of business that operates or would operate as a fraud or deceit upon any person, in connection with the purchase or sale of any security.[16]

1. Scope of Application. Rule 10b-5 applies to all securities, whether registered or not, as long as use is made of the mails, interstate commerce, or a national stock exchange. Under this rule, a civil action for damages may be brought by any injured party who purchased or sold securities because of false, misleading, or undisclosed information. Criminal penalties may also be imposed for willful violation of the Act or SEC regulations promulgated under the Act.

2. Overlap Between the Acts. In some instances there is an overlap between the provisions of the 1933 Act and the 1934 Act. Thus, purchasers of registered securities who allege they were defrauded by misrepresentations in a registration statement filed under the 1933 Act may bring an action under the catchall antifraud provision of Section 10(b) of the 1934 Act and SEC Rule 10b-5, notwithstanding the express remedy for misstatements in registration statements provided by Section 11 of the 1933 Act.[17]

3. Liability for "Material Misstatements or Omissions of Fact." Rule 10b-5 prohibits the making of any untrue statement of a "material" fact or the omission of a material fact necessary to render statements made not misleading. In every Rule 10b-5 case, the plaintiff must show "reliance" on the misrepresentation and resulting injury.

In a merger context, "materiality" depends on the probability that the transaction will be consummated and on the significance to the issuer of the securities. That is, "materiality" depends on the facts and must be determined on a case-by-case basis. Assume that Corporation *A*, while involved in merger discussions with Corporation *B*, made public statements denying that any merger negotiations were taking place or that it knew of any corporate developments that would account for heavy trading activity in its stock. In this case Corporation *A* may be held liable for damages to its shareholders who sold their stock after the public denial of merger activity and before the merger announcement.

The "reliance" issue must also be dealt with in such a lawsuit by the shareholders of Corporation *A* who sold their stock. Reliance is an element of a Rule 10b-5 case. However, there is a presumption of reliance in such a case. This presumption is supported by the "fraud-on-the-market theory" that the price of a company's stock is determined by available information. Misleading information may defraud those who buy or sell the stock in the market during the period of time in question. Corporation *A* may rebut the presumption of reliance by showing that news of the merger discussions credibly entered the market and dissipated the effects of its misstatements.

In *Basic Inc. v. Levinson* the Supreme Court dealt with the question of what should be the standard of "materiality" applied in merger cases.

---

[16]   17 CFR § 240, 10b-5 (1982).
[17]   Herman & MacLean v Huddleston, 459 US 375 (1983).

BASIC INC. v LEVINSON
485 US 224 (1988)

In December of 1978, Combustion Engineering Inc. and Basic Inc. agreed to merge. During the preceding two years, representatives of the two companies had meetings regarding the possibility of a merger. During this time, Basic made three public statements denying that any merger negotiations were taking place or that it knew of any corporate developments that would account for the heavy trading activity in its stock. Certain former shareholders who sold this stock between Basic's first public denial of merger activity and the public announcement of the merger brought a Section 10(b) and Rule 10b-5 action against Basic and some of its directors, contending that material misrepresentation had been made by Basic in its public statements denying merger activity. Basic raised the defense that the alleged misrepresentations were not material and that there was no showing of reliance by the shareholders on Basic's statements. The Court of Appeals reversed the district court's summary judgment for Basic that preliminary merger discussions are not material information. Basic appealed to the U.S. Supreme Court.

BLACKMUN, J. . . . The 1934 Act was designed to protect investors against manipulation of stock prices. . . . Underlying the adoption of extensive disclosure requirements was a legislative philosophy: "There cannot be honest markets without honest publicity. Manipulation and dishonest practices of the market place thrive upon mystery and secrecy." H.R.Rep. No. 1383, 73d Cong. 2d Sess., 11 (1934). This Court "repeatedly has described the 'fundamental purpose' of the Act as implementing a 'philosophy of full disclosure.' " . . .

Pursuant to its authority under § 10(b) of the 1934 Act, 15 U.S.C. § 78j, the Securities and Exchange Commission promulgated Rule 10b-5. Judicial interpretation and application, legislative acquiescence, and the passage of time have removed any doubt that a private cause of action exists for a violation of § 10(b) and Rule 10b-5, and constitutes an essential tool for enforcement of the 1934 Act's requirements. . . .

The Court previously has addressed various positive and common-law requirements for a violation of § 10(b) or of Rule 10b-5. . . . The Court also explicitly has defined a standard of materiality under the securities laws, see *TSC Industries, Inc. v. Northway, Inc.*, 426 U.S. 438, 96 S.Ct. 2126, 48 L.Ed.2d 757 (1976), concluding in the proxy-solicitation context that "[a]n omitted fact is material if there is a substantial likelihood that a reasonable shareholder would consider it important in deciding how to vote." . . . Acknowledging that certain information concerning corporate developments could well be of "dubious significance," . . . the Court was careful not to set too low a standard of materiality; it was concerned that a minimal standard might bring an overabundance of information within its reach, and lead management "simply to bury the shareholders in an avalanche of trivial information—a result that is hardly conducive to informed decisionmaking." . . . It further explained that to fulfill the materiality requirement "there must be a substantial likelihood that the disclosure of the omitted fact would have been viewed by the reasonable investor as having significantly altered the 'total mix' of information made available." . . . We now expressly adopt the *TSC Industries* standard of materiality for the § 10(b) and Rule 10b-5 context. . . .

Even before this Court's decision in *TSC Industries*, the Second Circuit had explained the role of the materiality requirement of Rule 10b-5, with respect to contingent or speculative information or events, in a manner that gave the term meaning that is independent of the other provisions of the Rule. Under such circumstances, materiality "will depend at any given time upon a balancing of both the indicated probability that the event will occur and the anticipated magnitude of the event in light of the totality of the company activity." *SEC v. Texas Gulf Sulphur Co.*, 401 F.2d, at 849. . . .

In a subsequent decision, the late Judge Friendly, writing for a Second Circuit panel, applied the *Texas Gulf Sulphur* probability/magnitude approach in the specific context of preliminary merger negotiations. . . .

Whether merger discussions in any particular case are material therefore depends on the facts. Generally, in order to assess the probability that the event will occur, a factfinder will need to look to indicia of interest in the transaction at the highest corporate levels. Without attempting to catalog all such possible factors, we note by way of example that board resolutions, instructions to investment bankers, and actual negotiations between principals or their intermediaries may serve as indicia of interest. To assess the magnitute of the transaction to the issuer of the securities allegedly manipulated, a factfinder will need to consider such facts as the size of the two corporate entities and of the potential premiums over market value. No particular event or factor short of closing the transaction need be either necessary or sufficient by itself to render merger discussions material.

As we clarify today, materiality depends on the significance the reasonable investor would place on the withheld or misrepresented information. . . . Because the standard of materiality we have adopted differs from that used by both courts below, we remand the case for reconsideration of the question whether a grant of summary judgment is appropriate on this record.

We turn to the question of reliance and the fraud-on-the-market theory. Succinctly put:

> The fraud on the market theory is based on the hypothesis that, in an open and developed securities market, the price of a company's stock is determined by the available material information regarding the company and its business. . . . Misleading statements will therefore defraud purchasers of stock even if the purchasers do not directly rely on the misstatements. . . . The causal connection between the defendants' fraud and the plaintiffs' purchase of stock in such a case is no less significant than in a case of direct reliance on misrepresentations. *Peil v. Speiser,* 806 F.2d 1154, 160–1161 (CA3 1986). . . .

Requiring proof of individualized reliance from each member of the proposed plaintiff class effectively would have prevented respondents from proceeding with a class action, since individual issues then would have overwhelmed the common ones. The District Court found that the presumption of reliance created by the fraud-on-the-market theory provided "a practical resolution to the problem of balancing the substantive requirement of proof of reliance in securities cases against the procedural requisites of [Fed.Rule Civ.Proc.] 23." The District Court thus concluded that with reference to each public statement and its impact upon the open market for Basic shares, common questions are predominated over individual questions, as required by Fed.Rule Civ.Proc. 23(a)(2) and (b)(3) . . . the fraud-on-the-market theory effectively eliminates the requirement that a plaintiff asserting a claim under Rule 10b-5 prove reliance.

We agree that reliance is an element of a Rule 10b-5 cause of action. . . . Reliance provides the requisite causal connection between a defendant's misrepresentation and a plaintiff's injury. . . . Commentators generally have applauded the adoption of one variation or another of the fraud-on-the-market theory. An investor who buys or sells stock at the price set by the market does so in reliance on the integrity of that price. Because most publicly available information is reflected in market price, an investor's reliance on any public material misrepresentations, therefore, may be presumed for purposes of a Rule 10b-5 action. . . .

Any showing that severs the link between the alleged misrepresentation and either the price received (or paid) by the plaintiff, or his decision to trade at a fair market price, will be sufficient to rebut the presumption of reliance. For example, if petitioners could show that the "market makers" were privy to the truth about the merger discussions here with Combustion, and thus that the market price would not have been affected by their misrepresentations, the causal connection could be broken: the basis for finding that the fraud had been transmitted through market price would be gone. Similarly, if, despite petitioners' allegedly fraudulent attempt to manipulate market price, news of the merger discussions credibly entered the market and dissipated the effects of the misstatements, those who traded Basic shares after the corrective statements would have no direct or indirect connection with the fraud. Petitioners also could rebut the presumption of reliance as to plaintiffs who would have divested themselves of their Basic shares without relying on the integrity of the market. For example, a plaintiff who believed that Basic's statements were false and that Basic was indeed engaged in merger discussions, and who consequently believed that Basic stock was artificially underpriced, but sold his shares nevertheless because of other unrelated concerns, *e.g.*, potential antitrust problems, or political pressures to divest from shares of certain businesses, could not be said to have relied on the integrity of a price he knew had been manipulated.

In summary:

We specifically adopt, for the § 10(b) and Rule 10b-5 context, the standard of materiality set forth in *TSC Industries, Inc. v. Northway, Inc.*, 426 U.S., at 449. . . .

Materiality in the merger context depends on the probability that the transaction will be consummated, and its significance to the issuer of the securities. Materiality depends on the facts and thus is to be determined on a case-by-case basis.

It is not inappropriate to apply a presumption of reliance supported by the fraud-on-the-market theory.

That presumption, however, is rebuttable.

[Judgment vacated and action remanded]

QUESTIONS

1. What was the legislative philosphy underlying the adoption of the extensive disclosure requirements of the 1934 Act?
2. What is the standard of materiality to be applied in a merger-related context?
3. What is the "fraud-on-the-market theory"?

7.   Trading on Insider Information

The SEC and the courts have relied on Section 10(b) and Rule 10b-5 as the legal basis for imposing sanctions for trading on **insider information.** Under the Insider Trading Sanctions Act of 1984, which amended the 1934 Act, the SEC may now bring an action against an individual purchasing or selling a security while in possession of material, inside information. The court may impose a civil penalty of up to three times the profit gained or loss avoided as a result of the unlawful sale.[18] Persons who "aid or abet" in the violation may also be held liable under the Act.

Under the 1988 Insider Trading Act "controlling persons," including employers whose lax supervision may allow employees to commit insider trading violations, are subject to civil penalties.[19] The SEC must establish

---

[18]   PL 98–376, 58 Stat 1264, 15 USC § 780.
[19]   PL 100–704, 102 Stat 4677, 15 USC § 78 u A (b)(2).

"knowing" or "reckless" behavior by the controlling person.

The 1988 law establishes bounty programs that allow the SEC to reward informants giving information on insider trading activity. The reward is up to 10 percent of any penalty imposed.

(a) TRADING BY INSIDERS AND TIPPEES. An **insider** may be a director or corporate employee. A **temporary insider** is someone retained by the corporation for professional services, such as an attorney, accountant, or investment banker. Insiders or temporary insiders are liable for inside trading when they fail to disclose material, nonpublic information before trading on it and thus make a secret profit. A **tippee** is an individual who receives information from an insider or temporary insider. A tippee is subject to the insider's fiduciary duty to shareholders when the insider has breached the fiduciary duty to shareholders by improperly disclosing the information to the tippee and when the tippee knows or should know there has been a breach.[20] Such a breach occurs when an insider benefits personally from his or her disclosure.

In the *Dirks* case the Supreme Court discussed the factors that subject a tippee to liability.

[20]   U.S. v Chestman (CA2 NY) 903 F2d 75 (1990).

DIRKS v SECURITIES AND EXCHANGE COMMISSION
463 US 646 (1983)

On March 6, 1973, Raymond Dirks, an investment analyst, received information from Ronald Secrist, a former officer of Equity Funding of America, alleging that the assets of Equity Funding were vastly overstated as the result of fraudulent corporate practices. Upon investigation Dirks received only denials from senior management, but certain corporation employees corroborated the charges of fraud. Neither Dirks nor his firm owned or traded any Equity Funding stock, but throughout his investigation he openly discussed the information he had obtained with a number of clients and investors, causing liquidation of Equity Fund stock in excess of $16 million. Dirks urged *The Wall Street Journal* to publish a story on the fraud allegations. However, it declined because it feared that publishing damaging hearsay might be libelous. Dirks continued his investigation and spread word of Secrist's charges during the next two weeks. During this time, Equity Funding stock fell from $26 per share to less than $15 per share. On March 27, the NYSE halted trading of Equity Funding stock, and a subsequent investigation revealed the vast fraud that had taken place. The SEC, investigating Dirks' role in the exposure of the fraud, found that Dirks had aided and abetted violations of the Securities Act of 1933, the Securities Exchange Act of 1934, and SEC Rule 10b-5 by repeating the allegations of fraud to members of the investment community who later sold their Equity Funding stock. Upon appeal by Dirks, the decision of the lower court was upheld by the U.S. Court of Appeals. An appeal was taken to the Supreme Court.

POWELL, J. . . . In the seminal case of *In re Cady, Roberts & Co.*, 40 S.E.C. 907 (1961), the SEC recognized that the common law in some jurisdictions imposes on "corporate 'insiders', particularly officers, directors, or controlling stockholders" an "affirmative duty of disclosure . . . when dealing in securities." The SEC found that not only did breach of this common-law duty also establish the elements of a Rule 10b-5 violation, but that individuals other than corporate insiders could be obligated either to disclose material nonpublic information before trading or to abstain from trading altogether. In *Chiarella* [445 U.S. 222 (1980)], we accepted the two elements set out in *Cady, Roberts* for establishing a Rule 10b-5 violation: "(i) the existence of a relationship affording access to inside information intended to be available only for a corporate purpose, and (ii) the unfairness of allowing a corporate insider to take advantage of that information by trading without disclosure." In examining whether Chiarella had an obligation to disclose or abstain, the Court found that there is no general duty to disclose before trading on material nonpublic information, and held that "a duty to disclose under § 10(b) does not arise from the mere possession of nonpublic market information." Such a duty arises rather from the existence of a fiduciary relationship.

Not "all breaches of fiduciary duty in connection with a securities transaction," however, come within the ambit of Rule 10b-5. There must also be "manipulation or deception." In an inside-trading case this fraud derives from the "inherent unfairness involved where one takes advantage" of "information intended to be available only for a corporate purpose and not for the personal benefit of anyone." Thus, an insider will be liable under Rule 10b-5 for inside trading only where he fails to disclose material nonpublic information before trading on it and thus makes "secret profits."

We were explicit in *Chiarella* in saying that there can be no duty to disclose where the person who has traded on inside information "was not [the corporation's] agent, . . . was not a fiduciary, [or] was not a person in whom the sellers [of the securities] had placed their trust and confidence." Not to require such a fiduciary relationship, we recognized, would "depart radically from the established doctrine that duty arises from a specific relationship between two parties" and would amount to "recognizing a general duty between all participants in market transactions to forgo actions based on material, nonpublic information." This requirement of a specific relationship between the shareholders and the individual trading on inside information has created analytical difficulties for the SEC and courts in policing tippees who trade on inside information. Unlike insiders who have independent fiduciary duties to both the corporation and its shareholders, the typical tippee has no such relationships.* In view of this absence, it has been unclear how a tippee acquires the *Cady, Roberts* duty to refrain from trading on inside information.

The SEC's position, as stated in its opinion in this case, is that a tippee "inherits" the *Cady, Roberts* obligation to shareholders whenever he receives inside information from an insider. . . .

In effect, the SEC's theory of tippee liability . . . appears rooted in the idea that the antifraud provisions required equal information among all traders. This conflicts with the principle set forth in *Chiarella* that only some persons, under some circumstances, will be barred from trading while in possession of material nonpublic information. . . .

Imposing a duty to disclose or abstain solely because a person knowingly receives

---

* Under certain circumstances, such as where corporate information is revealed legitimately to an underwriter, accountant, lawyer, or consultant working for the corporation, these outsiders may become fiduciaries of the shareholders. The basis for recognizing this fiduciary duty is not simply that such persons acquired nonpublic corporate information, but rather that they have entered into a special confidential relationship in the conduct of the business of the enterprise and are given access to information solely for corporate purposes. . . . When such a person breaches his fiduciary relationship, he may be treated more properly as a tipper than a tippee. . . . For such a duty to be imposed, however, the corporation must expect the outsider to keep the disclosed nonpublic information confidential, and the relationship at least must imply such a duty.

material nonpublic information from an insider and trades on it could have an inhibiting influence on the role of market analysts, which the SEC itself recognizes is necessary to the preservation of a healthy market. It is commonplace for analysts to "ferret out and analyze information," and this often is done by meeting with and questioning corporate officers and others who are insiders. And information that the analysts obtain normally may be the basis for judgments as to the market worth of a corporation's securities. The analyst's judgment in this respect is made available in market letters or otherwise to clients of the firm. It is the nature of this type of information, and indeed of the markets themselves, that such information cannot be made simultaneously available to all of the corporation's stockholders or the public generally.

The conclusion that recipients of inside information do not invariably acquire a duty to disclose or abstain does not mean that such tippees always are free to trade on the information. The need for a ban on some tippee trading is clear. Not only are insiders forbidden by their fiduciary relationship from personally using undisclosed corporate information to their advantage, but they may not give such information to an outsider for the same improper purpose of exploiting the information for their personal gain. See 15 U.S.C. § 78t(b) (making it unlawful to do indirectly "by means of any other person" any act made unlawful by the federal securities laws). Similarly, the transactions of those who knowingly participate with the fiduciary in such a breach are "as forbidden" as transactions "on behalf of the trustee himself." . . .

Thus, some tippees must assume an insider's duty to the shareholders not because they receive inside information, but rather because it has been made available to them *improperly*. And for Rule 10b-5 purposes, the insider's disclosure is improper only where it would violate his *Cady, Roberts* duty. Thus, a tippee assumes a fiduciary duty to the shareholders of a corporation not to trade on material nonpublic information only when the insider has breached his fiduciary duty to the shareholders by disclosing the information to the tippee and the tippee knows or should know that there has been a breach.

In determining whether a tippee is under an obligation to disclose or abstain, it thus is necessary to determine whether the insider's "tip" constituted a breach of the insider's fiduciary duty. All disclosures of confidential corporate information are not inconsistent with the duty insiders owe to shareholders. . . . Thus, the test is whether the insider personally will benefit, directly or indirectly, from his disclosure. Absent some personal gain, there has been no breach of duty to stockholders. And absent a breach by the insider, there is no derivative breach. . . .

Under the inside-trading and tipping rules set forth above, we find that there was no actionable violation by Dirks. It is undisputed that Dirks himself was a stranger to Equity Funding, with no pre-existing fiduciary duty to its shareholders. He took no action, directly or indirectly, that induced the shareholders or officers of Equity Funding to repose trust or confidence in him. There was no expectation by Dirks' sources that he would keep their information in confidence. Nor did Dirks misappropriate or illegally obtain the information about Equity Funding. Unless the insiders breached their *Cady, Roberts* duty to shareholders in disclosing the nonpublic information to Dirks, he breached no duty when he passed it on to investors as well as to *The Wall Street Journal*.

It is clear that neither Secrist nor the other Equity Funding employees violated their *Cady, Roberts* duty to the corporation's shareholders by providing information to Dirks. The tippers received no monetary or personal benefit for revealing Equity Funding's secrets, nor was their purpose to make a gift of valuable information to Dirks. As the facts of this case clearly indicate, the tippers were motivated by a desire to expose the fraud.

[Judgment reversed]

BLACKMUN, J. (dissenting) . . . The Court today takes still another step to limit the protections provided investors by § 10(b) of the Securities Exchange Act of 1934. . . . The device employed in this case engrafts a special motivational requirement on the fiduciary duty doctrine. This innovation excuses a knowing and intentional violation of an insider's duty to shareholders if the insider does not act from a motive of personal gain. Even on the extraordinary facts of this case, such an innovation is not justified. . . .

In my view, Secrist violated his duty to Equity Funding shareholders by transmitting material nonpublic information to Dirks with the intention that Dirks would cause his clients to trade on that information. Dirks, therefore, was under a duty to make the information publicly available or to refrain from actions that he knew would lead to trading. Because Dirks caused his clients to trade, he violated § 10(b) and Rule 10b-5. Any other result is a disservice to this country's attempt to provide fair and efficient capital markets.

QUESTIONS

1. State the SEC's theory of tippee liability. Would such a theory have an inhibiting influence on the role of market analysts?
2. When is a tippee subject to a fiduciary duty to the shareholders not to trade on material nonpublic information?
3. Does the court establish a "constructive insider" rule in its footnote?

(b) MISAPPROPRIATORS. Individuals who misappropriate or steal valuable nonpublic information in breach of a fiduciary duty to their employer and trade in securities on that information are guilty of insider trading as so-called misappropriators.[21] Thus, an employee working for a financial printing firm who, while proofreading a financial document being prepared for a client firm, was able to figure out the identity of certain tender offer targets and, soon thereafter, traded on such valuable nonpublic information to his advantage was found guilty of insider trading under Section 10(b) and Rule 10b-5.[22]

It is no defense to a Section 10(b) and Rule 10b-5 criminal charge of participating in a "scheme to defraud" that the victim of the fraud had no economic interest in the securities traded. The convictions of a columnist for *The Wall Street Journal* and a stockbroker were upheld under Section 10(b) of the 1934 Act when the columnist violated his fiduciary duty to his employer by revealing prepublication information about his column to the stockbroker. The stockbroker then used the information to trade in the securities identified in the column.[23]

(c) REMEDY FOR INVESTORS. Investors who lack inside information possessed by the insider and have sold their stock during the relevant time period may recover damages from any insider who has made use of the undisclosed information. Recovery is through a civil action based on Rule 10b-5.

[21]   U.S. v Willis (SD NY) 737 F Supp 269 (1990).
[22]   SEC v Materia (CA2 NY) 745 F2d 197 (1984).
[23]   Carpenter v U.S. 484 US 19 (1987).

8.   Disclosure of Ownership and Short-Swing Profit

Corporate directors and officers owning equity securities in their corporation and any shareholder owning more than 10 percent of any class of the corporation's equity securities must file a disclosure statement as to such ownership with the SEC under § 16(a) of the 1934 Act.

Section 16 is designed to prevent the unfair use of information available to these corporate insiders by preventing them from participating in short-term trading in their corporation's equity securities.

If such a person sells at a profit any of such securities in less than six months after their purchase, the profit is called a **short-swing profit.** Under § 16(b) the corporation may sue the director, officer, or major stockholder for the short-swing profit and may recover that profit even though there was no fraudulent intent in acquiring and selling the securities.

9.   Tender Offers

A corporation or group of investors may seek to acquire control of another corporation by making a general offer to all shareholders of the target corporation to purchase their shares for cash at a specified price, subject to a minimum or maximum number of shares that the offeror will accept. This is called a **cash tender offer.** The offer to purchase is usually contingent on the tender of a fixed number of shares sufficient to ensure takeover. The bid price is set at a premium over the prevailing market price. Should more shares be tendered than the offeror is willing to purchase, the tender offeror must purchase shares from each shareholder on a *pro rata* basis.

The Williams Act, which amended the 1934 Act,[24] was passed in order to ensure that public shareholders who are confronted with a cash tender offer will not be required to respond without adequate information. Under § 14(d) of the Williams Act, a person making a tender offer must ordinarily file appropriate SEC forms providing information about the

background and identity of the person filing, the source of funds used to make purchases of stock, the amount of stock beneficially owned, the purpose of the purchases, any plan the purchaser proposes to implement if it gains control over the target corporation, and any contracts or understandings that it has with other persons concerning the target corporation.[25]

Section 14(e) of the Williams Act is the antifraud section, which prohibits fraudulent, deceptive, or manipulative practices. SEC Rule 14e-1 requires any tender offer to remain open for a minimum of 20 business days from the date it is first published or given to security holders. The SEC believes that tender offers that do not stay open for a reasonable length of time increase the likelihood of hasty, ill-considered decision making on the basis of inadequate or incomplete information, as well as the possibility for fraudulent, deceptive, or manipulative acts or practices by a bidder and others.

Corporations themselves have adopted antitakeover measures to ward off tender offers. Most states have enacted laws that make it more difficult for tender offers to succeed.

The courts are not inclined to subject every tender offer to close judicial scrutiny. Such a practice could generally inhibit shareholders from taking advantage of favorable offerings. Fairness or unfairness of the offer may not be the basis of a Section 14(e) action; rather, it is essential to allege and prove misrepresentation.

10.   Regulation of Accountants by the SEC

Accountants play a vital role in financial re-

---

[24]   PL 90–439, 82 Stat 454, 15 USC §§ 78m(d), (e).

[25]   Section 14(d) requires a filing by any person making a tender offer that, if successful, would result in the acquisition of 5 percent of any class of an equity security required to be registered under the 1934 Act. Section 13(d) of the Act requires disclosure to the issuer, the SEC, and the appropriate stock exchange when a person acquires 5 percent of a class of equity security through stock purchases on exchanges or through private purchases. The person may have acquired the stock for investment purpose and not for control, but must still file disclosure forms under Section 13(d). Section 14(d) applies only to shares to be acquired by tender offer.

porting under the federal securities laws administered by the SEC. Accountants are subject to liability under Sections 11, 12, 17, and 24 of the 1933 Act and may also be liable under Section 10(b) of the 1934 Act. An accountant who prepares any statement, opinion, or other legal paper filed with the SEC with the preparer's consent is deemed to be practicing before the SEC.[26] Because accountants are relied on so heavily by the SEC, the SEC has promulgated Rule 2(e) to regulate and discipline the many accountants (as well as attorneys and consultants) who practice be-

fore it. Under Rule 2(e) the SEC may suspend or disbar from practice before it those who are unqualified or unethical or who have violated federal securities laws or SEC rules.[27]

[26]   17 CFR § 201.2e (1979).

[27]   Rule 2(e) provides in pertinent part: "Suspension and disbarment. (1) The Commission may deny, temporarily or permanently, the privilege of appearing or practicing before it in any way to any person who is found by the Commission after notice of an opportunity for hearing in the matter (i) not to possess the requisite qualifications to represent others, or (ii) to be lacking in character or integrity or to have engaged in unethical or improper professional conduct, or (iii) to have willfully violated, or willfully aided and abetted the violation of any provision of the federal securities laws (15 U.S.C. 77a to 80B-20), or the rules and regulations thereunder." 17 CFR § 201.2(e) (1979).
   The authority of the SEC to promulgate the rule was upheld in Touche Ross v SEC (CA2 NY) 609 F2d 570 (1979).

SUMMARY

State blue sky laws, which apply only to intrastate transactions, protect the public from the sale of fraudulent securities. The term *security* is defined sufficiently broadly to encompass not only stocks and bonds, but any conceivable kind of corporate interest that has investment characteristics. There are two principal laws providing the basic framework for federal regulation of the sale of securities in interstate commerce. The Securities Act of 1933 deals with the original distribution of securities by the issuing corporations. The Securities Exchange Act of 1934 is concerned with the secondary distribution of securities on the exchanges. These Acts are administered by the Securities and Exchange Commission. Except for certain private and limited offerings, the

1933 Act requires that a registration statement be filed with the SEC and that a prospectus be provided to each potential purchaser. Criminal and civil penalties exist for fraudulent statements made in this process. The 1934 Act provides reporting requirements for companies whose securities are listed on a national exchange and unlisted companies that have assets in excess of $3 million and 500 or more shareholders. Rule 10b-5 is the principal antifraud rule under the 1934 Act. Trading on "inside information" is unlawful and may subject those involved to a civil penalty of three times the profit made on the improperly disclosed information. Cash tender offers are regulated by the SEC under authority of the Williams Act, which amended the 1934 Act.

QUESTIONS AND CASE PROBLEMS

1. What social forces are affected by the rule of law that prohibits corporate insiders from participating in short-term trading of their company's stock?
2. What is the major distinction between the Securities Act of 1933 and the Securities Exchange Act of 1934?
3. On what rationale does the SEC allow for the private placement of securities with accredited

investors, without any limitation on the amount that may be raised?
4. Mark Magnison, a state lottery game million-dollar winner, reviewed the registration statement and prospectus of the Northern Sprinkler Supply Co., which had been timely filed with the SEC. He tells you that he cannot make much sense of these documents, but that he is going to invest in the company, because "the SEC ap-

proved the securities, and the federal government would not knowingly approve a bad investment." Is Mark correct?

5. The following transactions in Heritage Cosmetics Co., Inc. stock took place: On January 21, Jones, the corporation's vice president of marketing, purchased 1,000 shares of stock at $25 per share. On January 24, Sylvan, a local banker and director of Heritage, purchased 500 shares of stock at $26 per share. On January 30, McCarthy, a secretary at Heritage, purchased 300 shares of stock at $26½. On February 12, Winfried, a rich investor from New England, purchased 25,000 shares at an average price of $26 per share. At that time, Heritage had a total of 200,000 shares of stock outstanding. On June 14, Winfried sold his entire position in Heritage at an average price of $35 per share. In a local newspaper interview, Winfried was quoted regarding his reasons for selling the stock: "I have not had the pleasure of meeting any person from Heritage, but I have the highest regard for the Heritage Company. . . . I sold my stock simply because the market has gone too high and in my view is due for a correction." After independently reading Winfried's prediction on the stock market, Jones, Sylvan, and McCarthy sold their shares on June 15 for $33 per share. On June 20, Heritage Corp. demands that Jones, Sylvan, McCarthy, and Winfried remit to the corporation the profits made on the sale of the stock. Is the corporation correct in making such a demand on each of these individuals?

6. The Canadian Express Club solicited buyers to purchase shares in a group comprised of shareholders, whose money is pooled to purchase lottery tickets in Canada. Total winnings from tickets are split among shareholders, with Canadian Express administering the purchasing, recordkeeping and disbursements. The securities commission contended that Canadian Express was selling securities, arguing that this was an investment contract. Canadian Express contended that playing the lottery was simply not an "investment" of money. Decide. [Ontario, Inc. v Mays (Kan App) 780 P2d 1126]

7. Marsha Dale worked at the law office of Emory Stone, an attorney practicing securities law. In going over the typing of a document relating to the merger of two computer software companies, he joked to Marsha, "If I weren't so ethical, I could make a few bucks on this info. Nomac Software stock prices are going to take off when this news hits *The Street*." That evening Marsha told her friend Rick Needleworth, a stockbroker, all of what her boss had said. Needleworth bought 500 shares of Nomac Software stock the next day and sold it three days later when the news of the merger was made public. He made a profit of $3,500. Did Dale, Stone, or Needleworth violate any securities law(s) as to the small profit made by Needleworth?

8. International Advertising Inc. (IA) would like to raise $10 million in new capital in order to open new, full-service offices in Poland, Czechoslovakia, and the Soviet Union. It believes it could raise the capital by selling shares of stock to its directors and executive officers, as well to its bank and a large insurance company whose home office is located near IA's headquarters. Opposition to the financing plan exists because of the trouble, time, and cost involved with registering with the SEC. Advise IA how best to proceed with the registration of the new issue of stock.

9. Dubois sold Hocking a condominium that included an option to participate in a rental pool arrangement. Hocking elected to participate in the arrangement. Under it, the rental pool's agent rented condominiums, pooled the income, and after deducting a management fee, distributed the income to the owners on a *pro rata* basis. Hocking brought a Rule 10b-5 fraud action against Dubois. Dubois contended that the sale of the condominium was not a "security under the Securities Acts," so Hocking had no status to bring a securities suit against her. Was Dubois correct? [Hocking v Dubois (CA9 Hawaii) 839 F2d 290]

10. William Rubin, president of Tri-State Mining Co., sought a loan from Bankers Trust Co. To secure the loan, he pledged worthless stock in six companies and represented that the stock was worth $1.7 million. Moreover, he arranged for fictitious quotations to appear in an investment reporting service used by the bank to value the pledged securities. The bank loaned Rubin $475,000 and took the securities as pledged collateral. In a criminal action against Rubin under § 17(a) of the 1933 Act, Rubin defended that pledging of securities did not constitute an "offer or sale" of securities under the Act. Was Rubin correct? [Rubin v U.S., 449 US 424]

11. J.C. Cowdin, a director of the Curtis-Wright Co., phoned Robert Gintel, a partner of Cady, Roberts & Co., a stock brokerage house, and advised him that Curtis Wright's quarterly dividend had been cut. Gintel immediately entered

orders selling Curtis-Wright shares for his customers' accounts. The stock was selling at over $40 a share when the orders were executed but fell to $30 soon after the dividend cut was announced to the public. The SEC contended that the firm, Cady, Roberts & Co., and Gintel violated § 10(b) of the 1934 Act, Rule 10b-5, and § 17(a) of the 1933 Act. Gintel and Cady, Roberts & Co. disagreed. Decide. [In re Cady, Roberts & Co. 40 SEC 907]

12. The Baileys bought shares in a real estate limited partnership from Blarney Castle, Ltd., in reliance on false representations by Joan Casey that "Blarney Castle was qualified by the IRS as an IRS-approved tax shelter" and that "Blarney Castle would return their investment plus a profit in a reasonable period of time . . . that Blarney Castle was a secure investment, a sure thing." The offering memorandum Casey provided to the Baileys stated that Blarney Castle limited partnership interests were a risky investment, the IRS had not approved and would probably challenge some of the deductions, and buyers should not rely on oral descriptions of this security. The Baileys did not read this document before investing. The limited partnership went into bankruptcy, and Baileys sued Casey for making material misrepresentations in violation of § 12(2) of the 1933 Act. Casey defended that her statements were innocuous "puffery" or mere statements of opinion and were not actionable. Casey asserted that the Baileys are bound by the offering memorandum, which fully informed the Baileys of all relevant facts. Decide.

13. Douglas Hansen, Leo Borrell, and Bobby Lawrence were three psychiatrists who recognized the need for an inpatient treatment facility for adolescents and children in their community. They became limited partners in the building of a for-profit psychiatric facility. Each had a 6.25 percent interest in the partnership. Healthcare International Inc., the general partner with a 75 percent interest, had expertise in hospital construction, management, and operation. All three assert that the managerial control of the partnership was undertaken and operated by the general partner to the exclusion of the limited partners. The three doctors sent a meager number of patients in the total pool of admittees to the facility. The doctors claimed that their interest was a security—"investment contracts"—so as to give them status to file a securities suit against the general partner under the 1934 Act.

The general partner disagreed. Decide. [L & B Hospial Ventures Inc. v Healthcare International Inc. (CA5 Tex) 894 F2d 150]

14. Texas International Speedway, Inc. (TIS) filed a registration statement and prospectus with the Securities and Exchange Commission, offering a total of $4,398,900 in securities to the public. The proceeds of the sale were to be used to finance the construction of an automobile speedway. The entire issue was sold on the offering date. TIS did not meet with success, however, and the corporation filed a petition for bankruptcy. Huddleston and Bradley instituted a class action in the U.S. district court on behalf of themselves and other purchasers of TIS securities. The complaint alleged violations of § 10(b) of the 1934 Act. They sued most of the participants in the offering, including the accounting firm, Herman & MacLean, which had issued an opinion concerning certain financial statements and a *pro forma* balance sheet that were contained in the registration statement and prospectus. They claimed that the defendants had engaged in a fraudulent scheme to misrepresent or conceal material facts regarding the financial condition of TIS, including the costs incurred in building the speedway. Herman & MacLean defended that the case should be dismissed because § 11 of the 1933 Act provides an express remedy for a misrepresentation in a registration statement, so an action under § 10(b) of the 1934 Act is precluded. Decide. [Herman & MacLean v Huddleston, 459 US 375]

15. Ira Walbaum executed a stock purchase agreement to tender a controlling interest in Walbaum, Inc. to A&P stores. On November 24, 1986, Ira Waldbaum told his sister, Shirley Wilkins, in strict confidence. Wilkins told her daughter, Susan Loeb, in strict confidence, and Loeb told her husband Keith in strict confidence. Keith called his broker, Robert Chestman, on the morning of November 26, 1986, stating only that he had some "accurate information" that Waldbaum's was being sold at a "substantially higher" price than the market value of the stock. On the morning of November 26, Chestman bought 3,000 shares of Waldbaum's at $24.65 per share. After the announcement of the tender offer, the stock closed at $49 per share. The SEC brought a § 10(b), Rule 10b-5 securities fraud action against Chestman, alleging that Chestman was a tippee who received information from an insider and was therefore subject to the insider's fiduciary duty.

Chestman contended that the information was merely "family gossip" when Susan Loeb received it, and that he had no knowledge that Keith Loeb was breaking a confidential relationship. Did Keith Loeb reveal the information in breach of a duty of confidence known to Chestman? Decide the SEC case. [U.S. v Chestman (CA2 NY) 903 F2d 75]

49

MANAGEMENT OF CORPORATIONS

A corporation is managed, directly or indirectly, by its shareholders, board of directors, and officers.

In the large corporation it is common to find that the owners (the shareholders) are not to any appreciable extent the managers (directors and officers). In a closely held corporation, however, the owners commonly serve on the board of directors and hold corporate offices.

A. SHAREHOLDERS

Shareholders' management functions are usually very limited and take the form of voting at shareholders' meetings to elect directors whose management philosophies and interests best coincide with their own. In this sense shareholders indirectly determine the management policies of the business. Also, they may vote at shareholders' meetings to amend bylaws, approve shareholder resolutions, or vote on so-called extraordinary corporate matters. Extraordinary matters include the sale of corporate assets outside the regular course of the corporation's business or the merger or dissolution of the corporation.

1.   Meetings of Shareholders

To have legal effect, action by the shareholders must be taken at a regular or special meeting.

(a) REGULAR MEETINGS. The time and place of regular or stated meetings are usually prescribed by the articles of incorporation or bylaws. Notice to shareholders of such meetings is ordinarily not required, but it is usually given as a matter of good business practice. Some statutes require that notice be given of all meetings.

(b) SPECIAL MEETINGS. Generally, notice must be given specifying the subject matter when the meeting is of an unusual character. Unless otherwise prescribed, special meetings are called by the directors. It is sometimes provided that a special meeting may be called by a certain percentage of shareholders.[1] Notice of the day, hour, and place of a special meeting must be given to all shareholders. The notice must also include a statement of the nature of the business to be transacted. No other business may be transacted at such a meeting.

(c) QUORUM. A valid meeting requires the presence of a quorum of the voting shareholders. In order to constitute a **quorum,** usually a specified number of shareholders, or a number authorized to vote a stated proportion of the voting stock, must attend. If a quorum is present, a majority of those present may act with respect to any matter, unless there is an express requirement of a greater affirmative vote.

When a meeting opens with a quorum, the quorum is generally not broken if shareholders leave the meeting and those remaining are not sufficient to constitute a quorum.

2.   Action Without Meeting

A number of statutes provide for corporate action by shareholders without holding a meeting. The RMBCA provides that "action required or permitted by this Act to be taken at a shareholder's meeting may be taken without a meeting if the action is taken by all shareholders entitled to vote on the action."[2] The action must be evidenced by a written consent describing the action taken, signed by all the shareholders entitled to vote on the action, and delivered to the corporation for inclusion in the minutes. Such provisions give flexibility of operation, which is needed by the small or close corporation.

B.   DIRECTORS

The management of a corporation is usually under the control of a board of directors elected by the shareholders. Most states now permit the number of directors to be fixed by the bylaws. Many specify that the board of directors shall consist of not less than three directors. A few authorize one or more directors.[3] Professional corporation legislation often authorizes or is interpreted as authorizing a one- or two-person board of directors.

3.   Qualifications

Eligibility for membership on a board of directors is determined by statute, articles of incorporation, or bylaws. In the absence of a contrary provision, any person (including a nonresident, a minor, or even a person who is not a shareholder) is eligible for membership.

Bylaws may require that a director own stock in the corporation, although this requirement is not ordinarily imposed.

4.   Powers of Directors

The board of directors has authority to manage the corporation. The court will not interfere with the board's discretion in the absence

---

[1]   NY Bus. Corp. Law § 603.

[2]   RMBCA § 7.04 (a).
[3]   Del. Code § 141 (b). See Also ABA MBCA § 36.

FIGURE 49-1   POWERS OF DIRECTORS

of (a) illegal conduct or (b) fraud harming the rights of creditors, shareholders, or the corporation.[4]

The board of directors may enter into any contract or transaction necessary to carry out the business for which the corporation was formed. The board may appoint officers and other agents to act for the company, or it may

appoint several of its own members as an executive committee to act for the board between board meetings.

Broad delegation of authority to a single individual may, however, run the risk of being treated as an unlawful abdication of the board's management function.

In the *Boston Athletic Association* case the court considered whether the board improperly delegated authority to an individual officer.

[4]   Iwasaki v Iwasaki Bros., Inc. 58 Or App 543, 649 P2d 598 (1982).

BOSTON ATHLETIC ASSOCIATION v INTERNATIONAL MARATHON, INC.
292 Mass 356, 467 NE2d 58 (1984)

On April 27, 1981, the board of the Boston Athletic Association (BAA), a non-profit corporation whose principal activity is the presentation of an annual road race (the Boston Marathon), approved the following proposal:

> That William T. Cloney, as President of the Association, be and hereby is authorized and directed to negotiate and to execute in the name of and in behalf of this Association such agreements as he deems in the best interest of the Association for the perpetuation, sponsorship, or underwriting of the Boston A.A. Marathon.

There was no mention at this meeting of hiring an exclusive promoter. In the past all sponsorship and broadcast coverage contracts were negotiated between Cloney and individual sponsors. On September 23, 1981, Cloney executed an agreement on behalf of the BAA with Marshall Medoff, an attorney and president of IMI (a business corporation headed by Medoff). The agreement designated Medoff as the exclusive promoter of the Marathon, with the BAA transferring all right to the use of the Boston Marathon name and logos to IMI. The agreement's financial terms were extremely favorable to IMI. The agreement was automatically renewable year to year, at the option of IMI, with no way for the BAA to end the relationship. A majority of the Board members learned of the existence of the agreement in late February, 1982. By a vote taken on September 9, 1982, the board declared the agreement to be beyond the authorization vested in Cloney on April 27, 1981. The board brought an action to have the agreement set aside. IMI defended that Cloney had been given authority to make the contract with IMI, so the contract bound the corporation. From a judgment for the BAA, IMI (Medoff) appealed.

LYNCH, J. . . . Whether the board intended by its vote of April 27, 1981, to confer upon Cloney the authority to enter into the sponsorship agreement with IMI, that contract is void. The board of directors of a corporation cannot delegate total control of the corporation to an individual officer. . . . Neither can it delegate authority which is so broad that it enables the officer to bind the corporation to extraordinary commitments or significantly to encumber the principal asset or function of the corporation.

The contract seriously encumbers the manner in which the BAA may conduct the Marathon. The BAA is obliged to produce the race in its traditional form and to pay the entire bill. But it is not entitled to "present" the race. That right, as well as the right to use the name and logo of the BAA, belongs to IMI or its assignee. The BAA may not use its own logo in any way "inconsistent" with IMI's rights pursuant to the contract. The right to enter into sponsorship agreements belongs exclusively to IMI, although the BAA can reasonably withhold its approval. The BAA may not make independent agreements without written permission from IMI. Finally, the contract between IMI and the BAA is automatically renewable at the option of IMI. Under the plain language of the agreement, there is no way for the BAA to end the relationship.

In return for carrying out its obligations under the contract, the BAA is to be paid a $400,000 fee. Any revenues in excess of $400,000 are directly payable to IMI, and there is no limit to the number of sponsors who may be solicited or to the amount of money which may be raised. The annual fee is to be paid prior to the actual running of the race, but if the Marathon should not be run for some reason, the fee is to be returned to IMI.

According to the traditional principles of corporate governance, the board of governors of the BAA does not have the power to delegate to an individual officer authority to enter into a contract which so totally encumbers the most significant purpose of the BAA, the presentation of the Marathon. The by-laws of the BAA indicate that its organization and operation are, in all material respects, the same as those of a Massachusetts business corporation. Principles of corporate governance with respect to the power of the board of governors to delegate authority to individual officers are applicable to profit and nonprofit corporations alike. In fact, the powers of an officer of a charitable corporation to bind the corporation without specific ratification by the board of governors or directors are more strictly construed than would be similar powers of an officer of a business corporation. The validity of the board's purported delegation of authority to Cloney must be analyzed in this context.

Corporate officers are generally empowered, by delegation of authority of the board of directors, with general managerial functions. They are responsible for the day to day operation of the corporation. Courts are usually flexible and accommodating in allowing boards to delegate authority as necessary or expedient. But certain powers cannot be delegated generally. Certain transactions require specific authorization by the board in order to be valid. For example, in *Stoneman v. Fox Film Corp.*, 295 Mass. 419, 4 NE2d 63 (1936), the court found that the president, although authorized to act as a general manager on behalf of a film company, was not authorized to commit the company to the purchase of a theatre, an extraordinary transaction which involved a large financial commitment. The court indicated that delegation of authority to conduct such business was a "course of conduct manifestly ... unusual and extraordinary in the management of a corporation." It was an abdication of "the entire control" of the corporation and "[t]he functions of directors may not be abdicated." ...

The power of officers to bind charitable corporations is even more narrowly construed. ...

In light of these principles, it is clear that if the delegation to Cloney was so broad as to enable him to commit the BAA to an extraordinary contract which encumbered substantially all its assets, the board would have delegated away control of the very essence of the BAA's corporate existence. ... It is the obligation of the board of governors to oversee the presentation of the Marathon, not to surrender virtually complete control of the event to another organization. The fact that the agreement is automatically renewable and thus potentially perpetual demonstrates the pervasive nature of the limitation on the main purpose of the BAA. Authority to make such a contract was beyond the power of the board to delegate to Cloney.

Furthermore, the contract between IMI and the BAA is especially vulnerable because it is antithetical to the BAA's nature as a nonprofit corporation inasmuch as this agreement turns the solicitation of sponsors from a way to support the Marathon to a way for IMI to make a profit. It is entirely inconsistent with the nonprofit nature of the organization to permit such a substantial segment of the revenue earning capacity of the Marathon to be used as a vehicle for personal gain. ...

Although the promotion contract between IMI and the BAA is unenforceable, nevertheless as the BAA concedes IMI is entitled to recover the fair value of its services. ...

[Judgment affirmed]

QUESTIONS

1. Is there any difference between a business corporation and a nonprofit corporation with respect to the power of the board of directors to delegate authority to a corporate officer?
2. May a board of directors delegate control of a corporation to an individual officer?
3. Assess the September 23, 1981, contract negotiated by Cloney and Medoff as to its basic fairness.

5. Conflict of Interests

A director is disqualified from taking part in corporate action with respect to a matter in which the director has a conflicting interest. Since it cannot be known how the other directors would have acted if they had known of the conflict of interests, the corporation generally may avoid any transaction because of the director's disqualification.

A number of states provide by statute that the conflict of interests of a director does not impair the transaction or contract entered into or authorized by the board of directors if the disqualified director disclosed the interest and if the contract or transaction is fair and reasonable with respect to the corporation.

The *Dunbar* case sets forth an application of a state statute governing corporate transactions in which an officer or director has a personal interest.

DUNBAR v WILLIAMS

(La App) 554 So 2d 56 (1989)

Childs E. Dunbar, Jr. was a minority shareholder of Algiers Ironworks and Dry Dock Co., Inc. (AIW). He brought a shareholder's derivative action against the majority shareholders to recover damages on behalf of the corporation, AIW. Thomas S. Williams was the president and director of AIW. His wife served as a director of AIW. Mr. and Mrs. Williams also owned Tower Crane Co. Tower used AIW's phones, address, land for storage of cranes, and some personnel but Tower did not pay for them. Tower sold two cranes to AIW, and AIW's board did not consider or approve these transactions. Williams personally bought the yacht PATTY JEAN. He testified that work valued at $43,303 was expended on the vessel by AIW and that over $50,000 worth of business entertaining on behalf of AIW was rendered on the vessel. Mr. and Mrs. Williams charged $17,583 on an AIW credit card. Williams admitted that $4,571.45 was not business-related. Williams also admitted that $4,590.56 in gasoline charges to AIW were not business-related. The trial court issued a judgment against Williams for $9,162, reflecting these two admissions, and the minority shareholders appealed.

BARRY, J. . . . [A Louisiana statute provides that]

No contract or transaction between a corporation and one or more of its directors or officers, or between a corporation and any other business . . . in which one or more of its directors or officers are directors or officers or have a financial interest, shall be void or voidable solely for this reason . . . or solely because his or their votes were counted for such purpose, if:

1. The material facts as to his interest and as to the contract or transaction were disclosed or known to the board of directors or the committee, and the board or committee in good faith authorized the contract or transaction by a vote sufficient for such purpose without counting the vote of the interested director or directors; or
2. The material facts as to his interest and as to the contract or transaction were disclosed or known to the shareholders entitled to vote thereon, and the contract or transaction was approved in good faith by vote of the shareholders; or
3. The contract or transaction was fair as to the corporation as of the time it was authorized, approved or ratified by the board of directors, committee, or shareholders.

The questioned officer or director has the burden to establish that the transaction was fair and in good faith, essentially that it was at arms length. . . . *Noe v. Roussel,* 310

So.2d 806, 818–19 (La.1975). The *Noe* court explained: "[T]he agent or fiduciary may not take even the slightest advantage, but must zealously, diligently and honestly guard and champion the rights of his principal. . . ."

. . . The two crane purchases by Williams (as President of AIW) from his company (Tower) were not authorized by AIW's Board, hence, both purchases fail the test of [the statute]. . . . [On rehearing, May 9, 1989, on the issue of the Tower crane transactions, the district court was reversed. On second rehearing on the crane transactions held on November 16, 1989, the amount owed AIW was set at $15,000, which represented the profit gained by Tower from the sale to AIW.]

The use of AIW's premises, services, and personnel by Tower was clearly improper. AIW received no payment or discernible benefit and Williams' actions on behalf of Tower violated his fiduciary duty to AIW. . . .

We therefore remand for the trial court to conduct a hearing to determine the value of the various benefits and to enter a judgment in favor of AIW and against Williams. . . .

Williams personally bought the PATTY JEAN for $5,000 in August or September, 1977, apparently in very poor condition. Williams testified that he informally told [members of the board of directors] Dr. and Mrs. Grundmeyer and Edgar Williams that he intended to use the yacht to entertain customers and they approved. Williams did not discuss the matter with Dunbar, the other Board member. . . .

The trial court adjusted all of Williams' estimates [of amounts spent to refurbish, repair, and maintain the yacht] to reflect the costs of a regular customer and concluded the work should be valued at $43,303. We have no basis to find manifest error in that valuation.

As for the alleged benefits AIW received from the PATTY JEAN, twenty-one fishing trips were made entertaining approximately 152 people. Plaintiffs complain that not all of those trips were business related. Dunbar acknowledged the necessity for AIW to entertain, but maintained it would have been cheaper to charter a boat.

Jack Faulkner, an expert on overnight charters in the Gulf Coast area, testified that the standard charter fee for a vessel similar to the PATTY JEAN for a three-day fishing trip would be $125 per person per day with a four person minimum (not including alcohol) or $1,500. According to Williams, a trip cost approximately $600 to $800 and he computed the value of all the trips at over $50,000.

We disagree that a promotional trip is not business related, or that a guest unrelated to the shipping industry constitutes nonbusiness usage. It appears that the value of the trips fairly approximates the expense incurred by AIW to repair the vessel.

We conclude there was no fiduciary breach by Williams or manifest error in the trial court's finding that use of the PATTY JEAN by AIW in exchange for repairs, maintenance and refurbishing was reasonable and carried out in good faith. . . .

Plaintiffs claim the defendants breached their fiduciary duties by giving themselves unearned compensation in the form of . . . fringe benefits. . . .

The questioned benefits are (a) American Express charges (b) gas charges (c) charges at service stations, restaurants and food stores (d) company cars (e) home phone bills (f) Grundmeyer's country club bills and Williams' carnival club dues.

Plaintiffs contend those personal expenses were paid by AIW and are not business related, and the failure to keep records as to the business purpose constitutes a fiduciary breach. There is no question that AIW paid the expenses and the defendants must show their connection to AIW's business.

Mr. and Mrs. Williams, according to two ledger sheets in evidence, charged

$17,583.97 on an AIW American Express account from February 1980 through August 1985. Of that amount Williams admitted $4,571.45 was not business related. As to gasoline charges from 1980 to 1984, Williams admitted that he or his family charged $4,590.56 which was not business related. The trial court judgment against Williams for $9,162.01, reflecting those two sums, was not appealed and is final.

As for Williams' carnival club dues, . . . a local businessman testified for the defense that he considered them to be legitimate business expenses. . . .

Carnival dues are not, ipso facto, business related. Nor is there proof that Williams' membership in a carnival organization produced any revenue to AIW. The record and briefs are unclear as to which organizations Williams belonged to and at what costs to AIW.

We remand to the trial court to determine the amounts paid by AIW for carnival club dues and to enter the appropriate judgment in favor of AIW and against Williams.

[Judgment affirmed in part; reversed and action remanded in part]

QUESTIONS

1. Did a state law set guidelines to validate a corporate transaction in which an officer or director had a personal interest?
2. Did the board of directors have to approve the crane purchases in order to satisfy the state conflict of interest law?
3. Review the ethical principles set forth in Figure 1 of the preliminary pages of this book and express an opinion on the ethics of the following conduct: (1) sale of the cranes to AIW; (2) use of AIW facilities and personnel by Tower Crane Co.; (3) AIW's payment to refurbish the yacht PATTY JEAN; and (4) AIW's payment of fringe benefits, including carnival club dues.

6. Meetings of Directors

Theoretically, action by directors can be taken only at a proper meeting of the board. Bylaws sometimes require the meeting to be held at a particular place. Most states expressly provide that the directors may meet either in or out of the state of incorporation. Directors who participate without objection in a meeting irregularly held as to place or time other than as specified in the bylaws cannot object later. Generally, a director is not allowed to vote by proxy.

Most states permit action to be taken by the board of directors without the holding of an actual meeting. It is commonly provided when such action is taken that it be set forth in writing and signed by all the directors.

7. Liability of Directors

In dealing with the corporation the directors act in a fiduciary capacity. It is to their care

that the stockholders have entrusted the control of the corporate property and the management of the business.[5]

(a) THE BUSINESS JUDGMENT RULE. Courts recognize that the decisions of corporate directors often involve the weighing and balancing of legal, ethical, commercial, promotional, public relations, and other factors. Courts generally are reluctant to become involved in judicial second-guessing or to become enmeshed in complex corporate decision making, a task that they state they are ill-equipped to handle.[6] Some decisions of corporate directors, although made in good faith and in the best interest of the corporation when made, may eventually prove to be erroneous. The business judgment rule shields

---

[5]   Tillis v United Parts, Inc. (Fla App) 395 So 2d 518 (1981).
[6]   Auerback v Bennett, 47 NY2d 619, 419 NYS2d 920 (1979).

corporate directors from liability for informed business decisions made in good faith and in the best interest of the corporation.

(1) The Traditional Rule. Courts apply the business judgment rule as a presumption that in making a business decision the directors acted (a) on an informed basis, (b) in good faith, and (c) in the honest belief that the action taken was in the best interest of the corporation.[7] Thus, the party challenging the directors' actions has the difficult initial burden of proving that the directors did not act on an informed basis or in good faith or that the directors acted in self-interest rather than in the interest of the corporation.[8]

(2) Application in Corporate Control Transactions. When a corporation receives a hostile or nonhostile takeover bid, the target board of directors may tend to take actions that are in their own self-interests and not in the interests of the shareholders (owners). Courts have recognized the potential for director self-interest in these situations and, in order to protect the interests of shareholders, have taken a more active role under the business judgment rule in reviewing control-related board decisions.

In the *Smith v Van Gorkom* case the directors relied upon the business judgment rule to shield themselves from individual liability in a lawsuit charging that the directors did not act on an "informed basis" in accepting and recommending a merger at a price per share that was less than the "intrinsic value" of the shares.

---

[7]   Alford v Shaw, 318 NC 289, 349 SE2d 41 (1986).
[8]   Saillard v Natmos Co. 208 Cal App 3d 1250, 256 Cal Rptr 702 (1989).

SMITH v VAN GORKOM
(Del) 488 A2d 858 (1985)

On September 13, Jerome Van Gorkom as chairman and chief executive officer of Trans Union Inc., a holding company in the railcar leasing business, arranged a meeting with Jay Pritzker, a well-known takeover specialist and a social acquaintance, to determine his interest in acquiring Trans Union. On Thursday, September 18, Pritzker made an offer of $55 per share (a price suggested by Van Gorkom) with a decision to be made by the Board no later than Sunday, September 21. On Friday, Van Gorkom called a special meeting of the board of directors for noon the following day; no agenda was announced. At the directors' meeting Van Gorkom made a 20-minute oral analysis of the merger transaction, showed that the company was having difficulty generating sufficient income to offset its increasingly large investment tax credits, and discussed his meeting with Pritzker and the reasons for the meeting. Copies of the proposed merger agreement were delivered too late to be studied before or during the meeting. No consultants or investment advisers were called upon to support the merger price of $55 per share. The merger was approved at the end of the two-hour meeting. Certain shareholders brought a class action suit against the directors, contending that the board's decision was not the product of informed business judgment. The directors responded that their good faith decision was shielded by the business judgment rule. From a decision for the directors, the shareholders appealed.

HORSEY, J. . . . Under Delaware law, the business judgment rule is the offspring of the fundamental principle, codified in 8 *Del. C.* § 141(a), that the business and affairs of a

Delaware corporation are managed by or under its board of directors. In carrying out their managerial roles, directors are charged with an unyielding fiduciary duty to the corporation and its shareholders. The business judgment rule exists to protect and promote the full and free exercise of the managerial power granted to Delaware directors. The rule itself "is a presumption that in making a business decision, the directors of a corporation acted on an informed basis, in good faith and in the honest belief that the action taken was in the best interests of the company." *Aronson* [*v. Lewis*, Del. Supr., 473 A2d 805,] 812. Thus, the party attacking a board decision as uninformed must rebut the presumption that its business judgment was an informed one.

The determination of whether a business judgment is an informed one turns on whether the directors have informed themselves "prior to making a business decision, of all material information reasonably available to them." *Id.* . . .

Thus, a director's duty to exercise an informed business judgment is in the nature of a duty of care, as distinguished from a duty of loyalty. . . .

The standard of care applicable to a director's duty of care has also been recently restated by this Court. In *Aronson, supra,* we stated:

> While the Delaware cases use a variety of terms to describe the applicable standard of care, our analysis satisfies us that under the business judgment rule director liability is predicated upon concepts of gross negligence.

473 A.2d at 812.

We again confirm that view. We think the concept of gross negligence is also the proper standard for determining whether a business judgment reached by a board of directors was an informed one.

In the specific context of a proposed merger of domestic corporations, a director has a duty under 8 *Del. C.* 251(b), along with his fellow directors, to act in an informed and deliberate manner in determining whether to approve an agreement of merger before submitting the proposal to the stockholders. Certainly in the merger context, a director may not abdicate that duty by leaving to the shareholders alone the decision to approve or disapprove the agreement. . . .

It is against those standards that the conduct of the directors of Trans Union must be tested, as a matter of law and as a matter of fact, regarding their exercise of an informed business judgment in voting to approve the Pritzker merger proposal.

. . . The issue of whether the directors reached an informed decision to "sell" the Company on September 20, 1980 must be determined only upon the basis of the information then reasonably available to the directors and relevant to their decision to accept the Pritzker merger proposal. . . .

On the record before us, we must conclude that the Board of Directors did not reach an informed business judgment on September 20, 1980 in voting to "sell" the Company for $55 per share pursuant to the Pritzker cash-out merger proposal. Our reasons, in summary, are as follows:

The directors (1) did not adequately inform themselves as to Van Gorkom's role in forcing the "sale" of the Company and in establishing the per share purchase price; (2) were uninformed as to the intrinsic value of the Company; and (3) given these circumstances, at a minimum, were grossly negligent in approving the "sale" of the Company upon two hours' consideration, without prior notice, and without the exigency of a crisis or emergency.

As has been noted, the Board based its September 20 decision to approve the cash-out merger primarily on Van Gorkom's representations. None of the directors, other than Van Gorkom and Chelberg, had any prior knowledge that the purpose of the meeting was to propose a cash-out merger of Trans Union. No members of Senior Management were present, other than Chelberg, Romans and Peterson; and the latter two had only learned of the proposed sale an hour earlier. Both general counsel Moore and former general counsel Browder attended the meeting, but were equally uninformed as to the purpose of the meeting and the documents to be acted upon.

Without any documents before them concerning the proposed transaction, the members of the Board were required to rely entirely upon Van Gorkom's 20-minute oral presentation of the proposal. No written summary of the terms of the merger was presented; the directors were given no documentation to support the adequacy of $55 price per share for sale of the Company; and the Board had before it nothing more than Van Gorkom's statement of his understanding of the substance of an agreement which he admittedly had never read, nor which any member of the Board had ever seen. . . .

We hold, therefore, that the Trial Court committed reversible error in applying the business judgment rule in favor of the director defendants in this case.

On remand, the Court of Chancery shall conduct an evidentiary hearing to determine the fair value of the shares represented by the plaintiffs' class, based on the intrinsic value of Trans Union on September 20, 1980. . . . Thereafter, an award of damages may be entered to the extent that the fair value of Trans Union exceeds $55 per share.

[Judgment reversed and action remanded]

QUESTIONS

1. Did the court hold that the business judgment rule shielded the directors from personal liability in this case?
2. Upon what facts did the court rely in reaching its decision in this case?
3. Describe the applicable standard of care for determining whether a board of directors' decision was an informed one?

In a takeover situation in which an auction for control of the company develops, market forces must be allowed to operate freely to bring the target's shareholders the best price available for their shares.[9] Still, the business judgment rule will apply to shield board of directors' decisions on how to maximize the price of the shares once the auction has begun.

(3) Protection of Directors. In the wake of court decisions holding directors personally liable for damages for gross negligence and in the wake of the resulting general reluctance of individuals to serve as directors, states have passed statutes modernizing the laws protecting directors. The aim of the various state laws is essentially the same: to alleviate the risk of

personal liability for directors who act in good faith but whose decisions are retrospectively challenged. The laws permit a corporation, by a stockholder-approved amendment to its charter or certificate of incorporation, to protect its directors from monetary liability for duty of care violations (gross negligence), provided they have not acted in bad faith, breached their duty of loyalty, or gained an improper personal benefit.[10] The laws provide for indemnification and advancement of expenses.

(b) ACTION AGAINST DIRECTOR. Actions against directors should be brought by

---

[9]   Forbes Holding v Revlon Inc. (Del Ch) 501 A2d 1239 (1985), aff'd (Del) 506 A2d 173 (1986).

[10]   See Del. Code § 102(b)(7) (1987); NY Bus. Corp. Law § 721–723 (1987); Ohio Gen. Corp. Law § 1701.59 (1986); Ind. Bus. Corp. Law, Ch 35, § 1 (e) (1986); and Mo. Gen. Bus. Corp. Law 351.355 § 2, 7.

the corporation. If the corporation fails to act, as is the case when the directors alleged to be liable control the corporation, shareholders may bring the action in a representative capacity for the corporation.[11]

(c) REMOVAL OF DIRECTOR. Ordinarily, directors are removed by the vote of the shareholders. In some states the board of directors may remove a director and elect a successor on the ground that the director removed (1) did not accept office; (2) failed to satisfy the qualifications for office; (3) was continually absent from the state without a leave of absence granted by the board, generally for a period of six months or more; (4) received a discharge in bankruptcy; (5) was convicted of a felony; (6) was unable to perform the duties of director because of any illness or disability, generally for a period of six months or more; or (7) has been judicially declared of unsound mind.[12]

The RMBCA provides for removal of directors "with or without cause" by a majority vote of the shareholders, unless the articles of incorporation provide that directors may be removed only for cause.[13]

C. OFFICERS, AGENTS, AND EMPLOYEES

Corporations generally have a president, at least one vice president, a secretary, and a treasurer. The duties of these officers are generally set forth in the corporation's bylaws. Commonly included is the duty of the secretary to keep minutes of the proceedings of shareholders and directors. Corporation codes generally expressly permit the same person to be both secretary and treasurer. In larger corporations there is often a recording secretary and a corresponding secretary.

Sometimes the officers are elected by the shareholders, but usually they are appointed by the board of directors. The RMBCA follows the general pattern of providing for the appointment of officers by the board of directors.[14] Ordinarily, no particular formality need be observed in making such appointments. Unless prohibited, a director may hold an executive office.

Officers ordinarily hire the employees and agents of the corporation.

8. Powers of Officers

The officers of a corporation are its agents. Consequently, their powers are controlled by the laws of agency. As in the case of any other agency, the third person has the burden of proving that a particular officer has the authority that such officer purports to have.

The fact that the officer or employee acting on behalf of the corporation is a major shareholder does not give the officer or employee any greater agency powers. Moreover, the person dealing with the officer or employee is charged with knowledge of any limitation on authority contained in the recorded corporate charter.

When the nature of the transaction is unusual, that unusual nature should alert a third person to the necessity of specific authorization from the corporation.[15]

(a) PRESIDENT. It is sometimes held that in the absence of some limitation on authority, the president of a corporation has by virtue of that office the authority to act as agent on behalf of the corporation within the scope of the business in which the corporation is empowered to engage. It has also been held, however, that the president has such broad powers only when the president is the general manager of the corporation. Then such powers stem from the office of general manager, not from that of president. In any event the president does not have authority by virtue of that office to make a contract that, because of its unusual character, would require action by the board of directors.[16] The president, therefore, cannot make a

[11] John v John (Wis App) 450 NW2d 795 (1989).
[12] See California Corporations Code § 807, recognizing grounds (1), (2), (5), and (7).
[13] RMBCA § 8.08 (a).
[14] RMBCA § 8.40 (a).
[15] Kanavos v Hancock Bank & Trust Co. 14 Mass App 326, 439 NE2d 311 (1982).
[16] Molasky Enterprises, Inc. v Carps, Inc. (Mo App) 615 SW2d 83 (1981).

contract to fix long-term or unusual contracts of employment, to bind the corporation as a guarantor, to release a claim of the corporation, or to promise that the corporation will later repurchase shares when issued to a subscriber.

It is ordinarily held that the president of a business corporation is not authorized to execute commercial paper in the name of the corporation. However, the president may do so when authorized by the board of directors to borrow money for the corporation.

(b) OTHER OFFICERS AND EMPLOYEES. The authority of corporate employees and other officers, such as secretary or treasurer, is generally limited to the duties of their offices. However, the authority may be extended by the conduct of the corporation, in accordance with the general principles governing apparent authority based on the con-

duct of the principal. An unauthorized act may, of course, be ratified. The authority of the general manager of the corporation is determined by principles of ordinary agency law.

9.   Liability of Officers

The relationship of the officers to the corporation, like that of the directors, is a fiduciary one. For this reason, the officers are liable for secret profits made in connection with or at the expense of the business of the corporation.

If an officer diverts a corporate opportunity, the corporation may recover from the officer the profit of which the corporation has been thus deprived.

The *Klinicki* case was an action to recover lost profits caused by the diversion of a corporate business opportunity by an officer and majority shareholder.

KLINICKI v LUNDGREN

298 Or 662, 695 P2d 906 (1985)

In April of 1977, F. R. Klinicki and Kim Lundgren incorporated Berlinair, Inc., a closely held Oregon corporation. Lundgren was president and was responsible for developing business. Klinicki was vice president and director and was responsible for operations and maintenance. Klinicki owned one-third of the stock, and Lundgren controlled the remaining stock. Both men were former Pan American pilots who had been laid off while stationed in West Germany. In November of 1977, they met with BFR, a consortium of Berlin travel agents that contract charter flights to warmer climates. The contract with BFR was considered a lucrative business opportunity. After the initial meeting all contacts with BFR were made by Lundgren. In early June, 1978, Lundgren learned that there was a good chance that the BFR contract might be available. He informed a BFR representative that he would make a proposal on behalf of a new company. On July 7, 1978, he incorporated Air Berlin Charter Company (ABC) and was its sole owner. On August 20, 1978, ABC presented BFR with a contract proposal, and after a series of discussions, it was awarded the contract on September 1, 1978. Lundgren effectively concealed from Klinicki his negotiations with BFR and his diversion of the BFR contract to ABC, even though he used Berlinair working time, staff, money, and facilities. Klinicki, as a minority stockholder in Berlinair, brought a derivative action against ABC for diverting a corporate opportunity of Berlinair. ABC and Lundgren defended that there was no diversion of a corporate opportunity because Berlinair did not have the financial ability to undertake the contract. The court ordered the defendants to hold the profit made from the contract and return it to the plaintiff and also ordered that a computation be made of the amount of such profit. The defendants took this decision to the court of appeals, which affirmed the trial court. The matter was thereafter appealed to the Supreme Court of Oregon.

JONES, J. . . . There is no dispute that the corporate opportunity doctrine precludes corporate fiduciaries from diverting to themselves business opportunities in which the corporation has an expectancy, property interest or right, or which in fairness should otherwise belong to the corporation. The doctrine follows from a corporate fiduciary's duty of undivided loyalty to the corporation. ABC agrees that, unless Berlinair's financial inability to undertake the contract makes a difference, the BFR contract was a corporate opportunity of Berlinair.

We first address the issue, resolved by the Court of Appeals in Berlinair's favor, of the relevance of a corporation's financial ability to undertake a business opportunity to proving a diversion of corporate opportunity claim. This is an issue of first impression in Oregon.

The Court of Appeals held that a corporation's financial ability to undertake a business opportunity is not a factor in determining the existence of a corporate opportunity unless the defendant demonstrates that the corporation is technically or de facto insolvent. Without defining these terms, the Court of Appeals specifically placed the burden of proof as to this issue on the fiduciary by saying: "To avoid liability for usurping a corporate opportunity on the basis that the corporation was insolvent, the fiduciary must prove insolvency." The Court of Appeals then concluded "that ABC usurped a corporate opportunity belonging to Berlinair when, acting through Lundgren, the BFR contract was diverted" because nothing in Lundgren's testimony or otherwise in the record suggested that Berlinair was insolvent or was no longer a viable corporate entity. Accordingly, the Court of Appeals held that the constructive trust, injunction, duty to account and other relief granted by the trial court against ABC were appropriate remedies. . . .

One aspect of corporate fiduciary responsibility that has particularly troubled the courts in their search for a rule of thumb is that relating to so-called corporate opportunities. *What are the legal rules to be applied in determining when a corporate official, given an opportunity to make a profitable acquisition (business, lease, land, stock, whatever), can take it for himself rather than turning it over to the corporation?* . . .

[A rule proposed by the American Law Institute in 1984 in a tentative draft concerning principles of corporate governance] permits a director or principal senior executive to deal with his corporation so long as he deals fairly with full disclosure and bears the burden of proving fairness unless the corporate opportunity was rejected by disinterested directors or shareholders. . . .

Where a director or principal senior executive of a close corporation wishes to take personal advantage of a "corporate opportunity," as defined by the proposed rule, the director or principal senior executive must comply strictly with the following procedure:

(1) the director or principal senior executive must promptly offer the opportunity and disclose all material facts known regarding the opportunity to the disinterested directors or, if there is no disinterested director, to the disinterested shareholders. If the director or principal senior executive learns of other material facts after such disclosure, the director or principal senior executive must disclose these additional facts in a like manner before personally taking the opportunity.

The director or principal senior executive may take advantage of the corporate opportunity only after full disclosure and only if the opportunity is rejected by a majority of the disinterested directors or, if there are no disinterested directors, by a majority of the disinterested shareholders. If, after full disclosure, the disinterested directors or shareholders unreasonably fail to reject the offer, the interested director or principal senior executive may proceed to take the opportunity if he can prove the taking was otherwise "fair" to the corporation. Full disclosure to the appropriate corporate body is, however, an absolute condition precedent to the validity of any forthcoming rejection as well as to the availability to the director or principal senior executive of the defense of fairness. . . .

Applying these rules to the facts in this case, we conclude:

1. Lundgren, as director and principal executive officer of Berlinair, owed a fiduciary duty to Berlinair.
2. The BFR contract was a "corporate opportunity" of Berlinair.
3. Lundgren formed ABC for the purpose of usurping the opportunity presented to Berlinair by the BFR contract.
4. Lundgren did not offer Berlinair the BFR contract.
5. Lundgren did not attempt to obtain the consent of Berlinair to his taking of the BFR corporate opportunity.
6. Lundgren did not fully disclose to Berlinair his intent to appropriate the opportunity for himself and ABC.
7. Berlinair never rejected the opportunity presented by the BFR contract.
8. Berlinair never ratified the appropriation of the BFR contract.
9. Lundgren, acting for ABC, misappropriated the BFR contract.

Because of the above, the defendant may not now contend that Berlinair did not have the financial ability to successfully pursue the BFR contract. As stated in proposed Section 5.12(c) of the Principles of Corporate Governance, *supra*, "If the challenging party satisfies the burden of proving that a corporate opportunity was taken without being offered to the corporation, the challenging party will prevail."

This specific conclusion is also backed by what some might call a legal platitude and others might call a legal classic. When placing special burdens on those in positions of trust, it is worthwhile to recall the well-known admonition of Chief Justice Cardozo speaking for the New York Court of Appeals:

> Joint adventurers, like copartners, owe to one another, while the enterprise continues, the duty of the finest loyalty. Many forms of conduct permissible in a workaday world for those acting at arm's length, are forbidden to those bound by fiduciary ties. A trustee is held to something stricter than the morals of the market place. Not honesty alone, but the punctilio of an honor the most sensitive, is then the standard of behavior. As to this there has developed a tradition that is unbending and inveterate. Uncompromising rigidity has been the attitude of courts of equity when petitioned to undermine the rule of undivided loyalty by the "disintegrating erosion" of particular exceptions. . . . Only thus has the level of conduct for fiduciaries been kept at a level higher than that trodden by the crowd. It will not consciously be lowered by any judgment of this court. *Meinhard v. Salmon*, 249 NY 458, 164 NE 545 (1928). . . .

[Judgment affirmed]

Under some state statutes regulating the sale of corporate securities, an officer taking part in a sale that violates the statute is liable without regard to knowledge or lack of knowledge that the sale violated the statute. When the corporation has violated a statute designed to protect health or environment, corporate officers may be held liable for having failed to prevent the violation.

Officers are liable for willful or negligent acts that cause a loss to the corporation.[17] On the other hand, they are not liable for mere errors in judgment committed while exercising their discretion, provided they have acted with reasonable prudence and care.

10.   Agents and Employees

The authority, rights, and liabilities of an agent of a corporation are governed by the same rules applicable as when the principal is a natural person. The authority of corporate employees also is governed by general agency principles.

The fact that a person is acting on behalf of a corporation does not act as a shield from the liability that would be imposed for such acts if done on behalf of a natural person.[18]

D.   LIABILITY

Limited liability is a major reason for utilizing the corporate form of business organization. However, management is not free from all civil and criminal liability simply because the corporate form is used.

11.   Liability of Management to Third Persons

Ordinarily, the management of a corporation (its directors, officers, and executive employees) is not liable to third persons for the effect on such third persons of their management or advice. The liability of a director or officer for misconduct may ordinarily be enforced only by the corporation or by shareholders bringing a derivative action on behalf of the corporation. Ordinarily, directors or officers are not liable to a third person for loss caused by the negligent performance of their duties as directors or officers, even if, because of such negligence the corporation is in turn liable to the third person to whom the corporation owed the duty to use care or was under a contract obligation to render a particular service.

Officers and managers of a corporation are not liable for the economic consequence of their advice on third persons, even if they cause the corporation to refuse to deal with or to break its contract with such third persons, as long as the officers and managers act in good faith to advance the interests of the corporation.

12.   Criminal Liability

Officers and directors, as in the case of agents generally, are personally responsible for any crimes committed by them, even when they act in behalf of the corporation. At the local level they may be criminally responsible for violation of ordinances relating to sanitation, safety, and hours of closing. At the state level they may be criminally liable for conducting a business without obtaining necessary licenses or after the corporate certificate of incorporation has been forfeited.

Some statutes designed to regulate corporate activity provide specifically for fines and

[17]   Bellinzoni v Seland, 128 App Div 2d 583, 512 NYS2d 847 (1987).
[18]   Smith v NiteLife Inc. (Ky.) 777 SW2d 912 (1989).

imprisonment of corporate officers and other individuals responsible for corporate violations. For example, the president of a national food chain corporation was held criminally liable under the federal Food, Drug, and Cosmetic Act on the ground that food in the corporation's warehouse had been exposed to rodent contamination.

The Foreign Corrupt Practices Act makes it a crime to bribe a foreign official or political candidate to use influence to obtain business for an American corporation. The American corporation is subject to a fine, and officers and other individuals are subject to fine and imprisonment.[19]

A corporation itself may be convicted of a criminal offense if it is shown beyond a reasonable doubt that the offense was committed by its agent acting within the scope of the agent's authority.[20] Thus, an incorporated nursing home may be found guilty of criminal recklessness concerning the neglect of a patient.[21] Moreover, a corporation itself may be convicted of a crime involving specific intent, such as theft by swindle or forgery, when it is shown beyond a reasonable doubt that (a) the agent was acting at least in part in furtherance of the corporation's business interests and (b) corporate management authorized, tolerated, or ratified the criminal activity.

13.   Indemnification of Officers, Directors, Employees, and Agents

While performing what they believe to be their duty, officers, directors, employees, and agents of corporations may commit acts for which they are later sued or criminally prosecuted. The RMBCA broadly authorizes the corporation to indemnify such persons if they acted in good faith and in a manner reasonably believed to be in or not opposed to the interests of the corporation and had no reason to believe that their conduct was unlawful.

In some states statutory provision is made requiring the corporation to indemnify directors and officers for reasonable expenses incurred by them in defending unwarranted suits brought against them by shareholders. Such statutes have been adopted to encourage responsible persons to accept positions of corporate responsibility.

14.   Liability for Corporate Debts

Since the corporation is a separate legal person, debts owed by the corporation are ordinarily the obligations of the corporation only. Consequently, neither directors nor officers are individually liable for the corporate debts, even though it may have been their acts that gave rise to the debts.

In some states civil liability for corporate debts is imposed on the officers and directors of the corporation when it improperly engages in business.

15.   Protection of Shareholders

Various devices and limitations have been developed to protect shareholders both from misconduct by management and from the action of the majority of the shareholders. Shareholders may protect themselves by voting at the next annual election for new directors and also for new officers, if the latter are elected. Shareholders may take remedial action at a special meeting called for that purpose. In any case the objecting shareholders may bring a legal action when the management misconduct complained of constitutes a legal wrong.[22]

16.   Civil Liability

A corporation is liable to third persons for the acts of its officers, employees, and agents to the same extent as a natural person is liable for the acts of agents and employees. This means that the ordinary rules of agency law determine the extent to which the corporation is liable to a third person for a contract made or a tort committed by management personnel, employees, and agents.[23]

---

[19]   PL 95–213, 91 Stat 1494, 15 USC § 78m et seq.
[20]   People v Film Recovery Systems Inc. 194 Ill App 3d 79, 141 Ill Dec 44, 550 NE2d 1090 (1990).
[21]   State v Monticello Developers Inc. (Ind App) 502 NE2d 927 (1987).

[22]   Christner v Anderson, Nietzke & Co. 433 Mich 1, 444 NW2d 779 (1989).
[23]   Jenson v Alaska Valuation Service, Inc. (Alaska) 688 P2d 161 (1984).

SUMMARY

To have legal effect, shareholder action must be taken at a regular meeting as specified in the bylaws, or at a special meeting after due notice to shareholders. The presence of a quorum of the voting shareholders is required.

Management of a corporation is under the control of a board of directors elected by the shareholders. The courts will not interfere with the board's discretion in the absence of unusual conduct such as fraud. A director is disqualified from taking part in corporate action when the director has a conflict of interests. Action by directors is usually taken at a properly called meeting of the board. Directors act in a fiduciary capacity in dealing with the corporation. Directors who act in good faith and have exercised reasonable care are not liable for losses resulting from their management decisions. Ordinarily, directors are removed by shareholders.

Officers of a corporation, including a president, vice president, secretary, and treasurer, are usually selected and removed by the board of directors. Officers are agents of the corporation and their powers are governed by the law of agency. Their relations with the corporation are fiduciary in nature, and they are liable for any secret profits and for diverting corporate opportunities to their own advantage.

Directors and officers, as in the case of agents generally, are personally responsible for any crimes they commit, even if they act on behalf of the corporation. The corporation itself may be prosecuted for crimes and is subject to fines if convicted.

The ordinary rules of agency law determine the extent to which a corporation is liable for a contract made or tort committed by a director, officer, corporate agent, or employee.

QUESTIONS AND CASE PROBLEMS

1. What social forces are affected by the rule that a person dealing with a corporate officer is charged with knowledge of any limitation on the officer's authority contained in the recorded corporate charter?
2. What constitutes a quorum at a meeting of shareholders?
3. Roxanne owns 100 of the 10,000 outstanding shares of Microchip International Inc. She disagrees with the future plans of the board of directors. Should she bring a lawsuit against the directors?
4. Larry Phillips was hired for a two-year period as executive secretary of the Montana Education Association (MEA). Six months later he was fired. He then sued MEA for breach of contract and sued the directors and some of the other employees of MEA on the theory that they had caused MEA to break the contract with him and were therefore guilty of the tort of maliciously interfering with his contract with MEA. The evidence showed that the individual defendants, without malice, had induced the corporation to break the contract with Phillips but that this had been done in order to further the welfare of the corporation. Was MEA liable for breach of contract? Were the individual defendants shielded

from personal liability? [Phillips v Montana Education Association, 187 Mont 419, 610 P2d 154]
5. Christy Pontiac, a corporation, was indicted for theft by swindle and forgery involving a GM cash rebate program. Hesli, a middle-management employee of Christy Pontiac, had forged the cash rebate applications for two cars, so that the rebate money was paid to Christy Pontiac instead of to its customers. When confronted by a customer who should have received a rebate, the president of the dealership attempted to negotiate a settlement. The president did not contact GM headquarters until after an investigation was begun by the state attorney general. Christy Pontiac argued that it could not be held liable for a specific intent because since only "natural" persons, as opposed to corporations, can form such intent. Decide. [State v Christy Pontiac-GMC, Inc. (Minn) 354 NW2d 17]
6. Directors must always own stock of the corporation in order to ensure that they will be attentive to their duties. Appraise this statement.
7. Discuss the power of a corporation president to employ a sales manager and to agree that the manager should be paid a stated amount per year plus a percentage of any increase in the dollar volume of sales that might take place.

8. Thywissen owned 60 percent of Flexbin Corp., and Cron owned 40 percent. When they formed the corporation, Thywissen obtained a right of first refusal on a note, which was taken in his own name. He saw this right as a means of protecting Flexbin Corporation and increasing the value of Flexbin's corporate stocks. Due to lack of success, the Flexbin Corp. was liquidated. The "right of first refusal" was worth $92,000. Cron expected to received 40 percent of the proceeds. Thywissen claimed that since the right of first refusal was in his own name, it was a personal right, not a corporate asset. He claimed that he had no legal obligation to Cron, only a "moral obligation" to him. He offered him $7,200. Cron bought suit against Thywissen, claiming that Thywissen had breached his fiduciary duty to him by taking this corporate asset for himself. Decide.

9. Ponder was the president of the Long Beach Motel Hotel Corporation. He requested a quotation from General Electric on air conditioners for the hotel. He was sent a quotation, on the basis of which he sent in a purchase order on behalf of the corporation. General Electric rejected this order made in the name of the corporation and in effect stated that it would sell only to Ponder personally. Ponder was sent a new purchase order that showed him individually as the buyer. He signed his name but then added "Pres." When General Electric sued him for the purchase price, he claimed that he had signed on behalf of the corporation and that General Electric knew that it was dealing with the corporation. Was he bound by the contract? [General Electric Co. v Ponder (La App) 234 So 2d 786]

10. A director of a corporation cannot lend money to the corporation, because that would create the danger of a conflict of interests between the director's status as a director and status as a creditor. Appraise this statement.

11. Hamway and other minority shareholders brought an action against majority shareholders of the Libbie Rehabilitation Center, Inc. (Libbie), including Frank Giannotti, CEO-director, Alex Grossman, president-director, Henry Miller, vice president-director, Ernest Dervishian, secretary and corporate attorney, and Lewis Cowardin, treasurer-director. The minority shareholders contended that the corporation paid excessive salaries to these director-officers and were wasting corporate assets. Prior to coming to Libbie, Giannotti had been a carpet and tile retailer, Grossman a pharmacist, Miller a real estate developer, Dervishian a lawyer, and Cowardin a jeweler. The evidence showed that the extent of their work for the corporation was very limited. For example, Cowardin, Libbie's finance officer who was paid $78,121 in 1985 demonstrated no knowledge of the Medicare and Medicaid programs, the principle source of Libbie's income. Although he claimed to have spent 20 to 25 hours per week on corporate duties, he reported on the tax return for his jewelry business that he spent 75 percent of his working time in that business in 1984. One expert witness of the plaintiff testified that the five men were performing the management function of one individual. The director-officers contend that the business was making a profit and that all salaries were approved by a board of directors that had extensive business experience. Were the directors within their rights to elect themselves officers and set pay for themselves as they saw fit? Did they violate any duty to their shareholders?

12. Anthony Yee was the president of the Waipahu Auto Exchange, a corporation. As part of his corporate duties, he arranged financing for the company. The Federal Services Finance Corporation drew 12 checks payable to the order of the Waipahu Auto Exchange. These were then indorsed by its president, "Waipahu Auto Exchange, Limited, by Anthony Yee, President," and were cashed at two different banks. The Bishop National Bank of Hawaii, on which the checks were drawn, charged its depositor, Federal Services, with the amount of the checks. Federal Services then sued Bishop National Bank to restore to its account the amount of the 12 checks, on the theory that Bishop National Bank had improperly made payment on the checks, because Anthony Yee had no authority to cash them. Did Yee have authority to indorse and cash the checks? [Federal Services Finance Corp. v Bishop National Bank of Hawaii (CA9 Hawaii) 190 F2d 442]

13. E. P. Fournier Co. is a closely held corporation engaged in the sale of new and used automobiles. The board of directors hired Paul Fournier and agreed that he "shall act as general manager with full authority to hire, approve sales, and contribute to policy decisions affecting the interests of the corporation." On the same date Roland Fournier was hired by the board to act as assistant general manager. Paul was president and treasurer of the corporation, and Roland was vice president and secretary. Paul and Roland had a dispute about the roles of their re-

spective sons, who were also employed in the business. Soon thereafter Paul informed Roland that "his services with the company were no longer required" and removed two vehicles from Roland's garage; these vehicles were owned by the corporation but used by Roland. Roland sued the corporation for back pay and benefits, claiming that Paul did not have authority to terminate him unilaterally without authorization from the board of directors. Paul argued that his employment agreement with the board clearly delegated to him all of the board's authority to manage the business, including the power to remove Roland. Decide. [Fournier v Fournier (RI) 479 A2d 708]

14. Rudolph Redmont was the president of Abbott Thinlite Corporation. He left that corporation to run the Circle Corporation, in competition with his former employer. It was claimed that he diverted contracts from his former employer to his new one, having gained the advantage of the specific information of the deals in progress while employed by Abbott. The former employer sued Redmont and Circle Corporation to recover lost profits. Redmont contended that all of the contracts in question were made after he left Abbott, at which time his fiduciary duty to Abbott had ceased. Decide. [Abbott Thinlite Corp. v Redmont (CA2 NY) 475 F2d 85]

15. William Gurtler was president and a board member of Unichem Corporation, which produced and sold chemical laundry products. While president of Unichem, he encouraged his plant manager to leave to join a rival business, which Gurtler was going to join in the near future. Moreover, Gurtler sold Unichem products to his son, G. B. Gurtler, in January of 1982, at a figure substantially below their normal price and on credit, even though G. B. had no credit history. Gurtler made the sales with full knowledge that G. B. was going to start a rival business. Also at that time, Gurtler was aware that his wife was soliciting Unichem employees to join the new Gurtler Chemical Co., and he helped her design Gurtler's label so that it would mirror Unichem's. On February 9, 1982, Gurtler guaranteed a $100,000 loan for Gurtler Chemical Co. with funds to be disbursed after he left Unichem, which occurred on March 12, 1982. On March 15, 1982, he became president of Gurtler Chemical Co. Unichem sued Gurtler for breach of fiduciary duty and for the loss of profits that resulted. Gurtler contended that his sales to G. B. guaranteed needed revenues to Unichem and constituted a sound business decision that should be applauded and that was protected under the business judgment rule. Decide. [Unichem Corp v Gurtler, 148 Ill App 3d 284, 101 Ill Dec 400, 498 NE2d 724]

PART NINE

REAL PROPERTY
AND ESTATES

50

REAL PROPERTY

The law of real property is technical and to a large extent uses a vocabulary drawn from the days of feudalism. Much of the earlier law of real property is no longer of practical importance in the modern business world. The following is therefore a simplified presentation of the subject.

A.   NATURE OF REAL PROPERTY

Real property has special characteristics of permanence and uniqueness. These characteristics have strongly influenced the rules that society has developed to resolve disputes concerning real property.

1.   Definitions

Real property includes (a) land, (b) buildings and fixtures, and (c) rights in the land of another.

(a) LAND. **Land** means more than the surface of the earth. It comprises the soil and all things of a permanent nature affixed to the ground, such as herbs, grass, or trees, and other growing, natural products. The term also includes the waters upon the ground and things that are embedded beneath the surface. For example, coal, oil, and marble embedded beneath the surface are part of the land.

Technically, land is considered to extend downward to the earth's center and upward indefinitely. The Uniform Aeronautics Act states that the owner of the land owns the space above, subject to the right of aircraft in flight that do not interfere with the use of the land and are not dangerous to persons or property lawfully on the land.[1]

(b) BUILDINGS AND FIXTURES. A **building** includes any structure placed on or beneath the surface of land, without regard to its purpose or use. A **fixture** is personal property that has been attached to the earth or placed in a building in such a way or under such circumstances that it is deemed part of the real property.

(c) RIGHTS IN LAND OF ANOTHER. These rights include easements, such as the right to cross another's land, and **profits**, such as the right to take coal from another's land.

2.   Easements

An **easement** is not only a right in the land of another, but also a right that belongs to the land that is benefited. The benefited land is called the **dominant tenement,** and the land that is subject to the easement is called the **servient tenement.**

Since an easement is an interest in land, an oral promise to create an easement is not binding, because of the statute of frauds.

(a) CREATION OF EASEMENT. An easement may be created in several ways:

1.   An easement may be created by deed.
2.   An easement may be created by implication when one conveys part of the land that has been used as a dominant estate in relation to the part retained. To illustrate, if water or drain pipes run from the part conveyed through the part retained, there is an implied right to have such use continued. In order for an easement to be implied in such a case, the use must be apparent, continuous, and reasonably necessary.
3.   An easement may also be created by implication when the easement is necessary to the use of the land conveyed. This ordinarily arises when one subdivides land and sells a portion to which no entry can be made except over the land retained or over the land of a stranger. The grantee's right to use the land retained by the grantor for the purpose of going to and from the land conveyed is known as a **way of necessity.**[2]
4.   An easement may be created by estoppel,

---

[1]   The Uniform Aeronautics Act (UAA) has been adopted in Arizona, Delaware, Georgia, Hawaii, Idaho, Indiana, Maryland, Minnesota, Missouri, Montana, Nevada, New Jersey, North Carolina, North Dakota, Pennsylvania, South Carolina, South Dakota, Tennessee, Utah, Vermont, and Wisconsin, but was withdrawn by the Commissioners on Uniform State Laws in 1943.

[2]   Canei v Cullex (W Va) 374 SE2d 523 (1988).

as when the grantor states that the plot conveyed is bounded by a street. In such a case, if the grantor owns the adjoining land, the public cannot be denied the right to use the area that the owner has described as a street.

5. An easement may be created by prescription by adverse use for a statutory period. No easement is acquired if the use of the land is with the permission of the owner. This adverse use by which an easement is acquired is similar to the adverse possession by which title is acquired, as discussed in Section 26 of this chapter.

(b) TERMINATION OF EASEMENT. Once an easement has been granted, it cannot be destroyed by the act of the grantor. A "revocation" attempted without the easement owner's consent has no effect.

An easement may be lost by nonuse when there are surrounding circumstances that show an intent to abandon the easement.[3] For example, when a surface transit system had an easement to maintain trolley tracks, it could be found that there was an abandonment of the easement when the tracks were removed and when all surface transportation was discontinued. Likewise, when the owner of the easement planted a flower bed on the land across the end of the path of the easement, the intent to abandon the easement was evident.

3. Licenses

A **license** is a personal, revocable privilege to perform an act or series of acts upon the land of another. Unlike an easement, a license is not an interest in land. The person allowed to come into the house to use the telephone has a license. The advertising company that has permission to paint a sign on the side of a building also has a license.

A license may be terminated at the will of the licensor and continues only as long as the licensor is the owner of the land.

4. Liens

Real property may be subject to liens that arise by the voluntary act of the owner of the land. For example, the lien of a mortgage is created when the owner voluntarily borrows money and the land is made security for the repayment of the debt. Liens may also arise involuntarily, as in the case of tax liens, judgment liens, and mechanics' liens. In the case of taxes and judgments the liens provide a means for enforcing the obligations of the owner of the land to pay the taxes or the judgment.

Mechanics' liens give persons furnishing labor and materials in the improvement of real estate the right to proceed against the real estate for the collection of the amounts due them.

5. Duration and Extent of Ownership

A person's interest in real property may be defined in terms of the period of time for which the person will remain the owner, as (a) a fee simple estate or (b) a life estate. These estates are termed **freehold estates.** At the time of creation of a freehold estate, a termination date is not known. A life estate may be subject to a condition or may expire or terminate upon the happening of a specified contingency. Although a person may own property for a specified number of years, this interest is not regarded as a freehold estate; it is a **leasehold estate,** subject to special rules of law.

(a) FEE SIMPLE ESTATE. An **estate in fee,** a **fee simple,** or a **fee simple absolute** lasts forever. The owner of such a fee has the absolute and entire interest in the land. The important characteristics of this estate are as follows: (1) it is alienable, or transferable, during life; (2) it is alienable by will; (3) it descends to heirs generally if not devised (transferred by will); (4) it is subject to rights of the owner's surviving spouse; and (5) it is liable for debts of the owner before or after death.

(b) LIFE ESTATE. A **life estate** (or life tenancy), as its name indicates, lasts only during the life of a person (ordinarily, its owner).

[3]   Dean v Mod Properties, Ltd. (Fla App) 528 So 2d 432 (1988).

Upon the death of the person by whose life the estate was measured, the owner of the life estate has no interest remaining to pass to heirs or by will.

B. FIXTURES

By the concept of fixtures, personal property changes to real property, and third persons and creditors may acquire rights therein.

6. Definition

A **fixture** is personal property that is attached to the earth or placed in a building in such a way or under such circumstances that it is deemed part of the real property.

A person buys a refrigerator, an air conditioner, a furnace, or some other item that is used in a building, and then has the item installed. The question of whether the item is a fixture and therefore part of the building can arise in a variety of situations. (a) The real estate tax assessor assesses the building and adds in the value of the item, on the theory that it is part of the building. (b) The buyer of the item owns and then sells the building, and the new owner of the building claims that the item stays with the building. (c) The buyer places a mortgage on the building, and the mortgagee claims that the item is bound by the mortgage. (d) The buyer is a tenant in the building in which the item is installed, and the landlord claims that the item must stay in the building when the tenant leaves. (e) The buyer does not pay in full for the item, and the seller of the item has a security interest that the seller asserts against the buyer of the item or against the landlord of the building in which the buyer installs the item. The seller of the item may also be asserting a claim against the mortgagee of the building or against the buyer of the building.

The determination of the rights of these parties depends upon the common law of fixtures, as occasionally modified by statute.

7. Tests of a Fixture

In the absence of an agreement between the parties, the courts apply three tests to determine whether the personal property has become a fixture.

(a) ANNEXATION. Generally, the personal property becomes a fixture if it is so attached to the realty that it cannot be removed without materially damaging the realty or destroying the personal property itself. If the property is so affixed as to lose its specific identity, such as bricks in a wall, it becomes part of the realty. When railroad tracks are so placed as to be immovable, they are fixtures.

(b) ADAPTATION. Personal property especially adapted or suited to the use made of the building may constitute a fixture.

(c) INTENT. The true test is the intention of the person affixing the property.[4] Intent is considered as of the time the property was affixed. In the absence of direct proof of such intent, it is necessary to resort to the nature of the property, the method of its attachment, and all the surrounding circumstances to determine the intent.

In the *Premonstratensian Fathers* case the court considered all three tests in deciding if refrigeration equipment had become a fixture.

---

[4]   Harris v Rapke, 138 Misc 2d 429, 524 NYS2d 1005 (1988).

PREMONSTRATENSIAN FATHERS v BADGER MUTUAL FIRE INS. CO.

46 Wis 2d 362, 175 NW2d 337 (1970)

In 1958, a supermarket was constructed by Jacobs Realty Corporation and was owned by that corporation. The market contained five large walk-in coolers or refrigerators. Title to the market was thereafter transferred to the Premonstratensian Fathers and was insured against fire by Badger Mutual Insurance Company. The building was severely damaged by fire, and the insurer paid approximately $80,000 for the building damage. The Fathers claimed an additional $20,000 for the destruction of the coolers. The insurer refused to pay this amount, asserting that the coolers were not owned by the Fathers. From a judgment for the Fathers, the insurer appealed.

HANSE, J. . . . If the coolers are determined to be common-law fixtures, and were such at the time of the construction of the building and the installation of the coolers, then they would have passed to the Fathers under the warranty deed of March 7, 1960, and they would be insured under the terms of the policy. The issue then is whether these coolers constitute fixtures.

The rule which has developed . . . as to what constitutes a fixture is not really a comprehensive definition, but rather a statement of the factors which are to be applied to the facts and circumstances of a particular case to determine whether or not the property in question does constitute a fixture. . . .

Annexation

. . . An object will not acquire the status of a fixture unless it is in some manner or means . . . attached or affixed, either actually or constructively, to the realty. . . . The trial court ably pointed out the physical facts which led to its conclusion that there is indeed annexation in this case. The more important of these are as follows: (1) The exterior walls of the cooler, in four instances, constituted the interior wall of another room. (2) In the two meat coolers, a meat hanging and tracking system was built into the coolers. These tracks were used to move large cuts of meats from the cooler area into the meat preparation areas, and were suspended from the steel girders of the building structure by means of large steel bolts. These bolts penetrated through the roof of the cooler supporting wooden beams, which, in turn, supported the tracking system. The tracking in the coolers was a part of a system of tracking throughout the rear portion of the supermarket. (3) The coolers were attached to hardwood plank which was, in turn, attached to the concrete floor of the supermarket. The attachment of the plank to the floor was accomplished through the use of a ramsetting gun. The planks were laid on the floor, and the bolts were driven through them into the concrete floor, where they then exploded, firmly fixing the coolers into place. There was a material placed on the planks which served both as an adhesive and as an insulation. (4) The floor of the coolers was specially sloped during the construction of the building so that the slope would carry drainage into a specially constructed drain in the concrete. In addition, four of the coolers were coated with a protective coating to seal the floors. In the freezer, a special concrete buildup was constructed in the nature of a trough, the purpose of which was to carry away moisture as frozen chickens melted. (5) A refrigeration unit was built into each cooler. The unit was suspended from the ceiling of the cooler, and tubing was run through the wall of the cooler to compressors located elsewhere in the store. (6) Electric lights and power receptacles were built into each cooler and were connected by electrical wiring through the walls and the ceiling of the cooler to the store's electrical power supply. (7) The walls of the cooler were interlocked, and set into the splines, the hardwood planks ramset into the concrete floor, in tongue and groove fashion.

These factors adequately support the conclusion that the coolers were indeed physically annexed to the premises. The insurers argue that the coolers were removable without material injury to the premises, which detracts from the annexation. There was a dispute in the evidence introduced at the trial, with the insurers' expert testifying that this type of cooler was easily severable from the building, while one of the members of the Jacobs family testified that when he removed some of the bolts from the floor following the fire, large sections of concrete would crack on the floor. This was a conflict for resolution by the trial court. In any event, the element of removability without material damage to the building no longer enjoys the position of prominence in the law of fixtures which it once held. It is now only one of the factors which is to be considered by the trial court. . . .

Adaptation

Adaptation refers to the relationship between the chattel and the use which is made of the realty to which the chattel is annexed. The use of the realty was that of a retail grocery, commonly known as a supermarket. This was the intent of the parties at the time of the construction of the building, and the intent of the parties throughout the entire history of the business. The fact of operation has borne out this intent. In a business which carries fresh foods, frozen foods, produce, meats and butter, coolers used for storage and handling of these perishables are patently related to the use of the building. In fact, it would be hard to picture any equipment more closely related to the operation of a supermarket, where large quantities of perishables must, of necessity, be purchased for storage and processing.

The insurers raise a number of points to dispute this finding. They state: The coolers were not custom made; the coolers are useful not to the building, but to the use to which the building is put; the coolers could have been used anywhere; other coolers could have been used. There is no requirement that the coolers be custom made, but only that they be adapted to the use to which the building is put. The test here is not the adaptability to the building, but the adaptability to the use to which the building is put. The fact that other coolers could have been used, or that these coolers could have been used elsewhere, does not alter the fact that there was a close connection between these coolers and the retail grocery business conducted on the property. . . .

Intent

This court has repeatedly held that intent is the primary determinant of whether a certain piece of property has become a fixture. . . .

In its decision, the trial court found, as a reasonable and legitimate inference from all the facts and circumstances surrounding the placement of the coolers onto the realty, that there was an intention that the coolers become a permanent accession to the realty; that when Jacobs Realty Corporation conveyed the land together with all buildings and improvements thereon to Jacobs Brothers Stores, Inc., the intention still prevailed that the coolers were a permanent accession to the realty; and that the same intention still prevailed when Jacobs Brothers Stores, Inc., conveyed the building and improvements to the plaintiff, and when the plaintiff leased the premises (the land, with all buildings and improvements thereon) back to the corporation as lessee. . . .

The coolers were fixtures when installed; passed to Jacobs Brothers Stores, Inc., through the warranty deed; subsequently passed to the Fathers through that warranty deed; and are in fact fixtures within the meaning of the coverage clause of the insurance policy in this case. . . .

[Judgment affirmed]

QUESTIONS

1. Which party to the lawsuit had installed the coolers?
2. What difference would it make whether the coolers were or were not fixtures?
3. Does the adaptation test require that the goods be made especially for use in the particular building?

The fact that machinery installed in a plant would be very difficult and expensive to move and so delicate that the moving would cause damage and unbalancing is significant in reaching the conclusion that the owner of the plant had installed the equipment as a permanent addition and thus had the intent that would make the equipment become fixtures. When the floors in a large apartment house are of concrete that is covered with a thin sheet of plywood to which is stapled wall-to-wall carpeting, the carpeting constitutes a fixture that cannot be removed from the building. Removal would probably destroy the carpeting, since it was cut to size. In addition, the carpeting is necessary to make the building livable as an apartment.

8. Movable Machinery and Equipment

Machinery and equipment that is movable is ordinarily held not to constitute fixtures, even though, in order to move it, it is necessary to unbolt it from the floor or to disconnect electrical wires or water pipes.

It is ordinarily held that refrigerators, freezers, and gas and electric ranges are not fixtures and do not lose their character as personal property when they are readily removable after disconnecting pipes or unplugging wires. A portable window air conditioner that rests on a rack that is affixed to the window sill by two screws and is connected directly to the building only by an electric cord plug is not a fixture.

The mere fact that an item may be unplugged, however, does not establish that it is not a fixture. For example, a computer and its related hardware constituted fixtures when there was such a mass of wires and cables under the floor that the installation gave the impression of permanence.

9. Trade Fixtures

Equipment attached by a tenant to a rented building and used in a trade or business is ordinarily removable by the tenant when the tenant permanently leaves the premises. Such equipment is commonly called a **trade fixture.**[5]

C. LIABILITY TO THIRD PERSONS FOR CONDITION OF REAL PROPERTY

In the case of real estate, liability is ordinarily based upon occupancy. That is, the person in possession may be liable for harm caused to third persons by a condition of the premises, even though the occupant is not the owner but is merely a tenant renting the premises.

---

[5]   B. Kreisman & Co. v First Arlington National Bank, 91 Ill App 3d 47, 47 Ill Dec 757, 415 NE2d 1070 (1981).

10.   Status-of-Plaintiff Common Law Rule

Under the common law, liability to a person injured on real estate was controlled by the status of the injured person, that is, whether the person injured was a trespasser, a licensee, or an invitee. A different duty was owed by the occupier of land to persons in each of these three categories.[6]

(a) TRESPASSERS. As to **trespassers**, the occupier ordinarily owes only the duty of refraining from causing intentional harm once the presence of the trespasser is known. The occupier is not under any duty to warn of dangers or to make the premises safe to protect the trespasser from harm. The most significant exception to this rule arises in the case of small children. Even when they are trespassers, they are generally afforded greater protection through the **attractive nuisance doctrine.** For example, the owner of a private residential swimming pool was liable for the drowning of a 5-year-old trespasser when the owner did not maintain adequate fencing around the pool. The court reasoned that the placing of such fencing would not have imposed a great burden.

(b) LICENSEES. As to **licensees**, who are on the premises with the permission of the occupier, the latter owes the duty of warning of nonobvious dangers that are known to the occupier. For example, a host must warn a guest of such dangers. When a sliding glass door is "invisible" if the patio lights are on and the house lights are off, the host must warn guests of the presence of the glass and is liable if the guest is injured in shattering the glass.

However, the occupier owes no duty to the licensee to take any steps to learn of the presence of dangers unknown to the occupier.

(c) INVITEES. **Invitees** are persons whose presence is sought to further the economic interest of the occupier. For example, customers are invitees. An occupier has a duty to take reasonable steps to discover any danger and a duty to warn the invitee or to correct the danger. For example, a store must make a reasonable inspection of the premises to determine that there is nothing on the floor that would be dangerous, such as a slippery substance that might cause a patron to fall. The store must either correct the condition or appropriately rope off the danger area or give suitable warning. If the occupier of the premises fails to conform to the degree of care described and if harm results to an invitee on the premises, the occupier is liable for such harm.

In most states the courts have expanded the concept of invitees beyond the category of those persons whose presence will economically benefit the occupier. Invitees now usually include members of the public who are invited when it is apparent that such persons cannot be reasonably expected to make an inspection of the premises before making use of them and that they would not be making repairs to correct any dangerous condition. Some courts have also made inroads into the prior law by treating a recurring licensee, such as a letter carrier, as an invitee.

In the *Lucas* case the court was asked to abolish the distinction between an invitee and a licensee.

---

[6]   Huyck v Hecla Mining Co. 101 Idaho 299, 612 P2d 142 (1980).

LUCAS v B. JONES FORD LINCOLN MERCURY
(Miss App) 518 So 2d 646 (1988)

Joyce Lucas left her youngest son, Mark, at the Buddy Jones Ford dealership so that her husband, an employee there, could babysit Mark while Joyce kept an appointment with her doctor. After her appointment, Joyce returned for Mark.

> She parked her automobile and walked across the lot toward the service area of the dealership, where her husband worked. When she reached the freight ramp, she slipped and fell on ice that had accumulated because of a severe winter storm earlier in the day. Joyce injured her arm when she fell. She charged Buddy Jones with the negligent maintenance of the entrances to its business. Jones argued that Joyce was a licensee, not an invitee as she contended. From a judgment in favor of Buddy Jones, Joyce appealed.

ZUCCARO, J. . . . Lucas argues that she was not a licensee, but was instead an invitee. The basis for this contention is the fact that Buddy Jones Ford had on occasion encouraged the relatives of employees to pick up payment checks, so that the employee would not have to leave the job site. Thus, as Lucas had an implied invitation, Buddy Jones Ford owed to her a duty of ordinary care to make the premises safe. . . .

In looking to the facts presented in the case, we must note that on the date in question, Lucas was not going to Buddy Jones Ford to pick up her husband's check. Instead, as she stated in her deposition, she was on her way to a doctor's appointment, and had dropped her son off so that her husband might "babysit." When the accident occurred, Lucas was simply in the process of picking up her son so that they could go home. Further, in her deposition, Lucas admitted that there was no business purpose in her visit to Buddy Jones Ford, and that the business derived no benefit from her visit. The stop was made simply for her personal convenience.

In drawing the long standing, and traditional distinction between a "licensee" and an "invitee" it must be noted that a licensee is a person who enters upon the property of another for his own convenience, pleasure or benefit pursuant to the licenses or implied permission of the owner. . . . On the other hand, an invitee is a person who goes upon the premises of another in answer to an express or implied invitation of the owner or occupier for their *mutual advantage*. . . . From this distinction, and as can be seen from Lucas' own testimony, she clearly falls into the category of a "licensee."

The significance in drawing the above distinction can be found in the duty owed by the landowner, in the present case Buddy Jones Ford, to a licensee. A landowner owes a licensee the bare duty to refrain from willfully or wantonly injuring him. There is one recognized exception, in that ordinary reasonable care is required where the landowner engages in active conduct and the plaintiff's presence is known to him. This exception is not applicable where the licensee is injured as a result of the condition of the premises, or passive negligence. Conversely, a landowner always owes to a business invitee the duty to exercise reasonable care for said invitee's safety. As Lucas was a mere licensee, not falling within the above exception, Buddy Jones Ford owed to her only the duty not to willfully or wantonly harm her. The failure of Buddy Jones Ford to warn her of the open and obvious ice could hardly be said to rise to this level.

In *Graves v. Massey*, 227 Miss. 848, 87 So.2d 270 (1956), this Court stated that where the undisputed facts disclose that a plaintiff was a mere licensee, the court should not allow the jury to consider the question of whether or not his status was otherwise. The case presently at bar presents a similar situation, in that Lucas, in her own deposition, admitted that Buddy Jones Ford derived no advantage from her husband being allowed to babysit their son. As such, the lower court was correct in finding Lucas a licensee. Summary judgment was properly granted.

Additionally, we feel compelled to add that the views expressed in this opinion should not be construed as an indication that Buddy Jones Ford would be liable to Lucas if she were an invitee. Were appellant an invitee, (which as previously stated she obviously was not), Buddy Jones Ford would have only owed her the duty of exercising reasonable care to keep the premises safe, or of warning Lucas of *hidden or concealed perils* of which appellee knew or should have known in the exercise of reasonable care. The ice which caused Lucas to fall was in no way hidden or concealed.

Lucas next argues that if this Court cannot find her to be an invitee, that it should abolish the long-held distinction between an invitee and a licensee. In this context it must be noted that this Court has continuously and regularly adhered to the common law distinction between an invitee and a licensee since the world was young. Further, in very recent decisions, we have specifically refused to abandon our long-held recognition of the categories now in question.

Prosser and Keeton note that recently courts considering abandoning the distinction between an invitee and a licensee have refused to do so. *Prosser and Keeton on Torts,* § 62 (5th ed. 1984). As such, this Court will not at this time do away with a legal principle so long held and thoroughly developed. The assignment of error is meritless. . . .

[Judgment affirmed]

QUESTIONS

1. Was Lucas an invitee or a licensee?
2. Upon what basis did she allege she was an invitee?
3. Did the court abolish the distinction between an invitee and a licensee? Explain.

11.   Negligence Rule

A number of courts have begun ignoring these common law distinctions and holding the occupier liable according to ordinary negligence standards. That is, when the occupier as a reasonable person should foresee from the circumstances that harm would be caused a third person, the occupier has the duty to take reasonable steps to prevent such harm, without regard to whether the potential victim would be traditionally classified as a trespasser, a licensee, or an invitee.[7]

12.   Intermediate Rule

Some courts have taken an intermediate position. They have merely abolished the distinction between licensees and invitees, so that the occupier owes the same duty of care to all lawful visitors. Whether one is a licensee or an invitee is merely a circumstance to be considered by the jury in applying the ordinary rule of negligence.

In some states the distinction between licensees and invitees has been retained in name but destroyed in fact. In these states an occupier is required to warn the licensee of unknown dangers of which the occupier in the exercise of reasonable care should have known. Or a licensee may be classified as an invitee.[8]

13.   Recreational Use Statutes

Most states have enacted a statute commonly referred to as a **recreational use** statute. Such statutes provide that a landowner owes to persons using the property for recreational purposes and without charge, no duty to keep the property safe for entry or use. In addition, no duty is imposed on the landowner to give any warning of a dangerous condition or structure on the property.

In the *Monteville* case an action was brought against a parish for injuries sustained as a result of a defect in a boat ramp at a public boat-launching facility.

---

[7]   Rowland v Christian, 69 Cal 2d 108, 70 Cal Rptr 97, 443 P2d 561 (1968).

[8]   Caroff v Liberty Lumber Co. 146 NJ Super 353, 369 A2d 983 (1977) (holding that a public officer, such as a police officer or health inspector, who enters premises in the performance of official duties, has the same status as a business invitee when injured because of a condition of the premises).

MONTEVILLE v TERREBONNE PARISH CON. GOV.

(La) 567 So 2d 1097 (1990)

Monteville launched his boat from a trailer at the Cocodrie boat launching and vehicle/trailer parking facility, which is operated by the Terrebonne Parish Consolidated Government. One wheel of the trailer became caught in an underwater hole as he was pulling the trailer out of the water. Monteville tried to pull the trailer out of the hole by rapidly accelerating the truck, but this maneuver caused a sudden jerk of the vehicle as the wheel was pulled from the hole. As a result of this episode, Monteville suffered both property damage to his trailer and injuries to his back. The premises where the injury took place include a fisherman's landing store, a cement ramp, and clam shell driveways and parking areas. Monteville sued the parish government and its insurer, alleging that the parish's negligent maintenance of the boat launch caused his injuries. The parish government moved for summary judgment on the grounds that the Recreational Use Statutes absolve it from any mere negligence in maintaining the facility. From a judgment in favor of the parish, Monteville appealed.

DENNIS, J. . . . The Recreational Use Statutes are in derogation of common or natural right and, therefore, are to be strictly interpreted, and must not be extended beyond their obvious meaning. . . .

The stated goal of the Recreational Use Statutes is "to encourage owners of land to make land and water areas available to the public for recreational purposes by limiting their liability toward persons entering thereon for such purposes". . . . If a suitable tract is properly dedicated to one or more of the specified recreational purposes, the landowner or occupier's exposure to liability to a person who enters or uses the premises for such a recreational purpose is drastically limited. In such cases, the owner owes no duty of care to keep the premises safe or to give warnings of hazards, use, structure or activity on the premises. However, there is no limitation of liability for willful or malicious failure to guard or warn against a dangerous condition, structure, use or activity, or for injury when the premises are used as a commercial recreational development or facility or used primarily for a commercial, recreational enterprise for profit. . . .

The purpose of the Recreational Use Statutes, their legislative history and the state of the law at the time of original enactment indicate that the legislature intended to confer immunity only on owners of private lands. The texts of the statutes are silent on the subjects of sovereign, state, or governmental immunity. Consequently, there being at least a reasonable doubt about the meaning of the Recreational Use Statutes on this issue, the Statutes must be strictly construed as making the least rather than the most change in the preexisting general law. Accordingly, we conclude that the qualified immunity offered by the Recreational Use Statutes must be interpreted strictly as a legislated inducement granted only to the owners of large acreages of private land to open them to the public as outdoor recreational areas.

As other courts and commentators have noted, many aspects of the enactment of the recreational use-immunity legislation strongly indicate that it was intended to benefit only private land owners. The history of the legislative movement indicates that it began as a response to the efforts of individual forest owners, sportsmen and conservationists who wanted to make private lands more available for recreational purposes. . . . The purpose of limiting liability is explicitly stated in the commentary of the model act, from which virtually all states' acts are derived, to be that of encouraging private owners to make their land available for the recreation of the public. . . .

Construing the Recreational Use Statute strictly . . . we conclude that the Recreational Use Statutes were not intended to apply to public lands or to grant immunity to the state, its agencies or subdivisions. . . .

Because the purpose of the Recreational Use Statutes was to induce owners of large, remote acreages to dedicate suitable tracts for these particular recreational purposes, and because it was unrealistic to expect owners of farms, forests or other large, remote tracts to undertake the heavy cost of monitoring and maintaining these vast and remote lands for safe public use, it was thought necessary to free the owners of this burden by granting them limited tort immunity in order to persuade them to dedicate large acreages for these recreational purposes. By contrast, smaller readily accessible tracts of land are less apt to be suitable for the specified recreational purposes and are less costly for the owner to have monitored and maintained due to their size and proximity to population and urban services. Consequently, in view of the purpose and underlying policy considerations of the Recreational Use Statutes, and in light of the many cogent reasons for construing them narrowly and in keeping with their purpose, the statutes must be strictly interpreted to limit liability only when the recreational activity takes place on large, remote acreage dedicated to and suitable for one of the specified recreational purposes. . . .

Accordingly, this court [has] held that the legislature did not intend to grant tort immunity to all premises open for swimming, even though "swimming" is included within the statutory definition of "recreational purposes," because the purpose of the statutes is to confer immunity only on "open and undeveloped expanses of property" suitable for the type of recreational activities enumerated.

By the same token, in instances when the activity of the entrant is not one of those enumerated by the statute that can be accommodated only on large expanses of open and undeveloped lands, courts have held that the recreational use acts do not apply. . . .

Moreover, an owner who does not evidence an intent to permit the public to enter without charge for recreational use may not invoke the recreational use statute's protective benefits against liability. *Gibson v. Keith*, 492 A.2d 241 (Del.1985). This case arose from a swimming accident at a water hole in a gravel pit in an isolated area. The plaintiff, a 17 year old minor, suffered paralytic injuries when he dove into shallow water from a rope swing affixed to a nearby tree. The defendants denied giving him permission to enter and swim in the borrow pit. The Delaware Supreme Court held that the recreational use statute may only be invoked to limit the liability of real property owners who directly or indirectly invite or permit without charge the public at large to use their property for recreational purposes. . . .

Applying the foregoing precepts, we conclude that, even if the boat launching facility had been privately owned, the Recreational Use Statutes would not be applicable to afford qualified immunity in the present case. The premises which the defendant opened to the public was not a large, remote or open and undeveloped expanse of land. It was instead a fully developed 5.21 acre boat launching and vehicle/trailer parking facility containing a fisherman's landing store, a cement ramp and clam shell driveways and parking areas, located strategically between a state highway and a navigable bayou. The premises was small, readily accessible and, thus, much less costly to maintain and monitor than a large, remote tract more difficult in approach, size and arrangement. Construing the Recreational Use Statutes strictly and in conformity with the legislative purpose, it is evident that the parish government's facility is not the type of open and undeveloped expanse of land that the legislature sought to induce owners to dedicate to ultimate recreational purposes.

Although we conclude that the Recreational Use Statutes are not applicable to the parish government or to the particular tract of land involved for the reasons assigned, it should be noted that the summary judgment was incorrectly granted for an additional reason. Even if the Recreational Use Statutes were applicable, the moving party, the parish government, did not carry its burden of showing that the plaintiff entered or used the premises for a recreational purpose. The summary judgment evidence shows only that he launched and retrieved a boat. It does not sustain the mover's burden of proof that the plaintiff entered or used the premises for recreational, as opposed to commercial or work-related, boating activities.

[Judgment reversed and action remanded]

QUESTIONS

1. What is the purpose of limiting liability under recreational use statutes?
2. When will an owner of property not be able to invoke the recreational use statute?
3. What was the basis for the court's decision?

D.   CO-OWNERSHIP OF REAL PROPERTY

All interests in particular real property may be held in severalty, that is, by one person alone. As explained in Chapter 20, ownership in severalty also exists when title is held in the form of "*A* or *B*."

14.   Multiple Ownership

Several persons may have concurrent interests in the same real property. The forms of multiple ownership for real property are the same as those for personal property.[9]

When co-owners sell property, they hold the proceeds of sale by the same kind of tenancy as they held the original property.

15.   Condominiums

A **condominium** is a combination of co-ownership and individual ownership. For example, persons owning an office building or an apartment house by condominium are co-owners of the land and of the halls, lobby, elevators, stairways, exits, surrounding land, in-

cinerator, laundry rooms, and other areas used in common. Each apartment or office in the building, however, is individually owned by its occupant.

(a) CONTROL AND EXPENSE. In some states the owners of the various units in the condominium have equal voice in the management and share an equal part of its expenses. In others, control and liability for expenses are shared by a unit owner in the same ratio that the value of the unit bears to the value of the entire condominium project. In all states the unit owners have an equal right to use the common areas.

The owner of each condominium unit makes such repairs as are required by the owner's deed or contract of ownership, and the owner is prohibited from making any major change that would impair or damage the safety or value of an adjoining unit.

(b) COLLECTION OF EXPENSES FROM UNIT OWNER. When a unit owner fails to pay the owner's share of taxes, operating expenses, and repairs, it is commonly provided that a lien may be entered against that owner's unit for the amount due.

(c) TORT LIABILITY. Most condominium projects fail to make provision as to the liabil-

---

[9]   See Chapter 20.

ity of unit owners for a tort occurring in the common areas. A few states expressly provide that when a third person is injured in the common areas, a suit may only be brought against the condominium association, and any judgment recovered is a charge against the association, to be paid off as a common expense. When the condominium association is incorporated, the same result should be obtained by applying ordinary principles of corporation law, under which liability for torts occurring on the premises of the corporation are not the liability of the individual shareholders.

(d) COOPERATIVES DISTINGUISHED. Ownership in a condominium is to be distinguished from ownership in a **cooperative**. An apartment cooperative is typically a corporation renting apartments to persons who are also owners of stock of the corporation. The apartment complex is owned only by the corporation. The only "ownership" interests of the stockholders are as tenants of their respective apartments or offices.

(e) ADVANTAGES OF CONDOMINIUM OWNERSHIP. The owner of a condominium unit has the benefits of limited liability, tax deductions, and the ownership of property that can be transferred or sold.

(1) Freedom from Enterprise Liability. The owner of a unit is not personally liable for an enterprise liability, nor may the unit of the owner be taken to pay for such a liability.

(2) Transferability of Unit. The condominium unit is property that the unit owner can transfer as freely as any other kind of property.

(3) Tax Deductions. A deduction for a share of the mortgage interest and property taxes paid may be claimed by the unit owners on their individual income tax returns. Over a period of time, the unit owner can thus enjoy a tax savings that in effect will lower the cost of the condominium unit.

E.   TRANSFER OF REAL PROPERTY BY DEED

Although many of the technical limitations of the feudal and earlier common law days have disappeared, much of the law relating to the modern deed originated in those days.

16.   Definitions

A **deed** is an instrument or writing by which an owner or **grantor** transfers or conveys an interest in land to a new owner, called a **grantee** or transferee.

Unlike a contract, no consideration is required to make a deed effective. Although consideration is not required to make a valid deed or transfer of title by deed, the absence of consideration may be evidence to show that the transfer is made by the owner in fraud of creditors, who may then be able to set aside the transfer.

Real property may either be sold or given as a gift. However, a deed is necessary to transfer title to land, even if it is a gift.

17.   Classification of Deeds

Deeds may be classified in terms of the interest conveyed as (a) a **quitclaim deed,** which transfers merely whatever interest, if any, the grantor may have in the property, without specifying that interest in any way, and (b) a **warranty deed,** which purports to transfer a specified interest and which warrants or guarantees that such interest is transferred.

A deed may also be classified as a common law deed or a statutory deed. A **common law deed** is a long form that sets forth the details of the transaction. A **statutory deed** in substance merely recites that a named person is making a certain conveyance to a named grantee.

18.   Execution of Deeds

Ordinarily, a deed must be signed, by signature or mark, or sealed by the grantor. In order to have the deed recorded, statutes generally require that two or more witnesses sign the deed and that the grantor then acknowledge the deed before a notary public or other officer. In the interest of legibility, it is frequently required that the signature of the parties be followed by their printed or typewritten names.

In many states the statute that authorizes a

short or simplified form of deed also declares that no seal is required to make effective a writing that purports to convey an interest in land.

A deed must be executed and delivered by a person having capacity. It may be set aside by the grantor on the ground of the fraud of the grantee, provided that innocent third persons have not acquired rights in the land.

The deed remains binding as between the grantor and the grantee even if it has not been acknowledged or recorded.

19.   Delivery and Acceptance of Deeds

A deed has no effect, and title does not pass, until the deed has been delivered. Delivery is a matter of intent as shown by words and conduct;[10] no particular form of ceremony is required. The essential intent in delivering a deed is not merely that the grantor intends to hand over physical control and possession of the paper upon which the deed is written, but that the grantor intends thereby to transfer the

ownership of the property described in the deed. That is, the grantor must deliver the deed with the intent that it should take effect as a deed and convey an interest in the property.

A deed is ordinarily made effective by handing it to the grantee with the intention that the grantee should thenceforth be the owner of the property described in the deed. A delivery may also be made by placing the deed, addressed to the grantee, in the mail or by giving it to a third person with directions to hand it to the grantee.

When a deed is delivered to a third person for the purpose of delivery to the grantee upon the happening of some event or contingency, the transaction is called a **delivery in escrow.** No title passes until the fulfillment of the condition or the happening of the event or contingency.

An effective delivery of a deed may be made symbolically, as by delivering to the grantee the key to a locked box and informing the grantee that the deed to the property is in the box.

In the *Green* case it was claimed that the delivery of a safety deposit box key was a delivery of a deed that was in the box.

[10]   Smith v Smith (Tex Civ App) 607 SW2d 617 (1980).

GREEN v STANFILL
(Mo App) 612 SW2d 435 (1981)

Charlsie Green and her husband executed a deed of property to their son Frankie Green. She put the deed in a safety deposit box. Attached to the deed was a slip of paper stating that Frankie was not to "bother" with the deed until his parents were dead. Thereafter, the mother rented a new safety deposit box, put the deed and other papers in it, and gave one of the two keys for the box to Frankie. Unknown to the mother, Frankie thereafter removed the deed from the box and recorded it. He then executed a deed transferring the property to himself and his wife. The mother was never told that the deed had been taken from the safety deposit box and recorded. Later Frankie was killed. His wife remarried and was then known as Violet Green Stanfill. The mother sued Violet to set aside the deed to Frankie on the ground that it had never been delivered. From a judgment against the mother, she appealed.

PREWITT, P.J. . . . Whether there is delivery of a deed depends upon the facts of each case and all relevant facts and circumstances should be considered in determining the question. "Whether or not a deed has been delivered is a mixed question of law and fact. The element which controls the resolution of that question is the intention of the parties, especially the intention of the grantor. The vital inquiry is whether the grantor intended a complete transfer—whether the grantor *parted with dominion over the instrument* with the intention of relinquishing *all* dominion over it and of making it presently operative as a conveyance of the title to the land." *Meadows v Brich*, 606 SW2d 258 (Mo App 1980). Intention of the parties may be manifested by words or acts or both. . . .

Defendant Stanfill contends that the trial court's determination of the effect of giving the key to Frankie was correct, citing *McBride v Mercantile-Commerce Bank & Trust Co.* 330 Mo 259, 48 SW2d 922 (banc 1932), and *Foley v Harrison*, 233 Mo 460, 136 SW 354 (1911). However, in those cases there was evidence that the donor intended to make a present gift of the contents of the box. Here there was contrary evidence as to plaintiff's intention. Plaintiff's acts, as described in her testimony, indicated that by giving Frankie the key to the safety deposit box she did not then intend to deliver the deed and make a present conveyance of the property. She had the deed with her and deposited it in the box instead of giving it to her son. A note, apparently still attached to it, said he was not to take it until her death. It is essential to a valid delivery that the grantor part with the deed without reservation, with intention that it take effect at that time as a transfer of title. . . . Placing an executed and acknowledged deed in a place where the grantee has access and from which he can, without hindrance, transfer it to his possession, but with the intent that the grantee not take it and have it recorded until after the grantor's death, does not constitute a delivery. . . .

We hold that the delivery of the key to the safety deposit box did not constitute delivery of the deed as a matter of law and that plaintiff made a prima facie case. The judgment of dismissal is reversed and the cause remanded for a new trial.

[Judgment reversed and action remanded]

QUESTIONS

1. Does this case hold that there can never be a delivery of a deed by making a delivery of a key to a safety deposit box containing the deed?
2. What additional evidence would have changed the result in the *Green* case?
3. What was the significance of the fact that the mother was not told that the deed had been taken from the box and recorded?

Generally, there must be an acceptance by the grantee. In all cases an acceptance is presumed. However, the grantee may disclaim the transfer if the grantee acts within a reasonable time after learning that the transfer has been made.

20. Recording of Deeds

The owner of land may record the deed in the office of a public official, sometimes called a *recorder* or *commissioner of deeds*. The recording is not required to make the deed effective to pass title, but it is done so that the public will know that the grantee is the present owner and thereby prevent the former owner from making any other transaction relating to the property. The recording statutes provide that a person purchasing land from the last holder of record will take title free of any unrecorded claim to the land of which the purchaser does not have notice or knowledge.

The fact that a deed is recorded charges everyone with knowledge of its existence, even if they in fact do not know of it because they have neglected to examine the record. The recording of a deed, however, is only such notice if the deed was properly executed. Likewise, the grantee of land cannot claim any protection by virtue of the recording of a deed when (a) a claim is made by one whose title is superior to that of the owner of record; (b) the grantee had notice or knowledge of the adverse claim when title was acquired; (c) a person acting under a hostile claim was then in possession of the land; (d) the grantee received the land as a gift; or (e) the transfer to the grantee was fraudulent.

21.   Additional Protection of Buyers

Apart from the protection given to buyers and third persons by the recorded title to property, a buyer may generally also be protected by procuring title insurance or an abstract of title. An **abstract of title** is a summarized report of the title to the property as shown by the records, together with a report of all judgments, mortgages, and similar recorded claims against the property.

22.   Cancellation of Deeds

A deed, although delivered, acknowledged, and recorded, may be set aside or canceled by the grantor upon proof of such circumstances as would warrant the setting aside of a contract. For example, when a conveyance is made in consideration of a promise to support the grantor, the failure of the grantee to perform will ordinarily justify cancellation of the deed.

23.   Grantor's Warranties

The warranties of the grantor relate to the title transferred by the grantor and to the fitness of the property for use.

(a) WARRANTIES OF TITLE. In the common law deed the grantor may expressly warrant or make certain covenants as to the title conveyed. The statutes authorizing a short form of deed provide that unless otherwise stated in the deed, the grantor shall be pre-

sumed to have made certain warranties of title.

The more important of the covenants or warranties of title that the grantor may make are (1) **covenant of seisin,** or guarantee that the grantor owns the estate conveyed; (2) **covenant of right to convey,** or guarantee that the grantor—if not the owner, as in the case of an agent—has the right or authority to make the conveyance; (3) **covenant against encumbrances,** or guarantee that the land is not subject to any right or interest of a third person, such as a lien or easement; (4) **covenant of quiet enjoyment,** or covenant by the grantor that the grantee's possession of the land shall not be disturbed either by the grantor, in the case of a limited covenant, or by the grantor or any person claiming title under the grantor, in the case of a general covenant; and (5) **covenant of further assurances,** or promise that the grantor will execute any additional documents that may be required to perfect the title of the grantee.

(b) FITNESS FOR USE. In the absence of an express warranty in the deed, no warranty as to fitness arises under the common law in the sale or conveyance of real estate. Thus, by the common law there is no implied warranty that a house is reasonably fit for habitation, even though it is a new house sold by the builder.

In accord with a modern trend, however, courts in most states hold that when a builder or real estate developer sells a new house to a home buyer, an implied warranty that the house and foundation are fit for occupancy or use arises, without regard to whether the house was purchased before, during, or after completion of construction.[11] This warranty will not be implied against the first buyer when the house is resold, but there is authority that the second buyer may sue the original contractor for breach of the implied warranty, even though there is no privity of contract.

[11]   The buyer of a house should give notice to the seller of any defects within a reasonable time after the buyer learns or should have learned of the defects. Pollard v Saxe & Yolles Development Co. 12 Cal 3d 374, 115 Cal Rptr 648, 525 P2d 88 (1974) (extending the concept of UCC § 2–607(3), although recognizing that it was applicable only to the sale of goods).

FIGURE 50-1   FORM OF WARRANTY DEED

THIS DEED, made the twentieth day of November, nineteen hundred and... between James K. Damron, residing at 132 Spring Street in the Borough of Manhattan, City and State of New York, party of the first part, and Terrence S. Bloemker, residing at 14 Steinway Street in the Borough of Queens, City and State of New York, party of the second part,

WITNESSETH, that the party of the first part, in consideration of the sum of one dollar ($1), lawful money of the United States, and other good and valuable consideration paid by the party of the second part, does hereby grant and release unto the party of the second part, his heirs and assigns forever,

ALL that certain lot, piece, and parcel of land situated in the Borough of Manhattan, City and County of New York, and State of New York, and bounded and described as follows:

Beginning at a point on the northerly side of Spring Street, distant two hundred (200) feet westerly from the corner formed by the intersection of the northerly side of Spring Street with the westerly side of 6th Avenue, running thence northerly parallel with 6th Avenue one hundred (100) feet, thence westerly and parallel with said Spring Street one hundred (100) feet; thence southerly, again parallel with said 6th Avenue one hundred (100) feet to the northerly side of Spring Street, and thence easterly along the said northerly side of Spring Street one hundred (100) feet to the point or place of beginning.

Together with the appurtenances and all the estate and rights of the party of the first part in and to said premises.

TO HAVE AND TO HOLD the premises herein granted unto the party of the second part, his heirs and assigns forever.

AND the party of the first part covenants as follows:

First. That the party of the first part is seised of the said premises in fee simple, and has good right to convey the same;

Second. That the party of the second part shall quietly enjoy the said premises;

Third. That the said premises are free from encumbrances except as expressly stated;

Fourth. That the party of the first part will execute or procure any further necessary assurance of the title to said premises;

IN WITNESS WHEREOF, the party of the first part has hereunto set his hand and seal the day and year first above written.

JAMES K. DAMRON (L.S.)

In presence of:

DIANA L. REILMAN

State of New York } ss.:
County of New York

On the twentieth day of November in the year nineteen hundred and ..., before me personally came James K. Damron, to me known and known to me to be the individual described in, and who executed, the foregoing instrument, and he acknowledged that he executed the same.

DIANA L. REILMAN
Notary Public, New York County

[AUTHORS' NOTE: ACKNOWLEDGEMENT BEFORE A NOTARY PUBLIC IS NOT ESSENTIAL TO THE EFFECTIVENESS OF A DEED, BUT IT IS TYPICALLY REQUIRED IN ORDER TO QUALIFY THE DEED FOR RECORDING.]

---

24.   Grantee's Covenants

In a deed, the grantee may agree to do or to refrain from doing certain acts. Such an agreement becomes a binding contract between the grantor and the grantee. The grantor may sue the grantee for its breach.

(a) COVENANTS RUNNING WITH THE LAND. When the covenant of the grantee relates directly to the property conveyed, such as an agreement to maintain fences on the property or that the property shall be used only for residential purposes, it is said not only that the covenant is binding between the grantor and the grantee but also that it **runs with the land.** This means that anyone acquiring the land from the grantee is also bound by the covenant of the grantee, even though the subsequent owner has not made any such agreement with anyone.

The right to enforce the covenant also runs with the land owned by the grantor to whom the promise was made. Thus, if *A* owns adjoining tracts of land and conveys one of them to *B*, and if *B* covenants to maintain the surface drainage on the land so that it will not flood *A*'s land, the benefit of this covenant will run with the land retained by *A*. If *A* sells the remaining tract of land to *C*, *B* is bound to perform the covenant so as to benefit the neighboring tract. This is true even though the tract is now owned by *C*.

(b) RESTRICTIVE AND AFFIRMATIVE COVENANTS. A covenant that provides that the grantee shall refrain from certain conduct is termed a **restrictive** (or negative) **covenant.** It runs with the land in the same manner as a covenant that calls for the performance of an act, that is, an **affirmative covenant.**

A restrictive covenant may impose a limitation on the kind of structure that can be erected on the land and may also impose a limitation on the use that may be made of the land.

(1) General Building Scheme. When a tract of land is developed and when individual lots or homes are sold to separate purchasers, it is common to use the same restrictive covenants in all deeds, in order to impose uniform restrictions and patterns on the property. Any person acquiring a lot within the tract is bound by the restrictions if they are in the deed or a prior recorded deed, or if the grantee has notice or knowledge of such restrictions. Any person owning one of the lots in the tract may bring suit against another lot owner to enforce the restrictive covenant. The effect

is to create a zoning code based upon the agreement of the parties in their deeds, as distinguished from one based upon government regulation.

(2) Restraints on Alienation. Covenants may restrict the sale or transfer of the property. It is lawful to provide that the grantor shall have the option to repurchase the property, or that if the grantee offers to sell it to anyone, the grantor will be given an opportunity to match the price that a third person is willing to pay. Restrictions on the grantee's right to sell the property are not enforceable when the restriction discriminates against potential buyers because of race, color, creed, or national origin.

F.   OTHER METHODS OF TRANSFERRING REAL PROPERTY

Title to real property can also be acquired by eminent domain and by adverse possession.

25.   Eminent Domain

By **eminent domain** property is taken from its private owner and the title is acquired by the taking government or public authority. Two important questions arise: whether there is a taking of property and whether the property is taken for a public use. In respect to the first, it is not necessary that the owner be physically deprived of the property. It is sufficient that the normal use of the property has been impaired or lost. As to the second, it is not necessary that the public at large actually use the property. It is sufficient that it is appropriated for the public benefit.

26.   Adverse Possession

Title to land may be acquired by holding it adversely to the true owner for a certain period of time. In such a case, the possessor gains title by **adverse possession.** If such possession is maintained, the possessor automatically becomes the owner of the property, even though the possessor admittedly had no lawful claim to the land.

In order to acquire title in this manner, possession must be (a) actual, (b) visible and notorious, (c) exclusive, (d) hostile, and (e) continuous for a required period of time.[12]

---

[12]   Perivoliotis v Pierson, 167 Ill App 3d 259, 181 Ill Dec 186, 521 NE2d 254 (1988).

Commonly the period of time is 21 years, but state statutes may provide 10 to 20 years. Occupation of land in the mistaken belief that one is the owner is a "hostile" possession.

A claim of hostile possession was made in the *Meyers* case.

MEYERS v MEYERS
(Minn App) 368 NW2d 391 (1985)

Bernadine Meyers and Robert Meyers moved into the latter's house in 1947 after their marriage. In 1948, Robert enlisted in the army and moved to California. Bernadine remained in the home and cared for Robert's father until his death in 1950. When Robert returned for the funeral of his father, he and Bernadine had a violent argument. Robert was removed from the house by the police. He subsequently obtained a divorce from Bernadine in 1954. There was no mention in the divorce decree about the real estate. Numerous improvements were made to the house by Bernadine, and she paid taxes on the property for many years. When Robert instructed the taxing authorities to send property tax statements to his California address, Bernadine brought an action contending that she owned the property by adverse possession. From a judgment in favor of Bernadine, Robert appealed.

RANDALL, P. J. . . . Robert paid child support until 1957. In 1957 a dispute arose over the support. In a mediation attempt, a United States Army officer wrote Bernadine on Robert's behalf. He proposed that Robert pay $100 per month as child support, and deed the house to Bernadine. In exchange, she would return some personal property to Robert. Bernadine never replied to the offer. She testified that she made no reply on an attorney's advice.

Bernadine made significant improvements to the house in 1950. In addition, she has maintained the house and made minor repairs since that time. Robert paid the property taxes on the house through the first half of 1960, but Bernadine has paid the taxes since then.

Robert did not return to Minnesota from the time of his father's funeral in 1950 until 1979. In 1979 he indicated to Bernadine and the children that he thought he had deeded the house to the children. When informed otherwise, he told them he wanted the children to have it. When the children suggested he deed it to Bernadine instead, he said, "I'll burn it down first." Robert instructed local authorities to begin sending property tax statements to his California address, and Bernadine brought this action asking either for an equitable division of the property or reimbursement for improvements made, or for a declaration that she owned the property by virtue of adverse possession.

The trial court ruled only on the adverse possession issue, finding that Bernadine owned the property.

Was the evidence sufficient to sustain the trial court's finding that Bernadine acquired ownership of appellant's house by adverse possession?

To establish title by adverse possession, the adverse possessor must show by clear and convincing evidence an actual, open, hostile, continuous, and exclusive possession for 15 years. *Wojahn v. Johnson*, 297 N.W.2d 298 (Minn.1980). At least from 1950 to 1979, Bernadine's possession was actual, open, continuous, and exclusive. All five elements are equally necessary, however, and if her possession was not hostile to Robert's title, her claim must fail.

Robert contends Bernadine's possession of the house throughout the more than 15 years was permissive. The *Wojahn* court said:

> The general rule of law is that the existence of a family relationship between the claimant of land and the record owner . . . creates the inference, if not the presumption, that the original possession by the claimant of the other's land was permissive and not adverse . . . ; and that when such original use was thus permissive, it would be presumed permissive, rather than hostile, until the contrary was affirmatively shown.

Here, the facts, as well as the "inference" referred to in *Wojahn*, establish that Bernadine's initial possession of the property was permissive. Once initial possession is permissive, proof of the inception of possession which is hostile to the record owner's title must be clear and unequivocal.

> Where the original entry is permissive, the statute does not begin to run against the legal owner until an adverse holding is declared and notice of such change is brought to the knowledge of the owner. . . . While it is true that assertion of adverse title need not be always expressly or affirmatively declared, but may be shown by circumstances, . . . proof of inception of hostility must in all cases be clear and unequivocal. *Johnson v. Raddohl*, 226 Minn. 343, 32 N.W.2d 860 (1948).

The trial court found that the 1950 argument after which Robert was removed from the house was a declaration of Bernadine's adverse holding, of which Robert had notice. We disagree. Because one spouse has the other removed from the home during a domestic dispute does not mean that the spouse who remains in the home now possesses the house adversely to the ejected spouse's title. Such a holding could substantially interfere in property rights between married couples. Courts could become reluctant to allow the legitimate temporary relief of ejectment that spouses are entitled to if they show domestic abuse because of concerns over alienating title.

Robert continuously paid all real estate taxes due until 1960, which period includes ten years after the argument in the home. During those ten years, there was neither oral nor written indication from Bernadine that she claimed the house as hers, and she allowed Robert to pay the real estate taxes while she and the children continued to live there. The 1950 incident simply did not rise to the level of a declaration of an adverse holding strong enough to commence the 15-year period needed to claim under adverse possession.

Bernadine argues that, even if the 1950 incident did not rise to that level, her failure to respond to the 1957 offer Robert made through a mediating army officer did. The *Johnson* court stated, however, the *notice* of a declaration of an adverse holding must be brought to the attention of the record owner. If Bernadine's silence was, in her own mind, a declaration that she held the property adversely to Robert's title, she never gave him notice of her intent. Again, for at least three years after Robert's offer he continuously paid the real estate taxes on the home with no indication by her that she claimed partial or full ownership adversely to Robert. The 1957 support and property settlement negotiations could not, therefore, start the running of the 15-year period.

After 1960, Robert stopped paying the property taxes. Bernadine never took any steps, however, to give him notice that she was claiming the property as her own. Although equitably a strong argument can be made that Robert abandoned the property, the law is clear that legal title to realty is never lost by abandonment.

At trial, Bernadine testified that she never told Robert prior to the commencement of this lawsuit that she felt she owned the house, and that she never told anyone else that she felt she owned the house. She testified that she, in fact, never claimed to have title to the property, and that neither while raising the children nor after they grew up did she do anything different with the house that might reasonably put Robert or anyone else on notice that she was asserting an ownership claim. Bernadine has failed to show that her permissive use of the property became hostile, and thus the finding of adverse possession cannot be sustained. . . .

[Judgment reversed and action remanded]

QUESTIONS

1. Were all the elements present to constitute adverse possession?
2. Can silence amount to a notice of a declaration of holding property adversely?
3. Did Robert abandon the property?

G.   MORTGAGES

An agreement that creates an interest in real property as security for an obligation, which interest to cease upon the performance of the obligation, is a **mortgage**. The person whose interest in the property is given as security is the **mortgagor**. The person who receives the security is the **mortgagee**.

27.   Characteristics of a Mortgage

There are three characteristics of a mortgage: (a) the termination of the mortgagee's interest upon the performance of the obligation secured by the mortgage; (b) the right of the mortgagee to enforce the mortgage by foreclosure upon the mortgagor's failure to perform; and (c) the mortgagor's right to redeem or regain the property. In any case, however, the intention of the parties determines whether there is a mortgage.

28.   Property Subject to Mortgage

In general, any form of property that may be sold or conveyed may be mortgaged. It is immaterial whether the right is a present right or a future interest, or merely a right in the land of another. It is not necessary that the mortgagor have complete or absolute ownership in the property. The mortgagor may mortgage any interest, legal or equitable, divided or undivided.

29.   Form of Mortgage

As a mortgage upon real property transfers an interest in the property, it must be in writing by virtue of the statute of frauds.

As a general rule, no particular form of language is required, provided the language used expresses the intent of the parties to create a mortgage. In many states the substance of a mortgage is practically identical to that of a deed, with the exception that a mortgage contains a defeasance clause, a description of the obligation secured, and sometimes a covenant to pay or perform the obligation. The **defeasance clause** states that the mortgage shall cease to have any effect when the obligation is performed, as when the debt of the mortgagor is paid. In many states statutes provide a standardized form of mortgage that may be used.

30.   Recording or Filing of Mortgage

An unrecorded mortgage is valid and binding between the parties to it. The heirs or donees of a mortgagor cannot defend against the mortgage on the ground that it has not been recorded. Recording statutes in most states, however, provide that purchasers or creditors who give value and act in good faith in ignorance of an unrecorded mortgage may enforce their respective rights against the property without regard to the existence of the unrecorded mortgage. Accordingly, the purchaser of the land in good faith for value from the mortgagor holds the land free of the unrecorded mortgage, and the mortgagee's only remedy is against the mortgagor on the debt due the mortgagee. The mortgagee can proceed against the transferee only if the mortgagee can prove that the transferee of the land did not purchase it in good faith, for value, and in ignorance of the unrecorded mortgage.

31.   Responsibilities of the Parties

The mortgagor and mortgagee have the following duties and liabilities when a mortgage is placed upon real estate.

(a) REPAIRS AND IMPROVEMENTS. In the absence of an agreement to the contrary, a mortgagor is under no duty to make improvements or to restore or repair parts of the premises that are destroyed or damaged through no fault of the mortgagor.

A mortgagee, when in possession, must make reasonable and necessary repairs in order to preserve the property. The mortgagee is entitled to reimbursement for such repairs. Ordinarily, however, the mortgagee may not

charge to the mortgagor expenditures for valuable or enduring improvements.

(b) TAXES, ASSESSMENTS, AND INSURANCE. The duty to pay taxes and assessments rests upon the mortgagor. In the absence of an agreement, neither party is under a duty to insure the mortgaged property. Both parties, however, may insure their respective interests. It is common practice for the mortgagor to obtain a single policy of insurance on the property payable to the mortgagee and the mortgagor as their interests may appear.[13]

(c) IMPAIRMENT OF SECURITY. The mortgagor is liable to the mortgagee for any damage to the property, caused by the mortgagor's fault, that impairs the security of the mortgage by materially reducing the value of the property. Both the mortgagor and the mortgagee have a right of action against a third person who wrongfully injures the property.

32.   Transfer of Interest

Questions arise as to transfers by the mortgagor and the mortgagee of their respective interests and of the liability of a transferee of the mortgagor.

(a) TRANSFER BY MORTGAGOR. The mortgagor may ordinarily transfer the land without the consent of the mortgagee. Such a transfer passes only the interest of the mortgagor and does not divest or impair the mortgage if properly recorded.

The transfer of the property by the mortgagor does not affect the liability of the mortgagor to the mortgagee. Unless the latter has agreed to substitute the mortgagor's grantee for the mortgagor, the latter remains liable for the mortgage debt as though no transfer had been made.

(b) LIABILITY OF MORTGAGOR'S TRANSFEREE. The purchaser of mortgaged property does not become personally liable for the mortgage debt unless the purchaser ex-

[13]   Beneficial Standard Life Insurance Co. v Trinity National Bank (Tex App) 763 SW2d 52 (1988).

pressly assumes that debt. Such an assumption of the debt does not release the mortgagor from liability to the mortgagee unless the mortgagee agrees to such substitution of parties.

(c) TRANSFER BY MORTGAGEE. In most states a mortgage may be transferred or assigned by the mortgagee.

33. Rights of Mortgagee After Default

Upon the mortgagor's default, the mortgagee in some states is entitled to obtain possession of the property and collect the rents or to have a receiver appointed for that purpose. In all states the mortgagee may enforce the mortgage by **foreclosure,** a procedure to enforce the mortgage resulting in sale of the mortgaged property.

Generally, it is provided that upon any default under the terms of the mortgage agreement, the mortgagee has the right to declare that the entire mortgage debt is due, even though the default related only to an installment or to the doing of some act, such as maintaining insurance on the property or producing receipts for taxes.

A sale on the foreclosure of the mortgage destroys the mortgage, and the property passes free of the mortgage to the buyer at the sale. However, the extinction of the mortgage by foreclosure does not destroy the debt that was secured by the mortgage. The mortgagor remains liable for any unpaid balance or deficiency, although by statute the mortgagor is generally given credit for the fair value of the property if it was purchased by the mortgagee.

34. Rights of Mortgagor After Default

After default the mortgagor may seek to stop or stay foreclosure or to redeem the mortgaged land.

(a) STAY OF FORECLOSURE. In certain cases, authorized by statute, a **stay** (or delay) **of foreclosure** may be obtained by the mortgagor to prevent undue hardship.

(b) REDEMPTION. The **right of redemption** means the right of the mortgagor to free the property of the mortgage lien after default. By statute in many states, the right may be exercised during a certain time following foreclosure and sale of the mortgaged land.

SUMMARY

Real property includes land, buildings and fixtures, and rights in the land of another, such as easements.

The interest held by a person in real property may be defined in terms of the period of time for which the person will remain the owner. The interest may be a fee simple estate, which lasts forever, or a life estate, which lasts for the life of a person. These estates are known as freehold estates. If the ownership interest exists for a specified number of days, months, or years, the interest is a leasehold estate.

Personal property may be attached to or associated with real property in such a way that it becomes real property. In such a case it is called a *fixture*. To determine whether property has in fact become a fixture, the courts look to the method of attachment, to how the property is adapted to the realty, and to the intent of the person originally owning the personal property.

Under common law, the liability of an occupier of land for injury to third persons on the premises is dependent upon the status of the third persons as trespassers, licensees, or invitees. Many jurisdictions are ignoring these common law distinctions, however, in favor of an ordinary negligence standard, or giving licensees the same protection as invitees. Recreational use statutes limit or eliminate a landowner's liability for personal injuries to a person using the landowner's land for recreational purposes.

Real property may be the subject of multiple ownership. The forms of multiple ownership are the same as for personal property. In addition, there are special forms of co-ownership for real property, such as condominiums and cooperatives.

A deed is an instrument transferring an interest in land by a grantor to a grantee. A deed can be a quitclaim deed, a warranty deed, or a statutory deed. To be effective, a deed must be signed or sealed by the grantor and delivered to the grantee. Recording the deed is not required to make the deed effective to pass title, but recording provides notice to the public that the grantee is the present owner. The warranties of the grantor relate to the title transferred by the grantor and to the fitness of the property for use. Absent any express warranty in the deed, no warranty of fitness arises under the common law in the sale or the conveyance of real estate. Most states today hold that when a builder or real estate developer sells a new home to a buyer, an implied warranty of habitability arises. Title to real estate may also be acquired by eminent domain and adverse possession.

An agreement that creates an interest in real property as security for an obligation and that ends upon the performance of the obligation is a mortgage. A mortgage must be in writing under the statute of frauds. If the mortgage is unrecorded, it is valid between the parties. The mortgage should be recorded to put good faith purchasers on notice of the mortgage. A purchaser of the mortgaged property does not become liable for the mortgaged debt unless such purchaser assumes the mortgage. The mortgagor still remains liable unless the mortgagee agrees to a substitution of parties. If the mortgagor defaults, the mortgagee may enforce the mortgage by foreclosure. Such foreclosure may be delayed because of undue hardship.

QUESTIONS AND CASE PROBLEMS

1. What social forces are affected by recognizing the right of aircraft to fly over land at such a height that the flight does not interfere with the use of the land and is not dangerous to persons or property on the land?

2. Price sued Whisnant for cutting and removing trees from certain land. Price claimed title to the land by adverse possession. He proved that for over 20 years he had from time to time entered on the land and cut and removed trees. Was Price the owner of the land by adverse possession? [Price v Whisnant, 236 NC 381, 72 SE2d 851]

3. Richard sold land to Smith by a warranty deed. Smith did not record his deed. Some time thereafter Richard sold the same land to Wayne by a warranty deed. Wayne was a good faith purchaser for value who had no knowledge of the prior unrecorded deed. Who owns the land, Smith or Wayne? Why?

4. Compare (a) an easement, (b) a profit, and (c) a fixture.

5. Compare the status of an "apartment owner" in (a) a condominium and (b) a cooperative.

6. What is the most important difference between a license and an easement?

7. Bradham and others, trustees of the Mount Olivet Church, brought an action to cancel a mortgage on the church property that had been executed by Davis and others as trustees of the church and given to Robinson as mortgagee. It was found by the court that the church was not indebted to the mortgagee for any amount. Should the mortgage be canceled? [Bradham v Robinson, 236 NC 589, 73 SE2d 555]

8. Miller executed a deed to real estate, naming Mary Zieg as grantee. He placed the deed in an envelope upon which was written, "To be filed at my death," and put the envelope and deed in a safe deposit box in the National Bank. The box had been rented in the names of Miller and Mary Zieg. After Miller's death Mary removed the deed from the safe deposit box. Moseley, as executor under Miller's will, brought an action against Mary to declare the deed void. Decide. [Moseley v Zieg, 180 Neb 810, 146 NW2d 72]

9. Henry Lile owned a house. When the land on which it was situated was condemned for a highway, he removed the house to the land of his daughter, Sarah Crick. In the course of construction work, blasting damaged the house. Sarah Crick sued the contractors, Terry &

Wright. They claimed that Henry should be joined in the action as a plaintiff and that Sarah could not sue by herself, because it was Henry's house. Were the defendants correct? [Terry & Wright v Crick (Ky) 418 SW2d 217]

10. Stanley moved onto David's undeveloped land without permission to do so. Shortly thereafter, David learned about Stanley but said that Stanley could remain there indefinitely without paying rent if he would keep the property in good condition. Stanley did so for a period of fifteen years, which was the statutory period for obtaining property by adverse possession in the state. Subsequently, Stanley claimed title by adverse possession. Decide.

11. Larry Wiersema was building a house for himself in the country. He made a contract with Workman Plumbing, Heating & Cooling, Inc., to do most of the plumbing and heating work in the new house. This work included the installation of a septic tank. Workman performed the contract correctly. However, because of the peculiar kind of clay surrounding the house, the drainage from the septic tank system was very poor, and the basement of Larry's house was frequently flooded. He sued Workman for breach of the implied warranty of habitability. Was Workman liable? [Wiersema v Workman Plumbing, Heating & Cooling, Inc. 87 Ill App 3d 535, 42 Ill Dec 664, 409 NE2d 159]

12. Davis Store Fixtures sold certain equipment on credit to Head, who installed it in a building that was later owned by the Cadillac Club. When payment was not made, Davis sought to repossess the equipment. If the equipment constituted fixtures, this could not be done. The equipment consisted of a bar for serving drinks, a bench, and a drain board. The first two were attached to the floor or wall with screws, and the drain board was connected to water and drainage pipes. Did the equipment constitute fixtures?

13. Smikahl sold to Hansen a tract of land on which there were two houses and four trailer lots equipped with concrete patios and necessary connections for utility lines. The tract purchased by Hansen was completely surrounded by the land owned by Smikahl and third persons. In order to get onto the highway, it was necessary to cross the Smikahl tract. Several years later, Smikahl put a barbed wire fence around his land. Hansen sued to prevent obstruction to travel between his land and the highway over the Smikahl land. Smikahl defended on the ground that no such right of travel had been given to Hansen. Was he correct? [Hansen v Smikahl, 173 Neb 309, 113 NW2d 210]

14. Martin Manufacturing decided to raise additional long-term capital by mortgaging an industrial park that it owned. First National Loan Company agreed to lend Martin $1 million and to take a note and first mortgage on the land and building. The mortgage was duly recorded. Martin sold the property to Marshall, who took the property and assumed the mortgage debt. Does Marshall have any personal liability on the mortgage debt? Is Martin still liable on the mortgage debt? Explain.

15. In 1980, Ortleb, Inc., a Delaware corporation, purchased certain land in Montana from the Alberts but neglected to record the deed. In 1988, the Alberts sold the same property to Bently, a resident of Montana, who purchased in good faith and recorded his deed. Ortleb sues Bently to resolve the title question. Who will win? Explain.

51

ENVIRONMENTAL LAW AND COMMUNITY PLANNING

A. PREVENTION OF POLLUTION
1. Statutory Environmental Protection
2. Waste Control
3. Environmental Impact Statements
4. Regulation by Administrative Agencies
5. Litigation
6. Criminal Liability

B. COMMUNITY PLANNING
7. Restrictive Covenants in Private Contracts
8. Public Zoning
9. Eminent Domain
10. Definition of Nuisance
11. The Technological Environment of the Law of Nuisance

For the first two centuries of national existence, Americans looked upon their country as one of unlimited resources. To them, there was no need to conserve or protect these resources. The answer to any shortage problem was always very easy—just move westward, where there was more of everything. As long as the open West was available, there was no need to protect the environment. In 1912, the territories of New Mexico and Arizona became the 47th and 48th states, and the United States then stretched from the Atlantic to the Pacific. Americans and American industry were thus locked into a land area that re-mained constant. Although Hawaii and Alaska later became states, the geographical limits of the continental United States remained unchanged.

Increasing population and industrialization consumed national resources and created waste that threatened to destroy much of what was left. The result was that America had to begin to conserve resources and stop polluting the environment. The desire to protect people from the harmful effects of pollution and the desire to protect America from a shortage of resources led to the movement for environmental protection at the governmental level. At the private level added impetus was given to the concept of community planning.

Underlying these trends was the basic policy decision to restrict freedom of enterprise, the freedom of the use of property, and freedom of personal action, in the interest of the general welfare.

FIGURE 51-1   THE LEGAL ENVIRONMENT OF RESOURCE PROTECTION AND COMMUNITY PLANNING

	ENVIRONMENTAL ISSUES	
	---	---
	RESOURCE PROTECTION	COMMUNITY PLANNING
LEGAL BODY EXERCISING CONTROL	INTERNATIONAL GOVERNMENTS U.S. GOVERNMENT STATE GOVERNMENTS LOCAL GOVERNMENTS	STATE GOVERNMENTS LOCAL GOVERNMENTS
TYPE OF CONTROL AND DEVICES USED	DIRECT CONTROL THROUGH STATUTES AND ORDINANCES LIMITED OR INCIDENTAL STATE GOVERNMENTAL CONTROL THROUGH NUISANCE LAW AND RESTRICTIVE COVENANTS	DIRECT CONTROL THROUGH STATUTES, ORDINANCES, AND RESTRICTIVE COVENANTS

A.   PREVENTION OF POLLUTION

As America changed from a rural and agricultural society to an urban and industrial one, new laws were needed to prevent the pollution of the environment.

1.   Statutory Environmental Protection

Beginning with the National Environmental Policy Act of 1969 (NEPA), Congress has adopted a series of laws designed to prevent the pollution of the air and water and to reduce noise.[1] Congress has adopted other statutes designed to reduce the problem of waste disposal by encouraging recycling or reuse of various products.[2]

State legislatures have also been active in this area, and many states have laws that are similar to the federal laws. Statutes may require that before a permit may be issued for earth removal and similar operations requiring blasting, the contractor and the permit-issuing agency must agree on "satisfactory dust control provisions."[3] A state law must not (a) conflict with a federal statute or (b) place an unreasonable burden on interstate commerce.

[1]   For example, see the Clean Air Act, 42 USC §§ 1857 et seq.; the National Motor Vehicles Emissions Standards Act, 42 USC §§ 1857f-1 et seq.; the Noise Control Acts of 1970 and 1972, 42 USC § 4901; the Water Pollution Control Act Amendments of 1972, 33 USC §§ 1251 et seq. The pollution of navigable waters had already been prohibited by the River and Harbor Appropriations Act of 1899. See also the Wildfire Disaster Recovery Act of 1989, Act of May 9, 1990, PL 101–286, 104 Stat 171, ____ USC §§ ____ et seq.; The Oil Pollution Act of 1990, Act of August 18, 1990, PL 101–380, 104 Stat 484, ____ USC §§ ____ , increases the maximum liability of persons causing oil spills, establishes a clean-up fund to pay for clean-up expenses when produced by an unknown person or the person liable has paid the maximum amount of liability, and requires that all oil tankers built hereafter or in use after the year 2015 be constructed with double hulls.

[2]   See, for example, the Solid Waste Disposal Act, Act of October 20, 1965, 79 Stat 997, 42 USC §§ 3251 et seq.; the Resource Recovery and Policy Act of 1970, Act of October 26, 1970, PL 91–512, 84 Stat 1227, 42 USC §§ 3251 et seq.; the Resource Conservation and Recovery Act of 1976, Act of October 21, 1976, PL 94–580, 90 Stat 2795, 42 USC §§ 6901 et seq. These statutes have been amended many times.

[3]   Tebo v Board of Appeals of Shrewsbury, 22 Mass App 618, 495 NE2d 892 (1986).

2.   Waste Control

Modern industries and life-styles produce a large quantity of waste materials. Some of the industrial waste can be used to make by-products. Some can be used again or recycled. Some wastes are biodegradable.

In contrast, some waste materials remain, and some are dangerous to life, both human and animal, and to vegetation and water supplies. The state and federal governments have adopted programs for protecting the nation and the public from harmful wastes.[4] A license may be required for the disposal of radioactive wastes. A state law providing for a spill fund to compensate persons for damage from hazardous waste disposal is valid.[5]

The Comprehensive Environmental Response, Compensation and Liability Act of 1980 (CERCLA)[6] provides for the establishment of a national inventory of inactive hazardous waste sites. It also provides for the creation of a multimillion-dollar Hazardous Waste Fund, commonly called *Superfund*, to pay the cost of eliminating or containing the condemned waste sites.

Under CERCLA, a private enterprise may sue a state to recover the cost of cleanup made necessary by state action.[7]

3.   Environmental Impact Statements

Environmental protection legislation generally requires that any activity that might have a significant effect upon the environment be supported by an environmental impact statement (EIS). Whenever a bill is proposed in Congress, and whenever federal action significantly affecting the quality of the human environment is considered, a statement must be prepared as to the environmental impact of the action. A number of states impose the same requirement on government officials, and some require an environmental impact statement for the construction of any large, private building.

In the *Chinese Staff* case the underlying question was what was included in the environment.

---

[4]   See, for example, the Nuclear Waste Policy Act of 1982, Act of January 7, 1983, PL 97–425, 42 USC §§ 10101–10226; Minnesota v Gerring (Minn App) 418 NW2d 517 (1988).
[5]   Exxon Corp. v Hunt, 475 US 355 (1986).
[6]   Act of December 11, 1980, PL 96–510, 94 Stat 2767, 42 USC §§ 9601 et seq.

[7]   Pennsylvania v Union Gas Co. 491 US ____, 105 L Ed 2d 1 (1989).

CHINESE STAFF AND WORKERS ASS'N v NEW YORK
68 NY2d 359, 502 NE2d 176 (1986)

Henry Street Partners wished to build a high-rise luxury condominium on a vacant lot in the Chinatown section of New York City. The appropriate city agencies issued a permit allowing the construction of the building. The issuance of the permit was then attacked by a lawsuit brought by the Chinese Staff and Workers Association and others, protesting on the ground that the proposed building would have a harmful effect on the Chinatown section by driving out the poorer residents and businesses. From a judgment against the objectors, they appealed.

ALEXANDER, J. . . . The regulations promulgated by the City of New York (Executive Order No. 91, Aug. 24, 1977, entitled City Environmental Quality Review [CEQR]) as authorized by and in implementation of the State Environmental Quality Review Act (ECL art. 8 [SEQRA]) require lead agencies to consider both the short- and long-term and primary and secondary effects of a proposed action in determining whether the action may have a significant effect on the environment so as to require the preparation of an Environmental Impact Statement (EIS). . . .

In reviewing administrative proceedings in general and SEQRA determinations in particular, we are limited to considering "whether a determination was made in violation of lawful procedure, was affected by an error of law or was arbitrary and capricious or an abuse of discretion." . . . The limited issue presented for our review is whether the respondents identified the relevant areas of environmental concern, took a "hard look" at them, and made a "reasoned elaboration" of the basis for their determination. . . .

The initial determination to be made under SEQRA and CEQR is whether an EIS is required, which in turn depends on whether an action may or will not have a significant effect on the environment. In making this initial environmental analysis, the lead agencies must study the same areas of environmental impacts as would be contained in an EIS, including both the short-term and long-term effects as well as the primary and secondary effects of an action on the environment. The threshold at which the requirement that an EIS be prepared is triggered is relatively low: it need only be demonstrated that the action may have a significant effect on the environment. . . .

The dispute here concerns the reach of the term "environment," which is defined [in the State Environmental Quality Review Act and the city regulations] as "the *physical conditions* which will be affected by a proposed action, *including* land, air, water, minerals, flora, fauna, noise, objects of historic or aesthetic significance, *existing patterns of population concentration, distribution, or growth, and existing community or neighborhood character*" [emphasis supplied]. Petitioners argue that the displacement of neighborhood residents and businesses caused by a proposed project is an environmental impact within the purview of SEQRA and CEQR, and the failure of respondents to consider these potential effects renders their environmental analysis invalid. Respondents contend that any impacts that are not either directly related to a primary physical impact or will not impinge upon the physical environment in a significant manner are outside the scope of the definition of "environment," and that the lead agencies were therefore not required to investigate the potential effects alleged by petitioners.

. . . It is clear from the express terms of the statute and the regulations that environment is broadly defined . . . and expressly includes as physical conditions such considerations as "existing patterns of population concentration, distribution, or growth, and existing community or neighborhood character." Thus, the impact that a project may have on population patterns or existing community character, with or without a separate impact on the physical environment, is a relevant concern in an environmental analysis since the statute includes these concerns as elements of the environment. That these factors might generally be regarded as social or economic is irrelevant in view of this explicit definition. By their express terms, therefore, both SEQRA and CEQR require a lead agency to consider more than impacts upon the physical environment in determining whether to require the preparation of an EIS. In sum, population patterns and neighborhood character are physical conditions of the environment under SEQRA and CEQR regardless of whether there is any impact on the physical environment. . . .

Turning to the specific allegations in this case, we conclude that under CEQR the potential displacement of local residents and businesses is an effect on population patterns and neighborhood character which must be considered in determining whether the requirement for an EIS is triggered. A significant effect on the environment may be found if a proposed project impairs "the character or quality of . . . existing community or neighborhood character" (CEQR 6[a][5]) or impacts upon "existing patterns of population concentration, distribution, or growth" (ECL 8–0105[6]; *see*, CEQR 6[a][10]). It is not relevant whether the proposed project may effect these concerns primarily or secondarily or in the short term or in the long term since the regulations expressly include all such effects (CEQR 1[g]).

The potential acceleration of the displacement of local residents and businesses is a secondary long-term effect on population patterns, community goals and neighborhood character such that CEQR requires these impacts on the environment to be considered in an environmental analysis. . . .

We do not decide whether these impacts will in fact flow from the construction of Henry Street Tower nor do we express any opinion on the merits of the proposed project. Our holding is limited to a determination that existing patterns of population concentration, distribution or growth and existing community or neighborhood character are physical conditions such that the regulations adopted by the City of New York pursuant to SEQRA require an agency to consider the potential long-term secondary displacement of residents and businesses in determining whether a proposed project may have a significant effect on the environment. Since respondents did not consider these potential effects on the environment in their environmental analysis, their determination does not comply with the statutory mandate and therefore is arbitrary and capricious. . . .

[Judgment reversed]

QUESTIONS

1. What was the basic controversy in the *Chinese Staff* case?
2. Which interpretation was adopted by the court? What reason did the court give for its position?
3. How did the court describe the action of issuing the permit for the construction of the high-rise building?

While an EIS must consider alternative methods, it is not required to discuss every alternative that could be imagined. It is only required to consider alternatives that are practical and feasible.[8]

When the law requires that an environmental impact statement be filed before a particular construction or improvement can be made, a court will prohibit the construction or improvement if no statement has been filed. It will also do so if a statement has been filed but is so deficient or poor that, in effect, it is no statement at all.

The duty of a federal agency does not end with its issuance of an EIS. It has a continuing duty to gather relevant information, to evalu-

ate such information, and to issue a revised or supplemental EIS if the new information indicates such course of action.

4.   Regulation by Administrative Agencies

For the most part, the law against pollution is a matter of the adoption and enforcement of regulations by administrative agencies, such as the federal Environmental Protection Agency (EPA). Administrative agency control is likely to increase in the future because of the technical nature of the problems involved and because of the interrelationship of pollution problems and nonpollution problems.

5.   Litigation

A private person may bring a lawsuit to recov-

---

[8]   Bowman v City of Petaluma, 185 Cal App 3d 1065, 230 Cal Rptr 413 (1986).

er damages or obtain an injunction against a polluter if damages peculiar to such a plaintiff can be shown. This requirement of harm to the plaintiff has to some extent been relaxed, so that a person may sometimes sue without proving any harm different than that sustained by any other member of the general public. For example, federal statutes authorize a private suit by any person in a federal district court to stop a violation of the air, water, and noise pollution standards. Courts have been increasingly willing to recognize the right of organizations to sue on behalf of their members.

A private person does not always have the right to sue for violation of an environmental protection control. In some instances the right to sue is restricted to a particular government agency or to the attorney general of the United States.

It is reasonable to expect that courts will not take an active part in the solution of pollution problems. It is likely that on these technical problems they will defer to the decisions made or to be made by the appropriate administrative agency.[9] This is true particularly when the matter is merely a small segment of the total pollution problem or when jurisdiction by a court could hamper or disrupt the work of administrative agencies and study groups.[10]

6.   Criminal Liability

Knowingly doing an act prohibited by an environmental protection statute is generally a crime. For example, the dumping of hazardous wastes without a federal permit is a crime.

In a prosecution for such a crime, it is no defense that the defendant did not intend to violate the law or was not negligent. It is also no defense that the defendant operated a business in the customary way and did not produce a greater amount of pollution than other, similar enterprises.

The *Arizona Mines* case involved the question of whether good intentions is a defense to a criminal prosecution for air pollution.

---

[9]   Boomer v Atlantic Cement Co. 26 NY2d 219, 309 NYS2d 312, 257 NE2d 870 (1970).

[10]   Ohio v Wyandotte Chemicals Corp. 401 US 493 (1971) (Ohio sought to enjoin Canada, Michigan, and Delaware corporations from dumping mercury into tributaries of Lake Erie. This dumping allegedly polluted the lake used by parts of Ohio as a water supply. The Supreme Court refused to decide the case).

ARIZONA v ARIZONA MINES SUPPLY CO.
107 Ariz 199, 484 P2d 619 (1971)

Maricopa County, Arizona adopted an air pollution control regulation. The Arizona Mines Supply Company operated a mine within the county. It installed equipment in its mine in order to meet the standards of the regulation. In spite of these efforts, Arizona Mines polluted the air. It was prosecuted by Arizona for violating the regulation. It raised the defense that it was not guilty because it had not violated the regulation intentionally. To back up this argument, it showed that it had done its best to comply with the regulation by installing the special equipment. The prosecution objected to the admission of this evidence on the ground that it was sufficient to show that the defendant had violated the law. That is, the prosecution claimed that it was not necessary to show that the defendant had intentionally violated the law. The trial court admitted the evidence of the defendant's attempt to comply with the law. The prosecution claimed that this was wrong and filed a petition with the state supreme court to review the decision of the trial judge admitting such evidence.

UDALL, J. . . . [The defendant contends] that the State must prove knowledge or intent as a prerequisite to conviction. [The] Maricopa County Air Pollution Control Regulation . . . provides that:

> No person shall cause, suffer, allow or permit the discharge into the atmosphere from any single source of emission whatsoever any air contaminants for a period or periods aggregating more than three minutes in any one hour which is:
> a. As dark as or darker in shade than that designated as No. 2 on the Ringelmann Chart as published by the U.S. Bureau of Mines, or
> b. Of an opacity equal to or greater than an air contaminant designated as No. 2 on the Ringelmann Chart.

Nowhere does this regulation (or the Air Pollution Act, for that matter) provide, either expressly or impliedly, that before the state may convict someone of "air pollution" it must first prove that the air contaminant was discharged knowingly or intentionally. Defendant argues that some degree of knowledge or intent is prerequisite to conviction. The State, on the other hand, contends that it need not prove intent or knowledge since this offense is more in the nature of "malum prohibitum."

After having carefully considered the apparent intent of legislature, . . . and the consequences of unabated air pollution to public health; we find that the state need not prove intent or knowledge on the part of the accused as a prerequisite to conviction. That the legislature may make the doing of an act or the neglect to do something a crime without requiring criminal intent is well-settled. *Troutner v State*, 17 Ariz 506, 154 P 1048 (1916). . . .

> Whether a criminal intent or guilty knowledge is a necessary element of a statutory offense is a matter of construction to be determined from the language of the statute, *in view of its manifest purpose and design.* There are many instances in recent times where the legislature in the exercise of the police power has prohibited, under penalty, the performance of a specific act. *The doing of the inhibited act constitutes the crime,* and the moral turpitude or *purity of the motive* by which it was prompted *and knowledge or ignorance* of its criminal character *are immaterial circumstances* on the question of guilt. The only fact to be determined in these cases is whether the defendant did the act.

With regard to the introduction by a defendant of evidence of expenditures made in installing pollution control equipment and precautions taken to avoid pollution, such will not constitute a defense to prosecution and conviction, and are, therefore, inadmissible at trial. Evidence of "extenuating circumstances" may, however, be presented to the court *after verdict* in mitigation of the penalty to be imposed. ". . . *Although extenuating circumstances would be no legal bar to conviction, they would certainly be important factors in determining a penalty, and might even warrant granting of probation."* [Emphasis added.] *Fitzpatrick v Board of Examiners*, 96 Ariz 309 at 315, 394 P2d 423 at 427.

[Admission of evidence sustained for limited purpose of determining the penalty to be imposed after the guilt of the defendant was established]

QUESTIONS

1. Why did Arizona Mines Supply Company claim that it was not guilty of violating the regulation?

B. COMMUNITY PLANNING

In order to provide for the orderly growth of communities, some planning and control is necessary. Community planning may be classified as private (restrictive covenants) and public (zoning).

7. Restrictive Covenants in Private Contracts

In the case of private planning, a real estate developer will take an undeveloped tract or area of land, map out on paper an "ideal" community, and then construct the buildings shown on the plan. These are then sold to private purchasers. The buyers deeds' will contain **restrictive covenants** that obligate the buyers to observe certain limitations in the use of their property, the nature of buildings that will be maintained or constructed on the land, and so on. If a restrictive covenant is valid, it binds anyone becoming the owner of the land if the covenant is stated in a recorded deed or if the buyer has notice or knowledge of the restriction. Consequently, the owner of any one of the tracts may sue another owner for violating the covenant, even though there is no contract between the property owners. If a restrictive covenant violates a statute, rule of law, or public policy, it is not valid and will not be enforced.

A restrictive covenant is to be construed by the same rules of construction that are applied in interpreting contracts.[11] A restrictive covenant will be given its ordinary meaning. If there is any uncertainty, the covenant will be construed strictly in favor of the free use of the land. When there is no uncertainty and no reason to depart from the meaning of the words of the covenant, a court will enforce those words.

The social forces favoring freedom of action and the free use of property cause courts to interpret restrictive covenants narrowly, so as to permit the greatest use of the land possible. For example, a restrictive covenant that expressly permits "retail" business is held to permit the use of the land as a bowling center, as against the claim that a retail business was only one that sold tangible goods to the public.[12]

8. Public Zoning

By **zoning,** a governmental unit, such as a city, adopts an ordinance imposing restrictions on the use of the land. The object of zoning is to ensure an orderly physical development of the regulated area. In effect, zoning is the same as the restrictive covenants; the difference is in the source of authority. In most cases zoning is based on an ordinance of a local political subdivision, such as a municipality or a county. Restrictive covenants, on the other hand, are created by agreement of the parties.

The zoning power permits any regulation that is conducive to advancing public health, welfare, and safety. The object of a particular zoning regulation may be to prevent high density of population.

Some zoning ordinances may be conservation-inspired. Thus, the ordinance may prohibit the extraction of natural resources from any land within the zoned area.[13]

The fact that a house is designed for the landowner by an internationally known architect does not give the landowner the right to

---

[11]   Scoville v Springpark Homeowner's Ass'n, Inc. (Tex App) 784 SW2d 498 (1990).

[12]   Westminster Co. v Union Mut. Stock Life Ins. Co. 95 NC App 117, 381 SE2d 857 (1989).
[13]   American Aggregates Corp. v Highland Township, 151 Mich App 37, 390 NW2d 192 (1986).

build the house when it violates the local zoning ordinance on a number of points.[14]

(a) NONCONFORMING USE. When the use of the land is in conflict with a zoning ordinance at the time the ordinance goes into effect, such use is described as a **nonconforming use.** For example, when a zoning ordinance is adopted that requires a setback of 25 feet from the boundary line, an existing building that has a 10-foot setback is a nonconforming use.

A nonconforming use has a constitutionally protected right to continue. If the nonconforming use is discontinued, however, it cannot be resumed. The right to a nonconforming use may thus be lost by abandonment. If the owner of a garage stops using it as a garage and uses it for storing goods, a return to the use of the property as a garage will be barred by abandonment.

(b) VARIANCE. The administrative agency charged with the enforcement of a zoning ordinance may grant a **variance.** This permits the owner of the land to use it in a specified manner that is inconsistent with the zoning ordinance.

The agency will ordinarily be reluctant to permit a variance when neighboring property owners object, because to the extent that variation is permitted, the basic plan of the zoning ordinance is defeated. Likewise, the allowance of an individual variation may result in such inequality as to be condemned by the courts as **spot zoning.** In addition, there is a consideration of practical expediency: If variances are readily granted, every property owner will request a variance and thus flood the agency with such requests.

When the desired use of the land is in harmony with the general nature of the surrounding areas, it is probable that a zoning variance will be granted. A zoning variance will not be granted on the ground of hardship when the landowner created the hardship by purchasing land that was subject to a zoning ordinance later claimed to create the hard-

ship.[15] Hardship may have been created by purchasing a lot that was too small to satisfy the zoning requirements, or by selling portions of a tract and leaving the remaining part undersized.

It is unlikely that a variance from the zoning standard will be granted when the only reason advanced for the variance is that it would enable the owner to make more money. For example, a variance would not be granted to an outdoor advertiser on the basis that it would permit the construction of billboards that would produce more money.

9.   Eminent Domain

Eminent domain is the power of government to take private property for a public purpose. The power of eminent domain plays an important role in community planning, because it is the means by which the land required for public housing, redevelopment, and other projects may be acquired. Eminent domain has not become important in the area of environmental protection, although it is always present as a possible alternative. The theory would be that the operators of a government-owned plant would be more concerned than private owners with the protection of the environment.

When property is taken by government through eminent domain, it must be taken for a public purpose and the government must pay the owner the fair value of the property taken. The taking of property for a private purpose is void as a deprivation of property without due process of law.

The fact that a zoning restriction may have the effect of preventing the landowner from making the most profitable use of the land, and may thereby lower the value of the land, does not constitute an eminent domain "taking" of the land. It does not entitle the landowner to compensation.

---

[14]   Burroughs v Town of Paradise Valley (App) 150 Ariz 570, 724 P2d 1239 (1986).

[15]   City of Merriam v Board of Zoning Appeals, 242 Kan 532, 748 P2d 883 (1988).

C. NUISANCES

The common law, supplemented by statutes, prohibits conduct constituting a nuisance.

10. Definition of Nuisance

Conduct that unreasonably interferes with the enjoyment or use of land is a **nuisance.** This may be smoke from a chemical plant that damages the paint on neighboring houses. It may be noise, dirt, and vibration from the passing of heavy trucks. Some conduct is clearly so great an interference with others that it is easy to conclude that it constitutes a nuisance, but not every interference is a nuisance. Furthermore, it is frequently difficult to determine whether the interference is sufficiently great to be condemned as unreasonable and therefore a nuisance. The fact that the activity or business of the defendant is lawful and is conducted in a lawful manner does not establish that it is not a nuisance. It is the effect on others that determines whether there is a nuisance. Thus, a landfill may be a nuisance even though operated by a city in a nonnegligent manner and in accordance with the state's solid waste disposal statutes.[16]

The courts attempt to balance the social utility of the protection of a plaintiff with the social utility of the activity of the defendant. Thus, the mere fact that the plaintiff shows

harm does not establish that the defendant's conduct is a nuisance. The court may believe that the conduct is socially desirable and therefore should be allowed to continue at the expense of the plaintiff's interest. For example, it has been held that smoke, fumes, and noise from public utilities and power plants were not nuisances, although they harmed the complaining plaintiffs. The courts believed that the interests of the community in the activity of the defendants outweighed the interests of the plaintiffs affected. Similarly, the proper use of land does not constitute a nuisance as to a neighbor, even though the neighbor does not like the use. In any case, to constitute a nuisance, the plaintiff must sustain a harm that goes beyond mere inconvenience or annoyance with the defendant's activity.[17] For example, when trees and underbrush on the landowner's land served as a screen to hide the neighbor's backyard from public view, the neighbor has no legal ground for objecting to the landowner's removing such trees and underbrush, even though the neighbor has lost the privacy that such trees and underbrush had given.

The use of the land made by its owner may restrict the freedom of use of neighboring land. In the *Hendricks* case the court was faced with the claim that digging a water well was a nuisance.

---

[16]   Wilhelm v Great Falls, 225 Mont 251, 732 P2d 1315 (1987).

[17]   Crites v Sho-Me Dragways, Inc. (Mo App) 725 SW2d 90 (1987).

HENDRICKS v STALNAKER
(W Va App) 380 SE2d 198 (1989)

Stalnaker dug a water well on his land. Hendricks, the owner of the neighboring land, applied to the Health Department for a permit to construct a septic system on his land. The permit was refused because it would place the system too near the water well on Stalnaker's land. The Hendrickses brought a suit to have the water well declared a nuisance because it restricted their use of their land. The lower court held that the water well was a nuisance and Stalnaker appealed.

NEELY, J. . . . We define a private nuisance as a substantial and unreasonable interference with the private use and enjoyment of another's land. The definition of private nuisance includes conduct that is intentional and unreasonable, negligent or reckless, or that results in abnormally dangerous conditions or activities in an inappropriate place.

Early West Virginia cases indicate that the existence of a private nuisance was determined primarily by the harm caused. . . . Gradually the focus included an examination of the reasonableness of the property's use. . . .

Any determination of liability for a private nuisance must include an examination of the private use and enjoyment of the land seeking protection and the nature of the interference.

Because the present case concerns conduct that is not a negligent, reckless, or abnormally dangerous activity, our discussion of private nuisance is limited to conduct that is intentional and unreasonable. An interference is intentional when the actor knows or should know that the conduct is causing a substantial and unreasonable interference. Restatement (Second) of Torts § 825 (1979). The unreasonableness of an intentional interference must be determined by a balancing of the landowners' interests. An interference is unreasonable when the gravity of the harm outweighs the social value of the activity alleged to cause the harm. . . . Restatement (Second) of Torts §§ 827 and 828 (1979) list some of the factors to be considered in determining the gravity of the harm and the social value of the activity alleged to cause the harm.* However, this balancing to determine unreasonableness is not absolute. Additional consideration might include the malicious or indecent conduct of the actor. Restatement (Second) of Torts § 829.

. . . In the case before us, the Hendrickses' inability to operate a septic system on their property is clearly a substantial interference with the use and enjoyment of their land. The record indicates that the installation of the water well was intentional, but there was no evidence that the installation was done so as maliciously to deprive the Hendrickses of a septic system. Mr. Stalnaker wanted to insure himself of an adequate water supply and found no alternative to the well he dug.

The critical question is whether the interference, the installation of a water well, was unreasonable. Unreasonableness is determined by balancing the competing landholders' interests. We note that either use, well or septic system, burdens the adjacent property. Under Health Department regulations, a water well merely requires noninterference within 100 feet of its location. In the case of a septic system, however, the 100 foot safety zone, extending from the edge of the absorption field, may intrude on adjacent property. Thus, the septic system, with its potential for drainage, places a more invasive burden on adjacent property. Clearly both uses present similar considerations of gravity of harm and social value of the activity alleged to cause the harm. Both a water well and a septic system are necessary to use this land for housing; together they constitute the in and out of many water systems. Neither party has an inexpensive and practical alternative. The site of the water well means quality water

---

* The Restatement (Second) of Torts § 827 (1979) lists the following "gravity of harm" factors: (a) The extent of the harm involved; (b) the character of the harm involved; (c) the social value that the law attaches to the type or use or enjoyment invaded; (d) the suitability of the particular use or enjoyment invaded to the character of the locality; and (e) the burden on the person harmed of avoiding the harm.

The Restatement (Second) of Torts § 828 lists the following "utility factors: (a) the social value that the law attaches to the primary purpose of the conduct; (b) the suitability of the conduct to the character of the locality; and (c) the impracticability of preventing or avoiding the invasion.

for Mr. Stalnaker and the Hendrickses have only one location available for their septic system.

In the case before us, we are asked to determine if the water well is a private nuisance. But if the septic system were operational, the same question could be asked about the septic system. Because of the similar competing interests, the balancing of these landowners' interests is at least equal or, perhaps, slightly in favor of the water well. Thus, the Hendrickses have not shown that the balancing of interests favors their septic system. We find that the evidence presented clearly does not demonstrate that the water well is an unreasonable use of land and, therefore, does not constitute a private nuisance.

... Because the evidence is not disputed and only one interference is reasonable, the trial court should have held as a matter of law that the water well was not a private nuisance. . . .

[Judgment reversed]

QUESTIONS

1. The *Hendricks* case states a clear rule that makes it easy to determine whether there is a private nuisance. Appraise this statement.
2. Is conduct of *A* a nuisance because *A* interferes with *B*'s use of neighboring land?
3. What is the significance of whether conduct of the actor that affects the use of neighboring property is intentional?

If conduct is held to constitute a nuisance, the persons affected may be awarded monetary damages for the harm caused and may obtain an injunction or court order to stop the offending conduct.

(a) PRIVATE AND PUBLIC NUISANCES. When a nuisance affects only one or a few persons, it is called a **private nuisance.** When it affects the community or public at large, it is called a **public nuisance.** At this point the law of nuisance is very close to environmental protection, although there is a difference between the two. Environmental protection law is more concerned with harm to the environment and less concerned with the social utility of the defendant's conduct than is the law of nuisance.

The existence of a statutory environmental protection procedure may bar or supersede the prior common law of nuisance.[18]

(b) CRIMINAL NUISANCE. Distinct from the nuisance that is harmful to other persons or to the enjoyment of the use of their land is the nuisance classified as such because it is a place where criminal acts repeatedly occur. Either by virtue of common law principles or express provisions of statute, places conducting illegal gambling or the illegal sale of liquor or narcotics are declared to be nuisances.[19]

The reason for this classification is one of practical expediency. In addition to prosecuting individuals involved in crime, the place may be shut down in the same way that any nuisance may be stopped or closed by the police.[20]

(c) PERMANENT AND CONTINUING NUISANCES. A nuisance may be classified as permanent or continuing. A **permanent nuisance** consists of a single act that has caused permanent harm to the plaintiff. A **continuing nuisance** is a series of related acts or a continuation of an activity, such as the emission of smoke from a factory.

[18]   Milwaukee v Illinois, 451 US 304 (1981).

[19]   Colorado v Garner (Colo) 732 P2d 1194 (1987).
[20]   New York v Castro, 542 NYS2d 101 (1989).

(d) NUISANCES *PER SE* AND NUI-SANCES IN FACT. Nuisances may also be classified as nuisances *per se* and nuisances in fact. A **nuisance *per se*** is an act, occupation, or structure that is a nuisance at all times and under any circumstances. In contrast, a **nuisance in fact** is situational. Whether there is a nuisance in fact depends on the surrounding circumstances viewed objectively, that is, by the effect they would have on a normal person of ordinary sensitivity.[21] For example, the raising of pigs in a farming area is not a nuisance. The same activity in a large city would be a nuisance. It is therefore not a nuisance *per se* and could only be a nuisance in fact.

Noise is not a nuisance *per se* but may be of such a character or so excessive as to become one, even though it arises from a lawful activity or business.[22]

11.   The Technological Environment of the Law of Nuisance

As technology changes, new ways of manufacturing, new methods of transportation, and new ways of living develop. As the environment changes, corresponding changes are reflected in the law.

In the *Prah* case the ancient law of property rights was tested against the modern need for solar heating.

---

[21]   Statler v Catalano, 167 Ill App 3d 397, 118 Ill Dec 283, 521 NE2d 565 (1988).

[22]   Racine v Glendale Shooting Club, Inc. (Mo App) 755 SW2d 369 (1988).

PRAH v MARETTI
108 Wis 2d 223, 321 NW2d 182 (1982)

Prah bought one of two vacant lots. On his lot he built a house heated by solar energy. Maretti purchased the neighboring vacant lot and made plans to build a house on it. If Maretti built according to his plans, his house would interfere with the solar energy utilized by Prah's house. Prah requested Maretti to build his house a few feet further away from the boundary line. There was no evidence that Maretti would be harmed if he relocated his proposed house as requested. However, Maretti refused. His proposed location satisfied the zoning law and the restrictive covenant in his deed. Prah then sued to enjoin Maretti from building his house in such a way as to interfere with the solar energy of Prah's house. From a decision against Prah, he appealed.

ABRAHAMSON, J. . . . The defendant asserts that he has a right to develop his property in compliance with statutes, ordinances and private covenants without regard to the effect of such development upon the plaintiff's access to sunlight. In essence, the defendant is asking this court to hold that the private nuisance doctrine is not applicable in the instant case and that his right to develop his land is a right which is *per se* superior to his neighbor's interest in access to sunlight. This position is expressed in the maxim "cujus est solum, ejus est usque ad coelum et ad infernos," that is, the owner of land owns up to the sky and down to the center of the earth. The rights of the surface owner are, however, not unlimited.

The defendant is not completely correct in asserting that the common law did not protect a landowner's access to sunlight across adjoining property. At English common law a landowner could acquire a right to receive sunlight across adjoining land by both express agreement and under the judge-made doctrine of "ancient lights." Under the doctrine of ancient lights if the landowner had received sunlight across adjoining property for a specified period of time, the landowner was entitled to continue to receive unobstructed access to sunlight across the adjoining property. Under the doctrine the landowner acquired a negative prescriptive easement and could prevent the adjoining landowner from obstructing access to light.

Although American courts have not been as receptive to protecting a landowner's access to sunlight as the English courts, American courts have afforded some protection to a landowner's interest in access to sunlight. American courts honor express easements to sunlight. American courts initially enforced the English common law doctrine of ancient lights, but later every state which considered the doctrine repudiated it as inconsistent with the needs of a developing country. Indeed, for just that reason this court concluded that an easement to light and air over adjacent property could not be created or acquired by prescription and has been unwilling to recognize such as easement by implication.

Many jurisdictions in this country have protected a landowner from malicious obstruction of access to light (the spite fence cases) under the common law private nuisance doctrine. If an activity is motivated by malice it lacks utility and the harm it causes others outweighs any social values. This court was reluctant to protect a landowner's interest in sunlight even against a spite fence, only to be overruled by the legislature. Shortly after this court upheld a landowner's right to erect a useless and unsightly sixteen-foot spite fence four feet from his neighbor's windows, *Metzger v. Hochrein*, 107 Wis. 267, 83 N.W. 208 (1900), the legislature enacted a law specifically defining a spite fence as an actionable private nuisance. Thus a landowner's interest in sunlight has been protected in this country by common law private nuisance law at least in the narrow context of the modern American rule invalidating spite fences.

This court's reluctance in the nineteenth and early part of the twentieth century to provide broader protection for a landowner's access to sunlight was premised on three policy considerations. First, the right of landowners to use their property as they wished, as long as they did not cause physical damage to a neighbor, was jealously guarded.

Second, sunlight was valued only for aesthetic enjoyment or as illumination. Since artificial light could be used for illumination, loss of sunlight was at most a personal annoyance which was given little, if any, weight by society.

Third, society had a significant interest in not restricting or impeding land development. . . . These three policies are no longer fully accepted or applicable. They reflect factual circumstances and social priorities that are now obsolete.

First, society has increasingly regulated the use of land by the landowner for the general welfare.

Second, access to sunlight has taken on a new significance in recent years. In this case the plaintiff seeks to protect access to sunlight, not for aesthetic reasons or as a source of illumination but as a source of energy. Access to sunlight as an energy source is of significance both to the landowner who invests in solar collectors and to a society which has an interest in developing alternative sources of energy.

Third, the policy of favoring unhindered private development in an expanding economy is no longer in harmony with the realities of our society. The need for easy and rapid development is not as great today as it once was, while our perception of the value of sunlight as a source of energy has increased significantly.

Courts should not implement obsolete policies that have lost their vigor over the course of the years. The law of private nuisance is better suited to resolve landowners' disputes about property development in the 1980's than is a rigid rule which does not recognize a landowner's interest in access to sunlight. As we said in *Ballstadt v. Pagel*, 202 Wis. 484, 489, 232 N.W. 862 (1930), "What is regarded in law as constituting a nuisance in modern times would no doubt have been tolerated without question in former times." . . .

Yet the defendant would have us ignore the flexible private nuisance law as a means of resolving the dispute between the landowners in this case and would have us adopt an approach . . . of favoring the unrestricted development of land and of applying a rigid and inflexible rule protecting his right to build on his land and disregarding any interest of the plaintiff in the use and enjoyment of his land. This we refuse to do.

[Judgment reversed and action remanded]

QUESTIONS

1. Was the nuisance involved in the *Prah* case a public or private nuisance?
2. In its opinion the court states that the American courts have repudiated the doctrine of ancient lights as "inconsistent with the needs of a developing country." What does this statement tell you as to the nature and the development of the law?
3. In its opinion, the court states that, by using private nuisance law, it is departing from the narrow protection of a landowner's access to sunlight because that law is obsolete. What factors does the court give in support of this conclusion?

The *Prah* case is a departure from American property law. However, the movements in favor of environmental protection and fuel conservation will probably lead other courts to follow its conclusion in the next century.[23]

[23] The *Prah* case has been rejected in Sher v Herbert, 181 Cal App 3d 867, 226 Cal Rptr 698 (1986).

SUMMARY

America has awakened to the fact that resources are not unlimited and that the misuse of resources can be harmful to life. This realization has led to the adoption of numerous state and federal laws aimed at preventing the pollution of air, water, and earth. With the advent of the nuclear age, the problem of disposing of wastes in such a way as to avoid environmental pollution has become increasingly acute. A person violating an environmental protection law is subject to administrative agency action, civil suit, and criminal prosecution.

Community planning has both governmental and private aspects. With respect to government, community planning ordinarily takes the form of a zoning statute or ordinance that regulates the kind of use to which land may be put. When a zoning ordinance is adopted, there may be some spots in the zoned area that are being used in a manner that violates the zoning plan. Such a nonconforming use cannot be outlawed by the zoning ordinance. As the converse of allowing the nonconforming use to continue, a person wishing to use land in a way not permitted by the zoning ordinance may petition the zoning board or authority for a variance from the general zoning plan. Government may also take part in community planning by taking land by eminent domain for use for a public purpose. At the private level community planning is accomplished by means of restrictive covenants in the deeds given by the planning owner of a large tract to the purchasers of individual lots of the tract.

Traditional equity power authorizes enjoining (stopping) of nuisances. A public nuisance may also be stopped by direct government action.

QUESTIONS AND CASE PROBLEMS

1. "Smoke, fumes, and noise from public utilities and power plants are not to be condemned as nuisances merely because some harm is sustained from their activity by a particular plaintiff." Which of the objectives of the law listed in Chapter 2 are operative?

2. What is the purpose of an environmental impact statement?

3. The Federal Oil Company was loading a tanker with fuel oil. The loading hose snapped for some unknown reason, and about 1,000 gallons of oil poured into the ocean. The Federal Oil Company was prosecuted for water pollution. It raised the defense that it had exercised due care, was not at fault in any way, and had not intended to pollute the water. Was it guilty?

4. Annabel purchased a building in an area in the city that was zoned residential. She wanted to run a quick-printing shop in the building. She was informed that she could not do so, because of the zoning regulation. She replied that she could do so, because the deed that transferred ownership of the property to her did not contain any restriction prohibiting such use. Was she correct?

5. Magnolia City wanted to build a thruway from one side of the city to the other in order to facilitate thru traffic. To acquire the land for such a highway, it purchased various parcels of land from private owners. Thompson refused to sell his land. The city tendered to Thompson the fair value of his land and demanded that he surrender the land to the city. Thompson claimed that the city could not require him to sell the land. Was Thompson correct?

6. The McConnells bought a home in the Sherwood Estates. The land was subject to a restrictive covenant that "no building, fence, or other structure could be built on the land without the approval" of the developer of the property. The McConnells built a dog pen in their yard. It consisted of a cement base with fencing surrounding the base. They claimed that approval was not required, on the theory that the restrictive

covenant did not apply because it showed an intent to restrict only major construction, not minor additions to the landscape. A lawsuit was brought to compel the McConnells to remove the dog pen because prior approval had not been obtained. Decide. [Sherwood Estates Homes Ass'n, Inc. v McConnell (Mo App) 714 SW2d 848]

7. Carlotta owns a grocery store. It is located in an area that is later zoned as exclusively residential. Can Carlotta continue to run the grocery store after the city's adoption of the zoning regulation?

8. Mark divides a large tract of land into small lots. He then sells the lots. In the deed to each buyer is a provision stating that the buyer will not build a house closer than 6 feet to any boundary line of the lot. Madeline buys one of these lots and begins to build 2 feet from the boundary line. Her neighbor, Jason, protests that Madeline cannot do this because of the 6-foot restriction in her deed. Madeline replies that this restriction was made with Mark and has no effect between Jason and Madeline. Is Madeline correct?

9. A zoning ordinance of the city of Dallas, Texas, prohibited the use of property in a residential district for gasoline filling stations. Lombardo brought an action against the city to test the validity of the ordinance. He contended that the ordinance violated the rights of the owners of property in such districts. Do you agree with this contention? [Lombardo v City of Dallas, 124 Tex 1, 73 SW2d 475]

10. Taback began building a vacation home on a parcel of wooded land. It was to be a three-story house, 31 feet high. This violated the local zoning ordinance that limited residential homes to $2\frac{1}{2}$ stories, not exceeding 35 feet. When Taback learned of this violation, he applied for a zoning variance. Because of the delay of the zoning board and because winter was approaching, Taback finished the construction of the building as a 3-story house. At the later hearing before the zoning board, he showed that it would be nec-

essary for him to rebuild the third floor in order to convert the house into a $2\frac{1}{2}$-story house. The zoning board recognized that the violation of Taback could not be seen from neighboring properties. Was Taback entitled to a zoning variance? [Taback v Town of Woodstock Zoning Board of Appeals, 134 App Div 2d 733, 521 NYS2d 838]

11. The Belmar Drive-In Theatre Co. brought an action against the Illinois State Toll Highway Commission because the bright lights of the toll road station interfered with the showing of motion pictures at the drive-in. Decide. [Belmar Drive-In Theatre Co. v Illinois State Toll Highway Commission, 34 Ill 2d 544, 216 NE2d 788]

12. The Stallcups lived in a rural section of the state. In front of their house ran a relatively unused, unimproved public county road. Wales Trucking Co. transported concrete pipe from the plant where it was made to a lake where the pipe was used to construct a water line to bring water to a nearby city. In the course of four months Wales made 825 trips over the road, carrying from 58,000 to 72,000 pounds of pipe per trip and making the same number of empty return trips. The heavy use of the road by Wales cut up the dirt and made it like ashes. The Stallcups sued Wales for damages caused by the deposit of dust on their house and for the physical annoyance and discomfort caused by the dust. Wales defended on the ground that it had not been negligent and that its use of the road was not unlawful. Decide. [Wales Trucking Co. v Stallcup (Tex Civ App) 465 SE2d 44]

13. Some sections of the city of Manitou Springs have hills of varying degrees of slope. In order to protect from water drainage and erosion, the city adopted a "hillside" zoning ordinance that required homes on hillsides to be surrounded by more open land than in the balance of the city. Sellon owned land on a hillside and claimed that the hillside ordinance was unconstitutional because it did not treat all homeowners equally. Was the ordinance valid? [Sellon v City of Manitou Springs (Colo) 745 P2d 229]

14. A modular home is a home that is constructed in two or more parts. The parts are then moved to a particular tract of land, where they are fastened together. When completed, the house is as immobile as, and has the same appearance as, an ordinary house that is constructed piece by piece. The modular home, however, costs less. The Town of Fishkill adopted a zoning ordinance that prohibited mobile homes unless they were placed in trailer parks. Did the ordinance apply to a modular home? [Kyritsis v Fenny, 310 NYS2d 702]

15. Patrick Bossenberry owned a house in a planned community area. Each lot in the area was limited by a restrictive covenant to use for a single-family dwelling. The covenant defined family so as to require blood or marital relationship between most of the occupants. Bossenberry rented his building to Kay-Jan, Inc. Kay-Jan wanted to use the building as a care home for not more than six adult mentally retarded persons. The neighbors sought to enjoin this use as a breach of the covenant. A number of Michigan statutes had been adopted, advancing the public policy of providing care for mentally retarded persons. Could the neighbors prevent the use of the property as a care home for mentally retarded adults? [Craig v Bossenberry, 134 Mich App 543, 351 NW2d 596]

52

LEASES

A lease is an arrangement by which one person has for a time the possession and benefit of real property owned by another.

A. CREATION AND TERMINATION

Leases are governed by the common law of property as modified by judicial decisions and statutes.[1]

---

[1] A uniform act, the Uniform Residential Landlord and Tenant Act (URLTA), has been adopted in Alaska, Arizona, Connecticut, Florida, Hawaii, Iowa, Kansas, Kentucky, Michigan, Montana, Nebraska, New Mexico, Oklahoma, Oregon, Rhode Island, South Carolina, Tennessee, Virginia, and Washington.

1. Definition and Nature

The agreement by which one person holds possession of the real property owned by another is a **lease**.

The person who owns the real property and permits the occupation of the premises is known as the **lessor** or **landlord**. The **lessee**, or **tenant**, is the one who occupies the property. A lease establishes the relationship of landlord and tenant.

Basically, a lease parallels a bailment, in which there is an agreement to make the bailment and a subsequent transfer of possession to carry out that agreement. In the case of a lease there is the lease contract and the interest thereafter acquired by the tenant when possession is delivered under the lease contract. The common law looked at the transfer of possession and regarded the lease as merely the creation of an interest in land. The modern law looks at the contract and regards the lease as the same as the renting of an automobile. With this new approach, typical contract law concepts of unconscionability, mitigation of damages, and the implication of warranties are brought into the law of leases.

2. Creation of the Lease Relationship

The relationship of landlord and tenant is created by an express or implied contract. An oral lease is valid at common law, but statutes in most states require written leases for certain tenancies. Many states provide that a lease for a term exceeding three years must be in writing. Statutes in other states require written leases when the term exceeds one year.

(a) ANTIDISCRIMINATION. Statutes in many states prohibit an owner who rents property for profit from discriminating against prospective tenants on the basis of race, color, religion, or national origin. Enforcement of such statutes is generally entrusted to an administrative agency.

(b) COVENANTS AND CONDITIONS. Some obligations of the parties in the lease are described as covenants. Thus, a promise by the tenant to make repairs is called a **covenant to repair.** Sometimes it is provided that the lease shall be forfeited or terminated upon a breach of a promise. That provision is then called a **condition** rather than a covenant.

(c) OTHER AGREEMENTS. The lease may be the only agreement between the parties. In contrast, there may also be a separate guaranty or a letter of credit to protect the landlord from breach by the tenant. The tenant, in addition to holding under the lease, may also hold a franchise from the lessor.

(d) UNCONSCIONABILITY. At common law, the parties to a lease had relatively uncontrolled freedom to include such terms as they chose. As the lease is increasingly treated as a contract, some states require that leases conform to the concept of conscionability and follow the pattern of UCC § 2-302.[2] A provision in a residential lease stating that curtailment of services by the landlord will not constitute an eviction unless caused willfully or by gross negligence and that such interruption will not entitle the tenant to any compensation is unconscionable. It does not bar the tenant from suing for breach of the implied warranty of habitability. Similarly, a provision in a lease declaring that the landlord is not responsible for interruptions in the various services provided tenants will not protect the landlord when the air-conditioning system is out of operation for six weeks in midsummer.

3. Essential Elements

The following elements are necessary to the establishment of the relationship of landlord and tenant:

(a) The occupying of the land must be with the express or implied consent of the landlord.
(b) The tenant must occupy the premises in subordination to the rights of the landlord.
(c) A reversionary interest in the land must remain in the landlord. That is, the landlord must be entitled to retake the possession of the land upon the expiration of the lease.

---

[2]   Flam v Herrmann, 90 Misc 2d 434, 395 NYS2d 136 (1977); URLTA § 1.303.

(d) The tenant must have an estate of present possession in the land. This means a right to be in possession of the land now.

4.   Classification of Tenancies

Tenancies are classified by duration as tenancies for years, from year to year, at will, and by sufferance.

(a) TENANCY FOR YEARS. A **tenancy for years** is one under which the tenant has an estate of definite duration. The term "for years" is used to describe such a tenancy even if the duration of the tenancy is for only one year or for less than a year.

(b) TENANCY FROM YEAR TO YEAR. A **tenancy from year to year** is one under which a tenant, holding an estate in land for an indefinite duration, pays an annual, monthly, or weekly rent. A distinguishing feature of this tenancy is the fact that it does not terminate at the end of a year, month, or week, except upon proper notice.

In almost all states a tenancy from year to year is implied if the tenant holds over after a tenancy for years with the consent of the landlord. This consent may be shown by an express statement or by conduct such as continuing to accept rent.[3] The lease frequently states that a holding over shall give rise to a tenancy from year to year unless written notice to the contrary is given.

(c) TENANCY AT WILL. When land is held for an indefinite period, which may be terminated at any time by the landlord or the tenant, a **tenancy at will** exists. A person who enters into possession of land for an indefinite period, with the owner's permission but without any agreement as to rent, is a tenant at will.

Statutes in some states and decisions in others, require advance notice of termination of this kind of tenancy.

---

[3]   In some jurisdictions, when rent is accepted from a tenant holding over after the expiration of the term of the lease and there is no agreement to the contrary, there results only a periodic tenancy from month to month rather than a tenancy from year to year. S.D.G. v Inventory Control Co. 178 NJ Super 411, 429 A2d 394 (1981).

(d) TENANCY BY SUFFERANCE. When a tenant holds over without permission of the landlord, the latter may treat the tenant as a trespasser or as a tenant. Until the landlord elects to do one or the other, a **tenancy by sufferance** exists.

5.   Termination of Lease

A lease is generally not terminated by the death, insanity, or bankruptcy of either party, except in the case of a tenancy at will. Provisions in a lease giving the landlord the right to terminate the lease under certain conditions are generally strictly construed.

Leases may be terminated in the following ways.

(a) TERMINATION BY NOTICE. A lease may give the landlord the power to terminate it by giving notice to the tenant. In states that follow the common law, it is immaterial why the landlord terminates the lease by notice.

(b) EXPIRATION OF TERM IN A TENANCY FOR YEARS. When a tenancy for years exists, the relation of landlord and tenant ceases upon the expiration of the term, without any requirement that one party give the other any notice of termination. Express notice to end the term may be required of either or both parties by provisions of the lease, except when a statute prohibits the landlord from imposing such a requirement.

(c) NOTICE IN A TENANCY FROM YEAR TO YEAR. In the absence of an agreement of the parties, notice is now usually governed by statute. It is common practice for the parties to require 30 or 60 days' notice to end a tenancy from year to year. As to tenancies for periods of less than a year, the provisions of the statutes commonly require notice of only one week.

(d) RELEASE. The relation of landlord and tenant is terminated if the landlord makes a release or conveyance of the landlord's interest in the land to the tenant.

(e) MERGER. If the tenant acquires the landlord's interest in any manner, as by inheritance or purchase, the leasehold interest is said to disappear by merger into the title to the land now held by the former tenant.

The lease may give the tenant an option to purchase the property at any time or upon the expiration of the term of the lease. The lease may provide that the lessor shall offer to sell to the tenant before offering to sell the property to anyone else.[4]

(f) SURRENDER. A surrender or giving up of the tenant's estate to the landlord terminates the tenancy if the surrender is accepted by the landlord.[5] A surrender may be made expressly or may be implied. An express surrender must, under the statute of frauds, be in writing and be signed by the person making the surrender or by an authorized agent.

(g) FORFEITURE. The landlord may terminate the lease by forfeiting the relationship because of the tenant's misconduct or breach of a condition, if a term of the lease or a statute so provides. In the absence of such a provision, the landlord may only claim damages for the breach. Terminating the relationship by forfeiture is not favored by the courts.

(h) DESTRUCTION OF PROPERTY. If a lot and a building on it are leased, either an express provision in the lease or a statute generally releases the tenant from liability if the building is destroyed. Alternatively, the amount of rent may be reduced in proportion to the loss sustained. Such statutes do not impose upon the landlord any duty to repair or restore the property to its former condition.

When the lease covers rooms or an apartment in a building, a destruction of the leased premises terminates the lease.

(i) FRAUD. Since a lease is based upon a contract, a lease may be avoided when the circumstances are such that a contract could be avoided for fraud.

(j) TRANSFER OF THE TENANT. Residential leases may contain a provision for termination upon the tenant's being transferred by an employer to another city or upon the tenant's being called into military service. Such provisions are often strictly construed against the tenant. Therefore, when entering a lease, the tenant should exercise care to see that the provision is sufficiently broad to cover the situations that may arise.

6.   Notice of Termination

When notice of termination is required, no particular words are necessary to constitute a sufficient notice, provided the words used clearly indicate the intention of the party. The notice, whether given by the landlord or the tenant, must be definite. Statutes sometimes require that the notice be in writing. In the absence of such a provision, however, oral notice is generally held to be sufficient.

7.   Renewal of Lease

When a lease terminates for any reason, it is ordinarily a matter for the landlord and the tenant to enter into a new agreement if they wish to extend or renew the lease. The power to renew the lease may be stated negatively in the original lease by declaring that the lease runs indefinitely, as from year to year, subject to being terminated by either party by giving written notice a specified number of days or months before the termination date.

The lease may require the tenant to give written notice of the intention to renew the lease. In such a case there is no renewal if the tenant does not give the required notice but merely remains on the premises after the expiration of the original term.[6]

B.   RIGHTS AND DUTIES OF PARTIES

The rights and duties of the landlord and tenant are based upon principles of real estate law and contract law. With the rising tide of consumer protectionism, there is an increasing tendency to treat the relationship as mere-

---

[4]   Moore v Dodge (Tex Civ App) 603 SW2d 236 (1980).
[5]   Roosen v Schaffer, 127 Ariz App 346, 621 P2d 33 (1980).

[6]   Ahmed v Scott, 65 Ohio App 2d 271, 418 NE2d 406 (1979).

ly a contract and to govern the rights and duties of the parties by general principles of contract law.

8.   Possession

Possession involves both the right to acquire possession at the beginning of the lease and the right to retain possession until the lease is ended.

(a) TENANT'S RIGHT TO ACQUIRE POSSESSION. By making a lease, the lessor covenants by implication to give possession of the premises to the tenant at the agreed time. If the landlord rents a building that is being constructed, there is an implied covenant that it will be ready for occupancy at the commencement of the term of the lease.

(b) TENANT'S RIGHT TO RETAIN POSSESSION. After the tenant has entered into possession, the tenant has the exclusive possession and control of the premises. This right exists as long as the lease continues and so long as there is no default under the lease, unless the lease otherwise provides. Thus, the tenant can refuse to allow the lessor to enter the property for the purpose of showing it to prospective customers, although today most leases expressly give this right to the landlord.

If the landlord interferes with this possession by evicting the tenant, the landlord commits a wrong for which the tenant is afforded legal redress. An **eviction** occurs when the tenant is deprived of the possession, use, and enjoyment of the premises by the interference of the lessor or the lessor's agent. If the landlord wrongfully deprives the tenant of the use of one room when the tenant is entitled to use an entire apartment or building, there is a **partial eviction.**

(c) COVENANT OF QUIET ENJOYMENT. Most written leases today contain an express promise by the landlord to respect the possession of the tenant, called a **covenant of quiet enjoyment.** Such a provision protects the tenant from interference with possession by the landlord or the landlord's agent, but it does not impose liability upon the landlord for the

unlawful acts of third persons.[7] Thus, such a covenant does not require the landlord to protect a tenant from damages by a rioting mob.

(d) CONSTRUCTIVE EVICTION. An eviction may be actual or constructive. It is a **constructive eviction** when some act or omission of the landlord substantially deprives the tenant of the use and enjoyment of the premises.

It is essential in a constructive eviction that the landlord intended to deprive the tenant of the use and enjoyment of the premises. This intent may, however, be inferred from conduct. There is no constructive eviction unless the tenant leaves the premises. If the tenant continues to occupy the premises for more than a reasonable time after the acts claimed to constitute a constructive eviction, the tenant waives or loses the right to object to the conduct of the landlord. The tenant cannot thereafter abandon the premises and claim to have been evicted.[8]

9.   Use of Premises

The lease generally specifies the use to which the tenant may put the property. The landlord is often authorized by the lease to adopt regulations with respect to the use of the premises. These regulations are binding upon the tenant as long as they are reasonable, lawful, and not in conflict with the terms of the lease. In the absence of express or implied restrictions, a tenant is entitled to use the premises for any lawful purpose for which they are adapted or for which they are ordinarily employed or in a manner contemplated by the parties in executing the lease. A provision specifying the use to be made of the property is strictly construed against the tenant.

(a) CHANGE OF USE. The modern lease will in substance make a change of use a con-

---

[7]   Rittenbert v Donohoe Construction Co. (Dist Col App) 426 A2d 338 (1981).
[8]   Some states prohibit a landlord of residential property from "willfully" turning off the utilities of a tenant for the purpose of evicting the tenant. Kinney v Vaccari, 23 Cal 3d 348, 165 Cal Rptr 787, 612 P2d 877 (1980) (imposing civil penalty of $100 a day for every day utilities are shut off). Such conduct is also a violation of URLTA §§ 2.104, 4.105.

dition subsequent. That is, if the tenant uses the property for any purpose other than the one specified, the landlord has the option of declaring the lease terminated.

(b) CONTINUED USE OF PROPERTY. The modern lease will ordinarily require the tenant to give the landlord notice of nonuse or vacancy of the premises. This is because of the increased danger of damage to the premises by vandalism or fire when the building is vacant. Also, there is commonly an insurance provision making a fire insurance policy void when a vacancy continues for a specified time.

(c) RULES. The modern lease generally contains a blanket agreement by the tenant to abide by the provisions of rules and regulations adopted by the landlord. These rules are generally binding on the tenant whether they exist at the time the lease was made or are adopted thereafter.

(d) PROHIBITION OF PETS. A restriction in a lease prohibiting the keeping of pets is valid.

10. Rent

The tenant is under a duty to pay rent as compensation to the landlord. The amount of rent agreed to by the parties may be subject to governmental limitations establishing maximum amounts that can be charged.

(a) TIME OF PAYMENT. The time of payment of rent is ordinarily fixed by the lease. When the lease does not control, rent generally is not due until the end of the term. However, statutes or custom may require rent to be paid in advance when the agreement of the parties does not regulate the point. Rent that is payable in crops is generally payable at the end of the term.

(b) ASSIGNMENT. If the lease is assigned, the assignee is liable to the landlord for the rent. However, the assignment does not in itself discharge the tenant from the duty to pay the rent. The landlord thus may bring an action for the rent against either the original tenant or the assignee, or both, but is entitled to only one satisfaction. A sublessee ordinarily is not liable to the original lessor for rent, unless that liability has been expressly assumed or is imposed by statute.

(c) RENT ESCALATION. When property is rented for a long term, it is common to include some provision for the automatic increase of the rent at periodic intervals. Such a provision is often tied to increases in the cost of living or in the landlord's operating costs. Such a provision is called an **escalation clause**.

In the *George Backer* case the tenant claimed that it was not bound by the escalation clause.

GEORGE BACKER MANAGEMENT CORP. v ACME QUILTING CO., INC.
413 NYS2d 135, 46 NY2d 211, 385 NE2d 1062 (1978)

George Backer Management owned an office building. It rented office space to Acme Quilting Co. The lease contained a rent escalation clause, providing for the increase of rent when the wage scale fixed by the Realty Advisory Board (RAB) rose. After the lease was executed, the wage scale was increased by RAB. George Backer did not belong to the group that was bound by the RAB wage scale and, in fact, paid its employees below the RAB scale. Nevertheless, George Backer demanded that Acme pay additional rent based upon the RAB scale. Acme refused to pay the increase in the rent. George Backer sued Acme for the amount of the increase in the rent. Judgment was entered in favor of George Backer, and Acme appealed.

FUCHSBERG, J. [The rent escalation clause in the Backer-Acme lease] was not a novel provision, but one commonly found in New York City commercial leases. . . .

The purpose . . . was to relate additional rent increases to a fluctuating factor beyond the control of either party, namely, the RAB wage rate. . . .

Significantly, the lease contains no requirement that rent escalations be measured by actual costs as opposed to the common industry-wide criterion chosen by the parties here. . . .

Nor was the operation of the clause unconscionable. Acme assumed the precise risk of which it now complains—that the RAB labor rate would rise so as to substantially increase its monthly rental payments. But parties are free to make their own contracts. Here Backer no doubt believed that it was to its economic advantage to tie the rent escalation clause to the RAB rate; though it needed no other reason, perhaps Backer also believed that if it were able to operate the building at lower than prevailing cost, it and not the tenants should be the beneficiary of its enterprise. Acme's view, fueled by its own self-interest, understandably would be the opposite.

Once a contract is made, only in unusual circumstances will a court relieve the parties of the duty of abiding by it. By no means did such circumstances exist here. Indeed, the indexing of rent or wage increases to outside factors, such as, for instance, the cost of living index which may or may not directly affect particular parties, is commonplace. So, a cost of living clause in a lease would certainly be enforceable. . . . Thus, the wage rate clause here contravened no principle of public policy nor is its effect so onerous as to shock the conscience. Hence, judicial interpretation will not relieve Acme of what it may now regard as a burdensome bargain.

We turn now to Acme's claim for reformation. . . .

Reformation is not granted for the purpose of alleviating a hard or oppressive bargain, but rather to restate the intended terms of an agreement when the writing that memorializes that agreement is at variance with the intent of both parties. . . .

The history of the lease negotiations between Backer and Acme discloses continuing awareness on the prospective tenant's part that the wage rate escalation provision might be potentially disadvantageous. The negotiations were conducted in a most businesslike, meticulous and unhurried manner by both sides. These produced substantial economic modifications to Acme's advantage. And, only a month before the culmination of the negotiations, when [Acme advised Backer that it] was not satisfied with the clause, the latter remained steadfast and the lease containing the now objectionable provision was accepted by the tenant in unchanged form.

Furthermore, [Backer's] purported oral interpretation of the clause as limiting Acme's liability to about "four or five percent" of the actual wage rate sets forth no reasonable ground for reliance. The very indefiniteness of the figures confirms this statement as an expression of opinion rather than of fact. Above all, it did not relate to a concrete fact or a past or existing event. At best, it was no more than an expression of expectations as to labor agreements which had not yet been negotiated and the outcome of which, as both parties knew, could not be foretold. As a matter of law, then, it cannot form the basis for a claim of misrepresentation. . . .

[Judgment affirmed]

QUESTIONS

1. Was the rent due to George Backer fixed in amount?
2. Was the rent escalation clause limited to the wages paid by George Backer?
3. Was the escalation clause unconscionable because it employed the RAB wage scale rather than the wages actually paid by George Backer?

11. Repairs and Condition of Premises

In the absence of an agreement to the contrary, the tenant has no duty to make repairs. When the landlord makes repairs, reasonable care must be exercised to make them in a proper manner. The tenant is ordinarily liable for any damage to the premises caused by willful or negligent acts of the tenant.[9]

(a) INSPECTION OF PREMISES. Most states deny the landlord the right to enter the leased premises except when the right is expressly reserved in the lease.

(b) HOUSING LAWS. Various laws protect tenants, as by requiring landlords to observe specified safety, health, and fire prevention standards. Some statutes require that a landlord who leases a building for dwelling purposes must keep it in a condition fit for habi-

tation. Leases commonly require the tenant to obey local ordinances and laws relating to the care and use of the premises.

(c) WARRANTY OF HABITABILITY. At common law a landlord was not bound by any obligation that the premises be fit for use unless the lease contained an express warranty to that effect. Most jurisdictions now reject this view and infer from residential leases of furnished and unfurnished property a warranty that the premises are habitable. If the landlord breaches this warranty, the tenant is entitled to damages. These damages may be set off against the rent that is due, or if no rent is due, the tenant may bring an independent lawsuit to recover damages from the landlord.[10]

In the *Abram* case a tenant whose personal property was destroyed in a fire sued the landlord for property damage based upon a breach of the implied warranty of habitability.

---

[9]   Baird-Warner, Inc. v Al-Par, Inc. (Ill App) 539 NE2d 192 (1989); URLTA § 3.101.

[10]   Knight v Hallsthammar, 171 Cal Rptr 707, 623 P2d 268 (1981).

ABRAM v LITMAN
150 Ill App 3d 174, 103 Ill Dec 349, 501 NE2d 370 (1986)

Abram lived at property owned and operated by Litman. A fire, resulting from faulty wiring, occurred on the premises. The tenant's personal possessions were destroyed. Abram sued Litman, alleging a breach of the implied warranty of habitability. Litman argued that Abram did not show that Litman had notice of the alleged defects or dangerous condition, nor had he received such notice. Litman also argued that the implied warranty of habitability cannot serve as a basis of recovery for property damage. From a judgment in favor of Litman, Abram appealed.

WEBER, J. . . . In *Jack Spring, Inc. v. Little* (1972), 50 Ill.2d 351, 280 N.E.2d 208, the Supreme Court of Illinois held that the implied warranty of habitability applied to leases, both oral and written, of multiple-unit dwellings. In *Jack Spring* the court stated that the warranty was fulfilled by substantial compliance with the pertinent provisions of the applicable building code. Subsequently several districts of the appellate court of Illinois interpreted the court's statement in *Jack Spring* to mean that the implied warranty of habitability is only fulfilled by substantial compliance with a building code. In *Glasoe* [*v. Trinkle* (1985)] our supreme court clarified this confusion by holding "that the implied warranty of habitability applies to all leases of residential real estate regardless of the existence of housing or building codes." . . . The *Glasoe* court continued by examining the scope of the implied warranty of habitability. In so doing, the court stated:

> As did the Pennsylvania court, we decline to establish rigid standards for determining habitability and its breach. However, we think the guidelines above stated, which have been enunciated in other jurisdictions, will be helpful to the fact finder in determining the extent of the warranty of habitability and whether there has been a breach thereof in a particular case. *In addition to the guidelines stated, there, of course, must be notice of the alleged defects given by the tenant to the landlord and the landlord must have had a reasonable time within which to correct the alleged deficiencies.*

The trial court relied on the above-quoted statement in determining that plaintiff was required to plead and prove that she gave notice of the alleged defects to defendants.

Plaintiff argues that the above-quoted statement is mere dicta and that we should follow our holding in *Jarrell v. Hartman* (1977), 48 Ill.App.3d 985, 6 Ill.Dec. 812, 363 N.E.2d 626. In *Jarrell* we rejected the argument that a tenant seeking to establish a breach of the implied warranty of habitability is first required to give the landlord notice of the defect and an opportunity to repair. Our [principal] reason for rejecting defendants' argument was that no such requirement had been discussed in *Jack Spring*. This question was resolved in *Glasoe*.

In our opinion the trial court interpreted the statement of the supreme court in *Glasoe* concerning notice too broadly. *Glasoe* involved patent defects. Even in the case of such defects the court laid down no precise rule as to the nature of the required notice, only that some notice must be given. The court was not called upon to decide the matter of notice in the context of latent defects of the type involved in the instant case. If such defects were not apparent nor discoverable by either the landlord or the tenant until after the damage had occurred, it is at once apparent that notice of them would be logically impossible to give. We find that *Glasoe* is factually distinguishable from the instant case.

A short discussion of how other jurisdictions have treated the question of notice is in order.

. . . Some jurisdictions have stated that a landlord's knowledge may be either actual knowledge or constructive knowledge. . . .

We believe that one of the soundest approaches was that taken in *Old Town Development*. In *Old Town Development* the court held that the notice requirement may be satisfied in various ways depending upon the facts and circumstances of the case. Actual notice of the alleged defect given to the landlord by the tenant would always be sufficient. In addition, actual knowledge of the alleged defect on the part of the landlord would also be sufficient. In some instances the landlord could be charged with constructive knowledge of the alleged defect. For example, where the alleged defect is a latent defect and the landlord was also the builder of the premises, the landlord could properly be charged with constructive knowledge of the alleged defect. *(Old Town.)* However, defendants herein could not be charged with constructive knowledge of the faulty wiring since plaintiff did not allege that defendants were the builders of the premises leased to plaintiff. See *W.C. Haas Realty Management* (noting that liability could not be imposed on a nonbuilder landlord for a breach of the implied warranty of habitability which allegedly resulted from faulty wiring which had caused a fire on the premises).

Because the instant case concerns a latent defect about which the tenant knew nothing and because there is no allegation in the pleadings upon which the landlord could be charged with constructive notice of the defect, we find that the trial court properly dismissed the complaint. While its reliance upon the broad language in *Glasoe* was perhaps misplaced, its result was correct. As we have pointed out, the instant case differs from *Glasoe*, which was concerned with patent defects. An additional reason for the proper dismissal of the complaint is that the warranty of habitability cannot serve as a basis for recovery of property damage. *Auburn v. Amoco Oil Co.* (1982), 106 Ill.App.3d 60, 61 Ill.Dec. 939, 435 N.E.2d 780.

In *Auburn* the plaintiffs' complaint alleged that the defendant landlords breached the implied warranty of habitability by providing in the leased house a furnace which was neither in working order nor reasonably safe for its intended purpose. The complaint alleged further that as a result of the landlord's breach, an explosion occurred destroying the house and causing the plaintiffs to suffer personal injury and property damage. The complaint sought damages. Stating that no cause of action exists for personal injuries resulting from a breach of the implied warranty of habitability, the trial court dismissed the complaint. On appeal we affirmed, holding that the warranty of habitability implied in a lease of a dwelling does not give rise to a cause of action for personal injuries or property damage. We noted that although the implied warranty of habitability may be used as a sword as well as a shield and that an independent action for a landlord's breach of warranty may stand, such claims are "for a deterioration in the benefits from the lease rather than for personal injuries or property damage arising from a catastrophe." . . . Because the complaint herein seeks recovery of damages for property damage, the court below properly dismissed the action. . . .

[Judgment affirmed]

QUESTIONS

1. How may notice of breach of implied warranty of habitability be satisfied?
2. Was proper notice given?
3. Why did the court refuse to give recovery for property damage?

(d) ABATEMENT AND ESCROW PAYMENT OF RENT. In order to protect tenants from unsound living conditions, statutes sometimes provide that a tenant is not required to pay rent as long as the premises are not fit to live in. As a compromise, some statutes require the tenant to continue to pay the rent but require that it be paid into an escrow or agency account. The money in the escrow account is paid to the landlord only upon proof that the necessary repairs have been made to the premises.

12.   Improvements

In the absence of special agreement, neither the tenant nor the landlord is under the duty to make improvements, as contrasted with repairs. Either party may, as a term of the original lease, agree or covenant to make improvements, in which case a failure to perform will result in liability in an action for damages for breach of contract brought by the other party. In the absence of an agreement to the contrary, improvements that are attached to the land become part of the realty and belong to the landlord.

13.   Taxes and Assessments

In the absence of an agreement to the contrary, the landlord, not the tenant, is usually under a duty to pay taxes or assessments. The lease may provide for an increase in rent if taxes on the rented property are increased.[11]

If taxes or assessments are increased because of improvements made by the tenant, the landlord is liable for such increases if the improvements remain with the property. If the improvements can be removed by the tenant, the amount of the increase must be paid by the tenant.

14.   Tenant's Deposit

A landlord may require a tenant to make a deposit to protect the landlord from any default on the part of the tenant.

(a) CUSTODY. In some states protection is given the tenant who is required to make a payment to the landlord as a deposit to ensure compliance with the lease. It is sometimes provided that the landlord holds such payment as a trust fund and must inform the tenant of the bank in which the money is deposited; the landlord becomes subject to a penalty if the money is used before the tenant has breached the lease.

(b) REFUND. It may happen that the landlord will keep the entire deposit paid by the tenant, even though it is in excess of any claim against the tenant, and tenants will not bring suit because the amount involved is too small to justify an action. Tenant protection statutes sometimes remedy this situation by requiring the landlord to refund any part of the deposit in excess of the amount actually needed to compensate for the tenant's breach.

15.   Protection from Retaliation

There is a modern trend to protect tenants from retaliation by the landlord for the tenants' exercising their lawful rights or reporting the landlord for violating a housing and sanitation code.[12] The retaliation of the lessor may take the form of refusing to renew a lease or evicting the tenant.

16.   Remedies of Landlord

If a tenant fails to pay rent, the landlord may bring an ordinary lawsuit to collect the amount due and in some states may seize and hold the property of the tenant.

(a) LANDLORD'S LIEN. In the absence of an agreement or statute so providing, the landlord does not have a lien upon the personal property or crops of the tenant for money due for rent. The parties may create by express or implied contract a lien in favor of the landlord for rent and also for advances, taxes, or damages for failure to make repairs.

In the absence of a statutory provision, the lien of the landlord is superior to the claims of all other persons, except prior lienors and good faith purchasers without notice.

(b) SUIT FOR RENT. Whether or not the landlord has a lien for unpaid rent, the landlord may sue the tenant on the latter's obligation to pay rent as specified in the lease. Or, if payment of rent is not specified, the landlord may enforce a quasi-contractual obligation to pay the reasonable value of the use and occupation of the property. In some jurisdictions the landlord is permitted to bring a combined

---

[11]   Brazelton v. Jackson Drug Co., Inc. (Wyo) 796 P2d 808 (1990).

[12]   Mobil Oil Corp. v Handly, 76 Cal App 3d 956, 143 Cal Rptr 321 (1978); URLTA § 5.101.

action to recover the possession of the land and the overdue rent at the same time.

(c) DISTRESS. The common law devised a speedy remedy to aid the landlord in collecting rent. It permitted seizure of personal property found on the premises and allowed the landlord to hold such property until the arrears of rent were paid. This right was known as **distress**. It was not an action against the tenant for rent but merely a right to retain the property as security until the rent was paid. Statutes have generally either abolished or greatly modified the remedy of distress.[13]

(d) RECOVERY OF POSSESSION. The lease commonly provides that upon the breach of any of its provisions by the tenant, such as the failure to pay rent, the lease shall terminate or the landlord may exercise the option to declare the lease terminated. When the lease is terminated for any reason, the landlord then has the right to evict the tenant and retake possession of the property.

At common law, the landlord, when entitled to possession, could regain it without resorting to legal proceedings. This **right of re-entry** is available in many states even when the employment of force is necessary. Other states deny the right to use force.

Modern cases hold that a landlord cannot lock out a tenant for overdue rent and must employ legal process to regain possession,

even if the lease expressly gives the landlord the right to self-help.

The landlord may resort to legal process to evict the tenant in order to enforce the right to possession of the premises. The action of ejectment is ordinarily used. In addition to the common law remedies, statutes in many states provide a summary remedy to recover possession that is much more efficient than the slow common law remedies.

(e) LANDLORD'S DUTY TO MITIGATE DAMAGES. If the tenant leaves the premises before the expiration of the lease, is the landlord under any duty to rent the premises again in order to reduce the rent or damages for which the departing tenant will be liable? By the common law and majority rule, a tenant owns an estate in land, and if the tenant abandons it, there is no duty upon the landlord to seek to find a new tenant for the premises. A growing minority view places greater emphasis upon the contractual aspects of a lease. Thus, when the tenant abandons the property and thereby defaults or breaks the contract, the landlord is under the duty to seek to mitigate the damages caused by the tenant's breach and must make a reasonable effort to rent the abandoned property.

In the *Sommer* case a tenant who abandoned a rented apartment asserted that the landlord was required to make reasonable efforts to rent the apartment to someone else in order to reduce the rent owed by the tenant.

---

[13] It is abolished by the URLTA § 4.205(b). Callen v Sherman's, Inc. 182 NJ Super 438, 442 A2d 626 (1982).

SOMMER v KRIDEL
74 NJ 446, 378 A2d 767 (1977)

Abraham Sommer owned an apartment building. He rented one of the apartments to James Kridel for two years. Kridel intended to marry and move into the apartment with his bride. The engagement was broken. Kridel did not marry and never moved into the apartment. He never received any keys to the apartment. In May of 1972, he wrote to Sommer explaining the situation and requesting to be released from the obligations of the lease. Sommer never replied to this letter. Shortly thereafter, a stranger asked to rent the Kridel apartment. She was admittedly a proper applicant but the Kridel apartment was not rented to her because it was under the lease to Kridel. In October of 1972, Sommer sued Kridel and claimed the rent for the entire two years that the lease would have run. Sommer did not show the Kridel apartment to anyone until the next year, when the apartment was relet to a tenant under a lease beginning September 1, 1973. In the lawsuit brought by Sommer, Kridel claimed that the amount due to Sommer should be reduced because Sommer had failed to mitigate the damages by attempting to relet the apartment. From a judgment against Kridel, he appealed.

PASHMAN, J. . . . The weight of authority in this State supports the rule that a landlord is under no duty to mitigate damages caused by a defaulting tenant. . . . This rule has been followed in a majority of states, and has been tentatively adopted in the American Law Institute's Restatement of Property, *Restatement (Second) of Property,* § 11.1(3) (Tent. Draft No 3, 1975).

Nevertheless, while there is still a split of authority over this question, the trend among recent cases appears to be in favor of a mitigation requirement. . . .

The majority rule is based on principles of property law which equate a lease with a transfer of a property interest in the owner's estate. Under this rationale the lease conveys to a tenant an interest in the property which forecloses any control by the landlord; thus, it would be anomalous to require the landlord to concern himself with the tenant's abandonment of his own property.

For instance, in *Muller v Beck,* [94 NJL 311, 110 A 831 (Sup Ct 1920)] where essentially the same issue was posed, the court clearly treated the lease as governed by property, as opposed to contract, precepts. The court there observed that the "tenant had an estate for years, but it was an estate qualified by this right of the landlord to prevent its transfer," and that "the tenant has an estate with which the landlord may not interfere."

Yet the distinction between a lease for ordinary residential purposes and an ordinary contract can no longer be considered viable. As Professor Powell observed, evolving "social factors have exerted increasing influence on the law of estates for years." 2 *Powell on Real Property* (1977 ed), § 221 [1] at 180–81. The result has been that[:]

the complexities of city life, and the proliferated problems of modern society in general, have created new problems for lessors and lessees and these have been commonly handled by specific clauses in leases. This growth in the number and detail of specific lease covenants has reintroduced into the law of estates for years a predominantly contractual ingredient.

Thus in 6 *Williston on Contracts* (3 ed 1962), § 890A at 592, it is stated:

There is a clearly discernible tendency on the part of courts to cast aside technicalities in the interpretation of leases and to concentrate their attention, as in the case of other contracts, on the intention of the parties, . . .

Application of the contract rule requiring mitigation of damages to a residential lease may be justified as a matter of basic fairness. Professor McCormick first commented upon the inequity under the majority rule when he predicted in 1925 that eventually:

the logic, inescapable according to the standards of a "jurisprudence of conceptions" which permits the landlord to stand idly by the vacant, abandoned premises and treat them as the property of the tenant and recover full rent, [will] yield to the more realistic notions of social advantage which in other fields of the law have forbidden a recovery for damages which the plaintiff by reasonable efforts could have avoided. [McCormick, "The Rights of the Landlord Upon Abandonment of the Premises by the Tenant," 23 *MichLRev* 211 (1925)]

Various courts have adopted this position. . . .

We therefore hold that antiquated real property concepts which served as the basis for the pre-existing rule, shall no longer be controlling where there is a claim for damages under a residential lease. Such claims must be governed by more modern notions of fairness and equity. A landlord has a duty to mitigate damages where he seeks to recover rents due from a defaulting tenant.

If the landlord has other vacant apartments besides the one which the tenant has abandoned, the landlord's duty to mitigate consists of making reasonable efforts to re-let the apartment. In such cases he must treat the apartment in question as if it was one of his vacant stock.

As part of his cause of action, the landlord shall be required to carry the burden of proving that he used reasonable diligence in attempting to re-let the premises. . . .

The landlord will be in a better position to demonstrate whether he exercised reasonable diligence in attempting to re-let the premises. . . .

The *Sommer v Kridel* case presents a classic example of the unfairness which occurs when a landlord has no responsibility to minimize damages. Sommer waited 15 months and allowed $4658.50 in damages to accrue before attempting to re-let the apartment. Despite the availability of a tenant who was ready, willing and able to rent the apartment, the landlord needlessly increased the damages by turning her away. . . .

Here there has been no showing that the new tenant would not have been suitable. We therefore find that plaintiff could have avoided the damages which eventually accrued, and that the defendant was relieved of his duty to continue paying rent. Ordinarily we would require the tenant to bear the cost of any reasonable expenses incurred by a landlord in attempting to re-let the premises, but no such expenses were incurred in this case.

In assessing whether the landlord has satisfactorily carried his burden, the trial court shall consider, among other factors, whether the landlord, either personally or through an agency, offered or showed the apartment to any prospective tenants, or advertised it in local newspapers. Additionally, the tenant may attempt to rebut such evidence by showing that he proffered suitable tenants who were rejected. However, there is no standard formula for measuring whether the landlord has utilized satisfactory efforts in attempting to mitigate damages, and each case must be judged upon its own facts.

[Judgment reversed]

QUESTIONS

1. What did the plaintiff claim?
2. Was the landlord entitled to recover the agreed rental specified in the lease for the two-year term of the lease?
3. Did the lessor act in a reasonable manner?

C.   LIABILITY FOR INJURY ON PREMISES

When the tenant, a member of the tenant's family, or a third person is injured because of the condition of the premises, the question arises as to who is liable for the damages sustained by the injured person.

17.   Landlord's Liability to Tenant

In the absence of a covenant to keep the premises in repair, the landlord is ordinarily not liable to the tenant for the latter's personal injuries caused by the defective condition of the premises that are placed under the control of the tenant by the lease. Likewise, the landlord is not liable for the harm caused by an obvious condition that was known to the tenant at the time the lease was made. For example, a landlord is not liable for the fatal burning of a tenant whose clothing was set on fire by an open-faced radiant gas heater.

The landlord is liable to the tenant for injuries caused by latent defects, or defects that are not apparent, of which the landlord has knowledge.[14] A new trend is beginning to appear that makes foreseeability of harm, rather than the mechanical test of whether the landlord had control of the part of the premises involved, the test of the landlord's liability.

In a number of states, by decision or statute, a landlord is liable to a tenant or a child or guest of the tenant when there is a defect that makes the premises dangerously defective, even if the landlord did not have any knowledge of the defect. Other states refuse to apply this strict tort liability concept.

(a) CRIMES OF THIRD PERSONS. Ordinarily, the landlord is not liable to the tenant for crimes committed on the premises by third persons, as when a third person enters the premises and commits larceny or murder.[15] The landlord is not required to establish any security system to protect the tenant from crimes of third persons.

In contrast, when the criminal acts of third persons are reasonably foreseeable, the landlord may be held liable for the harm thereby caused a tenant. Consequently, when a tenant has repeatedly reported that the dead bolt on the apartment door is broken, the landlord is liable for the tenant's loss when a thief enters through the door, because such criminal conduct is foreseeable. Likewise, when the landlord of a large apartment complex does not take reasonable steps to prevent repeated criminal acts, the landlord is liable to the tenant for the harm caused by the foreseeable criminal act of a third person.

In the *Rivera* case the court takes up the issue of a social hall owner's ability to foresee criminal acts occurring on the premises.

---

[14]   Alvarez v DeAguirre (Fla App) 395 So 2d 213 (1981).

[15]   Rowe v State Bank of Lombard, 125 Ill 2d 203, 126 Ill Dec 519, 531 NE2d 1358 (1988).

RIVERA v UNITED AUTO WORKERS LOCAL 179
(Cal App 2d Dist.) 266 Cal Rptr 262 (1990)

Rivera attended a birthday party at a union meeting hall owned by defendant. The hall was leased by a Maria Garcia, a resident of the area. Some members of two rival teenage gangs came to the party. Those from one gang had been invited by the lessee. The members of the rival gang had not been invited. During the course of the evening, a fight between members of the two gangs erupted. Shots were fired. Rivera was struck by one of the bullets. Rivera argued that the incident was foreseeable and that the defendant, by failing to protect him, breached a duty owed to him as an invited guest on defendant's premises. From summary judgment in favor of the defendant, Rivera appealed.

COMPTON, J. . . . Defendant in the past had leased the building to over 100 different individuals and organizations for various functions. Defendant, however, provided nothing more than permission to use the premises. Garcia was in complete control of the party. Defendant did not undertake to control the guest list or to regulate the party in any way. Defendants had no representative on the premises and had no knowledge of who would attend the party. . . .

Plaintiff's position is that the incident was foreseeable and that the defendant, by failing to protect plaintiff, breached a duty owed to him as an invited guest on defendant's premises.

Plaintiff's claim of foreseeability is premised on the assertion that certain members of the . . . Police Department would provide depositions and testify at a trial that the [area in which the party was held] has experienced a high level of teenage gang violence . . . and that the police were aware of a number of instances of "gang violence" in the area where the union hall was located. In the past, some, but not all, of the lessees of the building had hired off-duty policemen to act as security guards.

. . . Plaintiff argues that defendant was chargeable with constructive knowledge of the information possessed by the police.

It is undisputed, of course, that plaintiff was completely unknown to defendant and was not invited to the hall by defendant. Similarly, plaintiff's assailant was neither known to nor invited by defendant. . . .

The basic law of property owner's liability is easily stated but its application to a particular set of circumstances is not easily determined: "A possessor of land who holds it open to the public for entry for his business purposes is subject to liability to members of the public while they are upon the land for such a purpose, for physical harm caused by accidental, negligent, or intentionally harmful acts of third persons. . . ." (Rest. 2d. Torts, § 344, pp. 223–224.) Section 315 of Restatement Second of Torts provides: "There is no duty to control the conduct of a third person as to prevent him from causing physical harm to another unless (a) a special relation exists between the actor and the third person which imposes a duty upon the actor to control the third person's conduct or (b) a special relation exists between the actor and the other which gives to the other a right to protection." . . .

Earlier cases applying these principles involved situations where the conduct of the third person was overt and in the presence of the property owner and the property owner had clear knowledge of the threat and the ability to prevent it. . . .

The zeal with which injured persons have sought a "deep pocket" and the tendency of some courts to socialize losses resulting from criminal conduct has produced some decisions which appear to have expanded the original precepts by creation of a duty of a property owner to somehow deter and prevent crime in general. . . .

As we pointed out in *7735 Hollywood Blvd. Venture v. Superior Court*, 116 Cal.App.3d 901, 906, 172 Cal. Rptr. 528, "anyone can foresee that a crime may be committed anywhere at any time. But that foreseeability which the owners of rental property or the proprietors of public premises share with the public at large, does not per se, impose a duty on such property owners or proprietors to [institute security measures]."

Furthermore, since the identity of those youth gangs and their membership is generally not a matter of public knowledge and is learned only through police intelligence channels, the average citizen would be hard pressed to know just when and where conflict between these gangs might erupt.

In *Totten v. More Oakland Residential Housing, Inc.* (1976) 63 Cal.App.3d 538, 543, 134 Cal.Rptr. 29, the court observed: "A landlord is not bound to anticipate the criminal activities of third persons, especially where . . . the wrongdoers were complete strangers to both the landlord and the victim, and where the fight and the shooting incident leading to the injury came about precipitously. . . ."

To our mind there is a qualitative difference between the recognized duty to control the conduct of an identifiable person or persons engaged in overt conduct which threatens particular individuals under circumstances where the property owner has the duty to control that conduct and the ability to exercise effective control, and the creation of a duty to take measures aimed at affording protection from an amorphous threat of violent crime by unknown individuals.

This latter concept of crime prevention and deterrence is the primary basis for maintaining a regular police establishment. As we pointed out in [an earlier case]

> Government Code section 845 provides that: 'Neither a public entity nor a public employee is liable for failure to establish a police department or otherwise provide police protection service or, *if police protection service is provided, for failure to provide sufficient police protection service*' (Emphasis added.) ¶ That section is clear recognition of the difficulty, if not impossibility, of assessing the efficacy of a particular policing pattern and is designed to immunize public entities from speculative law suits such as the case at bench. ¶ It seems anomalous to us that a public entity which has the primary role in providing police protection is so immunized while persons not generally considered to have that general responsibility are not so immunized.

In the case at bench, defendant can be said to have known of the potential for gang violence in the . . . area—the knowledge which it shared with the public in general. The question is whether it had any additional knowledge which would create a duty to protect this plaintiff. There is no question that both plaintiff and his assailant were unknown to defendant.

Defendant did nothing more than rent the premises to a [young woman] whose avowed purpose was to hold a birthday party and who would presumptively invite her friends and acquaintances. Nothing in that situation could create any special relationship between defendant and plaintiff which would support the establishment of a duty to protect plaintiff.

Plaintiff's case also founders on the issue of causation since plaintiff's injuries did not result from any defective condition of the premises itself nor any affirmative conduct on the part of defendant or its agents. The question is what inaction on the part of defendant caused plaintiff's injury? As noted earlier, the identity and the plans of these gangs to which plaintiff attributes the violence are generally unknown except to certain police specialists and since neither the penal statutes of California nor the efforts of the . . . Police Department in the area have served to deter the numerous violent confrontations that plaintiff alleges have occurred, there is obviously no reasonable action which defendant could have taken that would have prevented the violence that did occur.

Tragic as this case is, it must be remembered that the primary cause of plaintiff's injury was the person who did the shooting and not the defendant.

Based upon the foregoing, the trial court correctly concluded that there was no tri-

able issue of fact which would have supported plaintiff's case.
[Judgment affirmed]

QUESTIONS

1. Did the defendant have knowledge of the potential for violence in his area?
2. Is a landlord bound to anticipate the criminal activities of third persons?
3. Was the landlord guilty of negligence?

(b) LIMITATION OF LIABILITY. A provision in a lease excusing or exonerating the landlord from liability is generally valid, regardless of the cause of the tenant's loss. A number of courts, however, have restricted the landlord's power to limit liability in the case of residential, as distinguished from commercial, leasing. A provision in a residential lease that the landlord shall not be liable for damage caused by water, snow, or ice is void. A modern trend holds that clauses limiting liability of the landlord are void with respect to harm caused by the negligence of the landlord when the tenant is a residential tenant generally or is in a government low-cost housing project.

Third persons on the premises, even with the consent of the tenant, are generally not bound by a clause exonerating the landlord. Such third persons may therefore sue the landlord when they sustain injuries. Thus, it has been held that members of the tenant's family, employees, and guests, are not bound when they do not sign the lease. However, there is authority to the contrary.

(c) INDEMNIFICATION OF LANDLORD. The modern lease commonly contains a provision declaring that the tenant will indemnify the landlord for any liability (of the landlord to a third person) that arises in connection with the rented premises.

18. Landlord's Liability to Third Persons

The landlord is ordinarily not liable to third persons injured because of the condition of any part of the rented premises that is in the possession of a tenant by virtue of a lease.[16]

If the landlord retains control over a portion of the premises, such as hallways or stairways, however, liability exists for injuries to third persons caused by failure to exercise proper care in connection with that part of the premises. The modern trend of cases imposes liability upon the landlord when a third person is harmed by a condition that the landlord, under a contract with the tenant, was obligated to correct or when the landlord was obligated, under a contract with the tenant, to keep the premises in repair.

19. Tenant's Liability to Third Persons

A tenant in complete possession has control of the property and is therefore liable when the tenant's failure to use due care under the circumstances causes harm to (a) licensees, such as a person allowed to use a telephone, and (b) invitees, such as customers entering a store. With respect to both classes, the liability is the same as that of an owner in possession of property. It is likewise immaterial whether the property is used for residential or business purposes, provided the tenant has control of the area where the injury occurs.

The liability of the tenant to third persons is not affected by the fact that the landlord may have contracted in the lease to make repairs, which, if made, would have avoided the

---

16 Gilbreath v J. H. Greenwalt, 88 Ill App 3d 265, 43 Ill Dec 533, 410 NE2d 539 (1980).

injury. The tenant can be protected, however, in the same manner that the landlord can, by procuring liability insurance for indemnity against loss from claims of third persons.

D.   TRANSFER OF RIGHTS

Both the landlord and the tenant have property and contract rights with respect to the lease. When either makes a transfer of them, questions arise as to the rights and liabilities of the transferee.

20.   Transfer of Landlord's Reversionary Interest

The reversionary interest of the landlord may be transferred voluntarily by the landlord, or involuntarily by a judicial or execution sale. The tenant then becomes the tenant of the new owner of the reversionary interest, and the new owner is bound by the terms of the lease.

When the landlord assigns the reversion, the assignee is, in the absence of an agreement to the contrary, entitled to subsequent accruals of rent. The rent may, however, be reserved in an assignment or a reversion. The landlord also has the right to assign the lease independent of the reversion or to assign the rent independent of the lease.

21.   Tenant's Assignment of Lease and Sublease

An **assignment of a lease** is a transfer by the tenant of the tenant's entire interest in the premises to a third person. A tenancy for years may be assigned by the tenant unless the latter is restricted from so doing by the terms of the lease or by a statute. A **sublease** is a transfer to a third person, the **sublessee**, of less than the tenant's entire interest.[17]

Whether the transaction between the tenant and the third person is a sublease or an assignment is determined by the effect of the transaction. If the entire interest of the tenant is transferred to the third person, the transaction is an assignment of the lease, without re-

gard to whether the parties have described the transaction as a sublease or as an assignment. In contrast, if there is some interest left over after the interest of the third person expires or if possession of only part of the premises is transferred, the relationship is a sublease.

(a) LIMITATIONS ON RIGHTS. The lease may contain provisions denying the right to assign or sublet or may contain provisions imposing specified restrictions upon the privilege of assigning or subletting. Such restrictions enable the landlord to obtain protection from new tenants who would damage the property or be financially irresponsible.

Restrictions in the lease are construed liberally in favor of the tenant. An ineffectual attempt to assign or sublet does not violate a provision prohibiting such acts. Likewise, there is no violation when the tenant merely permits someone else to use the premises.

(b) EFFECT OF ASSIGNMENT OR SUBLEASE. An express covenant or promise by the sublessee is necessary to impose liability upon the sublessee for the obligations of the lease. In contrast, when the lease is assigned, the assignee becomes bound by the terms of the lease upon taking possession of the property. In any case the rights of a sublessee and those of an assignee can rise no higher than the rights of the original lessee under the lease.[18]

Neither the act of subletting nor the landlord's agreement to it releases the original tenant from liability under the terms of the original lease.

When a lease is assigned, the original tenant remains liable for the rent that becomes due thereafter. If the assignee renews or extends the lease by virtue of an option contained therein, the original tenant is likewise liable for the rent for such extended period in the absence of a contrary agreement or novation by which the landlord agrees that the assignee shall be deemed substituted as tenant and that the original tenant shall be released from further liability.

---

[17]   Diamond v Menasche, 535 NYS2d 335 (1988).

[18]   Gulden v Newberry Wrecker Service, Inc. 154 Ga App 130, 267 SE2d 763 (1980).

It is customary and desirable for the tenant to require the sublessee to covenant or promise to perform all obligations under the original lease and to indemnify the tenant for any loss caused by the default of the sublessee. An express covenant or promise by the sublessee is necessary to impose such liability. The fact that the sublease is made "subject" to the terms of the original lease merely recognizes the superiority of the original lease but does not impose any duty upon the sublessee to perform the tenant's obligation under the original lease. If the sublessee promises to assume the obligations of the original lease, the landlord, as a third party beneficiary, may sue the sublessee for breach of the provisions of the original lease.

SUMMARY

The agreement between a lessor and a lessee by which one person holds possession of real property owned by another is a lease. Statutes in many states prohibit discrimination by an owner who rents property and require that the lease not be unconscionable. Tenancies are classified as to duration as tenancies for years, from year to year, at will, and by sufferance. A lease is generally not terminated by the death, insanity, or bankruptcy of either party, except for a tenancy at will. Leases are usually terminated by notice, release, merger, surrender, forfeiture, destruction of the property, or because of fraud. A tenant has the right to acquire possession at the beginning of the lease and has the right to retain possession until the lease is ended. Evictions may be either actual or constructive. The tenant is under a duty to pay rent as compensation for the landlord. In the event the lease is assigned, the assignee is liable to the landlord for the rent. Such an assignment, however, does not discharge the tenant from the duty to pay rent. In a sublease, the sublessee ordinarily is not liable to the original lessor for rent unless that liability has been assumed or is imposed by statute. In long-term leases, rent escalation clauses are often included.

The tenant need not make repairs to the premises, absent agreement to the contrary. A warranty of habitability was not implied at common law. Many states now reject this view and infer from residential leases a warranty that the premises are fit for habitation.

A landlord is usually liable to the tenant only for injuries caused by latent defects, or those that are not apparent, of which the landlord had knowledge. Some states apply a strict tort liability, holding the landlord liable to a tenant or a child or guest of the tenant when there is a defect that makes the premises dangerously defective, even if the landlord does not have any knowledge of the defect. The landlord is not liable to the tenant for crimes of third persons unless they are reasonably foreseeable.

An assignment of a lease by the tenant is a transfer of the tenant's entire interest in the property to a third person; a sublease is a transfer of less than an entire interest—either in space or time. A lease may prohibit both an assignment and a sublease. In the event of an assignment, the assignee becomes bound by the terms of the lease upon taking possession of the property; a sublessee is not liable for the lease obligations unless there is a promise by the sublessee to assume such obligations.

QUESTIONS AND CASE PROBLEMS

1. What social forces are affected by the rule governing the duty of a landlord to relet premises wrongfully abandoned by a tenant?

2. Jacqueline rented a house from Harvey for two years. At the end of the two years, she remained in the house and offered to pay the next month's rent. Harvey refused to take the rent, told Jacqueline to leave, and stated that she was a tres-

passer and could be thrown out. She claimed that she was not a trespasser, because she had lawfully entered the premises under the lease. Was she correct?

3. Rod had a five-year lease in a building owned by Darwood. Rod agreed to pay $800 a month rent. After two years Rod assigned his rights under the lease to Kelly. Kelly moved in and paid the rent for a year. Kelly then moved out without Darwood's knowledge or consent, owing two months' rent. Darwood demanded that Rod pay him the past due rent. Must Rod do so? Why?

4. Maralyn rented a farm from Dale for 20 years. She rented the south part of the land to Ching-ya for 5 of the 20 years. Was Ching-ya an assignee or a sublessee?

5. Compare (a) an actual eviction of the tenant, (b) a constructive eviction of the tenant, and (c) a breach of the warranty of habitability.

6. Clay owned a tract of land. Clay permitted Hartney to live in a cabin on the land. Nothing was said as to the length of time that it could be used by Hartney. Nothing was said as to Hartney's paying anything for the use of the cabin. Hartney died. The next day Clay closed up the cabin and put Hartney's possessions outside the door. Paddock was appointed the executor of Hartney's will. Paddock claimed the right to use the cabin. Was he entitled to do so?

7. Phillips Petroleum, Inc., leased a service station to Prather. McWilliam was a customer at the service station. A rusted window fell from the wall, injuring her. She sued Phillips Petroleum. Was Phillips liable? [McWilliam v Phillips Petroleum, Inc. 269 Or 526, 525 P2d 1011]

8. Morgan rented an apartment in the Melrose Apartments. A number of crimes were committed in the apartment house. Morgan notified Melrose that it was required to hire additional security guards in order to protect the lessees in the apartment house from crimes. Was Morgan correct?

9. The Old Dover Tavern, Inc., rented a building from Amershadian to conduct a "business under the style and trade name of 'Old Dover Tavern, Inc.' engaging in the serving and selling [of] cigars, tobacco and all kinds of drinks and beverages of any name, nature and description." Thereafter, the tenant claimed that it was entitled to sell cold foods, such as sandwiches, on the theory that such sale was "incidental to the sale of beverages." The corporation brought an action to establish that it was so entitled. Was it? [Old Dover Tavern, Inc. v Amershadian, 2 Mass App 882, 318 NE2d 191]

10. Cantanese leased a drugstore building from Saputa. Cantanese moved his store from the rented store to another location but continued to pay the rent to Saputa. Saputa, fearing that he was losing his tenant, entered the premises without the permission of Cantanese and made extensive alterations to the premises to suit two physicians who had agreed to rent the premises from Saputa. Cantanese informed Saputa that he regarded the making of the unauthorized repairs as ground for canceling the lease. Saputa then claimed that Cantanese was liable for the difference between the rent that Cantanese had agreed to pay and the rent that the doctors would pay for the remainder of the term of the Cantanese lease. Was Cantanese liable for such rent? [Saputa v Cantanese (La App) 182 So 2d 826]

11. Sargent rented a second-floor apartment in an apartment house owned by Ross. Anna, the four-year-old daughter of Sargent, fell from an outdoor stairway and was killed. Suit was brought against Ross for her death. Ross defended on the ground that she did not have control over the stairway and therefore was not liable for its condition. Was this defense valid? [Sargent v Ross, 113 NH 388, 308 A2d 528]

12. What is the liability of the landlord to the tenant for crimes committed on the premises by third parties?

13. Green rented an apartment from Stockton Realty. The three-story building had a washroom and clothesline on the roof for use by the tenants. The clothesline ran very near the skylight. There was no guardrail between the clothesline and the skylight. Mrs. Green's friend, who was fourteen years old, was helping her remove clothes from the line. Her friend tripped on an object and fell against the skylight. The glass was too weak to support her weight and she fell to the floor below sustaining serious injuries. Is the landlord responsible for damages for the injury sustained? Decide. [Reiman v Moore, 42 Cal 2d 130, 180 P2d 452]

14. What is the purpose of antidiscrimination statutes in relation to rental of real property?

15. Williams rented an apartment in the Parker House. He was an elderly man who was sensitive to heat. His apartment was fully air-conditioned, which enabled him to stand the otherwise unbearable heat of the summer. The landlord was dissatisfied with the current rental

and, although the lease had a year to run, insisted that Williams agree to an increase. Williams refused. The landlord attempted to force Williams to pay the increase by turning off the electricity and thereby stopping the apartment's air conditioners. He also sent up heat on the hot days. After one week of such treatment Williams, claiming that he had been evicted, moved out. Has there been an eviction? Explain.

53

DECEDENTS' ESTATES AND TRUSTS

Public policy dictates that when an individual dies, the cost of proper burial and other expenses that may arise in connection with death be paid. Public policy also dictates that just debts contracted before death be settled, that property owned at the time of death be taken care of and applied to the payment of expenses and the debts mentioned, and that any remainder be distributed among those entitled to receive it.

The law of decedents' estates is governed by state statutes and court decisions. The general principles and the procedures that will be discussed herein may be considered typical; but state variations exist. A step toward national uniformity has been taken by the American Bar Association and the National Conference of Commissioners on Uniform Laws by approving a Uniform Probate Code (UPC) and submitting it to the states for adoption.[1]

A.   WILLS

After all of the debts of a decedent are paid, distribution is made of any balance of the estate to those entitled to receive it. If the decedent made a valid will, the will determines which persons are entitled to receive the property. If the decedent did not make a valid will, the distribution is determined by intestate law.

1.   Definitions

Testate distribution describes the distribution that is made when the decedent leaves a valid will. A **will** is ordinarily a writing that provides for a distribution of property upon the death of the writer but which confers no rights prior to that time. A man who makes a will is called a **testator**; a woman, a **testatrix**.

The person to whom property is left by a will is a **beneficiary**. A gift of personal property by will is a **legacy** or **bequest**, in which case the beneficiary may also be called a **legatee**. A gift of real property by will is a **devise**, in which case the beneficiary may be called a **devisee**.

2.   Parties to Will

Each state has a right to prescribe the qualifications of persons who wish to make a will.

There are some variations among the states, but the following is typical.

(a) TESTATOR. Generally, the right to make a will is limited to persons 18 or older. The testator must have **testamentary capacity**.[2] In order to have testamentary capacity, a person must have sufficient mental capacity to understand that the writing that is being executed is a will, that is, that it disposes of the person's property after death. The testator must also have a reasonable appreciation of the identity of relatives and friends and of the nature and extent of the property that may exist at death.

The excessive and continued use of alcohol, producing mental deterioration, may be sufficient to justify the conclusion that the decedent lacked testamentary capacity.

(b) BENEFICIARY. Generally, there is no restriction with respect to the capacity of the beneficiary. However, when part of a decedent's estate passes to a minor, it is ordinarily necessary to appoint a guardian to administer such interest for the minor. There are two common exceptions. If there is a will that directs that any share payable to a minor be held by a particular person as trustee for the minor, the minor's interest will be so held, and a guardian is not required. Statutes often provide that if the estate or interest of the minor is not large, it may be paid directly to the minor or to the parent or person by whom the minor is maintained.

3.   Testamentary Intent

There cannot be a will unless the testator manifests an intention to make a provision that will be effective only upon death. This is called a **testamentary intent**.[3] Ordinarily, this is an intention that certain persons shall become the owners of certain property upon the death of the testator. However, a writing also manifests a testamentary intent when the testator only designates an executor and does not make any disposition of property.

---

[1]   The Uniform Probate Code has been adopted in Alaska, Arizona, Colorado, Florida, Hawaii, Idaho, Maine, Michigan, Minnesota, Montana, Nebraska, New Mexico, North Dakota, South Carolina, and Utah. A number of minor amendments have since been made. Kentucky has adopted only Article VII, Part I, of the UPC. Alabama has adopted substantial portions of Articles I and II.

[2]   Succession of Cahn (La App) 552 So 2d 1160 (1988).
[3]   Thomas v Copenhaver, 235 Va 124, 365 SE2d 760 (1988).

4. Form

Since the privilege of disposing of property by will is purely statutory, the will must be executed in the manner and with the formalities required by state statutes. Unless statutory requirements are met, the will is invalid, and the testator is considered to have died intestate. In such a case the decedent's property will be distributed according to the laws of intestacy of the particular state.

(a) WRITING. Ordinarily, a will must be in writing. Some state statutes, however, permit oral wills made by soldiers and sailors.

(b) SIGNATURE. A written will must be signed by the testator. In the absence of a provision of the statute stating that the will must be signed "in writing," a rubber stamp signature has been held sufficient. It is common, however, to require a written signature.

Generally, a will must be signed at the bottom or end. The purpose of this requirement is to prevent unscrupulous persons from taking a will that has been validly signed and writing or typing additional provisions in the space below the signature.

(c) ATTESTATION AND PUBLICATION. **Attestation** is the act of witnessing the execution of a will. Generally, it includes signing the will as a witness, after a clause that recites that the witness has observed either the execution of the will or the testator's acknowledgment of the writing as the testator's will. This clause is commonly called an **attestation clause.** Statutes often require that attestation be made by the witnesses in the presence of the testator and in the presence of each other.

Publication is the act of the testator of informing the attesting witnesses that the document that is signed before them or is shown to them is the testator's will. Some states require publication.

In some states witnesses are not required. Some states require two witnesses, and some states require three.

(d) DATE. There is generally no requirement that a testator must date a will, but it is advisable to do so. When there are several wills, the most recent prevails with respect to conflicting provisions.

5. Modification of Will

A will may be modified by executing a codicil. A **codicil** is a separate writing that amends a will. The will, except as changed by the codicil, remains the same. The result is as though the testator rewrote the will, substituting the provisions of the codicil for those provisions of the will that are inconsistent with the codicil. A codicil must be executed with all the formality of a will and is treated in all other respects the same as a will.

A will cannot be modified merely by crossing out a clause and writing in what the testator wishes. Such an interlineation is not operative unless it is executed with the same formality required of a will, or in some states unless the will is republished in its interlineated form. This was the problem in the *Currier* case.

CURRIER GALLERY OF ART v PACKARD
23 Mass App 989, 504 NE2d 368 (1987)

The will of Marjorie T. Packard, dated September 4, 1969, and a first codicil thereto, dated December 1, 1970, were admitted to probate on May 4, 1978. In August, 1985, the Currier Gallery of Art offered a document for probate as a second codicil. It was typed on what appeared to be the decedent's personal stationery, was dated November 15, 1971, and was addressed "To whom it may concern."

Before an interlineation, this document stated in part: "I give and bequeath—at my direction or if still in my possession at my death—to the Trustees of the Currier Gallery . . . my maple New Hampshire chest . . . in memory of my brother Donald Kingman Packard." The decedent had signed the instrument, and it was attested by two witnesses. On January 15, 1975, the decedent drew lines through the words "if still in my possession" and wrote by hand, in apparent substitution, the words "when I can no longer use it or." She initialed and dated the alterations but did not have the paper attested by witnesses. The executors of the will and first codicil argued that the instrument as altered could not qualify for probate because, first, it was too informal to serve as a codicil, and second, it was not testamentary in content, but declared an intention to make an *inter vivos* gift of the piece. From a decision of the probate court admitting the second codicil, the executors appealed.

GREANEY, J. . . . As it stood on November 15, 1971, the instrument was in writing, signed by the decedent (whose capacity is not challenged), and attested by two witnesses. No more was required on the formal side to make an effective codicil (or will). It did not matter for this purpose that the paper was not labelled "codicil," did not refer to the will or first codicil, and generally lacked sophistication. Moreover, the substance was testamentary. "At my direction" may be read as the equivalent or, indeed, as a reinforcement of the expression "give and bequeath" (the will used "direct" repeatedly in such a testamentary sense). The words "if still in my possession" then merely note the possibility that the piece may pass from the testatrix and be unavailable for disposition at her death; the same would apply even if the bequest was in unqualified terms. Another, perhaps more difficult, way to read the text is that the testatrix may by her direction choose to give the piece to the Gallery before her death, but if it remains in her possession at her death it shall pass to the Gallery. In that view, too, testamentary character and intention are preserved.

We turn to the possible effects of the handwritten changes. Being unattested, they were not themselves effective. What would have been the testatrix's intention in that circumstance? That the attempt at change should have at least the result of cancelling (revoking) the crossed-out words, leaving the rest of the original instrument intact? Or that the original instrument should remain wholly intact, cancellation of the crossed-out words being desired only if the changes were effective.

We need not attempt a choice because the result in either case is testamentary. On the latter, we have a testamentary gift as explained above. On the former, we have the text "I give and bequeath—at my direction or at my death—to the Trustees." The executors, by evident mistake, elide or disregard the words "or at my death." Restoring those words, we have—giving the executors the benefit of a difficult reading—a statement that the testatrix may choose to "direct" the piece to the Gallery before she dies, otherwise it passes to the Gallery at her death. This is little different from the meaning of the original instrument, and is sufficiently testamentary. . . .

[Judgment affirmed]

QUESTIONS

1. What is the purpose of a codicil?
2. Were Packard's handwritten changes to the codicil admissible to probate?
3. Did the codicil qualify for probate?

6.   Revocation of Will

At any time during the testator's life, the testator may revoke the will made or may make changes in its terms. It may be revoked by act of the testator or by operation of law.

(a) REVOCATION BY ACT OF TESTATOR. A will is revoked when the testator destroys, burns, or tears the will, or crosses out the provisions of the will with the intention to revoke it. The revocation may be in whole or in part.

A testator must have the same degree of mental capacity to revoke a will as is required to make a will.[4]

(b) REVOCATION BY OPERATION OF LAW. In certain instances statutes provide that a change of circumstances has the effect of a revocation. Thus it may be provided that when a person marries after executing a will, the will is revoked or is presumed revoked, unless it was made in contemplation of marriage or unless it provided for the future spouse. In some states the revocation is not total but only to the extent of allowing the spouse to take such share of the estate as that to which the spouse would have been entitled had there been no will.

It is also commonly provided that the birth or adoption of a child after the execution of a will works a revocation or partial revocation of the will as to that child. In the case of a partial revocation, the child is entitled to receive the same share as if the testator had died intestate.

The divorce of the testator does not in itself work a revocation, but the majority of courts hold that if a property settlement is carried out on the basis of the divorce, a prior will of the testator is revoked, at least to the extent of the legacy given to the divorced spouse.

7.   Probate of Will

Probate is the act by which the proper court or official accepts a will and declares that the instrument satisfies the statutory requirements as the will of the testator. Until a will is probated, it has no legal effect.

When witnesses have signed a will, generally they must appear and state that they saw the testator sign the will. If those witnesses cannot be found, have died, or are outside the jurisdiction, the will may be probated nevertheless. When no witnesses are required, it is customary to require two or more persons to identify the signature of the testator at time of probate.

After the probate witnesses have made their statements under oath, the officer or court will ordinarily admit the will to probate, in the absence of any particular circumstances indicating that the writing should not be probated. A certificate or decree that officially declares that the will is the will of the testator and has been admitted to probate is then issued.

Any qualified person wishing to object to the probate of the will on the ground that it is not a proper will may appear before the official or court prior to the entry of the decree of probate. A person may petition after probate to have the probate of the will set aside.

8.   Will Contest

The probate of a will may be refused or set aside on the ground that the will is not the free expression of the intention of the testator. It may be attacked on the ground of (a) lack of mental capacity to execute a will; (b) undue influence, duress, fraud, or mistake existing at the time of the execution of the will that induced or led to its execution; or (c) forgery. With the exception of mental capacity, these terms mean the same as they do in contract law.

If it is found that any one of these elements exists, the probate of the will is refused or set aside. The decedent's estate is then distributed as if there had been no will unless an earlier will can be probated.

The *Bailey* case involved a will contest.

---

[4]   May v Estate of McCormick (Wyo) 769 P2d 395 (1989).

BAILEY v CLARK

_____ Ill App 3d _____, _____ Ill Dec _____, 561 NE2d 367 (1990)

Everett Clark died March 28, 1987. Harold Clark, a nephew of the decedent, filed a petition to have the will declared invalid. Everett Clark had lived with his sister Lola. Everett Clark met with his attorney Wham to discuss preparation of his last will and testament. He was to return the next day and execute the instrument. He was unable to do so because he developed complications from a perforated ulcer and was hospitalized. He underwent surgery. From that time until his death, he was in intensive care and was provided with an endotracheal tube attached to a ventilator to help him breathe. The placement of this tube made it impossible for him to speak. Everett Clark's cousin John Bailey and Vera Horton, John Bailey's sister-in-law, retrieved the will prepared by Wham. They took it to another attorney, Frank Walker, to have him finalize the execution of the will. Everett Clark was asked a few questions at the hospital to determine whether he understood what he was doing. Everett Clark marked "X" on the will with the assistance of Walker but in no way acknowledged that it was his will or that he knew the contents of the instrument. From a decision in favor of Harold Clark, Bailey filed a petition contesting the denial of the will to probate.

CHAPMAN, J. . . . Dr. Martin, the emergency room physician who attended Clark when he was admitted to the hospital, testified that he followed Clark's case and saw him every day while Clark was in the hospital. Dr. Martin testified that in his medical opinion, on March 25 Everett Clark was alert, competent, and capable of executing legal documents. It was revealed during cross-examination that Everett Clark passed into a coma on March 26. Dr. Martin testified, however, that it was possible that the decedent could have been perfectly competent before noon on March 25, and could have passed into a coma on March 26.

Dorothy Smith, an attesting witness to the will, testified that she had known Everett Clark for eight years, and believed him to be of "sound mind and memory and under no undue influence" when she was asked to witness the signing of the will. Immediately prior to signing the will she spoke with Everett Clark. Smith testified that "he couldn't talk verbally, but he could answer in a different way by nodding his head yes and no." She asked Clark "if he knew me and if he knew we were all there and he shook his head yes." Dorothy Smith testified that Mr. Walker then talked with Clark and said, "this is your will and testament, asked if John Bailey was his cousin. He asked if he wanted to leave everything to John Bailey; if he knew everything about this will." When asked by counsel whether Everett Clark indicated to Walker that he knew all about the will, Smith testified that he "didn't indicate that as such. He gave me the impression and I believed the man knew what was going on."

The second attesting witness, Vera Mae Horton, also testified that she had known Clark for eight years, and that at the time the will was executed she believed Everett Clark to be of sound mind and memory. She answered affirmatively when asked whether she believed Clark was capable of understanding ordinary business transactions and competent to make a will at the time he signed the document.

When a person executes a will he must possess sufficient mental capacity to know the natural objects of his bounty, to comprehend the character and extent of his property, to understand the particular business in which he is engaged, and to dispose of said property pursuant to a plan formed in his mind. . . . Lay persons may testify in a will contest concerning the issue of testamentary capacity as long as they testify to sufficient facts and circumstances indicating that their opinion is not a guess, speculation or suspicion. . . . No witness testified that he or she believed Everett Clark was lacking in the elements of testamentary capacity on March 25, 1987. All of the witnesses who testified as to the decedent's mental state declared their belief that Clark was of sound mind and memory at the time he signed the will. We find that there was sufficient evidence from which the jury could conclude that the decedent possessed the requisite testamentary capacity to make a will.

Section 4-3 of the Probate Act of 1975 (Ill.Rev.Stat.1987, ch. 110½, par. 4-3) provides that "Every will shall be in writing, signed by the testator or by some person in his presence and by his direction and attested in the presence of the testator by 2 or more credible witnesses." There is no question that the will was in written form. Evidence was presented, however, which raised the question of whether the will was signed as contemplated by section 4-3.

The will consists of two pages. At the bottom of page one is a typed signature line with the name Everett J. Clark typed underneath. Above the signature line is a handwritten "X". Although it is not designated on the instrument that the "X" represents the testator's mark, this is not enough to invalidate the will. A will may be valid where it is signed by mark even though the mark is not accompanied by the testator's name or by the words "his mark." . . .

There was testimony that Everett Clark did not mark the "X" without assistance. It was Dr. Martin's testimony that "from the first night post-operative, Mr. Clark pulled his [endotracheal] tube out, so his arms were restrained throughout the time." Attorney Walker testified that when the will was executed he placed a pencil in Everett Clark's hand because Clark's hand was tied down. Walker testified that he helped Everett Clark "find the line and we guided his hand and he made an "X" and I held the pen in his hand." Dorothy Smith and Vera Mae Horton each confirmed Walker's assisting Everett Clark mark the "X" on the will. Dorothy Smith could not recall whether Clark was asked to make the mark himself, but recalled that he was given a pencil and helped to mark.

If a guided or assisted signature is placed on a will at the request of the person making the will and such person thereafter in the presence of two witnesses acknowledges the instrument to be his will, voluntarily made, the requirements of the statute have been met. There was no testimony presented that Everett Clark requested assistance in marking the "X". There was sufficient evidence presented, however, that Everett Clark's condition necessitated that he be assisted in marking the "X". The greatest dispute in the testimony is whether the testator, in the presence of the attesting witnesses, acknowledged the instrument as his will or was aware of the contents of the document.

William Wham, the attorney who prepared the will, testified that after he prepared the instrument he never had the opportunity to read or review the will with Everett Clark.

Vera Mae Horton testified that prior to March 25, 1987, the will was never read to Everett Clark in her presence. She further testified that she did not know whether the will was read to Everett Clark on March 25. When counsel asked her whether Clark ever told her by any means on March 25, 1987, that the document was his last will and testament, she testified, "no, not me." Horton did testify, however, "When Mr. Walker asked him if this is what—if this was his will and if this is what he wanted and he shook his head, yes."

Smith, the other attesting witness, testified that just prior to Everett Clark's signing the will, she asked him if he knew that the attorney was there, and he responded by nodding affirmatively. She testified that Walker then spoke with Everett Clark, and explained to him that "he was there at the last will and testament. . . . He said, this is your will and testament, asked if John Bailey was his cousin . . . if he wanted to leave everything to John Bailey; if he knew everything about the will." When counsel asked Smith whether Clark indicated to the attorney that he knew all about the will, Smith testified, "he didn't indicate that as such . . . I believed the man knew what was going on."

The only witness who testified that the will was read to Everett Clark and that Clark was asked if he wanted to sign the will, was attorney Frank Walker. Walker, who represents the proponent in this case, testified that when he asked Clark, after reading the will to him, whether that is what Clark wanted, Clark shook his head yes.

The testimony of the witnesses who attested the execution of the will was not wholly conclusive on the issues of whether Everett Clark acknowledged the instrument as his will or knew the contents of the instrument executed as his will. Although Clark's physical disability alone cannot be considered as evidence that he did not know the contents of the instrument which he executed . . . based on the testimony presented in the instant case, it was entirely reasonable for the jury to find that Everett Clark did not acknowledge that the instrument was his will, and did not know the contents of the instrument.

On the question of the valid execution of a will in a proceeding for its probate, the question of the credibility of the witnesses is for the court hearing the case, and where it has given credit to the testimony of subscribing witnesses, this court will not disturb its judgment. . . . The credibility of witnesses and the weight to be accorded their testimony are matters for the jury to determine, and unless its determination is manifestly against the weight of the evidence, it will not be disturbed on appeal. . . . We conclude that the record does not support the proponent's contention that the verdict was against the manifest weight of the evidence, and therefore the judgment must be affirmed.

[Judgment affirmed]

QUESTIONS

1. Did the decedent possess the requisite testamentary capacity to make a will?
2. Is a will valid where it is signed by a mark?
3. What was the basis for the court's decision?

9. Special Kinds of Wills

A **holographic will** is an unwitnessed will that is written by the testator entirely by hand. In some states no distinction is made between holographic and other wills. In other states the general body of the law of wills applies, but certain variations are established. Thus, it may be required that a holographic will be dated.

A **nuncupative will** is an oral will made and declared by the testator in the presence of witnesses to be a will. Generally, it can be made only with respect to personal property during the last illness of the testator. It is commonly provided that a nuncupative will cannot be probated unless the witnesses reduce it to writing and sign the writing within a certain period of time after the declaring of the will.

Soldiers and sailors generally may make an oral or a written will of their personal estates without complying with the formalities required of other wills. It is sufficient that testamentary intent be shown. A will made by a soldier or sailor is not revoked by the termination of the testator's period of service. It can only be revoked in the same manner as any other will.

Self-proved wills are wills that eliminate some formalities of proof by being executed in the way set forth by statute. Self-proved wills are recognized in those states following the Uniform Probate Code. A will may be simultaneously executed, attested, and made self-proved, by acknowledgement by the testator and by affidavits of the witnesses. The acknowledgment and affidavits must each be made before an officer authorized to administer oaths under the laws of the state in which execution occurs. They must be evidenced by the officer's certificate, under official seal.

The self-proving provisions attached to the will are not a part of the will. They concern only the matter of its proof. The only purpose served by self-proving provisions is to admit a will to probate without the testimony of a subscribing witness. It was not the purpose of legislatures, upon enacting the statute permitting self-proving wills, to amend or repeal the requirement that the will itself must meet the requirements of the law. The execution of a valid will is a condition precedent to the use of the self-proving provisions.

Living wills, which allow individuals to make their wishes known regarding life-sustaining medical treatments, are legal in most states. Personal wishes are entitled to constitutional protection, as long as they are expressed clearly.

B. DISTRIBUTION UNDER THE WILL

If the decedent died leaving a valid will, the last phase of the administration of the estate by the decedent's personal representative is the distribution of property remaining after the payment of all debts and taxes, in accordance with the provisions of the will.

10. Legacies

The testator will ordinarily bequeath to named persons certain sums of money, called **general legacies** because no particular money is specified. The testator may bequeath identified property, called **specific legacies** or **specific devises.** Thus, the testator may say, "$1,000 to *A*; $1,000 to *B*; my auto to *C*." The first two bequests are general, the third is specific. After such bequests, the testator may make a bequest of everything remaining, called a **residuary bequest,** such as "the balance of my estate to *D*."

(a) ABATEMENT OF LEGACIES. Assume in the preceding example that after all debts are paid, there remains only $1,500 and the auto. What disposition is to be made? Legacies **abate** or bear loss in the following order: (1) residuary, (2) general, (3) specific. The law also holds that legacies of the same class abate proportionately. Accordingly, in the hypothetical case, *C*, the specific legatee, would receive the auto; *A* and *B*, the general legatees, would each receive $750, and *D*, the residuary legatee, would receive nothing.

(b) ADEMPTION OF PROPERTY. When specifically bequeathed property is sold or given away by the testator prior to death, the bequest is considered **adeemed** or canceled. The specific legatee is not entitled to receive any property or money. Ademption has the same consequence as though the testator had formally canceled the bequest.

(c) ANTILAPSE STATUTES. If the beneficiary named in the testator's will has died before the testator and the testator did not make any alternate provision applicable in such a case, the gift ordinarily does not lapse. **Antilapse** statutes commonly provide that the gift to the deceased beneficiary shall not lapse but that the children or heirs of that beneficiary may take the legacy in the place of the de-

FIGURE 53-1   NEW YORK LIVING WILL

New York Living Will

I,   *John Jones*   , being of sound mind, make this statement as a directive to be followed if I become permanently unable to participate in decisions regarding my medical care. These instructions reflect my firm and settled commitment to decline medical treatment under the circumstances indicated below:

I direct my attending physician to withhold or withdraw treatment that serves only to prolong the process of my dying, if I should be in an incurable or irreversible mental or physical condition with no reasonable expectation of recovery.

These instructions apply if I am a) in a terminal condition; b) permanently unconscious; or c) if I am conscious but have irreversible brain damage and will never regain the ability to make decisions and express my wishes.

I direct that treatment be limited to measures to keep me comfortable and to relieve pain, including any pain that might occur by withholding or withdrawing treatment.

While I understand that I am not legally required to be specific about future treatments, if I am in the condition(s) described above I feel especially strongly about the following forms of treatment:

I do not want cardiac resuscitation.
I do not want mechanical respiration.
I do not want tube feeding.
I do not want antibiotics.

I do want maximum pain relief.

Other directions (insert personal instructions):   *NONE*

These directions express my legal right to refuse treatment, under the law of New York. I intend my instructions to be carried out, unless I have rescinded them in a new writing or by clearly indicating that I have changed my mind.

Signed: *John Jones*
Witness: *Earl Hummel*
Address: *7852 Bailey Avenue*
Buffalo, New York
Witness: *Ramona Valey*
Address: *8921 Clinton Street*
Buffalo, New York

Keep the signed original with your personal papers at home. Give copies of the signed original to your doctor, family, lawyer and others who might be involved in your care.

ceased beneficiary.[5] An antilapse statute does not apply if the testator specifies a disposition that should be made of the gift if the original legatee has died.

11. Election to Take Against the Will

In order to protect the husband or wife of a testator, the surviving spouse may generally ignore the provisions of a will and elect to take against the will. In such a case the surviving spouse receives the share of the estate he or she would have received had the testator died without leaving a will, or a fractional share specified by statute.

The right to take against the will is generally barred by certain kinds of misconduct of the surviving spouse. Thus, if the spouse is guilty of such desertion or nonsupport as would have justified the decedent's obtaining a divorce, the surviving spouse usually cannot elect to take against the will.

12. Disinheritance

With two exceptions,[6] any person may be disinherited or excluded from sharing in the estate of a decedent. A person who would inherit if there were no will is excluded from receiving any part of a decedent's estate if the decedent has left a will giving everything to other persons.

13. Construction of Will

The will of a decedent is to be interpreted according to the ordinary or plain meaning evidenced by its words. The court will strive to give effect to every provision of the will in order to avoid concluding that any part of the decedent's estate was not disposed of by the will.[7]

C. INTESTACY

If the decedent does not effectively dispose of all property by will or does not have a will, the decedent's property is distributed to certain relatives. Since such persons acquire or succeed to the rights of the decedent and since the circumstance under which they do so is the absence of an effective will, it is said that they acquire title by **intestate succession.**

The right of intestate succession or inheritance is not a basic right of the citizen or an inalienable right. It exists only because the state legislature so provides. It is within the power of the state legislature to modify or destroy the right to inherit property.

14. Plan of Intestate Distribution

Although wide variations exist among the statutory provisions of the states, a common pattern of intestate distribution can be observed.

(a) SPOUSES. The surviving spouse of the decedent, whether husband or wife, shares in the estate. Generally, the amount received is a fraction that varies with the number of children. If no children survive, the spouse is generally entitled to take the entire estate. Otherwise, the surviving spouse ordinarily receives a one-half or one-third share of the estate.

(b) LINEALS. **Lineals** or **lineal descendants** are blood descendants of the decedent. That portion of the estate that is not distributed to the surviving spouse is generally distributed to lineals.

(c) PARENTS. If the estate has not been fully distributed by this time, the remainder is commonly distributed to the decedent's parents.

(d) COLLATERAL HEIRS. These are persons who are not descendants of the decedent but who are related through a common ancestor. Generally, brothers and sisters and their descendants share any part of the estate that has not already been distributed.

Statutes vary as to how far distribution will be made to the descendants of brothers

---

[5] Malecki's Estate, 79 App Div 2d 799, 435 NYS2d 112 (1980).

[6] The exceptions to this rule are based (a) upon the election of a spouse to take against the will and (b) in certain cases upon the partial revocation of a will by a subsequent marriage, birth, or adoption.

[7] Estate of Christensen (Iowa App) 461 NW2d 469 (1990).

and sisters. Under some statutes a degree of relationship is specified, such as first cousins, and no person more remotely related to the decedent is permitted to share in the estate. If the entire estate is not distributed within the permitted degree of relationship, the property that has not been distributed is given to the state government. This right of the state to take the property is the **right of escheat.** Under some statutes the right of escheat arises only when there is no relative of the decedent, however remotely related.

(e) DISTRIBUTION *PER CAPITA* AND *PER STIRPES.* The fact that different generations of distributees may be entitled to receive the estate creates a problem of determining the proportions in which distribution is to be made. When all the distributees stand in the same degree of relationship to the decedent, **distribution** is made **per capita,** each receiving the same share. Thus, if the decedent is survived by three children, *A, B,* and *C,* each of them is entitled to receive one-third of the estate.

If the distributees stand in different degrees of relationship, distribution is made in as many equal parts as there are family lines or *stirpes* represented in the nearest generation. Parents take to the exclusion of their children or subsequent descendants; and when members of the nearest generation have died, their descendants take by way of representation. This is called **distribution per stirpes** or **stipital distribution.**

FIGURE 53-2   DISTRIBUTION *PER CAPITA* AND *PER STIRPES*

(f) MURDER OF DECEDENT. Statutes generally provide that a person who murders the decedent cannot inherit from the victim by intestacy. In the absence of such a statute, courts are divided as to whether the heir may inherit.

(g) DEATH OF DISTRIBUTEE AFTER DECEDENT. The persons entitled to distribution of a decedent's estate are determined as of the date of death. If a distributee dies thereafter, the rights of the distributee are not lost but pass from the original decedent's estate to the deceased distributee's estate.

(h) SIMULTANEOUS DEATH. The Uniform Simultaneous Death Act[8] provides that

8   This Act has been adopted for the District of Columbia and the Panama Canal Zone and in every state except Louisiana and Ohio.

when survivorship cannot be established, "the property of each person shall be disposed of as if he had survived the other."[9]

D.   ADMINISTRATION OF DECEDENTS' ESTATES

A decedent's estate consists of the assets that a person owns at death. It must be determined who is entitled to receive that property. If the decedent owed debts, those debts must be paid first. After that, any balance is to be distributed according to the terms of any will, or by the intestate law if the decedent did not leave a will.

15.   Definitions

The decedent has the privilege of naming in the will the person who will administer the estate. A man named in a will to administer the estate of the decedent is an **executor**; a woman, an **executrix**. If the decedent failed to name an executor or did not leave a will, the law permits another person, usually a close relative, to obtain the appointment of someone to wind up the estate. This person is an **administrator** or **administratrix**.

In certain special instances a temporary administrator may be appointed. Thus, if there is a will contest, an **administrator** *pendente lite* may be appointed. This is an administrator who serves during the litigation for the purpose of preserving the estate.

Administrators and executors are often referred to generally as **personal representatives** of the decedents, since they represent the decedents or stand in their place.

16.   When Administration Is Not Necessary

No administration is required when the decedent did not own any property at the time of death or when all the property owned was jointly owned with another person who acquired the decedent's interest by right of survivorship. Thus, if all of the property of a husband and wife is held as tenants by the entireties, no administration is required upon the death of either of them. The other automatically acquires the entire estate free of any debts or liabilities of the decedent.

In some states special statutes provide for a simplified administration when the decedent leaves only a small estate.

17.   Appointment of Personal Representative

Both executors and administrators must be appointed to act as such by a court or officer designated by law. The appointment is made by granting to the personal representative **letters testamentary,** in the case of an executor, or **letters of administration,** in the case of an administrator. For the appointment of a personal representative, an application or petition is filed with the court or officer, setting forth the details of the decedent's death, stating that the decedent, if a resident of the state, lived within the county or, if a nonresident, that property of the decedent is within the county, and reciting the facts that justify the appointment of the personal representative.

(a) PERSON ENTITLED TO ACT AS PERSONAL REPRESENTATIVE. If the decedent has named an executor, that person has the right to act as personal representative or to decline to do so. If no executor has been named, an administrator is appointed.

The right to act as administrator is regulated by statutes, which generally give the right to administer to the surviving spouse. If there is no surviving spouse or if the spouse declines, the right is given to the next of kin.

(b) OATH AND BOND. A personal representative who is appointed is required to take an oath and to file a bond that the estate will be properly administered according to law. In some states an executor is not required to furnish a bond if a resident of the state and in sound financial condition or if the testator has expressly directed that no bond be required.

---

[9]   Special provision is made in the case of beneficiaries, joint tenants, tenants by entireties, community property, and insurance policies.

18.   Proof of Claims Against the Estate

The statutes vary widely with respect to the presentation of claims against a decedent's estate. In very general terms the statutes provide for some form of public notice of the grant of letters, as by advertisement. Creditors are then required to give notice of their claims within a period specified either by statute or a court order (for example, within six months). In most states the failure to present the claim within the specified time bars the claim.

E.   TRUSTS

A **trust** is a legal device by which property, real or personal, is held by one person for the benefit of another. Legal problems in the area of trusts invariably require a determination as to the nature of the relationship created by the trust and the rights and obligations of the parties with respect to that relationship.

19.   Definitions

The property owner who creates the trust is the **settlor**. (The word *settlor* is taken from the old legal language of "settling the property in trust.") The settlor is sometimes called the *donor* or *trustor*. The person to whom the property is transferred in trust is the **trustee**. The person for whose benefit the trustee holds the property is the **beneficiary** (or *cestui que trust*).

Property held in trust is sometimes called the **trust corpus, trust fund, trust estate,** or **trust res.** A distinction is made between the **principal**, or the property in trust, and the **income** that is earned by the principal and distributed by the trustee.

Although an express trust is ordinarily created by a transfer of property, the settlor may retain the property as trustee for the beneficiary. The fact that there is a duty to make a payment does not create a trust.

If the trust is created to take effect within the lifetime of the settlor, it is a **living trust** or an **inter vivos trust.** If the trust is provided for in the settlor's will and is to become effective only when the will takes effect after death, the trust is called a **testamentary trust.**

20.   Creation of Trusts

The requirements to create a trust are not uniform, but the following are typical of what is or is not required.

(a) CONSIDERATION. Since a trust is a transfer of property, consideration is not required, although the absence of consideration may show that the trust is a transfer in fraud of creditors.

(b) LEGALITY. A trust may generally be created for any lawful purpose. A trust is invalid when it is for an unlawful purpose or is in fraud of creditors.

(c) CAPACITY OF BENEFICIARY. The capacity of the beneficiary of the trust to hold property or to contract is immaterial. Many trusts are created because the beneficiary lacks legal or actual capacity to manage the property.

(d) FORMALITY. In creating a trust, it is common practice to execute a writing, called a **trust agreement** or **deed of trust.** No particular form of language is necessary to create a trust, so long as the property, the trust purpose, and the beneficiaries are designated. If an inter vivos trust relates to an interest in land, the statute of frauds requires that the trust be evidenced by a writing setting forth the details of the trust. A writing, signed by the trustee and referring to a deed from the trustor can satisfy this requirement, as the *McCaffrey* case illustrates. When the trust depends upon a transfer of title to land, there must be a valid transfer of the title to the trustee.

A trust in personal property may be declared orally without any writing. If a trust is created by the will of the settlor, there must be a writing that meets the requirements of a will. The same is true when the trust is not intended to come into existence until the death of the settlor.

In the absence of a specific requirement of the statute of frauds as to land or of the statutes setting forth the formal requirements for wills, any conduct or writing that shows an intent to create a trust will be given effect.

McCAFFREY v LAURSEN
215 Mont 305, 697 P2d 103 (1985)

T. K. Laursen executed a deed that purported to convey his Lincoln County property to his son Orville. On the day the deed was executed, Orville Laursen executed an affidavit acknowledging a transfer of property from T. K. Laursen and agreeing that the property would be held in trust for T. K., that T. K. was to receive all rents and profits from the property, and that the property would be reconveyed upon trustor's request or death. Because of the father's mental and physical condition, a conservator was appointed to manage his affairs. McCaffrey, the conservator, sued Orville to recover title to the property. Orville contended that no trust existed. From a judgment in favor of the conservator of the father's estate, Orville appealed.

SHEEHY, J. . . . On July 21, 1981, T. K. executed a deed which purported to convey all title and interest in his Lincoln County property to his son Orville A. Laursen, defendant-appellant herein. On the same day, a separate document, defendant's Exhibit B, was executed and signed by Orville A. Laursen. The document provided:

The undersigned acknowledges that as of this date his father, T. K. LAURSEN, did by written Deed convey certain property to him to be held by him in Trust for the said T. K. Laursen (a copy of said Deed is attached hereto). Undersigned covenants and agrees that all income from such properties shall belong to T. K. Laursen and that he, the affiant will re-convey the property to T. K. Laursen at anytime the said T. K. Laursen requests and that if the said T. K. Laursen should die while the property is still in the name of affiant such property shall be considered as an asset of T. K. Laursen's estate and be disposed of in accordance with T. K. Laursen's Will.

This document was delivered by appellant to Shelton R. Williams, T. K.'s attorney.

Based on these documents and the testimony of defendant, the District Court ruled that defendant holds the properties in trust for his father and by the terms of the trust, defendant is obligated to reconvey the property to T. K. and to account for all income from the properties. Appellant appeals this order and contends that there is no evidence that a trust existed. . . .

The creation of a voluntary trust as to the trustor is governed by § 72-20-107, MCA. Section 72-20-108, MCA, governs as to the trustee. They provide:

72-20-107. *Voluntary trust—how created as to trustor*. Subject to the provisions of 72-24-102, a voluntary trust is created, as to the trustor and beneficiary, by any words or acts of the trustor indicating with reasonable certainty:
(1) an intention on the part of the trustor to create a trust; and
(2) the subject, purpose, and beneficiary of the trust.

72-20-108. *Voluntary trust—how created as to trustee.* Subject to the provisions of 72-24-102, a voluntary trust is created, as to the trustee, by any words or acts of his indicating with reasonable certainty:
(1) his acceptance of the trust or his acknowledgment, made upon sufficient consideration, of its existence; and
(2) the subject, purpose, and beneficiary of the trust.

Section 72-24-102, MCA, refers to trusts concerning real property. It provides:

No trust in relation to real property is valid unless created or declared by:
(1) a written instrument subscribed by the trustee or his agent thereto authorized in writing;
(2) the instrument under which the trustee claims the estate affected; or
(3) operation of law.

The status of Orville A. Laursen, the appellant in this action, is that of trustee. He was entrusted with the property of T. K. Laursen. Exhibit B previously set forth herein and signed by appellant acknowledges that T. K. will receive all rents and profits from the properties and that appellant promises to reconvey the property on request. Together with the deed referred to therein, they satisfy the requirements of § 72-24-102, MCA. This instrument on its face conclusively proves that appellant accepted the deed from his father with the intent of holding the property for the benefit of his father. Appellant promised to convey the property to T. K. on request. He also promised to convey the property to T. K.'s estate if T. K. should die without demanding its return. These promises show appellant's intent to act as trustee for his father's property. Appellant's testimony concerning his intent was consistent with the document. He stated that the purpose of the transaction was estate planning. We hold appellant met the requirements of § 72-20-108, MCA.

T. K. Laursen did not sign Exhibit B, the aforementioned document. However, he was not required to sign the document to meet the requirements of § 72-24-102, MCA. Once those requirements are met by the actions of the trustee, the trustor, T. K., must by words or acts indicate with reasonable certainty: (1) an intention to create a trust; and (2) the subject, purpose, and beneficiary of the trust.

The fact that the document was given to T. K.'s now deceased attorney, Shelton Williams, for safekeeping is an act that tends to show T. K. intended a trust to be created. Appellant testified that he believed T. K. deeded the property to appellant because T. K. wanted someone to take care of the property and to take care of him; that T. K. wanted to make it more difficult for his wife to get the property in T. K.'s upcoming divorce action; and that T. K. deeded the property to appellant for estate planning purposes. Appellant's testimony taken with the circumstances of this case show with reasonable certainty that T. K.'s intention was to create a trust when he deeded his property to appellant. We hold the District Court's finding to be factually sound and legally correct.
[Judgment affirmed]

QUESTIONS

1. What are the essential elements that constitute a valid trust?
2. Was the father required to sign the affidavit executed by his son?
3. Did the court find a trust was created?

(e) INTENTION. An intention to impose a duty upon the trustee with respect to specific property must be expressed. It is not necessary, however, that the word *trust* or *trustee* be used. The settlor will ordinarily name a trustee, but failure to do so is not fatal to the trust, because a trustee will be appointed by the court.

(f) ACTIVE DUTY. A trust does not exist unless an active duty is placed upon the trustee to manage the property in some manner or to exercise discretion or judgment. A bare direction to hold the property in trust, without any direction as to its use or distribution, is not sufficient for an active duty. Thus, when a decedent transferred $5,000 to a trustee to be held in trust for *A*, no trust was created. In such a case the intended beneficiary is entitled to receive the property outright as though the decedent had not attempted to create a trust.

(g) IDENTITY OF BENEFICIARY. Every trust must have a beneficiary. In a private trust the beneficiaries must be identified by name, description, or designation of the class to which the beneficiaries belong.[10] In a charitable trust it is sufficient that the beneficiaries be members of the public at large or a general class of the public.

Trusts for religious masses, for the maintenance of grave monuments, or for the care of particular animals are technically invalid because there is no human, identified beneficiary. Such trusts are nevertheless enforced because of the social interests that are involved.

(h) ACCEPTANCE OF TRUST. As the performance of a trust imposes duties upon the trustee, a trustee may renounce or reject the trust. Acceptance will be presumed in the absence of a disclaimer. A renunciation does not affect the validity of the trust, because a court will appoint a substitute trustee if the settlor does not do so.

21.   Nature of Beneficiary's Interest

The effect of a transfer in trust is to divide the property so that the legal title is given to the trustee and the **equitable title** or beneficial interest is given to the beneficiary. The beneficiary may ordinarily transfer or assign such interest in the trust. The beneficiary's creditors may reach that interest in satisfaction of their claims. An exception arises when the settlor has restricted the trust in such a way that the beneficiary cannot assign nor creditors reach the interest. This is commonly called a **spendthrift trust.**

22.   Powers of Trustee

A trustee can exercise only those powers that are given by law or the trust instrument or those that the court will construe as being given by implication. Modern trusts commonly give the trustee discretion to make decisions on matters that could not be foreseen by the settlor. For example, the trustee may be authorized to expend principal as well as income when, in the trustee's opinion, it is necessary for the education or medical care of a beneficiary. The trustee must exercise discretion in a reasonable manner.

23.   Duties of Trustee

The duty of a trustee is to administer the trust. The trustee who accepts the appointment must take all the necessary steps to carry out the trust in a proper manner.

(a) PERFORMANCE. A trustee is under a duty to carry out the trust according to its terms and is personally liable for any loss sustained from an unjustified failure to perform such duties. A trustee cannot delegate the performance of personal duties.

(b) DUE CARE. The trustee is under a duty to use reasonable skill, prudence, and diligence in the performance of trust duties. More simply stated, the trustee must use the care that would be exercised by a reasonable person under the circumstances.[11]

(c) LOYALTY. A trustee is not permitted to profit personally from the position of trustee,

---

[10]   Schroeder v Herbert C. Coe Trust (SD) 437 NW2d 178 (1989).

[11]   Matter of Green Charitable Trust, 172 Mich App 298, 431 NW2d 492 (1988).

other than to receive the compensation allowed by contract or law.

(d) POSSESSION AND PRESERVATION OF TRUST PROPERTY. The trustee is under a duty to take possession of trust property and to preserve it from loss or damage. If the property includes accounts receivable or outstanding debts, the trustee is under the duty to collect them.

(e) DEFENSE OF TRUST. The trustee must defend the trust when its validity is disputed in court.

(f) PRODUCTION OF INCOME. By either express or implied direction, the trustee is required to invest the money or property in enterprises or transactions that will yield an income to the estate.

A trustee is generally permitted to invest in bonds of the United States or of instrumentalities of the United States; bonds of states, cities, and counties, subject to certain restrictions; first mortgages on real estate when the mortgage does not represent more than a specified percentage of the value of the land; and mortgage bonds of certain kinds of corporations. Most states now permit a trustee to invest in corporate stocks. Court approval is generally required for investments in real estate.

(g) ACCOUNTING AND INFORMATION. A trustee must keep accurate records so that it can be determined whether the trust has been properly administered. Upon request by a beneficiary, the trustee must furnish information with respect to the trust. Periodically, or at certain times, as determined by the law in each state, a trustee must file an account in court. At such time the court passes upon the stewardship of the trust.

24.   Remedies for Breach of Trust

A breach of trust may occur in a variety of ways, which in turn affects the remedies available. These remedies include:

(a) Money judgment against trustee for loss caused
(b) Injunction or order to compel the trustee to do or refrain from doing an act
(c) Criminal prosecution of the trustee for misconduct
(d) Tracing and recovery of trust property that has been converted by the trustee, unless the property had been acquired by a bona fide purchaser who gave value and purchased without notice of the breach of trust
(e) Judgment against surety on the trustee's bond for loss caused the trust by the trustee's default
(f) Removal of the trustee for misconduct, and
(g) Suit against third persons who participated in a breach of trust

25.   Termination of Trust

A trust may be terminated (a) in accordance with its terms,[12] (b) because of the impossibility of attaining the object of the trust; (c) via revocation by the settlor, when allowed by the terms of the trust; (d) by merger of all interests in the same person; and (e) upon the request of all the beneficiaries when there is no express purpose that requires continuation of the trust.

[12]   Schwartzkopf v American Heart Ass'n (Fla App) 541 So 2d 1348 (1989).

SUMMARY

A will is a disposition of property, to take effect upon death. A man who makes a will is called a *testator*; a woman, a *testatrix*. The person to whom property is left by will is a beneficiary. A legacy is a gift of personal property by will; a gift of real property by will is known as a devise.

A testator must have testamentary capacity to make a will and must manifest some intention that the will be effective only upon death.

The will must ordinarily be in writing and must be signed by the testator and be witnessed. Some states require publication—

some declaration that the document that is signed before the witnesses is the testator's will.

A will may be modified by a codicil or revoked either by the act of the testator or by operation of law.

Probate is the act by which a proper court official accepts a will. Probate may be refused or set aside on grounds that the will is not the free expression of the testator.

A holographic will is an unwitnessed will written entirely in the handwriting of the testator. A nuncupative will is an oral one. A self-proved will may be admitted to probate without the testimony of subscribing witnesses. A living will allows a person to make wishes known regarding life-sustaining medical treatment.

If there is a valid will, the last phase of administration of the estate is the distribution of property after the payment of all debts and taxes. General legacies are bequests of money, whereas specific legacies or specific devises are gifts of identified personal or real property. Legacies abate in the following order: residuary, general, and specific. If a beneficiary named in the will has died before the testator and no alternate provision has been made for such beneficiary, antilapse statutes provide that the gift will not lapse. In that event the children or heirs of the beneficiary may take the legacy in the place of the deceased beneficiary.

If the decedent does not dispose of all property by will or does not have a will, the property will be distributed according to state intestacy statutes. A surviving spouse may generally elect to take the statutory allocation instead of that provided in the will.

The estate of the testator will be administered by the person appointed in the will (the executor) or, if there is no will, by a person appointed by the court (an administrator). Creditors who have claims against the estate are required to give notice of their claim to the personal representative; otherwise, the claim will be barred.

A trust is a legal device by which property is held by one person for the benefit of another. The settlor creates the trust, and the person for whose benefit the trustee holds the property is the beneficiary. Property held in trust is called the *trust corpus, trust fund, trust estate*, or *res*.

A trust is usually created by a writing called a *trust agreement* or *deed of trust*. No particular form or language is required. A trust is not created unless an active duty is placed upon the trustee to manage the property in some manner. Acceptance of duties under a trust is presumed.

Legal title to trust property is given to the trustee, but equitable title is held by the beneficiary. A beneficiary may transfer an interest in the trust, except in the case of a spendthrift trust.

The trustee can exercise only those powers that are given by law or the trust instrument. The trustee must administer the trust and carry out the trust in a proper manner. A trustee may be sued for breach of the terms of the trust agreement. A trust comes to an end when its terms so provide or when it becomes impossible to attain the object of the trust.

QUESTIONS AND CASE PROBLEMS

1. What social forces are affected by allowing a person to give property after death by means of leaving a will?

2. Jean repeatedly told her best friend Dinah and their neighbors that Jean would leave her house to Dinah when she died. Jean died without having written any will. Dinah claimed the house, and the neighbors testified in court that Jean had repeatedly declared that she would leave the house to Dinah. Is Dinah entitled to the house?

3. Iona wrote her will. The following year she wrote another will that expressly revoked the earlier will. Later, while cleaning house, she came across the second will. She mistakenly thought that it was the first will and tore it up because the first will had been revoked. Iona died shortly thereafter. The beneficiaries named

in the second will claimed that the second will should be probated. The beneficiaries named in the first will claimed that the second will had been revoked when it was torn up. Had the second will been revoked?

4. Logsdon, who had three children, disliked one of them without any reason. In his will he left only a small amount to the child he disliked and gave the bulk of his estate to the remaining two. Upon his death, the disliked child claimed that the will was void and had been obtained by undue influence. Do you agree? [Logsdon v Logsdon, 412 Ill 19, 104 NE2d 622]

5. Field executed a will. Upon her death the will was found in her safe deposit box, but the part of the will containing the fifth bequest was torn from the will. This torn fragment was also found in the box. There was no evidence that anyone other than Field had ever opened the box. A proceeding was brought to determine whether the will was entitled to be probated. Decide. [Flora v Hughes, 312 Ky 478, 228 SW2d 27]

6. Anna Miller wrote a will 11 pages long and enclosed it in an envelope, which she sealed. She then wrote on the envelope, "My last will & testament," and signed her name below this statement. This was the only place where she signed her name on any of the papers. Was this signature sufficient to allow this writing to be admitted to probate as her will? [Miller's Executor v Shannon (Ky) 299 SW2d 103]

7. Probate of the will of Vivian Lingenfelter was opposed. It was shown that the testatrix was sick, highly nervous, and extremely jealous and that she committed suicide a week after executing the will. In support of the will, it was shown that she understood the will when she discussed it with an attorney, that her husband was seriously ill when she wrote the will, that he died the following day, and that she grieved his death. A proceeding was brought to determine whether the will was entitled to probate. Decide. [Lingenfelter's Estate, 38 Cal 2d 571, 241 P2d 990]

8. By his original will, Leon bequeathed one-third of his estate to Andrew. When the will was probated, it was found that the bequest to Andrew had been crossed out, and at the bottom of the will was a typewritten statement: "Under no condition do I wish Andrew to be included in this will." There was no evidence as to where the will had been kept at any time, nor any evidence as to when or under what circumstances the changes had been made to the will. Was Andrew entitled to the legacy? Explain.

9. Dolores states in her will, "I leave $10,000 to the First National Bank in trust for my niece, Clara." After the death of Dolores, the will is probated. Is the trust for Clara valid?

10. What is the difference between an inter vivos trust and a testamentary trust?

11. State three ways a trust may be terminated.

12. Rachael conveyed certain land to Roland in trust for her daughter, Mary. Roland refused to accept the trust. What effect does this refusal have on the rights of her daughter, Mary?

13. By her will, Hendricks provided: "I give, devise, and bequeath [the balance of my estate] to the City of Brookfield, Missouri, for the sole purpose of building and equipping and maintaining a city hospital. . . ." The city claimed that this was an absolute gift to the city, subject to a condition as to its use. Do you agree? [Ramsey v City of Brookfield, 361 Mo 857, 237 SW2d 143]

14. The Pioneer Trust and Savings Bank was trustee of certain land for the benefit of Harmon. Under the terms of the trust, Harmon could require the trustee to sell the land as he directed. Schneider wrote Pioneer Trust, offering to buy the land. Harmon made a written notation on the letter that he accepted the offer and sent it back to Schneider. Schneider withdrew his offer and claimed that there was no contract. Harmon claimed that Schneider was bound by a contract. Decide. [Schneider v Pioneer Trust and Savings Bank, 26 Ill App 2d 463, 168 NE2d 808]

15. Owens owned a 2,000-acre ranch that was very valuable. He decided that he wanted his daughter, Dorothy, to have this property after his death. He thereupon conveyed this land to Lockridge "in trust for my daughter, Dorothy, but Lockridge is to have no duties or burdens with respect to the land." When Owens died, Dorothy claimed she owned the land. Is she correct? Explain.

APPENDICES

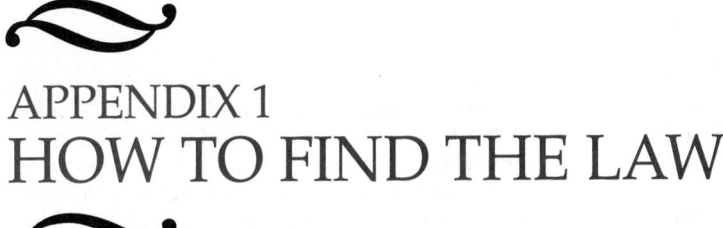

APPENDIX 1
HOW TO FIND THE LAW

In order to determine what the law on a particular question or issue is, it may be necessary to examine (1) compilations of constitutions, treaties, statutes, executive orders, proclamations, and administrative regulations; (2) reports of state and federal court decisions; (3) digests of opinions; (4) treatises on the law; and (5) loose-leaf services.

COMPILATIONS

In the consideration of a legal problem in business it is necessary to determine whether the matter is affected or controlled by the Constitution, national or state; by a national treaty; by an Act of Congress or a state legislature, or by a city ordinance; by a decree or proclamation of the President of the United States, a governor, or a mayor; or by a regulation of a federal, state, or local administrative agency.

Each body or person that makes laws, regulations, or ordinances usually compiles and publishes at the end of each year or session all of the matter that it has adopted. In addition to the periodical or annual volumes, it is common to compile all the treaties, statutes, regulations, or ordinances in separate volumes. To illustrate, the federal Anti-Injunction Act may be cited as the Act of March 23, 1932, 47 Stat 70, 29 USC Sections 101 et seq. This means that this law was enacted on March 23, 1932, and that it can be found at page 70 in Volume 47 of the reports that contain all of the statutes adopted by the Congress.

The second part of the citation, 29 USC Sections 101 et seq., means that in the collection of all of the federal statutes, which is known as the United States Code, the full text of the statute can be found in the sections of the 29th title beginning with Section 101.

COURT DECISIONS

For complicated or important legal cases or when an appeal is to be taken, a court will generally write an *opinion*, which explains why the court made the decision. Appellate courts as a rule write opinions. The great majority of these decisions, particularly in the case of the appellate courts, are collected and printed. In order to avoid confusion, the opinions of each court are ordinarily printed in a separate set of reports, either by official reporters or private publishers.

In the reference "Pennoyer v Neff, 95 US 714, 24 LEd 565," the first part states the names of the parties. It does not necessarily tell who was the plaintiff and who was the defendant. When an action is begun in a lower court, the first name is that of the plaintiff and the second name that of the defendant. When the case is appealed, generally the name of the person taking the appeal appears on the records of the higher court as the first one and that of the adverse party as the second. Sometimes, therefore, the original order of the names of the parties is reversed.

The balance of the reference consists of two citations. The first citation, 95 US 714, means that the opinion which the court filed in the case of Pennoyer and Neff may be found on page 714 of the 95th volume of a series of books in which are printed officially the opinions of the United States Supreme Court. Sometimes the same opinion is printed in two different sets of volumes. In the example, 24 LEd 565 means that in the 24th volume of another set of books, called *Lawyer's Edition,* of the United States Supreme Court Reports, the same opinion begins on page 565.

In opinions by a state court there are also generally two citations, as in the case of "Morrow v Corbin, 122 Tex 553, 62 SW2d 641." This means that the opinion in the lawsuit between Morrow and Corbin may be found in the 122d volume of the reports of the highest court of Texas, beginning on page 553; and also in Volume 62 of the *Southwestern Reporter,* Second Series, at page 641.

The West Publishing Company publishes a set of sectional reporters covering the entire United States. They are called "sectional" because each reporter, instead of being limited to a particular court or a particular state, covers the decisions of the courts of a particular section of the country. Thus the decisions of the courts of Arkansas, Kentucky, Missouri, Tennessee, and Texas are printed by the West Publishing company as a group in a sectional reporter called the

Southwestern Reporter.[1] Because of the large number of decisions involved, generally only the opinions of the state appellate courts are printed. A number of states[2] have discontinued publication of the opinions of their courts, and those opinions are now found only in the West reporters.

The reason for the "Second Series" in the Southwestern citation is that when there were 300 volumes in the original series, instead of calling the next volume 301, the publisher called it Volume 1, Second Series. Thus 62 SW2d Series really means the 362d volume of the *Southwestern Reporter*. Six to eight volumes appear in a year for each geographic section.

In addition to these state reporters, the West Publishing Company publishes a *Federal Supplement*, which primarily reports the opinions of the Federal District Courts; the *Federal Reporter*, which primarily reports the decisions of the United States Courts of Appeals; and the *Supreme Court Reporter*, which reports the decisions of the United States Supreme Court. The Supreme Court decisions are also reported in a separate set called the *Lawyers' Edition*, published by the Lawyers Cooperative Publishing Company.

The reports published by the West Publishing Company and Lawyers Cooperative Publishing Company are unofficial reports, while those bearing the name or abbreviation of the United States or of a state, such as "95 US 714" or "122 Tex 553" are official reports. This means that in the case of the latter, the particular court, such as the United States Supreme Court, has officially authorized that its decisions be printed and that by federal statute such official printing is made. In the case of the unofficial reporters, the publisher prints the decisions of a court on its own initiative. Such opinions are part of the public domain and not subject to any copyright or similar restriction.

DIGESTS OF OPINIONS

The reports of court decisions are useful only if one has the citation—that is, the name and volume number of the book and the page number of the opinion one is seeking.

For this reason, digests of the decisions have been prepared. These digests organize the entire field of law under major headings, which are then arranged in alphabetical order. Under each heading, such as "Contracts," the subject is divided into the different questions that can arise with respect to that field. A master outline is thus created on the subject. This outline includes short paragraphs describing what each case holds and giving its citation.

TREATISES AND RESTATEMENTS

Very helpful in finding a case or a statute are the treatises on the law. These may be special books, each written by an author on a particular subject, such as *Williston on Contracts, Bogert on Trusts, Fletcher on Corporations*, or they may be general encyclopedias, as in the case of *American Jurisprudence, American Jurisprudence, Second*, and *Corpus Juris Secundum*.

Another type of treatise is found in the restatements of the law prepared by the American Law Institute. Each restatement consists of one or more volumes devoted to a particular phase of the law, such as the *Restatement of the Law of Contracts, Restatement of the Law of Agency*, and *Restatement of the Law of Property*. In each restatement the American Law Institute, acting through special committees of judges, lawyers, and professors of law, has set forth what the law is; and in many areas where there is no law or the present rule is regarded as unsatisfactory, the restatement specifies what the Institute deems to be the desirable rule.

LOOSE-LEAF SERVICES

A number of private publishers, notably Commerce Clearing House and Prentice-Hall, publish loose-leaf books devoted to particular branches of the law. Periodically, the publisher sends to the purchaser a number of pages that set forth any decision, regulation, or statute made or adopted since the prior set of pages was prepared. Such services are unofficial.

COMPUTERS AND LEGAL RESEARCH

National and local computer services are providing constantly widening assistance for legal research. The database in such a system may be opinions, statutes, or administrative regulations stored word for word; or the later history of a particular case giving its full citation and showing whether the case has been followed by other courts; or the text of forms and documents. By means of a terminal connected to the system, the user can retrieve the above information at a great saving of time and with the assurance that it is up-to-date.

---

[1]   The sectional reporters are: Atlantic—A. (Connecticut, Delaware, District of Columbia, Maine, Maryland, New Hampshire, New Jersey, Pennsylvania, Rhode Island, Vermont); Northeastern—N.E. (Illinois, Indiana, Massachusetts, New York, Ohio); Northwestern—N.W. (Iowa, Michigan, Minnesota, Nebraska, North Dakota, South Dakota, Wisconsin); Pacific—P. (Alaska, Arizona, California, Colorado, Hawaii, Idaho, Kansas, Montana, Nevada, New Mexico, Oklahoma, Oregon, Utah, Washington, Wyoming); Southeastern—S.E. (Georgia, North Carolina, South Carolina, Virginia, West Virginia); Southwestern—S.W. (Arkansas, Kentucky, Missouri, Tennessee, Texas); and Southern—So. (Alabama, Florida, Louisiana, Mississippi). There is also a special New York State reporter known as the New York Supplement and a special California State reporter known as the California Reporter.

[2]   See, for example, Alaska, Florida, Iowa, Kentucky, Louisiana, Maine, Mississippi, Missouri, North Dakota, Oklahoma, Texas, and Wyoming.

There are two leading national systems for computer aid to research. Listed alphabetically, they are LEXIS and WESTLAW.

A specialized service of legal forms for business is provided by Shepard's BUSINESS LAW CASE MANAGEMENT SYSTEM.

The computer field has expanded to such an extent that there is now a *Legal Software Review* of over 500 pages prepared by Lawyers Library, 12761 New Hall Ferry, Florissant, MO 63033.

APPENDIX 2
THE CONSTITUTION OF THE UNITED STATES

We the people of the United States, in order to form a more perfect union, establish justice, insure domestic tranquillity, provide for the common defense, promote the general welfare, and secure the blessings of liberty to ourselves and our posterity, do ordain and establish this Constitution for the United States of America.

Article I

Section 1. All legislative powers herein granted shall be vested in a Congress of the United States, which shall consist of a Senate and House of Representatives.

Section 2. 1. The House of Representatives shall be composed of members chosen every second year by the people of the several States, and the electors in each State shall have the qualifications requisite for electors of the most numerous branch of the State legislature.

2. No person shall be a representative who shall not have attained to the age of twenty-five years, and been seven years a citizen of the United States, and who shall not, when elected, be an inhabitant of that State in which he shall be chosen.

3. Representatives and direct taxes[1] shall be apportioned among the several States which may be included within this Union, according to their respective numbers, which shall be determined by adding to the whole number of free persons, including those bound to service for a term of years, and excluding Indians not taxed, *three fifths of all other persons.*[2] The actual enumeration shall be made within three years after the first meeting of the Congress of the United States, and within every subsequent term of ten years, in such manner as they shall by law direct. The number of representatives shall not exceed one for every thirty thousand, but each State shall have at least one representative; and until such enumeration shall be made, the State of New Hampshire shall be entitled to choose three, Massachusetts eight, Rhode Island and Providence Plantations one, Connecticut five, New York six, New Jersey four, Pennsylvania

eight, Delaware one, Maryland six, Virginia ten, North Carolina five, South Carolina five, and Georgia three.

4. When vacancies happen in the representation from any State, the executive authority thereof shall issue writs of election to fill such vacancies.

5. The House of Representatives shall choose their speaker and other officers; and shall have the sole power of impeachment.

Section 3. 1. The Senate of the United States shall be composed of two senators from each State, *chosen by the legislature thereof,*[1] for six years; and each senator shall have one vote.

2. Immediately after they shall be assembled in consequence of the first election, they shall be divided as equally as may be into three classes. The seats of the senators of the first class shall be vacated at the expiration of the second year, of the second class at the expiration of the fourth year, and of the third class at the expiration of the fourth year, and of the third class at the expiration of the sixth year, so that one third may be chosen every second year; and if vacancies happen by resignation, or otherwise, during the recess of the legislature of any State, the executive thereof may make temporary appointments until the next meeting of the legislature, which shall then fill such vacancies.[3]

3. No person shall be a senator who shall not have attained to the age of thirty years, and been nine years a citizen of the United States, and who shall not, when elected, be an inhabitant of that State for which he shall be chosen.

4. The Vice President of the United States shall be President of the Senate, but shall have no vote, unless they be equally divided.

5. The Senate shall choose their other officers, and also a

---

[1] See the 16th Amendment.
[2] See the 14th Amendment.

[3] See the 17th Amendment.

president *pro tempore,* in the absence of the Vice President, or when he shall exercise the office of the President of the United States.

6. The Senate shall have the sole power to try all impeachments. When sitting for that purpose, they shall be on oath or affirmation. When the President of the United States is tried, the chief justice shall preside: and no person shall be convicted without the concurrence of two thirds of the members present.

7. Judgment in cases of impeachment shall not extend further than to removal from office, and disqualifications to hold and enjoy any office of honor, trust or profit under the United States: but the party convicted shall nevertheless be liable and subject to indictment, trial, judgment and punishment, according to law.

Section 4.   1. The times, places, and manner of holding elections for senators and representatives, shall be prescribed in each State by the legislature thereof; but the Congress may at any time by law make or alter such regulations, except as to the places of choosing senators.

2. The Congress shall assemble at least once in every year, and such meeting shall be on the first Monday in December, unless they shall by law appoint a different day.

Section 5.   1. Each House shall be the judge of the elections, returns and qualifications of its own members, and a majority of each shall constitute a quorum to do business; but a smaller number may adjourn from day to day, and may be authorized to compel the attendance of absent members, in such manner, and under such penalties as each House may provide.

2. Each House may determine the rules of its proceedings, punish its members for disorderly behavior, and, with the concurrence of two thirds, expel a member.

3. Each House shall keep a journal of its proceedings, and from time to time publish the same, excepting such parts as may in their judgment require secrecy; and the yeas and nays of the members of either House on any question shall, at the desire of one fifth of those present, be entered on the journal.

4. Neither House, during the session of Congress, shall, without the consent of the other, adjourn for more than three days, nor to any other place than that in which the two Houses shall be sitting.

Section 6.   1. The senators and representatives shall receive a compensation for their services, to be ascertained by law, and paid out of the Treasury of the United States. They shall in all cases, except treason, felony, and breach of the peace, be privileged from arrest during their attendance at the session of their respective Houses, and in going to and returning from the same; and for any speech or debate in either House, they shall not be questioned in any other place.

2. No senator or representative shall, during the time for which he was elected, be appointed to any civil office under the authority of the United States, which shall have been created, or the emoluments whereof shall have been in-

creased during such time; and no person holding any office under the United States shall be a member of either House during his continuance in office.

Section 7.   1. All bills for raising revenue shall originate in the House of Representatives; but the Senate may propose or concur with amendments as on other bills.

2. Every bill which shall have passed the House of Representatives and the Senate, shall, before it becomes a law, be presented to the President of the United States; if he approves he shall sign it, but if not he shall return it, with his objections to that House in which it shall have originated, who shall enter the objections at large on their journal, and proceed to reconsider it. If after such reconsideration two thirds of that House shall agree to pass the bill, it shall be sent, together with the objections, to the other House, by which it shall likewise be reconsidered, and if approved by two thirds of that House, it shall become a law. But in all such cases the votes of both Houses shall be determined by yeas and nays, and the names of the persons voting for and against the bill shall be entered on the journal of each House respectively. If any bill shall not be returned by the President within ten days (Sundays excepted) after it shall have been presented to him, the same shall be a law, in like manner as if he had signed it, unless the Congress by their adjournment prevent its return, in which case it shall not be a law.

3. Every order, resolution, or vote to which the concurrence of the Senate and the House of Representatives may be necessary (except on a question of adjournment) shall be presented to the President of the United States; and before the same shall take effect, shall be approved by him, or being disapproved by him, shall be repassed by two thirds of the Senate and House of Representatives, according to the rules and limitations prescribed in the case of a bill.

Section 8.   The Congress shall have the power

1. To lay and collect taxes, duties, imposts, and excises, to pay the debts and provide for the common defense and general welfare of the United States; but all duties, imposts, and excises shall be uniform throughout the United States;

2. To borrow money on the credit of the United States;

3. To regulate commerce with foreign nations, and among the several States, and with the Indian tribes;

4. To establish a uniform rule of naturalization, and uniform laws on the subject of bankruptcies throughout the United States;

5. To coin money, regulate the value thereof, and of foreign coin, and fix the standard of weights and measures;

6. To provide for the punishment of counterfeiting the securities and current coin of the United States;

7. To establish post offices and post roads;

8. To promote the progress of science and useful arts, by securing for limited times to authors and inventors the exclusive rights to their respective writings and discoveries;

9. To constitute tribunals inferior to the Supreme Court;

10. To define and punish piracies and felonies committed on the high seas, and offenses against the law of nations;

11. To declare war, grant letters of marque and reprisal, and make rules concerning captures on land and water;

12. To raise and support armies, but no appropriation of money to that use shall be for a longer term than two years;

13. To provide and maintain a navy;

14. To make rules for the government and regulation of the land and naval forces;

15. To provide for calling forth the militia to execute the laws of the Union, suppress insurrections and repel invasions;

16. To provide for organizing, arming, and disciplining the militia, and for governing such part of them as may be employed in the service of the United States, reserving to the States respectively, the appointment of the officers, and the authority of training the militia according to the discipline prescribed by Congress.

17. To exercise exclusive legislation in all cases whatsoever, over such distinct (not exceeding ten miles square) as may, by cession of particular States, and the acceptance of Congress, become the seat of the government of the United States, and to exercise like authority over all places purchased by the consent of the legislature of the State in which the same shall be, for the erection of forts, magazines, arsenals, dockyards, and other needful buildings; and

18. To make all laws which shall be necessary and proper for carrying into execution the foregoing powers, and all other powers vested by this Constitution in the government of the United States, or in any department or officer thereof.

Section 9. 1. The migration or importation of such persons as any of the States now existing shall think proper to admit, shall not be prohibited by the Congress prior to the year one thousand eight hundred and eight, but a tax or duty may be imposed on such importation, not exceeding ten dollars for each person.

2. The privilege of the writ of *habeas corpus* shall not be suspended, unless when in cases of rebellion or invasion the public safety may require it.

3. No bill of attainder or *ex post facto* law shall be passed.

4. No capitation, or other direct, tax shall be laid, unless in proportion to the census or enumeration hereinbefore directed to be taken.[4]

5. No tax or duty shall be laid on articles exported from any State.

6. No preference shall be given by any regulation of commerce or revenue to the ports of one State over those of another: nor shall vessels bound to, or from, one State be obliged to enter, clear, or pay duties in another.

7. No money shall be drawn from the treasury, but in consequence of appropriations made by law; and a regular statement and account of the receipts and expenditures of all public money shall be published from time to time.

8. No title of nobility shall be granted by the United States: and no person holding any office of profit or trust under them, shall, without the consent of the Congress, accept of any present, emolument, office, or title, of any kind whatever, from any king, prince, or foreign State.

Section 10. 1. No State shall enter into any treaty, alliance, or confederation; grant letters of marque and reprisal; coin money; emit bills of credit; make anything but gold and silver coin a tender in payment of debts; pass any bill of attainder, *ex post facto* law, or law impairing the obligation of contracts, or grant any title of nobility.

2. No State shall, without the consent of the Congress, lay any imposts or duties on imports or exports, except what may be absolutely necessary for executing its inspection laws: and the net produce of all duties and imposts laid by any State on imports or exports, shall be for the use of the treasury of the United States; and all such laws shall be subject to the revision and control of the Congress.

3. No State shall, without the consent of the Congress, lay any duty of tonnage, keep troops, or ships of war in time of peace, enter into any agreement or compact with another State, or with a foreign power, or engage in war, unless actually invaded, or in such imminent danger as will not admit of delay.

Article II

Section 1. 1. The executive power shall be vested in a President of the United States of America. He shall hold his office during the term of four years, and, together with the Vice President, chosen for the same term, be elected as follows:

2. Each State shall appoint, in such manner as the legislature thereof may direct, a number of electors, equal to the whole number of senators and representatives to which the State may be entitled in the Congress: but no senator or representative, or person holding an office of trust or profit under the United States, shall be appointed an elector.

The electors shall meet in their respective States, and vote by ballot for two persons, of whom one at least shall not be an inhabitant of the same State with themselves. And they shall make a list of all the persons voted for, and of the number of votes for each; which list they shall sign and certify, and transmit sealed to the seat of the government of the United States, directed to the president of the Senate. The president of the Senate shall, in the presence of the Senate and House of Representatives, open all the certificates, and the votes shall then be counted. The person having the greatest number of votes shall be the President, if such number be a majority of the whole number of electors appointed; and if there be more than one who have such majority, and have an equal number of votes, then the House of Representatives shall immediately choose by ballot one of them for President; and if no person have a majority, then from the five highest on the list the said House shall in like manner choose the President. But in choosing the President, the votes shall be taken by States, the representation from each State having one vote; a quorum for this purpose shall consist of a member or members from two thirds of the States,

---

4　See the 16th Amendment.

and a majority of all the States shall be necessary to a choice. In every case, after the choice of the President, the person having the greatest number of votes of the electors shall be the Vice President. But if there should remain two or more who have equal votes, the Senate shall choose from them by ballot the Vice President.[5]

3. The Congress may determine the time of choosing the electors, and the day on which they shall give their votes; which day shall be the same throughout the United States.

4. No person except a natural born citizen, or a citizen of the United States, at the time of the adoption of this Constitution, shall be eligible to the office of President; neither shall any person be eligible to that office who shall not have attained to the age of thirty-five years, and been fourteen years a resident within the United States.

5. In the case of removal of the President from office, or of his death, resignation, or inability to discharge the powers and duties of the said office, the same shall devolve on the Vice President, and the Congress may by law provide for the case of removal, death, resignation, or inability, both of the President and Vice President, declaring what officer shall then act as President, and such officer shall act accordingly, until the disability be removed, or a President shall be elected.

6. The President shall, at stated times, receive for his services a compensation, which shall neither be increased nor diminished during the period for which he shall have been elected, and he shall not receive within that period any other emolument from the United States, or any of them.

7. Before he enter on the execution of his office, he shall take the following oath or affirmation:—"I do solemnly swear (or affirm) that I will faithfully execute the office of President of the United States, and will to the best of my ability, preserve, protect and defend the Constitution of the United States."

Section 2.   1. The President shall be commander in chief of the army and navy of the United States, and of the militia of the several States, when called into the actual service of the United States; when called into the actual service of the United States; he may require the opinion, in writing, of the principal officer in each of the executive departments, upon any subject relating to the duties of their respective office, and he shall have power to grant reprieves and pardons for offenses against the United States, except in cases of impeachment.

2. He shall have power, by and with the advice and consent of the Senate, to make treaties, provided two thirds of the senators present concur; and he shall nominate, and by and with the advice and consent of the Senate, shall appoint ambassadors, other public ministers and consuls, judges of the Supreme Court, and all other officers of the United States, whose appointments are not herein otherwise provided for, and which shall be established by law: but the Congress may by law vest the appointment of such inferior officers, as they think proper, in the President alone, in the courts of law, or in the heads of departments.

3. The President shall have power to fill up all vacancies that may happen during the recess of the Senate, by granting commissions which shall expire at the end of their next session.

Section 3.   He shall from time to time give to the Congress information of the state of the Union, and recommend to their consideration such measures as he shall judge necessary and expedient; he may, on extraordinary occasions, convene both Houses, or either of them, and in case of disagreement between them with respect to the time of adjournment, he may adjourn them to such time as he shall think proper; he shall receive ambassadors and other public ministers; he shall take care that the laws be faithfully executed, and shall commission all the officers of the United States.

Section 4.   The President, Vice President, and all civil officers of the United States, shall be removed from office on impeachment for, and conviction of, treason, bribery, or other high crimes and misdemeanors.

Article III

Section 1.   The judicial power of the United States shall be vested in one Supreme Court, and in such inferior courts as the Congress may from time to time ordain and establish. The judges, both of the Supreme and inferior courts, shall hold their offices during good behavior, and shall, at stated times, receive for their services, a compensation, which shall not be diminished during their continuance in office.

Section 2.   1. The judicial power shall extend to all cases, in law and equity, arising under this Constitution, the laws of the United States, and treaties made, or which shall be made, under their authority;—to all cases affecting ambassadors, other public ministers and consuls;—to all cases of admiralty and maritime jurisdiction;—to controversies to which the United States shall be a party;—to controversies between two or more States; between a State and citizens of another State;[6]—between citizens of different States;—between citizens of the same State claiming lands under grants of different States, and between a State, or the citizens thereof, and foreign States citizens or subjects.

2. In all cases affecting ambassadors, other public ministers and consuls, and those in which a State shall be party, the Supreme Court shall have original jurisdiction. In all the other cases before mentioned, the Supreme Court shall have appellate jurisdiction, both as to law and to fact, with such exceptions, and under such regulations as the Congress shall make.

3. The trial of all crimes, except in cases of impeachment, shall be by jury; and such trial shall be held in the State where the said crimes shall have been committed; but when

---

[5]   Superseded by the 12th Amendment.

[6]   See the 11th Amendment.

not committed within any State, the trial shall be at such place or places as the Congress may by law have directed.

Section 3.   1. Treason against the United States shall consist only in levying war against them, or in adhering to their enemies, giving them aid and comfort. No person shall be convicted of treason unless on the testimony of two witnesses to the same overt act, or on confession in open court.

2. The Congress shall have power to declare the punishment of treason, but no attainder of treason shall work corruption of blood, or forfeiture except during the life of the person attained.

Article IV

Section 1.   Full faith and credit shall be given in each State to the public acts, records, and judicial proceedings of every other State. And the Congress may by general laws prescribe the manner in which such acts, records and proceedings shall be proved, and the effect thereof.

Section 2.   1. The citizens of each State shall be entitled to all privileges and immunities of citizens in the several States.[7]

2. A person charged in any State with treason, felony, or other crime, who shall flee from justice, and be found in another State, shall on demand of the executive authority of the State from which he fled, be delivered up to be removed to the State having jurisdiction of the crime.

3. No person held to service or labor in one State under the laws thereof, escaping into another, shall in consequence of any law or regulation therein, be discharged from such service or labor, but shall be delivered up on claim of the party to whom such service or labor may be due.[8]

Section 3.   1. New States may be admitted by the Congress into this Union; but no new State shall be formed or erected within the jurisdiction of any other State, nor any State be formed by the junction of two or more States, or parts of States, without the consent of the legislatures of the States concerned as well as of the Congress.

2. The Congress shall have power to dispose of and make all needful rules and regulations respecting the territory or other property belonging to the United States; and nothing in this Constitution shall be so construed as to prejudice any claims of the United States, or of any particular State.

Section 4.   The United States shall guarantee to every State in this Union a republican form of government, and shall protect each of them against invasion; and on application of the legislature, or of the executive (when the legislature cannot be convened) against domestic violence.

Article V

The Congress, whenever two thirds of both Houses shall deem it necessary, shall propose amendments to this Constitution, or, on the application of the legislature of two thirds of the several States, shall call a convention for pro-

---

posing amendments, which in either case, shall be valid to all intents and purposes, as part of this Constitution when ratified by the legislatures of three fourths of the several States, or by conventions in three fourths thereof, as the one or the other mode of ratification may be proposed by the Congress; Provided that no amendment which may be made prior to the year one thousand eight hundred and eight shall in any manner affect the first and fourth clauses in the ninth section of the first article; and that no State, without its consent, shall be deprived of its equal suffrage in the Senate.

Article VI

1. All debts contracted and engagements entered into, before the adoption of this Constitution, shall be as valid against the United States under this Constitution, as under the Confederation.[9]

2. This Constitution, and the laws of the United States which shall be made in pursuance thereof; and all treaties made, or which shall be made, under the authority of the United States, shall be the supreme law of the land; and the Judges in every State shall be bound thereby, anything in the Constitution or laws of any State to the contrary notwithstanding.

3. The senators and representatives before mentioned, and the members of the several State legislatures, and all executive and judicial officers, both of the United States and of the several States, shall be bound by oath or affirmation to support this Constitution; but no religious test shall ever be required as a qualification to any office or public trust under the United States.

Article VII

The ratification of the conventions of nine States shall be sufficient for the establishment of this Constitution between the States so ratifying the same.

Done in Convention by the unanimous consent of the States present the seventeenth day of September in the year of our Lord one thousand seven hundred and eighty-seven, and of the independence of the United States of America the twelfth. In witness whereof we have hereunto subscribed our names.

AMENDMENTS

First Ten Amendments passed by Congress Sept. 25, 1789.
Ratified by three-fourths of the States December 15, 1791.

Article I

Congress shall make no law respecting an establishment of religion, or prohibiting the free exercise thereof; or abridging the freedom of speech, or of the press; or the right of the people peaceably to assemble, and to petition the government for a redress of grievances.

---

[7]   See the 14th Amendment, Sec. 1.
[8]   See the 13th Amendment.

[9]   See the 14th Amendment, Sec. 4.

Article II

A well regulated militia, being necessary to the security of a free State, the right of the people to keep and bear arms, shall not be infringed.

Article III

No soldier shall, in time of peace be quartered in any house, without the consent of the owner, nor in time of war, but in a manner to be prescribed by law.

Article IV

The right of the people to be secure in their persons, houses, papers, and effects, against unreasonable searches and seizures, shall not be violated, and no warrants shall issue, but upon probable cause, supported by oath or affirmation, and particularly describing the place to be searched, and he person or things to be seized.

Article V

No person shall be held to answer for a capital, or otherwise infamous crime, unless on a presentment or indictment of a grand jury, except in cases arising in the land or naval forces, or in the militia, when in actual service in time of war or public danger; nor shall any person be subject for the same offense to be twice put in jeopardy of life or limb; nor shall be compelled in any criminal case to be a witness against himself, nor be deprived of life, liberty, or property, without due process of law; nor shall private property be taken for public use without just compensation.

Article VI

In all criminal prosecutions, the accused shall enjoy the right to a speedy and public trial, by an impartial jury of the State and district wherein the crime shall have been committed, which district shall have been previously ascertained by law, and to be informed of the nature and cause of the accusation; to be confronted with the witnesses against him; to have compulsory process for obtaining witnesses in his favor, and to have the assistance of counsel for his defense.

Article VII

In suits at common law, where the value in controversy shall exceed twenty dollars, the right of trial by jury shall be preserved, and no fact tried by a jury shall be preserved, and no fact tried by a jury shall be otherwise reexamined in any court of the United States, then according to the rules of the common law.

Article VIII

Excessive bail shall not be required, nor excessive fines imposed, nor cruel and unusual punishments inflicted.

Article IX

The enumeration in the Constitution of certain rights shall not be construed to deny or disparage others retained by the people.

Article X

The powers not delegated to the United States by the Constitution, nor prohibited by it to the States, are reserved to the States respectively, or to the people.

Article XI

Passed by Congress March 5, 1794. Ratified January 8, 1798.

The judicial power of the United States shall not be construed to extend to any suit in law or equity, commenced or prosecuted against one of the United States by citizens of another State, or by citizens or subjects of any foreign State.

Article XII

Passed by Congress December 12, 1803. Ratified September 25, 1804.

The electors shall meet in their respective States, and vote by ballot for President and Vice President, one of whom, at least, shall not be an inhabitant of the same State with themselves; they shall name in their ballots the person voted for as President, and in distinct ballots, the person voted for as Vice President, and they shall make distinct lists of all persons voted for as President and of all persons voted for as Vice President, and of the number of votes for each, which lists they shall sign and certify, and transmit sealed to the seat of the government of the United States, directed to the President of the Senate;—The President of the Senate shall, in the presence of the Senate and House of Representatives, open all the certificates and the votes shall then be counted;—The person having the greatest number of votes for President, shall be the President, if such number be a majority of the whole number of electors appointed; and if no person have such majority, then from the persons having the highest numbers not exceeding three on the list of those voted for as President, the House of Representatives shall choose immediately, by ballot, the President. But in choosing the President, the votes shall be taken by States, the representation from each State having one vote; a quorum for this purpose shall consist of a member or members from two thirds of the States, and a majority of all the States shall be necessary to a choice. And if the House of Representatives shall not choose a President whenever the right of choice shall devolve upon them, before the fourth day of March next following, then the Vice President shall act as President, as in the case of the death or other constitutional disability of the President. The person having the greatest number of votes as Vice President shall be the Vice President, if such number be a majority of the whole number of electors appointed, and if no person have a majority, then from the two highest numbers on the list, the Senate shall choose the Vice President; a quorum for the purpose shall consist of two thirds of the whole number of Senators, and a majority of the whole number shall be necessary to a choice. But no person constitutionally ineligible to the office of President shall be eligible to that of Vice President of the United States.

Article XIII

Passed by Congress February 1, 1865. Ratified December 18, 1865.

Section 1.   Neither slavery nor involuntary servitude, except as punishment for crime whereof the party shall have been duly convicted, shall exist within the United States, or any place subject to their jurisdiction.

Section 2.   Congress shall have power to enforce this article by appropriate legislation.

Article XIV

Passed by Congress June 16, 1866. Ratified July 23, 1868.

Section 1.   All persons born or naturalized in the United States, and subject to the jurisdiction thereof, are citizens of the United States and of the State wherein they reside. No State shall make or enforce any law which shall abridge the privileges or immunities of citizens of the United States; nor shall any State deprive any person of life, liberty, or property, without due process of law; nor deny to any person within its jurisdiction the equal protection of the laws.

Section 2.   Representatives shall be apportioned among the several States according to their respective numbers, counting the whole number of persons in each State, excluding Indians not taxed. But when the right to vote at any election for the choice of electors for President and Vice President of the United States, representatives in Congress, the executive and judicial officers of a State, or the members of the legislature thereof, is denied to any of the male inhabitants of such State, being twenty-one years of age, and citizens of the United States, or in any way abridged, except for participation in rebellion, or other crime, the basis of representation therein shall be reduced in the proportion which the number of such male citizens shall bear to the whole number of male citizens twenty-one years of age in such State.

Section 3.   No person shall be a senator or representative in Congress, or elector of President and Vice President, or hold any office, civil or military, under the United States, or under any State, who having previously taken an oath, as a member of Congress, or as an officer of the United States, or as a member of any State legislature, or as an executive or judicial officer of any State, to support the Constitution of the United States, shall have engaged in insurrection or rebellion against the same, or given aid or comfort to the enemies thereof. But Congress may by a vote of two thirds of each House, remove such disability.

Section 4.   The validity of the public debt of the United States, authorized by law, including debts incurred for payment of pensions and bounties for services in suppressing insurrection or rebellion, shall not be questioned. But nei-

ther the United States nor any State shall assume or pay any debt or obligation incurred in aid of insurrection or rebellion against the United States, or any claim for the loss or emancipation of any slave; but all such debts, obligations, and claims shall be held illegal and void.

Section 5.   The Congress shall have power to enforce, by appropriate legislation, the provisions of this article.

Article XV

Passed by Congress February 27, 1869. Ratified March 30, 1870.

Section 1.   The right of citizens of the United States to vote shall not be denied or abridged by the United States or by any State on account of race, color, or previous condition of servitude.

Section 2.   The Congress shall have power to enforce this article by appropriate legislation.

Article XVI

Passed by Congress July 12, 1909. Ratified February 25, 1913.

The Congress shall have power to lay and collect taxes on incomes, from whatever source derived, without apportionment among the several States, and without regard to any census or enumeration.

Article XVII

Passed by Congress May 16, 1912. Ratified May 31, 1913.

The Senate of the United States shall be composed of two senators from each State, elected by the people thereof, for six years; and each senator shall have one vote. The electors in each State shall have the qualifications requisite for electors of the most numerous branch of the State legislature.

When vacancies happen in the representation of any State in the Senate, the executive authority of such State shall issue writs of election to fill such vacancies: *Provided,* That the legislature of any State may empower the executive thereof to make temporary appointments until the people fill the vacancies by election as the legislature may direct.

This amendment shall not be so construed as to affect the election or term of any senator chosen before it becomes valid as part of the Constitution.

Article XVIII

Passed by Congress December 17, 1917. Ratified January 29, 1919.

After one year from the ratification of this article, the manufacture, sale, or transportation of intoxicating liquors within, the importation thereof into, or the exportation thereof from the United States and all territory subject to the jurisdiction thereof for beverage purposes is hereby prohibited.

The Congress and the several States shall have concurrent power to enforce this article by appropriate legislation.

This article shall be inoperative unless it shall have been ratified as an amendment to the Constitution by the legislatures of the several States, as provided in the Constitution, within seven years from the date of the submission hereof to the States by Congress.

Article XIX

Passed by Congress June 5, 1919. Ratified August 26, 1920.

The right of citizens of the United States to vote shall not be denied or abridged by the United States or by any State on account of sex.

The Congress shall have power by appropriate legislation to enforce the provisions of this article.

Article XX

Passed by Congress March 3, 1932. Ratified January 23, 1933.

Section 1.   The terms of the President and Vice President shall end at noon on the 20th day of January, and the terms of Senators and Representatives at noon on the 3d day of January, of the years in which such terms would have ended if this article had not been ratified; and the terms of their successors shall then begin.

Section 2.   The Congress shall assemble at least once in every year, and such meeting shall begin at noon on the 3d day of January, unless they shall by law appoint a different day.

Section 3.   If, at the time fixed for the beginning of the term of the President, the President-elect shall have died, the Vice President-elect shall become President. If a President shall not have been chosen before the time fixed for the beginning of his term, or if the President-elect shall have failed to qualify, then the Vice President-elect shall act as President until a President shall have qualified; and the Congress may by law provide for the case wherein neither a President-elect nor a Vice President-elect shall have qualified, declaring who shall then act as President, or the manner in which one who is to act shall be selected, and such person shall act accordingly until a President or Vice President shall have qualified.

Section 4.   The Congress may by law provide for the case of the death of any of the persons from whom the House of Representatives may choose a President whenever the right of choice shall have devolved upon them, and for the case of the death of any of the persons from whom the Senate may choose a Vice President whenever the right of choice shall have devolved upon them.

Section 5.   Sections 1 and 2 shall take effect on the 15th day of October following the ratification of this article.

Section 6.   This article shall be inoperative unless it shall have been ratified as an amendment to the Constitution by the legislatures of three-fourths of the several States within seven years from the date of its submission.

Article XXI

Passed by Congress February 20, 1933. Ratified December 5, 1933.

Section 1.   The Eighteenth Article of amendment to the Constitution of the United States is hereby repealed.

Section 2.   The transportation or importation into any State, Territory, or possession of the United States for delivery or use therein of intoxicating liquors in violation of the laws thereof, is hereby prohibited.

Section 3.   This article shall be inoperative unless it shall have been ratified as an amendment to the Constitution by conventions in the several States, as provided in the Constitution, within seven years form the date of the submission thereof to the States by the Congress.

Article XXII

Passed by Congress March 24, 1947. Ratified February 26, 1951.

Section 1.   No person shall be elected to the office of the President more than twice, and no person who has held the office of President, or acted as President, for more than two years of a term to which some other person was elected President shall be elected to the office of the President more than once. But this article shall not apply to any person holding the office of President when this article was proposed by the Congress, and shall not prevent any person who may be holding the office of President, or acting as President, during the term within which this article becomes operative from holding the office of President or acting as President during the remainder of such term.

Section 2.   This article shall be inoperative unless it shall have been ratified as an amendment to the Constitution by the legislatures of three-fourths of the several States within seven years from the date of its submission to the States by the Congress.

Article XXIII

Passed by Congress June 16, 1960. Ratified April 3, 1961.

Section 1.   The District constituting the seat of Government of the United States shall appoint in such manner as the Congress may direct:

A number of electors of President and Vice President equal to the whole number of Senators and Representatives in Congress to which the District would be entitled if it were a State, but in no event more than the least populous State; they shall be in addition to those appointed by the States, but they shall be considered, for the purposes of the election of President and Vice President, to be electors appointed by a State; and they shall meet in the District and perform such duties as provided by the twelfth article of amendment.

Section 2.   The Congress shall have power to enforce this article by appropriate legislation.

Article XXIV

Passed by Congress August 27, 1962. Ratified February 4, 1964.

Section 1.   The right of citizens of the United States to vote in any primary or other election for President or Vice President, for electors for President or Vice President, or for Senator or Representative in Congress, shall not be denied or abridged by the United States or any State by reason of failure to pay any poll tax or other tax.

Section 2. The Congress shall have power to enforce this article by appropriate legislation.

Article XXV

Passed by Congress July 6, 1965. Ratified February 23, 1967.

Section 1. In case of the removal of the President from office or of his death or resignation, the Vice President shall become President.

Section 2. Whenever there is a vacancy in the office of the Vice President, the President shall nominate a Vice President who shall take office upon confirmation by a majority vote of both Houses of Congress.

Section 3. Whenever the President transmits to the President pro tempore of the Senate and the Speaker of the House of Representatives has written declaration that he is unable to discharge the powers and duties of his office, and until he transmits to them a written declaration to the contrary, such powers and duties shall be discharged by the Vice President as Acting President.

Section 4. Whenever the Vice President and a majority of either the principal officers of the executive departments or of such other body as Congress may by law provide, transmit to the President pro tempore of the Senate and the Speaker of the House of Representatives their written declaration that the President is unable to discharge the powers and duties of his office, the Vice President shall immediately assume the powers and duties of the office as Acting President.

Thereafter, when the President transmits to the President pro tempore of the Senate and the Speaker of the House of Representatives his written declaration that no inability exists, he shall resume the powers and duties of his office unless the Vice President and a majority of either the principal officers of the executive department or of such other body as Congress may by law provide, transmit within four days to the President pro tempore of the Senate and the Speaker of the House of Representatives their written declaration that the President is unable to discharge the powers and duties of his office. Thereupon Congress shall decide the issue, assembling within forty-eight hours for that purpose if not in session. If the Congress, within twenty-one days after receipt of the latter written declaration, or, if Congress is not in session, within twenty-one days after Congress is required to assemble, determines by two-thirds vote of both Houses that the President is unable to discharge the powers and duties of his office, the Vice President shall continue to discharge the same as Acting President; otherwise, the President shall resume the powers and duties of his office.

Article XXVI

Passed by Congress March 23, 1971. Ratified July 5, 1971.

Section 1. The right of citizens of the United States, who are eighteen years of age or older, to vote shall not be denied or abridged by the United States or by any State on account of age.

APPENDIX 3
1990 UNIFORM
COMMERCIAL CODE*
(EXCERPTS)

ARTICLE 1

GENERAL PROVISIONS

Part 1

Short Title, Construction, Application and Subject Matter of the Act

§ 1—102. Purposes; Rules of Construction; Variation by Agreement

(1) This Act shall be liberally construed and applied to promote its underlying purposes and policies.

(2) Underlying purposes and policies of this Act are
    (a) to simplify, clarify and modernize the law governing commercial transactions;
    (b) to permit the continued expansion of commercial practices through custom, usage and agreement of the parties;
    (c) to make uniform the law among the various jurisdictions.

(3) The effect of provisions of this Act may be varied by agreement, except as otherwise provided in this Act and except that the obligations of good faith, diligence, reasonableness and care prescribed by this Act may not be disclaimed by agreement, but the parties may by agreement determine the standards by which the performance of such obligations is to be measured if such standards are not manifestly unreasonable.

. . .

§ 1—103. Supplementary General Principles of Law Applicable

Unless displaced by the particular provisions of this Act, the principles of law and equity, including the law merchant and the law relative to capacity to contract, principal and agent, estoppel, fraud, misrepresentation, duress, coer-

* The Code has been adopted in every state except Louisiana. It has also been adopted for Guam, the Virgin Islands, and the District of Columbia. Louisiana has adopted Articles 1 and 3 and 9, of the Code.

In 1972, a group of Amendments to the Code was recommended. These have been adopted in all states except Louisiana and Vermont. The 1972 Amendments have also been adopted for Guam. The changes made by the 1972 Amendments to the UCC are confined mainly to Article 9 on secured transactions.

In 1977, Article 8 of the Code, relating to investment securities, was amended. This amended version has been adopted in Arkansas, California, Colorado, Connecticut, Delaware, Florida, Hawaii, Idaho, Illinois, Indiana, Kansas, Kentucky, Maine, Maryland, Massachusetts, Michigan, Minnesota, Montana, Nevada, New Hampshire, New Mexico, New York, North Dakota, Ohio, Oklahoma, Oregon, Rhode Island, South Dakota, Tennessee, Texas, Virginia, Washington, West Virginia, Wisconsin, and Wyoming.

Article 2A on leases was promulgated recently; it has been adopted by California, Florida, Hawaii, Indiana, Kansas, Kentucky,

Minnesota, Montana, Nebraska, Nevada, North Dakota, Oklahoma, South Dakota, Utah, Virginia, and Wyoming.

Article 4A, Funds Transfers, has been adopted in Arizona, Arkansas, California, Colorado, Connecticut, Florida, Hawaii, Idaho, Illinois, Indiana, Kansas, Louisiana, Minnesota, Mississippi, Montana, Nebraska, New York, North Dakota, Oklahoma, South Dakota, Tennessee, Utah, Virginia, Washington, West Virginia, and Wyoming.

The 1989 Article 6, Bulk Sales, Alternative A (repeal) has been adopted in Arkansas, Minnesota, Montana, Nebraska, Oregon, and Wyoming. Alternative B (revision) has been adopted in California, Hawaii, Oklahoma, and Utah.

The 1990 Article 3, Negotiable Instruments, has been adopted in Arkansas, Connecticut, Hawaii, Kansas, Montana, Nebraska, North Dakota, Oklahoma, and Wyoming.

The 1990 Article 4, Bank Collections, has been adopted in Arkansas, Connecticut, Hawaii, Kansas, Montana, Nebraska, North Dakota, Oklahoma, and Wyoming.

cion, mistake, bankruptcy, or other validating or invalidating cause shall supplement its provisions.

§ 1—106.   Remedies to Be Liberally Administered

(1) The remedies provided by this Act shall be liberally administered to the end that the aggrieved party may be put in as good a position as if the other party had fully performed, but neither consequential or special nor penal damages may be had except as specifically provided in this Act or by other rule of law.

(2) Any right or obligation declared by this Act is enforceable by action unless the provision declaring it specifies a different and limited effect.

§ 1—107.   Waiver or Renunciation of Claim or Right After Breach

Any claim or right arising out of an alleged breach can be discharged in whole or in part without consideration by a written waiver or renunciation signed and delivered by the aggrieved party.

Part 2

General Definitions and Principles of Interpretation

§ 1—201.   General Definitions

Subject to additional definitions contained in the subsequent Articles of this Act which are applicable to specific Articles or Parts thereof, and unless the context otherwise requires, in this Act:

(1) "Action" in the sense of a judicial proceeding includes recoupment, counterclaim, set-off, suit in equity and any other proceedings in which rights are determined.

(2) "Aggrieved party" means a party entitled to resort to a remedy.

(3) "Agreement" means the bargain of the parties in fact as found in their language or by implication from other circumstances including course of dealing or usage of trade or course of performance as provided in this Act (Sections 1—205 and 2—208). Whether an agreement has legal consequences is determined by the provisions of this Act, if applicable; otherwise by the law of contracts (Section 1—103). (Compare "Contract.")

. . .

(5) "Bearer" means the person in possession of an instrument, document of title, or certificated security payable to bearer or indorsed in blank.

(6) "Bill of lading" means a document evidencing the receipt of goods for shipment issued by a person engaged in the business of transporting or forwarding goods, and includes an airbill. "Airbill" means a document serving for air transportation as a bill of lading does for marine or rail transportation, and includes an air consignment note or air waybill.

. . .

(8) "Burden of establishing" a fact means the burden of persuading the triers of fact that the existence of the fact is more probable than its nonexistence.

(9) "Buyer in ordinary course of business" means a person who in good faith and without knowledge that the sale to him is in violation of the ownership rights or security interest of a third party in the goods buys in ordinary course from a person in the business of selling goods of that kind but does not include a pawnbroker. All persons who sell minerals or the like (including oil and gas) at wellhead or minehead shall be deemed to be persons in the business of selling goods of that kind. "Buying" may be for cash or by exchange of other property or on secured or unsecured credit and includes receiving goods or documents of title under a preexisting contract for sale but does not include a transfer in bulk or as security for or in total or partial satisfaction of a money debt.

(10) "Conspicuous": A term or clause is conspicuous when it is so written that a reasonable person against whom it is to operate ought to have noticed it. A printed heading in capitals (as: NON-NEGOTIABLE BILL OF LADING) is conspicuous. Language in the body of a form is "conspicuous" if it is in larger or other contrasting type or color. But in a telegram any stated term is "conspicuous." Whether a term or clause is "conspicuous" or not is for decision by the court.

(11) "Contract" means the total legal obligation which results from the parties' agreement as affected by this Act and any other applicable rules of law. (Compare "Agreement.")

. . .

(15) "Document of title" includes bill of lading, dock warrant, dock receipt, warehouse receipt or order for the delivery of goods, and also any other document which in the regular course of business or financing is treated as adequately evidencing that the person in possession of it is entitled to receive, hold and dispose of the document and the goods it covers. To be a document of title a document must purport to be issued by or addressed to a bailee and purport to cover goods in the bailee's possession which are either identified or are fungible portions of an identified mass.

. . .

(18) "Genuine" means free of forgery or counterfeiting.

(19) "Good faith" means honesty in fact in the conduct or transaction concerned.

(20) "Holder" means a person who is in possession of a document of title or an instrument or a certificated investment security drawn, issued or indorsed to him or to his order or to bearer or in blank.

. . .

(25) A person has "notice" of a fact when
   (a) he has actual knowledge of it; or
   (b) he has received a notice or notification of it; or
   (c) from all the facts and circumstances known to him at the time in question he has reason to know that it exists.

A person "knows" or has "knowledge" of a fact when he has actual knowledge of it. "Discover" or "learn" or a word or phrase of similar import refers to knowledge rather than to reason to know. The time and circumstances under which a notice or notification may cease to be effective are not determined by this Act.

(26) A person "notifies" or "gives" a notice or notification to another by taking such steps as may be reasonably required to inform the other in ordinary course whether or not such other actually comes to know of it. A person "receives" a notice or notification when

      (a) it comes to his attention; or

      (b) it is duly delivered at the place of business through which the contract was made or at any other place held out by him as the place for receipt of such communications.

(27) Notice, knowledge or a notice or notification received by an organization is effective for a particular transaction from the time when it is brought to the attention of the individual conducting that transaction, and in any event from the time when it would have been brought to his attention if the organization had exercised due diligence. An organization exercises due diligence if it maintains reasonable routines for communicating significant information to the person conducting the transaction and there is reasonable compliance with the routines. Due diligence does not require an individual acting for the organization to communicate information unless such communication is part of his regular duties or unless he has reason to know of the transaction and that the transaction would be materially affected by the information.

(28) "Organization" includes a corporation, government or governmental subdivision or agency, business trust, estate, trust, partnership or association, two or more persons having a joint or common interest, or any other legal or commercial entity.

. . .

(31) "Presumption" or "presumed" means that the trier of fact must find the existence of the fact presumed unless and until evidence is introduced which would support a finding of its nonexistence.

(32) "Purchase" includes taking by sale, discount, negotiation, mortgage, pledge, hen, issue or re-issue, gift or any other voluntary transaction creating an interest in property.

(33) "Purchaser" means a person who takes by purchase.

. . .

(37) "Security interest" means an interest in personal property or fixtures which secures payment or performance of an obligation. The retention or reservation of title by a seller of goods notwithstanding shipment or delivery to the buyer (Section 2—401) is limited in effect to a reservation of a "security interest." The term also includes any interest of a buyer of accounts or chattel paper which is subject to Article 9. The special property interest of a buyer of goods on identification of such goods to a contract for sale under Section 2—401 is not a "security interest," but a buyer may also acquire a "security interest" by complying with Article 9. Unless a lease or consignment is intended as security, reservation of title thereunder is not a "security interest" but a consignment is in any event subject to the provisions on consignment sales (Section 2—326). Whether a lease is intended as security is to be determined by the facts of each case; however, (a) the inclusion of an option to purchase does not of itself make the lease one intended for security, and (b) an agreement that upon compliance with the terms of the lease the lessee shall become or has the option to become the owner of the property for no additional consideration or for a nominal consideration does make the lease one intended for security.

(38) "Send" in connection with any writing or notice means to deposit in the mail or deliver for transmission by any other usual means of communication with postage or cost of transmission provided for and properly addressed and in the case of an instrument to an address specified thereon or otherwise agreed, or if there be none to any address reasonable under the circumstances. The receipt of any writing or notice within the time at which it would have arrived if properly sent has the effect of a proper sending.

(39) "Signed" includes any symbol executed or adopted by a party with present intention to authenticate a writing.

. . .

(46) "Written" or "writing" includes printing, typewriting or any other intentional reduction to tangible form.

§ 1—203.   Obligation of Good Faith

Every contract or duty within this Act imposes an obligation of good faith in its performance or enforcement.

§ 1—204.   Time; Reasonable Time; "Seasonably"

(1) Whenever this Act requires any action to be taken within a reasonable time, any time which is not manifestly unreasonable may be fixed by agreement.

(2) What is a reasonable time for taking any action depends on the nature, purpose and circumstances of such action.

(3) An action is taken "seasonably" when it is taken at or within the time agreed or, if no time is agreed, at or within a reasonable time.

§ 1—205.   Course of Dealing and Usage of Trade

(1) A course of dealing is a sequence of previous conduct between the parties to a particular transaction which is fairly to be regarded as establishing a common basis of understanding for interpreting their expressions and other conduct.

(2) A usage of trade is any practice or method of dealing having such regularity of observance in a place, vocation or trade as to justify an expectation that it will be observed with respect to the transaction in question. The existence and scope of such a usage are to be proved as facts. If it is established that such a usage is embodied in a written

trade code or similar writing the interpretation of the writing is for the court.

(3) A course of dealing between parties and any usage of trade in the vocation or trade in which they are engaged or of which they are or should be aware give particular meaning to and supplement or qualify terms of an agreement.

(4) The express terms of an agreement and an applicable course of dealing or usage of trade shall be construed wherever reasonable as consistent with each other; but when such construction is unreasonable, express terms control both course of dealing and usage of trade and course of dealing controls usage of trade.

(5) An applicable usage of trade in the place where any part of performance is to occur shall be used in interpreting the agreement as to that part of the performance.

(6) Evidence of a relevant usage of trade offered by one party is not admissible unless and until he has given the other party such notice as the court finds sufficient to prevent unfair surprise to the latter.

§ 1—206.   Statute of Frauds for Kinds of Personal Property Not Otherwise Covered

(1) Except in the cases described in subsection (2) of this section, a contract for the sale of personal property is not enforceable by way of action or defense beyond five thousand dollars in amount or value of remedy unless there is some writing which indicates that a contract for sale has been made between the parties at a defined or stated price, reasonably identifies the subject matter, and is signed by the party against whom enforcement is sought or by his authorized agent.

(2) Subsection (1) of this section does not apply to contracts for the sale of goods (Section 2—201) nor of securities (Section 8—319) nor to security agreements (Section 9—203).

§ 1—207.   Performance or Acceptance Under Reservation of Rights

A party who with explicit reservation of rights performs or promises performance or assents to performance in a manner demanded or offered by the other party does not thereby prejudice the rights reserved. Such words as "without prejudice," "under protest" or the like are sufficient.

§ 1—208.   Option to Accelerate at Will

A term providing that one party or his successor in interest may accelerate payment or performance or require collateral or additional collateral "at will" or "when he deems himself insecure" or in words of similar import shall be construed to mean that he shall have power to do so only if he in good faith believes that the prospect of payment or performance is impaired. The burden of establishing lack of good faith is on the party against whom the power has been exercised.

ARTICLE 2

SALES

Part 1

Short Title, General Construction and Subject Matter

§ 2—103.   Definitions and Index of Definitions

(1) In this Article, unless the context otherwise requires,

   (a) "Buyer" means a person who buys or contracts to buy goods.
   (b) "Good faith" in the case of a merchant means honesty in fact and the observance of reasonable commercial standards of fair dealing in the trade.
   (c) "Receipt" of goods means taking physical possession of them.
   (d) "Seller" means a person who sells or contracts to sell goods.

. . .

§ 2—104.   Definitions: "Merchant"; "Between Merchants"; "Financing Agency"

(1) "Merchant" means a person who deals in goods of the kind or otherwise by his occupation holds himself out as having knowledge or skill peculiar to the practices or goods involved in the transaction or to whom such knowledge or skill may be attributed by his employment of an agent or broker or other intermediary who by his occupation holds himself out as having such knowledge or skill.

   . . .

(3) "Between merchants" means in any transaction with respect to which both parties are chargeable with the knowledge or skill of merchants.

§ 2—105.   Definitions: Transferability; "Goods"; "Future" Goods; "Lot"; "Commercial Unit"

(1) "Goods" means all things (including specially manufactured goods) which are movable at the time of identification to the contract for sale other than the money

in which the price is to be paid, investment securities (Article 8) and things in action. "Goods" also includes the unborn young of animals and growing crops and other identified things attached to realty as described in the section on goods to be severed from realty (Section 2—107).

(2) Goods must be both existing and identified before any interest in them can pass. Goods which are not both existing and identified are "future" goods. A purported present sale of future goods or of any interest therein operates as a contract to sell.

. . .

(5) "Lot" means a parcel or a single article which is the subject matter of a separate sale or delivery, whether or not it is sufficient to perform the contract.

(6) "Commercial unit" means such a unit of goods as by commercial usage is a single whole for purposes of sale and division of which materially impairs its character or value on the market or in use. A commercial unit may be a single article (as a machine) or a set of articles (as a suite of furniture or an assortment of sizes) or a quantity (as a bale, gross, or carload) or any other unit treated in use or in the relevant market as a single whole.

§ 2—106.   Definitions: "Contract"; "Agreement"; "Contract for Sale"; "Sale"; "Present Sale"; "Conforming" to Contract; "Termination"; "Cancellation"

(1) In this Article unless the context otherwise requires, "contract" and "agreement" are limited to those relating to the present or future sale of goods. "Contract for sale" includes both a present sale of goods and a contract to sell goods at a future time. A "sale" consists in the passing of title from the seller to the buyer for a price (Section 2—401). A "present sale" means a sale which is accomplished by the making of the contract.

(2) Goods or conduct, including any part of a performance, are "conforming" or conform to the contract when they are in accordance with the obligations under the contract.

. . .

Part 2

Form, Formation and Readjustment of Contract

§ 2—201.   Formal Requirements; Statute of Frauds

(1) Except as otherwise provided in this section, a contract for the sale of goods for the price of $500 or more is not enforceable by way of action or defense unless there is some writing sufficient to indicate that a contract for sale has been made between the parties and signed by the party against whom enforcement is sought or by his authorized agent or broker. A writing is not insufficient because it omits or incorrectly states a term agreed upon but the contract is not enforceable under this paragraph beyond the quantity of goods shown in such writing.

(2) Between merchants, if within a reasonable time a writing in confirmation of the contract and sufficient against the sender is received and the party receiving it has reason to know its contents, it satisfies the requirements of subsection (1) against such party unless written notice of objection to its contents is given within 10 days after it is received.

(3) A contract which does not satisfy the requirements of subsection (1) but which is valid in other respects is enforceable

(a) if the goods are to be specially manufactured for the buyer and are not suitable for sale to others in the ordinary course of the seller's business and the seller, before notice of repudiation is received and under circumstances which reasonably indicate that the goods are for the buyer, has made either a substantial beginning of their manufacture or commitments for their procurement; or

(b) if the party against whom enforcement is sought admits in his pleading, testimony or otherwise in court that a contract for sale was made, but the contract is not enforceable under this provision beyond the quantity of goods admitted; or

(c) with respect to goods for which payment has been made and accepted or which have been received and accepted (Sec. 2—606).

§ 2—202.   Final Written Expression: Parol or Extrinsic Evidence

Terms with respect to which the confirmatory memoranda of the parties agree or which are otherwise set forth in a writing intended by the parties as a final expression of their agreement with respect to such terms as are included therein may not be contradicted by evidence of any prior agreement or of a contemporaneous oral agreement but may be explained or supplemented

(a) by course of dealing or usage of trade (Section 1—205) or by course of performance (Section 2—208); and

(b) by evidence of consistent additional terms unless the court finds the writing to have been intended also as a complete and exclusive statement of the terms of the agreement.

§ 2—204.   Formation in General

(1) A contract for sale of goods may be made in any manner sufficient to show agreement, including conduct by both parties which recognizes the existence of such a contract.

(2) An agreement sufficient to constitute a contract for sale may be found even though the moment of its making is undetermined.

(3) Even though one or more terms are left open a contract for sale does not fail for indefiniteness if the parties have intended to make a contract and there is a reasonably certain basis for giving an appropriate remedy.

§ 2—205.   Firm Offers

An offer by a merchant to buy or sell goods in a signed writing which by its terms gives assurance that it will be held open is not revocable, for lack of consideration, during the time stated or if no time is stated for a reasonable time, but in no event may such period of irrevocability exceed three months; but any such term of assurance on a form supplied by the offeree must be separately signed by the offeror.

§ 2—206.   Offer and Acceptance in Formation of Contract

(1) Unless otherwise unambiguously indicated by the language or circumstances

    (a) an offer to make a contract shall be construed as inviting acceptance in any manner and by any medium reasonable in the circumstances;

    (b) an order or other offer to buy goods for prompt or current shipment shall be construed as inviting acceptance either by a prompt promise to ship or by the prompt or current shipment of conforming or non-conforming goods, but such a shipment of nonconforming goods does not constitute an acceptance if the seller seasonably notifies the buyer that the shipment is offered only as an accommodation to the buyer.

(2) Where the beginning of a requested performance is a reasonable mode of acceptance, an offeror who is not notified of acceptance within a reasonable time may treat the offer as having lapsed before acceptance.

§ 2—207.   Additional Terms in Acceptance or Confirmation

(1) A definite and seasonable expression of acceptance or a written confirmation which is sent within a reasonable time operates as an acceptance even though it states terms additional to or different from those offered or agreed upon, unless acceptance is expressly made conditional on assent to the additional or different terms.

(2) The additional terms are to be construed as proposals for addition to the contract. Between merchants such terms become part of the contract unless:

    (a) the offer expressly limits acceptance to the terms of the offer;

    (b) they materially alter it; or

    (c) notification of objection to them has already been given or is given within a reasonable time after notice of them is received.

(3) Conduct by both parties which recognizes the existence of a contract is sufficient to establish a contract for sale although the writings of the parties do not otherwise establish a contract. In such case the terms of the particular contract consist of those terms on which the writings of the parties agree, together with any supplementary terms incorporated under any other provisions of this Act.

§ 2—208.   Course of Performance or Practical Construction

(1) Where the contract for sale involves repeated occasions for performance by either party with knowledge of the nature of the performance and opportunity for objection to it by the other, any course of performance accepted or acquiesced in without objection shall be relevant to determine the meaning of the agreement.

(2) The express terms of the agreement and any such course of performance, as well as any course of dealing and usage of trade, shall be construed whenever reasonable as consistent with each other; but when such construction is unreasonable, express terms shall control course of performance and course of performance shall control both course of dealing and usage of trade (Section 1—205).

(3) Subject to the provisions of the next section on modification and waiver, such course of performance shall be relevant to show a waiver or modification of any term inconsistent with such course of performance.

§ 2—209.   Modification, Rescission and Waiver

(1) An agreement modifying a contract within this Article needs no consideration to be binding.

(2) A signed agreement which excludes modification or rescission except by a signed writing cannot be otherwise modified or rescinded, but except as between merchants such a requirement on a form supplied by the merchant must be separately signed by the other party.

(3) The requirements of the statute of frauds section of this Article (Section 2—201) must be satisfied if the contract as modified is within its provisions.

(4) Although an attempt at modification or rescission does not satisfy the requirements of subsection (2) or (3) it can operate as a waiver.

(5) A party who has made a waiver affecting an executory portion of the contract may retract the waiver by reasonable notification received by the other party that strict performance will be required of any term waived, unless the retraction would be unjust in view of a material change of position in reliance on the waiver.

§ 2—210.   Delegation of Performance; Assignment of Rights

(1) A party may perform his duty through a delegate unless otherwise agreed or unless the other party has a substantial interest in having his original promisor perform or control the acts required by the contract. No delegation of performance relieves the party delegating of any duty to perform or any liability for breach.

(2) Unless otherwise agreed, all rights of either seller or buyer can be assigned except where the assignment would materially change the duty of the other party, or increase materially the burden or risk imposed on him by his contract, or impair materially his chance of obtaining return performance. A right to damages for breach of the whole contract or a right arising out of the assignor's due perfor-

mance of his entire obligation can be assigned despite agreement otherwise.

(3) Unless the circumstances indicate the contrary, a prohibition of assignment of "the contract" is to be construed as barring only the delegation to the assignee of the assignor's performance.

(4) An assignment of "the contract" or of "all my rights under the contract" or an assignment in similar general terms is an assignment of rights and, unless the language or the circumstances (as in an assignment for security) indicate the contrary, it is a delegation of performance of the duties of the assignor, and its acceptance by the assignee constitutes a promise by him to perform those duties. This promise is enforceable by either the assignor or the other party to the original contract.

(5) The other party may treat any assignment which delegates performance as creating reasonable grounds for insecurity and may without prejudice to his rights against the assignor demand assurances from the assignee (Section 2—609).

Part 3

General Obligation and Construction of Contract

§ 2—301.   General Obligations of Parties

The obligation of the seller is to transfer and deliver and that of the buyer is to accept and pay in accordance with the contract.

§ 2—302.   Unconscionable Contract or Clause

(1) If the court as a matter of law finds the contract or any clause of the contract to have been unconscionable at the time it was made, the court may refuse to enforce the contract, or it may enforce the remainder of the contract without the unconscionable clause, or it may so limit the application of any unconscionable clause as to avoid any unconscionable result.

(2) When it is claimed or appears to the court that the contract or any clause thereof may be unconscionable, the parties shall be afforded a reasonable opportunity to present evidence as to its commercial setting, purpose and effect to aid the court in making the determination.

§ 2—303.   Allocation or Division of Risks

Where this Article allocates a risk or a burden as between the parties "unless otherwise agreed," the agreement may not only shift the allocation but may also divide the risk or burden.

§ 2—305.   Open Price Term

(1) The parties, if they so intend, can conclude a contract for sale even though the price is not settled. In such a case, the price is a reasonable price at the time for delivery if

(a)   nothing is said as to price; or

(b)   the price is left to be agreed by the parties and they fail to agree; or

(c)   the price is to be fixed in terms of some agreed market or other standard as set or recorded by a third person or agency and it is not so set or recorded.

(2) A price to be fixed by the seller or by the buyer means a price for him to fix in good faith.

(3) When a price left to be fixed otherwise than by agreement of the parties fails to be fixed through fault of one party, the other may at his option treat the contract as cancelled or himself fix a reasonable price.

(4) Where, however, the parties intend not to be bound unless the price be fixed or agreed and it is not fixed or agreed, there is no contract. In such a case, the buyer must return any goods already received or if unable so to do must pay their reasonable value at the time of delivery and the seller must return any portion of the price paid on account.

§ 2—306.   Output, Requirements and Exclusive Dealings

(1) A term which measures the quantity by the output of the seller or the requirements of the buyer means such actual output or requirements as may occur in good faith, except that no quantity unreasonably disproportionate to any stated estimate or in the absence of a stated estimate to any normal or otherwise comparable prior output or requirements may be tendered or demanded.

(2) A lawful agreement by either the seller or the buyer for exclusive dealing in the kind of goods concerned imposes, unless otherwise agreed, an obligation by the seller to use best efforts to supply the goods and by the buyer to use best efforts to promote their sale.

§ 2—312.   Warranty of Title and Against Infringement; Buyer's Obligation Against Infringement

(1) Subject to subsection (2), there is in a contract for sale a warranty by the seller that

(a)   the title conveyed shall be good, and its transfer rightful; and

(b)   the goods shall be delivered free from any security interest or other lien or encumbrance of which the buyer at the time of contracting has no knowledge.

(2) A warranty under subsection (1) will be excluded or modified only by specific language or by circumstances which give the buyer reason to know that the person selling does not claim title in himself or that he is purporting to sell only such right or title as he or a third person may have.

(3) Unless otherwise agreed a seller who is a merchant regularly dealing in goods of the kind warrants that the goods shall be delivered free of the rightful claim of any third person by way of infringement or the like but a buyer who furnishes specifications to the seller must hold the sell-

er harmless against any such claim which arises out of compliance with the specifications.

§ 2—313.   Express Warranties by Affirmation, Promise, Description, Sample

(1) Express warranties by the seller are created as follows:

(a) Any affirmation of fact or promise made by the seller to the buyer which relates to the goods and becomes part of the basis of the bargain creates an express warranty that the goods shall conform to the affirmation or promise.

(b) Any description of the goods which is made part of the basis of the bargain creates an express warranty that the goods shall conform to the description.

(c) Any sample or model which is made part of the basis of the bargain creates an express warranty that the whole of the goods shall conform to the sample or model.

(2) It is not necessary to the creation of an express warranty that the seller use formal words such as "warrant" or "guarantee" or that he have a specific intention to make a warranty, but an affirmation merely of the value of the goods or a statement purporting to be merely the seller's opinion or commendation of the goods does not create a warranty.

§ 2—314.   Implied Warranty; Merchantability; Usage of Trade

(1) Unless excluded or modified (Section 2—316), a warranty that the goods shall be merchantable is implied in a contract for their sale if the seller is a merchant with respect to goods of that kind. Under this section, the serving for value of food or drink to be consumed either on the premises or elsewhere is a sale.

(2) Goods to be merchantable must be at least such as

(a) pass without objection in the trade under the contract description; and

(b) in the case of fungible goods, are of fair average quality within the description; and

(c) are fit for the ordinary purposes for which such goods are used; and

(d) run, within the variations permitted by the agreement, of even kind, quality and quantity within each unit and among all units involved; and

(e) are adequately contained, packaged, and labeled as the agreement may require; and

(f) conform to the promises or affirmations of fact made on the container or label if any.

(3) Unless excluded or modified (Section 2—316), other implied warranties may arise from course of dealing or usage of trade.

§ 2—315.   Implied Warranty: Fitness for Particular Purpose

Where the seller at the time of contracting has reason to know any particular purpose for which the goods are required and that the buyer is relying on the seller's skill or judgment to select or furnish suitable goods, there is unless excluded or modified under the next section an implied warranty that the goods shall be fit for such purpose.

§ 2—326.   Sale on Approval and Sale or Return; Consignment Sales and Rights of Creditors

(1) Unless otherwise agreed, if delivered goods may be returned by the buyer even though they conform to the contract, the transaction is

(a) a "sale on approval" if the goods are delivered primarily for use, and

(b) a "sale or return" if the goods are delivered primarily for resale.

(2) Except as provided in subsection (3), goods held on approval are not subject to the claims of the buyer's creditors until acceptance; goods held on sale or return are subject to such claims while in the buyer's possession.

(3) Where goods are delivered to a person for sale and such person maintains a place of business at which he deals in goods of the kind involved, under a name other than the name of the person making delivery, then with respect to claims of creditors of the person conducting the business the goods are deemed to be on sale or return. The provisions of this subsection are applicable even though an agreement purports to reserve title to the person making delivery until payment or resale or uses such words as "on consignment" or "on memorandum." However, this subsection is not applicable if the person making delivery

(a) complies with an applicable law providing for a consignor's interest or the like to be evidenced by a sign, or

(b) establishes that the person conducting the business is generally known by his creditors to be substantially engaged in selling the goods of others, or

(c) complies with the filing provisions of the Article on secured Transactions (Article 9).

(4) Any "or return" term of a contract for sale is to be treated as a separate contract for sale within the statute of frauds section of this Article (Section 2—201) and as contradicting the sale aspect of the contract within the provisions of this Article on parol or extrinsic evidence (Section 2—202).

§ 2—327.   Special Incidents of Sale on Approval and Sale or Return

(1) Under a sale on approval, unless otherwise agreed

(a) although the goods are identified to the contract, the risk of loss and the title do not pass to the buyer until acceptance; and

(b) use of the goods consistent with the purpose of trial is not acceptance but failure seasonably to notify the seller of election to return the goods is acceptance, and if the goods conform to the contract acceptance of any part is acceptance of the whole; and

(c) after due notification of election to return, the

return is at the seller's risk and expense but a merchant buyer must follow any reasonable instructions.

(2) Under a sale or return, unless otherwise agreed
    (a) the option to return extends to the whole or any commercial unit of the goods while in substantially their original condition, but must be exercised seasonably; and
    (b) the return is at the buyer's risk and expense.

Part 4

Title, Creditors and Good Faith Purchasers

§ 2—401.   Passing of Title; Reservation for Security; Limited Application of This Section

Each provision of this Article with regard to the rights, obligations and remedies of the seller, the buyer, purchasers or other third parties applies irrespective of title to the goods except where the provision refers to such title. Insofar as situations are not covered by the other provisions of this Article and matters concerning title become material the following rules apply:

(1) Title to goods cannot pass under a contract for sale prior to their identification to the contract (Section 2—501), and unless otherwise explicitly agreed the buyer acquires by their identification a special property as limited by this Act. Any retention or reservation by the seller of the title (property) in goods shipped or delivered to the buyer is limited in effect to a reservation of a security interest. Subject to these provisions and to the provisions of the Article on Secured Transactions (Article 9), title to goods passes from the seller to the buyer in any manner and on any conditions explicitly agreed on by the parties.

(2) Unless otherwise explicitly agreed, title passes to the buyer at the time and place at which the seller completes his performance with reference to the physical delivery of the goods, despite any reservation of security interest and even though a document of title is to be delivered at a different time or place; and in particular and despite any reservation of a security interest by the bill of lading
    (a) if the contract requires or authorizes the seller to send the goods to the buyer but does not require him to deliver them at destination, title passes to the buyer at the time and place of shipment; but
    (b) if the contract requires delivery at destination, title passes on tender there.

(3) Unless otherwise explicitly agreed, where delivery is to be made without moving the goods,
    (a) if the seller is to deliver a document of title, title passes at the time when and the place where he delivers such documents; or
    (b) if the goods are at the time of contracting already identified and no documents are to be delivered, title passes at the time and place of contracting.

(4) A rejection or other refusal by the buyer to receive or retain the goods, whether or not justified, or a justified revocation of acceptance revests title to the goods in the seller. Such revesting occurs by operation of law and is not a "sale."

§ 2—403.   Power to Transfer; Good Faith Purchase of Goods; "Entrusting"

(1) A purchaser of goods acquires all title which his transferor had or had power to transfer except that a purchaser of a limited interest acquires rights only to the extent of the interest purchased. A person with voidable title has power to transfer a good title to a good faith purchaser for value. When goods have been delivered under a transaction of purchase, the purchaser has such power even though
    (a) the transferor was deceived as to the identity of the purchaser, or
    (b) the delivery was in exchange for a check which is later dishonored, or
    (c) it was agreed that the transaction was to be a "cash sale" or
    (d) the delivery was procured through fraud punishable as larcenous under the criminal law.

(2) Any entrusting of possession of goods to a merchant who deals in goods of that kind gives him power to transfer all rights of the entruster to a buyer in ordinary course of business.

(3) "Entrusting" includes any delivery and any acquiescence in retention of possession regardless of any condition expressed between the parties to the delivery or acquiescence and regardless of whether the procurement of the entrusting or the possessor's disposition of the goods have been such as to be larcenous under the criminal law.

(4) The rights of other purchasers of goods and of lien creditors are governed by the Articles on Secured Transactions (Article 9), Bulk Transfers (Article 6) and Documents of Title (Article 7).

Part 5

Performance

§ 2—501.   Insurable Interest in Goods; Manner of Identification of Goods

(1) The buyer obtains a special property and an insurable interest in goods by identification of existing goods as goods to which the contract refers even though the goods so identified are non-conforming and he has an option to return or reject them. . . .

(2) The seller retains an insurable interest in goods so long as title to or any security interest in the goods remains in him; and where the identification is by the seller alone, he may until default or insolvency or notification to the buyer that the identification is final substitute other goods for those identified.

. . .

§ 2—503.   Manner of Seller's Tender of Delivery

(1) Tender of delivery requires that the seller put and hold conforming goods at the buyer's disposition and give the buyer any notification reasonably necessary to enable him to take delivery. The manner, time and place for tender are determined by the agreement and this Article, and in particular

    (a) tender must be at a reasonable hour, and, if it is of goods, they must be kept available for the period reasonably necessary to enable the buyer to take possession; but

    (b) unless otherwise agreed, the buyer must furnish facilities reasonably suited to the receipt of the goods.

(2) Where the case is within the next section respecting shipment, tender requires that the seller comply with its provisions.

(3) Where the seller is required to deliver at a particular destination, tender requires that he comply with subsection (1) and also, in any appropriate case, tender documents as described in subsections (4) and (5) of this section.

(4) Where goods are in the possession of a bailee and are to be delivered without being moved

    (a) tender requires that the seller either tender a negotiable document of title covering such goods or procure acknowledgment by the bailee of the buyer's right to possession of the goods; but

    (b) tender to the buyer of a nonnegotiable document of title or of a written direction to the bailee to deliver is sufficient tender unless the buyer seasonably objects, and receipt by the bailee of notification of the buyer's rights fixes those rights as against the bailee and all third persons; but risk of loss of the goods and of any failure by the bailee to honor the nonnegotiable document of title or to obey the direction remains on the seller until the buyer has had a reasonable time to present the document or direction, and a refusal by the bailee to honor the document or to obey the direction defeats the tender.

(5) Where the contract requires the seller to deliver documents

    (a) he must tender all such documents in correct form, except as provided in this Article with respect to bills of lading in a set (subsection (2) of Section 2—323); and

    (b) tender through customary banking channels is sufficient and dishonor of a draft accompanying the documents constitutes nonacceptance or rejection.

§ 2—504.   Shipment by Seller

Where the seller is required or authorized to send the goods to the buyer and the contract does not require him to deliver them at a particular destination, then, unless otherwise agreed, he must

    (a) put the goods in the possession of such a carrier and make such a contract for their transportation as may be reasonable having regard to the nature of the goods and other circumstances of the case; and

    (b) obtain and promptly deliver or tender in due form any document necessary to enable the buyer to obtain possession of the goods or otherwise required by the agreement or by usage of trade; and

    (c) promptly notify the buyer of the shipment.

Failure to notify the buyer under paragraph (c) or to make a proper contract under paragraph (a) is a ground for rejection only if material delay or loss ensues.

§ 2—508.   Cure by Seller of Improper Tender or Delivery; Replacement

(1) Where any tender or delivery by the seller is rejected because non-conforming and the time for performance has not yet expired, the seller may seasonably notify the buyer of his intention to cure and may then within the contract time make a conforming delivery.

(2) Where the buyer rejects a non-conforming tender which the seller had reasonable grounds to believe would be acceptable with or without money allowance, the seller may if he seasonably notifies the buyer have a further reasonable time to substitute a conforming tender.

§ 2—509.   Risk of Loss in the Absence of Breach

(1) Where the contract requires or authorizes the seller to ship the goods by carrier

    (a) if it does not require him to deliver them at a particular destination, the risk of loss passes to the buyer when the goods are duly delivered to the carrier even though the shipment is under reservation (Section 2—505); but

    (b) if it does require him to deliver them at a particular destination and the goods are there duly tendered while in the possession of the carrier, the risk of loss passes to the buyer when the goods are there duly so tendered as to enable the buyer to take delivery.

(2) Where the goods are held by a bailee to be delivered without being moved, the risk of loss passes to the buyer

    (a) on his receipt of a negotiable document of title covering the goods; or

    (b) on acknowledgment by the bailee of the buyer's right to possession of the goods; or

    (c) after his receipt of a nonnegotiable document of title or other written direction to deliver, as provided in subsection (4)(b) of Section 2—503.

(3) In any case not within subsection (1) or (2), the risk of loss passes to the buyer on his receipt of the goods if the seller is a merchant; otherwise the risk passes to the buyer on tender of delivery.

(4) The provisions of this section are subject to con-

trary agreement of the parties and to the provisions of this Article on sale on approval (Section 2—327) and on effect of breach on risk of loss (Section 2—510).

§ 2—510.   Effect of Breach on Risk of Loss

(1) Where a tender or delivery of goods so fails to conform to the contract as to give a right of rejection, the risk of their loss remains on the seller until cure or acceptance.

(2) Where the buyer rightfully revokes acceptance, he may to the extent of any deficiency in his effective insurance coverage treat the risk of loss as having rested on the seller from the beginning.

(3) Where the buyer, as to conforming goods already identified to the contract for sale, repudiates or is otherwise in breach before risk of their loss has passed to him, the seller may to the extent of any deficiency in his effective insurance coverage treat the risk of loss as resting on the buyer for a commercially reasonable time.

Part 6

Breach, Repudiation and Excuse

§ 2—601.   Buyer's Rights on Improper Delivery

Subject to the provisions of this Article on breach in installment contracts (Section 2—612) and unless otherwise agreed under the sections on contractual limitations of remedy (Sections 2—718 and 2—719), if the goods or the tender of delivery fail in any respect to conform to the contract, the buyer may

   (a) reject the whole; or

   (b) accept the whole; or

   (c) accept any commercial unit or units and reject the rest.

§ 2—602.   Manner and Effect of Rightful Rejection

(1) Rejection of goods must be within a reasonable time after their delivery or tender. It is ineffective unless the buyer seasonably notifies the seller.

(2) Subject to the provisions of the two following sections on rejected goods (Sections 2—603 and 2—604),

   (a) after rejection any exercise of ownership by the buyer with respect to any commercial unit is wrongful as against the seller; and

   (b) if the buyer has before rejection taken physical possession of goods in which he does not have a security interest under the provisions of this Article (subsection (3) of Section 2—711), he is under a duty after rejection to hold them with reasonable care at the seller's disposition for a time sufficient to permit the seller to remove them; but

   (c) the buyer has no further obligations with regard to goods rightfully rejected.

(3) The seller's rights with respect to goods wrongfully rejected are governed by the provisions of this Article on Seller's remedies in general (Section 2—703).

§ 2—605.   Waiver of Buyer's Objections by Failure to Particularize

(1) The buyer's failure to state in connection with rejection a particular defect which is ascertainable by reasonable inspection precludes him from relying on the unstated defect to justify rejection or to establish breach

   (a) where the seller could have cured it if stated seasonably; or

   (b) between merchants when the seller has after rejection made a request in writing for a full and final written statement of all defects on which the buyer proposes to rely.

(2) Payment against documents made without reservation of rights precludes recovery of the payment for defects apparent on the face of the documents.

§ 2—606.   What Constitutes Acceptance of Goods

(1) Acceptance of goods occurs when the buyer

   (a) after a reasonable opportunity to inspect the goods signifies to the seller that the goods are conforming or that he will take or retain them in spite of their non-conformity; or

   (b) fails to make an effective rejection (subsection (1) of Section 2—602), but such acceptance does not occur until the buyer has had a reasonable opportunity to inspect them; or

   (c) does any act inconsistent with the seller's ownership; but if such act is wrongful as against the seller it is an acceptance only if ratified by him.

(2) Acceptance of a part of any commercial unit is acceptance of that entire unit.

§ 2—607.   Effect of Acceptance; Notice of Breach; Burden of Establishing Breach After Acceptance; Notice of Claim or Litigation to Person Answerable Over

(1) The buyer must pay at the contract rate for any goods accepted.

(2) Acceptance of goods by the buyer precludes rejection of the goods accepted and if made with knowledge of a non-conformity cannot be revoked because of it unless the acceptance was on the reasonable assumption that the non-conformity would be seasonably cured but acceptance does not of itself impair any other remedy provided by this Article for non-conformity.

(3) Where a tender has been accepted

   (a) the buyer must within a reasonable time after he discovers or should have discovered any breach notify the seller of breach or be barred from any remedy; and

   (b) if the claim is one for infringement or the like (subsection (3) of Section 2—312) and the buyer is sued as a result of such a breach, he must so notify the seller within a reasonable time after he receives notice of the litigation or be barred from any remedy over for liability established by the litigation.

(4) The burden is on the buyer to establish any breach with respect to the goods accepted.

(5) Where the buyer is sued for breach of a warranty or other obligation for which his seller is answerable over

   (a) he may give his seller written notice of the litigation. If the notice states that the seller may come in and defend and that if the seller does not do so he will be bound in any action against him by his buyer by any determination of fact common to the two litigations, then unless the seller after seasonable receipt of the notice does come in and defend he is so bound.

   (b) if the claim is one for infringement or the like (subsection (3) of Section 2—312), the original seller may demand in writing that his buyer turn over to him control of the litigation including settlement or else be barred from any remedy over and if he also agrees to bear all expense and to satisfy any adverse judgment, then unless the buyer after seasonable receipt of the demand does turn over control the buyer is so barred.

(6) The provisions of subsections (3), (4) and (5) apply to any obligation of a buyer to hold the seller harmless against infringement or the like (subsection (3) of Section 2—312).

§ 2—608.   Revocation of Acceptance in Whole or in Part

(1) The buyer may revoke his acceptance of a lot or commercial unit whose non-conformity substantially impairs its value to him if he has accepted it

   (a) on the reasonable assumption that its nonconformity would be cured and it has not been seasonably cured; or

   (b) without discovery of such non-conformity if his acceptance was reasonably induced either by the difficulty of discovery before acceptance or by the seller's assurances.

(2) Revocation of acceptance must occur within a reasonable time after the buyer discovers or should have discovered the ground for it and before any substantial change in condition of the goods which is not caused by their own defects. It is not effective until the buyer notifies the seller of it.

(3) A buyer who so revokes has the same rights and duties with regard to the goods involved as if he had rejected them.

§ 2—615.   Excuse by Failure of Presupposed Conditions

Except so far as a seller may have assumed a greater obligation and subject to the preceding section on substituted performance:

   (a) Delay in delivery or nondelivery in whole or in part by a seller who complies with paragraphs (b) and (c) is not a breach of his duty under a contract for sale if performance as

agreed has been made impracticable by the occurrence of a contingency the non-occurrence of which was a basic assumption on which the contract was made or by compliance in good faith with any applicable foreign or domestic governmental regulation or order whether or not it later proves to be invalid.

   (b) Where the causes mentioned in paragraph (a) affect only a part of the seller's capacity to perform, he must allocate production and deliveries among his customers but may at his option include regular customers not then under contract as well as his own requirements for further manufacture. He may so allocate in any manner which is fair and reasonable.

   (c) The seller must notify the buyer seasonally that there will be delay or non-delivery and, when allocation is required under paragraph (b), of the estimated quota thus made available for the buyer.

Part 7

Remedies

§ 2—701.   Remedies for Breach of Collateral Contracts Not Impaired

Remedies for breach of any obligation or promise collateral or ancillary to a contract for sale are not impaired by the provisions of this Article.

§ 2—706.   Seller's Resale Including Contract for Resale

. . . The seller may resell the goods concerned or the undelivered balance thereof. Where the resale is made in good faith and in a commercially reasonable manner, the seller may recover the difference between the resale price and the contract price together with any incidental damages allowed under the provisions of this Article (Section 2—710), but less expenses saved in consequence of the buyer's breach.

(2) Except as otherwise provided in subsection (3) or unless otherwise agreed, resale may be at public or private sale including sale by way of one or more contracts to sell or of identification to an existing contract of the seller. Sale may be as a unit or in parcels and at any time and place and on any terms but every aspect of the sale including the method, manner, time, place and terms must be commercially reasonable. The resale must be reasonably identified as referring to the broken contract, but it is not necessary that the goods be in existence or that any or all of them have been identified to the contract before the breach.

(3) Where the resale is at private sale, the seller must give the buyer reasonable notification of his intention to resell.

(4) Where the resale is at public sale
    (a) only identified goods can be sold except where there is a recognized market for a public sale of futures in goods of the kind; and
    (b) it must be made at a usual place or market for public sale if one is reasonably available and except in the case of goods which are perishable or threaten to decline in value speedily the seller must give the buyer reasonable notice of the time and place of the resale; and
    (c) if the goods are not to be within the view of those attending the sale, the notification of sale must state the place where the goods are located and provide for their reasonable inspection by prospective bidders; and
    (d) the seller may buy.

(5) A purchaser who buys in good faith at a resale takes the goods free of any rights of the original buyer even though the seller fails to comply with one or more of the requirements of this section.

(6) The seller is not accountable to the buyer for any profit made on any resale. . . .

§ 2—711.   Buyer's Remedies in General; Buyer's Security Interest in Rejected Goods

(1) Where the seller fails to make delivery or repudiates or the buyer rightfully rejects or justifiably revokes acceptance, then with respect to any goods involved, and with respect to the whole if the breach goes to the whole contract (Section 2—612), the buyer may cancel and whether or not he has done so may in addition to recovering so much of the price as has been paid
    (a) "cover" and have damages under the next section as to all the goods affected whether or not they have been identified to the contract; or
    (b) recover damages for nondelivery as provided in this Article (Section 2—713).

(2) Where the seller fails to deliver or repudiates, the buyer may also
    (a) if the goods have been identified recover them as provided in this Article (Section 2—502); or
    (b) in a proper case obtain specific performance or replevy the goods as provided in this Article (Section 2—716).

(3) On rightful rejection or justifiable revocation of acceptance, a buyer has a security interest in goods in his possession or control for any payments made on their price and any expenses reasonably incurred in their inspection, receipt, transportation, care and custody and may hold such goods and resell them in like manner as an aggrieved seller (Section 2—706).

§ 2—712.   "Cover"; Buyer's Procurement of Substitute Goods

(1) After a breach within the preceding section, the buyer may "cover" by making in good faith and without unreasonable delay any reasonable purchase of or contract to purchase goods in substitution for those due from the seller.

(2) The buyer may recover from the seller as damages the difference between the cost of cover and the contract price together with any incidental or consequential damages as hereinafter defined (Section 2—715), but less expenses saved in consequence of the seller's breach.

(3) Failure of the buyer to effect cover within this section does not bar him from any other remedy.

§ 2—713.   Buyer's Damages for Nondelivery or Repudiation

(1) Subject to the provisions of this Article with respect to proof of market price (Section 2—723), the measure of damages for nondelivery or repudiation by the seller is the difference between the market price at the time when the buyer learned of the breach and the contract price together with any incidental and consequential damages provided in this Article (Section 2—715), but less expenses saved in consequence of the seller's breach.

(2) Market price is to be determined as of the place for tender or, in cases of rejection after arrival or revocation of acceptance, as of the place of arrival.

§ 2—714.   Buyer's Damages for Breach in Regard to Accepted Goods

(1) Where the buyer has accepted goods and given notification (subsection (3) of Section 2—607), he may recover as damages for any non-conformity of tender the loss resulting in the ordinary course of events from the seller's breach as determined in any manner which is reasonable.

(2) The measure of damages for breach of warranty is the difference at the time and place of acceptance between the value of the goods accepted and the value they would have had if they had been as warranted, unless special circumstances show proximate damages of a different amount.

(3) In a proper case any incidental and consequential damages under the next section may also be recovered.

§ 2—715.   Buyer's Incidental and Consequential Damages

(1) Incidental damages resulting from the seller's breach include expenses reasonably incurred in inspection, receipt, transportation and care and custody of goods rightfully rejected, any commercially reasonable charges, expenses or commissions in connection with effecting cover and any other reasonable expense incident to the delay or other breach.

(2) Consequential damages resulting from the seller's breach include
    (a) any loss resulting from general or particular requirements and needs of which the seller at the time of contracting had reason to know and which could not reasonably be prevented by cover or otherwise; and
    (b) injury to person or property proximately resulting from any breach of warranty.

§ 2—719.   Contractual Modification or Limitation of Remedy

(1) ...

    (a) the agreement may provide for remedies in addition to or in substitution for those provided in this Article and may limit or alter the measure of damages recoverable under this Article, as by limiting the buyer's remedies to return of the goods and repayment of the price or to repair and replacement of nonconforming goods or parts; and

    (b) resort to a remedy as provided is optional unless the remedy is expressly agreed to be exclusive, in which case it is the sole remedy.

(2) Where circumstances cause an exclusive or limited remedy to fail of its essential purpose, remedy may be had as provided in this Act.

(3) Consequential damages may be limited or excluded unless the limitation or exclusion is unconscionable. Limitation of consequential damages for injury to the person in the case of consumer goods is prima facie unconscionable but limitation of damages where the loss is commercial is not.

§ 2—725.   Statute of Limitations in Contracts for Sale

(1) An action for breach of any contract for sale must be commenced within four years after the cause of action has accrued. By the original agreement, the parties may reduce the period of limitation to not less than one year but may not extend it.

(2) A cause of action accrues when the breach occurs, regardless of the aggrieved party's lack of knowledge of the breach. A breach of warranty occurs when tender of delivery is made, except that where a warranty explicitly extends to future performance of the goods and discovery of the breach must await the time of such performance the cause of action accrues when the breach is or should have been discovered.

. . .

ARTICLE 2A

LEASES

Part 1

General Provisions

§ 2A—103.   Definitions and Index of Definitions

(1) In this Article unless the context otherwise requires:

    . . .

    (e) "Consumer lease" means a lease that a lessor regularly engaged in the business of leasing or selling makes to a lessee, except an organization, who takes under the lease primarily for a personal, family, or household purpose, if the total payments to be made under the lease contract, excluding payments for options to renew or buy, do not exceed $25,000.

    . . .

    (g) "Finance lease" means a lease in which (i) the lessor does not select, manufacture or supply the goods, (ii) the lessor acquires the goods or the right to possession and use of the goods in connection with the lease, and (iii) either the lessee receives a copy of the contract evidencing the lessor's purchase of the goods on or before signing the lease contract, or the lessee's approval of the contract evidencing the lessor's purchase of the goods is a condition to effectiveness of the lease contract.

    . . .

    (j) "Lease" means a transfer of the right to possession and use of goods for a term in return for consideration, but a sale, including a sale on approval or a sale or return, or retention or creation of a security interest is not a lease. Unless the context clearly indicates otherwise, the term includes a sublease.

    (k) "Lease agreement" means the bargain, with respect to the lease, of the lessor and the lessee in fact as found in their language or by implication from other circumstances including course of dealing or usage of trade or course of performance as provided in this Article. Unless the context clearly indicates otherwise, the term includes a sublease agreement.

    (l) "Lease contract" means the total legal obligation that results from the lease agreement as affected by this Article and any other applicable rules of law. Unless the context clearly indicates otherwise, the term includes a sublease contract.

    . . .

    (o) "Lessee in ordinary course of business" means a person who in good faith and without knowledge that the lease to him [or her] is in violation of the ownership rights or security interest or leasehold interest of a third party in the goods leases in ordinary course from a person in the business of selling or leasing goods of that kind but does not include a pawnbroker. "Leasing" may be for cash or by exchange of other property or on secured or unsecured credit and includes receiving goods or documents of title under a pre-existing lease contract but does not include a transfer in bulk or as security for or in total or partial satisfaction of a money debt.

. . .

(t) "Merchant lessee" means a lessee that is a merchant with respect to goods of the kind subject to the lease.

. . .

§ 2A—106.   Limitation on Power of Parties to Consumer Lease to Choose Applicable Law and Judicial Forum

(1) If the law chosen by the parties to a consumer lease is that of a jurisdiction other than a jurisdiction in which the lessee resides at the time the lease agreement becomes enforceable or within 30 days thereafter or in which the goods are to be used, the choice is not enforceable.

(2) If the judicial forum chosen by the parties to a consumer lease is a forum that would not otherwise have jurisdiction over the lessee, the choice is not enforceable.

Part 2

Formation and Construction of Lease Contract

§ 2A—209.   Lessee Under Finance Lease as Beneficiary of Supply Contract

(1) The benefit of the supplier's promises to the lessor under the supply contract and of all warranties, whether express or implied, under the supply contract, extends to the lessee to the extent of the lessee's leasehold interest under a finance lease related to the supply contract, but subject to the terms of the supply contract and all of the supplier's defenses or claims arising therefrom.

(2) The extension of the benefit of the supplier's promises and warranties to the lessee (Section 2A—209(1)) does not: (a) modify the rights and obligations of the parties to the supply contract, whether arising therefrom or otherwise, or (b) impose any duty or liability under the supply contract on the lessee.

(3) Any modification or rescission of the supply contract by the supplier and the lessor is effective against the lessee unless, prior to the modification or rescission, the supplier has received notice that the lessee has entered into a finance lease related to the supply contract. If the supply contract is modified or rescinded after the lessee enters the finance lease, the lessee has a cause of action against the lessor, and against the supplier if the supplier has notice of the lessee's entering the finance lease when the supply contract is modified or rescinded. The lessee's recovery from such action shall put the lessee in as good a position as if the modification or rescission had not occurred.

§ 2A—210.   Express Warranties

(1) Express warranties by the lessor are created as follows:

(a) Any affirmation of fact or promise made by the lessor to the lessee which relates to the goods and becomes part of the basis of the bargain creates an express warranty that the goods will conform to the affirmation or promise.

(b) Any description of the goods which is made part of the basis of the bargain creates an express warranty that the goods will conform to the description.

(c) Any sample or model that is made part of the basis of the bargain creates an express warranty that the whole of the goods will conform to the sample or model.

(2) It is not necessary to the creation of an express warranty that the lessor use formal words, such as "warrant" or "guarantee," or that the lessor have a specific intention to make a warranty, but an affirmation merely of the value of the goods or a statement purporting to be merely the lessor's opinion or commendation of the goods does not create a warranty.

§ 2A—219.   Risk of Loss

(1) Except in the case of a finance lease, risk of loss is retained by the lessor and does not pass to the lessee. In the case of a finance lease, risk of loss passes to the lessee.

(2) Subject to the provisions of this Article on the effect of default on risk of loss (Section 2A—220), if risk of loss is to pass to the lessee and the time of passage is not stated the following rules apply:

(a) If the lease contract requires or authorizes the goods to be shipped by carrier

   (i) and it does not require delivery at a particular destination, the risk of loss passes to the lessee when the goods are duly delivered to the carrier; but

   (ii) if it does require delivery at a particular destination and the goods are there duly tendered while in the possession of the carrier, the risk of loss passes to the lessee when the goods are there duly so tendered as to enable the lessee to take delivery.

(b) If the goods are held by a bailee to be delivered without being moved, the risk of loss passes to the lessee on acknowledgment by the bailee of the lessee's right to possession of the goods.

(c) In any case not within subsection (a) or (b), the risk of loss passes to the lessee on the lessee's receipt of the goods if the lessor, or, in the case of a finance lease, the supplier, is a merchant: otherwise the risk passes to the lessee on tender of delivery.

§ 2A—220.   Effect of Default on Risk of Loss

(1) Where risk of loss is to pass to the lessee and the time of passage is not stated:

(a) If a tender or delivery of goods so fails to conform to the lease contract as to give a right of rejection, the risk of their loss remains with the lessor, or, in the case of a finance lease, the supplier, until cure or acceptance.

    (b) If the lessee rightfully revokes acceptance, he [or she], to the extent of any deficiency in his [or her] effective insurance coverage, may treat the risk of loss as having remained with the lessor from the beginning.

    (2) Whether or not risk of loss is to pass to the lessee, if the lessee as to conforming goods already identified to a lease contract repudiates or is otherwise in default under the lease contract, the lessor, or, in the case of a finance lease, the supplier, to the extent of any deficiency in his [or her] effective insurance coverage may treat the risk of loss as resting on the lessee for a commercially reasonable time.

§ 2A—221.   Casualty to Identified Goods

    If a lease contract requires goods identified when the lease contract is made, and the goods suffer casualty without fault of the lessee, the lessor or the supplier before delivery, or the goods suffer casualty before risk of loss passes to the lessee pursuant to the lease agreement or Section 2A—219, then:

    (a) if the loss is total, the lease contract is avoided; and

    (b) if the loss is partial or the goods have so deteriorated as to no longer conform to the lease contract, the lessee may nevertheless demand inspection and at his [or her] option either treat the lease contract as avoided or, except in a finance lease that is not a consumer lease, accept the goods with due allowance from the rent payable for the balance of the lease term for the deterioration or the deficiency in quantity but without further right against the lessor.

Part 3

Effect of Lease Contract

§ 2A—301.   Enforceability of Lease Contract

    Except as otherwise provided in this Article, a lease contract is effective and enforceable according to its terms between the parties, against purchasers of the goods, and against creditors of the parties.

§ 2A—303.   Alienability of Party's Interest Under Lease Contract or of Lessor's Residual Interest in Goods; Delegation of Performance; Assignment of Rights

    (1) Any interest of a party under a lease contract and the lessor's residual interest in the goods may be transferred unless

    (a) the transfer is voluntary and the lease contract prohibits the transfer; or

    (b) the transfer materially changes the duty of or materially increases the burden or risk imposed on the other party to the lease contract,

and within a reasonable time after notice of the transfer the other party demands that the transferee comply with subsection (2) and the transferee fails to comply.

    (2) Within a reasonable time after demand pursuant to subsection (1)(b), the transferee shall:

    (a) cure or provide adequate assurance that he [or she] will promptly cure any default other than one arising from the transfer;

    (b) compensate or provide adequate assurance that he [or she] will promptly compensate the other party to the lease contract and any other person holding an interest in the lease contract, except the party whose interest is being transferred, for any loss to that party resulting from the transfer;

    (c) Provide adequate assurance of future due performance under the lease contract; and

    (d) assume the lease contract.

    (3) Demand pursuant to subsection (1)(b) is without prejudice to the other party's rights against the transferee and the party whose interest is transferred.

    (4) An assignment of "the lease" or of "all my rights under the lease" or an assignment in similar general terms is a transfer of rights, and unless the language or the circumstances, as in an assignment for security, indicate the contrary, the assignment is a delegation of duties by the assignor to the assignee and acceptance by the assignee constitutes a promise by him [or her] to perform those duties. This promise is enforceable by either the assignor or the other party to the lease contract.

    (5) Unless otherwise agreed by the lessor and the lessee, no delegation of performance relieves the assignor as against the other party of any duty to perform or any liability for default.

    (6) A right to damages for default with respect to the whole lease contract or a right arising out of the assignor's due performance of his [or her] entire obligation can be assigned despite agreement otherwise.

    (7) To prohibit the transfer of an interest of a party under a lease contract, the language of prohibition must be specific, by a writing, and conspicuous.

§ 2A—304.   Subsequent Lease of Goods by Lessor

    (1) Subject to the provisions of Section 2A—303, a subsequent lessee from a lessor of goods under an existing lease contract obtains, to the extent of the leasehold interest transferred, the leasehold interest in the goods that the lessor had or had power to transfer, and except as provided in subsection (2) and Section 2A—527(4), takes subject to the existing lease contract. A lessor with voidable title has power to transfer a good leasehold interest to a good faith subsequent lessee for value, but only to the extent set forth in the preceding sentence. When goods have been delivered under a transaction of purchase the lessor has that power even though:

(a) the lessor's transferor was deceived as to the identity of the lessor;

(b) the delivery was in exchange for a check which is later dishonored;

(c) it was agreed that the transaction was to be a "cash sale"; or

(d) the delivery was procured through fraud punishable as larcenous under the criminal law.

(2) A subsequent lessee in the ordinary course of business from a lessor who is a merchant dealing in goods of that kind to whom the goods were entrusted by the existing lessee before the interest of the subsequent lessee became enforceable against the lessor obtains, to the extent of the leasehold interest transferred, all of the lessor's and the existing lessee's rights to the goods, and takes free of the existing lease contract.

(3) A subsequent lessee from the lessor of goods that are subject to an existing lease contract and are covered by a certificate of title issued under a statute of this State or of another jurisdiction takes no greater rights than those provided both by this section and by the certificate of title statute.

§ 2A—305.   Sale or Sublease of Goods by Lessee

(1) Subject to the provisions of Section 2A—303, a buyer or sublessee from the lessee of goods under an existing lease contract obtains, to the extent of the interest transferred, the leasehold interest in the goods that the lessee had or had power to transfer, and except as provided in subsection (2) and Section 2A—511(4), takes subject to the existing lease contract. A lessee with a voidable leasehold interest has power to transfer a good leasehold interest to a good faith buyer for value or a good faith sublessee for value, but only to the extent set forth in the preceding sentence. When goods have been delivered under a transaction of lease the lessee has that power even though:

(a) the lessor was deceived as to the identity of the lessee;

(b) the delivery was in exchange for a check which is later dishonored; or

(c) the delivery was procured through fraud punishable as larcenous under the criminal law.

(2) A buyer in the ordinary course of business or a sublessee in the ordinary course of business from a lessee who is a merchant dealing in goods of that kind to whom the goods were entrusted by the lessor obtains, to the extent of the interest transferred, all of the lessor's and lessee's rights to the goods, and takes free of the existing lease contract.

(3) A buyer or sublessee from the lessee of goods that are subject to an existing lease contract and are covered by a certificate of title issued under a statute of this State or of another jurisdiction takes no greater rights than those provided both by this section and by the certificate of title statute.

Part 4

Performance of Lease Contract: Repudiated, Substituted and Excused

§ 2A—401.   Insecurity: Adequate Assurance of Performance

(1) A lease contract imposes an obligation on each party that the other's expectation of receiving due performance will not be impaired.

(2) If reasonable grounds for insecurity arise with respect to the performance of either party, the insecure party may demand in writing adequate assurance of due performance. . . .

(4) Between merchants, the reasonableness of grounds for insecurity and the adequacy of any assurance offered must be determined according to commercial standards.

(5) Acceptance of any nonconforming delivery or payment does not prejudice the aggrieved party's right to demand adequate assurance of future performance.

§ 2A—407.   Irrevocable Promises: Finance Leases

(1) In the case of a finance lease that is not a consumer lease the lessee's promises under the lease contract become irrevocable and independent upon the lessee's acceptance of the goods.

(2) A promise that has become irrevocable and independent under subsection (1):

(a) is effective and enforceable between the parties, and by or against third parties including assignees of the parties, and

(b) is not subject to cancellation, termination, modification, repudiation, excuse, or substitution without the consent of the party to whom the promise runs.

Part 5

Default

A. In General

§ 2A—501.   Default: Procedure

(1) Whether the lessor or the lessee is in default under a lease contract is determined by the lease agreement and this Article.

(2) If the lessor or the lessee is in default under the lease contract, the party seeking enforcement has rights and remedies as provided in this Article and, except as limited by this Article, as provided in the lease agreement.

(3) If the lessor or the lessee is in default under the lease contract, the party seeking enforcement may reduce the party's claim to judgment, or otherwise enforce the lease contract by self-help or any available judicial procedure or

nonjudicial procedure, including administrative proceeding, arbitration, or the like, in accordance with this Article.

(4) Except as otherwise provided in this Article or the lease Agreement, the rights and remedies referred to in subsections (2) and (3) are cumulative.

(5) If the lease agreement covers both real property and goods, the party seeking enforcement may proceed under this Part as to the goods, or under other applicable law as to both the real property and the goods in accordance with his [or her] rights and remedies in respect of the real property, in which case this Part does not apply.

§ 2A—502. Notice After Default

Except as otherwise provided in this Article or the lease agreement, the lessor or lessee in default under the lease contract is not entitled to notice of default or notice of enforcement from the other party to the lease agreement.

§ 2A—503. Modification or Impairment of Rights and Remedies

(1) Except as otherwise provided in this Article, the lease agreement may include rights and remedies for default in addition to or in substitution for those provided in this Article and may limit or alter the measure of damages recoverable under this Article.

(2) Resort to a remedy provided under this Article or in the lease agreement is optional unless the remedy is expressly agreed to be exclusive. If circumstances cause an exclusive or limited remedy to fail of its essential purpose, or provision for an exclusive remedy is unconscionable, remedy may be had as provided in this Article.

. . .

§ 2A—506. Statute of Limitations

(1) An action for default under a lease contract, including breach of warranty or indemnity, must be commenced within 4 years after the cause of action accrued. By the original lease contract the parties may reduce the period of limitation to not less that one year.

(2) A cause of action for default accrues when the act or omission on which the default or breach of warranty is based is or should have been discovered by the aggrieved party, or when the default occurs, whichever is later. A cause of action for indemnity accrues when the act or omission on which the claim for indemnity is based is or should have been discovered by the indemnified party, whichever is later.

. . .

B. Default by Lessor

§ 2A—513. Cure by Lessor of Improper Tender or Delivery; Replacement

(1) If any tender or delivery by the lessor or the supplier is rejected because nonconforming and the time for performance has not yet expired, the lessor or the supplier may seasonably notify the lessee of the lessor's or the sup-

plier's intention to cure and may then make a conforming delivery within the time provided in the lease contract.

(2) If the lessee rejects a nonconforming tender that the lessor or the supplier had reasonable grounds to believe would be acceptable with or without money allowance, the lessor or the supplier may have a further reasonable time to substitute a conforming tender if he [or she] seasonably notifies the lessee.

§ 2A—514. Waiver of Lessee's Objections

(1) In rejecting goods, a lessee's failure to state a particular defect that is ascertainable by reasonable inspection precludes the lessee from relying on the defect to justify rejection or to establish default:

(a) if, states seasonably, the lessor or the supplier could have cured it (Section 2A—513); or

(b) between merchants if the lessor or the supplier after rejection has made a request in writing for a full and final written statement of all defects on which the lessee proposes to rely.

(2) A lessee's failure to reserve rights when paying rent or other consideration against documents precludes recovery of the payment for defects apparent on the face of the documents.

§ 2A—515. Acceptance of Goods

(1) Acceptance of goods occurs after the lessee has had a reasonable opportunity to inspect the goods and

(a) the lessee signifies or acts with respect to the goods in a manner that signifies to the lessor or the supplier that the goods are conforming or that the lessee will take or retain them in spite of their nonconformity; or

(b) the lessee fails to make an effective rejection of the goods (Section 2A—509(2)).

(2) Acceptance of a part of any commercial unit is acceptance of that entire unit.

§ 2A—518. Cover; Substitute Goods

(1) After default by a lessor under the lease contract . . . , the lessee may cover by making any purchase or lease of or contract to purchase or lease goods in substitution for those due from the lessor.

. . .

§ 2A—519. Lessee's Damages for Nondelivery, Repudiation, Default and Breach of Warranty in Regard to Accepted Goods

(1) Except as otherwise provided with respect to damages liquidated in the lease agreement . . . or determined by agreement of the parties (Section 1–102(3)), if a lessee elects not to cover or a lessee elects to cover and the cover . . . is by purchase or otherwise, the measure of damages for non-delivery or repudiation by the lessor or for rejection or revocation of acceptance by the lessee is the present value as of the date of the default of the difference between the then market rent and the original rent, computed for the remaining lease term of the original lease agree-

ment together with incidental and consequential damages, less expenses saved in consequence of the lessor's default.

. . .

(4) The measure of damages for breach of warranty is the present value at the time and place of acceptance of the difference between the value of the use of the goods accepted and the value if they had been as warranted for the lease term, unless special circumstances show proximate damages of a different amount, together with incidental and consequential damages, less expenses saved in consequence of the lessor's default or breach of warranty.

§ 2A—520.   Lessee's Incidental and Consequential Damages

(1) Incidental damages resulting from a lessor's default include expenses reasonably incurred in inspection, receipt, transportation, and care and custody of goods rightfully rejected or goods the acceptance of which is justifiably revoked, any commercially reasonable charges, expenses or commissions in connection with effecting cover, and any other reasonable expense incident to the default.

(2) Consequential damages resulting from a lessor's default include:

(a) any loss resulting from general or particular requirements and needs of which the lessor at the time of contracting had reason to know and which could not reasonably be prevented by cover or otherwise; and

(b) injury to person or property proximately resulting from any breach of warranty.

C. Default by Lessee

§ 2A—525.   Lessor's Right to Possession of Goods

(1) If a lessor discovers the lessee to be insolvent, the lessor may refuse to deliver the goods.

(2) The lessor has on default by the lessee under the lease contract the right to take possession of the goods. If the lease contract so provides, the lessor may require the lessee to assemble the goods and make them available to the lessor at a place to be designated by the lessor which is reasonably convenient to both parties. Without removal, the lessor may render unusable any goods employed in trade or business, and may dispose of goods on the lessee's premises (Section 2A—527).

(3) The lessor may proceed under subsection (2) without judicial process if that can be done without breach of the peace or the lessor may proceed by action.

§ 2A—527.   Lessor's Rights to Dispose of Goods

(1) After a default by a lessee under the lease contract . . . or after the lessor refuses to deliver or takes possession of goods . . . , the lessor may dispose of the goods concerned or the undelivered balance thereof by lease, sale or otherwise.

(2) Except as otherwise provided with respect to damages liquidated in the lease agreement . . . or determined by agreement of the parties (Section 1—102(3)), if the disposition is by lease agreement substantially similar to the original lease agreement and the lease agreement is made in good faith and in a commercially reasonable manner, the lessor may recover from the lessee as damages (a) accrued and unpaid rent as of the date of default, (b) the present value as of the date of default of the difference between the total rent for the remaining lease term of the original lease agreement and the total rent for the lease term of the new lease agreement, and (c) any incidental damages allowed under Section 2A—530, less expenses saved in consequence of the lessee's default.

. . .

(4) A subsequent buyer or lessee who buys or leases from the lessor in good faith for value as a result of a disposition under this section takes the goods free of the original lease contract and any rights of the original lessee even though the lessor fails to comply with one or more of the requirements of this Article.

(5) The lessor is not accountable to the lessee for any profit made on any disposition. . . .

§ 2A—529.   Lessor's Action for the Rent

(1) After default by the lessee under the lease contract . . . , if the lessor complies with subsection (2), the lessor may recover from the lessee as damages:

(a) for goods accepted by the lessee and for conforming goods lost or damaged within a commercially reasonable time after risk of loss passes to the lessee . . . , (i) accrued and unpaid rent as of the date of default, (ii) the present value as of the date of default of the rent for the remaining lease term of the lease agreement, and (iii) any incidental damages allowed under Section 2A—530, less expenses saved in consequence of the lessee's default; and

(b) for goods identified to the lease contract if the lessor is unable after reasonable effort to dispose of them at a reasonable price or the circumstances reasonably indicate that effort will be unavailing, (i) accrued and unpaid rent as of the date of default, (ii) the present value as of the date of default of the rent for the remaining lease term of the lease agreement, and (iii) any incidental damages allowed under Section 2A—530, less expenses saved in consequence of the lessee's default.

(2) Except as provided in subsection (3), the lessor shall hold for the lessee for the remaining lease term of the lease agreement any goods that have been identified to the lease contract and are in the lessor's control.

(3) The lessor may dispose of the goods at any time before collection of the judgment for damages obtained pursuant to subsection (1). . . .

(4) Payment of the judgment for damages obtained

pursuant to subsection (1) entitles the lessee to use and possession of the goods not then disposed of for the remaining lease term of the lease agreement.

...

§ 2A—530.   Lessor's Incidental Damages

Incidental damages to an aggrieved lessor include any commercially reasonable charges, expenses, or commissions incurred in stopping delivery, in the transportation, care and custody of goods after the lessee's default, in connection with return or disposition of the goods, or otherwise resulting from the default.

ARTICLE 3

COMMERCIAL PAPER

Part 1

Short Title, Form and Interpretation

§ 3—102.   Definitions and Index of Definitions

(1) In this Article unless the context otherwise requires

    (a) "Issue" means the first delivery of an instrument to a holder or a remitter.

    (b) An "order" is a direction to pay and must be more than an authorization or request. It must identify the person to pay with reasonable certainty. It may be addressed to one or more such persons jointly or in the alternative but not in succession.

    (c) A "promise" is an undertaking to pay and must be more than an acknowledgment of an obligation.

    (d) "Secondary party" means a drawer or indorser.

    (e) "Instrument" means a negotiable instrument.

...

§ 3—104.   Form of Negotiable Instruments; "Draft"; "Check"; "Certificate of Deposit"; "Note"

(1) Any writing to be a negotiable instrument within this Article must

    (a) be signed by the maker or drawer; and

    (b) contain an unconditional promise or order to pay a sum certain in money and no other promise, order, obligation or power given by the maker or drawer except as authorized by this Article; and

    (c) be payable on demand or at a definite time; and

    (d) be payable to order or to bearer.

(2) A writing which complies with the requirements of this section is

    (a) a "draft" ("bill of exchange") if it is an order;

    (b) a "check" if it is a draft drawn on a bank and payable on demand;

    (c) a "certificate of deposit" if it is an acknowledgment by a bank of receipt of money with an engagement to repay it;

    (d) a "note" if it is a promise other than a certificate of deposit.

(3) As used in other Articles of this Act, and as the context may require, the terms "draft," "check," "certificate of deposit" and "note" may refer to instruments which are not negotiable within this Article as well as to instruments which are so negotiable.

Part 2

Transfer and Negotiation

§ 3—201.   Transfer: Right to Indorsement

(1) Transfer of an instrument vests in the transferee such rights as the transferor has therein, except that a transferee who has himself been a party to any fraud or illegality affecting the instrument or who as a prior holder had notice of a defense or claim against it cannot improve his position by taking from a later holder in due course.

(2) A transfer of a security interest in an instrument vests the foregoing rights in the transferee to the extent of the interest transferred.

(3) Unless otherwise agreed, any transfer for value of an instrument not then payable to bearer gives the transferee the specifically enforceable right to have the unqualified indorsement of the transferor. Negotiation takes effect only when the indorsement is made and until that time there is no presumption that the transferee is the owner.

§ 3—202.   Negotiation

(1) Negotiation is the transfer of an instrument in such form that the transferee becomes a holder. If the instrument is payable to order, it is negotiated by delivery with any necessary indorsement; if payable to bearer, it is negotiated by delivery.

(2) An indorsement must be written by or on behalf of the holder and on the instrument or on a paper so firmly affixed thereto as to become a part thereof.

(3) An indorsement is effective for negotiation only when it conveys the entire instrument or any unpaid residue. If it purports to be of less, it operates only as a partial assignment.

(4) Words of assignment, condition, waiver, guaranty, limitation or disclaimer of liability and the like accompanying an indorsement do not affect its character as an indorsement.

Part 3

Rights of a Holder

§ 3—301.   Rights of a Holder

The holder of an instrument whether or not he is the owner may transfer or negotiate it and, except as otherwise provided in Section 3—603 on payment or satisfaction, discharge it or enforce payment in his own name.

§ 3—302.   Holder in Due Course

(1) A holder in due course is a holder who takes the instrument

    (a) for value; and

    (b) in good faith; and

    (c) without notice that it is overdue or has been dishonored or of any defense against or claim to it on the part of any person.

(2) A payee may be a holder in due course.

(3) A holder does not become a holder in due course of an instrument:

    (a) by purchase of it at judicial sale or by taking it under legal process; or

    (b) by acquiring it in taking over an estate; or

    (c) by purchasing it as part of a bulk transaction not in regular course of business of the transferor.

(4) A purchaser of a limited interest can be a holder in due course only to the extent of the interest purchased.

§ 3—305.   Rights of a Holder in Due Course

To the extent that a holder is a holder in due course, he takes the instrument free from

(1) all claims to it on the part of any person; and

(2) all defenses of any party to the instrument with whom the holder has not dealt except

    (a) infancy, to the extent that it is a defense to a simple contract; and

    (b) such other incapacity, or duress, or illegality of the transaction, as renders the obligation of the party a nullity; and

    (c) such misrepresentation as has induced the party to sign the instrument with neither knowledge nor reasonable opportunity to obtain knowledge of its character or its essential terms; and

    (d) discharge in insolvency proceedings; and

    (e) any other discharge of which the holder has notice when he takes the instrument.

§ 3—306.   Rights of One Not Holder in Due Course

Unless he has the rights of a holder in due course, any person takes the instrument subject to

    (a) all valid claims to it on the part of any person; and

    (b) all defenses of any party which would be available in an action on a simple contract and

    (c) the defenses of want or failure of consideration, nonperformance of any condition precedent, nondelivery, or delivery for a special purpose (Section 3—408); and

    (d) the defense that he, or a person through whom he holds the instrument, acquired it by theft, or that payment or satisfaction to such holder would be inconsistent with the terms of a restrictive indorsement. The claim of any third person to the instrument is not otherwise available as a defense to any party liable thereon unless the third person himself defends the action for such party.

§ 3—307.   Burden of Establishing Signatures, Defenses and Due Course

(1) Unless specifically denied in the pleadings, each signature on an instrument is admitted. When the effectiveness of a signature is put in issue

    (a) the burden of establishing it is on the party claiming under the signature; but

    (b) the signature is presumed to be genuine or authorized except where the action is to enforce the obligation of a purported signer who has died or become incompetent before proof is required.

(2) When signatures are admitted or established, production of the instrument entitles a holder to recover on it unless the defendant establishes a defense.

(3) After it is shown that a defense exists, a person claiming the rights of a holder in due course has the burden of establishing that he or some person under whom he claims is in all respects a holder in due course.

Part 4

Liability of Parties

§ 3—401.   Signature

(1) No person is liable on an instrument unless his signature appears thereon.

(2) A signature is made by use of any name, including any trade or assumed name, upon an instrument, or by any word or mark used in lieu of a written signature.

§ 3—405.   Impostors; Signature in Name of Payee

(1) An indorsement by any person in the name of a named payee is effective if

(a) an impostor by use of the mails or otherwise has induced the maker or drawer to issue the instrument to him or his confederate in the name of the payee; or

(b) a person signing as or on behalf of a maker or drawer intends the payee to have no interest in the instrument; or

(c) an agent or employee of the maker or drawer has supplied him with the name of the payee intending the latter to have no such interest.

(2) Nothing in this section shall affect the criminal or civil liability of the person so indorsing.

§ 3—406.   Negligence Contributing to Alteration or Unauthorized Signature

Any person who by his negligence substantially contributes to a material alteration of the instrument or to the making of an unauthorized signature is precluded from asserting the alteration or lack of authority against a holder in due course or against a drawee or other payor who pays the instrument in good faith and in accordance with the reasonable commercial standards of the drawee's or payor's business.

§ 3—407.   Alteration

(1) Any alteration of an instrument is material which changes the contract of any party thereto in any respect, including any such change in

(a) the number or relations of the parties; or

(b) an incomplete instrument, by completing it otherwise than as authorized; or

(c) the writing as signed, by adding to it or by removing any part of it.

(2) As against any person other than a subsequent holder in due course.

(a) alteration by the holder which is both fraudulent and material discharges any party whose contract is thereby changed unless that party assents or is precluded from asserting the defense;

(b) no other alteration discharges any party and the instrument may be enforced according to its original tenor, or as to incomplete instruments, according to the authority given.

(3) A subsequent holder in due course may in all cases enforce the instrument according to its original tenor, and when an incomplete instrument has been completed, he may enforce it as completed.

§ 3—419.   Conversion of Instrument; Innocent Representative

(1) An instrument is converted when

(a) a drawee to whom it is delivered for acceptance refuses to return it on demand; or

(b) any person to whom it is delivered for payment refuses on demand either to pay or to return it; or

(c) it is paid on a forged indorsement.

(2) In an action against a drawee under subsection (1), the measure of the drawee's liability is the face amount of the instrument. In any other action under subsection (1), the measure of liability is presumed to be the face amount of the instrument.

(3) Subject to the provisions of this Act concerning restrictive indorsements, a representative, including a depositary or collecting bank, who has in good faith and in accordance with the reasonable commercial standards applicable to the business of such representative dealt with an instrument or its proceeds on behalf of one who was not the true owner, is not liable in conversion or otherwise to the true owner beyond the amount of any proceeds remaining in his hands.

(4) An intermediary bank or payor bank which is not a depositary bank is not liable in conversion solely by reason of the fact that proceeds of an item indorsed restrictively (Sections 3—205 and 3—206) are not paid or applied consistently with the restrictive indorsement of an indorser other than its immediate transferor.

Part 5

Presentment, Notice of Dishonor and Protest

§ 3—501.   When Presentment, Notice of Dishonor, and Protest Necessary or Permissible

(1) Unless excused (Section 3—511), presentment is necessary to charge secondary parties as follows:

(a) presentment for acceptance is necessary to charge the drawer and indorsers of a draft where the draft so provides, or is payable elsewhere than at the residence or place of business of the drawee, or its date of payment depends upon such presentment. The holder may at his option present for acceptance any other draft payable at a stated date;

(b) presentment for payment is necessary to charge any indorser;

(c) in the case of any drawer, the acceptor of a draft payable at a bank or the maker of a note payable at a bank, presentment for payment is necessary, but failure to make presentment discharges such drawer, acceptor, or maker only as stated in Section 3—502(1) (b).

(2) Unless excused (Section 3—511)

(a) notice of any dishonor is necessary to charge any indorser;

(b) in the case of any drawer, the acceptor of a draft payable at a bank or the maker of a note payable at a bank, notice of any dishonor is necessary, but failure to give such notice discharges such drawer, acceptor or maker only as stated in Section 3—502(1)(b).

(3) Unless excused (Section 3—511), protest of any dishonor is necessary to charge the drawer and indorsers of any draft which on its face appears to be drawn or payable

outside of the states, territories, dependencies and possessions of the Unites States, the District of Columbia and the Commonwealth of Puerto Rico. The holder may at his option make protest of any dishonor of any other instrument and in the case of a foreign draft may on insolvency of the acceptor before maturity make protest for better security.

(4) Notwithstanding any provision of this section, neither presentment nor notice of dishonor nor protest is necessary to charge an indorser who has indorsed an instrument after maturity.

§ 3—504.   How Presentment Made

(1) Presentment is a demand for acceptance or payment made upon the maker, acceptor, drawee or other payor by or on behalf of the holder.

(2) Presentment may be made
  (a) by mail, in which event the time of presentment is determined by the time of receipt of the mail; or
  (b) through a clearing house; or
  (c) at the place of acceptance or payment specified in the instrument or, if there be none, at the place of business or residence of the party to accept or pay. If neither the party to accept or pay nor anyone authorized to act for him is present or accessible at such place, presentment is excused.

(3) It may be made
  (a) to any one of two or more makers, acceptors, drawees or other payors; or
  (b) to any person who has authority to make or refuse the acceptance or payment.

(4) A draft accepted or a note made payable at a bank in the United States must be presented at such bank.

(5) In the cases described in Section 4—210 presentment may be made in the manner and with the result stated in that section.

§ 3—507.   Dishonor; Holder's Right of Recourse; Term Allowing Re-Presentment

(1) An instrument is dishonored when
  (a) a necessary or optional presentment is duly made and due acceptance or payment is refused or cannot be obtained within the prescribed time or in case of bank collections the instrument is seasonably returned by the midnight deadline (Section 4—301); or
  (b) presentment is excused and the instrument is not duly accepted or paid.

(2) Subject to any necessary notice of dishonor and protest, the holder has upon dishonor an immediate right of recourse against the drawers and indorsers.

(3) Return of an instrument for lack of proper indorsement is not dishonor.

(4) A term in a draft or an indorsement thereof allowing a stated time for re-presentment in the event of any dishonor of the draft by nonacceptance if a time draft or by nonpayment if a sight draft gives the holder as against any secondary party bound by the term an option to waive the dishonor without affecting the liability of the secondary party and he may present again up to the end of the stated time.

Part 6

Discharge

§ 3—602.   Effect of Discharge Against Holder in Due Course

No discharge of any party provided by this Article is effective against a subsequent holder in due course unless he has notice thereof when he takes the instrument.

§ 3—603.   Payment or Satisfaction

(1) The liability of any party is discharged to the extent of his payment or satisfaction to the holder even though it is made with knowledge of a claim of another person to the instrument unless prior to such payment or satisfaction the person making the claim either supplies indemnity deemed adequate by the party seeking the discharge or enjoins payment or satisfaction by order of a court of competent jurisdiction in an action in which the adverse claimant and the holder are parties. This subsection does not, however, result in the discharge of the liability
  (a) of a party who in bad faith pays or satisfies a holder who acquired the instrument by theft or who (unless having the rights of a holder in due course) holds through one who so acquired it; or
  (b) of a party (other than an intermediary bank or a payor bank which is not a depositary bank) who pays or satisfies the holder of an instrument which has been restrictively indorsed in a manner not consistent with the terms of such restrictive indorsement.

(2) Payment or satisfaction may be made with the consent of the holder by any person including a stranger to the instrument. Surrender of the instrument to such a person gives him the rights of a transferee (Section 3—201).

§ 3—606.   Impairment of Recourse or of Collateral

(1) The holder discharges any party to the instrument to the extent that, without such party's consent, the holder
  (a) without express reservation of rights releases or agrees not to sue any person against whom the party has to the knowledge of the holder a right of recourse or agrees to suspend the right to enforce against such person the instrument or collateral or otherwise discharges such person, except that failure or delay in effecting any required presentment, protest or notice of dishonor with respect to any such person does not discharge any party as to whom presentment, protest or notice of dishonor is effective or unnecessary; or

(b) unjustifiably impairs any collateral for the instrument given by or on behalf of the party or any person against whom he has a right of recourse.

(2) By express reservation of rights against a party with a right of recourse, the holder preserves

(a) all his rights against such party as of the time when the instrument was originally due; and

(b) the right of the party to pay the instrument as of that time; and

(c) all rights of such party to recourse against others.

ARTICLE 3 [1990 Revision]

NEGOTIABLE INSTRUMENTS

Part 1

General Provisions and Definitions

§ 3—102.   Subject Matter

(a) This Article applies to negotiable instruments. It does not apply to money, to payment orders governed by Article 4A, or to securities governed by Article 8.

. . .

§ 3—103.   Definitions

(a) In this Article:

. . .

(4) "Good faith" means honesty in fact and the observance of reasonable commercial standards of fair dealing.

. . .

(7) "Ordinary care" in the case of a person engaged in business means observance of reasonable commercial standards, prevailing in the area in which the person is located, with respect to the business in which the person is engaged. In the case of a bank that takes an instrument for processing for collection or payment by automated means, reasonable commercial standards do not require the bank to examine the instrument if the failure to examine does not violate the bank's prescribed procedures and the bank's procedures do not vary unreasonably from general banking usage not disapproved by this Article or Article 4.

. . .

(11) "Remitter" means a person who purchases an instrument from its issuer if the instrument is payable to an identified person other than the purchaser.

. . .

§ 3—104.   Negotiable Instrument

(a) Except as provided in subsections (c) and (d), "negotiable instrument" means an unconditional promise or order to pay a fixed amount of money, with or without interest or other charges described in the promise or order, if it:

(1) is payable to bearer or to order at the time it is issued or first comes into possession of a holder;

(2) is payable on demand or at a definite time; and

(3) does not state any other undertaking or instruction by the person promising or ordering payment to do any act in addition to the payment of money, but the promise or order may contain (i) an undertaking or power to give, maintain, or protect collateral, to secure payment, (ii) an authorization or power to the holder to confess judgment or realize on or dispose of collateral, or (iii) a waiver of the benefit of any law intended for the advantage or protection of an obligor.

(b) "Instrument" means a negotiable instrument.

(c) An order that meets all of the requirements of subsection (a), except paragraph (1), and otherwise falls within the definition of "check" in subsection (f) is a negotiable instrument and a check.

(d) A promise or order other than a check is not an instrument if, at the time it is issued or first comes into possession of a holder, it contains a conspicuous statement, however expressed, to the effect that the promise or order is not negotiable or is not an instrument governed by this Article.

(e) An instrument is a "note" if it is a promise and is a "draft" if it is an order. If an instrument falls within the definition of both "note" and "draft," a person entitled to enforce the instrument may treat it as either.

(f) "Check" means (i) a draft, other than a documentary draft, payable on demand and drawn on a bank or (ii) a cashier's check or teller's check. An instrument may be a check even though it is described on its face by another term, such as "money order."

(g) "Cashier's check" means a draft with respect to which the drawer and drawee are the same bank or branches of the same bank.

(h) "Teller's check" means a draft drawn by a bank (i) on another bank, or (ii) payable at or through a bank.

(i) "Traveler's check" means an instrument that (i) is payable on demand, (ii) is drawn on or payable at or through a bank, (iii) is designated by the term "traveler's check" or by a substantially similar term, and (iv) requires, as a condition to payment, a countersignature by a person whose specimen signature appears on the instrument.

(j) "Certificate of deposit" means an instrument containing an acknowledgment by a bank that a sum of money has been received by the bank and a promise by the bank to repay the sum of money. A certificate of deposit is a note of the bank.

§ 3—105.   Issue of Instrument

(a) "Issue" means the first delivery of an instrument by the maker or drawer, whether to a holder or nonholder, for the purpose of giving rights on the instrument to any person.

. . .

§ 3—106.   Unconditional Promise or Order

(a) Except as provided in this section, for the purposes of Section 3—104(a), a promise or order is unconditional unless it states (i) an express condition to payment, (ii) that the promise or order is subject to or governed by another writing, or (iii) that rights or obligations with respect to the promise or order are stated in another writing. A reference to another writing does not of itself make the promise or order conditional.

(b) A promise or order is not made conditional (i) by a reference to another writing for a statement of rights with respect to collateral, prepayment, or acceleration, or (ii) because payment is limited to resort to a particular fund or source.

(c) If a promise or order requires, as a condition to payment, a countersignature by a person whose specimen signature appears on the promise or order, the condition does not make the promise or order conditional for the purposes of Section 3—104(a).

. . .

(d) If a promise or order at the time it is issued or first comes into possession of a holder contains a statement, required by applicable statutory or administrative law, to the effect that the rights of a holder or transferee are subject to claims or defenses that the issuer could assert against the original payee, the promise or order is not thereby made conditional for the purposes of Section 3—104(a); but if the promise or order is an instrument, there cannot be a holder in due course of the instrument.

§ 3—110.   Identification of Person to Whom Instrument Is Payable

(a) The person to whom an instrument is initially payable is determined by the intent of the person, whether or not authorized, signing as, or in the name or behalf of, the issuer of the instrument. The instrument is payable to the person intended by the signer even if that person is identified in the instrument by a name or other identification that is not that of the intended person. If more than one person signs in the name or behalf of the issuer of an instrument and all the signers do not intend the same person as

payee, the instrument is payable to any person intended by one or more of the signers.

(b) If the signature of the issuer of an instrument is made by automated means, such as a check-writing machine, the payee of the instrument is determined by the intent of the person who supplied the name or identification of the payee, whether or not authorized to do so.

(c) A person to whom an instrument is payable may be identified in any way, including by name, identifying number, office, or account number. For the purpose of determining the holder of an instrument, the following rules apply:

> (1) If an instrument is payable to an account and the account is identified only by number, the instrument is payable to the person to whom the account is payable. If an instrument is payable to an account identified by number and by the name of a person, the instrument is payable to the named person, whether or not that person is the owner of the account identified by number.

. . .

§ 3—118.   Statute of Limitations

(a) Except as provided in subsection (e), an action to enforce the obligation of a party to pay a note payable at a definite time must be commenced within six years after the due date or dates stated in the note or, if a due date is accelerated, within six years after the accelerated due date.

(b) Except as provided in subsection (d) or (e), if demand for payment is made to the maker of a note payable on demand, an action to enforce the obligation of a party to pay the note must be commenced within six years after the demand. If no demand for payment is made to the maker, an action to enforce the note is barred if neither principal nor interest on the note has been paid for a continuous period of 10 years.

(c) Except as provided in subsection (d), an action to enforce the obligation of a party to an unaccepted draft to pay the draft must be commenced within three years after dishonor of the draft or 10 years after the date of the draft, whichever period expires first.

(d) An action to enforce the obligation of the acceptor of a certified check or the issuer of a teller's check, cashier's check, or traveler's check must be commenced within three years after demand for payment is made to the acceptor or issuer, as the case may be.

(e) An action to enforce the obligation of a party to a certificate of deposit to pay the instrument must be commenced within six years after demand for payment is made to the maker, but if the instrument states a due date and the maker is not required to pay before that date, the six-year period begins when a demand for payment is in effect and the due date has passed.

(f) An action to enforce the obligation of a party to pay an accepted draft, other than a certified check, must be commenced (i) within six years after the due date or dates stated in the draft or acceptance if the obligation of the acceptor is payable at a definite time, or (ii) within six years after the date of the acceptance if the obligation of the acceptor is payable on demand.

(g) Unless governed by other law regarding claims for indemnity or contribution, an action (i) for conversion of an instrument, for money had and received, or like action based on conversion, (ii) for breach of warranty, or (iii) to enforce an obligation, duty, or right arising under this Article and not governed by this section must be commenced within three years after the [cause of action] accrues.

Part 2
Negotiation, Transfer, and Indorsement

§ 3—201.   Negotiation

(a) "Negotiation" means a transfer of possession, whether voluntary or involuntary, of an instrument by a person other than the issuer to a person who thereby becomes its holder.

(b) Except for negotiation by a remitter, if an instrument is payable to an identified person, negotiation requires transfer of possession of the instrument and its indorsement by the holder. If an instrument is payable to bearer, it may be negotiated by transfer of possession alone.

§ 3–203.   Transfer of Instrument; Rights Acquired by Transfer

(a) An instrument is transferred when it is delivered by a person other than its issuer for the purpose of giving to the person receiving delivery the right to enforce the instrument.

(b) Transfer of an instrument, whether or not the transfer is a negotiation, vests in the transferee any right of the transferor to enforce the instrument, including any right as a holder in due course, but the transferee cannot acquire rights of a holder in due course by a transfer, directly or indirectly, from a holder in due course if the transferee engaged in fraud or illegality affecting the instrument.

(c) Unless otherwise agreed, if an instrument is transferred for value and the transferee does not become a holder because of lack of indorsement by the transferor, the transferee has a specifically enforceable right to the unqualified indorsement of the transferor, but negotiation of the instrument does not occur until the indorsement is made.

(d) If a transferor purports to transfer less than the entire instrument, negotiation of the instrument does not occur. The transferee obtains no rights under this Article and has only the rights of a partial assignee.

§ 3–204.   Indorsement

(a) "Indorsement" means a signature, other than that of a signer as maker, drawer, or acceptor, that alone or accompanied by other words is made on an instrument for the purpose of (i) negotiating the instrument, (ii) restricting payment of the instrument, or (iii) incurring indorser's liability on the instrument, but regardless of the intent of the signer, a signature and its accompanying words is an indorsement unless the accompanying words, terms of the instrument, place of the signature, or other circumstances unambiguously indicate that the signature was made for a purpose other than indorsement. For the purpose of determining whether a signature is made on an instrument, a paper affixed to the instrument is a part of the instrument.

. . .

§ 3—205.   Special Indorsement; Blank Indorsement; Anomalous Indorsement

(a) If an endorsement is made by the holder of an instrument, whether payable to an identified person or payable to bearer, and the indorsement identifies a person to whom it makes the instrument payable, it is a "special indorsement." When specially indorsed, an instrument becomes payable to the identified person and may be negotiated only by the indorsement of that person. The principles stated in Section 3—110 apply to special indorsements.

(b) If an endorsement is made by the holder of an instrument and it is not a special indorsement, it is a "blank indorsement." When indorsed in blank, an instrument becomes payable to bearer and may be negotiated by transfer of possession alone until specially indorsed.

(c) The holder may convert a blank indorsement that consists only of a signature into a special indorsement by writing, above the signature of the indorser, words identifying the person to whom the instrument is made payable.

(d) "Anomalous indorsement" means an indorsement made by a person who is not the holder of the instrument. An anomalous indorsement does not affect the manner in which the instrument may be negotiated.

Part 3
Enforcement of Instruments

§ 3—301.   Person Entitled to Enforce Instrument

"Person entitled to enforce" an instrument means (i) the holder of the instrument, (ii) a nonholder in possession of the instrument who has the rights of a holder, or (iii) a person not in possession of the instrument who is entitled to enforce the instrument pursuant to Section 3—309 or 3—418(d). A person may be a person entitled to enforce the instrument even though the person is not the owner of the instrument or is in wrongful possession of the instrument.

§ 3—302.   Holder in Due Course

(a) Subject to subsection (c) and Section 3—106(d), "holder in due course" means the holder of an instrument if:

(1) the instrument when issued or negotiated to the holder does not bear such apparent evidence of forgery or alteration or is not otherwise so irregular or incomplete as to call into question its authenticity; and

(2) the holder took the instrument (i) for value, (ii) in good faith, (iii) without notice that the instrument is overdue or has been dishonored or that there is an uncured default with respect to payment of another instrument issued as part of the same series, (iv) without notice that the instrument contains an unauthorized signature or has been altered, (v) without notice of any claim to the instrument described in Section 3—306, and (vi) without notice that any party has a defense or claim in recoupment described in Section 3—305(a).

(b) Notice of discharge of a party, other than discharge in an insolvency proceeding, is not notice of a defense under subsection (a), but discharge is effective against a person who became a holder in due course with notice of the discharge. Public filing or recording of a document does not of itself constitute notice of a defense, claim in recoupment, or claim to the instrument.

(c) Except to the extent a transferor or predecessor in interest has rights as a holder in due course, a person does not acquire rights of a holder in due course of an instrument taken (i) by legal process or by purchase in an execution, bankruptcy, or creditor's sale or similar proceeding, (ii) by purchase as part of a bulk transaction not in ordinary course of business of the transferor, or (iii) as the successor in interest to an estate or other organization.

(d) If, under Section 3—303(a)(1), the promise of performance that is the consideration for an instrument has been partially performed, the holder may assert rights as a holder in due course of the instrument only to the fraction of the amount payable under the instrument equal to the value of the partial performance divided by the value of the promised performance.

(e) If (i) the person entitled to enforce an instrument has only a security interest in the instrument and (ii) the person obliged to pay the instrument has a defense, claim in recoupment, or claim to the instrument that may be asserted against the person who granted the security interest, the person entitled to enforce the instrument may assert rights as a holder in due course only to an amount payable under the instrument which, at the time of enforcement of the instrument, does not exceed the amount of the unpaid obligation secured.

(f) To be effective, notice must be received at a time and in a manner that gives a reasonable opportunity to act on it.

(g) This section is subject to any law limiting status as a holder in due course in particular classes of transactions.

§ 3—305. Defenses and Claims in Recoupment

(a) Except as stated in subsection (b), the right to enforce the obligation of a party to pay an instrument is subject to the following:

(1) a defense of the obligor based on (i) infancy of the obligor to the extent it is a defense to a simple contract, (ii) duress, lack of legal capacity, or illegality of the transaction which, under other law, nullifies the obligation of the obligor, (iii) fraud that induced the obligor to sign the instrument with neither knowledge nor reasonable opportunity to learn of its character or its essential terms, or (iv) discharge of the obligor in insolvency proceedings;

(2) a defense of the obligor stated in another section of this Article or a defense of the obligor that would be available if the person entitled to enforce the instrument were enforcing a right to payment under a simple contract; and

(3) a claim in recoupment of the obligor against the original payee of the instrument if the claim arose from the transaction that gave rise to the instrument; but the claim of the obligor may be asserted against a transferee of the instrument only to reduce the amount owing on the instrument at the time the action is brought.

(b) The right of a holder in due course to enforce the obligation of a party to pay the instrument is subject to defenses of the obligor stated in subsection (a)(1), but is not subject to defenses of the obligor stated in subsection (a)(2) or claims in recoupment stated in subsection (a)(3) against a person other than the holder.

(c) Except as stated in subsection (d), in an action to enforce the obligation of a party to pay the instrument, the obligor may not assert against the person entitled to enforce the instrument a defense, claim in recoupment, or claim to the instrument (Section 3—306) of another person, but the other person's claim to the instrument may be asserted by the obligor if the other person is joined in the action and personally asserts the claim against the person entitled to enforce the instrument. An obligor is not obliged to pay the instrument if the person seeking enforcement of the instrument does not have rights of a holder in due course and the obligor proves that the instrument is a lost or stolen instrument.

(d) In an action to enforce the obligation of an accommodation party to pay an instrument, the accommodation party may assert against the person entitled to enforce the instrument any defense or claim in recoupment under subsection (a) that the accommodated party could assert against the person entitled to enforce the instrument, except the defenses of discharge in insolvency proceedings, infancy, and lack of legal capacity.

§ 3—306. Claims to an Instrument

A person taking an instrument, other than a person having rights of a holder in due course, is subject to a claim of a property or possessory rights in the instrument or its proceeds, including a claim to rescind a negotiation and to recover the instrument or its proceeds. A person having rights of a holder in due course takes free of the claim to the instrument.

§ 3—310.   Effect of Instrument on Obligation for Which Taken

(a) Unless otherwise agreed, if a certified check, cashier's check, or teller's check is taken for an obligation, the obligation is discharged to the same extent discharge would result if an amount of money equal to the amount of the instrument were taken in payment of the obligation. Discharge of the obligation does not affect any liability that the obligor may have as an indorser of the instrument.

(b) Unless otherwise agreed and except as provided in subsection (a), if a note or an uncertified check is taken for an obligation, the obligation is suspended to the same extent the obligation would be discharged if an amount of money equal to the amount of the instrument were taken, and the following rules apply:

(1) In the case of an uncertified check, suspension of the obligation continues until dishonor of the check or until it is paid or certified. Payment or certification of the check results in discharge of the obligation to the extent of the amount of the check.

(2) In the case of a note, suspension of the obligation continues until dishonor of the note or until it is paid. Payment of the note results in discharge of the obligation to the extent of the payment.

(3) Except as provided in paragraph (4), if the check or note is dishonored and the obligee of the obligation for which the instrument was taken is the person entitled to enforce the instrument, the obligee may enforce either the instrument or the obligation. In the case of an instrument of a third person which is negotiated to the obligee by the obligor, discharge of the obligor on the instrument also discharges the obligation.

(4) If the person entitled to enforce the instrument taken for an obligation is a person other than the obligee, the obliges may not enforce the obligation to the extent the obligation is suspended. If the obligee is the person entitled to enforce the instrument but no longer has possession of it because it was lost, stolen, or destroyed, the obligation may not be enforced to the extent of the amount payable on the instrument, and to that extent the obligee's rights against the obligor are limited to enforcement of the instrument.

(c) If an instrument other than one described in subsection (a) or (b) is taken for an obligation, the effect is (i) that stated in subsection (a) if the instrument is one on which a bank is liable as maker or acceptor, or (ii) that stated in subsection (b) in any other case.

§ 3—311.   Accord and Satisfaction by Use of Instrument

(a) If a person against whom a claim is asserted proves that (i) that person in good faith tendered an instrument to the claimant as full satisfaction of the claim, (ii) the amount of the claim was unliquidated or subject to a bona fide dispute, and (iii) the claimant obtained payment of the instrument, the following subsections apply.

(b) Unless subsection (c) applies, the claim is discharged if the person against whom the claim is asserted proves that the instrument or an accompanying written communication contained a conspicuous statement to the effect that the instrument was tendered as full satisfaction to the claim.

(c) Subject to subsection (d), a claim is not discharged under subsection (b) if either of the following applies:

(1) The claimant, if an organization, proves that (i) within a reasonable time before the tender, the claimant sent a conspicuous statement to the person against whom the claim is asserted that communications concerning disputed debts, including an instrument tendered as full satisfaction of a debt, are to be sent to a designated person, office, or place, and (ii) the instrument or accompanying communication was not received by that designated person, office, or place.

(2) The claimant, whether or not an organization, proves that within 90 days after payment of the instrument, the claimant tendered repayment of the amount of the instrument to the person against whom the claim is asserted. This paragraph does not apply if the claimant is an organization that sent a statement complying with paragraph (1)(i).

(d) A claim is discharged if the person against whom the claim is asserted proves that within a reasonable time before collection of the instrument was initiated, the claimant, or an agent of the claimant having direct responsibility with respect to the disputed obligation, knew that the instrument was tendered in full satisfaction of the claim.

Part 4

Liability of Parties

§ 3—401.   Signature

(a) A person is not liable on an instrument unless (i) the person signed the instrument, or (ii) the person is represented by an agent or representative who signed the instrument and the signature is binding on the represented person under Section 3—402.

(b) A signature may be made (i) manually or by means of a device or machine, and (ii) by the use of any name, including a trade or assumed name, or by a word, mark, or symbol executed or adopted by a person with present intention to authenticate a writing.

§ 3—402.   Signature by Representative

(a) If a person acting, or purporting to act, as a representative signs an instrument by signing either the name of the represented person or the name of the signer, the represented person is bound by the signature to the same extent the represented person would be bound if the signature were on a simple contract. If the represented person is bound, the signature of the representative is the "authorized signature of the represented person" and the represented person is liable on the instrument, whether or not identified in the instrument.

(b) If a representative signs the name of the representative to an instrument and the signature is an authorized signature of the represented person, the following rules apply:

(1) If the form of the signature shows unambiguously that the signature is made on behalf of the represented person who is identified in the instrument, the representative is not liable on the instrument.

(2) Subject to subsection (c), if (i) the form of the signature does not show unambiguously that the signature is made in a representative capacity or (ii) the represented person is not identified in the instrument, the representative is liable on the instrument to a holder in due course that took the instrument without notice that the representative was not intended to be liable on the instrument. With respect to any other person, the representative is liable on the instrument unless the representative proves that the original parties did not intend the representative to be liable on the instrument.

(c) If a representative signs the name of the representative as drawer of a check without indication of the representative status and the check is payable from an account of the represented person who is identified on the check, the signer is not liable on the check if the signature is an authorized signature of the represented person.

§ 3—403.   Unauthorized Signature

(a) Unless otherwise provided in this Article or Article 4, an unauthorized signature is ineffective except as the signature of the unauthorized signer in favor of a person who in good faith pays the instrument or takes it for value. An unauthorized signature may be ratified for all purposes of this Article.

(b) If the signature of more than one person is required to constitute the authorized signature of an organization, the signature of the organization is unauthorized if one of the required signatures is lacking.

(c) The civil or criminal liability of a person who makes an unauthorized signature is not affected by any provision of this Article which makes the unauthorized signature effective for the purposes of this Article.

§ 3—404.   Imposters; Fictitious Payees

(a) If an impostor, by use of the mails or otherwise, induces the issuer of an instrument to issue the instrument to the impostor, or to a person acting in concert with the impostor, by impersonating the payee of the instrument or a person authorized to act for the payee, an indorsement of the instrument by any person in the name of the payee is effective as the indorsement of the payee in favor of a person who, in good faith, pays the instrument or takes it for value or for collection.

(b) If (i) a person whose intent determines to whom an instrument is payable (Section 3—110(a) or (b)) does not intend the person identified as payee to have any interest in the instrument, or (ii) the person identified as payee of an instrument is a fictitious person, the following rules apply until the instrument is negotiated by special indorsement:

(1) Any person in possession of the instrument is its holder.

(2) An indorsement by any person in the name of the payee stated in the instrument is effective as the indorsement of the payee in favor of a person who, in good faith, pays the instrument or takes it for value or for collection.

(c) Under subsection (a) or (b), an indorsement is made in the name of a payee if (i) it is made in a name substantially similar to that of the payee or (ii) the instrument, whether or not indorsed, is deposited in a depository bank to an account in a name substantially similar to that of the payee.

(d) With respect to an instrument to which subsection (a) or (b) applies, if a person paying the instrument or taking it for value or for collection fails to exercise ordinary care in paying or taking the instrument and that failure substantially contributes to loss resulting from payment of the instrument, the person bearing the loss may recover from the person failing to exercise ordinary care to the extent the failure to exercise ordinary care contributed to the loss.

§ 3—405.   Employer's Responsibility for Fraudulent Indorsement by Employee

(a) In this section:

(1) "Employee" includes an independent contractor and employee of an independent contractor retained by the employer.

(2) "Fraudulent indorsement" means (i) in the case of an instrument payable to the employer, a forged indorsement purporting to be that of the employer, or (ii) in the case of an instrument with respect to which the employer is the issuer, a forged indorsement purporting to be that of the person identified as payee.

(3) "Responsibility" with respect to instruments

means authority (i) to sign or indorse instruments on behalf of the employer, (ii) to process instruments received by the employer for bookkeeping purposes, for deposit to an account, or for other disposition, (iii) to prepare or process instruments for issue in the name of the employer, (iv) to supply information determining the names or addresses of payees of instruments to be issued in the name of the employer, (v) to control the disposition of instruments to be issued in the name of the employer, or (vi) to act otherwise with respect to instruments in a responsible capacity. "Responsibility" does not include authority that merely allows an employee to have access to instruments or blank or incomplete instrument forms that are being stored or transported or are part of incoming or outgoing mail, or similar access.

(b) For the purpose of determining the rights and liabilities of a person who, in good faith, pays an instrument or takes it for value or for collection, if an employer entrusted an employee with responsibility with respect to the instrument and the employee or a person acting in concert with the employee makes a fraudulent indorsement of the instrument, the indorsement is effective as the indorsement of the person to whom the instrument is payable if it is made in the name of that person. If the person paying the instrument or taking it for value or for collection fails to exercise ordinary care in paying or taking the instrument and that failure substantially contributes to loss resulting from the fraud, the person bearing the loss may recover from the person failing to exercise ordinary care to the extent the failure to exercise ordinary care contributed to the loss.

(c) Under subsection (b), an indorsement is made in the name of the person to whom an instrument is payable if (i) it is made in a name substantially similar to the name of that person or (ii) the instrument, whether or not indorsed, is deposited in a depository bank to an account in a name substantially similar to the name of that person.

§ 3—406. Negligence Contributing to Forged Signature or Alteration of Instrument

(a) A person whose failure to exercise ordinary care substantially contributes to an alteration of an instrument or to the making of a forged signature on an instrument is precluded from asserting the alteration or the forgery against a person who, in good faith, pays the instrument or takes it for value or for collection.

(b) Under subsection (a), if the person asserting the preclusion fails to exercise ordinary care in paying or taking the instrument and that failure substantially contributes to loss, the loss is allocated between the person precluded and the person asserting the preclusion according to the extent to which the failure of each to exercise ordinary care contributed to the loss.

(c) Under subsection (a), the burden of proving failure to exercise ordinary care is on the person asserting the preclusion. Under subsection (b), the burden of proving failure to exercise ordinary care is on the person precluded.

§ 3—407. Alteration

(a) "Alteration" means (i) an unauthorized change in an instrument that purports to modify in any respect the obligation of a party, or (ii) an unauthorized addition of words or numbers or other change to an incomplete instrument relating to the obligation of a party.

(b) Except as provided in subsection (c), an alteration fraudulently made discharges a party whose obligation is affected by the alteration unless that party assents or is precluded from asserting the alteration. No other alteration discharges a party, and the instrument may be enforced according to its original terms.

(c) A payor bank or drawee paying a fraudulently altered instrument or a person taking it for value, in good faith and without notice of the alteration, may enforce rights with respect to the instrument (i) according to its original terms, or (ii) in the case of an incomplete instrument altered by unauthorized completion, according to its terms as completed.

§ 3—411. Refusal to Pay Cashier's Checks, Teller's Checks, and Certified Checks

(a) In this section, "obligated bank" means the acceptor of a certified check or the issuer of a cashier's check or teller's check bought from the issuer.

(b) If the obligated bank wrongfully (i) refuses to pay a cashier's check or certified check, (ii) stops payment of a teller's check, or (iii) refuses to pay a dishonored teller's check, the person asserting the right to enforce the check is entitled to compensation for expenses and loss of interest resulting from the nonpayment and may recover consequential damages if the obligated bank refuses to pay after receiving notice of particular circumstances giving rise to the damages.

(c) Expenses or consequential damages under subsection (b) are not recoverable if the refusal of the obligated bank to pay occurs because (i) the bank suspends payments, (ii) the obligated bank asserts a claim or defense of the bank that it has reasonable grounds to believe is available against the person entitled to enforce the instrument, (iii) the obligated bank has a reasonable doubt whether the person demanding payment is the person entitled to enforce the instrument or (iv) payment is prohibited by law.

§ 3—412. Obligation of Issuer of Note or Cashier's Check

The issuer of a note or cashier's check or other draft drawn on the drawer is obliged to pay the instrument (i) according to its terms at the time it was issued or, if not issued, at the time it first came into the possession of a holder, or (ii) if the issuer signed an incomplete instrument, according to its terms when completed, to the extent stated in Sections 3—115 and 3—407. The obligation is owed to a person entitled to enforce the instrument or to an indorser who paid the instrument under Section 3—415.

§ 3—413.   Obligation of Acceptor

(a) The acceptor of a draft is obliged to pay the draft (i) according to its terms at the time it was accepted, even though the acceptance states that the draft is payable "as originally drawn" or equivalent terms, (ii) if the acceptance varies the terms of the draft, according to the terms of the draft as varied, or (iii) if the acceptance is of a draft that is an incomplete instrument, according to its terms when completed, to the extent stated in Sections 3—115 and 3—407. The obligation is owed to a person entitled to enforce the draft or to the drawer or an indorser who paid the draft under Section 3—414 or 3—415.

(b) If the certification of a check or other acceptance of a draft states the amount certified or accepted, the obligation of the acceptor is that amount. If (i) the certification or acceptance does not state an amount, (ii) the amount of the instrument is subsequently raised, and (iii) the instrument is then negotiated to a holder in due course, the obligation of the acceptor is the amount of the instrument at the time it was taken by the holder in due course.

§ 3—416.   Transfer Warranties

(a) A person who transfers an instrument for consideration warrants to the transferee and, if the transfer is by indorsement, to any subsequent transferee that:

(1) the warrantor is a person entitled to enforce the instrument;

(2) all signatures on the instrument are authentic and authorized;

(3) the instrument has not been altered;

(4) the instrument is not subject to a defense or claim in recoupment of any party which can be asserted against the warrantor; and

(5) the warrantor has no knowledge of any insolvency proceeding commenced with respect to the maker or acceptor or, in the case of an unaccepted draft, the drawer.

(b) A person to whom the warranties under subsection (a) are made and who took the instrument in good faith may recover from the warrantor as damages for breach of warranty an amount equal to the loss suffered as a result of the breach, but not more than the amount of the instrument plus expenses and loss of interest incurred as a result of the breach.

(c) The warranties stated in subsection (a) cannot be disclaimed with respect to checks. Unless notice of a claim for breach of warranty is given to the warrantor within 30 days after the claimant has reason to know of the breach and the identity of the warrantor, the liability of the warrantor under subsection (b) is discharged to the extent of any loss caused by the delay in giving notice of the claim.

(d) A [cause of action] for breach of warranty under this section accrues when the claimant has reason to know of the breach.

§ 3—417.   Presentment Warranties

(a) If an unaccepted draft is presented to the drawee for payment or acceptance and the drawee pays or accepts the draft, (i) the person obtaining payment or acceptance, at the time of presentment, and (ii) a previous transferor of the draft, at the time of transfer, warrant to the drawee making payment or accepting the draft in good faith that:

(1) the warrantor is, or was, at the time the warrantor transferred the draft, a person entitled to enforce the draft or authorized to obtain payment or acceptance of the draft on behalf of a person entitled to enforce the draft;

(2) the draft has not been altered; and

(3) the warrantor has no knowledge that the signature of the drawer of the draft is unauthorized.

(b) A drawee making payment may recover from any warrantor damages for breach of warranty equal to the amount paid by the drawee less the amount the drawee received or is entitled to receive from the drawer because of the payment. In addition, the drawee is entitled to compensation for expenses and loss of interest resulting from the breach. The right of the drawee to recover damages under this subsection is not affected by any failure of the drawee to exercise ordinary care in making payment. If the drawee accepts the draft, breach of warranty is a defense to the obligation of the acceptor. If the acceptor makes payment with respect to the draft, the acceptor is entitled to recover from any warrantor for breach of warranty the amounts stated in this subsection.

(c) If a drawee asserts a claim for breach of warranty under subsection (a) based on an unauthorized indorsement of the draft or an alteration of the draft, the warrantor may defend by proving that the indorsement is effective under Section 3—404 or 3—405 or the drawer is precluded under Section 3—406 or 4—406 from asserting against the drawee the unauthorized indorsement or alteration.

(d) If (i) a dishonored draft is presented for payment to the drawer or an indorser or (ii) any other instrument is presented for payment to a party obliged to pay the instrument, and (iii) payment is received, the following rules apply:

(1) The person obtaining payment and a prior transferor of the instrument warrant to the person making payment in good faith that the warrantor is, or was, at the time the warrantor transferred the instrument, a person entitled to enforce the instrument or authorized to obtain payment on behalf of a person entitled to enforce the instrument.

(2) The person making payment may recover from any warrantor for breach of warranty an amount equal to the amount paid plus expenses and loss of interest resulting from the breach.

(e) The warranties stated in subsections (a) and (d) cannot be disclaimed with respect to checks. Unless notice of a claim for breach of warranty is given to the warrantor within 30 days after the claimant has reason to know of the breach and the identity of the warrantor, the liability of the warrantor under subsection (b) or (d) is discharged to the extent of any loss caused by the delay in giving notice of the claim.

(f) A [cause of action] for breach of warranty under this section accrues when the claimant has reason to know of the breach.

§ 3—418. Payment or Acceptance by Mistake

(a) Except as provided in subsection (c), if the drawee of a draft pays or accepts the draft and the drawee acted on the mistaken belief that (i) payment of the draft had not been stopped pursuant to Section 4—403 or (ii) the signature of the drawer of the draft was authorized, the drawee may recover the amount of the draft from the person to whom or for whose benefit payment was made or, in the case of acceptance, may revoke the acceptance. Rights of the drawee under this subsection are not affected by failure of the drawee to exercise ordinary care in paying or accepting the draft.

(b) Except as provided in subsection (c), if an instrument has been paid or accepted by mistake and the case is not covered by subsection (a), the person paying or accepting may, to the extent permitted by the law governing mistake and restitution, (i) recover the payment from the person to whom or for whose benefit payment was made or (ii) in the case of acceptance, may revoke the acceptance.

(c) The remedies provided by subsection (a) or (b) may not be asserted against a person who took the instrument in good faith and for value or who in good faith changed position in reliance on the payment or acceptance. This subsection does not limit remedies provided by Section 3—417 or 4—407.

(d) Notwithstanding Section 4—215, if an instrument is paid or accepted by mistake and the payor or acceptor recovers payment or revokes acceptance under subsection (a) or (b), the instrument is deemed not to have been paid or accepted and is treated as dishonored, and the person from whom payment is recovered has rights as a person entitled to enforce the dishonored instrument.

§ 3—420. Conversion of Instrument

(a) The law applicable to conversion of personal property applies to instruments. An instrument is also converted if it is taken by transfer, other than a negotiation, from a person not entitled to enforce the instrument or a bank makes or obtains payment with respect to the instrument for a person not entitled to enforce the instrument or receive payment. An action for conversion of an instrument may not be brought by (i) the issuer or acceptor of the instrument or (ii) a payee or indorsee who did not receive delivery of the instrument either directly or through delivery to an agent or a co-payee.

(b) In an action under subsection (a), the measure of liability is presumed to be the amount payable on the instrument, but recovery may not exceed the amount of the plaintiff's interest in the instrument.

(c) A representative, other than a depository bank, who has in good faith dealt with an instrument or its proceeds on behalf of one who was not the person entitled to enforce the instrument is not liable in conversion to that person beyond the amount of any proceeds that it has not paid out.

Part 5

Dishonor

§ 3—501. Presentment

(a) "Presentment" means a demand made by or on behalf of a person entitled to enforce an instrument (i) to pay the instrument made to the drawee or a party obliged to pay the instrument or, in the case of a note or accepted draft payable at a bank, to the bank, or (ii) to accept a draft made to the drawee.

(b) The following rules are subject to Article 4, agreement of the parties, and clearing-house rules and the like:

(1) Presentment may be made at the place of payment of the instrument and must be made at the place of payment if the instrument is payable at a bank in the United States; may be made by any commercially reasonable means, including an oral, written, or electronic communication; is effective when the demand for payment or acceptance is received by the person to whom presentment is made; and is effective if made to any one of two or more makers, acceptors, drawees, or other payors.

(2) Upon demand of the person to whom presentment is made, the person making presentment must (i) exhibit the instrument, (ii) give reasonable identification and, if presentment is made on behalf of another person, reasonable evidence of authority to do so, and (iii) sign a receipt on the instrument for any payment made or surrender the instrument if full payment is made.

(3) Without dishonoring the instrument, the party to whom presentment is made may (i) return the instrument for lack of a necessary indorsement, or (ii) refuse payment or acceptance for failure of the presentment to comply with the terms of the instrument, an agreement of the parties, or other applicable law or rule.

(4) The party to whom presentment is made may treat presentment as occurring on the next business day after the day of presentment if the party to whom presentment is made has established a cut-off hour not earlier than 2 p.m. for the receipt and processing of instruments presented for payment or acceptance

and presentment is made after the cut-off hour.

§ 3—502. Dishonor

(a) Dishonor of a note is governed by the following rules:

(1) If the note is payable on demand, the note is dishonored if presentment is duly made to the maker and the note is not paid on the day of presentment.

(2) If the note is not payable on demand and is payable at or through a bank or the terms of the note require presentment, the note is dishonored if presentment is duly made and the note is not paid on the day it becomes payable or the day of presentment, whichever is later.

(3) If the note is not payable on demand and paragraph (2) does not apply, the note is dishonored if it is not paid on the day it becomes payable.

(b) Dishonor of an unaccepted draft other than a documentary draft is governed by the following rules:

(1) If a check is duly presented for payment to the payor bank otherwise than for immediate payment over the counter, the check is dishonored if the payor bank makes timely return of the check or sends timely notice of dishonor or nonpayment under Section 4—301 and 4—302, or becomes accountable for the amount of the check under Section 4—302.

(2) If a draft is payable on demand and paragraph (1) does not apply, the draft is dishonored if presentment for payment is duly made to the drawee and the draft is not paid on the day of presentment.

(3) If a draft is payable on a date stated in the draft, the draft is dishonored if (i) presentment for payment is duly made to the drawee and payment is not made on the day the draft becomes payable or the day of presentment, whichever is later, or (ii) presentment for acceptance is duly made before the day the draft becomes payable and the draft is not accepted on the day of presentment.

(4) If a draft is payable on elapse of a period of time after sight or acceptance, the draft is dishonored if presentment for acceptance is duly made and the draft is not accepted on the day of presentment.

(c) Dishonor of an unaccepted documentary draft occurs according to the rules stated in subsection (b)(2), (3), and (4), except that payment or acceptance may be delayed without dishonor until no later than the close of the third business day of the drawee following the day on which payment or acceptance is required by those paragraphs.

(d) Dishonor of an accepted draft is governed by the following rules:

(1) If the draft is payable on demand, the draft is dishonored if presentment for payment is duly made to the acceptor and the draft is not paid on the day of presentment.

(2) If the draft is not payable on demand, the draft is dishonored if presentment for payment is duly made to the acceptor and payment is not made on the day it becomes payable or the day of presentment, whichever is later.

(e) In any case in which presentment is otherwise required for dishonor under this section and presentment is excused under Section 3—504, dishonor occurs without presentment if the instrument is not duly accepted or paid.

(f) If a draft is dishonored because timely acceptance of the draft was not made and the person entitled to demand acceptance consents to a late acceptance, from the time of acceptance the draft is treated as never having been dishonored.

Part 6

Discharge and Payment

§ 3—601. Discharge and Effect of Discharge

(a) The obligation of a party to pay the instrument is discharged as stated in this Article or by an act or agreement with the party which would discharge an obligation to pay money under a simple contract.

(b) Discharge of the obligation of a party is not effective against a person acquiring rights of a holder in due course of the instrument without notice of the discharge.

§ 3—602. Payment

(a) Subject to subsection (b), an instrument is paid to the extent payment is made (i) by or on behalf of a party obliged to pay the instrument, and (ii) to a person entitled to enforce the instrument. To the extent of the payment, the obligation of the party obliged to pay the instrument is discharged even though payment is made with knowledge of a claim to the instrument under Section 3—306 by another person.

(b) The obligation of a party to pay the instrument is not discharged under subsection (a) if:

(1) a claim to the instrument under Section 3—306 is enforceable against the party receiving payment and (i) payment is made with knowledge by the payor that payment is prohibited by injunction or similar process of a court of competent jurisdiction, or (ii) in the case of an instrument other than a cashier's check, teller's check, or certified check, the party making payment accepted, from

the person having a claim to the instrument, indemnity against loss resulting from refusal to pay the person entitled to enforce the instrument; or

(2) the person making payment knows that the instrument is a stolen instrument and pays a person it knows is in wrongful possession of the instrument.

ARTICLE 4

BANK DEPOSITS AND COLLECTIONS

Part 1

General Provisions and Definitions

§ 4—103. Variation by Agreement; Measure of Damages; Certain Action Constituting Ordinary Care

(1) The effect of the provisions of this Article may be varied by agreement except that no agreement can disclaim a bank's responsibility for its own lack of good faith or failure to exercise ordinary care or can limit the measure of damages for such lack or failure; but the parties may by agreement determine the standards by which such responsibility is to be measured if such standards are not manifestly unreasonable.

(2) Federal Reserve regulations and operating letters, clearing house rules, and the like, have the effect of agreements under subsection (1), whether or not specifically assented to by all parties interested in items handled.

(3) Action or nonaction approved by this Article or pursuant to Federal Reserve regulations or operating letters constitutes the exercise of ordinary care and, in the absence of special instructions, action or nonaction consistent with clearing house rules and the like or with a general banking usage not disapproved by this Article, prima facie constitutes the exercise of ordinary care.

(4) The specification or approval of certain procedures by this Article does not constitute disapproval of other procedures which may be reasonable under the circumstances.

(5) The measure of damages for failure to exercise ordinary care in handling an item is the amount of the item reduced by an amount which could not have been realized by the use of ordinary care, and where there is bad faith it includes other damages, if any, suffered by the party as a proximate consequence.

§ 4—108. Delays

(1) Unless otherwise instructed, a collecting bank in a good faith effort to secure payment may, in the case of specific items and with or without the approval of any person involved, waive, modify or extend time limits imposed or permitted by this Act for a period not in excess of an additional banking day without discharge of secondary parties and without liability to its transferor or any prior party.

(2) Delay by a collecting bank or payor bank beyond time limits prescribed or permitted by this Act or by instructions is excused if caused by interruption of communication facilities, suspension of payments by another bank, war, emergency conditions or other circumstances beyond the control of the bank provided it exercises such diligence as the circumstances require.

Part 2

Collection of Items: Depositary and Collecting Banks

§ 4—204. Methods of Sending and Presenting; Sending Direct to Payor Bank

(1) A collecting bank must send items by reasonably prompt method taking into consideration any relevant instructions, the nature of the item, the number of such items on hand, and the cost of collection involved and the method generally used by it or others to present such items.

(2) A collecting bank may send
   (a) any item direct to the payor bank;
   (b) any item to any nonbank payor if authorized by its transferor; and
   (c) any item other than documentary drafts to any nonbank payor, if authorized by Federal Reserve regulation or operating letter, clearing house rule or the like.

(3) Presentment may be made by a presenting bank at a place where the payor bank has requested that presentment be made.

§ 4—205. Supplying Missing Indorsement; No Notice from Prior Indorsement

(1) A depositary bank which has taken an item for collection may supply any indorsement of the customer which is necessary to title unless the item contains the words "payee's indorsement required" or the like. In the absence of such a requirement, a statement placed on the item by the depositary bank to the effect that the item was deposited by a customer or credited to his account is effective as the customer's indorsement of.

(2) An intermediary bank, or payor bank which is not a depositary bank, is neither given notice nor otherwise

affected by a restrictive indorsement of any person except the bank's immediate transferor.

§ 4—206.   Transfer Between Banks

Any agreed method which identifies the transferor bank is sufficient for the item's further transfer to another bank.

§ 4—211.   Media of Remittance; Provisional and Final Settlement in Remittance Cases

(1) A collecting bank may take in settlement of an item

    (a) a check of the remitting bank or of another bank on any bank except the remitting bank; or

    (b) a cashier's check or similar primary obligation of a remitting bank which is a member of or clears through a member of the same clearing house or group as the collecting bank; or

    (c) appropriate authority to charge an account of the remitting bank or of another bank with the collecting bank; or

    (d) if the item is drawn upon or payable by a person other than a bank, a cashier's check, certified check or other bank check or obligation.

(2) If before its midnight deadline the collecting bank properly dishonors a remittance check or authorization to charge on itself or presents or forwards for collection a remittance instrument of or on another bank which is of a kind approved by subsection (1) or has not been authorized by it, the collecting bank is not liable to prior parties in the event of the dishonor of such check, instrument or authorization.

(3) A settlement for an item by means of a remittance instrument or authorization to charge is or becomes a final settlement as to both the person making and the person receiving the settlement

    (a) if the remittance instrument or authorization to charge is of a kind approved by subsection (1) or has not been authorized by the person receiving the settlement and in either case the person receiving the settlement acts seasonably before its midnight deadline in presenting, forwarding for collection or paying the instrument or authorization—at the time the remittance instrument or authorization is finally paid by the payor by which it is payable;

    (b) if the person receiving the settlement has authorized remittance by a nonbank check or obligation or by a cashier's check or similar primary obligation of or a check upon the payor or other remitting bank which is not of a kind approved by subsection (1)(b),—at the time of the receipt of such remittance check or obligation; or

    (c) if in a case not covered by subparagraphs (a) or (b) the person receiving the settlement fails to seasonably present, forward for collection, pay or return remittance instrument or au-

thorization to it to charge before its midnight deadline,—at such midnight deadline.

§ 4—213.   Final Payment of Item for Payor Bank; When Provisional Debits and Credits Become Final; When Certain Credits Become Available for Withdrawal

(1) An item is finally paid by a payor bank when the bank has done any of the following, whichever happens first:

    (a) paid the item in cash; or

    (b) settled for the item without reserving a right to revoke the settlement and without having such right under statute, clearing house rule or agreement; or

    (c) completed the process of posting the item to the indicated account of the drawer, maker or other person to be charged therewith; or

    (d) made a provisional settlement for the item and failed to revoke the settlement in the time and manner permitted by statute, clearing house rule or agreement.

Upon a final payment under subparagraphs (b), (c) or (d), the payor bank shall be accountable for the amount of the item.

(2) If provisional settlement for an item between the presenting and payor banks is made through a clearing house or by debits or credits in an account between them, then to the extent that provisional debits or credits for the item are entered in accounts between the presenting and payor banks or between the presenting and successive prior collecting banks seriatim, they become final upon final payment of the item by the payor bank.

(3) If a collecting bank receives a settlement for an item which is or becomes final (subsection 3) of Section 4—211, subsection (2) of Section 4—213), the bank is accountable to its customer for the amount of the item and any provisional credit given for the item in an account with its customer becomes final.

(4) Subject to any right of the bank to apply the credit to an obligation of the customer, credit given by a bank for an item in an account with its customer becomes available for withdrawal as of right

    (a) in any case where the bank has received a provisional settlement for the item,—when such settlement becomes final and the bank has had a reasonable time to learn that the settlement is final;

    (b) in any case where the bank is both a depositary bank and a payor bank and the item is finally paid,—at the opening of the bank's second banking day following receipt of the item.

(5) A deposit of money in a bank is final when made but, subject to any right of the bank to apply the deposit to an obligation of the customer, the deposit becomes available for withdrawal as of right at the opening of the bank's next banking day following receipt of the deposit.

Part 3

Collection of Items: Payor Banks

§ 4—301.   Deferred Posting; Recovery of Payment by Return of Items; Time of Dishonor

(1) Where an authorized settlement for a demand item (other than a documentary draft) received by a payor bank otherwise than for immediate payment over the counter has been made before midnight of the banking day of receipt, the payor bank may revoke the settlement and recover any payment if before it has made final payment (subsection (1) of Section 4—213) and before its midnight deadline it

    (a) returns the item; or

    (b) sends written notice of dishonor or non-payment if the item is held for protest or is otherwise unavailable for return.

(2) If a demand item is received by a payor bank for credit on its books, it may return such item or send notice of dishonor and may revoke any credit given or recover the amount thereof withdrawn by its customer, if it acts within the time limit and in the manner specified in the preceding subsection.

(3) Unless previous notice of dishonor has been sent, an item is dishonored at the time when for purposes of dishonor it is returned or notice sent in accordance with this section.

(4) An item is returned:

    (a) as to an item received through a clearing house, when it is delivered to the presenting or last collecting bank or to the clearing house or is sent or delivered in accordance with its rules; or

    (b) in all other cases, when it is sent or delivered to the bank's customer or transferor or pursuant to his instructions.

§ 4—302.   Payor Bank's Responsibility for Late Return of Item

In the absence of a valid defense such as breach of a presentment warranty (subsection (1) of Section 4—207), settlement effected or the like, if an item is presented on and received by a payor bank the bank is accountable for the amount of

    (a) a demand item other than a documentary draft whether properly payable or not if the bank, in any case where it is not also the depositary bank, retains the item beyond midnight of the banking day of receipt without settling for it or, regardless of whether it is also the depositary bank, does not pay or return the item or send notice of dishonor until after its midnight deadline; or

    (b) any other properly payable item unless within the time allowed for acceptance or payment of that item the bank either accepts or pays the item or returns it and accompanying documents.

Part 4

Relationship Between Payor Bank and Its Customer

§ 4—401.   When Bank May Charge Customer's Account

(1) As against its customer, a bank may charge against his account any item which is otherwise properly payable from that account even though the charge creates an overdraft.

(2) A bank which in good faith makes payment to a holder may charge the indicated account of its customer according to

    (a) the original tenor of his altered item; or

    (b) the tenor of his completed item, even though the bank knows the item has been completed unless the bank has notice that the completion was improper.

§ 4—407.   Payor Bank's Right to Subrogation on Improper Payment

If a payor bank has paid an item over the stop payment order of the drawer or maker or otherwise under circumstances giving a basis for objection by the drawer or maker, to prevent unjust enrichment and only to the extent necessary to prevent loss to the bank by reason of its payment of the item, the payor bank shall be subrogated to the rights

    (a) of any holder in due course on the item against the drawer or maker, and

    (b) of the payee or any other holder of the item against the drawer or maker either on the item or under the transaction out of which the item arose; and

    (c) of the drawer or maker against the payee or any other holder of the item with respect to the transaction out of which the item arose.

Part 5

Collection of Documentary Drafts

§ 4—501.   Handling of Documentary Drafts; Duty to Send for Presentment and to Notify Customer of Dishonor

A bank which takes a documentary draft for collection must present or send the draft and accompanying documents for presentment and, upon learning that the draft has not been paid or accepted in due course, must seasonably notify its customer of such fact even though it may have discounted or bought the draft or extended credit available for withdrawal as of right.

ARTICLE 4 [1990 Revision]

BANK DEPOSITS AND COLLECTIONS

§ 4—102.   Applicability

(a) To the extent that items within this Article are also within Articles 3 and 8, they are subject to those Articles. If there is conflict, this Article governs Article 3, but Article 8 governs this Article.

(b) The liability of a bank for action or non-action with respect to an item handled by it for purposes of presentment, payment or collection is governed by the law of the place where the bank is located. In the case of action or non-action by or at a branch or separate office of a bank, its liability is governed by the law of the place where the branch or separate office is located.

§ 4—103.   Variation by Agreement; Measure of Damages; Action Constituting Ordinary Care

(a) The effect of the provision of this Article may be varied by agreement, but the parties to the agreement cannot disclaim a bank's responsibility for its lack of good faith or failure to exercise ordinary care or limit the measure of damages for the lack or failure. However, the parties may determine by agreement the standards by which the bank's responsibility is to be measured if those standards are not manifestly unreasonable.

(b) Federal Reserve regulations and operating circulars, clearing-house rules, and the like have the effect of agreements under subsection (a), whether or not specifically assented to by all parties interested in items handled.

(c) Action or non-action approved by this Article or pursuant to Federal Reserve regulations or operating circulars is the exercise of ordinary care and, in the absence of special instructions, action or non-action consistent with clearing-house rules and the like or with a general banking usage not disapproved by this Article, is prima facie the exercise of ordinary care.

(d) The specification or approval of certain procedures by this Article is not disapproval of other procedures that may be reasonable under the circumstances.

(e) The measure of damages for failure to exercise ordinary care in handling an item is the amount of the item reduced by an amount that could not have been realized by the exercise of ordinary care. If there is also bad faith it includes any other damages the party suffered as a proximate consequence.

§ 4—107.   Separate Office of Bank

A branch or separate office of a bank is a separate bank for the purpose of computing the time within which and determining the place at or to which action may be taken or notice or orders must be given under this Article and under Article 3.

§ 4—109.   Delays

(a) Unless otherwise instructed, a collecting bank in a good faith effort to secure payment of a specific item drawn on a payor other than a bank, and with or without the approval of any person involved, may waive, modify, or extend time limits imposed or permitted by this Act for a period not exceeding two additional banking days without discharge of drawers or indorsers or liability to its transferor or a prior party.

(b) Delay by a collecting bank or payor bank beyond time limits prescribed or permitted by this Act or by instructions is excused if (i) the delay is caused by interruption of communication or computer facilities, suspension of payments by another bank, war, emergency conditions, failure of equipment, or other circumstances beyond the control of the bank, and (ii) the bank exercises such diligence as the circumstances require.

§ 4—110.   Electronic Presentment

(a) "Agreement for electronic presentment" means an agreement, clearing-house rule, or Federal Reserve regulation or operating circular, providing that presentment of an item may be made by transmission of an image of an item or information describing the item ("presentment notice") rather than delivery of the item itself. The agreement may provide for procedures governing retention, presentment, payment, dishonor, and other matters concerning items subject to the agreement.

(b) Presentment of an item pursuant to an agreement for presentment is made when the presentment notice is received.

(c) If presentment is made by presentment notice, a reference to "item" or "check" in this Article means the presentment notice unless the context otherwise indicates.

§ 4—111.   Statute of Limitations

An action to enforce an obligation, duty, or right arising under this Article must be commenced within three years after the [cause of action] accrues.

§ 4—204.   Methods of Sending and Presenting; Sending Directly to Payor Bank

(a) A collecting bank shall send items by a reasonably prompt method, taking into consideration relevant instructions, the nature of the item, the number of those items on hand, the cost of collection involved, and the method generally used by it or others to present those items.

(b) A collecting bank may send:
  (1) an item directly to the payor bank;
  (2) an item to a nonbank payor if authorized by its transferor; and

(3) an item other than documentary drafts to a nonbank payor, if authorized by Federal Reserve regulation or operating circular, clearing-house rule, or the like.

(c) Presentment may be made by a presenting bank at a place where the payor bank or other payor has requested that presentment be made.

§ 4—205.   Depository Bank Holder of Unindorsed Item

If a customer delivers an item to a depositary bank for collection:

(1) the depositary bank becomes a holder of the item at the time it receives the item for collection if the customer at the time of delivery was a holder of the item, whether or not the customer indorses the item, and, if the bank satisfies the other requirements of Section 3—302, it is a holder in due course; and

(2) the depositary bank warrants to collecting banks, the payor bank or other payor, and the drawer that the amount of the item was paid to the customer or deposited to the customer's account.

§ 4—207.   Transfer Warranties

(a) A Customer or collecting bank that transfers an item and receives a settlement or other consideration warrants to the transferee and to any subsequent collecting bank that:

(1) the warrantor is a person entitled to enforce the item;

(2) all signatures on the item are authentic and authorized;

(3) the item has not been altered;

(4) the item is not subject to a defense or claim in recoupment (Section 3—305(a)) of any party that can be asserted against the warrantor; and

(5) the warrantor has no knowledge of any insolvency proceeding commenced with respect to the maker or acceptor or, in the case of an unaccepted draft, the drawer.

(b) If an item is dishonored, a customer or collecting bank transferring the item and receiving settlement or other consideration is obliged to pay the amount due on the item (i) according to the terms of the item at the time it was transferred, or (ii) if the transfer was of an incomplete item, according to its terms when completed as stated in Sections 3—115 and 3—407. The obligation of a transferor is owed to the transferee and to any subsequent collecting bank that takes the item in good faith. A transferor cannot disclaim its obligation under this subsection by an indorsement stating that it is made "without recourse" or otherwise disclaiming liability.

(c) A person to whom the warranties under subsection (a) are made and who took the item in good faith may recover from the warrantor as damages for breach of warranty an amount equal to the loss suffered as a result of the breach, but not more than the amount of the item plus expenses and loss of interest incurred as a result of the breach.

(d) The warranties stated in subsection (a) cannot be disclaimed with respect to checks. Unless notice of a claim for breach of warranty is given to the warrantor within 30 days after the claimant has reason to know of the breach and the identity of the warrantor; the warrantor is discharged to the extent of any loss caused by the delay in giving notice of the claim.

(e) A cause of action for breach of warranty under this section accrues when the claimant has reason to know of the breach.

§ 4—208.   Presentment Warranties

(a) If an unaccepted draft is presented to the drawee for payment or acceptance and the drawee pays or accepts the draft, (i) the person obtaining payment or acceptance, at the time of presentment, and (ii) a previous transferor of the draft, at the time of transfer, warrant to the drawee that pays or accepts the draft in good faith that:

(1) the warrantor is, or was, at the time the warrantor transferred the draft, a person entitled to enforce the draft or authorized to obtain payment or acceptance of the draft on behalf of a person entitled to enforce the draft or authorized to obtain payment or acceptance of the draft on behalf of a person entitled to enforce the draft;

(2) the draft has not been altered; and

(3) the warrantor has no knowledge that the signature of the purported drawer of the draft is unauthorized.

(b) A drawee making payment may recover from a warrantor damages for breach of warranty equal to the amount paid by the drawee less the amount the drawee received or is entitled to receive from the drawer because of the payment. In addition, the drawee is entitled to compensation for expenses and loss of interest resulting from the breach. The right of the drawee to recover damages under this subsection is not affected by any failure of the drawee to exercise ordinary care in making payment. If the drawee accepts the draft (i) breach of warranty is a defense to the obligation of the acceptor, and (ii) if the acceptor makes payment with respect to the draft, the acceptor is entitled to recover from a warrantor for breach of warranty the amounts stated in this subsection.

(c) If a drawee asserts a claim for breach of warranty under subsection (a) based on an unauthorized indorsement of the draft or an alteration of the draft, the warrantor may defend by proving that the indorsement is effective under Section 3—404 or 3—405 or the drawer is precluded under Section 3—406 or 4—406 from asserting against the drawee the unauthorized indorsement or alteration.

(d) If (i) a dishonored draft is presented for payment to the drawer or an indorser or (ii) any other item is presented for payment to a party obliged to pay the item, and the item is paid, the person obtaining payment and a prior transferor of the item warrant to the person making payment in good faith that the warrantor is, or was, at the time the warrantor transferred the item, a person entitled to enforce the item or authorized to obtain payment on behalf of a person entitled to enforce the item. The person making payment may recover from any warrantor for breach of warranty an amount equal to the amount paid plus expenses and loss of interest resulting from the breach.

(e) The warranties stated in subsections (a) and (d) cannot be disclaimed with respect to checks. Unless notice of a claim for breach of warranty is given to the warrantor within 30 days after the claimant has reason to know of the breach and the identity of the warrantor, the warrantor is discharged to the extent of any loss caused by the delay in giving notice of the claim.

(f) A cause of action for breach of warranty under this section accrues when the claimant has reason to know of the breach.

§ 4—209. Encoding and Retention Warranties

(a) A person who encodes information on or with respect to an item after issue warrants to any subsequent collecting bank and to the payor bank or other payor that the information is correctly encoded. If the customer of a depositary bank encodes, that bank also makes the warranty.

(b) A person who undertakes to retain an item pursuant to an agreement for electronic presentment warrants to any subsequent collecting bank and to the payor bank or other payor that retention and presentment of the item comply with the agreement. If a customer of a depositary bank undertakes to retain an item, that bank also makes this warranty.

(c) A person to whom warranties are made under this section and who took the item in good faith may recover from the warrantor as damages for breach of warranty an amount equal to the loss suffered as a result of the breach, plus expenses and loss of interest incurred as a result of the breach.

§ 4—213. Medium and Time of Settlement by Bank

(a) With respect to settlement by a bank, the medium and time of settlement may be prescribed by Federal Reserve regulations or circulars, clearing-house rules, and the like, or agreement. In the absence of such prescription:

(1) the medium of settlement is cash or credit to an account in a Federal Reserve bank of or specified by the person to receive settlement; and

(2) the time of settlement is:

    (i) with respect to tender of settlement by cash, a cashier's check, or teller's check, when the cash or check is sent or delivered;

    (ii) with respect to tender of settlement by credit in an account in a Federal Reserve Bank, when the credit is made;

    (iii) with respect to tender of settlement by a

credit or debit to an account in a bank, when the credit or debit is made or, in the case of tender of settlement by authority to charge an account, when the authority is sent or delivered; or

    (iv) with respect to tender of settlement by a funds transfer, when payment is made pursuant to Section 4A—406(a) to the person receiving settlement.

(b) If the tender of settlement is not by a medium authorized by subsection (a) or the time of settlement is not fixed by subsection (a), no settlement occurs until the tender of settlement is accepted by the person receiving settlement.

(c) If settlement for an item is made by cashier's check or teller's check and the person receiving settlement, before its midnight deadline:

(1) presents or forwards the check for collection, settlement is final when the check is finally paid; or

(2) fails to present or forward the check for collection, settlement is final at the midnight deadline of the person receiving settlement.

(d) If settlement for an item is made by giving authority to charge the account of the bank giving settlement in the bank receiving settlement, settlement is final when the charge is made by the bank receiving settlement if there are funds available in the account for the amount of the item.

§ 4—214. Right of Charge-Back or Refund; Liability of Collecting Bank; Return of Item

(a) If a collecting bank has made provisional settlement with its customer for an item and fails by reason of dishonor, suspension of payments by a bank, or otherwise to receive a settlement for the item which is or becomes final, the bank may revoke the settlement given by it, charge back the amount of any credit given for the item to its customer's account, or obtain refund from its customer, whether or not it is able to return the item, if by its midnight deadline or within a longer reasonable time after it learns the facts it returns the item or sends notification of the facts. If the return or notice is delayed beyond the bank's midnight deadline or a longer reasonable time after it learns the facts, the bank may revoke the settlement, charge back the credit, or obtain refund from its customer, but it is liable for any loss resulting from the delay. These rights to revoke, charge back, and obtain refund terminate if and when a settlement for the item received by the bank is or becomes final.

(b) A collecting bank returns an item when it is sent or delivered to the bank's customer or transferor or pursuant to its instructions.

(c) A depositary bank that is also the payor may charge back the amount of an item to its customer's account or obtain refund in accordance with the section governing return of an item received by a payor bank for credit on its books (Section 4—301).

(d) The right to charge back is not affected by:

(1) previous use of a credit given for the item; or

(2) failure by any bank to exercise ordinary care with respect to the item, but a bank so failing remains liable.

(e) A failure to charge back or claim refund does not affect other rights of the bank against the customer or any other party.

(f) If credit is given in dollars as the equivalent of the value of an item payable in foreign money, the dollar amount of any charge-back or refund must be calculated on the basis of the bank-offered spot rate for the foreign money prevailing on the day when the person entitled to the charge-back or refund learns that it will not receive payment in ordinary course.

§ 4—215. Final Payment of Item by Payor Bank; When Provisional Debits and Credits Become Final; When Certain Credits Become Available for Withdrawal

(a) An item is finally paid by a payor bank when the bank has first done any of the following:

(1) paid the item in cash;

(2) settled for the item without having a right to revoke the settlement under statute, clearing-house rule, or agreement; or

(3) made a provisional settlement for the item and failed to revoke the settlement in the time and manner permitted by statute, clearing-house rule, or agreement.

(b) If provisional settlement for an item does not become final, the item is not finally paid.

(c) If provisional settlement for an item between the presenting and payor banks is made through a clearing house or by debits or credits in an accounting between them, then to the extent that provisional debits or credits for the item are entered in accounts between the presenting and payor banks or between the presenting and successive prior collecting banks seriatim, they become final upon final payment of the items by the payor bank.

(d) If a collecting bank receives a settlement for an item which is or becomes final, the bank is accountable to its customer for the amount of the item and any provisional credit given for the item in an account with its customer becomes final.

(e) Subject to (i) applicable law stating a time for availability of funds and (ii) any right of the bank to apply the credit to an obligation of the customer, credit given by a bank for an item in a customer's account becomes available for withdrawal as of right:

(1) if the bank has received a provisional settlement for the item, when the settlement becomes final and the bank has had a reasonable time to receive return of the item and the item has not been received within that time;

(2) if the bank is both the depositary bank and the payor bank, and the item is finally paid, at the opening of the bank's second banking day following receipt of the item.

(f) Subject to applicable law stating a time for availability of funds and any right of a bank to apply a deposit to an obligation of the depositor, a deposit of money becomes available for withdrawal as of right at the opening of the bank's next banking day after receipt of the deposit.

§ 4—302. Payor Bank's Responsibility for Late Return of Item

(a) If an item is presented to and received by a payor bank, the bank is accountable for the amount of:

(1) a demand item, other than a documentary draft, whether properly payable or not, if the bank, in any case in which it is not also the depositary bank, retains the item beyond midnight of the banking day of receipt without settling for it or, whether or not it is also the depositary bank, does not pay or return the item or send notice of dishonor until after its midnight deadline; or

(2) any other properly payable item unless, within the time allowed for acceptance or payment of that item, the bank either accepts or pays the item or return it and accompanying documents.

(b) The liability of a payor bank to pay an item pursuant to subsection (a) is subject to defenses based on breach of a presentment warranty (Section 4—208) or proof that the person seeking enforcement of the liability presented or transferred the item for the purpose of defrauding the payor bank.

§ 4—401. When Bank May Charge Customer's Account

(a) A bank may charge against the account of a customer an item that is properly payable from that account even though the charge creates an overdraft. An item is properly payable if it is authorized by the customer and is in accordance with any agreement between the customer and bank.

(b) A customer is not liable for the amount of an overdraft if the customer neither signed the item nor benefited from the proceeds of the item.

(c) A bank may charge against the account of a customer a check that is otherwise properly payable from the account, even though payment was made before the date of the check, unless the customer has given notice to the bank of the postdating describing the check with reasonable certainty. The notice is effective for the period stated in Section 4—403(b) for stop-payment orders, and must be received at such time and in such manner as to afford the bank a reasonable opportunity to act on it before the bank takes any action with respect to the check described in Section 4—303. If a bank charges against the account of a customer a check before the date stated in the notice of postdating, the bank is liable for damages for the loss resulting from its act. The loss may include damages for dishonor of subsequent items under Section 4—402.

(d) A bank that in good faith makes payment to a holder may charge the indicated account of its customer according to:

(1) the original terms of the altered item; or

(2) the terms of the completed item, even though the bank knows the item has been completed unless the bank has notice that the completion was improper.

§ 4—402. Bank's Liability to Customer for Wrongful Dishonor; Time of Determining Insufficiency of Account

(a) Except as otherwise provided in this Article, a payor bank wrongfully dishonors an item if it dishonors an item that is properly payable, but a bank may dishonor an item that would create an overdraft unless it has agreed to pay the overdraft.

(b) A payor bank is liable to its customer for damages proximately caused by the wrongful dishonor of an item. Liability is limited to actual damages proved and may include damages for an arrest or prosecution of the customer or other consequential damages. Whether any consequential damages are proximately caused by the wrongful dishonor is a question of fact to be determined in each case.

(c) A payor bank's determination of the customer's account balance on which a decision to dishonor for insufficiency of available funds is based may be made at any time between the time the item is received by the payor bank and the time that the payor bank returns the item or gives notice in lieu of return, and no more than one determination need be made. If, at the election of the payor bank, a subsequent balance determination is made for the purpose of reevaluating the bank's decision to dishonor the item, the account balance at that time is determinative of whether a dishonor for insufficiency of available funds is wrongful.

§ 4—403. Customer's Right to Stop Payment; Burden of Proof of Loss

(a) A customer or any person authorized to draw on the account if there is more than one person may stop payment of any item drawn on the customer's account or close the account by an order to the bank describing the item or account with reasonable certainty received at a time and in a manner that affords the bank a reasonable opportunity to act on it before any action by the bank with respect to the item described in Section 4—303. If the signature of more than one person is required to draw on an account, any of these persons may stop payment or close the account.

(b) A stop-payment order is effective for six months, but it lapses after 14 calendar days if the original order was oral and was not confirmed in writing within that period. A stop-payment order may be renewed for additional six-month periods by a writing given to the bank within a period during which the stop-payment order is effective.

(c) The burden of establishing the fact and amount of loss resulting from the payment of an item contrary to a stop-payment order or order to close an account is on the customer. The loss from payment of an item contrary to a stop-payment order may include damages for dishonor of subsequent items under Section 4—402.

§ 4—406. Customer's Duty to Discover and Report Unauthorized Signature or Alteration

(a) A bank that sends or makes available to a customer a statement of account showing payment of items for the account shall either return or make available to the customer the items paid or provide information in the statement of account sufficient to allow the customer reasonably to identify the items paid. The statement of account provides sufficient information if the item is described by item number, amount, and date of payment.

(b) If the items are not returned to the customer, the person retaining the items shall either retain the items or, if the items are destroyed, maintain the capacity to furnish legible copies of the items until the expiration of seven years after receipt of the items. A customer may request an item from the bank that paid the item, and that bank must provide in a reasonable time either the item or, if the item has been destroyed or is not otherwise obtainable, a legible copy of the item.

(c) If a bank sends or makes available a statement of account or items pursuant to subsection (a), the customer must exercise reasonable promptness in examining the statement or the items to determine whether any payment was not authorized because of an alteration of an item or because a purported signature by or on behalf of the customer was not authorized. If, based on the statement or items provided, the customer should reasonably have discovered the unauthorized payment, the customer must promptly notify the bank of the relevant facts.

(d) If the bank proves that the customer failed, with respect to an item, to comply with the duties imposed on the customer by subsection (c), the customer is precluded from asserting against the bank:

(1) the customer's unauthorized signature or any alteration on the item, if the bank also proves that it suffered a loss by reason of the failure; and

(2) the customer's unauthorized signature signature or alteration by the same wrongdoer on any other item paid in good faith by the bank if the payment was made before the bank received notice from the customer of the unauthorized signature or alteration and after the customer had been afforded a reasonable period of time, not exceeding 30 days, in which to examine the item or statement of account and notify the bank.

(e) If subsection (d) applies and the customer proves that the bank failed to exercise ordinary care in paying the item and that the failure substantially contributed to loss, the loss is allocated between the customer precluded and the bank asserting the preclusion according to the extent to which the failure of the customer to comply with subsection

(c) and the failure of the bank to exercise ordinary care contributed to the loss. If the customer proves that the bank did not pay the item in good faith, the preclusion under subsection (d) does not apply.

(f) Without regard to care or lack of care of either the customer or the bank, a customer who does not within one year after the statement or items are made available to the customer (subsection (a)) discover and report the custom-er's unauthorized signature on or any alteration on the item is precluded from asserting against the bank the unauthorized signature or alteration. If there is a preclusion under this subsection, the payor bank may not recover for breach of warranty under Section 4–208 with respect to the unauthorized signature or alteration to which the preclusion applies.

ARTICLE 4A

FUNDS TRANSFERS

Part 1

Subject Matter and Definitions

§ 4A—103.   Payment Order; Definitions

(a) In this Article:

(1) "Payment order" means an instruction of a sender to a receiving bank, transmitted orally, electronically, or in writing, to pay, or to cause another bank to pay, a fixed or determinable amount of money to a beneficiary if:

   (i) the instruction does not state a condition to payment to the beneficiary other than time of payment,

  (ii) the receiving bank is to be reimbursed by debiting an account of, or otherwise receiving payment from, the sender, and

 (iii) the instruction is transmitted by the sender directly to the receiving bank or to an agent, funds-transfer system, or communication system for transmittal to the receiving bank.

(2) "Beneficiary" means the person to be paid by the beneficiary's bank.

(3) "Beneficiary's bank" means the bank identified in a payment order in which an account of the beneficiary is to be credited pursuant to the order or which otherwise is to make payment to the beneficiary if the order does not provide for payment to an account.

(4) "Receiving bank" means the bank to which the sender's instruction is addressed.

(5) "Sender" means the person giving the instruction to the receiving bank.

(b) If an instruction complying with subsection (a)(1) is to make more than one payment to a beneficiary, the instruction is a separate payment order with respect to each payment.

(c) A payment order is issued when it is sent to the receiving bank.

§ 4A—104.   Funds Transfers; Definitions

In this Article:

(a) "Funds transfer" means the series of transactions, beginning with the originator's payment order, made for the purpose of making payment of the beneficiary of the order. The term includes any payment order issued by the originator's bank or an intermediary bank intended to carry out the originator's payment order. A funds transfer is completed by acceptance by the beneficiary's bank of a payment order for the benefit of the beneficiary of the originator's payment order.

(b) "Intermediary bank" means a receiving bank other than the originator's bank or the beneficiary's bank.

(c) "Originator" means the sender of the first payment order in a funds transfer.

(d) "Originator's bank" means (i) the receiving bank to which the payment order of the originator is issued if the originator is not a bank, or (ii) the originator if the originator is a bank.

§ 4A—105.   Other Definitions

(a) In this Article:

(1) "Authorized account" means a deposit account of a customer in a bank designated by the customer as a source of payment of payment orders issued by the customer to the bank. If a customer does not so designate an account, any account of the customer is an authorized account if payment of a payment order from that account is not inconsistent with a restriction on the use of that account.

(2) "Bank" means a person engaged in the business of banking and includes a savings bank, savings and loan association, credit union, and trust company. A branch or separate office of a bank is a separate bank for purposes of this Article.

(3) "Customer" means a person, including a bank, having an account with a bank or from

whom a bank has agreed to receive payment orders.

(4) "Funds-transfer business day" of a receiving bank means the part of a day during which the receiving bank is open for the receipt, processing, and transmittal of payment orders and cancellations and amendments of payment orders.

(5) "Funds-transfer system" means a wire transfer network, automated clearing house, or other communication system of a clearing house or other association of banks through which a payment order by a bank may be transmitted to the bank to which the order is addressed.

(6) "Good faith" means honesty in fact and the observance of reasonable commercial standards of fair dealing.

. . . .

§ 4A—108.   Exclusion of Consumer Transactions Governed by Federal Law

This Article does not apply to a funds transfer any part of which is governed by the Electronic Fund Transfer Act of 1978 (Title XX, Public Law 95–630, 92 Stat. 3728, 15 U.S.C. § 1693 et seq.) as amended from time to time.

Part 2

Issue and Acceptance of Payment Orders

§ 4A—201.   Security Procedure

"Security procedure" means a procedure established by agreement of a customer and a receiving bank for the purpose of (i) verifying that a payment order or communication amending or cancelling a payment order is that of the customer, or (ii) detecting error in the transmission or the content of the payment order or communication. A security procedure may require the use of algorithms or other codes, identifying words or numbers, encryption, callback procedures, or similar security devices. Comparisons of a signature on a payment order or communication with an authorized specimen signature of the customer is not by itself a security procedure.

§ 4A–202.   Authorized and Verified Payment Orders

(a) A payment order received by the receiving bank is the authorized order of the person identified as sender if that person authorized the order or is otherwise bound by it under the law of agency.

(b) If a bank and its customer have agreed that the authenticity of payment orders issued to the bank in the name of the customer as sender will be verified pursuant to a security procedure, a payment order received by the receiving bank is effective as the order of the customer, whether or not authorized, if (i) the security procedure is a commercially reasonable method of providing security against unauthorized payment orders, and (ii) the bank proves that it accepted the payment order in good faith and in compliance with the security procedure and any written agreement or instruction of the customer restricting acceptance of payment orders issued in the name of the customer. The bank is not required to follow an instruction that violates a written agreement with the customer or notice of which is not received at a time and in a manner affording the bank a reasonable opportunity to act on it before the payment order is accepted.

(c) Commercial reasonableness of a security procedure is a question of law to be determined by considering the wishes of the customer expressed to the bank, the circumstances of the customer known to the bank, including the size, type, and frequency of payment orders normally issued by the customer to the bank, alternative security procedures offered to the customer, and security procedures in general use by customers and receiving banks similarly situated. A security procedure is deemed to be commercially reasonable if (i) the security procedure was chosen by the customer after the bank offered, and the customer refused, a security procedure that was commercially reasonable for that customer, and (ii) the customer expressly agreed in writing to be bound by any payment order, whether or not authorized, issued in its name and accepted by the bank in compliance with the security procedure chosen by the customer.

(d) The term "sender" in this Article includes the customer in whose name a payment order is issued if the order is the authorized order of the customer under subsection (a), or it is effective as the order of the customer under subsection (b).

(e) This section applies to amendments and cancellations of payment orders to the same extent it applies to payment orders.

(f) Except as provided in this section and in Section 4A—203(a)(1), rights and obligations arising under this section or Section 4A—203 may not be varied by agreement.

§ 4A—204.   Refund of Payment and Duty of Customer to Report With Respect to Unauthorized Payment Orders

(a) If a receiving bank accepts a payment order issued in the name of its customer as sender which is (i) not authorized and most effective as the order of the customer under Section 4A—202, or (ii) not enforceable, in whole or in part, against the customer under Section 4A—203, the bank shall refund any payment of the payment order received from the customer to the extent the bank is not entitled to enforce payment and shall pay interest on the refundable amount calculated from the date the bank received payment to the date of the refund. However, the customer is not entitled to interest from the bank on the amount to be refunded if the customer fails to exercise ordinary care to determine that the order was not authorized by the customer and to notify the bank of the relevant facts within a reasonable time not exceeding 90 days after the date the customer received notification from the bank that the order was accepted or that the customer's account was debited with respect to the order. The bank is not entitled to any recovery from the customer on account of a failure by the customer to give notification as stated in this section.

(b) Reasonable time under subsection (a) may be fixed by agreement as stated in Section 1—204(1), but the obligation of a receiving bank to refund payment as stated in subsection (a) may not otherwise be varied by agreement.

§ 4A—205.   Erroneous Payment Orders

(a) If an accepted payment order was transmitted pursuant to a security procedure for the detection of error and the payment order (i) erroneously instructed payment to a beneficiary not intended by the sender, (ii) erroneously instructed payment in an amount greater than the amount intended by the sender, or (iii) was an erroneously transmitted duplicate of a payment order previously sent by the sender, the following rules apply:

> (1) If the sender proves that the sender or a person acting on behalf of the sender pursuant to Section 4A—206 complied with the security procedure and that the error would have been detected if the receiving bank had also complied, the sender is not obliged to pay the order to the extent stated in paragraphs (2) and (3).
>
> (2) If the funds transfer is completed on the basis of an erroneous payment order described in clause (i) or (iii) of subsection (a), the sender is not obliged to pay the order and the receiving bank is entitled to recover from the beneficiary any amount paid to the beneficiary to the extent allowed by the law governing mistake and restitution.
>
> (3) If the funds transfer is completed on the basis of a payment order described in clause (ii) if subsection (a), the sender is not obliged to pay the order to the extent the amount received by the beneficiary is greater than the amount intended by the sender. In that case, the receiving bank is entitled to recover from the beneficiary the excess amount received to the extent allowed by the law governing mistake and restitution.

(b) If (i) the sender of an erroneous payment order described in subsection (a) is not obliged to pay all or part of the order, and (ii) the sender receives notification from the receiving bank that the order was accepted by the bank or that the sender's account was debited with respect to the order, the sender has a duty to exercise ordinary care, on the basis of information available to the sender, to discover the error with respect to the order and to advise the bank of the relevant facts within a reasonable time, not exceeding 90 days, after the bank's notification was received by the sender. If the bank proves that the sender failed to perform that duty, the sender is liable to the bank for the loss the bank proves it incurred as a result of the failure, but the liability of the sender may not exceed the amount of the sender's order.

(c) This section applies to amendments to payment orders to the same extent it applies to payment orders.

§ 4A—206.   Transmission of Payment Order Through Funds-Transfer or Other Communication System

(a) If a payment order addressed to a receiving bank is transmitted to a funds-transfer system or other third-party communication system for transmittal to the bank, the system is deemed to be an agent of the sender for the purpose of transmitting the payment order to the bank. If there is a discrepancy between the terms of the payment order transmitted to the system and the terms of the payment order transmitted by the system to the bank, the terms of the payment order transmitted by the system to the bank, the terms of the payment order of the sender are those transmitted by the system. This section does not apply to a funds-transfer system of the Federal Reserve Banks.

(b) This section applies to cancellations and amendments of payment orders to the same extent it applies to payment orders.

§ 4A—209.   Acceptance of Payment Order

(a) Subject to subsection (d), a receiving bank other than the beneficiary's bank accepts a payment order when it executes the order.

(b) Subject to subsections (c) and (d), a beneficiary's bank accepts a payment order at the earliest of the following times:

> (1) when the bank (i) pays the beneficiary as stated in Section 4A—405(a) or 4A—405(b), or (ii) notifies the beneficiary of receipt of the order or that the account of the beneficiary has been credited with respect to the order unless the notice indicates that the bank is rejecting the order or that funds with respect to the order or that funds with respect to the order may not be withdrawn or used until receipt of payment from the sender of the order;
>
> (2) when the bank receives payment of the entire amount of the sender's order pursuant to Section 4A—403(a)(1) or 4A—403(a)(2); or
>
> (3) the opening of the next funds-transfer business day of the bank following the payment date of the order if, at that time, the amount of the sender's order is fully covered by a withdrawable credit balance in an authorized account of the sender or the bank has otherwise received full payment from the sender, unless the order was rejected before that time or is rejected within (i) one hour after that time, or (ii) one hour after the opening of the next business day of the sender following the payment date if that time is later.

If notice of rejection is received by the sender after the payment date and the authorized account of the sender does not bear interest, the bank is obliged to pay interest to the sender on the amount of the order for the number of days elapsing after the payment date to the day the sender receives notice or learns that the order was not accepted, counting that day as an elapsed day. If the withdrawable credit balance during that period falls below the amount of the order, the amount of interest payable is reduced accordingly.

(c) Acceptance of a payment order cannot occur before the order is received by the receiving bank. Acceptance does not occur under subsection (b)(2) or (b)(3) if the beneficiary of the payment order does not have an account with the receiving bank, the account has been closed, or the receiving bank is not permitted by law to receive credits for the beneficiary's account.

(d) A payment order issued to the originator's bank cannot be accepted until the payment date if the bank is the beneficiary's bank, or the execution date if the bank is not the beneficiary's bank. If the originator's bank executes the originator's payment order before the execution date or pays the beneficiary of the originator's payment order before the payment date and the payment order is subsequently canceled pursuant to Section 4A—211(b), the bank may recover from the beneficiary any payment received to the extent allowed by the law governing mistake and restitution.

Part 3

Execution of Sender's Payment Order by Receiving Bank

§ 4A—301.   Execution and Execution Date

(a) A payment order is "executed" by the receiving bank when it issues a payment order intended to carry out the payment order received by the bank. A payment order received by the beneficiary's bank can be accepted but cannot be executed.

(b) "Execution date" of a payment order means the day on which the receiving bank may properly issue a payment order in execution of the sender's order. The execution date may be determined by instruction of the sender but cannot be earlier than the day the order is received and, unless otherwise determined, is the day the order is received. If the sender's instruction states a payment date, the execution date is the payment date or an earlier date on which execution is reasonably necessary to allow payment to the beneficiary on the payment date.

§ 4A—302.   Obligations of Receiving Bank in Execution of Payment Orders

(a) Except as provided in subsections (b) through (d), if the receiving bank accepts a payment order pursuant to

Section 4A—209(a), the bank has the following obligations in executing the order:

(1) The receiving bank is obliged to issue, on the execution date, a payment order complying with the sender's order and to follow the sender's instructions concerning (i) any intermediary bank or funds-transfer system to be used in carrying out the funds transfer, or (ii) the means by which payment orders are to be transmitted in the funds transfer. If the originator's bank issues a payment order to an intermediary bank, the originator's bank is obliged to instruct the intermediary bank according to the instruction of the originator. An intermediary bank in the funds transfer is similarly bound by an instruction given to it by the sender of the payment order it accepts.

(2) If the sender's instruction states that the funds transfer is to be carried out telephonically or by wire transfer or otherwise indicates that the funds transfer is to be carried out by the most expeditious means, the receiving bank is obliged to transmit its payment order by the most expeditious available means, and to instruct any intermediary bank accordingly. If a sender's instruction states a payment date, the receiving bank is obliged to transmit its payment order at a time and by means reasonably necessary to allow payment to the beneficiary on the payment date or as soon thereafter as is feasible.

(b) Unless otherwise instructed, a receiving bank executing a payment order may (i) use any funds-transfer system if use of that system is reasonable in the circumstances, and (ii) issue a payment order to the beneficiary's bank or to an intermediary bank through which a payment order conforming to the sender's order can expeditiously be issued to the beneficiary's bank if the receiving bank exercises ordinary care in the selection of the intermediary bank. A receiving bank is not required to follow an instruction of the sender designating a funds-transfer system to be used in carrying out the funds transfer if the receiving bank, in good faith, determines that it is not feasible to follow the instruction or that following the instruction would unduly delay completion of the funds transfer.

(c) Unless subsection (a)(2) applies or the receiving bank is otherwise instructed, the bank may execute a payment order by transmitting its payment order by first class mail or by any means reasonable in the circumstances. If the receiving bank is instructed to execute the sender's order by transmitting its payment order by a particular means, the receiving bank may issue its payment order by the means stated or by any means as expeditious as the means stated.

(d) Unless instructed by the sender, (i) the receiving bank may not obtain payment of its charges for services and expenses in connection with the execution of the sender's order by issuing a payment order in an amount equal to the amount of the sender's order less the amount of the charges, and (ii) may not instruct a subsequent receiving bank to obtain payment of its charges in the same manner.

§ 4A—303. Erroneous Execution of Payment Order

(a) A receiving bank that (i) executes the payment order of the sender by issuing a payment order in an amount greater than the amount of the sender's order, or (ii) issues a payment order in execution of the sender's order and then issues a duplicate order, is entitled to payment of the amount of the sender's order under Section 4A—402(c) if that subsection is otherwise satisfied. The bank is entitled to recover from the beneficiary of the erroneous order the excess payment received to the extent allowed by the law governing mistake and restitution.

(b) A receiving bank that executes the payment order of the sender by issuing a payment order in an amount less than the amount of the sender's order is entitled to payment of the amount of the sender's order under Section 4A—402(c) if (i) that subsection is otherwise satisfied and (ii) the bank corrects its mistake by issuing an additional payment order for the benefit of the beneficiary of the sender's order. If the error is not corrected, the issuer of the erroneous order is entitled to receive or retain payment from the sender of the order it accepted only to the extent of the amount of the erroneous order. This subsection does not apply if the receiving bank executes the sender's payment order by issuing a payment order in an amount less than the amount of the sender's order for the purpose of obtaining payment of its charges for services and expenses pursuant to instruction of the sender.

(c) If a receiving bank executes the payment order of the sender by issuing a payment order to a beneficiary different from the beneficiary of the sender's order and the funds transfer is completed on the basis of that error, the sender of the payment order that was erroneously executed and all previous senders in the funds transfer are not obliged to pay the payment orders they issued. The issuer of the erroneous order is entitled to recover from the beneficiary of the order the payment received to the extent allowed by the law governing mistake and restitution.

§ 4A—305. Liability for Late or Improper Execution or Failure to Execute Payment Order

(a) If a funds transfer is completed but execution of a payment order by the receiving bank in breach of Section 4A—302 results in delay in payment to the beneficiary, the bank is obliged to pay interest to either the originator or the beneficiary of the funds transfer for the period of delay caused by the improper execution. Except as provided in subsection (c), additional damages are not recoverable.

(b) If execution of a payment order by a receiving bank in breach of Section 4A—302 results in (i) noncompletion of the funds transfer, (ii) failure to use an intermediary bank designated by the originator, or (iii) issuance of a payment order that does not comply with the terms of the payment order of the originator, the bank is liable to the origi-

nator for its expenses in the funds transfer and for incidental expenses and interest losses, to the extent not covered by subsection (a), resulting from the improper execution. Except as provided in subsection (c), additional damages are not recoverable.

(c) In addition to the amounts payable under subsections (a) and (b), damages, including consequential damages, are recoverable to the extent provided in an express written agreement of the receiving bank.

(d) If a receiving bank fails to execute a payment order it was obliged by express agreement to execute, the receiving bank is liable to the sender for its expenses in the transaction and for incidental expenses and interest losses resulting from the failure to execute. Additional damages, including consequential damages, are recoverable to the extent provided in an express written agreement of the receiving bank, but are not otherwise recoverable.

(e) Reasonable attorney's fees are recoverable if demand for compensation under subsection (a) or (b) is made and reused before an action is brought on the claim. If a claim is made for breach of an agreement under subsection (d) and the agreement does not provide for damages, reasonable attorney's fees are recoverable if demand for compensation under subsection (d) is made and refused before an action is brought on the claim.

(f) Except as stated in this section, the liability of a receiving bank under subsections (a) and (b) may not be varied by agreement.

Part 4

Payment

§ 4A—401. Payment Date

"Payment date" of a payment order means the day on which the amount of the order is payable to the beneficiary by the beneficiary's bank. The payment date may be determined by instruction of the sender but cannot be earlier than the day the order is received by the beneficiary's bank and, unless otherwise determined, is the day the order is received by the beneficiary's bank.

§ 4A—405. Payment by Beneficiary's Bank to Beneficiary

(a) If the beneficiary's bank credits an account of the beneficiary of a payment order, payment of the bank's obligation under Section 4A—404(a) occurs when and to the extent (i) the beneficiary is notified of the right to withdraw the credit, (ii) the bank lawfully applies the credit to a debt of the beneficiary, or (iii) funds with respect to the order are otherwise made available to the beneficiary by the bank.

(b) If the beneficiary's bank does not credit an account of the beneficiary of a payment order, the time when payment of the bank's obligation under Section 4A—404(a) occurs is governed by principles of law that determine when an obligation is satisfied.

(c) Except as stated in subsections (d) and (e), if the beneficiary's bank pays the beneficiary of a payment order under a condition to payment or agreement of the beneficiary giving the bank the right to recover payment from the beneficiary if the bank does not receive payment of the order, the condition to payment or agreement is not enforceable.

(d) A funds-transfer system rule may provide that payments made to beneficiaries of funds transfers made through the system are provisional until receipt of payment by the beneficiary's bank of the payment order it accepted. A beneficiary's bank that makes a payment that is provisional under the rule is entitled to refund from the beneficiary if (i) the rule requires that both the beneficiary and the originator be given notice of the provisional nature of the payment before the funds transfer is initiated, (ii) the beneficiary, the beneficiary's bank and the originator's bank agreed to be bound by the rule, and (iii) the beneficiary's bank did not receive payment of the payment order that it accepted. If the beneficiary is obliged to refund payment to the beneficiary's bank, acceptance of the payment order by the beneficiary's bank is nullified and no payment by the originator of the funds transfer to the beneficiary occurs under Section 4A—406.

. . .

§ 4A—406.   Payment by Originator to Beneficiary; Discharge of Underlying Obligation

(a) Subject to Sections 4A—211(e), 4A—405(d), and 4A—405(e), the originator of a funds transfer pays the beneficiary of the originator's payment order (i) at the time a payment order for the benefit of the beneficiary is accepted by the beneficiary's bank in the funds transfer and (ii) in an amount equal to the amount of the order accepted by the beneficiary's bank, but not more than the amount of the originator's order.

(b) If payment under subsection (a) is made to satisfy an obligation, the obligation is discharged to the same extent discharge would result from payment to the beneficiary of the same amount in money, unless (i) the payment under subsection (a) was made by a means prohibited by the contract of the beneficiary with respect to the obligation, (ii) the beneficiary, within a reasonable time after receiving notice of receipt of the order by the beneficiary's bank, notified the originator of the beneficiary's refusal of the payment, (iii) funds with respect to the order were not withdrawn by the beneficiary or applied to a debt of the beneficiary, and (iv) the beneficiary would suffer a loss that could reasonably have been avoided if payment had been made by a means complying with the contract. If payment by the originator does not result in discharge under this section, the originator is subrogated to the rights of the beneficiary to receive payment from the beneficiary's bank under Section 4A—404(a).

(c) For the purpose of determining whether discharge of an obligation occurs under subsection (b), if the beneficiary's bank accepts a payment order in an amount equal to the amount of the originator's payment order less charges of one or more receiving banks in the funds transfer, payment to the beneficiary is deemed to be in the amount of the originator's order unless upon demand by the beneficiary the originator does not pay the beneficiary the amount of the deducted charges.

(d) Rights of the originator or of the beneficiary of a funds transfer under this section may be varied only by agreement of the originator and the beneficiary.

Part 5
Miscellaneous Provisions

§ 4A—501.   Variation by Agreement and Effect of Funds-Transfer System Rule

(a) Except as otherwise provided in this Article, the rights and obligations of a party to a funds transfer may be varied by agreement of the affected party.

(b) "Funds-transfer system rule" means a rule of an association of banks (i) governing transmission of payment orders by means of a funds-transfer system of the association or rights and obligations with respect to those orders, or (ii) to the extent the rule governs rights and obligations between banks that are parties to a funds transfer in which a Federal Reserve Bank, acting as an intermediary bank, sends a payment order to the beneficiary's bank. Except as otherwise provided in this Article, a funds-transfer system rule governing rights and obligations between participating banks using the system may be effective even if the rule conflicts with this Article and indirectly affects another party to the funds transfer who does not consent to the rule. A funds-transfer system rule may also govern rights and obligations of parties other than participating banks using the system to the extent stated in Sections 4A—404(c), 4A—405(d), and 4A—507(c).

§ 4A—503.   Injunction or Restraining Order With Respect to Funds Transfer

For proper cause and in compliance with applicable law, a court may restrain (i) a person from issuing a payment order to initiate a funds transfer, (ii) an originator's bank from executing the payment order of the originator, or (iii) the beneficiary's bank from releasing funds to the beneficiary or the beneficiary from withdrawing the funds. A court may not otherwise restrain a person from issuing a payment order, paying or receiving payment of a payment order, or otherwise acting with respect to a funds transfer.

§ 4A—505.   Preclusion of Objection to Debit of Customer's Account

If a receiving bank has received payment from its customer with respect to a payment order issued in the name of the customer as sender and accepted by the bank, and the customer received notification reasonably identifying the order, the customer is precluded from asserting that the bank is not entitled to retain the payment unless the customer notifies the bank of the customer's objection to the payment within one year after the notification was received by the customer.

ARTICLE 5

LETTERS OF CREDIT

§ 5—102. Scope

(1) This Article applies

   (a) to a credit issued by a bank, if the credit requires a documentary draft or a documentary demand for payment; and

   (b) to a credit issued by a person other than a bank, if the credit requires that the draft or demand for payment be accompanied by a document of title; and

   (c) to a credit issued by a bank or other person, if the credit is not within subparagraphs (a) or (b) but conspicuously states that it is a letter of credit or is conspicuously so entitled.

(2) Unless the engagement meets the requirements of subsection (1), this Article does not apply to engagements to make advances or to honor drafts or demands for payment, to authorities to pay or purchase to guarantees or to general agreements.

(3) This Article deals with some but not all of the rules and concepts of letters of credit as such rules or concepts have developed prior to this act or may hereafter develop. The fact that this Article states a rule does not by itself require, imply or negate application of the same or a converse rule to a situation not provided for or to a person not specified by this Article.

§ 5—103. Definitions

(1) In this Article unless the context otherwise requires

   (a) "Credit" or "letter of credit" means an engagement by a bank or other person, made at the request of a customer and of a kind within the scope of this Article (Section 5—102), that the issuer will honor drafts or other demands for payment upon compliance with the conditions specified in the credit. A credit may be either revocable or irrevocable. The engagement may be either an agreement to honor or a statement that the bank or other person is authorized to honor.

   (b) A "documentary draft" or a "documentary demand for payment" is one honor of which is conditioned upon the presentation of a document or documents. "Document" means any paper including document of title, security, invoice, certificate, notice of default and the like.

   (c) An "issuer" is a bank or other person issuing a credit.

   (d) A "beneficiary" of a credit is a person who is entitled under its terms to draw or demand payment.

   (e) An "advising bank" is a bank which gives notification of the issuance of a credit by another bank.

   (f) A "confirming bank" is a bank which engages either that it will itself honor a credit already issued by another bank or that such a credit will be honored by the issuer or a third bank.

   (g) A "customer" is a buyer or other person who causes an issuer to issue a credit. The term also includes a bank which procures issuance or confirmation on behalf of that bank's customer.

. . .

§ 5—104. Formal Requirements; Signing

(1) Except as otherwise required in subsection (1)(c) of Section 5—102 on scope, no particular form of phrasing is required for a credit. A credit must be in writing and signed by the issuer, and a confirmation must be in writing and signed by the confirming bank. A modification of the terms of a credit or confirmation must be signed by the issuer or confirming bank.

(2) A telegram may be a sufficient signed writing if it identifies its sender by an authorized authentication. The authentication may be in code and the authorized naming of the issuer in an advice of credit is a sufficient signing.

§ 5—105. Consideration

No consideration is necessary to establish a credit or to enlarge or otherwise modify its terms.

§ 5—106. Time and Effect of Establishment of Credit

(1) Unless otherwise agreed, a credit is established

   (a) as regards the customer, as soon as a letter of credit is sent to him or the letter of credit or an authorized written advice of its issuance is sent to the beneficiary; and

   (b) as regards the beneficiary, when he receives a letter of credit or an authorized written advice of its issuance.

(2) Unless otherwise agreed, once an irrevocable credit is established as regards the customer, it can be modified or revoked only with the consent of the customer; and once it is established as regards the beneficiary, it can be modified or revoked only with his consent.

(3) Unless otherwise agreed after a revocable credit is established, it may be modified or revoked by the issuer without notice to or consent from the customer or beneficiary.

(4) Notwithstanding any modification or revocation of a revocable credit, any person authorized to honor or negotiate under the terms of the original credit is entitled to reimbursement for or honor of any draft or demand for payment duly honored or negotiated before receipt of notice of the modification or revocation and the issuer in turn is entitled to reimbursement from its customer.

§ 5—109.   Issuer's Obligation to Its Customer

(1) An issuer's obligation to its customer includes good faith and observance of any general banking usage but, unless otherwise agreed, does not include liability or responsibility

    (a) for performance of the underlying contract for sale or other transaction between the customer and the beneficiary; or

    (b) for any act or omission of any person other than itself or its own branch or for loss or destruction of a draft, demand or document in transit or in the possession of others; or

    (c) based on knowledge or lack of knowledge of any usage of any particular trade.

(2) An issuer must examine documents with care so as to ascertain that on their face they appear to comply with the terms of the credit but, unless otherwise agreed, assumes no liability or responsibility for the genuineness, falsification or effect of any document which appears on such examination to be regular on its face.

(3) A nonbank issuer is not bound by any banking usage of which it has no knowledge.

§ 5—114.   Issuer's Duty and Privilege to Honor; Right to Reimbursement

(1) An issuer must honor a draft or demand for payment which complies with the terms of the relevant credit regardless of whether the goods or documents conform to the underlying contract for sale or other contract between the customer and the beneficiary. The issuer is not excused from honor of such a draft or demand by reason of an additional general term that all documents must be satisfactory to the issuer, but an issuer may require that specified documents must be satisfactory to it.

(2) Unless otherwise agreed, when documents appear on their face to comply with the terms of a credit but a required document does not in fact conform to the warranties made on negotiation or transfer of a document of title (Section 7—507) or of a certificated security (Section 8—306) or is forged or fraudulent or there is fraud in the transaction

    (a) the issuer must honor the draft or demand for payment, if honor is demanded by a negotiating bank or other holder of the draft or demand which has taken the draft or demand under the credit and under circumstances which would make it a holder in due course (Section 3—302) and in an appropriate case would make it a person to whom a document of title has been duly negotiated (Section 7—502) or a bona fide purchaser of a certificated security (Section 8—302); and

    (b) in all other cases, as against its customer, an issuer acting in good faith may honor the draft or demand for payment despite notification from the customer of fraud, forgery or other defect not apparent on the face of the documents but a court of appropriate jurisdiction may enjoin such honor.

(3) Unless otherwise agreed, an issuer which has duly honored a draft or demand for payment is entitled to immediate reimbursement of any payment made under the credit and to be put in effectively available funds not later than the day before maturity of any acceptance made under the credit.

. . .

ARTICLE 6

BULK TRANSFERS

§ 6—101.   Short Title

This Article shall be known and may be cited as Uniform Commercial Code—Bulk Transfers.

§ 6—102.   "Bulk Transfers"; Transfers of Equipment; Enterprises Subject to This Article; Bulk Transfers Subject to This Article

(1) A "bulk transfer" is any transfer in bulk and not in the ordinary course of the transferor's business of a major part of the materials, supplies, merchandise or other inventory (Section 9—109) of an enterprise subject to this Article.

(2) A transfer of a substantial part of the equipment (Section 9—109) of such an enterprise is a bulk transfer if it is made in connection with a bulk transfer of inventory, but not otherwise.

(3) The enterprises subject to this Article are all those whose principal business is the sale of merchandise from stock, including those who manufacture what they sell.

(4) Except as limited by the following section, all bulk transfers of goods located within this state are subject to this Article.

§ 6—104.   Schedule of Property, List of Creditors

(1) Except as provided with respect to auction sales (Section 6—108), a bulk transfer subject to this Article is ineffective against any creditor of the transferor unless:

    (a) The transferee requires the transferor to furnish a list of his existing creditors prepared as stated in this section; and

    (b) The parties prepare a schedule of the property transferred sufficient to identify it; and

    (c) The transferee preserves the list and schedule for six months next following the transfer and permits inspection of either or both and copying therefrom at all reasonable hours by any creditor of the transferor, or files the list and schedule in (a public office to be here identified).

(2) The list of creditors must be signed and sworn to or affirmed by the transferor or his agent. It must contain the names and business addresses of all creditors of the transferor, with the amounts when known, and also the names of all persons who are known to the tr ansferor to assert claims against him even though such claims are disputed. If the transferor is the obligor of an outstanding issue of bonds, debentures or the like as to which there is an indenture trustee, the list of creditors need include only the name and address of the indenture trustee and the aggregate out standing principal amount of the issue.

(3) Responsibility for the completeness and accuracy of the list of creditors rests on the transferor, and the transfer is not rendered ineffective by errors or omissions therein unless the transferee is shown to have had knowledge.

§ 6—105.   Notice to Creditors

In addition to the requirements of the preceding section, any bulk transfer subject to this Article, except one made by auction sale (Section 6—108), is ineffective against any creditor of the transferor unless at least ten days before he takes possession of the goods or pays for them, whichever happens first, the transferee gives notice of the transfer in the manner and to the persons hereafter provided (Section 6—107).

§ 6—107.   The Notice

(1) The notice to creditors (Section 6—105) shall state:

    (a) that a bulk transfer is about to be made; and

    (b) the names and business addresses of the transferor and transferee, and all other business names and addresses used by the transferor within three years last past so far as known to the transferee; and

    (c) whether or not all the debts of the transferor are to be paid in full as they fall due as a result of the transaction, and if so, the address to which creditors should send their bills.

(2) If the debts of the transferor are not to be paid in full as they fall due or if the transferee is in doubt on that point, then the notice shall state further:

    (a) the location and general description of the property to be transferred and the estimated total of the transferor's debts;

    (b) the address where the schedule of property and list of creditors (Section 6—104) may be inspected;

    (c) whether the transfer is to pay existing debts and if so, the amount of such debts and to whom owing;

    (d) whether the transfer is for new consideration and if so, the amount of such consideration and the time and place of payment; [and]

    [(e) if for new consideration, the time and place where creditors of the transferor are to file their claims.]

(3) The notice in any case shall be delivered personally or sent by registered or certified mail to all the persons shown on the list of creditors furnished by the transferor (Section 6—104) and to all other persons who are known to the transferee to hold or assert claims against the transferor.

Note: *The words in brackets are optional.*

§ 6—110.   Subsequent Transfers

When the title of a transferee to property is subject to a defect by reason of his noncompliance with the requirements of this Article, then:

(1) a purchaser of any of such property from such transferee who pays no value or who takes with notice of such noncompliance takes subject to such defect, but

(2) a purchaser for value in good faith and without such notice takes free of such defect.

§ 6—111.   Limitation of Actions and Levies

No action under this Article shall be brought nor levy made more than six months after the date on which the transferee took possession of the goods unless the transfer has been concealed. If the transfer has been concealed, actions may be brought or levies made within six months after its discovery.

ARTICLE 6

BULK SALES [REVISION]

Alternative B

§ 6—102.   Definitions and Index of Definitions [Alternative B 1989]

(1) In this Article, unless the context otherwise requires:

    (a) "Assets" means the inventory that is the subject of a bulk sale and any tangible and intan-

gible personal property used or held for use primarily in, or arising from, the seller's business and sold in connection with that inventory, but the term does not include:

    (i) fixtures (Section 9—313(1)(a)) other than readily removable factory and office machines;

    (ii) the lessee's interest in a lease of real property; or

(iii) property to the extent it is generally exempt from creditor process under non-bankruptcy law.

...

(c) "Bulk sale" means:

(i) in the case of a sale by auction or a sale or series of sales conducted by a liquidator on the seller's behalf, a sale or series of sales not in the ordinary course of the seller's business of more than half of the seller's inventory, as measured by value on the date of the bulk-sale agreement, if on that date the auctioneer or liquidator has notice, or after reasonable inquiry would have had notice, that the seller will not continue to operate the same or a similar kind of business after the sale or series of sales; and

(ii) in all other cases, a sale not in the ordinary course of the seller's business of more than half the seller's inventory, as measured by value on the date of the bulk-sale agreement, if on that date the buyer has notice, or after reasonable inquiry would have had notice, that the seller will not continue to operate the same or a similar kind of business after the sale.

(d) Claim means a right to payment from the seller, whether or not the right is reduced to judgment, liquidated, fixed, matured, disputed, secured, legal, or equitable. The term includes costs of collection and attorney's fees only to the extent that the laws of this state permit the holder of the claim to recover them in an action against the obligor.

...

§ 6—103.   Applicability of Article [Alternative B 1989]

(1) Except as otherwise provided in subsection (3), this Article applies to a bulk sale if:

(a) the seller's principal business is the sale of inventory from stock; and

(b) on the date of the bulk-sale agreement the seller is located in this state or, if the seller is located in a jurisdiction that is not a part of the United States, the seller's major executive office in the United States is in this state.

(2) A seller is deemed to be located at his [or her] place of business. If a seller has more than one place of business, the seller is deemed located at his [or her] chief executive office.

(3) This Article does not apply to:

(a) a transfer made to secure payment or performance of an obligation;

(b) a transfer of collateral to a secured party pursuant to Section 9—503;

(c) a sale of collateral pursuant to Section 9—504;

(d) retention of collateral pursuant to Section 9—505;

(e) a sale of an asset encumbered by a security interest or item if (i) all the proceeds of the sale are applied in partial or total satisfaction of the debt secured by the security interest or lien or (ii) the security interest or lien is enforceable against the asset after it has been sold to the buyer and the net contract price is zero;

(f) a general assignment for the benefit of creditors or to a subsequent transfer by the assignee;

(g) a sale by an executor, administrator, receiver, trustee in bankruptcy, or any public officer under judicial process;

(h) a sale made in the course of judicial or administrative proceedings for the dissolution or reorganization of an organization;

(i) a sale to a buyer whose principal place of business is in the United States and who:

(i) not earlier than 21 days before the date of the bulk sale, (A) obtains from the seller a verified and dated list of claimants of whom the seller has notice three days before the seller sends or delivers the list to the buyer or (B) conducts a reasonable inquiry to discover the claimants;

(ii) assumes in full the debts owed to claimants of whom the buyer has knowledge on the date the buyer receives the list of claimants from the seller or on the date the buyer completes the reasonable inquiry, as the case may be:

(iii) is not insolvent after the assumption; and

(iv) gives written notice of the assumption not later than 30 days after the date of the bulk sale by sending or delivering a notice to the claimants identified in subparagraph (ii) or by filing a notice in the office of the [Secretary of State]:

(j) a sale to a buyer whose principal place of business is in the United States and who:

(i) assumes in full the debts that were incurred in the seller's business before the date of the bulk sale;

(ii) is not insolvent after the assumption; and

(iii) gives written notice of the assumption not later than 30 days after the date of the bulk sale by sending or delivering a notice to each creditor whose debt is assumed or by filing a notice in the office of the [Secretary of State];

(k) a sale to a new organization that is organized to take over and continue the business of the seller and that has its principal place of business in the United States if:

(i) the buyer assumes in full the debts that were incurred in the seller's business before the date of the bulk sale;

(ii) the seller receives nothing from the sale except an interest in the new organization that is subordinate to the claims against the organization arising from the assumption; and

(iii) the buyer gives written notice of the assumption not later than 30 days after the date of the bulk sale by sending or delivering a notice to each creditor whose debt is assumed or by filing a notice in the office of the [Secretary of State];

(l) a sale of assets having:

(i) a value, net of liens and security interests, of less than $10,000. If a debt is secured by assets and other property of the seller, the net value of the assets is determined by subtracting from their value an amount equal to the product of the debt multiplied by a fraction, the numerator of which is the value of the assets on the date of the bulk sale and the denominator of which is the value of all property securing the debt on the date of the bulk sale; or

(ii) a value of more than $25,000,000 on the date of the bulk-sale agreement; or

(m) a sale required by, and made pursuant to statute.

. . .

§ 6—104.   Obligations of Buyer [Alternative B 1989]

(1) In a bulk sale as defined in Section 6—102(1)(c)(ii) the buyer shall:

(a) obtain from the seller a list of all business names and addresses used by the seller within three years before the date the list is sent or delivered to the buyer;

(b) unless excused under subsection (2), obtain from the seller a verified and dated list of claimants of whom the seller has notice three days before the seller sends or delivers the list to the buyer and including, to the extent known by the seller, the address of and the amount claimed by each claimant;

(c) obtain from the seller or prepare a schedule of distribution (Section 6—106(1));

(d) give notice of the bulk sale in accordance with Section 6—105;

(e) unless excused under Section 6—106(4), distribute the net contract price in accordance with the undertakings of the buyer in the schedule of distribution; and

(f) unless excused under subsection (2), make

available the list of claimants (subsection (1)(b)) by:

(i) promptly sending or delivering a copy of the list without charge to any claimant whose written request is received by the buyer no later than six months after the date of the bulk sale;

(ii) permitting any claimant to inspect and copy the list at any reasonable hour upon request received by the buyer no later than six months after the date of the bulk sale; or

(iii) filing a copy of the list in the office of the [Secretary of State] no later than the time for giving a notice of the bulk sale (Section 6—105(5)). A list filed in accordance with this subparagraph must state the individual, partnership, or corporate name and a mailing address of the seller.

. . .

§ 6—105.   Notice to Claimants [Alternative B 1989]

(1) Except as otherwise provided in subsection (2), to comply with Section 6—104(1)(d) the buyer shall send or deliver a written notice of the bulk sale to each claimant on the list of claimants (Section 6—104(1)(b)) and to any other claimant of whom the buyer has knowledge at the time the notice of the bulk sale is sent or delivered.

(2) A buyer may comply with Section 6—104(1)(d) by filing a written notice of the bulk sale in the office of the [Secretary of State] if:

(a) on the date of the bulk-sale agreement the seller has 200 or more claimants, exclusive of claimants holding secured or matured claims for employment compensation and benefits, including commissions and vacation, severance, and sick-leave pay; or

(b) the buyer has received a verified statement from the seller stating that, as of the date of the bulk-sale agreement, the number of claimants, exclusive of claimants holding secured or matured claims for employment compensation and benefits, including commissions and vacation, severance, and sick-leave pay, is 200 or more.

(3) The written notice of the bulk sale must be accompanied by a copy of the schedule of distribution (Section 6—106(1)) and state at least:

(a) that the seller and buyer have entered into an agreement for a sale that may constitute a bulk sale under the laws of the State of _____;

(b) the date of the agreement;

(c) the date on or after which more than ten percent of the assets were or will be transferred;

(d) the date on or after which more than ten percent of the net contract price was or will be paid, if the date is not stated in the schedule of distribution;

(e) the name and a mailing address of the seller;

(f) any other business name and address listed by the seller pursuant to Section 6—104(1)(a);

(g) the name of the buyer and an address of the buyer from which information concerning the sale can be obtained;

(h) a statement indicating the type of assets or describing the assets item by item;

(i) the manner in which the buyer will make available the list of claimants (Section 6—104(1)(f)), if applicable; and

(j) if the sale is in total or partial satisfaction of an antecedent debt owed by the seller; the amount of the debt to be satisfied and the name of the person to whom it is owed.

(4) For purposes of subsections (3)(e) and (3)(g), the name of a person is the person's individual, partnership, or corporate name.

(5) The buyer shall give notice of the bulk sale not less than 45 days before the date of the bulk sale and, if the buyer gives notice in accordance with subsection (l), not more than 30 days after obtaining the list of claimants.

(6) A written notice substantially complying with the requirements of subsection (3) is effective even though it contains minor errors that are not seriously misleading.

. . .

§ 6—106.   Schedule of Distribution [Alternative B 1989]

(1) The seller and buyer shall agree on how the net contract price is to be distributed and set forth their agreement in a written schedule of distribution.

(2) The schedule of distribution may provide for distribution to any person at any time, including distribution of the entire net contract price to the seller.

(3) The buyer's undertakings in the schedule of distribution run only to the seller. However, a buyer who fails to distribute the net contract price in accordance with the buyer's undertakings in the schedule of distribution is liable to a creditor only as provided in Section 6—107(1).

. . .

§ 6—107.   Liability for Noncompliance [Alternative B 1989]

(1) Except as provided in subsection (3), and subject to the limitation in subsection (4):

(a) a buyer who fails to comply with the requirements of Section 6—104(1)(e) with respect to a creditor is liable to the creditor for damages in the amount of the claim, reduced by any amount that the creditor would not have realized if the buyer had complied; and

(b) a buyer who fails to comply with the requirements of any other subsection of Section 6—104 with respect to a claimant is liable to the claimant for damages in the amount of the claim, reduced by any amount that the claimant would not have realized if the buyer had complied.

(2) In an action under subsection (1), the creditor has the burden of establishing the validity and amount of the claim, and the buyer has the burden of establishing the amount that the creditor would not have realized if the buyer had complied.

(3) A buyer who:

(a) made a good faith and commercially reasonable effort to comply with the requirements of Section 6—104(1) or to exclude the sale from the application of this Article under Section 6—103(3); or

(b) on or after the date of the bulk sale agreement, but before the date of the bulk sale, held a good faith and commercially reasonable belief that this Article does not apply to the particular sale is not liable to creditors for failure to comply with the requirements of Section 6—104. The buyer has the burden of establishing the good faith and commercial reasonableness of the effort or belief.

(4) In a single bulk sale the cumulative liability of the buyer for failure to comply with the requirements of Section 6—104(1) may not exceed an amount equal to:

(a) if the assets consist only of inventory and equipment, twice the net contract price, less the amount of any part of the net contract price paid to or applied for the benefit of the seller or a creditor; or

(b) if the assets include property other than inventory and equipment, twice the net value of the inventory and equipment less the amount of the portion of any part of the net contract price paid to or applied for the benefit of the seller or a creditor which is allocable to the inventory and equipment.

. . .

§ 6—110.   Limitation of Actions [Alternative B 1989]

(1) Except as provided in subsection (2), an action under this Article against a buyer, auctioneer, or liquidator must be commenced within one year after the date of the bulk sale.

(2) If the buyer, auctioneer, or liquidator conceals the fact that the sale has occurred, the limitation is tolled and an action under this Article may be commenced within the earlier of (i) one year after the person bringing the action discovers that the sale has occurred or (ii) one year after the person bringing the action should have discovered that the sale has occurred, but no later than two years after the date of the bulk sale. Complete noncompliance with the requirements of this Article does not of itself constitute concealment.

. . .

Article 7

Warehouse Receipts, Bills of Lading and Other Documents of Title

Part 1
General

§ 7—104.   Negotiable and Nonnegotiable Warehouse Receipt, Bill of Lading or Other Document of Title

(1) A warehouse receipt, bill of lading or other document of title is negotiable

    (a) if by its terms the goods are to be delivered to bearer or to the order of a named person; or

    (b) where recognized in overseas trade, if it runs to a named person or assigns.

(2) Any other document is nonnegotiable. A bill of lading in which it is stated that the goods are consigned to a named person is not made negotiable by a provision that the goods are to be delivered only against a written order signed by the same or another named person.

Part 2
Warehouse Receipts: Special Provisions

§ 7—202.   Form of Warehouse Receipt; Essential Terms; Optional Terms

(1) A warehouse receipt need not be in any particular form.

(2) Unless a warehouse receipt embodies within its written or printed terms each of the following, the warehouseman is liable for damages caused by the omission to a person injured thereby:

    (a) the location of the warehouse where the goods are stored;

    (b) the date of issue of the receipt;

    (c) the consecutive number of the receipt;

    (d) a statement whether the goods received will be delivered to the bearer, to a specified person, or to a specified person or his order;

    (e) the rate of storage and handling charges, except that where goods are stored under a field warehousing arrangement a statement of that fact is sufficient on a non-negotiable receipt;

    (f) a description of the goods or of the packages containing them;

    (g) the signature of the warehouseman, which may be made by his authorized agent;

    (h) if the receipt is issued for goods of which the warehouseman is owner, either solely or jointly or in common with others, the fact of such ownership; and

        (i) a statement of the amount of advances made and of liabilities incurred for which the warehouseman claims a lien or security interest (Section 7—209). If the precise amount of such advances made or of such liabilities incurred is, at the time of the issue of the receipt, unknown to the warehouseman or to his agent who issues it, a statement of the fact that advances have been made or liabilities incurred and the purpose thereof is sufficient.

(3) A warehouseman may insert in his receipt any other terms which are not contrary to the provisions of this Act and do not impair his obligation of delivery (Section 7—403) or his duty of care (Section 7—204). Any contrary provisions shall be ineffective.

§ 7—203.   Liability for Non-Receipt or Misdescription

A party to or purchaser for value in good faith of a document of title other than a bill of lading relying in either case upon the description therein of the goods may recover from the issuer damages caused by the non-receipt or misdescription of the goods, except to the extent that the document conspicuously indicates that the issuer does not know whether any part or all of the goods in fact were received or conform to the description, as where the description is in terms of marks or labels or kind, quantity or condition, or the receipt or description is qualified by "contents, condition and quality unknown," "said to contain" or the like, if such indication be true, or the party or purchaser otherwise has notice.

§ 7—204.   Duty of Care; Contractual Limitation of Warehouseman's Liability

(1) A warehouseman is liable for damages for loss of or injury to the goods caused by his failure to exercise such care in regard to them as a reasonably careful man would exercise under like circumstances but, unless otherwise agreed, he is not liable for damages which could not have been avoided by the exercise of such care.

(2) Damages may be limited by a term in the warehouse receipt or storage agreement limiting the amount of liability in case of loss or damage, and setting forth a specific liability per article or item, or value per unit of weight, beyond which the warehouseman shall not be liable; provided, however, that such liability may on written request of the bailor at the time of signing such storage agreement or within a reasonable time after receipt of the warehouse receipt be increased on part or all of the goods thereunder, in which event increased rates may be charged based on such increased valuation, but that no such increase shall be permitted contrary to a lawful limitation of liability contained in the warehouseman's tariff, if any. No such limita-

tion is effective with respect to the warehouseman's liability for conversion to his own use.

(3) Reasonable provisions as to the time and manner of presenting claims and instituting actions based on the bailment may be included in the warehouse receipt or tariff.

§ 7—205. Title Under Warehouse Receipt Defeated in Certain Cases

A buyer in the ordinary course of business of fungible goods sold and delivered by a warehouseman who is also in the business of buying and selling such goods takes free of any claim under a warehouse receipt even though it has been duly negotiated.

§ 7—209. Lien of Warehouseman

(1) A warehouseman has a lien against the bailor on the goods covered by a warehouse receipt or on the proceeds thereof in his possession for charges for storage or transportation (including demurrage and terminal charges), insurance, labor, or charges present or future in relation to the goods, and for expenses necessary for preservation of the goods or reasonably incurred in their sale pursuant to law. If the person on whose account the goods are held is liable for like charges or expenses in relation to other goods whenever deposited and it is stated in the receipt that a lien is claimed for charges and expenses in relation to other goods, the warehouseman also has a lien against him for such charges and expenses whether or not the other goods have been delivered by the warehouseman. But against a person to whom a negotiable warehouse receipt is duly negotiated, a warehouseman's lien is limited to charges in an amount or at a rate specified on the receipt or if no charges are so specified then to a reasonable charge for storage of the goods covered by the receipt subsequent to the date of the receipt.

(2) The warehouseman may also reserve a security interest against the bailor for a maximum amount specified on the receipt for charges other than those specified in subsection (1), such as for money advanced and interest. Such a security interest is governed by the Article on Secured Transactions (Article 9).

(3) (a) A warehouseman's lien for charges and expenses under subsection (1) or a security interest under subsection (2) is also effective against any person who so entrusted the bailor with possession of the goods that a pledge of them by him to a good faith purchaser for value would have been valid but is not effective against a person as to whom the document confers no right in the goods covered by it under Section 7—503.

(b) A warehouseman's lien on household goods for charges and expenses in relation to the goods under subsection (1) is also effective against all persons if the depositor was the legal possessor of the goods at the time of deposit. "Household goods" means furniture, furnishings and personal effects used by the depositor in a dwelling.

(4) A warehouseman loses his lien on any goods which he voluntarily delivers or which he unjustifiably refuses to deliver.

Part 3
Bills of Lading: Special Provisions

§ 7—301. Liability for Non-Receipt or Misdescription; "Said to Contain"; "Shipper's Load and Count"; Improper Handling

(1) A consignee of a nonnegotiable bill who has given value in good faith or a holder to whom a negotiable bill has been duly negotiated relying in either case upon the description therein of the goods, or upon the date therein shown, may recover from the issuer damages caused by the misdating of the bill or the nonreceipt or misdescription of the goods, except to the extent that the document indicates that the issuer does not know whether any part or all of the goods in fact were received or conform to the description, as where the description is in terms of marks or labels or kind, quantity, or condition or the receipt or description is qualified by "contents or condition of contents of packages unknown," "said to contain," "shipper's weight, load and count" or the like, if such indication be true.

(2) When goods are loaded by an issuer who is a common carrier, the issuer must count the packages of goods if package freight and ascertain the kind and quantity if bulk freight. In such cases, "shipper's weight, load and count" or other words indicating that the description was made by the shipper are ineffective except as to freight concealed by packages.

(3) When bulk freight is loaded by a shipper who makes available to the issuer adequate facilities for weighing such freight, an issuer who is a common carrier must ascertain the kind and quantity within a reasonable time after receiving the written request of the shipper to do so. In such cases, "shipper's weight" or other words of like purport are ineffective.

(4) The issuer may by inserting in the bill the words "shipper's weight, load and count" or other words of like purport indicate that the goods were loaded by the shipper, and if such statement be true, the issuer shall not be liable for damages caused by the improper loading. But their omission does not imply liability for such damages.

(5) The shipper shall be deemed to have guaranteed to the issuer the accuracy at the time of shipment of the description, marks, labels, number, kind, quantity, condition and weight, as furnished by him; and the shipper shall indemnify the issuer against damage caused by inaccuracies in such particulars. The right of the issuer to such indemnity shall in no way limit his responsibility and liability under the contract of carriage to any person other than the shipper.

§ 7—307. Lien of Carrier

(1) A carrier has a lien on the goods covered by a bill of lading for charges subsequent to the date of its receipt of

the goods for storage or transportation (including demurrage and terminal charges) and for expenses necessary for preservation of the goods incident to their transportation or reasonably incurred in their sale pursuant to law. But against a purchaser for value of a negotiable bill of lading, a carrier's lien is limited to charges stated in the bill or the applicable tariffs, or if no charges are stated then to a reasonable charge.

(2) A lien for charges and expenses under subsection (1) on goods which the carrier was required by law to receive for transportation is effective against the consignor or any person entitled to the goods unless the carrier had notice that the consignor lacked authority to subject the goods to such charges and expenses. Any other lien under subsection (1) is effective against the consignor and any person who permitted the bailor to have control or possession of the goods unless the carrier had notice that the bailor lacked such authority.

(3) A carrier loses his lien on any goods which he voluntarily delivers or which he unjustifiably refuses to deliver.

§ 7—309.   Duty of Care; Contractual Limitation of Carrier's Liability

(1) A carrier who issues a bill of lading, whether negotiable or nonnegotiable, must exercise the degree of care in relation to the goods which a reasonably careful man would exercise under like circumstances. This subsection does not repeal or change any law or rule of law which imposes liability upon a common carrier for damages not caused by its negligence.

(2) Damages may be limited by a provision that the carrier's liability shall not exceed a value stated in the document if the carrier's rates are dependent upon value and the consignor by the carrier's tariff is afforded an opportunity to declare a higher value or a value as lawfully provided in the tariff, or, where no tariff is filed, he is otherwise advised of such opportunity; but no such limitation is effective with respect to the carrier's liability for conversion to its own use.

(3) Reasonable provisions as to the time and manner of presenting claims and instituting actions based on the shipment may be included in a bill of lading or tariff.

Part 4

Warehouse Receipts and Bills of Lading: General Obligations

§ 7—401.   Irregularities in Issue of Receipt or Bill or Conduct or Issuer

The obligations imposed by this Article on an issuer apply to a document of title regardless of the fact that

(a) the document may not comply with the requirements of this Article or of any other law or regulation regarding its issue, form or content; or

(b) the issuer may have violated laws regulating the conduct of his business; or

(c) the goods covered by the document were owned by the bailee at the time the document was issued; or

(d) the person issuing the document does not come within the definition of warehouseman, if it purports to be a warehouse receipt.

§ 7—403.   Obligation of Warehouseman or Carrier to Deliver; Excuse

(1) The bailee must deliver the goods to a person entitled under the document who complies with subsections (2) and (3), unless and to the extent that the bailee establishes any of the following:

(a) delivery of the goods to a person whose receipt was rightful as against the claimant;

(b) damage to or delay, loss or destruction of the goods for which the bailee is not liable [, but the burden of establishing negligence in such cases is on the person entitled under the document];

Note: *The brackets in (1)(b) indicate that State enactments may differ on this point without serious damage to the principle of uniformity.*

(c) previous sale or other disposition of the goods in lawful enforcement of a lien or on warehouseman's lawful termination of storage;

(d) the exercise by a seller of his right to stop delivery pursuant to the provisions of the Article on Sales (Section 2—705);

(e) a diversion, reconsignment or other disposition pursuant to the provisions of this Article (Section 7—303) or tariff regulating such right;

(f) release, satisfaction or any other fact affording a personal defense against the claimant;

(g) any other lawful excuse.

(2) A person claiming goods covered by a document of title must satisfy the bailee's lien where the bailee so requests or where the bailee is prohibited by law from delivering the goods until the charges are paid.

(3) Unless the person claiming is one against whom the document confers no right under Sec. 7—503(1), he must surrender for cancellation or notation of partial deliveries any outstanding negotiable document covering the goods, and the bailee must cancel the document or conspicuously note the partial delivery thereon or be liable to any person to whom the document is duly negotiated.

(4) "Person entitled under the document" means holder in the case of a negotiable document, or the person to whom delivery is to be made by the terms of or pursuant to written instructions under a non-negotiable document.

§ 7—404.   No Liability for Good Faith Delivery Pursuant to Receipt or Bill

A bailee who in good faith, including observance of reasonable commercial standards, has received goods and delivered or otherwise disposed of them according to the terms of the document of title or pursuant to this Article is not liable therefor. This rule applies even though the person from whom he received the goods had no authority to procure the document or to dispose of the goods and even though the person to whom he delivered the goods had no authority to receive them.

Part 5

Warehouse Receipts and Bills of Lading: Negotiation and Transfer

§ 7—501.   Form of Negotiation and Requirements of "Due Negotiation"

(1) A negotiable document of title running to the order of a named person is negotiated by his indorsement and delivery. After his indorsement in blank or to bearer, any person can negotiate it by delivery alone.

(2) (a)   A negotiable document of title is also negotiated by delivery alone when by its original terms it runs to bearer.

(b)   When a document running to the order of a named person is delivered to him, the effect is the same as if the document had been negotiated.

(3) Negotiation of a negotiable document of title after it has been indorsed to a specified person requires indorsement by the special indorsee as well as delivery.

(4) A negotiable document of title is "duly negotiated" when it is negotiated in the manner stated in this section to a holder who purchases it in good faith without notice of any defense against or claim to it on the part of any person and for value, unless it is established that the negotiation is not in the regular course of business or financing or involves receiving the document in settlement or payment of a money obligation.

(5) Indorsement of a nonnegotiable document neither makes it negotiable nor adds to the transferee's rights.

(6) The naming in a negotiable bill of a person to be notified of the arrival of the goods does not limit the negotiability of the bill nor constitute notice to a purchaser thereof of any interest of such person in the goods.

§ 7—502.   Rights Acquired by Due Negotiation

(1) Subject to the following section and to the provisions of Section 7—205 on fungible goods, a holder to whom a negotiable document of title has been duly negotiated acquires thereby:

(a)   title to the document;

(b)   title to the goods;

(c)   all rights accruing under the law of agency or estoppel, including rights to goods delivered to the bailee after the document was issued; and

(d)   the direct obligation of the issuer to hold or deliver the goods according to the terms of the document free of any defense or claim by him except those arising under the terms of

the document or under this Article. In the case of a delivery order, the bailee's obligation accrues only upon acceptance and the obligation acquired by the holder is that the issuer and any indorser will procure the acceptance of the bailee.

(2) Subject to the following section, title and rights so acquired are not defeated by any stoppage of the goods represented by the document or by surrender of such goods by the bailee, and are not impaired even though the negotiation or any prior negotiation constituted a breach of duty or even though any person has been deprived of possession of the document by misrepresentation, fraud, accident, mistake, duress, loss, theft or conversion, or even though a previous sale or other transfer of the goods or document has been made to a third person.

§ 7—507.   Warranties on Negotiation or Transfer of Receipt or Bill

Where a person negotiates or transfers a document of title for value otherwise than as a mere intermediary under the next following section, then unless otherwise agreed he warrants to his immediate purchaser only, in addition to any warranty made in selling the goods,

(a)   that the document is genuine; and

(b)   that he has no knowledge of any fact which would impair its validity or worth; and

(c)   that his negotiation or transfer is rightful and fully effective with respect to the title to the document and the goods it represents.

§ 7—508.   Warranties of Collecting Bank as to Documents

A collecting bank or other intermediary known to be entrusted with documents on behalf of another or with collection of a draft or other claim against delivery of documents warrants by such delivery of the documents only its own good faith and authority. This rule applies even though the intermediary has purchased or made advances against the claim or draft to be collected.

Part 6

Warehouse Receipts and Bills of Lading: Miscellaneous Provisions

§ 7—602.   Attachment of Goods Covered by a Negotiable Document

Except where the document was originally issued upon delivery of the goods by a person who had no power to dispose of them, no lien attaches by virtue of any judicial process to goods in the possession of a bailee for which a negotiable document of title is outstanding unless the document be first surrendered to the bailee or its negotiation enjoined, and the bailee shall not be compelled to deliver the goods pursuant to process until the document is surrendered to him or impounded by the court. One who purchases the document for value without notice of the process or injunction takes free of the lien imposed by judicial process.

ARTICLE 8

INVESTMENT SECURITIES

Part 1

Short Title and General Matters

§ 8—102.   Definitions and Index of Definitions

(1) In this Article, unless the context otherwise requires:

(a) A "certificated security" is a share, participation, or other interest in property of or an enterprise of the issuer or an obligation of the issuer which is

(i) represented by an instrument issued in bearer or registered form;

(ii) of a type commonly dealt in on securities exchanges or markets or commonly recognized in any area in which it is issued or dealt in as a medium for investment; and

(iii) either one of a class or series or by its terms divisible into a class or series of shares, participations, interests, or obligations.

(b) An "uncertificated security" is a share, participation, or other interest in property or an enterprise of the issuer or an obligation of the issuer which is

(i) not represented by an instrument and the transfer of which is registered upon books maintained for that purpose by or on behalf of the issuer;

(ii) of a type commonly dealt in on securities exchanges or markets; and

(iii) either one of a class or series or by its terms divisible into a class or series of shares, participations, interests, or obligations.

(c) A "security" is either a certificated or an uncertificated security. If a security is certificated, the terms "security" and "certificated security" may mean either the intangible interest, the instrument representing that interest, or both, as the context requires. A writing that is a certificated security is governed by this Article and not by Article 3, even though it also meets the requirements of that Article. This Article does not apply to money. If a certificated security has been retained by or surrendered to the issuer or its transfer agent for reasons other than registration of transfer, other temporary purpose, payment, exchange, or acquisition by the issuer, that security shall be treated as an uncertified security for purposes of this Article.

(d) A certificated security is in "registered form" if

(i) it specifies a person entitled to the security of the rights it represents; and

(ii) its transfer may be registered upon books maintained for that purpose by or on behalf of the issuer, or the security so states.

(e) A certified security is in "bearer form" if it runs to bearer according to its terms and not by reason of any indorsement.

. . .

§ 8—105.   Certificated Securities Negotiatable; Statements and Institutions Not Negotiable; Presumptions

(1) Certified securities governed by this Article are negotiable instruments.

(2) Statements (Section 8—408), notices, or the like, sent by the issuer of uncertificated securities and instructions (Section 8—308) are neither negotiable instruments nor certificated securities.

. . .

§ 8—107.   Securities Transferable; Action for Price

(1) Unless otherwise agreed and subject to any applicable law or regulation respecting short sales, a person obligated to transfer securities may transfer any certificated security of the specified issue in bearer form or registered in the name of the transferee, or indorsed to him or in blank, or he may transfer an equivalent uncertificated security to the transferee or a person designated by the transferee.

(2) If the buyer fails to pay the price as it comes due under a contract of sale, the seller may recover the price of:

(a) certificated securities accepted by the buyer;

(b) uncertificated securities that have been transferred to the buyer or a person designated by the buyer; and

(c) other securities if efforts at their resale would be unduly burdensome or if there is no readily available market for their resale.

Part 2

Issue—Issuer

§ 8—202.   Issuer's Responsibility and Defenses; Notice of Defect or Defense

(1) Even against a purchaser for value and without notice, the terms of a security include:

(a) if the security is certificated, those stated on the security;

(b) if the security is uncertificated, those contained in the initial transaction statement sent to such purchaser or, if his interest is transferred to him other than by registration of transfer, pledge, or release, the initial transaction statement sent to the registered owner or registered pledgee; and

(c) those made part of the security by reference, on the certificated security or in the initial transaction statement, to another instrument, indenture, or document or to a constitution, statute, ordinance, rule, regulation, order or the like, to the extent that the terms referred to do not conflict with the terms stated on the certificated security or contained in the statement. A reference under this paragraph does not of itself charge a purchaser for value with notice of a defect going to the validity of the security, even though the certificated security or statement expressly states that a person accepting it admits notice.

(2) A certificated security in the hands of a purchaser for value or an uncertificated security as to which an initial transaction statement has been sent to a purchaser for value, other than a security issued by a government or governmental agency or unit, even though issued with a defect going to its validity, is valid with respect to the purchaser if he is without notice of the particular defect unless the defect involves a violation of constitutional provisions, in which case the security is valid with respect to a subsequent purchaser for value and without notice of the defect. This subsection applies to an issuer that is a government or governmental agency or unit only if either there has been substantial compliance with the legal requirements governing the issue or the issuer has received a substantial consideration for the issue as a whole or for the particular security and a stated purpose of the issue is one for which the issuer has power to borrow money or issue the security.

(3) Except as provided in the case of certain unauthorized signatures (Section 8—205), lack of genuineness of a certificated security or an initial transaction statement is a complete defense, even against a purchaser for value and without notice.

(4) All other defenses of the issuer of a certificated or uncertificated security, including nondelivery and conditional delivery of a certificated security, are ineffective against a purchaser for value who has taken without notice of the particular defense.

(5) Nothing in this section shall be construed to affect the right of a party to a "when, as and if issued" or a "when distributed" contract to cancel the contract in the event of a material change in the character of the security that is the subject of the contract or in the plan or arrangement pursuant to which the security is to be issued or distributed.

§ 8—203.   Staleness as Notice of Defects or Defenses

(1) After an act or event creating a right to immediate performance of the principal obligation represented by a certificated security or that sets a date on or after which the security is to be presented or surrendered for redemption or exchange, a purchaser is charged with notice of any defect in its issue or defense of the issuer if:

(a) the act or event is one requiring the payment of money, the delivery of certificated securities, the registration of transfer of uncertificated securities, or any of these on presentation or surrender of the certificated security, the funds or securities are available on the date set for payment or exchange, and he takes the security more than one year after that date; and

(b) the act or event is not covered by paragraph (a) and he takes the security more than 2 years after the date set for surrender or presentation or the date on which performance became due.

(2) A call that has been revoked is not within subsection (1).

§ 8—204.   Effect of Issuer's Restrictions on Transfer

A restriction on transfer of a security imposed by the issuer, even if otherwise lawful, is ineffective against any person without actual knowledge of it unless:

(a) the security is certificated and the restriction is noted conspicuously thereon; or

(b) the security is uncertificated and a notation of the restriction is contained in the initial transaction statement sent to the person or, if his interest is transferred to him other than by registration of transfer, pledge, or release, the initial transaction statement sent to the registered owner or the registered pledgee.

§ 8—205.   Effect of Unauthorized Signature on Certificated Security or Initial Transaction Statement

An unauthorized signature placed on a certificated security prior to or in the course of issue or placed on an initial transaction statement is ineffective, but the signature is effective in favor of a purchaser for value of the certificated security or a purchaser for value of an uncertificated security to whom the initial transaction statement has been sent, if the purchaser is without notice of the lack of authority and the signing has been done by:

(a) an authenticating trustee, registrar, transfer agent, or other person entrusted by the issuer with the signing of the security, or similar securities, or of initial transaction statements or the immediate preparation for signing of any of them; or

(b) an employee of the issuer, or of any of the foregoing, entrusted with responsible handling of the security or initial transaction statement.

§ 8—208. Effect of Signature of Authenticating Trustee, Registrar, or Transfer Agent

(1) A person placing his signature upon a certificated security or an initial transaction statement as authenticating trustee, registrar, transfer agent, or the like, warrants to a purchaser for value of the certificated security or a purchaser for value of an uncertificated security to whom the initial transaction statement has been sent, if the purchaser is without notice of the particular defect, that:

(a) the certificated security or initial transaction statement is genuine;

(b) his own participation in the issue or registration of the transfer, pledge, or release of the security is within his capacity and within the scope of the authority received by him from the issuer; and

(c) he has reasonable grounds to believe the security is in the form and within the amount the issuer is authorized to issue.

(2) Unless otherwise agreed, a person by so placing his signature does not assume responsibility for the validity of the security in other respects.

Part 3

Transfer

§ 8—301. Rights Acquired by Purchaser

(1) Upon transfer of a security to a purchaser (Section 8—313), the purchaser acquires the rights in the security which his transferor had or had actual authority to convey unless the purchaser's rights are limited by Section 8—302(4).

. . .

§ 8—302. "Bona Fide Purchaser"; "Adverse Claim"; Title Acquired by Bona Fide Purchaser

(1) A "bona fide purchaser" is a purchaser for value in good faith and without notice of any adverse claim:

(a) who takes delivery of a certificated security in bearer form or in registered form, issued or indorsed to him or in blank;

(b) to whom the transfer, pledge, or release of an uncertificated security is registered on the books of the issuer; or

(c) to whom a security is transferred under the provisions of paragraph (c), (d), (i), or (g) of Section 8—313(1).

(2) "Adverse claim" includes a claim that a transfer was or would be wrongful or that a particular adverse person is the owner of or has an interest in the security.

(3) A bona fide purchaser in addition to acquiring the rights of a purchaser (Section 8—301) also acquires his interest in the security free of any adverse claim.

(4) Notwithstanding Section 8—301(1), the transfer-ee of a particular certificated security who has been a party to any fraud or illegality affecting the security, or who as a prior holder of that certificated security had notice of an adverse claim, cannot improve his position by taking from a bona fide purchaser.

§ 8—304. Notice to Purchaser of Adverse Claims

(1) A purchaser (including a broker for the seller or buyer, but excluding an intermediary bank) of a certificated security is charged with notice of adverse claims if:

(a) the security, whether in bearer or registered form, has been indorsed "for collection" or "for surrender" or for some other purpose not involving transfer; or

(b) the security is in bearer form and has on it an unambiguous statement that it is the property of a person other than the transferor. The mere writing of a name on a security is not such a statement.

(2) A purchaser (including a broker for the seller or buyer, but excluding an intermediary bank) to whom the transfer, pledge, or release of an uncertificated security is registered is charged with notice of adverse claims as to which the issuer has a duty under Section 8—403(4) at the time of registration and which are noted in the initial transaction statement sent to the purchaser or, if his interest is transferred to him other than by registration of transfer, pledge, or release, the initial transaction statement sent to the registered owner or the registered pledgee.

(3) The fact that the purchaser (including a broker for the seller or buyer) of a certificated or uncertificated security has notice that the security is held for a third person or is registered in the name of or indorsed by a fiduciary does not create a duty of inquiry into the rightfulness of the transfer or constitute constructive notice of adverse claims. However, if the purchaser (excluding an intermediary bank) has knowledge that the proceeds are being used or the transaction is for the individual benefit of the fiduciary or otherwise in breach of duty, the purchaser is charged with notice, of adverse claims.

§ 8—305. Staleness as Notice of Adverse Claims

An act or event that creates a right to immediate performance of the principal obligation represented by a certificated security, or sets a date on or after which a certificated security is to be presented or surrendered for redemption or exchange does not itself constitute any notice of adverse claims except in the case of a transfer;

(a) after one year from any date set for presentment or surrender for redemption or exchange; or

(b) after 6 months from any date set for payment of money against presentation or surrender of the security if funds are available for payment on that date.

§ 8—306.   Warranties on Presentment and Transfer of Certificated Securities; Warranties of Originators of Instructions

(1) A person who presents a certificated security for registration of transfer or for payment or exchange warrants to the issuer that he is entitled to the registration, payment, or exchange. But, a purchaser for value and without notice of adverse claims who receives a new, reissued, or re-registered certificated security on registration of transfer or receives an initial transaction statement confirming the registration of transfer of an equivalent uncertificated security to him warrants only that he has no knowledge of any unauthorized signature (Section 8—311) in a necessary indorsement.

(2) A person by transferring a certificated security to a purchaser for value warrants only that:

    (a)   his transfer is effective and rightful;

    (b)   the security is genuine and has not been materially altered; and

    (c)   he knows of no fact which might impair the validity of the security.

(3) If a certificated security is delivered by an intermediary known to be entrusted with delivery of the security on behalf of another or with collection of a draft or other claim against delivery, the intermediary by delivery warrants only his own good faith and authority, even though he has purchased or made advances against the claim to be collected against the delivery.

. . .

(5) A person who originates an instruction warrants to the issuer that:

    (a)   he is an appropriate person to originate the instruction; and

    (b)   at the time the instruction is presented to the issuer he will be entitled to the registration of transfer, pledge, or release.

(6) A person who originates an instruction warrants to any person specially guaranteeing his signature (subsection 8—312(3)) that:

    (a)   he is an appropriate person to originate the instruction; and

    (b)   at the time the instruction is presented to the issuer

        (i)   he will be entitled to the registration of transfer, pledge, or release; and

        (ii)   the transfer, pledge, or release requested in the instruction will be registered by the issuer free from all liens, security interests, restrictions, and claims other than those specified in the instruction.

(7) A person who originates an instruction warrants to a purchaser for value and to any person guaranteeing the instruction (Section 8—312(6)) that:

    (a)   he is an appropriate person to originate the instruction;

    (b)   the uncertificated security referred to therein is valid; and

    (c)   at the time the instruction is presented to the issuer

        (i)   the transferor will be entitled to the registration of transfer, pledge, or release;

        (ii)   the transfer, pledge, or release requested in the instruction will be registered by the issuer free from all liens, security interests, restrictions, and claims other than those specified in the instruction; and

        (iii)   the requested transfer, pledge, or release will be rightful.

. . .

(9) A person who transfers an uncertificated security to a purchaser for value and does not originate an instruction in connection with the transfer warrants only that:

    (a)   his transfer is effective and rightful; and

    (b)   the uncertificated security is valid.

(10) A broker gives to his customer and to the issuer and a purchaser the applicable warranties provided in this section and has the rights and privileges of a purchaser under this section. The warranties of and in favor of the broker, acting as an agent are in addition to applicable warranties given by and in favor of his customer.

§ 8—307.   Effect of Delivery Without Indorsement; Right to Compel Indorsement

If a certificated security in registered form has been delivered to a purchaser without a necessary indorsement he may become a bona fide purchaser only as of the time the indorsement is supplied; but against the transferor, the transfer is complete upon delivery and the purchaser has a specifically enforceable right to have any necessary indorsement supplied.

§ 8—308.   Indorsements; Instructions

(1) An indorsement of a certificated security in registered form is made when an appropriate person signs on it or on a separate document an assignment or transfer of the security or a power to assign or transfer it or his signature is written without more upon the back of the security.

(2) An indorsement may be in blank or special. An indorsement in blank includes an indorsement to bearer. A special indorsement specifies to whom the security is to be transferred, or who has power to transfer it. A holder may convert a blank indorsement into a special indorsement.

(3) An indorsement purporting to be only of part of a certificated security representing units intended by the issuer to be separately transferable is effective to the extent of the indorsement.

(4) An "instruction" is an order to the issuer of an uncertificated security requesting that the transfer, pledge, or release from pledge of the uncertificated security specified therein be registered.

(5) An instruction originated by an appropriate person is:

    (a)   a writing signed by an appropriate person; or

(b) a communication to the issuer in any form agreed upon in a writing signed by the issuer and an appropriate person.

If an instruction has been originated by an appropriate person but is incomplete in any other respect, any person may complete it as authorized and the issuer may rely on it as completed even though it has been completed incorrectly.

. . .

§ 8—309.   Effect of Indorsement Without Delivery

An indorsement of a certificated security, whether special or in blank, does not constitute a transfer until delivery of the certificated security on which it appears or, if the indorsement is on a separate document, until delivery of both the document and the certificated security.

§ 8—310.   Indorsement of Certificated Security in Bearer Form

An indorsement of a certificated security in bearer form may give notice of adverse claims (Section 8—304) but does not otherwise affect any right to registration the holder possesses.

§ 8—311.   Effect of Unauthorized Indorsement or Instruction

Unless the owner or pledgee has ratified an unauthorized indorsement or instruction or is otherwise precluded from asserting its effectiveness:

(a) he may assert its ineffectiveness against the issuer or any purchaser, other than a purchaser for value and without notice of adverse claims, who has in good faith received a new, reissued, or re-registered certificated security on registration of transfer or received an initial transaction statement confirming the registration of transfer, pledge, or release of an equivalent uncertificated security to him; and

(b) an issuer who registers the transfer of a certificated security upon the unauthorized indorsement or who registers the transfer, pledge, or release of an uncertificated security upon the unauthorized instruction is subject to liability for improper registration (Section 8—404).

§ 8—313.   When Transfer to Purchaser Occurs; Financial Intermediary as Bona Fide Purchaser; "Financial Intermediary"

(1) Transfer of a security or a limited interest (including a security interest) therein to a purchaser occurs only:

(a) at the time he or a person designated by him acquires possession of a certificated security;

(b) at the time the transfer, pledge, or release of an uncertificated security is registered to him or a person designated by him;

(c) at the time his financial intermediary acquires possession of a certificated security specially indorsed to or issued in the name of the purchaser;

(d) at the time a financial intermediary, not a clearing corporation, sends him confirmation of the purchase and also by book entry or otherwise identifies as belonging to the purchaser

(i) a specific certificated security in the financial intermediary's possession;

(ii) a quantity of securities that constitute or are part of a fungible bulk of certificated securities in the financial intermediary's possession or of uncertificated securities registered in the name of the financial intermediary; or

(iii) a quantity of securities that constitute or are part of a fungible bulk of securities shown on the account of the financial intermediary on the books of another financial intermediary;

(e) with respect to an identified certificated security to be delivered while still in the possession of a third person, not a financial intermediary, at the time that person acknowledges that he holds for the purchaser;

(f) with respect to a specific uncertificated security the pledge or transfer of which has been registered to a third person, not a financial intermediary, at the time that person acknowledges that he holds for the purchaser;

. . .

§ 8—314.   Duty to Transfer, When Completed

(1) Unless otherwise agreed, if a sale of a security is made on an exchange or otherwise through brokers:

(a) the selling customer fulfills his duty to transfer at the time he:

(i) places a certificated security in the possession of the selling broker or a person designated by the broker;

(ii) causes an uncertificated security to be registered in the name of the selling broker or a person designated by the broker;

(iii) if requested, causes an acknowledgment to be made to the selling broker that a certificated or uncertificated security is held for the broker; or

(iv) places in the possession of the selling broker or of a person designated by the broker a transfer instruction for an uncertificated security, providing the issuer does not refuse to register the requested transfer if the instruction is presented to the issuer for registration within 30 days thereafter; and

(b) the selling broker, including a correspondent broker acting for a selling customer, fulfills his duty to transfer at the time he:

   (i) places a certificated security in the possession of the buying broker or a person designated by the buying broker;

   (ii) causes an uncertificated security to be registered in the name of the buying broker or a person designated by the buying broker;

   (iii) places in the possession of the buying broker or of a person designated by the buying broker a transfer instruction for an uncertificated security, providing the issuer does not refuse to register the requested transfer if the instruction is presented to the issuer for registration within 30 days thereafter; or

   (iv) effects clearance of the sale in accordance with the rules of the exchange on which the transaction took place.

(2) Except as provided in this section or unless otherwise agreed, a transferor's duty to transfer a security under a contract of purchase is not fulfilled until he:

(a) places a certificated security in form to be negotiated by the purchaser in the possession of the purchaser or of a person designated by the purchaser;

(b) causes an uncertificated security to be registered in the name of the purchaser or a person designated by the purchaser; or

(c) if the purchaser requests, causes an acknowledgment to be made to the purchaser that a certificated or uncertificated security is held for the purchaser.

(3) Unless made on an exchange, a sale to a broker purchasing for his own account is within subsection (2) and not within subsection (1).

§ 8—315.   Action Against Transferee Based Upon Wrongful Transfer

(1) Any person against whom the transfer of a security is wrongful for any reason, including his incapacity, as against anyone except a bona fide purchaser, may:

(a) reclaim possession of the certificated security wrongfully transferred;

(b) obtain possession of any new certificated security representing all or part of the same rights;

(c) compel the origination of an instruction to transfer to him or a person designated by him an uncertificated security constituting all or part of the same rights; or

(d) have damages.

. . .

§ 8—318.   No Conversion by Good Faith Conduct

An agent or bailee who in good faith (including observance of reasonable commercial standards if he is in the business of buying, selling, or otherwise dealing with securities) has received certificated securities and sold, pledged, or delivered them or has sold or caused the transfer or pledge of uncertificated securities over which he had control according to the instructions of his principal, is not liable for conversion or for participation in breach of fiduciary duty although the principal had no right so to deal with the securities.

§ 8—319.   Statute of Frauds

A contract for the sale of securities is not enforceable by way of action or defense unless:

(a) there is some writing signed by the party against whom enforcement is sought or by his authorized agent or broker, sufficient to indicate that a contract has been made for sale of a stated quantity of described securities at a defined or stated price;

(b) delivery of a certificated security or transfer instruction has been accepted, or transfer of an uncertificated security has been registered and the transferee has failed to send written objection to the issuer within 10 days after receipt of the initial transaction statement confirming the registration, or payment has been made, but the contract is enforceable under this provision only to the extent of the delivery, registration, or payment;

(c) within a reasonable time a writing in confirmation of the sale or purchase and sufficient against the sender under paragraph (a) has been received by the party against whom enforcement is sought and he has failed to send written objection to its contents within 10 days after its receipt; or

(d) the party against whom enforcement is sought admits in his pleading, testimony, or otherwise in court that a contract was made for the sale of a stated quantity of described securities at a defined or stated price.

§ 8—320.   Transfer or Pledge Within Central Depository System

(1) In addition to other methods, a transfer, pledge, or release of a security or any interest therein may be effected by the making of appropriate entries on the books of a clearing corporation reducing the account of the transferor, pledgor, or pledgee and increasing the account of the transferee, pledgee, or pledgor by the amount of the obligation or the number of shares or rights transferred, pledged, or released, if the security is shown on the account of a transferor, pledgor, or pledgee on the books of the cleaning corporation; is subject to the control of the clearing corporation; and

(a) if certificated,

   (i) is in the custody of the clearing corporation, another clearing corporation, a custodian bank, or a nominee of any of them; and

      (ii) is in bearer form or indorsed in blank by an appropriate person or registered in the name of the cleaning corporation, a custodian bank, or a nominee of any of them; or

    (b) if uncertificated, is registered in the name of the clearing corporation, another clearing corporation, a custodian bank, or a nominee of any of them.

. . .

Part 4

Registration

§ 8—401. Duty of Issuer to Register Transfer, Pledge, or Release

(1) If a certificated security in registered form is presented to the issuer with a requent to register transfer or an instruction is presented to the issuer with a request to register transfer, pledge, or release, the issuer shall register the transfer, pledge, or release as requested if:

    (a) the security is indorsed or the instruction was originated by the appropriate person or persons (Section 8—308);

    (b) reasonable assurance is given that those indorsements or instructions are genuine and effective (Section 8—402);

    (c) the issuer has no duty as to adverse claims or has discharged the duty (Section 8—403);

    (d) any applicable law relating to the collection of taxes has been complied with; and

    (e) the transfer, pledge, or release is in fact rightful or is to a bona fide purchaser.

(2) If an issuer is under a duty to register a transfer pledge, or release of a security, the issuer is also liable to the person presenting a certificated security or an instruction for registration or his principal for loss resulting from any unreasonable delay in registration or from failure or refusal to register the transfer, pledge, or release.

§ 8—403. Issuer's Duty as to Adverse Claims

(1) An issuer to whom a certificated security is presented for registration shall inquire into adverse claims if:

    (a) a written notification of an adverse claim is received at a time and in a manner affording the issuer a reasonable opportunity to act on it prior to the issuance of a new, reissued, or re-registered certificated security, and the notification identifies the claimant, the registered owner, and the issue of which the security is a part, and provides an address for communications directed to the claimant; or

    (b) the issuer is charged with notice of an adverse claim from a controlling instrument it has elected to require under Section 8—4-402(4).

(2) The issuer may discharge any duty of inquiry by any reasonable means, including notifying an adverse claimant by registered or certified mail at the address furnished by him or, if there be no such address, at his residence or regular place of business that the certificated security has been presented for registration of transfer by a named person, and that the transfer will be registered unless within 30 days from the date of mailing the notification, either:

    (a) an appropriate restraining order, injunction, or other process issues from a court of competent jurisdiction; or

    (b) there is filed with the issuer an indemnity bond, sufficient in the issuer's judgment to protect the issuer and any transfer agent, registrar, or other agent of the issuer involved from any loss it or they may suffer by complying with the adverse claim.

. . .

§ 8—404. Liability and Non-Liability for Registration

(1) Except as provided in any law relating to the collection of taxes, the issuer is not liable to the owner, pledgee, or any other person suffering loss as a result of the registration of a transfer, pledge, or release of a security if:

    (a) there were on or with a certificated security the necessary indorsements or the issuer had received an instruction originated by an appropriate person (Section 8—308); and

    (b) the issuer had no duty as to adverse claims or has discharged the duty (Section 8—403).

(2) If an issuer has registered a transfer of a certificated security to a person not entitled to it, the issuer on demand shall deliver a like security to the true owner unless:

    (a) the registration was pursuant to subsection (1);

    (b) the owner is precluded from asserting any claim for registering the transfer under Section 8—405(1); or

    (c) the delivery would result in overissue, in which case the issuer's liability is governed by Section 8—104.

(3) If an issuer has improperly registered a transfer, pledge, or release of an uncertificated security, the issuer on demand from the injured party shall restore the records as to the injured party to the condition that would have obtained if the improper registration had not been made unless:

    (a) the registration was pursuant to subsection (1); or

    (b) the registration would result in overissue, in which case the issuer's liability is governed by Section 8—104.

§ 8—408. Statements of Uncertificated Securities

(1) Within 2 business days after the transfer of an uncertificated security has been registered, the issuer shall send to the new registered owner and, if the security has been transferred subject to a registered pledge, to the registered pledgee a written statement containing:

(a) a description of the issue of which the uncertificated security is a part;

(b) the number of shares or units transferred;

(c) the name and address and any taxpayer identification number of the new registered owner and, if the security has been transferred subject to a registered pledge, the name and address and any taxpayer identification number of the registered pledgee;

(d) a notation of any liens and restrictions of the issuer and any adverse claims (as to which the issuer has a duty under Section 8—403(4)) to which the uncertificated security is or may be subject at the time of registration or a statement that there are none of those liens, restrictions, or adverse claims; and

(e) the date the transfer was registered.

. . .

(6) At periodic intervals no less frequent than annually and at any time upon the reasonable written request of the registered owner, the issuer shall send to the registered owner of each uncertificated security a dated written statement containing:

(a) a description of the issue of which the uncertificated security is a part;

(b) the name and address and any taxpayer identification number of the registered owner;

(c) the number of shares or units of the uncertificated security registered in the name of the registered owner on the date of the statement;

(d) the name and address and any taxpayer identification number of any registered pledgee and the number of shares or units subject to the pledge; and

(e) a notation of any liens and restrictions of the issuer and any adverse claims (as to which the issuer has a duty under Section 8—403(4)) to which the uncertificated security is or may be subject or a statement that there are none of those liens, restrictions, or adverse claims.

. . .

(9) Each statement sent pursuant to this section must bear a conspicuous legend reading substantially as follows: "This statement is merely a record of the rights of the addressee as of the time of its issuance. Delivery of this statement, of itself, confers no rights on the recipient. This statement is neither a negotiable instrument nor a security."

ARTICLE 9

SECURED TRANSACTIONS; SALES OF ACCOUNTS AND CHATTEL PAPER

Part 1
Short Title, Applicability and Definitions

§ 9—102.   Policy and Subject Matter of Article

(1) Except as otherwise provided in Section 9—104 on excluded transactions, this Article applies

(a) to any transaction (regardless of its form) which is intended to create a security interest in personal property or fixtures including goods, documents, instruments, general intangibles, chattel paper or accounts; and also

(b) to any sale of accounts or chattel paper.

(2) This Article applies to security interests created by contract including pledge, assignment, chattel mortgage, chattel trust, trust deed, factor's lien, equipment trust, conditional sale, trust receipt, other lien or title retention contract and lease or consignment intended as security. This Article does not apply to statutory liens except as provided in Section 9—310.

(3) The application of this Article to a security interest in a secured obligation is not affected by the fact that the obligation is itself secured by a transaction or interest to which this Article does not apply.

§ 9—105.   Definitions and Index of Definitions

(1) In this Article unless the context otherwise requires:

(a) "Account debtor" means the person who is obligated on an account, chattel paper or general intangible;

(b) "Chattel paper" means a writing or writings which evidence both a monetary obligation and a security interest in or a lease of specific goods, but a charter or other contract involving the use or hire of a vessel is not chattel paper. When a transaction is evidenced both by such a security agreement or a lease and by an instrument or a series of instruments, the group of writings taken together constitutes chattel paper;

(c) "Collateral" means the property subject to a security interest, and includes accounts and chattel paper which have been sold;

(d) "Debtor" means the person who owes payment or other performance of the obligation secured, whether or not he owns or has rights in the collateral, and includes the seller of accounts or chattel paper. Where the debtor and the owner of the collateral are not the same person, the term "debtor" means the owner of the collateral in any provision of the article dealing with the collateral, the obligor in any provision dealing with the obligation, and may include both where the context so requires;

. . .

(f) "Document" means document of title as defined in the general definitions of Article 1 (Section 1—201), and a receipt of the kind described in subsection (2) of Section 7—201;

. . .

(i) "Instrument" means a negotiable instrument (defined in Section 3—104), or a certificated security (defined in Section 8—102) or any other writing which evidences a right to the payment of money and is not itself a security agreement or lease and is of a type which is in ordinary course of business transferred by delivery with any necessary indorsement or assignment;

. . .

§ 9—106.   Definitions: "Account"; "General Intangibles"

"Account" means any right to payment for goods sold or leased or for services rendered which is not evidenced by an instrument or chattel paper, whether or not it has been earned by performance. "General intangibles" means any personal property (including things in action) other than goods, accounts, chattel paper, documents, instruments, and money. All rights to payment earned or unearned under a charter or other contract involving the use or hire of a vessel and all rights incident to the charter or contract are accounts.

§ 9—107.   Definitions: "Purchase Money Security Interest"

A security interest is a "purchase money security interest" to the extent that it is

(a) taken or retained by the seller of the collateral to secure all or part of its price; or

(b) taken by a person who, by making advances or incurring an obligation, gives value to enable the debtor to acquire rights in or the use of collateral, if such value is in fact so used.

§ 9—109.   Classification of Goods; "Consumer Goods"; "Farm Products"; "Inventory"

Goods are

(1) "consumer goods" if they are used or bought for use primarily for personal, family or household purposes;

(2) "equipment" if they are used or bought for use primarily in business (including farming or a profession) or by a debtor who is a non-profit organization or a governmental subdivision or agency or if the goods are not included in the definitions of inventory, farm products or consumer goods;

(3) "farm products" if they are crops or livestock or supplies used or produced in farming operations or if they are products of crops or livestock in their unmanufactured states (such as ginned cotton, wool-clip, maple syrup, milk and eggs) and if they are in the possession of a debtor engaged in raising, fattening, grazing or other farming operations. If goods are farm products, they are neither equipment nor inventory;

(4) "inventory" if they are held by a person who holds them for sale or lease or to be furnished under contracts of service or if he has so furnished them, or if they are raw materials, work in process or materials used or consumed in a business. Inventory of a person is not to be classified as his equipment.

§ 9—110.   Sufficiency of Description

For the purposes of this Article, any description of personal property or real estate is sufficient whether or not it is specific if it reasonably identifies what is described.

§ 9—113.   Security Interests Arising Under Article on Sales

A security interest arising solely under the Article on Sales (Article 2) is subject to the provisions of this Article except that to the extent that and so long as the debtor does not have or does not lawfully obtain possession of the goods

(a) no security agreement is necessary to make the security interest enforceable; and

(b) no filing is required to perfect the security interest; and

(c) the rights of the secured party on default by the debtor are governed by the Article on Sales (Article 2).

Part 2

Validity of Security Agreement and Rights of Parties Thereto

§ 9—201.   General Validity of Security Agreement

Except as otherwise provided by this Act, a security agreement is effective according to its terms between the parties, against purchasers of the collateral and against creditors. Nothing in this Article validates any charge or practice illegal under any statute or regulation thereunder governing usury, small loans, retail installment sales, or the like, or extends the application of any such statute or regulation to any transaction not otherwise subject thereto.

§ 9—202.   Title to Collateral Immaterial

Each provision of this Article with regard to rights, obligations and remedies applies whether title to collateral is in the secured party or in the debtor.

§ 9—203.   Attachment and Enforceability of Security Interest; Proceeds; Formal Requisites

(1) Subject to the provisions of Section 4—208 on the security interest of a collecting bank, Section 8—321 on security interests in securities and Section 9—113 on a security

interest arising under the Article of Sales, a security interest is not enforceable against the debtor or third parties with respect to the collateral and does not attach unless

    (a) the collateral is in the possession of the secured party pursuant to agreement, or the debtor has signed a security agreement which contains a description of the collateral and in addition, when the security interest covers crops growing or to be grown or timber to be cut, a description of the land concerned; and

    (b) value has been given; and

    (c) the debtor has rights in the collateral.

(2) A security interest attaches when it becomes enforceable against the debtor with respect to the collateral. Attachment occurs as soon as all of the events specified in subsection (1) have taken place unless explicit agreement postpones the time of attaching.

(3) Unless otherwise agreed, a security agreement gives the secured party the rights to proceeds provided by Section 9—306.

(4) A transaction, although subject to this Article, is also subject to . . . .*, and in the case of conflict between the provisions of this Article and any such statute, the provisions of such statute control. Failure to comply with any applicable statute has only the effect which is specified therein.

Note: *At * in subsection (4) insert reference to any local statute regulating small loans, retail installment sales and the like.*

. . .

§ 9—204.   After-Acquired Property; Future Advances

(1) Except as provided in subsection (2), a security agreement may provide that any or all obligations covered by the security agreement are to be secured by after-acquired collateral.

(2) No security interest attaches under an after-acquired property clause to consumer goods other than accessions (Section 9—314) when given as additional security unless the debtor acquires rights in them within ten days after the secured party, gives value.

(3) Obligations covered by a security agreement may include future advances or other value whether or not the advances or value are given pursuant to commitment (subsection (1) of Section 9—105).

§ 9—205.   Use or Disposition of Collateral Without Accounting Permissible

A security interest is not invalid or fraudulent against creditors by reason of liberty in the debtor to use, commingle or dispose of all or part of the collateral (including returned or repossessed goods) or to collect or compromise accounts or chattel paper, or to accept the return of goods or make repossessions, or to use, commingle or dispose of proceeds or by reason of the failure of the secured party to require the debtor to account for proceeds or replace collateral. This section does not relax the requirements of

possession where perfection of a security interest depends upon possession of the collateral by the secured party, or by a bailee.

§ 9—206.   Agreement Not to Assert Defenses Against Assignee; Modification of Sales Warranties Where Security Agreement Exists

(1) Subject to any statute or decision which establishes a different rule for buyers or lessees of consumer goods, an agreement by a buyer or lessee that he will not assert against an assignee any claim or defense which he may have against the seller or lessor is enforceable by an assignee who takes his assignment for value, in good faith and without notice of a claim or defense, except as to defenses of a type which may be asserted against a holder in due course of a negotiable instrument under the Article on Commercial Paper (Article 3). A buyer who as part of one transaction signs both a negotiable instrument and a security agreement makes such an agreement.

(2) When a seller retains a purchase money security interest in goods, the Article on Sales (Article 2) governs the sale and any disclaimer, limitation or modification of the seller's warranties.

Part 3

Rights of Third Parties; Perfected and Unperfected Security Interests; Rules of Priority

§ 9—301.   Persons Who Take Priority Over Unperfected Security Interests; Rights of "Lien Creditor"

(1) Except as otherwise provided in subsection (2), an unperfected security interest is subordinate to the rights of

    (a) persons entitled to priority under Section 9—312;

    (b) a person who becomes a lien creditor before the security interest is perfected;

    (c) in the case of goods, instruments, documents, and chattel paper, a person who is not a secured party and who is a transferee in bulk or other buyer not in ordinary course of business or is a buyer of farm products in ordinary course of business, to the extent that he gives value and receives delivery of the collateral without knowledge of the security interest and before it is perfected;

    (d) in the case of accounts and general intangibles, a person who is not a secured party and who is a transferee, to the extent that he gives value without knowledge of the security interest and before it is perfected.

(2) If the secured party files with respect to a purchase money security interest before or within ten days after the debtor receives possession of the collateral, he takes priority over the rights of a transferee in bulk or of a lien cred-

itor which arise between the time the security interest attaches and the time of filing.

(3) A "lien creditor" means a creditor who has acquired a lien on the property involved by attachment, levy or the like and includes an assignee for benefit of creditors from the time of assignment, and a trustee in bankruptcy from the date of the filing of the petition or a receiver in equity from the time of appointment.

(4) A person who becomes a lien creditor while a security interest is perfected takes subject to the security interest only to the extent that it secures advances made before he becomes a lien creditor or within 45 days thereafter or made without knowledge of the lien or pursuant to a commitment entered into without knowledge of the lien.

§ 9—302. When Filing Is Required to Perfect Security Interest; Security Interests to Which Filing Provisions of This Article Do Not Apply

(1) A financing statement must be filed to perfect all security interests except the following:

(a) a security interest in collateral in possession of the secured party under Section 9—305;

(b) a security interest temporarily perfected in instruments or documents without delivery under Section 9—304 or in proceeds for a 10 day period under Section 9—306;

(c) a security interest created by an assignment of a beneficial interest in a trust or a decedent's estate;

(d) a purchase money security interest in consumer goods; but filing is required for a motor vehicle required to be registered; and fixture filing is required for priority over conflicting interests in fixtures to the extent provided in Section 9—313;

(e) an assignment of accounts which does not alone or in conjunction with other assignments to the same assignee transfer a significant part of the outstanding accounts of the assignor;

(f) a security interest of a collecting bank (Section 4—208) or in securities (Section 8—321) or arising under the Article on Sales (see Section 9—313) or covered in subsection (3) of this section;

(g) an assignment for the benefit of all the creditors of the transferor, and subsequent transfers by the assignee thereunder.

(2) If a secured party assigns a perfected security interest, no filing under this Article is required in order to continue the perfected status of the security interest against creditors of and transferees from the original debtor.

(3) The filing of a financing statement otherwise required by this Article is not necessary or effective to perfect a security interest in property subject to

(a) a statute or treaty of the United States which provides for a national or international registration or a national or international certificate of title or which specifies a place of filing different from that specified in this Article for filing of the security interest; or

(b) the following statutes of this state; [list any certificate of title statute covering automobiles, trailers, mobile homes, boats, farm tractors, or the like, and any central filing statute*.]; but during any period in which collateral is inventory held for sale by a person who is in the business of selling goods of that kind, the filing provisions of this Article (Part 4) apply to a security interest in that collateral created by him as debtor; or

(c) a certificate of title statute of another jurisdiction under the law of which indication of a security interest on the certificate is required as a condition of perfection (subsection (2) of Section 9—103).

(4) Compliance with a statute or treaty described in subsection (3) is equivalent to the filing of a financing statement under this Article, and a security interest in property subject to the statute or treaty can be perfected only by compliance therewith except as provided in Section 9—103 on multiple state transactions. Duration and renewal of perfection of a security interest perfected by compliance with the statute or treaty are governed by the provisions of the statute or treaty; in other respects the security interest is subject to this Article.

*Note: *It is recommended that the provisions of certificate of title acts for perfection of security interests by notation on the certificates should be amended to exclude coverage of inventory held for sale.*

§ 9—303. When Security Interest Is Perfected; Continuity of Perfection

(1) A security interest is perfected when it has attached and when all of the applicable steps required for perfection have been taken. Such steps are specified in Section 9—302, 9—304, 9—305 and 9—306. If such steps are taken before the security interest attaches, it is perfected at the time when it attaches,

(2) If a security interest is originally perfected in any way permitted under this Article and is subsequently perfected in some other way under this Article, without an intermediate period when it was unperfected, the security interest shall be deemed to be perfected continuously for the purposes of this Article.

§ 9—306. "Proceeds"; Secured Party's Rights on Disposition of Collateral

(1) "Proceeds" includes whatever is received upon the sale, exchange, collection or other disposition of collateral or proceeds. Insurance payable by reason of loss or damage to the collateral is proceeds, except to the extent that it is payable to a person other than a party to the secu-

rity agreement. Money, checks, deposit accounts, and the like are "cash proceeds." All other proceeds are "noncash proceeds."

(2) Except where this Article otherwise provides, a security interest continues in collateral notwithstanding sale, exchange or other disposition thereof unless the disposition was authorized by the secured party in the security agreement or otherwise, and also continues in any identifiable proceeds including collections received by the debtor.

(3) The security interest in proceeds is a continuously perfected security interest if the interest in the original collateral was perfected, but it ceases to be a perfected security interest and becomes unperfected ten days after receipt of the proceeds by the debtor unless

    (a) a filed financing statement covers the original collateral and the proceeds are collateral in which a security interest may be perfected by filing in the office or offices where the financing state ment has been filed and, if the proceeds are acquired with cash proceeds, the description of collateral in the financing statement indicates the types of property constituting the proceeds; or

    (b) a filed financing statement covers the original collateral and the proceeds are identifiable cash proceeds; or

    (c) the security interest in the proceeds is perfected before the expiration of the ten day period.

Except as provided in this section, a security interest in proceeds can be perfected only by the methods or under the circumstances permitted in this Article for original collateral of the same type.

. . .

§ 9—312. Priorities Among Conflicting Security Interests in the Same Collateral

(1) The rules of priority stated in other sections of this Part and in the following sections shall govern when applicable: Section 4—208 with respect to the security interests of collecting banks in items being collected, accompanying documents and proceeds; Section 9—103 on security interests related to other jurisdictions; Section 9—114 on consignments.

(2) A perfected security interest in crops for new value given to enable the debtor to produce the crops during the production season, and given not more than three months before the crops become growing crops by planting or otherwise, takes priority over an earlier perfected security interest to the extent that such earlier interest secures obligations due more than six months before the crops become growing crops by planting or otherwise, even though the person giving new value had knowledge of the earlier security interest.

(3) A perfected purchase money security interest in inventory has priority over a conflicting security interest in the same inventory and also has priority in identifiable cash proceeds received on or before the delivery of the inventory to a buyer if

    (a) the purchase money security interest is perfected at the time the debtor receives possession of the inventory; and

    (b) the purchase money secured party gives notification in writing to the holder of the conflicting security interest if the holder had filed a financing statement covering the same types of inventory (i) before the date of the filing made by the purchase money secured party, or (ii) before the beginning of the 21 day period where the purchase money security interest is temporarily perfected without filing or possession (subsection (5) of Section 9—304); and

    (c) the holder of the conflicting security interest receives the notification within five years before the debtor receives possession of the inventory; and

    (d) the notification states that the person giving the notice has or expects to acquire a purchase money security interest in inventory of the debtor, describing such inventory by item or type.

(4) A purchase money security interest in collateral other than inventory has priority over a conflicting security interest in the same collateral or its proceeds if the purchase money security interest is perfected at the time the debtor receives possession of the collateral or within ten days thereafter.

(5) In all cases not governed by other rules stated in this section (including cases of purchase money security interests which do not qualify for the special priorities set forth in subsections (3) and (4) of this section), priority between conflicting security interests in the same collateral shall be determined according to the following rules:

    (a) Conflicting security interests rank according to priority in time of filing or perfection. Priority dates from the time a filing is first made covering the collateral or the time the security interest is first perfected, whichever is earlier, provided that there is no period thereafter when there is neither filing nor perfection.

    (b) So long as conflicting security interests are unperfected, the first to attach has priority.

(6) For the purposes of subsection (5), a date of filing or perfection as to collateral is also a date of filing or perfection as to proceeds.

(7) If future advances are made while a security interest is perfected by filing or the taking of possession, or under Section 8—321 on securities, the security interest has the same priority for the purposes of subsection (5) with respect to the future advances as it does with respect to the first advance. If a commitment is made before or while the security interest is so perfected, the security interest has the same priority with respect to advances made pursuant thereto. In other cases, a perfected security interest has priority from the date the advance is made.

§ 9—318. Defenses Against Assignee; Modification of Contract After Notification of Assignment; Term Prohibiting Assignment Ineffective; Identification and Proof of Assignment

(1) Unless an account debtor has made an enforceable agreement not to assert defenses or claims arising out of a sale as provided in Section 9—206, the rights of an assignee are subject to

> (a) all the terms of the contract between the account debtor and assignor and any defense or claim arising therefrom; and
>
> (b) any other defense or claim of the account debtor against the assignor which accrues before the account debtor receives notification of the assignment.

(2) So far as the right to payment or a part thereof under an assigned contract has not been fully earned by performance, and notwithstanding notification of the assignment, any modification of or substitution for the contract made in good faith and in accordance with reasonable commercial standards is effective against an assignee unless the account debtor has otherwise agreed, but the assignee acquires corresponding rights under the modified or substituted contract. The assignment may provide that such modification or substitution is a breach by the assignor.

(3) The account debtor is authorized to pay the assignor until the account debtor receives notification that the amount due or to become due has been assigned and that payment is to be made to the assignee. A notification which does not reasonably identify the rights assigned is ineffective. If requested by the account debtor, the assignee must seasonably furnish reasonable proof that the assignment has been made; and unless he does so, the account debtor may pay the assignor.

(4) A term in any contract between an account debtor and an assignor is ineffective if it prohibits assignment of an account or prohibits creation of a security interest in a general intangible for money due or to become due or requires the account debtor's consent to such assignment or security interest.

Part 4

Filing

§ 9—401. Place of Filing; Erroneous Filing; Removal of Collateral

. . .

(2) A filing which is made in good faith in an improper place or not in all of the places required by this section is nevertheless effective with regard to any collateral as to which the filing complied with the requirements of this Article and is also effective with regard to collateral covered by the financing statement against any person who has knowledge of the contents of such financing statement.

(3) A filing which is made in the proper place in this state continues effective even though the debtor's residence or place of business or the location of the collateral or its use, whichever controlled the original filing, is thereafter changed.

Alternative Subsection (3)

[(3) A filing which is made in the proper county continues effective for four months after a change to another county of the debtor's residence or place of business or the location of the collateral, whichever controlled the original filing. It becomes ineffective thereafter unless a copy of the financing statement signed by the secured party is filed in the new county within said period. The security interest may also be perfected in the new county after the expiration of the four-month period; in such case, perfection dates from the time of perfection in the new county. A change in the use of the collateral does not impair the effectiveness of the original filing.]

. . .

§ 9—402. Formal Requisites of Financing Statement; Amendments; Mortgage as Financing Statement

(1) A financing statement is sufficient if it gives the names of the debtor and the secured party, is signed by the debtor, gives an address of the secured party from which information concerning the security interest may be obtained, gives a mailing address of the debtor and contains a statement indicating the types, or describing the items, of collateral. A financing statement may be filed before a security agreement is made or a security interest otherwise attaches. When the financing statement covers crops growing or to be grown, the statement must also contain a description of the real estate concerned. When the financing statement covers timber to be cut or covers minerals or the like (including oil and gas) or accounts subject to subsection (5) of Section 9—103, or when the financing statement is filed as a fixture filing (Section 9—313) and the collateral is goods which are or are to become fixtures, the statement must also comply with subsection (5). A copy of the security agreement is sufficient as a financing statement if it contains the above information and is signed by the debtor. A carbon, photographic or other reproduction of a security agreement or a financing statement is sufficient as a financing statement if the security agreement so provides or if the original has been filed in this state.

(2) A financing statement which otherwise complies with subsection (1) is sufficient when it is signed by the secured party instead of the debtor if it is filed to perfect a security interest in

> (a) collateral already subject to a security interest in another jurisdiction when it is brought into this state, or when the debtor's location is changed to this state. Such a financing statement must state that the collateral was brought into this state or that the debtor's location was changed to this state under such circumstances; or

(b) proceeds under Section 9—306 if the security interest in the original collateral was perfected. Such a financing statement must describe the original collateral; or

(c) collateral as to which the filing has lapsed; or

(d) collateral acquired after a change of name, identity or corporate structure of the debtor (subsection (7)).

. . .

(4) A financing statement may be amended by filing a writing signed by both the debtor and the secured party. An amendment does not extend the period of effectiveness of a financing statement. If any amendment adds collateral, it is effective as to the added collateral only from the filing date of the amendment. In this Article, unless the context otherwise requires, the term "financing statement" means the original financing statement and any amendments.

. . .

(7) A financing statement sufficiently shows the name of the debtor if it gives the individual, partnership or corporate name of the debtor, whether or not it adds other trade names or names of partners. Where the debtor so changes his name or, in the case of an organization, its name, identity or corporate structure that a filed financing statement becomes seriously misleading, the filing is not effective to perfect a security interest in collateral acquired by the debtor more than four months after the change, unless a new appropriate financing statement is filed before the expiration of that time. A filed financing statement remains effective with respect to collateral transferred by the debtor even though the secured party knows of or consents to the transfer.

(8) A financing statement substantially complying with the requirements of this section is effective even though it contains minor errors which are not seriously misleading.

Part 5

Default

§ 9—501.   Default; Procedure When Security Agreement Covers Both Real and Personal Property

(1)   When a debtor is in default under a security agreement, a secured party has the rights and remedies provided in this Part and, except as limited by subsection (3), those provided in the security agreement. He may reduce his claim to judgment, foreclose or otherwise enforce the security interest by any available judicial procedure. If the collateral is documents, the secured party may proceed either as to the documents or as to the goods covered thereby. A secured party in possession has the rights, remedies and duties provided in Section 9—207. The rights and remedies referred to in this subsection are cumulative.

(2)   After default, the debtor has the rights and reme-

dies provided in this Part, those provided in the security agreement and those provided in Section 9—207.

. . .

§ 9—502.   Collection Rights of Secured Party

(1)   When so agreed, and in any event on default, the secured party is entitled to notify an account debtor or the obligor on an instrument to make payment to him whether or not the assignor was theretofore making collections on the collateral, and also to take control of any proceeds to which he is entitled under Section 9—306.

(2)   A secured party who by agreement is entitled to charge back uncollected collateral or otherwise to full or limited recourse against the debtor and who undertakes to collect from the account debtors or obligors must proceed in a commercially reasonable manner and may deduct his reasonable expenses of realization from the collections. If the security agreement secures an indebtedness, the secured party must account to the debtor for any surplus, and unless otherwise agreed, the debtor is liable for any deficiency. But, if the underlying transaction was a sale of accounts or chattel paper, the debtor is entitled to any surplus or is liable for any deficiency only if the security agreement so provides.

§ 9—503.   Secured Party's Right to Take Possession After Default

Unless otherwise agreed, a secured party has on default the right to take possession of the collateral. In taking possession, a secured party may proceed without judicial process if this can be done without breach of the peace or may proceed by action. If the security agreement so provides, the secured party may require the debtor to assemble the collateral and make it available to the secured party at a place to be designated by the secured party which is reasonably convenient to both parties. Without removal, a secured party may render equipment unusable and may dispose of collateral on the debtor's premises under Section 9—504.

§ 9—504.   Secured Party's Right to Dispose of Collateral After Default; Effect of Disposition

(1)   A secured party after default may sell, lease or otherwise dispose of any or all of the collateral in its then condition or following any commercially reasonable preparation or processing. Any sale of goods is subject to the Article on Sales (Article 2). . . .

§ 9—505.   Compulsory Disposition of Collateral; Acceptance of the Collateral as Discharge of Obligation

(1)   If the debtor has paid sixty percent of the cash price in the case of a purchase money security interest in consumer goods or sixty percent of the loan in the case of another security interest in consumer goods and has not signed after default a statement renouncing or modifying his rights under this Part, a secured party who has taken possession of collateral must dispose of it under Section 9—504; and if he fails to do so within ninety days after he takes

possession, the debtor at his option may recover in conversion or under Section 9—507(1) on secured party's liability.

(2) In any other case involving consumer goods or any other collateral, a secured party in possession may, after default, propose to retain the collateral in satisfaction of the obligation. Written notice of such proposal shall be sent to the debtor if he has not signed after default a statement renouncing or modifying his rights under this subsection. In the case of consumer goods, no other notice need be given. In other cases, notice shall be sent to any other secured party from whom the secured party has received (before sending his notice to the debtor or before the debtor's renunciation of his rights) written notice of a claim of an interest in the collateral. If the secured party receives objection in writing from a person entitled to receive notification within twenty-one days after the notice was sent, the secured party must dispose of the collateral under Section 9—504. In the absence of such written objection, the secured party may retain the collateral in satisfaction of the debtor's obligation.

§ 9—507.   Secured Party's Liability for Failure to Comply With This Part

(1) If it is established that the secured party is not proceeding in accordance with the provisions of this Part, disposition may be ordered or restrained on appropriate terms and conditions. If the disposition has occurred, the debtor or any person entitled to notification or whose security interest has been made known to the secured party prior to the disposition has a right to recover from the secured party any loss caused by a failure to comply with the provisions of this Part. If the collateral is consumer goods, the debtor has a right to recover in any event an amount not less than the credit service charge plus ten percent of the principal amount of the debt or the time price differential plus 10 percent of the cash price.

. . .

APPENDIX 4
ANALYSIS OF UCC ARTICLE 2A

A. General Principles

In 1987, a new Article 2A, leases, was added to the Uniform Commercial Code to regulate the widespread modern practice of leasing personal property. At the date of publication of this book, Article 2A has been adopted by California, Florida, Hawaii, Indiana, Kansas, Kentucky, Minnesota, Montana, Nebraska, Nevada, North Dakota, Oklahoma, South Dakota, Utah, Virginia, and Wyoming.

§ 1. Subject of lease. The Article 2A lease is a lease of goods or of goods that are or become fixtures. Goods are defined in the same manner as in Article 2 as property that is movable. Whether property is a fixture is determined by the local non-Code law of real estate.

§ 2. Kinds of leases. Article 2A regulates the widely varied fact situations involved in leasing and makes special provision for (1) consumer leases, (2) nonconsumer or commercial leases, (3) finance leases, (4) nonfinance leases, and (5) subleases. These categories may overlap in some cases, as when there is a nonconsumer finance lease. There could also be a consumer finance lease.

In this appendix, consideration will first be given to principles applicable to all kinds of leases, and then special consideration will be given to consumer leases and finance leases.[1]

§ 3. Lease defined. A lease, for the purpose of Article 2A of the UCC, is "a transfer of the right to possession and use of goods [or fixtures] for a term in return for consideration. . . ."[2] A gratuitous bailment is thus excluded from the definition of *lease*. Also excluded are absolute sales and sales on approval or return. A lease that creates a security interest is also excluded.[3]

B. Formation and Effect of Lease

§ 4. Formation of the lease. A lease is formed when the parties reach an agreement to lease. The process specified by Article 2A is in substance a copy of the process described by Article 2 on the sale of goods. Article 2A repeats the firm offer provision as to merchants. It also nullifies the common-law effect of a seal. Offer and acceptance under Article 2A is the same as under Article 2, except that there is no provision for acceptance by shipment of goods or for additional terms in an acceptance or confirmation. The subject of modification, rescission, and waiver is treated by Article 2A in the same manner as Article 2.[4]

§ 5. Validity of lease. A lease is subject to the general rules of law that determine the validity of a contract. Article 2A repeats the prohibition against unconscionability[5] that is found in UCC § 2–302.

Article 2A recognizes that a lease may also be subject to a law of the United States, a title certificate statute of the local state or of a foreign state, and to consumer protection laws.[6]

§ 6. Interest of parties. As long as the lease continues, the lessor and the lessee both have property interests in the goods involved. As between the two of them, the lessor has a residual or reversionary interest that entitles the lessor to possession of the goods upon termination of the lease for any reason, and the lessee has the right to possess and use the goods while the lease continues.

Each party to the lease has an insurable interest in the goods and has standing to sue a third person for injury done to the goods.

§ 7. Assignment. Either party to a lease may make a voluntary transfer of that party's interest under the lease unless the lease contains an express prohibition against such transfer. However, even when a transfer is permitted, it may be nullified by a condition subsequent declared by the UCC. If the transfer will change the duty, burden, or risk

---

[1] Those wishing to go beyond the scope of this appendix will find an exhaustive, professional-level analysis of Article 2A in the 1989 Annotation to Volume 5 of *Anderson on the Uniform Commercial Code*, 3rd edition, Lawyers Co-operative Publishing Company, Rochester, New York, beginning with the 1989 annotation.

[2] UCC § 2A-103(1)(j).

[3] States adopting Article 2A will also adopt a 1987 Amendment to UCC § 1–103(37), redefining security interest in order to clarify the problem of when a lease is to be regarded as a secured transaction.

[4] UCC § 2A-208. No provision is made as to whether a lease as modified is required to satisfy the statute of frauds.

[5] UCC § 2A-108.

[6] UCC § 2A-104(1).

imposed upon the other party to the lease, that party may demand protection against such harm. If such a protective demand is not satisfied, the transfer made has no effect.[7]

It is not expressly stated whether duties may be delegated, but references to "duty" in the UCC[8] may be construed as including the delegation of duties. In any event, as there is no displacement by the UCC of the pre-Code law relating to the delegation of duties, it should be concluded that duties under a lease may be delegated, subject to the pre-Code limitations on delegation.

§ 8. Involuntary transfer. An involuntary transfer of the interest of any party to a lease may occur without regard to whether the lease contains a prohibition against transfer. Thus, the interest of a party under a lease may, in an otherwise proper case, be sold in execution on a creditor's judgment against that party. Likewise, if a party to a lease files a petition in bankruptcy court, the trustee in bankruptcy acquires the interest of the debtor.

The involuntary transfer of the interest of a party to a lease is subject to the same condition subsequent as discussed in § 7. That is, if the transfer will change the duty, burden, or risk imposed upon the other party to the lease, that party may make a protective demand, and if that demand is not satisfied, the transfer is nullified or canceled.

§ 9. Filing or recording. No filing or recording is required in the case of a lease in order to protect the rights of the parties thereto. An exception is made to this statement when the goods involved are or will become fixtures.[9]

The fact that a lease results in one person owning title to goods that are in the possession of another person is not fraudulent but is the very nature of a lease. Some jurisdictions have local statutes declaring the split of possession and title to be fraudulent or evidence of fraud. These statutes are overridden by Article 2A in states in which 2A is adopted.[10]

§ 10. Parol evidence. Article 2A repeats the parol evidence rule provision of Article 2 and permits a written lease to be supplemented or explained by evidence of a course of dealings, usage of trade, and course of performance.

§ 11. Statute of frauds. An oral lease is valid when the rental payments are less than $1,000. If $1,000 or more, the lease must be evidenced by a writing. If there is not a sufficient writing, the lease cannot be enforced by way of action or defense, although the lease is not in itself illegal and, when voluntarily performed, cannot be canceled on the claim that it was illegal.

The writing that is offered to satisfy the statute of frauds must be signed by the party against whom enforcement is sought. The content of the writing need only be "sufficient to indicate" that a lease contract has been made

and to describe the goods and state the term or duration of the lease.[11]

As in the case of transactions in goods under Article 2, the absence of a writing that satisfies the statute of frauds is excused when the goods cannot be disposed of by sale or lease, or there is a judicial admission of the existence of the oral lease, or the goods have been received and accepted by the lessee. The fact that the lessee makes payments under the lease does not excuse the absence of a writing.

§ 12. Identification of goods to lease. Article 2A follows the pattern of identification of goods made by Article 2.

§ 13. Insurable interest. The lease article follows the pattern of the sales article with respect to identification's giving rise to an insurable interest of the lessee. The lease article goes further and makes a more detailed regulation of insurable interest. The lessor, whether purchasing or leasing goods from the supplier, has an insurable interest in the goods that continues and is only terminated should the lessee purchase the goods. The lessee acquires an insurable interest in the leased goods when they are both existing and identified to the lease, even though the goods are so nonconforming that the lessee has the power to reject them.[12]

§ 14. Express and implied warranties. The express and implied warranty provisions of Article 2A parallel those of Article 2, except that the implied warranty of title is replaced under Article 2A by an implied warranty of quiet possession. This is a warranty that "for the lease term no person holds a claim to or interest in the goods that arose from an act or omission of the lessor . . . which will interfere with the lessee's enjoyment of its leasehold interest."[13]

When warranties are excluded by words, there must in all cases be a writing in which the exclusion is conspicuous, and "merchantability" must be expressly mentioned in order to exclude the implied warranty of merchantability.[14]

The subject of third party beneficiaries of warranties is regulated by UCC § 2A-216 in the same manner as in UCC § 2–318. In addition, the lessee of a finance lease is a beneficiary of the warranties of the supplier.[15]

§ 15. Performance of lease contract. Article 2A sets forth provisions paralleling those of Article 2 relating to insecurity and demand for assurance, the making and retracting of an anticipatory repudiation, and substituted and excused performance.[16]

C.   Rights of Third Persons

§ 16. Effect of lease. A lease passes to the lessee no greater interest than it purports to transfer. Thus, a lease for

---

[7]   UCC § 2A-303.
[8]   UCC § 2A-303(1)(b),(4).
[9]   UCC § 2A-309.
[10] UCC § 2A-302.

[11] UCC § 2A-201(b).
[12] UCC § 2A-219(1).
[13] UCC § 2A-211(1).
[14] UCC § 2A-214(20).
[15] See this Appendix, § 43.
[16] UCC § 2A-401 to § 2A-406.

one year passes only the right to possession for one year. At the same time, it ordinarily passes no greater right to the goods than possessed by the lessor. To illustrate, assume that *A* holds possession under a lease for 6 months. A sublease by *A* to *B* for 12 months could not have effect beyond 6 months. Ordinarily, third persons, such as purchasers from and creditors of the lessor and lessee, can acquire no greater right than possessed by the party to the lease.[17]

§ 17. Voidable title of lessor. When the lessee acts in good faith and gives value in entering into the lease, it is immaterial that the lessor had only a voidable title. The lessee then acquires "a good leasehold interest," meaning that the lessee's interest is not subject to avoidance on the ground on which the lessor's interest could have been avoided had there not been such a subsequent good faith lessee for value.

Whether the lessor's title is voidable depends upon continuing pre-Code law, as Article 2A does not define the term. It does, however, indicate that there is a voidable title when there has been an impersonation, a dishonored check, a cash sale, or criminal fraud.[18]

§ 18. Entrustment to lessor merchant. If the lessee entrusts the leased goods to the lessor from whom the goods have been leased and that lessor is a merchant who deals in goods of that kind, a lease of those goods made by the entrustee to a third person who leases in the ordinary course of business transfers the goods to such subsequent lessee free of the leasehold interest of the original lessee in the entrusted goods.[19]

If any element of this entrustment provision is not satisfied, a subsequent lease by the person in possession of the goods, whether or not an entrustee, passes merely the rights of that person, and the rights of the original lessee remain unchanged. Moreover, if the goods are covered by a certificate of title, the rights of the subsequent lessee are governed both by the Article 2A provision above noted and by the certificate of title statute.[20]

§ 19. Sale or lease by merchant lessee. If the lessee is a merchant dealing in goods of that kind, the lessee has the power to pass the title or interest of the lessor by a lease of the goods to a lessee in the ordinary course of business or by a sale of the goods to a buyer in the ordinary course of business. If the goods are subject to a certificate of title statute, the effect of the sale or lease by the lessee is governed by both Article 2A and by such statute.[21]

§ 20. Rights of creditors of the parties. The general creditors of either party to the lease must recognize the limited right of their debtor and the rights of the other party to the lease.

The claim of a creditor of the lessor is superior to the lease if the creditor holds a lien on or security interest in the goods that was perfected before the lease became binding or is able to avoid the lease as fraudulent under non-Code rules of law. The interest of a secured creditor that would otherwise be superior may be defeated if the entrustment provisions are applicable.[22]

§ 21. Fraudulent lease. If the creditor of the lessor can establish that the lease to the lessee was made to defraud creditors, the lease can be set aside. The mere fact that the lease gives possession of the goods to a person who is not its owner is not fraudulent. Likewise, the fact that the lessee in a given case allows the seller to retain possession of the leased goods for a commercially reasonable time does not constitute fraud, or as stated by the UCC, when goods are so left "in good faith and current course of trade." It is also declared that fraud is not established by showing that there was a sale of goods to a buyer who then made a lease back (a leaseback) to the seller.[23]

§ 22. Priority over hypothetical perfected secured creditor. In the absence of a contrary local non-Code consumer protection statute, a creditor of the lessor will prevail over the rights of the lessee if the creditor would have priority over a perfected hypothetical creditor. In order to satisfy this requirement, the creditor of the lessor must hold an Article 9 security interest in the leased goods, and, by virtue of UCC § 9–312, that interest would have priority over a hypothetical secured creditor who perfected his interest by filing at the time when the lease became enforceable. When these conditions are met, the creditor of the lessor may ignore the lease, even though it is a consumer lease, and treat the goods as belonging, without any limitation, to the lessor.[24]

§ 23. Bailee's lien for services and materials. Non-Code law in many jurisdictions gives a bailee for hire a lien upon goods for services or materials supplied in connection with the goods. When any party to the lease delivers the goods to a bailee who furnishes services or materials and this gives rise to a lien, that lien is binding on all parties to the lease unless the law declaring the existence of the lease expressly makes the lien inferior or subordinate to the leasehold interests.[25]

To illustrate, when the lessee takes the leased truck to a shop for repairs, the lien for repairs is superior to the right of both the lessee and the lessor in the truck. This means that the truck cannot be obtained from the repairer without making payment of the amount due for repairs and, under most statutes, that the repairer, after giving statutory notice, may sell the truck in spite of the lease in order to obtain payment of the amount due.

---

[17]   UCC § 2A-301.
[18]   UCC § 2A-304. The "cash sale" provision was apparently inadvertently included in Article 2A in disregard of the fact that UCC § 2–403 had abolished the view that a "cash sale" was a transaction subject to a condition subsequent of nonpayment.
[19]   UCC § 2A-304(2).
[20]   UCC § 2A-304(3).
[21]   UCC § 2A-305.

[22]   See this appendix, § § 18 et seq.
[23]   UCC § 2A-308. See Official Code Comment to that section, 4.
[24]   UCC § 2A-307(2)(b).
[25]   UCC § 2A-306.

D.   Remedies on Default

§ 24. Generally. Part 5 of Article 2A of the UCC specifies in detail the remedies available to a party to a lease upon breach by the other party. In addition to the remedies specified by the UCC, the parties in their lease may provide for other remedies. Such other remedies are to be regarded as cumulative, with those provided by the UCC unless expressly stated to be exclusive.

The power to provide for remedies in the lease includes the power to modify the UCC remedies and to liquidate or limit damages. When a limited remedy fails of its intended purpose, the aggrieved party, as under Article 2, may pursue any remedy authorized by the UCC or by the contract of the parties.[26]

When there is a default, the aggrieved party is not required to give the defaulting party any notice of the fact that there is a default or of the steps that the aggrieved party will take to enforce the obligations of the lease.[27]

§ 25. Statute of limitations. An action for breach of a lease must be brought within 4 years after the breach "was or should have been discovered by the aggrieved party or when the default occurs whichever is later."[28]

The same limitations period applies to a suit by a defendant against a third person, such as a suit by a lessor against a supplier, to obtain indemnity for the liability of the defendant to the plaintiff.

§ 26. Refund of payments to lessee. When the lessee is in default or when delivery of the goods to the lessee has been withheld or stopped because of the lessee's insolvency, the lessor must make a refund of part of the payments already made by the lessee to the lessor. If there is a valid limitation or liquidation of damages, the refund that must be made to the lessee is the difference between the amount of the payments made and the amount of the limitation. If there is no valid limitation or liquidation of damages, the refund is the difference between the total payments made by the lessee and 20 percent of the "then present value of the total rent the lessee was obligated to pay for the balance of the lease term."[29]

§ 27. Lessor's default. The default of the lessor may consist of a failure to deliver any goods under the lease, a repudiation of the lease, or delivery of nonconforming goods that were rightfully rejected by the lessee or the acceptance of which was rightfully revoked by the lessee.

§ 28. Lessee's remedies. When the lessor has defaulted under the provisions of the UCC or the lease contract, the lessee may employ the following remedies:

(1) rejection of improper tender of goods,

(2) revocation of acceptance of improper goods,

(3) cancellation of the lease,

(4) recovery of payments made to the lessor,

(5) cover and recovery of damages from the lessor,

(6) recovery of damages for nondelivery or breach of warranty,

(7) recovery of identified goods in case of nondelivery or repudiation by the lessor,

(8) specific performance, replevin, or other action to obtain the goods, and

(9) employment of the remedies provided by the lease contract or any collateral contract.

The above remedies are cumulative, and the use of one does not bar use of another, as long as the facts are such as to permit the use of the remedy in question.[30]

Although not strictly defined as a remedy, a lessee who has possession of nonconforming goods that have been rejected or as to which acceptance has been revoked has a security interest in such goods equal to any payments that should be refunded and any expenses reasonably incurred in the inspection of the goods and in their receipt, transportation, custody, and care.[31]

§ 29. Lessee's default. The default of the lessee may be an improper rejection or an improper revocation of the acceptance of conforming goods or nonpayment of the rent or a repudiation of the lease contract.[32]

§ 30. Lessor's remedies. When the lessee is in default, the lessor may

(1) employ the remedies specified in the lease,

(2) cancel the lease,

(3) identify to the lease goods in the lessor's possession and dispose of the goods,

(4) withhold delivery or stop delivery by a bailee or carrier,

(5) repossess the goods,

(6) retain the goods and recover damages,

(7) dispose of the goods and recover damages, and

(8) recover rent.[33]

As in the case of a lessee, the foregoing remedies of the lessor are cumulative and the lessor has the option to employ any remedy that is supported by the facts of the case. However, the lessor cannot be required to select one remedy and give up the others.

E.   Consumer Lease

§ 31. Consumer lease defined. A consumer lease is defined in terms of the character of the parties, the nature of the lessee's use of the goods, and the total rental payments due under the lease. The lessor must be a merchant who customarily sells or leases the kind of goods involved. The lessee must be a natural person and must obtain the goods

---

[26]   UCC § 2A-503(2).

[27]   Official Code Comment to UCC § 2A-501.

[28]   UCC § 2A-506(2). This may be described as a modified discovery rule and abandons the breach-on-tender rule of UCC § 2-725.

[29]   UCC § 2A-504(3)(b).

[30]   UCC § 2A-508 to § 2A-522.

[31]   UCC § 2A-508(5).

[32]   UCC § 2A-523(1). As to installment leases, see UCC § 2A-510.

[33]   UCC § 2A-523 to § 2A-530.

"primarily for a personal, family, or household use." Finally, the total rental payments required by the lease must be under $25,000.[34]

A consumer lease arises when a person leases a car from a car rental agency to take a vacation trip or to make daily trips to and from work or school. A consumer lease is, in general, subject to the provisions noted in the preceding parts of this appendix.[35] Article 2A makes certain exceptions or substitute provisions with respect to consumer leasing, and these are set forth in the following sections of this appendix.[36]

§ 32. Consumer protection laws. Article 2A does not displace or repeal any consumer protection law applicable to consumer leases. If there is no conflict between the provisions of such statutes and the provisions of Article 2A, the statutes and Article 2A will apply concurrently to a given consumer lease. In the event of an inconsistency, the consumer protection statute will prevail and displace the provisions of Article 2A.

§ 33. Choice of law. When the lease is a consumer lease, the parties do not have the full freedom given by UCC § 1–105 to designate the jurisdiction whose law is to govern. Instead, it must be a jurisdiction in which the goods are to be used or in which the lessee resides at the time the lease becomes binding or within 30 days thereafter.[37]

§ 34. Specification of forum. When the consumer lease specifies a forum in which suit may be brought against the lessee, that forum must be one that would have jurisdiction over the consumer even in the absence of such provision.[38] No provision is made as to the designation of the forum in which the consumer lessee is required to bring a suit against the lessor. If the effect of such a limitation is to place an unreasonable barrier that will bar a suit by the consumer lessee, it is likely that it will be held invalid as unconscionable.

§ 35. Statute of frauds. The statute of frauds provision applicable to leases[39] is equally applicable to consumer leases.

UCC § 2A-201 does not alter or affect a consumer protection statute that may require a more detailed writing than is required to satisfy the Article 2A statute of frauds. If the consumer protection statute is not satisfied, the consumer lease cannot be enforced even though the UCC provision is satisfied. This supremacy of the consumer protection statute is expressly declared by the UCC.[40]

§ 36. Unconscionability. Article 2A restates the protection against unconscionability made by UCC § 2–302 and, in the case of consumer leases, expands it to authorize judicial examination of preleasing and postleasing conduct

and to provide for the award of attorney's fees. If the consumer lease has been induced by "unconscionable conduct," the court may also grant appropriate relief when "unconscionable conduct has occurred in the collection of a claim arising from the lease contract." If the court finds that the lessee has been the victim of unconscionability, it shall award reasonable attorney's fees to the lessee. However, if the claim of unconscionability is groundless, the court shall award such fees to the lessor.[41]

§ 37. Acceleration of rent. When the lease permits the lessor to accelerate the balance of rent due for the remainder of the lease term when the lessee defaults, the lessor must act in the good faith belief that the default has made the lessor insecure. In the case of a consumer lease, the lessor has the burden of proving that the acceleration was made in good faith, as against the general rule that the lessee has the burden of proving that the lessor acted in bad faith.[42]

F.   Nonconsumer or Commercial Lease

§ 38. Nonconsumer or commercial lease defined. When a lease does not satisfy the definition of a consumer lease, it may be called a *nonconsumer* or *commercial* lease. For example, a contractor rents a truck for a year for the purpose of hauling building materials.

§ 39. Commercial nonfinance lease. When a lease is a commercial nonfinance lease, the provisions set forth in this appendix in the first four parts will govern the rights of the parties.[43]

G.   Finance Lease

1.   General principles

§ 40. Finance lease defined. In a finance lease, the customer knows exactly what is wanted and who makes or distributes it. Instead of going directly to the supplier, the customer goes to a financer and tells the financer where and what to obtain. The financer then purchases the goods from the supplier and leases the goods to the customer. As a variation of this pattern, the financer might lease the goods from the supplier and then sublet the goods to the customer. In either case the financer is in effect merely a paper channel, or conduit, between the supplier and the customer; the supplier and the customer are the real parties in interest. Article 2A emphasizes this character of the financer of a finance lease by defining a finance lease as a lease in which

(1) the lessor does not select, manufacture, or supply the goods,

(2) the financer acquires the goods in order to fill the lease to the customer, and

---

[34]   UCC § 2A-103(1)(e).
[35]   Parts A to D, inclusive.
[36]   See this appendix, § § 33 et seq.
[37]   UCC § 2A-106.
[38]   UCC § 2A-106.
[39]   See this appendix, § 11.
[40]   UCC § 2A-104(1)(d).

[41]   UCC § 2A-108.
[42]   UCC § 2A-109(2).
[43]   Parts A to D, inclusive.

(3) the lessee must approve the terms of the transaction between the supplier and the financer.[44]

§ 41. Independence-irrevocability concept. When the lessee of a nonconsumer finance lease accepts the goods, the lessee's obligations under the lease become irrevocable and independent from the obligations of the finance lessor.[45] This independence and irrevocability require the lessee to perform under the lease without regard to whether the finance lessor performs. This reverses the ordinary rule of contract law by which the obligations of the lessee and lessor would be mutually dependent, so that a default by the lessor would entitle the lessee to assert remedies for breach of contract. By virtue of the UCC provision the lessee cannot claim nonliability for a breach on the ground that the lessor has failed to perform its obligation under the lease. When suit is brought against the lessee by the finance lessor's assignee, the lessee is also barred from asserting that the finance lessor has not performed the lease.[46]

The waiver that the finance lessee makes by accepting the goods is irrevocable.[47] However, this finality does not bar avoiding the lease on such grounds as fraud, duress, or any other factor that by principles of contract law warrant avoiding a contract. The waiver that the lessee makes by accepting the goods is also canceled if the lessee makes a proper revocation of acceptance.

The independence-irrevocability concept is not applicable to a consumer finance lease and, therefore, does not bar the assertion by the consumer lessee of any defenses that would otherwise be available.

§ 42. Formation of supply contract. The finance lessor and the supplier of the lessor may make the supply contract on such terms as they decide. They may include in the supply contract any provision that is valid in a sales contract. In the making of the supply contract the parties can ignore the fact that there will be a lessee who will ultimately receive the goods supplied to the lessor. If the supply contract is a sale, as distinguished from a lease, any exclusion of warranties, any limitation of damages or remedies, and any modification of the statute of limitations that is valid under Article 2 may be properly included in the supply contract, and the lessee is bound thereby when asserting a claim against the supplier. This arrangement does not give the finance lessor and the supplier the power to impose upon the finance lessee a transaction that is not acceptable to the finance lessee. The finance lessee will not enter into the finance lease without first approving a copy of the supply contract, or a finance lease executed in advance of seeing the supply contract will include a provision that it shall be void if the lessee does not approve the supply contract. That is, the economic reality of the situation gives the finance lessee

a control over the supply contract that does not exist as a matter of law.

§ 43. Lessee as beneficiary of supply contract. Article 2A in effect makes the finance lessee the third party beneficiary of the supply contract. The lessee may bring suit in the lessee's own name directly against the supplier for breach by the supplier of any obligation of the supplier under the supply contract that would benefit the lessee if performed. This provision enables the finance lessee to sue the supplier directly for breach of any express or implied warranty of the supply contract.[48] As in the case of a third party beneficiary contract, the finance lessee is bound by the terms of the supply contract. Likewise, the fact that the lessee acquires rights under the supply contract does not constitute a delegation of any duties to the lessee.[49]

2.   Particular applications of status of finance lessee

§ 44. Generally. The effect of the independence-irrevocability concept[50] and the conferring on the lessee of the status of beneficiary of the supply contract[51] have the practical effect of making the finance lessee the other contracting party to the supply contract as far as the obligations of the supplier are concerned. This treatment of the parties to the finance lease is also seen in the following sections of this appendix.

§ 45. Exemption of finance lessor from implied warranties. The finance lessor does not make any implied warranty of freedom from infringement claims, merchantability, or fitness for a particular purpose.[52] Any warranty of a finance lessor must therefore rest on an express warranty made by the lessor.

§ 46. Restriction of revocation of acceptance. The finance lessee may revoke acceptance only when the lessee has accepted the goods because the lessor's assurance of conformity induced the lessee to accept the goods without discovering their nonconformity. Thus, the finance lessee is deprived of the right to revoke acceptance for the two other grounds that can be asserted by a nonfinance lessee:

(1) acceptance was made without knowledge of the nonconformity because of the difficulty of discovering the nonconformity before acceptance, or

(2) although the nonconformity was known by the lessee at the time of acceptance, the lessee accepted the goods on the reasonable assumption that the nonconformity would be seasonably cured, but it was not so cured.[53]

The nonconformity upon which the finance lessee's revocation is based is a nonconformity with respect to the finance lease as distinguished from the supply contract.[54]

---

[44]   UCC § 2A-103(1)(g). This third element is important, because the lessee is in effect a third party beneficiary of the contract between the supplier and the financer. See this appendix, § 43.

[45]   UCC § 2A-407(1).

[46]   UCC § 2A-307(2)(a).

[47]   UCC § 2A-407(2)(b).

[48]   UCC § 2A-209(1).

[49]   Official Code Comment to UCC § 2A-209, 3.

[50]   See this appendix, § 41.

[51]   See this appendix, § 43.

[52]   UCC § 2A-211(2), § 2A-212(1), and § 2A-213.

[53]   UCC § 2A-517(1).

[54]   Official Code Comment to § 2A-516, 1.

§ 47. Transfer of risk of loss. In a nonfinance lease, the risk of loss remains with the lessor and does not pass to the lessee. In contrast, in a finance lease the risk of loss passes to the lessee, and Article 2A makes detailed provisions similar to UCC § 2–509 as to when such risk of loss passes to the lessee when not specified in the finance lease.[55]

§ 48. Procedure on reduced performance. Article 2A follows the pattern of UCC § § 2–615 and 2–616 when complete performance cannot be made because of the failure of a presupposed condition. When the lease is a nonfinance lease, the lessee, upon being offered a partial performance, may elect to take such performance, but the acceptance thereof is a waiver of any claim for a deficiency. This procedure does not apply to a nonconsumer finance lessee.[56] The net result is that such finance lessee may accept the reduced performance but reserve the right to damages for the deficiency.

§ 49. Modification and rescission of supply contract. The finance lessor and the supplier may between themselves make any modification of the supply contract they choose. However, the making of a change that is harmful to the finance lessee imposes liability upon the party to the supply contract to the finance lessee for the amount of the loss caused thereby. With respect to the supplier this liability arises as to any harmful change made after the supplier has received notice that the finance lease has been entered into. In the case of the finance lessor the liability for harmful change arises as soon as the finance lease is entered into. In applying the above provisions it is immaterial that as a practical matter the finance lessor and the supplier had reason to know and contemplated that a finance lease would in fact be entered into.[57]

§ 50. Nondeduction of damage claims from rent due. If a nonfinance lessee has a right to recover damages from the lessor, the lessee may deduct all or part of such damage claim from any part of the rent "still due under the same lease contract."[58] In the case of a nonconsumer finance lessee, this deduction cannot be made if the lessee has already accepted the goods. This result follows from application of the independence-irrevocability concept.[59]

If the finance lease is a consumer lease, the lessee has the same right of setoff of a damage claim as in the case of a nonfinance lease.

---

[55]   UCC § 2A-219.
[56]   UCC § 2A-406.

[57]   UCC § 2A-209(3).
[58]   UCC § 2A-508(6).
[59]   See this appendix, § 41.

APPENDIX 5
ARTICLE 3 [1990 REVISION]
SECTIONAL CONCORDANCE

This table lists the sections of the 1990 revision of Article 3 that make significant changes or additions to Article 3 as set forth in the text. The column at the left of the page states the chapter and section number of this text that is involved. Each such reference is followed by a brief statement identifying the subject matter and the citation in brackets of the section of the 1990 revision of Article 3 relating thereto. For a complete professional-level analysis of revised Article 3, see the supplement to 6 *Anderson on the Uniform Commercial code* (3d Edition, Lawyers Co-operative Publishing Company).

Text Section	Subject matter and 1990 revision citation
Ch. 30	
1	Name changed to negotiable instruments [§ 3-101]
	Notation excluding nonchecks from Article 3 [§ 3-104(d)]
	Effect on underlying obligation [§ 3-310]
2	Drafts and notes only [§ 3-104]
	Same person drawer-drawee not a note [§ 3-103(a) (6)]
	Omission of nonnegotiable paper
	Checks, cashier's checks, teller's checks, bank money order [§ 3-104(f)]
	Travelers checks [§ 3-104(i)]
	Certificate of deposit [§ 3-104(j)]
3	Incomplete instrument [§ 3-110]
	Notice of right to defend action [§ 3-119]
	Definitions [§ 3-104]
	Remitter defined [§ 3-103(a) (11)]
3(d)	Identity of payee [§ 3-110]
	Joint and alternative payees [§ 3-110(d)]
3(e)	No liability of nonaccepting drawee [§ 3-408]
	Draft-varying acceptance [§ 3-410]
	Issuer [§ 3-105]
3(f)	No interest and floating interest [§ 3-112]
	Anomalous indorser [§ 3-116(a)]
3(g)	Delayed payment order of postdated check [see Appendix 6]
4	Statute of limitations [§ 3-118]
	Joint and several liability [§ 3-116]
	Contribution [§ 3-116]
	Liability of issuer of note or cashier's check [§ 3-412]
	Obligation of acceptor [§ 3-413]
	Obligation of drawer [§ 3-414]
	Obligation of indorser [§ 3-415]

APPENDIX 6
ARTICLE 4 [1990 REVISION] SECTIONAL CONCORDANCE

This table lists the sections of the 1990 revision of Article 4 that make significant changes or additions to Article 4 as set forth in this text. The column at the left of the page states the chapter and section number of this text that is involved. Each such reference is followed by a brief statement identifying the subject matter and the citation in brackets of the section of the 1990 revision relating thereto. For a complete professional-level analysis of revised Article 4, see supplement to 7 *Anderson on the Uniform Commercial Code* (3d Edition, Lawyers Co-operative Publishing Company).

Text Section	*Subject matter and 1990 revision citation*
Ch. 34	
4	Variation by agreement [§ 4-103]
	Effect of instructions [§ 4-203]
	Liability for premature payment of postdated check [§ 4-401]
	Physical examination of item by bank [see § 3-103(a) (7)]
6	Electronic presentment [§ 4-110]
	Sending to payor bank [§ 4-204]
	Transfer between banks [§ 4-206]
	Presentment by notice [§ 4-212]
7	Liability for wrongful dishonor [§ 4-402]
	Time for determining sufficiency of account [§ 4-402]
	Stale checks [§ 4-404]
	Incompetent or dead customer [§ 4-405]
8	Agency status [§ 4-201]
	Separate office of bank [§ 4-107]
	Unindorsed item [§ 4-205]
	Security interest of bank [§ 4-210]
	When bank gives value [§ 4-211]
	Medium and time of settlement [§ 4-213]
	Chargeback or refund [§ 4-214]
	Deferred posting [§ 4-301]
	Statute of limitations [§ 4-111]
	Transfer warranties [§ 4-208]
	Encoding and retention warranties [§ 4-209]
9	Right to stop payment [§ 4-403]
11	Duty of customer to examine and report forgery and alteration [§ 4-406]
15	Time of receipt of items [§ 4-108]
	Delays [§ 4-109]
	Responsibility for collection or return [§ 4-202]
	Late return liability [§ 4-302]

APPENDIX 7
1990 UCC SUPPLEMENT
TO COMMERCIAL PAPER

CHAPTER 30. KINDS OF PAPER, PARTIES, AND NEGOTIABILITY

The most significant changes made by the 1990 revision of Article 3 that relate to Chapter 30 follow.

§ 1. Definition

The 1990 Revision changes the name of Article 3 to "Negotiable Instruments."

The 1990 revision of Article 3 does not apply to money, transfer payment orders under Article 4A, nor to securities that come within the scope of Article 8. Documents of title are not expressly excluded but are excluded by definition as they do not call for the payment of money.

An instrument, other than a check, that would come within the scope of Article 3 may be excluded therefrom by a conspicuous notation that it is not to be controlled by Article 3. This may not be done in the case of checks. (UCC § 3-104(d), 1990 Revision.)

§ 2. Kinds of commercial paper

The 1990 revision of Article 3 divides negotiable instruments into drafts and notes. A certificate of deposit is merely a promissory note of the bank and not a separate category of negotiable instrument.

A draft or check remains such even though the drawer and the drawee are the same person. (UCC § 3-103(a) (6), 1990 Revision)

The draft or check does not automatically become a note and the possessor of the paper does not have to option to treat it as a note.

§ 3. Parties to commercial paper

The 1990 revision of Article 3 identifies the maker and the drawer as the issuer of the instrument and defines issue to require the delivery by such person of the instrument with the intent to give rights therein to the person to or for whom the paper is delivered. A paper handed to someone to see if it is satisfactory as to form is not an issuance of the instrument because the intent to then create rights is lacking.

§ 4. Liability of parties
§ 5. Requirements of negotiability

If an incomplete instrument is sufficiently complete to be a negotiable instrument, it is effective as such even though it is never completed. Thus, an instrument in which the installment schedule is left blank will be effective as demand paper. An instrument in which the payee's name is never filled in will be effective as bearer paper. If the incomplete instrument is so incomplete that it does not satisfy the requirements of Article 3, it is not governed by that Article and has no effect other than as possible evidence of the existence of a contract between the parties.

The 1990 revision of Article 3 abolishes coverage of nonnegotiable instruments. In order to come under revised Article 3, the instrument must be negotiable. If it is not, it is not under Article 3 and is then governed by contract and other pre-Code law.

When the instrument contains a preservation of defenses of a consumer, the instrument remains negotiable but there cannot be a holder in due course of such instrument.

(a) Signature. The signature of a party to a negotiable instrument may be made by hand or by any device or machine and may be made by the person involved or by an authorized agent.

The 1990 revision of Article 3 makes the practical exception to the rule of the earlier Article, by declaring that when the agent signs individually a check that bears the pre-printed name or account number of the principal, the agent is not bound thereby, even though he failed to comply with the requirements as to signing by a representative. (UCC § 3-402(c), 1990 Revision.)

(b) Unconditional order or promise. An order or a promise is conditional when it is subject to an express condition or to the terms of another instrument.

A reference to the consideration for which the paper has been given is not a condition, as no condition is to be implied that the consideration must be performed. An order or promise is unconditional even though it specifies that payment shall be made from a particular source or fund and does not impose liability on the issuer. (UCC § 3-106(b) (ii), 1990 Revision.) The requirement that the instrument be countersigned does not make the instrument conditional nor affect its negotiability. The requirement of the counter-signature is merely a condition precedent to the obligation of the issuer to pay the instrument.

(c) Payment in money. Money is defined as any medium of exchange authorized or adopted by a domestic state or a foreign government or an intergovernmental organization.

(d) Sum certain. An instrument bears no interest unless it states that interest is payable. Thus, no interest is payable if no statement as to interest is made. The interest may be stated as a fixed amount or as a variable or floating amount. In the latter case, the calculation of the interest day "may require reference to information not contained in the instrument." If the instrument states that interest is payable but does not specify the amount nor a formula for determining the amount, the interest rate is the judgment rate in effect at the place of payment when the interest first accrues. (UCC § 3-112, 1990 Revision.)

(e) Time of payment. The 1990 revision expands the definition of "payable at a definite time" to include payment at a time that is "readily ascertainable."

The holder of an instrument may extend the time of payment for any period of time and for any number of extensions. The instrument may also give the maker or acceptor the privilege of extending the time for payment. But in the latter case there may only be one extension and it must be to a definite date. In addition, the instrument may specify a time for payment and then further state that the instrument is automatically extended until another specified date if a specified act or event is done or takes place.

(f) Order or bearer. The requirement that a negotiable instrument be payable to order or bearer is abolished with respect to checks. (UCC § 3-104(c), 1990 Revision.)

An instrument payalbe to the order of a named person or bearer or payable to the order of bearer, or to cash or to the order of cash, or to the order of or to an impersonal payee is classified as a bearer instrument.

When an instrument does not name a payee it is payable to bearer even though there is no statement that it is a bearer instrument. (UCC § 3-109(a) (2), 1990 Revision.) If the instrument is not a bearer instrument and it is payable to a natural or artificial person or to a legal or commercial entity, it is order paper. this is described as being payable to an identified person. The payee may be identified in the instrument by name, number, account number, or by the title of an office.

CHAPTER 31. TRANSFER OF COMMERCIAL PAPER

Sections below state the significant changes made by the 1990 revision of Article 3.

§ 1.   Impostor rule (§ 5 of Chapter 31)

The 1990 revision reclassifies the subject of the former impostor rule by dividing the subject into impostors and fictitious payees. (UCC § 3-404, 1990 Revision.) In the impostor situation, a person or a confederate impersonates another person and thereby induces the maker or drawer to issue the instrument payable to the impersonated person. The impersonation may be made "by use of the mails or otherwise." The other impostor situations include those in which it is intended that the named payee should not have any interest in the instrument. This covers both the case where the drawer or maker has such intent and the case in which the employee supplying the name of the payee has such intent. In addition, it covers cases in which the intent is to make the instrument payable to a named payee who in fact has neither legal nor commercial existence. Such a non-existent payee is a fictitious payee. All of the above are governed by the 1990 impostor rule.

An impostor instrument may be effectively indorsed by any possessor of the instrument. The person who in good faith pays the instrument or who takes it for value or collection is immune from the defense that there had been an impersonation. In the other impostor situations, any person in possession of the instrument may indorse the name of the payee. Such indorsement is effective as to anyone who pays the instrument in good faith or takes it for value or for collection. The indorsement so made is effective as long as it is "substantially similar to the name of the payee." (UCC § 3-404, 1990 Revision.) Likewise, an employer cannot avoid liability on the ground that an indorsement made by an employee had been made to defraud the employer. Liability of the employer on the paper cannot be avoided as against a person who paid the paper in good faith or who took it for value or for collection. In order for this protection to arise, it is necessary that the wrongdoing employee had authority with respect to the signing or processing of instruments. UCC § 3-405, 1990 Revision)

§ 2.   Who may indorse

An indorsement made by a person who at the time is not the holder of the instrument is an "anomalous indorsement." It does not affect the manner in which the instrument may be negotiated thereafter by the holder. (UCC § 3-205, 1990 Revision.) Typically, the anomalous indorser will be an accommodation party.

A signature or an instrument made by any person other than a maker, drawer, or acceptor is held to be an indorsement in the absence of an unambiguous indication that it was not so intended.

§ 3. Restrictive indorsement (§ 11 of Chapter 31)

Bank deposit and collection indorsements are restrictive. These include "for deposit," "for collection," and "pay any bank." A nonbank taker of paper so indorsed must remit the proceeds of the paper to the indorser and is guilty of conversion of the instrument if this is not done.

When suit is brought on a negotiable instrument, the defendant may defend on the ground that making payment to the plaintiff would violate a restrictive indorsement on the instrument. But if the indorsement directs the payment to a named person upon the satisfaction of a condition, such condition has no effect and is ignored when payment is demanded by the transferee or by a person who paid the instrument or who took it for value. (UCC § 3-206, 1990 Revision.)

§ 4. Correction of name by indorsement (§ 12 of Chapter 31)

If the payee of an instrument is incorrectly named or is named by a trade, assumed, or fictitious name, such person may indorse the instrument in either the name stated therein or that person's correct name or in both the instrument name and the correct name. If the person taking the instrument gives value or takes it for collection, as a bank, the taker of the paper can require such double name indorsement.

§ 5. Assignment by act of parties (§ 16 of Chapter 31)

A transfer of possession gives the transferee the right to enforce the instrument. A transferee who gave value for the paper may bring an action to compel its indorsement by the transferor. (UCC § 3-203(c), 1990 Revision.)

CHAPER 32. RIGHTS OF HOLDERS AND DEFENSES

Sections below state the more significant provisions of the 1990 revision of Article 3 that apply to Chapter 32.

§ 1. Favored holders (§ 2 of Chapter 32)

The plaintiff is required to prove possession of the rights of a holder in due course only when the defendant asserts a defense or a claim in recoupment that may be asserted against an ordinary holder but that cannot be asserted against a person with the rights of a holder in due course. (UCC § 3-308(b), 1990 Revision.)

The shelter rule is preserved by the revised Article 3.

(a) Good faith. The concept of "good faith" is expanded beyond the honesty in fact of the prior version. There has been added the objective limitation of "observance of reasonable standards of fair dealing." (UCC § 3-103(a) (4), 1990 Revision.)

(b) Ignorance of defenses and adverse claims. To qualify as a holder in due course, the taker must not have notice of any defense, recoupment claim, or adverse claim. The fact that there are documents filed of record in a public office does not constitute notice of any defense or claim for the purpose of determining whether the taker of the instrument is a holder in due course.

Notice of any kind of an adverse claim bars the taker from being a holder in due course. This includes a claim of a former holder to rescind a negotiation or of a person claiming to be the owner or to have the right to possess the instrument. (UCC § 3-302(a) (2) (v), 1990 Revision.)

(c) Transfer by fiduciary. The fact that an indorsement describes the indorsee as a fiduciary does not impose any duty upon a person subsequently taking the instrument to inquire whether there has been a breach by the indorsee of a fiduciary duty. Such later taker of the paper is only affected by a fiduciary breach of which that later taker has actual knowledge. (UCC § 3-206, 1990 Revision.)

UCC § 3-307, 1990 Revision, lists specified transactions in which the terms of the instrument and the use to which it is put are declared to give the taker of the instrument notice that there has been a breach of a fiduciary duty.

(d) Knowledge of discharge. The fact that the taker of an instrument knows that a party has been discharged does not bar the taker from being a holder in due course but bars the taker from recovering from the person who was discharged.

§ 2. Limited defenses not available against a holder in due course (§ 4 of Chapter 32)

Nonissuance of the instrument is a limited defense. An incomplete instrument must be completed in accordance with the authority given by the signer of the instrument. If an unauthorized completion has been made, it is treated as an alteration of the instrument.

The 1990 revision describes the defense of "failure of consideration" as a "recoupment claim."

A transferor's claim to rescind a negotiation cannot be asserted against a holder in due course or a good faith payor of the paper. (UCC § 3-202, 1990 Revision.)

§ 3. Limitation of defenses of accommodation party under 1990 Revision of Article 3.

An accommodation party may not raise the defense that the accommodated party was a minor, lacked capacity, or had been discharged by insolvency proceedings. (UCC § 3-305(d), 1990 Revision.)

§ 4. Universal defenses against all plaintiffs (§ 5 of Chapter 32)

(a) Ordinary care. The standard of "ordinary care" is defined as the observance of reasonable commercial standards in the area in which the person in question is engaged. (UCC 3-103(a) (7), 1990 Revision.) No definition is made with respect to persons not engaged in business. As to them, the pre-Code law applies.

(b) Alteration. An "alteration" is an unauthorized change of an instrument. If fraudulently made, it discharges the person whose obligation is affected by the change. If not fraudulently made, the instrument may be enforced according to its original terms. Even if fraudulently made, it may be so enforced by a payor bank or drawee paying the instrument or a person taking the instrument in good faith and for value without notice of the alteration. When the alteration consists of an unauthorized completion of an incomplete instrument, such a bank, drawee, or taker, may enforce the instrument according to its terms as completed.

§ 5.   Statute of limitations

The original Article 3 does not contain any statue of limitations. Suits on commercial when subject to that Article are governed by local non-Code statutes. These may be dated in general terms as covering suits on written obligations or contracts or may specifically refer to notes, checks, or drafts.

The 1990 revision of Article 3 specifies in detail when different instruments are overdue and establishes a detailed statue of limitations. In general, suits on notes, accepted drafts, and certificates of deposit must be brought within six years. All other actions with respect to negotiable instruments must be brought within three years. (UCC § 3-118, 1990 Revision.)

CHAPTER 33. LIABILITY OF PARTIES AND DISCHARGE OF LIABILITY

The sections below state the significant changes made by the 1990 revisions of Articles 3 and 4 that apply to Chapter 33.

§ 1.   Presentment (§ 3 of Chapter 33)

In place of making a physical presentment of a negotiable instrument upon a bank, an electronic presentment must be made. This may be either an electronic transmission of an image of the instrument or of information relating to the terms of the instrument. When there is an agreement that presentment may be made in this manner, an instrument is deemed presented when the electronic communication is received. (UCC § 4-110, 1990 Revision.)

§ 2.   Notice of dishonor (§ 5 of Chapter 33)

The delay of a bank is excuted when caused by computer or equipment failure. (UCC § 4-109, 1990 Revision.)

A payor bank is excused for a late return of an item if there has been a breach of a presentment warranty or if fraud has been practiced upon the payor bank.

A branch or separate office of a bank is a separate bank for the purpose of time limitations established by Revised Article 4 without regard to whether deposit ledgers are maintained there. (UCC § 4-107, 1990 Revision.)

§ 9.   Discharge of individual parties (§ 6 of Chapter 33)

(a) Place of payment. If an instrument states that it is payable at a particular place, payment must there be made. If no such place is specified but the instrument does give an address of the drawee or maker, the instrument is payable at that address. If no place of payment nor address is stated in the instrument, it is payable at the business address of the drawee or maker, and if there is no place of business, at the residence of such party. (In the case of a check, the place of presentment and payment is governed by Federal Reserve Regulation CC § 229.36.)

(b) Tender of payment. The making of tender of payment stops the running of interest even though the tender is refused. Indorsers and accommodation parties having a right of recourse against the party making the tender are discharged pro tanto (to the extent of the amount tendered). (UCC § 3-603(b), 1990 Revision.)

An instrument is not discharged if the payor has actual knowledge that the possessor has wrongful possession and that the instrument had been stolen.

(c) Cancellation and Renunciation. The party entitled to enforce the instrument discharges any party thereto by a writing stating that such party will not be sued or that all rights against that party are renounced. No consideration is required for this agreement. A party is also discharged if the person entitled to enforce the instrument surrenders it to that party. Cancellation may be made by crossing out words or signatures on the instrument, in which case it is immaterial that the original signatures or terms can still be seen. (UCC § 3-604, 1990 Revision.)

(d) Impairment of right of recourse or collateral. Drawers and indorsers are discharged to the extent that a modification of the instrument made by the person having the right to enforce it causes them to lose a right of recourse. An accommodation party is also discharged if the person entitled to enforce the instrument knew or had notice of that party's accommodation status. The party claiming to be discharged by a modification has the burden of proving the extent to which there has been a loss of a right of recourse. There is no discharge by the modification if there has been no loss of a right of recourse or if the party losing such right had consented to the modification.

A drawer, indorser, or a known accommodation party is discharged by impairment of collateral. This may consist of a failing to file or record that bars acquiring perfection of a security interest, or that causes a loss of perfection, a release of collateral, a failure to preserve the value of the collateral, or an improper disposition of the collateral. (UCC § 3-605(g), 1990 Revision.)

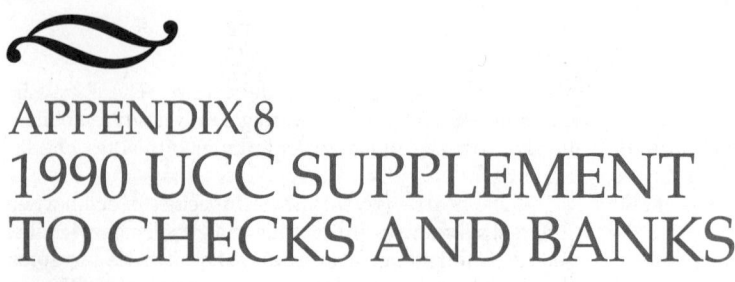

APPENDIX 8
1990 UCC SUPPLEMENT TO CHECKS AND BANKS

CHAPTER 34. CHECKS AND CUSTOMER-BANK RELATIONSHIP

The sections below state the significant changes made by the 1990 revisions of Articles 3 and 4 to material in Chapter 34.

§ 1. Nature of check

A check is a draft payable on demand and drawn on a bank and may be either the ordinary check, a cashier's check, or a teller's check. The name on the paper is not controlling and a bank "money order" payable to John Jones is a check and is negotiable. (UCC § 3-104(f), 1990 Revision.) A cashier's check is a check or draft drawn by a bank upon itself. If drawn on another bank in which the drawer bank has an account, it is a teller's check. Although the drawer and drawee are the same on a cashier's check, the holder does not have the option of treating the check as a note.

Unless otherwise agreed, a certified check, a cashier's check, or teller's check discharges the debt for which it is given to the amount of the check.

§ 2. Liability of drawer (§ 3 of Chapter 34)

If the account is the account of two or more persons, a person who does not sign the check that creates an overdraft is not liable for the amount of the overdraft if such person did not receive benefit from the proceeds of that check. (UCC § 4-401(b), 1990 Revision.)

§ 3. Time of presentment and payment (§ 6 of Chapter 34)

A check is overdue the day after demand for payment has been made or 90 days after the date of the check if no demand has been made, whichever date is the earlier. (UCC § 3-304(a), 1990 Revision.)

§ 4. Dishonor of check (§ 7 of Chapter 34)

An item is wrongfully dishonored if it is dishonored although (1) properly payable and the account on which it is drawn is sufficient to pay the item or (2) the customer has an agreeement with the bank to pay overdraft items.

§ 5. Agency status of collecting bank (§ 8 of Chapter 34)

The liability of a bank for its handling of an item is determined by the law of the state where the bank, branch, or separate office involved is located.

(a) Modification of bank duties. The parties in the bank collection process may modify their rights and duties by agreement but a bank cannot disclaim liability for lack of good faith or failure to exercise ordinary care nor can it limit the measure of damages for such lack of failure. When a bank handles checks by automated processes, the standard of ordinary care does not require the bank to make a physical examination of each item unless the bank's own procedures require such examination or general banking usage regards the absence of physical examination of the items as a lack of ordinary care.

(b) Encoding warranty and electronic presentment. In addition to transfer and presentment warranties, the revised Article 4 creates an encoding warranty by which anyone placing information on an item or transmitting the information electronically warrants that the information is correct. When there is an agreement for electronic presentment, a person making such a presentment warrants that it is made and that the item is retained in accordance with the terms of the agreement for such transmission. (UCC § 4-207 to § 4-209, 1990 Revision.)

§ 6. Premature payment of postdated check.

A check may be postdated but the bank is not liable for making payment on the check before the date stated unless the drawer has given the bank prior notice that a postdated check would be presented and that the bank should not make payment thereon until the stated date. (UCC § 4-401, 402, 1990 Revision. Nonchecks that are postdated may not be presented until the specified date has arrived. UCC § 3-113(a), 1990 Revision.)

§ 7. Payment over stop payment order (§ 9 of Chapter 34)

The 1990 revision of Article 4 expands the scope of the stop payment order to cover an order closing an account.

§ 8.   Payment on unauthorized signature of drawer (§ 10 of Chapter 34)

If the principal is an organization and has a requirement that two or more designated persons sign negotiable instruments on its behalf, a signing by less than the specified number is classified as "unauthorized."

A person cannot recover damages for forgery or alteration if the negligence of that person substantially contributed to the making of the forgery or alteration. If the other party in question was likewise negligent in failing to detect the forgery or alteration, the party must have paid the instrument in good faith or taken it for value or collection in order to be protected by the preclusion rule. (UCC § 3-406, 4-406(e), 1990 Revision.)

§ 9.   Payment on forged or missing indorsement (§ 11 of Chapter 34)

The depositary bank may take its customer's check without the indorsement of the customer and is not required to make an indorsement of the customer's name. (UCC § 4-205, 1990 Revision.) The depositary bank taking an unindorsed item also makes a warranty to the drawer that the proceeds of the item have been deposited to the account of the customer or paid directly to the customer.

§ 10.   Unauthorized collection of check (§ 13 of Chapter 34)

A collecting bank is protected from liability when it follows the instructions of its depositor. It is not required to inquire or verify that the depositor had the authority to give such instructins. (UCC § 4-203, 1990 Revision. This does not protect the bank if it converts the instrument by acting upon a forged or missing document or acts in violation of a restrictive indorsement.) In contrast, instructions do not protect a payor bank as it has an absolute duty to make proper payment. If it does not, it is liable unless it is protected by estoppel or by the preclusion rule. The person giving wrongful instructions is liable for the loss caused thereby.

§ 26.   Time limitations (§ 15 of Chapter 34)

Instead of returning cancelled checks and a bank statement to its customer, the Revised Article 4 provides that a customer and the bank may agree that the bank should retain cancelled checks and merely provide the customer with a list of paid items, identifying them by number, amount, and date of payment. The bank may then destroy paid items or make copies of them. In the latter case, it must be able for 7 years thereafter to furnish legible copies of paid items to the customer. On receiving the cancelled checks or a statement of the items paid, the customer must with reasonable promptness make an examination to see if any of the items were improperly paid because of an alteration or the customer's signature thereto was a forgery or was unauthorized. The customer must then report any unauthorized payments that he descovers or should have discovered by a reasonable examination.

The customer has one year from the date of receiving the disputed item or information relating thereto in which to notify the bank that the item was improperly paid. After that year, no claim for recrediting the improper payment can be made without regard to whether the bank had failed to exercise ordinary care.

If the bank's customer fails to make the examination for unauthorized payments or fails to report any alteration or unauthorized or forged signature of the customer, the customer is barred from requiring the bank to recredit the account with the amount of the authorized payment. The customer is not so barred if only one item is involved and the bank cannot show that it sustained a loss because of the breach of duty by the customer. If there is a series of improperly paid items and the same wrongdoer is involved, the customer is precluded only as to those items that were paid by the bank before it received notification from the customer and the customer had a reasonable amount of time in which to examine items or statements and to notify the bank. (UCC § 4-406, 1990 Revision.)

An action to enforce a liability imposed by Article 4 must be commenced within 3 years after the cause of action accrued.

APPENDIX 9
UNIFORM
PARTNERSHIP ACT

Part 1
Preliminary Provisions

§ 1. Name of Act
This act may be cited as Uniform Partnership Act.

§ 2. Definition of Terms
In this act, "Court" includes every court and judge having jurisdiction in the case.

"Business" includes every trade, occupation, or profession.

"Person" includes individuals, partnerships, corporations, and other associations.

"Bankrupt" includes bankrupt under the Federal Bankruptcy Actor insolvent under any state insolvent act.

"Conveyance" includes every assignment, lease, mortgage, or encumbrance.

"Real property" includes land and any interest or estate inland.

§ 3. Interpretation of Knowledge and Notice
(1) A person has "knowledge" of a fact within the meaning of this act not only when he has actual knowledge thereof, but also when he has knowledge of such other facts as in the circumstances shows bad faith.

(2) A person has "notice" of a fact within the meaning of this act when the person who claims the benefit of the notice

    (a) States the fact to such person, or

    (b) Delivers through the mail, or by other means of communication, a written statement of the fact to such person or to a proper person at his place of business or residence.

§ 4. Rules of Construction
(1) The rule that statutes in derogation of the common law are to be strictly construed shall have no application to this act.

(2) The law of estoppel shall apply under this act.

(3) The law of agency shall apply under this act.

(4) This act shall be so interpreted and construed as to effect its general purpose to make uniform the law of those states which enact it.

(5) This act shall not be construed so as to impair the obligations of any contract existing when the act goes into effect, nor to affect any action or proceedings begun or right accrued before this act takes effect.

§ 5. Rules for Cases Not Provided for in this Act
In any case not provided for in this act the rules of law and equity, including the law merchant, shall govern.

Part II
Nature of Partnership

§ 6. Partnership Defined
(1) A partnership is an association of two or more persons to carry on as co-owners a business for profit.

(2) But any association formed under any other statute of this state, or any statute adopted by authority, other than the authority of this state, is not a partnership under this act, unless such association would have been a partnership in this state prior to the adoption of this act; but this act shall apply to limited partnerships except in so far as the statutes relating to such partnerships are inconsistent herewith.

§ 7. Rules for Determining the Existence of a Partnership
In determining whether a partnership exists, these rules shall apply:

(1) Except as provided by Section 16 persons who are not partners as to each other are not partners as to third persons.

(2) Joint tenancy, tenancy in common, tenancy by the entireties, joint property, common property, or part ownership does not ofitself establish a partnership, whether such co-owners do or do not share any profits made by the use of the property.

(3) The sharing of gross returns does not of itself establish a partnership, whether or not the persons sharing

them have a joint or common right or interest in any property from which the returns are derived.

(4) The receipt by a person of a share of the profits of a business is prima facie evidence that he is a partner in the business, but no such inference shall be drawn if such profits were received in payment:

    (a) As a debt by installments or otherwise,

    (b) As wages of an employee or rent to a landlord,

    (c) As an annuity to a widow or representative of a deceased partner,

    (d) As interest on a loan, though the amount of payment vary with the profits of the business,

    (e) As the consideration for the sale of a goodwill of a business or other property by installments or otherwise.

§ 8.   Partnership Property

(1) All property originally brought into the partnership stock or subsequently acquired by purchase or otherwise, on account of the partnership, is partnership property.

(2) Unless the contrary intention appears, property acquired with partnership funds is partnership property.

(3) Any estate in real property may be acquired in the partnership name. Title so acquired can be conveyed only in the partnership name.

(4) A conveyance to a partnership in the partnership name, though without words of inheritance, passes the entire estate of the grantor unless a contrary intent appears.

Part III

Relations of Partners to Persons Dealing with the Partnership

§ 9.   Partner Agent of Partnership as to Partnership Business

(1) Every partner is an agent of the partnership for the purpose of its business, and the act of every partner, including the execution in the partnership name of any instrument, for apparently carrying on in the usual way the business of the partnership of which he is a member binds the partnership, unless the partner so acting has in fact no authority to act for the partnership in the particular matter, and the person with whom he is dealing has knowledge of the fact that he has no such authority.

(2) An act of a partner which is not apparently for the carrying on of the business of the partnership in the usual way does not bind the partnership unless authorized by the other partners.

(3) Unless authorized by the other partners or unless they have abandoned the business, one or more but less than all the partners have no authority to:

    (a) Assign the partnership property in trust for creditors or on the assignee's promise to pay the debts of the partnership,

    (b) Dispose of the goodwill of the business,

    (c) Do any other act which would make it impossible to carry on the ordinary business of a partnership,

    (d) Confess a judgment,

    (e) Submit a partnership claim or liability to arbitration or reference.

(4) No act of a partner in contravention of a restriction on authority shall bind the partnership to persons having knowledge of the restriction.

§ 10.   Conveyance of Real Property of the Partnership

(1) Where title to real property is in the partnership name, any partner may convey title to such property by a conveyance executed in the partnership name; but the partnership may recover such property unless the partner's act binds the partnership under the provisions of paragraph (1) of section 9 or unless such property has been conveyed by the grantee or a person claiming through such grantee to a holder for value without knowledge that the partner, in making the conveyance, has exceeded his authority.

(2) Where title to real property is in the name of the partnership, a conveyance executed by a partner, in his own name, passes the equitable interest of the partnership, provided the act is one within the authority of the partner under the provisions of paragraph (1) of Section 9.

(3) Where title to real property is in the name of one or more but not all the partners, and the record does not disclose the right of the partnership, the partners in whose name the title stands may convey title to such property, but the partnership may recover such property if the partners' act does not bind the partnership under the provisions of paragraph (1) of section 9, unless the purchaser or his assignee, is a holder for value, without knowledge.

(4) Where the title to real property is in the name of one or more or all the partners, or in a third person in trust for the partnership, a conveyance executed by a partner in the partnership name, or in his own name, passes the equitable interest of the partnership, provided the act is one within the authority of the partner under the provisions of paragraph (1) of section 9.

(5) Where the title to real property is in the names of all the partners a conveyance executed by all the partners passes all their rights in such property.

§ 11.   Partnership Bound by Admission of Partner

An admission or representation made by any partner concerning partnership affairs within the scope of his authority as conferred by this act is evidence against the partnership.

§ 12.   Partnership Charged with Knowledge of or Notice to Partner

Notice to any partner of any matter relating to partnership affairs, and the knowledge of the partner acting in the particular matter, acquired while a partner or then present to his mind, and the knowledge of any other partner who reasonably could and should have communicated it to the acting partner, operate as notice to or knowledge of the partnership, except in the case of a fraud on the partnership committed by or with the consent of that partner.

§ 13. Partnership Bound by Partner's Wrongful Act

Where, by any wrongful act or omission of any partner acting in the ordinary course of the business of the partnership or with the authority of his co-partners, loss or injury is caused to any person, not being a partner in the partnership, or any penalty is incurred, the partnership is liable therefor to the same extent as the partner so acting or omitting to act.

§ 14. Partnership Bound by Partner's Breach of Trust

The partnership is bound to make good the loss:

(a) Where one partner acting within the scope of his apparent authority receives money or property of a third person and misapplies it; and

(b) Where the partnership in the course of its business receives money or property of a third person and the money or property so received is misapplied by any partner while it is in the custody of the partnership.

§ 15. Nature of Partner's Liability

All partners are liable

(a) Jointly and severally for everything chargeable to the partnership under sections 13 and 14.

(b) Jointly for all other debts and obligations of the partnership; but any partner may enter into a separate obligation to perform a partnership contract.

§ 16. Partner by Estoppel

(1) When a person, by words spoken or written or by conduct, represents himself, or consents to another representing him to any one, as a partner in an existing partnership or with one or more persons not actual partners, he is liable to any such person to whom such representation has been made, who has, on the faith of such representation, given credit to the actual or apparent partnership, and if he has made such representation or consented to its being made in a public manner he is liable to such person, whether the representation has or has not been made or communicated to such person so giving credit by or with the knowledge of the apparent partner making the representation or consenting to its being made.

    (a) When a partnership liability results, he is liable as though he were an actual member of the partnership.

    (b) When no partnership liability results, he is liable jointly with the other persons, if any, so consenting to the contract or representation as to incur liability, otherwise separately.

(2) When a person has been thus represented to be a partner in an existing partnership, or with one or more persons not actual partners, he is an agent of the persons consenting to such representation to bind them to the same extent and in the same manner as though he were a partner in fact, with respect to persons who rely upon the representation. Where all the members of the existing partnership consent to the representation, a partnership act or obligation results; but in all other cases it is the joint act or obligation of the person acting and the persons consenting to the representation.

§ 17. Liability of Incoming Partner

A person admitted as a partner into an existing partnership is liable for all the obligations of the partnership arising before his admission as though he had been a partner when such obligations were incurred, except that this liability shall be satisfied only out of partnership property.

Part IV

Relations of Partners to One Another

§ 18. Rules Determining Rights and Duties of Partners

The rights and duties of the partners in relation to the partnership shall be determined, subject to any agreement between them, by the following rules:

    (a) Each partner shall be repaid his contributions, whether by way of capital or advances to the partnership property and share equally in the profits and surplus remaining after all liabilities, including those to partners, are satisfied; and must contribute toward the losses, whether of capital or otherwise, sustained by the partnership according to his share in the profits.

    (b) The partnership must indemnify every partner in respect of payments made and personal liabilities reasonably incurred by him in the ordinary and proper conduct of its business, or for the preservation of its business or property.

    (c) A partner, who in aid of the partnership makes any payment or advance beyond the amount of capital which he agreed to contribute, shall be paid interest from the date of the payment or advance.

    (d) A partner shall receive interest on the capital contributed by him only from the date when repayment should be made.

    (e) All partners have equal rights in the management and conduct of the partnership business.

    (f) No partner is entitled to remuneration for acting in the partnership business, except that a surviving partner is entitled to reasonable compensation for his services in winding up the partnership affairs.

    (g) No person can become a member of a partnership without the consent of all the partners.

    (h) Any difference arising as to ordinary matters

connected with the partnership business may be decided by a majority of the partners; but no act in contravention of any agreement between the partners may be done rightfully without the consent of all the partners.

§ 19.   Partnership Books

The partnership books shall be kept, subject to any agreement between the partners, at the principal place of business of the partnership, and every partner shall at all times have access to and may inspect and copy any of them.

§ 20.   Duty of Partners to Render

Information Partners shall render on demand true and full information of all things affecting the partnership to any partner or the legal representative of any deceased partner or partner under legal disability.

§ 21.   Partner Accountable as a Fiduciary

(1) Every partner must account to the partnership for any benefit, and hold as trustee for it any profits derived by him without the consent of the other partners from any transaction connected with the formation, conduct, or liquidation of the partnership or from any use by him of its property.

(2) This section applies also to the representatives of a deceased partner engaged in the liquidation of the affairs of the partnership as the personal representatives of the last surviving partner.

§ 22.   Right to an Account

Any partner shall have the right to a formal account as to partnership affairs:

(a) If he is wrongfully excluded from the partnership business or possession of its property by his co-partners,
(b) If the right exists under the terms of any agreement,
(c) As provided by Section 21,
(d) Whenever other circumstances render it just and reasonable.

§ 23.   Continuation of Partnership Beyond Fixed Term

(1) When a partnership for a fixed term or particular undertaking is continued after the termination of such term or particular undertaking without any express agreement, the rights and duties of the partners remain the same as they were at such termination, so far as is consistent with a partnership at will.

(2) A continuation of the business by the partners or such of them as habitually acted therein during the term, without any settlement or liquidation of the partnership affairs, is prima facie evidence of a continuation of the partnership.

Part V
Property Rights of a Partner

§ 24.   Extent of Property Rights of a Partner

The property rights of a partner are (1) his rights in specific partnership property, (2) his interest in the partnership, and (3) his right to participate in the management.

§ 25.   Nature of a Partner's Right in Specific Partnership Property

(1) A partner is co-owner with his partners of specific partnership property holding as a tenant in partnership.

(2) The incidents of this tenancy are such that:

(a) A partner, subject to the provisions of this act and to any agreement between the partners, has an equal right with his partners to possess specific partnership property for partnership purposes; but he has no right to possess such property, for any other purpose without the consent of his partners.
(b) A partner's right in specific partnership property is not assignable except in connection with the assignment of rights of all the partners in the same property.
(c) A partner's right in specific partnership property is not subject to attachment or execution, except on a claim against the partnership. When partnership property is attached for a partnership debt the partners, or any of them, or the representatives of a deceased partner, cannot claim any right under the homestead or exemption laws.
(d) On the death of a partner his right in specific partnership property vests in the surviving partner or partners, except where the deceased was the last surviving partner or partners, or the legal representative of the last surviving partner, has no right to possess the partnership property for any but a partnership purpose.
(e) A partner's right in specific partnership property is not subject to dower, courtesy, or allowances to widows, heirs, or next of kin.

§ 26.   Nature of Partner's Interest in the Partnership

A partner's interest in the partnership is his share of the profits and surplus, and the same is personal property.

§ 27.   Assignment of Partner's Interest

(1) A conveyance by a partner of his interest in the partnership does not of itself dissolve the partnership, nor, as against the other partners in the absence of agreement, entitle the assignee, during the continuance of the partner-

ship to interfere in the management or administration of the partnership business or affairs, or to require an information or account of partnership transactions, or to inspect the partnership books; but it merely entities the assignee to receive in accordance with his contract the profits to which the assigning partner would otherwise be entitled.

(2) In case of a dissolution of the partnership, the assignee is entitled to receive his assignor's interest and may require an account from the date only of the last account agreed to by all the partners.

§ 28.   Partner's Interest Subject to Charging Order

(1) On due application to a competent court by any judgment creditor of a partner, the court which entered the judgment, order, or decree, or any other court, may charge the interest of the debtor partner with payment of the unsatisfied amount of such judgment debt with interest thereon; and may then or later appoint a receiver of his share of the profits, and of any other money due or to fall due to him in respect of the partnership, and make all other orders, directions, accounts and inquiries which the debtor partner might have made, or which the circumstances of the case may require.

(2) The interest charged may be redeemed at any time before foreclosure, or in case of a sale being directed by the court may be purchased without thereby causing a dissolution:

(a) With separate property, by any one or more of the partners, or

(b) With partnership property, by any one or more of the partners with the consent of all the partners whose interests are not so charged or sold.

(3) Nothing in this act shall be held to deprive a partner of his right, if any, under the exemption laws, as regards his interest in the partnership.

Part VI

Dissolution and Winding Up

§ 29.   Dissolution Defined

The dissolution of a partnership is the change in the relation of the partners caused by any partner ceasing to be associated in the carrying on as distinguished from the winding up of the business.

§ 30.   Partnership Not Terminated by Dissolution

On dissolution the partnership is not terminated, but continues until the winding up of partnership affairs is completed.

§ 31.   Causes of Dissolution

Dissolution is caused: (1) Without violation of the agreementbetween the partners,

(a) By the termination of the definite term or particular undertaking specified in the agreement,

(b) By the express will of any partner when no definite term or particular undertaking is specified,

(c) By the express will of all the partners who have not assigned their interests or suffered them to be charged for their separate debts, either before or after the termination of any specified term or particular undertaking,

(d) By the expulsion of any partner from the business bona fide in accordance with such a power conferred by the agreement between the partners;

(2) In contravention of the agreement between the partners, where the circumstances do not permit a dissolution under any other provision of this section, by the express will of any partner at any time;

(3) By any event which makes it unlawful for the business of the partnership to be carried on or for the members to carry it on in partnership;

(4) By the death of any partner;

(5) By the bankruptcy of any partner or the partnership;

(6) By decree of court under Section 32.

§ 32.   Dissolution by Decree of Court

(1) On application by or for a partner the court shall decree a dissolution whenever:

(a) A partner has been declared a lunatic in any judicial proceedingor is shown to be of unsound mind,

(b) A partner becomes in any other way incapable of performing his part of the partnership contract,

(c) A partner has been guilty of such conduct as tends to affect prejudicially the carrying on of the business,

(d) A partner willfully or persistently commits a breach of the partnership agreement, or otherwise so conducts himself in matters relating to the partnership business that it is not reasonably practicable to carry on the business in partnership with him,

(e) The business of the partnership can only be carried on at a loss,

(f) Other circumstances render a dissolution equitable.

(2) On the application of the purchaser of a partner's interest under Sections 27 or 28:

(a) After the termination of the specified term or particular undertaking,

(b) At any time if the partnership was a partnership at will when the interest was assigned or when the charging order was issued.

§ 33.   General Effect of Dissolution on Authority of Partner

Except so far as may be necessary to wind up partnership affairs or to complete transactions begun but not then finished, dissolution terminates all authority of any partner to act for the partnership,

(1) With respect to the partners,

(a) When the dissolution is not by the act, bankruptcy or death of a partner, or

(b) When the dissolution is by such act, bankruptcy or death of a partner, in cases where Section 34 so requires.

(2) With respect to persons not partners, as declared in Section 35.

§ 34.   Right of Partner to Contribution from Copartners After Dissolution

Where the dissolution is caused by the act, death or bankruptcy of a partner, each partner is liable to his copartners for his share of any liability created by any partner acting for the partnership as if the partnership had not been dissolved unless

(a) The dissolution being by act of any partner, the partner acting for the partnership had knowledge of the dissolution, or

(b) The dissolution being by the death or bankruptcy of a partner, the partner acting for the partnership had knowledge or notice of the death or bankruptcy.

§ 35.   Power of Partner to Bind Partnership to Third Persons After Dissolution

(1) After dissolution a partner can bind the partnership except as provided in Paragraph (3)

(a) By any act appropriate for winding up partnership affairs or completing transactions unfinished by dissolution;

(b) By any transaction which would bind the partnership if dissolution had not taken place, provided the other party to the transaction

(I) Had extended credit to the partnership prior to dissolution and had no knowledge or notice of the dissolution; or

(II) Though he had not so extended credit, had nevertheless known of the partnership prior to dissolution, and, having no knowledge or notice of dissolution, the fact of dissolution had not been advertised in a newspaper of general circulation in the place (or in each place if more than one) at which the partnership business was regularly carried on.

(2) The liability of a partner under paragraph (1b) shall be satisfied out of partnership assets alone when such partner had been prior to dissolution.

(a) Unknown as a partner to the person with whom the contract is made; and

(b) So far unknown and inactive in partnership affairs that the business reputation of the partnership could not be said to have been in any degree due to his connection with it.

(3) The partnership is in no case bound by any act of a partner after dissolution.

(a) Where the partnership is dissolved because it is unlawful to carry on the business, unless the act is appropriate for winding up partnership affairs; or

(b) Where the partner has become bankrupt; or

(c) Where the partner has no authority to wind up partnership affairs; except by a transaction with one who

(I) Had extended credit to the partnership prior to dissolution and had no knowledge or notice of his want of authority; or

(II) Had not extended credit to the partnership prior to dissolution, and, having no knowledge or notice of his want of authority, the fact of his want of authority has not been advertised in the manner provided for advertising the fact of dissolution in paragraph (1bII).

(4) Nothing in this section shall affect the liability under section 16 of any person who after dissolution represents himself or consents to another representing him as a partner in a partnership engaged in carrying on business.

§ 36.   Effect of Dissolution on Partner's Existing Liability

(1) The dissolution of the partnership does not of itself discharge the existing liability of any partner.

(2) A partner is discharged from any existing liability upon dissolution of the partnership by an agreement to that effect between himself, the partnership creditor and the person or partnership continuing the business; and such agreement may be inferred from the course of dealing between the creditor having knowledge of the dissolution and the person or partnership continuing the business.

(3) Where a person agrees to assume the existing obligations of a dissolved partnership, the partners whose obligations have been assumed shall be discharged from any liability to any creditor of the partnership who, knowing of the agreement, consents to a material alteration in the nature or time of payment of such obligations.

(4) The individual property of a deceased partner shall be liable for all obligations of the partnership incurred while he was a partner but subject to the prior payment of his separate debts.

§ 37.   Right to Wind Up

Unless otherwise agreed the partners who have not wrongfully dissolved the partnership or the legal representative of the last surviving partner, not bankrupt, has the right to wind up the partnership affairs; provided, however, that any partner, his legal representative or his assignee, upon cause shown, may obtain winding up by the court.

§ 38.   Rights of Partners to Application of Partnership Property

(1) When dissolution is caused in any way, except in contravention of the partnership agreement, each partner as against his co-partners and all persons claiming through them in respect of their interests in the partnership, unless otherwise agreed, may have the partnership property applied to discharge its liabilities, and the surplus applied to pay in cash the net amount owing to the respective partners. But if dissolution is caused by expulsion of a partner, bona fide under the partnership agreement and if the expelled partner is discharged from all partnership liabilities, either by payment or agreement under Section 36(2), he shall receive in cash only the net amount due him from the partnership.

(2) When dissolution is caused in contravention of the partnership agreement the rights of the partners shall be as follows:

(a) Each partner who has not caused dissolution wrongfully shall have,
  (I) All the rights specified in paragraph (1) of this section, and
  (II) The right, as against each partner who has caused the dissolution wrongfully, to damages for breach of the agreement.

(b) The partners who have not caused the dissolution wrongfully, if they all desire to continue the business in the same name, either by themselves or jointly with others, may do so, during the agreed term for the partnership and for that purpose may possess the partnership property, provided they secure the payment by bond approved by the court, or pay to any partner who has caused the dissolution wrongfully, the value of his interest in the partnership at the dissolution, less any damages recoverable under clause (2aII) of the section, and in like manner indemnify him against all present or future partnership liabilities.

(c) A partner who has caused the dissolution wrongfully shall have:
  (I) If the business is not continued under the provisions of paragraph (2b) all the rights of a partner under paragraph (1), subject to clause (2aII), of this section,
  (II) If the business is continued under paragraph (2b) of this section the right as against his co-partners and all claiming through them in respect of their interests in the partnership, less any damages caused to his copartners by the dissolution, ascertained and paid to him in cash, or the payment secured by bond approved by the court, and to be released from all existing liabilities of the partnership; but in ascertaining the value of the partner's interest the value of the goodwill of the business shall not be considered.

§ 39.   Rights Where Partnership is Dissolved for Fraud or Misrepresentation

Where a partnership contract is rescinded on the ground of the fraud or misrepresentation of one of the parties thereto, the party entitled to rescind is, without prejudice to any other right, entitled,

(a) To a lien on, or right of retention of, the surplus of the partnership property after satisfying the partnership liabilities to third persons for any sum of money paid by him for the purchase of an interest in the partnership and for any capital or advances contributed by him; and

(b) To stand, after all liabilities to third persons have been satisfied, in the place of the creditors of the partnership for any payments made by him in respect of the partnership liabilities; and

(c) To be indemnified by the person guilty, of the fraud or making the representation against all debts and liabilities of the partnership.

§ 40.   Rules for Distribution

In settling accounts between the partners after dissolution, the following rules shall be observed, subject to any agreement to the contrary:

(a) The assets of the partnership are:
  (I) The partnership property,
  (II) The contributions of the partners necessary for the payment of all the liabilities specified in clause (b) of this paragraph.

(b) The liabilities of the partnership shall rank in order of payment, as follows:
  (I) Those owing to creditors other than partners,
  (II) Those owing to partners other than for capital and profits,
  (III) Those owing to partners in respect of capital,
  (IV) Those owing to partners in respect of profits.

(c) The assets shall be applied in the order of their declaration in clause (a) of this paragraph to the satisfaction of the liabilities.

(d) The partners shall contribute, as provided by Section 18(a) the amount necessary to satisfy the liabilities; but if any, but not all, of the partners are insolvent, or, not being subject to process, refuse to contribute, the other parties shall contribute their share of the liabilities, and, in the relative proportions in which they share the profits, the additional amount necessary to pay the liabilities.

(e) An assignee for the benefit of creditors or any person appointed by the court shall have the right to enforce the contributions specified in clause (d) of this paragraph.

(f) Any partner or his legal representative shall have the right to enforce the contributions specified in clause (d) of this paragraph, to the extent of the amount which he has paid in excess of his share of the liability.

(g) The individual property of a deceased partner shall be liable for the contributions specified in clause (d) of this paragraph.

(h) When partnership property and the individual properties of the partners are in possession of a court for distribution, partnership creditors shall have priority on partnership property and separate creditors on individual property, saving the rights of lien or secured creditors as heretofore.

(i) Where a partner has become bankrupt or his estate is insolvent the claims against his separate property shall rank in the following order:

(I)   Those owing to separate creditors,

(II) Those owing to partnership creditors,

(III) Those owing to partners by way of contribution.

§ 41.   Liability of Persons Continuing the Business in Certain Cases

(1) When any new partner is admitted into an existing partnership, or when any partner retires and assigns (or the representative of the deceased partner assigns) his rights in partnership property to two or more of the partners, or to one or more of the partners and one or more third persons, if the business is continued without liquidation of the partnership affairs, creditors of the first or dissolved partnership are also creditors of the partnership so continuing the business.

(2) When all but one partner retire and assign (or the representative of a deceased partner assigns) their rights in partnership property to the remaining partner, who continues the business without liquidation of partnership affairs, either alone or with others, creditors of the dissolved partnership are also creditors of the person or partnership so continuing the business.

(3) When any partner retires or dies and the business of the dissolved partnership is continued as set forth in paragraphs (1) and (2) of this section, with the consent of the retired partners or the representative of the deceased partner, but without any assignment of his right in partnership property, rights of creditors of the dissolved partnership and of the creditors of the person or partnership continuing the business shall be as if such assignment had been made.

(4) When all the partners or their representatives assign their rights in partnership property to one or more third persons who promise to pay the debts and who continue the business of the dissolved partnership, creditors of the dissolved partnership are also creditors of the person or partnership continuing the business.

(5) When any partner wrongfully causes a dissolution and the remaining partners continue the business under the provisions of Section 38(2b), either alone or with others, and without liquidation of the partnership affairs, creditors

of the dissolved partnership are also creditors of the person or partnership continuing the business.

(6) When a partner is expelled and the remaining partners continue the business either alone or with others, without liquidation of the partnership affairs, creditors of the dissolved partnership are also creditors of the person or partnership continuing the business.

(7) The liability of a third person becoming a partner in the partnership continuing the business, under this section, to the creditors of the dissolved partnership shall be satisfied out of partnership property only.

(8) When the business of a partnership after dissolution is continued under any conditions set forth in this section the creditors of the dissolved partnership, as against the separate creditors of the retiring or deceased partner or the representative of the deceased partner, have a prior right to any claim of the retired partner or the representative of the deceased partner against the person or partnership continuing the business, on account of the retired partner or the representative of the deceased partner against the person or partnership continuing the business, on account of the retired or deceased partner's interest in the dissolved partnership or on account of any consideration promised for such interest or for his right in partnership property.

(9) Nothing in this section shall be held to modify any right of creditors to set aside any assignment on the ground of fraud.

(10) The use by the person or partnership continuing the business of the partnership name, or the name of a deceased partner as part thereof, shall not of itself make the individual property of the deceased partner liable for any debts contracted by such person or partnership.

§ 42.   Rights of Retiring or Estate of Deceased Partner When the Business Is Continued

When any partner retires or dies, and the business is continued under any of the conditions set forth in Section 41 (1, 2, 3, 5, 6), or Section 38(2b), without any settlement of accounts as between him or his estate and the person or partnership continuing the business, unless otherwise agreed, he or his legal representative as against such persons or partnership may have the value of his interest at the date of dissolution ascertained, and shall receive as an ordinary creditor an amount equal to the value of his interest in the dissolved partnership with interest, or, at his option or at the option of his legal representative, in lieu of interest, the profits attributable to the use of his right in the property of the dissolved partnership as against the separate creditors, or the representative of the retired or deceased partner, shall have priority on any claim arising under this section, as provided by Section 41(8) of this act.

§ 43.   Accrual of Actions

The right to an account of his interest shall accrue to any partner, or his legal representative, as against the winding up partners or the surviving partners or the person or partnership continuing the business, at the date of dissolution, in the absence of any agreement to the contrary.

Part VII

Miscellaneous Provisions

§ 44.   When Act Takes Effect

This act shall take effect on the _____ day of _____ one thousand nine hundred and _____.

§ 45.   Legislation Repealed

All acts or parts of acts inconsistent with this act are hereby repealed.

APPENDIX 10
REVISED MODEL BUSINESS CORPORATION ACT
As Amended in 1986 and 1987 (EXCERPTS)

§ 1.20. FILING REQUIREMENTS

(a) A document must satisfy the requirements of this section, and of any other section that adds to or varies from these requirements, to be entitled to filing by the secretary of state.

(b) This Act must require or permit filing the document in the office of the secretary of state.

(c) The document must contain the information required by this Act. It may contain other information as well.

(d) The document must be typewritten or printed.

(e) The document must be in the English language. A corporate name need not be in English if written in English letters or Arabic or Roman numerals, and the certificate of existence required of foreign corporations need not be in English if accompanied by a reasonably authenticated English translation.

(f) The document must be executed:

    (1) by the chairman of the board of directors of a domestic or foreign corporation, by its president, or by another of its officers;

    (2) if directors have not been selected or the corporation has not been formed, by an incorporator; or

    (3) if the corporation is in the hands of a receiver, trustee, or other court-appointed fiduciary, by that fiduciary.

(g) The person executing the document shall sign it and state beneath or opposite his signature his name and the capacity in which he signs. The document may but need not contain:

    (1) the corporate seal,

    (2) an attestation by the secretary or an assistant secretary,

    (3) an acknowledgment, verification, or proof.

(h) If the secretary of state has prescribed a mandatory form for the document under section 1.21, the document must be in or on the prescribed form.

(i) The document must be delivered to the office of the secretary of state for filing and must be accompanied by one exact or conformed copy (except as provided in sections 5.03 and 15.09), the correct filing fee, and any franchise tax, license fee, or penalty required by this Act or other law.

§ 1.21. FORMS

(a) The secretary of state may prescribe and furnish on request forms for:

    (1) an application for a certificate of existence,

    (2) a foreign corporation's application for a certificate of authority to transact business in this state,

    (3) a foreign corporation's application for a certificate of withdrawal, and

    (4) the annual report. If the secretary of state so requires, use of these forms is mandatory.

(b) The secretary of state may prescribe and furnish on request forms for other documents required or permitted to be filed by this Act but their use is not mandatory.

§ 1.23. EFFECTIVE TIME AND DATE OF DOCUMENT

(a) Except as provided in subsection (b) and section 1.24(c), a document accepted for filing is effective:

    (1) at the time of filing on the date it is filed, as evidenced by the secretary of state's date and time endorsement on the original document; or

    (2) at the time specified in the document as its effective time on the date it is filed.

(b) A document may specify a delayed effective time and date, and if it does so the document becomes effective at the time and date specified. If a delayed effective date but no time is specified, the document is effective at the close of business on that date. A delayed effective date for a document may not be later than the 90th day after the date it is filed.

§ 1.25. FILING DUTY OF SECRETARY OF STATE

(a) If a document delivered to the office of the secretary of state for filing satisfies the requirements of section 1.20, the secretary of state shall file it.

(b) The secretary of state files a document by stamping or otherwise endorsing "Filed," together with his name and official title and the date and time of receipt, on both the original and the document copy and on the receipt for the filing fee. After filing a document, except as provided in sections 5.03 and 15.10, the secretary of state shall deliver the document copy, with the filing fee receipt (or acknowledgment of receipt if no fee is required) attached, to the domestic or foreign corporation or its representative.

(c) If the secretary of state refuses to file a document, he shall return it to the domestic or foreign corporation or its representative within five days after the document was delivered, together with a brief, written explanation of the reason for his refusal.

(d) The secretary of state's duty to file documents under this section is ministerial. His filing or refusing to file a document does not:

    (1) affect the validity or invalidity of the document in whole or part;

    (2) relate to the correctness or incorrectness of information contained in the document;

    (3) create a presumption that the document is valid or invalid or that information contained in the document is correct or incorrect.

§ 1.40.   ACT DEFINITIONS

In this Act:

(1) "Articles of incorporation" include amended and restated articles of incorporation and the articles of merger.

(2) "Authorized shares" means the shares of all classes a domestic or foreign corporation is authorized to issue.

(3) "Conspicuous" means so written that a reasonable person against whom the writing is to operate should have noticed it. For example, printing in italics or boldface or contrasting color, or typing in capitals or underlined, is conspicuous.

(4) "Corporation" or "domestic corporation" means a corporation for profit, which is not a foreign corporation, incorporated under or subject to the provisions of this Act.

(5) "Deliver" includes mail.

(6) "Distribution" means a direct or indirect transfer of money or other property (except its own shares) or incurrence of indebtedness by a corporation to or for the benefit of its shareholders in respect of any of its shares. A distribution may be in the form of a declaration or payment of a dividend; a purchase, redemption, or other acquisition of shares; a distribution of indebtedness; or otherwise.

(7) "Effective date of notice" is defined in section 1.41.

(8) "Employee" includes an officer but not a director. A director may accept duties that make him also an employee.

(9) "Entity" includes corporation and foreign corporation; not-for-profit corporation; profit and not-for-profit unincorporated association; business trust, estate, partnership, trust, and two or more persons having a joint or common economic interest; and state, United States, and foreign government.

(10) "Foreign corporation" means a corporation for profit incorporated under a law other than the law of this state.

(11) "Governmental subdivision" includes authority, county, district, and municipality.

(12) "Includes" denotes a partial definition.

(13) "Individual" includes the estate of an incompetent or deceased individual.

(14) "Means" denotes an exhaustive definition.

(15) "Notice" is defined in section 1.41.

(16) "Person" includes individual and entity.

(17) "Principal office" means the office (in or out of this state) so designated in the annual report where the principal executive offices of a domestic or foreign corporation are located.

(18) "Proceeding" includes civil suit and criminal, administrative, and investigatory action.

(19) "Record date" means the date established under chapter 6 or 7 on which a corporation determines the identity of its shareholders and their shareholdings for purposes of this Act. The determinations shall be made as of the close of business on the record date unless another time for doing so is specified when the record date is fixed.

(20) "Secretary" means the corporate officer to whom the board of directors has delegated responsibility under section 8.40(c) for custody of the minutes of the meetings of the board of directors and of the shareholders and for authenticating records of the corporation.

(21) "Shares" means the units into which the proprietary interests in a corporation are divided.

(22) "Shareholder" means the person in whose name shares are registered in the records of a corporation or the beneficial owner of shares to the extent of the rights granted by a nominee certificate on file with a corporation.

(23) "State," when referring to a part of the United States, includes a state and commonwealth (and their agencies and governmental subdivisions) and a territory and insular possession (and their agencies and governmental subdivisions) of the United States.

(24) "Subscriber" means a person who subscribes for shares in a corporation, whether before or after incorporation.

(25) "United States" includes district, authority, bureau, commission, department, and any other agency of the United States.

(26) "Voting group" means all shares of one or more classes or series that under the articles of incorporation or this Act are entitled to vote and be counted together collectively on a matter at a meeting of shareholders. All shares entitled by the articles of incorporation of this Act to vote generally on the matter are for that purpose a single voting group.

§ 1.41.   NOTICE

(a) Notice under this Act must be in writing unless oral notice is reasonable under the circumstances.

(b) Notice may be communicated in person; by telephone, telegraph, teletype, or other form of wire or wireless communication; or by mail or private carrier. If these forms of personal notice are impracticable, notice may be communicated by a newspaper of general circulation in the area where published; or by radio, television, or other form of public broadcast communication.

(c) Written notice by a domestic or foreign corporation to its shareholder, if in a comprehensible form, is effective when mailed, if mailed postpaid and correctly addressed to the shareholder's address shown in the corporation's current record of shareholders.

(d) Written notice to a domestic or foreign corporation (authorized to transact business in this state) may be addressed to its registered agent at its registered office or to the corporation or its secretary at its principal office shown in its most recent annual report or, in the case of a foreign corporation that has not yet delivered an annual report, in its application for a certificate of authority.

(e) Except as provided in subsection (c), written notice, if in a comprehensible form, is effective at the earliest of the following:

    (1) when received;

    (2) five days after its deposit in the United States Mail, as evidenced by the postmark, if mailed postpaid and correctly addressed;

    (3) on the date shown on the return receipt, if sent by registered or certified mail, return receipt requested, and the receipt is signed by or on behalf of the addressee.

(f) Oral notice is effective when communicated if communicated in a comprehensible manner.

(g) If this Act prescribes notice requirements for particular circumstances, those requirements govern. If articles of incorporation or bylaws prescribe notice requirements, not inconsistent with this section or other provisions of this Act, those requirements govern.

§ 1.42.   NUMBER OF SHAREHOLDERS

(a) For purposes of this Act, the following identified as a shareholder in a corporation's current record of shareholders constitutes one shareholder:

    (1) three or fewer co-owners;

    (2) a corporation, partnership, trust, estate, or other entity;

    (3) the trustees, guardians, custodians, or other fiduciaries of a single trust, estate, or account.

(b) For purposes of this Act, shareholdings registered in substantially similar names constitute one shareholder if it is reasonable to believe that the names represent the same person.

§ 2.01.   INCORPORATIONS

One or more persons may act as the incorporator or incorporators of a corporation by delivering articles of incorporation to the secretary of state for filing.

§ 2.02.   ARTICLES OF INCORPORATION

(a) The articles of incorporation must set forth:

    (1) a corporate name for the corporation that satisfies the requirements of section 4.01;

    (2) the number of shares the corporation is authorized to issue;

    (3) the street address of the corporation's initial registered office and the name of its initial registered agent at that office; and

    (4) the name and address of each incorporator.

(b) The articles of incorporation may set forth:

    (1) the names and addresses of the individuals who are to serve as the initial directors;

    (2) provisions not inconsistent with law regarding:

        (i) the purpose or purposes for which the corporation is organized;

        (ii) managing the business and regulating the affairs of the corporation;

        (iii) defining, limiting, and regulating the powers of the corporation, its board of directors, and shareholders;

        (iv) a par value for authorized shares or classes of shares;

        (v) the imposition of personal liability on shareholders for the debts of the corporation to a specified extent and upon specified conditions; and

    (3) any provision that under this Act is required or permitted to be set forth in the bylaws.

(c) The articles of incorporation need not set forth any of the corporate powers enumerated in this Act.

§ 2.03.   INCORPORATION

(a) Unless a delayed effective date is specified, the corporate existence begins when the articles of incorporation are filed.

(b) The secretary of state's filing of the articles of incorporation is conclusive proof that the incorporators satisfied all conditions precedent to incorporation except in a proceeding by the state to cancel or revoke the incorporation or involuntarily dissolve the corporation.

§ 2.04.   LIABILITY FOR PREINCORPORATION TRANSACTIONS

All persons purporting to act as or on behalf of a corporation, knowing there was no incorporation under this Act, are jointly and severally liable for all liabilities created while so acting.

§ 2.05.   ORGANIZATION OF CORPORATION

(a) After incorporation:

    (1) if initial directors are named in the articles of incorporation, the initial directors shall hold an organizational meeting, at the call of a majority of the directors, to complete the organization of the corporation by appointing officers, adopting bylaws, and carrying on any other business brought before the meeting;

    (2) if initial directors are not named in the articles, the incorporator or incorporators shall hold an organizational meeting at the call of a majority of the incorporators:

        (i) to elect directors and complete the organization of the corporation; or

        (ii) to elect a board of directors who shall complete the organization of the corporation.

(b) Action required or permitted by this Act to be taken by incorporators at an organizational meeting may be taken without a meeting if the action taken is evidenced by one or more written consents describing the action taken and signed by each incorporator.

(c) An organizational meeting may be held in or out of this state.

§ 2.06.   BYLAWS

(a) The incorporators or board of directors of a corporation shall adopt initial bylaws for the corporation.

(b) The bylaws of a corporation may contain any provision for managing the business and regulating the affairs of the corporation that is not inconsistent with law or the articles of incorporation.

§ 2.07.   EMERGENCY BYLAWS

(a) Unless the articles of incorporation provide otherwise, the board of directors of a corporation may adopt bylaws to be effective only in an emergency defined in subsection (d). The emergency bylaws, which are subject to amendment or repeal by the shareholders, may make all provisions necessary for managing the corporation during the emergency, including:

(1) procedures for calling a meeting of the board of directors;

(2) quorum requirements for the meeting; and

(3) designation of additional or substitute directors.

(b) All provisions of the regular bylaws consistent with the emergency bylaws remain effective during the emergency. The emergency bylaws are not effective after the emergency ends.

(c) Corporate action taken in good faith in accordance with the emergency bylaws:

(1) binds the corporation; and

(2) may not be used to impose liability on a corporate director, officer, employee, or agent.

(d) An emergency exists for purposes of this section if a quorum of the corporation's directors cannot readily be assembled because of some catastrophic event.

§ 3.01.   PURPOSES

(a) Every corporation incorporated under this Act has the purpose of engaging in any lawful business unless a more limited purpose is set forth in the articles of incorporation.

(b) A corporation engaging in a business that is subject to regulation under another statute of this state may incorporate under this Act only if permitted by, and subject to all limitations of, the other statute.

§ 3.02.   GENERAL POWERS

Unless its articles of incorporation provide otherwise, every corporation has perpetual duration and succession in its corporate name and has the same powers as an individual to do all things necessary or convenient to carry out its business and affairs, including without limitation power:

(1) to sue and be sued, complain and defend in its corporate name;

(2) to have a corporate seal, which may be altered at will, and to use it, or a facsimile of it, by impressing or affixing it or in any other manner reproducing it;

(3) to make and amend bylaws, not inconsistent with its articles of incorporation or with the laws of this state, for managing the business and regulating the affairs of the corporation;

(4) to purchase, receive, lease, or otherwise acquire, and own, hold, improve, use, and otherwise deal with, real or personal property, or any legal or equitable interest in property, wherever located;

(5) to sell, convey, mortgage, pledge, lease, exchange, and otherwise dispose of all or any part of its property;

(6) to purchase, receive, subscribe for, or otherwise acquire; own, hold, vote, use, sell, mortgage, lend, pledge, or otherwise dispose of; and deal in and with shares or other interests in, or obligations of, any other entity;

(7) to make contracts and guarantees, incur liabilities, borrow money, issue its notes, bonds, and other obligations (which may be convertible into or include the option to purchase other securities of the corporation), and secure any of its obligations by mortgage or pledge of any of its property, franchises, or income;

(8) to lend money, invest and reinvest its funds, and receive and hold real and personal property as security for repayment;

(9) to be a promoter, partner, member, associate, or manager of any partnership, joint venture, trust, or other entity;

(10) to conduct its business, locate offices, and exercise the powers granted by this Act within or without this state;

(11) to elect directors and appoint officers, employees, and agents of the corporation, define their duties, fix their compensation, and lend them money and credit;

(12) to pay pensions and establish pension plans, pension trusts, profit sharing plans, share bonus plans, share option plans, and benefit or incentive plans for any or all of its current or former directors, officers, employees, and agents;

(13) to make donations for the public welfare or for charitable, scientific, or educational purposes;

(14) to transact any lawful business that will aid governmental policy;

(15) to make payments or donations, or do any other act, not inconsistent with law, that furthers the business and affairs of the corporation.

§ 3.03.   EMERGENCY POWERS

(a) In anticipation of or during an emergency defined in subsection (d), the board of directors of a corporation may:

(1) modify lines of succession to accommodate the incapacity of any director, officer, employee, or agent; and

(2) relocate the principal office, designate alternative principal offices or regional offices, or authorize the officers to do so.

(b) During an emergency defined in subsection (d), unless emergency bylaws provide otherwise:

(1) notice of a meeting of the board of directors need be given only to those directors whom it is practicable to reach and may be given in any practicable manner, including by publication and radio; and

(2) one or more officers of the corporation present at a meeting of the board of directors may be deemed to be directors for the meeting, in order of rank and within the same rank in order of seniority, as necessary to achieve a quorum.

(c) Corporate action taken in good faith during an emergency under this section to further the ordinary business affairs of the corporation:

(1) binds the corporation; and

(2) may not be used to impose liability on a corporate director, officer, employee, or agent.

(d) An emergency exists for purposes of this section if a quorum of the corporation's directors cannot readily be assembled because of some catastrophic event.

§ 3.04.   ULTRA VIRES

(a) Except as provided in subsection (b), the validity of corporate action may not be challenged on the ground that the corporation lacks or lacked power to act.

(b) A corporation's power to act may be challenged:

(1) in a proceeding by a shareholder against the corporation to enjoin the act;

(2) in a proceeding by the corporation, directly, derivatively, or through a receiver, trustee, or other legal representative, against an incumbent or former director, officer, employee, or agent of the corporation; or

(3) in a proceeding by the Attorney General under section 14.30.

(c) In a shareholder's proceeding under subsection (b)(1) to enjoin an unauthorized corporate act, the court may enjoin or set aside the act, if equitable and if all affected persons are parties to the proceeding, and may award damages for loss (other than anticipated profits) suffered by the corporation or another party because of enjoining the unauthorized act.

§ 4.01.   CORPORATE NAME

(a) A corporate name:

(1) must contain the word "corporation," "incorporated," "company," or "limited," or the abbreviation "corp.," "inc.," "co." or "ltd.," or words or abbreviations of like import in another language; and

(2) may not contain language stating or implying that the corporation is organized for a purpose other than that permitted by section 3.01 and its articles of incorporation.

(b) Except as authorized by subsections (c) and (d), a corporate name must be distinguishable upon the records of the secretary of state from:

(1) the corporate name of a corporation incorporated or authorized to transact business in this state;

(2) a corporate name reserved or registered under section 4.02 or 4.03;

(3) the fictitious name adopted by a foreign corporation authorized to transact business in this state because its real name is unavailable; and

(4) the corporate name of a not-for-profit corporation incorporated or authorized to transact business in this state.

(c) A corporation may apply to the secretary of state for authorization to use a name that is not distinguishable upon his records from one or more of the names described in subsection (b). The secretary of state shall authorize use of the name applied for if:

(1) the other corporation consents to the use in writing and submits an undertaking in form satisfactory to the secretary of state to change its name to a name that is distinguishable upon the records of the secretary of state from the name of the applying corporation; or

(2) the applicant delivers to the secretary of state a certified copy of the final judgment of a court of competent jurisdiction establishing the applicant's right to use the name applied for in this state.

(d) A corporation may use the name (including the fictitious name) of another domestic or foreign corporation that is used in this state if the other corporation is incorporated or authorized to transact business in this state and the proposed user corporation:

(1) has merged with the other corporation;

(2) has been formed by reorganization of the other corporation; or

(3) has acquired all or substantially all of the assets, including the corporate name, of the other corporation.

(e) This Act does not control the use of fictitious names.

§ 5.01.   REGISTERED OFFICE AND REGISTERED AGENT

Each corporation must continuously maintain in this state:

(1) a registered office that may be the same as any of its places of business; and

(2) a registered agent, who may be:

(i) an individual who resides in this state and whose business office is identical with the registered office;

(ii) a domestic corporation or not-for-profit domestic corporation whose business

(iii) a foreign corporation or not-for-profit foreign corporation authorized to transact business in this state whose business office is identical with the registered office.

§ 6.03. ISSUED AND OUTSTANDING SHARES

(a) A corporation may issue the number of shares of each class or series authorized by the articles of incorporation. Shares that are issued are outstanding shares until they are reacquired, redeemed, converted, or canceled.

(b) The reacquisition, redemption, or conversion of outstanding shares is subject to the limitations of subsection (c) of this section and to section 6.40.

(c) At all times that shares of the corporation are outstanding, one or more shares that together have unlimited voting rights and one or more shares that together are entitled to receive the net assets of the corporation upon dissolution must be outstanding.

§ 6.20. SUBSCRIPTION FOR SHARES BEFORE INCORPORATION

(a) A subscription for shares entered into before incorporation is irrevocable for six months unless the subscription agreement provides a longer or shorter period or all the subscribers agree to revocation.

(b) The board of directors may determine the payment terms of subscriptions for shares that were entered into before incorporation, unless the subscription agreement specifies them. A call for payment by the board of directors must be uniform so far as practicable as to all shares of the same class or series, unless the subscription agreement specifies otherwise.

(c) Shares issued pursuant to subscriptions entered into before incorporation are fully paid and nonassessable when the corporation receives the consideration specified in the subscription agreement.

(d) If a subscriber defaults in payment of money or property under a subscription agreement entered into before incorporation, the corporation may collect the amount owed as any other debt. Alternatively, unless the subscription agreement provides otherwise, the corporation may rescind the agreement and may sell the shares if the debt remains unpaid more than 20 days after the corporation sends written demand for payment to the subscriber.

(e) A subscription agreement entered into after incorporation is a contract between the subscriber and the corporation subject to section 6.21.

§ 6.22. LIABILITY OF SHAREHOLDERS

(a) A purchaser from a corporation of its own shares is not liable to the corporation or its creditors with respect to the shares except to pay the consideration for which the shares were authorized to be issued (section 6.21) or specified in the subscription agreement (section 6.20).

(b) Unless otherwise provided in the articles of incorporation, a shareholder of a corporation is not personally liable for the acts or debts of the corporation except that he may become personally liable by reason of his own acts or conduct.

§ 7.01. ANNUAL MEETING

(a) A corporation shall hold a meeting of shareholders annually at a time stated in or fixed in accordance with the bylaws.

(b) Annual shareholders' meetings may be held in or out of this state at the place stated in or fixed in accordance with the bylaws. If no place is stated in or fixed in accordance with the bylaws, annual meetings shall be held at the corporation's principal office.

(c) The failure to hold an annual meeting at the time stated in or fixed in accordance with a corporation's bylaws does not affect the validity of any corporate action.

§ 7.04. ACTION WITHOUT MEETING

(a) Action required or permitted by this Act to be taken at a shareholders' meeting may be taken without a meeting if the action is taken by all the shareholders entitled to vote on the action. The action must be evidenced by one or more written consents describing the action taken, signed by all the shareholders entitled to vote on the action, and delivered to the corporation for inclusion in the minutes or filing with the corporate records.

(b) If not otherwise fixed under section 7.03 or 7.07, the record date for determining shareholders entitled to take action without a meeting is the date the first shareholder signs the consent under subsection (a).

(c) A consent signed under this section has the effect of a meeting vote and may be described as such in any document.

(d) If this Act requires that notice of proposed action be given to nonvoting shareholders and the action is to be taken by unanimous consent of the voting shareholders, the corporation must give its nonvoting shareholders written notice of the proposed action at least 10 days before the action is taken. The notice must contain or be accompanied by the same material that, under this Act, would have been required to be sent to nonvoting shareholders in a notice of meeting at which the proposed action would have been submitted to the shareholders for action.

§ 7.05. NOTICE OF MEETING

(a) A corporation shall notify shareholders of the date, time, and place of each annual and special shareholders' meeting no fewer than 10 nor more than 60 days before the meeting date. Unless this Act or the articles of incorporation require otherwise, the corporation is required to give notice only to shareholders entitled to vote at the meeting.

(b) Unless this Act or the articles of incorporation require otherwise, notice of an annual meeting need not include a description of the purpose or purposes for which the meeting is called.

(c) Notice of a special meeting must include a description of the purpose or purposes for which the meeting is called.

(d) If not otherwise fixed under section 7.03 or 7.07, the record date for determining shareholders entitled to notice of and to vote at an annual or special shareholders' meeting is the day before the first notice is delivered to shareholders.

(e) Unless the bylaws require otherwise, if an annual or special shareholders' meeting is adjourned to a different date, time, or place, notice need not be given of the new date, time, or place if the new date, time, or place is announced at the meeting before adjournment. If a new record date for the adjourned meeting is or must be fixed under section 7.07, however, notice of the adjourned meeting must be given under this section to persons who are shareholders as of the new record date.

§ 7.06.   WAIVER OF NOTICE

(a) A shareholder may waive any notice required by this Act, the articles of incorporation, or bylaws before or after the date and time stated in the notice. The waiver must be in writing, be signed by the shareholder entitled to the notice, and be delivered to the corporation for inclusion in the minutes or filing with the corporate records.

(b) A shareholder's attendance at a meeting:

   (1) waives objection to lack of notice or defective notice of the meeting, unless the shareholder at the beginning of the meeting objects to holding the meeting or transacting business at the meeting;

   (2) waives objection to consideration of a particular matter at the meeting that is not within the purpose or purposes described in the meeting notice, unless the shareholder objects to considering the matter when it is presented.

§ 7.07.   RECORD DATE

(a) The bylaws may fix or provide the manner of fixing the record date for one or more voting groups in order to determine the shareholders entitled to notice of a shareholders' meeting, to demand a special meeting, to vote, or to take any other action. If the bylaws do not fix or provide for fixing a record date, the board of directors of the corporation may fix a future date as the record date.

(b) A record date fixed under this section may not be more than 70 days before the meeting or action requiring a determination of shareholders.

(c) A determination of shareholders entitled to notice of or to vote at a shareholders' meeting is effective for any adjournment of the meeting unless the board of directors fixes a new record date, which it must do if the meeting is adjourned to a date more than 120 days after the date fixed for the original meeting.

(d) If a court orders a meeting adjourned to a date more than 120 days after the date fixed for the original meeting, it may provide that the original record date continues in effect or it may fix a new record date.

§ 7.21.   VOTING ENTITLEMENT OF SHARES

(a) Except as provided in subsections (b) and (c) or unless the articles of incorporation provide otherwise, each outstanding share, regardless of class, is entitled to one vote on each matter voted on at a shareholders' meeting. Only shares are entitled to vote.

(b) Absent special circumstances, the shares of a corporation are not entitled to vote if they are owned, directly or indirectly, by a second corporation, domestic or foreign, and the first corporation owns, directly or indirectly, a majority of the shares entitled to vote for directors of the second corporation.

(c) Subsection (b) does not limit the power of a corporation to vote any shares, including its own shares, held by it in a fiduciary capacity.

(d) Redeemable shares are not entitled to vote after notice of redemption is mailed to the holders and a sum sufficient to redeem the shares has been deposited with a bank, trust company, or other financial institution under an irrevocable obligation to pay the holders the redemption price on surrender of the shares.

§ 7.22.   PROXIES

(a) A shareholder may vote his shares in person or by proxy.

(b) A shareholder may appoint a proxy to vote or otherwise act for him by signing an appointment form, either personally or by his attorney-in-fact.

(c) An appointment of a proxy is effective when received by the secretary or other officer or agent authorized to tabulate votes. An appointment is valid for 11 months unless a longer period is expressly provided in the appointment form.

(d) An appointment of a proxy is revocable by the shareholder unless the appointment form conspicuously states that it is irrevocable and the appointment is coupled with an interest. Appointments coupled with an interest include the appointment of:

   (1) a pledgee;

   (2) a person who purchased or agreed to purchase the shares;

   (3) a creditor of the corporation who extended it credit under terms requiring the appointment;

   (4) an employee of the corporation whose employment contract requires the appointment; or

   (5) a party to a voting agreement created under section 7.31.

(e) The death or incapacity of the shareholder appointing a proxy does not affect the right of the corporation to accept the proxy's authority unless notice of the death or incapacity is received by the secretary or other officer or agent authorized to tabulate votes before the proxy exercises his authority under the appointment.

(f) An appointment made irrevocable under subsection (d) is revoked when the interest with which it is coupled is extinguished.

(g) A transferee for value of shares subject to an irrevocable appointment may revoke the appointment if he did not know of its existence when he acquired the shares and the existence of the irrevocable appointment was not noted conspicuously on the certificate representing the shares or on the information statement for shares without certificates.

(h) Subject to section 7.24 and to any express limitation on the proxy's authority appearing on the face of the appointment form, a corporation is entitled to accept the proxy's vote or other action as that of the shareholder making the appointment.

§ 8.01. REQUIREMENT FOR AND DUTIES OF BOARD OF DIRECTORS

(a) Except as provided in subsection (c), each corporation must have a board of directors.

(b) All corporate powers shall be exercised by or under the authority of, and the business and affairs of the corporation managed under the direction of, its board of directors, subject to any limitation set forth in the articles of incorporation.

(c) A corporation having 50 or fewer shareholders may dispense with or limit the authority of a board of directors by describing in its articles of incorporation who will perform some or all of the duties of a board of directors.

§ 8.03. NUMBER AND ELECTION OF DIRECTORS

(a) A board of directors must consist of one or more individuals, with the number specified in or fixed in accordance with the articles of incorporation or bylaws.

(b) If a board of directors has power to fix or change the number of directors, the board may increase or decrease by 30 percent or less the number of directors last approved by the shareholders, but only the shareholders may increase or decrease by more than 30 percent the number of directors last approved by the shareholders.

(c) The articles of incorporation or bylaws may establish a variable range for the size of the board of directors by fixing a minimum and maximum number of directors. If a variable range is established, the number of directors may be fixed or changed from time to time, within the minimum and maximum, by the shareholders or the board of directors. After shares are issued, only the shareholders may change the range for the size of the board or change from a fixed to a variable-range size board or vice versa.

(d) Directors are elected at the first annual shareholders' meeting and at each annual meeting thereafter unless their terms are staggered under section 8.06.

§ 8.04. ELECTION OF DIRECTORS BY CERTAIN CLASSES OF SHAREHOLDERS

If the articles of incorporation authorize dividing the shares into classes, the articles may also authorize the election of all or a specified number of directors by the holders of one or more authorized classes of shares. A class (or classes) of shares entitled to elect one or more directors is a separate voting group for purposes of the election of directors.

§ 8.05. TERMS OF DIRECTORS GENERALLY

(a) The terms of the initial directors of a corporation expire at the first shareholders' meeting at which directors are elected.

(b) The terms of all other directors expire at the next annual shareholders' meeting following their election unless their terms are staggered under section 8.06.

(c) A decrease in the number of directors does not shorten an incumbent director's term.

(d) The term of a director elected to fill a vacancy expires at the next shareholders' meeting at which directors are elected.

(e) Despite the expiration of a director's term, he continues to serve until his successor is elected and qualifies or until there is a decrease in the number of directors.

§ 8.06. STAGGERED TERMS FOR DIRECTORS

If there are nine or more directors, the articles of incorporation may provide for staggering their terms by dividing the total number of directors into two or three groups, with each group containing one half or one-third of the total, as near as may be. In that event, the terms of directors in the first group expire at the first annual shareholders' meeting after their election, the terms of the second group expire at the second annual shareholders' meeting after their election, and the terms of the third group, if any, expire at the third annual shareholders' meeting after their election. At each annual shareholders' meeting held thereafter, directors shall be chosen for a term of two years or three years, as the case may be, to succeed those whose terms expire.

§ 8.08. REMOVAL OF DIRECTORS BY SHAREHOLDERS

(a) The shareholders may remove one or more directors with or without cause unless the articles of incorporation provide that directors may be removed only for cause.

(b) If a director is elected by a voting group of shareholders, only the shareholders of that voting group may participate in the vote to remove him.

(c) If cumulative voting is authorized, a director may not be removed if the number of votes sufficient to elect him under cumulative voting is voted against his removal. If cumulative voting is not authorized, a director may be removed only if the number of votes cast to remove him exceeds the number of votes cast not to remove him.

(d) A director may be removed by the shareholders only at a meeting called for the purpose of removing him and the meeting notice must state that the purpose, or one of the purposes, of the meeting is removal of the director.

§ 8.20. MEETINGS

(a) The board of directors may hold regular or special meetings in or out of state.

(b) Unless the articles of incorporation or bylaws provide otherwise, the board of directors may permit any or all directors to participate in a regular or special meeting by, or conduct the meeting through the use of, any means of communication by which all directors participating may simultaneously hear each other during the meeting. A director participating in a meeting by this means is deemed to be present in person at the meeting.

§ 8.30.   GENERAL STANDARDS FOR DIRECTORS

(a) A director shall discharge his duties as a director, including his duties as a member on a committee:

    (1) in good faith;

    (2) with the care an ordinarily prudent person in a like position would exercise under similar circumstances; and

    (3) in a manner he reasonably believes to be in the best interests of the corporation.

(b) In discharging his duties a director is entitled to rely on information, opinions, reports, or statements, including financial statements and other financial data, if prepared or presented by:

    (1) one or more officers or employees of the corporation whom the director reasonably believes to be reliable and competent in the matters presented;

    (2) legal counsel, public accountants, or other persons as to matters the director reasonably believes are within the person's professional or expert competence; or

    (3) a committee of the board of directors of which he is not a member if the director reasonably believes the committee merits confidence.

(c) A director is not acting in good faith if he has knowledge concerning the matter in question that makes reliance otherwise permitted by subsection (b) unwarranted.

(d) A director is not liable for any action taken as a director, or any failure to take any action, if he performed the duties of his office in compliance with this section.

§ 8.31.   DIRECTOR CONFLICT OF INTEREST

(a) A conflict of interest transaction is a transaction with the corporation in which a director of the corporation has a direct or indirect interest. A conflict of interest transaction is not voidable by the corporation solely because of the director's interest in the transaction if any one of the following is true:

    (1) the material facts of the transaction and the director's interest were disclosed or known to the board of directors or a committee of the board of directors and the board of directors or committee authorized, approved, or ratified the transaction;

    (2) the material facts of the transaction and the director's interest were disclosed or known to the shareholders entitled to vote and they authorized, approved, or ratified the transaction; or

    (3) the transaction was fair to the corporation.

(b) For the purposes of this section, a director of the corporation has an indirect interest in a transaction if

    (1) another entity in which he has a material financial interest or in which he is a general partner is a party to the transaction or

    (2) another entity of which he is a director, officer, or trustee is a party to the transaction and the transaction is or should be considered by the board of directions of the corporation.

(c) For purposes of subsection (a)(1), a conflict of interest transaction is authorized, approved, or ratified if it receives the affirmative vote of a majority of the directors on the board of directors (or on the committee) who have no direct or indirect interest in the transaction, but a transaction may not be authorized, approved, or ratified under this section by a single director. If a majority of the directors who have no direct or indirect interest in the transaction vote to authorize, approve, or ratify the transaction, a quorum is present for the purpose of taking action under this section. The presence of, or a vote cast by, a director with a direct or indirect interest in the transaction does not affect the validity of any action taken under subsection (a)(1) if the transaction is otherwise authorized, approved, or ratified as provided in that subsection.

(d) For purposes of subsection (a)(2), a conflict of interest transaction is authorized, approved, or ratified if it receives the vote of a majority of the shares entitled to be counted under this subsection. Shares owned by or voted under the control of a director who has a direct or indirect interest in the transaction, and shares owned by or voted under the control of an entity described in subsection (b)(1), may not be counted in a vote of shareholders to determine whether to authorize, approve, or ratify a conflict of interest transaction under subsection (a)(2). The vote of those shares, however, is counted in determining whether the transaction is approved under other sections of this Act. A majority of the shares, whether or not present, that are entitled to be counted in a vote on the transaction under this subsection constituted a quorum for the purpose of taking action under this section.

§ 8.33.   LIABILITY FOR UNLAWFUL DISTRIBUTIONS

(a) A director who votes for or assents to a distribution made in violation of section 6.40 or the articles of incorporation is personally liable to the corporation for the amount of the distribution that exceeds what could have been distributed without violating section 6.40 or the articles of incorporation if it is established that he did not perform his duties in compliance with section 8.30. In any proceeding commenced under this section, a director has all of the defenses ordinarily available to a director.

(b) A director held liable under subsection (a) for an unlawful distribution is entitled to contribution:

    (1) from every other director who could be held liable under subsection (a) for the unlawful distribution; and

(2) from each shareholder for the amount the shareholder accepted knowing the distribution was made in violation of section 6.40 or the articles of incorporation.

(c) A proceeding under this section is barred unless it is commenced within two years after the date on which the effect of the distribution was measured under section 6.40(e) or (g).

§ 8.40.   REQUIRED OFFICERS

(a) A corporation has the officers described in its bylaws or appointed by the board of directors in accordance with the bylaws.

(b) A duly appointed officer may appoint one or more officers or assistant officers if authorized by the bylaws or the board of directors.

(c) The bylaws or the board of directors shall delegate to one of the officers responsibility for preparing minutes of the directors' and shareholders' meetings and for authenticating records of the corporation.

(d) The same individual may simultaneously hold more than one office in a corporation.

§ 8.41.   DUTIES OF OFFICERS

Each officer has the authority and shall perform the duties set forth in the bylaws or, to the extent consistent with the bylaws, the duties prescribed by the board of directors or by direction of an officer authorized by the board of directors to prescribe the duties of other officers.

§ 8.42.   STANDARDS OF CONDUCT FOR OFFICERS

(a) An officer with discretionary authority shall discharge his duties under that authority:

(1) in good faith;

(2) with the care an ordinarily prudent person in a like position would exercise under similar circumstances; and

(3) in a manner he reasonably believes to be in the best interests of the corporation.

(b) In discharging his duties an officer is entitled to rely on information, opinions, reports, or statements, including financial statements and other financial data, if prepared or presented by:

(1) one or more officers or employees of the corporation whom the officer reasonably believes to be reliable and competent in the matters presented; or

(2) legal counsel, public accountants, or other persons as to matters the officer reasonably believes are within the person's professional or expert competence.

(c) An officer is not acting in good faith if he has knowledge concerning the matter in question that makes reliance otherwise permitted by subsection (b) unwarranted.

(d) An officer is not liable for an action taken as an officer, or any failure to take any action, if he performed the duties of his office in compliance with this section.

§ 11.01.   MERGER

(a) One or more corporations may merge into another corporation if the board of directors of each corporation adopts and its shareholders (if required by section 11.03) approve a plan of merger.

(b) The plan of merger must set forth:

(1) the name of each corporation planning to merge and the name of the surviving corporation into which each other corporation plans to merge;

(2) the terms and conditions of the merger; and

(3) the manner and basis of converting the shares of each corporation into shares, obligations, or other securities of the surviving or any other corporation or into cash or other property in whole or part.

(c) The plan of merger may set forth:

(1) amendments to the articles of incorporation of the surviving corporation; and

(2) other provisions relating to the merger.

§ 13.02.   RIGHT TO DISSENT

(a) A shareholder is entitled to dissent from and obtain payment of the fair value of his shares in the event of, any of the following corporate actions:

(1) consummation of a plan of merger to which the corporation is a party (i) if shareholder approval is required for the merger by section 11.03 or the articles of incorporation and the shareholder is entitled to vote on the merger or (ii) if the corporation is a subsidiary that is merged with its parent under section 11.04;

(2) consummation of a plan of share exchange to which the corporation is a party as the corporation whose shares will be acquired, if the shareholder is entitled to vote on the plan;

(3) consummation of a sale or exchange of all, or substantially all, of the property of the corporation other than in the usual and regular course of business, if the shareholder is entitled to vote on the sale or exchange, including a sale in dissolution, but not including a sale pursuant to court order or a sale for cash pursuant to a plan by which all or substantially all of the net proceeds of the sale will be distributed to the shareholders within one year after the date of sale;

(4) an amendment of the articles of incorporation that materially and adversely affects rights in respect of a dissenter's shares because it:

(i) alters or abolishes a preferential right of the shares;

(ii) creates, alters, or abolishes a right in respect of redemption, including a provision respecting a sinking fund for the redemption or repurchase, of the shares;

(iii) alters or abolishes a preemptive right of

the holder of the shares to acquire shares or other securities;

   (iv) excludes or limits the right of the shares to vote on any matter, or to cumulate votes, other than a limitation by dilution through issuance of shares or other securities with similar voting rights; or

   (v) reduces the number of shares owned by the shareholder to a fraction of a share if the fractional share so created is to be acquired for cash under section 6.04; or

(5) any corporate action taken pursuant to a shareholder vote to the extent the articles of incorporation, bylaws, or a resolution of the board of directors provides that voting or nonvoting shareholders are entitled to dissent and obtain payment for their shares.

(b) A shareholder entitled to dissent and obtain payment for his shares under this chapter may not challenge the corporate action creating his entitlement unless the action is unlawful or fraudulent with respect to the shareholder or the corporation.

§ 16.01.   CORPORATE RECORDS

(a) A corporation shall keep as permanent records minutes of all meetings of its shareholders and board of directors, a record of all actions taken by the shareholders or board of directors without a meeting, and a record of all actions taken by a committee of the board of directors in place of the board of directors on behalf of the corporation.

(b) A corporation shall maintain appropriate accounting records.

(c) A corporation or its agent shall maintain a record of its shareholders, in a form that permits preparation of a list of the names and addresses of all shareholders, in alphabetical order by class of shares showing the number and class of shares held by each.

(d) A corporation shall maintain its records in written form or in another form capable of conversion into written form within a reasonable time.

(e) A corporation shall keep a copy of the following records at its principal office:

(1) its articles or restated articles of incorporation and all amendments to them currently in effect;

(2) its bylaws or restated bylaws and all amendments to them currently in effect;

(3) resolutions adopted by its board of directors creating one or more classes or series of shares, and fixing their relative rights, preferences, and limitations, if shares issued pursuant to those resolutions are outstanding;

(4) the minutes of all shareholders' meetings, and records of all action taken by shareholders without a meeting, for the past three years;

(5) all written communications to shareholders generally within the past three years, including the financial statements furnished for the past three years under section 16.20;

(6) a list of the names and business addresses of its current directors and officers; and

(7) its most recent annual report delivered to the secretary of state under section 16.22.

§ 16.02.   INSPECTION OF RECORDS BY SHAREHOLDERS

(a) A shareholder of a corporation is entitled to inspect and copy, during regular business hours at the corporation's principal office, any of the records of the corporation described in section 16.01(e) if he gives the corporation written notice of his demand at least five business days before the date on which he wishes to inspect and copy.

(b) A shareholder of a corporation is entitled to inspect and copy, during regular business hours at a reasonable location specified by the corporation, any of the following records of the corporation if the shareholder meets the requirements of subsection (c) and gives the corporation written notice of his demand at least five business days before the date on which he wishes to inspect and copy:

(1) excerpts from minutes of any meeting of the board of directors, records of any action of a committee of the board of directors while acting in place of the board of directors on behalf of the corporation, minutes of any meeting of the shareholders, and records of action taken by the shareholders or board of directors without a meeting, to the extent not subject to inspection under section 16.02(a);

(2) accounting records of the corporation; and

(3) the record of shareholders.

(c) A shareholder may inspect and copy the records described in subsection (b) only if:

(1) his demand is made in good faith and for a proper purpose;

(2) he describes with reasonable particularity his purpose and the records he desires to inspect; and

(3) the records are directly connected with his purpose.

(d) The right of inspection granted by this section may not be abolished or limited by a corporation's articles of incorporation or bylaws.

(e) This section does not affect:

(1) the right of a shareholder to inspect records under section 7.20 or, if the shareholder is in litigation with the corporation, to the same extent as any other litigant;

(2) the power of a court, independently of this Act, to compel the production of corporate records for examination.

(f) For purposes of this section, "shareholder" includes a beneficial owner whose shares are held in a voting trust or by a nominee on his behalf.

§ 16.20.   FINANCIAL STATEMENTS FOR SHAREHOLDERS

(a) A corporation shall furnish its shareholders annual financial statements, which may be consolidated or combined statements of the corporation and one or more of its subsidiaries, as appropriate, that include a balance sheet as of the end of the fiscal year, an income statement for that year, and a statement of changes in shareholders' equity for the year unless that information appears elsewhere in the financial statements. If financial statements are prepared for the corporation on the basis of generally accepted accounting principles, the annual financial statements must also be prepared on that basis.

(b) If the annual financial statements are reported upon by a public accountant, his report must accompany them. If not, the statements must be accompanied by a statement of the president or the person responsible for the corporation's accounting records:

(1) stating his reasonable belief whether the statements were prepared on the basis of generally accepted accounting principles and, if not, describing the basis of preparation; and

(2) describing any respects in which the statements were not prepared on a basis of accounting consistent with the statements prepared for the preceding year.

(c) A corporation shall mail the annual financial statements to each shareholder within 120 days after the close of each fiscal year. Thereafter, on written request from a shareholder who was not mailed the statements, the corporation shall mail him the latest financial statements.

GLOSSARY

GLOSSARY

A

abandon: give up or leave employment; relinquish possession of personal property with intent to disclaim title.

abate: put a stop to a nuisance; reduce or cancel a legacy because the estate of the decedent is insufficient to make payment in full.

ab initio: from the beginning.

abrogate: recall or repeal; make void or inoperative.

absolute liability: liability for an act that causes harm even though the actor was not at fault.

absolute privilege: protection from liability for slander or libel given under certain circumstances regardless of the fact that the statements are false or maliciously made.

abstract of title: history of the transfers of title to a given piece of land, briefly stating the parties to and the effect of all deeds, wills, and judicial proceedings relating to the land.

acceleration clause: provision in a contract or any legal instrument that upon a certain event the time for the performance of specified obligations shall be advanced; for example, a provision making the balance due upon debtor's default.

acceptance: unqualified assent to the act or proposal of another; as the acceptance of a draft (bill of exchange), of an offer to make a contract, of goods delivered by the seller, or of a gift or deed.

accession: acquisition of title to personal property by virtue of the fact that it has been attached to property already owned or was the offspring of an owned animal.

accessory after the fact: one who after the commission of a felony knowingly assists the felon.

accessory before the fact: one who is absent at the commission of the crime but who aided and abetted its commission.

accident: an event that occurs even though a reasonable person would not have foreseen its occurrence, because of which the law holds no one responsible for the harm caused.

accommodation party: a person who signs a commercial paper to lend credit to another party to the paper.

accord and satisfaction: an agreement to substitute a different performance for that called for in the contract and the performance of that substitute agreement.

accretion: the acquisition of title to additional land when the owner's land is built up by gradual deposits made by the natural action of water.

acknowledgment: an admission or confirmation, generally of an instrument and usually made before a person authorized to administer oaths, such as a notary public; the purpose being to declare that the instrument was executed by the person making the instrument, or that it was a voluntary act or that that person desires that it be recorded.

action: a proceeding to enforce any right.

action in personam: an action brought to impose liability upon a person, such as a money judgment.

action in rem: an action brought to declare the status of a thing, such as an action to declare the title to property to be forfeited because of its illegal use.

action of assumpsit: a common-law action brought to recover damages for breach of a contract.

action of ejectment: a common-law action brought to recover the possession of land.

action of mandamus: a common-law action

brought to compel the performance of a ministerial or clerical act by an officer.

action of quo warranto: a common-law action brought to challenge the authority of an officer to act or to hold office.

action of replevin: a common-law action brought to recover the possession of personal property.

action of trespass: a common-law action brought to recover damages for a tort.

Act of God: a natural phenomenon that is not reasonable foreseeable.

administrative agency: a governmental commission or board given authority to regulate particular matters.

administrator-administratrix: the person (manwoman) appointed to wind up and settle the estate of a person who has died without a will.

adverse possession: the hostile possession of real estate, which when actual, visible, notorious, exclusive, and continued for the required time, will vest the title to the land in the person in such adverse possession.

advisory opinion: an opinion that may be rendered in a few states when there is no actual controversy before the court and the matter is submitted by private persons, or in some instances by the governor of the state, to obtain the court's opinion.

affidavit: a statement of facts set forth in written form and supported by the oath or affirmation of the person making the statement setting forth that such facts are true on the basis of actual knowledge or on information and belief. The affidavit is executed before a notary public or other person authorized to administer oaths.

affinity: the relationship that exists by virtue of marriage.

affirmative covenant: an express undertaking or promise in a contract or deed to do an act.

agency: the relationship that exists between a person identified as a principal and another by virtue of which the latter may make contracts with third persons on behalf of the principal. (Parties—principal, agent, third person)

agency coupled with an interest in the authority: an agency in which the agent has given a consideration or has paid for the right to exercise the authority granted.

agency coupled with an interest in the subject matter: an agency in which for a consideration the agent is given an interest in the property to which the agency relates.

agency shop: a union contract provision requiring that nonunion employees pay to the union the equivalent of union dues in order to retain their employment.

agent: one who is authorized by the principal or by operation of law to make contracts with third persons on behalf of the principal.

allonge: a paper securely fastened to a commercial paper in order to provide additional space for endorsements.

alluvion: the additions made to land by accretion.

alteration: any material change of the terms of a writing fraudulently made by a party thereto.

ambulatory: not effective and therefore may be changed, as in the case of a will that is not final until its maker has died.

amicable action: an action that all parties agree should be brought and one that is begun by the filing of such an agreement, rather than by serving the adverse parties with process. Although the parties agree to litigate, the dispute is real, and the decision is not an advisory opinion.

amicus curiae: literally, a friend of the court; one who is appointed by the court to take part in litigation and to assist the court by furnishing an opinion in the matter.

annexation: attachment of personal property to realty in such a way as to make it become real property and part of the realty.

annuity: a contract by which the insured pays a lump sum to the insurer and later receives fixed annual payments.

anomalous indorser: a person who signs a commercial paper but is not otherwise a party to the instrument.

anticipatory breach: the repudiation by a promisor of the contract prior to the time that performance is required when such repudiation is accepted by the promisee as a breach of the contract.

anti-injunction acts: statutes prohibiting the use of injunctions in labor disputes except under exceptional circumstances; notably the federal Norris-La Guardia Act of 1932.

Anti-Pertrillo Act: a federal statute that makes it a crime to compel a radio broadcasting station to hire musicians not needed, to pay for services not performed, or to refrain from broadcasting music of school children or from foreign countries.

antitrust acts: statutes prohibiting combinations and contracts in restraint of trade, notably the federal Sherman Antitrust Act of 1890, now generally inapplicable to labor union activity.

appeal: taking a case to a reviewing court to determine whether the judgment of the lower court or administrative agency was correct. (Parties—appellant, appellee)

appellate jurisdiction: the power of a court to hear and decide a given class of cases on appeal from another court or administrative agency.

arbitration: the settlement of disputed questions, whether of law or fact, by one or more arbitrators by whose decision the parties agree to be bound. Increasingly used as a procedure for labor dispute settlement.

assignment: transfer of a right. Generally used in connection with personal property rights, as rights under a contract, commercial paper, an insurance policy, a mortgage, or a lease. (Parties—assignor, assignee)

assumption of risk: the common-law rule that an employee could not sue the employer for injuries caused by the ordinary risks of employment on the theory that the employee assumed such risks by undertaking the work. The rule has been abolished in those areas governed by workers' compensation laws and most employers' liability statutes.

attachment: the seizure of property of a debtor to secure satisfaction of a judgment.

attractive nuisance doctrine: a rule imposing liability upon a landowner for injuries sustained by small children playing on the land when the landowner permits a condition to exist or maintains equipment that a reasonable person should realize would attract small children who could not realize the danger. The rule does not apply if an unreasonable burden would be imposed upon the landowner in taking steps to protect the children.

authenticate: make or establish as genuine, official, or final, such as by signing, countersigning, sealing, or performing any other act indicating approval.

B

bad check laws: laws making it a criminal offense to issue a bad check with intent to defraud.

baggage: such articles of necessity or personal convenience as are usually carried for personal use by passengers of common carriers.

bail: variously used in connection with the release of a person or property from the custody of the law, referring (a) to the act of releasing or bailing, (b) to the persons who assume liability in the event that the released person does not appear or that it is held that the property should not be released, and (c) to the bond or sum of money that is furnished the court or other official as indemnity for nonperformance of the obligation.

bailee's lien: a specific, possessory lien of the bailee upon the goods for work done to them. Commonly extended by statute to any bailee's claim for compensation and eliminating the necessity of retention of possession.

bailment: the relationship that exists when personal property is delivered into the possession of another under an agreement, express or implied, that the identical property will be returned or will be delivered in accordance with the agreement. (Parties—bailor, bailee)

bankruptcy: a procedure by which one unable to pay debts may surrender to the court for administration and distribution to creditors all assets in excess of any exemption claim, and the debtor is given a discharge that releases from the unpaid balance due on most debts.

bearer: the person in physical possession of commercial paper payable to bearer, a document of title directing delivery to bearer, or an investment security in bearer form.

beneficiary: the person to whom the proceeds of a life insurance policy are payable, a person for whose benefit property is held in trust, or a person given property by a will.

bequest: a gift of personal property by will.

bill of exchange (draft): an unconditional order in writing by one person upon another, signed by the person giving it, and ordering the person to whom it is directed to pay upon demand or at a definite time a sum certain in money to order or to bearer.

bill of lading: a document issued by a carrier reciting the receipt of goods and the terms of the contract of transportation. Regulated by the federal Bills of Lading Act or the UCC.

bill of sale: a writing signed by the seller reciting that the personal property therein described has been sold to the buyer.

binder: a memorandum delivered to the insured stating the essential terms of a policy to be executed in the future, when it is agreed that the contract of insurance is to be effective before the written policy is executed.

blank indorsement: an indorsement that does not name the person to whom the paper, document of title, or investment security is negotiated.

blue sky laws: state statutes designed to protect the public from the sale of worthless stocks and bonds.

boardinghouse keeper: one regularly engaged in

the business of offering living accommodations to permanent lodgers or boarders.

bona fide: in good faith; without any fraud or deceit.

bond: an obligation or promise in writing and sealed, generally of corporations, personal representatives, and trustees; fidelity bonds.

boycott: a combination of two or more persons to cause harm to another by refraining from patronizing or dealing with such other person in any way or inducing others to so refrain; commonly an incident of labor disputes.

bulk sales acts: statutes to protect creditors of a bulk seller. Notice must be given creditors, and the bulk sale buyer is liable to the seller's creditors if the statute is not satisfied. Expanded to *bulk transfers* under the UCC.

business trust: a form of business organization in which the owners of the property to be devoted to the business transfer the title of the property to trustees with full power to operate the business.

C

cancellation: a crossing-out of a part of an instrument or a destruction of all legal effect of the instrument, whether by act of party, upon breach by the other party, or pursuant to agreement or decree of court.

capital: net assets of a corporation.

capital stock: the declared money value of the outstanding stock of the corporation.

cash surrender value: the sum paid the insured upon the surrender of a policy to the insurer.

cause of action: the right to damages or other judicial relief when a legally protected right of the plaintiff is violated by an unlawful act of the defendant.

caveat emptor: let the buyer beware. This maxim has been nearly abolished by warranty and strict tort liability concepts.

certificate of protest: a written statement by a notary public setting forth the fact that the holder had presented the commercial paper to the primary party and that the latter had failed to make payment.

certiorari: a review by a higher court of the regularity of proceedings before a lower court. Originally granted within the discretion of the reviewing court. The name is derived from the language of the writ, which was in Latin and directed the lower court to certify its record and transfer it to the higher court. In modern prac-

tice, the scope of review has often been expanded to include a review of the merits of the case and, also, to review the action of administrative agencies.

cestui que trust: the beneficiary or person for whose benefit the property is held in trust.

charter: the grant of authority from a government to exist as a corporation. Generally replaced today by a certificate of incorporation approving the articles of incorporation.

chattels personal: tangible personal property.

chattels real: leases of land and buildings.

check: an order by a depositor on a bank to pay a sum of money to a payee; a bill of exchange drawn on a bank and payable on demand.

chose in action: intangible personal property in the nature of claims against another, such as a claim for accounts receivable or wages.

chose in possession: tangible personal property.

circumstantial evidence: relates to circumstances surrounding the facts in dispute from which the trier of fact may deduce what has happened.

civil action: in many states a simplified form of action combining all or many of the former common-law actions.

civil court: a court with jurisdiction to hear and determine controversies relating to private rights and duties.

closed shop: a place of employment in which only union members may be employed. Now prohibited.

codicil: a testator's or testatrix's writing executed with all the formality of a will and treated as an addition to or modification of the will.

coinsurance: a clause requiring the insured to maintain insurance on property up to a stated amount and providing that to the extent that this is not done the insured is to be deemed a coinsurer with the insurer, so that the latter is liable only for its proportionate share of the amount of insurance required to be carried.

collateral note: a note accompanied by collateral security.

collective bargaining: the process by which the terms of employment are agreed upon through negotiations between the employer or employers within a given industry or industrial area and the union or the bargaining representative of the employees.

collective bargaining unit: the employment area within which employees are by statute authorized to select a bargaining representative, who is then to represent all the employees in bargaining with the employer.

collusion: an agreement between two or more persons to defraud the government or the courts, as by obtaining a divorce by collusion when no grounds for a divorce exist, or to defraud third persons of their rights.

color of title: circumstances that make a person appear to be the owner when in fact not the owner, as the existence of a deed appearing to convey the property to a given person gives color of title although the deed is worthless because it is in fact a forgery.

commission merchant: a bailee to whom goods are consigned for sale.

common carrier: a carrier that holds out its facilities to serve the general public for compensation without discrimination.

common law: the body of unwritten principles originally based upon the usages and customs of the community that were recognized and enforced by the courts.

common stock: stock that has no right or priority over any other stock of the corporation as to dividends or distribution of assets upon dissolution.

common trust fund: a plan by which the assets of small trust estates are pooled into a common fund, each trust being given certificates representing its proportionate ownership of the fund, and the pooled fund is then invested in investments of large size.

community property: the cotenancy held by husband and wife in property acquired during their marriage under the law of some of the states, principally in the southwestern United States.

complaint: the initial pleading filed by the plaintiff in many actions, which in many states may be served as original process to acquire jurisdiction over the defendant.

composition of creditors: an agreement among creditors that each shall accept a part payment as full payment in consideration of the other creditors doing the same.

concealment: the failure to volunteer information not requested.

conditional estate: an estate that will come into being upon the satisfaction of a condition precedent or that will be terminated upon the satisfaction of a condition subsequent.

confidential relationship: a relationship in which, because of the legal status of the parties or their respective physical or mental conditions or knowledge, one party places full confidence and trust in the other.

conflict of laws: the body of law that determines the law of which state is to apply when two or more states are involved in the facts of a given case.

confusion of goods: the mixing of goods of different owners that under certain circumstances results in one of the owners becoming the owner of all the goods.

consanguinity: relationship by blood.

consideration: the promise or performance that the promisor demands as the price of the promise.

consignment: a bailment made for the purpose of sale by the bailee. (Parties—consignor, consignee)

consolidation of corporations: a combining of two or more corporations in which the corporate existence of each one ceases and a new corporation is created.

constructive: an adjective employed to indicate that the instrument, described by the noun that is modified by the adjective, does not exist but the law disposes of the matter as though it did; as a constructive bailment or a constructive trust.

contingent beneficiary: the person to whom the proceeds of a life insurance policy are payable in the event that the primary beneficiary dies before the insured.

contract: a binding agreement based upon the genuine assent of the parties, made for a lawful object, between competent parties, in the form required by law, and generally supported by consideration.

contract carrier: a carrier that transports on the basis of individual contracts that it makes with each shipper.

contract to sell: a contract to make a transfer of title in the future as contrasted with a present transfer.

contribution: the right of a co-obligor who has paid more than a proportionate share to demand that the other obligor pay the amount of the excess payment made.

contributory negligence: negligence of the plaintiff that contributes to injury and at common law bars from recovery from the defendant although the defendant may have been more negligent than the plaintiff.

conveyance: a transfer of an interest in land, ordinarily by the execution and delivery of a deed.

cooling-off period: a procedure designed to avoid strikes by requiring a specified period of delay before the strike may begin during which negotiations for a settlement must continue.

cooperative: a group of two or more persons or enterprises that acts through a common agent with respect to a common objective, such as buying or selling.

copyright: a grant to an author or artist of an exclusive right to publish and sell the copyrighted work for the life of the author or artist and fifty years thereafter. For a "work made for hire," a grant of an exclusive right to publish and sell the copyrighted work for 100 years from its creation or 75 years from its publication, whichever is shorter.

corporation: an artificial being created by government grant, which for many purposes is treated as a natural person.

cost plus: a method of determining the purchase price or contract price by providing for the payment of an amount equal to the costs of the seller or contractor to which is added a stated percentage as the profit.

costs: the expenses of suing or being sued, recoverable in some actions by the successful party, and in others, subject to allocation by the court. Ordinarily, costs do not include attorney's fees or compensation for loss of time.

counterclaim: a claim that the defendant in an action may make against the plaintiff.

covenants of title: covenants of the grantor in a deed that guarantee such matters as the right to make the conveyance, to ownership of the property, to freedom of the property from encumbrances, or that the grantee will not be disturbed in the quiet enjoyment of the land.

crime: a violation of the law that is punished as an offense against the state or government.

cross complaint: a claim that the defendant may make against the plaintiff.

cross-examination: the examination made of a witness by the attorney for the adverse party.

cumulative voting: a system of voting for directors in which each shareholder has as many votes as the number of voting shares owned multiplied by the number of directors to be elected and such votes can be distributed for the various candidates as desired.

cy pres doctrine: the rule under which a charitable trust will be carried out as nearly as possible in the way the settlor desired, when for any reason it cannot be carried out exactly in the way or for the purposes expressed.

D

damages: a sum of money recovered to redress or make amends for the legal wrong or injury done.

damnum absque injuria: loss or damage without the violation of a legal right, or the mere fact that a person sustains a loss does not mean that legal rights have been violated.

declaratory judgment: a procedure for obtaining the decision of a court on a question before any action has been taken or loss sustained. It differs from an advisory opinion in that there must be an actual, imminent controversy.

dedication: acquisition by the public or a government of title to land when it is given over by its owner to use by the public and such gift is accepted.

deed: an instrument by which the grantor (owner of land) conveys or transfers the title to a grantee.

de facto: existing in fact as distinguished from as of right, as in the case of an officer or a corporation purporting to act as such without being elected to the office or having been properly incorporated.

deficiency judgment: a personal judgment entered against any person liable on the mortgage debt for the amount still remaining due on the mortgage after foreclosure. Statutes generally require the mortgagee to credit the fair value of the property against the balance due when the mortgagee has purchased the property. Also, a similar judgment entered by a creditor against a debtor in a secured transaction under Article 9 of the UCC.

del credere agent: an agent who sells goods for the principal and who guarantees to the principal that the buyer will pay for the goods.

delegation: the transfer to another of the right and power to do an act.

de minimis non curat lex: a maxim that the law is not concerned with trifles. Not always applied, as in the case of the encroachment of a building over the property line, in which case the law will protect the landowner regardless of the extent of the encroachment.

demonstrative evidence: evidence that consists of visible, physical objects, such as a sample taken from the wheat in controversy or a photograph of the subject matter involved.

demonstrative legacy: a legacy to be paid or distributed from a specified fund or property.

demurrage: a charge made by the carrier for the unreasonable detention of cars by the consignor or consignee.

demurrer: a pleading that may be filed to attack the sufficiency of the adverse party's pleading as not stating a cause of action or a defense.

dependent relative revocation: the doctrine recognized in some states that if a testator revokes or cancels a will in order to replace it with a later will, the earlier will is to be deemed revived if for any reason the later will does not take effect or no later will is executed.

deposition: the testimony of a witness taken out of court before a person authorized to administer oaths.

detrimental reliance: see *reliance* and *promissory estoppel.*

devise: a gift of real estate made by will.

directed verdict: a direction by the trial judge to the jury to return a verdict in favor of a specified party to the action.

directors: the persons vested with control of the corporation, subject to the elective power of the shareholders.

discharge in bankruptcy: an order of the bankruptcy court discharging the debtor from the unpaid balance of most claims.

discharge of contract: termination of a contract by performance, agreement, impossibility, acceptance of breach, or operation of law.

discovery: procedures for ascertaining facts prior to the time of trial in order to eliminate the element of surprise in litigation.

dishonor by nonacceptance: the refusal of the drawee to accept a draft (bill of exchange).

dishonor by nonpayment: the refusal to pay a commercial paper when properly presented for payment.

dismiss: a procedure to terminate an action by moving to dismiss on the ground that the plaintiff has not pleaded a cause of action entitling the plaintiff to relief.

disparagement of goods: the making of malicious, false statements as to the quality of the goods of another.

distress for rent: the common-law right of the lessor to enter the premises when the rent has not been paid and to seize all personal property found on the premises. Statutes have modified or abolished this right in many states.

distributive share: the proportionate part of the estate of the decedent that will be distributed to an heir or legatee, and also as devisee in those jurisdictions in which real estate is administered as part of the decedent's estate.

domestic bill of exchange: a draft drawn in one state and payable in the same or another state.

domestic corporation: a corporation that has been incorporated by the state in question as opposed to incorporation by another state.

domicile: the home of a person or the state of incorporation, to be distinguished from a place where a person lives but does not regard as home, or a state in which a corporation does business but in which it was not incorporated.

double indemnity: a provision for payment of double the amount specified by the insurance contract if death is caused by an accident and occurs under specified circumstances.

double jeopardy: the principle that a person who has once been placed in jeopardy by being brought to trial at which the proceedings progressed at least as far has having the jury sworn cannot thereafter be tried a second time for the same offense.

draft: see *bill of exchange.*

draft-varying acceptance: one in which the acceptor's agreement to pay is not exactly in conformity with the order of the instrument.

due care: the degree of care that a reasonable person would exercise to prevent the realization of harm, which under all the circumstances was reasonably foreseeable in the event that such care was not taken.

due process of law: the guarantee by the 5th and 14th Amendments to the U.S. Constitution and the guarantee of many state constitutions that no person shall be deprived of life, liberty, or property without due process of law. As currently interpreted, this process prohibits any law, either state or federal, that sets up an unfair procedure or the substance of which is arbitrary or capricious.

duress: conduct that deprives the victim of free will and that generally gives the victim the right to set aside any transaction entered into under such circumstances.

E

easement: a permanent right that one has in the land of another, as the right to cross another's land or an easement of way.

eleemosynary corporation: a corporation organized for a charitable or benevolent purpose.

embezzlement: a statutory offense consisting of the unlawful conversion of property entrusted to the wrongdoer.

eminent domain: the power of government and certain kinds of corporations to take private property against the objection of the owner, provided the taking is for a public purpose and just compensation is made therefor.

encumbrance: a right held by a third person in or a lien or charge against property, such as a mortgage or judgment lien on land.

equity: the body of principles that originally developed because of the inadequacy of the rules then applied by the common-law courts of England.

erosion: the loss of land through a gradual washing away by tides or currents, with the owner losing title to the lost land.

escheat: the transfer to the state of the title to a decedent's property when the owner of the property dies intestate not survived by anyone capable of taking the property as heir.

escrow: a conditional delivery of property or of a deed to a custodian or escrow holder, who in turn makes final delivery to the grantee or transferee when a specified condition has been satisfied.

estate: the extent and nature of one's interest in land; the assets constituting a decedent's property at the time of death; the assets of a debtor in bankruptcy proceedings.

estate in fee simple: the largest estate possible, in which the owner has absolute and entire property in the land.

estoppel: the principle by which a person is barred from pursuing a certain course of action or of disputing the truth of certain matters.

evidence: that which is presented to the trier of fact as the basis upon which the trier is to determine what happened.

exception: an objection, such as an exception to the admission of evidence on the ground that it is hearsay; a clause excluding particular property from the operation of a deed.

ex contractu: a claim or matter that is founded upon or arises out of a contract.

ex delicto: a claim or matter that is founded upon or arises out of a tort.

execution: the carrying out of a judgment of a court, generally directing that property owned by the defendant be sold and the proceeds first be used to pay the execution or judgment creditor.

exemplary damages: damages, in excess of the amount needed to compensate for the plaintiff's injury, that are awarded in order to punish the defendant for malicious or wanton conduct; also called punitive damages.

exoneration: an agreement or provision in an agreement that one party shall not be held liable for loss; the right of the surety to demand that those primarily liable pay the claim for which the surety is secondarily liable.

expert witness: one who has acquired special knowledge in a particular field as through practical experience or study, or both, whose opinion is admissible as an aid to the trier of fact.

ex post facto law: a law making criminal an act that was lawful when done or that increases the penalty when done. Such laws are generally prohibited by constitutional provisions.

extraordinary bailment: a bailment in which the bailee is subject to unusual duties and liabilities, such as a hotel keeper or common carrier.

F

factor: a bailee to whom goods are consigned for sale.

factors' acts: statutes protecting persons who buy in good faith for value from a factor although the goods had not been delivered to the factor with the consent or authorization of their owner.

fair employment practice acts: statutes designed to eliminate discrimination in employment on the basis of race, religion, national origin, or sex.

fair labor standards acts: statutes, particularly the federal statute, designed to prevent excessive hours of employment and low pay, the employment of young children, and other unsound practices.

featherbedding: the exaction of money for services not performed, which is made an unfair labor practice generally and a criminal offense in connection with radio broadcasting.

Federal Securities Act: a statute designed to protect the public from fraudulent securities.

Federal Securities Exchange Act: a statute prohibiting improper practices at and regulating security exchanges.

Federal Trade Commission Act: a statute prohibiting unfair methods of competition in interstate commerce.

fellow-servant rule: a common-law defense of the employer that barred an employee from suing an employer for injuries caused by a fellow employee.

felony: a criminal offense that is punishable by confinement in prison or by death, or that is expressly stated by statute to be a felony.

financial responsibility laws: statutes that require a driver involved in an automobile accident to prove financial responsibility in order to retain a license, such responsibility may be shown by procuring public liability insurance in a specified minimum amount.

financing factor: one who lends money to manufacturers on the security of goods to be manufactured thereafter.

firm offer: an offer stated to be held open for a specified time, which must be so held in some states even in the absence of an option contract, or under the UCC, with respect to merchants.

fixture: personal property that has become so attached to or adapted to real estate that it has lost its character as personal property and is part of the real estate.

Food, Drug, and Cosmetic Act: a federal statute prohibiting the interstate shipment of misbranded or adulterated foods, drugs, cosmetics, and therapeutic devices.

forbearance: refraining from doing an act.

foreclosure: procedure for enforcing a mortgage resulting in the public sale of the mortgaged property and, less commonly, in merely barring the right of the mortgagor to redeem the property from the mortgage.

foreign (international) bill of exchange: a bill of exchange made in one nation and payable in another.

foreign corporation: a corporation incorporated under the laws of another state.

forgery: the fraudulent making or altering of an instrument that apparently creates or alters a legal liability of another.

franchise: (a) a privilege or authorization, generally exclusive, to engage in a particular activity within a particular geographic area, such as a government franchise to operate a taxi company within a specified city, or a private franchise as the grant by a manufacturer of a right to sell products within a particular territory or for a particular number of years; (b) the right to vote.

fraud: the making of a false statement of a past or existing fact, with knowledge of its falsity or with reckless indifference as to its truth, with the intent to cause another to rely thereon, and such person does rely thereon and is harmed thereby.

freight forwarder: one who contracts to have goods transported and, in turn, contracts with carriers for such transportation.

fructus industriales: crops that are annually planted and raised.

fructus naturales: fruits from trees, bushes, and grasses growing from perennial roots.

fungible goods: goods of a homogeneous nature of which any unit is the equivalent of any other unit or is treated as such by mercantile usage.

future advance mortgage: a mortgage given to secure additional loans to be made in the future as well as to secure an original loan.

G

garnishment: the name given in some states to attachment proceedings.

general creditor: a creditor who has a claim against a debtor but does not have any lien on any of the debtor's property, whether as security for the debt or by way of a judgment or execution upon a judgment.

general damages: damages that in the ordinary course of events follow naturally and probably from the injury caused by the defendant.

general legacy: a legacy to be paid out of the decedent's assets generally without specifying any particular fund or source from which the payment is to be made.

general partnership: a partnership in which the partners conduct as co-owners a business for profit, and each partner has a right to take part in the management of the business and has unlimited liability.

gift causa mortis: a gift, made by the donor in the belief that death was immediate and impending, that is revoked or is revocable under certain circumstances.

grace period: a period generally of 30 or 31 days after the due date of a life insurance premium in which the payment may be made.

grand jury: a jury not exceeding 23 in number that considers evidence of the commission of crime and prepares indictments to bring offenders to trial before a petty jury.

grant: convey real property; an instrument by which such property has been conveyed, particularly in the case of a government.

gratuitous bailment: a bailment in which the bailee does not receive any compensation or advantage.

grievance settlement: the adjustment of disputes relating to the administration or application of existing contracts as compared with disputes over new terms of employment.

guarantor: one who undertakes the obligation of guaranty.

guaranty: an undertaking to pay the debt of another if the creditor first sues the debtor and is unable to recover the debt from the debtor or principal. (In some instances the liability is primary, in which case it is the same as suretyship.)

H

hearsay evidence: statements made out of court that are offered in court as proof of the information contained in the statements, and that, subject to many exceptions, are not admissible in evidence.

hedging: the making of simultaneous contracts to purchase and to sell a particular commodity at a future date with the intention that the loss on one transaction will be offset by the gain on the other.

heirs: those persons specified by statute to receive the estate of a decedent not disposed of by will.

holder: the person in possession of a commercial paper payable to that person as payee or indorsee, or the person in possession of a commercial paper payable to bearer.

holder in due course: a holder of a commercial paper who is favored and is given an immunity from certain defenses.

holder through a holder in due course: a person who is not a holder in due course but is a holder of the paper after it was held by some prior party who was a holder in due course, and who is given the same rights as a holder in due course.

holographic will: an unwitnessed will written by hand.

hotel keeper: one regularly engaged in the business of offering living accommodations to all transient persons.

hung jury: a petty jury that has been unable to agree upon a verdict.

I

ignorantia legis neminem excusat: ignorance of the law excuses no one.

implied contract: a contract expressed by conduct or implied or deduced from the facts. Also used to refer to a quasi contract.

imputed: vicariously attributed to or charged to another; for instance the knowledge of an agent obtained while acting in the scope of authority is imputed to the principal.

incidental authority: authority of an agent that is reasonably necessary to execute express authority.

incontestability clause: a provision that after the lapse of a specified time the insurer cannot dispute the policy on the ground of misrepresentation or fraud of the insured or similar wrongful conduct.

in custodia legis: in the custody of the law.

indemnity: the right of a person secondarily liable to require that a person primarily liable pay for loss sustained when the secondary party discharges the obligation that the primary party should have discharged; the right of an agent to be paid the amount of any loss or damage sustained without fault because of obedience to the principal's instructions; an undertaking by one person for a consideration to pay another person a sum of money to indemnify that person when a specified loss is incurred.

independent contractor: a contractor who undertakes to perform a specified task according to the terms of a contract but over whom the other contracting party has no control except as provided for by the contract.

indictment: a grand jury's formal accusation of crime, from which the accused is then tried by a petty or trial jury.

inheritance: the interest that passes from the decedent to the decedent's heirs.

injunction: an order of a court of equity to refrain from doing (negative injunction) or to do (affirmative or mandatory injunction) a specified act. Its use in labor disputes has been greatly restricted by statute.

in pari delicto: equally guilty; used in reference to a transaction as to which relief will not be granted to either party because both are equally guilty of wrongdoing.

insolvency: an excess of debts and liabilities over assets; or inability to pay debts as they mature.

insurable interest: an interest in the nonoccurrence of the risk insured against, generally because such occurrence would cause financial loss, although sometimes merely because of the close relationship between the insured and the beneficiary.

insurance: a plan of security against risks by charging the loss against a fund created by the payments made by policyholders.

intangible personal property: an interest in an enterprise, such as an interest in a partnership or stock of a corporation, and claims against other persons, whether based upon contract or tort.

interlineation: a writing between the lines or adding to the provisions of a document, the effect thereof depending upon the nature of the document.

interlocutory: an intermediate step or proceeding that does not make a final disposition of the action and from which ordinarily no appeal may be made.

international bill of exchange: a bill or draft made in one nation and payable in another.

interpleader: a form of action or proceeding by which a person against whom conflicting claims are made may bring the claimants into court to litigate their claims between themselves, as in the case of a bailee when two persons each claim to be the owner of the bailed property, or an insurer when two persons each claim to be the beneficiary.

inter se: among or between themselves, such as the rights of partners inter se or as between themselves.

inter vivos: any transaction which takes place between living persons and creates rights prior to the death of any of them.

intestate: the condition of dying without a will as to any property.

intestate succession: the distribution, made as directed by statute, of a decedent's property not effectively disposed of by will.

ipso facto: by the very act or fact in itself without any further action by any one.

irrebuttable presumption: a presumption that cannot be rebutted by proving that the facts are to the contrary; not a true presumption but merely a rule of law described in terms of a presumption.

irreparable injury to property: an injury that would be of such a nature or inflicted upon such an interest that it would not be reasonably possible to compensate the injured party by the payment of money damages because the property in question could not be purchased in the open market with the money damages that the defendant could be required to pay.

J

joint and several contract: a contract in which two or more persons are jointly and separately obligated or under which they are jointly and separately entitled to recover.

joint contract: a contract in which two or more persons are jointly liable or jointly entitled to performance under the contract.

joint stock company: an association in which the shares of the members are transferable and control is delegated to a group or board.

joint tenancy: the estate held by two or more jointly with the right of survivorship as between them, unless modified by statute.

joint venture: a relationship in which two or more persons combine their labor or property for a single undertaking and share profits and losses equally unless otherwise agreed.

judgment: the final sentence, order, or decision entered into at the conclusion of the action.

judgment note: a promissory note containing a clause authorizing the holder of the note to enter judgment against the maker of the note if it is not paid when due; also called a cognovit note.

judgment n.o.v.: a judgment that may be entered after verdict upon the motion of the losing party on the ground that the verdict is so wrong that a judgment should be entered the opposite of the verdict, or non obstante veredicto (notwithstanding the verdict).

judgment on the pleadings: a judgment that may be entered after all the pleadings are filed when it is clear from the pleadings that a particular party is entitled to win the action without proceeding any further.

judicial sale: a sale made under order of court by an officer appointed to make the sale or by an officer having such authority as incident to the office. The sale may have the effect of divesting liens on the property.

jurisdiction: the power of a court to hear and determine a given class of cases; the power to act over a particular defendant.

jurisdictional dispute: a dispute between rival labor unions that may take the form of each claiming that particular work should be assigned to it.

justifiable abandonment by employee: the right of an employee to abandon employment because of nonpayment of wages, wrongful assault, the demand for the performance of services not contemplated, or injurious working conditions.

justifiable discharge of employee: the right of an employer to discharge an employee for nonperformance of duties, fraud, disobedience, disloyalty, or incompetence.

L

laches: the rule that the enforcement of equitable rights will be denied when the party has delayed so long that rights of third persons have intervened or the death or disappearance of witnesses would prejudice any party through the loss of evidence.

land: earth, including all things embedded in or attached thereto, whether naturally or by the act of man.

last clear chance: the rule that a defendant who had the last clear chance to have avoided injuring the plaintiff is liable even though the plaintiff had also been contributorily negligent. In some states also called the humanitarian doctrine.

law of the case: matters decided in the course of litigation that are binding on the parties in the subsequent phases of litigation.

leading questions: questions that suggest the desired answer to the witness, or assume the existence of a fact that is in dispute.

lease: an agreement between the owner of property and a tenant by which the former agrees to give possession of the property to the latter in consideration of the payment of rent. (Parties—landlord or lessor, tenant or lessee)

leasehold: the estate or interest of a tenant in rented land.

legacy: a gift of personal property made by will.

legal tender: such form of money as the law recognizes as lawful and declares that a tender thereof in the proper amount is a proper tender that the creditor cannot refuse.

letter of credit: a written agreement by which the issuer of the letter, usually a bank, agrees with the other contracting party, its customer, that the issuer will honor drafts drawn upon it by the person named in the letter as the beneficiary. Domestic letters are regulated by the UCC, Article 5; international letters by the Customs and Practices for Commercial Documentary Credits. Commercial or payment letter: the customer is the buyer of goods sold by the beneficiary and the letter covers the purchase price of the goods. Standby letter: a letter obtained instead of a suretyship or guaranty contract requiring the issuer to honor drafts drawn by the beneficiary upon the issuer when the customer of the issuer fails to perform a contract between the customer and the beneficiary. Documentary letter: a letter of credit that does not obligate the issuer to honor drafts unless they are accompanied by the documents specified in the letter.

letters of administration: the written authorization given to an administrator of an estate as evidence of appointment and authority.

letters testamentary: the written authorization given to an executor of an estate as evidence of appointment and authority.

levy: a seizure of property by an officer of the court in execution of a judgment of the court, although in many states it is sufficient if the officer is physically in the presence of the property and announces the fact that it is "seized," but then allows the property to remain where it was found.

lex loci: the law of the place where the material facts occurred as governing the rights and liabilities of the parties.

lex loci contractus: the law of the place where the contract was made as governing the rights and liabilities of the parties to a contract with respect to certain matters.

lex loci fori: the law of the state in which the action is brought as determining the rules of procedure applicable to the action.

lex loci sitae rei: the law of the place where land is located as determining the validity of acts done relating thereto.

libel: written or visual defamation without legal justification.

license: a personal privilege to do some act or series of acts upon the land of another, as the placing of a sign thereon, not amounting to an easement or a right of possession.

lien: a claim or right, against property, existing by virtue of the entry of a judgment against its owner or by the entry of a judgment and a levy thereunder on the property, or because of the relationship of the claimant to the particular property, such as an unpaid seller.

life estate: an estate for the duration of a life.

limited jurisdiction: a court's power to hear and determine cases within certain restricted categories.

limited liability: loss of contributed capital or investment as maximum liability.

limited partnership: a partnership in which at least one partner has a liability limited to the loss of the capital contribution made to the partnership, and such a partner neither takes part in the management of the partnership nor appears to the public to be a general partner.

lineal consanguinity: the relationship that exists when one person is a direct descendant of the other.

liquidated damages: a provision stipulating the amount of damages to be paid in the event of default or breach of contract.

liquidation: the process of converting property into money whether of particular items of property or of all the assets of a business or an estate.

lis pendens: the doctrine that certain kinds of pending action are notice to everyone so that if any right is acquired from a party to such action, the transferee takes that right subject to the outcome of the pending action.

lobbying contract (illegal): a contract by which one party agrees to attempt to influence the action of a legislature or Congress, or any members thereof, by improper means.

lottery: any plan by which a consideration is given for a chance to win a prize.

lucri causa: with the motive of obtaining gain or pecuniary advantage.

M

majority: of age, as contrasted with being a minor; more than half of any group, as a majority of stockholders.

malice in fact: an intention to injure or cause harm.

malice in law: a presumed intention to injure or cause harm when there is no privilege or right to do the act in question, such presumption cannot be contradicted or rebutted.

maliciously inducing breach of contract: the wrong of inducing the breach of any kind of contract with knowledge of its existence and without justification.

malum in se: an offense that is criminal because it is contrary to the fundamental sense of a civilized community, such as murder.

malum prohibitum: an offense that is criminal not because inherently wrong but is prohibited for the convenience of society, such as overtime parking.

marshalling assets: the distribution of a debtor's assets in such a way as to give the greatest benefit to all creditors.

martial law: government exercised by a military commander over property and persons not in the armed forces, as contrasted with military law which governs military personnel.

mechanic's lien: protection afforded by statute to various kinds of laborers and persons supplying materials, by giving them a lien on the building and land that has been improved or added to by them.

mens rea: the mental state that must accompany an act to make the act a crime. Sometimes described as the guilty mind, although appreciation of guilt is not required.

merger by judgment: the discharge of a contract through being merged into a judgment that is entered in a suit on the contract.

merger of corporations: a combining of corporations by which one absorbs the other and continues to exist, preserving its original charter and identity while the other corporation ceases to exist.

misdemeanor: a criminal offense that is neither treason nor a felony.

misrepresentation: a false statement of fact although made innocently without any intent to deceive.

mobilia sequuntur personam: the maxim that personal property follows the owner and in the eyes of the law is located at the owner's domicile.

moratorium: a temporary suspension by statute of the enforcement of debts or the foreclosure of mortgages.

mortgage: an interest in land given by the owner to a creditor as security for the payment of the creditor for a debt, the nature of the interest depending upon the law of the state where the land is located. (Parties—mortgagor, mortgagee)

multiple insurers: insurers who agree to divide a risk so that each is only liable for a specified portion.

N

National Labor Management Relations Act: the federal statute, also known as the Taft-Hartley Act, designed to protect the organizational rights of labor and to prevent unfair labor practices by management or labor.

natural and probable consequences: those ordinary consequences of an act that a reasonable person would foresee.

negative covenant: an undertaking in a deed to refrain from doing an act.

negligence: the failure to exercise due care under the circumstances in consequence of which harm is proximately caused to one to whom the defendant owed a duty to exercise due care.

negligence per se: an action that is regarded as so improper that it is declared by law to be negligent in itself without regard to whether due care was otherwise exercised.

negotiable instruments: drafts, promissory notes, checks, and certificates of deposit in such form that greater rights may be acquired thereunder than by taking an assignment of a contract right; called negotiable commercial paper by the UCC.

negotiation: the transfer of a commercial paper by indorsement and delivery by the person to whom then payable in the case of order paper and by physical transfer in the case of bearer paper.

nominal damages: a nominal sum awarded the plaintiff in order to establish that legal rights have been violated although the plaintiff in fact has not sustained any actual loss or damages.

Norris-La Guardia Anti-Injunction Act: a federal statute prohibiting the use of the injunction in labor disputes, except in particular cases.

notice of dishonor: notice given to parties secondarily liable that the primary party to the instrument has refused to accept the instrument or to make payment when it was properly presented for that purpose.

novation: the discharge of a contract between two parties by their agreeing with a third person that such third person shall be substituted for one of the original parties to the contract, who shall thereupon be released.

nudum pactum: a mere promise for which there is not consideration given and which, therefore, is ordinarily not enforceable.

nuisance: any conduct that harms or prejudices another in the use of land or which harms or prejudices the public.

nuisance per se: an activity that is in itself a nuisance regardless of the time and place involved.

nuncupative will: an oral will made and declared to be a will by the testator in the presence of witnesses; generally made during the testator's last illness.

O

obiter dictum: that which is said in the opinion of a court in passing or by the way, but which is not necessary to the determination of the case and is therefore not regarded as authoritative as though it were actually involved in the decision.

obliteration: any erasing, writing upon, or crossing out that makes all or part of a will impossible to read, and which has the effect of revoking such part when done by the maker of the will with the intent of effecting a revocation.

occupation: taking and holding possession of property; a method of acquiring title to personal property after it has been abandoned.

open-end mortgage: a mortgage given to secure additional loans to be made in the future as well as to secure the original loan.

operation of law: the attaching of certain consequences to certain facts because of legal principles that operate automatically, as contrasted with consequences that arise because of the voluntary action of a party designed to create those consequences.

opinion evidence: evidence not of what the witness observed but the conclusion drawn from what the witness has observed; in the case of expert witnesses, what has been observed in tests or experiments or what has been heard in court.

option contract: a contract to hold an offer to make a contract open for a fixed period of time.

P

paper title: the title of a person evidenced only by deeds or matter appearing of record under the recording statutes.

parol evidence rule: the rule that prohibits the introduction in evidence of oral or written statements made prior to or contemporaneously with the execution of a complete written contract, deed, or instrument, in the absence of clear proof of fraud, accident, or mistake causing the omission of the statement in question.

passive trust: a trust that is created without imposing any duty to be performed by the trustee and is therefore treated as an absolute transfer of the title to the trust beneficiary.

past consideration: something that has been performed in the past and which, therefore, cannot be consideration for a promise made in the present.

patent: the grant to an inventor of an exclusive right to make and sell an invention for a nonrenewable period of 17 years; a deed to land given by a government to a private person.

pawn: a pledge of tangible personal property rather than of documents representing property rights.

pecuniary legacy: a general legacy of a specified amount of money without indicating the source from which payment is to be made.

per autre vie: limitation of an estate. An estate held by *A* during the lifetime of *B* is an estate of *A* per autre vie.

per curiam opinion: an opinion written by the court rather than by a named judge when all the judges of the court are in such agreement on the matter that it is not deemed to merit any discussion and may be simply disposed of.

perpetual succession: a phrase describing the continuing life of the corporation unaffected by the death of any stockholder or the transfer by stockholders of their stock.

perpetuities, rule against: a rule of law that prohibits the creation of an interest in property that will not become definite or vested until a date further away than 21 years after the death of persons alive at the time the owner of the property attempts to create the interest.

per se: in, through, or by itself.

person: a term that includes both natural persons, or living persons, and artificial persons, such as corporations which are created by act of government.

personal defenses: limited defenses that cannot be asserted by the defendant against a holder in due course. This term is not expressly used in UCC.

per stirpes: according to the root or by way of representation. Distribution among heirs related to the decedent in different degrees, the property being divided into lines of descent from the descendent and the share of each line then divided within the line by way of representation.

petit larceny: more commonly, petty larceny. At common law, the larceny of property having the value of 12 pence or less. When the property had a greater value, the crime was grand larceny and the punishment was death. In many states, degrees of larceny have replaced the common-law classification.

petty jury: the trial jury. Also, petit jury.

picketing: the placing of persons outside of places of employment or distribution so that by words or banners they may inform the public of the existence of a labor dispute or may influence employees or customers.

pleadings: the papers filed by the parties in an action in order to set forth the facts and frame the issues to be tried, although under some systems, the pleadings merely give notice or a general indication of the nature of the issues.

pledge: a bailment given as security for the payment of a debt or the performance of an obligation owed to the pledgee. (Parties—pledgor, pledgee)

police power: the power to govern; the power to adopt laws for the protection of the public heath, welfare, safety, and morals.

policy: the paper evidencing the contract of insurance.

polling the jury: the process of inquiring of each juror individually in open court as to whether the verdict announced in court was agreed to.

possession: exclusive dominion and control of property.

possessory lien: a right to retain possession of property of another as security for some debt or obligation owed the lienor, such right continues only as long as possession is retained.

possibility of reverter: the nature of the interest held by the grantor after conveying land outright but subject to a condition or provision that may cause the grantee's interest to become forfeited and the interest to revert to the grantor or heirs.

postdate: to insert or place on an instrument a later date than the actual date on which it was executed.

power of appointment: a power given to another, commonly a beneficiary of a trust, to designate or appoint who shall be beneficiary or receive the fund after the death of the grantor.

power of attorney: a written authorization to an agent by the principal.

precatory words: words indicating merely a desire or a wish that another use property for a particular purpose but which in law will not be enforced in the absence of an express declaration that the property shall be used for the specified purpose.

preemptive offer of shares: shareholder's right upon the increase of a corporation's capital stock to be allowed to subscribe to such a percentage of the new shares as the shareholder's old shares bore to the former total capital stock.

preferred creditor: a creditor who by some statute is given the right to be paid first or before other creditors.

preferred stock: stock that has a priority or preference as to payment of dividends or upon liquidation, or both.

preponderance of evidence: the degree or quantum of evidence in favor of the existence of a certain fact when from a review of all the evidence it appears more probable that the fact exists than that it does not. The actual number of witnesses involved is not material nor is the fact that the margin of probability is very slight.

prescription: the acquisition of a right to use the land of another, as an easement, through the making of hostile, visible, and notorious use of the land, continuing for the period specified by the local law.

presumption: a rule of proof that permits the existence of a fact to be assumed from the proof that another fact exists when there is a logical relationship between the two or when the means of disproving the assumed fact are more readily within the control or knowledge of the adverse party against whom the presumption operates.

presumption of death: the rebuttable presumption that a person has died when that person has been continuously absent and unheard of for a period of 7 years.

presumption of innocence: the presumption of fact that a person accused of crime is innocent until shown guilty of the offense charged.

presumption of payment: a rebuttable presumption that one performing continuing services that would normally be paid periodically, such as weekly or monthly, has in fact been paid when a number of years have passed without any objection or demand for payment having been made.

presumptive heir: a person who would be the heir if the ancestor should die at that moment.

pretrial conference: a conference, held prior to the trial, at which the court and the attorney seek to simplify the issues in controversy and eliminate matters not in dispute.

price: the consideration for sale of goods.

prima facie: evidence that, if believed, is sufficient by itself to lead to a particular conclusion.

primary beneficiary: the person designated as the first one to receive the proceeds of a life insurance policy, as distinguished from a contingent beneficiary who will receive the proceeds only if the primary beneficiary dies before the insured.

primary liability: the liability of a person whose act or omission gave rise to the cause of action and who in all fairness should, therefore, be the one to pay the victim even though others may also be liable for misconduct.

principal: one who employs an agent; the person who, with respect to a surety, is primarily liable to the third person or creditor.

principal in the first degree: one who actually engages in the commission or perpetration of a crime.

principal in the second degree: one who is actually or constructively present at the commission of the crime and who aids and abets in its commission.

private carrier: a carrier owned by the shipper, such as a company's own fleet of trucks.

privileged communication: information that the witness may refuse to testify to because of the relationship with the person furnishing the information, such as husband-wife or attorney-client.

privilege from arrest: the immunity from arrest of parties, witnesses, and attorneys while present within the jurisdiction for the purpose of taking part in other litigation.

privity: a succession or chain of relationship to the same thing or right, such as privity of contract, privity of estate, privity of possession.

probate: the procedure for formally establishing or proving that a given writing is the last will and testament of the person who purportedly signed it.

product liability: liability imposed upon the manufacturer or seller of goods for harm caused by a defect in the goods, comprising liability for (a) negligence, (b) fraud, (c) breach of warranty, and (d) strict tort.

profit prendre: the right to take a part of the soil or produce of another's land, such as timber or water.

promissory estoppel: the doctrine that a promise will be enforced although it is not supported by consideration when the promisor should have reasonably expected that the promise would induce action or forbearance of a definite and substantial character on the part of the promisee, and injustice can only be avoided by enforcement of the promise.

promissory note: an unconditional promise in writing made by one person to another, signed by the maker engaging to pay on demand, or at a definite time, a sum certain in money to order or to bearer. (Parties—maker, payee)

promissory representation: a representation made by the applicant to the insurer as to what is to occur in the future.

promissory warranty: a representation made by the applicant to the insurer as to what is to occur in the future that the applicant warrants will occur.

promoters: the persons who plan the formation of the corporation and sell or promote the idea to others.

proof: the probative effect of the evidence; the conclusion drawn from the evidence as to the existence of particular facts.

property: the rights and interests one has in anything subject to ownership.

pro rata: proportionately, or divided according to a rate or standard.

protest: the formal certificate by a notary public or other authorized person that proper presentment of a commercial paper was made to the primary party and that such party defaulted, the certificate commonly also including a recital that notice was given to secondary parties.

proximate cause: the act that is the natural and reasonably foreseeable cause of the harm or event that occurs and injures the plaintiff.

proximate damages: damages that in the ordinary course of events are the natural and reasonably foreseeable result of the defendant's violation of the plaintiff's rights.

proxy: a written authorization by a shareholder to another person to vote the stock owned by the shareholder; the person who is the holder of such a written authorization.

public charge: a person who because of personal disability or lack of means of support is dependent upon public charity or relief for sustenance.

public domain: public or government-owned lands.

public easement: a right of way for use by members of the public at large.

public policy: certain objectives relating to health, morals, and integrity of government that the law seeks to advance by declaring invalid any contract that conflicts with those objectives even though there is no statute expressly declaring such a contract illegal.

punitive damages: damages, in excess of those required to compensate the plaintiff for the wrong done, that are imposed in order to punish the defendant because of the particularly wanton or willful character of wrongdoing; also called exemplary damages.

purchase-money mortgage: a mortgage given by the purchaser of land to the seller to secure the seller for the payment of the unpaid balance of the purchase price, which the seller purports to lend the purchaser.

purchaser in good faith: a person who purchases without any notice or knowledge of any defect of title, misconduct, or defense.

Q

qualified acceptance: An acceptance of a draft that varies the order of the draft in some way.

qualified indorsement: an indorsement that includes words such as *without recourse* evidencing the intent that the indorser shall not be held liable for the failure of the primary party to pay the instrument.

quantum meruit: an action brought for the value of the services rendered the defendant when there was no express contract as to the purchase price.

quantum valebant: an action brought for the value of goods sold the defendant when there was no express contract as to the purchase price.

quasi: as if, as though it were, having the characteristics of; a modifier employed to indicate that the subject is to be treated as though it were in fact the noun that follows the word *quasi*, as in quasi contract, quasi corporation, quasi public corporation.

quid pro quo: literally "what for what." An early form of the concept of consideration by which an action for debt could not be brought unless the defendant had obtained something in return for the obligation sued upon.

quitclaim deed: a deed by which the grantor purports only to give up whatever right or title the grantor may have in the property without specifying or warranting transfer of any particular interest.

quorum: the minimum number of persons, shares represented, or directors who must be present at a meeting in order that business may be lawfully transacted.

R

ratification by minor: a minor's approval of a contract after the minor attains majority.

ratification of agency: the approval of the unauthorized act of an agent or of a person who is not an agent for any purpose. The approval occurs after the act has been done and has the same effect as though the act had been authorized before it was done.

ratio decidendi: the reason or basis for deciding the case in a particular way.

ratio legis: the reason for a principle or rule of law.

real defenses: certain defenses (universal) that are available against any holder of a commercial paper, although this term is not expressly used by the UCC.

real evidence: tangible objects that are presented in the courtroom for the observation of the trier of fact as proof of the facts in dispute or in support of the theory of a party.

real property: land and all rights in land.

reasonable care: the degree of care that a reasonable person would take under all the circumstances then known.

rebate: a refund, made by the seller or the carrier, of part of the purchase price or freight bill.

rebuttable presumption: a presumption that may be overcome or rebutted by proof that the actual facts were different from those presumed.

receiver: an impartial person appointed by a court to take possession of and manage property for the protection of all concerned.

recognizance: an obligation entered into before a court to do some act, such as to appear at a later date for a hearing. Also called a contract of record.

redemption: the buying back of one's property, which has been sold because of a default, upon paying the amount that had been originally due together with interest and costs.

referee: an impartial person selected by the parties or appointed by a court to determine facts or decide matters in dispute.

referee in bankruptcy: a referee appointed by a bankruptcy court to hear and determine various matters relating to bankruptcy proceedings.

reformation: a remedy by which a written instrument is corrected when it fails to express the actual intent of both parties because of fraud, accident, or mistake.

registration of titles: a system generally known as the Torrens system of permanent registration of title to all land within the state.

reimbursement: the right of one paying money on behalf of another, which such other person should have paid, to recover the amount of the payment from such other person.

release of liens: an agreement or instrument by which the holder of a lien of property such as a mortgage lien, releases the property from the lien although the debt itself is not discharged.

reliance: action taken or not taken by a person in the belief that the facts as stated by another are true or that the promise of another will be performed. Detrimental reliance: a term generally used to refer to reliance of such a degree that the person relying would sustain substantial damages that could not be compensated for by the payment of money; the same concept that underlies part performance as taking an oral contract out of the statute of frauds. In some cases, loosely used when merely reliance was present. See *promissory estoppel.*

remedy: the action or procedure that is followed in order to enforce a right or to obtain damages for injury to a right.

remote damages: damages that were in fact caused by the defendant's act but the possibility that such damages should occur seemed so improbable and unlikely to a reasonable person that the law does not impose liability for such damages.

renunciation of duty: the repudiation of one's contractual duty in advance of the time for performance.

renunciation of right: the surrender of a right or privilege, such as the right to act as administrator or the right to receive a legacy under the will of a decedent.

reorganization of corporation: procedure devised to restore insolvent corporations to financial stability through readjustment of debt and capital structure either under the supervision of a court of equity or of bankruptcy.

repossession: any taking again of possession although generally used in connection with the act of a secured seller in taking back the property upon the default of the credit buyer.

representations: any statements, whether oral or written, made to give the insurer the information that it needs in writing the insurance, and which if false and relating to a material fact will entitle the insurer to avoid the contract.

representative capacity: action taken by one on behalf of another, as the act of a personal representative on behalf of a decedent's estate, or action taken both on one's behalf and on behalf of others, as a shareholder bringing a representative action.

rescission upon agreement: the setting aside of a contract by the action of the parties as though the contract had never been made.

rescission upon breach: the action of one party to a contract to set the contract aside when the other party is guilty of a breach of the contract.

residuary estate: the balance of the decedent's estate available for distribution after all administrative expenses, exemptions, debts, taxes, and legacies have been paid.

res inter alios acta: the rule that transactions and declarations between strangers having no connection with the ending action are not admissible in evidence.

res ipsa loquitur: the permissible inference that the defendant was negligent in that the thing speaks for itself when the circumstances are such that ordinarily the plaintiff could not have been injured had the defendant not been at fault.

res judicata: the principle that once a final judgment is entered in an action between the parties, it is binding upon them and the matter cannot be litigated again by bringing a second action.

respondeat superior: the doctrine that the principal or employer is vicariously liable for the unauthorized torts committed by an agent or employee while acting within the scope of the agency or the course of the employment, respectively.

restraints on alienation: limitations on the ability of the owner to convey freely as the owner chooses. Such limitations are generally regarded as invalid.

restrictive covenants: covenants in a deed by which the grantee agrees to refrain from doing specified acts.

restrictive indorsement: an indorsement that prohibits the further transfer, constitutes the indorsee the agent of the indorser, vests the title in the indorsee in trust for or to the use of some other person, is conditional, or is for collection or deposit.

resulting trust: a trust that is created by implication of law to carry out the presumed intent of the parties.

retaliatory statute: a statute that provides that when a corporation of another state enters the state it shall be subject to the same taxes and restrictions as would be imposed upon a corporation from the retaliating state if it had entered the other state. Also known as reciprocity statutes.

reversible error: an error or defect in court proceedings of so serious a nature that on appeal the appellate court will set aside the proceedings of the lower court.

reversionary interest: the interest that a lessor has in property that is subject to an outstanding lease.

revival of judgment: the taking of appropriate action to preserve a judgment, in most instances to continue the lien of the judgment that would otherwise expire after a specified number of years.

revival of will: the restoration, by the writer, of a will that had previously been revoked.

rider: a slip of paper executed by the insurer and intended to be attached to the insurance policy for the purpose of changing it in some respect.

riparian rights: the right of a person through whose land runs a natural watercourse to use the water free from unreasonable pollution or diversion by upper riparian owners and blocking by lower riparian owners.

risk: the peril or contingency against which the insured is protected by the contract of insurance.

Robinson-Patman Act: a federal statute designed to eliminate price discrimination in interstate commerce.

run with the land: the concept that certain covenants in a deed to land are deemed to "run" or pass with the land so that whoever owns the land is bound by or entitled to the benefit of the covenants.

S

sale or return: a sale in which the title to the property passes to the buyer at the time of the transaction but the buyer is given the option of returning the property and restoring the title to the seller.

scienter: knowledge, referring to those wrongs or crimes that require a knowledge of wrong in order to constitute the offense.

scope of employment: the area within which the employee is authorized to act with the consequence that a tort committed while so acting imposes liability upon the employer.

seal: at common law an impression on wax or other tenacious material attached to the instrument. Under modern law, any mark not ordinarily part of the signature is a seal when so intended, including the letters *L.S.* and the word *seal*, or a pictorial representation of a seal, without regard to whether they had been printed or typed on the instrument before its signing.

sealed verdict: a verdict that is rendered when the jury returns to the courtroom during an adjournment of the court, the verdict then being written down and sealed and later affirmed before the court when the court is in session.

secondary evidence: copies of original writings or testimony as to the contents of such writings that are admissible when the original cannot be produced and the inability to do so is reasonably explained.

secured transaction: a credit sale of goods or a secured loan that provides special protection for the creditor.

securities: stock and bonds issued by a corporation. Under some investor protection laws, the term includes any interest in an enterprise that provides unearned income to its owner. Investment securities: under the UCC, Article 8, this term also includes any instrument representing an interest in property or an enterprise that is commonly dealt in or recognized as a medium of investment. Uncertificated securities: under the 1977 version of the UCC rights to securities that are not represented by a certificate but only by a record on a computer of the issuing enterprise.

settlor: one who settles property in trust or creates a trust estate.

severable contract: a contract the terms of which are such that one part may be separated or severed from the other so that a default as to one part is not necessarily a default as to the entire contract.

several contracts: separate or independent contracts made by different persons undertaking to perform the same obligation.

severalty: ownership of property by one person.

severed realty: real property that has been cut off and made movable, as by cutting down a tree, and which thereby loses its character as real property and becomes personal property.

shareholder's action: an action brought by one or more shareholders on behalf of themselves and on behalf of all shareholders generally and of the corporation to enforce a cause of action of the corporation against third persons.

sheriff's deed: the deed executed and delivered by the sheriff to the purchaser at a sale conducted by the sheriff.

Sherman Antitrust Act: a federal statute prohibiting combinations and contracts in restraint of interstate trade, now generally inapplicable to labor union activity.

shop right: the right of an employer to use in business without charge an invention discovered by an employee during working hours and with the employer's material and equipment.

sight draft: a draft or bill of exchange payable on sight or when presented for payment.

sit-down strike: a strike in which the employees remain in the plant and refuse to allow the employer to operate it.

slander: defamation of character by spoken words or gestures.

slander of title: the malicious making of false statements as to a seller's title.

slowdown: a slowing down of production by employees without actual stopping work.

social security acts: statutes providing for assistance for the aged, blind, unemployed, and similar classes of persons in need.

special agent: an agent authorized to transact a specific transaction or to do a specific act.

special damages: damages that do not necessarily result from the injury to the plaintiff but at the same time are not so remote that the defendant should not be held liable therefor provided that the claim for special damages is properly made in the action.

special indorsement: an indorsement that specifies the person to whom the instrument is indorsed.

special jurisdiction: a court with power to hear and determine cases within certain restricted categories.

specific (identified) goods: goods that are so identified to the contract that no other goods may be delivered in performance of the contract.

specific lien: the right of a creditor to hold particular property or assert a lien on particular property of the debtor because of the creditor's having done work on or having some other association with the property, as distinguished from having a lien generally against the assets of the debtor merely because the debtor is indebted to the lien holder.

specific performance: an action brought to compel the adverse party to perform a contract on the theory that merely suing for damages for its breach will not be an adequate remedy.

spendthrift trust: a trust that, to varying degrees, provides that creditors of the beneficiary shall not be able to reach the principal or income held by the trustee and that the beneficiary shall not be able to assign any interest in the trust.

spoliation: an alteration or change made to a written instrument by a person who has no relationship to or interest in the writing. It has no effect as long as the terms of the instrument can still be ascertained.

stare decisis: the principle that the decision of a court should serve as a guide or precedent and control the decision of a similar case in the future.

status quo ante: the original positions of the parties to a contract prior to the making of the contract or the doing of some other act.

Statute of Frauds: a statute that, in order to prevent fraud through the use of perjured testimony, requires that certain kinds of transactions be evidenced in writing in order to be binding or enforceable.

Statute of Limitations: a statute that restricts the period of time within which an action may be brought.

stop delivery: the right of an unpaid seller under certain conditions to prevent a carrier or a bailee from delivering goods to the buyer.

stop payment: an order by a depositor to the bank to refuse to make payment of a check when presented for payment.

strict tort liability: a product liability theory that imposes liability upon the manufacturer, seller, or distributor of goods for harm caused by defective goods.

sublease: a transfer of the premises by the lessee to a third person, the sublessee or subtenant, for a period of less than the term of the original lease.

subpoena: a court order directing a person to appear as a witness. In some states it is also the original process that is to be served on the defendant in order to give the court jurisdiction over the defendant.

subrogation: the right of a party secondarily liable to stand in the place of the creditor after making payment to the creditor and to enforce the creditor's right against the party primarily liable in order to obtain indemnity from such primary party.

subsidiary corporation: a corporation that is controlled by another corporation through the ownership by the latter of a controlling amount of the voting stock of the former.

subsidiary term: a provision of a contract that is not fundamental or does not go to the root of the contract.

substantial performance: the equitable doctrine that a contractor substantially performing a contract in good faith is entitled to recover the contract price less damages for noncompletion or defective work.

substantive law: the law that defines rights and liabilities.

substitution: discharge of a contract by substituting another in its place.

subtenant: one who rents the leased premises from the original tenant for a period of time less than the balance of the lease to the original tenant.

sui generis: in a class by itself, or its own kind.

sui juris: legally competent, possessing capacity.

summary judgment: a judgment entered by the court when no substantial dispute of fact is present, the court acting on the basis of affidavits or depositions that show that the claim or defense of a party is a sham.

summons: a writ by which an action was commenced under the common law.

supersedeas: a stay of proceedings pending the taking of an appeal or an order entered for the purpose of effecting such a stay.

suretyship: an undertaking to pay the debt or be liable for the default of another.

surrender: the yielding up of the tenant's leasehold estate to the lessor in consequence of which the lease terminates.

survival acts: statutes that provide that causes of action shall not terminate on death but shall survive and may be enforced by or against a decedent's estate.

survivorship: the right by which a surviving joint tenant or tenant by the entireties acquires the interest of the predeceasing tenant automatically upon the death of such tenant.

symbolic delivery: the delivery of goods by delivery of the means of control, such as a key or a relevant document of title, such as a negotiable bill of lading.

syndicate: an association of individuals formed to conduct a particular business transaction, generally of a financial nature.

T

tacking: adding together successive periods of adverse possession of persons in privity with each other in order to constitute a sufficient period of continuous adverse possession to vest title thereby.

Taft-Hartley Act: popular name for the Labor Management Relations Act of 1947.

tariff: domestically—a government-approved schedule of charges that may be made by a regulated business, such as a common carrier or warehouser. Internationally—a tax imposed by a country on goods crossing its borders, without regard to whether the purpose is to raise revenue or to discourage the traffic in the taxed goods.

tenancy at sufferance: a tenant's holding over of the rented land after a lease has expired without the permission of the landlord and prior to the time that the landlord has elected to treat such possessor as a trespasser or a tenant.

tenancy at will: the holding of land for an indefinite period that may be terminated at any time by the landlord or by the landlord and tenant acting together.

tenancy for years: a tenancy for a fixed period of time, even though the time is less than a year.

tenancy from year to year: a tenancy that continues indefinitely from year to year until terminated.

tenancy in common: the relationship that exists when two or more persons own undivided interests in property.

tenancy in partnership: the ownership relationship that exists between partners under the Uniform Partnership Act.

tender of payment: an unconditional offer to pay the exact amount of money due at the time and place specified by the contract.

tender of performance: an unconditional offer to perform at the time and in the manner specified by the contract.

tentative trust: a trust that arises when money is deposited in a bank account in the name of the depositor "in trust for" a named person.

terminable fee: an estate that terminates upon the happening of a contingency without any entry by the grantor or heirs, as a conveyance for "so long as" the land is used for a specified purpose.

testamentary: designed to take effect at death, as by disposing of property or appointing a personal representative.

testate: the condition of leaving a will upon death.

testate succession: the distribution of an estate in accordance with the will of the decedent.

testator-testatrix: a man-woman who makes a will.

testimonium clause: a concluding paragraph in a deed, contract, or other instrument, reciting that the instrument has been executed on a specified date by the parties.

testimony: the answers of witnesses under oath to questions given at the time of the trial in the presence of the trier of fact.

theory of the case: the rule that, when a case is tried on the basis of one theory, the appellant in taking an appeal cannot argue a different theory to the appellate court.

third party beneficiary: a third person whom the parties to a contract intend to benefit by the making of the contract and to confer upon such person the right to sue for breach of contract.

tie-in sale: the requirement imposed by the seller that the buyer of particular goods or equipment also purchase certain other goods from the seller in order to obtain the original property desired.

time draft: a bill of exchange payable at a stated time after sight or at a definite time.

title insurance: a form of insurance by which the insurer insures the buyer of real property against the risk of loss should the title acquired from the seller be defective in any way.

toll the statute: stop the running of the period of the Statute of Limitations by the doing of some act by the debtor.

Torrens system: see *registration of titles.*

tort: a private injury or wrong arising from a breach of a duty created by law.

trade acceptance: a draft or bill of exchange drawn by the seller of goods on the purchase at the time of sale and accepted by the purchaser.

trade fixtures: articles of personal property that have been attached to the freehold by a tenant and that are used for or are necessary to the carrying on of the tenant's trade.

trademark: a name, device, or symbol used by a manufacturer or seller to distinguish goods from those of other persons.

trade name: a name under which a business is carried on and, if fictitious, it must be registered.

trade secrets: secrets of any character peculiar and important to the business of the employer that have been communicated to the employee in the course of confidential employment.

treason: an attempt to overthrow or betray the government to which one owes allegiance.

treasury stock: corporate stock that the corporation has reacquired.

trier of fact: in most cases a jury, although it may be the judge alone in certain classes of cases (as in equity) or in any case when jury trial is waived, or when an administrative agency or commission is involved.

trust: a transfer of property by one person to another with the understanding or declaration that such property be held for the benefit of another; the holding of property by the owner in trust for another, upon a declaration of trust, without a transfer to another person. (Parties—settlor, trustee, beneficiary.)

trust corpus: the fund or property that is transferred to the trustee or held by the settlor as the body or subject matter of the trust.

trust deed: a form of deed that transfers the trust property to the trustee for the purposes therein stated, particularly used when the trustee is to hold the title to the mortgagor's land in trust for the benefit of the mortgage bondholders.

trustee de son tort: a person who is not a trustee but who has wrongly intermeddled with property of another and who is required to account for the property as though an actual trustee.

trustee in bankruptcy: an impartial person elected to administer the debtor's estate.

U

uberrima fides: utmost good faith, a duty to exercise the utmost good faith that arises in certain relationships, such as that between an insurer and the applicant for insurance.

ultra vires: an act or contract that the corporation does not have authority to do or make.

underwriter: an insurer.

undisclosed principal: a principal on whose behalf an agent acts without disclosing to the third person the fact of agency or the identity of the principal.

undue influence: the influence that is asserted upon another person by one who dominates that person.

unfair competition: the wrong of employing competitive methods that have been declared unfair by statute or an administrative agency.

unfair labor practice acts: statutes that prohibit certain labor practices and declare them to be unfair.

unincorporated association: a combination of two or more persons for the furtherance of a common nonprofit purpose.

union contract: a contract between a labor union and an employer or group of employers prescribing the general terms of employment of workers by the latter.

union shop: under present unfair labor practice statutes, a place of employment where nonunion workers may be employed for a trial period of not more than 30 days after which the nonunion workers must join the union or be discharged.

universal agent: an agent authorized by the principal to do all acts that can lawfully be delegated to a representative.

usury: the lending of money at greater than the maximum rate of interest allowed by law.

V

vacating of judgment: the setting aside of a judgment.

valid: legal.

verdict: the decision of the trial or petty jury.

void: of no legal effect and not binding on anyone.

voidable: a transaction that may be set aside by one party thereto because of fraud or similar reason but which is binding on the other party until the injured party elects to avoid.

voidable preference: a preference given by the debtor in bankruptcy to a creditor, but which may be set aside by the trustee in bankruptcy.

voir dire examination: the preliminary examination of a juror or a witness to ascertain fitness to act as such.

volenti non fit injuria: the maxim that the defendant's act cannot constitute a tort if the plaintiff has consented thereto.

voluntary nonsuit: a means of a plaintiff's stopping a trial at any time by moving for a voluntary nonsuit.

voting trust: the transfer by two or more persons of their shares of stock of a corporation to a trustee who is to vote the shares and act for such shareholders.

W

waiver: the release or relinquishment of a known right or objection.

warehouse receipt: a receipt issued by the warehouser for stored goods. Regulated by the UCC, which clothes the receipt with some degree of negotiability.

warranties of indorser of commercial paper: the implied covenants made by an indorser of a commercial paper distinct from any undertaking to pay upon the default of the primary party.

warranties of insured: statements or promises made by the applicant for insurance that, if false, will entitle the insurer to avoid the contract of insurance in many jurisdictions.

warranties of seller of goods: warranties consisting of express warranties that relate to matters forming part of the basis of the bargain; warranties as to title and right to sell; and the implied warranties that the law adds to a sale depending upon the nature of the transaction.

warranty deed: a deed by which the grantor conveys a specific estate or interest to the grantee and makes one or more of the covenants of title.

warranty of authority: an implied warranty of an agent of the authority exercised by the agent.

warranty of principal: an implied warranty of an agent that the agent is acting for an existing principal who has capacity to contract.

watered stock: stock issued by a corporation as fully paid when in fact it is not.

will: an instrument executed with the formality required by law, by which a person makes a disposition of property to take effect upon death or appoints a personal representative.

willful: intentional, as distinguished from accidental or involuntary. In penal statutes, with evil intent or legal malice, or without reasonable ground for believing one's act to be lawful.

Wool Products Labeling Act: a federal statute prohibiting the misbranding of woolen fabrics.

workers' compensation: a system providing for payments to workers because they have been injured from a risk arising out of the course of their employment while they were employed at their employment or who have contracted an occupational disease in that manner, payment being made without consideration of the negligence or lack of negligence of any party.

Y

year and a day: the common-law requirement that death result within a year and a day in order to impose criminal liability for homicide.

Z

zoning restrictions: restrictions imposed by government on the use of property for the advancement of the general welfare.

INDEXES

CASE INDEX

Principal cases are in boldface type; cited cases are in Roman type.

D

SUBJECT INDEX